THE WORLD ATLAS

EARTH is an epic publishing feat never to be repeated, proudly created by Millennium House

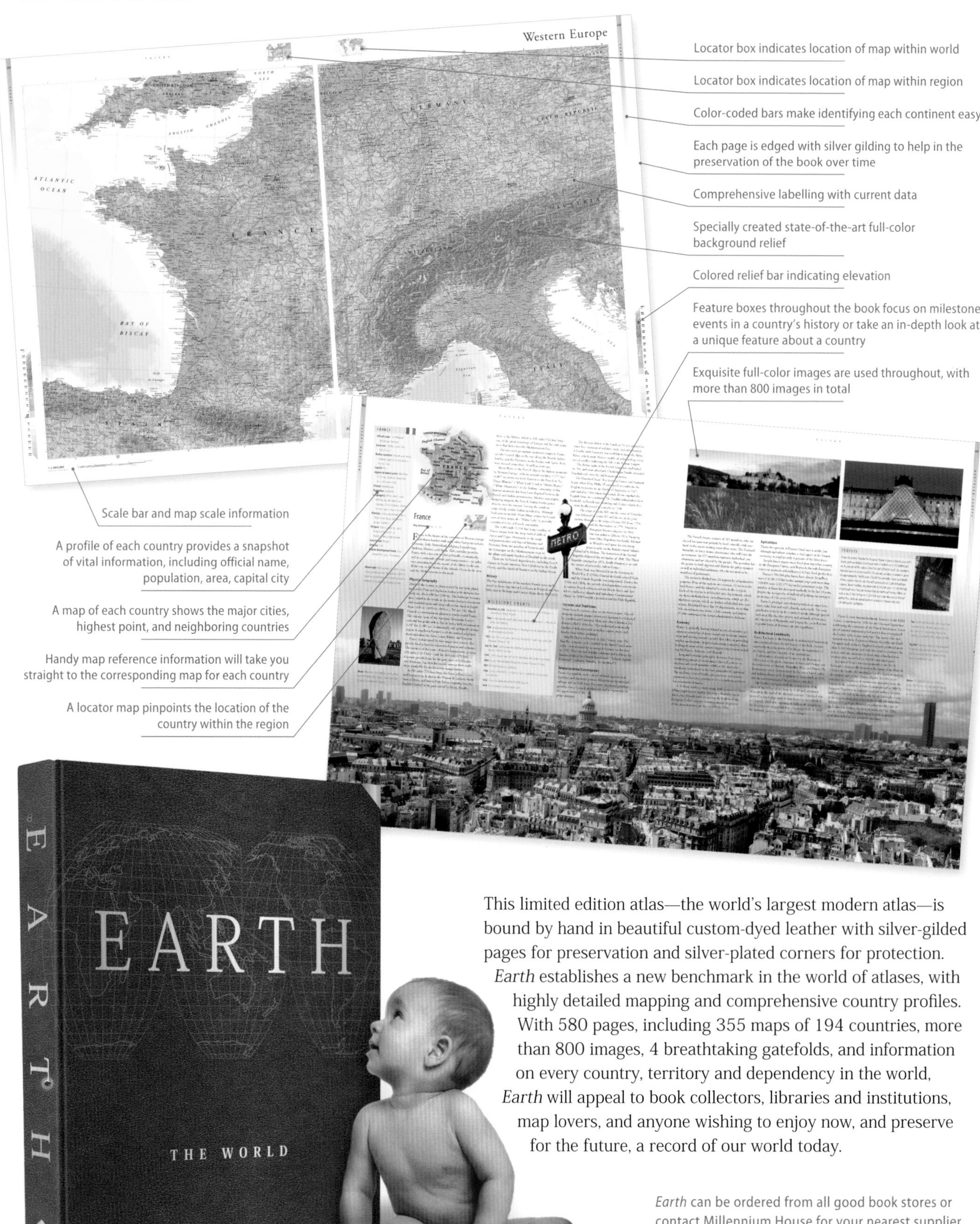
Western Europe
Locator box indicates location of map within world
Locator box indicates location of map within region
Color-coded bars make identifying each continent easy
Each page is edged with silver gilding to help in the preservation of the book over time
Comprehensive labelling with current data
Specially created state-of-the-art full-color background relief
Colored relief bar indicating elevation
Feature boxes throughout the book focus on milestone events in a country's history or take an in-depth look at a unique feature about a country
Exquisite full-color images are used throughout, with more than 800 images in total
Scale bar and map scale information
A profile of each country provides a snapshot of vital information, including official name, population, area, capital city
A map of each country shows the major cities, highest point, and neighboring countries
Handy map reference information will take you straight to the corresponding map for each country
A locator map pinpoints the location of the country within the region
France
EARTH
THE WORLD
This limited edition atlas—the world's largest modern atlas—is bound by hand in beautiful custom-dyed leather with silver-gilded pages for preservation and silver-plated corners for protection. *Earth* establishes a new benchmark in the world of atlases, with highly detailed mapping and comprehensive country profiles. With 580 pages, including 355 maps of 194 countries, more than 800 images, 4 breathtaking gatefolds, and information on every country, territory and dependency in the world, *Earth* will appeal to book collectors, libraries and institutions, map lovers, and anyone wishing to enjoy now, and preserve for the future, a record of our world today.
Earth can be ordered from all good book stores or contact Millennium House for your nearest supplier
www.millenniumhouse.com.au

THE WORLD ATLAS

Chief Consultant **Charles F. Gritzner**

MILLENNIUM HOUSE

Publisher Gordon Cheers
Associate Publisher Janet Parker
Art Director Stan Lamond
Project Managers Kate Etherington, Marie-Louise Taylor
Chief Consultant Charles F. Gritzner
Contributors Maria Alzate, Armen Asryan, Ann Marie B. Bahr, Donald J. Berg, Vonnie Calemine, Craig S. Campbell, Dr Robert R. Coenraads, Dr Lawrence W. Crissman, Nilson Crocia de Barros, Dr Julie Cupples, Christopher Cusack, Roman Cybriwsky, Paul Deans, Alan Dixon, Alasdair Drysdale, Bart Goins, Charles F. Gritzner, David Hamper, Reuel Hanks, Edward Patrick Hogan, Peter Holland, Ritva Kivikkokangas-Sandgren, Marijan M. Klemenčič, Dale Lightfoot, David McGonigal, Dr Bruce V. Millett, Francis Carleonet Nieves, Joseph R. Oppong, Thomas R. Paradise, Zoran Pavlović, Douglas A. Phillips, Michael Pretes, Noor Abdul Rahman, Carlos Rubinsky, Roger Sandall, Marianna Shahinyan, Dr R. B. Singh, Barry Stone, Daniel Wagner, Pornsawat Wathanakul, Alexander Wearing, Colonel (Ret.) Quintin Wight, Willow Wight, George Wingfield, Gamini G. Zoysa, Dr J. C. Zwaan
Cover Design Stan Lamond
Designers Lena Lowe, Hilda Mendham, Robert Taylor, Peta Zoubakin
Editors Loretta Barnard, Jo Black, Louise Buchanan, Helen Cooney, Chris Edwards, Denise Imwold, Heather Jackson, Carol Jacobson, Melody Lord, Susan Page, Anne Savage, Marie-Louise Taylor
Picture Research Gordon Cheers, Jane Cozens, Melody Lord, Susan Page, Marie-Louise Taylor, Debi Wager
Illustrators Andrew Davies, Warwick Jacobson, Glen Vause
Chief Cartographic Consultant Damien Demaj
Cartographic Consultant John Frith
Cartographers Munmun Adhikari, Will Adnams, Stewart Adrain, Imran Ahmad, Galen Barnett, Sushmita Bhaduri, Clare Brown, Sam Brown, Terry Bush, Vaclav Cerny, Indrajit Chakraborty, Ruth Coombs, Lawrence Crissman, Martin Darlison, Subhodip Ghosh Dastidar, Alison Davies, Linda Dawes, Damien Demaj, Adam Derringer, Liz Donnelly, Peeyush Dubey, Mark Eldridge, Alison Ewington, Mark Fairbairn, Kim Farrington, Heather Francisco, John Frith, Matt Goodchild, Erin Greb, Casey Greene, Alan Grimwade, Matthew Hampton, Paul Hyatt, Robin Hyatt, Jaibhagwan, Ravi Kant, Kevin Klein, Sanjay Kumar, Don Larsen, Scott Lockheed, Craig MacAlpine, Rob McCaleb, Laura McCormick, David McCutcheon, David Maltby, Ed Merritt, Greg Moore, Kate Morrill, Wayne Murphy, David Murray, Jatin Nankana, Lynn Neal, Joe Nunn, Alan Palfreyman, Nitin Pande, Amritanjan Pandey, Jerome Parkin, Alok Pathak, Jacob Patrylick, Max Peatman, Tim Rideout, Beth Robertson, Riju Roy, Kelly Sandefer, Julie Sheridan, Prem Singh, Alan Smith, Roger Smith, George Stoll, Matthew Townsend, Gail Townsley, Hans Van der Maarel, Clare Varney, Martin von Wyss, Allison Walls, Marcella Warner, Jonathan Wyss, Amelia Zander
Senior Map Editors Heather Jackson, Jan Watson
Map Editors Brenda Bartels, Louise Buchanan, Roger Bullen, Ngaio Chandler, Daniel Cheers, Hannah Cheers, Brett Constantine, Sam Diacos, Wayne Findlay, Sally Fitzgerald, Jackie Gilbert, Jo-Anne Gonsalves, Alicen Hunter, Denise Imwold, George Locke, Philippa Locke, Alicja Mosbauer, Anthony Pizzolato, Scott Quin, Val Russell, Andrew West, Natalie Wilson
Gazetteer John Cook
Production Simone Russell, Bernard Roberts
Publishing Assistants Michelle DiStefano, Rebecca Lamond

First published in 2009 as *Earth Condensed* by
Millennium House Pty Ltd
52 Bolwarra Road, Elanora Heights
NSW, 2101, Australia

ISBN: 978-1-921209-50-5
ISBN: 978-1-921209-46-8 (Cased)

Reprinted 2010

SALES
For all sales, please contact:
Millennium House Pty Ltd
52 Bolwarra Road, Elanora Heights
NSW, 2101, Australia
Ph: (612) 9970 6850 Fax: (612) 9913 3500
Email: info@millenniumhouse.com.au
Website: www.millenniumhouse.com.au

Printed in China by Sing Cheong Printing Co Ltd
Color Separation by Pica Digital Pte Ltd, Singapore

AUTHORS
Millennium House would be happy to receive submissions from authors. Please send brief submissions to: editor@millenniumhouse.com.au

PHOTOGRAPHERS AND ILLUSTRATORS
Millennium House would be happy to receive submissions from photographers or illustrators. Please send submissions to: editor@millenniumhouse.com.au

Pages 2–3: Along Greenland's western coast, a small field of glaciers surrounds Baffin Bay.
These pages: This enhanced image shows shallow lakes, mudflats, and salt marshes in the sinuous valleys of the Dasht-e-Kavir (Great Salt Desert) in Iran.
Pages 6–7: The peaks and ridges of the eastern Himalayas in southwestern China are shown in this digital land remote sensing image.

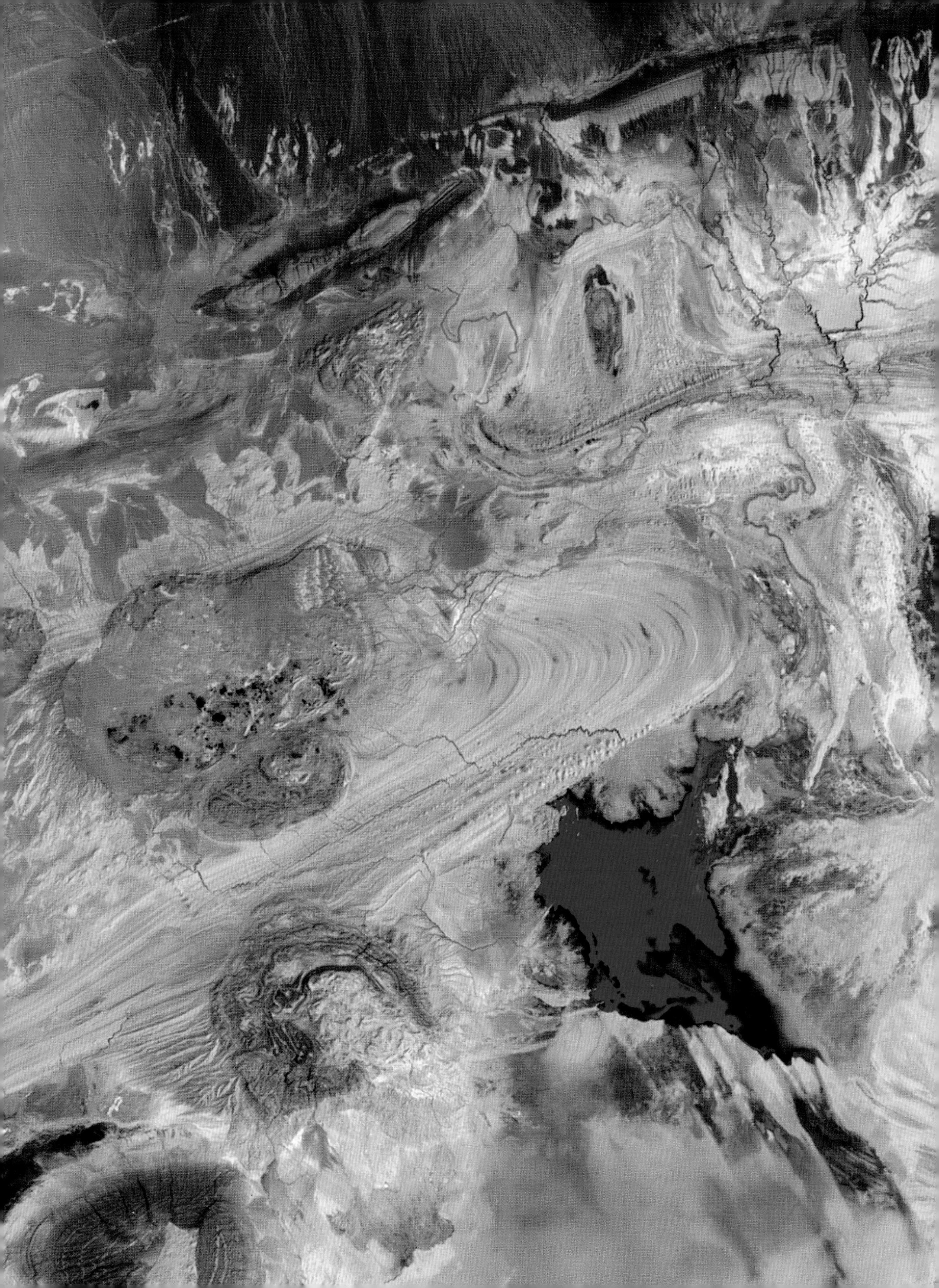

Preface

Journey from the balmy Pacific Islands to the Arctic tundra, from the deserts of Africa to the lush Amazon rainforest, from the rolling plains of North America to Asia's soaring Himalayas, and from the checkerboard farmland of Europe to the frozen expanses of Antarctica; discover the distribution of the human and animal populations, the religions of the world, the technology and expansion of global communications, and other topics of global importance. In a single comprehensive volume, *Earth Condensed* gives you the world in all its beauty, variety, and complexity.

It is an atlas—featuring 140 pages of detailed mapping produced by a team of international cartographers using state-of-the art techniques. The physical geography is beautifully illustrated with sophisticated topographic shading, while the place names and boundaries reflect the latest changes in political geography.

It is a geographic and scientific reference book—covering such topics as biodiversity and climate change. Information about our environment (how landforms come into being, how climatic systems operate, the unspoiled habitats of wildlife) and the interaction between humans and the environment (how we've used the natural resources, how we've spread across the land, the patterns of commerce and communication, the effects of natural disasters) is explained clearly with thematic maps and accessible text.

It is a social studies compendium—delving into the history, culture, politics, economy, religion, and government of every nation. *Earth Condensed* features interesting and informative easy-to-read text that tells the story of each country and dependency, accompanied by a wealth of colorful images carefully selected to capture its unique people, flora, fauna, landforms, and cityscapes.

Comprehensive cartography, special coverage of contemporary issues, detailed country information, and an extensive gazetteer make *Earth Condensed* an essential addition to every reference collection.

C o n t

Contributors 10

INTRODUCTION 14

Part One

THE WORLD WE LIVE IN 18

RECORDING EARTH 20
- Cartography and Satellite Imaging 22
- Modern Cartography and Satellite Imagery 24

PHYSICAL EARTH 26
- Our Place in Space 28
- Plate Tectonics 30
- Earth's Landforms 32
- Earth's Vital Statistics 34
- Temperature 36
- Precipitation 38
- Climate 40
- Climate Change 42
- Natural Hazards 44

LIFE ON EARTH 46
- Plant and Animal Diversity 48
- Wildlife and Habitats 50
- Natural Resources and World Energy 52
- Population 54
- Religions of the World 56
- Migration—People on the Move 58
- Human Impact on the Environment 60
- Global Communications and Trade 62

Part Two

COUNTRIES OF THE WORLD 64

THE WORLD 66
- World Overview 66
- *World Physical* 1:75,000,000 68
- *World Political* 1:75,000,000 70

OCEANS 72
- Introduction 74
- *Atlantic Ocean* 1:41,300,000 76
- *Pacific Ocean* 1:50,600,000 78
- *Indian Ocean* 1:37,500,000 80

NORTH AMERICA 82
- Introduction 84

NORTHERN AMERICA
- Canada 88
- USA 90

MEXICO
- Mexico 94

CENTRAL AMERICA
- Guatemala 96
- Belize 96
- El Salvador 97
- Honduras 98
- Nicaragua 98
- Costa Rica 99
- Panama 99

CARIBBEAN
- Cuba 100
- Jamaica 101
- Bahamas 102
- Haiti 102
- Dominican Republic 103
- St Kitts and Nevis 104
- Antigua and Barbuda 104
- Dominica 105
- St Lucia 105
- St Vincent and The Grenadines 106
- Barbados 106
- Grenada 107
- Trinidad and Tobago 107

DEPENDENCIES and TERRITORIES
- Greenland 108
- Bermuda 108
- Anguilla 108
- British Virgin Islands 109
- Cayman Islands 109
- Guadeloupe 109
- St Martin 109
- St Barthélemy 109
- Martinique 110
- Montserrat 110
- Navassa Island 110
- Netherlands Antilles 110
- Aruba 111
- Puerto Rico 111
- St Pierre and Miquelon 111
- Turks and Caicos Islands 111
- United States Virgin Islands 111

MAPPING
- *North America Physical* 1:25,300,000 112
- *North America Political* 1:25,300,000 114
- *Alaska, Northern Canada, and Greenland* 1:15,950,000 116
- *Western Canada* 1:5,630,000 118
- *Central Canada* 1:5,630,000 120
- *East Canada* 1:5,630,000 122
- *Northwestern USA* 1:5,630,000 124
- *Northeastern USA* 1:5,630,000 126
- *Southwestern USA* 1:5,630,000 128
- *Southeastern USA* 1:5,630,000 130
- *Mexico* 1:7,880,000 132
- *Central America and the Caribbean* 1:7,880,000 134

SOUTH AMERICA 136
- Introduction 138

NORTHERN SOUTH AMERICA
- Colombia 140
- Venezuela 140
- Guyana 141
- Suriname 141

CENTRAL SOUTH AMERICA
- Brazil 142
- Ecuador 144
- Bolivia 144
- Peru 145

SOUTHERN SOUTH AMERICA
- Argentina 146
- Chile 147
- Paraguay 148
- Uruguay 148

DEPENDENCIES and TERRITORIES
- French Guiana 149
- Falkland Islands 149
- South Georgia and the South Sandwich Islands 149

MAPPING
- *South America Physical* 1:20,600,000 150
- *South America Political* 1:20,600,000 152
- *Northwestern South America* 1:7,880,000 154
- *Eastern South America* 1:7,880,000 156
- *Central South America* 1:7,880,000 158
- *South Central South America* 1:7,880,000 160
- *Southern South America* 1:7,880,000 162
- *Islands around South America* 163

EUROPE 164
- Introduction 166

ICELAND and SCANDINAVIA
- Iceland 168
- Norway 169
- Sweden 170
- Finland 170
- Denmark 171

NORTHERN EUROPE
- United Kingdom 172
- Ireland 176
- Netherlands 177
- Belgium 178
- Luxembourg 179
- Liechtenstein 179
- France 180
- Austria 182
- Switzerland 183
- Germany 184

BALTIC STATES and RUSSIAN FEDERATION
- Lithuania 186
- Latvia 186
- Estonia 187
- Russian Federation 188

EASTERN EUROPE
- Poland 192
- Czech Republic 193
- Belarus 194
- Slovakia 195
- Hungary 196
- Ukraine 197
- Moldova 197

SOUTHERN EUROPE
- Portugal 198
- Andorra 199
- Spain 200
- Monaco 202
- Malta 202
- San Marino 203
- Vatican City 203
- Italy 204

SOUTHEASTERN EUROPE
- Slovenia 206
- Croatia 207
- Bosnia and Herzegovina 208
- Kosovo 208
- Serbia 209
- Romania 210
- Montenegro 210
- Bulgaria 211
- Albania 212
- Macedonia 212
- Greece 213

DEPENDENCIES and TERRITORIES
- Svalbard 214
- Faroe Islands 214
- Jan Mayen 215
- Åland Islands 215
- Isle of Man 215
- Gibraltar 216
- Guernsey 216
- Jersey 217

MAPPING
- *Europe Physical* 1:15,000,000 218
- *Europe Political* 1:15,000,000 220
- *Northern Scandinavia and Iceland* 1:3,750,000 222
- *Southern Scandinavia and the Baltic States* 1:3,750,000 224
- *Central Europe* 1:3,750,000 226
- *Western Europe* 1:3,750,000 228
- *Spain and Portugal* 1:3,750,000 230
- *Italy and Eastern Central Europe* 1:3,750,000 232
- *Southeastern Europe* 1:3,750,000 234
- *Russian Federation* 1:19,710,000 236
- *Western Russian Federation* 1:3,750,000 238
- *British Isles* 1:4,700,000 239
- *Southern England and Wales* 1:1,410,000 240
- *Northern England* 1:1,410,000 242
- *Scotland* 1:1,880,000 244
- *Ireland* 1:1,880,000 245

e n t s

AFRICA 246

Introduction 248

NORTH AFRICA
Morocco 250
Algeria 251
Tunisia 252
Libya 253
Egypt 254

WESTERN AFRICA
Mauritania 256
Senegal 256
Cape Verde 257
Gambia 258
Mali 258
Niger 259
Chad 260
Guinea-Bissau 260
Guinea 261
Burkina Faso 262
Sierra Leone 262
Liberia 263
Côte d'Ivoire 264
Ghana 265
Togo 266
Benin 266
Nigeria 267

CENTRAL AFRICA
Cameroon 268
Central African Republic 269
Equatorial Guinea 269
São Tomé and Príncipe 270
Gabon 270
Congo 271
Democratic Republic of Congo 272
Angola 273

EASTERN AFRICA
Sudan 274
Ethiopia 275
Djibouti 276
Eritrea 276
Somalia 277
Uganda 278
Kenya 279
Tanzania 280
Rwanda 280
Burundi 281

SOUTHERN AFRICA
Zambia 282
Malawi 283
Mozambique 284
Comoros 284
Seychelles 285
Madagascar 286
Mauritius 287
Namibia 288
Botswana 289
Zimbabwe 290
Swaziland 291
Lesotho 291
South Africa 292

DEPENDENCIES and TERRITORIES
Mayotte 294
Réunion 294
St Helena 294
Western Sahara 294
Ceuta 295
Canary Islands 295
Madeira 295
Melilla 295

MAPPING
Africa Physical 1:29,000,000 296
Africa Political 1:29,000,000 298
Northwestern Africa 1:10,320,000 300
Northeastern Africa and the Middle East 1:10,320,000 302
Western Central Africa 1:10,320,000 304
Eastern Central Africa 1:10,320,000 306
Southern Africa and Madagascar 1:10,320,000 308
Islands around Africa 310

ASIA 312

Introduction 314

WESTERN ASIA
Cyprus 318
Turkey 319
Georgia 320
Armenia 320
Azerbaijan 321

MIDDLE EAST
Lebanon 322
Syria 323
Israel 324
Jordan 325
Iraq 326
Iran 327
Saudi Arabia 328
Kuwait 329
Bahrain 329
Qatar 330
United Arab Emirates 330
Yemen 331
Oman 331

CENTRAL ASIA
Kazakhstan 332
Turkmenistan 332
Uzbekistan 333
Afghanistan 334
Tajikistan 335
Kyrgyzstan 335

INDIAN SUBCONTINENT
Pakistan 336
Maldives 337
India 338
Nepal 340
Sri Lanka 341
Bhutan 342
Bangladesh 343

EASTERN ASIA
China 344
Mongolia 349
North Korea 350
South Korea 351
Japan 352

SOUTHEAST ASIA
Myanmar (Burma) 354
Thailand 355
Laos 356
Cambodia 357
Vietnam 358
Malaysia 360
Brunei 361
Singapore 362
Philippines 363
Indonesia 364
Timor-Leste (East Timor) 365

DEPENDENCIES and TERRITORIES
Akrotiri and Dhekelia 366
British Indian Ocean Territory 366
Paracel Islands 366
Spratly Islands 366
Palestinian Territories 366
Palestine (Gaza Strip) 367
Palestine (West Bank) 367

MAPPING
Asia Physical 1:37,500,000 368
Asia Political 1:37,500,000 370
Eastern Indonesia and Papua New Guinea 1:9,390,000 372
Western Indonesia, Malaysia, and Singapore 1:9,390,000 374
Southeast Asia and Philippines 1:9,390,000 376
Western Central Asia 1:7,880,000 378
Eastern Central Asia 1:7,880,000 380
Central Asia 1:7,880,000 382
Northeastern China and Mongolia 1:7,880,000 384
Japan and Korea 1:7,880,000 386
Northwestern Asia 1:10,320,000 388
Middle East 1:10,320,000 390
India 1:10,320,000 392
Turkey and Eastern Europe 1:10,320,000 394

OCEANIA 396

Introduction 398

WESTERN OCEANIA
Australia 400
Papua New Guinea 402
Micronesia 403
Palau 403

CENTRAL OCEANIA
Nauru 404
Solomon Islands 404
Vanuatu 405
Marshall Islands 406
Tuvalu 406
Fiji 407

SOUTHERN OCEANIA
New Zealand 408

EASTERN OCEANIA
Tonga 410
Kiribati 410
Samoa 410

DEPENDENCIES and TERRITORIES
American Samoa 411
Ashmore and Cartier Islands 411
Christmas Island 411
Baker and Howland Islands 411
Cocos (Keeling) Islands 412
Cook Islands 412
Coral Sea Islands 412
French Polynesia 413
Guam 413
Jarvis Island 413
Johnston Atoll 414
Kingman Reef 414
Midway Islands 414
New Caledonia 414
Niue 415
Norfolk Island 415
Northern Mariana Islands 416
Palmyra Atoll 416
Pitcairn Islands 416
Tokelau 417
Wake Island 417
Wallis and Futuna 417

MAPPING
Oceania Physical 1:31,900,000 418
Oceania Political 1:31,900,000 420
New Zealand 1:3,750,000 422
Australia 1:14,080,000 424
Islands of the Pacific 426

THE POLES 428

Introduction 430

ANTARCTICA
Antarctica 432

DEPENDENCIES and TERRITORIES
Bouvet Island 433
French Southern and Antarctic Lands 433
Heard and McDonald Islands 433

MAPPING
Arctic 1:18,700,000 434
Antarctic 1:18,700,000 436

GAZETTEER 438

Credits and Acknowledgements 524

CHIEF CONSULTANT

CHARLES F. GRITZNER
"Fritz" Gritzner is Distinguished Professor of Geography at South Dakota State University in Brookings, South Dakota, USA. He is now in his fifth decade of college teaching and research. In addition to teaching, he enjoys research, travel, working with teachers, and writing to share his passion for geography with readers. Professor Gritzner has served as both president and executive director of the National Council for Geographic Education and has received the Council's highest honor—the George J. Miller Award for Distinguished Service to Geographic Education—as well as numerous other honors for teaching and research from the NCGE, the Association of American Geographers, and others.

CONTRIBUTORS

MARIA ALZATE
Maria Alzate studied geology at the Colombian National University. She was involved in government research on geological hazards in northwest Colombia, and worked for the National University in Medellin in environmental impact. Maria studied and worked in the gem industry, and is interested in all geological matters.

ARMEN ASRYAN
Armen Asryan is an expert in Geographical Information Systems. He has a wide range of academic qualifications and skills in such diverse fields as economics, information technology, natural resources, and environmental management and conservation, including climate change, biodiversity, forests, and anthropogenic impacts assessments. Armen completed his MSc in Applied GIS at Kingston University in London.

ANN MARIE B. BAHR
Ann Marie B. Bahr is Professor of Religious Studies at South Dakota State University, USA. She served as academic editor of Chelsea House's eleven-volume *Religions of the World* series, and is the author of *Christianity* and *Indigenous Religions*. Bahr is a member of Phi Beta Kappa, the American Academy of Religion, and the Society of Biblical Literature. She is on the American Academy of Religion's Task Force on Religion in the Schools.

DONALD J. BERG
Donald J. Berg is Professor of Geography at South Dakota State University, USA. He received his BA (History) and MA (History) from North Dakota State University, and his MA (Geography) and PhD (Geography) from University of California at Berkeley.

VONNIE CALEMINE
Vonnie Calemine graduated from the College of Charleston, South Carolina, USA, with a degree in Spanish and in History. She later pursued her Masters in Latin American Studies at San Diego State University, with an emphasis in political science and US–Latin American relations. She now teaches at Coastal Carolina University.

CRAIG S. CAMPBELL
Craig S. Campbell is Professor and Chair of the Department of Geography at Youngstown State University in Ohio, USA. He received his undergraduate degree in geography and Spanish from Indiana University–Purdue University at Indianapolis. His MA in Geography is from the University of Kentucky, and he received his PhD in Geography from University of Kansas. His interests are in the cultural geography of the United States, the Latter Day Saint movement, general and thematic cartography, and the regional geography of Europe and South America. He is author of *Images of the New Jerusalem: Latter Day Saint Faction Interpretations of Independence, Missouri.*

DR ROBERT R. COENRAADS
Dr Robert Coenraads is a consultant geoscientist, and author of four books and over 30 scientific publications. He has led archeology, natural history, and geology field trips to various corners of the globe. Dr Coenraads is currently President of FreeSchools World Literacy (Australia), and has established a support network to provide education for underprivileged children in Bihar State, India.

DR LAWRENCE W. CRISSMAN
Dr Lawrence W. Crissman is an anthropologist, concentrating his research on Chinese society. For the past twenty years he has been involved with GIS applications, having established the Australian Centre of the Asian Spatial Information and Analysis Network (ACASIAN) at Griffith University, in Queensland, Australia. He has been involved with the Electronic Cultural Atlas Initiative since its inception, and has produced digital versions of the Language Atlas of the Pacific Region and the Language Atlas of China for ECAI. He has also had a major role in the China Historical GIS Project.

NILSON CROCIA DE BARROS
Nilson Crocia de Barros is a lecturer at the Departamento de Geografia of the Universidade Federal de Pernambuco. He received Bachelor's and Master's degrees in geography from the Universidade Federal de Pernambuco and a PhD in geography from the Universidade de São Paulo, Brazil. He pursued post-doctoral studies at the University of Durham, UK, and was visiting lecturer at Radford University, Virginia. In 2004 he obtained the title of Free Lecturer (Livre Docente) from the University of São Paulo. Recently he has concentrated on the history of geographical thought and regional development in Northeast Brazil. He has published three books, a number of journal articles, and presented papers at academic meetings.

DR JULIE CUPPLES
Julie Cupples is a Senior Lecturer in Human Geography at the University of Canterbury in New Zealand. She has been conducting research in Central America since the early 1990s. Her work's themes include development and postdevelopment, neoliberalism, disasters, elections, and development fieldwork. It has been published in key edited collections and in leading geographical journals. Current research projects include the construction of citizenship, electoral geographies, the aftermath of Hurricane Felix, the struggle for electricity, and resistance to the Central American Free Trade Agreement (CAFTA).

CHRISTOPHER CUSACK
Christopher Cusack is an Associate Professor of Geography at Keene State College in New Hampshire, USA. His research includes publications on comparative urbanization, as well as urbanization in India, and development in Nunavut. His current research interests are focused on urban sustainability in the developing world, particularly East Africa. Cusack is past-president of the Regional Development and Planning Specialty group of the Association of American Geographers.

ROMAN CYBRIWSKY
Roman Cybriwsky is Professor of Geography and Urban Studies at Temple University, Philadelphia, USA. He has also taught for many years at Temple University's campus in Tokyo, Japan, where until recently he was Associate Dean and Director of the Undergraduate Program. He is the author of *Tokyo: The Shogun's City at the 21st Century*, and several other books about urban or Asian topics, as well as numerous journal articles, book chapters, and other publications. His current book project is about the social aspects of global economic interactions in Roppongi, one of Tokyo's international nightclub districts.

PAUL DEANS
Paul Deans was an associate editor for *Sky & Telescope* and *Night Sky* magazines and the editor of *SkyWatch* magazine before ending up as Sky Publishing's book editor. Now based in Edmonton, Canada, Paul is a freelance science writer/editor and the editor of two digital magazines: *Mercury* and *Travel Quest.*

ALAN DIXON
Alan Dixon is a human geographer with broad research interests in environment and development, and particularly the contribution of local knowledge and community institutions to sustainable livelihoods, and natural resource management in developing countries. He has worked extensively in East Africa and has been involved with the development of strategies for the sustainable management of wetland benefits. Before taking up his position at the University of Worcester, UK, Alan was a Research Fellow at the University of Otago, New Zealand, and a Lecturer in Geography at the University of Huddersfield, UK.

ALASDAIR DRYSDALE
Alasdair Drysdale is the co-author of *The Middle East and North Africa: A Political Geography* (Oxford University Press) and *Syria and the Middle East Peace Process* (Council on Foreign Relations). He has written articles for the *International Journal of Middle East Studies, Middle Eastern Studies, Middle East Report*, and *Middle East Journal,* and has contributed entries on Middle East topics to encyclopedias, yearbooks, and atlases. His current research focuses on the demography of Oman. He graduated with a BA in Modern Middle Eastern Studies at the University of Durham, UK, and received his PhD in geography from the University of Michigan, USA.

BART GOINS
Bart Goins is an undergraduate at the University of North Alabama, USA. He is majoring in geography with a specialization in Geographic Information Systems.

DAVID HAMPER
David Hamper is an experienced author and educator. He is currently Director of Staff Services at the International Grammar School in Sydney, Australia. David has been involved in curriculum development in geography, and has considerable experience in the education and professional development of geography teachers. He has authored and co-authored 15 texts on topics including physical and human geography, human rights, ecosystem management, and international relations and agreements. He has also contributed to several atlas projects and has had numerous articles published in professional journals.

REUEL HANKS
Dr Reuel Hanks is Associate Professor of Geography at Oklahoma State University, USA, and is the editor of the *Journal of Central Asian Studies.* Dr Hanks was a Fulbright Scholar in Tashkent, Uzbekistan, in 1995 and has published more than a dozen articles and book chapters on Central Asia, Islam, nationalism and identity, political geography, and ethnic geography. He is the author of *Uzbekistan* (World Bibliographical Series) and *Central Asia: A Global Studies Handbook.* He is currently writing the *Historical Dictionary of Uzbekistan.*

EDWARD PATRICK HOGAN
Edward Hogan is Professor Emeritus of Geography at South Dakota State University, USA, and State Geographer for South Dakota. Professor Hogan holds a PhD from Saint Louis University. He has written over 70 articles, and authored and co-authored books on the geography of South Dakota, Ireland, Sweden, and Norway.

PETER HOLLAND
Peter Holland is a geography graduate of the University of New Zealand (BSc) and the University of Canterbury (MSc). He completed the PhD in Biogeography at the Australian National University, Canberra, then joined McGill University in Montreal, Canada, before returning to the University of Canterbury, Christchurch. He was appointed Professor of Geography at the University of Otago, Dunedin, and was made an Emeritus Professor 20 years later in 2002. From 1982 to 2004 he was Associate Editor of the *Journal of Biogeography.* From 2002 to 2006 he was President of the New Zealand Geographical Society. His current research interests are landscape change and environmental learning in colonial New Zealand.

RITVA KIVIKKOKANGAS-SANDGREN
Ritva Kivikkokangas-Sandgren is Senior Lecturer of Development Geography at the University of Helsinki, Finland, and is an active member of the Association of Academics and the Faculty of Science. She specializes in development issues of Southeast Asia, Africa, and Latin America, particularly spatial, ecological, human and cultural change, and globalization and its sustainability.

MARIJAN M. KLEMENČIČ
Marijan M. Klemenčič is Associate Professor of Geography at University of Ljubljana, Slovenia, where he earned his PhD. His research is focused mainly on spatial and socio-economic problems of rural areas, typology of rural areas, and rural development. His areas of interest are theoretical

issues of geography, especially regionalization and space as geographical category. In 1990 he organized the symposium of the IGU Commission on Changing Rural Systems and Subcommission on Highlands and High-latitude Zones, and an international conference in 2001 on challenges and problems of rural areas.

DALE LIGHTFOOT
Dale Lightfoot is Professor and Head of the Department of Geography and is active in the School of International Studies at Oklahoma State University, USA. He received his PhD in geography at the University of Colorado–Boulder. His research maintains a strong fieldwork and geospatial technologies focus, oriented around historic landscapes, agriculture and water technology, and themes that emphasize human-environment relationships. He has authored or co-authored over 40 publications. Funded research has taken him to southwest USA, Central Asia, Morocco, Tunisia, Cyprus, and the Middle East.

DAVID MCGONIGAL
David McGonigal is an award-winning travel author and photographer. He has spent the last 15 years exploring the polar regions, most recently as an expedition leader on ships in Antarctica. He has degrees in geography and law. He is the author of more than a dozen books, mainly about Australia and Antarctica, and has contributed to many more.

BRUCE V. MILLETT
Dr Millett specializes in climatology, wetland ecology, Geographic Information Systems, and remote sensing. He is an Assistant Professor in the Department of Geography at South Dakota State University, USA. Dr Millett's research is focused on ecological modeling of northern prairie wetlands in North America. Dr Millett uses aerial photographs and satellite imagery to map and delineate the physical features of northern prairie wetlands on local and regional scales.

FRANCIS CARLEONET NIEVES
Francis Carleonet Nieves spent much of her early life in the rainforests bordering the Orinoco River, gaining an indepth knowledge of the country's native lore, food, medicinal plants, and animals, as well as practicing wilderness survival skills. Francis trained as a primary school teacher at the Universidad Nacional Abierta in Puerto Ayacucho in Amazon State, and taught at Morichote village in Cedeño District, Bolivar State.

JOSEPH R. OPPONG
Joseph R. Oppong is Associate Professor of Geography at the University of North Texas in Denton, Texas, USA. He has an MA and PhD in geography from the University of Alberta, Canada, and a BA in geography and sociology from the University of Ghana. He has university teaching experience in Ghana, Canada, and the USA. His research focuses on medical geography, the geography of disease and health care. He has written on HIV/AIDS in Africa and authored several books for the Chelsea House Modern World Nations and Major World Cultures series. He is a past chairperson of the Association of American Geographers Special Interest Groups on Africa and medical geography.

DR TOM PARADISE
Dr Tom Paradise is a Geography Professor and Director of the King Fahd Center for Middle East and Islamic Studies at the University of Arkansas, USA. He comes from a diverse background in the environmental sciences, architecture, Middle Eastern and North African geography, and cartography. Professor Paradise has published more than 40 articles, chapters, and books on the unique decaying architecture of Petra, Jordan, and advises foreign agencies on cultural heritage management. He has taught at universities in Rome, Venice, and Amman, as well as in Georgia, Hawaii, Arizona, and California, USA.

ZORAN PAVLOVIĆ
Zoran "Zok" Pavlović is a geographer whose area of professional interest and research is traditional cultural geography, primarily the landscape change in geography of viticulture, the evolution of geographic thought, and geographic education. He completed his Bachelor's and Master's degrees at South Dakota State University and is pursuing a doctorate in geography at the University of Minnesota. Since 2001 he has worked as a contributing author to Chelsea House Publishers/Facts on File series Modern World Nations, Modern World Cultures, and Global Connections.

DOUGLAS A. PHILLIPS
Douglas A. Phillips is a lifelong educator who worked in public education at elementary, secondary, college, and university levels for 26 years. His specializations are in civic education, geography, history, the other social sciences, and in curriculum development. He has facilitated and helped to write over 100 curricula including post-war national efforts in Macedonia and Bosnia and Herzegovina. He has been President of the National Council for Geographic Education and is the founder of the South Dakota and Alaska Councils for the Social Studies in the United States. Among the many awards he has received is the Outstanding Service Award from the National Council for the Social Studies. He has also been recognized by the US Congress for his contributions.

MICHAEL PRETES
Michael Pretes is Assistant Professor of Geography at the University of North Alabama, USA. He holds a BA from the University of California—Berkeley, an MA from Northwestern University, and a PhD from the Australian National University in Canberra. He has held research and teaching positions at the University of Calgary in Canada; the University of Lapland in Finland; Stanford University, the University of New Mexico, and the University of Hawaii–Hilo, in the United States, among others. He specializes in the development problems of remote regions, the geography of finance, and in tourism.

NOOR ABDUL RAHMAN
Noor Abdul Rahman is a Visiting Fellow at the Department of Geography at the National University of Singapore. Her research interests include migration and Asian transnational domestic workers. She has co-edited a book entitled *Asian Women as Transnational Domestic Workers* and has presented at numerous conferences and workshops on the subject. She is also an activist on migrant workers' issues.

CARLOS RUBINSKY
Carlos Rubinsky received his degree in Business Administration from the Universidad de Buenos Aires, Argentina. Also a keen artist, Carlos studied painting at the Betzalel Academy in Jerusalem, Israel. He has presented his artwork in collective exhibitions and one-man shows in Argentina and in Mexico and the USA.

ROGER SANDALL
Roger Sandall studied anthropology at the University of Auckland, then did postgraduate work in anthropology and fine arts at Columbia University in New York. He has written on literature, philosophy, and the arts in *Art International, Commentary, The New Criterion, Merkur, Social Science and Modern Society*, and *Encounter*. His book *The Culture Cult* was published in 2001.

MARIANNA SHAHINYAN
Marianna Shahinyan is a management consulting professional with particular expertise in the public utilities in countries with economies in transition. She worked in the development sector of the former Soviet Union republics on projects targeting water supply and sanitation, providing management consulting services to the World Bank and other major financial institutions. She completed her Bachelor's degree in political science and holds an MA in business management from the Kingston University in London.

DR R. B. SINGH
Dr R. B. Singh is reader and deputy coordinator in the Department of Geography at the Delhi School of Economics, University of Delhi, India. He is Secretary General of the National Association of Geographers, India (NAGI). Dr Singh has specialized in land and water management, mountain studies, land use/cover change, disaster management, remote sensing and GIS technology, and has served on many committees and research programs. He has to his credit 31 research volumes and books and more than 150 research papers in national and international journals.

BARRY STONE
Barry Stone is an author and travel writer and has contributed to reference books on topics ranging from history and an anthology of the world's greatest inventions to geology and cutting-edge residential architecture. A graduate of the Australian College of Journalism, he has written on the natural and built environment for some of Australia's largest daily newspapers.

DANIEL WAGNER
Daniel Wagner is an undergraduate student at the University of North Alabama, USA. He is majoring in geography and geology, and has traveled extensively in Europe, Africa, and South America.

PORNSAWAT WATHANAKUL
Pornsawat Wathanakul received her Dr. rer. nat. (Mineralogy and Geology of Mineral Deposits) from RWTH Aachen, Germany, in 1989. She is now head of the Department of Earth Sciences at Kasetsart University, Bangkok, Thailand. She also serves at the Gem and Jewelry Institute of Thailand as an academic adviser. Her research concentrates on mineral sciences and gem resources and characteristics and geographic origins of gem minerals.

ALEXANDER WEARING
Alexander Wearing is a geography graduate of the University of Canterbury (BSc Hons and MSc). He graduated MSc at Birkbeck College, University of London, and PhD in geography at the University of Otago. He has undertaken contracted research for the former New Zealand Forest Service, the Department of Lands and Survey, and more recently, the Agricultural Research Group on Sustainability, all of which involved mixtures of ecological and geomorphological surveys. Since 1999, he has been employed as a sessional lecturer in the Department of Geography at the University of Otago. His current research interests include plant ecology, changing landscapes, and environmental history.

COLONEL (RET.) QUINTIN WIGHT
With a background in science and English, Quintin spent 37 years as an engineering officer in the Royal Canadian Air Force and Canadian Forces. He has had a life-long interest in minerals, and lectures and writes extensively on the subject. The mineral quintinite was named for him in 1992, and his book, *The Complete Book of Micro-mounting* was published in 1993.

WILLOW WIGHT
After graduation from the University of Toronto as an organic chemist, Willow worked in research before switching careers to gemmology. She worked for three years with the gem collections of the Smithsonian Institution and for 32 years at the Canadian Museum of Nature in Ottawa. She was the editor of the quarterly journal *Canadian Gemmologist* for 25 years, and has just become Editor Emeritus.

GEORGE WINGFIELD
George Wingfield has a BA Hons Degree in Natural Sciences from Trinity College, Dublin. He has written and lectured on a number of subjects, such as prehistory and the ancient sites, astronomy, ufology, and crop circles. Recent titles include *Belgium* (Modern World Nations), *Glastonbury*, and *Prehistoric Sacred Sites of Wessex*. Recently, he has guided groups on tours of the ancient sites of the United Kingdom.

GAMINI G. ZOYSA
Gamini Zoysa attained a MSc in geology in Moscow and a Post Graduate Diploma in mineral exploration from ITC, Delft, Netherlands. He received a Diploma in Gemmology from FGA in London, and became a Graduate Gemologist at the Gemological Institute of America (GIA) in 2001. Mr Zoysa is a Fellow of the Gemmological Association of Great Britain, and a member of the Gemological Institute of America and the Institute of Mining and Metallurgy in London. He has lectured in gemology in Sri Lankan universities. Mr Zoysa has contributed to a variety of gemological books and journals.

HANCO ZWAAN
Dr Hanco Zwaan, FGA, joined the National Museum of Natural History Naturalis, Leiden, Netherlands, in 1995, as curator of minerals and gems and director of the Netherlands Gemmological Laboratory. After studying geology and mineralogy at university, Zwaan gained experience in gemmology and diamond grading. Dr Zwaan has a PhD in geology from Free University of Amsterdam.

INTRODUCTION

SL
SL

The Blue Planet

Earth, from distant space, appears as a small, fragile, marble-like sphere floating nearly alone through the dark and seemingly endless heavens. Yet like many marbles, upon closer inspection the planet exhibits a remarkable variety of colors and patterns. Illuminated and dark sides reveal that as a planet within the Solar System, it has a source of light and other energy. Dark patches appear in sharp contrast to areas of white; elsewhere shades of blue, green, and yellow appear. Even from a distant vantage point, the planet's remarkable diversity becomes apparent.

Far right Space exploration has enabled us to see our planet from far above. Pictured is the docked space shuttle *Atlantis* (STS-115). In 2006, *Atlantis* successfully transported six astronauts to the International Space Station.

Previous pages Isolated from the rest of the world until recently, the Longhorn Miao people of Guizhou, China, maintain long-held customs. Headwear made from horns–often adorned with long lengths of wool, hair or other textiles–has given these unique people thei r tribal name.

Right The Australian monolith Uluru (Ayers Rock) rises 1,130 feet (345 m) out of a vast, flat, arid plain of red soil. The rock itself changes color throughout the day—from a soft reddish brown, to a deep red, then a vibrant orange—as the sun strikes its surface from varying angles.

Below The Rocky Mountains in Glacier National Park, Montana, USA, show the shale layers that were originally laid down on an ancient seafloor. These mountains were sculpted over time by the erosional forces of glaciation.

A telescopic view clearly reveals Earth's four spheres. Clouds appear as patches of white and indicate that the planet has an atmosphere. Vast areas of dark blue and smaller areas of white scattered here and there indicate water and ice of the hydrosphere. The solid portion of Earth's surface, the lithosphere, appears in the outlines of landmasses. Various color changes appearing on the land give evidence of the various ecosystems that form the flora and diverse faunal habitats of the biosphere. Earth, among the planets, is distinctive in that the composition of its atmosphere and temperature, land and water, and plant life make possible the existence of animals—including *Homo sapiens*. This remarkable volume portrays in atlas format the fascinating geography of Earth, a unique planet and our home within the vast universe.

From a closer vantage point, a macroscopic view of Earth reveals many more details. Continents and oceans appear clearly. It becomes apparent that land (29 percent) and water (71 percent) are disproportionate in area, a reality that is recognized in Earth's nickname, "The Blue Planet."

Various colors, textures, and patterns clearly emerge on land surfaces. They range from the dark band of equatorial rainforests through the light colors of desert surfaces that are all but void of plant life. In some locations the surface is white, revealing a cover of glacial ice or snow. Each of these conditions is the

product of different temperature and moisture regimes. Even a distant view shows clearly that some areas of Earth's surface are warm whereas others are cold. The same holds true for the distribution of moisture, with some areas being very moist whereas others are parched. Details of the hydrosphere also emerge more clearly in a macroscopic view. Thousands of lakes, countless rivers and streams, and areas of frozen moisture now appear. So do seas, gulfs, and bays. Land features such as mountain ranges and vast plains also appear more clearly, as do peninsulas and islands.

A mesoscopic view of Earth provides a larger scale and much more detailed Earth view. Distinct patterns—some seemingly random and others in what appears to be an orderly

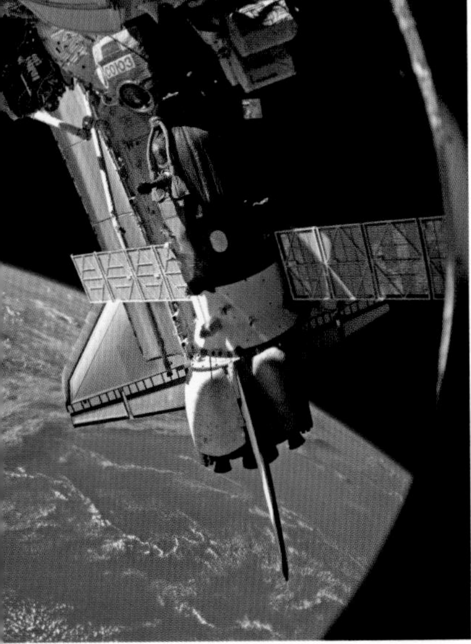

arrangement—begin to emerge. The distribution of vegetation, for example, suggests a close association with conditions of weather and climate. Rather than merely forests, grasslands, and deserts, each biome assumes its individual character. Woodlands become tropical rainforests, mid-latitude deciduous and evergreen forests, and poleward taiga. In turn, climate and flora have a profound effect upon soils and faunal habitat. Most natural lakes occur in poleward latitudes of the Northern hemisphere, or at high elevations, suggesting the glacial origin of perhaps 90 percent of all such bodies of water. Rivers and their basins are ubiquitous in humid areas and become sparse in arid lands. Yet the great importance of their life-giving moisture becomes evident in the narrow green strips that parallel their course through desert regions.

Numerous environmental interactions begin to appear with a mesoscopic view. Many mountain ranges, for example, have lush woodlands on one side and desert or scrub on the other, suggesting a relationship between prevailing winds, moisture availability, and plant life. Periodic changes in ground cover provide a hint of Earth's rhythmic seasonal oscillations. Here and there, changes in colors, textures, and patterns suggest yet another element of geographic complexity—humans and their imprint on Earth's surface.

Finally, a microscopic view affords a close-up look at the elements that contribute to the incredible diversity and complexity of Earth's surface. A close inspection soon reveals that no two locations on Earth's surface are identical. Rather, the physical and human elements appear as a quilted and seemingly bewildering mosaic of features and conditions. The land assumes myriad forms. Mountains give way to hills and plateaus and finally to broad plains. But each of these features is unique in its own right as a result of having been acted upon by various weathering agents and the sculpting work of moving ice, water, and wind, as well as the effect of gravity.

Conditions of weather and climate vary greatly from place to place. On the Hawaiian island of Kaua'i, one can stand in a semi-desert surrounded by cacti and watch rain falling on Mt Wai'ale'ale—one of the world's wettest spots—just a few miles away. On the nearby island of Maui, one can stand on the slope of 10,000-foot (3,050 m) Mt Pu'u'ula'ula and because of differences in elevation, slope, and exposure to sunlight, be within just a few miles of nearly all of Earth's climates and ecosystems from tropical rainforest to desert scrub and atop the mountain, subarctic tundra. Water features, soils, and animal habitat all correspond closely to climatic conditions. Only mineral resources are random in distribution, and even they correspond closely to past geologic conditions.

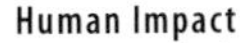

Human Impact

The microscopic view also reveals the agent that for many thousands of years has been most instrumental in altering the surface of Earth—humans and their cultural imprint. Humans are not evenly distributed across Earth's surface—in some areas, people are tightly clustered. Most such regions offer an environment that is conducive to agricultural development, or offer economic gain through employment in the industrial or service sector. Populations range from more than one billion in both China and India to about 800 in the smallest independent state, Vatican City.

Population density also varies greatly. Some areas, such as Bangladesh, support almost 2,700 people per square mile (1,050 per km^2) with an economy largely dependent upon subsistence farming of rice. Most of Siberia, the Sahara, northern Canada, much of Australia, and the Amazon Basin, on the other hand, support population densities of fewer than two people per square mile (less than one person per square kilometer). These places are remote, have challenging natural environments, and offer few economic opportunities.

Today, one-half of the world's population is urban, a figure that is expanding rapidly. Metropolitan Tokyo, home to an estimated 33 million people, is one of some 25 megacities—urban centers with populations that exceed 10 million. In Tokyo, the population is supported by the country's thriving industry, commerce, and service-related industries. In other cities, such as Mumbai (Bombay) in India, and Karachi in Pakistan, most of the people are impoverished. Surprisingly, perhaps, considering the concern expressed by many in regard to population growth, the majority of Earth's surface supports a very sparse population. People tend to avoid those areas where life is difficult.

Economic and land use practices also vary greatly from place to place. Some regions specialize in primary activities such as farming, mining, logging, and fishing.

Top Masai Mara women from Kenya wear traditional clothing and jewelry to sing and perform tribal dances. It is believed these warrior people migrated from North Africa, arriving in Kenya around the middle of the fifteenth century.

Above Humans have created many of the patterns visible from above Earth. We have carved terraces into mountainsides, for example, to allow us to use more land for agriculture. These workers in Japan are harvesting tea.

Above left A polar bear keeps her cubs warm in the snow of Hudson Bay, Manitoba, Canada. Manitoba's polar bears are listed as protected under the *Wildlife Act*, and threatened under the *Endangered Species Act*.

Left This aerial view shows a modern, crowded Yokohama. With a population of over 3 million, this port city on Honshu island grew from a small fishing village to become the second most populous urban area in Japan, after Tokyo.

Right *Louis XVI (1754–93) Giving Instructions to La Perouse, 29th June 1785* was painted by Nicolas Andre Monsiau in 1817. King Louis was a keen amateur cartographer and geographer, so he planned the three-year voyage of exploration to the Pacific Ocean for the naval hero La Perouse.

Bottom Though we have physical evidence that humans have been graphically representing their world since the third millennium BCE, it is quite likely that the earliest humans drew crude maps. Pictured is one of countless maps of the world still in existence.

Below La Sala delle Carte Geografiche (Hall of Geographical Maps) in the Palazzo Vecchio, Florence, Italy, houses a series of more than fifty, sixteenth-century paintings depicting maps of various parts of the world. This 1575 oil painting shows Japan at that time.

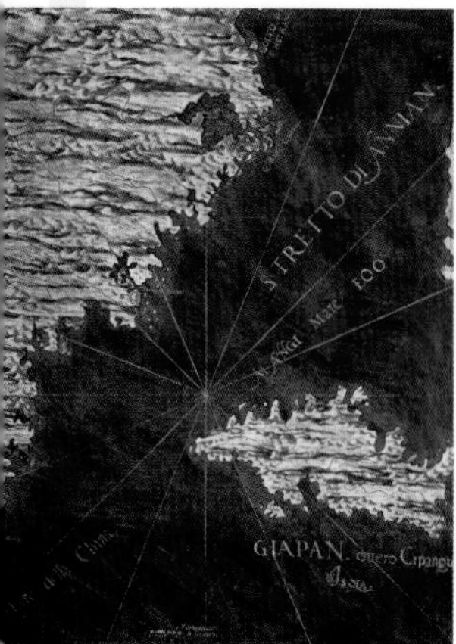
STRETTO DI ANIAN
GIAPAN

Agriculture alone can be classified under more than a dozen different systems, ranging from nomadic herding and low-yielding tropical shifting cultivation to dairying and specialized plantation agriculture.

Secondary industries are even more varied in their nature. They involve manufacturing and construction, as well as the processing and use of natural resources and raw materials. Many of the world's great cities began as manufacturing centers and grew in response to expanding trade and commerce. Today, much of the world's economy is post-industrial, or service related. Economic well-being varies significantly, ranging from Luxembourg's US$80,000 per year per capita gross domestic product to US$300 GDP in the Democratic Republic of Congo.

A microscopic view also reveals the great importance of political influences. Earth's surface is politically divided into almost 200 states. They range in size from Russia's nearly 6.6 million square miles (17 million km^2) to tiny 0.17 square-mile (0.44 km^2) Vatican City. Humans follow numerous religious faiths (more than 3,000), speak a veritable Babel of tongues (about 6,800), live in myriad types of dwellings, dine on an incredible array of foods, and drink a large number of different beverages. In *Earth* you will sample much of the world's fascinating diversity, both physical and cultural, and country by country.

Order from Chaos

Geography is the field of study that provides the methods, perspectives, tools, and techniques needed to make order from chaos in studying and seeking to explain the different conditions that exist on Earth's surface. As the oldest existing science—preceded only by Greek cosmography—this is the vital role geography has played since its inception among philosophers and cosmographers of classical Greek antiquity. As coined and defined by Eratosthenes in about 200 BCE, *geography* means "to describe the earth." But all sciences describe some aspect of the planet. What, then, sets geography apart from other sciences, arts, or humanities?

It is apparent that geographers focus attention on all the elements of Earth's surface, both physical and human. Certainly it is not a science based on the study of a particular phenomenon. This is the key to understanding the discipline: Geography is based not on what geographers study; rather, it stands apart from other sciences on the basis of how they organize, analyze, and present information pertaining to Earth's diverse features and conditions. Were the planet's surface homogeneous, there would be no raison d'être for geography.

A simple analogy can be drawn between geography and history, both of which are based on methodologies, the unique way each organizes and analyzes information. Fundamentally, historians organize information temporally, whereas geographers do so spatially. Historians ask "When?" Geographers ask "Where?"

Simply defined, geographers seek to explain three things: "What is where, why there, and why care?" in regard to the various physical and human features, conditions, distributions, and patterns to be found on Earth's surface.

ORBIS TERRARUM NOVA ET ACCURATISSIMA TABULA
POLUS ARCTICUS
POLUS ANTARCTICUS

The Language of Maps

Maps are a geographer's best friend. The single most important "tool" used in depicting and studying the world about us, they provide a graphic way of organizing the wonder we hold about the world's places. Maps help answer questions about places whether local and familiar or distant and unknown. Humans, by nature, are curious about places; we want and often need to know where they are, what they are like, how they got that way, how they are similar to or different from other places, and how we can get there. Poring over maps in search of such information, looking at maps as objects of art and history, making maps, being fascinated by maps, and collecting maps are all marks of a geographer.

A spatial perspective is the primary attribute that sets geographers apart from others. This unique way of viewing the world involves seeing places in terms of their location. But location is simply the beginning; to fully appreciate the geography of a place, one must know its physical and human conditions and how they relate to other features, conditions, and places. When an area is relatively homogeneous in regard to one or more environmental features, regions can be delineated. Regions are the geographer's primary method of classifying, organizing, and analyzing information pertaining to the diverse conditions of Earth's surface. All of these geographic elements can be portrayed cartographically (cartography is the science of mapping and a cartographer is one who makes maps).

Maps have been drawn and used for millennia. The oldest known and preserved maps were etched into clay tablets by Sumerians during the third millennium BCE. Many if not most ancient cultures created maps and used them for various purposes. Maps as we know them today, including the use of a system of coordinates and map projections, were first drafted by Greek geographers. Although there are earlier examples of maps being bound in a single volume, the credit for the first modern atlas is accorded to the Flemish geographer–cartographer, Abraham Ortelius. His *Theatrum Orbis Terrarum*, which appeared in 1570, was a compilation of 53 map-sheets covering countries of the known world. It was not until 1595 that another Flemish cartographer, Gerardus Mercator, used the term "atlas" in reference to a bound collection of maps.

It is true that maps have many uses and can reveal many things. They also vary greatly in their scale, style, content, and other salient features. It is essential, therefore, that maps be used in the appropriate context. Thematic maps, for example, are those that usually show a single topic, such as climate, ecosystem, population density, or primary economic activity. Many such maps appear in the topical introduction to this atlas. They are small-scale maps designed to convey a general impression of Earth's diverse natural and human conditions, their spatial distributions, and the ways in which many conditions—such as climate, precipitation, ecosystem, and population density—are intricately interrelated. Regional maps, on the other hand, usually show a variety of general information such as major political boundaries, terrain, water features, communities, and significant transportation linkages. The quantity and quality of detail, of course, varies greatly with scale or area covered. A typical world regional map would be of no use in planning a trip by motor vehicle, whereas the more detailed map of a country could be helpful.

Above This satellite image highlights the parallel ridges and deep gorges of northern Australia's MacDonnell Ranges. The mountains were formed some 350 million years ago when volcanic activity created a range of scarlet, iron oxide-saturated quartzite.

In addition to the various topical and regional information presented, many maps speak yet another language, that of *toponymy* (place names). Toponyms are often as revealing about a place as are more traditional forms of documentation. They can provide essential information about a place's history and geography. Terrain, vegetation, animal life, water features, minerals, and even soil conditions are often incorporated in toponyms. Additionally, they often provide clues regarding aboriginal heritage, ethnicity of settlers, significant historical events, aspects of transportation and accessibility, religion, and economic activity. Many others document factors of site selection, community function, and relative location.

Numerous maps are also designed to graphically present abstract ideas. Topical maps, for example, show distributions and patterns of specific features, including religion, language, land use, population and settlement, land forms, communication networks, and a vast array of other physical and human features. By comparing and/or contrasting sets of information, maps can bring many problems and ideas into sharp focus. A map showing the concentration of proven petroleum and natural gas reserves, for example, can raise many questions with respect to terrain, distribution routes, or political conditions.

Maps have served as a record for humankind over the centuries, and our fascination with maps and the world we live in is an ongoing interest. Between the covers of this book, the world will be revealed in mapping, information, and images. Take the opportunity to visit the fascinating places around our globe through the pages of *Earth*.

CHARLES F. GRITZNER

Above Vincenzo Coronelli, Cartographer to King Louis XIV, produced hundreds of maps, including this one of Africa. His maps and globes provided the most complete geographical knowledge of the world in the late seventeenth century.

Left This charming sixteenth-century illustrated map of Eskisehir is now held in Topkapi Palace Museum, Istanbul. The Turkish town of Eskisehir was founded on the Porsuk River in the first millennium; today it is a bustling industrial city.

Following pages New York as seen from the Empire State Building. This American city is famous across the globe as a symbol of the phenomenal human impact on planet Earth.

1
THE WORLD WE LIVE IN

IGNIS
Septentrio
AMERICA
Anno Domini 1492 a Christophoro Columbo nomine Regis Castellæ primum detecta, et ab Americo Vespucio nomen sortita 1499.
AME RICA
SEPTENTRIO
NALIS
Circul. Arctic.
MAR DEL NORT
Tropicus Cancri
Circulus Æquinoctialis
MAR DEL ZVR
OCEANVS PERVVI ENSIS.
AMERICA MERIDIONALIS
Tropicus Capricorni
MARE PACIFICVM
TERRA AVSTRA LIS INCOGNITA.
L.S.
Varias a variis et antehac editas esse, et quotidie edi tabulas totius Mundi situm depingentes, cuiq; notum est: hac tamen nullam accuratiorem elegantioremq; esse libere dico; quippe quæ succinctius quam omnes aliæ singula depingit, multosque errores aliarum tabular. corrigit. Imprimis vero in Oceano Tartarico et circa illum, multa aliter meliusq; delineat: nec non in nova Guinea, et India Orientali, ut et in America Sept. et Mar del Zur, ac versus Fretum Magellanicū plurima innovat mutatque. vale et fruere.
Circulus Antarcticus
Meridies
AQVA
Fretum Magellanicum
Nova Anglia
Nova Britannia
Fretum Davis
Frisland
Asores Ins.
I de Cabo Verde
Al. Flandricæ
Nova Albion
Florida
Nov Belgium
MARE VIRGI NIUM
SINVS MEXICANVS
Guaymures
Rio de la Plata
Fretum le Maire
Tierra del Fuego

RECORDING EARTH

AËR
CLAVDIVS PTOLOMÆVS
Septentrio
MARE
ATLAN
TICVM
MARE TARTA
RICVM
OCEANVS
ÆTHIOPICVS
MAR DI
INDIA
MARE LANT
CHIDOL
OCEANVS CHINENSIS
TERRA
AVS TRALIS IN
COG NITA
Doctissimis Ornatissimisq; Viris
D.D. Davidi Sanclaro, Antonio de
Willon, et D. Martinio, Matheseos
in illustriss. Academia Parisiensi
Professoribus eximiis in veræ
amicitiæ μνημόσυνον D.D.
Henr. Hondius Aº. 1630.
Meridies
TERRA
IODOCVS HONDIVS

Cartography

Cartography is the process of mapmaking: it is both an art and a science. Many maps from past eras were lavishly illustrated and often had a more aesthetic than functional role. Today, the process of mapmaking has never been so accurate, with technology allowing computer-generated maps using satellite tracking and aerial surveying.

Previous pages This seventeenth-century map divides the world into two hemispheres centered around the known landmasses. In tribute, great mapmakers such as Ptolemy and Mercator are depicted in its corners.

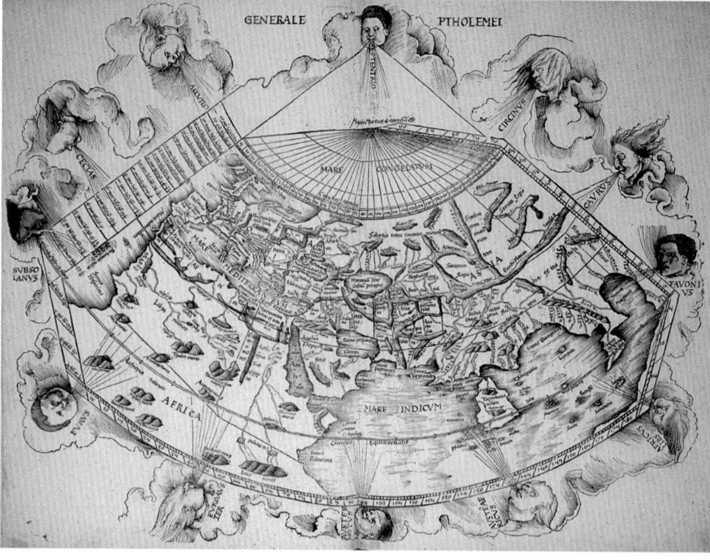
GENERALE
PTHOLEMEI
MARE
CONGELATVM
AFRICA
MARE INDICVM
SVBSOLANVS
FAVONIVS

Right Derived from the observations of Ptolemy in the second century CE, a sixteenth-century map of the world stretches from Britain in the west to Asia in the east.

The history of cartography is a long one. The oldest surviving maps are thought to have been developed in Babylon, in what is modern-day Iraq. Dating from about 2300 BCE, these maps were drawn on clay tablets. It is reasonable to assume, however, that humans were using crudely constructed maps long before this time.

It was in ancient Greece that cartography became a serious endeavor. Famous scholar Claudius Ptolemy wrote *Geographike hyphygesis* (Guide to Geography) in the first century of the common era. Many geographers see this book as the birth of their discipline; in it were numerous maps making the book not only a discussion of geography but also, perhaps, the first ever atlas. Ptolemy was the first to use a grid system on his maps, inventing the concept of latitude and longitude. Of course Ptolemy's *Geographike* contains many inaccuracies, reflecting the fact much of his cartography consisted of guesswork.

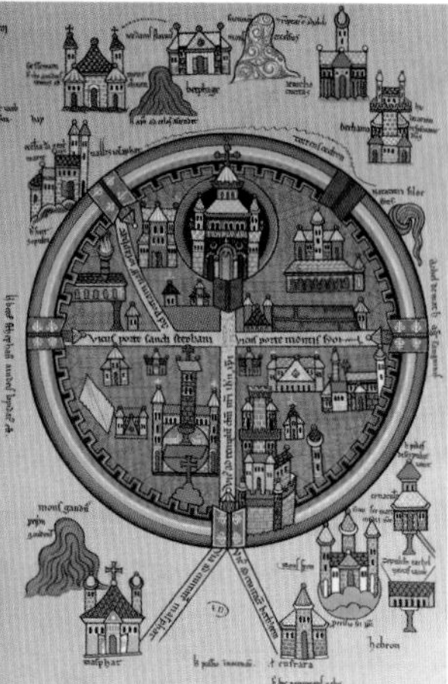

Above In medieval maps, Jerusalem was considered the center of the world and maps were illustrated figuratively rather than accurately. This map is a stylized depiction of the Holy Land with the Temple in the middle.

Right Based on the observations of Arabic cartographer al-Idrisi, this engraved copy of the original was made by Doctor Vincent for a thirteenth-century history of the voyage of Arrian.

Roman Maps

The Romans had a keen interest in geography, largely as a result of their extensive empire. Roman cartographers drew maps of the lands that they conquered. Their maps showed important detail, such as cities, rivers and other natural features, and road networks.

One of the more notable Roman maps is the Table of Peutinger (the existing map is thought to be a thirteenth-century copy of the original Roman map created in the first or second century CE), which is perhaps the world's first road map. It includes the location of cities and the roads connecting them, and the distances between important centers.

With the collapse of the Roman Empire, Europe entered the medieval period when cartography was dominated by religion and the power of the Church. Most European maps from this time were centered around Jerusalem and the Holy Land. These maps had little accuracy.

Arabic Cartography

While European cartographers were drawing religiously motivated maps, Arabic cartographers were generating remarkably accurate maps. Arabic cartography followed and advanced on the methods adopted by the Greeks. At this time in history the Arabs were trading as far afield as China and were developing a strong understanding of the physical world.

One of the most famous of the Arabic cartographers is Abu Abdullah ibn Idrisi, born in 1099. Al-Idrisi is said to have produced many works on geography that drew heavily on Greek studies of the world.

Chinese Cartography

As in many of the sciences, the contribution of Chinese scholars to cartography has not been widely acknowledged. By the third century CE, the Chinese were including a highly sophisticated system of graduated divisions on their maps to increase accuracy and detail. P'ei Hsui produced an 18-page atlas of the Chinese Empire in the year 267.

The Chinese continued to enhance their cartography throughout the centuries. During the Sung Dynasty (960–1279 CE), maps were developed that displayed North in the upper part of the map, a custom that continues in cartography today.

Printing Maps and Books

By the 1400s, the Renaissance was transforming all aspects of European society including science, religion, and culture.

The invention of the printing press by Johannes Gutenberg in 1440 meant that cartography could become a commercial enterprise. Copies of maps no longer had to be hand-drawn and, as a result, maps took on a more functional and less artistic aspect. By the mid 1500s, maps were being engraved on copper plates for printing, allowing for greater accuracy and detail in the copies.

King Alfonso V of Portugal commissioned Italian monk Fra Mauro to make a thorough map of the world. Taking two years, Fra Mauro completed the gigantic map (it was more than 4 meters [13 ft] square) in 1459. Although the map was inevitably inaccurate given that much of the world (particularly the Southern Hemisphere) remained unknown to Europeans at this time, it is significant because it was one of the first maps to attempt to illustrate the relative size of each of the continents.

Many of the Renaissance's greatest thinkers displayed an interest in cartography. Leonardo da Vinci and Peter Apian, for example, drew various maps of the world and their surrounds. It was, however, a Flemish maker of globes and navigational instrumentation who transformed cartography. Gerardus Mercator challenged accepted mapmaking methods when he introduced his cylindrical grid system, which became known as the Mercator projection.

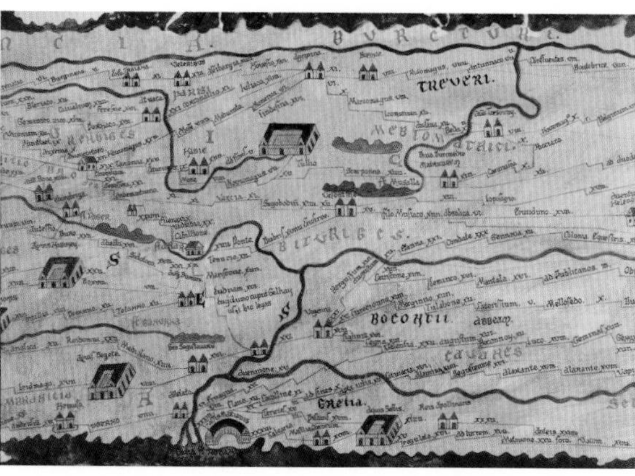
TREVERI

Left Dated 1763, this Chinese map claims to be a copy of a map made in 1418, coinciding with the voyages of Chinese explorer Zheng He (1405–1432). Mapmaking in China was an ancient scholarly tradition and this map adds evidence to recent claims that Chinese maps aided European explorers such as Columbus, da Gama, and Magellan.

Far left Detail of the Gallo-Roman segment of the Table of Peutinger, the world's first road map. This vellum facsimile of the third-century original is part of the collection of the Musée de la Poste in Paris.

THE MERCATOR PROJECTION

In 1569, the most famous map ever produced was released by Gerardus Mercator. The significance of his map lay in the grid that he used. All maps face the problem of displaying a spherical shape (Earth) on a flat two-dimensional surface (a sheet of paper). Invariably, the shapes and sizes of landmasses are distorted, making navigation using the map challenging.

Mercator's solution to the problem was to display all the compass lines and rhumb lines (curved lines that link the poles) as straight lines. Essentially, Mercator had squared the spherical earth, as in the eighteenth-century map below. He did this by systematically increasing the distance between the lines of latitude as they moved away from the equator.

The Mercator map projection does not accurately show the shape and size of the continents, as the scale changes as one moves away from the equator. However, the projection is the most widely used of map projections, possibly because of its popularity with navigators and because it neatly displays the world that most of us live in. The extreme north and south are largely misshapen but fewer people live in those parts of Earth.

Geographers have been critical of the projection, as it shows Europe to be substantially larger than it really is and downsizes Africa and other parts of the world. To some political and social geographers, it represents a colonialist notion, displaying power and authority centered around Europe. That Mercator actually set out to achieve this is unlikely; it is more likely that this anomaly is a consequence of the position of Europe. The real problem, however, is that so many maps use this projection that it has become the view that many people have of the world, encouraging people to misunderstand the real geography of Earth.

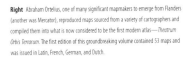

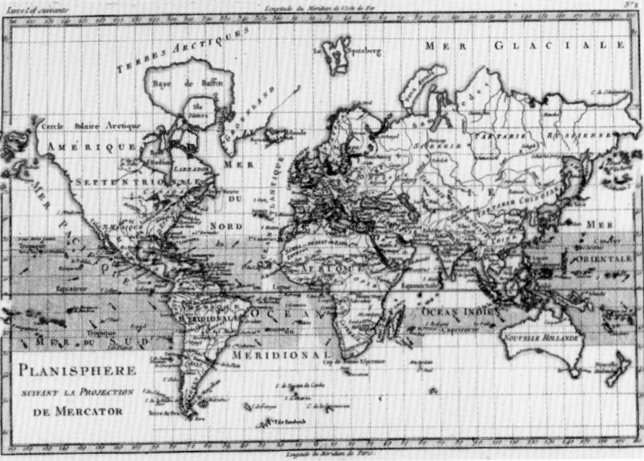
MER GLACIALE
PLANISPHERE
SUIVANT LA PROJECTION
DE MERCATOR
AMÉRIQUE
MERIDIONAL

Above The *Mappa Mundi* of Fra Mauro, a Camaldolese monk from Murano, was commissioned by King Alfonso V of Portugal. Fra Mauro took two years to complete this huge work, finishing his task in 1459. Despite its monastic author, the map has South at the top, as was typical of Muslim maps.

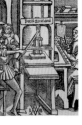

Near right The invention of the printing press by Johannes Gutenberg in 1440 meant that maps, engraved on copper plates, could be mass-produced in fine detail and without the risk of errors creeping in. It is no coincidence that some of the greatest strides in cartography and world exploration took place during this era.

Right Abraham Ortelius, one of many significant mapmakers to emerge from Flanders (another was Mercator), reproduced maps sourced from a variety of cartographers and compiled them into what is now considered to be the first modern atlas—*Theatrum Orbis Terrarum*. The first edition of this groundbreaking volume contained 53 maps and was issued in Latin, French, German, and Dutch.

EVROPAM
sive
CELTICAM
VETEREM.
sic describere conabar
Abrahamus Ortelius.
OCEANVS ATLANTICVS
MEDITERRANEVM
AFRICÆ PARS.
SCYTHIA
Evert Symons z. Hamers veldt sculpsit.

Theatrum Orbis Terrarum

Born in Antwerp, Flanders, in 1527, Abraham Ortelius produced one of the most famous atlases in *Theatrum Orbis Terrarum* (Theater of the World). This is considered to be the first true modern atlas, in that it contained uniform map sheets that were bound into a single volume. In the history of cartography, this work is without equal. From a wide variety of sources, Ortelius reproduced maps that he credited to the original 87 cartographers in an extensive source list included in the work.

Theatrum Orbis Terrarum was first released in 1570 and was republished in 31 editions in seven languages before finally going out of print in 1612. More than 3,700 copies of the work were sold, a truly remarkable figure.

The sixteenth, seventeenth, and eighteenth centuries are often referred to as the age of exploration. Navigators from Spain, Portugal, the Italian states, England, and the Netherlands crisscrossed the world in search of new territory and in the pursuit of great empires.

These voyages of discovery took Europeans around the globe and led to an explosion in cartography, as navigational charts and maps became essential to proving and sustaining ownership of vast territories around the world. Navigators such as Cook, Columbus, Tasman, Magellan, La Perouse, and da Gama, had little more to guide them than intuition and myth, and yet they discovered great lands thousands of miles from their homelands.

Modern cartography is perhaps less romantic and certainly less reliant on guesswork and chance. It is a science, complete with satellites and aircraft using complex arrays of sensors. Yet it still retains the sense of artistic expression that developed thousands of years ago.

Modern Cartography and Satellite Imagery

Technology has transformed the way we see the world. The first Moon landing in 1969 and the subsequent exploration of space gave humankind its first opportunity to view Earth from beyond the boundaries of our planet. Some people have gone so far as to suggest that the images of Earth taken from space have had a more profound effect on the environmental movement than any other event.

Right Images from satellite surveys are combined to create this color-coded topographic map of Earth, with dark blue areas representing the lowest points in the planet's surface (under the oceans) and dark brown representing the highest points (mountains).

Above Remote sensing by satellites in low-Earth orbits is often used for military reconnaissance as well as mapping. High-resolution cameras show remarkable detail from hundreds of miles out in space.

Above Geographic information systems (GIS) and satellite communications technology allow access to important maps and geographic information for modern-day explorers, even in very remote locations such as this mountaineer's base camp.

Today, maps are no longer created by guesswork, estimates, and second-hand information; instead they are precise and accurate representations of the world we live in.

Map Projections

Modern cartography produces maps using more complex and more accurate projections, giving us a better notion of the shape of the world. However, the maps in atlases today still face the problems of projecting the three-dimensional sphere that is Earth onto a flat two-dimensional page.

PETERS PROJECTION

Arno Peters, a German journalist, announced his new method of map projection in 1973. He claimed that this projection more fairly showed the world and undid the colonialist bias of maps using the Mercator projection.

The Peters projection does show the relative size of each of the continents far more accurately than previous flat maps. However, the Peters projection still creates an enormous amount of distortion and is not widely used.

ROBINSON PROJECTION

The Robinson projection has become one of the most commonly used projections. Robinson, a US geography professor, released his projection in 1963. Cartesian coordinates are used to create the projection, which uses a straight line for the prime meridian and curves the other meridians (lines of longitude). The lines of latitude are shown as parallel lines.

Robinson's projection avoids the extreme distortions common with most other projections; while the poles are extremely distorted, the distortion declines relatively soon after moving away from the poles.

WINKEL TRIPEL PROJECTION

This projection was developed by German cartographer Oswald Winkel in 1921. His projection attempts to minimize distortions of area, direction, and distance. By not attempting to eliminate any of these considerations, Winkel sought a compromised projection.

This projection was not widely adopted until 1998, when the National Geographic Society announced it was adopting the Winkel Tripel projection as the standard for all its maps. This has ensured that this projection is now one of the most popular.

This map projection has much in common with the Robinson projection (although it was developed years beforehand); however, Winkel uses curved lines for both the lines of longitude and the lines of latitude. Only the equator and the poles are shown as straight lines, along with the prime meridian. This helps to reduce the distortion of shape; although every part of the map suffers from some distortion, no part is extremely distorted.

WATERMAN PROJECTION

The Waterman projection—produced in 1996 by Steve Waterman—built on a method invented by Bernard Cahill called the Butterfly Map. It is based on Waterman's research into the close packing of spheres. The latitudes in the Waterman projection are drawn in three straight line sections. The projection shows reasonably accurate degrees of size, shape, and position. Antarctica has a separate smaller projection. Waterman continues to work on perfecting this projection.

OTHER PROJECTIONS

There are hundreds of map projections currently being used by mapmakers, each striving to overcome the problem of distortion, with no projection having arrived at a definitive solution. Mathematical and computer modelling has produced some radical projections. Polyhedron maps take different portions of the globe and project them onto different faces of the polyhedron (a figure with four or more faces).

These projections are very complex and produce maps that at first seem unrealistic as they are nothing like the projections commonly found in atlases. However, they are the closest we have come to solving the distortion problem in flat maps.

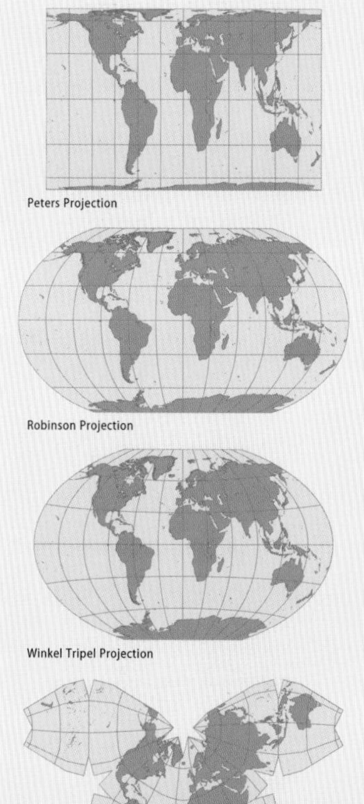
Peters Projection
Robinson Projection
Winkel Tripel Projection
Waterman Projection

Modern Mapping Technology

Remote sensing involves the collection of data about an object from a great distance away. Telescopes were the first remote-sensing instruments, allowing humans to view celestial objects far off in space. Today, remote sensing is also used in reverse, with instruments placed in space to look back at Earth. As well as allowing the first images of Earth from far above its surface, remote sensing is being used to give humans a better understanding of the whole planet.

Remote sensing has allowed cartographers to move into whole new areas of mapmaking. Using information from orbiting satellites, cartographers can now make maps showing the distribution of vegetation and changing patterns of growth. Environmental managers can, for example, use these types of maps and images to track the extent of deforestation. Agronomists can use the satellite images to examine the distribution of crop disease and die back. Meteorologists can use them to predict weather by tracking storms and other weather events, as well as seasonal temperature fluctuations and rainfall patterns.

Most of the satellite images we have come from the Landsat program. Begun in 1972 by the National Aeronautics and Space Administration (NASA) and the US Geological Survey, this program uses Earth-observing satellites to take digital photographs from space. Landsat satellites do not provide close-up images of small objects, such as a single house, but larger objects such as roads, bridges, and other infrastructure are clearly visible. This resolution allows for global coverage, while at the same time revealing the significant features of human activity. One of the useful features of the Landsat program is that individuals can have access to the images that are generated by the satellites for a relatively small cost.

Modern satellites are equipped with a wide variety of sensors and instruments. High-resolution cameras allow very detailed images to be taken from hundreds of miles above the ground. Infrared sensors are used to create heat images, which show variations in land use and vegetation patterns over large areas.

Geographic Information Systems (GIS)

Often referred to simply as GIS, geographic information systems have transformed cartography and geographic understanding. GIS uses computer technology to store, analyze, and present spatial information. These systems work by compiling layers of information; for example, one layer may contain data on the road network, another layer may show river systems, and yet another topography. Some GIS maps may contain hundreds of these layers, each compiled using extensive computer databases. GIS allows operators to analyse the interrelationships between the layers.

Above Nicknamed the "Blue Marble", this very detailed NASA image of Earth was assembled from multiple satellite observations. Viewing the planet from space inspires a new way of thinking about our place in the Solar System.

Right Satellite views, such as this one of the Himalaya mountains in Nepal, present opportunities for both mapmakers and meteorologists, who can use the information gleaned from such observations for more accurate cartography and weather reports.

Top right Some 400 bridges cross the labyrinth of canals that intersects the 120 islands of Venice, Italy, shown in this satellite image from the Advanced Spaceborne Thermal Emission and Reflection Radiometer (ASTER) on NASA's *Terra* satellite.

EXPLORING THE DEEP SEAS

Humans have long been fascinated by the ocean depths. It remains, however, one of the most challenging environments to explore. In many respects, exploring the very deep ocean is as difficult as space exploration. Despite this, over the centuries various instruments have been developed to assist in the mapping of the oceans.

One of the first major expeditions to study the oceans was undertaken when the British converted HMS *Challenger* into a floating laboratory. Between 1872 and 1876 British scientists sailed more than 68,890 nautical miles (127,584 km). They used wire line sounding equipment to systematically measure ocean depths and took thousands of samples (finding 4,700 new species) from every ocean except the Arctic.

In the twentieth century, deep sea exploration advanced dramatically with the development of sonar, which uses sound waves to detect objects in water. The development of ultra-deep submersibles has also been a very important technological advance. The bathysphere was the first real deep-sea submarine. Developed by William Beebe and Otis Barton, the bathysphere was a hollow steel ball about 7 feet (2 m) in diameter that was raised and lowered via a cable connected to the support ship. This cable also carried electrical power and oxygen. In 1934, Beebe and Barton dived to a depth of 3,028 feet (922 m) off the coast of Bermuda.

Although the bathysphere could dive to considerable depths it could only go up and down, with no lateral movement. Belgian scientist Auguste Piccard overcame this when he launched the bathyscaphe, which had far greater maneuverability. In 1953, Piccard and his son Jacques took the *Trieste* to a depth of 10,330 feet (3,148 m) in the Mediterranean Sea. The *Trieste* was then sold to the US Navy, who took the machine to the very bottom of the Mariana Trench (the lowest point in Earth's crust) off the coast of Guam in the Pacific Ocean, reaching a depth of 35,800 feet (10,911 m).

One of the most famous submersibles is *Alvin*, which is operated by the Woods Hole Oceanographic Institution. This is considered the most productive of all the machines, making around 150 dives every year. It was originally built in 1964 and has been rebuilt several times since. *Alvin*'s most famous mission was to retrieve a hydrogen bomb from a US bomber aircraft that had crashed in the Mediterranean Sea in 1966.

Today submersibles are designed with great maneuverability and dive time. These machines are becoming lighter and can stay underwater longer. A host of unmanned submersibles is used to collect samples and map the ocean floor.

Below, left to right Beebe and Barton's bathysphere allowed a single diver to reach 3,028 feet (922 m) below the sea in 1934, but this feat was eclipsed 20 years later by Auguste Piccard's *Trieste*, which reached the bottom of the Mariana Trench. Today, the submersible *Alvin* can reach similar depths and perform more complex tasks.

TRIESTE

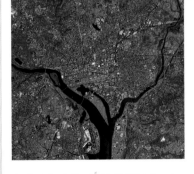

Above The White House, the Jefferson Memorial, and the Washington Monument with its shadow are all visible in this near-infrared image of Washington DC, USA. With 15-meter spatial resolution, NASA's Advanced Spaceborne Thermal Emission and Reflection Radiometer (ASTER) can see individual buildings.

Above center This satellite image, which was taken in August 2006, shows most of Greece, with its jagged coastline and many islands and peninsulas. Also shown are the countries that surround Greece. To the north are Albania, Macedonia, and Bulgaria, while Turkey lies to the east. The small gray patch at the bottom center of the image is the city of Athens.

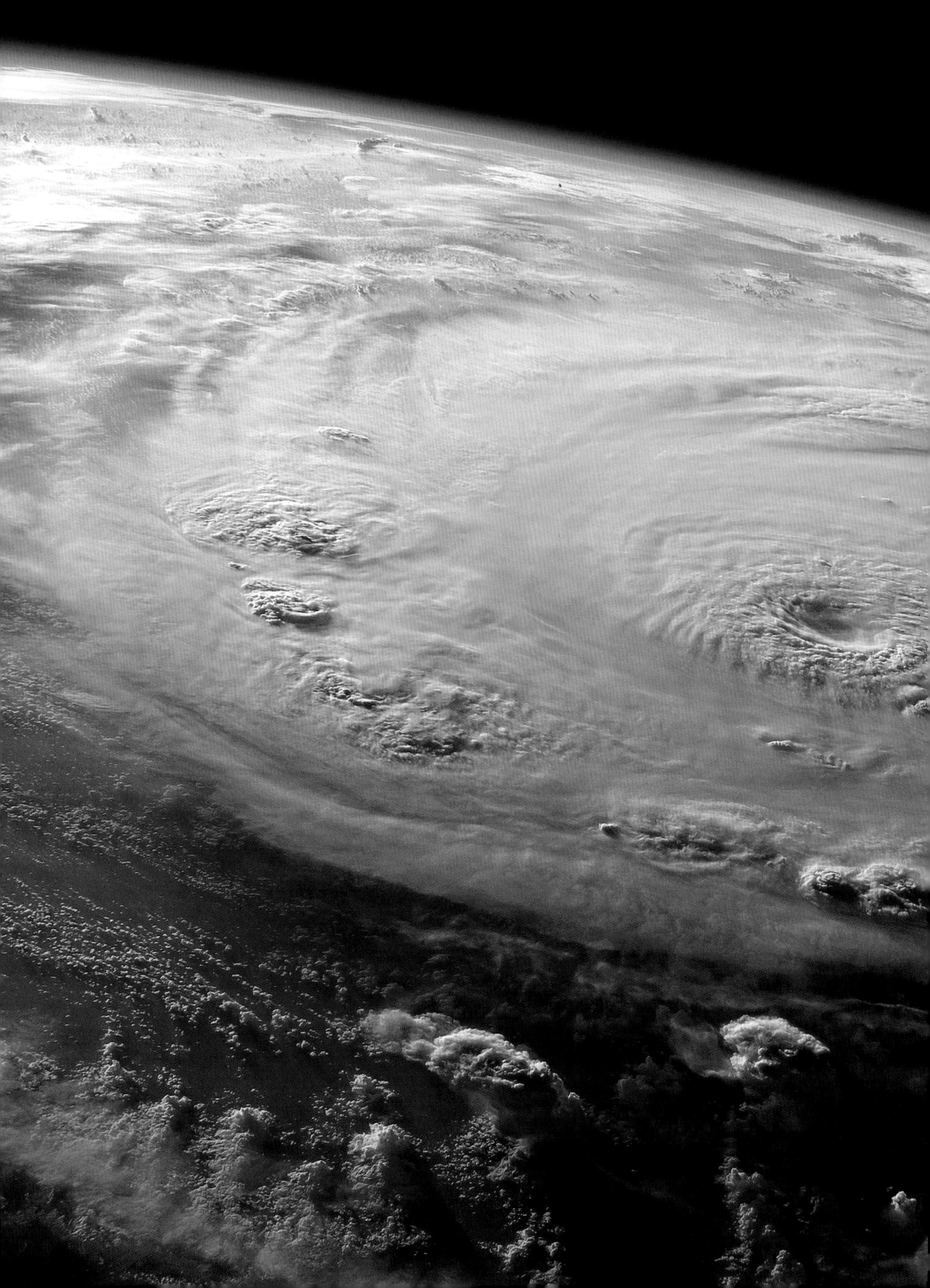

PHYSICAL EARTH

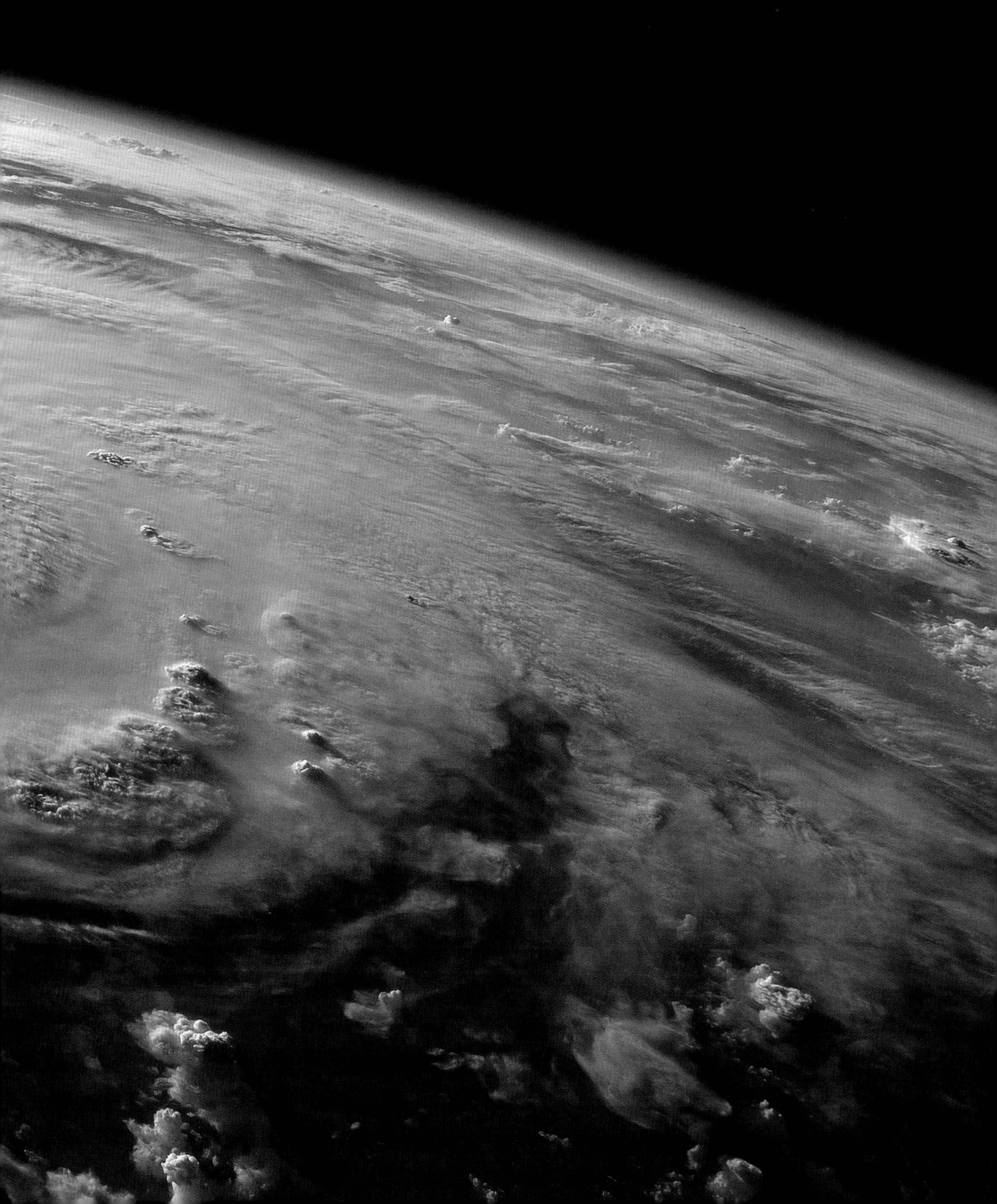

Our Place in Space

We live on a small blue orb, circling a nondescript sun in a spiral arm of a multibillion-star galaxy in an unimaginably large, 13.7 billion-year-old universe. This rather long sentence says much about our status in the cosmic scheme of things: Earth is merely an insignificant blue dot in the vastness of space.

Previous pages Hurricane Felix swirls over the Caribbean Sea in this satellite image, taken on September 3, 2007.

Top right This view of the rising Earth greeted the Apollo 8 astronauts as they came from behind the Moon after the lunar orbit insertion burn. The photo is displayed here in its original orientation.

Below An artist's conception of a young star system showing gas giant planets forming in the gap between the inner disk of dust and gas around the star (where the rocky planets of our Solar System formed). It also shows the outer ring of debris that may eventually form asteroids, comets, and possibly more planets.

Understanding our place in the universe has not come quickly or easily. For thousands of years, everyone simply assumed that Earth was the center of the universe and the Sun, Moon, planets, and stars all revolved around us. Less than 500 years ago the Sun replaced Earth as both the hub of the Solar System and the focal point of the cosmos. It was fewer than 100 years ago that astronomers realized there is more to the universe than just our Milky Way galaxy, and the Sun and Earth are nowhere near its core. Today we recognize that not only is there is no physical center to our vast universe, but the existence of dark matter and dark energy means we can't even detect most of it.

In our little corner of the cosmos, the Sun reigns supreme. It is the heart of the Solar System, and around it swirls a retinue of planets large and small, innumerable chunks of ice and rock, and bits of dusty debris.

In the Beginning

Our Sun was born 4.6 billion years ago in a collapsing cloud of gas and dust. A mere 10 million years later, it was already surrounded by planets.

The young Solar System was a violent place, with numerous rocky bodies swinging erratically around the Sun. Collisions were inevitable, as revealed by the crater-scarred surfaces of Mars and Mercury. A Mars-sized body is believed to have hit the young Earth, with the Moon forming as a byproduct of this collision. For all we know, the young Sun had many more planets than it does today.

Over time, the amount of interplanetary debris dwindled and the Solar System turned serene. But impacts still occur, sometimes with devastating consequences. Sixty-five million years ago an asteroid smashed into Earth, contributing to the demise of the dinosaurs. In 1994, astronomers on Earth had a ringside seat as 24 pieces of a broken comet (Shoemaker–Levy 9) slammed into Jupiter.

The Sun's Family

In 2006, professional astronomers attempted to define the meaning of "planet" as it applies to our Solar System. After much contentious debate, they decided that the Sun's family is composed of eight "traditional" planets, three dwarf planets (Pluto, Ceres, and Eris), plus thousands of asteroids and possibly trillions of comets that are collectively known as Small Solar System Bodies.

The vast outer fringe of our Solar System includes the Oort Cloud (a cloud of comets some eight trillion miles from the Sun) and the Kuiper Belt, a ring of small icy worlds and numerous dwarf planets. Pluto and Eris are two of the largest Kuiper Belt objects.

Closer to the Sun are the eight traditional planets (plus the dwarf planet Ceres, the largest

Left Artist's conception of the red dwarf star Gliese 581. Gliese 581 C, in the foreground, is the first exoplanet to be found in the "Goldilocks Zone," where the temperature is just right for liquid water. A "hot Jupiter," center, orbits even closer to the system's star.

SEARCHING FOR EARTH II

Anyone gazing into a sky full of stars can't help but wonder whether there are planets orbiting those stars, with intelligent beings on them looking up into their night sky wondering if there are other planets, circling other stars, with intelligent life on them. Until recently, astronomers couldn't even answer a fundamental question: Do exoplanets—planets beyond our Solar System—actually exist?

In 1995 the first exoplanet of a Sun-like star was discovered. Called 51 Pegasi b, it's about half the size of Jupiter and orbits close to its star. Since then, almost 300 exoplanets have been found. Most are so-called "hot Jupiters," because they're gas giant worlds orbiting very close to their star. To date, the smallest exoplanet known is more than five times the mass of Earth. Where are all the Earth-size, Earth-like, planets?

The problem is that the technology for spotting these small worlds still lags behind our ability to theorize their existence. For example, recent computer simulations have shown that terrestrial planets may have formed in the habitable zone of Alpha Centauri B, one of the stars in the nearby Alpha Centauri system. But it will take more than five years of observations by a dedicated telescope to determine if this is the case.

Still, the technology is improving. In early 2008, NASA's Spitzer Space Telescope looked for warm dust—the debris of planet formation—around Sun-like stars and found that upward of 60 percent of them are potential homes for rocky Earth-like worlds. Such results provide a positive background to the early 2009 launch of NASA's Kepler spacecraft. Its mission is to survey our region of the galaxy in search of Earth-size planets in or near the habitable zone of their stars.

Once a planet is discovered, its orbit can be calculated, and other telescopes will attempt to observe it directly. We won't see surface detail, but spectroscopy will determine the chemical composition of its atmosphere (if any). This has already been done, albeit for a large world. The Hubble Space Telescope's spectrometer recently found methane in the atmosphere of a Jupiter-size extrasolar planet.

Earth is the only rocky body in our Solar System with significant amounts of atmospheric oxygen and methane. These gases endure in our atmosphere only because of the existence of life. Their presence in the environment of an Earth-size exoplanet would be a tantalizing hint that we have found Earth II.

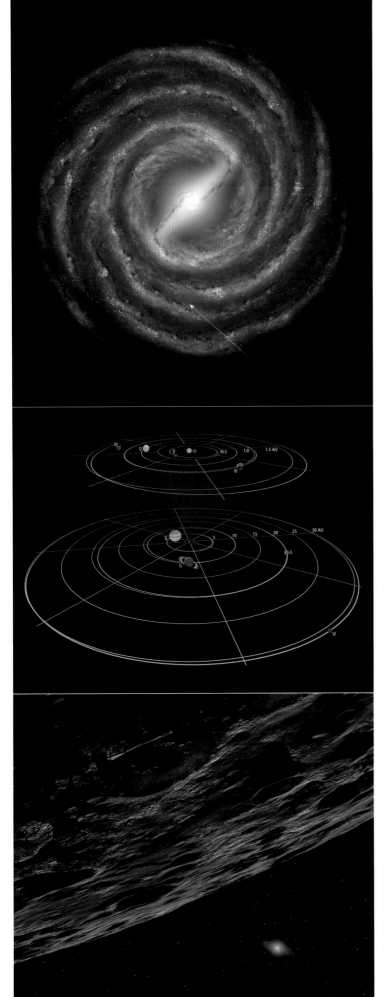

member of the Asteroid Belt). These range from Mercury with a diameter less than half that of Earth, to colossal Jupiter, with a mass that is 318 times greater than our world. Four are enormous gas globes; four are small rocky bodies. One is so close to the Sun that it needs a mere 88 days to complete a single orbit; one is so far removed that 165 years must pass before it finishes one circuit. Two have no natural satellites, while one (Jupiter) has 63 and counting.

The four giants (Jupiter, Saturn, Uranus, and Neptune) are each many times Earth's diameter (Jupiter, the largest, is 11 times wider than Earth) and are composed primarily of hydrogen gas. The four remaining planets (the "terrestrial" planets) orbit close to the Sun. Each is a small world of solid rock with a thin or non-existent atmosphere, few (or no) moons, and no rings.

The Goldilocks Planets

In the classic children's story *Goldilocks and the Three Bears*, one bowl of porridge in the bears' cottage is too hot, one is too cold, and one is just right. This tale is often used as an analogy for Venus, Earth, and Mars. While it's true that Venus is scorching and Mars is frigid, the differences go well beyond the obvious temperature analogy. For instance, Earth has a strong magnetic field, while Venus and Mars have next to none. But there's more.

The thin Martian atmosphere contains 95 percent carbon dioxide. The Venusian air also contains 95 percent carbon dioxide, but it's very thick with a high atmospheric pressure. Nitrogen (at 77 percent) is the main constituent of Earth's atmosphere, and our planet's atmospheric pressure and surface temperature are, well, just right.

All three worlds show evidence of vulcanism on the surface, but only on Earth is volcanic activity ongoing. And only Earth has plate tectonics. It appears that the surface of the other two planets consists of a single, immobile plate—the crust itself.

A Unique Planet

When compared to any other body in the Solar System, Earth possesses three unique features. It has liquid water on its surface, oxygen in its atmosphere, and life. Scientists think it's possible that other Solar System bodies may contain microscopic organisms (or hold the fossilized remains of ancient life). Mars has long been considered the frontrunner in the search for extraterrestrial life, since it's believed that the red planet was more Earth-like during its youth (before it lost most of its atmosphere, and froze). And if there are liquid oceans under the icy crusts of Europa (a large moon of Jupiter) or Enceladus (one of Saturn's moons), the possibility of microorganisms living in these extreme environments cannot be ruled out.

But the secret to Earth's abundant life lies in its location—93 million miles (149 million km) from our star. Earth orbits within the Sun's habitable zone, a region where sufficient solar energy reaches our planet to keep its surface temperature warm enough to sustain liquid water. And liquid water is essential for life as we know it.

Since its birth, Earth has undergone numerous changes. The release of oxygen by primitive bacteria altered its atmosphere. Continents emerged, joined, split, and vanished as the plates of Earth's crust moved. Extreme vulcanism, climate change, and impacts from space caused the fall, and rise, of countless species. And even as we try to understand the planet beneath our feet, we've begun looking up, to the stars, in search of other Earths.

Top left Artist's impression of the Milky Way as seen from outside. The location of the Sun and its surrounding planets is indicated on one of the spiral arms: The Orion Arm.

Center left The top illustration shows the orbits of the four terrestrial planets—Mercury, Venus, Earth, and Mars—around the Sun. The lower illustration, on a smaller scale, shows the orbits of the four gas giant planets—Jupiter, Saturn, Uranus, and Neptune. The dotted circle shows Earth's orbit in both illustrations. The planets are not drawn to scale.

Bottom left Kuiper Belt objects are debris left over from the formation of the Solar System, lying in a disk beyond the outskirts of the orbit of the planet Neptune.

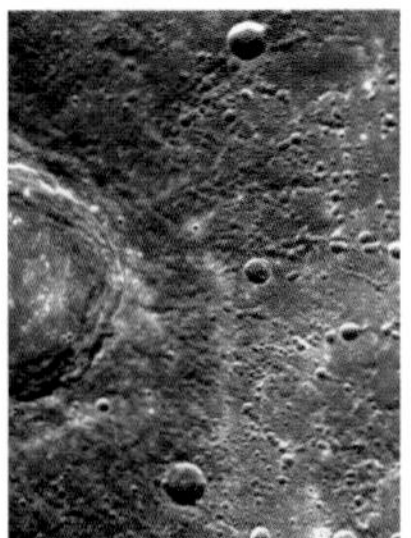

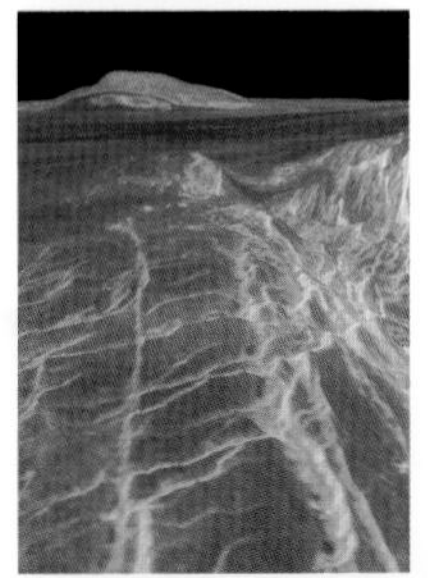

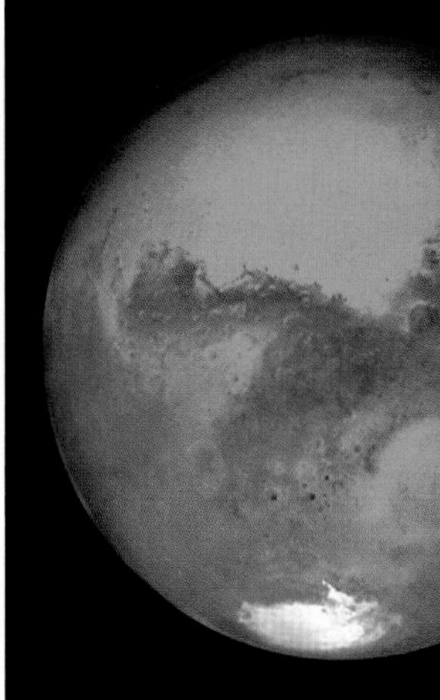

Above top The cratered surface of Mercury shows the scars of violent impacts from the time shortly after the birth of the Solar System.

Above center Sif Mons, a dormant volcano, rises 1.2 miles (2 km) above the surface of the planet Venus. Although the planet is masked by a thick atmosphere of sulfur clouds, a computer generated this view from radar mapping data.

Above bottom Although Mars is now considered barren, before it lost its atmosphere it may have been a home for living things.

Plate Tectonics

Earth's internal engine is fueled by a molten mantle, still boiling despite the billions of years that have passed since the tumultuous formation of this rocky world. On the surface where we live, however, the massive forces still working on our planet are mostly imperceptible to the human senses.

Left When tectonic plates collide, the result can cause folding on both sides. The effects of such folding can be seen on the surface of this mountain, Wildhauser Schafberg Peak in Switzerland.

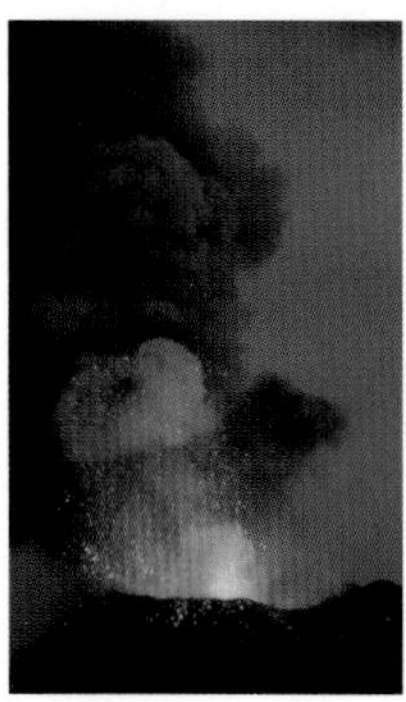

Above Mt Etna, Sicily, is in an almost constant state of eruption, as the heat of Earth's mantle sends molten rock to the surface where the Eurasian and African plates meet.

Below The Himalaya mountain range rises to the highest point on Earth, as a result of the Indian subcontinent pushing into the Asian mainland.

Bottom Dallol Volcano in Ethiopia is in the East African Rift. At 157 feet (48 m) below sea level, Dallol is one of the lowest points on Earth and also one of the hottest, reaching 145°F (63°C).

In the beginning, 4,600 million years ago, Earth formed by accretion in the flattened disk of debris that was spinning around the Sun. As it swept through the debris field in its orbit, the protoplanet slowly grew, heating up and finally becoming a molten ball.

A lighter mantle formed around a heavier core as gravity pulled the denser elements, such as iron, toward its center, while less dense elements, such as silicon and aluminum, were displaced toward the surface. Finally, a thin, brittle crust formed, still periodically smashed by incoming meteorites. A battle ensued, with the solid crust acting as an insulating blanket around a boiling interior trying to shed its heat into outer space. This is the basis of what is called Earth's internal heat engine or plate tectonic motor.

Earth's Plate Tectonic Motor

Earth's heat-driven internal engine is incredibly powerful yet, in human terms, it is imperceptibly slow. We cannot see any movement, although other evidence of its activity is everywhere around us.

Boiling plumes of hot material, pushing upward and outward beneath the crust, dome it up and eventually rip it apart in a quest for the surface. The lightest of materials (aluminum- and silicon-rich rocks) accumulate like a thickened scum on the surface and are not recycled back into the mantle—this is how Earth's first permanent continents were formed, and the planet's surface has been in constant motion since that time.

A Preposterous New Theory is Born

In the early 1900s, a young German meteorologist, Alfred Wegener, was particularly struck by the apparent jigsaw fit of the outlines of Earth's continents, and the interesting coincidence that the geology of South America matched that of Africa. In 1912 he proposed that all of the continents had once been joined together as a supercontinent he later named Pangea (meaning "all of Earth's lands").

EARTH'S SUPERCONTINENTS

Periodically, Earth's continents collide to form a great single landmass known as a supercontinent. This has happened several times since Earth's formation, with the last time being about 250 million years ago when the giant supercontinent, Pangea, came together. Surrounded by the Panthalassa Ocean, its habitable fringes encircled a vast, dry, desert interior. A supercontinent does not last too long, geologically speaking, as the heat buildup beneath its vast surface soon tears it apart again, starting the cycle anew. Pangaea began to break up about 240 million years ago, with narrow seaways forming between South America, Africa, and Antarctica as the continents began to migrate toward their present positions.

Life on Earth has thus always been on the move, as the continents have been pushed from equator to pole many times over. Living communities have moved in and out of contact with one another, and been placed in climates varying from glacial to desert. Different species have either adapted to these changes or perished. Biodiversity reaches a maximum when life is spread out over numerous smaller continents isolated by ocean. It drops to a minimum when life forms are forced to compete as all the continents are pushed together into one large supercontinent.

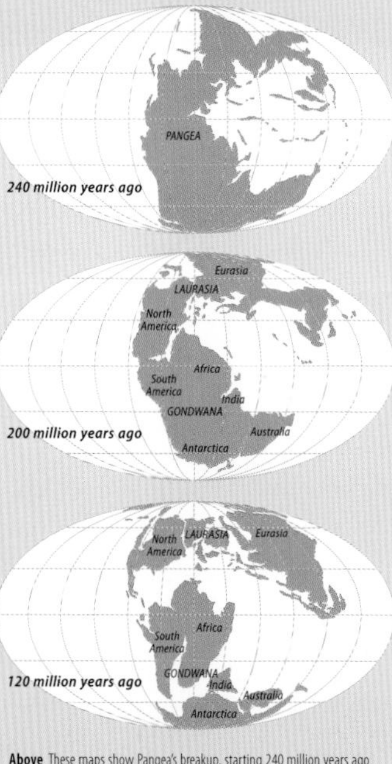
PANGEA
240 million years ago
Eurasia
LAURASIA
North America
Africa
South America
India
GONDWANA
Australia
Antarctica
200 million years ago
North America
LAURASIA
Eurasia
Africa
South America
GONDWANA
India
Australia
Antarctica
120 million years ago

Above These maps show Pangea's breakup, starting 240 million years ago (top). The separation of Gondwana and Laurasia was effective 200 million years ago (center), and 120 million years ago (bottom) the shapes of the present-day continents are beginning to be recognizable.

Wegener supported his ideas by demonstrating that the Appalachian Mountains in North America once lined up with the Scottish Highlands and that the coalfields of Europe matched up with those of North America. He correlated various deposits of identical fossils—such as the reptiles Mesosaurus and Lystrosaurus—all now separated by mighty oceans.

The theory created an uproar and outrage in the established scientific community of the day. In those times it was generally believed that rising and falling land bridges between the fixed continents had allowed the passage of different animals at different times. They could not imagine or explain how enormous land masses could just "drift" about in the oceans. It was not until the 1950s and 1960s, when new ocean-floor bathymetric data led to the discovery of oceanic spreading ridges and deep trough-like subduction trenches, that Wegener's theory was accepted as correct.

Spreading Ridges

Earth's tectonic plates, of which there are about 14, are being torn apart along fiery cracks, mostly hidden below sea level, and known as oceanic spreading ridges. Magma rises to the surface along these cracks to fill the gap, and hardens to make new crust, which is, in turn, split apart. Topographically, these spreading ridges are long, broad, submerged mountain chains, with the finest example, the Mid-Atlantic Ridge, running north–south down the length of the Atlantic Ocean.

Occasionally, these massive fracture zones are visible on land, in places such as Iceland or along the East African Rift, as steep valleys, basalt volcanoes, intense thermal activity, and deep, narrow lakes. In these places humans have been able to take advantage of Earth's abundant internal, or geothermal, heat to run power stations rather than use coal and oil.

Subduction Zones

Growing new crust along the ridges means that it must be destroyed in equal amounts elsewhere on Earth's surface. These lines of destruction, along which the tectonic plates are pushed together, are called subduction zones. One of the plates, usually the lighter one, slips over the top of the other, which is pushed down into the mantle and melted. Subduction zones are marked by deep, narrow, submarine trenches and bordered by explosive, classically cone-shaped volcanoes fed by the molten products of the descending plate. Such activity is abundant all around the edge of the Pacific Ocean, which is known as the "Rim of Fire." Here, the Pacific Plate is being steadily consumed on all sides by the encroaching neighboring plates.

Massive Collision Mountains

An interesting situation arises when the plates being pushed together are both buoyant, low-density, old continental crust, as neither is able to easily slip beneath the other. In these cases, the collision results in the land on both sides being crumpled and folded. The leading continental edges can be pushed miles skyward. The Himalaya mountain range is Earth's finest example of this process in action today, as the Indian subcontinent grinds steadily northward into the Asian mainland, pushing up Earth's tallest peaks. The Himalayas are part of an active collision mountain chain that includes the mountain ranges of the Hindu Kush, Zagros, Caucasus, Alps, Apennines, and Atlas, which have been squeezed like toothpaste between continental Eurasia and the northward traveling land-masses of Africa, the Arabian Peninsula, and India.

Many of Earth's less significant mountain ranges, such as the Caledonian Mountains of the UK, the Appalachians of the USA, and the Urals of Russia, were also once mighty, Himalaya-sized ranges. They were the result of much earlier continental collisions, but the forces of erosion have been slowly wearing away their grandeur ever since.

Above The volcanic origin of many Polynesian islands in the "Rim of Fire" is revealed by the steep slopes of the interior landscape, as well as by the reefs that skirt the islands, which may be remnants of older calderas.

Manifestations of Earth's Moving Plates

The fury of Earth's all too common and often devastating natural disasters reveals the way the planet's brittle thin crust responds to the driving forces of the internal heat engine. As the edges of the massive plates push and grind alongside one another, stresses may build for more than a hundred years and then release suddenly, with a resulting movement of several tens of feet, all in a few seconds.

Such a movement occurred along the San Andreas Fault (marking the edge of the Pacific and American plates) in the early morning of April 18, 1906. The rupture in the ground surface ran for a distance of some 200 miles (320 km) and the resultant shock waves manifested themselves as the most destructive earthquake ever experienced in the region.

Sudden ruptures in the sea floor crust may also manifest themselves in a disastrous way, by suddenly lifting or dropping a huge body of water. Like ripples generated by a pebble tossed into a calm pond, tsunami waves radiate out in concentric circles from the zone of undersea disturbance. Particular devastation can occur when the height of a tsunami is amplified by traveling over a shallow sea floor or by being funneled into a narrow inlet, such as happened in Valdez, Alaska, in 1964. Witnesses reported a 220-foot (67 m) wall of water rushing up the fjord and crashing into the Valdez pier. Dense coastal populations in Indonesia, Malaysia, Thailand, India, and Sri Lanka—and the lack of any warning system in the Indian Ocean—combined to cause a loss of more than 300,000 lives to a tsunami on December 26, 2004. Its source was a massive earthquake off the coast of Sumatra that was caused by a readjustment of the Indo–Australian and Eurasian plates.

Earth's Landforms

Our planet has a vast array of breathtaking landforms, including massive mountain chains, fiery volcanoes, deep canyons, powerful rivers, and magnificent waterfalls. These features are not just random—each is a result of predictable geologic circumstances, and all are caused by Earth's powerful internal heat engine.

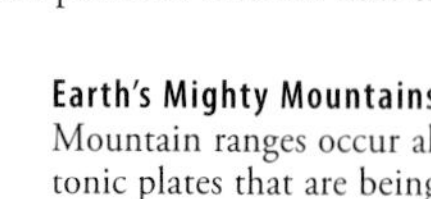

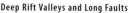

Imagine a completely different Earth—a swampy, monotonous landscape, flat as far as the eye can see, with indefinite, meandering, brackish coastlines melding into stagnant, muddy-bottomed, shallow seas. This is what a cold-cored Earth would look like—an Earth whose surface was not being folded, crumpled, and pushed by heat coming from within, from far below the surface.

The forces of erosion would quickly win their battle, reducing the landscape to its flattest, lowest energy state.

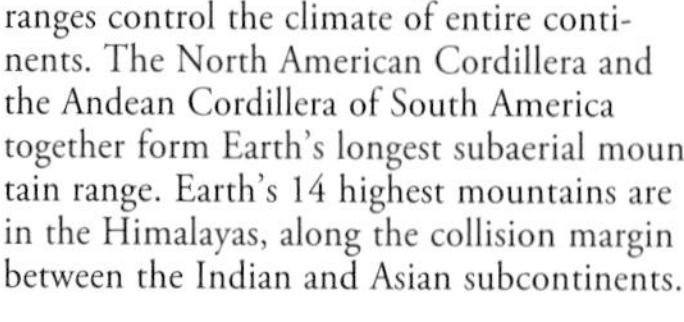

Below The Amazon River in South America is Earth's largest by volume, although the Nile is more than 100 miles (160 km) longer.

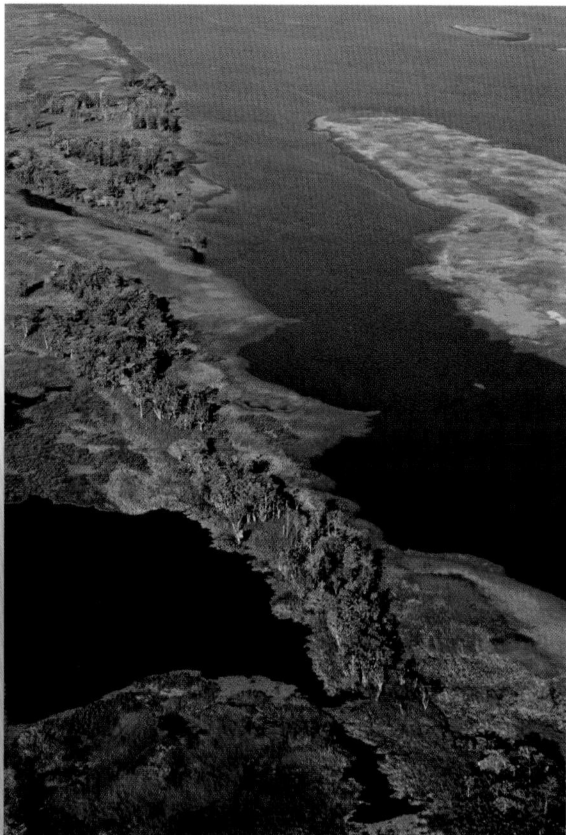

Earth's Mighty Mountains

Mountain ranges occur along the edges of tectonic plates that are being driven against one another. Crumpled together, their edges push upward as in the Himalayas, or overlap one another to melt and form volcanic arcs such as those of Japan, the Philippines, and Indonesia. In these places, the balance between the forces of erosion—wind, water, and ice—carving into the rapidly rising, folded rocks and growing volcanic peaks creates myriad interesting landforms.

The spines of Earth's mightiest mountain ranges control the climate of entire continents. The North American Cordillera and the Andean Cordillera of South America together form Earth's longest subaerial mountain range. Earth's 14 highest mountains are in the Himalayas, along the collision margin between the Indian and Asian subcontinents.

Earth's Biggest Rivers

Earth's most powerful rivers are those that drain the biggest mountain ranges. Their sources of water are derived from the disruption of moisture-laden air. Mountain barriers force air to rise, causing it to cool. The cooling air is forced to drop its moisture as precipitation on the mountain slopes.

The Amazon is, by far, the world's most powerful river, draining the forested eastern side of the northern Andean Cordillera and traveling the entire width of the South American continent before discharging into the Atlantic Ocean.

A river's power is determined by the volume of water discharged at its mouth, and is not related to its length. The Nile is the world's longest river; its water travels a total of 4,160 miles (6,700 km)—longer than the Amazon's 4,050 miles (6,516 km). But the Nile does not carry very much water. Its catchment is dry and it has been heavily dammed for agricultural use. In terms of volume of water discharged, the Nile River is ranked twenty-fourth.

Millions of tons of sediment carried by Earth's mightiest rivers are deposited in huge fan-shaped accumulations, known as deltas, at their mouths. The load is so heavy that it depresses the Earth's crust into enormous basins in these regions.

Deep Rift Valleys and Long Faults

Some of the lowest points on Earth's land surface are found where it has been stretched to breaking point by rising mantle currents acting on the base of the crust—a process known as rifting. Long cracks appear in the domed surface, accompanied by enormous slices of crust slipping vertically downward to form deep steep-walled valleys, clearly visible from space. Impressive examples include the East African Rift Valley, Australia's Spencer Gulf–Lake Torrens Rift, and the Jordan Valley–Dead Sea Rift. The lowest subaerial point on Earth is found on the shore of the Dead Sea, on the Israel–Jordan border. This point is 1,292 feet (394 m) below sea level. Ongoing irregular slippage along these fault planes is experienced in these regions in the form of abundant earthquakes. Some of the most dangerous and earthquake-prone areas are at the edges of major tectonic plates that slide sideways against one another. Large populations at risk include those living along California's San Andreas Fault and Turkey's North Anatolian Fault Zone.

Desert Landscapes

Deserts are perhaps Earth's most intriguing, yet least visited landscapes. About one-fifth of our planet's land surface is covered by deserts. They are defined as regions that receive very little precipitation—arbitrarily set at anything below 10 inches (250 mm), which means that cold dry regions of the world are also considered deserts. Antarctica contains the world's largest ice desert, although what snow does fall there tends not to melt. The Sahara Desert is the world's largest hot desert, and covers parts of Egypt, Libya, Mauritania,

Below The illustration shows plate tectonics in action: Convection currents rising and falling in Earth's interior drive the movement of its surface plates, producing all of the landforms around us.

Collision When light, thick continents collide, their edges buckle and fold, pushing up tall mountain ranges, such as the Himalayas and the Alps.

Hotspots Enormous volcanic islands grow on the sea floor above deep mantle hotspots until they are moved from their source by the continual movement of the tectonic plate. As each volcano dies and sinks, new islands grow.

Subduction volcanic islands Denser and thinner ocean crust pushes beneath lighter crust. The descending and melting oceanic plate gives rise to magma that rises to form arcs of volcanic islands, such as Indonesia and the Philippines.

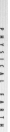

Left The Dead Sea, on the Israel–Jordan border, lies on a rift in Earth's crust. Its shore is the lowest dry-land point on Earth, which is still dropping as the salty waters slowly evaporate.

Far left The highest peaks of the Cordillera Sarmiento, in Patagonia, rise above clouds and icecaps. They are pushed up by the northward movement of the Antarctic Plate.

Chad, Morocco, and Algeria. Desert landscapes are mostly bare of vegetation, and may have a rocky or pebbly surface, or be traversed by mobile sand dunes. Surface water is practically nonexistent, and flows only as a sudden deluge following rare instances of torrential rainfall. Extremely high evaporation rates and low rainfall combine to transport soluble salts to temporary salt lakes, or playa lakes, that form at the deserts' lowest points. Salar de Uyuni, near Potosí in Bolivia, and Lake Eyre in Australia are extensive playa lakes.

Active Volcanoes and Volcanic Remnants

All of the classic volcanic peaks that we can see in Earth's landscape—such as Mt Fuji in Japan or Mt Etna in Italy—are essentially active, even though they may not have erupted in decades, centuries, or even millennia. There are about 1,500 such volcanoes on Earth. Geologically speaking, they could erupt any minute, as evidenced by the typical, clean-lined, conical peaks that are formed by periodic ash falls and lava flows, and have not yet been ravaged by the forces of erosion.

Extinct volcanoes are mostly unrecognizable to the untrained eye. Their soft ash cones have long been stripped away and the old lava flows broken into rubble and transported away in the rivers and streams draining radially outward from the ancient peak. Often it is only the volcano's internal "plumbing system" that stands proud above the landscape. This is the network of dykes and pipes that once transported lava to the surface from the magma chambers deep below. The molten rock, once cooled and set hard in the pipes and cracks, became much harder than the rocks of the surrounding landscape. Some of Earth's best known and most spectacular landforms are, in fact, eroded volcanic plumbing systems. Consider the much-visited US landmarks of Shiprock in New Mexico, and Devils Tower in Wyoming.

In the Old World, such volcanic remnants, being generally difficult to climb and therefore protected, have long been chosen as invincible sites on which to build fortresses and castles. Being isolated, such peaceful peaks have also made ideal sites for monasteries, churches, and temples throughout Europe and Asia. In France, the twelfth-century Chapelle St Michel d'Aiguilhe, in the town of Le Puy-en-Velay, is built atop a tall volcanic pinnacle. These days, monuments continue to be built on such landforms, such as the giant Christ the Redeemer statue—completed in 1931—which stands on top of Corcovado Mountain, welcoming visitors to Brazil's Rio de Janeiro with outstretched arms.

Sometimes, if erosion of an ancient volcano has been absolute, all that may remain is the imprint of the radial drainage pattern on an essentially flat landscape.

Below Known as the "Seven Summits," the list of the highest peak on each continent is a "to-do" list for any self-respecting mountaineer. In fact, there are 55 peaks in the Himalaya and contiguous ranges that are taller than Aconcagua.

m
ft
Everest
Aconcagua
McKinley
Kilimanjaro
Elbrus
Vinson Massif
Puncak Jaya
8000
6000
4000
2000
0
30,000
25,000
20,000
15,000
10,000
5,000
0

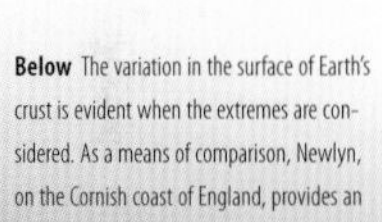

Below The variation in the surface of Earth's crust is evident when the extremes are considered. As a means of comparison, Newlyn, on the Cornish coast of England, provides an official measurement of sea level.

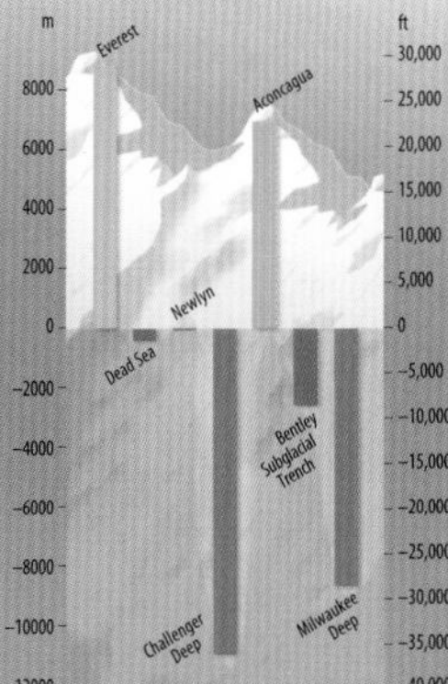

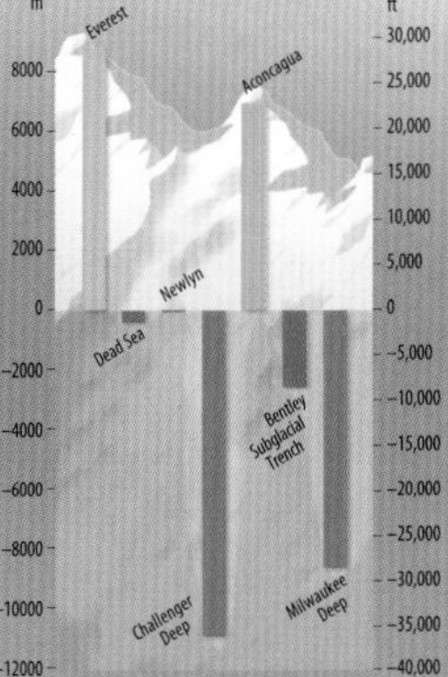

m
ft
Everest
Aconcagua
Newlyn
Dead Sea
Bentley Subglacial Trench
Challenger Deep
Milwaukee Deep
8000
6000
4000
2000
0
-2000
-4000
-6000
-8000
-10000
-12000
30,000
25,000
20,000
15,000
10,000
5,000
0
-5,000
-10,000
-15,000
-20,000
-25,000
-30,000
-35,000
-40,000

BEACHES AND COASTS

One can imagine many different beaches and coastlines, from an alluring coral atoll to the rugged steep inlets of New Zealand. Each coastal type is dependent on the tectonics of that region, combined with its geologic history. Areas of Earth that were once covered by a massive ice sheet, such as Canada's Hudson Bay, and Scandinavia's Gulf of Bothnia, are rising quite steadily now that they not weighted down. One can literally walk past hundreds of raised shorelines, complete with sand, rocks, and shells, on the way to the present water's edge.

Some of Earth's longest and most sinuous coastlines, such as those of northern Canada and Europe, are the result of heavy carving by glacial ice that has recently retreated. These coasts remain flooded by the sea for now, forming spectacular, deep, steep-walled fjords harboring abundant marine life.

Beaches lie in protected areas where the sea meets the land, and are doubtless some of Earth's most enchanting places. Sediment weathering from nearby rocks is what gives beaches their character—consider the variety, from pure white coral sand, golden yellow iron-tinted quartz sand, rare green mineral sand, through to the pitch black sand beaches of young volcanic islands.

Right The rocky weathered coastline of the Ligurian Sea at Manarola in Italy is no barrier to human civilization, which can find a foothold in almost any terrain.

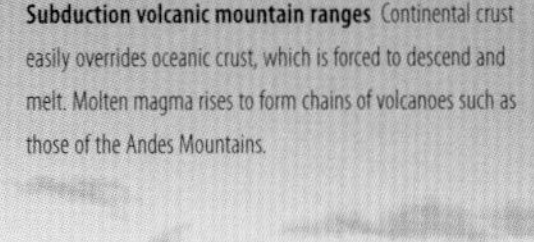

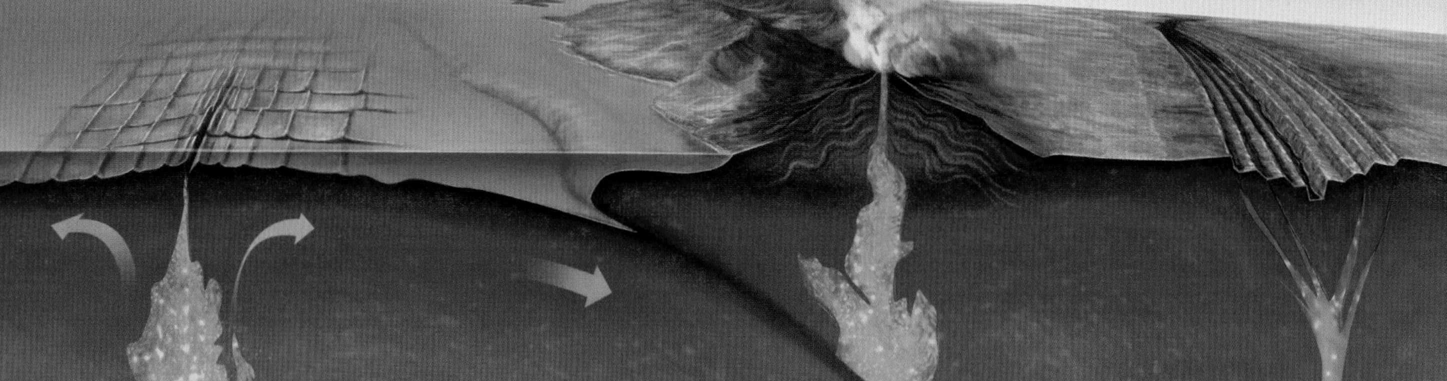

Mid-oceanic ridge New basaltic crust forms along the mid-oceanic ridges. Here, magma intrudes into the widening cracks and solidifies as the tectonic plates move apart.

Subduction volcanic mountain ranges Continental crust easily overrides oceanic crust, which is forced to descend and melt. Molten magma rises to form chains of volcanoes such as those of the Andes Mountains.

Rifting Rifting occurs in the middle of large continents sitting on top of rising convection plumes. The land is put under tension, which causes it to crack and move apart.

Earth's Vital Statistics

The world we live in is full of fascinating facts. From the top of the planet's highest mountain to the bottom of the deepest ocean trench, there are wonders to behold and exotic places to visit.

Earth is often referred to as the "blue planet," reflecting the fact that land covers less than 30 percent of the planet's surface. The land is divided into seven continents, each of which has unique physical and human environments. Asia is the biggest of these continents in both size and population, with 60 percent of humankind found in the countries of Asia. The smallest of the continents, Oceania, is centered around the vast landmass of Australia—the world's largest island—and includes thousands of small islands, some of which are among the world's smallest countries. Although vast in size, Antarctica—the most southerly of all the continents—has almost no human inhabitants, with just a tiny transient population of scientists living in bases.

More than 97 percent of all the water on Earth is saltwater, found in the oceans. The oceans remain the last great unexplored regions of planet Earth. Fresh water, the most vital element for human survival, accounts for less than three percent of Earth's water. It is mostly found in the polar icecaps and glaciers, with rivers and freshwater lakes containing just 0.02 percent. Rivers and lakes, however, are among the environments most degraded and damaged by human activities, despite their vital importance to our survival.

Human occupation of the continents reflects their capacity to support life. The fertile lands of Asia have allowed a massive population to develop there and it is here that China and India, the world's most populous countries, are found. The ancient landmass of Australia has a small population, reflecting its dry environment.

OUR PLANET

Dimension	Measurement	
Diameter at equator	7926.4 miles	12,756.3 km
Diameter between poles	7899.86 miles	12,713.6 km
Distance around equator	24,901.46 miles	40,075.02 km
Distance around poles	24,859.73 miles	40,007.86 km
Surface area	196,939,900 square miles	510,072,000 km^2
Mass	13.166 x 10^{24} lb	5.972 x 10^{24} kg

LARGEST AREA

Continent	Area (square miles)	Area (square km)
Asia	16,915,135	43,810,000
Africa	11,725,925	30,370,000
North America	9,455,640	24,490,000
South America	6,888,060	17,840,000
Antarctica	5,297,320	13,720,000
Europe	3,930,520	10,180,000
Oceania	3,478,780	9,010,000

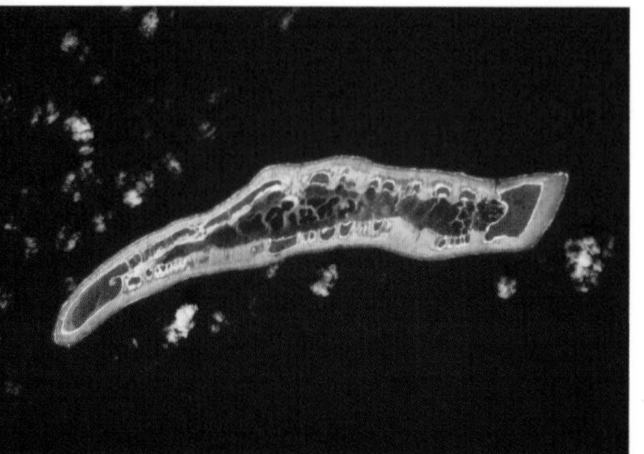

EXTREME EARTH

- The northernmost point on land is Kaffeklubben Island, east of Greenland (83°40'N, 29°50'W).
- The southernmost point on land is the geographic South Pole.
- The westernmost point on land, according to the path of the International Date Line, is Attu Island, Alaska.
- The easternmost point on land, according to the path of the International Date Line, is Caroline Atoll, Kiribati.

MERE MARVELS

- Lake Superior is the largest freshwater lake by surface area at 31,820 square miles (82,413.5 km^2).
- Lake Baikal is the deepest body of fresh water—5,022 feet (1,530 m)—but is only the 7th largest in surface area at 12,200 square miles (31,500 km^2).
- Lake Titicaca in Peru is the highest navigable lake at 12,500 feet (3,810 m) above sea level.
- Lake Vostok in Antarctica is the world's coldest lake, with an average temperature of 26.6°F (-3°C). The water remains liquid because of the pressure of the ice above its surface.

LARGEST FRESHWATER RESERVOIRS

Body	Country	Volume (cubic miles)	Volume (km^3)
Lake Baikal	Russia	5,700	23,600
Lake Tanganyika	Tanzania/DRC/Burundi/Zambia	4,500	18,900
Lake Superior	Canada/USA	2,900	12,100
Lake Michigan/Huron	Canada/USA	2,029	8,458
Lake Malawi	Malawi/Mozambique/Tanzania	2,000	8,400

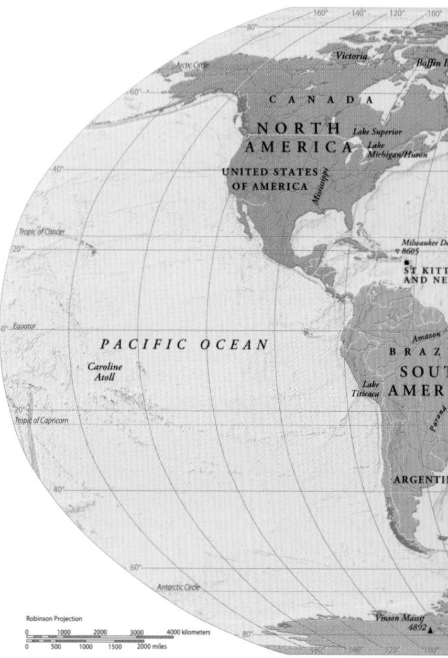
Victoria
CANADA
NORTH AMERICA
Lake Superior
Lake Michigan/Huron
UNITED STATES OF AMERICA
Mississippi
Tropic of Cancer
Milwaukee Deep 8605
Equator
PACIFIC OCEAN
Caroline Atoll
Amazon
Lake Titicaca
Tropic of Capricorn
Antarctic Circle
Vinson Massif 4892
Robinson Projection

Above This map shows the seven continents, using colors that are repeated in the tables on these pages and throughout this book. Some sources use different definitions for the continents, combining Europe and Asia, or North and South America, and sometimes naming Australia as a continent rather than the world's largest island.

LARGEST SALTWATER RESERVOIRS

Body of water	Area (square miles)	Area (km^2)	Greatest depth (feet)	Greatest depth (m)	Deepest point
Pacific Ocean	60,060,895	155,557,000	35,840	10,924	Challenger Deep, Mariana Trench
Atlantic Ocean	29,637,975	76,762,000	28,232	8,605	Milwaukee Deep, Puerto Rico Trench
Indian Ocean	26,469,620	68,556,000	23,812	7,258	Java Trench
Southern Ocean	7,848,300	20,327,000	23,737	7,235	South Sandwich Trench
Arctic Ocean	5,427,050	14,056,000	15,305	4,665	Fram Basin

Top At the dawn of a new day, the Sun's rays first touch land at the eastern point of Caroline Atoll, Kiribati, seen here in a photograph taken by an astronaut aboard the International Space Station.

Above Lake Baikal is the largest body of fresh water on the planet. It is nearly a mile (just over 1.5 km) deep, and forms part of the Yenisey river system—the fifth longest river in the world.

Right Although all of the world's oceans are really part of the same reservoir of saltwater, they are traditionally divided on geographic lines into five oceans. Of the five, the Pacific Ocean reigns supreme as the largest, covering an area more than double that of its nearest rival, the Atlantic, and also the deepest point in Earth's crust.

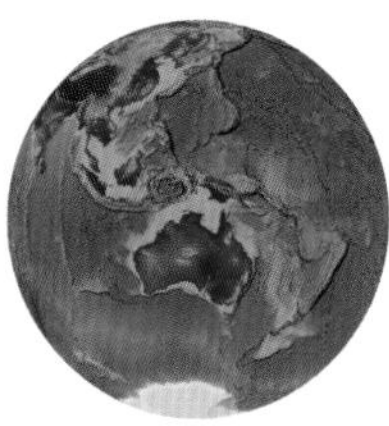

Above Three different views of Earth show how the continents are placed on the face of the globe. At left, Africa, Europe, and Asia are visible; in the center, Oceania dominates; and in the view at right, North and South America take pride of place.

NUMBER OF COUNTRIES

Continent	Countries
Africa	53
Asia	48
Europe	45
North America	23
Oceania	14
South America	12
Antarctica	0

LARGEST POPULATION

Continent	Global Population	Density mi² (km²)
Asia	61%	326 (126)
Africa	14%	80 (31)
Europe	11%	83 (32)
North America	8%	*39 (15)
South America	6%	**73 (28)
Oceania	<1%	†10 (4)
Antarctica	0.00002%	0.00007

* Indicates Anglo America ** Indicates Latin America † Indicates Australia

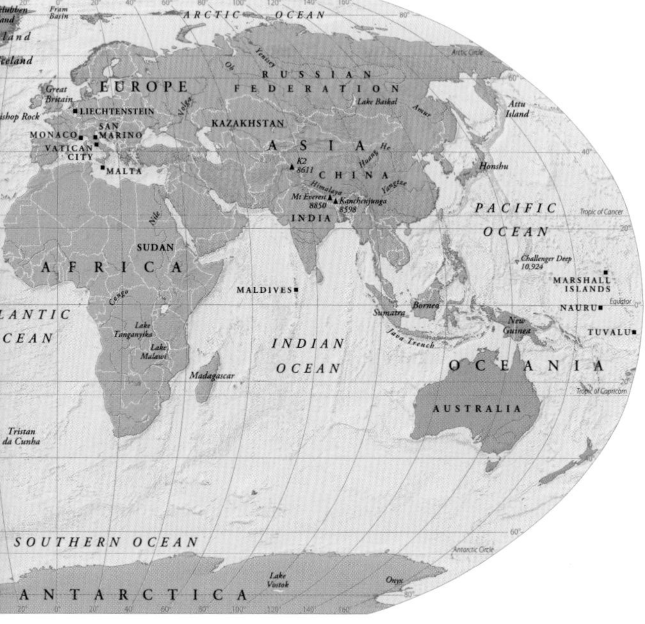
ARCTIC OCEAN
EUROPE
RUSSIAN FEDERATION
Lake Baikal
KAZAKHSTAN
LIECHTENSTEIN
SAN MARINO
MONACO
VATICAN CITY
MALTA
ASIA
CHINA
K2 8611
Mt Everest 8850
Kanchenjunga 8598
INDIA
Honshu
Attu Island
PACIFIC OCEAN
Challenger Deep 10,924
MARSHALL ISLANDS
NAURU
TUVALU
SUDAN
AFRICA
MALDIVES
Borneo
Sumatra
New Guinea
INDIAN OCEAN
OCEANIA
AUSTRALIA
Madagascar
Lake Tanganyika
Lake Malawi
Tristan da Cunha
SOUTHERN OCEAN
ANTARCTICA
Lake Vostok

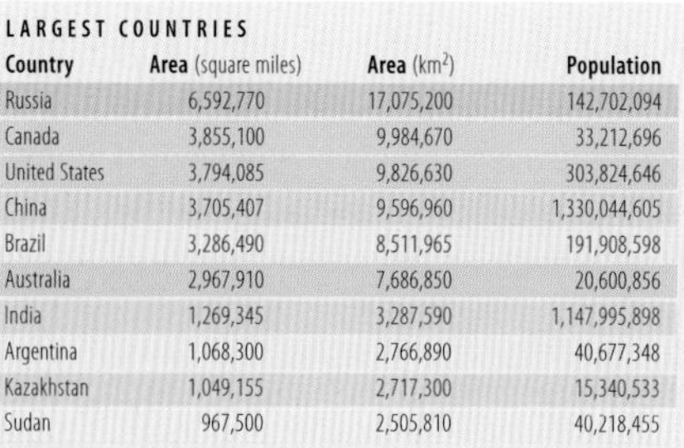

LARGEST COUNTRIES

Country	Area (square miles)	Area (km²)	Population
Russia	6,592,770	17,075,200	142,702,094
Canada	3,855,100	9,984,670	33,212,696
United States	3,794,085	9,826,630	303,824,646
China	3,705,407	9,596,960	1,330,044,605
Brazil	3,286,490	8,511,965	191,908,598
Australia	2,967,910	7,686,850	20,600,856
India	1,269,345	3,287,590	1,147,995,898
Argentina	1,068,300	2,766,890	40,677,348
Kazakhstan	1,049,155	2,717,300	15,340,533
Sudan	967,500	2,505,810	40,218,455

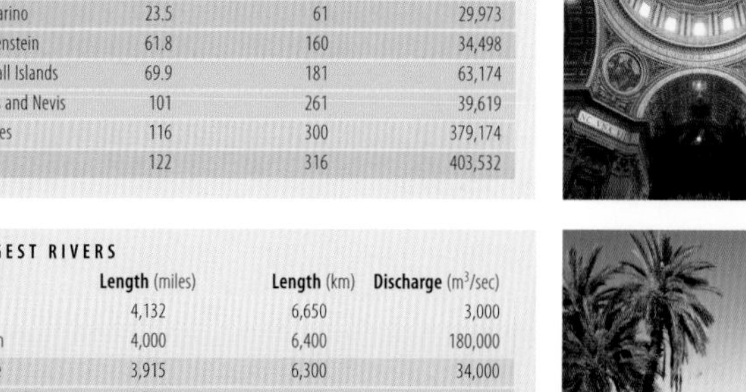

SMALLEST COUNTRIES

Country	Area (square miles)	Area (km²)	Population
Vatican City	0.17	0.45	824
Monaco	0.75	1.95	32,796
Nauru	8.11	21	13,770
Tuvalu	10	26	12,177
San Marino	23.5	61	29,973
Liechtenstein	61.8	160	34,498
Marshall Islands	69.9	181	63,174
St Kitts and Nevis	101	261	39,619
Maldives	116	300	379,174
Malta	122	316	403,532

LONGEST RIVERS

River	Length (miles)	Length (km)	Discharge (m³/sec)
Nile	4,132	6,650	3,000
Amazon	4,000	6,400	180,000
Yangtze	3,915	6,300	34,000
Mississippi/Missouri	3,710	5,970	18,000
Yenisey	3,442	5,540	19,000
Huang He (Yellow)	3,395	5,465	1,500
Ob/Irtysh	3,362	5,410	15,000
Paraná	3,032	4,880	22,000
Congo	2,900	4,700	41,000
Amur/Argun	2,755	4,425	12,000

HIGHEST MOUNTAINS

Mountain	Range	Height (feet)	Height (m)
Everest	Himalaya	29,035	8,850
K2	Karakoram	28,251	8,611
Kanchenjunga	Himalaya	28,209	8,598
Lhotse	Himalaya	27,923	8,511
Makalu	Himalaya	27,825	8,481
Cho Oyu	Himalaya	26,906	8,201
Dhaulagiri I	Himalaya	26,795	8,167
Manaslu I	Himalaya	26,781	8,163
Nanga Parbat	Himalaya	26,657	8,125
Annapurna I	Himalaya	26,545	8,091

Above top Russia, the world's largest country, is renowned for its onion-domed Orthodox churches—St Basil's Cathedral in Red Square, Moscow, is a typical example.

Above center St Peter's Cathedral is the focal point of Vatican City, both in physical terms and because it is the reason for the world's smallest country's existence.

Above The Nile is the world's longest river, although it is not even in the top ten by volume of water discharged.

LARGEST ISLANDS

Islands/Island groups	Area (square miles)	Area (km²)	Population (estimate)
Australia	2,967,910	7,686,850	20,600,850
Greenland, Denmark	836,330	2,166,085	56,325
New Guinea, Indonesia/PNG	341,630	884,820	7,990,170
Borneo, Brunei/Indonesia/Malaysia	285,330	739,000	16,000,000
Madagascar	226,655	587,040	20,042,550
Baffin Island, Canada	195,930	507,450	11,000
Sumatra, Indonesia	172,210	446,020	45,000,000
Great Britain, UK	88,985	230,465	59,210,912
Honshu, Japan	87,995	227,905	100,000,000
Victoria, Canada	83,895	217,290	750,000

ISLAND IDIOSYNCRACIES

- The smallest inhabited island in the world is Bishop Rock, UK. It has a lighthouse on it, and nothing else.
- The remotest inhabited island on Earth is Tristan da Cunha, 1,600 miles (2,575 km) from St Helena, its nearest neighbor.
- Nauru, in the Pacific Ocean, is the smallest independent island country, with an area of 8.2 square miles (21.28 km²).
- Iceland is mostly green, as geothermal activity melts the ice that would otherwise cover the island; Greenland, its nearest neighbor, is almost completely covered with ice.

Below left Australia is the world's largest island, stretching 2,704 miles (4,352 km) from the east coast to the west, a section of which (near Broome, Western Australia) is pictured here.

Below Everest—also known as Sagarmatha, in the Nepali language, and Chomolungma in Tibetan—rises above all of the other massive peaks in the Himalaya range.

Temperature

Air temperature affects many facets of our daily lives, from the clothes we choose to wear on a particular day to the types of vegetation we see growing in our immediate vicinity. It is also one of the most important determining factors of the climate. Understanding what causes variations in air temperature leads to a better knowledge of our planet.

Above The amount of sunlight that reaches Earth's surface is absorbed and scattered by particles and molecules in the atmosphere, such as the molecules of water in clouds.

Right Ellesmere Island, Canada, and Greenland are the northernmost points of land on Earth. The Sun does not set in summer, yet temperatures remain low because of the angle of the rays.

Below The maps show the change in mean average temperatures at different times in history.

The temperature of Earth's atmosphere varies with altitude. There are four atmospheric layers with distinguishing temperature profiles. The troposphere is the lowest layer of the atmosphere, extending from Earth's surface to about 4⅓ miles (7 km) at the poles and to 10½ miles (17 km) at the equator. It is in the lowest layer of our atmosphere that we experience the dynamic changes in temperature that occur on our planet.

Since the development of reliable means of measuring atmospheric temperatures using a standard scale some two centuries ago, official extremes have ranged from a high of 135.9°F (57.7°C) at Al'Aziziyah, Libya (on September 13, 1922) to a low of –128.6° F (–89.2°C) at Vostock II, Antarctica (on July 21, 1983).

Temperature on Earth is determined by energy balance at the surface. This balance is maintained because heat is transferred via conduction, convection, and radiation, or a combination thereof. Conduction is the transfer of thermal energy through matter, from a region of higher temperature to a region of lower temperature, and acts to equalize temperature differences. Convection transfers heat through the movement of currents within a fluid or gas. Warm air is less dense than cool air and this imbalance causes air movement, with warmer air rising and cooler air sinking. Radiation, or electromagnetic radiation, is emitted from the surface of an object due to the object's temperature. The balance of incoming electromagnetic energy from the Sun and outgoing electromagnetic energy from Earth helps to maintain the planet's temperature equilibrium.

Another important heat transfer process is latent heat, sometimes called hidden heat. It is hidden because it is energy that is taken up and stored in the form of molecular motion when a substance changes state. Matter basically exists in three states—solid, liquid, or gas. Earth's temperature range allows water to exist in all three states (as ice, water, and steam) and to change from one state to another. Because energy is stored in water and then either absorbed or released during the phase transitions, it can absorb energy in one location and transport it to another location where it is released.

Insolation

Our Sun has a surface temperature of about 11,000°F (6,000°C). It emits energy in the form of electromagnetic radiation. When this energy arrives at the top of Earth's atmosphere, it is referred to as INcoming SOLar radiATION, or insolation.

Solar radiation is absorbed, scattered, or reflected. Absorption occurs when solar radiation is intercepted by molecules and particles. The absorbed solar energy raises the temperature in the atmosphere, land, or ocean. Solar radiation passing through the atmosphere is

Global temperatures, 1850–1880

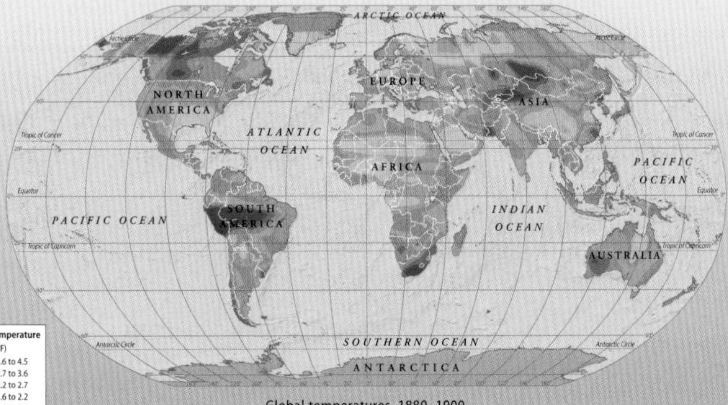

Global temperatures, 1880–1900

Change in Mean Temperature

(°C)	(°F)
2 to 2.5	3.6 to 4.5
1.5 to 2	2.7 to 3.6
1.2 to 1.5	2.2 to 2.7
0.9 to 1.2	1.6 to 2.2
0.6 to 0.9	1.1 to 1.6
0.3 to 0.6	0.5 to 1.1
0 to 0.3	0 to 0.5
-0.3 to 0	-0.5 to 0
-0.6 to -0.3	-1.1 to -0.5
-0.9 to -0.6	-1.6 to -1.1
-1.2 to -0.9	-2.2 to -1.6
-6 to -1.2	-10.8 to -2.2

Global temperatures, 1900–1950

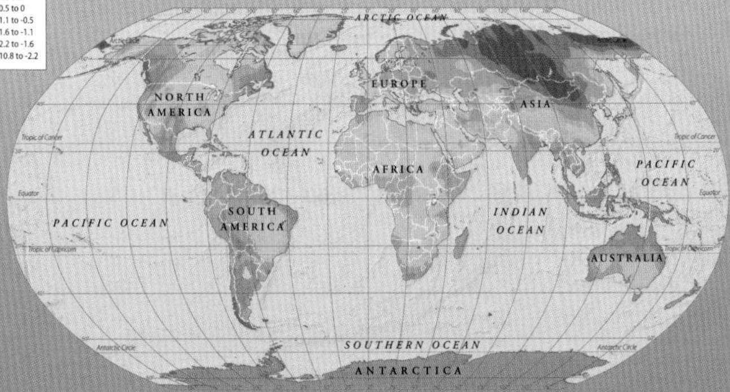

Global temperatures, 1950–2007

Right Evaporation is an important cooling mechanism on Earth. In the desert, where there is little water and water-retaining vegetation, temperatures can reach record highs.

scattered when it comes into contact with a molecule or particle. Scattered radiation changes the direction of the rays. Reflection occurs when radiation is scattered directly back into space. The proportion of radiation reflected or absorbed depends on the object's reflectivity, or albedo.

Latitude

Latitude determines the duration and intensity of insolation. The duration (both diurnal, or daily, and annual) alters very little throughout the year at the equator, 0° latitude. The greatest change in duration of solar radiation occurs at the poles, 90° North and South latitude. During the summer months, the Sun stays above the horizon throughout the 24-hour day and remains there for six months. Yet here the intensity of insolation is quite weak because solar rays strike the surface at a shallow angle and are thus spread out over a very large area.

At 45° North or South latitude, the duration of daylight hours changes seasonally, with many more hours of daylight in summer than winter. The intensity also changes because incoming insolation strikes Earth's surface at a shallower angle in winter.

Land and Water Distribution

Earth's temperature patterns are greatly affected by the different thermal characteristics and distribution of land and water. There are major differences in the rate of heating and cooling between a land surface and a water body. First, solar radiation does not penetrate below the surface of rock and soil on land surfaces. Solar radiation, however, can penetrate several meters through the upper layers of water. Second, dry land heats and cools about four times faster than water, and it takes four times the energy to raise the temperature of water by one degree than it does of rock. The same is true for cooling. Third, water is a fluid and therefore can mix warmer water at the surface with the cooler water below, creating a more uniform temperature through a more substantial portion of the water layer. Fourth, air over water surfaces can be cooled by evaporation. Evaporative cooling is limited over land surfaces because there is not as much water in soil and vegetation.

The thermal differences that exist between land and water cause continents to have strong diurnal and seasonal temperature contrasts, especially in interior locations. A place that has limited vegetation and soil moisture may experience intense heating during the day, but at night the same location will cool rapidly, thereby showing a large temperature range. This is a common occurrence over many arid regions around the world. In mid- and high-latitude continental regions, temperatures are lower because of the reduced incidence of solar radiation and also because insolation is reflected back to space by snow cover.

Temperature characteristics along coastal regions are influenced by proximity to the ocean. Temperature ranges are much more moderate where prevailing winds move air from water to land.

Elevation

Mountainous regions are cool to cold and typically have larger temperature ranges than surrounding lowlands. Temperature decreases on average at the environmental lapse rate of about 3.5°F per 1,000 foot increase in elevation (6.5°C/1,000 m). For example, the temperature at the base of a mountain in the tropics would be warm to hot, but the temperature at the summit would be cool to cold. At very high elevations, low temperatures persist throughout the year and the ground may be covered in ice or snow, even in the tropics.

Surface Type

Different types of land surfaces also contribute to temperature differences. Urban areas, for example, tend to be hotter than surrounding rural environments because of the different surface types. This is the urban heat-island effect, which has three main causes. First is the warming due to alterations on the land surface, with materials such as asphalt and cement absorbing more solar radiation. Second, urban environments lack the vegetation and moist soil that normally would provide a limited evaporative cooling effect. A third cause for urban warming is the heat generated by energy usage that escapes into the atmosphere.

Atmospheric and Ocean Currents

Large global atmospheric and oceanic circulation patterns transport heat from one region of the world to another. The Sun's energy is concentrated in the tropics.

The atmospheric circulation transports energy toward the poles, thereby reducing the equatorial and polar temperature contrast. Prevailing global wind systems also drive surface ocean currents, which transport warmer tropical water poleward and bring colder polar waters toward the tropics.

An example of an ocean current that modifies temperature patterns is the Gulf Stream. Warm water is transported from the tropics in the western Atlantic Ocean toward the coastal regions of northwestern Europe. The result is a range of temperatures that are much warmer than any other region at the same latitude.

Above top A body of water in an area can affect the local temperature, as evaporation cools the air above it. Dry land also heats about four times faster than water.

Above center Coastal areas have more moderate temperature ranges if the prevailing winds move from the water to land, such as at Big Sur, California, USA

Bottom Kilimanjaro rises above the hot dry plains of the Serengeti. This mountain is capped with snow all year round despite its location in equatorial latitudes. Due to its elevation, almost every climate type can be experienced as one climbs its slopes.

Top A satellite image of Phoenix, Arizona, USA, uses an infrared detector to reveal that built-up urban areas are significantly hotter than nearby undeveloped areas of land.

Above Wind, sometimes in hurricane form, transports energy from the warmer tropics, where the Sun's rays hit Earth at a steep angle, toward the polar regions where the temperature is colder.

MEASURING TEMPERATURE

Weather records, at best, convey a general impression of extreme conditions. It is extremely doubtful whether any record—whether of temperature, precipitation, wind, or other elements—actually represents the extreme. Consider the records listed for Antarctica, for example. The continent occupies an area of about 5.4 million square miles (14 million km²), yet there are only a small number of weather stations. The Sahara Desert is approximately the size of the United States or Brazil, and hundreds of thousands of square miles are without an official weather station. Are we really to believe that within that vast expanse the temperature has never risen above the "record"?

There are other problems. In locations subject to hot temperatures, a thermometer at ground level, on a dark surface, can soar well above 160°F (70°C). This is because official temperatures rarely, if ever, reflect the actual conditions in a location. To be official, a temperature must be recorded by a certified station under specific conditions; that is, shaded, several feet above the ground, over a neutral surface. When you are working in the sun, you are exposed to conditions many degrees higher than the temperature you will see or hear in a local weather report.

RECORD HIGH TEMPERATURES

Continent	Place	Highest Recorded Temperature	Date
Africa	Al'Aziziyah, Libya	135.9°F (57.7°C)	September 13, 1922
Antarctica	Hope Bay	58.3°F (14.6°C)	January 5, 1974
Asia	Tirat Tsvi, Israel	129.0°F (53.9°C)	June 21, 1942
Europe	Seville, Spain	122.0°F (50.0°C)	August 4, 1881
North America	Death Valley, USA	134.0°F (56.7°C)	July 10, 1913
Oceania	Cloncurry, Australia	123.3°F (50.7°C)	January 2, 1960
South America	Rivadavia, Argentina	120.0°F (48.9°C)	December 11, 1905

RECORD LOW TEMPERATURES

Continent	Place	Lowest Recorded Temperature	Date
Africa	Ifrane, Morocco	−11.0°F (−23.9°C)	February 11, 1935
Antarctica	Vostock II	−128.6°F (−89.2°C)	July 21, 1983
Asia	Verkhoyansk, Siberia	−93.6°F (−69.8°C)	February 7, 1892
Europe	Ust-Shchugor, Russia	−67.0°F (−55.0°C)	December 31, 1978
North America	Snag, Canada	−81.4°F (−63.0°C)	February 3, 1947
Oceania	Charlotte Pass, Australia	−9.4°F (−23.0°C)	June 29, 1994
South America	Sarmiento, Argentina	−27.4°F (−33.0°C)	June 1, 1907

Precipitation

From near space, Earth appears mostly blue, with small amounts of white. This is largely to do with the existence of water on the planet's surface in its many forms, including ice, liquid, and gas.

Above This view of Earth, as seen by astronauts on *Apollo 11*, shows the predominance of water on the planet's surface. Water is present in the oceans, clouds, and icecaps.

Right A series of mature thunderstorms near the Paraná River in southern Brazil. With warm temperatures and moisture-laden air abundant in this part of Brazil, large thunderstorms are common.

The predominant blue color of the planet results from the reflection of sunlight off the oceans, which cover 71 percent of Earth's surface. The white color is a reflection from the clouds that float over the oceans and continents, from the ice sheets of Greenland and Antarctica, and from scattered patches of ice and snow in mountainous regions.

Water is transported around the planet in a process called the hydrologic cycle that is essential for life on Earth. Precipitation is not, however, evenly distributed around the world. Some areas receive abundant amounts and are covered by dense green vegetation, whereas other areas appear to be parched, light brown, and void of any signs of life. The geographic pattern of precipitation is the result of unequal spatial distribution of air masses, distances from water sources, and uplift mechanisms.

Earth's Water Budget

Earth's hydrosphere consists of water in all forms that is stored in the atmosphere, oceans, lakes, rivers, glaciers, and groundwater. The largest reservoirs are the oceans, which account for 97.2 percent of the hydrosphere. Oceans are composed of saltwater; however, most of the remaining 2.8 percent of the planet's water is fresh. Ice sheets and mountain glaciers are the next largest freshwater reservoir. They contain about 2.15 percent of the total global water supply. Groundwater is the largest freshwater reservoir in liquid form. It comprises about 0.63 percent of the global total of water. The remaining 0.02 percent is found in saline lakes and inland seas, lakes, soil, the atmosphere, and streams.

Although the atmosphere is a very small portion of the hydrosphere, it is of enormous importance to the hydrologic cycle. The atmosphere is the primary transporter of water around the planet and replenishes other freshwater reservoirs. Water evaporates from the oceans and land surfaces and the resulting water vapor is transported elsewhere by the atmosphere. When condensation occurs, water precipitates as rain or snow. If it falls over a land surface, it is intercepted by soils and vegetation. Some of the water infiltrates into soils, where it is used by vegetation or recharges groundwater. The remaining water becomes runoff on the land surface and eventually discharges into streams or lakes. Eventually, the water returns to the oceans to complete the hydrologic cycle.

Earth contains a fixed amount of water, although the amount in each reservoir changes periodically. Alterations to the global water balance result in large-scale changes to weather and climate patterns.

Clouds

Clouds are common features in our atmosphere, covering about half the Earth at any given time. They are composed of water droplets and ice particles suspended in the air. Some are accompanied by precipitation in the form of rain, snow, hail, sleet, and freezing rain. Clouds are divided into two general types: Stratiform and cumuliform. Stratus clouds take their name from the Latin word for "layer," and cumulus clouds from the Latin term for "heap."

Stratus clouds are blanket-like and tend to cover large areas. They form when warm air overrides cold air. As the overriding air rises, it cools, and condensation produces the cloud. If warm air contains ample moisture the cloud will thicken and produce precipitation.

Cumulus clouds form by convection. Warm air rises because it is less dense than the surrounding air. As the air rises it cools and condenses, and clouds form. These clouds often have a cotton-ball appearance and are referred to as "fair-weather cumulus." Sometimes they continue to build vertically to form cumulonimbus, or thunderstorm clouds (nimbus is the Latin word for "rain").

Clouds also are divided into four groups based on their altitude. These are high clouds, middle clouds, low clouds, and clouds with vertical development. Fog is a cloud with its base in contact with the ground. It is another source of moisture in many dry regions.

Precipitation Process

In order to precipitate, air needs to be cooled, which—in nature—is accomplished by uplift. There are four mechanisms that force air upward to create atmospheric cooling and precipitation: Orographic, convectional, frontal, and cyclonic. The first lifting mechanism, orographic, is caused by moisture-bearing winds being forced up the side of a mountain. As the warm air ascends the mountain's windward side, temperature decreases. Eventually it reaches the dew point—the temperature at which condensation occurs—followed by

Above center Orographic cloud clings to the slopes of a mountain in Hornsund, Svalbard. Moisture-bearing air from the sea is forced upward by the rising ground until it reaches the dew point and condenses to form a cloud.

Above Typhoon Longwang approaches the island of Taiwan, on October 1, 2005. This typhoon began as a low-pressure system over the Mariana Islands in the western Pacific Ocean. Winds reached speeds of 150 miles per hour (130 knots). Making landfall twice, the storm killed 148 people in Taiwan and [illegible].

MEASURING RAINFALL

Unlike temperature, which tends to change rather gradually from place to place, precipitation is geographically spotty in nature. Understanding this characteristic becomes important when examining rainfall data.

Precipitation is measured using various types of rain gauges to measure the rainfall in either millimeters or hundredths of an inch. They collect precipitation at a particular point; however, they may not be representative of rainfall over the broader area, as when rain showers occur on one side of a street, while the other remains dry.

The areal extent of rainfall can be determined through numerous methods. One method is using a close network of rain gauges to draw estimated isohyets (lines of equal rainfall) over an area based on point measurements. Areal rainfall measurements also can be estimated from radar.

Problems with rainfall measurements occur when the temperature is below freezing. Freezing rain can accumulate around the top of the gauge and prevent subsequent rain from entering. Another problem occurs when strong winds drive rain at an angle to the gauge opening and therefore result in lower rainfall measurements. These limitations make reliable areal rainfall measurements difficult to obtain from ground-based monitoring stations. A new approach was taken by the National Aeronautics and Space Administration (NASA) and the National Space Development Agency of Japan (NASDA). The Tropical Rainfall Measuring Mission (TRMM) was the first satellite dedicated to rainfall measurement. The next generation of global precipitation satellites will provide more detailed information.

HIGHEST AVERAGE ANNUAL PRECIPITATION BY CONTINENT

Continent	Place	Highest Average (inches/mm)	Elevation (feet/m)	Years
Africa	Debundscha, Cameroon	405.0/10,287	30/9.1	32
Asia	Mawsynram, India	467.4/11,861	4,597/1,401	38
Europe	Crkvica, Bosnia–Herzegovina	183.0/4,648	3,337/1,017	22
North America	Henderson Lake, Canada	256.0/6,502	12/3.6	14
Oceania	Bellenden Ker, Australia	340.0/8,636	5,102/1,555	9
South America	Lloro, Colombia	523.6/13,299 *	520/158.5	29
South America	Quibdo, Colombia	354.0/8,991 *	120/36.5	16

* *The official greatest average annual precipitation for South America is 354 inches (8,991 mm) at Quibdo, Colombia. The 523.6 inches (13,299 mm) average at Lloro, Colombia (14 miles SE and at a higher elevation than Quibdo) is an estimated amount.*

LOWEST AVERAGE ANNUAL PRECIPITATION BY CONTINENT

Continent	Place	Lowest Average (inches/mm)	Elevation (feet/m)	Years
Africa	Wadi Halfa, Sudan	<0.1/<2.5	410/125	39
Antarctica	Amundsen–Scott Sth Pole Station	0.8/20.3	9,186/2,800	10
Asia	Aden, Yemen	1.8/45.7	22/6.7	50
Europe	Astrakhan, Russia	6.4/162.5	45/13.7	25
North America	Batagues, Mexico	1.2/30.5	16/4.9	14
Oceania	Mulka (Troudaninna), Australia	4.05/102.8	160/48.7	42
South America	Arica, Chile	0.03/0.7	95/28.9	59

Below Storm clouds over prairie farmland in Alberta, Canada, will deliver precipitation that may have been carried a great distance from its point of [illegible] by atmospheric movements.

ARCTIC OCEAN
Beaufort Sea
Baffin Bay
Greenland
Greenland Sea
Barents Sea
Laptev Sea
Arctic Circle
Anchorage
Gulf of Alaska
Vancouver
Hudson Bay
NORTH AMERICA
ROCKY MOUNTAINS
GREAT PLAINS
Toronto
New York
Appalachian Mountains
Los Angeles
Gulf of Mexico
Miami
Mexico City
Tropic of Cancer
Caribbean Sea
ATLANTIC OCEAN
Stockholm
Moskva (Moscow)
London
Paris
North European Plain
EUROPE
Budapest
Madrid
Roma (Rome)
Black Sea
Istanbul
Lisboa (Lisbon)
Rabat
Atlas Mountains
Mediterranean Sea
Al Qahirah (Cairo)
Beyrouth (Beirut)
Libyan Desert
SAHARA
Dakar
Sahel
El Khartûm (Khartoum)
Sudd
AFRICA
Lagos
Kinshasa
Nairobi
Lake Victoria
Kalahari Desert
Orange
Cape Town
Antananarivo
Arabian Peninsula
Ar Riyad (Riyadh)
Tehrān
Baghdād
Caspian Sea
Aral Sea
Ozero Balkhash
Ural Mountains
SIBERIA
Irtysh
Ob'
Yenisey
Lena
Ozero Baykal (Lake Baikal)
Amur
Sea of Okhotsk
Gobi
Tien Shan
ASIA
Plateau of Tibet
HIMALAYA
Lahore
New Delhi
Thar Desert
Karachi
Mumbai (Bombay)
Bengaluru (Bangalore)
Kolkata
Dhaka
Ganges
Brahmaputra
Chang Jiang
Huang He
Beijing
Sŏul (Seoul)
Tōkyō
Shanghai
Yangon (Rangoon)
Krung Thep (Bangkok)
South China Sea
Manila
Philippine Sea
PACIFIC OCEAN
Singapore
Borneo
Jakarta
New Guinea
INDIAN OCEAN
Coral Sea
Great Sandy Desert
AUSTRALIA
Great Victoria Desert
Darling
Sydney
Tasman Sea
Tropic of Capricorn
Equator
PACIFIC OCEAN
Bogotá
Amazon Basin
Amazon
SOUTH AMERICA
Lima
ANDES
Rio de Janeiro
São Paulo
Santiago
Buenos Aires
Punta Arenas
Scotia Sea
SOUTHERN OCEAN
Antarctic Circle
ANTARCTICA
Robinson Projection
0 1000 2000 3000 4000 kilometers
0 500 1000 1500 2000 miles
World Average Annual Rainfall (mm)
0–25
25–50
50–75
75–100
100–150
150–200
200–300
300–400
400–500
Above 500
no data available

Above center Ice and snow in the polar caps and glaciers contain just over two percent of Earth's supply of fresh water. Icebergs—like this spectacular example in Antarctica—break off from glaciers and ice sheets, carrying large reservoirs of fresh water into warmer parts of the ocean, where they melt.

Above After rain, mud flats crack and dry in Sossusvlei, Namibia. With so little precipitation in this area, when rain does fall it is quickly absorbed by the dry earth or evaporated by the hot Sun.

precipitation if there is sufficient moisture. On the leeward side of the mountain, the air contains less water vapor and is warmed by compression as it descends to lower elevations and higher atmospheric pressure. This process creates "rain shadow," or dry conditions on the leeward side of the mountain.

The second lifting mechanism, convection, is caused by unequal heating on the surface of the land. For example, a surface composed of dry sand will be much hotter than a surrounding forest, due to an evaporative cooling effect. Air over the dry sand is quickly heated by the Sun and becomes less dense than the surrounding air, rising like a hot-air balloon. This rising air cools until its temperature is equal to the dew point, condensation then occurs and billowing cumulus clouds with flat bases form.

The third mechanism is caused by frontal boundaries between air masses of different density. The warmer air is lifted, and then condenses to form clouds and precipitation.

The fourth lifting mechanism, cyclonic, is the result of the air flow associated with low-pressure systems. Air flows inward and upward near the center of low-pressure systems. These systems are associated with frontal systems in the middle and higher latitudes, but are seen by themselves in lower latitudes where there is not a contrast in air masses. At low latitudes these systems begin as tropical easterly waves that move westward; sometimes these waves start turning cyclonically.

When winds are less than 31 miles per hour (34 knots) the system is referred to as a tropical depression; when speeds are between 31 and 73 miles per hour (34 and 63 knots) it is called a tropical storm. Occasionally wind speeds exceed 73 miles per hour (64 knots) and air spirals in toward the center to form a tropical cyclone. These are called hurricanes in the Atlantic and eastern Pacific oceans, typhoons in the western Pacific Ocean, and cyclones in the Indian Ocean. These large atmospheric systems transport vast amounts of moisture from the oceans to land masses, often resulting in severe flooding.

Unequal Distribution of Precipitation

The global distribution of precipitation is the result of complex interactions of atmospheric circulation, temperature, and land/water distribution. Areas that receive less than 10 inches (250 mm) of rainfall each year are considered deserts, while regions receiving more than 80 inches (2,000 mm) are typically equatorial. Remote interior regions such as central Asia are dry throughout the year. Although there are large amounts of snow and ice in the Arctic and Antarctic, these areas are dry because cold air cannot hold as much moisture as warm air.

The Intertropical Convergence Zone (ITCZ) is an area of low pressure that forms where the northeast and southeast trade winds converge near the equator. The low pressure and converging winds force the moist air upward. Humidity is constantly high, often reaching 100 percent, and annual rainfall often exceeds 100 inches (2,540 mm). Rainfall is abundant throughout the year.

Monsoonal regions experience a distinct dry and wet season. These are caused by a reversal of wind-flow patterns: Winds flow from the continental interior and then out over the ocean during the dry season, but the reversal of flow brings air from over the ocean to the continents along with large amounts of moisture in the wet season.

Above This map shows the distribution of precipitation over land throughout the world. Inland areas of the continents are generally dry, while coastal and mountainous areas receive more rain. The Intertropical Convergence Zone (ITCZ) makes South America an exception.

Below When temperatures are below freezing, precipitation may take the form of snow or hail.

Bottom Bryce Canyon, Utah, USA, experiences a phenomenon known as the Arizona Monsoon—warm, moist air from the Gulf of Mexico, warmed by the summer Sun, creates convectional storms, which move quickly across the desert landscape.

Climate

Climate is the average and variations of weather in a region over long periods of time. Weather, on the other hand, is the measurement of air temperature, precipitation, pressure, and winds at this moment, or at some specific moment in the past.

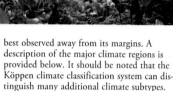

Above The Simpson Desert in central Australia is an example of an arid dry climate (group B in the Köppen system). Rain rarely falls, but some hardy plants survive nonetheless.

Above right Tropical rainforests benefit from warm wet conditions. The lush growth of plants and the ready availability of water allow a multiplicity of animals and insects to live here also.

Climate, in its basic sense, is the statistical analysis of weather: It combines weather record parameters into averages, ranges, and extremes. Climate zones are arbitrarily defined regions that share similar long-term weather elements such as temperature and precipitation.

Climate is one of the most important determining factors for the distribution of life on Earth. It is also an important factor in making informed economic and land use decisions, especially in agriculture and construction.

Climate Controls and Early Classification

Earth has a variety of climate types that range from tropical moist in equatorial regions to polar. There are seven factors that affect climate at a given location: Latitude, land/water distribution, ocean currents, wind patterns, high- and low-pressure circulations, mountain barriers, and elevation. These controls interact and produce a variety of climates. Each location on Earth's surface has its own climate that distinguishes it from other locations. In order to understand the general climate of a location, averages and ranges are used to group weather elements.

The Ancient Greeks grouped Earth's climates into three regions: The torrid zone, temperate zone, and frigid zone. This system of classifying climate was too general and excluded precipitation. Neither did it provide a way to differentiate wet from dry regions or consider the complex interactions of climate controls other than latitude.

Köppen Classification System

There have been many attempts to classify climate regions. The most widely used classification system for world climates was devised by German botanist-climatologist Wladimir Köppen (1846–1940), of the University of Graz in Austria. Published in 1918 and later revised by Rudolf Geiger and W. Pohl in 1953, the Köppen climate classification system applied a vegetation-based approach. This is based on the concept that natural vegetation reflects climatic conditions.

Global Climate Patterns

Major climate zones are subdivided into smaller regions. Each subdivision often has, within its boundaries, local differences brought about by changes in elevation, slope and aspect, and proximity to bodies of water. The edges of climate regions tend to gradually transition from one climate region to another. Therefore, the character of a climate region is best observed away from its margins. A description of the major climate regions is provided below. It should be noted that the Köppen climate classification system can distinguish many additional climate subtypes.

TROPICAL MOIST CLIMATES (GROUP A)

There are three major climate types found in the low latitudes. These are: Tropical wet climate (Af) rainforest, tropical monsoon climate (Am), and wet–dry tropical climate (Aw) savanna. These range from the equator to about 15° to 25° North and South. The tropical wet climate experiences heavy rainfall in all months with an annual rainfall often more than 60 inches (1,500 mm). Precipitation is associated with the Intertropical Convergence Zone (ITCZ). Monthly mean temperatures are above 64°F (18°C). The Amazon Basin of South America, the Congo basin of equatorial Africa, and the East Indies from Sumatra to New Guinea fall into this type. The great tropical rainforests cover less than six percent of Earth's land surface, yet they account for over half of the world's plant and animal species and produce 40 percent of Earth's oxygen.

The tropical monsoon climate has rainfall amounts comparable to those of the tropical wet climate, with a brief dry season in which precipitation drops below 2½ inches (60 mm) for one or two months. This type of climate is

CLIMATE SCALES

Climate is studied on four scales: Microclimate, mesoclimate, macroclimate, and global. Changes occur rapidly over smaller areas and slowly over larger areas, affecting the determination of climate averages, ranges, and cycles.

The smallest scale is the microclimate, typically ranging in size from a few square yards to a few square miles. Underlying surface properties cause changes in temperature and moisture characteristics. For example, the temperature and moisture of the air over an asphalt road would be very different than over a nearby pond. The asphalt road absorbs solar radiation and re-radiates heat, causing the air temperature to increase and moisture to decrease. Because of the unique properties of water (mixing, evaporation, and specific heat), the air temperature would be much cooler over the pond. Also, temperature and moisture can be affected by the direction in which a slope is facing (aspect) in relation to the Sun's rays. Temperature is determined by the length of time a surface is exposed—longer exposure and more direct sunlight translate to warmer temperatures.

The mesoclimate shows changes of temperature and moisture patterns at ranges between tens and hundreds of miles. The scale of the macroclimate delineates regions that are major subdivisions of continents, hundreds to thousands of miles across. The global climate extends over the entire planet and involves energy received from the Sun and large circulation patterns in the atmosphere and oceans.

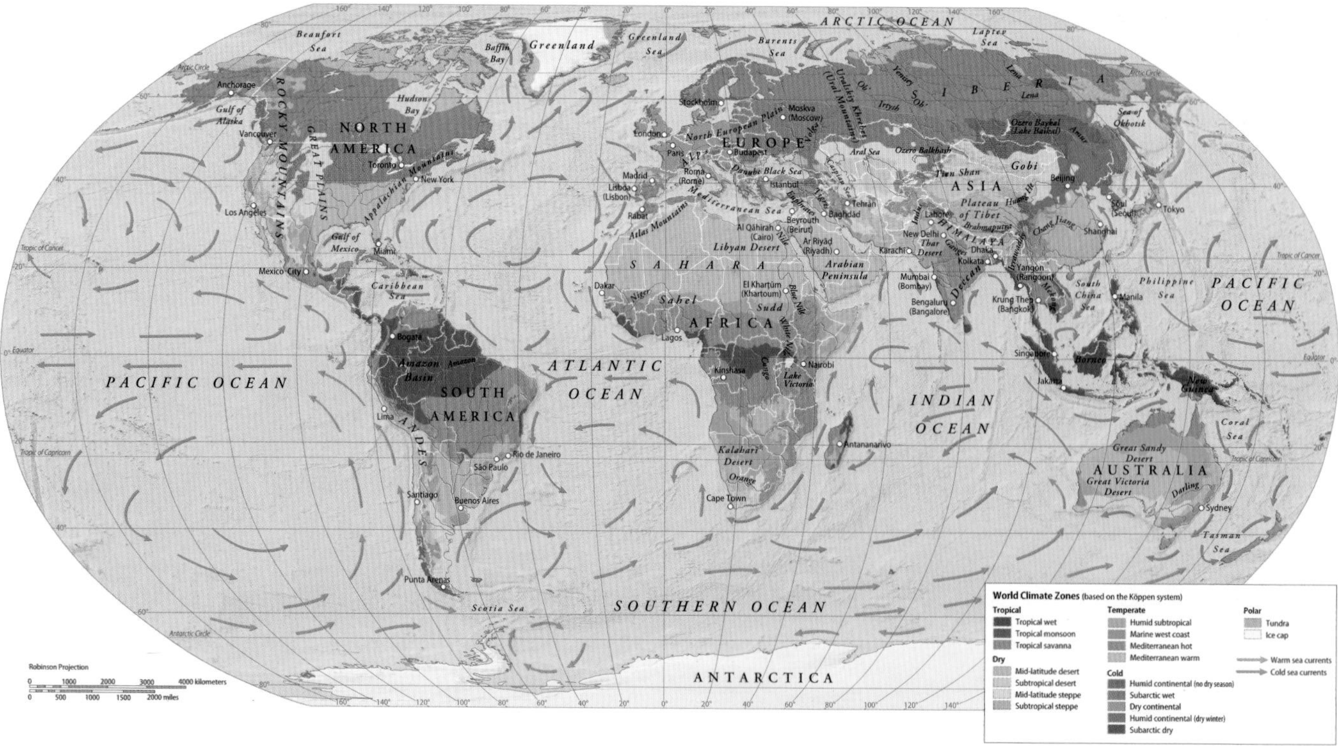
ARCTIC OCEAN
NORTH AMERICA
EUROPE
ASIA
AFRICA
SOUTH AMERICA
AUSTRALIA
ANTARCTICA
PACIFIC OCEAN
ATLANTIC OCEAN
INDIAN OCEAN
SOUTHERN OCEAN
Greenland
Hudson Bay
Gulf of Mexico
Caribbean Sea
Amazon Basin
Sahel
Libyan Desert
Arabian Peninsula
Plateau of Tibet
Gobi
Kalahari Desert
Great Sandy Desert
Great Victoria Desert
Tasman Sea
Coral Sea
Scotia Sea
Anchorage
Vancouver
Los Angeles
Toronto
New York
Mexico City
Miami
Bogotá
Lima
Rio de Janeiro
São Paulo
Santiago
Buenos Aires
Punta Arenas
London
Paris
Madrid
Stockholm
Budapest
Dakar
Lagos
Kinshasa
Nairobi
Cape Town
Antananarivo
Tehran
Karachi
Mumbai (Bombay)
Bengaluru (Bangalore)
Beijing
Shanghai
Tokyo
Manila
Singapore
Jakarta
Sydney
Robinson Projection
World Climate Zones (based on the Köppen system)
Tropical
Tropical wet
Tropical monsoon
Tropical savanna
Dry
Mid-latitude desert
Subtropical desert
Mid-latitude steppe
Subtropical steppe
Temperate
Humid subtropical
Marine west coast
Mediterranean hot
Mediterranean warm
Cold
Humid continental (no dry season)
Subarctic wet
Dry continental
Humid continental (dry winter)
Subarctic dry
Polar
Tundra
Ice cap
Warm sea currents
Cold sea currents

Far left Joshua trees *(Yucca brevifolia)* require hot summers, well-timed rains, and freezing winters to flower and develop their striking shapes. Their requirements limit them to a small area where conditions are suitable.

Center The Mediterranean region, with its dry summers and wet winters, has its own climate type. The vegetation is uniquely adapted to survive drought in summer, as well as coastal conditions such as moist sea air.

Left The bare branches of deciduous birches stand out against the evergreen pines and spruces in this boreal forest in Sweden. The trees provide shelter and food for animals, such as elks and wolves, to survive long cold winters.

experienced along the coasts of Southeast Asia, India, and in northeastern South America.

The wet–dry tropical climate is poleward of the tropical wet climate; total annual precipitation diminishes and becomes seasonal. Wet tropical air masses and dry tropical air masses bring about distinct wet and dry seasons. Temperatures are hottest in late spring, just prior to the arrival of the wet season. This climate is found in India, Indochina, western Africa, southern Africa, South America, and the north coast of Australia.

DRY CLIMATES (GROUP B)

The savanna environment gradually transitions into the desert environment. The two basic types of B climates are based on their degree of dryness, the arid (BW) and the semiarid or steppe (BS). Potential evaporation and transpiration exceed precipitation.

The tropical deserts extend roughly from 20° to 30° North and South latitude. The arid climates occupy about 12 percent of the world's land area. They are found along the west coasts of South America and Africa and interior portions of Australia. In North America, the arid climate extends from northern Mexico into the southern interior of the United States. The largest region is the Sahara–Saudi Arabia–Iran–Thar desert belt of North Africa and southern Asia. Surrounding most of these arid regions are semiarid steppes, with vegetation comprising short bunch grasses, thorny trees, and shrubs.

MOIST SUBTROPICAL MID-LATITUDE CLIMATES (GROUP C)

The moist subtropical mid-latitude climate is found on the eastern sides of continents between 20° to 35° North and South. These regions are noted for hot humid summers. Winters tend to be mild, especially in the lower latitudes. Poleward regions are colder and harsher. Rainfall is generally well distributed throughout the year, with annual averages of 30–65 inches (800–1,650 mm). Much of the natural vegetation consists of broadleaf deciduous forest. However, in southern China, southern Japan, and the US Gulf Coast, most of these forests are gone or greatly diminished.

Two other climate types, the marine west coast and Mediterranean, are included in the group C classification. Marine west-coast climates are located on the west coast of continents between 40° and 60° North and South. Prevailing westerly winds bring cool moist maritime air into these regions, moderating the climate. This climate does not extend far inland where mountains parallel coasts, such as in North and South America. However, the marine west-coast climate extends over extensive areas of Western Europe because the winds are unobstructed by mountains.

The Mediterranean climate is unique in that most precipitation is confined to the winter months while summers are dry. This climate is found around the borders of the Mediterranean Sea as well as the west coast of continents on the equatorial side of the marine west coast climate. Annual precipitation ranges from 12 to 35 inches (300 to 900 mm). Natural vegetation comprises trees and shrubs adapted to the long hot summer drought.

MOIST CONTINENTAL AND BOREAL FOREST CLIMATES (GROUP D)

The moist continental climate is found over great expanses of the temperate mid-latitudes. It experiences a large temperature range due to its interior location in mid-latitude continents. Annual precipitation typically ranges from 20 to 40 inches (500 to 1,000 mm) with the greatest monthly precipitation during summer. In regions of lower precipitation, grasses are the dominant natural vegetation. Colder and wetter regions are covered by forest under natural conditions.

The taiga or boreal forest region experiences bitterly cold winters and mild summers, and has the largest annual temperature range of any climate on Earth.

POLAR CLIMATES (GROUP E)

Polar climates are the tundra (ET) and ice cap (EF). The tundra climate is a transition from the boreal forest to its south and the northern ice-cap climate. Stunted trees gradually give way to sedges, mosses, and lichens. The tundra is characterized by very cold temperatures and generally dry conditions. Temperatures do not rise above 50°F (10°C) even during the summer. The ice-cap climate features Earth's coldest temperatures; it is bitterly cold throughout the year. Even though these regions are covered by snow and ice, they are extremely dry and snowfall is low. Climatologists describe these regions as "polar deserts."

HIGHLAND CLIMATES (GROUP H)

Highlands have many climate zones because temperature decreases as elevation increases. Climbing 1,000 feet (300 m) is equivalent to traveling poleward 186 miles (300 km), or about three degrees of latitude. The character of the climate is related to the surrounding lowlands. Temperature decreases with elevation, and temperature range and precipitation generally increase.

Below left Despite abundant water, the ice-cap climate is described as a desert because annual precipitation—in the form of snow—is actually quite low. Freezing temperatures ensure that the snow and ice do not melt and evaporate.

Below Highlands have climate zones that are quite different from the surrounding lowlands. This glacier-carved valley in Glencoe, Scotland, receives around 90 inches (2,300 mm) of rain each year and is whipped by racing winds.

Bottom In Banff National Park, Canada, the prevailing westerly winds bring moist air from the Pacific Ocean: As the air is forced up over the mountain peaks it cools, causing the moisture in the air to condense and precipitate.

Climate Change

Earth's climate is always changing. Evidence shows that climate has changed repeatedly in the past and there is no evidence to suggest that it will not change in the future. Understanding climate change and its causes involves scientists from many disciplines, including atmospheric science, climatology, geography, geology, biology, environmental science, human ecology, and other fields.

Above Stromatolites are rock-like outcrops formed by a type of cyanobacteria. Fossil evidence shows that these bacteria were among the earliest photosynthetic organisms on Earth, enriching the planet's atmosphere with oxygen.

Climate scientists study climatic variations on time scales from decades to millions of years. They also look for potential explanations for these changes. Some changes are the result of internal processes on Earth such as volcanic eruptions, or external forces such as variations in solar intensity. Many scientists believe the role of human activity has become increasingly important in climate change.

Earth's Changing Climate

Earth is estimated to be around 4.5 billion years old. Rock layers contain some of the oldest records of the climate in the past: Buried within them are the fossilized remains of plant life and, later, animal life that evolved over the last three billion years. Early life forms such as stromatolites transformed a carbon dioxide-rich atmosphere into an oxygen-rich atmosphere, similar to that of today, which allowed more complex life forms to gradually evolve. Paleoclimatologists use the fossilized remains of plants and animals as one indicator to estimate climatic conditions hundreds of millions of years ago.

Evidence shows that Earth's temperature has gone through warm (hothouse) and cold (icehouse) cycles. Ice ages occurred about 700 million years ago and again 300 million years ago. Much of the Mesozoic Era (255 to 65 million years ago), was warmer than today. After that, Earth entered a long, gradual, cooling trend and after millions of years ice began to accumulate at the polar regions. During the Pleistocene epoch (1.8 million to 11,500 years before present) the geological record provides evidence of 20 cycles of advancing and retreating continental glaciers.

Above Climate records from the Little Ice Age in Europe are imprecise, but many artists recorded the unusual weather, including James Stow in his engraving of a "Frost Fair" held on the frozen River Thames, London, in 1683–84.

The ice began to retreat about 14,000 years ago, as temperatures began to increase. There were two periods when temperatures dropped back toward glacial condition. The cold period ended and temperatures began to rise, reaching their warmest 6,000 years ago (known as the Holocene maximum, or climatic optimum). Cooling began again 5,000 years ago and alpine glaciers began to descend again.

Regional patterns began to be resolved over the last 1,000 years. In the Northern hemisphere some areas showed warming, while others were cooling. During the eleventh to fourteenth centuries, vineyards thrived in England and the Vikings colonized Greenland and Iceland, suggesting warmer and drier summers. This was followed by a cooling period from the fifteenth to the nineteenth centuries, called the Little Ice Age, affecting Europe and North America: The Thames River in England and the canals and rivers of the Netherlands regularly froze over during the winter.

Over the last century, temperatures have again increased. The Intergovernmental Panel on Climate Change reported that from 1906 to 2005 global surface temperature increased by 1.33°F (0.74°C) and that the 12 years from 1995 to 2006 rank among the 12 warmest years in the instrumental record of global surface temperature since 1850.

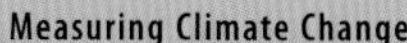

Measuring Climate Change

Paleoclimatologists use a variety of natural "proxy" sources to reconstruct past climatic conditions prior to instrument records. The two most common climatic proxies are biotic and geological–geochemical indicators.

Biotic proxies are based on changes in plants and animals. The presence of a single temperature-sensitive species provides important clues to ancient climate conditions. Another biotic proxy is measurement of the annual growth rates of trees and corals. Geological–geochemical proxies measure mass movements of materials by the processes of weathering, erosion, transportation, and deposition.

Dating Records

The best proxy records occur over long periods of time and provide a dense global coverage. Most records, however, have brief time series or are geographically limited. Dating is accomplished through numerous techniques.

Above The granite rocks of the Yosemite Valley, USA, weathered and eroded by Pleistocene glaciers, make the valley both a monument to and a record of the interaction of natural forces—geologic and meteorological—through millennia.

Top The Petrified Forest National Park in Arizona, USA, was once home to dinosaurs of the Triassic era. The growth rings of these fossilized trees in the park provide clues to climatologists about the conditions on Earth during that time.

Radiometric dating measures the decay of a radioactive isotope and provides the age of rocks and other geological features. These methods allow dating from a few thousand years to billions of years depending on the rate of radioactive decay for a particular element.

Some climate archives provide annual layers that can be manually counted. The annual layers form because of seasonal changes in accumulation or growth rates. Proxies that indicate year-to-year variations in climate include tree rings, ice cores, deep lake sediments, and coral reefs.

Dendrochronology (tree-ring dating) uses annual growth rings and relates them to past climate conditions by comparing several trees growing in the same place and at the same time. The trees usually show similar growth patterns.

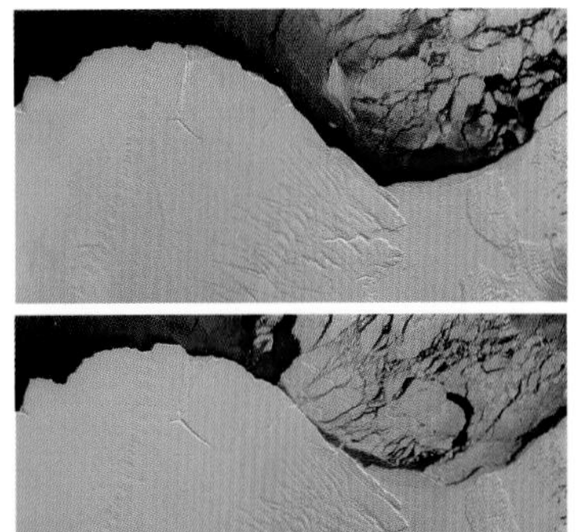

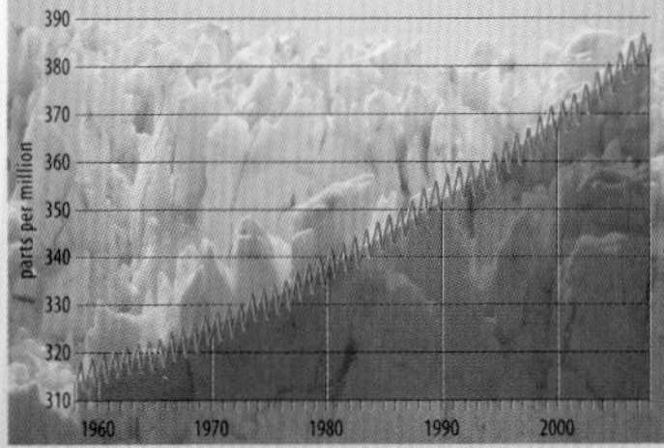
390
380
370
360
350
340
330
320
310
parts per million
1960
1970
1980
1990
2000

VOLCANIC ERUPTIONS

Large volcanic eruptions typically impact global climate for short time periods. Mt Tambora on Sumbawa Island, Indonesia, is in a subduction region. These are regions where one tectonic plate is sliding below another, creating conditions favorable for volcanic eruptions. Tambora's eruption in 1815 was the largest in recorded history. About 35 cubic miles (150 km^3) of ash was expelled and the explosion was heard on Sumatra, more than 1,200 miles (2,000 km) away. It released rock and ash called "tephra" along with sulfur dioxide (SO_2) 27 miles (43 km) into the stratosphere, where it was transported globally by strong upper atmospheric winds.

Sulfur dioxide produces very shiny water droplets that reflect incoming solar radiation back into space. The 1815 eruption of Tambora caused the "year without a summer." In fact, 1815 and 1816 were the coldest years in the last two centuries. Average global temperatures decreased about 0.7–1.3°F (0.4–0.7°C). Very cold and, in some locations, wet weather was documented globally. Over the next two years, crops failed in Europe and North America.

Several other major volcanic events have showed altered global temperature patterns lasting from one to three years. One of the more recent eruptions was of Mt Pinatubo in the Philippines in June 1991, pictured. It was the second largest eruption of the twentieth century and produced approximately 2.4 cubic miles (10 km^3) of rock and ash. Sulfur dioxide combined with water vapor reduced global surface temperatures by 0.9°F (0.5°C).

Another eruption, of El Chichón in northwestern Chiapas, Mexico, in March–April, 1982, coincided with a reduction in global temperatures of 0.36°F (0.2°C); however, this is within the limits of normal climate variation.

Supervolcanic eruptions are very rare, but result in stronger, long-term climate impacts. Thousands of times more powerful than any recent eruptions, their ash and gas can cover a continent. These eruptions cause volcanic depressions called "calderas" and spread ash over vast regions. On Toba, Sumatra, a caldera produced eruptions 840,000, 700,000, and 75,000 years ago. Scientists have estimated that the total amount of erupted material was about 670 cubic miles (2,800 km^3). Evidence from seashells and ice cores with high concentrations of sulfuric acid indicates that deep ocean temperatures dropped by almost 10°F (5°C) over a few thousand years. Many species, including humans, were pushed to the edge of extinction by these events.

Above Measurements of carbon dioxide in the atmosphere by the National Oceanic and Atmospheric Administration, USA, were started by C. David Keeling in 1958 and continue to date. Carbon dioxide is an important greenhouse gas.

Top Satellite images of the Amery Ice Shelf in Antarctica, taken a year apart, show a "loose tooth" of ice becoming looser. Scientists are monitoring iceberg calving in this area to determine whether the events are being affected by possible climate changes.

Annual layers (varves) are also present in lakes. These are alternating light and dark bands. The light layer is deposited in summer and the darker layer during winter. Material from varves can also be used to calibrate the radiocarbon time scale.

Potential Causes of Climate Change

Factors responsible for past episodes of climate change include variations in incoming solar radiation; changes in atmospheric composition; and changes in Earth's surface.

Variations in incoming solar radiation result from changes in Earth's orbit around the Sun. Because of the changing distances and angles, Earth receives varying amounts of energy from the Sun.

Recent measurements made by satellites show that the Sun's energy output also varies and changes with sunspot activity. Sunspots reach a maximum about every 11 years. During periods with maximum sunspot activity the Sun emits 0.1 percent more energy than during periods of minimum activity.

Changes in atmospheric composition are a result of both natural processes and human activities. The gases that affect surface temperatures are referred to as greenhouse gases: These gases trap radiation and prevent it from escaping back into space. The most important greenhouse gases are water vapor, carbon dioxide (CO_2), methane (CH_4), nitrous oxide (N_2O), and fluorinated gases.

Water vapor is responsible for warming Earth by about 54° F (30° C). Human activity does not directly affect water vapor concentrations except at local levels.

Carbon dioxide occurs naturally in the atmosphere and is emitted by processes such as the burning of fossil fuels. Atmospheric concentrations have increased from pre-industrial levels of 280 parts per million to current levels of 382 parts per million, a 36 percent increase.

Methane is emitted during the production and transport of coal, natural gas, and oil, as well as by livestock and agricultural activities. Methane concentrations increased during the twentieth century by 148 percent.

Nitrous oxide is emitted during agricultural and industrial activities, with combustion of fossil fuels, and from solid waste. Atmospheric levels have increased from pre-industrial levels of 270 parts per billion to current levels of 314 parts per billion.

Fluorinated gases include hydrofluorocarbons, perfluorocarbons, and sulfur hexafluoride. These are powerful synthetic gases that are emitted from a variety of industrial processes. They are potent greenhouse gases.

Changes in Earth's surface have occurred slowly over the geologic past but have had long-term effects on climate. Tectonic plates slide over subsurface molten material and intense geologic activity occurs along the plate boundaries. The Himalaya mountain range began rising about 50 million years ago when India collided with the Asian continent. They prevent warm moist air masses from entering the continental interior and affect monsoonal circulations in regions of the Indian Ocean.

In view of contemporary concerns related to potential global warming, it is important to remember that change, rather than stability, is the natural order of Earth's climate.

Above Sedimentary layers in the landscape of the Badlands National Park, South Dakota, USA, provide a clear geological "proxy" record for paleoclimatologists.

Above Tree rings are a biotic "proxy" climate record. This fossilized oak tree tells much about the Earth's climate at the time it was living.

Below Puerto Moreno Glacier in Patagonia loses a chunk of ice at its leading edge. Examples of glaciers retreating are often cited as evidence of climate change.

Natural Hazards

Earthquakes, volcanic eruptions, floods, and hurricanes are just some events that can have cataclysmic effects on a local or international scale. Life on this planet is in constant peril at the hand of the forces of nature.

Right A cloud of ash hangs over Vesuvius during a violent eruption in 1944. Naples, in the foreground, was largely unaffected, but the nearby towns of Massa and San Sebastiano were destroyed by the flow of lava.

Natural hazards are naturally occurring events that have significant impacts on humans. Sometimes referred to as "acts of God," natural hazards tend to occur suddenly, with little or no warning.

As the human population has grown, the risks of natural hazards have increased. Massive cities are located in areas known to be at great risk from earthquakes; for example, Los Angeles—a city of more than eight million people—lies on the highly active San Andreas Fault line. The city and surrounding areas of Naples in Italy, with a population of more than one million, are at risk of volcanic eruptions from Mount Vesuvius, the same mountain that destroyed the ancient city of Pompeii. Millions of people live in the flood-prone lowlands of Bangladesh and India.

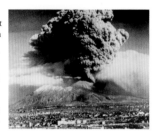

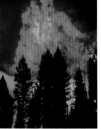

Above Lightning is frequently the cause of wildfires that can burn across the land. Some ecosystems need fire for regeneration, but it also burns out suburbs and cities.

Earthquakes

Earthquakes are the result of a build-up of enormous amounts of energy in Earth's crust. As the tectonic plates move around each other, stress increases. The area where the hard edges of the plates move against each other is known as a fault line, and the places most at risk from earthquake damage are those closest to the edges of tectonic plates.

The most at-risk locations tend to be those along the Pacific "Rim of Fire." Surrounding the vast Pacific Ocean, the "Rim of Fire" follows the fault line between the huge Pacific tectonic plate and a host of smaller plates adjacent to it. Another area particularly prone to earthquakes lies in the highly active tectonic zone of northern India and Nepal.

Above Drought can be as much of a natural disaster as flood. In rural Brazil, deep holes must be dug to reach scarce groundwater supplies during a long dry period.

Tsunamis

Tsunamis are often incorrectly called tidal waves, but tides have no role in the creation of tsunamis. They are most commonly the result of earthquakes taking place under or close to the ocean. Submarine landslides, volcanic activity, and meteorite strikes are other possible causes.

Tsunamis are thought of as enormous waves, but these only develop close to the shore. Out at sea, tsunamis are little more than a fast moving ripple on the surface. The first sign of a tsunami on shore is a dramatic retreat of the sea as water is pulled out to sea. This water then returns as part of the huge wave.

Tsunamis can occur in any ocean but are most common in the Pacific, as this is the most tectonically active ocean. High-tech buoys dot the Pacific Ocean, measuring any underwater activity that may spark a tsunami. The most devastating tsunami in history, the Boxing Day tsunami of 2004, occurred in the Indian Ocean where no early-warning system was in place.

Hurricanes, Cyclones, and Typhoons

Essentially different names for the same thing, hurricanes, cyclones, and typhoons are intense low-pressure systems that form over the ocean. These storms cause enormous damage across large areas in tropical and subtropical areas.

These storms begin as severe thunderstorms over warm ocean water at 81° F (27° C). As the storm develops, winds grow in strength and begin to move in a circular motion. Gradually a disk-shaped, three-dimensional structure forms that can reach heights of 9 miles (14.5 km) at its center and diameters of more than 600 miles (950 km).

The storms not only bring very strong winds, which can reach more than 150 miles per hour (250 km/h), they also create massive storm surges. The low pressures created by the storms "lift up" the water at the ocean's surface, causing very high tides to flow across the land. These storm surges are often more damaging than the storm itself.

Other Hazards

Other significant natural hazards include droughts, floods, tornadoes, fires, and snow storms. Droughts are defined as prolonged periods of below-average rainfall. The main impact of drought is on food production and the ability to obtain sufficient water. In developed nations, people do not die from drought because food and water can be obtained from elsewhere. In developing nations, however, droughts can have a devastating effect. A very long drought in India in 1875 to 1900 is estimated to have led to the deaths of more than 30 million people. Climate change is expected to increase the frequency and severity of droughts in many parts of the world, including Australia, central Africa, and parts of Asia.

The same hot dry conditions that give rise to droughts are also common causes of wildfires, although lightning and, in some cases, human actions are also sources of fire ignition. In many environments, fire is a necessary part of the regeneration of the ecosystem. However, it becomes a hazard when human activity gets in the way.

Floods are created when so much rain falls in an area that the natural drainage systems—rivers, streams, and creeks—cannot cope with the volume of water and it rises and flows across the landscape. Floods bring with them

THE BAM EARTHQUAKE, 2003

Bam is an historic city of around 90,000 people in Iran. Soon after dawn on December 26, 2003, the residents of Bam were awoken by an earthquake measuring 6.5 on the Richter Scale. The simple mud-brick houses of most of the inhabitants had no defense and most of the city's buildings collapsed. Bam's 2,000-year-old citadel (below, before and after the earthquake) crumbled.

After the initial destruction, the residents of Bam faced new challenges; with most of the infrastructure destroyed, the injured faced long trips by road or helicopter to the city of Kerman, around 100 miles (160 km) away. Adding to the city's woes, thousands of people from surrounding towns and villages flooded in, swelling the population to an estimated 120,000. Although local authorities and the international community sent considerable aid, the effects of disease, injuries, famine, and exposure—as well as the actual earthquake—resulted in more than 26,000 deaths.

HURRICANE KATRINA, 2005

Hurricane Katrina, shown in the satellite image at left, was one of the most destructive in US history. Katrina developed in the Gulf of Mexico and moved toward the US Gulf Coast, slamming into the land on August 29, 2005. On August 28, the US National Hurricane Center upgraded Katrina to a Category 5 storm with winds of around 175 miles per hour (282 km/h).

In the low-lying city of New Orleans, evacuation warnings were issued, calling on the residents to leave. However, as Katrina roared overhead many of the city's poor residents were unable to flee. New Orleans lies on the mighty Mississippi River with much of the city below sea level: A vast system of levee banks and barriers protects the city from flooding. The storm surge created by Katrina punched holes in this protection, leading to flooding of over 80 per cent of the city, right.

Katrina caused more than US$75 billion in damage; several thousand people were killed (many drowned in their New Orleans homes), and hundreds of thousands were left homeless. Years later, much of New Orleans still lies in ruins as the US government decides whether to rebuild the city and its complex barriers, or relocate it to higher ground.

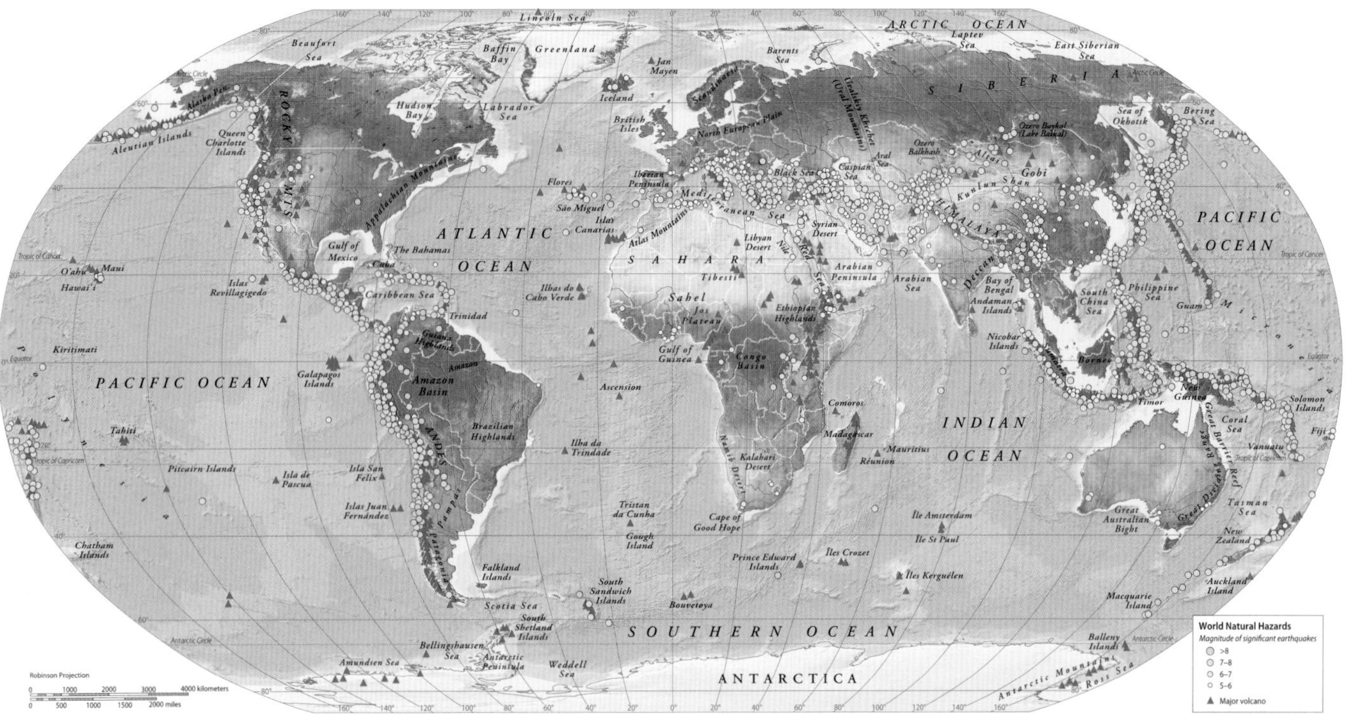
Lincoln Sea
ARCTIC OCEAN
Laptev Sea
East Siberian Sea
Beaufort Sea
Baffin Bay
Greenland
Jan Mayen
Barents Sea
Hudson Bay
Labrador Sea
Iceland
British Isles
SIBERIA
Sea of Okhotsk
Bering Sea
Aleutian Islands
Queen Charlotte Islands
ROCKY MTS
Ozero Baykal (Lake Baikal)
Ozero Balkhash
Aral Sea
Caspian Sea
Black Sea
Gobi
North European Plain
Flores
São Miguel
Islas Canarias
Iberian Peninsula
Mediterranean Sea
Atlas Mountains
ATLANTIC OCEAN
SAHARA
Libyan Desert
Syrian Desert
PACIFIC OCEAN
Gulf of Mexico
The Bahamas
Cuba
O'ahu
Maui
Hawai'i
Islas Revillagigedo
Caribbean Sea
Ilhas do Cabo Verde
Tibesti
Arabian Peninsula
Arabian Sea
Bay of Bengal
Andaman Islands
South China Sea
Philippine Sea
Guam
Sahel
Jos Plateau
Ethiopian Highlands
Trinidad
Kiritimati
Guiana Highlands
Gulf of Guinea
Congo Basin
Nicobar Islands
Borneo
Galapagos Islands
Amazon Basin
Ascension
Comoros
New Guinea
Timor
Solomon Islands
Tahiti
Brazilian Highlands
Ilha da Trindade
Madagascar
Mauritius
Réunion
INDIAN OCEAN
Coral Sea
Vanuatu
Fiji
Pitcairn Islands
Isla de Pascua
Isla San Félix
Kalahari Desert
ANDES
Islas Juan Fernández
Tristan da Cunha
Cape of Good Hope
Gough Island
Île Amsterdam
Île St Paul
Great Australian Bight
Tasman Sea
New Zealand
Chatham Islands
Falkland Islands
Prince Edward Islands
Îles Crozet
Îles Kerguélen
South Sandwich Islands
Bouvetøya
Scotia Sea
South Shetland Islands
Macquarie Island
Auckland Island
SOUTHERN OCEAN
Bellingshausen Sea
Antarctic Peninsula
Weddell Sea
Amundsen Sea
ANTARCTICA
Balleny Islands
Ross Sea
Robinson Projection
4000 kilometers
2000 miles
World Natural Hazards
Magnitude of significant earthquakes
>8
7–8
6–7
5–6
Major volcano

BOXING DAY TSUNAMI, 2004

Just before 8 a.m. on the morning of December 26, 2004, an earthquake measuring 9.1 on the Richter Scale rocked the sea floor off the northern coast of the large Indonesian island of Sumatra.

The resulting tsunami raced across the sea surface at around 500 miles per hour (800 km/h). Within half an hour, a 100-foot (30 m) high tsunami slammed into the Sumatran coastline, roaring up to 1.5 miles (2 km) inland. It only took one hour for the tsunami to reach the coasts of Thailand, Malaysia, and Myanmar (Burma). An hour later the eastern coasts of Sri Lanka and India were struck. Eight hours after the initial quake, the eastern coasts of Madagascar and Africa were also struck by the remnants of the wave.

Unlike the coastal dwellers of the Pacific, where tsunamis are more common, the people of the Indian Ocean shores did not recognise the telltale signs of the receding and boiling sea. Instead, intrigued by the sight, many people stood on the beaches watching the spectacle until, to their horror, the huge wave rolled in and swept them away. The final death toll will never be known, although an estimate by the US Geological Survey places the figure at around 300,000 deaths across 12 separate countries. As in most natural disasters, most of the deaths were the result of disease and starvation after the initial cataclysm.

Above The province of Aceh, Indonesia, was hit first by an earthquake and then by the resulting tsunami in late 2004. Fifty thousand people lost their lives and countless more lost their homes.

the potential for other hazards, including landslides and disease as sewerage and waste systems overflow. One of the worst floods in history took place in 1931 when China's Yangtze River flooded as a result of prolonged periods of rain: These floods led to more than 3.5 million deaths.

Global Destruction

One of the popular genres of Hollywood films is the disaster movie, and those involving global destruction have proved very successful. In reality, events that result in the destruction of most life on Earth are very rare. Yet Earth bears the scars of some past events and it is a question not of if, but when, such an event will happen again.

By studying the fossil record, scientists have learned that single events can result in a catastrophic decline in the number of species on Earth. The best known of these events took place in the Cretaceous Period (about 65 million years ago). Believed to be the result of a massive meteor strike, the Cretaceous Extinction saw over 85 percent of all species wiped out. Dinosaurs and marine reptiles disappeared at this time, leaving space for the smaller and more adaptable mammals to emerge and thrive.

While meteors are usually thought to be the cause of these mass disasters, volcanic activity can also be highly destructive. The Permian Period ended about 195 million years ago after what most scientists believe was a series of enormous volcanic eruptions in Siberia. These eruptions released greenhouse gases, dramatically altering the climate of the whole planet almost overnight. More than 95 percent of all species on Earth became extinct at this period.

The emergence of new species after these events highlights the resilience of Earth and its ability to recover. Astronomers scan space for meteors that might strike the Earth and vulcanologists monitor tectonic activity in the crust. In our lifetimes, Earth and its environment is far more at risk from the actions of humans than any natural disaster.

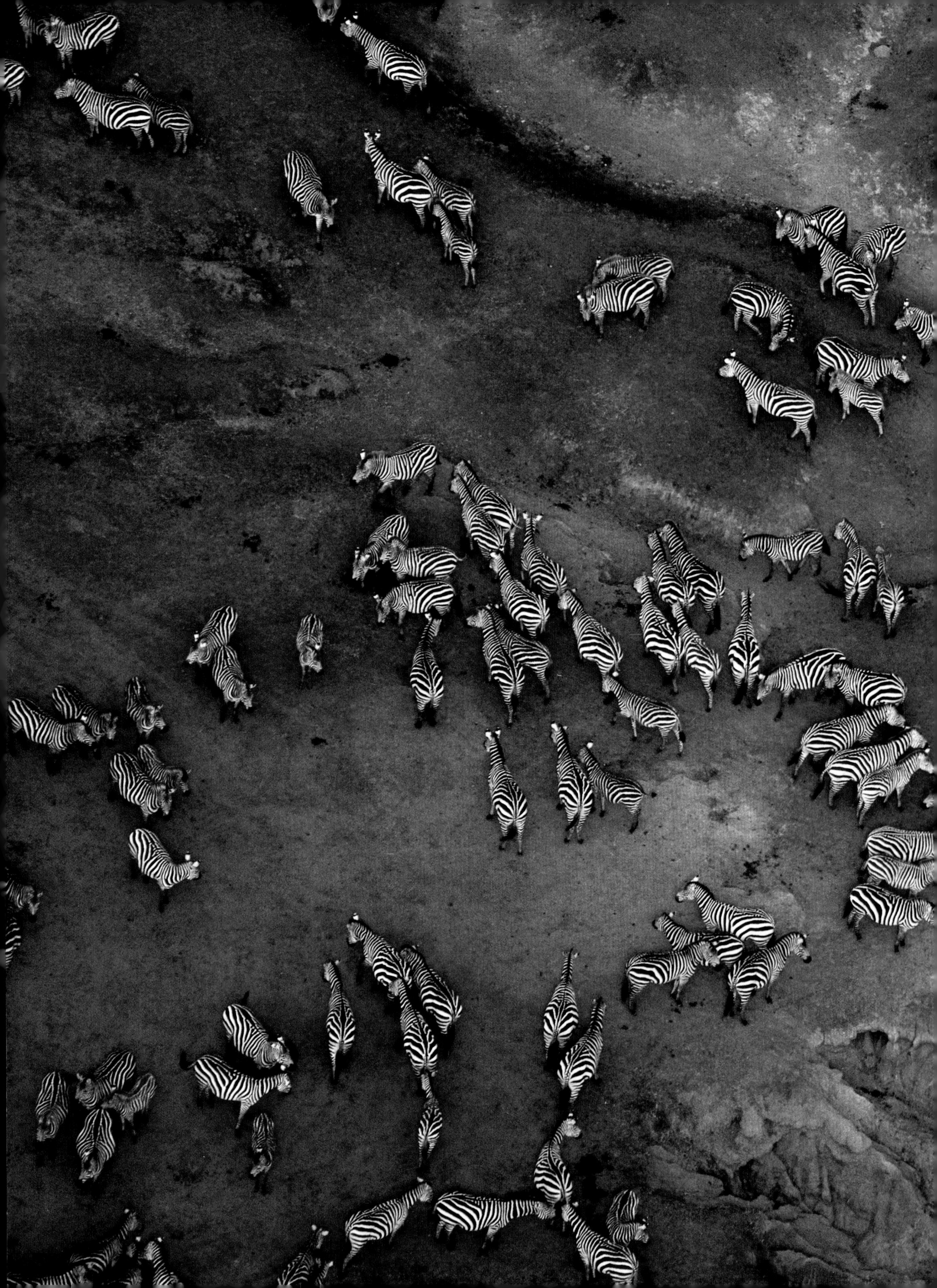

LIFE ON EARTH

Plant and Animal Diversity

The complexity of life on Earth is truly staggering. Estimates of the total number of plant and animal species differ greatly, with most scientists agreeing that the total figure is somewhere between five and 30 million individual species. About 1.75 million species have been formally identified and classified, of which around half are insects.

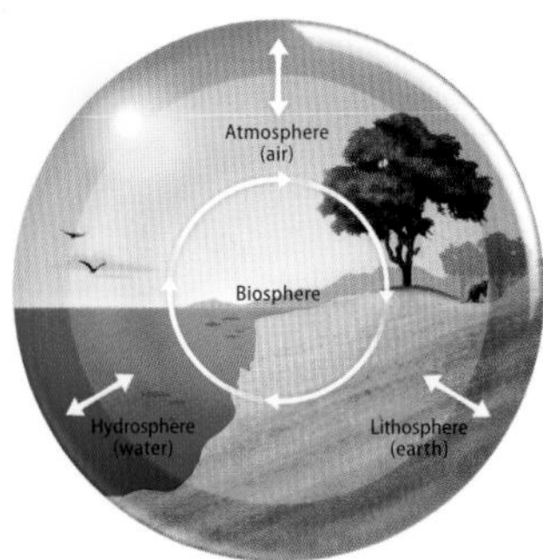
Atmosphere
(air)
Biosphere
Hydrosphere
(water)
Lithosphere
(earth)

Above This diagram shows the interconnectivity of the biophysical environment. The atmosphere, hydrosphere, and lithosphere all interact with each other and the biosphere, which represents all living things on Earth.

Above Coral reefs, such as this one in Milne Bay Province, Papua New Guinea, thrive in warm tropical waters. Despite their biodiversity, they are vulnerable to changes in sea water temperature.

Previous pages A herd of zebras in the bed of the Mara River, Masai Mara, Kenya. Like many herbivores, zebras congregate in large groups for added protection from carnivorous predators.

The surprisingly large number of unidentified species is the result of large areas of the planet remaining relatively unexplored as a result of rugged terrain, political factors which restrict access in certain parts of the world, and our limited ability to explore the deep oceans. In fact, it is often said that humans have a far better understanding of the environment of the moon than we do of the deep ocean.

Biodiversity is generally defined as "variability among living organisms". In this sense, biodiversity refers not only to variations between species but also to genetic variability within species.

Biodiversity is essential to the maintenance of a healthy environment at all scales, whether local, regional, or global. Generally, environments with high levels of biodiversity are more likely to cope with change—either caused by human factors or occurring naturally—than environments with low levels of diversity. Species with a small genetic pool, which often occurs as a species becomes endangered and its numbers fall, are highly vulnerable.

The Biophysical Environment

The biophysical environment is the collection of living (biotic) and non-living (abiotic) elements that make up the Earth. There are four such elements:

1. The biosphere—the collection of all living organisms, both plant and animal.
2. The atmosphere—the layer of gases that surround Earth.
3. The hydrosphere—water storages and the transfers between them, such as rain and snow.
4. The lithosphere—Earth's crust, including soils, rocks, landforms, and bedrock.

The ways these four "spheres" interact with each other create different environments and thus influence the biodiversity that is found in different locations. It is this complex interrelationship that creates the great number of ecosystems found on Earth.

At the heart of all ecosystems is the Sun. The Sun is the Earth's biophysical engine room, providing the energy that will be consumed and transferred throughout the biosphere. Solar energy is absorbed by plants and, through a process known as photosynthesis, is converted into energy. Plants are then consumed by herbivores (plant-eating animals) which are, in turn, consumed by carnivores (meat-eating animals), thus spreading energy through the ecosystem.

A host of other species then act as nature's cleaners. Known as decomposers, these plants and animals break down biological material and recycle it back into nutrients in the soil. Termites and fungi, for example, break down dead wood, returning the nutrients stored in it to the soil to support a new generation of life.

Thus each species exists in a finely tuned relationship with other species. The mightiest lions of the African savanna are as dependent on grasses as the animals they eat: Without the grass, the zebra dies, and without the zebra, the lion dies. This interrelationship is referred to as a food web, which is essentially a who-eats-who list.

At the base of all food webs are the producers; that is, those species that produce energy in an environment—plants. The next level comprises the secondary consumers: The herbivores that consume energy in the form of plants. Finally, at the top of the web we find the tertiary consumers, the carnivores.

In all ecosystems, there must be more energy produced than consumed or the system will collapse.For example, if the number of herbivores grew too large they would simply starve to death, as there would be insufficient vegetable matter for them to eat.

The Role of Latitude

Latitude is the single most important factor in determining climate and thus influences the plants and animals found in an area. In simple terms, the closer a location is to the equator, the more sun it will receive and therefore the more energy there will be for plants to use. The tropical zone is home to the most diverse ecosystems on earth, the rainforests, with thousands of species in a tiny area.

At the other extreme, the polar regions, beyond the Arctic Circle (65.5° North) and the Antarctic Circle (65.5° South), receive such small amounts of solar energy that they are virtually devoid of plant life on the land. Instead, highly adapted aquatic plants provide the basis of the polar food chains. Unlike the complex food webs of the tropical rainforests, the polar food chains are simple, making them extremely vulnerable to change.

Leopard seal
Killer whale
Crabeater seal
Petrel
Adelie penguin
Emperor penguin
Fish - Ice and Tooth fish
Humpback whale
Squid
Krill
Phytoplankton

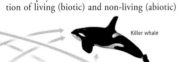

Above A diagram of an Antarctic food web. Even in this relatively unpopulated environment, there are complex interactions involved in the ecosystem. Different colored arrows reveal which animals get their energy directly from plants, and which eat other animals to obtain their share of the Sun's energy.

Right The pyramid shape indicates the number of organisms that are required to produce enough energy for the animals at each subsequent level of the food chain to survive. Many plants are needed to feed some herbivores which, in turn, will satisfy the needs of just a few carnivores.

Below left Royal penguins and elephant seals coexist in the relatively simple Antarctic ecosystem of Macquarie Island, Australia, sharing aquatic food resources.

Below Vegetation in Africa's grassy plains provides grazing land for herds of herbivores, such as these wildebeest. The grasses convert energy from the sun into food for animals.

Below right Around Mageni Cave in the Iso River Gorge, New Britain Island, Papua New Guinea, the tropical rainforest is a richly diverse ecosystem.

Below far right Deserts may seem barren, but many animals—such as these emus crossing Sturt's Stony Desert, South Australia—survive in this hostile environment.

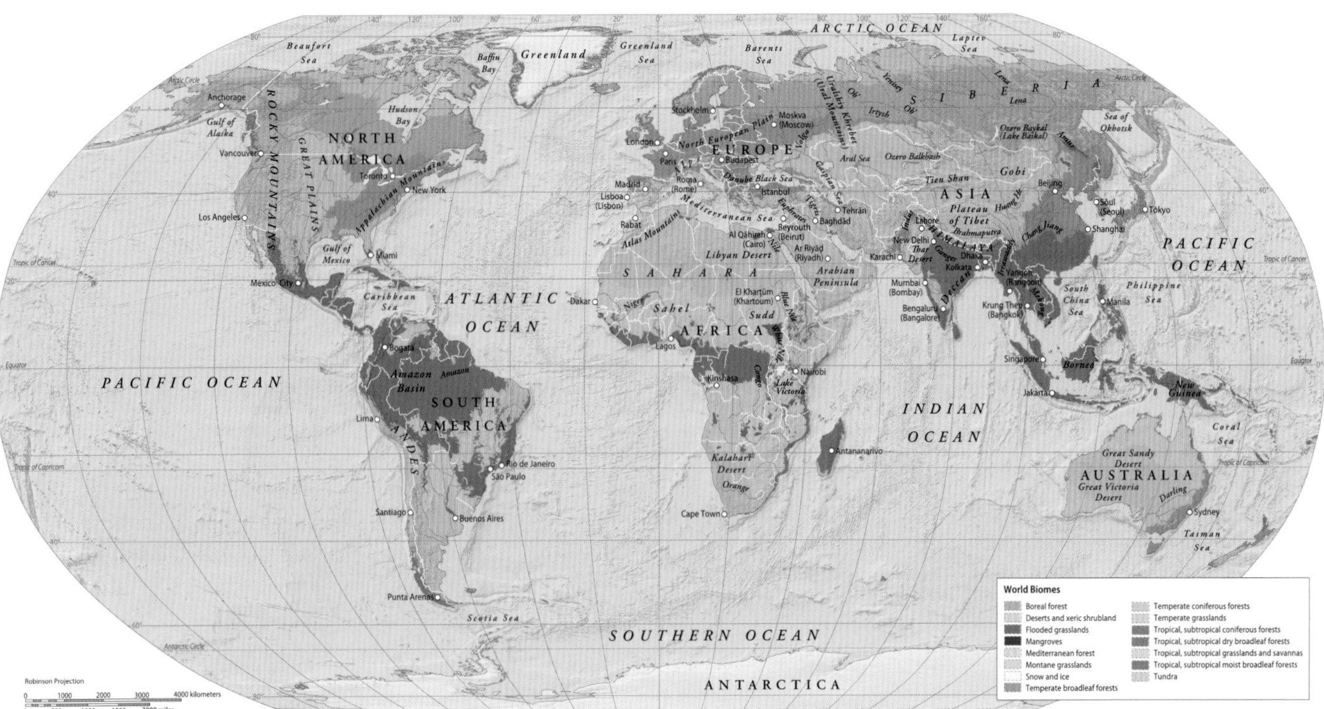
ARCTIC OCEAN
Beaufort Sea
Baffin Bay
Greenland
Greenland Sea
Barents Sea
Laptev Sea
Anchorage
Gulf of Alaska
ROCKY MOUNTAINS
Hudson Bay
NORTH AMERICA
GREAT PLAINS
Vancouver
Toronto
New York
Appalachian Mountains
Los Angeles
Gulf of Mexico
Miami
Mexico City
Caribbean Sea
ATLANTIC OCEAN
Stockholm
London
Paris
EUROPE
Budapest
Moskva (Moscow)
Madrid
Lisboa (Lisbon)
Roma (Rome)
Istanbul
Black Sea
Mediterranean Sea
Rabat
Atlas Mountains
Al Qahirah (Cairo)
Beyrouth (Beirut)
Baghdad
Tehran
Ar Riyad (Riyadh)
Libyan Desert
Arabian Peninsula
SAHARA
Dakar
Sahel
El Khartum (Khartoum)
Sudd
AFRICA
Lagos
Kinshasa
Nairobi
Lake Victoria
SIBERIA
Aral Sea
Ozero Balkhash
Ozero Baykal (Lake Baikal)
Sea of Okhotsk
Tien Shan
Gobi
ASIA
Plateau of Tibet
Beijing
Sŏul (Seoul)
Tōkyo
Shanghai
Lahore
New Delhi
Thar Desert
Karachi
Kolkata
Dhaka
Mumbai (Bombay)
Bengaluru (Bangalore)
Krung Thep (Bangkok)
Yangon (Rangoon)
Manila
South China Sea
Philippine Sea
PACIFIC OCEAN
Singapore
Borneo
Jakarta
New Guinea
PACIFIC OCEAN
Bogotá
Amazon Basin
SOUTH AMERICA
Lima
ANDES
Rio de Janeiro
São Paulo
Santiago
Buenos Aires
Punta Arenas
Scotia Sea
INDIAN OCEAN
Antananarivo
Kalahari Desert
Cape Town
Coral Sea
Great Sandy Desert
AUSTRALIA
Great Victoria Desert
Sydney
Tasman Sea
SOUTHERN OCEAN
ANTARCTICA
Robinson Projection
World Biomes
Boreal forest
Deserts and xeric shrubland
Flooded grasslands
Mangroves
Mediterranean forest
Montane grasslands
Snow and ice
Temperate broadleaf forests
Temperate coniferous forests
Temperate grasslands
Tropical, subtropical coniferous forests
Tropical, subtropical dry broadleaf forests
Tropical, subtropical grasslands and savannas
Tropical, subtropical moist broadleaf forests
Tundra

The Diversity of Forests

Forests are significant environments on Earth, covering huge areas of the continents. They are also among the environments that humans have most changed. Although there are thousands of forest types, there are three main groups of forests, each determined by latitude.

Around the equator the tropical rainforests are found. The combination of plentiful water and sunlight produces lush forests with year-round growing seasons. Trees in the rainforests grow close together, forming a dense canopy, reducing the sunlight that reaches the ground. This encourages plants to grow tall, in order to reach the sunlight, or to develop large leaves to capture whatever solar energy is available.

Beyond the tropics, in the mid-latitudes temperate forests dominate—these diverse forests once covered most of Western Europe, eastern North America, and Asia as well as eastern Australia. Trees tend to be broadleaf and hardwood. With a more open canopy, the forests support grazing animals—deer in Europe and kangaroos in Australia.

In Northern Europe, Siberia, and Canada the evergreen coniferous forests are prevalent. Growing in temperatures that rarely exceed 50°F (10°C) and are often well below –4°F (–20°C), conifers have tiny, needle-like leaves so that snow does not easily accumulate on their branches. The bears, squirrels and many other animals of these forests typically hibernate to survive the harsh winters.

Grasslands

More than 40 percent of Earth's land surface is covered by grassland. Grasses are one of the most prolific plant types on the planet, with some grasslands containing more than 250 separate grass species. Grasslands have evolved to support a complex interrelationship between plants and animals. Located in the center of the continents, grasslands are found in areas that have gradually dried out over thousands of years as forests retreated due to climate change.

Grazing animals became the dominant fauna. Some grazing species, such as South Africa's springbok, use speed for protection from carnivores. Many species, such as North America's bison, congregate in huge herds, using the approach of "safety in numbers." In turn, the carnivores evolved: Africa's cheetahs are the fastest animals on Earth, while other animals, such as African hunting dogs, hunt in packs to increase their chances of success.

Coral Reefs

Coral reefs are the most complex and diverse aquatic environments on Earth. They are very specialized, surviving in waters between 65°F (18°C) and 84°F (29°C), so they are generally found only in the tropics. Coral reefs are often thought of as geological features, but they are actually vast colonies of tiny animals called polyps. Australia's Great Barrier Reef is a series of interconnected reef systems stretching down the northeastern coast. The system is home to more than 330 species of coral, thousands of fish species, and more than 30 bird species.

THE GALAPAGOS ISLANDS

Located in the Pacific Ocean, the Galapagos Islands lie about 600 miles (965 km) off the coast of South America. The chain consists of 13 main islands and more than 100 smaller islands. Yet, from this small, isolated group of islands emerged one of the most significant theories in biology.

Although relatively close together, the islands of the Galapagos chain are quite different—some are covered in forest, some with grassland, and others have large active volcanoes. These very different environments present different challenges to the plants and animals that inhabit them.

In 1835, naturalist Charles Darwin visited the Galapagos Islands and was fascinated by the diversity of the plants and animals he found there. Species that seemed to have a common origin had different characteristics depending on the environment in which they were found. In perhaps the most significant of his findings, Darwin studied 14 species of finch, all of which had similar coloring, calls, reproductive strategies, and nesting habits. However, each of the species had different beak structures, different diets, and different body shape, depending on the plants characteristic of the islands they lived on.

Darwin theorized that, as the finches spread across the island chain, the ones that were best adapted to the unique habitat of each island survived while the rest died out. Darwin came to believe that species would evolve to suit the environment in which they live, with those individuals that possess the characteristics best suited to the environment thriving and producing adapted offspring, a theory that became known as "survival of the fittest." Darwin used his findings from the Galapagos Islands to derive his theory of evolution, which he presented to the world in his famous treatise *On the Origin of Species*.

Wildlife and Habitats

Life on Earth is complex and very diverse. Different ecosystems each have their own unique aspects providing habitats for a vast number of animals that humankind collectively calls wildlife.

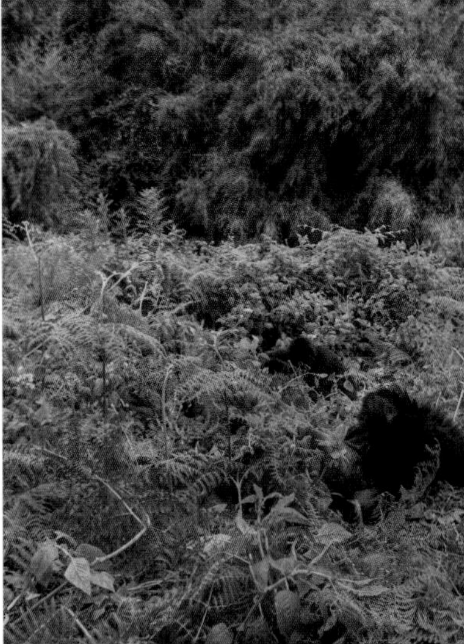

The diversity of life on Earth is truly amazing: Animals have evolved to fill almost every niche in nature, ensuring that living creatures are found in every environment from the extreme cold of Antarctica to the hottest deserts and the deepest oceans.

Environmental concerns often center around the potential impact of environmental disasters on humankind; for example, many of the arguments put forward in relation to dealing with global warming relate to the potential social and economic costs of this issue. Wildlife is often omitted from this equation, and yet human activity has led to the destruction of vast amounts of natural habitat; that is, the places where animals live and breed.

Above Blue whales are the largest animals ever to have existed, but their enormous size makes them vulnerable to changes in their habitat.

Endangered species are those that have suffered a dramatic decline in numbers and/or habitat. Recent research by the World Conservation Union found that 22 percent of mammal species, 12 percent of birds, 30 percent of reptiles, 31 percent of amphibians, and 39 percent of fish species are endangered. Furthermore, more than 50 percent of invertebrates, mostly insects, are endangered.

It is those animals that are found only in relatively small geographic areas that are the most threatened by human activity. In such small ranges, it is impossible for the animals to easily adapt to human activity by finding refuge. Other species that are particularly vulnerable are those with very low reproductive rates and those with very large body sizes, which require vast ranges from which to source food. Migratory animals, such as North America's bison or the many migratory birds, are also vulnerable because they rely on so many habitats to survive. As habitats shrink, or are altered by human intervention, so do the chances of survival for many species.

Above Beluga sturgeon eggs fetch a high price on the luxury goods market, but the fish that supply them may pay a higher price—extinction.

Animals that are perceived to be dangerous to humans, such as wolves and bears, or animals that are thought to interfere with human activities such as agriculture are also threatened by hunting. For example, in Australia the thylacine (often referred to as the Tasmanian Tiger) was hunted into extinction in the early twentieth century because it was believed to prey heavily on the sheep that European settlers introduced. Animals that provide valuable resources to humans are also at risk; as in the example of the threat to elephants created by the illegal ivory trade.

Endangered Species Around the World

THE BLACK RHINOCEROS

With fewer than 2,500 individual animals left, the black rhinoceros is regarded as one of the most endangered animals on Earth. Native to Africa, the rhino lives in the vast savanna grasslands, feeding on grass and small shrubs. Although the habitat of rhinos is being reduced by agriculture, it is illegal hunting that poses the greatest risk to this majestic animal. Some cultures believe that the powdered horn of the black rhino is a cure for numerous diseases and it is thus highly sought after.

THE GIANT PANDA

The giant panda has become a symbol for conservation organizations worldwide. There are thought to be only around 2,000 pandas left in the dense bamboo forests of central China. These solitary animals have very low reproductive rates, increasing their vulnerability. Loss of their habitat to forestry and agriculture is the major threat to this iconic species.

TIGERS OF ASIA

Originally found throughout much of Asia, numerous tiger subspecies are highly endangered. Estimates place the number of tigers in all of Asia in 1900 at more than 100,000; today there are between 3,000 and 4,500 individual animals—and the Caspian, Java, and Bali tigers are already extinct. Hunting for pelts and habitat loss have decimated tiger populations throughout the continent.

Above The black rhinoceros of Africa (this column, top) and the Asian tiger (above) are nearing extinction, due to animals being hunted for trophies or to prevent damage to crops and livestock. The giant panda of China (this column, center) is at risk because its geographically limited habitat is being cleared for forestry and agriculture.

BELUGA STURGEON

Prized worldwide for its eggs—caviar—this large ancient species of fish has been almost hunted into extinction. Found in the Caspian Sea between Russia and the Middle East, the sturgeon can grow up to 2,645 pounds (1,200 kg) and live for more than 150 years. The harvesting of the eggs for the gourmet market, however, means that few of these fish survive into old age.

ASIAN ELEPHANT

Across four subspecies, the Asian elephant has been reduced to fewer than 40,000 animals. Long used in southeast Asia, India, and Sri Lanka for work, elephants are hunted for the ivory in their tusks, while loss of habitat has further increased these animals' vulnerability.

Below African elephants roam the plains of the Masai Mara National Park in Kenya. They are still hunted and killed for the ivory in their tusks despite international bans on the product.

Above left A family of mountain gorillas *(Gorilla beringei beringei)* grooming each other, resting, and playing in the Virunga Mountains, Rwanda.

Above right Mahouts (elephant herders) and Indian elephants *(Elephas maximus)* in the river at the Thai Elephant Conservation Center.

TURTLES

Several species of turtle are highly endangered. In North America, the alligator snapping turtle—the world's largest freshwater turtle—has become threatened by development leading to the draining of the freshwater wetlands they inhabit. Harvesting for the pet trade and for export to Asia, where it is consumed as a delicacy, are also placing the species at risk. The hawksbill turtle, found in tropical waters of the Pacific, is threatened by fishing practices that tangle the animal in nets, direct hunting, and disturbance to breeding grounds.

MOUNTAIN GORILLA

The mountain gorillas of central Africa are found in some of the most politically unstable countries on Earth—such as Democratic Republic of Congo, Rwanda, and Uganda. These gorillas have been hunted for food by soldiers, shot by poachers, and decimated by human-borne diseases such as the Ebola virus.

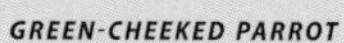

GREEN-CHEEKED PARROT

A native of Mexico, this colorful bird has become a victim of the illegal pet trade, which has almost led to the extinction of the species in the wild. Favored by bird collectors because of its ability to mimic the human voice, illegal trade across the US–Mexico border is rife.

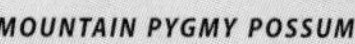

MOUNTAIN PYGMY POSSUM

This tiny possum lives in the alpine region of southeastern Australia. During the winter months, the possum burrows into the ground below the snow to hibernate. The development of ski resorts and agriculture has reduced their habitat, while climate change, which is reducing snow cover, presents a further threat.

MEDITERRANEAN MONK SEAL

Found in the waters of the one of the most intensely settled parts of the world, the Mediterranean Sea, the monk seal is highly endangered as it has long been hunted for its fur. Recently, as fish numbers in the Mediterranean have declined, it has become a target for some fishermen, who deliberately kill the seal as they see it competing with them for the fish that are becoming scarce.

Above Hawksbill sea turtles (this column, top) are often accidentally caught in fishing nets, while Mediterranean monk seals (above) are likely to be killed to prevent them taking the catch that is destined for human dinner tables. The Australian mountain pygmy possum (this column, center), is in danger of losing its habitat to winter tourism.

THE CONVENTION ON THE INTERNATIONAL TRADE IN ENDANGERED SPECIES OF WILD FAUNA AND FLORA (CITES)

Many of the world's endangered animals are threatened by illegal trade in the animals themselves for the pet industry or for valuable parts of the animal, such as ivory or fur. Most commonly, animals that are poached are traded internationally and this cruel and environmentally damaging industry is worth billions of dollars.

In 1973 the World Conservation Union proposed that an international treaty be developed that placed restrictions on the trade in endangered animals. Eighty countries attended the conference in Washington DC, USA, that debated the text of the treaty: In 1975 CITES came into force. Since then, the number of nations that are party to (that is, have signed and agreed to be bound by) CITES has grown to 172. Like all international agreements, countries cannot be forced to sign CITES and the Convention does not take precedence over national laws. This has created some problems in countries that do not recognize a species as being endangered and therefore allow trade in it to continue, even though other nations have ceased.

CITES does not automatically outlaw all trade in endangered species, but it creates a complex licensing system that aims to verify that the trade is legitimate and does not have a long-term effect on the viability of the species. For example, zoos often seek and are granted licences to buy or sell endangered animals to other reputable organizations for breeding programs. These programs are often designed to ensure the survival of a species.

Around 5,000 individual species of fauna and more than 28,000 plant species are protected by CITES. The species are listed in three different categories: Appendix One—highly endangered and close to extinction, with trade prohibition except for special circumstances, such as captive breeding programs in zoos; Appendix Two—species not necessarily threatened with extinction are protected from unsustainable trade; and Appendix Three—those species requiring special assistance for trade regulations, usually at the request of a particular member country.

Above The green-cheeked parrot *(Amazona viridigenalis)* has an adorable demeanor that makes it an attractive pet. This specimen lives in the Kansas City Zoo, Missouri, USA.

Natural Resources and World Energy

Energy is essential to all life. In the natural world it is the Sun that provides the primary source of energy. In modern human society, where energy is consumed on a vast scale, most of our energy is derived from burning fossil fuels.

Far right Oil rigs, like this one in the Gulf of Mexico, dot Earth's oceans, extracting the fossil fuel from beneath the sea bed.

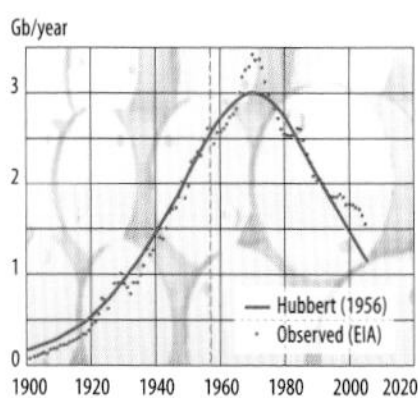
Gb/year
3
2
1
0
1900 1920 1940 1960 1980 2000 2020
— Hubbert (1956)
· Observed (EIA)

Above The predictions of M. King Hubbert have been borne out by reality. The "peak oil" curve that Hubbert predicted in the 1950s (blue line) is very close to actual production, marked by the red dots. By this estimation, the world peak will occur in 2010.

Demand for fossil fuels is currently doubling every 20 years. Natural gas, coal, and oil, although seemingly abundant, are in fact finite; as they are burned to make energy they are consumed and can never be replaced. Thus, they are non-renewable resources—eventually they will run out and humankind will need to find alternatives.

Renewable resources, on the other hand, are not exhaustible—energy derived from the Sun, wind, the power of waves, and running water comes from renewable resources.

In recent years, the energy requirements of developing nations—including much of Asia, particularly India and China—have grown considerably, with predictions that by the year 2030 the worldwide demand for energy will have risen by 66 percent compared with 2003 levels. Asia (with the exception of Japan) will account for nearly 40 percent of that growth.

Right Natural gas is clean and efficient; however, some experts believe that it, like oil, has already passed its production peak.

New energy sources will be required to meet the demands of these growing economies. Oil, natural gas, and uranium stores are facing depletion by the end of this century if current levels of consumption continue and no further reserves are found.

More than 50 of the world's 65 largest oil-producing nations have already passed their peak of production and are now in decline. The Association for the Study of Peak Oil estimates that the global peak for regular petroleum passed in 2004. If heavy oil, polar oil, and deepwater oil are considered, the peak is expected to occur in 2010. The resulting impacts on agriculture, lifestyles, geopolitics, and economic stability will soon follow.

The need for countries to switch to clean and sustainable sources of energy and reduce the world's dependence on fossil-based fuels has never been greater. Until recently, decisions about energy have been based solely on fundamental economic factors such as its cost and availability. The growing global debate on climate change, however, has increasingly brought non-economic environmental concerns into the equation. For example, at present rates, by 2030 carbon dioxide emissions will be 50 percent higher than they are today.

Nuclear Power Generation

Nuclear power is used in many countries as a source of energy. Globally, it accounts for around 16 percent of all power production, from about 450 nuclear power plants. It is a major source of energy in Europe, with almost 78 percent of France's power needs being currently met through nuclear power, 80 percent of Lithuania's energy needs, 57 percent of Slovakia's, and around half of Belgium's and Sweden's needs.

Nuclear power is considered a very clean technology in that there are no emissions from the actual site of generation. However, one of the main problems with nuclear power is the generation of highly toxic waste that needs to be stored in secure locations for thousands of years. The cost, both economically and socially, of this long-term waste problem is something that many nuclear power-using countries are yet to deal with.

Alternative Energy Sources

Since the growth of the environmental movement in the 1970s there has been an increasing awareness of the impact of human activities on the environment. The emergence of the climatic impacts of increasing levels of carbon dioxide associated with the use of fossil fuels has created an urgency and demand for research into viable energy alternatives. As renewable resources, such energy sources are inexhaustible and they represent long-term solutions to growing energy demands.

Solar energy is the most abundant alternative source. All plants derive their energy from the Sun, converting solar radiation into energy through a process called photosynthesis. Technology developed in the later part of the twentieth century to turn the power of the Sun into electricity now makes the use of solar power a very real option.

There are two main methods of solar-power generation. Photovoltaic cells are used for small- and medium-scale applications—these cells were first developed in the late nineteenth century, but it was not until the space program of the 1960s that research into making these small and efficient power sources was undertaken. Modern research is examining ways to make flexible cells that can be used to cover roof surfaces, allowing individual homes to become power stations.

For large-scale operations, solar energy is concentrated through very large arrays of mirrors. These arrays heat air, or sometimes water, which can then be used to power turbines and thus create electricity. Large-scale solar power stations are found in the dry sun-drenched regions of California, Australia, India, and Spain, with many more planned worldwide.

Below Each day, almost 80,300,00 barrels of oil a day are consumed across the world. Consumption of oil in the US accounts for about one-quarter of the total amount.

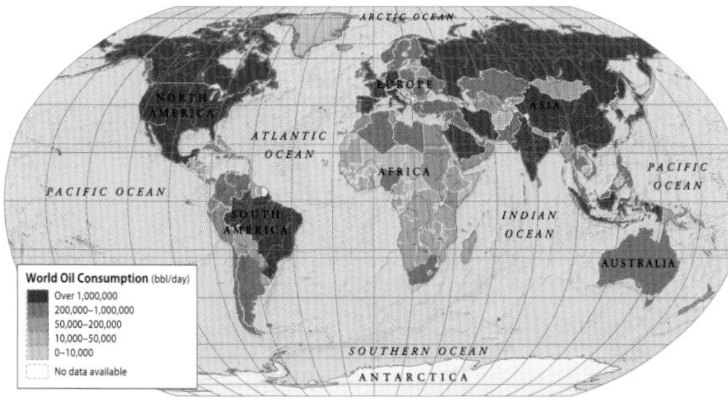
ARCTIC OCEAN
NORTH AMERICA
EUROPE
ASIA
ATLANTIC OCEAN
AFRICA
PACIFIC OCEAN
PACIFIC OCEAN
SOUTH AMERICA
INDIAN OCEAN
AUSTRALIA
SOUTHERN OCEAN
ANTARCTICA
World Oil Consumption (bbl/day)
Over 1,000,000
200,000–1,000,000
50,000–200,000
10,000–50,000
0–10,000
No data available

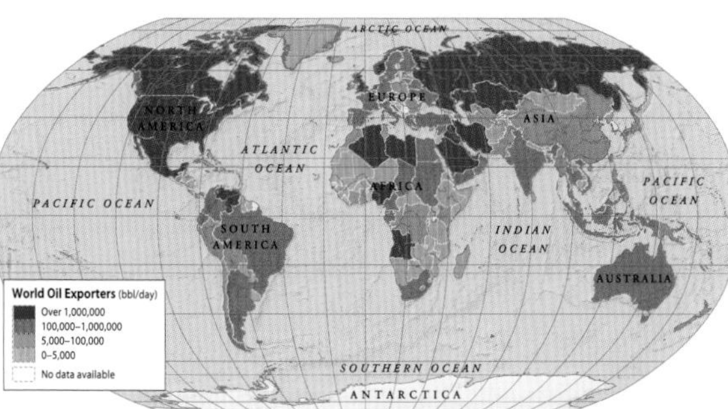
ARCTIC OCEAN
NORTH AMERICA
EUROPE
ASIA
ATLANTIC OCEAN
AFRICA
PACIFIC OCEAN
PACIFIC OCEAN
SOUTH AMERICA
INDIAN OCEAN
AUSTRALIA
SOUTHERN OCEAN
ANTARCTICA
World Oil Exporters (bbl/day)
Over 1,000,000
100,000–1,000,000
5,000–100,000
0–5,000
No data available

ENERGY FROM WASTE AND FROM FOOD

Human societies produce vast amounts of waste, much of which finds its way into landfill each year. Technology is now being investigated that will take this waste and make it into energy. Much of the waste that ends up in landfill is organic, including food scraps, garden clippings, and the like. As layers of new waste cover the old, these organics begin to break down and gases are produced. It is these gases that cause the strong odours we associated with landfill. One of the main gases emitted is methane, and this is a gas that can be burnt and converted into energy.

Sydney is Australia's largest city, with a population of more than four million people. The city produces thousands of tons of waste every week, with much of it going to landfill. The city's landfills have all but reached capacity and the waste is now compacted and loaded onto trains and taken to an abandoned mine about 125 miles (200 km) away. As the mine begins to fill with rubbish and methane is produced, it will be captured and fed into a bioreactor that will produce 25 megawatts of power. The same amount of energy from a coal-fired power station would produce more than 675,000 tons of carbon, the equivalent of about 20,000 cars annually.

Biomass is another alternative energy source that is attracting a great deal of attention. Biomass seeks to use naturally occurring renewable products for fuel. Waste generated by the timber industry is normally burnt and the resource is simply wasted. Some projects are now being developed to burn waste timber and other agricultural products in order to generate electricity.

Biofuels are also one of the most exciting advances in alternative energies. Crops such as maize and sugarcane are grown, not for food, but rather for energy, being harvested and fermented to produce ethanol, which can be used in much the same way as refined oil to power the internal combustion engines of cars.

For many years Brazil has used its vast sugarcane crop in this way, with many of the country's cars converted to run on ethanol. Many countries are blending up to 10 percent ethanol into conventional motor vehicle fuels to reduce their reliance on oil. Ethanol is also a clean-burning fuel, meaning that the impact of cars on the environment is greatly reduced.

Below Hoses suck methane from decomposing trash at a dump. Garbage feeds a growing market that recycles biomass and biogas into fuel.

World Energy Resources
- ▲ Oil
- ● Coal
- ⬮ Gas
- ▼ Uranium
- ◆ Wind
- ⬮ Hydroelectric

Robinson Projection
0 1000 2000 3000 4000 kilometers
0 500 1000 1500 2000 miles

Humans have harnessed the energy of the wind for centuries. Until the end of the nineteenth century, all sea transport was wind powered, and windmills have been used to pump water, crush grain, and create energy for hundreds of years. Wind power is now becoming fashionable again. At present around 1 percent of global electricity production is wind generated, although this is expected to grow considerably in coming years. Denmark, the world's leading user of wind turbines, expects to produce at least 40 percent of its power from wind within 20 years.

Like solar power, power generated by wind-driven turbines is pollution free, and wind is a ready source of energy, especially in coastal areas. Modern wind turbines are up to 200 feet (60 m) high and feature lightweight blades up to 100 feet (30 m) long. These giant turbines can produce up to one megawatt of power, and are capable of powering hundreds of homes. However, there has been some opposition to wind farms, on the grounds of noise and visual pollution.

Ocean waves are nothing more than energy flowing through a body of water. Engineers have now developed the technology to convert this energy into electricity. By using the power of a wave to turn a turbine, electricity is produced. A small wave plant installed in a harbor in the Australian coastal city of Wollongong produces around 450 kilowatts of energy per day, which is used to desalinate about 792,516 gallons (3,000,000 l) of water each day for the city's use.

Geothermal power is yet another attractive alternative to fossil fuels. This technology uses the heat of Earth's interior to superheat water and create steam for turning electricity turbines. Bores are sunk deep into the earth to reach "hot rocks;" water is then pumped down through the bore and heated by the rocks, turning it into steam.

Geothermal plants have long been used on the geologically active North Island of New Zealand and in Iceland (which has five geothermal power plants), and many more are planned throughout the world.

Above Geothermal energy provides more than a quarter of Iceland's electricity, as well as central heating and hot water for nearly 90 percent of homes.

Right Hydroelectricity provides some seven percent of the world's energy, as the massive forces of flowing water are harnessed by turbines for power generation.

Center right Photovoltaic cells harvest the Sun's rays in Mt Laguna, California, USA. It is thought that solar energy will supply 60 percent of Earth's energy needs by 2060.

Below Cooling towers are a familiar sight around power stations and nuclear power facilities. These towers release water vapor into the air in the energy production process.

Above Nuclear power is clean and efficient, but experience has shown that the waste products need to be handled and monitored very carefully. Many European countries derive more than half of their electricity from nuclear power.

Population

Earth is home to nearly seven billion human beings, a number that is projected to reach around 9.5 billion sometime during the middle of the twenty-first century, then plateau and perhaps decline. Some observers view these numbers and trends with alarm; others see no reason for concern. Certainly population is an issue that will continue to affect the global community in countless ways.

Left The Masai tribe of Kenya live in remote and arid regions of a country where less than a tenth of the land is arable. Yet Kenya's RNI is more than double the world average.

Above Major population centers are often on the coast, which offers a temperate climate, access for trade, and recreational opportunities.

Top Many factors contribute to a change in the rate of population increase. When this photograph was taken in 1938 in Melbourne, Australia, there had been a record number of births in the city.

Statistics and maps representing various population data reveal great differences in the spatial distribution of demographic conditions. In some places, population densities range in the thousands per square mile; elsewhere, huge areas remain almost uninhabited. Some areas have very high birth rates, fertility rates, and rates of natural population increase, whereas others experience declining populations. Life expectancy, age distribution, levels of educational attainment, income, and other indices of human wellbeing also vary greatly from place to place. So too do patterns of human migration.

Population Data

Although many countries conduct a regularly scheduled and detailed population census, some do not. The enumeration interval, types of data collected, and accuracy may also vary greatly from country to country. Population data, even for developed countries, can be widely off the mark. For less-developed countries (LDCs), data are often little more than "best guesses."

Demographic data must be viewed with extreme caution. Population statistics, regardless of their nature, can at best convey a general indication of conditions and trends.

However, world population data figures disclose some interesting information. For example, 61 percent of the world's population lives in Asia, home to six of the ten most populated countries. India, currently second in population and growing at an annual rate of 1.6 percent, will soon overtake China (0.6 percent) to become the most populated country. Several top 10 countries experience a rate of natural increase (RNI) twice that of the world's 1.2 percent average. Europe, on the other hand, has become the first continent in modern history to achieve sustained zero population growth. Russia is losing population and is one of the few countries on Earth experiencing a decline in life expectancy.

A population's rate of natural increase is a critical index of demographic, economic, and social conditions within a country. Generally speaking, regions with a low RNI tend to have a longer life expectancy, be more urban, and have a higher gross national product (GNP) than do countries with a high rate of growth. This has led to a widespread belief that high population growth contributes to poverty. In reality, the opposite is true. To poor, rural families, children are a vital capital resource; youngsters can gather firewood, fetch water, watch over flocks, or contribute in some other way to their family's material wellbeing. They also provide care for elderly parents. Hence, families in LDCs tend to be large.

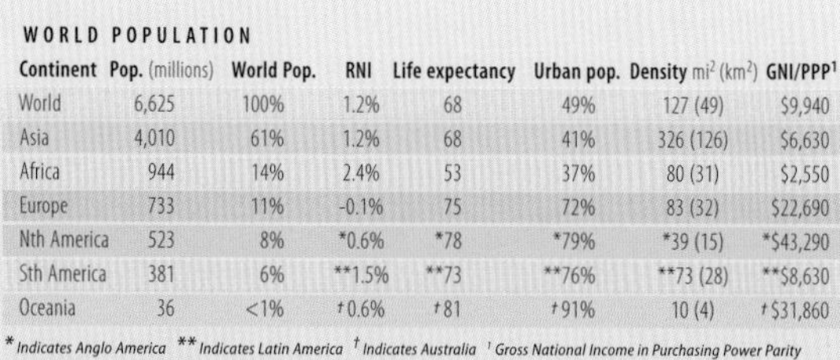

WORLD POPULATION

Continent	Pop. (millions)	World Pop.	RNI	Life expectancy	Urban pop.	Density mi² (km²)	GNI/PPP[1]
World	6,625	100%	1.2%	68	49%	127 (49)	$9,940
Asia	4,010	61%	1.2%	68	41%	326 (126)	$6,630
Africa	944	14%	2.4%	53	37%	80 (31)	$2,550
Europe	733	11%	-0.1%	75	72%	83 (32)	$22,690
Nth America	523	8%	*0.6%	*78	*79%	*39 (15)	*$43,290
Sth America	381	6%	**1.5%	**73	**76%	**73 (28)	**$8,630
Oceania	36	<1%	†0.6%	†81	†91%	10 (4)	†$31,860

** Indicates Anglo America ** Indicates Latin America † Indicates Australia [1] Gross National Income in Purchasing Power Parity (Jan 1, 2008 estimates)*

POPULATION BY COUNTRY (TOP 10)

Country	Pop. (millions)	RNI	Life expectancy	Urban pop.	Density mi² (km²)	GNI/PPP[1]
1 China	1,322	0.6%	73	44%	357 (138)	$7,730
2 India	1,132	1.6%	69	28%	891 (344)	$3,800
3 USA	303	0.6%	78	79%	80 (31)	$44,260
4 Indonesia	235	1.4%	70	42%	316 (122)	$3,950
5 Brazil	190	1.2%	72	81%	57 (22)	$8,800
6 Pakistan	169	2.3%	64	34%	552 (213)	$2,500
7 Bangladesh	150	2.0%	62	23%	2,681 (1,035)	$2,340
8 Nigeria	135	2.4%	47	44%	404 (156)	$1,050
9 Russia	141	-0.5%	66	73%	22 (8)	$11,620
10 Japan	127	0.0%	82	79%	876 (338)	$33,730

Data from various sources; most estimates current Jan 2008 [1] Gross National Income in Purchasing Power Parity (Jan 1, 2008 estimates)

Population Distribution and Density

A map of population distribution and density is perhaps the most revealing of all cartographic expressions. Generally speaking, people are attracted to areas where they can provide for their material needs and make an adequate living, regardless of the means. Where living is difficult, whether for environmental, economic, or other reasons, population densities tend to be low. Today, about two-thirds of Earth's land surface is inhabited and in some way productive.

Population density figures are quite often misleading. Europe has about 83 people per square mile (32/km²), but nearly the entire continent is settled. However in Asia—the most densely populated continent with about 326 people per square mile (126/km²)—about 75 percent of the territory is nearly inaccessible and largely unoccupied.

Many areas of low population density are "Too Lands"—places in which climatic conditions, terrain, or other physical features are too extreme to support economic development capable of sustaining extensive settlement. Areas of high population concentration—such as much of southern and eastern Asia, most of Europe, and eastern Northern America—generally offer a mild climate, good soils, ample water resources, and a relatively flat terrain.

There are, of course, anomalies. Deserts generally support sparse settlement, yet in the United States the desert Southwest has been the country's fastest-growing region during the past half-century. The nation's two driest cities of any size, Las Vegas and Phoenix, also are the fastest growing urban centers. Dubai is the world's fastest-growing city, yet the United Arab Emirates receives only about 6 inches (150 mm) of rainfall annually. Conversely, some very moist portions of Africa and South America support very low population densities. Yet a number of countries in tropical south and Southeast Asia support some of the world's highest population densities.

Rural-to-urban migration has resulted in one of the most remarkable shifts in settlement patterns during recent centuries. As industry and commerce have spread, so has urbanization. Today, approximately 50 percent of the world's population is urban. About 400 cities have more than one million residents, including 26 "megacities" with more than eight million inhabitants. The largest urban agglomeration is the Tokyo–Yokohama metropolitan area, with an estimated 33 million people. It is followed by New York City, São Paulo, Seoul, and Mexico City, each with 17 to 18 million residents. Urban growth shows no sign of slowing, suggesting that settlement will become increasingly concentrated spatially.

The "Population Explosion"

Throughout most of history, population grew very slowly: Birth and death rates were high and life expectancy was short. By the dawn of the contemporary era, the rate of increase was about 0.06 percent a year. A century ago, advances in hygiene, medicine and health care, and food production and distribution, combined to create a population explosion. By the 1970s, population was soaring at an unprecedented annual rate of two percent. Since 1960, world population has more than doubled—from 3.2 billion to nearly 6.7 billion in 2008.

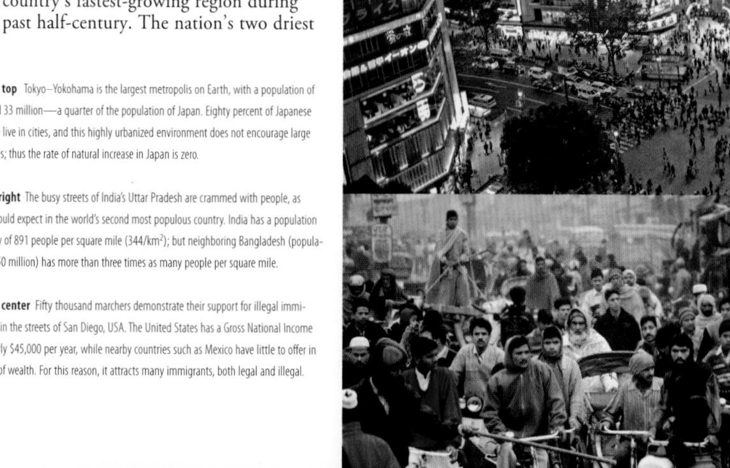

Right top Tokyo–Yokohama is the largest metropolis on Earth, with a population of around 33 million—a quarter of the population of Japan. Eighty percent of Japanese people live in cities, and this highly urbanized environment does not encourage large families; thus the rate of natural increase in Japan is zero.

Near right The busy streets of India's Uttar Pradesh are crammed with people, as one would expect in the world's second most populous country. India has a population density of 891 people per square mile (344/km²); but neighboring Bangladesh (population 150 million) has more than three times as many people per square mile.

Right center Fifty thousand marchers demonstrate their support for illegal immigrants in the streets of San Diego, USA. The United States has a Gross National Income of nearly $45,000 per year, while nearby countries such as Mexico have little to offer in terms of wealth. For this reason, it attracts many immigrants, both legal and illegal.

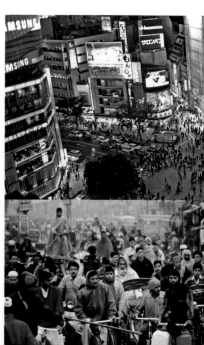

ARCTIC OCEAN
Beaufort Sea
Baffin Bay
Greenland Sea
Barents Sea
Laptev Sea
Hudson Bay
Gulf of Alaska
Sea of Okhotsk
NORTH AMERICA
EUROPE
ASIA
Sankt-Peterburg (St Petersburg)
Moskva (Moscow)
London
Berlin
Madrid
İstanbul
Ankara
Toronto
Montréal
New York
Los Angeles
Mexico City
Gulf of Mexico
Caribbean Sea
ATLANTIC OCEAN
Casablanca
Mediterranean Sea
Al Iskandarīya (Alexandria)
Al Qāhirah (Cairo)
Baghdād
Tehrān
Ar Riyāḍ
Jiddah (Jeddah)
Lahore
Karachi
New Delhi
Kanpur
Ahmadābād
Surat
Mumbai
Hyderābād
Kolkata
Dhaka
Chittagong
Bengaluru (Bangalore)
Chennai
Harbin
Shenyang
P'yŏngyang
Beijing
Tianjin
Sŏul (Seoul)
Tōkyō
Yokohama
Xian
Nanjing
Chengdu
Chongqing
Wuhan
Shanghai
Guangzhou
Yangon (Rangoon)
Krung Thep (Bangkok)
Ho Chi Minh City
Manila
South China Sea
Philippine Sea
PACIFIC OCEAN
AFRICA
Ibadan
Lagos
Abidjan
Adis Abeba (Addis Ababa)
Nairobi
Kinshasa
Durban
Cape Town
Bogotá
Lima
SOUTH AMERICA
Rio de Janeiro
São Paulo
Santiago
Buenos Aires
INDIAN OCEAN
Singapore
Jakarta
Coral Sea
AUSTRALIA
Sydney
Melbourne
Tasman Sea
SOUTHERN OCEAN
ANTARCTICA
Arctic Circle
Tropic of Cancer
Equator
Tropic of Capricorn
Antarctic Circle
Robinson Projection
0 1000 2000 3000 4000 kilometers
0 500 1000 1500 2000 miles
World Population Density
(persons per square kilometer)
500 +
250–500
100–250
50–100
25–50
5–25
1–5
0–1
No data
Populated Places
Over 10 million
5 million–10 million
4 million–5 million
3 million–4 million

Above Darker colors on this map represent a higher population density, and major cities are marked with symbols indicating their relative size.

Many people viewed this explosion of humanity with alarm. During the mid-twentieth century, a spate of book titles forecast an apocalyptic human and environmental catastrophe unless population growth was checked.

What happened? In the past three decades, the RNI has dropped from 2 percent annually to under 1.2 percent. Today, life expectancy is at an all-time high. Fewer people (as a percentage of the population) are suffering from acute hunger than ever before. Famine is far less common. Economic wellbeing, health, longevity, and overall quality of life have never been better for most of humanity. Clearly, people were not the only problem. In fact, if everyone in the world were to stand together as a closely packed group, they would occupy an area about the equivalent of a large city.

Overpopulation

Overpopulation is a condition reached when the human population of a defined geographic area exceeds the capacity of available land and other resources to provide the essential elements of survival under existing cultural (that is, social, political, technological, economic) and environmental conditions.

This definition can be illustrated by contrasting a very traditional, isolated society and an advanced industrial nation. What land and resources are available to each? A traditional group is limited to its immediate environment and what it offers. A country such as Japan, on the other hand, imports nearly all raw materials and natural resources used in its industry, nearly all of its fuel, and much of its food. Additionally, how might the essential elements of survival differ between a traditional and modern society?

Of greatest significance are a country's government and economy. With a stable democratic government, and viable free-market economy, a human society will prosper and thoughts of "overpopulation" will vanish.

Left Dubrovnik, Croatia, has been a thriving port since the fifteenth century CE, due to its situation on the coast of the Adriatic Sea. This made it an ideal place for traders to call, and for merchants to live in as they bought and sold their wares.

0120-999-119

Below In the world's most populous country, China, the government has legislated a one-child policy to help curb the rate of natural increase, in an attempt to maintain living standards.

Religions of the World

Religions shepherd individuals through birth, maturation and marriage, and death. They provide a sense of identity and a guide for action. They inspire, exhort, calm, and energize. They are a way of viewing the past, present, and future.

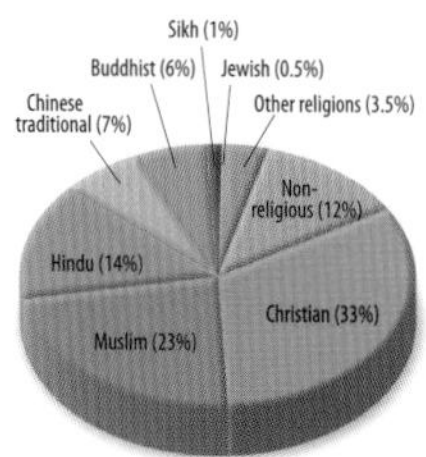
Sikh (1%)
Buddhist (6%)
Jewish (0.5%)
Chinese traditional (7%)
Other religions (3.5%)
Non-religious (12%)
Hindu (14%)
Christian (33%)
Muslim (23%)

Above A pie chart shows the relative numbers of followers of the world's major religions, including those who do not profess any religious beliefs—12 percent of the global population.

For most societies, religions provide shared narratives and mores, an integrated comprehensive view of the world, and an ethical code. In many cases, they are closely linked to cultural or ethnic identity.

Some religions had a global presence long before the term "globalization" was coined. Buddhism, Christianity, and Islam began spreading with missionary zeal almost as soon as they were born. Other religions, equally ancient, have such strong ties to a particular piece of geography that the majority of adherents live in that area even today.

Primal Religions

The 450 million practitioners of Primal Religions are 6 percent of the global population. Each tribe has its own beliefs and sacred sites.

Right A young Jewish man stands on a terrace in Jerusalem, Israel. Behind him is the Wailing Wall, the last remnant of the Jewish temple that once stood where the Dome of the Rock now sits.

The Adivasis of India find the sacred in the forest and its gifts. In African Traditional Religion, God is seen as the Great Ancestor, and one's own ancestors are revered as the custodians and enforcers of the traditional way of life. Among Australia's Aborigines, the spiritual insight known as the Dreaming both explains creation and determines a person's relation to living creatures and landforms. Mayan religion focuses on the calendar as determined by astronomical events.

Below Australian Aborigines perform an initiation ceremony in Arnhem Land. Primal religions such as theirs are closely linked to the geography and ethnicity of the practitioners.

The Quechua revere Pachamama (Mother Earth) on the Isla del Sol (Island of the Sun) in Lake Titicaca, and on sacred mountains such as Ausungate in southern Peru. Osun Sacred Grove, in southern Nigeria, is sacred to the Yoruba people of west Africa.

Hinduism

There are more than a billion Hindus (14 percent of the global population), 80 percent of whom live in India. Bali in Indonesia and Nepal are the only other areas of the world with a large Hindu majority.

A Hindu may worship many deities, while simultaneously espousing the view that all deities are ultimately the same. Some Hindus do not worship any deity at all. The key to these apparent contradictions is the Hindu belief that reality is ultimately one, without division into individual persons or objects. Hindus also believe in karma—good actions bear good fruit for the doer, evil actions bad fruit—and reincarnation.

Above An eight-year-old boy wears traditional makeup and costume for a Hindu celebration in Kumbh Mela, Allahabad, India.

Hinduism's sacred sites include the Ganga (Ganges) River, cleanser of sins; the Himalaya Mountains, abode of the gods; and Varanasi (Banaras), the holiest city.

Buddhism

There are about 400 million Buddhists in the world, comprising six percent of the global population. Buddhists share with Hindus a belief in karma, reincarnation, and the illusory nature of the phenomenal world. They emphasize the impermanence of everything, including the self. There is no "one behind the many" as in Hinduism, but only a flowing stream of psychological and physical states.

The sacred sites connected with the life of Siddhartha Gautama (the Buddha) are in northeastern India. They include Bodh Gaya, the place of his enlightenment, and the Deer Park at Sarnath, where he gave his first sermon.

From India, Mahayana Buddhism traveled along a northeastern route to Tibet, China, Korea, and Japan. Theravada followed a southeastern route encompassing Sri Lanka, Burma, Laos, Cambodia, and Thailand.

Judaism

The Jewish faith is espoused by 16.5 million people, less than 1 percent of the global population. The United States, with six million, has the world's largest Jewish population; Israel, with five million, the second largest. There are 2.5 million Jews in Russia, more than a million in Europe, about a million in Latin America, and less than a million in Canada.

Judaism's one God is both creator of the entire world and the God of Israel. Torah ("teaching," "law") includes the observance of 613 mitzvot (commandments) derived from the Bible. As land, "Israel" refers to a swathe of the modern Middle East that, according to the Bible, was promised to Abraham's descendants by God. As people, "Israel" is the descendants of Abraham through Isaac, participants in a unique covenantal relationship with God.

The most sacred place for Jews is the Temple Mount in Jerusalem, where the Temple once stood; however, the Mount is also the site of the Dome of the Rock, the oldest extant Muslim building in the world.

Christianity

Today, the followers of Jesus Christ (born in Bethlehem, around the year 6 BCE) have increased to more than two billion people, one-third of the global population.

Christians consider Jesus to be the second person of a triune God (Father, Son, and Holy Spirit—the "Trinity"), and they believe his death is the sacrifice through which anyone who believes in him is reconciled to God.

There are three main forms of Christianity: Orthodox, Roman Catholic, and Protestant.

Orthodox practice includes liturgical worship, seven sacraments, prayer to the saints, and veneration of icons.

Roman Catholics engage in liturgical worship, seven sacraments, devotions to the saints, and pilgrimages. The shrine of Our Lady of Guadalupe in Mexico City is the most visited pilgrimage site in the Americas.

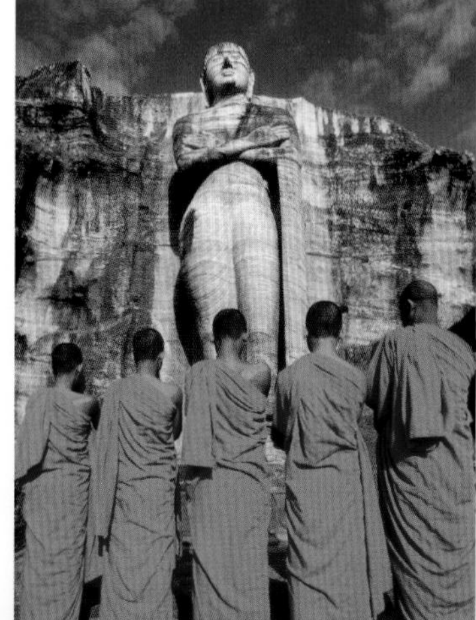

Right Buddhist monks pray before a giant statue of Buddha at Gal Vihara, Polonnaruwa, Sri Lanka. The saffron robes of Buddhist monks emulate the robes of the Buddha and represent humility.

Above In Brazil, where the population is mostly Roman Catholic, a massive statue of Christ the Redeemer overlooks the city and suburbs of Rio de Janeiro from the top of Mt Corcovado. The statue is 98½ feet (30 m) high.

Protestants emphasize the unmerited nature of the salvation that is found in Jesus Christ, and unmediated connection to God—having no Pope or saints as intercessors. Followers of the Protestant faith have few or no sacraments; their central practices are biblically based sermons and private reading of the scriptures.

Protestants are dominant in North America, northern Europe, Australia, and parts of Africa. Catholics dominate in Latin America, southern Europe, and parts of Africa. Orthodoxy is strongest in Russia, eastern Europe, and parts of the Middle East.

Islam

The Islamic religion began in the seventh century CE in what is now western Saudi Arabia. Most countries with Muslim majorities are in the Middle East or North Africa, but the largest Muslim populations are found in Indonesia, Pakistan, Bangladesh, and India.

Twenty-three percent of the global population, around 1.5 billion people, is Muslim. Most Muslims (83 percent) are Sunnis; 16 percent are Shi'ite.

Muslims believe in the absolute unity of Allah (God). Human beings are to submit to the will of God as revealed in the Qur'an. Muhammad is considered to be the last major prophet of God, but he is not seen as divine.

Islam's holy cities are Mecca (Makkah), Medina (al-Madinah)—both in Saudi Arabia—and Jerusalem (al-Quds). Every year, about two million pilgrims visit Mecca.

Sikhism

Of the 23 million Sikhs worldwide, 80 percent live in Punjab in northwest India. Sikhs are a substantial minority in the contiguous Indian states, in the United Kingdom, and also in Canada.

Sikhism, born in the fifteenth century CE, combines the monotheism of Islam with the Hindu concepts of maya, karma, and reincarnation. However, its followers consider it a new divine revelation, not merely a synthesis.

World Religions

Protestant Christianity
Catholic Christianity
Orthodox Christianity
Judaism
Sunni Islam
Shia Islam
Hinduism
Sikhism
Mahayana Buddhism
Theravada Buddhism
Chinese religions
Shinto
Primal religions
Sparsely populated areas

Major Holy Sites

Christianity
Judaism
Islam
Hindu
Sikh
Buddhism
Chinese
Shinto
Primal

Robinson Projection

The Golden Temple at Amritsar, which houses the Sikh scriptures, is in India.

Chinese Religions

China's 1.3 billion people are 20 percent of the global population. Early Chinese religious elements included the interplay of yin and yang energies as an explanation for the growth and decay of all things, the Dao ("way") as explanation for the order and harmony in nature, the worship of Heaven (performed by the emperor at the Temple of Heaven in Beijing), divination, and ancestor veneration.

From this ancient mix emerged two enduring traditions, Daoism and Confucianism. Both sought harmony, and both used the word "Dao" for the principle that established harmony, but Daoism looked to nature as a guide while Confucians sought the principle of harmony in human relations.

When Indian Buddhist monks reached China in the early centuries of the common era, the classical triad of traditions (Daoism, Confucianism, and Buddhism) was complete. The Chinese did not practice one of these traditions exclusively. Daoism was used for physical and psychological health, Confucianism dealt with family and ethical concerns, and Buddhist monks conducted funerals.

Wu-tai Shan (Mount Wu-tai), has been the center of Chinese Buddhism for two millennia. White Cloud Abbey in Beijing is where Daoist novices from all parts of mainland China train. Qufu is the hometown of Confucius.

Shinto

Shinto is the indigenous religion of Japan and at one time was the official state religion. It is difficult to estimate the number of adherents because there is no procedure for becoming a member. One is born Shinto simply by virtue of being born Japanese.

Shinto is confined almost exclusively to Japan. It has a reverence for the land, culture, people, and nation of Japan. There is no written code of ethics; the Shinto way of life is encoded in its rituals, which are an important part of daily life.

Amaterasu's shrine at Ise is Japan's most important pilgrimage site. Amaterasu is the Sun Goddess; members of the imperial family are believed to be her descendants.

Below left Muslim pilgrims encircle the holy Kaaba at Mecca's Grand Mosque in Saudi Arabia, during the annual hajj rituals. About two million pilgrims from around the world travel to Mecca to perform Al-Hajj or Bilgirame.

Below center Coils of incense hang from the ceiling of the Man Mo temple in Hong Kong, filling the air with fragrant smoke. Chinese believers often practice a combination of Confucianism, Daoism, and Buddhism.

Below right Sikhs in India gather to practice their beliefs in gurdwaras ("doors to the guru"). At Anandpur Sahib gurdwara, Punjab, Sikhs recently celebrated 300 years since the founding of the Khalsa (Order of the Pure).

Migration—People on the Move

In the animal kingdom, humans alone are not confined to a particular, biologically restricted, habitat. Culture is humankind's adaptive mechanism. It has allowed our species to occupy any of Earth's diverse environments. Currently, an estimated 200 million people—about three percent of the world's population—migrate across an international boundary each year.

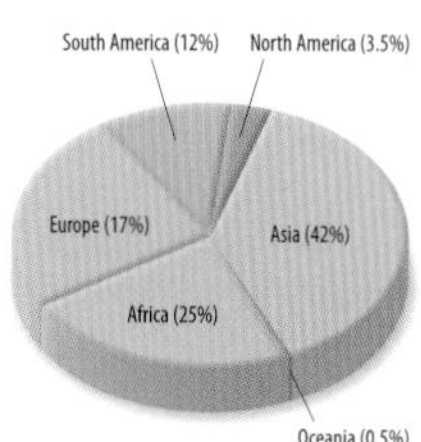
South America (12%)
North America (3.5%)
Europe (17%)
Asia (42%)
Africa (25%)
Oceania (0.5%)

Above This chart shows the relative proportion of refugees by continent of origin. The most populous continent, Asia, is the major source of refugees for both economic and political reasons.

Right "Liberty Enlightening the World" is the true name of the colossal statue in New York City. She overlooks Ellis Island, for many years a processing center for new immigrants to the USA and now a museum to their memory.

Below After the Holocaust of World War II, many Polish Jews found themselves in Displaced Persons (DP) camps set up by the United Nations, prior to being settled in new countries.

Above The nomads of eastern Tibet, China, still follow a pattern of seasonal migration, traveling to lower pastures in autumn each year before settling in their winter quarters.

Right The Moai statues on Easter Island are the remnants of an ancient Polynesian nation that was forced to leave its homeland because it had exhausted the natural resources of the island.

Far right Refugees from across central Europe queue for food at an Allied Forces refugee camp in Germany, after being displaced by the events of World War II.

Most migrants—about 120 million of them each year according to United Nations data—move from less developed to industrialized countries in search of a better life. Additionally, countless millions of people move, or change their location of residence, without crossing a political boundary. Still, given the physical ability to migrate, it seems somewhat paradoxical that perhaps three-quarters of the world's people never move further than a dozen or so miles from their birthplace.

Populations change as a result of four factors—births, deaths, in-migration, and out-migration. Today, population changes throughout much of the world are more dependent upon migration than they are on births and deaths. This is particularly true with regard to in-migration, which is the primary source of urban population growth worldwide.

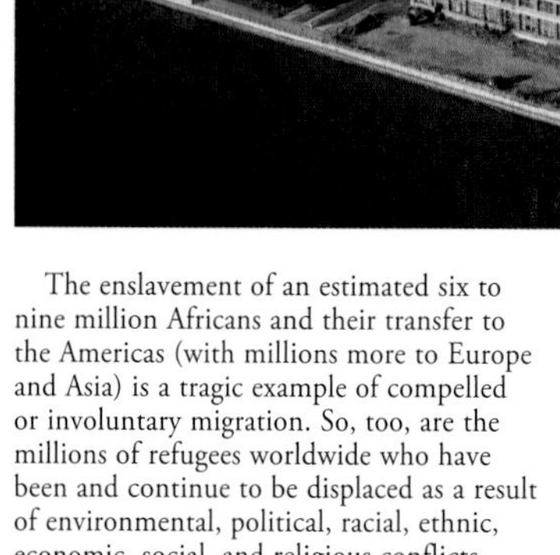

Push-and-Pull Factors

When people move, many factors can influence the decision. Migration is a two-stage process—leaving one location, followed by moving to another. Something must serve as a catalyst to the act of leaving; collectively, these are known as push factors. They may be self-determined, or beyond one's control. Once an individual decides to leave a location, any spot on Earth is a potential destination. Certain areas, however, tend to possess pull factors, conditions that lure migrants.

Throughout history, economic considerations have been the primary stimulus influencing migration. People leave a location because maintaining an adequate livelihood is difficult; they move to a place that offers greater opportunity for economic survival.

There are, of course, numerous other push-and-pull factors. Some physical factors include drought, natural disasters, loss of soil fertility, or mineral resources becoming exhausted. Human-induced conditions include war, ethnic cleansing, religious or political persecution, or other types of discrimination that can render life unbearable for a particular segment of the population.

History of Migration

There are many types of migration. Early humans migrated from place to place in search of a better food supply. Several thousand years ago, herders began to follow their flocks on seasonal migrations in search of better pasture. Seasonal migration continues to this day, particularly in places where winter conditions are harsh.

Occasionally, large numbers of people will relocate in a group, or mass, migration. The largest such migration involved more than 60 million Europeans who, over a span of several centuries, moved to the Americas, Australia and New Zealand, South Africa, and elsewhere. Their reasons varied, although nearly all of them sought a better life. For most, it was a quest for economic gain, including the prospect of land ownership; others sought freedom to practice their religion without persecution; many simply wanted to free themselves from the Old World's rigid socioeconomic system.

The enslavement of an estimated six to nine million Africans and their transfer to the Americas (with millions more to Europe and Asia) is a tragic example of compelled or involuntary migration. So, too, are the millions of refugees worldwide who have been and continue to be displaced as a result of environmental, political, racial, ethnic, economic, social, and religious conflicts.

Some countries restrict both immigration and emigration. Most countries, in fact, have laws that in some way limit immigration, in order to protect the national interest. The United States has had some of the world's most liberal immigration laws. Today, however, the country faces a contentious demographic, social, and political issue (some would call it a "crisis") resulting from a flood of undocumented immigrants. At present, an estimated 12 million residents are in the country illegally.

In a few countries—particularly in totalitarian Marxist states—emigration is severely limited if not prohibited outright. The regime in the former Soviet Union had such a policy and North Korea and Cuba are among the few societies that continue to restrict the free movement of their citizens to other countries.

Major Migrations

Equatorial East Africa is believed to be the homeland of humankind. Before *Homo sapiens* could leave this tropical hearth, certain cultural developments had to occur. Control of fire, protective clothing, and the invention of better tools, weapons, and containers rank among the more important developments that facilitated migration into more demanding climates and ecosystems.

Archeological evidence suggests that humans were living in mid-latitude climates of Europe and Asia as early as one million years ago. Open water was a much greater barrier to early migration than conditions on land. In fact, human settlement was limited to the "World Island" (the Afro-Eurasian landmass) throughout approximately 98 percent of human history.

The contemporary global distribution of physical features (DNA, blood type, stature, skin color, and so forth) and languages, in particular, amply document frequent and widespread human movements in the past.

Certainly, by the dawn of the Common Era, all of the world's ecumene (the two-thirds of Earth's land surface that is inhabited) was occupied. The Pacific Basin was the last settled frontier. Yet most islands in that vast expanse of water were inhabited by Polynesian peoples long before Magellan's epic voyage.

International Disputes and Disputed Borders

People migrate for reasons other than economic gain. Among the myriad other causes of human displacement are fear for one's life and the desperate search for a safe haven from political conflict. The number of such individuals worldwide is anyone's guess: The United Nations High Commissioner for Refugees (UNHCR) lists their number at between eight and nine million; the United States

Arctic
Disputed by: Canada, Denmark, Norway, Russia, United States of America

Transnistria
Disputed since: 1991
Disputed by: Moldova, Russia, Transnistria

Abkhazia and South Ossetia
Disputed since: 1991
Disputed by: Abkhazia, Georgia, Russia, South Ossetia

Nagorno-Kharabakh
Disputed since: 1988
Disputed by: Armenia, Azerbaijan

Cyprus
Disputed since: 1974
Disputed by: Republic of Cyprus, Turkish Republic of Northern Cyprus

Jammu and Kashmir
Disputed since: 1947
Disputed by: India, Pakistan

Aksai Chin
Disputed since: 1962
Disputed by: China, India

Kuril Islands
Disputed since: 1945
Disputed by: Japan, Russia

Gaza Strip and West Bank
Disputed since: 1948
Disputed by: Egypt, Israel, Jordan, Lebanon, Occupied Palestinian Territory, Syrian Arab Republic

Arunachal Pradesh
Disputed since: 1962
Disputed by: China, India

Taiwan
Disputed since: 1949
Disputed by: People's Republic of China, Taiwan

Western Sahara
Disputed since: 1976
Disputed by: Mauritania, Morocco, Western Sahara

Hala'ib Triangle
Disputed since: 1902/1992
Disputed by: Egypt, Sudan

Tibet
Disputed since: 1950
Disputed by: China, Tibet

Darfur (Sudan)
Disputed since: 2003
Disputed by: Sudan, Sudan Liberation Movement

Somaliland (Somalia)
Disputed since: 1991
Disputed by: Puntland, Somalia, Somaliland

Paracel Islands
Disputed since: 1974
Disputed by: China, Vietnam

Spratly Islands
Disputed since: 1951
Disputed by: China, Malaysia, Philippines, Taiwan, Vietnam

Falkland Islands (Islas Malvinas)
Disputed since: 1982
Disputed by: Argentina, United Kingdom

Antarctica
Disputed by: Argentina, Australia, Chile, France, New Zealand, Norway, United Kingdom

Robinson Projection

Committee for Refugees and Immigrants estimates that there are more than 12 million refugees and about 34 million internally displaced persons.

There are many types of political conflicts. The most serious are international disputes of various types, including those resulting from disputed borders. Ethnic cleansing often has a political catalyst. Some groups become politically marginalized and their wellbeing is threatened when a power shift occurs within a country. Countries may fail (for example, the former Soviet Union, Yugoslavia, and India prior to the original creation of a spatially divided Pakistan), resulting in massive demographic shifts.

Some contemporary conflicts are widely publicized and well known. Southwest Asia and northeastern Africa are the contemporary "hot spots" of conflict-caused migration. The ongoing dispute between Israel and the Palestinian Territories has resulted in tremendous human suffering and displacement of people. Nearly five million Iraqis have been forced from their homes since the invasion of their country in 2003. Since the 1980s, an estimated eight million people have been displaced in Afghanistan. In Africa, more than five million Sudanese are displaced, some internally and many to international destinations. The overspill of refugees from Darfur alone has had a severe impact on several neighboring countries, including Chad.

Not all of the hot spots are well known or widely reported; nonetheless, they are the source of considerable human suffering and migration. Conflict has lingered for decades in Jammu and Kashmir, control of which is contested by India and Pakistan; Russia has an ongoing territorial dispute with Japan over four of the Kuril Islands; and Transnistria (currently part of Moldova) and South Ossetia and Abkhazia in Georgia—among others around the world—are all striving for independence.

Future Migration

In regard to migration patterns, several trends appear likely during coming decades. First, migration will accelerate the mingling of races and cultures, paradoxically contributing to both greater diversity on a micro-scale and increasing homogeneity worldwide. Second, migration from less-developed to developed countries will accelerate because of a shortage of workers in developed lands created by a rapidly ageing population. Third, in developing countries, rural-to-urban migration will accelerate, whereas in developed nations the trend will be from large cities to smaller cities, suburbs, rural communities, and the countryside. Finally, as the world population expands toward the 9.5 billion mark, megacities will continue to grow because of in-migration; so too will many of the world's currently less populated areas.

Above The map shows the current major hot spots of international conflict or dispute, which result in the exodus of many people—by choice if they are fortunate, but more often simply in order to save their own lives in the face of war or starvation.

Right The movement of people from the country to the city will be one of the major forms of migration in the near future. Many cities will continue to grow as they absorb this influx, becoming hi-tech megacities like Shanghai in China.

Left, above A Russian peacekeeping officer (left), a Moldovan soldier (center) and a Transnistrian solder (right) stand guard in the security zone—over the Dniester River between Moldova and Transnistria—to monitor movement across the disputed border.

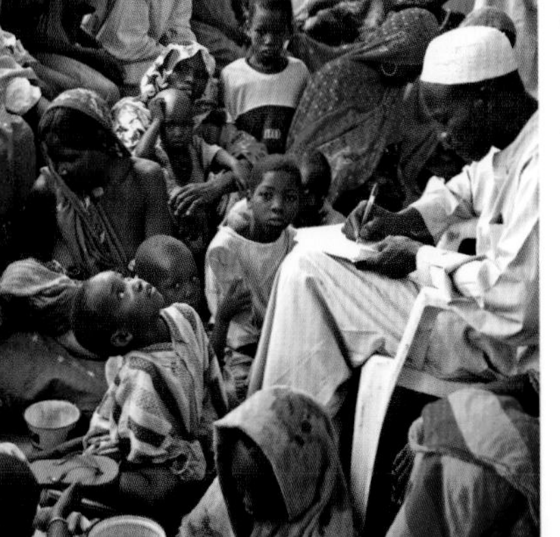

Left Sudanese refugees wait in a refugee camp in Koukou, Chad. Around 200,000 Sudanese refugees have fled to Chad from Darfur, and a further 100,000 citizens of Chad were forced to flee their homes when violence spilled across the border.

REFUGEES

People have been displaced from their place of residence throughout much of human history. Racial, religious, and ethnic persecution has long plagued the human population and resulted in millions of refugees. Millions of others have been forced from their homes for reasons ranging from drought to war and flood to famine. According to the United Nations, a refugee is:

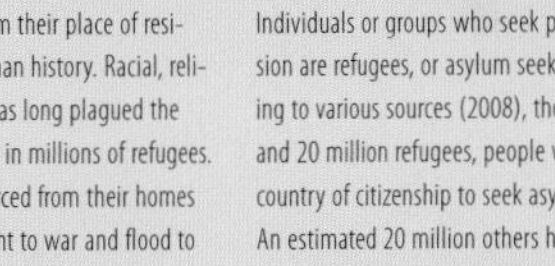

A person who, owing to a well-founded fear of being persecuted for reasons of race, religion, nationality, membership of a particular social group, or political opinion, is outside the country of their nationality, and is unable to or, owing to such fear, is unwilling to avail him/herself of the protection of that country.

Individuals or groups who seek protection from oppression are refugees, or asylum seekers (asylees). According to various sources (2008), there are between 10 and 20 million refugees, people who have left their country of citizenship to seek asylum in another land. An estimated 20 million others have been internally displaced within their own countries.

It is extremely difficult to determine numbers with any degree of accuracy and they vary widely. Paramount among the problems are legal vs. illegal status and accurate census documentation. In the United States, for example, there are an estimated 12 million to as many as 20 million undocumented residents, some of whom would certainly qualify for "refugee" status.

Right Refugee camps offer temporary shelter, along with food and medical care, to persons displaced by circumstances beyong their control. Up to 40 million people worldwide may be classed as refugees at any one time.

Human Impact on the Environment

Humans have altered the natural world in a far more dramatic way than any other species ever to have lived on Earth. The development of complex human societies has occurred through the taming and exploitation of Earth's environments and systems. Humans are perhaps the first species with the potential to destroy Earth.

Above A storm in the Black Sea wrecked five ships, causing a massive oil spill that poisoned wildlife in this environmentally sensitive area.

Above The lush green foliage in this photograph is water cabbage, which is encouraged in its rapid growth by the sewage disgorged into the Hongyan Reservoir, Chongqing, China.

Although many species can wreak havoc on the natural world, particularly when their numbers reach unsustainable proportions, the difference with humans is the scale of the impact. There is not a single place on Earth that is not influenced in some way by the activities of humans. Rubbish can be found throughout all the world's oceans, the global atmosphere has become a dump for the world's pollution, the rate of species extinction continues to increase, and environments the world over are showing signs of significant stress.

Most aspects of human activity impact on the environment. Every time we start our cars we contribute greenhouse gases to the atmosphere. The food we eat is most commonly grown with the application of fertilizers, which disrupt the nutrient cycle. Even if we choose to buy organic food, the food has been transported to the store using fossil fuels and it is likely we drove to the store to buy it. We will cook it using electricity that in most cases is generated through an environmentally damaging process.

Oil: Nature's Gift or Curse?

Oil is often said to be the single most important commodity in the world. It is certainly the most traded item and it has the power, like no other resource, to affect the world socially, politically, and environmentally. There are very few humans on Earth who aren't reliant on oil for some aspects of their daily existence. It is the major fuel source for transport, is used extensively for power generation, is a key ingredient in plastics, and is used in many different industrial applications.

For all of oil's benefits, it has exacted a heavy toll on the environment. Oil releases carbon dioxide into the atmosphere when burnt, contributing to the greenhouse effect.

Deforestation

Deforestation is one of humankind's more devastating impacts on the natural world. Forests are cleared to provide timber for construction and manufacturing or fiber for use in paper products and, most commonly, they are cleared to create large areas of land for agriculture. The annual rate of forest clearing is estimated to be around 18½ million acres (7.5 million ha) per year, although the rate may be much higher. Clearing is widespread in South America, particularly in the Amazon Basin, and in Southeast Asia, most notably in Indonesia, Malaysia, and Myanmar.

Logging for commercial timber and fiber is a controversial issue in many countries, including Australia, Canada, and New Zealand. The Amazon Basin is one of the most significant rainforest regions on Earth, but the forest has been widely cleared since the 1960s for timber, and there has been much land clearing associated with ranging. Estimates vary greatly, but between 15 and 40 percent of the forest has been cleared since the 1960s.

Because forests are such complex ecosystems, deforestation has a dramatic effect on a large number of species. Not only are tree-dwelling species directly affected, but the impacts of deforestation are seen in river systems where deforestation has increased soil erosion in surrounding areas. Forests are also seen as one solution to the problem of global warming. As plants absorb carbon dioxide, the main greenhouse gas, forests can play a powerful role in mitigating the effects of the greenhouse effect.

The World's Oceans

The planet's oceans have long been both a dumping ground and important food source

Above top Workers clean Huntingdon Beach, California, USA, after an oil spill. Toxic in its crude form, oil is also a major pollutant when it is burned to provide power.

Above center Fishing trawlers such as this one—off Lantau Island, Hong Kong—catch fish and other animals indiscriminately, throwing back the unsaleable bycatch.

Above Heavy industry and factories, cars and trucks, and population density (both domestic and corporate) make the air in many modern cities thick with pollution.

for millions of people. The oceans have been convenient places for humankind to dispose of all kinds of waste, ranging from sewage to unwanted radioactive materials.

Ocean currents, winds and tides carry rubbish around the planet. Mariners have for some time been aware of a coming together of winds and currents in the northern Pacific Ocean between San Francisco and Hawaii. These currents contrive to bring vast amounts of rubbish into the area in what some scientists have called a "plastic soup" that holds as much 2.5 percent of all the plastic manufactured worldwide since 1950.

Research conducted in 2007 found that the north Pacific "rubbish soup" had enlarged to join up with another massive concentration of rubbish in the western Pacific near Japan; the total area affected is bigger than the land area of the continental United States. Scientists have labelled the area the Pacific Garbage Patch. Toothbrushes, plastic bottles, plastic bags, and even hard hats are found in it.

The rubbish comes from all around the Pacific. At present, the patch lies well away from international shipping lanes and within international waters. Therefore, there is little political will to clean it up, although this may change as the patch gets closer to land.

The other major impact that humans have on the oceans is through commercial fishing. Seafood is a major part of the human diet and vast quantities of marine life are harvested from the seas every year: The average annual catch is estimated at around 90 million tons (80 million tonnes). Unsustainable fishing in the past has seen many species of fish become virtually extinct, taking with them the communities that depended on harvesting them.

As demand for seafood continues to grow, more pressure is being placed on marine environments. Many countries have adopted strict quotas for their fishing fleets, confining the amount that can be caught by each boat.

Bycatch is a term used within the fishing industry to describe the unwanted species caught while fishing. This unwanted catch is simply thrown overboard. As nets and lines get bigger and longer, bycatches have grown—research done into the North Sea fisheries found that as much as seven pounds (3 kg) of bycatch was taken for each pound (450 g) of commercial fish. When mammals such as dolphins and turtles rise to the surface to take in air they too may be caught in a net or hooked on a long line, and they simply drown.

Above top The beautiful rainbows of an oil slick belie its harmful effect. This incident in South Korea saw 10,000 tons (9,000 tonnes) of crude oil leak into the sea.

Above center Guitarfish, rays, and other bycatch are tossed from a shrimp boat in waters off La Paz, Mexico. Some fish will swim away, but many are already dead.

Above Plastics and other non-biodegradable rubbish are both an eyesore and an ongoing problem, since the waste will remain with us for a very long time.

THE CHERNOBYL NUCLEAR ACCIDENT

The world was shocked in April 1986 when the news broke of a massive nuclear accident in the remote Soviet city of Chernobyl.

Located in northern Ukraine, Chernobyl housed four large nuclear power generation plants. The Chernobyl power plant was scheduled for routine maintenance: On April 25, crews began preparing the reactor for maintenance, but on April 26, a series of mistakes led to coolant water in the reactor falling, allowing energy to increase within the reactor. Fuel elements within the reactor ruptured, leading to an explosion that lifted the cover plates off the reactor, releasing large amounts of radioactive material. Another explosion blew out further fragments of material, allowing air to rush into the reactor and set fire to the graphite moderator that surrounds the nuclear material. This graphite continued to burn for nine days, releasing vast amounts of radioactive material into the atmosphere.

Authorities reacted to the emergency by dropping more than 5,500 tons (5,000 tonnes) of boron, dolomite, clay sand and lead onto the reactor from helicopters in a vain attempt to douse the fires. On May 2 and 3, more than 45,000 people were evacuated from the area around the power station as nuclear fallout began to spread. Atmospheric winds carried the radioactive material some thousands of miles, spreading the environmental and health impacts of the nuclear disaster. It has been estimated that the Chernobyl accident released at least 100 times more radiation than the atomic bombs that were dropped on the Japanese cities of Nagasaki and Hiroshima in 1945.

Thirty people were killed at the time of the accident, but the scale of the disaster was not immediately obvious to staff at the plant, with many engaging in a clean-up operation without protective clothing, which would eventually see many die of acute radiation poisoning in the coming weeks.

Right A computer-enhanced satellite image of Chernobyl just after the disaster shows radioactivity in red. The town of Pripyat was evacuated and remains empty more than 20 years later.

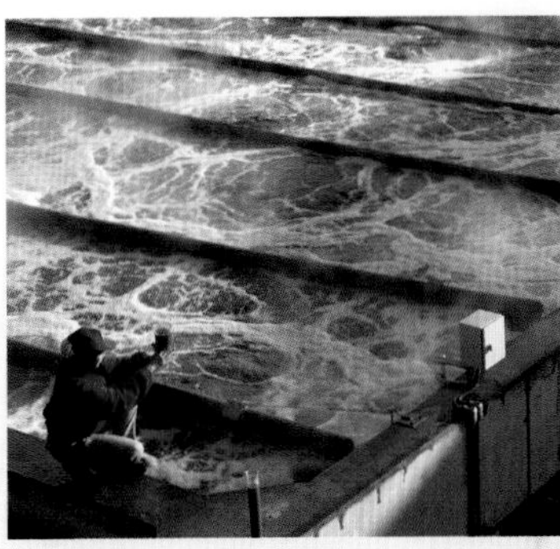

Left A scientist takes a sample from a water treatment plant in Mexico. Water treatment operations remove harmful chemicals and microorganisms from the water, making it suitable for human consumption, and for industrial and agricultural use.

International agreements—such as the Wellington Convention on Drift Net Fishing that seeks to control the size and use of large nets—and campaigns by environmental groups have attempted to reduce this horrific toll. Consumers of tuna, for example, are being encouraged to purchase only products that are endorsed as "dolphin-safe".

Below The scars on the landscape caused by logging in the Olympic National Forest, Washington State, USA, reveal in stark reality the effects of humans on the environment. Sustainable logging is the answer to preventing permanent damage to Earth's biosphere.

Global Communications and Trade

During the twentieth century the world became a much smaller place. Not literally, of course, but it is smaller in terms of the ability of humankind to communicate across the face of the planet, and to transport goods and services around it. Yet, while billions of people have multiple ways to communicate, there are still millions of people, particularly in Africa, who have never heard a telephone dial tone.

Above Cargo is transported around the world by massive container ships like this one, docked for loading at Khor Fakkhan, United Arab Emirates.

In 1900, the fastest that a newly arrived Irish migrant in the United States could communicate with their loved ones in Ireland was via a letter sent home by ship, a journey of several days. Today, that same message can be instantaneously transmitted by telephone.

There are now close to 1.5 billion mobile (cell) phone users worldwide, around a quarter of the world's population. Half the world's population (three billion people) lives in an area where mobile phone reception is available. The fastest growing regions for mobile phone use are China, India, and Russia—among the most populous countries on earth—places with rapidly developing economies.

While telecommunication advances have transformed much of the world, there are still very large gaps between access to this technology. For example, around 5 percent of Africa's population had Internet access in 2007, compared to approximately 72 percent of North Americans, 57 percent of Australians, and 44 percent of Europeans.

Above This engraving shows the laying of the first transatlantic telegraph cable from the *Agamemnon*, in 1857. The cable failed and was abandoned—it was some 10 years later that permanent communication links were established.

Undersea Cables

The vast majority of the world's voice and Internet traffic is carried by fiber optic cables. These cables are strung out across the ocean floor, linking the continents.

The first cables carried telegraph traffic—in 1850 a cable was laid beneath the English Channel, comprising only a length of copper wire, which was coated in 1851 with a protective covering. More cables were gradually laid, linking England to Ireland, and then England to the Netherlands. In 1866, the transatlantic cable allowed telegraph traffic to flow between Europe and the United States. In 1902 a cable was laid across the Pacific, linking the United States with Australia and New Zealand.

By the 1980s the cable technology had improved substantially, allowing more and more traffic to be carried. Using fiber optic cables, millions of separate data and voice transfers can now happen simultaneously.

Despite all the advances in technologies, the modern cables are still susceptible to damage. Fishing trawlers, ships' anchors, undersea landslides, and even shark attacks all take their toll. Often performed in very deep water, cable repairs are expensive and time consuming.

The World Wide Web

The World Wide Web is a global communication tool that has transformed the way that humans interact with one another. In a very short period of time the World Wide Web has changed the way people communicate, shop, search for information, and relax. In 1959, the famous science fiction author Isaac Asimov wrote a short story—*Anniversary*—in which people searched for information from computers in their own home. By 1990, this type of searching was no longer fiction and had become reality after Englishman Tim Berners-Lee created a computer web browser called the World Wide Web.

By 1996, use of the Web had continued to expand at such a rapid rate that most large companies were beginning to use it for commercial reasons, leading to the development of e-commerce. Since this time the Web has

Below The floor of the Tokyo Stock Exchange, Japan, is a hive of frenzied activity—modern communications mean that stock price rises and falls are transmitted around the globe instantly.

WORLD TRADE ORGANIZATION

Established in 1995 with headquarters in Geneva, Switzerland, the World Trade Organization (WTO) is a United Nations body that deals with the regulation of trade between nations. There are 150 member countries within the WTO. On becoming a member, each country agrees to be bound by the rules for international trade established through the international agreements and treaties the WTO enforces.

As with all United Nations institutions, the fundamental purpose of the WTO is to create a place where member nations can resolve their disputes with each other in a peaceful and constructive manner. So in reality, the WTO is a forum at which matters associated with international trade can be negotiated.

The WTO is most commonly associated with attempts to liberalize trade. For centuries, countries have tried to protect their domestic industries through the use of tariffs, a type of tax. Tariffs are placed on imported goods to make them more expensive, while domestically produced goods do not have this tax, making them cheaper than the imported product, or at least no more expensive. For those who support a global trading system, tariffs distort the process as they do not allow countries that can produce a product more cheaply to sell their products fairly. Those who oppose the removal of tariffs argue that in many cases those products that are produced at a cheaper rate are created through the exploitation of workers or the environment, and that trade liberalization simply exacerbates these problems.

Another element of trade liberalization has been the gradual removal of trade subsidies. These are special payments made by governments to specific industries to help them reduce the costs of their products. For example, a government might wish to support their country's poultry industry by helping farmers pay for the cost of chicken feed. By doing this the farmers' costs are reduced and they are able to sell their products more cheaply on the global market. Again, this is seen by supporters of global trade as creating an unequal market place where farmers from countries that don't offer subsidies cannot compete. Ultimately, it is argued, the consumer pays the price because prices are kept higher as there is no incentive for the subsidized farmers to find ways to reduce their costs, while the unsubsidized farmers go bankrupt.

Below Delegates attend the opening session of a 2007 World Trade Organization (WTO) Aid for Trade review summit at WTO headquarters in Geneva, Switzerland.

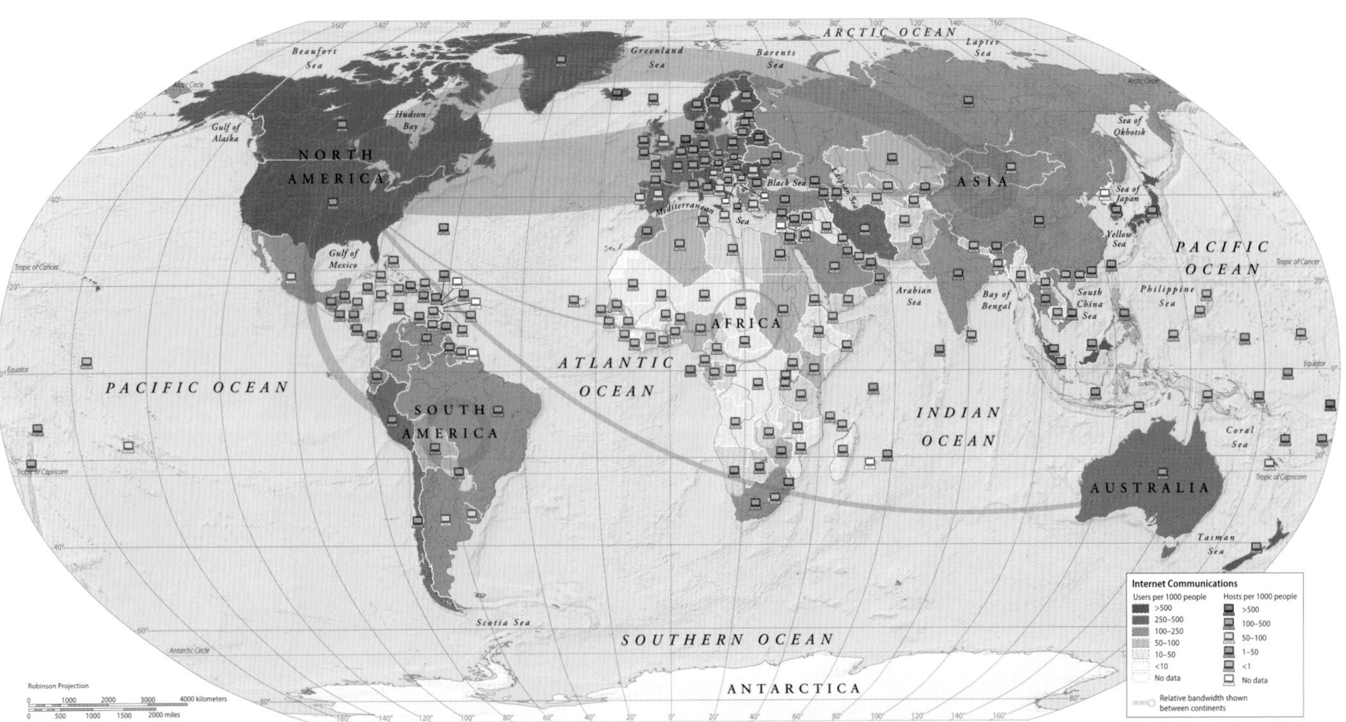
ARCTIC OCEAN
Beaufort Sea
Greenland Sea
Barents Sea
Laptev Sea
Hudson Bay
Gulf of Alaska
NORTH AMERICA
Sea of Okhotsk
Black Sea
Caspian Sea
ASIA
Sea of Japan
Mediterranean Sea
Yellow Sea
PACIFIC OCEAN
Gulf of Mexico
Arabian Sea
Bay of Bengal
South China Sea
Philippine Sea
AFRICA
ATLANTIC OCEAN
PACIFIC OCEAN
SOUTH AMERICA
INDIAN OCEAN
Coral Sea
AUSTRALIA
Tasman Sea
Scotia Sea
SOUTHERN OCEAN
ANTARCTICA
Robinson Projection
0 1000 2000 3000 4000 kilometers
0 500 1000 1500 2000 miles
Internet Communications
Users per 1000 people
>500
250–500
100–250
50–100
10–50
<10
No data
Hosts per 1000 people
>500
100–500
50–100
1–50
<1
No data
Relative bandwidth shown between continents

continued to grow, with most large companies offering their products for sale via websites.

The Web has also grown into an alternative recreational and news medium. The ability for individuals to create their own websites, using sites such as YouTube, has transformed the way that people receive information. Such citizen journalism, some of which has dubious authenticity, has meant that a single individual has the power to inform literally millions of people from a single desktop computer.

International Trade

Along with greater access and ease in global communications has come an ever greater ability to trade goods and services on a global scale. The complexity of the modern consumer world is such that no single country is able to produce all of the goods and services its citizens need or want. Every day, thousands of ships crisscross the world's oceans carrying a vast array of goods, ranging from cars to pencils, from television sets to shoes.

Trade has always been an important link between countries. The buying and selling of goods and services has brought countries together; indeed, some countries were actually created by trade. The modern state of Germany, for example, was founded in the late 1800s after the various smaller German-speaking states created a trading organization called the Zollverein. This trade led to political and social interactions between the states before they finally joined to create the unified Germany in 1871.

More recently a number of important trade organizations have emerged based on regional links. The North American Free Trade Agreement (NAFTA), established in 1993 between the United States, Canada, and Mexico, is designed to facilitate trade between these nations. The Asia Pacific Economic Cooperation (APEC) group, established in 1989, is a large organization that includes most of the nations of Asia and those that have a coastline on the Pacific Ocean.

The European Union

The European Union (EU) is one of the oldest and most complex trade organizations in the world. Formed in the years following World War II as the European Economic Community (EEC), the EU has evolved into a vast political, economic, social, and legal institution. The EU has its own parliament, court system, and central bank.

One of the most significant features of the EU is the concept of the single market. There are no import or export taxes between member nations and a single currency, the euro, is used by most of them. Moving between countries for work and leisure is unrestricted for citizens of any of the member nations.

While there have been many economic benefits, many Europeans have been frustrated by the desire to create uniform rules and regulations across all member countries. This has meant, some argue, that traditional methods and customs unique to certain regions have become diminished and, in some cases, lost.

Above The European Union Parliament building in Strasbourg, France, is an impressive symbol of the strength of this economic alliance.

2 COUNTRIES OF THE WORLD

The World

The world is a place of flourishing diversity that is, and will remain, enormously complex. Economic globalization and technological developments have ushered in a new age of prosperity for many people, even those in previously isolated corners of the globe. Nowadays, reindeer herders in the far distant lands of northeastern Russia use snowmobiles to corral their animals. The world, it can be said, is in rapid forward motion without any desire to look back. Road bumps, however, form part of any journey.

Previous pages At the annual Mt Hagen sing-sing in Papua New Guinea, hundreds of Western Highlands tribes come together to sing, dance, and make money from tourists and sponsors.

Right An open-pit gold mine in Utah, USA. Open-pit mines are used to extract minerals and rocks found near the surface, like gold. Mining has played a significant role in Utah's economic, industrial, political, and social development.

Far right Old traditions continue alongside thriving modern businesses in Grote Markt, in the medieval heart of Bruges, Belgium. Buildings were renovated and traffic was banned in 1996 to allow more room for celebrations.

Above Maun, Botswana, is a mix of modern buildings and native huts. A tourism center, it is home to many safari and air charter operations running trips into world-famous Okavango Delta.

Below right Nicknamed "The Marvelous City," Rio de Janeiro, Brazil, is known for its spectacular natural setting, its Carnival celebrations, its samba music, and its hotel-lined tourist beaches.

Below Rice paddies in Yunnan Province, China. Though rice is a staple food for many people, its cultivation can require copious amounts of water and produces methane, a greenhouse gas.

The big picture suggests that, in general, humanity is better off today than ever before in its history. It may not appear that way at first glance, given the negative side effects of global progress—increased pollution, widespread availability of drugs and weapons, and fast-spreading infectious diseases, for example. Anti-globalization movements criticize the developed nations for establishing low-wage factories in the developing world, exploiting local peoples and enlarging the income gap between wealthy and poor nations. Proponents of globalization argue that the path toward wealth is long, difficult and requires a great deal of sacrifice to change cultural systems set in place centuries ago. Overall, proponents say, the poor are in much better shape today than they were even several decades ago.

If developing countries are viewed in the context of their own historical experience, the scale of positive development is evident. India serves as a splendid example. The world's second most populous country has transformed itself from an undeveloped backwater into a food-exporting country whose economy is booming. Social changes have also been remarkable. The rigid social fabric of India's privileged upper-caste minority and hundreds of millions of lower-caste citizens is being slowly eroded, and for the first time, gender equality is becoming more than an impossible dream. Female emancipation is one of the global social changes breaking long-standing barriers in many cultures. It is not unusual to see rural schools filled with female pupils where a decade ago there were none.

Improved standards of living and the ability to have one's voice heard are universal aspirations held by all of humanity. This is why, after several disastrous attempts to bring their nation into the modern age following the path of communism, the Chinese had to introduce an outward-looking approach.

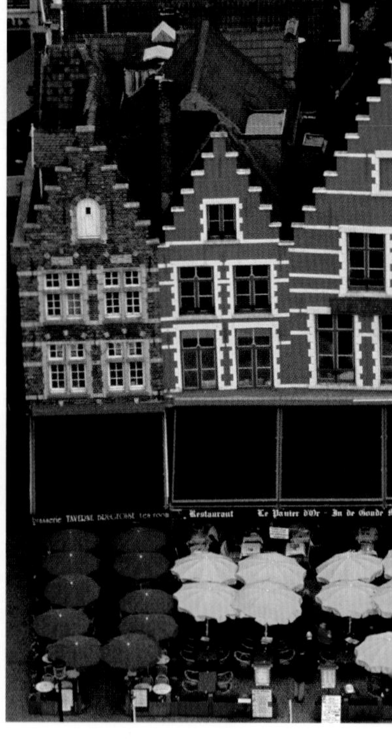

Their neighbor, North Korea, which continues to practice communism, battles recurring famine and remains one of the world's most impoverished and desperate places.

An inward-looking approach and inefficient management are the major causes of lack of improvement among nations that might otherwise shine. Zimbabwe is a timely example. Once the wealthy breadbasket of Africa, it collapsed after less than a decade of abysmal policies under an authoritarian government. Nearly 25 percent of Zimbabweans have left the country, striving for survival, while neighboring Botswana stands out as a role model for successful governance and more equitable distribution of wealth. Botswana was once a nation of cattle herders, but its government's appropriate management of mineral wealth has raised the standard of living to the highest levels in Africa.

Resources management is a growing global concern. The depletion of available resources such as fossil fuels or timber for the sake of economic growth is frequently noted as a cause of environmental problems. The pressure for regulations to help stabilize overconsumption of finite resources and bring pollution under control comes mainly from the developed world—because only an affluent society can afford the luxury of a clean and protected environment. In developing countries, a degraded environment is often regarded as a symbol of jobs, economic growth, a larger role on the global stage, and ultimately a better future for the next generation. The sea of plastic shopping bags littering the desert landscape on Mexico's side of the Rio Grande reflects an increase in the standard of living of ordinary Mexicans, no matter how horrendous the consequences for the natural environment.

Circumstances were certainly no different for Europeans and Americans in the early stages of the Industrial Revolution. With the passing of time and the increase in quality of life and wealth, the notion of environmental protection will successfully spread to the developing world as well.

Natural resources will not run out as quickly as many doomsayers predict. Oil did not replace coal as the main fuel because the world's coal deposits had been exhausted. At the time, oil was cheaper, more convenient, and cleaner to use than coal. Currently, oil and natural gas are still the most affordable energy options for the worldwide economy. Alternative energy will inevitably act as a driving force in the world's economy as soon as it becomes profitable enough to match fossil fuels and the various government impediments are removed.

Another indication that the world is getting better, rather than worse, is evident in the availability, prices, and variety of most foods compared with past trends. In both relative and absolute terms fewer people are malnourished, more have access to better quality food and, as the obesity epidemic in many developed countries illustrates, to larger amounts of high-calorie foods. Demographic data also indicates progress. Life expectancy is continually increasing, infant mortality rates continue to fall, and the rate of natural increase has dropped from a high of two percent per year during the 1970s to just over one percent today. Many previously incurable diseases have been either eradicated or contained. The death toll from conflicts around the globe is at its lowest point in modern history.

Despite these reasons for optimism, with the world population projected to increase from its current 6.6 billion to perhaps

SINT-JORIS
HOTEL-RESTAURANT "CENTRAL"
CAFE DES ARTS
stella artois
de gouden meermin

Left Pupusas, a thick hand-made tortilla made from corn or rice dough and stuffed with cheese, beans, and pork, being prepared at San Salvador's central market. Pupusas were first created by the Pipil tribes indigenous to the region now known as El Salvador.

Below left Ecotourism is on the rise in parts of Papua New Guinea. Milne Bay offers a beautiful coral garden with large plate corals in shallow water, an incredible forest of pink sea fans with red sea whips, black corals, barrel sponges, giant gorgonian sea fans, and colorful marine life. Because the coral reef systems of Milne Bay are some of the most biodiverse in the world, they attract the attention not only of dive operators and tourists but also of conservation groups.

Below The Sultan Ahmed Mosque in Istanbul, Turkey—also known as the Blue Mosque for the blue tiles adorning its interior—was built between 1609 and 1616, during the rule of Ahmed I. The culmination of two centuries of both Ottoman mosque and Byzantine church development, it is considered the last great mosque of the classical period. It also includes a tomb of the founder, a madrasah (school), and a hospice.

9.5 billion by mid-century there is also a need for caution, and indeed action in the case of looming problems like global warming. Natural resources must be conserved, alternative resources developed, pollution reduced, and human resources developed. This can only be achieved through good government, free markets, adequate education and health care, and respect for human rights.

Regions

To better understand the world, geographers systematize physical and cultural features into regional frameworks. They use the concept of regions to organize spatial data just as historians rely on eras, periods, and eons for systematizing chronological data. It is often said that regions are nothing more than successful examining tools for dissecting the world. The fact that they do not exist in reality but are invented explains why there are so many of them and why their boundaries fluctuate and often overlap, depending on human activity or natural processes. Each region has a core, a zone of highest distribution, and a periphery or transitional zone of overlap with surrounding regions. Natural regions can be based on landforms, vegetation, soils, climate, or other geographic criteria.

Criteria for a cultural region may comprise single or multiple cultural traits. For example, Americans tend to be of the Christian faith, but not all of them are Protestants. If we delineate a region in which Protestants represent a majority, its boundary will follow only one portion of US territory, spatial information that provides a deeper glimpse into the American geography of religion. Sub-regions can be created to more precisely map the distribution of particular denominations. Doing so reveals valuable information about the current distributions. For example, Baptists dominate the American South, Lutherans are the majority in Minnesota and neighboring states, and members of the Church of Jesus Christ of Latter-day Saints form a large block in the interior West.

Scholars frequently combine information from natural and cultural regions to expand their knowledge about people and places, cultural adaptation to natural environment, agriculture, and settlement, and to predict future patterns and distribution. When measuring economic activity or transportation, the concept of a "functional region" is applied—that is, a region created on the basis of a specific function. Examples of functional regions are areas covered by an airline carrier or the distributor of a newspaper. Finally, certain areas may be deemed to be regions by virtue of their residents' own perceptions of homogeneity. Some well-known examples of such vernacular, or perceptual, regions include Spain's Costa del Sol, Australia's Outback, and Canada's Maritime Provinces.

Below Earth's surface is longitudinally divided into 24 time zones. Each zone spans 15° of longitude, or one hour of time. Standard time zones are based on meridians divisible by 15, i.e., 15°E, 15°W, 30°E, 30°W, etc. Time zones extend 7½° east and west from each time meridian. Time begins at the prime meridian, or 0° longitude, arbitrarily located at the Royal Observatory in Greenwich, UK. Zones to the east and west range from Greenwich Mean Time (GMT) or Coordinated Universal Time (UTC) +12 hours (east) to -12 hours (west). Time zones often deviate from 15° for various practical reasons. The International Date Line coincides with the 180th meridian located in the mid-Pacific.

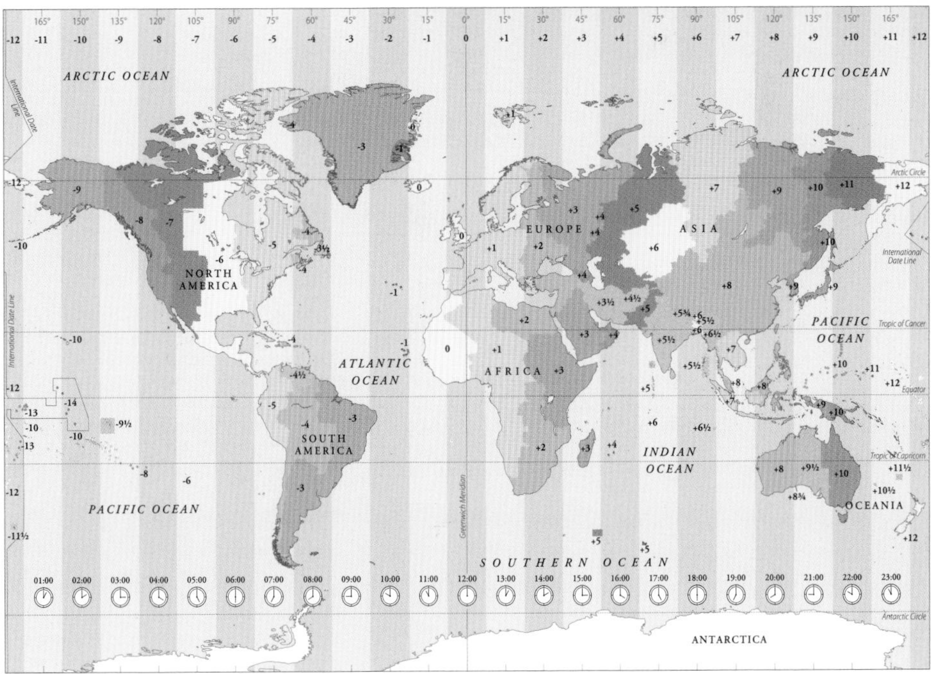
165° 150° 135° 120° 105° 90° 75° 60° 45° 30° 15° 0° 15° 30° 45° 60° 75° 90° 105° 120° 135° 150° 165°
-12 -11 -10 -9 -8 -7 -6 -5 -4 -3 -2 -1 0 +1 +2 +3 +4 +5 +6 +7 +8 +9 +10 +11 +12
ARCTIC OCEAN
ARCTIC OCEAN
NORTH AMERICA
EUROPE
ASIA
AFRICA
SOUTH AMERICA
ATLANTIC OCEAN
PACIFIC OCEAN
PACIFIC OCEAN
INDIAN OCEAN
OCEANIA
SOUTHERN OCEAN
ANTARCTICA
International Date Line
Greenwich Meridian
Arctic Circle
Tropic of Cancer
Equator
Tropic of Capricorn
Antarctic Circle
01:00 02:00 03:00 04:00 05:00 06:00 07:00 08:00 09:00 10:00 11:00 12:00 13:00 14:00 15:00 16:00 17:00 18:00 19:00 20:00 21:00 22:00 23:00

The black numbers on the map indicate the number of hours each time zone is ahead or behind Greenwich Mean Time (GMT). The clocks at the bottom of the map show the time in each time zone when it is 12:00 noon GMT.

NORTH AMERICA
SOUTH AMERICA
PACIFIC OCEAN
ATLANTIC OCEAN
ROCKY MTS
CANADIAN SHIELD
AMAZON BASIN
SELVAS
ANDES
PATAGONIA
PAMPAS
Beaufort Sea
Queen Elizabeth Islands
Baffin Bay
Greenland
Hudson Bay
Labrador Sea
BERING SEA
Gulf of Alaska
Aleutian Is
Aleutian Trench
Brooks Range
Alaska Range
Gulf of Mexico
Caribbean Sea
Greater Antilles
Lesser Antilles
Hawaiian Is
Line Is
POLYNESIA
Archipel des Tuamotu
Archipel de la Société
Archipel des Australes
Cook Islands
Galápagos
Guiana Highlands
Planalto do Mato Grosso
Planalto Central
Drake Passage
Scotia Sea
Falkland Islands
South Georgia
South Shetland Islands
South Orkney Islands
South Sandwich Islands
Bellingshausen Sea
Amundsen Sea
Weddell Sea
Ross Sea
Ross Ice Shelf
Ronne Ice Shelf
Marie Byrd Land
Ellsworth Land
Antarctic Peninsula
Pensacola Mountains
Iceland
Tristan da Cunha Group
Gough Island
Ascension Island
St Helena
Arquipélago dos Açores
Islas Canarias
Tropic of Cancer
Equator
Tropic of Capricorn
Antarctic Circle
1:75,000,000
Robinson Projection
0 1000 2000 3000 4000 kilometers
0 500 1000 1500 2000 miles

World Physical

EUROPE
ASIA
AFRICA
AUSTRALIA
ANTARCTICA
PACIFIC OCEAN
INDIAN OCEAN
SOUTHERN OCEAN
Svalbard
Barents Sea
Zemlya Frantsa-Iosifa
Karskoye More
Laptev Sea
Vostochno-Sibirskoye More
Severnaya Zemlya
Novosibirskiye Ostrova
SIBIR' (SIBERIA)
SREDNE-SIBIRSKOYE PLOSKOGOR'YE
ZAPADNO-SIBIRSKAYA RAVNINA
NORTHERN EUROPEAN PLAIN
ALPS
Black Sea
Caspian Sea
CAUCASUS
Mediterranean Sea
Aral Sea
Sea of Okhotsk
Karaginskiy Zaliv
Sakhalin
Hokkaido
Honshu
Sea of Japan (East Sea)
Yellow Sea
East China Sea
GOBI
TIEN SHAN
KUNLUN SHAN
HINDU KUSH
PAMIR
Taklimakan Shamo
QINGZANG GAOYUAN
HIMALAYA
Everest 8850
Tibesti
Libyan Desert
Nubian Desert
ARABIAN PENINSULA
Ar Rub' al Khali
Red Sea
Persian Gulf
G. of Oman
G. of Aden
Arabian Sea
Bay of Bengal
Andaman Sea
South China Sea
Philippine Sea
Taiwan
Hainan
Luzon
Borneo
Sumatera
Laut Jawa
Celebes Sea
New Guinea
Arafura Sea
Timor Sea
Coral Sea
Tasman Sea
Ethiopian Highlands
Somali Pen.
Congo Basin
Lake Victoria
Lake Tanganyika
Lake Nyasa
Madagascar
Mozambique Channel
Kalahari Desert
Namib Desert
Drakensberg
Great Karoo
Cape of Good Hope
Cape Agulhas
Mauritius
Réunion
Seychelles
Maldives
Sri Lanka
Lakshadweep
Cocos Islands
Christmas Island
Île Amsterdam
Île St-Paul
Îles Crozet
Île Kerguélen
McDonald Islands
Heard Island
Great Sandy Desert
Tanami Desert
Great Victoria Desert
Nullarbor Plain
Great Australian Bight
L. Eyre North
GREAT DIVIDING RA.
Macdonnell Ra.
Kimberley
Arnhem Land
Gulf of Carpentaria
Great Barrier Reef
Bass Str.
Tasmania
Kangaroo I.
Cape Leeuwin
North West Cape
New Zealand
North Island
South Island
Fiji Islands
New Caledonia
Solomon Sea
Bismarck Sea
MELANESIA
Caroline Is
Marshall Is
Ralik Chain
Ratak Chain
Gilbert Is
Mariana Is
Wake Islands
Ogasawara-shotō
Tropic of Cancer
Tropic of Capricorn
Equator
Arctic Circle
Antarctic Circle
Davis Sea
Queen Mary Land
WILKES LAND
Enderby Land
Victoria Land
Ross Sea
Ross Ice Shelf
Amery Ice Shelf
Balleny Islands
Adélie Coast
George V Coast
Princess Elizabeth Land
Prince Olav Coast
Princess Ragnhild Coast
20° 40° 60° 80° 100° 120° 140° 160°

160°
140°
120°
100°
80°
60°
40°
20°
Queen Elizabeth Islands
Ellesmere Island
Parry Islands
Greenland
(Kalaallit Nunaat)
(Denmark)
Beaufort Sea
Victoria Island
Baffin Bay
Baffin I.
Davis Strait
Denmark Strait
REYKJAVIK
ICELAND
RUS. FED.
ALASKA
(USA)
Barrow
Arctic Circle
Bering Str.
Seward Pen.
St Lawrence I.
St Matthew Island
Nunivak Island
Stebbins
Anchorage
Fairbanks
Whitehorse
Yellowknife
Great Bear Lake
Great Slave Lake
Hudson Bay
Hudson Strait
Labrador Sea
Nuuk
Bering Sea
Pribilof Islands
Alaska Pen.
Kodiak Island
Gulf of Alaska
Kenai Pen.
Aleutian Islands
Juneau
Queen Charlotte Is
ROCKY MTS
CANADA
Edmonton
Saskatoon
Calgary
Regina
Winnipeg
L. Winnipeg
Churchill
Gillam
Kamloops
Kelowna
Vancouver
Victoria
Seattle
Tacoma
Portland
Eugene
Boise
Helena
Bismarck
Billings
Pierre
Minneapolis
St Paul
Chicago
Detroit
Toronto
OTTAWA
Montreal
Quebec
Chicoutimi
Halifax
Newfoundland
St John's
Cape Race
St Pierre and Miquelon
(France)
Sault Ste Marie
L. Superior
L. Huron
L. Michigan
L. Ontario
L. Erie
Boston
Augusta
New York
Philadelphia
WASHINGTON DC
Baltimore
Pittsburgh
Columbus
Indianapolis
UNITED STATES OF AMERICA
Cape Mendocino
Reno
Sacramento
San Francisco
San Jose
Las Vegas
Denver
Los Angeles
San Diego
Tijuana
Mexicali
Albuquerque
Phoenix
Oklahoma City
Fort Worth
Dallas
Austin
Nashville
Memphis
Atlanta
Raleigh
Charlotte
Charleston
Savannah
Jacksonville
New Orleans
Houston
San Antonio
Ciudad Juárez
Chihuahua
Tampa
Orlando
Miami
Bermuda
(UK)
Midway Islands
(USA)
Tropic of Cancer
Necker Island
Nihoa
Kaua'i
O'ahu
Honolulu
Wailuku
Maui
Hilo
HAWAII
Hawai'i
Guadalupe
(Mexico)
Punta Eugenia
La Paz
Cabo Falso
Torreón
Monterrey
Saltillo
G. of Mexico
MEXICO
Guadalajara
León
CIUDAD DE MÉXICO
Puebla
Veracruz
Bahía de Campeche
Acapulco
Islas Revillagigedo
(Mexico)
Johnston Atoll
(USA)
LA HABANA
CUBA
Cancún
Cayman Is
JAMAICA
KINGSTON
PORT-AU-PRINCE
SANTO DOMINGO
Puerto Rico
San Juan
NASSAU
BAHAMAS
Turks and Caicos Islands
(UK)
British Virgin Islands
US Virgin Islands
Anguilla (UK)
Sint Maarten (Netherlands)
St Martin (France)
St Barthélemy (France)
ST KITTS AND NEVIS
ANTIGUA AND BARBUDA
Montserrat (UK)
Guadeloupe (France)
Martinique (France)
ST LUCIA
BARBADOS
ST VINCENT AND THE GRENADINES
GRENADA
TRINIDAD AND TOBAGO
BELMOPAN
BELIZE
GUATEMALA
HONDURAS
TEGUCIGALPA
SAN SALVADOR
EL SALVADOR
NICARAGUA
MANAGUA
SAN JOSÉ
COSTA RICA
PANAMÁ
PANAMA
Caribbean Sea
Aruba
Neth. Antilles
Barranquilla
Maracaibo
CARACAS
VENEZUELA
Cúcuta
Medellín
BOGOTÁ
Cali
COLOMBIA
GEORGETOWN
GUYANA
PARAMARIBO
SURINAME
Cayenne
French Guiana
ATLANTIC OCEAN
PACIFIC OCEAN
Kingman Reef
(USA)
Palmyra Atoll
(USA)
Tabuaeran
Kiritimati
Howland I.
Baker I.
Equator
KIRIBATI
Phoenix Islands
Line Islands
Malden Island
Starbuck Island
Tokelau
(New Zealand)
Penrhyn Atoll
Manihiki Atoll
Nassau
Caroline Island
Flint Island
Îles Marquises
Wallis and Futuna
(France)
SAMOA
APIA
Pago Pago
American Samoa
(USA)
FIJI
TONGA
NUKU'ALOFA
Niue
(New Zealand)
Cook Is
(New Zealand)
Papeete
Avarua
Archipel des Tuamotu
Archipel de la Société
French Polynesia
(France)
Archipel des Australes
Tropic of Capricorn
Henderson Island
Pitcairn Islands
(UK)
Rapa Nui
(Chile)
Kermadec Islands
(New Zealand)
Chatham Islands
(New Zealand)
Isla del Coco
(Costa Rica)
Isla de Malpelo
(Colombia)
Isla Fernandina
Isla Isabela
Isla Santa Cruz
Archipiélago de Colón
(Galapagos Islands)
(Ecuador)
QUITO
ECUADOR
Guayaquil
Iquitos
Boa Vista
Macapá
Belém
Mouths of the Amazon
Manaus
Santarém
Amazon Basin
São Luís
Fortaleza
Fernando de Noronha
(Brazil)
Teresina
Natal
João Pessoa
Recife
Maceió
Aracaju
Feira de Santana
Salvador
BRAZIL
Chiclayo
Trujillo
Huaraz
Callao
LIMA
PERU
Cajamarca
Rio Branco
Ariquemes
Cusco
Arequipa
LA PAZ
BOLIVIA
Cochabamba
SUCRE
Santa Cruz
Cuiabá
BRASÍLIA
Goiânia
Belo Horizonte
Porto Seguro
Campo Grande
Ribeirão Preto
Campinas
Rio de Janeiro
São Paulo
Curitiba
PARAGUAY
ASUNCIÓN
Iquique
Calama
Antofagasta
San Salvador de Jujuy
San Miguel de Tucumán
Isla San Felix
(Chile)
Isla San Ambrosio
(Chile)
Copiapó
Porto Alegre
Pelotas
Córdoba
Paysandú
URUGUAY
MONTEVIDEO
BUENOS AIRES
Río de la Plata
Mendoza
SANTIAGO
Archipiélago Juan Fernández
(Chile)
Concepción
Santa Rosa
Tandil
Mar del Plata
Bahía Blanca
Valdivia
Puerto Montt
CHILE
ARGENTINA
ANDES
PATAGONIA
Golfo San Matías
Comodoro Rivadavia
Falkland Islands
(UK)
Stanley
West Falkland
East Falkland
Punta Arenas
Isla Grande de Tierra del Fuego
Isla de los Estados
Cabo de Hornos
(Cape Horn)
Drake Passage
Scotia Sea
South Georgia
South Georgia and South Sandwich Islands
(UK)
South Sandwich Islands
South Shetland Islands
South Orkney Islands
Ilha da Trindade
(Brazil)
Ilhas Martin Vaz
(Brazil)
Ascension
(UK)
Tristan da Cunha Group
(UK)
Gough Island
(UK)
Antarctic Circle
Bellingshausen Sea
Amundsen Sea
Carney I.
Thurston Island
Alexander Island
Antarctic Peninsula
Weddell Sea
Ellsworth Land
Marie Byrd Land
Roosevelt Island
Ross Sea
Berkner Island
Azores
(Portugal)
Madeira
(Portugal)
Islas Canarias
(Spain)
Santa Cruz de Tenerife
Las Palmas de Gran Canaria
Western Sahara
(disputed)
Laâyoune
Ad Dakhla
PORTUGAL
LISBOA
Casablanca
RABAT
Marrakech
Agadir
MAURITANIA
NOUAKCHOTT
CAPE VERDE
PRAIA
Santiago
Santo Antão
DAKAR
Saint Louis
SENEGAL
BANJUL
GAMBIA
BISSAU
Arquipélago dos Bijagós
CONAKRY
FREETOWN
MONROVIA
LIBERIA
DUBLIN
IRELAND
Orkney
Outer Hebrides
Faroe Is
(Denmark)
1:75,000,000
Robinson Projection
0
1000
2000
3000
4000 kilometers
0
500
1000
1500
2000 miles

World Political

OCEANS

The Oceans

Most of planet Earth is covered with water; only 28 percent of our planet's surface is visible landmass, the other 72 percent is water. This enormous global ocean—oceanic currents gather all the world's oceans into one giant system—contains the majority of life, much more than has ever been present on land. Throughout geological history the ratio of land to water has continually changed, as has the distribution of the continents.

Previous pages The uninhabited Rock Islands of Palau are the ancient relics of coral reefs that violently surfaced at a unique crossroads of three of the world's major ocean currents.

Right Wild waves pounding rocks on Ojika Peninsula, Akita, Japan. Exposed to harsh natural conditions such as earthquakes, typhoons, and winter storms, the seacoasts in Japan are also vulnerable to tsunami, storm surges, and erosion.

Below right A colorful nembrotha nudibranch *(Nembrotha purpureolineolata)* photographed off the coast of Papua New Guinea. There are several thousand species of these gastropods worldwide.

Below Isolated from the mainland by a treacherous stretch of water, the lighthouse at Tevennec on the Brittany coast is now—like many of these beacons—solar-powered and unmanned.

Oceanic currents connect all oceanic water in a single giant system, creating conditions in which the oceans are continuously mixed and recharged. The Atlantic, the Pacific, and the Indian oceans are the main oceans; the Arctic and Southern (or Antarctic) oceans are sometimes counted separately, and sometimes included as part of the main three.

Physical and Biological Diversity

Oceans show remarkable diversity. With an average depth of over 12,000 feet (3,660 m), and the deepest locations over 35,000 feet (10,670 m), this variation in vertical range is too large to allow for uniformity. Modern technology has aided in mapping the physical geography of ocean floors and more accurately measuring depth. Biological make-up, however, remains to be fully explored, especially in the deeps beyond the continental shelf

zones. Oceans are primary catalysts in the global climatic cycle, directly influencing atmospheric changes and weather patterns.

The Pacific Ocean contains about half the world's entire volume of water, and stretches from the Arctic region of the north to 60° south latitude.

The western Pacific also holds the depth record. The Mariana Trench, where the Pacific Plate slides underneath the Philippine Plate, has reached a depth of 35,799 feet (10,911.5 m) so far, and may well become deeper. In the middle of the Pacific Ocean, continental rifting causes spreading of the ocean floor and expansion of the Pacific Plate. As a consequence, new, geologically younger islands are created near the rift by active vulcanism, while volcanic activity along the plate's peripheries also provides solid evidence of an active tectonic cycle.

Hawaii, for example, is a chain of islands created on the ocean floor along the Hawaiian Ridge. As the lithosphere rifts (opens), lava is released and a new island is created, while islands previously created in this fashion drift farther away. The oldest and seismically least active islands of the Hawaiian Archipelago are located farthest from the active hotspot. At the periphery, the contact of the Eurasian, North American, and Philippine plates with the expanding Pacific Plate creates ridges whose tips we know as Japan, the Philippines, the Aleutian Islands, and other archipelagos.

The term "Pacific Ring of Fire" is applied to areas where the collision of the Pacific Plate with the surrounding plates results in high levels of volcanic and seismic activity. Earthquakes, for example, are an everyday occurrence in countries such as Japan.

Oceanic Travel and Trade

Although evidence has surfaced of Asian travels to the Americas prior to Columbus's voyage in the sixteenth century, most early ocean travels were conducted between islands in the southern Pacific, for the purposes of trade and fishing in its western periphery. Once Europeans reached the New World, the Pacific became a transportation corridor. By the nineteenth century, the United States, in need of a mid-ocean refueling station, took control of Hawaii. In recent times globalization has gradually removed distance barriers, both real and perceived, and the concept of the "Pacific Rim" exemplifies the improvements in cooperation among countries bordering the Pacific Ocean.

The Atlantic Ocean, the second largest, reinforces the notion that seaports are the windows of the world. Even before the discovery of the Americas, the North Atlantic and its associated gulf, the Mediterranean Sea, enjoyed the status of the busiest waterways. Since then the Atlantic has been transformed into an avenue of trade and commerce between four continents. The Atlantic Ocean was created by the break-up of Pangaea about 130 million years ago. It is generally less prone to destructive physical processes than the Pacific, and where these occur they tend to be localized and isolated. It is quite possible that a volcano in the Canary Islands may eventually shatter into the ocean and result in a tsunami devastating to Northern America.

The Atlantic Ocean is better known for its climatic influences. The Gulf Stream, a warm

Left Baitfish school around a 10-foot pylon, Papua New Guinea. As juveniles, baitfish join large schools and spend almost their entire lives in these tightly packed formations, some of which are awe-inspiring in size. Their ability to move as one, with the precision of synchronized swimmers, may confuse some predators—viewed as a whole, the well-organized unit can appear to be one very intimidating creature. Other predators and fishermen, however, find schools easy prey.

Below Aldabra Atoll, the world's largest atoll, in the Republic of Seychelles in the Indian Ocean, is home to 200 plant species, 40 of which are unique to the region, as well as an abundance of avian and aquatic life. Snapper, surgeon-fish, stingrays, and sharks drift effortlessly through the vast lagoon, taking full advantage of the same tidal flows that have sculpted a mass of small mushroom-shaped limestone islands known as champignons, that sprout from the clear waters like hovering, plant-encrusted spaceships.

Left An oil drilling platform, with tanker, in the Mediterranean Sea. Some oil rigs are attached to the ocean floor, others are artificial islands, or free-floating. Most are on a continental shelf.

current that raises atmospheric temperatures, provides moisture to Western Europe and prevents freezing of Atlantic waters far into the northern latitudes. Near the Equator, just off the West African coast, water and wind currents move westward. As they come closer to North America they form conditions that result in severe weather patterns during summer and autumn months, known as hurricanes. The Atlantic south of the Equator displays less variety. Only a few significant islands are scattered in the South Atlantic and extreme storms are a rarity until one reaches latitudes close to the Antarctic region. The cold Benguela Current influences the desert environment in southwest Africa, similar to the way its Pacific equivalent, the Humboldt Current, cools the dry Chilean and Peruvian coasts of South America.

The smallest of the big three, the Indian Ocean is surrounded by the most culturally complex region, extending from Africa across the Middle East and South Asia to Australia. On its shores, anthropologists have suggested, humans first began practicing a sedentary lifestyle as they formed fishing communities. This ocean, unlike its larger counterparts, has been well traveled since antiquity. It never represented a physical or cultural barrier; rather, it acted as a cultural highway and excellent alternative to longer, much more dangerous overland travel.

The Indian Ocean's enclosed character plays a vital factor in the movement of the air masses that cause torrential rains in South Asia during the summer monsoons. These air masses originate near Mauritius. By the time they reach the Indian subcontinent, they are saturated with moisture. Most of the Indian Ocean is relatively stable in terms of its seismic activity, except where it borders Southeast Asia, as was well illustrated by the devastating tsunami of 2004. Tsunamis are created when earthquakes occur under the sea, but rarely do they result in such damage and loss of life as on that occasion. In the Pacific Ocean a tsunami must usually travel a much greater distance to reach densely populated coastlines, which gives authorities sufficient time to take some preventive measures. Indian Ocean distances are shorter and thus the timeframe for evacuation is limited.

Below A rogue iceberg about to crash into an oil drilling platform in the far North Atlantic is lassoed and towed away by one of the handful of crews who do this for a living.

Meters
Feet

0
LAND BELOW SEA LEVEL

100
328

200
656

1000
3281

2000
6562

4000
13123

6000
19685

1:41,300,000

Lambert Azimuthal Equal Area Projection

0 750 1500 2250 3000 kilometers

0 500 1000 1500 2000 miles

Atlantic Ocean

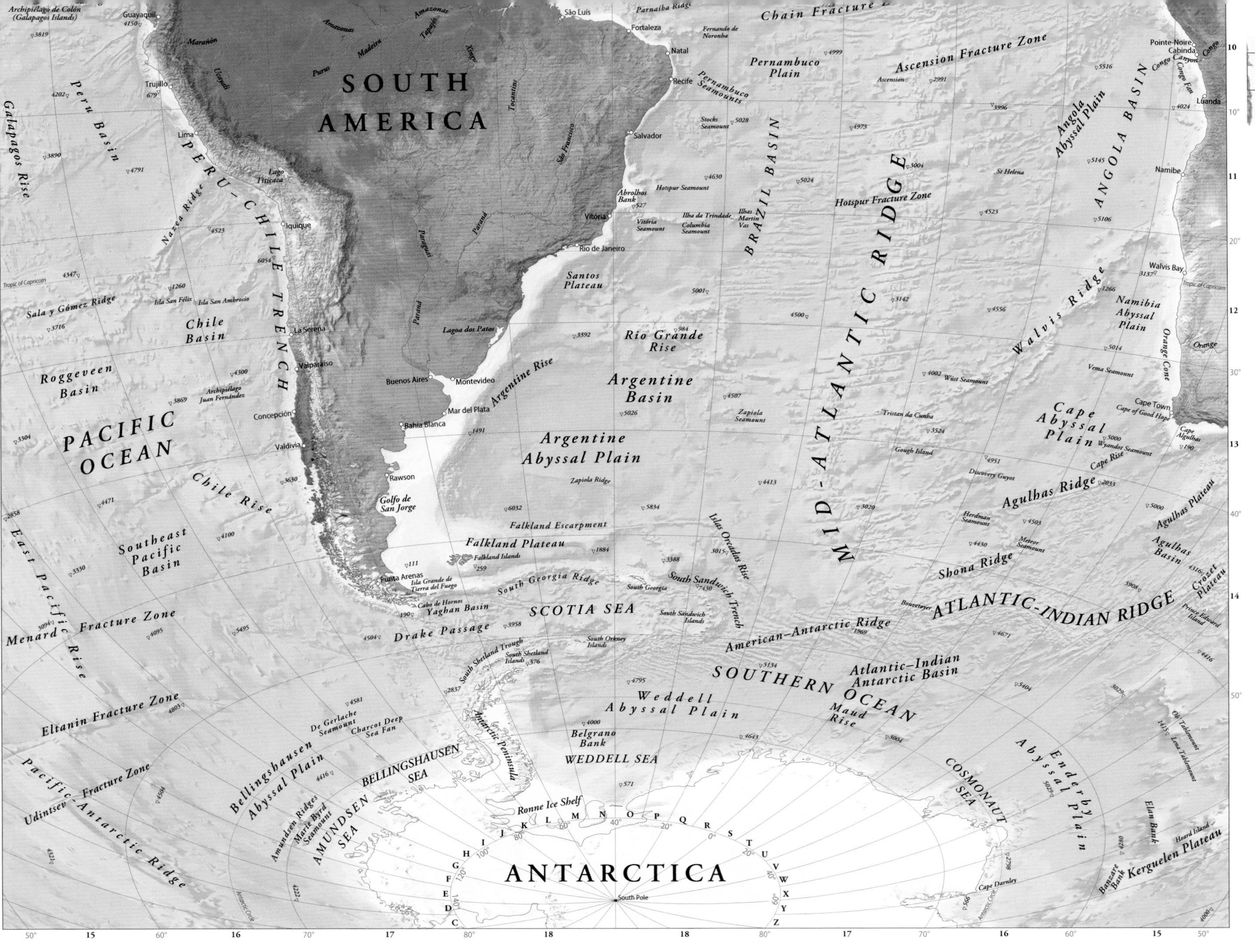
SOUTH AMERICA
ANTARCTICA
PACIFIC OCEAN
SOUTHERN OCEAN
MID-ATLANTIC RIDGE
ATLANTIC-INDIAN RIDGE
ANGOLA BASIN
BRAZIL BASIN
PERU-CHILE TRENCH
SCOTIA SEA
WEDDELL SEA
BELLINGSHAUSEN SEA
AMUNDSEN SEA
COSMONAUT SEA
Argentine Basin
Argentine Abyssal Plain
Cape Abyssal Plain
Angola Abyssal Plain
Namibia Abyssal Plain
Weddell Abyssal Plain
Enderby Abyssal Plain
Bellingshausen Abyssal Plain
Walvis Ridge
Agulhas Ridge
Agulhas Basin
Agulhas Plateau
Crozet Plateau
Shona Ridge
Rio Grande Rise
Santos Plateau
Falkland Plateau
Falkland Escarpment
South Georgia Ridge
South Sandwich Trench
Islas Orcadas Rise
American-Antarctic Ridge
Atlantic-Indian Antarctic Basin
Maud Rise
Drake Passage
Yaghan Basin
Pernambuco Plain
Pernambuco Seamounts
Ascension Fracture Zone
Chain Fracture Zone
Hotspur Fracture Zone
Argentine Rise
Chile Rise
Chile Basin
Southeast Pacific Basin
Roggeveen Basin
Peru Basin
Galapagos Rise
Nazca Ridge
Sala y Gómez Ridge
East Pacific Rise
Menard Fracture Zone
Eltanin Fracture Zone
Udintsev Fracture Zone
Pacific-Antarctic Ridge
Antarctic Peninsula
Ronne Ice Shelf
Belgrano Bank
Kerguelen Plateau
Elan Bank
Orange Cone
Golfo de San Jorge
Meters
Feet
0
LAND BELOW SEA LEVEL
100
328
200
656
1000
3281
2000
6562
4000
13123
6000
19685

40° A 50° B 60° C 70° D 80° E 90° F 100° G 110° H 120° I 130° J 140° K 150° L 160° M 170° N 180° O 170°

ASIA

Aral Sea
Ozero Balkhash
Ozero Baykal
Ob'
Lena
Amur
Ganges
Brahmaputra
Chang Jiang (Yangtze)
Huang He
Mekong
Tropic of Cancer

SEA OF OKHOTSK
Ostrov Sakhalin
Kuril Basin
Kuril'skiye Ostrova
Kuril-Kamchatka Trench
Petropavlovsk-Kamchatskiy
Kamchatka Basin
Shirshov Ridge
BERING SEA
Aleutian Basin
Bowers Ridge
Bowers Bank
Aleutian Islands
Aleutian Trench
St Matthew Island
Nunivak Island
Pribilof Islands

Vladivostok
Ch'ŏngjin
Japan Basin
SEA OF JAPAN (EAST SEA)
Hokkaidō
Honshū
Tokyo
Nagoya
Osaka
Hiroshima
Shikoku
Kyūshū
Kagoshima
Japan Trench
Dalian
Yantai
Inch'ŏn
Pusan
YELLOW SEA
Shanghai
EAST CHINA SEA
Nansei-shotō
Ryukyu Trench
Daitō Islands
Taiwan
Kaohsiung

NORTHWEST PACIFIC BASIN
Emperor Seamounts
Emperor Trough
Chinook Trough
Hess Rise
Izu Trench
Ogasawara-shotō
Bonin Trench
Kazan-rettō
Isakov Seamount
Joe Ferguson Seamount
Ann Judge Seamount
Makarov Seamount
Mapmaker Seamounts
Grosvenor Seamount
Minami Tori Shima
Liliuokalani Ridge
Kure Atoll
Midway Is
Pearl and Hermes Atoll
Lisianski I.
Gardner Pinnacles
Hawaiian Ridge
MID-PACIFIC MOUNTAINS
Mid-Pacific Seamount
Necker Ridge
Johnston Atoll
Wake I.

Chittagong
Sittwe
Puri
Kakinada
Chennai
Jaffna
Thiruvananthapuram
Sri Lanka
Sri Jayewardenepura Kotte
Gulf of Mannar
BAY OF BENGAL
Yangon
Mawlamyine
Andaman Islands
Andaman Sea
Andaman Basin
Nicobar Islands
GULF OF THAILAND
Chon Buri
Songkhla
Malay Peninsula
Strait of Malacca
George Town
Kuantan
Singapore
Qinzhou
Ha Long
Hai Phong
G. of Tonkin
Hainan
Haikou
Zhanjiang
Macau
Hong Kong
Vinh
Đồng Hới
Đà Nẵng
Nha Trang
Phan Thiết
Bạc Liêu
Paracel Is
Macclesfield Bank
SOUTH CHINA SEA
Spratly Is
Palawan Trough
Palawan
Sunda Shelf
Luzon Strait
Luzon
Benham Plateau
Philippine Basin
PHILIPPINE SEA
Manila
PHILIPPINE IS
Philippine Trench
Cebu
SULU SEA
Sulu Basin
Mindanao
Davao
Sandakan
Bandar Seri Begawan
Borneo
Kuching
Celebes Basin
CELEBES SEA
Manado
Halmahera
Laut Maluku (Molucca Sea)
Makassar Strait
Palu
Sulawesi
Laut Seram (Ceram Sea)
Buru
Seram
Ambon
LAUT BANDA (BANDA SEA)
Weber Basin
Makassar
LAUT JAWA (JAVA SEA)
Surabaya
Laut Bali (Bali Sea)
Laut Flores (Flores Sea)
Bali
Flores
Sumba
Timor
Dili
Timor Trough
Kupang
TIMOR SEA
Jawa
Java Ridge
Java Trench
Jakarta
Bandar Lampung
Sumatera
Padang
Siberut
Nias
Simeulue
Kepulauan Mentawai

Kyushu-Palau Ridge
West Mariana Basin
South Honshu Ridge
Mariana Trough
Mariana Ridge
Northern Mariana Islands
Saipan
Tinian
Rota
Guam
Mariana Trench
Challenger Deep
East Mariana Basin
Magellan Seamounts
MICRONESIA
Yap
Yap Trench
Palau Trench
Palau Islands
Ngulu Atoll
Woleai Atoll
Gaferut
Namonuito Atoll
Chuuk Islands
Pohnpei
Eauripik Atoll
Eauripik Rise
Caroline Islands
Mortlock Islands
Nukuoro Atoll
West Caroline Basin
East Caroline Basin
Kapingamarangi Atoll
Melanesian Basin
Marshall Islands
Enewetak Atoll
Bikini Atoll
Rongelap Atoll
Kwajalein Atoll
Jaluit Atoll
Majuro Atoll
Mili Atoll
Kosrae
Taongi Atoll
PACIFIC
CENTRAL PACIFIC BASIN
Magellan Rise
Palmyra
Butaritari
Tarawa
Gilbert Islands
Gilbert Ridge
Beru
Arorae
Nauru
Banaba
Howland I.
Baker I.
Kanton
Phoenix Is
McKean I.
Nikumaroro
Rawaki
Orona
Manra
Hilgard Deep
POLYNESIA
Nanumea
Tuvalu
Vaitupu
Nukufetau
Funafuti
Nukulaelae
Atafu
Nukunono
Fakaofo
Tokelau
Swains I.

New Guinea Trench
Admiralty Islands
Mussa I.
New Hanover
New Ireland
BISMARCK SEA
Bismarck Archipelago
New Britain
New Britain Trench
Bougainville I.
Solomon Islands
SOLOMON SEA
Jayapura
New Guinea
Lae
G. of Papua
Port Moresby
D'Entrecasteaux Islands
Louisiade Arch.
Rennell
Guadalcanal
Honiara
Torres Str.
C. York
MELANESIA
South Solomon Trench
Santa Cruz Is
Vityaz Trench
Rotuma
Îles Wallis
Îles de Hoorn
Samoa Is
Savai'i
Upolu
Samoa Basin
Tutuila
Rose Atoll
Nassau
Suwarrow
Banks Islands
Espiritu Santo
Malakula
Ambrym
New Hebrides Bank
Éfaté
Erromango
North Fiji Basin
Viti Levu
Vanua Levu
Fiji Is
Suva
Fiji Plateau
Lau Basin
Tonga Ridge
Tonga Trench
Tongatapu Group
'Ata
Niue
New Hebrides Trench
Hunter I. Ridge
Hunter I.
Anatom
Futuna
Loyalty Islands
Îles Loyauté
Nouvelle Calédonie
Nouméa
Îles Chesterfield
CORAL SEA
Coral Sea Basin
Queensland Plateau
Great Barrier Reef

ARAFURA SEA
Arafura Shelf
Darwin
Bonaparte Basin
Joseph Bonaparte Gulf
Bonaparte Archipelago
Browse Basin
Browse I.
GULF OF CARPENTARIA
Townsville
Argo Abyssal Plain
Gascoyne Plain
Exmouth Plateau
Northwest Shelf
Cuvier Plateau
Zenith Plateau
AUSTRALIA
Brisbane
Darling
Perth
Perth Basin
Naturaliste Plateau
Leeuwin Sill
Great Australian Bight
Adelaide
Murray
Sydney
Melbourne
Bass Strait
Tasmania
Hobart
South West Cape
South Australian Basin
East Tasman Plateau
South Tasman Rise
Tasman Fracture Zone
Tasman Plain
Tasman Sea
Lord Howe Island
Lord Howe Rise
Taupo Tablemount
Gascoyne Tablemount
New Caledonia Basin
Norfolk Ridge
Norfolk I.
Three Kings Basin
South Fiji Basin
South Fiji Ridge
Kermadec Islands
Kermadec Ridge
Kermadec Trench
Louisville Ridge
Auckland
North Island
Wellington
Christchurch
South Island
Dunedin
Stewart I.
Chatham Rise
Chatham Islands
Bounty Trough
Bounty Islands
Antipodes Islands
Bollons Tablemount
Campbell Plateau
Auckland Is
Campbell Island
Macquarie Ridge
New Zealand Plateau
Macquarie I.
Emerald Basin

INDIAN OCEAN
NINETYEAST RIDGE
Cocos Basin
Afanasij Nikitin Seamount
Investigator Ridge
Christmas Island
Christmas Rise
Cocos Is
Osborn Plateau
WHARTON BASIN
East Indiaman Ridge
Tropic of Capricorn
Equator
Broken Ridge
Diamantina Fracture Zone
Île Amsterdam
Île St.-Paul
SOUTHEAST INDIAN RIDGE
Kerguelen Plateau
Îles Kerguelen
Kohler Seamount
McDonald Islands
Heard Island
Williams Seamount
South Indian Basin
Elan Bank
Banzare Bank
ENDERBY ABYSSAL PLAIN
Australian–Antarctic Basin

Meters / Feet
0 — LAND BELOW SEA LEVEL
100 / 328
200 / 656
1000 / 3281
2000 / 6562
4000 / 13123
6000 / 19685

1:50,600,000
Eckert IV Projection

0 750 1500 2250 3000 kilometers
0 500 1000 1500 2000 miles

Pacific Ocean

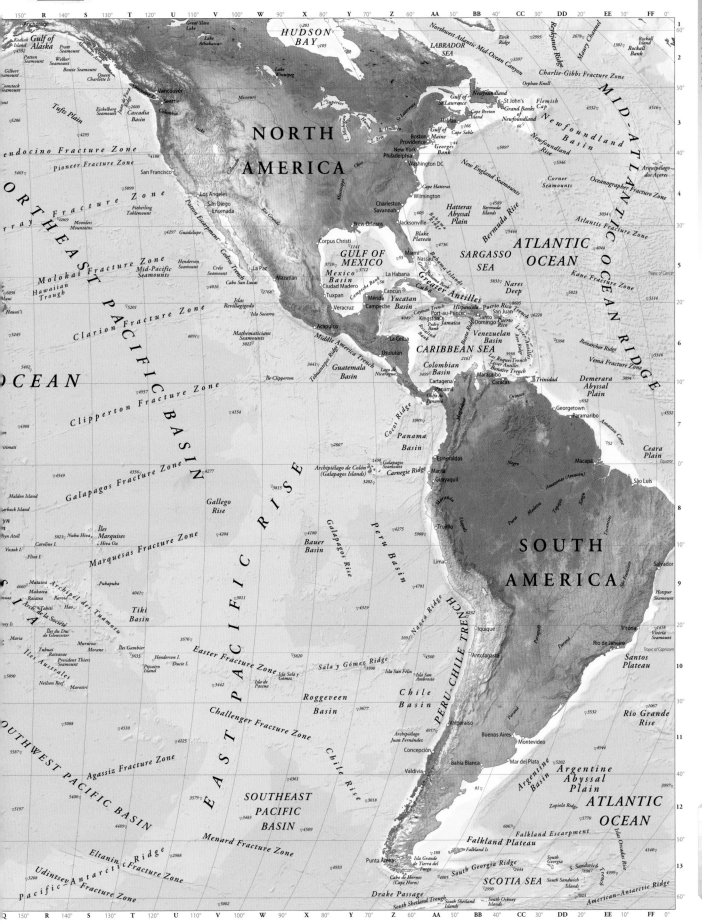

NORTH AMERICA
SOUTH AMERICA
HUDSON BAY
LABRADOR SEA
GULF OF MEXICO
CARIBBEAN SEA
SARGASSO SEA
ATLANTIC OCEAN
MID-ATLANTIC OCEAN RIDGE
NORTHEAST PACIFIC BASIN
EAST PACIFIC RISE
SOUTHEAST PACIFIC BASIN
SOUTHWEST PACIFIC BASIN
SCOTIA SEA
Drake Passage
PERU-CHILE TRENCH
Clarion Fracture Zone
Clipperton Fracture Zone
Galapagos Fracture Zone
Marquesas Fracture Zone
Easter Fracture Zone
Challenger Fracture Zone
Menard Fracture Zone
Eltanin Fracture Zone
Udintsev Fracture Zone
Pacific-Antarctic Ridge
Mendocino Fracture Zone
Pioneer Fracture Zone
Murray Fracture Zone
Molokai Fracture Zone
Agassiz Fracture Zone
Nazca Ridge
Cocos Ridge
Carnegie Ridge
Sala y Gómez Ridge
Chile Rise
Galapagos Rise
Panama Basin
Peru Basin
Chile Basin
Roggeveen Basin
Bauer Basin
Tiki Basin
Guatemala Basin
Argentine Basin
Argentine Abyssal Plain
Falkland Plateau
Falkland Escarpment
South Georgia Ridge
Rio Grande Rise
Santos Plateau
Ceara Plain
Demerara Abyssal Plain
Hatteras Abyssal Plain
Newfoundland Basin
Bermuda Rise
Charlie-Gibbs Fracture Zone
Atlantis Fracture Zone
Kane Fracture Zone
Vema Fracture Zone
American-Antarctic Ridge
Meters
Feet
LAND BELOW SEA LEVEL
100 328
200 656
1000 3281
2000 6562
4000 13123
6000 19685

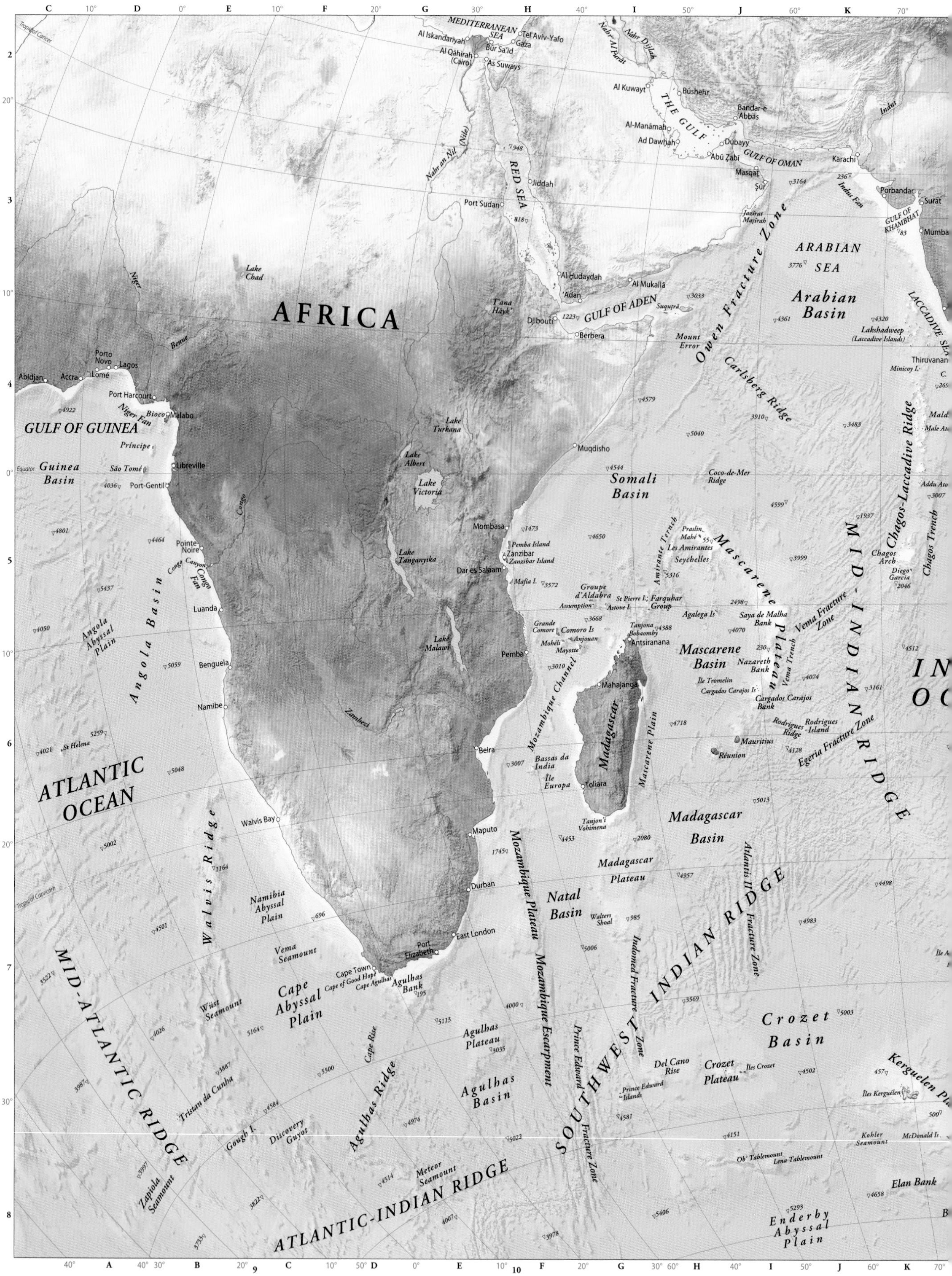

C 10° D 0° E 10° F 20° G 30° H 40° I 50° J 60° K 70°

Tropic of Cancer
MEDITERRANEAN SEA
Al Iskandarīyah
Tel Aviv-Yafo
Gaza
Būr Sa'īd
Al Qāhirah (Cairo)
As Suways
Nahr Al Furāt
Nahr Dijlah
Al Kuwayt
Būshehr
THE GULF
Bandar-e Abbās
Al-Manāmah
Ad Dawḩah
Dubayy
Abū Zabī
GULF OF OMAN
Karachi
Masqaţ
Şūr
Indus
Indus Fan
Porbandar
Surat
GULF OF KHAMBHAT
Mumbai
Nahr an Nil (Nile)
RED SEA
Jiddah
Port Sudan
Jazīrat Maşīrah
Owen Fracture Zone
ARABIAN SEA
Arabian Basin
Lake Chad
Niger
AFRICA
Al Ḩudaydah
'Adan
Al Mukallā
GULF OF ADEN
Suquţrā
Djibouti
Berbera
T'ana Hāyk'
Mount Error
Carlsberg Ridge
Lakshadweep (Laccadive Islands)
LACCADIVE SEA
Thiruvananthapuram
Minicoy I.
Benue
Porto Novo
Lagos
Lomé
Accra
Abidjan
Port Harcourt
Bioco
Malabo
Niger Fan
GULF OF GUINEA
Príncipe
São Tomé
Libreville
Port-Gentil
Equator
Guinea Basin
Lake Turkana
Lake Albert
Lake Victoria
Muqdisho
Somali Basin
Coco-de-Mer Ridge
Chagos-Laccadive Ridge
Maldives
Male Atoll
Addu Atoll
Congo
Mombasa
Pemba Island
Zanzibar
Zanzibar Island
Dar es Salaam
Mafia I.
Pointe-Noire
Congo Canyon
Congo Fan
Lake Tanganyika
Amirante Trench
Praslin
Mahé
Les Amirantes
Seychelles
Mascarene Plateau
MID-INDIAN RIDGE
Chagos Arch
Diego Garcia
Chagos Trench
Luanda
Angola Basin
Angola Abyssal Plain
Groupe d'Aldabra
Assumption
St Pierre I.
Astove I.
Farquhar Group
Agalega Is
Saya de Malha Bank
Vema Fracture Zone
Grande Comore
Comoro Is
Mohéli
Anjouan
Mayotte
Tanjona Bobaomby
Antsiranana
Lake Malawi
Pemba
Benguela
Mascarene Basin
Nazareth Bank
Vema Trench
Île Tromelin
Cargados Carajos Is
Cargados Carajos Bank
INDIAN OCEAN
Mahajanga
Mozambique Channel
Namibe
Zambezi
Madagascar
Mascarene Plain
Rodrigues Ridge
Rodrigues Island
Egeria Fracture Zone
Mauritius
Réunion
St Helena
Beira
Bassas da India
Île Europa
Toliara
ATLANTIC OCEAN
Tanjon'i Vohimena
Madagascar Basin
Walvis Bay
Walvis Ridge
Maputo
Mozambique Plateau
Madagascar Plateau
Atlantis II Fracture Zone
Tropic of Capricorn
Durban
Natal Basin
Walters Shoal
Namibia Abyssal Plain
East London
Port Elizabeth
Indomed Fracture Zone
SOUTHWEST INDIAN RIDGE
Vema Seamount
Cape Town
Cape of Good Hope
Cape Agulhas
Agulhas Bank
Cape Abyssal Plain
Mozambique Escarpment
MID-ATLANTIC RIDGE
Wüst Seamount
Agulhas Plateau
Prince Edward Fracture Zone
Crozet Basin
Cape Rise
Del Cano Rise
Crozet Plateau
Îles Crozet
Kerguelen Plateau
Tristan da Cunha
Agulhas Ridge
Agulhas Basin
Prince Edward Islands
Îles Kerguelen
Gough I.
Discovery Guyot
Kohler Seamount
McDonald Is.
Ob' Tablemount
Lena Tablemount
Meteor Seamount
ATLANTIC-INDIAN RIDGE
Zapiola Seamount
Elan Bank
Enderby Abyssal Plain

40° A 40° 30° B 20° 9 C 10° 50° D 0° E 10° 10 F 20° G 30° 60° H 40° I 50° J 60° K 70°

Meters / Feet
0 — LAND BELOW SEA LEVEL
100 / 328
200 / 656
1000 / 3281
2000 / 6562
4000 / 13123
6000 / 19685

1:37,500,000
Lambert Azimuthal Equal Area

0 500 1000 1500 2000 kilometers
0 250 500 750 1000 miles

Indian Ocean

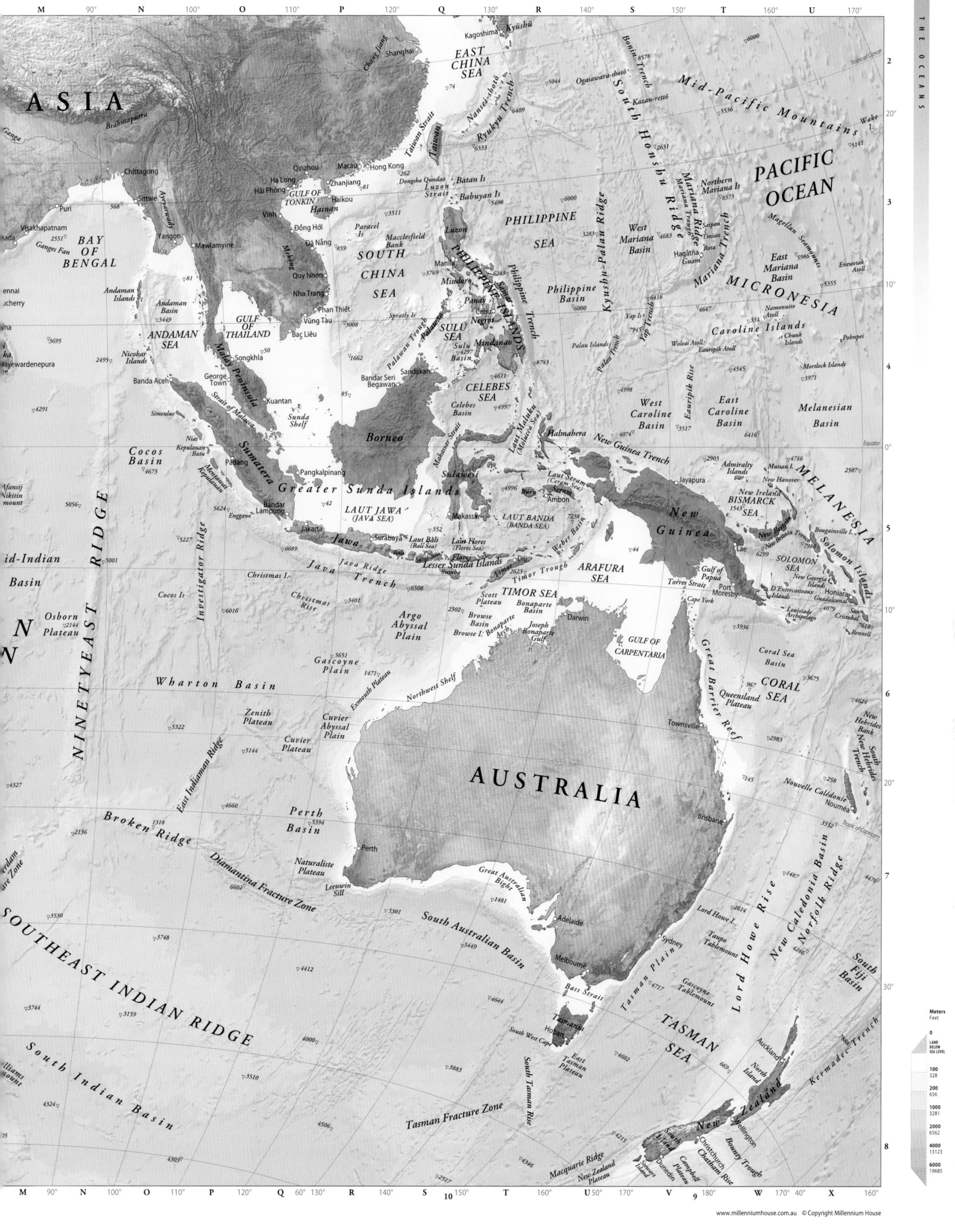

ASIA
PACIFIC OCEAN
AUSTRALIA
BAY OF BENGAL
ANDAMAN SEA
SOUTH CHINA SEA
EAST CHINA SEA
PHILIPPINE SEA
SULU SEA
CELEBES SEA
LAUT JAWA (JAVA SEA)
LAUT BANDA (BANDA SEA)
TIMOR SEA
ARAFURA SEA
CORAL SEA
SOLOMON SEA
BISMARCK SEA
TASMAN SEA
GULF OF THAILAND
GULF OF TONKIN
GULF OF CARPENTARIA
MICRONESIA
MELANESIA
NINETYEAST RIDGE
SOUTHEAST INDIAN RIDGE
Wharton Basin
South Indian Basin
Broken Ridge
Diamantina Fracture Zone
South Australian Basin
Tasman Fracture Zone
Lord Howe Rise
Borneo
Sumatera
Jawa
New Guinea
New Zealand
Greater Sunda Islands
Lesser Sunda Islands
Philippine Islands
Great Barrier Reef
Java Trench
Mariana Trench
Mid-Pacific Mountains
Tropic of Cancer
Tropic of Capricorn
Equator

NORTH AMERICA

Northern America

From the Arctic Ocean's shores to the Florida Keys, Northern America extends through almost all climatic regions except for equatorial tropical. Several major features clearly stand out on the map—interior plains, Appalachian Mountains, Rocky Mountains, and Pacific coastal ranges. Such a landform distribution, high elevation on both sides and enclosed flatlands in the middle, affects Northern America's climate in a drastic way by producing weather patterns that can frequently reach extreme conditions.

Previous pages Glen Canyon, USA, is one of the most geologically diverse areas in Northern America. Carved by the Colorado and San Juan rivers, it is the site of many dinosaur skeletons.

Above The mountain lion *(Felis concolor)*, able to live in many habitats, from desert to humid forest, is found throughout the Americas.

Just two countries—Canada and the United States—constitute the region of Northern America, which is relatively homogenous in cultural terms, yet quite diverse when it comes to its physical geography.

Tornadoes, and winters that produce heavy, long-lasting blizzards, are common across large areas of the plains. Taken together, the Jefferson, Mississippi, and Missouri rivers draining the interior form one of the longest river systems in the world.

Human impact began with the arrival of the Native Americans' ancestors from Asia many thousands of years ago, but the effect of their localized folk cultures on the environment was limited. It was not until Europeans firmly established their presence in the seventeenth century that conditions were set for the region to emerge in the global political and economic vanguard. The United States has managed to overcome historical odds by successfully integrating people of many diverse backgrounds into an independent nation. Canada, almost equally diverse, retains close ties with the United Kingdom.

Both nations benefited from the historical and geographic circumstances in which they were created. Capitalism, together with a free market economy, democratic institutions, and civil liberties, served as the foundation of rapid development in Northern America, while at the same time a substantial proportion of the Eastern hemisphere and Latin America struggled to overcome limitations created by long-lasting feudal patterns and territorial disputes.

Intraregional Cooperation

Productive cooperation has been the dominant focus of the relationship between the United States and Canada. The US defense installations designed to deter possible attacks during the years of the Cold War also control Canadian air space. The military forces of the two countries operate closely under international agreements in peacekeeping missions in Afghanistan and other turbulent places. Economic ties are equally strong. The North American Free Trade Agreement (NAFTA) has helped to facilitate the removal of trade barriers and further strengthen economic ties. Vast differences in population and economic size, however, are factors in the balance of trade turning in Canada's favor, especially as the US thirst for energy and fossil fuels continues to grow. The economy of the USA consumes one quarter of the world's energy and, unlike energy sourced from elsewhere, Canadian energy arrives from a neighboring and politically stable nation.

Intraregional differences are well illustrated by the geographical distribution of the population. Almost 90 percent of Northern Americans live in the United States and are fairly well dispersed. No single urban area dominates the country's economy, as is the case in many European countries. Americans are also incredibly mobile, in both geographic and social terms, and regional demographic patterns are in a continuous process of transformation. Since World War II, several major cross-country migrations have occurred, from

Above Vermont, USA, is synonymous with red barns (like the one pictured here at Craftsbury Common), as well as cows, hills, village greens, white-steepled churches, and winding country roads. Maple syrup is also produced from trees that turn the green hills gold every autumn. All this, in many eyes, represents traditional America.

Right Chicago, Illinois, was founded in 1833 on the shores of Lake Michigan at a site of portage between the Great Lakes and the Mississippi River watershed. It soon became a major transportation hub and the business and financial capital of the American midwest. Of the five Great Lakes of Northern America, Lake Michigan is the only one located entirely within the United States.

Above The mountainous terrain of Banff National Park, Alberta, Canada, incorporates numerous glaciers and ice fields, dense coniferous forest, and alpine landscapes.

the Rust Belt (northeast) to the Sun Belt (south and southwest), from the east coast to the west coast, and from California to the mountain states.

The Canadian population map has experienced less alteration. The majority still reside in the St Lawrence River valley and in southeastern Ontario, a region that has maintained its demographic, administrative, and economic advantages. Among the large urban areas in Canada, only Edmonton, Alberta, is more than a couple of hundred miles (300 km) from the American border—yet another example of economic imperatives. Canada's north remains sparsely populated and most settlements there are related to the activities of indigenous tribes or mining operations.

Urban Administration

Different national approaches toward the administration of cities has produced opposite urban patterns. Early on, US metropolitan areas were clearly delineated by the creation of numerous cities out of a single unit, each with the freedom to generate its own budget, collect income taxes, and administer local affairs. This caused uneven development, the expansion of suburbs, and a radical decline in quality of life for many inner-city residents.

BUILT
TOUGH

Left Rodeo grew out of the practices of Spanish ranchers and their Mexican ranch hands, whose mixture of cattle wrangling and bull fighting, and other displays of skill at annual roundups, drew on conquistador traditions.

As suburban living soon became a social imperative for many upper- and middle-class Americans, the core group of taxpayers in inner cities throughout the country gradually decreased in number. In more recent years, however, a return to downtown areas, and with it a push toward urban revitalization, has been underway.

Canadian cities exemplify a different approach to urban administration, based on the European principle of a city operating as a single administrative unit. In such a system local tax collection does not produce spatial anomalies and distribution of collected funds remains more balanced.

This example of differential urban development and administration is one of the few major departures from the almost identical lifestyles shared by the two countries. Although certain elements of socialism are welcomed in Canada, US citizens, leery of the federal government's intervention in local affairs, generally tend to prefer individualism over collectivism. Contemporary US citizens live where they want to instead of where they have to. Their argument is that individualism fosters civil liberties and generates reliance on self-responsibility; it creates healthy competition and wealth that ultimately benefit the entire society, while strong government involvement puts up barriers to capitalism and the flow of goods and people.

In the past, Europe was the main source of emigration to Northern America, but in more recent years, Latin American and Asian countries have taken over. Even as the native-born population's birth rates decrease, the impact of immigration is clearly visible in steady population growth, while the rest of the developed world is facing stagnant growth, skilled labor shortages and, in some cases, a decline in population. Migratory patterns and official migration data appear to suggest that by all measures Northern America is the most desirable destination. Its status as a global political and economic leader will remain unchanged in the foreseeable future.

Above Florida Keys, USA, is an archipelago of about 1,700 islands, the exposed portions of an ancient coral reef. Once the refuge of pirates, they are now connected to the Florida mainland by over 100 miles (160 km) of highway.

Left Monument Valley, Utah, USA, was carved out by meandering rivers over millions of years. Its buttes, especially the "Mittens" and the "Totem Pole," are among the best known icons of the Colorado Plateau. The valley's red color comes from iron oxide exposed in weathered siltstone.

Middle America

The narrow spine of land separating the Pacific and Atlantic oceans hosts seven countries which, combined, are smaller in area than Mexico. They share a similar physical landscape and climate, with high average elevation, volcanic activity, and tropical rainforests their best-known natural features. Mexico, because of its size, shows more physical and climatic variety and opens into valleys and deserts farther north. Apart from Cuba, most of the Caribbean islands are rather small.

Right Nestled in the mountains of central Mexico, the picturesque former silver mining town of Guanajuato derives its name from an indigenous word meaning "place of frogs."

Below A Tarahumara Indian woman with lamb, Chihuahua, Mexico. The Tarahumara retreated to Copper Canyon in the Sierra Madre on the arrival of Spanish explorers in the sixteenth century.

Middle America is a vernacular region that encompasses Mexico, Central America, and the Caribbean islands. Mexico and the Central American countries are part of the North American continent, which extends south to the border between Panama and Colombia, but these countries also belong to the cultural realm of Latin America. While this duality might initially sound confusing, it provides a key to understanding the cultural and historical development of the region.

Unifying factors for most of Middle America (and for Latin America in general) differ from those that unify North America. The first Europeans to populate the United States and Canada were people of northwest European stock, mainly from English and German speaking countries, while those who settled south of the Rio Grande predominantly came from Spain—and Portugal, in the case of Brazil. Their religion was Roman Catholicism, as opposed to a heavy Protestant presence in the north. The indigenous population of North America was quite small, and its remnants were for the most part successfully assimilated. South of Mexico, one finds an unmistakable Indian presence. Finally, the capitalist economic system that so dramatically transformed North America made minimal impact on Latin American nations, where many aspects of the old European feudal system were retained until recent times. The "God, gold, and glory" concept created a system of one-directional exploitation of local resources for the benefit of colonial powers, with little regard for any development or overall improvements in the colonies themselves. Industrialization also has by-passed Middle American nations, even though many of them have undergone significant urbanization. Due partly to these cultural conditions, ethnic diversity of the kind seen in the United States is difficult to find anywhere in Middle America, for none of these countries truly embrace the "melting pot" concept. Some degree of ethnic variation is found in the Caribbean, for many of the islands were previously in the hands of Britain and France.

Below At its height in the early part of the first millennium CE, Teotihuacan was the largest city in the Americas. Its name is also used to refer to the Mesoamerican civilization that was centered on the city between c. 150 BCE and c. 750 CE.

US Influence in Middle America

Despite proximity to the United States and its influence over the region for the past century, Middle America lags far behind in economic progress and the development of political institutions. For decades the region was a symbol of ineffective political organization and governmental corruption; Mexico serves as an example of a nation whose potential has never been properly fulfilled. In eight decades of domination by a single political party it struggled with continuous economic hardship, inflation, international debt, and saw only limited improvements in infrastructure.

As is the case in the rest of the region, society is heavily stratified in Mexico, favoring people of European (mainly Spanish) cultural background, who own a disproportionately large amount of the country's total wealth. These people are usually urban dwelling, middle-class or upper-class, and well educated, whereas unemployment, poverty, and illiteracy remain widespread throughout the rural areas inhabited by indigenous groups.

For much of the twentieth century the transition of power in Middle America revolved around the barrel of a gun, but the revolutions that toppled numerous dictatorships in the region merely established similar rules. The only difference was the side of the political spectrum to which the revolutionary forces belonged. The Cuban revolution, for example, was fought to replace right-wing Fulgencio Batista's dictatorship, yet it resulted in an equally restricting grip on power by the leftist dictator Fidel Castro.

Only Costa Rica, remarkably, evaded the obstacles its neighbors faced and remained

Left Fishing boats at Soufrière on St Lucia in the eastern Caribbean Sea, on the boundary with the Atlantic Ocean. The Pitons in the background are volcanic plugs. Like the sulfur springs and hot mud pools in the nearby Soufrière caldera, they are remnants of volcanic activity in the region. First visited by Europeans about 1500, St Lucia was colonized by France after a treaty was signed with the indigenous Carib peoples in 1660, but switched so often between French and British control that it was likened to the mythical Helen of Troy, and was sometimes referred to as the Helen of the West Indies. Since 1979, however, it has been an independent state of the Commonwealth of Nations.

Above The scarlet macaw *(Ara macao)* is the national bird of Honduras. Much valued by the pre-Columbian civilizations, it feeds on nectar, roots, and fruits from Bolivia up to Mexico.

Left Maya Indians in Chichicastenango, Guatemala, celebrate the festival of St Thomas. Mayan religious rites mingled with Catholicism can be witnessed at the 400-year-old Iglesio Santo Tomás, built atop a pre-Columbian base.

peaceful and democratic; it even became the first nation in the world to abolish its military.

American engagement in Middle America began in the nineteenth century, even before the Spanish–American War of 1898 effectively ended centuries of direct Spanish colonial influence. Military interventions across Middle America almost always aligned with the economic interests of some of the United States' largest corporations, such as United Fruit and Standard Oil. US corporations became more deeply involved in local political affairs and supported the large landowners; in the eyes of ordinary people this severely tarnished the image of the United States, helping to firm the resolve of the many leftist revolutionary movements advocating land reform and economic nationalization. This is one of the reasons for the traditionally negative perception of the United States throughout Latin America, which many populist leaders have successfully exploited for their own political gains and to cover the faults of ineffective governance. Conditions, however, are gradually changing for the better.

A Changing World

As Middle America enters a new age, one major change has stemmed from an understanding of the fact that participation in the global economic system will hugely benefit the region. The parochial lifestyle views and preservation of the status quo are finally losing ground. Individual farmers such as coffee growers in Central America now have status in the commodities business—something previously unheard of. Tourism, from the exploration of ecoregions to island hopping, is picking up in countries where the internal situation is stable, and the ideal of the tropical paradise is stronger today than the concept of the banana republic. Even the rule of law is being enforced, and corrupt politicians are prosecuted and imprisoned.

Change brings improvement—but improvements do not arrive without accompanying challenges and new burdens. This is especially obvious in relation to the social issues created under conditions in which Middle America, similarly to the rest of the developing world, is undergoing a transformation from folk to popular culture. Traditional values and perceptions are gradually weakening, more rapidly in urban than in rural areas. Even the overarching role of the Roman Catholic Church and its clergy in communal life is significantly smaller today than it was only a few decades ago. As changes occur in all aspects of culture, gender issues are entering the spotlight. In what was fiercely defended machismo territory, the emancipation of women is a new experience for Latin America, and rarely welcomed. Additionally, the region's drastic demographic transition in favor of younger generations exceeds the rate of economic growth and generates conditions favoring high unemployment and organized crime. The Central American gangs that rose to prominence in recent years are mainly composed of young disenfranchised people who have despaired of success by other means.

Below Christopher Columbus described the terrain of Dominica by crumpling a piece of paper. With valleys, gorges, and volcanic peaks covered in lush vegetation, the Caribbean island boasts 365 rivers, 29 waterfalls, 50 fumaroles and hot springs, freshwater lakes, and a "boiling" lake. It has been called the "nature isle" of the Caribbean because of its unspoiled natural beauty.

Canada

Map Reference Pages 116–123

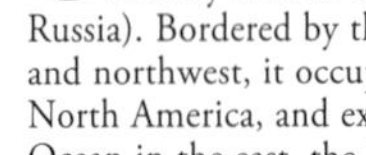

CANADA

Official name Canada
Land area 3,855,103 square miles (9,984,670 km²)
Border countries United States of America
Capital Ottawa
Highest point Mt Logan 19,551 feet (5,959 m)
Climate Temperate in south; subarctic to Arctic in the north
Population 33,390,000
Language(s) Official: English and French; other
Ethnicity British 28%; French 23%; other European 15%; Amerindian 2%; Asian, African, and Arab 6%; mixed background 26%
Religion Roman Catholic 42.6%, Protestant 23.3%, other Christian 4.4%, Muslim 1.9%, other/unspecified 11.8%, none 16%
Government Constitutional monarchy/parliamentary democracy/federation
Currency Canadian dollar
Human Development Index 0.961 (ranked 4th out of 177 countries)

Canada is the world's second largest country in total land area (just behind Russia). Bordered by the USA on the south and northwest, it occupies most of northern North America, and extends from the Atlantic Ocean in the east, the Pacific Ocean to the west, and the Arctic Ocean to the north. The terrain of this vast country varies from mostly plains and mountainous regions in the west and lowlands in the southeast. It has the longest coastline in the world (125,517 miles or 202,000 km), the world's largest estuary (Gulf of St Lawrence), the largest amount of lakes, and the world's greatest vertical tidal variation (Bay of Fundy). Approximately 90 percent of Canada's population is concentrated within 100 miles (160 km) of the US border.

Physical Geography

Canada's landscape reflects the two major divisions in its geology—a large core of massive, old, crystalline Precambrian rocks known as the Canadian Shield, and an outer rim of younger, mainly stratified rocks known collectively as the Borderlands.

The ancient, heavily glaciated surface of the Canadian Shield has relatively low relief, and for the most part the interior of Canada is a region of gently rolling landscapes with thousands of lakes. The geologically younger Borderlands has undergone a considerable amount of tectonic re-shaping, particularly in the west, where the Coast, Cascade, and Rocky mountain ranges offer high mountains and deep trenches before dropping to the Western Plains of Alberta. In the east, a series of high mountains have since eroded, leaving a rugged landscape of hills, valleys, and fjords.

In general, Canada's climate is warmer on the west coast than the east coast; the center has a true continental climate with extreme highs and lows. The north exhibits low precipitation and cold temperatures, and hence has large areas of permafrost and tundra.

Vegetation ranges from coniferous boreal forests (taiga) in the north to extensive prairies in the western provinces of Alberta and Saskatchewan. Temperate rainforests are a feature of the Pacific coast, and mixed deciduous forests cover the Atlantic seaboard.

History

Humans first crossed into present-day Canada via the Bering Strait from Asia, perhaps as early as 35,000 years ago. The first recorded landing of a European was by Viking seafarer Leif Ericson, in northern Newfoundland, in about 1000 CE. In 1497, Italian explorer Giovanni Caboto (John Cabot) at the behest of King Henry VII of England, explored the northeastern seaboard. By 1524, the French king Francis I was also sending explorers, including Jacques Cartier, who made several voyages from 1534 and a failed attempt to found a colony in Québec in 1541. It was not until 1605 that a successful colony was established at Port Royal in Nova Scotia. Samuel de Champlain founded the colony that became Québec City in 1608.

French trappers and missionaries advanced throughout much of what was to become the Canadian nation. The British founded colonies along the eastern coast to the south. They founded the Hudson's Bay Company in 1670 and began exploration and fur trading far to the north, establishing forts along the margin of the bay. In 1759, the English general Wolfe led a fleet of 140 ships and 9,000 soldiers against Québec. In 1763, the Treaty of Paris ended the so-called Seven Years' War in Europe and France ceded eastern North America to the British.

During the American Revolutionary War in 1775, the 13 American colonies dispatched two armies north to capture Canada, but one of their generals was killed, and the other was wounded. Both armies then retreated. Following the resumption of peace in 1783, 40,000 American colonists—the United Empire Loyalists—decided to leave the newly formed United States of America and moved to Canada because they wished to remain under British rule.

In 1791, the British Parliament passed the *Constitutional Act*, creating two provinces, Upper and Lower Canada (essentially, Ontario and Québec). The French colonists in Lower Canada were allowed to retain language, education, and their system of law. Exploration continued, and by the early nineteenth century formal settlement efforts were being made in the west. Two rival trading companies, the Hudson's Bay Company and the North West Company, had interests in the area, and occasional physical conflict broke out between them. In 1812, the first of waves of Scottish and Irish settlers sent by Thomas Douglas, Earl of Selkirk, began to arrive in the Red River Valley, but the conflicts prevented successful settlement until 1817. War broke out between Britain and the USA in 1812. Several attacks on Canada were repulsed, and by war's end Canada remained part of the Empire.

In 1870, the Northwest Territories were purchased from the Hudson's Bay Company. In 1871, the Treaty of Washington between Great Britain and the USA included de facto recognition of the Dominion of Canada. British Columbia entered the Dominion in the same year, and Prince Edward Island in 1873. Alberta and Saskatchewan both joined in 1905, and in 1949 the province of Newfoundland and Labrador completed the list.

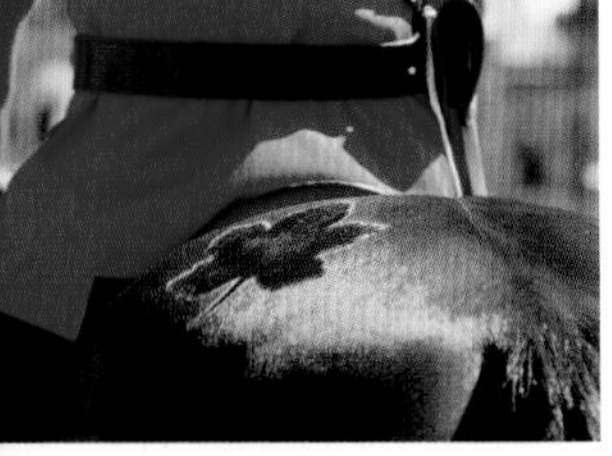

Above Two Canadian icons—the maple leaf and the Mountie—on a Canadian Mounted Police horse.

Above right The North American elk *(Cervus elaphus)* is also known as the wapiti. Over half of Canada's population of 72,000 elk are found in British Columbia.

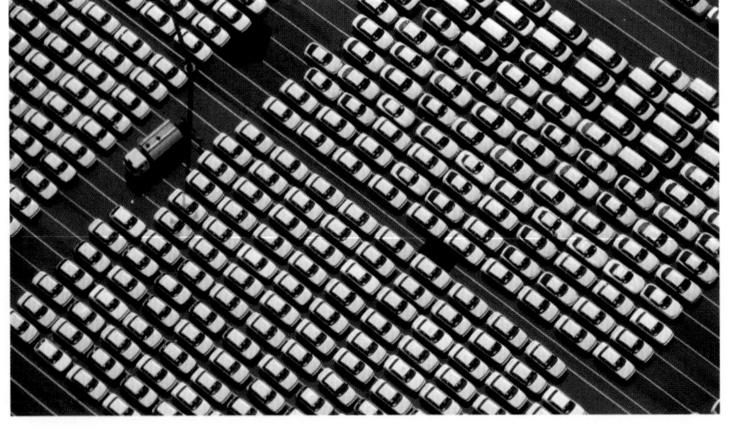

Right Aerial view of hundreds of new cars on a lot, Annacis Island, British Columbia. Part of Greater Vancouver, Annacis Island is a busy industrial center.

NORTHERN AMERICA

Left Winter sunrise on Bow River, with views of Castle Mountain, Banff National Park. Situated on the eastern slopes of the Rockies in Alberta, Banff is Canada's first national park.

FOOD FOR THOUGHT

Immigration introduced Canadians to a wide variety of cuisines, including the ubiquitous Chinese (mostly Cantonese) that followed the nineteenth-century railway workers from coast to coast. Although maple syrup is widely recognized as a Canadian symbol, it is also used commonly in other countries. There are a few specialties, however, that wear a truly Canadian stamp.

Poutine is an artery-clogging concoction of French-fried potatoes smothered with fresh cheese curds and gravy. It is the quintessential comfort food of Québec.

Tourtière is a meat pie made from ground pork and veal, or beef. A Québecois product, it is often served as Christmas or holiday fare. Some family variations include potatoes.

Nanaimo Bars are dessert slices with a crumb base covered in vanilla butter icing and/or custard, then topped with chocolate. They are named after the city of Nanaimo, Vancouver Island.

Fiddleheads are the young, unfurled fronds of certain varieties of fern.

Beaver Tails are made from deep-fried dough sprinkled with cinnamon, powdered sugar, or maple syrup. They are a particular favorite in Ottawa.

Arctic Char is a noted fish delicacy, native to glacial lakes in the far north. It is now being farmed commercially.

Cod Tongues are usually served breaded and fried. They are a popular specialty in Newfoundland.

Below Technicians dangle from ropes on an oil rig off Sable Island, 120 miles (180 km) southeast of Nova Scotia. Because of its long history of shipwrecks, Sable Island has been named "The Graveyard of the Atlantic."

Canada grew steadily during the early years of the twentieth century, primarily through immigration. In 1931, the Statute of Westminster established the British Commonwealth of Nations, and essentially set up Canada and other dominions as autonomous entities. On February 15, 1965, Canada raised the red-and-white maple leaf flag, replacing the former Red Ensign, and reducing symbolically the role of Britain in Canadian affairs. The final act of severing legal ties with Britain took place in 1982, when the *British North America Act* was replaced by the Canadian Constitution. The Northwest Territories (NWT) were split into two with the formal creation of Nunavut in 1999. Nunavut, the former eastern portion of the NWT, is classed as a self-governing homeland for the Inuit inhabitants.

Administration/Government

Canada is a federation that is comprised of ten provinces and three territories. The federal government has two houses: An elected House of Commons, and an appointed Senate that acts as an upper house. Each province and territory also has an elected legislative assembly. The leader of the federal government bears the title of Prime Minister, while the leaders of the provincial governments are known as Premiers. Canada's head of state is Queen Elizabeth II, who is represented at the federal level by a governor general. This position is appointed for a fixed term by the incumbent government.

MILESTONE EVENTS

35,000 BCE First inhabitants cross the Bering Strait from Asia into Canada

1000 CE First European contact by Viking seafarer Leif Ericson

1605 British establish colony at Port Royal, Nova Scotia

1608 Québec City founded

1763 Treaty of Paris ceded eastern North America to British

1774 *Québec Act* defined boundaries and rights

1867 Passage of *British North America Act* created the Dominion of Canada with four provinces

1871 Treaty of Washington recognizes Dominion of Canada; British Columbia joins Dominion

1885 Canadian Pacific Railway completed

1931 Statute of Westminster establishes British Commonwealth of Nations

1982 Canadian Constitution replaces *British North America Act*

1995 Failure of referendum on Québec separation

1999 Division of the Northwest Territories into Nunavut in the east, and Northwest Territories in the west

Economy

Canada is one of the world's wealthiest nations; in 2006, the International Monetary Fund reported that Canada ranked eighth worldwide, with a Gross Domestic Product (GDP) of US$1,275,273 million. The service industry occupies some three-quarters of the labor force, while 15 percent are in manufacturing, 5 percent in construction, and 3 percent in agriculture. Much of Canada's wealth is in the form of natural resources, particularly oil, timber, and minerals. There is also a large manufacturing sector concentrated primarily in the Windsor–Québec City corridor. The automobile industry of Ontario produces more than the US state of Michigan. Seven of the world's largest vehicle manufacturers operate 14 plants in Ontario. In the Québec portion, the emphasis is on aerospace and pharmaceuticals. The Canadarm, a mechanical arm used on the US Space Shuttle, was designed and built in Canada.

Newfoundland and Nova Scotia, both heavily reliant on fishing in the past, now have large revenues from offshore oil and gas deposits. British Columbia, New Brunswick, and Québec also have large forestry industries, and Prince Edward Island is famous for its potatoes. Alberta and Saskatchewan are well known for beef, wheat, and corn, but are also producers of oil and gas. The Alberta Tar Sands hold approximately 988 billion cubic feet (28 billion m^3) of recoverable crude bitumen, which amounts to three-quarters of North American petroleum reserves. Canada is the United States' largest trading partner, with yearly trade of over $620 billion Canadian dollars.

Population and Culture

When Europeans arrived in what is now Canada, they found two aboriginal peoples—the Inuit (formerly known as Eskimo) in the Arctic, and the Indifgdans in more southerly regions. In time, as European explorers worked their way westward, they intermarried with aboriginal people, creating a new population, the Métis. Métis come from many regions but are concentrated in the western provinces, particularly Manitoba. In the *Constitution Act* of 1982, all three groups are now classed legally as "Aboriginal Peoples of Canada." All Aboriginal Peoples of Canada, male and female, are guaranteed treaty rights under the Constitution, and in recent years many land claims made under such treaty rights have been settled across Canada; others are currently in process.

More recent cultural migrations were from English, Scottish, Irish, and French stock. Canada accepts about 200,000 immigrants per year from many ethnic groups—more than any other country in the world. The *Canadian Multiculturalism Act* was promulgated in 1985, which allows immigrants to practice (within reason) the traditional lifestyles of their countries of origin. A notable example of that has been allowing Sikh members of the Royal Canadian Mounted Police to wear their traditional turbans rather than the famous RCMP headgear.

Above Girls performing a fan dance during the Chinese New Year Parade in Vancouver.

CANADA
UNITED STATES OF AMERICA
PACIFIC OCEAN
ATLANTIC OCEAN
MEXICO
Gulf of Mexico
Seattle
Portland
Boise
Minneapolis
St. Paul
Salt Lake City
Sacramento
San Francisco
Denver
Kansas City
Los Angeles
San Diego
Phoenix
Santa Fe
Las Vegas
Detroit
Chicago
Cleveland
Pittsburgh
Indianapolis
Columbus
Cincinnati
St. Louis
Louisville
Nashville
Memphis
Little Rock
Oklahoma City
Atlanta
Dallas
Austin
Houston
San Antonio
New Orleans
Jacksonville
Orlando
Miami
Boston
New York
Philadelphia
Baltimore
WASHINGTON DC
Honolulu
HAWAII
RUSSIAN FEDERATION
Beaufort Sea
ALASKA
Anchorage
Juneau
Bering Sea

United States of America

Map Reference Pages 124–131

UNITED STATES OF AMERICA

Official name United States of America
Land area 3,794,066 square miles (9,826,630 km²)
Border countries Canada and Mexico
Capital Washington DC (District of Columbia)
Highest & lowest points Mt McKinley (Denali), Alaska 20,335 feet (6,198 m); Death Valley, California –282 feet (–86 m)
Climate Primarily temperate, but with polar, desert, and tropical extremes
Population 303,825,000
Language(s) English, Spanish, other
Ethnicity European 82%, African-American 13%, Asian 4%, Amerindian, Inuit, and Aleut 1%
Religion Protestant 52%, Roman Catholic 24%, none or other 24%
Government Constitution-based federal republic
Currency US dollar
Human Development Index 0.951 (ranked 12th out of 177 countries)

The United States of America (USA) occupies much of mid-latitude North America. The country is bordered by Canada to the north, and Mexico to the south, and faces the Atlantic, Pacific, and Arctic (in Alaska) oceans. More than 300 million people live within its 3,794,066 square miles (9,826,630 km^2), making the USA the world's third largest country in both population and area. Politically, the country is composed of 50 states, 48 of which are conterminous, plus Alaska and Hawaii. The capital, Washington, is located in the District of Columbia between Virginia and Maryland.

Physical Geography

The terrain of the USA includes vast expanses of mountains, plateaus, hills, and plains. Although it shares with Canada the world's largest network of freshwater lakes—the Great Lakes—much of the interior suffers from inadequate water supplies. The USA is endowed with large reserves of metals, fuels, good soils, and other essential natural resources.

The western third of the USA offers a mosaic of high mountains, extensive plateaus, broad basins, and fertile valleys. Erosional forces have etched jagged mountain peaks and scoured spectacular gorges, including Arizona's magnificent Grand Canyon.

The Hawaiian Islands are of volcanic origin, as are many peaks in Alaska and the Cascades. Sierra Nevada in California is of tilted fault block origin, as is the basin-and-range topography of the southwestern deserts. Farther inland, combined diastrophic and volcanic forces formed the Rocky Mountains. In the east, folding created the ancient ridge-and-valley terrain of the Appalachian Mountains.

The topography of the Interior West is dominated by the sedimentary Colorado Plateau in the Southwest, and the volcanic Columbia Plateau in the Pacific Northwest. Western lowlands include California's agriculturally productive Central Valley and the Great Basin, site of Great Salt Lake. Plains occupy most of the area between the Rocky Mountains and Appalachians. The drier Great Plains occupy the area generally lying west of the 100th meridian.

To the east, the Interior (Central) Plains (Lowlands) coincide with the Corn Belt and the Middle West. Large coastal plains border the Gulf of Mexico and the Atlantic Ocean.

Excluding tropical Hawaii and subarctic Alaska, most US territory lies in temperate mid-latitudes. Aridity is a problem—about 40 percent of the country receives less than 20 inches (50 cm) of rain annually.

East of the 100th meridian the USA experiences a moist climate—humid continental in the Northeast and humid subtropical in the Southeast. Moisture occurs year round with a summer peak. In the Northwest, winters are long, cold, and snowy, whereas the Southeast has long, hot, muggy summers. Eastern USA once supported a dense cover of broadleaf, needleleaf, and mixed forests. Most of the natural woodlands were cut for timber and agricultural clearing. The Midwestern Corn Belt has some of the world's most fertile soils.

MILESTONE EVENTS

1565 Spanish settle St Augustine, Florida
1607 British settle Jamestown, Virginia
1776 America declares independence on July 4
1803 USA buys Louisiana Territory from France
1848 Gold is discovered at Sutter's Mill in California
1861–1865 Civil War divides the country
1863 Emancipation Proclamation frees slaves
1865 President Abraham Lincoln is assassinated
1869 Completion of transcontinental railway
1941 USA enters World War II conflict when Japan bombs naval base at Pearl Harbor, Hawaii
1959 Alaska and Hawaii become 49th and 50th states
1963 President John F. Kennedy is assassinated
1973 Withdrawal of US troops from Vietnam
September 11, 2001 Terrorists strike World Trade Center in New York City and the Pentagon in Washington DC; a fourth hijacked plane crashes in Pennsylvania

Death Valley in California is the nation's driest location, receiving an annual average of less than 1½ inches (36 mm) of rain.

Temperatures vary greatly within the western interior. The desert Southwest experiences summer temperatures above 100°F (40°C). In the northern part of the region, winter temperatures often plunge below 0°F (–18°C).

Before Europeans arrived there, much of the central interior supported a grassland ecosystem that sustained an estimated 60 million American bison. Soil quality varies but is generally fertile in areas of plains and alluvium-filled river valleys and basins. This area supports the nation's Wheat Belt.

Climates within the Pacific region are generally mild. Southern California has a pleasant Mediterranean climate and can experience summer drought. Severe storms are limited to occasional heavy rains. Between November and April, an average 30 to 50 inches (75–125 cm) of precipitation occurs. Chaparral scrub and grassland dominate the natural vegetation, although exotic species such as cedars of Lebanon and Australian eucalypts dominate many urban landscapes.

The coastal Pacific Northwest and Alaskan Panhandle experience a moist temperate

THE TRANS-ALASKA PIPELINE

Oil was discovered at Prudhoe Bay, on Alaska's Arctic-facing North Slope, in 1968. It was North America's largest oil field, with reserves estimated at 24 billion barrels. Moving the petroleum posed a huge problem. Sea ice and other navigational hazards precluded oceanic transportation in the Arctic Ocean. The only feasible solution was to construct a pipeline. However, the nearest ice-free Pacific port was Valdez, a small town located 800 miles (1,287 km) to the south on Prince William Sound.

After several years of surveying and right-of-way litigation, President Richard Nixon signed the *Trans-Alaska Pipeline Authorization Act* into law in November 1973. Work began in March 1974 on what ultimately became one of the world's greatest and most costly engineering feats. Construction of the pipeline cost some US$8 billion. A consortium of seven petroleum companies hired five construction firms for the project. With as many as 21,000 employees working around-the-clock shifts throughout the year, the project was completed in a little over three years. Oil began flowing to the Valdez terminal in June 1977.

The construction of the pipeline faced huge physical obstacles. It passed through some of the world's most rugged, remote, and frigid terrain, crossing three mountain ranges, many active faults, and some 800 streams. Dealing with permafrost and its propensity to create an unstable boggy surface during the short summer thaw meant that 420 miles (676 km) of the pipeline was constructed above ground. This task involved building 78,000 supports at 60-foot (18 m) intervals.

The pipeline itself is an engineering marvel. At one point it plunges down a 2,800-foot (850 m) escarpment. The 48-inch (122 cm) diameter pipe segments are joined together by more than 100,000 welds. To allow for expansion and contraction resulting from temperature changes and earthquake-induced movements, the pipeline was built in a zigzag configuration. Eleven pumping stations facilitate the flow of oil, which moves through the pipeline at about 5½ miles per hour (9 km/h) and takes 5½ days to reach Valdez. At peak capacity, there are approximately nine million barrels of oil in the pipeline at any time. Alaska's oil production peaked in 1988 and is now in decline. The pipeline had a projected useful age of 30 years when built, a span now exceeded. Although its future is now uncertain, during its peak it carried a quarter of America's petroleum supply.

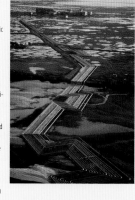

Above The distinctive eroded formations in Bryce Canyon, southern Utah, were created by wind, water, and ice erosion of the sedimentary rocks. The red, orange, and white colors of the rocks provide spectacular views to visitors.

Opposite page, top With its world famous beaches and welcoming climate, Honolulu, the capital city of Hawaii, is one of the USA's most popular tourist destinations.

marine climate. Summer temperatures are much cooler and winter temperatures milder than conditions inland. West-facing mountain slopes are the wettest part of continental USA, receiving up to 150 inches (380 cm) of precipitation annually. This region supports some of the nation's major forests, including giant redwoods, sequoia, and Douglas fir.

Hawaii is classified as humid tropical, yet has a variety of microclimates and ecosystems. Due to the orographic effect, it is possible to stand in a near-desert landscape in Kaua'i and watch rain falling over Mt Wai'ale'ale, one of the world's wettest spots, several miles away. Hot humid weather and tropical rainforest vegetation occur in many low-lying areas.

Away from its southern coast, most of Alaska experiences short cool summers and severe winters. Inland and at high elevations temperatures can drop to as low as –78°F (–61°C). Precipitation occurs year round, most falling as snow during any month in most locations. Taiga (boreal) forest and tundra are Alaska's dominant ecosystems. The state's local wildlife includes bears, moose, caribou, deer, in addition to plentiful marine life species.

The USA experiences all environmental hazards, including hurricanes, tornadoes, blizzards, hail, sleet, lightning, flood-causing rains, and drought. In 2005, Hurricane Katrina inflicted an estimated US$80 billion damage to the Gulf Coast and swamped the city of New Orleans.

The Pacific region is subject to seismic and volcanic activity, earth-creep, and landslides. San Francisco, Los Angeles, Seattle, and Anchorage sit atop active faults. In 1980, the eruption of Washington's Mt St Helens resulted in 57 deaths. Wildfires pose a major threat to many areas, particularly summer-parched and densely populated southern California.

History

When Europeans arrived in the fifteenth century, they found a land long occupied by indigenous peoples whose ancestors probably arrived from Asia some 13,000 to perhaps 30,000 years ago. Their cultures varied greatly from region to region, and they inhabited all areas of present-day USA. Some, such as the Iroquois and Cherokee in the East, were advanced farmers. Specialized bison hunters roamed the Interior Plains. The Southwest was home to farming peoples. Much of southern California and the Great Basin had scattered groups of nomadic hunter-gatherers. The Northwest was home to specialized fishing peoples. Northern groups included Alaska's Inuit and Aleut. Sea-faring Polynesians occupied the Hawaiian Islands.

The first documented European explorer to reach present-day USA was Italian Giovanni Caboto (John Cabot), who sailed the New England coast in 1497. Many others followed, including British, Dutch, and French explorers. In 1565, the Spanish settled St Augustine in Florida, which is the oldest continuously inhabited European settlement in the USA. In 1607, the British settled Jamestown, Virginia. In the Southwest, the Spanish settled Santa Fe (New Mexico) in 1610, a decade before the Pilgrims established their community in Plymouth, Massachusetts.

By the eighteenth century, Europeans were well established along the eastern seaboard. Cities such New York, Philadelphia, and Boston were built on harbors and grew as commercial centers.

NEW
YORKER

Below The Manhattan skyline at sunset. Some of Manhattan's famous landmarks include the Empire State Building, Madison Square Garden, Times Square, Wall Street, and Central Park.

Above The bald eagle (*Haliaeetus leucocephalus*) is one of the USA's most recognizable symbols. Long before it was adopted as the national bird, the bald eagle was spiritually significant to Native Americans.

THE MELTING POT

Give me your tired, your poor,
Your huddled masses yearning to breathe free. . .

America's human history is succinctly summarized by the foregoing segment of the inscription that appears on a bronze plaque mounted on the Statue of Liberty. Originally, the inhabitants varied by language, religion, social background, economic condition, political orientation, and countless other traits. Throughout the passage of time, this heterogeneous society blended to become the "Americans," with a culture composed of the diverse traits contributed by numerous peoples.

E Pluribus Unum—"From many, one"—is an American motto. As the maxim suggests, through time diverse populations melded together to become culturally unified in a process recognized as the American "melting pot." The uniqueness of this cultural and ethnic fusion was recognized as early as the late eighteenth century. In 1782, Crevecoeur, in *Letters from an American Farmer*, asked, "What then is the American, this new man?" In answering his own question, Crevecoeur replied, "He is an American, who, [left] behind him all his ancient prejudices and manners . . . [to become] incorporated into one of the finest systems . . . which has ever appeared." As a widely recognized expression, "The Melting Pot" first appeared in 1908 as title of a play by Israel Zangwill.

Since 1700, an estimated 45 million Europeans migrated to America. Another half-million African slaves were brought to the USA unwillingly. Millions more came from Asia and Latin America. Americans have ancestral links to every country on Earth in what became a grand and unparalleled human experiment conducted on a colossal scale. Biologically, 82 percent of the population is Caucasian (white), 12 percent is Negroid (black), 4 percent is Mongoloid (primarily of East Asian origin), and about 2 percent traces its ancestry to Amerindian, Alaskan, Hawaiian, or some other group. Such figures are misleading, because many Americans are of mixed ancestry. According to the 2000 Census, the US population is descended from immigrants tracing their national heritage to the following locations: Germany 19.2 percent, Latin America 12.5 percent, Africa 12.1 percent, Ireland 10.8 percent, England 7.7 percent, and Italy 5.6 percent. Most Americans, regardless of biological, ethnic, or country heritage, have willingly integrated into the American cultural "melting pot."

Above Commuters at Grand Central Terminal, New York City. Popularly known as Grand Central Station, it opened in 1871 and is the largest train station in the world.

In the subtropical South, cotton, indigo, and tobacco were produced by slave labor, resulting in an estimated 500,000 Africans being brought unwillingly to Colonial America. French trappers penetrated the country's central interior in pursuit of beaver pelts. Spain claimed the territory from Florida westward to the Pacific Coast and much of the western interior. By the mid-1700s, lands between the Appalachians and Atlantic were under British control, but relations between the original 13 colonies were strained. The resulting American Revolution was a long and bitter conflict that resulted in the United States declaring its independence from Britain on July 4, 1776.

The nineteenth century was a period of expansion, consolidation, and conflict. In 1803, the Louisiana Territory was purchased from France. Pioneer settlers spilled across the Appalachians, particularly into the Ohio River Valley. In 1848, gold was discovered east of Sacramento, California. The ensuing rush attracted thousands of prospectors.

Although slave trading was outlawed in 1808, slavery continued—a practice that sharply divided the country. Slavery was a key issue contributing to the Civil War (1861–1865), the bitter conflict between North and South that resulted in the loss of perhaps 600,000 lives. In 1863, President Abraham Lincoln terminated slavery with his Emancipation Proclamation.

By 1900, millions of European immigrants swelled the country's population. Industries, businesses, and agriculture were expanding and thriving, but this era of prosperity and stability was short-lived. By 1917, the USA was drawn into World War I. American troops played a vital role in ending the war a year later, but at a cost of more than 120,000 lives. In October 1929, the New York stock market crashed. During the ensuing Great Depression, the US economy declined by nearly 90 percent. Much of the interior USA also experienced the devastating Dust Bowl drought during the 1930s. On December 7, 1941, Japanese planes bombed the US military base in Pearl Harbor, Hawaii. The event drew the USA into both the Atlantic and Pacific theaters of World War II, with the loss of 400,000 lives.

By the mid-twentieth century, the USA was the world's leading technological, economic, and military power. The Soviet Union challenged the latter claim during the Cold War, but with the USSR's collapse in 1991, the USA emerged as the world's lone superpower. The USA's economy was one of those most affected by the 2008 world financial crisis.

Population and Settlement

The US population of over 303 million is exceeded only by China and India. Although its area covers some 3.7 million square miles (9.6 million km^2), 90 percent of the population is clustered in about 10 percent of the area. The population is growing at an annual rate of 1.2 percent, both from natural increase (0.9 percent) and immigration (0.3 percent). With the fertility rate now below the 2.1 replacement level, the US faces problems of an ageing population. Paradoxically, demographers project a US population of 420 million—a 40 percent gain—by 2050, most of which will come from immigration.

Life expectancy and the median age in the USA are 78 years and 36.6 years, respectively. Only 20 percent of the population is under 15 years and 13 percent is over 65 years. An ageing population will have an impact on the labor force, health care, and retirement programs. Increasingly, the US depends on

immigrant laborers, particularly at entry-level and minimum-wage jobs. With an estimated 12 million undocumented immigrants in the country, finding a fair and workable solution to the problem is of vital concern.

About 80 percent of the population is urbanized and lives within 200 miles (320 km) of the oceans or Great Lakes. Ten percent of the population is clustered in the greater New York and Los Angeles metropolitan areas. California is the most populous state with some 36.5 million people, whereas Wyoming has just over 500,000 people. Since the mid-1900s, urban-to-suburban migration has resulted in metropolitan area growth, but decline within the city proper. A second movement has been from the northern Snowbelt or Rustbelt to the Sunbelt of the South, Southwest, and West Coast.

Culture

Americans (including its indigenous peoples) form a complex mosaic of races, cultures, and ethnicities. Ninety-nine percent of the population can trace its ancestry to a foreign land. No other nation can match the diversity of ancestral origins represented.

Right A Vermont farmhouse set against a breathtaking backdrop of autumn trees ablaze with reds, oranges, yellows, and golds.

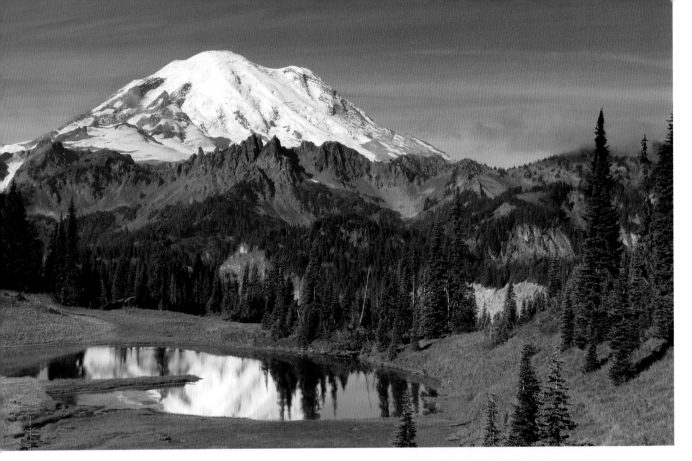

Language bonds a society. Although fewer than 8 percent of Americans claim English ancestry, English is the dominant language and is the primary tongue of 82 percent of Americans; 11 percent are Spanish-speaking.

America's tradition of religious tolerance has resulted in the practice of nearly 2,900 different organized faiths. About 50 percent of Americans are Protestant, the leading denominations being Baptist, Methodist, Lutheran, and Presbyterian. Almost 25 percent of the population is Roman Catholic.

Americans enjoy varied diets. Each of the world's major cuisines has contributed to the country's food culture. There are many specialized regional cuisines, including Southern, Louisiana Cajun, and Southwestern Tex-Mex.

America has had a profound impact on global popular culture. Its music, motion pictures, television programs, and printed media have diffused worldwide. Sports such as basketball and baseball have gained widespread acceptance. American tourists, technologies, corporations, products, and services also have a global reach and influence.

Administration/Government

The United States, a federal republic, gained independence from Britain in 1776. A constitution, adopted in 1789, established three branches of government (Executive, Legislative, and Judicial). The President heads the executive branch and is head-of-state charged with enforcing laws, administering government, and serving as Commander-in-Chief of the Armed Forces. The legislative branch, or Congress, comprises a 100-member Senate and 435-member House of Representatives and is responsible for making laws. The judicial branch is the system of justice.

Government has played a critical role in the country's remarkable economic growth and development. It has built, supported, or regulated vital transportation and communication linkages, and plays an important role in supporting agriculture, manufacturing, and service industries. Government acts that have altered the nation's cultural landscape include:

Land Ordnance Survey (1785) that created the American Rectangular Survey System, giving rise to a "checkerboard" system of land division, roads, field patterns, and other cultural traits aligned in the cardinal directions.

Public Lands Acts (various dates) placed about a third of the country's land in public ownership, restricting development and thus protecting lands for public use. Federal lands include parks and wilderness areas, Indian Trust lands, National Forests and Grasslands, and military bases.

The Homestead Act (1862) gave homesteaders title to 160 acres (about 65 hectares) of land. The lure of free land to eligible applicants drew hundreds of thousands of people westward, where they developed largely virgin lands and populated the countryside in a dispersed pattern of settlement.

Railroad Federal Land Grants (1862–1871) encouraged railroad building. Companies received a 400-foot (122 m) right-of-way, plus 10 square miles (25.9 km^2) of land for each mile (1.6 km) of track built. Eventually, a network of rail provided access to most developed sections of the country.

The National Park Service (1916) protects America's natural, historical, and cultural treasures, including national parks, memorials, seashores, trails, and other historical features.

The Federal Highway Act (1956) created the 50,000-mile (80,000 km) Interstate Highway System, a network of divided "super highways" that crisscrosses the country. This has had a massive impact on transportation, settlement, and both rural and urban landscapes.

Economy

The USA generates an annual US$14 trillion gross national product (GNP), about 30 percent of the world's total value of products and services. If California were an independent country, its economy would rank fifth among the world's nations. In 2008, per capita GDP-Purchasing Power Parity stood at US$46,000.

Many factors have contributed to US economic strength, including political stability and a free-market economy. Economic development has been assisted by an abundance of land and water, good soil, timber, metals, building materials, and fossil fuels. The USA also has benefited from a well-educated, healthy, and skilled labor force.

Less than 1 percent of the US workforce is engaged in agriculture; crop and livestock production accounts for less than 1 percent of the gross domestic product (GDP). Yet America is the world's leading agricultural producer. Manufacturing contributes only about 20 percent of the GDP, but the USA remains the world's leading industrial power. Some 80 percent of the GDP is generated by various services of products and services.

Top Reflected image of trees and a snow-capped Mt Rainier in a mountain lake, Mt Rainier National Park, Washington.

Above Cotton harvest at Sikeston, Missouri. The USA produces 20 percent of the world's cotton.

Left Sometimes referred to as the "national pastime," baseball is the second most popular sport in America. The Major League baseball season runs from early April to late September.

MEXICO

Official name United Mexican States (Mexico) (Estados Unidos Mexicanos)
Land area 761,606 square miles (1,972,550 km²)
Border countries United States of America, Belize, Guatemala
Capital Mexico City (México)
Highest & lowest points Mt Orizaba (Volcan Pico de Orizaba) 18,406 feet (5,610 m); Laguna Salada −33 feet (−10 m)
Climate Arid to semiarid in north, rainy tropical in south
Population 108,700,891
Language(s) Spanish; Mayan, Nahuatl, other regional indigenous languages
Ethnicity Mestizo (Amerindian–Spanish) 60%, Amerindian 30%, European 9%, other 1%
Religion Roman Catholic 77%, Protestant 7%, other 16%
Government Federal republic
Currency Mexican peso
Human Development Index 0.829 (ranked 52nd out of 177 countries)

UNITED STATES OF AMERICA
Tijuana
Mexicali
Ciudad Juárez
Isla Guadalupe
Hermosillo
Chihuahua
Los Mochis
Torreón
Monterrey
Gulf of Mexico
MEXICO
PACIFIC OCEAN
Mazatlán
San Luis Potosí
Ciudad Victoria
Tampico
Guadalajara
León
CIUDAD DE MÉXICO
(MÉXICO)
Mérida
Morelia
Toluca
Campeche
Pico de Orizaba
Islas Revillagigedo
Puebla
Coatzacoalcos
BELIZE
Acapulco
Oaxaca
Tuxtla Gutiérrez
GUATEMALA

Mexico

Map Reference Pages 132–133

Mexico is the northernmost country in Latin and Middle America. To the north it is bordered by the United States, on the east by the Atlantic Ocean (Gulf of Mexico and Caribbean Sea), Guatemala and Belize to the southeast, and the Pacific Ocean (and Gulf of California) to the south and west.

Physical Geography

Mexico's physical environment offers considerable variety. Three-quarters of the country features rugged mountains, plateaus and mesas, bolsons (basins of interior drainage), canyons, and narrow valleys. The Sierra Madre Occidental and Sierra Madre Oriental extend southward from the USA–Mexico border and join south of Mexico City.

Volcanic peaks, including Ixtaccihuatl (Iztaccíhuatl) (17,338 feet/5,286 m), Mt Orizaba (18,406 feet/5,610 m), and Popocatéptl (17,802 feet/5,426 m), rise near the capital and continue southward into Central America. The Mexican Plateau lies between the two sierras and rises in elevation from north to south. Relatively narrow coastal plains border both oceans. Northeast of the Isthmus of Tehuantepec lies the low, rather featureless limestone plain of the Yucatán Peninsula. Peninsular Baja California is a mountainous desert landscape. The rugged terrain means that only about 12 percent of Mexico is suitable for agriculture. Across much of the country, land-hungry peasants farm steep mountain slopes, resulting in serious erosion and stream siltation.

Weather and climate in Mexico are influenced more by elevation than by latitude. Climate and associated ecosystems vary from parched desert in the north and northwest to humid tropical, with lush tropical rainforest vegetation in the southeast. Between these extremes, undifferentiated highland climates prevail throughout much of the country.

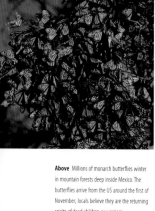

Above Millions of monarch butterflies winter in mountain forests deep inside Mexico. The butterflies arrive from the US around the first of November; locals believe they are the returning spirits of dead children or warriors.

Below The Pyramid of the Magician in Uxmal, Yucatán, is a sacred site of the Mayans.

GARDENS AFLOAT

When Spaniards arrived in the Valley of Mexico in 1519, they were amazed by a unique agricultural system employed by the Aztecs—the chinampas, or "floating gardens." Most farming methods in Europe at that time were primitive by comparison.

Before the Spanish conquest, much of the basin now occupied by Mexico City was filled by large, shallow lakes, including Texcoco, Chalco, and Xochimilco. Chinampas consisted of land reclaimed from—or more correctly, actually built within—the bottom of the lakes and marshes. Mud was scooped up from the lake or marsh bed and piled onto reed mats. These mounds reached about 3 feet (1 m) above water upon completion, and were surrounded by canals on several boundaries.

The sides of the plots were held in place by posts, mats, or vines and were stabilized by water-tolerant willow trees to help prevent erosion. Because chinampas were surrounded by water, there was constant seepage of moisture into the soil at root level. The outer canals allowed access throughout the network of fields and were a source of fish, crustaceans, and waterfowl to supplement native diets.

The primary crops grown were maize (corn), beans, squash, amaranth (a seed crop), tomatoes, chilies, and flowers. Most crops were transplanted from seedbeds. This allowed selection of only the hardiest plants and also made possible the harvest of two to three crops each year.

Mexico is subject to various environmental hazards. The country's Pacific-facing side lies within the geologically unstable Pacific Ring of Fire. Seismic activity is commonplace and often destructive. Low-lying lands fronting on to the Pacific also face the threat of tsunamis. Volcanic activity is frequent, especially in the mountains extending southward from Mexico City. The 1982 eruption of El Chicón in Chiapas killed 2,000 people and caused global cooling for several years. The most famous eruption was that of Paracutín (Paricutín), in Michoacán. Between 1943 and 1952 the volcano grew from a smoking vent in a cornfield to a 1,391-foot (424 m) cinder cone. Hurricanes along the Atlantic and Pacific coasts can bring torrential rain, damaging winds, and both inland and coastal flooding.

History

Humans may have reached Mexico 15,000 to 20,000 years ago. By 7000 BCE some Mesoamerican Amerindians were beginning to domesticate and cultivate plants. Crops such as maize, beans, squash, pumpkins, tomatoes, and chilies became the foundation of Mexico's early civilizations.

The Olmec flourished in the coastal lowlands of present-day Veracruz and Tabasco between 1500 BCE and 200 CE. Their achievements include early pottery, a simple written language, and America's first pyramids. They are best known for giant carved stone heads and for giving the world chocolate. The Olmec also possessed the wheel.

Mayan civilization thrived in Guatemala, Belize, and the Yucatán Peninsula from about 1100 BCE to 900 CE. These skilled farmers ultimately developed the most advanced culture in Mesoamerica. Mayan ruins attest to the civilization's high level of development. They constructed stone pyramids, plazas, and underground reservoirs without metal tools. They were skilled mathematicians and made accurate astronomical observations. Mayans were the first Amerindians to create a well-developed written language that allowed them to record their knowledge and history.

By the thirteenth century, the Mexica, a tribal group from northern Mexico (later known as the Aztecs), arrived in the Valley of Mexico. In 1325, they began to build Tenochtitlán, a magnificent city on an island in Lake Texcoco. Their empire gradually brought some 30 million people under Aztec rule. Farmland was scarce, which led to the farming system known as chinampa, the practice of growing crops in small, rectangular areas of land reclaimed from shallow lake beds. This method produced over half the food consumed by Tenochtitlán's population. It is now recognized by many scientists as the most productive system of crop growing.

Among other accomplishments, the Aztecs had an accurate calendar, a highly evolved written language, and monumental architecture. They were also brutal, practicing human sacrifice on a huge scale to appease their gods.

In April 1519, Hernán Cortés, accompanied by 508 soldiers, 14 cannons, and 16 horses, arrived on the Gulf Coast. By August 1521, he had conquered the Aztecs. At the time, Tenochtitlán was home to perhaps half a million people and possibly the world's largest city. Cortés selected the site as his capital, Mexico City, in 1522.

During the next three centuries, Spain expanded its hold on Mexico into much of what is now the western United States. The

MILESTONE EVENTS

c. 20,000 BCE Earliest human settlement
c. 7,000 BCE Dawn of plant domestication and cultivation
1100 BCE–1500 CE Various high cultures, including Olmec, Mayan, and Aztec thrive
1521 Cortés conquers Tenochtitlán, ending Aztec civilization
1546 Silver mining boom begins
1821 Mexico declares independence from Spain
1846–1848 Mexican–American War (Mexican War of Independence)
1910–1920 Mexican Revolution
1994 North American Free Trade Agreement (NAFTA)

Far left Named a UNESCO World Heritage site in 1988, Guanajuato boasts an underground road network that winds it way beneath the city's colorful houses. Strict rules govern all building work in the city.

Left Chess tables spread out in Mexico City's main square (Zócalo), on October 22, 2006, during an attempt to set a Guinness Record on simultaneous chess games. More than 13,000 games took place during the event.

vast wealth produced by Mexico's silver mines supported much of Spain's economy. By the early nineteenth century, Mexico began to tire of the one-way flow of wealth and other forms of colonial oppression. In September 1810, Mexico declared independence from Spain. The bitter War of Independence followed, with Mexico ultimately winning autonomy on September 27, 1821.

Population and Settlement

Mexico is the world's largest Spanish-speaking country and the eleventh most populous nation. Both its 1.2 percent annual rate of natural increase and 2.39 percent total fertility rate (TFR) suggest that the once explosive population growth has been checked. The population is relatively young; the median age is 25.6 years and 30 percent is under 15 years of age. Life expectancy of nearly 76 years and literacy exceeding 90 percent suggest a fairly high standard of living.

In recent decades, rural-to-urban migration has changed settlement patterns. Today, about half of all Mexicans live in the nation's 55 largest cities. Greater Mexico City, with over 19 million people, is one of the world's largest urban centers. Nine other cities have populations greater than one million. In recent decades, a second major migration flow has been south to north, particularly to cities near the USA–Mexico border. An estimated 12 to 20 million undocumented foreigners, half of whom are believed to be Mexicans, have crossed the border illegally into the USA.

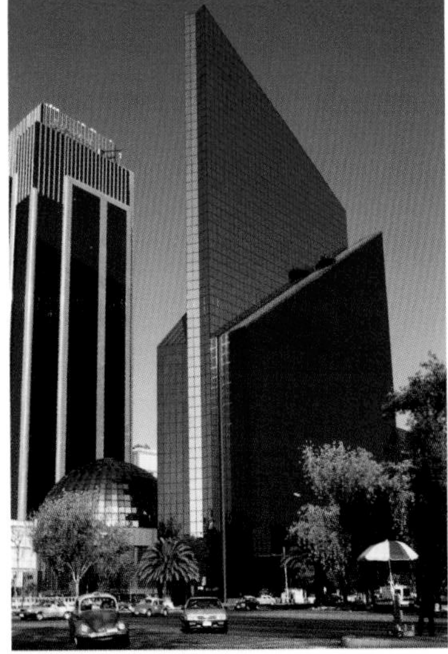

Culture

Mexican culture is a blend of Old World Spanish, New World Amerindian, and contemporary Western (mainly American) popular culture. Sixty percent of the population is mestizo (Amerindian–Spanish) and 30 percent is all or mainly Amerindian. Only 9 percent of the population is of European descent—mostly Spanish. Less than one percent of all Mexicans are of African, Asian, or other racial or ethnic origin.

Despite Mexico's Amerindian demographic dominance, its culture shows a strong Spanish imprint. Language, religion, customs, law, and many other traits are European in origin.

Roman Catholic clergy arrived with the Spanish conquerors. Catholicism continues to have a very powerful presence upon the cultural landscape and on the lives of many Mexicans. Seven percent of the population is Protestant. A small number of people continue to practice Amerindian religious traditions, although they often are incorporated into Catholic liturgy.

Mexican popular culture has spread beyond the borders of the country and Mexicans have also adopted many foreign popular culture traits. Mexican food, music, and art have gained widespread popularity. So too have rodeos, the guitar and country music, and beverages such as tequila. Domestically, bullfighting, fútbol (soccer), charreria (a type of rodeo), boxing, and baseball are very popular.

Administration/Government

Estados Unidos Mexicanos, or Mexico, is a federal republic governed under a constitution adopted in 1917. Mexico City is the capital. The country is divided into 31 states and one federal district. There are three branches of government. The executive branch is headed by a president, elected to a single six-year term, who is both the chief of state and the head of government. The bicameral legislative branch is divided into a 128-seat Senate and 500-seat Federal Chamber of Deputies. The judicial branch is represented at the federal level by the Supreme Court of Justice.

Economy/Industry

Mexico's economy ranks third in the Americas behind the USA and Brazil. Its free-market economy is increasingly dominated by the private sector, but the state continues to control power production and Petróleos Mexicanos (PEMEX). Seventy percent of the economy is generated by the service sector, although only 58 percent of the labor force is engaged in service industries. Conversely, 18 percent of the labor force works in agriculture, which produces 5 percent of the country's GDP.

Industries based on agriculture include those producing foodstuffs, tobacco products, and fabrics. Resource-based industries include mining, petroleum production, and chemicals. Motor vehicle production and the border maquiladora assembly plants are also important. Tourism is big business. With 20 million tourists annually, Mexico is the world's eighth most-visited country.

Above The Cardon cactus *(Pachycereus pringlei)* is the largest of the cactus species. The Catavina Desert, located in the heart of Baja California, has some of the most dramatic stands of Cardon.

Far left The futuristic headquarters of the Bolsa Mexicana de Valores, Mexico's only stock exchange, is located on the prestigious Paseo de la Reforma in central Mexico City.

Left Woman carrying an clay pot on her head, Chiapas, Mexico. About 25 percent of people in Chiapas have Mayan ancestry.

GUATEMALA

Official name Republic of Guatemala (República de Guatemala)
Land area 42,139 square miles (109,117 km²)
Border countries Mexico, Belize, Honduras, El Salvador
Capital Guatemala
Highest point Volcán Tajumulco 13,816 feet (4,211 m)
Climate Tropical
Population 12,728,000
Language(s) Spanish; Amerindian languages, including Quiché, Cakchiquel, Kekchi
Ethnicity Maya Indian 65%, Mestizo 35%
Religion Roman Catholic 60%, Protestant 25%, indigenous Mayan beliefs 15%
Government Constitutional democratic republic
Currency Quetzal
Human Development Index 0.689 (ranked 118th out of 177 countries)

MEXICO
BELIZE
Flores
GUATEMALA
Gulf of Honduras
Puerto Barrios
Huehuetenango
Cobán
Volcán Tajumulco
Salamá
Quetzaltenango
Sololá
Guastatoya
Zacapa
Chiquimula
Mazatenango
Champerico
GUATEMALA
Escuintla
Puerto San José
HONDURAS
EL SALVADOR
PACIFIC OCEAN

Guatemala

Map Reference Pages 134–135

Located in Central America, Guatemala is bordered by Mexico to the northwest, Belize and the Caribbean Sea to the northeast, Honduras and El Salvador to the southeast, and the North Pacific Ocean to the southwest. It has the largest population of Amerindians in the region. Guatemala's abundant biodiversity and unique ecosystems attract scientists and ecotourists from around the world.

Physical Geography

Guatemala's Altos Cuchumatanes and Sierra Madre are mountain ranges that dominate the lower two-thirds of the country. Much of Guatemala is forested. Its position on the Pacific Ring of Fire explains its almost daily seismic activity; it is home to 33 volcanoes.

The highest elevation communities are in Quezaltenango and Huehuetenango, facing the steep coast of the Pacific Ocean. The east coast faces the Caribbean Sea and has a tropical climate with high precipitation (200 to 300 inches/500–760 cm). Vegetation ranges from rainforests to tropical savannas. Subtropical regions under the influence of trade winds remain humid throughout the year. The country's altitudinal belts range from sea level, tierra caliente (hot land) to the alpine belt, tierra helada (freezing land).

History

Guatemala is located in the heartland of ancient Mayan culture (300–400 CE), although the first evidence of settlers reaches back to 10,000 BCE. Spain colonized Guatemala in the early sixteenth century, but after nearly three centuries of colonial rule, it became part of the Mexican Empire in 1821.

Military dictatorships dominated the Guatemalan political landscape after independence. Government repression and social inequities led to the 36-year Guatemalan Civil War (1960–1996), during which more than 250,000 people were killed, Mayan villages were razed to the ground, and about one million people became refugees. The integration of guerrilla groups back into civil society at the end of the war was a huge challenge. Many men began new lives as police in the Maya highlands.

The issue of land ownership for refugees was a big problem well into the 1990s. From 1981 to 1983 approximately 200,000 people crossed the border into Mexico seeking asylum and refugee status. Ultimately, one million people were forced to flee the country.

Population/Culture

Sixty-five percent of the Guatemalan population is Maya Indian, which is the highest ethnic percentage in Central American countries. The remaining 35 percent is of Mestizo (Amerindian–Spanish) background. The country's culture has its origins in the land's myriad biodiversity and unique landscapes. In ancient Maya civilization, the departemento of El Petén, or "country of eternal spring," was a region famous for scientific developments in architecture, mathematics, and astronomy.

La Ruta Maya is a rich cultural region that encompasses a zone from El Petén in the north of Guatemala, south to Copan in Honduras. It is a UNESCO World Heritage area. Twenty ruined cities of Mayan culture have been excavated in El Petén.

Mayan culture is still alive in festivals, clothing, and crafts. The highland culture of Guatemala's Amerindians stems from their agricultural lifestyle and the remoteness of their mountain farms and villages.

Administration/Government

Guatemala is a constitutional democratic republic. The president is both head of state and head of government. There are 22 departementos (similar to states). The unicameral Congress of the Republic has 158 members who are elected for a term of four years. The judiciary is independent from the president and congress.

Economy/Industry

Guatemala's relative political stability since the end of the civil war in 1996 has seen steady economic growth. The main economic sectors are services (51.8%), agriculture (22.8%), and industry (19.1%). Coffee, bananas, sugar, lumber, fisheries, and chicle (the raw material for chewing gum) are the chief exports. Other resources include oil, nickel, gold, and silver. More than half the population works in agriculture. Many of the nation's Amerindians are impoverished, earning their living on small plots of their own land, or as tenants on farms. Bartering is still common in the countryside. By contrast, ethnic people often live as street vendors in big cities as part of the money economy.

MILESTONE EVENTS

c. 10,000 BCE Earliest human settlement
c. 250–900 CE Classic period of Mayan culture
1523–1524 Maya-Quiché conquered by Spanish armies
1821 Independence from Spain; becomes part of the Mexican Empire
1823 Joins United Provinces of Central America (with Costa Rica, Honduras, Nicaragua, and El Salvador)
1839 Republic of Guatemala declared
1859 Treaty between Britain and Guatemala defines the boundaries of Belize
1959 Guatemala and Belize sign a border treaty
1960–1996 Guatemalan Civil War
February 4, 1976 Approximately 23,000 Guatemalans die when an earthquake hits
1992 Social activist Rigoberta Menchú Tum awarded Nobel Peace Prize
2004 DR–Central American Free Trade Agreement (DR–CAFTA) signed

WOMAN OF SUBSTANCE

The dark days of Guatemala's 36-year civil war not only witnessed terrible bloodshed, but also saw the emergence of the nation's women as a positive social and political force. Violence escalated in 1982 when Brigadier-General Rios Montt overthrew the president, General Fernando Romeo Lucas Garcia, in a military coup. Montt dissolved the parliament, annulled the constitution, and outlawed all political parties. Government repression was exercised through the use of torture, and many indigenous people were massacred, villages destroyed, and women and girls raped in numerous government-sanctioned raids. Rigoberta Menchú Tum, social activist and champion of Maya Indian rights, helped form the United Representation of the Guatemalan Opposition in order to expose and oppose the human rights violations committed by the military against the Mayan people. For this she was awarded the Nobel Prize for Peace in 1992. She subsequently became a candidate in the 2007 presidential elections, but was unsuccessful, receiving only three percent of the vote.

Above Close-up of a glyph on a Mayan pot from Burial Tomb 19 at Rio Azul, Guatemala. Vessels filled with cacao were decorated with such artwork and placed inside tombs, to provide nourishment for the deceased in the afterlife.

Right Christianity was introduced to the continent by the conquistadores and colonial powers, and the Catholic religion is still the dominant one in Guatemala. Symbols of the virgin and child have notable indigenous features.

Below A Guatemalan girl poses against a backdrop of patterned fabric. Although Guatemalan textile artists are among the world's finest, they live in extremely poor conditions.

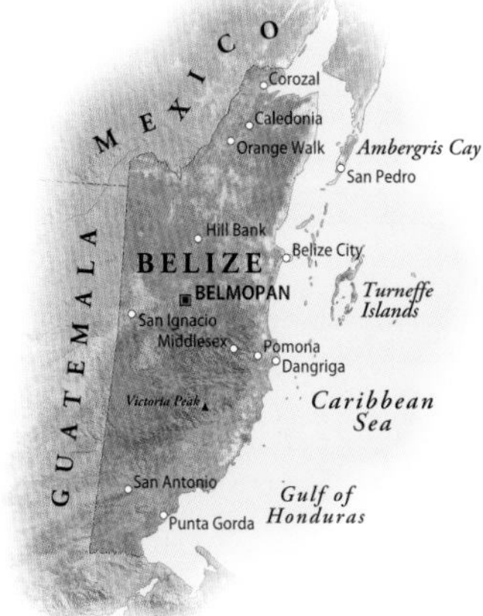
MEXICO
Corozal
Caledonia
Orange Walk
Ambergris Cay
San Pedro
Hill Bank
BELIZE
Belize City
BELMOPAN
San Ignacio
Middlesex
Turneffe Islands
Pomona
Dangriga
GUATEMALA
Victoria Peak
Caribbean Sea
San Antonio
Punta Gorda
Gulf of Honduras

Belize

Map Reference Pages 134–135

Belize, a small country on the southern part of the Yucatan Peninsula, is bordered by the Caribbean Sea and the Gulf of Honduras to the east, Guatemala to the west and south, and a corner of Mexico to the north.

Physical Geography

The north of Belize is mostly flat and low-lying; in the south the terrain is shaped by the low Maya Mountains. About 60 percent of the land is forested. Some 450 tiny islands and coral reefs form the 186-mile-long (300-km) Belize Barrier Reef, the world's second largest coral reef system. The climate is tropical, hot and humid, with hurricanes common from July to November.

History

The original inhabitants were Maya Indians. English privateers and settlers began to arrive in the seventeenth century, calling their de facto colony British Honduras. First logwood, then mahogany were exported, followed in the early twentieth century by sugar, bananas,

Left Inactive since 1966, Volcan Izalco is located on the southern flank of the Santa Ana volcano, in western El Salvador.

and other plantation crops. British Honduras became a Crown colony in 1871. Full independence came in 1981. Guatemala had long claimed the territory as its own and did not recognize Belize until 1991. Sometimes Guatemalan maps still show Belize as the twenty-third departemento of Guatemala.

Population/Culture

Belize is one of the least densely settled nations in the world. Belize City is the largest metropolis and former capital, with a population of approximately 71,000. Because of repeated hurricane damage, the capital was moved inland in 1970 to a new planned garden city named Belmopan. With a population of only 12,000, it is one of the smallest national capitals in the world.

Belize has a great variety of indigenous and immigrant cultures, languages, and ethnic and racial groups. The population is 48.7 percent Mestizo (mixed Amerindian and Spanish), 24.9 percent Belizean Kriol (mixed white and African ancestry), 10.6 percent Maya Indian, and 6.1 percent Garifuna (mixed Amerindian and African ancestries). Others include Asian–Belizeans (descendants from earlier labor migrations from India, China, and Korea), Latin Americans, and Caucasians. The official language of Belize is English.

Administration/Government

Belize is a parliamentary democracy. The head of state is Queen Elizabeth II, who is represented by a governor general. The legislative branch is a bicameral National Assembly made up of a Senate and a House of Representatives. The judicial branch is headed by a chief justice, appointed by the governor general on the prime minister's advice.

Economy/Industry

Belize is a poor country, with about one-third of its population living in poverty. The major employers are agri-business producers of sugar and bananas for export, and a growing citrus industry. There are also apparel manufacturing plants in Belize City and growing foreign investment in exploiting petroleum deposits in western Belize. Tourism promotion is a key part of Belize's economic development strategy.

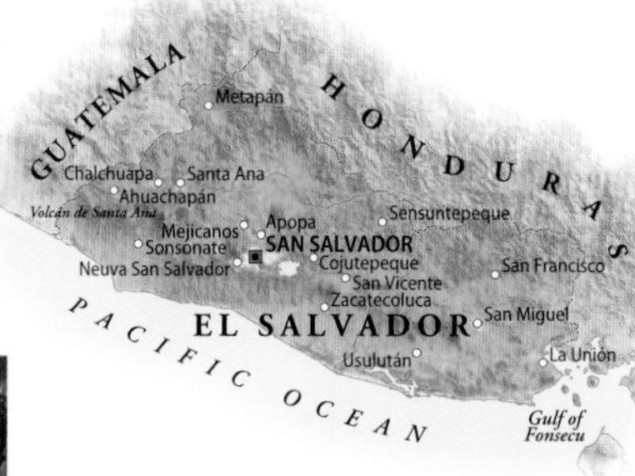
GUATEMALA
HONDURAS
Metapán
Chalchuapa
Santa Ana
Ahuachapán
Volcán de Santa Ana
Mejicanos
Sonsonate
Apopa
SAN SALVADOR
Sensuntepeque
Neuva San Salvador
Cojutepeque
San Vicente
Zacatecoluca
San Francisco
San Miguel
EL SALVADOR
Usulután
La Unión
PACIFIC OCEAN
Gulf of Fonsecu

El Salvador

Map Reference Pages 134–135

El Salvador is bordered by the North Pacific Ocean to the southwest, Guatemala to the northwest, and Honduras to the northeast. It is the only Central American country without a coastline on the Caribbean Sea.

Physical Geography

El Salvador's mountainous terrain dissects the country into three distinct regions: A coastal belt with average temperatures of 77–84°F (25–29°C); a central valley and plateau region with an average temperature of 73°F (23°C); and the colder northern mountains, averaging temperatures of 54–73°F (12–23°C). Part of the Pacific Ring of Fire, it is susceptible to earthquakes and has several active volcanoes.

History

The Pipil Indians were the first major inhabitants. In 1522, Spanish explorers became the first Europeans to set foot there. The country started its struggle for independence in 1811, which was eventually declared in 1821.

As with many Latin American countries, El Salvador experienced a turbulent period after independence. Some stability was achieved in the early twentieth century but after a period of democratic deterioration, civil war broke out in 1980 and lasted for 12 years.

Population/Culture

Ninety percent of Salvadorans are Mestizo (of mixed Amerindian and Spanish descent). Population density is high—approximately 6.9 million people inhabit the small land area (8,124 square miles/21,040 km^2). Almost all people speak Spanish, which includes a smattering of Pipil Indian words.

About 57 percent of Salvadorans are Catholic; about 21 percent of the remaining population attend a Protestant church, while 17 percent are non-affiliated. Many indigenous people renounced their heritage during La Matanza, the peasant uprising of the 1930s, and indigenous beliefs do not play a large part in Salvadoran life.

Corn, beans, and rice are staples of the local diet. Corn is most commonly served as a tortilla with every meal. Coffee and sugared fruit juices are the main drinks.

Administration/Government

El Salvador is a democratic republic governed by a president and an 84-member unicameral Legislative Assembly. The president—who is both head of state and head of government—is directly elected by popular vote, and serves a five-year term. Legislators are also elected directly through popular vote and serve a three-year term. The independent judicial branch is the Supreme Court. It is divided into four chambers—constitutional, civil, penal, and administrative.

Economy/Industry

For many years El Salvador's economy relied on coffee, its major export. Since the end of the civil war the economy has diversified and is now mostly dependent on services and industry. The services sector is the largest employer. El Salvador no longer has its own currency but uses the US dollar. The economy also relies on remittances from emigrants.

BELIZE

Official name Belize
Land area 8,867 square miles (22,966 km^2)
Border countries Mexico, Guatemala
Capital Belmopan
Highest point 3,806 feet (1,160 m)
Climate Tropical
Population 294,385
Language(s) Spanish, Creole (Kriol), Mayan dialects, English (official), Garifuna (Carib), German, other
Ethnicity Mestizo 48.7%, Creole (Kriol) 24.9%, Maya Indian 10.6%, Garifuna 6.1%, other 9.7%
Religion Roman Catholic 49.6%, Protestant 27%, other 14%, none 9.4%
Government Parliamentary democracy
Currency Belize dollar
Human Development Index 0.778 (ranked 80th out of 177 countries)

EL SALVADOR

Official name Republic of El Salvador (República de El Salvador)
Land area 8,124 square miles (21,040 km^2)
Border countries Guatemala, Honduras
Capital San Salvador
Highest point Cerro El Pital 8,957 feet (2,730 m)
Climate Tropical
Population 6,948,073
Language(s) Spanish, Nahua (among some Amerindians)
Ethnicity Mestizo 90%, European 9%, Amerindian 1%
Religion Roman Catholic 57%, Protestant 21%, non-affiliated 17%, other 5%
Government Presidential democracy
Currency Salvadoran colón; US dollar
Human Development Index 0.735 (ranked 103rd out of 177 countries)

Left A worker employed by a Malaysian company cuts a rainforest tree in Belize. Asian logging companies threaten one of the world's last standing rainforests.

Below Green coffee berries are spread out to dry on clay patios at El Beneficio de la Majada, El Salvador.

HONDURAS

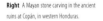

Official name Republic of Honduras (República de Honduras)
Land area 43,201 square miles (111,890 km²)
Border countries Guatemala, El Salvador, Nicaragua
Capital Tegucigalpa
Highest point Cerro Las Minas 9,416 feet (2,870 m)
Climate Subtropical by the coast, temperate inland
Population 7,639,000
Language(s) Official: Spanish; Amerindian dialects
Ethnicity Mestizo 90%, Amerindian 7%, African 2%, European 1%
Religion Roman Catholic 97%, Protestant 3%
Government Democratic constitutional republic
Currency Lempira
Human Development Index 0.700 (ranked 115th out of 177 countries)

Right A Mayan stone carving in the ancient ruins at Copán, in western Honduras.

Far right From an aerial view, the Wawu River makes numerous twists and turns as it cuts through the lush rainforest of Nicaragua.

NICARAGUA

Official name Republic of Nicaragua (República de Nicaragua)
Land area 46,430 square miles (120,254 km²)
Border countries Honduras, Costa Rica
Capital Managua
Highest point Pico Mogotón 7,999 feet (2,438 m)
Climate Tropical
Population 5,786,000
Language(s) Official: Spanish; Miskito, Creole English, Sumo–Mayanga, Rama, Garífuna
Ethnicity Mestizo (mixed European–Amerindian) 69%, European 17%, Afro-Nicaraguan–African 9%, indigenous (Miskitos, Ramas, and Mayangas) 5%
Religion Roman Catholic 75%, Evangelical Protestant 25%
Government Presidential democracy
Currency Gold córdoba
Human Development Index 0.710 (ranked 110th out of 177 countries)

Islas Santanilla
Islas de la Bahía
Gulf of Honduras
Roatán
Caribbean Sea
Trujillo
La Ceiba
San Pedro Sula
Yoro
Santa Bárbara
HONDURAS
Puerto Lempira
GUATEMALA
Santa Rosa de Copán
Juticalpa
Cerro Las Minas
Comayagua
Nueva Ocotepeque
La Paz
TEGUCIGALPA
EL SALVADOR
Yuscarán
Nacaome
Choluteca
Gulf of Fonseca
NICARAGUA

Honduras

Map Reference Pages 134–135

Honduras is bordered by the Caribbean Sea, between Guatemala and Nicaragua, and the Gulf of Fonseca, between El Salvador and Nicaragua. It has a tropical climate in the coastal areas and a temperate climate in the inland mountains. Honduras is also home to the Rio Platano Biosphere Reserve, set up to preserve Central American tropical rainforests.

The Maya and the Lenca were the first inhabitants of Honduras. Spain ruled Honduras for about three centuries until it granted independence in 1821. In 1823, Honduras joined the newly formed United Provinces of Central America, which collapsed in 1838. From the mid-1900s until the 1980s the country was ruled by military generals but returned to civilian rule peacefully. Honduras hosted the US military in the 1980s to help train Contra fighters for Nicaragua and El Salvador. The country was spared most of the turbulence experienced by its neighbors.

The population is primarily mestizo, but it also includes people of Amerindian and African descent. Lenca, Garífuna, and Miskito cultures are prominent in Honduran society. The Lenca inhabited the area before Spanish colonization, the Garífuna are a blend of African and Amerindian people, and the Miskito are an indigenous tribe that intermingled with runaway slaves.

Most Hondurans speak Spanish, although there is a sizable population of Garífuna and Miskito speakers. Other languages exist, but are spoken by only a few thousand people. Most Hondurans are Catholic. Like many Central American nations, Honduran cuisine is based on corn tortillas, beans, and rice.

Honduras is a democratic constitutional republic. The executive is a president who is both head of government and chief of state and is elected for four years. The legislative branch is unicameral. The representatives are elected for four years through proportional representation. The Supreme Court justices are elected for seven years by the National Congress.

Having relied on bananas as its major export for many years, the Honduran economy has diversified and now has a growing textile industry. Yet Honduras remains one of the ten poorest countries in the Western hemisphere, with many people relying on subsistence farming and remittances from the USA.

HONDURAS
Pico Mogotón
Ocotal
Somoto
Siuna
Puerto Cabezas
Estelí
Jinotega
Matagalpa
La Cruz de Río Grande
Chinandega
NICARAGUA
León
Boaco
MANAGUA
Masaya
Juigalpa
Jinotepe
Granada
Bluefields
Rivas
San Carlos
PACIFIC OCEAN
Caribbean Sea
COSTA RICA

Nicaragua

Map Reference Pages 134–135

Nicaragua is the largest country in Central America. It has three distinct geographical areas: The lowland plains of the Pacific; the cooler central northern highlands; and the Atlantic region, where the majority of the rainforests are found. Because of its geographical location, and its position on the Pacific Ring of Fire, Nicaragua experiences not only hurricanes, droughts, and floods, but also volcanic eruptions and earthquakes.

Nicaragua has two distinct cultural regions: The Pacific region, which is made up largely of Spanish-speaking mestizos; and the Atlantic region, which is home to Nicaragua's indigenous peoples (the Miskitos, the Mayangas, and the Ramas), as well as to a large English-speaking Afro-Caribbean population.

Nicaragua gained its independence from Spain in 1821, and by the end of the century had incorporated the Atlantic region into the nation. The early twentieth century was marked by US intervention, guerrilla warfare led by Augusto César Sandino, and the establishment of the Somoza dictatorship. After almost two decades of struggle, the Sandinista Front for National Liberation (FSLN) overthrew the dictatorship in 1979 and embarked on a project of revolutionary transformation.

Early achievements in areas such as literacy, health, and agrarian reform were curtailed by the US-backed counter-revolutionary forces known as the Contras. The Contra War caused widespread ruin. It ended after the 1990 elections when the FSLN was defeated. Since 1990, Nicaragua has experienced moderate economic growth along with political corruption and high levels of poverty.

Nicaragua is a presidential representative democracy governed by the 1987 Constitution. It is administratively divided into 15 departments and two autonomous regions. Nicaragua has four branches of government: The executive, the legislative, the judicial, and the electoral.

Famous for its revolutionary heritage, its literature, poetry (including world-renowned poet Rubén Darío) art, and music, Nicaragua celebrates many folkloric and religious festivals.

Since colonial times, the economy has been dominated by commodity trade. Coffee is the most important export, with beef, gold, sugar, bananas, seafood, and sesame also contributing. Most small farmers grow basic grains such as corn and rice, as well as beans for domestic consumption, while many urban Nicaraguans work in assembly factories (maquilas) in the country's free-trade zones. Nicaragua has a small but growing tourist industry.

Above Found throughout Central America, the jaguar is a protected species in Honduras.

Right Founded in 1529, Convento y Iglesia de San Francisco, Granada, Nicaragua, is now a museum.

NICARAGUA
La Cruz
Upala
Liberia
Colorado
Puerto Viejo
Caribbean Sea
Nicoya
COSTA RICA
Puntarenas
Alajuela
Heredia
Puerto Limón
SAN JOSÉ
Cartago
Cerro Chirripó
Puerto Quepos
San Isidro
PACIFIC OCEAN
Palmar Sur
Golfito
PANAMA

Costa Rica

Map Reference Pages 134–135

Costa Rica is the smallest country in Central America in terms of population, but is also the most affluent. Costa Ricans generally tend to be healthier and better educated than their neighbors.

The Caribbean and Pacific coastal plains are separated from north to south by a volcanic mountain chain. Costa Rica's climate is tropical and subtropical. The rainy season runs from May to November and the dry season from November to April.

Considered a world leader in environmental protection, Costa Rica has the greatest biodiversity in the world. Many areas are under protection, although problems such as deforestation and soil erosion persist.

Costa Rica's indigenous populations were decimated after colonization by Spain in the sixteenth century. It gained independence in 1821. Following the 1948 civil war, Costa Rica abolished the army and established democratic government, managing to escape the military rule, human rights abuses, and guerrilla warfare that afflicted most of its neighbors. This stability facilitated extensive public sector investment in social services, telecommunications, and banking. In 2007, widespread social opposition to the Central American Free Trade Agreement (CAFTA) with the USA led to the calling of a referendum, in which CAFTA triumphed with a very narrow margin.

Traditional export crops are coffee, sugar, bananas, and pineapples, but recently the export economy has diversified into electronic components, pharmaceuticals, medical equipment, and textiles. Corn, rice, and beans are grown for domestic use. Ecotourism is the most important industry. Many Nicaraguan immigrants work as seasonal labor in agriculture or as domestic servants.

Costa Rica is a representative democracy governed by its 1949 Constitution. It has three branches of government—executive, legislative, and judicial—and elections are held every four years. The country is administratively divided into seven provinces.

Costa Rica has varied local cultures, with significant differences between the mestizos who live in the Guanacaste region, the Afro-Caribbean population, descended from Jamaican slaves, who live in the Caribbean province of Limón, and the small indigenous populations. The country's most popular sport is football, and the national team often participates in the World Cup.

PASSING SHIPS

Since the early sixteenth century, visionaries dreamed of a canal that would allow ships to pass between the Atlantic and Pacific oceans. In 1880, the French began construction of a sea-level canal. Their effort ended in costly failure and the deaths of some 22,000 workers.

In 1903, Panama became independent from Colombia and gave the USA permission to build a canal. Work began in 1904 and the project—one of history's greatest and most difficult engineering feats—was completed in 1914. Ships no longer had to make the long, costly, and often treacherous journey around the southern tip of South America. Sailing distance between the US east and west coasts was reduced by about 8,000 miles (12,875 km).

More than 14,000 vessels pass through the canal annually. They are lifted 85 feet (26 m) above sea level by three sets of locks as they pass through the 48-mile (77 km) canal. Water for the locks is provided by 17 reservoirs. The fresh water also serves as a natural filter that blocks passage of marine organisms between oceans. Since the 1960s, many ships have been too large to pass through the canal. In 2007, work began to increase its size to accommodate even the largest of vessels.

COSTA RICA
Changuinola
Bocas del Toro
Caribbean Sea
Colón
El Porvenir
PANAMÁ
San Miguelito
La Chorrera
Volcán Barú
La Concepción
PANAMA
David
Aguadulce
Penonomé
Isla del Rey
La Palma
Santiago
Chitré
Golfo de Panamá
Isla de Coiba
Las Tablas
PACIFIC OCEAN
COLOMBIA

Panama

Map Reference Pages 134–135

The Republic of Panama occupies a narrow isthmus located between Costa Rica in Central America and Colombia at the northwestern tip of South America. Panama's small size and population of about 3.2 million belies the country's global importance as one of the world's most strategic crossroads.

At its narrowest point, the Isthmus of Panama (also Isthmus of Darién) separates the Caribbean Sea (Atlantic Ocean) and Pacific Ocean by only 38 miles (60 km). Mountains and hills dominate the terrain, with only about 7 percent being lowland plains suitable for mechanized agriculture. Nearly 2,000 islands dot the waters adjacent to the mainland. Panama has a hot, muggy, maritime tropical climate. About 50 percent of the country is covered by tropical rainforest. The dense forests, swamps, and marshes of eastern Panama's Darién Gap have contributed to the only land break in the Pan-American Highway.

The Spanish claimed Panama in 1502, but it was not until 1513 that the land's potential importance was realized when Vasco Nuñez de Balboa crossed the isthmus and discovered the Pacific Ocean. As Spain increased its grip on Latin America, Panama's importance as a crossroads between oceans and colonies grew.

Panama gained independence in 1821, but its destiny has long been controlled by outside forces because of its strategic importance—its isthmian position between oceans. In 1999, Panama gained control of the Panama Canal.

Panamanian culture offers a rich mix of Amerindian, Spanish, African, and other traits. Before the arrival of Europeans, Panama was settled by the Chocoan, Chibchan, and Cueva tribes. Language and religion strongly reflect its early Spanish influences. Panama now has an extensive international community that helped make the Canal Zone one of the most cosmopolitan areas in Latin America.

Panama is a presidential representative democratic republic. The president is both chief of state and head of government. The elected government exercises executive power, the unicameral National Assembly and government wields legislative power, and the judiciary is independent.

Panama's economy has long been tied to the canal. Today, the service sector, which includes the canal, contributes 80 percent of GDP. Tourism, banking, the Colón Free Trade Zone, and ship registry are service-based industries. About one-third of Panama's population lives in the capital, Panama City.

COSTA RICA

Official name Republic of Costa Rica (República de Costa Rica)
Land area 19,560 square miles (50,660 km²)
Border countries Nicaragua, Panama
Capital San José
Highest point Cerro Chirripó 12,500 feet (3,810 m)
Climate Tropical and subtropical
Population 4,196,000
Language(s) Official: Spanish; English, Limón Creole, Bribri, Cabécar, Maléku Jaíka, Plautdeutsch, Boruca, Teribe
Ethnicity European and Mestizo 94%, Afro-Caribbean 3%, indigenous 1%, Chinese 1%, other 1%
Religion Roman Catholic 75%, Evangelical Protestant 15%, other 3%, none 7%
Government Presidential democracy
Currency Costa Rican colón
Human Development Index 0.846 (ranked 48th out of 177 countries)

Above The keel-billed toucan *(Ramphastos sulfuratus)*—found throughout Central America and northern South America—is a rainforest-canopy dweller.

PANAMA

Official name Republic of Panama (República de Panamá)
Land area 29,340 square miles (75,990 km²)
Border countries Colombia, Costa Rica
Capital Panama City (Panamá)
Highest point Volcán Barú 11,400 feet (3,475 m)
Climate Tropical maritime
Population 3,293,000
Language(s) Official: Spanish; other: English
Ethnicity Mestizo (mixed Amerindian–European) 70%, European 10%, African and other 20%
Religion Roman Catholic 85%, Protestant 15%
Government Constitutional democracy
Currency Balboa; US dollar
Human Development Index 0.812 (ranked 62nd out of 177 countries)

Far left Rainforest waterfall, Costa Rica. The country's incredible biodiversity has made it a leading ecotourism destination.

Left Guaymi Indian woman harvesting coffee, Boquete, Panama. The best Panama coffee comes from this region.

CUBA

Official name Republic of Cuba (República de Cuba)
Land area 42,803 square miles (110,860 km²)
Capital Havana (La Habana)
Highest point Pico Turquino 6,578 feet (2,005 m)
Climate Subtropical
Population 11,424,000
Language(s) Official: Spanish; other: English, Russian, and Haitian Creole
Ethnicity Mulatto 51%, European 37%, African 11%, Chinese 1%
Religion Roman Catholic, Protestant, Santería, and Jewish
Government Communist
Currency Cuban peso (for Cubans only); Convertible peso
Human Development Index 0.838 (ranked 51st out of 177 countries)

Top right Once the seat of government in Cuba, the Capitolio Nacional in Havana, shown behind a busy street, is now the home of the Cuban Academy of Sciences.

Above Horseman riding past a vintage pink Chevrolet in Trinidad de Cuba, Cuba. Once the hub of the sugar boom, Trinidad de Cuba is now a major tourist center.

Right A Havana woman holds out a large cigar. Cuban cigars are world famous for their quality.

Below Limestone cliffs called "mogotes" tower above tobacco farms in the lush valley of Viñales.

Gulf of Mexico
LA HABANA (HAVANA)
Matanzas
Archipiélago de Sabana
BAHAMAS
Archipiélago de Camagüey
Pinar del Río
Santa Clara
Cienfuegos
Neuva Gerona
Sancti Spíritus
Ciego de Avila
Camagüey
Isla de la Juventud
CUBA
La Tunas
Holguín
Caribbean Sea
Archipiélago de los Jardines de la Reina
Pico Turquino
Bayamo
Guantanamo
Santiago de Cuba
UNITED STATES OF AMERICA

Cuba

Map Reference Pages 134–135

The nation of Cuba is an archipelago of islands in the Caribbean Sea; Cuba is the principal island. Situated about 90 miles (145 km) south of Key West, and 50 miles (80 km) west of Haiti through the Wayward Passage, Cuba is the largest island in area and the second largest in population in the Greater Antilles, which includes Haiti/Dominican Republic, Jamaica, and Puerto Rico.

Physical Geography

Cuba is a long narrow island, about 766 miles (1,233 km) from the westernmost tip to the eastern tip. About half of its 42,803 square miles (110,860 km²) is rolling plains, punctuated by four major mountain ranges: In the west, the Guaniguanico Mountains; in the central region, the Guamuhaya Mountains; and in the east, the Sagua-Baracoa and the Sierra Maestra ranges, the latter home to the country's highest peak, Pico Turquino (6,578 feet/2,005 m). Cuba's landscape ranges from semi-deserts to tropical rainforests, and contains well-preserved ecosystems and a large biodiversity.

The Cuban climate is classified as mild subtropical. Most rainfall occurs during the rainy season, which is May to October.

History

The first humans arrived in Cuba in about 3500 BCE. By around 1250 CE, the Arawak-speaking Taíno Indians, believed to be from South America, settled on the islands. Columbus came ashore on October 14, 1492, presuming he had landed on the Asian mainland. He subsequently claimed the islands for Spain on October 29. Gold was the primary objective for the Spanish in the New World colonies, and when Cuba's gold reserves proved less than prodigious, most settlers turned to growing sugar and tobacco in order to make their fortunes. The native population was decimated by war and disease after European contact, and the Spanish imported thousands of slaves from Africa.

Cuba gained independence from Spain in 1898 with the help and intervention of the USA during their involvement in the Spanish–American War. The Treaty of Paris established full Cuban independence, which was granted in 1902 after a three-year transition period. However, the USA retained the right to intervene in Cuban affairs and to supervise its foreign relations and financial affairs. An addition to the Platt Amendment meant Cuba also agreed to lease the naval base at Guantánamo Bay to the USA. Fidel Castro and his many supporters attacked the Moncada Barracks in protest over suspended elections. Castro was eventually exiled to Mexico where the 26th of July Movement was born. It overthrew the Fulgencio Batista government on January 1, 1959.

The USA broke off diplomatic relations in January 1961 and imposed an embargo on the nation in February 1962. From this point onward, Cuba's alliance with the Soviet Union became stronger. With the Soviet Union's dissolution in 1991, many thought the collapse of the Cuban system was imminent. In the early 1990s, with its extended economic crisis, Cuba entered the "Special Period in a Time of Peace." This was a testing time for Cuba, but one it survived by expanding tourism and joint ventures.

Population/Culture

The majority of Cubans are of African and Spanish origin. Most people fall into the category of mulatto (an African–European mix), with the remainder being of European background. There is a small percentage of African and Chinese people. Of the 11,424,000 people who live in Cuba, more than three-quarters live in urban areas. Spanish is the main language, but English and Russian are also widely spoken, although the popularity of Russian is declining.

Practice of religion was not encouraged for several decades after the Revolution, and active religious involvement precluded membership in the Communist Party. In 1991, however, Cuba lifted this prohibition and in 1992 the constitution was amended to make Cuba a secular state. Several religions are practiced.

Administration/Government

Cuba is a socialist republic. The highest executive and administrative body is the Council of Ministers. The leader of the Council is the president, who is both chief of state and head of government. The only political party is the Communist Party of Cuba.

Economy/Industry

Sugar has long been Cuba's major export, but tourism is now the leading industry. During the Special Period, Cuba introduced some liberalization policies to the economy, including joint ventures and special economic zones.

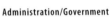

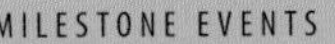

MILESTONE EVENTS

c. 3500 BCE First humans arrive in Cuba

c. 1250 CE Taíno Indians arrive

October 1492 Christopher Columbus claims Cuba as Spanish territory

1762–1763 British capture Havana

1868–1878 First War of Independence

1902 Cuba swears in its first independent president, Tomas Estrada Palma

1953 Revolutionary Fidel Castro fails at overthrowing Batista and is exiled to Mexico

1959 Castro leads guerrilla army of 9,000 into Havana, forcing Batista to leave Cuba; Castro becomes prime minister

1962 Cuban missile crisis occurs when Castro allows the USSR to deploy nuclear missiles in Cuba

1976 The communist party approves a new socialist constitution and Fidel Castro is elected president

1993 The USA continues its embargo; Cuba enters the Special Period in the Time of Peace

2008 Raul Castro officially takes power as president of the Council of State and Council of Ministers after elections

CHILDREN OF OLIFI

Santería is a religion widely practiced in Cuba. It is a syncretic religion, blending the traditions of the Yoruba people of West Africa and the Catholic traditions of the Spanish. The Yoruba were brought to Cuba as slaves and forced to convert to Catholicism. The slaves disguised the continued practice of their traditional religion (called Lucumi or La Regla de Ocha in Spanish) from slave owners by incorporating the veneration of Catholic saints into their rituals. For example, when praying to St Barbara, most Santeros were actually praying to Chango, one of the orishas.

Santería has one god only (Olifi), but because he is so vast and beyond human grasp, orishas act as intermediaries to communicate with the deity. Orishas are the embodiment of all aspects of nature and human characteristics, for example, Yemaya represents seas and motherhood; Chango is associated with virility, strength, and sexuality; Oggun deals with iron, metals, and war; and Babaluaye with disease and sickness.

Santeros speak to orishas in two ways: Ita and physical possession. Ita is the act of throwing 16 cowry stones and using them to interpret what an orisha is saying. Physical possession can also occur during this ritual. The orisha "mounts" the person and this person then becomes the orisha. This is particularly important during a drumming ceremony because it signifies that the Santeros' prayers have reached their god. Although drumming ceremonies are a form of community worship, Santería is a very personal religion. It focuses on an individual's communication with the orishas. Sacrifice plays an important role. Simple things such as candles or flowers are commonly used, but in extreme cases, sacrificial animals are offered.

All newborns are accompanied by an orisha. It is important to find out your orisha at the time of initiation into the religion in order to have a harmonious life. Highly trained priests perform a ceremony that discovers a person's orisha. The initiate has no say in selecting their orisha. The relationship is revealed through consulting oracles, the characteristics peculiar to the "children" of a particular orisha, and through the direct intervention of the orisha. When a person is initiated, they become a member of their godparents' Ilé or house. This makes the person a member of an extended family known as the Godfamily. Whichever orisha adopts the person determines the membership of the Godfamily.

Montego Bay
Falmouth
St Ann's Bay
Lucea
Ocho Rios
Port Maria
JAMAICA
Frankfield
Ewarton
Port Antonio
Mandeville
Spanish Town
Blue Mountain Peak
Black River
May Pen
Portmore
KINGSTON
Morant Bay
Jamaica Channel
Caribbean Sea

Jamaica

Map Reference Pages 134–135

Located 90 miles (144 km) south of eastern Cuba, Jamaica is the third largest island of the Greater Antilles, and has the largest English-speaking population of any island in the Caribbean. It is an exotic tropical vacation paradise, a place with a fascinating history (especially in relation to piracy), and a player in the international illegal drug trade.

Physical Geography

Jamaica's physical landscape is composed largely of a limestone plateau that averages 3,000 feet (1,800 m) in elevation. The coastal plain is narrow and discontinuous.

Jamaica has the highest concentration of caves per square mile of any place on Earth. Two-thirds of the island consists of a labyrinth of limestone caves that overlie vast deposits of older rocks. More than 1,200 caves, passageways, and sinkholes have so far been cataloged. Major parts of the interior terrain present classic karst topography (a landform produced by the dissolving of limestone), with sinks as the main surface features. Large-scale solution basins or valleys have also been formed. The karstification of white and yellow limestone groups in the island's northwestern region—known as Cockpit Country—began 12 million years ago with the erosion of a faulted limestone plateau. The region is dominated by "conekarst," where domed hills enclose closed lobed depressions—known as dolines—that drain to nearby aquifers via sinkholes.

Jamaica's climate is tropical, with temperate conditions found in the interior regions. Rainfall is most abundant on the northeastern side of the island. Jamaica is centrally located on the southern hurricane tracks taken by western Atlantic Ocean tropical storms.

Above A clifftop café at sunset, in Negril, Jamaica. Negril's Seven Mile Beach is considered one of the best in the world.

History

The Arawak (or possibly their seafaring relatives the Taínos Indians from South America) settled on the island of Jamaica between 4000 and 1000 BCE. Christopher Columbus encountered Jamaica on his second voyage to the West Indies in 1494, claiming the country for Spain. The Spanish gradually colonized during the sixteenth century. The native Taínos were exterminated over time, and were replaced by African slaves. Because of the relatively few Spaniards occupying the island on a permanent basis, an English army conquered Jamaica in 1655 with little resistance.

A plantation economy developed, based on sugar, cocoa, and coffee. With the abolition of slavery in 1834, many freed slaves became small farmers. Jamaica achieved full independence from the United Kingdom in 1962.

Population/Culture

Jamaica's population is predominantly of African origins (91.2 percent). Population growth rate is less than one percent per annum. Many Jamaicans have emigrated to countries such as the USA, Canada, and the UK in search of work or other opportunities, and they provide substantial remittances to family members living at home.

A significant part of the Jamaican subculture (and the agricultural sector as well) is the cultivation of illegal marijuana/cannabis (ganja). Producers generate incomes that far exceed the legal incomes of other farmers and also avoid being taxed in the process. Because of the clandestine nature of the marijuana business, most of the crop is grown in the island's interior, especially in the Cockpit Country. Ganja is consumed both internally and exported from Jamaica, principally to the USA. In recent times, Jamaicans have also been caught up in other aspects of the international illegal drug trade; the country is a transshipment point for cocaine from South America to North America and Europe. Government corruption has become a major concern and substantial money-laundering activity takes place, a situation that is favored by the Colombian narcotics traffickers.

MILESTONE EVENTS

c. 4,000–1000 BCE First inhabitants arrive (Arawaks/Taínos)

1494 Christopher Columbus claims Jamaica for Spain on his second voyage to the West Indies

1655 English seize control of Jamaica from Spain

1670 Jamaica officially ceded to England in Treaty of Madrid

1760 The most serious slave revolt, Tacky's Rebellion, begins

1834 Abolition of slavery

1907 Earthquake destroys the capital, Kingston

1958 Federation of the West Indies

1962 Jamaica gains independence from United Kingdom

Administration/Government

Jamaica's government is a constitutional parliamentary democracy with a bicameral parliament consisting of a 21-member Senate and a 60-seat House of Representatives, who serve five-year terms.

Economy/Industry

Jamaica's service sector accounts for more than 60 percent of GDP. Foreign exchange is obtained mostly from tourism, remittances, and bauxite/alumina. Jamaica was the world's leading producer of bauxite (an ore of aluminum) between 1957 and 1971, and remains a major producer with significant reserves. Other important industries include light manufacturing, agricultural processing, rum, cement, metals, paper, chemical products, and telecommunications.

Tourism is important to the economy, and the island is promoted as a tropical vacation destination. Many rural and resort areas are considered to be relatively safe and many tourists from North America and the United Kingdom visit beach resorts such as Montego Bay and Ocho Rios.

JAMAICA 

Official name Jamaica

Land area 4,182 square miles (10,831 km²)

Capital Kingston

Highest point Blue Mountain Peak 7,402 feet (2,256 m)

Climate Tropical, hot and humid; temperate interior

Population 2,804,000

Language(s) English, English patois

Ethnicity African descent 91.2%, mixed 6.2%, other or unknown 2.6%

Religion Protestant 62.5%, Roman Catholic 2.6%, other or unspecified 14.2%, none 20.7%

Government Constitutional parliamentary democracy

Currency Jamaican dollar

Human Development Index 0.735 (ranked 101st out of 177 countries)

Above The hulk of an old boat lies wrecked on a white-sand beach at Negril, Jamaica.

Left A shanty town sprawls up a hillside on the outskirts of Montego Bay. Until the mid-twentieth century, Montego Bay served as a major sugar port.

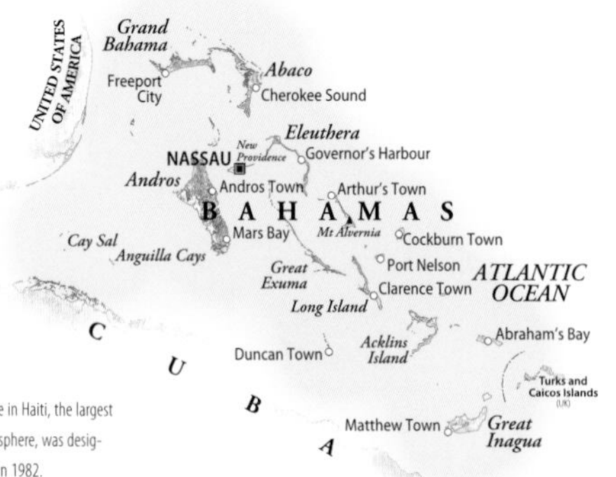
Grand Bahama
UNITED STATES OF AMERICA
Freeport City
Abaco
Cherokee Sound
Eleuthera
New Providence
NASSAU
Governor's Harbour
Andros
Andros Town
Arthur's Town
BAHAMAS
Mars Bay
Mt Alvernia
Cockburn Town
Cay Sal
Anguilla Cays
Great Exuma
Port Nelson
ATLANTIC OCEAN
Clarence Town
Long Island
Acklins Island
Abraham's Bay
Duncan Town
Turks and Caicos Islands
Matthew Town
Great Inagua
CUBA

Right La Citadelle Laferrière in Haiti, the largest fortress in the Western hemisphere, was designated a World Heritage Site in 1982.

BAHAMAS

Official name Commonwealth of The Bahamas
Land area 3,888 square miles (10,070 km²)
Border countries None
Capital Nassau
Highest point Mt Alvernia (Cat Island) 207 feet (63 m)
Climate Tropical marine, moderated by warm waters of Gulf Stream
Population 307,451
Language(s) English, Creole
Ethnicity African descent 85%, European 12%, Asian/Hispanic 3%
Religion Christian 96.3%, none or unspecified 2.9%, other 0.8%
Government Constitutional parliamentary democracy
Currency Bahamian dollar
Human Development Index 0.845 (ranked 49th out of 177 countries)

Right A Caribbean reef shark swims over a coral reef in the Bahama Islands. The warm waters and abundance of marine life make the Bahamas a haven for divers.

Below View of Elbow Cay from the top of the lighthouse at the historic village of Hope Town, Bahamas.

Bahamas

Map Reference Pages 134–135

The Bahamas includes some 700 islands and 2,000 small cays located in the North Atlantic Ocean. The Bahamian archipelago is scattered over a distance of some 500 miles (805 km), extending from Grand Bahama in the northwest, southeastward to Great Inagua, located just north of Haiti. Bimini, a group of islands lying approximately 50 miles (80 km) off Florida's southeast coast, claims the title Gateway to the Bahamas. Andros is the largest island of the group, and New Providence—on which the capital and largest city, Nassau—is located, is the most populous with about 70 percent of the country's inhabitants. Only 23 of the islands are inhabited.

Physical Geography

Three banks, or coral-formed limestone platforms that rise above sea level, form the islands and cays of the Bahamas. They are relatively flat and average only 10 feet (3 m) in elevation; as a result, most islands are vulnerable to hurricane-created storm surges. The highest elevation is only 207 feet (63 m) atop Mt Alvernia on Cat Island. The climate is seasonally wet-and-dry tropical in the south and subtropical in the north. Temperatures are moderated by the Gulf Stream and are generally mild throughout the year, seldom rising above 86°F (30°C) or dropping below 60°F (16°C). Freezing conditions are unknown. The islands average about 50 inches (130 cm) of rainfall annually, most of which occurs during the summer season as brief, but often intense, thundery showers. Extremely clear water, extensive coral reefs, and numerous sandy beaches have helped the Bahamas become a major tourist destination.

History

The country's European history began with Christopher Columbus' October 12, 1492, landfall on San Salvador (Watling), a small island in the eastern Bahamas. Columbus and his crew were greeted by Amerindians, various groups of whom have occupied the islands intermittently for perhaps 7,000 years. The British, who arrived in 1648, were the first Europeans to settle the islands. In 1717, the Bahamas became a British Crown colony. In 1973, the Bahamas gained independence.

Population/Culture

Bahamian culture offers a synthesis of African and European influences. Latter influences include the English language and Christianity. African peoples contributed dance, musical styles and instruments, linguistic influences, ancestor stories, and much more.

Administration/Government

The Bahamas is a constitutional democracy with a bicameral Parliament with a 16-seat Senate and 41-seat House of Assembly. Senate members are appointed by the governor general on the recommendation of the prime minister. The head of government is the prime minister; the chief of state is Queen Elizabeth ll, represented by the governor general.

Economy/Industry

A stable system of parliamentary democratic government has facilitated rapid economic growth, particularly tourism, which employs about half the workforce and contributes about two-thirds of the country's GDP.

Today, Bahamians enjoy the third highest per capita GNP in Latin America. Because of its proximity to the USA, the Bahamas has become a major stepping-stone for illegal migrants seeking entry into the country and for the international drug trade.

Windward Passage
Île de la Tortue
Port-de-Paix
Cap-Haïtien
Fort-Liberté
Gonaïves
Golfe de la Gonâve
HAITI
Hinche
Saint-Marc
Thomonde
Île de la Gonâve
Anse-à-Galets
Dame-Marie
Jérémie
PORT-AU-PRINCE
Petit-Goâve
Jacmel
Chaîne de la Selle
Coteaux
Les Cayes
Caribbean Sea
DOMINICAN REPUBLIC

Haiti

Map Reference Pages 134–135

The Republic of Haiti comprises the western one-third of the island of Hispaniola located in the central Caribbean Sea near the eastern tip of Cuba, and several islands off the Hispaniola coast. It shares Hispaniola with the Dominican Republic in the east. Haiti has the dubious distinction of being the poorest country in the Western hemisphere.

Physical Geography

Most of Haiti consists of rugged mountains, the Massif du Nord in the north, the Massif de la Selle and the Massif de la Hotte in the south. The Artibonite River cuts through the center of the country, flowing from mountains in the Dominican Republic into the Gulf of Gonâve. It is a source of irrigation and hydro-electricity. Plaine du Cul-de-Sac in the south is a rift valley, parts of which are below sea level, including the large saline lake Étang Saumâtre, also known as Lake Azuei.

Much of Haiti was heavily forested; but because of logging and land clearance for agriculture, forest cover is now less than two percent, with attendant increases in soil erosion, flooding, and other environmental problems.

History

The original inhabitants of Haiti were Taíno Indians, but their population was decimated by disease soon after the arrival of Spaniards in 1492. Santo Domingo—as Haiti was then known—became a French colony in 1697 and developed a plantation economy based on sugar and indigo. A series of rebellions led to the abolition of slavery in 1793 followed by independence from France in 1804. Haiti was the second country in the Americas, after the USA, to become independent and the first in the world to abolish slavery.

Haiti's history has been mostly one of political turmoil, bloody coups, and strong-armed dictatorships. Recent elections have been more democratic, resulting in a greater voice for Haiti's poor—80 percent of the population live below the poverty line.

Population/Culture

Most of Haiti's population is of predominantly African descent. With environmental devastation in the countryside, increasing numbers of Haitians have migrated to cities, most notably Port-au-Prince, which now has 1,200,000 inhabitants and nearly 2,000,000 more in surrounding slums.

The country is famous for its cuisine, which is a blend of French, African, and Taíno cooking; lively carnival celebrations; and distinctive art, especially the colorful and imaginative naïve or intuitive art forms.

Administration/Government

Haiti has a bicameral National Assembly comprising the Senate and Chamber of Deputies. The president is elected by popular vote, and together with the Chamber of Deputies appoints the prime minister. After 20 years of political instability, Haiti returned to constitutional rule in 2006.

Economy/Industry

About two-thirds of the population works in agriculture, mostly as small-scale subsistence farmers. Coffee and mangoes are the main export crops. Other exports include sisal, rum, automotive parts, and clothing items. The USA has provided tariff-free access to its markets, which helps exports. Haiti's main source of foreign earnings is remittances from nationals working overseas. Haiti relies heavily on international aid to stay afloat.

VOODOO IN HAITI

Haiti is said to be around 70 percent Roman Catholic, 30 percent Protestant, and 100 percent voodoo. So true, as most Haitians comfortably combine the doctrines of major world religions with beliefs and rituals associated with the spirits of their deceased ancestors. The spirits, called loua, can be good, bad, or demanding, and need to be "fed" during rituals that bring them food, drinks, and other offerings.

Because loua who are angry are believed to bring sicknesses to people who have done wrong, voodoo specialists are employed to diagnose illnesses and prescribe herbal treatments. Voodoo priests can also mediate between a family and its loua to meet other needs. Another belief is that loua can take over the body of a descendant, putting that person into a trance during which he or she displays the unique characteristics of that particular ancestral sprit. Trances take place spontaneously, usually during voodoo ceremonies or ritual dances, and are observed and responded to by others who are present. The individuals who have been possessed, however, do not remember anything about what transpired while they were in the trance.

The need to appease spirits underlies the elaborate nature of funeral and mourning rites in Haitian society, and the resplendent nature of Haitian cemeteries. A loua mask is fed money (pictured above).

Left Yanigua River, Los Haitises National Park, Dominican Republic. The park is home to over 78 species of birds and 400 types of flora.

HAITI

Official name Republic of Haiti (Republique d'Haiti/Repiblik d' Ayiti)
Land area 10,641 square miles (27,560 km2)
Border countries Dominican Republic
Capital Port-au-Prince
Highest point Chaine de la Selle 8,793 feet (2,680 m)
Climate Tropical; semiarid where mountains in east cut off trade winds
Population 8,925,000
Language(s) French, Haitian Creole
Ethnicity African descent 95%, mixed (mulatto) and European 5%
Religion Roman Catholic 70%, Protestant 30% (most of the population also practices voodoo)
Government Republic
Currency Gourde
Human Development Index 0.529 (ranked 146th out of 177 countries)

Monte Cristi
Puerto Plata
ATLANTIC OCEAN
Mao
Santiago
Nagua
La Vega
San Francisco de Macorís
Sabana de la Mar
Jarabacoa
Pico Duarte
Bonao
San Juan
El Seibo
HAITI
DOMINICAN REPUBLIC
Higüey
SANTO DOMINGO
San Pedro de Macorís
La Romana
San Cristóbal
Barahona
Isla Saona
Caribbean Sea
Isla Beata

Dominican Republic

Map Reference Pages 134–135

The Dominican Republic comprises the eastern two-thirds of the island of Hispaniola in the Caribbean Sea between Cuba and Puerto Rico. Its only land border is with Haiti to the west. The nation's capital, Santo Domingo, was founded in 1494, making it the oldest continuously occupied European settlement in the Americas.

Physical Geography

The topography is dominated by three main mountain chains running approximately parallel to each other. The highest peaks in the West Indies are located in the Dominican Republic.

The fertile Cibao Valley, formed by the country's two longest rivers, occupies much of the northern zone and is heavily farmed. The Neiba Valley (known in Haiti as the Cul-de-Sac) in the southwest is low-lying and arid. Lago Enriquillo, a lake of variable salinity, is the lowest point in the Caribbean. It shelters a large population of American crocodiles *(Crocodylus acuta)*, iguanas, and other fauna. The country has a tropical maritime climate, with a hurricane season between June and November.

History

Christopher Columbus, who landed on the north coast in what is now Haiti, claimed the island of Hispaniola for Spain in 1492. Spain ceded the Haitian part of the island to France in 1697, but France gained control of the entire island in 1795. French rule was followed by Haitian rule of the whole island. The Dominican Republic gained its independence in 1844, but there was continued conflict with Haiti and a brief reversion to Spanish rule between 1861 and 1863.

Beginning in 1906, the USA exerted increasing influence in the internal affairs of the Dominican Republic, citing a need to protect its interests in the Panama Canal, then under construction. From 1916 to 1924, US Marines took possession of the country. Dictator Rafael Trujillo ruled from 1930 until his assassination in 1961. US marines again occupied the country from 1965 to 1966 to restore order and oversee a return to multi-party democracy. The Dominican Republic continues to have close relations with the USA.

Population/Culture

Most Dominicans are of mixed racial ancestry, with around 80 percent being descendants, at least in part, of African slaves brought to Hispaniola during the colonial period. Dominican culture is a blend of European, African, Taíno, Haitian, and now American influences. Spanish is the dominant language, although Haitian Creole is also common. The country is noted for its distinctive music and dance forms, including merengue.

Administration/Government

Dominica is a democratic republic with a bicameral national Congress comprising the Senate with 32 seats, and the House of Representatives with 178 seats. The president, elected by popular vote for a maximum of two four-year terms, is both the chief of state and head of government.

Economy/Industry

Much of the population works in agriculture, the tourism industry, apparel, and other manufacturing in specially designated free trade zones. Exports include nickel, gold, sugar, and cacao. Remittances from Dominicans abroad contribute one-tenth to GDP.

Above A close-up view of a jumping spider (*Anasaitis* sp.), Dominican Republic.

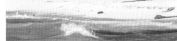

DOMINICAN REPUBLIC

Official name Dominican Republic (República Dominicana)
Land area 18,680 square miles (48,380 km²)
Border countries Haiti
Capital Santo Domingo
Highest & lowest points Pico Duarte 10,417 feet (3,175 m); Lago Enriquillo –151 feet (–46 m)
Climate Tropical maritime
Population 9,507,000
Language(s) Spanish, Haitian Creole
Ethnicity Mixed (mulatto) 73%, European 16%, African descent 11%
Religion Roman Catholic 95%, other 5%
Government Democratic republic
Currency Dominican peso
Human Development Index 0.779 (ranked 79th out of 177 countries)

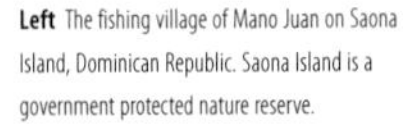

Left The fishing village of Mano Juan on Saona Island, Dominican Republic. Saona Island is a government protected nature reserve.

Right Sunset view of Saba Island—nearby Saba Marine Park is renowned for the variety of marine life that is protected within its waters.

Dieppe Bay Town
Saint Paul's
Sadlers
St Kitts
Mt Liamuiga
Sandy Point Town
Cayon
Middle Island
BASSETERRE
Caribbean Sea
ST KITTS AND NEVIS
The Narrows
Newcastle
Nevis
Nelson Spring
Charlestown
Zion
Fig Tree

ST KITTS AND NEVIS

Official name Federation of St Kitts and Nevis
Land area 101 square miles (261 km²)
Capital Basseterre
Highest point Mt Liamuiga (Mt Misery) 3,792 feet (1,156 m)
Climate Tropical wet-and-dry
Population 39,619
Language(s) English
Ethnicity Predominantly Afro-Caribbean; some British, Portuguese, and Lebanese
Religion Anglican and other Protestant; Roman Catholic
Government Parliamentary democracy
Currency East Caribbean dollar
Human Development Index 0.821 (ranked 54th out of 177 countries)

ANTIGUA AND BARBUDA

Official name Antigua and Barbuda
Land area 170 square miles (441 km²)
Capital St John's
Highest point Boggy Peak 1,319 feet (402 m)
Climate Tropical maritime
Population 69,842
Language(s) Official: English; other: local dialects
Ethnicity African 91%, mixed 4.4%, European 1.7%, other 2.9%
Religion Anglican 25.7%, Seventh Day Adventist 12.3%, Pentecostal 10.6%, Moravian 10.5%, Roman Catholic 10.4%, Methodist 7.9%, Baptist 4.9%, Church of God 4.5%, other Christian 5.4%, other 2%, none or unspecified 5.8%
Government Constitutional monarchy with parliamentary system
Currency East Caribbean dollar
Human Development Index 0.815 (ranked 57th out of 177 countries)

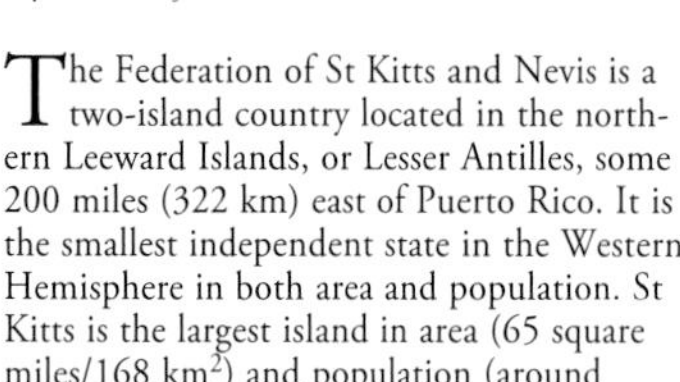

St Kitts and Nevis

Map Reference Pages 134–135

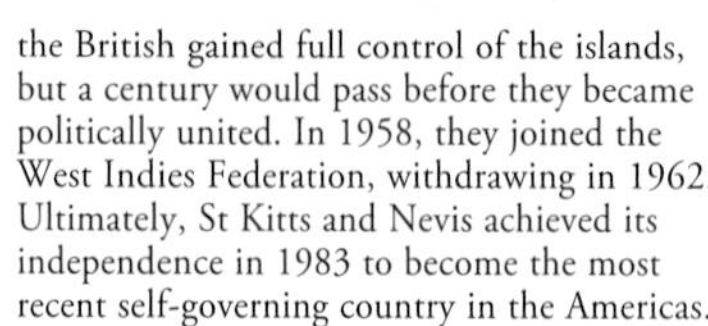

The Federation of St Kitts and Nevis is a two-island country located in the northern Leeward Islands, or Lesser Antilles, some 200 miles (322 km) east of Puerto Rico. It is the smallest independent state in the Western Hemisphere in both area and population. St Kitts is the largest island in area (65 square miles/168 km²) and population (around 27,500), with Nevis totaling 36 square miles (93 km²) in area and 12,000 in population. Basseterre, the country's capital and largest city, is also located on St Kitts.

Both islands are of volcanic origin. About 80 percent of the terrain is far too rugged for crop farming. The climate is wet-and-dry tropical. Temperatures average in the high 70s (26°C); precipitation varies greatly. Northern and eastern mountain slopes receive abundant rainfall that supports rainforest vegetation. Their leeward flanks are drier, as are coastal lowlands. The fertile soils of the narrow coastal plains support most agricultural activity and settlement. The islands lie within the Atlantic hurricane track.

Right Nelson's Dockyard viewed from Shirley Heights, Antigua. The dockyard was the British Royal Navy's repair facility in the Caribbean during the eighteenth century.

Amerindians settled St Kitts and Nevis about 5,000 years ago. In 1624, St Kitts became the first British island colony in the Caribbean. In 1625, it became the first French colony in the region, when it was divided between the two European powers. From their bases on St Kitts, the British and French expanded their respective territories within the Lesser Antilles.

By the late 1620s, settlement had spread from St Kitts to Nevis. Sugar was the mainstay of the economy and plantations depended upon African slave labor. In 1782, the British gained full control of the islands, but a century would pass before they became politically united. In 1958, they joined the West Indies Federation, withdrawing in 1962. Ultimately, St Kitts and Nevis achieved its independence in 1983 to become the most recent self-governing country in the Americas.

St Kitts and Nevis is one of the few Caribbean nations losing population from out-migration. In 1960, there were 51,000 people; today, there are fewer than 40,000 inhabitants. Historically, sugar was the economic mainstay. Today, tourism, clothing, electronics assembly, and offshore banking are attempts toward economic diversification.

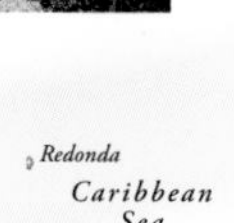
Codrington
Barbuda
ANTIGUA AND BARBUDA
Cedar Grove
ST JOHN'S
Parham
Willikies
Antigua
Bolans
Boggy Peak
Freetown
Old Road
Falmouth
Redonda
Caribbean Sea

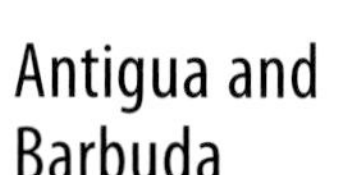

Antigua and Barbuda

Map Reference Pages 134–135

Antigua and Barbuda is a small Caribbean country located in the northern Lesser Antilles, or Leeward Islands. Antigua is the largest island both in population and area (108 square miles/280 km²). The smaller island of Barbuda (62 square miles/161 km²) lies about 30 miles (50 km) north of Antigua.

Southwestern Antigua, including Boggy Peak and the small uninhabited island of Redonda, is of volcanic origin. Elsewhere, the islands feature low, flat to gently rolling terrain composed mainly of limestone. The shoreline is indented with many natural harbors, while Barbuda possesses a large western harbor. Climate is seasonally wet-and-dry tropical. Pleasant temperatures, relatively low humidity, sunny skies, cooling northeast trade winds, and 365 sandy beaches help to make Antigua and Barbuda the leading tourist destination of the Lesser Antilles. The islands lie within the track of Atlantic hurricanes, which occasionally cause devastation.

The first inhabitants reached Antigua and Barbuda about 4,500 years ago. Various groups, including Arawaks and Caribs, have lived on the islands at different times. Their crops included maize (corn), sweet potatoes, chilies, cotton, and tobacco. The indigenous population experienced a sharp decline soon after the arrival of Europeans and Africans.

The British colonized the islands in 1632 and established a thriving sugar-based plantation economy. African slaves provided labor. With the emancipation of slaves in 1834, the economy experienced a gradual decline. After decades of perceived neglect, Antigua and Barbuda gained independence from the UK in 1981. It is now a constitutional monarchy with a parliamentary system of government. It is also a member of the British Commonwealth of Nations.

Most of the country's almost 70,000 people live on Antigua, including about 30,000 in or near the capital, St John's. More than 90 percent of the population is of African descent. Nonetheless, language, religion, and many other customs and practices are remnants of the colonial era and manifest a strong British cultural imprint. Today, the European population is growing because the country has become an attractive retirement destination.

One of the most famous Antiguans is Sir Vivian ("Viv") Richards, who played for, and captained, the West Indies cricket team.

Antigua has a relatively high GDP per capita in comparison to most other Caribbean nations. It is experiencing economic growth based on a thriving tourist industry.

EYE OF THE STORM

Since 1995, an average eight hurricanes have formed each year in tropical Atlantic waters. On September 21, 1998, Hurricane George struck St Kitts and Nevis with winds of 115 miles per hour (185 km/h), torrential rains that caused widespread flooding, and a high surge of storm-driven seawater water along the coast.

The destruction was widespread and devastating. George left five people dead and hundreds injured on the islands. It damaged or destroyed more than 80 percent of the country's homes, businesses, and public buildings and left the islands' communications, energy, and tourism infrastructure in shambles. It inflicted damage estimated at US$500 million, nearly $13,000 per resident.

Below Chattel house, St Kitts. Chattel houses were built by freed slaves, and could be quickly dismantled and moved when necessary.

Calibishie
Portsmouth
Wesley
Marigot
Colihaut
Morne Diablatins
Caribbean Sea
DOMINICA
Castle Bruce
Saint Joseph
ATLANTIC OCEAN
Mahaut
Canefield Estate
La Plaine
ROSEAU
Délices
Pointe Michel
Petite Savane
Soufrière
Berekua

Dominica

Map Reference Pages 134–135

Dominica is the northernmost of the Windward Islands in the Caribbean Sea. The geothermal activity that formed the island remains an important shaping element today. Geyser-fed Boiling Lake, the world's second largest boiling lake, has contaminated and harmed the surrounding forest area with sulfurous gases. Two-thirds of the island is covered by tropical rainforest.

Dominica's lush mountainous terrain is better preserved and more pristine than on most Caribbean islands. Morne Trois Pitons National Park was the first UNESCO World Heritage Site listed in the eastern Caribbean. The steep cliffs, waterfalls, and rivers provide hydropower. Dominica has a tropical climate with an average temperature of 80°F (27°C).

Dominica's first inhabitants, the Arawaks, were wiped out by the Caribs in the fourteenth century. Spanish attempts to colonize the island were resisted by the Caribs. The British took control in 1763 under the Treaty of Paris, and the island became a colony in 1805. Independence was gained in 1978.

The new nation was tested in 1979 and 1980 when severe hurricanes struck. Dominica was led from disaster by Prime Minister Mary Eugenia Charles who diversified the economy and redistributed land to farmers.

Most of the population is descended from slaves who were brought to the island during the eighteenth century. A notable minority is the Carib Indians who trace their ancestors back to pre-Columbian times. Numbering about 3,000, these people mostly live in villages on the east side of the island.

The literacy rate is is 94 percent, and life expectancy is about 75 years. English is the official language, but most speak a French-based Creole language. Dominica has been influenced by Christian faiths and the mixture of cultures on the island.

Dominica is a parliamentary democracy with a uni-cameral legislative body called the House of Assembly. The prime minister is the head of the government and a president serves as the chief of state.

Dominica's main income comes from the banana industry; other tropical crops such as citrus, mangoes, and coconuts are also grown. Unemployment is at 23 percent, and 30 percent of the population live below the poverty line. Dominica relies on tourism, and is promoting itself as an ecotourism destination.

Left Local fishermen on the west coast of Dominica. The country has significant fishery potential, but so far remains unexploited except on a small scale.

DOMINICA

Official name Commonwealth of Dominica
Land area 291 square miles (754 km²)
Capital Roseau
Highest point Morne Diablatins 4,747 feet (1,447 m)
Climate Tropical
Population 72,514
Language(s) Official: English; other: French patois
Ethnicity African 86.8%, mixed 8.9%, Carib Amerindian 2.9%, European 0.8%, other 0.6%
Religion Roman Catholic 61.4%, Seventh Day Adventist 6%, Pentecostal 5.6%, Baptist 4.1%, Methodist 3.7%, Church of God 1.2%, Jehovah's Witnesses 1.2%, other Christian 7.7%, Rastafarian 1.3%, other 1.6%, none 6.2%
Government Parliamentary democracy
Currency East Caribbean dollar
Human Development Index 0.798 (ranked 71st out of 177 countries)

Gros Islet
ATLANTIC OCEAN
ST LUCIA
CASTRIES
Marigot Bay
Anse-la-Raye
Caribbean Sea
Saint Lucia
Dennery
Praslin
Mt Gimie
Soufrière
Micoud
Choiseul
Laborie
Vieux Fort
Maria Islands

St Lucia

Map Reference Pages 134–135

St Lucia is one of the Windward Islands in the Lesser Antilles. It lies between Martinique, 22 miles (35 km) north across the St Lucia Channel, and St Vincent and the Grenadines, 30 miles (50 km) south across St Vincent Passage. Castries, the capital and largest city, is located on the northwest coast. One-third of St Lucia's total population of 170,000 live in Castries.

Rainforest, rugged terrain, and mountains of volcanic origin characterize the island. The best-known landmark is the Pitons, steep-sided twin peaks that rise 2,000 feet (610 m) almost vertically from the sea. Mt Soufrière, the "Drive-In Volcano," offers a roadside tour of bubbling springs and the stench of sulfur. Most settlements and farms occupy small valleys or narrow coastal plains.

The island has several splendid sandy beaches. St Lucia experiences a wet-and-dry tropical climate. Coastal temperatures average 80°F (27°C). Cooler temperatures prevail in the interior highlands. Annual precipitation averages 50 inches (130 cm) along the coast to nearly 160 inches (400 cm) in some mountainous areas. June to December is the wet season. Infrequent hurricanes strike the island.

Before European settlement during the sixteenth century, the island was home to several native groups including Arawaks and later Caribs. France claimed the island in 1635, but was displaced by the British in 1663. During the next 150 years, control of the island changed hands numerous times between the two European powers. Great Britain finally gained control in 1814.

St Lucia became self-governing in 1967 and an independent state within the British Commonwealth of Nations in 1979. It is a full member of the Caribbean Community (CARICOM) and the Organization of Eastern Caribbean States (OECS).

English is the country's official language, although most people speak a Creole derived from combined African, French, English, and Amerindian tongues. Nearly 70 percent of the people are Catholic; 23 percent are Protestant.

St Lucia's economy, long tied to plantation agriculture, is experiencing rapid diversification. The island has turned to tourism to boost its revenue. It has a great deal to offer, including spectacular terrain, lush tropical vegetation, sandy beaches, warm waters, and adequate tourist facilities.

Tourism is the leading source of income, with manufacturing, offshore banking, and a number of other international business activities growing in importance.

Above A St Lucian woman wearing traditional knotted headwear.

ST LUCIA

Official name St Lucia
Land area 234 square miles (606 km²)
Capital Castries
Highest point Mt Gimie 3,117 feet (950 m)
Climate Tropical wet-and-dry
Population 172,884
Language(s) Official: English; other: French patois
Ethnicity African 82.5%, mixed 11.9%, East Indian 2.4%, other or unspecified 3.2%
Religion Roman Catholic 67.5%, Protestant 23.3%, Rastafarian 2.1%, other 2.6%, none 4.5%
Government Parliamentary democracy
Currency East Caribbean dollar
Human Development Index 0.795 (ranked 72nd out of 177 countries)

Left During the period of French rule, Soufrière was the capital of St Lucia. Its beautiful bay is in the southwest, on the sheltered Caribbean side of the island and offers some excellent dive sites, such as Scotts Head/Soufrière Marine Reserve.

ST VINCENT AND THE GRENADINES

Official name Saint Vincent and the Grenadines
Land area 150 square miles (389 km²)
Border countries None
Capital Kingstown
Highest point La Soufrière 4,049 feet (1,234 m)
Climate Tropical
Population 90,343
Language(s) English, French patois
Ethnicity Afro-Caribbean 66%, mixed 19%, East Indian 6%, Carib Amerindian 2%, other 7%
Religion Christian 88%, other 12%
Government Parliamentary democracy
Currency East Caribbean dollar
Human Development Index 0.761 (ranked 93rd out of 177 countries)

Above right Aerial view of Tobago Cays, with Canouan in the distance. The Tobago Cays, surrounded by a horseshoe reef, are a snorkeler's paradise.

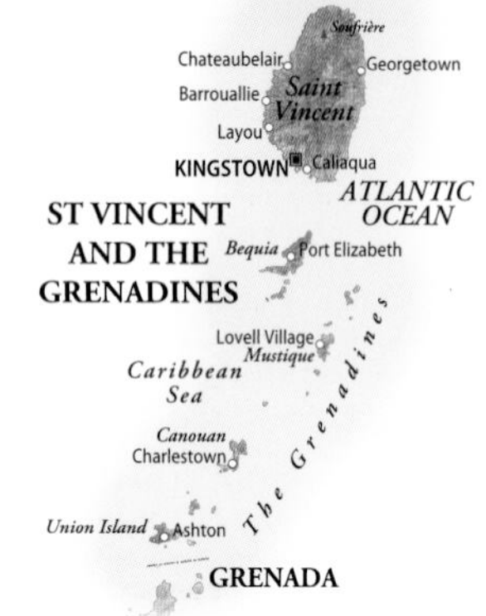
Soufrière
Chateaubelair
Georgetown
Barrouallie
Saint Vincent
Layou
KINGSTOWN
Calliaqua
ATLANTIC OCEAN
ST VINCENT AND THE GRENADINES
Bequia
Port Elizabeth
Lovell Village
Mustique
Caribbean Sea
Canouan
Charlestown
The Grenadines
Union Island
Ashton
GRENADA

Right Detailed view of a red ginger flower, *Alpinia purpurata*, Barbados. This plant is also known as the ostrich plume.

Below Palm Island Beach Club, St Vincent and the Grenadines. A travel magazine named Palm Island "one of the best places to stay in the world."

Right Women dancing in the Grand Kadooment, the finale of the Barbados Crop Over Festival.

St Vincent and the Grenadines

Map Reference Pages 134–135

St Vincent and the Grenadines is located in the southern Lesser Antilles. The country is composed of St Vincent, which occupies nearly 90 percent of the total land area, and the northern two-thirds of the Grenadines, small islands extending southward about 60 miles (100 km) toward Grenada. The capital and largest city, Kingstown, is located on St Vincent's southwest coast.

St Vincent and most of the Grenadines are of volcanic origin. La Soufrière, on St Vincent, has erupted five times during the past three centuries. An eruption in 1902 killed nearly 1,700 people and devastated the island's economy. A 1979 eruption caused widespread destruction, but no fatalities. The Grenadines is an archipelago of nearly 600 small islands and cays, of which only a few are settled.

The islands experience a seasonally wet-and-dry tropical climate. Annual temperatures range from 82°F (28°C) to 79°F (26°C). Rainfall varies from 50 inches (130 cm) in some coastal areas to more than 150 inches (375 cm) in the interior highlands. Hurricanes frequently sweep across the islands.

Ciboney Amerindians reached St Vincent some 7,000 years ago. Arawaks replaced them about 2,000 years ago and they were removed by Caribs around 1000 CE. When Europeans arrived, they met with fierce Carib resistance. St Vincent was one of the last Caribbean islands to be colonized by Europeans in 1719. France and Britain jockeyed for control during much of the eighteenth century. Finally, in 1783, the island was ceded to the British.

Before colonization, the ethnic isolation of Caribs changed in 1675 when a Dutch slave ship was wrecked nearby. Many Africans reached shore and were made welcome. Soon, the Africans took Carib wives, their offspring being the Afro-Caribs of St Vincent. Today, about 2,000 Vincentians claim Amerindian ethnicity, most of whom are Afro-Caribs.

The islands became self-governing in 1969 and an independent country within the Commonwealth of Nations in 1979. The government is a parliamentary democracy with a unicameral 21-seat House of Representatives. The head of government is the prime minister.

About 85 percent of the inhabitants are of African or mixed African and other ancestry. Ninety percent of the population lives on St Vincent. Agriculture, dominated by banana production, remains economically important. Service industries, led by tourism, are developing slowly. Per capita income of under US$3,000 and an unemployment rate of over 20 percent are negative figures exceeded only by Haiti within the Caribbean region.

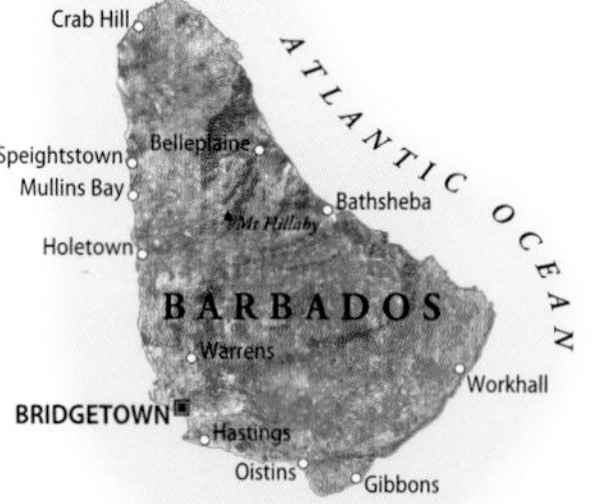
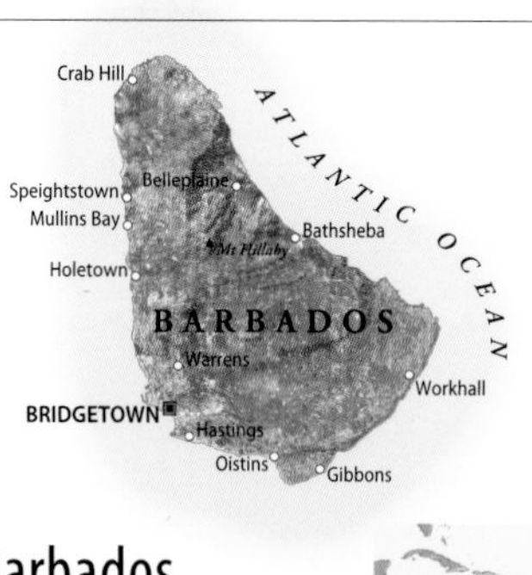
Crab Hill
ATLANTIC OCEAN
Speightstown
Belleplaine
Mullins Bay
Bathsheba
Mt Hillaby
Holetown
BARBADOS
Warrens
Workhall
BRIDGETOWN
Hastings
Oistins
Gibbons

Barbados

Map Reference Pages 134–135

Barbados is a prosperous island country located in the Atlantic Ocean. It is the most easterly island of the Lesser Antilles, its nearest neighbor being St Vincent and the Grenadines to the west. Despite its small area, Barbados has played a very important role in the region's history and economy.

The island is a coral-formed limestone platform that has been repeatedly uplifted, thus creating a series of steps and terraces. It has a seasonally wet-and-dry tropical climate. Average monthly temperatures range from 75°F to 82°F (24°C to 28°C). Annual rainfall varies from 50 inches (125 cm) along the coast to 75 inches (190 cm) in the interior. Barbados lies south of the Atlantic storm track, yet hurricanes have struck the island on occasion. Most soil is limestone based and generally fertile. Many fine beaches, cooling trade winds, and excellent conditions for surfing have contributed to the island's thriving tourist industry.

When British settlers arrived in 1627, Barbados was uninhabited. Indigenous populations may have died from diseases introduced by Portuguese settlers in the second half of the sixteenth century. By the 1640s a sugar-based plantation economy was established that within a century developed into one of the world's most lucrative plantation economies. In 1807, the British abolished the slave trade, but not slavery, which resulted in the violent revolt of some 20,000 slaves. Following emancipation in 1834, many former slaves continued to work on the plantations. Sugar and rum remained the mainstay of the economy until the mid-twentieth century. In 1966, Barbados gained independence.

Although 90 percent of Barbados's inhabitants are of African origin, the country bears the nickname of "little England" because of its continuing strong ties to the UK. Barbados has benefited from political stability based on parliamentary democracy. Tourism and other service-based industries account for about 80 percent of GDP. Barbados is fast becoming one of the Western Hemisphere's most prosperous countries.

BARBADOS

Official name Barbados
Land area 166 square miles (431 km²)
Border countries None
Capital Bridgetown
Highest point Mt Hillaby 1,102 feet (336 m)
Climate Tropical
Population 281,968
Language(s) English
Ethnicity Afro-Caribbean 90%, Asian/mixed 6%, European 4%
Religion Christian 71%, none 17%, other 12%
Government Parliamentary democracy
Currency Barbadian dollar
Human Development Index 0.892 (ranked 31st out of 177 countries)

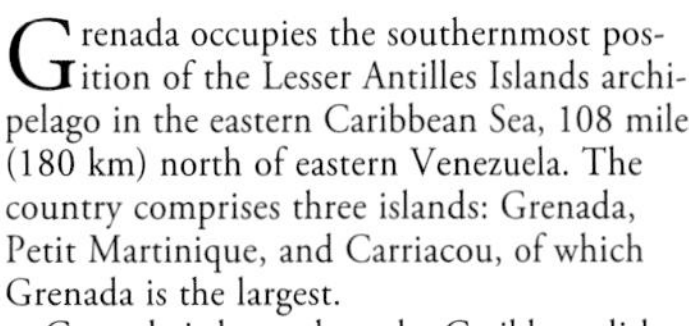
ST VINCENT AND THE GRENADINES
Petite Saint Vincent
Windward
Petite Martinique
Hillsborough
Argyle
Carriacou
GRENADA
Ronde Island
Caribbean Sea
Caille Island
ATLANTIC OCEAN
Sauteurs
Victoria
Gouyave
Mt Saint Catherine
Grenville
Grenada
ST GEORGE'S
Grand Anse

Grenada

Map Reference Pages 134–135

Grenada occupies the southernmost position of the Lesser Antilles Islands archipelago in the eastern Caribbean Sea, 108 miles (180 km) north of eastern Venezuela. The country comprises three islands: Grenada, Petit Martinique, and Carriacou, of which Grenada is the largest.

Grenada is located on the Caribbean lithospheric plate, near an active subduction zone. The interior of the main island is dominated by mountainous terrain of volcanic origin and is where the country's highest peak, Mt St Catherine, is located.

Tropical climatic conditions are moderated by northeast trade winds. The islands lie on the margin of the western Atlantic Ocean hurricane belt and are subject to storms during the hurricane season.

Christopher Columbus observed the islands during his third voyage to the West Indies in 1498. The French became the first Europeans to occupy the islands 152 years later in 1650. France and England traded control several times over the next 124 years, with England asserting sovereignty in 1784. Full independence was achieved on February 7, 1974; Grenada advertises itself as the smallest independent nation in the Western hemisphere.

Grenada is a parliamentary democracy with a bicameral legislature. The prime minister is appointed from the majority political party.

After internal political problems overwhelmed the country in 1983, President Ronald Reagan ordered the US military, along with token support from six nations from the area, to invade the main island. Combat against the Grenadian army with its Cuban advisors was brief, but US forces occupied the island until June 1985. The invasion context became part of the story line for the film *Heartbreak Ridge*, released in 1986.

Grenada's population consists largely of people of African descent, with some mixed races, Europeans and East Indians, as well as a vestige of Arawak/Carib Amerindians.

In the seventeenth century, French settlers established sugar plantations worked by African slaves. The agricultural economy became diversified along with some industrial activities. Today, tourism is the main source of foreign exchange.

Caribbean Sea
Tobago
Charlotteville
Plymouth
Scarborough
TRINIDAD AND TOBAGO
ATLANTIC OCEAN
Toco
Maracas
El Cerro del Aripo
PORT-OF-SPAIN
Arima
Sangre Grande
Chaguanas
Gulf of Paria
Trinidad
Rio Claro
La Brea
San Fernando
Point Fortin
Siparia
Fullarton
Moruga
VENEZUELA

Trinidad and Tobago

Map Reference Pages 134–135

Trinidad and Tobago lies between the Caribbean Sea and the Atlantic Ocean just 7 miles (11 km) from mainland Venezuela at the closest point. The country is composed of 23 islands, the largest being Trinidad, which occupies 94 percent of the combined territory. Tobago lies 50 miles (80 km) to the northeast of Trinidad. The capital and largest city, Port-of-Spain, is located on Trinidad's northwest coast.

QUEEN'S ROYAL COLLEGE
1904

Left The clock tower of Queen's Royal College, Port-of-Spain, Trinidad. The college is the alma mater of several notable citizens, including Dr Eric Williams, the country's first prime minister.

Geologically, the islands are extensions of the South American continent. Mountain ranges that rise above the sea form Trinidad's three large peninsulas. Tobago, too, is an emergent mountain ridge. Trinidad has large expanses of relatively low, flat land with fertile soils. The climate is hot and humid; average temperatures range from 77°F (25°C) to 81°F (27°C). Annual rainfall averages 83 inches (211 cm). The rainy season extends from June through November; most precipitation falls as brief but often torrential thundery showers. The islands lie south of the hurricane belt, but tropical storms occasionally strike.

Amerindian peoples had occupied Trinidad and Tobago for 7,000 years when Columbus came upon the islands in 1498. The islands came under British control by the early nineteenth century. Sugar was the primary industry. When African slaves were emancipated in 1834, laborers from India replaced them. In 1888, the islands of Trinidad and Tobago were combined as a single British Crown colony. Independence was gained in 1962 and the country became a republic in 1976.

The population is very cosmopolitan, and is unique in that 40 percent are of South Asian rather than African descent. About 38 percent of the population claims African ancestry and another 20 percent is mixed. This diversity is evident in the country's languages and religions.

English is the official language, but Caribbean Hindustani (Hindi dialect), Spanish, French, and Chinese are also spoken. Christian groups claim 57.6 percent of the population, but there are many Hindus, Muslims, and followers of other religions.

The islands are the home of calypso and steelpan (steelband, steeldrum), both of which have become popular across the Caribbean and beyond. Calypso began as a form of communication among slaves. In the 1900s, it became a pop culture medium for disseminating news and social protest. Steelpan is music created by pannists playing percussion instruments made from 55-gallon oil drums.

The government is a parliamentary democracy with a bicameral parliament made up of a 31-seat Senate, and a 41-seat House of Representatives. The chief of state is the president; the head of government is the prime minister.

In 1910, oil was discovered in Trinidad. Petroleum and natural gas production, some manufacturing, agriculture, and tourism are mainstays of the country's growing economy.

GRENADA

Official name Grenada
Land area 133 square miles (344 km²)
Border countries None
Capital St George's
Highest point Mt St Catherine 2,756 feet (840 m)
Climate Tropical tempered by northeast trade winds
Population 90,343
Language(s) English, French patois
Ethnicity Afro-Caribbean 82%, mixed 13%, European/East Indian 5%, trace Arawak/Carib Amerindian
Religion Christian 100%
Government Parliamentary democracy
Currency East Caribbean dollar
Human Development Index 0.777 (ranked 82nd out of 177 countries)

Below A young girl in carnival costume, Port-of-Spain, Trinidad. The five-day carnival features calypso, steelpan, and masquerade, and culminates with the Parade of the Bands.

TRINIDAD AND TOBAGO

Official name Republic of Trinidad and Tobago
Land area 1,980 square miles (5,128 km²)
Border countries None
Capital Port-of-Spain
Highest point El Cerro del Aripo 3,084 feet (940 m)
Climate Tropical
Population 1,047,000
Language(s) English, Caribbean Hindustani, French, Spanish, Chinese
Ethnicity Indian (South Asian) 40%, Afro-Caribbean 37.5%, mixed 20.5%, other 1.2%, unspecified 0.8%
Religion Christian 57.6%, Hindu 22.5%, Muslim 5.8%, other 12.2%, none 1.9%
Government Parliamentary democracy
Currency Trinidad and Tobago dollar
Human Development Index 0.814 (ranked 59th out of 177 countries)

Left A busy street market in Grenada. Market Square is the bustling hub of St George's and the focal point for community and social events.

GREENLAND

Official name Greenland (Kalaallit Nunaat)
Land area 836,330 square miles (2.16 million km²)
Capital Nuuk (Godthåb)
Climate Arctic to subarctic
Population 56,326
Government Self-governing overseas administrative division of the Kingdom of Denmark
Currency Danish krone

BERMUDA

Official name Bermuda
Land area 21 square miles (54 km²)
Capital Hamilton
Climate Subtropical
Population 66,536
Government Overseas territory of the United Kingdom; self-governing autonomous territory
Currency Bermudian dollar

ANGUILLA

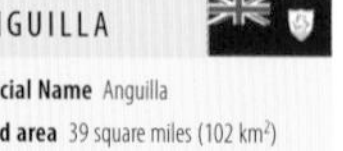

Official Name Anguilla
Land area 39 square miles (102 km²)
Capital The Valley
Climate Tropical
Population 14,108
Language Official: English
Government Overseas territory of the United Kingdom (parliamentary representative democratic)
Currency East Caribbean dollar

Right Since 1983, when he was 60 years old, Johnny Barnes has stood every weekday morning at the busiest roundabout in Hamilton, Bermuda, greeting commuters with a never-ending chorus of "Good morning," "God bless you," and "I love you." There whatever the weather, he greets everyone who passes individually, and it is considered good luck to tag him. A retired bus driver born of parents who migrated from the West Indies island of St Kitts, Mr Barnes is known as the "Happy Man." Bermuda's most famous resident, he has been honored with a 6½-foot statue depicting him in his most famous pose.

Greenland

Map Reference Pages 116–117

Greenland, the world's coldest inhabited country and one of the world's largest islands, is located between the Arctic and North Atlantic oceans. The country is linked physically and ethnically to North America, but has closer historical and political ties to Europe. Eighty-one percent of Greenland is covered in ice, with glaciers reaching a thickness of 9,850 feet (3 km). Recent warming has slightly reduced the ice mass, thereby expanding the area that is suitable for human habitation.

North American Eskimo (Inuit) reached Greenland about 2500 BCE. Vikings from Iceland and Scandinavia arrived by 984 CE. Since the 1500s, Greenland has had close ties with Denmark. In 1979 it became a self-governing territory; the Danish monarch is its head of state.

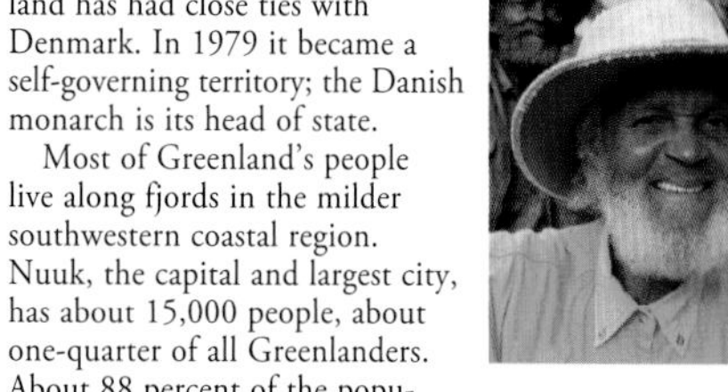

Most of Greenland's people live along fjords in the milder southwestern coastal region. Nuuk, the capital and largest city, has about 15,000 people, about one-quarter of all Greenlanders. About 88 percent of the population is pure or mixed Inuit. Greenlanders have long depended on the sea's marine life. Greenland's economy depends on fishing exports; with few other exports or services to offer, it relies on Danish subsidies and aid.

Bermuda

Map Reference Page 134–135

Located in the western North Atlantic Ocean 640 miles (1,030 km) east–southeast of Cape Hatteras, North Carolina, USA, the tiny British dependency of Bermuda consists of some 150 small coral islands and islets.

Bermudians enjoy a subtropical climate and the world's highest per capita income.

The warm waters of the Gulf Stream have promoted the growth of the abundant coral formations that make up the island group. It is located atop a volcanic cone extending more than 14,000 feet (4,267 m) from the ocean floor, part of the Bermuda Rise. These coral reefs are among the world's most northerly.

Bermuda's subtropical climate is mild and humid, with strong winds in winter and an annual mean temperature of 70°F (21°C).

The uninhabited islands were first visited by the Spanish in 1515 and named for Juan de Bermúdez. Englishmen on their westward passage were shipwrecked on Bermuda in 1609 and named the group the Somers Islands. British colonization began in 1612; under private oversight initially, Bermuda became a modified Crown colony in 1684.

A referendum on independence was defeated in 1995. Most of the population is of African descent, with a minority of European, mixed, and other ethnicities.

Bermuda sits at the apex of the infamous Bermuda Triangle, with Florida and Puerto Rico as the other vertexes. The Triangle is the site of numerous reported disappearances of ships and planes.

Bermuda is a parliamentary, self-governing territory, and an overseas territory of the United Kingdom. Its economy is based largely on providing financial services for international businesses and luxury facilities for tourists, over 80 percent of whom come from the USA.

Anguilla

Map Reference Pages 134–135

Anguilla, the northernmost of the Leeward Islands, or Lesser Antilles, is roughly 240 miles (386 km) due east of Puerto Rico. The small island is a low-lying, rather featureless limestone platform. Solution weathering has created one of its major attractions—a large cave offering a constant supply of fresh water, called the Fountain.

The climate is tropical, moderated by trade winds, with an annual average temperature of 80°F (27°C) and annual average rainfall of 35 inches (89 cm). The island features several coral reefs and over 30 coral sand beaches.

Amerindians lived on Anguilla as early as 1500 BCE. Carib Indians came later. The Spanish bestowed the name Anguilla ("eel") due to its shape. In 1650 England established the first permanent European settlement.

Due to its small size, lack of natural resources, low rainfall, and small population, the British Crown Colony has languished economically. Since 1981, Anguilla has been a semi-independent British Overseas Territory.

Over 90 percent of Anguilla's 13,700 population are of African descent. Only 3.7 percent of the people is European, yet European cultural traits dominate. English is the official language. Government is by parliamentary democracy. In the early twenty-first century, the luxury tourism industry boomed, as has a thriving offshore banking industry.

BRITISH VIRGIN ISLANDS

Official name British Virgin Islands
Land area 59 square miles (153 km²)
Capital Road Town
Climate Subtropical
Population 22,004
Government Overseas territory of the United Kingdom; self-governing autonomous territory
Currency US dollar

Right The territory of Greenland extends south as far as Cape Farewell (Kap Farvel in Danish, Uummannarsuaq in Greenlandic), a headland on the southern shore of Egger Island that projects out into the North Atlantic Ocean and the Labrador Sea at the same latitude as Stockholm and the Scottish Orkney Islands. Egger and the other small islands associated with it are known as the Farewell Archipelago.

British Virgin Islands

Map Reference Pages 134–135

The British Virgin Islands lie approximately 60 miles (100 km) east of Puerto Rico. They include Virgin Gorda, Tortola, the largest island, Anegada, Jost Van Dyke, and over 50 smaller islands and cays, some 15 of which are inhabited.

The terrain is rugged and mainly of volcanic origin. The climate is seasonally subtropical and humid, with conditions and temperatures influenced by northeast trade winds. Summer temperatures range from 75 to 90°F (24–32°C) and in winter from 70 to 75°F (21–24°C). Average annual rainfall, with an August to November maximum, is 40 to 50 inches (102–125 cm). Hurricanes occasionally sweep the islands.

Columbus saw and named the Virgin Islands on his second voyage in 1493, although the Spanish never settled there. Their location astride the Sir Francis Drake Channel and the Anegada Passage—natural routes between the Caribbean and Atlantic—played an important role in their history. They became a haven for pirates. Over time, the British, Danish, Dutch, French, Spanish, and Americans competed for control over various islands. The British Virgin Islands became a self-governing autonomous territory of the United Kingdom in 1967.

Most of the population lives on Tortola, with nearly 10,000 residing in Road Town, the capital. The growing economy is based mainly on tourism and financial services, including registration of more than half a million offshore companies.

Cayman Islands

Map Reference Pages 134–135

The Cayman Islands—Grand Cayman, Cayman Brac, and Little Cayman—are located in the West Indies, south of Cuba and northwest of Jamaica. The territory is a tourist and investment haven, with cruise ships and international investors visiting in recent years.

The Cayman Islands were settled by the British in the eighteenth century, and administered from Jamaica until Jamaica's independence in 1962.

The climate is classified tropical, with warm rainy summers and cool, relatively dry winters. In 2004, the islands were devastated by Hurricane Ivan, which hit with winds of nearly 200 miles per hour (322 km/h).

The culture is a rich mix of European, African, and American. Approximately 60 percent of the population is of mixed (usually African and European) heritage. Of the remaining 40 percent, about half are European and half African in descent.

The Cayman Islands are an overseas territory of the UK, with an appointed governor to represent the chief of state, Queen Elizabeth II. The Legislative Assembly handles domestic affairs.

The Cayman Islands is a world financial center for offshore banks because there is no direct taxation. In 2003, the islands had more than 68,000 registered companies—this figure exceeds the population by more than twenty thousand. Tourism is also vital, accounting for about 70 percent of GDP. Caymanians enjoy one of the world's highest standards of living, with a per capita GDP of US$43,800.

Guadeloupe

Map Reference Pages 134–135

Guadeloupe is a group of several small volcanic islands among the Windward Islands group in the eastern Caribbean Sea. The group consists of Basse-Terre and Grande-Terre (sometimes referred to as Guadeloupe proper); two smaller islands, Marie-Galante and La Désirade; and a cluster of still smaller islands called Les Saintes. A sea channel separates Basse-Terre and Grande-Terre. An active volcano, La Grande Soufrière, dominates the topography of Basse-Terre. The climate is subtropical, with moderately high humidity tempered by trade winds.

Guadeloupe has been a French possession since 1635; it is now administered as an overseas department of France, and as such, it is part of the European Union and its islands are mapped on euro banknotes.

The island of St Barthélemy and the French portion of the island of St Martin were part of Guadeloupe until 2007, when they became separate French overseas collectivities.

The population is approximately 408,000. Most residents are descendants of African slaves brought to the islands in the eighteenth century to work on sugar plantations. About 10 percent of the population is European, mostly French, and 11 percent is of East Indian descent. Sugar, bananas, and eggplants are important in the agricultural economy. There is also a light manufacturing sector, notably rum production. However, the largest part of the economy comprises overseas tourism.

St Martin

Map Reference Pages 134–135

St Martin, volcanic in origin, is one of the Leeward Islands, located about 186 miles (300 km) east of Puerto Rico. The island's northern half is French territory; the southern half is Dutch territory and referred to as St Maarten. The French zone is a first-order administrative district of France, referred to as an overseas collectivity; St Maarten is presently part of the Netherlands Antilles (see page 110), but eventually will become an autonomous Dutch territory.

In the eighteenth century, the economy was based on French sugar plantations using African slave labor. The modern economy focuses mainly on tourism, with the island's beaches attracting about one million visitors per year. The French zone is famous for its secluded beaches and its upscale restaurants and accommodations, while the Dutch zone has a bustling cruise-ship port and a commercial district with tourist shops and nightlife in the port town, Philipsburg.

St Barthélemy

Map Reference Pages 134–135

St Barthélemy is a small volcanic island in the Leeward Islands chain of the eastern Caribbean. It is surrounded by shallow reefs and its terrain is mostly hilly. St Barthélemy is an overseas collectivity of France and thus part of the European Union. Its territory includes a number of tiny islets. It was a part of French Guadeloupe until 2007; it became a separate collectivity in 2003. Unusually in the Caribbean, its population mainly comprises people of European descent.

The island became French territory in 1648, but was thought less desirable than other West Indies sites because steep slopes and a lack of fresh water limited agricultural possibilities. In 1784 it was sold to Sweden; St Barthélemy's main town, Gustavia, is named after Sweden's Gustav III. The island was used mainly for slave trading. France bought the island back in 1878.

The economy is based on high-end tourism. There are about 20 beaches on the island, as well as slopes that have been terraced for villas and hotels.

CAYMAN ISLANDS

Official name Cayman Islands
Land area 100 square miles (262 km²)
Capital George Town
Climate Tropical marine
Population 47,862
Government British Crown colony; overseas territory of the United Kingdom
Currency Caymanian dollar

Above left Tourism accounts for around 45 percent of national income for British Virgin Islands. A large proportion of visitors are US citizens, who relax on the numerous white sand beaches, visit the baths on Virgin Gorda, go snorkeling around the coral reefs near Anegada, experience the bars of Jost Van Dyke, or charter yachts to explore the less accessible islands. Cruise ships also visit.

Left A view of Marigot Bay from the St Louis Fort in St Martin. This historic fort was built by the French in the 1760s to protect the island against potential English invaders.

GUADELOUPE

Official name Department of Guadeloupe (Département de la Guadeloupe)
Land area 629 square miles (1,629 km²)
Capital Basse-Terre
Climate Subtropical
Population 408,000
Government Overseas department of France
Currency Euro

Left Gustavia, the main town on St Barthélemy, was named after King Gustav III of Sweden, and is a reminder of the island's Swedish period. Though the native language is Creole, many of St Barthélemy's residents are French citizens.

ST MARTIN

Official name Overseas Collectivity of Saint-Martin (Collectivite d'outre mer de Saint-Martin)
Land area 21 square miles (54.4 km²)
Capital Marigot
Climate Tropical
Population 29,376
Government Overseas collectivity of France
Currency Euro

ST BARTHELEMY

Official name Overseas Collectivity of Saint-Barthélemy (Collectivite d'outre mer de Saint-Barthélemy)
Land area 8 square miles (21 km²)
Capital Gustavia
Climate Tropical
Population 7,492
Government Overseas collectivity of France
Currency Euro

Left Guadeloupe is the center of the Caribbean's creole culture, which shows French, African, East Indian and West Indian influences. A bright plaid accompanied by matching headdress is typical of traditional creole dress.

MARTINIQUE

Official name Département de Martinique
Land area 436 square miles (1,128 km²)
Capital Fort-de-France
Climate Subtropical
Government Overseas department of France
Currency Euro

MONTSERRAT

Official name Montserrat
Land area 39 square miles (102 km²)
Capital Plymouth until 1997, interim government structures have been built at Brades Estate, Little Bay
Climate Tropical
Population 9,638
Government Self-governing possession of the United Kingdom
Currency East Caribbean dollar

NAVASSA ISLAND

Official name Navassa Island
Land area 2 square miles (5.4 km²)
Climate Marine, tropical
Population Uninhabited
Government Unorganized, unincorporated territory of the USA

Right Montserrat's Soufrière Hills volcano rumbled to life and buried the island's capital in July 1995, but since 1997 its activity has been confined to infrequent ventings of ash into the now uninhabited areas in the south.

NETHERLANDS ANTILLES

Official name Netherlands Antilles (Nederlandse Antillen)
Land area 371 square miles (960 km²); includes Bonaire, Curaçao, Saba, St Eustatius, and St Maarten (Dutch part of the island of St Martin)
Capital Willemstad
Climate Tropical
Population 225,369
Government Parliamentary; autonomous country within the Kingdom of the Netherlands
Currency Netherlands Antilles guilder

ARUBA

Official name Aruba
Land area 74½ square miles (193 km²)
Capital Oranjestad
Climate Tropical marine
Population 101,541
Government Parliamentary democracy
Currency Aruban guilder/florin

Right The Anse Cafard Slave Memorial pays tribute to slaves drowned on the night of April 7, 1830, when a storm sent their ship crashing into rocks off Le Diamant, Martinique. Slavery had been abolished in 1815, but an illegal trade continued.

Far right Stores in the center of Willemstad on Curaçao, Netherlands Antilles, bear testimony to centuries of Dutch influence, adapted to Caribbean conditions. In 1817, the port town banned white buildings as too dazzling in their effect.

UNITED STATES OF AMERICA
CANADA
St Pierre and Miquelon (France)
UNITED STATES OF AMERICA
PACIFIC OCEAN
ATLANTIC OCEAN
US Virgin Islands (US)
Netherlands Antilles (Netherlands)
BAHAMAS
Puerto Rico (US)
Turks and Caicos Islands (UK)
Montserrat (UK)
Martinique (France)
MEXICO
CUBA
DOM. REP.
HAITI
ST LUCIA
Navassa Island (US)
BARBADOS
JAMAICA
DOMINICA
ST V. AND THE G.
BELIZE
Caribbean Sea
TRIN. AND TOB.
GUATEMALA
HONDURAS
Aruba (Netherlands)
Netherlands Antilles (Netherlands)
EL SALVADOR
NICARAGUA
COSTA RICA
PANAMA

Martinique

Map Reference Pages 134–135

Martinique, in the Lesser Antilles Islands archipelago, is located in the eastern edge of the Caribbean. Dominica is its northern neighbor and St Lucia is just to the south.

Mountainous Martinique is on the eastern margin of the Caribbean Plate, with an active subduction zone just to the west of the island. Its highest point is the volcano Mt Pelée.

Before European colonization, Martinique was inhabited by at least two waves of Amerindian settlements, but by the time Columbus visited in 1502, Carib Indians lived there. France founded a permanent colony there in 1635. It was captured twice by the British, but in each case it was returned to France. The capital, Saint-Pierre, was devastated when Mt Pelée erupted on May 8, 1902, generating a pyroclastic flow—a *nuée ardente* (a glowing cloud of super-heated gases). An estimated 30,000 people who had taken refuge in Saint-Pierre were incinerated within minutes. The capital was relocated to Fort-de-France, the island eventually recovered, and the affected areas were later resettled. Mt Pelée exhibited new activity in 1929, but this ceased in 1932.

Over 90 percent of Martinique's population is of mixed ethnicity (African–European–Asian); others are of French, East Indian, Syro-Lebanese, or Chinese origin.

Martinique became an overseas department of France in 1946. Although France largely supports the economy, Martinique's industries include sugarcane, bananas, and tourism.

Montserrat

Map Reference Pages 134–135

Montserrat lies in the northern sector of the Lesser Antilles Islands archipelago on the eastern margin of the Caribbean. Its nearest neighbor is Antigua. Montserrat is part of an island arc framing the eastern end of the Caribbean Plate; a subduction zone lies just to the west. The Soufrière Hills stratovolcano began erupting on July 18, 1995, for the first time in recorded history, and has remained active ever since.

English and Irish colonists settled on Montserrat in 1632. African slaves were imported 30 years later for the sugarcane industry. France and Great Britain fought for control in the 1700s; in 1783 it became a British possession.

Until 1995, Montserrat was a secure place to visit; tourism is still an important part of the economy. The people are mainly of African descent; some are of mixed ancestry, or European.

The island's economic and social structures were shattered by the eruptions beginning in 1995, its airport and docking facilities destroyed. Plymouth, the capital, was abandoned in 1997 because of a destructive eruption. About 9,000 people fled, many going to England.

The UK government granted the people of Montserrat citizenship in 2002, and launched an aid program to help reconstruct the island's economy. A new capital is being built at Brades Estate, Little Bay, out of reach of volcanic activity. The island's southern half is expected to remain uninhabitable for another decade or so.

Navassa Island

Map Reference Pages 134–135

Navassa is a tiny uninhabited island of two square miles (5 km²) in the Caribbean, roughly 30 miles (48 km) west of Haiti's Cape Tiburon and about 100 miles (160 km) south of the US military base at Guantánamo Bay, Cuba. Ownership is disputed between the USA and Haiti, although control has been American since the island was claimed in 1857.

The island's rich guano deposits were mined by American interests between 1865 and 1898 for the manufacture of chemical fertilizers and explosives. After the opening of the Panama Canal in 1914, Navassa Island was the site of a strategic lighthouse along a main shipping lane, and was administered by the US Coast Guard from 1917 to 1996, when the lighthouse was finally dismantled.

Since 1999 the US Fish and Wildlife Service has run the island as a wildlife refuge, aiming to protect the marine environment, and to restore native wildlife and plants. Access is prohibited and special permission to visit the island is hard to obtain.

Netherlands Antilles

Map Reference Pages 134–135

The Netherlands Antilles, once known as the Dutch West Indies or Netherlands West Indies, comprises two island groups in the Caribbean: Curaçao and Bonaire in the Lesser Antilles near Venezuela; and Saba, St Eustatius, and St Maarten (the southern half of St Martin) in the northeast Caribbean.

The islands were acquired for the Netherlands in the seventeenth century by the Dutch West Indies Company and were used as military outposts and, until slavery was abolished in 1863, as bases for slave trading.

Today, the Netherlands Antilles is an autonomous part of the Kingdom of the Netherlands. Aruba was also part of the country until gaining separate status in 1986. Changes to the status of the other islands are in progress, with the Netherlands Antilles eventually to be dismantled. The economy depends on tourism.

There is also offshore financing and, on Curaçao and Bonaire, petroleum refining. The population includes descendants of European colonists, African slaves, and Asian laborers.

Aruba

Map Reference Pages 134–135

Aruba is a tiny island just off the coast of Venezuela. The Arawak people, native to the island, predate the arrival of Europeans by 500 years; remnants of their culture date back to 1000 CE.

Aruba is mostly flat; its highest point, Mt Jamanota, is only 617 feet (188 m) high. The island has no rivers and lies outside the hurricane routes of the Caribbean. Because the temperature is consistently warm it provides a very welcoming climate for tourists.

Amerigo Vespucci and Alonso de Ojeda arrived in 1499, claiming Aruba for Spain, which later colonized the island. The Dutch arrived in 1636 and, with minor exceptions, have administered Aruba ever since.

Aruba has over 100,000 people living in an area slightly larger than the US city of Washington DC. The population consists mainly of mixed Arawak–European peoples. The island has a mix of cultural elements, but Dutch influences are very much evident.

Aruba is self-governing with a unicameral legislature. The prime minister is the head of the government; the Dutch monarch is the chief of state. Aruba controls internal affairs; the Dutch government is responsible for defense and foreign affairs.Tourism is a big revenue source, with well over one million visitors arriving each year.

PENHA
PENHA
PENHA
YOU ARE HERE

Puerto Rico

Map Reference Pages 134–135

Puerto Rico, one of the four Greater Antilles islands in the northern Caribbean, is located between Hispaniola to the west and the US Virgin Islands to the east. A territory of the USA, it has had Commonwealth status since 1952. Its residents are American citizens. The USA acquired Puerto Rico, along with Cuba, the Philippines, and Guam, in 1898 after the Spanish–American War.

The population is about four million, with 434,000 residing in the capital San Juan, the largest city. The economy during the Spanish colonial period was agricultural. Sugar was the chief crop and African slaves the laborers. The island experienced considerable industrial growth in the twentieth century, notably in petrochemicals and pharmaceuticals. Tourism is important, with about five million visitors arriving annually, mostly from the USA.

There is roughly equal support among Puerto Ricans for continuation of US Commonwealth status, and a move to US statehood; a minority favors independence.

Most Puerto Ricans speak Spanish as a first language, but English is also spoken widely.

Turks and Caicos Islands

Map Reference Pages 134–135

The Turks and Caicos Islands are two small neighboring island groups in the West Indies, north of Hispaniola and south of the Bahamas, in the Atlantic Ocean, rather than the Caribbean. There are eight main islands and more than 20 smaller ones. The total land area is 166 square miles (430 km²). The Caicos group has 96 percent of the territory and 82 percent of the population. Most of the low-lying islands are limestone-based, and vegetation includes marshes, mangrove swamps, and sandy beaches. They are subject to severe hurricanes and shortages of fresh water.

The Turks and Caicos Islands are possessions of the United Kingdom and are administered as a British Overseas Territory. The islands were once administered as part of the UK's Jamaican colony and then as part of the Bahamas until those islands became independent. The islands were scheduled for independence in 1982 but the plans were reversed. There is support there, and in Canada, for the islands to become a province of Canada or a part of Nova Scotia.

The population totals 22,352. Tourism, fishing, and offshore financial services are mainstays of the economy.

United States Virgin Islands

Map Reference Pages 134–135

The US Virgin Islands are located among the Leeward Islands of the Lesser Antilles in the northeastern Caribbean. The group consists of three main islands—St Croix, St John and St Thomas, and Water Island—and many tiny islands. Except for Water Island, the group has been US territory since its purchase from Denmark in 1917. Water Island was purchased, also from Denmark, in 1944 for $10,000. About three-quarters of the population are descended from African slaves. Residents are citizens of the US but do not vote in presidential elections. Another part of the archipelago is controlled by the UK and is referred to as the British Virgin Islands.

Most of the islands are volcanic and hilly, although St Croix is mostly flat. Tourism is the largest part of the economy, with about two million visitors each year. Industries include garment manufacture, electronics assembly, rum, and pharmaceuticals; a petroleum refinery on St Croix processes Venezuelan crude oil for American markets.

St Pierre and Miquelon

Map Reference Pages 122–123

Strategically situated on the northern part of the Gulf of St Lawrence, St Pierre and Miquelon is the only French-controlled territory in North America, operating as a self-governing overseas collectivity of France. Covering 10 square miles (26 km²) and 83 square miles (215 km²) respectively, St Pierre and Miquelon are primarily land bases for fishing operations. The islands are important because of their proximity to the Grand Banks fishery resource in the western Atlantic Ocean. The climate is cold and wet, with a great deal of mist and fog.

Located off the southern coast of the huge Canadian island of Newfoundland, the islands were retained by France under the Treaty of Paris in 1763. Subsequently, St Pierre and Miquelon functioned as a French overseas territory from 1811 to 1976, as a French department from 1976 to 1985, and as a French overseas territorial collectivity from 1985. The President of the Territorial Council is the head of government, which has executive power in a multiparty system.

The population are primarily Basques and Bretons who are strongly involved in the fishing industry. However, fishery sustainability problems and territorial issues with Canada have seen recent economic declines. France subsidizes the islands' economy.

Far left As well as unusual flora and over 200 species of birds, Aruba boasts such cultural curiosities as De Olde Molen, an old Dutch windmill transported from Holland.

Left Trunk Bay Beach, on the United States Virgin Islands, "the most beautiful beach in the world" some say, where white sands fringed with lush tropical vegetation give onto a heart-shaped cay.

PUERTO RICO

Official name Commonwealth of Puerto Rico
Land area 3,425 square miles (8,870 km²)
Capital San Juan
Climate Tropical marine
Population 3,958,000
Government Commonwealth; unincorporated, organized territory of the USA
Currency US dollar

TURKS AND CAICOS ISLANDS

Official name Turks and Caicos Islands
Land area 166 square miles (430 km²)
Capital Grand Turk (Cockburn Town)
Climate Tropical; marine
Population 22,352
Government Overseas territory of United Kingdom
Currency US dollar

Left In the week leading up to Ash Wednesday, Ponce in Puerto Rico stages its annual Carnival celebrations, as it has done for around 150 years. Devilish "vejigantes" patrol the streets in masks and colorful costumes, whacking anyone who comes close enough with their vejigas (animal bladders). The "Funeral of the Sardine" marks Shrove Tuesday.

UNITED STATES VIRGIN ISLANDS

Official name United States Virgin Islands
Land area 134 square miles (346 km²)
Capital Charlotte Amalie
Climate Subtropical
Population 108,210
Government Organized, unincorporated territory of the USA
Currency US dollar

Left Loggerhead sea turtles *(Caretta caretta)* can change the seabed by "mining" its sediments for prey. These turtles carry entire colonies of animals and plants with them. This one, photographed off South Caicos Island, has a remora attached to its shell, no doubt feeding on the turtle's many smaller passengers.

ST PIERRE AND MIQUELON

Official name Saint Pierre and Miquelon (Collectivité territoriale de Saint-Pierre-et-Miquelon)
Land area 93 square miles (241 km²)
Capital Saint-Pierre
Climate Cold and wet, abundant fog, seasonal winds
Population 7,044
Government Self-governing overseas territorial collectivity of France
Currency Euro

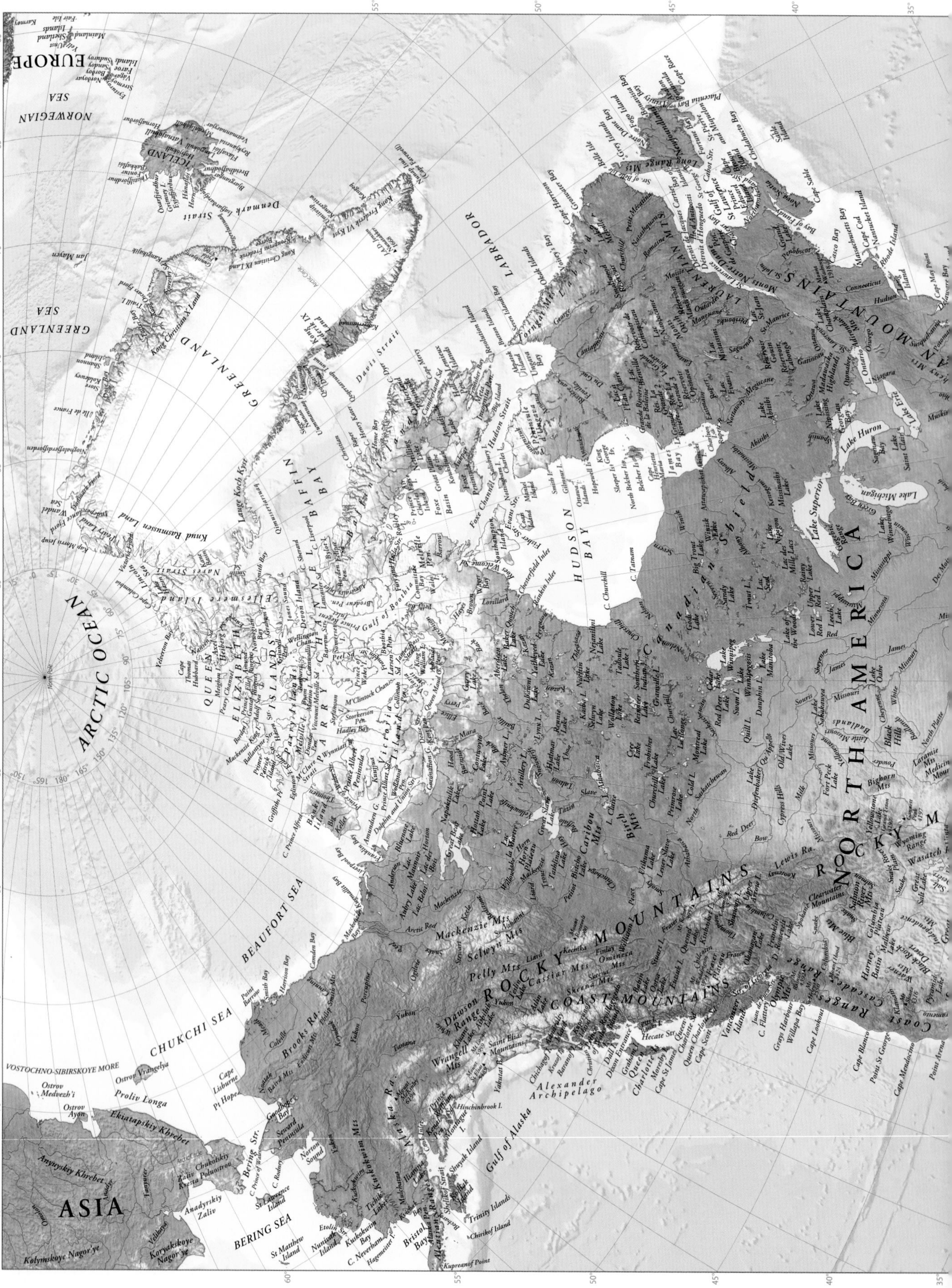

1:25,300,000

Lambert Azimuthal Equal Area

0 250 500 750 1000 kilometers

0 125 250 375 500 miles

North America Physical

ATLANTIC OCEAN
PACIFIC OCEAN
GULF OF MEXICO
CARIBBEAN SEA
SOUTH AMERICA
WEST INDIES
GREATER ANTILLES
LESSER ANTILLES
BAHAMAS
CUBA
HISPANIOLA
Sierra Madre Oriental
Sierra Madre Occidental
Sierra Madre del Sur
Golfo de California
Baja California
Bahía de Campeche
Yucatan
Istmo de Tehuantepec
Archipiélago de Colón (Galapagos Islands)
Clipperton Island
Isla del Coco
Equator
Tropic of Cancer
THE CARIBBEAN
Same scale as main map

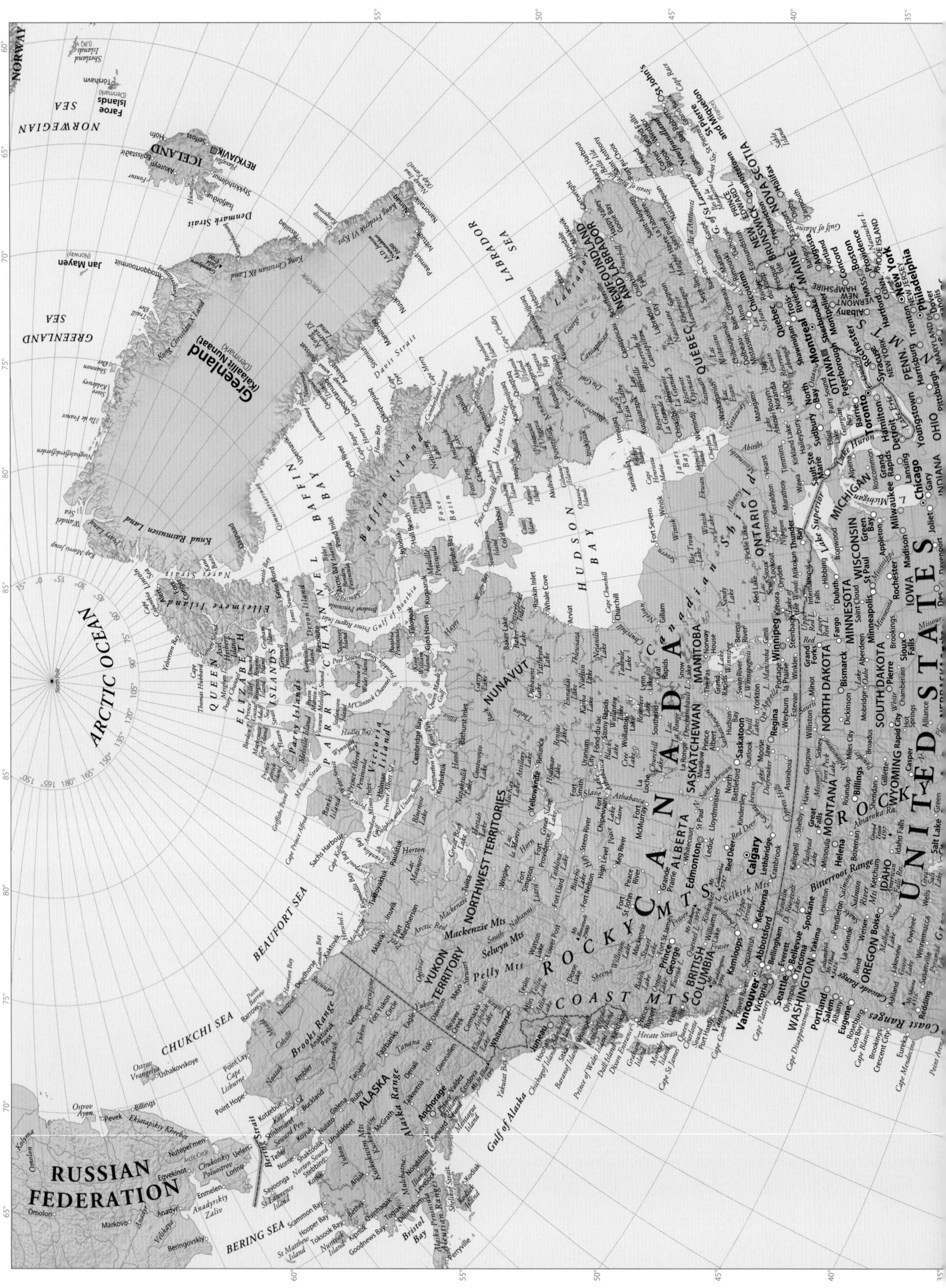
ARCTIC OCEAN
NORWEGIAN SEA
GREENLAND SEA
Greenland
(Kalaallit Nunaat)
(Denmark)
ICELAND
REYKJAVIK
Faroe Islands
(Denmark)
Jan Mayen
(Norway)
Denmark Strait
LABRADOR SEA
Davis Strait
BAFFIN BAY
Baffin Island
HUDSON BAY
Hudson Strait
Foxe Basin
James Bay
Ellesmere Island
QUEEN ELIZABETH ISLANDS
PARRY CHANNEL
Parry Islands
Victoria Island
BEAUFORT SEA
CHUKCHI SEA
BERING SEA
Bering Strait
Gulf of Alaska
Bristol Bay
RUSSIAN FEDERATION
ALASKA
Brooks Range
Alaska Range
Anchorage
Fairbanks
Juneau
YUKON TERRITORY
Whitehorse
NORTHWEST TERRITORIES
Yellowknife
NUNAVUT
Mackenzie Mts
Selwyn Mts
Pelly Mts
ROCKY MTS
COAST MTS
BRITISH COLUMBIA
Vancouver
Victoria
Prince George
ALBERTA
Edmonton
Calgary
SASKATCHEWAN
Saskatoon
Regina
MANITOBA
Winnipeg
ONTARIO
Canadian Shield
OTTAWA
Toronto
QUEBEC
Quebec
Montreal
NEWFOUNDLAND AND LABRADOR
St John's
NEW BRUNSWICK
NOVA SCOTIA
Halifax
PRINCE EDWARD ISLAND
St Pierre and Miquelon
(France)
CANADA
UNITED STATES
WASHINGTON
Seattle
OREGON
Portland
IDAHO
MONTANA
WYOMING
NORTH DAKOTA
SOUTH DAKOTA
MINNESOTA
WISCONSIN
MICHIGAN
IOWA
ILLINOIS
Chicago
INDIANA
OHIO
PENN.
NEW YORK
New York
Philadelphia
Boston
MAINE
Lake Superior
Lake Huron
Lake Michigan
Lake Winnipeg
Great Slave Lake
Great Bear Lake

1:25,300,000
Lambert Azimuthal Equal Area

0 250 500 750 1000 kilometers
0 125 250 375 500 miles

North America Political

ATLANTIC OCEAN
PACIFIC OCEAN
GULF OF MEXICO
CARIBBEAN SEA
MEXICO
CUBA
BAHAMAS
JAMAICA
HAITI
DOMINICAN REPUBLIC
BELIZE
GUATEMALA
HONDURAS
EL SALVADOR
NICARAGUA
COSTA RICA
PANAMA
COLOMBIA
VENEZUELA
ECUADOR
PERU
BRAZIL
CIUDAD DE MÉXICO
LA HABANA (HAVANA)
KINGSTON
PORT-AU-PRINCE
SANTO DOMINGO
BELMOPAN
TEGUCIGALPA
MANAGUA
SAN JOSÉ
BOGOTÁ
QUITO
LIMA
CARACAS
Clipperton Island (France)
THE CARIBBEAN
Same scale as main map

Meters / Feet
6000 19685
5000 16404
4000 13123
3000 9843
2000 6562
1000 3281
500 1640
200 656
100 328
0
LAND BELOW SEA LEVEL
100 328
200 656
1000 3281
2000 6562
4000 13123
6000 19685

1:15,950,000

Lambert Conic Conformal Projection

0 200 400 600 800 kilometers

0 100 200 300 400 miles

237

124

Alaska, Northern Canada, and Greenland

Meters
Feet

Meters	Feet
6000	19685
5000	16404
4000	13123
3000	9843
2000	6562
1000	3281
500	1640
200	656
100	328
0	LAND BELOW SEA LEVEL
100	328
200	656
1000	3281
2000	6562
4000	13123
6000	19685

127

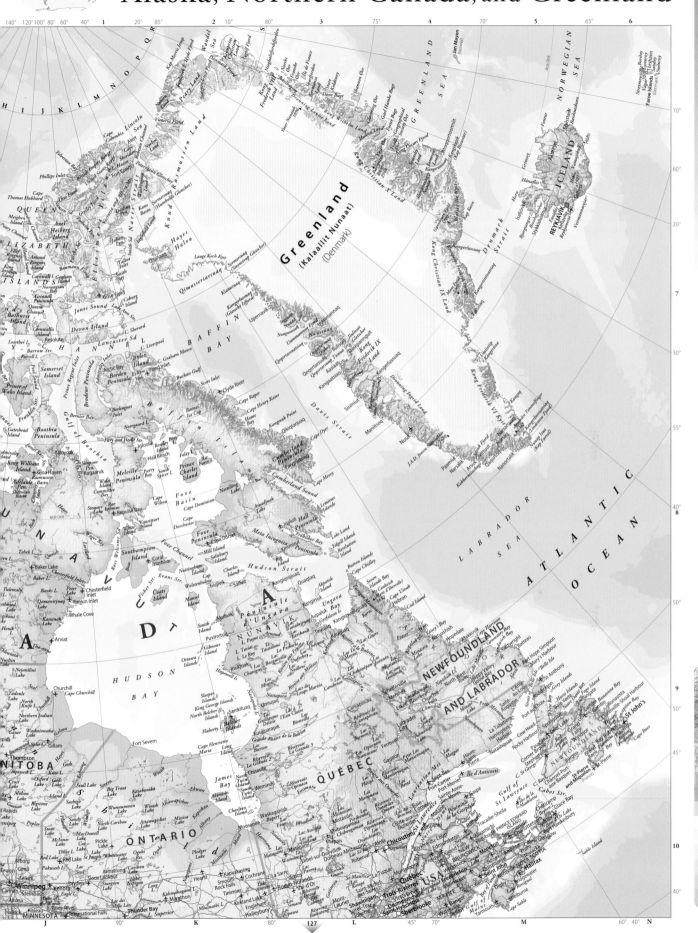

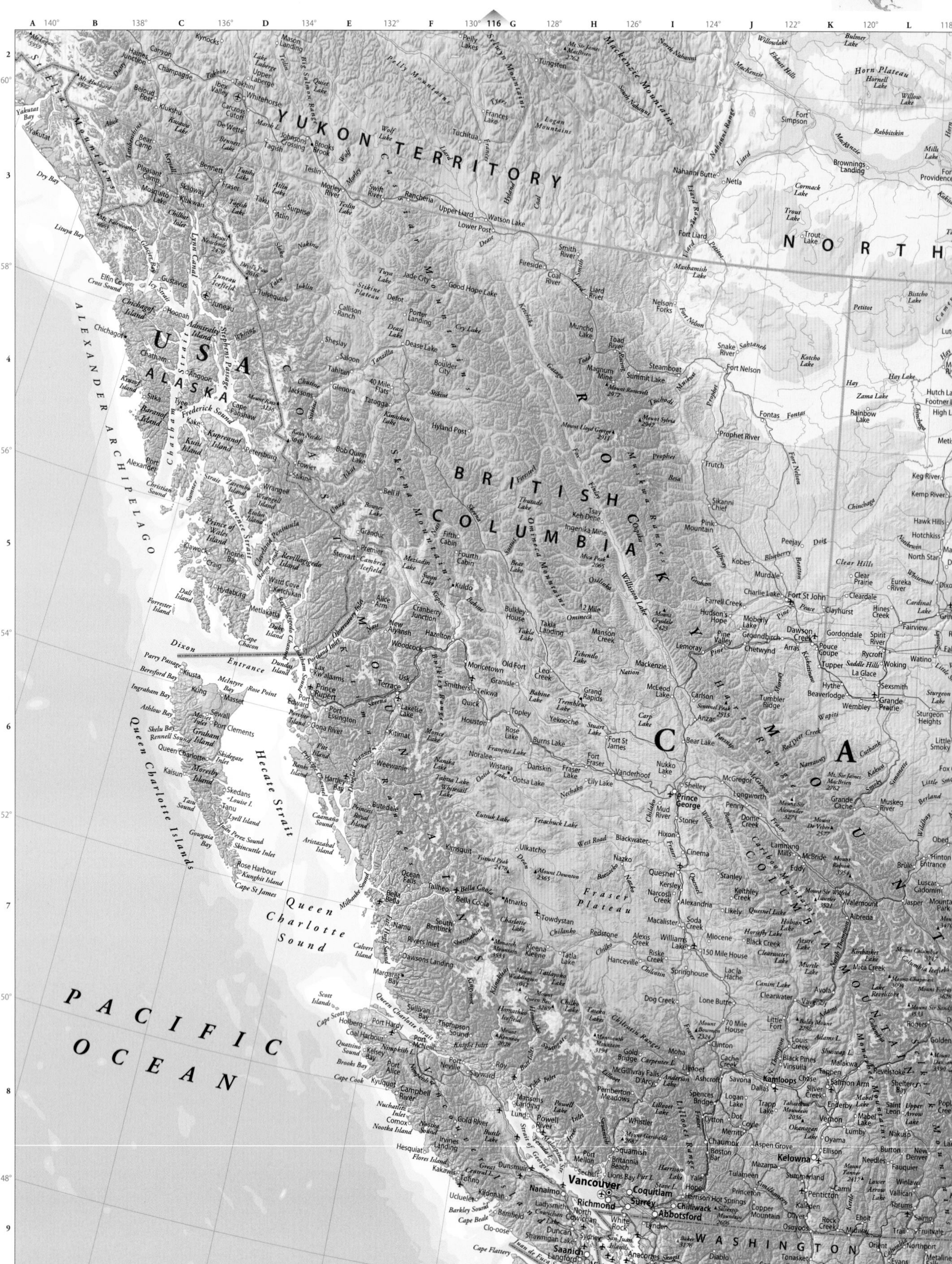
YUKON TERRITORY
BRITISH COLUMBIA
USA
ALASKA
PACIFIC OCEAN
ALEXANDER ARCHIPELAGO
Queen Charlotte Islands
Hecate Strait
Queen Charlotte Sound
Dixon Entrance
WASHINGTON
COAST MOUNTAINS
ROCKY MOUNTAINS
CARIBOO MOUNTAINS
Fraser Plateau
Mackenzie Mountains
Pelly Mountains
Skeena Mountains
Omineca Mountains
Stikine Plateau
Whitehorse
Juneau
Prince Rupert
Prince George
Vancouver
Victoria
Kamloops
Kelowna
Fort Nelson
Fort St John
Dawson Creek
Grande Prairie
Fort Simpson
Watson Lake
Williams Lake
Quesnel
Nanaimo
Richmond
Surrey
Coquitlam
Abbotsford
Saanich
Sitka
Ketchikan
Skagway
Haines
Petersburg
Wrangell
Terrace
Smithers
Kitimat
Campbell River
Port Hardy
Bella Coola
Penticton
Vernon
Revelstoke
Chilliwack
Squamish
Powell River
Vancouver Island
Williston Lake
NORTH

1:5,630,000
Lambert Conic Conformal Projection

0 50 100 150 200 kilometers
0 25 50 75 100 miles

Meters / Feet
6000 19685
5000 16404
4000 13123
3000 9843
2000 6562
1000 3281
500 1640
200 656
100 328
0
LAND BELOW SEA LEVEL
100 328
200 656
1000 3281
2000 6562
4000 13123
6000 19685

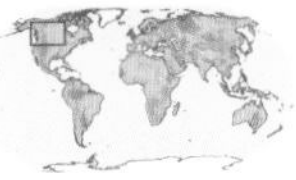

Western Canada

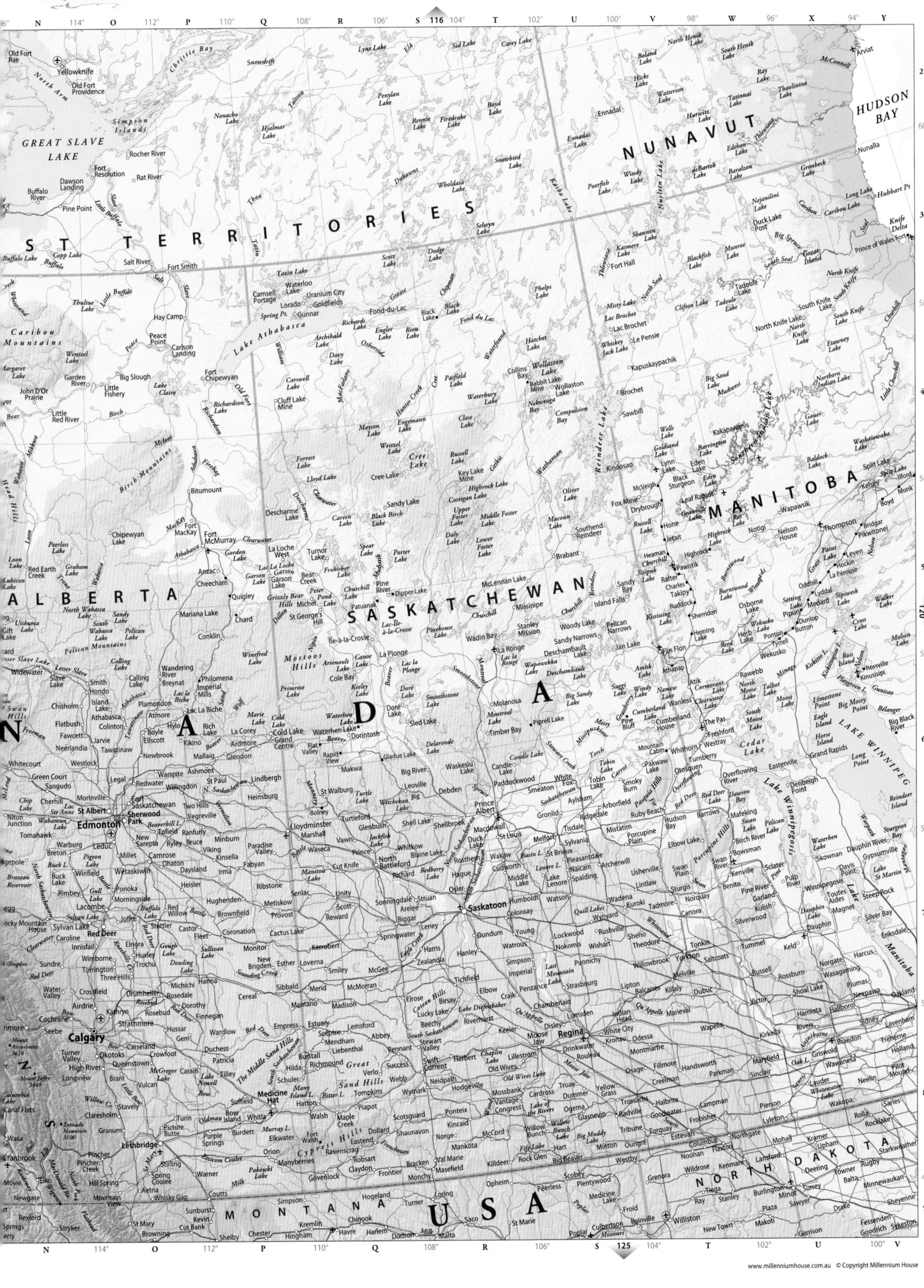

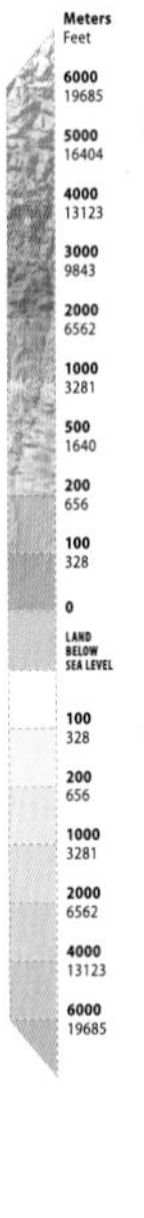

NORTHWEST TERRITORIES

NUNAVUT

ALBERTA

SASKATCHEWAN

MANITOBA

CANADA

HUDSON BAY

GREAT SLAVE LAKE

LAKE WINNIPEG

MONTANA

NORTH DAKOTA

USA

116

120

125

Meters / Feet

6000 19685

5000 16404

4000 13123

3000 9843

2000 6562

1000 3281

500 1640

200 656

100 328

0

LAND BELOW SEA LEVEL

100 328

200 656

1000 3281

2000 6562

4000 13123

6000 19685

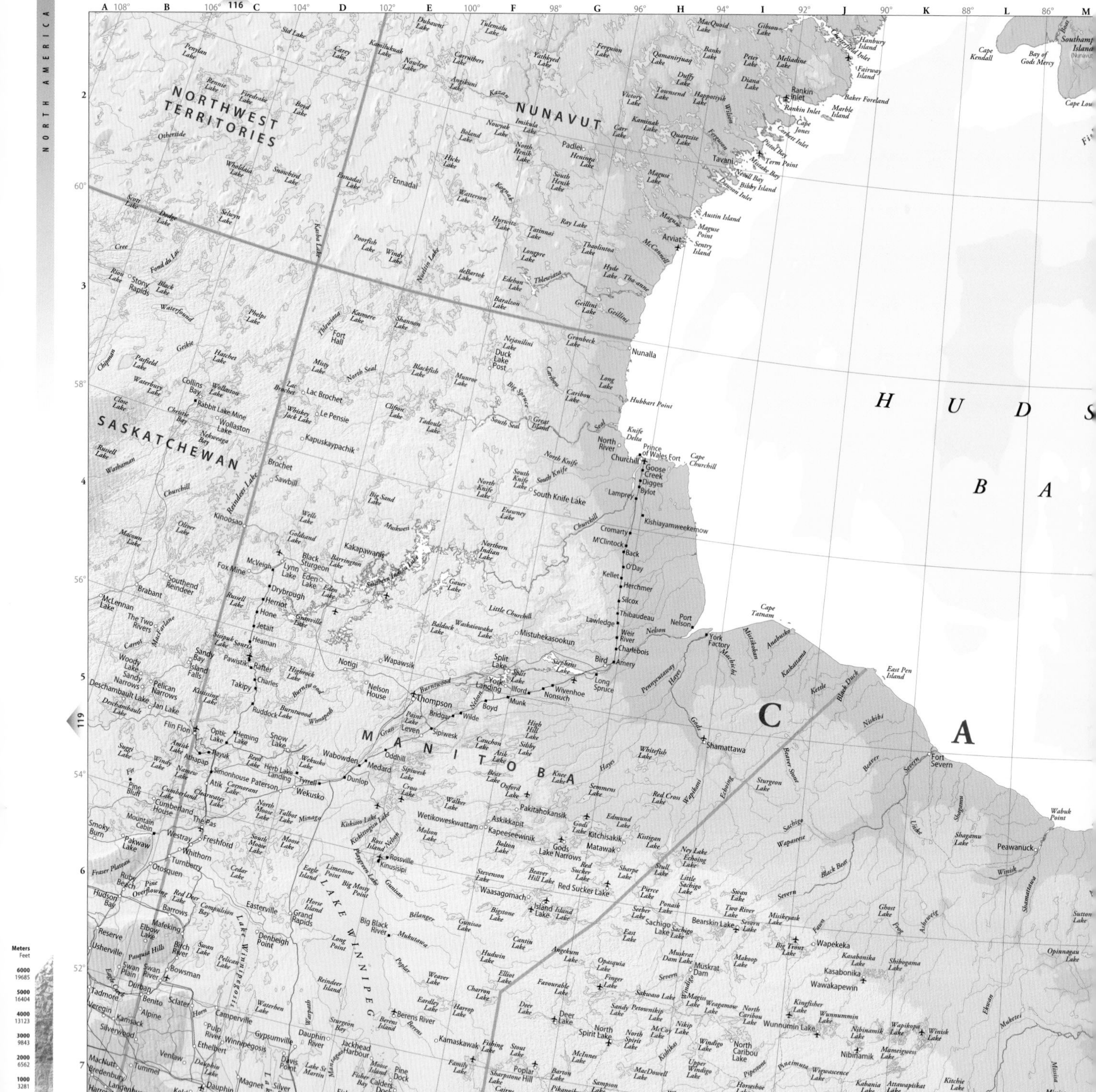

NORTHWEST TERRITORIES

NUNAVUT

SASKATCHEWAN

MANITOBA

ONTARIO

CANADA

HUDSON BAY

LAKE WINNIPEG

Lake Winnipegosis

Lake Manitoba

NORTH DAKOTA

USA

MINNESOTA

Winnipeg

Thompson

Churchill

The Pas

Flin Flon

Brandon

Arviat

Rankin Inlet

Fort Severn

Peawanuck

Meters / Feet

Meters	Feet
6000	19685
5000	16404
4000	13123
3000	9843
2000	6562
1000	3281
500	1640
200	656
100	328
0	
LAND BELOW SEA LEVEL	
100	328
200	656
1000	3281
2000	6562
4000	13123
6000	19685

1:5,630,000

Lambert Conic Conformal Projection

0 50 100 150 200 kilometers

0 25 50 75 100 miles

116 119 126

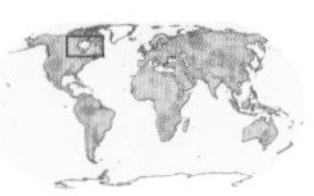

Central Canada

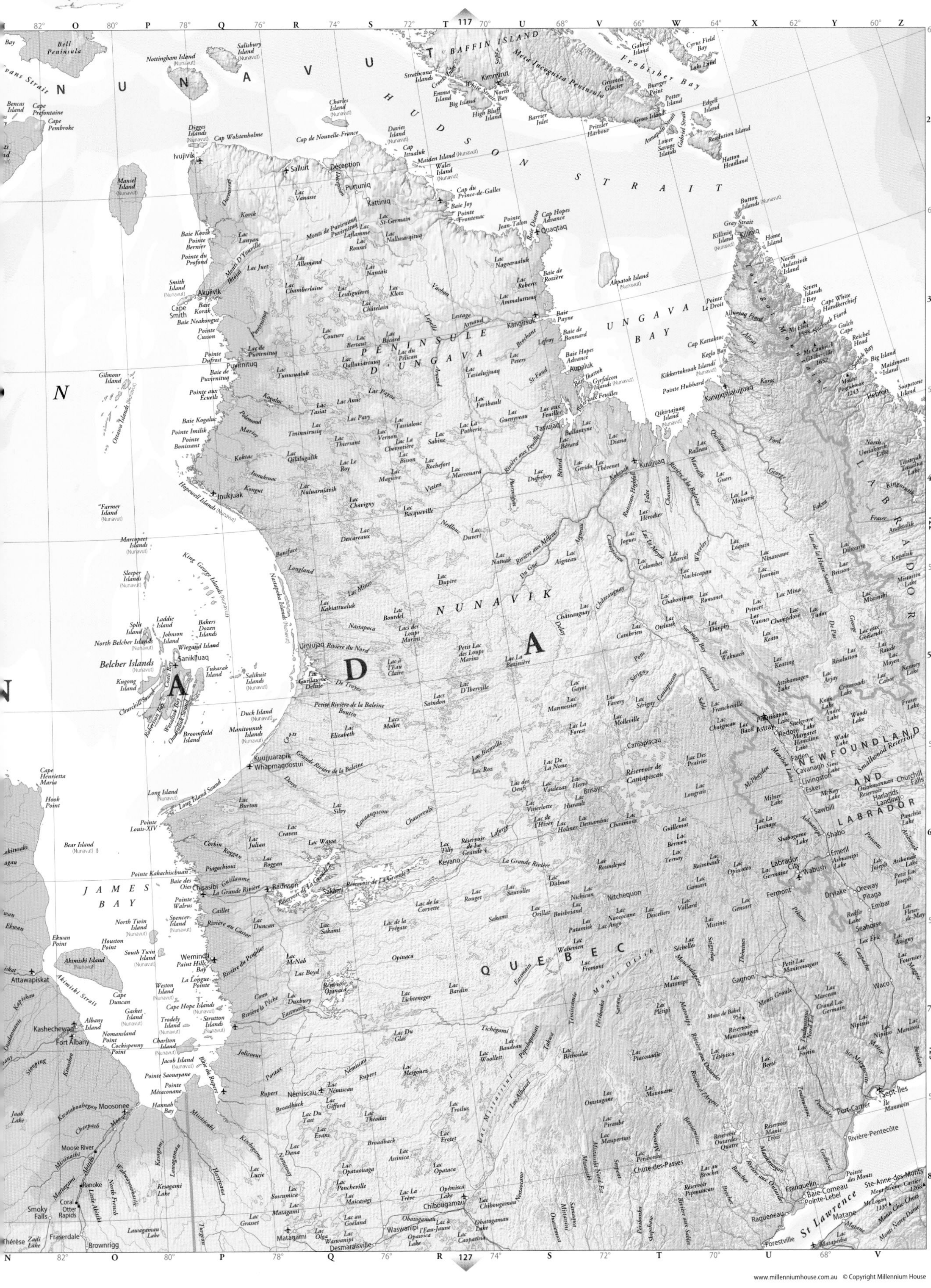

NUNAVUT
CANADA
HUDSON STRAIT
UNGAVA BAY
JAMES BAY
BAFFIN ISLAND
PENINSULE D'UNGAVA
NUNAVIK
QUEBEC
NEWFOUNDLAND AND LABRADOR
LABRADOR
Belcher Islands
Mansel Island
Akimiski Island
St Lawrence
Réservoir de Caniapiscau
Kuujjuaq
Inukjuak
Kuujjuarapik
Whapmagoostui
Chisasibi
Radisson
Moosonee
Fort Albany
Attawapiskat
Labrador City
Wabush
Fermont
Sept-Îles
Baie-Comeau
Chibougamau
Matagami
Schefferville
Kangiqsualujjuaq
Salluit
Ivujivik
Puvirnituq
Akulivik
Kangirsuk
Aupaluk
Tasiujaq
Quaqtaq
Kimmirut
Hebron
Churchill Falls
Gagnon
Port-Cartier
Meters / Feet
6000 19685
5000 16404
4000 13123
3000 9843
2000 6562
1000 3281
500 1640
200 656
100 328
0
LAND BELOW SEA LEVEL
117
122
123
127

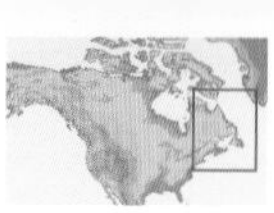

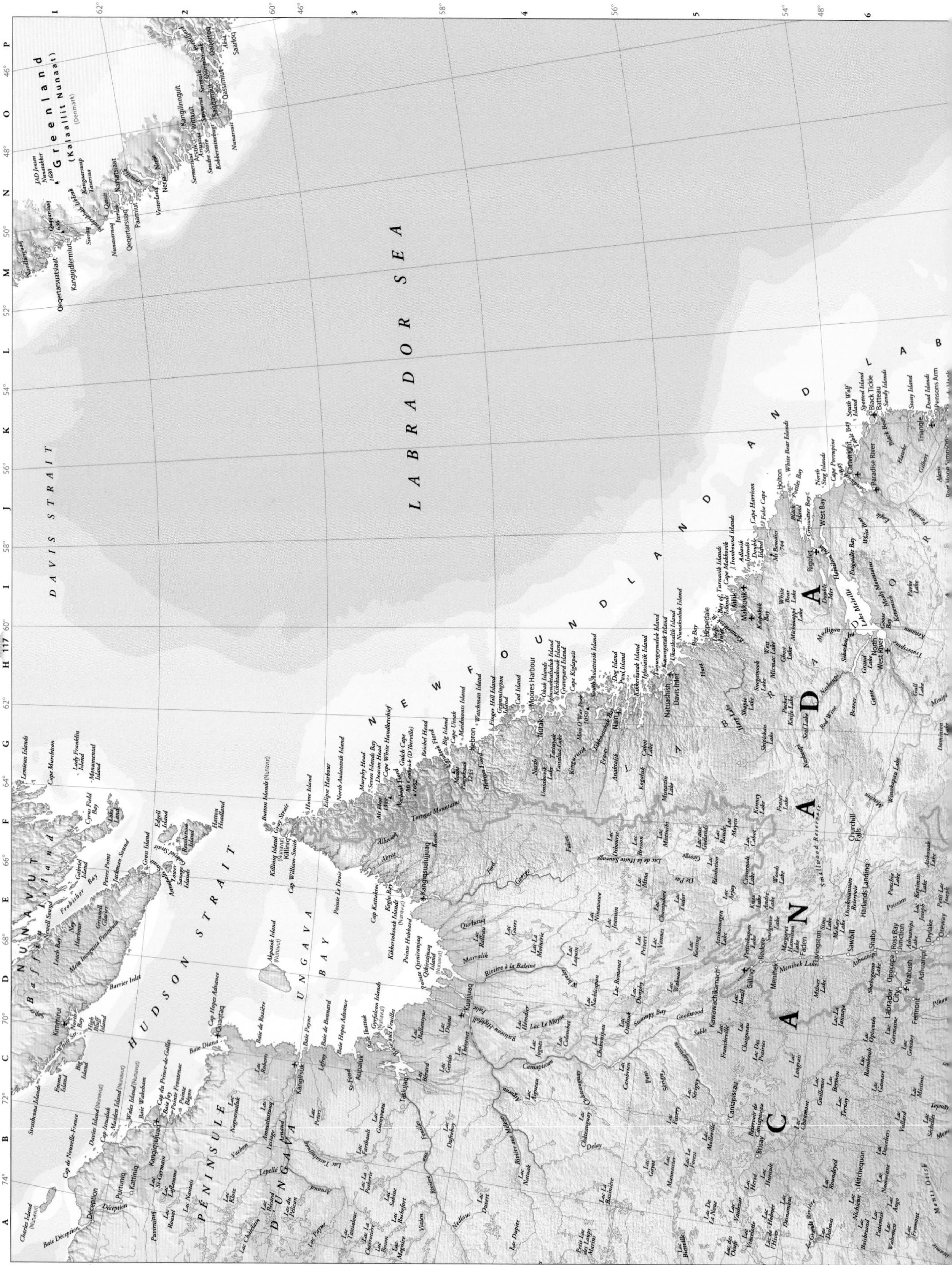

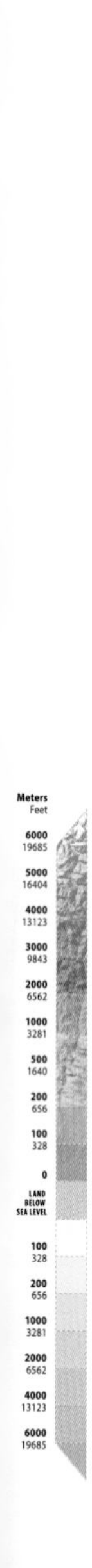

Greenland
(Kalaallit Nunaat)
(Denmark)
DAVIS STRAIT
LABRADOR SEA
NUNAVUT
Baffin Island
HUDSON STRAIT
UNGAVA BAY
PÉNINSULE D'UNGAVA
NEWFOUNDLAND AND LABRADOR
CANADA

117

121

Meters	Feet
6000	19685
5000	16404
4000	13123
3000	9843
2000	6562
1000	3281
500	1640
200	656
100	328
0	
LAND BELOW SEA LEVEL	
100	328
200	656
1000	3281
2000	6562
4000	13123
6000	19685

1:5,630,000

Lambert Conic Conformal Projection

0 50 100 150 200 kilometers

0 25 50 75 100 miles

Eastern Canada

Meters / Feet

6000 / 19685

5000 / 16404

4000 / 13123

3000 / 9843

2000 / 6562

1000 / 3281

500 / 1640

200 / 656

100 / 328

0 / LAND BELOW SEA LEVEL

100 / 328

200 / 656

1000 / 3281

2000 / 6562

4000 / 13123

6000 / 19685

127

PACIFIC OCEAN
UNITED STAT
BRITISH COLUMBIA
ALBERTA
WASHINGTON
OREGON
IDAHO
NEVADA
CALIFORNIA
CASCADE RANGE
COLUMBIA PLATEAU
BITTERROOT RANGE
COAST RANGES
ROCKY MOUNTAINS
Vancouver Island
Great Salt Lake Desert
Great Salt Lake
Vancouver
Victoria
Seattle
Tacoma
Spokane
Portland
Salem
Eugene
Boise
Sacramento
San Francisco
Oakland
San Jose
Reno
Calgary
Kelowna
Kamloops
Missoula
Pocatello
118
128
Meters
Feet
LAND BELOW SEA LEVEL

1:5,630,000

Lambert Conic Conformal Projection

0 50 100 150 200 kilometers

0 25 50 75 100 miles

Northwestern USA

119

126

129

Meters	Feet
6000	19685
5000	16404
4000	13123
3000	9843
2000	6562
1000	3281
500	1640
200	656
100	328
0	
LAND BELOW SEA LEVEL	
100	328
200	656
1000	3281
2000	6562
4000	13123
6000	19685

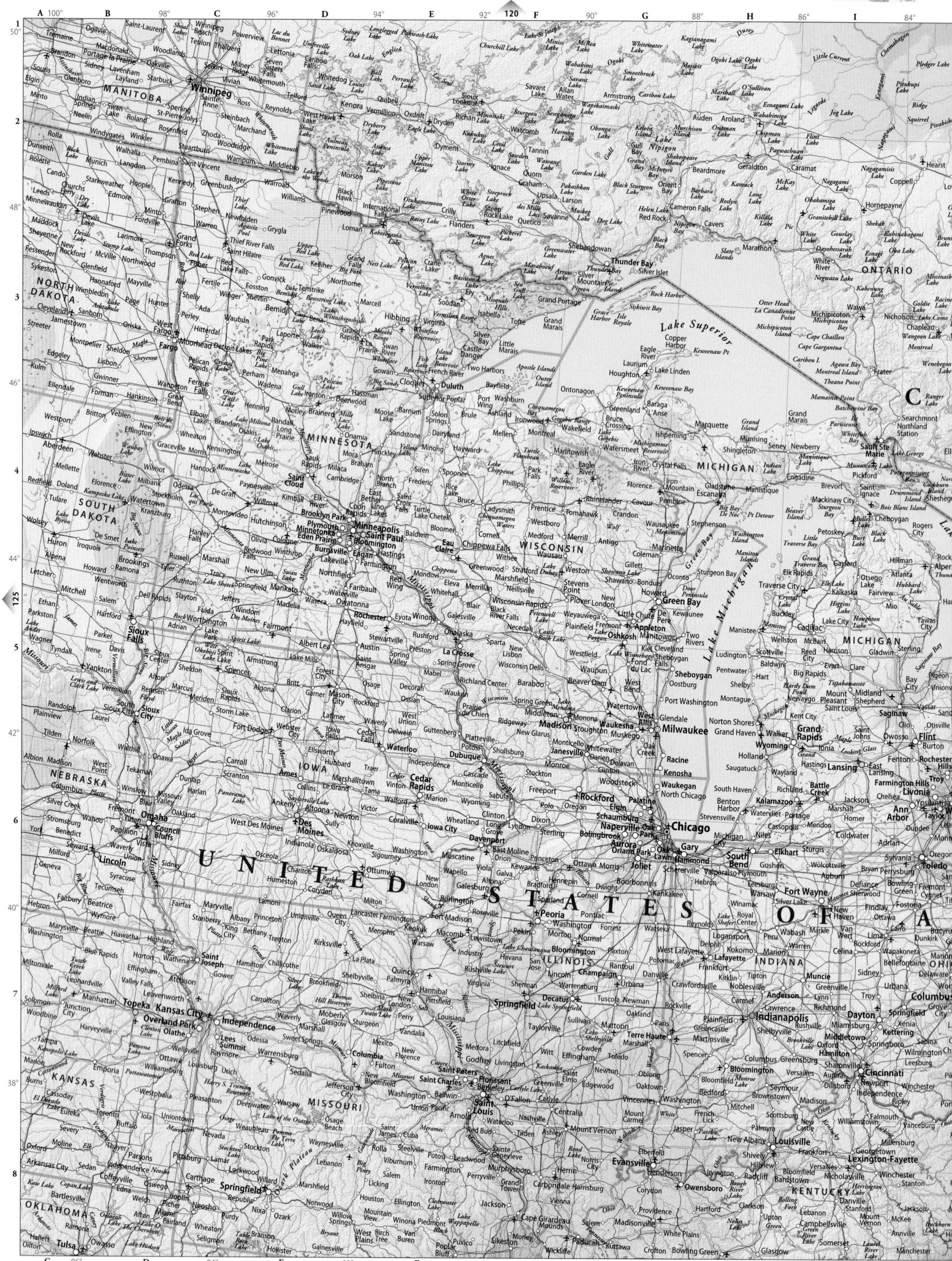
MANITOBA
ONTARIO
NORTH DAKOTA
SOUTH DAKOTA
MINNESOTA
WISCONSIN
MICHIGAN
IOWA
NEBRASKA
ILLINOIS
INDIANA
KANSAS
MISSOURI
KENTUCKY
OKLAHOMA
UNITED STATES OF A
Lake Superior
Lake Michigan
Winnipeg
Minneapolis
Saint Paul
Chicago
Milwaukee
Indianapolis
Kansas City
Omaha
Des Moines
Saint Louis
Thunder Bay
Duluth
120
125
130

Meters / Feet

Meters	Feet
6000	19685
5000	16404
4000	13123
3000	9843
2000	6562
1000	3281
500	1640
200	656
100	328
0	
LAND BELOW SEA LEVEL	
100	328
200	656
1000	3281
2000	6562
4000	13123
6000	19685

1:5,630,000

Lambert Conic Conformal Projection

0 50 100 150 200 kilometers

0 25 50 75 100 miles

Northeastern USA

121

123

131

CANADA

QUÉBEC

NEW BRUNSWICK

MAINE

NEW HAMPSHIRE

VERMONT

MASSACHUSETTS

RHODE ISLAND

CONNECTICUT

NEW YORK

NEW JERSEY

PENNSYLVANIA

DELAWARE

MARYLAND

DISTRICT OF COLUMBIA

WEST VIRGINIA

VIRGINIA

AMERICA

Gulf of Maine

ATLANTIC OCEAN

Lake Ontario

Lake Erie

APPALACHIAN MOUNTAINS

ALLEGHENY MOUNTAINS

BERMUDA
(UK)
1:938,600

ATLANTIC OCEAN

St George's I.
St Catherine Pt
St George
St David's I.
Harrington Sound
Castle Harbour
Flatts Village
Ireland I. North
Ireland I. South
Somerset
Somerset I.
Great Sound
Hamilton
Main Island
Gibb's Hill 75
32°20′
64°50′
64°40′

Meters / Feet

Meters	Feet
6000	19685
5000	16404
4000	13123
3000	9843
2000	6562
1000	3281
500	1640
200	656
100	328
0	LAND BELOW SEA LEVEL
100	328
200	656
1000	3281
2000	6562
4000	13123
6000	19685

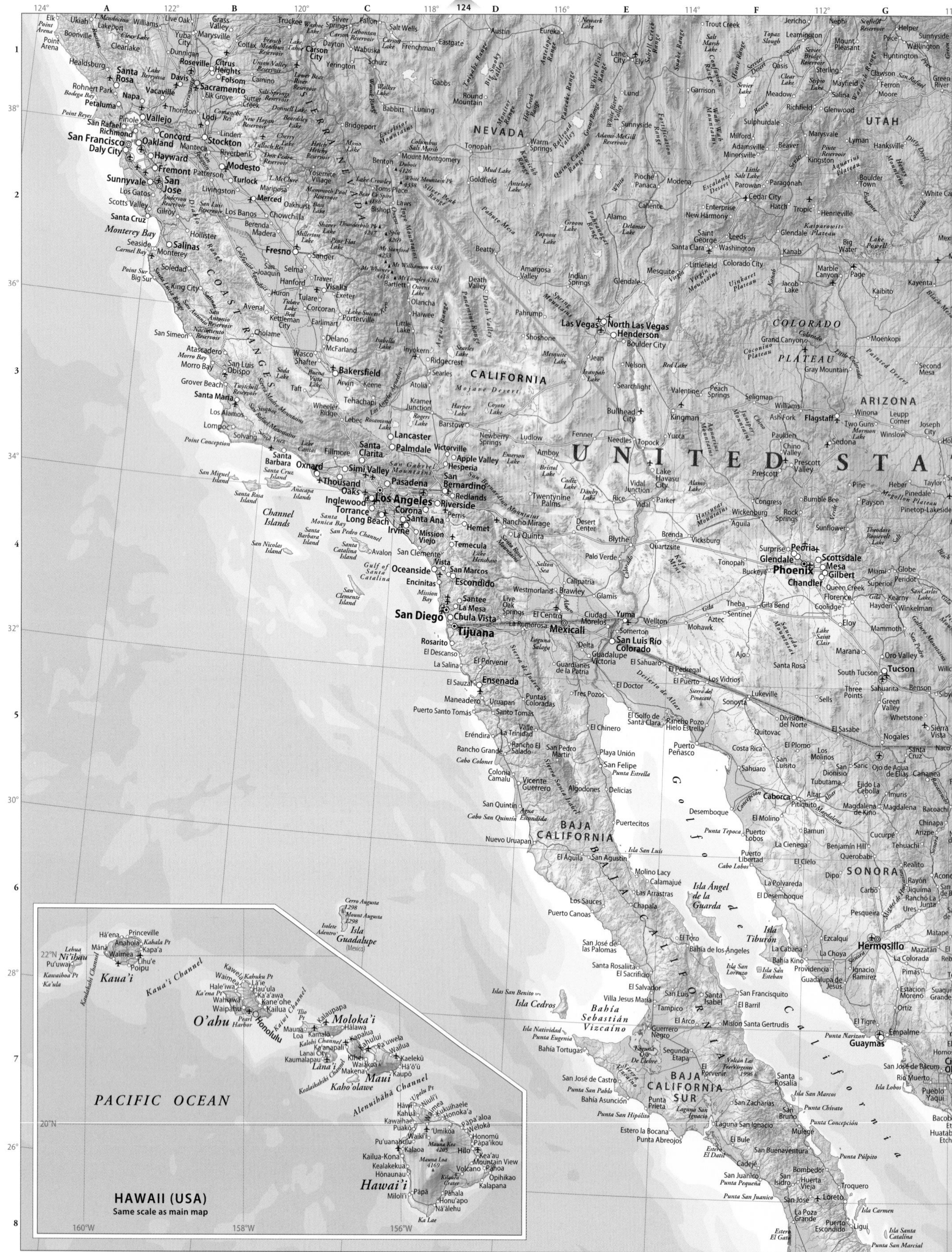
124
132
NEVADA
UTAH
CALIFORNIA
ARIZONA
UNITED STA
COLORADO PLATEAU
SONORA
BAJA CALIFORNIA
BAJA CALIFORNIA SUR
Golfo de California
Mojave Desert
COAST RANGES
SIERRA NEVADA
Channel Islands
Gulf of Santa Catalina
Monterey Bay
Isla Guadalupe (Mexico)
Isla Cedros
Bahía Sebastián Vizcaíno
Isla Ángel de la Guarda
Isla Tiburón
San Francisco
Oakland
Sacramento
Stockton
Modesto
Fresno
San Jose
Santa Rosa
Salinas
Bakersfield
Los Angeles
Long Beach
Santa Ana
Riverside
San Bernardino
Pasadena
Oxnard
San Diego
Chula Vista
Tijuana
Mexicali
Ensenada
Las Vegas
North Las Vegas
Henderson
Phoenix
Scottsdale
Mesa
Chandler
Glendale
Peoria
Tucson
Yuma
Flagstaff
Hermosillo
Guaymas
Empalme
Caborca
Nogales
Reno
Carson City
HAWAII (USA)
Same scale as main map
PACIFIC OCEAN
Ni'ihau
Kaua'i
O'ahu
Honolulu
Moloka'i
Lāna'i
Maui
Kaho'olawe
Hawai'i
Kaua'i Channel
Kaiwi Channel
Alenuihāhā Channel
160°W
158°W
156°W
22°N
20°N
Meters
Feet
6000 19685
5000 16404
4000 13123
3000 9843
2000 6562
1000 3281
500 1640
200 656
100 328
0
LAND BELOW SEA LEVEL
100 328
200 656
1000 3281
2000 6562
4000 13123
6000 19685

1:5,630,000

Lambert Conic Conformal Projection

0 50 100 150 200 kilometers

0 25 50 75 100 miles

Southwestern USA

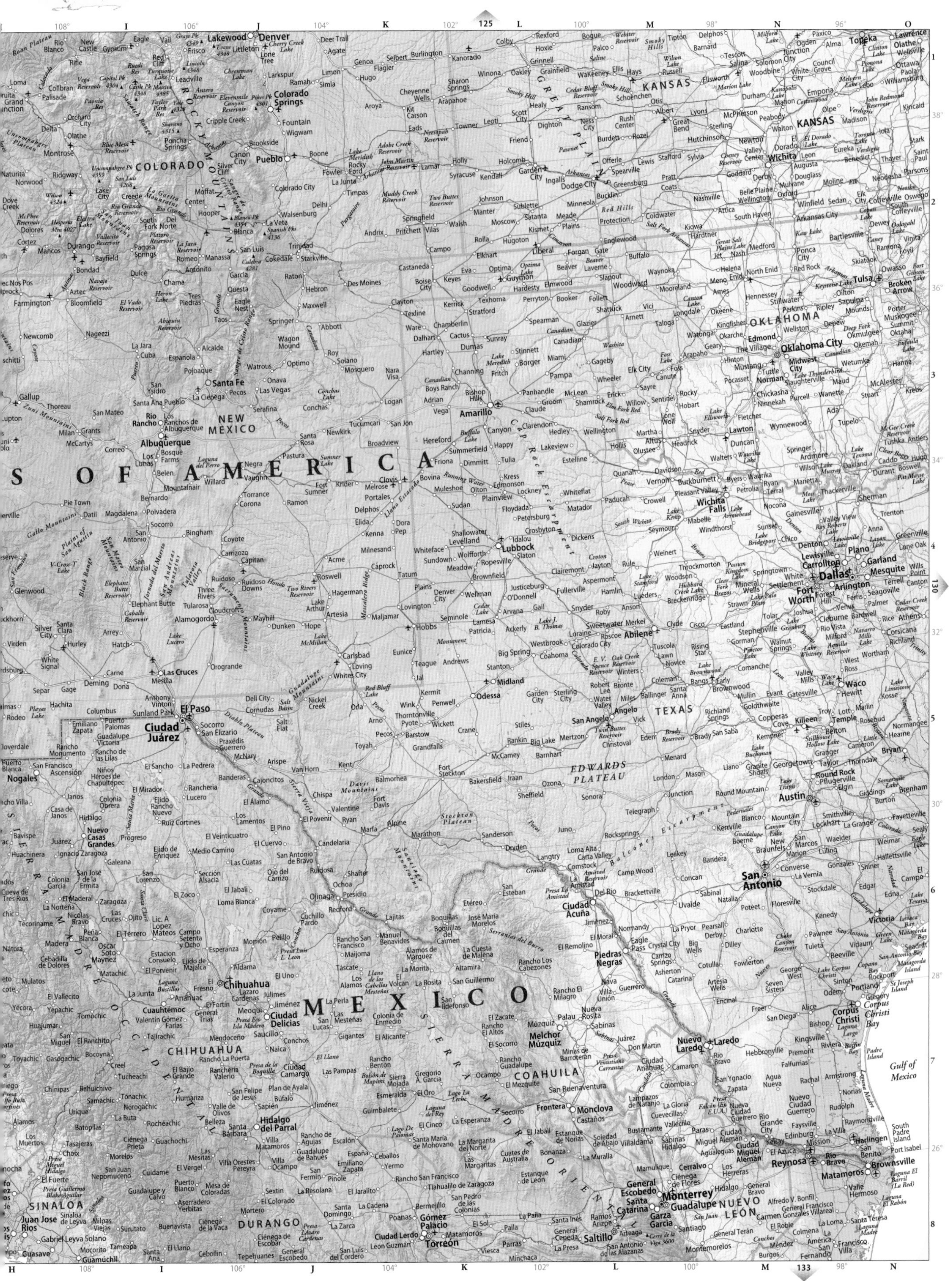
COLORADO
KANSAS
OKLAHOMA
NEW MEXICO
TEXAS
S OF AMERICA
MEXICO
CHIHUAHUA
COAHUILA
DURANGO
NUEVO LEÓN
SINALOA
ROCKY MOUNTAINS
GREAT PLAINS
EDWARDS PLATEAU
SIERRA MADRE OCCIDENTAL
SIERRA MADRE ORIENTAL
Denver
Lakewood
Colorado Springs
Pueblo
Topeka
Wichita
Oklahoma City
Tulsa
Santa Fe
Albuquerque
Amarillo
Lubbock
El Paso
Ciudad Juárez
Dallas
Fort Worth
Arlington
Austin
San Antonio
Corpus Christi
Laredo
Nuevo Laredo
Chihuahua
Monterrey
Saltillo
Torreón
Gulf of Mexico
Meters
Feet
LAND BELOW SEA LEVEL
125
130
133

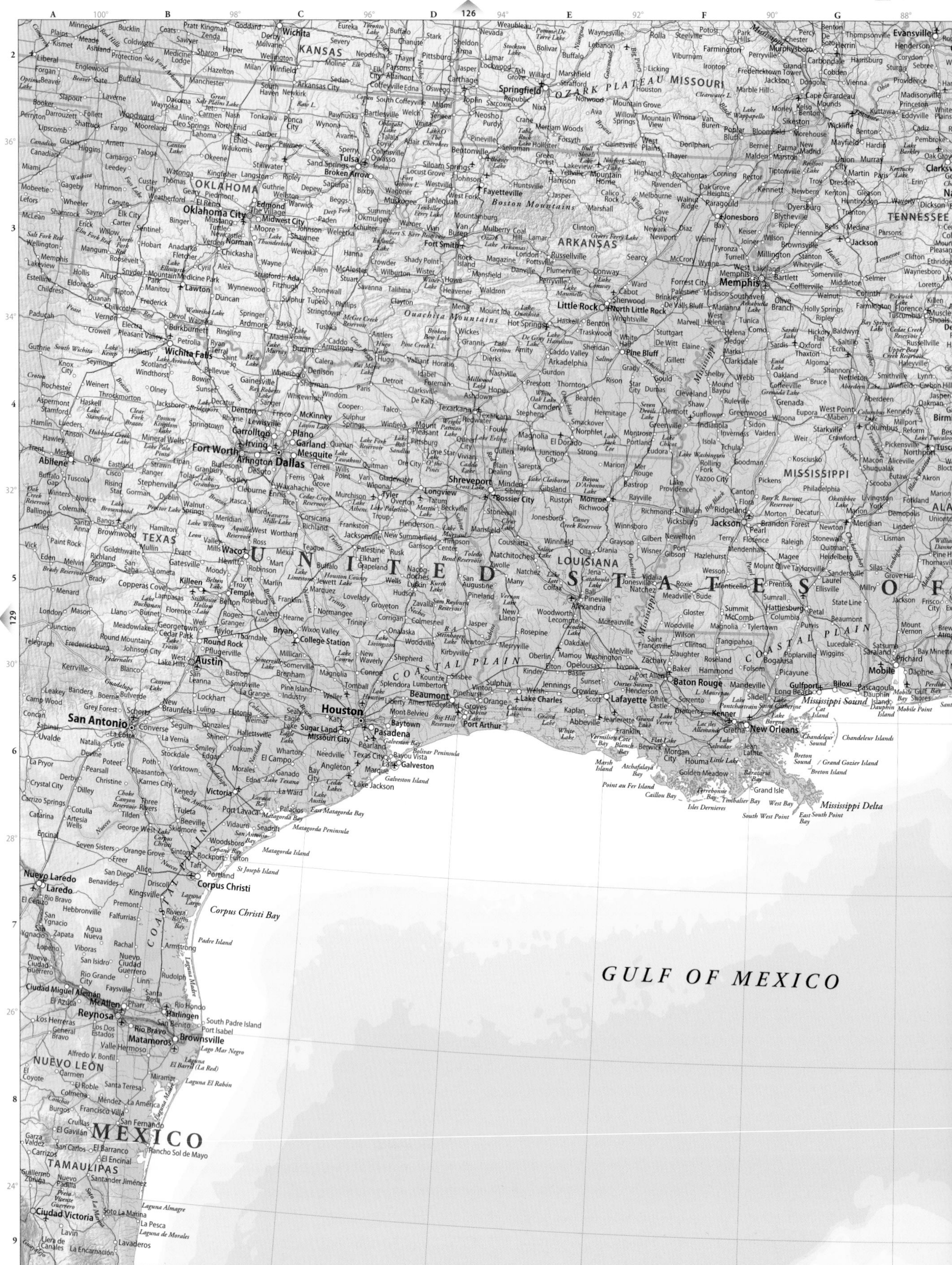
126
129
133
A
B
C
D
E
F
G
100°
98°
96°
94°
92°
90°
88°
36°
34°
32°
30°
28°
26°
24°
KANSAS
MISSOURI
OKLAHOMA
ARKANSAS
TENNESSEE
TEXAS
LOUISIANA
MISSISSIPPI
UNITED STATES OF
MEXICO
NUEVO LEON
TAMAULIPAS
GULF OF MEXICO
OZARK PLATEAU
Boston Mountains
Ouachita Mountains
COASTAL PLAIN
Mississippi Delta
Mississippi Sound
Chandeleur Islands
Corpus Christi Bay
Padre Island
Matagorda Island
Galveston Island
Laguna Madre
Wichita
Tulsa
Springfield
Oklahoma City
Fort Smith
Little Rock
Memphis
Jackson
Shreveport
Dallas
Fort Worth
Arlington
Abilene
Wichita Falls
Waco
Austin
San Antonio
Houston
Beaumont
Port Arthur
Baton Rouge
New Orleans
Lafayette
Lake Charles
Mobile
Biloxi
Gulfport
Corpus Christi
Laredo
Nuevo Laredo
McAllen
Reynosa
Brownsville
Matamoros
Ciudad Victoria
Evansville
Jonesboro
Pine Bluff
Texarkana
Tyler
Longview
Killeen
Bryan
College Station
Victoria
Galveston
Pasadena

1:5,630,000

Lambert Conic Conformal Projection

0 50 100 150 200 kilometers

0 25 50 75 100 miles

Meters / Feet
6000 19685
5000 16404
4000 13123
3000 9843
2000 6562
1000 3281
500 1640
200 656
100 328
0
LAND BELOW SEA LEVEL
100 328
200 656
1000 3281
2000 6562
4000 13123
6000 19685

Southeastern USA

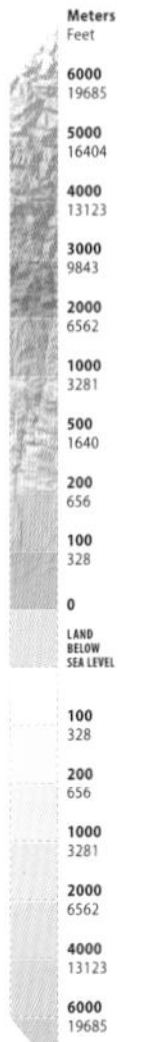

KENTUCKY
VIRGINIA
WEST VIRGINIA
NORTH CAROLINA
SOUTH CAROLINA
GEORGIA
FLORIDA
AMERICA
BAHAMAS
ATLANTIC OCEAN
APPALACHIAN MOUNTAINS
BLUE RIDGE
CUMBERLAND PLATEAU
Straits of Florida
Great Bahama Bank
Little Bahama Bank
Florida Keys
Florida Bay
Grand Bahama
Grand Abaco
Andros
Eleuthera
Cat Island
New Providence
NASSAU
Richmond
Norfolk
Virginia Beach
Raleigh
Charlotte
Columbia
Atlanta
Savannah
Jacksonville
Tallahassee
Orlando
Tampa
Miami
Key West
Chesapeake Bay
Pamlico Sound
Albemarle Sd
Onslow Bay
Raleigh Bay
Long Bay
Cape Hatteras
Cape Lookout
Cape Fear
Cape Canaveral
Cape Sable
Northwest Providence Channel
Northeast Providence Channel
Tongue of the Ocean
Santaren Channel

Meters / Feet
6000 19685
5000 16404
4000 13123
3000 9843
2000 6562
1000 3281
500 1640
200 656
100 328
0
LAND BELOW SEA LEVEL
100 328
200 656
1000 3281
2000 6562
4000 13123
6000 19685

127
134

128
A
B
C
D
E
116°
112°
108°
104°
32°
28°
24°
20°
16°
1
2
3
4
5
6
PACIFIC OCEAN
CALIFORNIA
ARIZONA
NEW MEXICO
UNITED
MEXICO
BAJA CALIFORNIA
BAJA CALIFORNIA SUR
SONORA
CHIHUAHUA
COAHUILA
DURANGO
SINALOA
NAYARIT
ZACATECAS
SAN LUIS P
AGUASCALIENTES
JALISCO
COLIMA
GUANAJU
MICHOA
SIERRA MADRE OCCIDENTAL
SIERRA MADRE ORIENTAL
EDWARDS PLATEA
Golfo de California
San Diego
Tijuana
Mexicali
Phoenix
Tucson
Ciudad Juárez
El Paso
Chihuahua
Hermosillo
Guaymas
Ciudad Obregón
Los Mochis
Culiacán
Mazatlán
Durango
Torreón
Gómez Palacio
Zacatecas
Aguascalients
Tepic
Guadalajara
Zapopan
Puerto Vallarta
Manzanillo
Colima
La Paz
San Lucas
Isla Guadalupe (Mexico)
Isla Cedros
Isla Tiburón
Isla Angel de la Guarda
Islas Marías
Islas Revillagigedo (Mexico)
Isla Clarión
Isla San Benedicto
Rocas Alijos
Tropic of Cancer
Lubbock
Odessa
Midland
Saltillo
Monc
Lázaro Cárdenas

1:7,880,000
Lambert Conic Conformal Projection

0 50 100 150 200 250 300 kilometers
0 25 50 75 100 125 150 miles

Meters
Feet
6000 19685
5000 16404
4000 13123
3000 9843
2000 6562
1000 3281
500 1640
200 656
100 328
0
LAND BELOW SEA LEVEL
100 328
200 656
1000 3281
2000 6562
4000 13123
6000 19685

Mexico

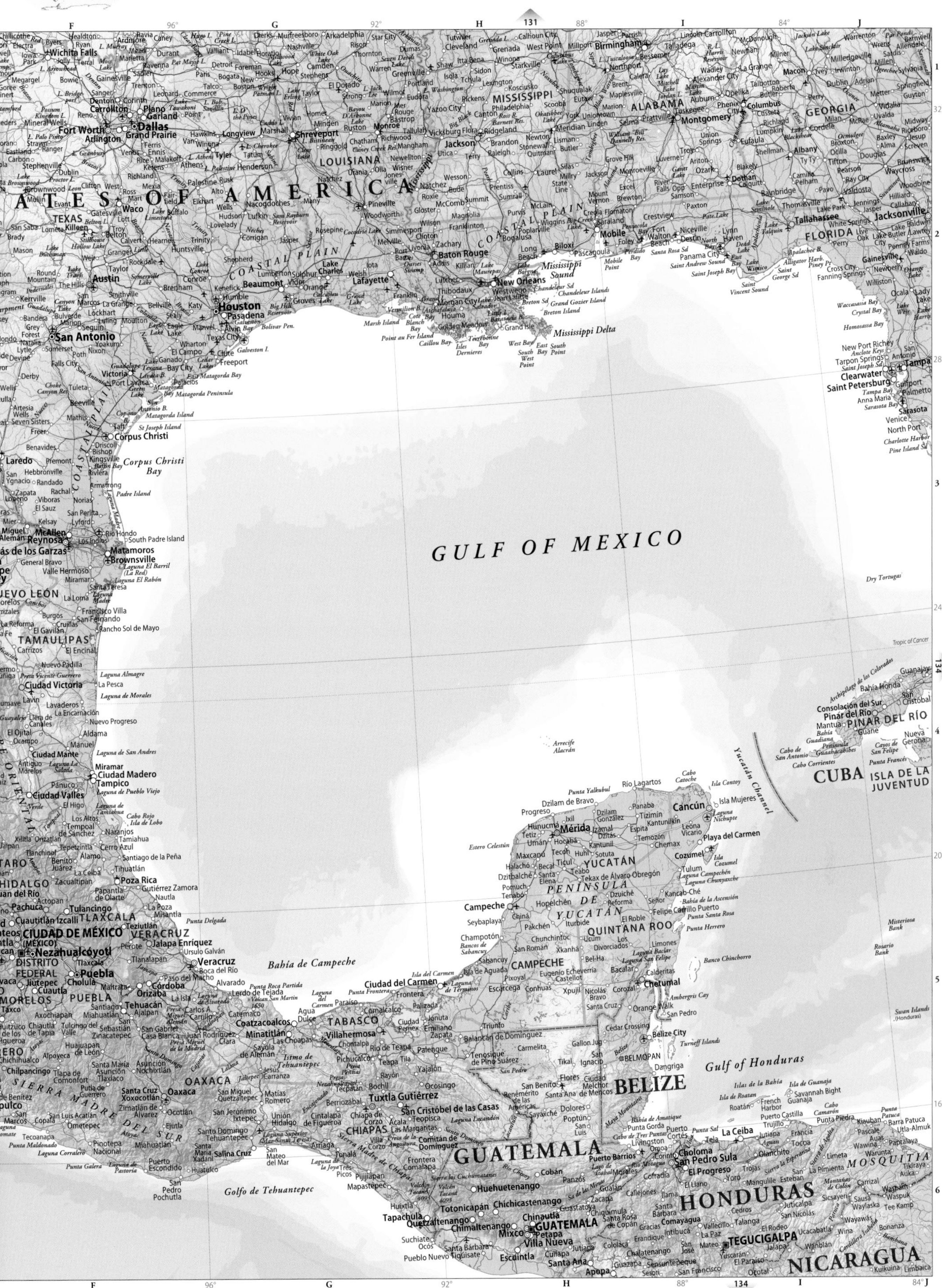
GULF OF MEXICO
UNITED STATES OF AMERICA
TEXAS
LOUISIANA
MISSISSIPPI
ALABAMA
GEORGIA
FLORIDA
COASTAL PLAIN
Mississippi Delta
CUBA
ISLA DE LA JUVENTUD
PINAR DEL RÍO
Yucatán Channel
YUCATÁN
PENÍNSULA DE YUCATÁN
QUINTANA ROO
CAMPECHE
Bahía de Campeche
TABASCO
CHIAPAS
OAXACA
VERACRUZ
PUEBLA
TLAXCALA
HIDALGO
TAMAULIPAS
NUEVO LEÓN
MORELOS
DISTRITO FEDERAL
CIUDAD DE MÉXICO
SIERRA MADRE DEL SUR
Golfo de Tehuantepec
GUATEMALA
BELIZE
HONDURAS
NICARAGUA
MOSQUITIA
Gulf of Honduras
Tropic of Cancer

GULF OF MEXICO

GREAT[er] ...

Gulf of Honduras

PACIFIC OCEAN

UNITED STATES OF AMERICA

MEXICO

BELIZE

GUATEMALA

HONDURAS

EL SALVADOR

NICARAGUA

COSTA RICA

PANAMA

CUBA

JAMAICA

Meters / Feet

Meters	Feet
6000	19685
5000	16404
4000	13123
3000	9843
2000	6562
1000	3281
500	1640
200	656
100	328
0	
LAND BELOW SEA LEVEL	
100	328
200	656
1000	3281
2000	6562
4000	13123
6000	19685

1:7,880,000

Lambert Conic Conformal Projection

0 50 100 150 200 250 300 kilometers

0 25 50 75 100 125 150 miles

Central America and the Caribbean

ATLANTIC OCEAN
CARIBBEAN SEA
WEST INDIES
ANTILLES
Leeward Islands
Windward Islands
Lesser Antilles
Tropic of Cancer
Turks and Caicos Islands (UK)
Hispaniola
HAITI
PORT-AU-PRINCE
Cap-Haïtien
Gonaïves
Pétionville
Les Cayes
Jacmel
DOMINICAN REPUBLIC
SANTO DOMINGO
Santiago de los Caballeros
San Felipe de Puerto Plata
La Romana
San Pedro de Macoris
Salvaleón de Higüey
Puerto Rico (USA)
San Juan
Bayamon
Carolina
Ponce
Mayagüez
Arecibo
British Virgin Islands (UK)
US Virgin Islands (USA)
Charlotte Amalie
Road Town
Frederiksted
Anguilla (UK)
St Martin (Fr.)
St Barthélemy (Fr.)
ST KITTS AND NEVIS
BASSETERRE
ANTIGUA AND BARBUDA
SAINT JOHN'S
Montserrat (UK)
Plymouth
Guadeloupe (Fr.)
Basse-Terre
Grand-Terre
Marie-Galante
DOMINICA
ROSEAU
Martinique (Fr.)
Fort-de-France
ST LUCIA
CASTRIES
ST VINCENT AND THE GRENADINES
KINGSTOWN
BARBADOS
BRIDGETOWN
GRENADA
ST GEORGE'S
TRINIDAD AND TOBAGO
PORT OF SPAIN
Tobago
Trinidad
Aves (Venezuela)
Aruba (Neth.)
Netherlands Antilles (Neth.)
Oranjestad
Willemstad
Bonaire
Kralendijk
Isla La Orchila
Islas Los Roques
Isla Blanquilla
NUEVA ESPARTA
Isla de Margarita
VENEZUELA
CARACAS
Maracaibo
Lago de Maracaibo
Golfo de Venezuela
Península de la Guajira
Península de Paraguaná
Punto Fijo
Coro
FALCÓN
LARA
Barquisimeto
Valencia
Maracay
Los Teques
ZULIA
TRUJILLO
MÉRIDA
Mérida
BARINAS
Barinas
PORTUGUESA
COJEDES
GUÁRICO
MIRANDA
ANZOÁTEGUI
Barcelona
Cumaná
SUCRE
MONAGAS
Maturín
DELTA AMACURO
Ciudad Guayana
Ciudad Bolívar
BOLÍVAR
APURE
San Fernando de Apure
AMAZONAS
Puerto Ayacucho
DISTRITO FEDERAL
GUYANA
BRAZIL
COLOMBIA
Barranquilla
Cartagena
Santa Marta
Valledupar
LA GUAJIRA
Riohacha
CESAR
MAGDALENA
Cúcuta
Bucaramanga
SANTANDER
Medellín
Tunja
BOYACÁ
ARAUCA
CASANARE
Cuba
Guantánamo
Guantánamo Bay Naval Base (USA)
Great Inagua Island
Acklins Island
Cat Island

SOUTH AMERICA

South America

The physical geography of South America broadly resembles that of North America—the high rugged mountain ranges of the Andes in the west and the older, less rugged mountains of the Brazilian Highlands in the east are separated by vast central plains drained by mighty river systems; and its landmass is almost totally surrounded by ocean.

Previous pages Machu Picchu, Peru, the small but extraordinary "Lost City of the Incas," is invisible from below and completely self-contained. Built around 1450, it was abandoned 100 years later at the time of the Spanish conquest.

Right Founded in 1548 by Spanish conquistador Alonso de Mendoza on the site of an indigenous settlement, La Paz, together with neighboring cities El Alto and Viacha, now comprises the largest urban area in Bolivia.

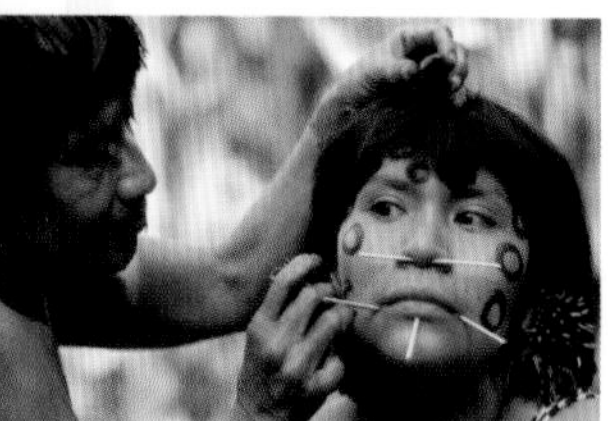

Above Yanomami tribal members decorating their faces for a dance in Hasubueteri, Venezuela. The Yanomami live primarily in the rainforests and mountains of northern Brazil and southern Venezuela. Today they number around 32,000.

Below Iguaça Falls, comprising 275 individual falls along almost 2 miles (3 km) of the Iguaça River on the border between Argentina and Brazil, are vastly larger than North America's Niagara Falls, and are rivalled in size and majesty only by Africa's Victoria Falls.

Climatic types range from dry deserts in the west to equatorial tropical (which North America lacks) in the Amazon Basin, and just about everything in between. South America is home to twelve nations.

The mighty Amazon River dominates its environment. It stretches across the equatorial regions of South America for some 4,000 miles (6,400 km), from its sources in the Peruvian highlands to the Atlantic Ocean. The river's watershed covers half of South America and the Amazon Basin is home to the world's largest tropical rainforest.

Continent of Contrasts

During a great deal of the twentieth century, most countries in South America languished economically and suffered politically, as transitions in political power tended to revolve around the barrel of a gun. The overall political situation now appears to be stabilizing and crippling hyperinflation, rampant corruption, and across-the-board mismanagement are giving way to sustainable economic development. Liberalization of the economic systems of Chile and Brazil has created success stories, with Brazil's remarkable transformation even more significant because it was accompanied by a peaceful transition of power, unlike Chile's dictatorial experiment of the Pinochet era. Cultural change takes time, but a middle class is gradually emerging within societies traditionally polarized between powerful minorities and huge masses of powerless poor.

Despite these overall changes, a few governments are flirting with populist policies that have historically resulted in economic and often social reversals. Venezuela's experiment with "twenty-first century socialism," as President Hugo Chavez describes it, has so far produced little in the way of improvements. Government coffers are filled with cash from a surge in oil revenues, but across the country people face empty shelves in grocery stores and rising prices for staple foods. Latin American populism is making a comeback in Bolivia and Ecuador as well.

The contrasts in wealth are mainly caused by the ongoing conflict between social and cultural systems based on the Iberian cultural legacy, and contemporary globalization. The social structure traditionally focuses on cohesive yet rigid social forces such as church, family, and the military. The machismo system favors individuals over the community, creating excellent conditions for the development of the personality cults so common in South American history.

The Industrial Revolution was late in reaching most of South America and so diversification remained inside the boundaries of major urban centers. Millions still survive on subsistence agriculture in remote villages of Peru and neighboring countries. Economic diversification is the leading priority for South America overall. Many countries still depend heavily on a monocultural economy based on non-renewable resources. Chilean copper production provides half the national income, while Bolivia counts on natural gas exports. Venezuela is an example of a country whose economy is almost entirely dependent on the production and export of one resource—deposits of oil in the sands of the Orinoco Delta, which equal the rest of the world's conventional oil reserves. Yet Brazil has shown that with adequate policy and a vision for the future, diversification can be a reality.

Another imperative is the development of transportation infrastructure. The Trans-Amazonian Highway, completed in 1972, connected Brazil's coastal cities with the vast interior. This is one of the few road systems, a good portion of which is still unpaved, to intersect the continent. Still needed, however, is a network of all-weather connections between the Atlantic and Pacific coasts, which would allow the South American countries to fully connect with the Pan-American Highway system, and a network of internal roads that would benefit the entire region. Because fully operational roads that connect east and west are few and far between, maritime transport of goods is still one of the more affordable options for intraregional trade. However, natural harbors are a rarity in South America. Shallow estuaries with continuously strong deposition of silt create problems on the

Atlantic side, while the rugged coast on the Pacific has few viable locations for ports and no continental shelf for offshore anchorage.

Colonial Legacies

The distribution and composition of South America's population reflects colonial legacies. The Portuguese, who never intended to colonize Brazil, focused on plantation agriculture and sugarcane production on the coast. Slaves were imported from Africa to work on the plantations, and the interior remained sparsely populated for centuries. The Brazilian government has been trying to increase migration to the interior, and took the lead by relocating the capital to Brasília in 1960; but this was only modestly successful. Spain's approach was different, for the Spanish idea of conquest included integration of all colonial lands into the Spanish Empire and forced conversion to Catholicism, while the extraction of gold and silver was their primary economic concern. Landless Indians were used for mine labor, their status equal to that of slaves. The local Spanish aristocracy owned most of the land, but tended to see it as a status symbol rather than use it for agriculture. Spain's colonies received little freedom in running their affairs; this resulted in the many nineteenth-century revolutions for independence.

When twentieth-century governments conducted land reforms they usually had in mind social equality rather than economic productivity; the outcome was that rural areas experienced a rapid loss of population as peasants migrated to cities to seek work. Many South American cities are surrounded by slums. Most South Americans now live in or near urban centers. Even the least urbanized countries such as Bolivia and Ecuador have urban populations of over 60 percent.

Generally, when economic conditions and standards of living improve, fertility rates decline. Brazil, the most populous country, after several decades of sharp population growth, will record an increase to only about 260 million people by 2050. Overall, South American countries enjoy above-average life expectancy, and this continues to increase.

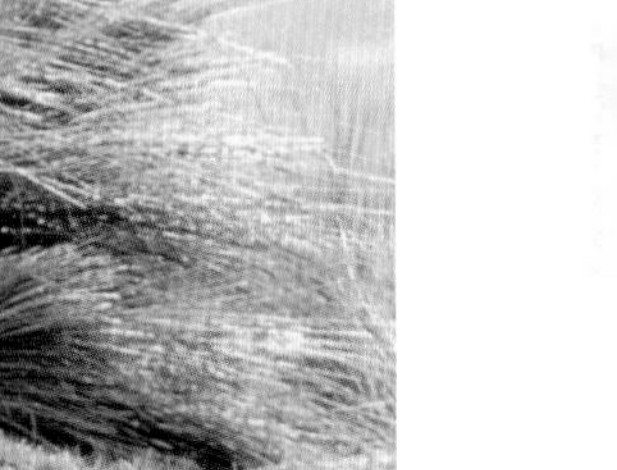

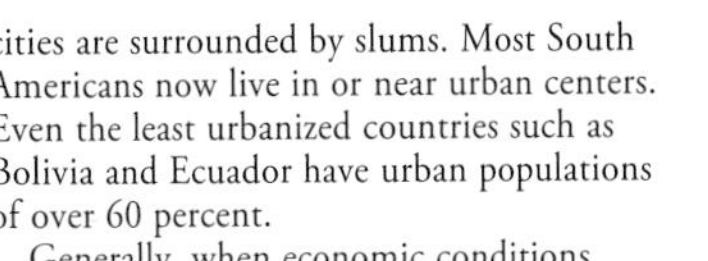

Above Quechua Indian women and children, Cotopaxi, Ecuador. Quechua was the official language of the Incan Empire. Reserved and dignified, these people have retained many elements of their traditional culture.

Left Water lilies in the Amazon rainforest, Brazil. These giants, found in the calmer parts of rivers, can reach 6 feet (1.8 m) in diameter.

Below Mostly nocturnal and very territorial, the ocelot *(Leopardus pardalis)* is distributed over South and Central America and Mexico, though it has been reported as far north as Texas.

Far left Torres del Paine National Park, in southern Patagonia, Chile, is a wonderland of snow-clad granite peaks, glacier-fed lakes, waterfalls, rivers, meadows, and thick forests.

COLOMBIA

Official name Republic of Colombia (Republica de Colombia)
Land area 401,044 square miles (1,038,700 km²)
Border countries Venezuela, Brazil, Peru, Ecuador, Panama
Capital Bogotá
Highest point Pico Cristobal Colon 18,945 feet (5,775 m)
Climate Tropical along coast and eastern plains; cooler in highlands
Population 45,014,000
Language(s) Spanish, 75 Amerindic languages
Ethnicity Mestizo 58%, European descent 20%, mulatto (European and African descent) 14%, African descent 4%, African and Amerindian descent 3%, Amerindian 1%
Religion Christian 90%, other 10%
Government Republic
Currency Colombian peso
Human Development Index 0.791 (ranked 75th out of 177 countries)

Above right The World Heritage-listed walled city of Cartagena, Colombia, has the most substantial fortifications in South America.

Below right Colombia's Embera Choco people hunt using blowguns armed with poison-tipped darts. The poison used exudes from the skin of the golden poison dart frog *(Phyllobates terribilis)*.

VENEZUELA

Official name Bolivarian Republic of Venezuela (Republica Bolivariana de Venezuela)
Land area 340,561 square miles (882,050 km²)
Border countries Guyana, Brazil, Colombia
Capital Caracas
Highest point Pico Bolivar 16,427 feet (5,007 m)
Climate Tropical; hot, humid; moderate to cold in highlands
Population 26,415,000
Language(s) Official: Spanish; other: Wayuu, Warao, Piaroa, Yanomami, Kahlihna, Manduhuaca, Panaré, Pemón, Guahibo, Nhengtu
Ethnicity Mestizo 68%, European descent 21%, African descent 10%, Amerindian 1%
Religion Christian 98%, other 2%
Government Federal republic
Currency Bolivar
Human Development Index 0.792 (ranked 74th out of 177 countries)

Above The colonial Spanish fort on Cartagena's harbor repelled invaders and pirates attempting to pillage the precious metals shipped from the port.

Caribbean Sea
Santa Marta
Riohacha
Barranquilla
Pico Cristobal Colón
Cartagena
Valledupar
Sincelejo
Magangué
Montería
PANAMA
Cúcuta
VENEZUELA
Barrancabermeja
Bucaramanga
Medellín
PACIFIC OCEAN
Quibdó
Tunja
Sogamoso
Manizales
Pereira
BOGOTÁ
Armenia
Ibagué
Villavicencio
Inírida
Buga
Buenaventura
Palmira
Cali
COLOMBIA
Neiva
San José del Guaviare
Popayán
Florencia
Mitú
Pasto
ECUADOR
BRAZIL
PERU
Leticia

Colombia

Map Reference Pages 154–155

Colombia shares borders with Venezuela to the northeast and east, Ecuador and Peru to the south, Brazil to the southeast, and Panama to the west. The coastline borders the Caribbean to the north and Pacific Ocean to the west. The country is named after the great seafaring adventurer, Christopher Columbus.

Physical Geography

The diverse topography includes the Andes Mountains, with plains to the east of the Andes, and lowlands on the Caribbean and Pacific coasts. The country lies on the Pacific Ring of Fire and is subject to sometimes devastating earthquakes. There are also 15 major active volcanoes. In 2001 Nevada del Ruiz erupted, creating a mudslide that smothered the city of Armero and killed 20,000 people.

Colombia has the fifth greatest number of endemic vertebrates and fourth greatest number of vascular plant species in the world. The country's climate is tropical along the coast and eastern plains and cooler in the highlands.

History

Indigenous Indians, including the Chibchas, Tayronas, and Muiscas, originally inhabited Colombia. It was discovered by Spanish explorer Alonso de Ojeda in 1498. Simón Bolívar led the independence movement and Spanish control ceased in 1819 with the foundation of the Republic of New Granada—formed mainly by Colombia with smaller parts of surrounding countries. In 1886 the country adopted its current name, Republic of Colombia. Panama was a Colombian province until 1903, when it became independent in exchange for allowing the USA to build the Panama Canal.

Population/Culture

Colombia is an ethnic mosaic. The different traditions of indigenous Indians, Spaniards, and Africans have produced interesting fusions, particularly in crafts, sculpture, and music. Pre-Colombian art consists mainly of stone sculpture, pottery, gold-work, and basket ware. Music incorporates African rhythms of the Caribbean, Cuban salsa, and Spanish-influenced Andean music. Notable writers include literary giant Gabriel García Márquez.

Administration/Government

Colombia is a republic headed by the president who is also the chief of state. The president and vice-president are elected by popular vote. The bicameral Congress consists of a 102-seat Senate and a 106-seat House of Representatives.

After decades of violence and unrest the security situation inside Colombia is showing some improvement, but insurgents continue attacks against civilians and large areas of the countryside are under guerrilla influence. The government has stepped up efforts to reassert control across the country.

Economy/Industry

Colombia is a free-market economy with abundant reserves of natural resources and energy, which includes the largest coal reserves in Latin America, and huge hydroelectric potential. It also possesses significant reserves of petroleum and is an oil exporter. Chemicals and petrochemicals, cement, iron, steel products, and metalworking are among its many industries. Colombia exports high-quality emeralds and coffee, apparel, bananas, and cut flowers. A safer environment for business during the last administration has helped to reduce unemployment.

CIVIL CONFLICT *(LA VIOLENCIA)*

In 1948, armed conflict caused the complete destruction of Román Village in Santander, Colombia, and violence and brutality by the incumbent regime's police reached every corner of the country. The popular presidential candidate, Jorge Eliécer Gaitán, organized a procession for the untold number of victim's of violence and a collective prayer for peace. Sixty thousand people marched under the rallying cry of "absolute silence" and amazingly it was maintained. It has gone down in history as the March of Silence. A few months later, the assassination of Jorge Eliécer Gaitán triggered riots and violence in Bogota. In response, the military dictatorship of Rojas Pinilla introduced agrarian reforms in an effort to solve social disparities and appease armed peasants. In 1957, civilian rule was restored after the moderate Conservative and Liberal parties agreed to unite under a bipartisan coalition known as the National Front. The coalition heralded a period in the history of Colombia in which the two main political parties agreed to let each other govern, alternating presidential terms. Unfortunately this did not end all the violence in Colombia because since about 1964, guerrilla organizations have been waging war against the government, the military, and civilians.

Caribbean Sea
Isla de Margarita
Coro
Maracaibo
Cabimas
CARACAS
Cumaná
Carúpano
TRINIDAD & TOBAGO
Valencia
Carora
Barquisimeto
Barcelona
ATLANTIC OCEAN
Acarigua
Anaco
Maturín
El Tigre
Mérida
Guanare
Calabozo
Ciudad Guayana
Pico Bolívar
Barinas
San Fernando de Apure
Ciudad Bolívar
San Cristóbal
VENEZUELA
GUYANA
COLOMBIA
Puerto Ayacucho
BRAZIL

Venezuela

Map Reference Pages 154–155

Venezuela is South America's sixth largest country. Its coastline is bounded by the Caribbean Sea and Atlantic Ocean. It shares borders with Guyana in the east, Brazil in the south, and Colombia in the west. Despite a varied and often difficult history, Venezuelans are renowned for their easy-going natures.

Physical Geography

Venezuela has a wide variety of landscapes, from jungle to snow-capped mountains, and can be roughly divided into four regions: The fertile Maracaibo lowlands in the northwest; the Venezuelan Andes, that extend from the border with Colombia to the Caribbean Sea; the Guyana Highlands in the southeast; and the Orinoco plains (Los Llanos) in the center.

Venezuela's highest mountain, Pico Bolivar, is in the Andes. Nearby is Pico Espejo, the destination of the world's longest (8 miles/12.5 km) and highest at 15,633 feet (4,765 m) cable car. Tepuis (sheer-sided tabletop mountains) are an outstanding feature of the Guyana Highlands. Auyantepui in Canaima National Park is the site of Angel Falls, the world's highest waterfall, which plunges 3,212 feet (979 m) into the valley.

Although Venezuela is within the tropics, climate varies from tropical to alpine, depending on elevation and location. Average annual temperature in the tropical coastal plains is 81°F (27°C); at elevations of 6,562–9,843 feet (2,000–3,000 m) it drops to 50°F (10°C).

History

Columbus found Venezuela inhabited by Arawak, Carib (inventors of the hammock),

and Chibcha Indians. Spanish explorer Alonso de Ojeda was reminded of Venice when he saw the Indians' houses perched on stilts above Lake Maracaibo, so he called the place *Venezuela* (Little Venice). Initially part of Greater Colombia (together with Colombia, Ecuador, and Panama), Venezuela became an independent republic in 1830. Several unstable dictatorships followed until Antonio Guzman Blanco governed from 1870 to 1888. He developed infrastructure, expanded agriculture, and encouraged foreign investment, paving the way for today's prosperous nation.

Population/Culture

Venezuela is a rich multi-ethnic melting pot, with mestizos—descended from a combination of European, African, and Amerindian peoples—comprising the largest group. Spanish is the most widely used language; the most common indigenous languages are those of the Carib, Arawak, and Chibcha peoples.

Musical forms show many influences. In the Andes, music has distinctly Spanish–Arabic overtones. Joropo music from the Orinoco plains is played with a harp *(arpa llanera)*, four-string guitar *(cuatro)*, and maracas, while a singer carries the melody.

Administration/Government

The government is a federal republic administering 23 states and one federal dependency. The latter consists of 72 Caribbean islands. The country's president is both chief of state and head of government and is elected by popular vote. The unicameral National Assembly has 167 seats. Three seats are reserved for indigenous peoples.

Economy/Industry

Venezuela was an agricultural country until oil was discovered in the 1920s. Now the main commodity, oil provides 50 percent of government revenues and 70 percent of export earnings. The national oil corporation, Petróleos de Venezuela, S.A. (PDVSA), is the third largest international oil conglomerate. Venezuela is now also a significant producer of bauxite, iron ore, coal, and gold.

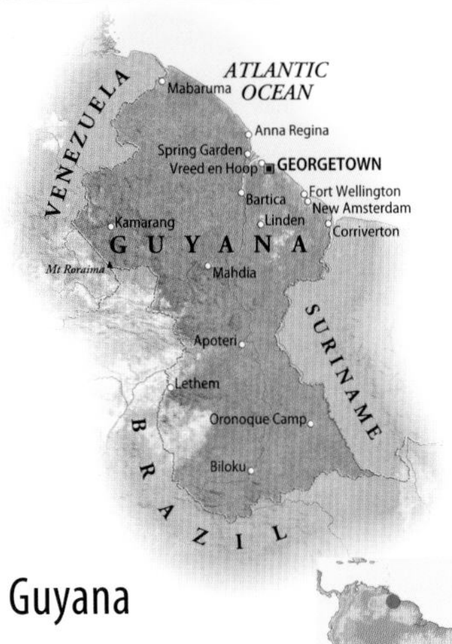
ATLANTIC OCEAN
Mabaruma
Anna Regina
Spring Garden
Vreed en Hoop
GEORGETOWN
Fort Wellington
New Amsterdam
Bartica
Linden
Corriverton
Kamarang
GUYANA
Mt Roraima
Mahdia
Apoteri
Lethem
Oronoque Camp
Biloku
VENEZUELA
SURINAME
BRAZIL

Guyana

Map Reference Pages 154–155

The Cooperative Republic of Guyana is bordered by Suriname to the east, Brazil to the south, and Venezuela to the northwest. The northeastern coastline lies on the Atlantic Ocean. It is the continent's third smallest country in area and population.

Guyana has a hot, humid, tropical climate. Occupying about 5 percent of total area is a narrow alluvial coastal plain, home to about 90 percent of the population. Further inland are rolling uplands rich in minerals, including gold, diamonds, manganese, and bauxite. In the western interior Mt Roraima is the highest peak in the Pacaraima Mountains.

Amerindian groups occupied the coastal area long before the Dutch arrived in 1616. Great Britain took control in 1815. In 1966 the former British Guiana gained independence as Guyana.

Guyana's colonial economy was based on coastal sugar plantations that used African slave labor. When slavery was abolished, most former slaves moved to urban areas and plantation owners turned to indentured labors from India, so 50 percent of the population is of East Indian ancestry, with 45 percent Hindu or Muslim. Since independence, the economy has struggled. Agriculture contributes about one-third of GDP, and the service sector slightly less than 50 percent.

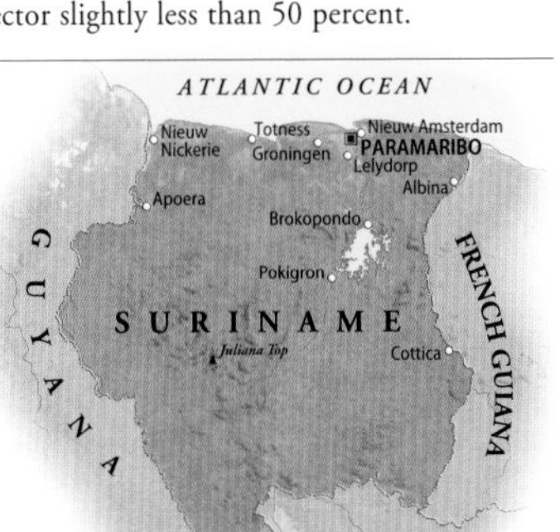
ATLANTIC OCEAN
Nieuw Nickerie
Totness
Groningen
Nieuw Amsterdam
PARAMARIBO
Lelydorp
Albina
Apoera
Brokopondo
Pokigron
SURINAME
Juliana Top
Cottica
GUYANA
FRENCH GUIANA
BRAZIL

Suriname

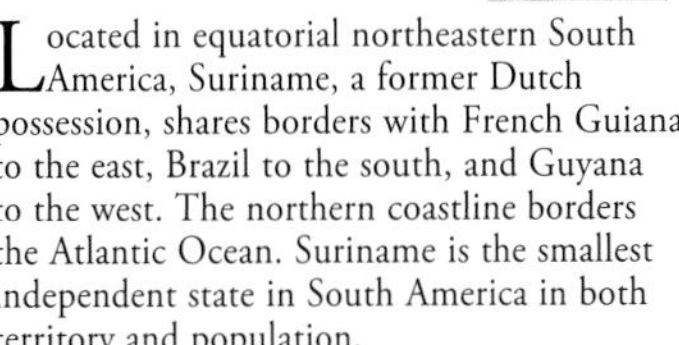

Map Reference Pages 154–155

Located in equatorial northeastern South America, Suriname, a former Dutch possession, shares borders with French Guiana to the east, Brazil to the south, and Guyana to the west. The northern coastline borders the Atlantic Ocean. Suriname is the smallest independent state in South America in both territory and population.

Suriname has a seasonal wet-and-dry tropical climate. Much of the coastal region supports tall grass savanna; tropical rainforest covers most of the interior. Hills and low mountains dominate the inaccessible interior.

Amerindians, primarily Caribs, had long occupied the region. In the seventeenth century, the Dutch and British established coastal plantations. In 1667, the Dutch gained control by exchanging their trading post at the mouth of the Hudson River for British territory in what is now Suriname. Dutch planters used African slave labor to produce sugar, cotton, and cocoa. With emancipation in 1863, planters contracted laborers from Southeast Asia and now Suriname is one of the world's most ethnically diverse populations. About 90 percent live on the narrow coastal plain, more than half in the capital city, Paramaribo.

Since independence in 1975, Suriname has suffered much political instability. About 75 percent of income is from bauxite mining.

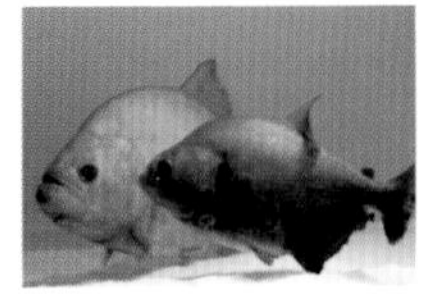

Above Known in popular culture for their sharp teeth and voracious meat-eating habits, piranha *(Serrasalmus* sp.*)* are a South American freshwater species found in rivers and the Amazon Basin.

Left The majestic Kukenan Tepui rises out of dense jungle in southeast Venezuela. Mt Roraima, a nearby flat-topped mesa or tepui, marks the Brazil–Guyana–Venezuela border.

GUYANA

Official name Cooperative Republic of Guyana
Land area 76,004 square miles (196,850 km²)
Border countries Suriname, Brazil, Venezuela
Capital Georgetown
Highest point Mt Roraima 9,301 feet (2,835 m)
Climate Tropical, moderated by northeast trade winds
Population 770,794
Language(s) English, Amerindian languages, Creole, Caribbean Hindustani (a dialect of Hindi), Urdu
Ethnicity East Indian 50%, African descent 36%, Amerindian 7%, European descent/Chinese descent/other 7%
Religion Christian 50%, Hindu 35%, Muslim 10%, other 5%
Government Republic
Currency Guyanese dollar
Human Development Index 0.750 (ranked 97th out of 177 countries)

SURINAME

Official name Republic of Suriname (Republiek Suriname)
Land area 62,344 square miles (161,470 km²)
Border countries French Guiana, Brazil, Guyana
Capital Paramaribo
Highest point Juliana Top 4,035 feet (1,230 m)
Climate Tropical
Population 475,996
Language(s) Official: Dutch; other: English, Sranang Tongo, Caribbean Hindustani (a dialect of Hindi), Javanese
Ethnicity East Indian 37%, Creole 31%, Javanese 15%, Maroons (African descent) 10%, Amerindian 2%, Chinese 2%, European descent 1%, other 2%
Religion Christian 48%, Hindu 27.4%, Muslim 19.6%, indigenous beliefs 5%
Government Constitutional democracy
Currency Surinam dollar
Human Development Index 0.774 (ranked 85th out of 177 countries)

Far left Georgetown, Guyana's capital and largest city, is at the mouth of the Demerara River. The city's street names and wards reflect times under Dutch, French, and English administration.

Left Javanese women gather at the Festival of Id-ul-Fitr in Surina, Suriname, to mark the end of Ramadan, the month-long Muslim fasting period.

COLOMBIA
VENEZUELA
GUYANA
SURINAME
FRENCH GUIANA
Boa Vista
Serra da Neblina
Macapá
ATLANTIC OCEAN
Belém
Manaus
Santarém
São Luís
Fortaleza
Marabá
Teresina
Cruzeiro do Sul
Porto Velho
B R A Z I L
Juazeiro do Norte
Natal
João Pessoa
PERU
Rio Branco
Ariquemes
Palmas
Petrolina
Recife
Maceió
Aracaju
Salvador
BOLIVIA
Cuiabá
BRASÍLIA
Ilhéus
Goiânia
Campo Grande
Belo Horizonte
Vitória
PARAGUAY
Campinas
São Paulo
Nova Iguaçu
Rio de Janeiro
Santos
Curitiba
ARGENTINA
Florianópolis
Porto Alegre
URUGUAY

Far right Completed in 1722, the Capela de Santa Rita is the oldest church in the town of Paraty, a gem of colonial architecture that is now World Heritage listed.

Below right The large, tree-dwelling Amazonian milk frog (*Phrynohyas resinifictrix*) was first discovered near the Maracanã River, Brazil.

BRAZIL

Official name Federative Republic of Brazil (República Federativa do Brasil)
Land area 3,300,000 square miles (8,514,877 km^2)
Border countries Colombia, Venezuela, Guyana, Suriname, French Guyana, Uruguay, Argentina, Paraguay, Bolivia, Peru
Capital Brasília
Highest point Pico da Neblina 10,184 feet (3,014 m)
Climate Mostly tropical; temperate in south; summer wet season
Population 191,909,000
Language(s) Official: Portuguese; other: Spanish, Italian, German, Japanese, English, French, numerous indigenous Amerindian languages (includes Apalaí, Arara, Bororo, Canela, Carajá, Caribe, Guarani, Kaingang, Nadëb, Nheengatu, Terena, Tucano, Tupiniquim)
Ethnicity European descent 53.7%, mulatto (mixed race) 38.5%, African descent 6.2%, other (includes Japanese, Arab, Amerindian) 0.9%, unspecified 0.7%
Religion Christian (Catholic and Protestant) 89%, spiritualist 1.3%, African/voodoo 0.3%, other 9.4%
Government Federative presidential republic
Currency Real
Human Development Index 0.800 (ranked 70th out of 177 countries)

Brazil

Map Reference Pages 154–159

Covering almost half the South American continent, Brazil is the fourth largest country in the world in terms of both population and surface area. The country was named after the *pau do brasil* (the brazilwood tree), from which a valued red dye was extracted.

With a long Atlantic coastline, Brazil shares borders with every other South American country except Chile and Ecuador. Extending north above the Equator and south below the Tropic of Capricorn, it is home to a diverse array of natural environments, and considerable natural resources. It is also famous for *Carnaval*, a joyous form of celebration held in the four days before Lent, and not limited solely to Rio de Janeiro. Brasília, the capital, is the only twentieth-century city in the world that has been awarded (in 1987) the status of Historical and Cultural Heritage of Humanity by UNESCO. The city is just one of the 17 World Heritage sites across the country.

Physical Geography

The landscape is largely formed by flat plateaus and lowlands, ringed by mountains. Brazil has five major geographic areas: In the north the dissected high plateau of the Guyana Highlands; in the east the dissected plateau of the Brazilian Highlands; the vast Amazon River Basin stretching between these two highland regions, from the foothills of the Andes Cordillera in the west to the river's mouths in an intricate delta to the east; in the center the grassy plains of Mato Grosso rising gently to the low plateau of the Planalto and the Pantanal wetlands in the southwest; and the often rugged Southern Highlands, which stretch from the Tropic of Capricorn south to the Uruguayan border.

An astonishing variety of tropical forests, grasslands, and fertile farmlands is found across the country, and white sand beaches fringe the coast. The dry *cerrado* (savanna) of the northeast is an open woodland, where agricultural prospects are limited. The Pantanal wetlands in the states of Mato Grosso and Mato Grosso do Sul, extending into Bolivia and Paraguay, are an internal delta where several rivers converge. In the wet season the rivers flood 80 percent of the area's 75,000 square miles (195,000 km^2) to a depth of 10 feet (3 m), nurturing the richest collection of aquatic plants in the world, over 3,500 species. The ecosystem also supports over 2,200 species of birds, fish, mammals, and reptiles, and is as vital and interesting as the better-known Amazon ecosystem.

Tropical and subtropical climates, from very wet to very dry, with most of the rainfall occurring in summer, dominate except in the south, where the climate transitions from subtropical to temperate, temperatures at the highest altitudes may drop below freezing.

History

The original inhabitants of Brazil are thought to be the Amerindians descended from the wave of North Asian migrants that crossed the Bering Strait land bridge around 9000 BCE and moved down through the Americas, but evidence provided by cave paintings in Serra da Capivara National Park in the northeastern state of Piauí indicate human habitation over 25,000 years ago, by an unknown people. In 1500 CE, when Portuguese explorers led by Pedro Alvares Cabral claimed the region for Portugal, the indigenous peoples were mostly semi-nomadic, living in tribal groups along the coast and major rivers.

The early colonizers were more interested in trade and subsistence agriculture than territorial expansion, but eventually sugarcane was grown as a plantation crop, and with it came the importation of African slaves. In 1690, a move to explore the interior was strengthened by the discovery of

MILESTONE EVENTS

1500 Pedro Alvares Cabral lands in Brazil and claims the country for Portugal
1630 The Dutch invade Brazil, and are driven out in 1654
1750 Portugal and Spain sign Treaty of Tordesillas dividing the Americas between them
1808–1815 Portuguese royal family rule Portugal and the Portuguese Empire from Rio de Janeiro
1822 Brazil declares independence
1888 Slavery abolished
1889 Brazil proclaimed a republic
1917 Brazil declares war on Germany in World War I
1942 Brazil declares war on the Axis powers in World War II
1960 The capital is moved from Rio de Janeiro to the new city of Brasília
1964 Military leaders take control
1985 Government returned to civilian rule
1988 New constitution provides for direct election of the president

gold and diamonds in Minais Gerais, but by the end of the eighteenth century the deposits became unprofitable and attention once again turned to coastal agriculture.

In 1808, following Napoleon Bonaparte's invasion of Portugal, the entire Portuguese court fled to Rio de Janeiro, establishing the city as the seat of government of Portugal and the entire Portuguese Empire until Napoleon was defeated at Waterloo. Brazil achieved independence in 1822 as the Empire of Brazil, and remained under monarchic leadership until Pedro II was deposed in November 1889 by a military coup led by Deodara do Fonseca and the Republic of the United States of Brazil was established. In 1930 a military junta took control, leading to dictatorial presidential rule. Military forces staged another coup in 1964, and the country was renamed the Federative Republic of Brazil in 1967. Democracy was re-established when the current Constitution was enacted on October 5, 1988.

Population

The indigenous peoples had a rich cultural life when the Portuguese arrived. Fewer than 20,000 Amerindians, compared to a sixteenth-century population of possibly 3 million, survive, mostly in the jungles of the Amazon. In Brazil, far more so than in the other South American colonies, the European settlers intermarried with the local people and with their slaves; there were also marriages between local people and slaves.

From the late nineteenth century immigrants from over 60 countries were welcomed—mostly from southern Europe and Germany in the first wave; Japan and the Middle East in the second. The end result is that today's population is intermingled to a degree seen in no other country.

Despite Brazil's relatively high HDI rating, millions of its people live in poverty in the *favelas* (slums) of the major cities, and in the more remote parts of the country most are unskilled and poorly educated. The wealth gap is large. State primary and secondary school education is free; the literacy rate for those over 15 years of age is 88.8 percent.

About 80 percent of Brazilians live in the major cities and within 200 miles (320 km) of the coast; the interior is sparsely populated. The current birth rate is 1.86 children per woman, and life expectancy is 72.24 years.

Culture

Brazil's official language is Portuguese, but this is greatly influenced by local Amerindian languages and the African languages of the slaves who worked the early sugar plantations; this linguistic environment was further enriched by the immigration programs which drew people from many countries.

European immigrants of the late nineteenth and early twentieth centuries mostly worked in coastal coffee plantations that succeeded the sugar plantations, and joined in the industrial expansion of the cities, or established themselves as small landholders in the south. Here they formed communities retaining much of their old culture, where even today Italian and German dialects, for example, are informally spoken. Their food, music, festivals, and religion are mirrors of their Old World origins, attracting many tourists.

The country is overwhelmingly Christian, includes the greatest number of Buddhists in South America, due to the presence of the largest Japanese population outside Japan, and is home to numerous smaller religious groups.

Above At a height of 262 feet (80 m) and a span of 8,858 feet (2,700 m) the thundering, semicircular Iguaçu Falls, on the border of Brazil and Argentina, is one of the world's most spectacular waterfalls.

Administration/Government

Brazil is a federal republic with 26 states and the federal district of the capital city, Brasília, bordered by the states of Goiás and Minas Gerais. Brasília is the seat of all three branches of government. In 1960, after a construction period of only 41 months, it formally replaced Rio de Janeiro as the national capital.

The bicameral National Congress consists of the Federal Senate, with 81 seats and the Chamber of Deputies, with 513 seats. The president and vice-president are popularly elected for five-year terms.

Above A Mebengokre (Kayapo) Indian elder wears a traditional headdress made from macaw and stork feathers. The Mebengokre live on the vast Mato Grosso plains of Brazil, located south of the Amazon Basin.

Economy/Industry

The economy has been growing steadily since the end of the nineteenth century, when coffee took over from sugar as the leading export.

Today Brazil has an up-to-date and complex manufacturing structure and thriving service industries. It exports quality manufactured goods and commodities. The agricultural sector focuses on coffee, soybeans, beef, wheat, rice, corn, sugarcane, cocoa, and citrus. Brazil is the world's biggest beef exporter, and second largest soy exporter after the United States.

The profitable manufacturing and service industries, and the ability to exploit vast natural resources, have made Brazil into South America's leading economic power.

THE AMAZON'S VANISHING ECOLOGY

The huge, mostly remote region known to the world as "the Amazon" encompasses over 2 million square miles (5 million km^2), or nearly 60 percent of Brazil's total land area, taking in all or part of the states of Roraima, Marapa, Amazonas, Para, Maranhao, Acre, Rondonia, Mato Grosso, and Tocantins. Of enormous environmental importance with its uniquely diverse ecosystems, the Amazon Basin and its ecosystems include one of the world's largest tropical rainforests as well as extensive savannas (*cerrado*). The Amazon itself is the largest river in the world by volume, and has the world's largest drainage basin.

The Amazon rainforest contains the largest collection of living plant and animal species in the world. Some 438,000 plant species of economic and social interest have been identified, and many more are yet to be cataloged. Over a million species of animals—ranging from tarantulas to monkeys to jaguars—are found there, more than 500,000 of them insects and spiders, and hundreds of thousands more are yet to be classified scientifically.

Despite its remote location, relative lack of physical and economic development, and having only 8 percent of the country's population, the Amazon region is an important and growing agricultural zone. Commercial farmers are converting frontier cattle ranches to soybean farms in northeastern Mato Grosso and southeastern Para states. Since 1978, roughly 150 million acres (60 million hectares) of forest have been lost to logging, mining, human settlement, construction of transportation infrastructure, and the establishment of subsistence and large-scale commercial agricultural enterprises, a loss representing more than 13 percent of the original ecosystem and the fragmentation of a much larger portion. Despite this, vast areas remain intact, with the northern Amazon Basin and Guyana Shield estimated to be the largest tropical frontier forest anywhere in the world.

The government has tried to reduce environmental impacts by using advanced remote monitoring technology to identify spots of fire and deforestation, and creating large national parks and forest reserves, which by 2006 covered 113 million acres (45.8 million hectares) of the region.

Below A view of Rio de Janeiro, looking toward Sugarloaf Mountain and Guanabara Bay. Rio is Brazil's second major city after São Paulo. It boasts beautiful beaches and lush urban forests.

ECUADOR

Official name Republic of Ecuador (Republica del Ecuador)
Land area 106,889 square miles (276,840 km²)
Border countries Colombia, Peru
Capital Quito
Highest point Chimborazo 20,561 feet (6,267 m)
Climate Hot tropical along coast and eastern lowlands; varies with elevation inland
Population 13,928,000
Language(s) Official: Spanish; other: Quechua, various Amerindian languages
Ethnicity Mestizo 65%, Amerindian 25%, Spanish 5%, Afro-Ecuadorian 3%, other 2%
Religion Roman Catholic 95%, other 5%
Government Republic
Currency US dollar
Human Development Index 0.772 (ranked 89th out of 177 countries)

COLOMBIA
Esmeraldas
Tulcán
Ibarra
Nueva Loja
PACIFIC OCEAN
QUITO
ECUADOR
Manta
Portoviejo
Latacunga
Ambato
Chimborazo
Paján
Santa Lucía
Riobamba
Babahoyo
La Libertad
Guayaquil
Alausí
Macas
Azogues
Isla Puná
Cuenca
Machala
Loja
PERU

Ecuador

Map Reference Pages 154–155

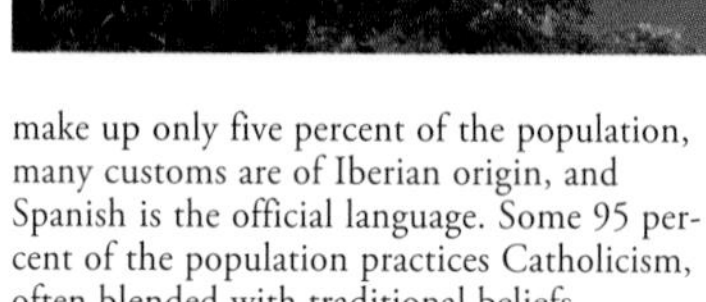

Above right Located near the active Volcán El Reventador, San Rafael Falls on the Quijos River are the highest in Ecuador, at 525 feet (160 m). The area is also known for its rich birdlife.

Above A Galápagos hawk *(Buteo galapagoensis)* hitches a ride on a Galapágos tortoise *(Geochelone elephantopus vandenburghi)* on the seahorse-shaped Isabella Island in the Galapágos, Ecuador. These are just two of the 38 species endemic to the exotic archipelago.

Ecuador takes its name from the Equator, which passes through this small country. Colombia borders the country on the north, Peru on the east and south, and the Pacific Ocean to the west. The Galápagos Islands (Archipiélago de Colón), about 600 miles (965 km) west, in the Pacific, belong to Ecuador. Quito, the capital, is located in the Andes at an elevation of 9,000 feet (2,750 m).

Physical Geography

Ecuador experiences great environmental diversity. The broad alluvial valleys and moist tropical climate make the La Costa, the low-lying coastal plain bordering the Pacific, well suited to plantation agriculture. The Golfo de Guayaquil forms the harbor on which Guayaquil—the largest city, chief port, and economic center—is located. The country's Andean backbone rises to elevations of more than 20,000 feet (6,000 m). Here, climate and ecosystems vary greatly. High mountain peaks, such as Chimborazo and Cotopaxi, despite their equatorial location, are capped with permanent glacial ice and snow. Occupying around half of Ecuador's territory, El Oriente lies within the humid tropical rainforest ecosystem of the upper Amazon Basin.

Ecuador is home to some 25,000 species of plants, 1,600 species of birds (15 percent of the world's total), 6,000 types of butterflies, and hundreds of reptiles, amphibians, and mammals. The Galápagos Islands, home of the unique fauna that inspired Charles Darwin's evolutionary theory, are a UNESCO World Heritage Site.

History

Ecuador's ancient Amerindian cultures were separated into distinct groups coinciding with the country's physiographic provinces. During the early fourteenth century, the expanding Inca Empire established its northern capital in Quito. By 1533, Spain had conquered the Inca; in 1563 a colonial government was established in Quito. Ecuador gained full independence in 1822 and then suffered greater political turbulence than any other Latin American country: There have been 20 constitutions and about 150 governments. As well, much of the country's original territory was lost in conflicts with Colombia and Peru.

Population/Culture

Ninety percent of Ecuador's inhabitants are Amerindian or mestizo. Although Spaniards make up only five percent of the population, many customs are of Iberian origin, and Spanish is the official language. Some 95 percent of the population practices Catholicism, often blended with traditional beliefs.

Music plays a central role in Ecuadorian culture, and possibly the most recognizable is the haunting sounds of bamboo panpipes and flutes—music that originates in the Andes. Also popular is the marimba music of Afro-Ecuadorians.

Administration/Government

Ecuador has a unicameral 100-seat National Congress (Congreso Nacional). The chief of state and head of government is the president who, with the vice-president, is popularly elected for four-year non-consecutive terms.

Economy/Industry

Guayaquil, with a metropolitan area population nearing four million, is the largest urban and economic center. Petroleum accounts for about one-third of the GDP and over 50 percent of export earnings. The service sector is the greatest contributor to GDP (54 percent). Ecuador exports coffee, hemp, shrimp, wood, and cut flowers. Political instability and repeated economic crises have led to Ecuador being one of South America's poorest nations.

Right The small mountain town of Otavalo at the foot of the soaring Andes, Ecuador, is known for its bustling market filled with colorful handcrafted goods. There is a strong cultural tradition also, maybe as a result of its isolated location.

BOLIVIA

Official name Republic of Bolivia (Republica de Bolivia)
Land area 418,685 square miles (1,084,390 km²)
Border countries Brazil, Paraguay, Argentina, Chile, Peru
Capital La Paz (administrative); Sucre (constitutional)
Highest & lowest points Nevado Sajama 21,463 feet (6,542 m); Rio Paraguay 295 feet (90 m)
Climate Varies with altitude; humid and tropical to cold and semi-arid
Population 9,248,000
Language(s) Spanish, Quechua, Aymara
Ethnicity Mestizo 30%, Quechua 30%, Aymara 25%, European descent 15%
Religion Roman Catholic 95%, Protestant (Evangelical, Methodist) 5%
Government Republic
Currency Boliviano
Human Development Index 0.695 (ranked 117th out of 177 countries)

Guayaramerín
Cobija
Riberalta
BRAZIL
PERU
San Borja
Trinidad
BOLIVIA
LA PAZ
Cochabamba
Charaña
Santa Cruz
Nevado Sajama
Oruro
Huanuni
SUCRE
Potosí
Camiri
CHILE
PARAGUAY
Tupiza
Tarija
Villazón
Yacuiba
ARGENTINA

Bolivia

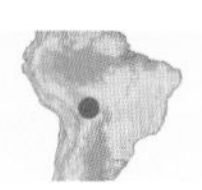

Map Reference Pages 158–159

Landlocked Bolivia in west-central South America is bordered by Brazil to the north and west, Chile and Peru to the east, and Paraguay and Argentina to the south. Bolivia is the highest country in South America, and its population contains the greatest percentage of indigenous people on the continent.

Physical Geography

Lowland plains dominate the northeast, and have a wet-and-dry tropical climate, with rainy summers. Vegetation ranges from rainforest near the Brazilian border to savanna grasslands on the eastern plains. In the southeast a landscape with slightly drier and cooler conditions supports scrub woodlands of the Chaco—a mostly uninhabited region rich in flora and fauna. The Andes dominate the western half of Bolivia, rising 21,000 feet (6,400 m) and include the Altiplano (high plateau). Climate and vegetation vary, from desert to permanent fields of snow and ice. Along its western border, Bolivia shares Lake Titicaca on the Altiplano with Peru. It is the world's highest large water body. Salar de Uyuni, in the southwest, is the world's largest intermittent lake and salt flat, formed when a prehistoric lake dried up 40,000 years ago.

History

Indigenous peoples inhabited the area perhaps 13,000 years ago. Agriculture, with potatoes as the staple crop, was practiced 5,000 years ago and provided the economic foundation of cultural development culminating in the Tiwanakan and later Aymara kingdoms that thrived around Lake Titicaca. By the mid-fifteenth century, Bolivia's highland peoples were conquered and drawn into the expanding Quechua-speaking Incan civilization.

Spaniards settled La Paz in 1548. During the colonial era, Bolivia's mines were the richest in the Americas. Cerro Rico (Rich Mountain), in Potosí, was the world's greatest source of silver and for many decades was the largest city in the Western hemisphere. The colony proclaimed independence in 1809. It became a republic in 1825 and adopted the name of its liberator, Simón Bolívar. During the 1879–1883 War of the Pacific, Bolivia lost its Pacific ports and rich nitrate deposits to Chile. Bolivia has had a long history of economic hardship and political turbulence.

Population/Culture

Most of Bolivia's population live in the highlands, with nearly two million within the La Paz metropolitan area. Eighty-five percent of the country's population is Amerindian or mestizo, many of whom live in poverty.

There are many pre-Colombian ruins, some yet to be explored. Ruins of note include Tiwinaku and Incallajta. Although Bolivia is almost wholly Christian, pagan rites are often interwoven in religious festivals. Amerindians and mestizos transformed the religious art of the Spanish into a distinct style known as Mestizo Baroque, characterized by vivid colors, and often overlaid with gold leaf.

Administration/Government

The Bolivian president is both head of government and chief of state, and is elected by popular vote for a single five-year term along with the vice-president. The bicameral National Congress comprises a 27-seat Chamber of Senators and a 130-seat Chamber of Deputies.

Economy/Industry

Much recent economic development has occurred in the eastern lowlands. Bolivia is one of South America's poorest countries and many residents practice a subsistence level folk economy. Manufacturing and services are poorly developed. Mining remains important and the recent discovery of petroleum and natural gas deposits offer hope for the future.

COLOMBIA
ECUADOR
Tumbes
Iquitos
Talara
Sullana
Piura
PERU
BRAZIL
Chiclayo
Tarapoto
Cajamarca
Pucallpa
Trujillo
Nevado Huascarán
Chimbote
Huaraz
Huánuco
PACIFIC OCEAN
Cerro de Pasco
Puerto Maldonado
Callao
LIMA
Huancayo
Ayacucho
Chincha Alta
Pisco
Ica
Cusco
Juliaca
Puno
Arequipa
Tacna
CHILE
BOLIVIA

Peru

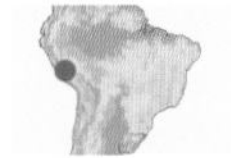

Map Reference Pages 158–159

The Republic of Peru, on the Pacific Coast of South America, is bordered by Colombia to the north, Chile to the south, Brazil and Bolivia to the east, and Ecuador to the northwest. Peru offers huge environmental contrasts, including desert landscapes bordering the Pacific, frigid polar conditions at high elevations, and sweltering humid tropics in the eastern lowlands.

Physical Geography

Peru's terrain is extremely varied. A narrow coastal plain gives way abruptly to the Andean cordillera. The Andes form a huge barrier to surface transportation. Only in the far southeast near Lake Titicaca do surface linkages join Peru to the east. Nevado Huascarán, the highest mountain, is also the site of the Western hemisphere's greatest natural disaster. In 1970, an earthquake unleashed a snow and rock avalanche that buried the towns of Yungay and Ranrahirca and resulted in the deaths of 66,000 people.

The Pacific Coastal Plain is primarily a desert landscape that increases in aridity from north to south. The climate and ecosystems of the Andean region vary greatly with elevation, while the eastern lowlands, within the upper Amazon basin, experience a humid tropical climate and rainforest ecosystem.

History

Peru was one of the world's earliest and most advanced centers of agriculture, urbanization, and civilization, culminating in the Inca empire (1438–1533). The Inca expanded northward to southern Colombia and southward into central Argentina and Chile. Other peoples adopted the Quechua language and Inca economic, political, and social customs.

The empire flourished for less than a century. Following the conquest by Francisco Pizarro and his force of 180 men together with Indian allies, Spain's grasp on much of South America tightened. Peru remained under Spanish control until independence in 1821. In the next 40 years, the country had 35 presidents and 15 different constitutions.

In the twentieth century, Peru suffered violent insurgencies, harsh military rule, rampant corruption, and ineffectual civilian governments. Democratic rule was re-established in 1980, but social cohesion is still lacking.

Population/Culture

Although people of European ancestry are outnumbered by Amerindians and mestizos, it is they who hold most power and wealth. This disparity is detrimental to the economy, society, and the government. Spanish and Quechua are both official languages, although several Amerindian languages are spoken by small numbers of people. Spanish is widely spoken by educated Peruvians, including those engaged in business and commerce.

Administration/Government

Members of the 120-seat unicameral Congress of the Republic of Peru are elected by popular vote for five-year terms. The president, also elected by popular vote, can serve non-consecutive five-year terms. The economic divide between rich and poor is a constant threat to political stability.

Economy/Industry

Peru, unlike many Latin American countries, has a diversified economy. Mining, agriculture, manufacturing, fishing, and services all contribute to GDP. An inadequate transportation infrastructure is a major obstacle to economic development. Despite steady economic growth, the number of people living below the poverty line remains high.

THE INCA EMPIRE

By the thirteenth century, Peru had experienced perhaps 10,000 years of cultural development. The region had developed into one of the world's most advanced centers of plant and animal domestication, urbanization, arts and architecture, science and technology, and social organization. It was in this environment that Inca civilization emerged. Legend suggests that an Andean tribe led by Manco Capac settled in the area of Cuzco around 1200 CE. In time, these people and their realm, *Tawantinsuyu* (Spanish: *Tahuantinsuyu*), became the Inca. In this context, it is important to distinguish between the Quechua-speaking culture, which evolved over thousands of years, and the short period of Inca rule that lasted less than a century. The first Inca (meaning Ruler) rose to power in 1438 and the civilization was conquered by Pizarro in 1533, 95 years later. During this short time, the Inca accomplished amazing feats and forged one of history's greatest empires.

Incan technology was among the world's most advanced of the time. Mountainsides were terraced and water for irrigation and domestic use was transferred great distances. An excellent network of roads linked the capital city of Cuzco to the far reaches of the empire. Llamas were the beasts of burden and *chasquis* (specially trained runners) transported information and light items up to 150 miles (240 km) a day. Their architecture was superb as was their stonework, exemplified by Sacsayhuaman—the Royal House of the Sun—a huge stone temple/fortress built near Cuzco, which has been declared a UNESCO World Heritage Site.

Among the many Incan ruins, none is better known or more apt to evoke awe than Machu Picchu. Also a World Heritage Site, it includes several hundred stone-built structures that cover an area of nearly 5 square miles (13 km²). The ruins are perched on a mountainside some 2,000 feet (610 m) above the Urubamba River. It is thought the city was built after 1400 CE, but why it was constructed remains a mystery. Location of the ruin was unknown to Europeans until 1911 when "discovered" by American adventurer, Hiram Bingham, who gave a local boy a dime to show his group some ruins.

PERU

Official name Peru (Republica del Peru)
Land area 463,323 square miles (1,280,000 km²)
Border countries Colombia, Brazil, Bolivia, Chile, Ecuador
Capital Lima
Highest point Nevado Huascarán 22,205 feet (6,768 m)
Climate Varies from tropical in east to dry desert in west; temperate to frigid in Andes
Population 29,181,000
Language(s) Official: Spanish, Quechua; other: Aymara, Amazonian languages
Ethnicity Amerindian 45%, mestizo 37%, European descent 15%, African/Japanese/Chinese descent/other 3%
Religion Christian 83.1%, other 0.6%, unspecified or none 16.3%
Government Constitutional republic
Currency Nuevo sol
Human Development Index 0.773 (ranked 87th out of 177 countries)

Center An Amerindian wears a traditional feather headdress, Sucre, Bolivia.

Far left A researcher catches the critically endangered Titicaca frog (*Telmatobius culeus*)—the world's largest aquatic frog—found only in Lake Titicaca, on the border of Bolivia and Peru.

Below Mist settles on Machu Picchu, Peru.

ARGENTINA

Official name Argentine Republic (República Argentina)

Land area 1,452,236 square miles (3,761,274 km²)

Border countries Bolivia, Paraguay, Brazil, Uruguay, Chile

Capital Buenos Aires

Highest & lowest points Cerro Aconcagua 22,831 feet (6,959 m); Laguna del Carbón −344 feet (−105 m)

Climate Mostly temperate; arid in southeast; subantarctic in southwest

Population 40,677,000

Language Official: Spanish; other: Italian, English, German, French

Ethnicity European descent (mainly Spanish and Italian) 97%, mestizo (mixed Amerindian–European descent), Amerindian/other 3%

Religion Nominally Roman Catholic 92% (less than 20% practicing), Protestant 2%, Jewish 2%, other 4%

Government Republic

Currency Argentine peso

Human Development Index 0.869 (ranked 38th out of 177 countries)

Above right Houses in the colorful port district of La Boca in Buenos Aires. The district was settled mainly by southern Italian immigrants (1860–1910), who painted their houses with leftover paint from ships.

Below right Gaucho (Argentinian cowboy) preparing his horses for the annual San Antonio de Areco Gaucho Festival, which lasts for three days. Horsemanship, parades, singing, and dancing are just some of the highlights of the festival.

Below Avenida 9 de Julio in Buenos Aires was named to commemorate Argentina's Independence Day, July 9. On that day in 1816, Argentina achieved independence from Spain.

BOLIVIA
PARAGUAY
BRAZIL
CHILE
San Salvador de Jujuy
San Miguel de Tucumán
Formosa
Corrientes
Posadas
Santiago del Estero
Catamarca
Reconquista
La Rioja
Córdoba
Santa Fé
Concordia
San Juan
Paraná
Cerro Aconcagua
Mendoza
San Luis
Rosario
URUGUAY
BUENOS AIRES
La Plata
San Rafael
ARGENTINA
Santa Rosa
Olavarria
Bahía Blanca
Neuquén
General Roca
Mar del Plata
San Carlos de Bariloche
Viedma
ATLANTIC OCEAN
Rawson
Comodoro Rivadavia
Río Gallegos
Ushuaia

Argentina

Map Reference Pages 160–162

The Argentine Republic occupies the southern part of South America. It stretches half the length of the continent, from the north above the Tropic of Capricorn, to Tierra del Fuego in the subantarctic zone in the south. It is the second largest country in South America after Brazil.

Physical Geography

There is great environmental diversity within Argentina, from subtropical forests to freezing conditions to dry desert. The South Atlantic Ocean fringes the east coast, and in the west the Andes form a formidable natural barrier. Lying within 186 miles (300 km) of two oceans would normally guarantee a moist climate, but the Patagonian Desert is the world's outstanding example of a rain-shadow desert, with the Andes shutting out rain-bearing westerly winds from the Pacific. Yet, this desert landscape with its year-round frosts, sparse precipitation, and unrelenting winds is home to a wide variety of flora and fauna.

MILESTONE EVENTS

1516 Spaniard, Juan Díaz de Solís, claims the region of Río de la Plata for the Spanish Crown

1535 Pedro de Mendoza founds Buenos Aires

1806 British fleet invades Buenos Aires, repelled by citizens militia

May 25, 1810 Spanish Viceroy removed from office in revolution that marks beginning of years of conflict

July 9, 1816 Country gains independence from Spain

1853 First constitution written; country named República Argentina

1916 Hipolito Yrigoyen becomes president and introduces a minimum wage

1930 President Yrigoyen is overthrown by military

1932 Civilian rule restored

1946 Juan Peron becomes the "people's" president

1952 Eva Peron, popular wife of the president, dies of cancer

July 1974 President Peron dies and his wife, Isabel Peron, becomes president; country is wracked by violence

1976 Military seizes power and "Dirty War" begins—30,000 citizens "disappear"

April 1982 Argentina invades Falkland Islands; beginning of six-week undeclared Falklands War

1983 Raul Alfonsin becomes civilian president; inflation reaches 900%

1989 Carlos Menem becomes president; economic reforms introduced

1992 Israeli embassy bombed killing 29 people

1994 Bombing of Jewish community center kills 86 and injures over 200

September 1996 General strike

June 1998 Former Dirty War dictator, Jorge Rafael Videla, arrested in connection with babies stolen from their mothers and given to his regime's supporters

July 2001 Country brought to standstill in general strike protesting proposed austerity measures

April 2002 Banking and foreign exchange activity suspended

September 2003 IMF agrees to refinance the country's debt

December 31, 2004 Fire kills 175 and injures 700 in nightclub

June 2005 Supreme Court overturns laws protecting former military officers from prosecution, in particular over human rights abuses committed between 1976 and 1983

January 2006 Argentina repays multi-billion-dollar debt to IMF

March 2008 Tax on soybeans increased for third time in six months, farmers strike in response causing food shortages; soybeans generate US$25 billion a year in export revenue

History

In 1516, Spanish sailor Juan Díaz de Solís arrived at the estuary of the Río de la Plata, claiming the region for the Spanish Crown. In 1535, Pedro de Mendoza founded Buenos Aires, the beginning of the colonization of what was later called Virreinato del Río de la Plata. *Plata* is Spanish for silver, which in Latin is *argentum*, from which Argentina derives its current name. Ships en route from mines in Peru to Spain had to stop here, hence the silver-related names.

In 1806 a British fleet invaded Buenos Aires unopposed by the Viceroy, who fled; shortly after, a popular militia led by Santiago de Liniers expelled the British. The following year another British fleet tried to lay siege to Buenos Aires and again was defeated; these events gave the local people a new understanding of their power and of the inability of the Spanish Crown to defend their interests.

Napoleon's invasion of Spain was the catalyst for open hostilities between locals and Spanish authorities. Revolution broke out on May 25, 1810, when the Viceroy was removed from office and replaced by a native junta. This marked the beginning of years of battles between royalists and republicans, which was part of the larger independence movement taking place over much of the Americas. In July 1816, the country gained independence.

The first constitution in 1853 included the nation's official name, República Argentina, but the political situation remained turbulent, the provinces struggling for hegemony. Not until 1880 did Buenos Aires become the nation's permanent capital.

Argentina's modern political history is built upon a succession of democratic and military governments. The most tragic era was from 1976 until 1982 when a military junta fought an illegal war against so-called subversives. This illegal war resulted in the "disappearance" of 30,000 citizens, a blight on the country's political history which remains a very painful issue. In 1982 Argentina invaded the disputed Falkland Islands; the British responded by sending in troops. An undeclared war lasted six weeks when the Argentine military surrendered to British troops. After this defeat the military government could no longer hold office and the country returned to a democratic government. Since then, successive elected civilian governments have held power.

Population/Culture

Argentina is seen as a "white" South American country, and indeed most inhabitants are of European descent, principally Spanish and Italian. Minority groups include mestizos, people of mixed European and Amerindian ancestry; descendants of African slaves; and Amerindians. Spanish conquistadors almost wiped out the indigenous population through violence, disease, and dispossession. Currently there are about 200,000 Amerindians belonging to 15 tribes, including the Mocovi, Toba, Abipone, and Guarani. These people tend to live on the fringes of society and fare poorly in health and education.

Culture is an eclectic mix of indigenous, European, and African traditions, reflected in art, literature, dance, and music. In Argentina music and dance are a fundamental part of life—the best known dance is the tango, which at one time was considered indecent because couples held each other in a "brazen and unrestained way." The tango originated in bars, cafes, and brothels in the poor districts of Buenos Aires in the 1880s.

Administration/Government

Argentina is a republic headed by the president who is also chief of state. The country is divided into 23 provinces and the federal capital district of Buenos Aires. The bicameral National Congress (Congreso Nacional) embodies the 72-seat Senate and 257-seat Chamber of Deputies. The president and vice-president are elected by popular vote for four-year terms and may serve a second term.

4962-1444

Left Chile's spectacular Torres del Paine National Park features mountains, glaciers, lakes, rivers, and waterfalls, and is home to unique wildlife and flora.

CHILE

Official name Republic of Chile (República de Chile)
Land area 292,260 square miles (756,950 km²)
Border countries Peru, Bolivia, Argentina
Capital Santiago
Highest point Nevado Ojos del Salados 22,572 feet (6,880 m)
Climate Temperate; desert in north; Mediterranean in central region; cool and damp to subantarctic in south
Population 16,454,000
Language(s) Official: Spanish; other: Mapudungun, German, English
Ethnicity European descent/mestizo (mixed Amerindian–European descent) 95%, Amerindian (Mapuche) 3%, other 2%
Religion Roman Catholic 70%, Evangelical 15.1%, Jehovah's Witness 1%, other Christian 1%, other 4.6%, none 8.3%
Government Republic
Currency Chilean peso
Human Development Index 0.867 (ranked 40th out of 177 countries)

Economy/Industry

Argentina's economy is the third largest in Latin America. It has rich natural resources, yet the mainstay of its wealth is agriculture and livestock. The most productive areas are the pampas, vast plains once used to graze cattle, but now used for crops. There is a solid fishing industry, a diversified industrial base, and a variety of minerals,. The economy has always been export oriented, with petroleum and gas, soybeans and soy products, vehicles, wheat, and corn being the major exports.

Despite great economic potential, there have been many ups and downs, depending on the administration and the world market. In 2001, a depression accompanied by a run on the banks saw 60 percent of the population living below the poverty line; today, that figure is just over 23 percent.

Chile

Map Reference Pages 160–162

Chile occupies most of the western side of South America between the Andes and the Pacific Ocean. It shares borders with three countries—Peru to the north, Bolivia to the northeast, and Argentina to the east. Chile is very long—2,700 miles (4,300 km) from north to south—but not very wide, averaging only 110 miles (177 km) east to west.

Physical Geography

Climate varies but overall is temperate. To the north is the dry Atacama Desert. In the middle of the country the large fertile valley that surrounds the capital, Santiago, has a Mediterranean climate and is a wine-growing area. South of the central valley are wet woodlands and beyond, reaching toward the tip of the continent, conditions are very cold. Extending the length of Chile are the Andes Mountains. Located on the Pacific Ring of Fire, the country is subject to earthquakes and has some active volcanoes—Chaitén violently erupted in May 2008 after being dormant for 9,000 years.

History

Chile was colonized by Spain in 1540 after the conquest of the Inca in Peru. Indigenous Indians, commonly referred to as the Mapuche, resisted the colonizers for over 300 years.

Independence from Spain was achieved in 1818. Chile did not experience instability in the post-independence years and became a leading economy in the region. Later in the 1800s, Chile claimed the Mapuche lands in the south and won the regions Antofagasta and Arica from Bolivia and Peru.

Following civil war (1891), a parliamentary government was in power from 1891 to 1924, when it was overthrown in a military coup. The military governed until 1932, after which the country was stable until socialist Salvador Allende was elected president in 1970. In 1973 General Augusto Pinochet and the CIA-backed military overthrew Allende's government in a military coup. Allende died during the fighting and thousands of people "disappeared." Pinochet's regime remained in power until 1990. Since then Chile has been a stable democratic republic that has elected its first female president.

Population/Culture

Chile's population comprises mestizos, of European and Amerindian descent; Mapuche, who make up three percent of the population; and Chileans of European descent, the largest group. Culture is a blend of European and Amerindian customs and beliefs.

Literature, festivals, music, and dance reflect the various cultural influences. Chile boasts two Nobel Prize winning authors—Gabriela Mistral and Pablo Neruda—as well as acclaimed author, Isabel Allende.

Administration/Government

The Republic of Chile has a bicameral National Congress and is divided into a 38-seat Senate and a 120-seat Chamber of Deputies. Members of both houses are elected by popular vote. The president is both chief of state and head of government, and is elected by popular vote to serve a single term.

RICHES OF THE ANDES

The continuous cycle of subduction, melting, and volcano-building along the South American Pacific coast leads to a concentration of elements, such as gold, silver, copper, tin, and other metals that are otherwise rare in the crust. Exploration in the Andes has uncovered some of the world's largest economic metal deposits and rarest gemstones, such as lapis lazuli. Chile produces about 30 percent of the world's copper from massive open-pit mines such as Chuquicamata and Escondida. These are the world's largest mines, with an annual production of 680,000 tons (616,886 tonnes) and 800,000 tons (725,748 tonnes) of copper metal respectively. The name "Chuquicamata" comes from the Aymara language and refers to the Chuqui Native South American group, who first worked the copper deposits to make tools and weapons. Today, enormous trucks carry low-grade copper-bearing rocks out of these colossal pits. In the weathered zones of these mines, many rare and unusual green copper minerals are commonplace, including antlerite and atacamite. Many are highly soluble minerals that can only survive in the region's dry deserts.

Economy/Industry

Chile has a free-market economy, with 57 bilateral and free-trade agreements—it does not rely heavily on any one trading partner. Copper is one of the most important industries and is a prime export commodity. In a farsighted move, the government set up the Social Stabilization Fund in 2006 to hold surplus copper revenues, so that in lean years social spending can be maintained.

Other important industries include iron and steel, wood and wood products, fish processing, and transport equipment. In addition to copper, Chile's exports include wine, fruit, paper, and chemicals.

Above Ready for a performance in Antofagasta, a city squeezed between the Pacific Ocean and the Cordillera de la Costa in the Atacama Desert. Antofagasta is one of the driest cities in the world.

Below Colorful dwellings are built on the steep slopes of Valparaiso, Chile's main seaport. This picturesque city is renowned for its funicular railways that climb the hills surrounding the port city.

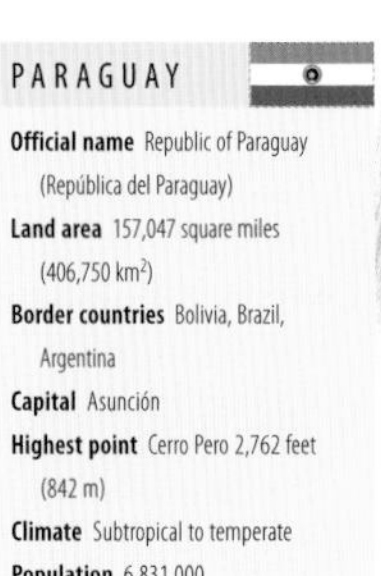

PARAGUAY

Official name Republic of Paraguay (República del Paraguay)
Land area 157,047 square miles (406,750 km²)
Border countries Bolivia, Brazil, Argentina
Capital Asunción
Highest point Cerro Pero 2,762 feet (842 m)
Climate Subtropical to temperate
Population 6,831,000
Languages Spanish, Guarani
Ethnicity Mestizo 95%, other 5%
Religion Christian 97%, other/unspecified 1.9%, none 1.1%
Government Constitutional republic
Currency Guarani
Human Development Index 0.755 (ranked 95th out of 177 countries)

Above right Performers dancing in the town square of Durazno, Uruguay, during a gaucho festival. The gaucho's courage and sense of freedom is associated with the struggle for independence.

URUGUAY

Official name Oriental Republic of Uruguay (República Oriental del Uruguay)
Land area 68,039 square miles (176,220 km²)
Border countries Brazil, Argentina
Capital Montevideo
Highest point Cerro Catedral 1,686 feet (514 m)
Climate Warm temperate
Population 3,478,000
Language(s) Spanish, Portunol or Brazilero (Portuguese–Spanish mix)
Ethnicity European descent 88%, mestizo 8%, African descent 4%
Religion Christian 68%, Jewish 1%, other/none 31%
Government Constitutional republic
Currency Uruguayan peso
Human Development Index 0.852 (ranked 46th out of 177 countries)

Below right The Communications Tower in Montevideo, capital city of Uruguay. With a population of over 1 million, this cosmopolitan city is a thriving tourist destination.

Below Asunción, the capital of Paraguay, was established in the sixteenth century, and named for the feast day of the Virgin Mary.

BOLIVIA
BRAZIL
ARGENTINA
PARAGUAY
Fuerte Olimpo
Filadelfia
Pedro Juan Caballero
Concepción
Salto del Guaira
ASUNCIÓN
Coronel Oviedo
Caaguazú
Villarrica
Cerro Perú
Caazapá
Pilar
San Juan Bautista
Encarnación

Paraguay

Map Reference Pages 160–161

Paraguay, in central South America, shares with neighboring Bolivia the distinction of being one of the Western hemisphere's two land-locked countries. Asunción, the capital, is located on the Paraguay River that borders Argentina and constitutes the country's primary water access to the Atlantic Ocean. Much of central Paraguay is swamp or marshland. In the far eastern and western parts of the country plains give way to uplands. The climate is temperate to subtropical, with frost rare and rainfall decreasing from east to west. The woodlands and savanna grasslands of the east give way to the marshes, thornbush, and semiarid scrublands of the Gran Chaco in the west. In the southeast, Itaipú Dam on the Paraná River powers one of the world's largest hydroelectric installations.

Before the arrival of Europeans in the early sixteenth century, Paraguay was inhabited by Tupi and Guarani Amerindians. Asunción was settled in 1537 as a Spanish administrative center, but because it lacked mineral wealth and lands suitable for agriculture, the colony languished. Paraguay gained its independence in 1811. In the War of the Triple Alliance (1865–1870), in which Paraguay fought Argentina, Brazil, and Uruguay, the country lost much of its territory and two-thirds of its adult male population. During the twentieth century, repeated conflicts and the 35-year dictatorship of Alfredo Stroessner further burdened the nation. Since a new constitution was drafted in 1992, Paraguay has held relatively free elections and now enjoys growing political and economic stability.

More than 90 percent of people live east of the Paraguay River, including 1.8 million in the Asunción metropolitan area. Annual population growth is 2.4 percent, the highest in South America. Ethnically, the population is homogeneous, with 95 percent being mestizo (Spanish–Amerindian ancestry). Spanish and Guarani are both official languages.

Paraguay's market economy has a large and important informal sector, including the re-export of goods to nearby countries, and many small enterprises. A large percentage of the population works directly or indirectly in agriculture, much at subsistence level. Poor infrastructure, lack of extensive industrial or agricultural resources, and decades of political turbulence have combined to make Paraguay one of the Western hemisphere's poorest countries. About 32 percent of the population live below the poverty line.

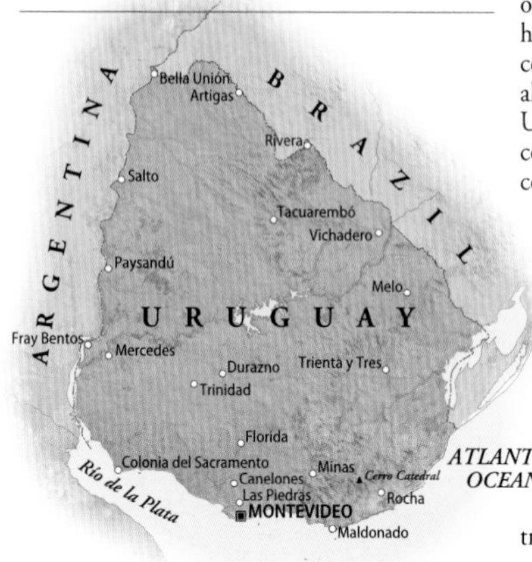
ARGENTINA
BRAZIL
URUGUAY
Bella Unión
Artigas
Rivera
Salto
Tacuarembó
Vichadero
Paysandú
Melo
Fray Bentos
Mercedes
Durazno
Trienta y Tres
Trinidad
Florida
Colonia del Sacramento
Minas
Cerro Catedral
Canelones
Las Piedras
Rocha
MONTEVIDEO
Maldonado
Río de la Plata
ATLANTIC OCEAN

Uruguay

Map Reference Pages 160–161

Uruguay is South America's smallest Spanish-speaking country in both area and population. Tucked between Brazil to the north and northeast and Argentina to the west, its coastline faces the South Atlantic Ocean. The capital and largest city, Montevideo, is located on the Rio de la Plata, the large estuary of the Paraná and Paraguay rivers.

Uruguay's terrain is dominated by rolling plains and scattered low hills. It is the only economically developed South American nation that is effectively served by transportation linkages. The climate is warm to temperate, and frosts are almost unknown. Soils are generally fertile and water resources adequate.

Few Amerindians occupied the area when Spaniards arrived in the early eighteenth century. Montevideo was founded as a military outpost in 1726, and because of its excellent harbor soon became an important commercial center. Neighboring Argentina and Brazil alternately claimed the territory, resulting in Uruguay finally freeing itself from Brazilian control in 1828. During the early twentieth century, widespread social, economic, and political reforms established Uruguay as the continent's most socialistic state.

By the 1960s the economy, which was primarily based on agriculture, was in decline and social unrest resulted in the formation of the Tupamaros, an urban guerrilla group. The Tupamaros gained popular support while robbing banks, kidnapping unpopular politicians and bureaucrats, and holding them for ransom. In 1973, the military assumed control and crushed the revolt. Democracy was restored in the mid-1980s and today Uruguay is one of the continent's most stable nations both politically and economically.

Some 44 percent of Uruguay's inhabitants live in the Montevideo metropolitan area. The population ranks among the continent's most literate and healthy, and enjoys excellent political and labor conditions. Eighty-eight percent of the population can trace ancestry to Europe, eight percent is mestizo, and four percent is of African descent. In 2007, Uruguay became the first Latin American country to recognize same-sex civil unions.

Although Uruguay has the continent's best-developed socioeconomic middle class, almost 28 percent of people live below the poverty line. The economy has depended on crops, livestock, and the processing of foods, beverages, wool, textiles, and hides. Today, the service sector is experiencing rapid growth, including a thriving tourist industry.

Caribbean Sea
VENEZUELA
GUYANA
SURINAME
French Guiana
(France)
COLOMBIA
ECUADOR
BRAZIL
PERU
BOLIVIA
PARAGUAY
CHILE
ARGENTINA
URUGUAY
PACIFIC OCEAN
ATLANTIC OCEAN
Falkland Islands
(UK)
South Georgia and
South Sandwich Islands
(UK)

French Guiana

Map Reference Pages 154–155

The territory of French Guiana faces the Atlantic Ocean. Bordered by Brazil to the south and Suriname to the west, it is the only political territory in South America that is not an independent country. The narrow Atlantic coastal plain rises to interior uplands and the Tumac-Humac Mountains in the south. Tropical forests cover most of the country. The hot humid tropical climate offers little seasonal variation, with annual temperatures averaging 80°F (27°C) and rainfall spread fairly evenly throughout the year.

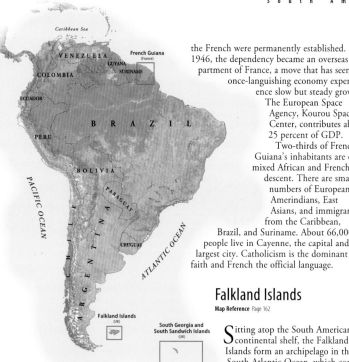

Arawak, Carib, and Tupi-Guarani Amerindians lived in the region long before French settlers arrived in the early 1600s. The territory then changed hands between the French, British, Dutch, and Portuguese, but by 1814, the French were permanently established. In 1946, the dependency became an overseas department of France, a move that has seen the once-languishing economy experience slow but steady growth. The European Space Agency, Kourou Space Center, contributes about 25 percent of GDP.

Two-thirds of French Guiana's inhabitants are of mixed African and French descent. There are small numbers of Europeans, Amerindians, East Asians, and immigrants from the Caribbean, Brazil, and Suriname. About 66,000 people live in Cayenne, the capital and largest city. Catholicism is the dominant faith and French the official language.

Falkland Islands

Map Reference Page 162

Sitting atop the South American continental shelf, the Falkland Islands form an archipelago in the South Atlantic Ocean, which comprises around 200 very small islands and two large islands, East and West Falkland, located 350 miles (560 km) east of southern Argentina.

The terrain of both large islands is rugged and mountainous. Good natural harbors provide safe havens from Atlantic storms. The climate is cold marine with strong winds, frequent rain, and occasional snow all year. Temperatures range from 48–55°F (9–13°C) in summer, and 36–39°F (2–4°C) in winter.

The first European explorer to see the islands is thought to have been Dutch sailor Sebald de Weert (1600). French navigator Louis Antoine de Bougainville founded St Louis, the first settlement, in East Falkland. This settlement was transferred to Spain in 1767 and renamed Puerto Soledad. About this time, British captain John Byron was establishing Port Egmont on West Falkland and claiming it for King George III, unaware of French presence on the eastern island.

When Argentina declared independence in 1816, it claimed the islands and later founded a settlement, subsequently destroyed by US warships (1831). Argentina sent another governor in 1832, and in 1833, British forces asserted British sovereignty. Since then the islands have been a self-governing Overseas Territory of the United Kingdom, but Argentina never relinquished its claim. On April 2, 1982, Argentina invaded and occupied the islands. A British task force quickly responded, compelling the Argentine military to surrender after six weeks. Falkland Islanders are almost exclusively of British birth or descent. Most live in the capital, Stanley. Once reliant on agriculture, the Falkland Islands now have several sources of income, including ecotourism.

Economic activity is tied with fishing. Licenses are sold to foreign-owned vessels to operate within the islands' fishing zone. Exports include wool, stamps, and coins, and surveys have pointed to significant reserves of oil offshore. Except for defense, the islands are now economically self-sufficient.

DEVIL'S ISLAND PENAL COLONY

French Guiana is synonymous with the notorious Devil's Island penal colony. Between 1852 and 1938, an estimated 80,000 French criminals were exiled to the infamous prison colony on the Guiana coast. Surprisingly, the name Devil's Island pre-dates the prison system by nearly a century. In 1763, France attempted to establish a dominantly European colony on the mainland of its tropical South American outpost. Most members of the colonizing party died within the first year, having succumbed to various tropical diseases. Others sought refuge on three offshore islands where conditions brought such relief that they were named Isles du Salut (Isles of Salvation). Treacherous currents and a steep rocky shore prevented the group from occupying the smallest island in the group, but their failure was said at the time to be the work of the devil, hence the island's name, Ile du Diable (Devil's Island).

France abolished slavery in 1848, an act that resulted in the destruction of the plantation economy. The government decided to fill the labor vacuum with prisoners from France. Of the approximately 80,000 convicts imprisoned between 1852 and 1939, 80 percent perished, hundreds escaped (although it is believed that less than one percent survived the attempt), about 2,500 were freed and returned to France. Around 18,000 became libérés—free, but confined to French Guiana. Relégués, another group of prisoners, were confined to the colony, but were free to resume their lives in the hope they would contribute to economic development. Of the 24,000 prisoners in this group, 19,000 died, some 2,500 escaped (most of whom died in the attempt), and a few took a wife—of mixed blood—and settled down. The prison system was a colossal failure and a tremendous embarrassment to France and was discontinued in 1938.

Left With a population of just over 2,000, Stanley is the only true city in the Falkland Islands.

FRENCH GUIANA

Official name Department of Guiana
Land area 34,421 square miles (89,150 km²)
Capital Cayenne
Climate Tropical
Population 209,000
Government Overseas department of France
Currency Euro, French franc

Below left The rocky, infamous, palm-covered Ile du Diable (Devil's Island) in French Guiana.

Below An abandoned former whaling station at Stromness Bay, South Georgia Island.

South Georgia and the South Sandwich Islands

Map Reference Page 163

South Georgia and the South Sandwich Islands is a remote and barren British overseas territory in the southern Atlantic Ocean some 808 miles (1,300 km) east of the tip of South America. It consists of South Georgia, the largest in the group, several small islands nearby, and the South Sandwich Islands, a long arc of 11 tiny volcanic islands more than 435 miles (700 km) to the southeast. All the islands are mountainous, and at higher elevations are permanently covered in snow. Argentina claims the islands and briefly occupied South Georgia in the Falklands War.

Captain James Cook claimed South Georgia and eight South Sandwich Islands for the British Crown in 1775, naming them for King George III. In the nineteenth century they became a base for sealing operations and, in the early twentieth century, for whaling. The last whaling station closed in 1965.

The islands are uninhabited except for a small contingent of British government officials, scientists on research expeditions, and support staff. There is no economy as such, but income is received from fishing licenses and port fees, and from postage stamps and coins produced in the UK. South Georgia is visited by cruise ships and environmental tourists—it is home to millions of penguins, colonies of seals, and other wildlife.

FALKLAND ISLANDS

Official name Falkland Islands (Islas Malvinas)
Land area 4,700 square miles (12,173 km²)
Capital Stanley
Climate Cold marine
Population 3,140
Government Overseas Territory of the United Kingdom
Currency Falkland pound

SOUTH GEORGIA AND THE SOUTH SANDWICH ISLANDS

Official name South Georgia and the South Sandwich Islands
Border countries None
Capital None
Climate Temperate to polar; nearly all precipitation falls as snow
Population Group of scientists of the British Antarctic Survey (South Georgia & Bird Island); South Sandwich Islands are uninhabited
Government Overseas territory of the United Kingdom
Currency None

ATLANTIC OCEAN
CARIBBEAN SEA
NORTH AMERICA
SOUTH AMERICA
WEST INDIES
GREATER ANTILLES
LESSER ANTILLES
BAHAMAS
HISPANIOLA
CUBA
AMAZON BASIN
SELVAS
GUIANA HIGHLANDS
BRAZILIAN HIGHLANDS
PLANALTO DO MATO GROSSO
ANDES
CORDILLERA ORIENTAL
CORDILLERA CENTRAL
CORDILLERA OCCIDENTAL
Orinoco Delta
Serra do Tombador
Serra dos Parecis
Chapada Diamantina

1:20,600,000

Lambert Azimuthal Equal Area Projection

0 250 500 750 1000 kilometers

0 125 250 375 500 miles

South America Physical

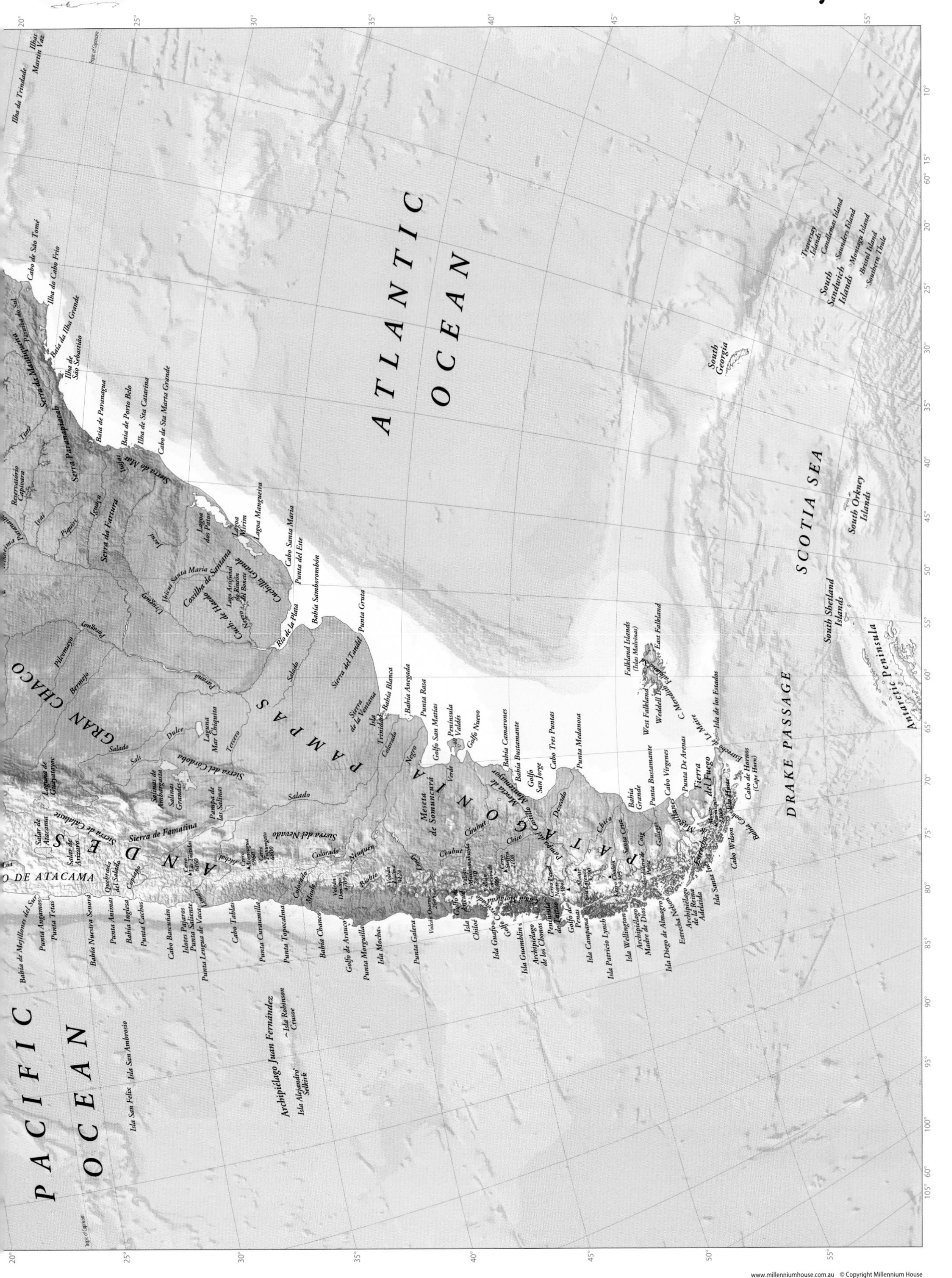
ATLANTIC OCEAN
PACIFIC OCEAN
SCOTIA SEA
DRAKE PASSAGE
GRAN CHACO
PAMPAS
PATAGONIA
ANDES
South Georgia
South Sandwich Islands
South Orkney Islands
South Shetland Islands
Antarctic Peninsula
Falkland Islands (Islas Malvinas)
West Falkland
East Falkland
Tierra del Fuego
Isla de los Estados
Cabo de Hornos (Cape Horn)
Archipiélago Juan Fernández
Isla Alejandro Selkirk
Isla Robinson Crusoe
Isla San Félix
Isla San Ambrosio
Ilha da Trindade
Ilhas Martin Vaz
Cabo de São Tomé
Ilha do Cabo Frio
Lagoa dos Patos
Lagoa Mirim
Lagoa Mangueira
Río de la Plata
Bahía Samborombón
Punta Gruta
Bahía Blanca
Golfo San Matías
Península Valdés
Golfo Nuevo
Bahía Camarones
Bahía Bustamante
Golfo San Jorge
Cabo Tres Puntas
Punta Medanosa
Bahía Grande
Cabo Vírgenes
Meseta de Somuncurá
Isla Chiloé
Isla Wellington
Isla Diego de Almagro
Isla Santa Inés
Cabo Wilson
Golfo de Arauco
Isla Mocha
Sierra de Famatina
Sierra del Nevado
Sierra de Córdoba
Laguna Mar Chiquita
Salinas Grandes
Pampa de las Salinas
Serra do Mar
Serra Paranapiacaba
Serra da Mantiqueira
Coxilha de Santana
Cuchilla Grande
Sierra del Tandil
Sierra de la Ventana
Bermejo
Pilcomayo
Paraná
Uruguay
Salado
Colorado
Negro
Chubut
Deseado
Dulce

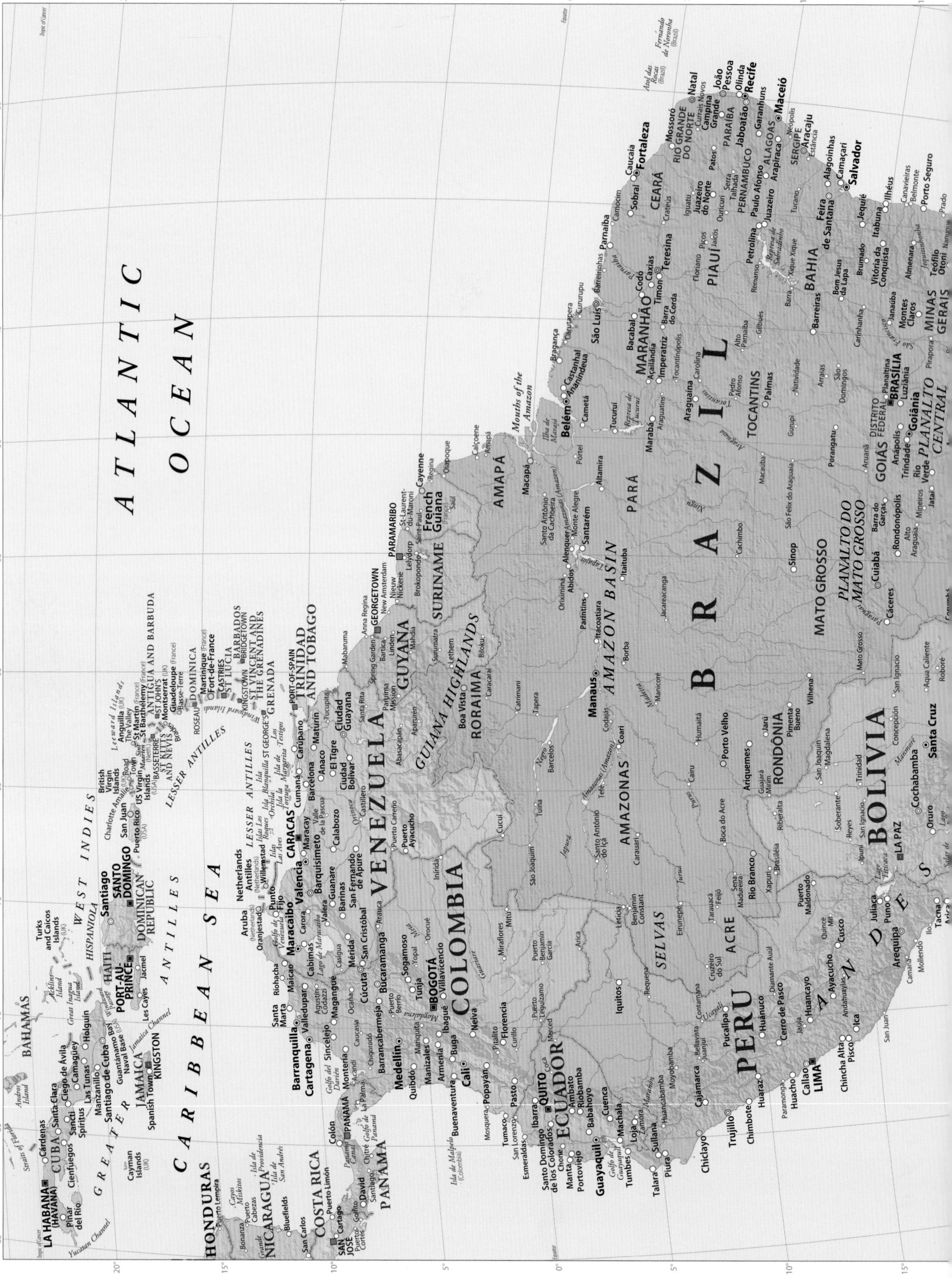

ATLANTIC OCEAN

CARIBBEAN SEA

WEST INDIES

GREATER ANTILLES

LESSER ANTILLES

BAHAMAS

CUBA

HAITI

DOMINICAN REPUBLIC

JAMAICA

HONDURAS

NICARAGUA

COSTA RICA

PANAMA

TRINIDAD AND TOBAGO

VENEZUELA

COLOMBIA

ECUADOR

PERU

BOLIVIA

GUYANA

SURINAME

French Guiana

BRAZIL

AMAZON BASIN

GUIANA HIGHLANDS

SELVAS

ANDES

PLANALTO DO MATO GROSSO

PLANALTO CENTRAL

1:20,600,000

Lambert Azimuthal Equal Area Projection

0 250 500 750 1000 kilometers

0 125 250 375 500 miles

South America Political

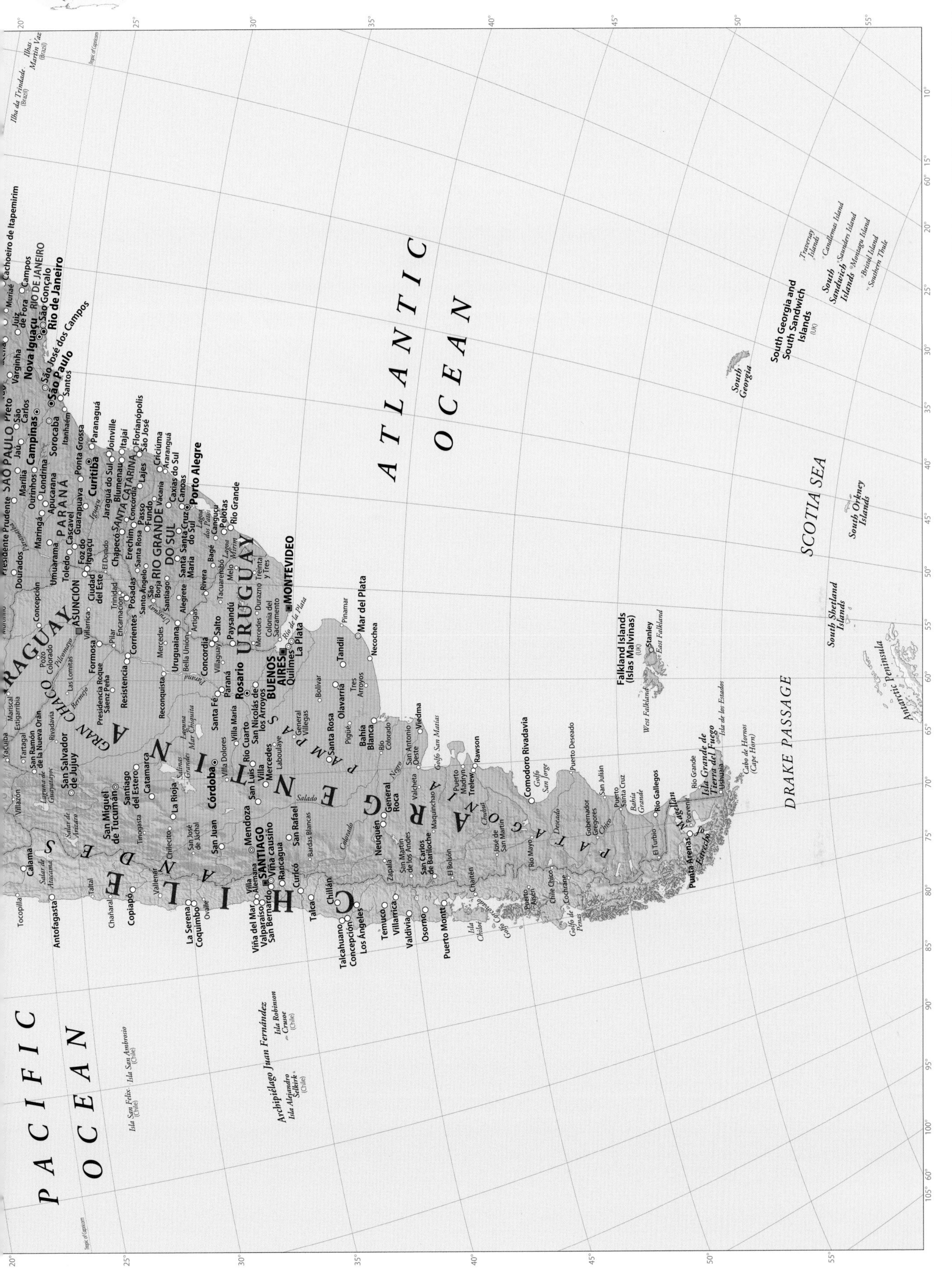
ATLANTIC OCEAN
PACIFIC OCEAN
SCOTIA SEA
DRAKE PASSAGE
ARGENTINA
CHILE
URUGUAY
PARAGUAY
PATAGONIA
PAMPAS
GRAN CHACO
BUENOS AIRES
MONTEVIDEO
SANTIAGO
ASUNCIÓN
Rio de Janeiro
São Paulo
Porto Alegre
Curitiba
Córdoba
Rosario
Mendoza
Mar del Plata
Bahía Blanca
Comodoro Rivadavia
Punta Arenas
Ushuaia
Falkland Islands (Islas Malvinas) (UK)
Stanley
East Falkland
West Falkland
South Georgia and South Sandwich Islands (UK)
South Georgia
South Sandwich Islands
South Orkney Islands
South Shetland Islands
Antarctic Peninsula
Isla Grande de Tierra del Fuego
Cabo de Hornos (Cape Horn)
Archipiélago Juan Fernández
Isla Robinson Crusoe (Chile)
Isla Alejandro Selkirk (Chile)
Isla San Félix (Chile)
Isla San Ambrosio (Chile)
Ilha da Trindade (Brazil)
Ilhas Martin Vaz (Brazil)
Tropic of Capricorn

CARIBBEAN SEA
PACIFIC OCEAN
PANAMA
COLOMBIA
ECUADOR
PERU
ANDES
LLANOS
SELVAS
Lesser Antilles
Netherlands Antilles
Aruba
Península de la Guajira
Golfo de Venezuela
Lago de Maracaibo
Golfo de Panamá
Golfo del Darién
Golfo de Guayaquil
Serrana Bank
Isla de Providencia
Isla de San Andrés
Isla de Malpelo
Isla de Coiba
Administrative regions in Ecuador numbered on the map:
1. SANTO DOMINGO DE LOS TSÁCHILAS
Administrative regions numbered on the map:
1. YARACUY
2. CARABOBO
3. ARAGUA
4. VARGAS
5. DISTRITO CA
PANAMÁ
Colón
Santiago
David
Barranquilla
Cartagena
Santa Marta
Medellín
BOGOTÁ
Cali
Bucaramanga
Cúcuta
Maracaibo
Valencia
CARACAS
Barquisimeto
Mérida
QUITO
Guayaquil
Cuenca
Iquitos
Leticia
Buenaventura
Manizales
Pereira
Ibagué
Neiva
Pasto
Popayán
Villavicencio
ANTIOQUIA
CHOCÓ
CÓRDOBA
SUCRE
BOLÍVAR
ATLÁNTICO
MAGDALENA
LA GUAJIRA
CESAR
NORTE DE SANTANDER
SANTANDER
BOYACÁ
CUNDINAMARCA
CALDAS
RISARALDA
QUINDÍO
TOLIMA
HUILA
VALLE DEL CAUCA
CAUCA
NARIÑO
PUTUMAYO
CAQUETÁ
META
ARAUCA
CASANARE
VICHADA
GUAINÍA
GUAVIARE
VAUPÉS
AMAZONAS
LORETO
ZULIA
FALCÓN
LARA
TRUJILLO
MÉRIDA
TÁCHIRA
BARINAS
APURE
PORTUGUESA
COJEDES
ESMERALDAS
MANABÍ
PICHINCHA
IMBABURA
CARCHI
SUCUMBÍOS
ORELLANA
NAPO
COTOPAXI
TUNGURAHUA
PASTAZA
CHIMBORAZO
BOLÍVAR
LOS RÍOS
GUAYAS
CAÑAR
AZUAY
EL ORO
LOJA
ZAMORA-CHINCHIPE
MORONA-SANTIAGO
TUMBES
PIURA
CAJAMARCA
AMAZONAS
BOCAS DEL TORO
CHIRIQUÍ
VERAGUAS
HERRERA
LOS SANTOS
COCLÉ
COLÓN
DARIÉN
KUNA YALA
Amazonas (Amazon)
Meters / Feet
6000 19685
5000 16404
4000 13123
3000 9843
2000 6562
1000 3281
500 1640
200 656
100 328
0
LAND BELOW SEA LEVEL
100 328
200 656
1000 3281
2000 6562
4000 13123
6000 19685

1:7,880,000
Lambert Conic Conformal Projection

0 50 100 150 200 250 300 kilometers
0 25 50 75 100 125 150 miles

Northwestern South America

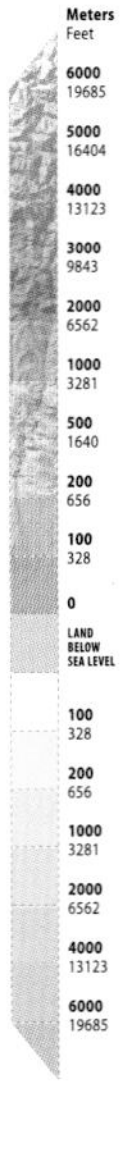

Administrative regions in Guyana numbered on the map:
1. ESSEQUIBO ISLANDS-WEST DEMERARA
2. DEMERARA-MAHAICA
3. MAHAICA-BERBICE

Administrative regions in Suriname numbered on the map:
1. SARAMACCA
2. WANICA
3. COMMEWIJNE

ATLANTIC OCEAN

Meters / Feet
6000 / 19685
5000 / 16404
4000 / 13123
3000 / 9843
2000 / 6562
1000 / 3281
500 / 1640
200 / 656
100 / 328
0 LAND BELOW SEA LEVEL
100 / 328
200 / 656
1000 / 3281
2000 / 6562
4000 / 13123
6000 / 19685

135
156
159

ATLANTIC OCEAN

Meters / Feet

Meters	Feet
6000	19685
5000	16404
4000	13123
3000	9843
2000	6562
1000	3281
500	1640
200	656
100	328
0	
LAND BELOW SEA LEVEL	
100	328
200	656
1000	3281
2000	6562
4000	13123
6000	19685

1:7,880,000

Lambert Conic Conformal Projection

0 50 100 150 200 250 300 kilometers

0 25 50 75 100 125 150 miles

155

Eastern South America

ATLANTIC OCEAN
BRAZIL
BAHIA
MINAS GERAIS
GOIÁS
DISTRITO FEDERAL
MATO GROSSO
MATO GROSSO DO SUL
SÃO PAULO
PARANÁ
RIO DE JANEIRO
ESPÍRITO SANTO
PLANALTO DO BRASIL
Brasília
Salvador
Belo Horizonte
Rio de Janeiro
São Paulo
Curitiba
Goiânia
Vitória
Campinas
Santos
Tropic of Capricorn
159
161

ECUADOR
PERU
CHILE
PACIFIC OCEAN
AMAZON BASIN
LIMA
Callao
Trujillo
Chiclayo
Arequipa
Iquitos
Pucallpa
Cusco
La Paz
Arica
Iquique
Antofagasta
Calama
Lago Titicaca
CORDILLERA CENTRAL
CORDILLERA OCCIDENTAL
CORDILLERA ORIENTAL
DESIERTO DE ATACAMA
154
160

1:7,880,000
Lambert Conic Conformal Projection

0 50 100 150 200 250 300 kilometers
0 25 50 75 100 125 150 miles

Meters / Feet: 6000 19685, 5000 16404, 4000 13123, 3000 9843, 2000 6562, 1000 3281, 500 1640, 200 656, 100 328, 0, LAND BELOW SEA LEVEL, 100 328, 200 656, 1000 3281, 2000 6562, 4000 13123, 6000 19685

Central South America

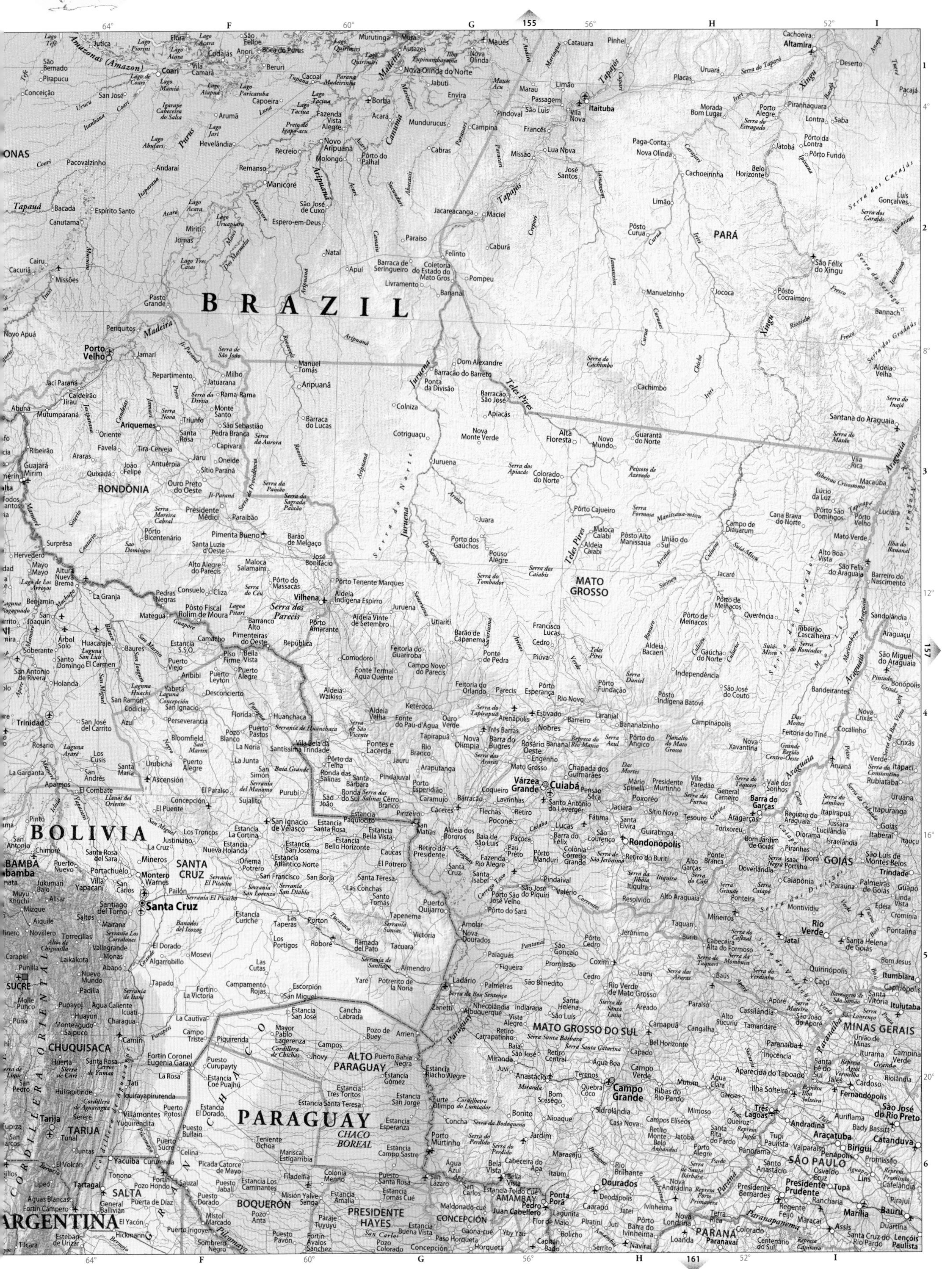
155
157
161
64°
60°
56°
52°
F
G
H
I
1
2
3
4
5
6
4°
8°
12°
16°
20°
BRAZIL
BOLIVIA
PARAGUAY
ARGENTINA
PARÁ
RONDÔNIA
MATO GROSSO
MATO GROSSO DO SUL
GOIÁS
MINAS GERAIS
SÃO PAULO
PARANÁ
SANTA CRUZ
CHUQUISACA
TARIJA
SALTA
ALTO PARAGUAY
BOQUERÓN
PRESIDENTE HAYES
CONCEPCIÓN
AMAMBAY
CHACO BOREAL
Porto Velho
Cuiabá
Várzea Grande
Campo Grande
Santa Cruz
Sucre
Trinidad
Rondonópolis
Itaituba
Altamira
Amazonas (Amazon)
Madeira
Tapajós
Xingu
Araguaia
Paraguay
Paraná
Juruena
Teles Pires
Serra dos Parecis
Meters
Feet
6000
19685
5000
16404
4000
13123
3000
9843
2000
6562
1000
3281
500
1640
200
656
100
328
0
LAND BELOW SEA LEVEL

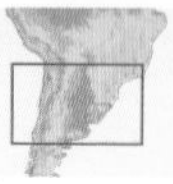

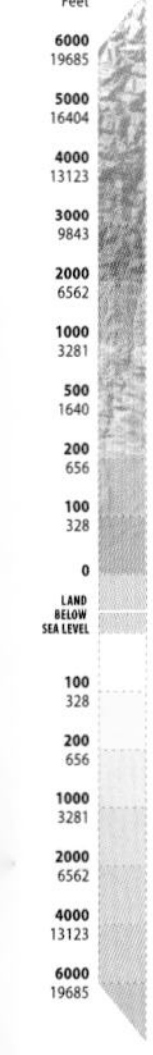

PACIFIC OCEAN

BOLIVIA

CHILE

ARGENTINA

ANDES

TARAPACÁ · ANTOFAGASTA · ATACAMA · COQUIMBO · VALPARAÍSO · REGIÓN METROPOLITANA · LIBERTADOR GENERAL BERNARDO O'HIGGINS · MAULE · BIOBÍO · ARAUCANÍA

POTOSÍ · CHUQUISACA · TARIJA · BOQUERÓN

JUJUY · SALTA · TUCUMÁN · CATAMARCA · SANTIAGO DEL ESTERO · LA RIOJA · SAN JUAN · CÓRDOBA · SAN LUIS · MENDOZA · LA PAMPA · NEUQUÉN · RÍO NEGRO

GRAN CHACO

DESIERTO DE ATACAMA

CORDILLERA OCCIDENTAL · CORDILLERA ORIENTAL · SIERRA DE CÓRDOBA

PAMPA SECA

Tropic of Capricorn

Iquique · Antofagasta · Calama · Tocopilla · Taltal · Chañaral · Copiapó · Vallenar · La Serena · Coquimbo · Viña del Mar · Valparaíso · SANTIAGO · San Antonio · Rancagua · Curicó · Talca · Linares · Chillán · Talcahuano · Concepción · Los Ángeles · Temuco

Tarija · San Salvador de Jujuy · Salta · San Miguel de Tucumán · Santiago del Estero · San Fernando del Valle de Catamarca · La Rioja · San Juan · Córdoba · Villa Carlos Paz · Río Tercero · Villa María · Río Cuarto · San Luis · Villa Mercedes · Mendoza · Godoy Cruz · Las Heras · San Rafael · General Pico · Santa Rosa · Neuquén · General Roca · Bahía Blanca · Punta Alta

El Yunque 915
Isla Robinson Crusoe (Chile)

Meters / Feet: 6000 19685 · 5000 16404 · 4000 13123 · 3000 9843 · 2000 6562 · 1000 3281 · 500 1640 · 200 656 · 100 328 · 0 · LAND BELOW SEA LEVEL · 100 328 · 200 656 · 1000 3281 · 2000 6562 · 4000 13123 · 6000 19685

1:7,880,000
Lambert Conic Conformal Projection

0 50 100 150 200 250 300 kilometers
0 25 50 75 100 125 150 miles

158 · 159 · 162

South Central South America

157

SOUTH AMERICA
BRAZIL
URUGUAY
ATLANTIC OCEAN
MATO GROSSO DO SUL
SÃO PAULO
MINAS GERAIS
PARANÁ
SANTA CATARINA
RIO GRANDE DO SUL
MISIONES
CORRIENTES
ENTRE RÍOS
DISTRITO FEDERAL
PRESIDENTE HAYES
CONCEPCIÓN
AMAMBAY
SAN PEDRO
CANINDEYÚ
CORDILLERA
CAAGUAZÚ
ALTO PARANÁ
GUAIRÁ
PARAGUARÍ
CAAZAPÁ
ITAPÚA
ÑEEMBUCÚ
CENTRAL
ARTIGAS
SALTO
RIVERA
PAYSANDÚ
TACUAREMBÓ
CERRO LARGO
RÍO NEGRO
DURAZNO
TREINTA Y TRES
SORIANO
FLORES
FLORIDA
LAVALLEJA
ROCHA
COLONIA
SAN JOSÉ
CANELONES
MALDONADO
ASUNCIÓN
BUENOS AIRES
MONTEVIDEO
La Plata
Quilmes
Mar del Plata
Tandil
Necochea
Campo Grande
Belo Horizonte
Rio de Janeiro
São Paulo
Campinas
Curitiba
Florianópolis
Porto Alegre
Pelotas
Rio Grande
Foz do Iguaçu
Ciudad del Este
Encarnación
Posadas
Corrientes
Formosa
Uruguaiana
Londrina
Maringá
Ponta Grossa
Joinville
Blumenau
Santa Maria
Passo Fundo
Caxias do Sul
Chapecó
Cascavel
Dourados
Ribeirão Preto
Uberaba
Juiz de Fora
Nova Iguaçu
Sorocaba
Santos
Paranaguá
Río de la Plata
Lagoa dos Patos
Lagoa Mirim
Tropic of Capricorn
Meters
Feet
6000
19685
5000
16404
4000
13123
3000
9843
2000
6562
1000
3281
500
1640
200
656
100
328
0
LAND BELOW SEA LEVEL
100
328
200
656
1000
3281
2000
6562
4000
13123
6000
19685

Southern South America

160
PACIFIC OCEAN
ATLANTIC OCEAN
ARGENTINA
LA PAMPA
BUENOS AIRES
NEUQUÉN
RÍO NEGRO
CHUBUT
SANTA CRUZ
TIERRA DEL FUEGO
BIOBÍO
ARAUCANÍA
LOS RÍOS
LOS LAGOS
AISÉN DEL GENERAL CARLOS IBÁÑEZ DEL CAMPO
MAGALLANES Y ANTÁRTICA CHILENA
Concepción
Los Ángeles
Temuco
Valdivia
Osorno
Puerto Montt
Coihaique
Punta Arenas
Ushuaia
Río Gallegos
Comodoro Rivadavia
Rawson
Trelew
Puerto Madryn
Viedma
Neuquén
General Roca
Bahía Blanca
Punta Alta
Mar del Plata
Tandil
Olavarría
Necochea
Golfo San Matías
Golfo Nuevo
Golfo San Jorge
Golfo de Penas
Golfo Coronados
Golfo Trinidad
Boca del Guafo
Isla Chiloé
Península de Taitao
Archipiélago de los Chonos
Archipiélago Wellington
Archipiélago Madre de Dios
Archipiélago de la Reina Adelaida
Isla Desolación
Isla Santa Inés
Isla Grande de Tierra del Fuego
Isla Hoste
Isla de los Estados
Bahía Grande
Roca Nassau
Cabo de Hornos (Cape Horn)
Islas Diego Ramírez
Falkland Islands (Islas Malvinas)
(UK)
Stanley
Meters
Feet
LAND BELOW SEA LEVEL

1:7,880,000
Lambert Conic Conformal Projection
0 50 100 150 200 250 300 kilometers
0 25 50 75 100 125 150 miles

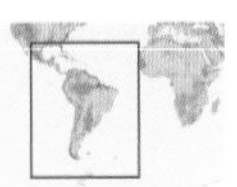

Islands around South America

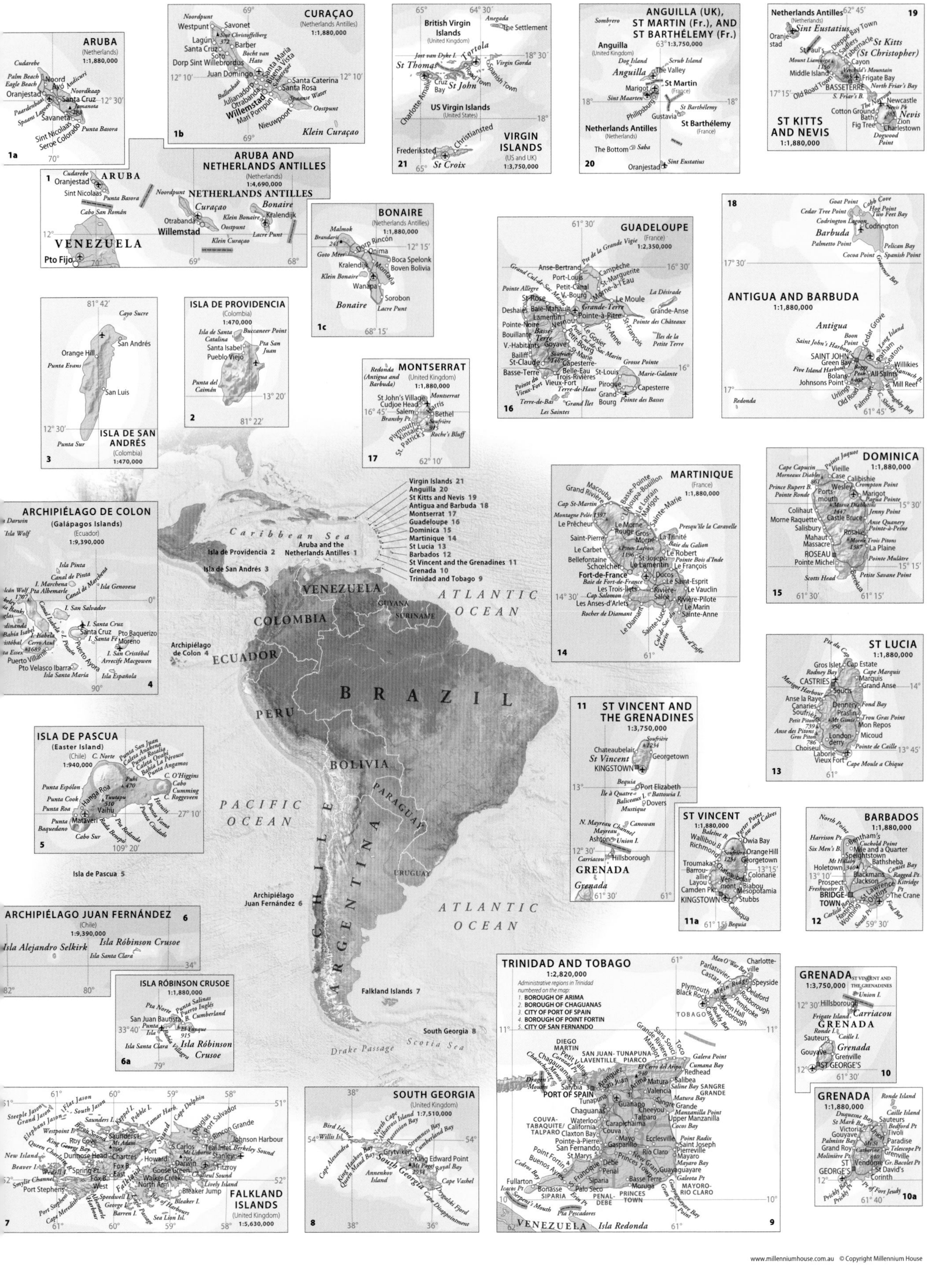

ARUBA (Netherlands) 1:1,880,000 — 1a

CURAÇAO (Netherlands Antilles) 1:1,880,000 — 1b

ARUBA AND NETHERLANDS ANTILLES (Netherlands) 1:4,690,000 — 1

BONAIRE (Netherlands Antilles) 1:1,880,000 — 1c

British Virgin Islands (United Kingdom); **US Virgin Islands** (United States); **VIRGIN ISLANDS** (US and UK) 1:3,750,000 — 21

ANGUILLA (UK), ST MARTIN (Fr.), AND ST BARTHÉLEMY (Fr.) 1:3,750,000 — 20

ST KITTS AND NEVIS 1:1,880,000 — 19

ISLA DE SAN ANDRÉS (Colombia) 1:470,000 — 3

ISLA DE PROVIDENCIA (Colombia) 1:470,000 — 2

MONTSERRAT (United Kingdom) 1:1,880,000 — 17

GUADELOUPE (France) 1:2,350,000 — 16

ANTIGUA AND BARBUDA 1:1,880,000 — 18

ARCHIPIÉLAGO DE COLON (Galápagos Islands) (Ecuador) 1:9,390,000 — 4

MARTINIQUE (France) 1:1,880,000 — 14

DOMINICA 1:1,880,000 — 15

ST LUCIA 1:1,880,000 — 13

ISLA DE PASCUA (Easter Island) (Chile) 1:940,000 — 5

ST VINCENT AND THE GRENADINES 1:3,750,000 — 11

ST VINCENT 1:1,880,000 — 11a

BARBADOS 1:1,880,000 — 12

ARCHIPIÉLAGO JUAN FERNÁNDEZ (Chile) 1:9,390,000 — 6

ISLA RÓBINSON CRUSOE 1:1,880,000 — 6a

TRINIDAD AND TOBAGO 1:2,820,000 — 9

Administrative regions in Trinidad numbered on the map:
1. BOROUGH OF ARIMA
2. BOROUGH OF CHAGUANAS
3. CITY OF PORT OF SPAIN
4. BOROUGH OF POINT FORTIN
5. CITY OF SAN FERNANDO

GRENADA 1:3,750,000 — 10

GRENADA 1:1,880,000 — 10a

FALKLAND ISLANDS (United Kingdom) 1:5,630,000 — 7

SOUTH GEORGIA (United Kingdom) 1:7,510,000 — 8

Virgin Islands 21
Anguilla 20
St Kitts and Nevis 19
Antigua and Barbuda 18
Montserrat 17
Guadeloupe 16
Dominica 15
Martinique 14
St Lucia 13
Barbados 12
St Vincent and the Grenadines 11
Grenada 10
Trinidad and Tobago 9
Aruba and the Netherlands Antilles 1
Isla de Providencia 2
Isla de San Andrés 3
Archipiélago de Colon 4
Isla de Pascua 5
Archipiélago Juan Fernández 6
Falkland Islands 7
South Georgia 8

EUROPE

Europe

The European continent is the westernmost extension of the world's largest landmass. Its mountain chains, which form the main physical barriers between northern and southern Europe, were created by global plate tectonics, primarily by the African Plate crashing into the Eurasian Plate. The best-known range is the Alps, although the Pyrenees, Carpathians, and mountains in southeastern Europe were all created under identical processes.

Previous pages An aerial view of the cathedral and rooftops of the old town of Cefalù on the north coast of Sicily. The Moorish-style cathedral was built in the 1100s by King Roger II, and features beautiful mosaic representations of Christ, the Madonna, and various saints and angels.

Right The Fiescherhorn Mountains in Bern, Switzerland, include the three peaks Gross Fiescherhorn, Hinter Fiescherhorn, and Ochs. The mountains are a popular trekking destination in the Swiss Alps. The Alps cover 61% of Switzerland's surface, making it the second most alpine country after Austria.

Above The town of Carrick-on-Shannon, in County Leitrim, Ireland, is typical of villages dotted around the British Isles. It has many historical buildings, including what is reputed to be the smallest chapel in Europe.

Below Oia, a village on Santorini, one of the Cyclades Islands in Greece, is known around the world for its blue-domed churches, whitewashed walls, spectacular sunsets, and sun-drenched balconies overlooking the Mediterranean Sea.

Europe's boundaries are defined in three directions by major bodies of water. The eastern boundary, however, obscures the exact point at which Europe begins because of the absence of a clear physical feature that would mark continental division. A notional line that follows the Ural Mountains south toward the Caspian Sea and the Caucasus Mountains is, however, generally accepted as the continent's boundary. Europe is also described as a peninsula of peninsulas, because much of its territory includes prominent peninsulas: Scandinavian, Iberian, Apennine, and Aegean. Almost all European residents live less than 300 miles (480 km) from a coast, a characteristic no other continent shares.

All of Europe's many mountain chains generally follow an east-west direction. The vast European Plain stretches from Belgium and the Netherlands into Russia.

Topography is a major factor in regional climate. Air masses from the Atlantic Ocean and Siberia encroach deep into the continent. The warm Gulf Stream contributes to the mild climate in Western Europe, while Siberian air masses bring bone-chilling winters into central Europe. The coastal areas of southern Europe are exposed to a Mediterranean climate, with relatively hot summers and precipitation occurring primarily during winter.

Europe's Cultural Mix

Most contemporary Europeans are of Indo-European cultural background. Linguistically, they belong to Germanic, Slavic, or Romanic language groups. Slavic peoples reside in eastern and southern Europe, Germanic peoples in the western and northern parts. With the exception of Romanian, Romanic languages are found between Italy and Portugal. Turks, Finns, and Hungarians are similarly related, except that their ancestry is Ural-Altaic. The Caucasus region is home to more than one hundred different ethnic groupings.

Europe is predominantly Christian. All three major branches of Christianity are represented; each has a traditionally distinct geographic distribution. Catholic Europe stretches from Lithuania through central Europe to Portugal. Protestants largely occupy northern Europe and the British Isles, while Eastern Orthodox Churches are concentrated in southeastern and eastern Europe. Islam, the most prominent non-Christian religion, forms a sizable population in the zone between Turkey and Bosnia and Herzegovina, though a number of Muslim groups also reside in the Caucasus. Immigrants of Islamic faith from Turkey, the Middle East, and Africa account for sizable minorities in France, Germany, and the United Kingdom. A growing bloc of atheists reflects an emphasis on secularization in the west and decades of communism in the east.

Expansion and Colonization

With the exception of the Mediterranean region, early European culture made only a minor contribution to global culture. This changed when exploration during the fifteenth and sixteenth centuries resulted in global linkages, commercial networks, colonization of other continents, and a worldwide export of European culture.

Another huge cultural change arrived with the Industrial Revolution, which began in the United Kingdom and gradually spread across Europe and around the globe. Unprecedented economic development influenced growth in urban areas, an increase in the quality of life and formal education, and an emphasis on establishing a society with genuine exercise of personal freedoms and liberties for all. Modern democratic institutions and political pluralism originated in Europe. European nations lead the world in terms of general well-being, according to UN socioeconomic indicators.

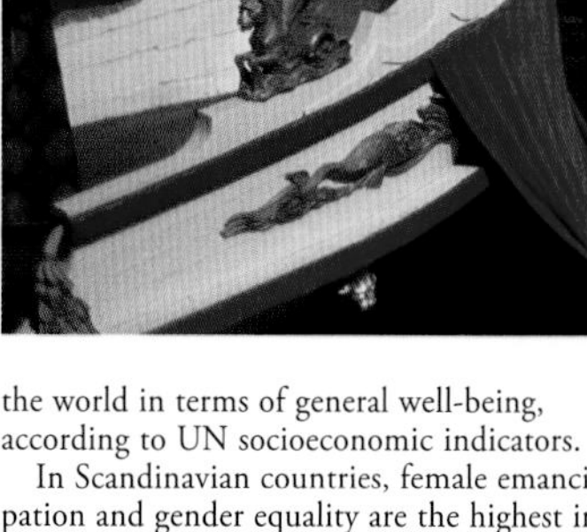
RISPARMIO VERDE

In Scandinavian countries, female emancipation and gender equality are the highest in the world, followed by neighboring countries such as the Netherlands. The Scandinavian countries are also the most generous donors to international aid funds, relative to GDP.

From Separation to Cooperation and the European Union

The concept of the modern nation state emerged in the seventeenth century after the Thirty Years' War (1618–48) ravaged Europe. European nation states have since fought two devastating world wars, among other conflicts, in order to dominate each other. The trend in recent times, however, has been toward cooperation rather than separation and isolation. From modest beginnings in the midst of the Cold War as an institution designed to help rebuild regional economies, the European Union has evolved into the world's most prominent example of economic and political integration. The success in overcoming a huge burden of history in order to accomplish such goals cannot be overstated. A common market, currency, and political institutions were unimaginable only several short decades ago.

A vision common to all Europeans is of a post-industrial society with a high quality of life. Protection of the natural environment and exploitation of alternative energy sources have become the core vision for future economic development, providing an answer to current fossil-fuel dependence. European nations were the first to embrace, ratify, and follow international agreements for greenhouse gas reduction.

Traditional agriculture and manufacturing are being phased out, with the implementation of the latest high-tech solutions to adequately increase the quality of products. The European service sector is among the most productive in the world, and the transportation and communication infrastructure is among the most efficient. The pendulum of wealth still leans heavily toward the western side, but the eastern parts are now progressing rapidly, and should eventually catch up.

The formation of a common European identity does not mean, however, that existing regional identities will somehow fade away. Ethnic and linguistic variations that are deeply embedded in peoples' collective memories mean that two complementary levels of identity will continue to exist.

Not everyone has achieved ethnic emancipation and freedom to run their own affairs, however. Many regional nationalist movements strive for political independence and at the same time look to their future as full members of the European Union. Political resolutions are not always peaceful and ethnic conflicts remain, yet long-term prosperity is a hallmark of Europe's future.

The best way to fully grasp Europe and its cultures is to look through the "big picture" lens. When an analysis of economic, demographic, political, and other factors is applied to each of its various geographic regions, one understands that the continent is indeed diverse and far from monolithic. It is, after all, home to both the largest and the smallest countries in the world.

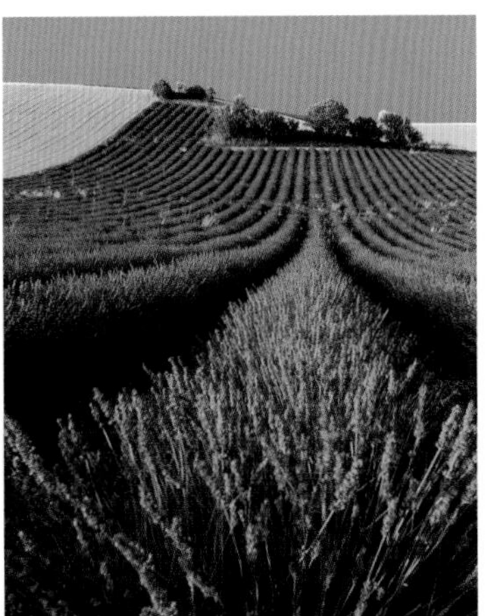

Above The Grand Canal carves an S-shaped swath through the enchanting Italian city of Venice. Believed to follow the course of an ancient river that emptied into the lagoon, the canal is a major city thoroughfare, but also the site of a centuries-old annual historical regatta.

Far left Bullfighting is synonymous with Spain: Though it was practiced in Knossos and ancient Rome, it was on the Iberian peninsula that contests were fully developed. Today the bullfight is much as it has been since 1726, when Francisco Romero of Ronda, Spain, introduced the *estoque* (the sword) and the *muleta* (the small cape used in the last part of the fight). Here, matador David Fandila "El Fandi" performs a pass to the bull.

Left A lavender field in Provence, France. In the sixteenth century, local peasants used lavender oil to heal wounds and expel intestinal worms. The true lavender *(Lavandula angustifolia)* that thrives in the chalky soils and hot dry climate of Provence was first picked systematically at the end of the nineteenthth century. At the beginning of the twentieth century, large fields of lavender were planted for commercial harvest.

ICELAND

Official name Republic of Iceland
Land area 38,706 square miles (100,250 km²)
Border countries None
Capital Reykjavík
Highest point Hvannadalshnúkur 6,952 feet (2,110 m)
Climate Temperate; mild on coast, cold in interior
Population 304,367
Language(s) Icelandic, German, English, Nordic languages
Ethnicity Icelandic 94%, other 6%
Religion Lutheran 85.5%, Reykjavík Free Church 2.1%, Roman Catholic 2%, other Christian 2.7%, Hafnarfjourour Free Church 1.5%, other or unspecified 3.8%, unaffiliated 2.4%
Government Parliamentary republic
Currency Icelandic króna
Human Development Index 0.968 (ranked 1st out of 177 countries)

Right Aerial view of a volcanic crater in Iceland. The Nordic Volcanological Center in Reykjavík is the center of European volcano research.

Grímsey
Ísafjörður
Dalvík
Húsavík
Sauðárkrókur
Akureyri
Egilsstaðir
Eskifjörður
Breiðafjörður
ICELAND
Borgarnes
Faxaflói
Akranes
Þingvellir
REYKJAVÍK
Höfn
Keflavík
Hafnarfjörður
Selfoss
Heimaey
Vík
Surtsey
ATLANTIC OCEAN

Iceland

Map Reference Pages 222–223

Iceland is an island country located just south of the Arctic Circle in the North Atlantic Ocean. Of Iceland's total land area, almost 68 percent is considered wasteland. Despite its northern location, Iceland's climate is very mild due to the warm Gulf Stream in the Atlantic Ocean, giving the country an average temperature of 28°F (–2°C) in January and 52°F (11°C) in July.

Physical Geography

At about only 100 million years old, Iceland is relatively young. Its geology is extremely volatile, with frequent earthquakes and volcanic activity. Glaciers cover about 11 percent of its surface, hence the nickname "the land of fire and ice." The largest glacier, Vatnajökull, covers 3,205 square miles (8,300 km²). The interior is a mix of volcanoes, glaciers, sand, and lava fields; the average elevation is around 3,208 feet (1,000 m) and mountain peaks reach around 6,560 feet (2,000 m).

History

Irish monks settled in Iceland in the eighth century CE and left when the Vikings arrived in 870. The first permanent settlement was in Reykjavík, established by Ingólfur Arnarson in 874. By 930 most good land had been claimed and the Althing, a form of parliament, was established in the Icelandic Free State.

The Icelandic Free State lasted until 1262, when the chieftains of Iceland became too powerful to govern through the Althing. This led to the signing of the Old Covenant, which brought Iceland directly under the Norwegian crown. Under the Kalmar Union (1397), Iceland was ruled by the unified crown of Denmark, Sweden, and Norway until the Treaty of Kiel in 1814, which gave control to Denmark.

Many Icelanders emigrated to North America around this time, but the seeds of independence had been planted. Iceland was granted home rule in 1874, and in 1918 Denmark signed the Act of Union, formally recognizing Iceland as a sovereign state within the Danish realm. During World War II Iceland was occupied by the British and later, the Americans. In 1944, Icelanders voted overwhelmingly for independence.

Population and Culture

The population of over 304,000 is centered on the capital city, Reykjavík. Over 285,000 are native Icelanders, though many nationalities are present through recent immigration.

Icelanders speak Icelandic, derived from Old Norse. Over 85 percent are members of the Lutheran Church of Iceland, yet only 10 percent regularly attend church service. Iceland is known for its sagas, a collection of historical narratives set during the time of exploration and settlement. In modern times Björk and Sigur Rós have helped to boost Icelandic music worldwide.

Administration/Government

The Republic of Iceland is a representative democracy and a parliamentary republic. The Althing is still the name of the modern parliament. Iceland has a president (a mainly ceremonial position) and a prime minister who controls the executive branch of government.

Economy/Industry

Fishing accounts for around 40 percent of the economy. Until recently Iceland was one of the poorer countries of Europe, but changes in policy and an influx of manufacturing has helped raise its status, giving it one of the highest standards of living in the world.

Above Turf roofs have been used in construction since the time of the first settlers in Iceland and are still in use today. This example is Oraefi Church, at Litlahof, a remote farming village on the south coast of Iceland.

Right The Blue Lagoon geothermal pools near Reykjavík in Iceland. The waters are famed for their restorative powers and the white silica mud is used for treating skin conditions.

Hammerfest
Vadsø
Tromsø
Hinnøya
Bodø
Norwegian Sea
NORWAY
SWEDEN
FINLAND
RUSSIAN FEDERATION
Trondheim
Molde
Ålesund
Galdhøpiggen
Lillehammer
Hamar
Bergen
Sandvika
OSLO
Drammen
Moss
Skien
Tønsberg
Stavanger
Arendal
Kristiansand
DENMARK

Norway

Map Reference Pages 222–225

Norway is located on the west coast of the Scandinavian Peninsula, and is bordered by Sweden to the east, and Finland and Russia to the northeast. It has coastlines on the North Sea and Skagerrak inlet to the south, the Norwegian Sea to the west, and the Barents Sea to the north.

Physical Geography

The interior is defined by the Scandinavian Mountains, which have an average elevation of 1,509 feet (460 m). Norway's most famous geological feature is its deep-water fjords—long narrow bays caused by glacial erosion—which are vital for travel and commerce.

Norway has a surprisingly temperate climate in relation to its geographical location. This is due to the combined warm North Atlantic and Norwegian ocean currents bringing warm air to the shore. The average temperature ranges from 42°F (5.5°C) in southern Norway, to 37°F (3°C) in the north.

History

The first humans arrived in Norway some 12,000 years ago, either from northern Germany or through the northeast from Finland or Russia, settling along the western coast. Norway's Viking Age started in 800 CE and continued to about 1200. This was the era of great sea voyages across the North Sea and Atlantic Ocean to the British Isles, Iceland, Greenland, and North America.

King Harald Fairhair unified the country around 872. After his death, Norway once again split into numerous smaller kingdoms. During this period Christianity was introduced by way of Great Britain. Viking expansion into Great Britain ended in 1066 with the death of King Harald Hardrada during a failed invasion attempt. Medieval Norway was also marked by a civil war from 1130 to 1240.

From 1349 to 1351, weakened by the Black Death, Norway was merged into the Danish realm, although it maintained its identity as a separate monarchy. It was a part of the Kalmar Union, with Sweden and Denmark from 1397 to 1814. After defeat by Sweden, the two countries were joined together by the Treaty of Kiel until 1905, when Sweden formally recognized Norway's independence. Norway remained neutral during World War I, though it gave some support to the Allied powers. Due to its strategic location on the North Atlantic and North Sea, Norway was occupied by Nazi Germany during World War II. Norway joined NATO in 1949, but declined to join the European Union.

Population

Most of Norway's population of 4.7 million are ethnic Norwegians; some are Sami, native to Norway, who live in the northern region of Lapland; others are Kven, natives of Finland, who reside in northern Norway. Immigration has accounted for a large spike in population.

Culture

The official languages are Norwegian and Sami. Norwegian has two different forms, Bokmål and Nynorsk. Over 85 percent belong to the Church of Norway (Lutheran).

A great body of literature is represented by authors such as Henrik Ibsen, Bjørnstjerne Bjørnson, Knut Hamsun, and Sigrid Undset—all but Ibsen have won the Nobel Prize for literature. Norway's musical output ranges from the symphonic music of Edvard Grieg to modern Death Metal. Artist Edvard Munch is best known for his 1893 painting *The Scream*.

Administration/Government

Norway is a constitutional monarchy with a parliamentary democracy. The parliament, called the Storting, has 169 members. When a vote is issued, the Storting divides into two groups—the Odelsting and the Lagting—turning the parliament into a bicameral legislature. After the 2009 general elections the division of the Storting will no longer be used.

Economy/Industry

Norway has the world's second highest GNP and the third highest GDP per capita, but the cost of living is high. The economy has both free-market and socialist elements. The government has large interests in the petroleum, telecommunications, energy production, and aluminum sectors. Oil and gas are the major exports. Norway also established a sovereign wealth fund in 1995, which has grown to around US$300 billion, the largest in Europe.

MILESTONE EVENTS

12,000 BCE First humans arrive in Norway

800 CE Viking Age begins

c. 872 Norway is unified under King Harald Fairhair

1000 Leif Eriksson reaches America

1030 Death of King Olaf II (later St Olaf) who is credited with Christianizing Norway

1066 Death of King Harald Hardrada marks the end of the Viking Age

1130–1240 Norwegian Civil War

1240–1319 Golden Age of Norwegian Kingdom

1299 The capital moves from Bergen to Oslo

1349–1351 Black Death

1397–1537 Kalmar Union of Denmark, Norway, and Sweden

1537–1814 Union with Denmark

1811 University of Oslo is established

1814 Treaty of Kiel cedes Norway to Sweden

1905 Norwegian independence granted

1918 Women gain the right to vote

1940 Germany occupies Norway

1945 Germany retreats from Norway; Norway joins United Nations

1949 Norway joins NATO

1968 Oil found in North Sea

1994 Norway refuses to join European Union; hosts XVII Winter Olympics in Lillehammer

2006 Nearly 200 barrels of oil are spilled from a chemical plant in southeastern Norway, threatening a nature preserve

NORWAY

Official name Kingdom of Norway
Land area 118,703 square miles (307,442 km²)
Border countries Russia, Finland, Sweden
Capital Oslo
Highest point Galdhoppigen 8,100 feet (2,469 m)
Climate Temperate on coast, colder inland, year-round rain on west coast
Population 4,644,000
Language(s) Official: Norwegian, Sami
Ethnicity Norwegian, Sami, Finnish
Religion Church of Norway (Evangelical Lutheran) 85.7%, other Christian 4.4%, Muslim 1.8%, other or unspecified 8.1%
Government Constitutional monarchy with parliamentary democracy
Currency Krone
Human Development Index 0.968 (ranked 2nd out of 177 countries)

Above left Scene looking down Ulvikfjord, in Hordaland County, with a church and the Norwegian flag in the foreground.

Left A row of UNESCO World Heritage-listed commercial buildings, known as the Bryggen, line the wharf at Bergen in Norway.

LAPLAND

The region of Lapland encompasses the northern parts of Norway, Sweden, Finland, and the Kola Peninsula in northwest Russia. Lapland has a subarctic climate, with short, warm summers and long, cold winters, though the warm Gulf Stream current in the Atlantic moderates the winter climate somewhat. Much of the region is situated above the Arctic Circle, and experiences 24 hours of daylight during June and July as well as near total darkness in December. Much of Lapland's territory is composed of boreal forest with pine, spruce, birches, and willow as the dominant trees; native animals include bears and wolves. Lapland contains important natural resources including iron, copper, fish, and timber, as well as hydroelectric power potential. The region is also important for reindeer herding.

Lapland is the home of the Sami people (also spelled Sámi, Saami, and Same, and formerly known as Lapps), who are indigenous to this region, which in their own language—also called Sami—they call Sápmi. Though estimates vary, many sources suggest that approximately 85,000 Sami live in the region, about half of whom live in Norway. Traditionally, Sami have been known for their shamanistic religion and reindeer herding but in the twenty-first century only about 10 percent of Sami herd reindeer for a living, though many others maintain herds in addition to their other jobs.

The Sami have lived in Lapland for at least 2,500 years. They were mentioned by the Roman author Tacitus in the first century CE, but until the nineteenth century the Sami were largely cut off from contact with southern Scandinavia and the rest of Europe. In the nineteenth century the Norwegian government encouraged cultural assimilation of the Sami as well as economic development in the region; Finland, Sweden, and Russia had similar policies, all of which led to a decline in Sami culture. The building of a hydroelectric dam in Alta, Norway, in 1979 brought the rights of the Sami people to the political forefront. In 1986 the Sami national anthem and flag were created, and Norway, Sweden, and Finland permitted the Sami to form parliaments allowing for some political expression. Sami culture is now enjoying a period of revival—the Sami man (right) is in traditional dress.

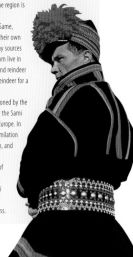

SWEDEN

Official name Kingdom of Sweden
Land area 158,662 square miles (410,934 km²)
Border countries Finland, Norway
Capital Stockholm
Highest & lowest points Kebnekaise 6,926 feet (2,111 m); Kristianstad −8 feet (−2.4 m)
Climate Temperate in south and central Sweden, subarctic in the north
Population 9,045,000
Language(s) Swedish
Ethnicity Swedes, Sami, other
Religion Church of Sweden (Lutheran) 87%, other (includes Roman Catholic, Orthodox, Baptist, Jewish, Buddhist, Muslim) 13%
Government Constitutional monarchy with parliamentary democracy
Currency Swedish krona
Human Development Index 0.986 (ranked 6th out of 177 countries)

NORWAY
SWEDEN
FINLAND
Kebnekaise
Luleå
Gulf of Bothnia
Umeå
Östersund
Härnösand
Falun
Gävle
Uppsala
Karlstad
Västerås
STOCKHOLM
Örebro
Norrköping
Linköping
Göteborg
Borås
Jönköping
Visby
Gotland
Halmstad
Öland
Helsingborg
Baltic Sea
Malmö
DENMARK

Sweden

Map Reference Pages 222–225

The Kingdom of Sweden is on the Scandinavian Peninsula in northern Europe, bordering Norway and Finland, and connected by a combined bridge and tunnel to Denmark.

Physical Geography

Sweden has coastline on the Baltic Sea and the Gulf of Bothnia, on the Kattegat and on several small straits that separate it from Denmark. To the west lie mountains that form the border with Norway.

Norrland in the north is mountainous and heavily wooded. It contains the majority of the 90,000 lakes in the country. Götaland, the southern portion, includes the stony Småland highlands and grasslands, and is an important agricultural region. Svealand, in central Sweden, has rolling hills and grasslands. Despite its high latitude, Sweden has a relatively temperate climate except in the far north above the Arctic Circle. Annual precipitation is about 28 inches (71 cm), with the greatest amount falling in the southwest.

Above right A man scans the horizon from the doorway of his igloo in Swedish Lapland. Igloos are dome-shaped structures built in a spiral pattern from blocks of snow. Sometimes a clear block of ice is added to let light into the interior. Igloos may be temporary or semi-permanent structures, depending on their purpose.

Below Stationed in the Royal Palace (Kungliga Slottet) in Stockholm, the Royal Guards have protected the Swedish royal family since 1523. The Swedish Royal House of Bernadotte is headed by King Carl XVI Gustaf Folke Hubertus (b. 1946).

History

From 1397 to 1523 Sweden was part of the Kalmar Union (Denmark, Norway, and Sweden). Modern Sweden emerged from the Kalmar Union in 1523 under King Gustav Vasa, when the country rejected Catholicism and became Protestant.

During the seventeenth century, Sweden became a great power after defeating Denmark, Russia, and Poland, but lost many of its imperial gains in the eighteenth and nineteenth centuries. Under King Charles XIII, a war was launched in 1814 against Norway, which forced Norway into union with Sweden. That war was the last that Sweden participated in as a combatant. Sweden was officially neutral during the two world wars.

Population/Culture

Sweden enjoys one of the highest life expectancies in Europe. The population is just over 9 million, consisting mainly of Swedes, along with Sami and a small number of Finnish–Swedes in the north. In the late twentieth century immigration increased, and Sweden now has large communities of Finns, Bosnians, Iranians, Danes, Iraqis, Norwegians, Turks, and others. More than 75 percent of the population lives in the southern part of Sweden.

Swedish culture is well known throughout the world, especially through literature, music, film, and architecture and design. The country has produced seven Nobel Prize winners. Motion picture directors including Victor Sjöström and Ingmar Bergman also have an international reputation, as do actresses such as Greta Garbo and Ingrid Bergman. The two major spectator sports in Sweden are football (soccer) and ice hockey.

Administration/Government

Sweden is a constitutional monarchy with a parliamentary democracy. The king is head of state, but has limited power. The Riksdag (parliament) has 349 members. The Riksdag holds supreme authority and has the responsibility of choosing a prime minister. The legislative power is shared between the prime minister and the Riksdag. The judiciary is independent and executive power is held by the government.

Economy/Industry

Sweden has an export-oriented market economy that is highly industrialized. It has a highly skilled labor force and excellent internal and external communications. Hydropower, iron ore, and timber are the main primary industries, with pharmaceuticals, telecommunications, and the automotive industry as the principal secondary ones.

More than 75 percent of the workforce in Sweden belongs to a trade union, and less than 5 percent of the population is unemployed. Since 1995 Sweden has been a member of the European Union.

MILESTONE EVENTS

1397 Kalmar Union begins union of Denmark, Norway, and Sweden
1523 Under King Gustav Vasa, Sweden separates from the Kalmar Union
1809 Sweden loses Finland to Russia
1814 Personal Union between Norway and Sweden
1901 Nobel Prizes established in Sweden by Alfred Nobel
1905 Norway separates from Sweden
1921 Women receive the right to vote
1971 Riksdag becomes unicameral
1995 Sweden joins the European Union
2003 A referendum decides against adopting the euro

NORWAY
Halti
SWEDEN
RUSSIAN FEDERATION
FINLAND
Rovaniemi
Oulu
Gulf of Bothnia
Kokkola
Kuopio
Vaasa
Varkaus
Jyväskylä
Mikkeli
Pori
Tampere
Hämeenlinna
Lahti
Turku
Vantaa
Åland
Espoo
HELSINKI
Gulf of Finland

Finland

Map Reference Pages 222–225

Finland is located in the east of Scandinavia in northern Europe. It is bordered by Norway, Russia, and Sweden. With a total area of 130,558 square miles (338,145 km²), it is the sixth-largest country in Europe.

Physical Geography

Finland has 187,888 lakes, including Saimaa, the fifth-largest lake in Europe, and is relatively flat. Most of Finland is covered with coniferous boreal forest. Finland has a northern temperate climate in the south and central regions and a subarctic climate in the area stretching north of the Arctic Circle.

History

Archeologists believe that the first humans came to the region around 8500 BCE. Sweden claimed Finland in the thirteenth century and established Swedish as the language of the nobility. The Finnish language—distantly related to Hungarian—was spoken mainly by peasants. War with Russia in the eighteenth century twice led to occupation by Russia, in the Greater Wrath (1714–1721) and the Lesser Wrath (1742–1743). Finland became a Grand Duchy of the Russian Empire in 1809.

Shortly after the 1917 Russian Revolution, Finland declared independence. A civil war in

Right Eurasian lynx *(Lynx lynx)*, Ranua Wildlife Park, Finland. The Eurasian lynx stands just over three feet (1 m) tall and weighs up to 49 pounds (22 kg). Although their numbers are limited in Western Europe, they are widely distributed from northeastern Europe to the Pacific Ocean and are the world's most widespread wild cat.

1917–1918 between the Whites (mainly the more conservative bourgeoisie) and the Reds (comprising radicalized peasantry and workers) was won by the Whites. Two wars against the Soviet Union between 1939 and 1944 led to Finland's alliance with Germany and loss of territory after World War II. In the postwar era, Finland experienced rapid economic growth, though the collapse of the Soviet Union in 1991 caused a recession because of the two countries' close trade relations.

Population/Culture

Over 5 million people live in Finland, mostly in the south. About 2.9 percent are immigrants. Most Finns speak Finnish; both Finnish and Swedish are official languages. The predominant religion is Lutheran.

Finns are very fond of sports and the country excels at ice hockey, ski jumping, and automobile racing. Finnish contributions to global culture include the composer Jean Sibelius, modern architects such as Alvar Aalto and Eero Saarinen, and many popular music groups. Finland has the world's highest per capita consumption of coffee.

Administration/Government

Finland is a parliamentary republic. The chief of state is the president, who is elected by popular vote every six years. The legislative branch is a unicameral parliament with 200 members, and is called the Eduskunta.

Economy/Industry

In recent years the economy has rebounded, especially since Finland joined the European Union in 1995. Finland produces timber, forest products, communications equipment, machinery, and ships. Major corporations include Nokia, Fiskars, Kone, and Marimekko.

THE SCANDINAVIAN SAUNA

The sauna is a steam bath of Finnish origin, popular throughout Scandinavia and other parts of the world. It is similar in some respects to the steam baths of other cultures. In Finland, the sauna is more than just a bath—it is an important part of Finnish culture and a place to relax with family or friends. Most invitations to dinners or parties will include a sauna.

The sauna itself is a small separate building or part of a room, usually the bathroom. It generally contains three areas: A dressing area, an area in which to shower and wash, and the steam room itself, which contains wooden benches to sit on. A stove called a kiuas is used to heat rocks to a high temperature, and water is then thrown on the rocks, creating steam. Traditionally stoves were wood-burning, but today most are electric. The temperature in the sauna is usually around 175°F (80°C) but can vary, as can the humidity.

Sometimes bathers use birch branches to lightly beat their skin, stimulating circulation. After spending time in the steam room, bathers will usually pour cold water on themselves to cool down—in some cases this may involve jumping into a river or lake.

Skagerrak
Kattegat
Ålborg
DENMARK
Viborg
Randers
Århus
Herning
Yding Skovhøj
Hillerød
KØBENHAVN
(COPENHAGEN)
Varde
Vejle
Roskilde
Esbjerg
Odense
Åbenrå
Rønne
Bornholm
Nykøbing
North Sea
Baltic Sea
SWEDEN
GERMANY

Denmark

Map Reference Pages 224–225

Home of Hans Christian Andersen and the Vikings, Denmark is about the same size as the Netherlands or Switzerland. It was once northern Europe's superpower.

Physical Geography

Denmark extends out from the European mainland, north of Germany, on the Jutland Peninsula. Many of its surrounding islands lie in the North Sea to the west and the Baltic Sea to the east. The landscape is mostly rolling lowlands, with average elevation only 100 feet (30 m) above sea level. The highest point, Yding Skovhøj, is a mere 568 feet (173 m). Fjords mark the eastern coast while sand and low dunes lie on the west coast.

History

Denmark dominated Scandinavia and the Baltic from 1200 to 1500 CE, and stretched its influence across the Atlantic, giving rise to modern Iceland and Greenland. In 1397, the Kalmar Union united Denmark, Sweden, and Norway under a single monarch. Sweden left the Kalmar Union in 1523, and the 1814 Treaty of Kiel awarded Norway to Sweden.

Greenland became a Danish province in 1729, and although today independently administered, is still under the political hegemony of Denmark.

Denmark remained neutral through both world wars, but endured German occupation in 1940–1945. In 1949, Denmark became a charter member of NATO.

Population/Culture

The capital and largest city of Copenhagen (nearly 2 million) contains over one-third of the country's population. Another 15 percent can be found on the central islands of Fyn, Lolland, Falster, Møn, Langeland, and Ærø. The remainder is distributed over the seven Jutland counties, in the country's east.

Denmark is a traditional European welfare state. Health care is free, pensions are good, and unemployment is fairly low. An example of the country's live-and-let-live mindset is Copenhagen's Christiania, a semi-autonomous commune of 1,000 people living largely untouched by Danish law, where the sale and use of marijuana and hashish is tolerated. Yet, Denmark has conservative leanings, especially with regard to the European Union. It joined rather late (1973) and has balked at some of the most important EU treaties.

Government

Denmark is a constitutional monarchy with an inherited monarch. The unicameral parliament is led by the prime minister. Thirty-eight percent of the Danish parliament is female, a typical Scandinavian trend.

Economy/Industry

Denmark has one of the most competitive economies in the world. The central region is a powerhouse of agriculture, particularly dairying, but the country's strength is just as much industrial. Dominance in manufacturing, electronics, renewable energy, and transportation infrastructure together make Denmark a tiny titan, with the second highest Gross National Income per person in Europe. Companies such as Polaris, BB, Ibsen, and Bang & Olufsen are just a few electronics names known worldwide.

In the Horns Rev shallows to the southwest, near Esbjerg, is the largest wind farm in the world. The grid of 80 modern windmills each with a diameter of 260 feet (80 m) produces enough electricity for 150,000 households.

Above Nyhavn in Copenhagen is now a popular recreational center, although for most of the time since its establishment in the 1670s it was a somewhat seedy service area for sailors..

FINLAND

Official name Republic of Finland
Land area 117,557 square miles (304,473 km²)
Border countries Norway, Russia, Sweden
Capital Helsinki
Highest point Halti 4,343 feet (1,324 m)
Climate Temperate, subarctic in north
Population 5,245,000
Language(s) Official: Finnish, Swedish
Ethnicity Finn 93.4%, Swede 5.7%, other 0.9%
Religion Lutheran 84.2%, Finnish Orthodox 1.1%, other 1.2%, unaffiliated 13.5%
Government Parliamentary republic
Currency Euro
Human Development Index 0.952 (ranked 11th out of 177 countries)

DENMARK

Official name Kingdom of Denmark
Land area 16,370 square miles (42,394 km²)
Border countries Germany
Capital Copenhagen (København)
Highest & lowest points Yding Skovhoej 568 feet (173 m); Lammefjord −23 feet (−7 m)
Climate Temperate
Population 5,485,000
Language(s) Danish, Faroese, Greenlandic, German, English
Ethnicity Scandinavian, Inuit, Faroese, German, Turkish, Iranian, Somali
Religion Evangelical Lutheran 95%, other Christian 3%, Muslim 2%
Government Constitutional monarchy
Currency Danish krone
Human Development Index 0.949 (ranked 14th out of 177 countries)

Far left Lapland today is a popular region with tourists, who seek its pristine forests, experiences of Sami culture, and, in winter, visits to the Santa Claus village in Rovaniemi, Finland, considered by some to be the real workshop of Santa Claus.

Left Formerly the royal residence of King Christian IV of Denmark, Frederiksborg Castle is now home to the Museum of National History.

UNITED KINGDOM

Official name United Kingdom of Great Britain and Northern Ireland
Land area 94,526 square miles (244,820 km²)
Border countries The only land border is the 225 mile (360 km) border between Northern Ireland and the Republic of Ireland
Capital London
Highest point Ben Nevis 4,406 feet (1,343 m)
Climate Temperate
Population 60,776,238
Language(s) Unofficial: English; plus Welsh, Scots Gaelic, Bengali, Punjabi, Hindi, Gujarati, Chinese, Italian, Polish, Greek, Turkish
Ethnicity English, Scottish, Welsh, Northern Irish 92.1%, African Caribbean 2%, Indian 1.8%, Pakistani 1.3%, mixed 1.2%, other 1.6%
Religion Christian 72%, Muslim 2.7%, Hindu 1%, Sikh 0.6%, Jewish 0.5%, none 15.5%, unspecified 7.7%
Government Parliamentary democracy and constitutional monarchy
Currency Pound sterling
Human Development Index 0.946 (ranked 16th out of 177 countries)

Shetland Islands
Orkney Islands
Ben Nevis
Aberdeen
Dundee
ATLANTIC OCEAN
Glasgow
Edinburgh
North Sea
UNITED KINGDOM
Belfast
Newcastle upon Tyne
IRELAND
Isle of Man
Douglas
Middlesbrough
Blackpool
Leeds
York
Irish Sea
Liverpool
Manchester
Sheffield
Derby
Nottingham
Birmingham
Leicester
Norwich
Coventry
Cambridge
Gloucester
Oxford
Ipswich
Swansea
Cardiff
Bristol
LONDON
Reading
Southampton
Portsmouth
Bournemouth
Brighton
Plymouth
English Channel
Channel Islands
St. Helier
FRANCE

United Kingdom

Map Reference Pages 239–244

Above right Coastline view of County Antrim in Northern Ireland.

The United Kingdom occupies the major part of the British Isles, the group of islands off the northwest coast of Europe. It is surrounded by the Atlantic Ocean, the North Sea, the English Channel, and the Irish Sea.

The United Kingdom's four constituent countries are England, Scotland, Wales, and Northern Ireland. Of these, England is the largest in area and also the most populous. Northern Ireland, also known as Ulster, comprises about one-sixth of the island of Ireland. The remainder of that island is the Republic of Ireland, partitioned in 1921.

Physical Geography

The island comprising England, Scotland, and Wales is the largest of the British Isles, and therefore is known as Great Britain. This island is of an irregular shape, roughly 600 miles (965 km) long from north to south and varying in width east-to-west from about 80 to 250 miles (130 to 400 km). No one in the UK lives more than 75 miles (120 km) from some part of the coast.

The northern third of the island is Scotland, and its southern two-thirds are England, and Wales to the west. Great Britain is joined to France by the 31-mile (50 km) Channel Tunnel, a rail link under the English Channel at its narrowest point.

Other islands which form part of the UK include the Orkneys and the Shetlands off the north of Scotland, and the Inner and Outer Hebrides (or Western Isles) to the west of Scotland. The Isle of Wight, off England's south coast, is part of the UK, as is Anglesey, off North Wales, and the Scilly Islands off Cornwall. The Crown Dependencies of the Channel Islands and the Isle of Man, formerly possessions of the British Crown, are not part of the UK but form a federacy with it. There are additionally 14 overseas territories, remnants of what was once the British Empire.

Southern England consists largely of rolling farmland, woodland, and some hilly regions. Population density is among the highest in Europe and the landscape is dotted with towns and villages including large areas of urban sprawl, especially near London.

A hundred miles (160 km) west of London is the ancient city of Bath and beyond that the port city of Bristol. The southwest of England is less populated. Cornwall and Devon have much wild moorland and rocky coastlines.

The English Midlands are also densely populated and industrialized. The countryside is mainly farmland, as are the fenlands further east. The north of England contains higher, more rugged country—the Yorkshire moors and the Pennines—and takes in the large industrial cities of Leeds and Sheffield. In the northwest, there is a further concentration of industry. This was once the hub of Britain's Industrial Revolution. Further northwest, in Cumbria, is the wild and picturesque Lake District. The industrialized northeast is centered around Newcastle and Middlesbrough.

The border between England and Scotland roughly follows the line of the Cheviot Hills.

Right Queen Elizabeth II smiles as she inspects Chelsea Pensioners on Founder's Day at the Royal Hospital Chelsea, London. The pensioners wear oak leaves on their lapels to commemorate King Charles I's escape from the Roundheads when he hid in an oak tree.

Below Westminster Bridge, a seven-arched bridge of wrought iron, was opened in 1862. It provides convenient access to the British Houses of Parliament (Palace of Westminster). Construction of the Gothic revival palace began in 1836 under the direction of Sir Charles Barry.

Further north are the Southern Uplands, then the central lowlands of Scotland. This central region contains the broad river valleys of the Forth and the Clyde on which the cities of Edinburgh and Glasgow are situated. Here is much of Scotland's urbanization and industry. Fifty miles (80 km) further north are the Grampian Mountains and the Scottish Highlands. The Highlands extend a further 150 miles (240 km) to the northern coast. The region is crossed by river valleys and many lochs. The rugged west coast is penetrated by long sea lochs. Beyond the coast are the numerous islands of the Inner and Outer Hebrides, including Skye and Mull, and Lewis and Harris.

Wales borders England to its west. It has some mountainous regions. Coastal areas are less hilly and there is much arable land across the country. Wales's industry is centered in the south near Cardiff, Swansea, and Newport.

Northern Ireland is in the northeast part of the island of Ireland, just across the Irish Sea from Scotland. It has some hilly regions near the coast, such as the Mountains of Antrim and the Mountains of Mourne. The largest urban and industrial center is Belfast. Lough Neagh, the largest lake in the British Isles at 159 square miles (412 km²), lies in the center of Northern Ireland.

The UK has a temperate climate due to the warming influence of the Gulf Stream. Temperatures reach 72–80°F (22–27°C) in July and August and dip to just above freezing in January. There is plentiful rainfall throughout the year and usually some snow in winter.

Early History

Early human remains date from about 500,000 BCE. During the last Ice Age and up to about 8,000 years ago Great Britain was joined to Europe by a wide land bridge. Hunter-gatherer tribes crossed into England and settled there. When Ice Age glaciers receded, rising sea levels swallowed the land bridge. England became more habitable but was cut off from Europe so that new techniques such as farming (from 4000 BCE), the use of bronze (2000–700 BCE), and the making of iron tools (from 500 BCE) were slow to arrive. During these times henges, dolmens, long barrows, and stone circles (such as Stonehenge) were built and, later, the Iron Age hill forts.

In 55 BCE Roman general Julius Caesar and his army landed in England. One hundred years later the Romans returned, subduing the native tribes and occupying the land as an outpost of the Roman Empire for the next 400 years. When Roman rule ended, England became disunited and suffered repeated invasions by Jutes, Angles, and Saxons from Germany and later by Viking and Norse raiders. In 927 CE King Athelstan of Wessex made England a single kingdom once again.

From 1066 to Today

In 1066, William I of Normandy invaded England, defeated King Harold and ushered in an era of Anglo–Norman rule. The Normans introduced the feudal system that structured society according to rank and gave the barons considerable power under the king. In 1215 many of England's barons rebelled against King John, forcing him to sign the Magna Carta, a bill of civil rights. The first recognizable parliament met under Edward I (reigned 1272–1307).

Ireland was conquered by England in the twelfth century and in 1284 Wales was made subject to the English Crown. England's Hundred Years' War with France (1337–1453), over claims to territories once owned by the Norman kings, eventually led to a withdrawal of all English armies from French lands.

Following the War of the Roses (1455–1485), a bloody internal battle for the crown, the first Tudor monarch, Henry VII, was enthroned. His son and heir Henry VIII broke with the Church of Rome in 1533. He is best known for having had six wives, two of whom were beheaded.

Under his daughter Elizabeth I (reigned 1558–1603), England enjoyed an age of unrivaled prosperity, exploration, and cultural achievement. In 1588, England defeated an attempted invasion by the Spanish Armada, intended to return the country to Catholic rule. This was also the time of William Shakespeare, and the founding of England's first colonies in North America.

Elizabeth's successor was the Stuart King James VI of Scotland (1566–1625) who became James I of England, uniting the two kingdoms. During his reign many Scottish and English Protestants settled in Northern Ireland. Resulting divisions between Catholics and Protestants in Ireland remain a source of conflict to this day. James's son, Charles I (1600–1649), fell out with parliament over the extent of his powers, resulting in civil war. After Charles's trial and execution in 1649, Oliver Cromwell ruled England as a Commonwealth (republic), but 11 years on, Charles's son, Charles II, was invited to return to the throne.

In 1707 England, Wales, and Scotland were formally united under the *Act of Union* as the Kingdom of Great Britain. A new dynasty of Hanoverian kings, Georges I through IV, followed. Two rebellions in Scotland to restore the Stuart line were suppressed by England, the last at the Battle of Culloden in 1746.

By 1770, when explorer James Cook discovered Australia, Britain

Above Oxford University's Radcliffe Camera (at left) once housed the Radcliffe Science Library. The Palladian-style building is now used as additional reading rooms for the Bodleian Library.

Left A stone carving from the great Roman baths in Bath, Somerset, England. The baths were built by the Romans over an older Celtic shrine dedicated to the goddess Sulis.

Below Snowdonia National Park in Wales covers 823 square miles (2,132 km²) in Gwynedd and Conwy counties, providing a huge range of habitats for a wide variety of plants and animals, including the gwyniad, a rare fish trapped in one of the lakes some 10,000 years ago.

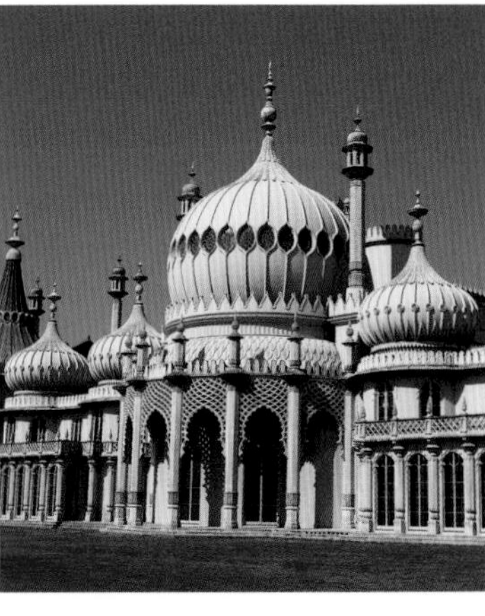

Above Queen Elizabeth II, accompanied by the Yeoman of the Guard, arrives in the Irish State Coach to open the new parliamentary year in the Palace of Westminster, London. This colorful annual ceremony dates back to medieval times.

Above right The Indo-Saracen Royal Pavilion in Brighton was built in the early nineteenth century as a seaside retreat for the Prince Regent, who went on to become King George IV.

Right A British Muslim mother and child in the East End of London. Nearly half of Britain's 1.6 million Muslims live in London. Currently, 50 percent of resident Muslims were born in Britain; the remainder come from the Middle East, Pakistan, and Bangladesh.

Below Men in clan tartans compete in a tug of war in Lonach, Strathdon, Scotland. The origins of tartan can be traced back to fifth century Ireland, where the "Scoti" originated.

Right Stonehenge, on Salisbury Plain in the English county of Wiltshire, England. It was constructed almost 4,500 years ago by people of the late Neolithic period. Its original purpose is unknown, but it is likely to have been a place of worship—it was not, as many believe, connected with the Druids.

had become a major colonial power. However, its American colonies rebelled in 1775 and seceded. Soon after, Britain was at war with France, then led by Emperor Napoleon I. Britain and its allies eventually defeated the French at the Battle of Waterloo in 1815.

Queen Victoria ruled from 1837 until her death in 1901. During her reign the empire was expanded in Asia and Africa, and Britain was acknowledged as the dominant world power. During this era the Industrial Revolution brought prosperity but also the start of movements for social change.

In 1914–1918 Britain, France, and their allies fought in World War I against Imperial Germany and Austria. Trench warfare resulted in the slaughter of 20 million soldiers and civilians. Germany lost, but the human and financial cost to Britain was immense.

During this period, rebellion in Ireland resulted in partition into the Irish Free State (soon renamed Ireland) and Northern Ireland (Ulster). Ulster's majority Protestants opted to remain part of the United Kingdom.

In 1931 the UK's self-governing overseas dominions of Australia, New Zealand, Canada, Ireland, and South Africa became known as the British Commonwealth. In 1949 this was renamed the Commonwealth of Nations and in that same year Ireland withdrew when it became a republic.

From 1939 to 1945 World War II was fought between the Allies and the Axis powers led by Nazi Germany. Only the heroism of RAF pilots and the resolve of Prime Minister Winston Churchill saved the UK from Nazi invasion in 1940. World War II became a global conflict involving the USA, the Commonwealth countries, Russia, Japan, and many other nations. After five years, Germany was again defeated but the UK was virtually bankrupt and unable to maintain its empire.

In 1947, a Labour government granted independence to India. It also created a welfare system in the UK, including a National Health Service. Since 1949, the UK has been a member nation of NATO. With its US allies and NATO, Britain has been engaged in military campaigns such as the Korean War, and more recently in Iraq and Afghanistan.

From 1979 to 1990 Margaret Thatcher's Conservative administration restructured many aspects of the British economy following the decline of heavy industry. A Labour government has held office since 1997.

Population and Religion

Some 92 percent of UK residents are of English, Scottish, Welsh, and Northern Irish extraction. Over 5 percent of the population comes from Africa, the Caribbean, India, and Pakistan; the remainder from other countries.

With more than 170 distinct religions, the religious makeup of the UK is diverse. While only about 50 percent of Britons told the 2001 census they believe in God, some 72 percent were Christian, although most had no connection to any church. Most indicators show continued secularization of British society similar to other European countries.

Culture

The UK population embraces four different countries whose people have over centuries moved, intermarried, and settled in different areas. As well as the many regional accents of England, one hears Scottish, Irish, and Welsh accents across the land. Immigration from the West Indies, the Indian subcontinent, and Africa has added to the rich cultural mix, but has also brought some racial tension.

Government

The British head of state and source of all political authority is the constitutional monarch, Queen Elizabeth II, who has reigned since 1952. In theory her powers are immense as leader of all three branches of government (the executive, the legislative, and the judiciary), commander-in-chief of the armed forces, and head of the Church of England. All holders of public office, civil servants, and members of the armed forces give a personal oath of loyalty to her. No law can be passed without her consent. In reality, power resides with the prime minister and his or her government, which exercises it through Crown Prerogative—that is, in the Queen's name.

The Parliament has two chambers, the elected House of Commons, and the hereditary House of Lords. There are 646 constituency seats in the House of Commons to which Members of Parliament (MPs) are elected by the public. After general elections, called every five years or sooner, the party that wins the majority of seats takes power and forms government.

The three largest political parties are Labour, Conservative, and the Liberal Democrats. Labour Prime Minister Tony Blair was succeeded in 2007 by his party colleague Gordon Brown.

In 1999 a Scottish Parliament was re-established in Edinburgh after nearly 300 years. Similarly, a National Assembly for Wales was established in Cardiff. In Belfast a power-sharing government that included both Unionists and Irish Republicans (former opponents) was agreed upon in 2007. These changes came about following demands for greater devolution of government and the rising influence of nationalist parties. MPs with seats in these three countries still sit in the UK Parliament in London; other representatives for the same electorates sit in their devolved national assemblies. Only England has no national assembly of its own.

Economy and Industry

The UK is one of the richest countries in the world today. In 2007, its GDP was estimated at £1.23 trillion (US$2.4 trillion). It was the first country to undergo an Industrial Revolution, which brought unprecedented commercial wealth. New industries depended on exploitation of

Left The Scottish Exhibition and Conference Center, located on the River Clyde in Glasgow, is Scotland's premier venue for public events. The center was constructed in 1984 on the site of the old Queens Dock, an area that has undergone major redevelopment.

natural resources, such as coal. This produced an economic base from which energy supplies, rail transport, and large-scale manufacturing could all be developed.

Since the 1970s, coal and other uncompetitive home products have been replaced by foreign imports, which has led to the decline of most heavy industry in the UK. The service sector—which includes information technology, computer software, banking, insurance, retail, entertainment, and tourism—has become the backbone of the economy. It now comprises about 73 percent of GDP, as against industry (26 percent) and agriculture (1 percent). Although coal mining has sharply declined, exploitation of North Sea oil and natural gas reserves, mainly off the Scottish coast, is a big factor in the UK economy.

The English Language

English began to be spoken in the British Isles from about the fifth century CE when Angles and Saxons from northern Germany invaded England's east coast. Their dialects gradually developed into what is called Old English. Six hundred years later, following the invasion by the Normans from northern France in 1066, Anglo-Norman, similar to Old French, became the dominant language. During the next three hundred years, Middle English developed as the spoken tongue, assimilating from Anglo-Norman many words of French origin. During the Renaissance, from about 1400 to 1700, large numbers of Latin and Greek words entered the English language.

The spread of English far beyond the shores of England was mainly due to the British Empire, which at its height (around 1900) embraced nearly one-quarter of the world's land surface. From that empire evolved the independent Commonwealth countries such as Australia, New Zealand, Canada, and many countries in Africa and the Caribbean where English had become established as the first language. Even after the decline of the British Empire, the rising influence of the United States—especially since World War II—has ensured that English has increasingly become the international language of choice.

Modern English is the preferred language of communications, airlines, the Internet, business, science, diplomacy, and entertainment. Many occupations and professions worldwide require knowledge of written and spoken English. Although English is not the most widely spoken language in the world, it is now the first language for approximately 375 million people according to figures for 2006, and a second language for between 200 million and a billion people.

MILESTONE EVENTS

500,000 BCE First signs of Paleolithic inhabitation of Great Britain

6,000 BCE Rising sea levels cut off Great Britain from European mainland

4,000 BCE First evidence of agriculture in Britain

2,450–2,100 BCE Construction of Stonehenge

2,000 BCE First evidence of bronze-working

700–300 BCE Celtic tribes move into England; evidence of iron-working

55 BCE Julius Caesar's Roman army raids southern England

43 BCE–410 CE Permanent Roman occupation of England (Britannia)

927 King Athelstan of Wessex reunites England as a single kingdom

1066 William of Normandy invades England and takes the throne

1215 King John signs the Magna Carta, a great charter limiting the actions of the monarchy and guaranteeing the rights of others

1282–1284 Wales is conquered and united with England (Statute of Rhuddlan)

1337–1453 Hundred Years War between England and France

1455–1485 War of the Roses between the Houses of York and Lancaster

1533 Henry VIII breaks with Rome and founds the Church of England

1558–1603 Reign of Elizabeth I

1603 James I (James VI of Scotland) succeeds to England's throne and becomes first King of Great Britain

1607 Jamestown, Virginia, is the first successful English settlement in North America

1641–1645 Civil War between Charles I and Parliament

1649–1660 After executing Charles I, Oliver Cromwell rules England as a republic

1660 Restoration of the monarchy under Charles II

1707 Act of Union between England and Scotland combines their parliaments and creates the United Kingdom

c. 1750–1850 Industrial Revolution

1770 James Cook lands in Australia and claims the land for Britain

1801 Act of Union: Ireland officially joins the "United Kingdom of Great Britain and Ireland"

1837–1901 Reign of Queen Victoria

1914–1918 World War I

1921–1922 Ireland given independence but Ulster remains part of UK

1939–1945 World War II

1947 India gains independence

1952 Coronation of Queen Elizabeth II

1973 The UK joins the European Economic Community (EEC)

1982 Falklands War: British troops defeat Argentine garrison at Port Stanley, Falkland Islands

1997 Princess Diana is killed in car accident in Paris

2005 Islamic suicide bombers detonate bombs in London Underground, killing 52 and wounding 700 people

Below The London Eye, also known as the Millennium Wheel, on the South Bank in London, is the tallest ferris wheel in Europe.

IRELAND

Official name Ireland (Éire)
Land area 27,136 square miles (70,282 km²) [Island of Ireland 32,589 square miles/84,405 km²]
Border countries Island surrounded by the Atlantic Ocean; the Republic of Ireland shares the island with Northern Ireland, part of the United Kingdom
Capital Dublin (Baile Átha Cliath)
Highest point Carrauntuohil, 3,414 feet (1,041 m)
Climate Marine west coast: mild, moist climate with narrow temperature variation
Population 4,109,086
Language(s) Official: English and Irish (Gaelic or Gaeilige)
Ethnicity Celtic, English 95%; other 5% includes nomadic Irish Travellers, Polish, Chinese and other Asians, Africans, and Caribbean people
Religion Roman Catholic 88.4%, Church of Ireland 3%, other Christian 1.6%, other 1.5%, unspecified 2%, none 3.5%
Government Republic, parliamentary democracy
Currency Euro
Human Development Index 0.959 (ranked 5th out of 177 countries)

Above right Heavy clouds mass as sheep graze in the foreground of the Rock of Cashel, in Cahir, County Tipperary, Ireland. The Rock of Cashel was once the seat of the kings of Munster.

Right The O'Connell Street Bridge over the River Liffey in Dublin is named after Daniel O'Connor, a leading political figure in the nineteenth century.

Below Dingle Peninsula, in County Kerry, is Ireland's most westerly point.

Donegal
UNITED KINGDOM
Sligo
Castlebar
Dundalk
Navan
Galway
Mullingar
Irish Sea
ATLANTIC OCEAN
IRELAND
DUBLIN (BAILE ÁTHA CLIATH)
Ennis
Limerick
Carlow
Tralee
Kilkenny
Clonmel
Killarney
Waterford
Wexford
Cork

Ireland

Map Reference Page 245

The Republic of Ireland, on the island of Ireland in the North Atlantic Ocean, occupies 83 percent of the island's landmass. The remaining 17 percent, Northern Ireland, is part of the United Kingdom.

Physical Geography

Ireland is rimmed by highlands, islands, and beaches. Its central lowland interior contains glacial landforms, lakes, and peat bogs. Wind and the River Shannon have also sculpted the landscape. The central lowlands are the major agricultural region of Ireland.

The Atlantic Ocean's warm waters create a marine west coast climate that is mild and moist with narrow temperature variations. Rainfall is consistent, although a bit heavier in winter. Total rainfall is highest in the western mountains and lowest around Dublin. Dense fog occurs up to 60 days a year in places.

History

Stone Age peoples arrived about 8,000–10,000 years ago—probably from Scotland. Some 4,000 years ago, the Celts arrived. Iron Age Celtic settlements dotted the landscape and were eventually organized into 200 small kingdoms, which over time aligned under more powerful rulers. The Hill of Tara was the seat of royal authority for 1,000 years, and is where St Patrick received King Laoghaire's approval to bring Christianity to the people.

Around 795 CE, Vikings began raiding Ireland and eventually built forts that became Ireland's first cities, including Dublin and Cork. In 1170, Henry II sent Anglo-Norman armies to claim Ireland for the British Crown, the beginning of more than 800 years of English domination.

Over the last 125 years, through civil war, rebellion, and compromise, Ireland has regained its independence. In 1921 the Irish Free State was established, with Northern Ireland remaining in the UK. The Irish Republican Army's efforts to return Northern Ireland to Irish control, and British responses, are known as "The Troubles." In 1949 the Republic of Ireland was established.

Population/Culture

Greater Dublin, home to over 1.6 million people, is the largest urban area. Travellers (Tinkers), a minority, number 21,000. Recent population growth is mainly a result of immigration comprised of returning Irish, UK residents, Polish, and Chinese.

Irish resistance to British colonial efforts to dominate their culture strengthened their resolve for cultural preservation and self-government. Today, social life revolves around the family, sporting teams, and pubs. There is a strong tradition of music and storytelling.

Administration/Government

Ireland is a republic with 26 counties and is governed as a parliamentary democracy. The Oireachtas (Parliament) consists of the 60-seat Senate and the 166-seat House of Representatives. The prime minister (Taoiseach) heads the executive power, while the president's position is largely ceremonial. The Supreme Court is in charge of judicial power.

Major political concerns include peaceful reunification, minorities and immigration, and continued economic growth.

Economy/Industry

Today, Ireland is among the world's most viable economies. The economic emergence of the "Celtic Tiger" is the result of farsighted leadership, a commitment to education and improved infrastructures, and membership of the European Union. Ireland's well-educated workforce supports its economic growth. Former Irish residents and foreign immigrants are attracted to employment opportunities in computer hardware and software, communications equipment, electrical goods, construction, pharmaceuticals, and tourism.

MILESTONE EVENTS

432 St Patrick establishes Christianity in Ireland
1170 King Henry II of England claims Ireland
1536 King Henry VIII establishes the Church of Ireland
1690 William of Orange defeats King James II at the Battle of Boyne
1845 Irish Potato Famine kills or forces migration of millions of people
1916 Easter Rising takes place in Dublin
1921 Ireland partitioned into Irish Free State and Northern Ireland
1949 Ireland becomes a republic
1973 Ireland joins European Economic Union
1998 Good Friday Agreement is signed
2008 Republicans and Unionists form a power-sharing government in Belfast

The Troubles

The source of "The Troubles" dates back to English efforts to destroy religious freedom in Ireland. Over time, this came to include destruction of economic, social, cultural, intellectual, civil, and political rights as well. The Irish resisted, and at times conflict occurred, but resistance did not end with independence and the creation of the Irish Free State in 1921. First there was civil war between independence forces, and then the Irish Republican Army (IRA) initiated efforts to regain the six counties of Northern Ireland. Protestant Northern Ireland resisted and reaffirmed its loyalty to the British Crown.

The conflicts resulting from these different loyalties are collectively referred to as "The Troubles." The worst period was from 1969 to the early 1990s, when over 3,000 Irish and British people lost their lives.

Often viewed as a religious conflict, The Troubles have also been struggles for civil rights and economic well-being. Historically, the Protestants in Northern Ireland were favored by the government, but following World War II they suffered massive unemployment and feared that equal competition between Protestant and Catholic would further erode the fragile economy. They tried to limit the Catholics' rights to education and jobs, which they hoped would result in more jobs for unemployed Protestants.

The people of Ireland—north and south—now seek to end the conflict. In 1998, the leaders of Nationalist, Unionist, and Republican forces, and government representatives of Northern Ireland, Great Britain, and the Republic of Ireland, signed the Good Friday Agreement. Unionists and Republicans are jointly involved in decommissioning their weapons and reducing conflict. The Peace Accord of 1998 and the establishment of a power-sharing government in 2007 are nurturing an effort to overcome hatreds, to establish equal rights, and most importantly to foster and protect peace in all of Ireland.

North Sea
Leeuwarden
Groningen
Assen
NETHERLANDS
Zaanstad
Haarlem
AMSTERDAM
Leiden
Enschede
'S-GRAVENHAGE/
DEN HAAG
(THE HAGUE)
Utrecht
Arnhem
Rotterdam
Nijmegen
Dordrecht
Breda
Tilburg
Eindhoven
GERMANY
BELGIUM
Maastricht
Vaalserberg

Netherlands

Map Reference Pages 226–227

The Netherlands is a small country with a dense population of 1,025 inhabitants per square mile (396 per km^2). It is part of the Kingdom of the Netherlands, which also includes the Netherlands Antilles and Aruba in the Caribbean. The Netherlands lies on the North Sea, largely on the deltas of the Rhine, Maas, and Schelde rivers.

Physical Geography

The country is typically flat, and roughly a third of it lies below sea level—reclaimed flat land ("polders") behind protective dikes. Glacial moorlands fill the northern and central part, with some hilly ridges, and there are coastal sand dunes. The foothills of the Ardennes Mountains rise in the southeastern tip of the country. The Netherlands has a moderate maritime climate, with cool summers and mild winters.

History

In 1579, during the Eighty Years' War with Spain, seven provinces declared independence and formed the Dutch Republic (Republic of the Seven United Netherlands). It became one of the major economic powers of the seventeenth century and established colonies all over the globe. Most notable were the Cape Colony (Cape Town area, South Africa) and the Dutch East Indies (now Indonesia).

Amsterdam became Europe's wealthiest trading center and it established the first full-time stock exchange. From 1810 to 1813 the Netherlands was part of the French Empire.

Nazi Germany invaded the Netherlands in 1940. During World War II, more than 100,000 Dutch Jews were transported to concentration camps and subsequently murdered. After suffering starvation during the "Hunger Winter," the Dutch population was freed by Allied forces in 1945.

A period of prosperity began but postwar reconstruction was disrupted in February 1953 by a flood disaster. Unusually high spring tides and gale-force winds caused the dikes protecting the southwest part of the country to break. More than 1,800 people were killed and 3,000 homes destroyed.

Left With its elaborate network of canals and more than 100 bridges, Amsterdam has been dubbed the "Venice of the North."

Population/Culture

Approximately 80 percent of the population is of Dutch and Frisian origin. The remaining 20 percent are immigrants from other parts of the European Union, as well as from Indonesia, Turkey, Morocco, and Suriname.

Dutch painters are famous worldwide; among them are Rembrandt van Rijn, Jan Steen, Johannes Vermeer, and Vincent van Gogh. People like Erasmus (philosopher) and Christiaan Huygens (scientist), to name just a few, have left their mark on the world. Anne Frank's *The Diary of a Young Girl*, published after this Holocaust victim died during the Nazi occupation, had a huge impact.

Windmills, tulips, wooden shoes, cheese, and pottery from Delft are traditional Dutch icons. The feast of Sinterklaas (St Nicholas) on December 5 is an unofficial holiday, celebrated with food, gifts, and merriment.

MILESTONE EVENTS

1584 William I of Orange, rebel leader against Philip II and founding father of the new state, is murdered

1612 Using 43 windwills, the Beemster polder is drained, an example of how the Dutch "created" large areas of their country

1637 First print of the Statenvertaling, a translation of the Bible in Dutch, has an enormous impact on Dutch culture and language

1655–1656 Christiaan Huygens discovers Saturn's ring and the moon Titan

1859 Multatuli writes Max Havelaar, a condemnation of the abuses of the Dutch colonial administration in the Dutch East Indies

1940–1945 World War II occupation by Nazi Germany, and liberation

1949 Under pressure, the Dutch government grants independence to Indonesia

1957 The Netherlands signs the Treaty of Rome, eventually making European Union a reality

1959 An enormous gasfield is discovered near Slochteren, Groningen

1975 Surinam, a former colony, becomes independent

2001 Laws are passed allowing homosexuals to marry and adopt children

2002 Pim Fortuyn, anti-immigration party leader, is killed

Administration/Government

The Netherlands is a constitutional monarchy. The head of state is the monarch, at present Queen Beatrix. In practice, her function is merely ceremonial, although officially she still has considerable powers.

The head of government is the prime minister, usually the leader of the largest party in the cabinet. Cabinet is responsible to the parliament, which is bicameral.

The judicial branch of government is represented by the Supreme Court. A long tradition of social tolerance has resulted in liberal policies on issues such as abortion, euthanasia, drugs, and prostitution.

Economy/Industry

Blessed with fertile soil and a highly educated population, the Netherlands has favorable conditions for a prosperous economy. It is the sixteenth largest economy in the world and has the lowest unemployment rate within the European Union. Industrial activity is based around petroleum refining, chemicals, electrical machinery, and food processing. One of the largest natural gasfields in the world is located near Slochteren.

A highly mechanized system enables the Netherlands to rank third worldwide in value of agricultural products. Banking and transportation are important. Rotterdam, the largest port in Europe, is a major distribution center for international trade.

NETHERLANDS

Official name Kingdom of the Netherlands (Koninkrijk der Nederlanden)
Land area 16,034 square miles (41,528 km^2) [including 18% water]
Border countries Belgium, Germany
Capital Amsterdam, The Hague ('s-Gravenhage/Den Haag)
Highest & lowest points Vaalserberg 1,053 feet (321 m); Nieuwerkerk aan den IJssel –22 feet (–6.7 m)
Climate Moderate maritime
Population 16,398,390
Language(s) Official: Dutch, Frisian
Ethnicity Dutch and Frisian 80.6%, other 19.4%
Religion Christian 43.7%, Muslim 5.8%, other 2.3%, unspecified 48.2%
Government Constitutional monarchy
Currency Euro
Human Development Index 0.953 (ranked 9th out of 177 countries)

Below A young woman wearing a traditional hat makes her way though a tulip field at Lisse. Tulips were brought to Europe from the Ottoman Empire in the sixteenth century.

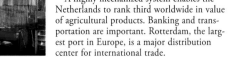

Left A Dutch fishing boat in Volendam, with its herring nets strung out to dry. According to a Dutch proverb, "if herring is around the doctor is far away."

BELGIUM

Official name Kingdom of Belgium
Land area 11,691 square miles (30,278 km²)
Border countries Netherlands, Germany, Luxembourg, France
Capital Brussels (Bruxelles/Brussel)
Highest point Signal de Botrange 2,277 feet (694 m)
Climate Temperate
Population 10,392,226
Language(s) Official: Dutch, French, German
Ethnicity Flemish 58%, Walloon 31%, other 11%
Religion Roman Catholic 75%, other (including Protestant and Muslim) 25%
Government Federal parliamentary democracy under constitutional monarchy
Currency Euro
Human Development Index 0.946 (ranked 17th out of 177 countries)

Above right A child wears a hat emblazoned with the colors of the Belgian flag during a protest march against the possible partition of Belgium.

Right A forest of European beech and blooms of bluebells outside Brussels.

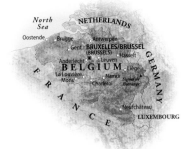

Below Bruges, seen from the belfry in Market Street. The historic city center was included on the UNESCO World Heritage list in 2000.

Belgium

Map Reference Pages 228–229

The Kingdom of Belgium, with about 10.4 million people, is two countries in one: French-speaking Wallonia to the south and Dutch (Flemish)-speaking Flanders to the north. The name Belgium comes from the ancient Belgae, a people of Celtic stock.

Physical Geography

The northern drift of the Atlantic Ocean into the North Sea moderates Belgium's climate.

Winter temperatures average around 37°F (3°C), summer temperatures average 65°F (18°C). Belgium ranges from sea level to elevations above 2,000 feet (600 m) in the eastern upland Ardennes. Belgium has very good road, rail, and canal systems. To the north it shares tributaries of the Rhine Delta with the Netherlands.

Cultural History: A Country of Two Minds

As part of the Habsburg Empire, the northern home of such Renaissance painters as Peter Paul Rubens, Anthony Van Dijck, and Pieter Brueghel grew in cultural and economic might in the sixteenth century. Positioned between Germanic northern interests and Romance southern ones, Belgium became a new state in 1830. From the Middle Ages, the French influence of the Catholic Church was dominant in hillier southern Wallonia compared with the less developed north.

Yet, from the Renaissance, the northern Flemings gained political clout and Antwerp (today a city of about 1.2 million) on the western Schelde River became a leading mercantile center. Uneasiness in the relationship between the once dominant south and the new powerful north has resulted in a trend toward increased federal devolution.

In 1993, a new constitution increased federalism. First, land use and economic issues were negotiated by regional authorities in Wallonia, Flanders, and the culturally mixed capital of Brussels. Second, cultural/linguistic communities were established for the Flemish, the French, and the small German-speaking community near the eastern border with Germany. Finally, a federal government for the entire country was established.

Population/Culture

Brussels (with a population of over 1 million) is the crux of the Belgian drama of contrasts. Its location in the middle of Flemish and Walloon interests led to its establishment as the capital of Belgium.

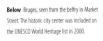

Belgium is one of the most densely populated and urban countries in the world and the most urban nation of all Europe. Ninety-seven percent of its population lives in cities.

Administration/Government

Belgium is a constitutional monarchy with a federal parliamentary democracy. Since 1993, when the constitution was revised, King Albert II (constitutional and hereditary monarch) has held the position of chief of state and head of the executive branch of the government. The legislative branch (parliament) consists of the Senate and the Chamber of Deputies.

Economy/Industry

Belgium shared coal and iron fields with the Netherlands, France, and Germany, but Flanders was the main beneficiary. These fields are depleted now, and the country depends on the import of raw materials and many other required goods. Through the 1900s, Antwerp grew as a trading center, gradually becoming the second largest port in Europe after Rotterdam. Important global connections in industry, commerce, and finance were established, and Antwerp is now the world's primary diamond center, brokering about half of stones sold anywhere.

The Hub of Europe

Following World War II, the governments of Belgium, the Netherlands, and Luxembourg, which had been in exile, formed the Benelux Union. In the mid-1950s, Belgium was a founding member, along with the Netherlands, Luxembourg, Germany, France, and Italy, of the European Coal and Steel Community (ECSC), established to ensure postwar interregional dependency and economic unity. This group was the core of the modern European Union (EU).

Brussels became the administrative capital of the European Economic Community (the EEC, later to become the EU) in 1962. It is the seat of the EU Council of Ministers, the European Commission, the Economic and Social Committee, and the Committee of the Regions. Though the EU parliament is officially seated in Strasbourg, France, most European parliament committee meetings are held in Brussels. While Belgium devolves as a country, Brussels remains the hub of European administration.

MILESTONE EVENTS

1530 Antwerp Exchange founded

***c.* 1810** Industrial revolution in textiles, coal, and iron gains force

1830 Belgium declares independence from the Netherlands

July 21, 1831 King Leopold I is crowned

1885 Berlin gives Congo to Belgium

August 3, 1914 Germany invades Belgium in World War I

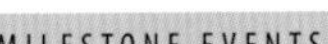

May 10, 1940 Germany starts blitzkrieg of Low Countries in World War II

April 4, 1949 Brussels becomes headquarters of NATO

April 17, 1958 World's Fair opens in Brussels

1960 The Congo gains independence from Belgium and becomes Zaire

1960s Construction of the Berlaymont Building, de facto headquarters of the EU

1990s Schengen and Maastricht treaties and adoption of euro further unify Europe; Brussels takes on more European Union "capital" functions

March 2006 Slobodan Milosevic, Serbian leader, dies in Belgium during proceedings of war crimes trial

Left Schloss Vaduz (Vaduz Castle) is the central landmark in Vaduz, Liechtenstein. Originally built as a medieval fortress, the castle was expanded in the sixteenth and seventeenth centuries; Schloss Vaduz is the official residence of the Prince Hans-Adam II of Liechtenstein.

BELGIUM
GERMANY
FRANCE
Buurgplaatz
Troisvierges
Wiltz
Ettelbruck
Diekirch
Colmar
Echternach
Mersch
LUXEMBOURG
Grevenmacher
Steinfort
LUXEMBOURG
Pétange
Bascharage
Esch-sur-Alzette
Mondorf-les-Bains

Luxembourg

Map Reference Pages 228–229

The Grand Duchy of Luxembourg is one of the smallest sovereign nations on Earth. With a land area measuring a mere 999 square miles (2,586 km²), this landlocked, constitutional monarchy has always been a key player on the European political scene, most recently as a founding member of the United Nations, the North Atlantic Treaty Organization (NATO), and the European Union (EU).

Luxembourg began its modern history as a castle. Luxembourg Castle was purchased by the Count of Ardennes in 963 CE, and soon a town established itself. A descendant bestowed upon himself the title Count of Luxembourg, and from the fifteenth to the eighteenth centuries the tiny nation was ruled in turn by Spain, France, and Austria. Luxembourg became a Grand Duchy in 1815 and had its independence confirmed by the First Treaty of London in 1839.

After World War II, Luxembourg entered into the Benelux economic union with Belgium and the Netherlands. Many see this union as a precursor to the European Union.

Luxembourg is home to a unicameral parliamentary system and overseen by a hereditary Grand Duke who is titular head of state.

The discovery of iron ore in the middle of the nineteenth century saw Luxembourg's economy explode. Tens of thousands of foreign workers were brought in to work its mines and factories, and today the country's largest single employer and world's largest steel company is the ArcelorMittal group. Luxembourg has diversified its economic base and specializes in financial services, which has seen it climb to third behind London and Paris as Europe's largest banking center.

The north of the country is characterized by the fertile uplands of the rugged Ardennes Mountains, while central and southern Luxembourg, known locally as the "Good Country," is a mix of broad valleys, rolling farmland, and extensive woodlands.

One in three people residing in the country is a foreign worker, the highest percentage of foreigners in the European Union. The ancient Germanic language Luxembourgish is widely spoken on the street, although French and German are the two official languages.

Liechtenstein

Map Reference Pages 226–227

The landlocked Principality of Liechtenstein is located in the Upper Rhine Valley between Switzerland and Austria. Liechtenstein is the world's sixth smallest nation, its boundaries measuring a mere 48 miles (77 km). Alpine terrain accounts for two-thirds of its territory. The dominant language is German. Its currency is the Swiss franc.

Liechtenstein's size, relative isolation, and distance from any remotely strategic location has seen it bypassed by the many massive conflagrations of European history.

The modern state of Liechtenstein came into being when the Liechtenstein dynasty purchased land near Schellenburg, and its capital Vaduz, from the Austrian town of Hohenems at the turn of the eighteenth century. It became a member of the Holy Roman Empire in 1719.

A constitution was granted in 1816, and the new nation continued to maintain close ties with the Austrian empire until the close of World War I. Liechtenstein chose a policy of neutrality in World War II.

In 2003 a national referendum saw the principality vote with a two-thirds majority to amend the 1921 Constitution. Overnight Liechtenstein's history as a constitutional monarchy had come to a close. The nation's monarch, Ruling Prince Hans-Adam II, has now been given authority by his citizens to hire and fire the government, in addition to his existing power of veto over all parliamentary legislation, which in turn has raised concerns that the Ruling Prince has been granted almost dictatorial status.

All legislative authority is vested in a 25-member unicameral parliament (Landtag) elected by proportional representation, and a National Committee is charged with the responsibility of overseeing the parliament.

A low rate of corporate tax has seen over 70,000 companies establish so-called "letter-box offices" in the country, which together account for almost a third of Liechtenstein's state revenue. A thriving financial sector gives its citizens a standard of living equal to its larger European Union neighbors.

LUXEMBOURG

Official name Grand Duchy of Luxembourg
Land area 999 square miles (2,586 km²)
Border countries Germany, France, Belgium
Capital Luxembourg
Highest point Buurgplaatz 1,843 feet (562 m)
Climate Temperate
Population 480,222
Language(s) Official: French, German; other: Luxembourgish
Ethnicity Luxembourger 67%, Portuguese 15%, Italian 5%, other 13%
Religion Roman Catholic 87%, other (includes Protestant, Jewish, and Muslim) 13%
Government Parliamentary democracy/Constitutional Grand Duchy
Currency Euro
Human Development Index 0.944 (ranked 18th out of 177 countries)

LIECHTENSTEIN

Official name Principality of Liechtenstein
Land area 61.8 square miles (160 km²)
Border countries Austria, Switzerland
Capital Vaduz
Highest point Vorder-Grauspitz 8,527 feet (2,599 m)
Climate Temperate
Population 34,247
Language(s) Official: German, Alemannic dialect
Ethnicity Alemannic 90%, other 10%
Religion Roman Catholic 76.2%, Protestant 7%, unspecified 10.6%, other 6.2%
Government Parliamentary democracy/absolute monarchy
Currency Swiss franc
Human Development Index Not available

Below Perched dramatically above the village of Vianden in northeastern Luxembourg, Vianden Castle, built between the eleventh and fourteenth centuries, has been restored to its former glory.

FRANCE

Official name French Republic (République Française)
Land area 210,668 square miles (545,630 km²)
Border countries Belgium, Luxembourg, Germany, Switzerland, Italy, Monaco, Andorra, Spain
Capital Paris
Highest & lowest points Mont Blanc 15,771 feet (4,807 m); Rhone River delta –6½ feet (–2 m)
Climate Mediterranean
Population 64,058,000
Language(s) Official: French; other: declining regional dialects and languages (Provencal, Breton, Alsatian, Corsican, Catalan, Basque, Flemish)
Ethnicity Celtic and Latin with Teutonic, Slavic, North African, Indochinese, Basque minorities
Religion Roman Catholic 83–88%, Protestant 2%, Jewish 1%, Muslim 5–10%, unaffiliated 4%
Government Republic
Currency Euro
Human Development Index 0.952 (ranked 10th out of 177 countries)

Above right The Paris Metro is a world-famous subway system that since its opening in 1900 has grown to provide cheap and efficient transport for approximately 6 million passengers each day.

Above More than 2,500 standing stones dating back to Neolithic times make an impressive sight at Carnac in northwestern France.

UNITED KINGDOM
English Channel
Le Havre
Lille
BELGIUM
Amiens
LUXEMBOURG
Brest
Caen
Rouen
Reims
GERMANY
PARIS
Metz
Rennes
Le Mans
Strasbourg
Troyes
Angers
Orléans
Nantes
Tours
Dijon
Besançon
Poitiers
FRANCE
SWITZERLAND
Bay of Biscay
Limoges
Clermont-Ferrand
Lyon
Mont Blanc
St-Étienne
Grenoble
Bordeaux
ITALY
Toulouse
Nîmes
Avignon
Nice
Pau
Montpellier
MONACO
Marseille
ANDORRA
Perpignan
Corse
SPAIN
Mediterranean Sea
Ajaccio

France

Map Reference Pages 228–229

France is the largest of the countries of Western Europe and shares borders with eight other European nations. This centrality provides France with a key role politically, economically, and as a crossroads of trade and transportation.

Physical Geography

Much of the country is characterized by low-lying plains such as the Paris and Aquitaine basins, where altitudes rarely rise more than 650 feet (200 m). The landscape becomes more varied in the south, featuring mountains with rounded peaks and steep valleys that range in height from 1,640 to 5,600 feet (500 to 1,700 m). The Massif Central is a mountainous plateau in south-central France, with the volcanic mass of the Auvergne Mountains at its core. This region supplies tributaries to the nation's mightiest rivers.

Four major river systems provide focal points for urban development and industry. The estuaries of the Loire—France's longest river, at some 630 miles (1,012 km)—and the 360-mile (575 km) Garonne provide bases for the port cities of St-Nazaire and Bordeaux, but their historically uneven flows make them unsuitable for modern river transportation.

At 482 miles (776 km), the Seine is France's second longest river. It rises in the Plateau de Langres, northwest of Dijon, and bisects Paris before emptying into the English Channel at the port city of Le Havre. Finally, there is the Rhône River, which is 325 miles (522 km) long—one of the great waterways of Europe and the only major river that flows into the Mediterranean Sea.

The two most prominent mountain ranges are the Central Alps in the east along the French–Italian border, and the Pyrenees on the border with Spain.

Mont Blanc in the French Alps is the highest mountain in Western Europe, reaching 15,771 feet (4,807 m) above sea level. Ownership of this famous mountain has long been disputed between France and Italy. Modern topographic mapping suggests the border passes directly over the summit, leaving the southeast ridge wholly within Italian jurisdiction. Although both nations include Mont Blanc within the boundaries of their maps, it is generally considered to be of French nationality.

The lengthy coastline includes the steep vertical cliffs of Artois and Upper Normandy; the sculpted promontories and bays of Brittany and Provence; the marshes of Poitevin and the Camargue; and the plains and sandy beaches of Dunkirk.

There are 16 French dependencies, including French Guiana in South America, New Caledonia in the Pacific Ocean, and the island of Réunion in the Indian Ocean.

History

The first inhabitants can be traced to Stone Age sites at Les Eyzies in Périgord and Neolithic sites in Brittany and Carnac.

MILESTONE EVENTS

December 25, 800 Charlemagne—having conquered much of Europe—is crowned Holy Roman Emperor
1066 French rule comes to England when William the Conqueror is victorious at the Battle of Hastings
1338 The Hundred Years' War begins—marking a time of intermittent warfare between England and France
1431 Joan of Arc is burned at the stake; she led the French troops against the English at Orleans in 1429
July 14, 1789 The French people, rebelling against the monarchy and its excesses, storm the Bastille
1793 French monarch Louis XVI and his wife Marie Antoinette are guillotined
1804 Corsican-born Napoleon Bonaparte is crowned Emperor of France
1871 The Third Republic is established
1940 The city of Paris falls to the German forces, and the Vichy Government is established
1958 Charles de Gaulle establishes the Fifth Republic
1968 Paris is rocked by violent student riots

The Roman defeat of the Gauls in 52 BCE ushered in some five centuries of stability, trade, and urbanization. A border with Germany was established along the Rhine River, which made France capable of withstanding centuries of conflict following the fall of the Roman Empire.

The Hundred Years' War between France and England began when King Philip VI tried to confiscate the English territories in the Duchy of Aquitaine in 1337, and ended in 1453 when the French all but expelled the English from the continent. The English retained only Calais, which they were finally forced to concede in 1558.

The reign of Louis XIV and the court of Versailles was followed by Louis XV and the era of the parlements, through to the reign of Louis XVI from 1774, until the Revolution of 1779. Napoleon Bonaparte became emperor in 1804, but was exiled to Elba in 1814. Escaping from Elba, Napoleon was finally defeated at Waterloo and spent his remaining years in exile on the British-owned Atlantic island of St Helena. The formation of the Second Republic followed the revolution of 1848. The Third Republic emerged in 1871, finally bringing to an end the system of monarchic rule in France.

When Paris was liberated from the Germans in World War II (1944), the Fourth Republic was inaugurated. Constitutional change in 1958 brought a president and the Fifth Republic.

Administration/Government

France is a republic with a clearly defined separation of legislative and executive powers. Elections are by universal suffrage and are held every five years. An elected president presides over a Council of Ministers and is responsible for the appointment of the nation's prime minister.

The French Senate consists of 321 members, with one-third of the senate retiring every three years. The National Assembly, or lower house, has 577 members elected by the people. The president has the power to both appoint and dismiss the prime minister as well as individual ministers, who do not need to be members of parliament.

The nation is divided into 26 regions for the purpose of administration.

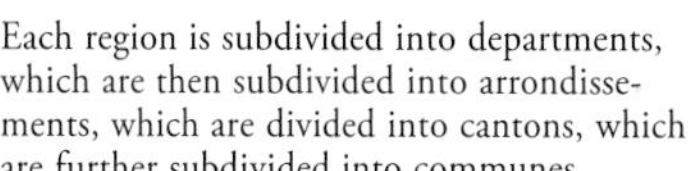

Each region is subdivided into departments, which are then subdivided into arrondissements, which are divided into cantons, which are further subdivided into communes.

Economy

France is gradually leaving behind an era of extensive government ownership of major social and economic institutions while moving toward a model that relies on prevailing market trends. However, it maintains a majority shareholding in some of the nation's largest corporations such as Air France and Renault.

Long-held socialist principles, however, have seen a continuing pursuit of social justice through policies on taxation and social spending. The escalating cost of health care provision and pension payments is, however, proving to be a significant problem for the government's finances.

A 35-hour working week, along with measures to boost falling employment figures, has seen a dramatic rise in labor costs. French taxes are among the highest of any European Union country, reaching almost 44 percent of the gross domestic product (GDP) in 2003.

Agriculture

Thirty-five percent of France's land area is arable, but although agriculture remains a vital aspect of the French economy, it employs only 4 percent of the labor force.

France exports more food than any of the other countries in the European Union, and is the only European nation to maintain self-sufficiency in basic food production.

The total number of farms has decreased markedly in the last 50 years or so, despite the average size of individual holdings increasing to an average of around 124 acres (50 ha).

The principal agricultural products are sugar beet, wine, milk, beef and veal, oilseeds, and cereals. The most productive areas lie in the north, but the olive groves and orchards of Provence, the vineyards of Burgundy and Languedoc, as well as the vegetable farms of Brittany, are also significant.

Architectural Landmarks

France has been at the forefront of architectural innovation since medieval times, its rich legacy of the built environment reflecting the power of its kings, the supremacy of its church, and the integrity of its institutions.

Colonization by the Romans in 120 CE led to the coliseums of Arles and Orange and the settlements at Glanum, Marseilles, Nice, and Fréjus. The Romanesque era is characterized by the stone barrel vaults and aisleless domes of St Trophime of Arles, built in 1150, and the ornamentation of Angoulême's cathedral.

The Gothic era began with the construction of the choir of the Abbey of St-Denis in 1140 and continued through to the end of the fifteenth century. Traceried windows of colored glass, such as those found in the great cathedral at Chartres, filled new expanses of walls made possible by the development of external flying buttresses.

France's most famous landmark, however, is the Eiffel Tower, constructed in 1889 for the Universal Exposition celebrating the centenary of the French Revolution. A new era of rational engineering had arrived that reinterpreted the Gothic style as pure structure. The tower's first raw material was iron. Engineers Maurice Koechlin and Emile Nouguier and architect Stephen Sauvestre produced more than 5,300 blueprints and took two years to construct the tower, with the assistance of more than a hundred ironworkers who assembled its 18,038 constituent parts.

Another of Paris's famous landmarks is the Arc de Triomphe, strategically located in the center of the Place de Charles de Gaulle, the meeting point of a dozen avenues at the western end of the Champs Elysées. It is the major structure in a sequence of monuments that stretches from the Louvre to the outskirts of Paris. Commissioned in 1806 by Emperor Napoleon to commemorate his military victories and those who fell in his wars, the Arc de Triomphe is one of the largest triumphal arches in the world, standing over 160 feet (50 m) high. Between its pillars lies the tomb of the Unknown Soldier, interred on Armistice Day 1920, and the Eternal Flame, which burns brightly in memory of all those killed in war and never identified.

FORESTS

France is ranked third in the European Union in terms of forest area, with forest and woodlands covering around 37 million acres (15 million ha) or 26 percent of the nation. Since the end of World War II, the country's forested areas have increased by 35 percent, and they continue to grow by approximately 74,000 acres (30,000 ha) annually. Some two-thirds of the country's forests are shared between almost 3,800,000 private owners. These holdings, together with 4,324,344 acres (1,750,000 ha) of national forest that are managed by the National Forestry Office, as well as the 7,042,500 acres (2,850,000 ha) under the control of local authorities, yield an annual harvest of almost 2 billion cubic feet (60 million m^3) of timber.

Top The old and the new lie side by side at the Louvre museum, with the original building—once a fortress—now accompanied by the stunning glass pyramid, which opened in 1989.

Top left Provence is world-famous for its fields of lavender and groves of olive trees. Herbs and olive oil are important export products for this region of southeastern France.

Below The distinctive cityscape of Paris, the largest city in France. Each year some 30 million foreign tourists visit the French capital, drawn by its many world famous attractions.

AUSTRIA

Official name Republic of Austria (Republik Oesterreich)
Land area 31,834 square miles (82,444 km²)
Border countries Czech Republic, Slovakia, Hungary, Slovenia, Italy, Switzerland, Lichtenstein, Germany
Capital Vienna (Wien)
Highest & lowest points Grossglockner 12,457 feet (3,797 m); Neusiedler See 377 feet (115 m)
Climate Humid continental to mountain
Population 8,206,000
Language(s) German, Turkish, Croatian, Hungarian, Serbian
Ethnicity Austrian 91.1%, former Yugoslavs (including Croatian, Slovene, Serb, Bosniak) 4%, Turk 1.6%, German 0.9%, other 2.4%
Religion Roman Catholic 73.6%, Protestant 4.7%, Muslim 4.2%, other 3.5%, unspecified 2%, none 12%
Government Federal republic with parliamentary democracy
Currency Euro
Human Development Index 0.948 (ranked 15th out of 177 countries)

Above right The colorful facade of Hundertwasser House, an apartment complex in Vienna.

Above The Alps provide a breathtaking backdrop to Stift Wilten, a Premonstratensian abbey founded in 1138 near Innsbruck, Austria.

Right Riegersburg Castle is the oldest castle in the Burgenland region of Austria. Built during the eleventh century on an extinct volcano, it remains unvanquished throughout its history.

Below A golden statue pays tribute to Johann Strauss II (1825–1899). Strauss composed the legendary "Blue Danube" and popularized the waltz in his home of Vienna.

CZECH REPUBLIC
GERMANY
Linz
St Pölten
WIEN (VIENNA)
Wels
Eisenstadt
Salzburg
Wiener Neustadt
SLOVAKIA
Bregenz
AUSTRIA
Bruck an der Mur
HUNGARY
Feldkirch
Innsbruck
Graz
LIECHTENSTEIN
Villach
Klagenfurt
SWITZERLAND
ITALY
SLOVENIA

Austria

Map Reference Pages 226–227

One of only a few landlocked countries in Europe, Austria, together with Switzerland, is an alpine oasis. Much of its territory is dominated by the eastern extension of the Alps. Its rich heritage includes Stone Age sites and a colorful imperial past.

Physical Geography

Glacial valleys and high mountain passes serve as narrow corridors between Europe's north and south. Toward the east, rugged mountain peaks turn into the lowlands of Burgenland. The widest part of Austria stretches between Switzerland and Hungary. In the north, the Danube, Austria's only waterway connection with the world, carves its way past declining mountains and continues into Hungary and toward the Black Sea. In the opposite direction navigation is possible into Germany and, eventually, the North Sea. The area near the Danube is the urban and economic core of Austria. Climatic boundaries generally follow topographic features, thus the climate varies from humid continental to montane.

History

Traces of many cultures and tribes have been found in Austria, but as a historical entity it owes its existence to the Kingdom of the Franks, who developed it as their eastern borderland during the ninth and tenth centuries.

Under the reign of the House of Habsburg, Austria evolved into a unit of Central Europe's largest multi-ethnic empire. The termination of the Habsburg monarchy in 1918 led to the creation of the Austrian nation-state, which lasted only until German annexation in 1938. In the aftermath of World War II, Allied forces occupied the country and split it into several occupied zones. Full independence was returned in 1955. In 1995, Austria became a member of the European Union.

Population/Culture

Most of the population resides in urban areas. The most heavily populated area is along the Danube between Salzburg and Vienna. Along with other countries in the region, Austria shares an uncertain demographic future and rapidly decreasing birth rates.

Austrians are the southern branch of the German ethnic group, with only variations in dialect differentiating them. They have traditionally formed a majority of the population in terms of numbers and distribution. Minority groups, such as Slovenians, Croats, and Hungarians reside in the border areas. Immigrants from southeastern European nations—Turkey and former Yugoslavia, in particular—have created a sizable population shift in recent decades. Catholicism is the predominant religion, but Muslims constitute a growing religious minority. Many pre-Christian (particularly Celtic and Germanic) religious traditions remain an integral part of annual festivals in the Alpine villages.

There is no single Austrian cuisine; rather it is a blend of Hungarian, Italian, and German influences, reflecting the extent of the once-mighty Habsburg Empire. Hearty stews, dumplings, goulash variations, some pasta, and fluffy dessert pastry are standard items on the menu.

Every summer, music lovers from all over the world flock to the birthplace of composer Wolfgang Amadeus Mozart for the Salzburg Festival. Other Austrians who have had a major impact on western culture include psychiatrist Sigmund Freud, artist Gustav Klimt, and composers Joseph Haydn, Gustav Mahler, and Franz Schubert.

Administration/Government

The structure of the national government varies little from others across Europe. At the core is a parliamentary democratic system with separation of powers and two chambers of national assembly. Presidential powers mainly fall in the ceremonial domain, which allows political parties to exercise their managerial skills in forming coalition governments.

Economy/Industry

Most economic indices list Austria among the world's most developed countries. Its ability to successfully diversify the service sector has been the key factor in a country with limited natural resources and raw materials.

Despite a landlocked position, Austria has managed to serve as the bridge between eastern and western European economies. A significant portion of domestic income comes from tourism, especially the highly developed sector that is based on winter sports.

Sound fiscal policies, low unemployment rates, and controlled inflation—supported by membership in the European Union—bode well for a positive economic outlook and bright future for Austria.

MILESTONE EVENTS

1918–1920 Formation of Austrian independent state
1938 German annexation of Austria
1939–1945 World War II
1955 Restoration of independence
1995 Austria joins the European Union
2002 The Danube bursts its banks; 100 people are killed in flood

SWITZERLAND

Official name Swiss Confederation (Schweiz [German]; Suisse [French]; Svizzera [Italian]; Svizra [Romansh])
Land area 15,355 square miles (39,770 km²)
Border countries Germany, Liechtenstein, Austria, Italy, France
Capital Bern
Highest & lowest points Dufourspitze (Monte Rosa) 15,200 feet (4,634 m); Lake Maggiore 640 feet (195 m)
Climate Temperate
Population 7,582,000
Language(s) Official: German, French, Italian, Romansh
Ethnicity German 65%, French 18%, Italian 10%, Roma 1%, other 6%
Religion Roman Catholic 41.8%, Protestant 35.3%, Muslim 4.3%, other Christian 2.2%, other 1%, unspecified 4.3%, none 11.1%
Government Federal democratic republic
Currency Swiss franc
Human Development Index 0.955 (ranked 7th out of 177 countries)

Above left The White Turf Tournament has taken place during February on the frozen St Moritz lake since 1907. There are trotting and short-distance flat races, as well as *skikjöring,* where a skier is towed around the track by a riderless horse.

GERMANY
FRANCE
AUSTRIA
LIECHTENSTEIN
SWITZERLAND
ITALY
Basel
Zürich
Sankt Gallen
Neuchâtel
BERN
Luzern
Chur
Lausanne
Genève
Sion
Locarno
Dufourspitze

Switzerland

Map Reference Pages 226–229

Switzerland is a small landlocked alpine country with many of its peaks reaching over 13,000 feet (4,000 m) above sea level. The most famous of these is the Matterhorn at 14,692 feet (4,478 m). The numerous passes through the Alps have long enabled movement between northern and southern Europe. Trains, cog railways, and aerial cable cars connect the mountain regions. Currently the world's largest railway base tunnel system through the St Gotthard massif is under construction. It is planned that the base tunnel will be ready in 2015 for high-speed trains to operate at 155 miles per hour (250 km/h), dramatically shortening commuting times between northern and southern Europe.

Physical Geography

Switzerland boasts over 1,158 square miles (3,000 km²) of mountain glaciers. The Aletschgletscher is the largest in Europe with an area of 46 square miles (118 km²). Swiss rivers flow into the North Sea, the Mediterranean, and the Black Sea. Hundreds of glacial lakes dot the landscape, the largest being Lake Geneva. Many other lakes result from the damming of rivers in the Alps and the northern Mittelland for hydroelectric power.

Switzerland's climate is temperate, varying from cooler alpine to warmer Mediterranean. Rainfall is moderate, and spread throughout the year. The "Föhn," a roaring south or north wind, crosses the Alps, typically raining out on the windward side and heating up when dropping into the leeward valleys.

History

The Swiss confederation can be traced back to August 1291, when three valleys—Uri, Schwyz, and Unterwalden—swore an oath to unite against Habsburg rule. This was recorded on parchment as "Bundesbrief." Over time more states joined, eventually leading to independence from the Holy Roman Empire in 1648 under the Treaty of Westphalia. Napoleon invaded Switzerland in 1798 and established the Helvetic Republic. This resulted in power being centralized, but the move was not liked by the Swiss.

The country regained self-rule through the 1803 *Act of Mediation,* and 19 cantons were established within a confederation. Following Napoleon's defeat in 1815, two of the terms of the Congress of Vienna were independence and neutrality for Switzerland. A further term of the treaty allowed the country to incorporate Valais, Neuchâtel, and Geneva as cantons, and thus increase its size.

Population/Language

There are four recognized national languages (German, French, Italian, and Romansh), and English is widely spoken. Switzerland's ethnic composition and culture has been strongly influenced by its neighboring countries.

Over centuries, Switzerland has been a refuge for many famous artists in times of political crisis or war. In recent years, there has been an influx of wealthy business people, artists, and sporting personalities from other countries (particularly Germany), especially to Geneva and Zurich.

Culture

The Swiss have a strong humanitarian culture. The Red Cross started here, and they host the United Nations Human Rights Council.

Small-scale traditional farming and herding still occurs in many areas. Many city people maintain a small garden plot or window boxes with flowers and kitchen herbs.

Traditional culture is expressed in poetry, folk music, dance, woodcarving, and embroidery. The well-known Alpine "yodel," which arose as a means of communication in the mountains, is a distinctive part of traditional Swiss music, along with the accordion or Schwiizerörgeli, and the long wooden trumpet-like alp-horn. The legend of Wilhelm Tell and the novel *Heidi* by Johanna Spyri (1827–1901) are two icons of Swiss folk-lore.

Administration/Government

Switzerland is a federal democratic republic consisting of 26 states called cantons. It adopted a federal constitution in 1848 that provided for a central authority while leaving the cantons the right to self-govern on local and regional issues. The constitution was revised in 1891 with very strong democratic elements, which remain unique even today. Continued political, economic, and social improvement has characterized Swiss history.

The capital city, Bern, is the seat of federal government. Zürich, Basel, and Geneva are economic centers. Geneva is also the seat of several agencies of the United Nations and other international institutions.

Economy/Industry

Switzerland has a stable modern market economy, one of the wealthiest, most powerful, and competitive in the world. Per capita GDP is higher than in the United States, Japan, and other major western European economies. Switzerland boasts several large multi-national corporations including UBS, Zurich Financial Services, Nestlé, Credit Suisse, and ABB.

The economy is based on banking, insurance services, tourism, the pharmaceutical industry, mechanical and electronic precision instruments, and the biotech industries.

MILESTONE EVENTS

1291 The states of Uri, Schwyz, and Unterwalden (known as the "Ur-Kantone") unite against surrounding aggressors
1648 Declaration of independence; Switzerland becomes an independent nation
1812 The Swiss Federation declares its neutrality
1848 The Swiss Federation changes from a union of states to a confederation; federal constitution ("Bundesverfassung") is set up
1864 Henri Dunant of Geneva founds the International Red Cross (IKRK)
1971 Swiss people vote for women's national suffrage
1978 Some villages in the Jurassic mountains leave the Canton of Bern and found the new French-speaking Canton Jura (capital Delémont JU)
October 1984 The combined/united Federal Assembly (Vereinigte Bundesversammlung) elects Elisabeth Kopp as the first woman Bundesrat (Federal Councillor)
1999 Ruth Dreifuss becomes first female president of the Bundesrat (Bundesratspräsident)
April 1999 Swiss people vote to accept a new federal constitution (Bundesverfassung)
September 2002 Switzerland becomes a full member of the United Nations

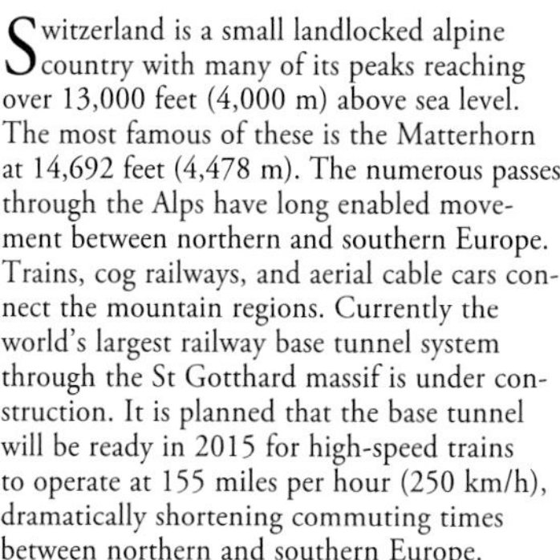

Above The Kapellbrücke (Chapel Bridge), built in 1333 over the Reuss River, Lucerne, is the oldest covered bridge in Europe. The octagonal brick Wasserturm (Water Tower) has variously been used as a prison, watchtower, treasury, and torture chamber.

Left This classic bucolic scene is dramatically punctuated by Schreckhorn, a peak in the Bernese Alps. Connection to the land and the agrarian–herder lifestyle is still deeply felt among Switzerland's rural residents.

GERMANY

Official name Federal Republic of Germany (Bundesrepublik Deutschland)
Land area 134,845 square miles (349,223 km²)
Border countries Denmark, Poland, Czech Republic, Austria, Luxembourg, Switzerland, France, Belgium, the Netherlands
Capital Berlin
Highest point Zugspitze 9,718 feet (2,962 m)
Climate Humid and moderate continental
Population 82,370,000
Language(s) Official: German; several minority languages recognized regionally
Ethnicity German 91.5%, Turkish 2.4%, other 6.1%
Religion Roman Catholic 34%, Protestant 34%, Muslim 3.7%, other or unaffiliated 28.3%
Government Republic
Currency Euro
Human Development Index 0.935 (ranked 22nd out of 177 countries)

DENMARK
Baltic Sea
North Sea
Kiel
Hamburg
Bremen
BERLIN
Potsdam
POLAND
NETHERLANDS
Hannover
Braunschweig
Magdeburg
Münster
Bielefeld
Duisburg
Dortmund
Halle
Leipzig
Dresden
Essen
Kassel
Düsseldorf
Leverkusen
Erfurt
Köln
BELGIUM
Aachen
Bonn
GERMANY
CZECH REPUBLIC
Koblenz
Mainz
Frankfurt am Main
Würzburg
LUXEMBOURG
Mannheim
Heidelberg
Nürnberg
Saarbrücken
Karlsruhe
FRANCE
Stuttgart
Ulm
München
Freiburg im Breisgau
Zugspitze
SWITZERLAND
AUSTRIA
LIECHTENSTEIN

Germany

Map Reference Pages 226–227

Right Sections of the Berlin Wall remain as a monument to this infamous symbol of division, isolation, and oppression. Dividing East and West Germany for 28 years, its dismantling saw Germany reunited as one nation.

Below Scenic Lake Königssee, in the extreme southeast of Bavaria, is the deepest lake in Germany. Formed by glacial action during the last ice age, the lake is reputed to have the cleanest water in the country.

Germany is one of the largest Western European countries. Except for the Benelux neighbors, its political boundaries mainly follow major features in the physical landscape. In the south the high slopes of the Alps form the border with Switzerland and Austria. The river Oder separates Germany and Poland, while the upper flow of the Rhine is the boundary with France. Just a short land bridge to Denmark interrupts the northern coastline.

Physical Geography

Until recent centuries the countryside was heavily forested. Rolling hills, mostly below 1,000 feet (304 m) in elevation, are the dominant landscape in southern and central Germany. Then the horizon opens into the North European Plain, Germany's northern third, with a minimal change in elevation. The influence of the Atlantic Ocean accounts for significant annual rainfall. A continental climate is found over most of Germany's territory, with noticeable seasonal regional variations. Bavaria and the rest of the southeast receive unequal rainfall distribution compared with the north and northeast. Melting snowfall in the spring and heavy summer rains often cause serious floods, especially in the northern lowlands and near the Rhine.

History

Germany's history is one of social and geographic separation. The Roman Empire controlled the present-day south, but the north was in the hands of various Celtic and Germanic tribes. Following the demise of the Roman Empire, the Franks eventually integrated most German lands into their sphere of interests. During the ninth century, the descendants of Charlemagne separated Germany into several kingdoms. Otto I reunified them in the mid-tenth century and Germany became part of the Holy Roman Empire.

The sixteenth century saw another separation of German lands, this time as the result of the Protestant Reformation. The 1555 Peace of Augsburg led to the religious division of Catholic (southern) and Protestant (northern) Germany, following the decision that the religion of a ruler should be the religion of his people. The Thirty Years' War (1618–1646) would also devastate Germany. Two centuries later the Prussians emerged as a force powerful enough to unify Germany as a nation-state in 1871.

As the German Empire the country grew in power, but the loss of World War I led to its replacement by the short-lived Weimar Republic. Germany's darkest age arrived with the election of Adolf Hitler as chancellor in 1933 and subsequent Nazi Party dictatorship, which lasted until 1945 and the end of World War II. In the aftermath of the war German lands were divided again into West (democratic) and East (communist) Germany. Finally, after the collapse of the Berlin Wall in 1989 and the end of the Cold War, Germany was united again.

Population

Germany is a rapidly ageing nation whose demographic trends resemble other post-industrial societies. Birth rates for German-born residents continue to decline and population models project the possibility of a serious decline in the near future. Only some immigrant groups have replacement-level or higher birth rates. Geographical distribution of population favors heavily industrialized and urbanized areas, such as the zones between Stuttgart and Frankfurt, Bonn and Dortmund, and the Chemnitz–Dresden–Leipzig triangle in former East Germany. Berlin is the largest metropolitan center. Westward migration from the former East Germany to the more economically developed West has been substantial.

Germany hosts large numbers of foreign workers and immigrants, some having resided in the country for decades. Demand for labor led to an open-door immigration policy during the 1960s and 1970s, particularly for workers from southeastern Europe, Italy, and Turkey. In the 1990s refugees from former Yugoslavia increased the number of immigrants, who account for up to 9 percent of the population.

Culture

Germans are of Indo-European background and speak a language closely related to English and the Scandinavian languages. Their ethnic identity did not evolve as a single unit; rather they represent an accumulation, over many centuries, of similar, but not identical, groups. They have successfully assimilated others into their cultural stock, especially Slavs, but Germans form over 90 percent of the population. Among the Slavic groups, Luzice Serbs are the most numerous; 100,000 reside near

Left Vines reach down to the historic half-timbered houses that line the streets of Assmannshausen, a quaint village in Rheingau, one of Germany's 13 wine regions. The area is renowned for its red wine, Assmannshäusser, which is made from pinot noir grapes.

the border of Poland and the Czech Republic. In regard to language, geographical differences are pronounced, with a strong north–south dialectical divide, to the degree that mutual understanding is sometimes difficult. The three main groups of dialects are southern or High German, Central, and northern or Low.

The general European trend toward secularization is seen in Germany. The country is almost equally divided between Protestants, Catholics, those of other faiths, or non-religious. Many former East Germans, impacted by half a century of communism, consider themselves agnostic or atheistic. Immigrants from Turkey, the Middle East, and North Africa form the second largest Muslim population in Western Europe.

Germans, the world's most passionate beer drinkers in terms of consumption, place a high emphasis on recreational activities. They enjoy more international leisure travel than any other nation.

MILESTONE EVENTS

1517 Martin Luther's 95 Theses signify the beginning of widespread Protestant reformation

1871 Germany is unified as an empire under Prussian dominance

1914 Germany declares war on France and Russia

1918 End of World War I—Germany is defeated by Allies

1933 Election victory lifts Nazis to power

1939–1945 World War II

1949 Creation of separate Federal Republic of Germany and German Democratic Republic

1961 Erection of the Berlin Wall, which remains until 1989

1990 Reunification of Germany

2002 Germany adopts the euro as its currency

2005 Angela Merkel becomes Germany's first woman chancellor

Administration/Government

Germany is a federal republic composed of 16 states, five of which have been added from former East Germany.

The political scene has been dominated for decades by two powerful parties: The center-left Social Democrats (SPD) and the center-right Christian Democrats (CDU). Because the electorate is always sharply divided, both parties draw support from smaller parties to form government, and thus coalition governments are very much the norm.

The chancellor (prime minister) is selected from the party winning the most votes, and assumes executive powers. The president of the republic holds ceremonial status and only sporadically assumes the power of the office.

Economy/Industry

Germany was late to enter the Industrial Revolution, but once it started, industrial development never ceased. It slowed during times of national hardship, but traditionally hard-working Germans have created the world's third-largest economy, emphasizing the expansion of the manufacturing sector and a close relationship with other European economies. Being a charter member of the European Coal and Steel Community elevated Germany to the status of a leading exporting country. Every year more than one trillion dollars worth of goods are exported worldwide, mostly expensive electronic items, machinery, and a variety of technologically advanced finished products.

A well-developed infrastructure supports economic needs. A network of expressways connects all corners of the country, and the high-speed railroad system is in the process of expansion. Waterways are highly utilized as well. The Rhine–Main–Danube canal connects the North Sea with the Black Sea and is Europe's most important inland waterway. Two continuing obstacles to even greater economic growth are the reconstruction of former East Germany and above-average unemployment rates.

Vineyards of Rhine and Mosel

A drive through the majestic river valleys of Mosel and middle Rhine shows an astonishing fusion of cultural and natural landscapes in the form of viticulture, or grape-growing. Although famous for its lager beers, Germany has a very long history of wine production. The Romans established the first vineyards in this region, using the waterways to transport wine to thirsty troops stationed in the British Isles and elsewhere. Cultivation here has changed little since ancient times. Very steep slopes do not allow large machinery to ease the back-breaking work of caring for the grapes. Labor-intensive viticulture throughout the season must be done on narrow terraces built to hold individual rows of vines. Manual harvest is the only option, especially for grapes producing the highest quality wines, which require gentle handling. The region is famous for the Riesling grape used mostly for white wines. Extra sweet *eiswein*, or ice wine, is another example of the struggle necessary to create a superb product. When temperatures fall well below freezing late in the year, workers climb the slopes to pick the frozen grapes scattered throughout the vineyard. The yield is limited but the grapes have a high sugar content. The best individual grapes are then selected to make the highly sought-after wine.

Above The neo-Romanesque Neuschwanstein Castle is spectacularly located on a mountain top near Hohenschwangau, Bavaria. It was built by King Ludwig II, partly to pay homage to famous German composer Richard Wagner. Tragically, the castle was nearing completion at the time of Ludwig's untimely death in 1886.

Autobahn

When Allied troops occupied Germany during World War II they were impressed with the well-organized transportation infrastructure. So impressive was the autobahn, the multi-lane highway that allowed high-speed transport of people and goods, that in the 1950s President Eisenhower used it as a model for the US Interstate highway system, as did other nations, to develop similar roads.

The first autobahn was built in 1935, connecting Frankfurt with Darmstadt. Today an extensive network of two- or three-lane autobahns connects the entire country. Except in potentially dangerous areas, construction zones, and junctions, a speed limit is not imposed and the left lane is reserved only for overtaking slower vehicles. Despite this lack of regulation, which many Germans with fast cars and motorcycles gladly take advantage of, the rate of accidents remains similar to that recorded on highways with strict speed limits.

Below An oom-pah band strikes up a tune in Traunstein, Bavaria. Often associated with beer halls, this lively Bavarian band music is also heard at celebrations and festivals.

LITHUANIA

Official name Republic of Lithuania (Lietuvos Respublika)
Land area 25,176 square miles (65,200 km²)
Border countries Latvia, Belarus, Poland, Russia
Capital Vilnius
Highest point Juozapines Kalnas 963 feet (293 m)
Climate Transitional, maritime, and continental
Population 3,565,000
Language(s) Official: Lithuanian, plus Russian and Polish
Ethnicity Lithuanian 83.4%, Polish 6.7%, Russian 6.3%, other 3.6%
Religion Roman Catholic 79%, Russian Orthodox 4.1%, Protestant (including Lutheran and Evangelical Christian Baptist) 1.9%, other or unspecified 5.5%, none 9.5%
Government Parliamentary democracy
Currency Litas
Human Development Index 0.862 (ranked 43rd out of 177 countries)

LATVIA
Biržai
Telšiai
Šiauliai
Baltic Sea
Klaipėda
Radviliškis
Panevėžys
Visaginas
LITHUANIA
Tauragė
Kėdainiai
Utena
Jonava
Kaunas
RUSSIAN FEDERATION
Marijampolė
VILNIUS
Alytus
Juozapinės Kalnas
POLAND
BELARUS

Lithuania

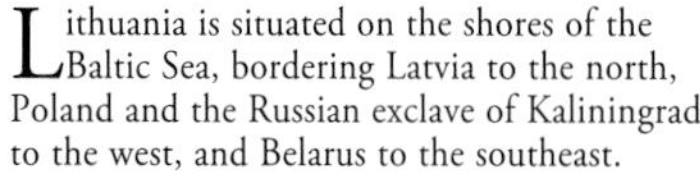

Map Reference Pages 224–225

Above right The beautiful lakeside village of Trakai, Lithuania, lies resplendent with its island castle. Commissioned by Grand Duke Kestutis, construction took place in three phases, beginning in the fourteenth century.

Below right This windmill is one of 140,000 items exhibited in the Latvian Open-Air Ethnographic Museum in Riga.

Below A group of dancers perform in Lithuania's capital, Vilnius. Traditional folk dancing reflects all aspects of Lithuanian life—its history, its morals, and the nation's character as a whole.

Lithuania is situated on the shores of the Baltic Sea, bordering Latvia to the north, Poland and the Russian exclave of Kaliningrad to the west, and Belarus to the southeast.

Physical Geography

The topography is dominated by lakes, wetlands, and forests, with maximum elevation below 1,000 feet (300 m). The climate is transitional between maritime and continental. Winters and summers are wet and moderate.

History

Lithuanian lands were united in 1236 by Mindaugas, the first known Grand Duke of Lithuania, who was crowned king in 1251, and is generally considered to be the founder of the Lithuanian state. During the fourteenth and early fifteenth centuries, the Grand Duchy of Lithuania was considerably larger, occupying the territories of present-day Belarus, Ukraine, and parts of Poland and Russia.

In 1569, Lithuania and Poland formed the Polish–Lithuanian Commonwealth. In 1795, the state was dissolved and its lands were taken over by the Russian Empire, Prussia, and Austria. Most of Lithuania was incorporated into the Russian Empire and the rest into Prussia. Lithuania re-established its independence in 1918.

In June 1940 Lithuania fell under the control of the Soviet Union and a year later came under Nazi German occupation. The Soviet Union regained control over Lithuania in 1944. Lithuania proclaimed independence from the USSR on March 11, 1990. In 2004 it joined NATO and the European Union.

Population

Ethnic Lithuanians make up the majority of population. Poles, Russians, and Belarusians are the main ethnic minorities representing 6.7 percent, 6.3 percent, and 1.1 percent of the total population respectively.

Culture

Lithuanian is the official language. Russian and Polish are spoken in their respective communities. Most Lithuanians belong to the Catholic Church, which has been the major denomination since the Christianization of the country at the end of the fourteenth century. The Russian minority belongs to the Russian Orthodox Church. Protestantism, Judaism, and Islam are also practiced.

Lithuania has a history of folk music, made up of romantic and wedding songs, as well as work and archaic war songs played on flutes, zithers, and other instruments. There are also many regional Baltic folk music festivals.

Lithuanian cuisine is based around potatoes and meat. One of the most popular dishes is *cepelinai*, an oval-shaped potato dumpling filled with ground meat. It got its name because it is shaped like the Zeppelin aircraft.

Administration/Government

The popularly elected president appoints the prime minister subject to approval by the parliament. The legislature is represented by the unicameral parliament (Seimas) with 141 members. The constitutional court, the supreme court, and the court of appeal make up the judiciary branch of the government.

Economy/Industry

The economy is increasing steadily, with annual GDP growth rate at 6–10 percent. The country's largest business operates in the field of oil refining, but industry is quite diversified, with information technology, biotechnology, plastics, high-tech machinery and electrical equipment, textiles and clothing, furniture and wood processing, food, construction, and tourism sectors. The combined service sector contributes about half of the national income and employs nearly two-thirds of the workforce.

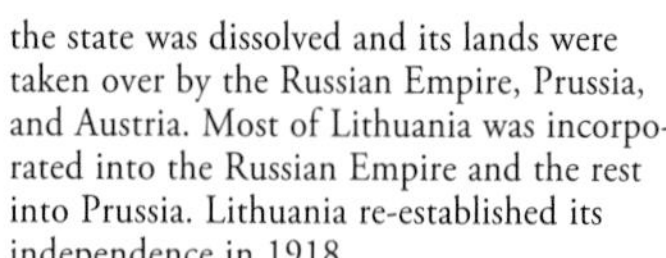

ESTONIA
Gulf of Riga
Valmiera
Alūksne
Ventspils
Talsi
Cēsis
Gulbene
Baltic Sea
Jūrmala
RIGA
Madona
Saldus
LATVIA
Liepāja
Jelgava
Aizkraukle
Rēzekne
Jēkabpils
RUSSIAN FEDERATION
LITHUANIA
Daugavpils
BELARUS

Latvia

Map Reference Pages 224–225

Latvia lies on the eastern shores of the Baltic Sea, bordered by Estonia to the north, Belarus and Lithuania to the south, and Russia to the east.

Physical Geography

Latvia is a low-lying country, mostly plains with some hills in the east. Woodlands cover about 40 percent and are a valuable economic resource. The climate is maritime: Wet, with quite moderate winters and mild summers.

History

Baltic tribes had settled in the region by around 900 CE. In the thirteenth century, a confederation of feudal nations known as Livonia developed. It included the territory that presently makes up Latvia and southern Estonia. After the Livonian War (1558–1583), the area fell under Polish and Lithuanian control. In 1795, the area was incorporated into the Russian Empire. Independence was proclaimed in 1918. Latvia was taken over by the USSR in 1940 but Nazi forces devastated the country. The Soviet Union regained control in 1944. Latvia re-established its independence in 1991, and joined both NATO and the European Union in 2004.

Population/Culture

Latvians comprise nearly 60 percent of the population. Russians are the second largest ethnic group, and Lithuanians, Ukranians, Poles, Baltic Germans, Jews, Estonians, and Belarusians make up the remainder. Latgalians, a culturally and linguistically distinct subgroup, inhabit the Latgale region in eastern Latvia. Another indigenous group is the Livonians, who speak the nearly extinct Finno-Ugric Livonian language.

Latvian, which belongs to the Baltic group of the Indo-European languages, is the official language. The Latgalian dialect is protected by law as a historical variation of the Latvian language. Russian is also widely spoken. Lutheranism is the main religion.

A distinctive feature of Latvian culture is the log house, which takes different forms in various parts of the country. Folk songs are an integral part of national identity and encompass the entire spectrum of life.

Administration/Government

The executive branch of the government is represented by the president, who is elected by the parliament for a four-year term without term limits. The head of the government, the prime minister, is appointed by the president. The legislature is the unicameral parliament (Saeima), with 100 members elected by proportional representation from party lists by popular vote to serve four-year terms. The judiciary branch consists of the supreme and constitutional courts.

Economy/Industry

The main component of Latvia's economy is the service sector, which contributes nearly three-quarters of the GDP, employing about two-thirds of the available workforce. The industrial sector is represented by the manufacturing of vehicles (such as buses, vans, automobiles, and railroad cars), agricultural machinery, synthetic fibers, fertilizers, washing machines, electronics, pharmaceuticals, processed foods, and textiles. Latvia has limited natural resources with deposits of peat, limestone, dolomite, and amber. Agriculture constitutes only a small part of the economy, producing grain, sugar beets, potatoes, other vegetables, beef, pork, milk, eggs, and fish.

LATVIA

Official name Republic of Latvia (Latvijas Republika)
Land area 24,554 square miles (63,589 km²)
Border countries Estonia, Russia, Belarus, Lithuania
Capital Riga
Highest point Galzina Kalns 1,024 feet (312 m)
Climate Maritime, wet
Population 2,245,000
Language(s) Official: Latvian, plus Russian, Lithuanian, Latgalian, Livonian
Ethnicity Latvian 57.7%, Russian 29.6%, Belarusian 4.1%, Ukrainian 2.7%, Polish 2.5%, Lithuanian 1.4%, other 2%
Religion Lutheran (majority), Roman Catholic, Russian Orthodox
Government Parliamentary democracy
Currency Lat
Human Development Index 0.855 (ranked 45th out of 177 countries)

Left Girls affirm Latvian national unity by wearing traditional costume for important holidays and events, including the Song and Dance Festival, held every five years since 1873.

Gulf of Finland
Baltic Sea
TALLINN
Kohtla-Järve
Sillamäe
Rakvere
Jõhvi
Kärdla
Haapsalu
Paide
Hiiumaa
ESTONIA
RUSSIAN FEDERATION
Pärnu
Tartu
Kuressaare
Viljandi
Saaremaa
Võru
Gulf of Riga
Valga
Suur Munamägi
LATVIA

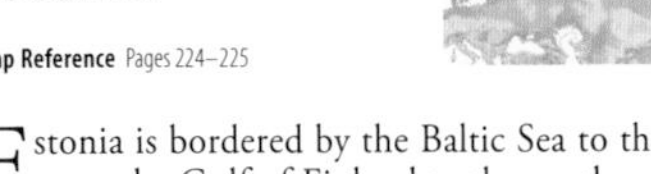

Estonia

Map Reference Pages 224–225

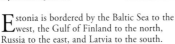

Estonia is bordered by the Baltic Sea to the west, the Gulf of Finland to the north, Russia to the east, and Latvia to the south.

Physical Geography

Estonia is a flat, low-lying country; the highest point is only 1,043 feet (318 m). Forests cover 47 percent of the land and play an important economic role. Estonia has around 1,500 islands, over 1,400 lakes, many rivers and bogs, and an extensive, indented coastline. The climate is maritime, with moderate winters and cool summers.

History

Hunting and fishing communities lived in the area that is now Estonia around 6500 BCE. In the Middle Ages, Estonia became part of the German Livonian Confederation, but after the Livonian War in 1561, fell under Swedish control. In 1721 the Swedish empire lost Estonia to Russia. Estonia achieved its independence in 1918, which lasted for 22 years. In August 1940, Estonia was formally incorporated into the Soviet Union.

During World War II the country was occupied by Nazi Germany. Soviet troops once again took control in 1944. Estonia formally declared independence on August 20, 1991, and regained its sovereignty following the dissolution of the USSR.

Population/Culture

Ethnic Estonians comprise close to 70 percent of the total population. Russians constitute about a quarter of the population. Minorities of Belarusians, Ukrainians, and Finns exist.

The official language is Estonian, a Finno-Ugric language closely related to Finnish. Russian is also widely spoken by the older generation. Estonians traditionally practice Evangelical Lutheranism.

Estonian culture draws from its rich indigenous heritage. Literature, theater, music, and other forms of the arts are important, while impressive churches reflect the deep-rooted traditions of Christianity.

Administration/Government

The executive branch is represented by the president who is elected by parliament for a five-year term and is eligible for a second term. The prime minister is nominated by the president and approved by parliament, which also approves the council of ministers appointed by the prime minister. The parliament (Riigikogu) has 101 members, elected by popular vote for a four-year term. The judiciary is represented by the national court, led by a chairperson who is appointed by parliament for life.

Economy/Industry

Estonian industry includes engineering, electronics, wood and wood products, and textiles. A growing information technology and telecommunications sector accounts for about 30 percent of GDP. Agricultural produce includes potatoes, other vegetables, livestock, dairy products, and fish.

ESTONIA

Official name Republic of Estonia (Eesti Vabariik)
Land area 16,685 square miles (43,211 km²)
Border countries Russia, Latvia
Capital Tallinn
Highest point Suur Munamagi 1,043 feet (318 m)
Climate Maritime, wet
Population 1,308,000
Language(s) Official: Estonian, plus Russian
Ethnicity Estonian 67.9%, Russian 25.6%, Ukrainian 2.1%, Belarusian 1.3%, Finn 0.9%, other 2.2%
Religion Evangelical Lutheran 13.6%, Orthodox 12.8%, other Christian 1.4%, unaffiliated 34.1%, other and unspecified 32%, none 6.1%
Government Parliamentary republic
Currency Kroon
Human Development Index 0.860 (ranked 44th out of 177 countries)

Above left A farmer drives his hay cart in rural Estonia. Almost one-third of Estonia's land is dedicated to agriculture. The main crops grown are potatoes, barley, and wheat.

Left The charming old town of Tallinn, the capital of Estonia. Dating back to the twelfth century, Tallinn is the country's most important cultural and industrial center.

RUSSIAN FEDERATION

Official name Russian Federation (Rossiyskaya Federatsiya)

Land area 6,562,591 square miles (16,995,800 km²)

Border countries China, North Korea, Mongolia, Kazakhstan, Azerbaijan, Georgia, Ukraine, Poland, Belarus, Lithuania (Kaliningrad Oblast), Latvia, Estonia, Finland, Norway

Capital Moscow (Moskva)

Highest & lowest points Gora El'brus 18,481 feet (5,633 m); Caspian Sea –92 feet (–28 m)

Climate Continental, with variations across the country

Population 140,702,000

Language(s) Russian, plus many minority languages

Ethnicity Russian 79.8%, Tatar 3.8%, Ukrainian 2%, Bashkir 1.2%, Chuvash 1.1%, other or unspecified 12.1%

Religion Russian Orthodox 20%, Muslim 15%, other Christian 2%, unaffiliated or unspecified 63%

Government Federation

Currency Russian ruble

Human Development Index 0.802 (ranked 67th out of 177 countries)

Russian Federation

Map Reference Pages 236–238

Russia is the largest country in the world, spanning 11 time zones from east to west. It is slightly less than twice the size of the United States and its territory includes one-eighth of Earth's inhabited land area. Largely part of northern Asia, the area to the west of the Urals is classified as part of Europe. It is bordered by the Arctic Ocean to the north and the Pacific Ocean to the east. Russia is also unique in that it is home to more than 160 ethnicities that speak around 100 languages.

Physical Geography

The country stretches from Kaliningrad, an exclave in the west, to the Bering Strait in the east. From the Arctic islands of Franz Josef Land in the north, the country extends for about 2,800 miles (4,500 km) to the Republic of Dagestan on the shores of the Caspian Sea in the south. Its border is the longest in the world, shared with 14 neighbor countries. Russia is traditionally divided into five natural zones: The tundra zone in Siberia; the taiga, a vast zone of coniferous forests; the steppe zone; the arid zone; and the mountain zone. Russian territory contains all the major vegetation zones of the world except for tropical rainforest. The bulk of the country consists of two plains, two lowlands, two plateaus, and mountainous areas mainly concentrated in the far northeast and along the southern border.

The climate ranges from continental in most of European Russia, to subarctic in Siberia, and tundra in the polar north. More than half of the country lies above 60° north latitude and extensive regions are covered with snow for half the year. Winters are cool along the Black Sea coast and freezing in Siberia. Summers are warm in the plains and cool along the Arctic coast. In most of Siberia, the average yearly temperature is below freezing. Summer temperatures in the southernmost regions—including the summer resort area on the Black Sea coast—average 68°F (20°C). The national low temperature record is –95.8°F (–71°C), set at Verkhoyansk in north central Siberia.

History

Greek merchants introduced classical civilization to the northern shores of the Black Sea as early as the eighth century BCE. Between the third and fifth centuries CE, nomadic invasions put an end to the Bosporus Kingdom, a successor state to the Greek colonies. Turkic tribes known as Khazars ruled the steppes between the Caspian and Black seas up until the eighth century. Early Slavs, the ancestors of the Russians, settled in what is now western Russia, gradually becoming the majority of the population from the seventh century.

The Vikings followed the waterways to the Black and Caspian seas and claimed tribute from the peoples there. By about 860 CE Rurik had established a settlement at Novgorod and ruled the area. His successors moved to the south, establishing authority over Kiev, once dominated by the Khazars.

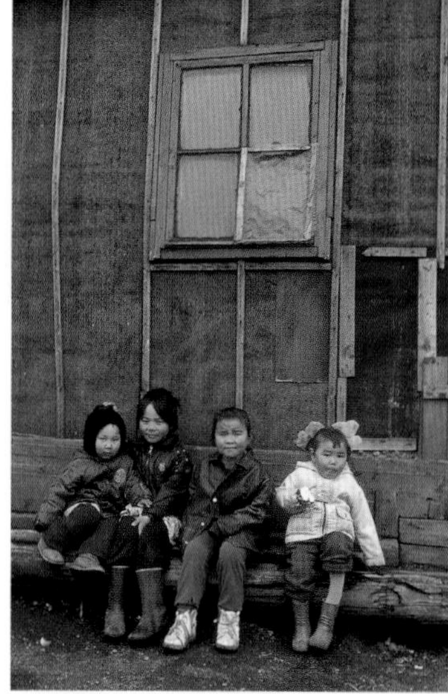

Kievan Rus', the first east Slavic state, was established along the Dnieper River valley in the ninth century and Prince Vladimir I of Kievan Rus' adopted Christianity in 988. By the eleventh century, during the reign of Yaroslav the Wise, Kievan Rus' was economically and culturally advanced, especially in architecture and literature. Kievan Rus' ceased to exist after its conquest by the Mongol Golden Horde in the thirteenth century. Only the Russian principality of Novgorod maintained its independence. The Russian army defeated the Golden Horde in a landmark battle at Kulikovo on the Don River in 1380.

In the late fifteenth and early sixteenth centuries, Ivan III (Ivan the Great) laid the foundations for a Russian national state, competing with the Grand Duchy of Lithuania for control of Novgorod, completing the defeat of the Golden Horde and establishing absolute sovereignty over all Russian princes and nobles. In the sixteenth century, Ivan IV, known as Ivan the Terrible for his autocratic and brutal rule, annexed territories to the east, including Siberia. A new code of laws was introduced in 1550 and the first Russian feudal representative body was established.

Following the death of Ivan IV, civil wars, invasions, and devastation—a time known as

Above right Of the approximately 15,000 Chukchi people worldwide, the majority live within the Chukotka Autonomous Okrug in Russia's Far Eastern Federal District.

Center The Siberian tiger *(Panthera tigris altaica)* is a critically endangered subspecies largely confined to a small area of the Amur region in Russia's Far East. The most recent census puts their numbers at between 480 and 520 individuals in the wild.

Right These buildings were the original headquarters of the Academy of Science in St Petersburg, founded by Peter the Great in 1724. The Academy was moved to Moscow in 1934.

MILESTONE EVENTS

9th century CE The first east Slavic state, Kievan Rus', established

13th–15th centuries Mongol invasion and dominance over most Russian principalities

1380 Russian army defeats the Golden Horde in landmark battle of Kulikovo

1721 Peter I (Peter the Great) defeats Sweden and opens access to the Baltic Sea; Russia becomes an empire

1812 Napoleon is defeated in his Russian campaign

1861 Serfdom is abolished

1914 Russian Empire enters World War I

1917 Bolsheviks come to power after October Revolution

December 1922 Soviet Union is established

June 22, 1941 Germany invades Soviet Union

May 1945 Soviet troops capture Berlin; end of World War II

October 4, 1957 Soviet Union launches the first satellite into outer space

April 12, 1961 A Soviet Russian cosmonaut becomes the first person in space

December 25, 1991 Formal dissolution of the Soviet Union; Russian Federation becomes the successor state

1998 Russian stock market crashes

2000 Vladimir Putin is elected president

2008 Dmitry Medvedev replaces Putin as president

the Time of Troubles—resulted in a loss of territory to the Polish-Lithuanian Commonwealth and the Swedish Empire. In 1613, a national assembly of representatives from Russian cities elected Michael Romanov as Tsar, starting a dynasty that would rule Russia until the Bolshevik Revolution in 1917.

Peter I (Peter the Great) further consolidated power in the early eighteenth century and brought about major changes to the governmental system, adopting western models. He is credited with laying the foundations of a modern state in Russia. During his reign Russia gained access to the Baltic Sea and the Gulf of Finland by defeating Sweden in the Great Northern War in 1721. Peter founded the new capital, St Petersburg, and assumed the title of emperor, transforming the Russian Tsardom into the Russian Empire in 1721.

The reign of Catherine II (Catherine the Great) during the second half of the eighteenth century extended Russian political influence over the Polish–Lithuanian Commonwealth and successfully fought the Ottoman Empire, pushing Russia's southern boundary to the Black Sea.

Napoleon Bonaparte declared war on Russia and launched an invasion in 1812. Although he briefly occupied Moscow, Russian troops drove the French all the way back to Paris.

In the early nineteenth century, Russia expanded into Transcaucasia and the North Caucasus. Alexander II came to the throne in 1855 and abolished serfdom in 1861. In the late 1870s Russia expanded into Central Asia and waged the Russo-Turkish War with the Ottoman Empire in the Balkans, supporting the independence of fellow Orthodox Slavs such as the Serbs and Bulgarians. Alexander III completed the conquest of Central Asia in the final years of the nineteenth century.

The unsuccessful Russo-Japanese War and economic downturns led to social unrest culminating in the "Bloody Sunday" of January 1905. A crowd marching to the Winter Palace in St Petersburg to present a petition to the tsar was brutally dispersed. Troops opened fire on civilians, leaving hundreds dead.

Under Nicholas II, Russia entered World War I in 1914 against Germany and Austria–Hungary. In 1917 strikes started in the capital Petrograd (formerly St Petersburg). Nicholas ordered a crackdown on demonstrators and disbanded the Duma, Russia's national assembly, triggering the February Revolution. On March 2, he abdicated and the Duma installed a provisional government. Public discontent continued with the deepening economic crisis and the continuation of the war. The socialist council (Soviet) in Petrograd, headed by Bolshevik Vladimir Lenin, created and led a national movement culminating in the seizure of power in November 1917, an event that became known as the October Revolution. The Bolshevik government withdrew from the war by signing the Treaty of Brest-Litovsk in 1918, gaining from Germany Finland, Estonia, Lithuania, Poland, parts of the territories of Latvia and Belarus, as well as the lands captured from the Ottoman Empire. The October Revolution was followed by a civil war between the Bolsheviks and their opponents, who were supported by the Allied powers. By 1921, the Red Army had secured control of the country. Land, industry, and small businesses were nationalized. A new economic policy allowed for small-scale commerce, while strategic sectors of the economy such as banking, transportation, heavy industry, and public utilities remained in the hands of the government.

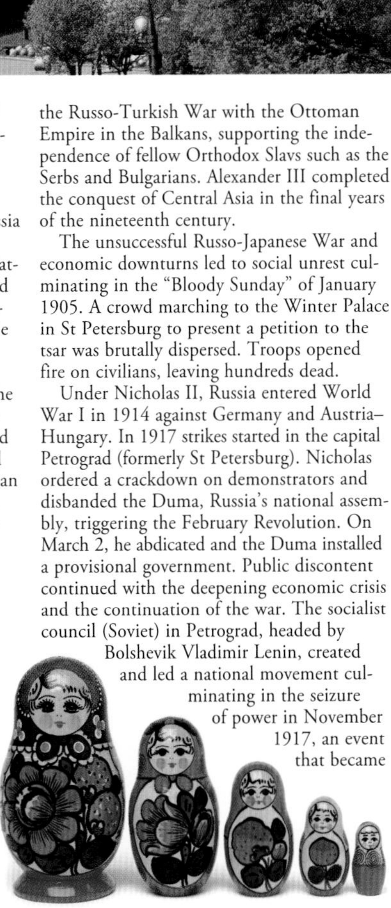

The Union of Soviet Socialist Republics (USSR or Soviet Union) was established in December 1922 by Russian Communist Party leaders. Following Lenin's death in 1924, Josef Stalin became the leader. His autocratic rule was associated with removal of political opponents and mass purges in the 1930s.

The Soviet Union became more assertive in its foreign policy, supporting the republican side in the Spanish Civil War (1936–1939) and in 1939, signed a non-aggression pact with Nazi Germany. In the same year, eastern portions of Poland were taken over by the Red Army and in December, the Soviet Union waged a costly war against Finland, gaining new northern territories. In 1940 the Soviet Union seized Bessarabia from Romania and occupied the three Baltic states of Estonia, Latvia, and Lithuania.

Above St Basil's Cathedral—officially the Cathedral of the Intercession of the Virgin by the Moat—sits on the edge of Red Square, Moscow. Built between 1555 and 1561 by order of Ivan the Terrible, it was commissioned to commemorate his victory over the Tatar Mongols in 1552.

Below A basalt plug spikes the frozen Arctic Ocean, Siberia, where volcanic activity is high.

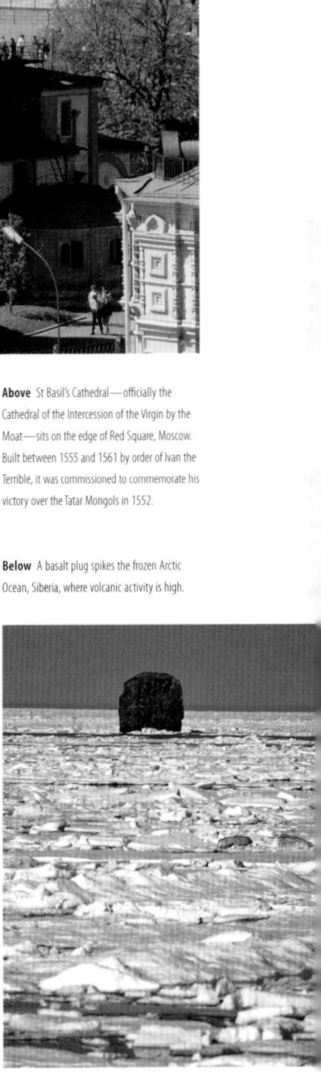

Left Russian nesting dolls *(matryoshka)* are arguably the federation's most popular souvenir. Sava Mamontov, an industrialist and arts patron, made the first set in 1890.

Right A captivating twilight settles on the Kamchatka Peninsula in Russia's Far East. The peninsula is home to more than 100 active volcanoes, making it one of the most volcanically active places on Earth.

On June 22, 1941, Germany attacked the Soviet Union without warning. In just a few months, German forces occupied the western part of the country, besieged Leningrad (formerly St Petersburg), and approached the city of Moscow. Though a successful counterattack threw the German forces back from Moscow, the Nazis retained the upper hand for another year until two major defeats in Stalingrad and Kursk turned the tide of the war.

By the end of 1943, the Red Army had managed to break through the German siege of Leningrad and liberate most of the occupied territories. By the end of 1944, they had driven the enemy into eastern Germany, and then captured Berlin in May 1945. The war claimed around 27 million lives and completely devastated the economy.

The Cold War followed World War II. The Warsaw Pact, similar to NATO, was established in 1955 between the Soviet Union and the countries of Eastern Europe. After Stalin's death in 1953, Nikita Khrushchev became leader. He was followed by Leonid Brezhnev. In the 1950s and 1960s the country was heavily industrialized and achieved remarkable success in a number of areas, most notably space exploration. The satellite *Sputnik 1* was launched in 1957, and in 1961 Major Yuri Gagarin became the first person to travel in space. A number of local wars and conflicts became arenas for rivalry between the United States and the Soviet Union including the Korean War, the Cuban Missile Crisis, and the wars in Vietnam and Afghanistan.

Above Forests of the adaptable larch *(Larix russica* and *L. gmelinii)* flourish across Siberia despite the extremes of temperature.

Above right Most indigenous Chukchis over the age of 30 can converse in their native language. However, there are concerns that younger people, particularly those living in urban areas, are losing the ability to speak their mother tongue.

In 1987 Mikhail Gorbachev started unsuccessful reforms (*perestroika)* to modernize the economy. In the 1989 revolutions, the Soviet Union lost its traditional allies in Eastern Europe. On August 19, 1991, a coup against Gorbachev, led by senior Soviet officials, failed. In the first Russian presidential election in 1991, Boris Yeltsin became president.

The Soviet Union officially was dissolved on December 25, 1991, and the Russian Federation became the successor state. In the 1990s, the country experienced severe economic crisis as a result of "shock therapy" reforms. A war in Chechnya between government forces and Chechen rebels added to the instability. In 2000 Vladimir Putin became president, bringing political stability and rapid economic growth. Putin's term ended in 2008; he was replaced by Dmitry Medvedev, who asked Putin to be prime minister.

Population

Russia is home to more than 160 distinct ethnic groups. Russians derive from the east Slavs, a group that gradually evolved into the Ukrainian, Belarusian, and Russian peoples. Russians account for nearly 80 percent of the population followed by other sizable ethnic groups of Tatars, Ukrainians, Bashkirs, Chuvashs, Chechens, and Armenians. The population is predominantly urban and has one of the lowest overall densities in the world. Density is highest in the heavily urbanized western part of Russia and is extremely low beyond the Urals and into Siberia to the east.

Culture

Russian is the official language and is the most geographically widespread language of Eurasia. It is spoken not only by the inhabitants of Russia but also by the populations of most of the former Soviet Union republics in Asia, Eastern Europe, and South Caucasus. About a quarter of the world's scientific literature is published in Russian. Russian is one of the six official languages of the United Nations, and is used for coding and storage of universal knowledge. Russia's 160 ethnic groups speak about 100 languages, and the constitution recognizes the native languages of the individual republics as official second languages.

The largest religious community is Eastern Orthodox Christianity, dominated by the Russian Orthodox Church. It is estimated that the number of believers ranges from 20 to 60 percent, a legacy of Soviet atheism. The second largest religion is Islam, whose followers comprise about 10 to 20 percent of the population. Other religions include Judaism, Protestantism, Catholicism, and Buddhism. Shamanism and a number of other pagan beliefs are practiced in remote regions by indigenous populations.

Early Russian literature consists of folk tales and a few military and religious works. The nineteenth century was the golden age of Russian culture, and literature in particular. The country boasts two of the world's greatest novelists: Leo Tolstoy *(War and Peace)* and Fyodor Dostoyevsky *(Crime and Punishment)*,

SPACE EXPLORATION

Space exploration is almost synonymous with Russia. A country with proven excellence in education and sciences became, along with the USA, one of the leading nations to push human frontiers far into outer space.

Russia, then the largest of the constituent republics of the Soviet Union, became the first country in the world to successfully launch an artificial satellite called *Sputnik 1* into outer space on October 4, 1957. This event is regarded as the start of the space race, an important part of the cultural, technological, and ideological competition between the USA and the Soviet Union during the Cold War.

On April 12, 1961, the Soviet Union astonished the world yet again by successfully launching the *Vostok 1* spaceship. Yuri Gagarin, the Soviet cosmonaut on board, became the first person in space and the first to orbit Earth.

The concept of space exploration was conceived during the Russian Empire before World War I, with the scientific writings of Konstantin Tsiolkovsky, a rocket scientist and pioneer of astronautic theory. After World War II, the quest for military dominance led both the USA and the Soviet Union to invest heavily in the development of new-generation intercontinental ballistic missiles that could carry nuclear warheads. The space exploration contest was seen as a matter of prestige and ideological supremacy.

The Soviet space program was highly classified and made up of a number of design groups responsible for various components of the program. Sergey Korolyov, a Soviet rocket engineer and designer, and a renowned figure in Russian space science, was the head of the principal design group. His identity, also classified, was made public only after his death in 1966. Successes were announced only after the fact, and failures were usually kept secret. In contrast, information about the US space program was generally available to the public. Only from the late 1980s did details about the Soviet space program become declassified.

As the space race evolved the Soviets achieved many "firsts." They obtained the first images of the moon's far side (1959); sent the first animals (dogs Belka and Strelka) to orbit Earth and return safely (1960); launched the first probes to Mars and Venus (1960–1961); completed the first spacewalk (1961); and sent the first woman (Valentina Tereshkova) into space (1963). Robotic space rover *Lunokhod 1* was the first wheeled vehicle to land on the moon (1970) and *Venera 9* became the first probe to orbit Venus and obtain photos from its surface (1975).

renowned poet Aleksandr Pushkin, and playwright Anton Chekhov. Leading twentieth-century figures include poets Boris Pasternak, Anna Akhmatova, and Joseph Brodsky, and novelists Vladimir Nabokov, Mikhail Bulgakov, and Alexandr Solzhenitsyn.

Russia is renowned for its classical music, opera, and ballet. Prominent composers include Tchaikovsky, Rachmaninoff, Stravinsky, Prokofiev, and Shostakovich. Tchaikovsky is by far the most famous. Some of his best works are the ballets *Swan Lake* and *The Nutcracker*. In the early twentieth century, musical romances—often a blend of Russian and Gypsy styles—became popular.

Thanks to its cultural and ethnic diversity, Russia has a rich folk music tradition, ranging from authentic Russian folk to the ethnic folk of Siberian tribes, with roots in shamanism. Traditional instruments include the balalaika—a three-stringed triangular sound-board played with the fingers—and the gusli. "Bard music" is a modern folk genre, often with political themes. Contemporary music—rock, heavy metal, and rap—is also popular.

Russian architecture has been influenced by Byzantine and later by Italian Renaissance and Rococo styles. St Basil's Cathedral in Moscow is one of many notable buildings in the country. The city of St Petersburg is representative of neoclassical architecture. One form of Russian traditional art is icon painting.

One of the most distinctive items of Russian art is the *matryoshka* nesting doll, a series of wooden, elaborately painted dolls that can be pulled apart to disclose another doll of a smaller size. Matryoshkas are cylindrical, rounded at the top, and without hands or legs. Most feature peasant girls in traditional dress, but images of Soviet and Russian leaders have become popular with tourists.

Also famous is Gzhel pottery, known from the fourteenth century and named after a village southeast of Moscow. It is mainly painted white with distinctive designs in blue. Over the years there have been several periods of disruption in production, but recently the quality pottery has undergone a revival and is being produced in its traditional colors.

Russian cuisine gradually incorporated western influences from the eighteenth century onward. Contact with the Caucasus, Persia, and the Ottoman Empire introduced an eastern flavor. Soups are among the main Russian dishes. They include *shchi*, a cabbage soup that has been the main first course in Russia for over millennia. *Ukha*, a hot watery fish broth, is another distinctive type of soup cooked with potatoes and other vegetables. *Pelmeni* is a traditional Eastern European (though mainly Russian) dish made with spiced minced meat filling, wrapped in thin dough made of flour. Pelmeni are boiled in water and served immediately with butter and sour cream.

Above The magnificent Rococo Catherine Palace near St Petersburg, built for Peter the Great's wife Catherine I, was ravaged during World War II, requiring extensive refurbishment to restore it to its former glory.

Administration/Government

Russia's executive branch is represented by the president, who is elected by popular vote for a four-year term and is eligible for a second term, and by the head of government, the premier, appointed by the president subject to parliamentary approval. The cabinet of ministers is also appointed by the president. The presidential administration and the security council are also part of the executive branch. The legislature consists of the federal assembly (Federalnoye Sobraniye), which is made up of the federation council (Sovet Federatsii) with 178 members appointed by the executive and legislative officials in each of the 88 federal administrative units for a four-year term, and the State Duma (Gosudarstvennaya Duma) with 450 members elected by a popular vote for a four-year term by proportional representation from party lists winning at least 7 percent of the vote.

The constitutional, supreme, and supreme arbitration courts make up the judiciary branch of the government with judges appointed for life by the federation council on the recommendation of the president.

Economy/Industry

Russia has been heavily industrialized since the first half of the twentieth century. Mining and extractive industries produce coal, oil, gas, metals, and chemicals. The manufacturing sector produces a wide range of machinery, including aircraft and space vehicles, road and rail transportation equipment, communications equipment, agricultural machinery, tractors, and construction equipment; electrical power generating and transmitting equipment; medical and scientific instruments; consumer durables; textiles; and foodstuffs. The industrial sector contributes around 40 percent to the national income and employs nearly one-third of the workforce. The defense industry, which produces ships, radar, missiles, and advanced electronic components, is one of the main branches of the economy. Armaments are the country's largest manufactured export.

Russia has the world's largest natural gas reserves, the second largest coal reserves, and eighth largest oil reserves. It is the world's leading natural gas exporter and the second leading oil exporter. Oil, natural gas, metals, and timber account for more than 80 percent of the country's exports.

Arid climate and low precipitation limit agriculture, which accounts for only about 5 percent of the GDP. The northern region focuses on livestock; the southern regions and Siberia produce grain. Agricultural produce includes grain, sugar beets, sunflower seeds, vegetables, fruits, beef, and milk. The service sector has about a 55 percent share in the GDP and employs approximately 60 percent of the available workforce.

Famous for its advanced educational system, Russia embraced the fundamental and applied sciences that serve as a basis for technological and scientific innovations. Information technologies are one of the fastest growing sectors of the economy. Software exports also contribute to the economy.

Above Russian ice dancers are among the most successful exponents of the sport, particularly at Olympic level. Alexei Sitnikov and Julia Zlobina are two of Russia's brightest stars.

Left A female Kamchatka brown bear accompanies her cubs along the edge of the Shumnaia River in Kronotsky State Biosphere Reserve. The reserve boasts the highest concentration of brown bears in the world.

POLAND

Official name Republic of Poland (Rzeczpospolita Polska)
Land area 117,563 square miles (304,465 km²)
Border countries Russia, Lithuania, Belarus, Ukraine, Slovakia, Czech Republic, Germany
Capital Warsaw (Warszawa)
Highest & lowest points Rysy 8,199 feet (2,499 m); near Raczki Elbalaskie –6½ feet (–2 m)
Climate Temperate: mild summers, frequently severe winters
Population 38,501,000
Language(s) Polish
Ethnicity Polish 96.7%, other 3.3%
Religion Roman Catholic 89.8%; Eastern Orthodox 1.3%; Protestant 0.3%; other and unspecified 8.6%
Government Republic
Currency Zloty
Human Development Index 0.870 (ranked 37th out of 177 countries)

Above right The young watch and learn: women offer sustenance to pilgrims on their way to venerate the famous religious icon, the Black Madonna of Częstochowa.

Below The sun rises on the village of Kluszkowce in the foothills of the rugged Tatra Mountains in southern Poland.

Baltic Sea
RUSSIAN FEDERATION
LITHUANIA
BELARUS
UKRAINE
GERMANY
CZECH REPUBLIC
SLOVAKIA
POLAND
Gdynia
Gdańsk
Koszalin
Elbląg
Szczecin
Olsztyn
Gorzów Wielkopolski
Bydgoszcz
Toruń
Białystok
Poznań
Płock
WARSZAWA (WARSAW)
Zielona Góra
Łódź
Radom
Lublin
Wrocław
Wałbrzych
Opole
Kielce
Katowice
Kraków
Tarnów
Rzeszów
Rysy

Poland

Map Reference Pages 226–227

Poland, on the south coast of the Baltic Sea, is bordered by Germany to the west, the Czech Republic and Slovakia to the south, Ukraine, Belarus, and Lithuania to the east, and the small Russian territory of Kaliningrad Oblast to the northeast. It is the ninth largest country in area in Europe.

Physical Geography

The north of Poland is a flat coastal plain along the Baltic Sea with sand dunes, depositional spits, and lakes that were once bays. South of this belt are several hilly regions dotted with thousands of small lakes. The Masurian Lake District in the northeast of Poland is the largest of these areas. Much of the center of the country consists of broad, fertile river valleys. To the south the terrain is increasingly mountainous. The most rugged ranges are the Sudetes, parts of the Carpathian Mountains, and the Tatra Mountains along the southern border.

History

The Polish state began in 966 CE when Mieszko I, the leader of a Slavic tribe called the Polans, was baptized into Christianity and established the Piast dynasty that governed Poland until 1370. In 1385 Poland entered into political partnership with the Grand Duchy of Lithuania, establishing the Jagiellon period, which governed until 1569 when the Polish–Lithuanian Commonwealth was formed.

Frequent and debilitating warfare against numerous tribes resulted in the partition of Polish lands in 1795 between Austria, Prussia, and Russia.

Poland declared independence in 1918 in the wake of World War I, creating the Second Polish Republic. In 1939 Poland was invaded by Nazi Germany. It suffered greatly during World War II, as more than 6 million of its citizens perished, including most of the country's 3.3 million Jews. The nation's boundaries were redrawn at the end of the war. The Soviet Union took over Polish territory in the east and Poland was given German territory in the west. A communist government took control in 1945. The Polish People's Republic was proclaimed in 1952.

In 1989–1990 the Solidarity movement triumphed in democratic elections and Lech Walesa became president. Poland is now a democratic country with a market economy. It joined NATO in 1999 and became a member of the European Union in 2004.

Population/Culture

Poland is one of the world's most ethnically and linguistically homogeneous countries. Around 97 percent of its people is Polish and speak the Polish language. Nearly 90 percent is Catholic. This homogeneity is largely a byproduct of its tragic history in World War II when the large Jewish minority was murdered during the Nazi occupation, and when Ukrainians and other minorities were repatriated by the redrawing of national boundaries.

Poland's population is now at a standstill or even in decline owing to a sharp drop in birth rates and considerable outmigration since 1990. The largest numbers of Polish émigrés live and work in the United States and in Ireland, Great Britain, and Germany.

Many of Poland's cultural traditions are linked to religious festivals. One such custom is the *Swieconka* basket, which is decorated and filled with sausages, eggs, horseradish, fruit, and bread, then taken to the church on Holy Saturday to be blessed.

MILESTONE EVENTS

966 CE Baptism of Mieszko I and start of Polish state under Piast dynasty
1385 Poland and Lithuania begin ruling partnership; start of Jagiellon Era
1569 Union of Lublin establishes Polish–Lithuanian Commonwealth
1795 Partition of Poland
1918 Polish independence and start of Second Polish Republic
1939 Invasion of Poland by Germany; start of World War II
1945 Poland reconfigured after World War II; start of Communist period
1989 Solidarity movement wins democratic elections
1990 Lech Walesa becomes president
2004 Poland joins the European Union

Administration/Government

Communist rule ended in 1989 after protests led by the labor union Solidarity *(Solidarność)* resulted in the holding of democratic elections. The president is elected by popular vote. A council of ministers is led by the prime minister. A bicameral legislature is comprised of the lower-house Sejm and the senate.

Economy/Industry

Poland's economy has grown rapidly since the market reforms of the 1980s and is considered the best example in the former Eastern bloc of successful transition from communism to a free market economy. Exports include iron and steel products, machinery, ships, automobiles, chemicals, and food products, mostly to other European Union countries.

ROMAN CATHOLICISM

The Catholic faith has been a major part of Polish life and identity since the baptism of Mieszko I in 966. In 1656, King Jan Casimir proclaimed that Mary, the mother of Jesus, would henceforth be "Queen of the Polish Crown," and that a shrine to her in Czestochowa would make the town the spiritual capital of Poland. Catholic clergy have long had high prestige and influence in Polish life. Poles took great pride in the 1978 election of their own Cardinal, Karol Wojtyla, as Pope John Paul II. In the 1980s, the Church played an important role alongside the Solidarity labor movement in the fall of communism in Poland, and has since had considerable influence in government policy.

The shrine in Czestochowa dates to the late fourteenth century. Its centerpiece is an icon of the Virgin Mary and Christ Child known as the Black Madonna. It is said to have been painted in the fifth century on wood that had come from a table belonging to the Holy Family. Polish Catholics attribute many miraculous cures to the Black Madonna, as well as the defeats of foreign invaders. The shrine attracts several million pilgrims each year.

SUB TVVM PRÆSIDIUM

GERMANY
POLAND
Liberec
Ústí nad Labem
Hradec Králové
Kladno
PRAHA
(PRAGUE)
Pardubice
Karlovy Vary
Opava
Ostrava
Olomouc
Plzeň
CZECH REPUBLIC
Jihlava
Brno
Zlín
České Budějovice
SLOVAKIA
AUSTRIA

Czech Republic

Map Reference Pages 226–227

The Czech Republic and neighboring Slovakia were created on January 1, 1993, when the nation of Czechoslovakia was dissolved and split in two. What came to be known colloquially in Eastern Europe as the "Velvet Divorce" was precipitated by a unilateral Declaration of Independence by the Slovakian parliament on July 17, 1992.

Physical Geography

The Czech Republic is ringed by a series of mountain ranges that form most of the country's borders. The Bohemian–Moravian highlands dominate the interior with the southwest characterized by the fertile valleys of the Moravian lowlands. The Czech Republic has a typical moderate continental climate with heavy rainfall in the summer.

History

The Czech identity emerged in the regions of Bohemia and Moravia in the fifth century. In 796 CE, after helping Charlemagne defeat the Avar Empire, Czech tribesmen from Moravia were granted a small fiefdom which grew to become the Great Moravian Empire, an amalgam of Czech and Slovak tribes. It lasted until the tenth century, leaving in its wake a great legacy of castles and fortified medieval towns. From 1526 until 1857 Bohemia, Moravia, and Slovakia were ruled by the Austrian Habsburgs.

The demise of the Austro-Hungarian Empire at the end of World War I led to the declaration of an independent Czechoslovakia on October 28, 1918. Tomas Garrigue Masaryk became the first president of the "First Republic," with Prague as its capital. The Nazis invaded Czechoslovakia in 1939 and remained there until the Soviet liberation of the city in 1945. Czechoslovakia was then drawn into the Soviet sphere of influence.

MILESTONE EVENTS

796 Moravian tribes granted fiefdom after helping Charlemagne defeat Avar Empire

1415 Jan Huss, populist reformer, burned as a heretic for challenging Church corruption

1419–1436 Hussite (Bohemian) Wars

1618–1648 Thirty Years' War

1745 Empress Maria Teresa expels Jews from Prague

August 23, 1866 Treaty of Prague ends Austro-Prussian War

October 28, 1918 Czechoslovakia gains independence from Austria–Hungary

1939 Nazis invade Czechoslovakia

May 1945 Prague Uprising attempts to free city from German occupation

1948 USSR takes over Czechoslovakia

1968 Prague Spring

January 1, 1993 Creation of Czech Republic

1999 Czech Republic joins NATO

August 2002 Floods ravage Prague and surrounding areas

2004 Czech Republic joins European Union

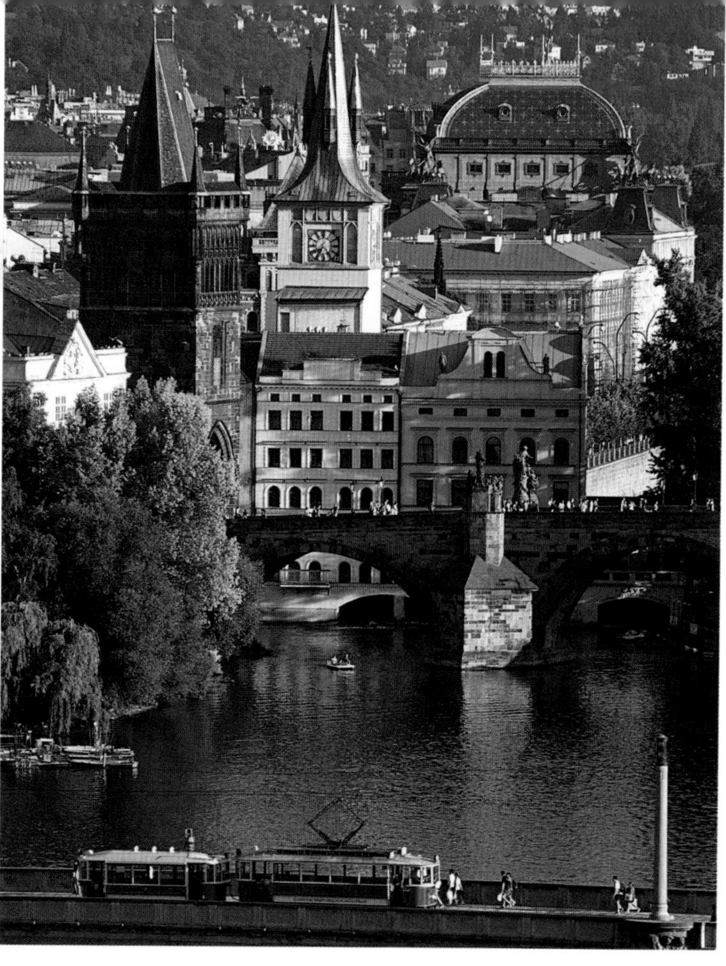

Left Built mostly during the fourteenth century under Holy Roman Emperor Charles IV, picturesque Prague possesses a host of inspiring monuments, churches, palaces, and bridges.

The "Prague Spring" of 1968 saw an attempt by the head of the Czechoslovakian Communist Party, Alexander Dubček, to give communism a "human face." His reforms included guaranteeing freedom of assembly and expression, reforming the electoral process, and the establishment of a multi-party system. On August 20 Soviet troops entered Czech territory, arrested Dubček and "accompanied him to Moscow for negotiations." Dubček was permitted to retain office until he was replaced in April 1969 by Gustav Husák, who reversed the reforms and brought Prague's bold social experiment to a close.

Population

Just over 90 percent of the population is Czech. Minorities include Slovaks, Poles, Germans, Vietnamese, and Roma. It is one of the most secular countries in Europe; 59 percent of people claim to be agnostic.

Prague: The Center of Culture

Prague's Old Town was built between the eleventh and eighteenth centuries, with excavations indicating an earlier settlement beneath Prague Castle dating to the ninth century Moravian empire. Prague became a bishopric in the tenth century. In the following 200 years the city saw the construction of truly monumental edifices such as the Romanesque Cathedral of St Vitus.

Despite a devastating by fire in 1541, the end of the 1600s saw the vestiges of the city reinvented in what is now called "Prague Baroque." Great architecture began to dominate the banks of the Vltava River, including monasteries, fortifications, and palaces. The redesigning of its streets and squares formed the basis of the Prague we know today. Prague was declared a World Heritage Site in 1992.

Administration/Government

The Czech Republic is a now multi-party parliamentary democracy with a bicameral parliament consisting of a Senate and a Chamber of Deputies, formally the Czech National Council. A Bill of Fundamental Rights and Freedoms guarantees human and civil rights.

The legal system was overhauled in 1992. The Supreme Court is the country's highest court of appeal and a separate constitutional court determines the outcome of proposed legislation. The military courts that existed in the old Czechoslovakia have now been abolished.

Economy/Industry

The Czech economy today bears very little resemblance to the state-controlled Soviet economic model of the 1960s. It has emerged as one of the fastest growing and most industrialized countries of the former USSR with minimal levels of foreign debt, a stable exchange rate, a vibrant and growing tourist industry, and total exports exceeding US$100 billion a year. The 1990s saw the privatization of many state-owned industries and today the Czech Republic receives more foreign investment dollars per head of population than any other country in Central Europe. It has negligible oil reserves and imports petroleum from Russia and Germany. Twenty percent of the country's electricity is provided by two nuclear power stations.

In 2004 the Czech Republic was admitted into the European Union, which has resulted in the reduction of trade barriers and the introduction of support mechanisms for its ailing agricultural sector, which has declined markedly and today contributes only around 4 percent of GDP.

CZECH REPUBLIC

Official name Czech Republic (Ceska Republika)

Land area 29,839 square miles (77,276 km²)

Border countries Poland, Slovakia, Austria, Germany

Capital Prague (Praha)

Highest & lowest points Mt Snezka 5,259 feet (1,602 m); Elbe River 377 feet (115 m)

Climate Temperate

Population 10,221,000

Language(s) Czech (primary), Slovak, Polish

Ethnicity Czech 90.4%, Moravian 3.7%, Slovak 1.9%, other 4%

Religion Roman Catholic 26.8%, Protestant 2.1%, other 3.3%, unspecified 8.8%, unaffiliated 59%

Government Parliamentary republic

Currency Czech koruna

Human Development Index 0.891 (ranked 32nd out of 177 countries)

Above The Gothic fifteenth-century Křivoklát Castle in Central Bohemia, Czech Republic, was founded centuries earlier in 1109. It was built primarily as a hunting lodge for the Premyslid kings. Charles IV spent his early childhood here, while later the Habsburgs used it as a prison.

Left Young women wear folk costume during celebrations to mark the Feast of St Wenceslas in Moravany, Czech Republic. The "Good King" of Christmas carol fame was, in reality, a duke. He is the patron saint of Prague.

BELARUS

Official name Republic of Belarus (Respublika Byelarus')
Land area 80,161 square miles (207,600 km²)
Border countries Latvia, Russia, Ukraine, Poland, Lithuania
Capital Minsk
Highest & lowest points Dzyarzhynskaya Hara 1,135 feet (346 m); Nyoman River 295 feet (90 m)
Climate Temperate, continental
Population 9,686,000
Language(s) Official: Belarusian, Russian; other: Polish, Ukranian, Lithuanian
Ethnicity Belarusian 81.2%, Russian 11.4%, Polish 3.9%, Ukrainian 2.4%, other 1.1%
Religion Eastern Orthodox 80%, other (including Roman Catholic, Protestant, Jewish, and Muslim) 20%
Government Republic
Currency Belarusian rouble
Human Development Index 0.804 (ranked 64th out of 177 countries)

Above right Wisent or European bison *(Bison bonasus)* can be seen in their natural habitat in the ancient woodland of Belaveskaya Forest. Once extinct in the wild, these bison were reintroduced to the forest in the 1950s, as a result of a successful breeding program using zoo animals.

zepter

Above Dmitry Meleshko of Belarus (right) and Niclas Wallin of Sweden battle it out during the International Ice Hockey Federation's World Ice Hockey Championship in Canada, 2008.

Belarus

Map Reference Pages 236–237

Belarus is bordered by Poland to the west, Latvia and Lithuania to the north, Russia to the east and Ukraine to the south. Of all the former Soviet countries, Belarus is the one most closely tied to Russia, both politically and economically. The nation's capital city, Minsk, is located on the Svislach River and is home to nearly two million people. This historic city was established before 1067 CE.

Physical Geography

The country is mostly flat, with highlands that span the country diagonally from west–southwest to east–northeast. One-third of the country is forested, and roughly another third of the land is arable. There are thousands of rivers and lakes. The climate is temperate continental. Winters are cold and summers tend to be cool and humid.

The Belaveskaya Pushcha (which continues into Poland as the Białowieża Primeval Forest), one of four World Heritage sites in Belarus, has been renowned for its virgin forest for centuries. The first recorded legislation to protect the forest, dated to 1538, instituted a death penalty for poaching wisent (European bison). The Belaveskaya Pushcha is also a Biosphere Reserve under UNESCO's Man and the Biosphere Program and is home to several internationally threatened species.

History

Slavic tribes settled in the area that is now Belarus in the sixth century CE. The history of the country goes back to the Kievan Rus' Slavic state in the ninth century. Over the centuries, the territory of present-day Belarus has come under the control of various states including the Grand Duchy of Lithuania, the Polish–Lithuanian Commonwealth, and finally the Russian Empire.

The Belarusian territories were held by the Russian Empire until their occupation by Germany during World War I. Belarus declared independence on March 25, 1918, as the Belarusian People's Republic, but was incorporated into the Soviet Union in 1919 under the name of Byelorussian Soviet Socialist Republic, or Byelorussia. Nazi Germany invaded the Soviet Union in June 1941 and occupied Byelorussia until 1944. A very heavy toll was exacted—nearly all the cities and most industry were destroyed. Much of the Jewish population was wiped out in the Holocaust.

In 1986, Byelorussia was greatly affected by the explosion at the Chernobyl nuclear power plant in neighboring Ukrainian SSR. The country's name was changed to the Republic of Belarus in 1991, and on December 8, 1991, the leaders of Belarus, Ukraine, and Russia met in Belavezskaya Pushcha to formally declare the dissolution of the Soviet Union and the formation of the Commonwealth of Independent States.

Population/Culture

Belarusians are the largest ethnic group, followed by Russians who make up about one-tenth of the population. Other groups include Poles and Ukrainians, with smaller communities of Jews, Lithuanians, and Lipka Tatars. Eighty percent of the population belongs to the Eastern Orthodox Church. Other religious groups include Catholics, Protestants, Jews, and Muslims.

Belarusian belongs to the group of East Slavonic languages. Russian, Ukrainian, Polish, and Lithuanian are also spoken by the members of their respective communities.

Belarus has its own unique brands of folk and religious music, and hosts numerous annual cultural events, one of which is the Slavianski Bazaar in Vitebsk. The Bazaar showcases talented performers in the fields of art, music, poetry, dance, and theater.

Belarus has always excelled in sports, and has won numerous medals in the Olympic Games since it was part of the Soviet Union. Ice hockey is the nation's most popular sport.

MILESTONE EVENTS

March 25, 1918 Belarus declares independence from Russia
1919 Belarus is incorporated into the Soviet Union
1941–1944 Belarus is occupied by Nazi Germany
July 27, 1990 Declaration of sovereignty from the Soviet Union
December 8, 1991 Formal dissolution of the Soviet Union; Commonwealth of Independent States is formed
March 2006 President Lukashenko wins another term

Administration/Government

The president is elected by popular vote. The presidency of Aleksandr Lukashenko, elected in 1994, was first extended to 2001 via referendum. A second referendum in 2004 ended the five-year term limits and allowed Lukashenko to stay in office. In 2006 he was re-elected with 82.6 percent of the vote in an election that was thought to be fraudulent. The prime minister and his deputies are appointed by the president.

The National Assembly (Natsionalnoye Sobranie) consists of the Council of the Republic (Soviet Respubliki) with 64 seats, and the Chamber of Representatives (Palata Predstaviteley) with 110 seats. The supreme and constitutional courts make up the judicial branch of government.

Economy/Industry

Manufacturing makes up about 40 percent of GDP and produces machine tools, tractors, trucks, earthmovers, motorcycles, televisions, chemical fibers, fertilizer, textiles, radios, and refrigerators. Belarus has few reserves of natural gas and insufficient oil reserves to meet its domestic needs. There are small deposits of iron ore, nonferrous metals, dolomite, potash, rock salt, and phosphorites. The service sector accounts for about half of the national income.

Above A reconstruction of a tenth-century Russian Orthodox church at Vitebsk, Belarus.

Right The Belaveskaya Pushcha, a remnant of the ancient European forest, is only partly held by Belarus; the border with Poland divides the forest. Both countries are working to protect this unspoiled habitat.

CZECH REPUBLIC
POLAND
SLOVAKIA
AUSTRIA
UKRAINE
HUNGARY
Žilina
Bardejov
Trenčín
Martin
Poprad
Prešov
Snina
Banská Bystrica
Zvolen
Košice
Trnava
Nitra
Lučenec
BRATISLAVA
Štúrovo

Slovakia

Map Reference Pages 226–227

Slovakia is a small landlocked country in Central Europe bordered by Poland to the north, Ukraine to the east, Hungary to the south, and Austria and the Czech Republic to the west. It was part of Czechoslovakia until January 1, 1993, when an agreement took effect dividing the country into the Czech Republic and the Slovak Republic.

Physical Geography

Most of northern Slovakia is mountainous, with the highest and most rugged peaks being in the High Tatras range of the Carpathian Mountains along the border with Poland. The Little Carpathians are foothills in the west of the country with vineyards, ski resorts, and trails for hiking and cycling. The fertile lowlands in the southwest produce grains, sugar beets, potatoes, and other crops.

History

Slovakian lands were settled by Slavic peoples in the fifth century and were ruled at various times as parts of the Kingdom of Great Moravia, the Kingdom of Hungary, and the Austrian and Austro–Hungarian empires.

In 1918 Slovakia became part of the newly independent state of Czechoslovakia. It was occupied by Nazi forces in World War II, and later became part of the communist eastern bloc of Europe. The Czechoslovak Socialist Republic was formed officially in 1960 and lasted until the so-called Velvet Revolution of 1989–1990 when a democratic government led by reformist President Vaclav Havel was introduced. Czechoslovakia was dissolved at the start of 1993 with the formation of the Czech Republic and the Slovak Republic.

Population/Culture

About 85 percent of the population are Slovaks. Ten percent are Hungarians. Roma people represent the second largest minority group.

Slovakia has a rich folkloric and material culture, including traditional regional costumes, folk art, and folk music. Between 1906 and 1918, Hungarian classical composer Bela Bartok recorded melodies to 3,409 Slovak folk tunes and lyrics for 4,500 songs as part of a wider project to catalogue the world's folk music.

The Slovak materials were published by the Matica Slovenska, and stand as a unique record of a people's past.

Administration/Government

Slovakia is a parliamentary democracy with multiple political parties. Vladimir Meciar served as prime minister from 1993 until he was unseated in the 1998 elections by reform leader Mikulas Dzurinda. After Dzurinda came to power, Slovakia was admitted into both the European Union and NATO, and foreign investment increased. Robert Fico was elected Slovakia's third prime minister in 2006.

Economy/Industry

Slovakia is undergoing a transition from a centrally planned economy to a market economy. Because of the comparatively low cost of labor with a high skills level, it has attracted considerable foreign investment in industry.

Manufacturing has focused on automobile assembly and machinery production. As car production increases, Slovakia is expected to manufacture more automobiles per capita than any other nation.

Slovakia's Historic Capital

Bratislava is Slovakia's capital city and leading financial center. It is divided by the Danube River and is the only capital city in the world bordered by foreign countries (Austria and Hungary). Built on a site where the first known permanent settlement dated back to 5000 BCE, the city was known by the German name Pressburg from the Middle Ages until 1919. The name is still occasionally used.

The Old Town of Bratislava has many buildings from the fourteenth and fifteenth centuries, most prominently the old Town Hall. There are baroque palaces from the Hungarian and Austrian periods and several historic churches. The tenth-century Bratislava Castle sits on a hill overlooking the Danube, and is classified as a National Cultural Monument.

SLOVAKIA

Official name Slovak Republic (Slovenska Republika)
Land area 18,843 square miles (48,800 km²)
Border countries Poland, Ukraine, Hungary, Austria, Czech Republic
Capital Bratislava
Highest & lowest points Gerlachovsky Stit 8,711 feet (2,655 m); Bodrok River 308 feet (94 m)
Climate Temperate
Population 5,455,000
Language(s) Official: Slovak; other: Hungarian, Roma, Ukrainian
Ethnicity Slovak 86%, Hungarian 10%, Roma 2%, Ukrainian 1%, other 1%
Religion Roman Catholic 69%, Protestant 11%, Greek Catholic 4%, other or unspecified 3%, none 13%
Government Parliamentary democracy
Currency Slovak koruna
Human Development Index 0.863 (ranked 42nd out of 177 countries)

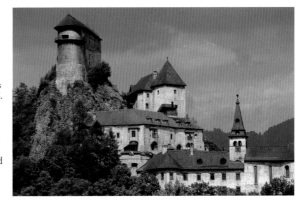

MILESTONE EVENTS

Fifth century CE Arrival of Slavic people
833 Kingdom of Great Moravia begins
1000 Start of the Kingdom of Hungary
1804 Start of Austrian Empire
1918 End of Austro-Hungarian Empire; formation of independent Czechoslovakia
1939 Czechoslovakia is invaded by forces of Nazi Germany
1948–1990 Communist period
1960 Formation of Czechoslovak Socialist Republic
1988 Candle Demonstration in Bratislava in favor of democracy
1989–1990 Velvet Revolution
1993 Velvet Divorce
2004 Slovakia joins NATO and European Union

Above A remarkable collection of fortifications, towers, and palaces make up the Orava Castle, located near the town of Oravský Podzámok in Slovakia. It was built on the site of wooden forts dating back to the Tartar invasion of 1241.

Above left Through the centuries Slovaks have fought hard to maintain their national identity, customs, and history, passing knowledge to younger generations through traditional food, music, dance, song, and poetry.

Left The stark beauty of the High Tatras mountain range, coupled with its large numbers of rare plants and animals, make this area one of the jewels of the Slovakian environment.

Top Houses dot a field in the beautiful Tatra Mountains of Slovakia. The country boasts some spectacular scenery, and its moderate climate makes it an attractive tourist destination.

HUNGARY

Official name Republic of Hungary (Magyar Koztarsasag)
Land area 35,655 square miles (92,340 km²)
Border countries Slovakia, Ukraine, Romania, Serbia, Croatia, Slovenia, Austria
Capital Budapest
Highest & lowest points Kekes 3,327 feet (1,014 m); Tisza River 256 feet (78 m)
Climate Temperate
Population 9,931,000
Language(s) Hungarian 94%, other 6%
Ethnicity Hungarian 92%, Roma 2%, other 6%
Religion Roman Catholic 52%, Calvinist 16%, Lutheran 3%, Greek Catholic 3%, other or unspecified 12%, unaffiliated 15%
Government Parliamentary democracy
Currency Forint
Human Development Index 0.874 (ranked 36th out of 177 countries)

SLOVAKIA
UKRAINE
AUSTRIA
Miskolc
Nyíregyháza
Eger
Győr
Tatabánya
BUDAPEST
Debrecen
Szombathely
Székesfehérvár
Veszprém
Szolnok
Dunaújváros
Kecskemét
SLOVENIA
HUNGARY
Békéscsaba
Kaposvár
Szeged
Pécs
ROMANIA
CROATIA
SERBIA

Hungary

Map Reference Pages 234–235

Hungary is a landlocked country bordered by Austria, Slovakia, Ukraine, Romania, Serbia, Croatia, and Slovenia. The Danube River forms part of its northern boundary with Slovakia and then turns south to bisect the country. The river also bisects the capital, Budapest, which has a population of about 1.7 million. Budapest is widely acclaimed as one of the most beautiful cities in the world. It is known as the "Paris of Central Europe," attracting up to 20 million tourists each year.

Right A Budapest cityscape showcasing the neo-Gothic Matthias Church (background).

Physical Geography

The basin of the Tisza River and the Great Hungarian Plain form much of eastern Hungary and the latter includes the Hortobagy, the largest natural grassland in Europe, deeply identified with the country's origins. The Little Hungarian Plain lies at the northwestern border with Austria and Slovakia. The highest land is in the Carpathian Mountains near another part of the border with Slovakia. Lake Balaton, the largest lake in Central Europe, is in western Hungary.

Above The white-stoned Fisherman's Bastion, located in the castle district of Budapest, incorporates seven towers, representing the seven Magyar tribes that settled in Hungary in 895 CE.

History

Hungary originated in 895 CE when Magyar tribes crossed the Carpathian Mountains under the leadership of Grand Prince Arpad and settled the central European plains. The Kingdom of Hungary was established at the start of 1001 under Stephen I, later canonized as St Stephen, a descendant of Arpad, who converted to Christianity and Christianized his subjects. The Arpad lineage ruled until 1301, but the kingdom survived with minor interruptions until 1946 under other family lines. The Mongol invasion in 1241, resulted in great devastation and loss of life.

Budapest can be traced to an ancient Celtic settlement named Aquincum. The Magyars also established a settlement on the site, naming it Buda after the brother of the first king. Across the river was a second Magyar town, Pest, named for the word for lime-kiln or oven. The union of the two towns under the combined name Budapest took place in 1873.

During the reign of Louis I (1342–1382), Hungary reached its zenith. The Ottoman Turks won a decisive battle against Hungarian troops in 1527, and most of Hungary was divided between Ottoman and Austrian Habsburg rule. The end of Ottoman rule came in 1718, and Louis Kossuth led an unsuccessful revolt against the Habsburgs in 1848. A dual Austro–Hungarian monarchy established in 1867 lasted until the end of World War I. The 1920 Treaty of Trianon set new, smaller boundaries for Hungary.

In World War II, Hungary allied with Nazi Germany and most of the Jews and Roma in the country were killed. Soviet troops occupied Hungary after the war. Communist rule began in 1948. A popular revolt against Soviet rule was crushed in 1956. A democratic constitution was enacted in 1989. Hungary joined NATO in 1999 and the European Union in 2004.

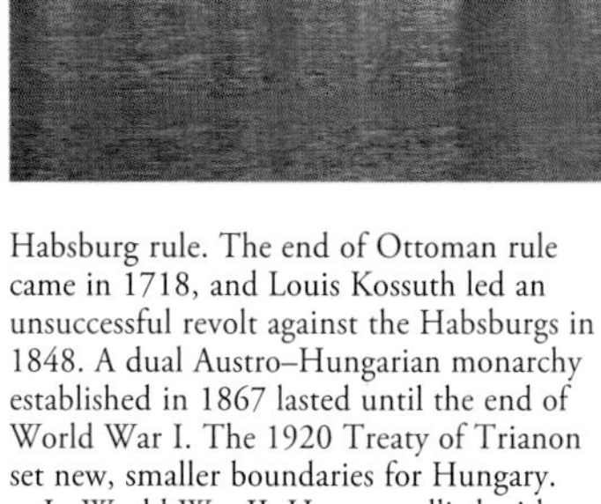

Center An organ grinder (*verklis*) busking on the streets of Budapest, Hungary.

Population/Culture

Ninety-two percent of the population is ethnic Hungarian; the remainder are Roma and people of German and Slovak descent.

The status of wife and mother has been a core ingredient of the national consciousness—expressed through the arts—for hundreds of years. But traditions are changing. Arranged marriages are now largely a thing of the past, and extended families living under one roof are now fairly rare.

Hungarian culinary specialties include beef goulash soup, sour cherry soup, *kolbász* (spicy sausage), paprika chicken, stuffed cabbage, and pancakes, both sweet and savory.

Right Hungarian artisans produce delicately hand-painted and lacquered dolls for sale in the many street markets of Budapest, Hungary.

Administration/Government

Hungary is governed by a unicameral national assembly consisting of 386 members The city of Pest houses the current government of Hungary. The spectacular parliament building is on the riverbank near the famous Chain Bridge. Built in a Gothic Revival style, the parliament building was dedicated in 1896 to coincide with Hungary's millennium. It is the third-largest parliament building in the world.

Economy/Industry

Fertile Hungary has long had a strong, diversified agricultural economy. Heavy industry, focused on metallurgy and machine production, was established during the communist period but collapsed after 1989 with the loss of Soviet markets. Subsequent privatization and the opening of new markets in the European Union have resulted in economic growth and a diversified economy in both agriculture and manufacturing. Foreign tourism to Budapest and to the country's many spa resorts is also a large part of the Hungarian economy.

BELARUS
RUSSIAN FEDERATION
POLAND
UKRAINE
KYIV/KYYIV (KIEV)
Kharkiv
Zhytomyr
Poltava
Luhans'k
L'viv
Ternopil'
Vinnytsya
Dniprodzerzhyns'k
Dnipropetrovs'k
Donets'k
Kirovohrad
Zaporizhzhya
Uzhhorod
Chernivtsi
Kryvyy Rih
Mariupol'
ROMANIA
MOLDOVA
Mykolayiv
Odesa
Sea of Azov
Simferopol'
Sevastopol'
Black Sea

Ukraine

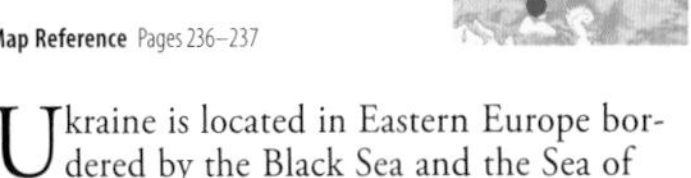

Map Reference Pages 236–237

Ukraine is located in Eastern Europe bordered by the Black Sea and the Sea of Azov to the south, Poland, Romania, and Moldova in the west, and Russia in the east.

Physical Geography

More than half the land is arable. Fertile plains and plateaus are crossed by rivers including the Dnieper, Dniester, and the Southern Buh. There are mountains in the west, and on the Crimean Peninsula in the south. The climate is temperate continental, and Mediterranean on the Crimean coast.

History

The earliest signs of human settlement date from around 4500 BCE. Ancient Greeks colonized the shores of the Black Sea from the sixth century BCE. Ukraine developed from Kievan Rus', a powerful eastern Slavic state founded in the ninth century CE, which thrived until the Mongol invasion in the thirteenth century. Ukraine then fell under the domination of Lithuania and later the Polish–Lithuanian Commonwealth. In the mid-seventeenth century the Cossacks established a state in what is now central Ukraine and allied with Russia, gradually incorporating Ukraine into the Russian Empire.

Ukraine was eventually incorporated into the Soviet Union in 1922. The country was completely devastated by World War II. On April 26, 1986, an explosion in the Chernobyl Nuclear Power Plant caused the worst nuclear reactor accident in history. The Ukrainian parliament declared independence from the Soviet Union on August 24, 1991.

Population/Culture

The majority of the population are ethnic Ukrainians; there are many ethnic minorities. Two-thirds of the population lives in urban areas. The state language is Ukrainian, and Russian is widely spoken, especially in the east and south. Eastern Orthodox Christianity has historically influenced culture and the arts.

Administration/Government

The president is elected by popular vote for a five-year term and eligible for a second term. The majority in parliament selects the prime minister. The legislative branch is represented by the supreme council (Verkhovna Rada) with 450 elected members. The supreme and constitutional courts comprise the judicial branch.

Economy/Industry

Industry contributes around one-third of GDP and includes coal mining; electric power; machinery and transport equipment; chemicals; and food processing. Agriculture employs a quarter of the workforce. Mineral deposits include iron ore, coal, manganese, salt, sulfur, graphite, titanium, magnesium, kaolin, nickel, and mercury. Ukraine imports most of its energy supplies, especially oil and natural gas. The service sector accounts for more than half the national income.

Left Swallow's Nest Castle is perched on the precipitous Aurora Cliffs, Cape Ai-Todor, Ukraine.

MOLDOVA 

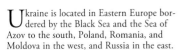

Official name Republic of Moldova (Republica Moldova)
Land area 12,886 square miles (33,371 km²)
Border countries Ukraine, Romania
Capital Kishinev (Chişinău)
Highest & lowest points Dealul Bălăneşti 1,411 feet (430 m); Dniester River 6½ feet (2 m)
Climate Mild and moderate continental
Population 4,324,000
Language(s) Official: Moldovan and Romanian; other: Russian
Ethnicity Moldovan/Romanian 78.2%, Ukrainian 8.4%, Russian 5.8%, Gagauz 4.4%, Bulgarian 1.9%, other 1.3%
Religion Eastern Orthodox 93.3%, Protestant 2.0%, other 4.7%
Currency Moldovan leu
Government Republic
Human Development Index 0.708 (ranked 111th out of 177 countries)

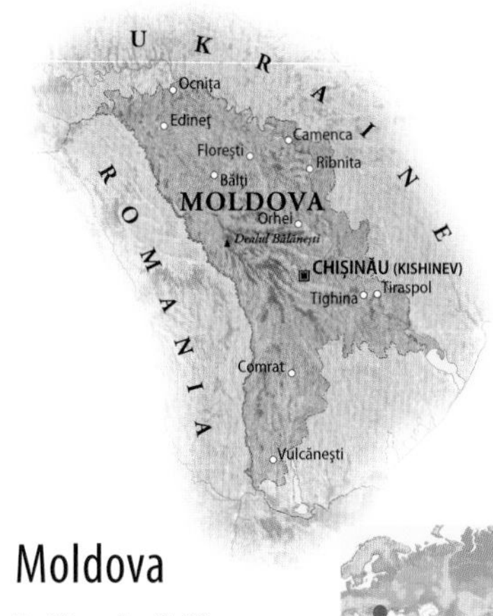

UKRAINE
ROMANIA
Ocniţa
Edineţ
Camenca
Floreşti
Rîbnita
Bălţi
MOLDOVA
Orhei
Dealul Bălăneşti
CHIŞINĂU (KISHINEV)
Tighina
Tiraspol
Comrat
Vulcăneşti

Moldova

Map Reference Pages 234–235

Moldova is a landlocked country sandwiched between Ukraine to the east and Romania to the west. The entire western border runs along the Prut River.

Physical Geography

Proximity to the Black Sea results in a moderate continental climate with warm summers and mild winters. Fertile soil and good climate make Moldova a key agricultural producer.

History

Inhabited since ancient times by the Dacians, the area was subject to continuous invasion by the Byzantine Empire, Slavs, Magyars, and Ottoman Turks. Much of the present-day Republic of Moldova incorporates Bessarabia, a historic region between the Dniester and Prut rivers, which was part of the Principality of Moldavia from the fourteenth century until 1812. When it was ceded to Russia a short-lived independence was declared by the National Council in 1917. The Moldavian Autonomous Soviet Socialist Republic was established in 1940. Following the collapse of the Soviet Union, Moldova declared its independence in 1991.

Population/Culture

Moldova's population of nearly 10 million comprises several ethnic groups. There has been some dispute as to whether Moldovans should constitute a distinct ethnic group, or be classed with Romanians.

Since the area was settled by the Dacians, the country was strongly influenced by the Romans and contact with neighboring Slavs, Magyars, and the Ottoman Turks. Moldovan folklore is of Dacian and Latin origin. Folk ballads play an important role in traditional culture. Decorative arts include ceramics, carpet weaving, traditional costumes, stonework, woodwork, leather, and metal working. Western culture influenced literature and arts in the nineteenth century. In 1989 Moldovan was declared the state language.

Administration/Government

The president is elected by the parliament. The prime minister is appointed by the president, subject to parliamentary approval. Members of the 101-seat unicameral parliament are elected by popular vote. The judicial branch is represented by the supreme and constitutional courts.

Economy/Industry

Agriculture (including fruit, vegetables, wine, and tobacco) is one of the main sectors of the Moldovan economy. Supplies of petroleum, coal, and natural gas come mainly from Russia. The service sector accounts for 56.5 percent of GDP, followed by industry at 22 percent and agriculture (21.5 percent). The economy is expanding with a 4 percent growth rate, but remains vulnerable to poor weather and fuel prices.

UKRAINE

Official name Ukraine (Ukrayina)
Land area 233,107 square miles (603,700 km²)
Border countries Belarus, Russia, Moldova, Romania, Hungary, Slovakia, Poland
Capital Kiev (Kyiv/Kyyiv)
Highest point Hora Hoverla 6,762 feet (2,061 m)
Climate Temperate continental and Mediterranean
Population 45,994,000
Language(s) Official: Ukrainian 67%; Russian 24%, other (including Romanian, Polish, Hungarian) 9%
Ethnicity Ukrainian 77.8%, Russian 17.3%, Belarusian 0.6%, Moldovan 0.5%, Crimean Tatar 0.5%, Bulgarian 0.4%, Hungarian 0.3%, Romanian 0.3%, Polish 0.3%, Jewish 0.2%, other 1.8%
Religion Ukrainian Eastern Orthodox 28%, Orthodox (no particular jurisdiction) 16%, Ukrainian Greek Catholic 6%, Ukrainian Autocephalous Orthodox 1.7%, Protestant, Jewish, none 38%, unspecified 10.3%
Government Republic
Currency Hryvnia
Human Development Index 0.788 (ranked 76th out of 177 countries)

Below The Răut (Reut) River, a tributary of the Dniester River, meanders its way through the Moldovan countryside.

PORTUGAL

Official name Portuguese Republic (República Portuguesa)
Land area 35,505 square miles (91,951 km²)
Border countries Spain
Capital Lisbon (Lisboa)
Highest point Ponta do Pico (Azores) 7,713 feet (2,351 m)
Climate Temperate
Population 10,677,000
Language(s) Official: Portuguese, Mirandese; other: Basque, Catalan, Galician
Ethnicity Portuguese; African and Eastern European immigrants
Religion Roman Catholic 84.5%, other Christian 2.2%, other or unspecified 13.3%
Government Parliamentary democracy
Currency Euro
Human Development Index 0.897 (ranked 29th out of 177 countries)

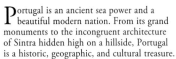

ATLANTIC OCEAN
PORTUGAL
SPAIN
Braga
Bragança
Vila Real
Porto
Aveiro
Viseu
Guarda
Coimbra
Malhão da Estrela
Leiria
Castelo Branco
Santarém
LISBOA (LISBON)
Portalegre
Setúbal
Évora
Beja
Faro

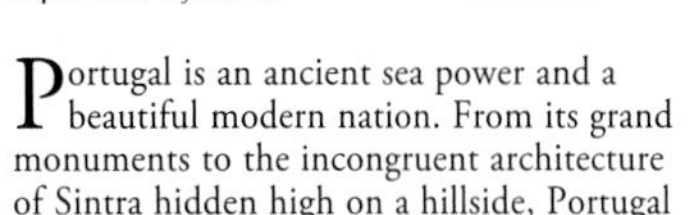

Portugal

Map Reference Pages 230–231

Portugal is an ancient sea power and a beautiful modern nation. From its grand monuments to the incongruent architecture of Sintra hidden high on a hillside, Portugal is a historic, geographic, and cultural treasure.

Right The island of Madeira, Portugal, known for its famous Madeira wine, was settled by the Portuguese in the 1400s. The Madeira Archipelago was also known to the Romans as the Purple Islands from as early as the first century CE.

Below Festivals (*festa*) feature prominently on the Portuguese calendar. Men and women wear traditional costume to celebrate their culture.

Right A fisherman mends his nets in the Algarve, Portugal. Big-game fishing is now big business with tourists, yet fisherman continue to ply their trade up and down the jagged coast.

Physical Geography

Located on the Iberian Peninsula, Portugal is mainland Europe's westernmost country, one that lies totally in the Western hemisphere, jutting into the Atlantic. Its beautiful natural harbors allowed Portuguese explorers to venture into the unknown. The port at Lisbon on the Tejo (Tagus) River is one of Europe's finest natural harbors.

The landscape exhibits enticing contrasts. South of the Tejo River, gentle rolling hills and vast plains are dominated by extensive estates coupled with large-scale agriculture. The north is populated with small farms and vineyards in the river valleys in the shadows of the Serra da Estrela—the largest mountain range in Portugal. The Serra da Estrela is the backbone of the Iberian Peninsula.

The Azores and Madeira—Portugal's two autonomous regions—are island groups in the Atlantic. Madeira is made up of eight mountainous islands, only two of them populated. The Azores Archipelago consists of nine islands formed by volcanic activity. The highest point in Portugal is Ponta do Pico in the Azores. Earthquakes sometimes rattle the autonomous regions and even Lisbon, where a devastating earthquake occurred in 1755.

History

Muslim invaders entered Portugal from Spain in 711 CE, after capturing the cities of Toledo and Cordoba. Their rule lasted four centuries until Portugal won its independence from Moorish Spain in 1143.

By the early fifteenth century, Portugal was unified by King John I, whose son, Prince Henry the Navigator, initiated the country's golden era of maritime adventures. In 1498, Bartolomeu Días rounded the Cape of Good Hope, and by 1498 Vasco da Gama had reached the west coast of India. By the early 1500s, Portuguese possessions extended from Africa to Brazil, and from Indochina south to the Malay Peninsula. The wealth from these outposts made the monarchy the richest in Europe, and Lisbon the commercial capital of the world.

Portuguese commerce and its colonies were devastated when Spain invaded in 1581. By 1640, England, Denmark, and France had divided up the bulk of Portuguese territories and Portugal began a time of imperial decline.

In the mid-twentieth century, Portugal was dominated by one man—Antonio de Oliveira Salazar. Appointed minister of finance after the 1926 revolution, he became prime minister in 1932, and ruled Portugal as a virtual dictator until 1968. On January 1, 1986, Portugal was elected to the European Economic Community. The following month, Mario Soares became the first civilian president in 60 years.

Population/Culture

Portuguese number more than 10.5 million, with one-quarter of the population living in or near Lisbon, the capital.

As a former colonial power, Portugal is adding to its population through immigration. Immigrants include Portuguese who have been living abroad and people from former colonies such as Brazil, Cape Verde, Angola, and Guinea Bissau. Immigrants from Eastern Europe began arriving in the 1990s to supplement the labor pool.

Portugal has experienced many cultures and religions during its history. Roman influences are evident in ancient architecture. The Moors left their indelible mark in the south on architecture and in place names like Lashbuna (Lisbon). Even the winding streets of the Alfama, Lisbon's oldest district, reflect the influence of the Moors.

Catholicism is the dominant religion. The impact of the church on culture and politics is readily evident in holidays and traditions.

Portuguese is the official language. Portuguese speakers in Brazil make this language the most prevalent in South America—not Spanish. Portuguese can be heard in Macau in China, in Goa in India, and in many parts of Africa. Cultural traditions include *fado*, a traditional folk music that is both sorrowful and melancholy like the American blues.

Manueline, a decorative architectural style, derives from colonial seagoing experiences, mixing shells and branches of coral with more traditional Christian iconography and religious symbols. It is often used over doorways, balustrades, and lintels.

Administration/Government

Portugal has had a wide variety of governments in its history, including a monarchy, constitutional monarchy, dictatorship, republic, and rule by many foreign powers. Today, Portugal is a parliamentary democracy with a unicameral parliament called the Assembly of the Republic (Assembleia da República) with 230 members elected to four-year terms. The president serves as the chief of state, and is elected in a popular vote for a five-year term. The head of the government is the prime minister who is appointed by the president and is usually the head of the majority political party or coalition.

PORTUGAL'S CASTLES

Centuries of occupation by the Romans and Moors made the Portuguese adept in the design and construction of castles. Many of its early castles date to the period after 1139 CE, when the young nation, emerging from the kingdoms of Castile and Leon under the leadership of the young King Afonso Henriques, began a crusade for liberation from Moorish occupation.

Dual-towered gatehouses and colorfully painted castellated walls of granite echoed older Roman and Moorish examples, but became increasingly ornate and imaginative, with the addition of oil spouts, archers' loops, and ever-higher towers and keeps. King Dinis I rebuilt almost every significant castle in Portugal in the thirteenth century, replete with staggered gates and multiple concentric walls. The fourteenth century saw increasing flamboyance such as pepper pots atop towers and decorative brickwork. In the fifteenth and sixteenth centuries, when the age of castles gave way to the age of forts that could withstand the advances made in cannon technology, Portugal's builders constructed hundreds of forts throughout the empire. From West Africa to Oman in the Middle East and from Asia to South America, Portuguese forts with their low stone walls built over mounds of earth as a defense against cannon fire can still be seen today, remnants of a brief but extensive maritime power.

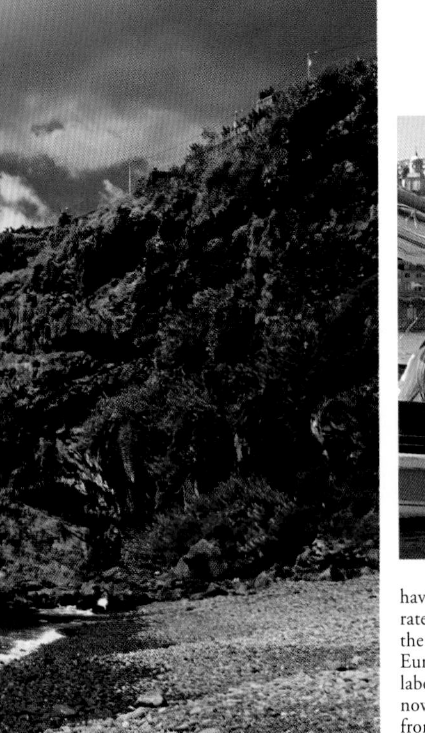

Economy/Industry

The economy has long struggled to maintain parity with wealthier European neighbors due to such factors as high levels of external debt and a per capita GDP among the lowest in the European Union. A legacy of the Salazar regime was that Portugal was perceived as having a workforce that was less educated and technically less proficient than other EU members. Its agricultural sector was seen as polarized, with small family-run farms in the north and large collectives in the south, both seemingly incapable of modernization and with a low productivity rate. As a result, many entrepreneurs and business elite left the country, preventing Portugal from resolving its economic nightmares, which included high inflation, fiscal deficits, and a burdensome foreign debt.

Since joining the EEC in 1986, the Portuguese economy has been transformed. Economic deregulation, debt reduction, tax reforms, and selective privatization have seen the Portuguese economy succeed in the exporting of automotive and electronic components. Joining the European Monetary Union in 1996 led to further structural reforms that have brought lower inflation, lower interest rates, and currency stability. However, when the European Union expanded into Eastern Europe, it erased Portugal's hold on low labor costs. The Portuguese government is now restructuring the economic foundation from one based on public consumption and public investment to one more focused on the development of technology, exports, and private investment.

Above left Although port wine is produced in the Douro region of Portugal, it is the seaport of Porto, at the mouth of the Douro River, that gives the sweet dessert wine its appellation.

MILESTONE EVENTS

711 CE Led by Tariq ibn Ziyad, the Moors invade Portugal

1143 The Treaty of Zamora acknowledges Portuguese independence from Moorish Spain

1498 Vasco da Gama reaches the west coast of India by navigating around Africa

1581 Spain invades Portugal; Philip II of Spain becomes Philip I of Portugal

1668 Portugal regains independence from Spain

1882 Brazil declares independence from Portugal

1908 After the assassination of King Carlos and his eldest son, King Carlos's second son Manuel is crowned

1910 Abdication of King Manuel II—Portugal becomes a republic

1916–1918 Portugal sides with Allies in World War I

1932 Antonio de Oliveira Salazar becomes prime minister

1970 Salazar dies, two years after a stroke forces him to resign

1975 Portuguese Timor declares independence and becomes East Timor

1986 Portugal joins European Economic Community (EEC)

2002 Euro becomes national currency

FRANCE
Pic de Coma Pedrosa
Llorts
El Serrat
ANDORRA
Soldeu
Ordino
Canillo
La Massana
Encamp
ANDORRA LA VELLA
Sant Julià de Lòria
SPAIN

Andorra

Map Reference Pages 230–231

The landlocked Principality of Andorra is the largest western European microstate. This enticing country is situated high in the eastern Pyrenees Mountains and pressed in between France and Spain.

Physical Geography

Andorra's terrain in the eastern Pyrenees is characterized by high peaks, tapered valleys, and deep gorges. Andorra was once heavily forested but most has been cleared and pastures have taken their place. The elevation promotes winter tourism with perfect conditions for alpine skiing and snowboarding.

History

With its challenging terrain, Andorra has avoided most European skirmishes over the centuries and has been an independent principality since the Middle Ages. From 1278 to 1993 it was governed under a unique arrangement which made it a co-principality, under French and Spanish leaders. Since then, the system has been modified to a parliamentary democracy, with French and Spanish influence.

Population/Culture

Andorra is one of the world's least populated countries with less than 73,000 people. Most of the population lives in the seven valleys that shape the country's political districts. Andorrans have the world's longest life expectancy at 83.52 years, and their literacy rate is 100 percent.

Andorra has a diverse population for its size. Native Andorrans, a minority in their own country, trace their heritage back to Catalonia and comprise about one-third of the population. The primary language is Catalan, the official language of the country. Spanish, French, and Portuguese immigrants comprise the majority of the population.

Nearly 90 percent of the population is Roman Catholic and the church plays a major role in social and cultural life. Andorra's isolation has allowed it to retain much of its folk culture, but improved transportation and communication have also introduced many elements from outside cultures.

Administration/Government

In 1993 Andorra became a parliamentary democracy with a unicameral legislature called the General Council of the Valleys. Each of the seven valleys is represented and the Council has 28 members with elected individuals. The executive role is carried out by two princes: The President of France serves as the French prince and the Bishop of Seu d'Urgell as the Spanish prince.

Economy/Industry

Andorra's isolation and impoverishment changed after World War II when a fledgling tourism industry was fostered by improved highway connections between France and Spain. Over 10 million tourists now visit annually, influenced by the country's duty-free status. Immigrants, legal and illegal, have also been attracted to Andorra because of its lack of income taxes.

ANDORRA

Official name Principality of Andorra (Principat d'Andorra)

Land area 181 square miles (469 km²)

Border countries France, Spain

Capital Andorra la Vella

Highest & lowest points Coma Pedrosa 9,665 feet (2,496 m); Riu Runer 2,756 feet (840 m)

Climate Temperate

Population 72,413

Language(s) Official: Catalan; other: French, Castilian, Portuguese

Ethnicity Spanish 43%, Andorran 33%, Portuguese 11%, French 7%, other 6%

Religion Roman Catholic almost 90%, other approximately 10%

Government Parliamentary democracy

Currency Euro

Human Development Index Not available

Above The mountain pass of Pas de la Casa (literally "pass of the house") is also home to a popular skiing and snowboarding resort on the Andorran–French border.

Below Perched on a 5,665-foot (1,727 m) slope, Andorra's Canillo is the highest inhabited village in Europe.

SPAIN

Official name Kingdom of Spain (Reino de España)
Land area 192,873 square miles (499,542 km²)
Border countries France, Andorra, Gibraltar, Portugal
Capital Madrid
Highest point Pico de Tiede (Tenerife) on Canary Islands 12,198 feet (3,718 m)
Climate Temperate
Population 40,491,000
Language(s) Official: Castilian Spanish; official regionally: Catalan, Galician, Basque
Ethnicity Mediterranean and Nordic
Religion Roman Catholic 94%, other 6%
Government Parliamentary monarchy
Currency Euro
Human Development Index 0.949 (ranked 13th out of 177 countries)

Right Tapas encompass a range of ingredients, and include many food combinations that are uniquely Spanish. Eating tapas is an everyday social activity in Spain.

Below Montefrío village, in Spain's Andalusian region, is a reminder of times long ago, with its whitewashed buildings clustered around a craggy outcrop. On this peak sits the Iglesia de la Villa; this church was built on the site of Nasrid castle.

Bay of Biscay
A Coruña
Gijón
Oviedo
Santander
Bilbao
Donostia-San Sebastián
Vigo
Ourense
León
Vitoria-Gasteiz
Pamplona
FRANCE
Burgos
Logroño
ANDORRA
Valladolid
Zaragoza
Lleida
Salamanca
Barcelona
Tarragona
PORTUGAL
MADRID
SPAIN
Menorca
Mallorca
Castelló de la Plana
Badajoz
Valencia
Palma de Mallorca
Albacete
Eivissa
Córdoba
Jaén
Murcia
Alicante
Huelva
Sevilla
Granada
Cartagena
Cádiz
Málaga
Almería
Mediterranean Sea
UNITED KINGDOM
SPAIN
SPAIN
MOROCCO

Spain

Map Reference Pages 230–231

Spain is the third largest country in Europe, and is divided into 17 historic and geographic regions that echo the boundaries of its Christian and Moorish past. Its capital of Madrid lies in the center of the country in the Meseta Central, a vast dissected plateau.

Physical Geography

The Sistema Central mountain range rings Madrid with peaks reaching up to 8,500 feet (2,600 m) high. Running east–west, the mountain range divides the plateau into its northern and southern parts called Old Castile (Castilla–León) and New Castile (Castilla–La Mancha) respectively.

The lowland regions include the Andalusian Plain in the southwest, the Ebro Basin in the northeast, and various coastal plains that are broadest along the Gulf of Cadiz.

The Balearic Islands are an archipelago off Spain's Mediterranean coast. Characterized by steep mountains and sharply indented coastlines, this picturesque group has a very long and violent history, involving Greeks, Romans, Arabs, and pirates.

The Canary Islands, 56 miles (90 km) off Africa's west coast, are a group of 13 volcanic islands with rugged mountainous terrain and Spain's tallest peak, Pico de Teide—at 12,198 feet (3,717 m)—on the island of Tenerife.

Spain has sovereignty over several island territories along the North African coast: Isla del Alboran, Islas de Alhucemas, Perejil, and Islas Chafarinas, the fortified enclave of Ceuta on the Moroccan coast opposite Gibraltar, and the town of Melilla, located on Morocco's Rif coast and joined by an isthmus to the African mainland.

Early History

The beginnings of human habitation on the Iberian Peninsula read like a "who's who" of the lost tribes of Europe—the Beaker People with their unique pottery and knowledge of metal work, the Vascons, the Los Millares of Andalusia, the El Argars, and the mysterious Tartessos—ancient navigators known only from fragmentary historical documents and scattered artefacts. Attracted by southern Spain's wealth of silver and tin, the Phoenicians established trading centers along the Spanish coast from around 800 BCE.

Following the fall of the Phoenician Empire, Spain was occupied by Carthage. After defeating Carthage in 146 BCE, the Romans ruled Spain into the early decades of the fifth century and left it with four priceless legacies: The Latin language, Christianity, Spain's municipalities, and Roman law.

A succession of invaders followed over the centuries until the arrival of the Arabs in the eighth century. Their rule lasted until 1492.

Modern History

The "Age of Expansion" in the mid-1500s saw the establishment of Spanish colonies from the Philippines to the Netherlands. By the mid-seventeenth century, Spain had become one of Europe's foremost economic and military powers, but in 1898 following a brief war with the United States, it lost its dependencies of Puerto Rico, Cuba, Guam, and the Philippines.

Spanish voters rejected the monarchy in the 1931 elections. In 1936, a devastating civil war broke out which ended in 1939 with victory for the fascists under General Franco. His 40-year dictatorship ended with his death in 1975—ironically paving the way for the restoration of the monarchy. King Juan Carlos I instituted democratic reforms. Spain became a member of NATO in 1982, joined the European Union in 1995, and was a founding member of the European Monetary Union in 1999.

Administration/Government

In a national referendum in 1978 the Spanish people overwhelmingly repealed the draconian laws of the Franco regime and reinvented Spain as a parliamentary monarchy. The king

Above These dancers in Salamanca wear traditional costume and carry castanets to accompany their dance.

Left The historic town of Ronda is surrounded by lush undulating agricultural land—a mainstay of the Andalusia region's economy. Ronda is also the birthplace of modern bullfighting in Spain.

became head of state and is invested with the power to ratify laws, dissolve the legislature, and appoint the president, vice-president, and ministers. Legislative authority was vested in a new Congress of Deputies with 350 members, and a Senate with 259 members.

The 1978 Constitution established an independent judiciary subject only to the rule of law. Its courts are organized hierarchically, with a system of appeals against the decisions of lower courts to higher courts and to the Supreme Court, which is the highest judicial body in the country.

Economy

From 1945, the Franco regime concentrated its efforts on rebuilding industrial infrastructure, which was decimated after the disastrous Civil War (1936–1939) and the isolation that followed the end of World War II.

The industrial sector has grown significantly, although as recently as 2001 Spain still ranked among the lowest nations of Western Europe in per capita income. Tourism is a major source of foreign exchange, now generating approximately 10 percent of GDP annually.

Spain and Roman Catholicism

Spain is a nation born of a religious struggle for power that had its beginnings in the *Reconquesta*—the retaking of Moorish Spain by the Christian kingdoms of northern Hispania that began with the Battle of Covadonga in 722, and ended with the capture of Granada by the Christians in 1492. The Inquisition that followed sought to complete the religious "purification" of the Iberian Peninsula by expelling Jews, Protestants, and other non-Catholics.

Catholicism became the state religion in 1851, when Madrid signed a concordat with the Vatican agreeing to fund the salaries of its clergy. The pact was renounced in 1931, when a series of anticlerical measures were incorporated into the secular constitution by the government of the Second Republic. General Franco restored the church's privileges, and Roman Catholicism was the only legalized religion during the Franco years. The 1978 constitution disestablished Catholicism and proclaimed religious liberty for non-Catholics to be a protected legal right.

MILESTONE EVENTS

1340 The Moors are defeated at the Battle of Salado, signalling the beginning of a slow withdrawal from Spain

August 3, 1492 Christopher Columbus sets sail on his history-making journey to the New World

September 20, 1519 Ferdinand Magellan sets out in search of the Spice Islands; his fleet brave the treacherous waters of the Magellan Straits

1560 Madrid is officially named as Spain's capital

1589 The Spanish Armada is defeated by the English fleet

1805 Spain is defeated at the Battle of Trafalgar

1868 The Spanish Revolution begins

1873 The first Spanish Republic is proclaimed

1898 Spain cedes Cuba, Puerto Rico, Guam, and the Philippines to the United States

1931 Following the revolution that began in 1930, the monarchy is ousted and a republic is established

1936 Spanish Civil War; General Franco becomes Spanish leader

1975 The monarchy is restored to Spain as Juan Carlos I takes the throne

Bullfighting

Bullfighting is an integral part of Spanish society. It is a controversial sport, with 24,000 bulls killed annually in front of a combined audience of more than 30 million people. The bullfighting season extends throughout the warmer months—from March to October.

The first recorded bullfight took place in 711 CE at the crowning of King Alfons VIII; it was long a sport of the aristocracy, played on horseback. Commoners soon adopted the practice; those could not afford horses dodged the bulls on foot and unarmed.

Festivals

Religious themes play out in many local and national festivals and celebrations. Each February in the town of Cuenca, in Castilla–La Mancha, the Festival of the Disguised Devils (La Endiablada) sees young boys dress up as "El Diablo." Wearing cardboard bishop's miters on their heads and large cowbells fastened around their waists, the boys dance and parade around the cathedral, then enter it and pretend to wash the statue of San Blais.

The famous Fallas de San Jose in Valencia dating from the Middle Ages, includes a night-time parade and a floral offering—often reaching a depth of many meters—to Our Lady of the Forsaken, the city's patroness.

In celebration of the longest day of the year during the Feast of San Juan in Alicante, Valencia, the streets are decorated with leaves and branches, and local boys serenade the town's young maidens. The festivities include the planting of pine and poplar trees in anticipation of the triumph of light over darkness.

Food and Wine

Eating in Spain is generally an inexpensive affair with meals substantial rather than gourmet—and the Spanish tradition of tapas is a good place to start. A tapa is a small dish of food that is generally served as a snack; eating tapas is a form of socializing that is very popular throughout Spain. There are countless tapa combinations including tripe with chickpeas *(callos)*, prawns in hot garlic oil *(gambas pil pil)*, and fresh white fish fillets in oil *(boquerones)*.

Another famous Spanish culinary favorite is paella, a one-dish meal of rice, seafood, vegetables, and chicken, tinted to a golden color with saffron.

The region of Andalucia boasts Spain's finest fruits and vegetables, hams, oils, and wine, with much of its local cuisine still echoing its Moorish origins.

Spain is the second largest wine producer in the world after France, with more than 40 regions specializing in their own marques. The region of Jerez in Andalucia is world famous for its sherries—from its pale dry finos to the darker, richer oloroso—while the Basque country of northern Spain produces a delightfully sour, sparkling green wine called *chacolí* or *txakoli*.

AN ARCHITECTURAL WONDER

Bilbao's Guggenheim Museum opened in 1997. This architectural marvel is located on the banks of the Nervión River, Bilbao's major waterway, and is a landmark edifice in the city. Designed by architect Frank O. Gehry, the building features limestone, glass, and titanium in sculptured forms, interconnecting to create a truly unique structure, while its ingenious design and situation ensures that it does not adversely impact on the Bilbao skyline. The building materials themselves were customized to ensure that artworks held in the museum are kept in optimum conditions.

Careful planning of the interior has afforded a massive 118,000 square feet (11,000 m^2) of exhibition space, and the museum has attracted thousands of visitors curious to view its interesting exterior as well as the myriad artworks on show in its 19 galleries. The museum is a major attraction in Spain's Basque region, and has injected some much-needed tourism income into the local economy.

FRANCE
Mediterranean Sea
MONACO
Sporting Monte Carlo
Grimaldi Forum
MONTE-CARLO
Casino
Centre de Congrès
Église Sainte-Dévote
Port de Monaco
LA CONDAMINE
Mt Agel
Palais Princier
Ministère d'Etat
MONACO-VILLE
Cathédrale de Monaco
Musée Océanographique
Centre Hospitalier Princesse Grace
Port de Fontvieille
FONTVIEILLE
Stade Louis II

MONACO

Official name Principality of Monaco
Land area ¾ square mile (1.95 km²)
Border countries France
Capital Monaco
Highest point Mont Agel 459 feet (140 m)
Climate Mediterranean
Population 32,671
Language(s) Official: French, English, Italian, Monegasque
Ethnicity French 47%, Monegasque 16%, Italian 16%, other 21%
Religion Roman Catholic 90%, other 10%
Government Constitutional monarchy
Currency Euro
Human Development Index Not available

Above right Coastline in the evening at Dwejra, Gozo, Malta. The area is a renowned dive site, with clear waters and many underwater caves and tunnels to explore.

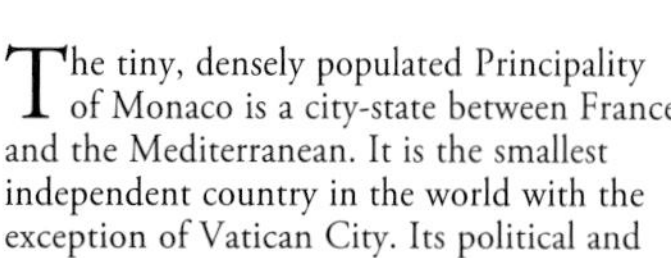

Monaco

Map Reference Pages 228–229

The tiny, densely populated Principality of Monaco is a city-state between France and the Mediterranean. It is the smallest independent country in the world with the exception of Vatican City. Its political and economic interests are very closely linked to France. Tourists flock to Monaco for its famous casinos, extravagant resorts, climate, scenery, and beautiful sandy beaches.

Monaco was founded as a colony of Genoa in 1215. Since 1297, the area has been ruled by the House of Grimaldi with the exception of a 25-year period (1793–1814) when it was ruled by France. Monaco became a sovereign country with the Franco–Monegasque Treaty of 1861, the Grimaldis ruling with absolute authority until 1911 when the first constitution was adopted.

Monaco signed an agreement with France in 1918 whereby France provided the country with protection. Monaco adopted a new constitution in 1962 that provided, among other things, for female suffrage and for greater protection of liberties. The House of Grimaldi serves as the royal family of the constitutional monarchy. Upon the death of his father, Prince Rainier, Albert became Prince of Monaco in 2005. He is the chief of state with a one-house national council comprising 24 members.

Monaco has a distinctly international flavor. French is the official language, but Monegasque, Italian, and English are also commonly spoken. Ninety percent of the country is Catholic. It is the most densely populated country in the world.

Luxury tourism is the key to Monaco's economy. The country also provides a tax haven for many companies and individuals.

Right A sea of red sun umbrellas at Larvotto Beach, Monte Carlo on a busy summer's day. This popular pebble beach is man-made.

MALTA

Official name Republic of Malta
Land area 122 square miles (316 km²)
Border countries None
Capital Valletta
Highest point Ta'Dmejrek 830 feet (253 m)
Climate Mediterranean
Population 401,880
Language(s) Official: Maltese, English
Ethnicity Maltese
Religion Roman Catholic 98%, other or unspecified 2%
Government Republic
Currency Euro
Human Development Index 0.878 (ranked 34th out of 177 countries)

Malta

Map Reference Pages 232–233

Malta is an island pearl in the heart of the Mediterranean Sea. It has a long history as a stop-over for early travelers who often stayed to occupy it, among them Phoenicians, Carthaginians, Romans, Byzantines, Arabs, Normans, Ottoman Turks, Crusaders, the French, and the British. Today most of the island's visitors are tourists, not conquerors. Malta gained its independence from the UK in 1964; ten years later it became a republic. Malta is a member of the Commonwealth.

With the second smallest land area in the European Union, the country consists of a handful of islands, of which only Malta, Gozo, and Comino are inhabited. The landscape is made up of low limestone hills and a craggy coastline. Agriculture is terraced, making use of land and scant rainfall. Climate is marked by hot dry summers and mild rainy winters.

The country is a history buff's paradise. Two sites at Ggantija, on Gozo Island, date back more than 1,000 years before the pyramids of Egypt. The temples of Hagar Qim, Mnajdra, and Tarxien on the island of Malta also predate the pyramids. The Apostle Paul is credited with bringing Christianity to Malta after being shipwrecked on St Paul's Island, and the Knights of St John of Jerusalem brought the symbol of the Maltese cross.

Ninety-eight percent of Maltese people are Catholic. Maltese is the national language and it has borrowed liberally from Italian. Both Maltese and English are official languages.

A republic since 1974, Malta has a parliamentary form of government but with a unicameral legislature that has 65 members. The president is elected by the parliament for a five-year term and is the chief of state. The prime minister is appointed by the president and serves as the head of government.

Except for limestone, the country has few natural resources. Farming is limited because of the small size of the country, which imports 80 percent of its food. Thus the economy revolves around trade, manufacturing, and tourism. Malta's entry into the European Union in 2004 is viewed as a positive step that will further enhance tourism.

ITALY
Serravalle
Domagnano
Acquaviva
Borgo Maggiore
SAN MARINO
Monte Titano
Faetano
SAN MARINO
Fiorentino
Montegiardino
Poggio di Chiesanuova
ITALY

San Marino

Map Reference Pages 232–233

San Marino is a landlocked microstate, the third smallest nation in Europe, 140 miles (225 km) due north of Rome, relatively close to the coast of the Adriatic Sea. It is situated in mountainous terrain on the slopes of Monte Titano, a limestone mass that has a triple summit, each with ancient fortifications. The climate is Mediterranean with mild to cool winters and warm sunny summers.

San Marino maintains that it is the world's oldest republic, established by a stonemason named Marino (St Marinus) together with a group of Christians on September 3, 301 CE.

Most of the population is Sammarinese, and there is an Italian minority. San Marino's foreign policy aligns itself with its dominant neighbor Italy, and social and political culture largely parallels Italian trends. San Marino is aware of the importance of preserving its venerable artefacts and traditions from 18 centuries of history that help to define its distinctive place in the international setting.

San Marino has a constitution dating from October 8, 1600, supplemented by an elec-toral law of 1926. There are nine municipalities (administrative subdivisions) in the republic. Two Captains Regent, selected from the parliament, function as the head of the government and serve six-month terms, while the head of government is the Secretary of State for Foreign and Political Affairs. Members of the popularly elected parliament, the Grand and General Council (Consiglio Grande e Generale), serve five-year terms. The next election is scheduled for June 2011.

Tourism is San Marino's economic mainstay, contributing more than 50 percent of the GDP and employing some 20 percent of the workforce.

The principal industries are banking, electronics, apparel, and ceramics. Wine, cheese, wheat, maize, and olives constitute the main agricultural products. Postage stamp sales to foreign collectors are another income producer. Living standards are on a par with those of the most prosperous northern Italian regions. San Marino maintains close relations with the European Union, has adopted the euro, but is not a member of the EU.

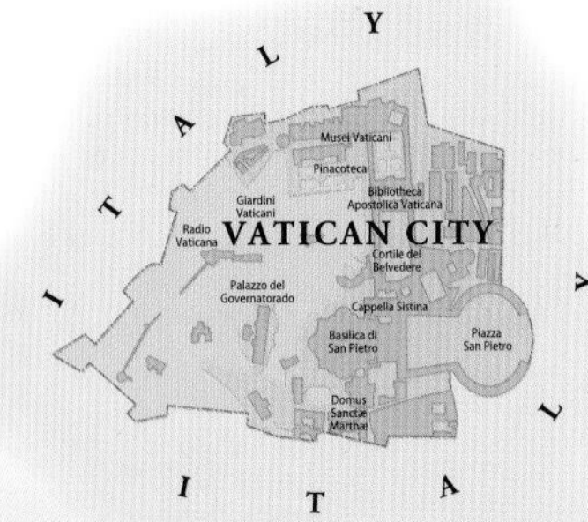
ITALY
Musei Vaticani
Pinacoteca
Giardini Vaticani
Biblioteca Apostolica Vaticana
Radio Vaticana
VATICAN CITY
Cortile del Belvedere
Palazzo del Governatorato
Cappella Sistina
Basilica di San Pietro
Piazza San Pietro
Domus Sanctae Marthae
ITALY

Vatican City

Map Reference Pages 232–233

Vatican City is the world's smallest country in both land area and population. In spite of its size, its impact extends to all corners of the globe. Vatican City is the home of the Roman Catholic Church, which has more than one billion followers worldwide.

Vatican City operates as a country; it has its own constitution, postal system, government, museums, and flag. It also had its own currency until the euro was adopted in 1999.

Located on Vatican Hill and enclosed by a medieval wall that opens at the entrance to St Peter's Square, the country is entirely surrounded by Rome.

Constantine the Great, the first Roman emperor to convert to Christianity, built the first basilica in 326 CE on Vatican Hill over the tomb of St Peter. Since then, the history of the Catholic Church has been tied very closely to the Vatican.

Most of the residents of Vatican City are members of religious orders, or connected to the Church in some way. The colorfully uniformed Swiss Guards, which number about 130, have protected the Pope since 1506.

The culture is based upon the tenets of the Catholic Church. Here even the "dead" language of Latin can be heard. St Peter's Basilica was until recently the world's largest church and houses the tombs of St Peter, Pope John Paul II, and many other Church leaders. The basilica, grounds, and adjacent museums hold many of the world's greatest art treasures, including the works of Bernini, Michelangelo, Raphael, da Vinci, and Titian.

In 1929, the Catholic Church and Italy's government signed agreements to create the State of the Vatican City. This agreement was revised in 1984. The Pope is the chief of state and holds all powers as an absolute monarch. However, many daily governance activities are carried on by others. The Holy See conducts diplomatic relations with 175 countries.

Vatican City's economy is unique in that most of its revenue comes from religious contributions from around the world. Other revenue comes from the sale of stamps, coins, religious objects, and museum entry fees.

Left St Peters Basilica in Vatican City was erected in the sixteenth century over the site of the original basilica, which was built in the fourth century by Emperor Constantine.

SAN MARINO

Official name Republic of San Marino
Land area 23½ square miles (61.2 km²)
Border countries Italy
Capital San Marino
Highest point Monte Titano 2,477 feet (755 m)
Climate Mediterranean
Population 29,615
Language(s) Italian
Ethnicity Sammarinese, Italian
Religion Roman Catholic
Government Republic
Currency Euro
Human Development Index Not available

VATICAN CITY

Official name Vatican City (Holy See)
Land area ⅙ square mile (0.44 km²)
Border countries Italy
Capital Vatican City (Città del Vaticano)
Highest point unnamed site 246 feet (75 m)
Climate Temperate with mild and rainy winters; hot and dry summers
Population 821
Language(s) Italian, Latin, French, other
Ethnicity Italian, Swiss, other
Religion Roman Catholic
Government Ecclesiastical
Currency Euro
Human Development Index Not available

Below Monte Titano has three summits, each with a tower and fortifications. At 2,477 feet (755 m) the mountaintop fortresses have sweeping views of San Marino below.

ITALY

Official name Republic of Italy (Repubblica Italiana)
Land area 113,530 square miles (294,020 km²)
Border countries Switzerland, Austria, Slovenia, San Marino, Vatican City, France
Capital Rome (Roma)
Highest point Monte Bianco de Courmayeur 15,577 feet (4,748 m)
Climate Mediterranean and humid continental
Population 58,145,000
Language(s) Official: Italian; other: German, French, Slovene
Ethnicity Italian, plus regional minority representation
Religion Roman Catholic 90%, other 10% (includes Protestant, Jewish, Muslim)
Government Republic
Currency Euro
Human Development Index 0.941 (ranked 20th out of 177 countries)

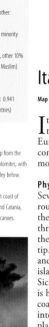

LIECHTENSTEIN
AUSTRIA
SWITZERLAND
Bolzano
SLOVENIA
Udine
Trieste
Monte Bianco
Brescia
Milano
Verona
Venezia
Torino
FRANCE
Piacenza
Modena
Bologna
Genova
SAN MARINO
Rimini
Pisa
Firenze
Ancona
Livorno
Perugia
Ligurian Sea
ITALY
Pescara
Adriatic Sea
ROMA (ROME)
Foggia
Bari
Napoli
Salerno
Taranto
Sassari
Sardegna
Tyrrhenian Sea
Cosenza
Catanzaro
Cagliari
Messina
Palermo
Reggio di Calabria
Sicilia
Catania
Mediterranean Sea
Siracusa
MALTA

Italy

Map Reference Pages 232–233

Italy owes its famous boot-like shape to the interaction between the African and Eurasian tectonic plates. This interaction has contributed to the formation of the Apennine mountain range, Italy's backbone.

Right The Geisler Mountains rise up from the Val Gardena near Ortisei in Italy's Dolomites, with St Jacob's nestled in the tranquil valley below.

Below Mt Etna, located on the east coast of Sicily near to the cities of Messina and Catania, is one of the world's most active volcanoes.

Physical Geography

Several gulfs of the Mediterranean Sea surround this narrow landmass. In the east, the Adriatic Sea follows the entire coast and, through the Strait of Otranto, connects to the Ionian Sea encompassing Italy's southern tip. Western Italy's coasts lie on the Ligurian and Tyrrhenian seas, facing two of the largest islands in the Mediterranean: Sardinia and Sicily. Most of central and southern Italy is hilly countryside. Except in "the heel," coastal plains rarely form incursions into the interior. In the north, the Po River's alluvial plain separates the Apennines from the Alps; it forms Italy's main lowlands and extends to the border with Slovenia. The Po is Italy's longest river and drains the largest watershed.

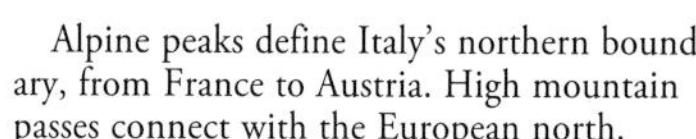

Alpine peaks define Italy's northern boundary, from France to Austria. High mountain passes connect with the European north.

The Apennines mountain chain contains four active volcanoes—Mt Vesuvius near Naples, Mt Etna near Catania in Sicily, and the Aeolian islands of Stromboli and Vulcano, north of Sicily. This volcanic unrest lies above the subduction zone where the African Plate is pushing northward beneath the Eurasian Plate. Naples, a city of over 3 million located on the flanks of Mt Vesuvius, is highly at risk. Italy also experiences numerous and sometimes devastating earthquakes.

The predominant climate is Mediterranean, with hot summers and wet winters. Northern areas experience both humid continental and mountain climates.

History

Archeological evidence suggests that Italy was inhabited in the Old Stone Age. Yet Italian culture truly began to evolve in the first millennium BCE, with the mysterious Etruscan civilization in central Italy and the establishment of Greek colonies in southern Italy and Sicily. In the following centuries Rome, created in 753 BCE, slowly emerged as a regional power and unified the entire country.

The Roman Republic, transformed into the Roman Empire during Augustus's reign (27–14 BCE), went on to conquer the entire Mediterranean realm. By 476 CE, however, it exited the stage after Germanic tribes conquered its last sections, took control of Rome, and replaced the empire's last ruler. It would take another 1,500 years to unify Italy again.

During the medieval period many outside and domestic powers controlled different regions. Venice and Genoa became city-states and merchants of the high seas; the Papacy controlled central Italy. Outside interests from all corners of the Mediterranean contributed to an influx of knowledge, education, and economic growth. In the Renaissance period (fifteenth to sixteenth centuries) Italy was the center of European culture. Only with the widespread growth of nationalism in the nineteenth century did the Italians—led by Giuseppe Garibaldi—finally manage to reunite most of their lands, and eventually form a monarchy in 1870.

The dark period of Italy's modern history lasted from 1922 until the end of World War II under the fascist dictatorship of Benito Mussolini, who abolished democracy and joined Nazi Germany's imperialism.

On June 2, 1946, Italy became a republic by referendum, and in 1949 became one of the founding members of NATO and an ally of the United States, thus receiving financial aid. Today, Italy participates in international missions and peacekeeping operations under the NATO and UN umbrellas.

VENICE

Scattered across numerous islands and intersected by canals, Venice is a living museum. For centuries this city, which evolved from a small fishing settlement, ruled the trade routes to every corner of the Mediterranean Sea. The Venetian republic's merchants had built their reputation as adventurers and uncompromising middlemen between east and west. They sailed eastward with the Crusaders to fight in the Holy Land, ravaged Constantinople, and searched for the land of the mythical Prester John. They brought back wealth and knowledge from many advanced eastern societies that eventually helped to make Italy the center of European culture.

The city's cultural landscape displays this wonderful symbiosis of Byzantine, Arab, and western traits especially in sacred architecture and the arts. For over a thousand years Venetians vigorously protected the independent status of their city-state, until Napoleon's forces occupied and abolished the republic in 1797.

Today a natural, rather than cultural, decline is on the mind of Venice's residents. Environmental mismanagement during the twentieth century has caused the city to gradually sink below sea level. In order to prevent Venice's brick and stone buildings, which were erected on wooden foundations, from being slowly eroded, some of the most expensive preservation projects in Italian history have been put in place.

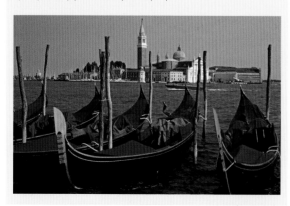

MILESTONE EVENTS

1860–1870 The process of Italian unification and formation of monarchy
1914 Italy joins Allies in World War I
1922 Mussolini's fascists take over political power; Italy becomes a dictatorship
1936 Italy allies with Nazi Germany
1940 Italy enters World War II
June 2, 1946 Proclamation of the Italian Republic
1951 Italy becomes founding member of the European Coal and Steel Community
1957 Italy becomes founding member of European Economic Community
1999 Italy joins Eurozone
2004 Nineteen Italian armed forces personnel are killed in a suicide bomb attack in southern Iraq

Population/Culture

Millions left Italy for the New World in the early twentieth century, mainly from the economically undeveloped south and islands.

From 1951 to 1971 more than 4 million Italians relocated to the industrial centers north of the Apennines. Population density remains highest in Lombardy, Piedmont, and Veneto, the provinces that are the most economically prosperous. The lowest population density remains in the rural countryside of the Apennine Mountains.

As Italy entered the postindustrial era, life expectancy rates have increased, yet birth rates for the native-born have drastically declined. Estimates that by 2050 Italy's total population may be reduced to near 50 million, from a current 58 million, are not unrealistic. It appears that Italy will have to rely on immigration to reverse negative trends. Albanians, Moroccans, and Romanians form the largest immigrant groups, mainly in urban areas.

On the surface, there appears to be a uniform ethnic structure, but there is a mix of regional identities. French, Austrian, and Slovenian minorities reside near the borders of their respective countries. Eastern Europeans are becoming increasingly represented. Sardinians track their roots to pre-Roman times, as do other indigenous peoples. Many northern Italians are of Germanic heritage, while Albanian and Greek ethnic backgrounds are not uncommon in the south.

Italy is still a stronghold of Catholicism. It is only recently that the Church's historically powerful influence over all aspects of life—from religious to political and social—has weakened. Rapid industrialization and urbanization, and formal education, have created more emphasis on individual rights. As in the other Catholic countries of Europe, active practice of religion has declined and church attendance generally remains low.

Italian is an official language and belongs to the Romanic (Romance) branch of Indo-European languages. Regional dialectical differences are pronounced, and to non-native speakers sometimes hard to comprehend.

Administration/Government

The political environment is perhaps the most turbulent of the world's developed countries. Italy has experienced 61 changes of national government since the restoration of democracy in 1946. The Roman tradition of continuously brewing political affairs continues today in a system of vast ideological differences. Most governments include multiparty coalitions that are prone to rapidly falling apart with the first shake-up in political equilibrium.

Despite this, Italy keeps evolving as one of the world's leading democracies. The president's role is mostly ceremonial; day-to-day executive power is in the hands of the prime minister and the cabinet.

The country is divided into twenty administrative divisions, of which five hold autonomous status in order to accommodate Italy's local minority populations: Friuli–Venezia Giulia, Trentino–South Tyrol, Sardinia, Sicily, and Aosta Valley.

Italy is a founding member of the European Coal and Steel Community, which later evolved into the European Union (EU).

Economy/Industry

In terms of economic performance, Italy ranks among the 10 leading countries in the world and has the world's seventh-highest GPD. Natural resources are limited, so fossil fuels must be imported from North Africa and other neighboring regions. Italy's leading trade partners are other EU members, especially Germany and France.

The economy is highly diverse, and renowned for luxury products. Milan is an international focus of fashion. Traditional manufacturing and heavy industry are declining, while the service sector accounts for over two-thirds of GDP. Numerous small-to-medium-sized companies employ skilled, highly productive staff. Italy ranks as one of the world's most visited destinations. Rome, Venice, and the Tuscan cities host millions of visitors each year, while many visitors are attracted to alpine centers during winter.

Infrastructure and communications are well developed and the highway network is among the best in Europe. Public debt, unemployment, and corruption are the main domestic economic issues, with strong regional differences between the northern and southern regions of the country. The agricultural south, historically known as the Mezzogiorno, still lags behind in development and is often perceived in the north as a region of uncontrolled organized crime and rampant corruption.

Italian Food

Italian cuisine is one of the hallmarks of the country's culture. A simple approach to meal preparation, fresh ingredients, and balanced portions are just several reasons for its worldwide appeal. Italy boasts many regional specialities and great emphasis is placed on the use of seasonal produce. Italians approach food seriously, not simply to satisfy hunger but as a way to enjoy life. Meals are to be savored and may last for hours, and are often accompanied by local wines and liqueurs.

The Italian diet, with an emphasis on cereals, grains, and vegetables, has evolved from the traditional peasant lifestyle. Throughout history, livestock were kept on small farms for the production of the milk and cheeses necessary to feed large families. Wheat and corn were affordable staple items that were used extensively in everyday cuisine.

Expensive high-quality cuts of meat were eaten only on special occasions, so Italians became masters of curing and preparing low-grade meats and turning them into tasty salamis and sausages.

Italians have also managed to capitalize on their diet's popularity and turn it into a major industry. Hams from Parma and San Danielle, cheeses, including Parmigiano Reggiano, and wines from Tuscany and Piedmont are some of the country's most popular culinary export items.

Italy's premium gourmet products are all very expensive and are controlled along strict geographic boundaries.

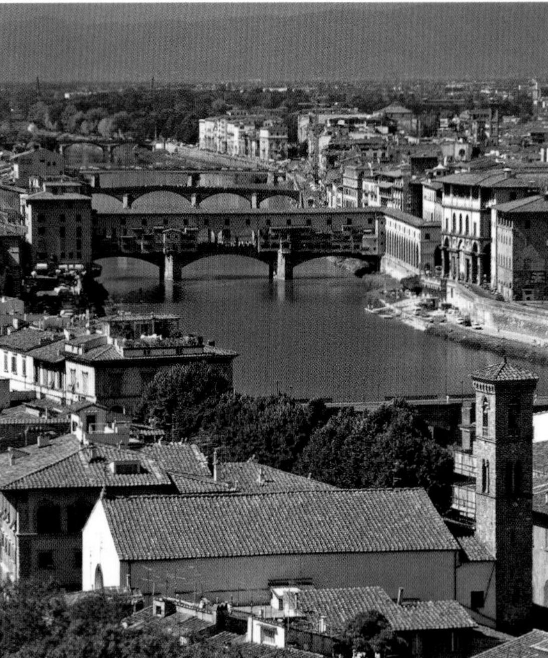

Above The River Arno flows under the Ponte Vecchio, Florence (Firenze). During medieval times the russet-roofed city was an important trade and financial center, and later became famous as the birthplace of the Italian Renaissance.

Left The exquisite masks worn at Venice Carnival time (Carnevale di Venezia) are traditionally fashioned from leather or papier mâché, but are now also made from painted acrylic gesso decorated with gold leaf, feathers, gems, and bells.

Above The Capitoline Museums in Rome house many ancient and Renaissance sculptures, artworks, and artefacts, including this hand, one of the remnants of a colossal marble statue of the Emperor Constantine (c. 272–337).

Far left The Colosseum, in the heart of the Eternal City, is an iconic symbol of the mighty Roman Empire. It was the largest amphitheater ever built by the Romans.

SLOVENIA

Official name Republic of Slovenia (Republika Slovenija)
Land area 7,781 square miles (20,151 km²)
Border countries Austria, Hungary, Croatia, Italy
Capital Ljubljana
Highest point Triglav 9,396 feet (2,864 m)
Climate Continental, Mediterranean, mountain
Population 2,008,000
Language(s) Slovenian, Serbian, Croatian, Italian, Hungarian
Ethnicity Slovene 83%, Serb 2%, Croat 2%, Bosniak 1%, other or unspecified 12%
Religion Catholic 57.8%, Muslim 2.4%, Orthodox 2.3%, other Christian 0.9%, unaffiliated 3.5%, other or unspecified 23%, none 10.1%
Government Parliamentary democracy
Currency Euro
Human Development Index 0.917 (ranked 27th out of 177 countries)

AUSTRIA
HUNGARY
ITALY
CROATIA
SLOVENIA
LJUBLJANA
Maribor
Sebota
Jesenice
Triglav
Celje
Kranj
Trbovlje
Škofja Loka
Nova Gorica
Novo Mesto
Izola
Koper

Slovenia

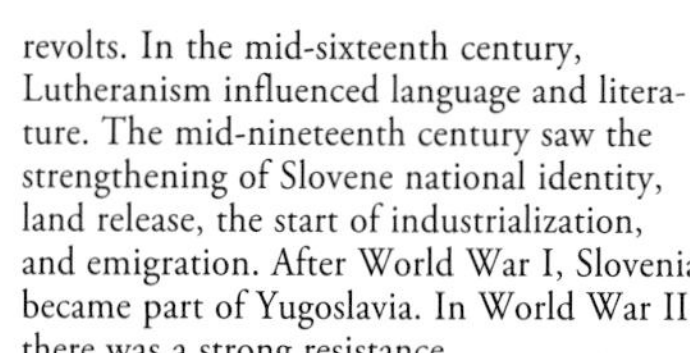

Map Reference Pages 226–227

Above right A view across the old town of Ljubljana, Slovenia's largest city and its capital. A Roman settlement known as Emona existed here from 15 CE until it was devastated by the Huns in 452 CE.

Right An woman slides past the finish line after completing the slalom race in the "Old-Fashioned Winter Olympics" in the northwestern Slovenian village of Krupa.

Below Located in the Julian Alps near Gorenjska, Slovenia, lies the beautiful glacial Lake Bled. Here, in blissful isolation, stands the Pilgrimage Church of Mary's Assumption, which was built in the fifteenth century.

Slovenia is located at the juncture of the Alps, the Adriatic Sea, the Pannonian Plain, and the Dinaric Mountain—an important crossroads between the Mediterranean and eastern Europe, and between western Europe and southeastern Europe.

Physical Geography

Slovenia is divided into five basic types of landscapes: Alpine in the north, subalpine in the center, Mediterranean in the southwest, Dinaric in the south, and Pannonian in the east. Mountains, hills, and karst plateaus are predominant relief features, and 60 percent of the country is covered with forests.

Among the many underground karst caves, one of the most fascinating is the Postojna Cave, famous for the "human fish" *(Proteus anguinus)*—a blind amphibian with human-like skin. The longest karst river, Ljubljanica, acquires seven names as its course appears and disappears seven times. Over half the country has a dense network of surface brooks and small rivers; the karst plateaus of limestone and dolomite have underground water.

The climate varies from moderate Mediterranean in the west, Alpine in the north and northwest, to moderate continental in the remainder of the country.

History

Slavic people settled the territory of the Slovenes in the sixth century. The independent duchy of Carantania in the territory of present-day Carinthia came under Frankish, and subsequently, German rule. From the end of the fifteenth century nearly all the Slovenian ethnic area was ruled by the Habsburgs until the end of World War I.

The fifteenth and sixteenth centuries were marked by Turkish incursions and peasant revolts. In the mid-sixteenth century, Lutheranism influenced language and literature. The mid-nineteenth century saw the strengthening of Slovene national identity, land release, the start of industrialization, and emigration. After World War I, Slovenia became part of Yugoslavia. In World War II there was a strong resistance movement against occupying Nazi and fascist troops, accompanied by social revolution.

The central government of postwar communist Yugoslavia stopped Slovenia's economic development. This, along with a desire for democracy, prompted the push for independence, which was achieved in 1991. Slovenia became a member of both the European Union and NATO in 2004.

Population/Culture

Half of the population lives in rural areas, most enjoying a high quality of life in a well-preserved natural environment. About 140,000 Slovenians live in neighboring countries, and a further 500,000 are scattered across the world, mostly in the United States.

Slovenia is a land of connection and transition—a meeting place of nations, languages, and cultures. The traditional Slovene Catholic culture was greatly altered at the end of the twentieth century due to immigrants from former Yugoslav republics, who settled mostly in the towns. In addition, some 2,500 Italians and 6,500 Hungarians live in bilingual territories along the state's border.

The native population uses 38 dialects, derived from landscape diversity, distribution of primary parishes, and the influence of other languages. Traditional architecture, cuisine, and customs reflect these variations.

A particularly well-loved cultural icon is the famous Lipizzaner horse, the compact muscular breed which originated in 1580 from Lipica in the country's Kras region.

Administration/Government

The Republic of Slovenia is a parliamentary democratic republic. The national assembly has 88 elected representatives of parliamentary parties and two representatives of Italian and Hungarian national communities. The national council has 40 elected representatives.

Economy/Industry

Slovenia was the most developed country of the former Yugoslavia, cooperating in the sphere of industry with western countries. Its economy developed and thrived during the transition period. Slovenia manufactures electrical, transport, and machine equipment, as well as metal, chemical, and food products, much of which are exported. Its agricultural products include meat, dairy, cereals, vegetables, and fruit, much of it organic. Superior natural conditions *(terroir)* make it possible to produce high-quality wines. Tourism is growing, with mountain and seaside wellness resorts becoming popular.

MILESTONE EVENTS

c. 568 Slavic people settle in the territory of Slovenia
976 Duchy of Carantania is established
c. 1000 Religious texts known as the Friesing Manuscripts become the earliest known document written in Slovenian
c. 1400s Habsburgs rule over most of the territory of Slovenia
1550 The first book in the Slovenian language is printed, a Lutheran catechism
1848 Unified Slovenia, the first Slovenian political program, comes into being
1918 Austro-Hungarian Empire is defeated, and the state of south Slavs (Slovenes, Croats, Serbs) is created
January 6, 1929 Kingdom of Yugoslavia is proclaimed
1945 The Federal People's Republic of Yugoslavia is formed, with Slovenia as one of its federal entities
June 25, 1991 Declaration of the independent Republic of Slovenia
2004 Slovenia becomes a member of NATO and the European Union

SLOVENIA
HUNGARY
Čakovec
Varaždin
Koprivnica
ZAGREB
Virovitica
Rijeka
Karlovac
Sisak
Osijek
CROATIA
Požega
Slavonski Brod
Pula
Cres
Krk
SERBIA
Pag
BOSNIA AND HERZEGOVINA
Zadar
Dinara
Adriatic Sea
Šibenik
Split
Brač
Hvar
Korčula
Dubrovnik
MONTENEGRO

Croatia

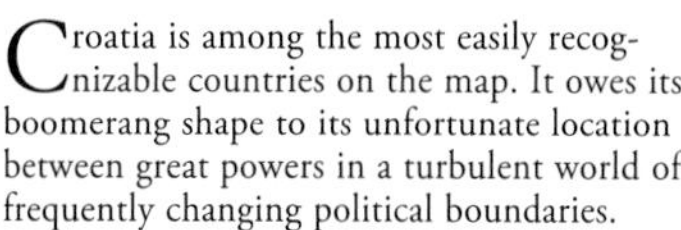

Map Reference Pages 232–233

Croatia is among the most easily recognizable countries on the map. It owes its boomerang shape to its unfortunate location between great powers in a turbulent world of frequently changing political boundaries.

Physical Geography

Two distinct geographic units, northern continental and southern coastal, are separated by the Dinaric Alps. The northern region is the extension of the Pannonian lowlands intersected with rolling hills and occasional mountains. This is the main agricultural belt.

Tectonic forces and the erosion of limestone and dolomite have created a unique landscape in the south, known as karst *(krš)*. The word derives from Croatian and Slovenian, and scientific terminology for karst features also come from these languages. Nowhere has nature combined its forces to form the karst landscape more remarkably than in Croatia. It is especially prevalent in Dalmatia where only two colors, the light gray of the karst and the blue of the Adriatic Sea, fill the horizon. A difficult environment for farming and livestock, with a limited amount of arable land, the karst region has traditionally been a place of emigration.

More than a thousand islands are scattered across the Croatian side of the Adriatic Sea. Few coastal plains exist and mountains literally rise from the sea. The interior highlands follow the line of the coast.

Climatic conditions correspond to regional division. A Mediterranean climate with hot summers and wet winters extends throughout Dalmatia and the rest of the Croatian coastal areas; the interior has a continental climate.

History

Modern-day Croatia has been populated since prehistoric times. The Romans were the first to utilize and urbanize the area, mainly on the coast and islands. The Croats, a Slavic tribe from Eastern Europe, settled around Dalmatia and founded a medieval kingdom that lasted until they entered a union with Hungarians at the beginning of the twelfth century. In various forms, association with Hungary and Austria lasted until the end of World War I and the demise of the Habsburg monarchy.

During this time Croatia acted as a fortified military belt against the advancing Ottoman Empire, which explains its current shape. In 1918 the Croats joined with other south Slavic nations into what later became known as Yugoslavia, first as a kingdom and then, between 1945 and 1991, a communist-led republic. Croatia became independent in 1991, triggering ethnic warfare between Croats and Croatia's Serbs that lasted until 1995.

DUBROVNIK

The city of Dubrovnik, along with Italy's Venice, is considered among the most visually appealing places on the shores of the Adriatic. Today recognized as the leading urban center of Croatia's southern tip and a major tourist destination, Dubrovnik has a rich heritage as an independent political entity and free republic that skillfully survived centuries of turbulent regional geopolitics. The first Slavic tribes settled this area around the seventh century. In the following centuries Dubrovnik became the economic center by utilizing its location near the mouth of the Adriatic Sea as a corridor to all corners of the Mediterranean realm. The wealth so generated helped to erect breathtaking architecture, much of which is still in remarkable condition, but also allowed the city to develop a cosmopolitan mentality. Dubrovnik implemented social and political measures vastly ahead of its time, such as abolishing the slave trade in the fifteenth century and providing medical benefits for local residents as early as the fourteenth century. In 1799 Napoleon Bonaparte's forces took over control and soon after his demise Dubrovnik was integrated into the Habsburg monarchy and eventually Croatia. In 1979 the entire old city of Dubrovnik was selected for addition to UNESCO's World Heritage list.

MILESTONE EVENTS

1102 Croatia forms joint kingdom with Hungary

1527 Habsburg monarchy integrates Croatia

1533 Military border "Vojna Krajina" created as defense against Ottoman Empire

1918 Formation of unified south Slavic kingdom

1945 Croatia becomes one of six republics of the Yugoslav socialist federation

1991 Independence from Yugoslavia triggers ethnic conflicts

2003 Croatia applies for membership of the European Union

Population/Culture

Croats are linguistically and ethnically related to their fellow south Slavs. Their language is moderately different from Slovenian and displays only a slight variation from Serbian. For a time these languages were known as Serbo-Croatian. Three clearly distinguished dialects, phonetically and geographically, are spoken: stokavski (the official dialect), cakavski (southern coastal region), and kajkavski (north–northwest).

Christianity is the dominant religion, with the vast majority of people practicing Roman Catholicism, although religious orientation is also separated along ethnic lines, because religion and ethnicity are synonymous throughout southeastern Europe. Ethnic Serbs follow Orthodox traditions and Bosniaks are Muslims.

Administration/Government

Political structure is a parliamentary democracy with a bicameral assembly, while the president, who appoints a prime minister, is elected to a maximum of two five-year terms. Two primary blocs, center-left and center-right, form the political factions on national and local levels. One of the most pressing priorities for the current government is to be granted full membership of the European Union. EU President José Manuel Barroso has promised to conclude membership talks with Croatia by November 2009, with 2010 being the likely entry date.

Economy/Industry

Croatia was one of the more prosperous former Yugoslav republics, but wartime activities stalled economic development for much of the 1990s. The transition from a centralized type of economy into a free-market system has been marked with obstacles, in particular an increase in cumulative debt and an inability to reduce the rate of unemployment, which is still over 11 percent. The service sector accounts for more than half of the workforce. Zagreb is the main economic center. The privatization of companies has allowed much-needed infrastructure and communication investment. Income from tourism, especially from summer tourism in the Adriatic area, represents the most important source of foreign currency income to the Croatian economy.

CROATIA

Official name Republic of Croatia (Republika Hrvatska)

Land area 21,781 square miles (56,414 km²)

Border countries Slovenia, Hungary, Serbia, Montenegro, Bosnia and Herzegovina

Capital Zagreb

Highest point Dinara 6,007 feet (1,831 m)

Climate Mediterranean and humid continental

Population 4,492,000

Language(s) Official: Croatian; other: Serbian and other

Ethnicity Croat 89.6%, Serb 4.5%, other 5.9% (including Bosniak, Hungarian, Slovene, Czech, Roma)

Religion Roman Catholic 87.8%, Orthodox 4.4%, other Christian 0.4%, Muslim 1.3%, other and unspecified 6.1%

Government Parliamentary democracy

Currency Kuna

Human Development Index 0.850 (ranked 47th out of 177 countries)

Top The hilltop location of the medieval Veliki Tabor Castle in Desinića, Croatia, commands expansive views across forests and rolling hills.

Above Dolphins are known to frolic in the clear waters of the Adriatic Sea close to shore. This calf, photographed off the southern Croatian town of Krilo Jesenice in 2007, was separated from its mother. According to reports, it was rescued by members of the pod some time later.

BOSNIA AND HERZEGOVINA

Official name Bosnia and Herzegovina (Bosna i Hercegovina)
Land area 19,742 square miles (51,129 km²)
Border countries Croatia, Serbia, Montenegro
Capital Sarajevo
Highest point Maglic 7,828 feet (2,386 m)
Climate Generally, hot summers and cold winters; colder year-round in higher areas; mild, wet winters along the coast
Population 3,842,537
Language(s) Bosnian, Serbian, Croatian
Ethnicity Bosniak, Serb, Croat
Religion Muslim 40%, Eastern Orthodox 31%, Roman Catholic 15%, other or unspecified 14%
Government Emerging federal democratic republic
Currency Convertible mark
Human Development Index 0.803 (ranked 66th out of 177 countries)

Above right Sarajevo, the capital of Bosnia and Herzegovina, at night. This historic city, which has endured the tumult and horror of war, became a member of the International Association of Peace Messenger Cities in 2005.

Right These young Bosnian women are wearing traditional Muslim clothing. These days, most urban Bosnians wear western-style clothing.

Below The renovated and revitalized historical part of Mostar is now a thriving business center. An international jury praised the sensitive and restrained way the more than 600-year-old town has been conserved.

Right Kosovar Bosnians wait for their son's turn to be circumcised as part of a festival of feasting, singing, and dancing in the village of Gornje Lubinje, near the border of Kosovo and Macedonia.

CROATIA
Bosanska Gradiška
Bihać
Banja Luka
Bijeljina
Tuzla
BOSNIA AND HERZEGOVINA
Zvornik
SERBIA
Zenica
Bugojno
SARAJEVO
Konjic
Mostar
Maglić
MONTENEGRO
Trebinje
Adriatic Sea

Bosnia and Herzegovina

Map Reference Pages 232–233

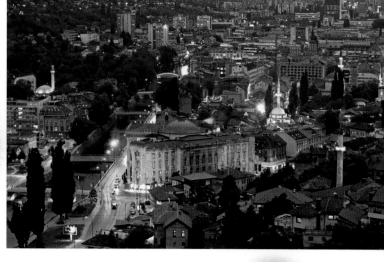

Named after the medieval political regions Bosnia (after the river Bosna) and Herzegovina (meaning dukedom), Bosnia and Herzegovina is the only former Yugoslav republic not named after its ethnic group.

Physical Geography

Despite modest territorial size, the country exemplifies the complexity of physical geography in this part of the world. The ranges of the Dinaric Alps predominate, intersected by river valleys, and forming natural barriers that are still an obstacle to transportation infrastructure. Main urban centers are located along rivers. Only in the north, bordering Croatia, have alluvial plains created potential for sizable agriculture.

A good portion of the country has forest cover, some of which is Europe's primeval forest. In Herzegovina, in the south, Mediterranean climate and dominance of sedimentary rocks have created a natural landscape similar to Dalmatia. A small sliver of coast that wedges into Croatian territory, around the city of Neum, is the only exit to the Adriatic Sea.

History

The small south Slavic kingdom of Bosnia reached its zenith in the fourteenth and early fifteenth centuries. King Tvrtko I (1338–1391) controlled territory extending to present-day boundaries. In 1463, the region fell to the Ottoman Empire. Four centuries later the Congress of Berlin ceded the lands of Bosnia and Herzegovina to the Habsburg Monarchy. They were annexed in 1908. In the aftermath of World War I, Bosnia joined the Kingdom of Serbs, Croats, and Slovenians, later Yugoslavia. After the wave of independence

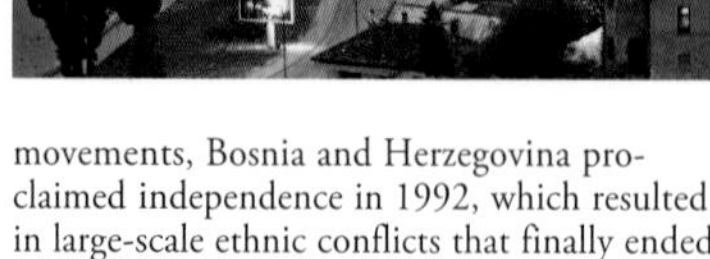

movements, Bosnia and Herzegovina proclaimed independence in 1992, which resulted in large-scale ethnic conflicts that finally ended with the Dayton Agreement in 1995.

Population/Culture

Population dynamics have been radically affected by wartime events, including forced and voluntary internal relocation.

At first sight Bosnia and Herzegovina appears as a complex ethnic mix. Almost all residents, however, are originally of Slavic stock and communicate in basically identical languages. Religion is the only major difference. Croats are Catholics, Serbs are Eastern Orthodox, and Bosniaks are Muslim Slavs (mainly Croats and Serbs, who converted to Islam during past centuries of Ottoman rule).

Many customs and traditions are similar. Some words display the historical influences of outside forces (mainly Turkish and German). Among young people, English is the main foreign language. In 1984 Sarajevo hosted the Winter Olympics, and put Bosnia and Herzegovina on the modern world map.

Administration/Government

In order to accommodate ethnic demands, administrative structure and political process are rather complicated. The country is composed of two political units of about equal size: The Federation of Bosnia and Herzegovina is Muslim–Croat, while the Republic of Srpska is controlled by ethnic Serbs. Each has a substantial amount of autonomy in regard to their internal affairs. The two rotate the national presidency and provide members to two chambers of assembly. The High Representative of the European Union oversees the entire political process with executive powers that prevent the country from straying from the Dayton Agreement.

Economy/Industry

During the Yugoslav era, Bosnia and Herzegovina was the center of mining and heavy industry, had defense-based industrial capacities, and exported raw materials. Despite rapid industrial development after World War II, it lagged behind the more developed republics Slovenia and Croatia, with a need for radical expansion in infrastructure and transportation. Atrocities during the civil war relegated output to pre-1990 levels, but a new currency, economic reforms, and foreign investment have created a positive impact. High unemployment rates, corruption, and geographically unequal distribution of investments block overall development.

MILESTONE EVENTS

1463 Ottoman Empire's rule begins
1908 Bosnia and Herzegovina becomes part of Austria–Hungary
1918 Bosnia and Herzegovina joins south Slavic state
1941 Hitler sends thousands of Serbs, Jews, Roma, and others to concentration camps
1945 Bosnia and Herzegovina becomes part of the Socialist Federal Republic of Yugoslavia
1991 Collapse of communism: Yugoslavia is dissolved
March 3, 1992 Independence declared
1995 The Dayton Agreement ends ethnic conflicts and forms the basis for the current political structure
2006 General elections reflect Serb and Muslim-Croat ethnic divisions

SERBIA
Leposavić
Kosovska Mitrovica
Podujevo
Vučitrn
MONTENEGRO
Peć
Klina
Kosovo Polje
PRIŠTINA
Daravica
KOSOVO
Gnjilane
Đakovica
Orahovac
Uroševac
Prizren
Kačanik
Dragaš
ALBANIA
MACEDONIA

Kosovo

Map Reference Pages 234–235

Until recently the province of Kosovo and Metohija within Serbia, Kosovo unilaterally proclaimed independence in February 2008. It has been officially recognized by a number of countries but denied recognition by others. Serbia rejected Kosovo's independence and filed a formal protest to the United Nations. When Serbia was one of the republics in the former Yugoslavia, Kosovo held the status of an autonomous province. A vast majority of Kosovo's population was ethnic Albanian and advocated separation from Serbia on that basis.

In 1999, after rebellion in Kosovo and Serbia's fierce response, NATO intervened in an air campaign against Serbia. Justification for armed intervention was the prevention of ethnic cleansing and the exodus of the Albanian civil population from Kosovo. Since then Kosovo has been subject to international supervision under an agreement with Serbia. Ethnic Serbs reside near the Serbian border in Kosovo's north. Because Albanians have boycotted the Serbian census for the past two decades, exact population numbers are estimates. Continuous population changes as a result of atrocities and emigration further complicate demographic studies.

While other ethnic groups experienced lowering birth rates, the close-knit Albanian society maintained the highest birth rates in Europe. Thus, by the 1980s Kosovo had become overwhelmingly Albanian. Most Albanians in Kosovo are Muslims and related to north Albania's tribesmen who were among the region's earliest settlers. Serbs (Eastern Orthodox Christians) are of Slavic ethnic background. They consider Kosovo the heart of their nation because it was the center of the Serbian medieval state and is home to several Eastern Orthodox monasteries. The linguistic relation between the two is loose; both languages belong to the Indo-European family, yet they are not mutually understandable.

Kosovo has two geographically different regions—rolling hillsides in the northeast, and a plateau in the southwest. The economy has always focused around small-scale agriculture and the mining of coal and metals, but poor infrastructure and corruption block rapid progress even in these sectors, making Kosovo the poorest nation in Europe.

HUNGARY
ROMANIA
CROATIA
Subotica
Sombor
Zrenjanin
Novi Sad
Zemun
Pančevo
Šabac
BEOGRAD (BELGRADE)
SERBIA
Valjevo
Kragujevac
Paraćin
Čačak
Kraljevo
Kruševac
Niš
Midžor
Novi Pazar
Leskovac
Pirot
BOSNIA AND HERZEGOVINA
MONTENEGRO
KOSOVO
BULGARIA
MACEDONIA

Serbia

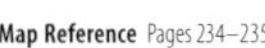

Map Reference Pages 234–235

The largest of the former Yugoslav republics, landlocked Serbia extends through the heart of southeastern Europe, well placed as a transportation route in an area where few natural corridors exist. Particularly valuable is the river valley of Morava, which connects Europe's southeast with the rest of the continent. The Danube River provides an indirect connection between Serbia and the ocean.

Physical Geography

Rolling hills and narrow river valleys dominate the landscape in the central and southern portions of the country. North of Belgrade the landscape transforms into the Pannonian lowlands of Vojvodina, the main agricultural region. The climate mainly falls into the category of humid continental. The highest rainfall occurs during the summer months.

The Romanian borderlands are in part defined by one of Europe's most breathtaking landscapes, the Djerdap Gorge. On its way to the sea, the Danube carves its way through a narrow corridor between the Carpathian Mountains' southern tip and the Balkan Mountains, where several canyons' impressive walls surpass 1,000 feet (304 m) in height.

History

The creation of Serbia has much in common with other south Slavic nations. In the early Middle Ages, a gradual emancipation from regional rulers allowed the Serbs to form an independent entity, which under Stephen IX Dusan's rule (1331–1355) reached the status of regional empire. By the end of the fourteenth century, the Turks were the strongest force across southeastern Europe and over the following decades, they conquered Serbia and its neighbors and occupied their lands.

In the early years of the nineteenth century, the debilitated Ottoman Empire granted Serbia autonomy, and full independence at the 1878 Congress of Berlin. After World War I, Serbia was a unit of the newly formed Kingdom of Serbs, Croats, and Slovenes, later renamed Yugoslavia. With the demise of socialist Yugoslavia in 1991, Serbia and Montenegro formed a union that lasted until their separation in 2006.

Population/Culture

Rapid transformation from an agrarian to an industrial nation has caused a strong increase in urban population, despite Serbia's overall population decline. Belgrade's metropolitan area has 20 percent of Serbia's almost 7.4 million residents. Yugoslav conflicts affected recent demographic changes in Serbia as well, through internal movements and external migrations. Thousands of refugees from Bosnia and Herzegovina, and Croatia, settled in Serbia, but thousands of Serbians emigrated elsewhere during the same period.

Serbia is composed of more than 24 ethnic groups. Serbs constitute two-thirds of the population. A sizable ethnic Hungarian minority resides in the north. Roma, who live throughout Eastern Europe, are also represented in substantial numbers. Religious orientation follows ethnic lines. The Serbian Orthodox Church has the largest membership. Ethnic Albanians mainly practice Islam, while Hungarians are Catholic and Protestant.

The linguistic structure is also complex. The Serbian language and Cyrillic alphabet are officially recognized, although other languages and the Latin alphabet enjoy widespread regional use. Regional variations in traditions, customs, daily life, and cuisine reflect strong cultural diversity, ranging from Turkish cultural traits in southern and central Serbia to Germanic and Hungarian in the north.

Administration/Government

Serbia is a republic with a unicameral national assembly that elects the prime minister and the president. It is currently working toward becoming a member of the European Union.

Economy/Industry

In the 1990s, escalation of political conflicts directly affected Serbia's economic performance. International sanctions caused the economy to plummet. Serbia suffered the highest inflation rates in Europe, and the highest rates of unemployment and underemployment.

In recent years, Serbia's economy has shown gradual economic improvements. Substantial amounts of foreign aid and debt forgiveness have helped; however, the slow process of privatization has remained an obstacle to more rapid development. Unemployment remains high. Trade balance projections indicate future trends in favor of imports. Serbia is currently pursuing membership of the World Trade Organization.

MILESTONE EVENTS

1878 Serbia granted full independence

1918 Kingdom of Serbia enters joint state with other south Slavs

1929 Kingdom of Serbs, Croats, and Slovenes becomes Yugoslavia

1945 Serbia joins the Socialist Federal Republic of Yugoslavia, led by Josip Tito

1989 Slobodan Milosevic becomes Serbian president

1991 Yugoslavia is dissolved

2000 After riots over election fraud, Milosevic resigns

2006 Serbia and Montenegro end short-lived federation

February 2008 Serbia protests Kosovo's declaration of independence

Left St Sava Orthodox church in Belgrade was consecrated in 1935, but due to World War II and other interruptions, it had to be reconsecrated in 1985. Construction work continues to this day.

KOSOVO

Official name Republic of Kosova (Republika e Kosoves or Republika Kosova)

Land area 4,203 square miles (10,887 km²)

Border countries Serbia, Macedonia, Albania, Montenegro

Capital Pristina

Highest & lowest points Gjeravica/Deravica 8,415 feet (2,565 m); Drini i Bardhe/Beli Drim 974 feet (297 m)

Climate Humid continental

Population 2,126,700

Language(s) Official: Albanian, Serbian; other: Bosniak, Turkish, Roma

Ethnicity Albanian 88%, Serb 7%, other (Bosniak, Gorani, Roma, Turk, Ashkali, Egyptian) 5%

Religion Muslim, Serbian Orthodox, Roman Catholic

Government Republic

Currency Euro; Serbian dinar also still in circulation

Human Development Index Not available

SERBIA

Official name Republic of Serbia (Republika Srbija)

Area 29,915 square miles (77,474 km²)

Border countries Hungary, Romania, Bulgaria, Macedonia, Kosovo, Montenegro, Bosnia and Herzegovina, Croatia

Capital Belgrade (Beograd)

Highest point Midzor 7,116 feet (2,169 m)

Climate Humid continental

Population 7,397,651

Language(s) Serbian, Albanian, Hungarian, Bosniak, Romansh

Ethnicity Serb, Albanian, Hungarian, Roma, Bosniak

Religion Serbian Orthodox 85%, Roman Catholic 5.5%, Muslim 3.2%, Protestant 1.1%, other and unaffiliated 5.2%

Government Republic

Currency Serbian dinar

Human Development Index Not available

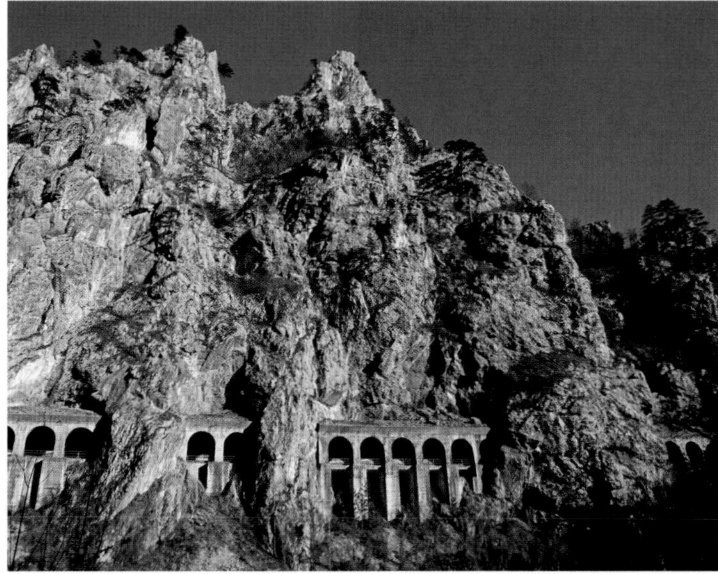

Left The Serbia–Montenegro railway line that connects Belgrade and Podgorica features stunning mountain passes. Also part of this line is the Mala Rijeka viaduct, said to be the highest viaduct in the world.

ROMANIA

Official name Romania
Land area 88,941 square miles (230,340 km²)
Border countries Ukraine, Moldova, Bulgaria, Serbia, Hungary
Capital Bucharest (Bucureşti)
Highest point Moldoveanu 8,346 feet (2,544 m)
Climate Temperate with cold winters and warm, wet summers
Population 22,247,000
Language(s) Official: Romanian; other: Hungarian, Romansh, German
Ethnicity Romanian 89.5%, Hungarian 6.6%, Roma 2.5%, other 1.4%
Religion Eastern Orthodox 87%, Protestant 8%, Roman Catholic 5%, other 1%
Government Republic
Currency Romanian leu
Human Development Index 0.813 (ranked 60th out of 177 countries)

UKRAINE
MOLDOVA
HUNGARY
SERBIA
BULGARIA
ROMANIA
Satu Mare
Suceava
Botoşani
Baia Mare
Iaşi
Oradea
Cluj-Napoca
Piatra Neamţ
Târgu Mureş
Bacău
Arad
Timişoara
Sibiu
Braşov
Galaţi
Brăila
Râmnicu Vâlcea
Buzău
Ploieşti
Piteşti
BUCUREŞTI
(BUCHAREST)
Craiova
Constanţa
Black Sea

Romania

Map Reference Pages 234–235

Romania is bordered by Ukraine, Bulgaria, Moldova, Serbia, and Hungary, and has an outlet to the Black Sea.

Physical Geography

The forested Carpathian Mountains occupy much of the center. The fertile valley of the Danube River covers much of the south and east, and a second agricultural lowland abuts the border with Hungary to the northwest.

At 1,771 miles (2,850 km), the Danube is the second longest river in Europe after the Volga in Russia. It originates in the Black Forest of Germany and flows through or borders 10 countries before breaking into a broad delta in Romania and emptying into the sea.

The Danube forms a large part of Romania's southern border, a part of the northern border, and cuts a south-to-north swath through the coastal plain before bending east and forming the delta. At the Serbian border, the river carves a spectacular gorge called the Iron Gate. In 1972, the Iron Gate Dam was opened as a joint hydroelectricity project by Romania and Yugoslavia.

The Danube Delta is a rich ecosystem that supports flocks of migratory birds and other fauna, but it has been damaged by the effects of channel dredging, industrial pollution, and earlier projects by the government to drain wetlands for agriculture. Since 1991, the delta has been a UNESCO World Heritage Site.

History

Romania's origins can be traced to the ancient Dacian Kingdom that reached its zenith in the first century BCE. During the Middle Ages, Romanian lands were divided into three principalities: Wallachia, Moldavia, and Transylvania. The three were briefly united in 1600. Later, Wallachia and Moldavia became parts of the Ottoman Empire until autonomy in 1856, when they united under the name Romania. In 1918 Transylvania joined Romania, along with parts of neighboring Bukovina and Bessarabia.

During World War II, Romania was initially allied with Nazi Germany, but sided with the Allies in 1944 after a change in leadership. Moldavia was annexed to the Soviet Union following World War II and became independent Moldova in 1991. From 1947 until 1989, Romania was part of the Soviet bloc. From 1965 until his assassination in 1989, Romania was ruled by the iron-fisted dictator Nicolae Ceausescu.

Population/Culture

Romania is a country of more than 22 million people whose ethnic origins are primarily Romanian, with strong Hungarian and Roma minorities. Romania is the only Orthodox Christian country in Europe where the people have Latin roots. Despite many decades of communism and political upheaval, Romanians have preserved their strong folk traditions, especially in music and dance.

Administration/Government

Romania is a republic whose chief of state is the president and head of government is the prime minister. The bicameral parliament is composed of the senate and chamber of deputies, both elected by popular vote.

The Palace of the Parliament in Bucharest is the largest building in Europe and the second largest government building in the world. It was built at enormous cost in 1983 during the dictatorship of Nicolae Ceausescu, and mockingly called the House of Ceausescu after the fall of his regime in 1989.

Economy/Industry

Romania is an emergent market economy following over 40 years of communist rule and ineffective state-run heavy industry. Much of the economy is now privatized and growing, with exports of precision machinery, motor vehicles, food products, clothing, and pharmaceuticals. The Black Sea port of Constanta is one of the busiest in the region, while beach resorts are popular holiday destinations.

Around 30 percent of Romanians work in the agricultural sector. The country produces a high volume of wine, and is the second largest grower of plums in the world.

Above right Bran Castle (or Dracula's Castle) in Transylvania was a stronghold built in 1212. It was given to the Romanian royal family in 1920 and renovated to transform it into a residence. The 187-foot (57 m) deep fountain in the central courtyard supplied their water.

Above These houses in the town of Sibiu, Transylvania, are very good examples of Saxon architecture. Sibiu was the largest and richest Saxon city; in 2007 it was declared European Cultural Capital for that year.

Right At 4,777 feet (1,456 m), Zabljak is said to be the highest city in the Balkans. It is located in Montenegro's Durmitor National Park, which is well known for its rich and varied flora.

BOSNIA AND HERZEGOVINA
SERBIA
KOSOVO
CROATIA
ALBANIA
MONTENEGRO
Pljevlja
Plužine
Bobotov Kuk
Bijelo Polje
Nikšić
Berane
Plav
Herceg-Novi
PODGORICA
Cetinje
Budva
Bar
Adriatic Sea

Montenegro

Map Reference Pages 232–233

Montenegro, on the Adriatic coast of the Balkan Peninsula, is a place where history and physical beauty collide. The country features the historic city of Cetinje and a beautiful and varied coastline that includes Kotar (Europe's southernmost fjord), beautiful beaches at Budva, and the remarkable island resort of Sveti Stefan.

Physical Geography

Montenegro is a land of stark beauty filled with breathtaking vistas and a coastline that rivals the Croatian coast to the north. The Gulf of Kotar is a spectacular World Heritage Site and the Tara River canyon is the deepest in Europe at 4,265 feet (1,300 m). The Dinaric Alps form a rugged wall behind the coastal plain. Durmitor National Park is in this range. Formed by glaciers and criss-crossed by undergound streams and rivers, the park was inscribed a World Heritage Site in 1980.

Montenegro has a Mediterranean climate with hot dry summers and winters that get cold enough for snowfall in non-coastal areas.

History

Illyrians were the first to settle in the region. The Principality of Montenegro was the last monarchy in the Balkans to be conquered by the Ottoman Turks, falling in 1499. Allowed moderate autonomy, Montenegro was ruled by bishop-princes in a theocracy. It was recognized as an independent country in 1878 at the Congress of Berlin. In 1922, Montenegro became part of the Kingdom of Serbs, Croats, and Slovenes which later became Yugoslavia. Montenegro gained independence from Serbia on June 3, 2006.

Population/Culture

The population is a variety of ethnic groups including Montenegrin, Serb, Bosniak, Albanian, Croat, Roma, and others. Serbian is the official language and is spoken by most citizens. Seventy-five percent of Montenegrins are Orthodox Christian. The Muslim and Catholic religions are also represented.

Many great treasures of Byzantine art and architecture are preserved in the Orthodox monasteries. The city of Cetinje is the artistic and cultural center of the country.

Administration/Government

Podgorica is the capital of the newborn republic. The constitution is currently being written. Interim governance is provided by the president who serves as chief of state and the prime minister who heads the government. The unicameral assembly serves as the legislative branch with 81 members.

Economy/Industry

Severing ties with Serbia in 2006 has caused economic disruptions. Unemployment is high at over 25 percent, but foreign investment is increasing. The euro is the currency of Montenegro. Tourism and a growing aluminum industry are important to the economy.

MONTENEGRO

Official name Montenegro (Crna Gora)
Land area 5,333 square miles (13,812 km²)
Border countries Serbia, Kosovo, Albania, Croatia, Bosnia and Herzegovina
Capital Podgorica
Highest point Bobotov Kuk 8,274 feet (2,522 m)
Climate Mediterranean
Population 678,177
Language(s) Official: Serbian; other: Bosnian, Albanian, Croatian
Ethnicity Montenegrin 43%, Serb 32%, Bosniak 8%, Albanian 5%, other (includes Croat and Roma) 12%
Religion Eastern Orthodox 75%, Muslim 20%, Roman Catholic and other 5%
Government Republic
Currency Euro
Human Development Index Not available

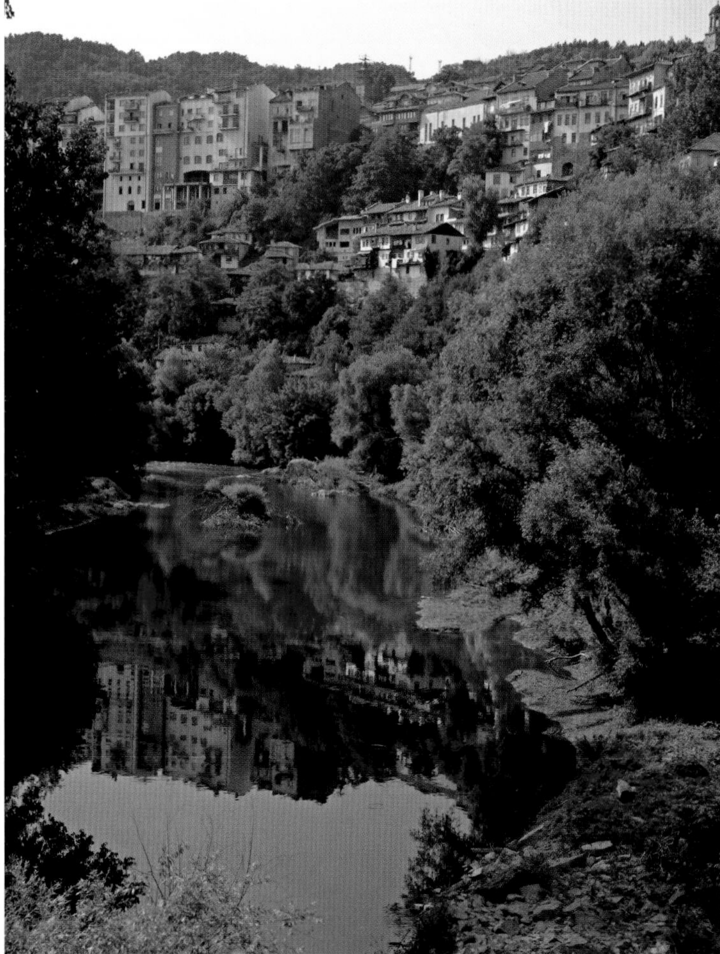

Left The ancient city of Veliko Turnovo is situated on the river Yantra in north-central Bulgaria. In medieval times, it was the capital of Bulgaria.

ROMANIA
SERBIA
BULGARIA
MACEDONIA
GREECE
TURKEY
Black Sea
Vidin
Silistra
Ruse
Dobrich
Montana
Pleven
Shumen
Vratsa
Varna
Veliko Turnovo
Gabrovo
Pernik
SOFIYA (SOFIA)
Sliven
Burgas
Stara Zagora
Kyustendil
Pazardzhik
Musala
Plovdiv
Blagoevgrad
Khaskovo
Kurdzhali

Bulgaria

Map Reference Pages 234–235

Bulgaria, a small country bordered by the Black Sea to the east, and surrounded by Romania, Turkey, Greece, Macedonia, and Serbia, was part of the communist eastern bloc from the end of World War II until 1991.

Physical Geography

Bulgaria has three mountain ranges and extensive lowlands. The Balkan Mountains extend east–west across the center, dividing the Danube valley from the lowlands in the south.

History

Bulgaria's long history can be traced to the early classical civilizations of Thrace, Moesia, and Macedonia many centuries BCE. Slavic people arrived in the mid-seventh century CE, and Orthodox Christianity was adopted in 864. The first and second Bulgarian kingdoms ruled expansive territories in southeastern Europe during the early Middle Ages, eventually giving way to almost 500 years of Ottoman rule. A third Bulgarian kingdom began in 1878 with the Treaty of San Stefano. Bulgaria became allied with the Soviet Union in 1946 until it became a republic in 1991. In 2004 Bulgaria joined NATO, and four years later became a member of the European Union.

Population/Culture

Because of its location at a cultural crossroads of east and west, Bulgaria is a great mix of cultural influences and traditions, including Turkish and Roma. It has many important archeological and historical sites, including ancient Thracian tombs, Greek and Roman ruins, churches and monasteries from medieval Bulgarian kingdoms, and architectural landmarks from the Ottoman period. It has nine UNESCO World Heritage Sites.

Administration/Government

Since 1991, Bulgaria has been a parliamentary democracy. The chief of state is the president, elected by popular vote. The council of ministers is chosen by the prime minister and elected by the unicameral national assembly.

Economy/Industry

Bulgaria is a fast-developing economy in transition from the communist period. Its heavy industry specializes in metallurgy, shipbuilding, and trucks, buses, and other motor vehicles. Tourism focuses on skiing and Black Sea beach resorts. Farm products are exported throughout the European Union.

Cyrillic Alphabet

The Cyrillic alphabet was developed in northeastern Bulgaria in the ninth century CE by Saints Cyril and Methodius, and by their disciple St Clement of Ohrid at the Preslav Literary School. The alphabet was disseminated in the early Middle Ages by the spread of Orthodox religious texts and Old Church Slavonic liturgical language, and became the writing system for many Slavic peoples throughout Eastern Europe. With only small differences in letter forms, Cyrillic is used to write Russian, Ukrainian, Serbian, and other Slavic languages, as well as modern Bulgarian.

Above A Bulgarian dancer called a "kukeri" participates in an ancient masquerade ritual that is held at the end of winter every year to drive away evil spirits and ensure the arrival of spring.

Below left Alexander Nevski Cathedral (left) and the National Assembly (right) in Sofia. The neo-Byzantine cathedral was completed in 1912.

BULGARIA

Official name Republic of Bulgaria (Republika Balgariya)
Land area 42,687 square miles (110,550 km²)
Border countries Romania, Turkey, Greece, Serbia, Macedonia
Capital Sofia (Sofiya)
Highest point Musala 9,596 feet (2,925 m)
Climate Temperate
Population 7,263,000
Language(s) Bulgarian, Turkish, Romansh
Ethnicity Bulgarian 84%, Turk 9%, Roma 5%, other 2%
Religion Bulgarian Orthodox 82.6%, Muslim 12.2%, other Christian 1.2%, other 4%
Government Parliamentary democracy
Currency Lev
Human Development Index 0.824 (ranked 53rd out of 177 countries)

ALBANIA

Official name Republic of Albania (Republika e Shqiperise)
Land area 10,579 square miles (27,398 km²)
Border countries Montenegro, Kosovo, Macedonia, Greece
Capital Tirana (Tiranë)
Highest point Maja e Korabit (Golem Korab) 9,068 feet (2,764 m)
Climate Mild temperate
Population 3,620,000
Language(s) Official: Albanian; other: Greek, Vlach, Romansh
Ethnicity Albanian 95%, Greek 3%, other 2%
Religion Muslim 70%, Albanian Orthodox 20%, Roman Catholic 10%
Government Emerging democracy
Currency Lek
Human Development Index 0.801 (ranked 68th out of 177 countries)

MONTENEGRO
KOSOVO
MACEDONIA
GREECE
Adriatic Sea
Shkodër
Kukës
Lezhë
Peshkopi
Laç
Burrel
ALBANIA
TIRANË
(TIRANA)
Durrës
Kavajë
Elbasan
Lushnjë
Pogradec
Korçë
Vlorë
Gjirokastër
Sarandë

Albania

Map Reference Pages 234–235

Albania, on the east coast of the Adriatic Sea, is bordered by Montenegro, Kosovo, Macedonia, and Greece. From 1944 until 1992 it was a communist state, but now it is a democracy with a growing capitalist economy.

Albanians trace their origins to the Illyrian Kingdom, which originated around 2000 BCE and reached its zenith in the fourth century BCE under King Bardyllis. Later, Albanian lands were ruled in turn by the Romans, the Byzantine Empire, and the Ottoman Turks. Gjergj Kastrioti Skanderbeg, who led the Albanian resistance against the Turks between 1443 and 1468, is a national hero.

From 1925 until 1939, Albania was a monarchy under King Zog I. It became a communist state after World War II until 1992. Since the 1991–92 fall of communism, Albania has become an emerging democracy and has embraced capitalism. The country aspires to membership of the European Union and NATO. In exile since his birth in 1939, Crown Prince Leka, son of Zog I, finally returned to Albania in 2002.

Albania is a poor country, and many people have emigrated to seek work. A market economy was introduced in 1992, and agriculture has been privatized. There is a growing tourism industry focused on Adriatic Sea beaches.

Most Albanians are Muslims, an outcome of nearly 500 years as part of the Ottoman Empire. There are also many Orthodox Christians and Catholics. During the years of the communist period, Albania was the world's only officially atheist state.

ARCHEOLOGY IN ALBANIA

Settled as far back as 2000 BCE and then occupied by a succession of powerful kingdoms, Albania is a treasure trove of antiquities and archeological digs. Centuries of European history are revealed in Albania, sometimes at a single site with multiple layers. Butrint National Park in southern Albania was opened in 2000 and is a UNESCO World Heritage Site with a long and detailed archeological sequence. From the fourth century BCE there is an example of a Greek-style theater, as well as a sanctuary dedicated to Asclepius, the god of medicine. From the early Christian period there is a baptistery that dates to the fifth century CE.

Above right Overlooking Macedonia's Lake Ohrid, St. John the Theologician-Kaneo church is a blend of Armenian and Byzantine architecture.

Above Muradite Mosque in Vlore, Albania, is one of over 300 structures designed by famous sixteenth-century architect Mimar Sinan.

Right Gjirokastra, in southern Albania, was inscribed a UNESCO World Heritage Site because it is a rare example of a preserved Ottoman town.

KOSOVO
SERBIA
BULGARIA
Kumanovo
Tetovo
SKOPJE
Kočani
Golem Korab
Gostivar
Veles
MACEDONIA
Debar
Kičevo
Prilep
Strumica
ALBANIA
Ohrid
Bitola
GREECE

Macedonia

Map Reference Pages 234–235

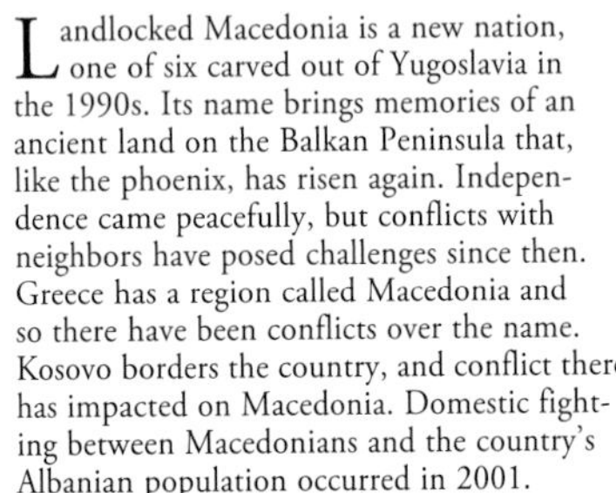

Landlocked Macedonia is a new nation, one of six carved out of Yugoslavia in the 1990s. Its name brings memories of an ancient land on the Balkan Peninsula that, like the phoenix, has risen again. Independence came peacefully, but conflicts with neighbors have posed challenges since then. Greece has a region called Macedonia and so there have been conflicts over the name. Kosovo borders the country, and conflict there has impacted on Macedonia. Domestic fighting between Macedonians and the country's Albanian population occurred in 2001.

Macedonia is mountainous, with the Rhodope Mountains in the east and the centrally located Babuna Mountains. Lake Ohrid in the southwest is one of the oldest lakes in the world and famous for the ancient Lake Ohrid trout, now in danger of extinction. The island of Golem Grad, in Lake Prespa, is a protected nature reserve.

Located at a historical crossroads between Asia and Europe, traders and invaders swept into and across this Balkan land with great frequency. Nationalist movements started late in the nineteenth century, but the region was incorporated into the Kingdom of Serbs, Croats, and Slovenes, and later Yugoslavia, in the twentieth century.

The people of Macedonia come from many ethnic groups including Macedonian, Albanian, Turkish, Roma, and Serb, and speak as many languages. Ethnic conflicts over perceived inequities for the Albanian population caused fighting in the hills near Skopje in 2001. Almost two-thirds of Macedonians are Orthodox Christians; one-third are Muslim.

Macedonia's new government is a parliamentary democracy. There is a unicameral assembly called the Sobranie, which has 120 elected members. The president is elected directly and serves as the chief of state. The head of government is the prime minister, who is elected by the Sobranie.

Unemployment, obsolete infrastructure, corruption, and an extensive gray market are difficulties facing Macedonia's transitioning economy. Unemployment has sometimes exceeded 40 percent. The underground economy is estimated to be 20 percent of GDP. Resulting corruption has hindered international investors and the development of a civil society. The government is working to crack down on this problem.

MACEDONIA

Official name Republic of Macedonia (Republika Makedonija)
Land area 9,493 square miles (24,586 km²)
Border countries Kosovo, Serbia, Bulgaria, Greece, Albania
Capital Skopje
Highest point Golem Korab 9,068 feet (2,764 m)
Climate Warm, dry summers and autumns; cold, snowy winters
Population 2,061,000
Language(s) Macedonian, Albanian, Turkish, Romansh, Serbian, other
Ethnicity Macedonian, Albanina, Turk, Roma, Serb, other
Religion Macedonian Orthodox 64.7%, Muslim 33.3%, other and unspecified 2%
Government Parliamentary democracy
Currency Macedonian denar
Human Development Index 0.801 (ranked 69th out of 177 countries)

MACEDONIA
BULGARIA
ALBANIA
Serres
Kavala
Thessaloniki
Kozani
Mt Olympus
Kerkyra
Kerkyra
Ioannina
Larisa
Limnos
TURKEY
Volos
Lesvos
Mytilini
GREECE
Lamia
Evvoia
Aegean Sea
Chalkida
Kefallonia
Patra
Chios
ATHINA
(ATHENS)
Zakynthos
Peiraias
Samos
Tripoli
Ionian Sea
Kalamata
Kyklades
Dodekanisa
Rodos
Rodos
Chania
Irakleio
Kriti
Mediterranean Sea

Greece

Map Reference Pages 234–235

As the heart of an ancient civilization that formed cultural bridges across the Mediterranean region, Greece's influence was far-reaching. Today, however, it is a medium-sized (by European standards) state tucked in the Aegean Peninsula.

Physical Geography

Numerous islands—from Corfu in the northwest to the boundary with Turkey—surround the rugged landscapes of the Greek mainland. Severely overgrazed dry hills and mountains dominate the horizon. There are only a few true fertile lowlands. This, combined with a

GREECE

Official name Hellenic Republic (Elliniki Dhimokratia)
Land area 50,505 square miles (130,800 km²)
Border countries Albania, Macedonia, Bulgaria, Turkey
Capital Athens (Athina)
Highest point Mt Olympus 9,570 feet (2,917 m)
Climate Mediterranean
Population 10,723,000
Language(s) Official: Greek
Ethnicity Greek 93%, other (including Albanian and Turk) 7%
Religion Greek Orthodox 98%, Muslim 1.3%, other 0.7%
Government Parliamentary republic
Currency Euro
Human Development Index 0.926 (ranked 24th out of 177 countries)

Left In 1640 BCE, the Minoan civilization was destroyed by a volcanic eruption. The explosion literally blew apart Santorini Island (seen here) in the Hellenic volcanic chain, and probably gave rise to the legend of the sunken city of Atlantis.

well-indented coastline and many harbors, explains why the Greeks were traditionally seafaring people. Vegetation throughout much of the country is a product of the Mediterranean climate and is well adjusted to long, hot, and dry summers with short periods of winter rainfall.

Vikos Gorge, in the North Pindus Mountains in Epirus, is one of Europe's deepest gorges. The Pindus gorges have beautiful turquoise or emerald rivers running between walls of red and gray limestone, and shelter many species of plants and animals. The surrounding deciduous forests contain orchids, beech and maple trees, and are home to bears, foxes, and deer.

A volcanic eruption destroyed Santorini Island in 1640 BCE. The volcano collapsed into its submarine magma chamber leaving only a ring of land—now the holiday isles of Thera, Therasia, and Aspronisi. In 197 BCE, a new cone was observed emerging from the sea, the first such event to be documented.

Several Greek islands have therapeutic hot mineral springs or spas. Hot water springs on Ikaria, for example, have been used for their curative properties since the fourth century BCE. Along Ikaria's coastline it is still possible to swim in warm water in places where the radiogenic hot springs flow into the sea.

MILESTONE EVENTS

1829 Formation of the Greek independent state
1896 Athens hosts first contemporary Olympic Games
1924 Greece abolishes monarchy
1935 Monarchy restored
1941 Greece succumbs to Nazi invasion
1944 Assisted by the British, Greece forces Nazi withdrawal
1952 Greece becomes parliamentary democracy and joins NATO
1967 Military coup—Colonel George Papadopoulous becomes prime minister
1974 Turks occupy northern Greece
1975 Greece becomes parliamentary republic under new constitution
1981 Greece joins the EEC
September 1999 Severe earthquake hits Athens
January 2002 Greece adopts the euro
August 2004 Athens hosts Summer Olympic Games

History

Greek tribes arrived from the north and established settlements throughout the Aegean Peninsula in the second and early first millennium BCE. The following centuries saw rapid expansion and colonization of Asia Minor and elsewhere. Never fully unified, Greece was a large number of city-states whose people shared a sense of common ancestry.

In the fifth century BCE the city-state of Athens briefly rose to prominence after protecting Greece against Persian invasion. Its unique governing structure, democracy, and other remarkable cultural traits were the foundation of western civilization. The era of Athens' dominance was short, however, and soon after Greece fell entirely under Macedonian rule. The Roman Empire controlled Greek lands for over a millennium, until the Ottoman Empire's occupation of Constantinople in 1453.

Between the fourteenth and nineteenth centuries the Turks actively ruled all of Greece's provinces. In 1829 the Greeks achieved independence, although it would take another century and several wars for Greece to consolidate political boundaries.

Population/Culture

Urban coastal centers, especially Athens, are home to half of the country's residents. Population density in the rural interior is low. Central and northern Greece and Peloponnesus remain traditional places of emigration.

The Greek language is related to other Indo-European tongues, but mutual understanding with neighboring peoples is limited. The national alphabet, one of the world's oldest, derives from the Phoenician alphabet and has been in continuous use for 3,000 years.

About 98 percent of citizens acknowledge Greek ancestry. Minorities (largely Albanian and Turkish) live in and near the borderlands. Christianity played a crucial role in integrating many of Ancient Greece's customs and traditions. The primary church is the Greek Orthodox, which holds independent status among other Eastern Orthodox Churches. Many other cultural traits, from art and architecture to customs, are of Greek origin.

As in 776 BCE when the first Olympic Games took place, contemporary Greeks cherish modern sporting events, mainly soccer.

Administration/Government

During the twentieth century, Greece endured turbulent periods, including civil war between royalists and communists, German invasion in World War II, conflict with Turks, and seven years of direct military control following a coup in 1967. It joined NATO in 1952 and the European Economic Community (now the European Union) in 1981.

Domestically Greece has had several decades of progressive parliamentary democracy. Geopolitical affairs are a substantial part of local political life. The relationship with Turkey has never been fully resolved, either in the Aegean or in Cyprus, which is still divided into Greek- and Turkish-controlled entities.

Economy/Industry

Lacking competitive amounts of natural resources, the economy has focused on the growing service sector. Tourism accounts for a sixth of GDP. Main trade partners are other members of the European Union, from which Greece has highly benefited, although the imports balance is much higher than exports. Unemployment, a need for infrastructure expansion, and difficulties in balancing the budget are among the main obstacles to be overcome. Development is highly uneven and favors Athens in particular.

Above The people of Mykonos are famous for their relaxed attitude to life. Their openness and hospitality have helped to make the island one of Greece's most popular holiday destinations.

Left This man wears the traditional and historically significant uniform of an elite unit of the Greek army known as the Evzones or Tsoliades. Today they serve the purely ceremonial role of guarding the Hellenic Parliament, the Tomb of the Unknown Soldier, and the Presidential Mansion, all of which are in Athens.

Below The Parthenon stands on the Acropolis and looks over the city of Athens. Named after the goddess Athena Parthenos, it was built around 2,500 years ago in gratitude for Athens having saved the Greeks from Persian invasion.

SVALBARD

Official name Svalbard
Land area 23,560 square miles (61,020 km²)
Capital Longyearbyen
Climate Polar
Population 2,214
Government Dependency of Norway
Currency Norwegian krone

FAROE ISLANDS

Official name Faroe Islands
Land area 540 square miles (1,399 km²)
Capital Thorshavn (Tørshavn)
Climate Temperate
Population 48,668
Government Autonomous province of Denmark
Currency Faroe króna

Svalbard
(Norway)
Jan Mayen
(Norway)
Barents Sea
ICELAND
Norwegian Sea
Faroe Islands
(Denmark)
NORWAY
SWEDEN
FINLAND
Åland
(Finland)
ESTONIA
RUSSIAN FEDERATION
Isle of Man
(UK)
North Sea
IRELAND
UNITED KINGDOM
DENMARK
Baltic Sea
LATVIA
LITHUANIA
RUS. FED.
ATLANTIC OCEAN
NETHERLANDS
BELARUS
GERMANY
POLAND
BELGIUM
LUXEMBOURG
CZECH REPUBLIC
UKRAINE
FRANCE
SLOVAKIA
LIECHT.
SWITZ.
AUSTRIA
HUNGARY
MOLD.
SLOVENIA
ROMANIA
PORTUGAL
ANDORRA
MONACO
SAN M.
CROATIA
BOS. AND HERZ.
SERBIA
Black Sea
SPAIN
ITALY
MONT.
KOS.
BULGARIA
VATICAN CITY
MACE.
TURKEY
ALBANIA
Mediterranean Sea
GREECE
MALTA

Above right A seabird wheels above the dramatic Smeerenburg Glacier on Spitsbergen Island, Svalbard. The Svalbard archipelago is an important breeding ground for seabirds, including auks and puffins.

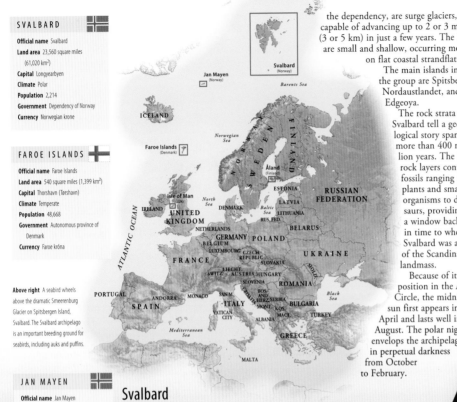

JAN MAYEN

Official name Jan Mayen
Land area 145 square miles (377 km²)
Capital Olonkinbyen (*de facto*)
Climate Arctic maritime
Population Seasonal
Government Norwegian territory
Currency Norwegian krone

Right A road sign outside Longyearbyen, Svalbard's administrative center, notifies motorists of the presence of polar bears. Longyearbyen is home to the world's northernmost art gallery, bank, cinema, and church.

Below A polar bear (*Ursus maritimus*) with its prey, Svalbard. Feeding almost exclusively on seals, polar bears have developed unique hunting skills for this challenging environment.

Svalbard

Map Reference Pages 236–237

A thousand miles north of Norway, halfway to the North Pole, lies the Svalbard Archipelago. Norse accounts suggest Vikings found the islands from as early as the twelfth century. Norway was granted sovereignty over Svalbard in the Svalbard Treaty of 1920.

Extending over some 23,560 square miles (61,020 km²) of the Arctic Ocean, the Svalbard Archipelago encompasses all islands, islets, and exposed rocks found between the latitudes 74–81°N and longitudes 10–35°E.

Svalbard is characterized by steep-flanked mountains, glacially formed fjords, and low coastal plains up to 6 miles (10 km) in width overlain with extensive marine deposits. Many of the glaciers, which cover over 60 percent of the dependency, are surge glaciers, capable of advancing up to 2 or 3 miles (3 or 5 km) in just a few years. The lakes are small and shallow, occurring mostly on flat coastal strandflats.

The main islands in the group are Spitsbergen, Nordaustlandet, and Edgeoya.

The rock strata of Svalbard tell a geological story spanning more than 400 million years. The bedrock layers contain fossils ranging from plants and small organisms to dinosaurs, providing a window back in time to when Svalbard was a part of the Scandinavian landmass.

Because of its position in the Arctic Circle, the midnight sun first appears in late April and lasts well into August. The polar night envelops the archipelago in perpetual darkness from October to February.

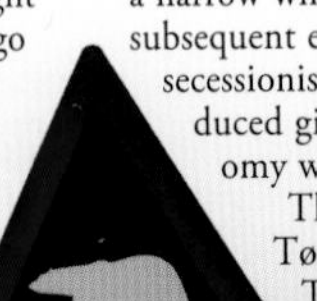
Gjelder hele
Svalbard

Faroe Islands

Map Reference Pages 76–77

The Faroes are an archipelago of 18 islands midway between Iceland and Norway, where the Norwegian Sea gives way to the North Atlantic. The main islands are Eysturoy and Streymoy. The topography is largely the result of volcanism and glaciation—deep valleys and fjords, with mountain ridges separated by steep bowl-shaped hollows, or cirques.

Irish ascetics settled the Faroe Islands in the sixth century CE. In the mid-seventh century Vikings brought the language and culture that have evolved into the modern Faroese traditions and language.

At the close of the ninth century CE, the Faroes were settled by Norwegian immigrants, and were administered by Norway until union with Denmark in 1380 saw them come under Danish influence; they have remained a Danish possession ever since.

In 1946 a referendum on independence saw a narrow win for the secessionists. Despite a subsequent election returning a fall in the secessionist vote, a home-rule law was introduced giving the Faroes increasing autonomy while keeping Danish sovereignty.

The capital of the Faroe Islands is Tørshavn, and it is located on the Tinganes Peninsula on the island of Streymoy. Founded in the tenth century, this city of 12,800 is home to the islands' parliament, the Logting. Its history dates back over a thousand years, having voted to approve the introduction of Christianity in 999. Tørshavn is a modern city with a historic heart seen in its many eighteenth- and nineteenth-century timber-framed, multicolored homes with turf roofs.

Once almost totally dependent upon fishing as a source of income, the Faroes are diversifying the economy by the introduction of IT services. However, the population is ageing due to the numbers of young people migrating to Europe in search of work.

THE GLOBAL SEED VAULT

Inside a mountain on the island of Spitsbergen in the Svalbard Archipelago, the Norwegian government has constructed a 394-foot-long (120 m) tunnel that descends to a chamber purposely constructed to store a selection of the world's crop seeds, thus protecting them from war, natural disasters, and the specter of genetic manipulation.

Seeds will be donated to this "Doomsday Vault" by participating nations and sealed behind a series of blast-proof doors and airlocks. The internal temperature of the mountain, a constant 21°F (–6°C) can be artificially lowered to –0.4°F (–18°C). The mountain's own layer of permafrost ensures the seeds will remain frozen.

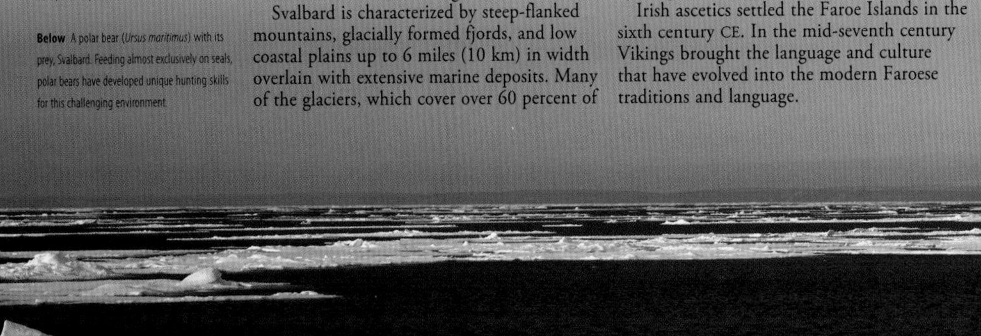

Jan Mayen

Map Reference Pages 236–237

The first authenticated sighting of the volcanic island of Jan Mayen dates to 1614, when Dutch whaler Jan Jacobs May van Schellinkhout sailed past. The island proved an ideal base for the establishment of oil boilers used for extracting oil from whale blubber.

Jan Mayen Island is actually two islands joined by a narrow isthmus, and is home, at its northern end, to Beerenberg, the world's northernmost active subaerial stratovolcano. Rising to 7,468 feet (2,276 m), its summit and upper elevations blanketed by glaciers, it has erupted on six occasions since 1732. The most recent eruption in 1985 saw Beerenberg eject over 247 million cubic feet (7 million m^3) of lava. Geologically, Beerenberg is a young volcano that has been formed over the last 700,000 years by seismic forces along the Jan Mayen fracture zone.

The island was appropriated by the Norwegian Meteorological Institute in 1922 and declared to be under Norwegian sovereignty in 1926. In September 1940, during World War II, the meteorological staff at the station was evacuated, and in 1943 the United States constructed a radio-locating station there. Jan Mayen's long tradition as a base for weather forecasting continues to this day.

In 1959 NATO built a LORAN (Long Range Navigation) transmitter on Jan Mayen, which was linked to transmitters in mainland Europe, Scandinavia, and Iceland to aid shipping in Arctic waters. Another transmitter added in 1960 required the construction of the island's first sealed runway. Scheduled flights began in 1961 and have since made life far less complicated for the defense force employees based there. Operating from Norway's Bodo Air Station, C-130 Hercules transports conduct over a dozen inbound flights a year, bringing supplies and equipment. The only settlement established on Jan Mayen is Olonkinbyen (Olonkin City).

The island is particularly mountainous but poor in natural resources. There is no natural or artificial harbor or significant infrastructure on the island, with all ships required to anchor offshore.

Åland Islands

Map Reference Pages 224–225

The Åland Islands are an archipelago of more than 6,500 islands and rocky outcrops located between Finland and Sweden in the Gulf of Bothnia. Despite an area of 572 square miles (1,481 km^2), 95 percent of Åland's more than 25,000 inhabitants live on the largest island, Fasta Aland, and half of those again live in the capital, Mariehamn.

There has been a steady decline in the number of inhabited islands, from 150 in 1905 to only 65 by the end of the twentieth century. The Åland Islands have a rich architectural heritage, with foundations of earlier houses as well as farm cemeteries from Viking settlements of 800 CE to 1000 CE still extant. Christianity arrived during the eleventh century as the Vikings established trade routes with the islands' European neighbors.

Ceded by Sweden to Russia in 1809, the Åland Islands were declared an autonomous region under Finnish sovereignty by the League of Nations in 1921. Finland agreed to safeguard the islands' culture, Swedish language, and self-determination. The Autonomy Act guaranteed neutrality and demilitarization, with Åland citizens exempt from serving in the Finnish military. Åland's first parliament was elected in 1922.

Åland received its own flag in 1954, has its own postage stamps, has become a full member of the Nordic Council, and has had its own airline since 2005. The islands are administered by a governor appointed by the Finnish government, while a state provincial office encompasses the bulk of Åland's municipal authorities and bureaucracy.

Isle of Man

Map Reference Pages 242–243

The Isle of Man is a self-governing dependency of the British Crown and incorporates the nearby islands of Chicken Rock, St Patrick's Isle, and Calf of Man. Located in the Irish Sea midway between England/Wales and Ireland, this tiny archipelago is a land of cliffs, wooded glens, and open moorlands.

The island was first settled by Celtic tribes around 700 BCE. At the close of the eighth century CE, the Vikings arrived. They established the parliament of Tynwald in 979, which is possibly the oldest continuously functioning parliament in the world.

From a traditional agricultural base, the economy has become a modern provider of financial services such as asset protection, life insurance, and corporate packaging, which together contribute more than a third of GDP. Agriculture still plays a vital role, with almost 80 percent of the island under cultivation. It is not a part of the European Union. Queen Elizabeth II is the head of state with the title Lord of Mann. Douglas on the east coast is the capital city and center of government with a population approaching 27,000.

The Isle of Man's rich culture is the result of its Celtic and Viking origins embellished over the centuries as it variously found itself under the sovereignty of Scotland, England, and Ireland. One of its more notable cultural oddities is the Manx language. With its origins lying deep in Old Irish, Manx is undergoing a revival after coming close to extinction in the 1970s.

Above Ramsey, the second largest town on the Isle of Man after Douglas, is located on the island's biggest harbor. In the past, the town was one of the main points of communication with Scotland.

ÅLAND ISLANDS

Official name Åland Islands
Land area 572 square miles (1,481 km^2)
Capital Mariehamn
Climate Mild to temperate
Population 25,226
Government Autonomous province
Currency Euro

ISLE OF MAN

Official name Isle of Man
Land area 221 square miles (572 km^2)
Capital Douglas
Climate Temperate
Population 75,831
Language(s) Manx (Gaelic), English
Government Parliamentary democracy/ British crown dependency
Currency Manx pound

Left The roofs of many traditional houses in the Faroe Islands are covered with shaggy turf or sod, a method of insulation that has been employed for a thousand years.

Barents Sea
ICELAND
Norwegian Sea
NORWAY
SWEDEN
FINLAND
ESTONIA
RUSSIAN FEDERATION
LATVIA
North Sea
IRELAND
UNITED KINGDOM
DENMARK
Baltic Sea
LITHUANIA
RUS. FED.
ATLANTIC OCEAN
NETHERLANDS
BELARUS
Guernsey (UK)
Jersey (UK)
GERMANY
POLAND
BELGIUM
LUXEMBOURG
CZECH REPUBLIC
UKRAINE
FRANCE
SLOVAKIA
LIECHT.
SWITZ.
AUSTRIA
HUNGARY
MOLD.
SLOVENIA
ROMANIA
PORTUGAL
ANDORRA
MONACO
SAN M.
CROATIA
BOS. AND HERZ.
SERBIA
Black Sea
SPAIN
ITALY
MONT.
BULGARIA
KOS.
VATICAN CITY
MACE.
TURKEY
ALBANIA
Gibraltar (UK)
Mediterranean Sea
GREECE
MALTA

Above right St Peter Port on the island of Guernsey has been an important trading center since Roman times, when it was part of the main Gaul–Britain trade route.

GIBRALTAR	
Official name	Gibraltar
Land area	2½ square miles (6.5 km^2)
Capital	Gibraltar
Climate	Mediterranean with mild winters and warm summers
Population	28,002
Government	Overseas territory of the United Kingdom
Currency	Gibraltar pound

GUERNSEY	
Official name	Bailiwick of Guernsey
Land area	30 square miles (78 km^2)
Capital	St Peter Port
Climate	Temperate
Population	65,726
Government	Parliamentary democracy/ British crown dependency
Currency	Guernsey pound/pound sterling

Above Gibraltar's Barbary macaques are one of the promontory's most famous attractions.

Right In Greek mythology, the limestone monolith we call the Rock of Gibraltar was one of the Pillars of Hercules. The Phoenicians considered the pillars to be the limit of the known world.

Gibraltar

Map Reference Pages 230–231

Thrusting boldly into the Mediterranean Sea is the Rock of Gibraltar, a rocky home for the British territory called Gibraltar. Its strategic position on the Iberian Peninsula has made it a key outpost for monitoring sea traffic through the Strait of Gibraltar.

Physical Geography

Gibraltar's west coast is more populated; the east has a few smaller settlements. The Rock itself is visible from the Mediterranean for great distances. Fresh water is limited.

History

Gibraltar has long been a jewel that many countries have sought to control. Gibraltar and Mt Acho in Ceuta—a Spanish enclave on the Moroccan coast—were the Pillars of Hercules of the ancients. For the past 2,000 years Gibraltar has been under the control of the Spanish, Moors, and British, who captured it during the Spanish War of Succession in 1704. In 1830, Gibraltar became a British colony. Britain provided for more local autonomy in the 1960s. Spain contested British control, leading to tensions between the two powers. The problem grew in 1969 when the people of Gibraltar voted to remain British. This resulted in Spain cutting off access to the narrow isthmus that connects the Rock with the mainland and preventing Spanish workers crossing into Gibraltar to work. After this, the economy switched to activities like tourism that would not need involvement with Spain.

MONKEYS GONE WILD

The famous hosts of Gibraltar are the tailless monkeys known as rock apes, or more correctly identified as Barbary macaques *(Macaca sylvanus)*. Legend says that if the macaques leave Gibraltar, then British rule will end.

However, a recent proliferation of the rock apes has created testy relationships with people. While the apes entertain visitors with their antics, they also jump on and into cars, and attack and terrorize tourists for food. Nearly every visitor to Gibraltar has a story about encounters with macaques. The government attempted to reduce the numbers but public outrage ensued. Thus both the numbers and the stories of the fabled rock apes of Gibraltar continue to grow.

Population/Culture

The population includes Spanish, Italian, English, Maltese, German, Portuguese, and North African people. Population density is high at 11,142 people per square mile (4,303 per km^2). Despite British influence, Gibraltar has an international flavor with its many nationalities and faiths. English is the official language but Spanish, Italian, and Portuguese are also spoken.

Administration/Government

Queen Elizabeth II is the head of state and is represented by a governor. There is a one-house parliament with 18 members who serve a term of four years. A chief minister is appointed by the governor from the majority party in parliament. The UK is responsible for defense, internal security, foreign relations, and financial stability.

Economy/Industry

Tourism, shipping, services, and a strong financial sector provide nearly three-quarters of Gibraltar's revenue, and it is a popular shopping destination for tourists.

Guernsey

Map Reference Pages 228–229

The Bailiwick of Guernsey in the Channel Islands, lying in the English Channel between the UK and France, includes the Island of Guernsey, the nearby islands of Sark, Herm, Alderney, and a number of islets.

Physical Geography

Geographically, Guernsey is divided into two principal regions—in the southern plateau area is the more rural Haut Pas; in the north a sandy low-lying expanse known as the Bas Pas is where the majority of the population lives.

History

Although the islands' position just off the northwest coast of France suggests they should be French territory, the Bailiwick of Guernsey first became a possession of the Crown when England was conquered by William, Duke of Normandy, in 1066, and has been under continuous British control since the end of the thirteenth century.

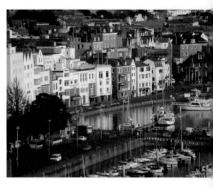

Much of Guernsey's history is reflected in the double-walled fortress of Vale Castle on the island's east coast, built between 1370 and 1400. Evidence of an Iron Age fort dating to 600 BCE was found beneath its foundations in 1980. In 1680, Vale Castle was abandoned and remained empty until 1778. A small British garrison was stationed in the castle during World War I, and during the German occupation of Guernsey in World War II, defensive fortifications were constructed around the fort's perimeter.

The German occupation made it illegal to own or operate a radio, and residents were ordered to hand them in. However, Eric Gill of Gill's Radio Service continued to supply crystal sets to those determined to stay informed of world events throughout the war.

Population/Culture

Guernsey is home to more than 65,000 citizens who are mainly of British and Norman–French descent. Others are Portuguese and, increasingly, Latvian. Culture and customs reflect this varied mix. The major harbor and capital, St Peter Port, is a graceful mix of Georgian- and Regency-style architecture. The great French author Victor Hugo made his home there from 1856 to 1870.

JERSEY'S WAR TUNNELS

Ho8 (Holhgangsanlage 8) was the name given to the subterranean hospital and associated complex network of tunnels constructed by the Germans during their occupation of Jersey in World War II. The tunnels were to become a part of Adolf Hitler's "Atlantic Wall," the Nazi's initial defensive line against an inevitable Allied assault upon the beaches of France.

Hitler was overjoyed to have captured a piece of the British Isles, albeit a tiny one, and he gave orders that Jersey be made impregnable. Fortifications were constructed across the island by thousands of laborers brought from Germany's occupied territories, but of particular interest are the tunnels. Almost 44,000 tons (44,706 tonnes) of rock was removed using nothing more than gunpowder and rudimentary hand tools. The tunnels were originally built as ammunition storage facilities but were converted into a hospital as the Allied landings in France drew near. Tunnels still in the process of construction were sealed, while wards, an operating theater, and a pharmacy were added.

Today the operating theater has been restored and is part of an exhibition that deals with the hardships of daily life on the island during the years of German occupation, which began in July 1940 and ended with the island's liberation on May 9, 1945.

Administration/Government

Today the Crown is represented on Guernsey by the office of lieutenant governor. Guernsey plays no part in British mainland politics, and most links to the UK are administered through the Home Office. Staunchly independent, Guernsey has its own constitution and legislative body known as The States, comprised of 45 deputies elected from within their local districts.

Economy/Industry

Guernsey's main revenue comes from financial services such as investment management. Its low tax rate makes it a haven for businesses looking to establish offshore offices.

Jersey

Map Reference Pages 228–229

Jersey Island, like Guernsey, is one of the group of islands known as the Channel Islands. Although only 12 miles (19) km) off France, English is the dominant language and Queen Elizabeth II is the chief of state. The UK is solely responsible for Jersey's defense. The Bailiwick of Jersey also includes a number of uninhabited rocky islets.

Physical Geography

Jersey is the Channel group's largest and southernmost island. A low plateau across the south rises to a series of small hills in the north, characterized by woodlands and open fields, and crisscrossed by country lanes bordered by hedgerows and granite walls. Jersey's designated green zones, agricultural zones, and strict development criteria have resulted in little change to its urban landscape since the end of World War II. The island enjoys both a temperate climate and several more days of sunshine each year than anywhere else in the British Isles.

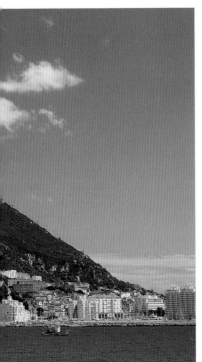

History

Jersey's strategic southerly position in the English Channel has bestowed upon it a long and colorful history. Nomadic hunters in search of mammoth were the first to settle the island more than 250,000 years ago, when it was joined to the European landmass. Permanent occupation did not occur until 4500 BCE. Its soils are replete with relics of Bronze Age and Iron Age settlements. Roman settlement is less certain, despite indications of Roman temple worship being uncovered on the coast at Le Pinacle.

Jersey became a Viking outpost in the ninth century CE before being annexed in 933 by William Longsword, Duke of Normandy. In 1204 it was retained as an English possession despite King John ceding his Normandy territories to France's King Philip II Augustus. During the nineteenth century Jersey became renowned throughout the British Isles as a center for shipbuilding, launching more than 900 wooden ships every year, and establishing a link with the Newfoundland fisheries.

Construction of Elizabeth Castle in St Aubin's Bay began in 1593 during the reign of King Edward VI in response to French and Spanish aggression. During the English Civil War of 1643 it was besieged by Parliamentary forces, and World War II saw it occupied by German forces for almost five years. The Germans constructed gun emplacements around the castle's base that can still be seen.

Culture

Although the dominant language is English, approximately 5,000 to 6,000 Jersey residents still speak Jerrais, an ancient tongue that is closely related to French but also with roots in original Norman English. Once spoken only by the older residents, something of a revival has been occurring in recent decades with Jerrais now being taught in Jersey schools. BBC Radio Jersey now broadcasts a weekly Jerrais program.

Above Mont Orgueil Castle overlooks Gorey Harbour, Jersey. Built in the early thirteenth century, it was England's frontline defense against its enemies.

Above left Famously captured on canvas by Renoir during his visit to Guernsey in 1883, Moulin Huet Bay is a picturesque area on the island's rugged southern coastline.

MILESTONE EVENTS

c. 4500 BCE Evidence of Bronze Age and Iron Age settlements

500s CE St Helier of Belgium brings Christianity to Jersey

803 Charlemagne sends emissary to Jersey

c. 800s Jersey becomes a Viking outpost

933 William Longsword, Duke of Normandy, annexes Jersey

1204 Jersey becomes a British possession

1643 Jersey is besieged by Parliamentary forces during English Civil War

1940–1945 German occupation

1960s Jersey becomes a tax haven

Administration/Government

As Jersey is a relatively small community, you could be forgiven for assuming its citizens are overgoverned. There are 53 elected members of the Jersey legislature, 12 constables, 29 deputies, a bailiff who is also the island's chief civil authority, and a chief minister. Organized political parties do not exist. Individuals work together to form coalitions, the makeup of which will vary from issue to issue. In effect, Jersey has come close to achieving truly representational government, being ruled by the people, for the people.

Economy/Industry

A very low income tax rate of 20 percent has attracted tens of thousands of registered companies to the island and financial services form the basis of 50 percent of revenues. Electronic commerce and tourism, boosted by its duty-free status, combine to underpin the economy. Tourism is big business on the island, which has more than 12,000 beds, golf courses, and a varied coastline. The milk of its famed Jersey cows is distributed throughout European Union countries.

JERSEY

Official name Bailiwick of Jersey

Land area 45 square miles (116 km²)

Capital St Helier

Highest point Les Platons 469 feet (143 m)

Climate Temperate

Population 91,533

Language(s) Official: English, plus French, Portuguese, Jerrais, other

Ethnicity Jersey 51%, British 35%, Irish and French 6.6%, Portuguese 6.4%, other 1%

Religion Christian 95%, Muslim 0.5%, other 4.5%

Government Parliamentary democracy/ British crown dependency

Currency Jersey pound/pound sterling

Left Jersey cattle have common ancestry with the Guernsey breed, as well as those found on the Brittany and Normandy coasts. The breed's purity is maintained by strict import bans that have been enforced for 150 years. There are no other breeds of cattle living on the island.

NORWEGIAN SEA
NORTH SEA
ATLANTIC OCEAN
MEDITERRANEAN SEA
Tyrrhenian Sea
Ionian Sea
Adriatic Sea
Baltic Sea
Bay of Biscay
English Channel
St George's Channel
Skagerrak
Kattegat
G. of Bothnia
Iceland
Faroe Islands
Shetland Islands
Orkney Is
British Isles
Ireland
Britain
Scandinavia
Iberian Peninsula
Pyrenees
ALPS
Appennino
Northern European Plain
AFRICA
Atlas Mountains
Strait of Gibraltar
Islas Baleares (Balearic Islands)
Corse (Corsica)
Sardegna (Sardinia)
Sicilia (Sicily)

1:15,000,000
Lambert Conformal Conic Projection
0 250 500 750 1000 kilometers
0 125 250 375 500 miles

Europe Physical

Barents Sea
Ostrov Kolguyev
Cheshskaya Guba
Poluostrov Kanin
Murmanskiy Bereg
Kol'skiy Poluostrov
Beloye More
Onezhskaya Guba
Timanskiy Kryazh
Ural'skiy Khrebet (Ural Mountains)
ZAPADNO-SIBIRSKAYA RAVNINA
Ob
Irtysh
Tobol
Ishim
Ishimskaya Ravnina
Kulundinskaya Steppe
Barabinskaya Nizmennost'
Pechora
Mezen
Severnaya Dvina
Onega
Sukhona
Vychegda
Kama
Kamskoye Vodokhranilishche
Chusovaya
Ufa
Vyatka
Volga
Onezhskoye Ozero
Ladozhskoye Ozero
Rybinskoye Vodokhranilishche
Gor'kovskoye Vodokhranilishche
Lake Peipus
Lake Pskov
Valdayskaya Vozvyshennost'
Zapadnaya Dvina
Oka
Yuzhnyy Ural
Turgayskaya Stolovaya Strana
Turgayskaya Dolina
Kazakhskiy Melkosopochnik
Privolzhskaya Vozvyshennost'
Samara
Ural
Ilek
Obshchiy Syrt
Sredne Russkaya Vozvyshennost'
Don
Volgogradskoye Vodokhranilishche
Tsimlyanskoye Vodoskhovyshche
Prikaspiyskaya Nizmennost'
Emba
Gory Mugodzhary
Plato Shagyray
Aral Sea
Peski Kyzyl Kum
TURANSKAYA NIZMENNOST
Syrdar'ya
Betpak-Dala
Chu
Amudar'ya
Plato Ustyurt
Plato Mangyshlak
Garabogazköl Aylagy
CASPIAN SEA
Garagum
Garagum Kanaly
Kopet Dag
Krasnovodskoye Plato
Dnieper
Desna
Pripet
Kyyivs'ke Vodoskhovyshche
Kremenchuts'ka Vodoskhovyshche
Dniprodzerzhyns'ke Vodoskhovyshche
Kakhovs'ke Vodoskhovyshche
Sivers'kyy Donets'
Pivdennyy Bug
Nistru (Dniester)
Prut
Sea of Azov
G. of Taganrog
Krums'kyy Pivostriv
BLACK SEA
Caucasus
Kuban
Terek
Kuma
Kura
Malyy Kavkaz
Kars Platosu
Sevana Lich
Araks
Daryācheh-ye Orūmīyeh (Lake Urmia)
Reshteh-ye Kūhhā-ye Alborz
Dasht-e Kavīr
Dasht-e Lūt
ASIA
IRANIAN PLATEAU
KŪHHĀ-YE ZAGROS
Küre Dağları
Anadolu Dağları
Köroğlu Dağları
Kızılırmak
Sakarya
Tuz Gölü
Toros Dağları
Güney Doğu Toroslar
Marmara Denizi
Bosporus
Aegean Sea
Lesvos
Chios
Samos
Rodos (Rhodes)
Kriti (Crete)
Cyprus
Euphrates
Tigris
Al Jazīrah
Bādiyat ash Shām (Syrian Desert)
Antalya Körfezi
Danube
BLACK SEA
35° 40° 45° 50° 55° 60° 65° 70° 75° 80° 85°
25° 30° 35° 40° 45° 50° 55°

ICELAND
REYKJAVÍK
Akureyri
Höfn
NORWEGIAN SEA
Faroe Islands (Denmark)
Tórshavn
Shetland Islands
Orkney Islands
NORTH SEA
ATLANTIC OCEAN
NORWAY
SWEDEN
Trondheim
Bergen
OSLO
Stavanger
Umeå
Uppsala
STOCKHOLM
Göteborg
Gulf of Bothnia
DENMARK
KØBENHAVN (COPENHAGEN)
Malmö
Odense
Århus
Ålborg
Skagerrak
Kattegat
Baltic Sea
Gotland
Öland
Bornholm
UNITED KINGDOM
SCOTLAND
ENGLAND
WALES
NORTHERN IRELAND
Aberdeen
Dundee
Glasgow
Edinburgh
Newcastle upon Tyne
Sunderland
Middlesbrough
Leeds
Manchester
Liverpool
Blackburn
Derby
Nottingham
Birmingham
Coventry
Norwich
Gloucester
Swansea
Cardiff
Bristol
Exeter
Plymouth
Southampton
Bournemouth
Portsmouth
Brighton
LONDON
Luton
Isle of Man (UK)
Belfast
IRELAND
DUBLIN (BAILE ATHA CLIATH)
Limerick
Cork
St George's Channel
English Channel
Channel Islands (UK)
Isles of Scilly
NETHERLANDS
AMSTERDAM
DEN HAAG/'S-GRAVENHAGE (THE HAGUE)
Rotterdam
Haarlem
Groningen
Arnhem
Antwerpen
BRUSSEL/BRUXELLES (BRUSSELS)
BELGIUM
Liège
Namur
LUXEMBOURG
LUX.
GERMANY
BERLIN
Hamburg
Bremen
Bremerhaven
Emmen
Hannover
Kiel
Lübeck
Rostock
Flensburg
Neumünster
Potsdam
Essen
Dortmund
Düsseldorf
Köln
Bonn
Siegen
Leipzig
Erfurt
Jena
Gera
Dresden
Chemnitz
Frankfurt am Main
Wiesbaden
Würzburg
Trier
Mannheim
Heidelberg
Karlsruhe
Heilbronn
Stuttgart
Nürnberg
Regensburg
Ingolstadt
Ulm
München (Munich)
POLAND
WARSZAWA (WARSAW)
Gdynia
Gdańsk
Elbląg
Olsztyn
Koszalin
Szczecin
Bydgoszcz
Toruń
Włocławek
Płock
Gorzów Wielkopolski
Poznań
Zielona Góra
Łódź
Legnica
Wrocław
Opole
Częstochowa
Katowice
Kraków
Rybnik
Bielsko-Biała
CZECH REPUBLIC
PRAHA (PRAGUE)
Plzeň
Ostrava
Olomouc
Brno
České Budějovice
Ústí nad Labem
SLOVAKIA
BRATISLAVA
Košice
AUSTRIA
WIEN (VIENNA)
Salzburg
Innsbruck
Klagenfurt
LIECH.
VADUZ
HUNGARY
BUDAPEST
Győr
Székesfehérvár
Kecskemét
Szeged
Pécs
Miskolc
Nyíregyháza
SWITZ.
BERN
Zürich
Basel
Lausanne
Genève
FRANCE
PARIS
Le Havre
Caen
Rouen
Amiens
Reims
Metz
Nancy
Strasbourg
Mulhouse
Brest
Rennes
Angers
Le Mans
Tours
Orléans
Nantes
La Rochelle
Dijon
Limoges
Clermont-Ferrand
Bordeaux
Lyon
St-Étienne
Grenoble
Toulouse
Montpellier
Nîmes
Marseille
Aix-en-Provence
Toulon
Nice
Perpignan
Bay of Biscay
Corse (Corsica)
Ajaccio
MONACO
ANDORRA
ANDORRA LA VELLA
SPAIN
MADRID
Getafe
Guadalajara
Toledo
A Coruña
Ferrol
Santiago de Compostela
Lugo
Ourense
Vigo
Oviedo
Gijón
Santander
Bilbao
San Sebastián
Vitoria-Gasteiz
León
Burgos
Logroño
Pamplona
Valladolid
Salamanca
Zaragoza
Lleida
Reus
Tarragona
Barcelona
Santa Coloma de Gramanet
El Prat de Llobregat
Girona
Castelló de la Plana
Valencia
Albacete
Alacant
Elx
Murcia
Cartagena
Badajoz
Cáceres
Sevilla
Huelva
Córdoba
Jaén
Granada
Málaga
Marbella
Cádiz
Jerez de la Frontera
Almería
Gibraltar (UK)
Ceuta (Spain)
Melilla (Spain)
Mallorca (Majorca)
Palma
Menorca (Minorca)
Mahón
Eivissa (Ibiza)
Islas Baleares (Balearic Islands)
PORTUGAL
LISBOA (LISBON)
Setúbal
Coimbra
Porto
Braga
ITALY
ROMA (ROME)
VATICAN CITY
SAN MARINO
Milano (Milan)
Torino (Turin)
Genoa
Novara
Bergamo
Brescia
Verona
Venezia (Venice)
Trento
Bolzano
Parma
Modena
Bologna
Ferrara
Forlì
Prato
Firenze (Florence)
Perugia
Pescara
Foggia
Bari
Andria
Napoli (Naples)
Salerno
Taranto
Brindisi
Lecce
Catanzaro
Reggio di Calabria
Messina
Palermo
Marsala
Sicilia (Sicily)
Catania
Syracuse
Ragusa
Gela
Sardegna (Sardinia)
Sassari
Cagliari
Tyrrhenian Sea
Ionian Sea
Adriatic Sea
Ligurian Sea
SLOVENIA
LJUBLJANA
Trieste
CROATIA
ZAGREB
Split
BOSNIA AND HERZEGOVINA
SARAJEVO
Mostar
Zenica
SERBIA
BEOGRAD (BELGRADE)
Novi Sad
MONTENEGRO
PODGORICA
KOSOVO
ALBANIA
TIRANË (TIRANA)
Durrës
Vlorë
MALTA
VALLETTA
MEDITERRANEAN SEA
MOROCCO
RABAT
Casablanca
Kénitra
Larache
Tangier
Tetouan
Fès
Meknès
Taza
Nador
Oujda
El Jadida
Settat
Khouribga
Safi
Essaouira
Marrakech
Agadir
Tiznit
Guelmim
Ouarzazate
Taroudannt
Er Rachidia
Atlas Mts
ALGERIA
ALGER (ALGIERS)
Oran
Mostaganem
Relizane
Chlef
Blida
Médéa
Tizi Ouzou
Bejaïa
Jijel
Skikda
Constantine
Annaba
Sétif
Batna
Biskra
Tlemcen
Saïda
Tiaret
Djelfa
Laghouat
Béchar
Ghardaïa
El Oued
TUNISIA
TUNIS
Bizerte
Sousse
Monastir
Kairouan
Sfax
Gabès
Gafsa
Tozeur
RUSS.
Kaliningrad
LIT.
Klaipeda
Liepāja
GREECE

1:15,000,000
Lambert Conformal Conic Projection

0 250 500 750 1000 kilometers
0 125 250 375 500 miles

Europe Political

Barents Sea
Beloye More
RUSSIAN FEDERATION
Ural'skiy Khrebet (Ural Mountains)
Timanskiy Kryazh
ZAPADNO-SIBIRSKAYA RAVNINA
KAZAKHSTAN
UZBEKISTAN
TURKMENISTAN
BELARUS
UKRAINE
MOLDOVA
GEORGIA
ARMENIA
AZERBAIJAN
TURKEY
SYRIA
IRAQ
IRAN
CYPRUS
LEBANON
ISRAEL
JORDAN
SAUDI ARABIA
KUWAIT
BLACK SEA
CASPIAN SEA
Sea of Azov
Aral Sea
Aegean Sea
The Gulf
KŪHHĀ-YE ZAGROS
IRANIAN PLATEAU
Caucasus
MOSKVA (MOSCOW)
Sankt-Peterburg (St Petersburg)
KYIV/KYYIV (KIEV)
CHIŞINĂU
BUCUREŞTI (BUCHAREST)
ANKARA
T'BILISI
YEREVAN
BAKI (BAKU)
TEHRĀN
BAGHDAD
DIMASHQ (DAMASCUS)
BEYROUTH (BEIRUT)
LEFKOSIA (NICOSIA)
AL KUWAYT (KUWAIT)
ASTANA
AŞGABAT (ASHGABAT)
Arkhangel'sk
Murmansk
Nizhniy Novgorod
Kazan'
Samara
Volgograd
Rostov-na-Donu
Yekaterinburg
Chelyabinsk
Perm'
Ufa
Omsk
Novosibirsk
Kharkiv
Dnipropetrovs'k
Odesa
İstanbul
Tabrīz
Eşfahān
Shīrāz
Al Başrah

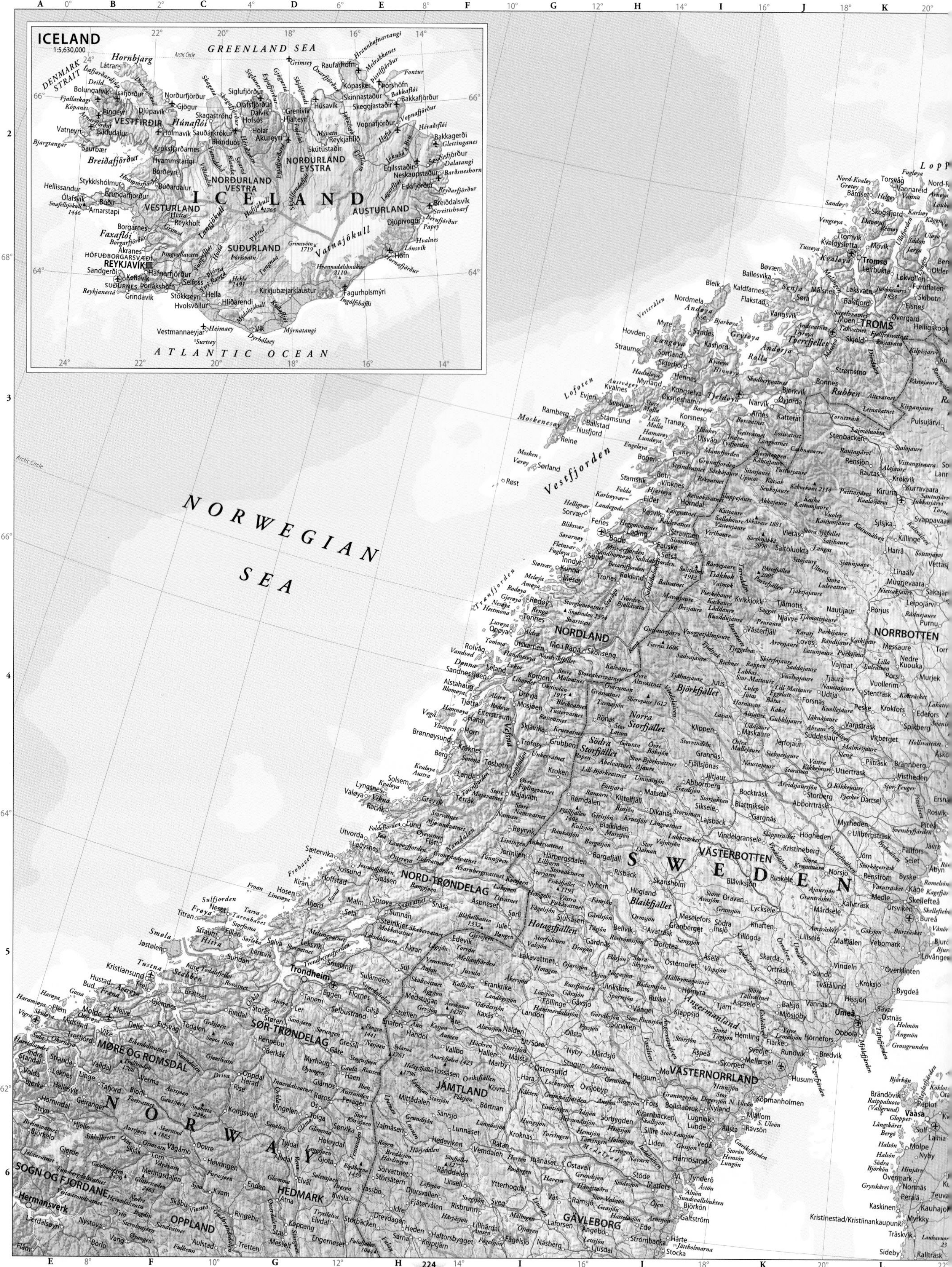
ICELAND
1:5,630,000
GREENLAND SEA
DENMARK STRAIT
ATLANTIC OCEAN
Arctic Circle
VESTFIRÐIR
NORÐURLAND VESTRA
NORÐURLAND EYSTRA
VESTURLAND
AUSTURLAND
SUÐURLAND
HÖFUÐBORGARSVÆÐI
SUÐURNES
REYKJAVÍK
Akureyri
Vatnajökull
Langjökull
Hofsjökull
NORWEGIAN SEA
Vestfjorden
Lofoten
TROMS
NORDLAND
NORD-TRØNDELAG
SØR-TRØNDELAG
MØRE OG ROMSDAL
SOGN OG FJORDANE
OPPLAND
HEDMARK
NORWAY
SWEDEN
NORRBOTTEN
VÄSTERBOTTEN
VÄSTERNORRLAND
JÄMTLAND
GÄVLEBORG
Tromsø
Narvik
Bodø
Trondheim
Umeå
Vaasa
Kiruna
Östersund

Meters
Feet

Meters	Feet
6000	19685
5000	16404
4000	13123
3000	9843
2000	6562
1000	3281
500	1640
200	656
100	328
0	
LAND BELOW SEA LEVEL	
100	328
200	656
1000	3281
2000	6562
4000	13123
6000	19685

224

1:3,750,000
Lambert Conic Conformal Projection

0 50 100 150 200 kilometers
0 25 50 75 100 miles

Northern Scandinavia and Iceland

BARENTS SEA
RUSSIAN FEDERATION
FINLAND
MURMANSKAYA OBLAST'
RESPUBLIKA KARELIYA
ARKHANGEL'SKAYA OBLAST'
FINNMARK
LAPPI
OULU
ITÄ-SUOMEN
SUOMEN
Lappland
Kol'skiy Poluostrov
Beloye More (White Sea)
Kandalakshskiya Guba
Onezhskaya Guba
Dvinskaya Guba
Varangerfjorden
Inarijärvi
Murmansk
Kandalaksha
Monchegorsk
Apatity
Kirovsk
Oulu
Kuopio
Joensuu
Jyväskylä
Petrozavodsk
Kemi
Hammerfest
Nordkapp
Kirkenes
Arctic Circle
Meters
Feet
6000
19685
5000
16404
4000
13123
3000
9843
2000
6562
1000
3281
500
1640
200
656
100
328
0
LAND BELOW SEA LEVEL
100
328
200
656
1000
3281
2000
6562
4000
13123
6000
19685
236
225
238

NORWAY
SWEDEN
DENMARK
GERMANY
NETHERLANDS
POLAND
NORTH SEA
SKAGERRAK
Kattegat
Deutsche Bucht
Kieler Bucht
Hanöbukten
Laholmsbukten
Ålborg Bugt
Pommersche Bucht (Zatoka Pomorska)
SØR-TRØNDELAG
MØRE OG ROMSDAL
SOGN OG FJORDANE
OPPLAND
HEDMARK
HORDALAND
BUSKERUD
AKERSHUS
ROGALAND
TELEMARK
VESTFOLD
ØSTFOLD
AUST-AGDER
VEST-AGDER
JÄMTLAND
HÄRJEDALEN
GÄVLEBORG
DALARNA
VÄRMLAND
VÄSTMANLAND
ÖREBRO
SÖDERMANLAND
VÄSTRA GÖTALAND
ÖSTERGÖTLAND
JÖNKÖPING
HALLAND
KRONOBERG
KALMAR
BLEKINGE
SKÅNE
NORDJYLLAND
MIDTJYLLAND
HOVEDSTADEN
SJÆLLAND
SYDDANMARK
SCHLESWIG-HOLSTEIN
MECKLENBURG-VORPOMMERN
NIEDERSACHSEN
ZACHODNIOPOMORSKI
OSLO
KØBENHAVN (COPENHAGEN)
Göteborg (Gothenburg)
Bergen
Stavanger
Kristiansand
Malmö
Hamburg
Kiel
Lübeck
Rostock
Bornholm (Denmark)
Anholt (Denmark)
Vänern
Vättern
Öland

1:3,750,000

Lambert Conic Conformal Projection

Southern Scandinavia and the Baltic States

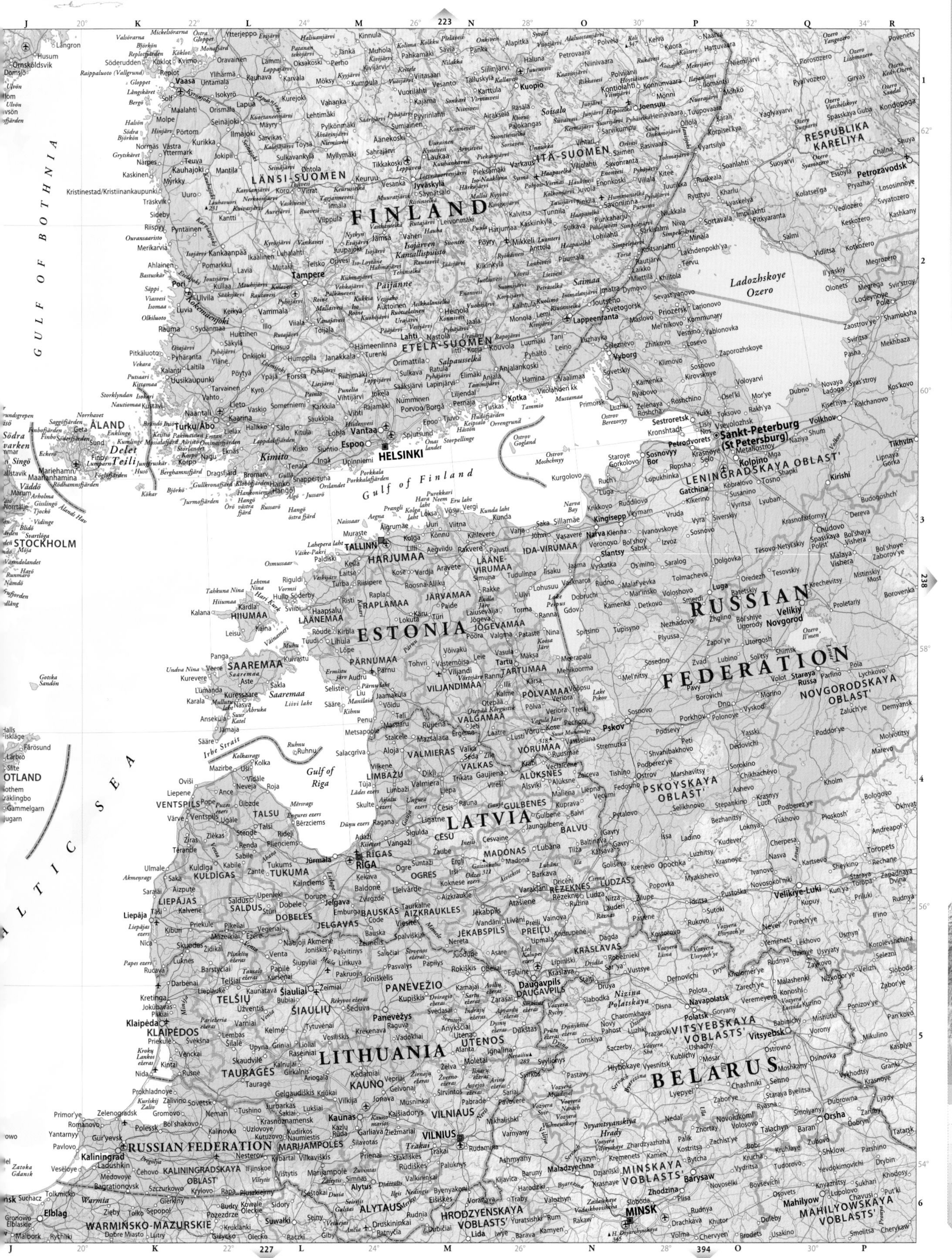
223
238
227
394
FINLAND
LÄNSI-SUOMEN
ITÄ-SUOMEN
ETELÄ-SUOMEN
ÅLAND
HELSINKI
Espoo
Vantaa
Tampere
Turku/Åbo
Pori
Vaasa
Kuopio
Joensuu
Jyväskylä
Lahti
Lappeenranta
Kotka
Mariehamn/Maarianhamina
STOCKHOLM
GULF OF BOTHNIA
Gulf of Finland
Gulf of Riga
BALTIC SEA
Irbe Strait
Ladozhskoye Ozero
Saimaa
Päijänne
REPUBLIKA KARELIYA
Petrozavodsk
Sankt-Peterburg (St Petersburg)
Vyborg
LENINGRADSKAYA OBLAST'
RUSSIAN FEDERATION
NOVGORODSKAYA OBLAST'
Velikiy Novgorod
PSKOVSKAYA OBLAST'
Pskov
Lake Peipus
Lake Pskov
Velikiye Luki
ESTONIA
TALLINN
HARJUMAA
IDA-VIRUMAA
SAAREMAA
HIIUMAA
PÄRNUMAA
Pärnu
Tartu
Narva
LATVIA
RIGA
Jūrmala
Liepāja
Ventspils
Daugavpils
LITHUANIA
VILNIUS
Kaunas
Klaipėda
Šiauliai
Panevėžys
RUSSIAN FEDERATION
Kaliningrad
KALININGRADSKAYA OBLAST'
WARMIŃSKO-MAZURSKIE
Elbląg
BELARUS
MINSK
MINSKAYA VOBLASTS'
VITSYEBSKAYA VOBLASTS'
Vitsyebsk
HRODZYENSKAYA VOBLASTS'
MAHILYOWSKAYA VOBLASTS'
Mahilyow
Meters
Feet
6000
19685
5000
16404
4000
13123
3000
9843
2000
6562
1000
3281
500
1640
200
656
100
328
0
LAND BELOW SEA LEVEL
100
328
200
656
1000
3281
2000
6562
4000
13123
6000
19685

UNITED KINGDOM
ENGLAND
SUFFOLK
NORTH SEA
NETHERLANDS
BELGIUM
LUXEMBOURG
GERMANY
NIEDERSACHSEN
NORDRHEIN-WESTFALEN
SACHSEN-ANHALT
MECKLENBURG-VORPOMMERN
HESSEN
THÜRINGEN
RHEINLAND-PFALZ
SAARLAND
BADEN-WÜRTTEMBERG
BAYERN
FRANCE
NORD-PAS-DE-CALAIS
PICARDIE
ÎLE-DE-FRANCE
CHAMPAGNE-ARDENNE
LORRAINE
ALSACE
CENTRE
BOURGOGNE
FRANCHE-COMTÉ
AUVERGNE
RHÔNE-ALPES
LANGUEDOC-ROUSSILLON
SWITZERLAND
LIECHTENSTEIN
VORARLBERG
TIROL
ITALY
VALLE D'AOSTA
PIEMONTE
LOMBARDIA
TRENTINO-ALTO ADIGE
VENETO
FRIULI-VENEZIA GIULIA
EMILIA-ROMAGNA
LIGURIA
Strait of Dover
Golfo di Venezia
Massif Central

Meters / Feet
6000 / 19685
5000 / 16404
4000 / 13123
3000 / 9843
2000 / 6562
1000 / 3281
500 / 1640
200 / 656
100 / 328
0
LAND BELOW SEA LEVEL
100 / 328
200 / 656
1000 / 3281
2000 / 6562
4000 / 13123
6000 / 19685

1:3,750,000

Lambert Conic Conformal Projection

0 50 100 150 200 kilometers

0 25 50 75 100 miles

224

228

232

Central Europe

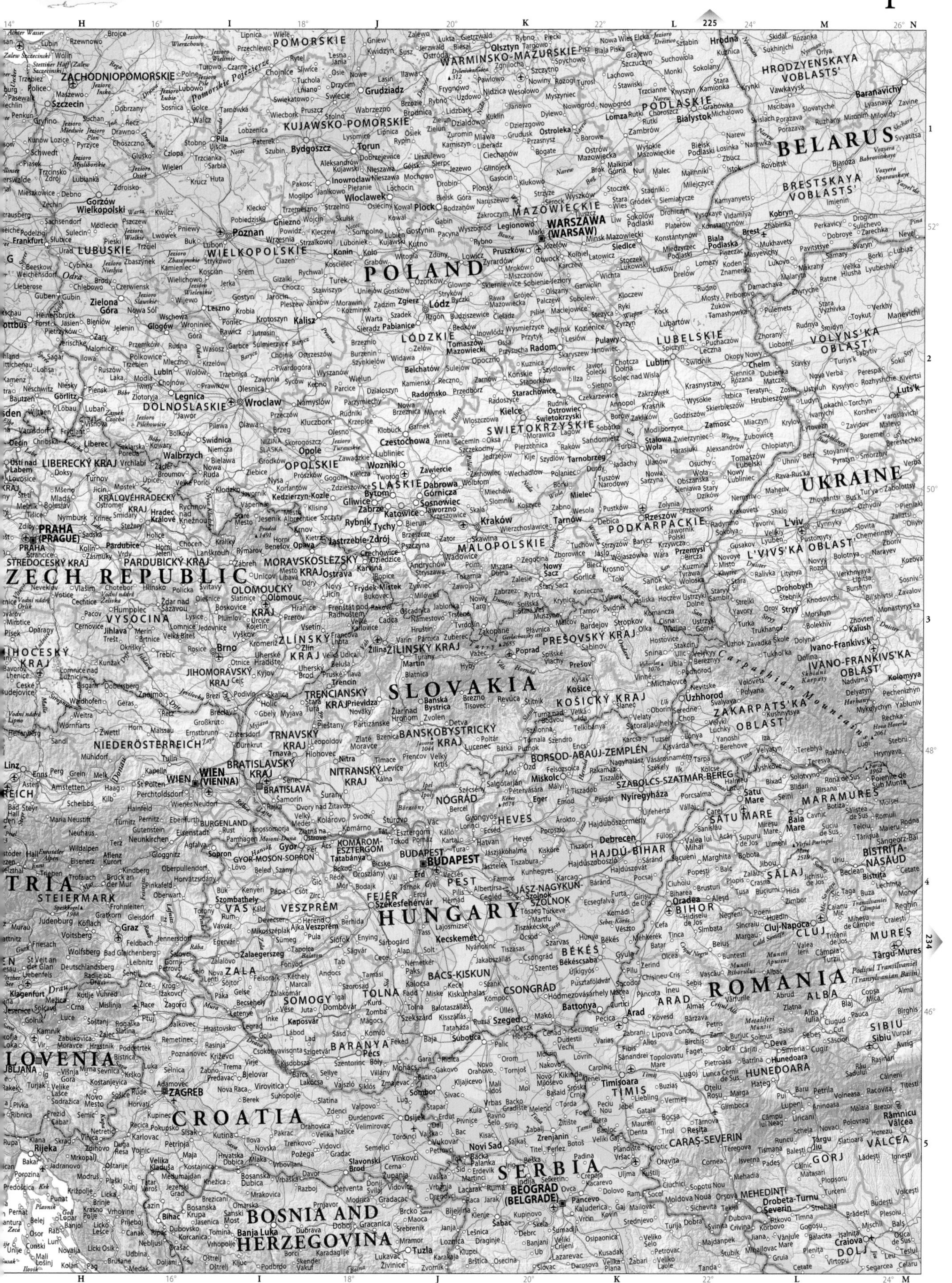
225
234
H
I
J
K
L
M
N
1
2
3
4
5
14°
16°
18°
20°
22°
24°
26°
52°
50°
48°
46°
POLAND
BELARUS
UKRAINE
SLOVAKIA
HUNGARY
ROMANIA
SERBIA
CROATIA
BOSNIA AND HERZEGOVINA
ZECH REPUBLIC
LOVENIA
TRIA
POMORSKIE
WARMINSKO-MAZURSKIE
ZACHODNIOPOMORSKIE
KUJAWSKO-POMORSKIE
PODLASKIE
HRODZYENSKAYA VOBLASTS'
BRESTSKAYA VOBLASTS'
MAZOWIECKIE
WIELKOPOLSKIE
LUBUSKIE
LÓDZKIE
LUBELSKIE
VOLYNS'KA OBLAST'
DOLNOSLASKIE
OPOLSKIE
SLASKIE
SWIETOKRZYSKIE
PODKARPACKIE
MALOPOLSKIE
L'VIVS'KA OBLAST
LIBERECKÝ KRAJ
KRÁLOVÉHRADECKÝ KRAJ
PARDUBICKÝ KRAJ
STREDOCESKÝ KRAJ
MORAVSKOSLEZSKÝ KRAJ
OLOMOUCKÝ KRAJ
VYSOCINA
ZLÍNSKÝ KRAJ
JIHOMORAVSKÝ KRAJ
IHOCESKÝ KRAJ
PRESOVSKÝ KRAJ
KOŠICKÝ KRAJ
ZILINSKÝ KRAJ
TRENCIANSKÝ KRAJ
BANSKOBYSTRICKÝ KRAJ
TRNAVSKÝ KRAJ
NITRANSKÝ KRAJ
BRATISLAVSKÝ KRAJ
NIEDERÖSTERREICH
BURGENLAND
STEIERMARK
IVANO-FRANKIVS'KA OBLAST'
ZAKARPATS'KA OBLAST
Carpathian Mountains
BORSOD-ABAÚJ-ZEMPLÉN
SZABOLCS-SZATMÁR-BEREG
NÓGRÁD
HEVES
HAJDÚ-BIHAR
PEST
JÁSZ-NAGYKUN-SZOLNOK
KOMÁROM-ESZTERGOM
GYOR-MOSON-SOPRON
VAS
VESZPRÉM
FEJÉR
ZALA
SOMOGY
TOLNA
BÁCS-KISKUN
CSONGRÁD
BÉKÉS
BARANYA
SATU MARE
MARAMURES
SĂLAJ
BISTRITA-NĂSĂUD
BIHOR
CLUJ
MURES
ARAD
ALBA
SIBIU
HUNEDOARA
TIMIS
CARAS-SEVERIN
MEHEDINTI
GORJ
VÂLCEA
DOLJ
Szczecin
Gdańsk
Olsztyn
Grudziadz
Bydgoszcz
Torun
Wloclawek
Plock
Ostroleka
Lomza
Bialystok
Hrodna
Baranavichy
Gorzów Wielkopolski
Poznan
Konin
Kalisz
Zielona Góra
Leszno
Glogów
Legnica
Wroclaw
Lódz
WARSZAWA (WARSAW)
Siedlce
Biala Podlaska
Brest
Kobryn
Radom
Lublin
Chelm
Lutsk
Kielce
Czestochowa
Opole
Katowice
Kraków
Tarnów
Rzeszów
Przemysl
L'viv
Bielsko-Biala
Ostrava
Olomouc
Brno
PRAHA (PRAGUE)
Pardubice
Hradec Králové
Liberec
Ústí nad Labem
Zilina
Poprad
Prešov
Košice
Uzhhorod
Ivano-Frankivs'k
Kolomyya
Trencin
Banská Bystrica
Nitra
BRATISLAVA
WIEN (VIENNA)
Linz
Graz
Klagenfurt
Gyor
Tatabánya
BUDAPEST
Miskolc
Eger
Nyíregyháza
Debrecen
Szolnok
Székesfehérvár
Veszprém
Szombathely
Zalaegerszeg
Kecskemét
Szeged
Békéscsaba
Kaposvár
Pécs
Szekszárd
Satu Mare
Baia Mare
Oradea
Cluj-Napoca
Târgu-Mures
Arad
Timisoara
Resita
Deva
Alba Iulia
Sibiu
Râmnicu Vâlcea
Târgu Jiu
Drobeta-Turnu Severin
Craiova
ZAGREB
Osijek
Subotica
Novi Sad
BEOGRAD (BELGRADE)
Zrenjanin
Pancevo
Banja Luka
Tuzla
Rijeka
Ljubljana
Meters
Feet
6000
19685
5000
16404
4000
13123
3000
9843
2000
6562
1000
3281
500
1640
200
656
100
328
0
LAND BELOW SEA LEVEL
100
328
200
656
1000
3281
2000
6562
4000
13123
6000
19685

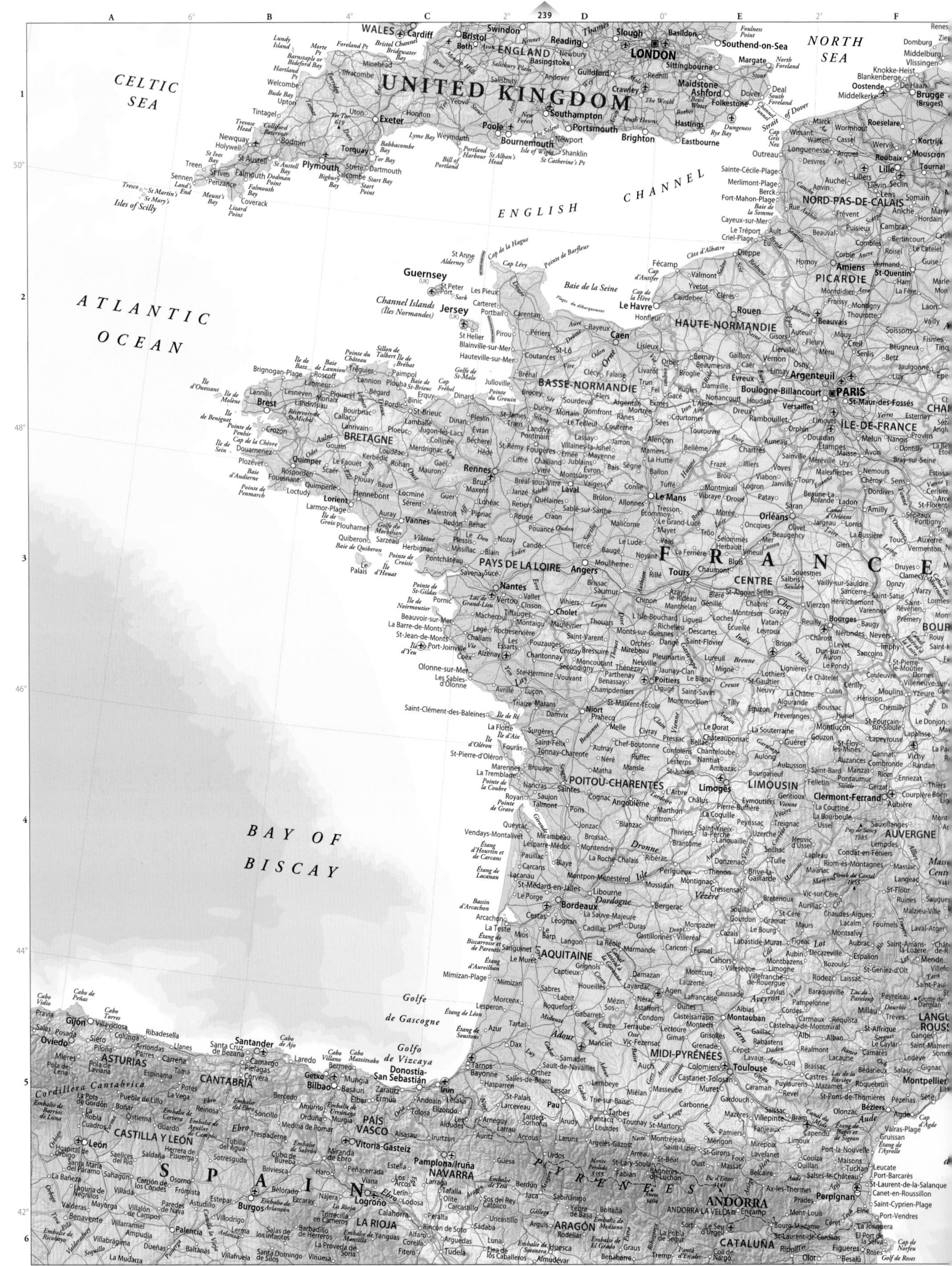
239
CELTIC SEA
ATLANTIC OCEAN
BAY OF BISCAY
NORTH SEA
ENGLISH CHANNEL
UNITED KINGDOM
WALES
ENGLAND
LONDON
Cardiff
Bristol
Bath
Swindon
Reading
Slough
Basildon
Southend-on-Sea
Margate
Maidstone
Ashford
Folkestone
Dover
Southampton
Portsmouth
Brighton
Hastings
Eastbourne
Bournemouth
Poole
Exeter
Plymouth
Torquay
Isles of Scilly
Channel Islands (Îles Normandes)
Guernsey (UK)
Jersey (UK)
Strait of Dover
Oostende
Brugge (Bruges)
Lille
FRANCE
PARIS
NORD-PAS-DE-CALAIS
PICARDIE
HAUTE-NORMANDIE
BASSE-NORMANDIE
BRETAGNE
ÎLE-DE-FRANCE
PAYS DE LA LOIRE
CENTRE
POITOU-CHARENTES
LIMOUSIN
AUVERGNE
AQUITAINE
MIDI-PYRÉNÉES
Le Havre
Rouen
Caen
Amiens
Brest
Rennes
Le Mans
Orléans
Tours
Angers
Nantes
Poitiers
Limoges
Clermont-Ferrand
Bordeaux
Toulouse
Montpellier
Perpignan
Golfe de Gascogne
Golfo de Vizcaya
PYRENEES
ANDORRA
SPAIN
ASTURIAS
CANTABRIA
PAÍS VASCO
NAVARRA
LA RIOJA
CASTILLA Y LEÓN
ARAGÓN
CATALUÑA
Cordillera Cantábrica
Oviedo
Gijón
Santander
Bilbao
Donostia-San Sebastián
Vitoria-Gasteiz
Pamplona/Iruña
Logroño
Burgos
León
Palencia
230
Meters / Feet
6000 19685
5000 16404
4000 13123
3000 9843
2000 6562
1000 3281
500 1640
200 656
100 328
0
LAND BELOW SEA LEVEL
100 328
200 656
1000 3281
2000 6562
4000 13123
6000 19685

1:3,750,000
Lambert Conic Conformal Projection
0 50 100 150 200 kilometers
0 25 50 75 100 miles

Western Europe

Meters / Feet

Meters	Feet
6000	19685
5000	16404
4000	13123
3000	9843
2000	6562
1000	3281
500	1640
200	656
100	328
0	
LAND BELOW SEA LEVEL	
100	328
200	656
1000	3281
2000	6562
4000	13123
6000	19685

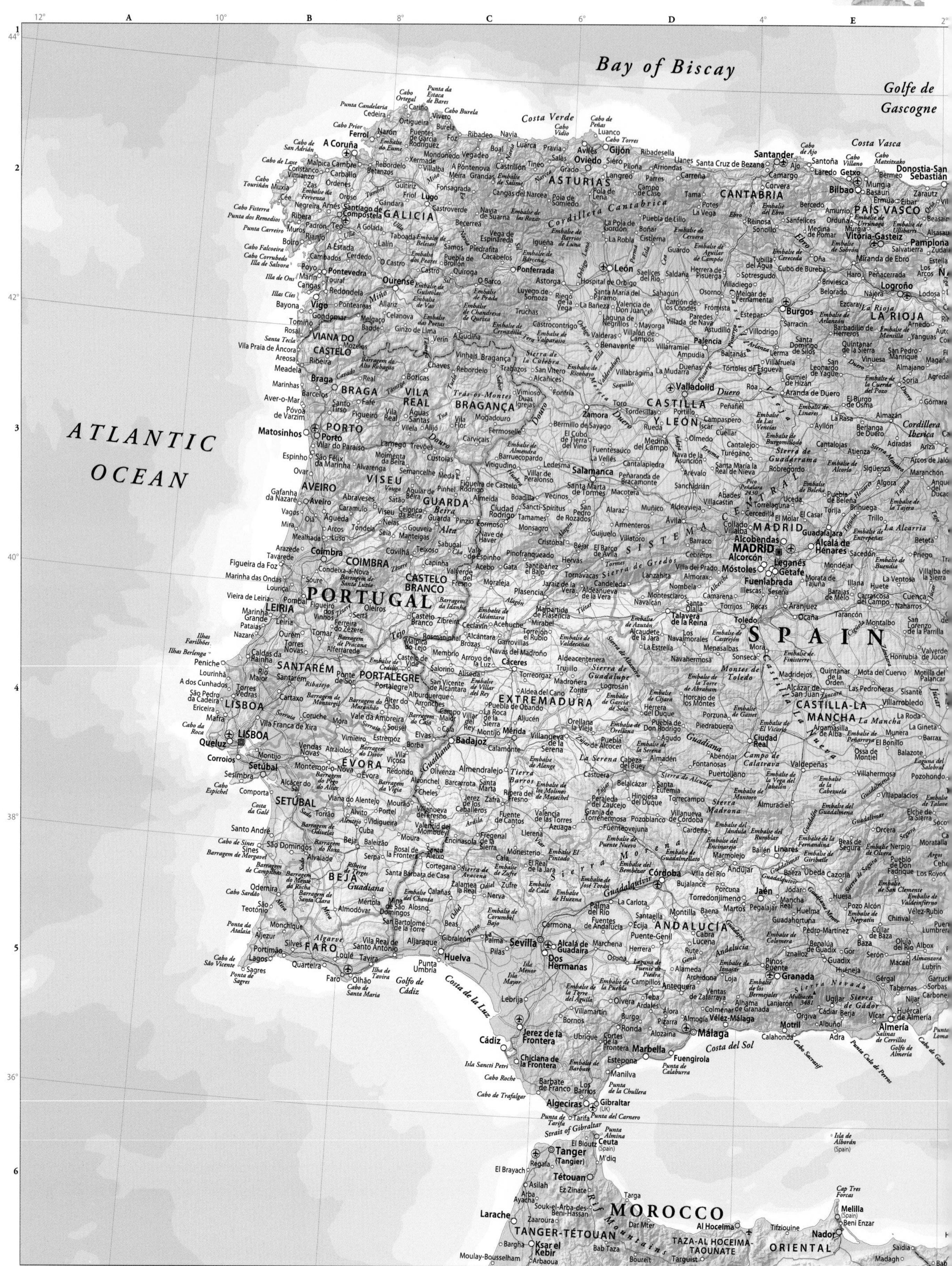
Bay of Biscay
Golfe de Gascogne
ATLANTIC OCEAN
Costa Verde
Costa Vasca
PORTUGAL
SPAIN
MOROCCO
GALICIA
ASTURIAS
CANTABRIA
PAÍS VASCO
LA RIOJA
CASTILLA Y LEÓN
CASTILLA-LA MANCHA
EXTREMADURA
ANDALUCÍA
MADRID
VIANA DO CASTELO
BRAGA
VILA REAL
BRAGANÇA
PORTO
AVEIRO
VISEU
GUARDA
COIMBRA
CASTELO BRANCO
LEIRIA
SANTARÉM
PORTALEGRE
LISBOA
SETÚBAL
ÉVORA
BEJA
FARO
TANGER-TÉTOUAN
TAZA-AL HOCEIMA-TAOUNATE
ORIENTAL
Cordillera Cantábrica
Sistema Central
Sierra de Gredos
Sierra Morena
Sierra Nevada
Montes de Toledo
Rif Mountains
Duero
Tajo
Guadiana
Guadalquivir
Miño
Ebro
Costa de la Luz
Costa del Sol
Golfo de Cádiz
Strait of Gibraltar
Cabo Ortegal
Cabo Finisterre
Cabo da Roca
Cabo de São Vicente
Cabo de Trafalgar
A Coruña
Ferrol
Santiago de Compostela
Lugo
Ourense
Vigo
Pontevedra
Oviedo
Gijón
Avilés
León
Santander
Bilbao
Donostia-San Sebastián
Vitoria-Gasteiz
Pamplona
Logroño
Burgos
Palencia
Valladolid
Zamora
Salamanca
Ávila
Segovia
Alcobendas
Alcorcón
Leganés
Getafe
Móstoles
Fuenlabrada
Alcalá de Henares
Toledo
Talavera de la Reina
Cáceres
Badajoz
Mérida
Ciudad Real
Córdoba
Jaén
Granada
Almería
Málaga
Marbella
Sevilla
Dos Hermanas
Huelva
Cádiz
Jerez de la Frontera
Algeciras
Gibraltar (UK)
Ceuta (Spain)
Melilla (Spain)
Tanger (Tangier)
Tétouan
Larache
Ksar el Kebir
Nador
Al Hoceima
Braga
Porto
Matosinhos
Aveiro
Coimbra
Leiria
Lisboa
Queluz
Setúbal
Faro
1:3,750,000

1:3,750,000
Lambert Conic Conformal Projection

0 50 100 150 200 kilometers
0 25 50 75 100 miles

Spain and Portugal

FRANCE

ITALY

MONACO

ANDORRA

ALGERIA

LIGURIAN SEA

Golfo di Genova

Golfe du Lion

MEDITERRANEAN SEA

Islas Baleares (Balearic Islands)

ISLAS BALEARES

Mallorca (Majorca)

Menorca (Minorca)

Eivissa (Ibiza)

Formentera

Cabrera

CORSE

SARDEGNA (Italy)

AQUITAINE

MIDI-PYRÉNÉES

LANGUEDOC-ROUSSILLON

PROVENCE-ALPES-CÔTE D'AZUR

CATALUÑA

ARAGÓN

VALENCIANA

Toulouse

Montpellier

Marseille

Toulon

Nice

Perpignan

Barcelona

Tarragona

Lleida

Zaragoza

Castelló de la Plana

Valencia

Alicante (Alacant)

Murcia

Cartagena

Palma

Mahón

ALGER (ALGIERS)

Oran

Constantine

Annaba

Sétif

Tellien Atlas

Hauts Plateaux

Meters / Feet

6000 / 19685

5000 / 16404

4000 / 13123

3000 / 9843

2000 / 6562

1000 / 3281

500 / 1640

200 / 656

100 / 328

0

LAND BELOW SEA LEVEL

100 / 328

200 / 656

1000 / 3281

2000 / 6562

4000 / 13123

6000 / 19685

228

233

301

Meters
Feet
6000 19685
5000 16404
4000 13123
3000 9843
2000 6562
1000 3281
500 1640
200 656
100 328
0
LAND BELOW SEA LEVEL
100 328
200 656
1000 3281
2000 6562
4000 13123
6000 19685

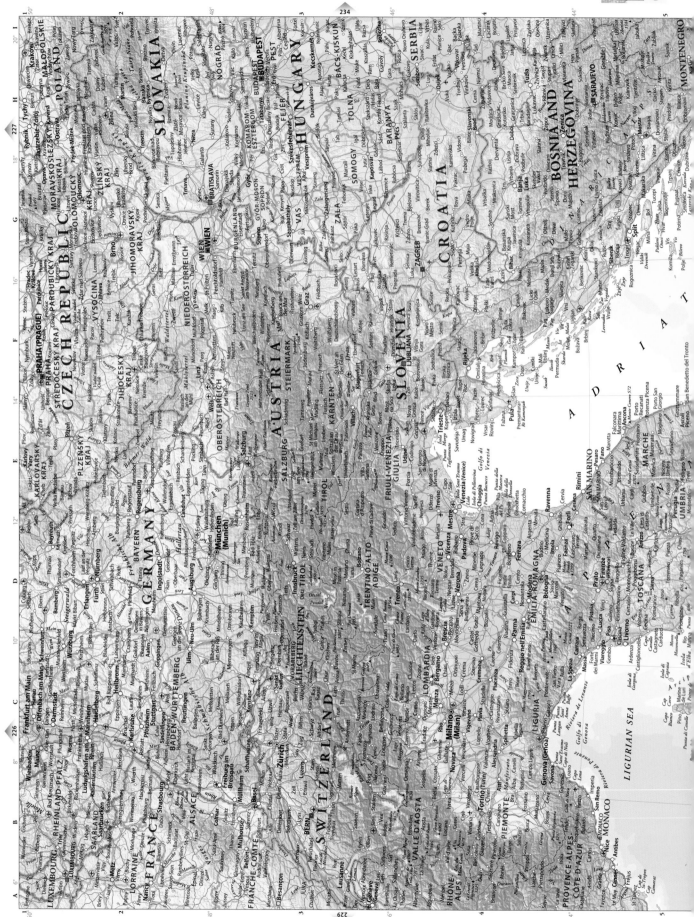

1:3,750,000
Lambert Conic Conformal Projection

0 50 100 150 200 kilometers
0 25 50 75 100 miles

Italy and Eastern Central Europe

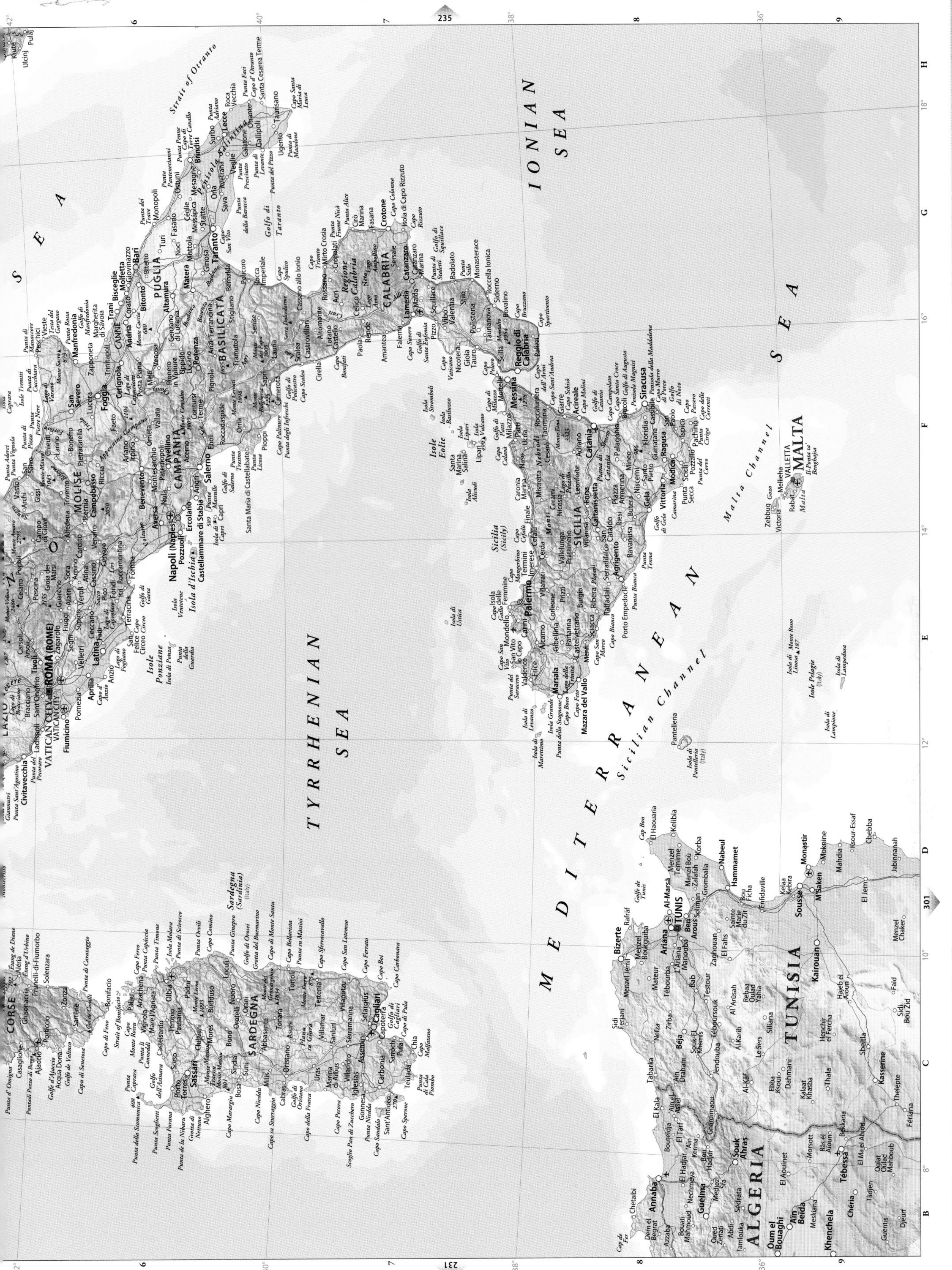
235
231
301
TYRRHENIAN SEA
IONIAN SEA
MEDITERRANEAN SEA
ADRIATIC SEA
Strait of Otranto
Golfo di Taranto
Sicilian Channel
Malta Channel
Strait of Bonifacio
SICILIA
SARDEGNA
CORSE
CALABRIA
BASILICATA
PUGLIA
CAMPANIA
MOLISE
LAZIO
TUNISIA
ALGERIA
MALTA
VALLETTA
ROMA (ROME)
VATICAN CITY
Napoli (Naples)
Palermo
Messina
Catania
Siracusa
Cagliari
Bari
Taranto
Reggio di Calabria
TUNIS
Isole Eolie
Isole Ponziane
Isole Pelagie (Italy)
Meters
Feet
6000 19685
5000 16404
4000 13123
3000 9843
2000 6562
1000 3281
500 1640
200 656
100 328
0
LAND BELOW SEA LEVEL
100 328
200 656
1000 3281
2000 6562
4000 13123
6000 19685

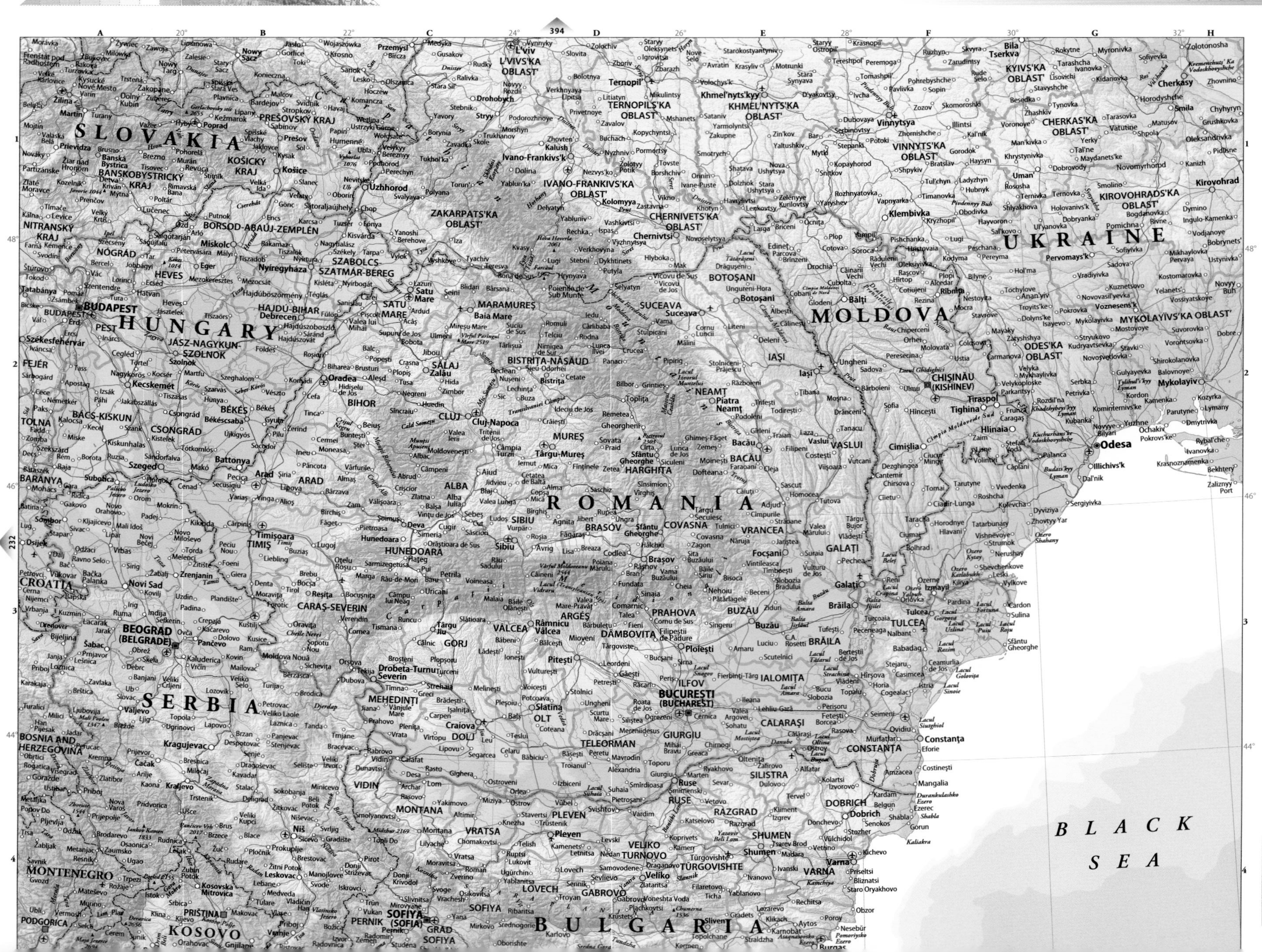
EUROPE
BLACK SEA
UKRAINE
MOLDOVA
ROMANIA
HUNGARY
SLOVAKIA
SERBIA
BULGARIA
CROATIA
BOSNIA AND HERZEGOVINA
MONTENEGRO
KOSOVO
BUCUREŞTI (BUCHAREST)
BUDAPEST
BEOGRAD (BELGRADE)
CHIŞINĂU (KISHINEV)
SOFIYA (SOFIA)
Odesa
Constanţa
394
232
Meters
Feet
6000
19685
5000
16404
4000
13123
3000
9843
2000
6562
1000
3281
500
1640
200
656
100
328
0
LAND BELOW SEA LEVEL
100
328
200
656
1000
3281
2000
6562
4000
13123
6000
19685

1:3,750,000
Lambert Conic Conformal Projection

0 50 100 150 200 kilometers
0 25 50 75 100 miles

Southeastern Europe

Meters
Feet

Meters	Feet
6000	19685
5000	16404
4000	13123
3000	9843
2000	6562
1000	3281
500	1640
200	656
100	328
0	
LAND BELOW SEA LEVEL	
100	328
200	656
1000	3281
2000	6562
4000	13123
6000	19685

394

233

EUROPE

394

390

392

Meters / Feet

Meters	Feet
6000	19685
5000	16404
4000	13123
3000	9843
2000	6562
1000	3281
500	1640
200	656
100	328
0	
LAND BELOW SEA LEVEL	
100	328
200	656
1000	3281
2000	6562
4000	13123
6000	19685

1:19,700,000

Conic Equidistant Projection

0 100 200 300 400 500 600 700 kilometers

0 100 200 300 400 miles

Russian Federation

Meters Feet
6000 19685
5000 16404
4000 13123
3000 9843
2000 6562
1000 3281
500 1640
200 656
100 328
0 LAND BELOW SEA LEVEL
100 328
200 656
1000 3281
2000 6562
4000 13123
6000 19685

116
380
381

Western Russian Federation

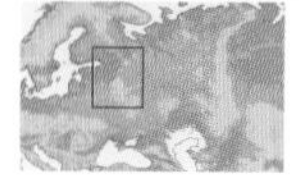

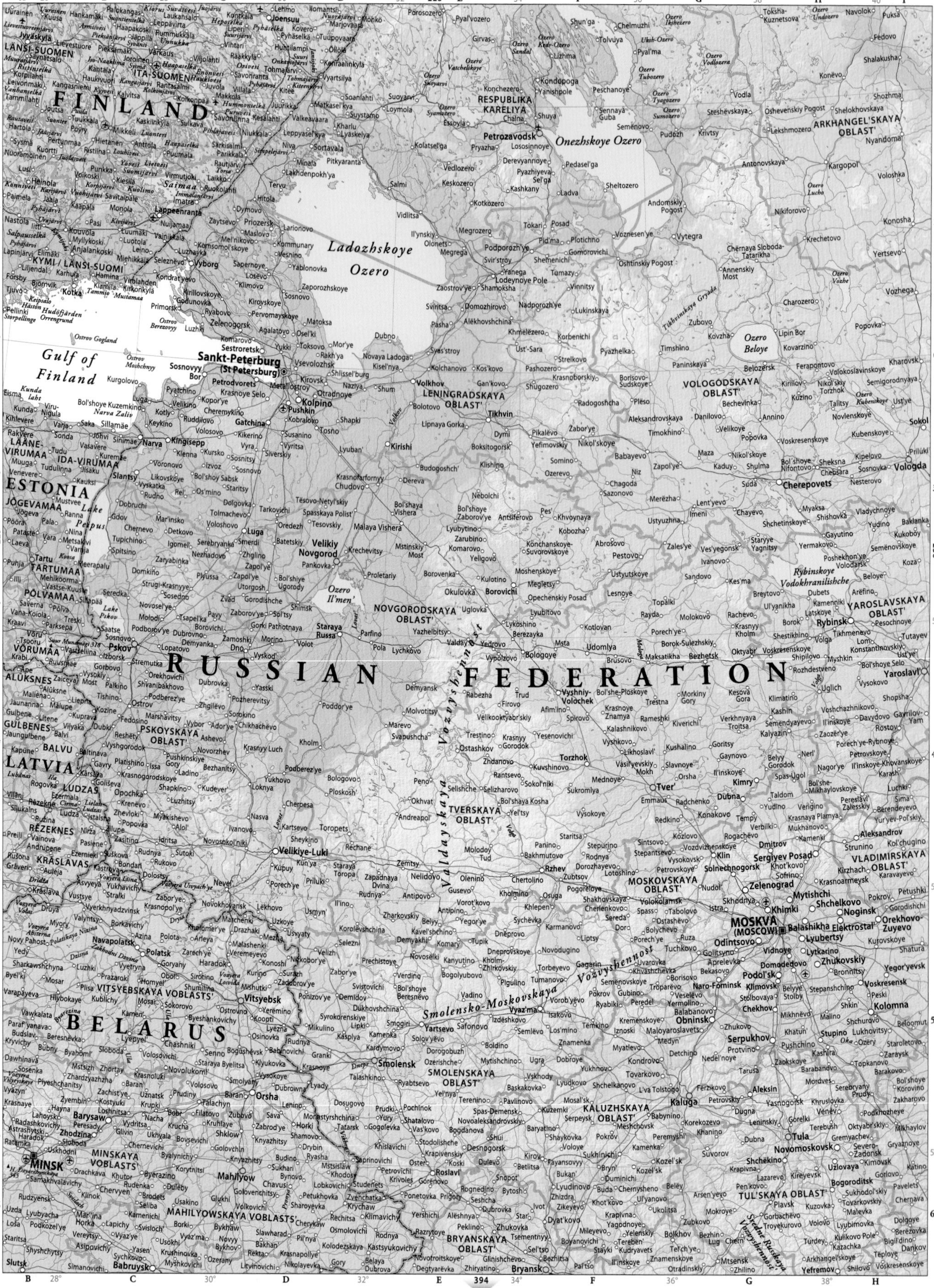

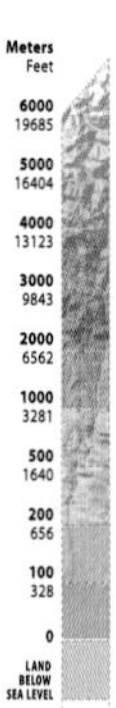

1:3,750,000

Lambert Conic Conformal Projection

0 50 100 150 200 kilometers

0 25 50 75 100 miles

223
225
236
394

British Isles

ATLANTIC OCEAN

NORTH SEA

CELTIC SEA

IRISH SEA

ST GEORGE'S CHANNEL

ENGLISH CHANNEL

UNITED KINGDOM

SCOTLAND

NORTHERN IRELAND

ENGLAND

WALES

IRELAND

FRANCE

NORWAY

Meters	Feet
6000	19685
5000	16404
4000	13123
3000	9843
2000	6562
1000	3281
500	1640
200	656
100	328
0	
LAND BELOW SEA LEVEL	
100	328
200	656
1000	3281
2000	6562
4000	13123
6000	19685

1:4,700,000

Lambert Conic Conformal Projection

0 50 100 150 200 250 kilometers

0 25 50 75 100 150 miles

242
245

7° A 6° B 5° C 4° D 3° E

1 2 3 4 5

53° 52° 51° 50°

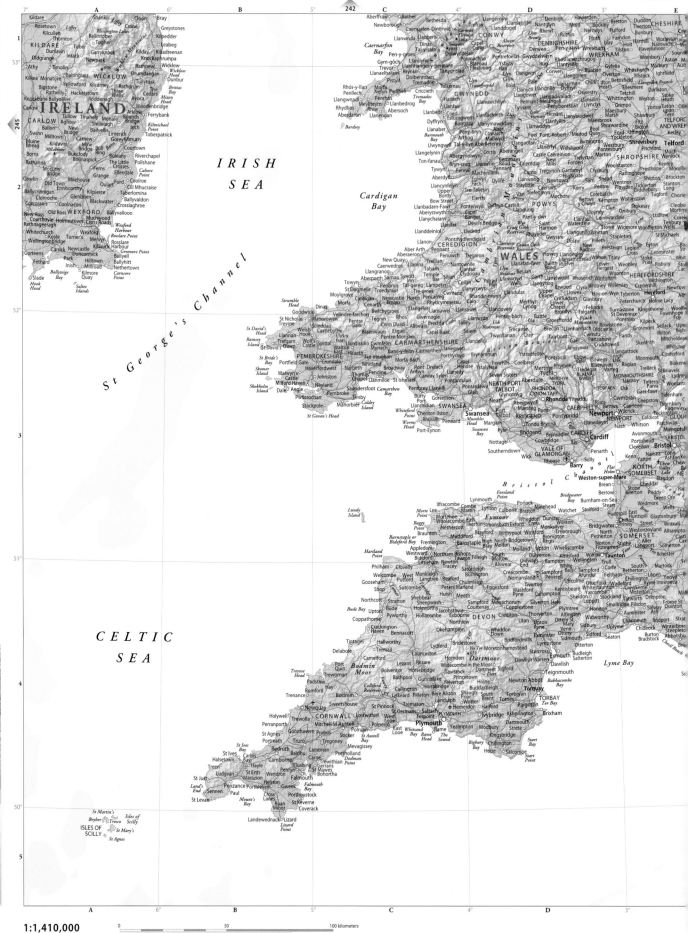

IRELAND
KILDARE
WICKLOW
CARLOW
WEXFORD
IRISH SEA
St George's Channel
CELTIC SEA
Cardigan Bay
Caernarfon Bay
WALES
CONWY
DENBIGHSHIRE
WREXHAM
GWYNEDD
POWYS
CEREDIGION
PEMBROKESHIRE
CARMARTHENSHIRE
SWANSEA
NEATH PORT TALBOT
RHONDDA CYNON TAFF
CAERPHILLY
BRIDGEND
VALE OF GLAMORGAN
MONMOUTHSHIRE
SHROPSHIRE
HEREFORDSHIRE
CHESHIRE
TELFORD AND WREKIN
Bristol Channel
NORTH SOMERSET
SOMERSET
DEVON
Exmoor
Dartmoor
Bodmin Moor
CORNWALL
TORBAY
Lyme Bay
ISLES OF SCILLY
Lundy Island
Cardiff
Swansea
Newport
Bristol
Plymouth
Taunton
Shrewsbury
Telford
Hereford
Weston-super-Mare
Torquay
Exeter

Meters / Feet
6000 19685
5000 16404
4000 13123
3000 9843
2000 6562
1000 3281
500 1640
200 656
100 328
0
LAND BELOW SEA LEVEL
100 328
200 656
1000 3281
2000 6562
4000 13123
6000 19685

1:1,410,000
Lambert Conic Conformal Projection

0 50 100 kilometers
0 25 50 miles

Southern England and Wales

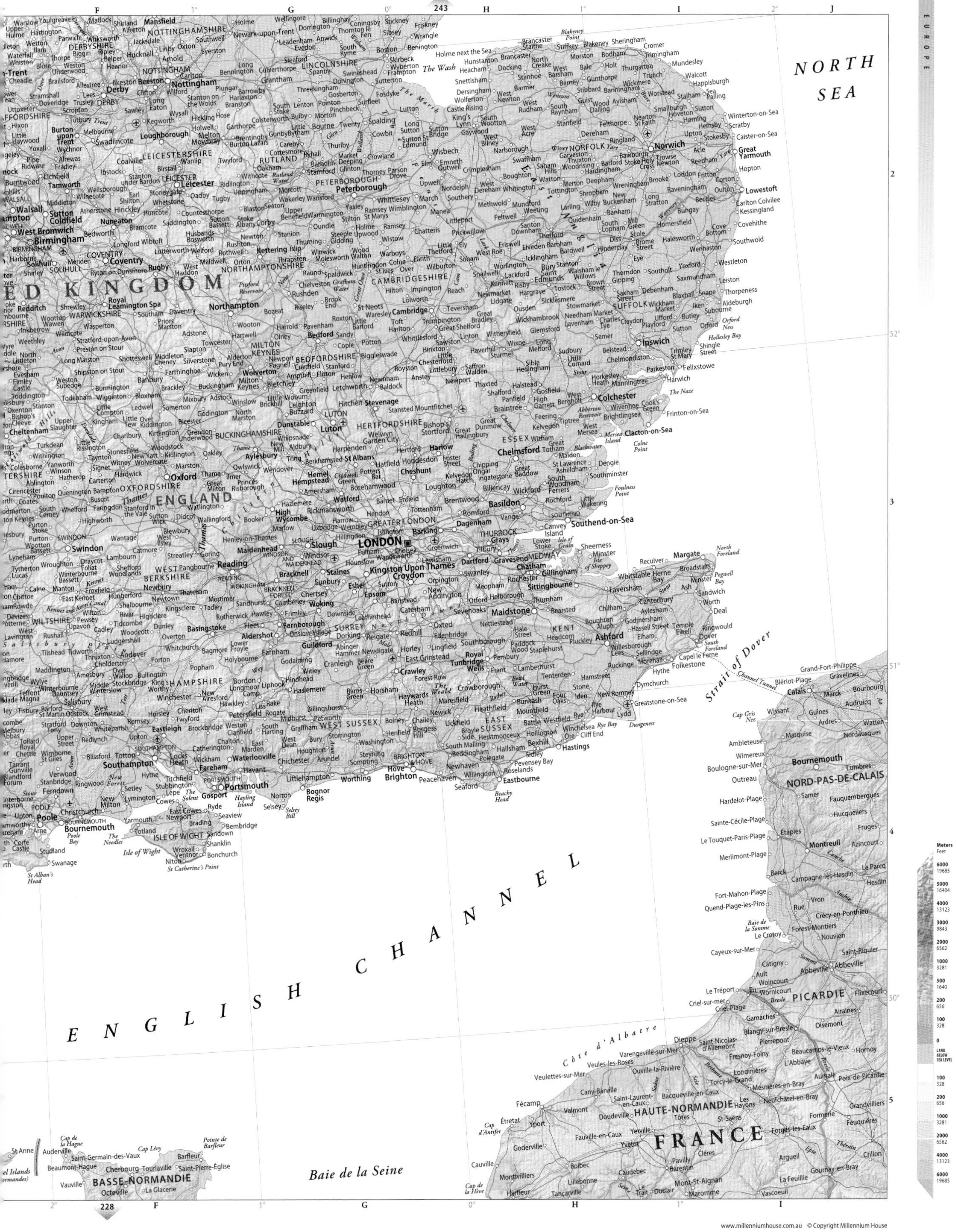

UNITED KINGDOM
NORTHERN IRELAND
IRELAND
SCOTLAND
WALES
IRISH SEA
North Channel
St George's Channel
Cardigan Bay
Solway Firth
Liverpool Bay
Isle of Man (UK)
DUBLIN (BAILE ÁTHA CLIATH)
Belfast
Londonderry
Dún Laoghaire
Douglas
Carlisle
Ayr
BLACKPOOL
Southport
Crosby
Wallasey
Morecambe
Aberystwyth
Holyhead
Rathlin Island
Mull of Kintyre
Mull of Galloway
Cardigan
Lambay Island
Saltee Islands
Bardsey
244
240
245
A
B
C
D
E
1
2
3
4
5
7°
6°
5°
4°
3°
55°
54°
53°
52°

Meters / Feet

6000 19685
5000 16404
4000 13123
3000 9843
2000 6562
1000 3281
500 1640
200 656
100 328
0
LAND BELOW SEA LEVEL
100 328
200 656
1000 3281
2000 6562
4000 13123
6000 19685

1:1,410,000

Lambert Conic Conformal Projection

0 50 100 kilometers

0 25 50 miles

Northern England

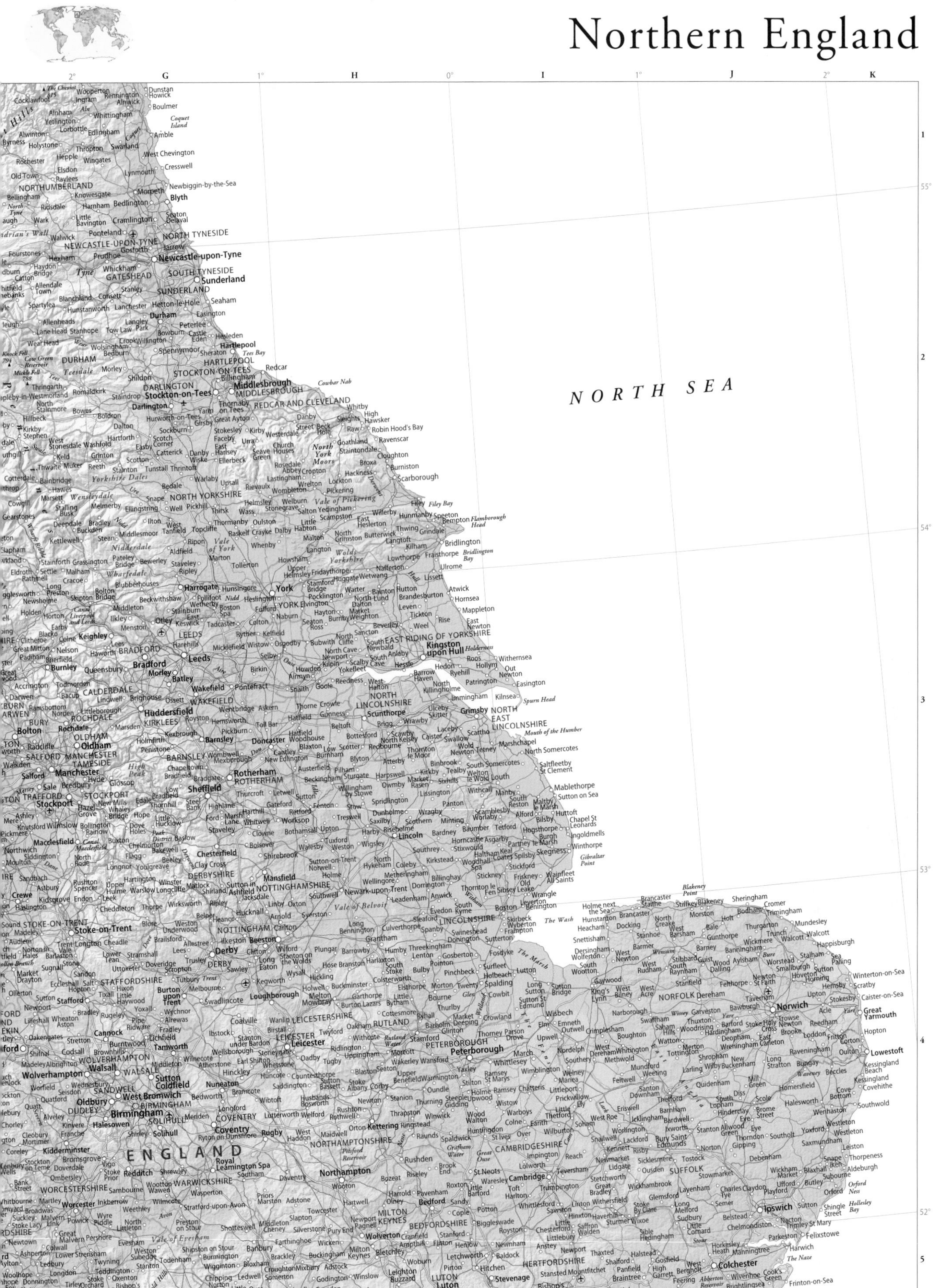
NORTH SEA
ENGLAND
NORTHUMBERLAND
NORTH TYNESIDE
NEWCASTLE-UPON-TYNE
Newcastle-upon-Tyne
GATESHEAD
SOUTH TYNESIDE
Sunderland
SUNDERLAND
Durham
DURHAM
Hartlepool
HARTLEPOOL
STOCKTON-ON-TEES
Stockton-on-Tees
DARLINGTON
Darlington
Middlesbrough
MIDDLESBROUGH
REDCAR AND CLEVELAND
NORTH YORKSHIRE
North York Moors
Yorkshire Dales
Vale of Pickering
Vale of York
Yorkshire Wolds
Scarborough
Whitby
Filey Bay
Flamborough Head
Bridlington
Bridlington Bay
Harrogate
York
YORK
EAST RIDING OF YORKSHIRE
Kingston upon Hull
Holderness
Spurn Head
Mouth of the Humber
LEEDS
Leeds
Bradford
BRADFORD
Wakefield
WAKEFIELD
CALDERDALE
KIRKLEES
Huddersfield
NORTH LINCOLNSHIRE
Scunthorpe
Grimsby
NORTH EAST LINCOLNSHIRE
Doncaster
Barnsley
BARNSLEY
Rotherham
ROTHERHAM
Sheffield
BURY
ROCHDALE
OLDHAM
Oldham
Bolton
SALFORD
MANCHESTER
Manchester
TAMESIDE
TRAFFORD
STOCKPORT
Stockport
High Peak
Peak District
Chesterfield
DERBYSHIRE
Lincoln
Skegness
Gibraltar Point
Mansfield
NOTTINGHAMSHIRE
Newark-upon-Trent
Vale of Belvoir
LINCOLNSHIRE
Boston
The Wash
NOTTINGHAM
Nottingham
Derby
DERBY
STOKE-ON-TRENT
Stoke-on-Trent
STAFFORDSHIRE
Stafford
Burton upon Trent
Loughborough
LEICESTERSHIRE
LEICESTER
Leicester
RUTLAND
Rutland Water
PETERBOROUGH
Peterborough
The Fens
Blakeney Point
NORFOLK
King's Lynn
Norwich
Great Yarmouth
Lowestoft
WOLVERHAMPTON
Wolverhampton
WALSALL
Walsall
Sutton Coldfield
SANDWELL
West Bromwich
BIRMINGHAM
Birmingham
DUDLEY
SOLIHULL
COVENTRY
Coventry
Nuneaton
Rugby
Kidderminster
WORCESTERSHIRE
Worcester
Vale of Evesham
Redditch
WARWICKSHIRE
Royal Leamington Spa
Stratford-upon-Avon
NORTHAMPTONSHIRE
Northampton
Kettering
CAMBRIDGESHIRE
Cambridge
Huntingdon
Grafham Water
SUFFOLK
Bury Saint Edmunds
Ipswich
Orford Ness
Hollesley Bay
Felixstowe
The Naze
MILTON KEYNES
Milton Keynes
BEDFORDSHIRE
Bedford
Wolverton
LUTON
Luton
Dunstable
HERTFORDSHIRE
Stevenage
Colchester
Frinton-on-Sea
Meters
Feet
6000
19685
5000
16404
4000
13123
3000
9843
2000
6562
1000
3281
500
1640
200
656
100
328
0
LAND BELOW SEA LEVEL
100
328
200
656
1000
3281
2000
6562
4000
13123
6000
19685

241

Scotland

ATLANTIC OCEAN

NORTH SEA

SCOTLAND

UNITED KINGDOM

IRELAND

NORTHERN IRELAND

ENGLAND

ORKNEY ISLANDS

Orkney Islands

Outer Hebrides

Inner Hebrides

Sea of the Hebrides

The Minch

Little Minch

North Channel

Firth of Clyde

Firth of Forth

Moray Firth

Pentland Firth

Solway Firth

Grampian Mountains

Southern Uplands

Cheviot Hills

NA H-EILEAN SAR

Na h-Eilean Siar (Western Isles)

HIGHLAND

MORAY

ABERDEENSHIRE

ANGUS

PERTH AND KINROSS

ARGYLL AND BUTE

STIRLING

FIFE

CLACKMANNANSHIRE

WEST DUNBARTONSHIRE

EAST DUNBARTONSHIRE

INVERCLYDE

RENFREWSHIRE

EAST RENFREWSHIRE

CITY OF GLASGOW

NORTH LANARKSHIRE

SOUTH LANARKSHIRE

NORTH AYRSHIRE

EAST AYRSHIRE

SOUTH AYRSHIRE

WEST LOTHIAN

EDINBURGH

MIDLOTHIAN

EAST LOTHIAN

SCOTTISH BORDERS

DUMFRIES AND GALLOWAY

NORTHUMBERLAND

CUMBRIA

DURHAM

Aberdeen

Dundee

Edinburgh

Glasgow

Inverness

Newcastle-upon-Tyne

SHETLAND ISLANDS (UK)

1:4,220,000

SHETLAND ISLANDS

Shetland Islands

Mainland

Meters / Feet

6000 19685 · 5000 16404 · 4000 13123 · 3000 9843 · 2000 6562 · 1000 3281 · 500 1640 · 200 656 · 100 328 · 0 LAND BELOW SEA LEVEL · 100 328 · 200 656 · 1000 3281 · 2000 6562 · 4000 13123 · 6000 19685

245

242

1:1,880,000

Lambert Conic Conformal Projection

0 50 100 kilometers

0 25 50 miles

Ireland

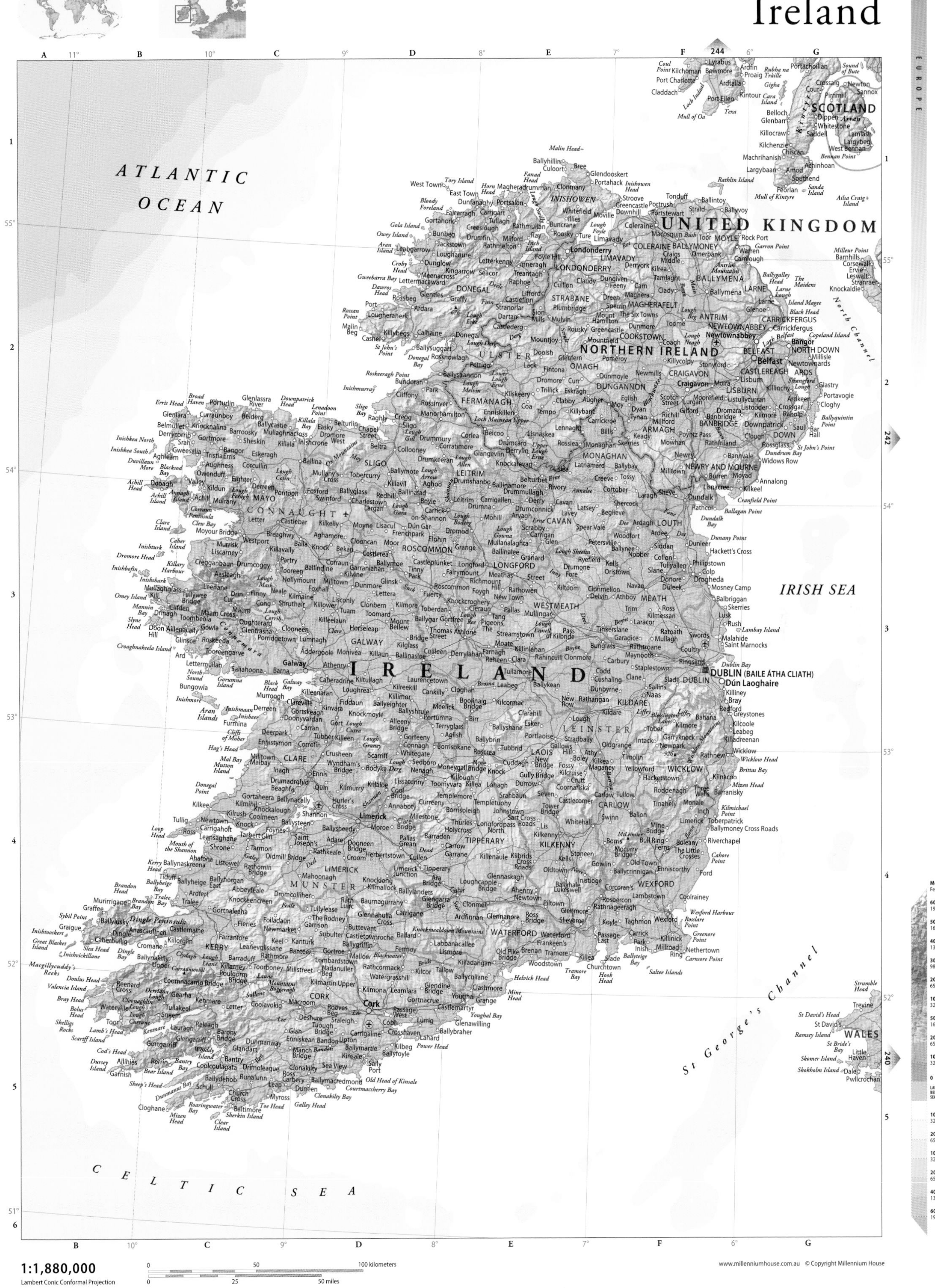

EUROPE
244
242
240
ATLANTIC OCEAN
CELTIC SEA
IRISH SEA
St George's Channel
North Channel
UNITED KINGDOM
SCOTLAND
NORTHERN IRELAND
WALES
IRELAND
ULSTER
CONNAUGHT
LEINSTER
MUNSTER
DUBLIN (BAILE ÁTHA CLIATH)
Dún Laoghaire
Belfast
Londonderry
Galway
Limerick
Cork
Waterford
Wexford
Kilkenny
Sligo
Dundalk
Drogheda
Tralee
Killarney
Athlone
Newry
Armagh
DONEGAL
SLIGO
MAYO
LEITRIM
ROSCOMMON
LONGFORD
WESTMEATH
MEATH
LOUTH
CAVAN
MONAGHAN
GALWAY
CLARE
OFFALY
LAOIS
KILDARE
WICKLOW
CARLOW
KILKENNY
WEXFORD
WATERFORD
TIPPERARY
LIMERICK
KERRY
CORK
FERMANAGH
OMAGH
LIMAVADY
COLERAINE
BALLYMONEY
MOYLE
BALLYMENA
LARNE
ANTRIM
NEWTOWNABBEY
CARRICKFERGUS
NORTH DOWN
ARDS
CASTLEREAGH
LISBURN
CRAIGAVON
BANBRIDGE
DOWN
NEWRY AND MOURNE
ARMAGH
DUNGANNON
COOKSTOWN
MAGHERAFELT
STRABANE
LONDONDERRY
INISHOWEN
Malin Head
Tory Island
Aran Islands
Achill Island
Clare Island
Inishbofin
Dingle Peninsula
Connemara
Lough Neagh
Lough Corrib
Lough Mask
Lough Derg
Lough Ree
Shannon
Mizen Head
Clear Island
Lambay Island
Rathlin Island
Mull of Kintyre
1:1,880,000
Lambert Conic Conformal Projection
0 50 100 kilometers
0 25 50 miles
Meters Feet
6000 19685
5000 16404
4000 13123
3000 9843
2000 6562
1000 3281
500 1640
200 656
100 328
0
LAND BELOW SEA LEVEL
100 328
200 656
1000 3281
2000 6562
4000 13123
6000 19685

www.millenniumhouse.com.au

AFRICA

Africa

Africa has a complex physical geography. In the east of the continent, the Great Rift Valley system stretches north from central Mozambique for 3,700 miles (6,000 km) to the Red Sea, and is home to some of the world's largest lakes and most notable volcanoes. To the north of the continent is the Sahara Desert, the world's largest hot desert, a vast region of sand seas, gravel plains, and plateaus. Savannas, tropical rainforests, highlands, lowlands, fertile and barren regions are all part of Africa's amazing diversity.

Previous pages The Himba women of Namibia coat their skin with an ocher mixture that protects against the sun while symbolizing earth and blood.

Above Rich in history, St Louis in Senegal is a bridge between savanna and desert, river and ocean, Christianity and Islam, Africa and Europe.

Below One example of the beautiful Muslim architecture found at Djenné, Mali, is this mud mosque, which can hold up to 3,000 people.

Africa is the second largest continent, almost equally divided between the Northern and Southern hemispheres by the equator. Until the opening of the Suez Canal in 1869, the only direct connection between Africa and Asia was a sliver of land in the northeast attached to Asia; the narrow Strait of Gibraltar separates Africa from Europe. Africa has few associated islands, with Madagascar in the Indian Ocean being the largest.

Land of Contrasts

The African continent encompasses a diversity of landscapes and features. The high plateaus in Ethiopia are known as "lands of eternal spring" because of their pleasant climate; their volcanic soils are nutrient-rich and highly productive. The Nile River is charged by the watershed formed by the Great Rift Valley region's highlands. This eastern region is known as "High Africa," because the average elevation is much higher than in the rest of the continent. Westward from the Rift Valley the landscape transforms into the tropical rainforests of the central Congo Basin, rainforests that continue to the coasts of the Gulf of Guinea and West Africa; to the northwest lie vast low plateau lands, and to the south savannas and deserts—these regions are known collectively as "Low Africa."

A transitional zone of savanna vegetation, the Sahel, separates the rainforests from the world's largest desert, the Sahara. The Sahel stretches from the Atlantic Ocean east to the Red Sea, from Senegal north to Sudan, and forms not only a physical transition but, in many ways, a cultural frontier. South of the Sahel is home to black African animist and Christian populations who live in settlements with agriculture and trade as their economic base. Northward, however, lies the treacherous Sahara. For centuries only well-supplied trade caravans crossed its burning sands and rocks; the only permanent residents were nomadic herders such as the Tuareg. The Sahara continues to be hazardous, but is no match for modern transportation. Northern Africa is populated by Caucasians of Semitic and Berber background, with the Arabic language and Islamic religion identifying the direction of cultural diffusion.

Most northern Africans live close to the Mediterranean coast or along the banks of the Nile. Below the Sahara's dunes, rich deposits of oil and natural gas form the economic backbone of several countries. Reservoirs of fresh water, or aquifers, are also trapped underground—the Sahara's future contribution to Africa. The southern corner of the continent

Above left Boundless stretches of sand are the main highways of Saharan Niger; dromedary camels are a favored means of transport due to their sobriety, endurance, and speed.

Above Zamalek, an island in the Nile between downtown Cairo and Giza, Egypt, is three miles (5 km) long. The northern half is residential, the southern half public gardens and sports grounds.

includes the Kalahari and Namib deserts, but also extensive natural diversity and an abundance of minerals and precious metals.

No continent suffers more from a poor image than Africa, in many ways unjustified, fueled by misinformed generalizations and stereotypes. This is not to say that Africa does not have a plethora of problems. The best description of contemporary Africa is the "continent of great potential." How long it will take to realize that potential depends on Africans themselves, for there are many obstacles to be confronted.

The colonial experiment of drawing political boundaries with disregard for ethnicity and tribal harmony has created huge potential for conflict. Since the 1960s, barely any African country has avoided some type of ethnically based atrocity. Driven by their interest in extracting Africa's riches, colonial powers did little toward the development of political and social institutions, and favored selective development of trading centers in coastal areas while leaving the interior undeveloped.

Postcolonial African leaders, beginning with Kwame Nkrumah in Ghana in 1960, made mistakes of their own, often implementing Marxist-type centralized economies with full oversight by government. Many countries saw democratically elected governments overthrown, to be replaced by ruthless dictators. In South Africa, institutionalized racism kept millions of non-whites in subjugation.

It did not help that Africa as a whole was a playground for the two Cold War superpowers, which exercised their respective geopolitical ambitions by fueling conflicts throughout the continent. The Democratic Republic of Congo's long-lasting ethnic conflicts, which began after the overthrow of a 32-year dictatorship, demonstrate the difficulty of finding an adequate political solution for Africa's multiethnic mosaic. Additionally, many newly independent nations severed connections with their former colonial rulers, cutting off the possibility of investments that could have helped their economies.

Left Samburu dancers in traditional clothing, Samburu National Park, Kenya. The Samburu, who share many customs with the Masai, inhabit an arid region in northern Kenya. Young girls have traditionally been the property of the community, with no need for schooling, but some Samburu women have begun challenging this view.

Africa also began to experience radical cultural and social changes. The traditional way of life was until recently the only reality for the vast majority, a setting in which self-sufficiency was acquired through farming and livestock herding, barter trade, and an allegiance to village and tribe. This way of life did not require literacy, or attainments in formal education, professional specialization, or the understanding of modern economic ways.

When the shift toward a modern economy occurred, the demand for a professional and educated labor force increased. In less than two generations Africa experienced an unprecedented demographic transition, making it the fastest growing and the youngest continent, because high birth rates remained steady while death rates decreased. This young population is one of the continent's biggest potential resources, as it can supply the human capital necessary for future economic development, in addition to its vast quantities of natural resources. Concurrently, however, a severe socioeconomic problem has arisen through widespread infection with HIV/AIDS, which has devastated some nations in sub-Saharan Africa. Another problem is rampant corruption and unequal distribution of wealth.

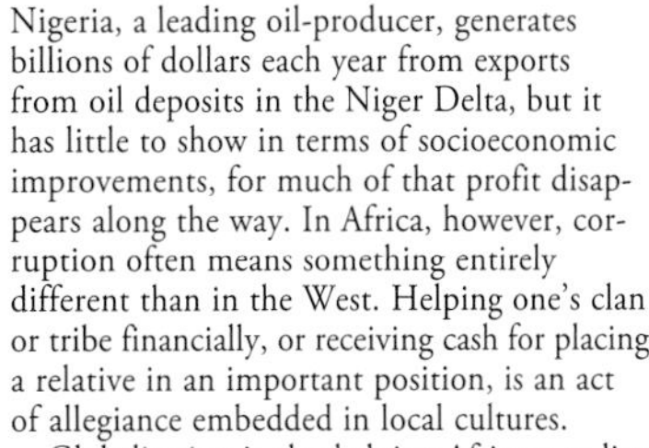

Nigeria, a leading oil-producer, generates billions of dollars each year from exports from oil deposits in the Niger Delta, but it has little to show in terms of socioeconomic improvements, for much of that profit disappears along the way. In Africa, however, corruption often means something entirely different than in the West. Helping one's clan or tribe financially, or receiving cash for placing a relative in an important position, is an act of allegiance embedded in local cultures.

Globalization is also helping Africans to live better than before. Communications technology has reached even the most remote villages. The revitalization of Rwanda after the worst genocide in recent history has been accomplished with a vision of its farmers as growers of world-class coffee. Economic opportunities are now gradually pushing aside historical differences so that Rwandans, together with other Africans, are increasingly concentrating on improving their future.

Above Sossusvlei is a salt pan in the central Namib Desert, Namibia, that lies within the Namib-Naukluft National Park. Fed by the Tsauchab River, it is known for the high red dunes that surround it, forming a sand sea.

Left A herd of giraffe grazing amid trees at Masai Mara, a large park reserve in southwestern Kenya. Along with the distinctive Masai giraffe, the common giraffe is also found here, as are lions, rhinoceros, hippopotamuses, cheetahs, many types of antelope, and wildebeest in their millions. The Great Migration, which sees many thousands of herbivores followed along their annual circular route by hungry predators, is one of the most impressive natural events worldwide.

MOROCCO

Official name Kingdom of Morocco (Al-Mamlaka al-Maghribiyya)
Land area 172,317 square miles (446,300 km²)
Border countries Spain (city enclaves of Ceuta and Melilla), Algeria, Western Sahara
Capital Rabat
Highest & lowest points Jebel Toubkal (Mt Toubkal) 13,665 feet (4,165 m); Sebkha Tah (Tah Depression) –180 feet (–55 m)
Climate Mediterranean, becoming more extreme in the interior
Population 34,343,000
Language(s) Arabic (official), Berber dialects, French
Ethnicity Arab-Berber 99.1%, other 0.7%, Jewish 0.2%
Religion Muslim 98.7%, Christian 1.1%, Jewish 0.2%
Government Constitutional monarchy
Currency Dirham
Human Development Index 0.646 (ranked 126th out of 177 countries)

SPAIN
Mediterranean Sea
Tanger
Tétouan
Nador
Oujda
ATLANTIC OCEAN
RABAT
Kénitra
Fès
Taza
Casablanca
Meknès
El Jadida
Settat
Khouribga
Safi
Beni Mellal
Figuig
Marrakech
MOROCCO
Jebel Toubkal
Ouarzazate
Agadir
ALGERIA
Tan-Tan
WESTERN SAHARA

Morocco

Map Reference Pages 300–301

Strategically located south of the Strait of Gibraltar on the Mediterranean Sea, Morocco overlooks the Atlantic Ocean from the northwest shoulder of Africa. It is the most westerly of the Maghreb countries (Morocco, Algeria, Tunisia, Libya, and Mauritania).

Physical Geography

Beautiful fertile plains cover the Atlantic coast on the west; the Mediterranean coast is mountainous. The Atlas Mountain system averages 11,000 feet (3,353 m) in elevation, and creates a rugged interior, with large areas of plateau and intermontane valleys. The rivers that flow toward the Sahara cut narrow valleys that support lush vegetation.

Coastal areas enjoy a Mediterranean climate, with warm summers and cool winters, but the interior experiences more extreme temperatures. Winter in the north is wet and rainy, but in the south, at the edge of the Moroccan Sahara, it is dry and bitterly cold. The Atlas Mountains are snow-capped most of the year.

History

Morocco's location and resources have always attracted fierce competition among European powers, beginning with the Portuguese, who captured the Atlantic coast in the fifteenth century. France and Spain also exerted some influence. The Treaty of Fes (1912) made Morocco a protectorate of France until 1956, when Sultan Mohammed became king. During his reign, Morocco regained control over certain Spanish-ruled areas, including Tangier. Mohammed VI, the current king, has introduced many economic, political, and social reforms, although retaining sweeping powers.

The long-term problem of Western Sahara, the territory annexed by Morocco in 1975, still remains unresolved.

Above Carpet weaving is the oldest handicraft in Morocco. There are two main types of carpet: Rural carpets (made for thousands of years by the Berbers) and urban carpets (made since the eighteenth century in the cities of Rabat, Fés, Meknès, and Marrakech).

Below The Oued Tahadart bird habitat site includes the estuarine river of the Oued Tahadart, the land around it, and part of the coastline between Tangier and Asilah, Morocco.

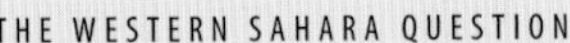

THE WESTERN SAHARA QUESTION

Western Sahara, a small, dry region in the Sahara Desert, continues to be a source of contention between Morocco and the indigenous Sahrawians. The legal status of territory and issue of sovereignty remains unresolved. Although the Polisario Front (Popular Front for the Liberation of the Saguia el Hamra and Rio de Oro) formally proclaimed a government-in-exile called the Sahrawi Arab Democratic Republic (SADR), led by President Mohamed Abdelaziz, Morocco claims the region as a territory.

Originally divided between Morocco and Mauritania in 1976, with Morocco acquiring the northern two-thirds, under pressure from Polisario guerrillas Mauritania abandoned all claims to its portion in 1979. Morocco quickly occupied the vacated part and has asserted administrative control since. Polisario's government-in-exile was recognized by the Organization of African Unity (OAU) in 1984, but Morocco refuses to relinquish control. UN attempts to broker a peace agreement have been unsuccessful, with Morocco generally rejecting any plan that might affect its sovereignty over the area.

Population/Culture

Ninety-nine percent of Moroccans are Sunni Muslims of Arab, Berber, or mixed Arab-Berber ancestry; there is also a tiny Christian minority. Casablanca, the largest city, center of commerce and industry and the leading port, has 3.4 million people. Rabat, the national capital, has 1.6 million. The Atlas Mountains separate the more densely populated coastal areas from the sparsely populated Sahara Desert to the east and south.

Islam is the state religion. Arabic is the official and most commonly spoken language, but French is often employed as the language of business, diplomacy, and government.

The family is the center of Moroccan life. Adult Moroccans are expected to marry, and marriage and childbearing are the life goals for most women who are usually married through an arrangement negotiated by their parents. Children live with their families until they in turn marry. The elderly are highly respected and are cared for by their families.

Moroccan arts, while based on Arabic and Berber traditions, also reflect Spanish influences in dance, and French influences in painting, sculpture, and drama. The country has long been known for its fine metalware, leather goods, rugs, and pottery.

Administration/Government

The government is a constitutional monarchy with a parliament and an independent judiciary. Ultimate authority rests with the king, who appoints the prime minister and all the members of the government, and who may terminate any minister, dissolve Parliament, call for new elections, or rule by decree. The king is also the head of the military, the country's religious leader, and presides over the Council of Ministers.

The bicameral legislature consists of a lower chamber which is directly elected, and an upper chamber, whose members comprise elected representatives of various regional, local, and professional councils.

Economy/Industry

Morocco has relative economic stability, low inflation, and slow economic growth. Agriculture employs 40 percent of the labor force, services another 45 percent, and industry the remaining 15 percent. The major industries include phosphate rock mining and processing, food processing, leather goods, textiles, construction, and tourism. Important natural resources include phosphates, iron ore, manganese, lead, zinc, fish, and salt. Morocco is the world's third largest producer of phosphates.

The major agricultural products include barley, wheat, citrus, wine, vegetables, olives, and livestock. Agricultural productivity is severely limited by poor and inconsistent rainfall and widespread drought in the southern part of the country. Rich fishing grounds lie off the Atlantic coast.

On the fertile Atlantic coastal plains, olives, citrus fruits, and wine grapes are grown, usually using water from artesian wells. Morocco also produces quite a significant amount of illicit hashish, much of which ends up in Western Europe. Rapidly expanding port facilities, and an expanding road and rail network, link Morocco's coastal areas and the mineral-producing interior.

Unemployment and underemployment are both at high levels, especially in the urban areas where they run at between 20 and 30 percent among the younger generation, although overall it stands at about 10 percent. Nevertheless, inflation runs at about 1 percent, which is low and certainly comparable to industrial country levels.

The Moroccan government is pursuing structural economic reforms in the labor market and financial sectors as well as privatization. For example, rules for oil and gas exploration have been liberalized. A bilateral Free Trade Agreement (FTA) with the United States came into effect in 2006. The FTA provides new trade and investment opportunities for Morocco and will encourage the ongoing economic reforms and liberalization efforts.

MILESTONE EVENTS

1786 Moroccan–American Treaty of Friendship signed
1884 Spain creates a protectorate in coastal areas of Morocco
1912 Morocco becomes a French protectorate under the Treaty of Fes
March 1956 End of French protectorate
1957 Sultan Mohammed becomes king
1961 King Hassan II comes to power
1971 Failed attempt to depose king and establish republic
1975 Moroccan and Polisario guerillas clash in Western Sahara
1998 Morocco's first opposition-led government comes to power
1999 King Hassan II is succeeded by his son, Mohammed VI
February 2004 A powerful earthquake hits the north; more than 500 people are killed
July 2004 Free trade agreement with the USA comes into effect
September–October 2005 Hundreds of African migrants try to storm Morocco's borders with the Spanish enclaves of Melilla and Ceuta
September 2007 Parliamentary elections held; the conservative Istiqlal party wins the most votes

Left The oasis town of Kerzaz is located in the Saoura Valley in the western Sahara Desert, Algeria. Traditional Saharan architecture here includes covered walkways between houses that protect residents from the blazing sun.

Mediterranean Sea
ALGER (ALGIERS)
Skikda
Annaba
Sétif
Constantine
Ech Chélif
Blida
Oran
Mostaganem
Sidi Bel Abbès
Batna
Tlemcen
Saïda
Biskra
Laghouat
El Oued
Ghardaïa
TUNISIA
MOROCCO
Béchar
ALGERIA
LIBYA
Adrar
MAURITANIA
Tahat
Tamanrasset
MALI
NIGER

Algeria

Map Reference Pages 300–301

From the sixteenth until the early nineteenth century the coastal regions of what are now Morocco, Algeria, Tunisia, and Libya were infamous as the Barbary Coast, home to pirates who attacked shipping and coastal settlements in the Mediterranean and the North Atlantic. They were also slave traders, trading captives from Europe and sub-Saharan Africa.

Physical Geography

Sloping up from the hilly Mediterranean coastline, Algeria's landscape evolves into the mountain ranges of the fertile Tell Atlas, backed by the Saharan Atlas. South of the mountains the landscape turns into the vast, sometimes rocky, most often erg (sand-dune) deserts of the Algerian Sahara. Parallel to the border with Niger rises the isolated, ancient volcanic massif of the Ahaggar Mountains, home to fascinating wildlife.

Mediterranean climate conditions extend to the north-facing slopes of the Atlas, with the majority of rainfall falling in winter. The desert interior sees its only rainfall arrive through scattered summer storms.

History

Artefacts prove the continuous habitation of Algeria since 10,000 BCE. The country's history shares similarities with neighboring countries along the Mediterranean coast. Greek and Phoenician colonists arrived first, later the Romans, in the seventh century the Arabs, and the Ottomans in the sixteenth century.

Algeria came under French control in 1830. Following a brutal war for independence, Algeria reached statehood in 1962. Three decades later the country exploded into another devastating conflict, the Civil War of 1992–2002 between secular and pro-Islamist forces, in which well over 100,000 people died.

Population/Culture

Algeria is a populous country with a large ratio of young people and strong population growth. Ninety percent of the population lives in the narrow strip along the coast. In the interior, many of the remaining 10 percent live in scattered oasis settlements, but some 1.5 million Berber practice a nomadic or semi-nomadic lifestyle.

People of Berber ethnic descent, heavily influenced by Arab culture, constitute almost the entire population. The Muslim religion and the Arabic and French languages are three of the most important forces in Algerian culture, and recently Tamazight (Berber) has been named a national language and is being taught in schools. Immediately following independence, 10 percent of the population, mostly those of French descent, emigrated. French is still the leading foreign language, particularly among the formally educated. Literacy rates are similar to those in neighboring countries, although lagging behind those of developed countries. While literacy rates are higher among males, 60 percent of university students in Algeria are women.

Much of Algeria's art and architecture, especially its wonderful domed mosques, reflect the influence of Islam, but modern painters are returning to traditional Berber and Arabic designs in their work.

Administration/Government

Ineffective governing processes and slow political, economic, and social reforms during the 1970s and 1980s were among the main background causes of the most recent civil conflict. Today, governments are elected by popular vote and the president, who holds five-year terms, appoints the prime minister. Political pluralism is also allowed and now there are dozens of parties that operate in the election process, which has been considerably improved in recent years.

Economy/Industry

The energy sector—production of oil and natural gas—serves as the primary source of national income. Algeria is among the leading exporters of fossil fuels to Western European and American markets.

The agricultural sector, which is concentrated in the coastal strip, employs 25 percent of the workforce. Other branches of the economy are not as well developed as the energy sector and the country is undergoing gradual privatization with the aim of stimulating faster development.

MILESTONE EVENTS

10,000 BCE Settlement by early Berber people

1,000 BCE Carthaginians establish coastal settlements

200 CE Roman Empire establishes control

700s Muslim Arabs conquer the region

1517 Ottoman Empire establishes Algeria's modern northern boundaries

1600s Rise of Barbary Coast pirates and slavers

1816 British and Dutch destroy Algiers and its pirate fleet

1830 France invades Algiers

1954 National Liberation Front (FLN) launches Algerian War of Independence

July 5, 1962 Independence from France

January 1992–June 2002 Algerian Civil War

April 27, 1999 Abdelaziz Bouteflika elected president

ALGERIA

Official name People's Democratic Republic of Algeria (Al Jumhuriyah al Jaza'iriyah ad Dimuqratiyah ash Sha'biyah)

Land area 919,595 square miles (2,381,740 km²)

Border countries Tunisia, Libya, Niger, Mali, Mauritania, Western Sahara, Morocco

Capital Algiers (Alger)

Highest & lowest points Jebel Tahat (Mt Tahat) 9,852 feet (3,003 m); Chott Melrhir (Lake Melhrir) –131 feet (–40 m)

Climate Mediterranean near the coast; desert in the interior

Population 33,770,000

Language(s) Arabic, Berber

Ethnicity Berber Arab 99%; other 1%

Religion Muslim 99%; Christian and Jewish 1%

Government Presidential republic

Currency Algerian dinar

Human Development Index 0.733 (ranked 104th out of 177 countries)

Above The majority of Algerians are Berbers. Around 80 percent of them live permanently in towns and cities; the remainder live a nomadic or semi-nomadic lifestyle in places such as the Great Eastern Erg in the Sahara Desert.

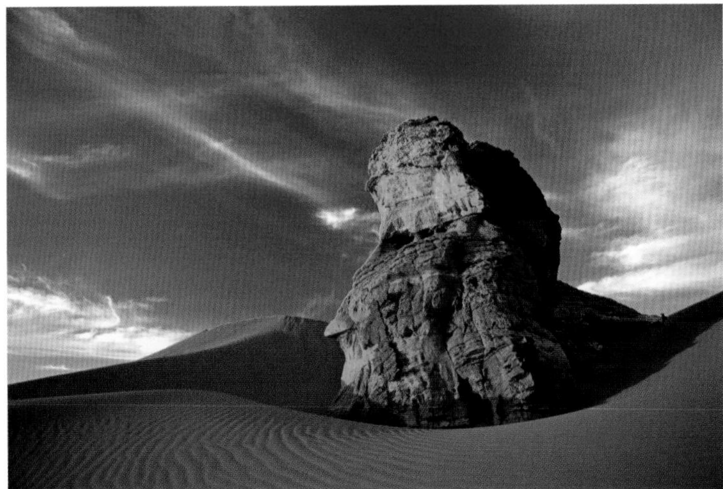

Left Tassili-n-Ajjer (meaning Creviced Plateau) is a region of desert plateaus and sand-dune plains in the Algerian Sahara. The sirocco, a strong, gusty, unpleasantly dust-laden south wind that blows off the desert, often reaches as far as southern Europe.

TUNISIA

Official name Tunisian Republic (Al Jumhuriyah at Tunisiyah)
Land area 63,170 square miles (163,610 km^2)
Border countries Libya, Algeria
Capital Tunis
Highest & lowest points Jebel ech Chambi (Mt Chambi) 5,064 feet (1,544 m); Shatt al Gharsah (Lake Gharsah) –56 feet (–17 m)
Climate Mediterranean near the coast; desert in the south
Population 10,384,000
Language(s) Arabic (official; one of the languages of commerce), French (commerce); Berber
Ethnicity Arab 98%, European 1%, Jewish and other 1%
Religion Muslim 98%, Christian 1%, Jewish and other 1%
Government Republic
Currency Tunisian dinar
Human Development Index 0.766 (ranked 91st out of 177 countries)

Mediterranean Sea
Menzel Bourguiba
Bizerte
Ariana
TUNIS
Ben Arous
Sousse
Kairouan
TUNISIA
Jebel ech Chambi
Kasserine
Sidi Bouzid
Gafsa
Sfax
Tozeur
Gabès
Kebili
Medenine
Tataouine
ALGERIA
LIBYA

Tunisia

Map Reference Pages 300–301

This small but diverse country at the northernmost point of Africa lies across the Mediterranean Sea from Sicily, with Algeria its western neighbor and Libya to the southeast. From its earliest days, Tunisia has been an important center of trade and politics.

Right This ornate doorway in the town of Sidi Bou Said reflects Tunisia's Arab Muslim heritage. Sitting on the cliffs overlooking the Bay of Tunis, the town was named after a Muslim saint who legend says fell in love with a Berber princess.

Physical Geography

More than 700 miles (1,000 km) of resort-edged beaches and cliffs line Tunisia's coastline. In the north, the eastern continuations of the Tell Atlas, the Northern Tell, and the High Tell are interspersed with fertile valleys. Most important is the Medjerda Valley, a notable cereal-producing area. From the High Tell, the land slopes to the semiarid, grassy plateau of central Tunisia, where cattle, sheep, and goats are raised, and to the Sahara Desert in the south, where oases support date palm plantations and huge seasonal salt lakes appear. The fertile coastal plain in the east is famous for its olive and citrus groves, and its vineyards. The climate is temperate along the coast with mild rainy winters and hot dry summers; in the interior and the desert, climatic extremes are common.

Above Once a week, Berbers congregate at the market in Douz to buy and sell animals such as camels and sheep. This oasis town on the edge of the Sahara Desert is a popular tourist stop.

History

First settled by Berber tribes, Tunisia has hosted several cultures over the centuries. Near Tunis, the powerful city of Carthage was founded by the Phoenicians in the tenth century BCE. After its destruction in 146 BCE, Rome re-established the city, which grew to a peak population of 500,000 since Tunisia (then the Africa Province) was a vital grain-producing area. Carthage became an early center of Christianity, hosting the Council of 397 CE. It was the region's most important port city until it was destroyed once again in 698 CE by Muslim marauders.

The Arab Muslims saw a succession of dynasties interrupted by Berber rebellions. During the sixteenth century, Tunisia's ports developed into the pirate strongholds of the eastern Barbary Coast. In the declining years of the Berber and Arab dynasties, Spain seized many of the ports, later losing them to the Ottoman Turks. During the mid-1800s, the Ottoman Beys borrowed heavily from France in an attempt to modernize the country; France used this influence to take control. In 1878, a secret deal between the United Kingdom and France gave control of Tunisia to France and control of Cyprus to Britain. Tunisia was formally declared a French protectorate on May 12, 1881.

French occupation benefited Tunisia with the development of a good road network, universities, and modern hospitals; but the desire for independence led to the establishment in 1920 of the Destour (Constitution) Party. The fiery Neo-Destour Party replaced it in 1934, and was deemed illegal, its leaders Habib Bourguiba, Tahar Sfar, Mahmoud Materi, and Bahri Guiga censured by the administration.

Bourguiba's imprisonment fueled momentum toward independence. He was moved from French to Italian to Tunisian prisons until his release in 1943 when Allied forces claimed the country. Bourguiba was incarcerated again in 1952, instigating violence by his supporters. In 1954, France removed direct authority, creating Tunisian autonomy with international relations managed by France. Full independence was granted on March 20, 1956. Bourguiba became the republic's first prime minister, then its first president one year later, molding a secular administration, modernizing the economy, and making improvements to the country's infrastructure.

In 1987, Zine el-Abidine Ben Ali was sworn in as the new president after physicians declared the 84-year-old Bourguiba unfit to govern. He has followed Bourguiba's hard line against religious extremists, while maintaining economic stability.

THE KASSERINE PASS: A TURNING POINT IN WORLD WAR II

During World War II, Tunisia saw a number of battles between Allied forces and the Axis powers. The British Army, led by Field Marshal Montgomery, advanced into Tunisia after their October 1942 victory at the Second Battle of el-Alamein in Egypt. They moved in from the south while other Allied troops invaded from the west following Operation Torch, the invasion of Algeria and Morocco. On February 19, 1943, the Axis' North African Commander, General Rommel, attacked Allied forces in the Kasserine Pass, a 2-mile (3 km) gap in the Grand Dorsal range of the Atlas Mountains. The strike was disastrous for the Allied forces, but they were able to reverse their retreat to penetrate the Axis line on March 20, linking up all Allied forces on April 8, 1943. The significance of this victory was that French, Polish, American, and British forces had won a major battle as an Allied army, thus forging an alliance that would be used later to liberate Western Europe.

Population/Culture

The majority of Tunisia's 10.3 million people lives in the towns and cities along the coast. Ninety-eight percent is Arab, and very few nomads remain. Since 1991, education for children between 6 and 16 years of age has been both compulsory and free, and the adult literacy rate is now approximately 75 percent.

Following independence, rights for women, unmatched in any other Arab nation, were established, and polygamy was abolished.

Tunisian culture largely reflects its Arab Muslim heritage, but it is also influenced by the fact that it is a secular state. International art festivals are held at Carthage, Dougga, and Hammamet while the International Festival of El Jem hosts classical music, the Andalusian Music Festival is held in Testour, and the Sahara Festival is held in Douz. International film festivals and the Theater Festival of Carthage also attract huge audiences.

Administration/Government

Appointed by the president, the executive cabinet reports to the National Assembly. Its 141 members face elections every five years.

Freedom of opinion is guaranteed by the constitution; nevertheless the press and broadcasting organizations are under tight government control. While Arab satellite television stations attract many viewers, Italian and British television channels are also widespread. There are many privately run journals, including two opposition party magazines.

Economy/Industry

Tunisia's economy is strong in many sectors due to its good trade links with Europe and the eastern Mediterranean. In 2006, agriculture represented 13 percent of economic gain through the production of grains, sugar beets, almonds, fruits, dates, and olives. Beef, dairy products, and wines are also available. Industry accounts for 33 percent of the economy with mining (iron, zinc, phosphates) and petroleum production. The service sector accounts for the remaining portion of GDP, mostly in tourism.

MILESTONE EVENTS

pre-10,000 BCE Tunisian region settled by early Berber tribes
800s BCE Founding of city of Carthage (legend has it by Queen Dido in 814 BCE)
146 BCE Carthage destroyed; re-established by Roman Empire
397 CE Council of Carthage establishes Biblical canon for Western Church
698 Carthage destroyed by Muslim invaders
1500s Tunisian coast is eastern stronghold of Barbary Coast pirates
May 12, 1881 Tunisia declared a French protectorate
March 20, 1956 Tunisia gains independence; Habib Bourguiba becomes prime minister; he becomes president the following year
1987 Zine el-Abidine Ben Ali becomes second president
1991 Compulsory education introduced

Right The Berbers of Tunisia built fortified grain storage structures of stone known as ksour, consisting of several cave-like rooms called ghorfa. The well-preserved Ksar Ouled Soltane near Tataouine is now a tourist attraction.

Above A young woman wearing traditional Berber clothing and jewelry participates in a folk festival in Kabaw. The town lies in a very fertile part of the Jebel Nafusa mountains.

Left Leptis Magna in Libya's Tripolitania region, is a World Heritage Site because it is one of Africa's finest examples of a well-preserved Roman city. Here we see Medusa Head and Severan Forum.

TUNISIA
Mediterranean Sea
Zuwārah
TARĀBULUS (TRIPOLI)
Az Zāwīyah
Al Khums
Miṣrātah
Gharyān
Bani Walid
Khalīj Surt
Surt
Al Baydā'
Banghāzī
Tubruq
Ajdābiyā
Hūn
LIBYA
Sabhā
ALGERIA
EGYPT
Al Jawf
NIGER
CHAD
SUDAN
Bikkū Bittī

Libya

Map Reference Pages 302–303

According to early Egyptian records, Libya's coastal plain has been inhabited for as long as Egypt has; evidence from the Tibesti Mountains in the south points to an even older human presence. These mountains are known for their cave paintings, dating from the fifth to the third millennia BCE, that feature elephants, leopards, and wolves, none of which are found in Libya today.

Physical Geography

Bordering the Mediterranean Sea, Libya has the longest coastline in North Africa, and is the fourth largest country on the continent, but over 90 percent of its area is desert. The arid rock and sand-dune landscapes of the great Sahara Desert extend right across the country. The coastal strip enjoys cool damp winters and warm dry summers, while the interior is dry and hot throughout the year. Like Algeria, Libya suffers from dust-laden desert winds. Elevation is modest except in the south, where the Tibesti Mountains extend into Libya, with some peaks above 7,000 feet (2,134 m) high. They receive more rainfall than the desert, supporting small settlements and wildlife.

History

In the seventh century BCE, the Phoenicians colonized the eastern part of Libya, known as Cyrenaica, and the Greeks colonized the western part, calling it Tripolitania. Both areas later came under Roman control, followed by Ottoman control. Until recent times the interior, the Fezzan, remained under the control of mostly nomadic Saharan tribes. Muslim Arabs, who entered the region in the seventh century CE, engraved the most permanent mark on local culture. The Italian occupation, which replaced almost four centuries of Turkish rule, began in 1911 and lasted until the end of World War II. In 1951, Libya became an independent monarchy and one of the few free African countries at the time. The monarchy was abolished in the aftermath of a 1969 military coup that propelled Muammar al-Gaddafi into power, which he holds to this day.

MILESTONE EVENTS

600s BCE Greek colonists settle the northeastern region

400s BCE Carthaginians establish trading centers in the northwest

500s CE Byzantine forces conquer the region

643 Arab forces occupy Tripoli

1551 Ottomans capture Tripoli

1911–1912 Italy takes control

December 24, 1951 Independence achieved as United Kingdom of Libya

September 1, 1969 Muammar al-Gaddafi stages coup; sets up Great Socialist People's Libyan Arab Jamahiriya and the Revolutionary Command Council

1972 Political parties banned

March 1992 UN sanctions imposed

September 2003 UN sanctions lifted

2007 Libya elected to nonpermanent seat on the United Nations Security Council for 2008–2009

Population/Culture

Despite its size, Libya has only a modest population, some 90 percent of which resides near the coast. Density is highest in the areas around Tripoli. There are few permanent interior settlements; they are found around oases and along old trans-Saharan trade routes. Urbanization and economic development have influenced steady population growth.

While traditional extended family households are suffering under the pressures of the country's largely urban lifestyle, traditional ways of life among nomadic Saharan tribes are still quite widely practiced.

Many cultures have left imprints in this region, most of them now integrated into the Arab–Berber cultural stock. The linguistic and religious structure is also simple. Arabic is the official language, with only minor regional variations; Islam is the dominant religion. Literacy rates rank among the highest in the Arab world and Africa.

Administration/Government

Since 1969 Muammar al-Gaddafi and a small network of leaders have overseen every aspect of the political environment. Libya's system relies on a symbiosis of Islamic and socialist ideas and the democratic electoral process is currently non-existent. Political parties are not allowed. Strict governmental control over politics, economics, and various aspects of social life has generated outside concerns about individual freedom. After years of a turbulent relationship with the west, Libya's foreign policy has recently shifted, allowing significant improvements in cooperation.

Economy/Industry

The economy revolves around oil exploration and production. Oil exports, primarily to Western European countries, account for almost all the country's trade profits. Although Libya is among Africa's leading countries in terms of relative wealth, its socialist policies block the speed of progress.

In order to diversify the economy and stimulate progress, the country is investing in the development of infrastructure and transportation, including a project called the Great Man-Made River, a giant underground network of pipes bringing water from aquifers below the Sahara to the coast for irrigation and drinking water.

LIBYA

Official name Great Socialist People's Libyan Arab Jamahiriya (Al Jumahiriyah al Arabiyah al Libiyah ash Shabiyah al Ishtirakiyah al Uzma)

Land area 679,359 square miles (1,759,540 km^2)

Border countries Egypt, Sudan, Chad, Niger, Algeria, Tunisia

Capital Tripoli (Ṭarābulus)

Highest & lowest points Bikku Bitti (Bette Peak) 7,437 feet (2,267 m); Sabkhat Ghuzayyil (Lake Ghuzayyil) −154 feet (−47 m)

Climate Mediterranean on the coast, desert in the interior

Population 6,174,000

Language(s) Arabic

Ethnicity Arab and Berber 97%; Greek, Maltese, Italian, Egyptian, Pakistani, Turkish, Indian, Tunisian 3%

Religion Muslim 97%; other 3%

Government Jamahiriya (neologism coined by Muammar al-Gaddafi)

Currency Libyan dinar

Human Development Index 0.818 (ranked 56th out of 177 countries)

Below The desert lake called Oum el Ma (or Umm el Ma) is situated in Mandara Valley, in Libya's southwestern desert region.

EGYPT

Official name Arab Republic of Egypt (Jumhuriyat Misr al-Arabiya)
Land area 384,344 square miles (995,450 km²)
Border countries Gaza Strip, Israel, Sudan, Libya
Capital Cairo (Al-Qāhirah)
Highest & lowest points Jabal Katrina (Mt Catherine) 8,623 feet (2,629 m); Munkhafad al Qattara (Qattara Depression) –436 feet (–133 m)
Climate Mediterranean on the coast; desert interior
Population 81,714,000
Language(s) Official: Arabic; other: English and French
Ethnicity Egyptian 98%; Berber, Nubian, Bedouin, Beja 1%; European 1%
Religion Sunni Muslim 90%, Eastern Orthodox (Coptic) Christian 9%, other Christian 1%
Government Republic
Currency Egyptian pound
Human Development Index 0.708 (ranked 112th out of 177 countries)

Mediterranean Sea
Al Iskandariya (Alexandria)
Dumyāt
Marsā Maṭrūḥ
Damanhūr
Ṭanṭā
Būr Sa'īd
Shibīn al Kawm
Al Ismā'īlīyah
Shubrā al Khaymah
AL QĀHIRAH (CAIRO)
Al Jīzah
As Suways (Suez)
Ḥulwān
Al Fayyūm
Banī Suwayf
Jabal Kātrinā (Mt Catherine)
ISRAEL
Al Minyā
Mallawī
Asyūṭ
Al Ghurdaqah
Sūhāj
Qinā
Al Uqṣur
Aswān
Red Sea
LIBYA
EGYPT
SUDAN

Egypt

Map Reference Pages 302–303

Although adjacent to two large bodies of water, the Mediterranean Sea and the Red Sea, Egypt is almost entirely a desert environment except for the great Nile River, the lifeblood of Egypt, and one of the world's longest rivers. It flows northward from its southernmost source, the Ruvironza River in Burundi, and its major source, Lake Victoria, through Sudan and Egypt, eventually discharging into the Mediterranean through a grand delta.

Physical Geography

The majority of Egypt's landmass covers the northeastern corner of the African continent. The Sinai Peninsula, the sizable eastern part of the country, lies on the Asian continent, separated by the Suez Canal and the Red Sea. Several major deserts, all part of the Sahara, stretch through the rest of the country—the Eastern Desert between the Nile and the Red Sea, the Libyan Desert in the southwest, and the Western Desert and the Great Sand Sea to the center-west. The Eastern Desert is a mountainous region with rocky peaks over 6,000 feet (1,942 m), while in the western deserts, rocky plateaus and sandy depressions, some below sea level, are the main features.

Despite its length, the coastline offers few islands and natural harbors. The coastal area enjoys a Mediterranean climate, but the rest of Egypt has an arid climatic regime. Almost all the fresh water that flows along the Nile is sourced in the Ethiopian highlands and central Africa. Fresh water in most desert oases is drilled from aquifers at great depths, as any water close to the surface is too salty to drink.

History

The earliest substantial sources providing a glimpse of political organization in ancient Egypt date beyond 3000 BCE. The civilization in the valley of the Nile evolved from two cores, one in the delta region, the other in the upper valley. Although they merged into a single kingdom and established a path for its early ruling dynasties, regional divisions remained throughout ancient Egypt's history. The Old Kingdom, centered in Memphis near the Nile delta, extended through much of the third millennium BCE, and is best known for the pyramids, popular tombs for pharaohs, their minions, and religious and military leaders during the Third Dynasty. Their initial construction was simple, but soon afterward the pharaohs of the Fourth Dynasty created the famously precise and complex pyramids at Giza, almost bankrupting the entire kingdom and accelerating its decline. Consolidation occurred with the Tenth Dynasty and the Middle Kingdom, which concentrated power in Thebes in central Egypt for another five centuries. A second decline and subsequent recovery would give birth to the New Kingdom. This era, especially the Eighteenth and Nineteenth dynasties, saw the zenith of the kingdom's power, reaching from Sudan to Syria. Ramses II, Hatshepsut, and Tutankhamen were among the most well-known historical figures of this period.

Rule over Egypt would soon be transferred to foreigners. From the Persians to Alexander the Great, followed by the Romans, Arabs, and the Ottoman Empire, foreign powers controlled Egypt for over two millennia. In the 1880s the imperial hand of Britain knocked on Egypt's door as well, although the country nominally remained in allegiance to Istanbul until World War I. In the postwar era, the United Kingdom proclaimed Egypt a British protectorate. In 1922 Egypt finally achieved independence, and continued as a monarchy until the revolution of 1952 and the proclamation of the republic. Two years later Gamal Abdel Nasser emerged as a national figure and celebrated president. Nasser's presidency and that of his successor Anwar Sadat were closely tied to regional geopolitics and several conflicts with Israel, a significant aspect of Egypt's recent history.

Population

Few other countries display similar settlement patterns. Nearly all Egyptians reside along the banks of the Nile or in its immediate proximity, leaving a vast emptiness in the rest of the country. Overall, Egypt's population density does not stand out, but if only the Nile Valley is taken into account it is among the highest in the world. Despite recent economic development, agriculture constitutes the main form of income for many in rural Egypt and the fertile river plain continues to be the prime location for settlement. In the rural regions, a large family of children forms valuable capital for a household as well as a status symbol. In the past half century Egypt's population rapidly increased, to become the most populated country in the Arab realm with more than 81 million residents. Despite the large urban,

THE VALLEY OF THE KINGS

The resting place for the New Kingdom's pharaohs on their journey from Thebes to the underworld, the Valley of the Kings is among Egypt's most excavated sites. During the second millennium BCE, dozens of pharaohs and high officials were laid to rest in limestone-carved graves, often accompanied by generous supplies of priceless artefacts. The valley's most celebrated resident, though a minor historical figure, was the pharaoh Tutankhamen, famous mainly because much of his tomb remained intact until discovery in 1922 (his funerary mask is pictured below). Many other tombs fell prey to the depredations of grave-robbers undaunted by any protective curses they might encounter. Thousands of tourists visit the Valley of the Kings each day, many of them brought by cruise ships sailing upstream from Cairo. Though not as monumental a landscape as the pyramids in Giza, the Valley of the Kings provides one of the most detailed insights into ancient Egypt's culture. After several centuries of active excavation, the site still yields new findings that help fill in the puzzle of early history.

Above Cairo is an ancient city with a rich and fascinating history. The site was originally settled during the Paleolithic period. In 973 CE, rulers of the Islamic sect called the Fatimids founded the city that was later named Al-Qāhirah (Cairo), meaning "The Triumphant City."

Right The pyramids of Giza, on the southern edge of Cairo, were built during the Fourth Dynasty. They are the burial grounds for three generations of pharaohs: Khufu (Cheops), Khafra (Chephren), and Menkaura (Mycerinus).

and remarkably cosmopolitan, areas of Cairo and Alexandria, which combined account for nearly 20 million people, over half of Egypt's population resides in a rural environment.

Culture

Ethnic structure is simple, with 98 percent being indigenous Egyptians. Other groups are found only in small numbers. The overwhelming majority of Egyptians are Sunni Muslims. Coptic Christians, an Eastern Orthodox group, account for 9 percent. The country's linguistic background is Afro-Asiatic, and Arabic serves as the official language and alphabet. The patriarchal structure of society is reflected in female literacy rates lagging far behind those of males, but major improvements in formal education have been recorded in the last couple of decades.

Administration/Government

Strong presidential powers and maintaining the status quo are the hallmarks of Egypt's political system. The current president, Hosni Mubarak, is in his fifth term. Calls for democratization have resulted in the creation of legislation with the aim of gradually loosening the electoral process, but real improvements are slow. The strong grip on executive power by the presidency has been a feature of Egyptian politics since the 1950s, as is the relationship between domestic and foreign affairs.

Since 1945, Cairo has been the headquarters for the Arab League. In the 1970s, Egypt ended an existing aid relationship with the Soviet Union in favor of the United States, and today it is among the largest recipients of American financial and military assistance.

Economy/Industry

Egypt began a rocky ride in the twentieth century with socialist plans to transform an economy based on agriculture into a modern industrial economy, but nationalization and state control proved only a limited success. It also paved a path to long-term economic instability. Heavy military expenditure and engagement in devastating conflicts further limited hope for rapid economic expansion, and increased borrowing and foreign debt. Recent liberalization of the economic system, mainly in terms of decentralization, has provided valuable benefits. Egypt's gross domestic product radically increased, followed by an influx of foreign investments.

However, development favors urban centers and many rural areas have received little benefit, keeping the pressure on government to continue providing costly subsidies to farming families and small agricultural businesses. About one-third of the workforce is involved in agriculture, yet Egypt continues to import staple foods such as wheat and corn. Natural gas exploration and its export is becoming an increasingly crucial factor and a vital source of hard currency. Income from tourism, which is quite well developed, provides the national account with the largest foreign currency contribution of any other element of the economy.

Aswan High Dam

In the 1960s, Egypt relied on the Soviet Union's financial assistance and the expertise of its engineers to construct the Aswan High Dam on the Nile. A major element in attempts to industrialize the nation, the dam was needed to regulate river flow, prevent the annual summer flooding of the agricultural areas on its banks, and produce much-needed electricity. The dam produces electricity for all of Egypt, and for Sudan.

The artificial Lake Nasser, created by the dam's completion in 1970, is the largest reservoir in the world, extending across the Sudanese border to a length of over 300 miles (480 km). Downstream, the seasonal flooding that so often devastated crops is a thing of the past. Lake water is released in sufficient quantity for year-round irrigation, but this is now causing serious environmental concerns. The dam blocks the distribution of the nutrients previously provided by the annual deposition of silt, and continuous irrigation, combined with the use of fertilizers, has increased the salinity of water returned to the river, leading to the near-destruction of the fishing industry.

MILESTONE EVENTS

3100 BCE King Menes unites Upper and Lower Egypt; he forms the world's first national government

3100–2900 BCE Irrigation begins; both ox-drawn plow and hieroglyphic writing develop

2686 BCE Old Kingdom founded

c. 2650 BCE Step Pyramid built at Saqqara

2600–2500 BCE Great Pyramid, and others, built at Giza

1991 BCE Middle Kingdom founded

1554 BCE New Kingdom founded

332 BCE Alexander the Great conquers Egypt; Ptolemaic Dynasty begins

30 BCE Ptolemaic Dynasty falls; Egypt comes under Roman rule

639–642 CE Muslim Arab conquest of Roman Egypt leads to adoption of Islam

973 Fatimid rulers found Al-Qâhirah (Cairo)

1100s Christian Crusaders from Europe invade Egypt

1168 Saladin drives out Crusaders

1250 Mamelukes seize control

1798 Napoleon Bonaparte defeats Mameluke forces in Battle of the Pyramids

1801 French withdraw

1805 Muhammad Ali begins process of modernization

1882 British forces defeat Egyptian army and install administrators

1922 Independence

1952 Revolution abolishes monarchy and establishes republic

1956 Suez Canal nationalized

1960–1970 Construction of Aswan High Dam

1967 Six-Day War with Israel

1973 Yom Kippur War with Israel

1978 Camp David Peace Accords with Israel

October 1981 Assassination of Anwar Sadat; Mubarak elected president

June 1995 Mubarak escapes assassination attempt by fundamentalists

Top Beautiful, steep-sided, white chalk inselbergs and other chalk formations rise out of the Farafra Depression southwest of Cairo. It is hoped they will soon be protected within the boundaries of a national park.

Above Tens of thousands of residents and entire precious archeological sites had to be relocated in order to form Lake Nasser. The temple of the pharaoh Ramses II at Abu Simbel (pictured here), one of ancient Egypt's most remarkable monuments, was cut out of the surrounding stone and moved block by block to higher ground.

Left A Nubian woman prepares for her wedding by having parts of her body decorated using henna. Wedding ceremonies are very important community events, and are a time for expressing deep emotions and celebrating traditions through costumes and jewelry as well as song, ululation, dance, and percussion.

ALGERIA
WESTERN SAHARA
Chegga
MALI
Fdérik
Zouérat
Kediet ej Jill
Nouâdhibou
Atâr
Akjoujt
ATLANTIC OCEAN
MAURITANIA
NOUAKCHOTT
Tidjikja
Boutilimit
Rosso
Aleg
Kaédi
Kiffa
'Ayoûn el 'Atroûs
Néma
SENEGAL

Mauritania

Map Reference Pages 300–301

MAURITANIA

Official name Islamic Republic of Mauritania (Al-Jumhuriyah al-Islamiyah al-Muritaniyah)
Land area 397,954 square miles (1,030,700 km²)
Border countries Algeria, Mali, Senegal, Western Sahara
Capital Nouakchott
Highest & lowest points Kediet Ijill (Mt Ijill) 3,002 feet (915 m); Sebkhet Te-n-Dghamcha (Lake Te-n-Dghamcha) −16 feet (−5 m)
Climate Desert; constantly hot, dry, dusty
Population 3,365,000
Language(s) Official: Arabic, French; other: Pulaar, Soninké, Hassaniya, Wolof
Ethnicity Black Moor 40%, White Moor 30%, African (Haalpulaar, Soninké, Wolof) 30%
Religion Muslim 100%
Government Republic
Currency Ouguiya
Human Development Index 0.550 (ranked 137th out of 177 countries)

Mauritania has suffered since the 1960s from the intrusion of the Sahara Desert into its Sahel zone. The Sahel is a semi-arid tropical savanna ecoregion stretching from the Atlantic coast to the Red Sea, the transition zone between the Sahara and the more fertile region to the south. The ongoing desertification of the entire Sahel is now understood to be the result of long-term poor land management practices that take no account of altered circumstances when drought strikes.

Physical Geography

Mauritania is mainly part of the vast Sahara, a sea of sand dunes with intermittent patches of scrubby vegetation, occasionally interrupted by rocky plateaus, and thinly scattered with small villages and oases. The central Adrar plateau rises to 1,640 feet (500 m), with the Tagant further south to 1,970 feet (600 m). The only region with permanent vegetation, supporting a wide variety of wildlife and most of the population, lies north of the Senegal River, which forms the southern border.

History

Mauritania was originally settled by the ancestors of the Soninké. From the fifth century, Berber tribes displaced them, followed by Moorish Islamic invaders. Explored by the Portuguese in the fifteenth century, in 1920 it became one of the colonies that constituted French West Africa. Mauritania achieved independence on November 28, 1960.

In 1976 Mauritania and Morocco divided the territory of Western Sahara. An indigenous Saharawi independence movement, the Polisario Front, fought against both countries. The war brought down Mauritania's civilian government, unleashed a series of military coups and forced withdrawal from Western Sahara in 1979.

From April 1992 a republican party dominated Mauritanian politics until another military coup in 2005, when a transitional government was appointed. A series of elections beginning in 2006 culminated on March 25, 2007, with the election of Sidi Ould Cheikh Abdellahi as president.

Population/Culture

About 30 percent of the population is White Moors of Arab-Berber ancestry, 40 percent Black Moors of Moorish-African heritage, and 30 percent African (Haalpulaar, Soninké, and Wolof). A nomadic lifestyle is still practiced in the north, but more than 90 percent of the people lives in the wetter southern quarter. The country is undergoing rapid urbanization, with Nouakchott, the capital, home to about 612,000 people.

Arabic and French are the official languages. Most people also speak Arabic dialects. Islam is the official religion. Theology, poetry, and music flourish, and Mauritania's artisans are famous for their goldsmithing.

Administration/Government

Control is tightly concentrated in the hands of the central government, although national and municipal elections since 1992 have produced some degree of decentralization. Political parties, illegal during the military period, were legalized in 1991.

Sharia (Islamic law) is followed for social and family matters, a western-style legal code in commercial and some criminal cases.

Economy/Industry

A majority of the population depends on agriculture for a livelihood, although in more recent times many subsistence farmers have been forced into urban areas by recurrent drought. Mauritania's coastal waters, among the world's richest fishing areas, are today threatened by overexploitation.

Extensive deposits of iron ore account for approximately 50 percent of total exports through the country's first deepwater port, which opened near Nouakchott in 1986.

Below Colorfully attired women in sand dunes close to the ancient city of Chinguetti in the Adrar region of Mauritania.

Below right A Bedik village in Senegal with typical grass-roofed houses. The Bedik are a minority ethnic group from Senegal's east.

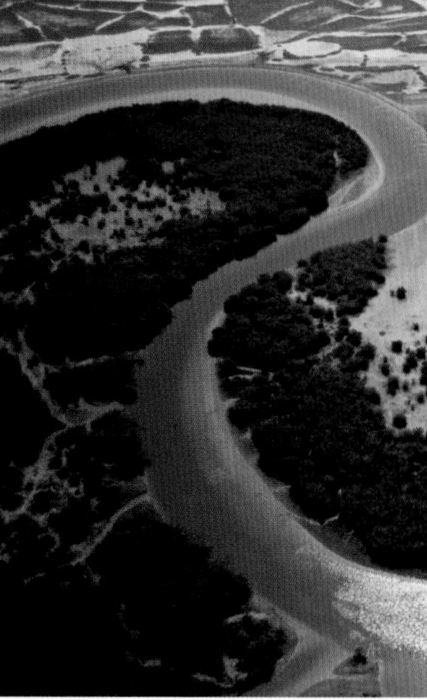

MAURITANIA
St-Louis
Dagana
Louga
Dara
Matam
DAKAR
Thiès
Diourbel
Fatick
SENEGAL
Bakel
Kaolack
ATLANTIC OCEAN
MALI
Tambacounda
GAMBIA
Médina Gounas
Kolda
Ziguinchor
GUINEA-BISSAU
unnamed
Kédougou
GUINEA

Senegal

Map Reference Pages 300–301

SENEGAL

Official name Republic of Senegal (République du Sénégal)
Land area 75,794 square miles (196,190 km²)
Border countries Mauritania, Mali, Guinea, Guinea-Bissau, Gambia
Capital Dakar
Highest point Unnamed feature in Fouta Djallon highlands 1,906 feet (581 m)
Climate Tropical; hot, humid; rainy season (May–November); dry season (December–April)
Population 12,853,000
Language(s) Official: French; other: Wolof, Pulaar, Jola, Mandinka
Ethnicity Wolof 43.3%, Pular 23.8%, Serer 14.7%, Jola 3.7%, Mandinka 3%, Soninké 1.1%, European and Lebanese 1%, other 9.4%
Religion Muslim 94%, Christian 5%, indigenous beliefs 1%
Government Republic
Currency Communauté Financière Africaine franc
Human Development Index 0.499 (ranked 156th out of 177 countries)

Senegal is sometimes called the "Gateway to Africa," and has been held up as one of Africa's model democracies due to its well-established multiparty system and tradition of civilian rule. The capital, Dakar, sits on Cap Vert, the westernmost point of the African continent, and the country almost entirely surrounds the tiny riverine nation of Gambia.

Physical Geography

The rolling, sandy grasslands of the Sahel rise to the foothills of the Fouta Djallon highlands in the southeast and to high sand dunes on the northern coast. Lying at an ecological boundary where semi-arid Sahel, coast, and tropical rainforest converge, Senegal is home to a wide variety of flora and fauna. The climate displays the well-defined dry winter and humid summer seasons common to tropical regions. Rainfall increases substantially to the south.

History

Senegal has a fascinating historical background, having at one time or another been part of the ancient Empire of Ghana, the Mandingo empires, and the Jolof Empire. In the nineteenth century it was colonized by France and became part of French West Africa. In 1960, independence saw Senegal and French Sudan form the Mali Federation, which broke apart within six months to become the independent republics of Senegal and Mali. In 1982 Senegal joined with Gambia as a federation called Senegambia, but this association was dissolved in 1989. Senegal has never experienced a military coup.

Culture
Islam was brought to Senegal in the eleventh century, and is the leading religion, followed by about 94 percent of the total population. Christians (mainly Roman Catholics) comprise another 5 percent and the remaining 1 percent follows indigenous beliefs.

Family ties are very important, particularly in the rural areas, where groups of related families live in separate houses within a compound. The Senegalese are noted for their striking artwork, particularly their carved wooden masks, and traditional dance and music. Mbalax, a Wolof form of percussive music, is known throughout West Africa.

Administration/Government
Senegal has experienced one of the most successful transitions from colonialism to independence in Africa, with a strongly democratic political culture. It has 11 administrative regions, each headed by a governor appointed by the elected president. The 120 members of the National Assembly are elected separately. The generally tolerant culture, largely free from ethnic or religious tensions, has provided a resilient base for democratic politics.

The current leader, President Wade, has advanced a liberal agenda for Senegal, which includes privatization and other market-opening measures. Liberalization of the economy is proceeding, slowly. Senegal enjoys a flourishing independent media.

Economy/Industry
Senegal is a predominantly rural country with limited natural resources, earning foreign exchange from fish, phosphates, peanuts, iron ore, tourism, and services. Agriculture, including peanuts, millet, sorghum, manioc, rice, and cotton, represents 17 percent of GDP; industry and mining 19.7 percent.

Senegal has one of the best road and rail networks in West Africa, good port facilities, an international airport, and an advanced telecommunications infrastructure.

Ponta do Sol
Santo Antão
Porto Novo
Mindelo
São Vicente
Vila da Ribeira Brava
Sal
São Nicolau
Santa Maria
CAPE VERDE
Sal Rei
ATLANTIC OCEAN
Boa Vista
Santiago
Pedra Badejo
Maio
Fogo
Tarrafal
Mt Fogo
Vila Nova Sintra
Brava
São Filipe
Porto Inglês
PRAIA

Cape Verde

Map Reference Page 310

The Cape Verde Islands lie in the mid-Atlantic Ocean about 385 miles (500 km) west of Senegal in two archipelagic groups—the Barlavento in the north and Sotavento in the south. Because of the islands' isolation they are home to many endemic species of birds and reptiles. The country is poor in natural resources and prone to drought, with little arable land.

Physical Geography
The volcanic islands are mostly mountainous, displaying deep scars and gullies created by erosion, while Sal, Boa Vista, and Maio are generally flat. Fogo has an active volcano. Sheer jagged cliffs rise from the sea on several of the mountainous islands, and the Barlavento group is notable for its spectacular rock formations. Vegetation is sparse in the semi-arid uplands and coast, but interior valleys support much denser growth.

Rainfall is irregular; periodic droughts are the norm, and food shortages are endemic.

History
The then-uninhabited islands were colonized by the Portuguese in 1642. They planted sugar cane, and prospered from the trans-Atlantic slave trade. When slave trading was abolished in the nineteenth century, Cape Verde became an important resupply location for ships traveling the mid-Atlantic shipping lanes and Mindelo, an excellent natural harbor on São Vicente, became a major commercial center. Cape Verde became independent in 1975.

Culture
Seventy-one percent of the population is Creole, offspring of Europeans and the African slaves brought to work on the plantations. The influence of African culture is most pronounced on the island of Santiago, where half the population resides. The official language is Portuguese, but most Cape Verdeans also speak Crioulo, which is based on archaic Portuguese and influenced by African and European languages. They enjoy rich traditions in literature and music. Because of a long history of emigration, more Cape Verdeans live abroad than on the islands.

Administration/Government
Cape Verde enjoys a stable democracy. In 1980 the African Party for the Independence of Cape Verde (PAICV) founded a one-party system and ruled until 1990. Responding to growing pressure for multiparty democracy, the first multiparty elections were held in 1991, and the Movement for Democracy captured a governing majority in the National Assembly, gaining an even larger majority in the general elections held in 1995. The PAICV regained power in 2001.

Economy/Industry
Cape Verde has few natural resources, and suffers from persistent drought and limited fresh water. Only Santiago, Santo Antão, Fogo, and Brava support significant agricultural production, and the country is heavily dependent on food imports. Mineral resources include salt and limestone. Fish and shellfish are plentiful, and small quantities are exported. The economy is service-oriented, with commerce, transport, and public services accounting for over 70 percent of GDP, and agriculture and fishing about 10 percent. An important source of foreign exchange is remittances, an estimated 20 percent of GDP, from expatriate Cape Verdeans. While tourism is increasing, it threatens the rich marine life, including nesting sites for loggerhead turtles and feeding grounds for humpback whales.

CAPE VERDE

Official name Republic of Cape Verde (República de Cabo Verde)
Land area 1,556 square miles (4,030 km²)
Border countries None
Capital Praia
Highest point Mt Fogo 9,281 feet (2,829 m)
Climate Temperate; warm dry summer; precipitation meager and very erratic
Population 426,998
Language(s) Official: Portuguese; Crioulo
Ethnicity Creole 71%, African 28%, European 1%
Religion Roman Catholic, Protestant (mostly Church of the Nazarene)
Government Republic
Currency Cape Verdean escudo
Human Development Index 0.736 (ranked 102nd out of 177 countries)

Top left A winding river channel among mangroves and dyeing pits in the Sine-Saloum Delta, Senegal. The area, once the haven of backpackers, now caters for a more exclusive market.

Above Men fish in the abundant but often treacherous waters around Cape Verde; women sort and sell the catches.

Above left A Bassari woman in southern Senegal wears the traditional hair adornment of the Ohamana age-passage ceremony.

Below Lighthouse perched atop a rocky islet in Porto Grande Bay, Mindelo, Cape Verde.

GAMBIA

Official name Republic of the Gambia
Land area 4,363 square miles (11,300 km²)
Border country Senegal
Capital Banjul
Highest point Unnamed location in the east 173 feet (53 m)
Climate Tropical, hot, rainy season (June–November); cooler, dry season (November–May)
Population 1,735,000
Language(s) Official: English; other: Mandinka, Wolof, Fula, other indigenous vernaculars
Ethnicity African 99% (Mandinka 42%, Fula 18%, Wolof 16%, Jola 10%, Serahuli 9%, other 4%), non-African 1%
Religion Muslim 90%, Christian 9%, indigenous beliefs 1%
Government Republic
Currency Dalasi
Human Development Index 0.502 (ranked 155th out of 177 countries)

Above right The Grand Mosque of Djenné is the largest mud-brick building in the world. Each year after the rainy season a new layer of mud is applied to preserve the building.

Above Gambian man playing the kora, a 21-stringed instrument. The sound of the kora can resemble both the harp and flamenco guitar.

ATLANTIC OCEAN
SENEGAL
GAMBIA
BANJUL
Brikama
Gunjur
Kerewan
Farafenni
Kanifing
Mansa Konko
Georgetown
Basse Santa Su
unnamed
SENEGAL

Gambia

Map Reference Pages 304–305

Gambia, the African mainland's smallest country, is almost completely surrounded by Senegal. The river Gambia runs through the middle. Its small economic base, dependence on rain-fed agriculture, and drought make it one of Africa's poorest countries.

Physical Geography

Gambia's terrain is simple—the floodplain of the Gambia River is flanked by low hills. Climate is tropical. The rainy season is from June to November; the dry season is from November to May.

History

Once part of the ancient Mali Empire, and a major player in the trans-Saharan trade in gold, ivory, and slaves, Gambia became a British Crown colony in 1889, achieved independence in 1965, and became a republic on April 24, 1970. Gambia has enjoyed relative political stability since independence, although authoritarian rule still tends to be the norm. An unsuccessful coup in 1981, resulting in several hundred deaths, led Senegal and Gambia to sign the 1982 Treaty of Confederation, but Gambia withdrew from the arrangement in 1989. Lieutenant Jammeh, who deposed the president and became head of state in 1994, has ruled since.

Population/Culture

Although home to a great number of ethnic groups that proudly preserve their own traditions and language, the population is generally free of intertribal friction. The literacy rate is low, at just 40.1 percent.

Tiny Gambia has an amazing cultural diversity. Most ethnic groups present in western Africa are represented here, including the offspring of European slave traders from the fifteenth through seventeenth centuries. Some of this history was popularized in Alex Haley's book *Roots*, and the TV series, which was set in Gambia. The government aims to serve as a cultural center for the African diaspora and for those seeking to better understand the rich heritage of African peoples.

English is the official language, making for a long narrow strip of English speakers surrounded by French-speaking Senegal. The majority of Gambians are Muslims.

Administration/Government

Gambia's constitution provides for a strong presidential government, a National Assembly with 53 seats. An independent judiciary, and the protection of human rights. Tribal chiefs also retain some traditional powers which are authorized by customary law.

Economy/Industry

Gambia's liberal market-based economy depends on traditional subsistence agriculture, employing 75 percent of the labor force, the export of peanuts, trade (relying on its ocean port and low import duties), and tourism. It has few natural resources. Limited manufacturing is primarily agriculturally based (such as peanut processing, bakeries, a brewery, and a tannery). Other manufacturing activities include soap, and clothing.

MALI

Official name Republic of Mali (République du Mali)
Area 475,000 square miles (1,230,244 km²)
Border countries Algeria, Niger, Burkina Faso, Cote d'Ivoire, Guinea, Senegal, Mauritania
Capital Bamako
Highest & lowest points Hombori Tondo (Mt Hombori) 3,789 feet (1,155 m), Senegal River 75 feet (23 m)
Climate Arid subtropical; hot and dry (February–June); rainy, humid, and mild (June–November); cool and dry (November–February)
Population 12,324,000
Language(s) Official: French; other: Bambara 80%, numerous African languages
Ethnicity Mandé 50% (Bambara, Malinké, Soninké), Peul 17%, Voltaic 12%, Songhai 6%, Tuareg and Moor 10%, other 5%
Religion Muslim 90%, Christian 1%, indigenous beliefs 9%
Government Republic
Currency Communauté Financière Africaine franc
Human Development Index 0.380 (ranked 173rd out of 177 countries)

ALGERIA
MAURITANIA
Taoudenni
Kidal
MALI
Tombouctou
Gao
Hombori Tondo
NIGER
SENEGAL
Kayes
Nioro du Sahel
Niono
Mopti
Djenné
Ségou
San
Kita
Koulikoro
Koutiala
BAMAKO
Bougouni
Sikasso
BURKINA FASO
GUINEA
CÔTE D'IVOIRE

Mali

Map Reference Pages 300–301

Mali is the cultural heir to the ancient African empires—Ghana, Malinké (Mali), and Songhai—that from 700 to 1600 CE controlled trans-Saharan trade and connected with Mediterranean and Middle Eastern centers of civilization. Along with Djenné, the fabled city of Timbuktu in central Mali (today a small trading town) was a center of commerce and learning, particularly of law and the Islamic faith, and priceless manuscripts from the era are preserved there.

Physical Geography

Mali is the seventh largest country in Africa. The Sahara Desert covers most of the northern half; the majority of the population lives in the relatively wetter grasslands of the south. The Niger, Africa's third longest river, crosses the Malian Sahel in the vast Niger Inland Delta. Its seasonal wetlands and lakes are important to migratory birds, and these have been included in UNESCO's Ramsar Convention on Wetlands.

History

Colonized by France in the late 1800s, Mali became independent in 1960, and under its first president, Modibo Keita, became a one-party state committed to socialist policies and nationalization of commercial enterprises. In 1968 Keita was removed in a military coup by Lieutenant Moussa Traoré, whose efforts at economic reform were thwarted by internal political struggles and the severe Sahelian drought of 1968–74. Mali's first democratic election, held in 1992, was won by Alpha Oumar Konaré, who implemented key political and economic reforms. Amadou Touré succeeded him and was elected to a second five-year term in 2007.

Population/Culture

The people are largely sub-Saharan ethnic groups with numerous similarities of religion, culture, history, and language. Around 70 percent is rural; up to 10 percent nomadic.

Mali is a site of transition between the Arab world and the black African nations. Music and dance are an especially rich heritage

among the Songhai and Malinké peoples. Local architectural forms are distinctive, their shapes and construction materials varying by ethnic group. Most notable are the mud-brick mosques, which have beams and tree-branches sticking out of them to aid annual repairs after the summer rains. Local handicrafts include the distinctive jewelry of the Mandingo people, leatherwork in the Niger Bend region, the mud-dyed cotton cloth with geometric designs from Djenné, and wooden carvings.

Administration/Government

Mali's constitution provides for a multiparty democracy in which all parties must transcend ethnic, religious, regional, or gender lines. The president is elected and appoints the prime minister as head of government. The president chairs the Council of Ministers, which adopts proposals for laws submitted to the National Assembly for approval.

Mali's legal system is based on codes that were inherited at independence from France.

Economy/Industry

Mali's landlocked status and harsh physical environment are major obstacles to development. Having few mineral resources, and plagued by drought, Mali is always vulnerable to economic crisis. Most Malians depend on subsistence agriculture. Mali exports some gold, phosphates, salt, and uranium. The Niger River is an important source of fish, but production is declining due to drought and diversion of river water for agriculture.

LIBYA
ALGERIA
MALI
NIGER
CHAD
NIGERIA
BURKINA FASO
BENIN
Arlit
Bilma
Mt Bagzane
Agadez
Tahoua
Tillabéri
Dogondoutchi
Birnin Konni
NIAMEY
Dosso
Maradi
Zinder
Tessaoua
Diffa

Niger

Map Reference Pages 300–301

Niger is one of the poorest countries in the world. It has minimal government services and insufficient funds to develop its resource base. The predominantly agrarian and subsistence-based economy is frequently disrupted by the extended droughts common to the Sahel region.

Physical Geography

Landlocked Niger has some of the hottest temperatures on Earth. The northern four-fifths is desert plains and sand dunes, interrupted by the Air Mountains; the southern fifth is savanna, with flat to rolling plains. Environmental concerns include overgrazing, soil erosion, deforestation, desertification, poaching of wildlife, and habitat destruction.

History

Niger was colonized by the French, became an autonomous state within the French Community in 1958, and gained independence in August 1960. For its first 14 years, Niger was ruled by President Hamani Diori and a single-party civilian regime. Following a military coup, Colonel Seyni Kountché and a small group ruled the country until his death in 1987. Colonel Ibrahim Baré Maïnassara overthrew the Third Republic in 1996.

In 1999, Baré was in turn overthrown in a coup led by Major Daouda Mallam Wanké, who established a French-style semi-presidential system. Mamadou Tandja won the presidency in 1999 and was re-elected in 2004.

Population/Culture

Niger's population lives mostly in the southern part of the country and in scattered oases in the north. Niger forms part of the vast Sahelian cultural region of West Africa. While 80 percent of the population is Muslim, pre-Islamic cultural traditions, including ancestor worship and animism, remain strong.

Over 21 languages are spoken. Hausa, spoken by over half the population, is the lingua franca, but French is the official language. Many people speak more than one language. The government has recently recognized ten languages as national languages.

Many different styles of musical instrument are encountered. The women of the nomadic Tuareg in the north accompany their songs with a drum played by three women together, the men use a one-stringed viol; both clap as well. The Djerma Sonrai, generally playing solo, utilize a variety of lutes, fiddles, and flutes, while the Hausa use drums, shawm, lute and trumpet.

Administration/Government

The president is elected by universal suffrage for a five-year term; a prime minister who is named by the president, shares executive power. Political parties must attain at least 5 percent of the vote to gain a seat in the legislature. The independent judicial system is composed of four higher courts—the Court of Appeals, the Supreme Court, the High Court of Justice, and the Constitutional Court.

Economy/Industry

Traditional subsistence farming, herding, small trading, seasonal migration, and informal markets dominate an economy that generates very few formal sector jobs. About 90 percent of the workforce is involved in agriculture. Niger does, however, have some of the world's largest deposits of uranium.

Limited arable land is found mainly along its southern border with Nigeria. The persistent drought and variable rainfall make it very difficult for the country to feed its population, compelling it to rely on food aid. Locust plagues are also a frequent problem. Millet and sorghum are the principal subsistence crops. Export crops include cowpeas, onions, and limited quantities of garlic, peppers, and sesame seeds.

Uranium, which provides 55 percent of export revenue, is the leading foreign exchange earner—Niger is the fourth largest exporter of uranium in the world. Exploitable gold deposits are also known to exist. Niger also has oil potential. Substantial deposits of phosphates, iron, limestone, and gypsum have also been found.

WHO HOLDS YOUR HISTORY? THE GRIOTS OF WEST AFRICA

The history of many West African peoples, in Niger, Mali, Gambia, Guinea, and Senegal, has traditionally been kept by griots—oral historians, messengers, and musically talented praise-singers whose profession is passed from one generation to the next. Griots are both respected and feared for their wisdom and way with words, for they can sing a person's praises and their doom. Praise-singing is accompanied by a variety of instruments, the most important of which is the kora, a 21-stringed bridge-harp (cora) with a long neck and its body made from half a calabash. In Gambia, they also use the balafon, which is similar to a xylophone, and the ngoni, a small traditional lute. In Gambia's Fula and Wolof tradition there are many stories about Hyena (an unworthy character) and Hare, the character who becomes Brer Rabbit in the folklore of the United States. In the Wolof stories, Hare came from the griot caste.

NIGER

Official name Republic of Niger (République du Niger)
Land area 489,678 square miles (1,266,700 km²)
Border countries Algeria, Libya, Chad, Nigeria, Benin, Burkina Faso, Mali
Capital Niamey
Highest & lowest points Mont Bagzane 6,633 feet (2,022 m); Niger River 656 feet (200 m)
Climate Desert; mostly hot, dry, dusty; tropical in extreme south
Population 13,273,000
Language(s) Official: French; other: Hausa, Djerma, many minority languages
Ethnicity Haoussa 55.4%, Djerma Sonrai 21%, Tuareg 9.3%, Peuhl 8.5%, Kanouri Manga 4.7%, other 1.1%
Religion Muslim 80%, other (includes indigenous beliefs and Christian) 20%
Government Republic
Currency Communauté Financière Africaine franc
Human Development Index 0.374 (ranked 174th out of 177 countries)

Left Banjul, formerly Bathurst, is the capital of Gambia. The city is located on St Marys Island between the Atlantic Ocean and the Gambia River.

Above The mud-brick Grand Mosque in Agadez, the largest city in northern Niger and a center of trade for Tuareg nomads.

Far left Masked Dogon men from the Bandiagara Escarpment in Mali. Originally, the masks were part of an elaborate ceremony for the souls of the dead, but now they are more likely part of tourist entertainment.

CHAD

Official name Republic of Chad (République du Tchad; Jumhuriyyat Tshad)
Land area 486,178 square miles (1,259,200 km²)
Border countries Libya, Sudan, Central African Republic, Cameroon, Nigeria, Niger
Capital N'Djamena (Ndjamena)
Highest & lowest points Emi Koussi 11,204 feet (3,415 m); Djourab Depression 524 feet (160 m)
Climate Tropical in south, desert in north
Population 10,111,000
Languages Official: French; other: Arabic, Sara (in south), more than 120 different languages and dialects
Ethnicity Sara 27.7%, Arab 12.3%, Mayo-Kebbi 11.5%, Kanem-Bornou 9%, Ouaddai 8.7%, Hadjarai 6.7%, Tandjile 6.5%, Gorane 6.3%, Fitri-Batha 4.7%, other 6.4%, unknown 0.2%
Religion Muslim 53.1%, Christian 34.3% (Catholic 20.1%, Protestant 14.2%), animist 7.3%, other 0.5%, unknown 1.7%, atheist 3.1%
Government Republic
Currency Communauté Financière Africaine franc
Human Development Index 0.388 (rated 170th out of 177 countries)

Right This child comes from a village near the Doba oilfields in Chad. The town's inhabitants have been compensated for any disturbance they experience during construction of the 665-mile (1,070 km) long pipeline from southern Chad to the Cameroon coast.

GUINEA-BISSAU

Official name Republic of Guinea-Bissau (República da Guiné-Bissau)
Land area 10,811 square miles (28,000 km²)
Border countries Senegal, Guinea
Capital Bissau
Highest point Unnamed location in northeast corner 984 feet (300 m)
Climate Tropical; generally hot and humid; monsoon-type rainy season (June–November) with southwesterly winds; dry season (December–May) with northeasterly harmattan winds
Population 1,503,000
Languages Official: Portuguese; other: Crioulo, African languages
Ethnicity African 98% (includes Balanta, Fulani, Manjaca, Mandinga, Pepel), European, Middle Eastern, and Cape Verdean mulatto 2%
Religion Indigenous beliefs 50%, Muslim 45%, Christian 5%
Government Republic
Currency Communauté Financière Africaine franc
Human Development Index 0.374 (ranked 175th out of 177 countries)

Right The lakes of Ounianga have been nominated for World Heritage listing. Rocky outcrops punctuate the landscape around the salt lakes of the region, which is a stopping point for migratory birds and supports a range of wildlife and vegetation.

LIBYA
NIGER
SUDAN
CHAD
Emi Koussi
Faya-Largeau
Mao
Bol
Biltine
Abéché
Ati
NIGERIA
NDJAMENA
(N'DJAMENA)
Mongo
Am Timan
Bongor
Fianga
Pala
Laï
Kélo
Bénoy
Sarh
Doba
Moundou
CAMEROON
CENTRAL AFRICAN REPUBLIC

Chad

Map Reference Pages 300–305

Landlocked Chad, often called the "dead heart of Africa," is the largest and least accessible of the West African Sahelian states. Its lack of infrastructure limits economic growth, as does the almost constant state of civil war since the mid-1960s.

Physical Geography
Chad is generally flat, with elevation gradually increasing north and east from Lake Chad. There are fertile lowlands and marshlands in the south, semiarid plains in the center, and deserts to the north, broken by the Tibesti Mountains in the northwest. Lake Chad is the second largest lake in West Africa and a very important wetland. Unfortunately, it has shrunk dramatically since the 1970s due to increased water use and decreased rainfall.

History
The Sao people, who have lived along the Chari River for thousands of years, suffered severely under Arab slave raids between 1500 and 1900. Chad became a French colony in 1920, and an independent nation under President François Tombalbaye in 1960. He was killed in a coup in 1975 and a government headed by Goukouni Oueddei assumed power. Hissène Habré took power in 1982 but Oueddei's forces continued their resistance. Idriss Déby toppled Habré's regime in 1990 and won Chad's first multiparty presidential election in 1996. He won again in 2001, and after the constitution was amended, won a third term in 2006. Guerrilla and opposition attacks against Déby's government continue.

EMI KOUSSI AND THE TIBESTI MOUNTAINS: ANCIENT VOLCANOS

A group of ancient dormant volcanoes called the Tibesti Mountains form the largest and highest range in the Sahara Desert. Emi Koussi, the highest mountain in Chad, indeed in the whole Sahara, is a shield volcano lying at the southern end of the Tibesti Mountains. The outer of the two calderas capping Emi Koussi is approximately 5 miles wide by 9 miles long (12 by 15 km); the inner one, on the southeast side, is smaller, about 2 miles (3 km) wide. Numerous lava flows and lava domes, cinder cones, and maars are visible within the calderas and along the flanks of the shield.

The Tibesti Mountains ecoregion has a substantially wetter climate than the surrounding desert. It supports a range of tropical vegetation along with populations of several important large desert mammals as well as a number of smaller creatures.

Population/Culture
Most of Chad's ethnically and linguistically diverse population lives in the south, where population densities are high. The arid north—sparsely populated and poor—is isolated and has traditionally opposed political domination by the south.

Just over half the population, mainly in the north and east, is Muslim; almost 35 percent, mostly in the south, is Christian. The rest, mainly in the south, follow traditional religions, usually combined with allegiance to Islam or Christianity. Ancestor veneration, the use of oracles, and divination, are almost universal. School attendance is compulsory, but only about 68 percent of boys moves on to secondary education, and literacy rates are low.

Administration/Government
Chad's government centers on a strong executive branch headed by the president. The president appoints the prime minister and the Council of State (Cabinet), as well as influencing appointments of provincial officials and the heads of state-owned firms. The president also names most key judicial officials. The Constitution recognizes traditional law in certain locales.

Industry/Economy
Chad has traditionally depended on cotton as its major cash crop, but this is changing thanks in large part to the discovery of large reserves of petroleum. A pipeline has been constructed from the oil fields to the coast of Cameroon. Besides oil and cotton, Chad exports maize, tubers, meat, and gum arabic. Subsistence agriculture currently employs 80 percent of the workforce.

SENEGAL
Cacheu
Bissorã
Bafatá
Gabú
GUINEA-BISSAU
Quinhámel
BISSAU
Fulacunda
ATLANTIC
OCEAN
unnamed
Catió
Arquipélago
dos Bijagós
GUINEA

Guinea-Bissau

Map Reference Pages 304–305

Once hailed as a model for African development, Guinea-Bissau is now one of the poorest countries in the world, with massive foreign debt and an economy that relies on foreign aid. A civil war in the late 1990s saw thousands killed, wounded, and displaced.

Physical Geography
A largely low-lying coastal region of rainforests, swamps, and mangrove-covered wetlands rises to savanna in the north and east. The Bijagós Archipelago of over 80 islands, only 25 or so of them inhabited, extends out to sea. Almost all the low-lying area is affected daily by tidal inflows reaching far inland.

Guinea-Bissau has a hot and humid tropical climate, with a rainy season from mid-May to mid-November and a cooler dry season. Rainfall generally exceeds 78 inches (198 cm), but droughts have long been a recurrent problem during the dry season.

History
After 500 years of Portuguese rule as a military and slave-trading center, and 10 years of guerrilla warfare, Guinea-Bissau became independent in 1974 under President Luis Cabral. In 1980, João Bernardo Vieira headed a military coup that deposed Cabral. Vieira was deposed in 1999. Following a period of military rule, Kumba Yalá was elected president in 2000. In 2003, he was removed in another military coup. In 2005, former president Vieira was elected president.

Population/Culture
About 24 percent of Guineans live in urban areas, but most live in small farming communities or fishing towns. Bissau, the capital city, has a population of around 274,000.

Left Dromedary camels come to drink at the ancient rock pool called Guelta d'Archei. Located in the Ennedi Massif in the Sahara Desert region of northeastern Chad, the guelta is inhabited by other wildlife including the Nile crocodile.

Guinea-Bissau's population includes five main ethnic groups. The Balanta live mainly in the central region; the Fulani in the north; the Manjaca, Mandinga, and Pepel on the coast. There are many smaller ethnic groups. The Cape Verdean mulatto community, about 2 per cent of the population, has disproportionate political and commercial influence.

Portuguese is the official language, but Crioulo (a Portuguese creole) and a number of African languages are also widely spoken. Half the people practice indigenous religions; about 45 percent is Muslim, and there is a small Christian minority.

Administration/Government

The Assembly and the regional councils are the nation's representative bodies. The president of this council automatically becomes head of state, head of government, and commander in chief. Before multiple parties were authorized in 1991, all Assembly members had to be members of the ruling African Party for the Independence of Guinea and Cape Verde (PAIGC).

Industry/Economy

Almost 90 percent of the population depends on agriculture, which also accounts for about 90 percent of exports, though only 11 percent of the land is arable. Major staples include rice, maize, cassava, beans, and potatoes. Cashews account for 95 per cent of export revenue. Guinea-Bissau is generally resource poor, and prospects for economic development are quite grim. Large reserves of bauxite are known to exist but are not exploited; and high recovery costs preclude the exploitation of offshore petroleum deposits.

Left A woman from the Bijagós Archipelago in Guinea-Bissau sells crabs at a market. Some islands in the archipelago follow a matriarchal social system in which women choose their husbands and the priesthood is female.

SENEGAL
M A L I
GUINEA-BISSAU
Mali
Labé
Boké
G U I N E A
Siguiri
Dalaba
Dabola
Mamou
Fria
Kindia
Coyah
ATLANTIC OCEAN
CONAKRY
SIERRA LEONE
Kankan
Kissidougou
Guéckédou
Beyla
Nzérékoré
Mont Nimba
LIBERIA
CÔTE D'IVOIRE

Guinea

Map Reference Pages 304–305

One of the larger countries in West Africa, Guinea's unusual shape gives it multiple and complex land borders. This has created some instability at various times as a result of fighting and unrest in neighboring nations spilling across the border into Guinea.

Physical Geography

Guinea has a short coastline of just 199 miles (320 km), consisting of extensive marshlands and intertidal wetlands. The narrow coastal plain quickly gives way to hilly savanna grasslands, then to densely vegetated mountainous terrain. The Niger River and its tributary the Milo have their headwaters in these mountains.

History

The area today occupied by Guinea has been the site of two significant African empires, that of the Susu from approximately 900 CE, and the Fulani Empire during the sixteenth century. The French declared Guinea a protectorate in 1849; in 1895 it was incorporated into French West Africa.

Independence came in 1958, with Marxist leader Sékou Touré becoming president. The Soviet Union became Guinea's chief source of economic assistance. In 1984, Colonel Lansana Conté seized control and set up a military dictatorship. Under a new constitution allowing for multiparty elections, in 1993 Conté was elected Guinea's civilian president. He then altered the constitution so he could stand for re-election an unlimited number of times, and he still rules through repression.

Civil war and unrest in neighboring Liberia and Sierra Leone spilled over into Guinea on several occasions during the 1990s and again in the early twenty-first century. A massive influx of refugees from these wars has destabilized the economy. Continued unrest under Conté's repressive rule saw nationwide protests in 2006, which continued with large-scale strikes in early 2007. Some analysts have predicted the possibility of civil war.

Population/Culture

With a median age of 17.7 years, Guinea is a country of young people. Only around 35 percent of the population is literate. Although the country has a relatively high prevalence of HIV/AIDS, the rate of infection is considerably lower than in most countries in the region. High incidences of waterborne infection, mainly typhoid fever, create a low life expectancy.

The three main ethnic groups are the Peuhl from mountainous regions, the Malinké from the savanna plateau, and the Soussou who inhabit the coastal regions. There is a small but commercially significant non-African population, mostly French and Lebanese.

Islam has been the dominant religion for some time. Less than one-tenth of the population follows one of the Christian faiths. Traditional tribal religions have been largely supplanted by the major organized religions, but they do manage to survive in small pockets in parts of the countryside.

Administration/Government

Since independence, Guinea has had only two presidents, who have tended to rule by decree. More recently, the National Assembly has begun to assert its authority more strongly, and following widespread civil unrest in 2007 there is now some movement toward a more representative style of government. Repression of opposition parties continues; corruption and nepotism remain a serious problem.

Economy/Industry

Guinea is rich in mineral resources, with about half of the world's known bauxite reserves as well as extensive gold and diamond deposits. Since the 1990s the government has been gradually privatizing industries, and trade reforms have encouraged foreign investment; but corruption, poorly developed infrastructure, and political instability continue to hinder large-scale investment.

GUINEA

Official name Republic of Guinea (République de Guinée)
Land area 94,526 square miles (245,857 km²)
Border countries Guinea-Bissau, Senegal, Mali, Côte d'Ivoire, Liberia, Sierra Leone
Capital Conakry
Highest point Mont Nimba 5,748 feet (1,752 m)
Climate Predominantly tropical; summer monsoonal rain season, cooler dry season
Population 10,211,000
Languages Official: French; other: wide range of indigenous languages
Ethnicity Peuhl 40%, Malinké 30%, Soussou 20%, other smaller indigenous groups 10%
Religion Muslim 85%, Christian 8%, indigenous religions 7%
Government Republic
Currency Guinean franc
Human Development Index 0.456 (ranked 160th out of 177 countries)

Above Devotees pray at Faisal Mosque, Conakry, Guinea. Built at great cost, the mosque is said to be the largest in West Africa.

BURKINA FASO

Country name Burkina Faso
Land area 105,714 square miles (273,800 km²)
Border countries Mali, Niger, Benin, Togo, Ghana, Côte d'Ivoire
Capital Ouagadougou
Highest & lowest points Tena Kourou 2,457 feet (749 m); Mouhoun (Black Volta) River 656 feet (200 m)
Climate Tropical; warm dry winters; hot wet summers
Population 15,265,000
Languages Official: French; other: African languages belonging to Sudanic family spoken by 90% of the population
Ethnicity Mossi over 40%, other (includes Gurunsi, Senufo, Lobi, Bobo, Mande, Fulani) approximately 60%
Religion Muslim 50%, indigenous beliefs 40%, Christian 10%
Government Parliamentary republic
Currency Communauté Financière Africaine franc
Human Development Index 0.370 (ranked 176th out of 177 countries)

Right The Mossi people of Burkina Faso are famous for their painted wooden masks.

SIERRA LEONE

Official name Republic of Sierra Leone
Land area 27,653 square miles (71,620 km²)
Border countries Guinea, Liberia
Capital Freetown
Highest point Loma Mansa (Mt Bintimani) 6,391 feet (1,948 m)
Climate Tropical in most of the country
Population 6,295,000
Languages Official: English; other: Mende spoken in the south, Temne in the north, Krio (English-derived Creole) widely understood throughout the country
Ethnicity Temne 30%, Mende 30%, Creole (descendents of freed Jamaican slaves) 10%, smaller indigenous groups and others 30%
Religion Muslim 60%, indigenous religions 30%, Christian 10%
Government Republic
Currency Leone
Human Development Index 0.336 (ranked 177th out of 177 countries)

Below This grand mosque in Burkina Faso was built in the Sahel style, out of mud bricks. Half the country's population are Muslim.

MALI
NIGER
BURKINA FASO
OUAGADOUGOU
Djibo
Dori
Gourcy
Nouna
Dédougou
Koudougou
Fada-N'Gourma
Diapaga
Manga
Tenkodogo
Tena Kourou
Bobo-Dioulasso
Léo
Pô
Orodara
Banfora
TOGO
BENIN
GHANA
CÔTE D'IVOIRE

Burkina Faso

Map Reference Pages 304–305

Burkina Faso, a secular state in West Africa, is one of the poorest countries in the world. It suffered very badly from the civil war in neighboring Côte d'Ivoire in 2002–2007, which led to a massive return of Burkinabés working in that country.

Physical Geography

This landlocked nation has a relatively flat savanna landscape, rising to the west. The northern zone, adjacent to the Sahara Desert, is very dry. In the south, highly variable May–October rains typically fall during short violent thunderstorms. During the driest months, extreme heat and the harmattan (a strong and dusty Saharan wind) combine with human activity to create massive catastrophic bushfires. Overgrazing and deforestation of the fragile, infertile, tropical soil have produced serious soil degradation, erosion, and desertification.

History

Colonized by France in the nineteenth century as Upper Volta, the country attained independence under that name in 1960. In 1983 Thomas Sankara, whose Marxist views radically changed society, toppled the government. He challenged the chiefs, advocated women's liberation, allied with North Korea, Libya, and Cuba, and renamed the country Burkina Faso, "country of the upright."

The current president, Blaise Compaoré, came to power in a coup in 1987 and has won three elections. He has embarked on a program of privatization and austerity measures, and disarmed local militias. He portrays himself as the guarantor of political stability and economic progress for Burkina Faso, and is working to make schooling more accessible.

Population/Culture

The population is concentrated in the south and center of the country, where fertile land supports mostly farming communities whose density sometimes exceeds 125 per square mile (48 per km²). Thousands of workers migrate seasonally to the gold mines and plantations of Côte d'Ivoire and Ghana.

The country has more than 50 ethnic groups, the principal one being the Mossi. Other dominant groups include the Fulani, Gurma, Lobi, Mande, Bobo, Senufo, and Gurunsi. Despite this diversity, ethnic conflict has never been a huge concern.

Approximately 20 percent of the people exclusively practice traditional African religions, particularly ancestral worship. Many Muslims and Christians include elements of indigenous religion in their religious practice.

Life in Burkina Faso centers around ceremonies and celebrations. The Mossi people express joy and suffering, or fulfill responsibilities to ancestors, through ceremonies that involve special masks and dancing. At Bobo funerals, masked dancers exhort the dead to depart their earthly abode.

Administration/Government

Burkina Faso has a semi-presidential government with a bicameral parliament (l'Assemblée Nationale or lower house; and la Chambre des Représentants or upper house). Both president and representatives are elected for five-year terms. The legal system is based on French civil law and customary law.

Economy/Industry

The few natural resources include manganese, limestone, gold, marble, phosphates, pumice, and salt; however, gold is the only economically viable one. Cotton, vulnerable to fluctuations in rainfall and world prices, is the country's economic mainstay. Migrant workers' remittances also provide an important income source. Most of the population is engaged in subsistence agriculture, where recurring drought is a dangerous natural hazard.

BURKINABÉ CUISINE

In Burkina Faso meat is considered a luxury in the villages, and is usually replaced with fish or eggs, eaten with rice, beans, or maize. Chicken is a delicacy, and prepared as brochettes (cooked on skewers). Vegetables include potatoes, yams, beans, and okra, and the strawberries are notable for their flavor. In the capital city Ouagadougou, where meat is more affordable, every dish seems to come with sauce, like *riz gras* (vegetable sauce), *sauce de poisson* (fish-based sauce), *boeuf sauce aubergine* (beef and eggplant sauce), and *mouton sauce tomatoe* (sauce with mutton and tomatoes). These sauces are served with *toh*, a porridge of pearl millet and maize.

GUINEA
Falaba
Mansa Loma
Makeni
Port Loko
Lunsar
Magburaka
Yengema
Koidu
FREETOWN
SIERRA LEONE
Kailahun
Bo
Kenema
Bonthe
Sherbro Island
Sulima
LIBERIA
ATLANTIC OCEAN

Sierra Leone

Map Reference Pages 304–305

Though for many years a British colony, Sierra Leone got its name from the Portuguese words meaning "Lion Mountain." A relatively small country that stretches along the Atlantic coast, Sierra Leone has been beset by civil war, rampant corruption, and violence for much of its history, and for the last few years has been declared to be the world's least livable country by the United Nations.

Physical Geography

Extensive barrier systems with intertidal wetlands line the coastline. The flat coastal plain stretches inland and then gives way to thickly wooded hills and eventually plateau uplands and mountainous regions in the east.

History

The British established a settlement for freed slaves at Freetown in 1787, and the coastal area became a British colony in 1808. In 1896, Sierra Leone was declared a British Protectorate. Independence came in 1961. Ten years later, Sierra Leone became a republic. In 1978 the Prime Minister Siaka Stevens declared a one-party state.

A coup in 1992 saw Stevens' successor Joseph Momoh replaced by military rulers who promised a return to representative government. Another coup was staged in 1996, but an election was held that year and Ahma

Tejan Kabbah became the country's first democratically elected leader. Yet another coup in 1997 saw Kabbah replaced by Johnny Paul Koroma. A UN peacekeeping force was sent in and Kabbah was re-established as leader in 1998. Rebel forces, supported by Liberia, continued to wage resistance in a bid to gain control of the rich diamond fields. In 2000, rebel leader Foday Sankoh was arrested and subsequently charged with war crimes. The United Nations declared the decade-long conflict over in 2002, the civil war having claimed an estimated 50,000 lives.

Democratic elections were held in 2007 and Ernest Bai Koroma was elected president, but the country remains highly unstable.

Population/Culture

With a median age of 17.7 years, Sierra Leone has a young population. Seven percent of the population is infected with HIV/AIDS, and diseases like typhoid are prevalent.

There are approximately 20 ethnic groups, the Temne and Mende being the two most significant. Approximately 10 percent of the population is Creole, and there are also small populations of Europeans, Pakistanis, and Indians, mostly living in the cities.

Islam is gradually taking over from traditional indigenous religions, although these remain strong outside the cities. English, the official language, is not widely used outside the educated elite; Krio and indigenous languages are used more commonly.

Administration/Government

Sierra Leone's unicameral parliament has 124 seats. The president is elected by popular vote for a five-year term. The legal system is based on English law and customary indigenous laws.

Economy/Industry

Sierra Leone is one of the poorest countries in the world and experiences significant income inequalities. Almost 50 percent of the working-age population is engaged in subsistence agriculture.

Despite significant mineral and agricultural resources, poor and damaged infrastructure, combined with civil unrest, hinder economic development. Diamond mining accounts for nearly half of all exports, and large deposits of bauxite and rutile are known to exist.

GUINEA
SIERRA LEONE
Voinjama
Sanniquellie
Gbarnga
Tubmanburg
Robertsport
LIBERIA
MONROVIA
CÔTE D'IVOIRE
Buchanan
Zwedru
River Cess
Greenville
Barclayville
Harper
ATLANTIC OCEAN

Liberia

Map Reference Pages 304–305

Liberia ("Land of the Free") was founded as a colony for freed African-American slaves, and has been independent since the mid-nineteenth century. Today it is best known as a "flag of convenience" for the world's shipping industry.

Physical Geography

Liberia's extensive coastline is lined with mangrove wetlands, an extensive lagoon system, and sandbars, along which the majority of the population lives. The coastal plain gives way to a gently rising plateau, with the highest elevations near the border with Guinea. The interior is mostly dominated by dense tropical rainforest with pockets of tropical savanna grasslands in the northern part of the country.

History

Freed African-American slaves were landed on the coast of modern-day Liberia in 1822, at a settlement called Monrovia, now the capital. Liberia gained independence in 1847. Especially under the leadership of President William Tubman (1944–1971), the economy grew and social reforms were implemented.

Bringing an end to Africa's first republic, a military coup led by Master Sergeant Samuel Doe led to his seizing power in 1980. Doe instituted a brutal regime that saw the economy falter. Civil war erupted in 1989 when Charles Taylor invaded from his base in neighboring Côte d'Ivoire, leading to more than 150,000 deaths by 1994. Taylor gained control and in 1997 won a resounding electoral victory. By 2002 fighting along the border with Guinea had intensified, and Taylor declared a state of emergency and introduced further repression. After negotiations with the United Nations and other bodies, Taylor went into exile. He was subsequently arrested and is facing war crimes charges.

Democratic elections were held in 2006 and Ellen Johnson-Sirleaf won the presidency, making her the first female elected head of state in Africa. Johnson-Sirleaf has established a Truth and Reconciliation Commission to address civil war crimes. Despite this, and the presence of a 15,000-strong UN peacekeeping mission, the security situation remains fragile.

Population/Culture

Liberia has a very young population, with 43.6 percent aged under 15 years. A high prevalence of disease, including HIV/AIDS, has led to a low life expectancy and a high infant mortality rate. Literacy rates were traditionally higher than in many African nations, but the legacy of war has left many younger Liberians with little or no education.

Most of the population belongs to one of 16 ethnic groups. Tribal religions are practiced widely. Descendants of freed US slaves, the Americo-Liberians, account for less than 3 percent of the population but have great political influence.

Administration/Government

Liberia's National Assembly has two chambers, the 30-member Senate and the 64 members of the House of Representatives. Liberia has a dual legal system, with statutory law based on Anglo-American common law, and customary law based on unwritten tribal practices.

Economy/Industry

While once Liberia had a strong economy, years of civil war and government corruption have destroyed much of the infrastructure. Since the democratic elections of 2006, however, some capital is returning.

Rich in natural resources, including iron ore, timber, diamonds, gold, and hydropower, and with a favorable agricultural climate, Liberia has considerable economic potential.

Left Sierra Leone's capital and largest city, Freetown, sits on the tip of a peninsula facing the Atlantic Ocean. The nearby Western Area Peninsula Forest is remnant rainforest; a survey found more than 50 mammal species living in the reserve, including five threatened primate species.

LIBERIA

Official name Republic of Liberia
Land area 37,189 square miles (96,320 km²)
Border countries Sierra Leone, Guinea, Côte d'Ivoire
Capital Monrovia
Highest point Mt Wuteve 4,528 feet (1,380 m)
Climate Tropical with hot wet summers; cooler winters with harmattan winds
Population 3,335,000
Languages Official: English; other: wide range of tribal languages
Ethnicity Indigenous African (Kpelle, Bassa, Gio, Kru, Grebo, Mano, Krahn, Gola, Gbandi, Loma, Kissi, Vai, Dei, Bella, Mandingo, and Mende) 95%, Americo-Liberians 2.5% (descendants of freed slaves from the USA), Congo People 2.5% (descendants of freed slaves from the Caribbean)
Religion Christian 40%, indigenous religions 40%, Muslim 20%,
Government Republic
Currency Liberian dollar
Human Development Index Not available

Above An adult chimpanzee in Liberia. In just a quarter of a century, the chimpanzee population in Liberia has dropped from around 200,000 to only a few thousand. Chimps can still be found in the Nimba Mountains.

Left UNICEF puts the number of HIV/AIDS orphans in Liberia at more than 36,000, which is over 15 percent of the total number of orphans in the country. Civil war has also left thousands of Liberian children without one or both parents.

CÔTE D'IVOIRE

Official name Republic of Côte d'Ivoire (République du Côte d'Ivoire)
Land area 122,780 square miles (318,000 km^2)
Border countries Mali, Burkina Faso, Ghana, Liberia, Guinea
Capital Yamoussoukro
Highest point Mont Nimba 5,748 feet (1,752 m)
Climate Tropical along the coastline, becoming semiarid in the far north
Population 18,373,000
Languages Official: French; other: more than 60 indigenous languages with Dioula the most common
Ethnicity Akan (Baoulé) 42.1%, Gur 17.6%, Northern Mandé 16.5%, Kru 11%, Southern Mandé 10%, other (includes French and Lebanese) 2.8%
Religion Indigenous tribal religions 40%, Muslim 35%, Christian 25%
Government Republic
Currency Communauté Financière Africaine franc
Human Development Index 0.432 (ranked 166th out of 177 countries)

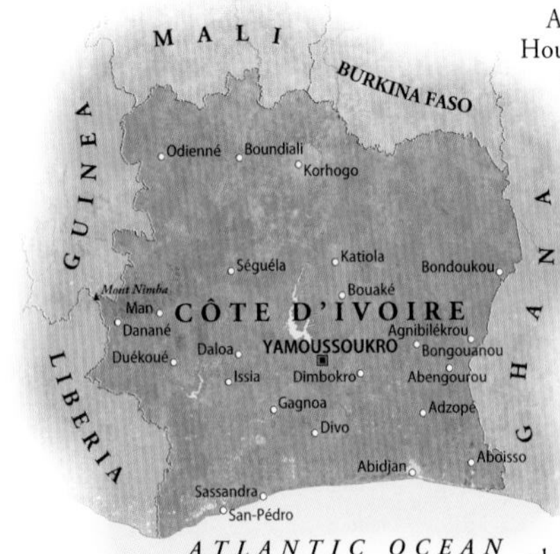
MALI
BURKINA FASO
GUINEA
LIBERIA
GHANA
Odienné
Boundiali
Korhogo
Séguéla
Katiola
Bondoukou
Bouaké
Mont Nimba
Man
CÔTE D'IVOIRE
Danané
Agnibilékrou
Duékoué
Daloa
YAMOUSSOUKRO
Bongouanou
Issia
Dimbokro
Abengourou
Gagnoa
Adzopé
Divo
Abidjan
Aboisso
Sassandra
San-Pédro
ATLANTIC OCEAN

Côte d'Ivoire

Map Reference Pages 304–305

Côte d'Ivoire is one of the more prosperous West African states. It is second only to Nigeria in size in the region. It has recently suffered from political instability with bloodshed and the overthrow of governments.

Below Côte d'Ivoire is the largest producer of cocoa in the world. Cocoa bean pods *(Theobroma cacao)* come in shades of yellow, green, and red. The pods will be split and processed.

Physical Geography

Much of Côte d'Ivoire is flat, with well-watered plains giving way to mountainous regions in the northwest. The coastal lowlands have extensive lagoon and wetland systems. The central part is dominated by a densely vegetated plateau. Upland savanna grasslands are found in the drier north. In 1950, the Vridi Canal connected Abidjan, situated on a coastal lagoon, to the sea, and the city became the major shipping and financial center of French-speaking West Africa.

History

Côte d'Ivoire received its name during the late fifteenth century, when French sailors began to trade for ivory there. In the sixteenth century, Portuguese traders set up trading posts, and other European nations cashed in on the slave trade to the Americas. In 1842, France established a protectorate across the coastal zone of Côte d'Ivoire and reinforced it with a significant military presence. In 1893 they announced a protectorate over the whole country, and Côte d'Ivoire was incorporated into French West Africa.

Below One of the main ports in Côte d'Ivoire is Sassandra, which was founded by the Portuguese and later run as a timber port by the British then the French. Fishing and light industries are both important in Sassandra.

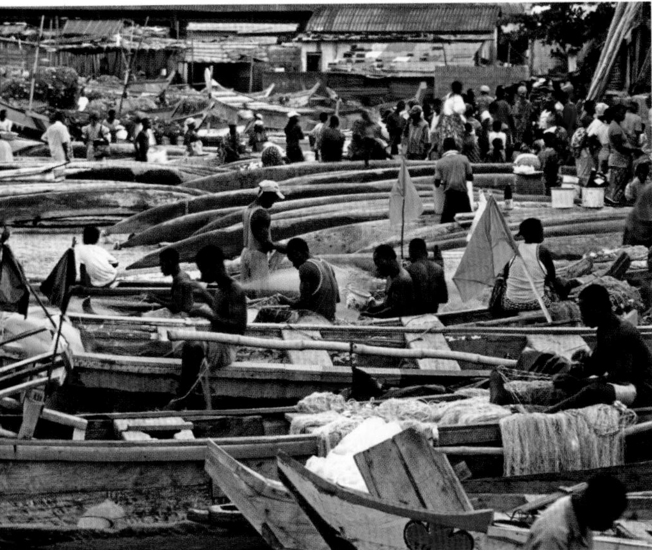

A nationalist group led by Félix Houphouët-Boigny was formed in 1946 to push claims for independence, and in 1958, Côte d'Ivoire elected to become an autonomous region within the French Community. In 1960, Côte d'Ivoire declared itself independent. By 1980, the once-prosperous country was gripped by high unemployment.

Houphouët-Boigny, who had headed the government since independence and was a force for unity, was widely criticized for his development of large-scale projects, particularly for spending millions of dollars to transform his home village of Yamoussoukro into the new capital; others, however, lauded his vision of developing a center for peace, education, and religion in the country's heart.

The 1990 elections were the first truly multiparty elections, and Houphouët-Boigny won a seventh term. After his death in 1993, Henri Konan Bédié became leader. He exploited ethnic differences by seeking support from the Christian-dominated south and isolating the Muslim and indigenous populations.

Civil war broke out in 2002, with rebel Muslim groups seizing parts of the north. A truce signed in 2003 led to a power-sharing government, but a comprehensive ceasefire was not achieved and the new government collapsed. In April 2004, a UN peacekeeping mission was established and South African President Thabo Mbeki played a key role in brokering a peace deal. Peace remains fragile, however, with rebel forces still controlling large parts of the country.

Population/Culture

With around 7 percent of the population infected with HIV/AIDS, Côte d'Ivoire has a low life expectancy and is dominated by a young population with a median age of just 19 years. High fertility rates are indicative of the lower levels of development throughout much of the country. There are, however, pockets of affluence, especially in the cities.

Of the over 60 ethnic groups within Côte d'Ivoire, the main one is the Akan (including the Baoulé, Dan, Anyi, Senufo, Beti, and Malinké). Relative prosperity has encouraged extensive work-related migration from neighboring countries. The free and open trade policies of Côte d'Ivoire, and its French links, are expressed in small French and Lebanese populations within the cities with significant interests in the retailing and trade sector.

About 35 percent of the population is Muslim. Indigenous languages and religions remain dominant in the countryside.

Yamoussoukro has been the official capital of Côte d'Ivoire since 1983, but Abidjan, sometimes described as a mini-Manhattan because of its impressive skyline, remains the nation's commercial and administrative center.

MILESTONE EVENTS

1500s Portuguese begin to establish trading posts along the coastline of Côte d'Ivoire
1842 France sends a military force to Côte d'Ivoire and claims the coastal area as a protectorate
1893 Côte d'Ivoire is declared a French Protectorate and incorporated into French West Africa
1920s France gains effective control
1946 Nationalist group Le Parti Démocratique de la Côte d'Ivoire (PDCI) is formed to push for independence
1950 The Vridi Canal is completed, creating an extensive deep-water port at the city of Abidjan and making it a major West African trade center
1958 Côte d'Ivoire elects to become an autonomous region within the French Community
December 7, 1960 Independence is declared
1963 Côte d'Ivoire joins Organization for African Unity
1980 First attempted coup caused by high unemployment
1980s Widespread civil unrest led by students and the unemployed
1990 Opposition parties are allowed to run in elections
1993 Côte d'Ivoire's first president, Félix Houphouët-Boigny dies, and is replaced by Henri Konan Bédié
1995 National elections are marred by vote-rigging and violence
1999 General Robert Guéï seizes power in Côte d'Ivoire's first military coup
2000 Guéï declares victory in national elections but is forced from power after widespread protest and military desertions
2002 Civil war erupts as rebel groups seize parts of the north
January 2003 A truce is signed but the ceasefire is fragile
April 2004 UN peacekeeping mission established to create stability
2006 Extensive oil and natural gas fields begin to generate significant foreign investment
June 2007 Rocket is unsuccessfully fired at the prime ministerial plane by rebels

Administration/Government

Côte d'Ivoire has a unicameral National Assembly with 225 members who are elected in single- and multi-district elections by direct popular vote to serve five-year terms. The president is also elected by popular vote for a five-year term with no limits on the number of terms. The judicial system is based on the French civil law system and customary law.

Economy/Industry

Agricultural exports (cocoa beans, coffee, and palm oil) account for some 70 percent of total export earnings. Over 65 percent of the population is employed in the agricultural sector.

In 2005, the UN Security Council banned the export of Ivorian diamonds on the basis that they were being used to finance arms purchases as part of the civil war. Since 2006, oil and natural gas reserves have begun to be exploited, generating US$1.3 billion in revenue in 2006. However, political instability is hampering further exploration and investment of this valuable income source.

THE BASILICA OF OUR LADY OF PEACE OF YAMOUSSOUKRO

President Félix Houphouët-Boigny declared his home town of Yamoussoukro the capital of Côte d'Ivoire in 1983. He apparently planned it to be a reflection of the country's grandeur; some say he also wanted to demonstrate his own importance.

In 1985, construction of the Basilica of Our Lady of Peace of Yamoussoukro (La Basilique de Notre Dame de la Paix de Yamoussoukro) began. This remarkable building is modeled on St Peter's Basilica in Rome and regarded as the world's largest church. The dome is 518 feet (158 m) high, slightly lower than St Peter's, although the surmounting cross is higher; its interior is lined with marble imported from Italy and 75,347 square feet (7,000 m^2) of imported French stained glass.

The nave seats 7,000 people with room for 11,000 more to stand. There are two other equally ornate and lavish buildings in the complex, a rectory and a papal villa. The villa is reserved for the Pope's exclusive use, but in the life of the Basilica so far only one Pope, John Paul II, has visited, to consecrate the church in 1990.

The building of the basilica more than doubled the national debt of Côte d'Ivoire overnight. It sits in the middle of the country surrounded by shanty towns where most of the people live without running water or electricity. While most Catholics are proud of the basilica, the majority of the population is not even Christian.

Far left Ghana's Krobo people mark a young girl's coming of age with a series of initiation rites known as Dipo. Here we see initiates of varying ages waiting to perform the Klama dance at their Outdooring Ceremony, which presents the girls to their community and to potential husbands.

Left The historic town of Cape Coast in central Ghana was once the country's capital city. The castle there was one of the largest trade and slave castles on the Ghanaian coast. Countless captives were transported to the New World through the "Gate of No Return" at Cape Coast.

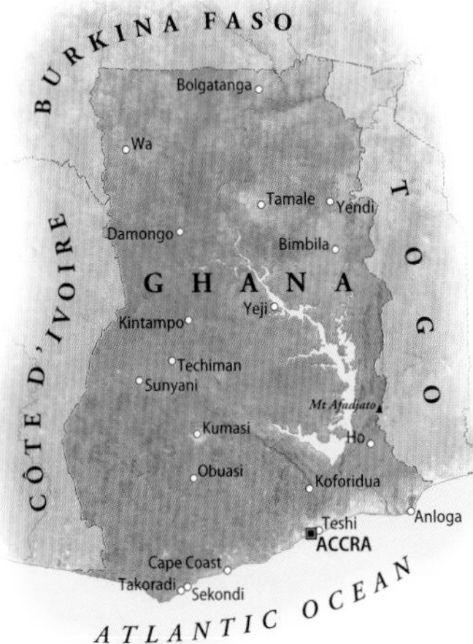
BURKINA FASO
Bolgatanga
Wa
Tamale
Yendi
Damongo
Bimbila
GHANA
TOGO
CÔTE D'IVOIRE
Yeji
Kintampo
Techiman
Sunyani
Mt Afadjato
Kumasi
Ho
Obuasi
Koforidua
Anloga
Teshi
ACCRA
Cape Coast
Takoradi
Sekondi
ATLANTIC OCEAN

Ghana

Map Reference Pages 304–305

Ghana, long known as the Gold Coast, was the first sub-Saharan country to gain its independence from a European power in 1957 when it separated from Britain. The name was chosen after the powerful West African Empire of Ghana, which existed during medieval times.

Physical Geography

Ghana is a few degrees north of the equator, and consists primarily of lowlands, flat plains, and rolling hills. Forests cover about one-quarter of the country; another quarter is used for agriculture. A significant portion of the coastline is sandy and dotted with lagoons. Tema, east of Accra, is the primary port city.

Ghana has the largest artificial lake in the world, Lake Volta, created in 1965 when Akosombo Dam was constructed on the Volta River. It provides inland transportation as well as hydroelectric power for much of the country. Ghana's only natural lake is the almost circular Lake Bosumtwi. Formed in an ancient meteorite impact crater northwest of Accra, it is approximately 13 miles (8 km) across. The Ashanti people consider it to be a sacred place, where the souls of the dead come to bid farewell to the god Twi.

History

Oral histories relate that, starting in the tenth century, Ghana's early people migrated from the regions of Mauritania and Mali, extensions of the Kingdom of Ghana that emerged about 500 CE. Various groups such as the Ga and Ewe settled in the area and were there when the Portuguese arrived in 1471.

The Portuguese established a permanent trading post at Elmina in 1482 and a built a fortress there. Gold, ivory, and pepper were their first economic interests, but soon slavery was included. It is estimated that 5,000 slaves were shipped from the Gold Coast each year during the eighteenth and early nineteenth centuries. In 1807, the British and Americans banned the slave trade. Unfortunately, this did not stop the slave traders.

British influence grew in the nineteenth century after a series of wars with the Ashanti that ended with a peace treaty in 1831. The British proclaimed the Gold Coast Colony in 1874, and ruled the area until Ghana's independence in 1957.

Kwame Nkrumah was selected as the first prime minister, but his repressive policies led to a military coup that ousted him in 1966, the first of a series that ended in 1991 with a coup led by Jerry Rawlings. His leadership invigorated the failing economy and led to a new democratic constitution in 1992. Rawlings was elected president and served two terms. He was succeeded by John Kufuor in 2001. This was the first time that power had exchanged hands peacefully in Ghana's civilian democratic government.

Population/Culture

Ghana's population exceeds 23 million. Population numbers are greater than at the time of independence, when the total was less than five million. The population is very young; the median age is only 20.4, almost eight years lower than the world median.

There are over 100 different languages spoken in Ghana, although English is the official language. This tremendous diversity has allowed English to prevail in government, business, education, and in radio and television. Akan languages (Akyem, Asante Twi, Akwapim Twi, and Fanti) are spoken by approximately half the population, with Mole-Dagbani, Ewe, Ga-Adangbe, and Guan spoken by significant segments.

Islam is prevalent in the north, while the south is mainly Christian. Indigenous faiths are practiced by less than 10 percent of people.

Government spending on education has varied from 28 to 40 percent of the annual budget over the last decade. Most Ghanaians have fairly easy access to primary and secondary schooling, where all instruction is in English.

Administration/Government

Ghana is a constitutional democracy with multiple political parties active in its unicameral parliament, which has 230 elected members. The New Patriotic Party and the National Party Congress are the two strongest political parties, but many others are active in contesting elections. The president, who is also head of state, heads the executive branch and is elected for a four-year term with a limit of two terms. Ghana's Supreme Court is the highest court in its judicial branch.

Economy/Industry

Rich in natural resources, Ghana is better off than most West African countries. However, the per capita GDP is still only US$1,400 per year. Over half the population works in agriculture, with cocoa, rice, cassava, peanuts, corn, bananas, and timber being major products. Ghana is one of the world's leading nations in the production of gold and cocoa.

MILESTONE EVENTS

500–1100 Kingdom of Ghana

1471 Portuguese land in Ghana, region named Gold Coast

1500s Slave trade begins in West Africa

1637 Dutch invade and seize Portuguese settlement at Elmina

1821 British government takes over British trading forts on the Gold Coast

1874 British establish Gold Coast Colony

March 6, 1957 Ghana gains independence from the British; Kwame Nkrumah becomes first prime minister

July 1, 1960 Republic declared

1965 Akosombo Dam built creating Volta Lake, the world's largest artificial lake

1979 New constitution

1991 Successful coup led by Flight Lieutenant Jerry Rawlings amid an era of corruption and a declining economy

April 28, 1992 New constitution promulgated, Rawlings elected president

2001 Peaceful democratic transition to civilian government as John Kufuor is elected president

2007 Ghana celebrates fiftieth anniversary of independence

GHANA

Official name Republic of Ghana

Land area 89,166 square miles (230,940 km²)

Border countries Burkina Faso, Togo, Côte d'Ivoire

Capital Accra

Highest point Mt Afadjato 2,887 feet (880 m)

Climate Tropical; warm and drier along southeast coast; hot and humid in southwest; hot and dry in north

Population 23,383,000

Languages Official: English; other: Asante Twi, Akwapim Twi, Akyem, Fanti, Mole-Dagbani, Ewe, Ga-Adangbe, Guan

Ethnicity Akan 45.3%, Mole-Dagbon 15.2%, Ewe 11.7%, Ga-Dangme 7.3%, Guan 4%, Gurma 3.6%, Grusi 2.6%, Mande-Busanga 1%, other tribes 1.4%, other 7.9%

Religion Christian 68.8%, Muslim 15.9%, traditional 8.5%, other 0.7%, none 6.1%

Government Constitutional democracy

Currency Ghana Cedi

Human Development Index 0.553 (ranked 135th out of 177 countries)

Above A critical part of the Krobo people's Dipo initiation rites is the blessing of the Tekpete, or sacred stone of virginity. The girls wear strips of pure white fabric and hold a leaf between their teeth to remind them to turn their thoughts inward and be silent. The Krobo people are part of the Ga-Adangbe ethnolinguistic group.

TOGO

Official name Togolese Republic (République Togolaise)
Land area 20,998 square miles (54,385 km²)
Border countries Burkina Faso, Benin, Ghana
Capital Lomé
Highest point Mont Agou 2,335 feet (986 m)
Climate Tropical: Hot and humid in the south; semi-arid in the north
Population 5,859,000
Languages Official: French; other: Ewe and Mina in the south; Kabyé and Dagomba in the north
Ethnicity African tribal groups (Ewe, Mina and Kabré the most dominant) 99%, European and Syrian-Lebanese less than 1%
Religion Indigenous religions 51%, Christian 29%, Muslim 20%
Government Republic
Currency Communauté Financière Africaine franc
Human Development Index 0.512 (ranked 152nd out of 177 countries)

BURKINA FASO
Dapaong
Sansanné-Mango
GHANA
BENIN
Kara
Bafilo
Bassar
Sokodé
Tchamba
TOGO
Badou
Atakpamé
Kpalimé
Mont Agou
Tabligbo
Tsévié
Aného
LOMÉ
Bight of Benin

Togo

Map Reference Pages 304–305

Togo is a tiny country located on the Gulf of Guinea in West Africa. Ruled by military dictatorship for much of its recent history, it has started to move toward representative government.

Physical Geography

Northern Togo is dominated by gently undulating savanna grasslands. The Togo–Atacora Mountains run from the southwest to the northeast, effectively dividing the country. The south has a much more tropical environment, with marshland and extensive lagoon systems along the 40-mile (64-km) coastline.

History

The Germans colonized Togoland in 1884, an area that included the eastern section of present-day Ghana. The League of Nations partitioned Togoland between France and Britain in 1922, with France taking control of the area that was to become Togo.

In 1960 the Togolese Republic was proclaimed. The last of several failed governments was eventually toppled in 1967 in a bloodless coup by Gnassingbé Eyadéma, who installed military rule. His regime became increasingly intolerant of any opposition and a new constitution in 1979 formalized one-party rule. Eyadéma died in early 2005 after 38 years in power. The immediate installation of his son, Faure Gnassingbé, as president provoked international condemnation. Faure stood down and called elections, which he won, two months later. In October 2007, the first free and fair elections were held.

Population/Culture

Togo has a young population. HIV/AIDS infection affects more than 4 percent of the population. Typical of many less developed nations, Togo has a high fertility rate, but also has high rates of infant mortality.

Togo has over 35 ethnic–linguistic groups. The Ewe and the Mina mostly live in the south, and the Kabré in the north. Tribal cultures are important, particularly outside the cities where traditional religions are preferred.

Administration/Government

Representative government is comparatively new to Togo and the country is still in a phase of transition toward open democracy. The legal system is based on that of the French, though it is only very recently that the courts have become free from political interference.

Economy/Industry

Togo's economy is agriculture-based, employing more than 65 percent of the population. Cocoa, coffee, and cotton are the main exports and Togo is the world's fourth largest producer of phosphate. The government, together with the World Bank and the IMF, has been reforming the economy over the past decade to encourage more foreign investment.

Above Tata house in northern Togo. No tools are used in the construction of these houses, which are made of unfired clay, straw (used as a binder), and wood. The roofs are used for storage.

BENIN

Official name Republic of Benin (République du Benin)
Land area 42,710 square miles (110,620 km²)
Border countries Burkina Faso, Niger, Nigeria, Togo
Capital Porto-Novo
Highest point Mont Sokbaro 2,159 feet (658 m)
Climate Tropical: Hot and humid in the south; semiarid in the north
Population 8,295,000
Languages Official: French; other: Fon, Yoruba and a range of tribal languages
Ethnicity Fon 39.2%, Adja 15.2%, Yoruba 12.3%, Bariba 9.2%, Peulh 7%, Ottamari 6.1%, Yoa-Lokpa 4%, Dendi 2.5%, other (includes Europeans) 1.6%, unspecified 2.9%
Religion Christian 42.8%, Muslim 24.4%, Vodoun 17.3%, other 15.5%
Government Republic
Currency Communauté Financière Africaine franc
Human Development Index 0.437 (ranked 163rd out of 177 countries)

NIGER
BURKINA FASO
Malanville
Kandi
BENIN
Natitingou
Djougou
Ndali
Mont Sokbaro
Parakou
TOGO
NIGERIA
Savalou
Abomey
Bohicon
Lokossa
Sakété
PORTO-NOVO
Ouidah
Cotonou
Bight of Benin

Benin

Map Reference Pages 304–305

Located on the Gulf of Guinea in West Africa, Benin (formerly known as Dahomey), is a small country stretching inland from a coastline only 62 miles (100 km) long. Porto-Novo is the capital; nearby Cotonou is the seat of government.

Physical Geography

Benin is a country of mostly low relief. The marshes and lagoons of the coastal plain give way to foothills rising gently to the Atacora Mountains of the northwest. The climate is tropical; coastal areas are more fertile and have higher rainfall. The north becomes semi-arid, and from December to March may experience the harmattan desert winds.

History

From the seventeenth century, the Dahomey Empire occupied the region of modern-day Benin. The empire was renowned for using women (Amazons) as royal guards. European slave-traders transported several million slaves from the ports here. France declared Dahomey a colony in 1892 and incorporated it into French West Africa in 1904.

Dahomey achieved full independence in 1960. Military leaders overthrew the government several times, and a 1972 coup led by Mathieu Kérékou saw the establishment of a socialist government. The government nationalized the economy; in 1975, Dahomey was renamed the People's Republic of Benin.

In 1990, following weeks of civil unrest, a new constitution was created and power transferred to a representative government. In 1991 the country was renamed the Republic of Benin. In 2006, Kérékou was succeeded as president by Thomas Yayi Boni.

Population/Culture

Close to 44 percent of Benin's population is aged under 14 years. Approximately 68,000 people suffer from HIV/AIDS, with most of those affected aged between 18 and 35 years.

The population comprises over 50 linguistic groups and nearly as many ethnic groups. The Fon are the biggest group; along with the Yoruba they dominate the more fertile south. In the less fertile central and northern regions the Bariba are the dominant group.

Administration/Government

Benin's unicameral Assemblée Nationale (National Assembly) has 83 members elected by direct popular vote. The president is also elected by popular vote. The legal system is based on French civil law and customary law.

Economy/Industry

Benin hopes to increase tourism revenue through sensitive exploitation of two large national parks in the north. The main exports include palm oil, cotton, shea butter, and peanuts. The country's small industrial base depends on textiles, food processing, construction materials, and cement. Offshore oil reserves have begun to be exploited.

MULTINATIONAL NATIONAL PARKS

Benin, Burkina Faso, and Niger have jointly declared two large national parks that overlap their borders to form a vast protected area, the Arli–W–Singou complex. The Pendjari National Park in northwest Benin is contiguous with the Arli National Park in Burkina Faso, and is known for its wildlife including elephants, monkeys, lions, hippopotamus, buffalo, various antelope, and most particularly the birds that flock to its wetlands. The W National Park in the north of Benin, extending through parts of Niger and Burkina Faso, incorporates a meander in the River Niger shaped like a W. The largest part of this park is in Niger. Known for its large mammals, including aardvarks, baboons, buffalo, caracal, cheetahs, elephants, hippopotamus, leopards, lions, serval, and warthogs, the W National Park was named a UNESCO World Heritage Site in 1996. Both parks became Ramsar Convention sites in 2007.

Right At a ceremony held at Glidji, Togo, to introduce new voodoo priestesses to the Ewe community, older priestesses clap and chant to encourage the young initiates, who, as they dance, become fully possessed by the gods.

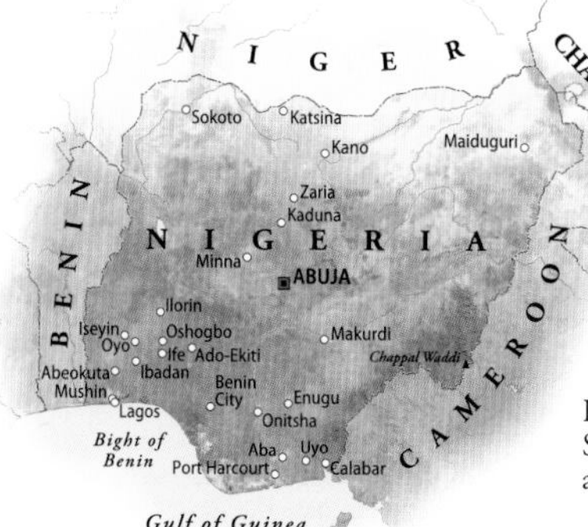
NIGER
CHAD
Sokoto
Katsina
Kano
Maiduguri
Zaria
Kaduna
NIGERIA
Minna
ABUJA
BENIN
Ilorin
Iseyin
Oyo
Oshogbo
Ife
Ado-Ekiti
Makurdi
Chappal Waddi
Abeokuta
Ibadan
Mushin
Lagos
Benin City
Enugu
Onitsha
Bight of Benin
Aba
Uyo
Port Harcourt
Calabar
CAMEROON
Gulf of Guinea

Nigeria

Map Reference Pages 304–305

Nigeria is Africa's most populated country and home to one out of seven Africans. A mix of more than 250 different ethnic groups means problems often arise between them. On the other hand, such diversity provides a cultural heritage unmatched in Africa.

Physical Geography

Nigeria is blessed with many rivers. The major rivers are the Niger and the Benue, which join near Lokoja and then run through the massive Niger Delta into the Atlantic Ocean. The terrain of the country varies, with coastal swamps and southern lowlands merging into the central hills and the Jos Plateau, before giving onto the plains of the Chad Basin in the north; mountains are found in the southeast and uplands in the west. There are rainforests, semi-desert, woodlands, and grasslands. Desertification, deforestation, air and water pollution, and soil degradation are major environmental problems.

History

Ancient kingdoms marked the early history of Nigeria: The Hausa kingdoms in Kano and Katsina, the Yoruba Oyo kingdom, and the Kingdom of Benin—which reached its peak between the fifteenth and nineteenth centuries.

Nigeria became a colony under the British, achieving independence in 1960. Since then, both military and civilian governments have held power. Disputes between larger groups, including the Hausa, Igbo, and Yoruba, are responsible for Nigeria's present division into 36 states. These disputes also led to the Igbo secession attempt and the short-lived Republic of Biafra (1967–1970). The country has had democratic civilian governments since 1999.

Nigeria is a fragile democracy whose history has been marked by corruption and beset by a number of military takeovers. Progress was made under President Olusegun Obasanjo, who left office in 2007. Umaru Yar'Adua was elected president in voting marred by widespread malfeasance and has promised to reform the election process.

Population/Culture

Nigeria's rapidly increasing population is a challenge, as the resources required to meet basic needs are becoming scarcer. HIV/AIDS is an increasing problem, along with a very high birth rate. The median age is only 18.7, thus over half the population is just reaching childbearing age.

Islam, the predominant religion in the north, is practiced by half of the country's people. Christians of many denominations live mainly in the south, and comprise 40 percent of the population. Over 500 languages are spoken; English is the official language.

Nigeria has long been famous for the variety and quality of its art. The oldest known African sculptures are terracotta figures created by the Nok civilization in central Nigeria as far back as 500 BCE. Famous traditional sculptures include the bronze and brass figures of Ife, and the wood carvings of the Yoruba, influenced by the Yoruba's many different forms of worship. Traditional Nigerian painting is mostly done on sculptures and textiles. In 1986 playwright, poet, and novelist Wole Soyinka became the first African writer to be awarded the Nobel Prize for literature.

Administration/Government

Nigeria is a federal republic with 36 states and the federal territory of Abuja. Abuja, which became the capital in 1991, is more central than the previous capital, Lagos, which was jammed by traffic and marked by violence. Abuja also stands on relatively neutral ground between the country's major ethnic factions.

Nigeria's president is elected by popular vote, and serves as both chief and head of state. The legislative branch is bicameral, collectively called the National Assembly, with a 360-member House of Representatives and a 109-member Senate. In many northern states where the population is Muslim, Sharia law is practiced. However, the Supreme Court has authority over Sharia court decisions.

Economy/Industry

Oil is a key resource in Nigeria, with most being exported. Conflicts between the oil industry and the people living in Nigeria's Delta state are frequent as they compete for revenues from the industry.

Oil and natural gas are the main exports (the primary recipients are the United Kingdom and the United States) and the main revenue source. Since the discovery of oil in the Niger Delta in the 1970s, Nigeria has neglected other sectors such as agriculture and manufacturing. It is the world's twelfth largest producer and eighth largest exporter of oil.

The bulk of employment, however, is in agriculture, where 70 percent of people work. In addition to a developed lumber industry, a wide variety of crops are grown including cocoa, peanuts, palm oil, corn, rice, yams, sorghum, millet, cassava, and rubber. Limited infrastructure is the main obstacle to growth.

MILESTONE EVENTS

c. 500 BCE–200 CE The Nok civilization thrives in central Nigeria

1000–1400s Development of the Benin, Kanem-Bornu, and Ife kingdoms, and the Hausa states

late 1400s The Portuguese reach Nigeria

1851 Great Britain seizes control of Lagos

1914 Great Britain forms Colony and Protectorate of Nigeria

1956 Oil discovered at Oloibiri in the Niger Delta

October 1, 1960 Nigeria becomes independent federation

January 1966 Military revolt overthrows government; in July a second revolt establishes new military government

1967 Eastern Region unilaterally declares independence as Republic of Biafra; civil war ensues

1970 Biafra surrenders

1979 Civilian rule restored in Nigeria

1983 Military leaders take control of the government

1999 Democracy regained when Olusegun Obasanjo is elected president

2007 Umaru Yar'Adua elected president

Left Market vendors on canoes in Ganvié ("the Venice of West Africa") in Benin. The village, which lies in Lake Nokoué, is built entirely on stilts and is home to 20,000–30,000 people.

Above A young female drill *(Mandrillus leucophaeus)* in Pandrillus Drill Sanctuary in Calabar, Cross River State, Nigeria. The drill is one of Africa's most endangered primates.

NIGERIA

Official name Federal Republic of Nigeria

Land area 356,669 square miles (923,768 km²)

Border countries Niger, Chad, Cameroon, Benin

Capital Abuja

Highest point Chappal Waddi 7,936 feet (2,419 m)

Climate Equatorial in the south, tropical in the center, arid in the north

Population 138,283,000

Languages Official: English; other: Hausa, Yoruba, Igbo (Ibo), Fulani

Ethnicity More than 250 ethnic groups; Hausa and Fulani, Yoruba, Igbo, Ijaw, Kanuri, Ibibio, Tiv are the largest

Religion Muslim, Christian, indigenous beliefs

Government Federal republic

Currency Naira

Human Development Index 0.470 (ranked 158th out of 177 countries)

Below A small village on the Jos Plateau, in Plateau State, Nigeria. Popular with tourists and dotted with extinct volcanoes, the Jos Plateau is also Africa's chief tin-mining region.

Right The Mandara Mountains region in the far north of Cameroon is home to a number of ethnic groups who depend on agriculture and forestry for their livelihoods. They live in villages of small circular adobe huts.

CAMEROON

Official name Republic of Cameroon (République du Cameroun)
Land area 183,568 square miles (475,440 km²)
Border countries Nigeria, Chad, Central African Republic, Republic of the Congo, Gabon, Equatorial Guinea
Capital Yaoundé
Highest point Fako (higher of two peaks on Mt Cameroon) 13,435 feet (4,095 m)
Climate Varies with terrain, from tropical along coast to semiarid and hot in north
Population 18,468,000
Language(s) Official: English, French; other: 24 major African language groups
Ethnicity Cameroon Highlanders (includes Bamiléké) 31%, Equatorial Bantu 19%, Kirdi 11%, Fulani 10%, Northwestern Bantu 8%, Eastern Nigritic 7%, other African 13%, non-African less than 1%
Religion Indigenous beliefs 40%, Christian 40%, Muslim 20%
Government Republic; multiparty presidential regime
Currency Communauté Financière Africaine franc
Human Development Index 0.532 (ranked 144th out of 177 countries)

Above With its rich volcanic soils, high altitude, and plentiful rainfall, Cameroon is the perfect place to grow good coffee beans. The country benefits greatly from its exports of different varieties of coffee, especially robusta and arabica.

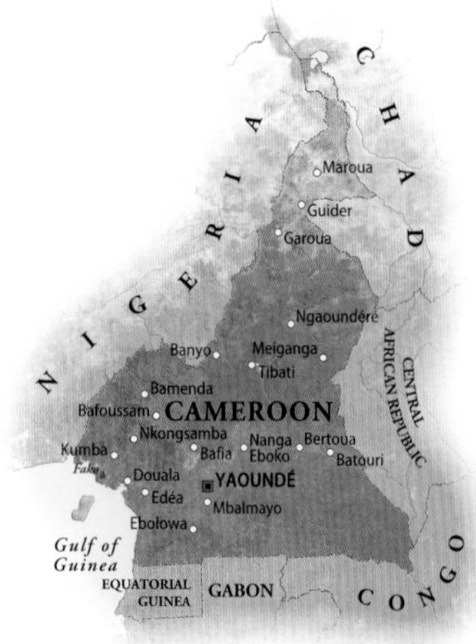
CHAD
NIGERIA
Maroua
Guider
Garoua
Ngaoundéré
Banyo
Meiganga
Tibati
Bamenda
Bafoussam
CAMEROON
Nkongsamba
Nanga Eboko
Bertoua
Bafia
Batouri
Kumba
Fako
Douala
Edéa
YAOUNDÉ
Mbalmayo
Ebolowa
CENTRAL AFRICAN REPUBLIC
Gulf of Guinea
EQUATORIAL GUINEA
GABON
CONGO

Cameroon

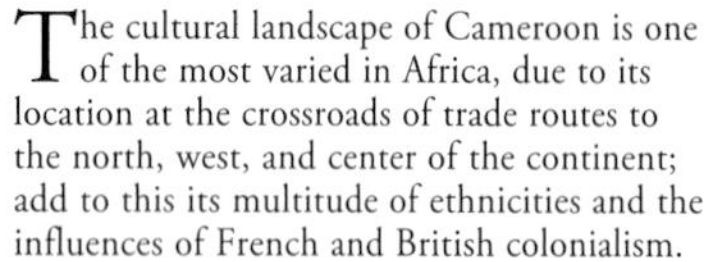

Map Reference Pages 304–305

The cultural landscape of Cameroon is one of the most varied in Africa, due to its location at the crossroads of trade routes to the north, west, and center of the continent; add to this its multitude of ethnicities and the influences of French and British colonialism.

Physical Geography

Extending from Lake Chad in the north to the Shanga River in the south, Cameroon has been called "Africa in miniature" because of its physical features—including rainforest, desert, savanna, beach, and mountain ranges. The lowlands of the south, including the narrow coastal belt, support dense rainforest, but the north is mostly hot semiarid savanna. The active volcano, Mt Cameroon (which is also known as Mongo ma Ndemi, or the Mountain of Greatness), rises near the coast.

History

Cameroon came under German domination in 1884. Following World War I, the League of Nations granted France a mandate over 80 percent of the area, and Great Britain the other 20 percent. Cameroon became an independent republic in 1960. In 1961 the southern part of the British territory joined the new Federal Republic of Cameroon while the northern part united with Nigeria. In 1994 and 1996, Cameroon and Nigeria fought over the oil-rich Bakassi Peninsula, but in compliance with the World Court rulings Nigeria handed over the disputed land in 2006.

Population/Culture

Cameroon's population is centered in the more densely populated western, British-colonized southwest. The capital, Yaoundé, and the major seaport, Douala, are both here. Cameroon is home to more than 200 ethnic and linguistic groups. The Bamiléké, the most populous group in the western highlands and one of the largest communities in Douala, control a large portion of the economy.

As well as its two official languages, French and English, Cameroon has many African languages. French is more widely spoken, especially in Yaoundé and Douala, but about 10 percent of the country relies primarily on varieties of Kamtok, an English-based Creole language. The literacy rate for those over 15 years of age is high, at about 68 percent.

Southern Cameroon has been influenced by European countries for over 500 years, but the isolated north was dominated by Muslim Fulani kingdoms, centered in Nigeria until the twentieth century. Tradition, and resistance to outside influence, remain very strong in the north of the country and have kept Western-style development to the minimum.

Administration/Government

The 180 members of Cameroon's National Assembly are elected for five-year terms. The authority of the traditional chiefs to govern at local level and resolve disputes is recognized. After 20 years of repressive one-party government under Ahmadou Ahidjo, the first president, he was succeeded by Paul Biya. Pressured by popular discontent, Biya allowed multiparty presidential elections in 1992, which he won, and again in 1997. His administration has been authoritarian.

Economy/Industry

Agriculture employs 70 percent of the population. Petroleum is the main source of export revenue, and large reserves of bauxite and natural gas await exploitation. Hydroelectric power stations on the rivers provide electricity for the country's needs. Cocoa, coffee, and cotton are the main agricultural exports.

The US$3.7 billion pipeline, 665 miles (1,070 km) long, connects the Doba oilfields in nearby Chad with offshore loading facilities on the Atlantic coast and is expected to bring employment and prosperity to Cameroon.

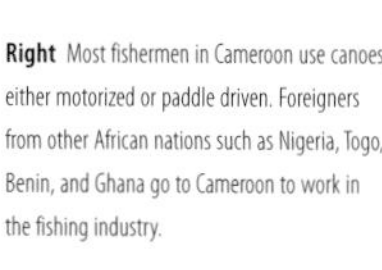

Right Most fishermen in Cameroon use canoes, either motorized or paddle driven. Foreigners from other African nations such as Nigeria, Togo, Benin, and Ghana go to Cameroon to work in the fishing industry.

Far right Cameroon boasts a diverse cultural tradition, which encompasses music, theater, poetry, and dance. Each region is famous for specific types of folklore. Pictured are two tribal dancers; a popular saying in Cameroon is "If you dance, you vibrate—and he who vibrates lives."

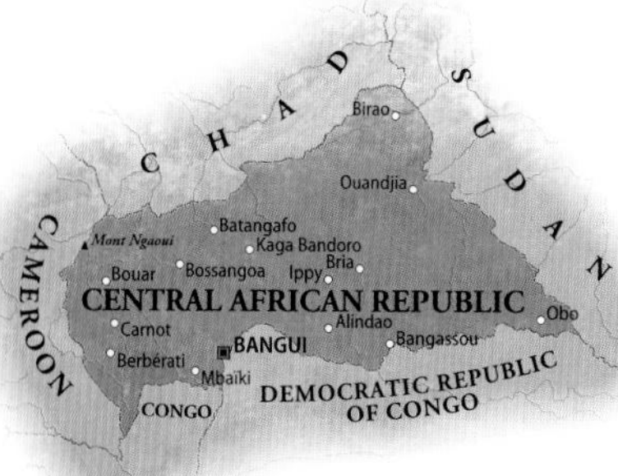
CHAD
SUDAN
CAMEROON
Birao
Ouandjia
Mont Ngaoui
Batangafo
Kaga Bandoro
Bria
Bouar
Bossangoa
Ippy
CENTRAL AFRICAN REPUBLIC
Obo
Carnot
Alindao
BANGUI
Bangassou
Berbérati
Mbaiki
DEMOCRATIC REPUBLIC OF CONGO
CONGO

Central African Republic

Map Reference Pages 304–305

The Central African Republic (CAR) is sparsely populated, especially in the east, due to severe and extensive raiding during the slave trade era. It is the only major Central African country to lack petroleum resources.

Physical Geography

Desert and Sahelian grasslands in the north grade to rainforest in the south. Along the Cameroon border rise the highlands of the Yadé Massif; the rest of the country is mostly rolling hills and plateaus, with mountains in the northeast. The Oubangui and Mbomou rivers form most of the southern border. The rainforests shelter important lowland gorilla and forest elephant populations.

The generally high elevation contributes to a cooler climate in the central region that limits the prevalence of the tsetse fly, allowing some cattle-rearing to take place; however, severe soil erosion resulting from clearing forests for farming is a serious problem.

History

Beginning around 1000 BCE, the region was settled in succession by Adamawa, Bantu, and Sudanic peoples. Europeans arrived in 1885. The French consolidated their claim to the area in 1910. Self-rule began in 1958, with Barthélémy Boganda as head of government. David Dacko oversaw the declaration of independence in 1960. Dacko was removed in a coup in 1966 by Jean-Bédel Bokassa, who abolished the constitution; in 1976 he crowned himself emperor. Dacko removed Bokassa in a military coup in 1979. After multiparty elections in 1993, Ange-Félix Patassé was elected president. In 2003, François Bozizé overthrew Patassé and declared himself president. The new constitution was ratified in 2004, and in 2005 Bozizé was elected president.

Population/Culture

The population is largely black African, divided into several ethnic groups covering at least 80 subgroups. Years of political chaos have seen many thousands of people displaced, many crossing the border into Chad. Periodic skirmishes occur along the border with Sudan over water and grazing rights.

French is the official language, but Sangho is the national language, widely used on radio and in official situations. There are pockets of Islam in the north of the country, and Christians and animists are in roughly equal numbers. Good and bad magic, and spirits, play a big role in local religions. Life usually centers on special events such as baptisms, weddings, funerals, and village fêtes.

Administration/Government

Under the 2004 Constitution, the 109 members of the multiparty National Assembly are elected for five-year terms. The country is divided into 14 administrative prefectures, based on the French system, and the legal system is also based on that of France.

Economy/Industry

Though the CAR has good agricultural, water, and mineral resources, including timber, diamonds, gold, and uranium, decades of political and economic misrule have left it one of the world's least developed countries. The primary occupation is subsistence farming. Main exports are diamonds, timber, cotton, coffee, and tobacco. A major limitation to development is high transportation costs arising from the country's landlocked position and poor infrastructure.

Left African forest elephants live in the Central African Republic's rainforests. Poaching of the diverse wildlife in the three large national parks has diminished the county's reputation as one of the last great wildlife refuges, and with it the potential for tourism.

CENTRAL AFRICAN REPUBLIC

Official name Central African Republic (Kodorosese ti Beafrika)
Land area 240, 534 square miles (622,984 km²)
Border countries Chad, Sudan, Democratic Republic of Congo, Republic of the Congo, Cameroon
Capital Bangui
Highest & lowest points Mont Ngaoui 4,658 feet (1,420 m); Oubangui River 1,099 feet (335 m)
Climate Tropical, modified by altitude; hot dry winters; mild to hot wet summers
Population 4,435,000
Language(s) Official: French; other: Sangho (lingua franca and national language), tribal languages, Arabic
Ethnicity Baya 33%, Banda 27%, Mandjia 13%, Sara 10%, Mboum 7%, M'Baka 4%, Yakoma 4%, other 2%
Religion Christian 50%, indigenous beliefs 35%, Muslim 15%
Government Republic
Currency Communauté Financière Africaine franc
Human Development Index 0.384 (ranked 171st out of 177 countries)

Above The grand Notre Dame Cathedral in Bangui, capital of Central African Republic, is a reminder of the country's French colonial history.

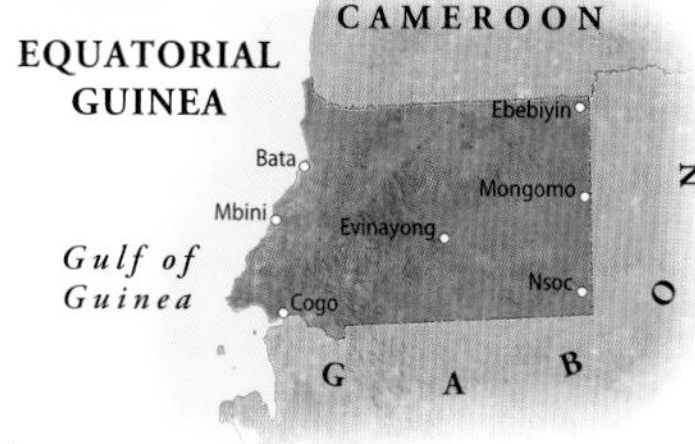
MALABO
Bioco
Pico Basile
Luba
EQUATORIAL GUINEA
CAMEROON
Ebebiyin
Bata
Mongomo
Mbini
Evinayong
Gulf of Guinea
Nsoc
Cogo
GABON

Equatorial Guinea

Map Reference Pages 304–305

Equatorial Guinea is made up of mainland Río Muni and several islands in the Gulf of Guinea, including Bioko (the largest), Annobón, Corisco, Elobey Grande, and Elobey Chico. The economic windfall from recent offshore oil discoveries has produced massive increases in revenue; however, the people have seen few improvements in living standards.

Physical Geography

Río Muni has a fairly flat coastal strip, with the interior rising to more than 3,600 feet (1,100 m). Bioko Island has the country's highest point; its extinct volcanoes, crater lakes, and rich lava soils form a rugged contrast with the mainland. Half the continental enclave is covered with rainforest. The climate is tropical; hot and humid with thunderstorms occurring especially during the wettest season, from December through February.

History

The mainland region was originally inhabited by Pygmy peoples. The Fang and Bubi arrived in the seventeenth century. Portugal, then Spain, Britain, and Spain again administered Bioko. Spanish Guinea, as it was then called, gained independence in 1968, when President Francisco Nguema, one of the worst despots in African history, began a brutal reign that destroyed the economy, abused human rights, and led to the death or exile of up to one-third of the population. He was overthrown by Teodoro Obiang in 1979, but dictatorial practices and widespread corruption continue.

Population/Culture

In Africa's only Spanish-speaking nation, the official language is Spanish, but most people speak Bantu languages. The population of Bioko, about a quarter of the country's total, is primarily Bubi, who practice matrilineal inheritance. Polygamy is permitted, despite the majority being nominally Catholic. Indigenous religious practices are widespread, and among the Fang, witchcraft is particularly important.

Cocoyam, plantains, and rice are the staple foods, supplemented with home-grown vegetables, fish and a little meat.

Folk art is rich and ethnically varied. Some groups produce baskets so finely woven that they hold liquids such as palm oil. The Bubi people are known for their colorful wooden bells embellished with intricate designs.

Administration/Government

Nominally a constitutional democracy with a 100-seat House of People's Representatives, President Obiang controls most opposition parties through patronage. He initially ruled with the aid of a Supreme Military Council, but abolished it in 1982. There are seven provinces, and the legal system is based partly on Spanish civil law, partly on tribal customs.

Economy/Industry

Oil and gas exports have produced huge economic growth, and in 2004 Equatorial Guinea had the world's fastest-growing economy. Yet few people beyond the president and his family have benefited from the riches and the country ranks near the bottom of the human development index. Government officials and their family members own most businesses. Other unexploited resources include fertile soils, deepwater ports, titanium, iron ore, manganese, uranium, and alluvial gold. The agricultural sector, once known for cocoa of the highest quality, is in disarray.

EQUATORIAL GUINEA

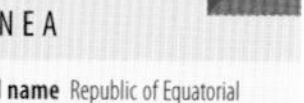

Official name Republic of Equatorial Guinea (República de Guinea Ecuatorial)
Land area 10,830 square miles (28,051 km²)
Border countries Cameroon, Gabon
Capital Malabo (on Bioko)
Highest point Pico Basile (on Bioko) 9,870 feet (3,008 m)
Climate Tropical, always hot and humid
Population 616,459
Languages Official: Spanish, French; other: Fang, Bubi, and Igbo
Ethnicity Fang 85.7%, Bubi 6.5%, Mdowe 3.6%, Annobón 1.6%, Bujeba 1.1%, other 1.5%
Religion Nominally Christian and predominantly Roman Catholic plus indigenous beliefs
Government Republic
Currency Communauté Financière Africaine franc
Human Development Index 0.642 (ranked 127th out of 177 countries)

SÃO TOMÉ AND PRÍNCIPE

Official name Democratic Republic of São Tomé and Príncipe (República Democrática de São Tomé e Príncipe)
Area 386 square miles (1,001 km²)
Border countries None
Capital São Tomé
Climate Tropical; hot, humid; rainy season October to May
Highest point Pico de São Tomé 6,639 feet (2,024 m)
Population 206,178
Languages Official: Portuguese; other: Creoles (Forro, Angolar, and Principense), French
Ethnicity Mestiço (descendants of Portuguese colonists and African slaves), Angolare (descendants of Angolan slaves), Forro (descendants of freed slaves), Serviçais (contract laborers from Angola, Mozambique, and Cape Verde), Tonga (children of Serviçais born on the islands), European (primarily Portuguese), Asian
Religion Catholic 70.3%, Protestant 7.2% (Evangelical 3.4%, New Apostolic 2%, Adventist 1.8%), other 3.1%, none 19.4%
Government Republic
Currency Dobra
Human Development Index 0.654 (ranked 123rd out of 177 countries)

Above right Fort São Sebastião, in São Tomé, was built by the Portuguese in 1575 to guard the entrance to the Bay of Ana Chaves. It now houses the São Tomé National Museum.

GABON

Official name Gabonese Republic (République Gabonais)
Area 103,346 square miles (267,667 km²)
Border countries Equatorial Guinea, Cameroon, Republic of the Congo
Capital Libreville
Highest point Mont Iboundji 5,166 feet (1,575 m)
Climate Tropical; always hot, humid
Population 1,486,000
Languages Official: French; other: Fang, Myene, Nzebi, Bapunu/Eschira, Bandjabi, other Bantu languages
Ethnicity At least 40 Bantu ethnic groups 90% (the largest are the Fang, Bapunu, Nzebi, Obamba), French 10%
Religion Christian (Roman Catholic and Protestant), animist/traditional indigenous religion, Muslim
Government Republic; multiparty presidential regime
Currency Communauté Financière Africaine franc
Human Development Index 0.677 (ranked 119th out of 177 countries)

Right An adult male mandrill *(Mandrillus sphinx)*, Gabon. Males have colorful faces and rumps; females have duller colors. The male's coloration, which becomes more pronounced when the animal is excited, grows stronger with sexual maturity.

Far right Women performing an initiation ceremony, Gabon. It has sometimes been said that Gabon is to Africa what Tibet is to Asia, the spiritual center of religious initiation.

Sundi
Santo António
Príncipe
Infante
Dom Henrique
Tinhosa Pequena
Tinhosa Grande
Gulf of Guinea
SÃO TOMÉ AND PRÍNCIPE
São Tomé
Neves
SÃO TOMÉ
Santa Catarina
Pico de São Tomé
Ribeira Afonso
Ribeira Peixa
Porto Alegre

São Tomé and Príncipe

Map Reference Pages 304–305

São Tomé and Príncipe, once a leading cocoa producer, is poised to profit from the recent discovery of large offshore oil reserves. One of Africa's smallest countries, it consists of two fertile islands of volcanic origin in the Gulf of Guinea, and some islets.

Physical Geography

The islands of São Tomé and Príncipe lie in the equatorial Atlantic, west of Gabon. São Tomé, the more mountainous of the two, is 30 miles (48 km) long and 20 miles (32 km) wide. Príncipe is about 10 miles (16 km) long and 4 miles (6 km) wide. Both are dissected by streams radiating down the mountains through lush forest and cropland to the sea.

The climate is tropical—hot and humid from September to May, and hot and dry from June to August.

History

Originally uninhabited, the islands were colonized by Portugal in the late fifteenth century. By the mid-sixteenth century, it had become Africa's largest exporter of sugar, and by the mid-seventeenth century yet another staging point for the export of slaves to the Americas. When slavery was banned, colonists turned to coffee and cocoa, cash crops ideally suited to the rich volcanic soils.

São Tomé and Príncipe achieved independence in 1975, choosing as its first president Manuel Pinto da Costa. It embraced multiparty democracy in 1990, and since then has had four democratic, multiparty elections.

Population/Culture

The homogeneous culture is deeply marked by centuries of colonialism and intermarriage, but the government is keen to stress African heritage. Language, family structure, and religion are basically Portuguese, while many African elements are found in cooking, customs, beliefs, and dress. Education is compulsory to the end of sixth grade (age 12).

Administration/Government

The unicameral Assembleia Naçional (National Assembly) has 55 members elected for four-year terms. The popularly elected president appoints the prime minister, who in turn names the 14 members of the Cabinet. Justice is administered by an independent judiciary.

Industry/Economy

Previously dependent on plantation agriculture, São Tomé is now poised to profit from the exploitation of large offshore oil reserves. Export crops include cocoa, copra, palm kernels, and coffee. Tourist infrastructure is improving in the hope of attracting more visitors.

CAMEROON
EQUATORIAL GUINEA
Oyem
Makokou
LIBREVILLE
Booué
GABON
Lambaréné
Port-Gentil
Mont Iboundji
Koulamoutou
Moanda
Pana
Franceville
Mouila
Ndendé
Tchibanga
CONGO
ATLANTIC OCEAN

Gabon

Map Reference Pages 304–305

Rich in natural resources, Gabon is a small country with rapid population growth, high rates of urbanization, and relative political stability.

Physical Geography

The tropical climate is always hot and humid. A narrow coastal plain with swamps and lagoons rises gradually to a hilly interior with savanna grasslands in the east and south, cut through by the Ogooué River and its tributaries. Gabon is famous for its environmental preservation efforts, having the largest percentage area of national parks in the world.

History

Bantu ethnic groups were the first settlers before Portuguese traders arrived in the fifteenth century. Gabon became a major center of the slave trade. In 1910, Gabon became one of the four territories of French Equatorial Africa, and achieved independence in 1960.

Under Leon M'Ba, the first president, Gabon became a one-party state. After his death in 1967, Omar Bongo became president, and has been president ever since. Bongo has sought to forge a national movement in support of the government's development policies. In 1990, economic discontent and a strong desire for a multiparty system led to sweeping political reforms. A new constitution was enacted in March 1991.

Population/Culture

French is the official language and the most widely spoken of more than 45 languages. Many young Gabonese cannot speak any language other than French.

A large percentage identifies themselves as Roman Catholic, a lesser percentage as Protestant. In reality, many hold animist beliefs but also practice Christianity. Belief in evil spirits and in sorcerers who can call and use them is common.

Administration/Government

Gabon is a republic with a presidential form of government. The National Assembly has 120 deputies. The president is elected by universal suffrage and can appoint and dismiss the prime minister, the Cabinet, the judges of the independent Supreme Court, and even dissolve the National Assembly.

Industry/Economy

Gabon's economy is dominated by oil, though production is declining. Oil revenues comprise 65 percent of the budget, 43 percent of GDP, and 81 percent of exports. Other natural resources include natural gas, diamonds, manganese, uranium, gold, timber, iron ore, and hydropower. Although GDP is high by African standards, about a third of Gabonese live in poverty. After oil, logging and manganese mining are the other major sectors.

CENTRAL AFRICAN REPUBLIC
CAMEROON
Ouésso
Impfondo
GABON
Etoumbi
Owando
CONGO
DEMOCRATIC REPUBLIC OF CONGO
Mayoko
Djambala
Mossendjo
Ngabé
Sibiti
Loubomo
Mindouli
BRAZZAVILLE
Madingou
Kinkala
TLANTIC
OCEAN
Pointe-Noire
ANGOLA

Congo

Map Reference Pages 304–305

Formerly the French colony of Middle Congo, the Republic of the Congo is virtually landlocked. It is one of Africa's biggest producers of oil, but declining reserves present a threat to economic prosperity.

Physical Geography

Much of Congo is covered by dense tropical rainforest, interspersed with open wooded grasslands, and marshlands in the north. The coastal plain and drainage basin of the Kouili-Niari River rises to a central plateau, which falls away to the drainage basin of the Congo River. Extensive river systems, notably those of the Congo and Ubangi, facilitate trade with the interior. The capital, Brazzaville, lies at the mouth of Pool Malebo (Stanley Pool) on the Congo River, opposite Kinshasa, the capital of the Democratic Republic of Congo.

History

The original inhabitants, the Pygmies, were largely replaced by Bantu tribes. Portuguese navigators explored the coastline in 1482 and soon the interior was being regularly raided for slaves. The Portuguese remained dominant until Frenchman Pierre Savorgnan de Brazza (after whom the capital is named) led expeditions up the Congo River in 1875 and 1883. De Brazza declared the north bank of the river a French Protectorate in 1880.

Initially called French Congo, then Middle Congo, the new protectorate was exploited for its rubber and ivory resources. At the French Constitutional Referendum held in 1958, Congo opted for autonomy within the wider French Community.

Congo was granted independence in 1960. In 1963, the first president, Fulbert Youlou, was forced out in a coup led by Alphonse Massamba-Débat. In 1964 a socialist state was established based on Marxist–Leninist ideals. In a policy reminiscent of pre-war Stalinist USSR, a Five Year Plan was developed and large swaths of arable land were nationalized.

In 1968 Marien Ngouabi seized control in a military coup. He was assassinated in 1977. A series of failed governments followed, and the military again seized control in 1979 under Denis Sassou-Nguesso. He maintained close trading ties with both the capitalist west and the communist east, and the country remained relatively stable during the 1980s.

A new constitution granting multiparty elections was approved in 1992, with Pascal Lissouba becoming the first democratically elected president. Civil war erupted in 1997. Former president Sassou-Nguesso captured the capital and was appointed president, but fighting continued well into 1999.

Fighting erupted again in the southern region of Pool in 2002, where rebel militias remain in control in some areas. In April 2007, a new power-sharing arrangement was entered into but peace remains very fragile.

Population/Culture

Congo has a very young population with a median age of less than 17 years. Life expectancy rates have been affected by high rates of HIV/AIDS infection involving about 4.5 percent of the population.

About half the population lives in the cities and larger towns with much of the inland sparsely populated. There are 15 major ethnic groups, and 75 subgroups. Pygmies (known as the Teke, the Ake, or forest-dwellers), who are often heavily discriminated against, live in the forests in the north in isolated groups of 40 to 50 people. Traditional cultures and religions are still widely practiced, particularly the monotheistic religion of Nzambi among the Bakongo. French is the official language, but traditional languages are more commonly used.

The people take pride in their appearance, no matter how poor they may be, and a certain formality characterizes most social interactions. Respect is shown to older people through physical gestures, and to agree with their opinions is often more important than being frank. Generosity is a deep-rooted tradition, even when it causes hardship to the giver.

Administration/Government

The upper house in Congo's bicameral Parliament is the 66-member Senate; the lower house is the 137-member National Assembly; in both houses members are elected by popular vote. The president is also elected by popular vote. The judicial branch is headed by the Supreme Court; the legal system is based on French civil law and customary law.

Economy/Industry

Oil production, in which France maintains a significant stake, accounts for almost 90 percent of all government revenues. Forestry and agriculture are also important. Major economic activity is centered around the capital, Brazzaville. Congo has diamond fields, but an embargo on the diamond trade was established in 2004 as most diamonds were illegally mined. Subsistence farming employs about one-third of the Congolese workforce.

Above Okapi *(Okapia johnstoni)* parent with young, Congo. Although its striped markings are reminiscent of the zebra, the okapi is most closely related to the giraffe. Both species have long, flexible, blue tongues that they use to strip leaves and buds from trees; it is one of the few mammals that can lick its own ears. Until 1901, the okapi had only been seen by local people, but it had legendary status in Europe, where it was known as the "African unicorn." Male okapi have short skin-covered horns called ossicones.

Below left These mountain gorillas *(Gorilla beringei beringei)* live at high altitudes in the Virunga Mountains, part of the Great Rift Valley in the Republic of the Congo. Their diet consists mainly of vegetation, including flowers, fruit, stems, and tree bark.

CONGO

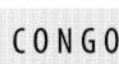

Official name Republic of the Congo (République du Congo)

Land area 131,854 square miles (341,500 km²)

Border countries Central African Republic, Democratic Republic of Congo (DRC), Cabinda (Angola), Gabon

Capital Brazzaville

Highest point Mt Berongou 2,963 feet (903 m)

Climate Predominantly tropical; constant high temperatures, humidity and rainfall

Population 3,903,000

Languages Official: French; other: over 60 indigenous languages, Kikongo, Sangha, and Bateke dominant

Ethnicity Bakongo 48%, Sangha 20%, Teke 17%, M'Bochi 12%, other (includes European) 3%

Religion Christian 50%, animist 48%, Muslim 2%

Government Republic

Currency Communauté Financière Africaine franc

Human Development Index 0.548 (ranked 139th out of 177 countries)

MILESTONE EVENTS

1400 CE Indigenous tribes, including the Pygmy, migrate into the area of modern-day Congo

1480s Portuguese navigators establish trading relations with the indigenous population

1500s–1700s Dutch, British, and French establish trading posts on the coast

1875 Italian-born French explorer Pierre Savorgnan de Brazza penetrates inland along the Congo River

1880 The northern bank of the Congo River declared a French Protectorate

1883 De Brazza undertakes his second great exploration of the interior

1907 French Government restricts the activities of French companies and landholders in Congo following abusive treatment of indigenous laborers

1958 Congo elects to accept autonomy within the French Community

August 15, 1960 Full independence gained from France

1963 President Fulbert Youlou loses office in a coup to Alphonse Massamba-Débat

1964 Socialist state using Marxist–Leninist ideals is established

1968 The military under Marien Ngouabi seize control

1977 Ngouabi is assassinated

1979 The military regain power through a coup led by Colonel Denis Sassou-Nguesso

1992 Multiparty elections take place electing Pascal Lissouba

1997 Civil war erupts and Sassou-Nguesso regains power with the help of Angolan troops

1999 Ceasefire announced

2002 Rebels in the Pool region of the country launch attacks on the government

2005 Fighting erupts in the capital

2007 New power-sharing government formed with representatives of the Pool militias

Left A aerial view of Odzala National Park, Republic of the Congo. One of Africa's more remarkable tropical forest ecosystems, the park, which comprises a mosaic of forest and savanna landscapes, is home to a rich diversity of wildlife: Grimm's duiker, spotted hyenas and lions, forest elephants, buffalo, bongos, leopards, gorillas, and other forest mammal species.

DEMOCRATIC REPUBLIC OF CONGO

Official name Democratic Republic of Congo (République Démocratique du Congo)
Area 90, 5568 square miles (2,345,410 km²)
Border countries Central African Republic, Sudan, Uganda, Rwanda, Burundi, Tanzania, Zambia, Angola, Republic of the Congo
Capital Kinshasa (Xinshasa)
Highest point Pic Marguerite on Mont Ngaliema (Mt Stanley) 16,761 feet (5,110 m)
Climate Tropical; hot and humid in equatorial river basin; cooler and drier in southern highlands; cooler and wetter in eastern highlands
Population 66,515,000
Languages Official: French; other: Lingala (lingua franca trade language), Kingwana (dialect of Kiswahili or Swahili), Kikongo, Tshiluba
Ethnicity Over 200 groups; Mono, Luba, Kongo, and Mangbetu-Azande constitute 40% of the population
Religion Roman Catholic 50%, Protestant 20%, Kimbanguist 10%, Muslim 10%, other sects and indigenous beliefs 10%
Government Republic
Currency Congolese franc
Human Development Index 0.411 (ranked 168th out of 177 countries)

Above left A canoe crosses one of the many tributaries of the Congo River, its banks overflowing with vegetation. Due to its equatorial location, the Congo experiences large amounts of rainfall, with an annual total of over 80 inches (200 cm) in some places. The massive expanse of lush jungle covering most of the Congo Basin constitutes the second largest rainforest in the world, after the Amazon.

Below left Mikeno Volcano, seen here from Rwanda, belongs to a chain of mostly dormant volcanoes comprising the Virunga Mountains. Mikeno is one of the oldest of these volcanoes, dating from the early part of the Pleistocene Epoch. The Virunga Mountains mark the borders between the DRC on one side and Uganda and Rwanda on the other.

CENTRAL AFRICAN REPUBLIC
SUDAN
Buta
Lisala
Mbandaka
Kisangani
Pic Marguerite
UGANDA
DEMOCRATIC REPUBLIC OF CONGO
CONGO
Inongo
Goma
RWANDA
Bukavu
BURUNDI
Bandundu
Kindu
XINSHASA (KINSHASA)
Kikwit
ANGOLA
Matadi
ATLANTIC OCEAN
Kananga
Mbuji-Mayi
Kabinda
Kalemie
TANZANIA
Kamina
ANGOLA
Dilolo
Kolwezi
Likasi
Lubumbashi
ZAMBIA

Democratic Republic of Congo

Map Reference Pages 306–307

Democratic Republic of Congo (DRC) is the third largest country in Africa, comparable in size to Western Europe, and is dominated by the drainage basin of the River Congo, much of which is sparsely populated and covered in dense rainforest. The area's mineral and natural resources have for many years fuelled conflict throughout the region, leading to widespread poverty, economic instability, and migration.

Physical Geography

The River Congo flows westward through the country toward the Atlantic. Most of the river is navigable. To the east, the border with Uganda and Rwanda is marked by high steep-sided mountains, one of the last remaining habitats of the endangered mountain gorilla. To the south, the forest gives way to upland plateau dominated by open savanna. The northern border with Congo and the Central African Republic is characterized by dense grasslands. Here the majority of Africa's last remaining natural rainforest, second only in size to the Amazon rainforest, has been subjected to a rapid increase in land clearance and illegal logging in recent years.

History

In the fifth century CE, Nilotic peoples from the north introduced agriculture to the area, and by the fourteenth century several kingdoms had developed. The Kingdom of Kongo was arguably the most significant. Historical evidence suggests a booming slave trade between Kongo and the Portuguese from this period until the mid-nineteenth century.

Little was known of inland DRC until Henry Morton Stanley, under the instruction of King Leopold II of Belgium, explored the interior in 1878. At the Berlin Conference of 1884–85, King Leopold persuaded other European powers that the Congo Free State be recognized as his personal territory, and in the years that followed millions of Congolese died as a result of their enslavement in the rubber industry. The Belgian government took over in 1908. In 1960, the country gained its independence.

Patrice Lumumba was appointed prime minister and Joseph Kasavubu president, but later that year Kasavubu authorized Lumumba's execution. Under Joseph-Désiré Mobutu, the military seized power in 1965 with the support of the United States, which felt the renamed Zaire important in the fight against communism. Mobutu opened up the country to exploitation and foreign investment, yet much of the income generated went into his personal accounts. By 1997, when Mobutu was overthrown by Laurent Kabila, DRC's development status had declined significantly.

Conflict between Kabila's forces and Rwanda and Uganda erupted during 1998, and led to regional conflict. In 2001 Kabila was assassinated. His son, Joseph Kabila, succeeded him as head of state, and established a transitional government. He was re-elected following multiparty elections in 2006, but deadly conflicts and displacement continue uncontrolled.

Population/Culture

HIV/AIDS and persistent conflict have accounted for the deaths of at least 5.4 million people during the last decade.

Around 250 different ethnic groups live in the DRC, most with their own distinct languages and traditions of storytelling, music, and arts. Soukous music, which developed in urban areas, is a unique fusion of traditional Congolese music with Latin American and Caribbean rhythms.

Administration/Government

The popularly elected president is the head of state. The prime minister, currently Antoine Gizenga, is head of the government and is appointed by the president. Parliament consists of two chambers: The National Assembly with 500 elected members; and the Senate, with 108 members.

Industry/Economy

Despite a wealth of natural resources including diamonds, copper, oil, gold, zinc, silver, cobalt, and coltan (used in mobile telephones), the DRC's economy has declined significantly since the 1980s. Conflict during the 1990s largely destroyed the country's mineral extraction, transport, and processing industries; widespread political instability has also resulted in a decline in foreign aid and investment, and huge external debt.

Around 60 per cent of the population engages in agriculture, forestry, or fishing, though much is subsistence oriented. Cash crops include tea, coffee, cocoa, and cotton. An active yet informal sector provides jobs for tailors, cobblers, construction workers, drivers, and small-scale retailers.

MILESTONE EVENTS

1200s CE Rise of Kongo Empire
1482 Portuguese navigator Diogo Cão visits the Congo; Portugal establishes diplomatic relations with the King of Kongo
1500s–1800s Europe engages in slave trade through Kongo intermediaries
1870s Belgian King Leopold II sets up private venture to colonize Kongo
1878 Leopold commissions Henry Morton Stanley to explore the Congo Basin
1884–85 European powers at the Conference of Berlin recognize Leopold's claim to the Congo Basin (renamed the Congo Free State)
1908 Belgium takes over the administration of Congo following reports of exploitation by Leopold's agents
June 30, 1960 Independence from Belgium; Patrice Lumumba becomes prime minister; Joseph Kasavubu is president
February, 1961 Lumumba executed
1965 Joseph-Désiré Mobutu leads coup d'état, ousting Kasavubu
1971 Mobutu renames the country Zaire
1973–74 Mobutu nationalizes many foreign-owned firms and forces European investors out of the country
1977 Mobutu invites foreign investors back
1989 Zaire defaults on loans from Belgium, resulting in a cancellation of development programs and further deterioration of the economy
1990 Mobutu ends ban on multiparty politics and appoints transitional government
1996–97 Tutsi rebels capture much of eastern Zaire
1997 Tutsi and other anti-Mobutu rebels capture Kinshasa; Zaire renamed the Democratic Republic of Congo; Laurent Kabila installed as president
1998 Rebel groups, supported by Rwanda and Uganda, take control of the east of DRC; Zimbabwe, Namibia, and Angola lend support to Kabila
1999 Ceasefire is signed in Lusaka
2000 UN force monitors the ceasefire but fighting continues between rebels and government forces, and between Rwandan and Ugandan forces
2001 President Kabila is shot dead by a bodyguard; his son Joseph Kabila succeeds him
2001 UN panel suggests that conflict is being prolonged to plunder gold, diamonds, lumber, and coltan
2002 DRC signs a peace accord first with Rwanda and Uganda, and then with the main rebel groups in the country; rebel leaders are invited into government
April, 2003 President Kabila signs a transitional constitution, and an interim parliament is inaugurated
2004 Attempted coup in Kinshasa
2005 New constitution is adopted by Parliament
2006 Presidential and parliamentary elections are held; Joseph Kabila is declared winner of a run-off presidential election
2007 Major outbreak of Ebola virus

BUSHMEAT AND BIODIVERSITY

Widespread poverty, fuelled by regional conflict and a lack of basic food production infrastructure, has led to an increase in the hunting of wild animals in the Congo Basin in recent years, much to the concern of conservationists. Bushmeat hunting, as it is known, has become a significant source of food and income for forest-dwelling communities; recent estimates are that 0.5 ounce (16 g) of bushmeat is consumed per person every day. Although hunting may have been sustainable on a small scale in the past, the expansion of logging activities and associated road construction have opened up new markets. It is now common to find bushmeat for sale in most towns and cities.

Although pigs, deer, and rodents are the most commonly hunted groups of animals, it is the hunting of primates such as gorilla, chimpanzee, and bonobo that has caused concern in the West. Concerns have also been raised regarding the role of bushmeat in the transmission of infectious diseases, such as Ebola, to human populations. The challenge for conservationists concerned about fragile biodiversity is to reduce the demand for bushmeat. While environmental education is one way to do so, it is only likely to be effective in cases where bushmeat is perceived as a luxury item, for example in urban areas. Elsewhere, when it is the main component of household income or food consumption, persuading people to find alternatives (with few other food sources available) is problematic. A range of management approaches has been suggested, from taxing or confiscating bushmeat, to paying local people to conserve areas of forest. But because of the DRC's fragile political and economic situation, few initiatives have in fact been implemented or funded, and the trade continues.

Left A church rises above the village of Catumbela, Angola. In 1650 there was talk of moving the provincial capital to Catembula because of its excellent water and friendly climate. Though this did not happen, Catembula played an important role in the large-scale rubber trade that began in 1888.

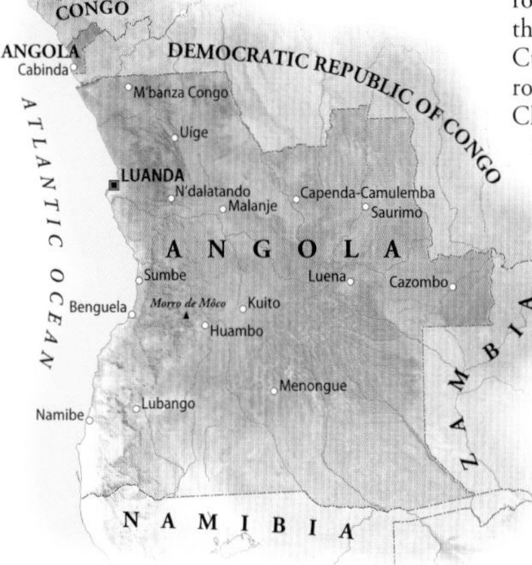
CONGO
ANGOLA
Cabinda
DEMOCRATIC REPUBLIC OF CONGO
M'banza Congo
Uige
LUANDA
N'dalatando
Malanje
Capenda-Camulemba
Saurimo
ATLANTIC OCEAN
A N G O L A
Sumbe
Luena
Cazombo
Benguela
Morro de Môco
Kuito
Huambo
Menongue
Lubango
Namibe
ZAMBIA
N A M I B I A

Angola

Map Reference Pages 308–309

Angola is an African paradox. Although rich in natural resources and pristine beauty, much of its past has been a nightmare—most recently because of civil war, earlier because of slavery and forced labor. Twenty-seven years of civil war ended in 2002.

Physical Geography

The name Angola comes from Ngola, a local word for a traditional ruler. On the southwest coast of Africa, facing the Atlantic, Angola shares borders with Democratic Republic of Congo, Republic of the Congo, Namibia, and Zambia. Cabinda province is set apart from the rest of the country by a narrow corridor, formed by a fraction of Democratic Republic of Congo and the Congo River.

Angola's narrow coastal plain rises sharply to a vast plateau that covers nearly two-thirds of the country. The plateau tapers away into tropical lowland forests in the north, barren rocky desert in the south, and grasslands in the east. The most important rivers are the Cuanza and Cunene—which are transport routes to the interior—and the Kwango. Climate in the south and along the coast to Luanda is semiarid, while the north has a rainy season from November to April and a cool dry season from May to October.

MILESTONE EVENTS

600–700 ce Bantu people arrive from the north

1483 Portuguese arrive at the Kongo Kingdom

1622 Portuguese attack Kongo Kingdom

1665 Kongo Kingdom disintegrates into smaller pieces after Portuguese victory

1671 Ndongo Kingdom defeated by Portugal

1961 Angolan guerrilla warfare against Portugal begins, forced labor ends

1974 Portugal's government falls in a military coup

November 11, 1975 Angola becomes independent, civil war begins

1992 Constitution promulgated

2002 Luena Memorandum of Understanding provides for a ceasefire to end civil war

2006 Memorandum of Understanding for Peace and Reconciliation in Cabinda

History

The Stone Age people who once roamed the area were replaced in the seventh century by Bantu peoples from the north, who worked with metal and by the end of the fourteenth century had established the Kingdom of Kongo.

The Portuguese landed in 1483 near the present northern border, and traded with Kongo. In 1506, the Kingdom's new ruler took the Christian name Afonso when he assumed the throne. By the nineteenth century the Portuguese colony of Angola was the world's leading source of slaves. A forced labor system on Portuguese-owned plantations followed slavery and lasted until 1961.

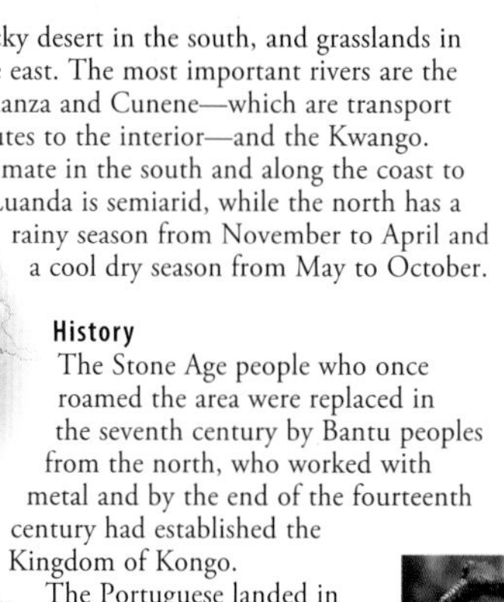

Left This girl is adorned in a traditional Mwila manner—the hair smeared with oil, and molded with mud and cow dung, the forehead shaved to make an even hairline, and the head and neck encircled with ropes of colored beads and shells.

Resistance to Portuguese rule became armed guerilla warfare in 1961. The resistance movement was led by three separate groups, each with powerful outside supporters.

When Portugal's government fell to a military coup in 1974, Angola soon declared independence, in 1975. Many divisions still existed, however, and two competing governments were established. The extended civil war resulted from these divisions.

In 2002 the Luena Memorandum of Understanding initiated a lasting ceasefire. The Memorandum of Understanding for Peace and Reconciliation in Cabinda was signed in 2006, but low-level fighting continues in that region. Over 1.5 million people died in the war and another 4 million were displaced. Many lasting effects of the war remain, with a crushed national infrastructure, a countryside littered with millions of land mines, and a scarred population, many of them amputees from land-mine explosions.

Population/Culture

Population data reflects some of the problems: The life expectancy at birth is only 37.92 years, the second worst in the world. The infant mortality rate is a horrific 182 out of 1,000 births, and the average woman has 6.2 children in her lifetime. Malaria, typhoid fever, hepatitis A, and sleeping sickness, along with many other diseases, are rife.

The primary ethnic groups are the Ovimbundu, Kimbundu, and Bakongo. Portuguese has been retained as the official language as Angola has over 90 ethnic groups. However, Bantu languages are commonly spoken by more than 90 percent of the population.

The Portuguese colonists left Christianity as one of their legacies. Today many Angolans mix Catholic or Protestant practices with traditional indigenous beliefs.

Administration/Government

Angola's embryonic and fragile government is a republic headed by a multiparty presidency created by the 1992 constitution. Legislative elections to the 220-member National Assembly were held in September 2008. Presidential elections are planned for 2009.

Economy/Industry

Angola's economic recovery since the war has been extraordinary, moving from disaster to the second fastest growing economy in Africa, almost entirely driven by the expanding oil industry. Oil contributes about 85 percent of GDP. Yet 85 percent of the people labor in subsistence farming and 70 percent of the population falls below the poverty line, with unemployment and underunemployment affecting more than half of the population. Reduced corruption and increased government transparency could lead to the development of other natural resources, including diamonds, iron, bauxite, uranium, and gold.

With continuing stability, adventure tourism will be possible, for Angola boasts Africa's second largest waterfall, the Kalandula Falls in Malanje province, a truly spectacular sight.

ANGOLA

Official name Republic of Angola (República de Angola)

Area 481,354 square miles (1,246,700 km²)

Border countries Republic of the Congo, Democratic Republic of Congo, Zambia, Namibia

Capital Luanda

Highest point Morro de Môco (Mt Moco) 8,596 feet (2,620 m)

Climate Semiarid in south and along coast to Luanda; north has cool, dry season and hot, rainy season

Population 12,531,000

Languages Official: Portuguese; other: Bantu and other African languages

Ethnicity Ovimbundu 37%, Kimbundu 25%, Bakongo 13%, Mestiço (mixed European and native African descent) 2%, European 1%, other ethnic groups 22%

Religion Christian 53% (Roman Catholic 38%, Protestant 15%), indigenous beliefs 47%

Government Republic; multiparty presidential regime

Currency Kwanza

Human Development Index 0.446 (ranked 162nd out of 177 countries)

Below Of the numerous waterfalls found in Angola, the Kalandula Falls (formerly the Duque de Bragança Falls) are perhaps the most impressive. Located on the Lucala River in Malanje Province, they are an estimated 344 feet (105 m) high.

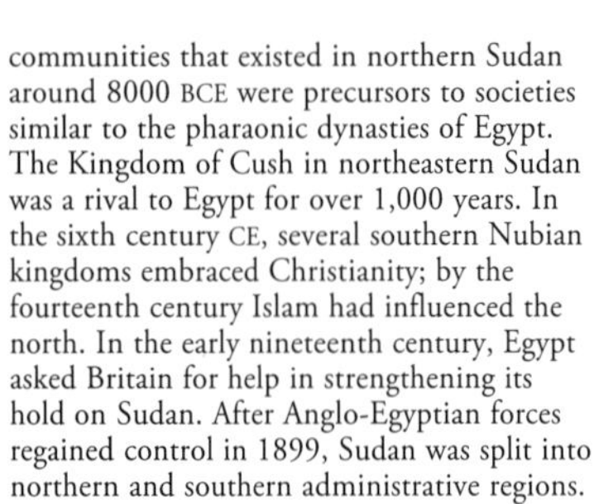

Right Khatmiyah Mosque at Kassala, northeastern Sudan, is a place of worship for Sufi pilgrims. A military post for various foreign forces in the past, Kassala—with its spectacular backdrop of the Tara Mountains—is now a railroad hub and trade center famous for its fruit gardens.

EGYPT
LIBYA
Red Sea
Wadi Halfa'
Bûr Sûdân (Port Sudan)
Dongola
Ed Damer
Atbara
CHAD
Omdurman
Khartoum North
AL KHARTŪM (KHARTOUM)
ERITREA
Kassala
Wad Medani
Gedaref
SUDAN
Al Fāshir
Al Ubayyiḍ
Nyala
Ad Damazin
ETHIOPIA
Kadugli
Malakāl
Warab
Wāw
Rumbek
CENTRAL AFRICAN REPUBLIC
Juba
Kinyeti
KENYA
UGANDA
DEMOCRATIC REPUBLIC OF THE CONGO

SUDAN

Official name Republic of the Sudan (Jumhuriyyat as-Sudan)
Area 967,499 square miles (2,505,810 km²)
Border countries Egypt, Eritrea, Ethiopia, Kenya, Uganda, Democratic Republic of the Congo, Central African Republic, Chad, Libya
Capital Khartoum (Al Kharṭūm)
Highest point Mt Kinyeti 10,456 feet (3,187 m)
Climate Tropical in south, desert in north
Population 40,218,000
Languages Official: Arabic; other: Nubian, Ta Bedawie, English, over 130 local languages
Ethnicity Black African tribes 52%, Arab 39%, Beja 6%, others 3%
Religion Sunni Muslim 70%, indigenous beliefs 25%, Christian 5%
Government Republic
Currency Sudanese dinar (currently replacing Sudanese pound)
Human Development Index 0.526 (ranked 147th out of 177 countries)

Sudan

Map Reference Pages 302–303

Located south of Egypt, bordering the Red Sea and spanning the eastern Sahara Desert, Sudan (from the Arabic *bilad al-sudan*, "land of the blackened") is the largest country in Africa. The Nile flows north through the country and has sustained human settlement for thousands of years. The Arab-influenced Muslim north and the African-dominated, animist and Christian south have fought sporadic civil war for most of the last 50 years.

Physical Geography

The capital, Khartoum, lies at the confluence of the Blue and White Niles. To the north lie the sparsely populated Libyan and Nubian deserts; to the west and northeast are low-lying mountains. Here, daily temperatures frequently reach 104°F (40°C), rainfall is rare, and apart from several oases in the northwest, the fresh water supply is limited to the Nile. Along the Nile valley, human settlement is concentrated in a strip of irrigable land only 1¼ miles (2 km) wide. South of Khartoum the landscape becomes more tropical, with savanna woodlands giving way to lush rainforests in the southwest.

Below right Egyptian-influenced carvings on one of the pyramids at Meroë, on the east bank of the Nile about 125 miles (200 km) northeast of Khartoum, Sudan. Once the southern capital of the Kingdom of Cush, Meroë was the burial site for its kings between c. 300 BCE and c. 300 CE. It was also the hub of a flourishing iron industry involving trade with India and China.

History

Human settlement along the Nile dates back thousands of years. The hunting and fishing communities that existed in northern Sudan around 8000 BCE were precursors to societies similar to the pharaonic dynasties of Egypt. The Kingdom of Cush in northeastern Sudan was a rival to Egypt for over 1,000 years. In the sixth century CE, several southern Nubian kingdoms embraced Christianity; by the fourteenth century Islam had influenced the north. In the early nineteenth century, Egypt asked Britain for help in strengthening its hold on Sudan. After Anglo-Egyptian forces regained control in 1899, Sudan was split into northern and southern administrative regions.

Almost immediately after independence in 1956, Sudan was plunged into a bitter civil war as the south pushed for autonomy. A 1972 agreement to move toward southern independence was broken in 1983 when President Gaafar Nimeiri attempted to create a federal structure and imposed Sharia law. The Islamic government forces and the Christian Sudanese People's Liberation Army signed a peace treaty in 2005. Inter-ethnic violence has overtaken many parts since then, particularly in the Darfur region in the northwest.

THE SUDD

The Sudd inland delta, on the White Nile in southern Sudan, is one of the largest wetlands in the world, with impenetrable papyrus, reed swamps, and marshland stretching over 125 miles (200 km) from east to west and 310 miles (500 km) from north to south between Mongalla and Malakal. A complex of huge significance to the hydrology of the Nile Basin, the wetland acts as a giant sponge that regulates the flow of water downstream and ensures the constant and reliable provision of water resources to Khartoum and beyond. It is also a major source of water for domestic livestock, and its annual flooding ensures the regeneration of surrounding grasslands that help sustain the livelihoods of the pastoralist Dinka, Nuer, and Shilluk peoples. During the dry season, these communities leave the highland areas and bring their cattle to the edges of the swamp to graze.

In 2006 the Sudd was designated a Wetland of International Importance by the Ramsar Convention due to its hydrological, socioeconomic, and ecological importance. Rich in biodiversity, and with a range of different ecosystems, the area is a wintering ground for rare bird species, and home to endemic fish, birds, mammals, and plants. It faces numerous threats, however. Plans were drawn up in the 1950s to build a canal bypassing the Sudd to reduce water loss (via evapotranspiration) from the Nile Basin. Work began in 1978 but was brought to a halt by the civil war in 1984. Environmentalists argue that completion of the canal would result in severe land degradation and loss of habitat, with catastrophic implications for local people, biodiversity, and water security in the Nile Basin.

MILESTONE EVENTS

750 BCE Cushite kingdom invades Egypt
590 BCE Egypt attacks Cushite kingdom, which is displaced to Meroë
500–600 CE Three dominant Nubian kingdoms in the north: Nobatia, Muqurra, Alawa
540 Christianity brought to Sudan
1315 First Muslim Nubian king
1820 Egyptian ruler Muhammad Ali Pasha invades Sudan
1881 Revolt against the Turco-Egyptian administration
1898 Battle of Omdurman, in which General Kitchener defeats the army of Abdullah al-Taashi
1899–1955 Sudan comes under joint British–Egyptian rule
January 1, 1956 Sudan becomes independent
1962 Start of civil war in the south
1972 South becomes a self-governing region after the Addis Ababa peace agreement
1978 Oil discovered in Bentiu in southern Sudan
1983 Outbreak of civil war in the south in opposition to the government's planned federalism
1983 President Numayri declares introduction of Sharia (Islamic law)
1985 President Numayri deposed and replaced by Transitional Military Council
1986 Formation of coalition government following general elections
1989 National Salvation Revolution takes over in military coup
1993 Omar al-Bashir appointed president
1998 US launches missile attack on a pharmaceutical plant in Khartoum; alleges it was making materials for chemical weapons
1998 New constitution endorsed by over 96% of voters in referendum
1999 President Bashir declares a state of emergency
1999 Sudan begins to export oil
2000 Bashir re-elected for another five years in elections boycotted by the main opposition parties
2001 UN lifts sanctions against Sudan
2002 Government accepts right of south to seek self-determination after six-year interim period
2003 Rebels in western Darfur rise up against the government
2004 Army and Arab militias pursue rebels in western Darfur and hundreds of thousands of refugees flee to neighboring Chad
2005 The government and southern rebels sign a peace agreement; former southern rebel leader John Garang is sworn in as first vice-president but killed in plane crash one month later
2007 SPLM temporarily suspends participation in national unity government

Population/Culture

The majority of the population lives along the Nile valley, and in the more tropical south, with possibly 66 percent within 200 miles (300 km) of Khartoum.

Sudan is ethnically diverse even within the northern and southern regions. The non-Arabic speaking, non-Muslim section of the population rejects attempts to impose Islamic Sharia law on the whole country. Many southern peoples uphold indigenous animist beliefs, and continue to practice rituals ranging from animal sacrifice to body scarification.

Administration/Government

A Government of National Unity was formed in 2005. President Omar Hassan Ahmad al-Bashir is the current head of government. Parliament consists of a 50-seat Council of States and a 450-seat National Assembly. Al-Bashir's National Congress Party dominates both the executive and legislative branches of government. Elections are scheduled for 2009.

Economy/Industry

Eighty percent of the workforce is employed in agricultural production, but Sudan has vast oil reserves, and has been exporting oil since 1999. This has had a positive impact on GDP, which is one of the highest in Africa. State farms in central Sudan produce cotton for export; livestock, peanuts, and sugar are exported in smaller quantities. Despite this active economy, most of the population still lives in poverty.

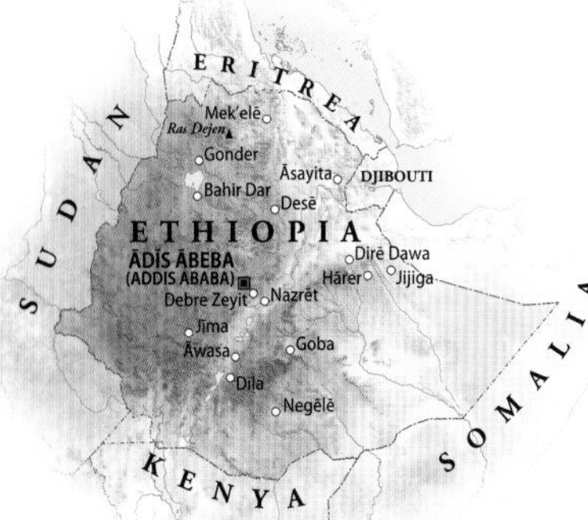
ERITREA
Mek'elē
Ras Dejen
Gonder
Bahir Dar
Āsayita
DJIBOUTI
Desē
ETHIOPIA
ĀDĪS ĀBEBA
(ADDIS ABABA)
Dirē Dawa
Hārer
Jijiga
Debre Zeyit
Nazrēt
Jīma
Āwasa
Goba
Dīla
Negēlē
SUDAN
SOMALIA
KENYA

Ethiopia

Map Reference Pages 306–307

Ethiopia is one of the oldest nations in the world. Its dynastic history is traditionally believed to have begun with the reign of Emperor Menelik I in 1000 BCE.

Physical Geography

Landlocked Ethiopia's landscape ranges from lowland desert in the Denakil (Afar) Depression, to dissected highland plateaus divided by the Great Rift Valley, and some of the highest mountains in Africa—the Semien Mountains, home to a number of rare species, including the Ethiopian wolf (or Semien fox), Gelada baboon, and Walia ibex.

Climate varies geographically, but most highland areas experience intermittent rains in February and March, with the main rainy season lasting from June to September. In recent years the rains have become far less predictable, causing major food security problems. Because the central highland plateau receives an annual average of 60 inches (150 cm), Ethiopia has been described as the "water tower of Africa." Lake Tana in these highlands is the source of the Blue Nile, which contributes about 70 to 80 percent of the flow of the Nile at Khartoum.

History

Some of the earliest remains of human ancestors have been found in Ethiopia, most famously the skeleton of Lucy, discovered in the Afar desert in 1974, and estimated to be some 3.18 million years old. The earliest civilizations were the kingdoms of D'mt (800–500 BCE) and Axum (100–700 CE). The latter left through the conversion of the country to Christianity. A series of small Christian states claiming lineage from the Axumite kings persisted to the modern era despite the rise of Islam in the seventh century.

By the sixteenth century there were frequent incursions by Oromo peoples from the south. Only in the nineteenth century, during the reign of Emperor Menelik II, did re-unification and expansion westward and southward begin, forging the modern Ethiopian state.

In the first half of the twentieth century, under Emperor Haile Selassie, Ethiopia abolished slavery and joined the League of Nations. Despite his presence on the world stage, his popularity waned due to the lack of development. In 1974 a military coup led by Mengistu Haile Mariam installed a socialist junta known as the Derg, but the killing of hundreds of thousands of people, forced deportations, deliberate starvation, and failure once again to address development issues, resulted in the junta's overthrow in 1991 by the Ethiopian People's Revolutionary Democratic Front (EPRDF). Eritrean independence was granted in 1993 and Ethiopia's first multiparty elections were held in 1995.

Population/Culture

The population has grown rapidly of late, more than doubling since 1983. The rate of HIV/AIDS infection is high, at about 4.4 percent.

Ethiopian culture reflects the diversity of its more than 80 ethnic groups and the historical influence of Islam and Christianity. Ethnic diversity is evident in food preferences, the design of traditional houses, and clothing. Common cultural elements include the strong emphasis placed on kinship ties and the deep respect for elders.

The traditional food of the highlands is a flat pancake-like bread known as injera, which is used as a base on which spicy stews or wat, of vegetables or meat, are served; strips of injera are torn off and used as scoops for the wat. Cutlery is not used.

The Orthodox Christian festival of Timkat (Epiphany) in January is one of the most colorful displays of Ethiopian culture. On the eve of the festival priests remove a symbolic Ark of the Covenant from their church and proceed to a public area where water is blessed for the following day's ceremony. In Addis Ababa, the event regularly attracts thousands of colorfully dressed people.

Administration/Government

The current constitution was adopted in 1994 with the election of 547 members of the House of People's Representatives following in 1995. Meles Zenawi, leader of the EPRDF, was elected as prime minister and head of government. The president, currently Girma Wolde-Giyorgis, is the ceremonial head of state. The House of Federation has 108 representative members. The judicial system is independent from government.

Economy/Industry

Ethiopia is one of the poorest countries in the world; in 2007 it had a per capita GDP of US$1,055. Most of the population is engaged in subsistence agriculture (cereals, pulses, vegetables, and fruit); agriculture, dominated by coffee, accounts for 60 percent of all exports.

Other exports include livestock, leather products, and, recently, the psychoactive plant qat, which produces feelings of euphoria, to Djibouti and Somalia, where it is also legal.

MILESTONE EVENTS

3.18 million years BCE Hominid remains laid down as fossils in Afar region

1000 CE Ethiopian dynastic history begins with reign of Emperor Menelik I

200 CE Christian Axum Kingdom established

600s Axum's power declines as Muslim traders stop its foreign trade

1137 Christian Zagwé dynasty rises to power; 11 magnificent churches carved out of solid rock at Lalibela

1270 Yekuno Amlak overthrows Zagwé dynasty

1500s Ethiopian Empire breaks up into smaller kingdoms

1855 Emperor Tewodros II reunifies Ethiopian Empire

1889 Menelik II becomes emperor; begins process of modernization

1896 Menelik's troops defeat occupying Italian forces at Battle of Adwa

1913 Menelik's grandson, Lij Iyasu, ascends the throne

1916 Menelik's daughter Zauditu becomes empress after unpopular Lij Iyasu removed from throne; she rules with Ras Tafari, who is named heir to throne

1930 Ras Tafari, taking the name Haile Selassie I, becomes emperor after Zauditu's death; continues modernization

1936 Italy invades, conquers Addis Ababa; Haile Selassie goes into exile in Britain

1941 British troops help drive out Italian forces; Haile Selassie returns

1942 Haile Selassie outlaws slavery

1952 Ethiopia regains control of Eritrea, held by Italy since the 1880s

1961 Eritrean nationalists demand independence

1972–73 Severe drought in northeast; critics claim government ignores the victims

1974 Haile Selassie deposed by pro-Soviet Marxist–Leninist military junta, the Derg, led by Mengistu Haile Mariam; one-party communist state established

1978 Ethiopia defeats Somalia in Ogaden War

1987 New constitution provides for return to civilian government

May 24, 1993 Eritrea gains independence from Ethiopia

1995 First multiparty elections held in Ethiopia

2006 Mengistu found guilty of genocide

Above Priest holding a Merkorios cross at Lalibela, in northern Ethiopia. Lalibela, a holy city, is a center of pilgrimage for much of the country.

ETHIOPIA

Official name Federal Democratic Republic of Ethiopia (Ityop'iya Federalawi Demokrasiyawi Ripeblik)

Area 435,184 square miles (1,127,127 km^2)

Border countries Eritrea, Djibouti, Somalia, Kenya, Sudan

Capital Addis Ababa (Ādīs Ābeba)

Highest & lowest points Ras Dashen ("Head Guard") 15,154 feet (4,620 m); Denakil Depression –410 feet (–125 m)

Population 78,254,000

Languages Official: Amharic; other: Orominya, Tigrinya, Somaligna, Guragigna, Sidamigna, Hadiyigna, plus approximately 70 others including English (which is taught in schools)

Ethnicity Oromo 32.1%, Amhara 30.1%, Tigrayan 6.2%, Somali 5.9%, Gurage 4.3%, Sidama 3.5%, Welaita 2.4%, other 15.5%

Religion Christian 60.8% (Orthodox 50.6%, Protestant 10.2%), Muslim 32.8%, traditional 4.6%, other 1.8%

Government Federal parliamentary republic

Currency Birr

Human Development Index 0.406 (ranked 169th out of 177 countries)

Below Denakil Depression, Ethiopia. As the sides of the Great African Rift Valley move farther apart, a "Y" has formed in northern Ethiopia, its arms encompassing the Denakil Desert. The lowest part of this desert is the Denakil Depression.

DJIBOUTI

Official name Republic of Djibouti (République de Djibouti/Jumhuriyat Jibuti)
Area 8,960 square miles (23,201 km²)
Border countries Eritrea, Somalia, Ethiopia
Capital Djibouti
Highest & lowest points Moussa Ali 6,652 feet (2,028 m); Lake Assal −502 feet (−153 m)
Climate Semiarid; desert; torrid, dry
Population 506,221
Languages Official: French; other: Arabic, Somali, Afar
Ethnicity Somali (Issa, Isaaq, and Gadabursi) 60%, Afar 35%, other 5% (includes French, Arab, Ethiopian, and Italian)
Religion Muslim 94%, Christian 6%
Government Republic
Currency Djiboutian franc
Human Development Index 0.516 (ranked 149th out of 177 countries)

ERITREA

Official name State of Eritrea (Hagere Ertra)
Area 46,842 square miles (121,320 km²)
Border countries Djibouti, Ethiopia, Sudan
Capital Asmara
Highest & lowest points Soira 9,900 feet (3,018 m); near Kulul, within the Denakil (Afar) Depression, −246 feet (−75 m)
Climate Temperate in highlands; semiarid in western hills and lowlands; desert strip along Red Sea coast
Population 5,028,000
Languages Tigrinya and Arabic ("working languages"), Afar, Tigre and Kunama, other Cushitic languages, English
Ethnicity Tigrinya 50%, Tigre and Kunama 40%, Afar 4%, Saho (Red Sea coast dwellers) 3%, other 3%
Religion Muslim 45%, Christian (Coptic Orthodox, Roman Catholic, Protestant) 45%, other (includes indigenous beliefs) 10%
Government Transitional government
Currency Nakfa
Human Development Index 0.483 (ranked 157th out of 177 countries)

ERITREA
ETHIOPIA
Moussa 'Ali
Moulhoulé
Khôr 'Angar
Dadda'to
Gulf of Aden
Dorra
Balho
Obock
Randa
Tadjoura
DJIBOUTI
Golfe de Tadjoura
DJIBOUTI
Yoboki
'Arta
Holhol
Dikhil
'Ali Sabieh
'As 'Ela
SOMALIA
ETHIOPIA

Djibouti

Map Reference Pages 302–303

Djibouti is a small country in the Horn of Africa. Its eastern coastline overlooks the Red Sea and the Gulf of Aden. Despite its small size, its location at the crossroads of Africa and the Middle East have made it strategically important.

Physical Geography

Much of Djibouti is volcanic plateau and stony desert, with mountain ranges inland. In the east is the arid, saline Denakil (Afar) Depression, at −502 feet (−153 m) the lowest point in Africa. Djibouti has one of the hottest and driest climates in the world, with average annual temperatures exceeding 90°F (32°C). Vegetation is mostly acacia scrub with patches of perennial forest in the north.

History

Djibouti has been home to nomadic Afar and Issas pastoralists for centuries. In 1862 local leaders in the region signed a treaty with the French that led to the creation of French Somaliland. In the early twentieth century the colonial government funded the construction of roads, administrative outposts, and a railway linking the city of Djibouti with Addis Ababa in Ethiopia.

Spurred by the independence of Somalia in 1960, anti-colonial demonstrations continued up to the 1970s. In 1976 a referendum was held in which 85 percent of the population voted for independence. This was granted in 1977. Ethnic tensions, along with accusations of discrimination,resulted in an armed uprising by the Afar in 1991, although a peace accord was signed in 1994. Despite its colonial legacy, Djibouti maintains close links with France and more recently the United States.

Population/Culture

The majority of the population lives in the city of Djibouti, where a small but significant expatriate population includes Ethiopians, French, and Yemenis. Most of the rest of the population are nomadic herders.

The culture of the two dominant ethnic groups, the Somali Issas and the Afar, reflects their historical nomadic pastoralist roots. A key cultural feature is the consumption of the mild narcotic qat. The Issas and Afar were among the first peoples in Africa to convert to Islam. French and Islamic influences are seen in the architecture, which includes decorative plasterwork and Islamic calligraphy.

Administration/Government

Djibouti is a presidential republic currently headed by Ismail Omar Guelleh. The president is elected by direct universal suffrage for a six-year term, renewable only once. The legislative arm of government consists of a 65-member Chamber of Deputies, universally elected for five-year terms.

Economy/Industry

The economy is dominated by service industries associated with the country's strategic location and its status as a free trade zone. The city of Djibouti serves as a regional port and international refueling and transshipment center. Imports and exports, particularly from landlocked Ethiopia, make up 85 percent of the container terminal's activity. The lack of rainfall restricts agriculture, and the country depends on food imports and foreign aid.

QAT CHEWING

Qat is the common name for the small evergreen shrub *Catha edulis*, which is believed to be native to either Ethiopia or Yemen, but is now cultivated extensively throughout East Africa. The chewing of the leaves, which induces feelings of elation and euphoria, is a significant social activity in Djibouti society. A qat chewing session typically involves the assembly of a small group of men, usually in the afternoon, who chew the leaves while discussing a topical issue or world event. A session may last between two to four hours. Qat chewing is also common among laborers and drivers, who use it to help maintain energy levels and concentration.

The increasing popularity of qat has led to a significant rise in demand; hence the more extensive cultivation of the shrub throughout the region. Qat is also imported from Ethiopia. Cultivation of the shrub has had economic benefits for those employed in its transport and distribution, and also for the many small-scale producers now moving away from traditional crop production to the more lucrative crop, which can be cultivated year round. However, recent studies have highlighted a range of negatives associated with the demand for qat. The shrub itself is highly demanding of water, and in many regions irrigation is required for its successful cultivation. In East Africa and Yemen, its production has implications for regional water security. Studies have also highlighted the social costs of qat production; those involved with its cultivation and sale are more likely to be users, or at worst, addicts. The conversion of agricultural land for qat production has also raised concerns regarding food security, especially in areas vulnerable to drought and famine.

SUDAN
Mersa Tehlay
Red Sea
Nakfa
Kerkebet
Mersa Gulbub
Dahlak Archipelago
ERITREA
Akordat
Keren
Massawa
Teseney
Barentu
ASMARA
Mendefera
Adi Keyih
Soyra
Koluli
Omhajer
Ed
ETHIOPIA
Assab
DJIBOUTI

Eritrea

Map Reference Pages 302–303

Eritrea faces many problems, including a border conflict with Ethiopia, food shortages, and an economy struggling due to the need to support a huge military effort. Most Eritreans depend on food aid, and serve in the army rather than the workforce.

Physical Geography

Mountainous for the most part, Eritrea has a high central plateau bisected by the Great Rift Valley, with a narrow coastal plain, lowlands in the west, and some 350 islands, mostly in the Dahlak Archipelago. To the south lies the Denakil (Afar) Depression, which also extends into parts of Ethiopia and Djibouti.

The climate is extremely hot and dry, but altitude moderates temperatures in some areas. The meager rains occur between February and April and again between late June and mid-September. Eritrea has no year-round rivers.

History

Eritrea was the site of ancient Egyptian expeditions to the fabled land of Punt, the most famous that sent by Hatshepsut, which brought back myrrh trees for her funerary temple. Before Italian colonization in 1885, a series of local and international powers dominated the region. After Italy's surrender in World War II, Eritrea was placed under British military administration. In 1952, a United Nations resolution federated Eritrea with Ethiopia, ignoring Eritrean pleas for independence. Defeating Ethiopian forces after a 30-year struggle, Eritrea became independent in 1993. The border remains hotly contested, and a security zone, patrolled by UN forces, separates the two countries.

Population/Culture

Eritrea's major ethnic groups are the Tigrinya, who comprise half the population, and the Tigre and Kunama, who together comprise

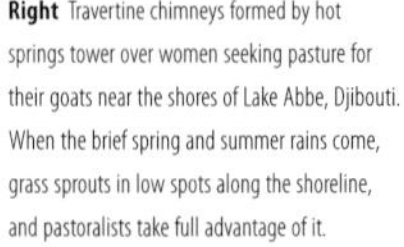
Right Travertine chimneys formed by hot springs tower over women seeking pasture for their goats near the shores of Lake Abbe, Djibouti. When the brief spring and summer rains come, grass sprouts in low spots along the shoreline, and pastoralists take full advantage of it.

Far right Rashaida women dance at a wedding, Eritrea. The Rashaida, who came to Eritrea in the nineteenth century from the Arabian Coast, are a relatively recent addition to the nation's ethnic mix. Typically nomadic, they seldom intermarry and comprise less than 1% of the population.

40 percent. Tigrinya and Arabic are used in official government business, and English is the language of instruction beyond fifth grade. Most Eritreans are Muslim, Coptic Orthodox Christian, Catholic, or Protestant.

Italian architecture dominates Asmara, reflecting the nation's Italian heritage. Other cities, including Agordet, display Turkish and Egyptian styles. Traditional handicrafts and art forms include woodcarvings, pottery, basketry and textiles, leather goods, and silver and gold jewelry.

Administration/Government

The long war of independence left Eritrea's government facing formidable challenges. For security reasons, the government strictly controls political, social, and economic systems; there are almost no civil liberties. A new constitution, ratified in 1997, has not been implemented, and National Assembly elections that were due to take place in December 2001 remain postponed.

The present government structure includes legislative, executive, and judicial bodies. The Transitional National Assembly is the highest power until the establishment of a democratic constitutional government. The president nominates individuals to head the various ministries, authorities, and offices.

Economy/Industry

Rain-fed agriculture employs 80 percent of the population, but erratic rainfall and prolonged drought have lowered productivity. Conflict compounds the economic crisis: When Ethiopia occupied territory in the agriculturally important west and south of Eritrea in 2007, livestock worth some $225 million, together with 55,000 homes, were destroyed. Public buildings, including hospitals, were also damaged. Extremely high levels of spending on defense have inflated the national debt.

DJIBOUTI
Gulf of Aden
Boosaaso
Shimbiris
Ceerigaabo
Berbera
Hargeysa
Burco
Garoowe
ETHIOPIA
SOMALIA
Gaalkacyo
Dhuusamarreeb
Beledweyne
Xuddur
Garbahaarrey
Baydhabo
Jawhar
MUQDISHO
(MOGADISHU)
Marka
KENYA
Jilib
Kismaayo
INDIAN OCEAN

Somalia

Map Reference Pages 306–307

Somalia, on the outer edge of the Horn of Africa, is bordered by Djibouti to the north, Kenya to the south and Ethiopia to the west. Its coastline is the longest in Africa, at 1,891 miles (3,025 km). Civil war together with inter-clan rivalry over the last two decades has decimated the country.

Physical Geography

Somalia is dominated by low undulating topography. Thorny scrubland and open savanna occupy most of the country, with a mountain range rising behind the narrow coastal plain in the north. The average annual rainfall is around 12 inches (300 mm). Across the country, temperatures can be in excess of 104°F (40°C), although December–February northeast monsoon winds bring cooler temperatures. Agriculture is restricted to areas of higher rainfall in the southwest and northwest, and nomadic and semi-nomadic grazing dominates the rest of the country.

History

Modern-day Somalia has been inhabited by Cushitic and Somali ethnic groups for at least 2,000 years. The arrival of the British, French, and Italians led to the formation of British Somaliland to the north, Italian Somaliland to the south and east, and French Somaliland in modern-day Djibouti. Unification and independence occurred in June 1960; nine years later a socialist government headed by Mohammed Siad Barre came to power. A war with Ethiopia over the disputed Ogaden region in 1977–78 ended in defeat for Somalia.

Opposition to Barre led to his ousting in 1991, resulting in anarchy. Somaliland in the north declared independence also in 1991, but this has not been recognized by the international community. Since 2000 civil war has continued, and in 2007 Ethiopian forces invaded Somalia to remove the influential Islamic Courts Union and restore the authority of the Transitional Federal Government (TFG).

Population/Culture

Due to widespread instability, there are few reliable statistics on Somalia's population, although the US Census Bureau estimates the 2008 mid-year figure at about 9,559,000. Nomads and semi-pastoralists make up a large portion of the population, although urbanization is increasing. Millions have emigrated to escape from the war.

The majority of Somalis belong to a single ethnic group, which is made up of six major clans—the Daarood, Isaaq, Hawiye, Dir, Digil, and Rahanwayn. The Isaaq and Daarood are traditionally pastoralists, the Hawiye and Rahanwayn, who live mostly in the south, engage in peasant farming.

Administration/Government

Somalia lacks a functioning government although the Transitional Federal Government was set up in 2004 under President Abdullahi Yusuf Ahmed and Prime Minister Nur Hassan Hussein. It controls only parts of southern Somalia. Customary and Islamic law form the basis of the judiciary.

Economy/Industry

There is no functioning formal economy in Somalia; most economic activities are undertaken by entrepreneurs, often with the aid of overseas financing. Agriculture is the single largest national contributor to GDP, with livestock, fish, charcoal, and bananas constituting the main exports. The small industrial sector, based on the processing of agricultural products, has largely been looted for scrap metal.

Left Eritrea is traversed by the Great Rift Valley, which began forming some 30 to 40 million years ago due to movements in Earth's tectonic plates. The highlands in the south of the country are slightly drier and cooler than other parts.

Below Somali women wait in line for food in Mogadishu. Inflation and civil war have made food increasingly difficult to come by, and relief agencies have been warning of an impending humanitarian catastrophe.

SOMALIA ★

Official name Somalia (Jamhuuriyada Demuqraadiga Soomaaliyeed)
Area 246,201 square miles (637,657 km²)
Border countries Djibouti, Kenya, Ethiopia
Capital Mogadishu (Muqdisho)
Highest point Mt Shimbiris 7,927 feet (2,416 m)
Climate Mainly desert
Population 9,559,000
Languages Official: Somali; other: Arabic, English, Italian, minority languages
Ethnicity Somali 85%, Bantu and other non-Somali 15%
Religion Sunni Muslim
Government Transitional government
Currency Somali shilling
Human Development Index Not available

Below Located in the coastal Benadir region of Somalia on the Indian Ocean, Mogadishu has served for centuries as an important regional port. Though civil unrest and insurgencies have made it one of the most dangerous and lawless cities in the world, international traders can benefit from its de facto duty-free status.

UGANDA

Official name Republic of Uganda
Land area 77,108 square miles (199,710 km²)
Border countries Sudan, Kenya, Tanzania, Rwanda, Democratic Republic of Congo
Capital Kampala
Highest & lowest points Margherita Peak on Mt Stanley 16,762 feet (5,109 m); Lake Albert 2,037 feet (621 m)
Climate Tropical, semiarid to northeast
Population 31,368,000
Language(s) Official: English and Swahili; other: Ganda or Luganda, other Niger-Congo languages, Nilo-Saharan languages, Arabic
Ethnicity Baganda 16.9%, Banyakole 9.5%, Basoga 8.4%, Bakiga 6.9%, Iteso 6.4%, Langi 6.1%, Acholi 4.7%, Bagisu 4.6%, Lugbara 4.2%, Bunyoro 2.7%, other 29.6%
Religion Christian 83.9%, Muslim 12.1%, other 3.1%, none 0.9%
Government Republic
Currency Ugandan shilling
Human Development Index 0.505 (ranked 154th out of 177 countries)

SUDAN
KENYA
UGANDA
TANZANIA
RWANDA
DEMOCRATIC REPUBLIC OF CONGO
Moyo
Kitgum
Arua
Kotido
Gulu
Nakapiripirit
Masindi
Soroti
Mbale
Luwero
Tororo
Bundibugyo
Margherita Peak
Kasese
KAMPALA
Jinja
Masaka
Bushenyi
Kabale

Uganda

Map Reference Pages 306–307

Uganda is a landlocked East African nation on the equator. It shares borders with Sudan, Kenya, Tanzania, Rwanda, and Democratic Republic of Congo. The country is a land of large lakes, several of which are located on the country's borders, including the freshwater Lake Victoria in the southeast.

Physical Geography

Much of Uganda lies on a plateau that rises some 4,300 feet (1,311 m) in the south and descends in the north to an elevation of 2,460 feet (750 m). Margherita Peak, Mt Stanley is the third highest peak in Africa. Forests prevail in the south, although many have been cleared for farming. Grasslands dominate the country's north.

Lake Victoria is the primary source of the River Nile, and the largest tropical lake in the world. Half of the lake is in Ugandan territory. It has more than 3,000 islands; its immense size moderates the country's climate in the southeast. Overall, Uganda's climate is mostly tropical except in the northeast, which is semiarid.

Right Uganda's wetland regions are home to the shoebill stork *(Balaeniceps rex)*, a protected species in a number of countries in its distribution range. This unusual bird is named for its shoe-shaped beak.

History

Bantu-speaking peoples began arriving from central and western Africa about 1,500 years ago. Several highly organized kingdoms arose during the middle of the second millennium, including the Kitara, Buganda, and Ankole. In 1830 a disgruntled royal son formed the Kingdom of Toro north of Lake Victoria.

Outsiders had scant interest in Uganda until Arab traders from Zanzibar arrived in 1844. The British East Africa Company ruled the area as a protectorate from 1888. In 1894, the British Crown consolidated kingdoms in the region and ruled directly.

The British introduced cotton and coffee, still important today. Ugandan nationalists became active after World War II and were allowed some democratic local governance. The formation of the Ugandan National Congress in 1952 led to independence in 1962.

The early years of independence were marked by struggles between the old kingdoms and the authority of the central government. In 1971 Idi Amin Dada overthrew Milton Obote's government. Amin's rule was murderous and an economic disaster, and he was ousted in 1979. Obote returned to govern in 1980, only to subject the populace to even more human rights' violations—estimates put the number of deaths under Obote at 100,000, and 300,000 under Amin. In 1986 Yoweri Kaguta Museveni seized power and the problem of the government's authority over the older kingdom constituencies resurfaced. Museveni has been president since then.

Below These Ugandan children have each lost a father to AIDS. Although a government education program has reduced the number of people dying from AIDS in Uganda, the disease continues to take tens of thousands of lives every year, mostly young adults who are the core of the labor force.

Population/Culture

Life expectancy is just over 52 years, with a median age of 15 years. Infant mortality and population growth rates are both high. HIV/AIDS is a major health issue, with over 4 percent of the population infected; however, the government has responded with good health and education programs. The official figure for the number of infections has been questioned; it seems likely that it is significantly higher.

Uganda is culturally diverse, with 34 different ethnic groups and many different languages. Approximately two-thirds of the people speak Bantu languages and live in the south of the country.

Traditional beliefs and practices are still important, though often fused with Christian teachings. Christianity accounts for almost 84 percent of the population; 12 percent of the inhabitants are Muslim.

Administration/Government

In the unicameral National Assembly of 332 members, 215 are elected by popular vote, while legally established interest groups nominate the remaining 105 members. The president, elected by popular vote, is head of government and chief of state. However, the constitution does not limit the number of terms the president serves. Since 2005, when diverse political parties were allowed, a plethora of parties has sprung up.

THE BUTCHER OF UGANDA

The first time some people heard about Uganda was when Idi Amin Dada became president. He seized power in 1971, overthrowing the government of Prime Minister Obote when he found out that he was about to be arrested for stealing military funds.

Born in the rural village of Koboko in 1923, Amin was a former Ugandan boxing champion who held the title from 1951 to 1960. He rose in the military and used his authority to gain power and money by smuggling arms. As president, Amin embarked on a program of murder, ethnic persecution, and political suppression. He expelled more than 70,000 Indians and Pakistanis in 1972, and 300,000 Ugandans were murdered during his rule. Among the victims were ministers, religious leaders, military leaders, ethnic groups, educated elites, and ordinary citizens.

In 1978, Amin's forces invaded Tanzania in an attempt to take the northern province of Kagera. Tanzania retaliated by uniting with dissident Ugandan forces who wanted Amin ousted. Their combined efforts were successful in 1979 when Tanzanian and rebel forces took the Ugandan capital, Kampala. Amin retreated to Libya for a decade and then sought refuge in Saudi Arabia where he died on August 16, 2003. His reign of terror gained him the nickname, "The Butcher of Uganda."

MILESTONE EVENTS

c. 500 CE Bantu-speaking peoples arrive and introduce agriculture
1844 Arab traders arrive from Zanzibar
1862 British explorers arrive seeking the source of the River Nile
1888 British East Africa Company rules the region as a protectorate
1894 British Crown directly rules the region of Uganda as a protectorate
1962 Uganda becomes independent; Milton Obote becomes prime minister
1971–1979 Dictatorship era of Idi Amin
1972 Amin expels Ugandan Indians and Pakistanis
1980 Obote regains power following the overthrow of Amin
1986 Lieutenant General Yoweri Kaguta Museveni seizes power
1995 The constitution is ratified and promulgated
1996 Museveni elected president
2001 President Museveni re-elected
2002 Rebel group Lord's Resistance Army (LRA), led by Joseph Kony, kidnaps thousands of children and displaces and attacks many civilians
2004 LRA rebels kill more than 200 displaced civilians
2005 Uganda adopts a multiparty system
2006 President Museveni re-elected, again defeating Kizza Besigye
2008 After years of conflict, government and LRA sign permanent ceasefire

Economy/Industry

Uganda's economy crashed under Idi Amin and it has struggled to recover ever since. Agriculture is the most important sector, employing 82 percent of the population. Coffee is the main export, followed by fish and fish products, tea, cotton, horticultural products, and gold. Timber and fishing are significant industries along with a rising service sector. The country has substantial natural resources, including copper, cobalt, gold, and other mineral deposits.

While communication and transportation systems are improving in Uganda, they are still somewhat inadequate; economic growth has increased recently to around 6 percent annually. Infrastructure is a major problem in many African nations because colonial powers built roads and railways that went straight to seaports on the coast, thus leaving a dearth of internal networks.

Left Lake Bunyonyi in southwestern Uganda is said to be the deepest crater lake in Africa. The Bakiga people live in the surrounding hills.

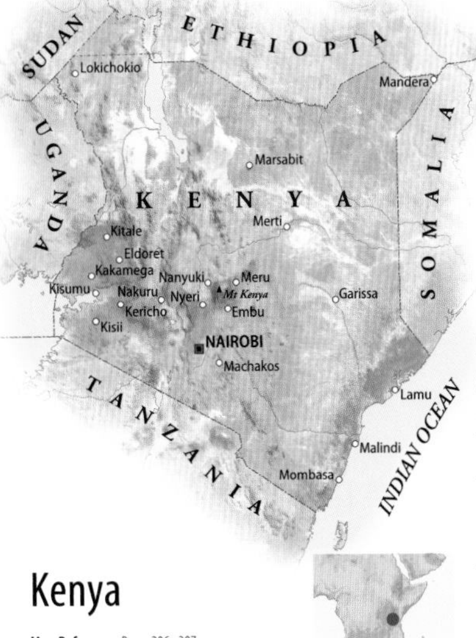

SUDAN
ETHIOPIA
UGANDA
SOMALIA
KENYA
TANZANIA
INDIAN OCEAN
Lokichokio
Mandera
Marsabit
Merti
Kitale
Eldoret
Kakamega
Nanyuki
Meru
Kisumu
Nakuru
Nyeri
Mt Kenya
Garissa
Kericho
Embu
Kisii
NAIROBI
Machakos
Lamu
Malindi
Mombasa

Kenya

Map Reference Pages 306–307

Located on Africa's east coast, Kenya is bordered by Ethiopia, Somalia, Tanzania, and Uganda. It is the hub of much economic and financial activity in East Africa. Its peoples include the Kikuyu, who fought for political independence in the 1950s, and the nomadic Masai on the southern border. The country is famous for its splendid parks and wildlife.

Physical Geography

From the Indian Ocean, low plains gradually rise to the Central Highlands, a fertile plateau formed by volcanic lava flows, and dissected by the East African Rift Valley. The Western Highlands fall away toward Lake Victoria and its densely populated plains. The Eastern Highlands descend to the valleys of the Tana and Galana rivers. Mangrove swamps, small islands, and coral reefs fringe the fertile coastal belt. In the far northeast, in the vicinity of Lake Turkana, semi-desert conditions prevail.

History

Archeological finds near Lake Turkana show the presence of hominids *(Homo habilis* and *H. erectus)* around 2.5 to 1.8 million years ago. Arabs set up trading colonies along the coast around the seventh century CE. In the first millennium Bantu and Nilotic peoples, who now comprise 75 percent of the population, moved inland.

The Portuguese navigator Vasco da Gama arrived in 1498, and for 150 years the Portuguese dominated the coast. In the nineteenth century British exploration led to the establishment in 1895 of Britain's East African Protectorate. In 1920 Kenya became a British Crown colony. The pleasant highlands climate attracted English immigrants, who took the best land and displaced Kikuyu farmers. The resentment this aroused led to the bloody Mau Mau rebellion (1952–1959) and to other efforts at independence, which was eventually obtained in 1963.

Under Jomo Kenyatta, an ethnic Kikuyu and leader of the political party the Kenya African National Union (KANU), a new direction evolved. Tribal divisions and enmities have bedeviled Kenyan politics from the beginning. When the Kenya People's Union, a small party under a Luo tribe elder, showed signs of strength in the 1970s, its leader was jailed. The National Assembly declared KANU Kenya's sole political party in 1982.

In 1991, constitutional changes abolished one-party rule, which was followed by Kenya's first multiparty elections. KANU retained power, and legitimate opposition has not yet produced the hoped-for effects. Disputed returns following the December 2007 elections led to rioting, the deaths of 1,000 people, and the displacement of 600,000 others.

Population/Culture

The huge variety of Kenya's present population derives mainly from the Cushitic peoples who moved into the region from Sudan and Ethiopia; and later groups of Bantu and Nilotic origin. Major ethnic groups include the Kikuyu, Luhya, Luo, Kalenjin, Kamba, Kisii, Meru, Masai, Turkana, and Embu.

Three groups illustrate the variety of Kenya's indigenous cultures. Traditional Kikuyu live as farmers. In the past they were polygamous because many wives lightened the burden of farm work. The Masai are herders, and each man's wealth is measured in cattle and children. The Turkana are camel-keepers and live in the semi-desert in Kenya's far northwest. They spend a large part of the long dry season searching for water for their livestock and themselves.

MILESTONE EVENTS

2000 BCE Arrival of Cushitic peoples from Sudan and Ethiopia

c. 800 CE Arab and Persian traders found settlements on coast

1498 Portuguese explorer Vasco da Gama visits Mombasa

1895 British East African Protectorate established

1920 Kenya becomes a British Crown colony

1952–1959 Mau Mau rebel against white settlers; a thousand killed, mostly indigenes

1963 Kenyan independence; Jomo Kenyatta becomes first prime minister

1978 Jomo Kenyatta dies; Vice-President Daniel arap Moi succeeds him

1992 First multiparty elections held

August 1998 Bomb explodes at US embassy, killing 224 and injuring many thousands

2001 Fossils of pre-human hominids found near Lake Turkana dating as far back as 2.5 million years ago

2002 President Daniel arap Moi unseated in a landslide victory headed by Mwai Kibaki

2007 Unprecedented violence and destruction follows contested election results

April 30, 2008 Privatization of Safaricom attracts US$194 million from investors, over twice as much as the government requires; investors can expect a refund

Administration/Government

The Kenyan president is elected by popular vote and is eligible for a second term. The unicameral National Assembly consists of 224 members, 210 being elected by popular vote. The remaining 12 members are appointed by the president. Unprecedented violence followed the disputed 2007 presidential election between incumbent President Kibaki and opposition leader Raila Odinga. It was then agreed to establish a coalition government, and to create the position of prime minister.

Economy/Industry

Most Kenyans are employed in agriculture, producing tea, coffee, corn, wheat, sugarcane, fruit, and vegetables as well as dairy products, beef, pork, and poultry—the Kenyan highlands are one of the continent's most productive agricultural areas. A small industrial sector produces consumer goods, agricultural products, aluminum, steel, lead, and cement. Hydropower and wildlife are two of Kenya's most valuable resources. Imports are twice the value of the largely agricultural exports on which the country mainly depends.

About 50 percent of the population lives below the poverty line, but endemic corruption has long made aid institutions very wary of involvement in Kenya.

KENYA

Official name Republic of Kenya (Republic of Kenya/Jamhuri y Kenya)

Land area 219,789 square miles (569,250 km²)

Border countries Ethiopia, Somalia, Sudan, Tanzania, Uganda

Capital Nairobi

Highest point Mt Kenya 17,057 feet (5,199 m)

Climate Tropical along coastal regions; arid in interior

Population 37,954,000

Language(s) Official: English and Kiswahili; other: numerous indigenous languages

Ethnicity Kikuyu 22%, Luhya 14%, Luo 13%, Kalenjin 12%, Kamba 11%, Kisii 6%, Meru 6%, other African 15%, Asian/European/Arab 1%

Religion Christian 78%, Muslim 10%, indigenous beliefs 10%, other 2%

Government Republic

Currency Kenyan shilling

Human Development Index 0.521 (ranked 148th out of 177 countries)

Above This Masai woman lives in the Masai Mara National Reserve. Agricultural expansion and wildlife conservation issues have reduced the Masai's grazing land. A Masai man's wealth is measured by the numbers of cattle and children he has.

Below Looking across the Tanzanian border to Mt Kilimanjaro. Due to Kilimanjaro's near-equatorial location as well as its height, climbers begin their ascent in tropical rainforest and pass through every conceivable climate before reaching ice-covered alpine desert at the summit.

TANZANIA

Official name United Republic of Tanzania (Jamhuri ya Muungano wa Tanzania)
Land area 342,101 miles (886,037 km²)
Border countries Uganda, Kenya, Mozambique, Malawi, Zambia, Democratic Republic of Congo, Burundi, Rwanda
Capitals Dar es Salaam (executive); Dodoma (legislative)
Highest point Mt Kilimanjaro 19,000 feet (5,895 m)
Climate Tropical on the coast; temperate in the highlands
Population 40,213,000
Language(s) Kiswahili or Swahili, English, Arabic, indigenous languages
Ethnicity Mainland: Bantu (130 ethnic groups) 95%, other African 4%, Asian/European/Arab 1%; Zanzibar: Arab, African, mixed Arab and African
Religion Mainland: Christian 30%, Muslim 35%, indigenous beliefs 35%; Zanzibar: more than 99% Muslim
Government Republic
Currency Tanzanian shilling
Human Development Index 0.467 (ranked 159th out of 177 countries)

Right A young Swahili woman is framed by an ornate doorway in the historic coastal town of Bagamoyo, Tanzania. Situated north of Dar es Salaam and not far from Zanzibar, the town developed as a trading center in the 1800s; slaves and ivory both passed through the port.

UGANDA
KENYA
RWANDA
BURUNDI
Bukoba
Musoma
Mwanza
Mt Kilimanjaro
Arusha
Moshi
DEMOCRATIC REPUBLIC OF THE CONGO
Kigoma
Tabora
Singida
Kondoa
Tanga
Wete
Pemba Island
TANZANIA
DODOMA
Morogoro
Zanzibar
Zanzibar Island
DAR ES SALAAM
Sumbawanga
Iringa
Mafia Island
Mbeya
INDIAN OCEAN
ZAMBIA
Lindi
Mtwara
Songea
MALAWI
MOZAMBIQUE

Tanzania

Map Reference Pages 306–307

One of the larger African states, Tanzania includes the island of Zanzibar in the Indian Ocean in the east and stretches to Lake Tanganyika in the west. The nation shares borders with eight countries, and is world famous for the wildlife of Serengeti National Park.

Physical Geography

Rising from its Indian Ocean coastline, Tanzania largely consists of a plateau averaging about 3,300 feet (1,000 m) in elevation. To the plateau's west are the large East African Rift Valley lakes of Nyasa and Tanganyika. Africa's biggest lake, Lake Victoria, lies on the boundary with Uganda to the north. Africa's highest point, Mt Kilimanjaro, is close to the Kenyan border in the northeast.

History

The history of mankind may have begun in this region: Tanzania's Olduvai Gorge has produced some of the earliest human fossil remains. By the eighth century CE the first Arabs had arrived, and by the twelfth century traders were coming from as far away as India. Increasing German and British intervention, control, and settlement provoked an unsuccessful nationalist rebellion in 1905–07. After World War II Tanzania was a UN trust territory until 1961, when it became independent under prime minister (later president), Julius Nyerere, whose socialist government ruled from 1961 till 1985. A revered president, Nyerere was a man of integrity, who scorned the trappings of power.

Population/Culture

Tanzania's peoples are diverse, comprising over 120 ethnic groups. The predominant cultural stock is Bantu; the nomadic Masai and the Luo are of Nilotic origin. Zanzibar's population combines Africans and non-Africans, the latter mainly Arab. There are numerous specific languages, but the lingua franca is Kiswahili—a language with an African foundation augmented and strongly influenced by Arabic borrowings.

Cultural life ranges from modern academic studies to a variety of traditional and modern musical forms. The string-based indigenous musical genre of taarab is found along with a distinctive hip-hop style, bongo flava. One of the best known of Tanzania's artists was George Lilanga (1934–2005) whose paintings and *shetani* sculptures have been shown in many international exhibitions.

Administration/Government

The president is both chief of state and head of government. A unicameral National Assembly consists of 274 seats, 37 of which are allocated to women nominated by the president. The president, vice-president, and 232 National Assembly members are all elected by popular vote. Because Zanzibar is politically sensitive—Islamic dissent from mainland policies is a possible source of division—it has its own House of Representatives responsible for special legislation with 50 seats elected by universal suffrage.

Economy/Industry

Only about 4 percent of land is arable, yet agriculture generates more than 40 percent of GDP, employs 80 percent of the workforce, and provides 85 percent of exports. Cash crops include coffee, tea, sisal, and cotton; food crops include maize, wheat, and cassava. Light industry processes farm products and produces small consumer goods. Overseas donations and loans are helping to rebuild infrastructure.

Right The spectacular glacier at the top of Mt Kilimanjaro is shrinking rapidly. Ice that once thwarted climbers at its summit has shrunk by more than 80 percent and has almost completely disappeared. Current speculation is that it will be completely gone by 2015.

OLDUVAI GORGE

Tanzania's Olduvai Gorge is the source of the oldest known human remains. A 31-mile (50 km) long ravine, it is located in the eastern Serengeti Plains. A happy combination of geological events proved ideal for fossil preservation. This included lake sediments, together with quickly deposited layers of ash and lava from volcanic eruptions over several million years. These conditions preserved such astonishing relics of the past as 3.5 million-year-old hominid footprints. The footprints could have remained deeply buried and invisible, but Pleistocene faulting and subsequent erosion cut through the rock strata revealing humankind's earliest traces.

In 1960 the famous archeologists Mary Leakey and her son discovered the fossil remains of *Homo habilis* (handy human), dating from 2 million years ago. Numerous ancient cultural relics have also been found, including hand axes made from stones and bones. Excavation has also discovered 150 species of extinct mammals, as well as prehistoric birds, reptiles, amphibians, and a variety of plants. Research is ongoing, and among those inclined to historical speculation, the range of early human material found at Olduvai justifies calling the region "the cradle of humankind."

RWANDA

Official name Republic of Rwanda (Republika y'u Rwanda)
Land area 9,632 square miles (24,948 km²)
Border countries Uganda, Democratic Republic of Congo, Tanzania, Burundi
Capital Kigali
Highest & lowest points Volcan Karisimbi 14,826 feet (4,519 m); Rusizi River 3,117 feet (950 m)
Climate Temperate; mild in mountains with frost and snow possible
Population 10,186,000
Language(s) Kinyarwanda (universal Bantu vernacular), French, English, Kiswahili (Swahili)
Ethnicity Hutu 84%, Tutsi 15%, Twa (Pygmy) 1%
Religion Christian 93.6%, Muslim 4.6%, indigenous beliefs 0.1%, none 1.7%
Government Republic
Currency Rwandan Franc
Human Development Index 0.452 (ranked 161st out of 177 countries)

UGANDA
TANZANIA
DEMOCRATIC REPUBLIC OF CONGO
Ruhengeri
Volcan Karisimbi
Byumba
Gisenyi
RWANDA
Murambi
KIGALI
Kabuga
Kibuye
Gitarama
Kibungo
Gatare
Nyabisindu
Cyangugu
Gikongoro
Butare
BURUNDI

Rwanda

Map Reference Pages 306–307

Rwanda is a landlocked country in Central Africa, bounded by Uganda, Tanzania, Burundi, and Democratic Republic of Congo. It is the continent's most populous country, and in the twentieth century, was one of the most violent and tragic.

Physical Geography

Often referred to as the "land of a thousand hills," Rwanda has a diverse terrain ranging from active volcanoes and high altitude forest, to grasslands and papyrus swamps. Its many rivers and lakes contribute to both the Congo and Nile drainage basins. Climate is temperate, with moderate rainfall. The majority of the countryside is under smallholder cultivation, and deforestation has emerged as a serious environmental issue in recent years.

History

Twa (Pygmies), the original inhabitants, have probably been in the region for about 35,000 years, but are now a marginalized group. Precolonial Rwandan society was a centralized feudal kingdom whose inhabitants were tied together by a common language, culture, and religion, and lived in relative harmony. Originally a German acquisition, Rwanda was handed to Belgium at the end of World War I. The Belgian administration decided to

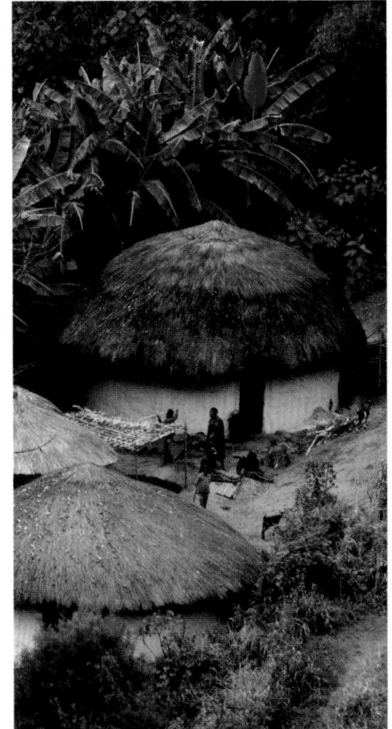

Far left Momela Lakes, in Tanzania's Arusha National Park, are surrounded by rolling green hills. Each lake is a different shade of blue or green, and often tinged pink because of the huge flocks of flamingoes that feed in the shallows.

Left Most people in Burundi live in rural areas, relying on subsistence agriculture. As a result of population pressure, deforestation has become a major environmental issue for the country.

classify the population into three distinct ethnic groups, the Tutsi, Hutu, and Twa.

Rwanda gained its independence in 1962. Former colonial support for the minority Tutsi, and later for the Hutu, created the conditions for ethnic unrest that culminated in the genocide of 1994 when over a million people (both Tutsi and Hutu) were killed by Hutu militias. Further violence was prevented by the invasion of the Rwanda Patriotic Front from neighboring Uganda, and the installation of a multi-ethnic transitional government which has sought to rebuild trust and to facilitate reconciliation among its population.

Population/Culture

Genocide impoverished Rwanda; today 60 percent of the population lives below the poverty line, and over 5 percent has HIV/AIDS. Life expectancy has dropped to 50 years.

Music and dance are culturally important. Traditional *intore* dancing was originally performed by returning warriors who were celebrating victory in battle. A range of traditional instruments includes the *inanga*, a 12-string guitar constructed from cow hide.

Administration/Government

Parliament has two chambers: A 26-seat Senate and an 80-seat Chamber of Deputies. Senators are variously appointed by the president, local councils, universities, and political organizations; the Chamber of Deputies is composed of those elected by popular vote (53), women elected by local bodies (24), and three elected by youth and disability organizations. The president is elected by popular vote.

Economy/Industry

With very few resources, Rwanda is one of the poorest countries in the world. Ninety percent of people are engaged in subsistence production (fruit, vegetables, and cereals), with some cash cropping. Exports are limited to small quantities of tea, coffee, flowers, and minerals.

In recent years more tourists have been visiting Rwanda, particularly the Parc National des Volcans (Volcanoes National Park), one of the few remaining habitats of the endangered mountain gorilla.

RWANDA
TANZANIA
DEMOCRATIC REPUBLIC OF CONGO
Kirundo
Citiboke
Buganda
Kayanza
Muyinga
Bubanza
Karuzi
BURUNDI
Cankuzo
BUJUMBURA
Gitega
Ruyigi
Heha
Mugamba
Bururi
Rutana
Makamba

Burundi

Map Reference Pages 306–307

Burundi is a small landlocked country in the heart of Africa. The capital, Bujumbura, is located in the northern highlands. Burundi has one of the highest population densities in the world along with high levels of poverty and HIV infection.

Physical Geography

Much of Burundi has a mountainous terrain ranging from 2,620 feet to 6,560 feet (800–2,000 m), falling to a lowland plateau along the eastern border with Tanzania. Burundi is situated along the East African Rift Valley and experiences earth tremors and earthquakes. It receives about 59 inches (150 cm) of rainfall per year, most of which falls in the north and west. The landscape is dominated by subsistence agriculture.

History

The original inhabitants were the Twa (Pygmies) who were gradually displaced by the settlement of Hutu and Tutsi from about 1000 CE. Prior to its colonization by Germany in 1903, Burundi was ruled by Tutsi *mwami* (kings) in a feudal system in which the numerically superior Hutu sold their services in return for cattle. This tense relationship was supported by indirect Belgian rule after World War II, and continued until political parties were established in the run-up to independence in 1962. Ethnic tensions and civil unrest continued into the 1990s despite Burundi's first democratic elections taking place in 1993, spilling over into civil war and the death of over 300,000 people. A peace agreement led to a power-sharing government in 2003. In 2007, an inclusive Government of National Unity was finally established.

Population/Culture

Tutsi and Hutu make up most of the population; they have lived together for centuries and have much in common culturally, yet their relationship is extremely antagonistic. Another major problem for the country is HIV/AIDS. Birth rates, death rates, and infant mortality are among the highest in the world.

Storytelling, music, and poetry are integral to Burundi culture. The world-famous Royal Drummers of Burundi showcase a tradition in which a group of drummers would accompany the king and perform wherever he traveled. Now, they perform at rites of passage—births, marriages, and deaths.

Administration/Government

The president, who is also chief of state, heads the government and nominates the first and second vice-presidents. The Parliament is bicameral: A 100-seat National Assembly elected by popular vote, and a 54-seat Senate elected by representatives of the country's 17 provinces. The president and the members of both chambers serve five-year terms.

Economy/Industry

Burundi is resource poor, and approximately 90 percent of the population is dependent on subsistence agriculture.

Burundi's small manufacturing sector is confined primarily to light consumer goods and food processing. Tea and coffee are the country's only major exports, but investment in these sectors has been limited due to the poor security situation. Economic growth is further hampered by shortages of food, medicine, and electricity.

BURUNDI

Official name Republic of Burundi (Republique du Burundi/Republika y'u Burundi)
Land area 9,904 square miles (25,650 km^2)
Border countries Rwanda, Tanzania, Democratic Republic of Congo
Capital Bujumbura
Highest & lowest points Mt Heha 8,760 feet (2,670 m), Lake Tanganyika 2,533 feet (772 m)
Climate Equatorial
Population 8,691,000
Language(s) Kirundi, French, Swahili
Ethnicity Hutu (Bantu) 84.94%, Tutsi (Hamitic) 14%, Twa (Pygmy) 1%, Europeans/South Asians 0.06%
Religion Christian 67%, indigenous beliefs 23%, Muslim 10%
Government Republic
Currency Burundi Franc
Human Development Index 0.413 (ranked 167th out of 177 countries)

Above The Royal Drummers of Burundi perform around the world. The men play a variety of drums, including the huge *ingoma* drums made from hollowed-out tree trunks. Drumming skills are usually passed down from father to son.

ZAMBIA

Official name Republic of Zambia
Land area 285,994 square miles (740,724 km²)
Border countries Democratic Republic of Congo, Tanzania, Malawi, Botswana, Mozambique, Zimbabwe, Namibia, Angola
Capital Lusaka
Highest & lowest points Unnamed location in Mafinga Hills, 7,549 feet (2,301 m); Zambezi River 1,079 feet (329 m)
Climate Tropical modified by altitude
Population 11,670,000
Language(s) English, Bemba, Kaonda, Lozi, Lunda, Luvale, Nyanja, Tonga, other (about 70 other indigenous languages)
Ethnicity Bemba, Nyanja-Chewa, Tonga, Tumbuka, Lunda, Luvale, Kaonde, Nkoya, Lozi, other (about 75 ethnic groups) 98.7%, European 1.1%, other 0.2%
Religion Christian 50–75%, Muslim/Hindu 24–49%, animistic beliefs 1%
Government Republic
Currency Zambian kwacha
Human Development Index 0.434 (ranked 165th out of 177 countries)

Above A Lozi woman sifts grain. Concentrated around the Zambezi River plain, the Lozi people follow a subsistence lifestyle, with the women doing most of the work in agriculture. The main crops are millet, cassava, maize, and sorghum.

Zambia

Map Reference Pages 308–309

Landlocked in south-central Africa, Zambia is encircled by eight countries. Formerly Northern Rhodesia, Zambia became independent in 1964 under the leadership of Kenneth Kaunda. More urbanized and industrialized than many of its neighbors, it is one of the world's leading producers of copper.

Physical Geography

Zambia stretches from Lake Tanganyika in the north to Victoria Falls in the south. Much of the country consists of high plateaus intersected by scattered valleys and mountains. The tallest peak is in the Mafinga Hills. Western Zambia is flat with broad plains, and the Rift Valley cuts through the southwest. The Zambezi River forms the boundary with Namibia and Zimbabwe. The river has been dammed at the Kariba Gorge (for hydroelectric purposes) and now forms Lake Kariba, the largest artificial lake in Africa. Several game parks protect a variety of flora and fauna; however, poaching is still a problem. Climate is tropical but varies with altitude.

History

Originally inhabited by Khoisan peoples who were similar to the San (or Bushmen) of the Kalahari, from the twelfth century the area was the destination of migrating Bantu-speaking groups. In 1888 Cecil Rhodes and the British South Africa Company managed to secure mineral rights from the Lozi tribe. The British Colonial Office assumed administrative control of the region in 1924, and in 1953 Northern Rhodesia became briefly a part of the Federation of Rhodesia and Nyasaland (Malawi). Following elections for both the Legislative Council (1962) and the presidency (1963), Northern Rhodesia became the Republic of Zambia in October 1964, with Kenneth Kaunda as the new nation's first president.

A doctrinaire socialist, Kaunda spent the next 25 years nationalizing commerce and industry and setting up a one-party state. Zambia's economic decline was precipitous: Once rich from copper revenues, the nation squandered its fortune on high-cost, loss-making state corporations. Since 1991, when the country's first free elections were held, there has been a change in political policy and economic management.

Population/Culture

Zambia's population consists of about 75 ethnic groups, most of them Bantu-speaking. Despite ethnic diversity there exists a strong sense of national identity among the people, more so than in many other African states.

While there is an overall Bantu cultural pattern there are variations, expressed in the beliefs and ceremonies of the different ethnic groups. The Kuomboka festival of the Lozi takes place each year at the end of the rainy season when the upper reaches of the Zambezi River flood nearby plains. Kuomboka means "to climb up out of the water" and celebrates the movement of the Lozi king, or Litunga, from his compound on the floodplain to the safety of higher ground. A special state barge used by the king bears a replica of a black elephant whose ears can be made to move from within the vessel.

There is also a vigorous arts and crafts tradition; Zambian basket weaving is considered among the best in Africa.

Administration/Government

The Zambian government has been a multiparty democracy since 1991. It is headed by the president who is also chief of state. Under the 1991 constitution the president is elected by popular vote, and then appoints the vice-president and members of cabinet from the unicameral National Assembly. One hundred and fifty members of the assembly are popularly elected, with the president appointing the remaining eight. Zambia's legal system is based on English common law and customary law. Court justices are appointed by the president.

ENDANGERED WILDLIFE IN ZAMBIA

Zambia's wildlife is increasingly endangered; the so-called "big five" animals—rhinoceros, elephant, lion (pictured below), buffalo, and leopard—could often be found outside of parks and reserves, but not now. Today, the rhinoceros is almost extinct, and only by visiting parks are you likely to see elephants or lions. Leopards, however, are better able to conceal themselves, and being creatures of the night they manage to maintain an independent existence in the wider world. The riverine habitat of hippos and crocodiles also gives them an immunity not enjoyed by large land animals needing expansive savannas.

Loss of habitat in Zambia, as elsewhere, is responsible for the decline in wildlife numbers. In the last 50 years there has been a four-fold increase in the number of Zambians competing for land, especially forest and woodland. Traditional farming practices of shifting cultivation, or *chitemene*, have been responsible for woodland deforestation estimated at 3,475 square miles (9,000 km²) per year. In addition, charcoal production for family cooking fires has been responsible for deforesting another 772 square miles (2,000 km²) annually.

Economy/Industry

During the 1990s there was some attempt at privatization and budgetary reform, and in recent years there have been encouraging signs of modest growth, with a real GDP increase of between 5 and 6 percent per year. Rich in copper, Zambia is one of the world's main sources of this metal, and though production has fluctuated over time, copper and cobalt remain indispensable exports. Higher copper prices and increasing foreign investment have stimulated a steady increase in copper production since 2004, though external debt is still very high, exacerbated by having to import all petroleum products. In 2005, Zambia qualified for debt relief under the Highly Indebted Poor Country Initiative, which amounted to US$6 billion. Good harvests in recent years have helped boost trade levels and GDP, but poverty is still a major issue.

MILESTONE EVENTS

c. 1150 Waves of immigrants arrive during Bantu expansion—Tonga the first to settle the area
1855 David Livingstone arrives and names the Victoria Falls for Queen Victoria
1888 Cecil Rhodes obtains mining rights from the king of the Lozi
1923 British government assumes control of Northern Rhodesia (to be later known as Zambia)
1924 Administration of Northern Rhodesia transferred to British Colonial Office
1953 Northern Rhodesia, Southern Rhodesia, and Nyasaland (Malawi) joined in short-lived federation
1962 Elections held for future Legislative Council
October 1964 Zambian independence; Kenneth Kaunda becomes nation's first president
1991 Movement for multiparty democracy wins election; Kaunda defeated
2002 President Mwanawasa launches major anti-corruption campaign
April 12, 2008 As chairperson of the Southern African Development Community (SADC), President Mwanawasa holds summit to discuss Zimbabwe's mounting crisis over disputed polls

Right *Mosi-oa-Tunya*, "the smoke that thunders," is the local name for Victoria Falls, which form part of the border between southern Zambia and northwestern Zimbabwe. These spectacular falls channel more than 300,000 cubic feet (9,000 m³) per second of water into the narrow 100-foot (30 m) wide Batoka Gorge.

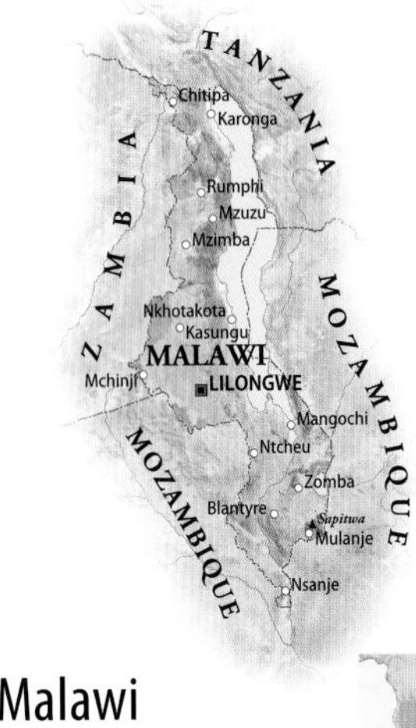
TANZANIA
ZAMBIA
MOZAMBIQUE
Chitipa
Karonga
Rumphi
Mzuzu
Mzimba
Nkhotakota
Kasungu
MALAWI
Mchinji
LILONGWE
Mangochi
Ntcheu
Zomba
Blantyre
Sapitwa
Mulanje
Nsanje

Malawi

Map Reference Pages 308–309

Left The floor of the East African Rift Valley is marked by a necklace of lakes. One of the larger freshwater lakes, Lake Nyasa (also known as Lake Malawi), is pictured here. In the distance is Likoma Island.

Malawi is a long, narrow, landlocked country that measures about 400 miles (644 km) from north to south. Lake Nyasa (also called Lake Malawi) forms part of the border with Mozambique and Tanzania. Densely populated, and ethnically diverse, Malawi was from 1963 run by Dr Hastings Kamuzu Banda as a one-party socialist state. In 1994, the people voted overwhelmingly for a multiparty democracy.

Physical Geography

The East African Rift Valley crosses Malawi north to south, with Lake Nyasa lying in the deep trough formed by the valley. West of the lake the land rises to a plateau with an elevation of 3,000–4,000 feet (900–1,200 m). From the southern end of Lake Nyasa the Shire River flows down to join the Zambezi River in Mozambique. The Shire Highlands, also in the south, reach a height of 2,000–5,000 feet (600–1,500 m). The Zomba Plateau and the Mulanje Massif have elevations of 7,000–10,000 feet (2,100–3,000 m). The west face of Chambe Peak provides visitors with the longest rock climb in Africa.

The climate is generally subtropical, but from June through August, evenings are cool in the north. The wet season is November to May; the dry season is May to November.

History

The earliest inhabitants are thought to have been Khoisan hunter-gatherers like the San (or Bushmen) of the Kalahari Desert. Over the last millennia Bantu-speaking peoples migrated into the area, with the Chewa ethnic group founding the Maravi state in the sixteenth century. In 1907 the British government established the Nyasaland Protectorate, which lasted until independence in 1964. Dr Hastings Banda, who appointed himself President for Life in 1971, ruled the country as a one-party state. In 1992, his tyranny was challenged by the bishops of the Catholic Church in Malawi and the leaders of the Church of Scotland to which Banda belonged. After belatedly agreeing to hold elections in 1994, Banda, aged 96, was defeated by one of his former ministers. Sixty-three percent of people voted for a new multiparty system.

Population/Culture

Regional differences and tribal rivalries stopped the development of a cohesive Malawian identity in the pre-colonial and colonial periods. Since independence, the main groups have developed a more unified sense of being Malawian. Still, ethnic groups tend to congregate in specific areas: The Chewa comprise 90 percent of the population in the central region; the south is mainly peopled by the Nyanja; and the north by the Tumbuka. In addition, there are numbers of Tonga in the north, while the Ngoni, who came from further south in the early 1800s, live in the lower northern and lower central regions.

The traditional rural culture of Malawi combines agriculture and herding. The Ngoni are herders of Zulu origin with a fierce reputation for cattle raiding: Their young men were once formed into age grades for military purposes. The Tongas, also cattle-herding people, place great importance on livestock as symbols of wealth. Among the matrilineal Chewa, women have a special place, with all property and land rights inherited through the mother's line.

Administration/Government

Under the constitution that came into effect in 1995 the president of Malawi is both the chief of state and the head of government. Elections for the presidency are held every five years, and the president is responsible for naming a 46-member cabinet. A unicameral National Assembly consists of 193 seats, the members elected by popular vote. There is an independent judiciary, with lower magisterial courts, a High Court, and a Supreme Court of Appeal. Any recent efforts to bring about economic and political reform have been obstructed by political deadlock because no one party has a majority.

MILESTONE EVENTS

1000–2000 Period of Bantu migrations

c. 1550 Chewa people found the Maravi state

1859 David Livingstone visits Lake Malawi

1883 British government establishes consular representation to "the kings and chiefs of central Africa"

1891 British Central African Protectorate established

1907 Nyasaland Protectorate established

1964 Malawi becomes a fully independent member of British Commonwealth

1971 Dr Hastings Banda declares himself President for Life

1994 People vote for multiparty democracy; Bakili Muluzi is elected president

1997 Bakili Muluzi commutes all death sentences and promises there will be no executions under his presidency

2006 Malawi approved for relief under Heavily Indebted Poor Countries program

Economy/Industry

Approximately 85 percent of the people in this densely populated country live in the countryside. Agriculture provides a third of GDP and 90 percent of export revenue. Tobacco production accounts for over half of the exports. There are small reserves of bauxite and uranium. No petroleum or natural gas reserves exist and all fuel must be imported. South Africa is Malawi's main trading partner. Since the 1980s the once prosperous economy has been crippled by debt. Now the nation depends heavily on economic assistance from the IMF, the World Bank, and from individual donor nations.

AIDS is an additional burden—there are more than a million orphans, and unofficial estimates rate HIV infection at a staggering 30 percent of the total population.

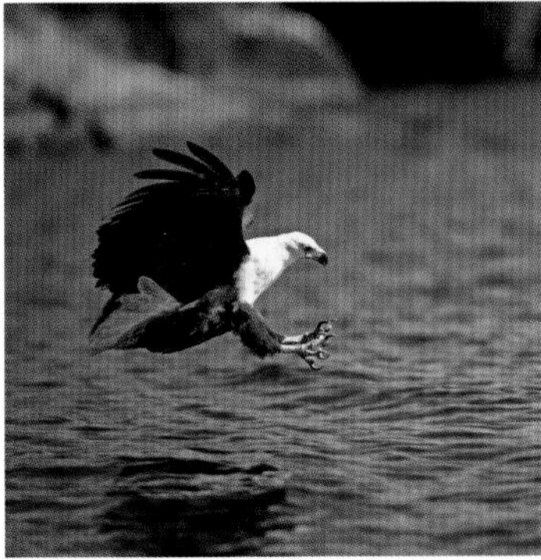

Left An African fish eagle *(Haliaeetus vocifer)* about to catch a fish in Lake Nyasa. These raptors with a distinctive call have been known to prey on flamingoes and other water birds, and even carrion, to supplement their main diet of fish.

MALAWI

Official name Republic of Malawi (Dziko la Malawi)

Land area 36,324 miles (94,080 km²)

Border countries Tanzania, Mozambique, Zambia

Capital Lilongwe

Highest & lowest points Sapitwa (Mt Mlanje) 9,849 feet (3,002 m); junction of Shire River and international boundary with Mozambique 121 feet (37 m)

Climate Subtropical

Population 13,932,000

Language(s) Chichewa, Chinyanja, Chiyao, Chitumbuka, Chisena, Chilomwe, Chitonga, other indigenous languages

Ethnicity Chewa, Nyanja, Tumbuka, Yao, Lomwe, Sena, Tonga, Ngoni, Ngonde, Asian, European

Religion Christian 79.9%, Muslim 12.8%, other 3%, none 4.3%

Government Multiparty democracy

Currency Malawian kwacha

Human Development Index 0.437 (ranked 164th out of 177 countries)

Above This woman comes from Nsanje District in the south of Malawi. In 2007, the region was devastated by heavy rain and flash flooding.

MOZAMBIQUE

Official name Republic of Mozambique (Republica de Moçambique)
Land area 302,739 square miles (784,090 km²)
Border countries Malawi, South Africa, Swaziland, Tanzania, Zambia, Zimbabwe
Capital Maputo
Highest point Monte Binga 7,992 feet (2,436 m)
Climate Tropical to subtropical
Population 21,285,000
Language(s) Emakhuwa, Xichangana, Portuguese, Elomwe, Cisena, Echuwabo, other Mozambican languages, others
Ethnicity Makhuwa/Tsonga/Lomwe/Sena/others 99.66%, Europeans 0.06%, Afro-European 0.2%, South Asian 0.08%
Religion Christian 23.8%, Muslim 17.8%, Zionist Christian 17.5%, other 17.8%, none 23.1%
Government Republic
Currency Metical
Human Development Index 0.384 (ranked 172nd out of 177 countries)

Right Many of Mozambique's diverse cultural traditions have survived centuries of colonialism. A Mozambican woman applies ceremonial makeup wearing the brightly colored and patterned clothing of her country.

COMOROS

Official Name Union of the Comoros (Union des Comores)
Land area 838 square miles (2,170 km²)
Border countries None
Capital Moroni
Highest point Le Kartala (Mt Karthala) 7,743 feet (2,360 m)
Climate Tropical marine
Population 732,000
Language(s) Arabic, French, Shikomoro (mix of Swahili and Arabic)
Ethnicity Antalote, Cafre, Makoa, Oimatsaha, Sakalava
Religion Muslim 98%, Christian 2%
Government Republic
Currency Comoran franc
Human Development Index 0.561 (ranked of 134th out of 177 countries)

Above Although there have been significant improvements in the quality of education in Mozambique over the past few years, standards are low. Drop-out rates are high, with the completion of primary school remaining well below the average of other countries in the region.

Right The bustling seaport of Inhambane Bay, which straddles the Tropic of Capricorn in southeastern Mozambique, was settled by the Portuguese in 1543. It has the largest fleet of working *dhows* on the coast of east Africa.

TANZANIA
ZAMBIA
MALAWI
Lichinga
Pemba
Lúrio
Nacala
Nampula
Ilha de Moçambique
Songo
Tete
Angoche
Mocuba
Quelimane
MOZAMBIQUE
ZIMBABWE
Chimoio
Monte Binga
Beira
Machanga
Mozambique Channel
SOUTH AFRICA
Inhambane
Chókwè
Xai-Xai
MAPUTO
SWAZILAND

Mozambique

Map Reference Pages 308–309

Mozambique, on the southeast coast of Africa, has borders with six countries. The Mozambique Channel lies to the east. Mozambique has beautiful beaches, colonial remnants, and fascinating cultural diversity, and a tragic past. Torn apart by a civil war that lasted from independence in 1975 until the Rome General Peace Accords in 1992, it has struggled to regain some semblance of stability under a fledgling democratic government.

Physical Geography

Mozambique runs in a slender Y-shape from north to south for 1,200 miles (1,930 km). Coastal lowlands give way to elevated regions of grasslands and forests inland. High plateaus dominate the northwest with mountainous regions further inland. The highest point, Monte Binga, is situated on the border with Zimbabwe. The Zambezi River valleys contain some of the most fertile soils in Mozambique.

Climate is tropical with a dry season from April to September and a wet season from October to March. Droughts are a major hazard with cyclones and flooding affecting the central and southern parts of the country.

History

Mozambique's first people were San hunters and gatherers. In the first four centuries CE, Bantu peoples migrated to the region from the north. By the end of the first millennium, merchants from northeast Africa and the Middle East traded with people in the region. A slave trade had developed prior to the arrival of the Portuguese in 1498.

After World War II, Portugal tried to hold onto Mozambique but was strongly resisted, and fighting continued until independence in 1975. A ruinous civil war followed, which finally ended in 1992.

Population/Culture

Mozambique's population faces some sizable demographic problems, including a high rate of HIV/AIDS (12.2 percent) and a low life expectancy. Literacy is less than 50 percent and the birth rate is high.

Cultural and linguistic diversity marks Mozambique's population. Four million Makhuwa reside in the north; the Sena and Ndau dominate the Zambezi River valley area. The major groups in the south are the Tsonga and Shangaan. There are eight local languages used in daily life; Portuguese serves as the official language. The Makonde people in northern Mozambique are particularly renowned for their carved wooden sculptures.

Administration/Government

The legislature is a unicameral Assembly of the Republic with 250 members elected by popular vote. The president, who heads the executive branch, is also elected, and appoints the prime minister. The Supreme Court is the country's highest body. Some judges are appointed by the president, others elected by members of the Assembly.

Economy/Industry

Huge economic problems faced the country after the civil war, including floods, inflation, foreign debt, the resettling of refugees, and trade deficits. The country is poor with a per capita GDP of only US$900. Seventy percent of the population falls below the poverty line. Four out of five workers work in subsistence agriculture. Exports include aluminum, fish, cotton, sugar, and timber. Currently there is an export/import imbalance; however, there are valuable resources, such as titanium, waiting to be exploited.

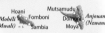

POISONED LAND

After a decade-long war against the Portuguese by the Front for Libration of Mozambique (FRELIMO), the country won its independence in 1975. However, independence did not end the fighting because an insurrection led by the Mozambique Resistance Movement extended into a devastating civil war that lasted for 17 years. Over a million people died and another 1.7 million fled the country during the fighting that finally ended in 1992. By 1995, most of the people who had fled returned but many problems followed.

One of the most insidious legacies is that of the land mines. Estimates indicate as many as three million land mines were placed during the civil war—the mines came from more than 15 countries. At their worst they blanketed approximately 70 percent of the land. A vast area of agricultural land was rendered unusable and an average of 20 people stepped on land mines each month—60 percent of those died, the remainder usually crippled for life because of loss of limbs. With the help of the United Nations and other international support, mine clearing began in 1992 and soon the country should be mine-free.

Mitsamiouli
Mbeni
Grande Comore (Njazidja)
MORONI
Le Kartala
INDIAN OCEAN
Dembéni
Foumbouni
COMOROS
Hoani
Mutsamudu
Mohéli (Mwali)
Fomboni
Domoni
Anjouan (Nzwani)
Nioumachoua
Moya

Comoros

Map Reference Pages 308–310

Situated between northern Madagascar and Mozambique in the Indian Ocean are the Comoros Islands, an archipelago of four islands of volcanic origin. Three islands—Grande Comore, Anjouan, and Mohéli—comprise the Union of the Comoros. Mayotte, the fourth island, is a French dependency.

Physical Geography

The interiors of the islands vary from low hills to steep mountains. Rainforests, once abundant, are disappearing rapidly. Le Kartala on Grande Comore is the highest peak in the republic, and one of the world's most active volcanoes. More than 20 eruptions have been recorded since the nineteenth century.

Climate is generally tropical. The islands are subject to cyclones in the summer rainy season; tsunamis are also a major threat.

Far left Moroni is the largest city on the island of Grand Comore and is the national capital of Comoros. Its harbor provides regular transport to other islands in the archipelago, as well as to the African mainland and Madagascar.

Left The jewel of the Seychelles Inner Islands and part of the Curieuse Marine National Park, the tiny St Pierre Island is a snorkeling paradise.

History

Populated by successive waves of immigrants from Africa, Indonesia, Madagascar, and Arabia, the islands remained under Arab domination until France established colonial rule in 1912. In 1975, three of the islands declared unilateral independence, but Mayotte remained a French dependency. Following independence, France stopped aid to the islands, and Comoros was jolted with a series of military takeovers. The small nation has experienced 19 successful and unsuccessful military coups.

Population/Culture

With fewer than a million people, Comoros is one of the world's least populous countries, but is also one of the most densely populated, with an average of 712 people per square mile (275 people per km^2).

Outmigration, particularly of the young and skilled to Madagascar, is a major concern. There is a shortage of medical personnel, modern health facilities, and supplies. Safe drinking water is scarce, and tuberculosis and malaria are endemic.

Islam is the dominant religion and Koranic schools reinforce its influence. The most common language is Shikomoro, a mix of Swahili and Arabic. French and Arabic are also spoken. Despite the dominance of Islam, Comorans practice matrilineal social organization. After marriage the husband moves to join the bride's family. Social life is characterized by a widespread system of exchange, which generates numerous customary ceremonies and rituals, particularly great weddings.

Administration/Government

In 1998, Anjouan and Mohéli voted for independence, but a compromise reached in 2001 produced a new federal governmental system, whereby each island elects its own president. The federation is headed by a presidency that rotates every four years among the three presidents. The unicameral Assembly of the Union has 33 seats. Despite these changes, political stability remains elusive.

Economy

Comoros is overpopulated and among the world's poorest and least developed nations. Subsistence agriculture is the main economic activity for more than 80 percent of the population. Agricultural products include vanilla, cloves, perfume essences, and copra; the islands are no longer self-sufficient in food, which must be imported. Industry accounts for only 4 percent of GNP and is essentially represented by companies that prepare spices and fragrant plants for exportation.

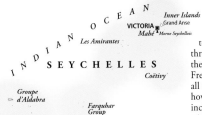

INDIAN OCEAN
Inner Islands
VICTORIA
Grand Anse
Mahé
Morne Seychellois
Les Amirantes
SEYCHELLES
Coëtivy
Groupe d'Aldabra
Farquhar Group

Seychelles

Map Reference Page 310

The Republic of Seychelles is an archipelago of about 100 islands located in the Indian Ocean, 994 miles (1,600 km) east of Kenya. The principal islands are Mahé, Praslin, and La Digue. Since independence (1976) the country has had both successful and unsuccessful coup attempts, invasion by mercenaries, and an abortive army mutiny.

Physical Geography

The archipelago has two distinct types of islands: One type is composed of granite, and the other of coral. Most islands have a narrow coastal strip and a central range of hills rising to 3,000 feet (900 m). The coral atolls are flat and barely rise above sea level, they lack fresh water, and are mostly uninhabited. The climate is tropical marine and is consistent throughout the year.

History

From the time of annexation by the French in 1756, the islands were regarded as a dependency of Mauritius until the British took control after the Napoleonic wars. Self-government in 1975 was followed by independence in 1976. The Prime Minister France-Albert René established a socialist state and a one-party system after a coup in 1977.

In 1981, an attempted coup by a group of mercenaries was quelled. A year later, an army mutiny was also put down after two days when loyal troops, reinforced by Tanzanian forces, recaptured rebel-held installations. Similar acts of opposition and international pressure finally led to the introduction of a multiparty system and other reforms in 1993.

Population/Culture

Originally settled by French colonists and African slaves, with a later infusion of Asians from China, India, and Malaya, the Republic of Seychelles today has a population of mixed descent. About 90 percent of people live on Mahé, and mostly in the capital city.

Creole (or Seselwa) is the mother tongue of most Seychellois, and one of three official languages. While English is the language of government and commerce, French is the language of the Church. Almost all inhabitants of the islands are Christian; however, many traditional religious practices, including magic, witchcraft, and sorcery, are widespread across the country.

Administration/Government

The president is both the chief of state and head of government and is elected by popular vote. The unicameral 34-seat National Assembly has 25 members who are elected by popular vote; the remaining nine members are appointed from parties with a minimum of 10 percent of the vote. The legal system is based on English common law, French civil law, and customary law. A multiparty system became law under the new constitution adopted in 1992.

Economy

The country's economy rests on tourism and fishing. Fine beaches, turquoise seas, and an array of wildlife are among the main attractions. Due to a dearth of arable land, agriculture contributes little to the economy. Coconuts, cinnamon bark, vanilla, and essential oils are the main agricultural products. Tuna fishing supplies domestic and foreign markets. Economic mismanagement has produced high inflation, foreign exchange shortages, and a parallel market currency exchange rate double the official rate.

SEYCHELLES

Official name Republic of Seychelles
Land area 176 square miles (455 km^2)
Border countries None
Capital Victoria
Climate Tropical marine
Highest point Morne Seychellois 2,969 feet (905 m)
Population 82,247
Language(s) Creole (Seselwa), English, French, other
Ethnicity Mixed French, African, Indian, Chinese, Arab
Religion Christian 93.2%, Hindu 2.1%, Muslim 1.1%, others 1.5%, unspecified 1.5%, none 0.6%
Government Republic
Currency Seychelles rupee
Human Development Index 0.843 (ranked 50th out of 177 countries)

Left The candy-striped sea star *(Fromia monilis)* is a denizen of Seychellois coral reefs.

Below The deepwater port at Victoria in Seychelles accommodates many large vessels.

MADAGASCAR

Official name Republic of Madagascar (République de Madagascar/ Repoblikan'i Madagasikara)
Land area 224,534 square miles (581,540 km²)
Border countries None
Capital Antananarivo
Highest point Maromokotro 9,436 feet (2,876 m)
Climate Tropical along coast, temperate inland, arid in south
Population 20,043,000
Language(s) Official: French, English, Malagasy
Ethnicity Malayo-Indonesian (Merina and related Betsileo), Cotiers (mixed African, Malayo-Indonesian, and Arab ancestry), French, Indian, Creole, Comoran
Religion Indigenous beliefs 52%, Christian 41%, Muslim 7%
Government Republic
Currency Ariary
Human Development Index 0.533 (ranked 143rd out of 177 countries)

Antsiranana
Andoany
Maromokotro
Bealanana
Sambava
Mahajanga
Marovoay
Maroantsetra
Mozambique Channel
Ambatondrazaka
MADAGASCAR
Toamasina
ANTANANARIVO
INDIAN OCEAN
Morondava
Antsirabe
Fianarantsoa
Toliara
Farafangana
Vangaindrano
Amboasary

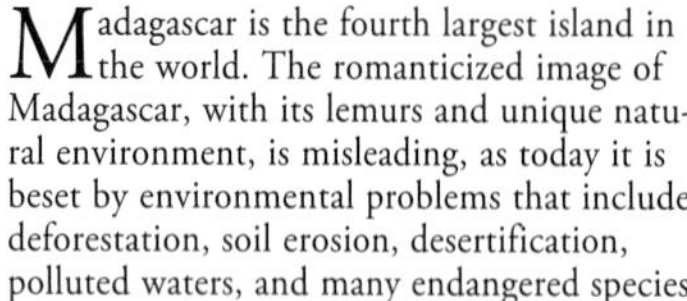

Madagascar

Map Reference Pages 308–309

Madagascar is the fourth largest island in the world. The romanticized image of Madagascar, with its lemurs and unique natural environment, is misleading, as today it is beset by environmental problems that include deforestation, soil erosion, desertification, polluted waters, and many endangered species.

Visitors take a step back in time when they travel outside the capital city of Antananarivo, which locals refer to as "Tana." For example, the major highway, running north to south between Tana and Fianarantsoa, carries only a few vehicles. Visitors will see people walking to market—with live ducks, vegetables, and other goods carried in baskets balanced on the heads of the women—or driving long-horned, humped zebu oxen pulling carts filled with items to sell. Many Malagasy still live at a subsistence level, practicing slash-and-burn agriculture *(tavy)*, which has contributed greatly to severe deforestation and erosion in many parts of the highlands.

Physical Geography

Madagascar's topography is dominated by a central plateau that runs the length of the island, and is divided into three distinct regions. The narrow coastal plain on the east ends abruptly with steep slopes and a few beaches facing the Indian Ocean. The central plateau and highland region is where Antananarivo is located. The wide coastal plain in the west ends with beaches and coral reefs facing the Mozambique Channel. The climate is tropical near the coast and inland. The south of the country is arid.

Although many species are endangered, Madagascar has a rich variety of plant life, with some 90 percent of its 10,000 species endemic to the island, including the distinctively shaped baobab trees. Much of the animal life is also unique, including the charming lemurs and the cat-like carnivorous fossa. Sadly, 12 bird and animal species are endangered and another 20 are at risk due to habitat loss.

History

Early Malagasy were primarily Malayo-Indonesians who arrived by sea, probably by way of East Africa, from the first to the thirteenth century CE, bringing with them African wives and slaves. Early colonization attempts were successfully resisted, but the French eventually prevailed in 1896 when Queen Ranavalona III was forced into exile. Madagascar remained a French colony until it became independent on June 26, 1960.

Presidential elections in 2001 divided the country, with the results not accepted by the candidates. Fighting ensued with Didier Ratsiraka setting up a capital in the coastal city of Toamasina and Marc Ravalomanana in control of Antananarivo. The High Constitutional Court and the international community ended the conflict by recognizing the election of Ravalomanana in 2002.

Population/Culture

Madagascar's population is increasing rapidly. Forward estimates are that the country will have nearly 42 million people by 2050, more than double the 2008 population. The use of contraceptives is low and the average births per mother, at 5.2, is very high. This rate of increase poses further difficulties for survival in rural subsistence areas.

The culture of Madagascar is an amazing mix of indigenous beliefs, religions, and languages introduced by outsiders. Malagasy, French, and English are all official languages. French is spoken by many educated Malagasy but they often resent needing to use a European language instead of their native tongue. Unfortunately, Malagasy doesn't always have the words necessary to convey modern ideas and technology. Christianity and Islam are widely practiced, but traditional beliefs, *fady*, dominate, and often color other religious practice. Malagasy have a great reverence for their ancestors and many participate in the ritual of Turning Over the Dead.

Administration/Government

Madagascar is a republic. The president is elected by a popular vote. The bicameral legislature is composed of the National Assembly and the Senate. The 127 National Assembly members are elected; two-thirds of the 100 senators are appointed by regional assemblies and the remainder appointed by the president.

Economy/Industry

Agriculture employs 80 percent of the population: Madagascar is the world's greatest producer of vanilla and cloves. The government is working to attract foreign investment and recent oil discoveries are a prelude to the development of the industry in the northwest. Madagascar has one of the lowest standards of living in the world, with a per capita GDP of US$900 per year.

FAMADIHANA: TURNING OVER THE DEAD

Famadihana is the Malagasy festival of turning the bones of dead relatives. Originally a practice of the Merina and Betsileo people of the highlands, it has spread to other groups. Many Malagasy believe that dead ancestors remain a part of the family, their link to Zanahary (God). A tomb may be better kept than the family home.

A family may save for years to conduct *famadihana*, which takes place in the dry cool season between June and September. Relatives may come from hundreds of miles away. It begins with the ancestor being removed, feet first, from the tomb. The body is removed from its shroud *(lamba)*, washed, and rewrapped. Red silk is the most desirable fabric, but as the cost can be prohibitive undyed cotton is often substituted. The festival culminates with the family carrying the rewrapped body around the village and back to the tomb, where it is circled seven times.

The festival is a giant party, often lasting several days, with singing, eating, drinking, and even dancing with the dead. The size of the festival demonstrates the family's status, but it can cause financial hardship. *Famadihana* takes place every seven to ten years unless a crisis requiring help from an ancestor calls for it to be held sooner. For example, if a woman in the family is having a difficult time getting pregnant, *famadihana*, which is believed to be more important than the husband for pregnancy, may be conducted to increase her fertility.

MILESTONE EVENTS

Up to c.1400s CE The highlands settled by waves of Malayo-Indonesian immigrants; immigrants from Africa and Arabian Peninsula settle on the coasts
1600s–1700s Popular base for sea pirates
Early 1800s Merina kingdom gains control of most of island
1817 King Radama I outlaws foreign slave trade
1840s Queen Ranavalona I expels Europeans
1861 Queen Ranavalona I dies; Europeans return
1896 Queen Ranavalona III exiled; Madagascar becomes French colony
1960 Malagasy Republic gains independence from France
1975 Country renamed Democratic Republic of Madagascar
April 27, 2007 New constitution establishes three official languages

Above The ring-tailed lemur *(Lemur catta)* is a vulnerable species found only on Madagascar.

Below left A patchwork of rice paddies near Mahajanga in western Madagascar.

Below right The imposing and endangered Grandidier's baobab tree *(Adansonia grandidieri)* is one of six species endemic to Madagascar.

Left Mark Twain noted in his travelogue, *Following the Equator*: "You gather the idea that Mauritius was made first and then heaven, and that heaven was copied after Mauritius." The awe-inspiring Le Morne Brabant is on the extreme southwestern tip of Mauritius.

MAURITIUS

Official name Republic of Mauritius
Land area 784 square miles (2,030 km^2)
Border countries None
Capital Port Louis
Highest point Mont Piton 2,717 feet (828 m)
Climate Tropical, warm, dry winter; hot, wet, humid summer
Population 1,274,000
Language(s) Creole, Bhojpuri, French, English (official; spoken by less than 1% of the population); other
Ethnicity Indo-Mauritian 68%, Creole 27%, Sino-Mauritian 3%, Franco-Mauritian 2%
Religion Hindu 48%, Roman Catholic 23.6%, Muslim 16.6%, other Christian 8.6%, other 2.5%, unspecified 0.3%, none 0.4%
Government Parliamentary democracy
Currency Mauritian rupee
Human Development Index 0.804 (ranked 65th out of 177 countries)

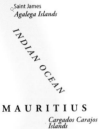

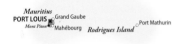

Saint James
Agalega Islands
INDIAN OCEAN
MAURITIUS
Cargados Carajos Islands
Mauritius
PORT LOUIS
Grand Gaube
Mont Piton
Mahébourg
Rodrigues Island
Port Mathurin

Mauritius

Map Reference Page 310

Mauritius is one of the most compact countries in the world, with a land area of only 784 square miles (2,030 km^2). It is a tropical paradise that was only permanently inhabited in the seventeenth century. Lying about 1,300 miles (800 km) east of Madagascar in the Indian Ocean, Mauritius is volcanic in origin, with a lush environment. Besides beautiful beaches, there are forests, mountains, and waterfalls, as well as rare plants, animals, and birds.

Physical Geography

Bare black volcanic peaks rise in the center of the island, which is surrounded by coral reefs. The country includes the island of Mauritius itself and the nearby Agalega Islands, Cargados Carajos Shoals (Saint Brandon), and Rodrigues Island. Mauritius is a part of the Mascarene Archipelago, formed in a series of undersea volcanic explosions 8–10 million years ago. The country has few rivers; most of them are very short. It has a tropical rainy climate. Cyclones are a natural hazard, but they very rarely strike.

History

Most likely first visited by Arab and Malay sailors around the tenth century, the island had many visitors and colonial masters. The Portuguese claimed Mauritius early in the sixteenth century but never settled on the unpopulated island. The Dutch then gained possession in 1598 and built a fort at Grand Port; they withdrew in 1710 leaving slavery, tobacco, and sugarcane as their legacy.

The French arrived in the guise of the French East India Company, claiming the island in 1715. Their rule lasted until the British took the island in 1810 in action related to the Napoleonic wars. Mauritius was officially ceded to the British in 1814.

The British ended slavery in 1835. To counteract the resulting labor shortage when most of the freed slaves refused to continue working on the sugar plantations, indentured servants were imported from India. These Indians' descendants make up the majority of Mauritians today.

Mauritius gained independence in 1968 as a constitutional monarchy. In 1992 the country became a republic and since that time it has been a very stable democracy.

MILESTONE EVENTS

1500s Portuguese sailors are the first Europeans to visit the uninhabited island
1598 The Dutch claim the island and name it after Prince Maurice of Nassau
1715 France takes possession
1810 Britain captures the island; names the new colony Mauritius
March, 1968 Mauritius achieves independence

Population/Culture

Mauritius has a high population density with 1,588 people per square mile (613 per km^2). Indo-Mauritians make up more than two-thirds of the people. Creoles, a mixture of French and African, make up over a quarter of the population. Other ethnic groups include Chinese, European, and Malagasy. English is the official language although French is dominant in the media. Mauritian Creole, a local variation of French, is commonly spoken, and Hindi is also common. Indian roots are evident in the predominant Hindu religion, followed by nearly half the population. Christians and Muslims make up the next largest religious groups.

There are frequent celebrations and festivals, reflecting the country's complex mix of ethnic origins. *Sega*, the popular local music style, has largely African roots. Its songs originally described the miseries of slavery, and today are often adapted as social satire.

Administration/Government

The Republic of Mauritius has rapidly developed strong democratic traditions. It has a unicameral parliament—the National Assembly, with 70 members, 62 elected by popular vote and 8 appointed by the election commission to assure the participation of ethnic groups. A president is elected to a five-year term by the National Assembly and serves as the chief of state. The president appoints the prime minister who serves as the head of government.

The country has nine districts and three dependencies; and Mauritius also has claims on the Chagos Archipelago and Tromelin Island which, respectively, are under the administration of Britain and France.

Economy/Industry

Since independence, the economy has diversified from agriculture and fishing into industrial, financial, and tourist sectors. Sugarcane is still the primary agricultural crop providing 25 percent of export earnings. Textiles are an important manufacturing industry along with food processing.

In order to maximize tourist numbers and provide residents with access to imports at lower prices, Mauritius is working toward becoming a duty-free state.

Far left A young devotee carries a "cavadee" decorated with flowers during the Cavadee Festival, a major celebration for the Tamils of Mauritius. Participants also have their tongue, cheeks, or body pierced as part of the rituals.

Below A Mauritian man passes the enormous banyan trees of Grande Case Noyale in the Black River district of Mauritius.

NAMIBIA

Official name Republic of Namibia
Land area 318,694 square miles (825,418 km²)
Border countries Angola, Zambia, Botswana, South Africa
Capital Windhoek
Highest point Königstein, tip of the Brandberg Massif 8,411 feet (2,606 m)
Climate Desert; hot, dry; rainfall sparse, higher inland
Population 2,089,000
Language English (official), Afrikaans, German, indigenous languages
Ethnicity Ovambo 50%, Kavango 9%, Herero 7%, Damara 7%, Nama 5%, Caprivian 4%, Bushmen 3%, Baster 2%, Tswana 0.5%, mixed 6.5%, European 6%
Religion Christian 85%, indigenous beliefs 15%
Government Republic with two legislative bodies (National Council and National Assembly)
Currency Namibian dollar
Human Development Index 0.650 (ranked 125th out of 177 countries)

ANGOLA
ZAMBIA
Oshakati
Opuwo
Rundu
Katima Mulilo
Tsumeb
Grootfontein
Otjiwarongo
Königstein
NAMIBIA
WINDHOEK
Gobabis
Swakopmund
Walvis Bay
Rehoboth
BOTSWANA
ATLANTIC OCEAN
Mariental
Keetmanshoop
Lüderitz
Oranjemund
SOUTH AFRICA

Namibia

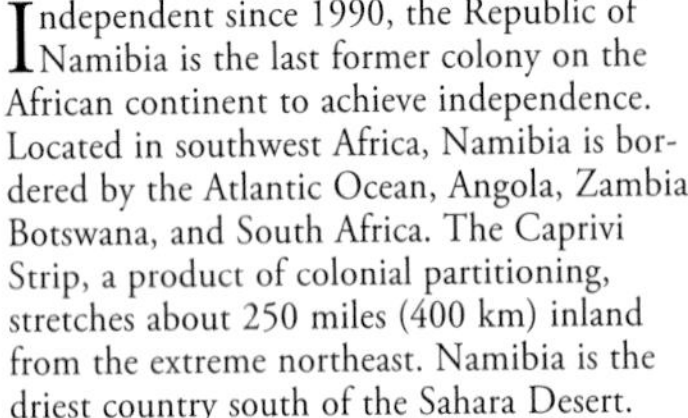

Map Reference Pages 308–309

Independent since 1990, the Republic of Namibia is the last former colony on the African continent to achieve independence. Located in southwest Africa, Namibia is bordered by the Atlantic Ocean, Angola, Zambia, Botswana, and South Africa. The Caprivi Strip, a product of colonial partitioning, stretches about 250 miles (400 km) inland from the extreme northeast. Namibia is the driest country south of the Sahara Desert.

Above The nomadic Himba people of Kaokoland in northern Namibia are cattle and goat breeders. Himba women coat their bodies and braid their hair with a thick mixture of butter fat, ocher, and herbs to provide sun protection, the ocher giving the skin a reddish tinge.

Above right Namibia has been called "a dry place located between two deserts." Sand dunes snake down to the rugged shores of the Skeleton Coast on Namibia's northern seaboard, so named for its shipwreck-strewn sands.

Below Election time and voters swamp the streets. Namibia has enjoyed more than a decade of political stability under founding president and freedom fighter Sam Nujoma, who led the campaign for independence from South Africa. His successor, President Pohamba, took over in 2005.

Physical Geography

The Namib Desert, after which the country is named, extends along the Atlantic coast. It is one of the world's oldest deserts. Desert gives way abruptly to the Great Escarpment, which extends parallel to the desert the entire length of the country. Beyond the escarpment lies the Central Plateau region at an average elevation of 5,000 feet (1,500 m). A spectacular feature of north–central Namibia is the Etosha Pan, a huge wet-season shallow lake that evaporates to a salty wasteland in the dry. The eastern part of the country is defined by the Kalahari Desert's sandy plains and grasses.

History

The area of Namibia was originally inhabited by the San (Bushmen), Namaqua, and Damara peoples. The nomadic Herero people arrived in the 1600s. The region became a German protectorate in 1884, called South West Africa. An uprising against German rule led to a vicious crackdown in 1904 that resulted in the death of 80 percent of the Herero population. Following World War I, control of the territory was ceded to South Africa. A system of apartheid was imposed and a bitter 23-year struggle for independence, beginning in 1966, was fought. In 1989, the political arm of the South West African People's Organization (SWAPO) won a historic election and the following year came independence.

SKELETON COAST

So treacherous are the waters off the Namibian coast, and so barren and inhospitable is the coastal strip that meets them, primarily rocky desert with interspersed belts of sand dunes, that the region has long been known as the Skeleton Coast. Although broadly associated with the entire coastline, the name specifically refers to the region from the mouth of the Swakop River in central Namibia north to the Kunene River, which forms part of the Angolan border. Here the upwelling of the cold Benguela Current, which flows north from Antarctica and generates a dense coastal fog bank, combines with the rocky, sandy shallows to create a perilous situation.

Testament to the dangers of these waters are the skeletal shipwrecks that litter the coast. Even if a sailor made it to shore, faced with one of the driest and most desolate landscapes on earth the choice was stark—either perish at the water's edge or strike inland to perish in the desert. The bony remains of seals and whales provide a visceral reminder of the days when the whaling industry was active, and reinforce the suitability of the region's name.

Today the entirety of the Skeleton Coast is becoming more accessible and is increasingly looked to as a vacation destination, although the fragile desert ecosystem limits travel. To protect this unique landscape, in 1971 Namibia designated a stretch of the northern coast between the Ugab and Kunene rivers as the Skeleton Coast Park.

Population/Culture

Namibia has the second lowest population density in the world (behind Mongolia). The distribution is very uneven; the northern regions of the Central Plateau account for only 16 percent of the land area but 54 percent of the population. The country has been hard hit by HIV/AIDS, which has reduced the average life expectancy from 61 years at independence to an estimated 46 years. It is also the third worst tuberculosis-affected country in the world, and malaria is the leading cause of illness and death in children aged under five.

The Ovambo constitute more than half the total population and share the northern region of Ovamboland with numerous other ethnic groups. Africans comprise 84 percent of the population; the remaining 16 percent is fairly evenly split between the European and mixed-race populations. Namibia has 24 indigenous languages and major dialects. English is the official language, but is the principal language spoken in only 2 percent of households. Most Namibians speak Herero, Nama, or Kwanyama, the main language of the Ovambo. Afrikaans remains the lingua franca south of Ovamboland.

Administration/Government

Namibia is a constitutional democracy and is notable as the first country in the world to incorporate environmental protection into its constitution. Fully 14 percent of its land, including virtually all of the Namib Desert, is protected. Every adult has the right to vote and opposition parties are free to criticize the ruling party and government. The government's principal objective has been land reform. About 2½ million acres (1 million hectares) of commercial farms have been purchased and transferred from white to black Namibians. With multiparty elections and separation of government powers, Namibia is recognized as one of the few "free" and "clean" countries on the African continent.

Economy/Industry

Namibia is categorized as a lower middle-income country, although glaring divisions remain between the wealthy white minority and the much poorer multi-ethnic majority, large numbers of whom depend on subsistence agriculture. Ecotourism provides important employment opportunities. Commercial agricultural activity is limited by climatic conditions. Cattle are raised in the northern and central plateau, and karakul (Persian) sheep are raised in the south. Namibia is the world's leading exporter of karakul products. Diamonds, the country's most valuable mineral, are principally found at the mouth of the Orange River. Namibia is also one of the world's leading producers of lead and uranium, and its fishing industry trawls one of the most productive fishing areas in the world.

MILESTONE EVENTS

1884 Berlin Conference, where Germany is given right to colonize Namibia
1904–1907 Suppression of Herero, Nama, and Damara rebellions; some 80 percent of all Herero are killed
1920 League of Nations grants South Africa a mandate to govern South West Africa (SWA)
1966 UN General Assembly revokes 1920 South African mandate; SWAPO begins war for independence
1990 Namibia gains independence with Sam Nujoma as president
1994 South African exclave of Walvis Bay is ceded to Namibia
2004 Opening of bridge across Zambezi River, raising hopes of increased regional trade
2004 Germany formally apologizes for century-old killings of Herero
2005 Government begins land reform program in which white-owned farms are appropriated for redistribution

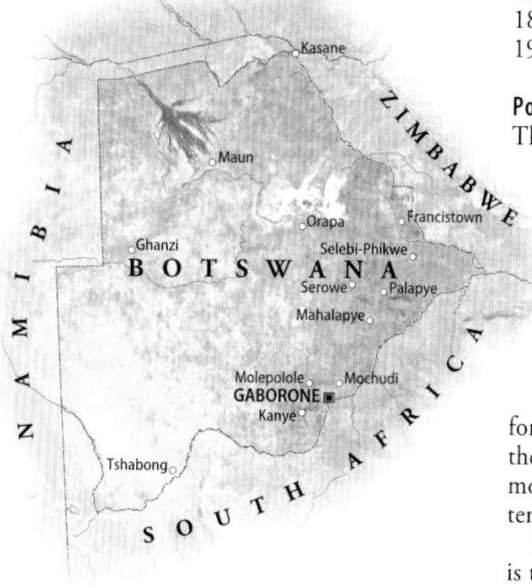
Kasane
NAMIBIA
ZIMBABWE
Maun
Orapa
Francistown
Ghanzi
Selebi-Phikwe
BOTSWANA
Serowe
Palapye
Mahalapye
Molepolole
Mochudi
GABORONE
Kanye
Tshabong
SOUTH AFRICA

Botswana

Map Reference Pages 308–309

Situated in southern Africa, the landlocked Republic of Botswana is a semi-arid tableland which is bordered by Namibia, Zambia, Zimbabwe, and South Africa, with which it maintains close economic ties. Formerly the British protectorate of Bechuanaland, Botswana achieved independence in 1966 and initially was among the poorest countries in the world. Since its independence, and following the discovery of rich diamond fields, Botswana has enjoyed the world's fastest economic growth rate and today is one of the wealthiest and most globalized countries on the African continent. However, facilitated by the country's impressive transportation network, Botswana is also being ravaged by the spread of HIV/AIDS. The 1980 movie *The Gods Must Be Crazy* was filmed on location in Botswana, which is also the setting for popular *The No. 1 Ladies' Detective Agency* stories.

Physical Geography

A plateau country with little topographic relief, much of Botswana's landscape is dominated by the Kalahari Desert, stretching across the center and southwest. The desert sands support scrub brush, acacias, and grasses, but the fertile eastern part of the country supports savanna grassland. There is little surface water and only three permanent rivers: The Limpopo, forming part of the southeastern border with South Africa; the Chobe, forming part of the northern border with Namibia and abutting Chobe National Park, home of the world's largest elephant herds; and the Okavango, terminating in the Okavango Delta, a huge wetlands on the northern edge of the Kalahari. The largest inland delta in the world with a rich diversity of wildlife, it has been called "Africa's last Eden." East of the delta lies the Makgadikgadi Pan, the world's largest salt flat complex, home to one of Africa's biggest zebra populations.

History

Originally inhabited by the nomadic San (Bushmen), the fertile eastern region was settled some time before 1000 CE by Bantu Tswana from the north, who drove the San out into the Kalahari. In the late nineteenth century, the discovery of gold resulted in the encroachment of Boers (Afrikaners) from neighboring South Africa into what was then British-controlled territory. The region was designated the British Bechuanaland Protectorate in 1885. Self-government was granted in 1965 and full independence in 1966.

Population/Culture

The largest cities and a majority of the population are located in the fertile east. The capital, Gaborone, (population 195,000), has more than twice the population of Francistown, the second largest city. Vast expanses of the country, particularly in the Kalahari Desert and the Okavango Delta, remain devoid of human settlement.

With about one-third of the critical workforce population infected with HIV/AIDS, the disease has become the leading cause of morbidity and mortality, and has resulted in tens of thousands of AIDS orphans.

Setswana, the language of the Tswana, is the primary language of a majority of the people and is understood by 95 percent of the population. In addition to the eight subgroups of Batswana (the national name for the Tswana people), San, Hereros, Asians, and Europeans also reside in the country.

Most Batswana are Christians, though small pockets of Muslims, Hindus, and Baha'is are present, as are traditional churches led by local prophets. Deference is accorded by the younger generation to the elderly, and it is customary and polite to greet senior men and women as *Rra* and *Mma* (which mean, literally, father and mother).

Administration/Government

As a multiparty democracy since gaining independence in 1966, Botswana represents Africa's longest continuous multi-party democracy. Elections are held every five years to the National Assembly, with the Botswana Democratic Party dominating election results since independence.

Generally free of corruption, the government maintains an estimable record on human rights issues and is noted for its fiscal conservatism. Through this approach, Botswana has sustained the most profitable diamond mines in the world and is one of the world's largest exporters of gemstone diamonds.

Economy/Industry

Botswana's diamond mines are jointly owned and operated with De Beers Consolidated Mines, and diamonds account for 80 percent of the country's export earnings.

Tourism is an important source of income and employment, as are agricultural activities, with maize, beans, and sorghum among the primary crops grown. Raising cattle for beef and hides is also an important activity. One of the African continent's economic success stories, Botswana's wealth generation has been used, in part, for social equity programs and infrastructural improvements. However, income inequality, which tends to follow a rural–urban division, remains a significant concern.

MILESTONE EVENTS

Pre-1000 CE Original San inhabitants driven from fertile eastern region by Tswana encroaching from the north

1852–1853 Batswana defeat Boer invaders

1885 British establish colonial rule over the protectorate of Bechuanaland

1960 Bechuanaland People's Party (BPP) is established

1965 Gaborone becomes seat of administrative power

1966 Bechuanaland gains independence as the Republic of Botswana; Seretse Khama is first president

1967 Discovery of diamonds at Orapa

1995 Government begins relocation of thousands of Bushmen to settlements beyond borders of Central Kalahari Game Reserve

2006 Bushmen win legal battle to retain their ancestral homelands

Below left A yellow-billed oxpecker *(Buphagus africanus)* picks insects and ticks from the neck of a giraffe *(Giraffa camelopardalis)* in Botswana's Chobe National Park.

BOTSWANA

Official name Republic of Botswana (Lefatshe la Botswana)

Land area 226,013 square miles (585,370 km²)

Border countries Zambia, Zimbabwe, South Africa, Namibia

Capital Gaborone

Highest & lowest points Tsodilo Hills 4,885 feet (1,489 m); junction of Limpopo and Shashe rivers 1,683 feet (513 m)

Climate Semi-arid to arid continental; warm winters and hot summers

Population 1,842,000

Language(s) Official: English; other: Setswana, Kalanga, Sekgalagadi, other indigenous languages

Ethnicity Tswana (or Setswana) 79%; Kalanga 11%; Basarwa 3%; other, including Kgalagadi and European 7%

Religion Christian 71.6%, Badimo 6%, other 1.4%, unspecified 0.4%, none 20.6%

Government Parliamentary republic with two legislative bodies (House of Chiefs and National Assembly)

Currency Pula

Human Development Index 0.654 (ranked 124th out of 177 countries)

Below The attentive gazes of lionesses *(Panthera leo)* lying in the grass, Botswana. Lions spend up to twenty hours resting, especially in the heat of the day, while the cooler hours at dawn and dusk are spent hunting and maintaining territory.

Left The Ministry of Minerals, Energy, and Water Resources in Botswana's capital, Gaborone, is a shimmering symbol of the country's economic success, generated mostly from diamond mining and maintained through sound fiscal policies.

ZIMBABWE

Official name Republic of Zimbabwe
Land area 149,294 square miles (386,670 km²)
Border countries Zambia, Mozambique, South Africa, Botswana
Capital Harare
Highest & lowest points Mt Inyangani 8,504 feet (2,592 m); junction of Runde and Save rivers 531 feet (162 m)
Climate Tropical, moderated by altitude
Population 12,383,000
Languages Official: English; other: Shona, Sindebele, numerous tribal dialects
Ethnicity Shona 82%, Ndebele 14%, other African 2%, mixed and Asian 1%, European less than 1%
Religion Mixed Christian–indigenous beliefs 50%, Christian 25%, indigenous beliefs 24%, Muslim and other 1%
Government Parliamentary democracy
Currency Zimbabwean dollar
Human Development Index 0.513 (ranked 151st out of 177 countries)

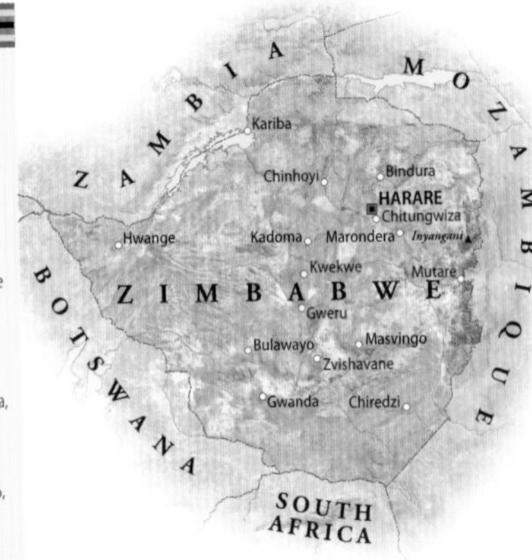
ZAMBIA
MOZAMBIQUE
ZIMBABWE
BOTSWANA
SOUTH AFRICA
Kariba
Chinhoyi
Bindura
HARARE
Chitungwiza
Hwange
Kadoma
Marondera
Inyangani
Kwekwe
Mutare
Gweru
Bulawayo
Masvingo
Zvishavane
Gwanda
Chiredzi

Zimbabwe

Map Reference Pages 308–309

The landlocked Republic of Zimbabwe in southern Africa was formerly known as Rhodesia, named for businessman, politician, and mining magnate Cecil Rhodes. Upon independence in 1980, it was renamed Zimbabwe ("place of stones") after the stone ruins—the largest stone structures in Africa south of the pyramids—known as Great Zimbabwe.

Below A wisp of rainbow hangs over the thunderous Victoria Falls, Zimbabwe.

Below right Zimbabwe's *mbira* consists of metal keys mounted on a wooden soundboard.

Physical Geography

Zimbabwe is largely a plateau country located between the Zambezi and Limpopo rivers, with desert landscape to the west and the Great Escarpment and Inyanga Mountains to the east. Approximately 25 percent of the country is high veld, a broad mountainous ridge that extends across the country from the southwest to the northeast. Zimbabwe enjoys a tropical climate moderated by the country's altitude, with a summer rainy season between November and March. At the height of the rainy season, the Zambezi River reaches full flood and bounds over the massive Victoria Falls, the world's largest waterfall. The local name for the falls is *Musi-oa-Tunya* (the smoke that thunders).

History

British activity in the area began in 1890, with administrative responsibility and commercial rights granted to the British South Africa Company. Land apportionment was based on the apartheid system, with the black areas, which were known as Tribal Trust Lands, characterized by generally infertile soils and a lack of rainfall. In 1965, the Rhodesian government, led by Ian Smith, declared independence from the United Kingdom. Armed struggle with the black African majority began the following year, with Zimbabwe finally achieving formal independence in 1980 with Robert Mugabe as president.

Population/Culture

Zimbabwe has relative ethnic homogeneity, with the majority Shona comprising 82 percent of the population. The emigration of white Zimbabweans since independence has reduced their number to less than 50,000. Black Zimbabweans have also emigrated in large numbers, seeking work and safety. Zimbabwe has one of the world's highest HIV/AIDS infection rates, estimated at around 30 percent. Life expectancy has fallen from 60 years to 40, and fertility rates have also declined markedly.

Black Zimbabweans, who comprise 98 percent of the total population, are subdivided into two major language groups: Shona and Ndebele. English is the official language. Christianity is the principal religion. Traditional arts of basketry, weaving, pottery, and jewelry are practiced, and Shona soapstone carvings and sculptures are justifiably famous. The staple food is sadza, a cornmeal mixture akin to thick grits. Family celebrations are usually marked with a feast featuring a barbecued goat or cow.

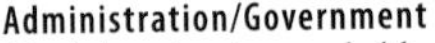

Administration/Government

Zimbabwe has been ruled by Robert Mugabe and his Zimbabwean African National Union-Patriotic Front (ZANU-PF) since independence. Declaration of a perpetual "state of emergency" gave the authorities widespread powers including the right to detain persons without charge, and kept political opposition to a minimum. Mugabe began radical land reform efforts in 2000 whereby white farmers were stripped of their land—much of it was subsequently given to members of the military or to Mugabe's own family.

Elections held in March 2008 saw the opposition leader Morgan Tsvangirai receive 49 percent of the vote, and Mugabe 42 percent. On April 3, it was revealed that ZANU-PF had lost control of parliament for the first time since independence. Mugabe and Tsvangirai signed a power-sharing deal, but little has yet come of it.

GREAT ZIMBABWE

The past glory of the peoples of Zimbabwe is nowhere more apparent than in the ruins popularly known as Great Zimbabwe, the largest stone structures in sub-Saharan Africa. These ancient ruins are the greatest of a series of some 300 known stone enclosure sites, known as *zimbabwes* or "places of stones," on the Zimbabwe plateau. Their sheer size and sophisticated structure led the first Europeans to see them to attribute their construction to foreign powers, perhaps Egyptians, Phoenicians, even the legendary Prester John, rather than the actual architects, the Bantu-speaking ancestors of the Shona.

The overall complex spreads over some 1,800 acres (730 ha). The elaborate main structure is enclosed by curvilinear granite walls about 20 feet (6 m) thick and 35 feet (11 m) high, and took an estimated 300 years to build. The individual slabs were fitted together without mortar at the apex of a hill rising 330 feet (100 m) above the surrounding landscape. Coinciding with its completion in the fourteenth century, the kingdom of Great Zimbabwe was reaching its zenith. The people were skilled metalworkers, and the kingdom flourished through its gold, ivory, and copper trade. Artefacts from as far away as China and India have been found among the ruins. The likeness of the distinctive carved soapstone birds found within the walls has become a symbol of modern Zimbabwe.

Economy/Industry

Having been an agrarian-based economy, Zimbabwe has seen its backbone of commercial agriculture collapse under the government's land reform policy. Tobacco continues to be the largest export earner, with $437 million in revenue. Mineral exports include chromium, copper, and gold. Economic mismanagement and hyperinflation mean that Zimbabwe is now a net importer of food, and the unemployment rate is running at 80 percent. Tourism has traditionally been important to the economy, but political instability and a declining international image have substantially reduced visitor numbers.

MILESTONE EVENTS

1200s–1500s Era of Great Zimbabwe and the trading empire

1855 David Livingstone sees the Zambezi River waterfalls, which he names Victoria Falls

1889 Cecil Rhodes' British South Africa Company gains British mandate to colonize what is to become Southern Rhodesia

1890 Pioneer column of British (white) settlers arrives

1924 Local government of Southern Rhodesia is placed in the hands of white settlers

1965 Unilateral declaration of independence

1966 Armed struggle begins

1980 Independence as the Republic of Zimbabwe, with veteran pro-independence leader Robert Mugabe as prime minister

1987 Mugabe changes constitution and becomes executive president

2000 Violent seizure of white-owned farms in a land redistribution policy

2008 Opposition MDC party claims victory in elections; ruling ZANU-PF disputes results

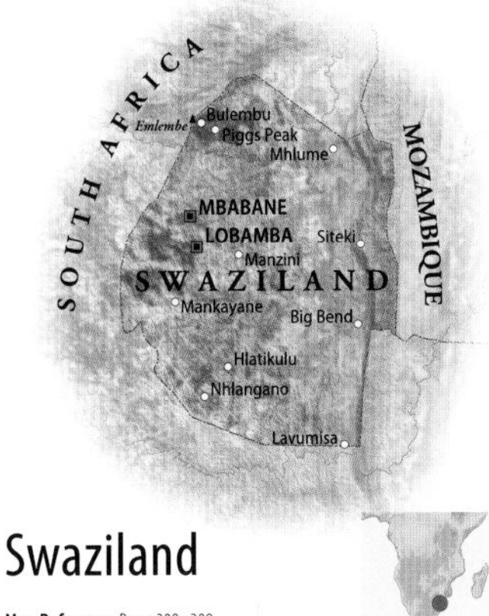
SOUTH AFRICA
Emlembe
Bulembu
Piggs Peak
Mhlume
MOZAMBIQUE
MBABANE
LOBAMBA
Siteki
Manzini
SWAZILAND
Mankayane
Big Bend
Hlatikulu
Nhlangano
Lavumisa

Swaziland

Map Reference Pages 308–309

The Kingdom of Swaziland is the last remaining absolute monarchy in Africa. It is a small, landlocked country bordered by Mozambique on the east, and by South Africa to the north, south, and west. It encompasses a variety of landscapes, from rainforest to rolling savannas and mountain ranges.

Physical Geography

In the mountainous temperate west, plantations of pines and eucalypts predominate. These highlands slope to the densely settled subtropical middle veld, which gives way to the hot, semiarid low veld bounded by the Lebombo Mountains along the eastern border.

History

In the late 1700s chief Ngwane II and subsequent leaders united the people of the region. In the 1880s Boer settlers from South Africa discovered gold and induced the chiefs into giving up control of the land.

Becoming a British protectorate in 1902, Swaziland achieved independence in 1968 as a constitutional monarchy under King Sobhuza II. In 1973, Sobhuza suspended the constitution and initiated rule by monarchy that was more closely aligned with Swazi traditionalism. Sobhuza was succeeded by his son, Mswati III, in 1982. Student and labor unrest in the 1990s pressured Mswati III to allow a greater degree of democracy, although political parties remain banned.

Population/Culture

About 1.1 million Swazi live in Swaziland proper, and many thousands live and work in an area of South Africa that formerly was part of the kingdom. It has the lowest life expectancy in the world, at a little over 32 years; Swaziland is firmly gripped by the HIV/AIDS pandemic, at 38 percent surpassing Botswana as the country with the highest rate of infection.

SiSwati and English are the official languages, with government and commercial business conducted in English. Nearly 60 percent of the country is held by the crown, and every adult male has the right to land under the *khonta* system. While the monarch (the *Ngwenyama*, hereditary leader) rules, the *Ndlovukazi* (queen mother) is in charge of the nation's rituals. A man may have more than one wife, and traditionally the king, who has many wives, may choose a wife from the participants in the annual Reed Dance. Cattle are highly valued in rural areas.

Administration/Government

The monarch appoints the prime minister and several representatives for both houses of parliament; the remainder are elected.

Economy/Industry

The small economy is based on soft drink (it is home to Coca-Cola's concentrate plant), sugar, and wood pulp and lumber from eucalypt plantations. Other major foreign exchange earners are cotton, coal, and diamonds. Efforts are underway to expand the industrial base, with textile, garment, and light manufacturing plants. Bolstered by its rich wildlife and scenery as well as very good road and rail infrastructure, Swaziland is a popular tourist destination, especially for South Africans.

SOUTH AFRICA
Hlotse
Maputsoe
Pitseng
Teyateyaneng
MASERU
Mokhotlong
Thabana Ntlenyana
LESOTHO
Thaba-Tseka
Mafeteng
Semonkong
Sehlabathebe
Qacha's Nek
Mohale's Hoek
Quthing
SOUTH AFRICA

Lesotho

Map Reference Pages 308–309

A relatively small country surrounded by South Africa, Lesotho is one of only a few monarchies in Africa, although the king has no political power and serves only a symbolic role. Previously known as Basutoland, it is a member of the Commonwealth of Nations.

Physical Geography

Lethoso's terrain is largely rugged and mountainous. In the east, the steep slopes of the Drakensberg Mountains are often blanketed in snow and eroded by heavy summer rains. The Maluti Mountains and associated ranges traverse the center. The rolling plateau of the west leads to the Caledon River, defining the western border and flanked by a thin strip of arable land. Here, the capital city of Maseru is connected to the district capitals of Mafeteng and Hlotse by the country's only paved road.

History

Victims of tribal wars in southern Africa in the late 1700s–early 1800s fled into the highlands of the area that is now Lesotho and were given protection by Chief Moshoeshoe, who in 1824 united them into the Basotho nation. In 1868 Moshoeshoe asked for British protection from Boer (Afrikaner) settlers, and Britain established the protectorate of Basutoland, which gained independence as the Kingdom of Lesotho in 1966.

Population/Culture

Lesotho is one of the most ethnically homogenous nations in Africa. Traditional religions of the non-Christian minority are based on ancestor worship. Lesotho is afflicted by HIV/AIDS, with a prevalence of about 29 percent.

Administration/Government

Lesotho is a parliamentary constitutional monarchy with two legislative houses (Senate and National Assembly). Administratively, Lesotho is divided into 10 districts, each headed by a district administrator.

Economy/Industry

About 86 percent of the population works in subsistence agriculture, but frequent drought means that food must be imported. Unemployment is estimated at nearly 50 percent, and up to one-half of active male wage earners work in South Africa. The Lesotho Highlands Water Project (LHWP) has made the country nearly self-sufficient in energy, and through exports of water and electricity to South Africa, generates one-quarter of export revenue. This has not translated into big employment opportunities and even the country's status as the sub-Sahara's largest exporter of clothing to the United States does little to bolster its weak industrial base. Lesotho is one of the least developed nations in the world.

LESOTHO

Official name Kingdom of Lesotho
Land area 11,720 square miles (30,355 km²)
Border countries South Africa
Capital Maseru
Highest & lowest points Mt Thabana-Ntlenyana 11,424 feet (3,482 m); junction of the Orange and Makhaleng Rivers 4,593 feet (1,400 m)
Climate Temperate; cool to cold, dry winters; hot, wet summers
Population 2,128,000
Language(s) Official: English; other: Sesotho, Zulu, Xhosa
Ethnicity Sotho 99.7%; Europeans, Asians, and other 0.3%
Religion Christian 80%, indigenous beliefs 20%
Government Parliamentary constitutional monarchy
Currency Loti
Human Development Index 0.549 (ranked 138th out of 177 countries)

Above left Dramatic clouds loom over the Maluti (Maloti) Mountains in central Lesotho.

Below Dressed in traditional costumes and headdresses, women attend a wedding in Lesotho's capital, Maseru.

SWAZILAND

Official name Kingdom of Swaziland (Umbuso weSwatini)
Land area 6,642 square miles (17,203 km²)
Border countries Mozambique, South Africa
Capital Mbabane (administrative); Lobamba (legislative))
Highest & lowest points Mt Emlembe 6,109 feet (1,862 m); Great Usutu River 70 feet (21 m)
Climate Tropical to temperate; wet season November to March
Population 1,129,000
Language(s) Official: English, siSwati; other: Zulu, Tsonga
Ethnicity African 97%, European 3%
Religion Mixed Christian-indigenous beliefs 40%, Roman Catholic 20%, Muslim 10%, other (includes Anglican, Bahai, Methodist, Mormon, Jewish) 30%
Government Monarchy with two legislative bodies (Senate and House of Assembly)
Currency Lilangeni
Human Development Index 0.547 (ranked 141st out of 177 countries)

Left The last remaining absolute monarch in Africa, King Mswati III of Swaziland and his entourage in the Lobamba Royal Village.

SOUTH AFRICA

Official name Republic of South Africa
Land area 471,008 square miles (1,219,912 km²)
Border countries Botswana, Zimbabwe, Mozambique, Swaziland, Namibia
Capitals Pretoria (Tshwane) (administrative), Cape Town (legislative), Bloemfontein (judicial)
Highest point Njesuthi 11,181 feet (3,408 m)
Climate Temperate, arid in west, semiarid in center; subtropical along east coast
Population 43,786,000
Language(s) Eleven official languages: Sepedi, Sesotho, Setswana, SiSwati, Tshivenda, Xitsonga, Afrikaans, English, IsiNdebele, IsiXhosa and IsiZulu; 8 non-official languages
Ethnicity Bantu (Zulu, Xhosa, Basotho or South Sotho, Bapedi or North Sotho, Venda, Tswana, Tsonga, Swazi, Ndebele) 79%, European 9.6%, Mixed 8.9%, Indian/Asian 2.5%
Religion Christian 79.7%, Muslim 1.5%, other 2.3%, unspecified 1.4%, none 15.1%
Government Republic
Currency Rand
Human Development Index 0.674 (ranked 121st out of 177 countries)

Above right South Africa's world-class wine-producing areas are centered around Cape Town, particularly Paarl, Stellenbosch, and Worcester.

Right The Zulu are the dominant ethnic group in South Africa, with approximately 10–11 million people residing mainly in the KwaZulu-Natal province, the Zulu homeland.

Below Ndebele tribeswoman Esther Mahlangu paints a mural, Gauteng province. The horizontal blue and mauve motif (center left) is based on a pattern found on the beaded apron worn by married women.

ZIMBABWE
BOTSWANA
MOZAMBIQUE
Polokwane
Soshanguve
PRETORIA (TSHWANE)
Soweto
Evaton
Johannesburg
Sasolburg
SWAZILAND
NAMIBIA
SOUTH AFRICA
Kimberley
Njesuthi
BLOEMFONTEIN
LESOTHO
Pietermaritzburg
Durban
Umlazi
INDIAN OCEAN
ATLANTIC OCEAN
Mdantsane
East London
CAPE TOWN
Bellville
Khayelitsha
Port Elizabeth

South Africa

Map Reference Pages 308–309

The key feature of today's South Africa is diversity—diversity of community, which resulted in Archbishop Desmond Tutu bestowing on it the label "Rainbow Nation," and sees 11 languages recognized as official, diversity of landscape, diversity of animal and plant life, and diversity of natural resources. Close to Cape Town, the Table Mountain National Park (one of 21 national parks) is home to more plant species than either the British Isles or New Zealand. South Africa hosts seven UNESCO World Heritage sites, places of "outstanding value to humanity," both natural and cultural. These include the 2 billion-year-old Vredefort Dome meteor impact site, the Cape Floral Region, Robben Island (for nearly 400 years a place of banishment and exile), the St Lucia Wetlands, the archeological site of Mapungubwe in Limpopo province (the center of the largest kingdom in Africa 1,000 years ago, where a sophisticated people traded gold and ivory with China, India, and Egypt), and the uKhahlamba–Drakensberg National Park which houses the world's greatest collection of rock art, over 35,000 individual images at some 600 sites.

Physical Geography

South Africa's lengthy coastline is washed by the Indian Ocean on the east and the Atlantic Ocean on the west. Cape Agulhas, 100 miles (160 km) southeast of the Cape of Good Hope, is the southernmost tip of the African continent, where the waters of the two oceans meet. South Africa is unusual in having another country, the landlocked Kingdom of Lesotho, wholly enclosed within it.

Nearly two-thirds of the country is flat or rolling plateau covered with grass and small shrubs—the veld. The south-central Highveld is the largest of the veld regions, part of the great African Plateau that continues northward to the Sahara Desert. Here agriculture and cattle-raising are practiced. Njesuthi, the highest point in South Africa, is part of the Drakensberg Mountains which form the Highveld's southeastern edge. From the Drakensbergs the land steps down to the ocean via the Great and Little Karoo, small plateaus separated by the Swartberg Mountains. West of the Highveld lies the arid Middleveld, which includes a section of the Kalahari Desert, and is mainly used for grazing sheep. The Bushveld to the north of the Highveld is also referred to as the Transvaal Basin. This region of mixed dry forests is famous for its abundant wildlife—including lion, leopard, blue wildebeest, white rhino, giraffe, hippopotamus, kudu, impala, and hyena. To the east are the wetter coastal plains of the Lowveld supporting extensive subtropical agriculture and cattle-raising.

The westward-flowing Orange River and the eastern-flowing Limpopo are the two major rivers of South Africa.

History

Fossil remains of the earliest hominid so far known, *Australopithecus africanus*, dating back 2.5–3 million years, have been found in South Africa, along with fossils of the ancestors of modern humans dating back over 50,000 years.

South Africa's written history begins with the arrival of the Portuguese, late in the fifteenth century. Colonization began with the Dutch East India Company in 1652 when a supply station was founded in the area where Cape Town would be established. The Company encouraged farmers to settle in the hinterland, and many arrived not only from the Netherlands but Germany and France. The site was called Cape Colony, and the settlers termed Boers or Afrikaners.

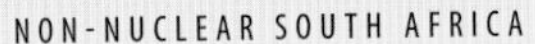

These early settlers had a tragic impact on native peoples, subjugating them or forcing them off their land. From the seventeenth to the nineteenth centuries, many hundreds of thousands of Bantu-speaking peoples, Khoikhoi, Xhosa, and others were killed by introduced diseases or died in wars with the Afrikaners and later the British.

In 1795 the British seized the Cape of Good Hope area and in 1806 annexed Cape Colony, leading to continuing conflict with the Afrikaners. With the discovery of diamonds at Kimberley in 1870 and gold in Transvaal in 1886, British miners and settlers arrived in greater numbers. This furthered conflict with the Boers, who had made independent republics in Transvaal (1852) and the Orange Free State (1854). The Anglo-Boer Wars of 1880–1881 and 1899–1902 saw the British winning and incorporating the independent republics, along with the British colony of Natal, and Cape Colony, to create the Union of South Africa, a self-governing dominion, on May 31, 1910. All political power was left in the hands of whites. Resistance to white rule became organized in 1912 with the creation of the forerunner of the African National Congress (ANC). Apartheid laws separating the races were created in 1948 by the white National Party (NP). For most of the next 30 years, ANC members like Nelson Mandela, and others who resisted apartheid, were imprisoned for treason—but they never gave up.

In May 1961, a whites-only referendum saw the Union become the Republic of South

NON-NUCLEAR SOUTH AFRICA

In a generation where the proliferation of nuclear weapons is a major global concern, many have forgotten that South Africa once developed and possessed nuclear technology, most likely conducted nuclear tests, and then voluntarily gave up its nuclear weapons program—the only country in the world ever to do so.

The seeds of South Africa's nuclear program were planted during World War II when the country discovered major deposits of uranium. A nuclear research project was initiated in 1959 and by the early 1970s the country was producing weapons-grade enriched uranium. In 1979 a US satellite detected an intense double flash of light near the southern part of Africa. Most today believe this was a nuclear test carried out by South Africa, perhaps in cooperation with Israel—an amazing development in that the country had suffered under international sanctions since 1962 as a result of the policy of apartheid.

The nuclear weapons program continued to develop during the 1980s until President F. W. de Klerk, elected in September, 1989, sought to have South Africa accepted back into the international community. He recognized that to achieve this goal, both apartheid and speculation about South Africa's nuclear program would need to end. The official termination date was February 26, 1990; dismantling activities continued until 1994, when South Africa was allowed to reclaim its seat in the United Nations.

Africa and leave the British Commonwealth. The ANC and other black political parties were banned but continued to resist NP rule and apartheid by both violent and non-violent means. Anti-apartheid political parties were legitimized in 1989 and, following years of international ostracism and boycotts, in 1990 Mandela was released from prison on Robben Island after 27 years. Most of the apartheid laws were rescinded in 1991. The first multi-racial elections were held in 1994, with the ANC winning by an overwhelming majority. Mandela was elected president, and South Africa rejoined the Commonwealth.

In 1996, Mandela's government created the Truth and Reconciliation Commission, chaired by Archbishop Desmond Tutu to reveal the truth about human rights violations and atrocities under the earlier governments and to work to promote racial healing.

Population/Culture

South Africa is a multi-ethnic nation with Bantu-speaking peoples comprising 79 percent of the population; whites 9.6 percent; Asians (mostly Indian) 2.5 percent; other non-whites 8.9 percent. The major tribal groups include the Zulu, Xhosa, Sotho (north and south), Tswana, and Tsonga. Afrikaners make up more than half of the white population, with the remainder of British heritage.

Life expectancy is low at only 42.45 years, in part due to HIV/AIDS, which affects over 20 percent of the adult population.

Linguistically South Africa is a vibrant mixture, with 11 official languages and eight non-official languages. IsiZulu is spoken by nearly a quarter of the population. IsiXhosa is the second most common language, followed by Afrikaans, English, Setswana, Sesotho, and others. Large numbers of young people migrate to the cities in search of work; most of them speak English or Afrikaans as well as their native tongue.

About 80 percent practice some form of Christianity; 2 percent are Hindu, and less than 2 percent are Muslim. Others probably adhere to traditional indigenous beliefs.

Ethnic diversity means that there are many different cultures within black South Africa, each with its own cuisine, music, and dance.

Apartheid has ended, but its effects are only very slowly being erased. There is a high correlation between race and prosperity. Millions of black South Africans still live in poverty. Half the population falls below the poverty line, and nearly one-quarter are unemployed.

Administration/Government

South Africa is unique in that each of the three branches of government is located in a different city. Cape Town is the legislative capital, Bloemfontein the judicial capital, and Pretoria the administrative capital, where the president presides as chief of state and head of government. The mining and manufacturing town of Johannesburg is the largest city.

The two houses of parliament are the National Council of Provinces (upper house, with 90 members elected by the provincial legislatures) and the National Assembly (lower house, with 400 members elected by popular vote. The president is elected by the National Assembly for a five-year term.

MILESTONE EVENTS

c. 3 million years BCE *Australopithecus africanus* emerges

50,000 BCE First species of the genus *Homo* emerges

100s CE Khoikhoi herders begin to displace San hunter-gatherers

400s Bantu-speaking farmers enter eastern South Africa from the north

1652 Dutch settlers arrive at site of Cape Town

1814 Netherlands give Cape Colony to Britain

1902 Britain wins second Anglo–Boer War

May 31, 1910 Union of South Africa is formed; white rule

1912 African National Congress (ANC) founded to seek equality

1948 Segregationist National Party comes to power

May 31, 1961 South Africa becomes a republic and leaves the Commonwealth of Nations

1990 President F.W. de Klerk terminates nuclear program; Nelson Mandela released from prison

1991 Apartheid abolished

1994 First multi-racial elections held; Mandela elected president; South Africa rejoins Commonwealth

1996 Truth and Reconciliation Commission formed

1999 Thabo Mbeki replaces Mandela as president

Economy/Industry

South Africa has long been recognized as a leading producer of natural resources. It is not only the world's largest producer of gold but also a major producer of diamonds, coal, uranium, platinum, manganese, and a variety of other minerals.

The economy has moved beyond simple exploitation of natural resources; today South Africa's stockmarket is the seventeenth largest in the world and the service sector makes up nearly two-thirds of the economy. South Africa also has modern and well-developed energy, communications, transportation, financial, and legal sectors. A well-developed road and rail infrastructure provides the platform for ground transportation deep into sub-Saharan Africa. Major shipping lanes pass along the South African coastline in the south Atlantic and Indian oceans. The country's seven commercial ports form the largest, best equipped, and most efficient network on the African continent.

Substantial revenue is earned by the tourist industry. Visitors are lured by the many game reserves and associated safari tours, the rich flora of the Fynbos Biome of the southern Cape region (one of six floral kingdoms), the multitude of national parks, the heritage sites, and the long-established and highly regarded wine industry, which accounts for 3.1 percent of world wine production.

Above During spring the Strandveld in West Coast National Park is blanketed with thousands of multi-hued daisies and a multitude of other colorful floral species.

Above left A herd of African elephants *(Loxodonta africana)* in Kruger National Park, South Africa's largest game reserve. The park's existing habitats can sustain 8,000 individuals only.

Above Giraffes *(Giraffa camelopardalis)* inhabit the savannas and grasslands of South Africa. Here, males engage in a "necking" duel—among other functions, this ritualized fighting helps establish dominance and access to females.

Below Nestled at the foot of Table Mountain on the Cape Peninsula, Cape Town was the site of the first European settlement of the Republic of South Africa. With a population of 3.5 million, it is South Africa's second largest city.

Right St Helena island is notable as the site of Napoleon Bonaparte's exile from 1815 until his death in 1821. Napoleon rode horses from Mount Pleasant estate (pictured here).

MAYOTTE

Official name Territorial Collectivity of Mayotte (Collectivité départementale de Mayotte)
Land area 145 square miles (374 km²)
Capital Dzaoudzi or Mamoudzou
Climate Tropical, marine; hot, humid rainy season (November–May); cooler dry season (May–November)
Population 216,306
Government French dependency
Currency Euro

RÉUNION

Official name Réunion (Région Réunion)
Land area 966 square miles (2,502 km²)
Capital St-Denis
Climate Tropical
Population 777,000
Government Republic (an overseas department of France)
Currency Euro

ST HELENA

Official name St Helena
Land area Total: 160 square miles (413 km²)
Capital Jamestown
Climate Tropical, moderated by trade winds; Tristan da Cunha cooler
Population 7,601 (includes Ascension and Tristan da Cunha)
Government Overseas territory of the United Kingdom
Currency Saint Helenian pound

WESTERN SAHARA

Official name Western Sahara (As-Sahra al-Garbiyah)
Land area 102,702 square miles (266,000 km²)
Capital El Aaiún (Laâyoune)
Climate Hot, dry desert; rain is rare; cold offshore currents produce fog and heavy dew
Population 393,831
Currency Moroccan dirham

Above right Located near St Suzanne, Réunion, Cascade Niagara falls from some 82 feet (25 m).

Below right El-Aaiún, Western Sahara, is just 8 miles (13 km) from the Atlantic Ocean.

Below Locals fish for a living opposite Mayotte's biggest city Mamoudzou. Mayotte's remote location inhibits the development of tourism.

Madeira
(Portugal)
Ceuta
(Spain)
Melilla
(Spain)
TUNISIA
Mediterranean Sea
Canary Islands
(Spain)
MOROCCO
ALGERIA
LIBYA
EGYPT
Western Sahara
Red Sea
CAPE VERDE
MAURITANIA
MALI
NIGER
CHAD
SUDAN
ERITREA
SENEGAL
GAMBIA
GUINEA-BISSAU
GUINEA
BURKINA FASO
TOGO
BENIN
NIGERIA
DJIBOUTI
SIERRA LEONE
CÔTE D'IVOIRE
GHANA
LIBERIA
CAMEROON
CENTRAL AFRICAN REPUBLIC
ETHIOPIA
SOMALIA
EQUATORIAL GUINEA
SÃO TOMÉ AND PRÍNCIPE
GABON
CONGO
UGANDA
KENYA
DEMOCRATIC REPUBLIC OF CONGO
RWANDA
BURUNDI
TANZANIA
INDIAN OCEAN
SEYCHELLES
Ascension
(UK)
ATLANTIC OCEAN
COMOROS
ANGOLA
ZAMBIA
MALAWI
Mayotte
(France)
St Helena
(UK)
MOZAMBIQUE
NAMIBIA
ZIMBABWE
MADAGASCAR
MAURITIUS
BOTSWANA
Réunion
(France)
SWAZILAND
SOUTH AFRICA
LESOTHO
Tristan da Cunha
(St Helena)
Gough Island
(Tristan da Cunha)

Mayotte

Map Reference Page 310

Mayotte (the islands of Grande Terre or Mayotte, Petite Terre or Pamanzi, and numerous islets) lies at the southeast end of the Comoros archipelago, in the northern Mozambique Channel. A volcanic mountain range forms a north–south chain on Mayotte, the main island. The terrain is generally undulating, with deep ravines and ancient volcanic peaks.

Surrounding coral reefs some distance from the shore provide protected waters for shipping and fishing. The warm maritime climate and plentiful year-round rainfall support the tropical forest.

Most of the people in Mayotte are Comoran of Malagasy origin, and predominantly Muslim. French culture is pre-eminent and French is the official language. A very high birth rate, with the result that around 50 percent of the population is under 15 years of age, is a major problem. Principal towns are Mamoudzou on Mayotte and Dzaoudzi on Île Pamanzi.

Agriculture is the main economic activity. Vanilla, ylang-ylang, coffee, coconuts, and copra are important exports. However, Mayotte imports most of its food needs from France, and development depends on French subsidies.

Mayotte did not join with the rest of the Comoros at independence from France in 1975, and is a dependency administered by a French-appointed prefect and an elected 17-member General Council. French law applies unless altered by local custom. The Comoros Republic claims Mayotte as a territory.

Réunion

Map Reference Page 310

Réunion is a small island in the Mascarene Archipelago east of Madagascar in the Indian Ocean. The densely populated, heavily forested island rises steeply out of the sea. A volcanic hotspot, it has one of the most active volcanoes in the world, Piton de la Fournaise, recording over 170 eruptions since 1640.

The French settled the uninhabited island, naming it Île Bourbon in 1649 and Réunion in 1793. Réunion was a colony until 1947 when it became an overseas department of France. Its residents are French citizens.

The population is an ethnic mix similar to that of Mauritius: Indian, Chinese, Malagasy, African, and French. People born on Réunion—Creoles—make up most of the population.

Most people are Roman Catholic, and French is the official language. Réunionnaise Creole, a localized version of French, is the daily language of the people. The culture is an interesting amalgamation with French, Indian, Chinese, and African influences.

As an overseas French department, Réunion sends three representatives to the French Senate and five to the National Assembly in Paris. Tourism and sugar production are the economy's main elements. Exports include sugar and rum, lobster, perfume essence, and vanilla.

St Helena

Map Reference Page 310

St Helena, a British overseas territory, is made up of the island of St Helena and the dependencies of Ascension Island and the Tristan da Cunha group. St Helena is located 1,152 miles (1,920 km) west of Angola and is one of the world's most isolated places. All the islands of the territory sit atop the Mid-Atlantic Ocean Ridge system and are volcanic and mountainous. Isolation means St Helena is home to at least 40 endemic plant species.

St Helena was discovered in 1502 by the Portuguese, garrisoned by British troops in 1659, and served as a confinement for South African Boer prisoners of war in 1900–1902.

St Helenians earn income from fishing, raising livestock, and sales of handicrafts to tourists. Because of the isolation and dearth of employment opportunities, one-quarter of the labor force has left to seek work overseas, and financial assistance from the United Kingdom largely supports the economy.

Western Sahara

Map Reference Pages 300–301

Located in northwest Africa on the Atlantic Ocean, Western Sahara is mostly low, flat, rocky and sandy desert with some low mountains in the south and northeast. The climate is hot and dry, and dust and sand-laden sirocco winds occur regularly during the winter and spring.

Western Sahara is occupied by Morocco. The main towns are El Aaiún (Laâyoune), the capital, as well as Dakhla, Boujdour, and Essemara. The traditional economy of the mostly nomadic Berber (Arabic-speaking Muslim Bedouin) people depends on raising goats, camels, and sheep, with date palm cultivation and some fishing. Rich deposits of phosphates were first exploited in the 1970s; potash and iron have also been found.

The area became a Spanish protectorate in 1884 and a colony (Spanish Sahara) in 1958. When Spain left in 1976, the territory was divided between Morocco and Mauritania. The indigenous Sahrawis, led by the Polisario Front, promptly declared a government-in-exile (the Sahrawi Arab Democratic Republic) from a base in Algeria. Polisario reached a peace agreement with Mauritania in 1979, but Morocco quickly seized the land given up and now controls the entire region. Morocco rejects any measure that will lead to independence, and the Polisario Front remains unwavering in its support for an independent state. Many Sahrawis are refugees in Algeria.

Most food is imported. Economic activities are controlled by Morocco. In 2001, Moroccan energy interests signed contracts to explore for oil off the coast, which has angered the Polisario. Standards of living in Western Sahara are well below Moroccan levels.

Left The towns on Tenerife in the Canary Islands are well known for their unique architecture, including pastel-colored houses with traditional balconies as well as castles and towers that once defended the towns from attack by pirates.

CEUTA

Official name Ceuta (Plaza de Soberania, "Place of Sovereignty")
Land area 7¾ square miles (20 km^2)
Capital Autonomous City of Ceuta (Ciudad Autónoma de Ceuta)
Climate Mediterranean; hot dry summer, mild damp winter
Population 75,861
Government Parliamentary monarchy/ autonomous town council
Currency Euro

CANARY ISLANDS

Official name Autonomous Community of the Canary Islands (Comunidad Autónoma de Canarias)
Land area 3,000 square miles (7,770 km^2)
Co-capitals Las Palmas de Gran Canaria, Santa Cruz de Tenerife
Climate Dry, warm, often windy
Population 1,996,000
Government Autonomous region of Spain (a constitutional monarchy)
Currency Euro

Ceuta

Map Reference Pages 300

Ceuta, at the east end of the Strait of Gibraltar, is one of two tiny Spanish enclaves on the northern coast of Africa, bordered by Morocco and the Mediterranean Sea. The other is Melilla, some 185 miles (300 km) to the east.

Monte Hacho is the highest point. Either it or Jebel Sidi Moussa, nearby in Morocco, is believed to be ancient Abila, the southern Pillar of Hercules. The Rock of Gibraltar (ancient Calpe) is the northern pillar.

Ceuta was claimed by Portugal in 1415 and seized by Spain in 1580. Since 1978 Morocco has made claims on both Ceuta and Melilla.

The east of Ceuta is Spanish-influenced; the west Moroccan and Islamic-influenced. Historic fortifications and monuments date back to medieval times. Tourism is a primary business; the scenic city is connected to the Spanish mainland by a 90-minute ferry trip.

Governed by a local council, Cueta has senators and representatives in the Spanish parliament. The city is a free port; shipyards and fish processing are important.

Canary Islands

Map Reference Pages 310

Lying some 75 miles (120 km) off the northwest coast of Africa, the Canary Islands are a very popular tourist destination. The archipelago includes seven major islands (Gran Canaria, Fuerteventura, Lanzarote, Tenerife, La Palma, Gomera, Hierro), remnants of steep extinct volcanoes, and several smaller islands. The ideal weather conditions and the beautiful beaches make the Canaries a perfect tourist escape from cold European winters. The islands' name is thought to be derived from Latin *Insula canaria*, "Island of the Dogs," referring to Gran Canaria, the home of a breed of large fierce dog.

The Canaries were declared a province of Spain in 1821, with Santa Cruz de Tenerife the capital. They became an autonomous region of Spain in 1982, as two provinces—Las Palmas and Santa Cruz de Tenerife. The islands have 13 seats in the Spanish Senate.

The original inhabitants, the Guanches, relied on limited farming, herding, hunting, and gathering for subsistence. Today's leading exports include bananas, sugarcane, tomatoes, potatoes, and tobacco. There is some fishing, but tourism, with an estimated 10 million tourists each year, is the major economic activity at 32 percent of GDP. An oil refinery and other large-scale industries are located at Santa Cruz de Tenerife.

Their extreme popularity as a tourist location has produced considerable nationalist sentiment on the islands. The Canaries are also a popular route and intermediate target for thousands of economic immigrants from sub-Saharan Africa seeking to enter Europe.

Madeira

Map Reference Pages 310

The Madeira archipelago in the Atlantic Ocean, 310 miles (500 km) west of North Africa, includes the islands of Porto Santo and Madeira, and two uninhabited groups. The largest in area, Madeira is a rugged mountainous island of volcanic origin, with a coastline of stony beaches and vertical rocks. Porto Santo (the Golden Island), is lower lying and has long sandy beaches.

The subtropical climate varies between the main island and smaller islands such as Porto Santo and the Selvagens. The main island is a popular tourist resort, noted for its wine (known as Madeira), flowers, and embroidery, and for big New Year's Eve celebrations.

Tourism contributes about 20 percent of GDP, and provides support for other important economic activities such as commercial transport. Agricultural produce apart from grapes includes bananas, mangoes, pawpaws, guavas, pineapples, sugarcane, and avocados.

Madeira became an autonomous political region of Portugal in 1976, and today has a separate government and legislative assembly. Most of the population lives on Madeira Island.

Melilla

Map Reference Pages 300

The autonomous city of Melilla is a small Spanish enclave on the Tres Forcas Peninsula, surrounded by Morocco and the Mediterranean Sea. Like its sister city of Ceuta, Melilla is enclosed on its landward side by a double border fence 20 feet (6 m) high to deter illegal immigrants attempting to reach Europe.

Like many other cities along the North African coast, Melilla had been conquered and reconquered by outsiders, including the Carthaginians, Romans, Vandals, Byzantines, and Berbers, before it was taken by Spain in 1497. A mixture of Moorish and Spanish elements can be seen in Melilla; Arabic and Spanish are commonly spoken. The diverse population has Christian, Muslim, Jewish, and Hindu communities.

Melilla is governed as a part of Spain, electing senators and deputies to the parliament in Madrid and administered locally by a council.

Tourism is a major money-earner, with the city's duty-free status being a big attraction. Melilla has Spain's second most important collection of Modernist art. Fishing is also an important component of the economy.

Left A Muslim man from Africa attends Friday prayers at the Center for the Temporary Residence of Immigrants (CETI) in Melilla. The facility is overcrowded with people trying to get to Europe.

MADEIRA

Official name Madeira Autonomous Region (Região Autónoma da Madeira)
Land area Madeira island: 320 square miles (828 km^2)
Capital Funchal
Climate Subtropical, with warm summers and extremely mild winters
Population 250,000
Government Autonomous region of the Portuguese Republic
Currency Euro

MELILLA

Official name Melilla (Plaza de Soberania, "Place of Sovereignty")
Land area 4½ square miles (12 km^2)
Capital Autonomous City of Melilla (Ciudad Autónoma de Melilla)
Climate Mediterranean; hot dry summer, mild damp winter
Population 66,871
Government Parliamentary monarchy/ autonomous town council
Currency Euro

Left The traditional fishing village of Câmara de Lobos, on the island of Madeira, is now a city. It was named by the explorers João Gonçalves Zarco and Tristão Vaz Teixeira, partly for the many *lobos* (sea lions) they saw in the bay.

ATLANTIC OCEAN
NORWEGIAN SEA
NORTH SEA
Barents Sea
EUROPE
ASIA
MEDITERRANEAN SEA
BLACK SEA
CASPIAN SEA
RED SEA
ARABIAN PENINSULA
SAHARA
SAHEL
Libyan Desert
Baltic Sea
Bay of Biscay
Ionian Sea
Tyrrhenian Sea
Adriatic Sea
Aegean Sea
Aral Sea
CAUCASUS
ALPS
Pyrenees
Iberian Peninsula
Ural'skiy Khrebet (Ural Mountains)
ZAPADNO-SIBIRSKAYA RAVNINA
Northern European Plain
ATLAS MOUNTAINS
GREENLAND
Iceland
Denmark Strait
Davis Strait
Shetland Islands
Faroe Islands
Orkney Islands
British Isles
Ireland
English Channel
Sicilia (Sicily)
Cyprus
Kriti (Crete)
Sinai
The Gulf
Jabal Tuwayq
Ar Rub' al Khali
Nubian Desert
Tibesti
Hoggar
Erg Iguidi
El Djouf
Ennedi
BODÉLÉ
Arquipélago da Madeira
Islas Canarias (Canary Islands)

1:29,000,000
Lambert Azimuthal Equal Area Projection

0 250 500 750 1000 kilometers
0 125 250 375 500 miles

Africa Physical

AFRICA
Congo Basin
ATLANTIC OCEAN
INDIAN OCEAN
Gulf of Guinea
Bight of Benin
Madagascar
Mozambique Channel
Kalahari Desert
Namib Desert
Okavango Delta
Drakensberg
Lake Victoria
Lake Tanganyika
Lake Nyasa
Lake Turkana
Lake Kariba
Lake Volta
Chalbi Desert
Masai Steppe
Sardendida Plain
Cameroon Highlands
Plateaux Batéké
Zambezi Escarpment
Muchinga Escarpment
Cape of Good Hope
Cape Agulhas
Cape Columbine
Cape Palmas
Cape Three Points
Dolphin Head
St Helena
Ascension
Tristan da Cunha
Gough Island
Mauritius
Réunion
Île Tromelin
Les Amirantes
Farquhar Group
Group d'Aldabra
Grande Comore
Mayotte
Îles Glorieuses
Île Europa
Bassas da India
Pemba Island
Zanzibar Island
Mafia Island
Prince Edward Islands
Îles Crozet
Annobón
São Tomé
Principe
Etosha Pan
Great Karoo
Ghaap Plateau

ATLANTIC OCEAN
NORWEGIAN SEA
NORTH SEA
Barents Sea
Greenland (Kalaallit Nunaat) (Denmark)
ICELAND
NORWAY
SWEDEN
FINLAND
RUSSIAN FEDERATION
KAZAKHSTAN
UZBEKISTAN
TURKMENISTAN
AFGHAN.
IRAN
IRAQ
SYRIA
TURKEY
BLACK SEA
CASPIAN SEA
MEDITERRANEAN SEA
RED SEA
SAUDI ARABIA
ARABIAN PENINSULA
YEMEN
OMAN
UNITED ARAB EMIRATES
KUWAIT
The Gulf
EGYPT
SUDAN
ERITREA
LIBYA
CHAD
NIGER
ALGERIA
SAHARA
MALI
MAURITANIA
SENEGAL
Western Sahara
MOROCCO
TUNISIA
SPAIN
PORTUGAL
FRANCE
ITALY
GERMANY
POLAND
UKRAINE
BELARUS
ROMANIA
GREECE
UNITED KINGDOM
IRELAND
Libyan Desert
Nubian Desert

1:29,000,000
Lambert Azimuthal Equal Area Projection
0 250 500 750 1000 kilometers
0 125 250 375 500 miles

Africa Political

ATLANTIC OCEAN
INDIAN OCEAN
Gulf of Guinea
Mozambique Channel
SIERRA LEONE
LIBERIA
CÔTE D'IVOIRE
GHANA
TOGO
CAMEROON
EQUATORIAL GUINEA
SÃO TOMÉ AND PRÍNCIPE
GABON
CONGO
CENTRAL AFRICAN REPUBLIC
DEMOCRATIC REPUBLIC OF CONGO
ETHIOPIA
SOMALIA
UGANDA
KENYA
RWANDA
BURUNDI
TANZANIA
MALAWI
ZAMBIA
ANGOLA
MOZAMBIQUE
ZIMBABWE
NAMIBIA
BOTSWANA
SOUTH AFRICA
LESOTHO
SWAZILAND
MADAGASCAR
COMOROS
SEYCHELLES
MAURITIUS
FREETOWN
MONROVIA
YAMOUSSOUKRO
ACCRA
LOMÉ
PORTO NOVO
YAOUNDÉ
MALABO
LIBREVILLE
SÃO TOMÉ
BRAZZAVILLE
KINSHASA
BANGUI
LUANDA
KAMPALA
NAIROBI
KIGALI
BUJUMBURA
DODOMA
DAR ES SALAAM
MUQDISHO (MOGADISHU)
LILONGWE
LUSAKA
HARARE
MAPUTO
WINDHOEK
GABORONE
PRETORIA (TSHWANE)
MBABANE
LOBAMBA
MASERU
BLOEMFONTEIN
CAPE TOWN
MORONI
ANTANANARIVO
VICTORIA
PORT LOUIS
Namib Desert
Kalahari Desert
Jamestown
Saint Helena (UK)
Georgetown
Ascension (UK)
Tristan da Cunha (St Helena)
Gough Island (St Helena)
Prince Edward Islands (South Africa)
Îles Crozet (French Southern and Antarctic Territories)
Saint Denis
Réunion (France)
Cape of Good Hope
Cape Agulhas

A 25° B 20° C 15° D 230 10° E 5°

1 2 3 4 5 6

35° 30° 25° 20° 15°

Azores (Portugal) Sao Miguel

LISBOA (LISBON) Queluz ÉVORA Badajoz Mérida Setúbal Évora EXTREMADURA Cabo Espichel SETÚBAL Costa da Galé Cabo de Sines Beja BEJA PORTUGAL Huelva Sevilla Córdoba Dos Hermanas FARO Faro Cabo de São Vicente Sagres Golfo de Cádiz Cabo de Santa Maria Jerez de la Frontera Cádiz Marbella Cabo de Trafalgar Algeciras Tanger (Tangier) Ceuta M'diq Asilah Tétouan Larache Ksar el Kebir Bargha Moulay- Bousselham Ouezzane Kénitra Sidi Slimane Sidi Kacem RABAT Meknès Fès Mohammedia Casablanca Khemisset Sefrou Rommani Berrechid El Hajeb Boulemane El Jadida Settat Oued Zem Jemaa de Mrirt Sidi Smail Khouribga Boujad Khenifra Khemis Zemamra Midelt Safi Fkih Ben Salah El Kelaâ des Srarhna Beni Mellal Er Rachidia Chemaia Essaouira Ounara Chichaoua Marrakech MOROCCO Boumaine Dadès Tinerhir Tamanar Ouarzazate Cap Rhir Jbel Toubkal 4167 Agadir Biougra Oued Sous Foum Zguid Zagora Tazzarine Tiznit Tafraoute Irherm Tata Hassi el Khebi Sidi Ifni Guelmim Tan-Tan Cap Drâa Oued Drâa Assa Jbel Ouarkziz Hamada du Drâa Tinfouchy Oued Tigzerte

Arquipélago de Madeira Ilha de Porto Santo Pico Ruivo 1862 Madeira Funchal Madeira (Portugal) Ilhas Desertas

ATLANTIC OCEAN

Ilhas Selvagens (Madeira)

Canary Islands (Spain) Roque de los Muchachos 2426 La Palma Las Indias San Cristóbal de la Laguna Santa Cruz de Tenerife Pico del Teide Calera La Gomera Tenerife Puerto de la Estaca El Hierro Frontera Agaete Las Palmas de Gran Canaria Pico de las Nieves 1949 Gran Canaria Playa del Ingles Islas Canarias Alegranza Lanzarote Graciosa Orzola Playa Blanca Arrecife Tindaya Puerto del Rosario Fuerteventura Tarfaya Cap Juby

Sabkhat Oum Dba Sabkhat Tah Al Haggounia Laâyoune As Saquia al Hamra Es Semara Boukra Al Mahbas Tindouf Sebkha de Tindouf Hamada Tounassine Hamada ed Douakel Cap Boujdour Sabkhat Aridal Aoufist Zemmour Bir Mogrein Aïn Ben Tili Sebkhet Iguetti Skaymat Zamlat Amagraj Galtat Zemmour Chegga Western Sahara (disputed) RIO DE ORO TIRIS ZEMMOUR GHALLAMANE Ad Dakhla Bahia de Rio de Oro Imlili Sabkhet Doumas Fdérik Zouérat Awserd El Hammâmi Bir Gandouz Tichla Touajil Agâraktem Erg Iguidi El Eglab Mcherrah

Tropic of Cancer

Nouâdhibou Ras Nouâdhibou Ras Agâdir DAKHLET NOUÂDHIBOU Azefal MAQTEIR Choûm Sebkhet Chemchâm Guelb er Richât 485 Atâr ADRAR El Mreyyé Iouik EtTidra Châmi Cap Timiris Nouâmghâr INCHIRI AKCHÂR Akjoujt Chinguetti Dhar Adrar El Djouf Boû Rjeimât El Mhaijrat MAURITANIA Elb el Frâl TOMBO Aghouavil El Gçaib

NOUAKCHOTT Afroût Faï TRARZA Ouâd Nâga Tidjikja TAGANT Dhar Tîchît Lekhcheb Tîchît Dhar Oualâta Tiguent Boutilimit Magta Lahjar Moudjéria Aoukâr Araouane HODH ECH CHARGUI Mederdra Rkîz Nbâk Cangrâfa Boumdeïd Tâmchekket BRAKNA Aleg Rosso Lexeiba Bogué Barkéwol el Abiod Guérou HODH EL GHARBI Ayoun el Atroûs Oualâta Dagana Podor Bababé Monguel Kiffa ASSABA Gleibat Boukenni St-Louis Kankossa Tintâne Néma Louga Lagbar Thilogne Kaédi Mbout GORGOL Kébémer Linguère Matam Sive Maghama Timbedgha Ndande Tivaouane Dara Kanel Kobenni Amourj Bassikounou DAKAR Cap Vert Mékhé Mbacké Touba Tiel Mamari GUIDIMAKA Sélibabi Nagara Aourou Touil Djiguéni Adel Bagrou Mbour Thiès Diourbel Gossas Gassane Vélingara Gouraye Kirané Yélimané Nioro Sanpaka Nara Joal-Fadiout Fatick Kaolack Mbar SENEGAL Toubéré Bafal Bakel Ambidédi Diangounté Kamara Diéma Dilli Nampala Youvarou Sokone Nioro du Rip Nganda Koungheul Bala Kidira Kayes KAYES Mourdiah GAMBIA BANJUL Serekunda Farafenni Maka Kaussanar Koussane Diamou Bafoulabé KOULIKORO Diafarabé Mopti Bwiam Tambacounda Sadiola Mahina Didiéni Djenné Sévaré Gambia Sutukoba Dialakoto Oualia Toukoto Kolokani Banamba SÉGOU Bankass Bignona Ziguinchor Kolda Dabo Fatoto Boutougou Fara Kita Tioribougou Ségou Zinzana San Tominian Kabrousse Sédhiou Wassadou Saraya Kéniéba Niamina Barouéli Tamani GUINEA-BISSAU Mansaba Kédougou Sébékoro Kangaba Koulikoro Mandiakui Cacheu Bafatá Dalaba Massif du Tamgué Satadougou Konrokota Faraba Négala Kati Sanando Fana Yallo Ilha de Jeta Ilha de Pecixe BISSAU Gabú Koulamori Lébékéré GUINEA Galé BAMAKO Mpessoba Kimparana

CAPE VERDE Santo Antão São Vicente Mindelo São Nicolau Pedra Lume Sal Fundo das Figuerias Sal Rei 390 Boa Vista Ilhas do Cabo Verde Curral Velho Tarrafal Fogo 2828 Fogo São Filipe 1392 Santiago Maio PRAIA

Meters Feet
6000 19685
5000 16404
4000 13123
3000 9843
2000 6562
1000 3281
500 1640
200 656
100 328
0 LAND BELOW SEA LEVEL
100 328
200 656
1000 3281
2000 6562
4000 13123
6000 19685

B 20° C 15° D 304 10° E 5°

1:10,320,000
Lambert Conic Conformal Projection

0 100 200 300 400 500 kilometers
0 50 100 150 200 250 300 miles

Northwestern Africa

231

233

302

305

MEDITERRANEAN SEA

ALGERIA

TUNISIA

LIBYA

NIGER

CHAD

NIGERIA

SAHARA

Meters	Feet
6000	19685
5000	16404
4000	13123
3000	9843
2000	6562
1000	3281
500	1640
200	656
100	328
0	LAND BELOW SEA LEVEL
100	328
200	656
1000	3281
2000	6562
4000	13123
6000	19685

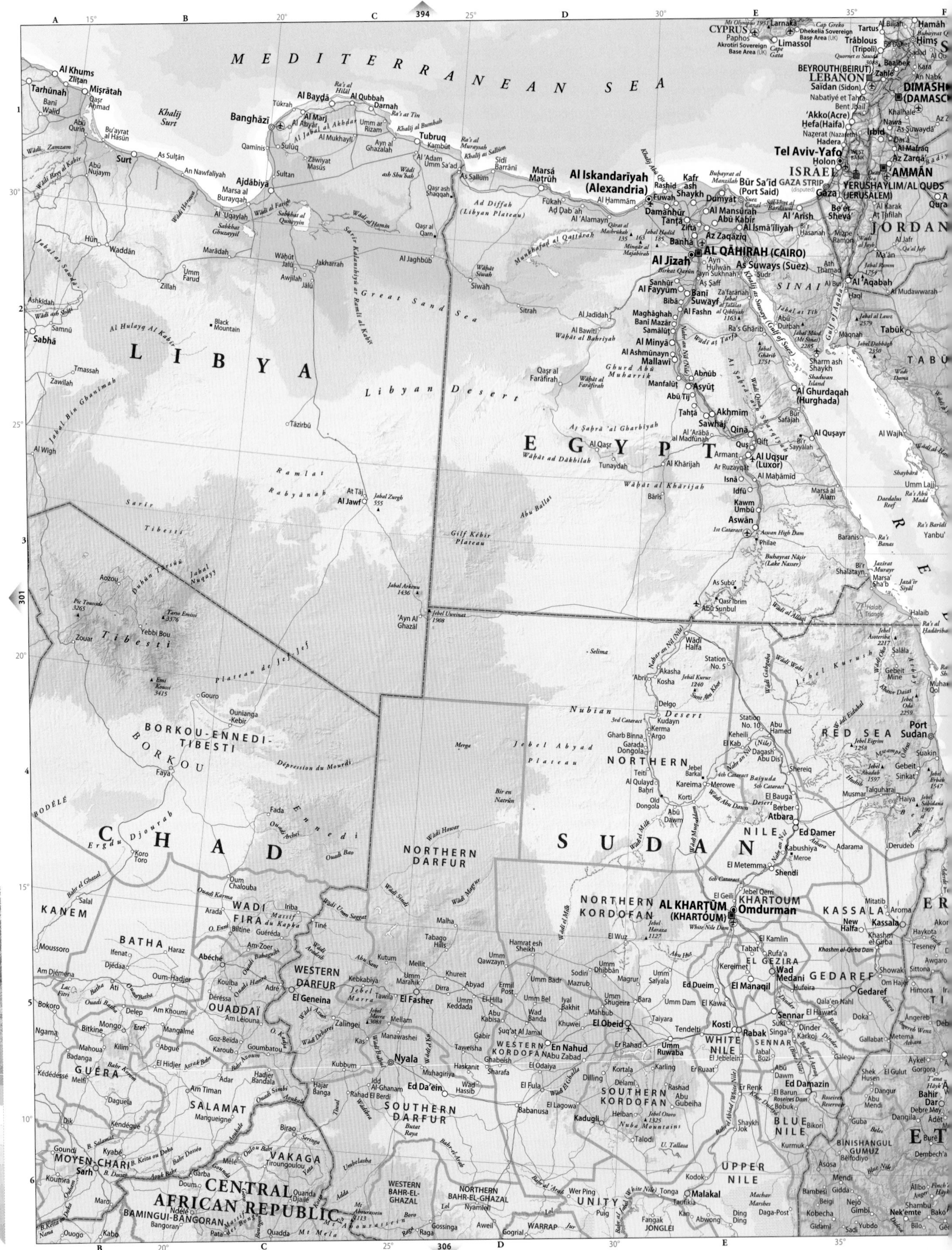
MEDITERRANEAN SEA
LIBYA
EGYPT
CHAD
SUDAN
Libyan Desert
Great Sand Sea
Al Qāhirah (Cairo)
Al Iskandarīyah (Alexandria)
Al Khartūm (Khartoum)
Omdurman
Banghāzī
Port Sudan
Tibesti
394
301
306

1:10,320,000
Lambert Conic Conformal Projection
0 100 200 300 400 500 kilometers
0 50 100 150 200 250 300 miles

Northeastern Africa and the Middle East

300

SENEGAL
GAMBIA
GUINEA-BISSAU
GUINEA
SIERRA LEONE
LIBERIA
MALI
BURKINA FASO
CÔTE D'IVOIRE
GHANA
TOGO

DAKAR
BANJUL
BISSAU
CONAKRY
FREETOWN
MONROVIA
BAMAKO
OUAGADOUGOU
YAMOUSSOUKRO
ACCRA
LOMÉ
NIAMEY

Bight of Benin
GULF OF GUINEA
ATLANTIC OCEAN
Equator

Ascension (United Kingdom)
Two Boats Village
Georgetown

Meters / Feet
6000 19685
5000 16404
4000 13123
3000 9843
2000 6562
1000 3281
500 1640
200 656
100 328
0
LAND BELOW SEA LEVEL
100 328
200 656
1000 3281
2000 6562
4000 13123
6000 19685

1:10,320,000
Lambert Conic Conformal Projection

0 100 200 300 400 500 kilometers
0 50 100 150 200 250 300 miles

Western Central Africa

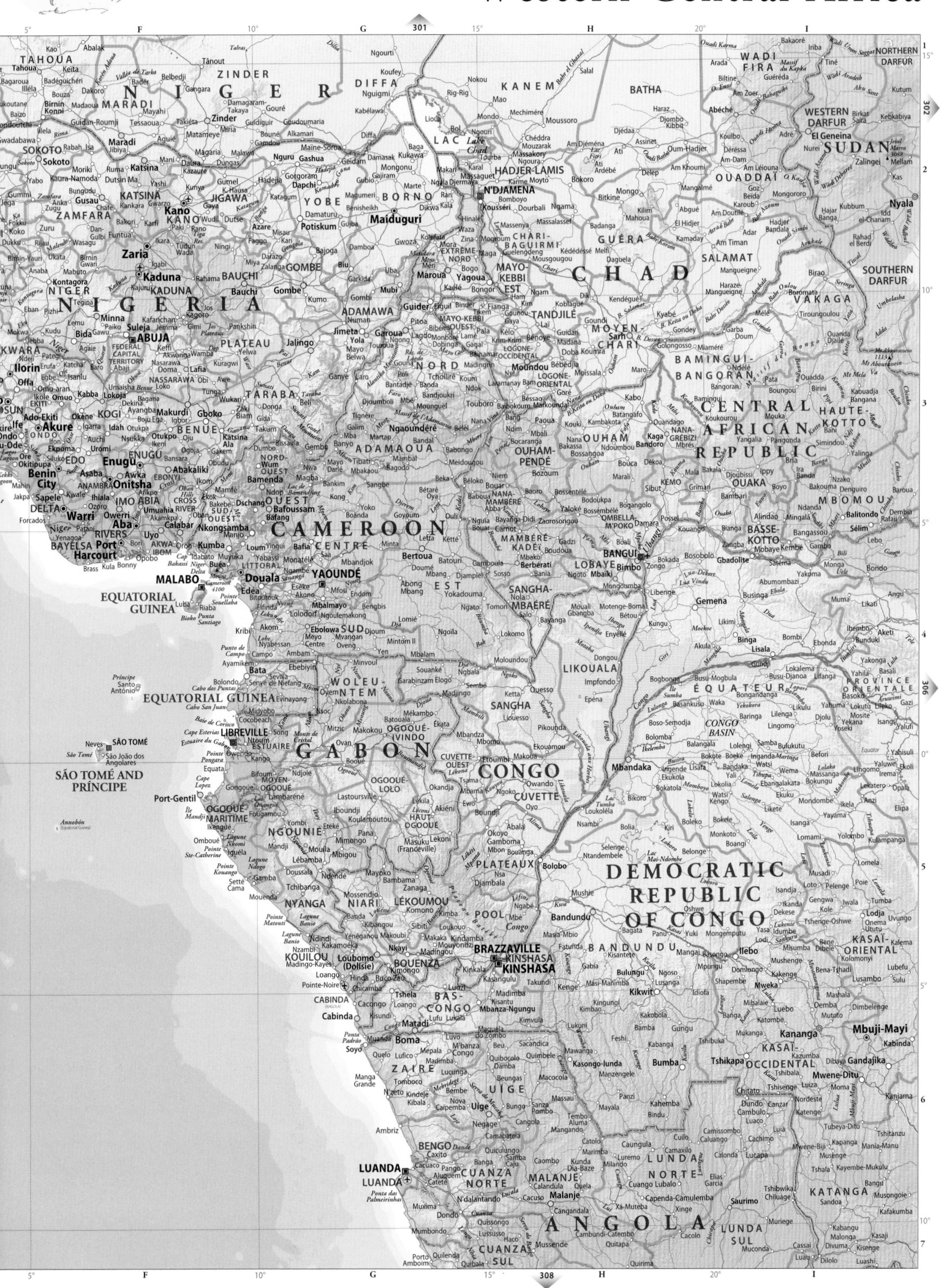
301
302
306
308
AFRICA
NIGER
NIGERIA
CHAD
SUDAN
CAMEROON
CENTRAL AFRICAN REPUBLIC
EQUATORIAL GUINEA
SÃO TOMÉ AND PRÍNCIPE
GABON
CONGO
DEMOCRATIC REPUBLIC OF CONGO
ANGOLA
CABINDA
ABUJA
N'DJAMENA
YAOUNDÉ
MALABO
SÃO TOMÉ
LIBREVILLE
BANGUI
BRAZZAVILLE
KINSHASA
LUANDA
Douala
Kano
Kaduna
Maiduguri
Port Harcourt
Pointe-Noire
Matadi
Mbuji-Mayi
Kananga
Meters
Feet
LAND BELOW SEA LEVEL

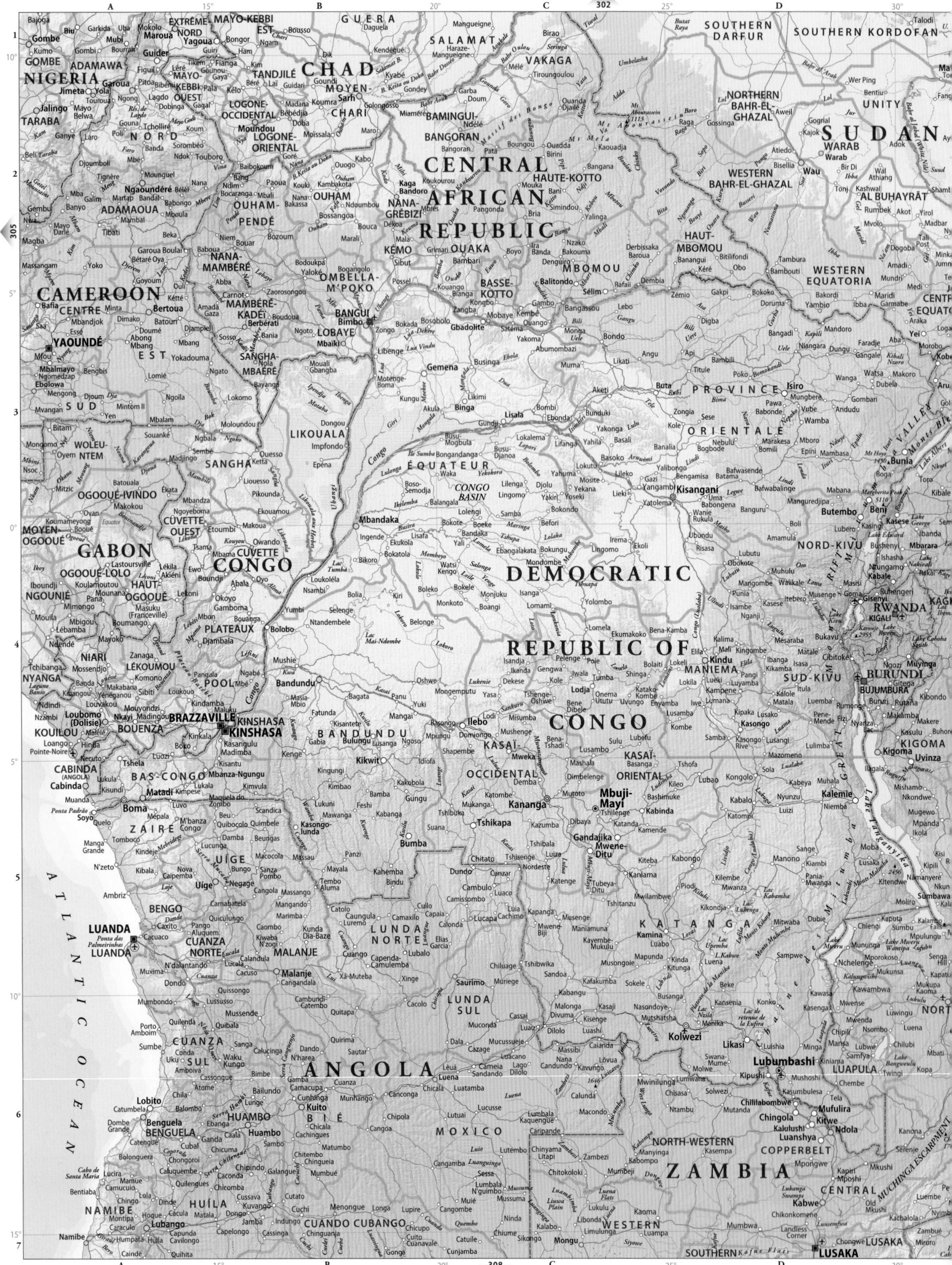
CHAD
NIGERIA
CAMEROON
CENTRAL AFRICAN REPUBLIC
SUDAN
GABON
CONGO
DEMOCRATIC REPUBLIC OF CONGO
ANGOLA
ZAMBIA
RWANDA
BURUNDI
ATLANTIC OCEAN
SOUTHERN DARFUR
SOUTHERN KORDOFAN
NORTHERN BAHR-EL-GHAZAL
WESTERN BAHR-EL-GHAZAL
WESTERN EQUATORIA
PROVINCE ORIENTALE
ÉQUATEUR
CONGO BASIN
BANDUNDU
KASAÏ-OCCIDENTAL
KASAÏ-ORIENTAL
MANIEMA
NORD-KIVU
SUD-KIVU
KATANGA
BAS-CONGO
LUNDA NORTE
LUNDA SUL
MOXICO
NORTH-WESTERN
COPPERBELT
YAOUNDÉ
BANGUI
BRAZZAVILLE
KINSHASA
LUANDA
KIGALI
BUJUMBURA
LUSAKA
302
305
308

1:10,320,000

Lambert Conic Conformal Projection

Eastern Central Africa

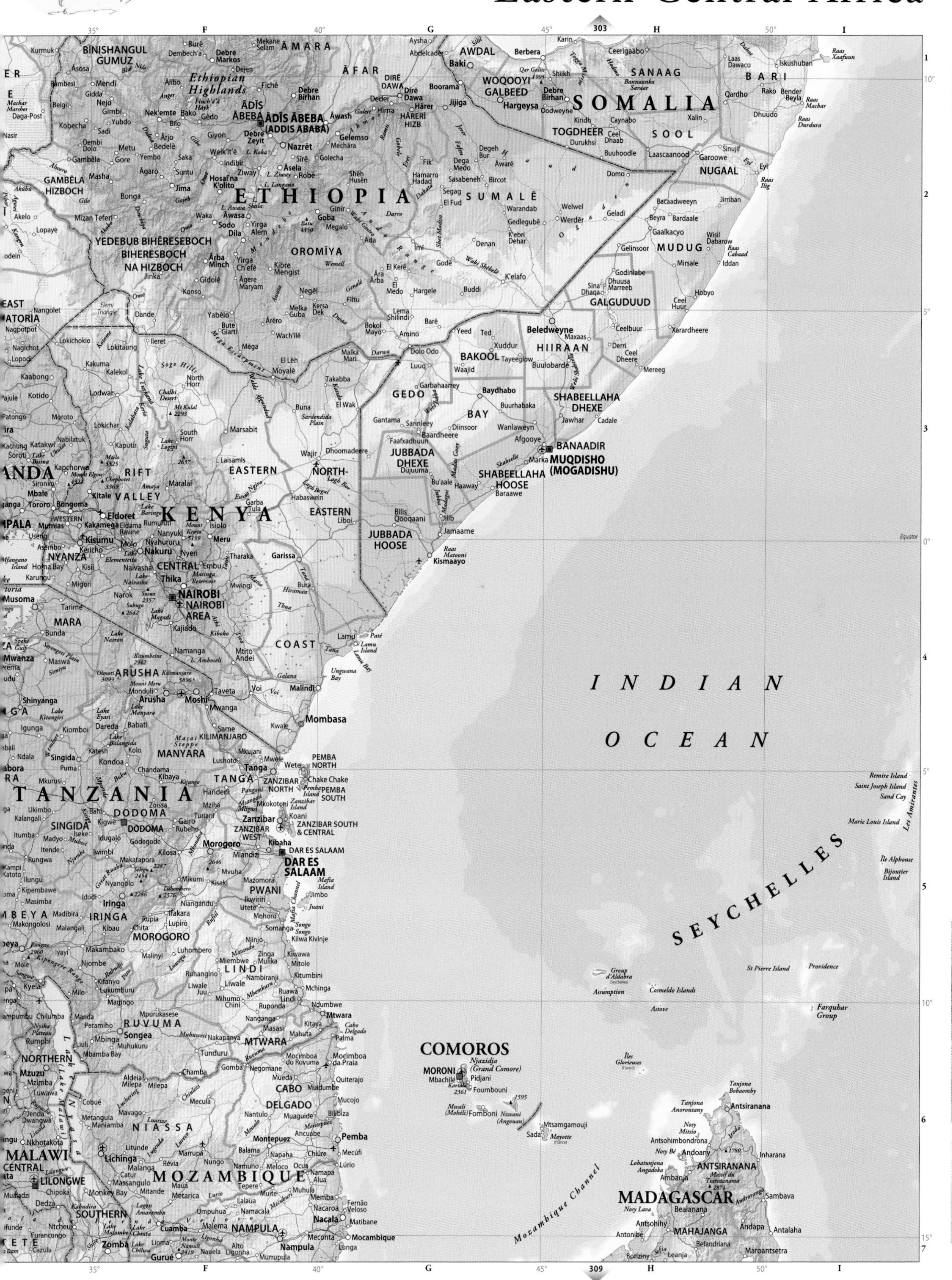
303
309
ETHIOPIA
SOMALIA
KENYA
TANZANIA
MOZAMBIQUE
MALAWI
COMOROS
MADAGASCAR
SEYCHELLES
INDIAN
OCEAN
ĀDĪS ĀBEBA (ADDIS ABABA)
MUQDISHO (MOGADISHU)
NAIROBI
DODOMA
DAR ES SALAAM
MORONI
LILONGWE
Ethiopian Highlands
AWDAL
WOQOOYI GALBEED
TOGDHEER
SANAAG
BARI
SOOL
NUGAAL
MUDUG
GALGUDUUD
HIIRAAN
BAKOOL
GEDO
BAY
SHABEELLAHA DHEXE
SHABEELLAHA HOOSE
BANAADIR
JUBBADA DHEXE
JUBBADA HOOSE
ĀFAR
ĀMARA
OROMĪYA
SUMALĒ
GAMBĒLA HIZBOCH
YEDEBUB BIHĒRESEBOCH BIHERESBOCH NA HIZBOCH
HĀRERĪ HIZB
DIRĒ DAWA
BĪNISHANGUL GUMUZ
RIFT VALLEY
EASTERN
NORTH-EASTERN
CENTRAL
NAIROBI AREA
COAST
NYANZA
WESTERN
ARUSHA
KILIMANJARO
MANYARA
TANGA
DODOMA
SINGIDA
IRINGA
MOROGORO
PWANI
LINDI
MTWARA
RUVUMA
NIASSA
CABO DELGADO
NAMPULA
ANTSIRANANA
MAHAJANGA
Berbera
Hargeysa
Garoowe
Kismaayo
Mombasa
Zanzibar
Lindi
Mtwara
Pemba
Nampula
Antsiranana
Mozambique Channel
Lake Turkana
Lake Nyasa (Lake Malawi)
Mayotte (France)
Group d'Aldabra
Cosmoldo Islands
Farquhar Group
Les Amirantes
Equator

ATLANTIC OCEAN

ANGOLA

ZAMBIA

NAMIBIA

BOTSWANA

SOUTH AFRICA

ZIMBABWE

LESOTHO

Meters / Feet

Meters	Feet
6000	19685
5000	16404
4000	13123
3000	9843
2000	6562
1000	3281
500	1640
200	656
100	328
0	
LAND BELOW SEA LEVEL	
100	328
200	656
1000	3281
2000	6562
4000	13123
6000	19685

1:10,320,000

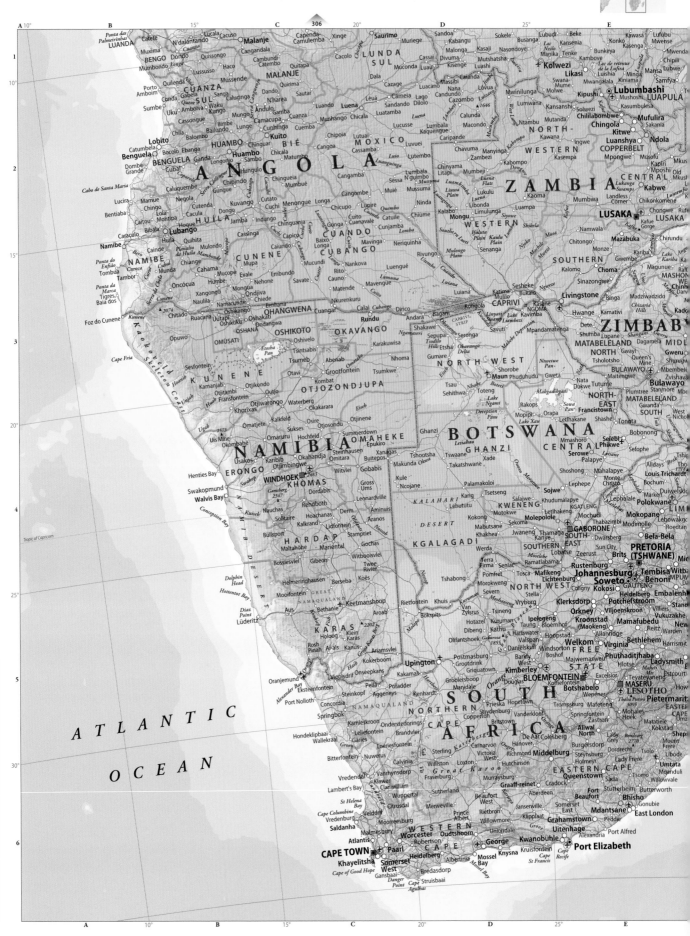

Lambert Conic Conformal Projection

0 100 200 300 400 500 kilometers

0 50 100 150 200 250 300 miles

Southern Africa and Madagascar

SEYCHELLES
Group d'Aldabra
COMOROS
MORONI
MOZAMBIQUE CHANNEL
MALAWI
LILONGWE
MOZAMBIQUE
MADAGASCAR
ANTANANARIVO
MAPUTO
INDIAN OCEAN
Tropic of Capricorn

Islands around Africa

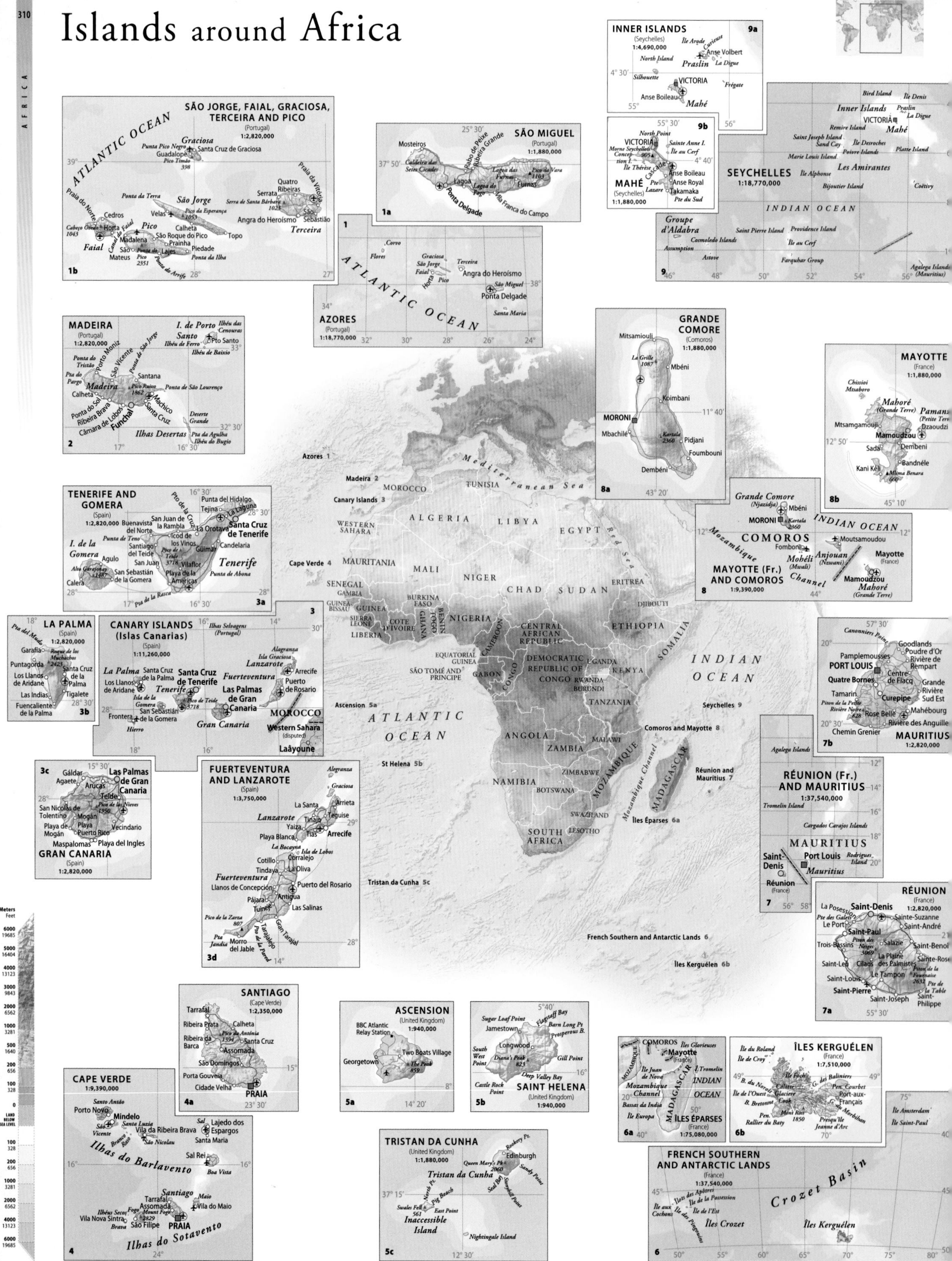
SÃO JORGE, FAIAL, GRACIOSA, TERCEIRA AND PICO
(Portugal)
1:2,820,000
ATLANTIC OCEAN
SÃO MIGUEL
(Portugal)
1:1,880,000
Ponta Delgada
AZORES
(Portugal)
1:18,770,000
ATLANTIC OCEAN
INNER ISLANDS
(Seychelles)
1:4,690,000
VICTORIA
Praslin
Mahé
MAHÉ
(Seychelles)
1:1,880,000
SEYCHELLES
1:18,770,000
INDIAN OCEAN
Groupe d'Aldabra
MADEIRA
(Portugal)
1:2,820,000
Funchal
Ilhas Desertas
GRANDE COMORE
(Comoros)
1:1,880,000
MORONI
MAYOTTE
(France)
1:1,880,000
Mamoudzou
TENERIFE AND GOMERA
(Spain)
1:2,820,000
Santa Cruz de Tenerife
Tenerife
LA PALMA
(Spain)
1:2,820,000
CANARY ISLANDS (Islas Canarias)
(Spain)
1:11,260,000
Lanzarote
Fuerteventura
Las Palmas de Gran Canaria
Gran Canaria
MOROCCO
Western Sahara (disputed)
Laâyoune
COMOROS
MAYOTTE (Fr.) AND COMOROS
1:9,390,000
Mozambique Channel
INDIAN OCEAN
PORT LOUIS
MAURITIUS
1:2,820,000
RÉUNION (Fr.) AND MAURITIUS
1:37,540,000
RÉUNION
(France)
1:2,820,000
Saint-Denis
Saint-Pierre
Mediterranean Sea
MOROCCO
ALGERIA
LIBYA
EGYPT
TUNISIA
WESTERN SAHARA
MAURITANIA
MALI
NIGER
CHAD
SUDAN
ERITREA
DJIBOUTI
ETHIOPIA
SOMALIA
SENEGAL
GAMBIA
GUINEA-BISSAU
GUINEA
SIERRA LEONE
LIBERIA
COTE D'IVOIRE
GHANA
TOGO
BENIN
BURKINA FASO
NIGERIA
CAMEROON
CENTRAL AFRICAN REPUBLIC
EQUATORIAL GUINEA
SÃO TOMÉ AND PRINCIPE
GABON
CONGO
DEMOCRATIC REPUBLIC OF CONGO
UGANDA
KENYA
RWANDA
BURUNDI
TANZANIA
ANGOLA
ZAMBIA
MALAWI
MOZAMBIQUE
ZIMBABWE
NAMIBIA
BOTSWANA
SWAZILAND
LESOTHO
SOUTH AFRICA
MADAGASCAR
ATLANTIC OCEAN
INDIAN OCEAN
Azores 1
Madeira 2
Canary Islands 3
Cape Verde 4
Ascension 5a
St Helena 5b
Tristan da Cunha 5c
Seychelles 9
Comoros and Mayotte 8
Réunion and Mauritius 7
Îles Éparses 6a
French Southern and Antarctic Lands 6
Îles Kerguélen 6b
FUERTEVENTURA AND LANZAROTE
(Spain)
1:3,750,000
GRAN CANARIA
(Spain)
1:2,820,000
SANTIAGO
(Cape Verde)
1:2,350,000
PRAIA
CAPE VERDE
1:9,390,000
Ilhas do Barlavento
Ilhas do Sotavento
ASCENSION
(United Kingdom)
1:940,000
Georgetown
SAINT HELENA
(United Kingdom)
1:940,000
Jamestown
TRISTAN DA CUNHA
(United Kingdom)
1:1,880,000
Edinburgh
Inaccessible Island
ÎLES ÉPARSES
(France)
1:75,080,000
ÎLES KERGUÉLEN
(France)
1:7,510,000
FRENCH SOUTHERN AND ANTARCTIC LANDS
(France)
1:37,540,000
Crozet Basin
Îles Crozet
Îles Kerguélen
Meters Feet
LAND BELOW SEA LEVEL

ASIA

INTRODUCTION

Asia

Asia extends from the Arctic Circle into the Southern hemisphere, and through all climatic zones. It spreads across the largest number of time zones of any continent and is home to over half of Earth's population. In many categories Asia is a place of extremes in regard to physical and cultural variety, yet the number of countries it encompasses is relatively low compared to the continents of Europe and Africa.

Previous pages A monk prays next to Phra Achana, the famous Buddha statue at Wat Si Chum in Thailand's Sukhothai Province. The Buddha's lap spans 37 feet (11.3 m).

Right The Himalayas stretch across Bhutan, China, India, Nepal, and Pakistan, and form part of a continuous mountain range running across Central Asia and Europe. The name Himalaya means "land of snow" and derives from the Sanskrit words *hima* (snow) and *alaya* (abode).

Asia's population is unevenly distributed, with large, dense clusters in some parts and almost endless emptiness in others. China and India alone account for more than 2 billion people, while the Asian part of Russia is filled with trees and is very sparsely populated.

Geographic and Cultural Diversity

There are significant settlements in Siberia and the Russian Far East, mainly along the Trans-Siberian railroad and near the Pacific coast. To the north of the railroad huge swathes of permanently frozen ground, or permafrost, serve as a significant barrier to settlement. Because the upper layer of permafrost thaws and moves with seasonal changes of temperature, the construction and maintenance of infrastructure are financially demanding, so settlements in the region are predominantly limited to mining communities and military bases.

Regardless of the difficulties caused by climate and physical geography, investment in North Asia is growing. Its vast and virtually untouched natural resources, from fossil fuels to precious metals and timber, are of great interest to booming economies in other parts of Asia. Oil and gas pipelines are being constructed to reach Chinese and Japanese customers as economic focus shifts toward East Asia. Dissolution of the Soviet Union and the end of the Cold War entirely altered geopolitical circumstances in North Asia—Russia and China are no longer overtly suspicious of each other and have entered an age of cooperation.

Above India's economy is changing rapidly, demanding flexibility and adaptation. One small example can be found in Varanasi, where weavers who recently lost their jobs due to a downturn in the sari industry are being offered the chance to become rickshaw owner/drivers.

Below right Hirosaki Castle, in Japan's Aomori Prefecture, was built in 1611 but has been modified and added to since then. It is now a popular place to see the spring cherry blossoms.

Below The people of southern China's Guangxi Zhuang Autonomous Region have made the most of the mountainous terrain by carving out countless terraces for rice growing.

The former Soviet republics in Central Asia—Kazakhstan, Uzbekistan, Turkmenistan, Tajikistan, and Kyrgyzstan—are of mixed fortune, and enjoy unequal potential. The physical geography of this region is not especially complex, with its open spaces of grassy treeless steppe and barren desert, and high elevations only in the extreme southeast. Yet, similar to Asia in its entirety, population distribution is highly skewed. Densities are highest along the ancient Silk Road route in the south and near Kazakhstan's boundary with Russia in the north. Only two rivers provide water for most of this area, which is not nearly enough, and is now a sensitive geopolitical issue. Energy production and export are leading forces in regional economic development, mainly in Kazakhstan.

South of the Himalayas, India is in rapid economic transformation, Pakistan is engaged in major geopolitical affairs, and Sri Lanka is wracked by a separatist guerilla movement. After three decades of various conflicts, a peaceful resolution in Afghanistan is still beyond the horizon. Millions of refugees are scattered across the region. Fortunately for India, its democratic electoral process has largely subdued regional separatist tendencies and the country has concentrated on economic progress. Soon to equal or even surpass China in population, India's future depends on human capital, which it has in abundance.

Globalization and Development

India's rapid transition from an agricultural nation to a modern society will be a gold mine for future sociological research in a country where hundreds of millions enjoy basically no rights because of their low caste status and live in abject poverty. Since independence in 1947, the government has made many attempts to eradicate the problems caused by the caste system and provide equal civil liberties, but success has been limited.

Similarly, protecting the natural environment still falls into the "less important" category. Industrial and human waste, the pollution of rivers and soils, and uncontrolled urban expansion are creeping up as unpaid bills for the price of progress—however, the alternatives to India's current path are even less desirable.

Wealth is a relative term in Southeast Asia. In all its forms, globalization has helped establish a system in which physical distance forms no barrier to economic success, but has also exposed how easily internal political inadequacy can create unbridgeable cultural barriers. In Laos and Myanmar, the preservation of an unproductive political system

topples the imperative of the economic liberalization needed to join the developed world. That a symbiosis between the two is possible is obvious in the example of Vietnam. After years of modest performance, economic reforms approved by the ruling communists have propelled Vietnam's economy to a flourishing state. To the south, the world's most populous Muslim country, Indonesia, and Asia's largest Christian country save Russia, the Philippines, stretch across an arc of thousands of islands encompassing the southeastern Asian mainland.

Then there is China, a country that in many ways exemplifies the big picture of contemporary Asia in both positive and negative terms. China's economic expansion during the past several decades has been astonishing, an expansion now felt not only in East Asia but increasingly throughout the world. At the same time China, similarly to the rest of the continent, carries substantial cultural and historical burdens. After the failed reforms of the Great Leap Forward and the Cultural Revolution, which cost never-to-be-known numbers of lives, the Chinese realized that instead of looking inward they should look outside their boundaries. The totalitarian communist regime, which still effectively rules China, is today less of a threat to the west's governments than are inexpensive Chinese products to the west's economies.

Rural China, where most people reside, many in harsh poverty, illustrates how geographically irregular is the distribution of wealth in this country. Population control measures, designed during the 1970s, have created huge social problems because the one-child policy combined with the traditional preference for male children has produced a gender imbalance measured in many millions of bachelors. (Following the devastating 2008 earthquake in southwestern China, the government relaxed the one-child policy for parents who had lost their only child in the disaster.) The issues of Tibetan and Taiwanese independence are still unresolved. As in India, environmental protection is not allowed to block China's road to economic growth.

In the rest of East Asia the two Koreas, side by side yet worlds apart, are tucked between China and another economic giant. Japan's postwar economic miracle made it the first Asian post-industrial society. Severely limited in natural resources and land-use potential, the Japanese turned to education, innovation, and service. It is difficult to imagine that as recently as the mid-nineteenth century Japan was entirely closed to the rest of the world and has gone through the process that Bhutan and Mongolia are now slowly entering.

Above India is a land of incredible contrast—geographically, culturally, and economically. Here we see the world-famous historic landmark, the Taj Mahal, which is a far cry from the thriving metropolis of Mumbai, for example.

Left Though China is officially an atheist nation, religion plays an important part in the lives of many of its people. These Buddhist monks are on a pilgrimage to the Chaga Sacred Mountain in Sichuan Province in the country's southwest.

Left Moon Village in Yangshuo County, southern China, is nestled in a valley surrounded by limestone mountains. Today, tourism is an invaluable source of income for the people who live in this region of spectacular landscapes.

Middle East

Climatically, nearly two-thirds of the Middle East is classified as arid to semiarid. Its topography varies from the mountains of Iran in the north to the flat plains and plateaus of the south. From the junction with the African continent at the Sinai Peninsula, it crosses mostly desert landscape to the Ar Rub'al-Khali Desert (also known as the Empty Quarter) on the Arabian Peninsula. This enormous desert is the world's largest continuous body of sand, and extends over a third of the Arabian Peninsula.

Far right Wadi Rum in southern Jordan is home to several Bedouin tribes, nomadic pastoralists who survive in this harsh desert landscape. The classic movie *Lawrence of Arabia* was filmed here.

Right Dome of the Rock on Temple Mount in Jerusalem, Israel, was built in the late 600s CE by the Muslim Caliph Abd al-Malik. This sacred site is said to be exactly where previously the Romans had erected a temple, and before that two Jewish temples had been built.

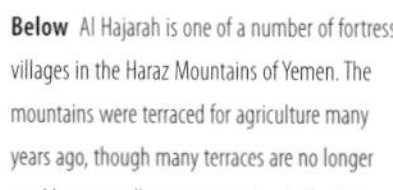

Below Al Hajarah is one of a number of fortress villages in the Haraz Mountains of Yemen. The mountains were terraced for agriculture many years ago, though many terraces are no longer used because villagers are moving to the cities.

The Middle East is a cultural region, a designation that indicates its boundaries are not fixed and are open to geographic interpretation. The traditionally accepted view is that the Middle East includes the countries in southwest Asia between the Mediterranean Sea and Afghanistan. Turkey, or Asia Minor, is accepted by some as part of the Middle East, but is excluded here.

Several elements combine to create the case for the Middle East. In terms of physical geography its boundaries encompass an arid environment, with only slight climatic variations near coastlines and at higher elevations. Deserts cover large areas; average precipitation is low, and the number of major streams and lakes is limited. Hot summers easily exceed 100°F (38°F) for prolonged periods of time, and in some parts years can pass without significant rainfall. Most of the water utilized for agriculture and consumption derives from underground aquifers, and rivers with sources in the mountain regions, like the Euphrates, Tigris, and Jordan.

Cradle of Civilization

The river valleys of the Middle East hold historic significance as the cradle of civilization. Ancient Mesopotamia's Fertile Crescent, in particular, was the home of early plant and animal domestication and the beginning of the agricultural revolution. Sedentary oasis farming set the scene for the growth of early cities and centers of commerce. The early Middle East was the site of developments in political organization and religious organization that have changed little since then, and saw the rise of the world's largest monotheistic religions: Judaism, Christianity, and Islam. The region's varied ethnic composition includes numerous groups of Semitic origin, including Arabs and Jews, and Indo-European Iranians, Kurds, Armenians, and others.

In medieval times, while Western Europe was struggling to overcome the ravages of plague and loss of population, the Middle East reached another cultural pinnacle. The Arab language became the regional lingua franca, Islam the dominant religion, and the scientific discoveries made at the time were later to set the west on the road to modernity. The Middle East's institutional structures remained unchanged, however, and blocked acceptance of western economic and political values once the Industrial Revolution had transformed Western Europe into a new cultural hearth. This swing of the pendulum further isolated an already inward-looking region. It did not help that the Ottoman Empire, which controlled provinces between Mesopotamia and the Mediterranean coast until the end of World War I, was reluctant to impose radical reforms. Local conditions favored the elite and hindered diversification of the economic base, and outside influence was considered a threat to the existing system.

connections still form the foundation of social organization. At the same time, most Middle Eastern nations are home to burgeoning young populations that tend to embrace the value of socio-economic reforms and political changes.

Lack of experience with political pluralism and the peaceful transition of power, the absence of democratic institutions, and gender inequality are all clouds over the Middle East's horizon. Despite unprecedented accumulation of wealth from oil and gas revenues, civil rights and personal liberties are often neglected, sometimes openly suppressed.

Islamic states are built on the ideal of symbiosis between religion and society. Religious leaders in the Middle East are often expected to participate in all aspects of social and political life. Any attempt to separate church and state is almost impossible in this system, and any attempt at reform can easily be perceived as a direct attack on Islam.

Oil and Geopolitics

As the Middle East entered the era of modern nation-state creation, it became clear that geopolitical factors would determine its future. The discovery of enormous deposits of oil further complicated regional geopolitics, given that former colonial powers realized their value only after artificial political boundaries had been drawn and autocratic rulers installed. The creation of a Jewish state in Palestine, in the aftermath of World War II, destroyed the chance of peaceful coexistence; sadly, this has been illustrated by the ensuing decades of armed conflict between Israel and its many Arab neighbors.

The Middle East is currently undergoing the almost inevitable transition from folk to popular culture. Traditional values are deeply entrenched among peoples reluctant to accept the modern lifestyle for fear of losing their identities. This is particularly obvious in rural areas, where cosmopolitan views are all but absent and ancient tribal

Water Resources

The geography of the Middle East displays a peculiar irony. Below the surface in Saudi Arabia, Iraq, and Iran lie the largest proven reserves of oil. Gasoline and oil appear to be coming from everywhere while water, the most inexpensive natural resource, is often difficult to find.

With continuing urbanization and population growth, demand for water is becoming a very serious geopolitical issue. The major rivers and their watersheds are shared by nations that have different visions of how to utilize water potentials. The headwaters of the Tigris and Euphrates are in southeastern Turkey, outside the Middle East, where their use in electrical power generation is the country's primary concern. Turkey is less fortunate in regard to fossil fuels and sees the building of dams, especially on the Euphrates, as an excellent source of electrical power for a nation with a rapidly emerging economy. Downstream in Syria, but particularly Iraq, water is needed for human consumption and for agriculture and industry. The diversion and accumulation of water in Turkey's artificial lakes, and lack of seasonal discharge when countries downstream are in need, are generating serious tensions in a region already prone to instability and conflict.

Similar problems face the nations that share water from the Jordan River, which has provided water since biblical times. Israel, Syria, and Jordan are now much thirstier, their populations measured in millions not thousands, yet the amount of water remains the same.

Israel's outstanding record in turning the desert into an agricultural heaven is based on effective irrigation. The tiny nation can now supply almost two-thirds of its own food, and has extended the range of crops grown. Other countries are less inclined to follow Israel's lead, because it is an expensive and difficult system to implement. The source of the Jordan River is the Sea of Galilee in the borderland of Israel and Syria, an area for which the two countries fought bitterly during the Arab–Israeli wars. Israel still occupies the Golan Heights east of the lake to ensure, among other things, that any attempts to disrupt water supply can be prevented.

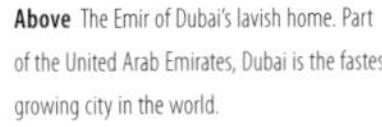

Above The Emir of Dubai's lavish home. Part of the United Arab Emirates, Dubai is the fastest growing city in the world.

Left Nearly three-quarters of Oman's population are Arabs who are also Ibadhi Muslims. Sunni and Shi'ite are the two most common forms of Islam.

Above Arab peoples known as the Nabataeans settled in the Petra region of Jordan over 2,000 years ago. They carved a huge city into the rock face, and turned Petra into a vital crossroad for the silk, spice, and other trade routes that connected China, India, and southern Arabia with Egypt, Syria, Greece, and Rome.

Left Kuwaiti Towers, consisting of three towers and three spheres in Kuwait City, blend Arabic and contemporary architectural design. The towers are used to store water for use in homes and businesses across the city.

CYPRUS

Official name Republic of Cyprus (Kypriaki Dimokratia/Kibris Cumhuriyeti)
Land area 3,570 square miles (9,250 km²) of which 1,295 square miles (3,355 km²) are in northern Cyprus
Border countries None (an island) but Turkey established and recognizes northern Cyprus as a separate country (Turkish Republic of Northern Cyprus)
Capital Nicosia (Lefkosia)
Highest point Mt Olympus 6,400 feet (1,950 m)
Climate Mediterranean
Population 792,604
Language(s) Greek, Turkish, English
Ethnicity Greek 77%, Turkish 18%, other 5%
Religion Greek Orthodox 78%, Muslim 18%, other 4%
Government Republic
Currency Cypriot pound (Turkish lira used in northern Cyprus)
Human Development Index 0.903 (ranked 28th out of 177 countries)

CYPRUS
Rizokarpaso
Aigialousa
Lapithos
Keryneia
Morfou
LEFKOSIA
(NICOSIA)
Ammochostos
Lefka
Dali
Dhekelia Sovereign Base Area
Polis
Mt Olympus
Larnaka
Pafos
Lemesos
Akrotiri Sovereign Base Area
Mediterranean Sea

Cyprus

Map Reference Pages 390–391

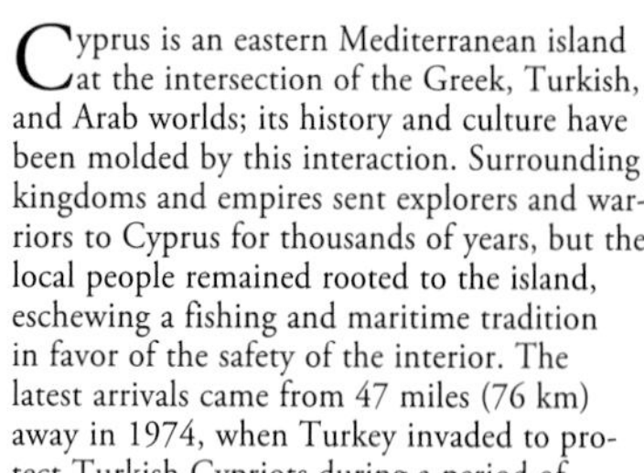

Cyprus is an eastern Mediterranean island at the intersection of the Greek, Turkish, and Arab worlds; its history and culture have been molded by this interaction. Surrounding kingdoms and empires sent explorers and warriors to Cyprus for thousands of years, but the local people remained rooted to the island, eschewing a fishing and maritime tradition in favor of the safety of the interior. The latest arrivals came from 47 miles (76 km) away in 1974, when Turkey invaded to protect Turkish Cypriots during a period of ethnic and political turmoil on the island.

Physical Geography

Two prominent mountain ranges define the northern and southern skylines of Cyprus. The Kyrenia (Girne) range is a long spine of hard crystalline limestone that parallels the northern coast and rises abruptly to heights of 1,970–2,950 feet (600–900 m). The pine-covered Troodos Mountains in the south, comprised of intrusive volcanic rock, are higher, averaging 2,300 feet (700 m) and rising to 6,400 feet (1,950 m) around the ski areas of Mt Olympus. Between these ranges lies the broad alluvial Mesaoria Plain, a semi-arid region with irrigated agriculture and a large concentration of towns and cities, including the capital city of Nicosia (Lefkosia).

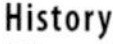

History

The island passed through many hands as empires waxed and waned in the eastern Mediterranean. Early Phoenicians and Greeks established colonies on Cyprus, and the Romans built several notable cities. The Byzantine Empire was a dominant influence in the Middle Ages. Arab raiders came and went. In 1191, en route to the third crusade in the Holy Land, Richard the Lionheart landed on Cyprus and briefly controlled the island before selling his claim to the French Crusader Guy de Lusignon, whose descendants ruled Cyprus for 300 years as the Lusignon Dynasty. The Venetians established colonial control for almost a century until Cyprus fell to the Ottoman Turks in 1571. Britain occupied Cyprus in 1878, then in 1925 annexed the island and declared it a Crown colony. Many Greek Cypriots regarded Greece as their mother country and sought union with Greece. Turkish Cypriots demanded the island be partitioned between the Greek and Turkish populations. Into this milieu of racial tension the independent state of Cyprus was born in 1960.

In 1974 the government was overthrown by a military coup in a second attempt to unite with Greece. Turkey promptly invaded the island to protect the interests of the Turkish Cypriot minority. Many Turkish Cypriots fled to the north, from where Greek Cypriots either fled or were evicted by Turkish authorities. The United Nations intervened and established a UN-patrolled buffer zone. The northern Turkish-held area declared itself the Turkish Republic of Northern Cyprus (TRNC), a political status recognized only by Turkey.

Border restrictions along the buffer zone were eased in 2003 and Greek and Turkish Cypriots began crossing to the other side after almost 30 years of isolation. Businessmen and scholars have been developing collaborative projects. Both sides continue to work through dialogue, but a climate of mistrust still exists, further confounding attempts at resolution. The Greek Cypriot south joined the European Union in 2004.

Population/Culture

Cypriots today are a mostly Greek- or Turkish-speaking people who identify themselves as Greek Cypriot (77%) or Turkish Cypriot (18%). Greek Cypriots are mostly Greek Orthodox in faith and Turkish Cypriots are mostly Muslim. Added to the historic blend are Turkish migrants who have arrived in Turkish-controlled northern Cyprus since 1974, and European inhabitants, mostly from Eastern Europe, who have arrived since Greek Cyprus joined the European Union.

Administration/Government

The constitution remains unchanged since Cyprus gained independence from the British in 1960. The president is elected by popular vote. The post of vice-president is reserved for a Turkish Cypriot. The legislative branch has 56 seats assigned to Greek Cypriots and 24 to Turkish Cypriots but, because of the partition of Cyprus, only seats assigned to Greek Cypriots are currently filled. Turkish Cypriots proclaimed self-rule in 1975, creating their own constitution within the Turkish Republic of Northern Cyprus (TRNC). The only internationally recognized government is that controlled by Greek Cypriots.

Economy/Industry

The economy is dominated by the service sector, which accounts for three-quarters of national earnings. Tourism and financial services are the most important activities, although retail sales and agricultural exports are also significant. Agriculture and services employ more than half of the workforce. Since EU accession in 2004, the economy has been growing at well above the EU average. The Turkish Cypriot economy is less robust, more volatile, and has less than half of the per capita GDP of the south. It is heavily dependent on investments and direct aid from the Turkish government.

Above Perched on the cliff top near Limassol, the Kourion Archeological Site provides a breathtaking vista of coastal Cyprus. The ruin of this fifth-century Christian basilica sits alongside earlier Roman relics, including an amphitheater, bathhouses, villas, and a U-shaped stadium.

Right The picturesque town of Paphos, nestled in the lee of the western Troodos Mountains, boasts an impressive medieval fort and harbor. Legend has it that the goddess Aphrodite was born on the town's shoreline.

MILESTONE EVENTS

1571 Cyprus falls to the Ottoman Turks
1878 Britain occupies Cyprus
1925 Britain declares Cyprus a Crown colony
1960 The independent state of Cyprus is born
1964 Following violent clashes between Greek and Turkish Cypriots, the UN deploys peacekeepers to the island
1974 A coup by the Greek military tries to seize control of the island; Turkey responds militarily and gains control of more than a third of Cyprus
1983 The Turkish Republic of Northern Cyprus (TRNC) is declared
2003 Border restrictions along the UN-controlled buffer zone are eased
April 2004 A referendum seeking to resolve the unification issue fails
2004 Greek Cyprus joins the European Union

Black Sea
BULGARIA
GREECE
Aegean Sea
İstanbul
Sea of Marmara
Zonguldak
Kocaeli (İzmit)
Samsun
Trabzon
GEORGIA
ARMENIA
Bursa
Balıkesir
Eskişehir
ANKARA
Kütahya
Sivas
Erzurum
Mt Ararat
İzmir
TURKEY
Kayseri
Elazığ
Van
IRAN
Denizli
Konya
Malatya
Diyarbakır
Antalya
Adana
İçel
Gaziantep
Mediterranean Sea
SYRIA
IRAQ
CYPRUS

Turkey

Map Reference Page 394

Turkey covers the landmass commonly known as Asia Minor, a subregion of Southwest Asia, with 3 percent of its territory in Europe. The Sea of Marmara and the Turkish Straits narrowly separate the two continents. The Mediterranean, Black, and Aegean seas surround the country and contribute to its almost peninsular form. Turkey has been attractive to numerous civilizations for its location and as a migratory route for nomads and invaders.

Physical Geography

Turkey's physical geography is the product of interaction between the African and Eurasian tectonic plates, which has created fault zones and often devastating earthquakes, and caused the east–west direction of the mountain ranges. A number of the mountain formations are old volcanoes, such as Mt Ararat.

The west and south enjoy a Mediterranean climate; the interior has a continental climate with hot dry summers and cold winters. The climate has influenced population trends. The interior evolved as predominantly agricultural while coastal areas became urbanized, a trend that continues today.

History

The Agricultural Revolution, the domestication of plants and animals, and the earliest evolution of Indo-European languages began in Asia Minor c. 8,000–10,000 BCE. Numerous civilizations have dominated this region, including the Hittites who controlled Anatolia for most of the second millennium BCE. Later, Greeks established a large network of trading settlements and permanent colonies, mainly on the Aegean coast. Istanbul, now the largest and most important urban center, was established in the sixth century BCE as a Greek city. The Roman Empire and Eastern Roman Empire controlled much of present-day Turkey for over a millennium, until Osman Turks occupied Constantinople in 1453 and renamed it Istanbul.

For the following five centuries cultural hegemony led to the geographical and numerical expansion of Turkish ethnicity. In this period a majority of the population accepted Islam, which accelerated assimilation.

In the aftermath of World War I the Republic of Turkey emerged as a modern nation-state from the Ottoman Empire's ashes, and proclaimed independence in 1923. Mustafa Kemal, the charismatic first president, implemented radical cultural transformation in order to modernize the country. Measures included secularization and implementation of western cultural traits such as the Latin alphabet, dress codes, and democracy.

Population/Culture

Population density is highest near the coasts, home to half of Turkey's residents. Istanbul and Ankara are leading destinations for those from the interior, while several million Turks live and work in Western Europe.

Unlike most of their neighbors, Turks are of Ural-Altaic ethnic stock. They share linguistic roots with Central Asian peoples. The Kurds in eastern and southeastern Turkey and most other minorities, except Arabs, are of Indo-European origin.

About 95 percent of the country's Muslims follow Sunni traditions. Christians make up only a fraction of the population, mainly belonging to Greek and Armenian Eastern Orthodox churches. Turks have acquired many elements of the eastern Mediterranean culture and diet.

Administration/Government

Turkey's political system is founded on a republican parliamentary democracy with separation of powers. During the second part of the twentieth century several political crises, including coups, temporarily stalled the development of democracy, but stability has been a hallmark in recent years.

Economy/Industry

Cyclical misfortunes have been one of Turkey's economic realities for a good portion of the twentieth century. In the past decade its overall economy has rebounded followed by an increased presence in the global economy, which ultimately has helped increase individual quality of life. Compared with the developed world economies, woes still remain because of a high unemployment rate of over 10 percent (2007), insufficient infrastructure and communication, and the need for complete liberalization of all economic sectors.

Geographic location appears to be the key to future economic development. Turkey's main trade partners are the European Union and Russia, both emerging economies. Turkey also has a young workforce that offers the prospect of a bright economic future.

Cappadocian Dwellings

Cappadocia, in the very heart of the country, is home to remarkable conical and pyramidal rock formations that have been carved into dwellings. This tradition dates back to ancient times when the local residents found the soft volcanic rock, called tufa, easy to penetrate. They created a large network of caverns and used them for various purposes, ranging from homes to sanctuaries during wartime or religious persecution.

Cappadocia's remoteness was popular with early Christians who sought peace and solace in these caverns. Today they represent one of Turkey's main tourist destinations.

MILESTONE EVENTS

1453 Ottoman Empire captures Constantinople

1923 Turkish independence proclaimed

1938 Mustafa Kemal (Atatürk) dies

1952 Turkey becomes a member of NATO

1960, 1971, 1980 Military intervention in Turkish politics

1993 Tansu Çiller is elected first female prime minister

TURKEY

Official name Republic of Turkey (Türkiye Cumhuriyeti)
Land area 301,380 square miles (780,580 km²)
Border countries Georgia, Armenia, Azerbaijan, Iran, Iraq, Syria, Greece, Bulgaria
Capital Ankara
Highest point Mt Ararat 16,948 feet (5,166 m)
Climate Temperate Mediterranean
Population 71,893,000
Language(s) Official: Turkish; other: Kurdish, Dimli (or Zaza), Azeri, Kabardian
Ethnicity Turkish 80%, Kurdish 20%
Religion Muslim 99.8%, other 0.2%
Government Republican parliamentary democracy
Currency Turkish lira
Human Development Index 0.775 (ranked 84th out of 177 countries)

Left Turkey's Cappadocia region is famous for its unique tapered dwellings and underground labyrinths of tunnels. Arising from the rocky landscape, the ancient fortress at Üçhisar is a formidable vantage point that affords a breathtaking panoramic view not only across the surrounding countryside, but across to Erciyes Dağı—a snow-capped volcano, and Turkey's third highest peak—which lies in the distance.

Left A Turkish fruit and vegetable vendor displays colorful produce in the Saturday morning market in Safranbolu, once an important caravan stop on the ancient East–West trade route.

Below Whirling dervishes perform a Sema, a form of *dhikr* (commemoration of Allah), in Istanbul. Dervishes are devotees of the Mevlevi sect of Sufism, a mystical form of Islam that extols the virtues of tolerance and understanding.

Right Vendors serve customers in the crowded vegetable market in Kutaisi, Georgia's second-largest city. Kutaisi was the capital of the ancient Kingdom of Colchis.

GEORGIA

Official name Georgia (Sak'art'velo)
Land area 26,911 square miles (69,700 km²)
Border countries Russia, Azerbaijan, Armenia, Turkey
Capital T'bilisi
Highest point Mt Shkhara 16,627 feet (5,068 m)
Climate Warm, Mediterranean
Population 4,631,000
Language(s) Georgian, Russian, Armenian, Azerbaijani, Abkhaz
Ethnicity Georgian 83.8%, Azerbaijani 6.5%, Armenian 5.7%, Russian 1.5%, Ossetian 0.9%, other 1.6%
Religion Orthodox Christian 83.9%, Muslim 9.9%, Armenian Orthodox 3.9%, Roman Catholic 0.8%, other 1.5%
Government Republic
Currency Lari
Human Development Index 0.754 (ranked 96th out of 177 countries)

RUSSIAN FEDERATION
Sokhumi
Black Sea
Zugdidi
P'ot'i
K'ut'aisi
Ts'khinvali
GEORGIA
Khashuri
Gori
T'elavi
T'BILISI
Bat'umi
Akhalts'ikhe
Sagarejo
Rust'avi
Dedop'listsqaro
TURKEY
ARMENIA
AZERBAIJAN

Georgia

Map Reference Pages 388–389

Right Herodotus and Marco Polo are among the noted historians and travelers who are said to have admired the exquisite beauty and craftsmanship of Armenian carpets.

Georgia, in southwest Asia, is bordered by Russia, Azerbaijan, Armenia, and Turkey. The Black Sea forms the entire western border. Georgia has an ancient culture and a unique alphabet found nowhere else in the world. Ethnic conflict and periodic civil war have marred its more recent history.

Physical Geography

Georgia is protected from more extreme climatic influences by the Greater Caucasus mountains in the north, and the Lesser Caucasus in the south. Numerous peaks rising well above 15,000 feet (4,572 m) dominate the Greater Caucasus; the Lesser Caucasus are lower, barely topping 11,000 feet (3,353 m). The Lesser Caucasus mountains are volcanic in origin and the region is earthquake-prone. Eastern Georgia has a continental climate, with low humidity, hot summers, and cold winters. Western Georgia tends to be subtropical with heavy rainfall, and the Black Sea coast has a Mediterranean-like climate.

History

The unified kingdom of Georgia was formed from the states of Colchis and Iberia in the fourth century BCE. Christianity was adopted as a state religion in 337 CE. At various times Georgia was dominated by Turks, Arabs, Persians, and Mongols. In 1918 the Democratic Republic of Georgia was established but was taken over by Bolshevik Russia in 1921. Independence was gained once again in 1991, followed by a civil war that ended in 1995. In 2003 the Rose Revolution brought a pro-Western government to power. Ethnic strife and unrest persists in the Abkhazia and South Ossetia regions. In 2008, Russia sent troops to Georgia to support South Ossetia separatists.

Population/Culture

Georgia's population is ethnically diverse with Georgians forming the majority. The unique Georgian alphabet was developed in the fifth century CE, and together with a strong literary tradition has served to cement the nation's culture and identity. Medieval culture was influenced by Orthodox Christianity, and is reflected in the country's numerous churches and monasteries. Performing arts have a long tradition: The national theater was founded in 1791 and the State Theater of Opera and Ballet in 1851. Georgian dances and polyphonic music are world famous.

Administration/Government

The president heads the executive branch of government and is voted in for a maximum of two five-year terms. The president is both chief of state and head of government for the power ministries (state security and defense). A prime minister heads the remaining ministries and is answerable to the president. The unicameral parliament or Umaghlesi Sabcho has 235 seats, elected by popular vote for a five-year term. The legal system is based on civil law, and the judiciary has two branches, being the supreme and constitutional courts.

Economy/Industry

Georgia's main economic activities are agriculture and mining, with a small industrial sector. Grapes, citrus fruits, and hazelnuts are major products of agriculture. The mining sector extracts manganese, iron ore, and copper. Other industry includes wine, machinery, and chemicals. Georgia's strategic location has greatly influenced its development as an international transportation center through its Black Sea ports. A pipeline from Azerbaijan transports oil through Georgia to Ceyhan, a port on the Mediterranean coast of Turkey.

GEORGIA
Tashir
Vanadzor
Ijevan
Gyumri
Dilijan
ARMENIA
Hrazdan
Kamo
Ashtarak
YEREVAN
Vardenis
Ejmiatsin
Artashat
Yeghegnadzor
Sisian
Kapan
TURKEY
AZERBAIJAN
IRAN

Armenia

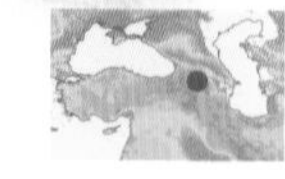

Map Reference Pages 388–389

Armenia is a landlocked country dominated by the Lesser Caucasus Mountain range. It shares borders with Georgia, Azerbaijan, Iran, and Turkey. Armenia has the distinction of being the oldest Christian country in the world as well as being home to the world's oldest Christian cathedral.

Physical Geography

The mountainous terrain encompasses ecosystems and landscapes ranging from mountainous ridges to deep valleys, from deserts to alpine meadows and forests. Canyons, the craters of extinct volcanoes, and hundreds of mineral springs dot the landscape. Armenia is also home to Lake Sevan, one of the largest alpine and freshwater lakes in the world. Climate varies from subtropical to continental; in the southern plain it is arid.

History

The Armenian highlands are rich in archeological finds from Neolithic and Bronze Age cultures. For four centuries (c. 1000–600 BCE) the Kingdom of Urartu extended over the Armenian Highlands before the Kingdom of Armenia was established. The country's strategic location between Roman, Middle Eastern, and Asian empires led to repeated invasions. After the fall of the Kingdom of Armenia in 428 CE successive neighboring empires that included Arab, Mongol, Persian, Ottoman, and Russian ruled the country.

During World War I, Armenians were subjected to forced resettlement and organized killings on a genocidal scale by the collapsing Ottoman Empire. Armenia was declared an independent republic in 1918. In 1922 the country was incorporated into the Union of Soviet Socialist Republics. Independence was gained once again in 1991. Conflict escalated through the early 1990s with neighboring Azerbaijan over Nagorno-Karabakh, a region with a majority Armenian population. This conflict remains unresolved despite the ceasefire that came into effect in 1994.

Population/Culture

Whether Armenian, Ezid, Russian, or a member of one of the minority ethnic groups,

Below The Khor Virap Monastery in the village of Lusarvat, Armenia is dwarfed by the majesty of Mt Ararat. The monastery dates from the twelfth century and is the legendary prison of St Gregory the Illuminator, who was incarcerated for 12 years for practicing Christianity. In 301 CE, Armenia became the first Christian state.

most of the population speaks Armenian. About two-thirds are urban residents, the majority of whom live in Yerevan, the capital, or the larger city of Leninakan. An estimated 10 million Armenians are scattered around the world, many the descendants of those who fled during the Great Calamity (genocide). The population also declined when Armenia regained independence in 1991 as a result of the falling birth rate and people migrating to countries such as the USA and Australia.

The Armenian language is a separate branch of the Indo-European family and features its own distinctive alphabet that was created in 405 CE and consists of 38 letters.

The material culture is expressed through exquisite handmade rugs and carpets along with other art forms, including needlework, carvings, and paintings.

Administration/Government

The Republic of Armenia was established in 1991. The constitution was adopted through a national referendum in July 1995. The highest executive authority is the president, who appoints a prime minister. The president is elected by popular vote. The legislative branch is the National Assembly, which has 135 elected parliamentarians.

Economy/Industry

Since the collapse of the Soviet Union, the economy has shifted from traditional industries—chemicals, electronics, food processing, textiles—that were dependent on the importation of resources and raw materials, to local skills-based sectors, including precious stone processing, and information and communications technology. Tourism is now playing an increasingly important role. Agriculture accounts for 20 percent of GDP and services generate 30 percent.

ARMENIA

Official name Republic of Armenia (Hayastani Hanrapetoutyoun)
Land area 10,965 square miles (28,400 km²)
Border countries Georgia, Azerbaijan, Iran, Turkey
Capital Yerevan
Highest & lowest points Mt Aragats 13,419 feet (4,090 m); Debed River 1,312 feet (400 m)
Climate Highland continental; hot summers, cold winters
Population 2,969,000
Language(s) Armenian, Russian, Ezid
Ethnicity Armenian 97.9%, Ezid 1.3%, Russian 0.4%, other 0.4%
Religion Armenian Apostolic 94.7%, Christian 4%, monotheist 1.3%
Government Republic
Currency Dram
Human Development Index 0.775 (ranked 83rd out of 177 countries)

Left Built during the fifteenth century by Ibrahim I of Shirvan, the Palace of Shirvanshah is located in the World Heritage-listed walled city of Baku, Azerbaijan. The complex of buildings includes a mosque, mausoleum, and bathhouse.

AZERBAIJAN

Official name Republic of Azerbaijan (Azarbaycan Respublikasi)
Land area 33,243 square miles (86,100 km²)
Border countries Russia, Iran, Armenia, Georgia
Capital Baku (Bakı)
Highest & lowest points Mt Bazarduzu 14,652 feet (4,466 m); Caspian Sea −92 feet (−28 m) below sea level
Climate Dry, semiarid steppe
Population 8,178,000
Language(s) Azerbaijani (Azeri), Russian
Ethnicity Azerbaijani 90.6%, Lezgi 2.2%, Russian 1.8%, Armenian 1.5%, Talish 1.0%, other 2.9%
Religion Muslim 93.4%, Russian Orthodox 1.1%, Armenian Orthodox 1.1%, other 4.4%
Government Republic
Currency Azerbaijani manat
Human Development Index 0.746 (ranked 98th out of 177 countries)

RUSSIAN FEDERATION
GEORGIA
Zaqatala
Qax
Xaçmaz
Quba
Şaki
Bazarduzu Dagi
Tovuz
Gäncä
Mingäçevir
Sumqayit
AZERBAIJAN
BAKI (BAKU)
Bärdä
Kürdämir
Äli Bayramli
ARMENIA
Xankändi
Beylaqan
TURKEY
AZERBAIJAN
Naxçivan
IRAN
Länkäran
Caspian Sea

Azerbaijan

Map Reference Pages 388–389

This ethnically diverse nation is located in the Southern Caucasus and shares borders with Georgia, Russia, Iran, and Armenia. The entire eastern border lies on the Caspian Sea. Famous for its oil and gas reserves, Azerbaijan is nevertheless beset by problems ranging from corruption and the uneven distribution of wealth to conflict with Armenia, and serious air, water, and soil pollution.

Physical Geography

The topography is diverse, ranging from the Caspian Sea at 92 feet (28 m) below sea level to steppe grasslands, mud volcanoes, and imposing Mt Bazarduzu. The Greater and Lesser Caucasus and Talysh mountain ranges cover half of the country. Climate is warm and dry in the central and eastern part, subtropical and humid in the southeast, cold in the mountains, and mostly temperate along the shores of the Caspian Sea. The Mingechaur Reservoir, the largest body of water in Azerbaijan, provides hydroelectric power and water for irrigating the dry Kura-Aras plain.

History

A people identified as Caucasian Albanians inhabited present-day Azerbaijan and founded a kingdom in the fourth century BCE. Much later (*c.* 300 CE) Christianity was adopted and remained the dominant religion until the Islamic conquest in the eighth century CE. The territory was conquered by Turkic tribes from Central Asia around 1000 CE. Various dynasties ruled throughout the Middle Ages until it was incorporated into the Russian Empire in the nineteenth century.

After the collapse of Tsarist Russia, Azerbaijan declared its independence, which was short-lived because the Bolsheviks took control in 1920. In 1936, the country became a member state of the USSR. In 1991, it again declared its independence. Conflict with neighboring Armenia over the Armenian-populated Nagorno-Karabakh enclave broke out in 1988. Although a ceasefire was declared in 1994, the conflict remains unresolved.

Population/Culture

Azerbaijan's population is a rich mix of ethnic groups of whom about 93 percent are nominally Muslim. There are large Christian communities in the capital, Baku. The official language, Azerbaijani (Azeri), is a member of the Turkic language family, and is spoken by approximately 95 percent of the population. The influence of Turkic, Persian, Islamic, Caucasus, and Russian cultures are evident in Azerbaijan's colorful culture, including the local cuisine, which features a delicious variety of soups and sweet syrup-saturated pastries.

Administration/Government

The president, elected by a popular vote, represents the executive power of Azerbaijan. The prime minister and the council of ministers are appointed by the president and approved by the unicameral National Assembly, which has 125 members elected by popular vote. Judges are nominated by the president.

Economy/Industry

The economy is largely based on oil, natural gas, and the production of oilfield equipment and petrochemicals. The Baku-Tbilisi-Ceyhan pipeline, which was designed to transport crude oil from the Caspian Sea to global markets, extends for 1,102 miles (1,774 km) from Azerbaijan to Turkey.

Below Traditional costume is often worn on special occasions. Here, Azerbaijani girls chatter during a pre-election rally for the presidential election of 2003 in the capital, Baku.

LEBANON

Official name Lebanese Republic (Al Jumhuriyah al Lubnaniyah)
Land area 3,950 square miles (10,230 km²)
Border countries Syria, Israel
Capital Beirut (Beyrouth)
Highest point Qornet es Saouda 10,131 feet (3,088 m)
Climate Mediterranean
Population 3,972,000
Language(s) Official: Arabic; other: French, English, Armenian
Ethnicity Arab 95%, Armenian 4%, other 1%
Religion Muslim 59.7% (Shi'a, Sunni, Druze, Isma'ilite, Alawite or Nusayri), Christian 39% (Maronite Catholic, Greek Orthodox, Melkite Catholic, Armenian Orthodox, Syrian Catholic, Armenian Catholic, Syrian Orthodox, Roman Catholic, Chaldean, Assyrian, Copt, Protestant), other 1.3%
Government Republic
Currency Lebanese pound
Human Development Index 0.772 (ranked 88th out of 177 countries)

Mediterranean Sea
SYRIA
LEBANON
Trâblous (Tripoli)
Qornet es Saouda
Adonis
Joûnié
Baalbek
BEYROUTH
(BEIRUT)
Zahlé
Aaley
Rayak
Saïda
(Sidon)
Nabatîyé et Tahta
Soûr
(Tyre)
ISRAEL

Lebanon

Map Reference Pages 390–391

Lebanon is located in Western Asia, bordering the Mediterranean Sea to the west, Syria to the east and north, and Israel to the south. It is a country of rich ethnic, religious, and cultural diversity.

Physical Geography

Most of Lebanon is mountainous except for the narrow coastline and the Beqaa Valley. The country has a moderate Mediterranean climate with cool wet winters and hot humid summers in coastal areas. In the mountainous regions, temperatures drop below zero with snowfalls, and summers are hot and dry.

In ancient times, Lebanon was famously home to large cedar forests, which have been depleted due to heavy use of lumber for boat construction and few reforestation efforts.

History

Phoenicians made the area that is now Lebanon their homeland and flourished through sea trade for about 2,000 years until the fifth century BCE. Phoenicia was conquered by the Achaemenid (Persian) Empire and made into a vassal state. It was subsequently conquered by Alexander the Great in 332 BCE and then fell under the control of the Seleucid Empire. Rome ruled from the first century CE until the Arab Caliphate took over. Lebanon became involved in the Crusader Wars in the twelfth century CE. In the early sixteenth century, Lebanon fell to the Ottoman Empire, and after World War I, became part of the French Mandate for Syria. The State of Greater Lebanon, within Syrian borders, was formed in 1920 and a Lebanese Republic was established in 1926. Full independence was achieved in 1943. The region remained under Allied control until the end of World War II.

The second half of the twentieth century was marked by many periods of turmoil. In 1948 Lebanon joined the Arab League and invaded Israel during the 1948 Arab–Israeli War and took part in the Six-Day War in 1967. Civil war broke out in 1975 and lasted for 15 years, devastating the economy and causing hundreds of thousands of casualties. The Palestine Liberation Organization launched attacks against Israel using Lebanese territory, and the country was twice (in 1978 and 1982) invaded by Israel, which controlled southern Lebanon up until 2000. In February 2005, former Prime Minister Rafik Hariri was assassinated, deepening political and societal divisions and destabilizing the country. In 2006, after the kidnapping of two Israeli soldiers by Hezbollah (Party of God), Israel launched a series of air strikes over Lebanon. In August the same year, the United Nations brokered an at times uncertain ceasefire.

Right The recently restored Al-Omari Mosque in central Beirut was originally the Crusader Cathedral of St John (1113–1115). It was transformed into the city's Grand Mosque in 1291 by Mamluks—soldier slaves who had converted to Islam.

Population/Culture

Most Lebanese people are considered to be Arab, although ethnic identity has come to be defined by religious and cultural affiliations rather than genetics. Only a small fraction of the population forms more or less distinct ethnic groups, such as Armenians, Assyrians, Jews, Kurds, and Persians. Lebanon also has large numbers of people who are descendants of the Palestinian refugees from the 1948 Arab–Israeli War.

Religious divisions are similarly complicated and there are many religious groups and sects. The constitution recognizes 18 religious groups with the right to practice family law in their own courts, and are the basic players in Lebanon's politics. Muslims constitute the religious majority at 60 percent; Christians account for 40 percent.

Lebanon is one of a few countries with a diaspora larger than the country's population. Estimates range from 4 to 5 million and rising.

Arabic is the official language. English and French are taught in many universities.

Lebanese cuisine is shared with many countries in the Eastern Mediterranean region. The national dish is *kibbe*, a meat pie made from finely minced lamb and wheat. The national drink is *arak*, a strong anise-flavored liquor made from fermented grape juice.

Administration/Government

The executive branch is represented by the president, who is elected by the National Assembly (elected by popular vote), and the prime minister, who is appointed by the president in consultation with the National Assembly. The agreement stipulates that the president is a Maronite Christian, the prime minister is a Sunni Muslim, and the speaker of the National Assembly is a Shi'a Muslim. The Constitutional Council, Supreme Council, and four Courts of Cassation represent the judicial branch.

Economy/Industry

Agriculture accounts for only a fraction of national income despite fertile soil, adequate water, and a high proportion of cultivated land. Fruit is a major agricultural product. Industry is represented by small businesses engaged primarily in reassembly and packaging of imported parts and contributes about 20 percent of Lebanon's GDP. The thriving service industry accounts for three-quarters of the national income due to the strong financial and banking sector and growing tourism.

Below Charming red-roofed houses in the village of Hasrun in northern Lebanon overlook the picturesque Qannoubine Valley.

MILESTONE EVENTS

1918 Becomes part of the French Mandate for Syria following World War I
1920 The State of Greater Lebanon is formed by France
1926 Lebanese Republic is formed by France, administered through the French Mandate for Syria
1943 Full independence is achieved
1948 Lebanon joins the Arab League and invades Israel in the Arab–Israeli War
1967 Lebanon participates in the Six-Day War
1975 Civil war breaks out
1978 and 1982 Israel invades and occupies southern Lebanon
1990 Civil war ends
February 14, 2005 Former Prime Minister Rafik Hariri is assassinated in Beirut
2006 Israel launches air strikes over Lebanon; the UN brokers a ceasefire

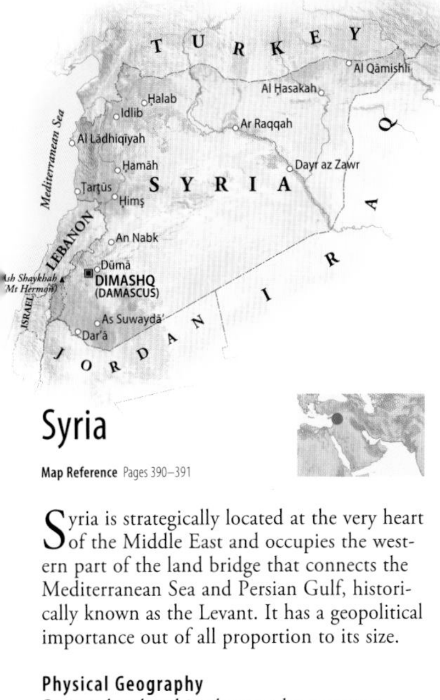

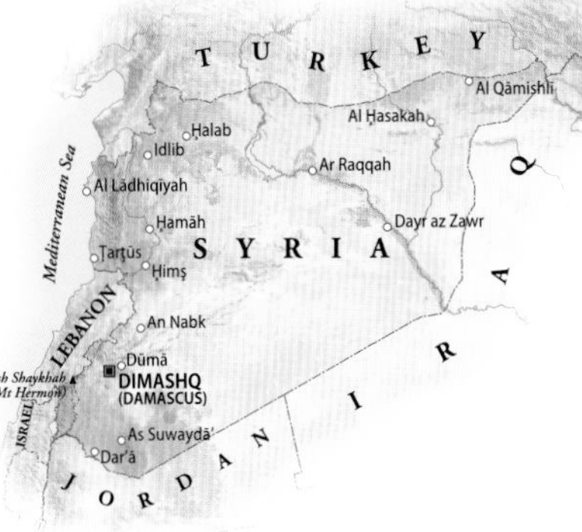
TURKEY
Al Qāmishlī
Al Ḩasakah
Ḩalab
Idlib
Ar Raqqah
Al Lādhiqīyah
Ḩamāh
Dayr az Zawr
Mediterranean Sea
Ţarţūs
SYRIA
Ḩimş
IRAQ
LEBANON
An Nabk
Dūmā
DIMASHQ
(DAMASCUS)
ISRAEL
As Suwaydā'
Dar'ā
JORDAN

Syria

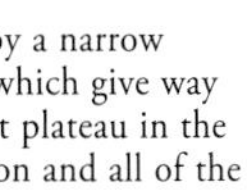

Map Reference Pages 390–391

Syria is strategically located at the very heart of the Middle East and occupies the western part of the land bridge that connects the Mediterranean Sea and Persian Gulf, historically known as the Levant. It has a geopolitical importance out of all proportion to its size.

Physical Geography

Syria is bordered in the west by a narrow coastal plain and mountains, which give way to a large, semi-arid and desert plateau in the interior. Most of the population and all of the major cities are concentrated in the west, in an axis extending between Damascus and Aleppo. While most of Syria is dry and the interior experiences extreme heat in summer, coastal areas have mild wet winters.

History

Syria falls within the Fertile Crescent, the ancient cradle of civilization that extended from Egypt to Mesopotamia. Over the centuries, Syria was incorporated into a series of empires and occupied by a succession of invaders, including the Canaanites, Phoenicians, Hebrews, Aramaeans, Assyrians, Babylonians, Persians, Greeks, Romans, Nabataeans, the Byzantines, and Crusaders. After Islam arrived in the seventh century, it became the capital of the Umayyad Empire, which stretched from Spain to India. The Levant was incorporated into the Ottoman Empire in 1517.

Modern Syria emerged following World War I. Between 1920 and 1946 France ruled it under a mandate awarded by the League of Nations. Following independence, Syria experienced more than two decades of upheaval and instability. In 1958 it merged with Egypt in the United Arab Republic, an unsuccessful experiment that ended in 1961.

Since 1963 the Ba'th Party has governed Syria under Emergency Law. Military coups in 1966 and 1970 consolidated Ba'thist control and Hafiz al-Asad emerged as president and dictator. He ruled with an iron fist until his death in 2000, when his son, Bashar, succeeded him. The secular Ba'thist regime has never been popular, because it is seen as repressive and gives disproportionate power to members of the Alawi minority sect over the Sunni majority. Many Syrians also blamed the regime for the loss of the Golan Heights to Israel in 1967. Recovering this territory has been the most important objective of Syria's rulers for over three decades, prompting Syria to attack its neighbor in 1973.

Under Hafiz al-Asad, Syria emerged as one of the most powerful and influential countries in the Arab world, a key frontline state in the struggle with Israel. It has exercised this power in neighboring Lebanon particularly, intervening in its civil war in 1976 and playing kingpin in its political life ever since.

Population/Culture

Most Syrians are Arabs and followers of Islam. Ten percent are Christian, and there are also some small Jewish communities.

Most Syrians follow a traditional lifestyle, and many crafts are made the way they have been for thousands of years. Syria is known for its embroidery, pottery, ceramics, and jewelry. In some old cities, such as Damascus and Aleppo, traditional housing with a central courtyard has been preserved.

Administration/Government

Syria is a republic run by a military dictatorship. The chief of state is the president, who governs the country's 14 provinces. The 250 members of the People's Council, or Majlis al-Shaab, are popularly elected.

Economy/Industry

A middle-income developing country, Syria has a relatively broad-based economy, with a large agricultural sector, some manufacturing, a growing tourist industry, and oil production. Lack of foreign investment, declining oil production, and international sanctions have had a detrimental effect on the economy.

Above The sun rises on tombs at the ancient oasis of Palmyra, northeast of Damascus in central Syria. Also known as the Bride of the Desert, this once prosperous and elegant city held a vital position on the caravan route linking Persia with Roman Syria and Phoenicia.

Left The impressive ruin of the Great Colonnade is testimony to the esteem in which Palmyra was held by Rome. The location was made a UNESCO World Heritage Site in 1980.

SYRIA

Official name Syrian Arab Republic (Al Jumhuriyah al Arabiyah as Suriyah)
Land area 71,062 square miles (184,050 km^2)
Border countries Turkey, Iraq, Jordan, Israel, Lebanon
Capital Damascus (Dimashq)
Highest & lowest points Mt Hermon 9,232 feet (2,814 m); unknown site near Lake Tiberias –656 feet (–200 m)
Climate Mostly desert; Mediterranean
Population 19,748,000
Language(s) Official: Arabic; others: Kurdish, Armenian, Aramaic, Circassian
Ethnicity Arab 90%; Kurdish, Armenian, Circassian, Turkoman, Jewish 10%
Religion Sunni Muslim 74%, Alawiti 12%, Christian 10%, Druze 3%, other including Jewish 1%
Government Republic under a military dictatorship
Currency Syrian pound
Human Development Index 0.724 (ranked 108th out of 177 countries)

Left A young Syrian woman tends her goats. A recent sociological study showed that married rural women spent an average of six hours working outside the home on agricultural tasks, as well as considerable time on household duties such as baking bread and looking after children.

MIDDLE EAST

ISRAEL

Official name State of Israel (Medinat Yisra'el)
Land area 7,849 square miles (20,330 km²)
Border countries Lebanon, Syria, West Bank, Jordan, Egypt, Gaza Strip
Capital Jerusalem (Yerushalayim/Al Quds)
Highest & lowest points Har Meron 3,963 feet (1,208 m); Dead Sea –1,339 feet (–408 m)
Climate Temperate
Population 7,112,000
Language(s) Official: Hebrew, Arabic used officially for Arab minority; English most commonly used foreign language
Ethnicity Jewish 76.4% (Israel-born 67.1%, Europe/US-born 22.6%, Africa-born 5.9%, Asia-born 4.2%), non-Jewish 23.6% (mostly Arab)
Religion Jewish 76.4%, Muslim 16%, Christian Arabs 1.7%, other Christian 0.4%, Druze 1.6%, unspecified 3.9%
Government Parliamentary democracy
Currency New Israeli shekel
Human Development Index 0.932 (ranked 23rd out of 177 countries)

Above right The ancient port of Jaffa stands proudly alongside the modern city of Tel Aviv.

Below The natural sandstone arches and caves at Timna National Park, north of Eliat, Israel, were the site of copper mining some 6,000 years ago.

Bottom Worshippers gather at the Wailing Wall in Jerusalem, a worldwide symbol of Judaism.

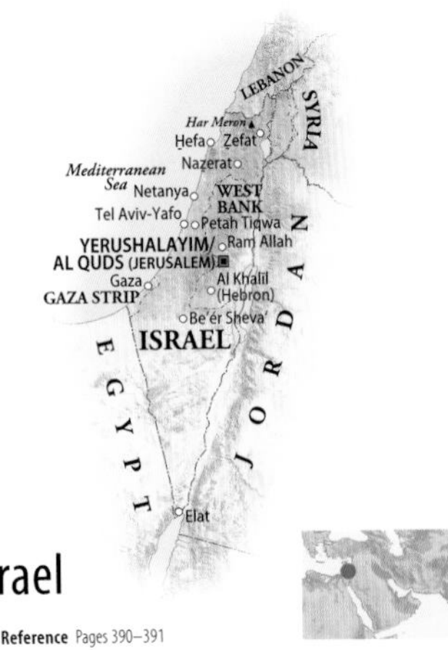
LEBANON
SYRIA
Har Meron
Hefa
Zefat
Mediterranean Sea
Nazerat
Netanya
WEST BANK
Tel Aviv-Yafo
Petah Tiqwa
YERUSHALAYIM/
AL QUDS (JERUSALEM)
Ram Allah
Gaza
GAZA STRIP
Al Khalil (Hebron)
Be'er Sheva'
ISRAEL
EGYPT
JORDAN
Elat

Israel

Map Reference Pages 390–391

In many ways Israel's economic, population, and cultural indicators do not match those of its neighbors, a regional mismatch that presents continual tensions without and within its borders.

Physical Geography

Northern Israel was part of the ancient Fertile Crescent. Today most of the country is rocky and stark, yet hauntingly beautiful. Climate varies from Mediterranean in the north and west to arid in the virtually uninhabited Negev Desert in the south. Israel shares with Jordan the world's lowest point below sea level at the Dead Sea at –1,339 feet (–408 m).

History

Israel was created amid the post-Holocaust sympathies of World War II, as a homeland for the Jewish people. A United Nations plan backed the establishment of two new states in the Middle East, one for the Jews and one for the Arabs, under which the religiously charged city of Jerusalem, sacred to Jews, Muslims, and Christians, was to be a neutral zone controlled by neither of the new countries.

The plan failed. From independence in 1948 through the mid-1970s, Israel and its neighbors fought several wars, Israel emerging from each one with more territory than before. The Arab state proposed was not established, nor was Jerusalem made a neutral zone. The Mediterranean port city of Tel Aviv was the official capital, but Israel gradually moved capital functions to Jerusalem, further fueling regional tensions. Today, Israel controls the Mediterranean Gaza Strip and the kidney-shaped West Bank—land where Arabs still aspire to independence. The northern sliver of the Golan Heights was taken from Syria in 1967, as was the entire Sinai Peninsula from Egypt, which was returned in phases.

Population/Culture

Israel's internal makeup is quite complex. The population is around 76 percent Jewish, with a range of diversity from the most secular and western of lifestyles to the most orthodox. At least 12 parties in parliament represent various Jewish interests. Israel's 1.4 million Muslims are divided among Arab, Druze, and Bedouin constituents. Not including Palestinian Arabs of the Gaza Strip, West Bank, and Golan Heights, nearly a million Israeli Arabs hold Israeli citizenship. Over 400,000 Israelis are Christian Arabs, other Christians, or of other religious affiliation.

Administration/Government

Israel is a parliamentary democracy which is governed by the Knesset, which sits in Jerusalem. Members of this 120-seat parliament are elected via general, national, proportional elections. The president is head of state, but the prime minister and cabinet run the country. Israel is working toward an official constitution; the Basic Laws of the State of Israel have since 1968 (with amendments) served as the nation's unofficial constitution.

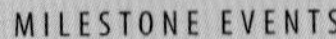

MILESTONE EVENTS

May 14, 1948 State of Israel is declared; the British withdraw from the region
May 15, 1948 Israel is invaded by five Arab states thus beginning the War of Independence
July 1948 War of Independence ends
1949 Israel is admitted to the United Nations
June 1967 As a result of the Six-Day War, Israel gains the Golan Heights
October 6, 1973 Syria and Egypt attack Israel in what becomes known as the Yom Kippur War
September 1978 Camp David Accords are signed between Israel and Egypt
1980s Palestinian intifada begins
November 4, 1995 Prime Minister Yitzhak Rabin assassinated by Jewish terrorist
2000 Palestinian intifada is renewed
July 2006 Israel launches air strikes over Lebanon for two weeks
May 2008 Israel and Jordan holding peace talks mediated by Turkey

The main political issue Israel faces is how much autonomy to give to the West Bank and Gaza Strip. Since about 1980, Arab unrest and violence against Israeli occupation has increased. Arabs wish for a sovereign Palestine, with East Jerusalem as its capital, but Israel rarely mentions independence as a main goal; leaders prefer more conservative phrasings like "the plan for peace." The proposition that a free Palestine might one day occur does not find favor among a population that has had to defend the country's territorial integrity since day one. Thus, Israel has taken a gradual course toward Palestinian independence, depending on the degree of conservatism of contemporary leadership.

Economy/Industry

The USA, UK, and France have continually supported Israel, thus the country has the mightiest military, the best agriculture, and the wealthiest economy in the region. The population is predominantly Jewish, made up of historic migrants from Europe, the USA, Russia, and elsewhere. The population is growing at a rate of 1.5 percent, with an infant mortality rate of about 3.9 and a life expectancy of 80 years. In comparison, neighboring Jordan has a growth rate of 2.4 percent, an infant mortality rate of 24 and a life expectancy of 72. Israel's gross national income per person is US$25,500 while Jordan's is US$6,200. Jordan claims that 90 percent of people 15 years and older are literate, while Israel claims 97 percent.

Better irrigation techniques and hardier crops have improved agriculture, and Israel has increased cropland area threefold since independence in 1948, managing to supply nearly two-thirds of its own food. This is startling considering the rapidly increasing need for water. Adding to the age-old Mediterranean staples of figs and olives, specialties now include out-of-season vegetables, avocados, and a variety of exotic fruits.

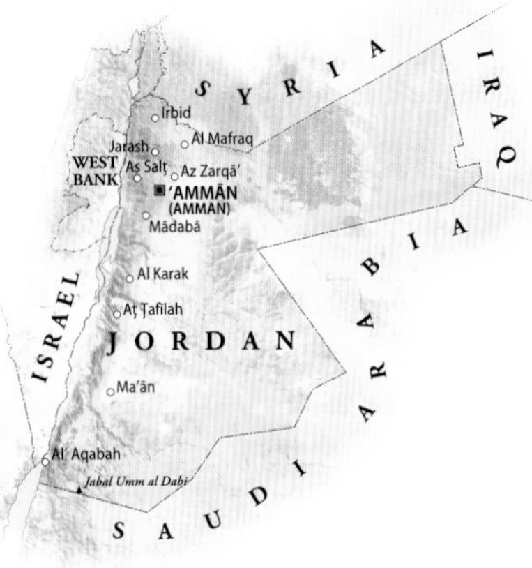
SYRIA
IRAQ
Irbid
Jarash
Al Mafraq
WEST BANK
As Salt
Az Zarqā'
'AMMĀN (AMMAN)
Mādabā
Al Karak
Aṭ Ṭafīlah
ISRAEL
JORDAN
Ma'ān
Al 'Aqabah
Jabal Umm al Dabi
SAUDI ARABIA

Jordan

Map Reference Pages 390–391

Jordan, officially the Hashemite Kingdom of Jordan, is located in western Asia and has borders with Syria to the north, Iraq to the northeast, Israel and the West Bank to the west, and Saudi Arabia to the east and south.

Above Blending Eastern culture with Hellenistic architectural traditions, the Jordanian city of Petra is one of the world's most famous archeological sites. Half-built, half-hewn from the surrounding rose-tinged rock, it was strategically positioned at the crossroads of the major trade routes of Arabia, Egypt, and Syria-Phoenicia.

Physical Geography

Jordan consists mostly of arid desert plateau in the east with highlands in the west. A mere 16 miles (26 km) of shoreline in the south, give access to the Red Sea. The climate is dry and hot for most of the year, with summer temperatures peaking in August.

History

The history of this part of the Middle East dates back to around 2000 BCE with Semitic settlements along the Jordan River. From then until the Middle Ages the region was in turn invaded and settled by Hittites, Egyptians, Israelites, Assyrians, Babylonians, Persians, Greeks, Romans, Arabs, Christian Crusaders, and Ottoman Turks. Following World War I, the territory that at present comprises Israel, Jordan, the West Bank, the Gaza Strip, and Jerusalem was given to the United Kingdom by the League of Nations as the mandate of Palestine Trans-Jordan. The mandate ended in May 1946, and became the independent Hashemite Kingdom of Trans-Jordan.

Opposed to the creation of Israel in 1948, Trans-Jordan took part in the war between the Arab states and the newly founded Israel. Trans-Jordan became Jordan in 1950. Its participation in the 1967 war between Israel and the Arab states resulted in a drastic increase in the number of Palestinians living in Jordan. In 1991 Jordan, along with Syria, Lebanon, and Palestinian representatives, participated in direct peace negotiations with Israel, which resulted in an end to hostilities and the signing of an Israeli–Jordanian peace treaty in 1994.

Population/Culture

Most Jordanians are of Bedouin origin; the Arabic word for Bedouin, *bedu*, means "desert dweller." Yet today, only a small number of Bedouin follow the traditional nomadic lifestyle.

More than half the population are Jordanian Arabs, and approximately 40 percent are Arabs of Palestinian origin as a result of mass migration during the Arab-Israeli wars in 1948 and 1967. Ethnic minorities include Circassians, Chechens, Armenians, Druze, and Kurds who are integrated into the Arab culture.

Arabic is the official language and English is also widely spoken. French is also understood in mostly business, government, and education circles. Jordan's culture is based on Arab and Islamic elements.

Art is ever present in exhibitions and at art galleries. The music of Jordan has a strong Bedouin influence. Rural songs and poetry are popular and are performed with accompanying ensembles. Alternative and rock music have recently become more popular, blending western and eastern influences.

Jordanian cuisine shares much with Arab cooking and is influenced by the cuisines of Lebanon, Egypt, India, and Turkey. It features meat ingredients such as chicken and lamb, usually delicately spiced with herbs, as well as an array of dairy products, yogurt, cheese, and vegetables.

Administration/Government

Jordan is a constitutional monarchy and King Abdullah II is the current chief of state. Abdullah II is the son of long-time monarch King Hussein, whose reign spanned 47 years. The king appoints the prime minister who assigns the ministers in consultation with the former. The National Assembly (Majlis al-'Umma) is a bicameral body and consists of the 55-seat Senate (also called the House of Notables, the members of which are appointed by the monarch for four-year terms) and the Chamber of Deputies (also called the House of Representatives or Majlis al-Nuwaab, with 110 members elected by a popular vote). Six seats are reserved for women and are assigned by an electoral panel if no women are elected.

Left Only a small proportion of Jordan's Bedouin population live a traditional nomadic existence.

Economy/Industry

Jordan's limited natural resources extend to water and oil. Only about 10 percent of the land is arable and even that depends on the water supply. Agriculture accounts for a mere 3.5 percent of GDP; the services sector contributes two-thirds. Phosphates, potash, and agricultural products are the main items of export. Poverty, unemployment, and inflation are among the major problems Jordan faces. The liberalization of trade in 1999 helped to boost the economy. Foreign aid and overseas transfers are among the main sources of income. Tourism is an important component of the economy due to the abundance of ancient sites, places of religious significance, and areas of great natural beauty.

MILESTONE EVENTS

1921 The British hand over the semi-autonomous control of Trans-Jordan to the future king, Abdullah I of Jordan

May 22, 1946 British mandate over Trans-Jordan ends

January 8, 1952 Constitution is adopted

1967 Jordan, along with the Arab states of Syria, Egypt, and Iraq, participates in the war with Israel

1991 King Hussein ends martial law and the following year legalizes political parties

October 26, 1994 An Israeli-Jordanian peace treaty is concluded

JORDAN

Official name Hashemite Kingdom of Jordan (Al Mamlakah al Urduniyah al Hashimiyah)

Land area 35,637 square miles (92,300 km²)

Border countries Syria, Iraq, Saudi Arabia, Israel, West Bank

Capital Amman

Highest & lowest points Jabal Ram 5,689 feet (1,734 m); Dead Sea –1,339 feet (–408 m)

Climate Arid desert

Population 6,199,000

Language(s) Official: Arabic

Ethnicity Arab 98%, other (Circassian, Armenian, Chechen, Druze, Kurdish) 2%

Religion Sunni Muslim 92%, Christian 6%, other 2%

Government Constitutional monarchy

Currency Jordanian dinar

Human Development Index 0.773 (ranked 86th out of 177 countries)

Left The intricate needlework and vibrant colors used in Jordanian embroidery incorporate motifs of cultural and regional significance.

IRAQ

Official name Republic of Iraq (Al Jumhuriyah al-Iraqiyah)
Land area 166,859 square miles (432,162 km²)
Border countries Turkey, Kuwait, Saudi Arabia, Iran, Jordan, Syria
Capital Baghdad
Highest point Unnamed peak 11,847 feet (3,611 m)
Climate Mostly desert; mild to cool winters, dry, hot summers
Population 28,221,000
Language(s) Arabic, Kurdish, Assyrian, Armenian
Ethnicity Arab 75–80%; Kurdish 15–20%; Turkmen, Assyrian, and other 5%
Religion Muslim 97%, Christian and other 3%
Government Parliamentary democracy
Currency New Iraqi dinar
Human Development Index Not available

Above right The split turquoise dome of the Martyr's Monument (Al-Shaheed Monument) in Baghdad commemorates the Iraqi soldiers who lost their lives during the Iraq–Iran War of 1980.

Right An Iraqi shepherd's flock graze along the banks of the Euphrates River. Since neighboring Syria built a dam upriver, water flow has decreased, affecting the growth of crops and the amount of fodder available for livestock.

Below A small oasis hamlet, north of the city of Haditha in the Al Ånbar district of Iraq, stands in defiance of the expansive desert beyond.

TURKEY
SYRIA
IRAN
IRAQ
JORDAN
SAUDI ARABIA
KUWAIT
The Gulf
Al Mawşil
Arbīl
Kirkūk
As Sulaymānīyah
Al Muqdādiyah
Ba'qūbah
BAGHDĀD
Ar Ramādī
Karbalā'
Al Hillah
An Najaf
Al 'Amārah
Ad Dīwānīyah
An Nāşirīyah
Sūq ash Shuyūkh
Al Başrah
Ābādān

Iraq

Map Reference Pages 390–391

Iraq is bounded by Turkey, Kuwait, Saudi Arabia, Iran, Jordan, and Syria. A narrow strip of coastline between Kuwait and Iran hugs The Gulf. Iraq is a young state in a very old land. The birthplace of western civilization is now home to a modern human tragedy.

Physical Geography

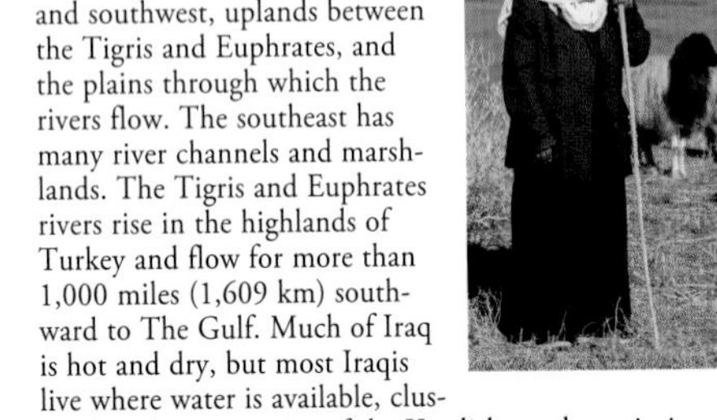

There are four distinct geographic regions: Highlands to the north and northeast, desert in the west and southwest, uplands between the Tigris and Euphrates, and the plains through which the rivers flow. The southeast has many river channels and marshlands. The Tigris and Euphrates rivers rise in the highlands of Turkey and flow for more than 1,000 miles (1,609 km) southward to The Gulf. Much of Iraq is hot and dry, but most Iraqis live where water is available, clustered in the mountains of the Kurdish northeast, or along the Tigris and Euphrates rivers. Silt from flooding and water for irrigation are essential to agriculture.

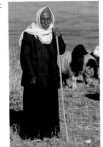

IRAQ IN TRANSITION

Iraq is a country in transition and its future is uncertain. Saddam Hussein was removed from power during the American- and British-led invasion of Iraq (2003). However, disagreements between Sunni Arabs, Shi'a Arabs, and Kurds were held in check by Saddam's tight control. Now, these groups are challenged to find ways of living together peaceably.

Iraq was once an economic and political powerhouse in the Middle East. However, it has suffered enormously from the problems brought about by three wars in three decades. International response to Iraq's aggression included devastating sanctions. The invasion of Iraq, justified by its alleged manufacture of weapons of mass destruction (WMDs), destroyed infrastructure and shattered the economy and has caused Iraqis immeasurable suffering. According to studies by *The Lancet*, a prestigious British medical journal, between the 2003 invasion and June 2006 there were 654,965 excess Iraqi deaths.

Since 2003, billions of dollars have been poured into the country to rebuild it, yet the deaths continue to mount. The speed of political change, and the violent nature of that change, created a power vacuum and instability that did not previously exist. The government has a difficult task in trying to create a balance of power in the new Iraq.

History

Settled agriculture began around 10,000 BCE, spurred on by the abundance of resources in the area between the Tigris and Euphrates rivers. Much of Iraq is part of ancient Mesopotamia—which means "between the two rivers"—where the civilizations of Sumer, Babylon, and Assyria flourished. These cultures developed mathematics, laws, philosophies, science, and early forms of writing.

Over the past 2,500 years, the region of Iraq has been contested and occupied by Persians, Greeks, Arabs, and Turks. It acquired its present name and current borders in the early twentieth century, when the British inherited the territory from the Ottoman Turks and drew boundaries that included the oilfields in the far south, where Shi'a Arabs are the majority population, and in the far north where the Kurdish population lives. Sunni Arabs occupied the gap between the oilfields and controlled the city of Baghdad in the center of the new country.

Iraqi kings and presidents, who ruled after the British departed in 1932, inherited the British-delineated borders. The most famous recent ruler—Saddam Hussein—was a central figure in Iraq's conflicts with neighboring countries. Two disagreements led to costly wars, the first a protracted war with Iran in the 1980s—the First Gulf War. The second was Iraq's invasion of Kuwait in 1990; coalition forces responded by bombing Iraq in January 1991, which was the beginning of the Second Gulf War. This latter misstep eventually led to the overthrow of Saddam Hussein during the British- and American-led invasion and occupation of Iraq in 2003.

Population/Culture

Most of the inhabitants of Iraq are Arabs, but there is a large Kurdish population, as well as Assyrians, Armenians, and Turkmen, many of whom live in northeast Iraq. Most people are Muslim. Iraq is one of three countries in the Middle East where the Shi'a branch of Islam is the majority faith (the others are Iran and Bahrain). Most Shi'a Arabs live in southern Iraq and have been politically dominated by a Sunni minority for a long time. The Sunni–Shi'a divide plays a big role in political and social relations.

Administration/Government

A new Iraqi government to replace the Ba'thist government of Saddam Hussein was created progressively in the period 2003 to 2005. The Iraqi constitution was completed in August 2005 and enshrined the principles of democracy and a federal system for Iraq. This system allows different groups—Sunni, Shi'a, and Kurd—to have regional control of their territory and to decide how much power to give the central government. Passage of the constitution paved the way for a federal government, which was established through national elections in December 2005.

MILESTONE EVENTS

10,000 BCE Beginning of agricultural settlement in Mesopotamia
August 23, 1932 Independent state of Iraq comes into being
July 14, 1958 Military coup overthrows the monarchy; Iraq declared a republic
1972 Treaty of Friendship signed between Iraq and Soviet Union
1972 Iraq Petroleum Company nationalized
July 16, 1979 Vice President Saddam Hussein becomes the country's leader
September 4, 1980 Iran shells Iraqi border towns—beginning of First Gulf War
June 7, 1981 Israel attacks nuclear research center in Baghdad
March 16, 1988 Chemical weapons used against the Kurds
August 20, 1988 Ceasefire between Iran and Iraq
August 2, 1990 Iraq invades Kuwait
August 6, 1990 Economic sanctions imposed on Iraq
January 1991 Coalition forces begin bombing Iraq—the Second Gulf War begins
March 3, 1991 Ceasefire comes into force
April 14, 1995 Oil for food program begins
February 19, 1999 Grand Ayatollah Sayyis Muhammad Sadiq al-Sadir assassinated
February 2001 Britain and USA bomb Iraq's air defenses
September 2002 US President George W. Bush accuses Iraq of being a grave danger to humanity
November 2002 Nuclear weapons inspectors return to Iraq
March 17, 2003 President George W. Bush warns Saddam Hussein to leave the country within 48 hours
March 20, 2003 Missiles launched against Baghdad
April 9, 2003 US forces enter Baghdad
December 14, 2003 Saddam Hussein captured
December 15, 2005 Eight million Iraqis vote for a transitional national assembly
December 30, 2006 Saddam Hussein hanged for crimes against humanity
December 2007 Turkey launches air strikes against Kurds in Iraq
March 2008 Suicide bombing in market kills 50; such bombings have continued unabated since beginning of US-led invasion

Economy/Industry

Iraq is steward to 10 percent of the world's oil reserves. The oil sector provides 90 percent of foreign exchange earnings. The largest oilfields are located in the southeast, around Basra and The Gulf, and in the northern plains and foothills around Kirkuk.

ARMENIA
AZERBAIJAN
TURKEY
Tabriz
Ardabil
Orumiyeh
Rasht
Caspian Sea
TURKMENISTAN
Zanjan
Gorgan
Bojnurd
Sari
Kuh-e Damavand
Mashhad
Sanandaj
TEHRAN
Kermanshah
Qom
Borujerd
Kashan
Khorramabad
Najafabad
Esfahan
Birjand
Yazd
IRAQ
Ahvaz
IRAN
AFGHANISTAN
Kerman
Shiraz
Sirjan
Zahedan
PAKISTAN
The Gulf
Bandar-e 'Abbas
Gulf of Oman

Iran

Map Reference Pages 390–391

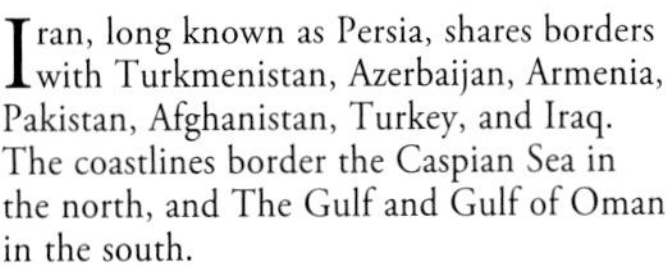

Iran, long known as Persia, shares borders with Turkmenistan, Azerbaijan, Armenia, Pakistan, Afghanistan, Turkey, and Iraq. The coastlines border the Caspian Sea in the north, and The Gulf and Gulf of Oman in the south.

Physical Geography

The topography is dominated by rugged mountain ranges, including the Zagros range that stretches from Armenia to The Gulf, and the Khorassan range, where Kuh-e Damavand, the highest peak, is located. An arid plateau in the interior contains an almost impassable salt wasteland, known as the *kavir*, which is approximately 200 miles long (320 km) by 100 miles (160 km) wide. Occasional plains are dotted along the coastlines. Around one-sixth of Iran is barren desert. The climate is mainly arid and semi-arid, but subtropical along the Caspian coast. Winters are harsh with sub-zero temperatures and heavy snowfall in mountainous regions. The coastal plains along The Gulf have mild winters and relatively high humidity.

History

Ancient cultures and settlements have existed on the Iranian plateau since the fourth millennium BCE. Many great Persian empires came and went, including Median, Achaemenid, Parthian, and Sassanid, before Persia was absorbed into the Arab Umayyad Caliphate. In the thirteenth century the Mongols invaded and razed many important cities. They also destroyed whole regions such as Mazandaran by demolishing irrigation channels and crops. The following centuries were marked by constant wars with neighboring states.

A constitutional monarchy and Persia's first parliament were established in 1906. In 1925 Reza Shah replaced the ruling Qajar Dynasty, founding the Pahlavi Dynasty. Persia was renamed Iran in 1935. Reza Shah was exiled in 1941 and replaced by his son, Mohammad Reza Shah. The Pahlavis are credited with the development of Iran's modern industry, transportation, and national education system, but their autocratic rule alienated their countrymen. In 1979, Ayatollah Khomeini's Islamic Revolution overthrew the Pahlavi Dynasty.

Population/Culture

Iran's population is diverse and consists of people of many religions and ethnic backgrounds. Persians make up the majority of the population. Azerbaijanis and Kurds constitute the largest ethnic groups, accounting for 24 percent and 7 percent of the population respectively. Other minorities include Arabs, Turkmen, Lurs, Baloch, Armenians, and Assyrians. Most Iranians are Muslims belonging to the Shi'a branch of Islam, the official state religion.

Multi-faceted Iranian culture is very old and one of the richest in the world. Religion, arts, poetry, and carpet weaving have been developed to a high degree. The Zoroastrian Avesta, the sacred texts of the Zoroastrians, was composed between 1700 BCE and 400 CE. Zoroastrianism was the state religion of the Achaemenid Empire and later the Persian empires, until the arrival of Islam in the seventh century CE. Persian belongs to the Indo-European family of languages and the earliest records of Old Persian date back to the sixth century BCE. Arabic influenced the language after the Islamic conquest of Persia.

Iranian New Year (Navruz) is an ancient tradition that is celebrated on March 21 or 22 (vernal equinox) and marks the arrival of spring. Modern Iranian cinema has gained worldwide recognition.

MILESTONE EVENTS

800 BCE Medians establish an empire

522–486 BCE King Darius rules the Achaemenid Empire

334 BCE Alexander the Great conquers the Achaemenid Empire

248 BCE–651 CE Rule of the Parthian and Sassanid empires

1906 Constitutional monarchy with the nation's first parliament established

1921 A coup is supported by Reza Khan and his troops

1925 Reza Khan becomes Reza Shah, replacing the ruling Qajar Dynasty and founding Pahlavi Dynasty

1941 Reza Shah is exiled and replaced by his son Mohammad Reza Shah

January 1979 Overthrow of Pahlavi Dynasty by Khomeini's Islamic Revolution

1980 Iran–Iraq war erupts

1988 Iran–Iraq war ends; the Iranian death toll is between 450,000 to 750,000

Administration/Government

The Supreme Leader, appointed for life, and the popularly elected president, represent the executive branch of government. The Assembly of Experts, a popularly elected body of 86 religious scholars, determines the succession of the Supreme Leader. The Islamic Consultative Assembly, or Majles, with 290 members, is elected by popular vote. The Supreme Court and the High Council of the Judiciary supervise the enforcement of laws.

Economy/Industry

Industry is largely based on mining, manufacturing, and construction. It contributes over 40 percent to GDP, and employs around one-third of the workforce. Iran has vast deposits of oil and natural gas; other natural resources include coal, chromium, copper, iron ore, lead, manganese, zinc, and sulfur. Oil generates around 80 percent of export earnings. The leading industrial sectors are car manufacturing, construction materials, home appliances, food and agricultural products, armaments, pharmaceuticals, and information technology. Agricultural produce contributes about one-tenth of GDP, but employs about one-third of the workforce. The service sector accounts for 44 percent of GDP. Efforts are being made to diversify by investing oil revenues into other sectors of the economy.

Above The originally nomadic Qashqai people are of Turkic origin and now mostly live a settled or semi-settled existence in the Iranian provinces of Fars, Khuzestan, and Isfahan.

IRAN

Official name Islamic Republic of Iran (Jomhuri-ye Eslami-ye Iran)

Land area 631,663 square miles (1,636,000 km²)

Border countries Turkmenistan, Afghanistan, Pakistan, Iraq, Turkey, Armenia, Azerbaijan

Capital Tehran

Highest & lowest points Kuh-e Damavand 18,606 feet (5,671 m); Caspian Sea −92 feet (−28 m)

Climate Arid and semi-arid; subtropical on Caspian coast

Population 65,875,000

Language(s) Persian and Persian dialects, Turkic and Turkic dialects , Kurdish, Luri, Balochi, Arabic, Turkish, other

Ethnicity Persian 51%, Azeri 24%, Gilaki/Mazandarani 8%, Kurd 7%, Arab 3%, Lur 2%, Baloch 2%, Turkmen 2%, other 1%

Religion Muslim 98%, Zoroastrian/Jewish/Christian/Baha'i 2%

Government Theocratic republic

Currency Iranian rial

Human Development Index 0.759 (ranked 94th out of 177 countries)

Above The Qashqai people of Iran are renowned for their carpet- and rug-making skills. Vibrant natural dyes are used to color the wool gathered from their sheep, and centuries-old spinning techniques are employed.

Left Established in the Sassanid period (226–651 CE), the World Heritage-listed Arg-é Bam (Citadel of Bam) in southeastern Iran was located on important silk and cotton trade routes. It was badly damaged by an earthquake in 2003.

SAUDI ARABIA

Official name Kingdom of Saudi Arabia (al-Mamlakah al-Arabiyah as Suudiyah)
Land area 830,000 square miles (2,149,690 km²)
Border Countries Jordan, Iraq, Kuwait, Oman, United Arab Emirates, Yemen
Capital Riyadh (Ar Riyāḑ)
Highest point Jabal Sawda 10,279 feet (3,133 m)
Climate Harsh, dry desert with temperature extremes
Population 28,161,000
Language(s) Arabic, English
Ethnicity Saudi Arab 75%, other 25%
Religion Muslim
Government Absolute monarchy
Currency Saudi riyal
Human Development Index 0.812 (61st out of 177 countries)

JORDAN
IRAQ
KUWAIT
Tabūk
Al Qayşūmah
Ḩā'il
The Gulf
Buraydah
Al Jubayl
Ad Dammām
BAHRAIN
QATAR
Al Hufūf
Yanbu' al Baḩr
Al Madīnah (Medina)
AR RIYĀḐ (RIYADH)
Haraḑ
SAUDI ARABIA
UNITED ARAB EMIRATES
Red Sea
Jiddah
Makkah (Mecca)
At Tā'if
Jabal Sawda'
Abhā
Abā as Su'ūd
OMAN
YEMEN

Saudi Arabia

Map Reference Pages 390–391

The Kingdom of Saudi Arabia, often referred to simply as The Kingdom, is on the Arabian Peninsula. It shares borders with Jordan, Iraq, Kuwait, Oman, the United Arab Emirates, and Yemen. The Saudi nation is one of the most influential and closely watched countries on Earth. The birthplace of Islam, it is the custodian of the two holiest shrines in the Muslim world at Mecca and Medina, and the steward of 25 percent of the world's proven reserves of petroleum.

Physical Geography

Saudi Arabia occupies around 80 percent of the Arabian Peninsula, mostly desert and largely uninhabited. Arable land accounts for less than 2 percent of land area. The barren Rub' al-Khali, or Empty Quarter, one of the largest sand deserts in the world, stretches for 1,000 miles (2,590 km) along Saudi Arabia's border with Yemen, from Oman almost to the shores of the Red Sea. With temperatures routinely reaching a scorching 131°F (55°C) in summer, and sand dunes over 1,000 feet (300 m) in height, it is one of the world's most forbidding environments.

History

Saudi Arabia is ruled by the Saudi royal family, the House of Saud. King Abdullah bin Abdul Aziz al-Saud became ruler in 2005. The House of Saud emerged in 1744 with an alliance between a local ruler, Muhammad bin Saud, and the reformist cleric, Muhammad bin Abdul Wahhab. The political entity they formed battled for control of the peninsula until 1902, when Abdul Aziz ibn Saud captured the capital Riyadh. By 1932 Abdul Aziz had united the disparate regions of the Arabian Peninsula and the Kingdom of Saudi Arabia was born.

Population/Culture

One-quarter of the population are non-national) from regions as different as Africa and South Asia. This cultural diversity is evident in the rich variety of cuisines on offer. Although ethnically diverse, most inhabitants are unified by Islam.

Administration/Government

Saudi Arabia is an absolute monarchy. There are no political parties or scheduled elections. The government gains its legitimacy not only from its long line of hereditary rulers but from its strict observance of Islamic Sharia law. The king appoints his own Council of Ministers, which often includes members of the royal family. Also, there is a 90-member legislative branch consisting of royal appointees who serve very strict four-year terms. The country has no constitution or bill of rights in the traditional western sense; nevertheless, the Qur'an together with the Traditions of the Prophet are accepted in Saudi society as providing the foundations for proper and correct human conduct.

The country has a less than outstanding record on human rights. Arbitrary arrests, closed trials, restrictions on freedom of speech and freedom of the press, and little in the way of government transparency, are all part of life in Saudi Arabia.

MILESTONE EVENTS

570 CE The Prophet Muhammad is born
1744 Muhammad bin Abdul Wahhab and Muhammad bin Saud take an oath to bring Arabian Peninsula Arabs back to the true Muslim faith
1792 Muhammad bin Abdul Wahhab dies
1902 Abdul Aziz ibn Saud captures Riyadh
1927 Abdul Aziz ibn Saud signs Treaty of Jedda
September, 1932 Kingdom of Saudi Arabia is founded
1938 Oil is discovered in the Eastern Province
1964 King Saud abdicates in favor of his half-brother, Faisal
1969 Islamic Development Bank is founded
1975 King Faisal is assassinated
1980 Saudi Arabia buys its oil company, ARAMCO, from western interests
April, 2005 The first municipal elections in 50 years are held
August 1, 2005 Abdullah bin Abdul Aziz al-Saud becomes the nation's sixth king
December, 2005 Saudi Arabia joins the World Trade Organization (WTO)

Economy/Industry

In 1938 oil was discovered in the country's Eastern Province, and oil-based economic development began in earnest in the 1960s. The country soon became the world's leading exporter of petroleum, which now accounts for over 90 percent of export earnings and almost half of the country's GDP.

Just how much oil remains in Saudi fields is crucial to the continuing growth and stability of the world economy. The Saudi government purchased the national oil company, ARAMCO, from western interests in 1980; it is impossible to acquire data on the status of their ageing fields or on their success or otherwise in locating new deposits. The Ghawar field, the country's largest, is running out. It has always been taken for granted that The Kingdom could increase oil production to cover any crisis, but this is now questionable. Many industry analysts believe that all seven of the major Saudi fields have passed their production peaks.

Wahhabism

The strain of Sunni Islam known today as Wahhabism started as a peculiarly Saudi interpretation of the teachings of the Prophet. Its primary belief is the unique nature and oneness of Allah, hardly an unorthodox view, but it began to assume very nationalistic elements and was to prove effective as a moral weapon against the rule of the Ottoman Empire in the early twentieth century. It later formed a perceived association with the more extreme elements of Islam, and colonial powers saw the movement as a threat to their rule. Wahhabism has evolved into a fundamentalist branch of Islam that is increasingly pervading every level of Saudi society.

Above Saudi Arabia has the largest oil reserves in the world, at a proven 264.3 million barrels—approximately 25 percent of the world's total. It looks set to remain the biggest oil producer in the Organization of Petroleum Exporting Countries (OPEC).

Right Mecca's Great Mosque is thronged with pilgrims during the Hajj, the largest annual pilgrimage in the world. An estimated two million attend each year to take part in rituals and pay homage to the life of Muhummad. All able-bodied Muslims are expected to attend at least once in their lifetime, if they can afford it.

SAUDI ARABIA
AL MANĀMAH (MANAMA)
Al Muharraq
Al Hadd
The Gulf
Al Budayyi'
Madīnat 'Īsá
Sitrah
Umm an Na'sān
BAHRAIN
Karzakkān
'Awālī
Az Zallāq
'Askar
Jabal ad Dukhān
Jaww
Am Mamtalah
Ar Rumaythah
Gulf of Bahrain
Hawār
QATAR

Bahrain

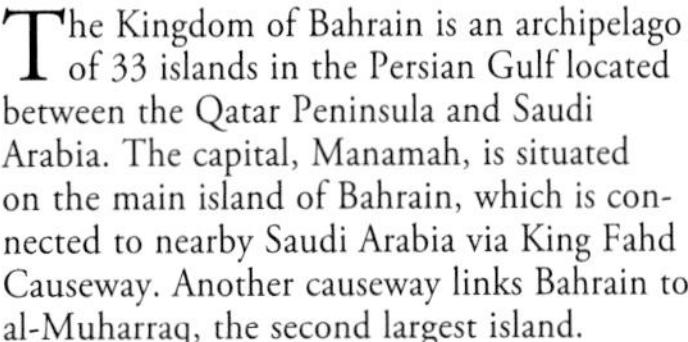

Map Reference Pages 390–391

The Kingdom of Bahrain is an archipelago of 33 islands in the Persian Gulf located between the Qatar Peninsula and Saudi Arabia. The capital, Manamah, is situated on the main island of Bahrain, which is connected to nearby Saudi Arabia via King Fahd Causeway. Another causeway links Bahrain to al-Muharraq, the second largest island.

The islands are low-lying, largely barren expanses of rock and sand. There is little arable land, and some of that is threatened by desertification. There is virtually no rainfall from June to late November. Summers are hot and humid, and winters are mild. The only sources of fresh water are ground water and desalinated sea water. Coastal degradation, caused mainly by oil spills, is a problem.

Bahrain has been at the crossroads of trade and commerce for millennia. The Portuguese conquered it in 1541 and in 1820 it became a British protectorate. Oil was discovered in 1931, but Bahrain is one of the smallest Gulf producers, compensating for this by having a more diversified economy than any of its neighbors. Shipbuilding and repair yards include a dry dock for the area's supertankers. To take advantage of its central location, efforts were made to transform the banking and financial services center, and Bahrain now holds a position similar to that held by Beirut before the Lebanese civil war.

Since 1869 Bahrain has been ruled by the al-Khalifa dynasty. Independence from Britain came in 1971. The present ruler is Shaikh Hamad bin Isa al-Khalifa, who took the title of King in 2002. There are no political parties; the King attends regular public gatherings where he listens to grievances, and intervenes in the bureaucracy when necessary.

Bahrainis are hospitable people with a long history of welcoming foreigners to their shores. The lifestyle is cosmopolitan with almost half the population under the age of twenty. Bahrain is also a place of religious tolerance: It is home to Jewish synagogues, various Sikh and Hindu temples, and a small indigenous Christian community.

The Causeway

In 1982 construction began on the four-lane, 15½-mile (25 km) King Fahd Causeway, connecting the island of Bahrain to the city of al-Khobar in Saudi Arabia. The causeway was officially opened in 1986. The cost of US$1.2 billion—financed in its entirety by Saudi Arabia—made it one of the world's most expensive "bridges." The project included the building of dams and five bridges with a combined span of 40,780 feet (12,430 m).

IRAQ
Abdali
Jazīrat Būbiyān
Faylakah
Al Jahrā'
Hawallī
AL KUWAYT (KUWAIT)
KUWAIT
Al Aḥmadī
Şubayḩiyah
The Gulf
Al Wafrah
SAUDI ARABIA

Kuwait

Map Reference Pages 390–391

The State of Kuwait is located on the extreme western shoreline of The Gulf, and shares borders with Iraq and the Kingdom of Saudi Arabia. The terrain is flat, mildly undulating desert with scattered shallow depressions and mud flats, varying little in terms of elevation. Its territory also includes nine small offshore islands, one of which, Bubiyan, is connected by a bridge to the mainland. Maximum temperatures of 124°F (51°C) are not uncommon in the summer months of June to August, and hail and thunderstorms are frequent during the spring, in March and April.

The region of Kuwait was first settled in 1613 by a loose association of Middle Eastern tribes. After World War I Kuwait went from being an autonomous zone, under the control of the crippled Ottoman Empire, to an independent sheikhdom under the protection of the United Kingdom. Today, it is a hereditary constitutional emirate that has been ruled by descendants of the al-Sabah family since 1756. The current amir is Shaikh Sabah al-Ahmad al-Jaber al-Sabah, who ascended the throne in January 1978.

Kuwait is an industrialized, highly developed nation. Oil was discovered in 1938 and exporting began in 1946. At the time it was estimated that Kuwait held about 10 percent of the world's reserves. By 1949 the nation had established a 25,000-barrel-a-day refinery and a desalination plant. Additional fields were discovered at Rawhatain and Minagish in the 1950s, and in 1980 the Kuwait Petroleum Corporation was formed. When Iraq invaded Kuwait in 1990, Kuwait's oil production had peaked at three million barrels a day. Kuwaiti officials have declared the

country has about 104 billion barrels of crude oil reserves. Ten percent of Kuwait's oil revenue is invested into a Future Generations Fund, to prepare for the day when its reserves are depleted. Currently, petroleum exports account for almost 50 percent of GDP, and oil revenues contribute over 90 percent of Kuwait's state budget—in 2006 that exceeded US$56 billion. Despite the country's wealth, long-term power shortages are a problem, which indicates that not enough money has been invested in infrastructure, and in particular, power generation.

Foreign nationals, mainly expatriate groups from the Philippines, Pakistan, and especially India, make up two-thirds of the population, thus making Kuwaiti nationals a minority in their own country. Most immigrants have few skills and are in the lowest paying jobs, with few, if any, safeguards. Allegations of slave labor conditions and sexual abuse are very common. To date, the government has failed to address these problems. Neighboring Saudi Arabia and Bahrain have also failed to address similar problems.

KUWAIT

Official name State of Kuwait (Dawlat al-Kuwayt)
Land area 6,880 square miles (17,820 km²)
Border countries Iraq, Saudi Arabia
Capital Kuwait City (Al Kuwayt)
Highest point Unnamed site 1,004 feet (306 m)
Climate Intensely hot summers, short cool winters
Population 2,597,000
Language(s) Arabic, English
Ethnicity Kuwaiti Arab 45%, other Arab 35%, South Asian 9%, Iranian 4%, other 7%
Religion Muslim 85%, Christian 6%, Hindu 6%, other 3%
Government Constitutional emirate
Currency Kuwaiti dinar
Human Development Index 0.891 (ranked 33rd out of 177 countries)

Above Camel racing is a popular sport in Kuwait and throughout the Middle East. The practice of using child jockeys has been internationally condemned by human rights activists, and has subsequently led to a ban in some countries.

Left The spectacle of Kuwait City's skyline at night, featuring the city's tallest structure, Liberation Tower. Originally called Kuwait City Telecommunications Tower, it was renamed when Saddam Hussein's forces were expelled from Kuwait in 1991 during its construction.

BAHRAIN

Official name Kingdom of Bahrain (Mamlakat al Bahrayn)
Land area 257 square miles (665 km²)
Capital Manama (Al-Manāmah)
Highest point Jabal ad Dukhan 400 feet (122 m)
Climate Arid, mild winters, very hot humid summers
Population 718,306
Language(s) Arabic, English, Farsi, Urdu
Ethnicity Bahraini Arab 66%, other 34%
Religion Muslim 81.2%, Christian 9%, other 9.8%
Government Constitutional monarchy
Currency Bahraini dinar
Human Development Index 0.866 (ranked 44th out of 177 countries)

Above The faces of football: Bahraini children wear their nation's colors during a Gulf Clubs championship between Bahrain's Al-Maharraq club and Oman's Al-Nasr club in Kuwait.

QATAR

Official name State of Qatar (Dawlat Qatar)
Land area 4,416 square miles (11,437 km²)
Border country Saudi Arabia
Capital Doha (Ad Dawḩah)
Highest point Qurayn Abū al Bawl 338 feet (103 m)
Climate Arid; mild, pleasant winters; very hot, humid summers
Population 929,000
Language(s) Arabic, English
Ethnicity Qatari Arab 40%, South Asian 36%, Iranian 10%, other 14%
Religion Muslim 77.5%, Christian 8.5%, other 14%
Government Emirate
Currency Qatari riyal
Human Development Index 0.875 (ranked 35th out of 177 countries)

UNITED ARAB EMIRATES

Official name United Arab Emirates (UAE) (Al Imarat al Arabiyah al Muttahidah)
Land area 32,278 square miles (83,600 km²)
Border countries Oman, Saudi Arabia
Capital Abu Dhabi (Abū Ẓabī)
Highest point Jabal Yibir 5,010 feet (1,527 m)
Climate Desert; cooler in eastern mountains
Population 4,621,000
Language(s) Official: Arabic; other: Persian, English, Hindi, Urdu
Ethnicity Emirati Arabic 19%, Arabic/Iranian 23%, South Asian 50%, other 8%
Religion Muslim 95%, Christian 2%, Hindu 2%, other 1%
Government Federation of Emirates
Currency Emirati dirham
Human Development Index 0.868 (ranked 39th out of 177 countries)

Above right The Burj Al Arab in Dubai held the record as the world's tallest hotel until 2007, when it was topped by the emirate's Rose Tower.

Below Doha, Qatar's capital, is a glittering beacon of the country's modernity, prosperity, and tourism growth in recent years. The city is now studded with five-star hotels and restaurants.

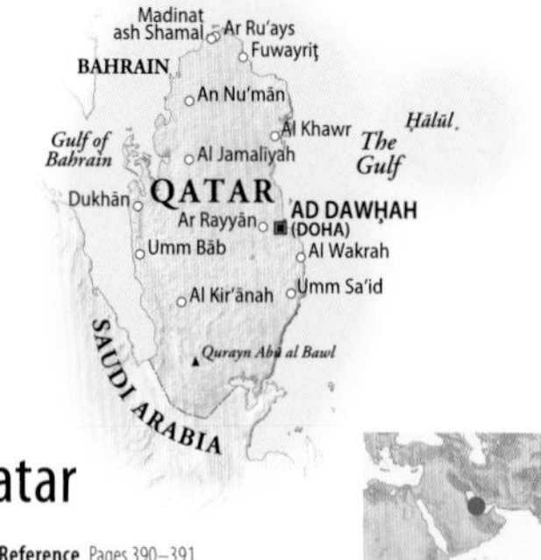
Madinat ash Shamal
Ar Ru'ays
Fuwayriţ
BAHRAIN
An Nu'mān
Al Khawr
Ḩālūl
The Gulf
Gulf of Bahrain
Al Jamaliyah
QATAR
Dukhān
Ar Rayyān
AD DAWḨAH (DOHA)
Umm Bāb
Al Wakrah
Al Kir'ānah
Umm Sa'īd
Qurayn Abū al Bawl
SAUDI ARABIA

Qatar

Map Reference Pages 390–391

Qatar is almost entirely surrounded by the waters of The Gulf, save for a 35 mile (56 km) land boundary with Saudi Arabia. The landscape is mostly flat and rocky, with some sand dunes and low hills. In the north and central areas a few drainage basins are suitable for agricultural production. The climate is hot at the height of summer—around 113°F (45°C)—and cool in winter, with temperatures around 45°F (7°C) in January.

The discovery of oil in 1939 transformed what was once an impoverished British protectorate into a nation with over US$130 billion worth of projects in the planning or construction stages. Qatar also has about one-third of the world's natural gas reserves, which contributes significantly to earnings.

Eight out of ten people live in Doha, the capital. Doha was founded in 1850, and declared the capital when Qatar gained independence from the British in 1971. The cultural and financial heart of the region, Doha is a mix of the old and new. Its ancient sukh and many mosques coexist with modern commercial buildings and a thriving international port. Doha is also the headquarters of the al-Jazeera television station.

The al-Thani dynasty has been a Qatari ruling family since the 1850s. Shaikh Mohammed bin Thani bin Mohammed established al-Bidd, modern-day Doha. The current ruler is Shaikh Hamad bin Khalifa al-Thani, who, before becoming the new emir in 1995, was commander-in-chief of the Qatari Armed Forces. In 2003, the country adopted a new constitution, allowing the creation of a 45-member parliament. Thirty members are elected, the remainder are appointed. In Qatar, women vote and hold office.

Despite its relatively small size, Qatar has a wealth of historic architecture and defense structures. Marroub Fort on the west coast is a superb example of the Abbassid architectural style. The four-towered, al-Thughb Fort in the northwest is typical of desert forts built between the seventeenth and nineteenth centuries. Fort Umm Salal Mohammed is known for its decorative facade and high thick walls.

Qatar's Natural Resources

Oil accounts for almost a third of Qatar's GDP, and has given its citizens a standard of living comparable to the wealthiest nations of the European Union. In the 1950s, the ruling al-Thani family began demanding equal shares of oil company profits, though it would be years until oil revenues started generating any real wealth.

In 1972 the Qatar National Petroleum Company was created in which the government had a 25 percent share, and by 1977 all offshore and onshore interests had been nationalized. In 1990 it was estimated that the country's known reserves of four-and-a-half billion barrels of oil would be exhausted by the year 2010. However, subsequent discoveries point to 2027.

The nation also has abundant reserves of natural gas. The North Gas Field, discovered in 1971, is thought to be the world's largest single concentration of gas.

United Arab Emirates

Map Reference Pages 390–391

Located on The Gulf, the United Arab Emirates (UAE) shares borders with Oman and Saudi Arabia. The landscape in the south and west is dominated by sand dunes and salt flats, and in the north dunes give way to stony plains and the Hajar Mountains. The eastern coast is a fertile plain, cultivated for millennia.

The UAE is a constitutional federation of seven emirates—Abu Dhabi, Dubai, Sharjah, Ajman, Umm al-Qaiwain, Ras al-Khaimah, and Fujairah. Established in December 1971 with six member states, it was joined by Ras al-Khaimah in January 1972.

Oil was discovered in 1958 off the coast of Abu Dhabi and commercial production began in 1962. The UAE is steadily shifting its reliance away from this finite natural resource, and recently, non-oil based sectors have grown by up to 20 percent per annum.

Dubai is one of the world's fastest growing cities, with many visionary projects underway, including an artificial offshore peninsula; Burj Dubai, the world's tallest building; Dubailand, a Middle Eastern version of Disneyland; and the world's largest waterfront development, which will extend Dubai's coast by 492 miles (792 km). Relatively oil-poor, Dubai is creating a new role for itself as a center of trade and international tourism, and as a shopper's paradise, while Abu Dhabi is the hub of the region's oil and gas industry. Together, Dubai and Abu Dhabi account for nearly 80 percent of the UAE's income.

Though sharing many traditions, such as falconry and camel-racing, each emirate has unique cultural resources. Abu Dhabi has two main centers: Al Ain, home to the UAE University and a major archeological museum; and the city of Abu Dhabi, housing many national institutions and soon to become a major international arts destination. Dubai's cosmopolitan culture centers on mega-malls, diverse cuisine, and the Middle East's liveliest nightlife. Sharjah has museums focusing on everything from commercial, military, and religious life to Islamic art, as well as several restored buildings. Fujairah shares many traditions with Oman, several linked to the sea; while the emirates of Umm-al-Quwain, Ajman, and the mountainous Ras-al-Khaimah have many reminders of their maritime heritage.

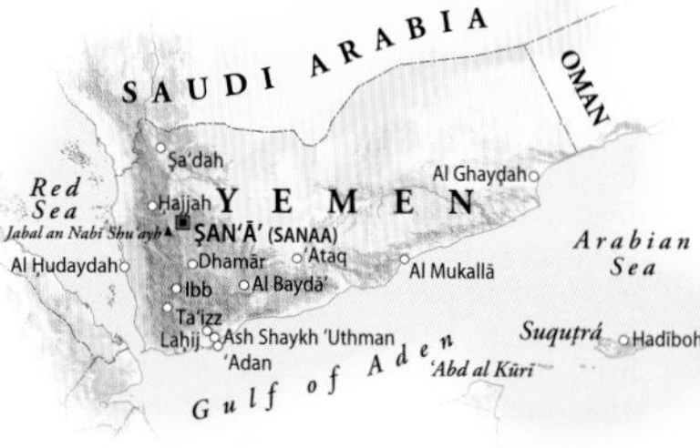
SAUDI ARABIA
OMAN
Ṣa'dah
Al Ghaydah
Red Sea
Ḩajjah
YEMEN
Jabal an Nabī Shu'ayb
ṢAN'Ā' (SANAA)
Al Ḩudaydah
Dhamār
'Ataq
Al Mukallā
Arabian Sea
Ibb
Al Bayḑā'
Ta'izz
Laḩij
Ash Shaykh 'Uthman
'Adan
Suquṭrá
Hadiboh
'Abd al Kūrī
Gulf of Aden

Yemen

Map Reference Pages 390–391

Located in the southwestern corner of the Arabian Peninsula, Yemen is bounded by Saudi Arabia and Oman. Its coastline adjoins the Gulf of Aden in the east and south, and the Red Sea in the west. Its territory includes over 200 islands. Socotra in the Indian Ocean is the largest and is home to around 700 endemic species of flora and fauna, including nine species of dragon's blood tree.

Yemen is a country of extremes—the interior desert contains extensive sand dunes while the western highlands are rainy throughout summer. The capital, Sana'a, sits on a broad plateau at an altitude of 7,200 feet (2,195 m). Yemen's highland settlements are some of the most isolated in the world, while its coastal

Left Dramatically sited atop jagged rocky outcrops, the mud-brick mountain village of Al Karn in Yemen stands sentinel over the surrounding countryside of the Al Mahwit governorate.

YEMEN

Official name Republic of Yemen (Al Jumhuriyah al Yamaniyah)
Land area 203,850 square miles (527,970 km²)
Border countries Saudi Arabia, Oman
Capital Sanaa (Şan'ā')
Highest point Jabal an Nabi Shu'ayb 12,336 feet (3,760 m)
Climate Mostly desert; hot and humid along west coast; temperate in western mountains; very hot, dry, desert in east
Population 23,013,000
Language(s) Arabic
Ethnicity Arabic 90%, East African/Afro-Arab/South Asian/European 10%
Religion Muslim 99.9%, Jewish/Christian/Hindu 0.1%
Government Republic
Currency Yemeni rial
Human Development Index 0.508 (ranked 153rd out of 177 countries)

ports have facilitated travel and trade between Arabia, Africa, and Asia for millennia.

The area of Yemen was known to the ancient Greeks and Romans as Arabia Felix (prosperous Arabia), because it was the source of frankincense and myrrh, resins obtained from dragon's blood trees and used in the Egyptian embalming process, Roman funerary rites, and perfumes. Yemen is believed to be the source of spices, silks, and precious stones that came from South and Southeast Asia.

The ancient kingdom of Saba, also known as Sheba, flourished between the tenth and sixth centuries BCE, and is known to have occupied the present-day region of Yemen. Islam arrived in the seventh century CE. In the 1800s, Britain occupied south Yemen and the port of Aden to better secure trade routes to India and the Far East. North Yemen was under Turkish control until the collapse of the Ottoman Empire in 1918. In 1967 the British left South Yemen. The establishment of a Marxist government resulted in the flight of hundreds of thousands of refugees to North Yemen, and for the next 20 years relations between north and south were hostile. In 1990, they unified as the Republic of Yemen.

Yemen is a traditional Arab country, but the oil trade and tourism increasingly tie Yemen into wider patterns of globalization. Yemen is 99.9 percent Muslim. Around 90 percent are Arabic. Most people live in the more humid and richer agricultural areas of western Yemen.

Democratic Yemen has a multi-party political system under a constitution guaranteeing free elections, the right to own private property, equality under the law, and respect of basic human rights. Executive power is held by the directly elected president who appoints a prime minister and a Council of Ministers.

Yemen is the least developed country in the Arab world. Oil production is modest compared to other countries in the region. Yemen is heavily dependent on foreign aid and remittances sent home from Yemenis who work abroad. It is an agricultural country with crops grown in western, highland Yemen. Coffee, cereal grains, cotton, fruit, and vegetables, and a narcotic leaf—qat *(Katha edulis)*—are the principal cash crops.

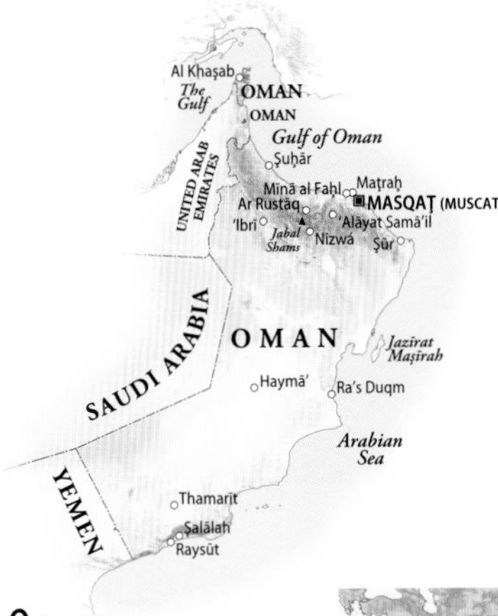
Al Khaşab
The Gulf
OMAN
OMAN
Gulf of Oman
Şuḩār
UNITED ARAB EMIRATES
Mīnā al Fahl
Maţraḩ
Ar Rustāq
MASQAŢ (MUSCAT)
'Ibrī
Jabal Shams
Nizwá
Alāyat Samā'il
Şūr
SAUDI ARABIA
OMAN
Jazīrat Maşīrah
Haymā'
Ra's Duqm
Arabian Sea
YEMEN
Thamarīt
Şalālah
Raysūt

Oman

Map Reference Pages 390–391

Oman occupies the southeastern quadrant of the Arabian Peninsula, facing the Arabian Sea. Oman shares borders with the United Arab Emirates, Yemen, and Saudi Arabia. Its northernmost point, the Musandam Peninsula, serves as a sentinel to the strategically vital Strait of Hormuz at the entrance to The Gulf. Some 20 percent of the world's oil passes through this narrow waterway, which separates Oman from Iran. The peninsula itself is an exclave, separated from the rest of the country by the United Arab Emirates.

Most of Oman's small population is concentrated along the fertile, irrigated Batinah coastal plain, wedged between the high Hajar Mountains and the Gulf of Oman. West and south of the Hajar mountain spine lies a vast desert with scattered oases. Muscat, the capital, lies on the Gulf of Oman. Some of the world's hottest temperatures are experienced in the arid interior during summer. High temperatures and humidity produce extremely uncomfortable conditions along the coastal plain.

Historically, Oman was the center of a maritime trading empire that extended from India to the coast of East Africa. Although Oman never became a colony, British influence prevailed from the nineteenth century. The current ruler, Sultan Qaboos, came to power in 1970, overthrowing his tyrannical father with British assistance, and initiating an ambitious program of modernization and economic and social development that has transformed the country. Although not a large producer by Middle Eastern standards, oil wealth has propelled Oman into the ranks of middle-income countries. Because reserves are comparatively small, the government has encouraged economic diversification.

Rapid economic development has drawn over half a million foreign workers to Oman, largely from Pakistan, India, and Bangladesh. According to official figures foreigners account for a quarter of the population, but the actual figure may be far higher. Oman is the only country in which most people belong to the Ibadhi branch of Islam, neither Sunni nor Shi'ite, and conservative although moderate.

Left Arabian oryx are extinct in the wild, the last herd being wiped out in the 1970s by indiscriminate hunting. A captive breeding program and reintroduction into Oman in the 1980s has been successful in bringing this handsome antelope back from the brink.

OMAN

Official name Sultanate of Oman (Saltanat Uman)
Land area 82,031 square miles (212,460 km²)
Border countries United Arab Emirates, Yemen, Saudi Arabia
Capital Muscat (Masqaţ)
Highest point Jabal Shams 9,777 feet (2,980 m)
Climate Dry desert; hot, humid along coast; hot, dry interior; summer monsoon in far south
Population 3,312,000
Language(s) Official: Arabic; other English, Baluchi, Urdu, Swahili, Indian dialects
Ethnicity Omani Arab 73%, South Asian 20%, East African 2%, other 5%
Religion Ibadhi Muslim 75%, other Muslim 13%, Hindu 7%, Christian 4%, other 1%
Government Monarchy
Currency Omani rial
Human Development Index 0.814 (ranked 58th out of 177 countries)

Left Traditional dress for Yemeni women in Hadhramout features a style known as "thail and kodma" (tail and front); the material trailing from the back of the garment is longer than the front.

KAZAKHSTAN

Official name Republic of Kazakhstan (Qazaqstan Respublikasy)
Land area 1,030,816 square miles (2,669,800 km²)
Border countries Russia, China, Kyrgyzstan, Uzbekistan, Turkmenistan
Capital Astana
Highest & lowest points Khan Tangiri Shyngy 22,949 feet (6,995 m); Vpadina Kaundy –433 feet (–132 m)
Climate Continental, arid and semiarid
Population 15,341,000
Language(s) Kazakh, Russian
Ethnicity Kazakh 53.4%, Russian 30%, Ukrainian 3.7%, Uzbek 2.5%, German 2.4%, Tatar 1.7%, Uygur 1.4%, other 4.9%
Religion Muslim 47%, Russian Orthodox 44%, Christian 2%, other 7%
Government Republic; authoritarian presidential rule, with little power outside the executive branch
Currency Tenge
Human Development Index 0.794 (ranked 73rd out of 177 countries)

RUSSIAN FEDERATION
Uralsk
Rudnyy
Kostanay
Petropavlovsk
Kokshetau
Aktobe
Atyrau
ASTANA
Pavlodar
Karaganda
Semipalatinsk
Ust-Kamenogorsk
Caspian Sea
KAZAKHSTAN
Aktau
Baykonyr
Kyzylorda
Taldykorgan
UZBEKISTAN
CHINA
Shymkent
Taraz
Almaty
KYRGYZSTAN
Khan Tangiri Shyngy

Kazakhstan

Map Reference Pages 388–389

Kazakhstan, in Central Asia, is a large landlocked country comparable in size to India. It is bordered by Russia, China, Kyrgyzstan, Uzbekistan, and Turkmenistan, and by the shrinking Aral Sea, and the great Caspian Sea to the west.

Physical Geography

The terrain is diverse, with semi-desert and desert accounting for 66 percent of the land. The nation's highest peak, Khan Tangiri Shyngy, rises out of the Tian Shan Mountains on the border with Kyrgyzstan. The Tian Shan and Altai mountains are wild, almost untouched landscapes that protect fauna such as the Tian Shan bear and Siberian ibex. The climate is continental, with very hot summers when temperatures can reach 104°F (40°C), and extremely cold winters when the temperature can sink to –58°F (–50°C).

History

In 1219, the region was invaded by Mongols led by Chinggis (Genghis) Khan. Although Khan's conquests were savage, wherever he went he introduced order in the form of taxes and communications in order to encourage trade. This led to the rejuvenation of the Silk Road trade. At the end of the fourteenth century Timur the Lame (Tamerlane), descended from the Mongols, created an empire that stretched from Delhi to the Mediterranean Sea. His armies were drawn from the nomadic tribes of central Asia, including Kazakhs, all recognized for their exceptional horsemanship. Timur's empire was replaced by the Zhungarian Empire, in turn replaced by the Russian Empire. In 1917, Kazakhstan was incorporated into the Soviet Union. Kazakhstan proclaimed its independence in 1991 after the collapse of the USSR.

Population/Culture

Kazakh is the official state language, although almost everyone speaks Russian, especially in business matters. Respect for elders and hospitality to guests and strangers are among the many time-honored traditions and values held by Kazakhs. To this day, honored guests in rural areas are treated to a feast of freshly killed lamb, but first it must be blessed and permission to eat the meat sought from the lamb's spirit.

Administration/Government

Kazakhstan is under authoritarian rule, with almost no power outside the executive branch, represented by the president. The president is elected by popular vote for a seven-year term (no term limits); the prime minister and the Council of Ministers are appointed by the president. The bicameral parliament consists of the Senate with 47 members and the Mazhilis with 107 members. The judiciary is represented by the Supreme Court and the Constitutional Council.

Economy/Industry

Kazakhstan has the largest economy in Central Asia, and has huge fossil fuel reserves as well as 90 valuable minerals and metals. The service sector employs about half the workforce. The industrial sector specializes in construction equipment and agricultural machinery. It accounts for 40 percent of GDP, and employs about 30 percent of the workforce. Agriculture is limited to growing grain and cotton, and raising livestock.

Above The Kazakhs trace their history back to when Mongol hordes invaded in the thirteenth century CE. On the plains, tradition runs deep—a farmer hunts quarry such as ducks, pigeons, and partridge with his hand-raised eagle, a centuries-old pursuit.

Right Kazakhstan's tsarist-era Zenkov Russian Orthodox Cathedral in Almaty was constructed from wood without using nails. Remarkably, it survived an earthquake that hit the area in 1911.

TURKMENISTAN

Official name Turkmenistan
Land area 188,456 square miles (488,100 km²)
Border countries Kazakhstan, Uzbekistan, Afghanistan, Iran
Capital Ashgabat (Aşgabat)
Highest & lowest points Gora Ayribaba 10,299 feet (3,139 m); Vpadina Akchanaya –266 feet (–81 m)
Climate Subtropical desert
Population 5,180,000
Language(s) Turkmen, Russian, Uzbek, other
Ethnicity Turkmen 85%, Uzbek 5%, Russian 4%, other 6%
Religion Muslim 89%, Eastern Orthodox 9%, unknown 2%
Government Republic, authoritarian presidential rule, with little power outside the executive branch
Currency Turkmen manat
Human Development Index 0.713 (ranked 109th out of 177 countries)

KAZAKHSTAN
UZBEKISTAN
Köneürgenç
Boldumsaz
Daşoguz
Caspian Sea
Türkmenbaşy
Balkanabat
TURKMENISTAN
Baherden
Türkmenabat
AŞGABAT (ASHGABAT)
Atamyrat
Mary
Bayramaly
Tejen
Yolöten
Sarahs
IRAN
AFGHANISTAN

Turkmenistan

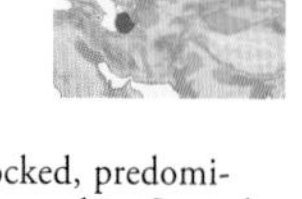

Map Reference Pages 388–389

Turkmenistan is a landlocked, predominantly desert country located in Central Asia. It is bordered by Kazakhstan, Uzbekistan, Afghanistan, and Iran. The Caspian Sea marks the western boundary. The country has relatively large reserves of gas and oil.

Physical Geography

The Kara Kum desert covers over 80 percent of the country. Gora Ayribaba, the highest peak, lies in the Kughinang Mountains near the eastern border with Uzbekistan. Poor irrigation practices have severely reduced the flow of water from the Amu Darya River into the Aral Sea, with the result that the sea is now half its original size and heavily polluted. Spreading desertification is another consequence. Turkmenistan's climate is mostly arid subtropical desert, with little precipitation.

History

Conquerors mostly passed through Turkmenistan on their way elsewhere. The Arab conquest of the late seventh and early eighth centuries brought Islam to the region. Seljuk Turks ruled from the early eleventh century, followed by Mongol invaders in the thirteenth century. Throughout all this, Turkmenistan's nomadic tribes moved from oasis to oasis grazing their flocks and breeding horses. Eventually, tribal marauding and kidnapping brought down the wrath of the Russian Empire, which secured the region in 1894, but only after much bloodletting. Following the Bolshevik Revolution of 1917 in Russia, the Turkmen Soviet Socialist Republic was formed in 1924, but it faced fierce opposition until 1936. Turkmenistan became independent again in October, 1991, after the break-up of the Soviet Union.

Left A clear blue sky enhances the beauty of the snow-capped Chatkal Range, part of the Chatkal National Park in Uzbekistan. The park preserves areas of environmental significance, from mountain steppes and alpine meadows to river valleys and forest floodplains.

Population/Culture

Ethnic Turkmen form the majority of the country's inhabitants, with sizable minorities of Uzbeks and Russians. Tribally based social structure and ethnic diversity make a cohesive national identity difficult to attain.

Turkmen are famous for their hand-loomed rugs—Bukharas—that differ between clans. Apart from their esthetic value, Bukharas were used by nomadic tribes to cover the floors and walls of yurts. The national dress for men comprises tall, shaggy sheepskin hats and red robes over white shirts; women wear long sack-like dresses over trousers.

Administration/Government

The chief of state is the president, who is also the head of the government, and is elected by popular vote. The president appoints the Cabinet of Ministers. The People's Council has up to 2,500 delegates, some elected and some appointed. The National Assembly has 50 members elected by popular vote. Opposition parties are illegal under the authoritarian ex-communist regime. Judges, appointed by the president, and the Supreme Court represent the government's judiciary branch.

Economy/Industry

Turkmenistan is largely desert, with irrigated oases making up just over 4 percent of arable land. About half the arable land is used to grow cotton. Turkmenistan has large reserves of natural gas and substantial oil reserves.

The economy has revived since oil and gas prices increased, but a poor educational system and the government's lack of reforms contribute to entrenched poverty. GDP is unknown because the government does not disclose the country's financial status. Some reforms are occurring, with increased foreign investment and privatization of state-owned enterprises.

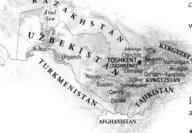

Left Women sell flatbread *(chorek)* at the market in Mary, Turkmenistan's fourth-largest city and an oasis on the edge of the Karakum Desert.

KAZAKHSTAN
Aral Sea
UZBEKISTAN
TURKMENISTAN
KYRGYZSTAN
TAJIKISTAN
AFGHANISTAN
Nukus
Urganch
Adelunga Toghi
Chirchiq
TOSHKENT (TASHKENT)
Angren
Namangan
Andijon
Olmaliq
Qo'qon
Farg'ona
Jizzax
Navoiy
Buxoro
Samarqand
Qarshi
Denov

Uzbekistan

Map Reference Pages 388–389

Uzbekistan is bordered by Kazakhstan, Kyrgyzstan, Tajikistan, Afghanistan, and Turkmenistan. A dry, landlocked country located in Central Asia, it is, nevertheless, one of the most populous countries in the region.

Physical Geography

A diverse topography ranges from flattish deserts with dunes, comprising nearly 80 percent of the territory, to mountains in the east. Water resources are scarce and unevenly distributed. The Amu Darya and Syr Darya rivers are used for irrigation along their valleys. In the northwest the border cuts across the shrinking and polluted Aral Sea. The climate is continental with little precipitation. Summers are very hot, and winters very cold. The country is earthquake-prone—the last major earthquake in 1966 devastated the capital, Tashkent.

History

The area that is now Uzbekistan has been subjected to repeated conquests since ancient times. As well as conquering Sogdiana and Bactria in 327 BCE—the area east of present-day Uzbekistan—Alexander the Great married the daughter of a local dignitary. Later, the region came under the control of the Parthians, Arabs, Sassanids, and Mongols. Timur the Lame (Tamerlane) built an empire in the fourteenth century CE that stretched as far as the Middle East. In the nineteenth century, the region became part of the Russian Empire, then a Soviet Socialist Republic. After the collapse of communism in the Soviet Union, Uzbekistan declared independence in 1991.

Population/Culture

More than 60 percent of the population lives in rural communities. Uzbeks make up the majority of the population, but there are several sizable ethnic communities.

The country has a literacy rate of 99.3 percent—a legacy of the Soviet educational system.

Regional classical music called *shashmaqam*, which originated in Bukhara in the sixteenth century, plays an important role in cultural life. *Shashmaqam*, which translates as "six maqams" (suites), is based on Sufi poetry about divine love adapted to beautiful lyric melodies. Several instruments accompany a group of singers, including long-necked lutes, the tambourine-like *dayra*, and the *tanbor*, similar to a bass fiddle.

Administration/Government

The president is elected by popular vote and represents the executive branch of government—there is almost no power outside of the executive. The prime minister and the cabinet of ministers are appointed by the president, subject to approval by the Supreme Assembly. The Supreme Assembly, or Oliy Majlis, consists of an upper house with 100 members elected by regional governing councils, and a lower house with 120 members, both elected for a five-year term. The judicial branch is represented by the Supreme Court.

Economy/Industry

Cotton is a key component of the country's economy—Uzbekistan is the world's second largest exporter of this commodity. Agriculture accounts for nearly 40 percent of the national income and employs 44 percent of the labor force. However, the heavy use of chemical fertilizers and pesticides is cause for environmental concern. Uzbekistan is rich in mineral resources, including gold, natural gas, coal, copper, oil, silver, and uranium. Favorable prices for major export commodities such as cotton, gold, and gas contribute to GDP growth. The service sector accounts for about one-third of the national income.

UZBEKISTAN

Official name Republic of Uzbekistan (Ozbekiston Respublikasi)
Land area 164,248 square miles (425,400 km²)
Border countries Kazakhstan, Kyrgyzstan, Tajikistan, Afghanistan, Turkmenistan
Capital Tashkent (Toshkent)
Highest & lowest points Adelunga Toghi 14,111 feet (4,301 m); Sariqarnish Kuli −39 feet (−12 m)
Climate Mostly midlatitude desert, long hot summers, mild winters; semiarid grassland in east
Population 28,268,000
Language(s) Uzbek, Russian
Ethnicity Uzbek 80%, Russian 5.5%, Tajik 5%, Kazakh 3%, Karakalpak 2.5%, Tatar 1.5%, other 2.5%
Religion Muslim 88%, Eastern Orthodox 9%, other 3%
Government Republic; authoritarian presidential rule, with little power outside the executive branch
Currency Soum
Human Development Index 0.702 (ranked 113th out of 177 countries)

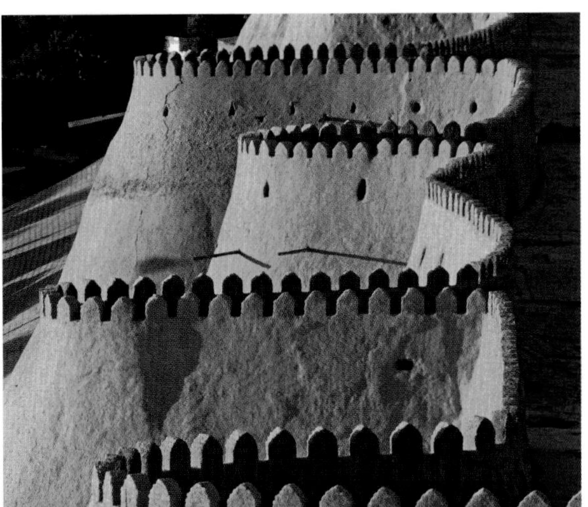

Below Massive clay ramparts encircle the inner city of Ichon-Qala (Itchan Kala), part of the Khiva oasis, which is located in present-day Uzbekistan. Khiva was the last stop on the caravan route before traders crossed the desert to Iran.

AFGHANISTAN

Official name Afghanistan (Jomhuri-ye Eslami-ye Afghanestan)
Land area 250,001 square miles (647,500 km²)
Border countries Uzbekistan, Tajikistan, China, Pakistan, Iran, Turkmenistan
Capital Kabul (Kābol)
Highest & lowest points Nowshak 24,557 feet (7,486 m); Amu Darya 846 feet (258 m)
Climate Arid to semiarid; cold winters, hot summers
Population 32,738,000
Language(s) Afghan Persian (Dari), Pashto, Turkic languages, Balochi, Pashai
Ethnicity Pashtun 42%, Tajik 27%, Hazara 9%, Uzbek 9%, Aimak 4%, Turkmen 3%, Baloch 2%, other 4%
Religion Muslim 99%, other 1%
Government Islamic republic
Currency Afghani
Human Development Index Not available

UZBEKISTAN
TAJIKISTAN
CHINA
TURKMENISTAN
Mazār-e Sharif
Sheberghān
Tāloqān
Nowshak
Baghlān
Meymaneh
Chārīkār
KĀBOL
(KABUL)
Jalālābād
Herāt
AFGHANISTAN
Ghaznī
Gardīz
IRAN
Farāh
Lashkar Gāh
Kandahār
PAKISTAN

Above right A pilgrim visits the sanctuary and mosque at Mazār-e Sharif, Afghanistan. Afghanis believe it is the tomb of Ali ibn Abi Talib, the Prophet Muhammad's cousin and son-in-law.

Above Women wait for treatment at a health clinic. According to the World Health Organization, more women die in childbirth in Afghanistan than in any other country, bar Sierra Leone.

Below Hewn from the cliffs at Bamiyan in the Hazarajat region of Afghanistan, some of the world's largest statues of Buddha were destroyed by the Taliban in 2001 because they were to be considered "un-Islamic."

Afghanistan

Map Reference Pages 390–391

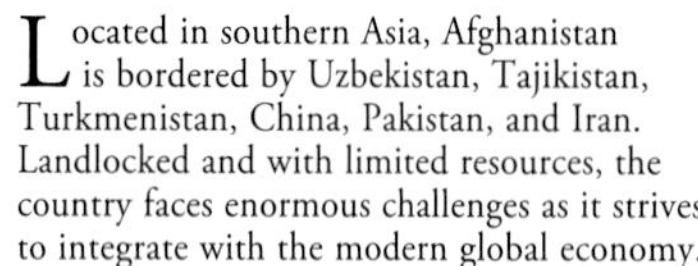

Located in southern Asia, Afghanistan is bordered by Uzbekistan, Tajikistan, Turkmenistan, China, Pakistan, and Iran. Landlocked and with limited resources, the country faces enormous challenges as it strives to integrate with the modern global economy.

Physical Geography

The landscape is one of the most forbidding and rugged in the world. Half of the country lies above 5,000 feet (1,500 m), and almost 15 percent is above 10,000 feet (3,000 m).

The earthquake-prone Hindu Kush mountain range divides the country into three geographic areas. The Northern Plateau, with an average elevation of 2,000 feet (600 m), has fertile plains and foothills where agriculture flourishes, and resources include natural gas and minerals. The Central Highlands is an extensive region of mountains and valleys, with dry desert plains and grass plains. The Southern Plateau has an average altitude of 3,000 feet (900 m), and comprises high plateaus, sandy deserts, and arid plains.

History

Located at the crossroads of the Middle East, Asia, and Europe, Afghanistan has experienced invasion by some of history's most powerful conquerors, all of whom left their mark. Arab invaders in the seventh century had perhaps the most profound and lasting influence.

Afghanistan's identity as a nation-state emerged in the eighteenth and nineteenth centuries, when British colonial interests in South Asia met Russian imperial ambitions in Central Asia. The Durand Line of 1893 identified the political boundary between British colonial India and Afghanistan. An agreement between Britain and Russia established the border between Russian Central Asia and Afghanistan.

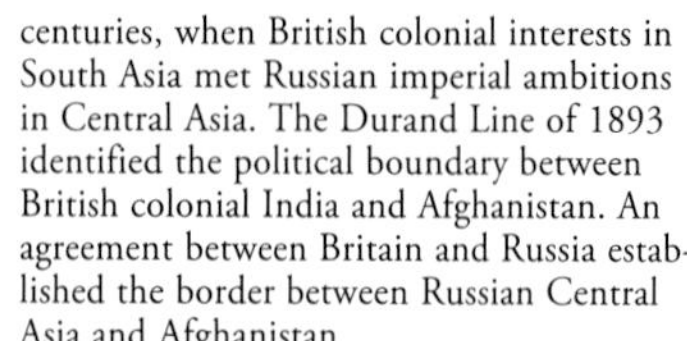

Formed as a buffer state between two empires, Afghanistan faced huge challenges. After World War II, increasing Soviet interest culminated in a coup in 1978 that brought a Marxist government to power, resulting in a Soviet invasion and two disastrous decades of civil war. The rise of the Taliban in 1996 brought only further violence, as the Uzbeks and Tajiks violently resisted this mostly Pashtun movement. Taliban support of Osama bin Laden and al-Qaida resulted in an American bombing campaign in 2001 that brought down the Taliban, but peace has proved elusive and the Taliban are gaining influence once again.

Population/Culture

Afghanistan's multi-ethnic population has made it difficult to forge a national identity. The country's complex amalgam of cultures almost all share the overarching framework of Islam. But this is not to suggest that all share exactly the same values, rituals, beliefs, or behaviors. The Hazaras, for example, are mostly Shi'ite and have suffered persecution periodically at the hands of the Sunni majority in years past, and significant differences exist even among the Sunnis. The various ethnic groups can often be distinguished on the basis of apparel, especially headgear. Uzbek men, for example, typically wear a skullcap called a *doppa*, while Pashtun and Hazara men wear a wound turban called the *shamlah*. Women typically cover their hair with a scarf in public, and more traditional women wear the *burqa*, a hooded, veiled garment that covers the body from head to toe.

Administration/Government

After the fall of the Taliban regime in 2001, Afghanistan officially became an Islamic republic, and for the first time in its history experienced representative, democratic government. The head of state is the president, who is elected by direct vote; two vice-presidents are also elected by direct ballot. The legislative branch consists of a bicameral National Assembly of the Council of People, whose members are directly elected for five-year terms; and the Council of Elders, who are either appointed from regional councils or named to the body by the president. The Supreme Court is composed of nine judges.

Economy/Industry

The Afghan economy is one of the most underdeveloped in the world. Constant warfare and political turmoil since 1979 have prevented economic growth and inhibited foreign investment. There are few industries except for food processing and light industry. The leading cash crop is opium.

There are few paved roads and no railway system. Since 2001 foreign assistance has reconstructed the famous Ring Road that connects the various regions, and living standards are gradually improving.

GAMES AND TEA

Afghani culture is famous for its unique games and contests. Two of the best known are *buzkashi* and *gudiparan bazi*. Buzkashi is a competition between two teams of mounted riders who attempt to carry the carcass of a goat to the opposing team's goal. The contest requires great skill on the part of both rider and mount. The game is often played at festivals and on holidays. Gudiparan bazi is competitive kite flying. Each kite is made by hand, and the object of the game is to cut the string of the opposing player's kite while maintaining control of one's own kite. Kite strings are usually coated with ground glass to make it easier to cut an opponent's string—the winner is the flier of the last kite in the air.

Much of the social and cultural life of men in Afghanistan revolves around two institutions: The mosque and the *chaikona*, or teahouse. The chaikona provides a forum for socializing, as well as for business transactions. In the chaikona men usually sit on the floor around a low table on which the tea is served. Guests in the chaikona may play chess, backgammon, or card games.

MILESTONE EVENTS

330 BCE Alexander the Great invades territory of modern Afghanistan
652 CE Muslim armies enter Central Asia, leading to mass conversion of population
962 Establishment of Ghaznavid Empire
1220 Mongols destroy Herat and other Afghan cities
1526 Babur sends forces into India from his capital at Kabul
1809 British conclude formal relations with Afghan king, Shuja
1839 First Anglo-Afghan war
1878 Second Anglo-Afghan war
1893 Durand Line Treaty signed between Afghanistan and Great Britain
1919 Third Anglo-Afghan war
1978 Soviet-backed coup, followed by Soviet invasion the next year
1988 Soviet forces withdraw from Afghanistan
1996 Taliban takes control of much of the country
2001 American-led invasion removes Taliban from power
2004 New constitution approved; democratic elections held for president
2005 National Assembly elections
October 2006 Security of Afghanistan becomes resposibility of NATO
July 24, 2007 Mohammad Zahir Shah, former king and "ceremonial father of the nation" dies aged 92 of unknown causes

UZBEKISTAN
Taboshar
Khujand
Nov
Isfara
Uroteppa
KYRGYZSTAN
Panjakent
CHINA
TAJIKISTAN
Pik Imeni Ismail Samani
Hisor
DUSHANBE
Norak
Alichur
Kulob
Qurghonteppa
Khorugh
Farkhor
Shahrtuz
AFGHANISTAN

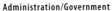

Tajikistan

Map Reference Pages 388–389

Tajikistan is a landlocked, mountainous country bordered by Kyrgyzstan, Uzbekistan, China, and Afghanistan. Like several other former Soviet republics in Central Asia, Tajikistan is an impoverished nation.

Physical Geography

Ninety-three percent of Tajikistan's territory is mountainous; over 50 percent lies above 10,000 feet (3,000 m). Numerous glaciers and rivers have carved deep valleys. The Fedchenko glacier has an area of 700 square miles (1,813 km^2), the biggest expanse of glacier outside of polar regions. Spring snowmelts often cause heavy flooding and consequent loss of life. Tajikistan lies on a fault line and is earthquake-prone. The climate is mainly continental, but there are marked variations according to elevation.

History

The territory of present-day Tajikistan came under the rule of various empire-building people, including Persians, Mongols, Arabs, and Russians. In 1929 Tajikistan became a Soviet Socialist Republic, its boundaries drawn to fragment communities and political loyalties. Civil war raged for five years after independence in 1991. Since 1999, Tajikistan has pursued democratic reforms and is in transition to a free-market economy.

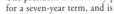

Population/Culture

Tajiks, the majority ethnic group, belong to an Indo-European family of Turkic-Persian descent. Modern Tajiks share much of their language and cuisine with Persians. Navruz or New Day is an extremely important celebration that dates back to the tenth century BCE. Held in March on the vernal equinox, Navruz celebrates the arrival of spring by exchanging gifts, family and community gatherings, singing, dancing, and colorful games.

Administration/Government

The president is elected by popular vote for a seven-year term, and is eligible for a second term. The president appoints the prime minister and cabinet or Council of Ministers. The Supreme Assembly comprises the upper chamber or National Assembly (Majlisi Milliy) with 34 seats, and the lower chamber or Assembly of Representatives (Majlisi Namoyandagon) with 63 seats.

Economy/Industry

Only seven percent of land in Tajikistan is arable and much of that is used to grow cotton. The state-owned aluminum plant, Talco, is the only sizable industry. At 984 feet (300 m), the Nurek dam is the tallest in the world. It supports nine hydroelectric generators that supply 98 percent of the country's electricity. Remittances from migrant workers abroad represent around one-third of GDP.

KAZAKHSTAN
Kara-Balta
BISHKEK
Tokmok
Kyzyl-Adyr
Talas
Balykchy
Karakol
Jengish Chokusu
Toktogul
KYRGYZSTAN
Naryn
Kerben
Mayluu-Suu
Jalal-Abad
UZBEKISTAN
Osh
CHINA
Sulukta
TAJIKISTAN

Kyrgyzstan

Map Reference Pages 388–389

Kyrgyzstan is a landlocked nation in Central Asia. It shares common borders with Kazakhstan, China, Tajikistan, and Uzbekistan. It is a deeply impoverished nation that relies heavily on exporting gold.

Physical Geography

Kyrgyzstan is dominated by the Tian Shan and Pamir mountain ranges. Among the snow-capped peaks of the Tian Shan range lies Ysyk-Köl, the world's second highest mountain lake—about 5,250 feet (1,600 m) above sea level. It is an enclosed lake, from which no water escapes. It is a Ramsar site of global biodiversity, part of the Ysyk-Köl Biosphere Reserve.

History

The early Kyrgyz, a nomadic people, were originally from Siberia, and were among the marauding nomads who gave Chinese rulers the impetus to build the Great Wall of China. Numerous invaders overran Kyrgyz territory until it was subsumed into the Russian Empire in 1876. A revolt against Russia in 1916 was brutally crushed, resulting in one-sixth of the population being killed. After the collapse of the Soviet Union, Kyrgyzstan declared independence in 1991.

Population/Culture

Approximately two-thirds of the inhabitants identify themselves as Kyrgyz; there are also large numbers of Uzbeks and Russians. Kyrgyz, a Turkic language, is the official language along with Russian.

Kyrgyz national pride and identity are expressed through the traditional epic poem *Manas*, a trilogy of three generations of heroes. The poem is also a moral tale that has evolved and been added to since its origins in the eighth or ninth century. Highly esteemed *manaschi* (storytellers) often sing or recite parts of the poem at festivities—at half a million lines, the whole poem takes about three days to perform.

Administration/Government

The president and prime minister represent the executive branch of government. The cabinet is appointed by the president on the recommendation of the prime minister. Kyrgyzstan's Supreme Council is elected by a popular vote. The judicial branch is represented by Supreme and Constitutional courts.

Economy/Industry

The economy is based primarily on farming, which employs almost half the labor force and accounts for about one-third of GDP. The industrial sector produces cement, small machinery, and textiles, and accounts for about a quarter of GDP. Significant water resources enable the country to export hydroelectric energy. Mineral deposits include coal, rare earth metals, uranium, and gold.

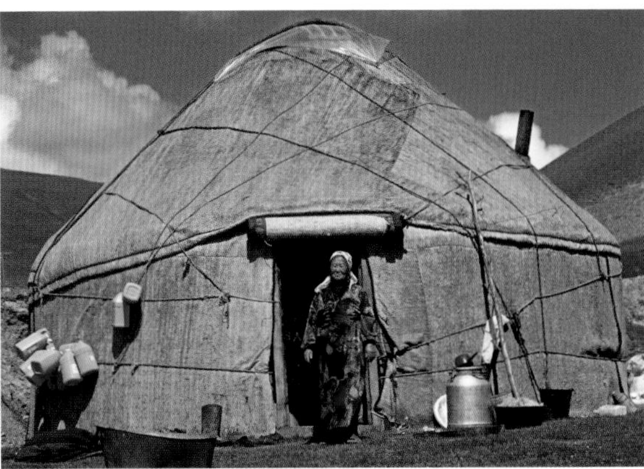

Above The yurt is the traditional home of the nomadic Kyrgyz. Covered in sheep's felt, it can be quickly packed and loaded onto horseback.

Above left The Pamir Mountains, centered mainly in Tajikistan, are snow covered all year.

TAJIKISTAN

Official name Republic of Tajikistan (Jumhurii Tojikiston)
Land area 55,097 square miles (142,700 km^2)
Border countries Kyrgyzstan, China, Afghanistan, Uzbekistan
Capital Dushanbe
Highest & lowest points Qullai Ismoili Somoni 24,590 feet (7,495 m); Syr Darya (Sirdaryo) 984 feet (300 m)
Climate Mid-latitude continental, hot summers, mild winters; semiarid to polar in Pamir Mountains
Population 7,212,000
Language(s) Tajik, Russian
Ethnicity Tajik 79.9%, Uzbek 15.3%, Russian 1.1%, Kyrgyz 1.1%, other 2.6%
Religion Muslim 90%, other 10%
Government Republic
Currency Somoni
Human Development Index 0.673 (ranked 122nd out of 177 countries)

KYRGYZSTAN

Official name Kyrgyz Republic (Kyrgyz Respublikasy)
Land area 73,861 square miles (191,300 km^2)
Border countries Kazakhstan, China, Tajikistan, Uzbekistan
Capital Bishkek
Highest & lowest points Jengish Chokusu Peak 24,406 feet (7,439 m); Kara-Darya 433 feet (132 m)
Climate Continental with local variations
Population 5,357,000
Language(s) Kyrgyz, Uzbek, Russian, Dungun, other
Ethnicity Kyrgyz 64.9%, Uzbek 13.8%, Russian 12.5%, Dungan 1.1%, Ukrainian 1%, Uygur 1%, other 5.7%
Religion Muslim 75%, Russian Orthodox 20%, other 5%
Government Republic
Currency Som
Human Development Index 0.696 (ranked 116th out of 177 countries)

Left Kyrgyzstan's Lake Ysyk-Köl ("warm lake") never freezes, even though temperatures around the Tian Shan Mountains get extremely low.

PAKISTAN

Official name Islamic Republic of Pakistan (Jamhuryat Islami Pakistan)
Land area 300,665 square miles (778,720 km²)
Border countries China, India, Iran, Afghanistan
Capital Islamabad
Highest point K2 (Mt Godwin-Austen) 28,251 feet (8,611 m)
Climate Mostly hot, dry desert; temperate in northwest; arctic in north
Population 166,488,000
Language(s) Punjabi, Sindhi, Siraiki, Pashtu, Urdu, Balochi, Hindko, Brahui, English, Burushaski 92%; other 8%
Ethnicity Punjabi 59.1%, Sindhi 12.1%, Pashtun 13.8%, Baloch 4.3%, Muhajir 7.7%, other 3%
Religion Muslim 97%, other 3%
Government Federal republic
Currency Pakistani rupee
Human Development Index 0.551 (ranked 136th out of 177 countries)

CHINA
K2 (Mt Godwin-Austen)
AFGHANISTAN
Peshawar
Mardan
ISLAMABAD
Rawalpindi
Gujrat
Sialkot
Sargodha
Gujranwala
Chiniot
Lahore
Faisalabad
Kasur
Okara
Quetta
Multan
Dera Ghazi Khan
Bahawalpur
PAKISTAN
Rahimyar Khan
IRAN
INDIA
Nawabshah
Hyderabad
Karachi
Arabian Sea

Above right The Karakoram Highway traverses the collision plates of Asia and India beneath the towering walls of the Hunza Valley, an area characterized by weathered fractured rock, meltwater surges, and unstable slopes.

Right This unicorn seal, now held in Pakistan's Karachi Museum, is one of hundreds that were unearthed at Mohenjo-Daro, an Indus Valley civilization site of great archeological importance.

Below Hiran Minar, near Sheikhupura, Pakistan, was a hunting complex built by Mogul Emperor Jahangir in 1606. The large water tank has an octagonal pavilion with a minaret at its center.

Pakistan

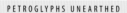

Map Reference Pages 390–391

Pakistan is located in the Indus Valley in the northwest of the Indian subcontinent and shares borders with China, India, Iran, and Afghanistan. The coastline is bounded by the Arabian Sea. The Indus Valley was once home to the great Indus Valley civilization, which dates back at least 5,000 years.

Physical Geography

Pakistan has distinct three geographic regions. The mountainous north has glaciers, mountain lakes, and 35 peaks above 24,000 feet (7,315 m), including K2, the world's second highest mountain. To the west, the Balochistan Plateau has highlands and ridges. The Indus River Basin, an alluvial plain formed by silt from the Indus River, overlies an important aquifer. The Indus Basin has the world's largest contiguous expanse of irrigation.

Climate varies from the warm coastal areas of the Arabian Sea coastline to the highlands. In the mountainous north, arctic conditions prevail. It is a mostly arid climate with little rainfall outside of the southwest monsoon period, from June through September.

Pakistan experiences frequent earthquakes: In 2005, an earthquake in Pakistan-controlled Kashmir claimed the lives of around 80,000 people and left some 3,300,000 homeless. Flooding in the Indus Valley is also a threat.

History

Evidence of Stone Age humans dating back 50,000 years has been found in the Soan Valley near Rawalpindi. Mohenjo-Daro in the Indus Valley was a flourishing metropolis from 2600 to 1900 BCE and is believed to be one of the world's first cities. Mohenjo-Daro displays many ideas common to contemporary urban planning such as a grid-like street pattern, houses insulated from noise and built around a central marketplace, and streets with covered drains to carry away water.

Graziers arrived from Central Asia around 1700 BCE and brought with them a primitive caste system that eventually evolved into Hinduism. Alexander the Great conquered the region in 326 BCE and was followed by the Scythians, Parthians, Huns, and significantly the Turks, who imparted to modern Pakistan its ethnic and cultural identity. In the early eighth century Islam brought both a new faith and a new architecture. Countless tombs, gardens, and mosques were constructed over the next thousand years, bestowing upon Pakistan much of its built environment.

The British arrived in 1857 and banned the teaching of Islamic religious studies in schools across British India. They also brought the doctrine of "territorial nationalism." The region's Muslims strongly opposed statehood as envisaged by the British, fearing that the creation of a modern state would reduce them to minority status, and in 1940 declared their resolve for an independent homeland.

The nation of Pakistan was created in 1947 after the partitioning of British India and became a Dominion in the Commonwealth of Nations until the Islamic Republic of Pakistan was created in 1956. Until 1971, the country was split into East and West Pakistan; after a civil war, the former became Bangladesh.

In 1977, General Zia-ul-Haq became Pakistan's Chief Martial Law Administrator, heralding an era of increased Islamization. Changes included the setting up of Sharia courts, the imposition of new taxes for distribution among the nation's poor, and the annihilation of women's rights.

Zia gave refuge to an estimated three million refugees displaced during the Russian invasion and occupation of neighboring Afghanistan in 1979. A philosophy of anticommunism shared with the USA saw huge amounts of aid given to Pakistan, which helped to prop up Zia's faltering regime. Military rule ended in 1988 when Zia was killed in a suspicious plane crash.

Civilian government returned during the 1990s with a series of election battles between Nawaz Sharif, leader of the Islamic Democratic Alliance, and Benazir Bhutto, leader of the Pakistan People's Party (PPP). Their parties alternately won government, but neither could escape persistent accusations of nepotism and corruption. General Pervez Musharraf seized control from the civilian government of Nawaz Sharif in 1999. Bhutto left Pakistan in 1999, returning in 2007 to campaign for the PPP in the 2008 elections. She was assassinated on December 27, 2007.

The PPP won the majority vote in the elections and Yousaf Raza Gilani was sworn in as the country's new prime minister. One of his first acts was to order the release of 48 judges and 13 Supreme Court judges who had been imprisoned by Musharraf.

Population/Culture

Ingrained divisions between various religious groups (mostly Islamic sects), ethnic and language groups, and a disparate gulf between the wealthy and the poor, bedevil the nation. Culturally it is a hierarchical society with the

PETROGLYPHS UNEARTHED

The Karakoram Highway that connects Pakistan to China has dramatically increased access to previously isolated areas. This in turn has led to the discovery of thousands of petroglyphs throughout the upper Indus Valley, most particularly near the village of Chilas. To date over 30,000 petroglyphs have been discovered that reveal over a dozen different writing styles recording the passage of invaders, traders, monks, and pilgrims over the centuries. The earliest examples of rock art date from prehistoric times with more recent finds dating from the fourteenth and fifteenth centuries. The greatest concentration of Buddhist petroglyphs found anywhere is located near Chilas. They date from the first to the eighth century and document the progression of ideas, attitudes, and beliefs of Buddhist monks.

MILESTONE EVENTS

1947 Pakistan declares independence; Liaquat Ali Khan becomes prime minister

1947 First India–Pakistan war over Kashmir begins

1951 Liaquat Ali Khan assassinated

1965 Second India–Pakistan war over Kashmir begins

1973 A new constitution comes into effect; Zulfiqar Ali Bhutto becomes prime minister

1977 General Mohammad Zia overthrows Zulfiqar Ali Bhutto and proclaims martial law

1978 Zia ul-Haq becomes president

1979 Zulfiqar Ali Bhutto hanged

1983 Zia announces martial law to be lifted, but army will maintain a role in future governments

1985 General elections held

1988 Zia dismisses the government; Zia dies in suspicious plane crash; elections are held and Benazir Bhutto becomes the first female prime minister of a Muslim nation

1990 Benazir Bhutto's Pakistan People's Party loses the election to a coalition of right-wing parties; Nawaz Sharif becomes prime minister

1993 Nawaz Sharif government dismissed; Benazir Bhutto's PPP wins election; Benazir Bhutto becomes prime minister again

1996 Benazir Bhutto's government dismissed over allegations of corruption and nepotism

1997 Elections held and Sharif comes to power again

October 1999 Sharif arrested by army citing corruption; General Pervez Musharraf becomes chief executive

2005 Earthquake kills 80,000 people

March 9, 2007 Musharraf suspends Chief Justice Chaudhry alleging misconduct

July 10, 2007 Pakistani security forces storm Islamabad's Red Mosque; 100 people killed

July 20, 2007 Supreme Court reinstates Chaudhry

July 27, 2007 Musharraf meets with Benazir Bhutto to discuss sharing power

September 10, 2007 Sharif returns from exile but is immediately sent back to Saudi Arabia

October 6, 2007 Musharraf wins presidential re-election

October 18, 2007 Benazir Bhutto returns from exile; suicide bomber attacks her convoy killing 100 people—she is unhurt

November 3, 2007 Musharraf declares state of emergency

November 29, 2007 Musharraf resigns his military post

December 15, 2007 Emergency rule ends

December 29, 2007 Benazir Bhutto is assassinated

February 18, 2008 The PPP wins parliamentary elections

March 25, 2008 Yousaf Raza Gilani sworn in as new prime minister and immediately releases imprisoned court judges

extended family underpinning social structures as well as the individual's identity. Islam governs every single aspect of people's lives from politics to business relationships and all legal matters.

Older people are highly regarded in Pakistani society, and the elderly are always the first to be served, and to be introduced in social settings. Etiquette when greeting someone often involves asking after the health of the person involved and their family.

Administration/Government

Though officially a democratic federal republic, Pakistan has in fact been governed under various military dictatorships for all but 16 years since it gained independence in 1947. Its lack of a democratic tradition has led to great periods of instability.

The constitution guarantees a bicameral Parliament, which comprises a 100-member Senate and a 342-seat National Assembly, with directly elected members representing Pakistan's provinces. The Supreme Court is the final court of appeal and its chief justice is appointed directly by the president. There are also provincial high courts and a Federal Sharia court to judge on laws that may be repugnant to the tenets of Islam.

Economy/Industry

Agriculture is centered on the Indus Valley and is the dominant sector of Pakistan's economy, employing 42 percent of the workforce and contributing almost 20 percent to GDP. The primary crops are wheat, cotton, and rice. Industry employs about 20 percent of the workforce and produces pharmaceuticals, fertilizer, construction materials, textiles, apparel, and food processing; industry contributes almost 27 percent to GDP. The service sector employs 38 percent of the workforce and contributes almost 54 percent to GDP. Remittances from a global expatriate workforce represent Pakistan's second largest source of foreign exchange.

Reforms such as the privatization of the banking sector, a tighter monetary policy, and an improved taxation system have helped to reduce poverty from 34 percent of the population in 2001 to its present rate of 24 percent. Inflation and a widening trade gap as imports outstrip exports are cause for concern.

In 2008, the government announced a three-year upgrade and expansion of the Karakoram Highway (KKH) to facilitate trade with China and also with the Central Asian republics. The construction of the highway—the world's highest paved road—was a collaborative effort by the Pakistan and Chinese governments. It connects the Pakistani town of Hassan Abdal, some 25 miles (40 km) from Islamabad, to the ancient town of Kashgar on the edge of China's inhospitable Taklamakan Desert via the 15,518 feet (4,730 m) Khunjerab Pass. Construction began in 1966; the Pakistan section was officially opened in 1982 and the Chinese section in 1986.

The highway is an engineering marvel that snakes for an incredible 800 miles (1,280 km) along a network of ancient Silk Road routes through the Karakoram and Pamir mountain ranges. It is at its most spectacular as it passes the base of the Hispar Range near the town of Ganesh, surrounded by six peaks rising above 23,000 feet (7,000 m).

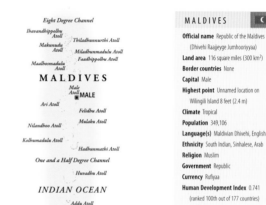

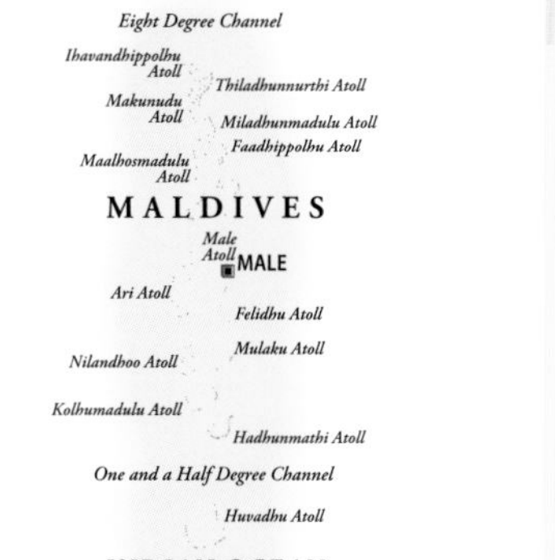
Eight Degree Channel
Ihavandhippolhu Atoll
Thiladhunmathi Atoll
Makunudu Atoll
Miladhunmadulu Atoll
Faadhippolhu Atoll
Maalhosmadulu Atoll
MALDIVES
Male Atoll
MALE
Ari Atoll
Felidhu Atoll
Mulaku Atoll
Nilandhoo Atoll
Kolhumadulu Atoll
Hadhunmathi Atoll
One and a Half Degree Channel
Huvadhu Atoll
INDIAN OCEAN
Addu Atoll

Maldives

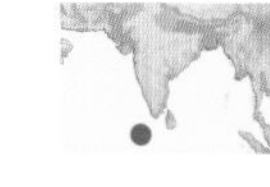

Map Reference Pages 392–393

Republic of the Maldives is a cluster of 26 atolls containing some 1,200 small islands in the Indian Ocean southwest of Sri Lanka. Only about 200 of the islands are inhabited. The islands barely rise above the surrounding ocean—the highest point is just 8 feet (2.4 m) above sea level. Thus, the very existence of the country is threatened by rising seas due to the effects of global warming.

In the second century BCE, the Maldivian islands became part of a Buddhist empire centered on the Indian subcontinent. Islam was introduced in 1153, and from that time until the establishment of a republic in 1968, they were ruled as an Islamic sultanate. They became a British protectorate in 1887, and in July 1965 gained their independence.

Fishing was the dominant occupation for centuries, but foreign tourism has grown from the 1970s into the country's largest source of revenue. Certain islands are set aside as tourist resorts, with scuba diving in the crystal-clear waters the major attraction. A growing crafts industry also caters to tourists. Agriculture is limited to taro, coconuts, and bananas.

The president is chief of state and head of government, and appoints a cabinet of ministers. The Majilis, or People's Council, has 50 members, 42 elected by popular vote; the president appoints the remainder. In 2004 there were protests and rioting in the capital, Malé, in favor of greater democracy, which was promised.

Republic of the Maldives is the smallest and least populated of the world's predominantly Islamic countries. Adherence to Islam is required for citizenship. Islamic law (Sharia) is used along with civil law. Many of the islands are essentially off-limits to foreigners.

MALDIVES

Official name Republic of the Maldives (Dhivehi Raajjeyge Jumhooriyyaa)

Land area 116 square miles (300 km²)

Border countries None

Capital Male

Highest point Unnamed location on Wilingili Island 8 feet (2.4 m)

Climate Tropical

Population 349,106

Language(s) Maldivian Dhivehi, English

Ethnicity South Indian, Sinhalese, Arab

Religion Muslim

Government Republic

Currency Rufiyaa

Human Development Index 0.741 (ranked 100th out of 177 countries)

Above The capital city Malé has the highest concentration of people in the Maldives. Though the island covers just ¾ of a square mile (2 km²), it is home to around 75,000 people.

Above Tourism is expanding in the Maldives. Visitors come to experience the beauty of its numerous tropical islands and the breathtaking underwater landscapes of colorful coral with accompanying marine life.

Left These girls live in Pakistan's remote mountain kingdom of Hunza, which was only opened up about 30 years ago when the Karakoram Highway was built. Hunzakuts speak Burushaski, a language that is thought to be unrelated to any other of the world's languages.

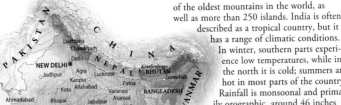

INDIA

Official name Republic of India (Bharatiya Ganarajya)
Land area 1,147,950 square miles (2,973,190 km²)
Border countries China, Nepal, Bhutan, Myanmar, Bangladesh, Pakistan
Capital New Delhi
Highest point Kanchenjunga 28,209 feet (8,598 m)
Climate Tropical to temperate
Population 1,148,000,000
Language(s) Official: Hindi; other: Bengali, Teluga, Marathi, Tamil, Urdu, Gujarati, Malayalam, Kannada, Oriya, Punjabi, Assamese, Kashmiri, Sindhi, and Sanskrit; widely spoken are English (for politics and commerce) and Hindustani (throughout northern India)
Ethnicity Indo-Aryan 72%, Dravidian 25%, Mongoloid and other 3%
Religion Hindu 80.5%, Muslim 13.4%, Christian 2.3%, Sikh 1.9%, other 1.8%, unspecified 0.1%
Government Federal republic
Currency Indian rupee
Human Development Index 0.619 (ranked 128th out of 177 countries)

Right Hindus believe ritual bathing in the sacred waters of the River Ganges will wash away sins and bring purification and healing.

Below Gandhi's doctrine of non-violent protest to effect social and political change led to India's independence from Britain in 1947.

PAKISTAN
CHINA
NEPAL
BHUTAN
BANGLADESH
MYANMAR
INDIA
Ludhiana
Chandigarh
Delhi
NEW DELHI
Jodhpur
Agra
Lucknow
Kanchenjunga
Guwahati
Kanpur
Patna
Kota
Allahabad
Varanasi
Ahmadabad
Bhopal
Jabalpur
Asansol
Kolkata
Surat
Nagpur
Mumbai
Pune
Hyderabad
Visakhapatnam
Arabian Sea
Vijayawada
Bay of Bengal
Bangalore
Chennai
Andaman Islands
Laccadive Islands
Kozhikode (Calicut)
Coimbatore
Madurai
Kochi (Cochin)
SRI LANKA
Nicobar Islands

India

Map Reference Pages 392–393

Situated between Myanmar (Burma) and Pakistan, India has the Bay of Bengal on the east and the Arabian Sea on the west. This South Asian nation features enormous geographical diversity together with plurality in language, religion, culture, and ethnicity.

Physical Geography

India is a vast country that extends up to 1,990 miles (3,200 km) from south to north and 1,860 miles (3,000 km) from east to west. This geologically ancient land is divided into the Himalaya and associated mountain chains, the Indus–Ganga–Brahmaputra plains, and the Peninsular plateau, including its coasts and islands. The Himalayan mountain region extends over 1,550 miles (2,500 km), from Karakoram in the west to Myanmar in the east, and boasts the world's 14 highest peaks and several large rivers. In the north, the Indus–Ganga–Brahmaputra plains extend for 1,990 miles (3,200 km) from west to east. The Peninsular plateau region of southern India has some of the oldest mountains in the world, as well as more than 250 islands. India is often described as a tropical country, but it has a range of climatic conditions. In winter, southern parts experience low temperatures, while in the north it is cold; summers are hot in most parts of the country. Rainfall is monsoonal and primarily orographic, around 46 inches (116 cm) annually, and is unevenly distributed. Maunsiram in eastern Meghalaya receives the world's highest annual rainfall; Jaisalmer is one of the world's driest regions.

India has one of the largest groundwater reservoirs in the world. Although only 30 percent of total groundwater has been harnessed, overuse has led to depletion in Punjab, Haryana, Rajasthan, Andhra Pradesh, and Uttar Pradesh. There is a plentiful supply of surface water from its many rivers, lakes, ponds, and canals. It has some of the largest rivers in the world, including the Brahmaputra, the Indus, and the Ganga (Ganges).

India is one of the most disaster-prone regions of the world—57 percent of its land is vulnerable to earthquakes, approximately 8 percent experiences cyclones of varying intensity, and much of the country suffers droughts and floods.

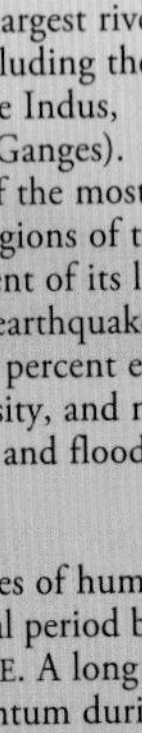

History

The earliest traces of humans date to the second Inter-Glacial period between 400,000 BCE and 200,000 BCE. A long period of evolution gathered momentum during the Indus Valley civilization, evidence for which has been excavated at Harappa and Mohenjo-Daro (now in Pakistan) where urbanization dates back to 3000 BCE. By 1700 BCE the Harappan culture had declined and migration of Indo-Aryans from the Middle East in about 1500 BCE introduced new features into the cultural background.

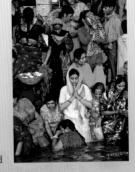

The two Hindu mythological epics, the *Ramayana* and the *Mahabharata*, refer to events that occurred between 1000–700 BCE, when Hinduism was taking root in India. India was ruled by the Mauryan kings and others in the Ancient period (321–185 BCE), the Mughals in the Medieval period (1526–1712), then the British until 1947, when India gained independence. The father of the nation, Mahatma Gandhi, worked throughout his life to achieve national unity and integrity through communal harmony and uplifting of the poor, and led the freedom movement.

Population/Culture

India has the second largest body of human resources in the world, accounting for around 16.8 percent of the world's population. There are 5,161 towns in India, as well as 35 cities with a population of at least one million and three cities with more than 10 million people: Mumbai, Kolkata, and Delhi. A major characteristic of Indian cities is the growth of slums, where 40.3 million people live.

A synthesis of cultures, religions, and languages of people belonging to different castes and communities characterizes the country. There exists great diversity in lifestyles, land tenure systems, inheritance and succession law, rites, rituals, and customs, but the notions of *dharma* (normative order), *karma* (personal moral commitment), and *jati* (caste) as the hierarchical principles of social stratification are basic to Indian society as a whole.

Most Indians follow the Hindu faith. Other religions are practiced, including Islam, Christianity, and Sikhism. Buddhism and Jainism are significant minority religions, and have influenced art, science, and philosophy.

The Constitution lists 23 languages, and more than 544 dialects are spoken. Sanskrit enjoyed the status of carrying Hindu culture throughout the country.

There are more than 285 tribal ethnic communities comprising 8.2 percent of the population, belonging to various racial groups.

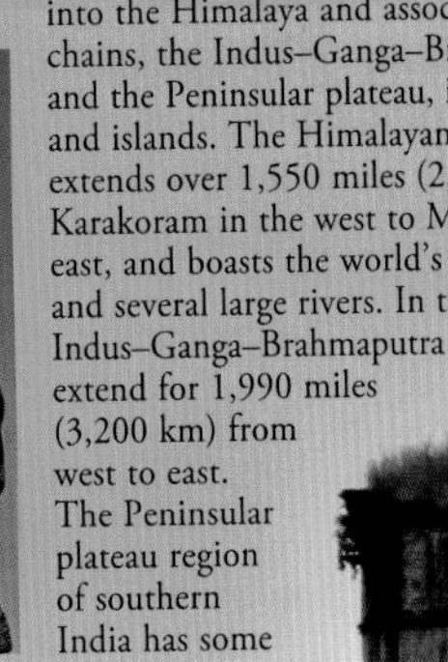

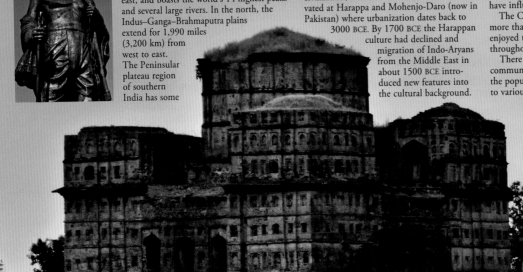

MILESTONE EVENTS

3000–1550 BCE Harappa and Mohenjo-Daro communities live in the Indus Valley

1500s BCE Aryan tribes migrate onto the Indus Plain; the four Vedas, texts that form the basis of Hindu religion and philosophy, are composed; the caste system is established

326 BCE Alexander the Great invades parts of India, bringing with him historians and scholars who document much of what they see and hear

c. 268 BCE The Mauryan king Ashoka comes to power and actively promotes Buddhism

320–647 CE The Gupta Dynasty rules India

1200s Muslims invade Indian territories

1526–1712 Mughals rule India; the Taj Mahal is built at Agra by the Mughal emperor, Shah Jahan

1600 The British East India Company is formed

1858–1947 The British Empire rules the Indian Subcontinent; the period is known as the British Raj

1885 The Indian National Congress (INC) is formed; it leads the independence movement

1920 Mohandas (Mahatma) Gandhi begins a mass movement to force the expulsion of the Raj

August 1947 India gains independence and is partitioned into the Republic of India and Pakistan; ensuing riots among Hindus, Muslims, and Sikhs lead to a death toll of around 50,000 people

1984 Indira Gandhi is assassinated

1998 India tests a nuclear device

Human development has become an important agenda in India, with a focus on literacy and health. Faced with low literacy rates (75.85 percent for males and 54.16 percent for females), the government is implementing various programs such as the National Literacy Mission.

Administration/Government

The process of nation building began after independence was achieved in 1947, and the Constitution of India was adopted in 1950. The Indian constitution is a living document and has been amended 106 times. India is a quasi-federal state with 28 states and seven union territories, and a multiparty system at both national and state levels.

The president, elected indirectly by an electoral college, is the head of state. The prime minister and leader of the majority party or coalition is the head of government. The bicameral parliament's upper house (the Council of States or Rajya Sabha) has 245 members, and the lower house (the House of the People or Lok Sabha) 545 members.

Economy/Industry

Agriculture is the backbone of the Indian economy. Agriculture and allied sectors such as forestry, logging, and fishing account for about 16 percent of GDP and employ about 60 percent of the population. Approximately 43 percent of the land is used for agriculture. Despite a steady decline in its share in GDP, agriculture remains the largest economic sector and plays a significant role in the overall socio-economic development.

Agriculture is dependent on the monsoons, referred to as the "Gamble of Monsoon." Among the non-food crops, oilseeds, fiber crops, several plantation crops, and forage crops are important. Rice and wheat are the principal food crops.

The country is moving toward rapid development of its industrial base from iron and steel, cotton, jute, and sugar to engineering, computers, information technology, communications, and biotechnical industries. The National Sample Survey for 2004–05 shows rural poverty at 28.3 percent and urban poverty at 25.7 percent. Altogether, 27.5 percent of India's population lives below the poverty line. The Five Year Plans and several other developmental schemes aim to uplift the poor and more vulnerable sections of society. Since 1991, liberalization of the economy and increasing integration with the global economy have helped GDP rates to grow to the current rate of more than 9 percent.

In 2000, India announced the introduction of Special Economic Zones (SEZs) which are designed to enhance foreign investments and promote exports. More than 500 SEZs have been proposed, 220 of which have been created to date.

Measured in terms of length, India has one of the largest road networks in the world. Roads, railway lines, waterways, and airports are vital carriers of goods and passengers across the country. Communication facilities— public phone booths, mobile phones, and the Internet—have grown phenomenally in India in recent years. There are about 217 million mobile phones in India today.

Forests and Biodiversity

India boasts a range of forest types, from tropical and subtropical forests in the western Ghats and eastern Himalaya, to temperate and alpine forests in central and western Himalaya, and desert forests, which are mostly found in arid and semi-arid regions of the country. Forests constitute 20.64 percent of India's geographical area. The country's mangroves make up 5 percent of the world's share.

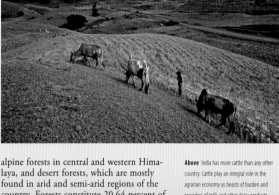

India's forests, wetlands, and marine areas boast a wealth of biodiversity. The western Ghats and eastern Himalaya are considered biodiversity hotspots. The country has an estimated 81,000 fauna species, which represents about 6.4 percent of the world's fauna, and 45,000 plant species (about 7 percent of the world's flora). However, 172 animal species are considered globally threatened. Of the 14 biosphere reserves, three of them—Sundarban, Gulf of Mannar, and the Nilgiri—are part of the world network of biosphere reserves.

Above India has more cattle than any other country. Cattle play an integral role in the agrarian economy as beasts of burden and providers of milk and other dairy products. Considered sacred by some Hindus, they cannot be slaughtered. Here, cattle graze on verdant pasture after the monsoonal rains.

Below Sun sets on the cenotaphs of the Bundela kings in the hamlet of Orchha, the former regal capital. In medieval times, these powerful kings reigned over a wide area, from the Ganga (Ganges) to Narmada.

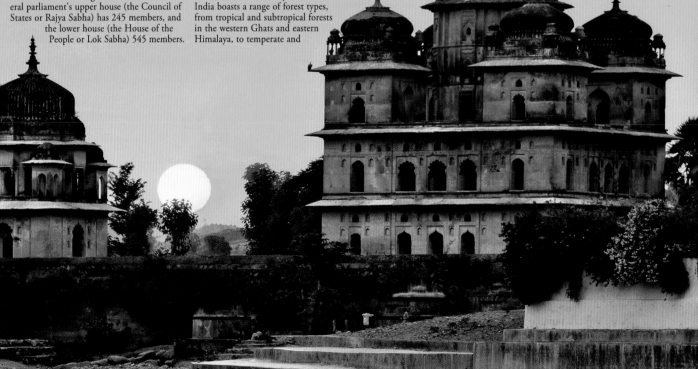

NEPAL

Official name Nepal
Land area 56,827 square miles (147,181 km²)
Border countries China (Tibet), India
Capital Kathmandu
Highest & lowest points Mt Everest (Sagarmatha) 29,035 feet (8,850 m); Kanchan Kalan 230 feet (70 m)
Climate Cool summers and harsh winters in the north; subtropical summers and mild winters in the south
Population 29,519,000
Language(s) Official: Nepali; other: Maithili, Bhojpuri, Tharu (Dagaura/Rana), Tamang, Newar , Magar, Awadhi
Ethnicity Over 50 ethnic groups including (in size order) Chhetri, Brahman, Magar, Tharu, Tamang, Newar, Muslim
Religion Hindu 86%, Buddhist 8%, Muslim 3%, other 3%
Government A federal democratic republic
Currency Nepali rupee
Human Development Index 0.534 (ranked 142nd out of 177 countries)

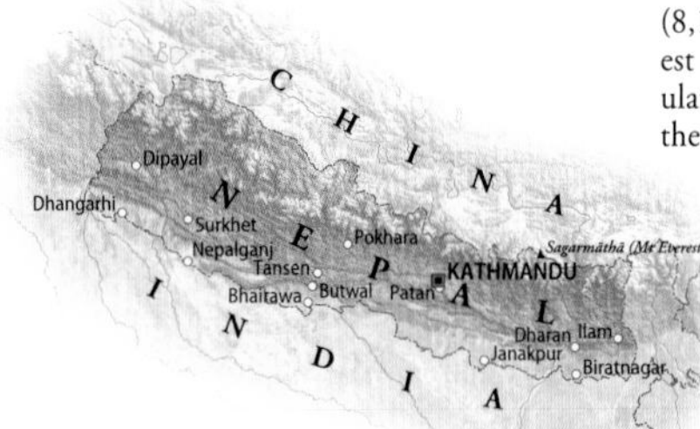
CHINA
NEPAL
INDIA
Dipayal
Dhangarhi
Surkhet
Nepalganj
Pokhara
Tansen
Bhairawa
Butwal
Patan
KATHMANDU
Sagarmatha (Mt Everest)
Dharan
Ilam
Janakpur
Biratnagar

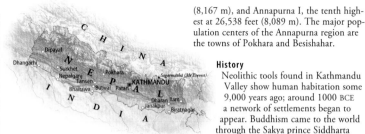

Nepal

Map Reference Pages 392–393

Although Nepal has an amazing diversity of geographic and ethnic regions, it will always be synonymous with the mountains and valleys of the great Himalayan range. Eight of the world's ten highest summits are found within its borders, attracting mountaineers and tourists from around the world.

Physical Geography

Nepal's geographic diversity is remarkable. An area of small ranges known as the Hills Region includes the Kathmandu Valley, the most heavily populated and fertile region, and ranges in elevations from 3,300 feet (1,005 m) to peaks over 13,000 feet (3,960 m). The Mountain Region runs along the northern border with China (Tibet) from Kanchenjunga on the border with India, through the Everest region to the Annapurna range in the west.

The Annapurna massif is one of the world's most popular trekking regions and is home to Dhaulagiri, the seventh highest mountain in the world with an elevation of 26,794 feet (8,167 m), and Annapurna I, the tenth highest at 26,538 feet (8,089 m). The major population centers of the Annapurna region are the towns of Pokhara and Besishahar.

History

Neolithic tools found in Kathmandu Valley show human habitation some 9,000 years ago; around 1000 BCE a network of settlements began to appear. Buddhism came to the world through the Sakya prince Siddharta Gautama (563–483 BCE), who was born in Kapilvastu in Nepal.

Over the next 19 centuries, the region came under the influence of a succession of Indian empires until the establishment in 1482 of three Newar kingdoms: Kath, Patan, and Bhadgaon. Nepal achieved nationhood in 1768 when a ruler named Prithvi Narayan Shah unified the three kingdoms.

The unmistakable architecture of the Newar period can still be seen in Kathmandu. Newar homes are generally built around a central courtyard, a *chowk*, often with elaborately decorated doors and windows, and with low ceiling heights. A Newar home is usually narrow and can be up to five stories high.

The Rana dynasty aligned itself with Britain in World War I, which led to formal recognition of Nepal in 1923. After the Chinese annexation of Tibet in 1950, the Indian government, fearful of an expansionist China, installed King Tribhavan on the Nepalese throne, where he ruled amid great division until 1959 when a non-political council was installed. However, the excessive constitutional powers of the monarchy remained. In May 2006, Nepal became a secular state.

Population/Culture

Nepal's population is made up of various ethnic groups, divided into different castes. The Newar people are the country's original inhabitants and are considered to be among the country's most cultured people. Around 1.2 million Newars live mainly in the Kathmandu Valley. They are predominantly Hindu, although most follow an amalgam of Hindu and Buddhist traditions.

Kathmandu, the nation's capital, has a population of approximately 750,000. It is located in the central Kathmandu Valley at an altitude of 4,500 feet (1,370 m). Established more than 1,500 years ago, it is the country's administrative, financial, and cultural hub.

Administration/Government

In 1996, leaders of the Maoist United People's Front began a violent insurgency with the aim of overthrowing the monarchy. The nation was plunged into further turmoil in 2001 when Crown Prince Dipendra massacred 10 members of the royal family, including his parents the King and Queen of Nepal; he then killed himself. The king's brother, Gyanendra, became king.

In 2006, the parliament voted to curtail the king's powers, and a peace agreement was signed to end the 10-year Maoist insurgency that had killed at least 12,500 people. An interim parliament was established in January 2007 that included Maoist leaders. Nepal held its first democratic elections in April 2008; the Communist Party of Nepal (Maoists) gained 36.6 percent of the votes. In May 2008, Nepal became a republic after a special assembly voted to abolish the monarchy.

Economy/Industry

Statistically, Nepal is Asia's poorest nation. Half the population lives below the poverty line, and half of the nation's children are undernourished. Unemployment averages 50 percent. Over 70 percent are engaged in agriculture. Economic development is hampered by an acute lack of infrastructure and a woefully inadequate road network. Nepal is almost wholly lacking an industrial sector.

Almost 750,000 Nepalese are forced to look overseas for work in countries such as the oil-rich Gulf states of the United Arab Emirates.

Above Children make up half of Nepal's population. After the country's first elections in 2008, all political parties promised to make children their number one priority in building a new Nepal.

Above right Namche Bazaar is well known as the last stop on the trek to Mt Everest Base Camp. Sitting 11,286 feet (3,440 m) above sea level, the village is the center of Nepal's Sherpa culture.

Below right Swayambhunath Stupa, the oldest holy shrine in Kathmandu Valley, is topped with a golden spire. On each side of the spire's base is a pair of eyes, symbolizing God's ability to see all. Hindus, Vajrayana Buddhists from northern Nepal and Tibet, and Newari Buddhists from central and southern Nepal all worship at the shrine.

MILESTONE EVENTS

Sixth century BCE Buddhism begins
1482 Newar kingdoms of Kath, Patan, and Bhadgaon established
1768 Newar kingdoms unified by Ghorka ruler Prithvi Narayan Shah
1923 Nepal formally recognized by the British
1950–1959 India-installed King Tribhavan rules Nepal
1959 Non-political council installed
1991 New parliament established
1996 Maoist insurgency begins
2001 Crown Prince Dipendra kills 10 members of Royal Family
2006 Peace agreement between government and Maoist rebels signed; Nepal becomes a secular state
2007 Interim parliament established
May 2008 Nepal becomes a republic

SIR EDMUND HILLARY'S HIMALAYAN TRUST

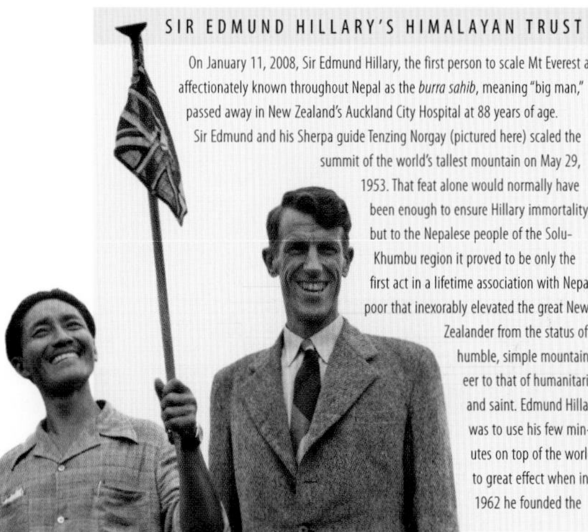

On January 11, 2008, Sir Edmund Hillary, the first person to scale Mt Everest and affectionately known throughout Nepal as the *burra sahib*, meaning "big man," passed away in New Zealand's Auckland City Hospital at 88 years of age.

Sir Edmund and his Sherpa guide Tenzing Norgay (pictured here) scaled the summit of the world's tallest mountain on May 29, 1953. That feat alone would normally have been enough to ensure Hillary immortality, but to the Nepalese people of the Solu-Khumbu region it proved to be only the first act in a lifetime association with Nepal's poor that inexorably elevated the great New Zealander from the status of humble, simple mountaineer to that of humanitarian and saint. Edmund Hillary was to use his few minutes on top of the world to great effect when in 1962 he founded the Himalayan Trust, a charitable organization that has improved the quality of life of the Sherpas of the Everest region with the construction of schools, hospitals, clinics, and the granting of scholarships for higher education. Sir Edmund's Himalayan Trust has been responsible for programs to control the spread of diseases such as smallpox and tuberculosis and has been instrumental in helping to reduce the rate of infant mortality and stillbirths.

The Trust has also established teacher-training programs, trained Sherpas to be wardens in Nepal's national parks, rebuilt infrastructure, and aided in the construction of new monasteries. The Trust's involvement in various reforestation programs includes the establishment of nurseries that have produced more than 100,000 endemic seedlings, which have helped regenerate forests that have been heavily degraded to provide, ironically, wood fires to keep trekkers warm at night and to cook their meals. The Trust nurseries' long-term goal is to stabilize local soils through the mass planting of native shrubs and trees in Nepal's Sagramatha National Park.

In 1964 the Trust constructed a new airfield at Lukla and it has been instrumental in helping the Sherpa community overcome the harsh extremes and challenges their environment presents to them, providing hope of a better future without compromising their fierce independence.

Sir Edmund continually emphasized that the Trust's projects were always pursued at the direct request of the local people and purpose-built to meet local needs. He continued to travel the world fundraising for the Trust until he was well into his eighties.He was also Honorary President of the non-profit American Himalayan Foundation.

INDIA
Kankesanturai
Jaffna
Mannar
Gulf of Mannar
Vavuniya
Trincomalee
Kinniyai
Mutur
Anuradhapura
SRI LANKA
Batticaloa
Chilaw
Kurunegala
Kandy
Negombo
Gampola
Pidurutalagala
SRI JAYEWARDENEPURA KOTTE
COLOMBO
Moratuwa
Ratnapura
Galle
INDIAN OCEAN

Sri Lanka

Map Reference Pages 392–393

Above The twice-restored Temple of the Tooth (Sri Dalada Maligawa) sits on Kandy Lake in central Sri Lanka. Inside the temple is a tooth that legend says was taken from the Buddha as he lay on his funeral pyre.

Sri Lanka is an island republic in the Indian Ocean off the southeast tip of India, separated from India by the Palk Strait. Adams Bridge, a mostly underwater atoll, almost links the two. Since antiquity, wayfarers have bequeathed several names to this beautiful island, among them Taprobane and Ceylon.

Physical Geography

Sri Lanka, a lush tropical island just north of the equator, is famous for its 494,200 acres (200,000 ha) of tea plantations scattered over rolling hill country. Low-lying coastal plains ring much of the island, and a mountain massif dominates the central and southern interior.

Forests, mostly in the interior, cover about 30 percent of the island, of which 10 percent is nature reserves that protect a huge diversity of flora and fauna. Over 3,000 species of plants grow in the tropical climate. Yala National Park in the southeast is renowned for its elephants, Wilpattu National Park in the northwest for leopards. Unfortunately, the habitats of many species of plants and animals are under threat from deforestation and poaching.

Although Sri Lanka's climate is tropical monsoon, it is moderated by sea breezes, especially in the lowlands.

History

Archeologists have dated cultivated barley and millet seeds from the central plateau of Horton Plains to around 5,000 BCE, and Paleolithic finds from around 100,000 BCE. For 23 centuries, Sri Lanka was ruled in part or whole by a monarchy, until 1972, with the appointment of the president of the Democratic Socialist Republic of Sri Lanka.

MILESTONE EVENTS

1505 Portuguese arrive in Colombo

1660 Dutch control all of Ceylon except for the kingdom of Kandy

1798 Island of Ceylon (excluding Kandy) becomes a British Crown colony

1802 Treaty of Amiens cedes Ceylon to Britain

1815 Britain annexes the kingdom of Kandy

1948 Independence

1956 Start of minority Tamil separatist movement; members of the Sinhalese majority attack Tamil civilians

1972 Ceylon declares itself the Democratic Socialist Republic of Sri Lanka; leads to greater discontent among Tamils and more violence

1978 Tamil recognized as a national language

1985 First peace talks between the government and Tamil Tiger rebels fail

2002 Tamil Tigers and government sign a ceasefire agreement, brokered by Norway; however, violence continues over next six years

2008 Government pulls out of ceasefire agreement; violence continues

Left The value of Sri Lanka's tea exports broke the US$1 billion mark in 2007, a 22 percent increase on the 2006 value. This was achieved despite a harsh drought and work stoppages by the Plantation Labour Unions.

From the sixteenth century, Sri Lanka was subjected to a number of western invaders. The first were the Portuguese, who by the end of the century controlled almost the entire coastal area of the island. About a century later, the Dutch were in control, followed in 1798 by the English, who made the island, except the hill kingdom of Kandy, the British Crown Colony of Ceylon. Kandy was finally annexed in 1815. Independence was declared in February 1948. Since then, intermittent strife between government forces and the Tamil separatist movement has marred the peace. The Hindu Tamil minority are fighting for an independent homeland, Tamil Eelam.

On December 26, 2004, a massive earthquake in the Indian Ocean off the island of Sumatra caused a tsunami, which hit the south and east coast of Sri Lanka with such ferocity that the areas were completely devastated and 31,000 people were killed.

Population/Culture

The population is multi-ethnic, divided mainly on the basis of language and religion into four groups. Sinhalese is the largest with 73.8 percent of the population, most of whom are Buddhist and speak Sinhali. Indian and Sri Lankan Tamils make up the second largest group with 8.5 percent of the population. Most are Hindu and speak Tamil. The third group, Moors with Arab origins, represent 7.2 percent of the population. The fourth group is the Burghers, a mixed group who are descended from Portuguese and Dutch colonizers and who practice Christianity.

Common to all four groups is the sacred peak of Sri Pada or Adam's Peak—the former name means "sacred footprint"—the island's second highest mountain. A rock formation near its summit resembles a footprint and pilgrims from four faiths—Buddhist, Hindu, Muslim, and Christian—climb thousands of steps to worship at the site. The footprint is variously attributed to Buddha, Shiva, Adam, and St Thomas.

Administration/Government

The president, who is both the chief of state and head of government, is elected by popular vote. The cabinet is appointed by the president in consultation with the prime minister. The latter's role is largely ceremonial. The 225 members of the unicameral parliament are elected by popular vote. The Supreme Court and the Court of Appeals represent the judiciary; Sri Lanka's president appoints judges in both courts.

Economy/Industry

Sri Lanka is a poor nation, with about 22 percent of people living below the poverty line. The government's economic approach to reducing poverty is to direct investment toward impoverished areas, develop small to medium businesses, and advance agriculture. The latter was the leading economic sector in the 1970s but accounts for only 16 percent of GDP while employing 34 percent of the labor force. The service sector is the country's largest employer, with over 40 percent of the labor force and contributing almost 57 percent to GDP. The industrial sector accounts for 27 percent of GDP and employs 25 percent of the labor force in activities such as petroleum refining, rubber manufacturing, textiles, and apparel. Diamonds, rubies, emeralds, tea, and spices are major export earners. Cash transfers home from migrant workers have also become a source of foreign currency.

Left These stilt fishermen at Koggala, on Sri Lanka's southern tip, have devised a simple way to stay above the water as they fish for sardines. The wooden poles are wedged into rock crevices.

SRI LANKA

Official name Democratic Socialist Republic of Sri Lanka (Shri Lamka Prajatantrika Samajaya di Janarajaya/Ilankai Jananayaka Choshalichak Kutiyarachu)

Land area 24,996 square miles (64,740 km²)

Border countries None

Capitals Colombo; Sri Jayewardenepura Kotte (legislative capital)

Highest point Mt Pidurutalagala 8,281 feet (2,524 m)

Climate Tropical monsoon

Population 21,129,000

Language(s) Sinhala, Tamil, other

Ethnicity Sinhalese 73.8%, Sri Lankan Moors 7.2%, Indian Tamil 4.6%, Sri Lankan Tamil 3.9%, other (including Burghers) 0.5%, unspecified 10%

Religion Buddhist 69.1%, Muslim 7.6%, Hindu 7.1%, Christian 6.2%, other 10%

Government Republic

Currency Sri Lankan rupee

Human Development Index 0.743 (ranked 99th out of 177 countries)

BHUTAN

Official name Kingdom of Bhutan (Druk Gyalkhap)
Land area 18,147 square miles (47,000 km²)
Border countries China, India
Capital Thimphu
Highest & lowest points Kula Kangri 24,780 feet (7,553 m); Drangme Chhu 318 feet (97 m)
Climate Tropical in southern plains; cool winters and hot summers in central valleys; severe winters and cool summers in Himalayas
Population 682,321
Language(s) Official: Dzongkha; other: Nepali and Tibetan dialects
Ethnicity Bhote 50%, ethnic Nepalese 35%, indigenous and migrant tribes 15%
Religion Buddhist 68%, Hindu 30%, other 2%
Government Constitutional monarchy
Currency Ngultrum; Indian rupee
Human Development Index 0.579 (ranked 133rd out of 177 countries)

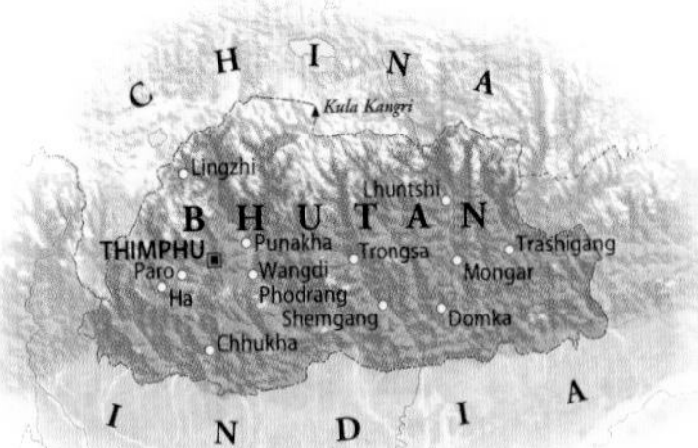
CHINA
Kula Kangri
Lingzhi
BHUTAN
Lhuntshi
THIMPHU
Punakha
Trongsa
Trashigang
Paro
Wangdi Phodrang
Mongar
Ha
Shemgang
Domka
Chhukha
INDIA

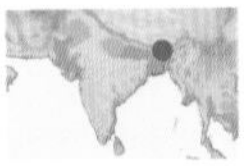

Above right Straddling the border between Tibet and Bhutan are the awe-inspiring mountain peaks of Chomolhari (left), Jitchudrake (center), and Tshering Gang (right).

Above Buddhist actors perform the *Chham* (sacred mask dance) at the Thimpu Festival, Bhutan. The five-day festival takes place within the walls of the Tashichhodzong fortress, the Bhutanese seat of government.

Below right Three smiling monks pay tribute to the Gross National Happiness, a concept introduced by the Bhutanese ruler in reaction to the standard economic indicator of a country's wealth, the Gross National Product.

Below Clinging to a 4,000-foot (1,200 m) precipice just outside Paro, Bhutan, the Taktsang Monastery is built around the cave where Guru Rinpoche (Guru Padmasambhava), the founder of Tibetan Buddhism, is said to have meditated.

Bhutan

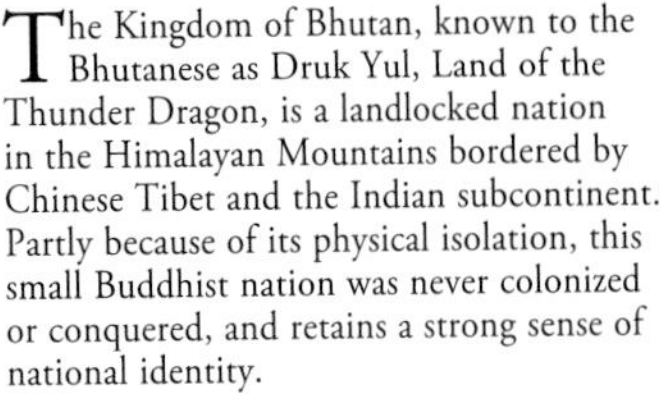

Map Reference Pages 392–393

The Kingdom of Bhutan, known to the Bhutanese as Druk Yul, Land of the Thunder Dragon, is a landlocked nation in the Himalayan Mountains bordered by Chinese Tibet and the Indian subcontinent. Partly because of its physical isolation, this small Buddhist nation was never colonized or conquered, and retains a strong sense of national identity.

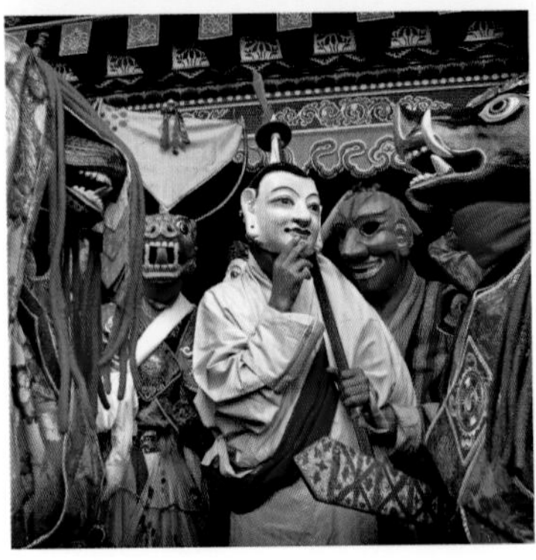

MILESTONE EVENTS

c. 2000 BCE Archeology indicates occupation of fertile valleys
747 CE Legendary visit of Guru Rinpoche, founder of Tibetan Buddhism
c. 1710 Bhutan unified under Tibetan lama and soldier Shabdrung Ngawang Namgyal; network of military fortresses built
1651 Beginning of civil wars; military incursions by Tibet
1759 After assaults by Tibetans and Mongols, armistice signed with Tibet
1865 Bhutan signs Treaty of Sinchula with British India; borderland ceded in exchange for annual subsidy of Rs 50,000
1907 Inauguration of Wangchuk royal line; Ugyen Wangchuk chosen as hereditary king by assembly of Buddhist monks
1953 King Jorgme Dorji Wangchuk establishes National Assembly
1971 Bhutan admitted to United Nations
2008 First general elections; deliberations take place on new constitution

Physical Geography

Bhutan is a land of mountains. Giant glaciated peaks in an arc stretching across the north of the country include Kula Kangri, the highest at 24,780 feet (7,553 m). Nearly three-quarters of Bhutan is covered in forest; only 6 percent of its land area is under cultivation. The south is lower in elevation and characterized by deciduous forests and alluvial river valleys.

History

Inhabited from 2000 BCE, and mainly Buddhist from the eighth or ninth century, records of Bhutan's early history are said to have been lost in a fire in 1827. Conflict with British India in the eighteenth and nineteenth centuries ended with the signing of the Treaty of Sinchulu in 1865, under which Bhutan ceded borderland to the British. In 1907 Britain established a monarchy. Three years later Bhutan was granted internal autonomy, with Britain retaining control of external affairs. In 1953, wishing to move toward democracy, the king established a National Assembly.

A general election held in 2008 resulted in a victory for the Bhutan United Party led by staunch royalist Jigme Thinley. This election was the latest stage of a long-term plan to replace the once absolute monarchy with a democratic constitutional monarchy.

Population/Culture

About 50 percent of the people are Bhote, with ethnic Nepalese (35 percent), indigenous and migrant tribes making up the remainder.

Bhutan's symbolic and highly ornamental arts and crafts traditions are deeply rooted in Buddhism. Religious works are mostly collaborative efforts, created by religious men or by groups under the supervision of monks.

In 1999 Bhutan became the last nation in the world to embrace television, and its introduction was greeted with furious debate. In 2002 a crime wave, Bhutan style, engulfed the kingdom with the vandalizing of religious stupas, accusations of corruption among government officials, and several instances of domestic violence, which led to calls for television to be censored. Cable television has since circumvented the state-controlled Bhutan Broadcasting Service and is a major challenge to the Bhutanese way of life.

Administration/Government

Bhutan's government has developed from an absolute monarchy to a constitutional monarchy. The hereditary chief of state of the Kingdom of Bhutan is King Jigme Khesar Namgyel Wangchuk. Beneath him is the head of the government, Prime Minister Jigme Thinley (since April 2008) and a cabinet consisting of a Council of Ministers nominated by the monarch and approved by the National Assembly. They serve fixed, five-year terms. Although the monarch is hereditary, the constitutional reforms of 1998 allow for his removal by a two-thirds vote of the National Assembly.

Economy/Industry

The economy is based on forestry and agriculture (mostly subsistence farming), which provides 60 percent of Bhutanese with their livelihoods. The domestic industry includes handicrafts—a small cottage industry supplies religious art for home altars—while heavy industry includes the production of cement. There is very little infrastructure, but the sale of hydroelectric power to India provides the government with much of its revenue. Bhutan must import all fuel and lubricants, and is not self-sufficient in rice.

The capital Thimphu is a showcase of Bhutanese art and tradition. Located in the Wang Chhu valley, Thimphu, though small by world standards, nonetheless faces problems of urban growth and town planning.

In 2003 the Thimphu Structure plan was approved and includes restrictions on building heights and the construction of urban villages to accommodate the growing population. In keeping with the country's approach to growth and the priority placed on individual happiness, the plan has been subject to intensive public consultation. Thimphu's urban growth is strictly controlled, and it is the only Asian capital city that has not a single set of traffic lights.

Gross National Happiness

One of the world's least developed societies, Bhutan may be one of its happiest. The philosophy of Gross National Happiness, developed by King Jigme Singye Wangchuk, has played a pivotal role in the nation's development. Rather than measuring a nation's worth by the material wealth it can generate, according to indicators such as Gross National Product, Bhutan gauges its success by the happiness and wellbeing of its citizens. By this philosophy the government seeks environmental sustainability and economic growth, while preserving the country's unique heritage.

INDIA
INDIA
Rangpur
Dinajpur
Bogra
Naogaon
Jamalpur
Mymensingh
Sylhet
BANGLADESH
Nawabganj
Rajshahi
Tangail
Pabna
Tungi
DHAKA
Brahmanbaria
Narayanganj
Comilla
Jessore
Khulna
Barisal
Chittagong
Keokradong
Mongla Port
Bay of Bengal
MYANMAR

Bangladesh

Map Reference Pages 392–393

Above Traffic congestion is the norm in Dhaka, the Bangladeshi capital. Throughout its history Dhaka has been a French, Dutch, and British trading post; today it is home to 11 million people.

Bangladesh in southern Asia shares its land border almost exclusively with India, except for a small area in the southeast bordered by Myanmar (Burma). The Bay of Bengal lies to the south. Regularly subjected to deadly floods, Bangladesh is one of the world's poorest and most densely populated nations.

Physical Geography

Ninety percent of Bangladesh's topography is characterized by fertile alluvial plains that seldom rise above 33 feet (10 m). Dividing the plains are two great rivers—the Ganga (Ganges) and the Brahmaputra. Together with the Meghna River, they flow into the Ganga Delta. The Sunderbans, an extensive area of mangrove forests bordering the Bay of Bengal, supports a rich variety of flora and fauna, including the majestic Bengal tiger. Low hills dot the landscape near the northern and eastern borders with India.

History

The history of the Bangladeshi region stretches back about 4,000 years. Its name may have originated from the Bang tribe, who arrived in the area around 1000 BCE. The region has been conquered by many different empires with competing religious ideologies. From the sixteenth to the mid-nineteenth century it was an eastern outpost of the Mughal Empire. The British East India Company took control of Bengal, which included Bangladesh and adjacent parts of India in 1757. In 1857 Bengal became a British Crown colony and was part of British India until the 1947 partition of India and Pakistan. Bangladesh was an eastern province of Pakistan until it gained independence in 1971, but not before almost 3 million Bangladeshis died in a civil war.

Population/Culture

Most Bangladeshis share the same ethnicity and religion. However, in the southeastern corner of the country, in the Chittagong Hills, there are several indigenous, non-Bengali tribal groups who comprise just 2 percent of the population. Conflict has arisen in this region between the indigenous population and the influx of Bangladeshis hungry for land.

Literature, dance, and music are important elements in the country's cultural tradition, and are often displayed in popular films—over 70 Bengali-language films are produced in the country each year. Bangladesh shares the Bengali language with neighboring West Bengal state in India, but unlike India it is mostly Muslim. Language was an important difference that led to the 1971 separation of Bangladesh from Pakistan.

Administration/Government

Bangladesh is a parliamentary democracy with a president as head of state—a ceremonial position only. The head of government is the prime minister who is selected by parliament from among its members. The unicameral parliament has 345 elected members, with 45 seats reserved for women. There has been tension in recent years involving radical Islamist parties and several deadly bomb attacks against political targets.

Economy/Industry

Bangladesh is primarily an agricultural economy and rice is the dominant crop. Jute was exported for most of the twentieth century, accounting for a large percentage of export income. However, the industry declined toward the end of the century as a result of competition from synthetic materials. Since around 1980, foreign firms have established factories in Bangladesh because of the low cost of labor. The garment industry has become the largest industrial sector and now accounts for over three-quarters of export earnings. About 90 percent of the workers in garment factories are poorly paid and female.

Many social programs and economic development efforts are being put in place by some 20,000 non-government organizations (NGOs). The best known is the Grameen Bank. It lends small amounts of money to poor individuals or groups, especially women. The aim is to build social capital by lending money to the poor, enabling them to open their own businesses, invest in livestock, or otherwise become more financially independent. It has been markedly successful, and has come to be a model for other micro-credit organizations in Bangladesh and elsewhere. In 2006, the bank's founder, Muhammad Yunus and the bank were jointly awarded the Nobel Peace Prize "for their efforts to create economic and social development from below."

THE GOLDEN TRIANGLE—DHAKA'S RICKSHAWS

Each day, as many as a quarter of a million rickshaw taxis ply the streets of the nation's capital, Dhaka, earning the city the nickname, Rickshaw Capital of the World. Runners on foot no longer pull rickshaws as in the past, because they are now bicycle-powered. There are also buses, automobiles, and other motor vehicles in the city, but rickshaws comprise more than half of the city's traffic, creating a unique urban character. There are other cities in Asia that still have rickshaws, most notably nearby Kolkota (Calcutta) in India, but those in Dhaka are distinctive for their bright, colorful individual designs, as well as for their large numbers.

An estimated five million of the city's residents subsist at least partially on income derived from rickshaw driving. Rickshaws have been especially helpful for the city's poor, both as a source of employment and as cheap transport. There are periodic sweeps of unlicensed rickshaws in Dhaka, and currently there is debate about whether or not the number of rickshaw permits should be reduced. On the one hand, removing rickshaws could improve the flow of traffic and help modernize the city. On the other hand, rickshaws are non-polluting, and can still be used when monsoon rains flood city streets because their high wheels keep the cabs, and hence passengers, dry.

MILESTONE EVENTS

1600s Bengal becomes part of the Mughal Empire

1757 British East India Company gains control of Bengal

1770 Famine claims around 3 million lives

1857 Bengal becomes a British Crown colony as part of British India

1947 Partition of India and establishment of Bangladesh as East Bengal province of Pakistan

1955 East Bengal is renamed East Pakistan

1971 Bangladesh declares independence from Pakistan after civil war

1974 Pakistan recognizes Bangladesh's independence

2006 Muhammad Yunus and Grameen Bank awarded the Nobel Peace Prize jointly

BANGLADESH

Official name People's Republic of Bangladesh (Gana Prajatantri Banladesh)

Land area 51,703 square miles (133,910 km²)

Border countries India, Myanmar

Capital Dhaka

Highest point Unnamed 3,488 feet (1,063 m)

Climate Tropical; mild winter (October to March); hot, humid summer (March to June); humid, warm rainy monsoon (June to October)

Population 153,547,000

Language(s) Bangla (Bengali), English

Ethnicity Bengali 98%, tribal groups 2%

Religion Muslim 83%, Hindu 16%, other 1%

Government Parliamentary democracy

Currency Taka

Human Development Index 0.547 (ranked 140th out of 177 countries)

Above Two-thirds of the population of Bangladesh works in the agricultural sector. A man plows a rice paddy with his precious yet clearly emaciated cattle to produce the country's dominant crop.

Left Bangladeshis cross a swollen river on a simple yet effective footbridge made from thick bamboo poles strung together with jute twine.

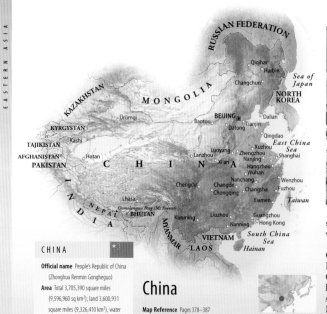

CHINA

Official name People's Republic of China (Zhonghua Renmin Gongheguo)
Area Total 3,705,390 square miles (9,596,960 sq km²); land 3,600,931 square miles (9,326,410 km²), water 104,460 square miles (270,550 km²)
Border countries Mongolia, Russia (northeast), North Korea, Vietnam, Laos, Myanmar, India, Bhutan, Nepal, Pakistan, Afghanistan, Tajikistan, Kyrgyzstan, Kazakhstan, Russia (northwest)
Capital Beijing
Highest & lowest points Mt Everest (Chomolungma) 29,035 feet (8,850 m); Moonlight Lake (Aydingkol) −505 feet (−154 m)
Climate Extremely diverse; tropical in south to subarctic in north
Population 1,330,044,605
Language(s) Standard Chinese or Mandarin (Putonghua, based on the Beijing dialect), Yue (Cantonese), Wu (Shanghainese), Minbei (Fuzhou), Minnan (Hokkien-Taiwanese), Xiang, Gan, Hakka dialects, minority languages
Ethnicity Han Chinese 91.9%; Zhuang, Uyghur, Hui, Yi, Tibetan, Miao, Manchu, Mongol, Buyi, Korean, and other nationalities 8.1%
Religion Officially atheist; Daoist (Taoist), Buddhist, Christian 3–4%, Muslim 1–2%
Government Communist state
Currency Renminbi
Human Development Index 0.777 (ranked 81st out of 177 countries)

China

Map Reference Pages 378–387

Occupying the eastern side of the Eurasian landmass, the People's Republic of China is roughly equivalent in size to Europe, but its population is nearly three times as large. China is as diverse as Europe in terms of climate, history, language, culture, and such things as cuisine. A major difference, however, is that since the second century BCE most of the core areas of eastern and central China have been united under a series of imperial dynasties.

Present-day China encompasses huge western, northern, and northeastern regions that were not part of traditional China proper. There are "two Chinas," the People's Republic of China (PRC) on the mainland and the Republic of China (ROC), which controls the Taiwan region. The former British Crown Colony of Hong Kong and the smaller Portuguese colony of Macau are now Special Administrative Regions.

Physical Geography

The climate is dominated by the great East Asian Monsoon, an inflow of warm moist southern winds producing hot wet summers in the south; an outflow of Siberian winds result in cold dry winters in the north.

The northern and western 60 percent of China consists of high mountains such as the Himalayas, high deserts such as those on the Qinghai–Tibetan Highland, sandy deserts like the Taklamakan in southern Xinjiang, and stony deserts like the Gobi in northern Inner Mongolia. Sparse grasslands cover northern Xinjiang and southern and eastern Inner Mongolia. These vast regions contain only 2 percent of the population.

China's greatest rivers are the flood-prone Yellow River in the north and the equally flood-prone, mighty Yangtze (Yangzi) that flows across the center. Other major drainages are the West River–Pearl River system in south China, and the Liao He and Sunghua–Heilong Jiang systems in Manchuria. The lowlands of these rivers, the plateau regions in the northwest and southwest, and the hilly southeast coast, comprise the remaining 40 percent of the land area and are home to the other 98 percent of the population.

History

China has the longest continuous history of any country, to at least the third millennium BCE. The numerous warring city-states of the first millennium BCE were unified by 221 BCE under the first imperial (Chin) dynasty. This soon collapsed due to excessive public works construction, including the joining up of various sections of the Great Wall. The Chin Dynasty was succeeded by the Han Dynasty (early second century BCE to late second century CE), which added northern and central Vietnam, southern Manchuria, and Korea to its domains. When the Han Dynasty collapsed, China split into three kingdoms. Another unified empire in the late sixth century became the Sui Dynasty, lasting only a few decades before being replaced by the great Tang Dynasty through to the ninth century. Again much of Vietnam and south Manchuria came under Chinese control. The following dynasty (Sung) governed a significantly smaller area. The Mongols incorporated all of China into their empire early in the fourteenth century, along with much of Central Asia, Russia, Vietnam, Yunnan, much of Tibet, and Myanmar (Burma), but lost it all within a hundred years. The Ming Dynasty expelled the Mongols and initially controlled all of China proper and southern Manchuria, but in its turn fell to Manchu invaders in the mid-seventeenth century. The Manchu Qing Dynasty also controlled eastern Siberia and Mongolia, and at one point occupied much of Central Asia and exercised suzerainty over Tibet, Burma, and Vietnam. It added Taiwan in the late seventeenth century.

Portugal established the small trading colony of Macau on the western edge of the Pearl River delta in

NEC NEC
RENESAS
中国平安
PING AN OF CHINA

Guangdong Province in the sixteenth century, and in 1841 Britain annexed a small island on the eastern edge of the delta, followed by the Kowloon Peninsula in 1860, and established the Crown Colony of Hong Kong. The neighboring New Territories, also part of Guangdong, were leased to Britain in 1897. In the nineteenth century Britain annexed Burma. France seized what is now Vietnam, Cambodia and Laos. Russia increasingly dominated the western parts of Central Asia, eventually forcing the Qing to cede territories north of the Heilong Jiang (Amur River) in the 1860s. Japan annexed Taiwan in 1895, less than ten years after it had become a province of China.

The Qing Dynasty collapsed in 1911. It was succeeded by the provisional Republic of China, but warlords controlled most of the countryside and paid little attention to the central government. The Kuomintang established a new Republic of China with the central government in the southern capital of Nanking (Nanjing) in the late 1920s, and occupied Peking (Beijing). They failed to stop the seizure of Manchuria by Japan in 1931, as they were devoting most of their energies to destroying the Chinese Communist Party (CCP). The CCP's Red Army was eventually driven to undertake the Long March, ending up at Yen'an on the Loess Plateau in Shaanxi, where Kuomintang forces could not pursue them. In 1937, a low-level civil war began, interrupted by Japan's invasion of much of eastern China. When Japan was defeated, the civil war resumed in earnest. When Beijing was occupied by the Red Army in late 1949 and the People's Republic of China established, the remnants of the Kuomintang government and its armies withdrew to Taiwan, where the Republic of China continues today.

Left Hanyu, a poet of the Tang Dynasty, described the Li River thus: "The river looks like a blue ribbon, and the mountains are emerald hairpins." The exquisite beauty of this region continues to charm visitors.

Opposite top Tiananmen Gate, or The Gate of Heavenly Peace, is the portal into the Forbidden City, which includes a mausoleum containing the remains of Mao Zedong. Tiananmen Square is the site of many major political events.

Opposite center A group of people practice tai chi, with the Shanghai skyline in the background. Tai chi chuan is an ancient martial art and moving meditation that promotes balance, health, and longevity.

Population

During the Han Dynasty, China's population reached approximately 50 million, about one-third of the world's population at the time. It roughly doubled during the Sung Dynasty due to the introduction of early-ripening rice from Vietnam. New World crops, including peanuts, maize, chilies, sweet and white potatoes, introduced via the Spanish Philippines, allowed the population to increase to 150 million by the mid-seventeenth century. Fighting associated with the change in dynasties saw the population fall by perhaps half, rising again to 150 million by the beginning of the eighteenth century.

The peace and prosperity of the early Qing Dynasty saw the population triple by 1850, to around 450 million. The Taiping Rebellion of the 1860s resulted in the death of about 50 million people. In the early twentieth century, the civil war and the Japanese invasion took a large toll. The first PRC census, held in 1952, enumerated around 580 million people, then a little less than one-quarter of the world's population.

In the first decade of the PRC, under Chairman Mao Zedong, the rural economy was increasingly collectivized culminating in the disastrous Great Leap Forward, a failed attempt to industrialize at local levels. This resulted in a famine in which around 30 million people died. The subsequent period of collectivized agriculture promoted population growth which was reinforced by a work point system that rewarded families with more sons. This lasted through the turbulent Great Proletarian Cultural Revolution until the downfall of the Gang of Four in 1976, and was abandoned under Deng Xiaoping. China's population had reached just over 1,000 million in the 1982 census. By then the One Child Policy had been implemented, and birth rates began to plummet. According to the last census in 2000, China's population was said to be "only" 1,300 million, not much changed from 1990, and now slightly more than a fifth of humanity.

Language/Culture

Almost 92 percent of the Chinese population is Han. Yet the Chinese people are far from homogenous, although they share a number of cultural principles and attitudes, mainly involving family values. There are also widespread commonalities in art, opera, cooking methods, and the writing system.

Everyone educated in the PRC has some proficiency in the national language (based on the Beijing dialect). But at home, and especially in villages, people use one of the dozen or so distinct, mutually unintelligible, Han Chinese languages. The other 8 percent or so of the population speak the languages of their minority nationalities.

There are 56 officially recognized ethnicities, including the majority Han. The other groups range in size from the nearly 15 million Zhuang in Guangxi to around 2,000 Hezhe people in northern Manchuria. Many smaller minorities, particularly in the more remote parts of southwest China, wear traditional dress, particularly the women. Tibetans generally wear traditional garments. Apart from those in poor rural areas, Han Chinese no longer wear the once so ubiquitous drab blue or khaki "Mao-style" uniform. The new urban middle class and newly rich dress in stylish modern fashions.

In the northeast, with its long cold winters and brief summers, spring wheat and maize

新宅地

Above This little girl is a member of the Miao ethnic minority group who live in the Shiqiao Village, Guizhou province. Shiqiao Village is famous for its craftspeople who practice the art of traditional papermaking.

Left Terracotta soldiers guard the first landing of the Great Wall of China, north of Beijing. The Great Wall extends 4,000 miles (6,437 km); it became a UNESCO World Heritage site in 1987.

Below Shanghai's skyscrapers and iconic buildings such as the Oriental Pearl TV Tower line the shores of the Huangpu River. This fast-growing city—a commercial hub and vital shipping port—is home to some 18 million people.

PHILIPS
Amway

Above Workers soldering components in a Shenzen factory. Once a small fishing village, Shenzen was designated a Special Economic Zone in 1979 and has since become the fastest growing city in the world.

are the dominant crops. The North China Plain, home to around 350 million people, is largely sown to winter wheat from October to April, and maize from May to September. Millet and sorghum, both drought resistant, are common on the northwestern Loess Plateau. In the north, the traditional staples are porridges and gruels made from assorted grains, wheat noodles, and steamed breads. Tibetan cuisine is based on barley. The central basins and delta of the Yangtze River have longer growing seasons in which winter wheat and rice alternate. Shanghai, in the Yangtze delta, has China's most sophisticated cuisine; in Hunan, further west, chilies are widely used. In the Red Basin of Sichuan, Sichuan peppercorns and chilies produce China's fieriest cuisine. The Cantonese, centered on Guangzhou and the Pearl River delta, are known to eat "anything that moves," but they also consume a great variety of vegetables and the semi-tropical and tropical fruits of the region. The poor people of southern China have for long subsisted mainly on sweet potatoes or manioc.

Right The giant panda *(Ailuropeda melanoleuca)*, native to southwest China, is an endangered species and symbol of the World Wildlife Federation. The Chinese government has established over 50 panda reserves in the hopes of saving this special creature from extinction.

Administration/Government

The CCP adopted Leninist-style "democratic centralism." The 2,987 members of the unicameral National People's Congress are elected by municipal, regional, and provincial people's congresses, and the People's Liberation Army, to serve five-year terms. The president and vice-president are elected by the National People's Congress; the premier is nominated by the president and is confirmed by the Congress. Congress. The CCP, the major party, also controls eight small registered parties.

Economy/Industry

There is no doubting the magnitude of economic growth and industrial development in the PRC since 1980. For example, during the 1980s the sleepy area of Shenzen just north of the Hong Kong border, where the railroad link into China was located, began to develop commercially, and by the end of the twentieth century had grown into one of the larger, and certainly one of the most prosperous, cities in the PRC, with a current population of approximately 6 million.

Since the 1990s, China has become the "factory of the world," using its abundant rural migrant labor to produce a significant percentage of the world's consumer goods, industrial parts, and machinery. Also China has transformed its cities into thriving metropolises with huge numbers of new high-rise commercial buildings and luxury apartment towers. The last ten years have seen the construction of a nationwide network of expressways that rivals the US system. Many railroads have been constructed, including the line across the Qinghai–Tibetan Highland. This line links Lhasa in Tibet to the national system.

China's foreign exchange reserves are now the largest of any country, and Chinese companies are making investments in financial and resource companies around the world. So great is the demand for electricity that the nation is now planning, and completing, multiple large coal-fired electric power plants each week. Further power-generating capacity came on line in 2006 with the completion of other large-scale developments, including the Three Gorges Dam across the Yangtze River. In 2007 energy officials agreed to purchase five third-generation nuclear reactors from the west. China has become a major importer of crude oil and petroleum products, along with coal, iron ore, and aluminum.

This rapid economic growth has not been achieved without serious social costs. Many older workers expected their "iron rice bowls" of permanent employment in state-owned factories to continue until their supported retirement. Now they are facing redundancy without meaningful pension entitlements as inefficient, first-generation plants are closing down in the older industrial centers, mainly in the north of the country.

The larger cities, particularly in the east, are home to up to 100 million rural migrants, a floating population with no legal right to an urban residence that would give them access to health care, and schooling for their children. In general, China's old people are as dependent as they have always been on their children for support, but younger generations with families of their own and living in small expensive apartments are much less willing to provide it, particularly only children married to other only children who could have four elderly parents to care for. The continued preference for boys over girls, combined with ultrasound imaging of embryos, has produced a surplus of males in younger age cohorts, with the result that 10 percent or more of young males will never be able to marry.

There are also health and environmental costs. A majority of Chinese, including many in the big cities, do not have access to a reticulated water supply, and even when they do the water is usually insufficiently purified, sometimes not at all, resulting in a high frequency of intestinal ailments. Much of the water supply in the older heavy industrial zones is contaminated by heavy metals and chemical effluent. The demands of industry, and of inefficient irrigation practices, mean that water supply of any kind is increasingly problematic for millions of people. Air pollution in the industrial cities is universally high, leading to high incidences of death from

MILESTONE EVENTS

c. 500 BCE The philosopher Confucius develops a system of moral values and responsible behavior that influences China for over 2,000 years

221 BCE Qin Dynasty establishes first strong central government

202 BCE–220 CE China becomes a powerful empire under Han Dynasty

581 Sui Dynasty reunifies China

618–907 Tang Dynasty rules during period of prosperity and cultural accomplishment

960–1279 Song Dynasty rules

1279 The Mongols control all China

1368 Ming Dynasty governs China

1644 Manchu Qing Dynasty rules China

1842 Treaty of Nanjing gives Hong Kong to Great Britain

1851 Millions die during Taiping Rebellion

1911 Qing Dynasty falls

1912 Republic of China established

1931 Japan seizes Manchuria

1934–35 Mao Zedong leads Red Army on Long March to Shaanxi

1949 The Chinese Communists establish the People's Republic of China (PRC); Mao Zedong becomes Chairman

1958 The Great Leap Forward is launched

1966–69 The Cultural Revolution disrupts daily life, government, and education

1971 China admitted to United Nations

1976 Chairman Mao Zedong dies

December 4, 1982 PRC adopts new constitution

1989 Demonstrations for democracy lead to Tiananmen Square massacre

May 12, 2008 Earthquake rocks southwestern China killing over 60,000 people and injuring 352,290; an estimated 26,221 are missing

August 2008 Beijing is the host city for the games of the XXIX Olympiad. These Olympics see the Chinese team lead the medal count

HONG KONG

Official name Hong Kong Special Administrative Region (Xianggang Tebie Xingzhengqu)

Area Total 422 square miles (1,092 km^2)

Border country People's Republic of China

Capital Hong Kong

Highest point Big Hat Mountain (Tai Mo Shan) 3,142 feet (958 m)

Climate Subtropical monsoon; cool and humid in winter, hot and rainy from spring through summer, warm and sunny in autumn

Population 7,018,636

Language(s) Cantonese (official), other Chinese dialects, English (official), other

Ethnicity Chinese 94.9%, Filipino 2.1%, other 3%

Religion Local religions 90%, Christian 10%

Government Limited democracy (special administrative region of China)

Currency Hong Kong dollar

Human Development Index 0.937 (ranked 21st out of 177 countries)

Right The magnificent karst peaks, the picturesque Yulong River, and the slow-paced, traditional way of life help make the Yangshuo region one of the loveliest areas in southern China.

Left Hong Kong harbor at dusk. A major center for international trade and finance, Hong Kong boasts the greatest number of skyscrapers in the world. From 1842 until 1997, it was a dependent territory of the United Kingdom.

respiratory disease. Crop yields around the industrial centers are now being affected by the particulate load. Basic food security is also threatened by the extent to which the most productive agricultural land is being alienated by urban growth. Along the southeast coast, the hills have been quarried for rubble to bury huge areas of rice paddies to make new factory sites where migrant laborers, many of them young women, work long hours for little pay.

Hong Kong

The Special Administrative Region of Hong Kong includes the islands of Hong Kong and Lantau, the Kowloon Peninsula, the New Territories, and about 260 small islands. The islands and the peninsula are hilly to mountainous with steep slopes, the New Territories largely low-lying. Much of the region remains undeveloped because of the difficult terrain and large areas of protected land.

Long serving as a trading post and naval base, Hong Kong was incorporated into China during the Qing Dynasty. After winning the first Opium War (1841), Britain annexed Hong Kong Island and founded Victoria City. In 1860—after winning the second Opium War—it took the Kowloon Peninsula to establish the Crown Colony of Hong Kong (Fragrant Harbour). In 1897 the neighboring New Territories were leased from China for 99 years.

Following a huge influx from Guangdong Province in the 1950s, Hong Kong grew as an international transshipment port, and developed light industries producing mainly consumer goods. As the PRC opened up to foreign investment in the 1980s, the first to take advantage were Hong Kong merchants and industrialists, who brought rapid prosperity to the colony.

Today, Hong Kong has a capitalist economy built on free markets, low taxation, and a policy of government non-intervention. It is an important center for international finance and trade, with services accounting for over 90 percent of GDP.

When it became clear that China intended to resume control over the New Territories when the 99-year lease expired, it was also clear that Kowloon and Hong Kong would not be viable without them. The New Territories contained huge apartment complexes and many of the factories and other facilities that the colony's wealth depended on. So, in 1997 Hong Kong became part of the PRC as a Special Administrative Region. The border with Guangdong Province is not completely open, but thousands of commuters from Hong Kong cross daily to the Special Economic Zone of Shenzen to work.

Macau

The recorded history of the Special Administrative Region of Macau can be traced back to the Qing Dynasty. Portugal established a small trading colony on the western edge of the Pearl River delta in the sixteenth century. Originally it consisted of three small islands—Macau, Taipa, and Coloane—but Macau Island is now linked to the mainland by a sandy isthmus, and the other islands are linked to Macau and each other by causeways. Portugal handed Macau back to the People's Republic of China in 1999, two years after Hong Kong was handed back to the Chinese government by the UK.

More than four centuries of mixed Portuguese and Chinese presence have left this tiny region with an extraordinary collection of events, holidays, and festivals from both cultures, and a style of cuisine that blends Cantonese and Portuguese influences. The historic center of Macau, listed as a World Heritage site by UNESCO in 2005, includes monuments, several fortresses, an ancient palace, historic buildings and churches, and public squares that bear witness to the unique co-existence of eastern and western culture, including the striking traditional Portuguese wave-patterned tiled pavement of Largo do Senado (Senado Square).

Macau (and Hong Kong) largely escaped the tumultuous events of the first 30 years of the PRC's existence. Macau's economy has long been based on casino gambling, and it is a major Chinese tourist destination because most gambling is prohibited in other parts of the country. Additional economic activities include textile and garment manufacturing, banking, and other financial services—Macau is an offshore financial center, tax haven, and free port with no foreign exchange controls.

MACAU

Official name Macau Special Administrative Region; Aomen Tebie Xingzhengqu (Chinese); Regiao Administrativa Especial de Macau (Portuguese)
Land area 11 square miles (28.2 km²)
Border country People's Republic of China
Capital Macau
Highest point Coloane Peak (Coloane Alto) 565½ feet (172.4 m)
Climate Subtropical; marine with cool winters, warm summers
Population 460,823
Language(s) Cantonese, Hokkien, Mandarin, other Chinese dialects, other
Ethnicity Chinese 95.7%, Macanese (mixed Portuguese and Asian ancestry) 1%, other 3.3%
Religion Buddhist 50%, Roman Catholic 15%, none and other 35%
Government Limited democracy (special administrative region of China)
Currency Macanese pataca
Human Development Index Not rated separately from People's Republic of China

Left Young people perform the dragon dance in Macau. The dragon is a sacred symbol in Chinese culture and is believed to bring health, power, and good fortune. Chinese people sometimes refer to themselves as "descendants of the dragon."

Below European-designed Senado Square in Macau was built in 1784, and was the municipal center of the Portuguese government. The square is paved in a mosaic of brightly colored stones, and is the center of community activity.

SANTA CASA DA MISERICORDIA

Above The Chiang Kai Shek memorial is the focal point of the National Theater and National Concert Hall, Taiwan. The performing arts center was commissioned following the death of Chiang Kai Shek in 1975, and completed in 1987.

Above right "Taipei 101" is 101 stories high, and was designed according to feng shui principles. Completed in 2001, it was the tallest building in the world until the completion of the Burj Dubai in the United Arab Emirates in 2007.

Republic of China (Taiwan)

When Portuguese sailors first saw the island of Taiwan in 1590, its wild, thickly forested mountainous beauty led them to name it Ilha Formosa, meaning "beautiful island," a name by which it was long known in the west.

Physical Geography

Taiwan is about 190 miles (300 km) from north to south and 95 miles (150 km) from east to west. The thinly populated eastern two-thirds is dominated by the rugged volcanic peaks of the Chungyang Shan Mountains. The densely populated western third, facing the Taiwan Strait, consists of hills and alluvial plains deposited by many small streams and rivers flowing from the mountains. The subtropical marine climate is characterized by summer and winter monsoons. The western section is a transportation corridor, crowded with rail lines and fast-moving expressways.

REPUBLIC OF CHINA (TAIWAN)

Official name Republic of China; commonly Taiwan
Land area 12,456 square miles (32,260 km²)
Border countries None
Capital Taipei
Highest point Yu Shan 12,966 feet (3,952 m)
Climate Tropical, marine
Population 22,858,872
Language(s) Mandarin Chinese, Taiwanese (Min), Hakka dialects
Ethnicity Hakka 84%, mainland Chinese 14%, aboriginal 2%
Religion Buddhist/Taoist 93%, Christian 4.5%, other 2.5%
Government Multi-party democracy
Currency Taiwan dollar
Human Development Index Not available

History

The ancestors of the island's aboriginal population, with ancient Malay and Polynesian origins, settled there about 4,000 years ago. Thirty-eight years of Dutch colonial rule commenced in 1624. Han Chinese from the nearby Fujian coast came to Taiwan as laborers to work on Dutch sugar plantations. Many settled permanently, often taking local wives, and were followed by many more. Incorporated into China after the Dutch were ousted in 1661, Taiwan became a province in 1887. After China's defeat in the First Sino-Japanese War (1895), Taiwan and the Penghu Islands were ceded to Japan and remained a Japanese colony until the end of World War II.

When the Kuomintang (KMT) was defeated by the Red Army in 1949, some government departments and Nationalist Chinese fled to Taiwan, forming the Republic of China (ROC). The Kuomintang also held some small islands off the coast of Fujian Province, principally Quemoy (Chinmen) and Matsu, along with the smaller Penghu Islands (Pescadores) in the Taiwan Strait, together making up the Taiwan Region of China. The ROC claims all the mainland provinces, Mongolia and parts of Siberia. The one thing that the PRC and ROC agree on is that Taiwan is part of China; they disagree over which is the legitimate government.

Population/Culture

Most of Taiwan's population is descended from the Han Chinese who migrated to the island centuries ago. They are referred to as native Taiwanese, distinguishing them from "mainlanders" or "new residents"—around 2 million post-civil war evacuees and their descendants. Fertility rates are declining as the economy and the cities continue to grow. Most aboriginal or First Nation Taiwanese live in the mountains.

Much of the indigenous inhabitants' cultural traditions have been altered by Taiwan's long history of Chinese occupation, while over one hundred years of political separation from mainland China has led to distinctive Taiwanese cultural traditions in areas such as cuisine, opera, and music.

Administration/Government

In the 1990s, Taiwan was transformed into an open democratic society through the popular election of a president and representatives. The unicameral Legislative Yuan has 113 seats, consisting of 73 elected district members, 34 members elected on the basis of the proportion of votes received by participating political parties, and six aboriginal representatives; all serve four-year terms.

The Kuomintang lost control of the government for the first time in 2000, and although they regained it in early 2008, are now only one of several parties. The primary political issue at present is whether Taiwan should seek eventual reunification with the "other China" or work toward an eventual declaration of independence. This is of tremendous interest and importance to the PRC, which has threatened military action whenever those who favor Taiwan's independence seem to be making headway.

Industry/Economy

During the Korean War and ensuing Cold War period, Taiwan was seen in the west as a bastion of "Free China" and received large amounts of American military and civil aid. One of the most successful post-World War II civilian aid programs, it laid the foundations for Taiwan's present prosperity by conducting meaningful land reform, establishing agricultural extension services, and promoting rural electrification. An import-substitution program supporting light industry began to show results in the 1960s. By the 1980s the economy had grown enormously and Taiwan was taking a lead in supplying inexpensive manufactured and electronic goods to world markets. Today the ROC is one of the members of the "Four Asian Tigers" (the others being Singapore, South Korea, and Hong Kong).

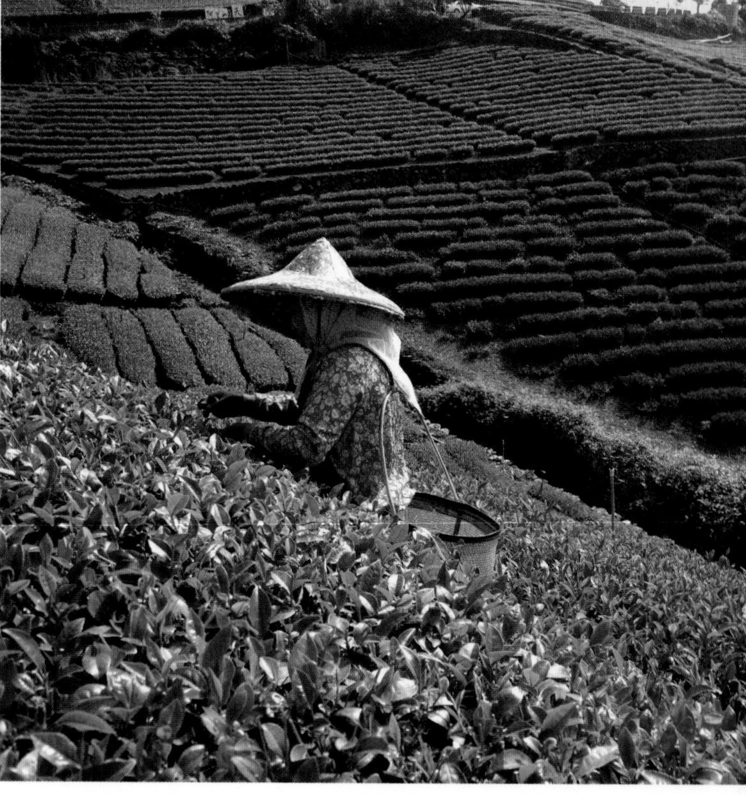

Right Tea picking in Taiwan. Native to Taiwan, tea has been grown commercially since the mid-1800s. Once a major export for the island, most teas are now grown for the domestic market.

MONGOLIA 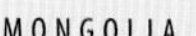

Official name Mongolia
Land area 603,906 square miles (1,564,116 km²)
Border countries Russia, China
Capital Ulan Bator (Ulaanbaatar)
Highest & lowest points Nayramadlin Orgil (Huyten Orgil) 14,350 feet (4,374 m); Hoh Nuur 1,699 feet (518 m)
Climate Desert, continental
Population 2,951,786
Language(s) Khalkha Mongol, Turkic, Russian
Ethnicity Mongol 95%, Kazakh 4%, Chinese 1%
Religion Lamaist 50%, Shamanist/Christian 6%, Muslim 4%, none 40%
Government Mixed parliamentary/presidential
Currency Tugrik
Human Development Index 0.700 (ranked 114th out of 177 countries)

Left With an average elevation of over 5,000 feet (1,524 m), Mongolia—the "land of the great blue sky"—is classed as one of the world's highest countries. Its extensive steppes provide grazing for horses, oxen, sheep, camels, and goats.

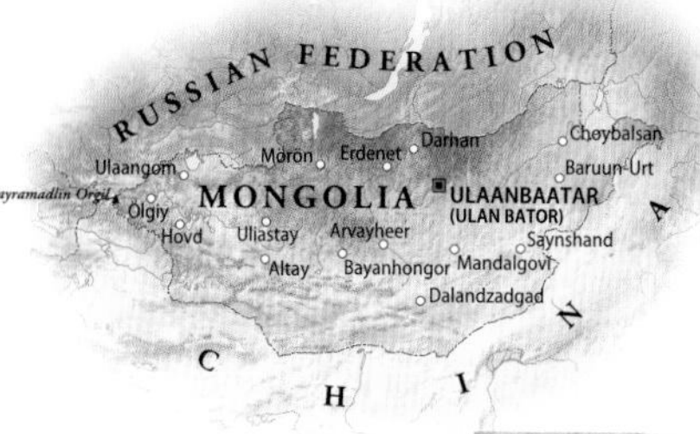
RUSSIAN FEDERATION
Ulaangom
Moron
Erdenet
Darhan
Choybalsan
Baruun-Urt
Nayramadlin Orgil
Olgiy
Hovd
Uliastay
Arvayheer
MONGOLIA
ULAANBAATAR (ULAN BATOR)
Saynshand
Altay
Bayanhongor
Mandalgovi
Dalandzadgad
CHINA

Mongolia

Map Reference Pages 382–385

Located in Northern Asia, Mongolia is a vast land with Russia to the north and China to the south. It is the largest landlocked country in the world, and has the lowest population density of any sovereign state.

Physical Geography

Mongolia's topography varies considerably, from taiga to steppe, and desert to mountain. There are three mountain ranges and high plateaus in the west and southwest. The highest and most remote is the Altai chain in the west. The Khangai Range is the source of the longest river, the Selenge, which eventually empties into Lake Baikal in Russia. Beyond the Khentii mountains, east of the capital, Ulan Bator, lie immense steppes and plains.

In the south, a semi-desert plain adjoins the stony Gobi Desert, a difficult environment that nevertheless provides a habitat for rare animals such as the mazalai (brown bear).

The climate is extreme continental, with the average temperature for much of the year freezing or below, although summer temperatures in the capital can reach 91°F (33°C).

History

Prior to the twelfth century, the Mongolian people were a loose collection of nomadic tribes grazing sheep, camels, and horses on the northern steppes. This changed radically with the rise of one of history's most successful conquerors, Chinggis Khan, who by the early 1200s had welded the tribes into a single confederation. By 1211 Chinggis Khan's army had invaded China, and within a few years, he had expanded his empire to the Caucasus mountains. His successors completed the construction of the largest land empire the world has ever seen, stretching all the way from China to the Middle East and Russia.

By the fifteenth century most of the massive Mongol empire had been absorbed into other states. The remote and landlocked steppe homeland of the Mongols lost influence as larger powers, principally Russia and China, expanded at its margins.

The Mongolian People's Republic, a communist state, was declared in 1924, and for most of the twentieth century was a satellite of the Soviet Union. In 1990 popular demonstrations by thousands of Mongolians led to multiparty democratic elections, and the dismantling of the communist state.

Population/Culture

The oldest Mongol traditions are rooted in the nomadic way of life that many still follow. Skills such as horseback riding and accuracy with a bow and arrow are greatly admired. Although much of the population now lives in urban areas, each summer, a national competition draws contestants from all over the country to showcase their expertise in horse racing, archery, and Mongolian wrestling.

Like many nomadic peoples, the Mongols recorded their history in oral epics. These were recounted by bards known as *khurchins*, who accompanied themselves on the *tovshuur*, a stringed lute, or on the *morin khuur*, Mongolia's famous horse-head violin. This two-stringed instrument features an intricate horse's head carved into the top of the fretboard—the bow is made from horsehair. A unique Mongolian musical form is the throat singing tradition known as *hoomii*, which involves producing two simultaneous tones.

Administration/Government

In 1990, the Mongolian constitution was amended to allow for parties other than the Mongolian Communist Party to field election candidates, and the first fully democratic elections were held. Over the next three years a new constitution was approved that enshrines basic human rights. The head of government is the prime minister, who is appointed by the president. The president serves as the head of state and chief of the country's armed forces. Both the prime minister and president serve four-year terms. Representatives are elected by direct vote to a unicameral body called the State Great Hural.

MILESTONE EVENTS

1211 Chinggis Khan attacks the Chinese Empire
1227 Death of Chinggis Khan and division of the Mongol Empire
1368 Collapse of the Mongol Yuan Dynasty in China
1500s Lamaism becomes dominant faith in Mongolia
1911 Outer Mongolia declares independence
1919 Chinese occupy Outer Mongolia (present-day Mongolia)
1921 Chinese driven out of the country
1924 Mongolian People's Republic proclaimed
1924–1937 Persecution of Buddhists and destruction of monasteries
1937 Prime Minister P. Genden executed in Moscow
July, 1941 Former Prime Minister Amar tortured and killed in Moscow
1952 Moscow-appointed Prime Minister Choibalsan, the "bloody butcher," dies in Moscow of poisoning
1990 Massive protests end political monopoly of communist party
November, 2005 President George W. Bush is the first incumbent US president to visit Mongolia

Economy/Industry

Economic reforms leading to a free-market economy were introduced throughout the 1990s. At the time of the establishment of the Mongolian People's Republic in 1924, the country's economy was almost entirely agrarian-based, with much of the population engaged in animal husbandry, and a smaller percentage raising a limited number of food crops, mostly wheat and barley.

The communist regime tried to develop industries in the decades between 1930 and 1990, but with limited success, and the Mongolian economy remained heavily dependent on subsidies from the Soviet Union. Following the fall of the communist regime in 1990, free market reforms were introduced, and since 2000 the economy has experienced significant growth. Much of the growth is due to foreign investment in the mining sector, especially in copper and gold, which are major exports.

Above The colorful interior of a Mongolian tent, known here as a ger and elsewhere as a yurt. Many Mongolians are semi-nomadic, and this type of portable dwelling can be easily taken apart and reassembled.

Left A Mongolian "cowboy" rounds up horses in the Gobi National Park. Horses are an intrinsic part of Mongolian life—a nomad's wealth is measured by the number of horses he owns. The national beverage is fermented mare's milk, known as airag.

NORTH KOREA

Official name Democratic People's Republic of Korea (Choson-minjujuui-inmin-konghwaguk)
Land area 46,490 square miles (120,410 km²)
Border countries China, South Korea, Russia
Capital Pyongyang
Highest point Paektu-san 9,003 feet (2,744 m)
Climate Temperate, rainfall concentrated in summer
Population 23,479,000
Language(s) Korean
Ethnicity Korean 99.9%, Chinese and Japanese 0.1%
Religion Traditionally Buddhist and Confucianist, some Christian and the syncretic, nationalist religious movement called Chondogyo (Religion of the Heavenly Way)
Government Communist state/one-man dictatorship
Currency North Korean won
Human Development Index Not available

CHINA
RUSSIAN FEDERATION
Najin
Paektu-san
Ch'ŏngjin
Hyesan
Kanggye
Ch'osan
Kimch'aek
Sea of Japan
Sinŭiju
Hamhŭng
Hŭngnam
NORTH KOREA
Wŏnsan
Korea Bay
P'YŎNGYANG
Namp'o
Songnim
Sariwŏn
Haeju
Kaesŏng
SOUTH KOREA

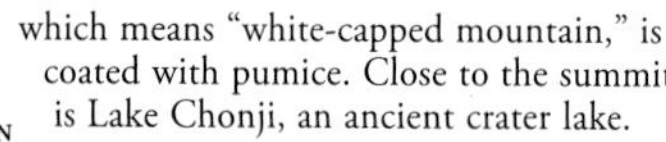

North Korea

Map Reference Pages 386–387

The Democratic People's Republic of Korea or, more commonly, North Korea, is bordered by China in the north and South Korea in the south. To the west is the Yellow Sea, and to the east the Sea of Japan. North and South Korea separated along ideological lines in 1945, and split permanently in 1953 as a result of the Korean War.

Physical Geography

Much of North Korea is rugged and mountainous, with relatively little arable land. The highest peak, Paektu-san, rises above the Kaema Plateau in the northeast, an area known as the "roof of Korea." Paektu-san, which means "white-capped mountain," is coated with pumice. Close to the summit is Lake Chonji, an ancient crater lake.

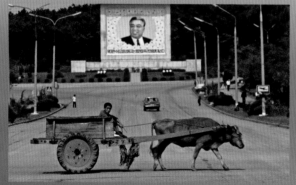

History

The history of North Korea parallels that of South Korea until the end of World War II, as the two were united until then. Three kingdoms dominated Korea from the first to the fifth century. The north of the peninsula was ruled by the Goryeo Dynasty (918–1392), for which Korea is named. The Joseon Dynasty (also spelled Chosun) succeeded Goreyo and ruled until the Japanese occupied the country in 1910. Japanese rule was harsh. Millions of Koreans were conscripted into forced labor, and some 200,000 women were forced into sexual slavery by the Japanese military.

After World War II, Korea became a battleground for conflicting geopolitical ambitions between the United States, and the Soviet Union and its Chinese ally. The Korean War (1950–1953) resulted in the division of the peninsula into two hostile nations. Several million people were killed, and cities and infrastructure were destroyed.

Population/Culture

Almost all the inhabitants are ethnic Korean. North Koreans still celebrate many aspects of their traditional culture, but increasingly the emphasis has been on a cult of personality centered on the late Kim Il-Sung and his son Kim Jong-Il. The most visible display of glorification is at the mass games, where thousands of people give spectacular synchronized dance performances in honor of the two leaders.

Administration/Government

North Korea is a communist, one-man dictatorship initiated by Kim Il-Sung. Leader of the country from 1948 until his death in 1994, Kim Il-Sung kept tight control over economic and political policies. He imposed a complex nationalistic ideology of self-sufficiency called the Juche Idea, which has led to long-term malnutrition and devastating famines. In 1998, four years after his death, Kim Il-Sung was proclaimed "eternal president."

The current leader is Kim Il-Sung's son, Kim Jong-Il, referred to as Dear Leader. Despite earlier promises that he would not do so, Kim Jong-Il made North Korea into a nuclear power. Human rights groups criticize North Korea for imprisoning political opponents. Kim Jong-Il is also criticized from abroad for his eccentric and lavish lifestyle despite the country's crushing poverty.

Above right A traditional North Korean farmhouse set in a grove of deciduous trees. Rural existence is often bleak, with scant resources limiting real agricultural growth.

Below A cart trundles through the streets of Pyongyang under the watchful eye of former president and cult figure Kim Il-Sung, the "Eternal President."

Economy/Industry

North Korea's per capita income is among the lowest in the world. The economy is state run, and in accordance with the military first policy espoused by Kim Jong-Il, industrial and collectivized agricultural production concentrate on the needs of the military. This has led to deep-rooted economic problems as well as long-term food shortages—in the 1990s as many as 2 million North Koreans starved to death as the result of famine. After the fall of communism and the dismantling of the USSR, Soviet aid disappeared. The government now accepts development aid and loans chiefly from South Korea and China.

MILESTONE EVENTS

100 BCE Three Kingdoms are founded
918 CE Goryeo Dynasty established
1392 Joseon Dynasty founded
1910 Japanese occupation begins
1945 End of Japanese rule and division of Korea
1948 Kim Il-Sung assumes leadership of North Korea
1950–1953 Korean War; division of Korea is cemented
1994 Death of Kim Il-Sung, Kim Jong-Il assumes leadership
1996 Severe flooding followed by terrible famine
1998 Kim Il-Sung declared "eternal president"
2000 North and South Korea summit meeting
2003 North Korea withdraws from the Nuclear Non-Proliferation Treaty
October, 2006 North Korea becomes a nuclear power
February, 2007 Pyongyang agrees to shut down main nuclear reactor in exchange for fuel aid
May, 2007 Trains pass the North-South border, the first time in over 50 years
February, 2008 Cultural diplomacy: New York Philharmonic performs in Pyongyang

NORTH KOREA
Ch'unch'on
Ullŭng-do
SŎUL (SEOUL)
P'uch'ŏn
Inch'ŏn
Wŏnju
Suwŏn
Ch'ungju
Sea of Japan
Ch'ŏngju
Andong
Yellow Sea
Taejŏn
P'ohang
SOUTH KOREA
Kunsan
Taegu
Ulsan
Masan
Kwangju
Pusan
Mokp'o
JAPAN
Cheju
Halla-san
Cheju-do

South Korea

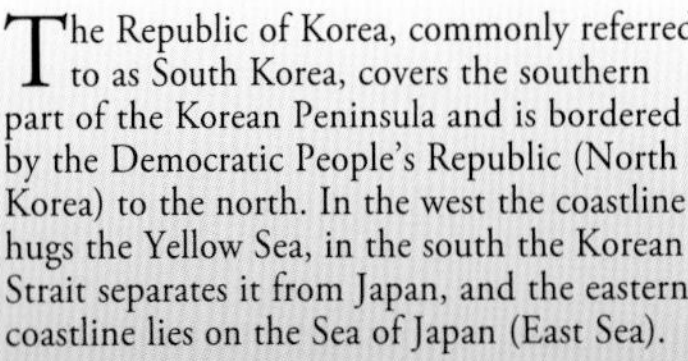

Map Reference Pages 386–387

The Republic of Korea, commonly referred to as South Korea, covers the southern part of the Korean Peninsula and is bordered by the Democratic People's Republic (North Korea) to the north. In the west the coastline hugs the Yellow Sea, in the south the Korean Strait separates it from Japan, and the eastern coastline lies on the Sea of Japan (East Sea).

Physical Geography

About 70 percent of South Korea is hilly or mountainous. At 6,398 feet (1,950 m) Mt Hallasan, an extinct volcano, is the highest peak. The remainder of the country is mostly coastal plain south and west and is densely settled. Seoul, the nation's capital, and Inchon, the nearby ocean port, are especially crowded and form one of the largest urban concentrations in the world. The Han and Nakdong are the longest rivers. The climate is temperate; the average temperature in winter is 23°F (–5°C), and in summer 79°F (26°C), varying according to altitude.

History

The nation's legendary founder, Dangun, is believed to have ruled around 2333 BCE. Much later Korea was divided into three kingdoms: Silla, Gogureyeo, and Baekje. Eventually, Silla became the most powerful, defeating the other two, ousting the Chinese and unifying the peninsula (671 CE). The Goryeo Dynasty replaced the Silla Kingdom in 918 and lasted until 1392. The Joseon Dynasty (also Chosun) succeeded the Goryeo, and ruled until the Japanese occupation began in 1910. Seoul became the capital in 1394. Under King Sejong the Great (1418–1450), Confucianism flourished and many creative advances were made. Because of an isolationist policy intended to protect the country from foreign domination, Joseon Korea was called the "Hermit Kingdom."

Japanese occupation lasted until the end of World War II; it was a brutal regime opposed by Korean resistance movements. Forced labor and sexual slavery were common, and the Korean language was suppressed.

The Korean tragedy continued after World War II when it became a Cold War battleground for the USA (together with UN troops), and the Soviet Union and its Chinese allies. The Korean War (1950–1953) resulted in the division of the peninsula near the 38th parallel, with a demilitarized zone (DMZ). Millions were killed, and there was great destruction of cities and infrastructure, particularly in the north. The two sides still face each other across the DMZ, and the USA is still there—around 25,000 US troops are deployed in South Korea.

Population/Culture

With the exception of a small community of Chinese, South Korea is one of the most ethnically homogenous nations in the world. Some 100 million people worldwide speak the Korean language, a distinctive tongue and probably a member of the Ural-Altaic family of languages, with many borrowings from Chinese. Korean is written with a novel script called Hangul, introduced by Sejong the Great.

Administration/Government

The government of South Korea is a democratic republic. The president, the head of state, is elected by popular vote, and appoints the prime minister, the head of government, and deputy prime ministers. The 299 members of the unicameral National Assembly are elected by popular vote. The justices of the Supreme Court and Constitutional Court are appointed by the president.

MILESTONE EVENTS

671 CE Silla Kingdom gains control of the Korean Peninsula

918 Establishment of the Goryeo Dynasty

1392 Start of the Joseon Dynasty

1910 Japanese occupation begins

1945 End of Japanese rule; division of Korea

1950–1953 Korean War

1980 Gwangju Massacre by government troops

1988 Seoul hosts Summer Olympics

2000 Leaders of North and South Korea hold summit meeting in Pyongyang; President Kim Dae Jung awarded Nobel Peace Prize

Economy/Industry

South Korea has undergone an amazing transformation—from a poor agricultural society to highly urbanized and industrialized—accomplished through close cooperation between the government and giant capitalist conglomerates called *chaebol*. Post-war industrial production emphasized garment making and textiles, later shifting to iron, steel, and chemicals. South Korea is now changing into a white-collar, post-industrial society.

The Sunshine Policy

Almost all Koreans, whether they live in the capitalist South, the communist North, or abroad, desire reunification. South Korea's current approach to relations with the North is referred to as the Sunshine Policy. It was first articulated in 1998 by President Kim Dae Jung, who argued that threats against North Korea by the USA and South Korea would only lead to a military buildup. He advocated instead, cooperative projects and help for the impoverished North Koreans. In 2000, Kim traveled to Pyongyang, capital of the North, for high-level talks with North Korean leader, Kim Jong-Il. Shortly after, Kim Dae Jung won the Nobel Peace Prize.

Above left Glowing paper lanterns hang from trees outside the Chogyesa Buddhist temple in Seoul, the main temple of the large Chogye sect.

SOUTH KOREA

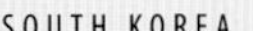

Official name Republic of Korea (Taehan-min'guk)
Land area 37,911 square miles (98,190 km²)
Border countries North Korea
Capital Seoul (Sŏul)
Highest point Mt Hallasan 6,398 feet (1,950 m)
Climate Temperate, with rainfall heavier in summer than winter
Population 49,233,000
Language(s) Korean, English
Ethnicity Korean 100% (except for 20,000 Chinese)
Religion None 46%, Buddhist 26%, Christian 26%, Confucianist 1%, other 1%
Government Republic
Currency South Korean won
Human Development Index 0.921 (ranked 26th out of 177 countries)

Above A musician plays a bamboo flute called a *daegeum* at Korea House, Myeong-dong, Seoul. This instrument was traditionally used for folk and royal court music.

Below A panoramic view of downtown Seoul, South Korea's capital, taken from Namsan Park. Seoul is one of the world's most populous cities, with more than ten million inhabitants.

Above Skyscrapers in Nishi-Shinjuku in Tokyo's business district are specially designed to withstand the effects of severe earthquakes.

JAPAN

Official name Japan (Nippon-koku)
Land area 145,882 square miles (377,835 km²)
Border countries None
Capital Tokyo
Highest & lowest points Mt Fuji 12,388 feet (3,776 m); Hachiro-gata −13 feet (−4 m)
Climate Tropical to cool temperate
Population 127,288,000
Language(s) Japanese
Ethnicity Japanese 98.5%, other 1.5% the most numerous of which are Koreans, Chinese, and Brazilians
Religion Observing both Shinto and Buddhism 84%, other 16%
Government Constitutional monarchy with a parliamentary government
Currency Yen
Human Development Index 0.953 (ranked 8th out of 177 countries)

RUSSIAN FEDERATION
Hokkaidō
Sapporo
Kushiro
Sea of Japan
Morioka
Akita
Honshū
Sendai
Niigata
JAPAN
Nagano
Maebashi
Kanazawa
TŌKYŌ
Yokohama
Matsue
Kobe
Kyōto
Shizuoka
Okayama
Ōsaka
Izu-shotō
SOUTH KOREA
Hiroshima
Wakayama
Kitakyūshū
Kōchi
Fukuoka
Shikoku
Nagasaki
Kyūshū
Kagoshima
PACIFIC OCEAN
East China Sea
Ogasawara-shotō (Bonin Islands)
Kazan-rettō (Volcano Islands)
Naha
Nansei-shotō (Ryukyu Islands)
Taiwan

Japan

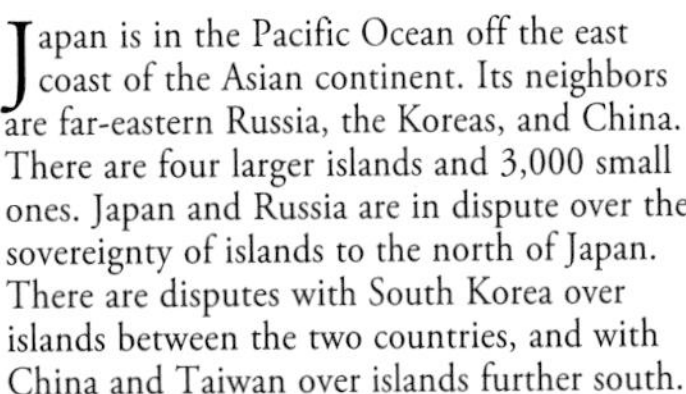

Map Reference Pages 386–387

Japan is in the Pacific Ocean off the east coast of the Asian continent. Its neighbors are far-eastern Russia, the Koreas, and China. There are four larger islands and 3,000 small ones. Japan and Russia are in dispute over the sovereignty of islands to the north of Japan. There are disputes with South Korea over islands between the two countries, and with China and Taiwan over islands further south.

Physical Geography

About 75 percent of the terrain is mountainous. Many islands have volcanoes, about 80 of them active. Mt Fuji on Honshu has been dormant for about 300 years. Honshu is the largest island and home to 80 percent of the population. Hokkaido was not settled until the nineteenth century and is still regarded as somewhat of a frontier, although the city of Sapporo is one of Japan's bigger metropolises.

History

The earliest culture is believed to be the Jomon, which dates from 14,000 to 300 BCE. Yayoi culture (300 BCE to 300 CE) brought agriculture from a rice-growing area in Asia. The origin of the Japanese nation specifically is traced to the fifth century CE, when the Yamato gained control of the islands.

Many cultural influences came from China and the Koreas, notably Buddhism. Japan's first permanent capital was Nara in south-central Honshu. Japan's emperors later ruled from nearby Kyoto, while warlords fought over control of various provinces. Unification came in 1590 and led to rule by the powerful Tokugawa family line of shoguns.

Under the shoguns, Japan was essentially closed to the world from 1600 until the collapse of their rule in 1868. By the early twentieth century, Japan had become an industrial nation and was powerful militarily, occupying Formosa (Republic of China), Korea, and southern Sakhalin. Expansion and militarism continued with the occupation of Chinese Manchuria in 1931 and the invasion further into China in 1937. On December 7, 1941, Japanese planes attacked the US naval base in Honolulu, Hawaii, bringing the USA and its allies into full-scale war against the country. Japan surrendered on August 15, 1945, soon after the atomic bombings of Hiroshima and Nagasaki by the USA.

A democratic and pacifist constitution was put into effect in 1947 and Allied occupation ended in 1952. Rebuilding emphasized industrial production. By the 1970s, Japan was on its way to becoming the world's second-largest economy, sustained by a highly profitable export economy. Urban areas remain crowded, but living conditions, environmental quality, and services are now much improved.

Population/Culture

Japan's culture is an interesting blend of long-standing traditions and newer styles, often from abroad. Early cultural influences arrived centuries ago from China and the Korean peninsula; later influences came from Europe and North America. A Japanese wedding, for example, could be a traditional Shinto-style ceremony in wedding kimonos or a western, Christian-type ceremony, even though neither bride nor groom is Christian. The Shinto ceremony is held in a Shinto shrine, with prayers to sacred spirits called *kami* and ritual sips of rice wine, officiated over by a Shinto priest. The western ceremony is staged in a wedding hall designed to resemble a church and performed by a mock priest or minister. The bride wears the traditional white wedding dress and the groom a stylish tuxedo, and they cut a multi-tiered wedding cake at the post-ceremony reception. Some couples have both types of ceremony in front of the same guests on the same day.

Above Japan's bullet trains, or Shinkansen, can reach speeds of up to 275 miles per hour (443 km/h). A network of these high-speed trains links Tokyo with most major cities on Honshu, and Fukuoka on the island of Kyushu.

EARTHQUAKES

Japan is located at the intersection of several of the globe's tectonic plates and is one of the most earthquake-prone regions of the world. Small tremors are common and there are occasional disasters. In 1995, the Great Hanshin Earthquake killed 6,000 people in the city of Kobe, while in 1923 more than 100,000 people died in the Tokyo-Yokohama area from the Great Kanto Earthquake and its resultant fires. Another giant shake could happen at any time at any location in the country. Consequently, Japan takes great care to educate its citizenry about disaster preparedness and leads the world in earthquake-safe construction technology.

Left Ember-red maples frame the riverbanks as a boat takes a leisurely punt down the river in Ranzan, Kyoto.

MILESTONE EVENTS

14,000 BCE Start of the Jomon Period

300 BCE Start of the Yayoi Period

400 CE Rise of the Yamato clan

712 Completion of the Kojiki chronicles

794 Imperial capital moves to Heiankyo (Kyoto)

1185–1333 Kamakura Period of rule by shoguns

1590 Unification of Japan's warring provinces by Toyotomi Hideyoshi

1603 Start of the Tokugawa Shogunate and Edo (Tokyo) as capital

1854 Arrival of "Black Ships" commanded by US Admiral Perry forces the opening of Japan

1868 End of the Shogunate and start of the Meiji Era of modernization

1894–1895 First Sino-Japanese War results in Japanese colonial expansion

1904–1905 Russo-Japanese War

1937 Japan invades China

1941 Japan attacks Pearl Harbor

1945 Atomic bombings of Hiroshima and Nagasaki; Japan surrenders

1952 End of Allied occupation of Japan

1964 Tokyo hosts summer Olympic Games

1980s Japan enjoys bubble economy

Similar observations can be made about other aspects of Japanese life. For example, for many city dwellers, any given meal could be meat or fish served with traditional staples of rice or noodles, or it could be a hamburger, fried chicken, or pizza from a fast-food restaurant. Likewise, we can think of two national sports. One is sumo, a tradition-rich wrestling contest with deep Shinto roots, and the other is baseball, a game imported from the US.

Administration/Government

Since the end of World War II, Japan's hereditary emperor has had symbolic duties only and government power has been with the democratically elected national Diet and a prime minister who is chosen from the majority party. For some decades, the Liberal Democratic Party has been the most powerful in the country; it has worked closely with Japanese industry and companies in order to advance national economic growth.

Economy/Industry

Japan is lacking many basic resources for an industrial society and imports much of what it needs from around the world. Oil comes from the Middle East, Africa, and Southeast Asia; timber comes from North America, Indonesia, and other countries; and food and mineral resources are imported from much of the world, including Australia.

To pay for the imports, Japan has developed its famous export economy that depends on high-quality products and the latest technology for markets worldwide. Japanese brand names are seen across the globe: Toyota, Sony, Nissan, and Toshiba are just a few of the best-known examples. Because of the high cost of labor in Japan, manufacturing and assembly are increasingly being performed in China, Southeast Asia, and other areas, while management, research and development, and other white-collar aspects of the economy stay at home. Japan's biggest metropolis, Tokyo, is especially noted for its concentration of corporate headquarters, financial institutions, and other companies that support Japan's manufacturing empire.

Rice and other crops are grown in Japan's countryside, to supplement food imports. Government subsidies for agriculture and protections against imports are common. Japan's fishing industry is one of the biggest and most advanced technologically in the world, and now accounts for approximately 15 percent of the world's catch.

Ageing Society and Immigration

Japan is the world's prime example of an ageing society. The combination of long life expectancy, now at about 82 years (85 years for women), and low birth rates, has resulted in an unusually large proportion of elderly people. Nearly one in five Japanese is aged 65 or older, but that proportion is expected to rise to about one in three by 2030.

This will mean increasing shortages in the future in a labor force that is already too small, and ever more financial strain on the already overburdened system of social security and services for the elderly. Without intervention the population of Japan as a whole is likely to decline from today's peak of 127 million to below 100 million after 2050.

The debates about how to ameliorate the situation are among the most urgent in Japan's public policy arena. Already, there have been tax increases to pay for the rising cost of caring for an older population, as well as calls to raise the customary retirement age. Many older people have re-entered the workforce part-time to stay active, as well as for financial support. There are proposals to increase fertility by offering women more public support for the care and education of offspring, as well as serious discussion about encouraging Japanese couples to become more amorous.

Other countries faced with similar demographic pressures have addressed their problems by permitting greater immigration from abroad. Japan, however, has been largely unwilling to allow much immigration. Of all the nations in the world, its population is among the most ethnically homogenous. Many Japanese people think that an infusion of foreigners would dilute their culture and increase social problems. It is not uncommon, for example, for people in Japan to blame the country's small population of foreigners for a disproportionate share of rising crime rates.

As Japan debates the merits of immigration, it has made provisions for foreign citizens of Japanese extraction to enter the country more easily and find work. As a result, some of the nation's leading industrial areas now have quite a few Japanese-Brazilians and other South Americans descended from earlier generations of emigrants from Japan working in factories, construction, and other difficult occupations. There are also increasing numbers of Chinese, Koreans, and Filipinos working in Japan. Nevertheless, the population of foreigners in Japan is still below 5 percent.

Below Traditional Kabuki theater—once performed by women only but now strictly a male domain—is characterized by dramatic make-up, historical and domestic plot lines, as well as stylized dance, song, and movement.

Bottom Originally built as a retirement villa for Shogun Ashikaga Yoshimitshu, the Golden Pavilion Temple (Kinkaku-ji) in Kyoto was completed in 1397. The two top stories of the pavilion are covered with shining gold leaf.

MYANMAR

Official name Union of Myanmar (also Union of Burma) (Pyidaungzu Myanma Naingngandaw)
Land area 253,955 square miles (657,740 km²)
Border countries China, India, Laos, Thailand, Bangladesh
Capitals Rangoon (Yangon), Naypyidaw
Highest point Hkakabo Razi 19,295 feet (5,881 m)
Climate Tropical monsoon
Population 47,400,000
Language(s) Burmese, Karen, other
Ethnicity Burman or Bamar 68%, Shan 9%, Karen 7%, Rakhine 4%, Chinese 3%, Indian 2%, Mon 2%, others 5%
Religion Buddhist 89%, Christian 4%, Muslim 4%, animist 1%, other 2%
Government Military junta
Currency Kyat
Human Development Index 0.583 (ranked 132nd out of 177 countries)

INDIA
CHINA
Hkakabo Razi
Myitkyina
MYANMAR
BANGLADESH
Monywa
Mandalay
Myingyan
Sagaing
Pakokku
Meiktila
Taunggyi
LAOS
Sittwe
Minbu
NAYPYIDAW
Bay of Bengal
Pyay
Hinthada
Pegu
THAILAND
Bassein
Thaton
YANGON (RANGOON)
Mawlamyine
Kyaikkami
Andaman Sea
Tavoy
Myeik Archipelago

Myanmar

Map Reference Pages 378–379

Above right Fisher folk on Inle Lake, Shan province, Myanmar. Inle Lake is relatively shallow—only about 10 feet (3 m) deep—and is surrounded by misty mountains. The native lake dwellers are known as the Intha, and live in stilt houses or on islands of floating vegetation.

Myanmar shares borders with China, India, Laos, Thailand, and Bangladesh. The southern coastline lies on the Bay of Bengal. The name Myanmar was applied to the country of Burma from 1989 when the ruling military junta declared that henceforth it would be the country's official name. The names are often used interchangeably, but Burma is preferred by those in opposition to the junta and by many users abroad.

Physical Geography

The core of Myanmar is the fertile valley of the Ayeyawady (Irrawaddy) River, which flows the length of the country from the mountains in the north to the Andaman Sea. The Ayeyawady bisects the country north–south and forms a broad and intensively farmed delta below the country's largest city, Yangon (Rangoon). This is the most important agricultural area, and is where most people live. The central valley and narrow coastal plain are ringed by rugged mountain ranges. Southeast Asia's highest mountain, Hkakabo Razi, rises in a remote corner of Kachin state. A treacherous mountain, it was climbed for the first time in 1996 by Takash Ozaki. Around half of Myanmar is covered in dense tropical forests. Myanmar's climate is tropical monsoon, although sheltered inland areas are not as wet as the coast.

History

Myanmar history can be traced back to the Mon kingdom of Sauwarnabhumi in 300 BCE. The most prominent kingdom was one centered on the central capital of Bagan. It began in 849 CE, and expanded and flourished from the eleventh century until its destruction by invading Mongol armies in 1287. The British invaded the country from neighboring India in 1824, then eventually conquered Burmese lands in 1886. Burma was incorporated into India and did not become a separate colony until 1937. The nationalist hero Aung San, who was assassinated in 1947, led the fight for independence, which was gained in 1948.

The Democratic Republic of Burma ended with a coup d'etat in 1962, led by General Ne Win who envisioned a unique Burmese Way to Socialism. A military junta has ruled since, even after free elections in 1990 gave victory to a democratic opposition led by Aung San Suu Kyi, daughter of the nationalist leader. The junta nullified those elections and democratic expression continues to be suppressed.

Population/Culture

Most of the people belong to the Burman (Bamar) ethnic group and practice Theravada Buddhism. Most young men spend a short period of their lives as Buddhist monks. Many of the most spectacular architectural landmarks are Buddhist temples. Ethnic minorities, including the Karen in the southeast and the Kachin in the north, tend to be Christian.

Right There are 1,200 monks in the Buddhist monastery at Bago, the largest in the country. Approximately 80 percent of the Myanmar population practice Theravada Buddhism.

THE GOLDEN TRIANGLE

The rugged mountainous area in the border zone of Myanmar, China, Laos, and Thailand is referred to as the Golden Triangle. It is home to various colorful hill tribe cultures, but is also an area of considerable poverty and environmental degradation. On the Myanmar side of the border, there is additional unrest between dissident minority groups and the government. Much of the world's opium production comes from the Golden Triangle, and efforts to eradicate the crop have failed. Poor farmers and villagers are guaranteed some income for raising opium poppies, an income they may not otherwise have. Powerful drug lords make enormous profits in processing the harvest and transporting the illicit cargo by mule caravan along the Myanmar–Thailand border, and then by ship and air to markets worldwide.

Administration/Government

Opposition to military rule is not allowed—opponents are imprisoned. The leading voice for democracy, Aung San Suu Kyi, has been under house arrest for much of the time since 1990. More recently, Buddhist monks have been at the fore of pro-democracy demonstrations in the country; many have been killed or imprisoned. Myanmar's constitution was suspended in 1988. Theoretically the legal system is based on English common law; the judiciary however is not independent.

Economy/Industry

Myanmar has fertile soils and considerable timber and mineral resources. Before military rule, it was the largest exporter of rice in the world, and a major supplier of teak and other natural resources. Since the junta nationalized industry, the economy has all but collapsed. Infrastructure and telecommunications are poorly developed. Much of the national income is from the illicit export of opium, and from the export of precious gems from government-controlled mines in the north.

Below The ancient city of Bagan (Pagan) was built between the eleventh and thirteenth centuries and is one of the world's richest archeological sites. As well as the pagodas and temples, the city is famous for its art, textiles, bamboo craft, and lacquer ware.

MILESTONE EVENTS

300 BCE Sauwarnabhumi Kingdom founded
1287 Invading Mongols destroy capital city of Bagan
1886 British colonial period begins
1947 Aung San assassinated
1948 Burma achieves independence
1948–1962 Years of the Democratic Republic of Burma
1962 Coup d'etat led by General Ne Win topples the democratic government
1988 Widespread pro-democracy demonstrations take place
1990 Aung San Suu Kyi's party wins first democratic election in 30 years; military junta refuses to hand over power
1991 Aung San Suu Kyi wins Nobel Peace Prize
2007 Large demonstrations led by monks leave many dead and untold numbers imprisoned
May 2–3, 2008 Deadly tropical cyclone *Nargis* batters five regions; over 130,000 people are dead or missing and many hundreds of thousands homeless

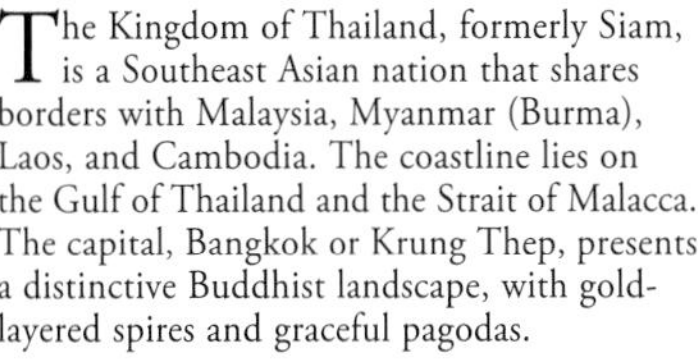
MYANMAR
LAOS
Chiang Mai
Doi Inthanon
Udon Thani
Phitsanulok
Khon Kaen
THAILAND
Nakhon Sawan
Ubon Ratchathani
Nakhon Ratchasima
Sara Buri
Nonthaburi
Ratchaburi
KRUNG THEP (BANGKOK)
Chon Buri
Chanthaburi
CAMBODIA
Prachuap Khiri Khan
Andaman Sea
Chumphon
Gulf of Thailand
Nakhon Si Thammarat
Phuket
Songkhla
MALAYSIA

Thailand

Map Reference Pages 376–377

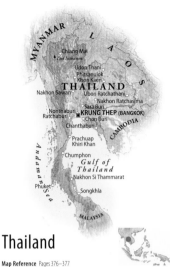

The Kingdom of Thailand, formerly Siam, is a Southeast Asian nation that shares borders with Malaysia, Myanmar (Burma), Laos, and Cambodia. The coastline lies on the Gulf of Thailand and the Strait of Malacca. The capital, Bangkok or Krung Thep, presents a distinctive Buddhist landscape, with gold-layered spires and graceful pagodas.

Physical Geography

The north is mountainous with well-watered intermontane valleys that support agriculture. The centre of Thailand is dominated by the flat Chao Phraya River basin, a very fertile rice-producing area. To the northeast is the Khorat Plateau, an arid to semiarid region with undulating hills and red soils, which contain huge underground stores of rock salts. The Mekong River lies to the east. The long southern region leading to Malaysia is mountainous and covered with tropical forests. The area supports rubber plantations and has rich deposits of tin ores. The peninsular southern region widens at the narrow Kra Isthmus until it reaches the border with Malaysia. Thailand has a warm tropical climate, with a rainy season from June to October.

History

The discovery of Bronze Age artefacts, dating back at least 3,500 years, has changed the theory that Thais came from northwestern Sichuan in China. It now appears they had their own thriving civilization and only later scattered to various parts of Asia, including China. From 1592 until 1939, and again from 1945 to 1949, Europeans knew the Kingdom of Thailand as Siam. The name was changed to Thailand in 1949—Thai means "free" and Thailand means "land of the free."

The Kingdom of Sukhothai, founded in 1238 was overshadowed by the Kingdom of Ayutthaya established in the mid-fourteenth century. King Rama I founded the current Chakri Dynasty in 1782.

After a brief and bloodless revolution in 1932, the absolutist monarchy was replaced by a constitutional monarchy. In 1946, King Bhumibol Adulayadej, Rama IX ascended the throne. Great celebrations were held in 2006 for the sixtieth anniversary of this much-loved king's accession to the throne.

MILESTONE EVENTS

1283 King Ramkhamhaeng the Great creates the first Thai alphabet with 44 consonants, 32 vowels, and 5 tones

1569 King Naresuan the Great declares the independence of Ayutthaya

1782 Bangkok is established

1905 King Rama V the Great abolishes slavery

1917 Change of the national flag, from a white elephant on a red background to five horizontal stripes of red, white, and blue

1932 Absolute monarchy becomes a constitutional monarchy

1949 Siam, the country's name, officially changes to Thailand

1967 ASEAN (Association of South East Asian Nations) is formed in Thailand

1982 Bicentennial Anniversary of Bangkok

September 28, 2006 Opening of Suvarnabhumi the new International Airport, one of the world's largest aviation hubs

Population/Culture

Thais make up the majority of the population, followed by Chinese, Malays, and various smaller groups, including hill tribes. Most people are followers of Theravada Buddhism.

Thailand has many festivals, including Songkran, the traditional Thai New Year, April 13, when it is customary for Thais to greet each other with water. Loy Kratong, or Festival of Light, originated in Sukhothai 800 years ago. Loy means to "float," and kratong is a lotus-shaped vessel traditionally made of banana leaves. On a full moon in November, people all over Thailand put flowers, coins, and lighted candles in kratongs, make wishes and let them float away in the hope that they also carry off bad luck and sins—thanks is given to the goddess of water. Young couples who make a wish together on Loy Kratong are believed to become lifelong partners. Thais celebrate New Year's Day (January 1) by giving flowers, food, and other essentials to monks and deprived members of society.

Administration/Government

Thailand is a constitutional monarchy and the chief of state is the king. The head of government is the prime minister, who is chosen by the members of the House of Representatives and is limited to two terms in office. There are 150 seats in the bicameral National Assembly, of which 76 are elected by popular vote and represent the country's 76 provinces. Non-partisan government bodies and judges appoint the remaining 74 members. Members of the National Assembly serve a six-year term. The House of Representatives has 480 seats, which represent 157 multi-seat constituencies. The Supreme Court and Court of Appeals represent the judiciary.

Economy/Industry

Thailand has a strong and robust economy that has recovered well from both the Asian financial crises of 1997–98 and the 2004 tsunami. The manufacturing sector is performing exceptionally well, especially export-oriented areas. Exports include textiles, footwear, jewelry, automobiles, computers, and electrical appliances. Industry employs 14 percent of the labor force and contributes over 45 percent to GDP.

Agriculture is also a significant export earner, and is the country's largest employer, with 49 percent of the labor force. It contributes 11 percent to GDP. The services sector, which includes Thailand's booming tourist industry, contributes 44 percent to GDP and employs 37 percent of the labor force. Recent bilateral free-trade agreements have been signed with Australia, China, and Japan.

THAILAND

Official name Kingdom of Thailand (Prathet Thai)
Land area 197,596 square miles (511,770 km²)
Border countries Laos, Myanmar (Burma), Malaysia, Cambodia
Capital Bangkok (Krung Thep)
Highest point Doi Inthanon 8,451 feet (2,576 m)
Climate Tropical monsoon
Population 65,070,000
Language(s) Thai, English
Ethnic composition Thai 75%, Chinese 14%, Malay 4%, other 7%
Religion Buddhism 94.6%, Muslim 4.6%, Christianity 0.7%, other 0.1%
Government Constitutional monarchy
Currency Thai baht
Human Development Index 0.781 (ranked 78th out of 177 countries)

Top Fishing village on one of the Phi Phi Islands, Thailand. This idyllic group of islands was severely affected by a tsunami in 2004.

Above left Indochinese tiger (*Panthera tigris corbetti*). The "Tiger Temple" in Kanchanaburi, two hours from Bangkok, is a tiger sanctuary run by Buddhist monks and has become a popular tourist attraction.

Left The Wat Phra Kaew (Temple of the Emerald Buddha) in Bangkok was built in 1785 by King Rama I. Legend has it that if the Emerald Buddha is destroyed, so too will Thailand be destroyed.

Above Krung Thep (Bangkok) is a huge, congested, polluted city of 10 million people. However, the drawbacks are offset by the abundance of tropical parklands within the city center.

LAOS

Official name Lao People's Democratic Republic (Sathalanalat Paxathipatai Paxaxon Lao)
Land area 89,112 square miles (230,800 km²)
Border countries China, Vietnam, Cambodia, Thailand, Myanmar (Burma)
Capital Vientiane (Viangchan)
Highest & lowest points Phou Bia 9,242 feet (2,817 m); Mekong River 230 feet (70 m)
Climate Tropical monsoonal
Population 6,678,000
Language(s) Lao, French, English, other
Ethnicity Lao Loum (lowland) 68%, Lao Theung (upland) 22%, Lao Soung (highland, including Hmong and Yao) 9%, Vietnamese/Chinese 1%
Religion Buddhist 65%, animist 32.9%, Christian/Muslim 1.3%, other 0.8%
Government Communist state
Currency Kip
Human Development Index 0.601 (ranked 130th out of 177 countries)

CHINA
MYANMAR
VIETNAM
THAILAND
CAMBODIA
LAOS
Phôngsali
Louang Namtha
Ban Houayxay
Xam Nua
Louangphrabang
Muang Xaignabouri
Phou Bia
Muang Phôn-Hông
Muang Pakxan
VIANGCHAN (VIENTIANE)
Muang Khammouan
Savannakhét
Salavan
Pakxé
Attapu

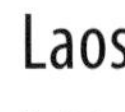

Laos

Map Reference Pages 376–377

Above right Visitors to the Buddha Park in Vientiane stroll among a curious collection of outdoor sculptures, including this impressive reclining Buddha. The communist government of Laos has not tried to subdue the practice of Buddhism to any great degree.

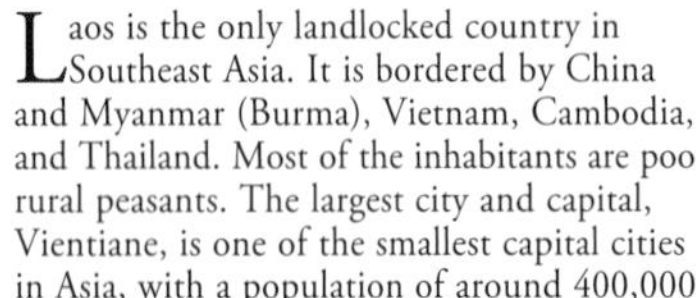

Laos is the only landlocked country in Southeast Asia. It is bordered by China and Myanmar (Burma), Vietnam, Cambodia, and Thailand. Most of the inhabitants are poor rural peasants. The largest city and capital, Vientiane, is one of the smallest capital cities in Asia, with a population of around 400,000.

Physical Geography

The landscape is mountainous and heavily forested. The Annamite Mountains form most of the border with Vietnam, while the Mekong River borders Thailand. The climate is tropical monsoonal.

Nam Ha Protected Area in Luang Namtha Province, declared an ASEAN Heritage Park in 2005, protects a vast array of flora and fauna, including 288 bird species, the Asian elephant, tiger, and two species of leopard.

History

The region that is now Laos was once a northern reach of the Khmer Empire. The first kingdom linked directly to Laos emerged in 1353 and was known as the Land of a Million Elephants. Later kingdoms often divided the region into northern and southern sectors. In 1893, Laos became part of French Indochina (formed in 1887 from the Kingdom of Cambodia and present-day Vietnam). Independence was achieved in 1954. During the Vietnam War, the Viet Cong used the rugged terrain of Laos as one of its bases. The communist Pathet Lao group took control of the country in 1975, renaming it the Lao People's Democratic Republic. Laos is still a socialist state and is closely allied with neighboring Vietnam. A policy of New Thinking, introduced in the 1990s, has liberalized private enterprise and made opportunities for foreign investment.

Population/Culture

The majority of people live in the lowlands; they are the Lao Loum, or "Lao people of the valley." More than half of them are ethnic Lao and almost all are Buddhist. Their villages have prominent wats, or temples, which also serve as social centers. Living at higher altitudes are the Lao Theung, "Lao people of the mountain slopes," comprising over 36 different ethnic groups and many languages. They grow rice and other crops following the age-old regime of shifting cultivation. The "Lao people of the mountain top," Lao Soung, are also farmers, but their language and ethnicity differ. Traditionally, the Lao Soung were animists, but many have converted to Christianity through missionary contact. The largest of the other six ethnic groups in the mountains are the Hmong, many of whom have emigrated as political refugees to countries abroad, most notably the United States.

Administration/Government

Laos is one of the world's few remaining communist states. The only political party is the Lao People's Revolutionary Party. The LPRP holds almost all the seats in the country's National Assembly and sets government policy through the 11-member Politburo, and the 55-member Central Committee. The president of Laos is the leader of the LPRP.

Economy/Industry

Laos is a poor country with very limited infrastructure. About 85 percent of the population is rural, mostly engaged in subsistence agriculture. Rice is the staple crop and accounts for around half the country's GDP. Resources include tin, gold, copper, gypsum, and gemstones. Exports include timber products and coffee. Laos has considerable hydropower potential. There are plans to build new dams to increase domestic electricity, and to export electricity to neighboring Thailand.

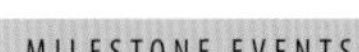

MILESTONE EVENTS

1353 The kingdom of Lan Xang emerges
1479 Vietnam invades Laos
1637 Soulinga Vongsa becomes king and a golden age begins
1713 Kingdom of Lan Xang disintegrates
1893 Laos becomes part of French Indochina
1941 Japanese invade the country
1946 French troops return to Laos
1954 Independence from France is attained
December 2, 1975 The Pathet Lao establishes the Lao People's Democratic Republic
1994 The LPDR's Constitution is promulgated
1997 Laos is admitted into ASEAN

The Mekong River

At just over 3,000 miles (4,828 km), the Mekong is one of the longest rivers in the world. It rises in the remote highlands of the Tibetan Plateau, flows through Myanmar into Laos and forms a major part of the Lao–Thai boundary. From Laos the Mekong flows through the heart of Cambodia, emptying into the South China Sea via a broad, densely settled delta region in southern Vietnam. In Laos and Thailand, it is called the Mother of all Rivers; in Cambodia it is referred to as the Great River; in Vietnam it is known as the River of Nine Dragons, referring to the nine principal channels flowing through the delta.

Over 90 million people rely on the river. It is not particularly navigable because narrow gorges, rock-strewn rapids, and shifting islands impede easy passage. The Mekong's value lies in the fresh soils brought by floods, and the huge variety of fish species—more than any other river in the world. The Mekong is also a source of water for crop irrigation.

During the rainy season, the river swells with so much water that, in Cambodia, some of its flow reverses direction and feeds into Tonlé Sap Lake, almost doubling its size. There are now serious environmental concerns about the Mekong, to do with the blasting of rapids and construction of dams.

Right below Many Hmong people, an ethnic minority in Laos, fought against the communist Pathet Lao during the Laotian Civil War (1960–75). Fearing post-war retribution, thousands fled to western countries, including the USA, France, Australia, and Canada in search of safe haven.

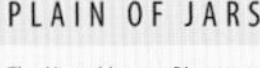

PLAIN OF JARS

The Xiangkhoang Plateau in north-central Laos is the site of thousands of mysterious, large stone jars thought to be some 1,500 to 2,000 years old. Research regarding their origin and purpose is inconclusive. They do, however, have similar features to stone jars found in northern India, and may have been used as funeral urns or as food storage jars.

Because of what seems to be a linear arrangement of jar clusters over a broad scale, experts theorize that the jars may be linked to an ancient trade route between India and China. Only three of the hundreds of jar clusters have been carefully studied and are accessible for viewing by tourists. Other clusters are too dangerous to visit because of the scale of unexploded ordnance embedded in the soil since the Vietnam War era. The Laos government is seeking help from the United Nations to clear the Plain of Jars of ordnance and preserve this important archeological site.

THAILAND
LAOS
VIETNAM
CAMBODIA
Phumi Sâmraông
Siĕmréab
Bătdâmbâng
Lumphăt
Kâmpóng Thum
Krâchéh
Kâmpóng Chhnăng
Phnum Aoral
Kâmpóng Cham
PHNUM PENH (PHNOM PENH)
Krŏng Kaôh Kŏng
Kâmpóng Spœ
Prey Vêng
Svay Riĕng
Gulf of Thailand
Takêv
Kâmpóng Saôm
Kâmpôt

Cambodia

Map Reference Pages 376–377

Cambodia is a small country on the mainland of Southeast Asia. It shares borders with Thailand, Laos, and Vietnam. The coastline hugs the Gulf of Thailand. Cambodia's tragic past continues to exact a heavy toll.

Physical Geography

The primary geographical features are the Mekong River and Tonlé Sap, a large central freshwater lake. Tonlé Sap nearly doubles in size during the May to October rainy season, when the flow of the Mekong is reversed and the broad lowlands surrounding the lake are flooded. Also dominating the heavily forested countryside is a series of low mountain ranges that rim the central lowlands.

History

From the ninth to the fifteenth centuries the region was the center of the flourishing Khmer Empire which controlled a large area of the Southeast Asian mainland. The ruins of Angkor Wat, an imposing temple complex near today's tourist town of Siem Reap, are testament to the power once wielded by the mighty Khmer Empire.

Cambodia became a French protectorate in 1863, and part of French Indochina in 1887. The decades following independence in 1953 were turbulent and bloody. Between 1969 and 1973, some 500,000 soldiers and civilians were killed in US carpet-bombing raids, purportedly to attack the Viet Cong's supply lines.

From 1975 until the Vietnamese invasion of 1978, Cambodia was ruled by the ruthless dictator Pol Pot, and the Khmer Rouge, a fanatical communist group. Under this cruel regime, an estimated one in five Cambodians died as a result of disease, malnutrition, overwork, or torture and execution. From 1978 to 1989 a further 65,000 people died as the US and UK-backed Khmer Rouge rebels fought the Vietnamese-backed government. The Paris Peace Accords of 1991 brought an end to years of bloodshed and suffering, and led to multiparty elections in 1993 under the supervision of the United Nations.

Population/Culture

The majority of the population is Khmer, with minorities of Chams, Chinese, Vietnamese, and various hill tribes. Even though there are also Muslims, Christians, and animists, the population is mostly Buddhist. Traditional Khmer culture retains influences of Hinduism from earlier periods, reflected in the Khmer language and in architecture, such as the main temple of Angkor Wat, and in traditional dance, art, and folklore.

MILESTONE EVENTS

c. 800–1600 Golden age of the Khmer Empire

1432 Angkor destroyed by invading Thais

1863 Cambodia becomes a French protectorate

1887 Cambodia is absorbed into French Indochina

November 9, 1953 Cambodia gains independence

April, 1975 Khmer Rouge take Phnom Penh and a reign of terror begins

1978 Vietnam invades and installs a new government

1991 Paris Peace Accords end civil war

1993 Elections are held

1993 Constitution promulgated

2004 Norodom Sihamoni becomes new king

Administration/Government

Cambodia's king is officially head of state but his powers are largely symbolic and ceremonial. The head of government is the prime minister, appointed by the king after being selected by the National Assembly from the majority party. The largest parties are the Cambodian People's Party, which governs in coalition with the royalist Funcinpec, and the opposition Sam Rainsy Party.

Economy/Industry

Since the 1990s, Cambodia has moved to a private enterprise economy, and has been attracting foreign investment in labor-intensive manufacturing and international tourism. The leading industrial sector is garment and textile manufacturing. Tourism development centers on the Angkor Wat complex, with nearby Siem Reap undergoing a facelift. There is also increasing foreign tourism to Phnom Penh and beach resorts in and near Sihanoukville. Since the start of the twenty-first century, Cambodia has once again become self-sufficient in rice production.

Despite recent progress, Cambodia remains one of the world's poorest nations. The country depends on various foreign aid donors and non-government organizations (NGOs) for funds and expertise to ameliorate its many social and environmental problems. It is seriously lacking in basic infrastructure, and rampant government corruption has hindered fuller economic development.

Landmines

There are an estimated four to six million landmines still hidden under Cambodian soil, more than in any other country in the world. The mines were set by different factions during three decades of civil war. The removal process is slow and dangerous, and may take as long as 100 years. More than 40,000 Cambodians have suffered amputations as a result of landmine injuries, with more casualities being added every year.

CAMBODIA

Official name Kingdom of Cambodia (Preahreacheanachakr Kampuchea)

Land area 68,155 square miles (176,520 km²)

Border countries Thailand, Laos, Vietnam

Capital Phnom Penh (Phnum Penh)

Highest point Phnum Aoral 5,938 feet (1,810 m)

Climate Tropical

Population 14,242,000

Language(s) Khmer, French, English

Ethnicity Khmer 90%, Vietnamese 5%, Chinese 1%, other 4%

Religion Buddhist 95%, other 5%

Government Democracy under a constitutional monarchy

Currency Riel

Human Development Index 0.598 (ranked 131st out of 177 countries)

Left The sandstone temple walls at Angkor Wat feature intricately carved bas-relief friezes of mystical deities, including dancing Apsaras, the celestial nymphs considered the embodiment of female beauty and grace.

Below Giant fig-tree roots take a stranglehold on the entrance to Ta Prohm temple at Angkor Wat. Ta Prohm was left as it was originally found to demonstrate the rainforest's power of encroachment in the absence of human contact.

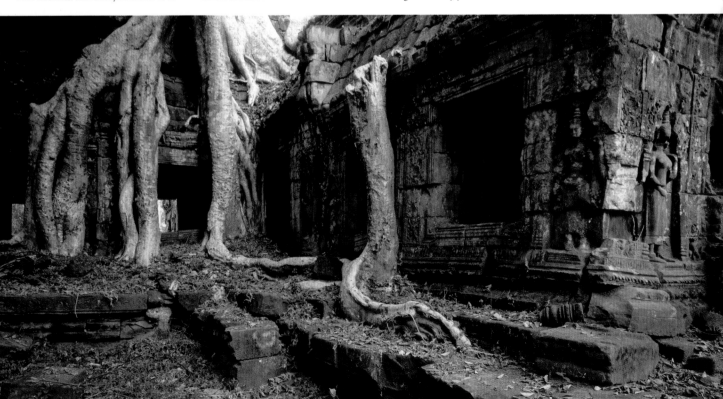

VIETNAM

Official name Socialist Republic of Vietnam (Cong Hoa Xa Hoi Chu Ngia Viet Nam)

Land area 125,622 square miles (325,360 km²)

Border countries China, Cambodia, Laos

Capital Hanoi (Hà Nội)

Highest point Fan Si Pan 10,315 feet (3,144 m)

Climate Tropical in the south, monsoonal in the north with a hot rainy season and a warm dry season

Population 86,117,000

Language(s) Official: Vietnamese; other: English (increasingly favored as second language), some French, Chinese, and Khmer; mountain area languages (Mon-Khmer and Malayo-Polynesian)

Ethnicity Kinh (Viet) 86.2%, Tay 1.9%, Thai 1.7%, Muong 1.5%, Khome 1.4%, Hoa 1.1%, Nun 1.1%, Hmong 1%, others 4.1%

Religion Buddhist 70%, other ("Tam Giao," Confucianist, Taoist, Protestant, Catholic, Hoa Hao, Cao Dai, Muslim, unaffiliated) 30%

Government Communist state

Currency Dong

Human Development Index 0.733 (ranked 105th out of 177 countries)

Right One of the country's 54 recognized ethnic minorities, the Hmong people are culturally, geographically, and economically isolated in Vietnam. They have low social status and live in the hilly and remote areas of the north.

Right Rice-growing occupies 94 percent of Vietnam's arable land. In the north, three crops per year are possible, thanks to an extensive irrigation system. In the south, single-cropping is more usual, relying on six months of heavy rain followed by six months of relatively dry conditions.

Below Rush hour in a Vietnamese city is a cacophony of horns, engines, and shouts. The streetscape teems with bicycles, mopeds, carts, and cyclos, all making their way through the intricate maze of streets and laneways.

CHINA
VIETNAM
LAOS
CAMBODIA
Fan Si Pan
Cao Bằng
Sơn La
Việt Trì
HÀ NỘI
(HANOI)
Hạ Long
Hải Phòng
Nam Định
Thanh Hóa
Gulf of Tonkin
Vinh
Huế
Đà Nẵng
South China Sea
Quy Nhơn
Buôn Ma Thuột
Nha Trang
Đà Lạt
Biên Hòa
Phan Thiết
Hồ Chí Minh
Long Xuyên
Mỹ Tho
Cần Thơ
Gulf of Thailand
Bạc Liêu

Vietnam

Map Reference Pages 376–377

Vietnam is located at what was a crossroads for early seafarers, merchants, and traders. Its extensive shoreline on the East Sea has long tempted invaders from Indonesia, Japan, and India. However, Vietnam's very rich cultural background is primarily linked to the Chinese civilization as a result of numerous invasions in the north by China.

Physical Geography

The natural landscapes are divided into coastline, two big rivers and deltas (Red River and Mekong River), mountainous regions with primeval rainforests (in the north), and lowlands. The terrain is not easily connected by roads and railways. An old tarmac highway along the coast connects the south to the north, and a new road is under construction over the mountain area. The lowlands consist of vast rice paddy fields.

In the northeast is the World Heritage site, Halong Bay. Its 1,600 or so limestone pillars (karst towers) create an awe-inspiring seascape.

All kinds of exotic fauna live in Vietnam's rainforests. In Cuc Phong Forest close to Hanoi, visitors may see flying lizards and yellow monkeys. Cat Ba Island, in the Cat Ba archipelago, is home to porcupines, deer, wild cats, boars, and monkeys. The island also features lakes, freshwater wetland areas, waterfalls, mangrove forests, and hot springs.

Eastern Vietnam has a tropical monsoonal climate with a south monsoon (rainy season) from May to September and a north monsoon (dry season) from October to April. Rainfall is abundant. In southern and central Vietnam, temperatures are high year round; the northern part of Vietnam has a distinct cooler season.

History

China conquered the Nam Viet kingdom in 111 BCE and remained there for the next 1,000 years, a period which is known as the Han Dynasty. The Chinese writing style, language, and lifestyle, as well as the cultivation of paddy rice, were absorbed by the Vietnamese. In 939 CE, Chinese armies were defeated, freeing Vietnam from Chinese rule. However, Chinese influence persisted; later in the millennium the Chinese model of the Imperial Forbidden Palace (City) was adopted by the Vietnamese regime of Dinh Bo Linh.

In 1858, the French navy attacked the coastal city of Da Nang, which marked the beginning of France's colonization of the country; in 1887, Vietnam became part of French Indochina (the protectorates of Annam, Cochin China, and Tonkin comprise modern Vietnam). A short period of Japanese rule (1940–1945) left a power vacuum filled by the Viet Minh, a nationalist group led by the communist guerrilla, Ho Chi Minh. Viet Minh defeated French colonial forces and declared its independence in 1945. Under the 1954 Geneva Agreement, Vietnam was formally separated into Communist North Vietnam, which had the support of China and the former USSR, and non-communist South Vietnam, backed by the USA. For more than two decades the northern forces waged a war against the south and its allies. This is considered to have been one of the most inhumane civil wars in modern history, because of the use of devastating napalm bombs that caused genetic mutations and the enormous loss of civilians—approximately four million people died during the Vietnam War.

The USA pulled its troops out of Vietnam in 1973 and the war officially ended with the fall of Saigon in South Vietnam in 1975. Vietnam became a communist (Maoist) republic. Privately owned production equipment, such as factories, farms, and businesses, were nationalized by the state. Even the ethnic groups of the highlands were forced to settle under the Vietnamese agricultural system.

Population

Around half the population is under 35 years of age. More than 75 percent of the population still lives in the countryside; but the cities with their greater educational and economic opportunities and their modern lifestyles are proving more attractive to young Vietnamese today.

Culture/Religion

Nam Viet was the name of the ancient kingdom that ruled the great part of present-day North Vietnam and South China. The Red River delta in northern Vietnam is traditionally the core region of Vietnamese culture. More than 80 percent of the population is ethnically Vietnamese. There are more than 50 other ethnic groups, such as those who live in the mountainous regions, including an estimated 600,000 Khmer people and 80,000 Cham people.

Religion has significantly influenced culture, especially attitudes to life and death. The eastern faiths of Buddhism (Vietnam's main religion), Confucianism, and Taoism have all played a role in the way these attitudes have developed. For example, Buddhism contributed the law of karma, which states that a person's fate in this life is determined by her or his actions in a past life. Unique to Vietnam is Tam Giao, a mix of popular Chinese beliefs, Taoism, and ancient Vietnamese animism. Some Vietnamese people follow Shamanism, Christianity, or Caodaism. In 2006, two Protestant sects in Ho Chi Minh City—the Vietnam Grace Baptist Church and the Vietnam Seventh Day Adventist Church—were given official certificates of religious practice.

During the economic renewal program started by the government in 1986, attitudes toward capitalism and global markets changed markedly. The desire to avoid poverty and stagnation by participating in more dynamic sectors of the economy has increased greatly. "The better standard of living, the better life quality" is the motto of most young people.

59.271-E

MILESTONE EVENTS

111 BCE China conquers the Nam Viet kingdom

939 CE Chinese armies are defeated thus liberating Vietnam

1858 The French navy attacks the coast of Vietnam at Da Nang; beginning of colonization by the French

1887 Vietnam becomes part of French Indochina

1940–1945 Japan rules Vietnam

1945 The Viet Minh, under the leadership of Ho Chi Minh, declare independence for Vietnam

1954 Ho Chi Minh wins the battle against France at Dien Bien Phu

1965 First US combat troops arrive to take part in Vietnam War

January 27, 1973 Paris Peace Accords are signed by North Vietnam, South Vietnam, the Viet Cong, and the United States thus ending the Vietnam War

1975 The US presence in Vietnam ends; Saigon falls to the Viet Cong and Vietnam gains independence as the Socialist Republic of Vietnam

1980s–1990s *Doi moi* economic reform program in place

2000s Vietnam takes rapid steps in information technology

The country's difficult but important history prevails in the war museums and in the stories told by the older generation.

Administration/Government

Vietnam is divided into 59 provinces and five urban regions. The National Assembly is at the top of a hierarchy of government organizations, including People's Councils, People's Committees, the Supreme People's Court, and the Supreme People's Organs of Control. A tiered voting system is used to elect members of these various bodies.

Economy/Industry

The most important natural resources are oil, timber, bauxite, manganese, coal, and phosphate. The country exports rice, unrefined oil, coffee (more recently), clothing, and shoes. Economically, Vietnam can be divided into agriculture (21 percent), the service sector (38 percent), and industry (41 percent).

Vietnam is a developing country that has experienced rapid economic change in recent years. By the early 1980s, the strict Marxist policies had stagnated the country's economic base through the decline of agriculture, lack of investments, and paucity of consumer goods. The new planned economy of *doi moi* was welcomed as an "economic renovation" that would open up the country to foreign investments and markets. The program liberalized the economy and privatized ownership of land and enterprises. The national government prescribed new laws at a faster pace than neighboring China, the model for Vietnam's market-based socialism. Vietnam largely avoided the Southeast Asian economic crisis of 1996 and experienced some of the highest economic growth rates in the region during the 1990s. The well-educated labor force, which included women entrepreneurs, faced new possibilities via the establishment of small enterprises such as hair salons, bakeries, and information technology companies. *Doi moi* enabled hundreds of thousands of people to rise above the poverty line by the beginning of the new millennium. Despite the rapid transformation toward market-based socialism, Vietnam still lacks notable foreign investments due to uncertainty surrounding government regulations.

Exploitation of natural resources, such as deforestation, has caused ecological hazards in the mountainous regions. Rehabilitation of the environment is a challenge that is recognized by the government.

The Bay of the Descending Dragon

According to one legend: A long time ago, when Vietnam was under siege from a great enemy, a dragon came down from the hills to assist the people. Using its mighty tail, the dragon lashed and split apart entire mountain ranges, impeding the advance of the enemy and creating "Vinh Halong"—the 1,969 dolomite islands that comprise Halong Bay—Vietnam's Bay of the Descending Dragon.

Halong Bay gained World Heritage status in 1994. It is located in northeastern Vietnam, bordered to the west by the Red River delta and to the southwest by the island of Cat Ba. Covering a total area of 600 square miles (1,553 km^2), Halong Bay contains 1,969 islands. The bay's seafloor is submerged karst plains—its islands emerging from a fine-grained carboniferous and permian limestone over 3,300 feet (1,000 m) thick—ideal for the development of caves, sinkholes, and underground drainage systems.

The bay's geologic substructure is complex, with drowned fault-guided valleys between the islands and bedding ranging from horizontal in its eastern region to small overfolds in the western part of the bay. Halong Bay's islands are a vast mix of individual karsts and karst clusters. Cluster towers can reach heights of 650 feet (200 m), with steep cone profiles, minimal lateral undercutting, and few vertical cliffs. The majority of the individual towers reach heights of between 165 and 330 feet (50 and 100 m) with vertical walls present on all or most of their faces.

An abundance of lakes exists on many of the limestone islands. Known as "hongs" or "rooms," they are mostly tidal, with seawater moving freely back and forth via sea-level caves or inaccessible networks of fissures.

Halong Bay has a variety of unique plants and wildlife. A recent expedition discovered more than 80 previously unknown species, including some cave-adapted spiders and 17 species of snails.

Above A young woman from the White Thai Lu hill tribe poses in traditional costume in Son La, Vietnam.

Left Jagged limestone monoliths pierce through the shallow waters of Vietnam's famous Halong Bay in the Gulf of Tonkin. Its scenic beauty and biological significance saw it recognized as a World Heritage site in 1994.

Below The crumbling vestiges of the My Son Sanctuary temple complex are located near Ho An in southern Vietnam. The "forest" of towers that once comprised this site pays homage to the spiritual and architectural influences of Indian Hinduism. My Son was the religious and political capital of the Champa Kingdom (300–1400 CE).

South China Sea
PHILIPPINES
THAILAND
Alor Setar
Kota Baharu
George Town
Kuala Terengganu
Strait of Malacca
Taiping
Ipoh
MALAYSIA
Kuantan
Kelang
KUALA LUMPUR
PUTRAJAYA
Seremban
Melaka
Johor Bahru
INDONESIA
Gunung Kinabalu
Kota Kinabalu
BRUNEI
Sulu Sea
Sandakan
Miri
Tawau
Celebes Sea
Sibu
Kuching
INDONESIA

Malaysia

Map Reference Pages 374–375

MALAYSIA

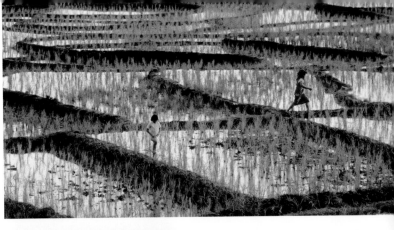

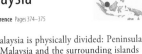

Official name Malaysia
Land area 126,854 square miles (328,550 km²)
Border countries Thailand, Brunei, Indonesia
Capital Kuala Lumpur
Highest point Gunung Kinabalu 13,451 feet (4,100 m)
Climate Tropical
Population 25,274,000
Language(s) Official: Bahasa Malaysia; other: English, Chinese (Cantonese, Mandarin, Hokkien, Hakka, Hainan, Foochow), Tamil, Telugu, Malayalam, Punjabi, Thai Iban, Kadazan, other indigenous languages
Ethnicity Malay 50.4%, Chinese 23.7%, indigenous 11%, Indian 7.1%, others 7.8%
Religion Muslim 60.4%, Buddhist 19.2%, Christian 9.1%, Hindu 6.3%, Confucianism/Taoism 2.6%, other/unknown 1.6%, none 0.8%
Government Constitutional monarchy
Currency Ringgit
Human Development Index 0.811 (ranked 63rd out of 177 countries)

Above top Rice paddies in Malaysia where productive double-cropping is commonly practiced.

Above right Designed by architect Cesar Pelli, the Petronas Twin Towers in Kuala Lumpur are two of the world's tallest buildings.

Above A master kite maker in Kota Bharu, Kelantan State, surrounded by his colorful and imaginative flying creations.

Right A Bidayuh girl from the southwestern part of Sarawak, in East Malaysia. Ethnic Bidayuh, formerly known as Land Dayak, represent 8 percent of Sarawak's population.

Malaysia is physically divided: Peninsular Malaysia and the surrounding islands are known as West Malaysia, while the states of Sarawak and Sabah in Borneo and nearby islands are called East Malaysia. West Malaysia is bordered by Thailand to the north; East Malaysia shares a small border with Brunei to the north and Indonesia to the south.

Physical Geography

Mountain ranges running on a north–south axis divide the northern part of peninsular Malaysia into a narrow coastal strip on one side and a broad fertile plain on the other. The country's tallest peak, Gunung Kinabalu, is located in the Crocker Range in East Malaysia's Kinabalu National Park World Heritage site. The park is home to a number of rare species of flora. National parks and extensive jungle cover and protect fauna such as the endangered orang-utan, bears, leopards, panthers, elephants, and many others. Malaysia has a tropical climate. Annual rainfall is over 79 inches (200 cm) depending on the region; East Malaysia's northern mountain slopes receive over 200 inches (500 cm).

History

Small kingdoms dominated the peninsula until Prince Parameswara, a convert to Islam, established the Kingdom of Malacca around 1400 CE. The Portuguese conquered the peninsula in 1511. In 1641, Malacca fell to the Dutch, who gave the area to the British in 1824. The British also acquired Sarawak and North Borneo as protectorates in the late nineteenth century, which gave them control of modern East Malaysia. During World War II, the British held Malaya until it was taken by Japanese troops.

The Federation of Malaya declared its independence in 1957. Sabah (then called North Borneo), Singapore, and Sarawak joined the federation in 1963. Singapore withdrew from the federation and declared independence in 1965. Mahathir bin Mohamad became the prime minister of Malaysia in 1981 and, in his 22 years in office, was a key player in Malaysia's rapid economic development in the late twentieth century.

Population/Culture

Malays comprise slightly more than half of a population that also includes Chinese, Indian, and indigenous peoples. The population of Australians, Europeans and others is increasing as Malaysia develops economically. The indigenous peoples are the oldest inhabitants of the country, and, while there are many different tribes, they are collectively referred to as Orang Asli, the original people. They inhabit Sarawak and Sabah, and most retain their traditional lifestyles.

Bahasa Malaysia, an Austronesian language, is the official language, but English is quite widely spoken. While around 60 percent of people are Muslim, there are large Buddhist, Christian, and Hindu constituencies along with followers of Taoism and Confucianism.

The kaleidoscope of cultures in Malaysia is manifested in many ways, including holidays, special celebrations, literature, theater, dance, and language. During religious festivals, each home has an open door policy and everyone is welcome, a practice that fosters religious tolerance and acceptance of other cultures.

Administration/Government

Malaysia is a constitutional monarchy and one of the most democratic Islamic nations in the world. The King is elected for a five-year term from among the states' rulers on a rotating basis decided by the Conference of Rulers. Since independence in 1957, Malaysia has developed a stable democratic government. The legislative branch of government is divided into two houses: The House of Representatives, which has 222 elected members, and the 70-member Senate. The prime minister serves as head of government.

Economy/Industry

During the last third of the twentieth century, the Malaysian economy rapidly changed from agricultural to industrial. In 1991, the Malaysian government adopted Mahathir's economic plan called Vision 2020. The goal of this farsighted plan is for Malaysia to become a fully developed nation by the year 2020. Now rapidly advancing on its path, the country is working in many areas of high technology, and exports advanced microchips and complex electrical components.

Traditional industries are still very important, including fishing, rubber plantations, palm oil production, tin mining, and logging. Foreign investors have enthusiastically put money into the country, which has a dependable workforce and strong productivity.

The most visible symbol of Malaysia's economic prosperity is the Petronas Twin Towers. Humans have been trying to create the tallest buildings since the biblical tower of Babel was constructed, which archeologists believe rose to 295 feet (90 m) in height. Today, the competition for the world's tallest building is global, and Malaysia is a major player. The Petronas Twin Towers opened in 1999 but the buildings were declared the world's tallest in 1996, but have since been overtaken by Taipei 101 which stands at 1,670 feet (509 m). The towers' tapered design and interior schemes reflect Islamic patterns created by Argentinean-born American Cesar Pelli, who served as the chief architect for the project.

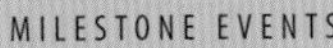

MILESTONE EVENTS

c. 1400 Prince Parameswara establishes the Kingdom of Malacca
1511 Portuguese conquer the peninsula
1641 Malacca falls to the Dutch
1824 Malacca passes to the British in the Anglo-Dutch Treaty
1895 Four states combine to form the Federated Malay States
1942–1945 Japanese invasion and occupation
1948–1960 State of emergency declared
August 31, 1957 Federation of Malaya declares independence and Tunku Abdul Rahman is first prime minister
1963 British colonies of Sabah (North Borneo), Singapore, and Sarawak join with Malaysia to form the Federation of Malaysia
1965 Singapore withdraws from the Federation of Malaysia; communist insurgency in Sarawak
1969 Malays stage anti-Chinese riots
1970 Tunku Abdul Rahman resigns and Tun Abdul Razak becomes prime minister
1971 Minimum quotas for Malays in education, the civil service, and business are introduced
1981 Mahathir bin Mohamad becomes prime minister
1989 Communist insurgents sign peace accord
1997 Asian financial crisis ends a decade of economic growth
1998 Prime Minister Mahathir bin Mohamad sacks his deputy, Anwar Ibrahim, on charges of sexual misconduct; Ibrahim arrested
2000 Ibrahim is found guilty of sodomy and a nine-year sentence is added to the six-year sentence for corruption he received in 1999
2001 Malays and ethnic Indians clash and many are arrested
October 2003 Abdullah Ahmad Badawi becomes prime minister as Mahathir bin Mohamad leaves after 22 years in office
September 2004 Anwar Ibrahim freed after court overturns his sodomy conviction
December 2004 Sixty-eight people killed in the Asian tsunami
March 2005 Illegal immigrants rounded up and deported; those who remain risk a fine, jail, or whipping
December 2006 Severe flooding displaces tens of thousands in the low-lying southern region
January 2007 Thousands evacuated as yet more floods inundate the south
February 2007 Malaysia, Brunei Darussalam, and Indonesia sign an agreement to protect 77,220 square miles (200,000 km²) of rainforest on Borneo
March 8, 2008 Prime Minister Abdullah Ahmad Badawi's Barisan Nasional coalition loses its two-thirds parliamentary majority, suffering its worst election result in decades

BRUNEI
BANDAR SERI BEGAWAN
Muara
South China Sea
Tutong
Seria
Kuala Belait
Kampong Layong
Bangar
Kampong Batan Duri
Labi
Sukang
Bukit Pagon
MALAYSIA

Brunei

Map Reference Pages 374–375

Oil-rich Brunei is a small tropical country on the northwest coast of Borneo only 4 degrees north of the Equator. Its two disconnected parts both face the South China Sea and are otherwise surrounded by Malaysia's Sarawak State. Most of the people live in the larger western portion near the capital, Bandar Seri Begawan, and along the coast.

Physical Geography

Sarawak State (East Malaysia) divides Brunei Darussalam into two separate parts. The west has the largest area, dominated by hilly lowlands, alluvial valleys, and swampy plains. The eastern part has a wide coastal plain that rises to mountains. Mangroves, important breeding grounds for fish and birds, fringe the rivers and estuaries that adjoin Brunei Bay and the South China Sea. Large areas of mangroves are designated reserves. Nearly 75 percent of the country is tropical jungle that provides habitat for a range of flora and fauna, such as the endangered proboscis monkey.

THE SULTAN'S WEALTH

The Sultan of Brunei, Hassanal Bolkiah, the 29th sultan of a family dynasty that has ruled Brunei without interruption since the fifteenth century, is the absolute ruler of his small oil-rich nation and one of the world's richest individuals. The total of his private wealth fluctuates with the world price of crude oil and was estimated by *Forbes* magazine to be US$22 billion in 2007. In 1997 it was estimated to have been US$38 billion, which was more than enough at the time to qualify him as world's richest man.

The Sultan shares his wealth with the citizens of Brunei, all of whom enjoy free health care, free education, subsidized rice and housing, and pay no income taxes. His personal charitable foundation, established in 1992, helps Bruneians in other ways. On the other hand, the sultan is also known for having an extravagant lifestyle. His palace, the Istana Nurul Iman, is the world's largest and has 1,788 rooms, 257 bathrooms, five swimming pools, and 564 chandeliers. It was built in 1984 at an estimated cost of US$1.4 billion. The Sultan also has as many 3,000 to 5,000 luxury automobiles, including many unique models, a Boeing 747-400 jet with gold-plated furniture, and some 200 polo ponies living in air-conditioned stables.

History

The Brunei Sultanate was powerful from the fifteenth through to the seventeenth centuries, but lost territory and influence during the European colonial period that came afterward. It resisted joining the Federation of Malaysia in 1963 and became independent in 1984.

Population/Culture

Most residents are ethnic Malays or Chinese descendants of earlier immigrants. A sizable minority of westerners work in the oil industry. Many of these expatriates live in compounds set aside for foreigners and are exempt from some of Brunei's strict Muslim rules, such as those prohibiting alcohol consumption.

Administration/Government

The Sultan of Brunei, whose inherited title has passed through a one-family line since the fifteenth century, rules single-handedly. Because of the enormous oil wealth in this small country, the Sultan is one of the richest men in the world. He is known for a lavish lifestyle and for exerting strong control over life in Brunei, including the media. Citizens are exempt from paying taxes and benefit from free education and health care, subsidized housing and other services.

Economy/Industry

The economy depends on oil production and on income from foreign investments of oil profits. The government is promoting tourism to diversify and widen the economic base.

Because of chronic shortages of labor, the economy depends heavily on workers who come from abroad for temporary jobs. Since 1992 foreigners have comprised more than half the approximately 150,000-strong workforce, particularly in the private sector. While some foreigners hold senior positions in the oil industry, many more labor on construction crews or at the docks, or work in low-paying service jobs. Bruneians dominate the public sector, working as civil servants, public officials, and other government employees.

The largest number of foreigners come from developing countries, such as Indonesia, Malaysia, Thailand, the Philippines, and Bangladesh. Many stay in special dormitories for temporary workers. Because the government is wary about any possible negative influences on Bruneian culture of large numbers of entrenched foreigners, it issues work permits for short durations only and administers heavy penalties, including imprisonment and caning, to guests who overstay.

BRUNEI

Official name Brunei Darussalam (Negara Brunei Darussalam)
Land area 2,035 square miles (5,270 km²)
Border countries Malaysia
Capital Bandar Seri Begawan
Highest point Bukit Pagon 6,070 feet (1,850 m)
Climate Tropical
Population 381,371
Language(s) Official: Malay; other: English, Chinese
Ethnicity Malay 67%, Chinese 15%, indigenous 6%, other 12%
Religion Muslim 67%, Buddhist 13%, Christian 10%, other (including indigenous beliefs) 10%
Government Constitutional sultanate
Currency Bruneian dollar
Human Development Index 0.894 (ranked 30th out of 177 countries)

Above left An orangutan mother and baby. The name orangutan is derived from *orang hutan*, which means "man or person of the forest" in Indonesian and Malay. As the name implies, these great apes live in rainforests, a habitat that is under threat from legal and illegal logging.

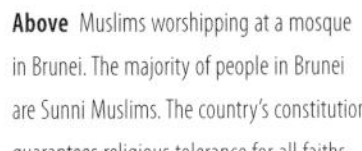

Above Muslims worshipping at a mosque in Brunei. The majority of people in Brunei are Sunni Muslims. The country's constitution guarantees religious tolerance for all faiths.

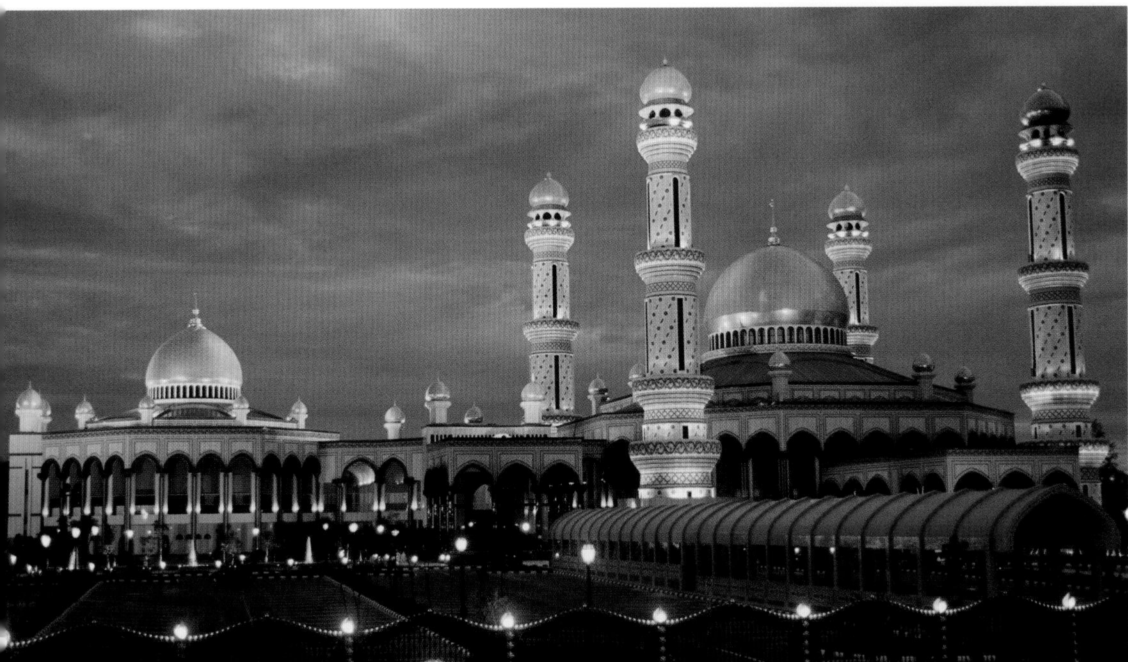

Left Jame'Asr Hassanil Bolkia Mosque (or Kariong Mosque) in Bandar Seri Begawan, the capital of Brunei, was built to commemorate the 25th anniversary of the Sultan's reign. This magnificent building with intricately carved minarets and golden domes towers over the surrounding area.

SINGAPORE

Official name Republic of Singapore
Land area 264 square miles (683 km²)
Border countries None
Capital Singapore
Highest point Bukit Timah Hill 545 feet (166 m)
Climate Tropical
Population 4,554,000
Language(s) Official: Mandarin, English, Malay, Tamil; other: Hokkien, Cantonese, Teochew, other Chinese dialects
Ethnicity Chinese 76.8%, Malay 13.9%, Indian 7.9%, other 1.4%
Religion Buddhist 42.5%, Muslim 14.9%, Taoist 8.5%, Hindu 4%, Christian 14.6%, other 0.7%, none 14.8%
Government Parliamentary republic
Currency Singapore dollar
Human Development Index 0.922 (ranked 25th out of 177 countries)

MALAYSIA
Woodlands
Sembawang
Yishun
Pulau Ubin
Pulau Tekong
SINGAPORE
Ang Mo Kio
Hougang
Bukit Timah
Bishan
Tampines
Jurong
Toa Payoh
Bedok
Queenstown
SINGAPORE
Jurong Island
Sentosa Island
Strait of Singapore
Southern Islands
INDONESIA

Singapore

Map Reference Pages 374–375

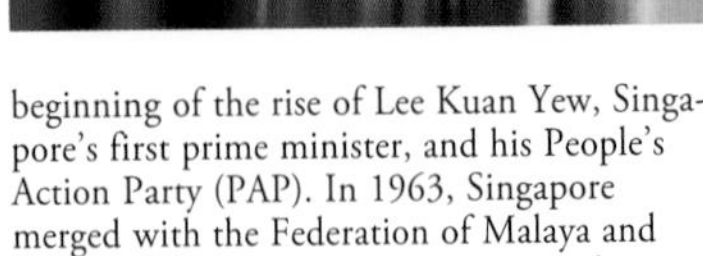

Above right View of Singapore across Marina Bay. The Marina Bay precinct is in the process of redevelopment, with plans underway for a Las Vegas-owned casino and state-of-the-art convention center.

The island of Singapore is a modern independent city-state separated from southern Malaysia by the narrow Strait of Johor, and from northern Indonesia by the more extensive Singapore Strait. Two bridges link Singapore to Johor State in Malaysia. The nation's bustling, highly mechanized port is one of the world's busiest.

Physical Geography

The diamond-shaped main island measures 29 miles (47 km) from east to west and 17 miles (28 km) from north to south. Singapore's land area includes 63 mostly uninhabited surrounding islands. Singapore Island's topography is diverse, with rounded granitic hills dotting the center. Low but steep ridges are found in the west and southeast, while alluvial soils and sediments characterize the flat coastal areas in the east. Singapore's tropical rainforest climate is moderated by sea breezes. Temperatures range from 75°F to 90°F (24–32°C) throughout the year, humidity is higher in mornings than in afternoons. Annual rainfall is 93 inches (236 cm).

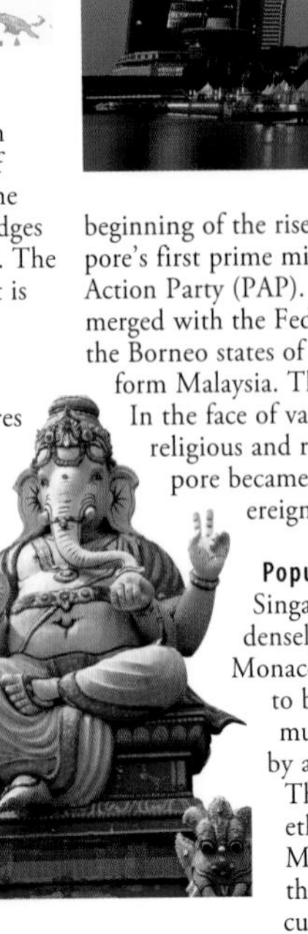

Right This carved temple figure of Ganesa, the Hindu god of prophecy, is one of the many sculptures of Hindu deities that adorn the Sri Mariamman Temple in Singapore City.

History

Located at the crossroads of sea routes between China and India, Singapore long ago became an entrepôt and trans-shipment point for traders from Asia, the Arabian Peninsula, and India. A new era started in 1819 when Sir Stamford Raffles, from the British East India trading company, established a free port there to rival the Dutch port in Batavia (Jakarta). The Suez Canal opening in 1869 and the introduction of steamships in the 1870s consolidated Singapore's dominance as a trade center, and the population became more diverse with the influx of European and Asian businessmen, and tens of thousands of immigrant laborers.

The Japanese occupied Singapore in 1942. When they surrendered in 1945 the colony pressed for independence. Self-governance was gained in 1959. The year also marked the beginning of the rise of Lee Kuan Yew, Singapore's first prime minister, and his People's Action Party (PAP). In 1963, Singapore merged with the Federation of Malaya and the Borneo states of Sabah and Sarawak to form Malaysia. The union was short lived. In the face of various policy conflicts and religious and racial animosities, Singapore became an independent and sovereign country in August 1965.

Population/Culture

Singapore is the world's most densely populated country after Monaco. The state has sought to build a multi-ethnic and multilingual nation unified by a Singaporean identity. The integration of the major ethnic groups—Chinese, Malays, and Indians—and the retention of their many customs and traditions are emphasized in education and housing policies, but the presence of a sizable population of workers from the Philippines, Thailand, Indonesia, and Bangladesh has contributed to the mushrooming of ethnic enclaves.

Administration/Government

Singapore's unicameral parliament has 83 elected representatives. The PAP has enjoyed continuous control of the government since 1959. The first opposition member of parliament was elected in 1981. In 1984, the government introduced the Non-constituted Member of Parliament scheme to allow opposition voices in parliament. The scheme allows for up to three members of opposition party losers—with the highest number of votes in the general election—to be admitted to parliament with restricted voting rights. Parliament also introduced the Nominated Member of Parliament scheme in 1990. The scheme allows for up to six individuals who do not represent any electoral district to participate in parliamentary debates.

Economy/Industry

The economy is strong, with a high per capita GDP. As it has neither natural resources nor a large domestic market to rely on, its twin engine of growth is export-oriented manufacturing and services—industry contributes 33.7 percent and the service sector 66.3 percent respectively to GDP. In the early 1960s, Singapore was a haven for low-cost, labor-intensive manufacturing. By the late 1980s, the economy was oriented toward developing high value-added manufacturing activities, and incentives were introduced to attract global corporations to the island. However, the recession of 2001–03 hit consumer electronics and information technology products. As a result of the downturn, the government has changed its emphasis and aims to attract businesses less affected by the peaks and troughs of global demand.

Above Festive lanterns decorate a street in Singapore's Chinatown. This vibrant area was established in 1821 when the first Chinese junk sailed in from Xiamen.

Below The legendary Raffles Hotel was declared a National Monument in 1987. Named for Sir Stamford Raffles, the father of modern Singapore, the hotel has hosted many of the rich and famous, and is renowned for the invention of the potent cocktail, the "Singapore Sling."

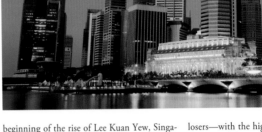

RAFFLES HOTEL

GARDEN CITY

Singapore is largely urban; its landscape consists mostly of built-up areas of skyscrapers and modern infrastructure. Despite this the island is renowned for its lush greenery: Its streetscapes are lined with shady trees, flowering shrubs, and many varied and interesting parks. The rooftops and walls of high-rise building are also green—some rooftop gardens are like tropical jungles. Lush tropical creepers adorn bridge pylons and similar structures to soften the jarring effect of concrete.

The island's luxuriant landscape is the result of state effort. The idea of turning the island into a garden city was driven by Prime Minister Lee Kuan Yew, beginning with a tree planting campaign in 1963. The idea was to ensure that rapid urbanization went hand-in-hand with a healthy, aesthetically pleasing environment. It was also expected that a quality urban environment would attract foreign investments into the country. The greening of Singapore's built environment enables the best use of the small island's limited land resources. The optimal use of land and space is deemed as central to the making of Singapore as a world city for a targeted population of 6,500,00 people. Today, the garden city hosts the renowned biennial Singapore Garden Festival, the only such festival in the tropics.

MILESTONE EVENTS

1819 Sir Stamford Raffles from the British East India trading company establishes a free port on Singapore Island
1826 Singapore, Malacca, and Penang become the British Straits Settlements
1832 Singapore becomes capital of Straits Settlements attracting thousands of migrants from Europe and Asia
1867 Straits Settlements become British Crown colony
1941 Singapore bombed by Japan
1942–45 Singapore falls to Japan
August 1945 Japan defeated, World War II ends
1946 Singapore becomes separate British Crown colony
1959 Self-government attained; Lee Kuan Yew becomes prime minister
1963 Singapore merges with Federation of Malaya
1965 After racial tensions and violence, Singapore withdraws from the federation and declares independence
1967 Singapore founder member of Association of Southeast Asian Nations (ASEAN)
1990 Prime Minister Lee Kuan Yew leaves office after 31 years
1993 Ong Teng Cheong becomes nation's first directly elected president
1998 Downturn in economy due to Asian financial crisis
April 2001 First legal demonstration outside of election campaigns takes place
April 2003 Outbreak of SARS virus
May 2003 Singapore signs free trade agreement with USA
2004 August Former Prime Minister Lee Kuan Yew's son, Lee Hsien Loong, is sworn in as prime minister
May 2006 Lee Hsien Loong's ruling People's Action Party wins general election
October 2007 The Airbus A380, the world's largest passenger plane, flies from Singapore to Sydney on its maiden commercial flight

Batan Islands
Babuyan Islands
Laoag
Luzon
Baguio
Philippine Sea
Dagupan
Cabanatuan
Angeles
Olongapo
Valenzuela
South China Sea
MANILA
Quezon City
Lucena
Batangas
Naga
Mindoro
Legaspi
PHILIPPINES
Calbayog
Samar
Panay
Cadiz
Tacloban
Iloilo
Palawan
Cebu
Negros
Butuan
Sulu Sea
Cagayan de Oro
Mindanao
Mt Apo
Davao
Zamboanga
General Santos
MALAYSIA
Celebes Sea
INDONESIA

Philippines

Map Reference Pages 376–377

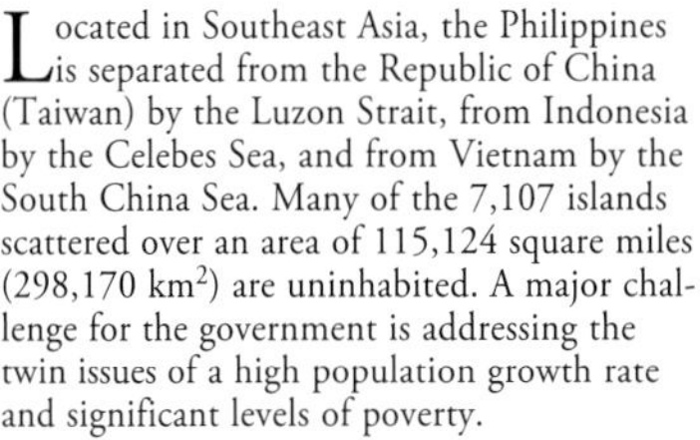

Above A wayside shrine on Luzon Island, with Mt Mayon in the distance. The most active volcano in the Philippines, Mt Mayon's most recent eruption occurred in 1993.

Located in Southeast Asia, the Philippines is separated from the Republic of China (Taiwan) by the Luzon Strait, from Indonesia by the Celebes Sea, and from Vietnam by the South China Sea. Many of the 7,107 islands scattered over an area of 115,124 square miles (298,170 km^2) are uninhabited. A major challenge for the government is addressing the twin issues of a high population growth rate and significant levels of poverty.

Physical Geography

The Philippines is one of the most hazardous countries in the world in terms of natural catastrophes. The mountainous landscape of rapidly flooding rivers (blizzard floods) is vulnerable to landslides and erosion that is made worse by deforestation. Many islands are at risk of earthquakes, volcanic eruptions, floods, typhoons, tidal waves, and drought.

Mt Apo on Mindanao is the highest peak. An active volcano, it is renowned for the biodiversity on its slopes. The climate is tropical marine with year-round high humidity and two distinct seasons—wet and dry.

History

Prior to colonization by Spain in 1521, the Philippines was an archipelago of independent island communities with a variety of belief systems. In 1898 Spain sold the Philippines to the USA as a result of the Spanish–American War. Although the Philippines gained its independence in 1946, the US maintained a military presence until 1992. Recent history has featured a series of rapid regime changes and the country is unbalanced politically, socially, and economically. A further source of instability has been decades of Muslim insurgency in the south of the country.

Population/Culture

The Philippines has several ethnic groups and about 65 cultural minorities that speak over 85 different dialects. A rich cultural heritage reflects the complexity of its history. Key influences include Hispanic music, dance, literature, food, language, and art. The Catholic Church's influence is apparent in religious celebrations and equal access to education. Sulu and Mindanao became Muslim in the thirteenth and fourteenth centuries. Chinese influence is especially visible in rural areas, while popular culture reflects the American influence. During the festival season people participate in vibrant barrio fiestas and street parades, and cockfights.

Administration/Government

The government is a parliamentary democracy. The president is both head of government and chief of state. The army has considerable influence on the administration. The president and vice-president are popularly elected (on separate tickets). The bicameral Congress consists of a House of Representatives with 239 seats and a Senate with 24 seats. The legal system is based on Spanish and Anglo-American law; the Supreme Court and Court of Appeals represent the judiciary.

Economy/Industry

The Philippines is economically linked to the Association of Southeast Asian Nations (ASEAN), and also belongs to the Newly Industrialized Economies (NIE) group of countries. Natural resources include nickel, cobalt, silver, gold, salt, copper, and timber, although only 20 percent of forests remain. Agriculture, which employs 35 percent of the workforce, produces sugarcane, pineapples, bananas, coconuts, rice, and corn, and contributes 14 percent to the national economy. The industrial sector, employing 15 percent of the workforce and contributing more than 31 percent to GDP, produces garments, footwear, pharmaceuticals, chemicals and more. The service sector is the largest employer and contributes over 54 percent to GDP. For historic reasons, the economy of the country is still very fragile, and conflict over landowning is one of the most critical issues faced by the nation. Migrant worker remittances also contribute significantly to the economy.

MILESTONE EVENTS

1521 Spain colonizes the Philippines

June 12, 1898 The Philippines proclaims independence from Spain

December 10, 1898 The Spanish–American War ends with Spain ceding the Philippines to the USA (the USA paid 20 billion dollars for the Philippines, Guam, and Puerto Rico)

July 4, 1901 The USA declares an end to military rule in the Philippines

1935 The Philippines becomes a self-governing commonwealth

1942–1945 Japan occupies the Philippines

1945 The USA regains control of the Philippines

July 4, 1946 The Philippines gains independence

1947 The Republic of the Philippines–United States Military Bases Agreement is signed allowing the USA to maintain bases in the Philippines for 99 years without paying rent

1965 The first president of the Fourth Philippine Republic, Ferdinand Marcos, is elected

1986 President Marcos is forced into exile by EDSA 1, a people's revolutionary movement; Corazon Aquino becomes president

1992 The USA closes its bases in the Philippines

2008 The government reiterates its commitment to the peace process with the Moro Islamic Liberation Front (MILF) in Mindanao in a bid to resolve decades of Muslim insurgency in the southern Philippines

PHILIPPINES

Official name Republic of the Philippines (Republika ng Pilipinas)

Land area 115,124 square miles (298,170 km^2)

Border countries None

Capital Manila

Highest point Mt Apo (Mindanao) 9,692 feet (2,954 m)

Climate Tropical marine

Population 91,077,287

Language(s) Official: Filipino, English; other: Tagalog, Cebuano, Ilocano, Hiligaynon (Ilonggo), Bicol, Waray, Pampango, Pangasinan, other dialects

Ethnicity Tagalog 28.1%, Cebuano 13.1%, Ilocano 9%, Bisaya/Binisaya 7.6%, Hiligaynon Ilonggo 7.5%, Bikol 6%, Waray 3.4%, other 25.3%

Religion Christian 88.2%, Muslim 5%, Iglesia ni Kristo 2.3%, Aglipayan 2%, other 2.4%, none 0.1%

Government Republic

Currency Philippine peso

Human Development Index 0.771 (ranked 90th out of 177 countries)

Above The Dinagyang Festival has been held in the city of Iloilo since 1968. It is celebrated on the fourth weekend in January to honor the Christ Child, and is a time of thanksgiving and joy.

Left A collection of stilt houses on the lush, unspoiled tropical island of Tawitawi, the southernmost island of the Philippines.

PHILIPPINES
Medan
MALAYSIA
Celebes Sea
PACIFIC OCEAN
Pekanbaru
SINGAPORE
Manado
Halmahera
Padang
Pontianak
Samarinda
Gorontalo
Jambi
Borneo
Balikpapan
Palembang
Bandjarmasin
Sulawesi
Ambon
New Guinea
Jayapura
Puncak Jaya
Sumatera
INDONESIA
PAPUA NEW GUINEA
Tanjungkarang-Telukbetung
JAKARTA
Java Sea
Makassar
Semarang
Surabaya
Malang
Banda Sea
INDIAN OCEAN
Yogyakarta
Denpasar
TIMOR-LESTE
Jawa
Sumba
Timor
Kupang
Arafura Sea
AUSTRALIA

INDONESIA

Official name Indonesia (Republik Indonesia)
Land area 741,096 square miles (1,919,440 km²)
Border countries Malaysia, Papua New Guinea, Timor-Leste
Capital Jakarta
Highest point Puncak Jaya (New Guinea) 16,503 feet (5,030 m)
Climate Tropical
Population 237,512,000
Language(s) Official: Bahasa Indonesia; other: English, Dutch, and more than 700 local languages (mostly widely spoken is Javanese)
Ethnicity Javanese 41.7%, Sundanese 15.4%, Malayan 3.5%, other or unspecified 39.4%
Religion Muslim 86% (largest in the world), Protestant 5%, Roman Catholic 3%, Hindu 5%, Buddhist 1%
Government Republic
Currency Rupia
Human Development Index 0.728 (ranked 107th out of 177 countries)

Indonesia

Map Reference Pages 372–375

Indonesia is a sweeping curve made up of 18,108 islands of which only 6,000 are inhabited. It is the most densely populated nation in Southeast Asia, and the archipelago is the biggest in the world. The western half of the island of New Guinea (Irian Jaya) was linked (via Dutch rule) to Indonesia in 1963. Years later, in 2002, the province of East Timor gained its independence and became a new nation called Timor-Leste.

Physical Geography

Indonesia is situated between the Philippines, Australia, and Indochina, and between the Indian and Pacific oceans. It is home to around 15 percent of the world's coral reefs, and is a popular destination for scuba divers.

The largest islands are Kalimantan, Java, and Sumatra. Indonesia sits in an extremely tectonically unstable region and has experienced many volcanic eruptions, earthquakes, and tsunamis. Of Indonesia's 400 or so volcanoes, around 100 are active. Krakatau volcano in the Sunda Straits erupted in August 1883, killing around 36,400 people. The eruption blew the top 4 cubic miles (18 km³) off the summit.

In December 1927, Javanese fishermen noticed plumes of steam and debris shooting from the sea. They were witnessing the birth of Anak Krakatau, "child of Krakatau," a new volcano rising from the caldera of the old one. Since 1927, Anak Krakatau has grown into a 100-foot (300-m) tall conical-shaped island. Anak still has quite a way to grow before it is ready to complete the next explosive cycle.

In more recent times, the subterranean earthquake on December 26, 2004 off the west coast of Sumatra and subsequent tsunami caused widespread devastation and led to the deaths of over 150,000 people in South Asia and East Africa, the greatest death toll from such an event in recorded history.

A rich diversity of flora is found in the archipelago. The world's largest flower—the stemless, parasitic *Rafflesia arnoldi*—and the largest orchid—the giant orchid—are both found in isolated pockets throughout Borneo and Sumatra, while the overall humus-rich soils provide a perfect habitat for rare luminescent varieties of fungus and black mildew.

Indonesia's indigenous fauna includes the Komodo dragons on the island of Flores, east of Bali, and one-horned and two-horned rhinoceroses that can still be spotted in West Java. The island of Sulawesi has evolved its own peculiar array of endemic mammals such as the dwarf buffalo and strange deer-like pigs, while its nutrient-poor serpentine soils host rare and endemic species of wildflowers.

The island of Bali off the east coast of Java is an anomaly: An overwhelmingly Hindu society in the world's most populous Muslim nation. The south is a mix of dry alluvial plains and shallow rivers with a string of mountains across its center.

History

The Portuguese invasion at the start of 1500 was only one episode in the archipelago's long history. There were many independent Buddhist and Hindu kingdoms on the islands of Sumatra and Java as early as 600 BCE. In 1600 the archipelago was united violently by the Dutch, who quelled the independence of the local kingdoms. The colony was under the rule of the Netherlands for 300 years.

In 1945, President Sukarno and his league claimed independence for Indonesia, but it took four years and the help of the United Nations to achieve it. After independence, Sukarno tried to unite the state through his own communist ideology of *Nasakom (Nationalism-Agama-Kommunism)* and autocratic leadership.

In September 1965, General Suharto suppressed a military coup by a small band of leftwing military officers, and over the next six months led a nationwide violent purge of Indonesians deemed to be communists and Islamists. Sukarno was deposed and hundreds of thousands of people lost their lives. The new dictator Suharto ruled by promoting the ideology of *Pancasila* (the Five Principles, which included the unity of Indonesia) and by using military force; the US covertly supported his actions against communists. In the 1990s, a groundswell of opposition to his rule by repression expressed itself in protests across the country, and in 1998, the man known as the "smiling general" was forced to step down.

Above right Built during the eighth and ninth centuries, the famous Borobudur temple in central Java is a shrine to the Lord Buddha and a place of pilgrimage.

Right Characters used in the Javanese shadow puppet theater *(Wayang Kulit)* are skilfully carved from leather and deftly manipulated by *dalang*, the superstar performers who command hefty fees for their puppeteering talents.

Suharto's 32-year reign saw Indonesia develop closer ties with the west, with both positive and negative results. Overseas investment boosted the economy but in some cases resulted in environmental destruction.

After Suharto's fall, the government strove toward a parliamentary democracy. In 2001, the People's Consultative Assembly moved toward a system whereby the president is directly elected by the people. Susilo Bambang Yudhoyono became the first president to be elected this way when he took office in 2004.

Population

A major problem facing Indonesia is population density. Most Indonesians live on either Java or Bali. Although it constitutes less than 10 percent of archipelago's land area, Java is the most crowded island, supporting almost 60 percent of the population. Government endeavors to move people from Java to other islands have faced resistance from hundreds of other ethnic groups in the islands.

Overall, the population is increasing at a rate of about 1.2 percent. Currently, it is the fourth-most populous country in the world (after China, India, and the USA).

Culture/Religion

There are over 700 languages and 300 ethnic groups across Indonesia. Many Javanese belong to the highest class of the social strata. Their privileges, inherited from the colonial times, have allowed them to dominate political, business, and academic arenas.

Most Indonesians are Muslim. The other major religions are Protestantism, Catholicism,

Below right Anak Krakatau rose, phoenix-like, from the Sunda Strait 80 years after the previous volcano, Krakatau, blew its top in 1883.

Below Ulun Danu is one of the most important Hindu temple complexes on Bali. It sits on a promontory jutting into the serene Beratan Lake, north of Denpasar.

Left Mt Bromo (left) and Mt Semeru (right) are active volcanoes in the Bromo–Tengger–Semeru National Park, Java. Mt Bromo has erupted more that 60 times since 1767—in 1996 an eruption killed 39 people and in 1994 another killed two tourists walking on the rim.

Below Quintessentially a traditional dance of grace and femininity, the *legong* is performed by very young Indonesian girls—by the age of 14 a dancer may be considering her retirement.

Hinduism, and Buddhism. These faiths are officially recognized. The ancient temple area of Borobudur in Yogyakarta, a religious center that dates back to the Buddhist era (1300 CE), is on UNESCO's World Heritage List.

Administration/Government

The president, who is the head of state and commander-in-chief, and the vice-presdent, are directly elected. The bicameral People's Consultative Assembly has 550 elected members in the lower house, and 128 elected members in the upper house. Military forces retain a major role in politics and government.

Pancasila remains the national philosophy; the national motto is Unity in Diversity. The government is faced with the ongoing task of striking a balance between recognizing and celebrating the heterogeneity of Indonesia and fostering a philosophy of cohesion and unity. Old problems of separatism still live among many guerrilla movements in Sulawesi and Ambon. In practice, the central government tries to keep politics out of religion.

Economy/Industry

Indonesia's natural resources include oil, gas, tin, nickel, bauxite, copper, and rubber; the country has the second largest tropical forests in the world. The major export countries are the USA, Singapore, Malaysia, Japan, and Australia. Profits from oil exports allowed Indonesia to enjoy good economic growth in the late 1980s and 1990s.

The economic crises of Southeast Asia were hazardous to Indonesia's fragile society and economy in the 1990s, and in part led to the rise of violent attacks between various ethnic and religious groups. Muslim attacks on Chinese merchants and entrepreneurs in the 1990s were as much economic as religious in nature because the Chinese minority owned most such businesses. Many Chinese people were obliged to migrate to Kalimantan province on the island of Borneo, which made it difficult for them to continue trading.

The big question is who is benefiting from the rich natural resources? Regions outside Java would like to use their resources for their own benefit and not send them to Java. The huge forest resources of the country are vital for the whole world as "safeguards" against climate change because of their capacity to absorb carbon dioxide, but at present the tropical forests are rapidly vanishing. The rehabilitation of forests challenges sustainable development. In Kalimantan illegal logging is a major problem and the vast forest regions have been transformed into fields of sugar cane, palm oil, and other export products, partly for use as biofuels. Only 20 percent of the trees felled are of commercial value. It is to be noted that large companies do carry out reforestation to supply their paper mills and for domestic purposes.

Merapi's Fury

Mt Merapi, one of the world's most dangerous volcanoes, is on the island of Java, on the border between central Java and Yogyakarta. No vegetation grows at the top because volcanic ash often falls there, and because of the *nuées ardentes* (avalanches of ash and pumice) resulting from crumbling of the summit lava dome. Dense vegetation covers the volcano's lower flanks, where many farmers live. The old volcanic ash makes rich soil for growing crops, but it is a dangerous place to live. A devastating eruption in 1930 killed 1,300 people. Another, in 1976, killed 28 people and left 1,176 people homeless. In 1979, 80 people were killed when heavy rainfall led to mudflows that surged 12 miles (20 km) down the flank of the volcano. In 1994, a dome collapse sent hot volcanic flows down the volcano's southern side, killing 43 people. Today, 50,000 people live on the volcano's flanks, and the city of Yogyakarta (population 3 million) lies only 22 miles (35 km) to the south.

In April 2006, Merapi again showed signs of activity. All residents were ordered off the mountain in early May. Volcanic activity had begun to calm by the middle of May, and villagers started to return. Then a large earthquake struck nearby, and Mt Merapi became active once again.

MILESTONE EVENTS

600 BCE–1300 CE Old Hindu and Buddhist kingdoms exist

1500 Portugal invades Indonesia

1600–1945 The archipelago is a Dutch colony

1945–1949 Indonesia moves to independence

1962 New Guinea is transferred from the Netherlands to Indonesia

1998 Suharto's rule comes to an end

2002 East Timor (Timor-Leste) gains its independence from Indonesia

2007 The World Conference on Climate Change is held in Bali

2008 Former president Suharto dies

INDONESIA
Selat Ombai
Pulau Atauro
TIMOR-LESTE
Atauro
Selat Wetar
Lautem
Tutuala
Pulau Jaco
Baucau
Los Palos
Liquica
DILI
Manatuto
TIMOR-LESTE
Ossu
Lore
Batugade
Maubisse
Viqueque
Foho Tatamailau
Maliana
Pante Makasar
TIMOR-LESTE
Timor Sea
Suai
INDONESIA
Timor

Timor-Leste

Map Reference Pages 372–373

Timor-Leste (East Timor), a nation of rugged tropical mountains, savanna, and grasslands, is located on the eastern half of the island of Timor, off the northwest coast of Australia. In May 2002 it was declared one of the world's newest independent nations.

Timor was a Portuguese colony from the sixteenth century. In 1859 the Dutch assumed sovereignty over its western half. When the Portuguese abandoned East Timor in 1975, the Indonesian military began a brutal occupation that lasted for 24 years. In a 1999 referendum most of Timor-Leste's population voted for independence. A violent and deadly backlash by anti-independence militia (backed by the Indonesian military) left the country and much of its infrastructure in ruins and forced some 300,000 people to flee to West Timor. In September 1999 the Australian-led International Force for East Timor (INTERFET) arrived and restored a measure of peace. Violence broke out again in 2006 causing the internal displacement of many thousands of people.

Timor-Leste experiences a tropical climate with distinct dry and rainy seasons. In the north there is little or no rain for much of the year, then landslides and flooding occur.

Timor-Leste is largely dependent on foreign aid, and forced to consider unorthodox approaches to revenue raising such as selling fishing rights to other nations. It is fostering its tourism potential and seeking international trade and investment opportunities. Agriculture is the main source of income, with coffee the only significant export. Abundant oil and gas reserves in the Timor Sea offers the nation, with an unemployment rate of 50 percent, the promise of future prosperity.

TIMOR-LESTE

Official name Democratic Republic of Timor-Leste (Repúblika Demokrátika Timor Lorosa'e; Republica Democratica de Timor-Leste)

Land area 5,794 square miles (15,007 km²)

Border countries Indonesia

Capital Dili

Highest point Foho Tatamailau 9,721 feet (2,963 m)

Climate Tropical; hot, humid; wet and dry seasons

Population 1,109,000

Language(s) Tetum, Portuguese, Indonesian, English, Tetum, Galole, Mambae, Kemak, 12 indigenous languages

Ethnicity Timorese 78%, Indonesian 20%, Chinese 2%

Religion(s) Christian 99%, Muslim 1%

Government Republic

Currency US dollar

Human Development Index 0.514 (ranked 150th out of 177 countries)

Above These dancers are wearing *tais*, a Tetum word meaning "cloth." These traditional textiles have been woven by women in Timor-Leste for centuries. The designs tell important stories.

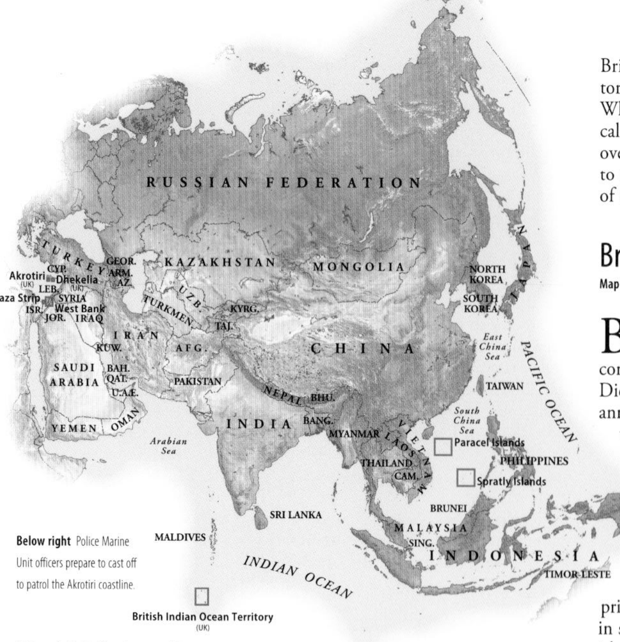
RUSSIAN FEDERATION
TURKEY
GEOR.
ARM.
AZ.
CYP.
Akrotiri (UK)
Dhekelia (UK)
LEB.
Gaza Strip
SYRIA
ISR.
West Bank
JOR.
IRAQ
KAZAKHSTAN
MONGOLIA
NORTH KOREA
SOUTH KOREA
JAPAN
UZB.
TURKMEN.
KYRG.
TAJ.
IRAN
KUW.
AFG.
CHINA
East China Sea
PACIFIC OCEAN
SAUDI ARABIA
BAH.
QAT.
U.A.E.
PAKISTAN
NEPAL
BHU.
TAIWAN
YEMEN
OMAN
INDIA
BANG.
MYANMAR
LAOS
VIETNAM
South China Sea
Paracel Islands
Arabian Sea
THAILAND
CAM.
PHILIPPINES
Spratly Islands
BRUNEI
SRI LANKA
MALAYSIA
SING.
MALDIVES
INDONESIA
TIMOR-LESTE
INDIAN OCEAN
British Indian Ocean Territory (UK)

Below right Police Marine Unit officers prepare to cast off to patrol the Akrotiri coastline.

Bottom right The fifteenth-century Ayios Elias Church is a prominent feature of Protaras, Cyprus. This town near Dhekelia Sovereign Base is now a haven for British tourists.

AKROTIRI AND DHEKELIA

Official name Akrotiri and Dhekelia Sovereign Base Areas
Land area 98 square miles (253.8 km²)
Capital Episkopi Cantonment
Climate Temperate Mediterranean
Population 14,000 (7,000 British military, 7,000 Cypriot)
Government Administered by British military personnel
Currency Cypriot pound

BRITISH INDIAN OCEAN TERRITORY

Official name British Indian Ocean Territory (BIOT)
Land area 23 square miles (60 km²)
Capital Diego Garcia
Climate Tropical marine
Population 4,000 (military personnel)
Government Military administration
Currency Pound Sterling

PARACEL ISLANDS

Official name Paracel Islands
Land area Not available
Capital None
Climate Tropical
Population Not available
Government Administered by People's Republic of China
Currency Chinese yuan

SPRATLY ISLANDS

Official name Spratly Islands
Land area 2 square miles (5 km²)
Capital None
Climate Tropical
Population No indigenous inhabitants
Government Disputed territory

Akrotiri and Dhekelia

Map Reference Pages 390–391

The Akrotiri and Dhekelia Sovereign Base Areas on the Mediterranean island of Cyprus are British territories retained by agreement with the UK when Cyprus gained independence from Britain in 1960. The Treaty of Establishment of the Republic of Cyprus guarantees Britain a continuing military presence in the region.

The bases cover 3 percent of the land area of Cyprus and with almost two-thirds privately owned and the remainder owned by the British Ministry of Defence. The administrator is an appointee of Queen Elizabeth II. Whoever holds this position possesses identical legislative and executive prerogatives of an overseas governor. The only economic activity to speak of is the provision of a limited degree of administrative support to the military.

British Indian Ocean Territory

Map Reference Pages 80–81

British Indian Ocean Territory is a group of 55 islands east of the Seychelles. They consist of the Chagos Archipelago (including Diego Garcia) and a number of other islands annexed by the British government in 1965 when their 1,200 residents were relocated.

Discovered by Vasco da Gama in the sixteenth century, the islands were administered by France until ceded, with Mauritius, to Britain in 1814. Mauritius continued to administer the islands until 1965.

The British Indian Ocean Territory's primary role is the provision of various services in support of the US military outpost on the island of Diego Garcia. Since the 1980s the Mauritian government has reasserted claims over the islands.

SBA POLICE
MARINE UNIT

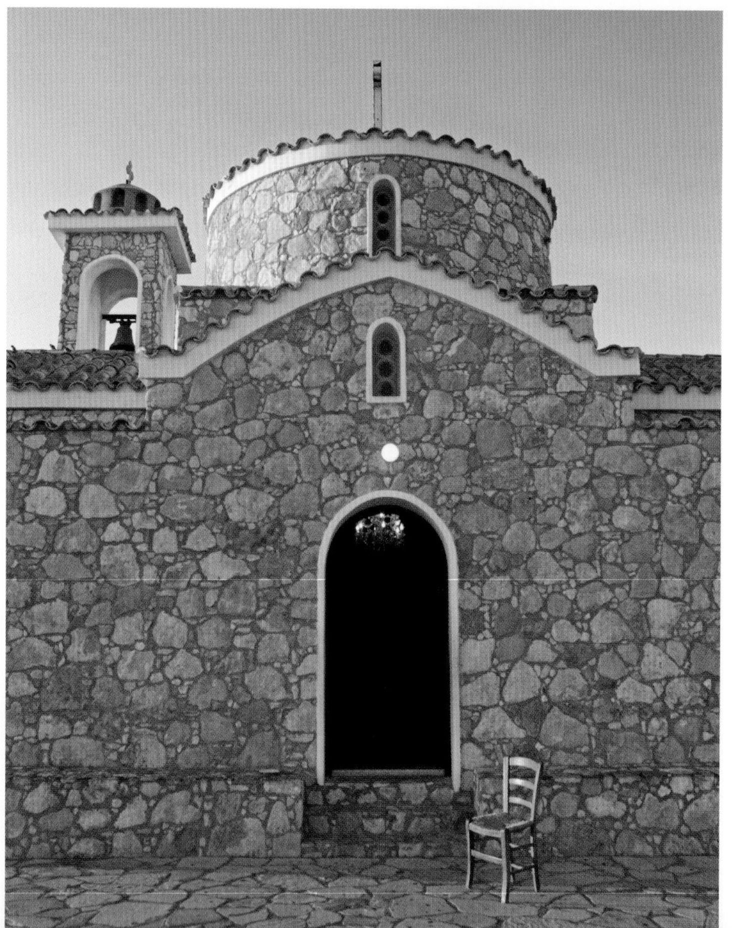

Paracel Islands

Map Reference Pages 376–377

The Paracel Islands—130 reefs and small coral islands in the South China Sea—have been subject to a long-running dispute over sovereignty between Vietnam, China, and Republic of China (Taiwan). South Vietnam claimed the islands in 1951 and annexed the group in October 1956. In 1974 Chinese forces invaded the Paracel Islands, overrunning Vietnamese garrisons in the Battle of Hoang Sa, and have administered the group ever since.

With the exception of two port facilities on Duncan and Woody islands and an airport with one paved runway, there is almost no infrastructure, although China is making moves to open the islands to tourism. There are no natural land-based resources, but potential natural gas and oil fields have been located offshore. There is no arable land on the islands.

Spratly Islands

Map Reference Pages 376–377

Located in the southern South China Sea, between the Philippines and Vietnam, Spratly Islands consist of about 600 coral reefs, islets, rocks, sand bars, shoals, and sea mounts, claimed all or in part by six nations. The Spratlys are spread over 158,300 square miles (410,000 km²). Commercial fishing around the Spratly Islands is highly productive.

The Spratlys have been the foci of intense geopolitical interest since the discovery of petroleum in 1968 in nearby subsea sedimentary basins. It has been speculated that up to US$1 trillion worth of oil and natural gas might be recovered. The People's Republic of China, Republic of China (Taiwan), and the Socialist Republic of Vietnam claim the Spratlys entirely. Brunei, the Republic of the Philippines, and Malaysia assert sovereignty over lesser areas. The People's Republic of China has been most assertive in advancing its claims, maintaining military garrisons on several islands. Some of the other claimant countries also have a military presence.

Palestinian Territories

Map Reference Pages 390–391

Palestine is not considered a country—it is physically and politically divided, and the entities of the Gaza Strip and the West Bank are unrecognized politically by most of the world. Uncertainty has become a way of life for Palestinians since this region in the Middle East was carved up in 1947 to create an Arab and Jewish state. Palestinians and other Arab nations rejected the plans. In 1948, Israel declared independence and now physically separates the West Bank and Gaza.

In 2006 Hamas, the Islamic Resistance Movement, won elections that gave the organization control of the Palestinian Legislative Council. As Hamas does not recognize Israel and refuses to abide by any peace agreements between Israel and the Palestinian Authority,

the international community does not recognize the Hamas government. Hamas has also failed to renounce violence, which is another factor that alienates most of the world.

Life became even more uncertain in 2007 as Gaza and the West Bank violently split over political differences, with Gaza under the control of Hamas and the West Bank dominated by Fatah, the party of the Palestinian Authority President Mahmud Abbas. Each group believes they hold the authority over all of Palestine.

Adding to the confusion are the Israeli settlements that dot the Palestinian landscape, self-contained communities often located on higher ground that overlooks Palestinian lands. Israel accumulated most of these lands after the 1967 Six-Day War. The settlements are a major barrier to peace, and Israel has been evacuating them, often by forcefully evicting residents. All the settlements in Gaza have been abandoned, but over 250,000 Israelis remain in settlements in the West Bank.

The Palestinians are largely dependent on Israel for basic daily needs like food, water, and electricity. Both Israel and Palestine seek to have Jerusalem as their capital. The religious significance of the city is a priority to Muslims, Christians, and Jews. Though all three faiths worship the God of Abraham, unity in the region is yet to be achieved.

Palestine (West Bank)

Map Reference Pages 390–391

The West Bank is pinched between Israel and Jordan. With its political division from Gaza in 2007, the West Bank faces an uncertain future. Israel occupies most of the territory and Israeli settlements punctuate the landscape.

There are three geographic regions in the West Bank. The Jordan Valley region runs along the Jordan River and the Dead Sea in the south, their waters forming the boundary with Jordan where two and half a million Palestinians live in exile. This region experiences hot summers, warm winters and little rainfall.

The Eastern Slopes region runs along the eastern edge of the West Bank. The climate is semi-dry and sheep and goats are farmed here. The Central Highlands region runs between the cities of Hebron in the south and Janin in the north. The topography is rugged with elevations over 3,300 feet (1,000 m). This is the wettest region, with an average rainfall of 15¾ to 27½ inches (400–700 mm) per year.

The West Bank's history traces back to the Canaanites over 4,000 years ago. Islam entered in the seventh century. The British forced out the Ottoman Turks and ruled the West Bank from 1917 until 1948 when war broke out over Israel's independence. The West Bank was under Jordanian authority until 1967 when the Six-Day War resulted in the territory being occupied by Israel. Israeli and Palestinian agreements in the 1990s set up the Palestinian Authority with the intention of creating a Palestinian state. The division of Gaza and the West Bank in 2007 has led to uncertainty over Palestinian independence.

Most people living in the West Bank are Palestinian Arabs. Three-quarters of the West Bank is Muslim, mostly Sunni, while 17 percent are Jewish and another 8 percent are Christian or some other faith. Arabic is the primary language; many Palestinians also speak English and Hebrew.

Currently, the West Bank is governed by the Fatah party. Recognition of the West Bank government continues to be negotiated with Israel and the international community.

The economy has suffered greatly since conflict with Israel escalated in 2000. Before this there had been extensive transborder trade that has now largely evaporated.

PALESTINE (WEST BANK)

Official name West Bank
Land area 2,178 square miles (5,640 km^2)
Capital (disputed)
Climate Temperate
Population 2,536,000
Government (Palestinian Authority)
Currency New Israeli shekel, Jordanian dinar

Left Bethlehem, on the west side of the Jordan River, relies heavily on income from pilgrims and tourists. Being part of the West Bank, Bethlehem is controlled by the Palestinian Authority.

Palestine (Gaza Strip)

Map Reference Pages 390–391

A million and a half people, with little fresh water or natural resources, are crushed into a tiny area lying on the Mediterranean Sea and squeezed between Egypt and Israel. The Gaza Strip creates a stir around the world out of proportion to its size, due to the ruling Hamas political party.

The flat coastal plain is carpeted with sand and dunes. The climate is semi-arid with hot dry summers, mild winters, and an average rainfall of 7¾ to 15¾ inches (200–400 mm).

Gaza, once called Canaan, was the home of the Egyptian governor during ancient times. In the late twelfth century BCE, after the Philistines arrived, the city of Gaza became an important port. Islam arrived during the seventh century. Outsiders ruled for many centuries, with the British assuming power after the Ottoman Turks in 1917. This lasted until 1947. Gaza was occupied by Egypt from 1948 until 1967, and then Israel; the last Israeli settlements were abandoned in 2005.

An enormous challenge for Gaza is the high population density, a staggering 10,665 people per square mile (4,118 per km^2). Combined with the West Bank, Gaza has an unemployment rate of 20.3 percent.

The people of the Gaza Strip are mostly Palestinian Arab and Muslim. There are also small Jewish and Christian populations. Since Hamas took control from the Palestinian Authority in 2007, many believe that the society has developed a dangerous culture of violence. Weapons are very easy to obtain and are openly visible on the streets, with children exposed to the problem and acculturated into the violence.

The international community continues efforts to broker a lasting peace agreement between Hamas and the Israeli government, with a number of ceasefire arrangements bringing temporary peace to the region.

Fishing is an important industry in the Gaza Strip, but Israel's navy often blockades the fishing areas. The primary natural resource is natural gas, and close to one-third of the land is arable; however, farming lands and fresh water are both increasing in salinity.

Above Date palms (pictured) and olive trees once grew in abundance in Gaza, but over the last two decades farming land has been levelled and some of it confiscated. The International Committee of the Red Cross is helping farmers rehabilitate their land and their livelihoods.

PALESTINE (GAZA STRIP)

Official name Gaza Strip
Land area 139 square miles (360 km^2)
Capital Gaza
Climate Temperate
Population 1,482,000
Government (disputed)
Currency New Israeli shekel

Left This Palestinian child lives in Jabalia in northern Gaza. A great many children have been killed here in the ongoing violence that is a tragic feature of daily life.

Below A Palestinian Arab man and a donkey, loaded with wheat straw, Nablus. Unemployment in the West Bank runs at over 20 percent and half of the population lives below the poverty line.

1:37,500,000

Lambert Azimuthal Equal Area Projection

0 500 1000 1500 2000 kilometers

0 250 500 750 1000 miles

Asia Physical

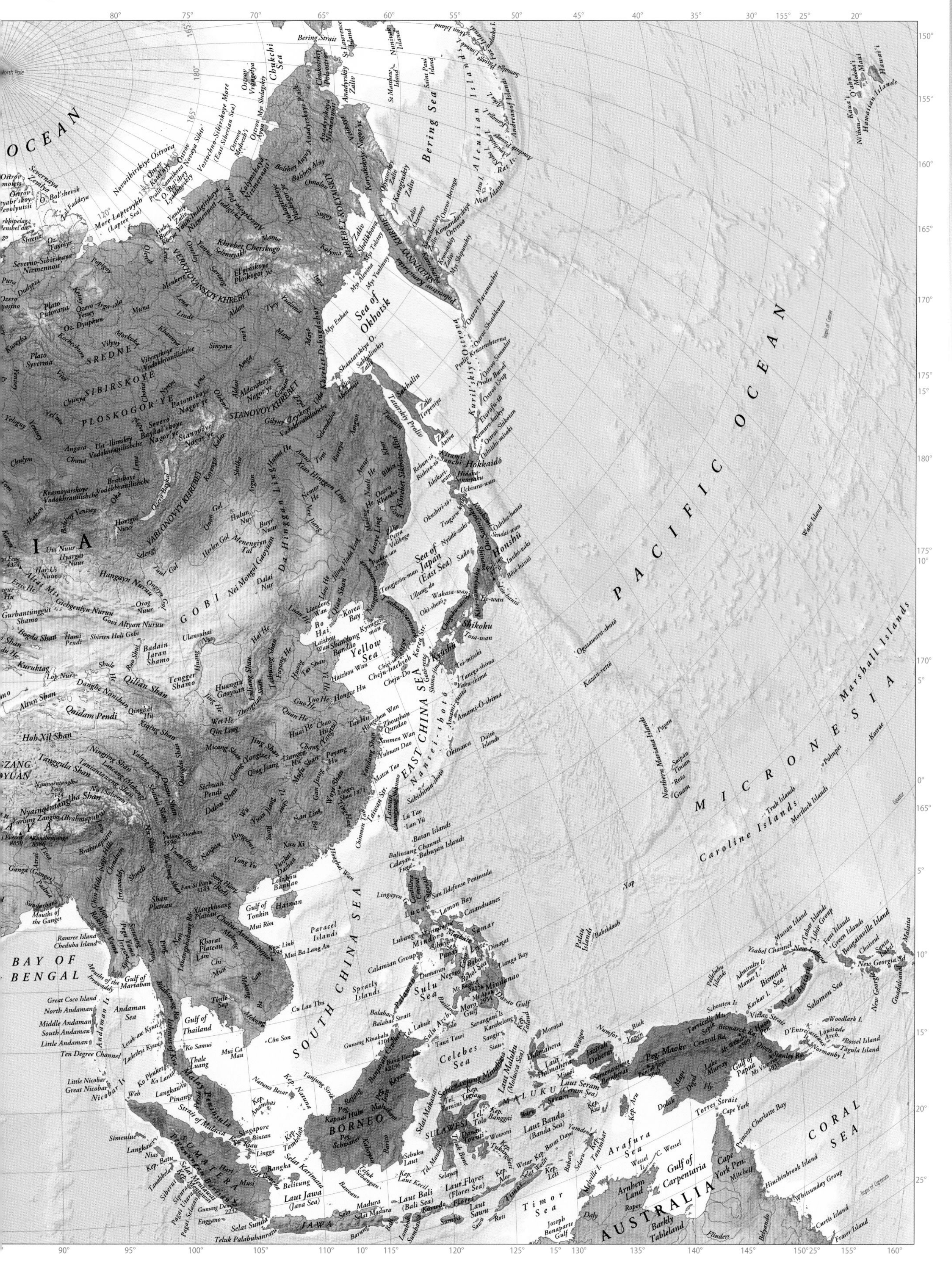
PACIFIC OCEAN
Sea of Okhotsk
Bering Sea
Sea of Japan (East Sea)
Yellow Sea
EAST CHINA SEA
SOUTH CHINA SEA
BAY OF BENGAL
Andaman Sea
Celebes Sea
Sulu Sea
CORAL SEA
Timor Sea
Arafura Sea
Gulf of Carpentaria
MICRONESIA
AUSTRALIA
BORNEO
SUMATERA
SULAWESI
Hokkaidō
Honshū
Shikoku
Kyūshū
Sakhalin
GOBI
Kuril'skiye Ostrova
Aleutian Islands
Caroline Islands
Marshall Islands
Hawaiian Islands
Bering Strait
Chukchi Sea
Gulf of Thailand
Gulf of Tonkin
Hainan
Luzon
Mindanao
Taiwan
Okinawa
Malay Peninsula
Strait of Malacca
Singapore
JAWA

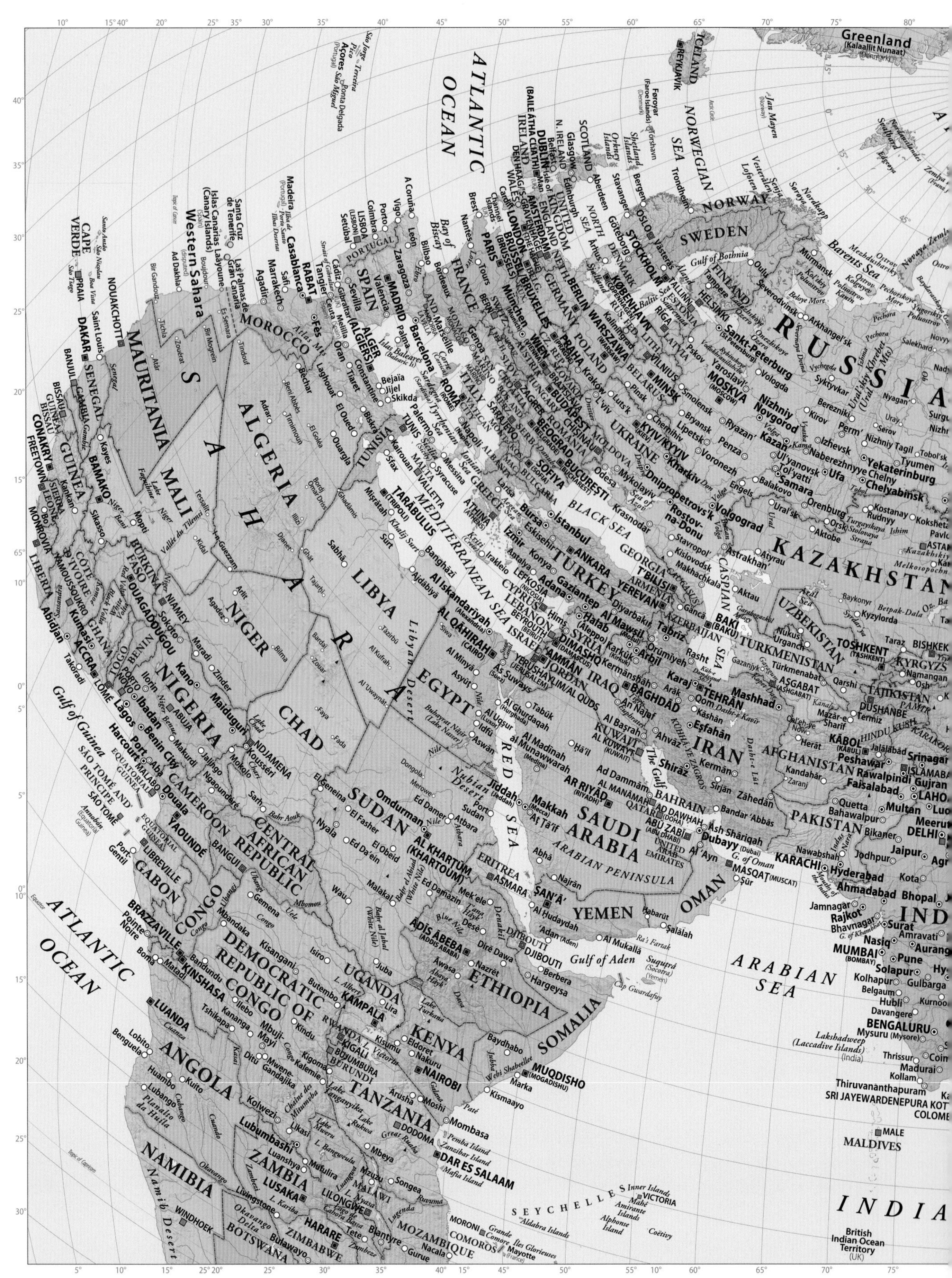
ATLANTIC OCEAN
NORWEGIAN SEA
NORTH SEA
Greenland
(Kalaallit Nunaat)
(Denmark)
ICELAND
REYKJAVÍK
NORWAY
SWEDEN
FINLAND
DENMARK
UNITED KINGDOM
IRELAND
FRANCE
SPAIN
PORTUGAL
GERMANY
POLAND
ITALY
GREECE
ESTONIA
LATVIA
LITH.
BELARUS
UKRAINE
ROMANIA
BULGARIA
MOLDOVA
RUSSIA
KAZAKHSTAN
UZBEKISTAN
TURKMENISTAN
KYRGYZSTAN
TAJIKISTAN
AFGHANISTAN
PAKISTAN
IRAN
IRAQ
SYRIA
TURKEY
GEORGIA
ARMENIA
AZERBAIJAN
CYPRUS
LEBANON
ISRAEL
JORDAN
KUWAIT
SAUDI ARABIA
BAHRAIN
QATAR
UNITED ARAB EMIRATES
OMAN
YEMEN
BLACK SEA
CASPIAN SEA
MEDITERRANEAN SEA
RED SEA
ARABIAN PENINSULA
ARABIAN SEA
Gulf of Aden
Gulf of Oman
Gulf of Bothnia
Baltic Sea
Barents Sea
Bay of Biscay
MOROCCO
ALGERIA
TUNISIA
LIBYA
EGYPT
SAHARA
Libyan Desert
Nubian Desert
Western Sahara
MAURITANIA
MALI
NIGER
CHAD
SUDAN
ERITREA
DJIBOUTI
ETHIOPIA
SOMALIA
KENYA
UGANDA
TANZANIA
RWANDA
BURUNDI
DEMOCRATIC REPUBLIC OF CONGO
CONGO
GABON
CAMEROON
CENTRAL AFRICAN REPUBLIC
NIGERIA
BENIN
TOGO
GHANA
BURKINA FASO
CÔTE D'IVOIRE
LIBERIA
SIERRA LEONE
GUINEA
GUINEA-BISSAU
SENEGAL
GAMBIA
CAPE VERDE
EQUATORIAL GUINEA
SÃO TOMÉ AND PRINCIPE
ANGOLA
ZAMBIA
MALAWI
MOZAMBIQUE
ZIMBABWE
BOTSWANA
NAMIBIA
Namib Desert
COMOROS
SEYCHELLES
MALDIVES
INDIA
INDIAN OCEAN
Gulf of Guinea
British Indian Ocean Territory
(UK)
Lakshadweep
(Laccadive Islands)
(India)
MOSKVA
(MOSCOW)
Sankt-Peterburg
İstanbul
ANKARA
AL QĀHIRAH
(CAIRO)
BAGHDĀD
TEHRĀN
AR RIYĀḌ
(RIYADH)
KARACHI
MUMBAI
(BOMBAY)
NAIROBI
KINSHASA
LUANDA
DAR ES SALAAM
MUQDISHO
(MOGADISHU)
ADDIS ABEBA
AL KHARṬŪM
(KHARTOUM)
LONDON
PARIS
MADRID
ROMA
BERLIN
DELHI

1:37,500,000
Lambert Azimuthal Equal Area Projection

0 500 1000 1500 2000 kilometers
0 250 500 750 1000 miles

Asia Political

PACIFIC OCEAN
FEDERATION
SIBIR' (SIBERIA)
SEA OF OKHOTSK
Bering Sea
Aleutian Islands
ALASKA
HAWAII
MONGOLIA
ULAANBAATAR
CHINA
BEIJING
Shanghai
Hong Kong
JAPAN
TOKYO
NORTH KOREA
P'YONGYANG
SOUTH KOREA
SOUL
EAST CHINA SEA
PHILIPPINE SEA
PHILIPPINES
MANILA
SOUTH CHINA SEA
VIETNAM
HA NOI
LAOS
THAILAND
KRUNG THEP
CAMBODIA
PHNUM PENH
MYANMAR
BANGLADESH
DHAKA
BHUTAN
THIMPHU
BAY OF BENGAL
ANDAMAN SEA
MALAYSIA
KUALA LUMPUR
SINGAPORE
BRUNEI
INDONESIA
JAKARTA
Borneo
Sumatera
CELEBES SEA
LAUT BANDA
TIMOR-LESTE
PAPUA NEW GUINEA
PORT MORESBY
SOLOMON ISLANDS
MELANESIA
FEDERATED STATES OF MICRONESIA
MARSHALL ISLANDS
PALAU
Northern Mariana Islands (USA)
Guam (USA)
Wake Island (USA)
CORAL SEA
AUSTRALIA
Taiwan
T'aipei

PHILIPPINES
PHILIPPINE SEA
PALAU
Sulu Sea
Celebes Sea
Laut Maluku (Molucca Sea)
Laut Seram (Ceram Sea)
Laut Banda (Banda Sea)
INDONESIA
Laut Flores (Flores Sea)
Laut Sawu (Savu Sea)
Timor Sea
Arafura Sea
TIMOR-LESTE (EAST TIMOR)
SULAWESI UTARA
GORONTALO
SULAWESI TENGAH
SULAWESI BARAT
SULAWESI SELATAN
SULAWESI TENGGARA
MALUKU UTARA
MALUKU
IRIAN JAYA BARAT
NUSA TENGGARA BARAT
NUSA TENGGARA TIMUR
NORTHERN TERRITORY
AUSTRALIA
WESTERN AUSTRALIA
ARNHEM LAND
Mindanao
Dumaguete
Cagayan de Oro
Zamboanga
Davao
General Santos
Manado
Gorontalo
Palu
Kendari
Makassar
Ambon
Sorong
Manokwari
Ternate
DILI
Kupang
Darwin
377
375
424
Meters
Feet
1:9,390,000
Mercator Projection
600 kilometers
400 miles

Eastern Indonesia and Papua New Guinea

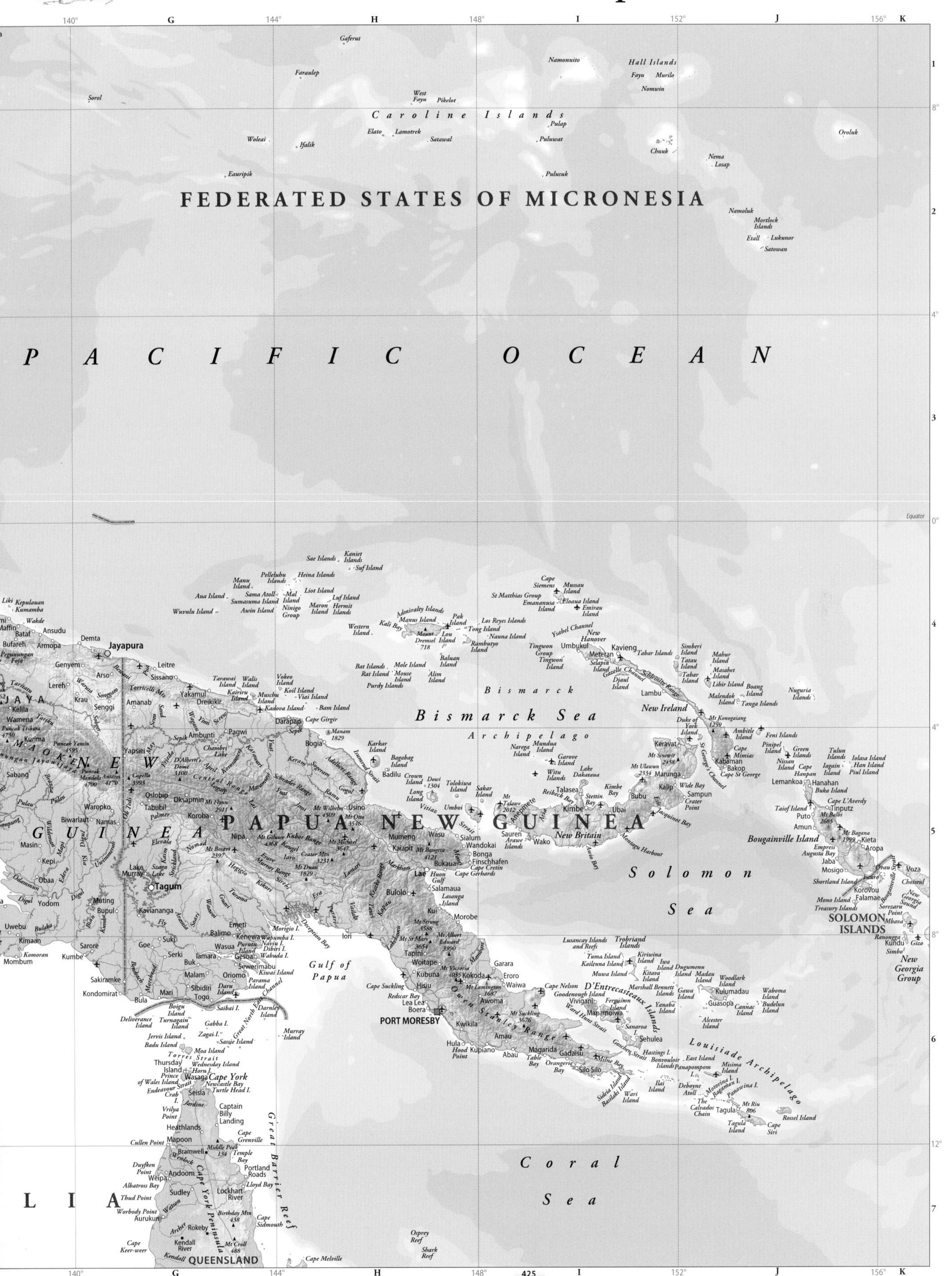
FEDERATED STATES OF MICRONESIA
Caroline Islands
PACIFIC OCEAN
Bismarck Sea
Bismarck Archipelago
PAPUA NEW GUINEA
New Britain
New Ireland
Bougainville Island
SOLOMON ISLANDS
Solomon Sea
Gulf of Papua
PORT MORESBY
Coral Sea
Louisiade Archipelago
Owen Stanley Range
Torres Strait
Cape York
QUEENSLAND
Great Barrier Reef
Jayapura
Equator

Andaman Sea
INDIAN OCEAN
SOUTH CHINA
THAILAND
MALAYSIA
Malay Peninsula
Strait of Malacca
Sumatra
SINGAPORE
KUALA LUMPUR
JAKARTA
Medan
Padang
Palembang
Pekanbaru
Jambi
Bengkulu
Banda Aceh
Bandar Lampung
Bandung
Christmas Island
Cocos (Keeling) Islands
North Keeling Island
ANDAMAN AND NICOBAR ISLANDS (India)
Nicobar Islands
KEPULAUAN RIAU
SINGAPORE 1:469,250
Lambert Conic Conformal Projection
Johore Strait
Singapore Strait
Main Strait
Jurong Island
Pulau Ubin
Pulau Tekong
Sentosa

1:9,390,000
Mercator Projection
0 150 300 450 600 kilometers
0 100 200 300 400 miles

Western Indonesia, Malaysia, and Singapore

112° G 116° H 377 120° I 124° J 128° K

PHILIPPINES
SPRATLY ISLANDS (disputed)
Spratly Island
Cuarteron Reef
Pearson Reef
Commodore Reef
Barque Canada Reef
Mariveles Reef
Amboyna Cay
Ardasier Reefs
Swallow Reef
Royal Charlotte Reef
Balabac
Balabac Strait
Cape Buliluyan
Brooke's Point
Cape Melville
Sulu Sea
Kota Kinabalu
Sandakan
Lahad Datu
Tawau
Semporna
SABAH
LABUAN
Labuan
BANDAR SERI BEGAWAN
BRUNEI
Miri
Bintulu
Mukah
Sibu
SARAWAK
Kuching
MALAYSIA
KALIMANTAN TIMUR
Borneo
KALIMANTAN BARAT
KALIMANTAN TENGAH
KALIMANTAN SELATAN
Tarakan
Tanjungredeb
Bontang
Samarinda
Balikpapan
Palangkaraya
Sampit
Banjarmasin
Kotabaru
Celebes Sea
Sulu Archipelago
Jolo
Zamboanga
Moro Gulf
Pagadian
Cotabato
Dumaguete
Dipolog
Dapitan
Iligan
Cagayan de Oro
Butuan
Mindanao
Davao
Digos
Koronadal
General Santos
Tagum
Philippine Sea
SEMENANJUNG MINAHASA
SULAWESI UTARA
Manado
Bitung
Gorontalo
GORONTALO
Teluk Tomini
SULAWESI TENGAH
Palu
Poso
Sulawesi (Celebes)
SULAWESI BARAT
Mamuju
SULAWESI SELATAN
Palopo
Parepare
Makassar
SULAWESI TENGGARA
Kendari
Baubau
Teluk Bone
Selat Makassar (Macassar Strait)
Laut Maluku (Molucca Sea)
Ternate
Halmahera
MALUKU UTARA
Maluku (Moloccas)
Obi
Laut Seram (Ceram Sea)
Buru
Ambon
Laut Banda (Banda Sea)
INDONESIA
Greater Sunda Islands
Jawa (Java Sea)
Java
Semarang
Surabaya
Surakarta
Madiun
Kediri
Malang
JAWA TIMUR
Banyuwangi
Madura
BALI
Bali
Denpasar
Singaraja
Laut Bali (Bali Sea)
Lombok
Mataram
Sumbawa
Bima
NUSA TENGGARA BARAT
Laut Flores (Flores Sea)
Flores
Maumere
Ende
Lesser Sunda Islands
NUSA TENGGARA TIMUR
Sumba
Waingapu
Laut Sawu (Savu Sea)
Kupang
TIMOR-LESTE (EAST TIMOR)
DILI
Timor
Timor Sea
Hibernia Reef
Ashmore Reef
Ashmore and Cartier Islands (Australia)
Cartier Island
Seringapatam Reef
Scott Reef
Bonaparte Archipelago
Joseph Bonaparte Gulf
AUSTRALIA

Meters	Feet
6000	19685
5000	16404
4000	13123
3000	9843
2000	6562
1000	3281
500	1640
200	656
100	328
0	
LAND BELOW SEA LEVEL	
100	328
200	656
1000	3281
2000	6562
4000	13123
6000	19685

372
424

112° G 116° H 120° I 124° J 128° K

A
92°
B
96°
C
380
100°
D
104°
E
108°
1
2
3
4
5
6
7
24°
20°
16°
12°
8°
4°
393
374
INDIA
CHINA
BANGLADESH
MYANMAR
LAOS
THAILAND
CAMBODIA
VIETNAM
MALAYSIA
INDONESIA
YUNNAN
GUIZHOU
SAGAING
KACHIN
SHAN
CHIN
MAGWAY
MANDALAY
RAKHINE
BAGO
KAYIN
KAYAH
YANGON
MON
AYEYARWADY
TANINTHARYI
NAGALAND
ACEH
SUMATERA UTARA
KEDAH
PERLIS
PINANG
PERAK
KELANTAN
TERENGGANU
PAHANG
SELANGOR
Bay of Bengal
Andaman Sea
INDIAN OCEAN
Gulf of Thailand
Gulf of Tonkin
SOUTH CHINA SEA
Malay Peninsula
Isthmus of Kra
Strait of Malacca
Mouth of the Ganges
Mouth of the Ayeyarwady (Irrawaddy)
Preparis North Channel
Preparis South Channel
Ten Degree Channel
Sombrero Channel
North Andaman
Middle Andaman
South Andaman
Andaman Islands (India)
Little Andaman
Nicobar Islands (India)
Car Nicobar
Great Nicobar Island
Preparis Island
Port Blair
Sumatera (Sumatra)
Dhaka
Chittagong
Comilla
Cox's Bazar
Guwahati
Dimapur
Kohima
Imphal
Shillong
Silchar
Aizawl
Agartala
Sittwe (Akyab)
Mandalay
NAYPYIDAW
YANGON (RANGOON)
Pathein (Bassein)
Bago (Pegu)
Mawlamyaing (Moulmein)
Dawei (Tavoy)
Myeik (Mergui)
Taunggyi
Myitkyina
Lashio
Pyay (Pri, Prome)
Magway (Magwe)
Toungoo
Hpa-an
Kunming
Dali
Qujing
Gejiu
Kaiyuan
Nanning
HÀ NỘI
Hải Phòng
Nam Định
Thanh Hóa
Vinh
Huế
Đà Nẵng
Hồ Chí Minh (Saigon)
Cần Thơ
Vũng Tàu
Buôn Ma Thuột
Đà Lạt
VIANGCHAN (VIENTIANE)
Louangphabang
Savannakhet
Pakxe
KRUNG THEP (BANGKOK)
Chiang Mai
Chiang Rai
Lampang
Phitsanulok
Nakhon Sawan
Khon Kaen
Udon Thani
Nakhon Ratchasima
Ubon Ratchathani
Surat Thani
Nakhon Si Thammarat
Hat Yai
Songkhla
Phuket
PHNUM PENH (PHNOM PENH)
Siemréab
Bătdâmbâng
Kâmpóng Saôm (Sihanoukville)
Alor Setar
George Town
Ipoh
Kota Bharu
Kuala Terengganu
Kuantan
Banda Aceh
Medan
Lhokseumawe

1:9,390,000
Mercator Projection

0 150 300 450 600 kilometers
0 100 200 300 400 miles

Southeast Asia and the Philippines

PACIFIC OCEAN
SOUTH CHINA SEA
Philippine Sea
Sulu Sea
Celebes Sea
Luzon Strait
Balintang Channel
Bashi Channel
Taiwan Strait
Moro Gulf
Bohol Sea
PHILIPPINES
TAIWAN
JAPAN
BRUNEI
MALAYSIA
INDONESIA
FUJIAN
GUANGDONG
JIANGXI
HUNAN
SABAH
SARAWAK
KALIMANTAN TIMUR
Borneo
Luzon
Mindanao
Panay
Negros
Samar
Leyte
Bohol
Palawan
Mindoro
Babuyan Islands
Batan Islands
Calamian Group
Cuyo Islands
Sulu Archipelago
Turtle Islands (Philippines)
Sarangani Islands
PARACEL ISLANDS (disputed)
SPRATLY ISLANDS (disputed)
Pratas Island
Scarborough Shoal
Macclesfield Bank
Nansei-shoto (Ryukyu Islands) (Japan)
Sakishima-shoto
Senkaku-shotō (disputed)
Tropic of Cancer
MANILA
Quezon City
Cebu
Davao
Zamboanga
Iloilo
Bacolod
Cagayan de Oro
Iligan
General Santos
Tacloban
Legazpi
Puerto Princesa
Baguio
Dagupan
Angeles
Antipolo
Batangas
Lucena
Naga
Butuan
Cotabato
Jolo
T'aipei
T'aichung
T'ainan
Kaohsiung
Hsinchu
Keelung
Hualien
T'aitung
Fuzhou
Xiamen
Quanzhou
Zhangzhou
Shantou
Guangzhou
Shenzhen
Dongguan
Foshan
Zhongshan
Hong Kong (Xianggang)
Kowloon
Macau (Aomen)
Zhanjiang
Haikou
Okinawa
Naha
Kota Kinabalu
Sandakan
Tawau
Lahad Datu
BANDAR SERI BEGAWAN
Labuan
Miri
112°
116°
120°
124°
128°
24°
20°
16°
12°
8°
4°
G
H
I
J
K
1
2
3
4
5
6
7
381
375
Meters
Feet
6000 19685
5000 16404
4000 13123
3000 9843
2000 6562
1000 3281
500 1640
200 656
100 328
0
LAND BELOW SEA LEVEL
100 328
200 656
1000 3281
2000 6562
4000 13123
6000 19685

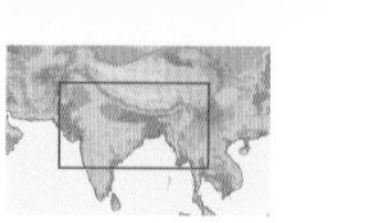

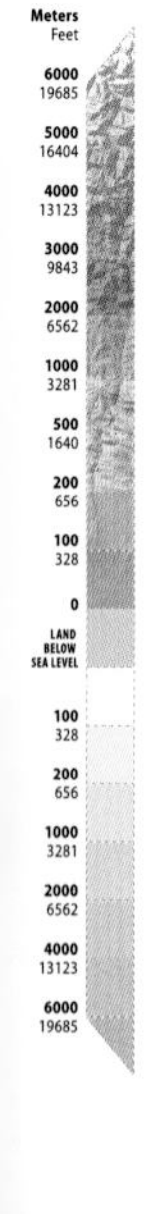

388

391

393

AFGHANISTAN

PAKISTAN

INDIA

NEPAL

JAMMU AND KASHMIR

AZAD KASHMIR

FEDERALLY ADMINISTERED TRIBAL AREAS

BALOCHISTAN

PUNJAB

SINDH

HIMACHAL PRADESH

UTTARANCHAL

HARYANA

RAJASTHAN

UTTAR PRADESH

GUJARAT

MADHYA PRADESH

CHHATTISGARH

ORISSA

JHARKHAND

MAHARASHTRA

DAMAN AND DIU

DADRA AND NAGAR HAVELI

GOA

KARNATAKA

ANDHRA PRADESH

ARABIAN SEA

Gulf of Kachchh

Gulf of Khambhat

Rann of Kachchh

Thar Desert

Islamabad · Rawalpindi · Peshawar · Srinagar · Lahore · Faisalabad · Multan · Quetta · Hyderabad · Karachi · Delhi · New Delhi · Chandigarh · Jaipur · Agra · Lucknow · Kanpur · Varanasi · Allahabad · Ahmadabad · Surat · Vadodara · Indore · Bhopal · Jabalpur · Nagpur · Raipur · Mumbai · Pune · Pimpri Chinchwad · Nashik · Aurangabad · Hyderabad · Secunderabad · Vishakhapatnam · Vijayawada · Guntur · Kathmandu

Meters / Feet

Meters	Feet
6000	19685
5000	16404
4000	13123
3000	9843
2000	6562
1000	3281
500	1640
200	656
100	328
0	LAND BELOW SEA LEVEL
100	328
200	656
1000	3281
2000	6562
4000	13123
6000	19685

1:7,880,000

Conic Equidistant Projection

0 50 100 150 200 250 300 kilometers

0 25 50 75 100 125 150 miles

Western Central Asia

C H I N A
XIZANG ZIZHIQU
QINGHAI
SICHUAN
PLATEAU OF TIBET
Tanggula (Dangla) Shan
Nyainqentanglha Shan
Hengduan Shan
Chengdu
Leshan
Xichang
Panzhihua
Kunming
Dali
YUNNAN
Lhasa
ARUNACHAL PRADESH
BHUTAN
THIMPHU
SIKKIM
Gangtok
ASSAM
Guwahati
NAGALAND
Dimapur
Kohima
MEGHALAYA
Shillong
MANIPUR
Imphal
MIZORAM
Aizawl
TRIPURA
Agartala
WEST BENGAL
Kolkata
Haora
Jamshedpur
BANGLADESH
DHAKA (DACCA)
RAJSHAHI
SYLHET
KHULNA
BARISAL
CHITTAGONG
Chittagong
Cox's Bazar
Mouths of the Ganges
BAY OF BENGAL
MYANMAR
KACHIN
Myitkyina
SAGAING
Mandalay
MANDALAY
Monywa
CHIN
RAKHINE
Sittwe (Akyab)
MAGWAY
NAYPYIDAW
SHAN
Shan Plateau
Taunggyi
Lashio
KAYAH
BAGO
Bago (Pegu)
YANGON (RANGOON)
YANGON
AYEYARWADY
Pathein (Bassein)
MON
Mawlamyaing (Moulmein)
KAYIN
TANINTHARYI
Dawei (Tavoy)
Mouth of the Ayeyarwady (Irrawaddy)
Gulf of Martaban
LAOS
Louangphabang
THAILAND
Chiang Mai
Chiang Rai
Lampang
Phitsanulok
KRUNG THEP (BANGKOK)
Nakhon Pathom
Meters
Feet
6000 19685
5000 16404
4000 13123
3000 9843
2000 6562
1000 3281
500 1640
200 656
100 328
0
LAND BELOW SEA LEVEL
100 328
200 656
1000 3281
2000 6562
4000 13123
6000 19685
384
376
380

384

379

376

Meters / Feet
6000 19685
5000 16404
4000 13123
3000 9843
2000 6562
1000 3281
500 1640
200 656
100 328
0
LAND BELOW SEA LEVEL
100 328
200 656
1000 3281
2000 6562
4000 13123
6000 19685

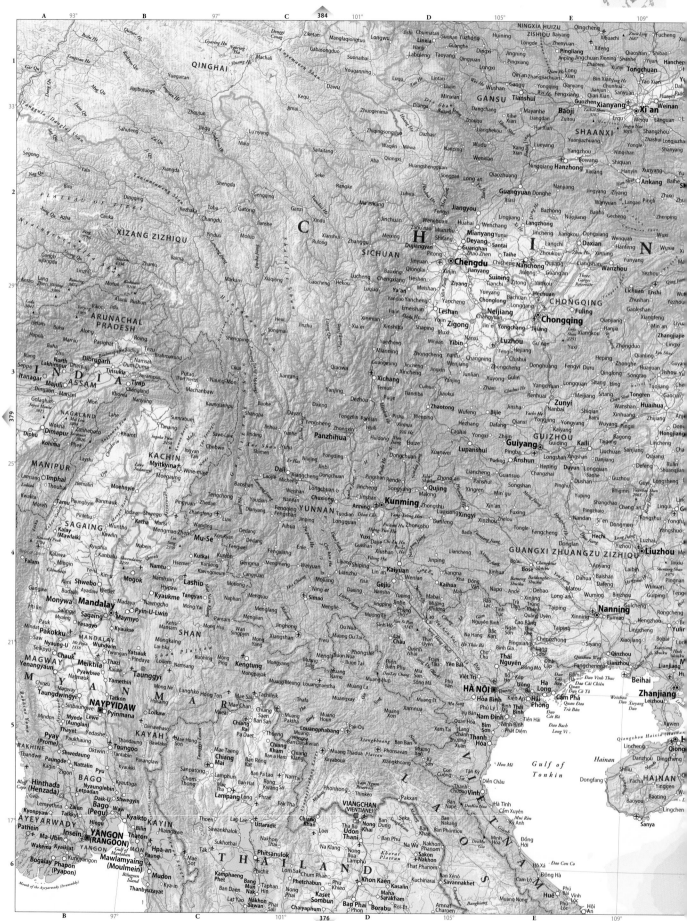

1:7,880,000
Conic Equidistant Projection

0 50 100 150 200 250 300 kilometers
0 25 50 75 100 125 150 miles

Eastern Central Asia

385
377
SHANGDONG
JIANGSU
ANHUI
SHANGHAI
ZHEJIANG
JIANGXI
FUJIAN
GUANGDONG
TAIWAN
SOUTH KOREA
JAPAN
PHILIPPINES
YELLOW SEA
(HUANG HAI)
EAST CHINA SEA
SOUTH CHINA SEA
PACIFIC OCEAN
PHILIPPINE SEA
Taiwan Strait
Luzon Strait
Bashi Channel
Korea Strait
Okinawa-shoto
Sakishima-shoto
Nansei-shoto (Ryukyu Islands)
Amami-shoto
Senkaku-shoto (disputed)
Tropic of Cancer
Shanghai
Nanjing
Hangzhou
Wuhan
Hefei
Nanchang
Changsha
Fuzhou
Xiamen
Shantou
Guangzhou
Dongguan
Shenzhen
Kowloon
Hong Kong (Xianggang)
HONG KONG (XIANGGANG) S.A.R.
Macau (Aomen)
Zhongshan
T'aipei
T'aichung
Kaohsiung
Xuzhou
Zhengzhou
Luoyang
Kaifeng
Linyi
Lianyungang
Huainan
Bengbu
Changzhou
Wuxi
Suzhou
Ningbo
Wenzhou
Taizhou
Pusan (Busan)
Kwangju
Cheju
Fukuoka
Nagasaki
Okinawa
Naha
Laoag
Baguio
Tuguegarao
Dagupan
Pratas Island
Amphitrite Group
PARACEL ISLANDS (disputed)
Meters
Feet
6000
19685
5000
16404
4000
13123
3000
9843
2000
6562
1000
3281
500
1640
200
656
100
328
0
LAND BELOW SEA LEVEL
100
328
200
656
1000
3281
2000
6562
4000
13123
6000
19685

Meters
Feet

6000 19685
5000 16404
4000 13123
3000 9843
2000 6562
1000 3281
500 1640
200 656
100 328
0
LAND BELOW SEA LEVEL
100 328
200 656
1000 3281
2000 6562
4000 13123
6000 19685

1:7,880,000

Conic Equidistant Projection

0 50 100 150 200 250 300 kilometers
0 25 50 75 100 125 150 miles

Central Asia

89° I 93° J 97° K 101° L 105° M 109° N
RESPUBLIKA KHAKASIYA
KEMEROVSKAYA OBLAST'
KRASNOYARSKIY KRAY
IRKUTSKAYA OBLAST'
Irkutsk
Ulan-Ude
Kyzyl
RESPUBLIKA TYVA
RUSSIAN FEDERATION
RESPUBLIKA BURYATIYA
CHITINSKAYA OBLAST'
Mikhaylovka
HÖVSGÖL
SELENGE
DARHAN-UUL
Darhan
ULAANBAATAR (ULAN BATOR)
HENTIY
BULGAN
ORHON
Erdenet
UVS
Ulaangom
BAYAN-ÖLGIY
DZAVHAN
ARHANGAY
TÖV
MONGOLIA
HOVD
Hovd
GOVĬSÜMBER
BAYANHONGOR
Bayanhongor
ÖVÖRHANGAY
DUNDGOVĬ
DORNOGOVĬ
GOVĬ-ALTAY
ÖMNÖGOVĬ
MONGOLIAN PLATEAU
GOBI
Ürümqi
BOGDA SHAN
TIAN SHAN
Hami
XINJIANG UYGUR ZIZHIQU
NEI MONGOL ZIZHIQU
Linhe
Wuhai
Yinchuan
NINGXIA HUIZU ZIZHIQU
Jiuquan
Jiayuguan
Yumen
Zhangye
Jinchang
Wuwei
QILIAN SHAN
Xining
Lanzhou
Baiyin
Tianshui
GANSU
CHINA
QINGHAI
KUNLUN SHAN
HOH XIL SHAN
SICHUAN
Meters Feet
6000 19685
5000 16404
4000 13123
3000 9843
2000 6562
1000 3281
500 1640
200 656
100 328
0
LAND BELOW SEA LEVEL
100 328
200 656
1000 3281
2000 6562
4000 13123
6000 19685

385

379

RUSSIAN FEDERATION

MONGOLIA

CHINA

KAZAK.

XINJIANG UYGUR ZIZHIQU

GANSU

QINGHAI

NEI MONGOL ZIZHIQU

NINGXIA HUIZU ZIZHIQU

SHAANXI

Mongolian Plateau

Gobi

236

389

380

Meters / Feet

6000 / 19685

5000 / 16404

4000 / 13123

3000 / 9843

2000 / 6562

1000 / 3281

500 / 1640

200 / 656

100 / 328

0

LAND BELOW SEA LEVEL

100 / 328

200 / 656

1000 / 3281

2000 / 6562

4000 / 13123

6000 / 19685

1:7,880,000

Conic Equidistant Projection

0 50 100 150 200 250 300 kilometers

0 25 50 75 100 125 150 miles

Northeastern China and Mongolia

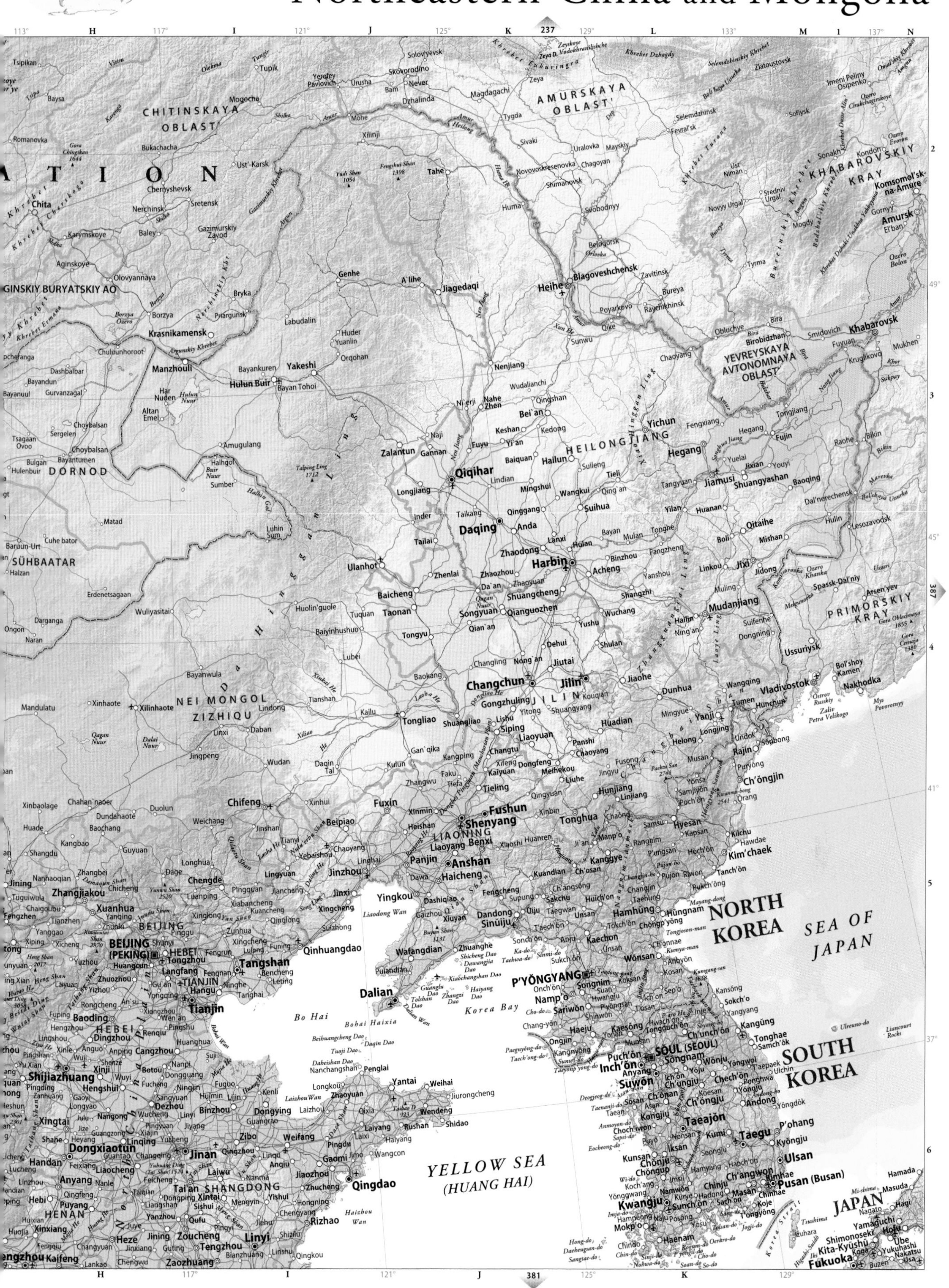
AMURSKAYA OBLAST'
CHITINSKAYA OBLAST'
KHABAROVSKIY KRAY
YEVREYSKAYA AVTONOMNAYA OBLAST'
PRIMORSKIY KRAY
HEILONGJIANG
JILIN
LIAONING
NEI MONGOL ZIZHIQU
HEBEI
BEIJING (PEKING)
TIANJIN
SHANGDONG
HENAN
DORNOD
SÜHBAATAR
NORTH KOREA
SOUTH KOREA
JAPAN
SEA OF JAPAN
YELLOW SEA (HUANG HAI)
Bo Hai
Korea Bay
Liaodong Wan
Harbin
Qiqihar
Daqing
Changchun
Jilin
Shenyang
Fushun
Anshan
Dalian
Tangshan
Qingdao
Jinan
Shijiazhuang
Vladivostok
Khabarovsk
Blagoveshchensk
P'YŎNGYANG
SŎUL (SEOUL)
Inch'ŏn
Taegu
Pusan (Busan)
Kwangju
Taejŏn
Ulsan
Fukuoka
Chita
Manzhouli
Hulun Buir
Heihe
Mudanjiang
Jiamusi
Yanji
Chifeng
Zhangjiakou
Baoding
Yantai
Weifang
Linyi
Meters
Feet
LAND BELOW SEA LEVEL
237
381
387

MONGOLIA

CHINA

NEI MONGOL ZIZHIQU

HEILONGJIANG

JILIN

LIAONING

HEBEI

SHANDONG

JIANGSU

ANHUI

ZHEJIANG

JIANGXI

SHANGHAI

NORTH KOREA

SOUTH KOREA

YEVREYSKAYA AVTONOMNAYA OBLAST'

Bo Hai

Korea Bay

YELLOW SEA (HUANG HAI)

EAST CHINA SEA

Da Hinggan Ling

BEIJING (PEKING)

Tianjin

Shenyang

Harbin

Changchun

Dalian

Qingdao

Nanjing

Shanghai

Hangzhou

P'YŎNGYANG

SŎUL (SEOUL)

Pusan (Busan)

Vladivostok

Fukuoka

Hiroshima

Kyūshū

Shikoku

Meters / Feet

6000 / 19685

5000 / 16404

4000 / 13123

3000 / 9843

2000 / 6562

1000 / 3281

500 / 1640

200 / 656

100 / 328

0

LAND BELOW SEA LEVEL

100 / 328

200 / 656

1000 / 3281

2000 / 6562

4000 / 13123

6000 / 19685

1:7,880,000

Conic Equidistant Projection

0 50 100 150 200 250 300 kilometers

0 25 50 75 100 125 150 miles

385

384

381

Japan and Korea

RUSSIAN FED.

SEA OF OKHOTSK (OKHOTSKOYE MORE)

SAKHALINSKAYA OBLAST'

Ostrov Sakhalin

La Perouse Strait

Hokkaidō

Kuril'skiye Ostrova (Kuril Islands)

Honshū

JAPAN

PACIFIC OCEAN

Sapporo
Asahikawa
Kitami
Obihiro
Kushiro
Otaru
Hakodate
Aomori
Hachinohe
Morioka
Akita
Sendai
Niigata
Kōriyama
Nagano
TŌKYŌ
Saitama
Kawasaki
Yokohama
Chiba
Shizuoka
Hamamatsu
Nagoya
Kyoto
Osaka
Yuzhno Sakhalinsk
Korsakov
Nevel'sk
Kholmsk
Dolinsk

Meters / Feet
6000 19685
5000 16404
4000 13123
3000 9843
2000 6562
1000 3281
500 1640
200 656
100 328
0
LAND BELOW SEA LEVEL
100 328
200 656
1000 3281
2000 6562
4000 13123
6000 19685

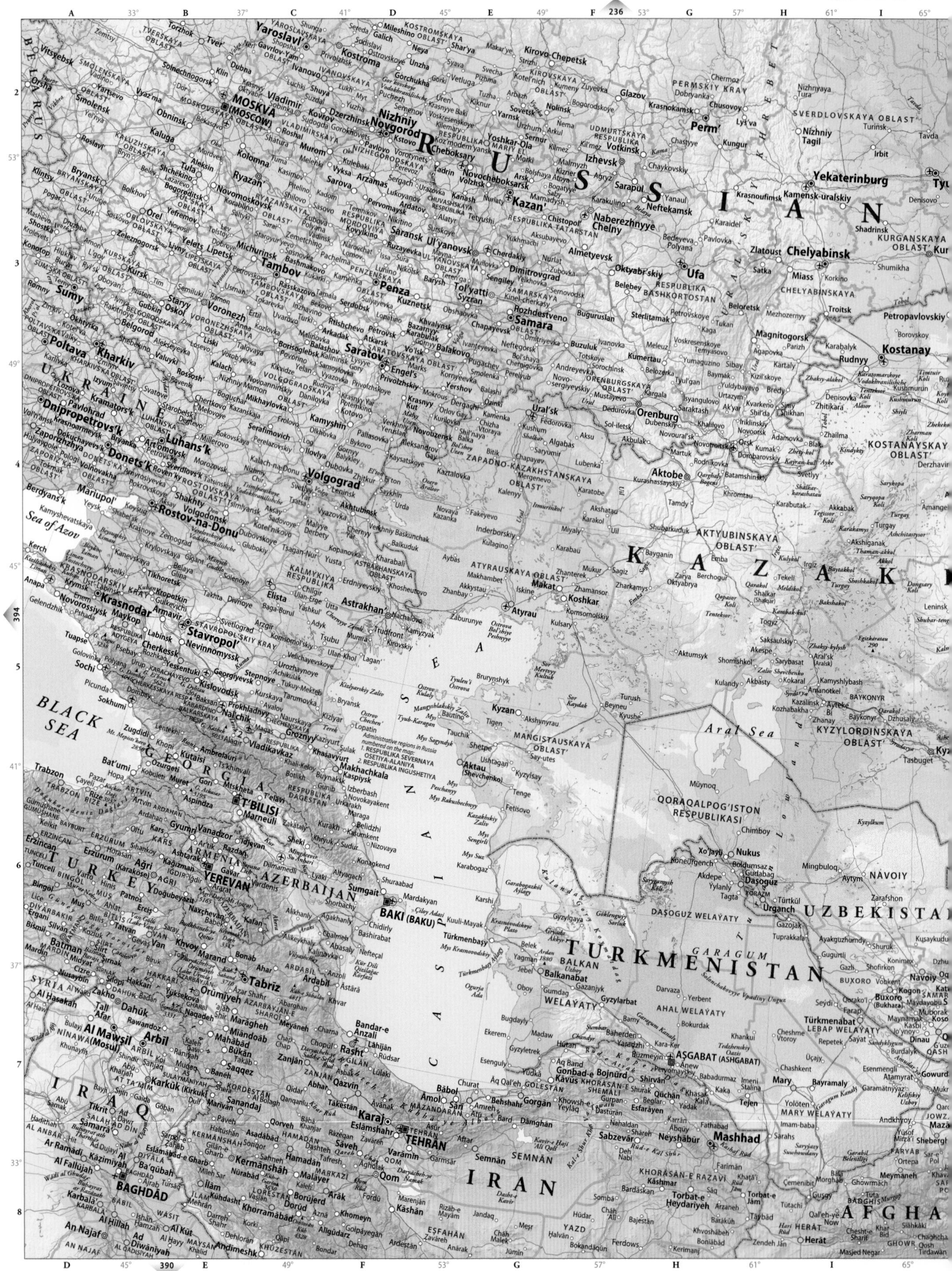
A
B
C
D
E
F
G
H
I
33°
37°
41°
45°
49°
53°
57°
61°
65°
236
394
390
2
3
4
5
6
7
8
RUSSIAN
KAZAK
UKRAINE
BELARUS
GEORGIA
ARMENIA
AZERBAIJAN
TURKEY
IRAQ
IRAN
TURKMENISTAN
UZBEKISTAN
SYRIA
AFGHA
BLACK SEA
Sea of Azov
CASPIAN SEA
Aral Sea
GARAGUM
MOSKVA (MOSCOW)
Nizhniy Novgorod
Yaroslavl'
Kostroma
Vladimir
Ivanovo
Tver'
Kazan'
Samara
Saratov
Volgograd
Astrakhan'
Rostov-na-Donu
Krasnodar
Stavropol'
Voronezh
Kharkiv
Dnipropetrovs'k
Donets'k
Luhans'k
Poltava
Sumy
Penza
Tambov
Ul'yanovsk
Izhevsk
Perm'
Ufa
Yekaterinburg
Chelyabinsk
Orenburg
Kostanay
Aktobe
Atyrau
Ural'sk
Makhachkala
Groznyy
T'BILISI
YEREVAN
BAKI (BAKU)
TEHRAN
Tabriz
Mashhad
AŞGABAT (ASHGABAT)
BAGHDĀD
Al Mawşil (Mosul)
Arbīl
Kirkūk
Nukus
Daşoguz
Turkmenbaşy
Aktau (Shevchenko)
Elista
Naberezhnyye Chelny
Tol'yatti
Syzran'
Engel's
Kursk
Belgorod
Lipetsk
Ryazan'
Tula
Kaluga
Smolensk
Bryansk
Orel
Vitsyebsk
Magnitogorsk
Bukhara
Navoiy
Gorgān
Rasht
Qazvīn
Kermānshāh
Hamadān
Qom
Herāt

Meters / Feet
6000 19685
5000 16404
4000 13123
3000 9843
2000 6562
1000 3281
500 1640
200 656
100 328
0
LAND BELOW SEA LEVEL
100 328
200 656
1000 3281
2000 6562
4000 13123
6000 19685

1:10,320,000

Conic Equidistant Projection

0 100 200 300 400 500 kilometers

0 50 100 150 200 250 300 miles

Northwestern Asia

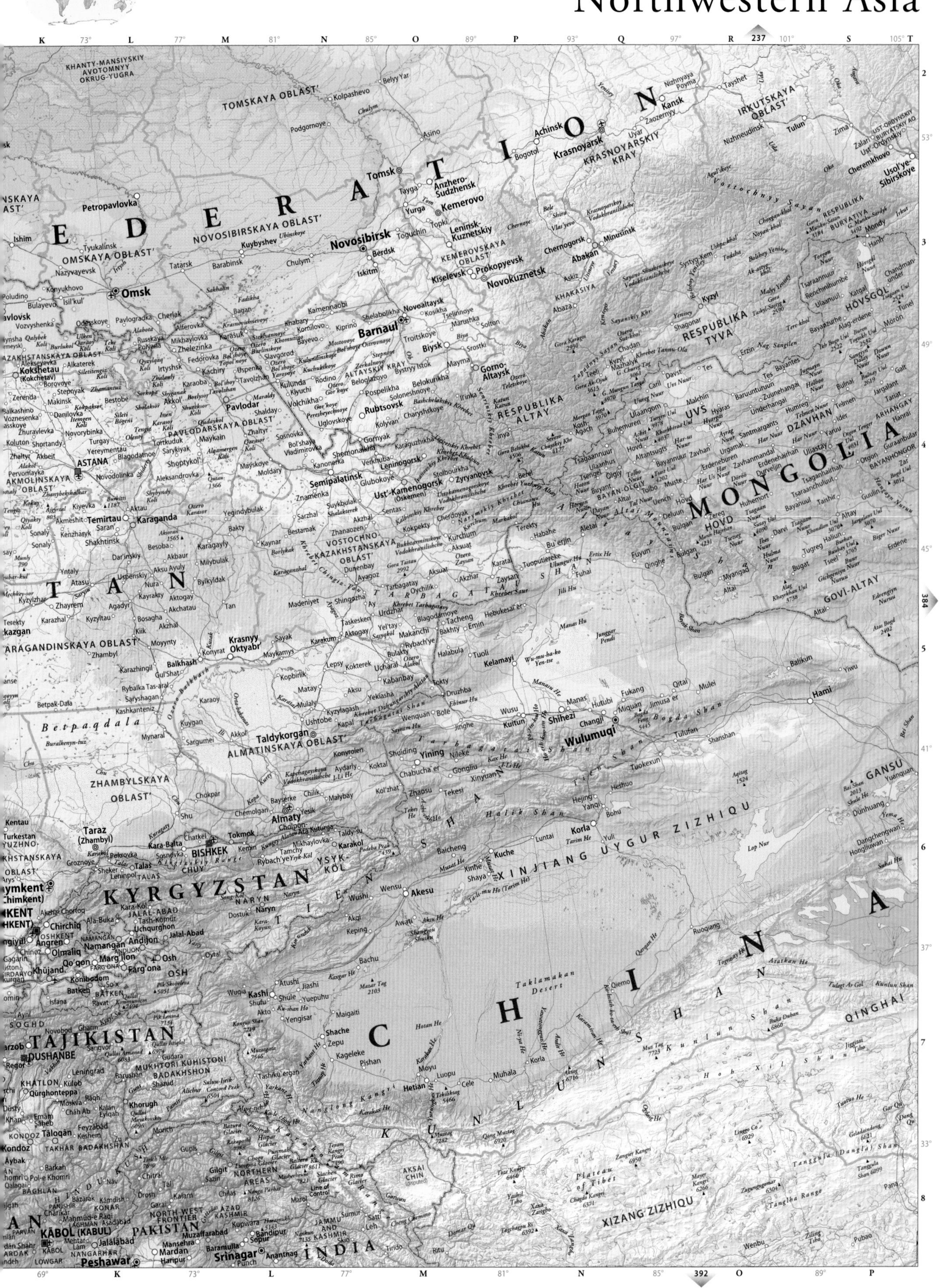
RUSSIAN FEDERATION
KAZAKHSTAN
MONGOLIA
CHINA
KYRGYZSTAN
TAJIKISTAN
PAKISTAN
INDIA
KHANTY-MANSIYSKIY AVTOMNYY OKRUG-YUGRA
TOMSKAYA OBLAST'
NOVOSIBIRSKAYA OBLAST'
OMSKAYA OBLAST'
KEMEROVSKAYA OBLAST'
KRASNOYARSKIY KRAY
IRKUTSKAYA OBLAST'
RESPUBLIKA BURYATIYA
RESPUBLIKA TYVA
RESPUBLIKA ALTAY
ALTAYSKIY KRAY
KHAKASIYA
PAVLODARSKAYA OBLAST'
AKMOLINSKAYA OBLAST'
VOSTOCHNO KAZAKHSTANSKAYA OBLAST'
KARAGANDINSKAYA OBLAST'
ALMATINSKAYA OBLAST'
ZHAMBYLSKAYA OBLAST'
XINJIANG UYGUR ZIZHIQU
XIZANG ZIZHIQU
GANSU
QINGHAI
GOVI-ALTAY
HOVD
UVS
DZAVHAN
ARKHANGAY
BAYANHONGOR
HÖVSGÖL
BAYAN-ÖLGIY
Tomsk
Novosibirsk
Omsk
Barnaul
Kemerovo
Novokuznetsk
Krasnoyarsk
Achinsk
Kansk
Abakan
Kyzyl
Biysk
Gorno-Altaysk
Semipalatinsk
Ust'-Kamenogorsk (Öskemen)
Pavlodar
Petropavlovka
ASTANA
Karaganda
Temirtau
Balkhash
Taldykorgan
Almaty
BISHKEK
Tokmok
Taraz (Zhambyl)
Naryn
Osh
Jalal-Abad
Andijon
Namangan
Farg'ona
Khujand
DUSHANBE
Khorugh
KĀBOL (KABUL)
Jalālābād
Peshawar
Srinagar
Gilgit
Leh
Wulumuqi
Shihezi
Kelamayi
Yining
Akesu
Kashi
Shache
Hetian
Korla
Hami
Dunhuang
Taklamakan Desert
Plateau of Tibet
Tien Shan
Kunlun Shan
Altai Mountains
Tarbagatai Shan
Bogda Shan
Betpaqdala
Lop Nur
Vostochnyy Sayan
Karakoram Range
HINDU KUSH
AKSAI CHIN
Line of Control
JAMMU AND KASHMIR
NORTHERN AREAS
AZAD KASHMIR
NORTH-WEST FRONTIER
Meters
Feet
6000
19685
5000
16404
4000
13123
3000
9843
2000
6562
1000
3281
500
1640
200
656
100
328
0
LAND BELOW SEA LEVEL
237
384
392

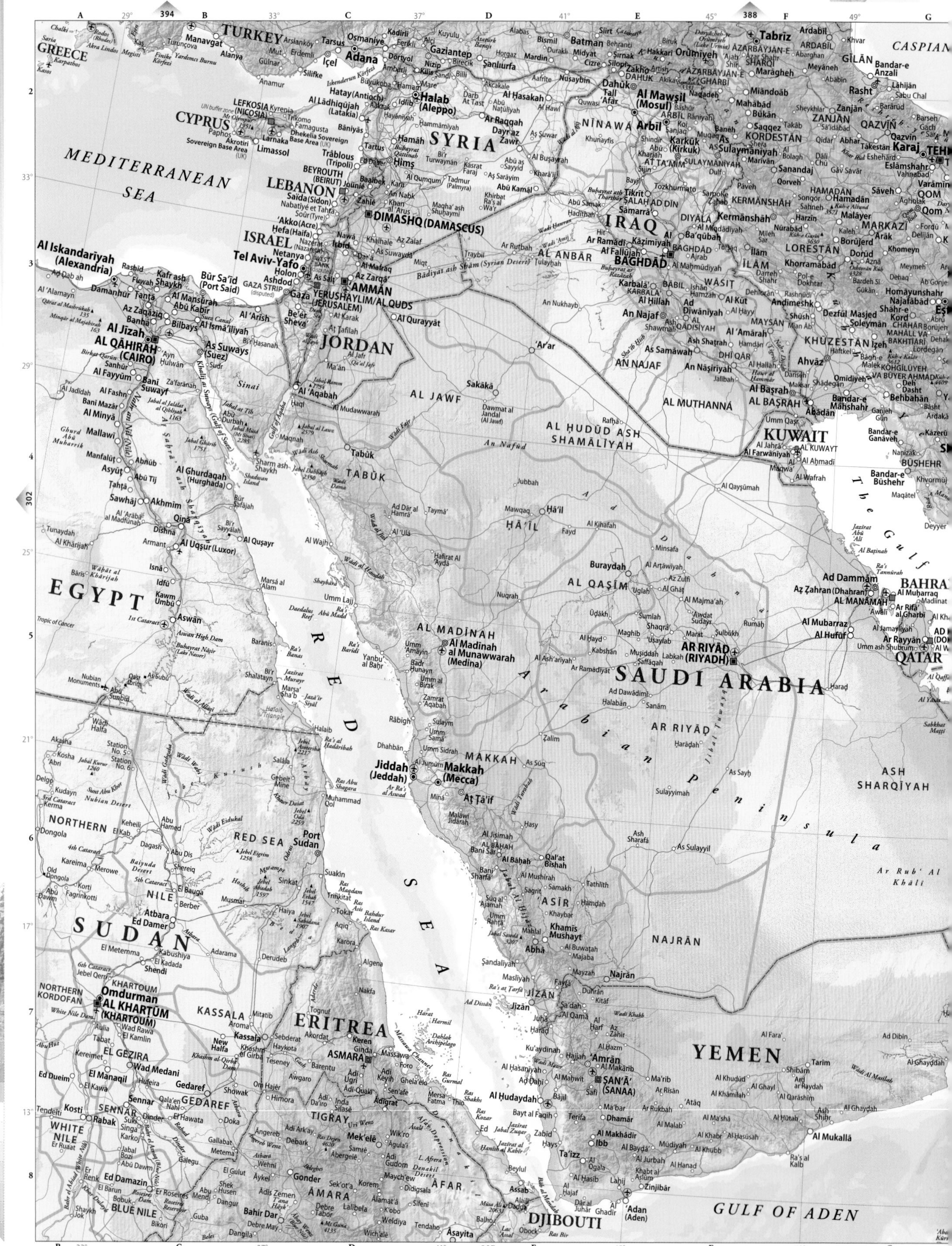
TURKEY
GREECE
CYPRUS
SYRIA
LEBANON
ISRAEL
JORDAN
IRAQ
KUWAIT
EGYPT
SAUDI ARABIA
QATAR
SUDAN
ERITREA
YEMEN
DJIBOUTI
MEDITERRANEAN SEA
RED SEA
GULF OF ADEN
CASPIAN
The Gulf
Arabian Peninsula
Ar Rub' Al Khālī
An Nafūd
Sinai
DIMASHQ (DAMASCUS)
BAGHDĀD
'AMMĀN
YERUSHALAYIM/AL QUDS (JERUSALEM)
AL QĀHIRAH (CAIRO)
AR RIYĀḌ (RIYADH)
AL KHARṬŪM (KHARTOUM)
ASMARA
ṢAN'Ā' (SANAA)
Makkah (Mecca)
Al Madīnah al Munawwarah (Medina)
Jiddah (Jeddah)
Al Iskandarīyah (Alexandria)
Ḥalab (Aleppo)
Al Mawṣil (Mosul)
Al Baṣrah
'Adan (Aden)
Port Sudan
Omdurman
Tropic of Cancer
A B C D E F G
29° 33° 37° 41° 45° 49°
394 388 302 307

1:10,320,000

Conic Equidistant Projection

0 100 200 300 400 500 kilometers

0 50 100 150 200 250 300 miles

Meters / Feet: 6000 19685; 5000 16404; 4000 13123; 3000 9843; 2000 6562; 1000 3281; 500 1640; 200 656; 100 328; 0; LAND BELOW SEA LEVEL; 100 328; 200 656; 1000 3281; 2000 6562; 4000 13123; 6000 19685

TURKMENISTAN
UZB.
TAJ.
CHINA
AFGHANISTAN
PAKISTAN
INDIA
OMAN
ARABIAN SEA
INDIAN OCEAN
Gulf of Oman
Laccadive Sea
Lakshadweep (Laccadive Islands)
LAKSHADWEEP
AŞGABAT (ASHGABAT)
Mashhad
Mary
Herāt
KĀBOL (KABUL)
ISLĀMĀBĀD
Peshawar
Rawalpindi
Srinagar
JAMMU AND KASHMIR
NORTHERN AREAS
NORTH-WEST FRONTIER
HIMACHAL PRADESH
Lahore
Faisalabad
Gujranwala
Amritsar
Ludhiana
Chandigarh
PUNJAB
HARYANA
Multan
Quetta
Kandahār
Zāhedān
Kermān
Bandar-'Abbās
Dubayy (Dubai)
Ash Shāriqah
Ra's al Khaymah
Al Fujayrah
Al 'Ayn
MASQAṬ (MUSCAT)
Şūr
Hyderabad
Karachi
SINDH
BALOCHISTAN
RAJASTHAN
Jodhpur
Jaipur
Ajmer
Bikaner
GUJARAT
Ahmadabad
Vadodara
Rajkot
Surat
Indore
MADHYA PRADESH
Nashik
Aurangabad
Mumbai
Pune
Pimpri Chinchwad
MAHARASHTRA
Kolhapur
Belgaum
GOA
KARNATAKA
DAMAN AND DIU
DADRA AND NAGAR HAVELI
Gwadar
Chāh Bahār
SĪSTĀN VA BALŪCHESTĀN
HORMOZGĀN
KERMĀN
KHORĀSĀN-E RAZAVĪ
KHORĀSĀN-E JANŪBĪ
YAZD
Yazd
SEMNĀN
GOLESTĀN
HELMAND
NĪMRŪZ
KANDAHĀR
ORŪZGĀN
ZĀBOL
PAKTĪKĀ
GHAZNĪ
BĀMĪĀN
BALKH
BADGHĪS
FARĀH
Mouths of the Indus
Gulf of Kachchh
Gulf of Khambhat
Rann of Kachchh
Thar Desert
Hindu Kush
Khalīj Maşīrah
Jazīrat Maşīrah
Tropic of Cancer

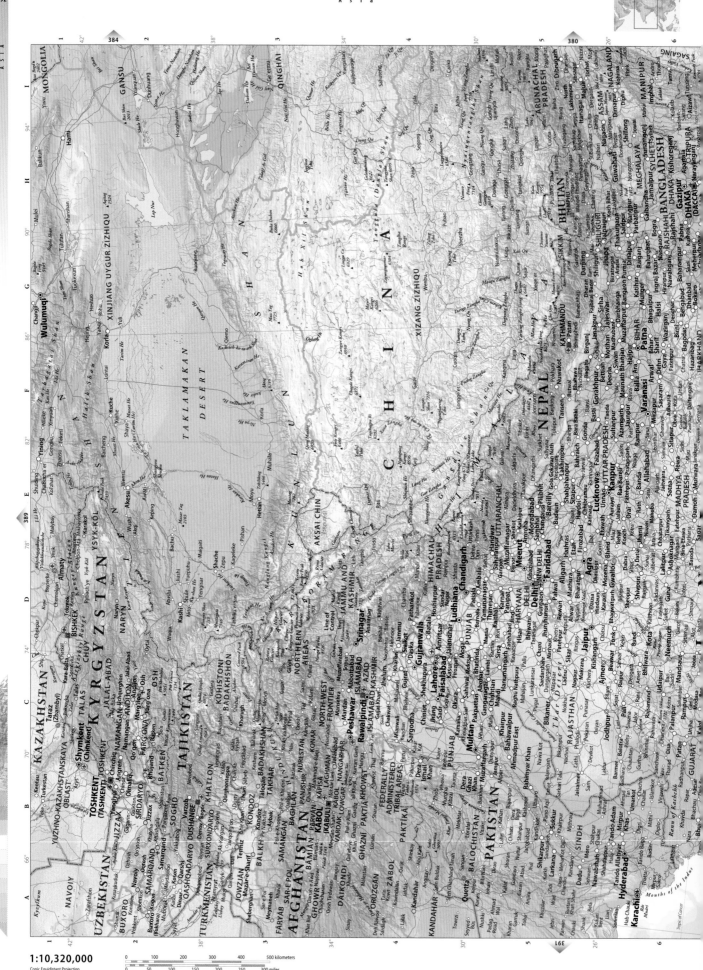

Meters / Feet

Meters	Feet
6000	19685
5000	16404
4000	13123
3000	9843
2000	6562
1000	3281
500	1640
200	656
100	328
0	
LAND BELOW SEA LEVEL	
100	328
200	656
1000	3281
2000	6562
4000	13123
6000	19685

1:10,320,000

Conic Equidistant Projection

0 100 200 300 400 500 kilometers

0 50 100 150 200 250 300 miles

BAY OF BENGAL
ARABIAN SEA
INDIAN OCEAN
ANDAMAN AND NICOBAR ISLANDS
(India)
LAKSHADWEEP
(India)
Laccadive Sea
SRI LANKA
MALDIVES
MYANMAR
MAGWAY
RAKHINE
CHHATTISGARH
ORISSA
MAHARASHTRA
ANDHRA PRADESH
KARNATAKA
TAMIL NADU
KERALA
GOA
DAMAN AND DIU
DADRA AND NAGAR HAVELI
Mumbai
Pune
Pimpri Chinchwad
Nashik
Surat
Aurangabad
Nagpur
Hyderabad
Secunderabad
Chennai
Bengaluru (Bangalore)
Vishakhapatnam
Vijayawada
Bhubaneshwar
Cuttack
Kochi
Thiruvananthapuram
Madurai
Coimbatore
Mysore
Hubli
Dharwad
Solapur
Kolhapur
Warangal
Guntur
Raipur
Bhilai
Puducherry (Puducherry)
SRI JAYEWARDENEPURA KOTTE
COLOMBO
Jaffna
Kandy
Trincomalee
Galle
MALE
Port Blair
Sittwe (Akyab)
Cox's Bazar
North Andaman
Middle Andaman
South Andaman
Little Andaman
Ten Degree Channel
Nine Degree Channel
Eight Degree Channel
Malabar Coast
Coromandel Coast
Mouths of the Ganges
Gulf of Mannar
Palk Bay
376

Turkey and Eastern Europe

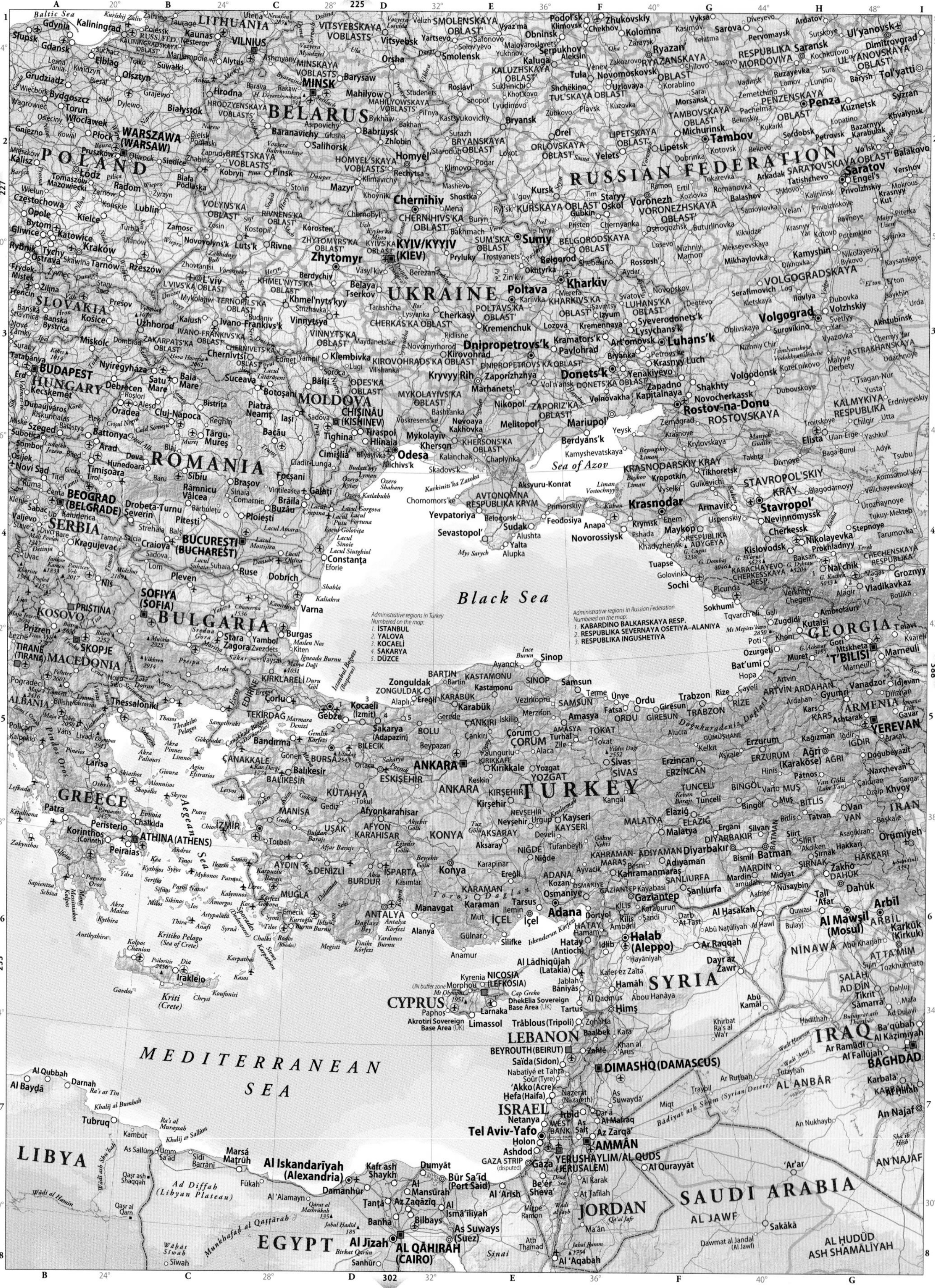
LITHUANIA
BELARUS
POLAND
UKRAINE
RUSSIAN FEDERATION
SLOVAKIA
HUNGARY
MOLDOVA
ROMANIA
SERBIA
KOSOVO
BULGARIA
MACEDONIA
ALBANIA
GREECE
GEORGIA
ARMENIA
TURKEY
SYRIA
CYPRUS
LEBANON
ISRAEL
JORDAN
IRAQ
IRAN
SAUDI ARABIA
EGYPT
LIBYA
Black Sea
Sea of Azov
MEDITERRANEAN SEA
Aegean Sea
Administrative regions in Turkey
Numbered on the map:
1. İSTANBUL
2. YALOVA
3. KOCAELİ
4. SAKARYA
5. DÜZCE
Administrative regions in Russian Federation
Numbered on the map:
1. KABARDINO BALKARSKAYA RESP.
2. RESPUBLIKA SEVERNAYA OSETIYA–ALANIYA
3. RESPUBLIKA INGUSHETIYA

Meters / Feet
6000 / 19685
5000 / 16404
4000 / 13123
3000 / 9843
2000 / 6562
1000 / 3281
500 / 1640
200 / 656
100 / 328
0 LAND BELOW SEA LEVEL
100 / 328
200 / 656
1000 / 3281
2000 / 6562
4000 / 13123
6000 / 19685

1:10,320,000

Conic Equidistant Projection

0 100 200 300 400 500 kilometers

0 50 100 150 200 250 300 miles

Oceania

Oceania covers a large area spattered with numerous islands, most of which are quite small and located far apart. The region today is taken to include the continent of Australia, the large islands of New Guinea and New Zealand, and the thousands of small, often tiny, islands that make up the cultural regions of Melanesia, Micronesia, and Polynesia. Australia and New Zealand account for over 90 percent of the land and population.

Previous pages Many sing-sings take place in the Western Highlands of Papua New Guinea. Most are ceremonial and private, but since 1961 the annual sing-sing at Mt Hagen has drawn many tribes, each uniquely adorned, to perform in public. A celebration of culture, the sing-sing is also a forum for friendly competition in place of war.

Above Boy befriends joey (baby kangaroo), Arnhem Land, Australia. The rocks behind him bear signs of past storytelling, ceremony, and passing on of knowledge.

Above right Baier River men, Papua New Guinea. An estimated 1,000 or more cultural groups live in PNG, and most have their own art, architecture, dance, weaponry, costumes, singing, music, and language. To help unify the nation, Tok Pisin (Pidgin English) is used as the lingua franca in parliament, the media, and elsewhere.

Right Bora Bora, French Polynesia, is a classic atoll structure—a barrier reef surrounding a lagoon, with a volcanic island in the center. The remnants of an extinct volcano rising to two peaks, Mt Pahia and Mt Otemanu, its Tahitian name *(Pora Pora)* means "First Born."

Below A white-bonnet anemonefish *(Amphiprion leucokranos)* and an orange-fin anemonefish *(Amphiprion chrysopterus)* occupy the same sea anemone at Milne Bay, Papua New Guinea, where ecotourism encompasses diving, snorkelling, bat caving, and rainforest walks.

Since the days of Ancient Greece the idea of a southern continent intrigued European geographers, who assumed that a landmass balancing the vast Eurasian landmass must lie south of the Equator. Ptolemy's atlas (c. 150 CE) depicted this supposed southern land as an extension of Asia, but it would be many centuries until the first Europeans reached Terra Australis Incognita, or the "unknown southern land," and proved that such a continent existed. It would take over two centuries after that for cartographers to completely map the waters of Australia and the Pacific Ocean.

Magellan's expedition of 1519–21, an attempt to create an alternative route to the Spice Islands, opened the way for exploration of Oceania, although this part of the world never generated much interest as a target for European colonization. The Portuguese, the first to establish their presence, declined as a world power soon afterward. The Dutch focused on economic exchange, and when the Spanish found no gold, they departed, leaving a significant presence only in the Philippines. The mostly tropical environment offered little prospect for traditional European agriculture, and if not for the British experiment of sending prisoners to penal settlements in Australia, and other countries making claims on various island groups for geopolitical reasons, the cultural geography of the region would today present a very different picture.

Oceania's climate is mainly tropical—apart from the higher southern latitudes of Australia and New Zealand. The Australian continent, because of its size, enjoys a variety of climates, including Mediterranean climatic regions in the south and southwest.

The First Colonizers

By the time Europeans arrived, the islands of Melanesia, Micronesia, and Polynesia were well populated, their inhabitants' navigational skills having amply compensated for the lack of large vessels. Through island-hopping, it took less than 1,000 years for human presence to diffuse from Southeast Asia to as far as Easter Island. Evidence suggests that a continuous human presence began in Australia much earlier than in the Americas, at least 50,000 years BCE, and new archeological findings are continuously moving the date even deeper into the Pleistocene. Until interaction with Europeans, indigenous populations practiced folk culture lifestyles, either hunter-gatherer or subsistence agriculture, and benefited from fishing.

A mix of British, American, French, New Zealand, and Australian possessions is scattered between New Guinea and Pitcairn Island, together with independent countries such as Fiji and Vanuatu.

After World War II, Oceania progressed as a peaceful region, but it is not completely free of turmoil. Atrocities on the Solomon Islands prompted the intervention of an Australian-led international peacekeeping force in 2003, and Fiji's record of power transition through coups rather than the electoral process is well known. However, political issues remain local.

Cultural Transformation

Oceania's peoples have experienced radical cultural transformations, undergoing economic and demographic transitions as they follow global trends. One obvious dichotomy is that Australia and New Zealand have highly developed service-focused economies, while the rest of the region is emerging at a much slower pace. Mining and agriculture also contribute in a major way to the national accounts of Australia and New Zealand; they depend on the latest technologies and require minimal involvement of traditional manual labor. Australia is among the world's largest exporters of

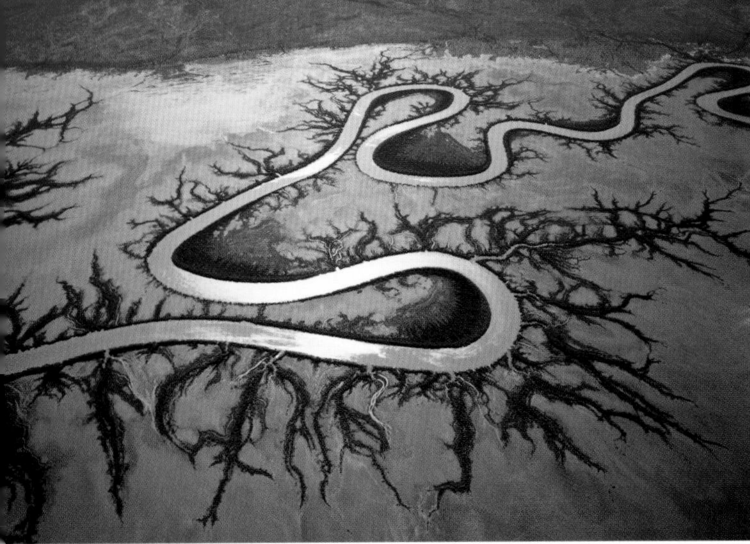

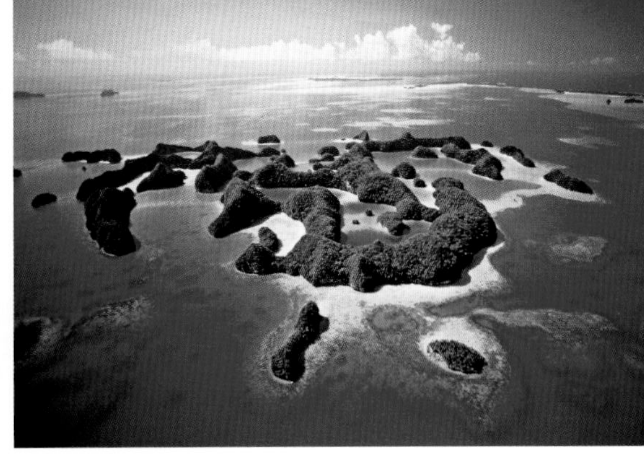

minerals, coal, and a variety of agricultural products. Residents of Australia and New Zealand live in a post-industrial environment and enjoy high standards of living, formal education, age expectancy, and low birth rates.

In the rest of the southern Pacific, circumstances are rather different. Most of the island nations have experienced rapid population growth and the penetration of modern values has shattered traditional cultural systems. The time of simple, self-sufficient, barter economies has ended, and globalization is affecting even those most reluctant to change. The only natural way to reduce population growth is to industrialize, urbanize, and provide formal education and genuine civil liberties.

The current gross national income for the rest of Oceania is only a fraction of that in Australia and New Zealand, and is likely to remain unchanged for some time. Natural resources other than sun, water, and sand are limited. Population growth is an important source of future human capital, but only so long as it is accompanied by successful social and economic reforms, which throughout this region are far from fully implemented. The disparity creates pressure on institutions and the environment, and generates dependence on foreign help. Difficult as it may be to overcome such obstacles, it is not impossible.

The current population distribution is heavily skewed in favor of Australia, which has 21 million of Oceania's 35 million residents. Just short of 11 million more reside in Papua New Guinea and New Zealand. The population map of Australia reveals, however, that the country, and the continent, is almost empty, for much of Australia is covered by desert and marginal savanna country. European settlers generally chose to settle in areas where they could enjoy a familiar climate, and southeastern Australia provided ideal environmental conditions. Further, Sydney's great harbor served as a valuable entrepôt. More than 90 percent of Australians reside in urban areas, and a majority of New Zealanders prefer the northern island. Both countries welcome immigrants who today are predominantly arriving from Asian countries.

Oceania's current ethnic mosaic is composed of a number of layers. The first layer is the indigenous populations of Polynesia, Micronesia, and Melanesia, who all share ancient cultural roots. The second is people of European background who arrived during colonial times, or who were born elsewhere and currently reside on territory owned by their countries, such as in French Polynesia. The final group comprises the descendants of non-Europeans who were transported to Oceania during the nineteenth century to work as laborers. They are a sizable group in places such as Fiji, where they form one-third of the country's population.

Above left The Kimberley is Western Australia's northernmost region, between the Indian Ocean, the Timor Sea, and the Great Sandy Desert. Spanning arid desert, sandy beaches, gorges, escarpments, cave systems, waterfalls, rainforests, river valleys, and open plains fed by meandering rivers, it is home to more than 30 Aboriginal language groups. Its tropical monsoon climate brings distinct wet and dry seasons.

Above The Rock Islands of Palau are for the most part uninhabited. Famous for their beaches, their blue lagoons, and their peculiar shapes, there may be as many as 300 of them. They, and the reefs around them, are popular tourist destinations. Some of the better known locations are the Blue Hole, the Blue Corner, the German Channel, and Jellyfish Lake—one of the many marine lakes in the islands that shelter several kinds of stingless jellyfish found only in Palau.

Above Maori carving in Otago Museum, Dunedin, New Zealand. Maori carvings often feature human figures, some naturalistic, others grotesque. The *manaia*, a bird-headed man, or bird, or serpent, or human figure in profile, is also common, as are spirals. Two sea monsters, the *marakihau* and the whale, are seen less frequently. Maori carvers seem to have had artistic licence to adapt their designs to the available space—often one of the broad slabs of timber used in Maori houses.

Left Sydney's Opera House is one of Australia's most distinctive icons, and one of the world's best-known buildings. Its Danish architect, Jørn Utzon, oversaw construction of the building's podium and its magnificent outer shells. The changes that were made to his plans for the interior after he resigned in 1966 are now seen as regrettable, though the Opera House lost none of its capacity to impress, and is a popular venue for opera, concerts, and other performing arts. Utzon was later involved in plans to rebuild the interior spaces to his original design until his death in 2008.

AUSTRALIA

Official name Commonwealth of Australia
Land area 2,941,299 square miles (7,617,930 km²)
Border countries None
Capital Canberra
Highest & lowest points Mt Kosciuszco 7,313 feet (2,229 m); Lake Eyre −49 feet (−15 m)
Climate Generally arid to semiarid; temperate in the south and east; tropical in the north
Population 20,434,000
Language(s) Official: English; other: Aboriginal languages, Cantonese, Italian, Greek, Arabic, Vietnamese
Ethnicity European (white) 92%, Asian 7%, Aboriginal and other 1%
Religions Christian 67.4%, Buddhist 1.9%, Muslim 1.5%, other 1.2%, unspecified 12.7%, none 15.3%
Government Federal parliamentary democracy
Currency Australian dollar
Human Development Index 0.962 (ranked 3rd out of 177 countries)

Right Australia's national animal emblem is the kangaroo, a marsupial unique to the continent.

Above In 2007, Australia celebrated 100 years of surf lifesaving. This movement, which includes competitive sport with surf rescue, has spread to New Zealand, South Africa, and the USA.

Below Sydney Harbour Bridge (opened in 1932) and the Opera House (opened in 1973) are both world-famous Australian icons.

INDONESIA
PAPUA NEW GUINEA
EAST TIMOR
Arafura Sea
Melville Island
Timor Sea
Darwin
Gulf of Carpentaria
Coral Sea
INDIAN OCEAN
Cairns
Townsville
Port Hedland
Mount Isa
Alice Springs
Rockhampton
AUSTRALIA
Toowoomba
Brisbane
Geraldton
Kalgoorlie
Perth
Broken Hill
Lord Howe Island
Whyalla
Newcastle
Great Australian Bight
Adelaide
Campbelltown
Sydney
CANBERRA
Wollongong
Albany
Kangaroo Island
Albury
Mt Kosciuszko
Ballarat
Melbourne
Tasman Sea
Geelong
Frankston
King Island
Flinders Island
Launceston
Tasmania
Hobart

Australia

Map Reference Pages 424–425

Australia is unique in being a single country (the world's sixth largest) occupying an entire continent. The coastline is bordered by seven oceans: The Timor, Arafura and Coral seas to the north, the South Pacific Ocean and Tasman Sea to the east, the wild Southern Ocean to the south, and the Indian Ocean to the west. Australia is also home to the oldest continuous culture in the world, that of the Australian Aborigines, who live side by side with a relatively young and multi-ethnic culture; unfortunately, the two don't always sit happily together.

Physical Geography

The Great Dividing Range runs along the eastern seaboard, stretching from Cape York Peninsula in the north to the island of Tasmania in the south. Mt Kosciuszko, the highest peak on the range, is 7,313 feet (2,229 m) above sea level, and is part of the small alpine region in the southeast. West of the range, the topography is predominately flat—a few low ranges are scattered across the continent, including the Grampians and the Flinders in the south, the MacDonnells in the center, and the Hammersley Range in the west.

The landmass is geologically stable, ancient, and heavily eroded, with an average elevation of just 1,083 feet (330 m) above sea level—which makes it the lowest continent in the world. The lowest point is 49 feet (15 m) below sea level at Lake Eyre, a dry salt pan in the south at the center of an extensive, and usually dry, inland drainage basin.

Australia is a semi-arid to arid land—ten deserts comprise almost 20 percent of the landmass. The majority of permanent rivers are in the eastern part of the continent. Inland river flows are erratic and salinity is a growing problem. The climate is affected by the irregular fluctuations of the El Niño and La Niña cycles of the Southern Oscillation that in some years result in droughts accompanied by bushfires, and in other years in heavy rains, flooding, and more frequent tropical cyclones in the north. Median annual rainfall ranges from 70 inches (180 cm) on the northeast coast to 8 inches (20 cm) in the arid center. Artesian (underground) water is often the only source of water for inland towns, although central Australia is inhospitable and very sparsely populated. Temperatures across the country vary with latitude.

History

The first inhabitants were the Aborigines, who migrated from Asia between 60,000 and 40,000 years ago. Before European settlement, there may have been between 500,000 and one million people living in Australia and speaking about 250 distinct languages. Some lived a relatively settled existence, but most had a nomadic to semi-nomadic hunter-gatherer lifestyle. Aboriginal oral history and legend stretches back to the time when giant marsupial megafauna roamed Australia. Connection with the past and oneness with the land form a strong part of Aboriginal culture and spiritual belief systems. Conflict with European settlers, dispossession, and introduced diseases to which they had no natural immunity, reduced their numbers. Today, there are some 350,000 Aborigines, with only about 20 of their languages being spoken.

Macassan traders from Sulawesi fished northern Australian waters for trepang (sea slugs) and traded with Aborigines centuries before Dutch, Portuguese, and Spanish sailors became aware of Australia. In 1606, Willem Janszoon, captain of the Dutch East India Company ship *Duyfken,* mapped part of the northern coastline. In 1616, Dirk Hartog, captain of the Dutch ship *Eendracht*, landed on what is now called Dirk Hartog Island at the entrance to Shark Bay in the west. The territory became known as New Holland. In 1770, Captain James Cook sailed along the east coast in the *Endeavour*. The first British penal settlement was established at Port Jackson (Sydney Harbour) in 1788 when Terra Australis was claimed for the British Crown.

The colony grew as free settlers and former convicts began to work the land. New settlements were founded in Van Diemen's Land (Tasmania), Victoria, Western Australia, South Australia, and Queensland. The 1850's gold rushes attracted more immigrants, while wheat and sheep farming soon increased economic prosperity. In 1901, the six separate British colonies federated to become the Commonwealth of Australia. Australia fought alongside the Allies in World War I (1914–1918) and World War II (1939–1945), which strengthened ties with both Britain and the United States.

In 1967 a referendum gave indigenous Australians full citizenship rights for the first time. In 1992 the High Court, in the landmark Mabo decision, overturned the doctrine of *terra nullius*—land that belongs to no one—which paved the way for Aboriginal land rights. In 2008, Prime Minister Kevin Rudd officially apologized—on behalf of both the government and the Australian people—to Aborigines for over two centuries of wrongs committed against them, including the policy of forcibly removing Aboriginal children from their families.

AUSTRALIA'S UNDERGROUND OPAL MINING TOWNS

Opal was discovered in the Great Australian Basin in the late 1800s. As a result, wild and unruly frontier towns sprang up in the most inhospitable desert settings. The best known of these are Coober Pedy, Andamooka, White Cliffs, and Lightning Ridge. "Ants nests" of shafts and a treeless moonscape of mine-waste dumps dominate the landscape, and bear witness to the fortunes and struggles of countless miners. Temperatures of over 130°F (55°C) are common followed by very chilly night-time temperatures. The oppressive heat combined with the high cost of freighting in building materials made old mine shafts look appealing places to live—cool in summer and warm in winter. Today, a digging machine can add new rooms to old mine shafts in the space of a few hours, and some of the desert homes (such as the Coober Pedy house pictured here) have become underground mansions replete with modern conveniences. There are underground hotels, shops, churches, and even swimming pools.

A peculiar feature of Coober Pedy is its grassless golf course, which looks more like a giant sand trap. Players usually carry a small square of artificial grass, which they use to tee off.

Left The beehive-shaped Bungle Bungle mountains rise up to 1,000 feet (300 m) above a plain of forest and grass in the Kimberley region of Western Australia. Ancient rivers shaped these mostly sandstone mounds.

Population/Culture

The hardship of convict life, the difficulties faced by the early settlers, followed by participation in two world wars, forged the national cultural identity of mateship, a type of loyal brotherhood, and a stubborn determination to work together to achieve common goals despite personal hardship.

In the 1960s and 1970s, changes to the immigration laws, which previously favored Europeans, heralded the diversification of the population from one with a primarily Anglo cultural heritage to one with influences from many countries, including Italy, Greece, China, Vietnam, the Middle East, and more recently, Africa. Nevertheless, Australians voted to retain formal allegiance to the British Crown in a referendum held in 1999.

The newer immigrant groups have had a profound influence on Australian society: Colorful festivals abound, and music, dance, theater, and literature resonate with multiethnic influences. Increasing diversity is also reflected in Australian cuisine, originally based on traditional British cooking.

Aboriginal culture and art has become a vital part of the national identity. People the world over are now familiar with the dot and X-ray style of traditional Aboriginal painting. The bassoon-like didgeridoo, made from a hollowed-out tree trunk, and the wing-shaped returning boomerang (originally a hunting tool) are recognizably Australian Aboriginal.

Two important holidays are January 26, Australia Day, which celebrates the country's founding in 1788, and Anzac Day. The latter, celebrated on April 25, commemorates the World War I landing of Australian and New Zealand forces at Gallipoli in 1915, and their courage in the face of overwhelming odds.

About 80 percent of the population lives in the main cities and towns in coastal regions.

MILESTONE EVENTS

60,000–40,000 BCE Arrival of first Australians

1606 CE Willem Janszoon lands on the shores of Gulf of Carpentaria

1616 Dirck Hartogh names New Holland (Western Australia)

1770 Captain James Cook takes possession of Australia in the name of Great Britain

1788 First European convicts arrive on the First Fleet

1817 "Australia" is formally adopted for the name of the country

1825 Colony of Tasmania (Van Diemen's Land) established

1829 Colony of Western Australia established

1834 Colony of South Australia established

1839 Convict penal settlement system suspended

1851 Colony of Victoria established

1851 Immigration associated with gold rushes begins

1859 Colony of Queensland established

1901 The six colonies of the United Kingdom federated to become the Commonwealth of Australia

1967 Australian Aborigines given full citizenship rights

1984 National anthem changed from "God Save the Queen" to "Advance Australia Fair"

1992 High Court overturns the doctrine of *terra nullius*

November 1999 Voters (11.6 million) reject a referendum to end Australia's allegiance to the British Crown

2003 Despite strong opposition, Prime Minister Howard sends 2,000 Australian troops to fight alongside American and British troops in Iraq

2008 Prime Minister Rudd officially apologizes to Australian Aborigines for wrongs committed against them

Administration/Government

Australia's eight administrative divisions, in order of population, are: New South Wales, Victoria, Queensland, Western Australia, South Australia, Tasmania, the Australian Capital Territory, and the Northern Territory. Australia's seven dependencies are: Ashmore and Cartier Islands, Christmas Island, Cocos (Keeling) Islands, Coral Sea Islands, Heard and McDonald Islands, Norfolk Island, and Macquarie Island.

Queen Elizabeth II is the symbolic head of the country and is represented by the Governor General, who is appointed by the government. The prime minister is head of federal parliament, which consists of the Senate and House of Representatives; below federal parliament are state parliaments headed by state premiers who are responsible for the running of the states. Democratic elections are held every three or four years and voting is compulsory. There are two major political parties, the more socialist-leaning Australian Labor Party and the conservative Liberal Party. Other important parties are the National Party (allied with the Liberal Party), Australian Democrats, and Greens Party.

Economy/Industry

The capitalist economy has a high per capita GDP, a stable currency, and strong business and consumer confidence. Australia comes third out of 177 countries on the Human Development Index, attesting to the high standard of living enjoyed by most people. The economy is fueled by the export of raw materials and agricultural products. Natural resources include coal, bauxite, iron ore, copper, tin, gold, silver, uranium, nickel, tungsten, mineral sands, lead, zinc, diamonds, natural gas, and oil. Agricultural products include wheat, barley, sugarcane, fruit, cattle, sheep, and poultry. Service industries are important, and hospitality and tourism have grown. Economic priorities are to maintain low inflation, and strengthen trade relations with China and other growing nations.

Environmental concerns include rising soil salinity and soil erosion from overgrazing and poor farming practices, as well as drought and desertification that have been induced by climate change. Land clearing, urbanization, pollution, and runoff threaten some of Australia's unique natural habitats.

Above An Aboriginal dancer takes part in a traditional Woggan-ma-gule Morning Ceremony, which opens Sydney's Australia Day celebrations each year. Sydney is located on sacred land of the indigenous Gadigal people.

Below Queensland's Great Barrier Reef, said to be the largest coral reef in the world, is one of numerous natural habitats in Australia that are under threat because of the negative impacts of human habitation.

PAPUA NEW GUINEA

Official name Independent State of Papua New Guinea
Land area 174,850 square miles (452,860 km²)
Border countries Indonesia
Capital Port Moresby
Highest point Mt Wilhelm 14,793 feet (4,509 m)
Climate Tropical
Population 5,932,000
Language(s) Melanesian Pidgin, English, Motu (Papua region), 820 indigenous languages
Ethnicity Papuan, Melanesian, Negrito, Micronesian, Polynesian
Religion Christian 66%, indigenous beliefs 34%
Government Constitutional parliamentary democracy
Currency Kina
Human Development Index 0.530 (ranked 145th out of 177 countries)

Above right Rabaul volcano, on the island of New Britain, is still active. In 1994 it erupted violently; volcanic ash destroyed much of Rabaul town and residents were forced to relocate permanently. Because of early warnings, however, few deaths resulted from the eruption.

Above Matschie's tree-kangaroo *(Dendrolagus matschiei)* is only found in the mountains of PNG's Huon Peninsula, on the nearby island of Umboi, and on Mt Agulupella in the west of New Britain island. Each individual tree-kangaroo has a unique facial pattern.

Right A wig-wearing Huli tribesman takes part in a ceremony. To witness traditional singing and dancing by a troop of PNG men or women in traditional regalia can be a breathtaking experience, and is all the more remarkable for its preservation in this age of globalization.

Admiralty Islands
Lorengau
Bismarck Sea
Kavieng
PACIFIC OCEAN
Wewak
New Ireland
Rabaul
PAPUA NEW GUINEA
INDONESIA
Mt Wilhelm
Madang
Bougainville Island
Mount Hagen
Goroka
Arawa
New Britain
New Guinea
Lae
Solomon Sea
SOLOMON ISLANDS
Kerema
Balimo
PORT MORESBY
Alotau
AUSTRALIA
Coral Sea

Papua New Guinea

Map Reference Pages 372–373

Papua New Guinea (PNG) occupies the eastern half of the island of New Guinea, sharing a border with Indonesian-controlled Irian Jaya. PNG includes hundreds of islands adjacent to the northeast and east coast. New Guinea lies just south of the Equator and north of Australia. The two landmasses, separated by the shallow Torres Strait, were connected during the Quaternary ice ages when sea levels were lower.

Physical Geography

A mountain mass with pinnacles higher than 13,123 feet (4,000 m) extends along the central axis. The mountains are flanked to the southwest by broad plains and to the north by wide valleys and lesser mountain ranges. The islands to the northeast and east are moderately mountainous and partly volcanic.

PNG has 22 active volcanoes: Rabaul volcano erupted in 1994, causing the evacuation of Rabaul town and forcing a relocation of most services to Kokopo to the southeast. Most inhabitants of Manam Island relocated to the mainland after increased activity in 2004–2005. The violent 1665 eruption of Long Island volcano cast an ash cloud that blocked out the sun over much of the highlands and is recalled in legend as a "time of darkness."

Climate for most of PNG is wet tropical with rainfall exceeding 98 inches (250 cm). Vegetation is mainly tropical rainforest, giving way to freshwater swamps in the lowlands and moss forest and alpine grassland on the higher peaks. Areas with elevations of 11,483 feet (3,500 m) and above were glaciated during the last glacial maximum, 20,000 years ago.

History

The first migrants reached PNG at least 50,000 years ago, arriving from the west during times of lower sea levels. Cultivation of edible plants began over 9,000 years ago and ranks with the earliest developments of cultivation worldwide. European contact began with navigators in the sixteenth century. Regular contact began in the nineteenth century with the arrival of missionaries, blackbirders who recruited (kidnapped) people for plantation labor, gold prospectors, and traders who sought bird of paradise plumes.

Germany claimed the northern mainland and the northeastern islands in 1884, followed by Britain's claim of the southern mainland and islands in 1888, the area later ceded to Australia as the Territory of Papua. The German territory became a League of Nations Mandate in 1919, administered by Australia. The two territories subsequently became the independent state of Papua New Guinea in 1975.

Population/Culture

The population comprises 700 to 1,000 ethnic groups with 820 indigenous languages. The population growth rate is 2.7 percent annually; but an estimated 2 percent (minimum) of the population is HIV positive.

The country's rich cultural heritage is expressed in song, dance, ritual, personal decoration, carving, and pottery. Most people describe themselves as Christians; at the same time many people retain a belief in ancestral spirits and sorcery.

Administration/Government

PNG is a constitutional parliamentary democracy with 109 seats in the unicameral National Parliament. As head of government the prime minister selects ministers; together they form the National Executive Council. There are 19 provinces, each governed by an assembly comprising the province's members in National Parliament, the president of each local-level government, and two appointed members representing women and churches. After 16 years of civil unrest and armed conflict, Bougainville Province achieved limited self-government in 2005 (as the Autonomous Bougainville Government) and has the option to negotiate for full independence at a future date. On June 15, 2005, members of the first Bougainville House of Representatives were officially sworn in.

Economy/Industry

Agriculture provides the major component of GDP; however, exports of extractable minerals are the backbone of PNG's monetized economy. Major exports include gold, oil, copper, and palm oil. Other valuable exports are forest products (mostly unprocessed logs), fish, coffee, cocoa, copra and copra oil, tea, and rubber. Eighty-five percent of people live by subsistence agriculture, many of them in remote areas, and 37 percent of the population lives below the poverty line.

Coral Terraces and Rising Seas

Raised coral terraces on the Huon Peninsula's north coast provide a detailed record of past changes in sea level and hence of climate change. At times of global warming, when ice sheets are melting, sea levels rise in concert with the land, permitting coral reefs to be established. As the land continues to rise, the reef is lifted out of the water to form an uplifted terrace.

At times of global cooling, when water from the oceans is being trapped in ice sheets, sea levels fall and coral reefs can develop only as a thin veneer. By determining the age of each terrace using isotopes, we can define the sequence of rise and fall of sea level and of global cooling and warming for the last 350,000 years.

MILESTONE EVENTS

1526 First European, Jorge de Meneses, visits islands and names them Ilhas dos Papuas

1884 Britain and Germany divide up New Guinea

1906 British New Guinea handed over to Commonwealth of Australia and renamed Territory of Papua

1914 German New Guinea occupied by Australian forces

1921 League of Nations grants Australia a mandate to govern German New Guinea

1933 Hundred of thousands of previously undiscovered people found living in remote mountain valleys

1942 Japanese forces occupy parts of the country

July 1949 Australia establishes joint administration over both territories named the Territory of Papua and New Guinea

May 1963 Control of West New Guinea (Papua) transferred to Indonesia by UN

June 1964 House of Assembly replaces Legislative Council with indigenous representatives elected to the majority of seats

July 1971 Country is renamed Papua New Guinea (PNG)

December 1973 Self-government granted and Michael Somare becomes head of the Executive Council

September 16, 1975 PNG gains independence with Sir Michael Somare as prime minister

1975 Bougainville votes to secede from PNG

June–July 1977 First parliamentary elections since independence

April 1989 Armed struggle begins for an independent Bougainville; Australian-owned Panguna copper mine forced to close

1994 Prime Minister Sir Julius Chan signs agreement with Bougainville secessionist leaders allowing for a transitional administration

April 1995 Bougainville Transitional Government, under leadership of Theodore Miriong, is sworn in

1996 Theodore Miriong assassinated, Gerard Sinato replaces him

March 1997 Prime Minister Chan is forced to resign over the hiring of mercenaries—from Sandline International—as support for government troops in Bougainville

April 1998 Permanent ceasefire signed in Bougainville

July 1998 Three tsunamis strike northwest coast killing over 3,000 people

December 1999 John Momis sworn in as Governor of Bougainville

November 2000 Low-lying Duke of York Atoll to be evacuated because of rising ocean levels

August 2001 Bougainville Peace Agreement signed, guaranteeing a referendum (in 10–15 years) on the island's political status

August 2002 Sir Michael Somare elected as prime minister for the third time

May 2005 Former separatist Joseph Kabui elected president of Bougainville's first autonomous government

August 2007 Sir Michael Somare is elected as premier for a second consecutive term

March 7, 2008 Australia pledges extra $13 million to help stop the spread of HIV/AIDS

Ngcheangel
Ollei
Ngetbong
Babeldaob
Mt Ngerchelchuus
MELEKEOK
Koror
Airai
Mecherchar
Peleliu
Ngaramasch
Angaur
PALAU
PACIFIC OCEAN
Sonsoral Island
Pulo Anna
Merir
Tobi
Helen Reef

Palau

Map Reference Pages 426–427

Located at the western end of the Micronesian Caroline chain of islands in the Pacific, the Republic of Palau lies 724 km (450 miles) east of the Philippine island of Mindanao. It is an archipelago of six groups of islands, with 26 islands and over 300 islets. The new capital, Melekeok, is on the island of Babelthuap. A UN trusteeship under US administration until 1994, Palau is one of the world's newest and smallest states.

Palau is home to a multi-ethnic population. The largest group is Palauan, a people of mixed Micronesian, Melanesian, and Malayan ancestry. Successively occupied and controlled from 1886 by Spain, Germany, Japan, and the USA, the modern history of the islands began in the turmoil of World War II, when they were fought over by Japanese and US forces.

In 1978 Palau faced incorporation into the Federated States of Micronesia. However, its leaders sought independent status, and in 1981 adopted their own constitution banning nuclear weapons and military bases. This provision was overturned in 1993, which enabled a Compact of Free Association to be signed with the USA in 1994, freeing the islands to become the independent Republic of Palau.

Palau's natural resources consist of timber, marine products, gold, and other onshore and offshore minerals. Agriculture produces coconuts, cassava, and sweet potatoes, and fishing supplies domestic and commercial markets. Craft industries produce items made from shell and wood. Exports include tuna, copra, trochus shell, and handicrafts.

The government is the leading employer, and the main source of revenue is US aid. High hopes are held for tourist development.

PALAU

Official name Republic of Palau (Beluu er a Belau)
Land area 177 square miles (458 km²)
Border countries None
Capital Melekeok
Highest point Mt Ngerchelchuus 794 feet (242 m)
Climate Tropical; hot and humid
Population 21,093
Language(s) Palauan, Sonsoralese, English, Tobi, Angaur, Japanese, Filipino, Chinese, Carolinian, Japanese, other
Ethnicity Palauan, 69.9%, Filipino 15.3%, Chinese 4.9%, other Asian 2.4%, European descent 1.9%, Carolinian 1.4%, other Micronesian 1.1%, other/unspecified 3.1%
Religion Christian 71.7%, Modekngei 8.8%, other 3.1%, unspecified/none 16.4%
Government Constitutional government in free association with the USA
Currency US dollar
Human Development Index Not available

Philippine Sea
Colonia
Yap
Hall Islands
PACIFIC OCEAN
FEDERATED STATES OF MICRONESIA
Weno
Chuuk
PALIKIR
Pohnpei
Kosrae
Caroline Islands
Nukuoro Atoll
Kapingamarangi Atoll

Micronesia

Map Reference Pages 426–427

Four major island groups make up the Federated States of Micronesia (FSM)—Pohnpei, Kosrae, Yap, and Chuuk (formerly Truk). Once known as the Caroline Islands, they lie north-northeast of Papua New Guinea in the North Pacific Ocean, some 607 islands scattered over a large area of ocean. Geologically they range from low coral atolls to mountainous islands. Climate is tropical with heavy year-round precipitation.

FSM lies on the edge of the typhoon belt. In 2002, Typhoon Chata'an (Gloria) struck Chuuk, causing destructive mudslides and killing dozens of people. In April 2004, Typhoon Sudal (Cosme) devastated Yap. There was no loss of life, but it knocked out power supplies and communications, and substantially damaged the infrastructure.

FSM has been inhabited for perhaps 3,000 years, as evidenced by the Lelu ruins in Kosrae (1400 CE) and the Nan Madol ruins of Pohnpei (1000 CE). The islands were annexed by Spain in 1874. In 1945 the United States took over Micronesia's administration. US governance ended in 1986 when the FSM and the USA signed a Compact of Free Association.

The majority of the population engage in fishing or subsistence farming. Industries are construction, fish processing and specialized aquaculture, and the making of handcrafted products. Exports include fish, bananas, and black pepper. In recent years foreign commercial fishing fleets have paid license fees for the right to operate in the territorial waters of Micronesia. These fees account for around 28 percent of government revenue.

FSM depends heavily on financial aid from the USA. However, trade links with China are currently being developed; recently China announced grants of US$2.5 million, while awarding the country Approved Destination Status. This could greatly improve the country's tourist prospects. The islands are a prime destination for scuba divers, although remoteness and poor infrastructure are ongoing tourist and travel liabilities.

MICRONESIA

Official name Federated States of Micronesia
Land area 271 square miles (702 km²)
Border countries None
Capital Palikir
Highest point Dolohmwar (Totolom) 2,595 feet (791 m)
Climate Tropical
Population 107,665
Language(s) English, Trukese, Pohnpeian, Yapese, Kosrean, Ulithian, Woleaian, Nukuoro, Kapingamarangi
Ethnicity Chuukese 48.8%, Pohnpeian 24.2%, Yapese 9.7%, Kosraean 6.2%, Asian 1.8%, Polynesian 1.5%, other 6.4%, unknown 1.4%
Religion Christian 97%, other 3%
Government Constitutional government in free association with the US
Currency US dollar
Human Development Index Not available

Below left Locals at Chamorro Bay, Yap Island, Micronesia, often build their houses on stilts.

Below right Scuba divers are drawn to the spectacular marine environments of Palau.

NAURU

Official name Republic of Nauru
Land area 8 square miles (21 km²)
Border countries None
Capital Yaren
Highest point Unnamed location 200 feet (61 m)
Climate Tropical with a monsoonal pattern
Population 13,770
Language(s) Nauruan, English
Ethnicity Nauruan 58%, other Pacific Islander 26%, Chinese 8%, European 8%
Religion Christian 100%
Government Republic
Currency Australian dollar
Human Development Index Not available

Right The island of Ghizo, Western Province, Solomon Islands, has the typical features of a tropical island. Its crystal clear waters attract scuba divers from around the world who are interested in marine life as well as shipwrecks.

SOLOMON ISLANDS

Official name Solomon Islands
Land area 10,633 square miles (27,450 km²)
Border countries None
Capital Honiara
Highest point Mt Makarakomburu 8,028 feet (2,447 m)
Climate Tropical monsoon
Population 581,318
Language(s) Solomons pijian or Melanesian pidgin, English, plus 120 indigenous languages
Ethnicity Melanesian 94.5%, Polynesian 3%, Micronesian 1.2%, other 1.1%, unspecified 0.2%
Religion Christian 97.1%, other 2.7%, none 0.2%
Government Parliamentary democracy
Currency Solomon Islands dollar
Human Development Index 0.602 (ranked 129th out of 177 countries)

Below In 1798, the British whaler John Fearn stopped at Nauru and named it Pleasant Island. Several decades later other whalers and traders began visiting the island to resupply their ships.

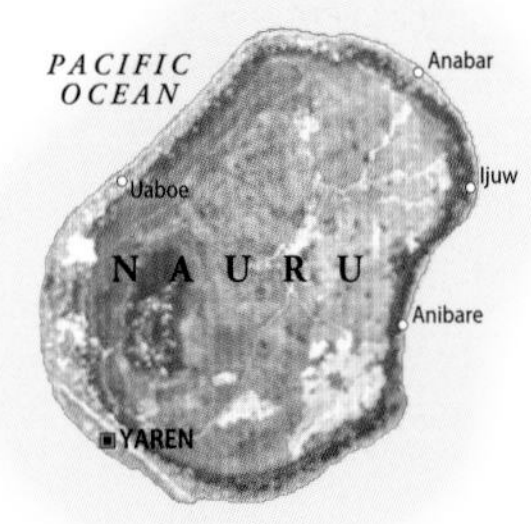
PACIFIC OCEAN
Anabar
Ijuw
Uaboe
NAURU
Anibare
YAREN

Nauru

Map Reference Pages 426–427

Nearly lost in the vast Pacific Ocean is the tiny country of Nauru, the world's smallest island nation and smallest republic. Nearly 80 percent of the island has been environmentally damaged by phosphate mining.

Nauru is a small, oval coral island just south of the Equator. The climate is tropical with a monsoon season from November to February. A narrow coastal strip surrounds a central plateau, which has been mined for phosphate for over a century. The coastal strip contains the only habitable and fertile land on the island, with the exception of the area surrounding Buada Lagoon. Bananas, pineapples, and some vegetables are grown, but almost everything else must be imported.

The first Nauruans traveled from Polynesia and Micronesia. The British arrived in 1798, and Germany annexed the island in 1888. Australia captured the island in 1914 during World War I; Japan seized it then lost it during World War II. Nauru gained its independence in 1968.

Nauru's population of 13,770 is increasing due to a high birth rate. Nauruans make up nearly 60 percent of the population. Other Pacific Islanders provide another 26 percent.

Nauru has a unicameral parliament with 18 seats. Members are elected for three-year terms. The president is elected by parliament for a three-year term and serves as both chief of state and head of government. The judiciary is represented by the Supreme Court.

Phosphate wealth has been a blessing and a curse. In 1975, Nauruans had the second highest per capita income in the world. At the time, phosphate prices and demand were high. Now, dwindling supplies and low prices have pushed the nation close to bankruptcy. Nauru's per capita income has plummeted to 132nd in the world. Nauru's greatest challenge now is to find other sources of income.

PAPUA NEW GUINEA
Ontong Java Atoll
PACIFIC OCEAN
Choiseul
Panggoe
Korovou
Shortland Islands
Gizo
Baolo
Santa Isabel
Buala
Stewart Islands
New Georgia Group
Auki
Malaita
SOLOMON ISLANDS
HONIARA
Tulaghi
Apio
Guadalcanal
Mt Makarakomburu
Makira
Kirakira
(San Cristobal)
Lata
Santa Cruz Islands
Solomon Sea
Rennell
Lavanggu
Tikopia
VANUATU

Solomon Islands

Map Reference Pages 426–427

Located in the southwestern Pacific, the Solomon Islands lie between the eastern shores of New Guinea and Vanuatu. Numbering about 1,000 in all, the six main islands of the archipelago are Guadalcanal, Malaita, New Georgia, Makira (also known as San Cristobal), Santa Isabel, and Choiseul. The capital city, Honiara, is on Guadalcanal.

Physical Geography

The larger islands have heavily forested mountain ranges with steep-sided river valleys, and are ringed by narrow coastal plains and coral reefs. The region is geologically active with several volcanoes and frequent earthquakes. In 2007, an undersea earthquake measuring 8.1 on the Richter scale occurred 214 miles (345 km) west–northwest of Honiara, resulting in a tsunami as high as 33 feet (10 m) striking coastal areas. Dozens of people were killed, thousands more were displaced.

History

The islands seem to have been first settled about 30,000 years ago. In 1568 the Spanish navigator Alvaro de Mendana named them in the belief that he had found "the riches of Solomon." In the 1870s and 1880s labor recruiters known as blackbirders arrived, luring or kidnapping islanders to work on sugarcane plantations in Australia. This resulted in the establishment, in 1893, of the British Solomon Islands Protectorate over the southern Solomons.

In World War II, Japanese forces occupied the islands, and in 1942, Allied forces launched naval bombardments and amphibious landings on Guadalcanal, the site of some of the most intense fighting in the Pacific. Following Japan's defeat, the Solomons became a major area for operations in the Pacific campaign.

A politically aware indigenous leadership did not accept the returning British colonial government after the war, but it was not until 1976 that self-government was granted, and the name Solomon Islands officially adopted.

The path of the new nation has not been smooth. There have been secessionist declarations by different provinces. Divisions based on tribes, locality, and language run deep, and ethnic tensions surfaced in 1998. On Guadalcanal the Isatabu Freedom Movement fought members of the Malaita Eagle Force. Lawlessness reached a point where the prime minister, then Sir Allen Kemakeza, asked Australia to intervene, which it did in 2003 with the Regional Assistance Mission to the Solomon Islands.

Even more serious was the situation on Bougainville. Although this island was culturally and geographically part of the Solomons, Bougainville had been treated politically as part of Papua New Guinea (PNG) for more than 100 years. When PNG was granted independence in 1975, Bougainville became part of that country. A violent secessionist campaign resulted in a 10-year civil war (1989–98). As part of its strategy to defeat the rebels, PNG blockaded the island, and many of the sick and injured traveled by open boat to the Solomons for treatment. Some have never returned.

Population/Culture

Most of the people are ethnically Melanesian. There were originally 74 languages spoken in the islands (four are now extinct), and English is the official language, although only 1 to 2

MAASINA RULE

World War II not only turned the Solomons upside down, it prompted a quasi-military egalitarian movement—Maasina Rule, or the Rule of the Brotherhood. Men who had witnessed US army organization and equipment decided to reshape their own communal life. Different tribal peoples were to join together, united by a council of nine head chiefs, to negotiate with the returning British administration. The islanders were to form communal villages based on military units, with roll-calls, chiefs to supervize communal labor, and daily drills with wooden rifles.

The plan was that the Rule of the Brotherhood would unite the Solomons into a new social, economic, and political order, free from colonial rule. On Malaita men refused to work on plantations, and large demonstrations took place where demands were voiced. The nine head chiefs were jailed, and warships and military aircraft demonstrated British power. Eventually the Rule of the Brotherhood communities disintegrated and the movement was driven underground. Although it had millenarian elements, Maasina Rule was basically a political rather than a religious movement.

percent of the population speak it. The lingua franca is a local form of English known as Solomons pijin or Melanesian pidgin.

The traditional culture involved a familiar western Pacific pattern of subsistence agriculture, growing root crops such as yams and taro, pig-keeping, and harvesting coconuts. Fishing was an important activity for some people. Coastal settlements tended to be larger: In the lagoons of northern Malaita villages housing up to 200 people were built upon coral platforms in the lagoons. The sexes were residentially separated, and men's clubhouses were the focus of solidarity.

Administration/Government

The Solomon Islands is formally a constitutional monarchy with a prime minister as head of government and Queen Elizabeth II as head of state. There are competing political parties, and the leader of the majority party is elected prime minister by parliament. In reality, however, a combination of tribal violence, economic mismanagement, and chronic corruption have weakened the nation's efforts to create a modern parliamentary democracy.

Economy/Industry

Some 75 percent of Solomon Islanders are engaged in subsistence agriculture, producing cocoa beans, palm kernels, and raising beef cattle. Agriculture contributes 42 percent to GDP as does the service sector, which employs 20 percent of the labor force. Industry, which processes products such as palm oil and copra, employs 5 percent of the labor force and contributes 11 percent to GDP. Export commodities include fish, copra, palm oil, cocoa, and timber. The country has an abundance of undeveloped mineral resources, including lead, zinc, nickel, gold, bauxite, and phosphate.

Political stability has returned—since 2003, more than 6,000 militants have been arrested and over 9,000 charges have been laid against those responsible for civil unrest—but economic stagnation persists.

MILESTONE EVENTS

c. 30,000 BCE First settlers arrive from Papua

800–1200 BCE Lapita culture arrives from the west

1568 CE Visit of Alvaro de Mendana

1893–1899 British Solomons Islands Protectorate

1942 Battle of Guadalcanal, World War II

1946 Maasina Rule active

1978 The islands gain independence

1997–1998 Inter-regional fighting

2003 Regional Assistance Mission to the Solomon Islands (RAMSI) goes into operation

2007 Major earthquake and tsunami

Left The Solomon Islands are made up of around a thousand islands that range from tiny to very large. Palm trees abound on Marovo Island, pictured, which is situated in Marovo Lagoon.

PACIFIC OCEAN
Torres Islands
Banks Islands
Sola
Espíritu Santo
Mt Tabwémasana
Luganville
Norsup
Malakula
Aoba
Naoné
Maéwo
Bwatnapné
Pentecost
Ranon
Ambrym
Lamap
Mélip
Epi
Lamengo
Coral Sea
PORT-VILA
Forari
Éfaté
VANUATU
Potnarvin
Erromango
Tanna
Isangel
Anatom

Vanuatu

Map Reference Pages 426–427

Lying west of Fiji and 300 miles (500 km) northeast of New Caledonia, Vanuatu consists of 13 large islands and 70 small islets. From around 1000 BCE, the islands were settled by successive waves of colonizers.

Physical Geography

The two largest islands, Espiritu Santo and Malakula, comprise half the total landmass of Vanuatu. These islands are volcanic, with lowlands, plateaus, and mountain peaks. Other volcanic islands in the archipelago have a stratum of limestone. Smaller islands are coral and limestone.

Most of Vanuatu's islands are mountainous and forested, and over the years have been unsustainably logged for trees such as sandalwood. Now the government limits harvesting of sandalwood to three months of the year.

History

Portuguese, the first Europeans, arrived in 1606; when Captain Cook visited in 1774 he named the islands the New Hebrides. France and Britain jointly administered the islands after 1887, which produced a lingering political and social division between the anglophone and francophone populations.

In World War II, Espiritu Santo and Port-Vila became major military bases for the Allied drive through the Pacific islands. By the 1960s locals were pushing for self-government and independence, which came in 1980.

Population/Culture

Most of the people are Christian and ethnically labeled Ni-Vanuatu. Over 100 indigenous languages are spoken on the islands.

Administration/Government

Vanuatu's chief of state is the president, and the head of government is the prime minister. The members of the 52-seat unicameral parliament are elected by popular vote. The National Council of Chiefs guides the government on issues regarding culture and language. The Supreme Court, headed by a chief justice and three judges, represents the judiciary.

Economy/Industry

Subsistence agriculture provides a living for 65 percent of the population. The beef industry comprises 130,000 head of cattle. All oil is imported because there are no known oil reserves and mineral deposits are insignificant. A small light industry caters to the local market. Tourism is important, while fishing and offshore financial services are other mainstays of the economy. The service sector employs 30 percent of the labor force and contributes 62 percent to GDP. Copra, beef, cocoa, timber, kava, and coffee bring export earnings.

Left Lopevi Volcano in Malampa Province, Vanuatu, is now uninhabited. Ongoing volcanic activity has made the island unsafe for human habitation. In April 2008, Lopevi sent up a thick gray plume of ash that was estimated to be at least 8,000 feet (2.4 km) tall, probably higher.

VANUATU

Official name Republic of Vanuatu (Ripablik blong Vanuatu)

Land area 4,710 square miles (12,200 km²)

Border countries None

Capital Port-Vila

Highest point Tabwemasana 6,158 feet (1,877 m)

Climate Tropical; may be affected by cyclones from December to April

Population 215,446

Language(s) Bislama or Bichelama (pidgin), local languages (more than 100), English, French, other

Ethnicity Ni-Vanuatu 98.5%, other 1.5%

Religion Christian 82.5%, indigenous beliefs 5.6%, other 10.9%, none 1%

Government Parliamentary republic

Currency Vatu

Human Development Index 0.674 (ranked 120th out of 177 countries)

Above A woman from Tanna Island, Vanuatu, waits for her son to return from his long seclusion following his circumcision. She wears traditional ceremonial dress.

MARSHALL ISLANDS

Official name Republic of the Marshall Islands
Land area 70 square miles (181.3 km^2)
Border countries None
Capital Majuro
Highest point Unnamed location on Likiep 33 feet (10 m)
Climate Tropical; hot and humid; islands border typhoon belt
Population 63,174
Language(s) Marshallese, English, other
Ethnicity Micronesian 100%
Religion Christian 97.5%, none 1.5%, other 1%
Government Constitutional government in free association with the USA
Currency US dollar
Human Development Index Not available

Taongi Atoll
PACIFIC OCEAN
Bikini Atoll
Enewetak Atoll
Rongelap Atoll
Ujelang Atoll
Wotje Atoll
Kwajalein Atoll
Maloelap Atoll
MARSHALL ISLANDS
Ailinglaplap Atoll
Majuro Atoll
MAJURO
Mili Atoll
Jaluit Atoll
Ebon Atoll

Marshall Islands

Map Reference Pages 426–427

The Republic of the Marshall Islands in the western Pacific consists of 5 islands, 31 coral atolls, and 1,152 islets; 10 atolls are uninhabited. Most of the important atolls and islands are arranged in two groups—the Ratak Chain to the east (sunrise islands), and the Ralik Chain to the west (sunset islands). Two-thirds of the population live in Majuro, the capital, and Ebeye (on Kwajalein Atoll).

Settled by Micronesian peoples as far back as 1000 BCE, the Marshall Islands were first sighted by Europeans in 1526. The next westerner to arrive, in 1788, was British naval captain John Marshall, after whom the islands are named. Under German control from 1885 to 1914, they were seized by Japan in World War I, and were administered after the war as a League of Nations mandate. In 1944 they were occupied by the USA. From 1946 to 1962 Bikini and Enewetak atolls were used by the USA as nuclear testing sites—compensation claims are still being heard. US army forces and the Ronald Reagan Ballistic Missile Defense site are located on Kwajalein Atoll.

In 1979 the Marshall Islands became self-governing, and in 1986 gained independence under a Compact of Free Association with the USA. In 1990 the UN officially ended the country's trusteeship status.

On the occupied outlying atolls a typical Pacific island subsistence economy is centered on agriculture and fishing. Commercial crops include coconuts, tomatoes, melons, and breadfruit. A few cattle ranches supply the domestic meat market. Industry consists of copra processing and handcraft items. Exports include copra and coconut oil products. The economic difficulties facing the nation can be seen in the tuna industry. Though there have been serious efforts by a number of nearby countries to establish viable processing plants, most have failed. As a result, most regional island states have decided to take what money they can from fishing license fees. The country depends on US foreign aid, and in 2006 had an external debt of US$86.5 million. Tourism is the best hope for added revenue.

Right Likiep Atoll is part of the Ratak Chain of Marshall Islands. The palm-studded islands and pristine coral reefs surround a large lagoon.

Far right Evacuated in 1954 due to fallout from nuclear tests on nearby islands, Rongelap Atoll in the Marshall Islands will soon be resettled.

Above Children swim in Funafuti Lagoon on Funafuti Atoll, Tuvalu. This tiny group of coral islets makes up one of the world's smallest nations.

TUVALU

Official name Tuvalu
Land area 10 square miles (26 km^2)
Border countries None
Capital Funafuti
Highest point Unnamed 16 feet (5 m)
Climate Tropical marine
Population 12,177
Language(s) Tuvaluan, English, Samoan, Kiribati (on the island of Nui)
Ethnicity Polynesian 96%, Micronesian 4%
Religion Christian 98.4%, Baha'i 1%, other 0.6%
Government Constitutional monarchy with a parliamentary democracy
Currency Australian dollar, Tuvaluan dollar
Human Development Index Not available

Nanumea Atoll
Niutao
Nanumanga
PACIFIC OCEAN
Nui Atoll
Vaitupu Vaitupu
TUVALU
Nukufetau Atoll
Funafuti Atoll
FUNAFUTI
Nukulaelae Atoll

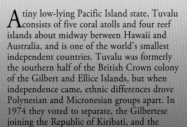

Tuvalu

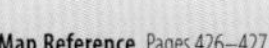

Map Reference Pages 426–427

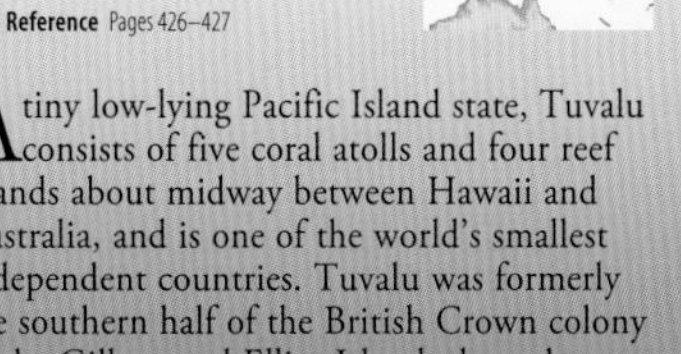

A tiny low-lying Pacific Island state, Tuvalu consists of five coral atolls and four reef islands about midway between Hawaii and Australia, and is one of the world's smallest independent countries. Tuvalu was formerly the southern half of the British Crown colony of the Gilbert and Ellice Islands, but when independence came, ethnic differences drove Polynesian and Micronesian groups apart. In 1974 they voted to separate, the Gilbertese joining the Republic of Kiribati, and the southern Ellice Islanders setting up as Tuvalu.

During the fourteenth century seafarers from Samoa and Tonga are believed to have populated Tuvalu. The islands were sighted in the sixteenth century by the Spanish. When labor recruiters known as blackbirders were luring and abducting islanders for work on Australian sugar plantations or in Peruvian mines, the population is believed to have

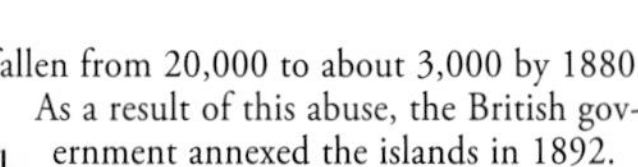

fallen from 20,000 to about 3,000 by 1880. As a result of this abuse, the British government annexed the islands in 1892.

With the smallest and most precarious economy in the world, life is not easy for the people of Tuvalu. There are no mineral resources, streams or rivers, and groundwater is unsuitable for human consumption. The soil is poor, and food crops like taro have to be grown in pits dug out of the coral. The value of imports exceeds exports by two hundred to one.

Elsewhere in the Pacific tourism helps support the economy, but Tuvalu is remote and tourists average fewer than 1,000 a year. Some revenue comes from selling stamps and coins, and from rich fishing grounds in its exclusive economic zone. Other revenue comes from license fees paid by fishing fleets from Korea, Taiwan, and the USA. Many Tuvaluan men work as seamen on merchant ships abroad and send remittances home. Most of Tuvalu's income comes from an international trust fund established in 1987 by Japan, South Korea, Australia, New Zealand, and the UK. Tuvalu derives some income from leasing its ".tv" internet domain name. It is possible that in the long run the islands may not be viable, either economically or geographically—there is mounting concern about rising sea levels. Should the situation become untenable, Tuvalu's population will be forced to move.

Rotuma
PACIFIC
OCEAN
Vanua Levu
Labasa
Bua
Somosomo
Taveuni
Nabouwalu
Tavua
Lautoka
Mt Tomanivi
Nadi
Viti
Levu
Levuka
Korovou
Koro
Sea
Gau
SUVA
FIJI
Naroi
Lau Group
Kadavu
Ono-i-Lau

Fiji

Map Reference Pages 426–427

The Republic of the Fiji Islands in the South Pacific is located about two-thirds of the way from Hawaii to New Zealand. Fiji covers an area of about 501,933 square miles (1,300,000 km^2), but only 7,054 square miles (18,270 km^2) is dry land. The idyllic setting and tropical climate attract tourists, bringing much-needed foreign currency to this less than politically stable developing nation.

Physical Geography

Fiji consists of about 332 islands, 110 of them uninhabited; there are many hundreds more islets in this large archipelago. Most of the larger islands are of volcanic origin; others are formed from coral or limestone. The two main islands of Viti Levu and Vanua Levu are mountainous, with dense tropical forests on their upper slopes. The latter island is known for earth tremors and geothermal activity—the archipelago is relatively close to a tectonic plate boundary. Fiji's tropical climate is warm throughout the year.

History

Fiji was already settled by people of the Lapita culture by about 800 BCE. From 1830, missionaries arrived and converted the people to Christianity. This did little to prevent persistent tribal warfare, which finally ended when Chief Cakobau ceded the islands to Britain in 1874. The British thought the islands were suited for growing sugarcane, and when the indigenous people declined to work in the plantations the colonial authorities imported contract labor from India. Since the 1870s, the country has produced sugar for New Zealand refineries. Fiji has been independent since 1970. The period of independence has been politically tumultuous, with ethnic tensions producing significant instability.

Population/Culture

The largest single group in the population is indigenous Fijians. Indo-Fijians, descended from contract laborers brought to the island in the nineteenth century, are the next largest group. Labor was also brought from the Solomon Islands. Europeans and Chinese make up the remainder of the population.

Fijians are a Melanesian people sharing cultural and linguistic traits with peoples further to the west. They grew yams and taro and fished the surrounding seas. They also built impressive sailing vessels, made fine bark cloth (or tapa) for clothing, and used a variety of hardwood clubs as weapons. Inter-tribal fighting was continuous, and forays were also made further across the ocean to Tonga.

Administration/Government

Fiji is nominally a democratic republic with multiple parties and regular elections. The prime minister is head of government; the president is head of state. But there have been four coups since independence in 1970. In 1987, a coup led by Colonel Sitiveni Rabuka initiated a period of instability that led to expulsion from the British Commonwealth. In 2000, the elected government of Indo-Fijian leader Mahendra Pal Chaudhry was overthrown by George Speight, an ethnic Fijian. Prime Minister Laisenia Qarase's government was ousted in a 2006 coup.

At the root of Fiji's political problems lies conflict between the claims of its two main ethnic communities—the indigenous Fijians, and the descendants of immigrant Indians. Tensions between the groups are proving intractable, and not easily reconciled by parliamentary means.

Economy/Industry

While Fiji is the most economically modern of the Pacific island nations, it is still a developing country with a sizable subsistence sector, and agriculture employs some 70 percent of the workforce. Sugar production provided Fiji with modest prosperity for many years, much of it resting on the work of Indian farmers whose leases are now under threat. Five-sixths of all land is owned communally by indigenous Fijians, and may only be leased to other indigenous Fijians. The Indian leases are now expiring.

In recent years insecurity of land tenure, combined with ongoing political turmoil and discouraging prospects for participation in government, has led many Indians to leave the country. A 2004 report of the OECD found that 61 percent of Fiji's skilled labor has emigrated. Sugar production has declined despite subsidies being provided by the European Union, but sugar processing still makes up one-third of all industrial activity. If the industry cannot compete with producers such as Brazil and Australia, numerous small farmers may lose their livelihoods. Sugar exports are still important, but the tourist industry now generates a greater percentage of GDP and is a major source of foreign exchange.

Nevertheless, serious economic problems remain in Fiji. The country runs a large trade deficit that is kept only roughly in balance by tourist revenue. Tourism, in turn, is sensitive to political uncertainty.

MILESTONE EVENTS

c. 800 BCE Arrival of Lapita culture and first settlers

1643 CE Dutch voyager Abel Tasman visits

1830 First missionaries arrive

1874 Fiji becomes a British Crown colony; Indian contract labor imported

1970 Independence granted

1987 Two coups; the nation becomes a republic replacing British monarchy

1990 New constitution adopted

1997 Name changed to Republic of the Fiji Islands

2000 Third coup; mutinies at Queen Elizabeth Barracks

2006 Coup led by Voreque Bainimarama; later he becomes interim prime minister

FIJI

Official name Republic of the Fiji Islands (Matanitu ko Viti)

Land area 7,054 square miles (18,270 km^2)

Border countries None

Capital Suva

Highest point Tomanivi 4,344 feet (1,324 m)

Climate Tropical marine

Population 932,000

Language(s) Official: English and Fijian; other: Hindustani

Ethnicity Fijian 54.8%, Indo-Fijian 37.4%, other 7.8%

Religion Christian 53%, Hindu 34%, Muslim 7%, other 5.7%, none 0.3%

Government Republic

Currency Fijian dollar

Human Development Index 0.762 (ranked 92nd out of 177 countries)

Left Men on Taveuni Island participate in a traditional Fijian kava ceremony. Kava or *yaqona* is a herb made from the ground roots of a pepper plant, and is used as a social drink or in ceremony to reconfirm the hierarchy within a group.

Above Featuring the thatched bures that epitomize Fiji, Navala Village in Nadi is one of the country's most traditional villages. The Ba River flows through this picturesque town.

TRADITIONAL SKILLS AND SOCIAL PRACTICES

Traditional Fijian houses were sturdily attractive, with pyramid-like thatched roofs and walls, so it is not surprising they have been revived for tourist beachside accommodation. Besides domestic buildings, each village contained a meeting-house and a spirit house with a variety of scented flora planted nearby. Fijians also built one of the Pacific's most remarkable war canoes—the drua. Double hulled, and very big, the drua was a masterpiece of design and workmanship. Fast and highly maneuverable, it was capable of carrying over 100 warriors. "It had a magnificent appearance with its immense sail of white mats," wrote one observer in 1840, "and its velocity was almost inconceivable."

Fijian society was traditionally aristocratic. Great importance was attached to the family unit, and above this stood a hierarchy of chiefs presiding over villages, clans, and tribes. Before the arrival of European missions in the early nineteenth century, religious ritual required human sacrifice, and victory in war demanded that enemy dead be eaten. Seru Epenisa Cakobau, the high chief who united the various tribes of Fiji in 1871, renounced this practice on his conversion to Christianity in 1854.

Below Fiji's Yasawa Islands are both a tropical paradise for tourists and a traditional home to locals. This group of more than 20 islands is situated off the west coast of Viti Levu.

NEW ZEALAND

Official name New Zealand
Land area 103,483 square miles (268,021 km²)
Border countries None
Capital Wellington
Highest point Aoraki (Mt Cook) 12,316 feet (3,754 m)
Population 4,230,000
Language(s) English, te reo Maori, sign language
Ethnicity European 69.8%, Maori 7.9%, Asian 5.7%, Pacific Islander 4.4%, other 0.5%, mixed 7.8%, unspecified 3.9%
Religion Christian 53.5%, other 3.3%, unspecified 17.2%, none 26%
Government Parliamentary democracy
Currency New Zealand dollar
Human Development Index 0.943 (ranked 19th out of 177 countries)

Three Kings Islands
Great Barrier Island
North Island
Auckland
Manukau
Hamilton
Tauranga
Rotorua
Taupo
Gisborne
New Plymouth
Napier
Hastings
NEW ZEALAND
Wanganui
Palmerston North
Lower Hutt
WELLINGTON
Nelson
Blenheim
South Island
Christchurch
Aoraki (Mt Cook)
Timaru
Dunedin
Invercargill
Stewart Island
Snares Islands
Tasman Sea
PACIFIC OCEAN

New Zealand

Map Reference Pages 422–423

New Zealand is a remote group of islands located in the South Pacific Ocean. The nearest significant landmass is Australia, 1,198 nautical miles west. The two main islands in the archipelago—North Island and South Island—are separated by stormy Cook Strait. It is a land of snow-capped mountains, deep fjords, bubbling mud pools, and excellent wine-growing regions. Its people enjoy a relatively high standard of living.

Above New Zealand players do the "haka," a traditional Maori war cry, before the start of a Rugby World Cup match between England and the New Zealand All Blacks. The haka is usually led by a player of Maori descent.

Physical Geography

This small, geographically isolated archipelago straddles two geophysical plates. Mountains and uplands are defining features, with about three-quarters of New Zealand's surface higher than 656 feet (200 m). Twenty million years ago the archipelago was low-lying or submerged; tectonic activity, which continues to this day, shaped the land. The mountain ranges are mostly soft metamorphic rocks. The only active volcanoes are located on the North Island, but there is evidence of volcanic activity on the South Island, where Dunedin and Christchurch lie on or beside long-extinct volcanoes and several smaller coastal settlements are sheltered by old lava flows.

The Southern Alps and the mountain ranges of the North Island are not very high, but a combination of length, height, and orientation ensures their interaction with prevailing westerly winds. Near the main divide, annual precipitation can exceed 197 inches (500 cm), but a few miles east may be just 20 inches (50 cm). Snow can accumulate on higher ground and there are about 448 square miles (1,160 km²) of ice in 360 glaciers along the Southern Alps. The tempering effect of the oceans is felt across the country.

From the 1840s to 1860s, land companies and the government promoted the image of a uniform Mediterranean environment where olives, grapes, and wheat would thrive. In the lowlands, conditions range from cool temperate to marginally subtropical, and from an almost continental temperature to dry inland basins, with persistently cool, wet weather on Stewart Island and the sub-Antarctic islands.

EXTINCTIONS

Until Polynesian settlers arrived in New Zealand the only land mammals were two species of bat, and they were also native to Australia. It was birds and insects that once dominated food webs in the country's extensive forests. Around 120 species of bird could be found when the Maori arrived, and 70 of those existed nowhere else on the planet. Birds varied in their size and habits and included ducks, perching birds, parrots, kiwis, moas, and Haast's eagles. Some were flightless, and others nested on the ground. All these creatures evolved in isolation, and it was only relatively recently that humans arrived, so it is likely that the animals had not become fearful of humans.

When Polynesians arrived with dogs and the Pacific rat, ground-nesting and flightless birds proved easy prey for man and beast. Haast's eagle, an enormous raptor weighing up to 31 pounds (14 kg), preyed on the moa, a flightless herbivorous bird weighing around 441 pounds (200 kg). Evidence from bone sites show that moas, an easy source of protein for Maori, were clubbed to death in huge numbers until they became extinct, as did Haast's eagle.

Many of the fauna that survived the arrival of Polynesians and introduced predators, failed to survive the Europeans, their farming practices, and the predators they introduced. By the 1900s other rat species, deer, cats, dogs, weasels, pigs, possums, sheep, and cattle are just some of the introduced species that have upset the ecological balance. Because extinctions occurred relatively recently, New Zealand can be seen as a laboratory situation from which lessons can be learnt.

History

Polynesian people (Maori), who voyaged southward from islands in the equatorial Pacific Ocean, settled New Zealand about 750 years ago, and until the late eighteenth century, had exclusive occupation of the land. The first Europeans known to have visited were the Dutch navigator Abel Tasman and his crew in 1642–43. A century later New Zealand was visited by English and French navigators, notably James Cook (1769–70) and Jean de Surville (1769). For 80 years safe havens around the coast provided base camps for Northern hemisphere sealers and whalers, and lowland swamps and forests were valued sources of flax fiber for ropes and wood for ships' spars.

Above right This statue of the late mountaineer and great humanitarian Sir Edmund Hillary stands outside the Hermitage Hotel in Mount Cook National Park. Famous New Zealanders such as Sir Edmund Hillary, opera singer Kiri Te Kanawa, writer Katherine Mansfield, and scientist Ernest Rutherford are celebrated at home for their successes on the international stage.

In 1840 the British Crown negotiated an agreement with Maori, the Treaty of Waitangi, which led to New Zealand becoming a British colony.

Land companies used agents to purchase blocks of land from their Maori occupants, though seldom on fair terms. Organized settlements were established in Wellington (1840), New Plymouth (1841), Nelson (1842), Otago (1848), and Canterbury (1850). Immigrants who had occupied parcels of land in the extensive tussock grasslands of both main islands quickly established productive operations, unlike those who chose land in the widespread lowland forests. Initially, the new colony produced wool, hides, grain, and other primary products for export to British, Australian, and other markets.

During the second half of the nineteenth century two events helped buffer the infant economy. The first was the discovery of gold; the second was refrigerated shipping between New Zealand and Great Britain. This began in 1882, allowing the country to export perishable primary products in bulk, chiefly meat, butter, cheese, and apples, to markets half a world away. The early colonists' visions of New Zealand as both Great Britain's farm and God's garden in the Antipodes began to be realized.

The colony was granted representative government in 1852, achieved Dominion status in 1907, and became a founder member of the United Nations in 1945. A charter member of the British Commonwealth of Nations, New Zealand has maintained legal, linguistic, political, economic, and familial ties to Great Britain. The war in the Pacific, especially the Battle of the Coral Sea in 1942, showed New Zealand's vulnerability and started six decades of political and economic realignment that would reshape the nation's economy, social and cultural structures, and ethnicity.

Since 1970 the country has assumed a more independent stance toward defense and external relations, and in 1987, took a stand

Right Ruapehu's crater lake in the Tongariro volcanic complex can indicate changes in the activity of the volcano's magma chamber. An increase in the amount of gas released alters the color of the lake. The striking blue-green color means there is no activity; gray indicates a change.

Far left Milford Sound near Queenstown on the South Island provides visitors with spectacular fjordland scenery as well as opportunities for adventure, such as alpine hiking and skiing.

Left Auckland, on the North Island, sits on a narrow isthmus between two harbors. Shown here is the view across Waitemata Harbour to the port and city; on the other side is Manukau Harbour. Auckland is New Zealand's largest city, and home to around a third of its population.

MILESTONE EVENTS

c. 1250 CE Arrival of first Polynesian settlers
1642–1643 Visit by Abel Tasman
1769–1770 First visit by Captain James Cook
1840 Treaty of Waitangi signed by Maori chiefs and Lieutenant-Governor Hobson; settlement by British begins in earnest
1840s Arrival of merino sheep from Australia
1855 Wellington earthquake
1860–1861 First land wars between British settlers and Maori
1865 Telegraphic communications established between North and South Islands
1907 New Zealand becomes a Dominion
1938 *Social Security Act*
1977 Establishment of the Waitangi Tribunal
1983 Closer Economic Relations Agreement negotiated with Australia
1987 te reo Maori formally recognized as an official language
1991 *Resource Management Act*

on nuclear disarmament, despite veiled economic threats from elsewhere, passing the *New Zealand Nuclear Free Zone, Disarmament, and Arms Control Act*. The act bans the state and its people from all association with nuclear weapons. As a result, the ANZUS Treaty (Australia, New Zealand, United States) ceased to apply between America and New Zealand. In 2005, New Zealand acceded to the Association of South-East Asian Nations Treaty of Amity and Cooperation.

Population/Culture

In the nineteenth century, commentators predicted the ultimate demise of Maori. A century later the situation has reversed, with demographers announcing that Pakeha (whites) are raising insufficient children to replace the dying. Of concern for New Zealand's future has been the steady out-migration of well-educated young people. Though the country has become increasingly secular since 1960, Christian churchgoers may follow the order of service in English or te reo Maori. The primacy of English is fading; in its place is emerging a multilingual, multicultural society.

Migrants have been able to place their marks on New Zealand society and culture through music, literature, entertainment, food, and new manufactures.

The franchise was extended to women in 1893; since then they have played significant roles in governance and society. In 2005 the prime minister, governor-general, and chief justice were all women, and those former bastions of male exclusiveness—the church, engineering, and the health sciences except nursing—are approaching gender balance.

Administration/Government

New Zealand is a parliamentary democracy with a constitutional monarchy. A mixed member proportional voting system has been in place since 1996. Elected representatives currently occupy 62 general seats in the unicameral parliament, 52 seats are allocated in proportion to party votes cast at the election, and 7 seats are reserved for Maori electorates. A Cabinet supports the prime minister, who is the leader and senior member of the group in power. The Supreme Court is the highest court; the judiciary includes the High Court, the Court of Appeal, and lower courts.

Economy/Industry

New Zealand's economy depends heavily on products from farms and forests, orchards and vineyards, commercial fisheries, and horticulture, and is sustained by both local and imported sources of energy. The nation actively cultivates markets across the world for its exports. During the 1980s the economy was opened to imported goods and foreign investment, and both government and the private sector have sought ways to diversify sources of national income. Reduction in tariffs and the removal of other instruments designed to protect local industry from international competition saw car assembly plants, clothing and footwear manufacturers, food processing operations, and light industry come under greater pressure to compete. Many amalgamated into larger and more efficient operations, closed, or relocated to sites closer to the market or to where production costs are lower. The impact of these and other changes has been felt across New Zealand, but especially in small rural centers. It has taken many of them two decades or longer to restructure their local economies.

Apart from one steel mill there is little heavy industry, but the lineaments of the new economy are evident everywhere. Education and immigration are of strategic importance as the country diversifies and modernizes its economy. Long a victim of the tyranny of distance, the best prospects for New Zealand lie in being seen as a reliable producer of added value items for export to the growing economies of the Pacific rim and South Asia.

Above New Zealand-born opera singer Dame Kiri Te Kanawa is famous across the globe. She has set up a foundation to mentor and assist young New Zealand singers and musicians to achieve international success.

Below Sheep graze on the South Island's lush green pastures. For about a century, the largest industrial operations in New Zealand were typically meat-packing plants. However, they are growing less common as sheep and cattle numbers decline.

Right Sopo'aga Falls and rainforest on the island of Upolu, Samoa. The falls drop 200 feet (60 m) into the valley below. Though much of Upolu's rainforest has been cleared, lush pockets remain in the mountainous interior and on the east coast.

TONGA

Official name Kingdom of Tonga (Pule'anga Tonga)
Land area 277 square miles (718 km²)
Border countries None
Capital Nuku'alofa
Highest point Unnamed location on Kao Island 3,389 feet (1,033 m)
Climate Tropical, modified by trade winds
Population 119,009
Language(s) Tongan, English
Ethnicity Polynesian, European
Religion Not available
Government Constitutional monarchy
Currency Pa'anga
Human Development Index 0.819 (ranked 55th out of 177 countries)

KIRIBATI

Official name Republic of Kiribati
Land area 313 square miles (811 km²)
Border countries None
Capital Bairiki
Highest point Unnamed location on Banaba 266 feet (81 m)
Climate Tropical marine, moderated by trade winds
Population 110,356
Language(s) I-Kiribati, English
Ethnicity Micronesian 98.8%, other 1.2%
Religion Christian 92%, other 8%
Government Republic
Currency Australian dollar
Human Development Index Not available

SAMOA

Official name Independent State of Samoa (Malo Sa'oloto Tuto'atasi o Samoa)
Land area 1,133 square miles (2,934 km²)
Border countries None
Capital Apia
Highest point Mauga Silisili (Savaii) 6,093 feet (1,857 m)
Climate Tropical
Population 217,083
Language(s) Samoan (Polynesian), English
Ethnicity Samoan 92.6%, Euronesians (mixed European and Polynesian) 7%, Europeans 0.4%
Religion Christian 98%, other 2%
Government Parliamentary democracy
Currency Tala
Human Development Index 0.785 (ranked 77th out of 177 countries)

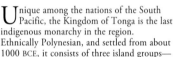

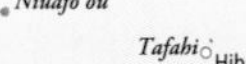
Niuafo'ou
Tafahi
Hihifo
PACIFIC OCEAN
TONGA
Vava'u Group
Vava'u Island
Neiafu
Late Island
Kao Island
Tofua
Foa
Pangai
Lifuka
Nomuka
Nomuka
Ha'apai Group
Tongatapu
NUKU'ALOFA
'Ohonua
Tongatapu Group
'Eua
'Ata Island

Tonga

Map Reference Pages 426–427

Unique among the nations of the South Pacific, the Kingdom of Tonga is the last indigenous monarchy in the region. Ethnically Polynesian, and settled from about 1000 BCE, it consists of three island groups—Tongatapu, Ha'apai, and Vava'u—lying one-third of the way from New Zealand to Hawaii. They were named the Friendly Isles by James Cook on his visit in the 1770s.

Two parallel belts of islands range south–north. The eastern belt consists of low coral-line limestone formations. The western belt, where the island of Kao rises to 3,389 feet (1,033 m), is higher and volcanic. A quarter of the land is arable, and most Tongans are subsistence farmers whose produce includes yams, squash, bananas, coffee, and coconuts. A large proportion of food is imported. The most significant sources of income are from nationals resident overseas, and from tourism. Tonga is dependent on external aid.

Not originally a kingdom, Tonga was united and became a constitutional monarchy only in 1845. In 1875, the king formally emancipated the serfs, adopted a code of law, and limited the power of the Tongan chiefs. A small group of hereditary nobles still dominates the Legislative Assembly, and there are persistent calls for more democracy. After King Tupou IV's death in 2006, demonstrations for political reform resulted in the capital, Nuku'alofa, being vandalized. King George Tupou V, who was crowned in August 2008, is expected to rebuild the city.

Right An aerial view of Vava'u, the main island of Tonga. Though it boasts one of the most beautiful natural harbors in the world, Vava'u still remains off the track of mass tourism.

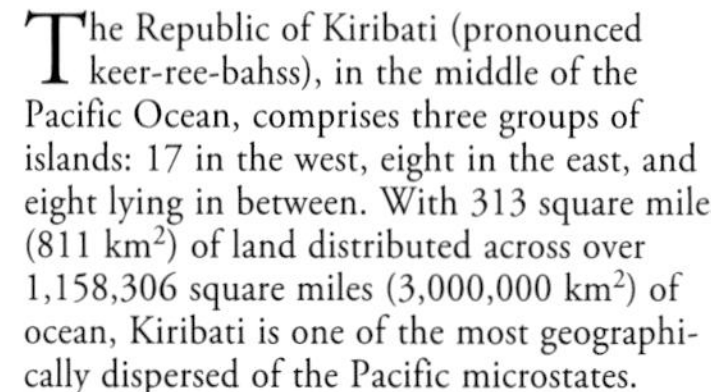
MARSHALL ISLANDS
PACIFIC OCEAN
Tarawa
BAIRIKI
Banaba
Gilbert Islands
KIRIBATI
Phoenix Islands
TUVALU
Teraina
Tabuaeran
London
Kiritimati
Line Islands
Malden Island
Starbuck Island
Millennium Island
Flint Island

Kiribati

Map Reference Pages 426–427

The Republic of Kiribati (pronounced keer-ree-bahss), in the middle of the Pacific Ocean, comprises three groups of islands: 17 in the west, eight in the east, and eight lying in between. With 313 square miles (811 km²) of land distributed across over 1,158,306 square miles (3,000,000 km²) of ocean, Kiribati is one of the most geographically dispersed of the Pacific microstates.

Indigenous peoples of the Pacific may have lived on the atolls for a thousand years before western voyagers began visiting them around 1537. In 1892 what were formerly the Gilbert and Ellice Islands became a British Protectorate, and from 1916 a British Crown colony. With the coming of independence in the 1970s the Polynesian Ellice Islanders voted to separate from the Micronesian Gilbertese, and formed the new state of Tuvalu; the Gilberts became self-governing in 1977, and then became the Republic of Kiribati in 1979.

The country has few natural resources. Mining of the ancient phosphate deposits on Banaba provided income during the colonial period, but this ceased in 1979. Copra and fish make up the bulk of exports, along with coconuts and seaweed. The country imports food, machinery, equipment, and fuel, and depends heavily on foreign aid.

In 2004, President Tong announced the creation of the world's biggest marine reserve: The Phoenix Islands Protected Area. With its eight coral atolls, the park covers 71,043 square miles (184,000 km²). Environmentalists have hailed the reserve as a major advance for marine conservation in the Pacific.

Far right Men tap out a rhythm with batons while singing along with the women on Canton Island, one of the Phoenix Islands that form part of the Republic of Kiribati.

SAMOANS AND WORLD SPORT

Samoans from both Samoa and American Samoa are prominent in sport. About 30 ethnic Samoans currently play in the US National Football League. In those islands culturally influenced by New Zealand, Rugby Union is popular. Samoa has participated in every Rugby World Cup contest since 1991, and has consistently equalled the performances of much bigger nations.

Savai'i
Fagamalo
Falealupo
Asau
Mt Silisili
Pu'apu'a
Tuasivi
SAMOA
Sala'ilua
Salelologa
Sale'imoa
Taga
Apolima
APIA
Manono
Mulifanua
Falefa
Upolu
Matautu
Poutasi
Salani
Nu'utele
PACIFIC OCEAN

Samoa

Map Reference Pages 426–427

The Independent State of Samoa lies in the South Pacific about halfway between Hawaii and New Zealand. It consists of nine islands. The two largest, Savai'i and Upolu, are volcanic, but only Savai'i is active, the last eruptions occurring early in the twentieth century. Fast-flowing rivers descend from the densely forested mountainous interiors to the narrow coastal plains. Coral reefs lie offshore.

Ancestral Polynesians first settled Samoa about 1000 BCE. In the late nineteenth century Germany, Britain, and the USA competed for influence. The eastern part of the archipelago became American Samoa. The western part, originally German Samoa, was administered by New Zealand after World War I as a League of Nations mandate, and in 1962 became the first Pacific Island nation to gain independence.

Traditional Samoan culture was aristocratic. The rank of chief still plays an important part in social and political life, and the leaders (matai) enjoy more power than commoners. Although Samoa had gained independence in 1962 it was not until 1991 that direct elections under a universal franchise were held, and even then only matai could be candidates.

The only natural resources are tropical hardwoods and fish. Yams, breadfruit, banana, and papaya are grown for local consumption. Cocoa, taro, and coconuts are grown for export. Tourism also plays an important role.

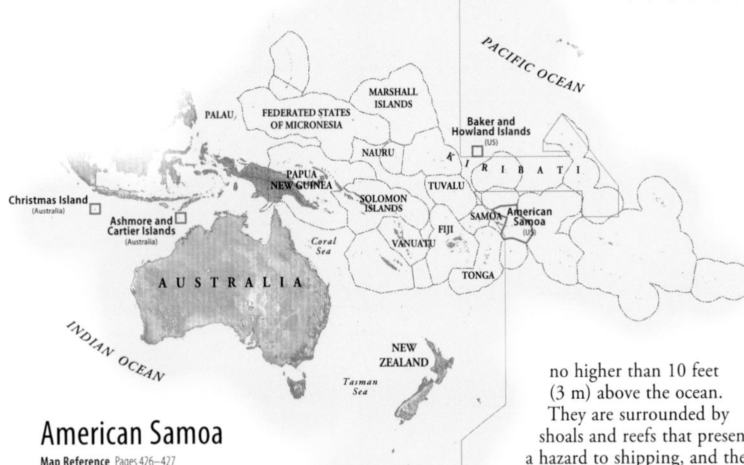
PACIFIC OCEAN
PALAU
FEDERATED STATES OF MICRONESIA
MARSHALL ISLANDS
Baker and Howland Islands (US)
NAURU
KIRIBATI
PAPUA NEW GUINEA
Christmas Island (Australia)
Ashmore and Cartier Islands (Australia)
SOLOMON ISLANDS
TUVALU
SAMOA
American Samoa (US)
FIJI
VANUATU
Coral Sea
TONGA
AUSTRALIA
INDIAN OCEAN
NEW ZEALAND
Tasman Sea

American Samoa

Map Reference Pages 426–427

Comprising two atolls and five volcanic islands, American Samoa lies about halfway between New Zealand and Hawaii. The first Polynesian people arrived on the islands around 800 BCE. European contact was first made by the Dutch in 1722; British missionaries later converted most of the people to Christianity. In the nineteenth century Germany and the USA divided the Samoan archipelago, America taking the eastern islands that included the harbor of Pago Pago. One of the few deepwater harbors in the region, Pago Pago is sheltered and provides a strategic base for the US Pacific Fleet.

Some 90 percent of land is communally owned and a traditional Polynesian subsistence economy produces bananas, coconuts, pineapples, and papayas. There are no commercially viable mineral deposits, and freshwater supplies are limited. Most trade is with the USA, which also provides financial aid. Tuna fishing and processing are important private sector industries, with canned tuna the main export. The remoteness of the islands, together with limited transport and climatic hazards, including fierce hurricanes, have frustrated efforts to build a more secure and broad-based economy.

Ashmore and Cartier Islands

Map Reference Pages 424–425

Located in the Indian Ocean, northwest of Australia, the Territory of Ashmore and Cartier Islands comprises two groups of uninhabited islands. Likely to be affected by rising sea levels, the sandy and coralline islands rise no higher than 10 feet (3 m) above the ocean. They are surrounded by shoals and reefs that present a hazard to shipping, and there is no safe port or harbor.

No economic activity takes place in the Territory, which is administered by Australia. In 1983 the Ashmore Reef Marine National Nature Reserve was established. Because the reef is located in the flow of current that runs from the Pacific Ocean through the Indonesian Archipelago to the Indian Ocean, its biodiversity is of great interest to marine biologists. The Cartier Island Marine Reserve was proclaimed in 2000.

In more recent years, Ashmore Reef became notorious for its involvement in people smuggling. Once asylum seekers landed on the reef they could claim to have entered Australian territory and ask to be processed through legal channels as refugees. To discourage this practice the Australian government excised the area from the legally defined Australian migration zone.

Christmas Island

Map Reference Pages 424–425

Christmas Island is a small Australian territory in the Indian Ocean about 200 miles (300 km) south of Java. The central plateau is the top of an ancient volcano. Uninhabited until late in the nineteenth century, it is home to unique species of fauna and flora. In the November breeding season the red crab cross-country migration—from forest to coast—is one of the most unusual spectacles in crustacean zoology. Two-thirds of the island is now national park.

Christmas Island was annexed by the British Crown in 1888. A small settlement was established to collect timber and supplies for the growing industry on the Cocos Islands. Phosphate mining began in the 1890s using indentured labor from China and Malaysia, and continued until relatively recently.

Sovereignty was transferred to Australia in 1957. In recent years the island has periodically received boatloads of asylum seekers. The government's handling of these people was a controversial issue in Australian politics and society. In response to migratory pressure the government at first removed the island from Australia's migration zone. It has now built an official reception and processing center to formalize immigration procedures.

Baker and Howland Islands

Map Reference Page 421

Baker and Howland Islands are uninhabited atolls with fringing reefs that lie just north of the equator, midway between Hawaii and Australia, and are 15 nautical miles apart. Neither island has natural freshwater resources and both have little rainfall. The USA took possession in 1857, and unsuccessful attempts were made to settle the islands. Both the territories are part of the Pacific Remote Islands National Wildlife Refuge Complex managed by the US Fish and Wildlife Service.

Baker Island—405 acres (164 ha)—was first named New Nantucket by American whaling captain Elisha Folger, who found it in 1818. Its present name comes from a visit by Captain Michael Baker in 1834.

Howland Island is some 455 acres (184 ha) in area. Archeological evidence indicates early intermittent Polynesian settlement. Guano deposits were mined until 1890. Barely visible by day, and not at all by night, Howland has been the scene of many shipwrecks. It is best known as the stopover that solo pilot Amelia Earhart never reached on the last leg of her round-the-world flight in 1937.

Left Howland Island shows no sign of human visitation save for a small boat landing area and a crumbling day beacon. Airstrips built to accommodate Amelia Earhart's planned stopover were not maintained, and have gradually disappeared.

AMERICAN SAMOA

Official name Territory of American Samoa
Land area 77 square miles (199 km^2)
Capital Pago Pago
Climate Tropical marine, moderated by southeast trade winds
Population 57,496
Government Unincorporated and unorganized territory of the USA
Currency US dollar

ASHMORE AND CARTIER ISLANDS

Official name Territory of Ashmore and Cartier Islands
Land area 2 square miles (5 km^2)
Capital None
Population None
Government Territory of Australia

CHRISTMAS ISLAND

Official name Territory of Christmas Island
Land area 52 square miles (135 km^2)
Capital The Settlement
Climate Tropical; heat and humidity moderated by trade winds
Population 1,402
Government Non-self governing territory of Australia
Currency Australian dollar

BAKER AND HOWLAND ISLANDS

Official name Baker and Howland Islands
Land area 2 square miles (4.7 km^2) combined
Capital None
Climate Equatorial; scant rainfall, constant wind, burning sun
Population None
Government Unincorporated territories of the USA

Above The white tern or fairy tern *(Gygis alba)*, seen here on Christmas Island, lays its eggs in the forks or hollows of bare thin branches.

Left The town of Fagatogo nestles between Pago Pago Harbor and the peaks of Tutuila, the largest island of American Samoa. A national park has been established on the other side of the island.

COCOS (KEELING) ISLANDS

Official name Territory of Cocos (Keeling) Islands
Land area 5 square miles (14 km²)
Capital West Island
Climate Tropical moderated by the southeast trade winds
Population 596
Government Non-self governing territory of Australia; administered from Canberra by the Australian Attorney-General's Department
Currency Australian dollar

COOK ISLANDS

Official name Cook Islands
Land area 92 square miles (237 km²)
Capital Avarua
Climate Tropical oceanic moderated by trade winds
Population 21,923
Government Self-governing parliamentary democracy
Currency New Zealand dollar

CORAL SEA ISLANDS

Official name Coral Sea Islands
Land area 1 square mile (3 km²)
Capital None
Climate Tropical
Population Uninhabited except for manned meteorological weather station
Government Territory of Australia administered from Canberra

Above right The people of the Cook Islands are descended from the Polynesian migrants who settled there from about 500 CE. The atmosphere is relaxed and friendly, and song and dance feature strongly in the local culture.

Below The waters of the Indian Ocean around the Cocos (Keeling) Islands are home to a huge range of sea life. Turtles, dolphins, and manta rays, often with remora fish attached, are very common sights.

PACIFIC OCEAN
Guam
(US)
PALAU
FEDERATED STATES OF MICRONESIA
MARSHALL ISLANDS
NAURU
KIRIBATI
Jarvis Island
(US)
PAPUA NEW GUINEA
SOLOMON ISLANDS
TUVALU
Cook Islands
(New Zealand)
SAMOA
Cocos Islands
(Australia)
Coral Sea
Coral Sea Islands
(Australia)
VANUATU
FIJI
French Polynesia
(France)
TONGA
AUSTRALIA
INDIAN OCEAN
NEW ZEALAND
Tasman Sea

Cocos (Keeling) Islands

Map Reference Pages 424–425

The Cocos (Keeling) Islands, located about halfway between Sri Lanka and Australia in the Indian Ocean, consist of two atolls and 27 coral islands. The Pulu Keeling National Park on the uninhabited atoll of North Keeling Island protects the island's unique biodiversity. The South Keeling Islands form an incomplete atoll ring. The only inhabited islands are Home and West islands, though some Home Island residents maintain weekend shacks on smaller islands.

The East India Company's Captain William Keeling discovered the islands in 1609. In 1826, the first settler, Alexander Hare, brought slaves to work a coconut plantation. When John Clunies-Ross established his own settlement in 1827, Hare's slaves deserted to join Clunies-Ross, who provided better conditions.

The Battle of Cocos in 1914 was one of the first naval battles of World War I. It began when the German light cruiser, *Emden*, attacked the telegraph station, and was in turn engaged and destroyed by an Australian cruiser, HMAS *Sydney*. During World War II the Cocos were an important communications center, and there were fears that the Japanese would invade and occupy the islands, but they merely sent a monthly reconnaissance aircraft to monitor the scene.

Ruled for over a century in semi-feudal style by the Clunies-Ross family, the islands were transferred to Australian control in 1955, and were administered by the Australian government. Local government is in the hands of a Shire Council with seven elected members.

The economy is limited and relies heavily on public sector employment. Small businesses provide goods and services for locals and a budding tourism industry. Foodstuffs and other essentials imported from Australia supplement local goods.

Cook Islands

Map Reference Page 421

Lying about 2,175 miles (3,500 km) northeast of New Zealand, the Cook Islands comprise 15 islands scattered over 849,424 square miles (2,200,000 km²) of the South Pacific Ocean. The seven northern islands are low-lying coral atolls with few inhabitants. The eight southern islands, including Rarotonga, the group's largest and most populous island, are volcanic with fertile soils. The Polynesian inhabitants are ethnically close to the New Zealand Maori.

It is believed that the first people to reach the Cook Islands came from Tahiti around 500 CE. When Fernando de Quiros landed on Rakahanga Island in 1606, he called the islands "the place of the beautiful people." James Cook visited in 1773 and 1779, naming them the Hervey Islands. They were renamed in honor of Cook in the nineteenth century.

In 1821, John Williams of the London Missionary Society arrived on Aitutaki. He used Tahitian Christian converts to help get his message across and before long, a once warlike culture was pacified, and cannibalism was suppressed. Between 1901 and 1965 the islands were a New Zealand protectorate. Today five times as many Cook Islanders live in New Zealand as in the Cook Islands.

Since 1965 the islands have been self-governing in free association with New Zealand, which retains responsibility for defense and external affairs. Although democracy has not been without its problems, a combination of universal suffrage and robust debate ensures political stability. Agriculture provides the main economic base; exports include copra, oranges, and black pearls. Tourism and remittances from nationals working overseas are also important sources of income.

Coral Sea Islands

Map Reference Page 420

Located northeast of Australia, the Coral Sea Islands comprise reefs, small low-lying islands, and cays spread over an area of 301,160 square miles (780,000 km²). Some islands and cays are sunken or partially sunken; others have low scrub and grass cover and provide nesting areas for birds and sea turtles.

The only inhabited island is Willis Island where there is a manned weather station. Lighthouses, beacons, and unmanned weather stations are on some islands; the area is a shipping hazard and contains many wrecks. Lihou Reef is a National Nature Reserve measuring 3,259 square miles (8,440 km²) of seabed with a reef system of around 18 cays.

First charted and mapped in 1803, the islands were mined for guano in the 1870s and 1880s. The lack of a permanent water supply has prevented long-term occupation. The Coral Sea Islands were declared Australian territory in 1969, and were later extended to include Elizabeth and Middleton reefs further south in the Tasman Sea.

The islands are perhaps best known for their connection with the Battle of the Coral Sea, May 4–8, 1942. This was the first aircraft carrier battle ever fought, notable as an engagement in which the ships on each side never saw or fired directly upon each other. The Battle of the Coral Sea checked Japan's military plans in the Pacific and may have saved Australia from being invaded.

Right Raratonga in the Cook Islands is surrounded by a lagoon that extends out to the reef, then slopes steeply to deep water. On the southeast of the island, around Matavera and Muri (seen here), it is at its widest and deepest.

Far left Kia Ora Resort, Rangiroa, Tuamotu Archipelago, French Polynesia. Rangiroa ("vast sky") is the largest atoll in the Tuamotus, and one of the largest in the world. It consists of about 250 individual islands.

Left Waterfront houses, Inarajan, Guam. The village, which predates the discovery of Guam by the Spanish in 1521, is the best preserved of the Spanish era villages and is known for its rich history and culture.

French Polynesia

Map Reference Pages 426–427

French Polynesia, located in the South Pacific about halfway between Australia and South America, consists of five groups of volcanic peaks and atolls. The best-known island is Tahiti in the Society Islands group, seat of the capital, Papeete. The other archipelagoes are the Austral, Gambier, Tuamotus, and Marquesas islands. It is believed that the Marquesas Islands were first settled by Polynesians around 300 CE, and the Society Islands around 800 CE.

A PAINTER'S PARADISE

The artist Paul Gauguin (1848–1903) lived in French Polynesia from 1891 to 1903, except for one brief period when he returned to France. It was during this latter part of his career as an artist that he produced many of his finest works. His paintings provide powerful images of French Polynesians—mainly women—and are haunted by religious questions and symbolism. His most famous work from this period is *Where Do We Come From? What Are We? Where Are We Going?* He sided emotionally with the Tahitian people, and wrote a book (*Noa Noa*) that included observations about Polynesian life combined with a general commentary on art and literature. His health ruined by syphilis and alcohol, Gauguin died in May 1903 at his home in the Marquesas Islands; he left behind his Danish wife and five children.

European contact began with the sighting of the Tuamotus by Ferdinand Magellan in 1521. In 1768 Louis-Antoine de Bougainville claimed Tahiti for France, naming it New Cythera. He also broadcast its charms and gave it its reputation as the paradise of the South Seas in his book, *Voyage*, published in 1771. James Cook's mission to the islands in June 1769 was to record the transit of the planet Venus across the Sun. Unfortunately, his astronomical observations were unsuccessful because the instruments were too crude.

Each island group in French Polynesia was culturally distinct and independent before France established a protectorate in 1889. For a time they were politically organized into a system of Polynesian chieftainships. Today the region is defined as a French "overseas collectivity," having its own unicameral Territorial Assembly comprising 57 members who are elected by popular vote.

Since 1962, when France sent out military personnel for nuclear testing on Mururoa Atoll, the economy has changed from one based on subsistence farming to one associated with the military or with tourism. Tourism is now a leading source of hard currency, and contributes about one-quarter of the total GDP. Pearl farming and commercial fishing are also important economic activities, with black Tahitian pearls a major export.

Guam

Map Reference Pages 426–427

Guam, a prosperous, multi-ethnic society strategically located in the western North Pacific Ocean, is the largest and southernmost island in the Mariana Islands archipelago. At the westernmost edge of US territory, it is called "the place where America's day begins."

Guam was formed by two volcanoes and has a surrounding coral reef and a narrow coastal plain. The northern part of the island is a limestone plateau with several volcanic peaks. The more rugged south is where Mt Lamlam, the highest peak, is located.

Guam was settled around 2000 BCE by ancestors of the Chamorros, a people from Southeast Asia. They were skilled craftsmen, seamen, and weavers with a complex culture. Their society was strongly matriarchal, and Chamorro culture survives to the present day. The Chamorros are the largest single ethnic group in a multi-ethnic society that includes Filipinos, other Pacific islanders, Asians, Europeans, and people of mixed descent.

In 1898 the island was ceded to the USA by Spain as a result of that country's defeat in the Spanish–American War. Captured by Imperial Japanese forces in 1941, Guam was liberated by the US military in 1944. The US government handles Guam's external affairs. Guamanians elect a governor, a lieutenant governor, and a 15-seat unicameral legislature.

Although tourism is the largest source of income, Guam's economy is heavily dependent on US military spending. Andersen Air Force Base, a major US military bastion, has the longest airstrip in the Pacific.

GUAM

Official name Territory of Guam (Guahan)
Land area 209 square miles (541 km²)
Capital Hagatna (Agana)
Climate Tropical marine moderated by northeast trade winds
Population 175,877
Government Organized, unincorporated territory of the USA
Currency US dollar

FRENCH POLYNESIA

Official name Overseas Lands of French Polynesia (Pays d'outre-mer de la Polynesie Francaise)
Land area 1,413 square miles (3,660 km²)
Capital Papeete
Climate Tropical but moderate
Population 283,019
Government Overseas collectivity of France
Currency Comptoirs Francais du Pacifique franc

JARVIS ISLAND

Official name Jarvis Island
Land area 2 square miles (4.5 km²)
Capital None
Climate Equatorial; scant rainfall
Population Uninhabited
Government Unincorporated territory of the USA

Jarvis Island

Map Reference Page 421

Jarvis Island is a sandy coral islet surrounded by a reef. Located close to the equator, it lies halfway between Hawaii and the Cook Islands. As the island has no natural fresh water and little rainfall, it is uninhabited, though the US Fish and Wildlife Service and the US Coast Guard visit occasionally. Vegetation is limited, with only bunch grass, prostrate vines, and some low shrubs, but is sufficient to provide a habitat for sea birds.

The first recorded sighting by Europeans was in 1821 by the crew of British ship *Eliza Francis* who named it after the Jarvis family, the ship's owners. In 1857 the USA claimed the island, and it was formally annexed in 1858. For the next 20 years guano was mined for fertilizer. In 1936 the island was colonized by the USA as part of the unsuccessful Baker, Howland, and Jarvis Colonization Scheme, and for a few years a tiny settlement named Millersville existed. The hamlet had a weather station, open-sided dwellings, and a landing strip but no plane ever landed there.

Four Hawaiians were living at Millersville early in World War II when a Japanese submarine surfaced off the coast. Thinking it was a US Navy craft approaching, the men ran to shore but were fired upon. In 1942 a US naval ship evacuated the men before shelling Millersville and destroying the remote settlement.

Above The largest tiki in French Polynesia can be found on Hiva Oa Island, part of the Marquesas Islands. Primitive Oceanic cultures gave spiritual attributes to their tikis, which became the faces of their ancestors, their gods.

Midway Islands
(US)
PACIFIC OCEAN
Johnston Atoll
(US)
Kingman Reef
(US)
MARSHALL ISLANDS
PALAU
FEDERATED STATES OF MICRONESIA
NAURU
KIRIBATI
PAPUA NEW GUINEA
TUVALU
SOLOMON ISLANDS
SAMOA
FIJI
Coral Sea
VANUATU
New Caledonia
(France)
TONGA
Niue
(New Zealand)
AUSTRALIA
Norfolk Island
(Australia)
INDIAN OCEAN
NEW ZEALAND
Tasman Sea

Right Lifou Island is prized for its stunning coral reefs and beaches, lush tropical vegetation, and huge caves. It is the largest of the four Loyalty Islands, which are part of New Caledonia. The other islands are Tiga, Maré, and Ouvéa.

JOHNSTON ATOLL

Official name Johnston Atoll
Land area 1 square mile (2.6 km^2)
Border countries None
Capital None
Climate Tropical, but generally dry
Population None
Government Unincorporated territory of the USA

KINGMAN REEF

Official name Kingman Reef
Land area 2½ acres (1 ha)
Capital None
Climate Tropical, but generally dry
Population None
Government Unincorporated territory of the USA

MIDWAY ISLANDS

Official name Midway Islands
Land area 2 square miles (6.2 km^2)
Capital None
Climate Subtropical
Population 40 staff from US Fish and Wildlife Service
Government Unincorporated territory of the USA
Currency US dollar

Above Today, Midway Islands are a wildlife refuge managed by staff from the US Fish and Wildlife Service. Anyone interested in wildlife may visit the atoll, which for much of the year is home to two million birds, including the Laysan albatross *(Diomedea immutabilis)* pictured here.

Right Hawaii's green sea turtles migrate as much as 800 miles (1,287 km) from their feeding grounds near Hawaii's main islands to the smaller northern islands such as Midway Islands, where they nest on the beaches.

Johnston Atoll

Map Reference Page 421

Located about 825 miles (1,400 km) west of Hawaii, Johnston Atoll has four islands. Two of them, Johnston Island and Sand Island, are natural but have been artificially enlarged through coral dredging. Akau (North) Island and Hikina (East) Island have been similarly created where nothing but submerged reef existed previously. There is no natural supply of fresh water, but low vegetation does provide shelter for a variety of birds. The climate is tropical, though generally dry.

In 1806, Captain Charles Johnston, of the naval ship *Cornwallis*, claimed the uninhabited atoll for the British Crown. This claim was followed by American and Hawaiian claims. Eventually, guano deposits on the atoll were mined by US interests until depleted. In 1926, the atoll was declared a Federal bird refuge; then, as tensions mounted in the Pacific during the 1930s, it became a seaplane base with an airstrip and associated facilities. In February 1941, it was designated a US Naval Defensive Sea Area and Airspace Reservation.

After World War II Johnston Atoll was successively a US nuclear weapons test site, a launch site for spy satellites, and the site of the Johnston Atoll Chemical Agent Disposal System, when up to 1,200 personnel lived there. Today, all military structures have been removed, the runway closed, and chemical weapons destroyed. The atoll is now part of the Pacific Island Wildlife Refuges controlled by the US Fish and Wildlife Service.

Kingman Reef

Map Reference Page 421

About halfway between Hawaii and Samoa, Kingman Reef is a roughly triangular shoal measuring about 9 miles (15 km) east to west and 5 miles (8 km) north to south. Inside the reef is a sheltered lagoon that in some places is as much as 219 feet (73 m) deep. Although areas at the eastern end of the reef are slightly above the water line, most of it is awash even at low tide. From the shoal at the western end of the reef the sides of the atoll drop steeply by more than 2,000 feet (610 m) to the ocean floor. The marine flora and fauna of the atoll are spectacular.

Captain Edmund Fanning, of the American ship *Betsy*, made the first recorded discovery of the reef in 1798; he had a premonition one night that his ship was in danger. He ordered the anchor to be dropped, and when daylight came found his ship was close to the reef.

Marked as Danger Rock on some charts in the early nineteenth century, it received its present name after a visit from Captain Kingman, of the American ship *Shooting Star*, in 1853. The US flag was raised in 1922 and a proclamation of annexation was read. It was described as "a pancake of dead coral" standing 6 feet (1.8 m) clear of the sea at low tide, which makes Kingman Reef a shipping hazard.

FLYING BOATS

Kingman Reef, in particular its sheltered lagoon, played a part in the pioneering flying boat routes flown by Pan-American Airways across the Pacific Ocean during the 1930s. In April 1937, a schooner chartered by Pan-Am anchored at the reef. This served as a base for a trial flight between Honolulu and Pago Pago (American Samoa). Captain Edwin C. Musick also visited the reef in his flying boat on his ill-fated last flight south in 1938. He and his plane were lost near Tutuila in January after taking off from Pago Pago for Auckland, New Zealand.

Midway Islands

Map Reference Page 420

Some 1,456 miles (2,334 km) northwest of Hawaii lie the two Midway Islands—Sand Island and Eastern Island. They and a few islets comprise the visible parts of an atoll at the extreme end of the Hawaii–Emperor chain, all that remain of an extinct shield volcano formed 28 million years ago. It gradually sank into the sea, and a coral reef formed at its crest. Today the reef and its islands form a shallow atoll 6 miles (10 km) wide.

The Midway Islands were annexed by the US government in 1867, and an unsuccessful attempt at settlement was made in 1871. In 1935, Pan-American Airlines began flights from San Francisco to China, using flying boats (clippers), which island-hopped across the Pacific; they were able to land in the calm waters of Midway's lagoon. Midway is roughly half the distance from North America to China, which is how it got its name.

In 1941, the Midway Islands were second only to Pearl Harbor as an important forward defense position in the Pacific. Fortifications were built and the airstrips and seaplane base were upgraded. In June 1942, a crucial naval battle took place nearby, resulting in a defeat for the Japanese. Today the islands are a National Wildlife Refuge administered by the US Fish and Wildlife Service.

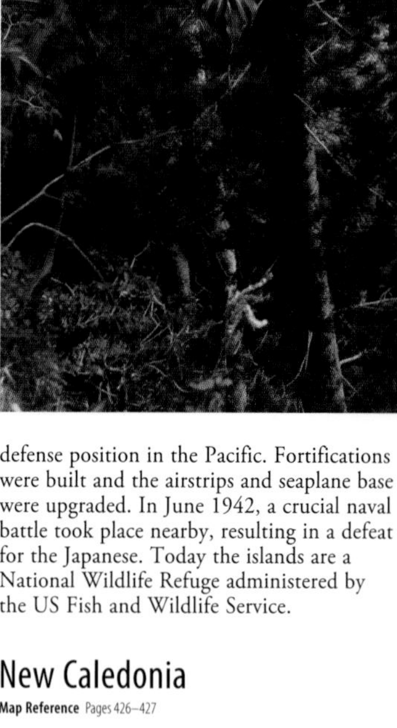

New Caledonia

Map Reference Pages 426–427

The island group called New Caledonia lies 746 miles (1,200 km) east of Australia; the Pacific nation of Vanuatu is to the northeast. Only 7 percent of the land area is dedicated to agriculture. The main island, Grand Terre, the third largest island in the Pacific region, is surrounded by 994 miles (1,600 km) of coral reef. A mountainous spine runs north–south down the center of Grand Terre, with several lower ranges running across the island. The varied topography results in a diversity of climatic zones and soils. Unlike the nearby islands of more recent volcanic

origin, Grande Terre was once part of the ancient landmass called Gondwanaland.

The agricultural Lapita people settled the islands of New Caledonia between 800 and 1300 BCE. During the eleventh century CE Polynesians arrived; the mixed population in recent times were known as Kanaks. Captain James Cook saw Grand Terre in 1774, naming it New Caledonia. In the first half of the nineteenth century, sandalwood traders visited the islands, and then in the second half blackbirders were active, luring Kanak laborers to work on sugar plantations in Australia and Fiji.

Between 1864 and 1922, France used New Caledonia as a penal colony, and 22,000 convicted felons were sent there. During the 1980s and 1990s there was a strong Kanak resistance movement, which ended with the 1998 Noumea Accord.

New Caledonia has about one-quarter of the world's proven nickel reserves, and nickel production is the foundation of the country's prosperity—it is the fourth largest economy in Oceania. As well as nickel, there are other economically important minerals and elements.

Niue

Map Reference Page 421

One of the world's largest coral atolls, Niue lies in the Pacific Ocean between Tonga, Samoa, and the Cook Islands. Roughly oval in shape, the island has a central limestone plateau ending in steep coastal cliffs. The only break in the surrounding coral reef occurs on the western side near Alofi, the capital city. The climate is tropical, modified by trade winds from the southeast. The area of arable land is limited—approximately 12 percent. The slash and burn agriculture practiced traditionally led to a serious loss of soil fertility.

Captain James Cook was the first European to sight the atoll, in 1774. The Polynesian inhabitants were painted with what Cook thought was blood, so he named the place Savage Island. For a short period before it was annexed by New Zealand in 1901, Niue was a British protectorate. Today it is a self-governing territory which is in free association with New Zealand.

Like other isolated Pacific islands, Niue faces great economic challenges. It has few resources, revenues are small and regularly exceeded by government expenditures. Most Niue Islanders are expatriates. About five out of six of Niue's population live and work in New Zealand. Recent attempts have been made to develop fisheries and to cultivate an edible fruit called noni. However, a destructive typhoon in 2004 set these ventures back, and since then Niue has been largely dependent on foreign aid.

Norfolk Island

Map Reference Pages 424–425

Norfolk Island lies 870 miles (1,400 km) east of Australia. Uninhabited at the time Captain James Cook visited in 1774, the volcanic remnant is surrounded by cliffs, making it difficult to access by sea, and it has no ports or harbors. The subtropical rainforest was cleared for pasture early in the nineteenth century, though small patches remain. The island's climate is subtropical, with little seasonal temperature variation.

Early Polynesian seafarers settled the island in the fourteenth or fifteenth century CE, but disappeared after a few generations. Cook believed that the Norfolk Island pine would make ideal timber for masts. In fact it proved unsuitable, but Britain's need for mast-timber was a reason for sending convicts there from Australia in 1788. The Norfolk Island convict settlement was notorious for punitive excess; however, despite difficulties of access and communication, it continued to serve as an offshore penal colony until 1855.

In 1856 the descendants of the *Bounty* mutineers, a population of British–Tahitian ancestry, were moved there from Pitcairn Island. They spoke a language known as Norfuk, a mixture of eighteenth-century English and Tahitian. Because of increasing tourism, this dialect is now in decline.

In 1979, the island was granted limited self-government by the Australian government. The *Norfolk Island Act* allows it to elect a nine-member body that runs most of the territory's affairs; however, Norfolk Island residents are not represented in the Australian Parliament.

Above The Old Military Barracks complex in Kingston, Norfolk Island, was built in the early nineteenth century. Officers' quarters are located on either side of the central soldiers' barracks.

NEW CALEDONIA

Official name Territory of New Caledonia and Dependencies (Territoire des Nouvelle-Caledonie et Dependances)
Land area 7,172 square miles (18,575 km²)
Capital Nouméa
Climate Tropical, modified by southeast trade winds
Population 224,824
Government Overseas territory of France
Currency Comptoirs Francais du Pacifique franc

NIUE

Official name Niue
Land area 260 square miles (100 km²)
Border countries None
Capital Alofi
Climate Tropical, modified by southeast trade winds
Population 1,492
Government Self-governing parliamentary democracy
Currency New Zealand dollar

NORFOLK ISLAND 

Official name Territory of Norfolk Island
Land area 13 square miles (34.6 km²)
Capital Kingston
Climate Subtropical
Population 2,114
Government Self-governing territory of Australia
Currency Australian dollar

Above left For centuries, people from Niue have used pandanus leaves to weave their baskets.

Far left In the northern provinces of New Caledonia's Grande Terre Island, the people live a more traditional village lifestyle than their compatriots in the south. This is the mission church in Poindimié on the northern coast.

Right A rusty World War II tank sits in the sea near a monument to the hundreds of Japanese civilians and soldiers who jumped to their deaths from Banzai Cliff, in the Northern Mariana Islands, to avoid capture by the invading US army.

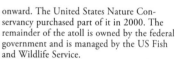

NORTHERN MARIANA ISLANDS

Official name Commonwealth of the Northern Mariana Islands
Land area 184 square miles (477 km²)
Capital Saipan
Climate Tropical marine, moderated by northeast trade winds
Population 86,616
Government Commonwealth in political union with the USA
Currency US dollar

PALMYRA ATOLL

Official name Palmyra Atoll
Land area 1½ square miles (4 km²)
Capital None
Climate Equatorial, extremely wet
Population No permanent population
Government Incorporated Territory of the USA

PITCAIRN ISLANDS

Official name Pitcairn, Henderson, Ducie, and Oeno Islands
Land area 18 square miles (47 km²)
Capital Adamstown
Climate Tropical, modified by southeast trade winds
Population 48
Government Overseas territory of the UK
Currency New Zealand dollar

Below right Abundant heavy rainfall means that Palmyra Atoll is covered with lush vegetation that includes the hala tree or screwpine *(Pandanus tectorius)*. The atoll is also home to one of the largest remaining undisturbed stands of *Pisonia* trees in the Pacific region.

Below Latte stones are ancient houses, remnants of the Chamorro culture, that can be seen across the Northern Mariana Islands. They are made up of two sections, a supporting column *(halagi)* with a capstone *(tasa)*. This limestone latte stone is at San Jose on Tinian Island.

Northern Mariana Islands (US)
Wake Island (US)
PACIFIC OCEAN
MARSHALL ISLANDS
PALAU
FEDERATED STATES OF MICRONESIA
Palmyra Atoll (US)
NAURU
KIRIBATI
PAPUA NEW GUINEA
TUVALU
Tokelau (New Zealand)
SOLOMON ISLANDS
Wallis and Futuna (France)
SAMOA
Pitcairn Islands (UK)
Coral Sea
VANUATU
FIJI
TONGA
AUSTRALIA
INDIAN OCEAN
NEW ZEALAND
Tasman Sea

Northern Mariana Islands

Map Reference Pages 426–427

Stretching some 500 miles (805 km) north from Guam in a gently curving arc are the 15 Northern Mariana Islands. The southern islands, including Rota, Tinian, and Saipan, are composed of limestone and feature terraces and fringing coral reefs. To the north the islands are volcanic; there are active volcanoes on Anatahan, Pagan, and Agrihan, the last rising 3,166 feet (965 m) above the sea. In May 2003, the stratovolcano on Anatahan erupted, and a column of volcanic ash and gas rose 33,000 feet (10,000 m) into the air. Volcanic activity has continued intermittently.

Ferdinand Magellan was the first European navigator to reach the area in 1521, landing on the nearby island of Guam and claiming it for the Spanish Crown. Japan occupied the Northern Marianas under a mandate of the League of Nations between 1919 and 1939. After World War II, the islands became part of the UN Trust Territory of the Pacific Islands. A constitution establishing a commonwealth in union became effective in 1978.

The indigenous Chamorro population is now mixed with a variety of peoples, which includes Filipinos, Spaniards, Micronesians, Japanese, and Chinese. A garment industry enjoying US duty and quota exemptions shows promise, but its labor practices have been criticized. Agriculture produces coconuts, melons, breadfruit, and tomatoes. Several cattle ranches produce beef. Tourism accounts for about one-quarter of GDP. Financial support from the USA remains important.

Palmyra Atoll

Map Reference Page 421

Palmyra Atoll consists of approximately 50 islets and sand bars grouped around two shallow lagoons, almost due south of Hawaii. The atoll has 9 miles (14.5 km) of coastline, a single anchorage at the western end, and is nowhere higher than 6 feet (1.8 m) above sea level. Dense vegetation includes coconut palms and stands of balsa-like trees (*Pisonia* species) that grow to about 100 feet (30 m) tall.

First sighted in 1798, the atoll was named in 1802 when the US ship *Palmyra* was wrecked on its uninhabited shores. In 1859 an American company claimed it for guano mining, only to find there was no guano. The atoll lies near the Intertropical Convergence Zone and rainfall is so heavy that bird droppings are washed away.

In 1898 the atoll was annexed to the USA, and was privately owned, either in whole or in part, by various families from 1912 onward. The United States Nature Conservancy purchased part of it in 2000. The remainder of the atoll is owned by the federal government and is managed by the US Fish and Wildlife Service.

Palmyra Atoll is now an important base for research on coral reef conservation and climate change. In 2005 a new research station was launched on Palmyra. Scientists from around the world joined with Nature Conservancy to participate in an international study of global warming, the degrading and disappearance of coral reefs, and the dangers posed by uncontrolled invasive species.

A MESSY PLACE

Pollution of various kinds has made Palmyra Atoll a rather messy place. When US military personnel were stationed there, goonie birds (albatrosses) were a problem. After feasting, these birds would sometimes be drenched by rain and unable to fly home to their roosting grounds. In order to get airborne they would regurgitate, spilling their malodorous stomach contents all around the military camp. More recently the abundance of floating trash in the ocean has piled up along Palmyra's shore. Located where the southern and northern currents meet, the atoll's beaches are littered with soft-drink bottles, detergent containers, plastic mooring buoys, and all manner of refuse.

Pitcairn Islands

Map Reference Pages 426–427

The United Kingdom's most isolated dependency, the Pitcairn Islands are located in the South Pacific Ocean midway between Peru and New Zealand. There are four islands—Oeno, Henderson, Ducie, and Pitcairn—only the last-named is permanently inhabited. Ruggedly volcanic and with a humid tropical climate, Pitcairn Island is surrounded by steep cliffs. Access is very difficult. Longboats ferry people from ships offshore to a landing at Bounty Bay; there is no harbor or airstrip. Henderson Island is an uplifted coral formation comprising 67 percent of the total area. It has enough usable land for a small community, but a shoreline of steep limestone cliffs makes settlement impractical.

An unidentified Polynesian people occupied the islands for some hundreds of years, but had died out by the time Europeans

Left In 1790, the *Bounty* mutineers, led by Fletcher Christian, reached Pitcairn Island. At what is now known as Bounty Bay, they stripped the vessel of its stores and fittings then destroyed it. Forty years later, some Pitcairn Islanders used copper bolts from the *Bounty* to pay for a ship to return them home from a brief stay in Tahiti.

Below left Pitcairn Island is one of the most isolated places on Earth. In 1814, a British frigate came across the island by chance. Finding the small settlement being run by the last surviving *Bounty* mutineer, John Adams, the ship's captain decided to leave them in peace.

arrived in the seventeenth century. The islands are best known as the refuge of the *Bounty* mutineers. After turning Lieutenant William Bligh, and 18 of his crew adrift in the ship's launch, the mutineers fled. The *Bounty's* crew of mutineers and kidnapped Tahitians reached Pitcairn in 1790 and stayed there. However, life on Pitcairn proved tumultuous, and many died of alcoholism, disease, or were murdered.

In 1856 the population was relocated to Norfolk Island, but some were unhappy with the move, and Pitcairn Islanders—who speak a part-Tahitian, part-English dialect—have moved to and from Pitcairn since. The island's mini economy functions through fishing and subsistence farming. Exports include fruit, stamps, and handicrafts. Iron, copper, gold, silver, zinc, and manganese, discovered offshore, await commercial development.

Tokelau

Map Reference Page 422

Tokelau, a self-administering territory of New Zealand, consists of three atolls in the South Pacific about halfway between Hawaii and New Zealand, some 300 miles (500 km) north of Samoa. There are no harbors or large areas of land over 7 feet (2 m) above high tide. The atolls are regularly struck by cyclones. In 2005, Cyclone Percy submerged two villages under 3 feet (1 m) of water and caused erosion on several islets.

The atolls—from north to south, Atafu, Nukunonu, and Fakaofo—are believed to have been settled about 1,000 years ago by Polynesians. In the mid-1800s, missionaries converted the islanders to Christianity. In 1863 Peruvian slave-traders took most of the able-bodied men to work as laborers in South America—most died of dysentery and smallpox. In 1926, the islands were placed under New Zealand administration, which assumed sovereignty over Tokelau in 1948. Moves are afoot to establish a relationship of free association with New Zealand, similar to that existing for Niue and the Cook Islands.

Tokelau has the smallest economy of any country, and depends almost entirely on New Zealand subsidies to survive. Natural resources are limited and the shrinking population ekes out a living growing coconuts, papaya, breadfruit, and bananas. Most Tokelauans now live in New Zealand and their remittances provide income for families back home. The geographic future of the island nation is uncertain because of changing sea levels; the economic future is more bleak—isolation and lack of facilities make tourism unlikely to provide relief.

Wake Island

Map Reference Page 420

Wake Island is about two-thirds of the way from Hawaii to Guam. Technically it is an atoll consisting of three small coral islets surrounding a lagoon and joined by causeways. The largest is Wake Island; the two smaller islets are Peale and Wilkes islands.

The uninhabited atoll was named for Captain William Wake, the master of a British schooner that visited in 1796. The atoll was annexed by the USA in 1899, and in 1935 Pan-American Airways constructed a settlement to service flights between the USA and China. On the same day as the attack on Pearl Harbor (December 7 HST, 1941), the Japanese carried out an air assault on the US marine garrison at Wake Island. An attempted landing resulted in heavy Japanese casualties, but eventually the Americans were overwhelmed; US military prisoners were sent to prisoner-of-war camps in Asia. In 1943, about 100 civilian prisoners were machine-gunned by order of the Japanese commander, Rear Admiral Shigematsu Sakaibara, who was later sentenced to death for this and other crimes.

After World War II, the island was used by the military for launching rockets and testing anti-missile systems. Following the fall of Saigon (1975), approximately 8,000 Vietnamese refugees camped on the island. There are no permanent residents, but US Army personnel and contractors are stationed on the island, and its 9,843-foot (3,000 m) runway is also used as an emergency runway for commercial flights.

Wallis and Futuna

Map Reference 426–427

Located between Fiji and Samoa, the Territory of Wallis and Futuna is a French collectivity made up of two island groups some 162 miles (260 km) apart. The northern, Wallis group (Îles Uvea) includes the main island (Wallis) and 20 islets in the nearby coral reef and lagoon. The southern, Futuna group, or Hoorn Islands, consists of Futuna and Alofi islands, the latter uninhabited. Both groups are volcanic in origin, but Futuna has the tallest peaks: Mt Singavi, also known as Mt Puke, reaches 2,510 feet (765 m). Futuna is the only main island that does not have a fringing reef. The climate is tropical and wet.

The Futuna group was discovered by the Dutch (in the seventeenth century), and the Wallis group by the British (in the eighteenth century); the French settled them in 1837. After 60 years under New Caledonian administrative control, the islanders voted in 1959 to become a French overseas territory.

Though its status as a French dependency is not a source of discord, chiefly authority and the role of native royalty is an issue. In 2005 the fiftieth king, Tomasi Kulimoetoke II, gave sanctuary to a delinquent grandson whom he believed should be tried by tribal law, not French law. Riots resulted, but the king's supporters won the day. When the king died in 2007, mention of a successor was prohibited.

About 80 percent of the workforce subsists by growing coconuts and vegetables, raising pigs, and fishing. Revenues from the licensing of fishing rights are also important.

TOKELAU

Official name Tokelau
Land area 4 square miles (10 km^2)
Capital None (each atoll has its own administrative center)
Climate Tropical, moderated by trade winds
Population 1,449
Government Self-administering territory of New Zealand
Currency New Zealand dollar

WAKE ISLAND

Official name Wake Island
Land area 2½ square miles (6.5 km^2)
Capital None
Climate Tropical
Population None
Government Unorganized, unincorporated territory of the USA

WALLIS AND FUTUNA

Official name Territory of the Wallis and Futuna Islands (Territoire des Îles Wallis et Futuna)
Land area 106 square miles (274 km^2) (combined)
Capital Mata-Utu
Climate Tropical
Population 16,448
Government Overseas territory of France
Currency Comptoirs Francais du Pacifique franc

Above In Tokelau, education is free for children aged between five and eighteen. Each of the three atolls has a primary school and a secondary school. Health care is also universally available.

110° 120° 130° 140° 150° 160° 170°

Tropic of Cancer
Haitan Dao
TAIWAN
Yu Shan 3950
Miyako Jima
Ishigaki Shima
Iriomote Jima
Lan Yu
Kita Daito Jima
Daito Islands
Okino Daito Jima
Kita Iwo To
Iwo To
Minami Iwo To
Kazan Retto
Minami Tori Shima
Shangchuan Dao
Weizhou Dao
Donghai Dao
Dongsha Qundao
Batan Islands
Luzon Strait
Calayan
Babuyan
Dalupiri
Babuyan Islands
Parece Vela
Maug Islands
Asuncion
Agrihan
Pagan
Mariana Islands
Anatahan
Saipan
Tinian
Rota
Guam
Wake Island
HAINAN
PHILIPPINE SEA
Crescent Group
Amphitrite Group
Lincoln Island
Passu Keah
Triton I.
Cu Lao Re
PARACEL IS
Mt Pulog 2929
Cagayan
Mt Pinatubo 1660
LUZON
Polillo Islands
PHILIPPINE IS
SOUTH CHINA SEA
ASIA
Lubang
Catanduanes
Mindoro
Calamian Gp
Masbate
Samar
Visayan Is
Panay
Leyte
Cebu
Negros
Bohol
MICRONESIA
Challenger Deep 10920
Taongi Atoll
Enewetak Atoll
Bikini Atoll
Rongelap Atoll
Utirik
Ailuk
Thitu I.
West York Island
Flat I.
Namyit I.
Union Atoll
Cu Lao Thu
Dumaran
Palawan
SPRATLY IS
Spratly Island
Amboyna Cay
Royal Charlotte Reef
Balabac Strait
Sulu Sea
MINDANAO
Mt Apo 2954
Basilan
Pangutaran Group
Ulithi Atoll
Yap Islands
Ngulu Atoll
Sorol Atoll
Babelthuap
Palau
CAROLINE ISLANDS
Gaferut
Namonuito Atoll
Pikelot
Satawal
Puluwat Atoll
Hall Is
Murilo Atoll
Nomwin Atoll
Pulap Atoll
Chuuk
Minto Reef
Oroluk Atoll
Pohnpei
Woleai Atoll
Eauripik Atoll
Losap Atoll
Namoluk Atoll
Satawan Atoll
Mortlock Islands
Nukuoro Atoll
Ngatik Atoll
Mokil Atoll
Pingelap Atoll
Kosrae
Ujelang Atoll
Ralik Chain
Likiep Atoll
Kwajalein Atoll
Ujae Atoll
Namu Atoll
Ailinglapalap Atoll
Jaluit Atoll
Majuro Atoll
Gunung Kinabalu 4095
Tapul Gp
Tawi Tawi
Sulu Arch.
Sarangani Islands
Kinabatangan
Natuna Besar
Kepulauan Natuna
Bukit Harden 2136
Celebes Sea
Sangir
Siau
Tabulandang
Karakelong
Kepulauan Talaud
Morotai
Kapingamarangi Atoll
BORNEO
Gunung Menyapa 2060
Maratua
Selat Makassar
Kapuas
Equator
0°
Maya
Karimata
Belitung
Unauna
Talatakoh
Kep. Togian
Laut Maluku (Molucca Sea)
Halmahera
Kepulauan Ayu
Kepulauan Mapia
Waigeo
Biak
Numfor
Yapen
Tanjung d'Urville
Wuvulu Island
Ninigo Gp
Admiralty Islands
Mussau Island
Manus I.
New Hanover
Tabar Islands
Lihir Gp
New Ireland
Tanga Is
Feni Islands
Nuguria Islands
Nauru
Banaba
SULAWESI
Peleng
Kep. Banggai
Taliabu
Mangole
Sanana
Kep. Obi
Obi
Bacan
Salawati
Misool
Laut Seram (Ceram Sea)
Seram
Ambon
Manawoka
Gorong
Buru
Wowoni
Muna
Buton
Kabaena
Gunung Kaplamada 2736
Gunung Rantemario 3478
Mamberamo
Puncak Jaya 5030
Puncak Trikora 4750
Puncak Mandala 4700
Pegunungan Maoke
NEW GUINEA
Sepik
Bismarck Sea
Bismarck Arch.
Mt Sinewit 2438
New Britain
Buka
Mt Balbi 2685
Bougainville
Choiseul
Nukumanu Islands
Ontong Java Atoll
Kepulauan Karimunjawa
Bawean
Laut Jawa (Java Sea)
Madura
Kep. Kangean
Kep. Tukangbesi
Laut Banda (Banda Sea)
Kep. Kai
Kep. Aru
Kobroor
Trangan
Mt Wilhelm 4509
Mt Giluwe 4368
Central Ra.
Cape Cretin
Huon Gulf
Solomon Sea
Santa Isabel
Vella Lavella
New Georgia
New Georgia Gp
Vangunu
Mt Sasari 1200
Malaita
Mt Kalourat 1450
Gunung Slamet 3428
Gunung Merapi 2911
Gunung Semeru 3676
JAVA
Kep. Tengah
Tanahjampea
Gunung Tambora 2851
Gunung Rinjani 3726
Lombok
Bali
Sumbawa
Flores
Selayar
Laut Flores (Flores Sea)
Damar
Romang
Wetar
Alor
Atauro
Babar
Kep. Leti
Sermata
Yamdena
Kep. Tanimbar
Moluccas
Tanjung Vals
Pulau Dolak
Digul
Fly
Strickland
Gulf of Papua
Mt Victoria 4073
Owen Stanley Range
Trobriand Is
Woodlark
Fergusson I.
D'Entrecasteaux Is
Normanby I.
Guadalcanal
Mt Popomanaseu 2330
Makira (San Cristobal)
Rennell
Duff Islands
Santa Cruz Islands
Tinakula
Nendo
Utupua
Vanikolo Is
Sumba
Savu Sea
Savu
Raijua
Roti
Timor
Timor Sea
Arafura Sea
Torres Strait
C. York
Great Barrier Reef
Melville I.
Bathurst I.
Croker I.
Goulburn Is
Wessel Is
Cape Wessel
Cape Arnhem
Arnhem Land
Ashmore Islands
Cartier Island
INDIAN OCEAN
Seringapatam Reef
Scott Reef
Joseph Bonaparte Gulf
Bonaparte Arch.
Groote Eylandt
Gulf of Carpentaria
Cape Grenville
Archer
C. Melville
Osprey Reef
CORAL SEA
Louisiade Archipelago
Rossel Island
Tagula
Indispensable Reefs
Torres Islands
Vanua Lava
Banks Islands
Santa Maria
Mt Garet 797
Espiritu Santo
Mt Tabwemasana 1879
Maewo
Pentecost
Ambrym
Malakula
Mt Marum 1270
Éfaté
Erromango
Mt Tukosmera 1084
Tanna
Aneityum
Buccaneer Archipelago
Cape Leveque
Kimberley
Drysdale
Daly
Victoria
Roper
McArthur
Wellesley Is
Cape Flattery
Holmes Reef
Moore Reefs
Mitchell
Staaten
Normanby
Gilbert
Norman
Einasleigh
Flinders
Leichhardt
Burdekin
Hinchinbrook I.
Flinders Reefs
Lihou Reef
Mellish Reef
Récifs d'Entrecasteaux
Île Huon
Marion Reef
Great Barrier Reef
Rowley Shoals
King Sound
Fitzroy
Sturt Creek
Barkly Tableland
Gregory Ra.
Whitsunday Island
Sandy Island
Îles Chesterfield
Îles Bélep
Ouvéa
Lifou
Îles Loyauté
Maré
Nouvelle Calédonie (New Caledonia)
Mont Humboldt 1618
Île des Pins
Grand Récif du Sud
Matthew Island
Dampier Archipelago
Barrow Island
Exmouth Gulf
North West Cape
De Grey
Fortescue
Hamersley Range
Great Sandy Desert
Tanami Desert
Lake Mackay
Georgina
Hay
Sutton
Swain Reefs
Capricorn Channel
Capricorn Group
Tropic of Capricorn
Ashburton
Little Sandy Desert
Mt Augustus 1106
Lyons
Gascoyne
Gibson Desert
Mt Liebig 1524
Macdonnell Ranges
Uluru (Ayers Rock) 867
Mt Woodroffe 1440
Musgrave Ranges
Simpson Desert
Diamantina
Thomson
Barcoo
Warrego
Drummond Range
Maranoa
Sandy Cape
Fraser Island
Cape Inscription
Dirk Hartog Island
Shark Bay
Murchison
Greenough
GREAT DIVIDING RANGE
AUSTRALIA
Grey Range
Paroo
Balonne
Moreton Island
North Stradbroke Island
Houtman Abrolhos
Great Victoria Desert
Lake Eyre North
Lake Eyre South
Sturt Stony Desert
Macintyre
Gwydir
Barwon
Namoi
Middleton Reef
Elizabeth Reef
Norfolk Island
Nullarbor Plain
Lake Torrens
Lake Gairdner
Lake Frome
Strzelecki Desert
Flinders Ranges
Gawler Ranges
Darling
Bogan
Macquarie
Liverpool Ra.
Mt Barrington 1586
Hunter
Lord Howe Island
Balls Pyramid
Rottnest Island
Darling Range
Great Australian Bight
Lachlan
Murrumbidgee
Murray
Snowy Mts
Mt Kosciuszko 2229
Three Kings Is
Cape Maria van Diemen
Cape Naturaliste
Cape Leeuwin
Point D'Entrecasteaux
Bald Island
Hood Point
Archipelago of the Recherche
Cape Pasley
Spencer G.
Mt Lofty Ranges
Cape Carnot
G. St Vincent
Kangaroo Island
Cape Jaffa
TASMAN SEA
Cape Howe
Cape Nelson
Cape Otway
Wilsons Promontory
King Island
Hunter Island
Bass Strait
Flinders Island
Furneaux Group
Cape Barren Island
Mt Ossa 1617
TASMANIA
INDIAN OCEAN
Tasman Peninsula
South West Cape
South East Cape
NEW ZEALAND
Aoraki (Mt Cook) 3754
Mt Aspiring 3033
Southern Alps
West Cape
Solander Island
South West Cape
Stewart Island
The Snares

110° 120° 130° 140° 150° 160° 170°

1:31,900,000
Mercator Projection

0 500 1000 1500 2000 kilometers
0 250 500 750 1000 miles

Oceania Physical

180° 170° 160° 150° 140° 130°

Laysan Island
Gardner Pinnacles
Northwestern Hawaiian Islands
French Frigate Shoals
Necker Island
Nihoa
Hawaiian Islands
Kaua'i
Kawaikini 1598
Ni'ihau
O'ahu
Ka'ala 1227
Moloka'i
Lāna'i
Maui
Kaho'olawe
Pu'u 'Ula'ula 3055
Hawai'i
Mauna Kea 4205
Mauna Loa 4169
Tropic of Cancer
20°
Johnston Atoll
P
PACIFIC OCEAN
O
10°
Kingman Reef
Palmyra Atoll
Teraina
Tabuaeran
Kiritimati
L
LINE ISLANDS
Y
Howland Island
Baker Island
Jarvis Island
Equator
0°
Beru
Arorae
Kanton Island
Enderbury Island
Phoenix Islands
Nikumaroro
Manra
Malden Island
N
Starbuck Island
Nanumea
Niutao
Nukufetau
Funafuti
Nukulaelae
Atafu
Nukunonu
Fakaofo
Tokelau Islands
Rakahanga
Penrhyn
Vostok Island
Caroline Island
S
E
Eiao
Marquesas Is
Nuku Hiva
Ua Huka
Ua Pou
Hiva Oa
Tahuata
Fatu Hiva
10°
Swains Island
Pukapuka
Nassau
Manihiki
Flint Island
Rotuma
Îles Wallis
Uvea
Mt Silisili 1858
Mt Fito 1133
Savai'i
Upolu
Samoa Islands
Tutuila
Tau
Rose Atoll
Cook Islands
Suwarrow
Îles du Désappointement
Futuna
Îles de Horne
Alofi
Îles du Roi Georges
Manihi
Takapoto
Takaroa
TUAMOTU ARCH.
Napuka
Pukapuka
FIJI ISLANDS
Cikobia
Niuafo'ou
Niuatoputapu
Tafahi
Îles Palliser
Rangiroa
Apataki
Kauehi
Takume
Fangatau
Fakahina
Society Is
Motu One
Vanua Levu 1032
Nasorolevu
Rabi
Lau Group
Tahaa
Huahine
Maupihaa
Bora-Bora
Îles Sous le Vent
Moorea
Tahiti
Orohena 2241
Mehetia
Kaukura
Fakarava
Katiu
Tuanake
Raroia
Nihiru
Makemo
Marutea
Taenga
Tatakoto
Koro
Vanua
Viti Levu
Gau
Nayau
Lakeba
Moala
Kadavu
Matuku
Fulaga
Vatoa
Vava'u Gp.
Palmerston Atoll
Tonga Islands
Niue
Aitutaki
Îles du Vent
Amanu
Hao
Marokau
Nengonengo
Vairaatea
Vahitahi
Nukutavake
Pinaki
Pukarua
Reao
Tofua
Kotu Gp.
Nomuka Gp.
Ha'apai Group
Tongatapu Group
Tongatapu
'Eua
Ono-i-Lau
Mitiaro
Atiu
Rarotonga
Mangaia
Austral Islands
Îles Maria
Rurutu
Rimatara
Tubuai
Raivavae
A
Hereheretue
Îles Duc de Gloucester
Nukutipipi
Tematagi
Moruroa
Groupe Actéon
Tenararo
Tenarunga
Marutea Sud
Îles Gambier
Morane
Taravai
Mangareva
Tropic of Capricorn
20°
Oeno Island
Pitcairn Island
Henderson Island
Ducie Island
PACIFIC OCEAN
Rapa Iti
Marotiri
Îles Marotiri
Kermadec Islands
Raoul Island
Macauley Island
Curtis Island
L'Esperance Rock
30°
Brett
Great Barrier Island
Bay of Plenty
East Cape
NORTH ISLAND
Lake Taupo
Mahia Peninsula
Cape Kidnappers
40°
Cape Palliser
Chatham Islands
Chatham Island
Pitt Island
D
Bounty Islands

180° 170° 160° 150° 140° 130°

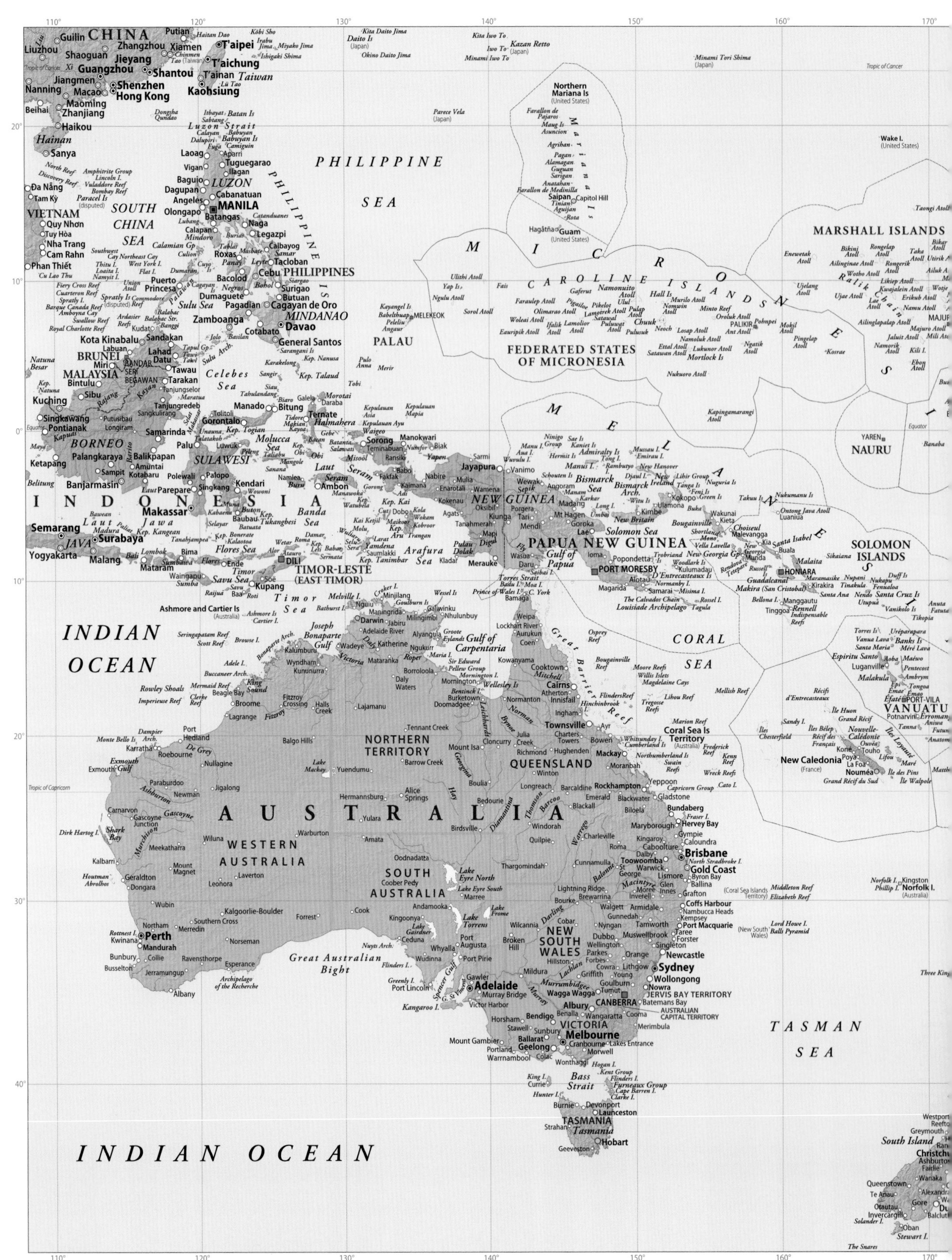
CHINA
T'aipei
Taiwan
Hong Kong
Kaohsiung
PHILIPPINE SEA
Northern Mariana Is
(United States)
Wake I.
(United States)
Hainan
LUZON
MANILA
SOUTH CHINA SEA
VIETNAM
PHILIPPINES
MINDANAO
Davao
MARSHALL ISLANDS
MICRONESIA
CAROLINE ISLANDS
FEDERATED STATES OF MICRONESIA
PALAU
Guam
(United States)
BRUNEI
MALAYSIA
Celebes Sea
BORNEO
SULAWESI
Molucca Sea
Halmahera
NAURU
INDONESIA
Java
Makassar
Semarang
Surabaya
Banda Sea
Flores Sea
DILI
TIMOR-LESTE
(EAST TIMOR)
Timor Sea
Arafura Sea
NEW GUINEA
PAPUA NEW GUINEA
PORT MORESBY
Solomon Sea
SOLOMON ISLANDS
HONIARA
MELANESIA
Gulf of Papua
Gulf of Carpentaria
CORAL SEA
Coral Sea Is
Territory
(Australia)
VANUATU
PORT-VILA
New Caledonia
(France)
Nouméa
INDIAN OCEAN
Ashmore and Cartier Is
(Australia)
Darwin
NORTHERN TERRITORY
QUEENSLAND
WESTERN AUSTRALIA
AUSTRALIA
SOUTH AUSTRALIA
NEW SOUTH WALES
VICTORIA
Brisbane
Gold Coast
Sydney
Newcastle
Wollongong
CANBERRA
JERVIS BAY TERRITORY
AUSTRALIAN CAPITAL TERRITORY
Melbourne
Adelaide
Perth
Great Australian Bight
Bass Strait
TASMANIA
Tasmania
Hobart
TASMAN SEA
Norfolk I.
(Australia)
South Island
INDIAN OCEAN
Tropic of Cancer
Tropic of Capricorn
Equator
110° 120° 130° 140° 150° 160° 170°

1:31,900,000

Mercator Projection

0 500 1000 1500 2000 kilometers

0 250 500 750 1000 miles

Oceania Political

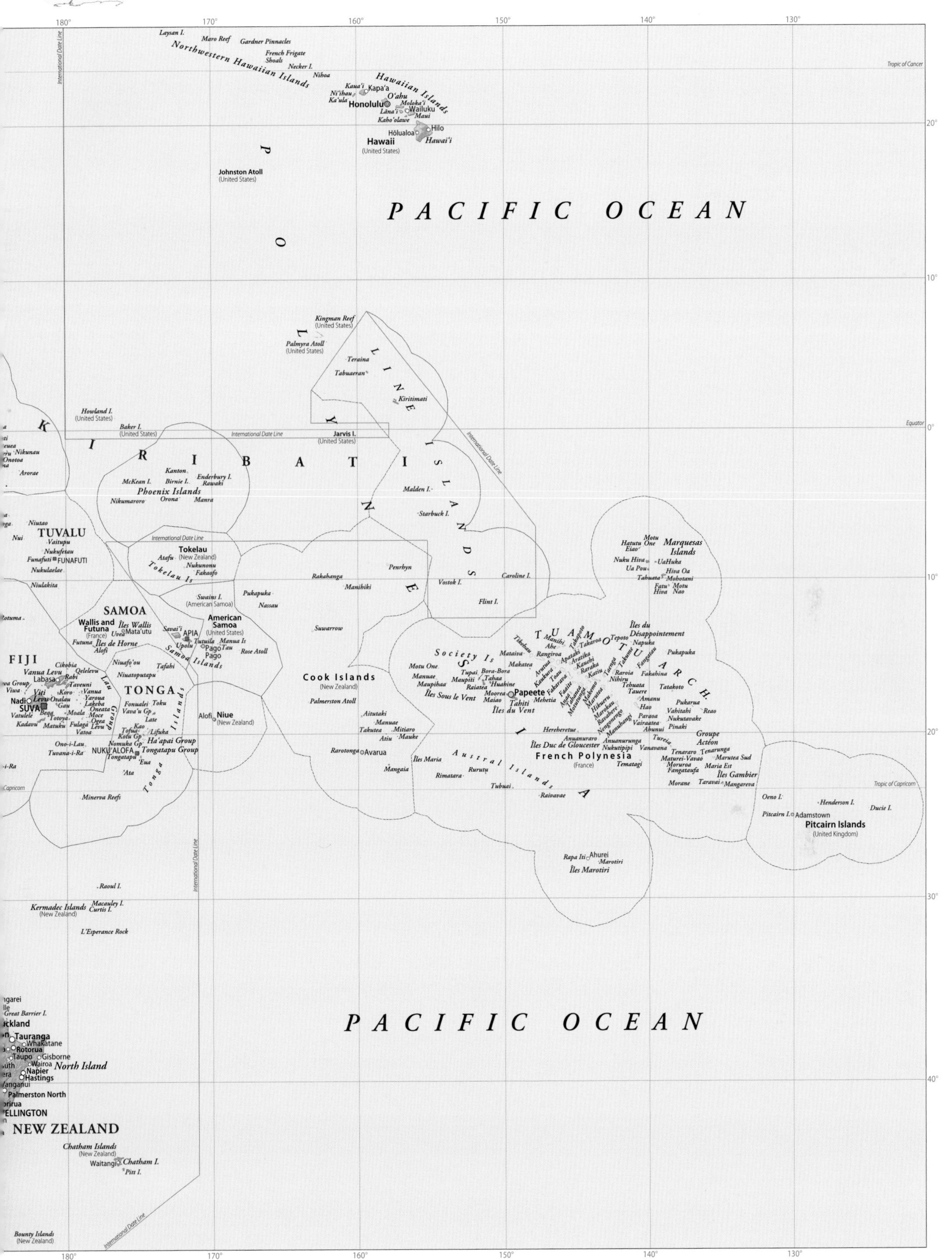
PACIFIC OCEAN
Hawaiian Islands
Northwestern Hawaiian Islands
Honolulu
Hawaii
(United States)
Johnston Atoll
(United States)
Kingman Reef
(United States)
Palmyra Atoll
(United States)
LINE ISLANDS
Kiritimati
Howland I.
(United States)
Baker I.
(United States)
Jarvis I.
(United States)
KIRIBATI
Phoenix Islands
TUVALU
FUNAFUTI
Tokelau
(New Zealand)
SAMOA
APIA
American Samoa
(United States)
Pago Pago
Wallis and Futuna
(France)
FIJI
SUVA
TONGA
NUKU'ALOFA
Niue
(New Zealand)
Cook Islands
(New Zealand)
Avarua
Marquesas Islands
TUAMOTU ARCH.
Society Is
Papeete
Tahiti
French Polynesia
(France)
Austral Islands
POLYNESIA
Pitcairn Islands
(United Kingdom)
Adamstown
Kermadec Islands
(New Zealand)
Chatham Islands
(New Zealand)
Bounty Islands
(New Zealand)
NEW ZEALAND
North Island
WELLINGTON
International Date Line
Tropic of Cancer
Equator
Tropic of Capricorn
PACIFIC OCEAN

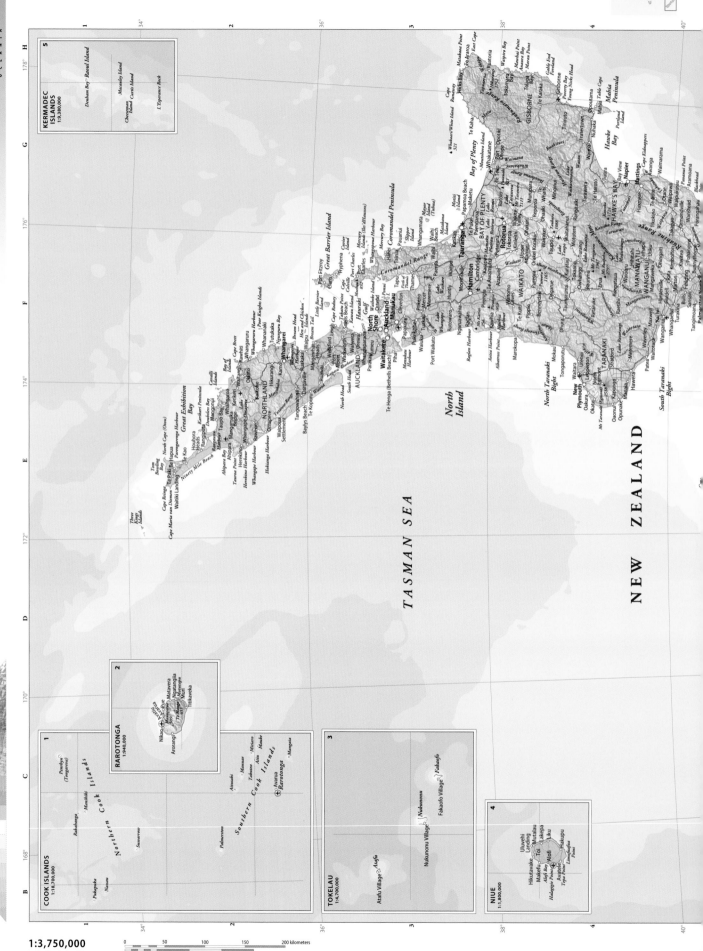

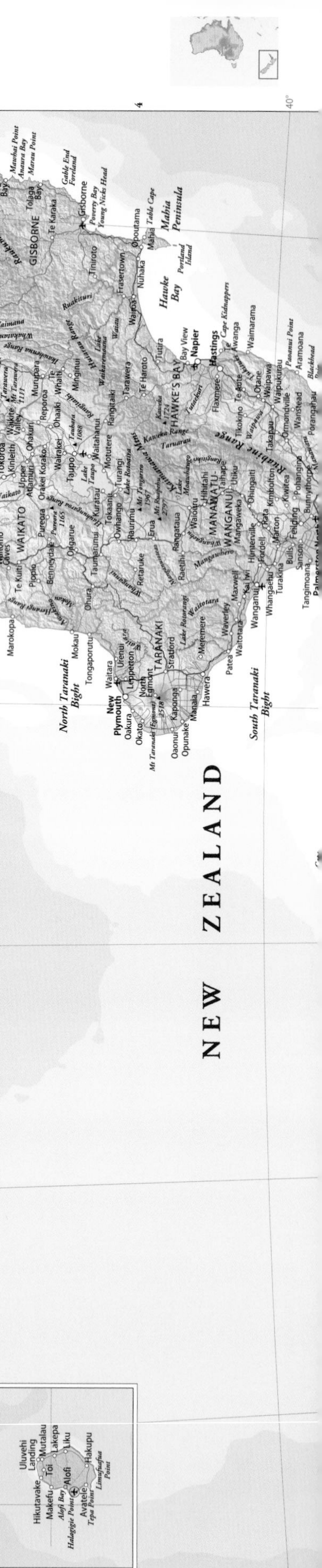
KERMADEC ISLANDS
1:9,380,000
Raoul Island
Denham Bay
Macauley Island
Curtis Island
Cheeseman Island
L'Esperance Rock
COOK ISLANDS
1:18,700,000
Northern Cook Islands
Southern Cook Islands
Penrhyn (Tongareva)
Manihiki
Rakahanga
Pukapuka
Nassau
Suwarrow
Palmerston
Aitutaki
Manuae
Takutea
Mitiaro
Atiu
Mauke
Mangaia
Rarotonga
Avarua
RAROTONGA
1:940,000
Nikao
Avarua
Pue
Matavera
Ngatangiia
Arorangi
Titikaveka
TOKELAU
1:4,700,000
Atafu
Atafu Village
Nukunonu
Nukunonu Village
Fakaofo
Fakaofo Village
NIUE
1:1,800,000
Alofi
Avatele
Hakupu
Liku
Lakepa
Mutalau
Tuapa
Makefu
Hikutavake
Toi
Uluvehi Landing
TASMAN SEA
NEW ZEALAND
North Island
Three Kings Islands
Cape Reinga
Cape Maria van Diemen
Ninety Mile Beach
Great Exhibition Bay
NORTHLAND
Whangarei
Great Barrier Island
AUCKLAND
Auckland
Manukau
Waitakere
North Shore
Hauraki Gulf
Coromandel Peninsula
Hamilton
WAIKATO
Bay of Plenty
BAY OF PLENTY
Tauranga
Rotorua
Taupo
Lake Taupo
GISBORNE
Gisborne
East Cape
Hawke Bay
HAWKE'S BAY
Napier
Hastings
Mahia Peninsula
TARANAKI
New Plymouth
North Taranaki Bight
South Taranaki Bight
MANAWATU-WANGANUI
Wanganui
Palmerston North
Meters
Feet
6000
19685
5000
16404
4000
13123
3000
9843
2000
6562
1000
3281
500
1640
200
656
100
328
0
LAND BELOW SEA LEVEL
100
328
200
656
1000
3281
2000
6562
4000
13123
6000
19685
1:3,750,000
Lambert Conic Conformal Projection
0
50
100
150
200 kilometers
0
25
50
75
100 miles

New Zealand

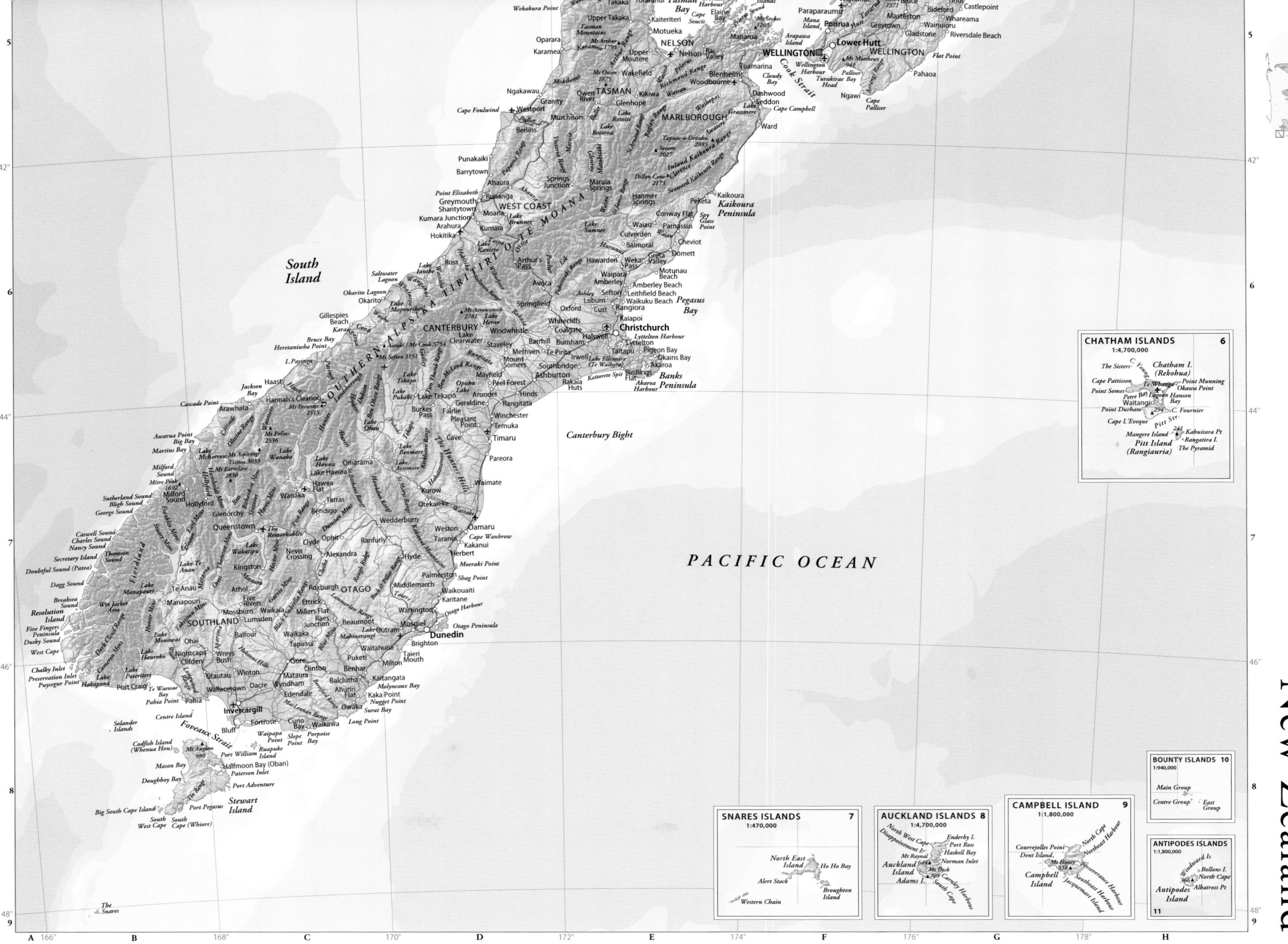
PACIFIC OCEAN
South Island
Canterbury Bight
Cook Strait
Foveaux Strait
Stewart Island
SOUTHERN ALPS KA TIRITIRI O TE MOANA
WEST COAST
CANTERBURY
OTAGO
SOUTHLAND
MARLBOROUGH
TASMAN
NELSON
WELLINGTON
Christchurch
Dunedin
Invercargill
Lower Hutt
Timaru
Oamaru
Queenstown
Greymouth
Blenheim
Kaikoura
Banks Peninsula
Kaikoura Peninsula
Pegasus Bay
CHATHAM ISLANDS 6
1:4,700,000
SNARES ISLANDS 7
1:470,000
AUCKLAND ISLANDS 8
1:4,700,000
CAMPBELL ISLAND 9
1:1,800,000
BOUNTY ISLANDS 10
1:940,000
ANTIPODES ISLANDS 11
1:1,800,000
Meters
Feet
LAND BELOW SEA LEVEL

375

INDONESIA

JAWA BARAT
YOGYAKARTA
JAWA TIMUR
JAWA TENGAH
BALI
NUSA TENGGARA BARAT
NUSA TENGGARA TIMUR
Jawa (Java)
Depok
Bogor
Bandung
Tasikmalaya
Purwokerto
Salatiga
Yogyakarta
Surakarta
Tulungagung
Kepanjen
Jombang
Malang
Probolinggo
Banyuwangi
Denpasar
Singaraja
Mataram
Lombok
Sumbawabesar
Sumbawa
Bima
Bangkulua
Ruteng
Flores
Ende
Waikelo
Memboro
Waingapu
Sumba
Gunung Wanggameti 1225
Ngalu
LAUT SAWU (SAVU SEA)
Seba
Kepulauan Sawu
Pulau Raijua
Roti
Kupang
Timor
Baa
Pulau Roti
Pulau Pamana
Atambua
Maliana
Halilulik
Besikama
Nikiniki
Gunung Mutis 2427
TIMOR-LESTE (EAST TIMOR)
TIMOR SEA

Hibernia Reef
Ashmore Reef
Ashmore and Cartier Islands (Australia)
Cartier Island
The Settlement
Christmas Island (Australia)
Seringapatam Reef
Scott Reef
Mermaid Reef
Rowley Shoals
Imperieuse Reef

INDIAN OCEAN

Cape Van Diemen
Pirlangimpi
Bathurst Island
Melville I.
Milikapiti
Mitchell Point
Nguiu
Paru
Beagle Gulf
Darwin
Palmerston
Humpty Doo
Point Blaze
Batchelor
Adelaide River
Cape Ford
Daly River
Sir Graham Moore Is.
Cape Londonderry
Cape Bougainville
Bonaparte Archipelago
Joseph Bonaparte Gulf
Kalumburu
Wadeye
Katherine
Bigge Island
York Sound
Cape Dussejour
Mt Hogarth 330
Victoria
Timber Creek
Heywood Is.
Wyndham
Ord
Kununurra
Victoria River Roadhouse
Adele Island
Buccaneer Archipelago
Mt Hann 779
Drysdale
Durack
Lake Argyle Village
Lake Argyle
Victoria River Downs
Mt Bebn 428
Bedford Is.
One Arm Point
Cape Leveque
Lombadina
KIMBERLEY
Mt Hart 667
Kupungarri
King Sound
King Leopold Ranges
Lacepede Is.
Derby
Mt Wells 983
Mt Napier 487
Kalkarindji
Broome
Roebuck Roadhouse
Fitzroy
Looma
Fitzroy Crossing
O'Donnell
Halls Creek
Lajamanu
Cape Latouche Treville
Bidyadanga Community
Sturt
Mt Bannerman 449
Eighty Mile Beach
GREAT SANDY DESERT
Balgo Hills
Lake Gregory
Rabbit Flat Roadhouse
Mt Davidson 457
TANAMI DESERT
Poissonnier Point
Pardoo Roadhouse
De Grey
Dampier Archipelago
Port Hedland
Percival Lakes
Lake Hazlett
Monte Bello Is.
Barrow I.
Dampier
Wickham
Karratha
Marble Bar
Nullagine
Oakover
Telfer
Lake Mackay
Yuendumu
Mary Anne Reef
Onslow
Mt Herbert 370
Chichester Range
Fortescue
Nullagine
Mt Isdell 389
Lake Dora
Lake Auld
Kunawaritji Community
North West Cape
Exmouth
Exmouth Gulf
Ashburton
Hamersley Range
Munjina
Mt Brockman 1132
Tom Price
Mt Meharry 1253
Mt Newman 1057
Newman
AUSTRALIA
Lake Disappointment
Lake MacDonald
Kintore
Glen Helen
GIBSON DESERT
Point Cloates
Coral Bay
PILBARA
Savory
Lake Hopkins
Kings Canyon Resort
Hermannsburg
Kaltukatjara (Docker River)
Lake Amadeus
Lyndon
Little Sandy Desert
Mt Augustus 1106
Warakurna Roadhouse
Yulara
Cape Farquhar
Mt Essendon 910
Kata Tjuta (Mt Olga) 1069
Uluru (Ayers Rock) 867
Lake MacLeod
Lyons
Gascoyne
Mt Aloysius 982
Quobba
Bernier I.
Carnarvon
Dorre I.
Gascoyne Junction
WESTERN AUSTRALIA
Warburton
Papulankutja (Blackstone)
Amata
Pipalyatjara
Musgrave
Tropic of Capricorn
Cape Inscription
Shark Bay
Dirk Hartog Island
Monkey Mia
Wooramel Roadhouse
Denham
Useless Loop
Overlander Roadhouse
Murchison
Mt Murchison
Meekatharra
Lake Annean
Wiluna
Lake Way
Lake Carnegie
Lake Wells
Tjukayirla Roadhouse
Lake Throssell
Ilturu
Billabong Roadhouse
Murchison
Cue
Lake Austin
Cosmo Newbery
Yeo Lake
Zuytdorp Cliffs
Sanford
Mount Magnet
Sandstone
Leinster
Kalbarri
Galena
Teutonic
Laverton
Mt Crawford 507
Lake Rason
GREAT VICTORIA DESERT
Serpentine Lakes
Emu Junction
Jubilee Lake
Northampton
Yalgoo
Lake Noondie
Lake Raeside
Leonora
Lake Carey
Lake Maurice
Gregory
Mullewa
Tardun
Mongers Lake
Lake Barlee
Lake Ballard
Houtman Abrolhos
Geraldton
Greenough
Dongara
Irwin
Morawa
Mingenew
Paynes Find
Lake Moore
Menzies
Nullarbor Plain
Cook
Eneabba
Bunjil
Broad Arrow
Forrest
Deakin
Coolimba
Marchagee
Jibberding
Mollerin
Bonnie Rock
Lake Deborah East
Kalgoorlie-Boulder
Green Head
Jurien Bay
Badgingarra
Wubin
Dalwallinu
Coolgardie
Nullarbor Roadhouse
Cervantes
Moora
Koorda
Mukinbudin
Southern Cross
Kambalda
Coonana
Rawlinna
Cataby
New Norcia
Nungarin
Boorabbin
Lake Lefroy
Eucla
Border Village
Head of Bight
Lancelin
Goomalling
Merredin
Cave Hill 455
Lake Cowan
Gingin
Yanchep
Northam
Cunderdin
Bruce Rock
Norseman
Balladonia
Caiguna
Cocklebiddy
Perth
Midland
Quairading
Fremantle
Corrigin
Hyden
Lake Hope
Lake Dundas
Rockingham
Kwinana
Brookton
Holt Rock
Salmon Gums
Mandurah
Pinjarra
Kulin
Great Australian Bight
Dwellingup
Williams
Lake Grace
Lake King
Harvey
Narrogin
Dumbleyung
Ravensthorpe
Mt Arid 357
Israelite Bay
Point Malcolm
Bunbury
Collie
Wagin
Nyabing
Esperance
Cape Pasley
Cape Naturaliste
Busselton
Donnybrook
Katanning
Kojonup
Gnowangerup
Fitzgerald
Hopetoun
Archipelago of the Recherche
Cape Le Grand
Margaret River
Bridgetown
Nannup
Manjimup
Bluff Knoll 1096
Bremer Bay
Cape Knob
Mount Barker
Cape Leeuwin
Augusta
Denmark
Albany
Windy Harbour
Walpole
Flinders Peninsula

CHRISTMAS ISLAND
1:1,400,000

105°40'
Flying Fish Cove
North East Point
North West Point
The Settlement
Hanitch Hill 509
Murray Hill 361
Low Point
Egeria Pt
Ross Hill 319
Smithson Bight
Jones Point
South Point
INDIAN OCEAN
10°30'

1

ASHMORE REEF AND CARTIER ISLAND
1:2,800,000

123°
12°
Hibernia Reef
Ashmore Reef
INDIAN OCEAN
West Islet
Middle Islet
East Islet
Johnson Bank
Woodbine Bank
Paxtoe Passage
Cartier Island

2

COCOS (KEELING) ISLANDS
1:1,400,000

3

96°50'
North Keeling Island
INDIAN OCEAN
12°
Horsburgh Island (Luar)
Western Entrance
Port Refuge
Direction Island (Tikus)
Home Island
South Keeling Islands
Pulo Pandang
West Island (Panjang)
Tanjong Pugi
South Island (Atas)
Kapia Tigu

HEARD ISLAND
1:2,800,000

73°30'
53°
Laurens Peninsula
Atlas Cove
Azorella Peninsula
Corinthian Bay
Shag Island
Anzac Peak 715
McDonald Island
South West Bay
Spit Bay
Cape Gazert
Mawson Peak 2745
Spit Point
Cape Labuan
Lambeth Bluff
SOUTHERN OCEAN

4

Meters	Feet
6000	19685
5000	16404
4000	13123
3000	9843
2000	6562
1000	3281
500	1640
200	656
100	328
0	LAND BELOW SEA LEVEL
100	328
200	656
1000	3281
2000	6562
4000	13123
6000	19685

1:14,000,000
Lambert Conic Conformal Projection

0 150 300 450 600 kilometers
0 75 150 225 300 miles

Australia

373

LORD HOWE ISLAND
1:950,000
7

MACQUARIE ISLAND
1:1,400,000
5

NORFOLK ISLAND
1:950,000
6

Meters
Feet

Meters	Feet
6000	19685
5000	16404
4000	13123
3000	9843
2000	6562
1000	3281
500	1640
200	656
100	328
0	LAND BELOW SEA LEVEL
100	328
200	656
1000	3281
2000	6562
4000	13123
6000	19685

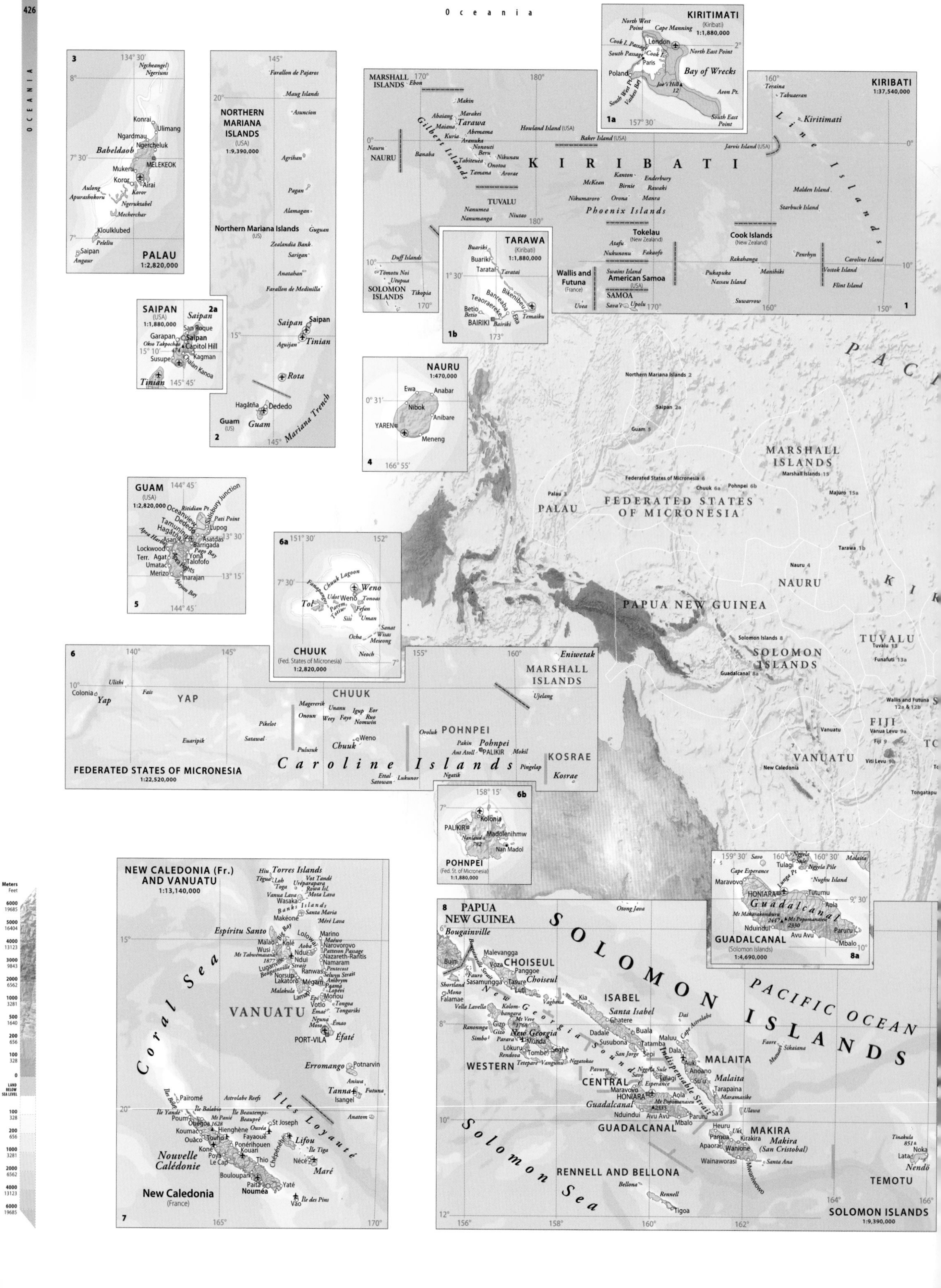

3
134° 30′
Ngcheangel) Ngeruns
8°
Konrai
Ulimang
Ngardmau
Ngercheluk
Babeldaob
7° 30′
MELEKEOK
Mukeru
Koror
Airai
Aulong
Koror
Apurashokoru
Ngeruktabel
Mecherchar
Kloulklubed
Peleliu
7°
Saipan
Angaur
PALAU
1:2,820,000

145°
Farallon de Pajaros
Maug Islands
20°
NORTHERN MARIANA ISLANDS
(USA)
1:9,390,000
Asuncion
Agrihan
Pagan
Alamagan
Northern Mariana Islands
(US)
Guguan
Zealandia Bank
Sarigan
Anatahan
Farallon de Medinilla
15°
Saipan
Saipan
Tinian
Aguijan
Rota
Hagåtña
Dededo
Guam
(US)
Guam
Mariana Trench
2
145°

SAIPAN
(USA)
1:1,880,000
2a
Saipan
San Roque
Garapan
Saipan
Okso Takpochao
15° 10′
Capitol Hill
474
Susupe
Kagman
Chalan Kanoa
Tinian
145° 45′

MARSHALL ISLANDS
170°
Ebon
180°
Makin
Abaiang
Marakei
Tarawa
Maiana
Abemama
Gilbert Islands
Kuria
Aranuka
Nonouti
Beru
Nikunau
Tabiteuea
Onotoa
Tamana
Arorae
0°
Nauru
NAURU
Banaba
Howland Island (USA)
Baker Island (USA)
KIRIBATI
Kanton
Enderbury
McKean
Birnie
Rawaki
Nikumaroro
Orona
Manra
Phoenix Islands
TUVALU
Nanumea
Niutao
Nanumanga
180°
10°
Duff Islands
Tömotu Noi
Utupua
SOLOMON ISLANDS
Tikopia
170°

KIRITIMATI
(Kiribati)
1:1,880,000
North West Point
Cape Manning
London
2°
Cook I. Passage
Cook I.
North East Point
South Passage
Paris
Bay of Wrecks
Poland
South West Pt.
Vaskess Bay
Joe's Hill
12
Aeon Pt.
1a
157° 30′
South East Point

160°
KIRIBATI
1:37,540,000
Teraina
Tabuaeran
Kiritimati
Line Islands
Jarvis Island (USA)
0°
Malden Island
Starbuck Island
Tokelau
(New Zealand)
Atafu
Nukunonu
Fakaofo
Cook Islands
(New Zealand)
Penrhyn
Rakahanga
Caroline Island
Manihiki
Vostok Island
10°
Wallis and Futuna
(France)
Swains Island
Pukapuka
Nassau Island
Flint Island
American Samoa
(USA)
SAMOA
Uvea
Sava'i
Upolu
170°
Suwarrow
160°
150°
1

TARAWA
(Kiribati)
1:1,880,000
Buariki
Buariki
Taratai
Taratai
1° 30′
Bikenibeu
Banreaba
Teaoraereke
Eita
Temaiku
Betio
Betio
BAIRIKI
Bairiki
1b
173°

NAURU
1:470,000
Ewa
Anabar
0° 31′
Nibok
Anibare
YAREN
Meneng
4
166° 55′

PACIFIC
Northern Mariana Islands 2
Saipan 2a
Guam 5
MARSHALL ISLANDS
Marshall Islands 15
Federated States of Micronesia 6
Chuuk 6a
Pohnpei 6b
Majuro 15a
Palau 3
PALAU
FEDERATED STATES OF MICRONESIA
Tarawa 1b
Nauru 4
NAURU
KI
PAPUA NEW GUINEA
TUVALU
Tuvalu 13
Funafuti 13a
Solomon Islands 8
SOLOMON ISLANDS
Guadalcanal 8a
Wallis and Futuna 12a & 12b
S
FIJI
Vanua Levu 9a
Vanuatu
Fiji 9
TC
VANUATU
Viti Levu 9b
New Caledonia
Tongatapu

GUAM
(USA)
144° 45′
1:2,820,000
Sinsbury Junction
Ritidian Pt
Oceanview
Pati Point
Dededo
Lupog
Tamuning
13° 30′
Apra Harbor
Hagåtña
Asatdas
Asan
Barrigada
Pago Bay
Lockwood Terr.
Agat
Yona
Talofofo
Umatac
Merizo
Inarajan
13° 15′
Mt. Lamlam
Achang Bay
5
144° 45′

6a
151° 30′
152°
Chuuk Lagoon
7° 30′
Fanapanges
Weno
Udot
Weno
Tonoas
Tol
Parem
Totiw
Fefan
Siis
Uman
Sanat
Wisas
Ocha
Mesesong
CHUUK
(Fed. States of Micronesia)
1:2,820,000
Neoch
7°

6
140°
145°
155°
160°
Eniwetak
10°
MARSHALL ISLANDS
Ulithi
Colonia
Yap
Fais
YAP
Ujelang
CHUUK
Magererik
Unanu
Igup
Eor
Onoun
Wrey
Fayo
Ruo
Nomwin
Pikelot
Oroluk
POHNPEI
Euaripik
Satawal
Weno
Chuuk
Pakin
Pohnpei
Pulusuk
Ant Atoll
PALIKIR
Mokil
KOSRAE
Caroline Islands
Pingelap
FEDERATED STATES OF MICRONESIA
1:22,520,000
Ettal
Satowan
Lukunor
Ngatik
Kosrae

158° 15′
6b
7°
Kolonia
PALIKIR
Madolenihmw
Nanlaud
782
Nan Madol
POHNPEI
(Fed. St. of Micronesia)
1:1,880,000

NEW CALEDONIA (Fr.) AND VANUATU
1:13,140,000
Hiu
Torres Islands
Tégua
Loh
Vot Tandé
Toga
Uréparapara
Rowa Isl.
Vanua Lava
Mota Lava
Wasaka
Banks Islands
Santa Maria
Makéone
Méré Lava
Espíritu Santo
15°
Big Bay
Lolowai
Marino
Malao
Kolé
Aoba
Maéwo
Narovorovo
Wusi
Mt Tabwemasana 1877
Patteson Passage
Nazareth-Rantis
Nduindui
Luganville
Ndui
Namaram
Bougainville Strait
Pentecost
Norsup
Ranwas
Selwyn Strait
Lakatoro
Mégam
Ambrym
Malakula
Paama
Lopévi
Lamap
Epi
Morlou
Coral Sea
VANUATU
Votlo
Tongoa
Émaé
Tongariki
Nguna
Moso
Émao
PORT-VILA
Éfaté
Erromango
Potnarvin
Aniwa
Tanna
Futuna
Isangel
Îles Belep
Pairomé
Astrolabe Reefs
Îles Loyauté
Île Balabio
Île Beautemps-Beaupré
20°
Île Yandé
Mt Panié 1628
Poum
Ouvéa
St Joseph
Anatom
Ouégoa
Touho
Hienghène
Koumac
Fayaoué
Lifou
Ouaco
Ponérihouen
Chépénéhé
Île Tiga
Koné
Kouari
Nouvelle Calédonie
Poya
Thio
Nécé
Le Cap
Maré
Bouloupari
Yaté
Païta
Nouméa
New Caledonia
(France)
Île des Pins
Vao
7
165°
170°

Meters / Feet
6000 19685
5000 16404
4000 13123
3000 9843
2000 6562
1000 3281
500 1640
200 656
100 328
0
LAND BELOW SEA LEVEL
100 328
200 656
1000 3281
2000 6562
4000 13123
6000 19685

159° 30′
Savo
160°
Nggela Sule
160° 30′
Malaita
Tulagi
Nggela Pile
Cape Esperance
Lunga Pt
Nughu Island
Maravovo
HONIARA
Tutumu
9° 30′
Guadalcanal
Mt Makarakomburu 2447
Mt Popomanaseu 2330
Nduindui
Paruru
Avu Avu
Mbalo
10°
GUADALCANAL
(Solomon Islands)
1:4,690,000
8a

8
PAPUA NEW GUINEA
Ontong Java
6°
Bougainville
SOLOMON ISLANDS
Bougainville Strait
Malevangga
Buin
Voza
CHOISEUL
Panggoe
Fauro
Choiseul
Sasamungga
Shortland
Tasure
Luti
Mono
New Georgia Sound
Falamae
Vaghena
Kia
ISABEL
PACIFIC OCEAN
Vella Lavella
Kolombangara
Santa Isabel
Ghatere
Dai
Mt Veve 1768
Cape Astrolabe
8°
Ranongga
Gizo
New Georgia
Buala
Gizo
Dadale
Maluu
Simbo
Parara
Munda
Susubona
Tatamba
Faore
Sikaiana
Lokuru
San Jorge
Sepi
Dala
Manaoba
Rendova
Tombe
Seghe
Indispensable Strait
MALAITA
Tetepare
Vangunu
Nggatokae
WESTERN
Auki
Anoano
Pavuvu
Nggela Sule
Savo
Malaita
CENTRAL
Tulagi
Su'u
Esperance
Tarapaina
Maravovo
Aola
Maramasike
HONIARA
Mt Popomanaseu 2335
Ulawa
Guadalcanal
10°
Nduindui
Avu Avu
Paruru
Sa'a
Mbalo
GUADALCANAL
Heuru
Uki
MAKIRA
Makira
Pamua
Kirakira
Tinakula 851
Solomon Sea
Apaoro
Wanione
(San Cristobal)
Noka
Lata
Wainaworasi
Santa Ana
Nendö
Mwaniwowo
RENNELL AND BELLONA
TEMOTU
Bellona
Rennell
164°
166°
12°
Tigoa
156°
158°
160°
162°
SOLOMON ISLANDS
1:9,390,000

Islands of the Pacific

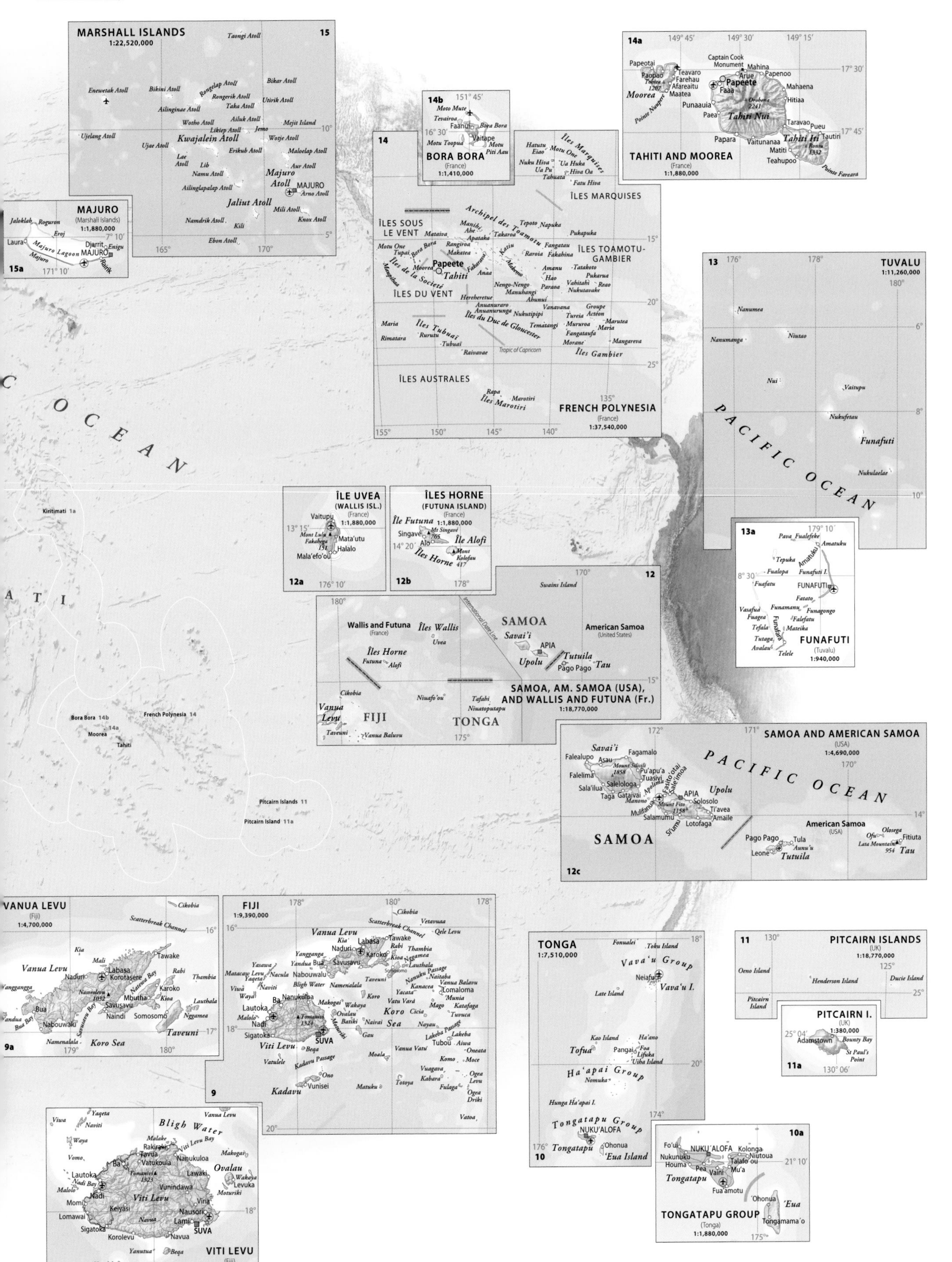
MARSHALL ISLANDS
1:22,520,000
15
Taongi Atoll
Enewetak Atoll
Bikini Atoll
Rongelap Atoll
Rongerik Atoll
Bikar Atoll
Utirik Atoll
Ailinginae Atoll
Taka Atoll
Wotho Atoll
Ailuk Atoll
Mejit Island
Likiep Atoll
Jemo
Ujelang Atoll
Kwajalein Atoll
Wotje Atoll
Ujae Atoll
Erikub Atoll
Maloelap Atoll
Lae Atoll
Lib
Aur Atoll
Namu Atoll
Majuro Atoll
MAJURO
Ailinglapalap Atoll
Arno Atoll
Jaluit Atoll
Mili Atoll
Namdrik Atoll
Kili
Knox Atoll
Ebon Atoll
MAJURO
(Marshall Islands)
1:1,880,000
Jaloklab
Roguron
Eroj
Laura
Majuro Lagoon
Djarrit
Enigu
MAJURO
Rairok
15a
14b
BORA BORA
(France)
1:1,410,000
Moto Mute
Tevairoa
Faanui
Bora Bora
Vaitape
Motu Toopua
Motu Piti Aau
14a
Papeetoai
Captain Cook Monument
Mahina
Papenoo
Teavaro
Arue
Paopao
Farehau
Papeete
Afareaitu
Faaa
Mahaena
Moorea
Maatea
Punaauia
Hitiaa
Paea
Orohena 2241
Tahiti Nui
Taravao
Pueu
Papara
Vaitunanaa
Tahiti Iti
Tautira
Matiti
Teahupoo
Pointe Fareara
TAHITI AND MOOREA
(France)
1:1,880,000
14
ÎLES MARQUISES
Hatutu
Eiao
Motu One
Nuku Hiva
Ua Huka
Ua Pu
Hiva Oa
Tahuata
Fatu Hiva
ÎLES SOUS LE VENT
Archipel des Tuamotu
Tepoto
Napuka
Manihi
Ahe
Takaroa
Pukapuka
Mataiva
Rangiroa
Fangatau
Motu One
Tupai
Makatea
Raroia
Fakahina
ÎLES TOAMOTU-GAMBIER
Papeete
Moorea
Tahiti
Anaa
Amanu
Hao
Tatakoto
Pukarua
Reao
Îles de la Société
Nengo-Nengo
Manuhangi
Paraoa
Vahitahi
Nukutavake
ÎLES DU VENT
Hereheretue
Ahunui
Anuanuraro
Anuanurunga
Nukutipipi
Vanavana
Groupe Actéon
Îles du Duc de Gloucester
Tematangi
Tureia
Mururoa
Marutea
Maria
Maria
Îles Tubuaï
Rurutu
Rimatara
Tubuaï
Raivavae
Fangataufa
Morane
Mangareva
Tropic of Capricorn
Îles Gambier
ÎLES AUSTRALES
Rapa
Marotiri
Îles Marotiri
FRENCH POLYNESIA
(France)
1:37,540,000
13
TUVALU
1:11,260,000
Nanumea
Nanumanga
Niutao
Nui
Vaitupu
Nukufetau
Funafuti
Nukulaelae
PACIFIC OCEAN
13a
Pava
Fualefeke
Amatuku
Tepuka
Fualopa
Funafuti I.
Fuafatu
FUNAFUTI
Fatato
Vasafua
Funamanu
Funagongo
Fuagea
Falefatu
Tefala
Mateika
Tutaga
Avalau
Telele
FUNAFUTI
(Tuvalu)
1:940,000
ÎLE UVEA
(WALLIS ISL.)
(France)
1:1,880,000
Vaitupu
Mont Lulu Fakahega 151
Mata'utu
Halalo
Mala'efo'ou
12a
ÎLES HORNE
(FUTUNA ISLAND)
(France)
1:1,880,000
Île Futuna
Mt Singavé 765
Singavé
Alo
Île Alofi
Mont Kolofau 417
Îles Horne
12b
12
Swains Island
Wallis and Futuna
(France)
Îles Wallis
Uvea
International Date Line
SAMOA
Savai'i
APIA
American Samoa
(United States)
Îles Horne
Futuna
Alofi
Upolu
Tutuila
Pago Pago
Tau
Cikobia
SAMOA, AM. SAMOA (USA), AND WALLIS AND FUTUNA (Fr.)
1:18,770,000
Niuafo'ou
Tafahi
Niuatoputapu
Vanua Levu
FIJI
TONGA
Taveuni
Vanua Balavu
SAMOA AND AMERICAN SAMOA
(USA)
1:4,690,000
Savai'i
Fagamalo
Falealupo
Asau
Mount Silisili 1858
Pu'apu'a
Tuasivi
Falelima
Salelologa
Sala'ilua
Taga
Manono
APIA
Upolu
Solosolo
Mount Fito 1158
Ti'avea
Mulifanua
Salamumu
Amaile
Si'umu
Lotofaga
SAMOA
PACIFIC OCEAN
American Samoa
(USA)
Ofu
Olosega
Fitiuta
Lata Mountain 954
Tau
Pago Pago
Tula
Leone
Aunu'u
Tutuila
12c
OCEAN
ATI
Kiritimati 1a
Bora Bora 14b
French Polynesia 14
Moorea 14a
Tahiti
Pitcairn Islands 11
Pitcairn Island 11a
VANUA LEVU
(Fiji)
1:4,700,000
Cikobia
Scatterbreak Channel
Kia
Mali
Tawake
Vanua Levu
Labasa
Rabi
Naduri
Korotasere
Thambia
Vanggangga
Natewa Bay
Karoko
Navoloau 1032
Bua
Mbutha
Kioa
Lauthala
Savusavu
Naindi
Somosomo
Ngamea
Bua Bay
Nabouwalu
Taveuni
Namenalala
Koro Sea
9a
FIJI
1:9,390,000
Cikobia
Vetauua
Qele Levu
Vanua Levu
Tawake
Labasa
Naduri
Thambia
Yanggangga
Karoko
Rabi
Yandua
Bua
Savusavu
Kioa
Yasawa
Matacawa Levu
Nacula
Nabouwalu
Lauthala
Yaqeta
Naviti
Bligh Water
Namenalala
Taveuni
Nanuku Passage
Naitaba
Vanua Balavu
Lomaloma
Waya
Nanukuloa
Koro
Kanacea
Yacata
Munia
Lautoka
Ba
Makogai
Vatu Vara
Mago
Katafaga
Malolo
Nadi
Tomanivi 1324
Wakaya
Ovalau
Koro Sea
Cicia
Tuvuca
Sigatoka
Batiki
Nairai
Nayau
Viti Levu
SUVA
Gau
Lakeba Passage
Lakeba
Tubou
Aiwa
Oneata
Vatulele
Beqa
Vanua Vatu
Moala
Komo
Moce
Kadavu Passage
Ono
Vuagava
Ogea Levu
Kabara
Totoya
Kadavu
Vunisei
Matuku
Fulaga
Ogea Driki
Vatoa
9
Yaqeta
Vanua Levu
Viwa
Naviti
Bligh Water
Waya
Malake
Rakiraki
Viti Levu Bay
Makogai
Vomo
Ba
Tavua
Vatukoula
Nanukuloa
Ovalau
Wakaya
Lautoka
Tomanivi 1323
Lawaki
Levuka
Nadi Bay
Vunindawa
Moturiki
Malolo
Nadi
Momi
Viti Levu
Viria
Keiyasi
Nausori
Lomawai
Navua
Lami
SUVA
Sigatoka
Korolevu
Navua
Yanutua
Beqa
VITI LEVU
(Fiji)
1:4,700,000
Vatulele
9b
TONGA
1:7,510,000
Fonualei
Toku Island
Vava'u Group
Neiafu
Vava'u I.
Late Island
Kao Island
Ha'ano
Tofua
Pangai
Foa
Lifuka
'Uiha Island
Ha'apai Group
Nomuka
Hunga Ha'apai I.
Tongatapu Group
NUKU'ALOFA
Tongatapu
'Ohonua
'Eua Island
10
10a
Fo'ui
NUKU'ALOFA
Kolonga
Nukunuku
Niutoua
Houma
Talafo'ou
Pea
Vaini
Mu'a
Tongatapu
Fua'amotu
'Ohonua
'Eua
Tongamama'o
TONGATAPU GROUP
(Tonga)
1:1,880,000
11
PITCAIRN ISLANDS
(UK)
1:18,770,000
Oeno Island
Henderson Island
Ducie Island
Pitcairn Island
PITCAIRN I.
(UK)
1:380,000
Adamstown
Bounty Bay
St Paul's Point
11a
Meters
Feet
6000 19685
5000 16404
4000 13123
3000 9843
2000 6562
1000 3281
500 1640
200 656
100 328
0
LAND BELOW SEA LEVEL
100 328
200 656
1000 3281
2000 6562
4000 13123
6000 19685

THE POLES

INTRODUCTION

The Poles

Far from the major centers of population of Europe and Asia, the Arctic was for a long time long viewed as a peripheral, barely inhabited, desolate place that offered little. Until the discovery of Antarctica in the nineteenth century, only geographic speculation had imagined the existence of an actual landmass surrounding the South Pole rather than a vast ice-covered ocean like that which surrounds the North Pole.

Previous pages Tourists sail on an inflatable raft through the dramatic arches of an iceberg on the Antarctic Peninsula. Most of the iceberg is underwater, leaving just the "tip" on the surface.

Right The most important zooplankton in the Antarctic food chain, krill *(Euphausia superba)*, a small shrimp-like crustacean, provides food for baleen whales and many other species of fish and birds; some feed almost exclusively on krill, which are also targets for commercial fishing.

Below Ammassalik District, covering an area of some 93,800 square miles (243,000 km²), lies on Greenland's eastern side. While hunting and fishing are the main activities in the district's few towns and settlements, tourism also plays a role in the local economy.

Bottom Polar bear *(Ursus maritimus)* mother and cubs, Svalbard. Polar bears range throughout the arctic region surrounding the North Pole, usually at the edge of the ice pack.

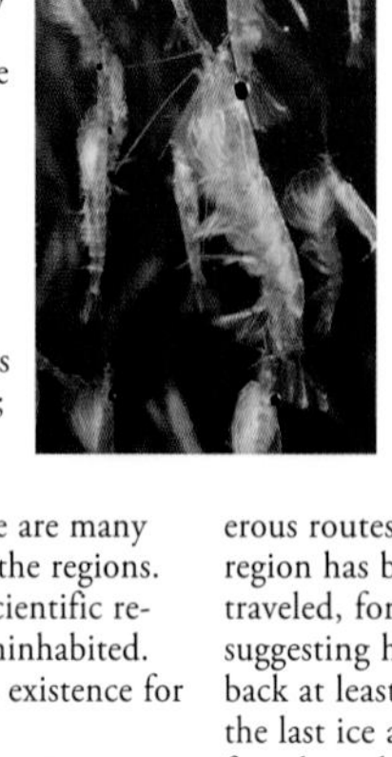

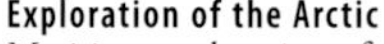

Harsh conditions, in which winter and darkness seem to last forever, is one of the more common beliefs about polar environments. Another is that there are continuous violent storms that produce huge snowfalls. Neither perception is entirely accurate. Daylight hours are limited in the long winters, but there are few days of total darkness, just as in the summers there are few days when the sun does not set. Violent blizzards are frequent, but heavy snow is not; both the Arctic and Antarctic regions receive less than 10 inches (250 mm) of precipitation a year; in the center of Antarctica this drops to 2 inches (50 mm).

Despite these similarities, there are many pronounced differences between the regions. Were it not for the presence of scientific researchers, Antarctica would be uninhabited. The Arctic has supported human existence for centuries. There are several reasons for this, to do with physical geography. The Southern hemisphere is predominantly ocean and the continental landmasses of South America and Australia are at huge distances from Antarctica. In the high southern latitudes, rough seas and complex weather patterns create difficult conditions for navigation, and shipping lanes have long bypassed this part of the globe in favor of less treacherous routes. In contrast, the Arctic region has been inhabited, and well traveled, for a long time. Evidence suggesting human presence dating back at least 30,000 years, before the last ice age developed, has been found on the Yana River in a remote corner of Siberia, 300 miles (480 km) north of the Arctic Circle. Today, about 8 million people, including some 250,000 indigenous people, live within the Arctic Circle.

Exploration of the Arctic

Maritime exploration of the Arctic began when Vikings ventured west from Scandinavia to Iceland in the ninth century. From permanent settlements on Iceland they reached Greenland and the coast of North America. The Greenland colony survived for centuries. It was not abandoned solely because of the effects of climate change, as conventional wisdom suggests, but also because of political changes in Scandinavia which led to Iceland and Greenland being economically marginalized.

When later Europeans discovered the Americas for a second time they were quick to recognize the difficulties of circumnavigating the globe in a westward direction. The dream of finding a Northwest Passage that would allow an undisturbed connection between Europe and East Asia arose as early as the sixteenth century. This inspired quite a few to undertake Arctic exploration, but it took a further four centuries and many ill-fated expeditions to prove that such a passage existed.

Due to the difficulties of navigating its shallow, rocky, and often-frozen waters, the Northwest Passage has never fulfilled expectations as a major trade route. Yet this may radically change in the not too distant future. If climate change continues to follow recent patterns, the ice-covered northern seas may open for business, which will influence life in the Arctic in both positive and negative ways. The economic possibilities are unlimited. Natural resources ranging from fossil fuels to minerals are found in the region in abundance. Alaska's gold rush opened the doors to wide-scale exploitation of the American side of the Arctic in the nineteenth century, recently replaced by large oil drilling operations along the Arctic coast. The potential for Russia, whose coastline along the Arctic Ocean is the longest, is even greater. With our increasing ability to extract minerals even in difficult conditions, the geopolitics of the northern polar world is entering a complex new stage.

Climate change may also produce many unfortunate consequences. Transportation and housing have always been problematic because of the permafrost, or permanently frozen ground, which covers immense areas of northern Russia, Canada, and Alaska. Summer temperatures thaw the upper layer of the soil, which becomes an active force whose movement damages infrastructure such as roads, railroads, and the foundations of buildings. The problem will worsen if increased temperatures due to climate change contribute to a deepening of the active layer.

The Farthest Corner of the World: Antarctica

Covered with thick glacial ice, and with temperatures that can fall below –100°F (–73°C), the continent of Antarctica remains in a true

Left Bylot Island is part of Sirmilik National Park, in Canada's High Arctic. Mountainous terrain, ice-caps, and glaciers form much of the island's landscape, and, though rugged, the island has ample tundra vegetation, and is a nesting and breeding ground for many species of birds.

Above Perhaps the best known of the Antarctic seals, the Weddell seal *(Leptonychotes weddellii)* lives farther south than any other mammal, as far as McMurdo Sound, 800 miles (1,280 km) from the South Pole. These placid creatures are often found in large groups on fast pack ice, and can easily be approached by humans, but spend most of their time safe from predators in the frigid waters below the ice. Hunted in the past for oil, food, and skins, their numbers are currently stable.

Below Icebergs undergo a constant process of sculpting by wind and water. The results are often astonishing, and usually photogenic. Tourists are sometimes tempted to sail close to arches like this one, or even sail through them, though they can collapse at any time under their own weight. Icebergs never stop changing shape as they lose balance, tip, then roll into new positions.

sense the farthest corner of the world. With its cover of ice it appears uniform, with only 2 percent of the continent not hidden by ice that on average is about 1½ miles (2.3 km) thick. Beneath that ice, however, lie mountain ranges, ice-scoured valleys, low plateaus, and numerous islands. The unknown though long guessed-at landmass was first sighted from a Russian vessel in 1820, and by the mid-1800s explorers who sailed along its coasts had realized it was large enough to be considered a continent. Including its icecap, it is larger in area than either Europe or Australia; without it, Antarctica would be the smallest continent.

Norwegian whaling master Henryk Johann Bull made the first known landing on Antarctica's shores in 1895, and inland exploration began in 1901. Roald Amundsen, benefitting from the survival skills he had learned in the Canadian Arctic, became the first to reach the South Pole in December 1911. He managed to return and tell his story, unlike his less fortunate British rival Robert Falcon Scott, who perished in the icy wastes along with his party in March 1912. Looking back at the history of polar explorations, the public remembers those who conquered the odds, yet there were many others who failed in their pursuit of fame. Reaching the South Pole today requires much less effort.

The undisturbed Antarctic environment offers an array of possibilities for scientific study of Earth's geological past, and some 64 stations and recording posts are currently operated by 26 countries. Although it could offer many natural resources, Antarctica has not been opened up to any form of commercial exploitation. In 1959 an international treaty intended to conserve existing conditions banned all activities related to commercial use and military activities.

Far left King penguins *(Aptenodytes patagonicus)* prefer breeding grounds on temperate–cool islands with low bare ground. They prefer to be close to the sea, a convenient food source, but will sometimes travel great distances from their breeding grounds to find food.

Bouvet Island
(Norway)
SOUTHERN
OCEAN
French Southern and
Antarctic Lands
(France)
Heard and
McDonald Islands
(Australia)
Peter I Island
(Norway)
South Pole
ANTARCTICA
South Geomagnetic
Pole (2003)
SOUTHERN
OCEAN
South Magnetic
Pole (2003)

Right The U-shape of Wright Valley is typical of glacially eroded valleys—ice-free valleys are a rarity in Antarctica.

ANTARCTICA

Official name Antarctica
Land area 5,482,651 square miles (14,200,000 km²)
Border countries None
Capital None
Highest & lowest points Vinson Massif 16,066 feet (4,897 m); Bentley Subglacial Trench –8,383 feet (–2,555 m)
Climate Cold polar desert
Population No permanent population
Government Antarctic Treaty
Currency None
Human Development Index Not available

Above right Despite cold dry conditions Antarctica supports many terrestrial plants, especially along the Antarctic Peninsula.

Below Deception Island is situated in the South Shetland Islands off the Antarctic Peninsula. An active volcano, the island has steaming beaches, ash-layered glaciers, and a flooded caldera that makes a perfect natural harbor for visiting ships.

Antarctica

Map Reference Pages 436–437

When Antarctica split from the rest of Gondwanaland and drifted southward over the South Pole, its role as the engine room of the world's weather fell into place. The ice cap grew to cover almost the entire continent and Antarctica is now the coldest, driest, highest, and windiest continent on Earth.

Physical Geography

Under the ice, Antarctica is formed of two very different landmasses. West Antarctica is largely low-lying land and islands, but also having the highest peak and the mountain spine of the Antarctic Peninsula. The Transantarctic Mountains delineate the boundary with East Antarctica.

The air is generally too cold to hold much moisture so Antarctica is a cold desert—the ice comes from innumerable small snowfalls over a long time. Most sunlight is reflected back by the ice into space. A series of cyclonic storms endlessly circles the continent from west to east, producing what sailors refer to as the roaring forties, the furious fifties, and the screaming sixties. The warmest and wettest part of the continent is the Antarctic Peninsula, where more land protrudes through the ice and wildlife can find places to establish breeding colonies.

Population/Culture

There is no indigenous Antarctic population. Only scientists and their support staff live there. Some 30,000 tourists visit during the summer months of November to March. Most scientists leave at the end of summer, too. There is no industry and mining has been prohibited until at least 2048 by the Madrid Protocol.

Administration/Government

The governance of the Antarctic is unique. After it was discovered numerous territorial claims were made, the largest of which was Australia's claim of 42 percent. Both Russia and the USA were very active in Antarctic exploration and science, but neither ever made a claim or accepted other claims.

After the International Geophysical Year (1957–1958) showed that scientists of many countries could work together, the Antarctic Treaty was signed by 12 participating nations. It now has 46 signatories. Effectively, the continent's affairs are run through the annual Antarctic Treaty Consultative Meeting and the Antarctic Treaty Secretariat in Argentina. Antarctic regulations are often legislated into the national law of signatories.

Even the area covered by the Antarctic Treaty is unusual. The Antarctic (as defined by the treaty) is the entire area south of 60°S parallel. The area within this is the Antarctic, the continent itself is Antarctica.

Wildlife

While the geopolitical boundary is 60°S, the physical boundary is the Antarctic Convergence—the circumpolar line around the bottom of the world between 40°S and 60°S where cold polar water meets the warmer water of the Southern Ocean.

There are many plants in Antarctica, but of some 800 species only two are vascular plants: Antarctic hair grass *(Deschampsia antarctica)* and pearlwort *(Colobanthus quitensis)*. The majority of plants growing in this harsh environment are lichens, mosses, liverworts, fungi, algae, and phytoplankton. Similarly, the only land fauna of the Antarctic are invertebrates and many of those are parasites found on seals and penguins. Some 45 bird species live in the Antarctic, and 18 of these are penguins. The emperor is the largest penguin; other penguin species found there include Adélies, gentoos, and chinstraps. The Southern Ocean is the habitat of the great albatross and the feeding ground for many whales, dolphins, and seals.

MILESTONE EVENTS

1773 James Cook is first to cross the Antarctic Circle

1820 First documented sightings of Antarctic Peninsula by Fabian von Bellingshausen, and Smith and Bransfield

1823 James Weddell, on the *Jane*, reaches 74°15'S in the Weddell Sea

1898 De Gerlache and Belgica expedition overwinter in Antarctica

1901 Robert Falcon Scott leads Discover expedition for first attempt to reach the South Pole

1908 Ernest Shackleton leads Nimrod expedition that comes to within 100 miles (161 km) of the South Pole

December 14, 1911 Roald Amundsen reaches the South Pole

1911 Scott leads Terra Nova expedition that reaches South Pole on January 17, but the whole party of six die on return trip

1914 Shackleton leads Endurance expedition to attempt crossing the Antarctic continent; the ship is crushed in the ice but all escape

1957 International Geophysical Year begins—much of Antarctica is surveyed

1958 Commonwealth Transantarctic Expedition under Dr Vivian Fuchs and Sir Edmund Hillary complete joint crossing of Antarctica

1959 Antarctic Treaty signed

1991 Madrid Protocol designates Antarctica as a "natural reserve, devoted to peace and science" until at least 2048

2007–08 International Polar Year

Bouvet Island

Map Reference Pages 76–77

Discovered in 1739 by French explorer Jean-Baptiste-Charles Bouvet de Lozier, this glacier-covered island was next seen in 1808, and the first landing on its rugged shore was by the American sealer Benjamin Morrell in 1822. Three years later, Captain Norris, a British whaler, claimed it for Britain, naming it Liverpool Island. In 1928 Britain relinquished its claim after Lars Christensen and his whaling crew spent a month there in 1927, and claimed it for Norway. Declared a nature reserve in 1971, it is administered by Norway's Polar Department of the Ministry of Justice and Police. It remains unoccupied and rarely visited. Volcanic Bouvet Island is the southernmost island of the Mid-Atlantic Ridge that extends from Norway's Jan Mayen Island in the High Arctic.

Bouvet Island is the sub-Antarctic's most remote island. The nearest people are in Cape Town 1,553 miles (2,500 km) to the northeast, nevertheless it has been assigned its own web prefix. Unexplained events have occurred on the island: In 1979 a US satellite detected a flash of light near the island that may have been a nuclear detonation, a meteor, or a misreading by the satellite. Equally odd was the discovery of a lifeboat and supplies in 1964.

French Southern and Antarctic Lands

Map Reference Page 310

Since 2007, the far-flung French Southern and Antarctic Lands have included the Îles Éparses, tropical islands scattered around Madagascar, as well as other islands, archipelagoes and the Adélie Coast on Antarctica. The largest port of the expanded territory is Îles Kerguélen, an archipelago of one large and 300 small islands with a total land area of about 2,786 square miles (7,215 km^2), populated by up to 100 scientists at Port-aux-Français. The Îles Crozet, an expansive archipelago with a land area of 125 square miles (325 km^2), was claimed for France in 1772. The main island, Île de la Possession, covers 58 square miles (150 km^2). Île Amsterdam et Île Saint-Paul consists of two islands. Île Amsterdam is volcanic, has an area

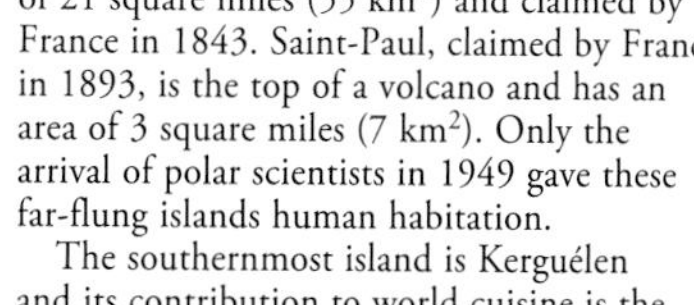

of 21 square miles (55 km^2) and claimed by France in 1843. Saint-Paul, claimed by France in 1893, is the top of a volcano and has an area of 3 square miles (7 km^2). Only the arrival of polar scientists in 1949 gave these far-flung islands human habitation.

The southernmost island is Kerguélen and its contribution to world cuisine is the Kerguélen cabbage *(Pringlea antiscorbutica)*, discovered by James Cook. It was eaten by early sailors as a dietary supplement to prevent scurvy: It contains an essential oil rich in vitamin C. Though most cabbages are insect pollinated, the Kerguélen cabbage has necessarily adapted to wind pollination.

Heard Island and McDonald Islands

Map Reference Pages 424–425

Inscribed onto the World Heritage List in 1997, this volcanic island group 2,485 miles (4,000 km) southwest of Western Australia consists of the small ice-free McDonald Islands and the much larger Heard Island, which is 80 percent glaciated. Mawson's Peak, located on the Beg Ben Massif that dominates Heard Island, is the highest mountain on Australian territory and an active volcano. The last major eruption was in 1992.

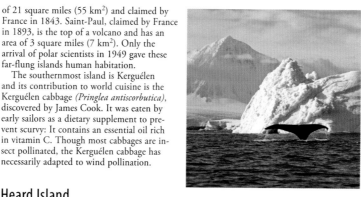

The first confirmed sighting of Heard Island by American Captain John Heard in 1853 and of the McDonalds by William McDonald in 1854 were followed by a period of intense sealing. Over 50 expeditions hunting elephant seals wiped out most of the animals by 1859, though sealers continued to visit until 1877. The islands were transferred from British to Australian control in 1947 and an Australian base was located there until 1955. There is no permanent human population and no introduced species. The wide range of wildlife includes the world's largest macaroni penguin colony and a rapidly expanding king penguin population.

At 25,096 square miles (65,000 km^2), when declared in 2002, the Heard Island and McDonald Islands Marine Reserve was the world's largest fully protected marine reserve. The largest colony of king penguins has over 25,000 breeding pairs. Gentoo and rockhopper penguins also breed there. The large macaroni penguin colony may have reached a million breeding pairs at its peak, with a similar number on McDonald Island. The Heard Island sheathbill and cormorant are the only birds endemic to the island.

Left Humpback whales are large and relatively slow-moving, making them easy prey for hunters, which brought them to the brink of extinction. In the last ten years their numbers have increased.

Left A Weddell seal *(Leptonychotes weddellii)* poking its head through a breathing hole in the Antarctic ice. In winter, seals use their teeth to create holes in the ice, sometimes wearing them down to the extent they are unable to feed or create new breathing holes and so drown.

BOUVET ISLAND

Official name Bouvet Island (Bouvetøya)
Land area 19 square miles (49 km^2)
Capital None
Climate Maritime Antarctic
Population No permanent population
Government Dependency of Norway
Currency None

FRENCH SOUTHERN AND ANTARCTIC LANDS

Official name Territory of the French Southern and Antarctic Lands (Territoire des Terres Australes et Antarctiques Françaises)
Land area 2,992 square miles (7,748 km^2)
Capital None
Climate Maritime Antarctic to tropical
Population No permanent population
Government Overseas territory of France
Currency None

HEARD ISLAND AND MCDONALD ISLANDS

Official name Territory of Heard Island and McDonald Islands
Land area 150 square miles (388 km^2)
Capital None
Climate Maritime Antarctic
Population No permanent population
Government Territory of Australia
Currency None

ADAPTIVE EVOLUTION

The building block of the numerically rich but species poor Antarctic wildlife pyramid is krill, the small crustacean that feeds on diatoms, which are microscopic single-celled plants. Krill are the food of fish, seals, whales, and birds and it's thought that there may be a greater biomass of krill than any other single species. It is typical of the Antarctic that of some 20,000 species of fish in the world only about 120 are found in Antarctic waters, and most of those live in Antarctic bottom waters. Antarctic fish have glycoproteins, anti-freeze compounds that depress the freezing point of the water in their bodies.

Another Southern Ocean adaptation is exhibited by albatross (pictured) that have hollow, yet strong wing bones reinforced by struts. When flying, albatross use the prevailing wind to keep them aloft, so they expend no more energy than when sitting on their nests. They are such exceptional flying machines that, even when they need to return regularly to feed their chicks, their far-ranging foraging flights can cover 5,000 miles (4,971 km) within a week.

But perhaps the most exceptional adaptation is that of the emperor penguin. As they don't fly, all penguins have developed heavy layers of fat, and the veins to their legs are located around their arteries so that warm blood is cooled before reaching the feet and cold blood is warmed before it reaches the penguin's heart. Only the emperor penguin stays on the ice over winter, where males nurse their chicks, balancing them on their feet under an insulating skin fold. To keep warm, colonies of males with their chicks huddle together, constantly changing position within the huddle so each bird gets equal time in the warm middle as well as at the exposed edges.

Below Emperor Penguins, Dawson-Lambton Glacier, Weddell Sea, Antarctica. Penguins are flightless; their feathers, adapted to freezing conditions, are waterproof, which keeps their skin dry and warm.

ASIA
NORTH AMERICA
SEA OF OKHOTSK
BERING SEA
CHUKCHI SEA
BEAUFORT SEA
ARCTIC OCEAN
PACIFIC OCEAN
VOSTOCHNO-SIBIRSKOYE MORE
(East Siberian Sea)
MORE LAPTEVYKH
(Laptev Sea)
POLUOSTROV KAMCHATKA
Ostrov Sakhalin
Kuril'skiye Ostrova
Kuril-Kamchatka Trench
Aleutian Trench
Aleutian Ridge
Aleutian Islands
Aleutian Basin
Shirshov Ridge
Bowers Bank
Bowers Ridge
Kamchatka Basin
Zaliv Shelikhova
Anadyrskiy Zaliv
Bering Strait
St Lawrence I.
Pribilof Islands
Bristol Bay
Gulf of Alaska
Cook Inlet
Kodiak I.
Alaska Peninsula
Fox Islands
Shumagin Islands
Patton Seamount
Kodiak Seamount
Pratt Seamount
Gilbert Seamount
Chichagof Island
Ostrov Vrangelya
Proliv Longa
Kucherov Terrace
Wrangel Abyssal Plain
Mendeleyev Ridge
Mendeleyev Ridge Abyssal Plain
Chukchi Abyssal Plain
Chukchi Plateau
Northwind Abyssal Plain
Northwind Ridge
Northwind Escarpment
Canada Abyssal Plain
CANADA BASIN
MAKAROV BASIN
Pole Abyssal Plain
Novosibirskiye Ostrova
Yanskiy Zaliv
Oleneksiy Zaliv
Point Barrow
Mackenzie Bay
Banks Island
Victoria Island
Amundsen Gulf
Prince of Wales Str.
Great Bear L.
Queen Maud Gulf
Lena
Aldan
Kolyma
Indigirka
Anadyr
Magadan
Mackenzie
North Magnetic

1:18,700,000
Lambert Conic Conformal Projection
0 200 400 600 800 kilometers
0 100 200 300 400 miles

Arctic

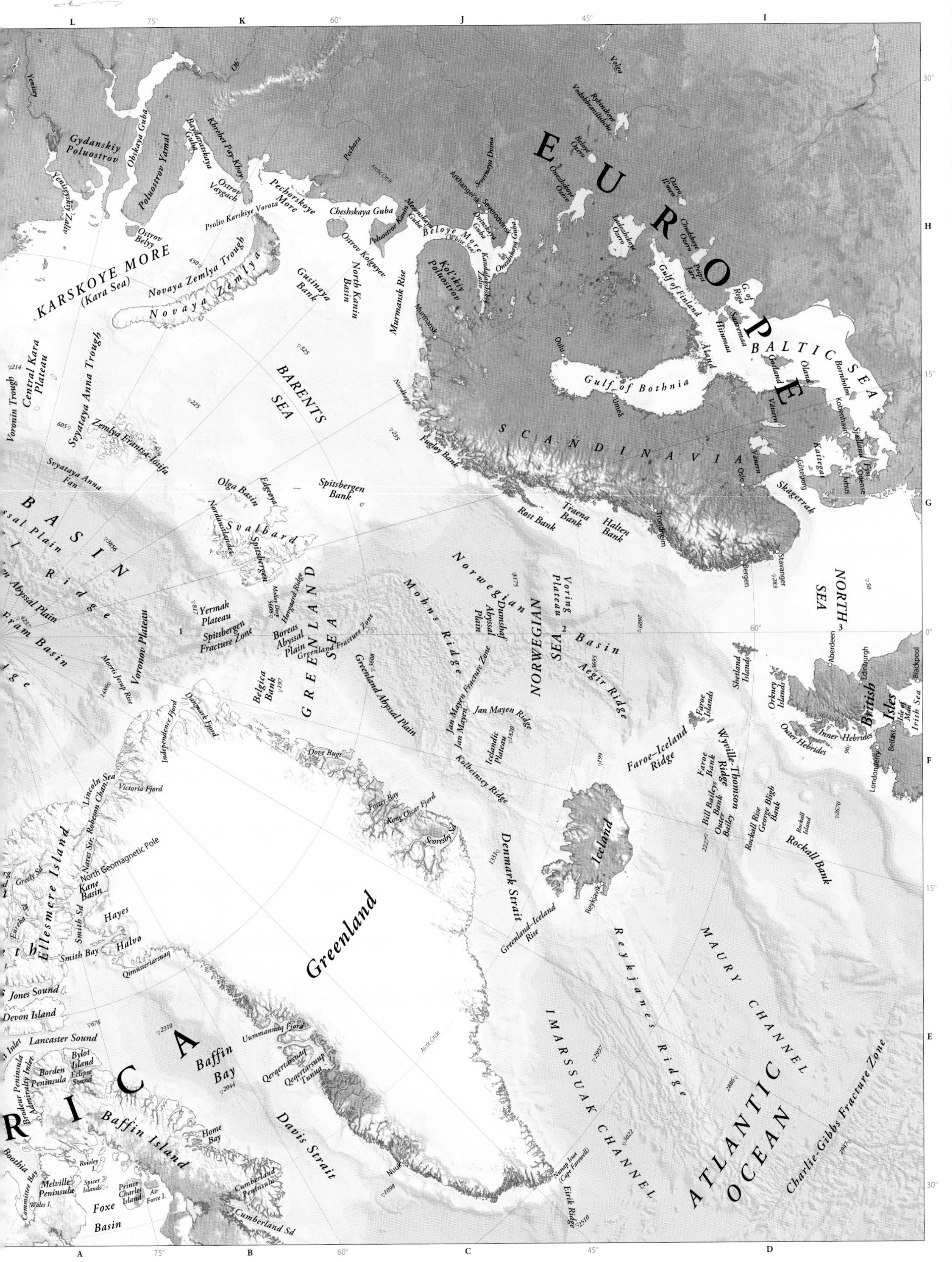
EUROPE
BARENTS SEA
KARSKOYE MORE (Kara Sea)
Novaya Zemlya
SCANDINAVIA
BALTIC SEA
Gulf of Bothnia
Gulf of Finland
NORWEGIAN SEA
GREENLAND SEA
NORTH SEA
British Isles
Iceland
Greenland
Baffin Bay
Davis Strait
Denmark Strait
ATLANTIC OCEAN
IMARSSUAK CHANNEL
MAURY CHANNEL
Reykjanes Ridge
Charlie-Gibbs Fracture Zone
Svalbard
Spitsbergen
Ellesmere Island
Baffin Island
Devon Island
Lancaster Sound
Jones Sound
Foxe Basin
Cumberland Sd
Nuuk
Reykjavik
Murmansk
Trondheim
Bergen
Stavanger
Oslo
Aberdeen
Edinburgh
Belfast
Meters
Feet

Research Stations
1. Arctowski (Poland)
2. Artigas (Uruguay)
3. Bellingshausen (Rus.)
4. Arturo Prat (Chile)
5. Comandante Ferraz (Brazil)
6. Escudero (Chile)
7. O'Higgins (Chile)
8. Great Wall (China)
9. Jubany (Arg.)
10. King Sejong (S. Korea)
11. Frei (Chile)
SOUTH AMERICA
Falkland Is
Stanley
East Falkland
West Falkland
SCOTIA SEA
South Sandwich Fracture Zone
South Orkney Is
Orcadas (Arg.)
Yaghan Basin
Drake Passage
Tierra del Fuego
Isla Grande de Tierra del Fuego
Cabo de Hornos (Cape Horn)
Río Grande
Río Gallegos
Argentinian claim (shared)
British claim (shared)
Chilean claim (shared)
South Shetland Is
Bransfield Str.
Esperanza (Arg.)
Marambio (Arg.)
Graham Land
Palmer Arch.
Vernadsky (Ukr.)
Rothera (UK)
San Martín (Arg.)
Antarctic Peninsula
Palmer Land
Black Coast
Larsen Ice Shelf
Wilkins Coast
Lassiter Coast
Orville Coast
Alexander I.
George VI Sd
English Coast
Ronne Entrance
Stange Sd
WEDDELL ABYSSAL PLAIN
Belgrano Bank
WEDDELL SEA
Ronne Ice Shelf
Korff Ice Rise
Henry Ice Rise
Zumberge Coast
Fowler Ice Rise
Carlson Inlet
Skytrain Ice Rise
Evans Ice Stream
Berkner I.
Filchner Ice Shelf
Halley (UK)
Brunt Ice Shelf
Caird Coast
Coats Land
Belgrano II (Arg.)
Riiser-Larsen Ice Shelf
Princess Martha Coast
Shackleton Range
Pensacola Mts
Patriot Hills (Chile)
Vinson Massif 4897
Ellsworth Mountains
Ellsworth Land
BELLINGSHAUSEN SEA
Charcot Deep Sea Fan
Peter I Island
De Gerlache Seamounts
SOUTHERN OCEAN
BELLINGSHAUSEN ABYSSAL PLAIN
unclaimed territory
Eights Coast
Abbot Ice Shelf
Thurston I.
Walgreen Coast
Pine Island B.
Thwaites Glacier Tongue
Kohler Ra.
AMUNDSEN SEA
Amundsen Ridges
Marie Byrd Seamounts
WEST ANTARCTICA
Hollick-Kenyon Plateau
Marie Byrd Land
Whitmore Mountains
Thiel Mts
ANTARCTICA
Rockefeller Plateau
Ford Ranges
Hobbs Coast
Ruppert Coast
Saunders Coast
Sulzberger Bay
Siple Coast
Shirase Coast
Roosevelt Island
Ross
Edward VII Pen.
Udintsev Fracture Zone
PACIFIC-ANTARCTIC RIDGE
Antarctic Circle
New Zealand

1:18,700,000
Polar Stereographic Projection

250 500 750 1000 kilometers
125 miles 250 miles 375 miles 500 miles

Antarctic

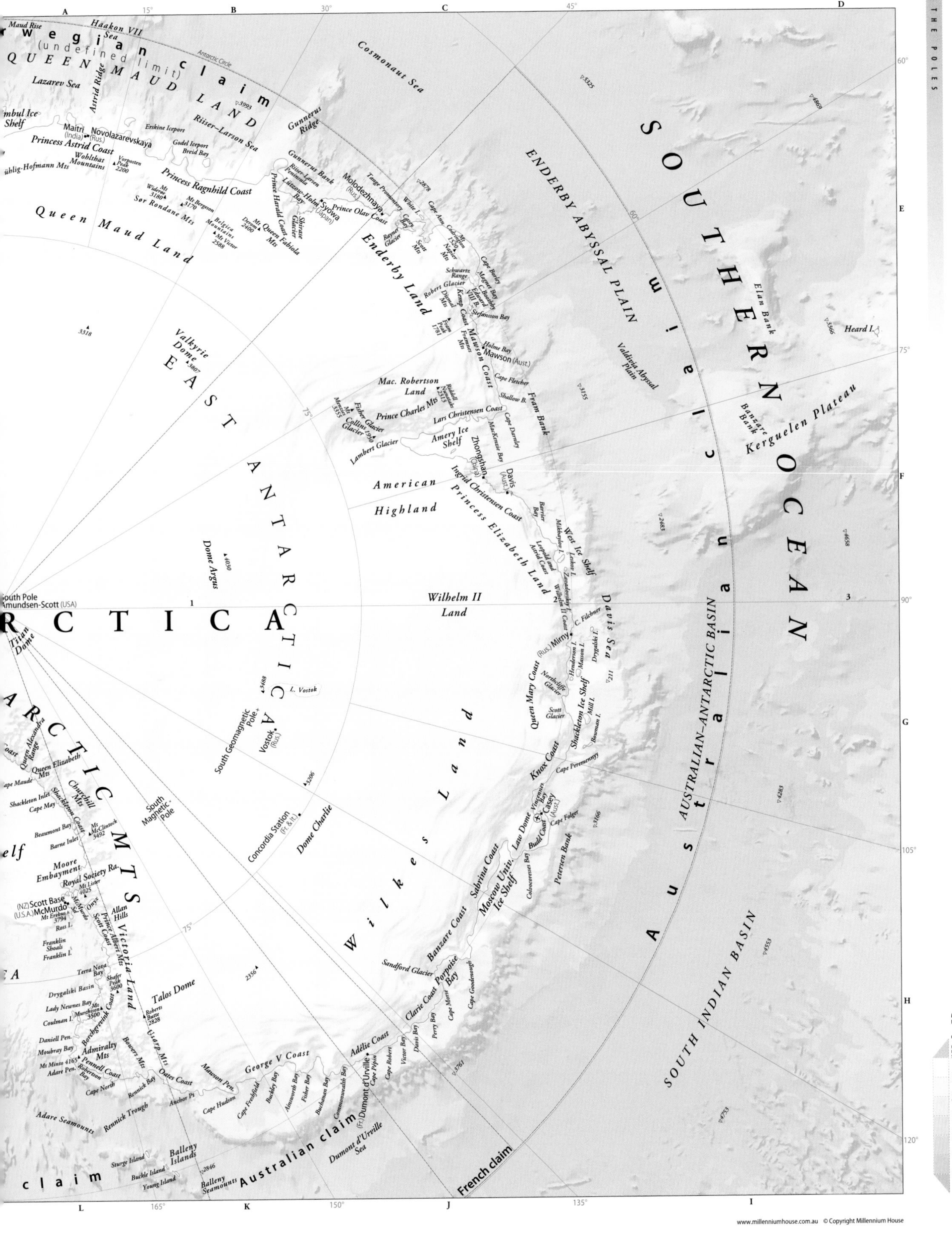

Cosmonaut Sea
SOUTHERN OCEAN
ENDERBY ABYSSAL PLAIN
Valdivia Abyssal Plain
Elan Bank
Heard I.
Banzare Bank
Kerguelen Plateau
AUSTRALIAN–ANTARCTIC BASIN
SOUTH INDIAN BASIN
Davis Sea
Fram Bank
Petersen Bank
Haakon VII Sea
Lazarev Sea
Riiser-Larsen Sea
Gunnerus Ridge
Gunnerus Bank
Astrid Ridge
Maud Rise
QUEEN MAUD LAND
Queen Maud Land
Princess Astrid Coast
Princess Ragnhild Coast
Prince Olav Coast
Prince Harald Coast
Enderby Land
Kemp Coast
Mawson Coast
Mac. Robertson Land
Prince Charles Mts
Lars Christensen Coast
Amery Ice Shelf
Lambert Glacier
Ingrid Christensen Coast
American Highland
Princess Elizabeth Land
West Ice Shelf
Wilhelm II Land
Wilhelm II Coast
Queen Mary Coast
Shackleton Ice Shelf
Knox Coast
Budd Coast
Sabrina Coast
Moscow Univ. Ice Shelf
Banzare Coast
Clarie Coast
Adélie Coast
George V Coast
Oates Coast
Pennell Coast
Wilkes Land
EAST ANTARCTICA
ANTARCTICA
TRANSANTARCTIC MTS
Valkyrie Dome
Dome Argus
Dome Charlie
Talos Dome
Titan Dome
South Pole Amundsen-Scott (USA)
South Geomagnetic Pole
South Magnetic Pole
Vostok (Rus.)
L. Vostok
Concordia Station (Fr. & It.)
Mawson (Aust.)
Davis (Aust.)
Zhongshan (China)
Mirnyy (Rus.)
Casey (Aust.)
Maitri (India)
Novolazarevskaya (Rus.)
Molodezhnaya (Rus.)
Syowa (Japan)
Dumont d'Urville (Fr.)
Dumont d'Urville Sea
(NZ) Scott Base
(U.S.A.) McMurdo
Mt Erebus 3794
Victoria Land
Queen Alexandra Range
Queen Elizabeth Mts
Churchill Mts
Shackleton Coast
Royal Society Ra.
Allan Hills
Prince Albert Mts
Scott Coast
Admiralty Mts
Borchgrevink Coast
Usarp Mts
Bowers Mts
Rennick Trough
Adare Seamounts
Balleny Islands
Balleny Seamounts
Sturge Island
Buckle Island
Young Island
Norwegian claim (undefined limit)
Australian claim
French claim
Antarctic Circle

Meters / Feet: 0; Land below sea level; 100 / 328; 200 / 656; 1000 / 3281; 2000 / 6562; 4000 / 13123; 6000 / 19685

Gazetteer

FOREIGN TERMS

Açude Reservoir or lake *PORTUGUESE*
Ada, Adası Island *TURKISH*
Adaları Islands *TURKISH*
Adrar Hill or mountain *BERBER*
Akra, Akrotirio Cape or point *GREEK*
Älv, -älv, -älven River *SWEDISH*
Archipel Archipelago *FRENCH*
Archipiélago Archipelago *SPANISH*
Arquipélago Archipelago *PORTUGUESE*
Arrecife Reef *SPANISH*
Arroio River *PORTUGUESE, SPANISH*
Bahía Bay *SPANISH*
Baḩr Sea or large body of water *ARABIC*
Baía Bay *PORTUGUESE*
Baie Bay *FRENCH*
Banco Reef *SPANISH*
Banjaran Range *MALAY*
Barragem Dam or reservoir *PORTUGUESE*
Boca River mouth *PORTUGUESE, SPANISH*
Buchta Bay *UKRAINIAN*
Bugt Bay *DANISH*
Bukit Hill *INDONESIAN, MALAY*
Burnu Cape or point *TURKISH*
Cabo Cape *PORTUGUESE, SPANISH*
Cachoeira Waterfall *PORTUGUESE*
Caleta Bay or inlet *SPANISH*
Câmpia Plain *ROMANIAN*
Caño River *SPANISH*
Cap Cape *FRENCH*
Capo Cape *ITALIAN*
Cayo, Cayos Island, Islands *SPANISH*
Cerro Mountain *SPANISH*
Chaîne Mountain range *FRENCH*
Chott Lake or swamp *ARABIC*
Cienago Swamp *SPANISH*
Cima Mountain *ITALIAN*
Cordillera Mountain chain *SPANISH*
Colle Pass *ITALIAN*
Collina Hill or mountain *ITALIAN*
Cordillera Mountain chain *SPANISH*
Costa Coast *SPANISH*
Côte Coast *FRENCH*
Cuchillo Mountain range *SPANISH*
Dağ, Dağı Mountain or mountain range *TURKISH*
Dağlar, Dağları Mountains *TURKISH*
Dahr Escarpment *ARABIC*
Danau Lake *INDONESIAN*
Dao Island *CHINESE*
Đao Island *VIETNAMESE*
Dasht Desert *PERSIAN*
Denizi Sea *TURKISH*
Desierto Desert *SPANISH*
-do Island *KOREAN*
Eilean Island *GAELIC*
Embalse Dam or reservoir *SPANISH*
Ensenada Bay or cove *SPANISH*
Erg Large sand-covered desert area or sand dunes *ARABIC*
Estero Estuary or inlet *SPANISH*
Estrecho Strait *SPANISH*
Étang Lagoon or lake *FRENCH*
Ežeras Lake *LITHUANIAN*
Fiume River *ITALIAN*
-fjell Mountain *NORWEGIAN*
Falaise Cliff or escarpment *FRENCH*
Fleuve River *FRENCH*
Ghard Sand dune or sand dunes *ARABIC*
Gjiri Bay *ALBANIAN*
Gletscher Glacier *DANISH, GERMAN*
Gol, Golü Lake *TURKISH*
Golfe Gulf *FRENCH*
Golfo Gulf *ITALIAN, PORTUGUESE, SPANISH*
Gora Mountain *BULGARIAN, CROATIAN, RUSSIAN, SERBIAN, SLOVENIAN*
Gory Mountain range *RUSSIAN*
Guba Bay *RUSSIAN*
Gunung Mountain *INDONESIAN, MALAY*
Hamada, Hammadat Rocky desert plateau *ARABIC*
-hana Point *JAPANESE*
He River *CHINESE*
Hòn Island *VIETNAMESE*
Hora Mountain *CZECH, UKRAINIAN*
Île Island *FRENCH*
Îles Islands *FRENCH*
Ilha Island *PORTUGUESE*
Ilhas Islands *PORTUGUESE*
Isla Island *SPANISH*
Islas Islands *SPANISH*
Isola Island *ITALIAN*
Isole Islands *ITALIAN*
Istmo Isthmus *SPANISH*
Jabal, Jebel Mountain *ARABIC*
-jarv, -jarvi Lake or lagoon *ESTONIAN*
-jarvi Lake or lagoon *FINNISH*
Jazīrat Island *ARABIC*
Jezero Lake *SLOVENIAN*
Jeziero Lake *POLISH*
Jiang River *CHINESE*
-jima Island *JAPANESE*
-jökull Glacier or ice cap *ICELANDIC*
Kap, Kapp Cape *DANISH, GERMAN, NORWEGIAN*
Kavir Salt desert *PERSIAN*
Kepulauan Archipelago or islands *INDONESIAN*
Khrebet Mountain range *RUSSIAN*
Khālij Bay or gulf *ARABIC*
Khao Mountain or peak *THAI*
Ko Island *THAI*
-ko Lake *JAPANESE*
Kolĭ Lake *KAZAKH*
Kólpos Gulf *GREEK*
Körfezi Gulf or bay *TURKISH*
Kuh, Kuh-e Mountains *PERSIAN*
Kūli Lake *UZBEK*
Kyun Island *BURMESE*
Lac Lake *FRENCH*
Lacul Lake *ROMANIAN*
Laem Cape or point *THAI*
Lago, Laguna Lake *ITALIAN, PORTUGUESE, SPANISH*
Laut Sea *INDONESIAN, MALAY*
Liedao Islands *CHINESE*
Limnothalassa Bay or inlet *GREEK*
Llano Plain *SPANISH*
Ormos Bay *GREEK*
Loch, Lough Lake *GAELIC*
Maja Mountain *ALBANIAN*
Mar Sea *SPANISH*
Mare Sea *ITALIAN*
Massif Mountain *FRENCH*
Meer Lake *DUTCH, GERMAN*
Mesa, Meseta Plateau or tableland *SPANISH*
Melkosopochnik Sandy plateau with small hills *RUSSIAN*
-misaki Point *JAPANESE*
Mont, Montagne Mountain *FRENCH*
Monte Mountain *ITALIAN, PORTUGUESE, SPANISH*
Monti Mountain *ITALIAN*
Monts Mountain range *FRENCH*
More Sea *RUSSIAN*
Mui Cape or Point *VIETNAMESE*
Mys Cape or Point *RUSSIAN*
Nam River *BURMESE, LAOTIAN*
Nehri Stream *TURKISH*
Nevado Mountain range *SPANISH*
Nisoi Islands *GREEK*
Nizmennost' Lowlands, plain *RUSSIAN*
Novaya New *BELORUSSIAN, RUSSIAN*
Nuur Lake **Mongolian**
Ø, Øer Island *DANISH*
Oblast' Administrative division *RUSSIAN*
Okrug Administrative area *RUSSIAN*
Ormos Bay *GREEK*
Oros Mountain or mountains *GREEK*
Ostrov, Ostrova Island, islands *RUSSIAN*
Ouad, Oued River or wadi *ARABIC*
-øy, -øya Island, islands *NORWEGIAN*
Ozero Lake *RUSSIAN*
Pantà Reservoir or lake *CATALAN*
Passo Pass *ITALIAN*
Pegunungan Mountain range *INDONESIAN, MALAY*
Pendi Basin *CHINESE*
Péninsula Peninsula *SPANISH*
Péninsule Peninsula *FRENCH*
Peski Desert or sands *RUSSIAN*
Pic Peak *FRENCH*
Pico Peak *SPANISH*
Pik Peak *RUSSIAN*
Pivostriv Peninsula *UKRAINIAN*
Plaine Plain *FRENCH*
Planalto Plateau *PORTUGUESE*
Planina Mountain, Mountains *BULGARIAN*
Pointe Cape or point *FRENCH*
Poluostrov Peninsula *RUSSIAN*
Ponta Cape or point *PORTUGUESE*
Porto Port *ITALIAN, PORTUGUESE, SPANISH*
Pôrto Port *PORTUGUESE*
Potamos River *GREEK*
Presa Dam, reservoir, or lake *SPANISH*
Proliv Strait *RUSSIAN*
Promontório Promontory *SPANISH*
Puerto Port *SPANISH*
Pulau Island *INDONESIAN, MALAY*
Punta Cape or point *ITALIAN*
Puy Hill or peak *FRENCH*
Ra's, Raas Cape or point *ARABIC*
Ramlat Desert *ARABIC*
Represa Dam or reservoir *PORTUGUESE*
Ribeirão, Rio River *PORTUGUESE*
Río River *SPANISH*
Rivière River *FRENCH*
Rubha Cape *GAELIC*
Sabkhat Salt flat or salt marsh *ARABIC*
Sainte Saint *FRENCH*
Salina, Salinas Salt pan *SPANISH*
San, Santa, Santo Saint *ITALIAN, PORTUGUESE, SPANISH*
-san Mountain or volcano *JAPANESE*
São Saint *PORTUGUESE*
Selat Strait *INDONESIAN*
Semenanjung Peninsula *INDONESIAN*
Serra Mountain range *PORTUGUESE*
Serranía, Sierra Mountain range *SPANISH*
Shamo Desert *CHINESE*
Shan Mountain or mountains *CHINESE*
-shima Island *JAPANESE*
-shotō Islands *JAPANESE*
Slieve Mountain *GAELIC*
Sud South *FRENCH*
Sul South *PORTUGUESE*
Sund Sound *DANISH, GERMAN, NORWEGIAN, SWEDISH*
Sur South *SPANISH*
Tanjona Cape or point *MALAGASY*
Tanjong Cape or point *MALAY*
Tanjung Cape or point *INDONESIAN*
Tasik Lake *MALAY*
Tassili Plateau *BERBER*
Techniti Limni Reservoir *GREEK*
Tell Mountain *ARABIC*
Teluk Bay or gulf *INDONESIAN, MALAY*
Tierra Land *SPANISH*
Ujung Cape or point *INDONESIAN*
Vinh Bay or gulf *VIETNAMESE*
Vodokhranilishche Dam or reservoir *RUSSIAN*
Volcan Volcano *FRENCH*
Volcán Volcano *SPANISH*
Vozyera Lake *BELORUSSIAN*
Vozvyshennost' Region *RUSSIAN*
Vūng Bay *VIETNAMESE*
Wadi Watercourse *ARABIC*
Wāḩāt Oasis *ARABIC*
-wan Bay *JAPANESE*
-zaki Cape *JAPANESE*
Zaliv Bay or gulf *RUSSIAN*
Zemlya Land *RUSSIAN*

ABBREVIATIONS

AO Avtonomnyy Okrug
Arch./Archip. Archipelago
At. Atoll
B. Bay
Bgt Bight
Bn Basin
Br. Bridge
C. Cape
Can. Canyon
Cd Ciudad
Chan. Channel
DC District of Columbia
Dep. Depression
E East, Eastern, Easterly
Esc. Escarpment
Est. Estuary
For. Forest
Ft. Fort
Fj. Fjord
Fr. France
FYROM Former Yugoslav Republic of Macedonia
G. Gulf
Harb. Harbor, Harbour
Hd Headland
I. Island
Is Islands
It. Italy
Isth. Isthmus
L. Lake
Lag. Lagoon
Mt Mount, Mountain
Mts Mountains
N North, Northern, Northerly
Neth. Netherlands
Pass. Passage
Pen. Peninsula
Pln Plain
Plat. Plateau
Pk Park
Pt Point
R. River, Rivers
Res. Reserve
Resr Reservoir
S South, Southern, Southerly
Sea Chan. Sea Channel
St/Ste Saint
Str. Strait
Terr. Territory
UAE United Arab Emirates
UK United Kingdom
USA United States of America
Vol. Crater Volcanic Crater
Vol. Volcano
W West, Western, Westerly

Australian States
ACT Australian Capital Territory
NSW New South Wales
NT Northern Territory
Qld Queensland
SA South Australia
Tas. Tasmania
Vic. Victoria
WA Western Australia

MAP LEGEND

POPULATED PLACES

Population	National capital	Administrative capital	Other city or town
Over 5 million	PARIS	Hyderabad	New York
1 million–5 million	BUDAPEST	Zürich	Vsevolozhsk
500,000–1 million	SKOPJE	Kraków	Argenteuil
100,000–500,000	PRIŠTINA	Ostrava	Korinthos
50,000–100,000	LUXEMBOURG	Zlín	Eastbourne
10,000–50,000	MONACO	Neuchâtel	Exmouth
Less than 10,000	VADUZ	Sarnen	Campodolcino

Research station, homestead, point of interest, historic site, tourist feature — Mawson
Built-up area

ADMINISTRATIVE FEATURES

Boundaries
International boundary – defined
International boundary – claimed, disputed, or undefined
Line of control, demarcation or ceasefire line
Internal administrative boundary – defined
Internal administrative boundary – claimed, disputed, or undefined
Other administrative boundary
Indication of extent of country or territory

Lettering Styles
ASIA — Continent name
KENYA — Country or independent nation
ALSACE — Main internal administrative area
DORSET — Other administrative area
New Caledonia (France) — Dependency (administering or parent country in parenthesis)
ARTOIS — Cultural region, historic area, or physical region or area

TRANSPORTATION

Motorway, freeway, expressway, or divided highway
Motorway, freeway, expressway, or divided highway (under construction)
Motorway, freeway, expressway, or divided highway (through a tunnel)
NOTE: Motorways are only shown at scales of 1:3 million or larger
Major road
Major road (under construction)
Major road (through a tunnel)
Secondary or minor road
Secondary or minor road (under construction)
Secondary or minor road (through a tunnel)
Track (shown in remote and sparsely populated areas only)
Primary or major railway
Primary or major railway (under contruction)
Primary or major railway (through a tunnel)
International airport
Major regional airport

OTHER FEATURES

Tropic of Cancer — Tropics and polar circles
International Date Line — International date line
50° — Graticule (lines of latitude and longitude) with value in degrees

PHYSICAL FEATURES

Lettering Styles
Holy Island — Small island or island group, peninsula, cape, reef, or other coastal feature
Shetland Islands — Major island or island group, peninsula, cape, reef, or other coastal feature
Mendip Hills — Small mountain range, plateau, valley, desert, or other landform
ANDES — Major or extensive mountain range, plateau, valley, desert, or other landform
Thames — Small hydrographic feature – river, lake, bay, gulf, glacier, channel
Loch Lomond — Large or extensive hydrographic feature – river, lake, bay, gulf, glacier, channel
Yellow Sea — Small sea name
North Sea — Large sea name
ARCTIC OCEAN — Ocean name
Chile Basin — Small ocean floor feature: ridge, trench, basin, or plateau (ocean maps only)
Perth Basin — Large ocean floor feature: ridge, trench, basin, or plateau (ocean maps only)

Hydrographic Features
Coastline or shoreline – definite
Coastline or shoreline – undefined, fluctuating, or indefinite
Major river
Minor or secondary river
Intermittent stream (main seasonal river)
Minor or secondary seasonal or intermittent river or wadi
Irrigation or drainage canal
Aqueduct
average extent of sea ice — Extent of sea ice or drift ice in polar regions
Significant waterfall, rapids, dam or barrage (major rivers only)
Reef or coral atoll
Perennial lake, reservoir, or other water body
Seasonal, intermittent or impermanent lake
Perennial salt lake (significant)
(salt) — Seasonal salt lake (significant)
(salt) — Mainly dry lake, salt pan, salt flat, or claypan
Glacier, ice cap, ice sheet, ice shelf, permanent ice, or snow
Area of swamp, marsh, or land subject to inundation
Important spring, well, waterhole, or oasis

Topographic Features
Mt Bogong 1986 — Mountain peak (height in meters above sea level)
Glacier Peak 3180 — Volcano – active or inactive (height in meters above sea level)
2025 — Ocean depth (meters below sea level) or land below sea level
Significant mountain pass
Significant escarpment or cliff
Great Wall — Significant wall or other linear man-made structure
Desert or significant area of sand

Relief
All maps portray relief using elevation layer tints based on the intervals in the diagram at right, overlaid with specially prepared hill shading to give a three- dimensional effect for the topography of the area being mapped.

Meters / Feet
6000 / 19685
5000 / 16404
4000 / 13123
3000 / 9843
2000 / 6562
1000 / 3281
500 / 1640
200 / 656
100 / 328
0
LAND BELOW SEA LEVEL
100 / 328
200 / 656
1000 / 3281
2000 / 6562
4000 / 13123
6000 / 19685

Iceland place names may incorporate two letters not used in the English language (Þ, þ and Ð, ð). The letters Þ, þ represent "Th" and are indexed as such.

118 I5 **12 Mile** British Columbia Canada
118 K6 **150 Mile House** British Columbia Canada
118 F4 **40 Mile Flats** British Columbia Canada
118 K7 **70 Mile House** British Columbia Canada

A

222 H3 **Å** Norway
382 G4 **A-chi-chih Ho** *watercourse* Xinjiang Uygur Zizhiqu China
230 B2 **A Coruña** Spain
230 B4 **A dos Cunhados** Portugal
230 B2 **A Estada** Spain
230 B2 **A Golada** Spain
230 C2 **A Gudiña** Spain
230 C2 **A Pontenova** Spain
376 F4 **A Yun Pa** Vietnam
385 J2 **A`lihe** Nei Mongol Zizhiqu China
228 F1 **Aa** *watercourse* France
226 D2 **Aachen** Germany
394 G6 **Aafrite** Syria
394 E6 **Aakrak** Syria
226 F3 **Aalen** Germany
223 P2 **Äälisjärvi** *lake* Finland
228 G1 **Aalst** Belgium
226 D2 **Aalten** Netherlands
223 N5 **Äänekoski** Finland
223 N3 **Aapajärvi** Finland
223 N3 **Aapajoki** Finland
223 M3 **Aapua** Sweden
229 I3 **Aarau** Switzerland
232 B3 **Aare** *watercourse* Switzerland
224 E5 **Aarre** Denmark
117 N5 **Aasiaat** Greenland
245 C3 **Aasleagh** Ireland
391 H3 **Āb Anbār-E Kān Sorkh** Iran
391 H4 **Āb Āqā** Iran
390 G3 **Āb-E Bāzoft** *watercourse* Iran
391 I3 **Āb-E Garm Va Sard** Iran
391 I4 **Āb Gazān** Iran
390 G3 **Āb Gonjeshk** Iran
391 H4 **Āb Kahūr** Iran
390 G3 **Āb Pardeh** Iran
391 H4 **Āb Sardū** Iran
391 I4 **Āb Shahr** Iran
391 H4 **Āb Zaminū** Iran
380 D2 **Aba** Sichuan China
305 H5 **Aba** Democratic Republic of Congo
305 F3 **Aba** Nigeria
388 E6 **Abābin** Iran
159 G2 **Abacaxis** *watercourse* Brazil
222 J4 **Abacka** Sweden
391 K4 **Abad** Pakistan
302 F4 **Abadab, Jebel** *mountain* Sudan
390 F3 **Ābādān** Iran
388 G6 **Ābādān Tappeh** Iran
390 G3 **Ābādeh** Iran
230 D3 **Abades** Spain
157 B7 **Abadiânia** Brazil
301 F2 **Abadla** Algeria
157 C7 **Abaeté** Brazil
156 B3 **Abaetetuba** Brazil
183 H3 **Abaí** Paraguay
426 1 **Abaiang** *island* Kiribati
305 F3 **Abaji** Nigeria
305 F3 **Abakaliki** Nigeria
389 P2 **Abakan** Russian Federation
389 O3 **Abakan** *watercourse* Russian Federation
305 H5 **Abala** Congo
301 G6 **Abala** Niger
301 H5 **Abalak** Niger
301 G4 **Abalessa** Algeria
237 U7 **Aban** Russian Federation
158 C4 **Abancay** Peru
391 I4 **Āband** Iran
154 B5 **Abanico** Ecuador
159 F5 **Abapó** Bolivia
388 E6 **Abarghan** Iran
391 H3 **Abarkūh** Iran
158 F5 **Abasacapán** Venezuela
388 E6 **Abasaly** Azerbaijan
387 J2 **Abashiri** Japan
132 E4 **Abasolo** Mexico
373 I6 **Abau** Papua New Guinea
225 L4 **Abava** *watercourse* Latvia
302 F5 **Abay Wenz (Blue Nile)** *watercourse* Ethiopia
389 F5 **Abaza** Russian Federation
305 H3 **Abba** Central African Republic
233 C6 **Abbasanta** Sardinia Italy
224 G5 **Abbekås** Sweden
241 H3 **Abberton Reservoir** England UK
241 I4 **Abbeville** France
130 E6 **Abbeville** Louisiana USA
119 Q7 **Abbey** Saskatchewan Canada
244 E3 **Abbey Head** *cape* Scotland UK
242 E2 **Abbey Town** Cumbria England UK
245 C4 **Abbeyfeale** Ireland
222 J4 **Abborrberg** Sweden
222 K4 **Abborrträsk** Sweden
436 R2 **Abbot Ice Shelf** Antarctica
425 M5 **Abbot Point** Qld Australia
240 E4 **Abbotsbury** Dorset England UK
118 J8 **Abbotsford** British Columbia Canada
129 J2 **Abbott** New Mexico USA
391 M2 **Abbottabad** Pakistan
303 I5 **Abd Al Kūrī** *island* Yemen
391 H3 **Ābdān Anjir** Iran
390 F3 **Ābdānān** Iran
391 H4 **Ābdasht** Iran
303 G5 **Abdelcader** Somalia
307 G1 **Abdelcader** Somalia
233 B8 **Abdi** Algeria
235 E5 **Abdürrahim** Turkey
302 C5 **Abéché** Chad
222 G4 **Abelvær** Norway
222 J4 **Abelvattnet** *lake* Sweden
426 1 **Abemama** *island* Kiribati
308 C3 **Abenab** Namibia
303 D3 **Abengourou** Côte d'Ivoire
230 D4 **Abenójar** Spain
224 E5 **Åbenrå** Denmark
226 F3 **Abens** *watercourse* Germany
226 F3 **Abensberg** Germany
304 E3 **Abeokuta** Nigeria
240 C3 **Aber Arth** Ceredigion Wales UK
240 D2 **Aber Cowarch** Gwynedd Wales UK
240 C2 **Aberaeron** Ceredigion Wales UK
240 D2 **Aberangell** Gwynedd Wales UK
244 F3 **Aberchirder** Aberdeenshire Scotland UK
240 D3 **Aberdare** Rhondda Cynon Taff Wales UK
240 C2 **Aberdaron** Gwynedd Wales UK
308 D6 **Aberdeen** South Africa
244 F3 **Aberdeen** Aberdeen Scotland UK
244 F3 **Aberdeen** *admin. area* Scotland UK
130 G4 **Aberdeen** Mississippi USA
125 P4 **Aberdeen** South Dakota USA
124 D3 **Aberdeen** Washington USA
117 J6 **Aberdeen Lake** Nunavut Canada
130 G4 **Aberdeen Lake** Mississippi USA
244 E3 **Aberdeenshire** *admin. area* Scotland UK
240 C2 **Aberdyfi** Gwynedd Wales UK
240 C1 **Aberffraw** Isle of Anglesey Wales UK
244 D4 **Aberfoyle** Stirling Scotland UK
303 F5 **Äbergelē** Ethiopia
240 D3 **Abergwynfi** Neath Port Talbot Wales UK
240 D2 **Abergynolwyn** Gwynedd Wales UK
244 F4 **Aberlady** East Lothian Scotland UK
240 D2 **Aberllefenni** Gwynedd Wales UK
129 L4 **Abernathy** Texas USA
240 C2 **Aberporth** Ceredigion Wales UK
228 B2 **Abers, Les** *region* France
240 C2 **Abersoch** Gwynedd Wales UK
124 E5 **Abert, Lake** Oregon USA
240 C2 **Aberystwyth** Ceredigion Wales UK
302 B5 **Abgué** Chad
390 E6 **Abhā** Saudi Arabia
388 F7 **Abhar** Iran
303 G5 **Abhe, Lac** *lake* Djibouti
305 F3 **Abia** *admin. area* Nigeria
302 E5 **Abiad, Bahr el (White Nile)** *watercourse* Sudan
155 E5 **Abico** Brazil
304 D3 **Abidjan** Côte d'Ivoire
155 F5 **Abidos** Brazil
130 B4 **Abilene** Texas USA
241 G3 **Abinger Hammer** Surrey England UK
244 E5 **Abington** South Lanarkshire Scotland UK
129 I2 **Abiquiu Reservoir** New Mexico USA
222 K2 **Abisko nationalpark** *park* Sweden
121 O7 **Abitibi** *watercourse* Ontario Canada
117 L9 **Abitibi, Lake** Ontario Canada
222 H4 **Åbjørvatnet** *lake* Norway
391 I2 **Ābkesht** Iran
241 F3 **Ablington** Gloucestershire England UK
302 E2 **Abnūb** Egypt
391 M3 **Abohar** Punjab India
304 D3 **Aboisso** Côte d'Ivoire
223 M2 **Abojávri** *lake* Norway
304 E3 **Abomey** Benin
310 3a **Abona, Punta de** *cape* Canary Islands
226 D4 **Abondance** France
305 G4 **Abong Mbang** Cameroon
374 C2 **Abongabong, Gunung** *mountain* Indonesia
377 H5 **Aborlan** Philippines
390 F6 **Abou Hanâya** Syria
306 C2 **Abourassein, Mont** *mountain* Sudan
244 F3 **Aboyne** Aberdeenshire Scotland UK
388 H7 **Ābqūy** Iran
377 I3 **Abra** *watercourse* Philippines
162 B5 **Abra, Canal** *strait* Chile
160 E2 **Abra Pampa** Argentina
119 M6 **Abraham Lake** Alberta Canada
127 F3 **Abrat** *watercourse* Québec Canada
222 K3 **Abraur** *lake* Sweden
230 C3 **Abraveses** Portugal
154 C2 **Ábrego** Colombia
302 E3 **'Abri** Sudan
244 D3 **Abriachan** Highland Scotland UK
232 B4 **Abriès** France
391 H3 **Ābrīz** Iran
77 O11 **Abrolhos Bank** *underwater feature* Atlantic Ocean
238 F3 **Abrosovo** Russian Federation
390 G3 **Ābrū** Iran
234 C2 **Abrud** Romania
225 L3 **Abruka** *island* Estonia
391 H3 **Ābrūn** Iran
233 E5 **Abruzzo** *admin. area* Italy
390 E7 **'Abs** Yemen
436 W1 **Absalom, Mount** *mountain* Antarctica
125 K4 **Absaroka Range** Wyoming USA
238 B5 **Absterna, Vozyera** *lake* Belarus
232 E3 **Abtenau** Austria
391 H5 **Abū al Abyaḑ** *island* United Arab Emirates
390 G4 **Abū 'Alī, Jazīrat** *island* Saudi Arabia
394 F6 **Abū as Sayyid** Syria
302 D3 **Abū Ballāş** *range* Egypt
302 E4 **Abū Dawm** Sudan
302 E5 **Abū Dawm** Sudan
302 E4 **Abū Dawn, Wādī** *watercourse* Sudan
Abu Dhabi *see* **Abū Ẓabī** United Arab Emirates
302 E4 **Abu Dis** Sudan
302 D4 **Abū Durbah** Egypt
302 E5 **Abu Gubeiha** Sudan
302 E4 **Abu Hamed** Sudan
302 E5 **Abū Ḩūt** *watercourse* Sudan
302 E1 **Abū Kabīr** Egypt
302 D5 **Abu Kabisa** Sudan
391 K3 **Abū Kalā** Afghanistan
394 G6 **Abū Kamāl** Syria
390 E2 **Abū Kharjah** Iraq
390 D5 **Abū Madd, Ra's** *cape* Saudi Arabia
302 F5 **Abu Mendi** Ethiopia
391 H4 **Abū Mūsā, Jazīreh-ye** *island* Iran
394 F6 **Abū Naţūliyah** Syria
301 J4 **Abū Nujaym** Libya
301 E2 **Abū Qīr, Khalīj** *bay* Egypt
301 J3 **Abū Qurin** Libya
392 C6 **Abu Road** Rajasthan India
302 D2 **Abū Samak** Iraq
305 I2 **Abū Sanţ** *watercourse* Sudan
302 F3 **Abu Shagara, Ras** *cape* Sudan
302 E3 **Abū Sunbul** Egypt
302 E3 **Abū Tij** Egypt
302 D5 **Abu Zabad** Sudan
391 H5 **Abū Ẓabī (Abu Dhabi)** United Arab Emirates
159 F2 **Abufari, Lago** *lake* Brazil
305 F3 **Abuja** Nigeria
377 I3 **Abulong** *watercourse* Philippines
306 C3 **Abumombazi** Democratic Republic of Congo
158 E3 **Abuna** *watercourse* Bolivia
159 E3 **Abunã** Brazil
154 E5 **Abunai** Brazil
304 D3 **Aburi** Ghana
304 D3 **Abuso** Ghana
377 J5 **Abuyog** Philippines
306 E2 **Abwong** Sudan
302 D5 **Abyad** Sudan
222 I4 **Åbyn** Sweden
154 C4 **Acacias** Colombia
436 U1 **Academy Glacier** *ice* Antarctica
119 P7 **Acadia Valley** Alberta Canada
156 C4 **Açailândia** Brazil
157 E5 **Acajutiba** Brazil
133 G5 **Acala** Mexico
132 E4 **Acámbaro** Mexico
154 B2 **Acandí** Colombia
132 D4 **Acaponeta** Mexico
133 F5 **Acapulco** Mexico
156 B3 **Acará** Brazil
156 B3 **Acará** *watercourse* Brazil
159 F2 **Acará, Lago** *lake* Brazil
156 B3 **Acará Miri** *watercourse* Brazil
156 D3 **Acaraú** Brazil
161 H3 **Acaray** *watercourse* Paraguay
159 G2 **Acari** *watercourse* Brazil
158 C3 **Acarí** Peru
158 C4 **Acari, Rio de** *watercourse* Peru
155 G4 **Acari, Serra** *mountains* Brazil
154 D4 **Acaricuara** Colombia
154 D2 **Acarigua** Venezuela
227 L4 **Acâş** Romania
232 B4 **Acceglio** France
127 N8 **Accomac** Virginia USA
228 D5 **Accous** France
304 D3 **Accra** Ghana
243 F3 **Accrington** Lancashire England UK
133 G6 **Acebo** Spain
129 K6 **Acebuches** Mexico
374 C2 **Aceh** *admin. area* Indonesia
230 C4 **Acehuche** Spain
233 F6 **Acerno** Italy
158 D5 **Achacachi** Bolivia
393 D7 **Achalpur** Maharashtra India
244 E2 **Achavanich** Highland Scotland UK
237 AJ6 **Achayvayam** Russian Federation
244 C3 **Achduart** Highland Scotland UK
235 B6 **Acheloös** *watercourse* Greece
385 K3 **Acheng** Heilongjiang China
226 E3 **Achenkirch** Austria
226 F4 **Achensee** *lake* Austria
235 C5 **Acheráda, Akra** *cape* Greece
226 E3 **Achern** Germany
244 D2 **Achfary** Highland Scotland UK
162 B2 **Achicó** Argentina
244 D2 **Achiemore** Highland Scotland UK
388 D5 **Achikulak** Russian Federation
245 C3 **Achill** Ireland
244 B3 **A'Chill** Highland Scotland UK
245 B3 **Achill Head** *cape* Ireland
244 B2 **Achiltibuie** Highland Scotland UK
244 C5 **Achinhoan** Argyll and Bute Scotland UK
389 P2 **Achinsk** Russian Federation
244 C3 **Achintee** Highland Scotland UK
383 I2 **Achit Nuur** *lake* Mongolia
244 C3 **Achmore** Highland Scotland UK
244 D3 **Achnairn** Highland Scotland UK
224 G6 **Achter Wasser** *bay* Germany
394 E5 **Achwa** *watercourse* Uganda
235 E6 **Aciçay** *watercourse* Turkey
235 F7 **Acıgöl** *lake* Turkey
235 F7 **Acıpayam** Turkey
233 F8 **Acireale** Italy
388 D5 **Ackasar, Gora** *mountain* Georgia
129 L4 **Ackerly** Texas USA
135 F2 **Acklins Island** Bahamas
241 I2 **Acle** Norfolk England UK
129 J4 **Acme** New Mexico USA
158 C3 **Acolla** Peru
160 D5 **Aconcagua, Cerro** *mountain* Argentina
128 G6 **Aconchi** Mexico
156 E4 **Acopiara** Brazil
158 C4 **Acoria** Peru
134 C5 **Acoyapa** Nicaragua
233 C6 **Acqua Doria** Corsica France
226 F5 **Acquanegra sul Chiese** Italy
226 E4 **Acquarossa** Switzerland
232 E5 **Acquasparta** Italy
425 J7 **Acraman, Lake** SA Australia
158 D3 **Acre** *admin. area* Brazil
159 I5 **Acreúna** Brazil
233 G7 **Acri** Italy
232 H3 **Ács** Hungary
427 14 **Actéon, Groupe** *island* French Polynesia
127 K5 **Acton** Ontario Canada
245 F2 **Acton** Armagh Northern Ireland UK
128 C3 **Acton** California USA
133 F4 **Actopan** Mexico
156 E4 **Açu** Brazil
156 C3 **Açu, Lago** *lake* Brazil
302 D1 **Aḑ Ḑab ah** Egypt
390 E7 **Aḑ Ḑahī** Yemen
390 F4 **Ad Dahnā'** Saudi Arabia
300 C4 **Ad Dakhla** Western Sahara
390 G4 **Ad Dammām** Saudi Arabia
390 D4 **Ad Dār al Ḩamrā** Saudi Arabia
390 E5 **Ad Dawādimī** Saudi Arabia
390 G4 **Ad Dawḩah (Doha)** Qatar
390 E2 **Ad Dawr** Iraq
390 G7 **Ad Dibin** Yemen
302 D1 **Aḑ Ḑiffah (Libyan Plateau)** *plateau* Egypt
390 E7 **Ad Dissān** *island* Saudi Arabia
390 E3 **Ad Dīwānīyah** Iraq
390 E2 **Ad Dujayl** Iraq
307 G2 **Ada** Ethiopia
125 Q3 **Ada** Minnesota USA
130 C3 **Ada** Oklahoma USA
384 F3 **Adaatsar** Mongolia
126 D8 **Adair** Oklahoma USA
131 I3 **Adairsville** Georgia USA
230 D3 **Adaja** *watercourse* Spain
237 AL8 **Adak Island** Alaska USA
163 7 **Adam, Mount** Falkland Islands
305 G3 **Adamaoua** *admin. area* Cameroon
305 G3 **Adamaoua, Massif de l'** *range* Cameroon
305 G3 **Adamawa** *admin. area* Nigeria
227 I5 **Adamovec** Croatia
388 H3 **Adamovka** Russian Federation
118 L7 **Adams** *watercourse* British Columbia Canada
124 F4 **Adams** Oregon USA
436 T1 **Adams, Cape** Antarctica
127 P4 **Adams, Mount** New Hampshire USA
393 E10 **Adam's Bridge** *island* Tamil Nadu India
423 8 **Adams Island** Auckland Islands New Zealand
118 L7 **Adams Lake** British Columbia Canada
128 E1 **Adams-McGill Reservoir** Nevada USA
427 11a **Adamstown** Pitcairn Islands
128 F1 **Adamsville** Utah USA
390 F8 **'Adan (Aden)** Yemen
394 E6 **Adana** Turkey
394 E6 **Adana** *admin. area* Turkey
375 H4 **Adang, Teluk** *bay* Indonesia
Adapazarı *see* **Sakarya** Turkey
302 C5 **Adar** Chad
302 E4 **Adarama** Sudan
245 D4 **Adare** Ireland
437 L2 **Adare, Cape** Antarctica
437 L2 **Adare Peninsula** Antarctica
437 L2 **Adare Seamounts** *underwater feature* Southern Ocean
425 M6 **Adavale** Qld Australia
225 M4 **Ādaži** Latvia
232 C3 **Adda** *watercourse* Italy
306 C2 **Adda** *watercourse* Sudan
245 C3 **Addergoole** Ireland
244 F5 **Addinston** Scottish Borders Scotland UK
130 F5 **Addis** Louisiana USA
Addis Ababa *see* **Ādis Ābeba** Ethiopia
300 E5 **Adel Bagrou** Mauritania
425 K8 **Adelaide** SA Australia
436 T2 **Adelaide Island** Antarctica
117 J5 **Adelaide Peninsula** Nunavut Canada
424 I3 **Adelaide River** NT Australia
128 D3 **Adelanto** California USA
373 H5 **Adelbert Range** Papua New Guinea
424 G3 **Adele Island** WA Australia
235 D6 **Adelfoi** *island* Greece
437 J2 **Adélie Coast** Antarctica
231 F3 **Ademuz** Spain
390 F8 **Aden, Gulf of** Middle East
301 H5 **Aderbissinat** Niger
233 F5 **Aderci, Punta** *cape* Italy
302 F4 **Aderde** *watercourse* Eritrea
392 C6 **Adesar** Gujarat India
302 F5 **Ādēt** Ethiopia
392 F6 **Adhaura** Bihar India
372 E5 **Adi** *island* Indonesia
302 F5 **Ādī Ark'ay** Ethiopia
302 F5 **Ādī Da'iro** Ethiopia
303 F5 **Adi Gudom** Ethiopia
303 F5 **Adi Keyh** Eritrea
303 F5 **Ādī-Quala** Eritrea
303 F5 **Ādī Ugri** Eritrea
304 D3 **Adiaso** Ghana
232 D4 **Adige** *watercourse* Italy
303 F5 **Ādīgrat** Ethiopia
393 D8 **Adilabad** Andhra Pradesh India
235 F6 **Adıgüzel Barajı** *lake* Turkey
307 F2 **Ādīs Ābeba** *admin. area* Ethiopia
307 F2 **Ādīs Ābeba (Addis Ababa)** Ethiopia
302 F5 **Ādīs Zemen** Ethiopia
394 F6 **Adıyaman** Turkey
394 F6 **Adiyaman** *admin. area* Turkey
234 E2 **Adjud** Romania
122 I5 **Adlavik Islands** Newfoundland and Labrador Canada
117 K4 **Admiralty Inlet** Nunavut Canada
117 I5 **Admiralty Island** Nunavut Canada
118 D4 **Admiralty Island** Alaska USA
425 inset **Admiralty Islands** Lord Howe Island Australia
373 H4 **Admiralty Islands** Papua New Guinea
437 L2 **Admiralty Mountains** Antarctica
129 N1 **Admire** Kansas USA
305 F3 **Ado-Ekiti** Nigeria
125 N7 **Adobe Creek Reservoir** Colorado USA
306 E2 **Adok** Sudan
129 H7 **Adolfo López Mateos** Mexico
132 D3 **Adolfo López Mateos, Presa** *lake* Mexico
132 C3 **Adolfo Ruíz Cortines** Mexico
222 J3 **Adolfsström** Sweden
372 B6 **Adonara** *island* Indonesia
393 D8 **Adoni** Andhra Pradesh India
226 G2 **Adorf** Germany
238 C4 **Ador'ye** Russian Federation
228 D5 **Adour** *watercourse* France
230 E5 **Adra** Spain
230 E3 **Adradas** Spain
233 F8 **Adrano** Italy
301 F3 **Adrar** Algeria
305 I2 **Adré** Chad
226 G5 **Adria** Italy
131 J4 **Adrian** Georgia USA
126 I6 **Adrian** Michigan USA
125 R5 **Adrian** Minnesota USA
129 K3 **Adrian** Texas USA
309 I4 **Adriandampy** Madagascar
233 H6 **Adriano, Punta** *cape* Italy
232 F5 **Adriatic Sea** *sea* Europe
241 G3 **Adstock** Buckinghamshire England UK
241 F2 **Adstone** Northamptonshire England UK
423 C8 **Adventure, Port** New Zealand
388 E4 **Adyk** Russian Federation
304 D3 **Adzopé** Côte d'Ivoire
236 N5 **Adz'va** *watercourse* Russian Federation
236 M5 **Adz'vavom** Russian Federation
224 F5 **Æbelø** *island* Denmark
235 D6 **Aegean Sea** *sea* Greece
76 R3 **Aegir Ridge** *underwater feature* Norwegian Sea
225 M3 **Aegna** *island* Estonia
225 M3 **Aegviidu** Estonia
426 1a **Aeon Point** Kiribati
224 F5 **Ærø** *island* Denmark
119 O8 **Aetna** Alberta Canada
303 F4 **Afabet** Eritrea
303 G5 **Āfambo Hāyk'** *lake* Ethiopia
78 E8 **Afansij Nikitin Seamount** *underwater feature* Indian Ocean
235 F7 **Afantou** Greece
307 G2 **Āfar** *admin. area* Ethiopia
303 G5 **Afar Depression** *pan* Ethiopia
427 14a **Afareaitu** French Polynesia
222 E5 **Åfarnes** Norway
228 C3 **Aff** *watercourse* France
304 D3 **Afferi** Côte d'Ivoire
388 J7 **Afghanistan** *country*
307 H3 **Afgooye** Somalia
307 F3 **Afgundud** *watercourse* Kenya
305 F3 **Afikpo** Nigeria
238 F4 **Afim'ino** Russian Federation
222 G5 **Åfjord** Norway
227 H4 **Aflenz Kurort** Austria
301 G2 **Aflou** Algeria
116 D7 **Afognak Island** Alaska USA
303 G5 **Afrera, Lac** *lake* Ethiopia
235 F6 **Afşar Barajı** *lake* Turkey
391 H2 **Aftar** Iran
129 I4 **Afton** New Mexico USA
127 N5 **Afton** New York USA
126 D8 **Afton** Oklahoma USA
125 J5 **Afton** Wyoming USA
156 B3 **Afuá** Brazil
394 D5 **Afyon Karahisar** *admin. area* Turkey
235 G6 **Afyonkarahisar** Turkey
393 D8 **Afzalpur** Karnataka India
301 H5 **Agadez** Niger
300 E2 **Agadir** Morocco
389 K4 **Agadyr** Kazakhstan
310 3b **Agaete** Canary Islands
305 F3 **Agaie** Nigeria
236 P5 **Agakhanly** Azerbaijan
238 D2 **Agalatovo** Russian Federation
310 7 **Agalega Islands** Mauritius
134 C4 **Agalta, Sierra de** *range* Honduras
236 Q6 **Agan** *watercourse* Russian Federation
236 S4 **Agapa** *watercourse* Russian Federation
235 G6 **Ağapınar** Turkey
236 S5 **Agapitovo** Russian Federation
388 H2 **Agapovka** Russian Federation
392 D6 **Agar** Madhya Pradesh India
307 F2 **Āgaro** Ethiopia
379 G4 **Agartala** Tripura India
79 S11 **Agassiz Fracture Zone** *underwater feature* Pacific Ocean
126 D2 **Agassiz Pool** *lake* Minnesota USA
426 5 **Agat** Guam
236 T5 **Agata, Ozero** *lake* Russian Federation
129 K1 **Agate** Colorado USA
235 E7 **Agathonisi** *island* Greece
393 C9 **Agatti Island** Lakshadweep India
237 AJ8 **Agattu Island** Alaska USA
126 I3 **Agawa Bay** Ontario Canada
304 D3 **Agboville** Côte d'Ivoire
237 Y6 **Agdary** Russian Federation
228 F5 **Agde** France
228 F5 **Agde, Cap d'** *cape* France
222 F5 **Agdenes** Norway
228 E4 **Agen** France
124 E5 **Agency Lake** Oregon USA
307 F2 **Āgere Maryam** Ethiopia
224 F5 **Agersø** *island* Denmark
227 I4 **Ágfalva** Hungary
308 C5 **Aggeneys** South Africa
224 E4 **Agger** Denmark
222 H5 **Äggsjön** *lake* Sweden
242 B2 **Aghalee** Armagh Northern Ireland UK
245 D3 **Aghamore** Ireland
242 B1 **Aghanloo** Limavady Northern Ireland UK
245 B2 **Aghleam** Ireland
242 B2 **Aghnagap** Ireland
390 G2 **Āgholak** Iran
245 D2 **Aghoo** Ireland
245 F4 **Aghow** Ireland
235 C6 **Agia** Greece
235 A6 **Agia Aikaterini, Akra** *cape* Greece
235 D6 **Agia Eirinis, Akra** *cape* Greece
235 D8 **Agia Galini** Greece
235 D6 **Agiásmata** Greece
385 H2 **Aginskiy Buryatskiy AO** *admin. area* Russian Federation
385 H2 **Aginskoye** Russian Federation
235 C6 **Agiokampos** Greece
235 D5 **Agion Oros** *range* Greece
235 D8 **Agios Charalampos** Greece
235 D6 **Agios Efstratios** *island* Greece
235 C7 **Agios Georgios** *island* Greece
235 D8 **Agios Ioannis, Akrotirio** *cape* Greece
235 E7 **Agios Minas** *island* Greece
235 D5 **Agiou Orous, Kolpos** *bay* Greece
235 C7 **Agkistri** *island* Greece
235 G7 **Ağlasun** Turkey
245 D3 **Aglish** Ireland
228 F5 **Agly** *watercourse* France
235 B6 **Agnanteron** Greece
126 F2 **Agnes Lake** Ontario Canada
425 N6 **Agnes Water** Qld Australia
127 K3 **Agnew Lake** Ontario Canada
162 C3 **Agnia, Laguna de** *bay* Argentina
234 D3 **Agnita** Romania
229 I4 **Agno** Switzerland
224 I2 **Agön** *island* Sweden
304 D3 **Agona** Ghana
229 K3 **Agordo** Italy
158 D3 **Agostinho** Brazil
228 E5 **Agout** *watercourse* France
392 E5 **Agra** Uttar Pradesh India
230 F3 **Agreda** Spain
233 F6 **Agri** *watercourse* Italy
394 G5 **Ağrı** *admin. area* Turkey
394 G5 **Ağrı (Karaköse)** Turkey
394 H5 **Ağrı Dagı (Mount Ararat)** *mountain* Turkey
233 E8 **Agrigento** Italy
426 2 **Agrihan** *island* Northern Mariana Islands
235 B6 **Agrinion** Greece
162 B2 **Agrio** *watercourse* Argentina
388 F2 **Agryz** Russian Federation
224 I2 **Ågsjön** *lake* Sweden
160 D4 **Agua Amarga** Chile
161 G2 **Água Azul** Brazil
161 H2 **Água Boa** Brazil
155 F4 **Água Boa do Univini** *watercourse* Brazil
157 B6 **Água Bonita** Brazil
156 D4 **Água Branca** Brazil
132 D4 **Agua Brava, Laguna** *lake* Mexico
159 E5 **Agua Caliente** Bolivia
158 E6 **Agua Castilla** Bolivia
157 A8 **Água Clara** Brazil
159 E4 **Agua Dulce** Bolivia
133 G5 **Agua Dulce** Mexico
160 D6 **Agua Escondida** Argentina
132 B2 **Agua Escondida** *watercourse* Mexico
154 D2 **Agua Larga de Dolores** Venezuela
154 D3 **Agua Linda** Venezuela
130 B7 **Agua Nueva** Texas USA
159 E3 **Agua Preta** Brazil
132 C2 **Agua Prieta** Mexico
132 D4 **Agua Verde** Mexico
157 B8 **Água Vermelha, Represa** *lake* Brazil
154 D2 **Agua Viva, Embalse de** *lake* Venezuela
154 A4 **Aguada, Punta** *cape* Ecuador
162 D2 **Aguada Cecilio** Argentina
162 C2 **Aguada de Guerra** Argentina
162 C2 **Aguada de Guzmán** Argentina
154 C3 **Aguadas** Colombia
135 H3 **Aguadilla** Puerto Rico
158 D4 **Aguajal** Peru
130 B7 **Agualeguas** Mexico
134 C4 **Aguan, Rio** *watercourse* Honduras
132 E3 **Aguanaval** *watercourse* Mexico
123 G7 **Aguanish** Québec Canada
157 B8 **Aguapeí** *watercourse* Brazil
161 G4 **Aguapey** *watercourse* Argentina
160 F2 **Aguaragüe, Cordillera de** *range* Bolivia
154 B4 **Aguarico** *watercourse* Ecuador
156 E5 **Águas Belas** Brazil
159 E6 **Aguas Blancas** Argentina
160 E2 **Aguas Calientes, Laguna** *lake* Chile
157 D7 **Águas Formosas** Brazil
230 C3 **Águas Santas** Portugal
157 D6 **Águas Vermelhas** Brazil
132 E4 **Aguascalientes** Mexico
132 E4 **Aguascalientes** *admin. area* Mexico
231 F3 **Aguaviva** Spain
158 C3 **Aguaytia** *watercourse* Peru
154 C3 **Aguazul** Colombia
230 D4 **Agudo** Spain
157 B8 **Agudos** Brazil
230 B3 **Agueda** Portugal
301 G5 **Aguelhok** Mali
157 D7 **Águia Branca** Brazil
230 C3 **Aguiar de Beira** Portugal
301 H6 **Aguié** Niger
426 2 **Aguijan** *island* Northern Mariana Islands
128 F4 **Aguila** Arizona USA
159 E6 **Aguilar, Cerro** *mountain* Argentina
230 D2 **Aguilar de Campóo, Embalse de** *lake* Spain
160 E3 **Aguilares** Argentina
230 F5 **Águilas** Spain
132 E5 **Aguililla** Mexico
162 D6 **Aguirre, Bahía** *bay* Argentina
158 A2 **Aguja, Punta** *cape* Peru
303 F5 **Āgula'i** Ethiopia
310 2 **Agulhas, Ponta da** *cape* Madeira
308 C6 **Agulhas, Cape** South Africa
80 G8 **Agulhas Bank** *underwater feature* Southern Ocean
157 C8 **Agulhas Negras** *mountain* Brazil
80 G9 **Agulhas Plateau** *underwater feature* Southern Ocean
80 F9 **Agulhas Ridge** *underwater feature* Southern Ocean
310 3a **Agulo** Canary Islands
389 Q2 **Agul'skoye** *lake* Russian Federation
381 J3 **Aguni-jima** *island* Japan
154 C2 **Agustín Codazzi** Colombia
377 I5 **Agutaya** *island* Philippines
235 F5 **Ağva** Turkey
302 F4 **Agwampt** *watercourse* Sudan
305 F3 **Agwara** Nigeria
307 E2 **Agwei** *watercourse* Sudan
245 C4 **Ahafona** Ireland
388 H6 **Ahal Welaýaty** *admin. area* Turkmenistan
388 E6 **Ahar** Iran
423 D6 **Ahaura** New Zealand
423 D6 **Ahaura** *watercourse* New Zealand
226 D1 **Ahaus** Germany
427 14 **Ahe** *island* French Polynesia
242 A4 **Ahenny** Ireland
422 E2 **Ahipara** New Zealand
422 E2 **Ahipara Bay** New Zealand
393 E7 **Ahiri** Maharashtra India
225 K2 **Ahlainen** Finland
394 G5 **Ahlat** Turkey
226 E1 **Ahlden** Germany
226 D2 **Ahlen** Germany
223 O3 **Ahma-aapa** *island* Finland
391 L4 **Ahmad Tar** Pakistan
391 K3 **Ahmad Wal** Pakistan
392 C6 **Ahmadabad** Gujarat India
392 D4 **Ahmadgarh** Punjab India
393 D7 **Ahmadnagar** Maharashtra India
391 L3 **Ahmadpur East** Pakistan
391 L3 **Ahmadpur Sial** Pakistan
307 G2 **Ahmar** *range* Ethiopia
223 O4 **Ahmas** Finland
223 O5 **Ahokylä** Finland
223 P3 **Ahola** Finland
226 D2 **Ahr** *watercourse* Germany
392 F6 **Ahraura** Uttar Pradesh India
223 N5 **Ähtäri** Finland
225 M1 **Ähtärinjärvi** *lake* Finland
132 D4 **Ahuacatlán** Mexico
134 B4 **Ahuachapán** El Salvador
132 E4 **Ahualulco** Mexico
427 14 **Ahunui** *island* French Polynesia
423 C7 **Ahuriri** *watercourse* New Zealand
423 C8 **Ahuriri Flat** New Zealand
390 F3 **Ahvāz** Iran
223 O5 **Ahveninen** Finland
223 P3 **Ahvenselkä** Finland
372 D5 **Ai** *island* Indonesia
308 C5 **Ai-ais** Namibia
159 F2 **Aiapuá, Lago** *lake* Brazil
154 D4 **Aiari** *watercourse* Brazil
372 E5 **Aiduma** *island* Indonesia
235 D7 **Aigiali** Greece
235 C7 **Aigina** *island* Greece
235 C6 **Aiginio** Greece
235 C6 **Aigio** Greece
229 H3 **Aigle** Switzerland
122 C4 **Aigneau** *watercourse* Québec Canada
122 C4 **Aigneau, Lac** *lake* Québec Canada
225 M3 **Aigrumäe** Estonia
161 H5 **Aiguá** Uruguay
229 H4 **Aiguebelle** France
226 C5 **Aigues** *watercourse* France
228 G5 **Aigues-Mortes** France
228 E3 **Aigurande** France
380 C4 **Aihua** Yunnan China
225 M4 **Aijažu ezers** *lake* Latvia
131 K4 **Aiken** South Carolina USA
244 F1 **Aikerness** Orkney Islands Scotland UK
242 F2 **Aiketgate** Cumbria England UK
425 J5 **Aileron** NT Australia
372 C6 **Aileu** Timor-Leste (East Timor)
154 B2 **Ailigandí** Panama
427 15 **Ailinginae Atoll** Marshall Islands
427 15 **Ailinglapalap Atoll** Marshall Islands
245 C3 **Aillenacally** Ireland
122 I5 **Aillik** Newfoundland and Labrador Canada
242 C1 **Ailsa Craig** *island* Scotland UK
427 15 **Ailuk Atoll** Marshall Islands
228 G5 **Aimargues** France
372 B6 **Aimere** Indonesia
157 D7 **Aimorés** Brazil
229 G4 **Ain** *watercourse* France
301 H1 **Aïn Beïda** Algeria
300 E3 **'Aïn Ben Tili** Mauritania
301 F2 **Aïn Beni Mathar** Morocco
301 G1 **Aïn Defla** Algeria
301 G1 **Aïn Defla** *admin. area* Algeria
301 G2 **Aïn Deheb** Algeria
233 C8 **Aïn Draham** Tunisia
233 C8 **'Aïn el Assel** Algeria
301 G1 **'Aïn el Hadjel** Algeria
301 G2 **'Aïn el Melh** Algeria
231 H6 **Aïn Feka** Algeria
231 J5 **Aïn Kechera** Algeria
233 C8 **'Aïn Kerma** Algeria
301 G2 **'Aïn Madhi** Algeria
301 H1 **Aïn-M'lila** Algeria
231 G6 **Aïn Nouissy** Algeria
301 H1 **Aïn Oulmene** Algeria
231 I6 **'Aïn Oum Chemel** Algeria
301 G1 **Aïn Oussera** Algeria
301 F2 **Aïn Sefra** Algeria
231 F6 **Aïn Temouchent** Algeria
235 B6 **Ainos** *cape* Greece
242 E3 **Ainsdale** Merseyside England UK
123 H9 **Ainslie, Lake** Nova Scotia Canada
125 P5 **Ainsworth** Nebraska USA
437 J2 **Ainsworth Bay** Antarctica
386 G4 **Aioi** Japan
384 G3 **Aipar** Mongolia
155 F5 **Aiparuça** Brazil
159 E5 **Aiquile** Bolivia
117 L5 **Air Force Island** Nunavut Canada
426 3 **Airai** Palau
241 I5 **Airaines** France
223 O5 **Airaksela** Finland
374 C3 **Airbangis** Indonesia
244 A3 **Aird** Na h-Eileanan Siar Scotland UK
244 B2 **Aird Dhail** Na h-Eileanan Siar Scotland UK
244 B3 **Aird Mhige** Na h-Eileanan Siar Scotland UK
244 B2 **Aird Thunga** Na h-Eileanan Siar Scotland UK
124 H1 **Airdrie** Alberta Canada
244 E5 **Airdrie** North Lanarkshire Scotland UK
229 G2 **Aire** *watercourse* France
243 G3 **Aire** *watercourse* England UK
228 D5 **Aire-sur-l'Adour** France
375 F4 **Airhitam** *watercourse* Indonesia
375 F4 **Airhitam, Teluk** *bay* Indonesia
225 L2 **Airisto** *bay* Finland
425 N5 **Airlie Beach** Qld Australia
243 H3 **Airmyn** East Riding of Yorkshire England UK
226 E4 **Airolo** Switzerland
375 J5 **Airpanas** Indonesia
244 E4 **Airth** Falkirk Scotland UK
379 G4 **Aisatung Mountain** Myanmar
372 F4 **Aisau** Indonesia
232 D2 **Aisch** *watercourse* Germany
162 B3 **Aisén del General Carlos Ibáñez del Campo** *admin. area* Chile
155 G4 **Aishalton** Guyana
116 F6 **Aishihik Lake** Yukon Territory Canada
222 J3 **Aisjaure** *bay* Sweden
162 C3 **Aisladores, Sierra de los** *range* Argentina
228 F2 **Aisne** *watercourse* France
226 D4 **Aissey** France
244 E1 **Aith** Orkney Islands Scotland UK
244 E3 **Aitnoch** Moray Scotland UK
223 O5 **Aittojärvi** Finland
422 1 **Aitutaki** *island* Cook Islands New Zealand
227 L4 **Aiud** Romania
225 N4 **Aiviekste** *watercourse* Latvia
427 9 **Aiwa** *island* Fiji
228 D3 **Aix, Île d'** *island* France
229 G5 **Aix-en-Provence** France
229 G4 **Aix-les-Bains** France
235 C6 **Aiyira** Greece
379 G4 **Aizawl** Mizoram India
228 D3 **Aizenay** France
225 M4 **Aizkraukle** Latvia
225 M4 **Aizkraukles Rajon** *admin. area* Latvia
225 K4 **Aizpute** Latvia
387 H4 **Aizuwakamatsu** Japan
388 E6 **'Ajab Shir** Iran
233 C6 **Ajaccio** Corsica France
233 C6 **Ajaccio, Golfe d'** *bay* Corsica France
392 E6 **Ajaigarh** Madhya Pradesh India
133 F5 **Ajalpan** Mexico
223 M3 **Ajankijärvi** *lake* Finland
222 I4 **Ajaure** *bay* Sweden
222 I4 **Ajaureforsen** Sweden
222 K4 **Ajaursjön** *lake* Sweden
426 5 **Ajayan Bay** Guam
302 C1 **Ajdābiyā** Libya
389 K3 **Ajgyrzal** *mountain* Kazakhstan
390 E2 **Ajij, Wādī al** *watercourse* Iraq
232 G3 **Ajka** Hungary

391 H4 **'Ajmān** United Arab Emirates
392 D5 **Ajmer** Rajasthan India
392 D4 **Ajnala** Punjab India
230 E2 **Ajo** Spain
128 F4 **Ajo** Arizona USA
228 C5 **Ajo, Cabo de** *cape* Spain
158 C4 **Ajpi** Peru
393 D8 **Ajra** Maharashtra India
390 E2 **Ajrab** Iraq
304 D3 **Ajumaku** Ghana
377 I5 **Ajuy** Philippines
389 R3 **Ak-attyg-khol'** *lake* Russian Federation
388 J6 **Ak-Kurgan** Uzbekistan
389 P3 **Ak-Ojuk, Gora** *mountain* Russian Federation
301 G3 **Akabli** Algeria
237 AC8 **Akademii, Zaliv** *bay* Russian Federation
393 F7 **Akaltara** Chhattisgarh India
305 F3 **Akamkpa** Nigeria
387 J2 **Akan-ko** *lake* Japan
423 E6 **Akaroa** New Zealand
423 E6 **Akaroa Harbour** New Zealand
302 E3 **Akasha** Sudan
387 G4 **Akashi** Japan
223 N3 **Äkäsjärvi** *lake* Finland
223 N3 **Äkäslompolo** Finland
235 E6 **Akbaş** Turkey
388 H4 **Akbasty** Kazakhstan
389 L3 **Akbaur** Kazakhstan
389 K3 **Akbeit** Kazakhstan
301 G1 **Akbou** Algeria
235 E7 **Akbük** Turkey
389 M3 **Akbulak** Kazakhstan
388 G3 **Akbulak** Russian Federation
394 F6 **Akçakale** Turkey
235 G5 **Akçakoca** Turkey
235 F7 **Akçapınar** Turkey
235 F7 **Akçay** Turkey
394 D6 **Akçay** *watercourse* Turkey
300 D5 **Akchâr** *region* Mauritania
389 L4 **Akchatau** Kazakhstan
235 F7 **Akdağlar** *range* Turkey
388 H5 **Akdepe** Turkmenistan
394 G6 **Akdiken** Turkey
372 D3 **Akelamo** Indonesia
307 E2 **Akelo** Sudan
388 E6 **Akera** *watercourse* Azerbaijan
222 L4 **Åkerholmen** Sweden
224 F2 **Akershus** *admin. area* Norway
222 I5 **Åkersjön** *lake* Sweden
224 F2 **Åkerstrømmen** Norway
388 H4 **Akespe** Kazakhstan
382 F4 **Akesu** Xinjiang Uygur Zizhiqu China
306 C3 **Aketi** Democratic Republic of Congo
302 E2 **Akhmim** Egypt
392 D4 **Akhnoor** Jammu and Kashmir India/Pakistan
391 M3 **Akhoor** Pakistan
235 E4 **Akhtopol** Bulgaria
388 E4 **Akhtubinsk** Russian Federation
386 G5 **Aki** Japan
122 O2 **Akia** *island* Greenland
305 G5 **Akiéni** Gabon
390 E1 **Akika** Iraq
117 K8 **Akimiski Island** Nunavut Canada
121 N6 **Akimiski Strait** Nunavut/Ontario Canada
387 H4 **Akimoto-ko** *lake* Japan
387 I3 **Akita** Japan
423 G5 **Akitio** New Zealand
300 D5 **Akjoujt** Mauritania
388 I3 **Akkabak** Kazakhstan
222 J3 **Akkajaure** *lake* Sweden
389 J4 **Akkanse** Kazakhstan
222 J3 **Akkavare** *mountain* Sweden
235 F6 **Akkent** Turkey
390 C3 **'Akko (Acre)** Israel
Akkol *see* **Alekseyevka** Kazakhstan
389 L3 **Akkol'** Kazakhstan
389 L4 **Akkol'** Kazakhstan
388 I4 **Akkol** *lake* Kazakhstan
235 E7 **Akköy** Turkey
389 M4 **Akkystau** Kazakhstan
116 F5 **Aklavik** Northwest Territories Canada
225 K4 **Akmeņrags** *cape* Latvia
389 K3 **Akmeshit** Kazakhstan
Akmola *see* **Astana** Kazakhstan
388 J3 **Akmola** *mountain* Kazakhstan
389 K3 **Akmolinskaya Oblast'** *admin. area* Kazakhstan
300 F2 **Aknoul** Morocco
155 G3 **Akobenang Mountains** Guyana
155 H3 **Akoelitatajepratti** Suriname
392 D6 **Akola** Rajasthan India
305 G4 **Akom** Cameroon
305 G4 **Akono** Cameroon
302 F4 **Akordat** Eritrea
393 D7 **Akot** Maharashtra India
306 D2 **Akot** Sudan
155 H4 **Akotipa** Brazil
122 D2 **Akpatok Island** Nunavut Canada
235 G6 **Akpınar** Turkey
382 F5 **Akqi** Xinjiang Uygur Zizhiqu China
222 H5 **Åkran** Norway
222 inset **Akranes** Iceland
235 D5 **Akrathos, Akra** *cape* Greece
235 B7 **Akritas, Akra** *cape* Greece
130 H4 **Akron** Alabama USA
125 N6 **Akron** Colorado USA
127 K6 **Akron** Ohio USA
394 E6 **Akrotiri Sovereign Base Area (UK)** Cyprus
235 C8 **Akrotirio Spatha** *cape* Greece
392 E3 **Aksai Chin (Disputed)** *admin. area* China
394 E5 **Aksaray** Turkey
394 E5 **Aksaray** *admin. area* Turkey
388 C4 **Aksay** Russian Federation
235 G6 **Akşehir Gölü** *lake* Turkey
388 G3 **Akshatau** Kazakhstan
388 I3 **Akshiganak** Kazakhstan
388 F5 **Akshynyrau** Kazakhstan
389 L3 **Aksoran** *mountain* Kazakhstan
388 G3 **Aksu** Kazakhstan
389 M4 **Aksu** Kazakhstan
235 G7 **Aksu** Turkey
235 G7 **Aksu** *watercourse* Turkey
389 L4 **Aksu Ayuly** Kazakhstan
382 F5 **Aksu He** *lake* Xinjiang Uygur Zizhiqu China
382 F5 **Aksu He** *watercourse* Xinjiang Uygur Zizhiqu China
389 N4 **Aksuat** Kazakhstan
388 F2 **Aksubayevo** Russian Federation
303 F5 **Āksum** Ethiopia
394 E4 **Aksyuru-Konrat** Ukraine
382 G6 **Aktag** *mountain* Xinjiang Uygur Zizhiqu China
389 L3 **Aktau** Kazakhstan
388 F5 **Aktau (Shevchenko)** Kazakhstan
382 E5 **Akto** Xinjiang Uygur Zizhiqu China
388 H3 **Aktobe** Kazakhstan
389 L4 **Aktogay** Kazakhstan
389 M4 **Aktogay** Kazakhstan
388 H4 **Aktumsyk** Kazakhstan
Aktyubinsk *see* **Aktobe** Kazakhstan
388 H3 **Aktyubinskaya Oblast'** *admin. area* Kazakhstan
307 F2 **Akūbū** *watercourse* Sudan
306 C3 **Akula** Democratic Republic of Congo
121 P2 **Akulivik** Québec Canada
222 L4 **Åkullsjön** Sweden
386 F5 **Akune** Japan
305 F3 **Akure** Nigeria
222 inset **Akureyri** Iceland
386 F6 **Akuseki-shima** *island* Japan
116 C8 **Akutan** Alaska USA
305 F4 **Akwa Ibom** *admin. area* Nigeria
305 F3 **Akwanga** Nigeria
389 L4 **Akzhal** Kazakhstan
389 K5 **Akzhar** Kazakhstan
389 N4 **Akzhar** Kazakhstan
301 I3 **Al Abyaḍ** Libya
302 C1 **Al Abyār** Libya
302 C1 **Al 'Adam** Libya
390 F3 **Al Aḥmadī** Kuwait
302 D1 **Al 'Alamayn** Egypt
390 F3 **Al 'Amārah** Iraq
390 C3 **Al 'Aqabah** Jordan
302 E2 **Al 'Arābā al Madfūnah** Egypt
302 E1 **Al 'Arīsh** Egypt
390 F4 **Al Arṭāwīyah** Saudi Arabia
233 C8 **Al 'Arūsah** Tunisia
390 E5 **Al Ash'arīyah** Saudi Arabia
302 E2 **Al Ashmūnayn** Egypt
391 H5 **Al 'Ayn** United Arab Emirates
301 I2 **Al 'Azīzīyah** Libya
390 E4 **Al Bāḥah** Saudi Arabia
302 E1 **Al Bardawīl, Sabkhat** *lake* Egypt
390 F3 **Al Baṣrah** Iraq
302 D2 **Al Bawīṭī** Egypt
302 C1 **Al Bayḍā** Libya
390 F7 **Al Bayḍā'** Yemen
390 E2 **Al Biljah** Syria
388 E7 **Al Bolagh** Iran
302 C1 **al Bumbah, Khalīj** *bay* Libya
391 H5 **Al Buraymī** Oman
390 C3 **Al Burj** Jordan
394 G6 **Al Buṣayrah** Syria
390 E5 **Al Buwaṭah** Saudi Arabia
390 E2 **Al Fallūjah** Iraq
390 F7 **Al Fara'** Yemen
390 F3 **Al Farwānīyah** Kuwait
302 E2 **Al Fashn** Egypt
302 E2 **Al Fayyūm** Egypt
391 H4 **Al Fujayrah** United Arab Emirates
390 E6 **Al Fukah** Saudi Arabia
390 E8 **Al Ghadir** Yemen
390 E4 **Al Ghāṭ** Saudi Arabia
390 G7 **Al Ghayḍah** Yemen
390 G7 **Al Ghayḍah** Yemen
390 F7 **Al Ghayl** Yemen
302 E2 **Al Ghurdaqah (Hurghada)** Egypt
390 E7 **Al Ḥadīd** Yemen
300 D3 **Al Haggounia** Western Sahara
390 F5 **Al Ḥā'ir** Saudi Arabia
390 E8 **Al Ḥajaf** Yemen
390 F3 **Al Ḥallah** Iraq
391 H6 **Al Ḥallānīyah** *island* Oman
302 D1 **Al Ḥammām** Egypt
390 F7 **Al Hanad** Yemen
390 E7 **Al Ḥarf** Yemen
394 G6 **Al Ḥasakah** Syria
390 E7 **Al Ḥasanīyah** Yemen
390 E7 **Al Ḥasib** Yemen
390 F7 **Al Ḥasūsah** Yemen
394 G6 **Al Hawl** Syria
390 E5 **Al Ḥayd** Saudi Arabia
390 F3 **Al Ḥayy** Iraq
390 E7 **Al Ḥazm** Yemen
390 E3 **Al Ḥillah** Iraq
390 F5 **Al Ḥillah** Saudi Arabia
300 F1 **Al Hoceima** Morocco
390 E3 **Al Ḥudūd Ash Shamālīyah** *admin. area* Saudi Arabia
390 E7 **Al Ḥudaydah** Yemen
390 G4 **Al Hufūf** Saudi Arabia
301 J3 **Al Ḥulayq al Kabīr** *range* Libya
390 F7 **Al Ḥūṭah** Yemen
302 D1 **Al Iskandarīyah (Alexandria)** Egypt
302 E1 **Al Ismā'īlīyah** Egypt
306 E2 **Al Jabal, Baḥr** *watercourse* Sudan
301 K2 **Al Jabal Al Akhḍar** *admin. area* Libya
302 D2 **Al Jadīdah** Egypt
390 C3 **Al Jafr** Jordan
302 C2 **Al Jaghbūb** Libya
390 F3 **Al Jahrā'** Kuwait
390 G4 **Al Jamaliyah** Qatar
302 C3 **Al Jawf** Libya
390 F5 **Al Jifārah** Saudi Arabia
390 E6 **Al Jisimah** Saudi Arabia
302 F2 **Al Jizah** Egypt
390 D5 **Al Jumūm** Saudi Arabia
390 F7 **Al Jurbah** Yemen
233 C8 **Al-Kāf** Tunisia
391 I5 **Al Kāmil** Oman
390 C3 **Al Karak** Jordan
233 C8 **Al Karib** Tunisia
390 E2 **Al Kāẓimīyah** Iraq
390 F7 **Al Khabr** Yemen
391 I5 **Al Khābūrah** Oman
390 F7 **Al Khāmilah** Yemen
302 E2 **Al Khārijah** Egypt
390 F5 **Al Kharj** Saudi Arabia
302 E4 **Al Kharṭūm** Sudan
390 G4 **Al Khawr** Qatar
391 H5 **Al Khaznah** United Arab Emirates
390 F7 **Al Khubb** Yemen
390 F7 **Al Khudūd** Yemen
301 I2 **Al Khums** Libya
390 E4 **Al Kihafah** Saudi Arabia
390 F3 **Al Kūt** Iraq
390 F3 **Al Kuwayt** Kuwait
394 E6 **Al Lādhiqīyah (Latakia)** Syria
390 F7 **Al Lazif** Yemen
390 D5 **Al Madīnah al Munawwarah (Medina)** Saudi Arabia
390 C3 **Al Mafraq** Jordan
302 E2 **Al Maḥāmīd** Egypt
300 E3 **Al Mahbas** Western Sahara
390 E2 **Al Maḥmūdīyah** Iraq
390 E7 **Al Maḥwīt** Yemen
390 F4 **Al Majma'ah** Saudi Arabia
390 E7 **Al Makārib** Yemen
390 E7 **Al Makhādir** Yemen
390 F7 **Al Malab** Yemen
390 G4 **Al Manāmah** Bahrain
302 E1 **Al Manṣūrah** Egypt
390 F3 **Al Maqwa'** Kuwait
390 E7 **Al Marāshi** Yemen
302 C1 **Al Marj** Libya
233 D8 **Al-Marsā** Tunisia
390 F7 **Al Ma'shā** Yemen
390 G7 **Al Masīlah, Wādī** *watercourse* Yemen
390 E7 **Al Maṭābif** Yemen
390 E2 **Al Mawṣil (Mosul)** Iraq
302 E2 **Al Minyā** Egypt
390 E2 **Al Miqdādīyah** Iraq
390 G4 **Al Mubarraz** Saudi Arabia
390 E2 **Al Mudawwarah** Jordan
391 I5 **Al Muḍaybī** Oman
390 G4 **Al Muḥarraq** Bahrain
390 G7 **Al Mukallā** Yemen
302 C1 **Al Mukhayli** Libya
390 F3 **Al Muṣandaq** Iraq
390 E6 **Al Mushirah** Saudi Arabia
390 E7 **Al Ogala** Yemen
394 F6 **Al Qadmus** Syria
302 E1 **Al Qāhirah (Cairo)** Egypt
390 F7 **Al Qamā** Yemen
390 F7 **Al Qarāshim** Yemen
301 I2 **Al Qaṣabāt** Libya
302 D2 **Al Qaṣr** Egypt
301 I4 **Al Qaṭrūn** Libya
390 F4 **Al Qayṣūmah** Saudi Arabia
302 C1 **Al Qubbah** Libya
Al Quds *see* **Yerushalayim (Jerusalem)** Israel
302 E4 **Al Qulayd Baḥrī** Sudan
394 F6 **Al Qumqum** Syria
301 K2 **Al Qunayyin, Sabkhat** *lake* Libya
390 E6 **Al Qunfundah** Saudi Arabia
390 D3 **Al Qurayyāt** Saudi Arabia
302 E2 **Al Quṣayr** Egypt
390 D4 **Al 'Ulā** Saudi Arabia
302 B1 **Al 'Uqaylah** Libya
302 E2 **Al Uqṣur (Luxor)** Egypt
301 I3 **Al 'Uwaynāt** Libya
391 I5 **Al Wāfī** Oman
390 F4 **Al Wafrah** Kuwait
390 C4 **Al Wajh** Saudi Arabia
390 G4 **Al Wakrah** Qatar
390 E2 **Al Walid** Syria
301 I4 **Al Wigh** Libya
229 J4 **Ala** Italy
225 J4 **Ala** Sweden
232 D5 **Ala, Punta** *cape* Italy
389 K5 **Ala-Buka** Uzbekistan
223 O3 **Ala-Nampa** Finland
223 O3 **Ala-Suolijärvi** *lake* Finland
223 M4 **Ala-Viirre** Finland
115 **Alabama** *admin. area* USA
131 H4 **Alabama** *watercourse* Alabama USA
394 G6 **Alabas** Turkey
130 H4 **Alabaster** Alabama USA
389 L2 **Alabota** *lake* Russian Federation
394 E5 **Alaca** Turkey
Alacant *see* **Alicante** Spain
133 H4 **Alacrán, Arrecife** *reef* Mexico
384 D2 **Alag-erdene** Mongolia
383 J3 **Alag Khayrkhan Uul** *mountain* Mongolia
155 F4 **Alagadiço** Brazil
388 D5 **Alagir** Russian Federation
228 F4 **Alagnon** *watercourse* France
156 E5 **Alagoas** *admin. area* Brazil
157 E6 **Alagoinhas** Brazil
231 F3 **Alagón** Spain
230 D3 **Alagón** *watercourse* Spain
310 3 **Alagranza** *island* Canary Islands
237 AG8 **Alaid** *volcano* Kuril Islands
228 F5 **Alaigne** France
303 G5 **Alaili Dadda'** Djibouti
231 I4 **Alaior** Spain
223 O2 **Alajärvi** *lake* Finland
222 L2 **Alajaure** *lake* Sweden
134 E5 **Alajuela, Lago** *lake* Panama
223 P3 **Alakitka** *lake* Finland
392 E4 **Alaknanda** *watercourse* Uttaranchal India
389 K3 **Alakol'** *lake* Kazakhstan
389 N4 **Alakol', Ozero** *lake* Kazakhstan
223 Q3 **Alakurtti** Russian Federation
223 N3 **Alakylä** Finland
155 G4 **Alalapadu** Suriname
155 F5 **Alalau** *watercourse* Brazil
223 O4 **Alalvo** Finland
223 P5 **Alaluostanjärvi** *lake* Finland
426 2 **Alamagan** *island* Northern Mariana Islands
303 F5 **Ālamat'ā** Ethiopia
125 N2 **Alameda** Saskatchewan Canada
230 D5 **Alameda** Spain
392 G6 **Alamnagar** Bihar India
133 F4 **Álamo** Mexico
128 E4 **Alamo** *watercourse* California USA
131 J4 **Alamo** Georgia USA
128 E2 **Alamo** Nevada USA
128 F3 **Alamo Lake** Arizona USA
129 J4 **Alamogordo** New Mexico USA
132 C3 **Álamos** Mexico
129 K6 **Álamos de Márquez** Mexico
125 M8 **Alamosa** Colorado USA
388 F2 **Alan-polyan** Russian Federation
223 P4 **Alanäljänkä** Finland
226 F1 **Åland** *watercourse* Germany
225 K2 **Åland** *Finnish autonomous state* Finland
224 H3 **Ålandern** *lake* Sweden
235 F6 **Alandız** Turkey
225 J3 **Ålands Hav** *bay* Sweden
374 D3 **Alang Besar** *island* Indonesia
230 C4 **Alange, Embalse de** *lake* Spain
374 E4 **Alanggantang** *island* Indonesia
223 N4 **Alaniemi** Finland
225 M5 **Alanta** Lithuania
305 G3 **Alantika Mountains** *range* Cameroon
394 E6 **Alanya** Turkey
234 A2 **Alap** Hungary
305 E3 **Alapa** Nigeria
223 O5 **Alapitkä** Finland
235 G5 **Alaplı** Turkey
393 D10 **Alappuzha** Kerala India
230 D3 **Alaraz** Spain
375 H6 **Alas** Indonesia
375 H6 **Alas, Selat** *strait* Indonesia
235 F6 **Alaşehir** Turkey
437 D2 **Alasheyev Bight** *bay* Antarctica
118 C3 **Alaska** *admin. area* USA
116 D7 **Alaska, Gulf of** Alaska USA
116 C7 **Alaska Peninsula** Alaska USA
116 D6 **Alaska Range** Alaska USA
388 I3 **Alasor** *lake* Kazakhstan
233 E6 **Alatri** Italy
388 E2 **Alatyr** Russian Federation
124 C2 **Alava, Cape** Washington USA
223 P4 **Alavuokki** Finland
242 D3 **Alaw, Llyn** *lake* Wales UK
235 G6 **Alayunt** Turkey
237 AF4 **Alazeya** *watercourse* Russian Federation
237 AE5 **Alazeyskoye Ploskogor'ye** *region* Russian Federation
226 E4 **Alb** *watercourse* Germany
226 E5 **Alba** Italy
234 C2 **Alba** *admin. area* Romania
234 C2 **Alba Iulia** Romania
234 C2 **Albac** Romania
230 F4 **Albacete** Spain
224 F4 **Ålbæk Bugt** *bay* Denmark
393 E7 **Albaka** Andhra Pradesh India
231 G3 **Albalate de Cinca** Spain
228 F5 **Alban** France
121 S7 **Albanel, Lac** *lake* Québec Canada
154 C2 **Albania** Colombia
154 C3 **Albania** Colombia
154 C4 **Albania** Colombia
235 B5 **Albania** *country* Europe
424 F8 **Albany** WA Australia
120 K7 **Albany** *watercourse* Ontario Canada
131 I5 **Albany** Georgia USA
131 I2 **Albany** Kentucky USA
126 D6 **Albany** Missouri USA
127 O5 **Albany** New York USA
121 O6 **Albany Island** Ontario Canada
231 I2 **Albaron** France
425 I3 **Albatross Bay** Qld Australia
163 8 **Albatross Island** South Georgia
423 11 **Albatross Point** Antipodes Islands New Zealand
233 D5 **Albegna** *watercourse* Italy
131 K3 **Albemarle** North Carolina USA
163 4 **Albemarle, Punta** *cape* Archipiélago de Colón (Galapagos Islands)
163 7 **Albemarle Harbour** Falkland Islands
131 M2 **Albemarle Sound** North Carolina USA
230 D3 **Alberche** *watercourse* Spain
222 G5 **Albergy** Norway
425 J6 **Alberga** *watercourse* SA Australia
231 F4 **Alberique** Spain
124 C2 **Alberni Inlet** British Columbia Canada
228 F1 **Albert** France
129 M1 **Albert** Kansas USA
306 E3 **Albert, Lake** Uganda
124 G1 **Albert Canyon** British Columbia Canada
373 H6 **Albert Edward, Mount** Papua New Guinea
126 E5 **Albert Lea** Minnesota USA
306 E3 **Albert Nile** *watercourse* Uganda
135 F2 **Albert Town** Bahamas
116 H7 **Alberta** *admin. area* Canada
308 D6 **Albertinia** South Africa
234 A2 **Albertirsa** Hungary
123 F9 **Alberton** Prince Edward Island Canada
124 H3 **Alberton** Montana USA
229 H4 **Albertville** France
131 H3 **Albertville** Alabama USA
234 E2 **Albeşti** Romania
228 F5 **Albi** France
228 E4 **Albias** France
226 F5 **Albignasego** Italy
125 M6 **Albin** Wyoming USA
155 H3 **Albina** Suriname
226 E5 **Albino** Italy
231 G3 **Albocácer** Spain
301 F1 **Alborán, Isla de** *island* Spain
224 E4 **Ålborg** Denmark
224 F4 **Ålborg Bugt** *bay* Denmark
230 E5 **Albox** Spain
118 L6 **Albreda** British Columbia Canada
240 E2 **Albrighton** Shropshire England UK
226 E3 **Albstadt** Germany
230 E5 **Albuñol** Spain
159 G5 **Albuquerque** Brazil
129 I3 **Albuquerque** New Mexico USA
154 A1 **Albuquerque, Cayos de** *island* Colombia
230 C4 **Alburquerque** Spain
425 M9 **Albury** NSW Australia
222 I5 **Alby** Sweden
230 B4 **Alcácer do Sal** Portugal
377 I3 **Alcala** Philippines
230 D5 **Alcalá de Guadaira** Spain
230 E3 **Alcalá de Henares** Spain
129 I2 **Alcalde** New Mexico USA
233 E8 **Alcamo** Italy
231 G3 **Alcanar** Spain
230 C3 **Alcañices** Spain
231 F3 **Alcañiz** Spain
156 C3 **Alcântara** Brazil
230 C4 **Alcántara** Spain
230 C4 **Alcántara, Embalse de** *lake* Spain
231 F5 **Alcantarilla** Spain
230 E3 **Alcarria, La** *region* Spain
230 D4 **Alcaudete de la Jara** Spain
230 E4 **Alcázar de San Juan** Spain
234 F2 **Alcedar** Moldova
373 J6 **Alcester Island** Papua New Guinea
394 F6 **Alçi** Turkey
160 F5 **Alcira** Argentina
230 E3 **Alcobendas** Spain
231 F4 **Alcoi** Spain
230 C4 **Alconchel** Spain
230 E3 **Alcorcón** Spain
231 F3 **Alcorisa** Spain
230 E3 **Alcorlo, Embalse de** *lake* Spain
231 G3 **Alcover** Spain
231 F3 **Alcubierre** Spain
231 H4 **Alcúdia** Spain
230 D4 **Alcudia, Sierra de** *range* Spain
310 9 **Aldabra, Groupe d'** *island* Seychelles
129 J6 **Aldama** Mexico
133 F4 **Aldama** Mexico
237 AA7 **Aldan** Russian Federation
237 AB6 **Aldan** *watercourse* Russian Federation
237 Z7 **Aldanskoye Nagor'ye** *region* Russian Federation
383 J3 **Aldarhaan** Mongolia
241 G3 **Aldbury** Hertfordshire England UK
242 F2 **Aldcliffe** Lancashire England UK
230 C4 **Aldea del Cano** Spain
230 D4 **Aldeacentenera** Spain
230 D3 **Aldeanueva de la Vera** Spain
230 D3 **Aldeavieja** Spain
241 I2 **Aldeburgh** Suffolk England UK
159 H4 **Aldeia Bacaeri** Brazil
159 H3 **Aldeia Caiabi** Brazil
159 G5 **Aldeia dos Bororos** Brazil
159 G4 **Aldeia Indígena Espirro** Brazil
309 G2 **Aldeia Milepa** Mozambique
159 G4 **Aldeia Velha** Brazil
159 I3 **Aldeia Velha** Brazil
159 G4 **Aldeia Vinte de Setembro** Brazil
159 G4 **Aldeia Waikiso** Brazil
437 J2 **Alden, Point** Antarctica
228 C2 **Alderney** *island* Channel Islands UK
241 G3 **Aldershot** Hampshire England UK
119 O7 **Aldersyde** Alberta Canada
241 G2 **Alderton** Northamptonshire England UK
243 G2 **Aldfield** North Yorkshire England UK
244 E3 **Aldivalloch** Moray Scotland UK
222 H3 **Aldra** *island* Norway
244 E3 **Aldunie** Moray Scotland UK
224 G4 **Åled** Sweden
300 D5 **Aleg** Mauritania
310 3d **Alegranza** *island* Canary Islands
161 H4 **Alegrete** Brazil
304 E3 **Aléhéride** Togo
163 6 **Alejandro Selkirk, Isla** *island* Juan Fernández Archipiélago
238 E2 **Alëkhovshchina** Russian Federation
238 H4 **Aleksandrov** Russian Federation
388 E3 **Aleksandrov Gay** Russian Federation
389 L3 **Aleksandrovka** Kazakhstan
237 AD8 **Aleksandrovsk Sakhalinskiy** Russian Federation
238 G3 **Aleksandrovskaya** Russian Federation
227 J1 **Aleksandrów Kujawski** Poland
389 K2 **Alekseyevka** Kazakhstan
394 F2 **Alekseyevka** Russian Federation
388 D3 **Alekseyevskaya** Russian Federation
238 G5 **Aleksin** Russian Federation
224 I4 **Ålem** Sweden
307 G2 **Alem Maya** Ethiopia
127 L2 **Alembert, Lac d'** *lake* Québec Canada
222 G5 **Ålen** Norway
228 E2 **Alençon** France
155 H5 **Alenquer** Brazil
230 C4 **Alentejo** *region* Portugal
128 inset **Alenuihāhā Channel** Hawai'i USA
233 C5 **Aléria** Corsica France
117 M2 **Alert** Nunavut Canada
423 7 **Alert Stack** *island* Snares Islands New Zealand
158 D3 **Alerta** Peru
228 G4 **Alès** France
227 L4 **Aleşd** Romania
238 E6 **Alëshnya** Russian Federation
226 E5 **Alessandria** Italy
232 E3 **Alesso** Italy
222 E5 **Ålesund** Norway
383 H3 **Aletai** Xinjiang Uygur Zizhiqu China
162 B3 **Aleusco, Laguna** *bay* Argentina
78 N2 **Aleutian Basin** *underwater feature* Pacific Ocean
237 AL8 **Aleutian Islands** Alaska USA
116 D7 **Aleutian Range** Alaska USA
78 O2 **Aleutian Ridge** *underwater feature* Pacific Ocean
78 N2 **Aleutian Trench** *underwater feature* Pacific Ocean
130 C3 **Alex** Oklahoma USA
125 N3 **Alexander** North Dakota USA
436 T2 **Alexander, Cape** Antarctica
118 C4 **Alexander Archipelago** Alaska USA
308 C5 **Alexander Bay** South Africa
131 I4 **Alexander City** Alabama USA
436 T2 **Alexander Island** Antarctica
423 C7 **Alexandra** New Zealand
163 8 **Alexandra, Cape** South Georgia
376 B4 **Alexandra Channel** Andaman and Nicobar Islands India
118 J6 **Alexandria** British Columbia Canada
134 E3 **Alexandria** Jamaica
308 E6 **Alexandria** South Africa
130 E5 **Alexandria** Louisiana USA
127 M7 **Alexandria** Virginia USA
154 E4 **Alexandrina** Brazil
235 D5 **Alexandropoulis** Greece
122 J6 **Alexis** *watercourse* Newfoundland and Labrador Canada
118 J6 **Alexis Creek** British Columbia Canada
227 L2 **Alexsandrów** Poland
389 N3 **Aleysk** Russian Federation
230 F2 **Alfaro** Spain
234 E4 **Alfatar** Bulgaria
233 F6 **Alfedena** Italy
235 B7 **Alfeios** *watercourse* Greece
157 C8 **Alfenas** Brazil
389 L2 **Alferovka** Russian Federation
230 B4 **Alferrarede** Portugal
240 D4 **Alfington** Devon England UK
244 F3 **Alford** Aberdeenshire Scotland UK
243 I3 **Alford** Lincolnshire England UK
157 D8 **Alfredo Chaves** Brazil
133 F3 **Alfredo V. Bonfil** Mexico
423 F5 **Alfredton** New Zealand
241 F1 **Alfreton** Derbyshire England UK
388 F3 **Algabas** Kazakhstan
229 I5 **Algajola** Corsica France
237 AJ6 **Alganskaya** Russian Federation
224 C3 **Ålgård** Norway
159 F5 **Algarrobillo** Bolivia
154 C2 **Algarrobo** Colombia
160 E6 **Algarrobo del Aguilla** Argentina
230 B5 **Algarve** *region* Portugal
154 C4 **Algeciras** Colombia
230 D5 **Algeciras** Spain
303 F4 **Algena** Eritrea
301 G1 **Alger** *admin. area* Algeria
301 G1 **Alger (Algiers)** Algeria
301 G3 **Algeria** *country* Africa
233 C6 **Alghero** Sardinia Italy
Algiers *see* **Alger** Algeria
225 L3 **Ålgö** *island* Finland
128 E5 **Algodones** Mexico
128 G7 **Algodones, Estero Los** *bay* Mexico
130 G3 **Algoma** Mississippi USA
126 D5 **Algona** Iowa USA
131 I2 **Algood** Tennessee USA
230 E3 **Algora** Spain
230 E5 **Alhama de Granada** Spain
231 F5 **Alhama de Murcia** Spain
222 L4 **Alhamn** Sweden
240 E3 **Alhampton** Somerset England UK
390 F3 **'Alī Al Gharbī** Iraq
391 L2 **'Alī Kheyl** Afghanistan
303 G5 **Ali Sabieh** Djibouti
231 F3 **Aliaga** Spain
158 B2 **Alianza** Peru
235 C6 **Aliartos** Greece
393 C7 **Alibag** Maharashtra India
235 E6 **Alibey** Turkey
235 E6 **Alibey Adası** *island* Turkey
307 F2 **Ālībo** Ethiopia
304 E2 **Alibori** *watercourse* Benin
231 F4 **Alicante (Alacant)** Spain
155 I4 **Alice** Brazil
130 B7 **Alice** Texas USA
233 G7 **Alice, Punta** *cape* Italy
118 G5 **Alice Arm** British Columbia Canada
425 M4 **Alice River** Qld Australia
425 J5 **Alice Springs** NT Australia
131 L8 **Alice Town** Bahamas
130 G4 **Aliceville** Alabama USA
389 L6 **Alichur** *watercourse* Tajikistan
377 I3 **Alicia** Philippines
233 F7 **Alicudi, Isola** *island* Italy
235 G5 **Alifuatpaşa** Turkey
392 E5 **Aliganj** Uttar Pradesh India
392 E5 **Aligarh** Uttar Pradesh India
390 G2 **Alīgūdarz** Iran
230 C3 **Alijó** Portugal
155 H4 **Alikéné, Monts** *range* French Guiana
388 E6 **Alikeykhaly** Azerbaijan
388 E6 **Alikhanly** Azerbaijan
235 D5 **Alikí** Greece
235 C8 **Alikianos** Greece
223 M5 **Alikylä** Finland
373 H4 **Alim Island** Papua New Guinea
305 H5 **Alima** *watercourse* Congo
235 E7 **Alimia** *island* Greece
305 I3 **Alindao** Central African Republic
130 B2 **Aline** Oklahoma USA
234 B2 **Alioş** Romania
394 D5 **Aliova** *watercourse* Turkey
391 L3 **Alipur** Pakistan
379 F3 **Alipurduar** West Bengal India
159 E5 **Alisar** Bolivia
230 C4 **Aliseda** Spain
308 E6 **Aliwal North** South Africa
305 E2 **Aljanare** Nigeria
230 C5 **Aljaraque** Spain
230 B5 **Aljezur** Portugal
230 C4 **Aljucén** Spain
124 I2 **Alkali Lake** Montana USA
125 P3 **Alkaline Lake** North Dakota USA
301 I6 **Alkamari** Niger
389 K2 **Alkaterek** Kazakhstan
224 H3 **Alkvettern** *bay* Sweden
235 C6 **Alkyonidon, Kolpos** *bay* Greece
163 18 **All Saints** Antigua and Barbuda
304 E3 **Allada** Benin
127 Q3 **Allagash** *watercourse* Maine USA
392 E6 **Allahabad** Uttar Pradesh India
437 K1 **Allan Hills** *mountain* Antarctica
120 J7 **Allan Water** Ontario Canada
308 E5 **Allanridge** South Africa
393 E7 **Allapalli** Maharashtra India
302 E3 **Allāqi, Wādī Al** *watercourse* Egypt
230 C2 **Allariz** Spain
244 A4 **Allathasdal** Na h-Eileanan Siar Scotland UK
131 I3 **Allatoona Lake** Georgia USA
308 E4 **Alldays** South Africa
229 H3 **Alle** Switzerland
245 D3 **Alleeny Bridge** Ireland
127 L7 **Allegheny Mountains** USA
163 16 **Allègre, Pointe** *cape* Guadeloupe
223 O3 **Allemalehto** Finland
121 R2 **Allemand, Lac** *lake* Québec Canada
130 F6 **Allemands, Lac des** *lake* Louisiana USA
130 C3 **Allen** Oklahoma USA
245 E2 **Allen, Lough** *lake* Ireland
131 K4 **Allendale** South Carolina USA
243 F2 **Allendale Town** Northumberland England UK
243 F2 **Allenheads** Northumberland England UK
127 N6 **Allentown** Pennsylvania USA
226 F1 **Aller** *watercourse* Germany
240 E3 **Aller** Somerset England UK
232 D2 **Allershausen** Germany
241 F2 **Allestree** Derby England UK
229 H4 **Allevard** France
224 H4 **Allgunnen** *lake* Sweden
233 G7 **Alli** *watercourse* Italy
125 N5 **Alliance** Nebraska USA
228 F4 **Allier** *watercourse* France
131 I6 **Alligator Harbor** Florida USA
245 B5 **Allihies** Ireland
162 C2 **Allipén** Chile
127 L4 **Alliston** Ontario Canada
244 E4 **Alloa** Clackmannanshire Scotland UK
228 E3 **Allonnes** France
229 H4 **Allos** France
223 M3 **Allsån** Sweden
222 J5 **Ållsjön** Sweden
222 K5 **Allsta** Sweden
226 F2 **Allstedt** Germany
240 C3 **Alltwalis** Carmarthenshire Wales UK
393 E8 **Allur** Andhra Pradesh India
122 F3 **Alluviaq** *watercourse* Québec Canada
122 F3 **Alluviaq Fiord** Québec Canada
241 I2 **Allwood Green** Suffolk England UK
117 L9 **Alma** Québec Canada
234 D2 **Alma** Romania
129 I1 **Alma** Colorado USA
131 J5 **Alma** Georgia USA
129 N1 **Alma** Kansas USA
125 P6 **Alma** Nebraska USA
Alma-Ata *see* **Almaty** Kazakhstan
231 G3 **Almacellas** Spain
230 D4 **Almadén** Spain
133 F4 **Almagre, Laguna** *lake* Mexico
230 E3 **Almajano** Spain
389 M4 **Almaly** Kazakhstan
231 F4 **Almansa** Spain
230 E5 **Almanzora** *watercourse* Spain
234 C2 **Almaş** Romania
157 B6 **Almas, Rio das** *watercourse* Brazil
389 M4 **Almatinskaya oblast'** *admin. area* Kazakhstan
389 M5 **Almaty** Kazakhstan
230 E3 **Almazán** Spain
230 C3 **Almeida** Portugal
156 A3 **Almeirim** Brazil
157 D7 **Almenara** Brazil
231 F4 **Almenara** Spain
230 C3 **Almendra, Embalse de** *lake* Spain
230 C4 **Almendralejo** Spain
159 G5 **Almendro** Bolivia
226 C1 **Almere** Netherlands
230 E5 **Almería** Spain
301 F1 **Almería, Golfe de** *bay* Spain
Al'met'yevsk *see* **Almetyevsk** Russian Federation
388 F2 **Almetyevsk** Russian Federation
224 H4 **Älmhult** Sweden
230 D6 **Almina, Punta** *cape* Morocco
162 C6 **Almirante Brown** Argentina
162 B5 **Almirante Montt, Golfo** *bay* Chile
230 B5 **Almodôvar** Portugal
230 D5 **Almogía** Spain
244 E4 **Almond** *watercourse* Scotland UK
129 I1 **Almont** Colorado USA
126 J5 **Almont** Michigan USA
127 M4 **Almonte** Ontario Canada
392 E5 **Almora** Uttaranchal India
230 D3 **Almorox** Spain
231 F4 **Almordi** Spain
222 J4 **Almsele** Sweden
231 F2 **Almudévar** Spain
230 E4 **Almuradiel** Spain
235 D8 **Almyrou, Ormos** *bay* Greece
243 G1 **Aln** *watercourse* England UK
393 D8 **Alnavar** Karnataka India
244 D3 **Alness** Highland Scotland UK
243 F1 **Alnham** Northumberland England UK
222 J5 **Alnö** Sweden
222 J5 **Alnön** *island* Sweden
243 G1 **Alnwick** Northumberland England UK
427 12a **Alo** Wallis and Futuna
155 H4 **Aloepi Twee** Suriname
422 4 **Alofi** Niue New Zealand
427 12a **Alofi, Île** *island* Wallis and Futuna
225 M4 **Aloja** Latvia
238 C4 **Alol'** Russian Federation
379 H3 **Along** Arunachal Pradesh India
235 C6 **Alonnisos** *island* Greece
372 C6 **Alor** *island* Indonesia
372 C5 **Alor, Kepulauan** *island* Indonesia
375 J6 **Alor, Selat** *strait* Indonesia
374 D2 **Alor Setar** Malaysia
230 D5 **Álora** Spain
230 C5 **Alosno** Spain
392 D6 **Alot** Madhya Pradesh India
424 I6 **Aloysius, Mount** WA Australia
230 D5 **Alozaina** Spain
126 J4 **Alpena** Michigan USA
125 P4 **Alpena** South Dakota USA
156 C4 **Alpercatas** *watercourse* Brazil
425 M5 **Alpha** Qld Australia
76 I1 **Alpha Ridge** *underwater feature* Arctic Ocean
310 9 **Alphonse, Île** *island* Seychelles
119 U7 **Alpine** Manitoba Canada
129 H4 **Alpine** Arizona USA
129 K5 **Alpine** Texas USA
125 J5 **Alpine** Wyoming USA
133 F5 **Alpoyeca** Mexico
229 I3 **Alps** *range* Switzerland
223 N4 **Alpua** Finland
235 G5 **Alpullu** Turkey
389 L3 **Alqamergen Koli** *lake* Kazakhstan
241 F2 **Alrewas** Staffordshire England UK
224 E5 **Als** *island* Denmark
229 H2 **Alsace** *region* France
230 E2 **Alsasau** Spain
125 K1 **Alsask** Saskatchewan Canada
118 C3 **Alsek** *watercourse* British Columbia Canada
116 F6 **Alsek** *watercourse* Yukon Territory Canada
222 H5 **Alsen** Sweden
226 E5 **Alseno** Italy
222 H5 **Alsensjön** *bay* Sweden
222 G5 **Alset** Norway
229 I1 **Alsfeld** Germany
222 J5 **Alsjö** Sweden
237 AC8 **Al'skiy Khrebet** *range* Russian Federation
222 I3 **Ålstad** Norway
222 H4 **Alstahaug** Norway
222 H4 **Alsten** *island* Norway
224 G3 **Alstern** *lake* Sweden
243 F2 **Alston** Cumbria England UK
225 N4 **Alsviķi** Latvia
240 D4 **Alswear** Devon England UK
223 M2 **Alta** Norway
230 C3 **Alta** *island* Portugal
224 J3 **Älta** Sweden
162 C3 **Alta, Pampa** *region* Argentina
159 H3 **Alta Floresta** Brazil
160 E4 **Alta Gracia** Argentina
223 M2 **Altaelv** *watercourse* Norway
223 M1 **Altafjorden** *bay* Norway
158 D3 **Altagracia** Bolivia
154 E2 **Altagracia de Orituco** Venezuela
383 I3 **Altai** Mongolia
383 I3 **Altai** Mongolia
383 J4 **Altai** Mongolia
383 I3 **Altai Mountains** Mongolia
133 J2 **Altamaha** *watercourse* Georgia USA
131 K5 **Altamaha Sound** Georgia USA
156 A3 **Altamira** Brazil
160 D3 **Altamira** Chile
132 E2 **Altamira** Mexico

230 D4 Altamira, Sierra de range Spain
126 D8 Altamont Kansas USA
233 G6 Altamura Italy
385 H3 Altan Emel Nei Mongol Zizhiqu China
384 G5 Altan Shiret Nei Mongol Zizhiqu China
384 F2 Altanbulag Mongolia
384 F3 Altanbulag Mongolia
244 D2 Altanduin Highland Scotland UK
157 A8 Altânia Brazil
384 G3 Altanshiree Mongolia
383 I3 Altantsögts Mongolia
132 C2 Altar Mexico
132 C2 Altar watercourse Mexico
128 F5 Altar, Desierto de desert Mexico
223 N4 Altarnen Finland
229 J4 Altavilla Vicentina Italy
127 L8 Altavista Virginia USA
383 J3 Altay Mongolia
389 O3 Altay admin. area Russian Federation
383 I3 Altay Shan range Xinjiang Uygur Zizhiqu China
389 M3 Altayskiy Kray admin. area Russian Federation
229 I3 Altdorf Switzerland
231 F4 Altea Spain
223 M1 Alteidet Norway
226 E2 Altenau watercourse Germany
229 K1 Altenburg Germany
230 C4 Alter do Chão Portugal
157 C8 Alterosa Brazil
222 K2 Altevatnet lake Norway
244 D6 Alticry Dumfries and Galloway Scotland UK
234 C4 Altimir Bulgaria
235 G6 Altıntaş Turkey
235 F7 Altınyayla Turkey
229 H3 Altkirch France
242 A2 Altmover Limavady Northern Ireland UK
232 D2 Altmühl watercourse Germany
244 D2 Altnaharra Highland Scotland UK
131 J3 Alto Georgia USA
130 D5 Alto Texas USA
159 F4 Alto Alegre do Parecis Brazil
157 A7 Alto Araguaia Brazil
154 D2 Alto Barinas Venezuela
159 I3 Alto Boa Vista Brazil
158 C3 Alto Conazo Peru
310 3a Alto Garajonay volcano Canary Islands
157 A7 Alto Garças Brazil
309 G3 Alto Ligonha Mozambique
156 D4 Alto Longá Brazil
154 D4 Alto Madre de Dios watercourse Peru
309 G3 Alto Mólocuè Mozambique
161 G2 Alto Paraguay admin. area Paraguay
161 H3 Alto Paraná admin. area Paraguay
158 H3 Alto Piquiri Brazil
158 D3 Alto Purus watercourse Peru
230 C3 Alto Rabagão, Barragem do lake Portugal
162 B3 Alto Río Senguer Argentina
154 C3 Alto San Mateo mountain Colombia
157 A7 Alto Sucuriú Brazil
233 G7 Altomonte Italy
125 R5 Alton Iowa USA
124 I8 Alton Utah USA
120 G8 Altona Manitoba Canada
126 F6 Altona Illinois USA
126 E6 Altoona Iowa USA
127 L6 Altoona Pennsylvania USA
226 G3 Altötting Germany
229 I3 Altstätten Switzerland
159 E4 Altura Nueva Brema Bolivia
124 E6 Alturas California USA
130 B3 Altus Oklahoma USA
388 E6 Altyagach Azerbaijan
309 G2 Alua Mozambique
394 F5 Alucra Turkey
225 N4 Alūksne Latvia
225 N4 Alūksnes admin. area Latvia
162 B2 Aluminé, Lago lake Argentina
394 E4 Alupka Ukraine
393 E8 Alur Andhra Pradesh India
394 E4 Alushta Ukraine
244 E4 Alva Clackmannanshire Scotland UK
223 N5 Alvajärvi Finland
230 B5 Alvalade Portugal
390 F2 Alvand, Kūh-e mountain Iran
224 G4 Älvängen Sweden
133 G5 Alvarado Mexico
133 G5 Alvarado, Laguna de lake Mexico
155 E5 Alvarães Brazil
230 B3 Alvarenga Portugal
157 B8 Álvares Machado Brazil
132 C3 Alvaro Obregón, Presa lake Mexico
222 G5 Alvdal Norway
240 E2 Alveley Shropshire England UK
233 E5 Alviano Italy
244 E3 Alvie Highland Scotland UK
222 L4 Alvik Sweden
224 D2 Ålvik Norway
130 D6 Alvin Texas USA
230 C4 Alvito Portugal
157 B6 Alvorada Brazil
124 F5 Alvord Lake Oregon USA
222 C4 Alvøy island Norway
222 I5 Älvros Sweden
222 L4 Älvsbyn Sweden
392 D5 Alwar Rajasthan India
240 D1 Alwen Reservoir Wales UK
237 E4 Alwero watercourse Ethiopia
243 F1 Alwinton Northumberland England UK
225 M5 Alytaus admin. area Lithuania
244 E4 Alyth Perth and Kinross Scotland UK
225 M5 Alytus Lithuania
226 G3 Alz watercourse Germany
226 E3 Alzey Germany
228 F5 Alzon France
305 I2 Am-Dam Chad
301 J6 Am Djéména Chad
305 J3 Am Doutilé Chad
302 B5 Am Khoumi Chad
302 C5 Am Léiouna Chad
305 I2 Am Léouna Chad
305 I2 Am Timan Chad
302 C5 Am-Zoer Chad
305 I2 Am Zoer Chad
305 H4 Amada Gaza Central African Republic
224 H2 Åmådalen Sweden
424 I6 Amadeus, Lake NT Australia
305 E2 Amadi Sudan
117 L5 Amadjuak Lake Nunavut Canada
128 G5 Amado Arizona USA
128 B1 Amador City California USA
224 G5 Amager island Denmark
427 12c Amaile Samoa
133 F4 Amajac watercourse Mexico
386 F5 Amakusa-shimoshima island Japan
224 G3 Åmål Sweden
393 F8 Amalapuram Andhra Pradesh India
393 D7 Amalner Maharashtra India
372 F5 Amamapare Indonesia
161 H2 Amambai watercourse Brazil
161 G2 Amambay admin. area Paraguay
381 J3 Amami-O-shima island Japan
381 J3 Amami-shotō island Japan
306 D4 Amamula Democratic Republic of Congo
155 F2 Amana watercourse Venezuela
155 E5 Amana, Lago lake Brazil
373 G4 Amanab Papua New Guinea
229 G2 Amance, Lac lake France
229 H3 Amancey France
392 E6 Amanganj Madhya Pradesh India
388 J3 Amangel'dy Kazakhstan
224 I3 Åmänningen lake Sweden
388 I4 Amanotkel Kazakhstan
233 G7 Amantea Italy
427 14 Amanu island French Polynesia
155 I4 Amapá Brazil
156 B2 Amapá admin. area Brazil
156 A2 Amapari watercourse Brazil
303 F5 Āmara admin. area Ethiopia
234 E3 Amara, Lacul lake Romania
156 F5 Amaraji Brazil
309 G2 Amaramba, Lagon lake Mozambique
156 D4 Amarante Brazil
156 C4 Amarante do Maranhão Brazil
162 C2 Amarga, Laguna La lake Argentina
128 D2 Amargosa Valley Nevada USA
129 L3 Amarillo Texas USA
160 D5 Amarillo, Cerro mountain Argentina
232 E3 Amaro Italy
229 L5 Amaro, Monte mountain Italy
392 E6 Amarpatan Madhya Pradesh India
379 G4 Amarpur Tripura India
234 E3 Amaru Romania
234 E4 Amaru, Danau lake Indonesia
393 E6 Amarwara Madhya Pradesh India
394 E5 Amasya Turkey
394 E5 Amasya admin. area Turkey
424 I6 Amata SA Australia
134 C3 Amatique, Bahía de bay Belize
232 E5 Amatrice Italy
427 13a Amatuku island Tuvalu
373 I6 Amau Papua New Guinea
307 F3 Amaya watercourse Kenya
156 B2 Amazon, Mouths of the Brazil
155 D2 Amazon Basin depression Brazil
79 BB7 Amazon Cone underwater feature Atlantic Ocean
155 I5 Amazon River watercourse Brazil
155 E5 Amazonas admin. area Brazil
156 B3 Amazonas watercourse Brazil
154 B6 Amazonas admin. area Peru
155 D5 Amazonas watercourse Peru
155 E4 Amazonas admin. area Venezuela
393 D7 Ambad Maharashtra India
372 F4 Ambai, Kepulauan island Indonesia
393 D7 Ambajogai Maharashtra India
392 D4 Ambala Haryana India
393 E10 Ambalangoda Sri Lanka
375 H3 Ambalat Indonesia
303 G4 Ambam Cameroon
309 I2 Ambanja Madagascar
237 AH5 Ambarchik Russian Federation
394 F6 Ambarli Syria
223 R4 Ambarnyy Russian Federation
309 I4 Ambatafinandrahama Madagascar
154 B5 Ambato Ecuador
309 I3 Ambato Boeny Madagascar
309 I3 Ambatolampy Madagascar
309 I3 Ambatondrazaka Madagascar
228 E4 Ambazac France
155 I4 Ambé Brazil
372 C4 Ambelau island Indonesia
226 F3 Amberg Germany
134 C3 Ambergris Cay island Belize
229 G4 Ambérieu-en-Bugey France
423 E6 Amberley New Zealand
423 E6 Amberley Beach New Zealand
228 F4 Ambert France
300 D6 Ambidédi Mali
392 F6 Ambikapur Chhattisgarh India
309 I2 Ambilobe Madagascar
309 I3 Ambinaninony Madagascar
373 J5 Ambitle Island Papua New Guinea
243 G1 Amble Northumberland England UK
116 D5 Ambler Alaska USA
242 F4 Ambleside Cumbria England UK
241 I4 Ambleteuse France
309 I3 Ambodifotatra Madagascar
309 I4 Ambohimanga Atsimo Madagascar
309 I4 Ambohinihaonana Madagascar
308 B2 Amboiva Angola
372 D4 Ambon Indonesia
372 D4 Ambon island Indonesia
307 F4 Amboseli, Lake Kenya
309 I4 Ambositra Madagascar
309 I5 Ambovombe Madagascar
128 E3 Amboy California USA
377 G6 Amboyna Cay island Spratly Islands
229 J5 Ambra Italy
306 A5 Ambriz Angola
388 D5 Ambrolauri Georgia
425 N5 Ambrose Qld Australia
426 7 Ambrym island Vanuatu
377 I4 Ambulong island Philippines
375 G6 Ambulu Indonesia
375 G5 Ambunten Indonesia
373 G5 Ambunti Papua New Guinea
237 AK8 Amchitka Island Alaska USA
237 AL8 Amchitka Pass strait Alaska USA
132 D4 Ameca Mexico
229 H1 Amel Belgium
226 C1 Ameland island Netherlands
233 E5 Amelia Italy
231 H4 Amer, Punta de n' cape Spain
157 D5 América Dourada Brazil
79 EE13 American-Antarctic Ridge underwater feature Southern Ocean
124 I5 American Falls Idaho USA
124 I5 American Falls Reservoir Idaho USA
437 F2 American Highland Antarctica
427 12c American Samoa unincorporated US territory Pacific Ocean
157 C8 Americana Brazil
131 I4 Americus Georgia USA
226 C1 Amerongen Netherlands
226 C1 Amersfoort Netherlands
241 G3 Amersham Buckinghamshire England UK
120 H4 Amery Manitoba Canada
437 E2 Amery Basin underwater feature Southern Ocean
437 E2 Amery Ice Shelf Antarctica
302 B2 Amés Spain
126 E5 Ames Iowa USA
130 B2 Ames Oklahoma USA
130 D5 Ames Texas USA
241 F3 Amesbury Wiltshire England UK
120 M8 Ameson Ontario Canada
392 C6 Amet Rajasthan India
235 B6 Amfilochia Greece
237 AB6 Amga watercourse Russian Federation
237 AL5 Amguema Russian Federation
237 AL5 Amguema watercourse Russian Federation
379 H3 Amguri Assam India
127 Q4 Amherst Maine USA
129 K3 Amherst Texas USA
127 M4 Amherst Island Ontario Canada
228 F2 Amiens France
127 L4 Amigo Beach Ontario Canada
390 E2 'Amij, Wādī watercourse Iraq
228 F3 Amilly France
393 C9 Amindivi Islands Lakshadweep India
393 C9 Amini Island Lakshadweep India
307 G3 Amino Ethiopia
308 C4 Aminuis Namibia
80 J5 Amirante Trench underwater feature Indian Ocean
310 9 Amirantes, Les islands Seychelles
120 D5 Amisk Lake Saskatchewan Canada
132 E2 Amistad, Presa La lake Mexico
132 E2 Amistad Reservoir Texas USA
130 E3 Amity Arkansas USA
393 D7 Amla Madhya Pradesh India
392 D6 Amli Rajasthan India
237 AM8 Amlia Island Alaska USA
242 D3 Amlwch Isle of Anglesey Wales UK
122 C2 Ammalluttuuq, Lac lake Québec Canada
390 C3 'Ammān Jordan
222 I3 Ammarfjället island Sweden
222 J4 Ammarnäs Sweden
222 J5 Ammer Sweden
226 D1 Ammerland region Germany
226 F3 Ammersee lake Germany
124 J5 Ammon Idaho USA
376 E4 Amnat Charoen Thailand
244 C5 Amod Argyll and Bute Scotland UK
388 F7 Āmol Iran
159 G5 Amolar Brazil
235 C5 Amolianí Greece
394 E2 Amon' Russian Federation
161 G4 Amores watercourse Argentina
235 E7 Amorgos island Greece
159 I5 Amorinópolis Brazil
117 L9 Amos Québec Canada
224 D3 Åmot Norway
231 I5 Amoucha Algeria
300 E5 Amourj Mauritania
304 D3 Amoya Ghana
222 H3 Amøya island Norway
375 G4 Ampah Indonesia
372 B4 Ampana Indonesia
393 F7 Ampani Orissa India
309 H4 Ampanihy Madagascar
393 E10 Amparai Sri Lanka
309 I3 Ampasimanolotra Madagascar
235 C6 Ampelonas Greece
226 F3 Amper watercourse Germany
161 H3 Ampére Brazil
76 Q6 Ampère Seamount underwater feature Atlantic Ocean
226 G4 Ampezzo Italy
377 G3 Amphitrite Group island Paracel Islands
372 B4 Ampoa Indonesia
233 G7 Ampollino, Lago lake Italy
231 G3 Amposta Spain
241 G3 Ampthill Bedfordshire England UK
230 D3 Ampudia Spain
223 O3 Ampuma-alue island Finland
121 V8 Amqui Québec Canada
390 E7 'Amrān Yemen
393 D7 Amravati Maharashtra India
388 G7 Amreh Iran
393 C7 Amreli Gujarat India
392 D4 Amritsar Punjab India
392 E5 Amroha Uttar Pradesh India
222 K4 Åmsele Sweden
222 H2 Amsen lake Sweden
226 C1 Amsterdam Netherlands
127 N5 Amsterdam New York USA
310 6 Amsterdam, Île island French Southern and Antarctic Lands
229 L2 Amstetten Austria
222 K4 Åmträsket lake Sweden
232 C3 Amtzell Germany
394 G6 'Āmūdah Syria
388 J6 Amudar'ya watercourse Turkmenistan
385 I3 Amugulang Nei Mongol Zizhiqu China
237 AM8 Amukta Pass strait Alaska USA
155 G4 Amuku Mountains Guyana
244 E4 Amulree Perth and Kinross Scotland UK
373 J5 Amun Papua New Guinea
117 J3 Amund Ringnes Island Nunavut Canada
434 M1 Amundsen Abyssal Plain underwater feature Arctic Ocean
437 D2 Amundsen Bay Antarctica
436 N1 Amundsen Coast Antarctica
116 G4 Amundsen Gulf Northwest Territories Canada
77 F16 Amundsen Ridges underwater feature Southern Ocean
437 G1 Amundsen-Scott (USA) research station Antarctica
436 P2 Amundsen Sea Antarctica
434 V2 Amundsen Trough underwater feature Beaufort Sea
224 H2 Amungen lake Sweden
375 G4 Amuntai Indonesia
237 AB9 Amur watercourse China
304 D3 Amur watercourse Ghana
237 AC8 Amur watercourse Russian Federation
372 C3 Amurang, Teluk bay Indonesia
231 I2 Amurrio Spain
385 M2 Amursk Russian Federation
237 AA8 Amurskaya Oblast' admin. area Russian Federation
235 B6 Amvrakikos Kolpos bay Greece
394 F3 Amvrosiyevka Ukraine
235 B5 Amyntaio Greece
234 F4 Amzacea Romania
376 F4 An Khê Vietnam
394 F7 An Nabk Syria
390 E3 An Najaf Iraq
390 E3 An Najaf admin. area Iraq
390 F3 An Nāşiriyah Iraq
301 J2 An Nawfaliyah Libya
390 E3 An Nukhayb Iraq
244 A3 An t-Òb Na h-Eileanan Siar Scotland UK
385 H5 An'su Hebei China
134 E2 Ana María, Golfo de bay Cuba
224 D3 Åna-Sira Norway
427 14 Anaa island French Polynesia
305 E2 Anaba Nigeria
426 4 Anabar Nauru
237 X4 Anabar watercourse Russian Federation
120 J4 Anabusko watercourse Manitoba Canada
128 C4 Anacapa Islands California USA
155 E2 Anaco Venezuela
124 I3 Anaconda Montana USA
124 I4 Anaconda Range Montana USA
124 D2 Anacortes Washington USA
130 B3 Anadarko Oklahoma USA
237 AK6 Anadyr' Russian Federation
237 AI6 Anadyr' watercourse Russian Federation
237 AJ6 Anadyrskaya Nizmennost' region Russian Federation
237 AL6 Anadyrskiy Zaliv bay Russian Federation
237 AJ5 Anadyrskoye Ploskogor'ye region Russian Federation
235 D7 Anafi island Greece
135 I3 Anagada Passage strait Caribbean Sea/Atlantic Ocean
157 D6 Anagé Brazil
128 D4 Anaheim California USA
128 inset Anahola Hawai'i USA
132 D2 Anáhuac Mexico
393 D9 Anai Mudi mountain Kerala India
156 C3 Anajatuba Brazil
309 H4 Anakao Madagascar
393 F8 Anakapalle Andhra Pradesh India
163 5 Anakena, Caleta bay Isla de Pascua (Easter Island)
122 G4 Anaktalik watercourse Newfoundland and Labrador Canada
116 D5 Anaktuvuk Pass Alaska USA
158 D5 Anallajchi, Cerro mountain Bolivia
237 U5 Anama, Ozero lake Russian Federation
374 E3 Anambas, Kepulauan island Indonesia
394 E6 Anamur Turkey
386 G5 Anan Japan
393 C6 Anand Gujarat India
393 G7 Anandapur Orissa India
389 M5 Anan'evo Kyrgyzstan
156 B3 Ananindeua Brazil
372 C5 Anano island Indonesia
393 D8 Anantapur Andhra Pradesh India
392 D4 Anantnag Jammu and Kashmir India/Pakistan
Ananyev see Anan'yiv Ukraine
234 F2 Anan'yiv Ukraine
388 C5 Anapa Russian Federation
157 B7 Anápolis Brazil
159 I1 Anapú watercourse Brazil
391 H2 Anārak Iran
437 L2 Anare Mountains Antarctica
425 inset Anare Station Macquarie Island Australia
222 H5 Anarisfjällen mountain Sweden
154 D2 Anaro, Caño watercourse Venezuela
245 B4 Anascaul Ireland
222 L4 Anäset Sweden
161 H2 Anastácio Brazil
426 2 Anatahan island Northern Mariana Islands
235 D5 Anatoliki Makedonia kai Thraki admin. area Greece
426 7 Anatom island Vanuatu
223 P4 Änättijärvi lake Finland
160 F4 Añatuya Argentina
155 F4 Anaua watercourse Brazil
422 H4 Anaura Bay New Zealand
155 F5 Anavilhanas, Arquipélago das island Brazil
235 C6 Anavra Greece
162 A3 Anay, Punta cape Chile
390 E3 Anbār, Al admin. area Iraq
386 E3 Anbyŏn North Korea
158 B3 Ancash admin. area Peru
225 L4 Ance Latvia
229 G2 Ancerville France
237 AC6 Ancha Russian Federation
158 C4 Anchivay Peru
162 A4 Ancho, Canal strait Chile
116 E6 Anchorage Alaska USA
225 L5 Ančia lake Lithuania
133 J2 Anclote Keys island Florida USA
154 A5 Ancón, Punta cape Ecuador
154 B4 Ancón de Sardinas, Bahía de bay Ecuador
232 E5 Ancona Italy
228 F5 Ancre watercourse France
309 G2 Ancuabe Mozambique
162 B2 Ancud Chile
385 K3 Anda Heilongjiang China
372 C2 Anda island Indonesia
158 C4 Andahuaylas Peru
309 I3 Andaingo Gara Madagascar
309 I4 Andalatanosy Madagascar
222 E5 Åndalsnes Norway
300 F1 Andalucía admin. area Spain
230 D5 Andalucía region Spain
162 D3 Andaluz, Pampa del region Argentina
391 I5 'Andām, Wādī watercourse Oman
393 H9 Andaman and Nicobar Islands (India) admin. area India
78 F6 Andaman Basin underwater feature Bay of Bengal
376 B4 Andaman Islands (India) India
376 B4 Andaman Sea
425 K7 Andamooka SA Australia
309 I2 Andapa Madagascar
308 D3 Andara Namibia
159 F2 Andaraí Brazil
380 E4 Ande Guangxi Zhuangzu Zizhiqu China
222 J2 Andenes Norway
225 H5 Andéramboukane Niger
222 J2 Ånderdalen Nasjonalpark park Norway
229 I3 Andermatt Switzerland
228 D4 Andernos-les-Bains France
426 5 Andersen Air Force Base Guam
116 G5 Anderson watercourse Northwest Territories Canada
116 E6 Anderson Alaska USA
124 D6 Anderson California USA
126 I6 Anderson Indiana USA
131 J3 Anderson South Carolina USA
124 H5 Anderson Ranch Reservoir Idaho USA
128 B2 Anderson Reservoir California USA
224 G4 Anderstorp Sweden
162 B2 Andes range Argentina
159 E6 Andes range Bolivia
162 B3 Andes range Chile
154 C3 Andes range Colombia
154 B4 Andes range Ecuador
158 C4 Andes range Peru
393 E8 Andhra Pradesh admin. area India
163 1a Andicuri bay Aruba
389 K6 Andijon Uzbekistan
389 K6 Andijon admin. area Uzbekistan
309 I3 Andilamena Madagascar
390 F3 Andimeshk Iran
382 G5 Andir He watercourse Xinjiang Uygur Zizhiqu China
159 G1 Andira watercourse Brazil
Andizhan see Andijon Uzbekistan
388 J7 Andkhvoy Afghanistan
228 C5 Andoain Spain
309 I2 Andoany Madagascar
232 G3 Andocs Hungary
238 G2 Andomskiy Pogost Russian Federation
386 F4 Andong South Korea
386 F4 Andong-ho lake South Korea
222 J2 Andørja Norway
222 J2 Andørja island Norway
231 G2 Andorra country Europe
231 F3 Andorra Spain
231 G2 Andorra La Vella Andorra
241 F3 Andover Hampshire England UK
222 J2 Andøya island Norway
128 E4 Andrade California USA
157 B8 Andradina Brazil
309 H4 Andranolava Madagascar
309 I3 Andranomavo Madagascar
122 F5 André Lake Newfoundland and Labrador Canada
309 H3 Andrea Madagascar
237 AL8 Andreanof Islands Alaska USA
225 Q4 Andreapol' Russian Federation
131 J3 Andrews North Carolina USA
131 L4 Andrews South Carolina USA
129 K4 Andrews Texas USA
388 F3 Andreyevka Russian Federation
233 G6 Andria Italy
129 K2 Andrix Colorado USA
379 H4 Andro Manipur India
309 H4 Androka Madagascar
309 I2 Androranga watercourse Madagascar
131 L8 Andros island Bahamas
235 D7 Andros island Greece
134 E1 Andros Town Bahamas
127 P4 Androscoggin watercourse Maine USA
393 C9 Andrott Island Lakshadweep India
225 N4 Andrupene Latvia
232 H2 Andrychów Poland
222 L1 Andsnes Norway
222 K2 Andsvatnet lake Norway
306 D3 Andudu Democratic Republic of Congo
230 D4 Andújar Spain
308 C2 Andulo Angola
237 Y6 Andyngda Russian Federation
301 G5 Anéfis Mali
163 21 Anegada island British Virgin Islands
162 E2 Anegada, Bahía bay Argentina
154 A3 Anegada, Punta cape Panama
160 D6 Añelo Argentina
373 I5 Anepmete Papua New Guinea
129 H2 Aneth Utah USA
231 G2 Aneto mountain Spain
388 H6 Änew Turkmenistan
162 B3 Anexo, Cerro mountain Argentina
301 I5 Aney Niger
226 F5 Anfo Italy
374 D3 Ang Mo Kio admin. area Singapore
376 D4 Ang Thong Thailand
309 I2 Angadoka, Lohatanjona cape Madagascar
162 A4 Angamos, Isla island Chile
163 5 Angamos, Punta cape Isla de Pascua (Easter Island)
384 E2 Angara watercourse Russian Federation
384 E2 Angarsk Russian Federation
237 V8 Angaul Russian Federation
426 3 Angaur island Palau
222 I5 Ånge Sweden
222 J6 Ängebo Sweden
120 I6 Angekum Lake Ontario Canada
132 B2 Ángel de la Guarda, Isla island Mexico
129 J2 Angel Fire New Mexico USA
377 I4 Angeles Philippines
224 G4 Ängelholm Sweden
223 N2 Angeli Finland
127 L5 Angelica New York USA
132 E2 Angelo Texas USA
373 F4 Angemuk, Gunung mountain Indonesia
307 F2 Anger watercourse Ethiopia
232 C4 Angera Italy
302 F5 Ångereb Ethiopia
302 F5 Ångereb Wenz watercourse Ethiopia
222 J5 Ångermanälven watercourse Sweden
222 J5 Ångermanland region Sweden
228 D3 Angers France
223 M3 Ängesån Sweden
222 L3 Ängesån watercourse Sweden
222 L5 Ängesön Sweden
222 L5 Ängesön island Sweden
375 H4 Anggana Indonesia
224 H4 Ånghultasjön lake Sweden
156 E4 Angicos Brazil
120 F1 Angikuni Lake Nunavut Canada
391 K3 Angizay Afghanistan
240 B3 Angle Pembrokeshire Wales UK
423 B8 Anglem, Mount New Zealand
242 D3 Anglesey, Isle of admin. area England UK
130 D6 Angleton Texas USA
228 E3 Anglin watercourse France
226 B3 Anglure France
122 C6 Ango, Lac lake Québec Canada
309 G3 Angoche Mozambique
391 I4 Angohrān Iran
160 C6 Angol Chile
308 C2 Angola country Africa
77 S11 Angola Abyssal Plain underwater feature Atlantic Ocean
77 S11 Angola Basin underwater feature Atlantic Ocean
118 D4 Angoon Alaska USA
132 C2 Angostura, Presa La lake Mexico
125 N5 Angostura Reservoir South Dakota USA
309 H2 Angouan (Nzwani) island Comoros
228 E4 Angoulême France
228 E4 Angoumois region France
379 H3 Angpawng Bum Myanmar
310 1b Angra do Heroísmo Azores
157 C8 Angra dos Reis Brazil
372 E4 Angra Meos island Indonesia
389 K5 Angren Uzbekistan
233 F6 Angri Italy
222 H5 Ångsfjärden bay Sweden
306 C3 Angu Democratic Republic of Congo
163 20 Anguilla British overseas territory Caribbean
134 E2 Anguilla Cays island Bahamas
385 H5 Anguo Hebei China
425 K3 Angurugu NT Australia
244 F4 Angus admin. area Scotland UK
222 F5 Angvik Norway
308 E3 Angwa watercourse Zimbabwe
161 H2 Anhanduí watercourse Brazil
224 F4 Anholt Denmark
381 H2 Anhui admin. area China
116 D6 Aniak Alaska USA
116 D7 Aniakchak National Monument and Preserve park Alaska USA
426 4 Anibare Nauru
228 F1 Aniche France
157 B7 Anicuns Brazil
304 E3 Anie Togo
244 D4 Anie Stirling Scotland UK
226 G4 Anif Austria
162 B4 Animales Chile
129 H5 Animas New Mexico USA
129 I2 Animas watercourse New Mexico USA
234 C3 Aninoasa Romania
235 G6 Anıtkaya Turkey
387 I1 Aniva Russian Federation
237 AD9 Aniva, Mys cape Russian Federation
387 I1 Aniva, Mys mountain Russian Federation
237 AD9 Aniva, Zaliv bay Russian Federation
426 7 Aniwa island Vanuatu
393 D6 Anjad Madhya Pradesh India
225 N2 Anjala Finland
225 N2 Anjalankoski Finland
222 H5 Anjan lake Sweden
393 D7 Anjangaon Maharashtra India
392 C6 Anjar Gujarat India
380 F3 Anjiang Hunan China
391 K4 Anjira Pakistan
310 8 Anjouan (Nzwani) island Comoros
309 I3 Anjozorobe Madagascar
386 E3 Anju North Korea
305 F2 Anka Nigeria
309 H4 Ankaboa, Tanjona cape Madagascar
380 F2 Ankang Shaanxi China
394 E5 Ankara Turkey
394 E5 Ankara admin. area Turkey
222 I4 Ankarede Kapell Sweden
222 I4 Ankarvattnet Sweden
222 I4 Ankarvattnet lake Sweden
309 I3 Ankavandra Madagascar
309 H4 Ankazoabo Madagascar
309 I3 Ankazobe Madagascar
126 E5 Ankeny Iowa USA
393 C7 Ankleshwar Gujarat India
393 D8 Ankola Karnataka India
243 H3 Anlaby East Riding of Yorkshire England UK
376 E4 Ånlong Vêng Cambodia
381 G2 Anlu Hubei China
386 E4 Anmoyon-do island South Korea
222 H5 Ånn lake Sweden
437 D2 Ann, Cape Antarctica
126 J5 Ann Arbor Michigan USA
78 N4 Ann Judge Seamount underwater feature Pacific Ocean
122 H6 Ann Marie Lake Newfoundland and Labrador Canada
388 C3 Anna Russian Federation
130 C4 Anna Texas USA
127 M7 Anna, Lake Virginia USA
131 J7 Anna Maria Florida USA
162 A3 Anna Pink, Bahía bay Chile
155 C3 Anna Regina Guyana
301 H1 Annaba Algeria
301 H1 Annaba admin. area Algeria
245 D4 Annaboty Ireland
424 I3 Annaburroo NT Australia
242 C2 Annacloy Down Northern Ireland UK
245 C3 Annagh Island Ireland
242 B2 Annahilt Lisburn Northern Ireland UK
242 A2 Annalee watercourse Ireland
242 C2 Annalong Newry and Mourne Northern Ireland UK
244 E6 Annan Dumfries and Galloway Scotland UK
244 E5 Annan watercourse Scotland UK
127 M7 Annapolis Maryland USA
122 E2 Annapolis Strait Nunavut Canada
242 E2 Annaside Cumbria England UK
244 C3 Annat Highland Scotland UK
424 F6 Annean, Lake WA Australia
229 H4 Annecy France
163 8 Annenkov Island South Georgia
238 G2 Annenskiy Most Russian Federation
380 D4 Anning Yunnan China
238 G3 Annino Russian Federation
305 F5 Annobón island Equatorial Guinea
226 C5 Annonay France
227 K2 Annopol Poland
229 H5 Annot France
134 E3 Annotto Bay Jamaica
126 J8 Annville Kentucky USA
229 H2 Annweiler Germany
162 C6 Año Nuevo, Seno bay Chile
235 D7 Ano Sagkri Greece
426 8 Anoano Solomon Islands
226 C2 Anor France
155 F5 Anori Brazil
307 H6 Anorontany, Tanjona cape Madagascar
224 F1 Anoya lake Norway
385 H5 Anping Hebei China
381 H2 Anqing Anhui China
385 I6 Anqiu Shandong China
230 E3 Anquela del Ducado Spain
379 G3 Anrao Xizang Zizhiqu China
229 K3 Anras Austria
381 G3 Anren Hunan China
372 E4 Ansas Indonesia
226 F3 Ansbach Germany
135 F3 Anse-à-Galets Haiti
163 16 Anse-Bertrand Guadeloupe
310 9a Anse Boileau Seychelles
163 13 Anse la Raye St Lucia
310 9b Anse Royal Seychelles
310 9a Anse Volbert Seychelles
233 D5 Ansedónia Italy
225 L3 Ansekūla Estonia
385 J4 Anshan Liaoning China
380 E3 Anshun Guizhou China
160 D4 Ansilta mountain Argentina
224 H1 Ansjön lake Sweden
125 P6 Ansley Nebraska USA
130 B4 Anson Texas USA
425 inset Anson Point Norfolk Island Australia
301 G5 Ansongo Mali
425 inset Ansons Bay Norfolk Island Australia
241 H3 Anstey Hertfordshire England UK
373 F4 Ansus Indonesia
426 6 Ant Atoll island Federated States of Micronesia
158 C4 Antabamba Peru
309 J2 Antalaha Madagascar
394 D6 Antalya Turkey
394 D6 Antalya admin. area Turkey
235 G7 Antalya Körfezi bay Turkey
309 I3 Antananarivo Madagascar
309 I3 Antananarivo admin. area Madagascar
436 T2 Antarctic Peninsula Antarctica
437 G1 Antarctica continent
373 G5 Antares mountain Indonesia
161 I4 Antas watercourse Brazil
374 E5 Antatai Indonesia
128 D2 Antelope Lake Nevada USA
128 D1 Antelope Range Nevada USA
124 G5 Antelope Reservoir Oregon USA
230 D5 Antequera Spain
129 J1 Antero Reservoir Colorado USA
232 E3 Anterselva Italy
129 I5 Anthony Texas USA
Anti-Taurus Mountains see Güney Doğu Toroslar Turkey
229 H5 Antibes France
155 F2 Antica, Isla island Venezuela
123 F8 Anticosti, Île d' island Québec Canada
228 E2 Antifer, Cap d' cape France
126 G4 Antigo Wisconsin USA
163 18 Antigua island Antigua and Barbuda
310 3d Antigua Canary Islands
135 I3 Antigua and Barbuda country Caribbean
133 F4 Antiguo Morelos Mexico
235 C6 Antikyras, Kolpos bay Greece
235 D7 Antimilos island Greece
124 J7 Antimony Utah USA
223 M3 Antinrova Sweden
Antioch see Hatay Turkey
154 C3 Antioquia Colombia
154 C3 Antioquia admin. area Colombia
235 D7 Antiparos island Greece
235 B6 Antipaxoi island Greece
236 Q5 Antipayuta Russian Federation
238 E5 Antipino Russian Federation
423 11 Antipodes Island New Zealand
377 I4 Antipolo Philippines
238 F4 Antipovo Russian Federation
154 B5 Antisana volcano Ecuador
130 C3 Antlers Oklahoma USA
160 D2 Antofagasta Chile
160 D2 Antofagasta admin. area Chile
160 E3 Antofagasta de la Sierra Argentina
160 E3 Antofalla, Salina de lake Argentina
160 D3 Antofalla, Volcán volcano Argentina
134 D5 Antón Panama
129 K4 Anton Texas USA
309 J3 Antongila, Helodranon' bay Madagascar
310 4a Antónia, Pico da volcano Cape Verde
309 I3 Antonibe Madagascar
162 C4 Antonio de Biedma Argentina
162 B5 Antonio Varas, Peninsula peninsula Chile
129 J2 Antonito Colorado USA
223 U6 Antonovskaya Russian Federation
242 B2 Antrim Antrim Northern Ireland UK
242 B2 Antrim admin. area Northern Ireland UK
242 B2 Antrim Mountains Northern Ireland UK
309 I3 Antsiafabositra Madagascar
238 E3 Antsiferovo Russian Federation
309 I3 Antsirabe Madagascar
309 I2 Antsiranana Madagascar
309 I2 Antsiranana admin. area Madagascar
309 H3 Antsoha Madagascar

309 I2 **Antsohihy** Madagascar
309 I2 **Antsohimbondrona** Madagascar
225 N2 **Anttola** Finland
392 E5 **Antu** Uttar Pradesh India
159 F3 **Antuérpia** Brazil
229 G1 **Antwerpen** Belgium
229 G1 **Antwerpen** *admin. area* Belgium
427 14 **Anuanuraro** *island* French Polynesia
427 14 **Anuanurunga** *island* French Polynesia
121 R3 **Anuc, Lac** *lake* Québec Canada
392 C5 **Anupgarh** Rajasthan India
392 D5 **Anupshahr** Rajasthan India
393 E10 **Anuradhapura** Sri Lanka
436 T2 **Anvers Island** Antarctica
228 F1 **Anvin** France
381 H2 **Anwen** Zhejiang China
241 G1 **Anwick** Lincolnshire England UK
385 H5 **Anxin** Hebei China
304 D3 **Anyama** Côte d'Ivoire
380 E4 **Anyang** Guangxi Zhuangzu Zizhiqu China
385 H6 **Anyang** Henan China
386 E4 **Anyang** South Korea
380 C1 **A'nyemaoen Shan** *range* Jiangsu China
381 H1 **Anyi** Jiangsu China
304 D3 **Anyinam** Ghana
225 M5 **Anykščiai** Lithuania
237 AI5 **Anyuyskiy Khrebet** *range* Russian Federation
119 P4 **Anzac** Alberta Canada
118 J5 **Anzac** British Columbia Canada
424 inset **Anzac Peak** Heard Island Australia
389 O2 **Anzhero-Sudzhensk** Russian Federation
306 C4 **Anzi** Democratic Republic of Congo
233 F6 **Anzi** Italy
233 E6 **Anzio** Italy
233 E6 **Anzio, Capo d'** *cape* Italy
160 F6 **Anzoátegui** Argentina
155 E2 **Anzoátegui** *admin. area* Venezuela
388 E6 **Anzoli** Azerbaijan
376 C5 **Ao Luk** Thailand
426 7 **Aoba** *island* Vanuatu
387 H5 **Aoga-shima** *island* Japan
231 I5 **Aokas** Algeria
426 8a **Aola** Solomon Islands
387 I3 **Aomori** Japan
423 D6 **Aoraki/Cook, Mount** New Zealand
423 F5 **Aorangi Range** New Zealand
423 E5 **Aorere** *watercourse* New Zealand
226 D5 **Aosta** Italy
422 F4 **Aotea Harbour** New Zealand
300 B5 **Aoufist** Western Sahara
306 B2 **Aouk, Bahr** *watercourse* Central African Republic
305 I2 **Aoukale** *watercourse* Central African Republic
305 I2 **Aoukale** *watercourse* Chad
300 D5 **Aourou** Mali
300 E2 **Aoutime, Jbel** *mountain* Morocco
381 G3 **Aoxi** Jiangxi China
381 H3 **Aoyang** Fujian China
381 G3 **Aoyang** Jiangxi China
301 J4 **Aozou** Chad
161 G2 **Apa** *watercourse* Brazil
307 E3 **Apac** Uganda
128 G4 **Apache Junction** Arizona USA
160 E2 **Apagado, Volcán** *volcano* Chile
133 I2 **Apalachee Bay** Florida USA
131 I6 **Apalachicola** Florida USA
133 I2 **Apalachicola** *watercourse* Florida USA
304 D3 **Apam** Ghana
155 G3 **Apanachi** Guyana
426 8 **Apaora** Solomon Islands
154 D5 **Apaporis, Rio** *watercourse* Brazil
375 H4 **Apar, Teluk** *bay* Indonesia
159 I5 **Aparecida do Rio Doce** Brazil
157 B8 **Aparecida do Taboado** Brazil
159 E4 **Aparejos** Bolivia
423 C7 **Aparima** *watercourse* New Zealand
377 I3 **Aparri** Philippines
154 B3 **Apartadó** Colombia
155 F3 **Apurén** Venezuela
162 C3 **Apas, Sierra** *range* Argentina
427 14 **Apataka** *island* French Polynesia
223 R3 **Apatity** Russian Federation
155 H3 **Apatou** French Guiana
132 E5 **Apatzingán** Mexico
226 C1 **Apeldoorn** Netherlands
159 E4 **Apere** *watercourse* Bolivia
306 D3 **Api** Democratic Republic of Congo
372 A6 **Api, Gunung** *volcano* Indonesia
372 B4 **Api, Tanjung** *cape* Indonesia
427 12c **Apia** Samoa
159 G3 **Apiacás** Brazil
159 G3 **Apiacás, Serra dos** *range* Brazil
157 B9 **Apiaí** Brazil
155 F4 **Apiaú, Serra do** *range* Brazil
377 J6 **Apo, Mount** *mountain* Philippines
132 E3 **Apodaca** Mexico
156 E4 **Apodi** Brazil
156 E4 **Apodi** *watercourse* Brazil
235 D7 **Apoikia** Greece
155 F3 **Apoipó** Venezuela
235 E7 **Apolakkia** Greece
427 12c **Apolima** *island* Samoa
425 L9 **Apollo Bay** Vic. Australia
235 D7 **Apollonia** Greece
134 B4 **Apopa** El Salvador
131 K6 **Apopka** Florida USA
131 K6 **Apopka, Lake** Florida USA
159 H5 **Apore** *watercourse* Brazil
159 I5 **Aporé** Brazil
158 D4 **Aporoma** Peru
234 A2 **Apostag** Hungary
117 O6 **Apostelen Tommelfinger** *mountain* Greenland
126 F3 **Apostle Islands** Wisconsin USA
161 H3 **Apóstoles** Argentina
310 6 **Apôtres, Îlots des** *island* French Southern and Antarctic Lands
132 E4 **Apozol** Mexico
127 M6 **Appalachian Mountains** USA
229 K5 **Appennino** *range* Italy
229 I3 **Appenzell** Switzerland
229 J3 **Appiano sulla Strada del Vino** Italy
244 E5 **Appin** Dumfries and Galloway Scotland UK
128 D3 **Apple Valley** California USA
243 F2 **Appleby-in-Westmorland** Cumbria England UK
240 C3 **Appledore** Devon England UK
126 G4 **Appleton** Wisconsin USA
156 A1 **Approuague** *watercourse* French Guiana
426 5 **Apra Harbor** Guam
426 5 **Apra Heights** Guam
238 G5 **Aprelevka** Russian Federation
373 G5 **April** *watercourse* Papua New Guinea
233 E6 **Aprilia** Italy
127 L4 **Apsley** Ontario Canada
229 G5 **Apt** France
157 B8 **Apucarana** Brazil
159 G2 **Apuí** Brazil
426 3 **Apurashokoru** *island* Palau
154 D3 **Apure** *admin. area* Venezuela
154 D3 **Apure** *watercourse* Venezuela
158 C4 **Apurímac** *admin. area* Peru
225 N5 **Apvardų ežeras** *lake* Lithuania
388 G6 **Aq Band** Iran
388 F7 **Aq Gadok Gardanehye** *pass* Iran
388 G6 **Aq Qal'eh** Iran
390 C4 **Aqaba, Gulf of** Red Sea
388 J7 **Āqchah** Afghanistan
302 F4 **Aqiq** Sudan
383 I4 **Aqitag** *mountain* Xinjiang Uygur Zizhiqu China
391 H4 **'Aqqah** United Arab Emirates
128 F3 **Aquarius Mountains** Arkansas USA
128 G1 **Aquarius Plateau** Utah USA
120 M5 **Aquatuk** *watercourse* Ontario Canada
158 D2 **Aquidabã** Brazil
226 G5 **Aquileia** Italy
135 C3 **Aquilla Reservoir** Texas USA
135 F3 **Aquin** Haiti
132 E3 **Aquiraz** Brazil
228 D4 **Aquitaine** *admin. area* France
154 C2 **Aquja, Cabo de la** *cape* Colombia
391 H5 **Ar Rajmi** Oman
390 E2 **Ar Ramādī** Iraq
390 E5 **Ar Ramādīyāt** Saudi Arabia
394 F6 **Ar Raqqah** Syria
390 G4 **Ar Rayyān** Qatar
390 G4 **Ar Rifā' al Gharbi** Bahrain
390 F7 **Ar Risān** Yemen
390 F5 **Ar Riyāḍ (Riyadh)** Saudi Arabia
390 F7 **Ar Rukbah** Yemen
390 D2 **Ar Ruṭbah** Iraq
390 G5 **Ar Ruways** United Arab Emirates
302 E2 **Ar Ruzayqāt** Egypt
392 F6 **Ara** Bihar India
307 G2 **Āra Ārba** Ethiopia
245 D4 **Ara Bridge** Ireland
131 H3 **Arab** Alabama USA
306 D1 **'Arab, Baḥr al** *watercourse* Sudan
80 K3 **Arabian Basin** *underwater feature* Arabian Sea
390 F5 **Arabian Peninsula** Saudi Arabia
391 J6 **Arabian Sea**
155 F3 **Arabopó** Venezuela
155 F4 **Araca** *watercourse* Brazil
157 E5 **Aracaju** Brazil
156 E4 **Aracati** Brazil
158 C3 **Aracati** Brazil
157 B8 **Araçatuba** Brazil
155 E5 **Araçatuba, Ilhas de** *island* Brazil
230 C5 **Aracena, Sierra de** *range* Spain
157 E5 **Araci** Brazil
157 D7 **Aracruz** Brazil
157 D7 **Araçuaí** Brazil
157 D7 **Araçuaí** *watercourse* Brazil
234 B2 **Arad** Romania
234 B2 **Arad** *admin. area* Romania
305 I2 **Arada** Chad
305 I2 **Aradeib, Wadi** *watercourse* Sudan
372 D6 **Arafura Sea** Australia
78 J9 **Arafura Shelf** *underwater feature* Arafura Sea
157 A6 **Aragarças** Brazil
231 F3 **Aragón** *admin. area* Spain
231 F2 **Aragón** *watercourse* Spain
154 E2 **Aragua** *admin. area* Venezuela
154 E2 **Aragua de Barcelona** Venezuela
157 B6 **Araguaçu** Brazil
157 A7 **Araguaia** *watercourse* Brazil
156 B5 **Araguaia, Arroios do** *watercourse* Brazil
157 B5 **Araguaia, Rio** *watercourse* Brazil
156 B4 **Araguaína** Brazil
155 F2 **Araguao, Boca** *bay* Venezuela
155 F2 **Araguapiche, Punta** *cape* Venezuela
157 B7 **Araguari** Brazil
155 I4 **Araguari** *watercourse* Brazil
156 B4 **Araguatins** Brazil
423 D6 **Arahura** New Zealand
156 D3 **Araioses** Brazil
223 O3 **Arajärvi** *lake* Finland
390 G2 **Arāk** Iran
306 E3 **Araka** Sudan
237 AM5 **Arakamchechen, Ostrov** *island* Russian Federation
388 E6 **Araks** *watercourse* Azerbaijan
388 H4 **Aral Sea** *lake* Kazakhstan
388 I4 **Aral'sk (Aralsk)** Kazakhstan
Aral'skoye More *see* **Aral Sea** Kazakhstan/Uzbekistan
388 E3 **Aralsor, Ozero** *lake* Kazakhstan
224 C1 **Aram** Norway
373 G5 **Aramia** *watercourse* Papua New Guinea
422 G5 **Aramoana** New Zealand
245 C3 **Aran Islands** Ireland
230 E3 **Aranda de Duero** Spain
163 9 **Aranguez** Trinidad and Tobago
393 E9 **Arani** Tamil Nadu India
230 E3 **Aranjuez** Spain
160 F6 **Arano** Argentina
308 C4 **Aranos** Namibia
157 B7 **Arantes** *watercourse* Brazil
426 1 **Aranuka** *island* Kiribati
300 F5 **Araouane** Mali
158 D4 **Arapa, Lago de** *lake* Peru
130 B3 **Arapaho** Oklahoma USA
129 K1 **Arapahoe** Colorado USA
125 P6 **Arapahoe** Nebraska USA
423 F5 **Arapawa Island** New Zealand
161 G4 **Arapey Grande** *watercourse* Uruguay
156 E5 **Arapiraca** Brazil
155 H5 **Arapiriri, Ilha** *island* Brazil
235 D5 **Arapis, Akra** *cape* Greece
155 H5 **Arapiuns** *watercourse* Brazil
422 F4 **Arapuni** New Zealand
159 G4 **Araputanga** Brazil
390 E3 **'Ar'ar** Saudi Arabia
156 F4 **Arara** Brazil
154 C5 **Araracuara, Mesa** *region* Colombia
161 I4 **Araranguá** Brazil
159 E3 **Araras** Brazil
157 A7 **Araras, Serra das** *range* Brazil
154 C5 **Araras de Coemas** Colombia
388 D6 **Ararat** Armenia
388 E6 **Ararat** *pass* Armenia
425 L9 **Ararat** Vic. Australia
159 E4 **Araré, Laguna** *lake* Bolivia
156 C3 **Arari** Brazil
156 B3 **Arari, Lago** *lake* Brazil
392 G5 **Araria** Bihar India
156 D4 **Araripe** Brazil
156 D4 **Araripina** Brazil
224 C2 **Arās** Norway
231 F4 **Aras de Alpuente** Spain
156 D4 **Aratas, Açude** *lake* Brazil
154 D3 **Arauca** *admin. area* Colombia
154 D3 **Arauca** Venezuela
135 G6 **Arauca** *watercourse* Venezuela
162 B2 **Araucania** *admin. area* Chile
157 B9 **Araucária** Brazil
392 C6 **Aravali Range** Rajasthan India
225 M3 **Aravete** Estonia
373 I5 **Arawe Islands** Papua New Guinea
423 C7 **Arawhata** New Zealand
157 C7 **Araxá** Brazil
235 B6 **Araxos, Akra** *cape* Greece
155 E2 **Araya, Punta de** *cape* Venezuela
230 B3 **Arazede** Portugal
230 D6 **Arba Ayacha** Morocco
307 F2 **Ārba Minch** Ethiopia
230 D6 **Arbaoua** Morocco
231 I5 **Arbaoun** Algeria
388 E1 **Arbazh** Russian Federation
390 F2 **Arbīl** Iraq
390 E2 **Arbīl** *admin. area* Iraq
224 H3 **Arboga** Sweden
229 G3 **Arbois** France
159 E4 **Árbol Solo** Bolivia
160 F6 **Arboledas** Argentina
154 B2 **Arboletes** Colombia
229 I3 **Arbon** Switzerland
119 T6 **Arborfield** Saskatchewan Canada
244 F4 **Arbroath** Angus Scotland UK
231 H3 **Arbúcies** Spain
128 A1 **Arbuckle** California USA
383 K2 **Arbulag** Mongolia
393 F4 **Arc** *watercourse* France
228 D4 **Arcachon** France
131 K7 **Arcadia** Florida USA
125 P6 **Arcadia** Nebraska USA
124 C6 **Arcata** California USA
132 E5 **Arcelia** Mexico
228 F2 **Arces** France
235 F7 **Archángelos** Greece
234 C4 **Archar** Bulgaria
302 C4 **Archeï, Ouadi** *watercourse* Chad
231 F4 **Archena** Spain
437 K2 **Archer Point** *cape* Antarctica
425 L3 **Archer River Roadhouse** Qld Australia
119 T6 **Archerwill** Saskatchewan Canada
128 H1 **Arches National Park** Utah USA
233 F5 **Archi** Italy
119 Q3 **Archibald Lake** Saskatchewan Canada
230 D5 **Archidona** Spain
226 F5 **Arco** Italy
124 I5 **Arco** Idaho USA
226 C4 **Arconce** *watercourse* France
157 C8 **Arcos** Brazil
230 B3 **Arcos** Portugal
230 E3 **Arcos de Jalón** Spain
156 E5 **Arcoverde** Brazil
117 K4 **Arctic Bay** Nunavut Canada
116 B3 **Arctic Ocean**
116 F5 **Arctic Red** *watercourse* Northwest Territories Canada
436 U2 **Arctowski (Poland)** *research station* Antarctica
226 E6 **Arcu, Punta di** *cape* Corsica France
245 C3 **Ard** Ireland
390 F7 **Arḍ ar Raydah** Yemen
235 D5 **Arda** *watercourse* Bulgaria
229 I4 **Arda** *watercourse* Italy
388 E6 **Ardabil** Iran
388 E6 **Ardabil** *admin. area* Iran
242 B3 **Ardagh** Ireland
242 B2 **Ardaghy** Ireland
394 G5 **Ardahan** Turkey
394 G5 **Ardahan** *admin. area* Turkey
390 G3 **Ardakān** Iran
391 H3 **Ardakān** Iran
230 D5 **Ardales** Spain
222 E6 **Årdalstangen** Norway
388 G6 **Ardan** *mountain* Turkmenistan
245 D2 **Ardara** Ireland
377 G6 **Ardasier Reefs** Spratly Islands
388 E2 **Ardatov** Russian Federation
242 B2 **Ardboe** Cookstown Northern Ireland UK
244 B4 **Ardchiavaig** Highland Scotland UK
229 G4 **Ardèche** *watercourse* France
245 F3 **Ardee** Ireland
244 D4 **Ardentinny** Argyll and Bute Scotland UK
232 D5 **Ardenza** Italy
244 D4 **Ardeonaig** Perth and Kinross Scotland UK
390 G2 **Ardestān** Iran
245 C4 **Ardfert** Ireland
244 B5 **Ardfin** Argyll and Bute Scotland UK
245 E4 **Ardfinnan** Ireland
300 E1 **Ardila** *watercourse* Spain
244 A3 **Ardivachar Point** Scotland UK
242 C2 **Ardkeen** Ards Northern Ireland UK
242 A4 **Ardlea** Ireland
244 D4 **Ardleish** Argyll and Bute Scotland UK
425 M8 **Ardlethan** NSW Australia
244 D4 **Ardlui** Argyll and Bute Scotland UK
119 P5 **Ardmore** Alberta Canada
244 D3 **Ardmore** Highland Scotland UK
130 H3 **Ardmore** Alabama USA
130 C3 **Ardmore** Oklahoma USA
244 B4 **Ardnamurchan, Point of** Scotland UK
244 B5 **Ardnave Point** Scotland UK
244 D4 **Ardoch** Stirling Scotland UK
229 H3 **Ardon** Switzerland
226 A2 **Ardres** France
242 C2 **Ards** *admin. area* Northern Ireland UK
244 B5 **Ardtalla** Argyll and Bute Scotland UK
232 D2 **Ardud** Romania
234 C3 **Ardvasar** Highland Scotland UK
244 D4 **Ardverikie** Highland Scotland UK
244 A3 **Ardvule, Rubha** *cape* Scotland UK
242 D2 **Ardwell** Dumfries and Galloway Scotland UK
222 H5 **Åre** Sweden
159 H5 **Areado** Brazil
157 D8 **Areal** Brazil
135 H3 **Arecibo** Puerto Rico
238 H3 **Arëfino** Russian Federation
161 G3 **Aregua** Paraguay
156 E4 **Areia Branca** Brazil
303 F5 **Arekwa** *watercourse* Ethiopia
119 R6 **Arelee** Saskatchewan Canada
224 F3 **Aremarksjøen** *lake* Norway
377 I5 **Arena** *island* Philippines
124 C7 **Arena, Point** California USA
132 C4 **Arena, Punta** *cape* Mexico
132 C3 **Arena de la Ventana, Punta** *cape* Mexico
154 C2 **Arenal** Colombia
134 C5 **Arenal, Laguna de** *lake* Costa Rica
162 B4 **Arenales, Cerro** *mountain* Chile
159 G4 **Arenápolis** Brazil
160 D2 **Arenas, Punta** *cape* Chile
154 B4 **Arenas, Punta** *cape* Ecuador
162 C5 **Arenas, Punta de** *cape* Argentina
224 E3 **Arendal** Norway
226 F1 **Arendsee** *lake* Germany
230 F3 **Arenys, Embalse de** *lake* Spain
235 C7 **Areopoli** Greece
230 B3 **Areosa** Portugal
158 D5 **Arequipa** Peru
158 C4 **Arequipa** *admin. area* Peru
155 H5 **Arere** Brazil
307 F3 **Ārēro** Ethiopia
156 F4 **Arês** Brazil
135 H5 **Areskutan** *mountain* Sweden
228 D5 **Arette** France
230 D3 **Arévalo** Spain
232 D5 **Arezzo** Italy
237 AE5 **Arga** Russian Federation
228 D5 **Arga** *watercourse* Spain
237 W5 **Arga-Sala** *watercourse* Russian Federation
384 F3 **Argalant** Mongolia
230 E4 **Argamasilla de Alba** Spain
224 G2 **Årgård** Norway
228 D5 **Argelès-Gazost** France
228 F5 **Argelès-sur-Mer** France
229 H5 **Argens** *watercourse* France
127 Q1 **Argent, Rivière à l'** *watercourse* Québec Canada
118 M7 **Argenta** British Columbia Canada
232 D4 **Argenta** Italy
228 D2 **Argentan** France
228 E4 **Argentat** France
232 B4 **Argentera, Cima dell'** *mountain* Italy
226 D5 **Argentera, Punta** *mountain* Italy
228 F2 **Argenteuil** France
159 E6 **Argentina** *country* South America
436 V1 **Argentina Range** Antarctica
79 BB12 **Argentine Abyssal Plain** *underwater feature* Atlantic Ocean
79 AA12 **Argentine Basin** *underwater feature* Atlantic Ocean
77 N13 **Argentine Rise** *underwater feature* Atlantic Ocean
234 D3 **Argeș** *admin. area* Romania
302 E4 **Argo** Sudan
78 H9 **Argo Abyssal Plain** *underwater feature* Indian Ocean
230 E4 **Argos** *watercourse* Spain
230 F2 **Arguedas** Spain
241 I5 **Argueil** France
157 E7 **Arguipélago dos Abrolhos** *island* Brazil
231 F2 **Arguís** Spain
385 I2 **Argun** *watercourse* Russian Federation
305 E2 **Argungu** Nigeria
372 E4 **Arguni, Teluk** *bay* Indonesia
385 I2 **Argunskiy Khrebet** *range* Russian Federation
437 F1 **Argus, Dome** *mountain* Antarctica
128 D2 **Argus Range** California USA
125 Q2 **Argyle** Minnesota USA
424 I4 **Argyle, Lake** WA Australia
242 C1 **Argyll and Bute** *admin. area* Scotland UK
384 E3 **Arhangay** *admin. area* Mongolia
225 J3 **Arholma** *island* Sweden
224 F4 **Århus** Denmark
384 F3 **Arhust** Mongolia
393 C11 **Ari Atoll** Maldives
373 I5 **Aria** *watercourse* Papua New Guinea
372 C2 **Ariaga** *island* Indonesia
308 C5 **Ariamsvlei** Namibia
233 D8 **Ariana** Tunisia
233 F6 **Ariano Irpino** Italy
154 C4 **Ariari** *watercourse* Colombia
159 F4 **Aribibi** Bolivia
304 D2 **Aribinda** Burkina Faso
158 D5 **Arica** Chile
154 D5 **Arica** Colombia
158 D5 **Arica, Bahía de** *lake* Peru
158 D5 **Arica-Parinacota** *admin. area* Chile
244 C4 **Arichamish** Argyll and Bute Scotland UK
154 D3 **Arichuna** *watercourse* Venezuela
424 G8 **Arid, Mount** WA Australia
387 G4 **Arida** Japan
235 C5 **Aridaia** Greece
228 E5 **Ariège** *watercourse* France
391 M3 **Arifwala** Pakistan
154 C2 **Ariguaní** Colombia
234 B4 **Arilje** Serbia
163 9 **Arima** Trinidad and Tobago
163 9 **Arima** *admin. area* Trinidad and Tobago
134 C4 **Arimís** Honduras
124 I5 **Arimo** Idaho USA
244 C4 **Arinagour** Highland Scotland UK
244 B4 **Arinambane** Na h-Eileanan Siar Scotland UK
233 E5 **Aringo** Italy
225 M5 **Arino ežeras** *lake* Lithuania
157 C6 **Arinos** Brazil
159 G3 **Arinos** *watercourse* Brazil
225 C5 **Ariogala** Lithuania
163 9 **Aripo, El Cerro del** *mountain* Trinidad and Tobago
154 D3 **Ariporo** *watercourse* Colombia
155 F6 **Aripuana** *watercourse* Brazil
159 F3 **Aripuanã** Brazil
159 F3 **Ariquemes** Brazil
244 C4 **Arisaig, Sound of** *bay* Scotland UK
129 J5 **Arispe** Texas USA
118 G6 **Aristazabal Island** British Columbia Canada
135 I5 **Ariton** Alabama USA
393 E9 **Ariyalur** Tamil Nadu India
230 E3 **Ariza** Spain
160 E3 **Arizaro, Salar de** *lake* Argentina
228 E5 **Arize** *watercourse* France
160 E5 **Arizona** Argentina
133 I6 **Arizona** Honduras
115 **Arizona** *admin. area* USA
128 G5 **Arizpe** Mexico
375 G5 **Arjasa** Indonesia
374 F5 **Arjawinangun** Indonesia
122 F5 **Arjay, Lac** *lake* Québec Canada
222 J3 **Arjeplog** Sweden
391 H3 **Arjnū** Iran
307 F2 **Ārjo** Ethiopia
154 C2 **Arjona** Colombia
237 AD6 **Arka** Russian Federation
130 F3 **Arkabutla Lake** Mississippi USA
388 D3 **Arkadak** Russian Federation
130 E3 **Arkadelphia** Arkansas USA
244 C4 **Arkaig, Loch** *lake* Scotland UK
393 D9 **Arkalgud** Karnataka India
388 J3 **Arkalyk** Kazakhstan
391 H3 **Arkān** Iran
115 **Arkansas** *admin. area* USA
130 E3 **Arkansas** *watercourse* Arkansas USA
129 I1 **Arkansas** *watercourse* Colorado USA
129 L2 **Arkansas** *watercourse* Kansas USA
125 Q8 **Arkansas City** Kansas USA
425 K7 **Arkaroola Village** SA Australia
302 C3 **Arkenu, Jabal** *mountain* Libya
235 D6 **Arkesini** Greece
236 J6 **Arkhangel'sk** Russian Federation
238 H2 **Arkhangel'skaya Oblast'** *admin. area* Russian Federation
245 F4 **Arklow** Ireland
224 I3 **Arkö** *island* Sweden
235 E7 **Arkoi** *island* Greece
224 G5 **Arkona Kap** *cape* Germany
235 D6 **Arkoudi** *island* Greece
236 Q3 **Arktichesкogo Instituta, Ostrova** *islands* Russian Federation
388 F1 **Arkul** Russian Federation
228 F4 **Arlanc** France
228 C5 **Arlanza** *watercourse* Spain
228 C5 **Arlanzón, Embalse de** *lake* Spain
229 G5 **Arles** France
228 F5 **Arles-sur-Tech** France
304 E2 **Arli** Burkina Faso
129 K1 **Arlington** Colorado USA
129 M2 **Arlington** Kansas USA
124 E4 **Arlington** Oregon USA
130 C4 **Arlington** Texas USA
124 D2 **Arlington** Washington USA
301 H5 **Arlit** Niger
227 K3 **Arló** Hungary
229 G2 **Arlon** Belgium
126 D8 **Arma** Kansas USA
424 F8 **Armadale** WA Australia
386 C2 **Armadires** *island* Indonesia
123 C9 **Armagh** Québec Canada
242 B2 **Armagh** Armagh Northern Ireland UK
242 B2 **Armagh** *admin. area* Northern Ireland UK
391 H4 **Armak** Iran
226 C4 **Armançon** *watercourse* France
302 E2 **Armant** Egypt
235 E8 **Armathia** *island* Greece
388 D6 **Armavir** *pass* Armenia
388 D5 **Armavir** Russian Federation
388 D6 **Armenia** *country*
154 C3 **Armenia** Colombia
154 B5 **Armenia** Ecuador
235 E7 **Armenistis** Greece
235 E7 **Armenistis, Akra** *cape* Greece
230 D3 **Armenteros** Spain
228 F1 **Armentières** France
233 F8 **Armi, Capo dell'** *cape* Italy
425 N7 **Armidale** NSW Australia
225 N1 **Armisvesi** *lake* Finland
373 F4 **Armopa** Indonesia
242 B1 **Armoy** Moyle Northern Ireland UK
222 J5 **Armsjön** *lake* Sweden
120 K7 **Armstrong** Ontario Canada
126 D5 **Armstrong** Iowa USA
130 C3 **Armstrong** Oklahoma USA
130 C7 **Armstrong** Texas USA
387 G1 **Armu** *watercourse* Russian Federation
393 E7 **Armur** Andhra Pradesh India
235 G5 **Armutcuk** Turkey
235 C7 **Arna** Greece
228 E4 **Arnac-Pompadour** France
222 inset **Arnarfjörður** *bay* Iceland
222 inset **Arnarstapi** Iceland
122 C2 **Arnaud** *watercourse* Québec Canada
389 K6 **Arnavad, Qullai** *mountain* Tajikistan
241 E4 **Arne** Dorset England UK
230 E2 **Arnedo** Spain
228 D5 **Arnéguy** France
222 J2 **Arnes** Norway
231 G3 **Arnes** Spain
222 F5 **Årnes** Norway
130 B2 **Arnett** Oklahoma USA
226 C2 **Arnhem** Netherlands
425 K3 **Arnhem, Cape** NT Australia
425 J3 **Arnhem Land** *region* NT Australia
244 B3 **Arnish** Highland Scotland UK
129 K5 **Arno** Texas USA
427 I5 **Arno Atoll** Marshall Islands
244 B2 **Arnol** Na h-Eileanan Siar Scotland UK
241 F1 **Arnold** Nottinghamshire England UK
128 B1 **Arnold** California USA
126 F7 **Arnold** Missouri USA
228 F3 **Arnon** *watercourse* France
222 L1 **Arnøya** *island* Norway
127 M4 **Arnprior** Ontario Canada
242 F2 **Arnside** Cumbria England UK
229 J1 **Arnstadt** Germany
226 G3 **Arnstorf** Germany
155 E3 **Aro** *watercourse* Venezuela
224 E5 **Arø** *island* Denmark
308 C5 **Aroab** Namibia
310 9a **Arode, Île** *island* Seychelles
227 K4 **Árokto** Hungary
120 L7 **Aroland** Ontario Canada
226 E2 **Arolsen** Germany
302 F4 **Aroma** Sudan
222 M5 **Aronkylä** Finland
373 J5 **Aropa** Papua New Guinea
426 1 **Arorae** *island* Kiribati
422 2 **Arorangi** Cook Islands New Zealand
232 C3 **Arosa** Switzerland
222 K3 **Årosjåkk** Sweden
129 K1 **Aroya** Colorado USA
228 B3 **Arpajon** France
223 E6 **Arpino** Italy
229 K5 **Arquata del Tronto** Italy
228 F1 **Arques** France
231 F3 **Arquillo de San Blás, Embalse del** *lake* Spain
159 H3 **Arraias** *watercourse* Brazil
134 E5 **Arraiján** Panama
230 C4 **Arraiolos** Portugal
242 C1 **Arran** *island* Scotland UK
118 K5 **Arras** British Columbia Canada
226 B2 **Arras** France
228 E5 **Arrats** *watercourse* France
228 F5 **Arre** France
228 E5 **Arreau** France
310 3d **Arrecife** Canary Islands
163 4 **Arrecife Macgowen** *reef* Archipiélago de Colón (Galapagos Islands)
160 F5 **Arrecifes** Argentina
129 I4 **Arrey** New Mexico USA
133 G5 **Arriaga** Mexico
125 N7 **Arriba** Colorado USA
159 G5 **Arrien** Paraguay
310 3d **Arrieta** Canary Islands
230 D2 **Arriondas** Spain
161 H5 **Arroio Grande** Brazil
230 C4 **Arronches** Portugal
228 G3 **Arroux** *watercourse* France
245 D2 **Arrow, Lough** *lake* Ireland
127 F2 **Arrow Lake** Ontario Canada
130 B4 **Arrowhead, Lake** Texas USA
124 H5 **Arrowrock Reservoir** Idaho USA
423 D6 **Arrowsmith, Mount** New Zealand
159 F4 **Arroyo Agustin** *watercourse* Bolivia
230 C4 **Arroyo de la Luz** Spain
162 C2 **Arroyo de la Ventana** Argentina
128 B3 **Arroyo Grande** California USA
162 C3 **Arroyo Perdido** *watercourse* Argentina
162 B3 **Arroyo Pescado** Argentina
162 C3 **Arroyo Verde** Argentina
159 E4 **Arroyos, Lago de los** *lake* Bolivia
222 H4 **Ärsand** Norway
391 H3 **Arsanjān** Iran
119 Q5 **Arsenault Lake** Saskatchewan Canada
387 I1 **Arsent'evka** Russian Federation
238 G6 **Arsen'yev** Russian Federation
387 G5 **Arsen'yevo** Russian Federation
226 F5 **Arsiè** Italy
388 F2 **Arsk** Russian Federation
394 E6 **Arslanköy** Turkey
373 G4 **Arso** Indonesia
233 E5 **Arsoli** Italy
229 G2 **Arsonval** France
222 J2 **Årstein** Norway
122 N2 **Arsuk** Greenland
122 N2 **Arsuutaa** *island* Greenland
226 B3 **Arsy** France
129 L8 **Arteaga** Mexico
132 E5 **Arteaga** Mexico
231 G3 **Artesa de Segre** Spain
129 J4 **Artesia** New Mexico USA
130 B6 **Artesia Wells** Texas USA
125 Q5 **Artesian** South Dakota USA
226 E4 **Arth** Switzerland
240 C2 **Arthog** Gwynedd Wales UK
125 O6 **Arthur** Nebraska USA
125 Q3 **Arthur** North Dakota USA
423 E5 **Arthur, Mount** New Zealand
423 E5 **Arthur Range** New Zealand
423 D6 **Arthur's Pass** New Zealand
135 F1 **Arthur's Town** Bahamas
161 G4 **Artigas** Uruguay
161 G4 **Artigas** *admin. area* Uruguay
436 U2 **Artigas (Uruguay)** *research station* Antarctica
388 D6 **Ar'tik** Armenia
116 I6 **Artillery Lake** Northwest Territories Canada
390 E1 **Artish** Iraq
239 F3 **Art'omovsk** Ukraine
237 X7 **Artomovskiy** Russian Federation
231 H3 **Artrutx, Cap d'** *cape* Spain
384 E4 **Arts Bogd Uul** Mongolia
389 H5 **Artuby** *watercourse* France
436 U2 **Arturo Prat (Chile)** *research station* Antarctica
394 G5 **Artvin** Turkey
394 G5 **Artvin** *admin. area* Turkey
237 AE6 **Artyk** Russian Federation
154 E4 **Aru** Brazil
372 E5 **Aru, Kepulauan** *island* Indonesia
306 E3 **Arua** Uganda
157 B6 **Aruanã** Brazil
154 D1 **Aruba** *admin. area* Caribbean Netherlands Antilles
310 3b **Arucas** Canary Islands
228 D5 **Arudy** France
427 14a **Arue** French Polynesia
159 F2 **Arumã** Brazil
155 F4 **Arumã, Serra do** *range* Brazil
155 F4 **Arumim** Brazil
392 G5 **Arun** *watercourse* Nepal
241 G4 **Arun** *watercourse* England UK
379 H3 **Arunachal Pradesh** *admin. area* India
241 G4 **Arundel** West Sussex England UK
372 B3 **Arus, Tanjung** *cape* Indonesia
307 F4 **Arusha** Tanzania
307 F4 **Arusha** *admin. area* Tanzania
375 F4 **Arut** *watercourse* Indonesia
306 C3 **Aruwimi** *watercourse* Democratic Republic of Congo
125 M7 **Arvada** Colorado USA
245 E3 **Arvagh** Ireland
129 L4 **Arvana** Texas USA
384 E3 **Arvayheer** Mongolia
162 A2 **Arvejas, Punta** *cape* Chile
222 K3 **Arvesjaure** *lake* Sweden
119 X2 **Arviat** Nunavut Canada
222 K4 **Arvidsjaur** Sweden
222 K4 **Arvidsjaursjön** *lake* Sweden
224 G3 **Arvika** Sweden
222 L1 **Årviksand** Norway
128 C3 **Arvin** California USA
233 G7 **Arvo, Lago** *lake* Italy
392 F6 **Arwal** Bihar India
372 C5 **Arwala** Indonesia
389 J5 **Arys'** Kazakhstan
233 C6 **Arzachena** Italy
228 D5 **Arzacq-Arraziquet** France
388 D2 **Arzamas** Russian Federation
390 G5 **Arzanah** *island* United Arab Emirates
391 I2 **Arzaneh** Iran
301 F1 **Arzew** Algeria
388 D4 **Arzgir** Russian Federation
229 H3 **Arzier** Switzerland
226 C2 **As** Belgium
226 G2 **Aš** Czech Republic
224 F3 **Ås** Norway
302 E2 **Aş Şaff** Egypt
302 D2 **Aş Şaḥrā' al Gharbiyah** *desert* Egypt
390 B4 **Aş Şaḥrā' Ash Sharqiyah** Egypt
302 D1 **As Sallūm** Egypt
390 C3 **As Salṭ** Jordan
390 F3 **As Samāwah** Iraq
394 F6 **As Sarāyim** Syria
390 F5 **As Sayḥ** Saudi Arabia
391 I5 **As Sīb** Oman
390 B5 **As Subū'** Egypt
390 F2 **As Sulaymānīyah** Iraq
390 F6 **As Sulayyil** Saudi Arabia
301 J2 **As Sulṭān** Libya
390 E5 **As Sūq** Saudi Arabia
394 G6 **Aş Şuwar** Syria
394 F7 **As Suwaydā'** Syria
391 I5 **As Suwayq** Oman
302 E2 **As Suways (Suez)** Egypt
306 D3 **Asa** *watercourse* Democratic Republic of Congo
224 F4 **Aså** Denmark
305 F3 **Asaba** Nigeria
391 L2 **Asadābād** Afghanistan
390 F2 **Asadābād** Iran
162 B4 **Asador, Pampa del** *region* Argentina
235 E5 **Aşağıinova** Turkey
394 H6 **Asagikiran** Turkey
374 C3 **Asahan** *watercourse* Indonesia
387 I4 **Asahi** Japan
387 I2 **Asahi-dake** *volcano* Japan
387 I2 **Asahikawa** Japan
391 J3 **Asaji** Iran
303 G5 **Āsalē** *lake* Ethiopia
426 5 **Asan** Guam
386 E4 **Asan** South Korea
386 E4 **Asan-man** *bay* South Korea
392 G6 **Asansol** West Bengal India
225 M4 **Asare** Latvia
222 I5 **Åsarna** Sweden
426 5 **Asatdas** Guam
427 12c **Asau** Samoa
303 G5 **Āsayita** Ethiopia
226 D2 **Asbach** Germany
388 F7 **Asbak** Iran
159 F4 **Ascensión** Bolivia
132 D2 **Ascensión** Mexico
134 C3 **Ascensión, Bahía de la** *bay* Mexico
77 R10 **Ascension Fracture Zone** *underwater feature* Atlantic Ocean
226 E3 **Aschaffenburg** Germany
231 G3 **Ascó** Spain
232 E5 **Ascoli Piceno** Italy
229 I3 **Ascona** Switzerland
158 B2 **Ascope** Peru
222 I2 **Åse** Norway
307 F2 **Āsela** Ethiopia
222 J4 **Åsele** Sweden
223 N4 **Asemankylä** Finland
307 E4 **Asembo** Kenya
224 G2 **Åsen** Sweden
162 C6 **Aserradero La Paciencia** Chile
129 I7 **Aserradero Yerbitas** Mexico
134 D5 **Aserrío de Gariché** Panama
388 H6 **Aşgabat (Ashgabat)** Turkmenistan
243 H3 **Asgarby** Lincolnshire England UK
383 J2 **Asgat** Mongolia
241 I3 **Ash** Kent England UK
128 F3 **Ash Fork** Arizona USA
126 E8 **Ash Grove** Missouri USA
390 E6 **Ash Sharafā** Saudi Arabia
391 H4 **Ash Shāriqah** United Arab Emirates
390 C4 **Ash Sharmah, Wādī** *watercourse* Saudi Arabia
390 G5 **Ash Sharqīyah** *admin. area* Saudi Arabia
390 F3 **Ash Shaṭrah** Iraq
390 E3 **Ash Shawmalī** Iraq
390 G7 **Ash Shiḥr** Yemen
301 I2 **Ash Shuwayrif** Libya
131 J5 **Ashburn** Georgia USA
424 E5 **Ashburton** *watercourse* WA Australia
423 D6 **Ashburton** New Zealand
388 J5 **Ashchikol'** *lake* Kazakhstan
388 I3 **Ashchitastysor** *lake* Kazakhstan
118 K7 **Ashcroft** British Columbia Canada
390 C3 **Ashdod** Israel
130 D4 **Ashdown** Arkansas USA
241 H3 **Asheldham** Essex England UK
130 B6 **Asherton** Texas USA
131 J3 **Asheville** North Carolina USA
225 O4 **Ashevo** Russian Federation
120 L5 **Asheweig** *watercourse* Ontario Canada
241 H3 **Ashford** Kent England UK
131 I5 **Ashford** Alabama USA
131 H4 **Ashikaga** Japan
386 F5 **Ashikita** Japan
301 I3 **Ashkidah** Libya
244 F5 **Ashkirk** Scottish Borders Scotland UK
125 P8 **Ashland** Kansas USA
126 J7 **Ashland** Kentucky USA
127 Q3 **Ashland** Maine USA
127 J6 **Ashland** Ohio USA
124 D5 **Ashland** Oregon USA
127 M8 **Ashland** Virginia USA
126 F3 **Ashland** Wisconsin USA
423 F6 **Ashley** *watercourse* New Zealand
243 E6 **Ashley** Cheshire England UK
126 G7 **Ashley** Illinois USA
125 P3 **Ashley** North Dakota USA
124 H2 **Ashley Lake** Montana USA
119 P5 **Ashmont** Alberta Canada
241 E4 **Ashmore** Dorset England UK
424 inset **Ashmore and Cartier Islands** *Australian territory* Australian

424 inset **Ashmore Reef** Ashmore Reef and Cartier Island Australia
225 M5 **Ashmyany** Belarus
392 D6 **Ashoknagar** Madhya Pradesh India
240 E2 **Ashperton** Herefordshire England UK
240 D4 **Ashprington** Devon England UK
392 D6 **Ashta** Madhya Pradesh India
127 K6 **Ashtabula** Ohio USA
126 C3 **Ashtabula, Lake** North Dakota USA
393 C7 **Ashtami** Maharashtra India
388 D6 **Ashtarak** Armenia
163 11 **Ashton** St Vincent and the Grenadines
124 J4 **Ashton** Idaho USA
241 F3 **Ashton Keynes** Wiltshire England UK
121 V6 **Ashuanipi** Newfoundland and Labrador Canada
122 E6 **Ashuanipi** *watercourse* Newfoundland and Labrador Canada
122 E6 **Ashuanipi Lake** Newfoundland and Labrador Canada
127 O2 **Ashuapmuchuan** *watercourse* Québec Canada
131 H4 **Ashville** Alabama USA
162 B5 **Asia, Estero** *bay* Chile
158 B4 **Asia, Isla** *island* Peru
372 D3 **Asia, Kepulauan** *island* Indonesia
232 D4 **Asiago** Italy
155 F4 **Asiasito** Venezuela
377 I4 **Asid Gulf** Philippines
393 E7 **Asifabad** Andhra Pradesh India
393 F7 **Asika** Orissa India
225 M2 **Asikkalanselkä** *bay* Finland
300 E1 **Asilah** Morocco
158 D4 **Asillo** Peru
233 C6 **Asinara, Golfo dell'** *bay* Italy
392 D6 **Asind** Rajasthan India
389 O2 **Asino** Russian Federation
238 C6 **Asipovichy** Belarus
390 E6 **'Asir** *admin. area* Saudi Arabia
302 F4 **Asis, Ras** *cape* Sudan
223 O3 **Aska** Finland
394 G5 **Aşkale** Turkey
224 F3 **Asker** Norway
243 G3 **Askern** South Yorkshire England UK
244 A3 **Askernish** Na h-Eileanan Siar Scotland UK
120 H5 **Askikkapit** Manitoba Canada
389 P2 **Askiz** Russian Federation
224 I3 **Askö** *island* Sweden
222 L4 **Åskogen** Sweden
224 C2 **Askøy** *island* Norway
391 L2 **Asmār** Afghanistan
303 F4 **Asmara** Eritrea
224 F5 **Asnæs** Denmark
224 H4 **Åsnen** *bay* Sweden
386 F5 **Aso** Japan
387 G4 **Aso-kai** *lake* Japan
386 F5 **Aso-san** *volcano* Japan
155 G4 **Asoenangka** Brazil
226 F5 **Asolo** Italy
379 H3 **Asonli** Arunachal Pradesh India
372 F4 **Asori** Indonesia
235 B6 **Ásos** Greece
302 E5 **Ásosa** Ethiopia
302 F3 **Asoteriba, Jebel** *mountain* Sudan
222 I5 **Aspås** Sweden
390 G3 **Aspās** Iran
242 E2 **Aspatria** Cumbria England UK
222 J5 **Aspeå** Sweden
125 L7 **Aspen** Colorado USA
118 K8 **Aspen Grove** British Columbia Canada
224 F3 **Asperen** *lake* Norway
130 A4 **Aspermont** Texas USA
388 D5 **Aspindza** Georgia
423 C7 **Aspiring/Tititea, Mount** New Zealand
222 H4 **Aspneset** Norway
224 H4 **Aspö** *island* Sweden
224 I3 **Aspöja** *island* Sweden
229 G4 **Aspres-sur-Buëch** France
235 A6 **Asprokavos, Akra** *cape* Greece
222 K5 **Aspsele** Sweden
384 F3 **Asralt Hairhan** *mountain* Mongolia
300 E3 **Assa** Morocco
303 G5 **Assab** Eritrea
158 D1 **Assacaio** Brazil
157 B8 **Assaí** Brazil
303 G5 **Assal, Lac'** *lake* Djibouti
379 G3 **Assam** *admin. area* India
156 E4 **Assaré** Brazil
226 C2 **Asse** Belgium
384 B2 **Asse** *watercourse* France
233 C7 **Assemini** Italy
226 D1 **Assen** Netherlands
228 F1 **Assenede** Belgium
123 F7 **Assigny, Lac** *lake* Newfoundland and Labrador Canada
305 H2 **Assinet** Chad
126 A2 **Assiniboine** *watercourse* Manitoba Canada
124 H1 **Assiniboine, Mount** British Columbia Canada
127 N1 **Assinica, Lac** *lake* Québec Canada
157 B8 **Assis** Brazil
232 E5 **Assisi** Italy
226 E2 **Aßlar** Germany
310 4a **Assomada** Cape Verde
310 9 **Assumption** *island* Seychelles
244 C2 **Assynt, Loch** *lake* Scotland UK
228 E4 **Astaffort** France
237 AC5 **Astakh** Russian Federation
390 A2 **Astakida** *island* Greece
389 K3 **Astana** Kazakhstan
222 J3 **Åstansjö** Sweden
388 E6 **Āstārā** Iran
240 E1 **Astbury** Cheshire England UK
225 L3 **Aste** Estonia
227 H3 **Asten** Austria
226 E5 **Asti** Italy
222 J5 **Åstön** *island* Sweden
240 E1 **Aston** Cheshire England UK
161 I2 **Astorga** Brazil
230 C2 **Astorga** Spain
310 9 **Astove** *island* Seychelles
388 E4 **Astrakhan'** Russian Federation
388 E4 **Astrakhanskaya** *admin. area* Russian Federation
238 B5 **Astrashytski Haradok** Belarus
224 K4 **Åsträsk** Sweden
121 V5 **Astray** Newfoundland and Labrador Canada
154 C2 **Astrea** Colombia
437 A2 **Astrid Ridge** *underwater feature* Southern Ocean
235 B6 **Astrochórion** Greece
426 8 **Astrolabe, Cape** Solomon Islands
426 7 **Astrolabe Reefs** Vanuatu
230 D2 **Astudillo** Spain
230 C2 **Asturias** *admin. area* Spain
235 E7 **Astypalaia** *island* Greece
426 2 **Asuncion** *island* Northern Mariana Islands
161 G3 **Asunción** Paraguay
134 B4 **Asunción Mita** Guatemala
133 F5 **Asunción Nochixtlán** Mexico
224 H4 **Åsunden** *lake* Sweden
233 C7 **Asuni** Italy
390 G2 **Āsūr** Iran
222 H3 **Åsvaer** *island* Norway
225 M5 **Asvejos ežeras** *lake* Lithuania
224 C4 **Asvyeya** Belarus
390 D5 **Aswad, Ar Ra's al** *cape* Saudi Arabia
302 E3 **Aswân** Egypt
302 E2 **Asyût** Egypt
376 D4 **At Samat** Thailand
390 C3 **Aţ Ţafilah** Jordan
390 D5 **Aţ Ţā'if** Saudi Arabia
302 C3 **At Tāj** Libya
390 D5 **Aţ Ţuwāl** Saudi Arabia
372 C6 **Atabae** Timor-Leste (East Timor)
160 D3 **Atacama** *admin. area* Chile
160 D3 **Atacama, Desierto de** *desert* Chile
160 D2 **Atacama, Salar de** *lake* Chile
155 H4 **Atachi Bakka, Monts** *range* French Guiana
154 C4 **Ataco** Colombia
422 3 **Atafu** *island* Tokelau New Zealand
422 3 **Atafu Village** Tokelau New Zealand
304 E2 **Atakora, Chaîne de l'** *range* Benin
304 E3 **Atakpamé** Togo
230 B5 **Atalaia, Ponta da** *cape* Portugal
160 E6 **Ataliva Roca** Argentina
372 C6 **Atambua** Indonesia
388 J6 **Atamyrat** Turkmenistan
375 H2 **Atap** Indonesia
158 D4 **Atapata** Peru
390 F7 **'Atāq** Yemen
234 E4 **Ataqnasovsko Ezero** *lake* Bulgaria
300 D4 **Atâr** Mauritania
154 D2 **Atarigua, Embalse** *lake* Venezuela
392 E6 **Atarra** Uttar Pradesh India
Atas *see* **South Island** Australia
383 J4 **Atas Bogd** *mountain* Mongolia
128 B3 **Atascadero** California USA
225 N4 **Atašiene** Latvia
389 K4 **Atasu** Kazakhstan
383 I5 **Atatkan He** *watercourse* Xinjiang Uygur Zizhiqu China
394 F6 **Atatürk Barajı** *lake* Turkey
302 F5 **Atbara** *watercourse* Ethiopia
302 E4 **Atbara** Sudan
302 E4 **Atbara** *watercourse* Sudan
389 J3 **Atbasar** Kazakhstan
302 F3 **Atbāy** *range* Sudan
130 F6 **Atchafalaya Bay** Louisiana USA
126 D7 **Atchison** Kansas USA
155 F3 **Atenas** Venezuela
233 F5 **Atessa** Italy
226 B2 **Ath** Belgium
244 B2 **Ath Linne** Na h-Eileanan Siar Scotland UK
302 E2 **Ath Thamad** Egypt
119 O5 **Athabasca** Alberta Canada
119 P3 **Athabasca, Lake** Alberta/Saskatchewan Canada
124 G1 **Athalmer** British Columbia Canada
119 U5 **Athapap** Manitoba Canada
245 F3 **Athboy** Ireland
245 D3 **Athenry** Ireland
Athens *see* **Athina** Greece
130 H3 **Athens** Alabama USA
131 J4 **Athens** Georgia USA
127 J7 **Athens** Ohio USA
131 I3 **Athens** Tennessee USA
130 D4 **Athens** Texas USA
130 D4 **Athens, Lake** Texas USA
235 B6 **Atheras** Greece
235 B6 **Atheras, Akra** *cape* Greece
241 F2 **Atherstone** Warwickshire England UK
425 M4 **Atherton** Qld Australia
307 F4 **Athi** *watercourse* Kenya
235 C7 **Athina (Athens)** Greece
245 E3 **Athlone** Ireland
118 E6 **Athlow Bay** British Columbia Canada
423 C7 **Athol** New Zealand
124 G3 **Athol** Idaho USA
245 F4 **Athy** Ireland
302 B5 **Ati** Chad
301 J6 **Ati Ardébé** Chad
305 E3 **Atiak** Uganda
157 C8 **Atibaia** Brazil
123 I7 **Aticonipi, Lac** *lake* Québec Canada
306 D2 **Atiedo** Sudan
230 E3 **Atienza** Spain
119 U5 **Atik** Manitoba Canada
120 H5 **Atik Lake** Manitoba Canada
119 N5 **Atikameg** Alberta Canada
121 N7 **Atikameg** *watercourse* Ontario Canada
122 F6 **Atikonak** *watercourse* Newfoundland and Labrador Canada
122 F6 **Atikonak Lake** Newfoundland and Labrador Canada
126 E2 **Atikwa Lake** Ontario Canada
162 B3 **Atilio, Isla** *island* Chile
233 E6 **Atina** Italy
422 1 **Atiu** *island* Cook Islands New Zealand
237 AF6 **Atka** Russian Federation
436 X2 **Atka Iceport** Antarctica
237 AL8 **Atka Island** Alaska USA
388 D3 **Atkarsk** Russian Federation
125 P5 **Atkinson** Nebraska USA
131 I4 **Atlanta** Georgia USA
126 I4 **Atlanta** Michigan USA
125 P6 **Atlanta** Nebraska USA
127 N7 **Atlantic City** New Jersey USA
77 S16 **Atlantic-Indian Antarctic Basin** *under-water feature* Southern Ocean
77 T15 **Atlantic-Indian Ridge** *underwater feature* Southern Ocean
76 **Atlantic Ocean** *ocean*
154 C2 **Atlantico** *admin. area* Colombia
308 C6 **Atlantis** South Africa
76 N6 **Atlantis Fracture Zone** *underwater feature* Atlantic Ocean
80 J8 **Atlantis II Fracture Zone** *underwater feature* Indian Ocean
162 D3 **Atlas, Punta** *cape* Argentina
237 AG8 **Atlasova, Ostrov** *island* Kuril Islands
125 J1 **Atlee** Alberta Canada
118 E3 **Atlin** British Columbia Canada
118 E3 **Atlin Lake** British Columbia Canada
118 E3 **Atlin Provincial Park** British Columbia Canada
224 C2 **Atløy** *island* Norway
119 O5 **Atmore** Alberta Canada
130 H5 **Atmore** Alabama USA
224 G2 **Atna** Norway
118 I6 **Atnarko** British Columbia Canada
222 G6 **Atnfoss** Norway
159 E6 **Atocha** Bolivia
235 B6 **Atokos** *island* Greece
128 D3 **Atolia** California USA
308 B2 **Atome** Angola
224 H3 **Åtorp** Sweden
133 F5 **Atoyac** *watercourse* Mexico
132 E5 **Atoyac de Álvarez** Mexico
116 D4 **Atqasuk** Alaska USA
224 G4 **Ätran** Sweden
224 G4 **Ätran** *watercourse* Sweden
154 B3 **Atrato** *watercourse* Colombia
160 F6 **Atreucó** Argentina
373 F5 **Atsy** Indonesia
244 C3 **Attadale** Highland Scotland UK
245 F4 **Attanagh** Ireland
376 E4 **Attapu** Laos
121 N6 **Attawapiskat** Ontario Canada
120 L6 **Attawapiskat Lake** Ontario Canada
127 P4 **Attean Pond** Maine USA
243 H3 **Atterby** Lincolnshire England UK
226 C3 **Attert** *watercourse* Luxembourg
125 P8 **Attica** Kansas USA
226 B3 **Attichy** France
229 G2 **Attigny** France
122 E5 **Attikamagen Lake** Newfoundland and Labrador Canada
235 C7 **Attiki** *admin. area* Greece
237 AJ8 **Attu** Alaska USA
237 AJ8 **Attu Island** Alaska USA
388 G7 **Atū** Iran
160 D5 **Atuel** *watercourse* Argentina
307 E3 **Atura** Uganda
383 E5 **Atushi** Xinjiang Uygur Zizhiqu China
119 T7 **Atwater** Saskatchewan Canada
125 R4 **Atwater** Minnesota USA
243 H3 **Atwick** East Riding of Yorkshire England UK
125 O7 **Atwood** Kansas USA
388 F4 **Atyrau** Kazakhstan
388 F4 **Atyrauskaya Oblast'** *admin. area* Kazakhstan
232 C3 **Au** Austria
226 F3 **Au** Germany
126 J4 **Au Sable** *watercourse* Michigan USA
373 G4 **Aua Island** Papua New Guinea
134 C4 **Auas** Honduras
229 G5 **Aubagne** France
377 I3 **Aubarede Point** Philippines
228 G2 **Aube** *watercourse* France
226 C2 **Aubel** Belgium
226 C5 **Aubenas** France
228 F4 **Aubière** France
228 F4 **Aubin** France
228 F4 **Aubrac** France
228 F4 **Aubrac** *region* France
116 G5 **Aubry Lake** Northwest Territories Canada
131 I4 **Auburn** Alabama USA
124 E7 **Auburn** California USA
126 I6 **Auburn** Indiana USA
127 M5 **Auburn** New York USA
228 F4 **Aubusson** France
160 D6 **Aucá Mahuida, Sierra de** *mountain* Argentina
228 E5 **Auch** France
244 D4 **Auch** Argyll and Bute Scotland UK
244 C5 **Auchamore** North Ayrshire Scotland UK
244 E4 **Auchavan** Angus Scotland UK
228 F1 **Auchel** France
244 E6 **Auchencairn** Dumfries and Galloway Scotland UK
305 F3 **Auchi** Nigeria
422 F3 **Auckland** New Zealand
422 F3 **Auckland** *admin. area* New Zealand
376 C4 **Auckland Bay** Myanmar
423 8 **Auckland Island** New Zealand
228 D5 **Aucun** France
228 F5 **Aude** *watercourse* France
120 L7 **Auden** Ontario Canada
241 F5 **Auderville** France
229 G3 **Audeux** France
228 B2 **Audierne** France
228 B2 **Audierne, Baie d'** *bay* France
232 B3 **Audincourt** France
240 E2 **Audlem** Cheshire England UK
307 G2 **Audo Range** *range* Ethiopia
225 M3 **Audru** Estonia
241 J4 **Audruicq** France
229 K1 **Aue** Germany
229 K1 **Auerbach** Germany
425 M6 **Augathella** Qld Australia
242 A2 **Augher** Dungannon Northern Ireland UK
242 B2 **Aughnacloy** Dungannon Northern Ireland UK
245 C2 **Aughness** Ireland
245 F4 **Aughrim** Ireland
226 F3 **Augsburg** Germany
424 E8 **Augusta** WA Australia
131 K4 **Augusta** Georgia USA
125 Q8 **Augusta** Kansas USA
127 Q4 **Augusta** Maine USA
233 F8 **Augusta, Golfo di** *bay* Italy
116 D7 **Augustine Island** Alaska USA
156 C3 **Augusto Corrêa** Brazil
424 F6 **Augustus, Mount** WA Australia
134 D4 **Auka** Honduras
222 F5 **Aukan** Norway
223 M3 **Aukea** Sweden
426 8 **Auki** Solomon Islands
222 E5 **Aukra** Norway
116 H4 **Aulavik National Park** Northwest Territories Canada
424 G5 **Auld, Lake** WA Australia
238 B4 **Auleja** Latvia
224 E4 **Aulia** Sudan
232 C4 **Aulla** Italy
228 D3 **Aulnay** France
228 D4 **Aulne** *watercourse* France
126 H2 **Aulneau Peninsula** Ontario Canada
228 E3 **Aulong** France
426 3 **Aulong** *island* Palau
222 G6 **Aulstad** Norway
228 E1 **Ault** France
244 C3 **Aultbea** Highland Scotland UK
241 I5 **Aumale** France
222 H5 **Aumen** *bay* Sweden
226 C3 **Aumetz** France
124 D4 **Aumsville** Oregon USA
305 E2 **Auna** Nigeria
393 E7 **Aundhi** Maharashtra India
228 E2 **Auneau** France
228 D3 **Aunis** *region* France
427 12c **Aunu'u** *island* American Samoa
121 U3 **Aupaluk** Québec Canada
372 C4 **Aupanda** Indonesia
229 H5 **Aups** France
374 E3 **Aur** *island* Malaysia
427 15 **Aur Atoll** Marshall Islands
392 E5 **Auraiya** Uttar Pradesh India
392 F6 **Aurangabad** Bihar India
393 D7 **Aurangabad** Maharashtra India
228 C3 **Auray** France
228 D2 **Aure** *watercourse* France
222 F5 **Aure** Norway
228 D4 **Aureilhan, Étang d'** *lake* France
223 M5 **Aurejärvi** *lake* Finland
372 E4 **Auri, Kepulauan** *island* Indonesia
226 D1 **Aurich** Germany
157 B8 **Auriflama** Brazil
228 E5 **Aurignac** France
228 F4 **Aurillac** France
231 I2 **Auriol** France
231 F2 **Auritz** Spain
228 F3 **Auron** *watercourse* France
156 E4 **Aurora** Brazil
155 G3 **Aurora** Guyana
125 M7 **Aurora** Colorado USA
126 G6 **Aurora** Illinois USA
126 I7 **Aurora** Indiana USA
131 M3 **Aurora** North Carolina USA
159 F3 **Aurora, Serra da** *range* Brazil
425 inset **Aurora Point** *cape* Macquarie Island Australia
222 K2 **Aursfjordgård** Norway
224 E2 **Aursjøen** *lake* Norway
222 F5 **Aursunden** *lake* Norway
425 L3 **Aurukun** Qld Australia
308 C5 **Aus** Namibia
392 G6 **Ausgram** West Bengal India
244 F1 **Auskerry** *island* Scotland UK
224 D3 **Aust-Agder** *admin. area* Norway
224 E3 **Austad** Norway
222 G4 **Austafjord** Norway
224 E3 **Austbø** Norway
222 H4 **Austborg** Norway
243 G3 **Austerfield** South Yorkshire England UK
223 P1 **Austertana** Norway
223 Q1 **Austhavet** *bay* Norway
125 P2 **Austin** Manitoba Canada
126 E5 **Austin** Minnesota USA
128 D1 **Austin** Nevada USA
130 C5 **Austin** Texas USA
424 F6 **Austin, Lake** WA Australia
130 D6 **Austin, Lake** Texas USA
120 I2 **Austin Island** Nunavut Canada
224 G2 **Austmarka** Norway
222 H4 **Austnes** Norway
222 G4 **Austra** *island* Norway
427 14 **Australes, Îles** *admin. area* French Polynesia
424 **Australia** *country* Oceania
78 F13 **Australian-Antarctic Basin** *underwater feature* Southern Ocean
425 N8 **Australian Capital Territory** *admin. area* Australia
224 C3 **Austre Bokn** *island* Norway
232 E3 **Austria** *country* Europe
222 inset **Austurland** *admin. area* Iceland
222 I2 **Austvågøy** *island* Norway
159 G1 **Autazes** Brazil
228 E5 **Auterive** France
228 F2 **Auteuil** France
228 E1 **Authie** *watercourse* France
228 E3 **Authion** *watercourse* France
230 E2 **Autol** Spain
394 E4 **Autonomous Republic of Krym** *admin. area* Ukraine
223 O3 **Autti** Finland
225 M2 **Auttoinen** Finland
228 F4 **Auvergne** *admin. area* France
228 F4 **Auvergne** *region* France
228 E4 **Auvézère** *watercourse* France
228 F3 **Auxerre** France
228 F2 **Auxon** France
155 F3 **Auyan-Tepui** *mountain* Venezuela
117 M5 **Auyuittuq National Park** Nunavut Canada
228 F3 **Auzances** France
126 E8 **Ava** Missouri USA
393 E9 **Avadi** Tamil Nadu India
222 M3 **Avafors** Sweden
427 13a **Avalau** *island* Tuvalu
228 F3 **Avallon** France
128 C4 **Avalon** California USA
123 L9 **Avalon Peninsula** Newfoundland and Labrador Canada
388 D5 **Avalov** Russian Federation
222 L4 **Avan** Sweden
388 F7 **Āvānak** Iran
390 G3 **Avanjān** Iran
130 C2 **Avant** Oklahoma USA
157 B8 **Avaré** Brazil
422 1 **Avarua** Cook Islands New Zealand
422 4 **Avatele** Niue New Zealand
422 2 **Avatiu** Cook Islands New Zealand
222 J4 **Avaträsk** Sweden
222 K4 **Avaviken** Sweden
391 H4 **Avaz** Iran
235 D5 **Avdira** Greece
155 F3 **Ave Chica** Venezuela
230 B3 **Aveiro** Portugal
230 B3 **Aveiro** *admin. area* Portugal
226 B2 **Avelgem** Belgium
233 F6 **Avellino** Italy
128 B3 **Avenal** California USA
391 H4 **Avenān** Iran
230 B3 **Aver-o-Mar** Portugal
224 H3 **Avern** *lake* Sweden
224 F5 **Avernakø** *island* Denmark
224 D1 **Averøya** *island* Norway
233 F6 **Aversa** Italy
135 I4 **Aves** *island* Venezuela
76 L8 **Aves Ridge** *underwater feature* Caribbean Sea
224 I2 **Avesta** Sweden
233 G6 **Avetrana** Italy
228 E4 **Aveyron** *watercourse* France
232 E3 **Aviano** Italy
244 E3 **Aviemore** Highland Scotland UK
423 D7 **Aviemore, Lake** New Zealand
229 G5 **Avignon** France
230 D3 **Ávila** Spain
230 D2 **Avilés** Spain
225 M5 **Aviliu ežeras** *lake* Lithuania
154 D3 **Avimi** Colombia
226 C3 **Avioth** France
235 E7 **Avlakia** Greece
235 C7 **Avlemonas** Greece
245 F4 **Avoca** Ireland
423 D6 **Avoca** New Zealand
244 D3 **Avoch** Highland Scotland UK
118 L7 **Avola** British Columbia Canada
226 B3 **Avon** France
241 E3 **Avon** *watercourse* England UK
244 E3 **Avon** *watercourse* Scotland UK
127 J6 **Avon** Ohio USA
131 K7 **Avon Park** Florida USA
240 E3 **Avonmouth** Bristol England UK
234 E1 **Avratin** Ukraine
228 E2 **Avre** *watercourse* France
234 D3 **Avrig** Romania
228 D3 **Avrillé** France
232 H5 **Avtovac** Bosnia and Herzegovina
426 8 **Avu Avu** Solomon Islands
422 F4 **Awakino** *watercourse* New Zealand
390 G4 **'Awālī** Bahrain
375 H6 **Awang** Indonesia
375 G5 **Awarange, Tanjung** *cape* Indonesia
307 G2 **Āwarē** Ethiopia
423 C7 **Awarua Point** *cape* New Zealand
155 G4 **Awaruwaunawa** Guyana
307 F2 **Āwasa** Ethiopia
307 F2 **Āwasa, Lake** Ethiopia
307 G2 **Āwash** Ethiopia
303 G5 **Āwāsh Wenz** *watercourse* Ethiopia
307 F2 **Awata** *watercourse* Ethiopia
423 E5 **Awatere** *watercourse* New Zealand
382 F5 **Awati** Xinjiang Uygur Zizhiqu China
303 I3 **Awbārī** Libya
301 G5 **Awdal** *admin. area* Somalia
390 F4 **'Awdat Sudayr** Saudi Arabia
305 F3 **Awe** Nigeria
244 C4 **Awe, Loch** *lake* Scotland UK
306 D2 **Aweil** Sudan
131 L4 **Awendaw** South Carolina USA
302 F5 **Awgaro** Eritrea
373 H4 **Awin Island** Papua New Guinea
373 I5 **Awio Bay** Papua New Guinea
302 C2 **Awjilah** Libya
305 F3 **Awka** Nigeria
373 H6 **Awoma** Papua New Guinea
300 D4 **Awserd** Western Sahara
305 E3 **Awun** *watercourse* Nigeria
228 E5 **Ax-les-Thermes** France
226 F4 **Axams** Austria
117 J3 **Axel Heiberg Island** Nunavut Canada
304 D4 **Axim** Ghana
235 C5 **Axios** *watercourse* Greece
224 I2 **Axmar** Sweden
240 E4 **Axminster** Devon England UK
133 F5 **Axochiapan** Mexico
389 M4 **Ay** Kazakhstan
158 B2 **Ayabaca** Peru
162 B3 **Ayacara** Chile
300 F2 **Ayachi, Jbel** *mountain* Morocco
161 G6 **Ayacucho** Argentina
158 C4 **Ayacucho** Peru
158 C4 **Ayacucho** *admin. area* Peru
179 H4 **Ayadaw** Myanmar
389 M4 **Ayagoz** Kazakhstan
389 M4 **Ayagoz** *watercourse* Kazakhstan
388 I6 **Ayakguzhumdy** Uzbekistan
237 U4 **Ayakli** *watercourse* Russian Federation
304 D3 **Ayamé** Côte d'Ivoire
304 D3 **Ayamé, Lac d'** *lake* Côte d'Ivoire
305 G4 **Ayamikem** Equatorial Guinea
154 A5 **Ayampe, Punta** *cape* Ecuador
237 AC7 **Ayan** Russian Federation
237 T5 **Ayan** *watercourse* Russian Federation
394 E5 **Ayancık** Turkey
304 D3 **Ayanfuri** Ghana
305 F3 **Ayangba** Nigeria
237 AI6 **Ayanka** Russian Federation
158 D4 **Ayapata** Peru
154 C2 **Ayapel** Colombia
154 B5 **Ayasa** Ecuador
237 V7 **Ayava** Russian Federation
389 J7 **Āybak** Afghanistan
388 F4 **Aybas** Kazakhstan
389 J3 **Aydabul** Kazakhstan
394 F2 **Aydar** Russian Federation
394 F3 **Aydar** *watercourse* Ukraine
388 J6 **Aydar Kŭl'i** *lake* Uzbekistan
389 M5 **Aydarly** Kazakhstan
394 D6 **Aydın** *admin. area* Turkey
226 D4 **Ayent** Switzerland
235 C7 **Ayeranós** Greece
Ayers Rock *see* **Uluru** Australia
376 B4 **Ayeyarwady** *admin. area* Myanmar
379 H4 **Ayeyarwady** *watercourse* Myanmar
235 D6 **Áyios Evstrátios** Greece
388 I3 **Ayke** *lake* Kazakhstan
302 F5 **Āykel** Ethiopia
243 F2 **Ayle** Cumbria England UK
125 M1 **Aylesbury** Saskatchewan Canada
241 G3 **Aylesbury** Buckinghamshire England UK
241 I3 **Aylesham** Kent England UK
230 E3 **Ayllón** Spain
116 I6 **Aylmer Lake** Northwest Territories Canada
119 T6 **Aylsham** Saskatchewan Canada
241 I2 **Aylsham** Norfolk England UK
240 E2 **Aylton** Herefordshire England UK
302 C3 **'Ayn Al Ghazāl** Libya
302 C1 **Ayn al Ghazalah** Libya
302 E2 **'Ayn Ḩulwān** Egypt
302 E2 **'Ayn Sukhnah** Egypt
158 C4 **Ayna** Peru
389 J6 **Aynī** Tajikistan
163 I4 **Ayó** Aruba
306 E2 **Ayod** Sudan
161 G3 **Ayolas** Paraguay
237 AI5 **Ayon** Russian Federation
237 AI4 **Ayon, Ostrov** *island* Russian Federation
231 F4 **Ayora** Spain
301 G6 **Ayorou** Niger
300 E5 **Ayoûn el Atroûs** Mauritania
425 M4 **Ayr** Qld Australia
242 D1 **Ayr** North Ayrshire Scotland UK
242 D1 **Ayr** *watercourse* Scotland UK
242 E3 **Ayr, Point of** *cape* England UK
383 J3 **Ayrag Nuur** *lake* Mongolia
242 D2 **Ayre, Point of** *cape* Isle of Man UK
228 F5 **Ayrolle, Étang de l'** *lake* France
388 J6 **Ayrybaba** *mountain* Uzbekistan
303 G5 **Aysha** Ethiopia
388 I4 **Ayteke Bi** Kazakhstan
234 E4 **Aytos** Bulgaria
388 I5 **Aytym** Uzbekistan
372 D3 **Ayu** *island* Indonesia
372 D3 **Ayu, Kepulauan** *islands* Indonesia
376 D4 **Ayutthaya** Thailand
394 F6 **Ayvacık** Turkey
229 G1 **Aywaille** Belgium
390 E7 **Az Zāhir** Yemen
390 G4 **Aẓ Ẓahran (Dharan)** Saudi Arabia
394 F7 **Az Zalaf** Syria
302 E1 **Az Zaqāziq** Egypt
390 C3 **Az Zarqā'** Jordan
301 I2 **Az Zāwiyah** Libya
390 E4 **Az Zulfī** Saudi Arabia
391 M2 **Azad Kashmir** *admin. area* Pakistan
231 F3 **Azaila** Spain
392 F5 **Azamgarh** Uttar Pradesh India
158 D4 **Azángaro** Peru
391 H3 **Āzar Shahr** Iran
388 E6 **Āzarbāyjān-e Gharbī** *admin. area* Iran
388 E6 **Āzarbāyjān-e Sharqī** *admin. area* Iran
305 G2 **Azare** Nigeria
228 E3 **Azay-le-Rideau** France
231 I5 **Azeffoun** Algeria
388 E6 **Azerbaijan** *country*
159 H3 **Azevedo, Peixoto de** *watercourse* Brazil
302 F5 **Āzezo** Ethiopia
379 G2 **Azha** Xizang Zizhiqu China
238 C5 **Azina** Belarus
241 J4 **Azincourt** France
127 P4 **Aziscohos Lake** Maine USA
390 G2 **Aznā** Iran
154 B5 **Azogues** Ecuador
424 inset **Azorella Peninsula** Heard Island Australia
76 Q5 **Azores-Biscay Rise** *underwater feature* Atlantic Ocean
76 P5 **Azores Plain** *underwater feature* Atlantic Ocean
158 E3 **Azotes** Bolivia
305 I2 **Azoum, Bahr** *watercourse* Chad
394 F3 **Azov, Sea of**
305 I2 **Azrak, Bahr** *watercourse* Chad
302 E5 **Azraq, Bahr el** *watercourse* Sudan
128 F4 **Aztec** Arizona USA
129 I2 **Aztec** New Mexico USA
230 D4 **Azuaga** Spain
231 F3 **Azuara** Spain
154 B5 **Azuay** *admin. area* Ecuador
160 D3 **Azúcar** *watercourse* Chile
154 B3 **Azuero, Peninsula de** *peninsula* Panama
160 D3 **Azufre, Cerro del** *mountain* Chile
161 G6 **Azul** Argentina
159 F4 **Azul** Bolivia
160 D5 **Azul** *volcano* Chile
163 4 **Azul, Cerro** *volcano* Archipiélago de Colón (Galapagos Islands)
160 E3 **Azul, Cerro** *mountain* Argentina
162 B4 **Azul, Cerro** *mountain* Chile
158 C3 **Azul, Cordillera d'** *range* Peru
159 H4 **Azul, Serra** *range* Brazil
305 I2 **Azum, Wadi** *watercourse* Sudan
387 I4 **Azuma-san** *volcano* Japan
228 D5 **Azur** France
118 L6 **Azure Lake** British Columbia Canada
230 D4 **Azután, Embalse de** *lake* Spain
233 B8 **Azzaba** Algeria
232 E4 **Azzano Decimo** Italy

B

130 D5 **B. A. Steinhagen Lake** Texas USA
131 L3 **B. Everett Jordan Lake** North Carolina USA
427 9 **Ba** Fiji
376 E5 **Ba Đông** Vietnam
372 B6 **Baa** Indonesia
390 C2 **Baalbek** Lebanon
229 I3 **Baar** Switzerland
307 G3 **Baardheere** Somalia
226 C2 **Baarle-Hertog** Netherlands
226 C1 **Baarn** Netherlands
384 D3 **Baatsagaan** Mongolia
233 C8 **Bab** Tunisia
230 E6 **Bab el Assa** Algeria
303 G5 **Bab el Mandeb** *strait* Djibouti
230 D6 **Bab Taza** Morocco
394 C5 **Baba Burnu** *cape* Turkey
390 F2 **Bābā Khanjar** Iran
300 D5 **Bababé** Mauritania
234 F3 **Babadag** Romania
374 E5 **Babadan** Indonesia
388 H6 **Babadurmaz** Turkmenistan
154 B5 **Babahoyo** Ecuador
154 B5 **Babahoyo** *watercourse* Ecuador
235 E6 **Babakale** Turkey
372 A4 **Babana** Indonesia
302 D5 **Babanusa** Sudan
231 J6 **Babar** Algeria
372 D5 **Babar** *islands* Indonesia
372 D6 **Babar, Kepulauan** *island* Indonesia
375 G5 **Babat** Indonesia
307 F4 **Babati** Tanzania
372 B6 **Babau** Indonesia
238 F3 **Babayevo** Russian Federation
240 D4 **Babbacombe Bay** England UK
128 C1 **Babbitt** Nevada USA
388 E6 **Babek** Azerbaijan
123 D7 **Babel, Mont de** *mountain* Québec Canada
426 3 **Babeldaob** *island* Palau
372 E2 **Babelthuap** *island* Palau
234 D3 **Băbeni** Romania
374 C3 **Babi** *island* Indonesia
234 D3 **Băbiciu** Romania
390 E3 **Bābil** *admin. area* Iraq
307 G2 **Babile** Ethiopia
116 G7 **Babine** *watercourse* British Columbia Canada
225 P5 **Babinichy** Belarus
238 D5 **Babinovichi** Belarus
372 E4 **Babo** Indonesia
232 G3 **Babócsa** Hungary
388 F7 **Bābol** Iran
306 D3 **Babonde** Democratic Republic of Congo
306 D3 **Babongena** Democratic Republic of Congo
305 G3 **Babongo** Cameroon
305 G3 **Baboua** Central African Republic
223 T3 **Babozero, Ozero** *lake* Russian Federation
227 M1 **Babrovitskaye, Vozyera** *lake* Belarus
238 C6 **Babruysk** Belarus
394 D2 **Babruysk** Belarus
384 F2 **Babushkin** Russian Federation
377 I3 **Babuyan** *island* Philippines
377 I3 **Babuyan Channel** Philippines
377 I3 **Babuyan Islands** Philippines
238 F5 **Babynino** Russian Federation
244 B2 **Bac** Na h-Eileanan Siar Scotland UK
235 B5 **Bač** Macedonia
234 A3 **Bač** Serbia
376 E2 **Bắc Giang** Vietnam
376 E2 **Bắc Kạn** Vietnam
376 E5 **Bac Liêu** Vietnam
307 H2 **Bacaadweeyn** Somalia
158 E2 **Bacaba** Brazil
156 C4 **Bacabal** Brazil
159 E2 **Bacada** Brazil
156 B3 **Bacajá** *watercourse* Brazil
133 H5 **Bacalar** Mexico
134 B3 **Bacalar, Laguna** *lake* Mexico
132 C2 **Bacanuchi** *watercourse* Mexico
372 C4 **Bacan** *island* Indonesia
372 C4 **Bacan, Kepulauan** *islands* Indonesia
128 G5 **Bacanuchi** Mexico
234 E2 **Bacău** Romania
234 E2 **Bacău** *admin. area* Romania
123 L8 **Baccalieu Island** Newfoundland and Labrador Canada
229 H2 **Baccarat** France
123 F11 **Baccaro Point** *cape* Nova Scotia Canada
226 E4 **Baceno** Italy
129 H5 **Bacerac** Mexico
376 E2 **Bach Long Vi, Dao** *island* Vietnam
124 E5 **Bachelor, Mount** *volcano* Oregon USA
392 E5 **Bachhrawan** Uttar Pradesh India
382 F5 **Bachu** Xinjiang Uygur Zizhiqu China
380 E2 **Bachuan** Chongqing China
120 H4 **Back** Manitoba Canada
117 J5 **Back** *watercourse* Nunavut Canada
224 G2 **Backa** Sweden
232 H4 **Bačka Palanka** Serbia
222 I6 **Bäckan** Sweden
224 H4 **Backaryd** Sweden
222 J5 **Backe** Sweden
224 G3 **Bäckefors** Sweden
224 H2 **Backesjön** *lake* Sweden
244 F3 **Backhill** Aberdeenshire Scotland UK
226 E3 **Backnang** Germany
234 B3 **Bačko Gradište** Serbia
125 R3 **Backus** Minnesota USA
128 F5 **Bacoachi** Mexico
128 H7 **Bacobampo** Mexico
377 I5 **Bacolod** Philippines
131 I5 **Baconton** Georgia USA
122 B3 **Bacqueville, Lac** *lake* Québec Canada
241 H5 **Bacqueville-en-Caux** France
234 A2 **Bács-Kiskun** *admin. area* Hungary
232 E4 **Bacucco, Punta** *cape* Italy
243 F3 **Bacup** Lancashire England UK
158 D2 **Bacuri** Brazil
125 O4 **Bad** *watercourse* South Dakota USA
226 G4 **Bad Aibling** Germany
229 J1 **Bad Berka** Germany
229 I2 **Bad Dürkheim** Germany
226 E3 **Bad Dürrheim** Germany
227 H4 **Bad Gleichenberg** Austria
229 I1 **Bad Hall** Austria
229 I1 **Bad Hersfeld** Germany
227 G4 **Bad Ischl** Austria
226 D3 **Bad Kreuznach** Germany
229 I1 **Bad Laasphe** Germany
226 E2 **Bad Orb** Germany
232 C3 **Bad Ragaz** Switzerland
226 E3 **Bad Rappenau** Germany
229 J1 **Bad Sachsa** Germany
229 L3 **Bad Sankt Leonhard** Austria
226 F4 **Bad Tölz** Germany
226 E2 **Bad Wildungen** Germany
229 J2 **Bad Wörishofen** Germany
226 E4 **Bad Wurzach** Germany
380 E4 **Bada** Guangxi Zhuangzu Zizhiqu China
393 D9 **Badagara** Kerala India
384 E5 **Badain Jaran Shamo** Nei Mongol Zizhiqu China
223 M2 **Badajokka** *watercourse* Norway
155 F5 **Badajos, Lago** *lake* Brazil
230 C4 **Badajoz** Spain
389 K7 **Badakhshān** *admin. area* Afghanistan
390 E1 **Badān** Iraq
305 H2 **Badanga** Chad
379 G4 **Badarpur** Assam India
392 D6 **Badarwas** Madhya Pradesh India
375 G2 **Badas** Brunei
374 E3 **Badas, Kepulauan** *island* Indonesia
244 C2 **Badcall** Highland Scotland UK
222 L2 **Badderfjorden** *bay* Norway
393 F7 **Bade Bacheli** Chhattisgarh India
301 H6 **Badéguichéri** Niger
229 I3 **Baden** Switzerland
226 E3 **Baden-Württemberg** *admin. area* Germany
231 F3 **Badenas** Spain

244 F3 **Badenscoth** Aberdeenshire Scotland UK
301 H6 **Badér** Niger
226 G4 **Badgastein** Austria
125 Q2 **Badger** Minnesota USA
391 J2 **Bādghīs** *admin. area* Afghanistan
424 E7 **Badgingarra** WA Australia
304 B2 **Badi** *watercourse* Guinea
229 K5 **Badia Tedalda** Italy
373 H5 **Badilu** Papua New Guinea
391 K5 **Badin** Pakistan
131 K3 **Badin Lake** North Carolina USA
132 D3 **Badiraguato** Mexico
390 D3 **Bādiyat ash Shām (Syrian Desert)** Jordan
125 N3 **Badlands** *range* North Dakota USA
125 N5 **Badlands** *range* South Dakota USA
393 C7 **Badlapur** Maharashtra India
244 E3 **Badnafrave** Moray Scotland UK
233 G7 **Badolato** Italy
304 E3 **Badou** Togo
390 D5 **Badr Ḩunayn** Saudi Arabia
244 C3 **Badrallach** Highland Scotland UK
373 G6 **Badu Island** Australia
393 E10 **Badulla** Sri Lanka
391 H4 **Bādūnī** Iran
393 E8 **Badvel** Andhra Pradesh India
157 B8 **Bady Bassitt** Brazil
237 AC8 **Badzhal'skiy Khrebet** *range* Russian Federation
231 G2 **Baells, Pantà de la** *lake* Spain
230 D5 **Baena** Spain
230 E5 **Baeza** Spain
118 I6 **Baezaeko** *watercourse* British Columbia Canada
305 G3 **Bafang** Cameroon
304 B2 **Bafatá** Guinea-Bissau
232 C4 **Baffe, Punta** *cape* Italy
117 L4 **Baffin Bay** Canada/Greenland
130 C7 **Baffin Bay** Texas USA
122 C1 **Baffin Island** Nunavut Canada
305 G4 **Bafia** Cameroon
304 B2 **Bafing** *watercourse* Guinea
304 B2 **Bafing-Makana** Mali
300 D6 **Bafoulabé** Mali
305 G3 **Bafoussam** Cameroon
391 H3 **Bāfq** Iran
391 H3 **Bāft** Iran
306 D3 **Bafwabalinge** Democratic Republic of Congo
306 D3 **Bafwasende** Democratic Republic of Congo
391 J4 **Bag** Iran
305 G2 **Baga** Nigeria
388 D4 **Baga-Burul** Russian Federation
373 H5 **Bagabag Island** Papua New Guinea
154 B3 **Bagadó** Colombia
392 F5 **Bagaha** Bihar India
393 D8 **Bagalkot** Karnataka India
373 J6 **Bagaman Island** Papua New Guinea
377 J4 **Bagamanoc** Philippines
389 M2 **Bagan** Russian Federation
374 D3 **Bagan Datuk** Malaysia
305 F3 **Bagana** Nigeria
373 J5 **Bagana, Mount** *volcano* Papua New Guinea
377 J6 **Baganga** Philippines
308 D3 **Bagani** Namibia
374 D3 **Bagansiapiapi** Indonesia
384 F3 **Baganuur** Mongolia
301 G6 **Bagaroua** Niger
306 B4 **Bagata** Democratic Republic of Congo
304 B3 **Bagbe** *watercourse* Sierra Leone
161 H4 **Bagé** Brazil
228 F5 **Bages et de Sigean, Étang de** *lake* France
392 E5 **Bageshwar** Uttaranchal India
222 L4 **Baggen** *island* Sweden
242 E2 **Baggrow** Cumbria England UK
125 L6 **Baggs** Wyoming USA
240 C3 **Baggy Point** *cape* England UK
391 H4 **Bāgh-e Chenār** *mountain* Iran
390 G3 **Bāgh-e Malek** Iran
391 I3 **Bāghārān, Kūh-e** *mountain* Iran
390 E2 **Baghdād** Iraq
390 E2 **Baghdād** *admin. area* Iraq
389 J7 **Baghlān** *admin. area* Afghanistan
379 G4 **Baghmara** Meghalaya India
242 E3 **Bagillt** Flintshire Wales UK
374 E4 **Baginda, Tanjung** *cape* Indonesia
235 G6 **Bağkonak** Turkey
125 R3 **Bagley** Minnesota USA
393 D6 **Bagli** Madhya Pradesh India
392 F5 **Baglung** Nepal
241 F3 **Bagmore** Hampshire England UK
228 E5 **Bagnères-de-Bigorre** France
228 E5 **Bagnères-de-Luchon** France
226 F5 **Bagnolo Mella** Italy
229 G4 **Bagnols-sur-Cèze** France
376 C3 **Bago** *admin. area* Myanmar
224 E5 **Bågø** *island* Denmark
376 C3 **Bago (Pegu)** Myanmar
392 F6 **Bagodar** Jharkhand India
305 G3 **Bagodo** Cameroon
304 C2 **Bagoé** *watercourse* Mali
380 E3 **Bagong** Guizhou China
225 K5 **Bagrationovsk** Russian Federation
Bagrax *see* **Bohu** China
155 I4 **Bagres, Lago dos** *lake* Brazil
158 B2 **Bagua Grande** Peru
377 I3 **Baguio** Philippines
301 H5 **Bagzane, Monts** *mountain* Niger
392 E5 **Bah** Uttar Pradesh India
390 E6 **Bāḩah, Al** *admin. area* Saudi Arabia
76 K6 **Bahama Ridge** *underwater feature* Atlantic Ocean
135 F2 **Bahamas** *country* Caribbean
245 F3 **Bahana** Ireland
393 G6 **Baharagora** Jharkhand India
389 K7 **Bahārak** Afghanistan
392 G6 **Baharampur** West Bengal India
375 G3 **Bahau** *watercourse* Indonesia
375 F4 **Bahaur** Indonesia
391 L3 **Bahawalpur** Pakistan
235 E5 **Bahçeköy** Turkey
303 F4 **Bahdur Island** *island* Sudan
388 H6 **Bāherden** Turkmenistan
307 F5 **Bahi** Tanzania
157 D6 **Bahia** *admin. area* Brazil
134 C3 **Bahía, Islas de la** *island* Honduras
375 E5 **Bahia, Tanjung** *cape* Indonesia
132 B3 **Bahía Asunción** Mexico
160 F6 **Bahía Blanca** Argentina
162 C3 **Bahía Bustamante** Argentina
154 A5 **Bahía de Caráquez** Ecuador
128 F6 **Bahía de los Ángeles** Mexico
134 D2 **Bahía Honda** Cuba
132 C2 **Bahía Kino** Mexico
162 C4 **Bahía Laura** Argentina
162 B2 **Bahía Mansa** Chile
162 B4 **Bahía Murta** Chile
162 D4 **Bahía Oso Marino** Argentina
162 D6 **Bahía Thetis** Argentina
132 B3 **Bahía Tortugas** Mexico
302 F5 **Bahir Dar** Ethiopia
391 I5 **Bahlā'** Oman
304 C3 **Bahn** Liberia
372 B4 **Bahomonte** Indonesia
301 J6 **Bahr el Ghazal** *watercourse* Chad
392 E5 **Bahraich** Uttar Pradesh India
390 G4 **Bahrain** *country*
302 D2 **Bahriyah, Wāḩāt Al** *spring* Egypt
372 B4 **Bahubulu** *island* Indonesia
129 H7 **Bahuichivo** Mexico
376 E5 **Bãi Cạnh, Hòn** *island* Vietnam
383 J5 **Bai Shan** *mountain* Gansu China
159 G5 **Baía** Brazil
159 G5 **Baía de São Luís** Brazil
155 I5 **Baía do Pracaí** *lake* Brazil
308 B3 **Baía dos Tigres** Angola
234 C2 **Baia Mare** Romania
156 B3 **Baião** Brazil
229 H5 **Baiardo** Italy
305 H3 **Baibokoum** Chad
381 G1 **Baicheng** Henan China
385 J3 **Baicheng** Jilin China
382 G4 **Baicheng** Xinjiang Uygur Zizhiqu China
380 E4 **Baidonghe Shuiku** *lake* Guangxi Zhuangzu Zizhiqu China
121 U8 **Baie-Comeau** Québec Canada
123 G7 **Baie-Johan-Beetz** Québec Canada
163 I6 **Baie-Mahault** Guadeloupe
123 C9 **Baie-St-Paul** Québec Canada
123 F8 **Baie-Ste-Claire** Québec Canada
121 V8 **Baie-Trinité** Québec Canada
123 J8 **Baie Verte** Newfoundland and Labrador Canada
380 F2 **Baihe** Shaanxi China
244 B2 **Baile Ailein** Na h-Eileanan Siar Scotland UK
244 B2 **Baile an Truiseil** Na h-Eileanan Siar Scotland UK
Baile Átha Cliath *see* **Dublin** Ireland
244 A3 **Baile nan Cailleach** Na h-Eileanan Siar Scotland UK
234 D3 **Băile Olănești** Romania
234 E3 **Băile Siriu** Romania
230 E4 **Bailén** Spain
163 I6 **Bailiff** Guadeloupe
384 G4 **Bailingmiao** Nei Mongol Zizhiqu China
156 B2 **Bailique, Ilha** *island* Brazil
380 D1 **Bailong Jiang** *watercourse* Jiangsu China
308 C2 **Bailundo** Angola
379 H2 **Baima** Xizang Zizhiqu China
124 C2 **Bainbridge** British Columbia Canada
243 F2 **Bainbridge** North Yorkshire England UK
131 I5 **Bainbridge** Georgia USA
380 E3 **Baini** Guizhou China
243 H3 **Bainton** East Riding of Yorkshire England UK
125 M2 **Bainville** Montana USA
385 K3 **Baiquan** Heilongjiang China
116 C5 **Baird Mountains** Alaska USA
426 1b **Bairiki** *island* Kiribati
425 M9 **Bairnsdale** Vic. Australia
228 D2 **Bais** France
377 I5 **Bais** Philippines
228 E5 **Baïse** *watercourse* France
380 E2 **Baisha** Sichuan China
380 E4 **Baishan** Guangxi Zhuangzu Zizhiqu China
381 H3 **Baishanzu** *mountain* Zhejiang China
380 F1 **Baishui** Shaanxi China
392 E5 **Baitadi** Nepal
310 2 **Baixio, Ilhéu de** *island* Madeira
308 C2 **Baixo Longa** Angola
384 F5 **Baiya Shan** *range* Shaanxi China
384 F6 **Baiyang** Zishiqu China
384 E6 **Baiyin** Gansu China
385 H4 **Baiyinchagan** Nei Mongol Zizhiqu China
385 J3 **Baiyinhushuo** Nei Mongol Zizhiqu China
302 E4 **Baiyuda Desert** *desert* Sudan
301 G6 **Baïzo** Niger
227 J4 **Baja** Hungary
162 A4 **Baja, Punta** *cape* Chile
128 E6 **Baja, Punta** *cape* Mexico
132 B2 **Baja California** *admin. area* Mexico
132 B2 **Baja California** *peninsula* Mexico
132 B3 **Baja California Sur** *admin. area* Mexico
374 E3 **Bajau** *island* Indonesia
372 B6 **Bajawa** Indonesia
391 I2 **Bajestān** Iran
391 K2 **Bājgāh** Afghanistan
390 E7 **Bājil** Yemen
162 B4 **Bajo Caracoles** Argentina
162 C4 **Bajo Picaso** Argentina
305 G2 **Bajoga** Nigeria
135 G3 **Bajos de Haina** Dominican Republic
393 F7 **Bajpur** Orissa India
375 G4 **Baka, Bukit** *mountain* Indonesia
305 I3 **Bakala** Central African Republic
392 D6 **Bakani** Rajasthan India
305 I1 **Bakaoré** Chad
232 F4 **Bakar** Croatia
305 F4 **Bakassi, Cap** *cape* Cameroon
375 H4 **Bakaucengal** Indonesia
305 F3 **Bakebe** Cameroon
300 D6 **Bakel** Senegal
130 F5 **Baker** Louisiana USA
125 M3 **Baker** Montana USA
426 1 **Baker and Howland Islands** *unincorporated US territory* Pacific Ocean
124 G4 **Baker City** Oregon USA
120 J1 **Baker Foreland** Nunavut Canada
426 1 **Baker Island** Pacific Ocean
117 J6 **Baker Lake** Nunavut Canada
121 P4 **Bakers Dozen Islands** Nunavut Canada
128 D3 **Bakersfield** California USA
129 K5 **Bakersfield** Texas USA
243 G3 **Bakewell** Derbyshire England UK
238 D6 **Bakhan'** Belarus
394 E2 **Bakhmach** Ukraine
236 S6 **Bakhta** Russian Federation
236 S6 **Bakhta** *watercourse* Russian Federation
391 H3 **Bakhtegan, Daryācheh-ye** *lake* Iran
382 G3 **Bakhty** Xinjiang Uygur Zizhiqu China
303 G5 **Baki** Somalia
388 F6 **Bakı (Baku)** Azerbaijan
235 E6 **Bakır** *watercourse* Turkey
222 inset **Bakkafjörður** Iceland
222 inset **Bakkaflói** *bay* Iceland
222 inset **Bakkagerði** Iceland
224 F3 **Bakke** Norway
222 L2 **Bakkeby** Norway
224 F3 **Bakko** Norway
235 F7 **Baklan** Turkey
238 I3 **Baklanka** Russian Federation
304 C3 **Bako** Côte d'Ivoire
307 F2 **Bako** Ethiopia
375 F3 **Bako National Park** Malaysia
374 C3 **Bakongan** Indonesia
307 G3 **Bakool** *admin. area* Somalia
373 J5 **Bakop** Papua New Guinea
306 D3 **Bakordi** Sudan
305 F2 **Bakori** Nigeria
305 I3 **Bakouma** Central African Republic
232 F4 **Bakovac** Croatia
155 H4 **Bakrakondre** Suriname
388 D5 **Baksan** Russian Federation
388 I4 **Bakshakol'** *lake* Kazakhstan
389 L3 **Bakty** Kazakhstan
Baku *see* **Bakı** Azerbaijan
374 E3 **Bakung** *island* Indonesia
436 P2 **Bakutis Coast** Antarctica
225 J4 **Bāl** Sweden
237 AB5 **Bala** Russian Federation
300 D6 **Bala** Senegal
240 D2 **Bala** Gwynedd Wales UK
391 I3 **Bālā Ḩowz** Iran
391 J2 **Bālā Morghāb** Afghanistan
377 H5 **Balabac** Philippines
375 H2 **Balabac** *island* Philippines
377 H6 **Balabac Strait** Malaysia
375 H1 **Balabac Strait North** Philippines
375 H4 **Balabalagan, Kepulauan** *island* Indonesia
238 G5 **Balabanovo** Russian Federation
426 7 **Balabio, Île** *island* New Caledonia
234 C3 **Bălăcița** Romania
237 AE7 **Balaganoye** Russian Federation
393 E7 **Balaghat** Madhya Pradesh India
231 G3 **Balaguer** Spain
375 F4 **Balaiberkuak** Indonesia
375 F3 **Balaikarangan** Indonesia
374 D3 **Balaipungut** Indonesia
375 F4 **Balairiam** Indonesia
379 E3 **Balaka** Malawi
388 E3 **Balakovo** Russian Federation
309 G2 **Balama** Mozambique
375 H2 **Balambangan** *island* Malaysia
133 H5 **Balancán de Domínguez** Mexico
306 B3 **Balangala** Democratic Republic of Congo
307 F4 **Balangida, Lake** *lake* Tanzania
393 F7 **Balangir** Orissa India
372 B4 **Balantak** Indonesia
154 B5 **Baláo** Ecuador
388 F3 **Balashi** Russian Federation
238 G5 **Balashikha** Russian Federation
388 D3 **Balashov** Russian Federation
234 B2 **Balástya** Hungary
232 G3 **Balaton** *lake* Hungary
377 I4 **Balayan** Philippines
230 E4 **Balazote** Spain
377 I3 **Balbalan** Philippines
373 J5 **Balbi, Mount** *volcano* Papua New Guinea
154 D5 **Balbina** Brazil
244 D3 **Balblair** Highland Scotland UK
245 F3 **Balbriggan** Ireland
227 L4 **Balc** Romania
125 N1 **Balcarres** Saskatchewan Canada
242 E2 **Balcary Point** *cape* Scotland UK
234 D3 **Bălcești** Romania
436 O1 **Balchen Glacier** *ice* Antarctica
423 C8 **Balclutha** New Zealand
130 B6 **Balcones Escarpment** Texas USA
235 E6 **Balçova** Turkey
127 K8 **Bald Knob** *mountain* Virginia USA
240 B4 **Baldhu** Cornwall England UK
241 G3 **Baldock** Hertfordshire England UK
120 G4 **Baldock Lake** Manitoba Canada
225 M4 **Baldone** Latvia
131 K5 **Baldwin** Florida USA
126 I5 **Baldwin** Michigan USA
126 E4 **Baldwin** Wisconsin USA
130 G3 **Baldwyn** Mississippi USA
118 L7 **Baldy Mount** British Columbia Canada
128 H4 **Baldy Peak** Arkansas USA
232 E4 **Bale** Croatia
304 B2 **Bale** *watercourse* Guinea
374 D4 **Bale** Indonesia
241 H2 **Bale** Norfolk England UK
231 H4 **Balearic Islands** *island* Spain
372 B4 **Balease, Gunung** *mountain* Indonesia
375 G3 **Baleh** *watercourse* Malaysia
157 E7 **Baleia, Ponta da** *cape* Brazil
121 Q5 **Baleine, Petite Rivière de la** *watercourse* Québec Canada
122 E4 **Baleine, Rivière à la** *watercourse* Québec Canada
163 11a **Baleine Bay** St Vincent and the Grenadines
228 D3 **Baleines, Pointe des** *cape* France
230 C4 **Baleizão** Portugal
244 B4 **Balemartine** Highland Scotland UK
229 G1 **Balen** Belgium
244 B4 **Balephuil** Highland Scotland UK
377 I4 **Baler** Philippines
377 I4 **Baler Bay** Philippines
244 A3 **Baleshare** *island* Scotland UK
393 G7 **Baleshwar** Orissa India
234 C3 **Bălești** Romania
244 B4 **Balevulin** Highland Scotland UK
385 H2 **Baley** Russian Federation
301 G6 **Baléyara** Niger
423 C7 **Balfour** New Zealand
244 D4 **Balfron** Stirling Scotland UK
424 H5 **Balgo Hills** WA Australia
155 G5 **Balhina, Represa de** *lake* Brazil
303 G5 **Balho** Djibouti
375 G6 **Bali** *admin. area* Indonesia
375 G6 **Bali** *island* Indonesia
375 G5 **Bali, Laut (Bali Sea)** Indonesia
375 G6 **Bali, Selat** *strait* Indonesia
375 G6 **Bali Barat, Taman Nasional** *park* Indonesia
Bali Sea *see* **Bali, Laut** Indonesia
163 11 **Baliceaux Island** St Vincent and the Grenadines
393 F7 **Baliguda** Orissa India
394 D5 **Balıkesir** *admin. area* Turkey
375 H4 **Balikpapan** Indonesia
375 H4 **Balikpapan, Teluk** *bay* Indonesia
383 J4 **Balikun** Xinjiang Uygur Zizhiqu China
377 H6 **Balimbing** Philippines
393 F7 **Balimela** Orissa India
373 G6 **Balimo** Papua New Guinea
377 J5 **Balingasag** Philippines
226 E3 **Balingen** Germany
375 G3 **Balingian** Malaysia
310 6b **Baliniers, Golfe des** *bay* French Southern and Antarctic Lands
377 I3 **Balintang** *island* Philippines
377 I3 **Balintang Channel** Philippines
244 D3 **Balintombuie** Highland Scotland UK
244 E3 **Balintore** Highland Scotland UK
305 I3 **Balitondo** Central African Republic
245 C4 **Baliynakilly Upper** Ireland
226 C1 **Balk** Netherlands
244 F4 **Balkaithly** Fife Scotland UK
388 G6 **Balkan Welaýaty** *admin. area* Turkmenistan
388 G6 **Balkanabat** Turkmenistan
389 J3 **Balkashino** Kazakhstan
389 J7 **Balkh** Afghanistan
391 K2 **Balkh** *admin. area* Afghanistan
391 K2 **Balkhāb** Afghanistan
389 L4 **Balkhash** Kazakhstan
389 L4 **Balkhash, Ozero** *lake* Kazakhstan
388 E4 **Balkuduk** Kazakhstan
130 E5 **Ball** Louisiana USA
126 D1 **Ball Lake** Ontario Canada
245 C3 **Balla** Ireland
424 G8 **Balladonia** WA Australia
242 B3 **Ballagan Point** *cape* Ireland
222 J2 **Ballangen** Norway
244 C5 **Ballantrae** South Ayrshire Scotland UK
122 D3 **Ballantyne, Lac** *lake* Québec Canada
116 H3 **Ballantyne Strait** Northwest Territories Canada
425 L9 **Ballarat** Vic. Australia
245 D4 **Ballard** Ireland
424 F7 **Ballard, Lake** WA Australia
393 E7 **Ballarpur** Maharashtra India
244 E3 **Ballater** Aberdeenshire Scotland UK
300 E5 **Ballé** Mali
160 D3 **Ballena, Punta** *cape* Chile
437 K2 **Balleny Islands** Antarctica
437 K2 **Balleny Seamounts** *underwater feature* Southern Ocean
222 J2 **Ballesvika** Norway
392 F6 **Ballia** Uttar Pradesh India
424 F7 **Ballidu** WA Australia
425 O7 **Ballina** NSW Australia
245 C2 **Ballina** Ireland
242 A3 **Ballinabrackey** Ireland
245 D2 **Ballinafad** Ireland
245 E3 **Ballinalack** Ireland
245 E3 **Ballinalee** Ireland
245 E2 **Ballinamore** Ireland
245 D3 **Ballinasloe** Ireland
245 D3 **Ballindine** Ireland
130 B5 **Ballinger** Texas USA
244 E4 **Ballinluig** Perth and Kinross Scotland UK
240 A1 **Ballintober** Ireland
242 B1 **Ballintoy** Moyle Northern Ireland UK
242 B3 **Ballivor** Ireland
244 B3 **Ballochan** Aberdeenshire Scotland UK
228 E2 **Ballon** France
245 F4 **Ballon** Ireland
229 J5 **Ballone Poggio** *mountain* Italy
425 inset **Balls Pyramid** Lord Howe Island Australia
235 A5 **Ballsh** Albania
222 H2 **Ballstad** Norway
126 F7 **Ballwin** Missouri USA
244 C5 **Ballyaurgan** Argyll and Bute Scotland UK
245 F2 **Ballybay** Ireland
242 A2 **Ballybegly** Ireland
245 D5 **Ballybraher** Ireland
245 E3 **Ballybrin** Ireland
245 C2 **Ballycastle** Ireland
242 B1 **Ballycastle** Moyle Northern Ireland UK
242 A3 **Ballycollin** Ireland
245 F4 **Ballycrinnigan** Ireland
245 E4 **Ballycullane** Ireland
245 C5 **Ballydehob** Ireland
245 D3 **Ballyeighter** Ireland
240 A2 **Ballyell** Ireland
242 B4 **Ballyellis** Ireland
245 E3 **Ballyfore** Ireland
245 D5 **Ballyfoyle** Ireland
242 C2 **Ballygalley Head** *cape* Northern Ireland UK
245 D3 **Ballygar** Ireland
245 D3 **Ballyglass** Ireland
242 C2 **Ballygowan** Ards Northern Ireland UK
245 D4 **Ballygriffin** Ireland
245 E4 **Ballyhale** Ireland
244 B4 **Ballyhaugh** Highland Scotland UK
245 C4 **Ballyheige** Ireland
245 C4 **Ballyheige Bay** Ireland
245 E1 **Ballyhillin** Ireland
242 B4 **Ballyhitt** Ireland
245 C4 **Ballyhorgan East** Ireland
245 E3 **Ballyjamesduff** Ireland
245 E3 **Ballykean** Ireland
245 D4 **Ballylanders** Ireland
245 B4 **Ballylusky** Ireland
245 E4 **Ballylynan** Ireland
245 D5 **Ballymacredmond** Ireland
242 A4 **Ballymartin** Ireland
245 D5 **Ballymartle** Ireland
242 B2 **Ballymena** Ballymena Northern Ireland UK
242 B2 **Ballymena** *admin. area* Northern Ireland UK
245 D3 **Ballymoe** Ireland
242 B1 **Ballymoney** Ballymoney Northern Ireland UK
242 B1 **Ballymoney** *admin. area* Northern Ireland UK
242 B4 **Ballymoney Cross Roads** Ireland
245 D2 **Ballymote** Ireland
245 C4 **Ballynacally** Ireland
242 C2 **Ballynahinch** Down Northern Ireland UK
245 C4 **Ballynaskreena** Ireland
242 B3 **Ballynee** Ireland
245 B4 **Ballyoliver** Ireland
242 C2 **Ballyquintin Point** *cape* Northern Ireland UK
245 E4 **Ballyragget** Ireland
245 E3 **Ballyshane** Ireland
245 D2 **Ballyshannon** Ireland
245 D4 **Ballysheedy** Ireland
245 D3 **Ballyshrule** Ireland
245 E3 **Ballysteen** Ireland
245 D2 **Ballysuggart** Ireland
242 B4 **Ballyteige Bay** Ireland
245 F4 **Ballyvaldon** Ireland
245 F4 **Ballyvalloo** Ireland
242 B1 **Ballyvoy** Moyle Northern Ireland UK
242 C2 **Ballywalter** Ards Northern Ireland UK
242 B2 **Ballyward** Banbridge Northern Ireland UK
160 D3 **Balmaceda** Chile
162 B5 **Balmaceda, Cerro** *mountain* Chile
244 E4 **Balmacneil** Perth and Kinross Scotland UK
244 D4 **Balmaha** Stirling Scotland UK
232 B4 **Balme** Italy
244 F3 **Balmedie** Aberdeenshire Scotland UK
423 E6 **Balmoral** New Zealand
129 K5 **Balmorhea** Texas USA
242 A3 **Balnacart** Ireland
244 C3 **Balnacra** Highland Scotland UK
244 B4 **Balnahard** Argyll and Bute Scotland UK
160 F4 **Balnearia** Argentina
162 D2 **Balneario Massini** Argentina
160 F6 **Balneario Monte Hermoso** Argentina
161 G6 **Balneario Orense** Argentina
160 F6 **Balneario Oriente** Argentina
391 J4 **Balochistan** *admin. area* Pakistan
393 E7 **Balod** Chhattisgarh India
393 F6 **Baloda** Chhattisgarh India
374 E4 **Balok, Teluk** *bay* Indonesia
308 B2 **Balombo** Angola
372 C3 **Balontohe** *island* Indonesia
232 H3 **Balotaszállás** Hungary
392 C6 **Balotra** Rajasthan India
155 H4 **Balourou** French Guiana
234 G2 **Balovnoye** Ukraine
392 E5 **Balrampur** Uttar Pradesh India
425 L8 **Balranald** NSW Australia
242 B3 **Balrath** Ireland
234 D3 **Balș** Romania
227 L4 **Balșa** Romania
156 C4 **Balsas** Brazil
132 E5 **Balsas** *watercourse* Mexico
156 C4 **Balsas, Rio das** *watercourse* Brazil
222 K2 **Balsfjord** Norway
228 F4 **Balsièges** France
222 K5 **Balsjö** Sweden
224 I2 **Bålsön** *island* Sweden
229 H3 **Balsthal** Switzerland
119 U8 **Balta** North Dakota USA
234 E3 **Balta Amara** *lake* Romania
234 F3 **Balta Jijilei** *lake* Romania
234 E3 **Balta Jirlăul** *lake* Romania
230 D3 **Baltanás** Spain
161 G4 **Baltasar Brum** Uruguay
244 inset **Baltasound** Shetland Scotland UK
234 E2 **Bălți** Moldova
225 J4 **Baltic Sea**
245 C5 **Baltimore** Ireland
127 M7 **Baltimore** Maryland USA
225 N4 **Baltinava** Latvia
245 F4 **Baltinglass** Ireland
391 M2 **Baltoro Glacier** Pakistan
163 4 **Baltra, Isla** *island* Archipiélago de Colón (Galapagos Islands)
226 D1 **Baltrum** *island* Germany
373 H4 **Baluan Island** Papua New Guinea
375 G3 **Balui** *watercourse* Malaysia
374 C3 **Balumundam** Indonesia
224 H2 **Balungen** *lake* Sweden
375 G5 **Baluran, Taman Nasional** *park* Indonesia
392 G6 **Balurghat** West Bengal India
377 J6 **Balut** *island* Philippines
222 I3 **Balvatnet** *lake* Norway
226 D2 **Balve** Germany
225 N4 **Balvi** Latvia
225 N4 **Balvu** *admin. area* Latvia
154 B5 **Balzar** Ecuador
232 E5 **Balzo** Italy
305 H3 **Bam** Chad
391 I3 **Bam** Iran
385 J1 **Bam** Russian Federation
373 H4 **Bam Island** Papua New Guinea
425 L2 **Bamaga** Qld Australia
120 J7 **Bamaji Lake** Ontario Canada
300 E6 **Bamako** Mali
305 I3 **Bamba** *watercourse* Central African Republic
306 B5 **Bamba** Democratic Republic of Congo
305 G5 **Bambama** Congo
158 B2 **Bambamarca** Peru
134 C4 **Bambana, Rio** *watercourse* Nicaragua
305 I3 **Bambari** Central African Republic
374 C3 **Bambel** Indonesia
232 D2 **Bamberg** Germany
302 E6 **Bambesi** Ethiopia
306 D3 **Bambili** Democratic Republic of Congo
304 D3 **Bamboi** Ghana
306 D2 **Bambouti** Sudan
157 C8 **Bambuí** Brazil
375 G4 **Bambulung** Indonesia
305 G3 **Bamenda** Cameroon
305 G3 **Bamendjing, Lac de** *lake* Cameroon
380 E4 **Bameng Shuiku** *lake* Guangxi Zhuangzu Zizhiqu China
124 C2 **Bamfield** British Columbia Canada
393 E6 **Bamhani** Madhya Pradesh India
391 K2 **Bāmīān** Afghanistan
391 K2 **Bāmīān** *admin. area* Afghanistan
305 I3 **Bamingui** Central African Republic
305 I3 **Bamingui-Bangoran** *admin. area* Central African Republic
376 D4 **Bamnet Narong** Thailand
129 H7 **Bamocha** Mexico
392 E6 **Bamori** Madhya Pradesh India
240 D4 **Bampton** Devon England UK
241 F3 **Bampton** Oxfordshire England UK
391 I2 **Bamrūd** Iran
128 E3 **Bamuri** Mexico
388 G6 **Bamy** Turkmenistan
304 D2 **Ban** Burkina Faso
376 D3 **Ban a Ham** Thailand
376 D3 **Ban a Hi** Thailand
376 D5 **Ban Ao Fat** Thailand
376 D4 **Ban Ao Yai** Thailand
376 D3 **Ban Ban** Laos
376 C4 **Ban Daen** Thailand
376 D3 **Ban Dan Kwian** Thailand
376 E3 **Ban Đao Hon Gom** *island* Vietnam
376 E4 **Bản Đôn** Vietnam
376 D4 **Ban Dung** Thailand
376 C3 **Ban Hat** Thailand
376 D4 **Ban Khae** Thailand
376 D4 **Ban Laem** Thailand
376 D4 **Ban Na** Thailand
376 E3 **Ban Nakang** Laos
376 E3 **Ban Napè** Laos
376 D4 **Ban Nong Tao** Thailand
376 D4 **Ban Pa Lao** Thailand
376 D3 **Ban Phai** Thailand
376 E3 **Ban Phôntiou** Laos
376 D3 **Ban Phu** Thailand
376 C3 **Ban Rong Kat** Thailand
376 C3 **Ban San** Thailand
376 D6 **Ban Sanam Chai** Thailand
376 E3 **Ban Xénô** Laos
390 F7 **Banā, Wādī** *watercourse* Yemen
307 H3 **Banaadir** *admin. area* Somalia
426 1 **Banaba** *island* Kiribati
156 E4 **Banabuiu** *watercourse* Brazil
306 D3 **Banalia** Democratic Republic of Congo
309 F4 **Banamana, Lago** *lake* Mozambique
300 E6 **Banamba** Mali
128 E5 **Banámichi** Mexico
425 N6 **Banana** Qld Australia
304 B3 **Banana Islands** Sierra Leone
159 H5 **Bananal** Brazil
157 B5 **Bananal, Ilha do** *island* Brazil
159 H4 **Bananalzinho** Brazil
376 B6 **Bananga** Andaman and Nicobar Islands India
306 D2 **Banangui** Central African Republic
163 I6 **Bananier** Guadeloupe
304 C3 **Banankoro** Guinea
392 D6 **Banas** *watercourse* Rajasthan India
302 F3 **Banās, Ra's** *cape* Egypt
372 A5 **Banawaya** *island* Indonesia
242 B2 **Banbridge** Banbridge Northern Ireland UK
242 B2 **Banbridge** *admin. area* Northern Ireland UK
241 F2 **Banbury** Oxfordshire England UK
240 C3 **Banc-y-felin** Carmarthenshire Wales UK
375 H1 **Bancalan** *island* Philippines
244 F3 **Banchory** Aberdeenshire Scotland UK
154 D3 **Banco las Piñas** Venezuela
375 H2 **Bancoran** *island* Philippines
124 J5 **Bancroft** Idaho USA
391 I3 **Band-e Kahnūj** Iran
305 G3 **Banda** Cameroon
305 G5 **Banda** Congo
392 E6 **Banda** Madhya Pradesh India
393 C8 **Banda** Maharashtra India
392 E6 **Banda** Uttar Pradesh India
372 D5 **Banda, Kepulauan** *island* Indonesia
372 C5 **Banda, Laut (Banda Sea)** Indonesia
374 B2 **Banda Aceh** Indonesia
Banda Sea *see* **Banda, Laut** Indonesia
374 C3 **Bandahara, Gunung** *mountain* Indonesia
224 E3 **Bandak** *lake* Norway
306 C4 **Bandaka** Democratic Republic of Congo
306 A2 **Bandal** Cameroon
304 D3 **Bandama, Vallée du** *admin. area* Côte d'Ivoire
304 C3 **Bandama Rouge** *watercourse* Côte d'Ivoire
372 D5 **Bandaneira** Indonesia
374 C3 **Bandar** Indonesia
391 H4 **Bandar-e 'Abbās** Iran
388 F6 **Bandar-e Anzalī** Iran
390 G4 **Bandar-e Būshehr** Iran
390 G3 **Bandar-e Ganāveh** Iran
391 H4 **Bandar-e Lengeh** Iran
390 G3 **Bandar-e Māhshahr** Iran
374 E5 **Bandar Lampung** Indonesia
375 G2 **Bandar Seri Begawan** Brunei
375 F3 **Bandar Sri Aman** Malaysia
374 E5 **Bandaragung** Indonesia
379 G4 **Bandarban** Bangladesh
392 E4 **Bandarpunch** *mountain* Uttaranchal India
393 F8 **Bandarulanka** Andhra Pradesh India
230 C2 **Bande** Spain
157 B6 **Bandeirantes** Brazil
157 D8 **Bandeiras, Pico de** *mountain* Brazil
130 B6 **Bandera** Texas USA
129 J5 **Banderas** Mexico
132 D4 **Banderas, Bahía de** *bay* Mexico
300 F6 **Bandiagara** Mali
304 D2 **Bandiagara, Falaise de** *range* Mali
392 D3 **Bandipur** Jammu and Kashmir India/Pakistan
235 E5 **Bandırma** Turkey
235 F5 **Bandırma Körfezi** *bay* Turkey
305 G3 **Bandjoukri** Cameroon
310 8b **Bandnéle** Mayotte
245 D5 **Bandon** Ireland
245 D5 **Bandon** *watercourse* Ireland
124 C5 **Bandon** Oregon USA
306 B4 **Bandundu** Democratic Republic of Congo
306 B4 **Bandundu** *admin. area* Democratic Republic of Congo
374 E5 **Bandung** Indonesia
388 E7 **Baneh** Iran
372 D3 **Banemo** Indonesia
135 F2 **Banes** Cuba
304 B2 **Banfélé** Guinea
124 H1 **Banff** Alberta Canada
304 D2 **Banfora** Burkina Faso
305 H3 **Bang** Central African Republic
376 D4 **Bang Lamung** Thailand
376 D3 **Bang Mun Nak** Thailand
376 D4 **Bang Sai** Thailand
376 C5 **Bang Saphan** Thailand
306 B5 **Banga** Angola
305 I3 **Banga** *watercourse* Central African Republic
306 C5 **Banga** Democratic Republic of Congo
392 D4 **Banga** Punjab India
377 J6 **Banga** Philippines
306 D3 **Bangadi** Democratic Republic of Congo
305 I3 **Banganga** Central African Republic
392 D5 **Banganga Nadi** *watercourse* Rajasthan India
392 G6 **Bangaon** Bihar India
375 G2 **Bangar** Brunei
377 I3 **Bangar** Philippines
305 I4 **Bangassou** Central African Republic
372 B5 **Bangbong** Indonesia
373 H5 **Bangeta, Mount** Papua New Guinea
372 B4 **Banggai, Kepulauan** *island* Indonesia
375 H2 **Banggi** *island* Malaysia
302 C1 **Banghāzī** Libya
376 E3 **Banghiang** *watercourse* Laos
372 C3 **Bangka** *island* Indonesia
372 C3 **Bangka, Selat** *strait* Indonesia
374 E4 **Bangka-Belitung** *admin. area* Indonesia
375 G4 **Bangkal** Indonesia
375 G5 **Bangkalan** Indonesia
374 C3 **Bangkaru** *island* Indonesia
374 D3 **Bangkinang** Indonesia
374 D4 **Bangko** Indonesia
375 G4 **Bangkuang** Indonesia
372 B4 **Bangkulu** *island* Indonesia
375 H6 **Bangkulua** Indonesia
379 G4 **Bangladesh** *country*
308 C2 **Bango, Serra do** *range* Angola
240 C2 **Bangor** Ceredigion Wales UK
242 C2 **Bangor** North Down Northern Ireland UK
127 Q4 **Bangor** Maine USA
245 C2 **Bangor Erris** Ireland
305 I3 **Bangoran** Central African Republic
130 B5 **Bangs** Texas USA
375 H4 **Bangsalsembera** Indonesia
222 G4 **Bangsjøen** *lake* Norway
222 G4 **Bangsund** Norway
306 C5 **Bangu** Democratic Republic of Congo
377 I3 **Bangued** Philippines
305 H4 **Bangui** Central African Republic
377 I3 **Bangui** Philippines
377 I3 **Bangui Bay** Philippines
306 D3 **Banguru** Democratic Republic of Congo
308 F2 **Bangweulu, Lake** *lake* Zambia
302 E1 **Banhā** Egypt
241 H2 **Banham** Norfolk England UK
304 D2 **Bani** Burkina Faso
305 I3 **Bani** Central African Republic
135 G3 **Baní** Dominican Republic
300 E6 **Bani** *watercourse* Mali
377 H3 **Bani** Philippines
301 G5 **Bani-Bangou** Niger
302 E2 **Banī Mazār** Egypt
390 E5 **Banī Sār** Saudi Arabia
390 E6 **Banī Sharfā'** Saudi Arabia
302 E2 **Banī Suwayf** Egypt
301 I2 **Banī Walīd** Libya
305 H4 **Bania** Central African Republic
231 J6 **Baniane** Algeria
304 B2 **Banie** *watercourse* Guinea
304 C2 **Banifing** *watercourse* Mali
392 D4 **Banihal** Jammu and Kashmir India/Pakistan
304 E2 **Banikoara** Benin
305 G5 **Banio, Lagune** *lake* Gabon
231 I6 **Baniou** Algeria
234 D4 **Baniski Lom** *watercourse* Bulgaria
235 D5 **Banite** Bulgaria
235 E6 **Bāniyās** Syria
232 G4 **Banja Luka** Bosnia and Herzegovina
234 A3 **Banjani** Serbia
374 E5 **Banjaran** Indonesia
375 G4 **Banjarmasin** Indonesia
227 H5 **Banjol** Croatia
304 A2 **Banjul** Gambia
240 E2 **Bank Street** Worcestershire England UK
392 G6 **Banka** Bihar India
393 D8 **Bankapur** Karnataka India
300 F6 **Bankass** Mali
244 E4 **Bankfoot** Perth and Kinross Scotland UK
301 G6 **Bankilare** Niger
305 G3 **Bankim** Cameroon
304 B2 **Banko, Massif du** *mountain* Guinea
375 H5 **Bankobankoang** *island* Indonesia
304 C2 **Bankon** Guinea
243 F3 **Banks** Lancashire England UK
163 4 **Banks, Bahía** *bay* Archipiélago de Colón (Galapagos Islands)
118 F6 **Banks Island** British Columbia Canada
426 7 **Banks Islands** Vanuatu
120 H1 **Banks Lake** Nunavut Canada
124 F3 **Banks Lake** Washington USA
423 E6 **Banks Peninsula** New Zealand
425 M10 **Banks Strait** Tas. Australia
425 N8 **Bankstown** NSW Australia
392 G6 **Bankura** West Bengal India
234 B3 **Banloc** Romania
379 H4 **Banmauk** Myanmar
242 B2 **Bann** *watercourse* Northern Ireland UK
159 I2 **Bannach** Brazil
424 H4 **Bannerman, Mount** WA Australia
128 D4 **Banning** California USA
241 I2 **Banningham** Norfolk England UK
391 L3 **Bannu** Pakistan
242 B2 **Bannvale** Newry and Mourne Northern Ireland UK
232 H2 **Bánovce nad Bebravou** Slovakia
376 E4 **Banphon** Laos
426 1b **Banreaba** Kiribati
305 F3 **Bansara** Nigeria
392 F5 **Bansi** Uttar Pradesh India

227 J3 **Banská Bystrica** Slovakia
227 J3 **Banská Štiavnica** Slovakia
227 J3 **Banskobystrický** *admin. area* Slovakia
241 G3 **Banstead** Surrey England UK
377 I4 **Bansud** Philippines
393 D7 **Banswada** Andhra Pradesh India
392 D6 **Banswara** Rajasthan India
305 G3 **Bantadjé** Cameroon
374 C7 **Bantam** Cocos (Keeling) Islands Australia
304 E3 **Banté** Benin
245 D4 **Banteer** Ireland
374 E5 **Banten** *admin. area* Indonesia
377 I4 **Banton** *island* Philippines
245 C5 **Bantry** Ireland
245 C5 **Bantry Bay** Ireland
234 D4 **Banya** Bulgaria
374 C3 **Banyak, Kepulauan** *island* Indonesia
305 G3 **Banyo** Cameroon
231 H2 **Banyoles** Spain
374 E4 **Banyuasin** *watercourse* Indonesia
375 G6 **Banyuwangi** Indonesia
78 D13 **Banzare Bank** *underwater feature* Southern Ocean
437 I2 **Banzare Coast** Antarctica
302 C4 **Bao, Ouadi** *watercourse* Chad
376 E2 **Bảo Lạc** Vietnam
376 E5 **Bảo Lộc** Vietnam
384 F6 **Bao'an** Shaanxi China
385 H4 **Baochang** Nei Mongol Zizhiqu China
385 I5 **Baodi** Tianjin China
385 H5 **Baoding** Hebei China
380 C3 **Baohe** Yunnan China
380 E1 **Baoji** Shaanxi China
381 F2 **Baokang** Hubei China
385 J4 **Baokang** Nei Mongol Zizhiqu China
385 L3 **Baoqing** Heilongjiang China
305 H3 **Baoro** Central African Republic
135 G3 **Baoruco, Sierra de** *range* Dominican Republic
380 C3 **Baoshan** Yunnan China
380 F5 **Baoting** Hainan China
384 G5 **Baotou** Nei Mongol Zizhiqu China
304 C2 **Baoulé** *watercourse* Mali
380 D2 **Baoxing** Sichuan China
380 F5 **Baoyou** Hainan China
393 E8 **Bapatla** Andhra Pradesh India
234 A3 **Bapska** Croatia
380 D3 **Bapu** Sichuan China
391 H3 **Baqījān** Iran
381 G3 **Baqiu** Jiangxi China
390 E2 **Ba'qūbah** Iraq
160 D2 **Baquedano** Chile
163 5 **Baquedano, Punta** *cape* Chile
233 H5 **Bar** Montenegro
234 E1 **Bar** Ukraine
242 C2 **Bar Hall** Ards Northern Ireland UK
123 D10 **Bar Harbor** Maine USA
240 E2 **Bar Hill** Staffordshire England UK
229 G2 **Bar-sur-Seine** France
302 E5 **Bara** Sudan
392 F5 **Bara Banki** Uttar Pradesh India
307 G3 **Baraawe** Somalia
375 G4 **Barabai** Indonesia
238 H5 **Barabanovo** Russian Federation
389 M2 **Barabinsk** Russian Federation
126 G5 **Baraboo** Wisconsin USA
233 G6 **Baracca, Punta della** *cape* Italy
135 F2 **Baracoa** Cuba
155 I5 **Barada** Brazil
126 G3 **Baraga** Michigan USA
154 D2 **Baragua, Sierra de** *range* Venezuela
230 E3 **Barajas de Melo** Spain
238 H5 **Barakovo** Russian Federation
391 I2 **Barākūh** Iran
120 G2 **Baralzon Lake** Nunavut Canada
375 G3 **Baram** *watercourse* Malaysia
375 G2 **Baram, Tanjong** *cape* Malaysia
393 D7 **Baramati** Maharashtra India
391 J4 **Barambah** Pakistan
392 D3 **Baramulla** Jammu and Kashmir India/Pakistan
225 P5 **Baran'** Belarus
391 I3 **Bārān, Kūh-e** *mountain* Iran
242 A2 **Baranailt** Limavady Northern Ireland UK
394 C2 **Baranavichy** Belarus
234 B2 **Báránd** Hungary
304 D2 **Barani** Burkina Faso
302 F3 **Baranis** Egypt
118 D4 **Baranof Island** Alaska USA
234 A2 **Baranya** *admin. area* Hungary
159 G4 **Barão de Capanema** Brazil
159 F3 **Barão de Melgaço** Brazil
300 E6 **Baraouéli** Mali
228 F4 **Baraqueville** France
388 F7 **Barārūd** Iran
377 J4 **Baras** Philippines
393 G6 **Barasat** West Bengal India
372 C5 **Barat Daya, Kepulauan** *island* Indonesia
376 B4 **Baratang Island** Andaman and Nicobar Islands India
130 G6 **Barataria Bay** Louisiana USA
156 E4 **Baraúna** Brazil
225 M6 **Barava** Belarus
154 C2 **Barbacás, Bahía de** *bay* Colombia
157 D8 **Barbacena** Brazil
230 E2 **Barbadillo de Herreros** Spain
155 G1 **Barbados** *country* Caribbean
76 M8 **Barbados Ridge** *underwater feature* Atlantic Ocean
156 E4 **Barbalha** Brazil
154 C5 **Bárbara** Colombia
126 H2 **Barbara Lake** Ontario Canada
230 E2 **Barbastro** Spain
230 D5 **Barbate, Embalse de** *lake* Spain
230 D5 **Barbate de Franco** Spain
228 D4 **Barbezieux-St-Hilaire** France
393 F6 **Barbil** Orissa India
234 F2 **Bărboieni** Moldova
243 F2 **Barbon** Cumbria England UK
154 C3 **Barbosa** Colombia
131 J2 **Barbourville** Kentucky USA
163 18 **Barbuda** *island* Antigua and Barbuda
234 D3 **Bărbuleţu** Romania
224 I4 **Bårby** Sweden
229 I5 **Barcaggio** France
244 C4 **Barcaldine** Argyll and Bute Scotland UK
425 M5 **Barcaldine** Qld Australia
156 B3 **Barcarena** Brazil
230 C4 **Barcarrota** Spain
157 D3 **Barcelona** Peru
231 H3 **Barcelona** Spain
155 E2 **Barcelona** Venezuela
229 H4 **Barcelonnette** France
155 F5 **Barcelos** Brazil
230 B3 **Barcelos** Portugal
230 C2 **Bárcena, Embalse de** *lake* Spain
154 B4 **Barcos** Colombia
232 G4 **Barcs** Hungary
388 G7 **Bard** Iran
162 C2 **Barda Negra, Meseta de la** *plateau* Argentina
307 H2 **Bardaale** Somalia
301 J4 **Bardaï** Chad
235 F6 **Bardakçı** Turkey
160 D5 **Bardas Blancas** Argentina
391 I2 **Bardāskan** Iran
392 G6 **Barddhaman** West Bengal India
390 G2 **Bardeh Sī** Iran
227 K3 **Bardejov** Slovakia
121 R6 **Bardin, Lac** *lake* Québec Canada
243 H3 **Bardney** Lincolnshire England UK
393 C7 **Bardoli** Gujarat India
242 D2 **Bardrochwood** Dumfries and Galloway Scotland UK
222 K1 **Bårdset** Norway
240 C2 **Bardsey** *island* Wales UK
391 H3 **Bardsīr** Iran
222 inset **Barðsneshorn** *cape* Iceland
126 I8 **Bardstown** Kentucky USA
222 K2 **Bardujord** Norway
241 H2 **Bardwell** Suffolk England UK
130 C4 **Bardwell** Texas USA
307 G3 **Barē** Ethiopia
234 B3 **Bare** Serbia
242 F2 **Bare** Lancashire England UK
392 E5 **Bareilly** Uttar Pradesh India
241 H5 **Barentin** France
435 L1 **Barents Abyssal Plain** *underwater feature* Arctic Ocean
434 I2 **Barents Sea**
236 F3 **Barentsøya** *island* Norway
302 F4 **Barentu** Eritrea
375 G3 **Bareo** Malaysia
241 F5 **Barfleur** France
228 D2 **Barfleur, Pointe de** *cape* France
241 I2 **Barford** Norfolk England UK
241 F3 **Barford St Martin** Wiltshire England UK
234 D4 **Barga** Italy
393 F7 **Bargarh** Orissa India
226 D5 **Barge** Italy
230 C6 **Bargha** Morocco
393 E6 **Barghat** Madhya Pradesh India
392 E6 **Bargi** Madhya Pradesh India
384 G1 **Barguzin** Russian Federation
237 X7 **Barguzinskiy Khrebet** *range* Russian Federation
393 E7 **Barhi** Chhattisgarh India
392 E6 **Barhi** Madhya Pradesh India
241 G2 **Barholm** Lincolnshire England UK
393 G7 **Bari** Orissa India
392 D6 **Bari** Rajasthan India
233 G6 **Bari** Italy
307 I1 **Bari** *admin. area* Somalia
392 D6 **Bari Sadri** Rajasthan India
390 D5 **Barīdī, Ra's** *cape* Saudi Arabia
301 H1 **Barika** Algeria
155 F2 **Barima** *watercourse* Venezuela
155 G3 **Barima-Waini** *admin. area* Guyana
154 D2 **Barinas** Venezuela
154 D2 **Barinas** *admin. area* Venezuela
305 I4 **Baringa** Democratic Republic of Congo
307 F3 **Baringo, Lake** *lake* Kenya
154 D2 **Barinitas** Venezuela
157 B8 **Bariri** Brazil
302 E3 **Bâris** Egypt
379 G4 **Barisal** Bangladesh
379 G4 **Barisal** *admin. area* Bangladesh
374 D5 **Barisan, Pegunungan** *range* Indonesia
233 E5 **Barisciano** Italy
375 G4 **Barito** *watercourse* Indonesia
229 G4 **Barjac** France
229 H5 **Barjols** France
391 I5 **Barkā'** Oman
391 K7 **Barkah** Afghanistan
302 E1 **Barkal, Jebel** *mountain* Sudan
155 H4 **Barkaref** French Guiana
225 N4 **Barkava** Latvia
300 D5 **Barkéwol el Abiod** Mauritania
391 L3 **Barkhan** Pakistan
241 H3 **Barking** Greater London England UK
130 H2 **Barkley, Lake** Kentucky USA
124 C2 **Barkley Sound** British Columbia Canada
425 J4 **Barkly Homestead** NT Australia
425 J4 **Barkly Tableland** NT Australia
308 D5 **Barkly West** South Africa
129 L6 **Barksdale** Texas USA
244 D6 **Barlae** Dumfries and Galloway Scotland UK
241 E2 **Barlaston** Staffordshire England UK
310 4 **Barlavento, Ilhas do** *islands* Cape Verde
226 F1 **Barleben** Germany
424 F7 **Barlee, Lake** WA Australia
304 B3 **Barlo Point** *cape* Sierra Leone
391 I3 **Barmenj** Iran
392 C6 **Barmer** Rajasthan India
241 H2 **Barmer** Norfolk England UK
240 C2 **Barmouth Bay** Wales UK
310 5b **Barn Long Point** *cape* St Helena
245 C3 **Barna** Ireland
242 A4 **Barnadown** Ireland
392 D4 **Barnala** Punjab India
245 E3 **Barnan** Ireland
129 M1 **Barnard** Kansas USA
232 E2 **Bărnau** Germany
389 N2 **Barnaul** Russian Federation
437 K1 **Barne Inlet** *bay* Antarctica
127 O7 **Barnegat Bay** New Jersey USA
127 N7 **Barnegat Light** New Jersey USA
125 Q7 **Barnes** Kansas USA
117 L4 **Barnes Ice Cap** Nunavut Canada
241 G3 **Barnet** Greater London England UK
162 C6 **Barnevelt, Islas** *islands* Chile
226 G1 **Barnewitz** Germany
241 H2 **Barney** Norfolk England UK
241 H2 **Barnham** Suffolk England UK
129 L5 **Barnhart** Texas USA
241 E3 **Barnhill** Moray Scotland UK
244 C5 **Barnhills** Dumfries and Galloway Scotland UK
241 G3 **Barns Green** West Sussex England UK
243 G3 **Barnsley** South Yorkshire England UK
240 C3 **Barnstaple** Devon England UK
240 C3 **Barnstaple or Bideford Bay** England UK
226 E1 **Barnstorf** Germany
126 E3 **Barnum** Minnesota USA
131 K4 **Barnwell** South Carolina USA
305 F3 **Baro** Nigeria
392 D6 **Baroda** Madhya Pradesh India
392 D6 **Baroda** Rajasthan India
391 M2 **Baroghil Pass** Pakistan
124 I2 **Barons** Alberta Canada
245 C5 **Barony Bridge** Ireland
306 C2 **Baroua** Central African Republic
222 I2 **Barøya** *island* Norway
377 G5 **Barque Canada Reef** Spratly Islands
154 D2 **Barquisimeto** Venezuela
244 D5 **Barr** South Ayrshire Scotland UK
157 D5 **Barra** Brazil
309 G4 **Barra, Ponta da** *cape* Mozambique
244 A3 **Barra, Sound of** *bay* Scotland UK
157 D6 **Barra da Estiva** Brazil
156 F5 **Barra de Santo Antônio** Brazil
157 D7 **Barra de São Francisco** Brazil
156 C4 **Barra do Corda** Brazil
159 H5 **Barra do Bugres** Brazil
156 C4 **Barra do Corda** Brazil
159 H5 **Barra do Félix** Brazil
157 A6 **Barra do Garças** Brazil
157 D8 **Barra do Piraí** Brazil
309 G4 **Barra Falsa, Ponta da** *cape* Mozambique
134 C4 **Barra Patuca** Honduras
157 B9 **Barra Velha** Brazil
159 G2 **Barraca de Seringueiro** Brazil
159 F3 **Barraca do Lucas** Brazil
159 G4 **Barracão** Brazil
159 G3 **Barracão do Barreto** Brazil
159 G3 **Barracão São José** Brazil
231 F3 **Barrachina** Spain
230 D3 **Barraco** Spain
245 D4 **Barraden** Ireland
245 C4 **Barraduff** Ireland
158 B2 **Barranca** Peru
154 C3 **Barranca de Upía** Colombia
154 C2 **Barrancabermeja** Colombia
160 D6 **Barrancas** *watercourse* Argentina
158 E6 **Barrancas** Bolivia
154 C2 **Barrancas** Colombia
132 D3 **Barranco** Mexico
159 F4 **Barranco Alto** Brazil
242 B4 **Barranisky** Ireland
154 C2 **Barranquilla** Colombia
154 D2 **Barranquitas** Venezuela
244 B4 **Barrapoll** Highland Scotland UK
156 D4 **Barras** Brazil
231 F4 **Barrax** Spain
228 F4 **Barre-des-Cévennes** France
159 I3 **Barreira do Campo** Brazil
157 C6 **Barreiras** Brazil
156 D3 **Barreirinhas** Brazil
159 H4 **Barreiro** Brazil
157 D6 **Barreiro do Jaíba** Brazil
157 D6 **Barreiro do Nascimento** Brazil
126 F2 **Barrel Lake** Ontario Canada
163 7 **Barren Island** Falkland Islands
376 B4 **Barren Island** Andaman and Nicobar Islands India
116 D7 **Barren Islands** Alaska USA
131 H2 **Barren River Lake** Kentucky USA
157 B8 **Barretos** Brazil
423 D6 **Barrhill** New Zealand
244 D5 **Barrhill** South Ayrshire Scotland UK
127 L4 **Barrie** Ontario Canada
162 E1 **Barrientos, Sierra de los** *range* Argentina
437 F2 **Barrier Bay** Antarctica
122 D1 **Barrier Inlet** Nunavut Canada
426 5 **Barrigada** Guam
133 F3 **Barril, Laguna El** *lake* Mexico
123 F11 **Barrington** Nova Scotia Canada
244 E4 **Barrington** Fife Scotland UK
120 E4 **Barrington Lake** Manitoba Canada
425 N8 **Barrington Tops** NSW Australia
425 M7 **Barringun** Qld Australia
228 B5 **Barrios de Luna, Embalse de** *lake* Spain
245 C2 **Barroosky** Ireland
156 D3 **Barroquinha** Brazil
158 D5 **Barroso** Brazil
158 D5 **Barroso, Nevado** *mountain* Peru
163 11a **Barrouallie** St Vincent and the Grenadines
160 F6 **Barrow** Argentina
242 B4 **Barrow** *watercourse* Ireland
116 D4 **Barrow** Alaska USA
116 D4 **Barrow, Point** Alaska USA
425 J5 **Barrow Creek** NT Australia
243 H3 **Barrow Haven** North Lincolnshire England UK
424 E5 **Barrow Island** WA Australia
117 J4 **Barrow Strait** Nunavut Canada
241 G2 **Barrowby** Lincolnshire England UK
119 U6 **Barrows** Manitoba Canada
230 C3 **Barruecopardo** Spain
155 H3 **Barruol, Monts** *range* French Guiana
240 D3 **Barry** Vale of Glamorgan Wales UK
423 D6 **Barrytown** New Zealand
304 D2 **Barsalogo** Burkina Faso
227 M4 **Bârsana** Romania
388 F7 **Barseh** Iran
393 D7 **Barsi** Maharashtra India
224 E5 **Barsø** *island* Denmark
128 D3 **Barstow** California USA
129 K5 **Barstow** Texas USA
225 K4 **Barstyčiai** Lithuania
222 J3 **Bartaurte** *mountain* Sweden
224 G5 **Barthe** *watercourse* Germany
155 G3 **Bartica** Guyana
394 E5 **Bartin** Turkey
394 E5 **Bartin** *admin. area* Turkey
425 M4 **Bartle Frere** *mountain* Qld Australia
126 D8 **Bartlesville** Oklahoma USA
128 C2 **Bartlett** California USA
125 P6 **Bartlett** Nebraska USA
130 G3 **Bartlett** Tennessee USA
127 O4 **Barton** Vermont USA
120 I6 **Barton Lake** Ontario Canada
131 K7 **Bartow** Florida USA
227 L5 **Baru** Romania
154 C2 **Baru, Isla de** *island* Colombia
154 C2 **Barú, Punta** *cape* Colombia
155 F4 **Barudene, Serra** *range* Brazil
157 C8 **Barueri** Brazil
374 C3 **Barumun** *watercourse* Indonesia
384 G2 **Barun-Sabartuj, Gora** *mountain* Russian Federation
375 G6 **Barung** *island* Indonesia
424 J3 **Barunga** NT Australia
225 N5 **Baruny** Belarus
374 C3 **Barus** Indonesia
389 K6 **Barushan** Tajikistan
227 G1 **Baruth** Germany
385 H3 **Baruun-Urt** Mongolia
384 E3 **Baruunbayan-ulaan** Mongolia
384 E2 **Baruunburen** Mongolia
383 J2 **Baruunturuun** Mongolia
393 C6 **Barwala** Gujarat India
393 D6 **Barwani** Madhya Pradesh India
425 M7 **Barwon** *watercourse* NSW Australia
238 F5 **Barybino** Russian Federation
227 L3 **Barycz** Poland
227 I2 **Barycz** *watercourse* Poland
237 AB5 **Barylas** Russian Federation
238 C5 **Barysaw** Belarus
388 E2 **Barysh** Russian Federation
234 B2 **Bârzava** Romania
306 A5 **Bas-Congo** *admin. area* Democratic Republic of Congo
234 B3 **Bašaid** Serbia
306 C3 **Basali** Democratic Republic of Congo
306 C5 **Basanga** Democratic Republic of Congo
306 B3 **Basankusu** Democratic Republic of Congo
230 E2 **Basauri** Spain
393 D8 **Basavakalyan** Karnataka India
377 I2 **Basco** Philippines
160 D4 **Bascuñán, Cabo** *cape* Chile
229 H3 **Basel** Switzerland
233 G6 **Basento** *watercourse* Italy
234 D3 **Băseşti** Romania
389 N3 **Bashchelakskiy Khrebet** *range* Russian Federation
381 I4 **Bashi Channel** *sea* Taiwan China
306 C5 **Bashimuke** Democratic Republic of Congo
388 F6 **Bashirabat** Azerbaijan
388 D2 **Bashmakovo** Russian Federation
390 G3 **Bāsht** Iran
234 H2 **Bashtanka** Ukraine
390 E2 **Bashur** Iraq
373 I6 **Basilaki Island** Papua New Guinea
377 I6 **Basilan** *island* Philippines
241 H3 **Basildon** Essex England UK
130 E5 **Basile** Louisiana USA
233 F6 **Basilicata** *admin. area* Italy
233 F7 **Basiluzzo, Isola** *island* Italy
125 K4 **Basin** Wyoming USA
119 S6 **Basin Lake** Saskatchewan Canada
224 I2 **Båsingen** *lake* Sweden
241 F3 **Basingstoke** Hampshire England UK
393 G6 **Basirhat** West Bengal India
127 R4 **Baskahegan Lake** Maine USA
238 F5 **Baskakovka** Russian Federation
394 H5 **Başkale** Turkey
117 L9 **Baskatong, Réservoir** Québec Canada
127 N3 **Baskatong Lake** Québec Canada
222 J4 **Bäsksjö** Sweden
243 G3 **Baslow** Derbyshire England UK
235 G7 **Başmakçı** Turkey
393 D7 **Basmat** Maharashtra India
393 F7 **Basna** Chhattisgarh India
374 D4 **Baso** *island* Indonesia
392 D6 **Basoda** Madhya Pradesh India
306 C3 **Basoko** Democratic Republic of Congo
306 C4 **Basongo** Democratic Republic of Congo
163 1a **Basora, Punta** *cape* Aruba
390 F3 **Başrah, Al** *admin. area* Iraq
128 C2 **Bass Lake** California USA
425 M9 **Bass Strait** *watercourse* Australia
232 D4 **Bassano del Grappa** Italy
310 6a **Bassas da India** Îles Éparses
305 I3 **Basse-Kotto** *admin. area* Central African Republic
228 D2 **Basse-Normandie** *admin. area* France
163 14 **Basse-Pointe** Martinique
304 B2 **Basse Santa Su** Gambia
163 16 **Basse-Terre** Guadeloupe
163 16 **Basse-Terre** *island* Guadeloupe
163 9 **Basse-Terre** Trinidad and Tobago
242 E2 **Bassenthwaite Lake** England UK
163 16 **Basses, Pointe des** *cape* Guadeloupe
163 19 **Basseterre** St Kitts and Nevis
125 P5 **Bassett** Nebraska USA
300 E5 **Bassikounou** Mauritania
228 D4 **Bassin d'Arcachon** *bay* France
226 E1 **Bassum** Germany
126 F2 **Basswood Lake** Ontario Canada
244 inset **Basta** Shetland Scotland UK
392 F5 **Basti** Uttar Pradesh India
229 I5 **Bastia** France
232 E5 **Bastia** Italy
123 H7 **Bastille, Lac** *lake* Québec Canada
229 G1 **Bastogne** Belgium
157 B8 **Bastos** Brazil
130 F4 **Bastrop** Louisiana USA
130 C5 **Bastrop** Texas USA
225 K2 **Bastuskär** *island* Finland
222 L4 **Bastuträsk** Sweden
374 D4 **Basu, Tanjung** *cape* Indonesia
393 G7 **Basudebpur** Orissa India
373 H4 **Bat Islands** Papua New Guinea
384 E3 **Bat ulzai** Mongolia
305 F4 **Bata** Equatorial Guinea
377 I4 **Bataan Peninsula** *cape* Philippines
134 D2 **Batabanó, Golfo de** *bay* Cuba
377 I3 **Batac** Philippines
373 F4 **Bataf** Indonesia
377 J4 **Batag** *island* Philippines
237 AB5 **Batagay-Alyta** Russian Federation
157 A8 **Bataiporã** Brazil
235 D5 **Batak** Bulgaria
375 G5 **Batakan** Indonesia
392 D4 **Batala** Punjab India
156 D4 **Batalha** Brazil
374 E3 **Batam** *island* Indonesia
306 D3 **Batama** Democratic Republic of Congo
388 H3 **Batamshinskiy** Kazakhstan
377 I2 **Batan Islands** Philippines
374 F5 **Batang** Indonesia
375 G3 **Batang Ai National Park** Malaysia
375 F3 **Batang Tarang** Indonesia
305 H3 **Batangafo** Central African Republic
377 I4 **Batangas** Philippines
374 C3 **Batangtoru** Indonesia
372 D4 **Batanta** *island* Indonesia
234 B2 **Bátar** Romania
234 A2 **Bátaszék** Hungary
155 G5 **Batata, Lagoa** *lake* Brazil
157 C8 **Batatais** Brazil
424 I3 **Batchelor** NT Australia
126 I3 **Batchewine Bay** Michigan USA
376 D5 **Bătdâmbâng** Cambodia
306 A4 **Batéké, Plateaux** *plain* Congo
425 N8 **Batemans Bay** NSW Australia
126 I7 **Batesville** Indiana USA
225 P3 **Batetskiy** Russian Federation
163 19 **Bath** St Kitts and Nevis
230 E3 **Bath** Bath and North East Somerset England UK
240 E3 **Bath and North East Somerset** *admin. area* England UK
305 H2 **Batha** *admin. area* Chad
305 H2 **Batha, Ouadi** *watercourse* Chad
240 C4 **Bathpool** Cornwall England UK
163 12 **Bathsheba** Barbados
425 N8 **Bathurst** NSW Australia
123 F9 **Bathurst** New Brunswick Canada
116 G4 **Bathurst, Cape** Northwest Territories Canada
116 I5 **Bathurst Inlet** Nunavut Canada
424 I2 **Bathurst Island** WA Australia
117 J3 **Bathurst Island** Nunavut Canada
303 F5 **Bati** Ethiopia
235 E7 **Batı Menteşe Dağları** *range* Turkey
304 E2 **Batia** Benin
304 D3 **Batié** Burkina Faso
427 9 **Batiki** *island* Fiji
232 H4 **Batina** Croatia
390 G4 **Baţinah, Al** *island* Saudi Arabia
227 K3 **Bátka** Slovakia
389 K6 **Batken** Kyrgyzstan
389 K6 **Batken** *admin. area* Kyrgyzstan
391 H3 **Bātlāq-e Gāvkhūnī** *lake* Iran
243 G3 **Batley** West Yorkshire England UK
394 G6 **Batman** Turkey
394 G6 **Batman** *admin. area* Turkey
394 G6 **Batman Barajı** *lake* Turkey
301 H1 **Batna** Algeria
301 H1 **Batna** *admin. area* Algeria
384 G3 **Batnarov** Mongolia
377 I2 **Baton** *island* Philippines
130 F5 **Baton Rouge** Louisiana USA
376 C6 **Baton, Ko** *island* Thailand
129 I7 **Batopilas** Mexico
392 D4 **Batote** Jammu and Kashmir India/Pakistan
305 G4 **Batouala** Gabon
305 G4 **Batouri** Cameroon
234 C3 **Bătrina** Romania
222 K3 **Båtsa** *lake* Sweden
223 P1 **Båtsfjord** Norway
384 G3 **Batshireet** Mongolia
235 D7 **Batsíon** Greece
222 J3 **Båtsjaur** Sweden
384 F3 **Batsumber** Mongolia
122 K6 **Batteau** Newfoundland and Labrador Canada
374 B1 **Batti Malv** *island* Andaman and Nicobar Islands India
376 B5 **Batti Malv** *island* Andaman and Nicobar Islands India
393 E10 **Batticaloa** Sri Lanka
119 Q6 **Battle** *watercourse* Alberta/Saskatchewan Canada
241 H4 **Battle** East Sussex England UK
240 D3 **Battle** Powys Wales UK
126 I5 **Battle Creek** Michigan USA
124 G6 **Battle Mountain** Nevada USA
234 B2 **Battonya** Hungary
384 E3 **Battsengel** Mongolia
307 F2 **Batu** *mountain* Ethiopia
375 G3 **Batu, Bukit** *mountain* Malaysia
374 C4 **Batu, Kepulauan** *island* Indonesia
375 H3 **Batu, Tanjung** *cape* Indonesia
374 E6 **Batu Ampar** Indonesia
374 D3 **Batu Besar** Indonesia
375 G3 **Batu Bora, Bukit** *mountain* Malaysia
374 D2 **Batu Gajah** Malaysia
374 D3 **Batu Pahat** Malaysia
374 D2 **Batu Puteh, Gunung** *mountain* Malaysia
372 B5 **Batuata** *island* Indonesia
375 G3 **Batuayau, Bukit** *mountain* Indonesia
374 E4 **Batubetumbang** Indonesia
372 B4 **Batudaka** *island* Indonesia
372 B4 **Batuhitam, Tanjung** *cape* Indonesia
375 H4 **Batulicin** Indonesia
375 G3 **Batulilangmebang, Gunung** *mountain* Indonesia
388 D5 **Bat'umi** Georgia
374 D4 **Batumonga** Indonesia
391 M2 **Batura Glacier** Pakistan
374 E5 **Baturaja** Indonesia
156 E4 **Baturité** Brazil
228 B2 **Batz, Île de** *island* France
375 F3 **Bau** Malaysia
372 B5 **Baubau** Indonesia
305 F2 **Bauchi** Nigeria
305 F2 **Bauchi** *admin. area* Nigeria
228 C3 **Baud** France
121 S7 **Baudeau, Lac** *lake* Québec Canada
393 F7 **Baudh** Orissa India
154 B3 **Baudó, Bahía de** *bay* Colombia
154 B3 **Baudó, Serranía de** *range* Colombia
79 V8 **Bauer Basin** *underwater feature* Pacific Ocean
425 inset **Bauer Bay** Macquarie Island Australia
228 D3 **Baugé** France
155 H3 **Baugé, Monts** *range* French Guiana
228 F3 **Baugy** France
372 C6 **Baukau** Timor-Leste (East Timor)
372 B5 **Baula** Indonesia
123 K7 **Bauld, Cape** Newfoundland and Labrador Canada
117 K3 **Baumann Fiord** Nunavut Canada
243 H3 **Baumber** Lincolnshire England UK
229 H3 **Baume-les-Dames** France
375 E5 **Baun** *island* Indonesia
159 F4 **Baures** Bolivia
245 D4 **Baurnagurrahy** Ireland
157 B8 **Bauru** Brazil
157 A7 **Baús** Brazil
392 G6 **Bausi** Bihar India
225 M4 **Bauska** Latvia
225 M4 **Bauskas** *admin. area* Latvia
388 F5 **Bautino** Kazakhstan
227 H2 **Bautzen** Germany
162 C4 **Bauzá, Punta** *cape* Argentina
226 B2 **Bavay** France
224 I3 **Båven** *lake* Sweden
132 C2 **Bavispe** Mexico
132 C2 **Bavispe** *watercourse* Mexico
232 F2 **Bavorov** Czech Republic
375 F4 **Bawal** *island* Indonesia
375 G4 **Bawan** Indonesia
375 F4 **Bawang, Tanjung** *cape* Indonesia
241 I2 **Bawburgh** Norfolk England UK
375 G5 **Bawean** *island* Indonesia
304 D2 **Bawku** Ghana
379 H5 **Bawlake** Myanmar
304 C3 **Bawo** Liberia
391 I5 **Bawshar** Oman
131 J5 **Baxley** Georgia USA
307 G3 **Bay** *admin. area* Somalia
130 F3 **Bay** Arkansas USA
123 L9 **Bay Bulls** Newfoundland and Labrador Canada
126 J5 **Bay City** Michigan USA
130 D6 **Bay City** Texas USA
130 H5 **Bay Minette** Alabama USA
422 G3 **Bay of Plenty** *admin. area* New Zealand
123 L9 **Bay Roberts** Newfoundland and Labrador Canada
123 H9 **Bay St Lawrence** Nova Scotia Canada
130 G3 **Bay Springs Lake** Mississippi USA
422 G4 **Bay View** New Zealand
374 E5 **Bayah** Indonesia
134 E2 **Bayamo** Cuba
135 H3 **Bayamón** Puerto Rico
385 K3 **Bayan** Heilongjiang China
384 D5 **Bayan** Qinghai China
384 E6 **Bayan** Qinghai China
375 H6 **Bayan** Indonesia
384 E2 **Bayan** Mongolia
384 G3 **Bayan-adarga** Mongolia
384 F5 **Bayan Hot** Nei Mongol Zizhiqu China
383 I2 **Bayan-Ölgiy** *admin. area* Mongolia
384 F4 **Bayan-ovoo** Mongolia
385 I2 **Bayan Tohoi** Nei Mongol Zizhiqu China
384 F3 **Bayan-unjuul** Mongolia
384 E4 **Bayandalai** Mongolia
385 G3 **Bayandelger** Mongolia
384 E3 **Bayandun** Mongolia
306 B3 **Bayanga** Central African Republic
305 H3 **Bayanga-Didi** Central African Republic
384 F5 **Bayangaole** Nei Mongol Zizhiqu China
384 E3 **Bayangol** Mongolia
384 D4 **Bayangov** Mongolia
383 J2 **Bayanhairhan** Mongolia
384 F3 **Bayanhangai** Mongolia
384 D3 **Bayanhongor** Mongolia
384 D3 **Bayanhongor** *admin. area* Mongolia
384 G3 **Bayanjargalan** Mongolia
384 F3 **Bayanjargalan** Mongolia
385 I2 **Bayankuren** Nei Mongol Zizhiqu China
384 D4 **Bayanlig** Mongolia
385 G3 **Bayanmunha** Mongolia
384 E3 **Bayannuur** Mongolia
154 B2 **Bayano, Lago** *lake* Panama
384 G3 **Bayanovoo** Mongolia
384 F3 **Bayantal** Mongolia
384 E3 **Bayanteeg** Mongolia
383 J2 **Bayantes** Mongolia
384 D3 **Bayantsagaan** Mongolia
384 F3 **Bayantsagaan** Mongolia
384 F3 **Bayantsogt** Mongolia
385 H3 **Bayantumen** Mongolia
384 E3 **Bayanunder** Mongolia
385 G2 **Bayanuul** Mongolia
385 I4 **Bayanwula** Nei Mongol Zizhiqu China
384 G3 **Bayanzurhe** Mongolia
125 N6 **Bayard** Nebraska USA
129 H4 **Bayard** New Mexico USA
235 G6 **Bayat** Turkey
131 M3 **Bayboro** North Carolina USA
242 E2 **Baycliff** Cumbria England UK
236 O5 **Baydaratskaya Guba** *bay* Russian Federation
307 G3 **Baydhabo** Somalia
305 F4 **Bayelsa** *admin. area* Nigeria
226 F4 **Bayern** *admin. area* Germany
228 D2 **Bayeux** France
389 M2 **Bayevo** Russian Federation
127 K5 **Bayfield** Ontario Canada
129 I2 **Bayfield** Colorado USA
126 F3 **Bayfield** Wisconsin USA
123 I7 **Bayfield, Île** *island* Québec Canada
388 G4 **Bayganin** Kazakhstan
390 E2 **Bayji** Iraq
384 F1 **Baykal, Ozero (Lake Baikal)**, *lake* Russian Federation
237 W7 **Baykal'skiy Khrebet** *range* Russian Federation
237 U6 **Baykit** Russian Federation
388 I4 **Baykonyr** Kazakhstan
422 E2 **Baylys Beach** New Zealand
388 H3 **Baymak** Russian Federation
229 H2 **Bayon** France
230 B2 **Bayona** Spain
228 D5 **Bayonne** France
130 E4 **Bayou D'Arbonne Lake** Louisiana USA
130 D6 **Bayou Vista** Texas USA
158 A2 **Bayovar** Peru
388 I4 **Bayqonyr** *admin. area* Kazakhstan
388 I6 **Bayramaly** Turkmenistan
226 F3 **Bayreuth** Germany
127 L4 **Bays, Lake of** Ontario Canada
385 H1 **Baysa** Russian Federation
389 M5 **Bayserke** Kazakhstan
390 E7 **Bayt al Faqīh** Yemen
388 I4 **Baytakkol'** *lake* Kazakhstan
383 I3 **Baytik Shan** *range* Xinjiang Uygur Zizhiqu China
130 D6 **Baytown** Texas USA
372 B4 **Bayu** Indonesia
374 D4 **Bayunglincir** Indonesia
230 E5 **Baza** Spain
391 L2 **Bāzārak** Afghanistan
388 E3 **Bazarnyy-Karabulak** Russian Federation
309 G4 **Bazaruto, Ilha do** *island* Mozambique
228 D4 **Bazas** France
380 E2 **Bazhong** Sichuan China
385 H5 **Bazhou** Hebei China
391 I4 **Bāzīgar** Iran
122 E5 **Bazil, Lac** *lake* Québec Canada
310 5a **BBC Atlantic Relay Station** Ascension
376 E5 **Be** *watercourse* Vietnam
309 I2 **Bé, Nosy** *island* Madagascar
244 C4 **Beach** Highland Scotland UK
125 N3 **Beach** North Dakota USA
425 K9 **Beachport** SA Australia
127 N7 **Beachwood** New Jersey USA
241 H4 **Beachy Head** *cape* England UK
127 O6 **Beacon** New York USA
240 C4 **Beaford** Devon England UK
245 C4 **Beaghfa** Ireland
162 C6 **Beagle, Canal** *strait* Chile
162 A5 **Beagle, Isla** *island* Chile
424 K3 **Beagle Gulf** NT Australia
309 I2 **Bealanana** Madagascar
124 C2 **Beale, Cape** British Columbia Canada
244 E4 **Beannie** Perth and Kinross Scotland UK
119 N3 **Bear** *watercourse* Alberta Canada
124 J5 **Bear** *watercourse* Idaho USA
118 C3 **Bear Camp** British Columbia Canada
120 M1 **Bear Cove** Nunavut Canada
119 Q4 **Bear Creek** Saskatchewan Canada
124 F8 **Bear Creek Spire** *mountain* California USA
121 O5 **Bear Island** Nunavut Canada
245 C5 **Bear Island** Ireland
118 J5 **Bear Lake** British Columbia Canada
120 H5 **Bear Lake** Manitoba Canada
124 J6 **Bear Lake** Utah USA
436 Q2 **Bear Peninsula** Antarctica
130 E4 **Bearden** Arkansas USA
126 H2 **Beardmore** Ontario Canada
128 B1 **Beardsley Lake** California USA
241 G3 **Beare Green** Surrey England UK
228 D5 **Béarn** *region* France
242 A2 **Bearney** Strabane Northern Ireland UK
125 K2 **Bears Paw Mountains** Montana USA
244 D5 **Bearsden** East Dunbartonshire Scotland UK
120 J6 **Bearskin Lake** Ontario Canada
241 H3 **Bearsted** Kent England UK
230 C5 **Beas** Spain
230 E4 **Beas de Segura** Spain
230 E3 **Beasain** Spain
135 G3 **Beata, Cabo** *cape* Dominican Republic
135 G3 **Beata, Isla** *island* Dominican Republic
76 K8 **Beata Ridge** *underwater feature* Caribbean Sea
125 Q6 **Beatrice** Nebraska USA
425 K3 **Beatrice, Cape** NT Australia
125 Q7 **Beattie** Kansas USA
244 E5 **Beattock** Dumfries and Galloway Scotland UK
118 K4 **Beatton** *watercourse* British Columbia Canada
128 D2 **Beatty** Nevada USA
229 G5 **Beaucaire** France
241 I5 **Beaucamps-le-Vieux** France
228 E2 **Beauce** *region* France
162 E5 **Beauchêne Island** Falkland Islands
228 F4 **Beaufort** France
375 G2 **Beaufort** Malaysia
131 M3 **Beaufort** North Carolina USA
131 K4 **Beaufort** South Carolina USA
116 D4 **Beaufort Sea** Canada/USA
308 D6 **Beaufort West** South Africa
228 E3 **Beaugency** France
244 D3 **Beauly** *watercourse* Scotland UK
242 D3 **Beaumaris** Isle of Anglesey Wales UK
228 E2 **Beaumesnil** France
229 G1 **Beaumont** Belgium
245 F3 **Beaumont** Ireland
423 C7 **Beaumont** New Zealand
130 G5 **Beaumont** Mississippi USA
130 E5 **Beaumont** Texas USA
437 K1 **Beaumont Bay** Antarctica
228 E4 **Beaumont-du-Périgord** France
229 G2 **Beaumont-en-Argonne** France
241 F5 **Beaumont-Hague** France
229 G3 **Beaune** France
228 F2 **Beaune-La Rolande** France
229 G1 **Beauraing** Belgium
426 7 **Beautemps-Beaupré, Île** *island* New Caledonia
228 F2 **Beauvais** France
228 F1 **Beauval** France
228 C3 **Beauvoir-sur-Mer** France
116 H/18 **Beaver** *watercourse* Alberta/Saskatchewan Canada
122 H6 **Beaver** *watercourse* Newfoundland and Labrador Canada
120 K5 **Beaver** *watercourse* Ontario Canada
125 O8 **Beaver** Oklahoma USA
130 A2 **Beaver** *watercourse* Oklahoma USA
124 I7 **Beaver** Utah USA
124 I7 **Beaver** *watercourse* Utah USA
116 E6 **Beaver Creek** Yukon Territory Canada
126 G5 **Beaver Dam** Wisconsin USA
120 H5 **Beaver Hill Lake** Manitoba Canada
163 7 **Beaver Island** Falkland Islands
126 I4 **Beaver Island** Michigan USA
118 M2 **Beaver Lake** Northwest Territories Canada
130 E2 **Beaver Lake** Arkansas USA
120 J5 **Beaver Stone** *watercourse* Ontario Canada
119 R8 **Beaver Valley** Saskatchewan Canada
124 I4 **Beaverhead Mountains** Montana USA
119 O6 **Beaverhill Lake** Alberta Canada
118 L5 **Beaverlodge** Alberta Canada
124 D4 **Beaverton** Oregon USA
392 D5 **Beawar** Rajasthan India
160 E5 **Beazley** Argentina
305 H3 **Bébédjia** Chad
157 B8 **Bebedouro** Brazil
156 E4 **Beberibe** Brazil
242 E3 **Bebington** Merseyside England UK

229 I1 **Bebra** Germany
231 H4 **Beca, Punta** *cape* Spain
133 H4 **Becal** Mexico
122 B2 **Bécard, Lac** *lake* Québec Canada
241 I2 **Beccles** Suffolk England UK
234 E3 **Beceni** Romania
230 C2 **Becerreá** Spain
154 C2 **Becerril** Colombia
301 F2 **Béchar** Algeria
116 D7 **Becharof Lake** Alaska USA
228 D2 **Bécherel** France
238 G3 **Bechevinka** Russian Federation
243 H2 **Beck Hole** North Yorkshire England UK
436 T1 **Becker, Mount** *mountain* Antarctica
243 H3 **Beckingham** Nottinghamshire England UK
127 K8 **Beckley** West Virginia USA
130 D4 **Beckville** Texas USA
243 G3 **Beckwithshaw** North Yorkshire England UK
234 D2 **Beclean** Romania
227 I4 **Becsehely** Hungary
242 B3 **Bective** Ireland
243 G2 **Bedale** North Yorkshire England UK
228 F5 **Bédarieux** France
243 G2 **Bedburn** Durham England UK
241 H4 **Beddingham** East Sussex England UK
119 U8 **Bede** Manitoba Canada
307 F2 **Bedelē** Ethiopia
388 G2 **Bedeyeva Polyana** Russian Federation
241 G2 **Bedford** Bedfordshire England UK
126 H7 **Bedford** Indiana USA
127 L6 **Bedford** Pennsylvania USA
127 L8 **Bedford** Virginia USA
424 G4 **Bedford Island** WA Australia
130 10a **Bedford Point** Grenada
241 G2 **Bedfordshire** *admin. area* England UK
391 K4 **Bedi** Pakistan
374 E4 **Bedinggong** Indonesia
302 F4 **Bedja** *range* Sudan
227 J2 **Będków** Poland
243 G1 **Bedlington** Northumberland England UK
237 U7 **Bedoba** Russian Federation
374 E4 **Bedok** *admin. area* Singapore
374 E3 **Bedok Reservoir** Singapore
374 E3 **Bedok Reservoir Park** Singapore
226 F4 **Bedole** Italy
425 K6 **Bedourie** Qld Australia
226 D1 **Bedum** Netherlands
374 D2 **Bedung** Malaysia
241 F2 **Bedworth** Warwickshire England UK
244 A3 **Bee, Loch** *bay* Scotland UK
127 L7 **Beech Flat Knob** *mountain* West Virginia USA
125 L1 **Beechy** Saskatchewan Canada
243 G3 **Beeley** Derbyshire England UK
425 K6 **Beenleighwah** Qld Australia
390 C3 **Be'ér Sheva'** Israel
425 O6 **Beerwah** Qld Australia
227 H1 **Beeskow** Germany
241 F2 **Beeston** Nottinghamshire England UK
436 T2 **Beethoven Peninsula** Antarctica
130 C6 **Beeville** Texas USA
309 I3 **Befandriana** Madagascar
306 C3 **Befori** Democratic Republic of Congo
309 I4 **Befotaka** Madagascar
242 B2 **Beg, Lough** *lake* Northern Ireland UK
425 N9 **Bega** NSW Australia
372 C4 **Bega** Indonesia
228 C2 **Bégard** France
130 C3 **Beggs** Oklahoma USA
388 H6 **Beglar** Iran
242 A3 **Beglieve** Ireland
224 E2 **Begna** *watercourse* Norway
122 C2 **Bégon, Pointe** *cape* Québec Canada
392 D6 **Begun** Rajasthan India
231 H3 **Begur, Cap de** *cape* Spain
156 B1 **Béhague, Pointe** *cape* French Guiana
392 E5 **Behat** Madhya Pradesh India
392 D4 **Behat** Uttar Pradesh India
390 G3 **Behbahān** Iran
118 F5 **Behm Canal** Alaska USA
424 I4 **Behn, Mount** WA Australia
394 G6 **Behranci** Turkey
436 T1 **Behrendt Mountains** Antarctica
388 G7 **Behshahr** Iran
383 J6 **Bei Huisan Hu** *lake* Qinghai China
381 F4 **Bei Jiang** *watercourse* Guangdong China
383 J4 **Bei Shan** *range* Gansu China
385 K3 **Bei'an** Heilongjiang China
222 I3 **Beiarnfjorden** *lake* Norway
384 D5 **Beida Shan** *range* Nei Mongol Zizhiqu China
307 E2 **Beigi** Ethiopia
381 H3 **Beiguan Dao** *island* Fujian China
380 F4 **Beihai** Guangxi Zhuangzu Zizhiqu China
385 I5 **Beihuangcheng Dao** *island* Shandong China
385 H5 **Beijing** *admin. area* China
385 H5 **Beijing (Peking)** Beijing China
226 D1 **Beilen** Netherlands
380 F4 **Beiliu** Guangxi Zhuangzu Zizhiqu China
380 F4 **Beiliu He** *watercourse* Guangxi Zhuangzu Zizhiqu China
381 I3 **Beilong Shan** *range* Zhejiang China
383 J6 **Beilu He** *lake* Qinghai China
305 H3 **Béinamar** Chad
244 E3 **Beinn Macduibh** *mountain* Scotland UK
244 D4 **Beinn Mhòr** *mountain* Scotland UK
385 I4 **Beipiao** Liaoning China
309 F3 **Beira** Mozambique
230 C3 **Beira** *island* Portugal
124 I1 **Beiseker** Alberta Canada
222 J2 **Beisfjord** Norway
381 F5 **Beishi Dao** *island* Hainan China
385 H5 **Beitai Ding** Shanxi China
385 H5 **Beitai Ding** *mountain* Shanxi China
308 E4 **Beitbridge** Zimbabwe
244 D5 **Beith** North Ayrshire Scotland UK
227 L4 **Beiuş** Romania
230 C4 **Beja** Portugal
230 C5 **Beja** *admin. area* Portugal
233 C8 **Béja** Tunisia
301 H1 **Bejaïa** Algeria
231 I5 **Béjaïa** *admin. area* Algeria
230 D3 **Béjar** Spain
305 G3 **Beka** Cameroon
245 D3 **Bekan** Ireland
374 E5 **Bekasi** Indonesia
238 G5 **Bekasovo** Russian Federation
306 D5 **Beke** Democratic Republic of Congo
234 B2 **Békés** Hungary
234 B2 **Békés** *admin. area* Hungary
234 B2 **Békéscsaba** Hungary
234 H2 **Bekhtery** Ukraine
235 F6 **Bekilli** Turkey
309 I4 **Bekily** Madagascar
309 I3 **Bekipay** Madagascar
309 I4 **Bekitro** Madagascar
233 C9 **Bekkaria** Algeria
309 H4 **Bekoropoka-Antongo** Madagascar
388 D3 **Bekovo** Russian Federation
127 M7 **Bel Air** Maryland USA
133 H5 **Bel-Ha** Mexico
159 H5 **Bel Horizonte** Brazil
391 K4 **Bela** Pakistan
308 E4 **Bela-Bela** South Africa
156 D3 **Bela Cruz** Brazil
161 G2 **Bela Vista** Brazil
157 B7 **Bela Vista de Goiás** Brazil
375 G3 **Belaga** Malaysia
389 M3 **Bel'agash** Kazakhstan
230 D4 **Belalcázar** Spain
393 E7 **Belampalli** Andhra Pradesh India
372 C3 **Belang** Indonesia
372 C4 **Belangbelang** *island* Indonesia
120 G6 **Bélanger** *watercourse* Manitoba Canada
231 F6 **Belarbi** Algeria
225 **Belarus** *country* Europe
374 C3 **Belawan** Indonesia
116 A5 **Belaya** *watercourse* Russian Federation
238 D6 **Belaya Dubrova** Belarus
388 C4 **Belaya Glina** Russian Federation
394 D3 **Belaya Tserkov** Ukraine
375 H3 **Belayan** *watercourse* Indonesia
301 H6 **Belbedji** Niger
228 E5 **Belcaire** France
227 J2 **Bełchatów** Poland
117 L7 **Belcher Islands** Nunavut Canada
231 F3 **Belchite** Spain
245 E2 **Belcoo** Fermanagh Northern Ireland UK
245 C2 **Belderg** Ireland
237 U5 **Bel'dunchana, Ozero** *lake* Russian Federation
389 P2 **Bele** *lake* Russian Federation
388 G2 **Belebey** Russian Federation
227 I4 **Beled** Hungary
307 H3 **Beledweyne** Somalia
303 F5 **Beleghes** *watercourse* Ethiopia
232 F4 **Belej** Croatia
388 G6 **Belek** Turkmenistan
304 C2 **Beleko** Mali
305 G3 **Bélél** Cameroon
156 B3 **Belém** Brazil
156 E5 **Belém de São Francisco** Brazil
162 B3 **Belén** Argentina
160 E3 **Belén** *watercourse* Argentina
134 C5 **Belén** Costa Rica
162 G2 **Belén** Paraguay
129 I3 **Belen** New Mexico USA
161 G4 **Belén** Uruguay
158 D5 **Belén, Cerro** *mountain* Chile
158 B3 **Belén de Umbría** Colombia
230 E3 **Beleña, Embalse de** *lake* Spain
426 7 **Bélep, Îles** *islands* New Caledonia
302 F5 **Beles** *watercourse* Ethiopia
230 C2 **Belesar, Embalse de** *lake* Spain
234 F3 **Beleţ, Lacul** *lake* Moldova
238 G6 **Belëv** Russian Federation
235 E6 **Belevi** Turkey
242 C2 **Belfast** Belfast Northern Ireland UK
242 C2 **Belfast** *admin. area* Northern Ireland UK
127 Q4 **Belfast** Maine USA
245 G2 **Belfast Lough** *bay* Northern Ireland UK
302 F5 **Bēlfodiyo** Ethiopia
229 H3 **Belfort** France
393 D8 **Belgaum** Karnataka India
229 K1 **Belgern** Germany
435 F1 **Belgica Bank** *underwater feature* Greenland Sea
437 C2 **Belgica Mountains** Antarctica
226 E5 **Belgioioso** Italy
226 C2 **Belgium** *country* Europe
394 F2 **Belgorod** Russian Federation
394 F2 **Belgorodskaya Oblast'** *admin. area* Russian Federation
Belgrade *see* **Beograd** Serbia
77 N17 **Belgrano Bank** *underwater feature* Southern Ocean
436 V1 **Belgrano II (Argentina)** *research station* Antarctica
234 F4 **Belgun** Bulgaria
244 D5 **Belhamie** South Ayrshire Scotland UK
131 M3 **Belhaven** North Carolina USA
301 H2 **Belhirane** Algeria
305 G3 **Beli** Nigeria
234 B4 **Beli Drim** *watercourse* Kosovo
234 E4 **Beli Lom** Bulgaria
234 E4 **Beli Lom, Yazovir** *reservoir* Bulgaria
234 B3 **Beli Potok** Serbia
234 C4 **Beli Timok** *watercourse* Serbia
388 E5 **Belidzhi** Russian Federation
374 E5 **Belimbing** Indonesia
388 D3 **Belinskiy** Russian Federation
374 E4 **Belinyu** Indonesia
374 E4 **Belitung** *island* Indonesia
134 B3 **Belize** *watercourse* Belize
134 B3 **Belize** *country* Central America
134 B3 **Belize City** Belize
127 M2 **Bell** *watercourse* Québec Canada
118 G4 **Bell II** British Columbia Canada
123 K7 **Bell Island** Newfoundland and Labrador Canada
121 O1 **Bell Peninsula** Nunavut Canada
160 F5 **Bell Ville** Argentina
118 G6 **Bella Bella** British Columbia Canada
118 H6 **Bella Coola** British Columbia Canada
161 G4 **Bella Unión** Uruguay
161 G4 **Bella Vista** Argentina
159 F4 **Bella Vista** Bolivia
161 G2 **Bella Vista** Paraguay
228 E3 **Bellac** France
226 E5 **Bellagio** Italy
232 C3 **Bellano** Italy
393 D8 **Bellary** Karnataka India
162 B2 **Bellavista** Chile
154 B3 **Bellavista** Colombia
158 B2 **Bellavista** Peru
233 C7 **Bellavista, Capo** *cape* Sardinia Italy
135 F3 **Belle-Anse** Haiti
123 K9 **Belle Bay** Newfoundland and Labrador Canada
125 N4 **Belle Fourche** South Dakota USA
125 M5 **Belle Fourche** *watercourse* Wyoming USA
125 N4 **Belle Fourche Reservoir** South Dakota USA
131 K7 **Belle Glade** Florida USA
228 C3 **Belle-Île** *island* France
123 K7 **Belle Isle** Newfoundland and Labrador Canada
123 J7 **Belle Isle, Strait of** Newfoundland and Labrador Canada
130 C2 **Belle Plaine** Kansas USA
242 B2 **Belleek** Newry and Mourne Northern Ireland UK
163 14 **Bellefontaine** Martinique
126 J6 **Bellefontaine** Ohio USA
228 F2 **Bellême** France
224 H4 **Bellen** *lake* Sweden
127 M4 **Belleville** Ontario Canada
229 G3 **Belleville** France
125 Q7 **Belleville** Kansas USA
127 J6 **Belleville** Ohio USA
124 H5 **Bellevue** Idaho USA
130 B4 **Bellevue** Texas USA
124 D3 **Bellevue** Washington USA
229 G4 **Belley** France
132 D3 **Belleza** Mexico
243 F1 **Bellingham** Northumberland England UK
436 U2 **Bellingshausen (Russia)** *research station* Antarctica
77 H16 **Bellingshausen Abyssal Plain** *underwater feature* Southern Ocean
436 S2 **Bellingshausen Sea** Antarctica
229 I3 **Bellinzona** Switzerland
154 C3 **Bello** Colombia
244 C5 **Belloch** Argyll and Bute Scotland UK
426 8 **Bellona** *island* Solomon Islands
127 O5 **Bellows Falls** Vermont USA
130 G3 **Bells** Tennessee USA
393 D9 **Belluru** Karnataka India
222 J3 **Bellvik** Sweden
130 C6 **Bellville** Texas USA
125 P2 **Belmont** Manitoba Canada
244 inset **Belmont** Shetland Scotland UK
157 E6 **Belmonte** Brazil
134 B3 **Belmopan** Belize
245 C2 **Belmullet** Ireland
309 H4 **Belo** Madagascar
156 A4 **Belo Horizonte** Brazil
157 D7 **Belo Oriente** Brazil
309 H3 **Belo-Tsiribihina** Madagascar
127 O2 **Beloeil** Québec Canada
389 N3 **Beloglazovo** Russian Federation
385 K2 **Belogorsk** Russian Federation
394 E4 **Belogorsk** Ukraine
309 I5 **Beloha** Madagascar
125 P7 **Beloit** Kansas USA
305 G3 **Béloko** Central African Republic
236 N3 **Belokurikha** Russian Federation
236 H6 **Belomorsk** Russian Federation
306 B4 **Belonge** Democratic Republic of Congo
379 G4 **Belonia** Tripura India
238 H5 **Beloomut** Russian Federation
230 E2 **Belorado** Spain
388 H2 **Beloretsk** Russian Federation
116 G5 **Belot, Lac** *lake* Northwest Territories Canada
118 C2 **Beloud Post** Yukon Territory Canada
238 H3 **Beloye** Russian Federation
238 G2 **Beloye, Ozero** *lake* Russian Federation
236 I5 **Beloye More (White Sea)** *sea* Russian Federation
388 G3 **Belozerka** Russian Federation
238 G2 **Belozersk** Russian Federation
228 E5 **Belpech** France
241 F1 **Belper** Derbyshire England UK
125 P8 **Belpre** Kansas USA
241 I2 **Belstead** Suffolk England UK
125 J3 **Belt** Montana USA
155 H5 **Belterra** Brazil
242 B3 **Beltichburne** Ireland
243 H3 **Beltoft** North Lincolnshire England UK
126 D7 **Belton** Missouri USA
131 J3 **Belton** South Carolina USA
130 C5 **Belton** Texas USA
130 C5 **Belton Lake** Texas USA
245 D2 **Beltra** Ireland
245 E2 **Belturbet** Ireland
245 D3 **Belturlin** Ireland
389 O3 **Belukha, Gora** *mountain* Kazakhstan
375 H2 **Beluran** Malaysia
227 J3 **Beluša** Slovakia
236 L4 **Belush'ya Guba** Russian Federation
241 G1 **Belvoir, Vale of** *valley* England UK
425 M5 **Belyando** *watercourse* Qld Australia
425 M5 **Belyando Crossing** Qld Australia
238 E5 **Belyy** Russian Federation
236 P4 **Belyy, Ostrov** *island* Russian Federation
238 G4 **Belyy Gorodok** Russian Federation
389 O1 **Belyy Yar** Russian Federation
227 M2 **Belz** Ukraine
126 G1 **Belzig** Germany
309 H3 **Bemaraha** *range* Madagascar
309 I3 **Bemarivo** *watercourse* Madagascar
306 A5 **Bembe** Angola
230 D5 **Bembézar, Embalse del** *lake* Spain
241 F4 **Bembridge** Isle of Wight England UK
126 R3 **Bemidji** Minnesota USA
126 D3 **Bemidji, Lake** Minnesota USA
243 H2 **Bempton** East Riding of Yorkshire England UK
244 D4 **Ben Alder Lodge** Highland Scotland UK
233 D8 **Ben Arous** Tunisia
231 F6 **Ben Badis** Algeria
376 E5 **Bên Cat** Vietnam
244 C4 **Ben Cruachan** *mountain* Scotland UK
301 I2 **Ben Guerdane** Tunisia
244 D2 **Ben Hope** *mountain* Scotland UK
244 D4 **Ben Lawers** *mountain* Scotland UK
244 D4 **Ben Lomond** *mountain* Scotland UK
423 D6 **Ben McLeod Range** New Zealand
244 B4 **Ben More** *mountain* Scotland UK
423 C7 **Ben Ohau Range** New Zealand
304 C3 **Ben Town** Liberia
244 D4 **Ben Vorlich** *mountain* Scotland UK
244 D3 **Ben Wyvis** *mountain* Scotland UK
125 R3 **Bena** Minnesota USA
306 D4 **Bena-Kamba** Democratic Republic of Congo
306 C4 **Bena-Tshadi** Democratic Republic of Congo
231 G2 **Benabarre** Spain
231 F4 **Benaguacil** Spain
230 E5 **Benalúa de Guadix** Spain
375 G4 **Benanga** Indonesia
375 G4 **Benangin** Indonesia
228 E3 **Benassay** France
230 D2 **Benavente** Spain
158 E4 **Benavides** Bolivia
130 B7 **Benavides** Texas USA
121 N1 **Bencas Island** Nunavut Canada
385 I5 **Bencheng** Hebei China
124 E4 **Bend** Oregon USA
375 F5 **Benda, Tanjung** *cape* Indonesia
308 E6 **Bendearg** *mountain* South Africa
307 I2 **Bender Beyla** Somalia
425 M9 **Bendigo** Vic. Australia
423 C7 **Bendigo** New Zealand
309 F3 **Bene** Mozambique
306 C4 **Bene Dibele** Democratic Republic of Congo
130 D2 **Benedict** Kansas USA
122 I5 **Benedict, Mount** Newfoundland and Labrador Canada
156 D4 **Benedittinos** Brazil
135 G3 **Benemérita de San Cristóbal** Dominican Republic
133 H5 **Benemérito de las Américas** Mexico
300 F6 **Bénéna** Mali
309 I4 **Benenitra** Madagascar
233 F6 **Benevento** Italy
156 B3 **Benevides** Brazil
229 H2 **Benfeld** France
376 D2 **Bèng** *watercourse* Laos
392 G6 **Bengabad** Jharkhand India
376 A3 **Bengal, Bay of**
393 D9 **Bengaluru (Bangalore)** Karnataka India
306 D3 **Bengamisa** Democratic Republic of Congo
305 G4 **Bengbis** Cameroon
381 H2 **Bengbu** Anhui China
Benghazi *see* **Banghāzī** Libya
374 D3 **Bengkalis** Indonesia
374 D3 **Bengkalis** *island* Indonesia
374 F3 **Bengkayang** Indonesia
374 D4 **Bengkulu** Indonesia
374 D4 **Bengkulu** *admin. area* Indonesia
375 H4 **Bengkung** Indonesia
306 A5 **Bengo** *admin. area* Angola
125 M2 **Bengough** Saskatchewan Canada
308 B2 **Benguela** Angola
308 B2 **Benguela** *admin. area* Angola
309 G4 **Benguérua, Ilha** *island* Mozambique
Benha *see* **Banhā** Egypt
78 I6 **Benham Plateau** *underwater feature* Philippine Sea
423 C8 **Benhar** New Zealand
159 E4 **Beni** *admin. area* Bolivia
158 E4 **Beni** *watercourse* Bolivia
306 D3 **Beni** Democratic Republic of Congo
301 F2 **Beni Abbès** Algeria
230 E6 **Beni Enzar** Morocco
300 E2 **Beni Mellal** Morocco
231 I5 **Beni Ouaggag** Algeria
301 F1 **Beni Saf** Algeria
Beni Suef *see* **Bani Suwayf** Egypt
231 G3 **Benicarló** Spain
231 G3 **Benicasim** Spain
159 E3 **Benicito** *watercourse* Bolivia
231 F4 **Benidorm** Spain
228 B2 **Beniguet, Île de** *island* France
304 E3 **Benin** *country* Africa
305 F3 **Benin** *watercourse* Nigeria
304 E4 **Benin, Bight of** *bay*
305 F3 **Benin City** Nigeria
241 H2 **Benington** Lincolnshire England UK
305 G2 **Benisheikh** Nigeria
119 T7 **Benito** Manitoba Canada
133 F4 **Benito Juárez** Mexico
159 E4 **Benjamín** Bolivia
161 G3 **Benjamín Aceval** Paraguay
158 D3 **Benjamin Constant** Brazil
159 I5 **Benjamin dos Santos** Brazil
132 C2 **Benjamín Hill** Mexico
124 E5 **Benjamin Lake** Oregon USA
160 E6 **Benjamín Zorrilla** Argentina
372 E5 **Benjina** Indonesia
125 O6 **Benkelman** Nebraska USA
232 F4 **Benkovac** Croatia
423 D7 **Benmore, Lake** New Zealand
240 C4 **Bennacott** Cornwall England UK
244 C5 **Bennan Point** Scotland UK
118 D3 **Bennett** British Columbia Canada
125 M7 **Bennett** Colorado USA
118 D2 **Bennett Lake** Yukon Territory Canada
237 AE3 **Bennetta, Ostrov** *island* Russian Federation
245 E4 **Bennettsbridge** Ireland
422 F4 **Benneydale** New Zealand
308 E5 **Benoni** South Africa
305 H3 **Bénoye** Chad
134 B3 **Benque Viejo del Carmen** Belize
373 G6 **Bensbach** *watercourse* Papua New Guinea
229 I2 **Bensheim** Germany
119 T8 **Benson** Saskatchewan Canada
128 G5 **Benson** Arizona USA
125 R4 **Benson** Minnesota USA
390 C2 **Bent Jbail** Lebanon
374 D2 **Benta** Malaysia
387 I2 **Benten-numa** *lake* Japan
372 B5 **Benteng** Indonesia
163 12 **Bentham's** Barbados
304 B3 **Benti** Guinea
308 B2 **Bentiaba** Angola
425 K4 **Bentinck Island** Qld Australia
376 C5 **Bentinck Island** Myanmar
161 I4 **Bento Gonçalves** Brazil
130 E3 **Benton** Arkansas USA
128 C2 **Benton** California USA
126 G8 **Benton** Illinois USA
130 G2 **Benton** Kentucky USA
126 G8 **Benton** Missouri USA
126 H5 **Benton Harbor** Michigan USA
124 J3 **Benton Lake** Montana USA
374 D3 **Bentong** Malaysia
130 D2 **Bentonville** Arkansas USA
242 E1 **Bentpath** Dumfries and Galloway Scotland UK
375 G3 **Bentung Kerihun National Park** Indonesia
372 B5 **Benua** Indonesia
374 E3 **Benua** *island* Indonesia
374 G3 **Benua Martinus** Indonesia
305 F3 **Benue** *admin. area* Nigeria
305 F3 **Benue** *watercourse* Nigeria
374 D3 **Benum, Gunung** *mountain* Malaysia
385 J4 **Benxi** Liaoning China
372 C2 **Beo** Indonesia
372 F4 **Beoga** Indonesia
234 B3 **Beograd (Belgrade)** Serbia
392 E6 **Beohari** Madhya Pradesh India
304 D3 **Béoumi** Côte d'Ivoire
372 E4 **Bepondi** *island* Indonesia
386 F5 **Beppu** Japan
427 9 **Beqa** *island* Fiji
163 11 **Bequia** *island* St Vincent and the Grenadines
156 C3 **Bequimão** Brazil
242 A2 **Beragh** Omagh Northern Ireland UK
309 I4 **Beraketa** Madagascar
375 H4 **Berangas** Indonesia
122 C3 **Bérard** *watercourse* Québec Canada
122 C3 **Bérard, Lac** *lake* Québec Canada
374 C3 **Berastagi** Indonesia
375 H4 **Beratus, Gunung** *mountain* Indonesia
375 H3 **Berau** *watercourse* Indonesia
309 I3 **Beravina** Madagascar
374 E4 **Berbak, Taman Nasional** *park* Indonesia
231 F3 **Berbegal** Spain
302 E4 **Berber** Sudan
307 G1 **Berbera** Somalia
305 H4 **Berbérati** Central African Republic
155 G3 **Berbice** *watercourse* Guyana
230 E2 **Bercedo** Spain
232 H3 **Bercel** Hungary
226 E5 **Bercelo** Italy
388 H4 **Berchogur** Kazakhstan
241 I4 **Berck** France
237 AK6 **Berdigestyakh** Russian Federation
389 N2 **Berdsk** Russian Federation
231 F2 **Berdún** Spain
394 F3 **Berdyans'k** Ukraine
394 D3 **Berdychiv** Ukraine
305 H3 **Béré** Chad
240 C4 **Bere Alston** Devon England UK
372 D3 **Berebere** Indonesia
303 I5 **Bereeda** Somalia
234 C1 **Berehove** Ukraine
227 I5 **Berek** Croatia
163 I5 **Berekua** Dominica
389 O3 **Berel** Kazakhstan
128 B2 **Berenda** California USA
238 H4 **Berendeyevo** Russian Federation
120 G6 **Berens** *watercourse* Manitoba Canada
120 G6 **Berens Island** Manitoba Canada
120 G6 **Berens River** Manitoba Canada
123 F9 **Beresford** New Brunswick Canada
118 E5 **Beresford Bay** Alaska USA
423 C8 **Beresford Range** New Zealand
238 C5 **Berešnëvka** Belarus
227 M2 **Berestechko** Ukraine
227 O2 **Berezan** Ukraine
238 E4 **Berezayka** Russian Federation
236 M7 **Berezniki** Russian Federation
223 R4 **Berëzovo** Russian Federation
225 O2 **Berezovyy, Ostrov** *island* Russian Federation
222 H4 **Berg** Norway
229 J1 **Berga** Germany
231 G2 **Berga** Spain
224 I4 **Berga** Sweden
235 E6 **Bergama** Turkey
226 E5 **Bergamo** Italy
226 D1 **Berge** Germany
222 I5 **Berge** Sweden
224 C2 **Bergen** Norway
127 M5 **Bergen** New York USA
226 C2 **Bergen op Zoom** Netherlands
228 E4 **Bergerac** France
437 B2 **Bergeson, Mount** Antarctica
225 K2 **Berghamnsfjärd** *bay* Finland
226 D2 **Bergisch Gladbach** Germany
222 L2 **Bergmo** Norway
222 M4 **Bergnäset** Sweden
222 K4 **Bergnäsudden/Bergnäs** Sweden
222 L5 **Bergö** Finland
223 M4 **Bergön** *island* Sweden
223 L1 **Bergsfjord** Norway
224 H3 **Bergslagen** *region* Sweden
224 H4 **Bergundasjön** *lake* Sweden
222 K3 **Bergviken** Sweden
224 I2 **Bergviken** *lake* Sweden
384 G3 **Berh** Mongolia
374 D4 **Berhala, Selat** *strait* Indonesia
232 H3 **Berhida** Hungary
374 E4 **Berikat, Tanjung** *cape* Indonesia
116 C5 **Bering Land Bridge National Preserve** *park* Alaska USA
116 A7 **Bering Sea** Russian Federation/USA
116 C6 **Bering Strait** Russian Federation/USA
237 AI8 **Beringa, Ostrov** *island* Russian Federation
229 G1 **Beringen** Belgium
237 AK6 **Beringovskiy** Russian Federation
230 E5 **Berja** Spain
222 G5 **Berkåk** Norway
237 Z7 **Berkakit** Russian Federation
226 D2 **Berkel** *watercourse* Netherlands/Germany
124 D8 **Berkeley** California USA
126 F7 **Berkeley** Missouri USA
163 4 **Berkeley, Cabo** *cape* Archipiélago de Colón (Galapagos Islands)
163 7 **Berkeley Sound** *bay* Falkland Islands
241 G3 **Berkhamsted** Hertfordshire England UK
241 E3 **Berkley** Somerset England UK
436 U1 **Berkner Island** Antarctica
127 O5 **Berkshire Hills** Massachusetts USA
118 M6 **Berland** *watercourse* Alberta Canada
230 E3 **Berlanga de Duero** Spain
224 C2 **Berle** Norway
230 B4 **Berlenga, Ilhas** *islands* Portugal
223 P1 **Berlevåg** Norway
226 G1 **Berlin** Germany
226 G1 **Berlin** *admin. area* Germany
133 H6 **Berlín** Honduras
127 N7 **Berlin** Maryland USA
127 P4 **Berlin** New Hampshire USA
126 G4 **Berlin** Wisconsin USA
436 O1 **Berlin, Mount** Antarctica
117 K4 **Berlinguet Inlet** Nunavut Canada
423 D5 **Berlins** New Zealand
425 N9 **Bermagui** NSW Australia
230 E5 **Bermejales, Embalse de los** *lake* Spain
132 E3 **Bermejillo** Mexico
160 E4 **Bermejo** *watercourse* Argentina
160 E2 **Bermejo** *watercourse* Bolivia
154 B5 **Bermejos** Ecuador
122 D6 **Bermen, Lac** *lake* Québec Canada
230 E2 **Bermeo** Spain
230 C3 **Bermillo de Sayago** Spain
127 inset **Bermuda Island** Bermuda
76 L6 **Bermuda Rise** *underwater feature* Atlantic Ocean
229 H3 **Bern** Switzerland
233 G6 **Bernalda** Italy
129 I3 **Bernalillo** New Mexico USA
129 I3 **Bernardo** New Mexico USA
160 F6 **Bernasconi** Argentina
227 G1 **Bernau** Germany
228 E2 **Bernay** France
227 F2 **Bernburg** Germany
226 D4 **Berner Alpen** *range* Switzerland
244 A4 **Berneray** *island* Scotland UK
130 G2 **Bernie** Missouri USA
121 Q2 **Bernier, Pointe** *cape* Québec Canada
117 K4 **Bernier Bay** Nunavut Canada
424 E6 **Bernier Island** WA Australia
127 P3 **Bernierville** Québec Canada
229 I3 **Bernina, Piz** *mountain* Switzerland
229 I3 **Bernina Gruppe** *mountain* Switzerland
308 B3 **Bero** *watercourse* Angola
309 I4 **Beroroha** Madagascar
232 F2 **Beroun** Czech Republic
227 G3 **Berounka** *watercourse* Czech Republic
229 G5 **Berre, Étang de** *lake* France
300 E2 **Berrechid** Morocco
425 L8 **Berri** SA Australia
301 G2 **Berriane** Algeria
244 E2 **Berriedale** Highland Scotland UK
133 G5 **Berriozábal** Mexico
301 G1 **Berrouaghia** Algeria
240 D3 **Berrow** Somerset England UK
228 F3 **Berry** *region* France
134 E1 **Berry Islands** Bahamas
124 D7 **Berryessa, Lake** California USA
308 C5 **Berseba** Namibia
162 B5 **Bersovio el Covacio** Chile
374 D2 **Bertam** Malaysia
122 A3 **Bertaut, Lac** *lake* Québec Canada
123 D7 **Berté, Lac** *lake* Québec Canada
234 E3 **Berteştii de Jos** Romania
129 I3 **Bertha** Minnesota USA
226 B2 **Bertincourt** France
232 A1 **Bertogne** Belgium
305 G4 **Bertoua** Cameroon
162 B4 **Bertrand, Cerro** *mountain* Argentina
226 C3 **Bertrix** Belgium
426 1 **Beru** *island* Kiribati
222 inset **Berufjörður** *bay* Iceland
159 F1 **Beruri** Brazil
393 E10 **Beruwala** Sri Lanka
130 F6 **Berwick** Louisiana USA
127 M6 **Berwick** Pennsylvania USA
125 P6 **Berwyn** Nebraska USA
234 B3 **Berzasca** Romania
225 L4 **Bērzciems** Latvia
232 G3 **Berzence** Hungary
228 F4 **Bès** *watercourse* France
118 J4 **Besa** *watercourse* British Columbia Canada
375 H3 **Besah** Indonesia
309 H3 **Besalampy** Madagascar
231 H2 **Besalú** Spain
228 H3 **Besançon** France
372 B6 **Besar** *island* Indonesia
374 D3 **Besar** *mountain* Malaysia
374 D2 **Besar, Gunung** *mountain* Malaysia
374 D3 **Besar Hantu** *mountain* Malaysia
228 F3 **Besbre** *watercourse* France
234 G1 **Besedka** Ukraine
374 D3 **Beserah** Malaysia
303 F5 **Beshio** *spring* Ethiopia
372 B6 **Besi, Tanjung** *cape* Indonesia
226 E3 **Besigheim** Germany
374 C2 **Besitang** Indonesia
227 K5 **Beška** Serbia
235 G7 **Beşkonak** Turkey
394 F6 **Besni** Turkey
389 L3 **Besoba** Kazakhstan
305 H3 **Béssao** Chad
130 H4 **Bessemer** Alabama USA
226 C2 **Best** Netherlands
389 M3 **Bestamak** Kazakhstan
389 L3 **Bestobe** Kazakhstan
236 J6 **Bestuzhevo** Russian Federation
309 I3 **Betafo** Madagascar
309 H3 **Betanatanana** Madagascar
309 I5 **Betanty** Madagascar
230 B2 **Betanzos** Spain
305 G3 **Bétaré Oya** Cameroon
304 E3 **Bétérou** Benin
230 E3 **Beteta** Spain
308 C5 **Bethanie** Namibia
126 D6 **Bethany** Missouri USA
228 D5 **Bétharram, Grottes de** *point of interest* France
163 17 **Bethel** Montserrat
240 C1 **Bethel** Isle of Anglesey Wales UK
116 C6 **Bethel** Alaska USA
131 M3 **Bethel** North Carolina USA
127 O5 **Bethel** Vermont USA
Bethells Beach *see* **Te Henga** New Zealand
240 C1 **Bethesda** Gwynedd Wales UK
308 E5 **Bethlehem** South Africa
121 S7 **Béthoulat, Lac** *lake* Québec Canada
129 K1 **Bethune** Colorado USA
228 E2 **Béthune** *watercourse* France
157 C7 **Betim** Brazil
426 1b **Betio** *island* Kiribati
309 H4 **Betioky** Madagascar
238 E5 **Betlitsa** Russian Federation
425 L6 **Betoota** Qld Australia
305 H4 **Bétou** Congo
389 K4 **Betpak-Dala** Kazakhstan
389 K4 **Betpaqdala** Kazakhstan
309 I4 **Betroka** Madagascar
121 U8 **Betsiamites** Québec Canada
123 C7 **Betsiamites** *watercourse* Québec Canada
309 I3 **Betsiboka** *watercourse* Madagascar
392 F5 **Bettiah** Bihar India
240 E2 **Bettisfield** Wrexham Wales UK
226 E5 **Bettola** Italy
240 D3 **Bettws** Newport Wales UK
240 D2 **Bettws y Crwyn** Shropshire England UK
244 D2 **Bettyhill** Highland Scotland UK
245 F3 **Bettystown** Ireland
393 D7 **Betul** Madhya Pradesh India
392 D6 **Betwa** *watercourse* Madhya Pradesh India
228 F2 **Betz** France
306 B5 **Beu** Angola
158 E4 **Beu, Serranía del** *range* Bolivia
228 F2 **Beugneux** France
240 D2 **Beulah** Powys Wales UK
125 O3 **Beulah** North Dakota USA
124 F5 **Beulah Reservoir** Oregon USA
306 B5 **Beungas** Angola
228 E3 **Beuvron** *watercourse* France
243 H3 **Beverley** East Riding of Yorkshire England UK
129 N1 **Beverly** Kansas USA
127 P5 **Beverly** Massachusetts USA
127 K7 **Beverly** Ohio USA
127 L7 **Beverly** West Virginia USA
373 G4 **Bewani** Papua New Guinea
373 G4 **Bewani** *watercourse* Papua New Guinea
243 G2 **Bewerley** North Yorkshire England UK
241 H3 **Bewl Water** *lake* England UK
229 H3 **Bex** Switzerland
241 H4 **Bexhill** East Sussex England UK
235 G7 **Bey Dağları** *range* Turkey
235 F6 **Beydilli** Turkey
235 F6 **Beyel** Turkey
304 C3 **Beyla** Guinea
303 G5 **Beylul** Eritrea
388 G4 **Beyneu** Kazakhstan
235 E6 **Beyoba** Turkey
394 D5 **Beypazari** Turkey
393 D9 **Beypore** Kerala India
307 H2 **Beyra** Somalia
390 C2 **Beyrouth (Beirut)** Lebanon
235 G7 **Beyşehir Gölü** *lake* Turkey
388 C4 **Beysugskiy Liman** *lake* Russian Federation
309 H4 **Bezaha** Madagascar
225 O4 **Bezhanitsy** Russian Federation
238 G4 **Bezhetsk** Russian Federation
238 G6 **Bezhin Lug** Russian Federation
238 F6 **Bezhitsa** Russian Federation
228 F5 **Béziers** France
392 C6 **Bhachau** Gujarat India
392 D4 **Bhadaur** Punjab India
392 D4 **Bhaderwah** Jammu and Kashmir India/Pakistan
393 E8 **Bhadrachalam** Andhra Pradesh India
393 G7 **Bhadrak** Orissa India
393 D9 **Bhadravati** Karnataka India
392 G6 **Bhagalpur** Bihar India
392 D5 **Bhagwatgarh** Rajasthan India
393 D7 **Bhainsdehi** Madhya Pradesh India
392 F5 **Bhairawa** Uttar Pradesh India
244 B3 **Bhalamus** Na h-Eileanan Siar Scotland UK
393 D7 **Bhalki** Karnataka India
391 L3 **Bhalwal** Pakistan
379 H4 **Bhamo** Myanmar
393 E7 **Bhamragad** Maharashtra India
391 K4 **Bhan** Pakistan
393 E7 **Bhandara** Maharashtra India
393 E7 **Bhanupratappur** Chhattisgarh India
393 B7 **Bhanvad** Gujarat India
392 D5 **Bharatpur** Rajasthan India
392 F6 **Bharno** Jharkhand India
393 C7 **Bharuch** Gujarat India
392 E6 **Bharwa Sumerpur** Uttar Pradesh India
392 E6 **Bharwari** Uttar Pradesh India
393 E7 **Bhatapara** Chhattisgarh India
244 A4 **Bhatarsaigh** Na h-Eileanan Siar Scotland UK
392 D4 **Bhatinda** Punjab India
393 D8 **Bhatkal** Karnataka India
393 D9 **Bhavani Sagar** *lake* Tamil Nadu India
393 C7 **Bhavnagar** Gujarat India
393 F7 **Bhawanipatna** Orissa India
244 A3 **Bhearnaraigh, Eilean** *island* Scotland UK
392 F5 **Bheri** *watercourse* Nepal
393 D7 **Bhikangaon** Madhya Pradesh India
393 E7 **Bhilai** Chhattisgarh India
392 D6 **Bhilwara** Rajasthan India
392 F5 **Bhimphedi** Nepal
393 F8 **Bhimunipatnam** Andhra Pradesh India
392 E5 **Bhind** Madhya Pradesh India
392 E5 **Bhinga** Uttar Pradesh India
392 C6 **Bhinmal** Rajasthan India
308 E6 **Bhisho** South Africa
393 C7 **Bhiwandi** Maharashtra India
392 D5 **Bhiwani** Haryana India
379 G4 **Bhola** Bangladesh
392 D6 **Bhopal** Madhya Pradesh India
393 C7 **Bhor** Maharashtra India
393 F7 **Bhubaneshwar** Orissa India
392 B6 **Bhuj** Gujarat India
393 D7 **Bhum** Maharashtra India
393 D7 **Bhusawal** Maharashtra India
379 G3 **Bhutan** *country*
158 E2 **Bia** *watercourse* Brazil
391 H3 **Biābānī** Iran
163 11a **Biabou** St Vincent and the Grenadines
372 E4 **Biak** *island* Indonesia
227 L1 **Biała Piska** Poland
227 L1 **Biała Podlaska** Poland
244 D3 **Biallaid** Highland Scotland UK
227 L1 **Białystok** Poland
373 G5 **Bian** *watercourse* Indonesia
229 I5 **Bianco, Capo** *cape* Corsica France

233 E8 **Bianco, Capo** *cape* Italy
381 H1 **Biandangang Kou** *sea* Jiangsu China
305 I4 **Bianga** Central African Republic
381 H1 **Bianzhuang** Shandong China
372 C3 **Biaro** *island* Indonesia
228 D5 **Biarritz** France
229 I3 **Biasca** Switzerland
302 E2 **Bibā** Egypt
308 B2 **Bibala** Angola
131 I4 **Bibb City** Georgia USA
232 D5 **Bibbiena** Italy
120 I2 **Bibby Island** Nunavut Canada
305 G3 **Bibémi** Cameroon
226 E3 **Biberach an der Riß** Germany
391 K3 **Bibi Nani** Pakistan
304 D3 **Bibiani** Ghana
235 B5 **Bicaj** Albania
157 D8 **Bicas** Brazil
241 F3 **Bicester** Oxfordshire England UK
116 H7 **Biche, Lac la** *lake* Alberta Canada
425 N10 **Bicheno** Tas Australia
372 D3 **Bicoli** Indonesia
232 H3 **Bicske** Hungary
240 E2 **Bicton** Shropshire England UK
393 D7 **Bid** Maharashtra India
391 I3 **Bīd** Iran
305 F3 **Bida** Nigeria
375 H2 **Bidadari, Tanjong** *cape* Malaysia
390 E6 **Bīdah, Wādī** *watercourse* Saudi Arabia
393 D8 **Bidar** Karnataka India
423 F5 **Bideford** New Zealand
240 C3 **Bideford** Devon England UK
392 E5 **Bidhuna** Uttar Pradesh India
223 M2 **Bidjovagge** Norway
424 G4 **Bidyadanga Community** WA Australia
385 L3 **Bidzhar** *watercourse* Russian Federation
308 C2 **Bié** *admin. area* Angola
227 K3 **Biecz** Poland
226 E2 **Biedenkopf** Germany
229 H3 **Biel** Switzerland
394 A2 **Bielawa** Poland
233 G2 **Biele Karpaty** *range* Slovakia
226 E1 **Bielefeld** Germany
226 E5 **Biella** Italy
227 J1 **Bielsk** Poland
227 L1 **Bielsk Podlaski** Poland
376 E5 **Biên Hòa** Vietnam
227 H2 **Bieniów** Poland
122 B5 **Bienville, Lac** *lake* Québec Canada
231 F2 **Bierge** Spain
227 J2 **Bieruń** Poland
227 K1 **Biesal** Poland
227 G1 **Biesenthal** Germany
229 G2 **Bièvre** Belgium
233 F6 **Biferno** *watercourse* Italy
305 G5 **Bifoum** Gabon
116 G4 **Big** *watercourse* Northwest Territories Canada
119 R6 **Big** *watercourse* Saskatchewan Canada
122 H5 **Big Bay** Newfoundland and Labrador Canada
423 C7 **Big Bay** New Zealand
426 7 **Big Bay** Vanuatu
126 H4 **Big Bay De Noc** Michigan USA
128 D3 **Big Bear Lake** California USA
119 S8 **Big Beaver** Saskatchewan Canada
125 J3 **Big Bell Mountains** Montana USA
130 F4 **Big Black** *watercourse* Mississippi USA
119 W6 **Big Black River** Manitoba Canada
126 C6 **Big Blue** *watercourse* Nebraska USA
130 G5 **Big Creek Lake** Alabama USA
125 S2 **Big Falls** Minnesota USA
126 E2 **Big Fork** *watercourse* Minnesota USA
130 D6 **Big Hill Reservoir** Texas USA
122 G3 **Big Island** Newfoundland and Labrador Canada
120 H8 **Big Island** Ontario Canada
127 R4 **Big Lake** Maine USA
125 K4 **Big Lake** Montana USA
129 L5 **Big Lake** Texas USA
120 G6 **Big Mossy Point** Manitoba Canada
119 S8 **Big Muddy Lake** Saskatchewan Canada
128 C2 **Big Pine** California USA
126 D3 **Big Pine Lake** Minnesota USA
130 E2 **Big Piney** *watercourse* Missouri USA
125 J5 **Big Piney** Wyoming USA
126 I5 **Big Rapids** Michigan USA
127 M4 **Big Rideau Lake** Ontario Canada
119 R6 **Big River** Saskatchewan Canada
124 E6 **Big Sage Reservoir** California USA
118 E2 **Big Salmon Range** Yukon Territory Canada
120 F4 **Big Sand Lake** Manitoba Canada
125 J2 **Big Sandy** Montana USA
119 S5 **Big Sandy Lake** Saskatchewan Canada
126 E3 **Big Sandy Lake** Minnesota USA
125 K5 **Big Sandy Reservoir** Wyoming USA
126 C4 **Big Sioux** *watercourse* South Dakota USA
119 O3 **Big Slough** Alberta Canada
128 E1 **Big Smoky Valley** Nevada USA
423 B8 **Big South Cape Island** New Zealand
129 L4 **Big Spring** Texas USA
125 N6 **Big Springs** Nebraska USA
120 G3 **Big Spruce** *watercourse* Manitoba Canada
119 P7 **Big Stone** Alberta Canada
128 B2 **Big Sur** California USA
125 K4 **Big Timber** Montana USA
120 K6 **Big Trout Lake** Ontario Canada
128 G2 **Big Water** Utah USA
130 B6 **Big Wells** Texas USA
372 D4 **Biga** Indonesia
240 D4 **Bigbury Bay** England UK
300 C6 **Bigene** Senegal
383 J3 **Biger Nuur** *lake* Mongolia
223 M2 **Biggajávri** *lake* Norway
119 Q6 **Biggar** Saskatchewan Canada
424 H3 **Bigge Island** WA Australia
241 F1 **Biggin** Derbyshire England UK
241 G2 **Biggleswade** Bedfordshire England UK
125 K5 **Bighorn** *watercourse* Wyoming USA
125 K4 **Bighorn Lake** Wyoming USA
125 L4 **Bighorn Mountains** Wyoming USA
376 D4 **Bight of Bangkok** *bay* Thailand
238 H6 **Bigil'dino** Russian Federation
229 I3 **Bignasco** Switzerland
305 C6 **Bignona** Senegal
234 A4 **Bigor** Montenegro
240 A2 **Bigstone** Ireland
120 H6 **Bigstone Lake** Manitoba Canada
161 I3 **Biguaçu** Brazil
127 K3 **Bigwood** Ontario Canada
234 B2 **Bihać** Bosnia and Herzegovina
392 F6 **Bihar** *admin. area* India
392 F6 **Bihar Sharif** Bihar India
306 E4 **Biharamulo** Tanzania
234 B2 **Biharea** Romania
234 C2 **Bihor** *admin. area* Romania
387 J2 **Bihoro** Japan
234 C2 **Bihorului, Munții** *range* Romania
158 D4 **Bihua** Bolivia
304 A2 **Bijagós, Arquipélago dos** *islands* Guinea-Bissau
392 D5 **Bijaipur** Madhya Pradesh India
393 E7 **Bijapur** Chhattisgarh India
393 D8 **Bijapur** Karnataka India
393 F7 **Bijapur** Orissa India
392 E6 **Bijawar** Madhya Pradesh India
232 H4 **Bijeljina** Bosnia and Herzegovina
380 E3 **Bijie** Guizhou China
379 G3 **Bijni** Assam India
392 E5 **Bijnor** Uttar Pradesh India
391 L4 **Bijnot** Pakistan
310 9 **Bijoutier Island** Seychelles
392 C5 **Bikampur** Rajasthan India
392 C5 **Bikaner** Rajasthan India
427 15 **Bikar Atoll** Marshall Islands
426 1b **Bikenibeu** Kiribati
386 G1 **Bikin** Russian Federation
386 G1 **Bikin** *watercourse* Russian Federation
427 15 **Bikini Atoll** Marshall Islands
309 F4 **Bikita** Zimbabwe
302 E5 **Bikori** Sudan
306 B4 **Bikoro** Democratic Republic of Congo
234 G1 **Bila Tserkva** Ukraine
372 A3 **Bilang Bilangan** *island* Indonesia
392 C5 **Bilara** Rajasthan India
393 F6 **Bilaspur** Chhattisgarh India
377 I6 **Bilatan** *island* Philippines
392 E5 **Bilaua** Madhya Pradesh India
376 C4 **Bilauktaung Range** Thailand
230 E2 **Bilbao** Spain
302 E1 **Bilbays** Egypt
245 E4 **Bilboa** Ireland
234 D2 **Bilbor** Romania
222 inset **Bildudalur** Iceland
232 H5 **Bileća** Bosnia and Herzegovina
394 D5 **Bilecik** *admin. area* Turkey
227 K5 **Biled** Romania
392 E5 **Bilhaur** Uttar Pradesh India
306 C3 **Bili** *watercourse* Democratic Republic of Congo
237 AI5 **Bilibino** Russian Federation
309 H2 **Bilibiza** Mozambique
232 G4 **Bilice** Croatia
393 C7 **Bilimora** Gujarat India
376 C3 **Bilin** Myanmar
227 G2 **Bílina** Czech Republic
377 J5 **Biliran** *island* Philippines
307 G3 **Bilis Qooqaani** Somalia
235 B5 **Bilisht** Albania
375 H2 **Bilit** Malaysia
229 K4 **Bilje** Slovenia
76 Q3 **Bill Baileys Bank** *underwater feature* Atlantic Ocean
240 E4 **Bill of Portland** *cape* England UK
424 E6 **Billabong Roadhouse** WA Australia
241 H3 **Billericay** Essex England UK
394 F6 **Billi** Syria
222 E5 **Billingen** Norway
243 G2 **Billingham** Stockton-on-Tees England UK
241 G1 **Billinghay** Lincolnshire England UK
237 AK5 **Billings** Russian Federation
125 K4 **Billings** Montana USA
241 G3 **Billingshurst** West Sussex England UK
242 B2 **Billis** Ireland
225 J1 **Billsta** Sweden
124 E4 **Billy Chinook, Lake** Oregon USA
305 I3 **Bilma** Niger
307 F2 **Bilo** Ethiopia
425 N6 **Biloela** Qld Australia
155 G4 **Biloku** Guyana
393 D7 **Biloli** Maharashtra India
232 H2 **Bilovec** Czech Republic
130 G5 **Biloxi** Mississippi USA
243 I3 **Bilsby** Lincolnshire England UK
234 D1 **Bil'shivtsi** Ukraine
227 M2 **Bil's'ka Volya** Ukraine
226 E4 **Bilten** Switzerland
302 C5 **Biltine** Chad
222 L2 **Bilto** Norway
243 G1 **Bilton** Northumberland England UK
376 C3 **Bilugyun Island** Myanmar
372 B3 **Bilungala** Indonesia
234 G2 **Bilyayivka** Ukraine
234 F2 **Bilyne** Ukraine
376 E2 **Bim Sơn** Vietnam
306 D3 **Bima** *watercourse* Democratic Republic of Congo
372 A6 **Bima** Indonesia
308 C2 **Bimbe** Angola
304 E3 **Bimbila** Ghana
305 H4 **Bimbo** Central African Republic
131 L8 **Bimini Islands** Bahamas
391 H5 **Bin Aḥmad** United Arab Emirates
380 E1 **Bin Xian** Shaanxi China
392 E6 **Bina-Etawa** Madhya Pradesh India
242 A1 **Binalt** Ireland
229 I4 **Binasco** Italy
243 H3 **Binbrook** Lincolnshire England UK
228 G1 **Binche** Belgium
305 G3 **Binder** Chad
384 G3 **Binder** Mongolia
392 F5 **Bindki** Uttar Pradesh India
125 J1 **Bindloss** Alberta Canada
306 B5 **Bindu** Democratic Republic of Congo
309 F3 **Bindura** Zimbabwe
304 D3 **Bineda** *watercourse* Côte d'Ivoire
230 F3 **Binefar** Spain
306 C3 **Binga** Democratic Republic of Congo
308 E3 **Binga** Zimbabwe
309 F3 **Binga, Monte** *mountain* Mozambique
393 C9 **Bingaram Island** Lakshadweep India
130 B3 **Binger** Oklahoma USA
129 I4 **Bingham** New Mexico USA
380 E3 **Bingmei** Guizhou China
394 G5 **Bingöl** Turkey
394 G5 **Bingöl** *admin. area* Turkey
224 H2 **Bingsjö** Sweden
381 H3 **Bingxi** Jiangxi China
376 E2 **Bình Gia** Vietnam
376 E2 **Bình Mỹ** Vietnam
228 C2 **Binic** France
393 F7 **Binika** Orissa India
231 H4 **Binisalem** Spain
374 C3 **Binjai** Indonesia
304 B3 **Binkolo** Sierra Leone
425 N7 **Binnaway** NSW Australia
303 I5 **Binne, Raas** *island* Somalia
307 F1 **Bīnshangul Gumuz** *admin. area* Ethiopia
374 E3 **Bintan** *island* Indonesia
374 D2 **Bintang, Banjaran** *range* Malaysia
374 D5 **Bintuhan** Indonesia
375 G3 **Bintulu** Malaysia
372 E4 **Bintuni, Teluk** *bay* Indonesia
380 E4 **Binzhou** Guangxi Zhuangzu Zizhiqu China
385 K3 **Binzhou** Heilongjiang China
385 I5 **Binzhou** Shandong China
160 D6 **Biobío** *admin. area* Chile
160 C6 **Biobío** *watercourse* Chile
305 F4 **Bioko** *island* Equatorial Guinea
300 E2 **Biougra** Morocco
372 C6 **Biquele** Timor-Leste (East Timor)
303 G5 **Bir, Ras** *cape* Djibouti
231 J6 **Bir Chouhada** Algeria
306 D2 **Bir Di** Sudan
302 D4 **Bir en Natrûn** *spring* Sudan
300 C4 **Bir Gandouz** Western Sahara
231 I6 **Bir Ghellalia** Algeria
302 E1 **Bi'r Ḥasanah** Egypt
300 D3 **Bîr Mogreïn** Mauritania
302 E2 **Bi'r Sayyālah** *place of interest* Egypt
302 F3 **Bi'r Shalatayn** Egypt
394 F6 **Bi'r Turwaynān** Syria
385 L2 **Bira** Russian Federation
385 M3 **Bira** *watercourse* Russian Federation
301 I3 **Birāk** Libya
223 T4 **Birandozero** Russian Federation
302 C5 **Birao** Central African Republic
392 G5 **Biratnagar** Nepal
119 O3 **Birch** *watercourse* Alberta Canada
127 K3 **Birch Island** Ontario Canada
119 M1 **Birch Lake** Northwest Territories Canada
120 I7 **Birch Lake** Ontario Canada
116 H7 **Birch Mountains** Alberta Canada
119 U6 **Birch River** Manitoba Canada
126 F8 **Birch Tree** Missouri USA
425 L8 **Birchip** Vic. Australia
234 C3 **Birchiș** Romania
307 G2 **Bircot** Ethiopia
227 L3 **Bircza** Poland
120 H4 **Bird** Manitoba Canada
125 O7 **Bird City** Kansas USA
123 J7 **Bird Cove** Newfoundland and Labrador Canada
310 9 **Bird Island** Seychelles
163 8 **Bird Island** South Georgia
423 E6 **Birdlings Flat** New Zealand
425 K6 **Birdsville** Qld Australia
119 U7 **Birdtail** Manitoba Canada
394 F5 **Birecik** Turkey
376 C6 **Bireun** Indonesia
391 J4 **Birg, Kūh-e** *mountain* Iran
392 F5 **Birganj** Nepal
234 D3 **Birghiș** Romania
235 F6 **Birgi** Turkey
377 J4 **Biri** *island* Philippines
306 D2 **Biri** *watercourse* Sudan
157 B8 **Birigui** Brazil
305 I3 **Birini** Central African Republic
391 I3 **Birjand** Iran
302 E2 **Birkat Qārūn** *lake* Egypt
305 I2 **Birkat Saira** Sudan
232 B2 **Birkenfeld** Germany
302 F5 **Birket** Denmark
242 E1 **Birkhill** Scottish Borders Scotland UK
243 G3 **Birkin** North Yorkshire England UK
241 F2 **Birmingham** West Midlands England UK
130 H4 **Birmingham** Alabama USA
393 F6 **Birmitrapur** Orissa India
392 F6 **Birni** Jharkhand India
426 1 **Birnie** *island* Kiribati
425 K5 **Birnie, Mount** Qld Australia
305 F2 **Birnin Gwari** Nigeria
305 F2 **Birnin Kebbi** Nigeria
301 H6 **Birnin Konni** Niger
305 F2 **Birnin-Yauri** Nigeria
385 L3 **Birobidzhan** Russian Federation
372 B5 **Birongko** *island* Indonesia
392 G5 **Birpur** Bihar India
245 E3 **Birr** Ireland
226 D4 **Birr** Switzerland
234 D2 **Birsana** Romania
125 L1 **Birsay** Saskatchewan Canada
244 E1 **Birsay** Orkney Islands Scotland UK
241 F2 **Birstall** Leicester England UK
226 E2 **Birstein** Germany
373 G7 **Birthday Mountain** Australia
379 G2 **Biru** Xizang Zizhiqu China
373 F5 **Birufu** Indonesia
394 G6 **Biruk** Turkey
393 D9 **Birur** Karnataka India
237 U7 **Biryusa** *watercourse* Russian Federation
372 C4 **Bisa** *island* Indonesia
128 H5 **Bisbee** Arizona USA
228 D4 **Biscarrosse** France
228 D4 **Biscarrosse et de Parentis, Étang de** *lake* France
228 D4 **Biscarrosse-Plage** France
228 C4 **Biscay, Bay of** Atlantic Ocean
76 R5 **Biscay Plain** *underwater feature* Atlantic Ocean
131 K8 **Biscayne Bay** Florida USA
233 G6 **Bisceglie** Italy
226 F3 **Bischofswiesen** Germany
229 H2 **Bischwiller** France
436 T2 **Biscoe Islands** Antarctica
127 J3 **Biscotasing** Ontario Canada
302 D4 **Bisellia** Sudan
235 D5 **Biser** Bulgaria
237 L7 **Biserovo** Russian Federation
232 G5 **Biševo** *island* Croatia
376 D3 **Bishan** *admin. area* Singapore
391 J2 **Bisheh** Afghanistan
389 L5 **Bishkek** Kyrgyzstan
128 F8 **Bishop** California USA
130 C7 **Bishop** Texas USA
124 H6 **Bishop Creek Reservoir** Nevada USA
129 L3 **Bishop Hills** Texas USA
241 E3 **Bishop's Cleeve** Gloucestershire England UK
241 H3 **Bishop's Stortford** Hertfordshire England UK
240 C3 **Bishops Tawton** Devon England UK
392 F6 **Bishrampur** Jharkhand India
381 G2 **Bishui** Henan China
392 F6 **Bishunpur** Jharkhand India
307 E3 **Bisina, Lake** Uganda
154 D3 **Bisinaca** Colombia
154 D5 **Bisira** Panama
127 J3 **Biskotasi Lake** Ontario Canada
301 H2 **Biskra** Algeria
301 H2 **Biskra** *admin. area* Algeria
377 J5 **Bislig** Philippines
125 O3 **Bismarck** North Dakota USA
373 I5 **Bismarck Archipelago** *islands* Papua New Guinea
373 I4 **Bismarck Sea** Papua New Guinea
394 G6 **Bismil** Turkey
222 F6 **Bismoen** Norway
234 E3 **Bisoca** Romania
125 N4 **Bison** South Dakota USA
119 M4 **Bison Lake** Alberta Canada
391 H3 **Bīsrom** Iran
304 A2 **Bissau** Guinea-Bissau
305 G3 **Bissaula** Nigeria
120 H7 **Bissett** Manitoba Canada
304 B2 **Bissikrima** Guinea
122 B3 **Bisson, Lac** *lake* Québec Canada
229 I4 **Bistagno** Italy
118 L3 **Bistcho Lake** Alberta Canada
130 E4 **Bistineau, Lake** Louisiana USA
234 B4 **Bistra** *mountain* Macedonia/Kosovo
234 D2 **Bistrața-Năsăud** *admin. area* Romania
232 F3 **Bistrica** Slovenia
234 D2 **Bistrița** Romania
234 D2 **Bistrița** *watercourse* Romania
306 C2 **Bita** *watercourse* Central African Republic
305 G4 **Bitam** Gabon
226 D3 **Bitburg** Germany
226 D3 **Bitche** France
233 G6 **Bitetto** Italy
388 F3 **Bitik** Kazakhstan
306 D2 **Bitilifondi** Central African Republic
301 J6 **Bitkine** Chad
394 G5 **Bitlis** Turkey
394 G5 **Bitlis** *admin. area* Turkey
233 G6 **Bitonto** Italy
305 G4 **Bitoutouk** Cameroon
393 C9 **Bitra Island** Lakshadweep India
119 Q7 **Bitter Lake** Saskatchewan Canada
125 N4 **Bitter Lake** South Dakota USA
308 C6 **Bitterfontein** South Africa
124 G3 **Bitterroot Range** Idaho USA
119 P4 **Bitumount** Alberta Canada
372 C3 **Bitung** Indonesia
305 G2 **Biu** Nigeria
373 F5 **Biwarlaut** Indonesia
234 C2 **Bixad** Romania
130 D3 **Bixby** Oklahoma USA
244 inset **Bixter** Shetland Scotland UK
389 O3 **Biya** *watercourse* Russian Federation
381 H2 **Biyang** Anhui China
388 J3 **Biyesoygan** *lake* Kazakhstan
389 O3 **Biysk** Russian Federation
301 H1 **Bizerte** Tunisia
222 inset **Bjargtangar** *cape* Iceland
222 J2 **Bjarkøya** *island* Norway
227 M1 **Bjaroza** Belarus
222 K5 **Bjästa** Sweden
224 D3 **Bjelland** Norway
232 G4 **Bjelovar** Croatia
222 H3 **Bjerka** Norway
222 J2 **Bjerkvik** Norway
224 E5 **Bjerregård** Denmark
224 D2 **Bjørgvin** *region* Norway
222 J5 **Björkå** Sweden
222 E5 **Bjørke** Norway
224 I2 **Björke** Sweden
224 F3 **Bjørkelangen** *lake* Norway
224 D2 **Bjørkelo** Norway
222 J3 **Björkfjället** *island* Sweden
223 M4 **Björkfors** Sweden
222 J5 **Björkhöjden** Sweden
222 G5 **Bjørklia** Norway
222 K2 **Björkliden** Sweden
225 K3 **Björkö** *island* Finland
222 L5 **Björköby** Finland
222 L5 **Björkön** *island* Finland
222 J5 **Björkön** Sweden
223 M4 **Björkön** *island* Sweden
222 K4 **Björksele** Sweden
222 F5 **Bjorli** Norway
222 K5 **Björna** Sweden
223 P2 **Bjørnevatn** Norway
222 I5 **Björnön** Sweden
236 E4 **Bjørnøya** *island* Norway
222 H4 **Bjørnstad** Norway
222 J2 **Bjørntoppen** *lake* Norway
238 B2 **Björnvik** Finland
224 G2 **Bjurberget** Sweden
222 L4 **Bjurfors** Sweden
222 L4 **Bjuröklubb** *cape* Sweden
222 L4 **Bjurön** Sweden
222 K4 **Bjurträsk** Sweden
224 G4 **Bjuv** Sweden
300 E6 **Bla** Mali
234 B4 **Blace** Serbia
120 G7 **Black** *watercourse* Manitoba Canada
128 G4 **Black** *watercourse* Arkansas USA
130 F2 **Black** *watercourse* Missouri USA
127 N5 **Black** *watercourse* New York USA
131 L3 **Black** *watercourse* North Carolina USA
126 G2 **Black Bay** Ontario Canada
120 K5 **Black Bear** *watercourse* Ontario Canada
119 R4 **Black Birch Lake** Saskatchewan Canada
124 D7 **Black Butte Lake** California USA
436 T2 **Black Coast** Antarctica
118 K6 **Black Creek** British Columbia Canada
120 K4 **Black Duck** *watercourse* Ontario Canada
126 E2 **Black Hawk** Ontario Canada
245 G2 **Black Head** *cape* Northern Ireland UK
125 N5 **Black Hills** South Dakota USA
122 J5 **Black Island** Newfoundland and Labrador Canada
119 S3 **Black Lake** Saskatchewan Canada
126 I4 **Black Lake** Michigan USA
127 N4 **Black Lake** New York USA
128 G2 **Black Mesa** Arkansas USA
425 K5 **Black Mountain** Qld Australia
301 J3 **Black Mountain** Libya
240 D3 **Black Mountains** Wales UK
124 E1 **Black Pines** British Columbia Canada
132 D1 **Black Range** New Mexico USA
126 F4 **Black River Falls** Wisconsin USA
163 9 **Black Rock** Trinidad and Tobago
388 C5 **Black Sea**
394 D4 **Black Sea** Asia/Europe
119 U4 **Black Sturgeon** Manitoba Canada
126 G2 **Black Sturgeon Lake** Ontario Canada
122 K6 **Black Tickle** Newfoundland and Labrador Canada
423 C7 **Black Umbrella Range** New Zealand
Black Volta *see* **Mouhoun** Ghana
130 H4 **Black Warrior** *watercourse* Alabama USA
425 M6 **Blackall** Qld Australia
243 F3 **Blackburn with Darwen** *admin. area* England UK
224 I3 **Blacken** *bay* Sweden
120 F3 **Blackfish Lake** Manitoba Canada
124 I5 **Blackfoot** Idaho USA
124 J5 **Blackfoot Reservoir** Idaho USA
242 B1 **Blackheath** Coleraine Northern Ireland UK
244 B3 **Blackhill** Highland Scotland UK
163 12 **Blackmans** Barbados
243 F3 **Blacko** Lancashire England UK
242 E3 **Blackpool** Blackpool England UK
242 E3 **Blackpool** *admin. area* England UK
242 F1 **Blackpool Gate** Cumbria England UK
123 E10 **Blacks Harbour** New Brunswick Canada
120 G7 **Blacks Point** Manitoba Canada
133 J2 **Blackshear, Lake** Georgia USA
245 B2 **Blacksod Bay** Ireland
Blackstone *see* **Papulankutja** Australia
123 F9 **Blackville** New Brunswick Canada
425 N5 **Blackwater** Qld Australia
118 J6 **Blackwater** British Columbia Canada
245 F4 **Blackwater** Ireland
245 D4 **Blackwater** *watercourse* Ireland
241 H3 **Blackwater** *watercourse* England UK
116 G6 **Blackwater Lake** Northwest Territories Canada
127 P5 **Blackwater Reservoir** New Hampshire USA
244 C5 **Blackwaterfoot** North Ayrshire Scotland UK
244 E5 **Blackwood** Dumfries and Galloway Scotland UK
240 D2 **Blaenau Ffestiniog** Gwynedd Wales UK
240 D3 **Blaenau Gwent** *admin. area* Wales UK
240 D3 **Blaenavon** Torfaen Wales UK
240 C3 **Blaenwaun** Carmarthenshire Wales UK
222 H4 **Blåfjellhatten** *mountain* Norway
232 G5 **Blagaj** Bosnia and Herzegovina
240 E3 **Blagdon** North Somerset England UK
389 N4 **Blagodarnoye** Kazakhstan
388 D4 **Blagodarnyy** Russian Federation
389 K3 **Blagodatnoe** Kazakhstan
Blagodatnoye *see* **Blagodatnoe** Kazakhstan
235 C4 **Blagoevgrad** Bulgaria
235 C5 **Blagoevgrad** *admin. area* Bulgaria
385 K2 **Blagoveshchensk** Russian Federation
222 J4 **Blaikfjället** *island* Sweden
222 I4 **Blaikliden** Sweden
228 D3 **Blain** France
131 J2 **Blaine** Tennessee USA
119 R6 **Blaine Lake** Saskatchewan Canada
228 D2 **Blainville-sur-Mer** France
125 Q6 **Blair** Nebraska USA
126 F4 **Blair** Wisconsin USA
242 D1 **Blairquhan** South Ayrshire Scotland UK
234 C2 **Blaj** Romania
388 I3 **Blak** Russian Federation
76 K7 **Blake Plateau** *underwater feature* Atlantic Ocean
131 I5 **Blakely** Georgia USA
240 E3 **Blakeney** Gloucestershire England UK
241 I2 **Blakeney** Norfolk England UK
241 H2 **Blakeney Point** England UK
224 F3 **Blaker** Norway
374 E5 **Blambangan** Indonesia
375 G6 **Blambangan, Semenanjung** *peninsula* Indonesia
232 B2 **Blâmont** France
231 H4 **Blanc, Cap** *cape* Spain
226 D5 **Blanc, Mont** *mountain* France/Italy
125 M8 **Blanca** Colorado USA
162 D2 **Blanca, Bahía** *bay* Argentina
158 B3 **Blanca, Cordillera** *range* Peru
231 F4 **Blanca, Costa** *region* Spain
162 B5 **Blanca, Laguna** *bay* Chile
162 D2 **Blanca Grande, Laguna La** *lake* Argentina
125 M8 **Blanca Peak** Colorado USA
160 D3 **Blancas** Chile
425 K7 **Blanche, Lake** SA Australia
243 F2 **Blanchland** Durham England UK
160 D4 **Blanco** *watercourse* Argentina
159 F4 **Blanco** *watercourse* Bolivia
158 C2 **Blanco** *watercourse* Peru
130 B5 **Blanco** Texas USA
162 D4 **Blanco, Cabo** *cape* Argentina
134 C5 **Blanco, Cabo** *cape* Costa Rica
124 C5 **Blanco, Cape** California USA
162 B5 **Blanco, Cerro** *mountain* Chile
162 C6 **Blanco, Lago** *lake* Chile
160 D3 **Blanco Encalada, Caleta** *bay* Chile
222 inset **Blanda** *watercourse* Iceland
425 N7 **Blandford** NSW Australia
241 E4 **Blandford Forum** Dorset England UK
125 K8 **Blanding** Utah USA
231 H3 **Blanes** Spain
374 C2 **Blangkejeren** Indonesia
374 C3 **Blangpidie** Indonesia
241 I5 **Blangy-sur-Bresle** France
228 F1 **Blankenberge** Belgium
155 E2 **Blanquilla, Isla** *island* Venezuela
309 F3 **Blantyre** Malawi
228 E4 **Blanzac** France
244 D4 **Blarstainge** Argyll and Bute Scotland UK
224 D3 **Blåsjø** *lake* Norway
241 G2 **Blaston** Leicester England UK
235 C5 **Blatec** Macedonia
227 G3 **Blatná** Czech Republic
234 A1 **Blatnica** Slovakia
222 J4 **Blattniksele** Sweden
226 E3 **Blaufelden** Germany
224 E5 **Blauort** *island* Germany
224 D5 **Blåvands Huk** *cape* Denmark
222 K4 **Blåviken** *bay* Sweden
222 K4 **Blåviksjön** Sweden
241 I2 **Blaxhall** Suffolk England UK
243 H3 **Blaxton** South Yorkshire England UK
228 D4 **Blaye** France
163 7 **Bleaker Island** Falkland Islands
163 7 **Bleaker Jump** Falkland Islands
226 F1 **Bleckede** Germany
227 H4 **Bled** Slovenia
244 F5 **Blegbie** East Lothian Scotland UK
226 D2 **Bleialf** Germany
222 I2 **Bleik** Norway
222 H4 **Bleikvasslia** Norway
222 I4 **Bleikvatnet** *lake* Norway
224 H4 **Blekinge** *admin. area* Sweden
304 C2 **Blendio** Mali
423 E5 **Blenheim** New Zealand
229 H4 **Bléone** *watercourse* France
228 E3 **Bléré** France
241 I4 **Blériot-Plage** France
224 D3 **Bleskestad** Norway
228 F4 **Blesle** France
242 B3 **Blessington Lakes** *watercourse* Ireland
241 G2 **Bletchley** Milton Keynes England UK
226 C4 **Bletterans** France
306 E3 **Bleus, Monts** *range* Democratic Republic of Congo
241 F3 **Blewbury** Oxfordshire England UK
131 L3 **Blewett Falls Lake** North Carolina USA
234 A1 **Blhovce** Slovakia
301 G1 **Blida** Algeria
301 G1 **Blida** *admin. area* Algeria
234 C2 **Blidari** Romania
232 G5 **Blidinje Jezero** *lake* Bosnia and Herzegovina
225 J3 **Blidö** *island* Sweden
232 B2 **Blies** *watercourse* Germany
423 B7 **Bligh Sound** New Zealand
427 9a **Bligh Water** *strait* Fiji
222 H3 **Bliksvær** *island* Norway
126 J3 **Blind River** Ontario Canada
226 E4 **Blindenhorn** *mountain* Switzerland
235 A5 **Blinisht** Albania
425 inset **Blinkenthorpe Bay** Lord Howe Island Australia
124 H5 **Bliss** Idaho USA
241 F4 **Blissford** Hampshire England UK
375 G6 **Blitar** Indonesia
234 E4 **Bliznatsi** Bulgaria
436 O1 **Block Bay** Antarctica
308 E5 **Bloemfontein** South Africa
308 E5 **Bloemhof** South Africa
228 E3 **Blois** France
224 E4 **Blokhus** Denmark
224 C2 **Blomøy** *island* Norway
222 inset **Blönduós** Iceland
375 H6 **Blongas** Indonesia
120 G7 **Bloodvein** *watercourse* Manitoba Canada
242 C2 **Bloody Bridge** Newry and Mourne Northern Ireland UK
245 D1 **Bloody Foreland** *cape* Ireland
126 F4 **Bloomer** Wisconsin USA
159 F4 **Bloomfield** Bolivia
126 H7 **Bloomfield** Indiana USA
126 I8 **Bloomfield** Kentucky USA
126 G8 **Bloomfield** Missouri USA
129 I2 **Bloomfield** New Mexico USA
126 G6 **Bloomington** Illinois USA
126 H7 **Bloomington** Indiana USA
126 E4 **Bloomington** Minnesota USA
127 M6 **Bloomsburg** Pennsylvania USA
375 F5 **Blora** Indonesia
241 F1 **Blore** Staffordshire England UK
117 Q5 **Blosseville Kyst** *coast* Greenland
237 AK4 **Blossom, Mys** *cape* Russian Federation
241 F2 **Bloxham** Oxfordshire England UK
243 G3 **Blubberhouses** North Yorkshire England UK
131 K7 **Blue Cypress Lake** Florida USA
125 P6 **Blue Hill** Nebraska USA
127 Q4 **Blue Hill Bay** Maine USA
124 D6 **Blue Lake** California USA
125 L7 **Blue Mesa Reservoir** Colorado USA
379 G4 **Blue Mountain** Mizoram India
423 C7 **Blue Mountains** New Zealand
124 F4 **Blue Mountains** Oregon USA
Blue Nile *see* **Abay Wenz and Azraq, Bahr el** Africa
307 F1 **Blue Nile** *watercourse* Ethiopia
125 Q7 **Blue Rapids** Kansas USA
131 I3 **Blue Ridge** Georgia USA
131 K2 **Blue Ridge** North Carolina USA
127 L8 **Blue Ridge** *range* Virginia USA
131 I3 **Blue Ridge Lake** Georgia USA
118 K4 **Blueberry** *watercourse* British Columbia Canada
127 K8 **Bluefield** West Virginia USA
134 E3 **Bluefields** Jamaica
134 D4 **Bluefields** Nicaragua
116 H5 **Bluenose Lake** Nunavut Canada
423 C8 **Bluff** New Zealand
128 H2 **Bluff** Utah USA
376 B3 **Bluff Cape** Myanmar
131 J2 **Bluff City** Tennessee USA
424 F8 **Bluff Knoll** *mountain* WA Australia
161 I3 **Blumenau** Brazil
125 P4 **Blunt** South Dakota USA
243 G1 **Blyth** Northumberland England UK
128 E4 **Blythe** California USA
131 J4 **Blythe** Georgia USA
130 G3 **Blytheville** Arkansas USA
243 H3 **Blyton** Lincolnshire England UK
304 B3 **Bo** Sierra Leone
376 E2 **Bố Hạ** Vietnam
385 I5 **Bo Hai** *bay* China
376 C4 **Bo Phloi** Thailand
157 C8 **Boa Esperança** Brazil
156 D4 **Boa Esperança, Açude** *lake* Brazil
159 G5 **Boa Sentença, Serra da** *range* Brazil
156 E4 **Boa Viagem** Brazil
158 C2 **Boa Vista** Brazil
310 4 **Boa Vista** *island* Cape Verde
154 D5 **Boa Vista, Ilhas** *islands* Brazil
157 B6 **Boa Vista, Serra da** *range* Brazil
377 I4 **Boac** Philippines
134 C4 **Boaco** Nicaragua
230 C3 **Boadilla** Spain
380 E4 **Bo'ai** Yunnan China
230 C2 **Boal** Spain
305 H4 **Boali** Central African Republic
305 G3 **Boanda** Cameroon
373 J4 **Boang Island** Papua New Guinea
306 C4 **Boangi** Democratic Republic of Congo
372 D4 **Boano, Selat** *strait* Indonesia
117 K6 **Boas** *watercourse* Nunavut Canada
425 inset **Boast Harbour** Lord Howe Island Australia
134 D3 **Boatswain Point** Cayman Islands
377 H5 **Boayan** *island* Philippines
131 H3 **Boaz** Alabama USA
118 F4 **Bob Quinn Lake** British Columbia Canada
130 D4 **Bob Sandlin, Lake** Texas USA
380 F4 **Bobai** Guangxi Zhuangzu Zizhiqu China
307 H6 **Bobaomby, Tanjona** *cape* Madagascar
393 F7 **Bobbili** Andhra Pradesh India
224 I6 **Bobięcińskie Wielkie, Jezioro** *lake* Poland
232 D2 **Bobingen** Germany
226 E3 **Böblingen** Germany
304 D2 **Bobo Dioulasso** Burkina Faso
308 E4 **Bobonong** Botswana
234 C2 **Bobota** Romania
225 O5 **Bobr** Belarus
227 H2 **Bóbr** *watercourse* Poland
234 H1 **Bobrynets'** Ukraine
302 E5 **Bobuk** Sudan
226 F1 **Böbzin** Germany
134 D1 **Boca Chica Key** *island* Florida USA
162 D2 **Boca de la Travesía** Argentina
162 D3 **Boca de la Zanja** Argentina
154 E3 **Boca de Paria** Venezuela
133 F5 **Boca del Río** Mexico
158 E3 **Boca do Acre** Brazil
158 D2 **Bôca do Mutum** Brazil
159 F1 **Boca do Purus** Brazil
155 E4 **Boca Mavaca** Venezuela
131 K7 **Boca Raton** Florida USA
163 1c **Boca Spelonk** Netherlands Antilles
154 B5 **Boca Suno** Ecuador
158 C3 **Boca Tiberi** Peru
157 D7 **Bocaiúva** Brazil
304 D3 **Bocanda** Côte d'Ivoire
305 H3 **Bocaranga** Central African Republic
154 D3 **Bocas del Guaturia** Colombia
134 D5 **Bocas del Toro** Panama
134 D5 **Bocas del Toro, Archipiélago de** *islands* Panama
133 G5 **Bochil** Mexico
226 D2 **Bocholt** Germany
226 D2 **Bochum** Germany
308 E4 **Bochum** South Africa
222 K4 **Bockträsk** Sweden
308 B2 **Bocoio** Angola
129 I7 **Bocoyna** Mexico
234 B3 **Bocșa** Romania
234 C3 **Bocușnița** Romania
227 J4 **Bodajk** Hungary
425 N9 **Bodalla** NSW Australia
224 G3 **Bodane** Sweden
244 G3 **Boddam** Aberdeenshire Scotland UK
244 inset **Boddam** Shetland Scotland UK
226 F2 **Bode** *watercourse* Germany
124 D7 **Bodega Bay** California USA
124 D7 **Bodega Head** *point* California USA
222 L4 **Boden** Sweden
226 E4 **Bodensee** *lake* Germany
245 D3 **Boderg, Lough** *lake* Ireland
224 H5 **Boderne** Denmark
241 I2 **Bodham** Norfolk England UK
393 D8 **Bodhan** Karnataka India
304 E3 **Bodi** Benin
240 C4 **Bodmin** Cornwall England UK
240 C4 **Bodmin Moor** Cornwall England UK
222 I3 **Bodø** Norway
161 G2 **Bodoquena, Serra da** *range* Brazil
305 H3 **Bodoukpa** Central African Republic
392 E6 **Bodri** Madhya Pradesh India
222 J5 **Bodumsjön** *lake* Sweden
391 H3 **Bodur Bahman** Iran
245 D4 **Bodyke** Ireland
227 K1 **Bodzanów** Poland
306 C3 **Boeke** Democratic Republic of Congo
228 F4 **Boën-sur-Lignon** France
233 E8 **Boeo, Capo** *cape* Italy
373 H6 **Boera** Papua New Guinea
130 B6 **Boerne** Texas USA
224 H3 **Boet** Sweden
306 D3 **Boga** Democratic Republic of Congo
376 B3 **Bogalay** Myanmar
130 G5 **Bogalusa** Louisiana USA
425 M7 **Bogan** *watercourse* NSW Australia
304 D2 **Bogandé** Burkina Faso
305 H3 **Bogangolo** Central African Republic
130 D4 **Bogata** Texas USA
227 K1 **Bogate** Poland
227 J5 **Bogatić** Serbia
388 F2 **Bogatyye Saby** Russian Federation
306 D3 **Bogbode** Democratic Republic of Congo
306 B3 **Bogbonga** Democratic Republic of Congo
384 D3 **Bogd** Mongolia
383 K3 **Bogd Uul** *mountain* Mongolia
383 H4 **Bogda Feng** *mountain* Xinjiang Uygur Zizhiqu China
383 I4 **Bogda Shan** *range* Xinjiang Uygur Zizhiqu China
238 E5 **Bogdanova** Russian Federation
234 G1 **Bogdanovka** Ukraine
226 G3 **Bogen** Germany
222 I3 **Bogen** Norway
425 N7 **Boggabri** NSW Australia
245 C4 **Boggeragh Mountains** Ireland
163 18 **Boggy Peak** *volcano* Antigua and Barbuda

244 F4 **Boghead** Aberdeenshire Scotland UK
373 H5 **Bogia** Papua New Guinea
386 E4 **Bogil-do** *island* South Korea
244 F3 **Bogniebrae** Aberdeenshire Scotland UK
241 G4 **Bognor Regis** West Sussex England UK
305 G2 **Bogo** Cameroon
224 G5 **Bogø** Denmark
387 G1 **Bogoladza, Khrebet** *range* Russian Federation
238 E5 **Bogolyubovo** Russian Federation
235 B5 **Bogomila** Macedonia
232 G5 **Bogomolje** Croatia
425 M9 **Bogong, Mount** Vic. Australia
374 E5 **Bogor** Indonesia
238 H6 **Bogoroditsk** Russian Federation
388 F1 **Bogorodskoye** Russian Federation
154 C3 **Bogotá** Colombia
389 P2 **Bogotol** Russian Federation
379 F4 **Bogra** Bangladesh
237 U7 **Boguchany** Russian Federation
388 C3 **Boguchar** Russian Federation
242 D1 **Bogue** Dumfries and Galloway Scotland UK
125 P7 **Bogue** Kansas USA
300 D5 **Bogué** Mauritania
238 D5 **Bogushëvsk** Belarus
229 M1 **Boguszów-Gorce** Poland
385 I5 **Bohai Haixia** *bay* China
385 I5 **Bohai Wan** *bay* Hebei China
242 B3 **Bohermeen** Ireland
304 E3 **Bohicon** Benin
229 K1 **Böhlen** Germany
232 E2 **Böhmer Wald** *region* Germany
377 J5 **Bohol** *island* Philippines
377 J5 **Bohol Sea** Philippines
240 C4 **Bohortha** Cornwall England UK
383 H4 **Bohu** Xinjiang Uygur Zizhiqu China
224 F3 **Bohuslan** *region* Sweden
233 C7 **Boi, Capo** *cape* Italy
373 G6 **Boigu Island** Australia
157 E6 **Boipeba, Ilha de** *island* Brazil
230 B2 **Boiro** Spain
157 B7 **Bois** *watercourse* Brazil
116 G5 **Bois, Lac des** *lake* Northwest Territories Canada
126 I4 **Bois Blanc Island** Michigan USA
126 C3 **Bois de Sioux** *watercourse* North Dakota USA
163 I4 **Bois d'Inde, Pointe** *cape* Martinique
122 C6 **Boisbriand, Lac** *lake* Québec Canada
124 G5 **Boise** Idaho USA
125 N8 **Boise City** Oklahoma USA
377 I3 **Bojeador, Cape** Philippines
388 H6 **Bojnūrd** Iran
375 F5 **Bojonegoro** Indonesia
374 E5 **Bojong** Indonesia
374 E5 **Bojong Gede** Indonesia
222 I4 **Bojtiken** Sweden
305 F3 **Boju Ega** Nigeria
305 G4 **Bok** *watercourse* Cameroon
306 B3 **Bokada** Democratic Republic of Congo
391 H2 **Bokandāqūn** Iran
392 G6 **Bokaro** Jharkhand India
372 B3 **Bokat** Indonesia
306 B4 **Bokatola** Democratic Republic of Congo
389 N3 **Boke** Kazakhstan
304 B2 **Boké** Guinea
306 C4 **Bokele** Democratic Republic of Congo
376 D2 **Bokeo** *admin. area* Laos
425 M7 **Bokhara** *watercourse* NSW Australia
304 D2 **Bokin** Burkina Faso
305 G5 **Boko** Congo
Boko *see* **Boke** Kazakhstan
227 J4 **Bokod** Hungary
306 D3 **Bokoko** Democratic Republic of Congo
307 G3 **Bokol Mayo** Ethiopia
306 C3 **Bokondo** Democratic Republic of Congo
301 J6 **Bokoro** Chad
306 C4 **Bokote** Democratic Republic of Congo
388 D3 **Bokovskaya** Russian Federation
376 C5 **Bokpyn** Myanmar
238 E3 **Boksitogorsk** Russian Federation
308 D5 **Bokspits** South Africa
306 C4 **Bokungu** Democratic Republic of Congo
388 H6 **Bokurdak** Turkmenistan
301 I6 **Bol** Chad
232 G5 **Bol** Croatia
372 B4 **Bolaang** Indonesia
306 C4 **Bolaiti** Democratic Republic of Congo
224 I2 **Bölan** Sweden
120 F2 **Boland Lake** Nunavut Canada
132 E4 **Bolaños** *watercourse* Mexico
163 I8 **Bolans** Antigua and Barbuda
156 C5 **Bolas, Rio das** *watercourse* Brazil
241 H5 **Bolbec** France
301 G6 **Bolbol** Niger
226 F5 **Bolca** Italy
238 E5 **Boldino** Russian Federation
243 G2 **Boldron** Durham England UK
388 H5 **Boldumsaz** Turkmenistan
382 G4 **Bole** Xinjiang Uygur Zizhiqu China
304 D3 **Bole** Ghana
222 L4 **Böle** Sweden
242 A2 **Boleany** Ireland
234 C1 **Bolekhiv** Ukraine
306 B4 **Boleko** Democratic Republic of Congo
372 B6 **Boleng, Ili** *volcano* Indonesia
242 A4 **Boley** Ireland
222 H3 **Bolga** Norway
304 D2 **Bolgatanga** Ghana
234 F3 **Bolhrad** Ukraine
385 L3 **Boli** Heilongjiang China
306 D4 **Boli** Democratic Republic of Congo
306 B4 **Bolia** Democratic Republic of Congo
162 C2 **Boliche** Argentina
161 H2 **Bolicho** Brazil
222 L4 **Boliden** Sweden
377 H3 **Bolinao** Philippines
245 F4 **Bolinaspick** Ireland
126 G6 **Bolingbrook** Illinois USA
372 B3 **Boliohutu, Gunung** *mountain* Indonesia
158 E4 **Bolívar** Bolivia
154 C2 **Bolívar** *admin. area* Colombia
126 E8 **Bolivar** Missouri USA
155 F3 **Bolívar** *admin. area* Venezuela
135 G5 **Bolívar, Pico** *mountain* Venezuela
130 D6 **Bolivar Peninsula** Texas USA
160 E2 **Bolivia** *country* South America
232 H5 **Boljanići** Montenegro
238 G6 **Bolkhov** Russian Federation
227 I2 **Bolków** Poland
231 I1 **Bollène** France
243 F3 **Bollington** Cheshire England UK
425 M7 **Bollon** Qld Australia
423 11 **Bollons Island** Antipodes Island New Zealand
78 O13 **Bollons Tablemount** *underwater feature* Southern Ocean
222 J5 **Bollstabruk** Sweden
224 G4 **Bolmen** *lake* Sweden
119 Q6 **Bolney** Saskatchewan Canada
241 G4 **Bolney** West Sussex England UK
306 B4 **Bolobo** Democratic Republic of Congo
226 F5 **Bologna** Italy
229 G2 **Bologne** France
225 P4 **Bologovo** Russian Federation
237 AB6 **Bologur** Russian Federation
306 B3 **Bolomba** Democratic Republic of Congo
306 C3 **Bolombo** *watercourse* Democratic Republic of Congo
237 AC9 **Bolon', Ozero** *lake* Russian Federation
133 H5 **Bolonchencahuich** Mexico
305 F4 **Bolondo** Equatorial Guinea
308 B2 **Bolonguera** Angola
234 D1 **Bolotnya** Ukraine
238 E3 **Bolotovo** Russian Federation
160 D4 **Bolsa, Cerro** *mountain* Argentina
233 D5 **Bolsena, Lago di** *lake* Italy
225 K5 **Bol'shakovo** Russian Federation
388 F2 **Bolshaya Atnya** Russian Federation
388 F3 **Bol'shaya Chernigovka** Russian Federation
238 E4 **Bol'shaya Kosha** Russian Federation
237 W5 **Bol'shaya Kuonamka** *watercourse* Russian Federation
385 L1 **Bos'haya Ussurka** *watercourse* Russian Federation
386 G2 **Bol'shaya Ussurka** *watercourse* Russian Federation
225 Q3 **Bol'shaya Vishera** Russian Federation
389 M3 **Bol'shaya Vladimirovka** Kazakhstan
238 H4 **Bol'she-Mikhaylovskoye** Russian Federation
238 F4 **Bol'she-Ploskoye** Russian Federation
237 AG8 **Bol'sheretsk** Russian Federation
237 W3 **Bol'shevik, Ostrov** *island* Russian Federation
236 M5 **Bol'shezemel'skaya Tundra** *region* Russian Federation
223 U4 **Bol'shiye Kozly** Russian Federation
388 F4 **Bol'shiye Peshnyye, Ostrova** *island* Kazakhstan
238 F3 **Bol'shiye Ugorody** Russian Federation
237 AH5 **Bol'shoy Anyuy** *watercourse* Russian Federation
237 X4 **Bol'shoy Begichev, Ostrov** *island* Russian Federation
386 G2 **Bol'shoy Kamen'** Russian Federation
237 AD4 **Bol'shoy Lyakhovskiy, Ostrov** *island* Russian Federation
237 AA7 **Bol'shoy Nimnyr** Russian Federation
225 O3 **Bol'shoy Sabsk** Russian Federation
237 AC8 **Bol'shoy Shantar, Ostrov** *island* Russian Federation
389 M3 **Bol'shoy Tavolzhan** *lake* Kazakhstan
388 F3 **Bol'shoy Uzen** *watercourse* Kazakhstan
389 Q3 **Bolshoy Yenisey** *watercourse* Russian Federation
237 X8 **Bol'shoy Yeravnoye, Ozero** *lake* Russian Federation
387 H1 **Bolshoya Ussurka** *watercourse* Russian Federation
238 E5 **Bol'shoye Beresnëvo** Russian Federation
238 H5 **Bol'shoye Korovino** Russian Federation
238 C3 **Bol'shoye Kuzemkino** Russian Federation
237 AH4 **Bol'shoye Morskoye, Ozero** *lake* Russian Federation
238 H3 **Bol'shoye Nifontovo** Russian Federation
389 N3 **Bol'shoye Ostrovnoye** *lake* Russian Federation
223 R2 **Bol'shoye Ozerko** Russian Federation
238 H4 **Bol'shoye Selo** Russian Federation
389 M2 **Bol'shoye Topol'noye, Ozero** *lake* Russian Federation
389 M3 **Bol'shoye Yarovoye, Ozero** *lake* Russian Federation
225 Q3 **Bol'shoye Zaborov'ye** Russian Federation
132 D3 **Bolsón de Mapimí** *region* Mexico
243 G3 **Bolsover** Derbyshire England UK
224 C2 **Bolstadfjorden** *lake* Norway
231 G2 **Boltaña** Spain
243 F3 **Bolton** Greater Manchester England UK
243 G3 **Bolton Bridge** North Yorkshire England UK
120 H5 **Bolton Lake** Manitoba Canada
242 F2 **Bolton le Sands** Lancashire England UK
394 D5 **Bolu** *admin. area* Turkey
222 inset **Bolungarvík** Iceland
245 B5 **Bolus Head** *cape* Ireland
240 C4 **Bolventor** Cornwall England UK
227 J5 **Bóly** Hungary
235 E4 **Bolyarovo** Bulgaria
238 F5 **Bolychevo** Russian Federation
232 D3 **Bolzano** Italy
156 E5 **Bom Conselho** Brazil
157 C7 **Bom Despacho** Brazil
156 C4 **Bom Jardim** Brazil
159 H5 **Bom Jardim de Goiás** Brazil
157 B7 **Bom Jesus** Brazil
157 D6 **Bom Jesus da Lapa** Brazil
161 H2 **Bom Sossêgo** Brazil
157 C8 **Bom Sucesso** Brazil
306 A5 **Boma** Democratic Republic of Congo
425 N9 **Bombala** NSW Australia
162 B5 **Bombalot** Chile
135 F3 **Bombardopolis** Haiti
Bombay *see* **Mumbai** India
377 G3 **Bombay Reef** Paracel Islands
132 C3 **Bombedor** Mexico
372 E4 **Bomberai** *watercourse* Indonesia
372 E4 **Bomberai, Semenanjung** *peninsula* Indonesia
306 C3 **Bombi** Democratic Republic of Congo
301 J6 **Bomboyo** Chad
379 G3 **Bomdila** Arunachal Pradesh India
306 D3 **Bomili** Democratic Republic of Congo
224 C3 **Bømlo** *island* Norway
306 D3 **Bomokandi** *watercourse* Democratic Republic of Congo
374 B1 **Bompoka** *island* India
376 B5 **Bompoka** *island* Andaman and Nicobar Islands India
222 I5 **Bomsterbo** Sweden
301 I1 **Bon, Cap** *cape* Tunisia
373 I6 **Bona Bona Island** Papua New Guinea
388 E6 **Bonāb** Iran
163 1 **Bonaire** *island* Netherlands Antilles
76 L8 **Bonaire Trench** *underwater feature* Caribbean Sea
223 P1 **Bonakas** Norway
132 E3 **Bonanza** Mexico
134 C4 **Bonanza** Nicaragua
124 E5 **Bonanza** Oregon USA
135 G3 **Bonao** Dominican Republic
424 H3 **Bonaparte Archipelago** *islands* WA Australia
78 I9 **Bonaparte Basin** *underwater feature* Timor Sea
230 D2 **Boñar** Spain
163 9 **Bonasse** Trinidad and Tobago
123 F8 **Bonaventure** Québec Canada
123 F8 **Bonaventure** *watercourse* Québec Canada
123 F8 **Bonaventure, Île** *island* Québec Canada
123 L8 **Bonavista** Newfoundland and Labrador Canada
123 L8 **Bonavista Bay** Newfoundland and Labrador Canada
123 L8 **Bonavista Peninsula** Newfoundland and Labrador Canada
241 F4 **Bonchurch** Isle of Wight England UK
232 B3 **Boncourt** Switzerland
129 I2 **Bondad** Colorado USA
390 G3 **Bondar** Iran
238 C4 **Bondari** Russian Federation
232 D4 **Bondeno** Italy
223 M4 **Bondersbyn** Sweden
306 C3 **Bondo** Democratic Republic of Congo
304 D3 **Bondoukou** Côte d'Ivoire
304 D2 **Bondoukui** Burkina Faso
375 G5 **Bondowoso** Indonesia
126 G4 **Bonduel** Wisconsin USA
372 B5 **Bone, Teluk** *bay* Indonesia
233 F6 **Bonefro** Italy
372 B5 **Bonerate** Indonesia
372 B5 **Bonerate** *island* Indonesia
372 B5 **Bonerate, Kepulauan** *islands* Indonesia
231 F4 **Bonete** Spain
160 D4 **Bonete, Cerro** *mountain* Argentina
155 I5 **Bonfim** Brazil
155 G4 **Bonfim** Guyana
307 F2 **Bonga** Ethiopia
373 H5 **Bonga** Papua New Guinea
379 G3 **Bongaigaon** Assam India
306 C3 **Bongandanga** Democratic Republic of Congo
377 H6 **Bongao** Philippines
425 O6 **Bongaree** Qld Australia
377 J6 **Bongo** *island* Philippines
305 I3 **Bongo, Massif des** *range* Central African Republic
309 I3 **Bongolava** *range* Madagascar
305 H2 **Bongor** Chad
301 F5 **Boni** Mali
391 I2 **Boniābād** Iran
304 D3 **Boniérédougou** Côte d'Ivoire
121 Q4 **Boniface** *watercourse* Québec Canada
233 C6 **Bonifacio** Corsica France
233 C6 **Bonifacio, Strait of** Corsica France
233 F7 **Bonifati, Capo** *cape* Italy
131 I5 **Bonifay** Florida USA
78 K5 **Bonin Trench** *underwater feature* Pacific Ocean
121 P3 **Bonissant, Pointe** *cape* Québec Canada
161 G2 **Bonito** Brazil
374 D4 **Bonjol** Indonesia
301 G6 **Bonkoukou** Niger
229 G3 **Bonlieu** France
229 H1 **Bonn** Germany
122 D3 **Bonnard, Baie de** *bay* Québec Canada
123 I8 **Bonne Bay** Newfoundland and Labrador Canada
123 J7 **Bonne-Espérance** Québec Canada
124 G2 **Bonners Ferry** Idaho USA
222 K2 **Bonnes** Norway
229 H3 **Bonneville** France
424 F7 **Bonnie Rock** WA Australia
305 F4 **Bonny** Nigeria
129 K1 **Bonny Reservoir** Colorado USA
233 C6 **Bono** Sardinia Italy
373 F4 **Bonoi** Indonesia
159 I4 **Bonópolis** Brazil
375 H3 **Bontang** Indonesia
240 D2 **Bontddu** Gwynedd Wales UK
304 B3 **Bonthe** Sierra Leone
372 A5 **Bontosunggu** Indonesia
222 L3 **Bönträsket** *lake* Sweden
373 I6 **Bonvouloir Islands** Papua New Guinea
304 C3 **Bonzo** Côte d'Ivoire
372 D4 **Boo, Kepulauan** *island* Indonesia
241 G3 **Booker** Buckinghamshire England UK
130 A2 **Booker** Texas USA
304 C3 **Boola** Guinea
425 M8 **Booligal** NSW Australia
245 E3 **Boolinaig Bridge** Ireland
163 I8 **Boon Point** Antigua and Barbuda
125 M7 **Boone** Colorado USA
131 K2 **Boone** North Carolina USA
131 J2 **Boone Lake** Tennessee USA
384 D3 **Bööntsagaan Nuur** *lake* Mongolia
128 A1 **Boonville** California USA
127 N5 **Boonville** New York USA
424 G7 **Boorabbin** WA Australia
307 G2 **Boorama** Somalia
303 H5 **Boosaaso** Somalia
242 E2 **Boot** Cumbria England UK
437 D2 **Boothby, Cape** Antarctica
117 J4 **Boothia, Gulf of** Nunavut Canada
117 J4 **Boothia Peninsula** Nunavut Canada
242 E2 **Bootle** Cumbria England UK
305 G5 **Booué** Gabon
425 O6 **Booyal** Qld Australia
156 E4 **Boqueirão** Brazil
157 C6 **Boqueirão, Serra do** *range* Brazil
159 F6 **Boquerón** *admin. area* Paraguay
132 D3 **Boquilla, Presa de la** *lake* Mexico
132 E3 **Boquillas** Mexico
132 E2 **Boquillas** Texas USA
132 E2 **Boquillas del Carmen** Mexico
157 D6 **Boquira** Brazil
306 E2 **Bor** Sudan
383 K4 **Bor Ul Shan** *range* Nei Mongol Zizhiqu China
427 14 **Bora Bora** *island* French Polynesia
376 D3 **Borabu** Thailand
309 I3 **Boraha, Nosy** *island* Madagascar
232 G5 **Boraja** Croatia
372 E5 **Borang, Tanjung** *cape* Indonesia
224 G4 **Borås** Sweden
390 G3 **Borāzjān** Iran
159 G2 **Borba** Brazil
230 C4 **Borba** Portugal
234 E3 **Borcea** Romania
437 L2 **Borchgrevink Coast** Antarctica
232 G4 **Borci** Bosnia and Herzegovina
226 D1 **Borculo** Netherlands
224 D3 **Bordalsvatnet** *lake* Norway
228 D4 **Bordeaux** France
116 H3 **Borden Island** Northwest Territories/Nunavut Canada
117 K4 **Borden Peninsula** Nunavut Canada
424 I7 **Border Village** SA Australia
425 L9 **Bordertown** SA Australia
222 inset **Borðeyri** Iceland
301 G1 **Bordj Bou Arréridj** Algeria
301 H1 **Bordj Bou Arréridj** *admin. area* Algeria
301 G1 **Bordj Bounaama** Algeria
301 H2 **Bordj de Chegga** Algeria
231 H5 **Bordj Emir Khaled** Algeria
301 H2 **Bordj Messouda** Algeria
301 G4 **Bordj Mokhtar** Algeria
231 H5 **Bordj Okhriss** Algeria
301 H3 **Bordj Omer Driss** Algeria
241 G3 **Bordon** Hampshire England UK
117 S6 **Borðoy** *island* Faroe Islands
232 C4 **Bore** Italy
300 F5 **Boré** Mali
435 F1 **Boreas Abyssal Plain** *underwater feature* Greenland Sea
436 X2 **Boreas Nunatak** *mountain* Antarctica
241 G3 **Borehamwood** Hertfordshire England UK
244 D6 **Boreland** Dumfries and Galloway Scotland UK
229 K4 **Borello** Italy
227 M2 **Boremel'** Ukraine
224 H3 **Boren** *lake* Sweden
244 A3 **Boreray** *island* Scotland UK
222 I4 **Borgafjäll** Sweden
222 inset **Borgarfjörður** *bay* Iceland
222 inset **Borgarnes** Iceland
222 I4 **Borgasjön** *lake* Sweden
129 L3 **Borger** Texas USA
244 A3 **Borgh** Na h-Eileanan Siar Scotland UK
130 G5 **Borgne, Lake** Louisiana USA
232 D3 **Borgo Valsugana** Italy
244 E2 **Borgue** Highland Scotland UK
224 G3 **Borgunda** Sweden
224 C3 **Borgundøy** *island* Norway
222 I5 **Borgvattnet** Sweden
305 F4 **Bori** Nigeria
162 A3 **Bories, Punta** *cape* Chile
376 D3 **Borikhan** Laos
135 H3 **Borinquen, Punta** *cape* Puerto Rico
388 D3 **Borisoglebsk** Russian Federation
238 G5 **Borisovo** Russian Federation
238 G3 **Borisovo-Sudskoye** Russian Federation
309 I3 **Boriziny** Madagascar
301 H2 **Borj Bourguiba** Tunisia
391 H3 **Borj-e Dargāh** Iran
238 C5 **Borkavichy** Belarus
238 C6 **Borki** Belarus
227 K2 **Borki** Poland
227 M2 **Borki** Ukraine
301 J5 **Borkou** *region* Chad
302 B4 **Borkou-Ennedi-Tibesti** *admin. area* Chad
226 D1 **Borkum** Germany
226 D1 **Borkum** *island* Germany
224 H2 **Borlänge** Sweden
437 D2 **Borley, Cape** Antarctica
222 E6 **Borlo** Norway
235 F6 **Borlu** Turkey
389 M4 **Borlykak** *lake* Kazakhstan
389 L3 **Borlysor** *lake* Kazakhstan
232 C4 **Bormida** *watercourse* Italy
229 K1 **Borna** Germany
301 H4 **Borne** Algeria
226 D1 **Borne** Netherlands
372 A3 **Borneo** *island* Indonesia
244 D6 **Borness** Dumfries and Galloway Scotland UK
224 H5 **Bornholm** *island* Denmark
224 H5 **Bornholmsgattet** *bay* Sweden
306 A1 **Borno** *admin. area* Nigeria
230 D5 **Bornos** Spain
384 F3 **Bornuur** Mongolia
306 D2 **Boro** *watercourse* Sudan
238 H3 **Borok** Russian Federation
238 G4 **Borok-Sulezhskiy** Russian Federation
372 B3 **Boroko** Indonesia
305 I2 **Boromata** Central African Republic
304 D2 **Boromo** Burkina Faso
304 C3 **Boron** Côte d'Ivoire
237 AD5 **Borong, Khrebet** *range* Russian Federation
234 A2 **Borota** Hungary
225 Q3 **Borovenka** Russian Federation
225 O4 **Borovichi** Russian Federation
389 N3 **Borovlyanka** Russian Federation
232 F4 **Borovnica** Slovenia
223 R4 **Borovoy** Russian Federation
389 K2 **Borovoye** Kazakhstan
388 I2 **Borovskoy** Kazakhstan
227 K2 **Borów** Poland
227 K1 **Borowe** Poland
154 A5 **Borrachos, Punta** *cape* Ecuador
224 H5 **Borrby** Sweden
224 F3 **Borre** Norway
132 D3 **Borrego** Mexico
245 F4 **Borris** Ireland
245 D4 **Borrisokane** Ireland
245 E4 **Borrisoleigh** Ireland
425 K4 **Borroloola** NT Australia
393 C6 **Borsad** Gujarat India
224 D3 **Borsæ** *lake* Norway
223 N1 **Børselv** Norway
223 N1 **Borselvjellet** *region* Norway
234 E1 **Borshchiv** Ukraine
385 G2 **Borshchovochnyy Khrebet** *range* Russian Federation
234 B1 **Borsod-Abaúj-Zemplén** *admin. area* Hungary
222 J2 **Børsvatnet** *lake* Norway
228 F4 **Bort-les-Orgues** France
Bortala *see* **Bole** China
222 H5 **Börtnan** Sweden
237 AD4 **Boru** Russian Federation
390 G3 **Borūjen** Iran
390 F2 **Borūjerd** Iran
244 B3 **Borve** Highland Scotland UK
242 F2 **Borwick** Lancashire England UK
234 C1 **Borynia** Ukraine
385 H2 **Borzya** Russian Federation
385 H2 **Borzya** *watercourse* Russian Federation
385 H2 **Borzya Ozero** *lake* Russian Federation
233 C6 **Bosa** Sardinia Italy
389 K4 **Bosagha** Kazakhstan
232 G4 **Bosanska Dubica** Bosnia and Herzegovina
227 I5 **Bosanska Krupa** Bosnia and Herzegovina
373 G5 **Bosavi, Mount** Papua New Guinea
226 E5 **Bosco Marengo** Italy
380 E4 **Bose** Guangxi Zhuangzu Zizhiqu China
308 E5 **Boshof** South Africa
391 I2 **Boshrūyeh** Iran
227 I3 **Boskovice** Czech Republic
232 H4 **Bosna** *watercourse* Bosnia and Herzegovina
232 G4 **Bosnia and Herzegovina** *country* Europe
306 B3 **Boso-Semodja** Democratic Republic of Congo
306 B3 **Bosobolo** Democratic Republic of Congo
129 I3 **Bosque Farms** New Mexico USA
305 H3 **Bossangoa** Central African Republic
306 B2 **Bossembélé** Central African Republic
305 H3 **Bossentélé** Central African Republic
301 G6 **Bossey Bangou** Niger
130 E4 **Bossier City** Louisiana USA
308 C4 **Bossiesvlei** Namibia
391 K3 **Bostan** Pakistan
241 G2 **Boston** Lincolnshire England UK
127 P5 **Boston** Massachusetts USA
118 K8 **Boston Bar** British Columbia Canada
130 D3 **Boston Mountains** Arkansas USA
243 G3 **Boston Spa** West Yorkshire England UK
130 D3 **Boswell** Oklahoma USA
127 L6 **Boswell** Pennsylvania USA
393 C6 **Botad** Gujarat India
158 D3 **Botafogo** Brazil
374 C4 **Botanic Gardens** *point of interest* Singapore
308 D4 **Boteti** *watercourse* Botswana
243 H3 **Bothamsall** Nottinghamshire England UK
225 J2 **Bothnia, Gulf of** Finland
425 M10 **Bothwell** Tas. Australia
230 C3 **Boticas** Portugal
234 D2 **Botiza** Romania
388 E5 **Botlikh** Russian Federation
222 I3 **Botn** Norway
222 F5 **Botngard** Norway
222 J2 **Botnhamn** Norway
234 B3 **Botoš** Serbia
234 E2 **Botoșani** Romania
234 E2 **Botoșani** Romania
234 E2 **Botoșani** *admin. area* Romania
385 H5 **Botou** Hebei China
304 C3 **Botro** Côte d'Ivoire
308 E5 **Botshabelo** South Africa
222 L4 **Botsmark** Sweden
308 D4 **Botswana** *country* Africa
243 H3 **Bottesford** North Lincolnshire England UK
157 B8 **Botucatu** Brazil
304 C3 **Bou** *watercourse* Côte d'Ivoire
233 D8 **Bou Ficha** Tunisia
233 C8 **Bou Hadjdr** Algeria
231 H5 **Bou Medfaa** Algeria
231 I6 **Bou Mellal** Algeria
300 F2 **Bou Naceur, Jbel** *mountain* Morocco
231 G6 **Bou Noual** Algeria
300 C5 **Boû Rjeïmât** Mauritania
301 G1 **Bou Saâda** Algeria
304 C3 **Bouaflé** Côte d'Ivoire
304 C3 **Bouaké** Côte d'Ivoire
301 G2 **Boualem** Algeria
301 F2 **Bouânane** Morocco
305 H5 **Bouanga** Congo
305 H3 **Bouar** Central African Republic
301 F2 **Bouârfa** Morocco
233 B8 **Bouati Mahmoud** Algeria
229 G5 **Bouc-Bel-Air** France
305 H3 **Bouca** Central African Republic
123 D8 **Boucher** *watercourse* Québec Canada
123 I7 **Boucher, Lac** *lake* Québec Canada
123 F9 **Bouctouche** New Brunswick Canada
300 F2 **Boudenib** Morocco
305 H4 **Boudoua** Central African Republic
305 G5 **Bouenza** *admin. area* Congo
305 G5 **Bouenza** *watercourse* Congo
301 H1 **Bougaa** Algeria
426 8 **Bougainville** *island* Papua New Guinea
424 H3 **Bougainville, Cape** WA Australia
372 D4 **Bougainville, Selat** *strait* Indonesia
426 8 **Bougainville Strait** Solomon Islands
426 7 **Bougainville Strait** Vanuatu
301 H1 **Bougaroûn, Cap** *cape* Algeria
301 G4 **Boughessa** Mali
241 H2 **Boughton** Norfolk England UK
241 H3 **Boughton Aluph** Kent England UK
304 C2 **Bougouni** Mali
301 G1 **Bougzoul** Algeria
231 J6 **Bouhamama** Algeria
163 16 **Bouillante** Guadeloupe
229 G2 **Bouillon** Belgium
226 C3 **Bouilly** France
305 G4 **Bouinandjé** *watercourse* Gabon
301 G1 **Bouira** Algeria
301 G1 **Bouira** *admin. area* Algeria
300 E2 **Boujad** Morocco
300 D3 **Boukra** Western Sahara
232 B2 **Boulay-Moselle** France
125 M7 **Boulder** Colorado USA
124 I3 **Boulder** Montana USA
118 G3 **Boulder City** British Columbia Canada
128 E3 **Boulder City** Nevada USA
128 G2 **Boulder Town** Utah USA
123 F7 **Bouleau** *watercourse* Québec Canada
231 J6 **Boulehilet** Algeria
300 F2 **Boulemane** Morocco
304 E2 **Boulgou** Burkina Faso
425 K5 **Boulia** Qld Australia
243 G1 **Boulmer** Northumberland England UK
228 F2 **Boulogne-Billancourt** France
228 E5 **Boulogne-sur-Gesse** France
241 I4 **Boulogne-sur-Mer** France
305 I3 **Boulou** *watercourse* Central African Republic
426 7 **Bouloupari** New Caledonia
304 D2 **Boulsa** Burkina Faso
300 E2 **Boumaine Dadès** Morocco
305 G5 **Boumango** Gabon
305 G4 **Boumba** *watercourse* Cameroon
305 H4 **Boumbé** *watercourse* Central African Republic
301 F5 **Boumboum** Mali
300 D5 **Boumdeït** Mauritania
301 G1 **Boumerdès** Algeria
301 G1 **Boumerdès** *admin. area* Algeria
304 D3 **Bouna** Côte d'Ivoire
127 P4 **Boundary Mountains** Maine USA
304 C3 **Boundiali** Côte d'Ivoire
305 H5 **Boundji** Congo
242 B4 **Bounds Bridge** Ireland
301 I6 **Bouné** Niger
305 I3 **Boungou** Central African Republic
305 I3 **Boungou** *watercourse* Central African Republic
300 C6 **Bounkiling** Senegal
427 11a **Bounty Bay** Pitcairn Islands
423 10 **Bounty Islands** New Zealand
78 N12 **Bounty Trough** *underwater feature* Pacific Ocean
304 D2 **Boura** Burkina Faso
228 F3 **Bourbonnais** *region* France
126 H6 **Bourbonnais** Illinois USA
229 G3 **Bourbonne-les-Bains** France
241 J4 **Bourbourg** France
228 C2 **Bourbriac** France
162 C6 **Bourchier, Bahía** *bay* Chile
229 G4 **Bourdeaux** France
121 R4 **Bourdel, Lac** *lake* Québec Canada
230 D6 **Boureït** Morocco
301 F5 **Bourem** Mali
229 G4 **Bourg-Argental** France
229 G3 **Bourg-en-Bresse** France
229 G4 **Bourg-lès-Valence** France
228 E5 **Bourg-Madame** Spain
229 H4 **Bourg-St-Maurice** France
228 E4 **Bourganeuf** France
228 F3 **Bourges** France
229 G4 **Bourget, Lac du** *lake* France
228 F3 **Bourgogne** *admin. area* France
229 G4 **Bourgoin-Jallieu** France
425 M7 **Bourke** NSW Australia
127 K2 **Bourkes** Ontario Canada
241 G2 **Bourne** Lincolnshire England UK
241 F4 **Bournemouth** Bournemouth England UK
241 F4 **Bournemouth** *admin. area* England UK
305 G2 **Bourrah** Cameroon
228 E4 **Bourran** France
304 D2 **Bourzanga** Burkina Faso
244 B4 **Bousd** Highland Scotland UK
231 H5 **Bouskene** Algeria
228 F3 **Boussac** France
305 H2 **Bousso** Chad
233 C8 **Bouteldja** Algeria
300 D5 **Boutilimit** Mauritania
121 R5 **Boutin** *watercourse* Québec Canada
228 D3 **Boutonne** *watercourse* France
77 I5 **Boutougou Fara** Senegal
Bouvet Island *see* **Bouvetøya** Antarctica
77 S15 **Bouvetøya** *dependency* Antarctica Norwegian
229 H2 **Bouxwiller** France
306 D2 **Bouyé** *watercourse* Central African Republic
301 H6 **Bouza** Niger
231 G5 **Bouzghaïa** Algeria
222 J2 **Bøvær** Norway
233 G7 **Bovalino** Italy
232 E3 **Bovec** Slovenia
229 J4 **Bovegno** Italy
163 1c **Boven Bolivia** Netherlands Antilles
155 H4 **Boven Tapanahoni** *watercourse* Suriname
226 E2 **Bovenden** Germany
222 F5 **Bøverfjorden** Norway
226 D5 **Boves** Italy
124 G3 **Bovill** Idaho USA
129 K3 **Bovina** Texas USA
225 O5 **Bovsevichi** Belarus
244 E2 **Bow** Orkney Islands Scotland UK
119 P8 **Bow Island** Alberta Canada
240 C2 **Bow Street** Ceredigion Wales UK
380 E1 **Bowang** Shaanxi China
125 N2 **Bowbells** North Dakota USA
243 G2 **Bowburn** Durham England UK
125 P4 **Bowdle** South Dakota USA
125 P3 **Bowdon** North Dakota USA
425 N5 **Bowen** Qld Australia
243 F1 **Bower** Northumberland England UK
78 N2 **Bowers Bank** *underwater feature* Bering Sea
437 K2 **Bowers Mountains** Antarctica
78 N2 **Bowers Ridge** *underwater feature* Bering Sea
243 F2 **Bowes** Durham England UK
127 M7 **Bowie** Maryland USA
130 C4 **Bowie** Texas USA
79 S2 **Bowie Seamount** *underwater feature* Pacific Ocean
126 H8 **Bowling Green** Kentucky USA
126 J6 **Bowling Green** Ohio USA
127 M7 **Bowling Green** Virginia USA
131 J3 **Bowman** Georgia USA
131 K4 **Bowman** South Carolina USA
118 K7 **Bowman, Mount** British Columbia Canada
436 T2 **Bowman Coast** Antarctica
125 N4 **Bowman-Haley Lake** North Dakota USA
437 G2 **Bowman Island** Antarctica
436 U2 **Bowman Peninsula** Antarctica
244 B5 **Bowmore** Argyll and Bute Scotland UK
425 N8 **Bowral** NSW Australia
118 K6 **Bowron** *watercourse* British Columbia Canada
118 K6 **Bowron Lake Provincial Park** British Columbia Canada
118 G4 **Bowser Lake** British Columbia Canada
119 U6 **Bowsman** Manitoba Canada
126 E3 **Bowstring Lake** Minnesota USA
241 E3 **Box** Wiltshire England UK
125 N4 **Box Elder** South Dakota USA
385 I5 **Boxing** Shandong China
154 C3 **Boyaca** *admin. area* Colombia
235 F5 **Boyalı** Turkey
238 F6 **Boyanovichi** Russian Federation
237 U4 **Boyarka** Russian Federation
119 W5 **Boyd** Manitoba Canada
121 Q6 **Boyd, Lac** *lake* Québec Canada
120 D2 **Boyd Lake** Northwest Territories Canada
124 H6 **Boyd Reservoir** Nevada USA
119 M3 **Boyer** Alberta Canada
126 D5 **Boyer** *watercourse* Iowa USA
388 C4 **Boykov Liman** *lake* Russian Federation
119 O5 **Boyle** Alberta Canada
245 D3 **Boyle** Ireland
242 A3 **Boyne** *watercourse* Ireland
131 K7 **Boynton Beach** Florida USA
305 I3 **Boyo** Central African Republic
375 F5 **Boyolali** Indonesia
129 K3 **Boys Ranch** Texas USA
125 K5 **Boysen Reservoir** Wyoming USA
389 J6 **Boysun** Uzbekistan
222 E6 **Bøyum** Norway
232 F4 **Božava** Croatia
235 E6 **Bozcaada** Turkey
235 D6 **Bozcaada** *island* Turkey
235 F7 **Bozdoğan** Turkey
241 G2 **Bozeat** Northamptonshire England UK
125 J4 **Bozeman** Montana USA
235 F6 **Bozen** Turkey
381 G1 **Bozhou** Anhui China
236 L6 **Bozhyudor** Russian Federation
234 C4 **Božica** Serbia
228 F4 **Bozouls** France
305 H3 **Bozoum** Central African Republic
235 G7 **Bozova** Turkey
389 L3 **Bozshakol'** Kazakhstan
388 J2 **Bozshakol** *lake* Kazakhstan
226 F5 **Bozzolo** Italy
226 D5 **Bra** Italy
155 H3 **Braams Punt** *cape* Suriname
229 G1 **Brabant** *admin. area* Belgium
119 T4 **Brabant** Saskatchewan Canada
436 T2 **Brabant Island** Antarctica
244 B3 **Bracadale, Loch** *bay* Scotland UK
233 E5 **Bracciano** Italy
233 E5 **Bracciano, Lago di** *lake* Italy
234 C3 **Braćevac** Serbia
222 I5 **Bräcke** Sweden
119 Q8 **Bracken** Saskatchewan Canada
129 L6 **Brackettville** Texas USA
244 D4 **Brackletter** Highland Scotland UK
241 F2 **Brackley** Northamptonshire England UK
241 G3 **Bracknell** Bracknell Forest England UK
241 G3 **Bracknell Forest** *admin. area* England UK
233 G6 **Bradano** *watercourse* Italy
131 J7 **Bradenton** Florida USA
234 C3 **Brădești** Romania
243 G3 **Bradfield** South Yorkshire England UK
243 G3 **Bradford** West Yorkshire England UK
126 G6 **Bradford** Illinois USA
127 O5 **Bradford** Vermont USA
240 E4 **Bradford Abbas** Dorset England UK
243 G3 **Bradgate** South Yorkshire England UK
241 F4 **Brading** Isle of Wight England UK
243 G2 **Bradley** North Yorkshire England UK
241 E2 **Bradley** Staffordshire England UK
128 B3 **Bradley** California USA
125 O6 **Brady** Nebraska USA
130 B5 **Brady** Texas USA
130 B5 **Brady Reservoir** Texas USA
244 D3 **Brae** Highland Scotland UK
244 inset **Brae** Shetland Scotland UK
244 D3 **Braeantra** Highland Scotland UK
244 E3 **Braemar** Aberdeenshire Scotland UK
244 E2 **Braemore** Highland Scotland UK
230 B3 **Braga** Portugal
230 B3 **Braga** *admin. area* Portugal
160 F5 **Bragado** Argentina
156 C3 **Bragança** Brazil
230 C3 **Bragança** Portugal
230 C3 **Bragança** *admin. area* Portugal
157 C8 **Bragança Paulista** Brazil
119 N7 **Bragg Creek** Alberta Canada
237 AK6 **Bragina** Russian Federation
154 D3 **Bragueta** Venezuela
126 E4 **Braham** Minnesota USA
379 H3 **Brahmakund** Arunachal Pradesh India
379 G4 **Brahmanbaria** Bangladesh
393 F7 **Brahmapur** Orissa India
379 H3 **Brahmaputra** *watercourse* Assam India
234 E3 **Brăila** Romania
234 E3 **Brăila** *admin. area* Romania
241 F2 **Brailsford** Derbyshire England UK
126 D3 **Brainerd** Minnesota USA
241 H3 **Braintree** Essex England UK
308 E4 **Brak** *watercourse* South Africa
226 E1 **Brake** Germany
224 G3 **Brålanda** Sweden
228 F5 **Bram** France
241 F2 **Bramcote** Warwickshire England UK
222 J5 **Brämön** *island* Sweden

242 F2 **Brampton** Cumbria England UK
226 D1 **Bramsche** Germany
224 I2 **Bramsöfjärden** *bay* Sweden
234 D3 **Bran** Romania
222 J4 **Brånaberg** Sweden
241 H2 **Brancaster** Norfolk England UK
241 H2 **Brancaster Staithe** Norfolk England UK
155 F4 **Branco** *watercourse* Brazil
310 4 **Branco** *island* Cape Verde
232 C3 **Brand** Austria
163 1c **Brandaris** *mountain* Netherlands Antilles
222 J5 **Brändbo** Sweden
222 F5 **Brandbu** Norway
226 G1 **Brandenburg** *admin. area* Germany
243 H3 **Brandesburton** East Riding of Yorkshire England UK
225 K2 **Brändö** *island* Finland
125 P2 **Brandon** Manitoba Canada
125 R4 **Brandon** Minnesota USA
130 G4 **Brandon** Mississippi USA
222 M4 **Brändön** Sweden
245 B4 **Brandon Bay** Ireland
245 B4 **Brandon Head** *cape* Ireland
222 L5 **Brändövik** Finland
224 E5 **Brandsø** *island* Denmark
308 D6 **Brandvlei** South Africa
131 J6 **Branford** Florida USA
374 D4 **Brani, Pulau** *island* Singapore
232 F4 **Branica** *watercourse* Slovenia
222 L4 **Brännberg** Sweden
222 L5 **Brännland** Sweden
163 I7 **Bransby Point** *cape* Montserrat
436 U2 **Bransfield Strait** Antarctica
126 E8 **Branson** Missouri USA
241 G2 **Branston** Leicester England UK
119 O7 **Brant** Alberta Canada
121 N5 **Brant** *watercourse* Ontario Canada
127 K5 **Brantford** Ontario Canada
242 E2 **Branthwaite** Cumbria England UK
228 E4 **Brantôme** France
372 E3 **Bras** *island* Indonesia
123 H10 **Bras d'Or Lake** Nova Scotia Canada
131 J3 **Braselton** Georgia USA
157 D7 **Brasil, Planalto do** *region* Brazil
158 D3 **Brasiléia** Brazil
157 C6 **Brasília** Brazil
234 D3 **Brașov** Romania
234 D3 **Brasóv** *admin. area* Romania
305 F4 **Brass** Nigeria
228 F5 **Brassac** France
229 G1 **Brasschaat** Belgium
375 H2 **Brassey, Banjaran** *range* Malaysia
227 I3 **Bratislava** Slovakia
227 I3 **Bratislavský** *admin. area* Slovakia
235 D4 **Bratsigovo** Bulgaria
237 V7 **Bratsk** Russian Federation
234 F1 **Bratslav** Ukraine
222 I4 **Brattbäcken** Sweden
222 I4 **Bratten** Sweden
127 O5 **Brattleboro** Vermont USA
240 D3 **Bratton** Somerset England UK
222 F5 **Brattset** Norway
222 E5 **Brattvåg** Norway
226 F1 **Braunschweig** Germany
240 C3 **Braunton** Devon England UK
310 4 **Brava** *island* Cape Verde
231 H3 **Brava, Costa** *region* Spain
154 A5 **Brava, Punta** *cape* Ecuador
224 I3 **Bråviken** *bay* Sweden
160 D3 **Bravo, Cerro** *mountain* Chile
128 E4 **Brawley** California USA
245 F3 **Bray** Ireland
245 B5 **Bray Head** *cape* Ireland
117 L5 **Bray Island** Nunavut Canada
228 F2 **Bray-sur-Seine** France
228 E3 **Braye** *watercourse* France
240 D3 **Brayford** Devon England UK
119 M6 **Brazeau** *watercourse* Alberta Canada
118 M6 **Brazeau, Mount** Alberta Canada
119 N6 **Brazeau Reservoir** Alberta Canada
304 B3 **Brazier Point** *cape* Liberia
157 C5 **Brazil** *country* South America
77 P11 **Brazil Basin** *underwater feature* Atlantic Ocean
130 B4 **Brazos** *watercourse* Texas USA
373 F5 **Brazza** *watercourse* Indonesia
305 H5 **Brazzaville** Congo
232 F4 **Brbinj** Croatia
234 A3 **Brčko** Bosnia and Herzegovina
227 G3 **Brdy** *range* Czech Republic
245 C3 **Breaghwy** Ireland
244 inset **Breakon** Shetland Scotland UK
423 B7 **Breaksea Sound** New Zealand
228 D2 **Bréal-sous-Vitré** France
422 F2 **Bream Head** *cape* New Zealand
422 F2 **Bream Tail** *cape* New Zealand
240 D3 **Brean** Somerset England UK
234 D3 **Breaza** Romania
374 F5 **Brebes** Indonesia
374 F5 **Brebes, Tanjung** *cape* Indonesia
234 B3 **Brebu** Romania
228 D2 **Brécey** France
240 C3 **Brechfa** Carmarthenshire Wales UK
244 F4 **Brechin** Angus Scotland UK
130 B4 **Breckenridge** Texas USA
227 I3 **Břeclav** Czech Republic
240 D3 **Brecon** Powys Wales UK
240 D3 **Brecon Beacons** *range* Wales UK
226 C2 **Breda** Netherlands
308 D6 **Bredasdorp** South Africa
224 G1 **Bredåsjön** *lake* Sweden
243 F3 **Bredbury** Greater Manchester England UK
222 I5 **Bredbyn** Sweden
122 P2 **Bredefjord** *bay* Greenland
125 N1 **Bredenbury** Saskatchewan Canada
224 E5 **Bredningen** *bay* Denmark
224 H2 **Bredsjön** *lake* Sweden
225 J1 **Bredvik** Sweden
388 H3 **Bredy** Russian Federation
229 G1 **Bree** Belgium
245 E1 **Bree** Ireland
235 C5 **Bregalnica** *watercourse* Macedonia
226 E4 **Bregenz** Austria
228 D2 **Bréhal** France
228 C2 **Bréhat, Île de** *island* France
224 H1 **Brehungen** *lake* Sweden
437 B2 **Breid Bay** Antarctica
222 inset **Breiðafjörður** *bay* Iceland
224 D1 **Breidalsvatn** *lake* Norway
222 inset **Breiðdalsvik** Iceland
229 H5 **Breil-sur-Roya** France
222 D4 **Breim** Norway
224 D2 **Breimsvatnet** *lake* Norway
223 M1 **Breivikbotn** Norway
222 K2 **Breivikeidet** Norway
156 C3 **Brejo** Brazil
156 D5 **Brejo** *watercourse* Brazil
156 E4 **Brejo Santo** Brazil
222 G5 **Brekken** Norway
224 C2 **Bremangerlandet** *island* Norway
232 C4 **Brembo** *watercourse* Italy
226 E1 **Bremen** Germany
226 E1 **Bremen** *admin. area* Germany
424 F8 **Bremer Bay** WA Australia
226 E1 **Bremerhaven** Germany
242 A4 **Brenan** Ireland
128 F4 **Brenda** Arizona USA
232 D4 **Brendola** Italy
130 C5 **Brenham** Texas USA
304 E3 **Breniase** Ghana
240 D1 **Brenig, Llyn** *lake* Wales UK
228 E3 **Brenne** *region* France
226 F4 **Brennero** Italy
226 F5 **Breno** Italy
226 C4 **Brénod** France
130 H4 **Brent** Alabama USA
226 F4 **Brenta, Cima** *mountain* Italy
241 G2 **Brentingby** Leicester England UK
241 H3 **Brentwood** Essex England UK
130 H2 **Brentwood** Tennessee USA
226 F5 **Brescia** Italy
228 E1 **Bresle** *watercourse* France
234 B4 **Bresnica** Serbia
226 F4 **Bressanone** Italy
229 G3 **Bresse** *region* France
228 D3 **Bressuire** France
394 B2 **Brest** Belarus
228 B2 **Brest** France
234 B4 **Brestovac** Serbia
394 C2 **Brestskaya Voblasts'** *admin. area* Belarus
228 C2 **Bretagne** *admin. area* France
228 C3 **Bretagne** *region* France
228 E4 **Bretenoux** France
119 N6 **Breton** Alberta Canada
133 H2 **Breton Island** *island* Louisiana USA
133 H2 **Breton Sound** Louisiana USA
310 6b **Bretonne, Baie** *bay* French Southern and Antarctic Lands
422 F2 **Brett, Cape** New Zealand
240 E1 **Bretton** Flintshire Wales UK
374 B2 **Breueh, Pulau** *island* Indonesia
156 B3 **Breves** Brazil
126 I3 **Brevort** Michigan USA
425 M7 **Brewarrina** NSW Australia
304 B3 **Brewerville** Liberia
129 L1 **Brewster** Kansas USA
124 F2 **Brewster** Washington USA
Brewster, Kap *see* **Kangikajik** Greenland
437 L2 **Brewster, Mount** Antarctica
423 C7 **Brewster, Mount** New Zealand
130 H5 **Brewton** Alabama USA
119 O5 **Breynat** Alberta Canada
238 G3 **Breytovo** Russian Federation
234 B3 **Brežde** Serbia
227 I3 **Březí** Czech Republic
227 I5 **Brezičani** Bosnia and Herzegovina
227 G3 **Březnice** Czech Republic
227 J3 **Brezno** Slovakia
234 D3 **Brezoi** Romania
232 G4 **Brezovac** Croatia
305 I3 **Bria** Central African Republic
128 F2 **Brian Head** Utah USA
229 H4 **Briançon** France
240 D2 **Brianne, Llyn** *lake* Wales UK
232 F4 **Bribir** Croatia
234 E1 **Briceni** Moldova
123 H7 **Briçonnet, Lac** *lake* Québec Canada
245 D4 **Bride** *watercourse* Ireland
240 C4 **Bridestowe** Devon England UK
240 D4 **Bridfordmills** Devon England UK
119 W5 **Bridgar** Manitoba Canada
244 E3 **Bridge of Dee** Aberdeenshire Scotland UK
244 F4 **Bridge of Dye** Aberdeenshire Scotland UK
244 E4 **Bridge of Earn** Perth and Kinross Scotland UK
244 D4 **Bridge of Orchy** Argyll and Bute Scotland UK
244 F3 **Bridgend** Aberdeenshire Scotland UK
240 D3 **Bridgend** Bridgend Wales UK
240 D3 **Bridgend** *admin. area* Wales UK
128 C1 **Bridgeport** California USA
127 O6 **Bridgeport** Connecticut USA
125 N6 **Bridgeport** Nebraska USA
124 F3 **Bridgeport** Washington USA
130 C4 **Bridgeport, Lake** Texas USA
128 C1 **Bridgeport Reservoir** California USA
125 K4 **Bridger** Montana USA
127 N7 **Bridgeton** New Jersey USA
424 F8 **Bridgetown** WA Australia
135 J4 **Bridgetown** Barbados
240 D3 **Bridgetown** Somerset England UK
240 D3 **Bridgwater** Somerset England UK
240 D3 **Bridgwater Bay** England UK
243 H2 **Bridlington** East Riding of Yorkshire England UK
243 H2 **Bridlington Bay** England UK
240 E4 **Bridport** Dorset England UK
228 B2 **Briec** France
123 E10 **Brier Island** Nova Scotia Canada
125 M1 **Briercrest** Saskatchewan Canada
243 F3 **Brierfield** Lancashire England UK
127 K7 **Briery Knob** *mountain* West Virginia USA
226 C3 **Briey** France
229 H3 **Brig** Switzerland
243 H3 **Brigg** North Lincolnshire England UK
124 I6 **Brigham City** Utah USA
243 G3 **Brighouse** West Yorkshire England UK
241 I3 **Brightlingsea** Essex England UK
423 D7 **Brighton** New Zealand
241 G4 **Brighton** Brighton and Hove England UK
241 G4 **Brighton and Hove** *admin. area* England UK
228 B2 **Brignogan-Plage** France
229 H5 **Brignoles** France
230 E2 **Brihuega** Spain
232 E3 **Brijuni** Croatia
161 H2 **Brilhante** *watercourse* Brazil
154 D5 **Brilla Nueva** Peru
244 E2 **Brims** Orkney Islands Scotland UK
129 I7 **Brincadero** Mexico
233 G6 **Brindisi** Italy
223 N1 **Bringnes** *island* Norway
244 E1 **Brinian** Orkney Islands Scotland UK
229 L4 **Brinje** Croatia
130 F3 **Brinkley** Arkansas USA
234 E1 **Brinzeni** Moldova
228 E3 **Brion** France
123 H9 **Brion, Île** *island* Québec Canada
228 F4 **Brioude** France
121 T5 **Brisay** Québec Canada
425 O6 **Brisbane** Qld Australia
119 M7 **Brisco** British Columbia Canada
228 D3 **Brissac** France
229 I3 **Brissago** Switzerland
122 F4 **Brisson, Lac** *lake* Québec Canada
123 E9 **Bristol** New Brunswick Canada
240 E3 **Bristol** Bristol England UK
240 E3 **Bristol** *admin. area* England UK
127 O6 **Bristol** Connecticut USA
116 D7 **Bristol Bay** Alaska USA
240 D3 **Bristol Channel** England UK
128 E3 **Bristol Lake** California USA
118 J8 **Britannia Beach** British Columbia Canada
117 K2 **British Empire Range** Nunavut Canada
239 **British Isles** Europe
135 H3 **British Virgin Islands (UK)** *admin. area* Caribbean
308 E5 **Brits** South Africa
308 D6 **Britstown** South Africa
126 E5 **Britt** Iowa USA
240 B2 **Brittas Bay** Ireland
125 Q4 **Britton** South Dakota USA
228 E4 **Brive-la-Gaillarde** France
230 E2 **Briviesca** Spain
240 D4 **Brixham** Torbay England UK
227 I3 **Brno** Czech Republic
224 I3 **Bro** Sweden
134 D2 **Broa, Ensenada de la** *bay* Cuba
424 G7 **Broad Arrow** WA Australia
245 C2 **Broad Haven** *bay* Ireland
244 E5 **Broad Law** *mountain* Scotland UK
131 K3 **Broad Run** *watercourse* South Carolina USA
127 L1 **Broadback** *watercourse* Québec Canada
226 A2 **Broadstairs** Kent UK
125 M4 **Broadus** Montana USA
129 K3 **Broadview** New Mexico USA
240 E2 **Broadwas** Worcestershire England UK
125 N6 **Broadwater** Nebraska USA
240 C3 **Broadway** Carmarthenshire Wales UK
240 E4 **Broadwey** Dorset England UK
224 H4 **Broby** Sweden
122 C3 **Brochant** *watercourse* Québec Canada
119 U4 **Brochet** Manitoba Canada
123 D8 **Brochet** *watercourse* Québec Canada
120 E3 **Brochet, Lac** *lake* Manitoba Canada
117 M9 **Brochet, Lac au** *lake* Québec Canada
119 Q7 **Brock** Saskatchewan Canada
116 H3 **Brock Island** Northwest Territories Canada
244 E1 **Brockan** Orkney Islands Scotland UK
241 F4 **Brockbridge** Hampshire England UK
226 F2 **Brocken** *mountain* Germany
424 F5 **Brockman, Mount** WA Australia
240 E2 **Brockton** Shropshire England UK
127 P5 **Brockton** Massachusetts USA
125 M2 **Brockton** Montana USA
127 N4 **Brockville** Ontario Canada
127 L5 **Brockton** New York USA
234 A4 **Brodarevo** Serbia
227 O6 **Brodets** Belarus
117 K4 **Brodeur Peninsula** Nunavut Canada
227 K5 **Brodica** Serbia
227 J1 **Brodnica** Poland
227 H1 **Brody** Poland
228 E2 **Broglie** France
227 H1 **Brojce** Poland
227 K1 **Brok** Poland
128 D2 **Broken Arrow** Oklahoma USA
130 D3 **Broken Bow Lake** Oklahoma USA
425 L7 **Broken Hill** NSW Australia
78 F11 **Broken Ridge** *underwater feature* Indian Ocean
237 AF7 **Brokhovo** Russian Federation
155 H3 **Brokopondo** Suriname
155 H3 **Brokopondo** *admin. area* Suriname
225 L3 **Bromarv** Finland
232 D2 **Brombachsee** *lake* Germany
226 F1 **Brome** Germany
241 I2 **Brome Street** Suffolk England UK
240 D3 **Brompton Regis** Somerset England UK
241 E2 **Bromsgrove** Worcestershire England UK
240 E2 **Bromyard** Herefordshire England UK
226 E5 **Broni** Italy
240 D2 **Bronllys** Powys Wales UK
236 O7 **Bronnikovo** Russian Federation
238 H5 **Bronnitsy** Russian Federation
222 H4 **Brønnøysund** Norway
131 J6 **Bronson** Florida USA
130 A5 **Bronte** Texas USA
241 G2 **Brook End** Bedfordshire England UK
241 I2 **Brooke** Norfolk England UK
377 H5 **Brooke's Point** Philippines
126 F7 **Brookfield** Missouri USA
125 Q4 **Brookings** South Dakota USA
123 F10 **Brooklyn** Nova Scotia Canada
126 E4 **Brooklyn Park** Minnesota USA
436 U2 **Brooks, Cape** Antarctica
118 H7 **Brooks Bay** British Columbia Canada
118 E2 **Brooks Brook** Yukon Territory Canada
116 D5 **Brooks Range** Alaska USA
129 J1 **Brookside** Colorado USA
131 J6 **Brooksville** Florida USA
424 F8 **Brookton** WA Australia
126 H7 **Brookville Lake** Indiana USA
424 G4 **Broome** WA Australia
121 P5 **Broomfield Island** Nunavut Canada
243 G1 **Broomhill** Northumberland England UK
425 O7 **Brooms Head** NSW Australia
244 E2 **Brora** Highland Scotland UK
244 D2 **Brora** *watercourse* Scotland UK
224 H5 **Brösarp** Sweden
242 A3 **Brosna** *watercourse* Ireland
228 D4 **Brossac** France
234 C3 **Broșteni** Romania
228 E2 **Brou** France
228 D3 **Brouage** France
244 E1 **Brough Head** *cape* Scotland UK
244 F2 **Brough Ness** *cape* Scotland UK
240 E1 **Broughton** Flintshire Wales UK
242 F3 **Broughton** Lancashire England UK
423 7 **Broughton Island** Snares Islands New Zealand
227 I2 **Broumov** Czech Republic
118 M7 **Brouse** British Columbia Canada
237 AF9 **Broutona, Ostrov** *island* Kuril Islands
241 I2 **Brown Street** Suffolk England UK
119 P6 **Brownfield** Alberta Canada
129 K4 **Brownfield** Texas USA
241 F2 **Brownhills** West Midlands England UK
125 J2 **Browning** Montana USA
118 L2 **Brownings Landing** Northwest Territories Canada
127 K2 **Brownrigg** Ontario Canada
127 H2 **Brownstown** Indiana USA
130 G3 **Brownsville** Tennessee USA
130 C8 **Brownsville** Texas USA
130 B3 **Brownwood** Texas USA
130 B5 **Brownwood, Lake** Texas USA
78 I9 **Browse Basin** *underwater feature* Indian Ocean
243 H2 **Broxa** North Yorkshire England UK
244 E5 **Broxburn** West Lothian Scotland UK
131 J5 **Broxton** Georgia USA
241 H3 **Broyle Side** East Sussex England UK
230 C4 **Brozas** Spain
234 A3 **Brštica** Serbia
232 F2 **Brtnice** Czech Republic
224 C3 **Bru** Norway
228 F1 **Bruay-la-Bussière** France
119 O6 **Bruce** Alberta Canada
130 G4 **Bruce** Mississippi USA
126 F4 **Bruce** Wisconsin USA
423 C6 **Bruce Bay** New Zealand
126 G3 **Bruce Crossing** Michigan USA
127 K4 **Bruce Peninsula** Ontario Canada
424 F7 **Bruce Rock** WA Australia
229 H2 **Bruche** *watercourse* France
226 E3 **Bruchsal** Germany
226 D2 **Brück** Germany
232 F3 **Bruck an der Mur** Austria
233 F8 **Brucoli** Italy
240 E3 **Brue** *watercourse* England UK
244 B2 **Brue** Na h-Eileanan Siar Scotland UK
228 F1 **Brugge** Belgium
226 D2 **Brühl** Germany
222 H5 **Bruksvallarna** Sweden
126 F3 **Brule** Wisconsin USA
118 M6 **Brûlé** Alberta Canada
122 G6 **Brûlé, Lac** *lake* Québec Canada
228 D3 **Brûlon** France
157 D6 **Brumado** Brazil
229 H2 **Brumath** France
226 F1 **Brunau** Germany
131 I5 **Brundidge** Alabama USA
124 H5 **Bruneau** *watercourse* Idaho USA
375 G2 **Brunei** *country* Asia
375 G2 **Brunei Bay** Brunei/Malaysia
123 K9 **Brunette Island** Newfoundland and Labrador Canada
226 F4 **Brunico** Italy
423 D6 **Brunner, Lake** New Zealand
131 K5 **Brunswick** Georgia USA
123 D11 **Brunswick** Maine USA
162 B5 **Brunswick, Península de** *peninsula* Chile
425 O7 **Brunswick Heads** NSW Australia
127 J2 **Brunswick Lake** Ontario Canada
436 W1 **Brunt Ice Shelf** Antarctica
232 G2 **Bruntál** Czech Republic
388 F4 **Brurynshyk** Kazakhstan
234 B4 **Brus** Serbia
227 H5 **Brušane** Croatia
125 N6 **Brush** Colorado USA
227 J3 **Brusno** Slovakia
238 F4 **Brusovo** Russian Federation
161 I3 **Brusque** Brazil
Brussels *see* **Bruxelles** Belgium
234 C2 **Brusturi** Romania
240 E3 **Bruton** Somerset England UK
226 C2 **Bruxelles (Brussels)** Belgium
228 D2 **Bruz** France
233 G7 **Bruzzano, Capo** *cape* Italy
126 I6 **Bryan** Ohio USA
130 C5 **Bryan** Texas USA
436 S2 **Bryan Coast** Antarctica
394 F3 **Bryanka** Ukraine
238 F6 **Bryansk** Russian Federation
388 E5 **Bryansk** Russian Federation
394 E2 **Bryansk** Russian Federation
394 E2 **Bryanskaya Oblast'** *admin. area* Russian Federation
Bryanskoye *see* **Bryansk** Russian Federation
130 E2 **Bryant** *watercourse* Missouri USA
436 U2 **Bryant, Cape** Antarctica
128 F2 **Bryce Canyon National Park** Utah USA
224 C2 **Bryggja** Norway
240 A5 **Bryher** *island* England UK
385 I2 **Bryka** Russian Federation
238 F5 **Bryn'** Russian Federation
240 C2 **Bryn-crug** Gwynedd Wales UK
240 D3 **Brynamman** Carmarthenshire Wales UK
240 C2 **Brynkir** Gwynedd Wales UK
240 D3 **Brynna** Rhondda Cynon Taff Wales UK
240 D3 **Brynsadler** Rhondda Cynon Taff Wales UK
242 D3 **Brynteg** Isle of Anglesey Wales UK
234 B3 **Brzan** Serbia
234 B4 **Brzeće** Serbia
227 I2 **Brzeg** Poland
232 H2 **Brzeszcze** Poland
227 K3 **Brzezie** Poland
227 I1 **Brzeźno** Poland
227 J1 **Brzozie** Poland
391 I4 **Bū Rang** Iran
383 H3 **Bu'erjin** Xinjiang Uygur Zizhiqu China
373 I5 **Bua** Fiji
376 D4 **Bua Yai** Thailand
307 G3 **Bu'aale** Somalia
244 D4 **Buachaille Etive Mòr-Stob Dearg** *mountain* Scotland UK
304 D3 **Buaka** Ghana
426 8 **Buala** Solomon Islands
244 B3 **Bualintur** Highland Scotland UK
372 B5 **Buapinang** Indonesia
426 1b **Buariki** *island* Kiribati
374 D3 **Buatan** Indonesia
301 J2 **Bu'ayrat al Hasūn** Libya
304 B2 **Buba** Guinea-Bissau
304 A2 **Bubaque** Guinea-Bissau
308 F4 **Bubi** *watercourse* Zimbabwe
225 L5 **Bubiai** Lithuania
390 F5 **Būbiyān, Jazirat** *island* Kuwait
238 B5 **Bubny** Belarus
373 I5 **Bubu** Papua New Guinea
307 F5 **Bubu** *watercourse* Tanzania
243 H3 **Bubwith** East Riding of Yorkshire England UK
235 G7 **Bucak** Turkey
154 C3 **Bucaramanga** Colombia
424 G3 **Buccaneer Archipelago** WA Australia
163 2 **Buccaneer Point** Isla de Providencia
234 D1 **Buchach** Ukraine
244 E4 **Buchal** Perth and Kinross Scotland UK
117 L4 **Buchan Gulf** Nunavut Canada
127 L8 **Buchanan** Virginia USA
130 B5 **Buchanan, Lake** Texas USA
437 J2 **Buchanan Bay** Antarctica
123 J8 **Buchans** Newfoundland and Labrador Canada
Bucharest *see* **București** Romania
232 C3 **Buchs** Switzerland
232 B2 **Buchy** France
232 D5 **Bucine** Italy
235 C5 **Bučište** Macedonia
234 C2 **Buciumi** Romania
119 N6 **Buck Lake** Alberta Canada
243 F2 **Buckden** North Yorkshire England UK
128 F4 **Buckeye** Arizona USA
240 D4 **Buckfastleigh** Devon England UK
244 E4 **Buckhaven** Fife Scotland UK
129 H4 **Buckhorn** New Mexico USA
131 J2 **Buckhorn Lake** Kentucky USA
127 N4 **Buckingham** Québec Canada
241 G3 **Buckingham** Buckinghamshire England UK
241 G3 **Buckinghamshire** *admin. area* England UK
116 C5 **Buckland** Alaska USA
437 K2 **Buckle Island** Antarctica
240 D1 **Buckley** Flintshire Wales UK
126 I4 **Buckley** Michigan USA
437 J2 **Buckley Bay** Antarctica
125 P8 **Bucklin** Kansas USA
241 G2 **Buckminster** Leicester England UK
241 F3 **Bucknell** Oxfordshire England UK
124 F7 **Bucks Lake** California USA
306 A4 **Buco Zau** Angola
234 D3 **Bucșani** Romania
234 E3 **Bucu** Romania
234 E3 **București (Bucharest)** Romania
126 J6 **Bucyrus** Ohio USA
222 E5 **Bud** Norway
238 F6 **Buda** Russian Federation
379 H4 **Budalin** Myanmar
234 D1 **Budaniv** Ukraine
232 H3 **Budaörs** Hungary
234 A2 **Budapest** Hungary
232 H3 **Budapest** *admin. area* Hungary
222 inset **Búðardalur** Iceland
234 G2 **Budats'kyy Lyman** *lake* Ukraine
392 E5 **Budaun** Uttar Pradesh India
437 H2 **Budd Coast** Antarctica
307 G2 **Buddi** Ethiopia
244 F4 **Buddon Ness** *cape* Scotland UK
233 C6 **Buddusò** Sardinia Italy
240 C4 **Bude** Cornwall England UK
130 F5 **Bude** Mississippi USA
240 C4 **Bude Bay** England UK
226 C2 **Budel** Netherlands
373 J6 **Budelun Island** Papua New Guinea
234 C3 **Budești** Romania
162 B2 **Budi, Lago del** *lake* Chile
372 E4 **Budidi** *watercourse* Indonesia
238 D6 **Budino** Belarus
222 inset **Búðir** Iceland
240 D4 **Budleigh Salterton** Devon England UK
225 Q3 **Budogoshch'** Russian Federation
232 D4 **Budrio** Italy
225 K5 **Budry** Poland
238 B5 **Budslav** Belarus
233 H5 **Budva** Montenegro
Budweis *see* **České Budějovice** Czech Republic
227 J2 **Budziszewice** Poland
305 F4 **Buéa** Cameroon
229 G4 **Buëch** *watercourse* France
128 B3 **Buellton** California USA
233 C6 **Buemarino, Grotta del** Sardinia Italy
162 C3 **Buen Pasto** Argentina
162 C5 **Buen Tiempo, Cabo** *cape* Argentina
127 N7 **Buena** New Jersey USA
160 E5 **Buena Esperanza** Argentina
158 E4 **Buena Hora** Bolivia
163 1b **Buena Vista** Netherlands Antilles
158 C2 **Buena Vista** Peru
134 E2 **Buena Vista, Bahía de** *bay* Cuba
128 C3 **Buena Vista Lake Bed** California USA
160 D2 **Buenaventura** Chile
154 B4 **Buenaventura** Colombia
132 D3 **Buenavista** Mexico
310 3a **Buenavista del Norte** Canary Islands
230 E3 **Buendia, Embalse de** *lake* Spain
161 J2 **Buenos Brandão** Brazil
161 G5 **Buenos Aires** Argentina
162 E1 **Buenos Aires** *admin. area* Argentina
134 D5 **Buenos Aires** Costa Rica
158 B2 **Buenos Aires** Peru
162 B4 **Buenos Aires, Lago** *lake* Argentina
163 9 **Buenos Ayres** Trinidad and Tobago
157 E6 **Buerarema** Brazil
122 E1 **Buerger Point** Nunavut Canada
132 D3 **Búfalo** Mexico
373 F4 **Bufareh** Indonesia
119 P7 **Buffalo** Alberta Canada
119 N2 **Buffalo** *watercourse* Northwest Territories Canada
130 D2 **Buffalo** Kansas USA
126 E8 **Buffalo** Missouri USA
127 L5 **Buffalo** New York USA
125 P8 **Buffalo** Oklahoma USA
125 N4 **Buffalo** South Dakota USA
130 C5 **Buffalo** Texas USA
127 K7 **Buffalo** West Virginia USA
125 L4 **Buffalo** Wyoming USA
125 K4 **Buffalo Bill Reservoir** Wyoming USA
125 N5 **Buffalo Gap** South Dakota USA
130 B4 **Buffalo Gap** Texas USA
119 M4 **Buffalo Head Hills** Alberta Canada
119 O6 **Buffalo Lake** Alberta Canada
116 H6 **Buffalo Lake** Northwest Territories Canada
129 K3 **Buffalo Lake** Texas USA
119 N2 **Buffalo River** Northwest Territories Canada
131 J3 **Buford** Georgia USA
227 K1 **Bug** *watercourse* Poland
154 B4 **Buga** Colombia
234 A2 **Bugac** Hungary
307 E4 **Bugala Island** Uganda
377 I5 **Bugasong** Philippines
383 J3 **Bugat** Mongolia
384 E2 **Bugat** Mongolia
388 G6 **Bugdayly** Turkmenistan
234 E3 **Bugeac, Lacul** *lake* Romania
310 2 **Bugio, Ilhéu do** *island* Madeira
232 G4 **Bugojno** Bosnia and Herzegovina
237 W6 **Bugorkan** Russian Federation
236 K5 **Bugrino** Russian Federation
375 H1 **Bugsuk** *island* Philippines
372 F4 **Buguba** Indonesia
393 F7 **Buguda** Orissa India
377 I4 **Bugui Point** Philippines
388 F2 **Buguruslan** Russian Federation
383 K5 **Buh He** *watercourse* Qinghai China
379 G3 **Buha** Arunachal Pradesh India
235 F7 **Buharkent** Turkey
390 E3 **Buḩayrat ar Razāzah** *lake* Iraq
390 E2 **Buḩayrat ath Tharthār** *lake* Iraq
394 F6 **Buhayrat Qattinah** *lake* Syria
383 I2 **Buhemuren** Mongolia
309 F3 **Buhera** Zimbabwe
226 E3 **Bühl** Germany
306 E4 **Buhoro** Tanzania
240 D2 **Builth Road** Powys Wales UK
156 E5 **Buíque** Brazil
385 I3 **Buir Nuur** *lake* Mongolia
308 C4 **Buitepos** Namibia
230 D5 **Bujalance** Spain
231 F3 **Bujaraloz** Spain
227 G5 **Buje** Croatia
306 D4 **Bujumbura** Burundi
373 G6 **Buk** Papua New Guinea
227 I1 **Buk** Poland
232 G3 **Bük** Hungary
383 I6 **Buka Daban** *mountain* Xinjiang Uygur Zizhiqu China
373 J5 **Buka Island** Papua New Guinea
385 H1 **Bukachacha** Russian Federation
308 D3 **Bukalo** Namibia
238 F6 **Bukan'** Russian Federation
388 E7 **Būkān** Iran
373 H5 **Bukaua** Papua New Guinea
306 D4 **Bukavu** Democratic Republic of Congo
Bukhara *see* **Buxoro** Uzbekistan
389 N4 **Bukhtarminskoye Vodokhranilishche** *lake* Kazakhstan
372 C3 **Bukide** *island* Indonesia
374 B3 **Bukit Batok** *admin. area* Singapore
376 D6 **Bukit Gajah Hutan** *mountain* Thailand
374 D2 **Bukit Mertajam** Malaysia
374 C3 **Bukit Panjang** *admin. area* Singapore
374 C3 **Bukit Timah** *admin. area* Singapore
374 C3 **Bukit Timah** *mountain* Singapore
374 D4 **Bukittinggi** Indonesia
306 E4 **Bukoba** Tanzania
227 J3 **Bukovec** Czech Republic
224 I5 **Bukowo, Jezioro** *bay* Poland
374 E4 **Buku, Tanjung** *cape* Indonesia
374 C5 **Bukum, Pulau** *island* Singapore
374 C5 **Bukum Kechil, Pulau** *island* Singapore
373 G6 **Bula** Papua New Guinea
229 I3 **Bülach** Switzerland
425 O8 **Bulahdelah** NSW Australia
384 G2 **Bulagansk** Russian Federation
373 F5 **Bulaka** *watercourse* Indonesia
389 N4 **Bulakty** Kazakhstan
377 I5 **Bulalacao** *island* Philippines
377 I4 **Bulan** Philippines
377 I6 **Bulan** *island* Philippines
308 E4 **Bulawayo** Zimbabwe
308 E4 **Bulawayo** *admin. area* Zimbabwe
389 K2 **Bulayevo** Kazakhstan
390 E2 **Bulayj** Iraq
305 I2 **Bulbul, Wadi** *watercourse* Sudan
241 G2 **Bulby** Lincolnshire England UK
235 F6 **Buldan** Turkey
235 F6 **Buldan Barajı** *lake* Turkey
393 D7 **Buldana** Maharashtra India
237 AK8 **Buldir Island** Alaska USA
304 D3 **Bulenga** Ghana
383 I3 **Bulgan** Mongolia
383 I3 **Bulgan** Mongolia
383 I3 **Bulgan** Mongolia
384 E3 **Bulgan** Mongolia
384 E4 **Bulgan** Mongolia
385 H3 **Bulgan** Mongolia
384 E2 **Bulgan** *admin. area* Mongolia
234 D4 **Bulgaria** *country* Europe
233 F6 **Bulgheria, Monte** *mountain* Italy
229 G2 **Bulgnéville** France
372 D3 **Buli** Indonesia
372 D3 **Buli, Teluk** *bay* Indonesia
375 H1 **Buliluyan, Cape** Philippines
118 H5 **Bulkley House** British Columbia Canada
118 G5 **Bulkley Ranges** British Columbia Canada
119 N8 **Bull** *watercourse* British Columbia Canada
242 B4 **Bull Ring** Ireland
124 G6 **Bull Run Reservoir** Nevada USA
130 E2 **Bull Shoals Lake** Arkansas USA
307 G1 **Bullaxaar** Somalia
163 1b **Bullenbaai** *bay* Netherlands Antilles
423 D5 **Buller** *watercourse* New Zealand
128 E3 **Bullhead City** Arizona USA
241 F3 **Bullington** Hampshire England UK
222 L4 **Bullmark** Sweden
425 L6 **Bulloo** *watercourse* Qld Australia
422 F5 **Bulls** New Zealand
131 L4 **Bulls Bay** South Carolina USA
131 J2 **Bulls Gap** Tennessee USA
308 C4 **Büllsport** Namibia
425 J3 **Bulman** NT Australia
118 K1 **Bulmer Lake** Northwest Territories Canada
383 K3 **Bulnai** Mongolia
383 K2 **Bulnay Uul** *mountain* Mongolia
160 C6 **Bulnes** Chile
373 H5 **Bulolo** Papua New Guinea
377 J6 **Buluan** Philippines
372 B5 **Bulubulu** Indonesia
372 B5 **Bulukumba** Indonesia
306 C3 **Bulukutu** Democratic Republic of Congo
306 B4 **Bulungu** Democratic Republic of Congo
377 J4 **Bulusan** Philippines
130 B6 **Bulverde** Texas USA
125 M1 **Bulyea** Saskatchewan Canada
306 B5 **Bumba** Democratic Republic of Congo
384 D3 **Bumbeger** Mongolia
306 E4 **Bumbire Island** Tanzania
128 F3 **Bumble Bee** Arizona USA
375 F5 **Bumiayu** Indonesia
307 F3 **Buna** Kenya
244 C4 **Bunavullin** Highland Scotland UK
377 J5 **Bunawan** Philippines
245 D1 **Bunbeg** Ireland
424 E8 **Bunbury** WA Australia
240 E1 **Bunbury** Cheshire England UK
154 A4 **Bunche** Ecuador
245 F4 **Bunclody** Ireland
245 E1 **Buncrana** Ireland
307 E4 **Bunda** Tanzania
425 O6 **Bundaberg** Qld Australia
425 J5 **Bundey** *watercourse* NT Australia
392 D6 **Bundi** Rajasthan India
245 D2 **Bundoran** Ireland
392 F6 **Bundu** Jharkhand India
306 C3 **Bunduki** Democratic Republic of Congo
244 B4 **Bunessan** Highland Scotland UK
305 F2 **Bunga** *watercourse* Nigeria
374 C4 **Bungalaut, Selat** *strait* Indonesia
241 I2 **Bungay** Suffolk England UK
437 G2 **Bunger Hills** *mountain* Antarctica
372 B4 **Bunginkela** *island* Indonesia
372 B4 **Bungku** Indonesia
242 B3 **Bunglass** Ireland
306 B5 **Bungo** Angola
386 G5 **Bungo-suidō** *strait* Japan
307 E3 **Bungoma** Kenya
245 C3 **Bungowla** Ireland
305 F2 **Bungudu** Nigeria
306 E3 **Bunia** Democratic Republic of Congo
424 F7 **Bunjil** WA Australia
129 M1 **Bunker Hill** Kansas USA
306 D6 **Bunkeya** Democratic Republic of Congo
245 E4 **Bunlacken** Ireland
131 K6 **Bunnell** Florida USA
422 F5 **Bunnythorpe** New Zealand
231 F4 **Buñol** Spain
234 C2 **Bunteşti** Romania
375 G4 **Buntok** Indonesia
375 G4 **Buntokecil** Indonesia
375 H3 **Bunyu** *island* Indonesia
223 N2 **Buollannjar'ga** Norway
376 F4 **Buôn Hồ** Vietnam
376 F4 **Buôn Ma Thuột** Vietnam
376 D2 **Buon Nao** Laos
376 D2 **Buon Tai** Laos
237 AB4 **Buor-Khaya, Guba** *bay* Russian Federation
237 AB4 **Buor-Khaya, Mys** *cape* Russian Federation
237 AA6 **Buotama** *watercourse* Russian Federation
373 G5 **Bupul** Indonesia
302 E2 **Būr Safājah** Egypt
302 E1 **Būr Sa'īd (Port Said)** Egypt
Bur Sudan *see* **Port Sudan** Sudan
307 F4 **Bura** Kenya
389 K4 **Buralkenyn-tuz** *lake* Kazakhstan
390 E4 **Buraydah** Saudi Arabia
127 M3 **Burbidge** Québec Canada
388 I6 **Burdalyk** Turkmenistan
119 P8 **Burdett** Alberta Canada
125 P7 **Burdett** Kansas USA
394 D6 **Burdur** *admin. area* Turkey
394 D6 **Burdur Gölü** *lake* Turkey
222 J4 **Bure** Sweden
241 I2 **Bure** *watercourse* England UK
307 F1 **Burē** Ethiopia
222 L4 **Bureå** Sweden
237 AB8 **Bureinskiy Khrebet** *range* Russian Federation
230 C2 **Burela** Spain
230 C2 **Burela, Cabo** *cape* Spain
384 D2 **Buren Togtokh Uul** *mountain* Mongolia
384 G3 **Burenhaan** Mongolia
384 E3 **Burenhangai** Mongolia
385 L2 **Bureya** Russian Federation
385 L2 **Bureya** *watercourse* Russian Federation
223 M2 **Burfjord** Norway
127 K5 **Burford** Ontario Canada
224 F5 **Burg** Germany
244 B4 **Burg** Highland Scotland UK
234 E4 **Burgas** Bulgaria
234 E4 **Burgas** *admin. area* Bulgaria
226 F3 **Burgau** Germany
229 H3 **Burgdorf** Switzerland
232 G3 **Burgenland** *admin. area* Austria
123 J9 **Burgeo** Newfoundland and Labrador Canada
308 E6 **Burgersdorp** South Africa
127 M8 **Burgess** Virginia USA
241 G4 **Burgess Hill** West Sussex England UK
243 I3 **Burgh le Marsh** Lincolnshire England UK
244 E3 **Burghead Bay** Scotland UK
233 E8 **Burgio** Italy
226 G3 **Burglengenfeld** Germany
230 D5 **Burgo** Spain
230 E3 **Burgomillodo, Embalse de** *lake* Spain
130 B8 **Burgos** Mexico
230 E2 **Burgos** Spain

226 E2 Burgsinn Germany
224 J4 Burgsvik Sweden
383 J3 Burhan Buubay Uul mountain Mongolia
393 D7 Burhanpur Madhya Pradesh India
226 E1 Burhave Germany
157 B8 Buri Brazil
391 J3 Buri Afghanistan
374 D4 Buriai Indonesia
377 I4 Burias island Philippines
134 D6 Burica, Punta cape Panama
306 E4 Burigi, Lake Tanzania
123 K9 Burin Peninsula Newfoundland and Labrador Canada
157 B8 Buritama Brazil
159 H5 Buriti Brazil
156 C5 Buriti, Cachoeira do watercourse Brazil
157 B7 Buriti Alegre Brazil
156 D4 Buriti Bravo Brazil
157 C6 Buritis Brazil
157 C7 Buritizeiro Brazil
231 F4 Burjassot Spain
234 C3 Burjuc Romania
130 B3 Burkburnett Texas USA
425 L4 Burke and Wills Roadhouse Qld Australia
436 Q2 Burke Island Antarctica
423 D7 Burkes Pass New Zealand
425 K4 Burketown Qld Australia
301 F6 Burkina Faso country Africa
389 K3 Burkitti mountain Kazakhstan
228 D5 Burlada Spain
232 C2 Burladingen Germany
130 C4 Burleson Texas USA
124 I5 Burley Idaho USA
125 N7 Burlington Colorado USA
126 F6 Burlington Iowa USA
125 Q2 Burlington North Dakota USA
125 K4 Burlington Wyoming USA
389 M2 Burlinskoye, Ozero lake Russian Federation
389 K2 Burlukol' lake Kazakhstan
Burma see Myanmar
236 N6 Burmantovo Russian Federation
241 F2 Burmington Warwickshire England UK
243 H3 Burnby East Riding of Yorkshire England UK
242 F2 Burneside Cumbria England UK
130 B5 Burnet Texas USA
423 E6 Burnham New Zealand
240 E3 Burnham-on-Sea Somerset England UK
425 M10 Burnie Tas. Australia
243 H2 Burniston North Yorkshire England UK
243 F3 Burnley Lancashire England UK
244 F5 Burnmouth Scottish Borders Scotland UK
125 Q7 Burns Kansas USA
124 F5 Burns Oregon USA
118 I5 Burns Lake British Columbia Canada
116 H5 Burnside watercourse Nunavut Canada
126 E4 Burnsville Minnesota USA
123 I9 Burnt Islands Newfoundland and Labrador Canada
425 inset Burnt Pine Norfolk Island Australia
120 E5 Burntwood watercourse Manitoba Canada
241 F2 Burntwood Staffordshire England UK
120 E5 Burntwood Lake Manitoba Canada
222 K1 Burøysund Norway
425 K8 Burra SA Australia
244 inset Burrafirth Shetland Scotland UK
244 inset Burravoe Shetland Scotland UK
244 F2 Burray island Scotland UK
235 B5 Burrel Albania
244 E4 Burrelton Perth and Kinross Scotland UK
245 F2 Burren Newry and Mourne Northern Ireland UK
231 F4 Burriana Spain
240 D4 Burrington Devon England UK
132 E2 Burro, Serranías del range Mexico
222 D2 Burrow Head cape Scotland UK
240 C3 Burry Port Carmarthenshire Wales UK
394 D5 Bursa admin. area Turkey
242 F3 Burscough Bridge Lancashire England UK
234 D1 Burshtyn Ukraine
125 K1 Burstall Saskatchewan Canada
126 I4 Burt Lake Michigan USA
233 H5 Burtaiši Montenegro
118 M8 Burton British Columbia Canada
126 J5 Burton Michigan USA
130 C5 Burton Texas USA
117 L8 Burton, Lac lake Québec Canada
131 J3 Burton, Lake Georgia USA
240 E4 Burton Bradstock Dorset England UK
241 G2 Burton Lazars Leicester England UK
241 F2 Burton upon Trent Staffordshire England UK
222 L4 Burträsk Sweden
222 L4 Burträsket lake Sweden
372 C4 Buru island Indonesia
306 D4 Burundi country Africa
306 D4 Bururi Burundi
241 H4 Burwash East Sussex England UK
125 P6 Burwell Nebraska USA
241 G4 Bury West Sussex England UK
241 H2 Bury St Edmunds Suffolk England UK
394 E2 Buryn Ukraine
227 J2 Burzenin Poland
306 D5 Busai Saudi Arabia
306 D6 Busanga Democratic Republic of Congo
226 D5 Busca Italy
226 F4 Busche Italy
241 F3 Buscot Oxfordshire England UK
242 B1 Bush watercourse Northern Ireland UK
390 G3 Būshehr admin. area Iran
306 E4 Bushenyi Uganda
131 J6 Bushnell Florida USA
374 B5 Busing, Pulau island Singapore
306 C3 Businga Democratic Republic of Congo
306 B4 Busira watercourse Democratic Republic of Congo
224 G2 Busjön lake Sweden
227 M3 Bus'k Ukraine
224 E2 Buskerud admin. area Norway
244 F5 Buskin Scottish Borders Scotland UK
232 F5 Buško Jezero lake Bosnia and Herzegovina
226 D4 Bussang France
424 E8 Busselton WA Australia
306 D2 Busseri watercourse Sudan
226 F5 Busseto Italy
237 AF9 Bussol', Proliv strait Kuril Islands
387 K1 Bussol', Proliv lake Russian Federation
232 B4 Bussoleno Italy
237 AD4 Bustakh, Ozero lake Russian Federation
132 E3 Bustamante Mexico
132 D2 Bustillos, Laguna lake Mexico
306 C3 Busu-Djanoa Democratic Republic of Congo
306 C3 Busu-Mogbula Democratic Republic of Congo
224 E5 Büsum Germany
306 C3 Buta Democratic Republic of Congo
160 D6 Buta Ranquil Argentina
306 D1 Butat Raya lake Sudan
244 C5 Bute island Scotland UK
244 C5 Bute, Sound of bay Scotland UK
307 F3 Bute Giarti Ethiopia
118 G6 Butedale British Columbia Canada
306 D3 Butembo Democratic Republic of Congo
233 F8 Butera Italy
379 G5 Buthidaung Myanmar
161 I4 Butiá Brazil
306 E3 Butiaba Uganda
130 G4 Butler Alabama USA
131 I4 Butler Georgia USA
127 L6 Butler Pennsylvania USA
245 E2 Butlers Bridge Ireland
241 I2 Butley Suffolk England UK
372 B5 Buton island Indonesia
372 B5 Buton, Selat strait Indonesia
232 D4 Buttapietra Italy
124 I4 Butte Montana USA
124 E6 Butte Lake California USA
242 E2 Buttermere Cumbria England UK
243 H2 Butterwick North Yorkshire England UK
374 D2 Butterworth Malaysia
308 E6 Butterworth South Africa
245 D4 Buttevant Ireland
240 D2 Buttington Powys Wales UK
229 I1 Buttlar Germany
119 V5 Button Manitoba Canada
122 F2 Button Islands Nunavut Canada
377 J5 Butuan Philippines
377 J5 Butuan Bay Philippines
388 C3 Buturlinovka Russian Federation
392 F5 Butwal Nepal
229 I1 Butzbach Germany
377 I6 Buug Philippines
307 H2 Buuhoodle Somalia
307 H3 Buulobarde Somalia
383 J3 Buur Nuur lake Mongolia
307 G3 Buurhabaka Somalia
383 K3 Buutsagaan Mongolia
222 I2 Buvåg Norway
222 G5 Buvika Norway
388 I6 Buxoro admin. area Uzbekistan
388 I6 Buxoro (Bukhara) Uzbekistan
243 G3 Buxton Derbyshire England UK
383 I3 Buyant Mongolia
383 I3 Buyant Mongolia
384 G4 Buyant-Uhaa Mongolia
388 E5 Buynaksk Russian Federation
304 C3 Buyo Côte d'Ivoire
304 C3 Buyo, Lac de lake Côte d'Ivoire
235 E7 Büyük Menderes Nehri watercourse Turkey
235 F5 Büyükada Turkey
394 E6 Büyükoba Turkey
235 F6 Büyükorhan Turkey
385 J5 Buyun Shan mountain Liaoning China
234 D2 Buza Romania
234 E3 Buzău Romania
234 E3 Buzău admin. area Romania
234 E3 Buzău watercourse Romania
386 F5 Buzen Japan
232 E4 Buzet Croatia
309 F3 Buzi Mozambique
234 B3 Buziaş Romania
236 H6 Büzmeýin Turkmenistan
388 F3 Buzuluk Russian Federation
373 J6 Bwagaoia Papua New Guinea
306 E4 Bwanga Tanzania
304 A2 Bwiam Gambia
240 C3 Bwlchygroes Pembrokeshire Wales UK
238 C5 Byahoml' Belarus
238 C6 Byalynichy Belarus
116 I3 Byam Martin Island Nunavut Canada
394 D2 Byarezina watercourse Belarus
227 K2 Byczki Poland
222 H5 Bydalen Sweden
227 J1 Bydgoszcz Poland
238 B5 Byel'ki Belarus
225 M5 Byenyakoni Belarus
130 B3 Byers Texas USA
238 C5 Byeshankovichy Belarus
222 L4 Bygdeå Sweden
222 L4 Bygdeträsket lake Sweden
224 E2 Bygdin lake Norway
224 F2 Bygdsiljum Sweden
224 D3 Byglandsfjorden lake Norway
238 D6 Bykhaw Belarus
224 D3 Bykle Norway
388 E2 Bykovo Russian Federation
237 AA4 Bykovskiy Russian Federation
389 L4 Bylkyldak Kazakhstan
425 N8 Bylong NSW Australia
120 H3 Bylot Manitoba Canada
117 L4 Bylot Island Nunavut Canada
127 K4 Byng Inlet Ontario Canada
238 D6 Bynovo Belarus
237 Z4 Byraya-Tas, Vozvyshennost' range Russian Federation
437 K1 Byrd Glacier ice Antarctica
222 C2 Byrknesøy island Norway
243 F1 Byrness Northumberland England UK
131 J4 Byron Georgia USA
162 A4 Byron, Isla island Chile
125 P4 Byron, Lake South Dakota USA
425 O7 Byron Bay NSW Australia
163 7 Byron Sound Falkland Islands
237 U4 Byrranga, Gory range Russian Federation
224 F4 Byrum Denmark
224 I2 Bysjön bay Sweden
222 L4 Byske Sweden
222 L4 Byskeälven watercourse Sweden
389 N3 Bystryy Istok Russian Federation
237 AB5 Bytantay watercourse Russian Federation
225 O5 Bytcha Belarus
227 J2 Bytom Poland
238 F6 Bytosh' Russian Federation
237 AD6 Byuchenyakh Russian Federation
227 J3 Bzenica Slovakia

C

234 E3 C. A. Rosetti Romania
124 H5 C. J. Strike Reservoir Idaho USA
376 E3 Ca watercourse Vietnam
376 E5 Cà Mau Vietnam
374 E1 Cà Mau, Mũi cape Vietnam
376 E5 Ca Mau Peninsula cape Vietnam
378 E2 Ca Qu watercourse Xizang Zizhiqu China
161 G3 Caacupe Paraguay
161 H3 Caaguazú admin. area Paraguay
308 C2 Caala Angola
118 G6 Caamaño Sound British Columbia Canada
156 F4 Caaporá Brazil
161 G3 Caapucú Paraguay
161 H2 Caarapó Brazil
161 G3 Caazapá Paraguay
161 G3 Caazapá admin. area Paraguay
307 H2 Cabaad, Raas cape Somalia
377 I3 Cabagan Philippines
158 C4 Caballas, Bahía de bay Peru
132 D1 Caballo Reservoir New Mexico USA
154 B4 Caballos Colombia
240 D2 Caban Coch Reservoir Wales UK
135 F2 Cabañas, Punta cape Cuba
377 I4 Cabanatuan Philippines
232 F4 Čabar Croatia
135 F3 Cabaret Haiti
159 H5 Cabeceira Alta do Formoso Brazil
161 H2 Cabeceira do Apa Brazil
155 F6 Cabeceira do Salsa, Igarapé watercourse Brazil
310 1b Cabeço Gordo volcano Azores
156 F4 Cabedelo Brazil
232 C4 Cabella Ligure Italy
132 D2 Cabellos Mesteños, Llano de los plain Mexico
228 F5 Cabestany France
230 D4 Cabeza del Buey Spain
230 E4 Cabezuela, Embalse de la lake Spain
154 D2 Cabimas Venezuela
306 A5 Cabinda Angola
306 A4 Cabinda admin. area Angola
436 T2 Cabinet Inlet bay Antarctica
124 G2 Cabinet Mountains Idaho USA
377 I6 Cabingan island Philippines
156 F5 Cabo Brazil
162 D4 Cabo Blanco Argentina
160 H5 Cabo Colorado Uruguay
309 G2 Cabo Delgado admin. area Mozambique
157 D8 Cabo Frio Brazil
157 D8 Cabo Frio, Ilha do island Brazil
162 D3 Cabo Raso Argentina
117 L9 Cabonga, Réservoir Québec Canada
132 B2 Caborca Mexico
130 E3 Cabot Arkansas USA
122 F5 Cabot, Lac lake Québec Canada
122 G4 Cabot Lake Newfoundland and Labrador Canada
376 B6 Cabra island Andaman and Nicobar Islands India
230 D5 Cabra Spain
135 G3 Cabral Dominican Republic
159 G2 Cabras Brazil
233 C7 Cabras Sardinia Italy
231 H4 Cabrera island Spain
160 C6 Cabrero Chile
231 F4 Cabriel watercourse Spain
156 E5 Cabrobó Brazil
304 B2 Cabuco Guinea-Bissau
377 I3 Cabugao Philippines
377 I5 Cabulauan island Philippines
159 G2 Caburá Brazil
162 B2 Caburga, Lago lake Chile
230 C2 Cacabelos Spain
161 I3 Caçador Brazil
234 B4 Čačak Serbia
231 D5 Cacao Colombia
161 H4 Caçapava do Sul Brazil
233 G6 Caccia, Monte mountain Italy
161 H4 Cacequi Brazil
159 G5 Cáceres Brazil
154 C3 Cáceres Colombia
230 C4 Cáceres Spain
158 B2 Cachachi Peru
118 K7 Cache Creek British Columbia Canada
304 A2 Cacheau watercourse Guinea-Bissau
162 B4 Cachet, Cerro mountain Chile
304 A2 Cacheu Guinea-Bissau
160 E3 Cachi Argentina
160 E3 Cachi watercourse Argentina
159 H3 Cachimbo Brazil
159 H3 Cachimbo, Serra do range Brazil
306 C5 Cachimo Angola
308 C2 Cachingues Angola
159 H1 Cachoeira Brazil
159 I5 Cachoeira Alta Brazil
161 H4 Cachoeira do Sul Brazil
159 H2 Cachoeirinha Brazil
157 D8 Cachoeiro de Itapemirim Brazil
160 D3 Cachos, Punta cape Chile
304 A2 Cacine Guinea-Bissau
156 B2 Caciporé watercourse Brazil
156 B2 Caciporé, Cabo cape Brazil
159 F2 Cacoal Brazil
308 C2 Cacolo Angola
308 C2 Caconda Angola
306 A5 Cacongo Angola
154 C3 Cácota Colombia
129 L2 Cactus Texas USA
119 Q6 Cactus Lake Saskatchewan Canada
157 B7 Caçu Brazil
306 A5 Cacuaco Angola
308 C2 Cacuchi watercourse Angola
306 B5 Cacula Angola
157 D6 Caculé Brazil
157 B7 Cacuriã Brazil
308 C1 Cacuso Angola
307 G2 Cadaadley Somalia
307 H3 Cadale Somalia
244 E3 Cadboll Highland Scotland UK
232 H2 Čadca Slovakia
244 E4 Caddam Angus Scotland UK
130 C3 Caddo Oklahoma USA
130 D3 Caddo Lake Texas USA
130 E3 Caddo Valley Arkansas USA
132 B3 Cadejé Mexico
376 B4 Cadell Point Andaman and Nicobar Islands India
229 G5 Cadenet France
129 M8 Cadereyta Jiménez Mexico
228 E5 Cadí, Serra del range Spain
230 E5 Cádiar Spain
127 L2 Cadillac Québec Canada
228 D4 Cadillac France
126 I4 Cadillac Michigan USA
377 I5 Cadiz Philippines
230 C5 Cádiz Spain
130 H2 Cadiz Kentucky USA
127 K6 Cadiz Ohio USA
128 E3 Cadiz Lake California USA
241 F3 Cadley Wiltshire England UK
425 J6 Cadney Park SA Australia
118 M6 Cadomin Alberta Canada
119 M4 Cadotte watercourse Alberta Canada
119 M4 Cadotte Lake Alberta Canada
228 D2 Caen France
222 E2 Caër France
240 E3 Caerleon Newport Wales UK
240 C1 Caernarfon Gwynedd Wales UK
240 C1 Caernarfon Bay Wales UK
240 D3 Caerphilly admin. area Wales UK
240 D2 Caersws Powys Wales UK
240 C2 Caerwedros Ceredigion Wales UK
158 D3 Caete watercourse Brazil
156 C3 Caeté, Baía do bay Brazil
156 E5 Caetés Brazil
157 D6 Caetité Brazil
157 D5 Cafarnaum Brazil
160 E3 Cafayate Argentina
159 H5 Café, Serra do range Brazil
157 B8 Cafelândia Brazil
159 H5 Cafêzal, Serra do range Brazil
155 G4 Cafuini watercourse Brazil
377 J3 Cagayan watercourse Philippines
377 J5 Cagayan de Oro Philippines
377 I5 Cagayan Islands Philippines
232 E5 Cagli Italy
233 C7 Cagliari Italy
233 C7 Cagliari, Golfo di bay Sardinia Italy
229 H5 Cagnes-sur-Mer France
154 C4 Caguan watercourse Colombia
135 H3 Caguas Puerto Rico
308 B3 Cahama Angola
245 B3 Caher Island Ireland
245 D3 Caheradrine Ireland
245 B4 Caherbullig Ireland
245 E4 Cahir Ireland
309 F3 Cahora Bassa, Lago de lake Mozambique
309 F3 Cahora Bassa Dam Mozambique
240 A2 Cahore Point Ireland
228 E4 Cahors France
134 D5 Cahuita Costa Rica
134 D5 Cahuita, Punta cape Costa Rica
376 E2 Cái Bầu, Đao island Vietnam
376 E2 Cái Chiên, Đao island Vietnam
230 C4 Caia Portugal
230 C4 Caia, Barragem do lake Portugal
159 G3 Caiabis, Serra dos range Brazil
308 D2 Caianda Angola
234 C2 Căianu Mic Romania
157 B7 Caiapó watercourse Brazil
159 H5 Caiapó, Serra range Brazil
157 B7 Caiapônia Brazil
156 E4 Caicó Brazil
135 G2 Caicos Islands Turks and Caicos Islands
135 F2 Caicos Passage channel Caribbean
424 H8 Caiguna WA Australia
222 K2 Caihnavarre island Norway
163 I3 Caille, Pointe de cape St Lucia
121 P6 Caillet watercourse Québec Canada
130 F6 Caillou Bay Louisiana USA
163 2 Caimán, Punta del cape Isla de Providencia
132 D4 Caimanero, Laguna del lake Mexico
234 F1 Căinarii Vechi Moldova
308 B3 Cainde Angola
234 D3 Căineni Romania
128 G1 Caineville Utah USA
240 D2 Caio Carmarthenshire Wales UK
436 W1 Caird Coast Antarctica
244 D5 Cairnderry Dumfries and Galloway Scotland UK
244 D4 Cairndow Argyll and Bute Scotland UK
244 C6 Cairnryan Dumfries and Galloway Scotland UK
425 M4 Cairns Qld Australia
120 H7 Cairns Lake Ontario Canada
244 E4 Cairnston Stirling Scotland UK
131 I5 Cairo Georgia USA
125 P6 Cairo Nebraska USA
126 I6 Cairo Ohio USA
159 E2 Cairu Brazil
241 I2 Caister-on-Sea Norfolk England UK
243 H3 Caistor Lincolnshire England UK
308 B2 Caitou Angola
308 C3 Caiundo Angola
234 E2 Căiuţi Romania
381 I2 Caiyuan Zhejiang China
158 B2 Cajabamba Peru
157 C8 Cajamar Brazil
158 B2 Cajamarca Peru
158 B2 Cajamarca admin. area Peru
157 B9 Cajati Brazil
154 C5 Cajón Colombia
128 D3 Cajon Junction California USA
129 J5 Cajoncitos Mexico
133 F5 Cajones watercourse Mexico
156 D3 Caju, Ilha do island Brazil
156 E5 Cajueiro Brazil
129 H6 Cajurichic Mexico
157 C8 Cajuru Brazil
235 F7 Çakmak Turkey
235 F6 Çal Turkey
230 C5 Cala Spain
230 C5 Cala, Embalse de lake Spain
231 H4 Cala Figuera, Cap de cape Spain
233 C7 Cala Piombo, Punta di cape Sardinia Italy
305 F4 Calabar Nigeria
154 E2 Calabozo Venezuela
233 F7 Calabria admin. area Italy
230 D5 Calaburra, Punta de cape Spain
231 G3 Calaceite Spain
158 C4 Calachane Peru
158 D5 Calacoto Bolivia
229 I5 Calacuccia Corsica France
234 C4 Calafat Romania
377 I4 Calagua Islands Philippines
230 E5 Calahonda Spain
230 F2 Calahorra Spain
308 C3 Calai Angola
241 I4 Calais France
160 E3 Calalaste, Sierra de range Argentina
160 D2 Calama Chile
128 E6 Calamajué Mexico
154 C4 Calamar Colombia
154 C3 Calambre, Cerros de mountains Colombia
377 H4 Calamian Group island Philippines
231 F3 Calamocha Spain
230 C4 Calamonte Spain
158 D5 Calana Peru
155 E5 Calanaque Brazil
230 C5 Calañas Spain
231 F3 Calanda Spain
377 I5 Calandagan island Philippines
306 B5 Calandula Angola
374 B2 Calang Indonesia
121 N1 Calanus Bay Nunavut Canada
377 I4 Calapan Philippines
234 E3 Călăraşi Romania
234 E3 Călăraşi admin. area Romania
230 F3 Calasparra Spain
230 F3 Calatayud Spain
160 D2 Calate Chile
231 F3 Calatorao Spain
230 E4 Calatrava, Campo de region Spain
233 F7 Calavà, Capo cape Italy
377 I4 Calavite, Cape Philippines
377 I3 Calayan island Philippines
377 J4 Calbayog Philippines
377 J5 Calbiga Philippines
162 B2 Calbuco Chile
158 D4 Calca Peru
130 E6 Calcasieu Lake Louisiana USA
162 C3 Calcatapul, Sierra range Argentina
154 A5 Calceta Ecuador
154 D2 Calceta Abajo Venezuela
160 F4 Calchaquí Argentina
155 I4 Calçoene Brazil
Calcutta see Kolkata India
154 C3 Caldas admin. area Colombia
230 B4 Caldas da Rainha Portugal
157 B7 Caldas Novas Brazil
159 E3 Caldeirão Brazil
244 E2 Calder, Loch lake Scotland UK
160 D3 Caldera Chile
243 G3 Calderdale admin. area England UK
133 H5 Calderitas Mexico
120 G7 Calders Dock Manitoba Canada
240 C3 Caldey Island Wales UK
240 E3 Caldicot Monmouthshire Wales UK
394 G5 Çaldıran Turkey
124 G5 Caldwell Idaho USA
242 B2 Caledon Dungannon Northern Ireland UK
310 3a Calera Canary Islands
130 H4 Calera Alabama USA
130 C4 Calera Oklahoma USA
135 F2 Caleta, Punta cape Cuba
162 B5 Caleta Clarencia Chile
162 B3 Caleta Condor Chile
160 D3 Caleta el Cobre Chile
162 C4 Caleta Olivia Argentina
162 B2 Caleufú Argentina
128 E4 Calexico California USA
242 D2 Calf of Man island Isle of Man UK
124 H1 Calgary Alberta Canada
245 D2 Calhaine Ireland
310 1b Calheta Azores
310 4a Calheta Cape Verde
310 2 Calheta Madeira
131 I3 Calhoun Georgia USA
130 G4 Calhoun City Mississippi USA
154 B4 Cali Colombia
244 B4 Caliach Highland Scotland UK
163 15 Calibishie Dominica
131 K4 Calibogue Sound South Carolina USA
377 J5 Calicoan island Philippines
124 H8 Caliente Nevada USA
163 9 California Trinidad and Tobago
115 California admin. area USA
132 B2 California, Golfo de bay Mexico
128 C3 California Aqueduct California USA
128 D3 California City California USA
231 G3 Cālig Spain
234 E2 Călineşti Moldova
128 D4 Calingasta Argentina
377 I4 Calintaan Philippines
128 E4 Calipatria California USA
228 C2 Callac France
131 K5 Callahan Florida USA
245 E4 Callan Ireland
244 D4 Callander Stirling Scotland UK
158 B4 Callao Peru
162 C4 Calle, Punta cape Argentina
134 B4 Callejones Honduras
163 11a Calliaqua St Vincent and the Grenadines
119 O5 Calling Lake Alberta Canada
240 C4 Callington Cornwall England UK
425 N6 Calliope Qld Australia
118 F3 Callison Ranch British Columbia Canada
241 E3 Calne Wiltshire England UK
234 C3 Călnic Romania
306 C5 Calonda Angola
231 H3 Calonge Spain
154 B4 Caloto Colombia
425 O6 Caloundra Qld Australia
120 M8 Calstock Ontario Canada
233 F8 Caltanissetta Italy
306 B5 Caluango Angola
308 C2 Calucinga Angola
308 D2 Calunda Angola
308 B2 Caluquembe Angola
303 I5 Caluula Somalia
377 I5 Caluya island Philippines
373 J6 Calvados Chain, The islands Papua New Guinea
130 C5 Calvert Texas USA
118 G7 Calvert Island British Columbia Canada
160 F5 Calvez Argentina
229 I5 Calvi Corsica France
231 H4 Calvià Spain
308 C6 Calvinia South Africa
226 F1 Calvörde Germany
226 E3 Calw Germany
241 H2 Cam watercourse England UK
376 E3 Cam Lộ Vietnam
376 E2 Cẩm Phả Vietnam
376 F5 Cam Rahn Vietnam
376 E3 Cẩm Xuyên Vietnam
306 B5 Camabatela Angola
157 E6 Camaçari Brazil
159 F4 Camacho Bolivia
161 I4 Camacho, Lagoa do lake Brazil
308 C2 Camacupa Angola
134 E2 Camagüey Cuba
134 E2 Camagüey admin. area Cuba
134 E2 Camagüey, Archipiélago de islands Cuba
374 D2 Camah, Gunung mountain Malaysia
155 I4 Camaipi Brazil
159 G2 Camaiu watercourse Brazil
235 G5 Çamalan Turkey
156 B3 Camaleão, Ilha island Brazil
157 E6 Camamu Brazil
158 C5 Camaná Peru
157 A7 Camapuã Brazil
161 I4 Camaquã Brazil
310 2 Câmara de Lobos Madeira
156 B3 Camaraipi watercourse Brazil
229 H5 Camarat, Cap cape France
230 D3 Camarena Spain
228 F5 Camarès France
228 B2 Camaret-sur-Mer France
230 F2 Camargo Spain
130 B2 Camargo Oklahoma USA
128 C3 Camarillo California USA
233 F8 Camarina bay Italy
129 L7 Camarón Mexico
134 C3 Camarón, Cabo cape Honduras
162 D3 Camarones Argentina
162 D3 Camarones, Bahía bay Argentina
240 C3 Camarthen Bay Wales UK
158 D4 Camata Bolivia
306 B5 Camaxilo Angola
230 B2 Cambados Spain
157 B8 Cambé Brazil
241 G3 Camberley Surrey England UK
228 D5 Cambo-les-Bains France
376 E4 Cambodia country
240 B4 Camborne Cornwall England UK
228 F1 Cambrai France
230 B2 Cambre Spain
128 B3 Cambria California USA
118 G5 Cambria Icefield British Columbia Canada
240 D2 Cambrian Mountains Wales UK
422 F3 Cambridge New Zealand
241 H2 Cambridge Cambridgeshire England UK
124 G4 Cambridge Idaho USA
127 M7 Cambridge Maryland USA
127 P5 Cambridge Massachusetts USA
126 E4 Cambridge Minnesota USA
116 I5 Cambridge Bay Nunavut Canada
241 H2 Cambridgeshire admin. area England UK
122 D4 Cambrien, Lac lake Québec Canada
306 C5 Cambulo Angola
308 C2 Cambundi-Catembo Angola
425 K3 Camburinga Village NT Australia
130 E4 Camden Arkansas USA
127 N7 Camden Maine USA
127 N5 Camden New York USA
131 K3 Camden South Carolina USA
116 E4 Camden Bay Alaska USA
163 11a Camden Park St Vincent and the Grenadines
116 I9 Camduff Saskatchewan Canada
308 D2 Cameia Angola
155 F3 Cameirán Venezuela
240 C4 Camelford Cornwall England UK
128 G3 Cameron Arizona USA
130 C5 Cameron Texas USA
127 K7 Cameron West Virginia USA
126 G2 Cameron Falls Ontario Canada
116 H6 Cameron Hills Northwest Territories Canada
117 I3 Cameron Island Nunavut Canada
126 I2 Cameron Lake Ontario Canada
423 B8 Cameron Mountains New Zealand
305 G3 Cameroon country Africa
305 F4 Cameroon, Mount Cameroon
233 F6 Camerota Italy
156 B3 Cametá Brazil
158 D5 Camiara Peru
377 I3 Camiguin island Philippines
131 I5 Camilla Georgia USA
128 B1 Camino California USA
159 F6 Camiri Bolivia
158 C3 Camisea watercourse Peru
306 C5 Camissombo Angola
134 C4 Camoapa Nicaragua
156 D3 Camocim Brazil
425 K4 Camooweal Qld Australia
155 H4 Camopi French Guiana
156 A2 Camopi watercourse French Guiana
376 B5 Camorta island Andaman and Nicobar Islands India
377 J5 Camotes Islands island Philippines
377 J5 Camotes Sea Philippines
131 I4 Camp Hill Alabama USA
128 G3 Camp Verde Arizona USA
130 A6 Camp Wood Texas USA
241 I4 Campagne-lès-Hesdin France
155 F4 Campamento El Gigante Brazil
159 F5 Campamento Rojas Bolivia
162 G5 Campana Argentina
162 A4 Campana, Isla island Chile
160 D6 Campana Mahuida Argentina
161 H2 Campanha Brazil
233 F6 Campania admin. area Italy
233 F6 Campano, Appennino range Italy
158 B1 Campanquiz, Cerro mountain Peru
230 D3 Campaspero Spain
125 Q3 Campbell Minnesota USA
423 F5 Campbell, Cape New Zealand
425 M6 Campbell, Mount Qld Australia
374 B2 Campbell Bay National Park India
9 Campbell Island New Zealand
124 F5 Campbell Lake Oregon USA
78 N12 Campbell Plateau underwater feature Pacific Ocean
124 C2 Campbell River British Columbia Canada
126 I8 Campbellsville Kentucky USA
123 E9 Campbellton New Brunswick Canada
425 N8 Campbelltown NSW Australia
133 H5 Campeche Mexico
134 B3 Campeche admin. area Mexico
163 16 Campêche Guadeloupe
134 A2 Campeche, Bahía de bay Mexico
76 I7 Campeche Bank underwater feature Gulf of Mexico
134 C2 Campechén, Laguna bay Mexico
134 E2 Campechuela Cuba
234 C2 Câmpeni Romania
119 U7 Camperville Manitoba Canada
234 C2 Câmpia Turzii Romania
230 B5 Campilhas, Barragem de lake Portugal
230 D5 Campillos Spain
155 G6 Campina Brazil
156 F4 Campina Grande Brazil
157 B7 Campina Verde Brazil
159 H4 Campinápolis Brazil
157 C8 Campinas Brazil
232 E5 Campli Italy
372 B6 Camplong Indonesia
305 F4 Campo Cameroon
231 G2 Campo Spain
125 N8 Campo Colorado USA
305 F4 Campo, Punto de cape Equatorial Guinea
156 E5 Campo Alegre Brazil
154 D3 Campo Alegre Colombia
157 C8 Campo Belo Brazil
230 D2 Campo de Caso Spain
157 A5 Campo de Diauarum Brazil
160 F3 Campo Gallo Argentina
132 D3 Campo Gobierno Mexico
229 I4 Campo Ligure Italy
156 D4 Campo Maior Brazil
230 C4 Campo Maior Portugal
157 A9 Campo Mourão Brazil
159 G4 Campo Novo do Parecis Brazil
154 C5 Campo Serio Peru
132 D2 Campo Setenta y Ocho Mexico
159 F6 Campo Triste Bolivia
157 A8 Campo Verde Brazil
154 C4 Campoalegre Colombia
233 F6 Campobasso Italy
123 E10 Campobello Island New Brunswick Canada
233 F8 Campolato, Capo cape Italy
157 D8 Campos Brazil
161 G2 Campos Paraguay
228 B5 Campos, Tierra de region Spain
157 C7 Campos Altos Brazil
157 C6 Campos Belos Brazil
161 H2 Campos Eliseos Brazil
156 D4 Campos Sales Brazil
158 C3 Campoverde Peru
234 C3 Câmpu lui Neag Romania
119 O6 Camrose Alberta Canada
119 Q3 Camsell Portage Saskatchewan Canada
235 F6 Çamsu Turkey
308 B2 Camucuio Angola
244 C3 Camusrory Highland Scotland UK
376 E5 Cần Thơ Vietnam
159 I3 Cana Brava do Norte Brazil
123 F10 Canaan watercourse New Brunswick Canada
163 9 Canaan Trinidad and Tobago
375 H1 Canabungan island Philippines
120 C5 Canada country North America
434 U1 Canada Abyssal Plain underwater feature Arctic Ocean
76 D2 Canada Basin underwater feature Arctic Ocean
123 J7 Canada Bay Newfoundland and Labrador Canada
160 F5 Cañada de Gómez Argentina
160 D4 Cañada Honda Argentina
129 J2 Canadian watercourse New Mexico USA
130 C3 Canadian watercourse Oklahoma USA
130 A3 Canadian Texas USA
116 I5 Canadian Shield region Canada
162 C5 Cañadón de las Vacas Argentina
162 C4 Cañadón Once de Septiembre Argentina
162 C4 Cañadón Seco Argentina
232 F4 Čanak Croatia
394 C5 Çanakkale admin. area Turkey
235 E5 Çanakkale Boğazı (Dardanelles) watercourse Turkey
119 N7 Canal Flats British Columbia Canada
160 D5 Canalejas Argentina
154 B2 Canalete Colombia
231 F4 Canals Spain
158 C2 Canamá Brazil
132 C2 Canamea Mexico
157 C9 Cananéia Brazil
154 B5 Cañar admin. area Ecuador
157 D5 Canarana Brazil
156 D3 Canárias, Baía das inlet Brazil
163 13 Canaries St Lucia
134 D2 Canarreos, Archipiélago de los islands Cuba
76 Q6 Canary Basin underwater feature Atlantic Ocean
134 C5 Cañas Costa Rica
127 N5 Canastota New York USA
161 J1 Canastra, Serra da range Brazil
132 D3 Canatlán Mexico
131 K6 Canaveral, Cape Florida USA

157 E6 **Canavieiras** Brazil
134 D5 **Cañazas** Panama
229 J3 **Canazei** Italy
425 N8 **Canberra** ACT Australia
162 B5 **Cancha Carrera** Argentina
159 G5 **Cancha Labrada** Paraguay
160 D3 **Canchas** Chile
228 E1 **Canche** *watercourse* France
228 E4 **Cancon** France
308 C2 **Canconga** Angola
133 I4 **Cancún** Mexico
235 E6 **Çandarlı** Turkey
228 D3 **Candé** France
159 F3 **Candeias** *watercourse* Brazil
132 E3 **Candela** *watercourse* Mexico
159 E3 **Candelaria** Bolivia
161 H4 **Candelária** Brazil
310 3a **Candelaria** Canary Islands
129 J5 **Candelaria** Texas USA
230 B2 **Candelaria, Punta** *cape* Spain
230 D3 **Candeleda** Spain
157 B9 **Cândido de Abreu** Brazil
156 C3 **Cândido Mendes** Brazil
226 D5 **Candiolo** Italy
119 S6 **Candle Lake** Saskatchewan Canada
125 P2 **Cando** North Dakota USA
377 I3 **Candon** Philippines
127 M5 **Candor** New York USA
155 H5 **Canea** Brazil
154 E2 **Caneio** Venezuela
160 D4 **Canela Baja** Chile
232 C5 **Canelle, Punta di** *cape* Corsica France
232 C4 **Canelli** Italy
161 G5 **Canelones** Uruguay
161 H5 **Canelones** *admin. area* Uruguay
154 B5 **Canelos** Ecuador
231 H2 **Canet-en-Roussillon** France
158 C4 **Canete** *watercourse* Peru
160 C6 **Cañete** Chile
230 F3 **Cañete** Spain
130 C3 **Caney** Oklahoma USA
126 D8 **Caney** *watercourse* Oklahoma USA
130 E4 **Caney Creek Reservoir** Louisiana USA
157 A7 **Cangalha** Brazil
308 C2 **Cangamba** Angola
308 C1 **Cangandala** Angola
230 B2 **Cangas** Spain
230 C2 **Cangas del Narcea** Spain
308 C2 **Cangoa** Angola
306 B5 **Cangola** Angola
308 C2 **Cangombe** Angola
300 D5 **Cangrâfa** Mauritania
160 E2 **Cangrejillos** Argentina
156 F4 **Canguaretama** Brazil
161 H4 **Canguçu** Brazil
308 C2 **Canguenjo, Serra** *range* Angola
380 C4 **Cangyuan** Yunnan China
385 H5 **Cangzhou** Hebei China
121 U5 **Caniapiscau** Québec Canada
122 D4 **Caniapiscau** *watercourse* Québec Canada
122 D5 **Caniapiscau, Réservoir de** Québec Canada
160 D6 **Cañicú** Chile
118 K7 **Canim Lake** British Columbia Canada
156 E4 **Canindé** Brazil
156 D4 **Canindé** *watercourse* Brazil
156 E5 **Canindé de São Francisco** Brazil
161 H3 **Canindeyú** *admin. area* Paraguay
377 I5 **Canipo** *island* Philippines
436 R2 **Canisteo Peninsula** Antarctica
245 D3 **Cankilly** Ireland
394 E5 **Çankiri** Turkey
394 E5 **Çankiri** *admin. area* Turkey
124 H1 **Canmore** Alberta Canada
425 N9 **Cann River** Vic. Australia
244 B3 **Canna** *island* Scotland UK
373 J6 **Cannac Island** Papua New Guinea
393 C9 **Cannanore Islands** Lakshadweep India
233 G6 **Canne** *ruin* Italy
233 C6 **Canneddi, Punta li** *cape* Sardinia Italy
229 H5 **Cannes** France
241 E2 **Cannock** Staffordshire England UK
124 D4 **Cannon Beach** Oregon USA
127 N5 **Cannonsville Reservoir** New York USA
154 C2 **Caño Blanco** Venezuela
154 D2 **Caño Hondo** Venezuela
154 C2 **Canoas, Punta** *cape* Colombia
161 I3 **Canõas, Rio das** *watercourse* Brazil
157 B9 **Canoinhas** Brazil
125 M7 **Canon City** Colorado USA
244 F5 **Canonbie** Dumfries and Galloway Scotland UK
160 F6 **Canónigo Gorriti** Argentina
310 7b **Canonniers Point** *cape* Mauritius
119 T7 **Canora** Saskatchewan Canada
155 F1 **Canouan** *island* St Vincent and the Grenadines
232 C4 **Canove** Italy
163 11 **Canowan** St Vincent and the Grenadines
162 C3 **Canquel** Argentina
158 D6 **Canquella** Bolivia
134 D5 **Canquintú** Panama
123 H10 **Canso** Nova Scotia Canada
123 H10 **Canso, Cape** Nova Scotia Canada
235 F5 **Çanta** Turkey
230 D2 **Cantabria** *admin. area* Spain
230 D2 **Cantabrica, Cordillera** *range* Spain
157 D8 **Cantagalo** Brazil
228 F4 **Cantal** *region* France
230 D3 **Cantalapiedra** Spain
230 E3 **Cantalejo** Spain
230 E3 **Cantalojas** Spain
160 E5 **Cantantal** Argentina
155 E2 **Cantaura** Venezuela
234 F2 **Cantemir** Moldova
241 I3 **Canterbury** Kent England UK
423 E7 **Canterbury Bight** New Zealand
377 J5 **Cantilan** Philippines
120 H6 **Cantin Lake** Manitoba Canada
243 G3 **Cantley** South Yorkshire England UK
156 D5 **Canto do Buriti** Brazil
130 F4 **Canton** Mississippi USA
127 N4 **Canton** New York USA
127 K6 **Canton** Ohio USA
130 D4 **Canton** Texas USA
130 B2 **Canton Lake** Oklahoma USA
119 Q7 **Cantuar** Saskatchewan Canada
116 E6 **Cantwell** Alaska USA
161 G5 **Cañuelas** Argentina
155 G6 **Canuma** *watercourse* Brazil
159 E2 **Canutama** Brazil
130 B3 **Canute** Oklahoma USA
129 J7 **Canutillo** Mexico
241 H3 **Canvey Island** Essex England UK
309 F3 **Canxixe** Mozambique
241 H5 **Cany-Barville** France
118 C2 **Canyon** Yukon Territory Canada
129 L3 **Canyon** Texas USA
124 J3 **Canyon Ferry Lake** Montana USA
130 B6 **Canyon Lake** Texas USA
128 H1 **Canyonlands National Park** Utah USA
124 D5 **Canyonville** Oregon USA
306 C5 **Canzar** Angola
376 E2 **Cao Bằng** Vietnam
376 F5 **Cao Nguyen Di Linh** Vietnam
380 D3 **Caohai** Guizhou China
381 G2 **Caohe** Hubei China
379 H2 **Caoka** Xizang Zizhiqu China
244 B4 **Caolas** Highland Scotland UK
306 B5 **Caombo** Angola
123 E7 **Caopacho** *watercourse* Québec Canada
127 N2 **Caopatina, Lac** *lake* Québec Canada
232 C4 **Caorso** Italy
377 I6 **Cap** *island* Philippines
163 13 **Cap, Pointe du** *cape* St Lucia
123 H9 **Cap aux Meules, Île du** *island* Québec Canada
163 13 **Cap Estate** St Lucia
135 F3 **Cap-Haïtien** Haiti
132 E1 **Cap Rock Escarpment** Texas USA
233 C6 **Capáccia, Punta** *cape* Sardinia Italy
233 F6 **Capacciotti, Lago di** *lake* Italy
161 H1 **Capado** Brazil
306 C5 **Capaia** Angola
372 C4 **Capalulu, Selat** *strait* Indonesia
154 D5 **Capana** Brazil
154 E3 **Capanaparo** *watercourse* Venezuela
157 B9 **Capão Bonito** Brazil
161 I4 **Capão da Canoa** Brazil
230 F2 **Caparroso** Spain
377 I4 **Capas** Philippines
158 E3 **Capatará** Brazil
228 D5 **Capbreton** France
80 E8 **Cape Abyssal Plain** *underwater feature* Atlantic Ocean
123 I9 **Cape Anguille** Newfoundland and Labrador Canada
425 N10 **Cape Barren Island** Tas. Australia
123 H9 **Cape Breton Island** Nova Scotia Canada
123 L9 **Cape Broyle** Newfoundland and Labrador Canada
304 D3 **Cape Coast** Ghana
131 K7 **Cape Coral** Florida USA
425 J4 **Cape Crawford** NT Australia
117 L6 **Cape Dorset** Nunavut Canada
118 E4 **Cape Fanshaw** Alaska USA
131 L3 **Cape Fear** *watercourse* North Carolina USA
126 G8 **Cape Girardeau** Missouri USA
163 7 **Cape Meredith** Falkland Islands
80 F8 **Cape Rise** *underwater feature* Atlantic Ocean
123 I8 **Cape St George** Newfoundland and Labrador Canada
121 P2 **Cape Smith** Nunavut Canada
308 C6 **Cape Town** South Africa
76 P7 **Cape Verde Abyssal Plain** *underwater feature* Atlantic Ocean
76 O8 **Cape Verde Fracture Zone** *underwater feature* Atlantic Ocean
76 P8 **Cape Verde Seamount** *underwater feature* Atlantic Ocean
123 F9 **Cape Wolfe** Prince Edward Island Canada
425 L3 **Cape York Peninsula** Qld Australia
240 D2 **Capel Bangor** Ceredigion Wales UK
240 D1 **Capel-Curig** Conwy Wales UK
240 C3 **Capel Hendre** Carmarthenshire Wales UK
240 C3 **Capel Isaac** Carmarthenshire Wales UK
241 I3 **Capel le Ferne** Kent England UK
156 E5 **Capela** Brazil
157 D7 **Capelinha** Brazil
425 M5 **Capella** Qld Australia
373 G5 **Capella** *mountain* Papua New Guinea
308 C2 **Capelongo** Angola
306 B5 **Capenda-Camulemba** Angola
228 F5 **Capendu** France
163 16 **Capesterre** Guadeloupe
163 16 **Capesterre-Belle-Eau** Guadeloupe
161 G3 **Capiatá** Paraguay
308 C3 **Capico** Angola
231 G3 **Capicorp, Punta de** *cape* Spain
158 E3 **Capihuara** Bolivia
156 B3 **Capim** *watercourse* Brazil
157 D5 **Capim Grosso** Brazil
230 C3 **Capinha** Portugal
157 B7 **Capinópolis** Brazil
134 E5 **Capira** Panama
129 J4 **Capitan** New Mexico USA
162 B6 **Capitán Aracena, Isla** *island* Chile
162 B5 **Capitán Eyroa** Argentina
162 A2 **Capitanes, Punta** *cape* Chile
156 C3 **Capitão Poço** Brazil
426 2 **Capitol Hill** Northern Mariana Islands
125 L7 **Capitol Peak** Colorado USA
159 F3 **Capivara** Brazil
161 I2 **Capivara, Reservatório** *lake* Brazil
123 F8 **Caplan** Québec Canada
234 F2 **Căplani** Moldova
226 G5 **Capo Sile** Italy
309 F2 **Capoche** *watercourse* Mozambique
159 F2 **Capoeira** Brazil
233 C7 **Capoterra** Sardinia Italy
377 J4 **Capotoah, Mount** *mountain* Philippines
242 E1 **Capplegill** Dumfries and Galloway Scotland UK
242 B3 **Cappoge** Ireland
232 C5 **Capraia, Isola di** *island* Italy
233 F5 **Caprara, Isola** *island* Italy
233 C6 **Caprara, Punta** *cape* Italy
233 F6 **Capri** Italy
233 F6 **Capri, Isola di** *island* Italy
308 D3 **Caprivi** *admin. area* Namibia
308 D3 **Caprivi Strip** *region* Botswana
129 K4 **Caprock** New Mexico USA
233 E6 **Caprolace, Lago di** *lake* Italy
427 14a **Captain Cook Monument** *landmark* French Polynesia
228 D4 **Captieux** France
163 15 **Capucin, Cape** Dominica
308 B2 **Capunda Cavilongo** Angola
158 E6 **Caquella, Cerro** *mountain* Bolivia
154 C4 **Caqueta** *admin. area* Colombia
154 C4 **Caqueta** *watercourse* Colombia
376 B5 **Car Nicobar** *island* Andaman and Nicobar Islands India
244 C5 **Cara Island** Scotland UK
154 D2 **Carabobo** *admin. area* Venezuela
155 F4 **Caracaraí** Brazil
154 E2 **Caracas** Venezuela
154 B3 **Caracoles, Punta** *cape* Panama
154 C3 **Caracolí** Colombia
160 D2 **Caracote** Chile
132 E5 **Carácuaro** Mexico
308 B2 **Caraculo** Angola
234 F2 **Caragaș** Moldova
229 H4 **Caraglio** Italy
161 H5 **Caraguatá** *watercourse* Uruguay
157 C8 **Caraguatatuba** Brazil
160 E2 **Carahuasi** Argentina
160 C6 **Carahue** Chile
157 D7 **Caraí** Brazil
159 H2 **Carajari** *watercourse* Brazil
156 B4 **Carajás** Brazil
156 B4 **Carajás, Serra dos** *range* Brazil
223 M2 **Cárájávri** *lake* Norway
231 G2 **Caraman** France
126 H2 **Caramat** Ontario Canada
160 D2 **Caramucho, Caleta** *bay* Chile
159 G4 **Caramujo** Brazil
230 B3 **Caramulo** Portugal
155 F4 **Caraná** Brazil
157 D8 **Carandaí** Brazil
157 D8 **Carangola** Brazil
163 9 **Carapichaima** Trinidad and Tobago
159 E5 **Carapiri** Bolivia
123 F9 **Caraquet, Baie de** *bay* New Brunswick Canada
158 B3 **Carás** Peru
234 C3 **Caraș-Severin** *admin. area* Romania
226 E5 **Carasco** Italy
158 E5 **Carasilla** Bolivia
374 E4 **Carat, Tanjung** *island* Indonesia
233 C6 **Carataggio, Punta di** *cape* Corsica France
134 D4 **Caratasca, Laguna de** *bay* Honduras
157 D7 **Caratinga** Brazil
158 E2 **Carauari** Brazil
156 E4 **Caraúbas** Brazil
157 E7 **Caravelas** Brazil
161 H4 **Carazinho** Brazil
230 B2 **Carballo** Spain
125 P2 **Carberry** Manitoba Canada
155 H4 **Carbet Maïs** French Guiana
155 H3 **Carbet Toukan** French Guiana
240 B4 **Carbis Bay** Cornwall England UK
128 G6 **Carbó** Mexico
130 B4 **Carbon** Texas USA
162 B4 **Carbón, Meseta** *plateau* Argentina
130 H4 **Carbon Hill** Alabama USA
233 C7 **Carbonara, Capo** *cape* Sardinia Italy
125 L7 **Carbondale** Colorado USA
126 G8 **Carbondale** Illinois USA
129 O1 **Carbondale** Kansas USA
230 F5 **Carboneras** Spain
230 F4 **Carboneras de Guadazaón** Spain
233 C7 **Carbonia** Sardinia Italy
232 E3 **Carbonin** Italy
228 E5 **Carbonne** France
244 B3 **Carbost** Highland Scotland UK
245 F3 **Carbury** Ireland
231 F4 **Carcaixent** Spain
228 D4 **Carcans** France
244 E5 **Carcant** Scottish Borders Scotland UK
160 F5 **Carcaraña** *watercourse* Argentina
226 E5 **Carcare** Italy
154 C3 **Carcasí** Colombia
228 F5 **Carcassonne** France
231 F2 **Carcastillo** Spain
118 D2 **Carcross Cutoff** Yukon Territory Canada
161 G5 **Cardal** Uruguay
393 C9 **Cardamum** *island* Lakshadweep India
230 D4 **Cardeña** Spain
134 D2 **Cárdenas** Cuba
133 F4 **Cárdenas** Mexico
134 C5 **Cárdenas** Nicaragua
162 B4 **Cardiel, Lago** *lake* Argentina
240 D3 **Cardiff** Wales UK
240 D3 **Cardiff** *admin. area* Wales UK
240 C2 **Cardigan** Ceredigion Wales UK
123 G9 **Cardigan Bay** Prince Edward Island Canada
240 C2 **Cardigan Bay** Wales UK
118 M4 **Cardinal Lake** Alberta Canada
233 E6 **Cardito** Italy
154 A5 **Cardo Grande, Punta** *cape* Peru
234 F3 **Cardon** Romania
231 G3 **Cardona** Spain
157 B8 **Cardoso** Brazil
125 M2 **Cardross** Saskatchewan Canada
242 E2 **Cardurnock** Cumbria England UK
425 M4 **Cardwell** Qld Australia
241 G2 **Careby** Lincolnshire England UK
119 Q4 **Careen Lake** Saskatchewan Canada
128 G4 **Carefree** Arizona USA
234 C2 **Carei** Romania
155 G5 **Careiro, Ilha do** *island* Brazil
155 G5 **Careiro da Várzea** Brazil
228 D2 **Carentan** France
154 B3 **Carepa** Colombia
124 I5 **Carey** Idaho USA
424 G7 **Carey, Lake** WA Australia
120 D1 **Carey Lake** Northwest Territories Canada
80 K6 **Cargados Carajos Bank** *underwater feature* Indian Ocean
310 7 **Cargados Carajos Islands** Mauritius
245 F2 **Cargan** Ballymena Northern Ireland UK
229 I5 **Cargèse** France
242 A1 **Carha** Ireland
158 B3 **Carhuamayo** Peru
158 C4 **Carhuanca** Peru
157 D8 **Cariacica** Brazil
155 E2 **Cariaco, Golfo de** *bay* Venezuela
154 B6 **Cariamanga** Ecuador
154 B2 **Caribana, Punta** *cape* Colombia
135 F4 **Caribbean Sea**
133 H5 **Caribe** *watercourse* Mexico
118 K6 **Cariboo Mountains** British Columbia Canada
120 G3 **Caribou** *watercourse* Manitoba Canada
120 H7 **Caribou Falls** Ontario Canada
126 I3 **Caribou Island** Ontario Canada
120 G3 **Caribou Lake** Manitoba Canada
126 G1 **Caribou Lake** Ontario Canada
127 Q4 **Caribou Lake** Maine USA
116 H7 **Caribou Mountains** Alberta Canada
135 G3 **Carice** Haiti
377 J5 **Carigara** Philippines
226 D5 **Carignano** Italy
383 I2 **Caril** Mongolia
425 M7 **Carinda** NSW Australia
231 F3 **Cariñena** Spain
157 D6 **Carinhanha** Brazil
157 C6 **Carinhanha** *watercourse* Brazil
233 E7 **Carini** Italy
244 A3 **Carinish** Na h-Eileanan Siar Scotland UK
230 C2 **Cariño** Spain
306 C6 **Caripande** Angola
158 D5 **Cariquima** Chile
157 E5 **Carira** Brazil
156 D3 **Cariré** Brazil
156 E4 **Caririaçu** Brazil
227 L5 **Cârjiti** Romania
245 F3 **Carlanstown** Ireland
132 E3 **Carleña** Mexico
377 I5 **Carles** Philippines
242 F2 **Carleton** Cumbria England UK
123 E9 **Carleton, Mount** New Brunswick Canada
123 G8 **Carleton, Pointe** *cape* Québec Canada
234 D2 **Cârlibaba** Romania
124 G6 **Carlin** Nevada USA
242 F2 **Carlisle** Cumbria England UK
127 M6 **Carlisle** Pennsylvania USA
163 12 **Carlisle Bay** Barbados
133 G5 **Carlos A. Carrillo** Mexico
160 F5 **Carlos Casares** Argentina
157 D7 **Carlos Chagas** Brazil
161 G5 **Carlos Reyles** Uruguay
160 F5 **Carlos Tejedor** Argentina
245 F4 **Carlow** Ireland
240 A2 **Carlow** *admin. area* Ireland
128 D4 **Carlsbad** California USA
129 J4 **Carlsbad** New Mexico USA
80 K4 **Carlsberg Ridge** *underwater feature* Indian Ocean
118 J5 **Carlson** British Columbia Canada
436 S1 **Carlson Inlet** *bay* Antarctica
119 P3 **Carlson Landing** Alberta Canada
241 F2 **Carlton** Nottinghamshire England UK
241 I2 **Carlton Colville** Suffolk England UK
126 G7 **Carlyle** Illinois USA
126 G7 **Carlyle Lake** Illinois USA
116 F6 **Carmacks** Yukon Territory Canada
120 G8 **Carman** Manitoba Canada
234 F2 **Carmanova** Moldova
240 C3 **Carmarthen** Carmarthenshire Wales UK
240 C3 **Carmarthenshire** *admin. area* Wales UK
228 F4 **Carmaux** France
126 H7 **Carmel** Indiana USA
128 A2 **Carmel Bay** California USA
242 D3 **Carmel Head** *cape* England UK
134 B3 **Carmelita** Guatemala
161 G5 **Carmelo** Uruguay
158 E3 **Carmen** Bolivia
130 B8 **Carmen** Mexico
377 J5 **Carmen** Philippines
125 P8 **Carmen** Oklahoma USA
134 B3 **Carmen, Isla del** *island* Mexico
133 G5 **Carmen, Laguna del** *lake* Mexico
158 D4 **Carmen de Toromonas** Bolivia
124 F2 **Carmi** British Columbia Canada
424 I6 **Carmichael Crag** *mountain* NT Australia
157 D8 **Carmo** Brazil
157 C8 **Carmo do Cajuru** Brazil
157 C7 **Carmo do Paranaíba** Brazil
161 J2 **Carmo do Rio Claro** Brazil
230 D5 **Carmona** Spain
244 F4 **Carmyllie** Angus Scotland UK
245 F2 **Carn** Limavady Northern Ireland UK
244 E3 **Càrn Gorm** *mountain* Scotland UK
242 B2 **Carnagh** Armagh Northern Ireland UK
156 E5 **Carnaíba** Brazil
242 B3 **Carnaross** Ireland
424 E6 **Carnarvon** WA Australia
308 D6 **Carnarvon** South Africa
245 E1 **Carndonagh** Ireland
240 C4 **Carne** Cornwall England UK
129 I4 **Carne** New Mexico USA
240 C1 **Carnedd Llewelyn** *mountain* Wales UK
424 G6 **Carnegie, Lake** WA Australia
77 J10 **Carnegie Ridge** *underwater feature* Pacific Ocean
157 B7 **Carneirinho** Brazil
230 D5 **Carnero, Punta del** *cape* Spain
242 B4 **Carnew** Ireland
436 P2 **Carney Island** Antarctica
242 F2 **Carnforth** Lancashire England UK
244 F3 **Carnichal** Aberdeenshire Scotland UK
423 8 **Carnley Harbour** Auckland Islands New Zealand
242 C2 **Carnlough** Larne Northern Ireland UK
240 D2 **Carno** Powys Wales UK
244 D3 **Carnoch** Highland Scotland UK
305 H4 **Carnot** Central African Republic
425 J8 **Carnot, Cape** SA Australia
240 A2 **Carnsore Point** Ireland
242 B2 **Carnteel** Dungannon Northern Ireland UK
244 E5 **Carnwath** South Lanarkshire Scotland UK
155 G4 **Caroebe** Brazil
156 C4 **Carolina** Brazil
158 D2 **Carolina** Peru
135 H3 **Carolina** Puerto Rico
119 N6 **Caroline** Alberta Canada
426 1 **Caroline Island** Kiribati
373 H2 **Caroline Islands** Federated States of Micronesia
155 F3 **Caroní, Río** *watercourse* Venezuela
233 F7 **Caronia Marina** Italy
154 D2 **Carora** Venezuela
154 D2 **Carora, Sabana de** *region* Venezuela
229 H3 **Carouge** France
118 J5 **Carp Lake** British Columbia Canada
162 B5 **Carpa Manzano** Chile
227 L3 **Carpathian Mountains** *range* Slovakia
234 D3 **Carpații Meridionali** *range* Romania
234 C3 **Carpen** Romania
425 K3 **Carpentaria, Gulf of** *bay* Australia
124 D1 **Carpenter Lake** British Columbia Canada
229 G4 **Carpentras** France
226 F5 **Carpi** Italy
156 F4 **Carpina** Brazil
234 B3 **Cărpiniș** Romania
128 C3 **Carpinteria** California USA
155 F2 **Carpintero** Venezuela
125 O2 **Carpio** North Dakota USA
158 B3 **Carpo Bajo, Cerro** *mountain* Peru
437 I2 **Carr, Cape** Antarctica
131 J2 **Carr Fork Lake** Kentucky USA
120 H1 **Carr Lake** Nunavut Canada
131 I6 **Carrabelle** Florida USA
245 C3 **Carran** Ireland
160 C5 **Carranza, Cabo** *cape* Chile
154 F4 **Carrao** *watercourse* Venezuela
232 D4 **Carrara** Italy
230 E3 **Carrascosa del Campo** Spain
245 E2 **Carraskea** Ireland
245 C4 **Carrauntoohil** *mountain* Ireland
244 E3 **Carrbridge** Highland Scotland UK
135 F3 **Carrefour** Haiti
230 B2 **Carreiro, Punta** *cape* Spain
230 D2 **Carreña** Spain
158 B4 **Carretas, Punta** *cape* Peru
163 10 **Carriacou** *island* Grenada
242 B4 **Carrick** Ireland
244 D4 **Carrick** Argyll and Bute Scotland UK
425 inset **Carrick Bay** Macquarie Island Australia
245 D3 **Carrick-on-Shannon** Ireland
242 C2 **Carrickfergus** Carrickfergus Northern Ireland UK
242 C2 **Carrickfergus** *admin. area* Northern Ireland UK
242 A2 **Carrickmore** Omagh Northern Ireland UK
242 A2 **Carrickroe** Ireland
245 C4 **Carrigaholt** Ireland
127 P4 **Carrigain, Mount** New Hampshire USA
245 D5 **Carrigaline** Ireland
245 E3 **Carrigallen** Ireland
242 A3 **Carrigan** Ireland
245 D4 **Carrigane** Ireland
242 B2 **Carrigans** Ireland
245 E1 **Carrigart** Ireland
242 A4 **Carrigeen** Ireland
125 P3 **Carrington** North Dakota USA
230 D2 **Carrión de los Condes** Spain
159 E4 **Carrito** Bolivia
134 C4 **Carrizal** Honduras
160 D4 **Carrizal Bajo** Chile
129 M6 **Carrizo Springs** Texas USA
130 B8 **Carrizos** Mexico
129 J4 **Carrizozo** New Mexico USA
126 D5 **Carroll** Iowa USA
120 H7 **Carroll Lake** Ontario Canada
131 I4 **Carrollton** Georgia USA
126 E7 **Carrollton** Missouri USA
130 C4 **Carrollton** Texas USA
244 C4 **Carron** Argyll and Bute Scotland UK
244 E4 **Carron** *watercourse* Scotland UK
244 E5 **Carronbridge** Dumfries and Galloway Scotland UK
231 J2 **Carros** France
119 T6 **Carrot** *watercourse* Saskatchewan Canada
245 D4 **Carrow** Ireland
120 E1 **Carruthers Lake** Nunavut Canada
127 N4 **Carry Falls Reservoir** New York USA
244 C4 **Carsaig** Highland Scotland UK
124 I1 **Carseland** Alberta Canada
244 D6 **Carseriggan** Dumfries and Galloway Scotland UK
244 D5 **Carskeoch** East Ayrshire Scotland UK
233 E5 **Carsoli** Italy
128 C1 **Carson** *watercourse* Nevada USA
125 O3 **Carson** North Dakota USA
124 F7 **Carson City** Nevada USA
244 E5 **Carstairs** South Lanarkshire Scotland UK
119 Q3 **Carswell Lake** Saskatchewan Canada
129 L6 **Carta Valley** Texas USA
154 C2 **Cartagena** Colombia
154 C5 **Cartagena** Peru
231 F5 **Cartagena** Spain
154 C4 **Cartagena del Chairá** Colombia
230 B4 **Cartaxo** Portugal
130 B3 **Carter** Oklahoma USA
228 D2 **Carteret** France
131 I3 **Carters Lake** Georgia USA
131 I3 **Cartersville** Georgia USA
241 F3 **Carterton** Oxfordshire England UK
126 D8 **Carthage** Missouri USA
125 Q4 **Carthage** South Dakota USA
424 inset **Cartier Island** Ashmore Reef and Cartier Island Australia
242 B3 **Carton** Ireland
122 J6 **Cartwright** Newfoundland and Labrador Canada
424 inset **Cartwright, Cape** Heard Island Australia
155 F3 **Caruana de Montaña** Venezuela
156 F5 **Caruaru** Brazil
155 F3 **Carunantabari** Venezuela
233 F6 **Carunchio** Italy
155 F2 **Carúpano** Venezuela
154 D4 **Carurú** Colombia
156 C3 **Carutapera** Brazil
230 C3 **Carviçais** Portugal
240 C3 **Carway** Carmarthenshire Wales UK
131 L3 **Cary** North Carolina USA
162 F5 **Carysfort, Cape** Falkland Islands
154 C4 **Casa Agapito** Colombia
128 G5 **Casa Blanca** Mexico
129 H5 **Casa de Janos** Mexico
158 E4 **Casa de Lienzo** Bolivia
162 D2 **Casa de Piedra, Embalse** *lake* Argentina
128 G4 **Casa Grande** Arizona USA
157 A8 **Casa Nova** Brazil
162 B2 **Casa Pangue** Chile
160 E2 **Casabindo, Cerro de** *mountain* Argentina
300 E2 **Casablanca** Morocco
233 C5 **Casaglione** Corsica France
226 D5 **Casalborgone** Italy
161 G6 **Casalins** Argentina
229 J4 **Casalmaggiore** Italy
300 C6 **Casamance** *watercourse* Senegal
229 I5 **Casamozza** Corsica France
154 D3 **Casanare** *watercourse* Colombia
230 F4 **Casas de Juan Núñez** Spain
231 F4 **Casas-Ibáñez** Spain
423 C7 **Cascade** *watercourse* New Zealand
425 inset **Cascade** Norfolk Island Australia
310 9b **Cascade** Seychelles
124 G4 **Cascade** Idaho USA
126 F5 **Cascade** Iowa USA
124 J3 **Cascade** Montana USA
423 C7 **Cascade Point** New Zealand
124 D5 **Cascade Range** Oregon/Washington USA
124 G4 **Cascade Reservoir** Idaho USA
155 H3 **Cascades, Plateau des** *region* Suriname
79 T3 **Cascadia Basin** *underwater feature* Pacific Ocean
158 A2 **Cascajal** *watercourse* Peru
123 E8 **Cascapédia** *watercourse* Québec Canada
158 B2 **Cascas** Peru
156 E4 **Cascavel** Brazil
157 A9 **Cascavel** Brazil
232 D5 **Cascina** Italy
127 Q5 **Casco Bay** Maine USA
229 H4 **Caselle Torinese** Italy
154 D3 **Caserío El Banco** Colombia
127 N3 **Casey** Québec Canada
437 H2 **Casey (Australia)** *research station* Antarctica
437 D2 **Casey Bay** Antarctica
245 D2 **Cashel** Ireland
124 E3 **Cashmere** Washington USA
154 D2 **Casigua** Venezuela
377 I4 **Casiguran Bay** Philippines
234 F3 **Casimcea** Romania
132 D5 **Casimiro Castillo** Mexico
425 O7 **Casino** NSW Australia
128 C3 **Casitas, Lake** California USA
227 H3 **Čáslav** Czech Republic
158 B3 **Casma** Peru
231 F3 **Caspe** Spain
125 L5 **Casper** Wyoming USA
388 F5 **Caspian Sea**
126 D3 **Cass Lake** Minnesota USA
309 F2 **Cassacatiza** Mozambique
308 D2 **Cassai** Angola
308 D2 **Cassamba** Angola
233 G7 **Cassano allo Ionio** Italy
228 F1 **Cassel** France
125 Q3 **Casselton** North Dakota USA
157 C8 **Cássia** Brazil
118 F2 **Cassiar Mountains** British Columbia/Yukon Territory Canada
233 F8 **Cassibile** Italy
124 D2 **Cassidy** British Columbia Canada
157 B7 **Cassilândia** Brazil
124 I1 **Cassils** Alberta Canada
308 C3 **Cassinga** Angola
233 E6 **Cassino** Italy
226 F5 **Cassio** Italy
155 I4 **Cassipore** *watercourse* Brazil
229 G5 **Cassis** France
244 D2 **Cassley** *watercourse* Scotland UK
125 Q7 **Cassoday** Kansas USA
308 C2 **Cassongue** Angola
126 H6 **Cassopolis** Michigan USA
232 D5 **Castagneto Carducci** Italy
129 K2 **Castaneda** Oklahoma USA
228 E5 **Castanet-Tolosan** France
156 C3 **Castanhal** Brazil
158 D3 **Castanheira** Brazil
132 E3 **Castaños** Mexico
163 9 **Castara** Trinidad and Tobago
232 C4 **Casteggio** Italy
229 J4 **Castel Goffredo** Italy
229 J4 **Castel Maggiore** Italy
232 D5 **Castelfiorentino** Italy
228 E4 **Casteljaloux** France
233 F6 **Castellammare di Stabia** Italy
229 H5 **Castellane** France
229 J4 **Castellarano** Italy
160 F3 **Castelli** Argentina
231 F4 **Castelló de la Plana** Spain
228 D4 **Castelnau-de-Médoc** France
231 G2 **Castelnau-de-Montmiral** France
228 F5 **Castelnau-le-Lez** France
228 E5 **Castelnau-Magnoac** France
228 E5 **Castelnaudary** France
232 D5 **Castelnuovo di Val di Cecina** Italy
157 D8 **Castelo** Brazil
230 C4 **Castelo Branco** Portugal
230 C3 **Castelo Branco** *admin. area* Portugal
230 C4 **Castelo de Vide** Portugal
156 D4 **Castelo do Piauí** Brazil
233 C6 **Castelsardo** Sardinia Italy
228 E4 **Castelsarrasin** France
233 E8 **Castelvetrano** Italy
425 L9 **Casterton** Vic. Australia
231 F2 **Castets** France
232 D5 **Castiglioncello** Italy
157 B8 **Castilho** Brazil
160 D3 **Castilla** Chile
230 E4 **Castilla-La Mancha** *admin. area* Spain
230 D4 **Castilla la Nueva** *region* Spain
230 D3 **Castilla la Vieja** *region* Spain
230 D3 **Castilla y Léon** *admin. area* Spain
155 E3 **Castillero** Venezuela
160 D5 **Castillo, Cerro del** *mountain* Chile
162 C3 **Castillo, Pampa del** *region* Argentina
228 E4 **Castillonnès** France
161 H5 **Castillos** Uruguay
158 D5 **Castilluma** Chile
240 D2 **Castle Caereinion** Powys Wales UK
242 F2 **Castle Carrock** Cumbria England UK
240 E3 **Castle Cary** Somerset England UK
125 J7 **Castle Dale** Utah USA
126 F3 **Castle Danger** Minnesota USA
244 E6 **Castle Douglas** Dumfries and Galloway Scotland UK
243 G2 **Castle Eden** Durham England UK
127 inset **Castle Harbour** Bermuda
125 L7 **Castle Peak** Colorado USA
241 H2 **Castle Rising** Norfolk England UK
125 M7 **Castle Rock** Colorado USA
126 G5 **Castle Rock Lake** Wisconsin USA
310 5b **Castle Rock Point** *cape* St Helena
244 D3 **Castle Stuart** Highland Scotland UK
129 H1 **Castle Valley** Utah USA
245 C3 **Castlebar** Ireland
245 F3 **Castlebellingham** Ireland
245 F2 **Castleblayney** Ireland
240 C3 **Castlebythe** Pembrokeshire Wales UK
245 E4 **Castlecomer** Ireland
242 A2 **Castlederg** Strabane Northern Ireland UK
245 E2 **Castlefinn** Ireland
425 M9 **Castlemaine** Qld Australia
245 C4 **Castlemaine** Ireland
245 D5 **Castlemartyr** Ireland
245 D3 **Castleplunket** Ireland
423 G5 **Castlepoint** New Zealand
245 D3 **Castlerea** Ireland
242 C2 **Castlereagh** *admin. area* Northern Ireland UK
242 A3 **Castlereban North** Ireland
245 F1 **Castlerock** Coleraine Northern Ireland UK
244 F5 **Castleton** Scottish Borders Scotland UK
242 D2 **Castletown** Isle of Man UK
245 D4 **Castletownroche** Ireland
242 C2 **Castlewellan** Banbridge Northern Ireland UK
119 P6 **Castor** Alberta Canada
121 P6 **Castor, Rivière au** *watercourse* Québec Canada
230 D4 **Castrejón, Embalse de** *lake* Spain
228 F5 **Castres** France
226 C1 **Castricum** Netherlands
163 13 **Castries** St Lucia
230 C2 **Castrillón** Spain
157 B9 **Castro** Brazil
162 B3 **Castro** Chile
230 C2 **Castro** Spain
157 E6 **Castro Alves** Brazil
229 J4 **Castrocaro Terme** Italy
230 C2 **Castrocontrigo** Spain
230 C2 **Castroverde** Spain
233 G7 **Castrovillari** Italy
230 D4 **Castuera** Spain
161 H5 **Casupá** Uruguay
423 B7 **Caswell Sound** New Zealand
376 E2 **Cát Bà, Đao** *island* Vietnam
135 F1 **Cat Island** Bahamas
133 H2 **Cat Island** Mississippi USA
131 L8 **Cat Keys** Bahamas
120 J7 **Cat Lake** Ontario Canada
424 E7 **Cataby** WA Australia
158 A2 **Catacaos** Peru
154 B6 **Catacocha** Ecuador
157 D8 **Cataguases** Brazil
130 E5 **Catahoula Lake** Louisiana USA
394 G6 **Çataksuyu** *watercourse* Turkey
157 C7 **Catalão** Brazil
235 F5 **Çatalca Yarımadası** *region* Turkey
123 L8 **Catalina** Newfoundland and Labrador Canada
231 G3 **Cataluña** *region* Spain
231 G3 **Cataluñya** *admin. area* Spain
160 E3 **Catamarca** *admin. area* Argentina
154 B5 **Catamayo** Ecuador
309 F3 **Catandica** Mozambique
377 J4 **Catanduanes** *island* Philippines
157 B8 **Catanduva** Brazil
233 F8 **Catania** Italy
233 F8 **Catania, Golfo di** *bay* Italy
233 F8 **Catania, Piana di** *island* Italy
233 G7 **Catanzaro** Italy
233 G7 **Catanzaro Marina** Italy
130 B6 **Catarina** Texas USA
377 J4 **Catarman** Philippines
231 F4 **Catarroja** Spain
155 G5 **Catauara** Brazil
309 F3 **Cataxa** Mozambique
377 J5 **Catbalogan** Philippines
162 B6 **Catedral de York, Cabo** *cape* Chile
377 J6 **Cateel** Philippines
377 J6 **Cateel Bay** Philippines
133 G5 **Catemaco** Mexico
308 B2 **Catengue** Angola
241 G3 **Caterham** Surrey England UK
308 B1 **Catete** Angola
128 D4 **Cathedral City** California USA
118 K8 **Cathedral Provincial Park** British Columbia Canada
241 F4 **Catherington** Hampshire England UK
128 B2 **Catheys Valley** California USA
154 E2 **Catia La Mar** Venezuela
233 E5 **Catignano** Italy
241 I4 **Catigny** France
228 F1 **Catillon** France
304 A2 **Catió** Guinea-Bissau
155 F4 **Catisimiña** Brazil
241 F3 **Catmore** West Berkshire England UK
134 C2 **Catoche, Cabo** *cape* Mexico
156 E4 **Catolé do Rocha** Brazil
306 B5 **Catolo** Angola
232 E5 **Catria, Monte** *mountain* Italy
160 E6 **Catriel** Argentina
160 F6 **Catriló** Argentina
155 F4 **Catrimani** Brazil
155 F4 **Catrimani** *watercourse* Brazil
154 B3 **Catripe, Ensenada** *bay* Colombia
127 N5 **Catskill Mountains** New York USA
243 G2 **Catterick** North Yorkshire England UK
242 F2 **Catterlen** Cumbria England UK
243 F2 **Catton** Northumberland England UK
157 E6 **Catu** Brazil
160 E2 **Catúa** Argentina
308 D3 **Catuile** Angola
308 B2 **Catumbela** Angola
309 G2 **Catur** Mozambique
376 E3 **Câu Giát** Vietnam
155 E4 **Cauaburi** *watercourse* Brazil
377 I3 **Cauayan** Philippines
122 G3 **Caubvick, Mount (D'Iberville)** Newfoundland and Labrador/Québec Canada
154 C2 **Cauca** *watercourse* Colombia
156 E3 **Caucaia** Brazil
159 G5 **Caucas** Bolivia
154 C3 **Caucasia** Colombia

388 D5 **Caucasus** *range* Russian Federation
160 D4 **Caucete** Argentina
160 E2 **Cauchari, Salar de** *lake* Argentina
162 C5 **Cauchicol** Argentina
120 G5 **Cauchon Lake** Manitoba Canada
123 D9 **Caucomgomoc Lake** Maine USA
241 H5 **Caudebec** France
377 J5 **Cauit Point** Philippines
306 B5 **Caungula** Angola
308 C3 **Cauno** Angola
160 C5 **Cauquenes** Chile
155 E3 **Caura** *watercourse* Venezuela
155 F5 **Caures** *watercourse* Brazil
123 E8 **Causapscal** Québec Canada
228 E4 **Caussade** France
159 E3 **Cautario** *watercourse* Brazil
228 D5 **Cauterets** France
241 H5 **Cauville** France
230 B3 **Cavado** *watercourse* Portugal
229 I4 **Cavaglià** Italy
231 I2 **Cavaillon** France
229 H5 **Cavalaire-sur-Mer** France
157 C6 **Cavalcante** Brazil
125 Q2 **Cavalier** North Dakota USA
231 I3 **Cavalleria, Cap de** *cape* Spain
422 E2 **Cavalli Islands** New Zealand
232 D5 **Cavallo, Capo** *cape* Italy
233 F5 **Cavalluccio, Punta di** *cape* Italy
304 C3/4 **Cavally** *watercourse* Côte d'Ivoire/Liberia
245 E3 **Cavan** Ireland
245 E3 **Cavan** *admin. area* Ireland
121 V5 **Cavanagh** Newfoundland and Labrador Canada
226 G5 **Cavarzere** Italy
423 D7 **Cave** New Zealand
130 F3 **Cave City** Arkansas USA
128 G4 **Cave Creek** Arizona USA
424 G7 **Cave Hill** WA Australia
124 D5 **Cave Junction** Oregon USA
126 J7 **Cave Run Lake** Kentucky USA
158 E4 **Cavedor** Bolivia
126 H2 **Cavers** Ontario Canada
377 I4 **Cavite** Philippines
234 C2 **Cavnic** Romania
229 H4 **Cavour** Italy
126 G4 **Cavour** Wisconsin USA
232 H5 **Cavtat** Croatia
157 C8 **Caxambu** Brazil
156 D4 **Caxias** Brazil
161 I4 **Caxias do Sul** Brazil
306 A5 **Caxito** Angola
155 I5 **Caxuana, Baia de** *bay* Brazil
235 G6 **Çay** Turkey
134 D2 **Cay Sal Bank** Bahamas
132 E5 **Cayacal, Punta** *cape* Mexico
154 B4 **Cayagama** Ecuador
127 M3 **Cayamant, Lac** *lake* Québec Canada
154 B4 **Cayambe** Ecuador
394 G5 **Çayeli** Turkey
155 H3 **Cayenne** French Guiana
155 H4 **Cayenne** *admin. area* French Guiana
241 I4 **Cayeux-sur-Mer** France
235 F6 **Çaygören Barajı** *lake* Turkey
235 F7 **Çayhisar** Turkey
235 G5 **Çayırhan** Turkey
228 E4 **Caylus** France
134 E3 **Cayman Brac** *island* Cayman Islands
134 D3 **Cayman Islands** *British overseas territory* Caribbean
76 K8 **Cayman Trench** *underwater feature* Caribbean
307 H2 **Caynabo** Somalia
154 A5 **Cayo, Ensenada de** *bay* Ecuador
163 19 **Cayon** St Kitts and Nevis
127 M5 **Cayuga Lake** New York USA
162 C2 **Cayuqueo** Argentina
161 G4 **Caza Pava** Argentina
308 D2 **Cazage** Angola
228 E4 **Cazals** France
232 F4 **Cazin** Bosnia and Herzegovina
232 C3 **Cazis** Switzerland
308 D2 **Cazombo** Angola
230 E5 **Cazorla** Spain
309 F3 **Cazula** Mozambique
158 D4 **Ccolo** Peru
230 D2 **Cea** *watercourse* Spain
234 F3 **Ceamurlia de Jos** Romania
244 B2 **Ceann Loch Shiphoirt** Na h-Eileanan Siar Scotland UK
156 E4 **Ceará** *admin. area* Brazil
76 N9 **Ceara Plain** *underwater feature* Atlantic Ocean
134 D6 **Cebaco, Isla de** *island* Panama
129 H6 **Cebadilla de Dolores** Mexico
129 J7 **Ceballos** Mexico
160 E4 **Cebollar** Argentina
129 I8 **Cebollin** Mexico
230 D3 **Cebreros** Spain
377 I5 **Cebu** Philippines
233 E6 **Ceccano** Italy
234 A2 **Cece** Hungary
227 H3 **Čechtice** Czech Republic
126 F2 **Cecil Lake** Ontario Canada
232 D5 **Cecina** Italy
232 D5 **Cecina** *watercourse* Italy
230 C4 **Ceclavín** Spain
118 J8 **Cedar** British Columbia Canada
126 F5 **Cedar** *watercourse* Iowa USA
129 L1 **Cedar Bluff Reservoir** Kansas USA
124 I8 **Cedar City** Utah USA
130 H3 **Cedar Creek Reservoir** Alabama USA
130 C4 **Cedar Creek Reservoir** Texas USA
134 B3 **Cedar Crossing** Belize
126 E5 **Cedar Falls** Iowa USA
163 18 **Cedar Grove** Antigua and Barbuda
131 J6 **Cedar Key** Florida USA
120 E6 **Cedar Lake** Manitoba Canada
132 E1 **Cedar Lake** Texas USA
130 D6 **Cedar Lakes** Texas USA
130 C5 **Cedar Park** Texas USA
126 F5 **Cedar Rapids** Iowa USA
163 18 **Cedar Tree Point** *cape* Antigua and Barbuda
230 B2 **Cedeira** Spain
230 C4 **Cedillo, Embalse de** *lake* Portugal
156 E4 **Cedro** Brazil
159 G4 **Cedro** Brazil
159 H5 **Cedro** Brazil
310 1b **Cedros** Azores
134 C4 **Cedros** Honduras
129 H7 **Cedros** Mexico
128 E6 **Cedros, Isla** *island* Mexico
163 9 **Cedros Bay** Trinidad and Tobago
79 U5 **Cedros Trench** *underwater feature* Pacific Ocean
425 J8 **Ceduna** SA Australia
230 B2 **Cée** Spain
307 H2 **Ceel Dhaab** Somalia
307 H3 **Ceel Dheere** Somalia
307 H3 **Ceel Huur** Somalia
307 H3 **Ceelbuur** Somalia
303 H5 **Ceerigaabo** Somalia
234 B2 **Cefa** Romania
233 F7 **Cefalù** Italy
233 F7 **Cefalù, Capo** *cape* Italy
234 A2 **Cegléd** Hungary
233 G6 **Céglie Messápica** Italy
230 F4 **Cehegín** Spain
225 K5 **Čehovo** Russian Federation
161 G5 **Ceibas** Argentina
227 I3 **Čejč** Czech Republic
233 E5 **Celano** Italy
230 C2 **Celanova** Spain
234 D3 **Celaru** Romania
132 E4 **Celaya** Mexico
245 F3 **Celbridge** Ireland
382 F6 **Cele** Xinjiang Uygur Zizhiqu China
228 E4 **Célé** *watercourse* France
Celebes *see* **Sulawesi** Indonesia
81 Q4 **Celebes Basin** *underwater feature* Celebes Sea
372 B3 **Celebes Sea** Indonesia/Philippines
158 B2 **Celendín** Peru
134 B2 **Celestún, Estero** *bay* Mexico
154 B6 **Celica** Ecuador
233 G7 **Celico** Italy
160 F2 **Celina** Paraguay
126 I6 **Celina** Ohio USA
231 F3 **Cella** Spain
240 C2 **Cellan** Ceredigion Wales UK
226 F1 **Celle** Germany
230 C3 **Celorico da Beira** Portugal
161 I3 **Celso Ramos** Brazil
245 C5 **Celtic Sea** Europe
235 G7 **Çeltikçi** Turkey
240 D2 **Celyn, Llyn** *lake* Wales UK
388 I7 **Çemenibit** Turkmenistan
240 D2 **Cemmaes Road** Powys Wales UK
375 H6 **Cempi, Teluk** *bay* Indonesia
234 B2 **Cenad** Romania
240 C2 **Cenarth** Carmarthenshire Wales UK
372 E4 **Cenderawasih, Teluk** *bay* Indonesia
227 K5 **Cenei** Romania
228 D4 **Cenon** France
133 H4 **Cenotillo** Mexico
310 2 **Cenouras, Ilhéu das** *island* Madeira
234 B3 **Čenta** Serbia
231 H3 **Centellas** Spain
157 B8 **Centenário do Sul** Brazil
309 F3 **Centenary** Zimbabwe
125 L8 **Center** Colorado USA
130 D5 **Center** Texas USA
131 I3 **Center Hill Lake** Tennessee USA
130 H3 **Centerville** Tennessee USA
232 D4 **Cento** Italy
308 E4 **Central** *admin. area* Botswana
155 I5 **Central** Brazil
307 F4 **Central** *admin. area* Kenya
309 F2 **Central** *admin. area* Malawi
160 F3 **Central** *admin. area* Paraguay
426 8 **Central** *admin. area* Solomon Islands
308 E2 **Central** *admin. area* Zambia
154 C3 **Central, Cordillera** *range* Colombia
135 G3 **Central, Cordillera** *range* Dominican Republic
158 B3 **Central, Cordillera** *range* Peru
377 I3 **Central, Cordillera** *range* Philippines
305 I3 **Central African Republic** *country* Africa
125 N4 **Central City** South Dakota USA
425 N4 **Central Diamond Islet** Coral Sea Islands Territory Australia
306 E3 **Central Equatoria** *admin. area* Sudan
435 L1 **Central Kara Plateau** *underwater feature* Arctic Ocean
78 O7 **Central Pacific Basin** *underwater feature* Pacific Ocean
120 J7 **Central Patricia** Ontario Canada
124 D5 **Central Point** Oregon USA
373 G5 **Central Range** Papua New Guinea
126 G7 **Centralia** Illinois USA
124 D3 **Centralia** Washington USA
157 B7 **Centralina** Brazil
305 G3 **Centre** *admin. area* Cameroon
226 B4 **Centre** *admin. area* France
229 G3 **Centre, Canal du** *watercourse* France
310 7b **Centre de Flacq** Mauritius
423 10 **Centre Group** *island* Bounty Islands New Zealand
423 B8 **Centre Island** New Zealand
127 M7 **Centreville** Maryland USA
123 L8 **Centreville-Wareham-Trinity** Newfoundland and Labrador Canada
158 D4 **Centro Firmeza** Bolivia
229 I5 **Centuri** Corsica France
130 H5 **Century** Florida USA
380 F4 **Cenxi** Guangxi Zhuangzu Zizhiqu China
381 H3 **Cenyang** Jiangxi China
228 E5 **Cépet** France
375 F5 **Cepu** Indonesia
Ceram Sea *see* **Seram, Laut** Indonesia
233 F8 **Cerami** Italy
230 D3 **Cercedilla** Spain
233 E8 **Cerda** Italy
228 E5 **Cerdanya** *region* Spain
230 B2 **Cerdedo** Spain
228 E4 **Cère** *watercourse* France
226 F5 **Cerea** Italy
119 P7 **Cereal** Alberta Canada
230 E2 **Cereceda, Embalse de** *lake* Spain
240 D2 **Ceredigion** *admin. area* Wales UK
234 A4 **Cerem** Albania
160 F4 **Ceres** Argentina
157 B6 **Ceres** Brazil
226 D5 **Ceres** Italy
226 F5 **Cerese** Italy
229 I4 **Cereseto** Italy
228 F5 **Céret** France
154 C2 **Cereté** Colombia
310 9 **Cerf, Île au** *island* Seychelles
226 E5 **Cergnago** Italy
233 F6 **Cerignola** Italy
226 B4 **Cérilly** France
154 C3 **Cerinza** Colombia
228 F2 **Cerisiers** France
228 D3 **Cerizay** France
235 F5 **Çerkezköy** Turkey
227 G4 **Cerkno** Slovenia
234 B2 **Cermei** Romania
227 J5 **Cerna** Croatia
230 C2 **Cernadilla, Embalse de** *lake* Spain
386 G2 **Cernaja, Gora** *mountain* Russian Federation
234 E3 **Cernica** Romania
229 K2 **Černošín** Czech Republic
227 H3 **Černovice** Czech Republic
162 D3 **Cero, Punta** *cape* Argentina
157 C8 **Cerquilho** Brazil
129 M7 **Cerralvo** Mexico
132 C3 **Cerralvo, Isla** *island* Mexico
235 A5 **Cërrik** Albania
230 E5 **Cerrillos, Salinas de** *lake* Spain
161 G3 **Cerrito** Paraguay
132 E4 **Cerritos** Mexico
162 C2 **Cerro Abanico** Argentina
133 F4 **Cerro Azul** Mexico
162 C4 **Cerro Blanco** Argentina
159 G4 **Cêrro Branco** Brazil
161 H5 **Cerro Colorado** Uruguay
158 B3 **Cerro de Pasco** Peru
155 E3 **Cerro Jaua, Meseta del** *mountain* Venezuela
161 H5 **Cerro Largo** *admin. area* Uruguay
160 D6 **Cerro Policía** Argentina
134 D5 **Cerro Punta** Panama
162 C2 **Cerros Colorados, Embalse** *lake* Argentina
232 D5 **Certaldo** Italy
424 E7 **Certes** WA Australia
233 E6 **Cervaro** Italy
233 F6 **Cervati, Monte** *mountain* Italy
230 D2 **Cervera, Embalse de** *lake* Spain
232 E4 **Cervia** Italy
233 F6 **Cervialto, Monte** *mountain* Italy
154 C2 **Cesar** *admin. area* Colombia
233 F8 **Cesarò** Italy
232 E4 **Cesena** Italy
232 E4 **Cesenatico** Italy
225 M4 **Cēsis** Latvia
227 H3 **České Budějovice (Budweis)** Czech Republic
227 J3 **Český Těšín** Czech Republic
437 I2 **Cesney, Cape** Antarctica
425 N8 **Cessnock** NSW Australia
228 D4 **Cestas** France
304 C3 **Cestos** *watercourse* Liberia
304 C3 **Cestos Point** *cape* Liberia
225 N4 **Cēsu** *admin. area* Latvia
225 M4 **Cesvaine** Latvia
234 C3 **Cetate** Romania
234 D2 **Cetate** Romania
234 D2 **Cetatea de Baltă** Romania
230 F3 **Cetina** Spain
159 F4 **Céu, Serra do** *range* Brazil
158 E2 **Céu Aberto** Brazil
230 D6 **Ceuta** *Spanish autonomous city* North Africa
226 E5 **Ceva** Italy
228 B6 **Cevico de la Torre** Spain
229 I3 **Cevio** Switzerland
226 C4 **Ceyzériat** France
378 E3 **Cha-hsieh Tsang-pu** *watercourse* Xizang Zizhiqu China
378 E2 **Cha-ko-mo Ho** *watercourse* Xizang Zizhiqu China
374 D3 **Chaah** Malaysia
228 F2 **Chaalis, Abbaye de** *point of interest* France
228 E3 **Chabris** France
382 G4 **Chabucha'er** Xinjiang Uygur Zizhiqu China
163 9 **Chacachacare** *island* Trinidad and Tobago
134 C5 **Chacarita** Costa Rica
162 C3 **Chacays, Sierra de los** *range* Argentina
162 C1 **Chachahuén, Sierra de** *range* Argentina
158 B2 **Chachapoyas** Peru
160 E6 **Chacharramendi** Argentina
376 D4 **Chachoengsao** Thailand
391 L4 **Chachro** Pakistan
160 F3 **Chaco** *admin. area* Argentina
160 F2 **Chaco Boreal** *region* Paraguay
118 E5 **Chacon, Cape** Alaska USA
154 B4 **Chacón, Punta** *cape* Colombia
306 B2 **Chad** *country* Africa
305 G2 **Chad, Lake** Chad
389 P3 **Chadan** Russian Federation
160 E6 **Chadileo** *watercourse* Argentina
309 F2 **Chadiza** Zambia
237 U7 **Chadobets** *watercourse* Russian Federation
125 N5 **Chadron** Nebraska USA
305 F2 **Chafe** Nigeria
162 B3 **Chaffers, Isla** *island* Chile
226 D4 **Chaffois** France
163 9 **Chagaunas** *admin. area* Trinidad and Tobago
163 9 **Chagauramas** Trinidad and Tobago
382 G6 **Chagdo Kangri** *mountain* Xizang Zizhiqu China
391 K2 **Chaghcharān** Afghanistan
238 F3 **Chagoda** Russian Federation
80 L4 **Chagos-Laccadive Ridge** *underwater feature* Indian Ocean
80 L5 **Chagos Trench** *underwater feature* Indian Ocean
385 K2 **Chagoyan** Russian Federation
163 9 **Chaguanas** Trinidad and Tobago
389 K6 **Chāh Āb** Afghanistan
391 I2 **Chāh 'Ali** Iran
391 I4 **Chāh Bahār** Iran
391 H3 **Chāh-e Dozdān** Iran
391 I3 **Chāh-e Sagak** Iran
391 H2 **Chāh Farsi** Iran
391 H4 **Chāh Gūni** Iran
391 H3 **Chāh Khāvar** Iran
391 I4 **Chāh Log** Iran
391 H2 **Chāh Malek** Iran
391 I3 **Chāh Mūsā** Iran
391 I3 **Chāh Sand** Iran
391 H3 **Chāh Shūr** Iran
134 B4 **Chahal** Guatemala
385 H4 **Chahan'naoer** Nei Mongol Zizhiqu China
383 K6 **Chahanwusu** Qinghai China
391 I3 **Chahār Farsakh** Iran
390 G3 **Chahār Maḥāll Va Bakhtiārī** *admin. area* Iran
301 G1 **Chahbounia** Algeria
309 H2 **Chai** Mozambique
376 D4 **Chai Nat** Thailand
393 F6 **Chaibasa** Jharkhand India
122 E5 **Chaigneau, Lac** *lake* Québec Canada
385 H5 **Chaigoubu** Hebei China
391 L5 **Chailar** Pakistan
241 G4 **Chailey** East Sussex England UK
228 D2 **Chailland** France
126 I3 **Chaillon, Cape** Ontario Canada
77 P10 **Chain Fracture Zone** *underwater feature* Atlantic Ocean
376 C4 **Chainat** *admin. area* Thailand
376 E4 **Chaîne Annamitique** *mountain* Vietnam
162 B3 **Chaitén** Chile
162 B3 **Chaitén, Ensenada** *bay* Chile
376 D4 **Chaiyaphum** Thailand
161 G4 **Chajarí** Argentina
134 B4 **Chajul** Guatemala
307 F5 **Chake Chake** Tanzania
122 D4 **Chakonipau, Lac** *lake* Québec Canada
393 F6 **Chakradharpur** Jharkhand India
391 L3 **Chakwal** Pakistan
426 2a **Chalan Kanoa** Northern Mariana Islands
134 B4 **Chalatenango** El Salvador
307 F3 **Chalbi Desert** Kenya
132 E4 **Chalchihuites** Mexico
123 F9 **Chaleur Bay** New Brunswick/Québec Canada
162 B4 **Chalía** *watercourse* Argentina
393 D7 **Chalisgaon** Maharashtra India
393 D9 **Chaliyar** *watercourse* Kerala India
235 E7 **Chalki** Greece
235 E7 **Chalki** *island* Greece
235 C6 **Chalkida** Greece
423 B8 **Chalky Inlet** New Zealand
228 D3 **Challans** France
158 E5 **Challapata** Bolivia
78 K6 **Challenger Deep** *underwater feature* Pacific Ocean
79 V11 **Challenger Fracture Zone** *underwater feature* Pacific Ocean
124 H4 **Challis** Idaho USA
388 E6 **Chalmeh** Iran
223 T3 **Chal'mny-Varre** Russian Federation
225 R2 **Chalna** Russian Federation
226 C4 **Chalon-sur-Saône** France
229 G2 **Châlons-en-Champagne** France
229 G2 **Châlons-sur-Marne** France
162 B4 **Chaltén, Cerro** *mountain* Argentina
393 C7 **Chalthan** Gujarat India
241 G4 **Chalton** Hampshire England UK
228 E4 **Châlus** France
229 I3 **Cham** Switzerland
125 L8 **Chama** New Mexico USA
309 F2 **Chama** Zambia
160 E5 **Chamaico** Argentina
226 G3 **Chamb** *watercourse* Germany
392 D4 **Chamba** Himachal Pradesh India
307 F6 **Chamba** Tanzania
392 E5 **Chambal** *watercourse* Madhya Pradesh India
392 D6 **Chambal** *watercourse* Rajasthan India
119 S7 **Chamberlain** Saskatchewan Canada
123 D9 **Chamberlain Lake** Maine USA
121 R2 **Chamberlaine, Lac** *lake* Québec Canada
129 K2 **Chamberlin** Texas USA
116 E5 **Chamberlin, Mount** Alaska USA
129 H3 **Chambers** Arizona USA
127 M7 **Chambersburg** Pennsylvania USA
229 G4 **Chambéry** France
309 F2 **Chambeshi** *watercourse* Zambia
154 B5 **Chambira** Peru
158 C2 **Chambira** *watercourse* Peru
373 G5 **Chambri Lake** Papua New Guinea
154 B2 **Chame, Punta** *cape* Panama
300 C5 **Châmi** Mauritania
160 E4 **Chamical** Argentina
235 E8 **Chamili** *island* Greece
118 C2 **Champagne** Yukon Territory Canada
226 C3 **Champagne-Ardenne** *admin. area* France
228 E4 **Champagne-Mouton** France
229 G3 **Champagnole** France
126 G6 **Champaign** Illinois USA
160 E5 **Champaqui, Cerro** *mountain* Argentina
376 E4 **Champasak** Laos
228 F2 **Champaubert** France
228 D3 **Champdeniers** France
122 F5 **Champdoré, Lac** *lake* Québec Canada
228 F4 **Champeix** France
376 E3 **Champhon** *watercourse* Laos
127 O4 **Champlain, Lake** Vermont USA
133 H5 **Champotón** Mexico
160 E4 **Chañar** Argentina
160 D3 **Chañaral** Chile
160 D4 **Chañaral** *watercourse* Chile
160 D4 **Chañaral, Isla** *island* Chile
158 B3 **Chancay** Peru
158 C3 **Chanchavocaia** Brazil
160 C5 **Chanco** Chile
160 C5 **Chanco, Bahía** *bay* Chile
307 F5 **Chandama** Tanzania
392 F6 **Chandauli** Uttar Pradesh India
392 E5 **Chandausi** Uttar Pradesh India
133 H2 **Chandeleur Islands** Louisiana USA
133 H2 **Chandeleur Sound** Louisiana USA
392 E6 **Chandia** Madhya Pradesh India
392 D4 **Chandigarh** Haryana India
392 G6 **Chandil** Jharkhand India
128 G4 **Chandler** Arizona USA
158 D3 **Chandless** *watercourse* Brazil
383 I3 **Chandman** Mongolia
383 K3 **Chandman** Mongolia
384 D2 **Chandman-under** Mongolia
379 G4 **Chandpur** Bangladesh
393 F7 **Chandpur** Orissa India
392 F5 **Chandpur** Uttar Pradesh India
393 E7 **Chandrapur** Maharashtra India
393 F7 **Chandrapur** Orissa India
230 C2 **Chandrexa de Queixa, Embalse de** *lake* Spain
393 E7 **Chandur** Maharashtra India
388 G6 **Chandyr** *watercourse* Turkmenistan
381 F2 **Chang Hu** *lake* Hubei China
381 H2 **Chang Jiang (Yangtze)** *watercourse* Anhui China
386 E3 **Chang-yŏn** North Korea
380 F3 **Chang'an** Guangxi Zhuangzu Zizhiqu China
309 F4 **Changane** *watercourse* Mozambique
385 K4 **Changbai Shan** *range* Jilin China
385 K4 **Changchun** Jilin China
381 F2 **Changde** Hunan China
379 H2 **Changdu** Xizang Zizhiqu China
381 G1 **Changge** Henan China
380 E5 **Changhua** *watercourse* Hainan China
381 H4 **Changhua** Taiwan China
374 F3 **Changi Beach Park** Singapore
374 E3 **Changi Village** *admin. area* Singapore
383 H4 **Changji** Xinjiang Uygur Zizhiqu China
386 E3 **Changjin** North Korea
386 E3 **Changjin-ho** *lake* North Korea
379 H3 **Changland** Arunachal Pradesh India
385 I5 **Changli** Hebei China
385 J4 **Changling** Jilin China
374 D2 **Changlun** Malaysia
381 F3 **Changning** Hunan China
381 G3 **Changning** Jiangxi China
380 D3 **Changning** Sichuan China
380 F3 **Changpu** Hunan China
385 H6 **Changqing** Shandong China
381 F3 **Changsha** Hunan China
381 H2 **Changshu** Jiangsu China
386 E3 **Ch'angsŏng** North Korea
385 J4 **Changtu** Liaoning China
386 F4 **Ch'angwon** South Korea
381 I2 **Changxing Dao** *island* Shanghai China
380 E2 **Changyuan** Chongqing China
381 G1 **Changyuan** Henan China
380 E3 **Changzhai** Guizhou China
385 H6 **Changzhi** Shanxi China
381 H2 **Changzhou** Jiangsu China
235 C8 **Chanion, Kolpos** *bay* Greece
128 C4 **Channel Islands** California USA
228 C2 **Channel Islands (Îles Normandes)** UK
128 C3 **Channel Islands National Park** California USA
241 I3 **Channel Tunnel** France/UK
129 K3 **Channing** Texas USA
228 E3 **Chanteloube** France
376 D4 **Chanthaburi** Thailand
228 D3 **Chantonnay** France
117 J5 **Chantrey Inlet** Nunavut Canada
374 B1 **Chanumla** India
376 B5 **Chanumla** Andaman and Nicobar Islands India
126 D8 **Chanute** Kansas USA
230 C5 **Chanza, Embalse del** *lake* Spain
381 H2 **Chao Hu** *lake* Anhui China
381 H2 **Chaohu** Anhui China
386 E3 **Chaŏng** North Korea
226 C3 **Chaource** France
381 G4 **Chaoyang** Guangdong China
385 L3 **Chaoyang** Heilongjiang China
385 K4 **Chaoyang** Jilin China
385 I4 **Chaoyang** Liaoning China
381 G4 **Chaozhou** Guangdong China
388 E6 **Chap Chap** Iran
159 H4 **Chapada dos Guimarães** Brazil
156 D4 **Chapada Grande** *region* Brazil
156 D3 **Chapadinha** Brazil
128 E6 **Chapala** Mexico
132 E4 **Chapala, Laguna de** *lake* Mexico
154 C4 **Chaparral** Colombia
388 F3 **Chapayev** Kazakhstan
388 F3 **Chapayevsk** Russian Federation
161 H3 **Chapecó** Brazil
161 H3 **Chapecó** *watercourse* Brazil
131 H3 **Chapel Hill** Tennessee USA
242 D2 **Chapel Rossan** Dumfries and Galloway Scotland UK
243 I3 **Chapel St Leonards** Lincolnshire England UK
245 D2 **Chapel Street** Ireland
242 C2 **Chapeltown** Down Northern Ireland UK
243 G3 **Chapeltown** South Yorkshire England UK
387 I1 **Chaplanovo** Russian Federation
126 J3 **Chapleau** Ontario Canada
125 L1 **Chaplin, Lake** Saskatchewan Canada
Chaplinka *see* **Chaplynka** Ukraine
394 E3 **Chaplynka** Ukraine
125 P6 **Chapman** Nebraska USA
118 L7 **Chapman, Mount** British Columbia Canada
223 U3 **Chapoma** Russian Federation
132 D3 **Chapotán** Mexico
125 N6 **Chappell** Nebraska USA
391 K2 **Chaqmāq** Afghanistan
158 D5 **Chaqui** Chile
160 E2 **Chaqui Laguna** *lake* Bolivia
392 D4 **Char** Jammu and Kashmir India/Pakistan
237 Y7 **Chara** *watercourse* Russian Federation
161 G3 **Charadai** Argentina
159 F5 **Charagua** Bolivia
154 B3 **Charambirá, Punta** *point* Colombia
154 A5 **Charapotó, Punta** *cape* Ecuador
160 F3 **Charata** Argentina
235 B5 **Charavgi** Greece
132 E4 **Charcas** Mexico
154 C4 **Charco Caimán** Colombia
436 S2 **Charcot Deep Sea Fan** *underwater feature* Southern Ocean
436 S2 **Charcot Island** Antarctica
119 P5 **Chard** Alberta Canada
240 E3 **Charfield** South Gloucestershire England UK
305 H2 **Chari** *watercourse* Chad
305 H2 **Chari-Baguirmi** *admin. area* Chad
391 L2 **Chārīkār** Afghanistan
392 G5 **Charikot** Nepal
126 E6 **Chariton** Iowa USA
126 E6 **Chariton** *watercourse* Missouri USA
236 L5 **Charkayuvom** Russian Federation
241 F3 **Charlbury** Oxfordshire England UK
120 H4 **Charlebois** Manitoba Canada
229 G1 **Charleroi** Belgium
119 U5 **Charles** Manitoba Canada
122 K6 **Charles, Cape** Newfoundland and Labrador Canada
422 F3 **Charles, Port** New Zealand
162 B5 **Charles Fuhr** Argentina
122 A1 **Charles Island** Nunavut Canada
423 B7 **Charles Sound** New Zealand
241 H2 **Charles Tye** Suffolk England UK
131 L4 **Charleston** South Carolina USA
131 I3 **Charleston** Tennessee USA
127 K7 **Charleston** West Virginia USA
131 L4 **Charleston Harbor** South Carolina USA
127 M4 **Charleston Lake** Ontario Canada
245 D3 **Charlestown** Ireland
163 19 **Charlestown** St Kitts and Nevis
425 M6 **Charleville** Qld Australia
437 I2 **Charlie, Dome** *mountain* Antarctica
76 O4 **Charlie-Gibbs Fracture Zone** *underwater feature* Atlantic Ocean
118 K4 **Charlie Lake** British Columbia Canada
131 K3 **Charlotte** North Carolina USA
130 B6 **Charlotte** Texas USA
155 H3 **Charlotte, Pointe** *cape* French Guiana
163 21 **Charlotte Amalie** US Virgin Islands
133 J3 **Charlotte Harbor** Florida USA
118 I6 **Charlotte Lake** British Columbia Canada
123 G9 **Charlottetown** Prince Edward Island Canada
163 9 **Charlotteville** Trinidad and Tobago
240 E3 **Charlton Horethorne** Somerset England UK
117 L8 **Charlton Island** Nunavut Canada
241 E3 **Charlton Kings** Gloucestershire England UK
226 D3 **Charmes** France
240 E4 **Charmouth** Dorset England UK
388 E6 **Charna** Iran
229 G3 **Charollais** *region* France
225 N5 **Charomkhava** Belarus
228 F3 **Chârost** France
238 H2 **Charozero** Russian Federation
120 H6 **Charron Lake** Manitoba Canada
425 M5 **Charters Towers** Qld Australia
163 7 **Chartres** Falkland Islands
228 E2 **Chartres** France
389 N3 **Charyshskoye** Russian Federation
161 G5 **Chas** Argentina
392 G6 **Chas** Jharkhand India
393 C7 **Chas** Maharashtra India
160 D3 **Chaschuil** Argentina
161 G5 **Chascomús** Argentina
118 L7 **Chase** British Columbia Canada
125 P7 **Chase** Kansas USA
388 I6 **Chashkent** Turkmenistan
391 H3 **Chashmeh Mārī** Iran
225 O5 **Chashniki** Belarus
304 D3 **Chasia** Ghana
162 C3 **Chasicó** Argentina
228 E4 **Chasseneuil-sur-Bonnieure** France
229 G3 **Chassigny** France
228 D3 **Chassiron, Pointe de** *cape* France
229 G1 **Chastre** Belgium
388 G1 **Chastyye** Russian Federation
228 C2 **Château, Pointe du** *cape* France
229 H2 **Château-Salins** France
127 O4 **Châteauguay** Québec Canada
122 D4 **Châteauguay** *watercourse* Québec Canada
122 C4 **Châteauguay, Lac** *lake* Québec Canada
228 F4 **Châteauneuf-de-Randon** France
228 E3 **Châteauponsac** France
229 G5 **Châteaurenard** France
226 C3 **Châteauvillain** France
163 16 **Châteaux, Pointe des** *cape* Guadeloupe
229 H3 **Châtel-St-Denis** Switzerland
228 D3 **Châtelaillon-Plage** France
122 A2 **Châtelain, Lac** *lake* Québec Canada
229 G1 **Châtelet** Belgium
226 C3 **Châtenois** France
125 P2 **Chater** Manitoba Canada
241 H3 **Chatham** Medway England UK
118 D4 **Chatham** Alaska USA
130 E4 **Chatham** Louisiana USA
162 A5 **Chatham, Isla** *island* Chile
423 6 **Chatham Island (Rekohua)** New Zealand
78 O12 **Chatham Rise** *underwater feature* Pacific Ocean
118 F5 **Chatham Sound** British Columbia/Alaska Canada/USA
118 D4 **Chatham Strait** Alaska USA
389 L5 **Chatkël** Kyrgyzstan
392 F6 **Chatra** Jharkhand India
392 D5 **Chatsu** Rajasthan India
131 I5 **Chattahoochee** Florida USA
133 I1 **Chattahoochee** *watercourse* Georgia USA
131 I3 **Chattanooga** Tennessee USA
241 H2 **Chatteris** Cambridgeshire England UK
376 D4 **Chatturat** Thailand
131 J3 **Chatuge Lake** North Carolina USA
376 E5 **Châu Đốc** Vietnam
228 F4 **Chaudes-Aigues** France
229 G3 **Chauffailles** France
392 C6 **Chauhtan** Rajasthan India
379 H5 **Chauk** Myanmar
392 E4 **Chaukhamba** *mountain* Uttaranchal India
391 K4 **Chauki** Pakistan
122 E4 **Chaumaux** *watercourse* Québec Canada
228 E3 **Chaumont** France
122 D6 **Chaumont, Lac** *lake* Québec Canada
118 K8 **Chaumox** British Columbia Canada
379 H5 **Chaung-U** Myanmar
237 AI5 **Chaunskaya Guba** *bay* Russian Federation
392 D4 **Chaupal** Himachal Pradesh India
226 C4 **Chaussin** France
126 F6 **Chautauqua, Lake** Illinois USA
121 R5 **Chauvreulx** *watercourse* Québec Canada
393 E10 **Chavakachcheri** Sri Lanka
223 T3 **Chavan'ga** Russian Federation
235 B7 **Chavarion** Greece
230 C3 **Chaves** Portugal
121 R3 **Chavigny, Lac** *lake* Québec Canada
308 D2 **Chavuma** Zambia
225 P6 **Chavusi** Belarus
393 D7 **Chawala** Maharashtra India
237 AC8 **Chayatyn, Khrebet** *range* Russian Federation
238 G3 **Chayevo** Russian Federation
388 G2 **Chaykovskiy** Russian Federation
237 AD8 **Chayvo, Zaliv** *bay* Russian Federation
160 F5 **Chazón** Argentina
158 B2 **Chazuta** Peru
376 E4 **Chbar** Cambodia
380 D4 **Che-kan Ho** *watercourse* Yunnan China
241 F2 **Cheadle** Staffordshire England UK
162 A4 **Cheap, Canal** *strait* Chile
130 H2 **Cheatham Lake** Tennessee USA
226 G2 **Cheb** Czech Republic
301 I1 **Chebba** Tunisia
388 E2 **Cheboksary** Russian Federation
126 I4 **Cheboygan** Michigan USA
238 H3 **Chebsara** Russian Federation
379 I4 **Chebwe** Myanmar
388 E5 **Chechen', Ostrov** *island* Russian Federation
388 E5 **Chechenskaya Respublika** *admin. area* Russian Federation
386 F4 **Chech'ŏn** South Korea
123 H10 **Chedabucto Bay** Nova Scotia Canada
240 E3 **Cheddar** Somerset England UK
241 E1 **Cheddleton** Staffordshire England UK
301 J6 **Chéddra** Chad
379 G5 **Cheduba Strait** Myanmar
119 P4 **Cheecham** Alberta Canada
127 K1 **Cheepash** *watercourse* Ontario Canada
126 J1 **Cheepay** *watercourse* Ontario Canada
422 5 **Cheeseman Island** Kermadec Islands New Zealand
129 J1 **Cheeseman Lake** Colorado USA
437 K2 **Cheetham, Cape** Antarctica
163 9 **Cheeyou** Trinidad and Tobago
228 D3 **Chef-Boutonne** France
300 E3 **Chegga** Mauritania
124 D3 **Chehalis** Washington USA
231 G6 **Chehama** Algeria
391 I3 **Chehel Tokhm** Iran
234 D3 **Cheia** Romania
234 B3 **Cheile Nerei** *range* Romania
386 E5 **Cheju** South Korea
386 E5 **Cheju-do** *island* South Korea
386 E5 **Cheju-Haehyŏp** *strait* South Korea
238 G5 **Chekhov** Russian Federation
387 I1 **Chekhov** Russian Federation
223 U5 **Chekuyevo** Russian Federation
308 B3 **Chela, Serra da** *range* Angola
124 E3 **Chelan** Washington USA
124 E2 **Chelan, Lake** Washington USA
230 C4 **Cheles** Spain
160 E6 **Chelforó** Argentina
301 H1 **Chelghoum el Aïd** Algeria
309 G4 **Cheline** Mozambique
227 L2 **Chełm** Poland
241 H3 **Chelmer** *watercourse* England UK
241 I3 **Chelmondiston** Suffolk England UK
243 G3 **Chelmorton** Derbyshire England UK
241 H3 **Chelmsford** Essex England UK
223 S5 **Chelmuzhi** Russian Federation
241 G3 **Chelsea** Greater London England UK
126 I5 **Chelsea** Michigan USA
241 E3 **Cheltenham** Gloucestershire England UK
241 G2 **Chelveston** Northamptonshire England UK
388 I2 **Chelyabinsk** Russian Federation
388 H2 **Chelyabinskaya** *admin. area* Russian Federation
126 I1 **Chemahagan** *watercourse* Ontario Canada
300 E2 **Chemaïa** Morocco
237 AD5 **Chemalginskiy Khrebet** *range* Russian Federation
133 I4 **Chemax** Mexico
308 E2 **Chembe** Zambia
227 M3 **Chemerintsy** Ukraine
228 F3 **Chemilly** France
310 7b **Chemin Grenier** Mauritius
231 J6 **Chemora** Algeria
229 K1 **Chemnitz** Germany
389 L5 **Chemolgan** Kazakhstan
380 E3 **Chen Shui** *watercourse* Guizhou China
391 M3 **Chenab** *watercourse* Pakistan
129 M2 **Cheney Reservoir** Kansas USA
392 E3 **Cheng Chemmo** *watercourse* Jammu and Kashmir India/Pakistan
393 E9 **Chengalpattu** Tamil Nadu India
380 E4 **Chengbine Shuiku** *lake* Guangxi Zhuangzu Zizhiqu China
385 I5 **Chengde** Hebei China
381 G2 **Chengdong Hu** *lake* Anhui China
380 D2 **Chengdu** Sichuan China
381 G4 **Chenghai** Guangdong China
381 G3 **Chengjiang** Jiangxi China
381 I2 **Chengqiao** Shanghai China
381 G1 **Chengwu** Shandong China
381 G4 **Chengxiang** Jiangxi China
380 D2 **Chengxiang** Sichuan China
385 I6 **Chengyang** Shandong China
380 E4 **Chengzhong** Guangxi Zhuangzu Zizhiqu China
393 E9 **Chennai** Tamil Nadu India
380 F3 **Chenyang** Hunan China
381 H3 **Chenying** Jiangxi China
381 G3 **Chenzhou** Hunan China
158 B2 **Chepén** Peru
426 7 **Chépénéhé** New Caledonia
160 E4 **Chepes** Argentina
307 F3 **Chephotet** *mountain* Kenya
158 E4 **Chepite, Serranía** *range* Bolivia
240 E3 **Chepstow** Monmouthshire Wales UK
162 B3 **Chepu** Chile
126 F3 **Chequamegon Bay** Wisconsin USA
126 F4 **Chequamegon Waters** *lake* Wisconsin USA
228 E3 **Cher** *watercourse* France
393 C9 **Cherbaniani Reef** Lakshadweep India
241 F5 **Cherbourg** France
301 G1 **Cherchell** Algeria
388 E2 **Cherdakly** Russian Federation
389 N4 **Cherdoyak** Kazakhstan
237 V8 **Cheremkhovo** Russian Federation
384 E1 **Cheremkhovo** Russian Federation
238 C3 **Cheremykino** Russian Federation
238 G3 **Cherepovets** Russian Federation
119 N6 **Cherhill** Alberta Canada
301 H1 **Chéria** Algeria
393 E8 **Cherial** Andhra Pradesh India
241 F3 **Cheriton** Hampshire England UK

240 C3 **Cheriton** Swansea Wales UK
127 N8 **Cheriton** Virginia USA
393 C9 **Cheriyam Island** Lakshadweep India
394 D3 **Cherkas'ka Oblast'** *admin. area* Ukraine
234 H1 **Cherkasy** Ukraine
388 D5 **Cherkessk** Russian Federation
393 E7 **Cherla** Andhra Pradesh India
389 L2 **Cherlak** Russian Federation
238 F5 **Cherlenkovo** Russian Federation
388 G1 **Chermoz** Russian Federation
238 G6 **Chern'** Russian Federation
238 H6 **Chernava** Russian Federation
238 G2 **Chërnaya Sloboda-Tatarikha** Russian Federation
238 C3 **Chernevo** Russian Federation
394 D2 **Chernihiv** Ukraine
394 D2 **Chernihivs'ka Oblast'** *admin. area* Ukraine
394 C3 **Chernivets'ka Oblast'** *admin. area* Ukraine
234 D1 **Chernivtsi** Ukraine
Chernobyl *see* **Chornobyl'** Ukraine
389 P2 **Chernogorsk** Russian Federation
389 O2 **Chernoye** *lake* Russian Federation
394 F2 **Chernyanka** Russian Federation
236 F2 **Chernysheno** Russian Federation
385 I2 **Chernyshevsk** Russian Federation
236 T6 **Chërnyy Ostrov** Russian Federation
223 R5 **Chërnyy Porog** Russian Federation
388 E4 **Chernyy Yar** Russian Federation
388 E4 **Chernyye Zemli** Russian Federation
130 D4 **Cherokee, Lake** Texas USA
131 J2 **Cherokee Lake** Tennessee USA
228 F2 **Chéroy** France
225 P4 **Cherpesa** Russian Federation
379 G4 **Cherra Punjee** Meghalaya India
129 J1 **Cherry Creek Lake** Colorado USA
128 C1 **Cherry Lake** California USA
237 X8 **Cherskogo, Khrebet** *range* Russian Federation
394 G3 **Chertkovo** Ukraine
238 E4 **Chertolino** Russian Federation
241 G3 **Chertsey** Surrey England UK
393 D10 **Cheruvalli** Kerala India
237 U7 **Chervyanka** Russian Federation
225 O6 **Chervyen'** Belarus
225 P6 **Cherykaw** Belarus
127 M8 **Chesapeake** Virginia USA
127 M7 **Chesapeake Bay** Maryland USA
131 N2 **Chesapeake Bay** Virginia USA
131 M2 **Chesdin, Lake** Virginia USA
243 F3 **Cheshire** *admin. area* England UK
388 I6 **Cheshme Vtoroy** Turkmenistan
236 K5 **Cheshskaya Guba** *bay* Russian Federation
391 J2 **Chesht-e Sharif** Afghanistan
241 G3 **Cheshunt** Hertfordshire England UK
240 E4 **Chesil Beach** Dorset England UK
391 I2 **Chesmeh Shāh** Iran
123 F10 **Chester** Nova Scotia Canada
242 F3 **Chester** Cheshire England UK
126 G8 **Chester** Illinois USA
125 J2 **Chester** Montana USA
125 Q7 **Chester** Nebraska USA
131 K3 **Chester** South Carolina USA
243 G2 **Chester-le-Street** Durham England UK
243 G3 **Chesterfield** Derbyshire England UK
120 J1 **Chesterfield Inlet** Nunavut Canada
123 D9 **Chesuncook Lake** Maine USA
231 J5 **Chetaibi** Algeria
376 B5 **Chetamale** Andaman and Nicobar Islands India
126 F4 **Chetek** Wisconsin USA
123 H9 **Chéticamp** Nova Scotia Canada
393 C9 **Chetlat Island** Lakshadweep India
241 E4 **Chettle** Dorset England UK
133 H5 **Chetumal** Mexico
423 F5 **Chetwode Islands** New Zealand
118 K5 **Chetwynd** British Columbia Canada
226 B4 **Chevagnes** France
159 E4 **Chevejécure** Bolivia
423 E6 **Cheviot** New Zealand
243 F1 **Cheviot, The** *mountain* England UK
244 F5 **Cheviot Hills** *range* England UK
228 B2 **Chèvre, Cap de la** *cape* France
240 E3 **Chew Magna** Bath and North East Somerset England UK
240 E3 **Chew Valley Lake** England UK
125 N5 **Cheyenne** *watercourse* South Dakota USA
125 M6 **Cheyenne** Wyoming USA
125 N7 **Cheyenne Wells** Colorado USA
376 D5 **Chhâk** *island* Cambodia
392 F6 **Chhapra** Bihar India
392 E6 **Chhatarpur** Madhya Pradesh India
391 K4 **Chhatr** Pakistan
393 F7 **Chhattisgarh** *admin. area* India
392 E5 **Chhibramau** Uttar Pradesh India
393 E6 **Chhindwara** Madhya Pradesh India
376 E4 **Chhlong** *watercourse* Cambodia
393 E7 **Chhuikhadan** Chhattisgarh India
379 F3 **Chhukha** Bhutan
381 H2 **Chi He** *watercourse* Anhui China
380 D4 **Chi-Lu Hu** *lake* Yunnan China
378 E3 **Chi-lung Ho** *watercourse* Xizang Zizhiqu China
381 H4 **Chi-Pei Tao** *island* Taiwan China
154 C3 **Chia** Colombia
233 C7 **Chia** Sardinia Italy
381 H4 **Chiai** Taiwan China
383 H3 **Chianassu Hu** *lake* Xinjiang Uygur Zizhiqu China
229 J5 **Chianciano Terme** Italy
376 D3 **Chiang Kham** Thailand
376 D3 **Chiang Khan** Thailand
376 D3 **Chiang Klang** Thailand
376 C3 **Chiang Mai** Thailand
376 C3 **Chiang Mai** *admin. area* Thailand
376 C3 **Chiang Rai** Thailand
376 D2 **Chiang Saen** Thailand
308 B3 **Chiange** Angola
232 D5 **Chianni** Italy
133 G5 **Chiapa de Corzo** Mexico
133 G5 **Chiapas** *admin. area* Mexico
134 A4 **Chiapas, Sierra Madre de** *range* Mexico
232 C4 **Chiari** Italy
133 F5 **Chiautla de Tapia** Mexico
232 F4 **Chiavenna** Italy
387 I4 **Chiba** Japan
381 G2 **Chibi** Hubei China
121 R8 **Chibougamau** Québec Canada
121 R8 **Chibougamau, Lac** *lake* Québec Canada
386 G4 **Chiburi-jima** *island* Japan
309 F4 **Chibuto** Mozambique
123 E8 **Chic-Chocs, Monts** *range* Québec Canada
160 D2 **Chica** Chile
162 C3 **Chica, Pampa** *region* Argentina
126 H6 **Chicago** Illinois USA
308 C2 **Chicala** Angola
308 C2 **Chicala** Angola
158 B2 **Chicama** Peru
305 G5 **Chicamba** Congo
309 F3 **Chicamba** Mozambique
308 C2 **Chicapa** *watercourse* Angola
154 B3 **Chicha Bay** Colombia
158 D4 **Chichacori** Peru
118 C4 **Chichagof** Alaska USA
118 C3 **Chichagof Island** Alaska USA
300 E2 **Chichaoua** Morocco
160 E/F2 **Chichas, Cordillera de** *range* Bolivia/Paraguay
159 H3 **Chiche** *watercourse* Brazil
385 H5 **Chicheng** Hebei China
380 E2 **Chicheng** Sichuan China
241 G4 **Chichester** West Sussex England UK
424 F5 **Chichester Range** WA Australia
134 D5 **Chichica** Panama
134 B4 **Chichicastenango** Guatemala
133 F5 **Chichihualco** Mexico
160 E6 **Chichinales** Argentina
154 B5 **Chichirota** Ecuador
393 D6 **Chicholi** Madhya Pradesh India
130 G5 **Chickasawhay** *watercourse* Mississippi USA
130 C3 **Chickasha** Oklahoma USA
241 E3 **Chicklade** Wiltshire England UK
230 C5 **Chiclana de la Frontera** Spain
158 B2 **Chiclayo** Peru
162 B4 **Chico** *watercourse* Argentina
124 E7 **Chico** California USA
130 C4 **Chico** Texas USA
161 G5 **Chico, Lago** *lake* Argentina
158 C3 **Chico Mana** Brazil
308 F2 **Chicoa** Mozambique
308 B2 **Chicomba** Angola
309 G2 **Chiconono** Mozambique
127 O5 **Chicopee** Massachusetts USA
130 F4 **Chicot, Lake** Mississippi USA
123 C8 **Chicoutimi** Québec Canada
308 B2 **Chicuma** Angola
306 B6 **Chicupo** Angola
393 E9 **Chidambaram** Tamil Nadu India
240 E4 **Chideock** Dorset England UK
388 F6 **Chidirly** Azerbaijan
117 M6 **Chidley, Cape** Nunavut Canada
308 C3 **Chiede** Angola
127 K4 **Chiefs Point** Ontario Canada
232 E3 **Chiemsee** *lake* Germany
306 D5 **Chiengi** Zambia
232 B4 **Chieri** Italy
229 G2 **Chiers** *watercourse* France
232 D3 **Chiese Fiume** *watercourse* Italy
233 F5 **Chieti** Italy
233 F6 **Chieuti** Italy
226 B2 **Chièvres** Belgium
385 I4 **Chifeng** Nei Mongol Zizhiqu China
309 F2 **Chifunde** Mozambique
116 D7 **Chiginagak, Mount** Alaska USA
123 F10 **Chignecto Bay** New Brunswick/Nova Scotia Canada
154 B3 **Chigorodó** Colombia
123 O2 **Chigoubiche, Lac** *lake* Québec Canada
159 E5 **Chiguailla, Altos de** *range* Bolivia
309 F4 **Chigubo** Mozambique
132 D2 **Chihuahua** Mexico
132 D3 **Chihuahua** *admin. area* Mexico
154 C2 **Chikepu** Colombia
225 O4 **Chikhachëvo** Russian Federation
393 E7 **Chikhli** Madhya Pradesh India
393 D7 **Chikhli** Maharashtra India
393 F7 **Chikiti** Orissa India
393 D9 **Chikmagalur** Karnataka India
308 E2 **Chikonkomene** Zambia
384 F2 **Chikoy** *watercourse* Russian Federation
237 AG8 **Chikurachki** *volcano* Kuril Islands
308 E2 **Chikwa** Zambia
308 B2 **Chila** Angola
158 B3 **Chila** Peru
158 C4 **Chila Pillune, Cerro** *mountain* Peru
118 J6 **Chilako** *watercourse* British Columbia Canada
116 G8 **Chilanko** *watercourse* British Columbia Canada
391 M2 **Chilas** Pakistan
393 E10 **Chilaw** Sri Lanka
158 B4 **Chilca** Peru
118 J7 **Chilcotin** *watercourse* British Columbia Canada
118 J7 **Chilcotin Ranges** British Columbia Canada
129 L3 **Childress** Texas USA
425 O6 **Childers** Qld Australia
158 D6 **Chile** *country* South America
79 Y11 **Chile Basin** *underwater feature* Pacific Ocean
79 X12 **Chile Rise** *underwater feature* Pacific Ocean
158 E6 **Chilena** Bolivia
306 B6 **Chilengue, Serra do** *range* Angola
158 B2 **Chilete** *watercourse* Peru
388 E4 **Chilgir** Russian Federation
241 H3 **Chilham** Kent England UK
389 M5 **Chilik** Kazakhstan
393 F7 **Chilika Lake** Orissa India
308 E2 **Chililabombwe** Zambia
233 C6 **Chilivani** Sardinia Italy
118 D3 **Chilkat Inlet** Alaska USA
116 G8 **Chilko** *watercourse* British Columbia Canada
118 I7 **Chilko Lake** British Columbia Canada
425 M4 **Chillagoe** Qld Australia
160 C6 **Chillán** Chile
126 E7 **Chillicothe** Missouri USA
126 J7 **Chillicothe** Ohio USA
128 E3 **Chillicothe** Texas USA
240 D4 **Chillington** Devon England UK
240 E3 **Chillington** Somerset England UK
118 K8 **Chilliwack** British Columbia Canada
162 B3 **Chiloé, Archipiélago de** *islands* Chile
162 B3 **Chiloé, Isla** *island* Chile
309 F2 **Chilonga** Zambia
124 E5 **Chiloquin** Oregon USA
133 F5 **Chilpancingo** Mexico
241 G3 **Chiltern Hills** *range* England UK
240 D3 **Chilton Trinity** Somerset England UK
306 C5 **Chiluage** Angola
308 E2 **Chilubi** Zambia
309 F2 **Chilumba** Malawi
309 G3 **Chilwa, Lake** Malawi
134 B4 **Chimaltenango** Guatemala
134 E5 **Chimán** Panama
155 E2 **Chimanas, Islas** *islands* Venezuela
229 G1 **Chimay** Belgium
158 B3 **Chimbote** Peru
158 B3 **Chimbote, Bahía** *bay* Peru
388 H5 **Chimboy** Uzbekistan
309 F2 **Chimbwingombe** *mountain* Zambia
305 I3 **Chimko** *watercourse* Central African Republic
389 J6 **Chimkurgan** Uzbekistan
124 G6 **Chimney Reservoir** Nevada USA
309 F3 **Chimoio** Mozambique
159 E5 **Chimoré** Bolivia
160 E6 **Chimpay** Argentina
379 G4 **Chin** *admin. area* Myanmar
386 E4 **Chin-do** *island* South Korea
379 G5 **Chin Hills** Myanmar
384 C4 **China** *country* Asia
133 H5 **Chiná** Mexico
134 C4 **Chinandega** Nicaragua
132 C2 **Chinapa** Mexico
374 D4 **Chinatown** *admin. area* Singapore
134 B4 **Chinautla** Guatemala
158 B4 **Chincha Alta** Peru
116 H7 **Chinchaga** *watercourse* Alberta Canada
134 C3 **Chinchorro, Banco** *reef* Mexico
160 D5 **Chincolco** Chile
127 N8 **Chincoteague** Virginia USA
127 N8 **Chincoteague Bay** Virginia USA
309 G3 **Chinde** Mozambique
386 E4 **Chindo** South Korea
379 H4 **Chindwin** *watercourse* Myanmar
385 H2 **Chingikan, Gora** *mountain* Russian Federation
389 M4 **Chingiz-Tau, Khrebet** *range* Kazakhstan
308 E2 **Chingo** Angola
308 E2 **Chingola** Zambia
308 C3 **Chinguanja** Angola
308 C2 **Chinguar** Angola
308 C2 **Chingueia** Angola
159 H6 **Chingüelo** Paraguay
300 D4 **Chinguetti** Mauritania
386 E4 **Chinhae** South Korea
309 F3 **Chinhanda** Mozambique
309 F3 **Chinhoyi** Zimbabwe
391 L3 **Chiniot** Pakistan
129 H7 **Chinipas** Mexico
158 E4 **Chiñiri** Bolivia
386 E4 **Chinju** South Korea
305 I3 **Chinko** *watercourse* Central African Republic
128 H2 **Chinle** Arizona USA
128 H2 **Chinle** *watercourse* Arkansas USA
381 H4 **Chinmen Tao (Quemoy) (Taiwan)** *island* Taiwan China
393 E8 **Chinna Ganjum** Andhra Pradesh India
393 E9 **Chinna Salem** Tamil Nadu India
128 F3 **Chino** *watercourse* Arkansas USA
128 F3 **Chino Valley** Arizona USA
228 E3 **Chinon** France
125 K2 **Chinook** Montana USA
78 O3 **Chinook Trough** *underwater feature* Pacific Ocean
158 B3 **Chinos, Bahía Los** *bay* Peru
389 K5 **Chinoz** Uzbekistan
309 F2 **Chinsali** Zambia
393 E9 **Chintamani** Karnataka India
154 C2 **Chinú** Colombia
229 G2 **Chiny** Belgium
308 D2 **Chinyama Litapi** Zambia
379 H5 **Chinzu** Myanmar
226 G5 **Chioggia** Italy
235 D6 **Chios** *island* Greece
119 N6 **Chip Lake** Alberta Canada
309 F2 **Chipata** Zambia
234 F2 **Chiperceni** Moldova
309 G3 **Chiperone, Mount** Mozambique
119 O4 **Chipewyan Lake** Alberta Canada
308 E2 **Chipili** Zambia
308 C2 **Chipindo** Angola
309 F4 **Chipinge** Zimbabwe
123 F9 **Chipman** New Brunswick Canada
119 S3 **Chipman** *watercourse* Saskatchewan Canada
126 H2 **Chipman Lake** Ontario Canada
308 C2 **Chipoia** Angola
309 F2 **Chipoka** Malawi
306 B6 **Chipola** Angola
126 F4 **Chippewa** *watercourse* Wisconsin USA
126 F4 **Chippewa Falls** Wisconsin USA
243 F3 **Chipping** Lancashire England UK
241 F3 **Chipping Norton** Oxfordshire England UK
241 H3 **Chipping Ongar** Essex England UK
229 H3 **Chippis** Switzerland
123 E10 **Chiputneticook Lakes** New Brunswick Canada
134 B4 **Chiquimula** Guatemala
160 D2 **Chiquinata, Bahía** *bay* Chile
393 E8 **Chirala** Andhra Pradesh India
379 G3 **Chirang** Bhutan
240 D2 **Chirbury** Shropshire England UK
389 K5 **Chirchiq** Uzbekistan
309 G3 **Chire** Mozambique
301 I4 **Chirfa** Niger
154 C2 **Chiriguaná** Colombia
116 D7 **Chirikof Island** Alaska USA
154 A3 **Chiriquí, Golfo de** *bay* Panama
154 A2 **Chiriquí, Laguna de** *bay* Panama
154 A2 **Chiriquí, Punta** *cape* Panama
154 A2 **Chiriquí, Volcán de** *volcano* Panama
134 D5 **Chiriquí Grande** Panama
230 E5 **Chirivel** Spain
240 D2 **Chirk** Wrexham Wales UK
234 E3 **Chirnogi** Romania
244 F5 **Chirnside** Scottish Borders Scotland UK
134 D5 **Chirripó, Cerro** *mountain* Costa Rica
134 D5 **Chirripó, Río** *watercourse* Costa Rica
234 F2 **Chirsova** Moldova
158 D4 **Chiru Choricha, Serranía** *range* Bolivia
308 E3 **Chirundu** Zimbabwe
308 E2 **Chisasa** Zambia
121 P6 **Chisasibi** Québec Canada
244 C5 **Chiscan** Argyll and Bute Scotland UK
154 C3 **Chiscas** Colombia
134 B4 **Chisec** Guatemala
309 F1 **Chisenga** Malawi
119 N5 **Chisholm** Alberta Canada
123 C10 **Chisholm** Maine USA
391 L3 **Chishtian Mandi** Pakistan
380 E3 **Chishui** Guizhou China
380 E3 **Chishui He** *watercourse* Sichuan China
234 F2 **Chişinău (Kishinev)** Moldova
227 K4 **Chişineu-Criş** Romania
129 J5 **Chispa** Texas USA
309 F4 **Chissibuca** Mozambique
309 F4 **Chissinguane** Mozambique
310 8b **Chissioua Mtsamboro** *island* Mayotte
388 F2 **Chistopol'** Russian Federation
241 G3 **Chiswell Green** Hertfordshire England UK
385 H2 **Chita** Russian Federation
307 F5 **Chita** Tanzania
308 B3 **Chitado** Angola
306 C5 **Chitato** Angola
308 C2 **Chitembo** Angola
237 Y8 **Chitinskaya Oblast'** *admin. area* Russian Federation
307 E5 **Chitipa** Malawi
392 E4 **Chitkul** Himachal Pradesh India
309 F4 **Chitobe** Mozambique
308 D2 **Chitokoloki** Zambia
308 D2 **Chitongo** Zambia
387 I2 **Chitose** Japan
393 D8 **Chitradurga** Karnataka India
391 L2 **Chitral** Pakistan
134 D6 **Chitré** Panama
379 G4 **Chittagong** Bangladesh
379 G4 **Chittagong** *admin. area* Bangladesh
392 D6 **Chittaurgarh** Rajasthan India
241 E3 **Chittoe** Wiltshire England UK
393 E9 **Chittoor** Andhra Pradesh India
309 F3 **Chitungwiza** Zimbabwe
309 G2 **Chiulezi** *watercourse* Mozambique
308 D3 **Chiume** Angola
309 G2 **Chiúre** Mozambique
226 F4 **Chiusa** Italy
232 D5 **Chiusi** Italy
309 G2 **Chiuta, Lake** Mozambique
226 D5 **Chivasso** Italy
132 C3 **Chivato, Punta** *cape* Mexico
309 F3 **Chivhu** Zimbabwe
161 F5 **Chivilcoy** Argentina
154 C2 **Chivolo** Colombia
162 C3 **Chivos, Pampa de los** *region* Argentina
133 H6 **Chixoy** *watercourse* Guatemala
308 E3 **Chizarira Hills** *range* Zimbabwe
388 F3 **Chizha Vtoraya** Kazakhstan
381 H2 **Chizhou** Anhui China
227 H1 **Chlebowo** Poland
301 G1 **Chlef** Algeria
301 G1 **Chlef** *admin. area* Algeria
227 L2 **Chłopiatyn** Poland
232 F2 **Chlum u Třeboně** Czech Republic
376 E2 **Chợ Chu** Vietnam
386 E3 **Cho-do** *island* North Korea
386 E4 **Cho-do** *island* South Korea
379 F3 **Cho Oyu** *mountain* Xizang Zizhiqu China
374 B3 **Choa Chu Kang** *admin. area* Singapore
376 E4 **Choâm Khsant** Cambodia
160 D4 **Choapa** *watercourse* Chile
387 I2 **Chobushi-numa** *lake* Japan
227 I2 **Choceň** Czech Republic
386 E4 **Choch'iwon** South Korea
154 B3 **Chocó** *admin. area* Colombia
154 B4 **Chocó, Bahía** *bay* Colombia
131 H5 **Choctawhatchee Bay** Florida USA
227 I2 **Chocz** Poland
391 I2 **Chodān** Iran
393 E8 **Chodavaram** Andhra Pradesh India
160 E6 **Choele Choel** Argentina
309 F2 **Chofombo** Mozambique
391 M2 **Chogo Lungma Glacier** Pakistan
384 F4 **Chogtovoo** Mongolia
384 F4 **Chogttsetsii** Mongolia
244 D2 **Choire, Loch** *lake* Scotland UK
426 8 **Choiseul** *admin. area* Solomon Islands
426 8 **Choiseul** *island* Solomon Islands
163 7 **Choiseul Sound** *bay* Falkland Islands
132 C3 **Choix** Mexico
227 I1 **Chojnice** Poland
227 I2 **Chojnik** Poland
227 H2 **Chojnów** Poland
376 D4 **Chok Chai** Thailand
387 I3 **Chōkai-zan** *volcano* Japan
130 B6 **Choke Canyon Reservoir** Texas USA
125 Q4 **Chokio** Minnesota USA
389 L5 **Chokpar** Kazakhstan
309 F4 **Chokwé** Mozambique
128 B3 **Cholame** California USA
241 F3 **Cholderton** Wiltshire England UK
228 D3 **Cholet** France
162 B3 **Cholila** Argentina
154 D3 **Chololobo** Colombia
134 C4 **Choloma** Honduras
389 M5 **Cholpon-Ata** Kyrgyzstan
133 F5 **Cholula** Mexico
386 E3 **Ch'ŏlwon** South Korea
376 C3 **Chom Thong** Thailand
308 E3 **Choma** Zambia
234 D4 **Chomakovtsi** Bulgaria
379 F3 **Chomo Yummo** *mountain* Xizang Zizhiqu China
379 G3 **Chomo Ganggar** *mountain* Xizang Zizhiqu China
379 F3 **Chomo Lhari** *mountain* Bhutan
376 E5 **Chơn Thành** Vietnam
237 W6 **Chona** *watercourse* Russian Federation
386 E4 **Ch'ŏnan** South Korea
376 D4 **Chonburi** Thailand
154 A5 **Chone** Ecuador
376 D4 **Chông Kal** Cambodia
386 F3 **Ch'ongjin** North Korea
386 E4 **Ch'ŏngju** South Korea
380 D2 **Chonglong** Sichuan China
381 I2 **Chongming Dao** *island* Shanghai China
308 B2 **Chongoroi** Angola
158 B2 **Chongoyape** Peru
386 E3 **Chŏngp'yŏng** North Korea
380 E2 **Chongqing** *admin. area* China
380 E2 **Chongqing** Chongqing China
386 E4 **Chŏngup** South Korea
308 E3 **Chongwe** Zambia
386 E4 **Chŏnju** South Korea
386 E3 **Ch'onnae** North Korea
162 A3 **Chonos, Archipiélago de los** *islands* Chile
154 B5 **Chontal** Ecuador
133 G5 **Chontalpa** Mexico
234 C1 **Chop** Ukraine
392 F6 **Chopan** Uttar Pradesh India
393 D7 **Chopda** Maharashtra India
157 A9 **Chopim** *watercourse* Brazil
157 A9 **Chopinzinho** Brazil
388 F6 **Chopūl** Iran
384 F3 **Chor** Mongolia
240 E2 **Chorley** Shropshire England UK
394 D2 **Chornobyl'** Ukraine
394 E4 **Chornomors'ke** Ukraine
159 E6 **Chorolque, Nevado** *mountain* Bolivia
160 D4 **Choros, Islas de los** *islands* Chile
227 J2 **Choroszcz** Poland
389 K5 **Chortoq** Uzbekistan
386 E3 **Ch'osan** North Korea
387 I4 **Chōshi** Japan
160 E5 **Chosmes** Argentina
227 H1 **Choszczno** Poland
158 B2 **Chota** Peru
227 K2 **Chotcza Dolna** Poland
124 I3 **Choteau** Montana USA
232 F2 **Chotěboř** Czech Republic
300 D4 **Choûm** Mauritania
124 E8 **Chowchilla** California USA
385 H3 **Choybalsan** Mongolia
229 G3 **Choye** France
389 R3 **Choygan-khol'** *lake* Russian Federation
231 H5 **Chrea** Algeria
227 H2 **Chřibská** Czech Republic
126 H7 **Chrisney** Indiana USA
423 E6 **Christchurch** New Zealand
241 F4 **Christchurch** Dorset England UK
118 D4 **Christian Sound** Alaska USA
127 K8 **Christiansburg** Virginia USA
163 21 **Christiansted** US Virgin Islands
119 P1 **Christie Bay** Northwest Territories Canada
376 C5 **Christie Island** Myanmar
125 Q3 **Christine** North Dakota USA
130 B6 **Christine** Texas USA
424 inset **Christmas Island** *Australian territory* Indian Ocean
374 E6 **Christmas Island National Park** Australia
124 E5 **Christmas Lake** Oregon USA
81 O6 **Christmas Rise** *underwater feature* Indian Ocean
129 L5 **Christoval** Texas USA
235 D8 **Chrysi** *island* Greece
235 D5 **Chrysoupoli** Greece
389 L5 **Chu** *watercourse* Kazakhstan
134 B4 **Chuacús, Sierra de** *range* Guatemala
379 F4 **Chuadanga** Bangladesh
128 B2 **Chualar** California USA
309 F4 **Chuáli, Lagoa** *lake* Mozambique
389 J4 **Chubar-kul'** *lake* Kazakhstan
381 I4 **Chubei** Taiwan China
162 C3 **Chubut** *admin. area* Argentina
162 C3 **Chubut** *watercourse* Argentina
158 C4 **Chuchaujasa, Cerro** *mountain* Peru
158 B2 **Chuchuhuasi** Peru
154 B2 **Chucunaque** *watercourse* Panama
225 P3 **Chudovo** Russian Federation
116 E6 **Chugach Mountains** Alaska USA
237 AM8 **Chuginadak Island** Alaska USA
125 M6 **Chugwater** Wyoming USA
384 E6 **Chuimatan** Gansu China
386 E5 **Chuja-gundo** *island* South Korea
381 F3 **Chujiang** Hunan China
237 AC8 **Chukchagirskoye, Ozero** *lake* Russian Federation
434 S1 **Chukchi Abyssal Plain** *underwater feature* Arctic Ocean
434 S1 **Chukchi Plateau** *underwater feature* Arctic Ocean
116 B5 **Chukchi Sea** Russian Federation/USA
237 AG5 **Chukoch'ye** *watercourse* Russian Federation
237 AM6 **Chukotskiy, Mys** *cape* Russian Federation
237 AJ5 **Chukotskiy Avtonomnyy Okrug** *admin. area* Russian Federation
237 AM5 **Chukotskiy Poluostrov** *peninsula* Russian Federation
237 AK5 **Chukotskoye Nagor'ye** *range* Russian Federation
128 D4 **Chula Vista** California USA
158 C4 **Chulca** Peru
230 D5 **Chullera, Punta de la** *cape* Spain
237 Z7 **Chul'man** Russian Federation
240 D4 **Chulmleigh** Devon England UK
158 A2 **Chulucanas** Peru
158 E5 **Chulumani** Bolivia
385 H2 **Chuluunhoroot** Mongolia
384 D3 **Chuluut** Mongolia
384 D3 **Chuluut Gol** *watercourse* Mongolia
389 M2 **Chulym** Russian Federation
389 N1 **Chulym** *watercourse* Russian Federation
236 N5 **Chum** Russian Federation
376 D3 **Chum Phae** Thailand
376 D4 **Chum Saeng** Thailand
160 E4 **Chumbicha** Argentina
389 O4 **Chumek** Kazakhstan
234 D4 **Chumerna** *mountain* Bulgaria
391 M3 **Chumian** Pakistan
237 AC8 **Chumikan** Russian Federation
376 C5 **Chumphon** Thailand
237 U7 **Chuna** *watercourse* Russian Federation
133 H5 **Chunchintoc** Mexico
386 E4 **Ch'unch'ŏn** South Korea
376 E5 **Chuối, Hòn** *island* Vietnam
158 D5 **Chuncoroco** Peru
376 E2 **Chung** *watercourse* Vietnam
386 E4 **Ch'ungju** South Korea
381 I4 **Chungyang Shanmo** *range* Taiwan China
380 E1 **Chunhua** Shaanxi China
381 H2 **Chunxi** Jiangsu China
237 V6 **Chunya** *watercourse* Russian Federation
133 I4 **Chunyaxche, Laguna** *lake* Mexico
376 D5 **Chuor Phnum Krâvanh** Cambodia
223 R3 **Chupa** Russian Federation
391 J3 **Chūqhak** Afghanistan
158 B3 **Chuquicara** *watercourse* Peru
159 E6 **Chuquisaca** *admin. area* Bolivia
158 D5 **Chuquitira** Peru
229 I3 **Chur** Switzerland
388 G7 **Churat** Iran
245 C5 **Church Cross** Ireland
243 H2 **Church Houses** North Yorkshire England UK
119 X3 **Churchill** Manitoba Canada
120 E5 **Churchill** *watercourse* Manitoba Canada
122 G6 **Churchill** *watercourse* Newfoundland and Labrador Canada
120 D5 **Churchill** *watercourse* Saskatchewan Canada
120 I3 **Churchill, Cape** Manitoba Canada
122 F6 **Churchill Falls** Newfoundland and Labrador Canada
126 F1 **Churchill Lake** Ontario Canada
119 Q4 **Churchill Lake** Saskatchewan Canada
437 K1 **Churchill Mountains** Antarctica
121 O4 **Churchill Sound** Nunavut Canada
119 V8 **Churchs Ferry** North Dakota USA
242 B4 **Churchtown** Ireland
162 B1 **Churriaca, Sierra** *range* Argentina
392 D5 **Churu** Rajasthan India
129 H2 **Chuska Mountains** New Mexico USA
388 H1 **Chusovoy** Russian Federation
121 T8 **Chute-des-Passes** Québec Canada
379 G3 **Chutia** Assam India
118 E4 **Chutine** *watercourse* British Columbia Canada
426 6 **Chuuk** *admin. area* Federated States of Micronesia
426 6 **Chuuk** *island* Federated States of Micronesia
426 6a **Chuuk Lagoon** Federated States of Micronesia
237 AI6 **Chuvanskiye Gory** *range* Russian Federation
388 E2 **Chuvashskaya Respublika** *admin. area* Russian Federation
380 D3 **Chuxiong** Yunnan China
389 L5 **Chüy** *admin. area* Kyrgyzstan
381 H2 **Chuzhou** Anhui China
394 E3 **Chyhyryn** Ukraine
234 F2 **Ciadîr-Lunga** Moldova
374 F5 **Ciamis** Indonesia
374 E5 **Cianjur** Indonesia
157 A8 **Cianorte** Brazil
227 I1 **Ciążeń** Poland
374 E5 **Cibadak** Indonesia
306 D4 **Cibitoke** Burundi
228 D5 **Ciboure** France
374 E5 **Cicalengka** Indonesia
427 9 **Cicia** *island* Fiji
310 4a **Cidade Velha** Cape Verde
161 I4 **Cidreira** Brazil
227 K1 **Ciechanów** Poland
134 E2 **Ciego de Ávila** Cuba
134 E2 **Ciego de Ávila** *admin. area* Cuba
227 K2 **Cielądz** Poland
374 E5 **Ciemas** Indonesia
154 C2 **Ciénaga** Colombia
129 J8 **Ciénega de Escobar** Mexico
132 E3 **Ciénega de Flores** Mexico
129 I8 **Ciénega de la Vaca** Mexico
129 I7 **Ciénega Prieta** Mexico
134 D2 **Cienfuegos** Cuba
134 D2 **Cienfuegos** *admin. area* Cuba
230 B2 **Cíes, Ilhas** *islands* Spain
231 F4 **Cieza** Spain
235 G6 **Çifteler** Turkey
230 E4 **Cigüela** *watercourse* Spain
132 D5 **Cihuatlán** Mexico
234 F2 **Ciietu** Moldova
230 D4 **Cijara, Embalse de** *lake* Spain
374 F5 **Cijulang** Indonesia
380 C3 **Cikai** Yunnan China
374 F5 **Cikalong** Indonesia
374 E5 **Cikampek** Indonesia
427 9 **Cikobia** *island* Fiji
374 F5 **Cilacap** Indonesia
310 7a **Cilaos** Réunion
374 E5 **Cilegon** Indonesia
235 G5 **Çilimli** Turkey
245 F4 **Cill Mhucraise** Ireland
244 A3 **Cille Pheadair** Na h-Eileanan Siar Scotland UK
388 F6 **Çiloy Adasi** *island* Azerbaijan
374 E5 **Cimahi** Indonesia
130 A2 **Cimarron** *watercourse* Kansas USA
129 J2 **Cimarron** New Mexico USA
234 F2 **Cimişlia** Moldova
154 C3 **Cimitarra** Colombia
234 E2 **Cimpia Moldovei de Nord** *range* Moldova
234 F2 **Cimpia Moldovei de Sud** *range* Moldova
234 E2 **Cimpurile** Romania
374 E5 **Cina, Tanjung** *cape* Indonesia
235 F5 **Çınarcık** Turkey
154 D3 **Cinaruco** *watercourse* Venezuela
231 G3 **Cinca** *watercourse* Spain
126 I7 **Cincinnati** Ohio USA
160 D6 **Cinco Saltos** Argentina
240 E3 **Cinderford** Gloucestershire England UK
118 J6 **Cinema** British Columbia Canada
229 G1 **Ciney** Belgium
372 A4 **Cinoka, Tanjung** *cape* Indonesia
376 B5 **Cinque Islands** Andaman and Nicobar Islands India
133 G5 **Cintalapa de Figueroa** Mexico
228 E5 **Cintegabelle** France
228 D5 **Cintruénigo** Spain
374 F5 **Cipatujah** Indonesia
157 E5 **Cipó** Brazil
155 H5 **Cipoal** Brazil
374 E5 **Ciputat** Indonesia
233 E6 **Circeo, Capo** *cape* Italy
116 E5 **Circle** Alaska USA
125 M3 **Circle** Montana USA
126 J7 **Circleville** Ohio USA
374 F5 **Cirebon** Indonesia
233 F7 **Cirella** Italy
241 F3 **Cirencester** Gloucestershire England UK
226 D3 **Cirey** France
158 C4 **Cirialo** Peru
226 D5 **Ciriè** Italy
233 F8 **Ciriga, Punta** *cape* Italy
225 N4 **Cirma** *lake* Latvia
233 G7 **Cirò Marina** Italy
228 D4 **Ciron** *watercourse* France
234 D2 **Cirța** Romania
374 E5 **Cirtasa** Indonesia
130 B4 **Cisco** Texas USA
227 L3 **Cisna** Poland
134 E2 **Cistern Point** Bahamas
230 D2 **Cistierna** Spain
124 F7 **Citrus Heights** California USA
308 C6 **Citrusdal** South Africa
232 E5 **Città di Castello** Italy
226 F5 **Cittadella** Italy
244 E5 **City of Edinburgh** *admin. area* Scotland UK
244 D5 **City of Glasgow** *admin. area* Scotland UK
234 B3 **Ciuchici** Romania
234 F2 **Ciucur-Mingir** Moldova
132 E2 **Ciudad Acuña** Mexico
130 B7 **Ciudad Alemán** Mexico
132 E5 **Ciudad Altamirano** Mexico
132 E3 **Ciudad Anáhuac** Mexico
134 B4 **Ciudad Arce** El Salvador
154 B3 **Ciudad Bolívar** Colombia
155 E2 **Ciudad Bolívar** Venezuela
129 M7 **Ciudad Camargo** Mexico
132 D3 **Ciudad Camargo** Mexico
134 C4 **Ciudad Choluteca** Honduras
132 C3 **Ciudad Constitución** Mexico
134 C4 **Ciudad Darío** Nicaragua
134 D2 **Ciudad de La Habana** *admin. area* Cuba
133 F5 **Ciudad de México (México City)** Mexico
133 H5 **Ciudad del Carmen** Mexico
160 H3 **Ciudad del Este** Paraguay
133 F4 **Ciudad del Maíz** Mexico
132 D2 **Ciudad Delicias** Mexico
155 F2 **Ciudad Guayana** Venezuela
129 I6 **Ciudad Guerrero** Mexico
133 F5 **Ciudad Guzmán** Mexico
132 D2 **Ciudad Juárez** Mexico
132 E3 **Ciudad Lerdo** Mexico
133 F5 **Ciudad López Mateos** Mexico
133 F4 **Ciudad Madero** Mexico
133 F4 **Ciudad Mante** Mexico
134 B3 **Ciudad Melchor de Mencos** Guatemala
133 F3 **Ciudad Miguel Alemán** Mexico
128 E4 **Ciudad Morelos** Mexico
132 C3 **Ciudad Obregón** Mexico
133 G5 **Ciudad Pemex** Mexico
230 E4 **Ciudad Real** Spain
230 C3 **Ciudad Rodrigo** Spain
134 C4 **Ciudad Sandino** Nicaragua
133 F4 **Ciudad Valles** Mexico
133 F4 **Ciudad Victoria** Mexico
163 5 **Ciudado, Punta** *cape* Isla de Pascua (Easter Island)
227 L4 **Ciugud** Romania
234 C2 **Ciuhoiu** Romania
234 F3 **Ciumai** Moldova
229 I5 **Ciuttone, Punta di** *cape* Corsica France
229 K3 **Cividale del Friuli** Italy
233 D5 **Civitavecchia** Italy
228 E3 **Civray** France
381 I2 **Cixi** Zhejiang China
394 G6 **Cizre** Turkey
242 A2 **Clabby** Fermanagh Northern Ireland UK
244 C5 **Clachan** Argyll and Bute Scotland UK
244 B3 **Clachan** Highland Scotland UK
244 C4 **Clachan of Glendaruel** Argyll and Bute Scotland UK
244 E4 **Clackmannanshire** *admin. area* Scotland UK
241 I3 **Clacton-on-Sea** Essex England UK
244 A3 **Cladach a' Chaolais** Na h-Eileanan Siar Scotland UK
244 B5 **Claddach** Argyll and Bute Scotland UK
244 C4 **Cladich** Argyll and Bute Scotland UK
242 B2 **Clady** Magherafelt Northern Ireland UK
240 D2 **Claerwen Reservoir** Wales UK
125 P7 **Claflin** Kansas USA
242 A1 **Claggan** Ireland
130 E4 **Claiborne, Lake** Louisiana USA
228 E3 **Clain** *watercourse* France
124 D6 **Clair Engle Lake** California USA
116 H7 **Claire, Lake** Alberta Canada
129 L4 **Clairemont** Texas USA
229 G3 **Clairvaux-les-Lacs** France
425 N5 **Clairview** Qld Australia
228 F3 **Clamecy** France
124 G7 **Clan Alpine Mountains** Nevada USA
245 F3 **Clane** Ireland
241 F4 **Clanfield** Hampshire England UK
131 H4 **Clanton** Alabama USA
308 C6 **Clanwilliam** South Africa
244 D2 **Claonel** Highland Scotland UK
243 F2 **Clapham** North Yorkshire England UK
245 E3 **Clara** Ireland
125 R4 **Clara City** Minnesota USA
376 C5 **Clara Island** Myanmar
245 E3 **Clarahill** Ireland
425 K8 **Clare** SA Australia
245 C4 **Clare** *admin. area* Ireland
245 D3 **Clare** *watercourse* Ireland
126 I5 **Clare** Michigan USA
245 D4 **Clare Bridge** Ireland
245 B3 **Clare Island** Ireland
127 O5 **Claremont** New Hampshire USA
423 F6 **Clarence** *watercourse* New Zealand
162 B6 **Clarence, Isla** *island* Chile
436 U2 **Clarence Island** Antarctica
118 E4 **Clarence Strait** Alaska USA
135 F2 **Clarence Town** Bahamas
129 L3 **Clarendon** Texas USA
119 O7 **Claresholm** Alberta Canada
245 C3 **Clareville** Ireland

437 I2 **Clarie Coast** Antarctica
126 E5 **Clarion** Iowa USA
127 L6 **Clarion** *watercourse* Pennsylvania USA
132 B5 **Clarión, Isla** *island* Mexico
79 S6 **Clarion Fracture Zone** *underwater feature* Pacific Ocean
422 F3 **Claris** New Zealand
116 D6 **Clark, Lake** Alaska USA
127 K4 **Clark, Point** Ontario Canada
124 G2 **Clark Fork** Idaho USA
436 O1 **Clark Mountains** Antarctica
128 F3 **Clarkdale** Arizona USA
121 V7 **Clarke City** Québec Canada
425 M4 **Clarke River** Qld Australia
123 F11 **Clark's Harbour** Nova Scotia Canada
127 K7 **Clarksburg** West Virginia USA
130 F3 **Clarksdale** Mississippi USA
126 H8 **Clarkson** Kentucky USA
124 G3 **Clarkston** Washington USA
130 H2 **Clarksville** Tennessee USA
130 D4 **Clarksville** Texas USA
131 L3 **Clarkton** North Carolina USA
157 B6 **Claro** *watercourse* Brazil
229 I3 **Claro** Switzerland
160 E3 **Claro, Lago** *lake* Argentina
242 A4 **Clasheen Bridge** Ireland
245 E4 **Clashmore** Ireland
124 D3 **Clatskanie** Oregon USA
242 D1 **Clatteringshaws Loch** *lake* Scotland UK
129 L3 **Claude** Texas USA
157 C8 **Cláudio** Brazil
242 A2 **Claudy** Londonderry Northern Ireland UK
117 Q4 **Clavering Øer** *island* Greenland
128 G1 **Clawson** Utah USA
163 9 **Claxton Bay** Trinidad and Tobago
125 Q7 **Clay Center** Kansas USA
243 G3 **Clay Cross** Derbyshire England UK
242 D2 **Clay Head** *cape* Isle of Man UK
119 Q8 **Claydon** Saskatchewan Canada
241 I2 **Claydon** Suffolk England UK
118 K4 **Clayhurst** British Columbia Canada
124 B2 **Clayoquot Sound** British Columbia Canada
127 N7 **Clayton** Delaware USA
129 K2 **Clayton** New Mexico USA
130 D3 **Clayton** Oklahoma USA
130 D3 **Clear Boggy** *watercourse* Oklahoma USA
130 B4 **Clear Fork Brazos** *watercourse* Texas USA
118 L4 **Clear Hills** Alberta Canada
245 C5 **Clear Island** Ireland
128 A1 **Clear Lake** California USA
130 E4 **Clear Lake** Louisiana USA
128 F1 **Clear Lake** Utah USA
124 E6 **Clear Lake Reservoir** California USA
118 L4 **Clear Prairie** Alberta Canada
118 L4 **Cleardale** Alberta Canada
116 E7 **Cleare, Cape** Alaska USA
124 D7 **Clearlake** California USA
125 L4 **Clearmont** Wyoming USA
116 H7 **Clearwater** *watercourse* Alberta Canada
118 K7 **Clearwater** British Columbia Canada
119 Q4 **Clearwater** *watercourse* Saskatchewan Canada
131 J7 **Clearwater** Florida USA
124 G3 **Clearwater** *watercourse* Idaho USA
118 K6 **Clearwater Lake** British Columbia Canada
130 F2 **Clearwater Lake** Missouri USA
124 H4 **Clearwater Mountains** Idaho USA
119 Q4 **Clearwater River Provincial Park** Saskatchewan Canada
242 E2 **Cleator Moor** Cumbria England UK
130 C4 **Cleburne** Texas USA
228 D2 **Clécy** France
226 C3 **Clefmont** France
234 E2 **Cleja** Romania
374 C4 **Clementi** *admin. area* Singapore
131 K2 **Clemmons** North Carolina USA
131 J3 **Clemson** South Carolina USA
127 K7 **Clendenin** West Virginia USA
130 B2 **Cleo Springs** Oklahoma USA
240 E2 **Cleobury Mortimer** Shropshire England UK
377 H5 **Cleopatra Needle** *mountain* Philippines
245 E3 **Cleraun** Ireland
241 I5 **Clères** France
425 M5 **Clermont** Qld Australia
123 C9 **Clermont** Québec Canada
226 B3 **Clermont** France
228 F4 **Clermont-Ferrand** France
228 F5 **Clermont-l'Hérault** France
229 H1 **Clervaux** Luxembourg
422 F3 **Clevedon** New Zealand
240 E3 **Clevedon** North Somerset England UK
131 H4 **Cleveland** Alabama USA
130 F4 **Cleveland** Mississippi USA
125 P3 **Cleveland** North Dakota USA
127 K6 **Cleveland** Ohio USA
131 I3 **Cleveland** Tennessee USA
126 H5 **Cleveland** Wisconsin USA
118 E5 **Cleveland Peninsula** Alaska USA
157 A9 **Clevelândia** Brazil
245 C3 **Clew Bay** Ireland
131 K7 **Clewiston** Florida USA
245 B3 **Clifden** Ireland
423 B8 **Clifden** New Zealand
244 C4 **Cliff** Highland Scotland UK
241 H4 **Cliff End** East Sussex England UK
245 D2 **Cliffony** Ireland
245 C4 **Cliffs of Moher** *point of interest* Ireland
242 F2 **Clifton** Cumbria England UK
241 F2 **Clifton** Nottingham England UK
129 H4 **Clifton** Arizona USA
124 I5 **Clifton** Idaho USA
130 H3 **Clifton** Tennessee USA
130 C5 **Clifton** Texas USA
127 L8 **Clifton Forge** Virginia USA
120 F3 **Clifton Lake** Manitoba Canada
119 Q8 **Climax** Saskatchewan Canada
118 M6 **Cline River** Alberta Canada
129 I3 **Clines Corners** New Mexico USA
131 J3 **Clingmans Dome** *mountain* North Carolina USA
129 I5 **Clint** Texas USA
118 K7 **Clinton** British Columbia Canada
127 K5 **Clinton** Ontario Canada
423 C8 **Clinton** New Zealand
130 E3 **Clinton** Arkansas USA
126 F6 **Clinton** Iowa USA
130 F5 **Clinton** Louisiana USA
126 G5 **Clinton** Wisconsin USA
126 D7 **Clinton Lake** Kansas USA
126 J5 **Clio** Michigan USA
79 S7 **Clipperton Fracture Zone** *underwater feature* Pacific Ocean
79 V6 **Clipperton Island** *French dependency* Pacific Ocean
228 D3 **Clisson** France
234 C2 **Clit** Romania
243 F3 **Clitheroe** Lancashire England UK
159 F4 **Cliza** Brazil
124 C2 **Clo-oose** British Columbia Canada
244 G3 **Clochtow** Aberdeenshire Scotland UK
242 B2 **Clogh** Ballymena Northern Ireland UK
242 B2 **Clogh Mills** Ballymena Northern Ireland UK
245 E3 **Cloghan** Ireland
245 C5 **Cloghane** Ireland
242 A2 **Clogher** Dungannon Northern Ireland UK
242 B2 **Cloghoge** Newry and Mourne Northern Ireland UK
242 C2 **Cloghy** Ards Northern Ireland UK
245 D5 **Clonakilty** Ireland
245 D5 **Clonakilty Bay** Ireland
242 B3 **Clonalvy** Ireland
242 A3 **Clonarrow** Ireland
245 D3 **Clonbern** Ireland
242 A3 **Cloncanon** Ireland
425 L5 **Cloncurry** Qld Australia
245 E2 **Clones** Ireland
242 B2 **Clonfeacle** Dungannon Northern Ireland UK
242 A2 **Clonleigh** Ireland
245 E1 **Clonmany** Ireland
245 E4 **Clonmel** Ireland
242 A3 **Clonmellon** Ireland
242 A3 **Clonmore** Ireland
245 F4 **Clonroche** Ireland
242 B3 **Cloon** Ireland
245 B5 **Cloonaghlin Lough** *lake* Ireland
245 D3 **Clooncan** Ireland
245 C3 **Clooneen** Ireland
128 E3 **Cloquet** Minnesota USA
437 D2 **Close, Cape** Antarctica
119 S4 **Close Lake** Saskatchewan Canada
244 E5 **Closeburn** Dumfries and Galloway Scotland UK
244 inset **Clothan** Shetland Scotland UK
125 L4 **Cloud Peak** Wyoming USA
129 J4 **Cloudcroft** New Mexico USA
423 F5 **Cloudy Bay** New Zealand
162 C6 **Cloué, Península** Chile
242 C2 **Clough** Down Northern Ireland UK
243 H2 **Cloughton** North Yorkshire England UK
244 C4 **Clounlaid** Highland Scotland UK
127 N2 **Clova** Québec Canada
244 F4 **Clova** Angus Scotland UK
240 C4 **Clovelly** Devon England UK
129 H5 **Cloverdale** New Mexico USA
126 H8 **Cloverport** Kentucky USA
124 F8 **Clovis** California USA
129 K3 **Clovis** New Mexico USA
244 C4 **Clovullin** Highland Scotland UK
243 G3 **Clowne** Derbyshire England UK
240 E2 **Clows Top** Worcestershire England UK
244 C3 **Cluanie, Loch** *lake* Scotland UK
119 Q3 **Cluff Lake Mine** Saskatchewan Canada
234 C2 **Cluj** *admin. area* Romania
234 C2 **Cluj-Napoca** Romania
240 D2 **Clun** Shropshire England UK
244 D4 **Clunes** Highland Scotland UK
244 E4 **Clunes Lodge** Perth and Kinross Scotland UK
229 H3 **Cluses** France
226 E5 **Clusone** Italy
130 D6 **Clute** Texas USA
423 C7 **Clutha** *watercourse* New Zealand
245 C4 **Clydagh** *watercourse* Ireland
423 C7 **Clyde** New Zealand
242 E1 **Clyde** *watercourse* Scotland UK
125 Q7 **Clyde** Kansas USA
130 B4 **Clyde** Texas USA
244 D5 **Clyde, Firth of** *bay* Scotland UK
125 J4 **Clyde Park** Montana USA
117 M4 **Clyde River** Nunavut Canada
244 D5 **Clydebank** West Dunbartonshire Scotland UK
240 D2 **Clyro** Powys Wales UK
242 A2 **Coa** Fermanagh Northern Ireland UK
230 C3 **Côa** *watercourse* Portugal
128 D4 **Coachella** California USA
242 B2 **Coagh** Cookstown Northern Ireland UK
129 L4 **Coahoma** Texas USA
132 E5 **Coahuayana** Mexico
132 E3 **Coahuila** *admin. area* Mexico
118 H2 **Coal** *watercourse* Yukon Territory Canada
118 H7 **Coal Harbour** British Columbia Canada
130 E3 **Coal Hill** Arkansas USA
116 G7 **Coal River** British Columbia Canada
243 F2 **Coalcleugh** Northumberland England UK
132 E5 **Coalcomán** Mexico
119 O8 **Coaldale** Alberta Canada
423 D6 **Coalgate** New Zealand
128 B2 **Coalinga** California USA
241 F2 **Coalville** Leicester England UK
124 J6 **Coalville** Utah USA
154 B5 **Coangos** Ecuador
157 E6 **Coaraci** Brazil
155 I4 **Coaracy Nunes** Brazil
159 F2 **Coari** Brazil
155 E6 **Coari** *watercourse* Brazil
155 F6 **Coari, Lago de** *lake* Brazil
307 F4 **Coast** *admin. area* Kenya
244 C3 **Coast** Highland Scotland UK
116 F7 **Coast Mountains** British Columbia Canada
128 B2 **Coast Ranges** California USA
130 G5 **Coastal Plain** Louisiana USA
130 C7 **Coastal Plain** Texas USA
244 D5 **Coatbridge** North Lanarkshire Scotland UK
241 E3 **Coates** Gloucestershire England UK
121 Q5 **Coats** *watercourse* Québec Canada
125 P8 **Coats** Kansas USA
121 P4 **Coats Bay** Nunavut Canada
117 K6 **Coats Island** Nunavut Canada
436 W1 **Coats Land** *plain* Antarctica
133 G5 **Coatzacoalcos** Mexico
134 B4 **Cobán** Guatemala
234 E2 **Cobani** Romania
425 M7 **Cobar** NSW Australia
154 C3 **Cobardes, Serranía Los** *range* Colombia
131 N2 **Cobb Bay** Virginia USA
163 18 **Cobb Cove** *bay* Antigua and Barbuda
127 M4 **Cobden** Ontario Canada
126 G8 **Cobden** Illinois USA
123 F10 **Cobequid Mountains** Nova Scotia Canada
245 D5 **Cóbh** Ireland
158 D3 **Cobija** Brazil
127 L5 **Cobourg** Ontario Canada
424 I2 **Cobourg Peninsula** NT Australia
160 C6 **Cobquecura** Chile
425 M8 **Cobram** Vic. Australia
309 F2 **Cobué** Mozambique
232 D1 **Coburg** Germany
117 L3 **Coburg Island** Nunavut Canada
154 B5 **Coca** *watercourse* Ecuador
226 E4 **Coca, Pizzo di** *mountain* Italy
158 D5 **Cocachacra** Peru
156 D3 **Cocal** Brazil
157 B6 **Cocalinho** Brazil
159 E5 **Cochabamba** Bolivia
159 E5 **Cochabamba** *admin. area* Bolivia
155 F2 **Coche, Isla** *island* Venezuela
232 B1 **Cochem** Germany
134 C5 **Cochinos, Bahía de** *bay* Cuba
310 6 **Cochons, Île aux** *island* French Southern and Antarctic Lands
127 Q2 **Cochons, Sault aux** *watercourse* Québec Canada
131 J4 **Cochran** Georgia USA
119 N7 **Cochrane** Alberta Canada
117 K9 **Cochrane** Ontario Canada
162 B6 **Cockburn, Canal** *strait* Chile
126 J4 **Cockburn Island** Ontario Canada
135 F1 **Cockburn Town** Bahamas
244 F5 **Cockburnspath** Scottish Borders Scotland UK
242 F3 **Cockerham** Lancashire England UK
121 O7 **Cockispenny Point** Ontario Canada
244 F5 **Cocklawfoot** Scottish Borders Scotland UK
424 H8 **Cocklebiddy** WA Australia
134 D5 **Coclé** Panama
134 E2 **Coco, Cayo** *island* Cuba
134 C6 **Coco, Isla de** *island* Costa Rica
154 B4 **Coco, Punta** *cape* Colombia
134 D4 **Coco, Río** *watercourse* Nicaragua
376 B4 **Coco Channel** Andaman and Nicobar Islands India
80 J4 **Coco-de-Mer Ridge** *underwater feature* Indian Ocean
131 K6 **Cocoa Beach** Florida USA
163 18 **Cocoa Point** *cape* Antigua and Barbuda
305 F4 **Cocobeach** Gabon
130 E5 **Cocodrie Lake** Louisiana USA
128 F3 **Coconino Plateau** Arkansas USA
424 inset **Cocos (Keeling) Islands** *Australian territory* Pacific Ocean
81 N5 **Cocos Basin** *underwater feature* Indian Ocean
163 9 **Cocos Bay** *bay* Trinidad and Tobago
79 X7 **Cocos Ridge** *underwater feature* Pacific Ocean
162 A2 **Cocotué, Bahía** *bay* Chile
127 Q6 **Cod, Cape** Massachusetts USA
127 P6 **Cod Bay, Cape** Massachusetts USA
122 H4 **Cod Island** Newfoundland and Labrador Canada
159 F1 **Codajás** Brazil
245 E3 **Codd** Ireland
225 M4 **Code** Latvia
155 E2 **Codera, Cabo** *cape* Venezuela
423 B8 **Codfish Island (Whenua Hou)** New Zealand
159 F4 **Codicia** Bolivia
226 G5 **Codigoro** Italy
160 D6 **Codihué** Argentina
234 D3 **Codlea** Romania
156 D4 **Codó** Brazil
226 E5 **Codogno** Italy
135 I3 **Codrington** Antigua and Barbuda
437 D2 **Codrington, Mount** Antarctica
163 18 **Codrington Lagoon** *lake* Antigua and Barbuda
232 E4 **Codroipo** Italy
245 B5 **Cod's Head** *cape* Ireland
241 E2 **Codsall** Staffordshire England UK
125 O5 **Cody** Nebraska USA
125 K4 **Cody** Wyoming USA
240 C2 **Coed Ystumgwern** Gwynedd Wales UK
240 D3 **Coelbren** Powys Wales UK
156 D4 **Coelho Neto** Brazil
425 L3 **Coen** Qld Australia
310 9 **Coëtivy** *island* Seychelles
124 G3 **Coeur d'Alene** Idaho USA
124 G3 **Coeur d'Alene Lake** Idaho USA
228 D3 **Coëx** France
130 G4 **Coffeeville** Mississippi USA
126 D8 **Coffeyville** Kansas USA
425 J8 **Coffin Bay** SA Australia
425 O7 **Coffs Harbour** NSW Australia
134 B4 **Cofradía** Honduras
234 F3 **Cogealac** Romania
228 D4 **Cognac** France
229 H5 **Cogolin** France
306 E4 **Cohoha South, Lake** Burundi
154 A3 **Coiba, Isla de** *island* Panama
162 C5 **Coig** *watercourse* Argentina
244 C2 **Coigeach, Rubha** *cape* Scotland UK
162 B3 **Coihaique** Chile
160 D6 **Coihueco** Chile
393 D9 **Coimbatore** Tamil Nadu India
230 B3 **Coimbra** Portugal
230 B3 **Coimbra** *admin. area* Portugal
158 D5 **Coipasa, Lago de** *lake* Bolivia
158 D5 **Coipasa, Salar de** *pan* Bolivia
154 D2 **Cojedes** *admin. area* Venezuela
154 A4 **Cojimíes, Punta** *cape* Ecuador
158 B3 **Cojup, Nevado** *mountain* Peru
125 M8 **Cokedale** Colorado USA
125 J5 **Cokeville** Wyoming USA
425 L9 **Colac** Vic. Australia
154 B5 **Colai, Cerro** *mountain* Ecuador
162 C3 **Colan Conhué** Argentina
157 D7 **Colatina** Brazil
436 N1 **Colbeck Basin** *underwater feature* Southern Ocean
125 O7 **Colby** Kansas USA
158 C4 **Colca** Peru
158 E5 **Colcha** Bolivia
241 H3 **Colchester** Essex England UK
119 P5 **Cold Lake** Alberta Canada
244 F5 **Coldstream** Scottish Borders Scotland UK
125 P8 **Coldwater** Kansas USA
126 I6 **Coldwater** Michigan USA
240 E3 **Cole** Somerset England UK
119 Q5 **Cole Bay** Saskatchewan Canada
436 T2 **Cole Peninsula** Antarctica
240 D2 **Colebatch** Shropshire England UK
127 P4 **Colebrook** New Hampshire USA
243 H3 **Coleby** Lincolnshire England UK
162 C3 **Colelache** Argentina
119 N8 **Coleman** Alberta Canada
130 B5 **Coleman** Texas USA
126 G4 **Coleman** Wisconsin USA
242 B1 **Coleraine** Coleraine Northern Ireland UK
245 F1 **Coleraine** *admin. area* Northern Ireland UK
308 E6 **Colesberg** South Africa
241 E3 **Colesborne** Gloucestershire England UK
159 G2 **Coletoria do Estado do Mato Gros** Brazil
124 E7 **Colfax** California USA
130 E5 **Colfax** Louisiana USA
124 G3 **Colfax** Washington USA
162 C3 **Colhué Huapí, Lago** *lake* Argentina
226 E4 **Colico** Italy
308 E5 **Coligny** South Africa
132 E5 **Colima** Mexico
132 D5 **Colima** *admin. area* Mexico
156 C4 **Colinas** Brazil
228 C5 **Colindres** Spain
119 O5 **Colinton** Alberta Canada
244 B4 **Coll** *island* Scotland UK
231 G2 **Coll de Nargó** Spain
230 E3 **Collado Villalba** Spain
232 E3 **Collalto** *mountain* Italy
425 N7 **Collarenebri** NSW Australia
125 L7 **Collbran** Colorado USA
131 I4 **College Park** Georgia USA
124 F3 **College Place** Washington USA
130 C5 **College Station** Texas USA
425 N7 **Collie** NSW Australia
424 F8 **Collie** WA Australia
436 T2 **Collier, Cape** Antarctica
130 G3 **Collierville** Tennessee USA
240 C4 **Colliford Reservoir** England UK
228 C2 **Collinée** France
126 E6 **Collins** Iowa USA
130 G5 **Collins** Mississippi USA
119 T3 **Collins Bay** Saskatchewan Canada
437 E2 **Collins Glacier** *ice* Antarctica
117 I4 **Collinson Peninsula** Nunavut Canada
425 M5 **Collinsville** Qld Australia
130 D2 **Collinsville** Oklahoma USA
160 C6 **Collipulli** Chile
301 H1 **Collo** Algeria
245 F3 **Collon** Ireland
245 D2 **Collooney** Ireland
129 L1 **Collyer** Kansas USA
229 H2 **Colmar** France
130 B8 **Colmena** Mexico
230 D5 **Colmenar** Spain
130 D5 **Colmesneil** Texas USA
162 A4 **Colmillo, Cabo** *cape* Chile
244 D5 **Colmonell** South Ayrshire Scotland UK
241 H2 **Colne** Cambridgeshire England UK
243 F3 **Colne** Lancashire England UK
241 I3 **Colne Point** England UK
159 G3 **Colniza** Brazil
158 E3 **Colocação Vertente** Brazil
126 D4 **Cologne** Minnesota USA
134 B4 **Cololaca** Honduras
122 D4 **Colombet, Lac** *lake* Québec Canada
130 B7 **Colombia** Mexico
154 D4 **Colombia** *country* South America
76 K8 **Colombian Basin** *underwater feature* Caribbean
157 B9 **Colombo** Brazil
393 E10 **Colombo** Sri Lanka
125 P5 **Colome** South Dakota USA
230 E5 **Colomera, Embalse de** *lake* Spain
228 E5 **Colomiers** France
154 B4 **Colón** Colombia
134 D2 **Colón** Cuba
134 E5 **Colón** Panama
163 4 **Colón, Archipiélago de (Galapagos Islands)** *islands* Ecuador Pacific Ocean
134 C4 **Colón, Montañas de** *range* Honduras
163 11a **Colonarie** St Vincent and the Grenadines
163 11a **Colonarie** *watercourse* St Vincent and the Grenadines
132 A2 **Colonet, Cabo** *cape* Mexico
426 6 **Colonia** Federated States of Micronesia
161 G5 **Colonia** *admin. area* Uruguay
158 C2 **Colonia Angamos** Peru
132 C2 **Colonia Aribabi** Mexico
128 D5 **Colonia Camalu** Mexico
159 H5 **Colônia Córrego Grande** Brazil
132 E2 **Colonia de Enmedio** Mexico
161 G5 **Colonia de Sacramento** Uruguay
160 F4 **Colonia Dora** Argentina
129 H6 **Colonia Garcia** Mexico
160 D6 **Colonia Gobernador Ayala** Argentina
160 E6 **Colonia Josefa** Argentina
161 G2 **Colonia Menno** Paraguay
160 F2 **Colonia Neuland** Paraguay
132 D2 **Colonia Obrera** Mexico
160 F6 **Colonia Santa Rosa** Argentina
127 M8 **Colonial Heights** Virginia USA
233 G6 **Colonna, Capo** *cape* Italy
119 S7 **Colonsay** Saskatchewan Canada
244 B4 **Colonsay** *island* Scotland UK
129 O1 **Colony** Kansas USA
160 F6 **Colorada Grande, Salina** *pan* Argentina
162 C2 **Colorado** *watercourse* Argentina
157 B8 **Colorado** Brazil
160 D5 **Colorado** *watercourse* Chile
132 B2 **Colorado** *lake* Mexico
115 **Colorado** *admin. area* USA
128 E4 **Colorado** *watercourse* Arkansas USA
129 H1 **Colorado** *watercourse* Colorado USA
130 C6 **Colorado** *watercourse* Texas USA
128 G2 **Colorado** *watercourse* Utah USA
154 C2 **Colorado, Cuchilla del** *range* Colombia
128 F2 **Colorado City** Arizona USA
129 J2 **Colorado City** Colorado USA
129 L4 **Colorado City** Texas USA
159 G3 **Colorado do Norte** Brazil
128 F2 **Colorado Plateau** Arkansas USA
125 M7 **Colorado Springs** Colorado USA
160 F6 **Colorado Viejo** *watercourse* Argentina
160 D3 **Colorados, Cerro** *mountain* Argentina
232 D4 **Colorno** Italy
234 F2 **Colosova** Moldova
132 E4 **Colotlán** Mexico
245 F3 **Colp** Ireland
227 G1 **Cölpin** Germany
158 E5 **Colquiri** Bolivia
131 I5 **Colquitt** Georgia USA
241 G2 **Colsterworth** Lincolnshire England UK
243 G3 **Colton** North Yorkshire England UK
128 D3 **Colton** California USA
116 H8 **Columbia** *watercourse* British Columbia Canada
126 I8 **Columbia** Kentucky USA
130 G5 **Columbia** Mississippi USA
126 E7 **Columbia** Missouri USA
131 M3 **Columbia** North Carolina USA
116 G9 **Columbia** *watercourse* Oregon USA
131 K4 **Columbia** South Carolina USA
130 H3 **Columbia** Tennessee USA
124 E3 **Columbia** *watercourse* Washington USA
117 M2 **Columbia, Cape** Nunavut Canada
116 H8 **Columbia, Mount** Alberta/British Columbia Canada
118 L6 **Columbia Icefield** British Columbia Canada
124 H1 **Columbia Lake** British Columbia Canada
116 G8 **Columbia Mountains** British Columbia Canada
124 F4 **Columbia Plateau** Oregon USA
77 O12 **Columbia Seamount** *underwater feature* Pacific Ocean
308 C6 **Columbine, Cape** South Africa
131 I4 **Columbus** Georgia USA
126 I7 **Columbus** Indiana USA
130 G4 **Columbus** Mississippi USA
125 K4 **Columbus** Montana USA
125 Q6 **Columbus** Nebraska USA
129 I5 **Columbus** New Mexico USA
125 N3 **Columbus** North Dakota USA
126 J7 **Columbus** Ohio USA
135 F2 **Columbus Bank** Bahamas
130 G4 **Columbus Lake** Mississippi USA
135 F1 **Columbus Point** Bahamas
128 C1 **Columbus Salt Marsh** Nevada USA
230 D2 **Colunga** Spain
160 D2 **Colupo, Cerro** *mountain* Chile
116 D5 **Colville** *watercourse* Alaska USA
124 G2 **Colville** Washington USA
422 F3 **Colville, Cape** New Zealand
116 G5 **Colville Lake** Northwest Territories Canada
437 H2 **Colvocoresses Bay** Antarctica
240 E2 **Colwall** Herefordshire England UK
242 E3 **Colwyn Bay** Conwy Wales UK
226 G5 **Comacchio** Italy
133 G5 **Comalcalco** Mexico
158 D5 **Comanche** Bolivia
130 B5 **Comanche** Texas USA
128 B1 **Comanche Reservoir** California USA
436 U2 **Comandante Ferraz (Brazil)** *research station* Antarctica
160 F3 **Comandante Fontana** Argentina
160 D5 **Comandante Salas** Argentina
234 D3 **Comarnic** Romania
162 B3 **Comau, Estero** *bay* Chile
134 C4 **Comayagua** Honduras
160 D4 **Combarbala** Chile
240 C3 **Combe Martin** Devon England UK
229 G3 **Combeaufontaine** France
242 C2 **Comber** Ards Northern Ireland UK
379 G5 **Combermere Bay** Myanmar
228 F1 **Combles** France
309 F4 **Combomune** Mozambique
228 F4 **Combronde** France
131 J3 **Comer** Georgia USA
379 G4 **Comilla** Bangladesh
233 C6 **Comino, Capo** *cape* Sardinia Italy
133 G5 **Comitán de Domínguez** Mexico
228 F3 **Commentry** France
130 D4 **Commerce** Texas USA
226 C3 **Commercy** France
127 O2 **Commissaires, Lac des** *lake* Québec Canada
117 K5 **Committee Bay** Nunavut Canada
377 G5 **Commodore Reef** Spratly Islands
437 J2 **Commonwealth Bay** Antarctica
226 E5 **Como** Italy
130 G3 **Como** Mississippi USA
232 C3 **Como, Lago di** *lake* Italy
126 J3 **Como, Lake** Ontario Canada
124 H3 **Como, Lake** Montana USA
159 G4 **Comodoro** Brazil
162 C3 **Comodoro Rivadavia** Argentina
393 D10 **Comorin, Cape** Tamil Nadu India
310 6a **Comoros** *country* Africa
124 C2 **Comox** British Columbia Canada
230 B4 **Comporta** Portugal
132 D4 **Compostela** Mexico
157 C9 **Comprida, Ilha** *island* Brazil
229 H5 **Comps-sur-Artuby** France
228 B5 **Compuerto, Embalse de** *lake* Spain
120 D4 **Compulsion Bay** Saskatchewan Canada
244 E4 **Comrie** Perth and Kinross Scotland UK
129 L6 **Comstock** Texas USA
79 Q2 **Comstock Seamount** *underwater feature* Pacific Ocean
229 K5 **Comunanza** Italy
155 F3 **Comunidad** Venezuela
376 E3 **Con Co, Đao** *island* Vietnam
376 E3 **Con Cuông** Vietnam
374 E1 **Côn Đảo National Park** Vietnam
374 E1 **Côn Sơn** *island* Vietnam
226 G5 **Cona** Italy
162 C2 **Cona Niyeo** Argentina
304 B3 **Conakry** Guinea
160 D4 **Conay** Chile
158 D4 **Concaj** Peru
130 B6 **Concan** Texas USA
159 E2 **Conceição** Brazil
157 B7 **Conceição das Alagoas** Brazil
156 B5 **Conceição do Araguaia** Brazil
157 D7 **Conceição do Mato Dentro** Brazil
155 G4 **Conceição do Maú** Brazil
160 E3 **Concepción** Argentina
159 F5 **Concepción** Bolivia
160 C6 **Concepción** Chile
132 B2 **Concepción** *watercourse* Mexico
161 G2 **Concepción** Paraguay
161 G2 **Concepción** *admin. area* Paraguay
158 C3 **Concepción** Peru
160 C6 **Concepción, Bahía** *bay* Chile
162 A5 **Concepción, Canal** *strait* Chile
159 F4 **Concepción, Laguna** *lake* Bolivia
132 C3 **Concepción, Punta** *cape* Mexico
135 G3 **Concepción de La Vega** Dominican Republic
132 E3 **Concepción del Oro** Mexico
128 B3 **Conception, Point** California USA
123 L9 **Conception Bay** Newfoundland and Labrador Canada
308 B4 **Conception Bay** Namibia
135 F2 **Conception Island** Bahamas
310 9b **Conception Island** Seychelles
159 G6 **Concha** Brazil
157 B8 **Conchas** Brazil
129 J3 **Conchas** New Mexico USA
129 K3 **Conchas Lake** New Mexico USA
160 D2 **Conchi** Chile
128 G3 **Concho** Arizona USA
129 J7 **Conchos** Mexico
130 B8 **Conchos** *watercourse* Mexico
124 F2 **Conconully** Washington USA
124 D8 **Concord** California USA
127 P5 **Concord** New Hampshire USA
131 K3 **Concord** North Carolina USA
389 L6 **Concord Peak** *mountain* Tajikistan
161 H3 **Concórdia** Brazil
134 C4 **Concordia** Honduras
132 D4 **Concordia** Mexico
308 C5 **Concordia** South Africa
161 G4 **Concordia** Uruguay
437 I1 **Concordia Station (France and Italy)** *research station* Antarctica
118 K8 **Concrete** Washington USA
308 B2 **Conda** Angola
134 E2 **Condado** Cuba
425 N6 **Condamine** Qld Australia
228 F4 **Condat-en-Féniers** France
157 E5 **Conde** Brazil
230 B3 **Condeixa-a-Nova** Portugal
229 J4 **Condino** Italy
425 M8 **Condobolin** NSW Australia
228 E5 **Condom** France
124 E4 **Condon** Oregon USA
158 B2 **Condor, Cordillera del** *range* Peru
232 B4 **Condove** Italy
232 E5 **Conero, Monte** *mountain* Italy
120 I7 **Confederation Lake** Ontario Canada
154 C3 **Confines** Colombia
228 E3 **Confolens** France
128 F1 **Confusion Range** Utah USA
161 G3 **Confuso** *watercourse* Paraguay
245 C3 **Cong** Ireland
376 E4 **Cong Tum Plateau** Vietnam
244 E3 **Congash** Highland Scotland UK
305 H5 **Congo** *country* Africa
305 G6 **Congo** *watercourse* Angola
305 H5 **Congo** *watercourse* Congo
306 C4 **Congo, Democratic Republic of** *country* Africa
306 D5 **Congo (Lualaba)** *watercourse* Democratic Republic of Congo
306 C3 **Congo Basin** Democratic Republic of Congo
80 F5 **Congo Canyon** *underwater feature* Atlantic Ocean
80 F5 **Congo Fan** *underwater feature* Atlantic Ocean
157 D8 **Congonhas** Brazil
119 R8 **Congress** Saskatchewan Canada
128 F3 **Congress** Arizona USA
133 H5 **Conhuas** Mexico
241 G1 **Coningsby** Lincolnshire England UK
242 E2 **Coniston** Cumbria England UK
242 E2 **Coniston Water** *lake* England UK
425 N8 **Conjola** NSW Australia
119 P5 **Conklin** Alberta Canada
228 D2 **Conlie** France
242 C2 **Conlig** Ards Northern Ireland UK
121 Q6 **Conn** *watercourse* Québec Canada
245 C2 **Conn, Lough** *lake* Ireland
245 D4 **Connagh** Ireland
127 K6 **Conneaut** Ohio USA
114 **Connecticut** *admin. area* USA
244 C4 **Connel** Argyll and Bute Scotland UK
245 C3 **Connemara** *region* Ireland
242 B2 **Connor** Ballymena Northern Ireland UK
234 B2 **Conop** Romania
154 E4 **Conorochite** *watercourse* Venezuela
157 D6 **Conquista** Brazil
124 J2 **Conrad** Montana USA
130 D5 **Conroe** Texas USA
130 D5 **Conroe, Lake** Texas USA
157 D8 **Conselheiro Lafaiete** Brazil
157 D7 **Conselheiro Pena** Brazil
163 12 **Conset Bay** Barbados
243 G2 **Consett** Durham England UK
155 F4 **Consolação** Brazil
134 D2 **Consolación del Sur** Cuba
234 F3 **Constanța** Romania
234 F3 **Constanța** *admin. area* Romania
301 H1 **Constantine** Algeria
116 D7 **Constantine, Cape** Alaska USA
157 B6 **Constantino, Serra do** *range* Brazil
160 C5 **Constitución** Chile
161 G4 **Constitución** Uruguay
159 F4 **Consuelo** Brazil
425 N6 **Consuelo Peak** Qld Australia
119 Q8 **Consul** Saskatchewan Canada
157 C7 **Contagem** Brazil
393 G7 **Contai** West Bengal India
158 C2 **Contamana** Peru
155 F4 **Contão** Brazil
157 D6 **Contas, Rio de** *watercourse* Brazil
233 H6 **Contessa, Punta della** *cape* Italy
244 D3 **Contin** Highland Scotland UK
124 F6 **Continental Lake** Nevada USA
129 I2 **Continental Reservoir** Colorado USA
133 I4 **Contoy, Isla** *island* Mexico
160 D6 **Contraalmirante Cordero** Argentina
162 A5 **Contraras, Isla** *island* Chile
230 F4 **Contreras, Embalse de** *lake* Spain
154 A3 **Contreras, Islas** *islands* Panama
160 C6 **Contulmo** Chile
158 B2 **Contumazá** Peru
233 F6 **Contursi Terme** Italy
116 H5 **Contwoyto Lake** Nunavut Canada
154 D4 **Conuco de Ciucar** Colombia
130 B6 **Converse** Texas USA
130 E3 **Conway** Arkansas USA
131 L4 **Conway** South Carolina USA
130 E3 **Conway, Lake** Arkansas USA
423 E6 **Conway Flat** New Zealand
242 E3 **Conwy** Conwy Wales UK
240 D1 **Conwy** *admin. area* Wales UK
240 D1 **Conwy** *watercourse* Wales UK
424 I7 **Cook** SA Australia
423 C6 **Cook** *watercourse* New Zealand
162 B6 **Cook, Bahía** *bay* Chile
310 6b **Cook, Calotte Glaciaire** *glacier* French Southern and Antarctic Lands
Cook, Mount *see* **Aoraki** New Zealand
163 5 **Cook, Punta** *cape* Isla de Pascua (Easter Island)
437 K2 **Cook Ice Shelf** Antarctica
116 D7 **Cook Inlet** Alaska USA
426 1a **Cook Island** Kiribati
426 1a **Cook Island Passage** *strait* Kiribati
422 1 **Cook Islands** *NZ territory* Pacific Ocean
423 F5 **Cook Strait** New Zealand
131 I2 **Cookeville** Tennessee USA
241 I3 **Cook's Green** Essex England UK
127 P4 **Cookshire** Québec Canada
245 F2 **Cookstown** Cookstown Northern Ireland UK
245 F2 **Cookstown** *admin. area* Northern Ireland UK
425 M3 **Cooktown** Qld Australia
245 D4 **Cool Bridge** Ireland
425 M7 **Coolabah** NSW Australia
425 M6 **Cooladdi** Qld Australia
425 O7 **Coolangatta-Tweed Heads** NSW Australia
425 N7 **Coolatai** NSW Australia
245 C5 **Coolavokig** Ireland
242 A3 **Coolayna Haggard** Ireland
245 C5 **Coolcoulagata** Ireland
242 A3 **Coole** Ireland
424 G7 **Coolgardie** WA Australia
128 G4 **Coolidge** Arizona USA
424 E7 **Coolimba** WA Australia
245 C4 **Coolmeen** Ireland
245 F4 **Coolnacon** Ireland
242 B4 **Coolnahorna** Ireland
245 B4 **Coolrainey** Ireland
245 F4 **Coolroe** Ireland
425 N9 **Cooma** NSW Australia
425 L8 **Coombah** NSW Australia
245 C5 **Coomnacarrig Bridge** Ireland
126 E4 **Coon Rapids** Minnesota USA
425 N7 **Coonabarabran** NSW Australia
425 N7 **Coonamble** NSW Australia
424 G7 **Coonana** WA Australia
242 A2 **Cooneen** Fermanagh Northern Ireland UK
393 D9 **Coonoor** Tamil Nadu India
425 L6 **Cooper** *watercourse* Qld Australia
425 K7 **Cooper** *watercourse* SA Australia
130 D4 **Cooper** Texas USA
125 M6 **Cooper Lake** Wyoming USA
131 M7 **Coopers Town** Bahamas
245 E4 **Coorlaghan** Ireland
242 A4 **Coornariska** Ireland
124 C5 **Coos Bay** Oregon USA
124 C5 **Coos Bay** Oregon USA
158 B3 **Copa, Nevado** *mountain* Peru
160 D6 **Copahue, Volcán** *volcano* Chile
133 F5 **Copala** Mexico
159 E3 **Copallora** Bolivia
130 D2 **Copan Lake** Oklahoma USA
130 C6 **Copano Bay** Texas USA
245 F5 **Cope, Cabo** *cape* Spain
125 O8 **Copeland** Kansas USA
242 C2 **Copeland Island** *island* Down Northern Ireland UK
134 C4 **Copén** Honduras
Copenhagen *see* **København** Denmark
160 D3 **Copiapó** Chile
160 D3 **Copiapó** *watercourse* Chile
160 D3 **Copiapo, Volcán** *volcano* Chile
244 F2 **Copinsay** *island* Scotland UK
241 G2 **Cople** Bedfordshire England UK
308 B2 **Coporolo** *watercourse* Angola
119 N2 **Copp Lake** Northwest Territories Canada
425 N5 **Coppabella** Qld Australia
242 A2 **Coppanagh Mills** Ireland
226 F5 **Copparo** Italy
240 C4 **Coppathorne** Cornwall England UK
126 J2 **Coppell** Ontario Canada
126 H3 **Copper Harbor** Michigan USA
124 E2 **Copper Mountain** British Columbia Canada
130 C5 **Copperas Cove** Texas USA
308 E2 **Copperbelt** *admin. area* Zambia
116 H5 **Coppermine** *watercourse* Nunavut Canada
308 D5 **Copperton** South Africa
240 D4 **Copplestone** Devon England UK
234 D2 **Copșa Mică** Romania
378 E2 **Coqen Zangbo** *watercourse* Xizang Zizhiqu China
159 G4 **Coqueiro** Brazil
243 G1 **Coquet** *watercourse* England UK
243 G1 **Coquet Island** England UK
124 C5 **Coquille** Oregon USA
160 D4 **Coquimbo** Chile
160 D4 **Coquimbo** *admin. area* Chile

118 J8 **Coquitlam** British Columbia Canada
157 C7 **Coração de Jesus** Brazil
135 F3 **Corail** Haiti
121 O7 **Coral** Ontario Canada
424 E5 **Coral Bay** WA Australia
375 H1 **Coral Bay** Philippines
117 K6 **Coral Harbour** Nunavut Canada
78 **Coral Sea** Oceania
78 K9 **Coral Sea Basin** *underwater feature* Coral Sea
425 N4 **Coral Sea Islands** *Australian territory* Pacific Ocean
131 K7 **Coral Springs** Florida USA
233 C6 **Coralli, Col de** *pass* Corsica France
126 F6 **Coralville** Iowa USA
155 G3 **Corantijn** *watercourse* Suriname
233 G6 **Corato** Italy
232 E5 **Corbara, Lago di** *lake* Italy
157 A9 **Corbélia** Brazil
120 I1 **Corbett Inlet** Nunavut Canada
228 F2 **Corbie** France
121 P5 **Corbin** *watercourse* Québec Canada
241 G2 **Corby** Northamptonshire England UK
128 C2 **Corcoran** California USA
242 B4 **Corcoran's** Ireland
162 B3 **Corcovado, Bahía de** *bay* Chile
245 C2 **Corcullin** Ireland
131 J5 **Cordele** Georgia USA
131 I2 **Cordell Hull Reservoir** Tennessee USA
228 E4 **Cordes** France
377 I5 **Cordilleras Range** Philippines
160 E4 **Córdoba** Argentina
160 F4 **Córdoba** *admin. area* Argentina
154 C2 **Córdoba** Colombia
154 C2 **Córdoba** *admin. area* Colombia
133 F5 **Córdoba** Mexico
230 D5 **Córdoba** Spain
160 E4 **Córdoba, Sierra de** *mountain* Argentina
244 C5 **Cordon** North Ayrshire Scotland UK
116 E6 **Cordova** Alaska USA
129 J3 **Cordova** New Mexico USA
156 D3 **Coreaú** Brazil
240 E2 **Coreley** Shropshire England UK
230 F2 **Corella** Spain
156 E4 **Coremas** Brazil
240 D4 **Corfe** Somerset England UK
241 E4 **Corfe Castle** Dorset England UK
Corfu *see* **Kerkyra** Greece
232 E5 **Corinaldo** Italy
Corinth *see* **Korinthos** Greece
163 10a **Corinth** Grenada
130 G3 **Corinth** Mississippi USA
130 C4 **Corinth** Texas USA
424 inset **Corinthian Bay** Heard Island Australia
157 C7 **Corinto** Brazil
154 C4 **Corinto** Colombia
134 C4 **Corinto** El Salvador
134 B4 **Corinto** Honduras
158 E5 **Coripata** Bolivia
305 F4 **Corisco, Baie de** *bay* Gabon
230 B2 **Coristanco** Spain
245 D5 **Cork** Ireland
245 D5 **Cork** *admin. area* Ireland
245 E2 **Corlea** Ireland
233 E8 **Corleone** Italy
235 E5 **Çorlu** Turkey
123 J8 **Cormack** Newfoundland and Labrador Canada
118 K2 **Cormack Lake** Northwest Territories Canada
226 C4 **Cormatin** France
229 K4 **Cormòns** Italy
120 E5 **Cormorant Lake** Manitoba Canada
226 C4 **Cormoz** France
129 M3 **Corn** Oklahoma USA
226 D4 **Cornaux** Switzerland
234 C3 **Cornea** Romania
126 G6 **Cornell** Illinois USA
126 F4 **Cornell** Wisconsin USA
231 H3 **Cornellà** Spain
123 J8 **Corner Brook** Newfoundland and Labrador Canada
76 N6 **Corner Seamounts** *underwater feature* Atlantic Ocean
130 H3 **Cornersville** Tennessee USA
232 D5 **Cornia** *watercourse* Italy
229 J4 **Cornicello** *mountain* Italy
226 D4 **Cornimont** France
130 F2 **Corning** Arkansas USA
124 D7 **Corning** California USA
127 M5 **Corning** New York USA
162 A4 **Cornish, Seno** *bay* Chile
229 I5 **Corno di Becco, Punta** *cape* Corsica France
244 F2 **Cornquoy** Orkney Islands Scotland UK
234 D3 **Cornu de Sus** Romania
234 E2 **Cornu Luncii** Romania
129 J5 **Cornudas** Texas USA
228 F5 **Cornus** France
127 N4 **Cornwall** Ontario Canada
240 C4 **Cornwall** *admin. area* England UK
117 J3 **Cornwall Island** Nunavut Canada
117 J3 **Cornwallis Island** Nunavut Canada
154 D2 **Coro** Venezuela
154 D2 **Coro, Golfete de** *bay* Venezuela
156 C4 **Coroatá** Brazil
158 E5 **Coroico** Bolivia
223 N2 **Corokjávri** *lake* Norway
157 C7 **Coromandel** Brazil
393 E9 **Coromandel Coast** Tamil Nadu India
422 F3 **Coromandel Peninsula** New Zealand
422 F3 **Coromandel Range** New Zealand
377 I5 **Coron** Philippines
377 I4 **Coron** *island* Philippines
128 D4 **Corona** California USA
129 J3 **Corona** New Mexico USA
119 S8 **Coronach** Saskatchewan Canada
128 D4 **Coronado** California USA
134 D5 **Coronado, Bahía de** *bay* Costa Rica
162 A2 **Coronados, Golfo** *bay* Chile
119 P6 **Coronation** Alberta Canada
116 H5 **Coronation Gulf** Nunavut Canada
160 C6 **Coronel** Chile
161 G3 **Coronel Oviedo** Paraguay
160 F6 **Coronel Suárez** Argentina
161 G6 **Coronel Vidal** Argentina
157 A9 **Coronel Vivida** Brazil
155 G3 **Coronie** *admin. area* Suriname
158 C4 **Coropuna, Nevado** *mountain* Peru
134 B3 **Corozal** Belize
155 E3 **Corozal** Venezuela
163 9 **Corozal Point** *cape* Trinidad and Tobago
244 C4 **Corpach** Highland Scotland UK
162 C4 **Corpen** Argentina
229 G4 **Corps** France
228 D3 **Corps-Nuds** France
130 C7 **Corpus Christi** Texas USA
130 C6 **Corpus Christi, Lake** Texas USA
130 C7 **Corpus Christi Bay** Texas USA
162 B2 **Corral** Chile
310 3d **Corralejo** Canary Islands
133 F5 **Corralero, Laguna** *lake* Mexico
129 I3 **Corrales** New Mexico USA
134 D2 **Corralillo** Cuba
159 F5 **Corralones, Serranía Los** *range* Bolivia
244 C3 **Corran** Highland Scotland UK
245 D2 **Corratimore** Ireland
245 D3 **Corraun** Ireland
245 C3 **Corraun Peninsula** Ireland
229 H3 **Corre** France
134 D5 **Corredor** Costa Rica
377 I4 **Corregidor** *island* Philippines
159 G5 **Corrego Taxo** *watercourse* Brazil
157 A7 **Correntes** *watercourse* Brazil
159 E3 **Correnteza** Bolivia
233 F8 **Correnti, Capo delle** *cape* Italy
157 C6 **Correntina** Brazil
129 I3 **Correo** New Mexico USA
228 E4 **Corrèze** *watercourse* France
245 C3 **Corrib, Lough** *lake* Ireland
244 C5 **Corrie** North Ayrshire Scotland UK
244 C5 **Corriecravie** North Ayrshire Scotland UK
244 D2 **Corriekinloch** Highland Scotland UK
161 G3 **Corrientes** Argentina
161 G4 **Corrientes** *admin. area* Argentina
161 G4 **Corrientes** *watercourse* Argentina
158 C1 **Corrientes** *watercourse* Peru
154 B3 **Corrientes, Cabo** *cape* Colombia
134 C2 **Corrientes, Cabo** *cape* Cuba
132 D4 **Corrientes, Cabo** *cape* Mexico
130 D5 **Corrigan** Texas USA
424 F8 **Corrigin** WA Australia
240 D2 **Corris** Gwynedd Wales UK
245 C4 **Corrofin** Ireland
230 B4 **Corroios** Portugal
244 D4 **Corrour Sta** Highland Scotland UK
230 B2 **Corrubedo, Cabo** *cape* Spain
244 C3 **Corry** Highland Scotland UK
231 K2 **Corse** *admin. area* Corsica France
232 C5 **Corse, Cap** *cape* France
242 C2 **Corsewall** Dumfries and Galloway Scotland UK
241 E3 **Corsham** Wiltshire England UK
130 C4 **Corsicana** Texas USA
160 D6 **Cortaderas** Argentina
132 E4 **Cortazar** Mexico
229 I5 **Corte** Corsica France
230 C5 **Cortegana** Spain
230 D5 **Cortes de la Frontera** Spain
125 K8 **Cortez** Colorado USA
124 G6 **Cortez Mountains** Nevada USA
232 E3 **Cortina d'Ampezzo** Italy
127 M5 **Cortland** New York USA
242 B2 **Cortober** Ireland
241 I2 **Corton** Suffolk England UK
232 D5 **Cortona** Italy
242 B3 **Cortown** Ireland
230 B4 **Coruche** Portugal
394 E5 **Çoruh** Turkey
394 E5 **Çorum** *admin. area* Turkey
157 B7 **Corumbá** *watercourse* Brazil
157 E7 **Corumbaú, Ponta** *cape* Brazil
230 C5 **Corumbel Bajo, Embalse de** *lake* Spain
156 E5 **Coruripe** Brazil
124 D4 **Corvallis** Oregon USA
230 E2 **Corvera** Spain
121 R6 **Corvette, Lac de la** *lake* Québec Canada
310 1 **Corvo** *island* Azores
233 F8 **Corvo, Punta del** *cape* Italy
240 D2 **Corwen** Denbighshire Wales UK
126 E6 **Corydon** Iowa USA
126 H8 **Corydon** Kentucky USA
132 D3 **Cosalá** Mexico
158 C2 **Cosca** Peru
127 K6 **Coshocton** Ohio USA
158 E4 **Cosincho** Bolivia
132 E4 **Cosío** Mexico
424 G6 **Cosmo Newbery** WA Australia
310 9 **Cosmoledo Islands** Seychelles
437 C2 **Cosmonaut Sea** Southern Ocean
226 E5 **Cossato** Italy
228 E3 **Cosson** *watercourse* France
154 E2 **Costa, Cordillera de la** *range* Venezuela
155 I3 **Costa, Ponta do** *cape* Brazil
230 D5 **Costa del Sol,** *region* Spain
231 H3 **Costa Dorada** *region* Spain
128 D4 **Costa Mesa** California USA
161 H2 **Costa Rica** Brazil
134 D5 **Costa Rica** *country* Central America
132 B2 **Costa Rica** Mexico
132 D3 **Costa Rica** Mexico
234 E2 **Costeşti** Romania
119 S4 **Costigan Lake** Saskatchewan Canada
234 F4 **Costineşti** Romania
377 J6 **Cotabato** Philippines
154 B4 **Cotacachi** Ecuador
158 E5 **Cotacajes** *watercourse* Bolivia
157 D7 **Cotaxé** *watercourse* Brazil
130 F6 **Cote Blanch Bay** Louisiana USA
228 E1 **Côte d'Albâtre** *region* France
228 C2 **Côte du Granit Rose** *region* France
234 D3 **Coteana** Romania
125 P4 **Coteau des Prairies** *valley* South Dakota USA
125 O3 **Coteau du Missouri** *valley* North Dakota USA
119 R7 **Coteau Hills** Saskatchewan Canada
135 F3 **Côtes-de-Fer** Haiti
240 C3 **Cothi** *watercourse* Wales UK
310 3d **Cotillo** Canary Islands
234 F2 **Cotiujeni** Moldova
304 E3 **Cotonou** Benin
154 B5 **Cotopaxi** *volcano* Ecuador
234 E1 **Cotova** Moldova
159 G3 **Cotriguaçu** Brazil
241 F3 **Cotswold Hills** England UK
124 D5 **Cottage Grove** Oregon USA
233 E5 **Cottanello** Italy
227 H2 **Cottbus** Germany
241 G2 **Cotterdale** North Yorkshire England UK
244 E4 **Cotterton** Perth and Kinross Scotland UK
241 G2 **Cottesmore** Rutland England UK
163 19 **Cotton Ground** St Kitts and Nevis
124 G3 **Cottonwood** Idaho USA
126 C7 **Cottonwood** *watercourse* Kansas USA
129 N1 **Cottonwood Falls** Kansas USA
135 G3 **Cotuí** Dominican Republic
130 B6 **Cotulla** Texas USA
228 D4 **Coubre, Pointe de la** *cape* France
127 P3 **Coudres, Île aux** *island* Québec Canada
228 F5 **Couiza** France
244 B5 **Coul Point** Scotland UK
244 C3 **Coulags** Highland Scotland UK
124 F3 **Coulee Dam** Washington USA
228 F3 **Couleuvre** France
437 L2 **Coulman Island** Antarctica
228 G3 **Coulmier-le-Sec** France
228 D4 **Coulon** *watercourse* France
127 M3 **Coulonge** *watercourse* Québec Canada
242 B3 **Coultry** Ireland
124 G3 **Council** Idaho USA
125 R6 **Council Bluffs** Iowa USA
125 Q7 **Council Grove** Kansas USA
240 E2 **Cound** Shropshire England UK
241 F2 **Countesthorpe** Leicester England UK
123 J9 **Coupé, Cap** *cape* St Pierre and Miquelon
244 C5 **Cour** Argyll and Bute Scotland UK
155 G3 **Courantyne** *watercourse* Guyana
310 6b **Courbet, Péninsule** *peninsula* French Southern and Antarctic Lands
226 D5 **Courchevel** France
228 F4 **Courpière** France
423 9 **Courrejolles Point** Campbell Island New Zealand
226 C4 **Cours** France
229 G4 **Courthézon** France
242 B4 **Courthoyle** Ireland
131 M2 **Courtland** Virginia USA
245 D5 **Courtmacsherry Bay** Ireland
228 E2 **Courtomer** France
245 F4 **Courtown** Ireland
130 E4 **Coushatta** Louisiana USA
228 D2 **Coutances** France
228 D2 **Couterne** France
119 P8 **Coutts** Alberta Canada
121 R2 **Couture, Lac** *lake* Québec Canada
163 9 **Couva** Trinidad and Tobago
163 9 **Couva-Tabaquite/Talparo** Trinidad and Tobago
226 C2 **Couvin** Belgium
234 E3 **Covasna** Romania
234 D3 **Covasna** *admin. area* Romania
244 C3 **Cove** Highland Scotland UK
241 I2 **Cove Bottom** Suffolk England UK
241 I2 **Covehithe** Suffolk England UK
241 F2 **Coventry** West Midlands England UK
240 B4 **Coverack** Cornwall England UK
230 C3 **Covilhã** Portugal
131 J4 **Covington** Georgia USA
163 11a **Cow and Calves** *cape* St Vincent and the Grenadines
243 F2 **Cow Green Reservoir** England UK
123 J8 **Cow Head** Newfoundland and Labrador Canada
424 G7 **Cowan, Lake** WA Australia
243 H2 **Cowbar Nab** *cape* England UK
241 G2 **Cowbit** Lincolnshire England UK
240 D3 **Cowbridge** Vale of Glamorgan Wales UK
126 G7 **Cowden** Illinois USA
425 K8 **Cowell** SA Australia
241 F4 **Cowes** Isle of Wight England UK
243 F2 **Cowgill** Cumbria England UK
244 E5 **Cowgill** South Lanarkshire Scotland UK
124 C2 **Cowichan Lake** British Columbia Canada
425 N8 **Cowra** NSW Australia
226 F3 **Cox** France
161 H4 **Coxilha Grande** *region* Brazil
159 H5 **Coxim** Brazil
123 I7 **Coxipi** *watercourse* Québec Canada
123 I7 **Coxipi, Lac** *lake* Québec Canada
379 G5 **Cox's Bazar** Bangladesh
162 C5 **Coy Aike** Argentina
160 D2 **Coya Sur** Chile
304 B3 **Coyah** Guinea
132 D2 **Coyame** Mexico
124 E1 **Coyle** British Columbia Canada
244 D5 **Coylton** Ayrshire Scotland UK
129 J4 **Coyote** New Mexico USA
129 H2 **Coyote** *watercourse* New Mexico USA
128 D3 **Coyote Lake** California USA
124 F5 **Coyote Lake** Oregon USA
128 E4 **Coyote Wells** California USA
132 E5 **Coyuca de Benítez** Mexico
125 P6 **Cozad** Nebraska USA
228 D4 **Cozes** France
133 H4 **Cozumel** Mexico
134 C2 **Cozumel, Isla** *island* Mexico
135 J4 **Crab Hill** Barbados
240 C4 **Crackington Haven** Cornwall England UK
243 F2 **Cracoe** North Yorkshire England UK
425 N6 **Cracow** Qld Australia
308 E6 **Cradock** South Africa
244 E4 **Craggie** Highland Scotland UK
234 D2 **Crăieşti** Romania
244 C3 **Craig** Highland Scotland UK
242 D1 **Craig** South Ayrshire Scotland UK
118 E1 **Craig** Alaska USA
125 L6 **Craig** Colorado USA
240 D2 **Craig Goch Reservoir** Wales UK
242 B2 **Craigavole** Coleraine Northern Ireland UK
242 B2 **Craigavon** Armagh Northern Ireland UK
245 F2 **Craigavon** *admin. area* Northern Ireland UK
242 D1 **Craigdarroch** East Ayrshire Scotland UK
244 E4 **Craignavar** Perth and Kinross Scotland UK
242 B2 **Craigs Middle** Ballymoney Northern Ireland UK
244 E2 **Craigtown** Highland Scotland UK
119 S7 **Craik** Saskatchewan Canada
244 F3 **Craik** Aberdeenshire Scotland UK
244 F4 **Crail** Fife Scotland UK
227 F5 **Crailsheim** Germany
234 C3 **Craiova** Romania
243 G1 **Cramlington** Northumberland England UK
244 E5 **Cramond** City of Edinburgh Scotland UK
245 E2 **Cranagh** Strabane Northern Ireland UK
118 G5 **Cranberry Junction** British Columbia Canada
425 M9 **Cranbourne** Vic. Australia
119 N8 **Cranbrook** British Columbia Canada
126 G4 **Crandon** Wisconsin USA
126 E8 **Crane** Missouri USA
129 K5 **Crane** Texas USA
125 K1 **Crane Lake** Saskatchewan Canada
126 E2 **Crane Lake** Minnesota USA
241 G2 **Cranfield** Bedfordshire England UK
245 G2 **Cranfield Point** Northern Ireland UK
241 G3 **Cranleigh** Surrey England UK
228 D3 **Craon** France
234 F3 **Crapina, Lacul** *lake* Ukraine
437 L2 **Crary Bank** *underwater feature* Ross Sea
436 M1 **Crary Ice Rise** Antarctica
436 P1 **Crary Mountains** Antarctica
244 D2 **Crask Inn** Highland Scotland UK
234 C2 **Crasna** Romania
124 D5 **Crater Lake** Oregon USA
373 H5 **Crater Mountain** Papua New Guinea
373 J5 **Crater Point** Papua New Guinea
156 D4 **Crateús** Brazil
244 E3 **Crathie** Aberdeenshire Scotland UK
233 G7 **Crati** *watercourse* Italy
156 E4 **Crato** Brazil
121 Q5 **Craven, Lac** *lake* Québec Canada
154 D3 **Cravo Norte** Colombia
154 D3 **Cravo Sur** *watercourse* Colombia
244 E5 **Crawford** South Lanarkshire Scotland UK
130 G4 **Crawford** Mississippi USA
125 N5 **Crawford** Nebraska USA
424 G7 **Crawford, Mount** WA Australia
244 E5 **Crawfordjohn** South Lanarkshire Scotland UK
126 H6 **Crawfordsville** Indiana USA
244 E5 **Crawick** Dumfries and Galloway Scotland UK
241 G3 **Crawley** West Sussex England UK
240 D3 **Cray** Powys Wales UK
243 G2 **Crayke** North Yorkshire England UK
125 J3 **Crazy Mountains** Montana USA
240 D4 **Creacombe** Devon England UK
226 B3 **Crécy** France
241 I4 **Crécy-en-Ponthieu** France
240 E2 **Credenhill** Herefordshire England UK
240 D4 **Crediton** Devon England UK
116 I7 **Cree** *watercourse* Saskatchewan Canada
116 I7 **Cree Lake** Saskatchewan Canada
119 R4 **Cree Lake** Saskatchewan Canada
125 L8 **Creede** Colorado USA
132 D3 **Creel** Mexico
119 T8 **Creelman** Saskatchewan Canada
245 E1 **Creeslough** Ireland
244 D6 **Creetown** Dumfries and Galloway Scotland UK
242 B2 **Creeve** Ireland
242 A2 **Creevelea** Ireland
245 D2 **Cregg** Ireland
242 A1 **Creggan** Londonderry Northern Ireland UK
245 C3 **Cregganbaun** Ireland
228 F2 **Creil** France
232 C4 **Crema** Italy
229 G4 **Crémieu** France
232 D4 **Cremona** Italy
130 G5 **Creola** Alabama USA
229 K3 **Crep Nudo** *mountain* Italy
234 B3 **Crepaja** Serbia
159 G2 **Crepori** *watercourse* Brazil
227 H5 **Cres** Croatia
124 D2 **Crescent, Lake** Washington USA
124 C6 **Crescent City** California USA
377 F3 **Crescent Group** *island* Paracel Islands
131 K6 **Crescent Lake** Florida USA
124 E5 **Crescent Lake** Oregon USA
226 B2 **Crespin** France
160 F5 **Crespo** Argentina
228 E4 **Cressensac** France
243 G1 **Cresswell** Northumberland England UK
229 G4 **Crest** France
79 U5 **Crest Seamount** *underwater feature* Pacific Ocean
118 M8 **Creston** British Columbia Canada
124 F3 **Creston** Washington USA
131 H5 **Crestview** Florida USA
124 D5 **Creswell** Oregon USA
Crete, Sea of *see* **Kritiko Pelago** Europe
373 I5 **Cretin, Cape** Papua New Guinea
228 F5 **Creus, Cap de** *cape* Spain
228 E3 **Creuse** *watercourse* France
226 F3 **Creußen** Germany
240 E1 **Crewe** Cheshire England UK
127 L8 **Crewe** Virginia USA
240 E4 **Crewkerne** Somerset England UK
240 C2 **Criccieth** Gwynedd Wales UK
161 I4 **Criciúma** Brazil
240 D2 **Crickadarn** Powys Wales UK
240 D3 **Crickhowell** Powys Wales UK
244 E4 **Crieff** Perth and Kinross Scotland UK
228 E1 **Criel-Plage** France
241 I4 **Criel-sur-mer** France
241 I5 **Crillon** France
126 E2 **Crilly** Ontario Canada
244 G3 **Crimond** Aberdeenshire Scotland UK
241 H2 **Crimplesham** Norfolk England UK
244 C4 **Crinan** Argyll and Bute Scotland UK
242 B1 **Crindle** Limavady Northern Ireland UK
125 M7 **Cripple Creek** Colorado USA
234 C2 **Crişcior** Romania
127 N8 **Crisfield** Maryland USA
305 G4 **Cristal, Monts de** *range* Gabon
157 C7 **Cristalina** Brazil
154 A3 **Cristo, Punta** *cape* Panama
230 D3 **Cristóbal** Spain
163 4 **Cristóbal, Punta** *cape* Archipiélago de Colón (Galapagos Islands)
154 C2 **Cristóbal Colón, Pico** *mountain* Colombia
234 C2 **Crişul Alb** *watercourse* Romania
234 C2 **Crişul Negru** *watercourse* Romania
234 C3 **Crivina** Romania
226 F1 **Crivitz** Germany
157 B6 **Crixás** Brazil
157 B6 **Crixás Açu** *watercourse* Brazil
232 G5 **Crkvice** Croatia
235 B5 **Crna** *watercourse* Macedonia
229 L3 **Črna** Slovenia
234 B4 **Crna Gora** *region* Serbia
234 A3 **Crnča** Serbia
235 B5 **Crni Drim** *watercourse* Macedonia
245 B3 **Croaghnakeela Island** Ireland
232 **Croatia** *country* Europe
226 F4 **Croce, Monte** *mountain* Italy
375 G2 **Crocker, Banjaran** *range* Malaysia
375 H2 **Crocker Range National Park** Malaysia
425 J2 **Crocodile Islands Group** NT Australia
126 H8 **Crofton** Kentucky USA
244 C4 **Croggan** Highland Scotland UK
245 D2 **Crohy Head** *cape* Ireland
244 D3 **Croick** Highland Scotland UK
228 C3 **Croisic, Pointe de** *cape* France
127 K4 **Croker, Cape** Ontario Canada
424 I2 **Croker Island** NT Australia
424 L3 **Croll, Mount** Qld Australia
226 C5 **Crolles** France
245 C4 **Cromane** Ireland
120 H4 **Cromarty** Manitoba Canada
244 D3 **Cromarty** Highland Scotland UK
241 I2 **Cromer** Norfolk England UK
159 I5 **Cromínia** Brazil
163 15 **Crompton Point** *cape* Dominica
244 D4 **Cromra** Highland Scotland UK
242 B3 **Crone** Ireland
243 G2 **Crook** Durham England UK
125 N6 **Crook** Colorado USA
135 F2 **Crooked Island Passage** Bahamas
123 J8 **Crooked Lake** Newfoundland and Labrador Canada
242 A3 **Crookedwood** Ireland
122 C1 **Crooks Inlet** Nunavut Canada
425 N8 **Crookwell** NSW Australia
245 D4 **Croom** Ireland
233 G7 **Cropalati** Italy
243 H2 **Cropton** North Yorkshire England UK
244 B2 **Crosbost** Na h-Eileanan Siar Scotland UK
242 E2 **Crosby** Cumbria England UK
242 E3 **Crosby** Merseyside England UK
242 E2 **Crosby Villa** Cumbria England UK
129 L4 **Crosbyton** Texas USA
305 F3 **Cross** *watercourse* Nigeria
131 J6 **Cross City** Florida USA
243 F2 **Cross Fell** *mountain* England UK
131 K3 **Cross Hill** South Carolina USA
120 G5 **Cross Lake** Manitoba Canada
130 D4 **Cross Lake** Louisiana USA
127 Q3 **Cross Lake** Maine USA
240 B4 **Cross Lanes** Cornwall England UK
305 F3 **Cross River** *admin. area* Nigeria
118 C3 **Cross Sound** Alaska USA
244 C5 **Crossaig** Argyll and Bute Scotland UK
244 B4 **Crossapolx** Highland Scotland UK
119 N7 **Crossfield** Alberta Canada
242 C2 **Crossgar** Down Northern Ireland UK
245 D5 **Crosshaven** Ireland
242 B4 **Crosslaghroe** Ireland
242 E1 **Crosslee** Scottish Borders Scotland UK
244 F3 **Crossroads** Aberdeenshire Scotland UK
122 F5 **Crossroads Lake** Newfoundland and Labrador Canada
130 A4 **Croton** *watercourse* Texas USA
233 G7 **Crotone** Italy
241 F3 **Croughton** Northamptonshire England UK
241 H3 **Crowborough** East Sussex England UK
130 D3 **Crowder** Oklahoma USA
425 O7 **Crowdy Head** NSW Australia
130 B4 **Crowell** Texas USA
124 I1 **Crowfoot** Alberta Canada
241 G2 **Crowland** Lincolnshire England UK
243 H3 **Crowle** North Lincolnshire England UK
130 E5 **Crowley** Louisiana USA
128 C2 **Crowley, Lake** California USA
373 H5 **Crown Island** Papua New Guinea
244 D3 **Croy** Highland Scotland UK
310 6b **Croy, Île de** *island* French Southern and Antarctic Lands
425 L4 **Croydon** Qld Australia
241 G3 **Croydon** Greater London England UK
310 6 **Crozet, Îles** *islands* French Southern and Antarctic Lands
80 J9 **Crozet Basin** *underwater feature* Southern Ocean
80 J9 **Crozet Plateau** *underwater feature* Southern Ocean
116 G3 **Crozier Channel** Northwest Territories Canada
228 B2 **Crozon** France
234 D2 **Crucea** Romania
155 E2 **Crucero Pardillal** Venezuela
154 B3 **Cruces, Punta** *cape* Colombia
244 G3 **Cruden Bay** Aberdeenshire Scotland UK
244 D6 **Cruggleton** Dumfries and Galloway Scotland UK
133 F3 **Cruillas** Mexico
76 P6 **Cruiser Seamount** *underwater feature* Atlantic Ocean
242 B3 **Cruisetown** Ireland
124 F5 **Crump Lake** Oregon USA
240 C3 **Crundale** Pembrokeshire Wales UK
245 D4 **Crusheen** Ireland
245 E4 **Crutt** Ireland
156 D3 **Cruz** Brazil
162 D3 **Cruz, Bahía** *bay* Argentina
158 A2 **Cruz, Bahía La** *bay* Peru
134 E3 **Cruz, Cabo** *cape* Cuba
160 F5 **Cruz Alta** Argentina
161 H4 **Cruz Alta** Brazil
163 21 **Cruz Bay** US Virgin Islands
160 E4 **Cruz del Eje** Argentina
158 D4 **Cruz Pampa** Peru
157 C8 **Cruzeiro** Brazil
158 C2 **Cruzeiro do Sul** Brazil
157 C8 **Cruzília** Brazil
118 G3 **Cry Lake** British Columbia Canada
118 K5 **Crysdale, Mount** British Columbia Canada
131 J6 **Crystal Bay** Florida USA
425 K8 **Crystal Brook** SA Australia
130 B6 **Crystal City** Texas USA
126 G3 **Crystal Falls** Michigan USA
126 H4 **Crystal Lake** Michigan USA
131 J6 **Crystal River** Florida USA
232 H3 **Csávoly** Hungary
227 K3 **Cserehát** *region* Hungary
227 I4 **Csokonyavisonta** Hungary
227 K4 **Csongrád** Hungary
227 K4 **Csongrád** *admin. area* Hungary
227 I4 **Csót** Hungary
376 F4 **Cu Lao Re** *island* Vietnam
376 F5 **Cu Lao Thu** *island* Vietnam
154 E2 **Cúa** Venezuela
374 E1 **Cua Lon** *watercourse* Vietnam
162 C3 **Cuadrada, Sierra** *range* Argentina
158 E6 **Cuadrilla Tres** Bolivia
230 D2 **Cuadros** Spain
244 C3 **Cuaig** Highland Scotland UK
309 G2 **Cuamba** Mozambique
308 D3 **Cuando** *watercourse* Angola
308 C3 **Cuando Cubango** *admin. area* Angola
308 C3 **Cuangar** Angola
306 B5 **Cuango** Angola
306 B5 **Cuango** *watercourse* Angola
306 B5 **Cuango** *watercourse* Democratic Republic of Congo
308 C2 **Cuanza** Angola
308 B1 **Cuanza** *watercourse* Angola
308 B1 **Cuanza Norte** *admin. area* Angola
308 C2 **Cuanza Sul** *admin. area* Angola
154 E3 **Cuao, Macizo del** *range* Venezuela
155 E3 **Cuao, Río** *watercourse* Venezuela
154 E3 **Cuao, Serranía de** *range* Venezuela
161 G4 **Cuaro** *watercourse* Uruguay
377 G5 **Cuarteron Reef** Spratly Islands
129 K7 **Cuates de Australia** Mexico
308 C3 **Cuatir** *watercourse* Angola
129 K7 **Cuatrociénegas de Carranza** Mexico
132 D2 **Cuauhtémoc** Mexico
133 F5 **Cuautitlán** Mexico
133 F5 **Cuautla** Mexico
134 E2 **Cuba** *country* Caribbean
230 C4 **Cuba** Portugal
126 F7 **Cuba** Missouri USA
129 I2 **Cuba** New Mexico USA
127 L5 **Cuba** New York USA
155 E2 **Cubagua, Isla** *island* Venezuela
308 B2 **Cubal** Angola
308 B3 **Cubal** *watercourse* Angola
306 B6 **Cubango** *watercourse* Angola
154 C3 **Cubará** Colombia
157 C8 **Cubatão** Brazil
157 B6 **Cubatão, Serra do** *range* Brazil
230 E2 **Cubo de Bureba** Spain
234 F2 **Cubolta** Moldova
162 A3 **Cucao, Bahía** *bay* Chile
233 F6 **Cucchiara, Punta di** *cape* Italy
308 C2 **Cuchi** Angola
308 C3 **Cuchi** *watercourse* Angola
160 E6 **Cuchillo Có** Argentina
129 J6 **Cuchillo Pardo** Mexico
134 B4 **Cuchumatanes, Sierra los** *range* Guatemala
163 12 **Cuckold Point** *cape* Barbados
154 E4 **Cucui** Venezuela
132 C2 **Cucurpé** Mexico
154 B3 **Cucurrupí** Colombia
154 C3 **Cúcuta** Colombia
163 1a **Cudarebe** *cape* Aruba
242 A4 **Cuddagh** Ireland
393 E9 **Cuddalore** Tamil Nadu India
393 E8 **Cuddapah** Andhra Pradesh India
228 A5 **Cudillero** Spain
163 17 **Cudjoe Head** Montserrat
119 S6 **Cudworth** Saskatchewan Canada
424 F6 **Cue** WA Australia
308 C3 **Cuebe** *watercourse* Angola
308 C3 **Cueio** *watercourse* Angola
308 C2 **Cuelei** *watercourse* Angola
230 D3 **Cuéllar** Spain
308 C2 **Cuemba** Angola
154 B5 **Cuenca** Ecuador
230 E3 **Cuenca** Spain
230 E3 **Cuenca, Serranía de** *range* Spain
230 E3 **Cuerda del Pozo, Embalse de la** *lake* Spain
133 F5 **Cuernavaca** Mexico
377 I5 **Cueros de Negros** *mountain* Philippines
231 J2 **Cuers** France
129 J6 **Cuerva, Laguna El** *lake* Mexico
135 F2 **Cueto** Cuba
133 F3 **Cuevecillas** Mexico
154 B3 **Cuevita, Bahía** *bay* Colombia
234 C3 **Cugir** Romania
388 C5 **Cugus, Gora** *mountain* Russian Federation
385 H3 **Cuhe bator** Mongolia
159 G4 **Cuiabá** Brazil
159 G5 **Cuiabá** *watercourse* Brazil
132 D3 **Cuidame** Mexico
244 B2 **Cuidhaseadair** Na h-Eileanan Siar Scotland UK
380 D3 **Cuihua** Yunnan China
381 G3 **Cuijiang** Fujian China
134 B4 **Cuilapa** Guatemala
245 D3 **Cuilleen** Ireland
244 B3 **Cuillin Sound** Scotland UK
306 B5 **Cuilo** Angola
156 E4 **Cuité** Brazil
308 C3 **Cuito** *watercourse* Angola
308 C3 **Cuito Cuanavale** Angola
132 E3 **Cuitzeo, Laguna de** *lake* Mexico
155 F5 **Cuiuni** *watercourse* Brazil
126 F7 **Cuivre** *watercourse* Missouri USA
374 D2 **Cukai** Malaysia
163 14 **Cul-de-Sac du Marin** *bay* Martinique
228 F3 **Culan** France
377 I5 **Culasi** Philippines
125 M2 **Culbertson** Montana USA
240 D3 **Culbone** Somerset England UK
425 M8 **Culcairn** NSW Australia
135 H3 **Culebra, Isla de** *island* Puerto Rico
129 J2 **Culebra, Mount** Colorado USA
230 C3 **Culebra, Sierra de la** *range* Spain
425 M7 **Culgoa** *watercourse* NSW Australia
132 D3 **Culiacán** Mexico
377 I5 **Culion** Philippines
377 H5 **Culion** *island* Philippines
159 H4 **Culiseu** *watercourse* Brazil
244 C2 **Culkein** Highland Scotland UK
231 F3 **Culla** Spain
230 E5 **Cúllar de Baza** Spain
162 C5 **Cullen** Argentina
245 D4 **Cullen** Ireland
244 F3 **Cullen** Moray Scotland UK
130 E4 **Cullen** Louisiana USA
231 F4 **Cullera** Spain
242 A2 **Cullion** Strabane Northern Ireland UK
130 H3 **Cullman** Alabama USA
240 D4 **Cullompton** Devon England UK
242 D2 **Culmalzie** Dumfries and Galloway Scotland UK
230 E5 **Culo de Perros, Punta** *cape* Spain
242 A1 **Culoort** Ireland
244 D3 **Culrain** Highland Scotland UK
242 D2 **Culshabbin** Dumfries and Galloway Scotland UK
244 inset **Culswick** Shetland Scotland UK
157 A6 **Culuene** *watercourse* Brazil
423 E6 **Culverden** New Zealand
241 G2 **Culverthorpe** Lincolnshire England UK
244 D5 **Culzean Bay** Scotland UK
156 C3 **Cumã, Baía do** *bay* Brazil
155 E2 **Cumaná** Venezuela
163 9 **Cumana Bay** *bay* Trinidad and Tobago
154 C3 **Cumaral** Colombia
154 D3 **Cumaribo** Colombia
131 J2 **Cumberland** Kentucky USA
131 I2 **Cumberland** *watercourse* Kentucky USA
127 L7 **Cumberland** Maryland USA
127 L8 **Cumberland** Virginia USA
163 6a **Cumberland, Bahía** *bay* Isla Róbinson Crusoe
131 I2 **Cumberland, Lake** Kentucky USA
163 8 **Cumberland Bay** South Georgia
119 T6 **Cumberland House** Saskatchewan Canada
425 N5 **Cumberland Islands** Qld Australia
120 D5 **Cumberland Lake** Saskatchewan Canada
131 J2 **Cumberland Mountains** Kentucky USA
117 M5 **Cumberland Peninsula** Nunavut Canada
131 I3 **Cumberland Plateau** Tennessee USA
117 M5 **Cumberland Sound** Nunavut Canada
131 K5 **Cumberland Sound** Georgia USA
244 E5 **Cumbernauld** North Lanarkshire Scotland UK
154 B4 **Cumbitara** Colombia
242 E2 **Cumbria** *admin. area* England UK
155 H5 **Cuminapanema** *watercourse* Brazil
163 5 **Cumming, Cabo** *cape* Isla de Pascua (Easter Island)
425 J8 **Cummins** SA Australia
244 D5 **Cumnock** East Ayrshire Scotland UK
155 I4 **Cunani** Brazil
160 C6 **Cunco** Chile
424 F7 **Cunderdin** WA Australia
308 C3 **Cunene** *admin. area* Angola
308 B3 **Cunene** *watercourse* Angola
308 C2 **Cunhinga** Angola
158 D3 **Cunhupuca** Brazil
231 G3 **Cunit** Spain
308 D3 **Cunjamba** Angola
425 M7 **Cunnamulla** Qld Australia
158 C2 **Cunshamayo** Peru
232 F4 **Čunski** Croatia
223 N2 **Čuokkaraš'ša** *mountain* Norway
379 G3 **Cuomei** Xizang Zizhiqu China
379 G3 **Cuona** Xizang Zizhiqu China
378 E2 **Cuoqin** Xizang Zizhiqu China
119 S7 **Cupar** Saskatchewan Canada
244 E4 **Cupar** Fife Scotland UK
159 H1 **Cupari** *watercourse* Brazil
154 B3 **Cupica, Golfo de** *bay* Colombia
155 I4 **Cupixi** Brazil
162 B3 **Cuptana, Isla** *island* Chile
228 F5 **Cuq** France
245 C3 **Cur** Ireland
134 D2 **Cura, Laguna del** *lake* Cuba
162 D1 **Cura Malal, Sierra de** *range* Argentina
156 E5 **Curaçá** Brazil
154 D2 **Curaçao** *island* Netherlands Antilles
162 E2 **Curacó** *watercourse* Argentina
155 E4 **Curamoni** Venezuela
160 C6 **Curanilahue** Chile
154 B5 **Curaray** *watercourse* Ecuador
154 C5 **Curaray** *watercourse* Peru
161 G4 **Curaya** *watercourse* Argentina
228 F3 **Cure** *watercourse* France
129 H6 **Curea** Mexico
129 I1 **Curecanti National Recreation Area** Colorado USA
310 7b **Curepipe** Mauritius
159 E3 **Curequete** *watercourse* Brazil
159 E6 **Curi, Sierra de** *range* Bolivia
158 D3 **Curichón** Bolivia
160 D5 **Curicó** Chile
154 E5 **Curicuriari** *watercourse* Brazil
310 9a **Curieuse** *island* Seychelles
154 C4 **Curillo** Colombia
154 D5 **Curinga** Peru
423 C8 **Curio Bay** New Zealand
157 B9 **Curitiba** Brazil
161 I3 **Curitibanos** Brazil
308 B3 **Curoca** *watercourse* Angola
242 A2 **Curr** Omagh Northern Ireland UK
245 F3 **Curragha** Ireland
245 E4 **Currahill** Ireland
155 G5 **Curral Velho** Brazil
300 B5 **Curral Velho** Cape Verde
157 E5 **Curralinho** Brazil
245 B5 **Currane, Lough** *lake* Ireland
245 C2 **Curraunboy** Ireland
245 D4 **Curreeny** Ireland
425 L9 **Currie** Tas. Australia
131 N2 **Currituck Sound** North Carolina USA
234 B2 **Curtici** Romania
125 O6 **Curtis** Nebraska USA
425 N5 **Curtis Island** Qld Australia

422 5 **Curtis Island** Kermadec Islands New Zealand
159 H2 **Curuá** *watercourse* Brazil
156 B2 **Curuá, Ilha** *island* Brazil
155 H5 **Curua do Sul** *watercourse* Brazil
159 H1 **Curua Una** *watercourse* Brazil
159 H2 **Curuaes** *watercourse* Brazil
155 H5 **Curuai, Lago Grande do** *lake* Brazil
377 I6 **Curuan** Philippines
158 C2 **Curuçá** *watercourse* Brazil
308 B3 **Curue** *watercourse* Angola
154 C2 **Curumani** Colombia
155 I5 **Curumu** Brazil
374 D4 **Curup** Indonesia
155 H5 **Curupari** Brazil
159 F6 **Cururenda** Bolivia
156 C3 **Cururupu** Brazil
161 G4 **Curuzú Cuatiá** Argentina
157 C7 **Curvelo** Brazil
134 D5 **Cusapín** Panama
158 D4 **Cusco** Peru
158 C4 **Cusco** *admin. area* Peru
158 C2 **Cushabatay** *watercourse* Peru
242 A3 **Cushaling** Ireland
242 B1 **Cushendun** Moyle Northern Ireland UK
154 C3 **Cusiana** *watercourse* Colombia
124 G2 **Cusick** Washington USA
232 D4 **Cusna, Monte** *mountain* Italy
308 C2 **Cussava** Angola
228 F3 **Cusset** France
131 I4 **Cusseta** Georgia USA
121 Q2 **Cusson, Pointe** *cape* Québec Canada
423 E6 **Cust** New Zealand
125 N5 **Custer** South Dakota USA
130 B3 **Custer City** Oklahoma USA
229 H2 **Custines** France
156 E5 **Custódia** Brazil
230 C3 **Custoias** Portugal
234 C3 **Cut** Romania
124 I2 **Cut Bank** Montana USA
119 Q6 **Cut Knife** Saskatchewan Canada
308 C2 **Cutato** Angola
118 L5 **Cutbank** *watercourse* Alberta Canada
242 D2 **Cutcloy** Dumfries and Galloway Scotland UK
308 C2 **Cutenda** Angola
131 I5 **Cuthbert** Georgia USA
244 D3 **Cuthill** Highland Scotland UK
245 D3 **Cutra, Lough** *lake* Ireland
160 D6 **Cutral-Có** Argentina
393 F7 **Cuttack** Orissa India
154 B5 **Cutucú, Cordillera de** *range* Ecuador
305 H5 **Cuvette** *admin. area* Congo
305 G4 **Cuvette-Ouest** *admin. area* Congo
81 P7 **Cuvier Abyssal Plain** *underwater feature* Indian Ocean
422 F3 **Cuvier Island** New Zealand
81 O7 **Cuvier Plateau** *underwater feature* Indian Ocean
226 E1 **Cuxhaven** Germany
377 I5 **Cuyo** *island* Philippines
377 I5 **Cuyo East Passage** *strait* Philippines
377 I5 **Cuyo West Passage** *strait* Philippines
155 F3 **Cuyuni** *watercourse* Guyana
242 E3 **Cwm** Denbighshire Wales UK
240 C3 **Cwm Duad** Carmarthenshire Wales UK
240 C2 **Cwmann** Carmarthenshire Wales UK
240 D3 **Cwmbran** Torfaen Wales UK
240 D3 **Cwmdu** Powys Wales UK
240 C3 **Cwmfelin Mynach** Carmarthenshire Wales UK
227 H1 **Cybinka** Poland
Cyclades *see* **Kyklades** Greece
126 J6 **Cygnet** Ohio USA
125 K2 **Cypress Hills** Saskatchewan Canada
125 K2 **Cypress Lake** Saskatchewan Canada
394 E6 **Cyprus** *country*
130 B3 **Cyril** Oklahoma USA
122 F1 **Cyrus Field Bay** Nunavut Canada
227 I1 **Czarne** Poland
227 H3 **Czech Republic** *country* Europe
227 J3 **Czechowice-Dziedzice** Poland
227 K2 **Czekarzewice** Poland
227 H1 **Czerwieńsk** Poland
227 J2 **Częstochowa** Poland
227 I1 **Człopa** Poland

D

385 I3 **Da Hinggan Ling** *range* Nei Mongol Zizhiqu China
376 F5 **Đà Lat** Vietnam
376 F3 **Đà Nẵng** Vietnam
376 F4 **Đa Răng** *watercourse* Vietnam
381 H1 **Da Yunhe (Grand Canal)** *watercourse* Jiangsu China
385 J3 **Da'an** Jilin China
384 G6 **Da'ning** Shanxi China
222 I6 **Dåasen** *lake* Sweden
380 E2 **Daba Shan** *range* Chongqing China
304 D3 **Dabakala** Côte d'Ivoire
385 I4 **Daban** Nei Mongol Zizhiqu China
390 C4 **Dabbāgh, Jabal** *mountain* Saudi Arabia
154 B3 **Dabeiba** Colombia
393 C6 **Dabhoi** Gujarat India
393 C8 **Dabhol** Maharashtra India
381 G2 **Dabie Shan** *range* Anhui China
230 D3 **Dabo** France
300 D6 **Dabo** Senegal
304 D3 **Dabou** Côte d'Ivoire
304 D3 **Daboya** Ghana
384 F5 **Dabqig** Nei Mongol Zizhiqu China
393 F7 **Dabra** Chhattisgarh India
392 E6 **Dabra** Madhya Pradesh India
227 J2 **Dąbrowa Górnicza** Poland
383 J5 **Dabsan Hu** *lake* Qinghai China
Dacca *see* **Dhaka** Bangladesh
381 I2 **Dachangtu Shan** *range* Zhejiang China
381 I2 **Dachu Shan** *range* Zhejiang China
130 B2 **Dacoma** Oklahoma USA
127 M4 **Dacre** Ontario Canada
423 C8 **Dacre** New Zealand
232 B4 **Dadal** Mongolia
426 8 **Dadale** Solomon Islands
131 J6 **Dade City** Florida USA
392 E5 **Dadeldhura** Nepal
391 K3 **Dadhar** Pakistan
372 D4 **Dadi, Tanjung** *cape* Indonesia
391 J4 **Dadigor** Pakistan
228 F5 **Dadou** *watercourse* France
393 C7 **Dadra and Nagar Haveli** *admin. area* India
391 K4 **Dadu** Pakistan
380 D2 **Dadu He** *watercourse* Sichuan China
390 C5 **Daedalus Reef** Saudi Arabia
Daegu *see* **Taegu** South Korea
386 E4 **Daeheugsan-do** *island* South Korea
235 C7 **Daemoniá** Greece
377 I4 **Daet** Philippines
380 E3 **Dafang** Guizhou China
380 E4 **Dafeng** Guangxi Zhuangzu Zizhiqu China
381 H1 **Dafeng** Jiangsu China
235 B6 **Dafnoudi, Akra** *cape* Greece
379 F3 **Daga** Bhutan
307 E2 **Daga-Post** Sudan
308 E3 **Dagamela** Zimbabwe
300 C5 **Dagana** Senegal
302 E4 **Dagash** Sudan
372 C3 **Dagasuli** *island* Indonesia
235 G7 **Dağbeli** Turkey
225 N4 **Dagda** Latvia
235 F6 **Dağdere** Turkey
385 H4 **Dage** Hebei China
241 H3 **Dagenham** Greater London England UK
423 B7 **Dagg Sound** New Zealand
224 H3 **Daglösen** *lake* Sweden
305 H2 **Daguela** Chad
377 I3 **Dagupan** Philippines
385 I5 **Daheishan Dao** *island* Shandong China
303 G4 **Dahlak Archipelago** *island* Eritrea
390 E2 **Dahlūj** Iraq
301 H1 **Dahmani** Tunisia
227 G2 **Dahme** *watercourse* Germany
224 F5 **Dahmeshöved** *cape* Germany
392 D6 **Dahod** Gujarat India
381 F2 **Dahong Shan** *mountain* Hubei China
307 H1 **Dahot** *watercourse* Somalia
380 E4 **Dahua** Guangxi Zhuangzu Zizhiqu China
390 E2 **Dahūk** Iraq
390 E2 **Dahūk** *admin. area* Iraq
372 D5 **Dai** *island* Indonesia
426 8 **Dai** *island* Solomon Islands
381 H3 **Dai Jiang** *watercourse* Fujian China
376 E5 **Đại Ngãi** Vietnam
386 G4 **Dai-sen** *volcano* Japan
381 H3 **Dai Xian** Shanxi China
374 E4 **Daik** Indonesia
376 C3 **Daik-U** Myanmar
222 J4 **Daikanvik** Sweden
391 K2 **Dāikondi** *admin. area* Afghanistan
392 E5 **Dailekh** Nepal
244 D5 **Dailly** South Ayrshire Scotland UK
425 M4 **Daintree** Qld Australia
244 F4 **Dairsie** Fife Scotland UK
126 E3 **Dairyland** Wisconsin USA
387 I3 **Daisengen-dake** *volcano* Japan
381 I2 **Daishan Dao** *island* Zhejiang China
393 F7 **Daitari** Orissa India
425 K5 **Dajarra** Qld Australia
380 D4 **Dajie** Yunnan China
380 D2 **Dajin Chuan** *watercourse* Sichuan China
381 F4 **Dajin Dao** *island* Guangdong China
391 I4 **Dak** Iran
376 E4 **Đắk Tô** Vietnam
300 C6 **Dakar** Senegal
300 C6 **Dakar** *admin. area* Senegal
307 G2 **Dakata** *watercourse* Ethiopia
373 I5 **Dakataua, Lake** Papua New Guinea
302 D2 **Dākhilah, Wāḥāt ad** *spring* Egypt
374 B2 **Dakoank** Andaman and Nicobar Islands India
301 H6 **Dakoro** Niger
234 B4 **Đakovica** Kosovo
224 F2 **Dal** Norway
308 D2 **Dala** Angola
426 8 **Dala** Solomon Islands
304 B2 **Dalaba** Guinea
300 D6 **Dalaba** Senegal
385 H4 **Dalai Nuur** *lake* Nei Mongol Zizhiqu China
383 J5 **Dalai Shan** *mountain* Gansu China
384 E4 **Dalain Hob** Nei Mongol Zizhiqu China
224 H2 **Dalälven** *watercourse* Sweden
235 F7 **Dalama** Turkey
235 F7 **Dalaman** *watercourse* Turkey
384 E4 **Dalandzadgad** Mongolia
384 G3 **Dalanjargalan** Mongolia
224 H2 **Dalarna** *admin. area* Sweden
375 F3 **Dalat** Malaysia
222 inset **Dalatangi** *cape* Iceland
244 C4 **Dalavich** Argyll and Bute Scotland UK
391 J4 **Dalbandin** Pakistan
244 E6 **Dalbeattie** Dumfries and Galloway Scotland UK
425 M5 **Dalbeg** Qld Australia
244 D3 **Dalbeg** Highland Scotland UK
373 G5 **D'Alberti's Dome** *mountain* Papua New Guinea
222 G3 **Dalbosjön** *bay* Sweden
425 N6 **Dalby** Qld Australia
243 G2 **Dalby** North Yorkshire England UK
224 C2 **Dale** Norway
240 B3 **Dale** Pembrokeshire Wales UK
131 I2 **Dale Hollow Lake** Tennessee USA
244 inset **Dale of Walls** Shetland Scotland UK
226 D1 **Dalen** Netherlands
224 E3 **Dalen** Norway
244 E3 **Daless** Highland Scotland UK
244 E3 **Dalestie** Moray Scotland UK
244 E3 **Dalfad** Aberdeenshire Scotland UK
391 I4 **Dalgān** Iran
129 K2 **Dalhart** Texas USA
222 F5 **Dalholen** Norway
116 G4 **Dalhousie, Cape** Northwest Territories Canada
380 F1 **Dali** Shaanxi China
380 C3 **Dali** Yunnan China
388 J6 **Dāli** Afghanistan
390 F2 **Dāli Chū** Iran
385 J5 **Dalian** Liaoning China
381 H3 **Dalian Dao** *island* Fujian China
385 J5 **Dalian Wan** *bay* Liaoning China
385 I4 **Daling He** *watercourse* Liaoning China
232 H4 **Dalj** Croatia
244 E5 **Dalkeith** Midlothian Scotland UK
118 E5 **Dall Island** Alaska USA
124 E1 **Dallas** British Columbia Canada
244 E3 **Dallas** Moray Scotland UK
131 K3 **Dallas** North Carolina USA
124 D4 **Dallas** Oregon USA
130 C4 **Dallas** Texas USA
301 G6 **Dallol Bosso** *watercourse* Niger
390 G5 **Dalmā** *island* United Arab Emirates
160 F5 **Dalmacio** Argentina
244 D4 **Dalmally** Argyll and Bute Scotland UK
122 C6 **Dalmas, Lac** *lake* Québec Canada
244 D5 **Dalmellington** East Ayrshire Scotland UK
244 D3 **Dalnavie** Highland Scotland UK
387 G2 **Dal'negorsk** Russian Federation
386 G1 **Dal'nerechensk** Russian Federation
244 D4 **Dalness** Highland Scotland UK
244 D2 **Dalnessie** Highland Scotland UK
234 G2 **Dal'nik** Ukraine
223 T2 **Dal'niye Zelentsy** Russian Federation
237 AD9 **Dal'nyaya** Russian Federation
387 I2 **Dal'nyaya** Russian Federation
304 C3 **Daloa** Côte d'Ivoire
244 E4 **Dalriech** Perth and Kinross Scotland UK
244 D5 **Dalrymple** East Ayrshire Scotland UK
425 M5 **Dalrymple, Lake** Qld Australia
224 F3 **Dalsland** *region* Sweden
237 AC6 **Dal'stroy** Russian Federation
392 F6 **Daltenganj** Jharkhand India
243 G2 **Dalton** North Yorkshire England UK
131 I3 **Dalton** Georgia USA
125 N6 **Dalton** Nebraska USA
242 E2 **Dalton-in-Furness** Cumbria England UK
244 E3 **Daltra** Highland Scotland UK
374 D3 **Daludalu** Indonesia
377 I3 **Dalupiri** *island* Philippines
377 J4 **Dalupiri** *island* Philippines
244 E4 **Dalvanie** Angus Scotland UK
222 inset **Dalvik** Iceland
244 D4 **Dalwhinnie** Highland Scotland UK
424 I3 **Daly** *watercourse* NT Australia
124 D8 **Daly City** California USA
119 S4 **Daly Lake** Saskatchewan Canada
424 I3 **Daly River** NT Australia
425 J4 **Daly Waters** NT Australia
235 F7 **Dalyan** Turkey
235 E6 **Dalyanköy** Turkey
376 E2 **Đầm Hà** Vietnam
379 G2 **Dam Qu** *watercourse* Qinghai China
390 C4 **Damā, Wādī** *watercourse* Saudi Arabia
227 L2 **Damachava** Belarus
301 H6 **Damagaram-Takaya** Niger
391 G5 **Damāgheh-ye Meydānī** *cape* Iran
393 C7 **Daman** Daman and Diu India
393 C7 **Daman and Diu** *admin. area* India
302 E1 **Damanhûr** Egypt
385 H4 **Damaqun Shan** *range* Hebei China
372 C3 **Damar** Indonesia
372 D4 **Damar** *island* Indonesia
129 M1 **Damar** Kansas USA
305 H4 **Damara** Central African Republic
235 F7 **Damarası** Turkey
305 G3 **Damasak** Nigeria
305 G2 **Damaturu** Nigeria
231 G1 **Damazan** France
306 B5 **Damba** Angola
304 E3 **Dambai** Ghana
235 E5 **Dambaslar** Turkey
305 G2 **Damboa** Nigeria
234 D3 **Dâmbovita** *admin. area* Romania
135 F3 **Dame Marie, Cap** *cape* Haiti
381 I3 **Damen Dao** *island* Zhejiang China
388 G7 **Dāmghān** Iran
385 H6 **Daming** Hebei China
377 I6 **Dammai** *island* Philippines
392 E6 **Damoh** Madhya Pradesh India
424 F5 **Dampier** WA Australia
372 D4 **Dampier, Selat** *strait* Indonesia
424 E5 **Dampier Archipelago** WA Australia
375 G6 **Dampit** Indonesia
393 E6 **Damua** Madhya Pradesh India
228 E2 **Damville** France
226 C3 **Damvillers** France
228 D3 **Damvix** France
225 P3 **Damyanitsa** Bulgaria
131 L2 **Dan** *watercourse* Virginia USA
305 F3 **Dan-Gulbi** Nigeria
380 F1 **Dan Jiang** *watercourse* Shaanxi China
376 D4 **Dan Khun Thot** Thailand
376 D3 **Dan Sai** Thailand
372 B6 **Dana** *island* Indonesia
127 M1 **Dana, Lac** *lake* Québec Canada
128 D4 **Dana Point** California USA
304 C3 **Danané** Côte d'Ivoire
377 J5 **Danao** Philippines
127 O6 **Danbury** Connecticut USA
125 O6 **Danbury** Nebraska USA
243 H2 **Danby** North Yorkshire England UK
128 E3 **Danby Lake** California USA
243 G2 **Danby Wiske** North Yorkshire England UK
381 G1 **Dancheng** Henan China
381 I2 **Dancheng** Zhejiang China
306 A5 **Dande** *watercourse* Angola
307 F3 **Dande** Ethiopia
393 D8 **Dandeli** Karnataka India
308 C2 **Dando** Angola
385 J5 **Dandong** Liaoning China
243 F3 **Dane** *watercourse* England UK
391 I4 **Dānel** Iran
380 D4 **Danfeng** Yunnan China
372 B6 **Danga** Indonesia
245 E4 **Dangan Bridge** Ireland
381 G4 **Dangan Dao** *island* Guangdong China
380 D1 **Dangchang** Gansu China
383 J5 **Dangchengwan** Gansu China
228 E3 **Dangé** France
308 C6 **Danger Point** *cape* South Africa
383 J5 **Danghe Nanshan** *range* Gansu China
302 F5 **Dangila** Ethiopia
Dangla Shan *see* **Tanggula Shan** China
379 E2 **Dangra Tssho** *lake* Xizang Zizhiqu China
134 B3 **Dangriga** Belize
381 G1 **Dangshan** Anhui China
302 F5 **Dangur** Ethiopia
159 H4 **Daniel, Serra** *range* Brazil
134 D5 **Daniel Flores** Costa Rica
437 L2 **Daniell Peninsula** Antarctica
123 J7 **Daniel's Harbour** Newfoundland and Labrador Canada
308 D5 **Danielskuil** South Africa
389 K3 **Danilovka** Kazakhstan
388 D3 **Danilovka** Russian Federation
238 G3 **Danilovo** Russian Federation
380 E3 **Danjiang** Guizhou China
381 F2 **Danjiangkou** Hubei China
381 F2 **Danjiangkou Shuiku** *lake* Hubei China
238 H6 **Dankov** Russian Federation
134 C4 **Danlí** Honduras
117 Q2 **Danmark Fjord** Greenland
304 D2 **Dano** Burkina Faso
162 C4 **Dañoso, Cabo** *cape* Argentina
118 I6 **Danskin** British Columbia Canada
376 B3 **Danson Bay** Myanmar
393 G7 **Dantan** West Bengal India
Danube *see* **Donau** Europe
376 B3 **Danubyu** Myanmar
375 G3 **Danumparai** Indonesia
127 O4 **Danville** Québec Canada
130 E3 **Danville** Arkansas USA
126 H6 **Danville** Illinois USA
126 I8 **Danville** Kentucky USA
381 H2 **Danyang** Jiangsu China
376 F5 **Danzhou** Hainan China
384 G6 **Danzhou** Shaanxi China
381 F3 **Daojiang** Hunan China
377 J5 **Dapa** Philippines
304 E2 **Dapaong** Togo
305 G2 **Dapchi** Nigeria
130 H5 **Daphne** Alabama USA
377 I5 **Dapitan** Philippines
393 C8 **Dapoli** Maharashtra India
380 F4 **Dapu** Guangxi Zhuangzu Zizhiqu China
385 J5 **Daqin Dao** *island* Shandong China
385 I4 **Daqin Tal** Nei Mongol Zizhiqu China
385 J3 **Daqing** Heilongjiang China
384 G5 **Daqing Shan** *range* Nei Mongol Zizhiqu China
390 E8 **Dār al Juhār** Yemen
388 H7 **Dar Beyaban** Iran
307 F5 **Dar es Salaam** Tanzania
307 F5 **Dar es Salaam** *admin. area* Tanzania
391 I4 **Dar Gol** Iran
230 D6 **Dar Mter** Morocco
300 C5 **Dara** Senegal
394 F7 **Dar'ā** Syria
391 H4 **Dārāb** Iran
301 I2 **Daraj** Libya
377 J5 **Daram** Philippines
372 D4 **Daram, Pulau** *island* Indonesia
373 H4 **Darapap** Papua New Guinea
305 G2 **Darazo** Nigeria
394 F6 **Darb At Tast** Syria
225 K4 **Darbėnai** Lithuania
392 F5 **Darbhanga** Bihar India
391 H3 **Darbid** Iran
124 H3 **Darby** Montana USA
118 J7 **D'Arcy** British Columbia Canada
Dardanelles *see* **Çanakkale Boğazı** Turkey
307 F4 **Dareda** Tanzania
232 D4 **Darfo** Italy
229 J4 **Darfo Boario Terme** Italy
385 H3 **Darganga** Mongolia
422 E2 **Dargaville** New Zealand
228 F4 **Dargilan, Grotte de** France
425 M9 **Dargo** Vic. Australia
304 D2 **Dargo** Burkina Faso
379 F2 **Dargo Zangbo** *watercourse* Xizang Zizhiqu China
301 G6 **Dargol** Niger
384 F2 **Darhan** Mongolia
384 G3 **Darhan** Mongolia
384 F2 **Darhan-Uul** *admin. area* Mongolia
131 K5 **Darien** Georgia USA
126 G5 **Darien** Wisconsin USA
154 B2 **Darién, Golfo del** *bay* Colombia/Panama
134 E5 **Darién, Serranía del** *range* Colombia/Panama
134 C4 **Dariense, Cordillera** *range* Nicaragua
389 K3 **Dar'inskiy** Kazakhstan
154 D5 **Dário** Brazil
390 F3 **Darisheh** Iran
392 G5 **Darjiling** West Bengal India
423 B7 **Dark Cloud Range** New Zealand
242 B2 **Darkley** Armagh Northern Ireland UK
376 F4 **Darlac Plateau** Vietnam
379 G4 **Darlawn** Mizoram India
425 L7 **Darling** *watercourse* NSW Australia
125 O2 **Darling, Lake** North Dakota USA
117 L3 **Darling Peninsula** Nunavut Canada
243 G2 **Darlington** Darlington England UK
243 G2 **Darlington** *admin. area* England UK
131 L3 **Darlington** South Carolina USA
240 E2 **Darliston** Shropshire England UK
226 E3 **Darmstadt** Germany
393 C7 **Darna** *watercourse* Maharashtra India
302 C1 **Darnah** Libya
229 H2 **Darney** France
244 F5 **Darnford** Aberdeenshire Scotland UK
437 E2 **Darnley, Cape** Antarctica
116 G5 **Darnley Bay** Northwest Territories Canada
373 G6 **Darnley Island** Qld Australia
231 F3 **Daroca** Spain
234 B3 **Darosova** Serbia
300 E6 **Darouma** *watercourse* Mali
391 K2 **Darrah-e Awd** Afghanistan
390 F2 **Darreh Shahr** Iran
307 G2 **Darro** *watercourse* Ethiopia
130 A2 **Darrouzett** Texas USA
303 I5 **Darsah** *island* Yemen
240 D4 **Dart** *watercourse* England UK
245 E2 **Dartan** Ireland
241 H3 **Dartford** Kent England UK
240 D4 **Dartmeet** Devon England UK
245 L9 **Dartmoor** Vic. Australia
123 G10 **Dartmouth** Nova Scotia Canada
123 F8 **Dartmouth** *watercourse* Québec Canada
240 D4 **Dartmouth** Devon England UK
222 L4 **Dartsel** Sweden
391 H4 **Darū** Iran
373 G6 **Daru Island** Papua New Guinea
304 B3 **Darul** Sierra Leone
388 H6 **Darvaza** Turkmenistan
376 H6 **Darvel, Teluk** *bay* Malaysia
383 J3 **Darvi** Mongolia
383 J3 **Darvi** Mongolia
307 G3 **Darwa** *watercourse* Ethiopia
243 F3 **Darwen** Blackburn with Darwen England UK
308 F3 **Darwendale** Zimbabwe
393 D7 **Darwha** Maharashtra India
160 E5 **Darwin** Argentina
424 I3 **Darwin** NT Australia
163 7 **Darwin** Falkland Islands
162 B5 **Darwin, Cordillera** *range* Chile
163 4 **Darwin, Isla** *island* Archipiélago de Colón (Galapagos Islands)
162 C6 **Darwin, Monte** *mountain* Chile
391 K2 **Daryā-ye Helmand** *watercourse* Afghanistan
391 L2 **Daryā-ye Kābul** *watercourse* Pakistan
388 F7 **Daryācheh-ye Sadd-e Sefid Rud** *lake* Iran
388 E6 **Daryācheh-ye Orūmiyeh (Lake Urmia)** *lake* Iran
385 H2 **Dashbalbar** Mongolia
384 E3 **Dashintsilen** Mongolia
385 J5 **Dashiqiao** Liaoning China
391 H2 **Dasht-e Kavir** *desert* Iran
391 I3 **Dasht-e Lūt** *desert* Iran
390 G2 **Dashteh** Iran
423 F5 **Dashwood** New Zealand
391 M3 **Daska** Pakistan
388 H5 **Daşoguz** Turkmenistan
388 H5 **Daşoguz Welaýaty** *admin. area* Turkmenistan
377 H4 **Dasol Bay** Philippines
377 I6 **Dassalan** *island* Philippines
226 F1 **Dassow** Germany
224 F5 **Dassower See** *bay* Germany
388 G7 **Dastūrān** Iran
392 D4 **Dasua** Punjab India
391 K4 **Data Chandio** Pakistan
375 G3 **Datadian** Indonesia
235 E7 **Datça** Turkey
387 I2 **Date** Japan
392 E6 **Datia** Madhya Pradesh India
381 F4 **Datian Ding** *mountain* Guangdong China
129 I3 **Datil** New Mexico USA
385 H5 **Datong** Shanxi China
237 AD9 **Datta** Russian Federation
224 G3 **Dättern** *bay* Sweden
374 F3 **Datu** *island* Indonesia
374 F3 **Datu, Tanjung** *cape* Indonesia
374 D4 **Datuk, Tanjung** *cape* Indonesia
227 G1 **Datze** *watercourse* Germany
391 H4 **Dāu** *island* United Arab Emirates
391 L3 **Daud Khel** Pakistan
225 N5 **Daugavpils** Latvia
225 N5 **Daugavpils** *admin. area* Latvia
229 H1 **Daun** Germany
393 D7 **Daund** Maharashtra India
119 U7 **Dauphin** Manitoba Canada
130 G5 **Dauphin Island** Alabama USA
120 F7 **Dauphin Lake** Manitoba Canada
119 V7 **Dauphin River** Manitoba Canada
305 F2 **Daura** Nigeria
384 G2 **Daurskiy Khrebet** *range* Russian Federation
392 D5 **Dausa** Rajasthan India
244 E3 **Dava** Moray Scotland UK
393 D8 **Davangere** Karnataka India
377 J6 **Davao** Philippines
377 J6 **Davao Gulf** *bay* Philippines
308 E5 **Davel** South Africa
128 A2 **Davenport** California USA
126 F6 **Davenport** Iowa USA
124 F3 **Davenport** Washington USA
241 F2 **Daventry** Northamptonshire England UK
134 D5 **David** Panama
125 Q6 **David City** Nebraska USA
130 B3 **Davidson** Oklahoma USA
424 I5 **Davidson, Mount** NT Australia
122 B1 **Davies Island** Nunavut Canada
244 D3 **Daviot** Highland Scotland UK
124 E7 **Davis** California USA
125 Q5 **Davis** South Dakota USA
437 F2 **Davis (Australia)** *research station* Antarctica
437 J2 **Davis Bay** Antarctica
122 H5 **Davis Inlet** Newfoundland and Labrador Canada
124 E5 **Davis Lake** Oregon USA
132 D2 **Davis Mountains** Texas USA
120 F7 **Davis Point** Manitoba Canada
437 G2 **Davis Sea** Antarctica
122 G1 **Davis Strait** Canada/Greenland
304 C3 **Davo** *watercourse* Côte d'Ivoire
232 G4 **Davor** Croatia
229 I3 **Davos** Switzerland
222 K1 **Davøya** *island* Norway
383 I2 **Davst** Mongolia
235 E7 **Davutlar** Turkey
119 Q3 **Davy Lake** Saskatchewan Canada
238 H4 **Davydovo** Russian Federation
385 J5 **Dawa** Liaoning China
385 J5 **Dawangjia Dao** *island* Liaoning China
376 C4 **Dawei (Tavoy)** Myanmar
376 C4 **Dawei Point** Myanmar
372 D5 **Daweloor** *island* Indonesia
391 I6 **Dawḥat Ṣawqirah** *sea* Oman
240 D4 **Dawlish** Devon England UK
240 D4 **Dawlish Warren** Devon England UK
390 D3 **Dawmat al Jandal (Al Jawf)** Saudi Arabia
376 C3 **Dawna Range** Myanmar
245 D2 **Dawros Head** *cape* Ireland
116 F6 **Dawson** Yukon Territory Canada
162 B6 **Dawson, Isla** *island* Chile
124 G1 **Dawson, Mount** British Columbia Canada
118 K5 **Dawson Creek** British Columbia Canada
120 I2 **Dawson Inlet** Nunavut Canada
119 N2 **Dawson Landing** Northwest Territories Canada
118 H7 **Dawsons Landing** British Columbia Canada
381 G2 **Dawu** Hubei China
380 C1 **Dawu** Qinghai China
391 I6 **Dawwah** Oman
228 D5 **Dax** France
380 E2 **Daxian** Sichuan China
381 I2 **Daxie Dao** *island* Zhejiang China
380 C3 **Daxing** Yunnan China
380 D4 **Daxing** Yunnan China
376 E2 **Đáy** *watercourse* Vietnam
380 C3 **Dayan** Yunnan China
383 H3 **Dayan Nuur** *lake* Mongolia
381 G2 **Daye Hu** *lake* Hubei China
161 G4 **Daymán** *watercourse* Uruguay
126 I2 **Dayohessarah Lake** Ontario Canada
394 G6 **Dayr az Zawr** Syria
119 O6 **Daysland** Alberta Canada
128 C1 **Dayton** Nevada USA
126 I7 **Dayton** Ohio USA
125 L4 **Dayton** Wyoming USA
131 K6 **Daytona Beach** Florida USA
375 G4 **Dayu** Indonesia
381 G3 **Dayu Ling** *range* Guangdong China
381 H3 **Dayu Shan** *range* Fujian China
124 F4 **Dayville** Oregon USA
385 I6 **Daze Shan** *range* Shandong China
380 D1 **Dazhasi** Sichuan China
380 F5 **Dazhou Dao** *island* Hainan China
308 D6 **De Aar** South Africa
132 D4 **De Acaponeta, Rio** *watercourse* Mexico
125 K7 **De Beque** Colorado USA
425 J4 **De Burgh, Lake** NT Australia
226 C1 **De Cocksdorp** Netherlands
131 H5 **De Funiak Springs** Florida USA
436 R2 **De Gerlache Seamounts** *underwater feature* Southern Ocean
125 R4 **De Graff** Minnesota USA
130 E3 **De Gray Lake** Arkansas USA
424 F5 **De Grey** *watercourse* WA Australia
228 F1 **De Haan** Belgium
130 D4 **De Kalb** Texas USA
226 C1 **De Koog** Netherlands
161 G6 **De la Canal** Argentina
160 F6 **De la Garma** Argentina
116 C5 **De Long Mountains** Alaska USA
122 F5 **De Pas** *watercourse* Québec Canada
126 G4 **De Pere** Wisconsin USA
226 B2 **De Pinte** Belgium
125 Q4 **De Smet** South Dakota USA
126 G8 **De Soto** Illinois USA
121 R4 **De Troyes** *watercourse* Québec Canada
130 F3 **De Valls Bluff** Arkansas USA
118 L6 **De Veber, Mount** Alberta Canada
118 D2 **De Wette** Yukon Territory Canada
130 F3 **De Witt** Arkansas USA
122 G3 **Deacon Head** Newfoundland and Labrador Canada
245 D4 **Dead** *watercourse* Ireland
122 K6 **Dead Islands** Newfoundland and Labrador Canada
131 I5 **Dead Lake** Florida USA
390 C3 **Dead Sea** Israel/Jordan
116 E4 **Deadhorse** Alaska USA
118 M4 **Deadwood** Alberta Canada
424 I7 **Deakin** WA Australia
437 K2 **Deakin Bay** Antarctica
241 I3 **Deal** Kent England UK
118 I6 **Dean** *watercourse* British Columbia Canada
436 P2 **Dean Island** Antarctica
118 G3 **Dease** *watercourse* British Columbia Canada
116 H5 **Dease Arm** Northwest Territories Canada
116 D4 **Dease Inlet** Alaska USA
118 F3 **Dease Lake** British Columbia Canada
118 F3 **Dease Lake** British Columbia Canada
116 I5 **Dease Strait** Nunavut Canada
128 D2 **Death Valley** California USA
375 F3 **Debak** Malaysia
380 E4 **Debao** Guangxi Zhuangzu Zizhiqu China
305 I2 **Debarei, Wadi** *watercourse* Sudan
302 F5 **Debark** Ethiopia
120 F2 **Debartok Lake** Nunavut Canada
119 R6 **Debden** Saskatchewan Canada
301 F2 **Debdou** Morocco
163 9 **Débé** Trinidad and Tobago
241 I2 **Debenham** Suffolk England UK
123 G10 **Debert** Nova Scotia Canada
227 K2 **Dębica** Poland
227 H1 **Dębno** Poland
300 F5 **Débo, Lac** *lake* Mali
424 F7 **Deborah East, Lake** WA Australia
373 J6 **Deboyne Atoll** *reef* Papua New Guinea
159 H6 **Debrasa** Brazil
234 A3 **Debrc** Serbia
307 F2 **Debre Birhan** Ethiopia
302 F2 **Debre Birhan** Somalia
307 F1 **Debre Markos** Ethiopia
302 F5 **Debre May** Ethiopia
302 F5 **Debre Tabor** Ethiopia
307 F2 **Debre Zeyit** Ethiopia
234 B2 **Debrecen** Hungary
130 H3 **Decatur** Alabama USA
126 G7 **Decatur** Illinois USA
130 G4 **Decatur** Mississippi USA
130 C4 **Decatur** Texas USA
228 F4 **Decazeville** France
162 C6 **Deceit, Cabo** *cape* Chile
121 R1 **Déception** Québec Canada
122 A1 **Déception** *watercourse* Québec Canada
122 A1 **Déception, Baie** *bay* Québec Canada
373 H5 **Deception Bay** Papua New Guinea
308 D4 **Deception Pans** *pan* Botswana
381 F4 **Decheng** Guangdong China
227 H2 **Děčín** Czech Republic
226 B4 **Decize** France
126 F5 **Decorah** Iowa USA
234 A2 **Decs** Hungary
234 A4 **Dedaj** Albania
380 C4 **Dedang** Yunnan China
376 B3 **Dedaya** Myanmar
426 5 **Dededo** Guam
235 C5 **Dedeli** Macedonia
307 G2 **Deder** Ethiopia
157 C9 **Dedo de Deus** *mountain* Brazil
304 D2 **Dédougou** Burkina Faso
225 O4 **Dedovichi** Russian Federation
388 G3 **Dedurovka** Russian Federation
307 E6 **Dedza** Malawi
242 B3 **Dee** *watercourse* Ireland
244 E4 **Dee** *watercourse* Scotland UK
240 D2 **Dee** *watercourse* Wales UK
242 A3 **Deel** *watercourse* Ireland
129 N3 **Deep** *watercourse* Oklahoma USA
119 M2 **Deep Bay** Northwest Territories Canada
124 I7 **Deep Creek Range** Utah USA
130 C3 **Deep Fork** *watercourse* Oklahoma USA
122 H5 **Deep Inlet** Newfoundland and Labrador Canada
127 M3 **Deep River** Ontario Canada
310 5b **Deep Valley Bay** St Helena
243 F2 **Deepdale** North Yorkshire England UK
425 N7 **Deepwater** NSW Australia
126 E7 **Deepwater** Missouri USA
123 E10 **Deer Island** New Brunswick Canada
116 C8 **Deer Island** Alaska USA
123 J8 **Deer Lake** Newfoundland and Labrador Canada
120 H6 **Deer Lake** Ontario Canada
120 H6 **Deer Lake** Ontario Canada
124 I3 **Deer Lodge** Montana USA
124 G3 **Deer Park** Washington USA
131 I5 **Deer Point Lake** Florida USA
123 K8 **Deer Pond** Newfoundland and Labrador Canada
125 M7 **Deer Trail** Colorado USA
131 K7 **Deerfield Beach** Florida USA
125 O2 **Deering** North Dakota USA
245 C3 **Deerpark** Ireland
126 E3 **Deerwood** Minnesota USA
380 F3 **Defeng** Guizhou China
161 G6 **Defferrari** Argentina
126 I6 **Defiance** Ohio USA
129 H3 **Defiance Plateau** Arkansas USA
118 F3 **Defot** British Columbia Canada
307 G2 **Dega Medo** Ethiopia
307 G2 **Degeh Bur** Ethiopia
123 D9 **Dégelis** Québec Canada
222 K5 **Degerfjärden** *bay* Sweden
222 L3 **Degerselet** *lake* Sweden
222 L3 **Degervattnet** *lake* Sweden
224 H2 **Deglunden** *lake* Sweden
155 H4 **Dégrad Claude** French Guiana
155 H4 **Dégrad Kwata** French Guiana
155 H3 **Dégrad Neuf** French Guiana
388 C3 **Degtevo** Russian Federation
238 E6 **Degtyarëvka** Russian Federation
390 G3 **Deh Dasht** Iran
391 I4 **Deh Dāti** Iran
391 H4 **Deh Hang** Iran
391 I2 **Deh Nabī** Iran
391 K3 **Deh Rāwod** Afghanistan
391 I3 **Deh Salm** Iran
391 I2 **Deh Tah** Iran
390 G3 **Dehak** Iran
390 G2 **Dehaq** Iran
390 F3 **Dehlorān** Iran
388 J6 **Dehqonobod** Uzbekistan
392 E4 **Dehra Dun** Uttaranchal India
392 F6 **Dehri** Bihar India
385 K4 **Dehui** Jilin China
222 inset **Deild** *cape* Iceland
228 F1 **Deinze** Belgium
391 I4 **Dejan-e Bālā** Iran
307 F1 **Dejen** Ethiopia
302 F5 **Dejen, Ras** *mountain* Ethiopia
235 B5 **Dejës, Maja e** *mountain* Albania
379 F3 **Dejilin** Xizang Zizhiqu China
232 E4 **Dekani** Slovenia
306 C4 **Dekese** Democratic Republic of Congo
305 F3 **Dekina** Nigeria
305 H3 **Dékoa** Central African Republic
119 O8 **Del Bonita** Alberta Canada
80 I9 **Del Cano Rise** *underwater feature* Southern Ocean
128 D4 **Del Mar** California USA
125 L8 **Del Norte** Colorado USA
129 L6 **Del Rio** Texas USA
240 C4 **Delabole** Cornwall England UK
163 9 **Delaford** Trinidad and Tobago
372 C6 **Delaki** Indonesia
128 E2 **Delamar Lake** Nevada USA
302 E5 **Delami** Sudan
128 C3 **Delano** California USA
237 AL8 **Delarof Islands** Alaska USA
119 R5 **Delaronde Lake** Saskatchewan Canada
114 **Delaware** *admin. area* USA
126 J6 **Delaware** Ohio USA
127 N6 **Delaware** *watercourse* Pennsylvania USA
127 N7 **Delaware Bay** Delaware USA
122 C4 **Delay** *watercourse* Québec Canada
244 E3 **Delbog** Highland Scotland UK
229 H3 **Delémont** Switzerland
234 E2 **Deleni** Romania
302 B5 **Delep** Chad
225 K2 **Delet Teili** *bay* Finland
162 D3 **Delfín, Punta** *cape* Argentina
160 F6 **Delfín Huergo** Argentina
226 D1 **Delfzijl** Netherlands
124 C6 **Delgada, Point** California USA
162 D3 **Delgada, Punta** *cape* Argentina
309 H2 **Delgado, Cabo** *cape* Mozambique
383 K3 **Delger** Mongolia
384 E3 **Delgereh** Mongolia
384 E3 **Delgerhaan** Mongolia
384 G3 **Delgerhaan** Mongolia
384 E3 **Delgerhangai** Mongolia
384 G3 **Delgerkhaan Uul** *mountain* Mongolia
384 F3 **Delgertsogt** Mongolia
302 E3 **Delgo** Sudan
392 D5 **Delhi** Delhi India
392 D5 **Delhi** *admin. area* India
129 J2 **Delhi** Colorado USA
127 N5 **Delhi** New York USA
374 E5 **Deli** *island* Indonesia
132 B2 **Delicias** Mexico
234 B4 **Deligrad** Serbia
390 G2 **Delījān** Iran
383 K5 **Delingha** Qinghai China
374 C3 **Delitua** Indonesia
373 G6 **Deliverance Island** Qld Australia
129 J5 **Dell City** Texas USA
125 Q5 **Dell Rapids** South Dakota USA
232 B3 **Delle** Switzerland
301 G1 **Dellys** Algeria
135 F3 **Delmas** Haiti
425 M10 **Deloraine** Tas. Australia
235 C6 **Delphi** Greece
126 H6 **Delphi** Indiana USA
125 Q7 **Delphos** Kansas USA
129 K3 **Delphos** New Mexico USA

131 K7 **Delray Beach** Florida USA
222 J6 **Delsbo** Sweden
132 B1 **Delta** Mexico
305 F3 **Delta** *admin. area* Nigeria
125 K7 **Delta** Colorado USA
155 F2 **Delta Amacuro** *admin. area* Venezuela
116 E6 **Delta Junction** Alaska USA
131 K6 **Deltona** Florida USA
383 I3 **Deluun** Mongolia
245 E3 **Delvin** Ireland
234 D1 **Delyatyn** Ukraine
231 J5 **Dem el Begrat** Algeria
436 R2 **Demas Ice Tongue** Antarctica
306 C5 **Demba** Democratic Republic of Congo
302 F5 **Dembech'a** Ethiopia
310 8b **Dembeni** Mayotte
310 8a **Dembéni** Comoros
307 E2 **Dembi Dolo** Ethiopia
305 I3 **Dembia** Central African Republic
155 F5 **Demeni** *watercourse* Brazil
76 M8 **Demerara Abyssal Plain** *underwater feature* Atlantic Ocean
76 M9 **Demerara Plateau** *underwater feature* Atlantic Ocean
156 D4 **Demerval Lobão** Brazil
238 D5 **Demidov** Russian Federation
129 I4 **Deming** New Mexico USA
155 F4 **Demini** *watercourse* Brazil
155 F4 **Demini, Serras do** *range* Brazil
235 B5 **Demir Hisar** Macedonia
235 F6 **Demirköprü Barajı** *lake* Turkey
235 E5 **Demirköy** Turkey
232 B4 **Demonte** Italy
130 H4 **Demopolis** Alabama USA
374 D5 **Dempo, Gunung** *volcano* Indonesia
373 G4 **Demta** Indonesia
238 E5 **Demyakhi** Russian Federation
238 C4 **Demyanka** Russian Federation
236 P7 **Dem'yanka** *watercourse* Russian Federation
225 Q4 **Demyansk** Russian Federation
236 O7 **Dem'yanskoye** Russian Federation
226 C1 **Den Burg** Netherlands
376 D3 **Den Chai** Thailand
Den Haag *see* **'s-Gravenhage (The Hague)** Netherlands
226 C1 **Den Helder** Netherlands
226 C1 **Den Oever** Netherlands
244 F3 **Den of Glasslaw** Aberdeenshire Scotland UK
303 G5 **Denakil** *range* Ethiopia
303 G5 **Denakil Desert** Ethiopia
Denali *see* **McKinley, Mt** USA
307 G2 **Denan** Ethiopia
119 V6 **Denbeigh Point** Manitoba Canada
127 M4 **Denbigh** Ontario Canada
240 D1 **Denbigh** Denbighshire Wales UK
240 D1 **Denbighshire** *admin. area* Wales UK
374 E4 **Dendang** Indonesia
226 D1 **Denekamp** Netherlands
305 F2 **Denge** Nigeria
241 H3 **Dengie** Essex England UK
385 J4 **Dengta** Liaoning China
305 I3 **Denguiro** Central African Republic
424 E6 **Denham** WA Australia
422 5 **Denham Bay** Kermadec Islands New Zealand
244 F5 **Denholm** Scottish Borders Scotland UK
231 G4 **Denia** Spain
425 M8 **Deniliquin** NSW Australia
310 9 **Denis, Île** *island* Seychelles
130 C4 **Denison** Texas USA
437 J2 **Denison, Cape** Antarctica
388 I3 **Denisovka** Kazakhstan
388 J2 **Denisovo** Russian Federation
393 E10 **Deniyaya** Sri Lanka
394 D6 **Denizli** *admin. area* Turkey
437 G2 **Denman Glacier** *ice* Antarctica
424 F8 **Denmark** WA Australia
224 F5 **Denmark** *country* Europe
131 K4 **Denmark** South Carolina USA
117 P5 **Denmark Strait** Greenland/Iceland
163 18 **Dennery** St Lucia
389 J6 **Denov** Uzbekistan
375 G6 **Denpasar** Indonesia
423 9 **Dent Island** Campbell Island New Zealand
234 B3 **Denta** Romania
125 K3 **Denton** Montana USA
130 C4 **Denton** Texas USA
133 F1 **Denton** *watercourse* Texas USA
373 I6 **D'Entrecasteaux Islands** Papua New Guinea
125 M7 **Denver** Colorado USA
129 K4 **Denver City** Texas USA
131 Q5 **Denys** *watercourse* Québec Canada
392 D5 **Deoband** Uttar Pradesh India
157 A8 **Deodápolis** Brazil
392 F6 **Deogarh** *mountain* Chhattisgarh India
393 F7 **Deogarh** Orissa India
392 C6 **Deogarh** Rajasthan India
392 G6 **Deoghar** Jharkhand India
386 E4 **Deogjeog-do** *island* South Korea
376 E3 **DeoKeo Nua** *mountain* Laos
393 E7 **Deolali** Maharashtra India
393 D7 **Deoli** Madhya Pradesh India
393 E7 **Deoli** Maharashtra India
376 E3 **DeoMu Gia** *mountain* Laos
241 I2 **Deopham** Norfolk England UK
393 F7 **Deori** Chhattisgarh India
393 E7 **Deori** Maharashtra India
392 F5 **Deoria** Uttar Pradesh India
376 D2 **DeoTay Chang** *mountain* Laos
305 F3 **Dep** *watercourse* Nigeria
385 L2 **Dep** *watercourse* Russian Federation
130 C3 **Depew** Oklahoma USA
124 C4 **Depoe Bay** Oregon USA
374 E5 **Depok** Indonesia
391 L3 **Dera Bugti** Pakistan
391 L3 **Dera Ghazi Khan** Pakistan
391 L3 **Dera Ismail Khan** Pakistan
234 B4 **Đeravica** *mountain* Kosovo
391 L4 **Derawar Fort** Pakistan
388 H7 **Deräz Āb** Iran
237 AC5 **Derbeke** *watercourse* Russian Federation
235 F6 **Derbent** Turkey
306 C2 **Derbissaka** Central African Republic
424 G4 **Derby** WA Australia
241 F2 **Derby** Derby England UK
241 F2 **Derby** *admin. area* England UK
125 Q8 **Derby** Kansas USA
130 B6 **Derby** Texas USA
127 O4 **Derby Line** Vermont USA
243 G3 **Derbyshire** *admin. area* England UK
235 G7 **Derebucak** Turkey
241 H2 **Dereham** Norfolk England UK
235 D5 **Dereköy** Turkey
384 F3 **Deren** Mongolia
302 C5 **Dérésa** Chad
225 Q3 **Dereva** Russian Federation
238 F2 **Derevyannoye** Russian Federation
372 F4 **Derewo** *watercourse* Indonesia
242 A2 **Derg** *watercourse* Northern Ireland UK
245 D4 **Derg, Lough** *lake* Ireland
388 E3 **Dergachi** Russian Federation
379 G3 **Dergaon** Assam India
308 C4 **Derm** Namibia
235 C6 **Dermatas, Akra** *cape* Greece
242 B3 **Dermotstown** Ireland
130 F4 **Dermott** Arkansas USA
133 H2 **Dernieres, Isles** *islands* Louisiana USA
225 O5 **Dernovichi** Belarus
437 C2 **Derom, Mount** Antarctica
231 H6 **Derrag** Algeria
309 G3 **Derre** Mozambique
245 C3 **Derreen** Ireland
307 H3 **Derri** Somalia
245 C5 **Derriana Lough** *lake* Ireland
242 A3 **Derry** Ireland
245 E2 **Derry** *admin. area* Northern Ireland UK
245 C2 **Derrycorrib** Ireland
242 A3 **Derrygolan** Ireland
245 D3 **Derrylahan** Ireland
242 A2 **Derrylin** Fermanagh Northern Ireland UK
242 B3 **Derrymullen** Ireland
242 B2 **Derryork** Limavady Northern Ireland UK
242 A3 **Derryrobinson** Ireland
241 H2 **Dersingham** Norfolk England UK
302 F4 **Derudeb** Sudan
244 B4 **Dervaig** Highland Scotland UK
232 G4 **Derventa** Bosnia and Herzegovina
242 B1 **Dervock** Ballymoney Northern Ireland UK
240 D1 **Derwen** Denbighshire Wales UK
243 H2 **Derwent** *watercourse* England UK
236 R4 **Deryabino** Russian Federation
388 J3 **Derzhavinsk** Kazakhstan
126 E6 **Des Moines** Iowa USA
126 D5 **Des Moines** *watercourse* Minnesota USA
129 K2 **Des Moines** New Mexico USA
130 F5 **Des Ourses Swamp** Louisiana USA
122 D5 **Des Prairies, Lac** *lake* Québec Canada
234 C4 **Desa** Romania
160 E5 **Desaguadero** *watercourse* Argentina
158 D5 **Desaguadero** *watercourse* Bolivia
158 D5 **Desaguadero** Peru
160 D5 **Desague, Cerro** *mountain* Argentina
393 E7 **Desaiganj** Maharashtra India
128 D4 **Descanso** California USA
121 R4 **Descareaux, Lac** *lake* Québec Canada
228 E3 **Descartes** France
122 C6 **Desceliers, Lac** *lake* Québec Canada
120 D5 **Deschambault Lake** Saskatchewan Canada
119 Q4 **Descharme** *watercourse* Saskatchewan Canada
119 Q4 **Descharme Lake** Saskatchewan Canada
124 E4 **Deschutes** *watercourse* Oregon USA
159 F4 **Desconcierto** Bolivia
162 C4 **Deseado** *watercourse* Argentina
162 A5 **Deseado, Cabo** *cape* Chile
128 F5 **Desemboque** Mexico
162 C4 **Desengaño, Punta** *cape* Argentina
127 M4 **Deseronto** Ontario Canada
128 E4 **Desert Center** California USA
128 D4 **Desert Hot Springs** California USA
124 G6 **Desert Ranch Reservoir** Nevada USA
124 F6 **Desert Valley** Nevada USA
310 2 **Desertas, Ilhas** *islands* Madeira
310 2 **Deserte Grande** *island* Madeira
159 I1 **Deserto** Brazil
163 16 **Deshaies** Guadeloupe
125 Q6 **Deshler** Nebraska USA
245 D5 **Deshure** Ireland
121 Q8 **Desmaraisville** Québec Canada
394 D2 **Desna** *watercourse* Ukraine
122 C5 **Desnambuc, Lac** *lake* Québec Canada
238 E5 **Desnogorsk** Russian Federation
162 A5 **Desolación, Isla** *island* Chile
162 B6 **Desolada, Bahía** *bay* Chile
130 C4 **DeSoto** Texas USA
235 D7 **Despotiko** *island* Greece
234 B3 **Despotovac** Serbia
310 9 **Desroches, Île** *island* Seychelles
135 F3 **Dessalines** Haiti
226 G2 **Dessau** Germany
226 C2 **Dessel** Belgium
131 H5 **Destin** Florida USA
162 D4 **Desvelos, Bahía** *bay* Argentina
228 E1 **Desvres** France
234 B2 **Deszk** Hungary
238 G5 **Detchino** Russian Federation
308 E3 **Dete** Zimbabwe
234 A4 **Đetinja** *watercourse* Serbia
225 O3 **Detkovo** Russian Federation
126 H4 **Detour, Point** Michigan USA
126 J5 **Detroit** Michigan USA
124 D4 **Detroit** Oregon USA
130 D4 **Detroit** Texas USA
125 R3 **Detroit Lakes** Minnesota USA
232 H2 **Detva** Slovakia
392 C6 **Detvas** Rajasthan India
226 D5 **Deutsche Bucht** *bay* Germany
227 H4 **Deutschlandsberg** Austria
234 C3 **Deva** Romania
393 D8 **Devadurga** Karnataka India
235 E5 **Deveçatağı** Turkey
232 G3 **Devecser** Hungary
394 E5 **Develi** Turkey
392 D6 **Devgarh** Maharashtra India
392 C5 **Devikot** Rajasthan India
240 D2 **Devil's Bridge** Ceredigion Wales UK
Devil's Island *see* **Diable, Île du** French Guiana
125 P2 **Devils Lake** North Dakota USA
118 E3 **Devil's Paw** *mountain* British Columbia/Alaska Canada/USA
130 B6 **Devine** Texas USA
241 F3 **Devizes** Wiltshire England UK
130 B3 **Devol** Oklahoma USA
240 D4 **Devon** *admin. area* England UK
117 K3 **Devon Island** Nunavut Canada
425 M10 **Devonport** Tas. Australia
309 F3 **Devure** *watercourse* Zimbabwe
374 B3 **Dewa, Tanjung** *cape* Indonesia
375 H5 **Dewakang Besar** *island* Indonesia
392 D6 **Dewas** Madhya Pradesh India
128 F3 **Dewey** Arizona USA
126 D8 **Dewey** Oklahoma USA
127 M8 **DeWitt** Virginia USA
241 E4 **Dewlish** Dorset England UK
381 H3 **Dexing** Jiangxi China
130 C2 **Dexter** Kansas USA
123 D10 **Dexter** Maine USA
129 J4 **Dexter** New Mexico USA
380 D2 **Deyang** Sichuan China
390 G4 **Deyyer** Iran
390 F3 **Dezfūl** Iran
234 F2 **Dezghingea** Moldova
116 C5 **Dezhneva, Mys** *cape* Russian Federation
385 H5 **Dezhou** Shandong China
380 D3 **Dezhou** Sichuan China
390 D5 **Dhahbān** Saudi Arabia
379 G4 **Dhaka** Bangladesh
379 G4 **Dhaka** *admin. area* Bangladesh
392 F5 **Dhaka** Bihar India
231 J6 **Dhalaa** Algeria
390 E7 **Dhamār** Yemen
393 E7 **Dhamtari** Chhattisgarh India
392 G6 **Dhanbad** Jharkhand India
393 C6 **Dhandhuka** Gujarat India
392 C6 **Dhanera** Gujarat India
392 E5 **Dhangarhi** Nepal
392 D5 **Dhansia** Rajasthan India
392 F6 **Dhanwar** Jharkhand India
393 D6 **Dhar** Madhya Pradesh India
393 F7 **Dharakota** Orissa India
392 G5 **Dharan Bazar** Nepal
379 G4 **Dharmanagar** Tripura India
393 E7 **Dharmapuri** Andhra Pradesh India
393 D8 **Dharmapuri** Maharashtra India
393 D8 **Dharmavaram** Andhra Pradesh India
393 F6 **Dharmjaygarh** Chhattisgarh India
393 E8 **Dharur** Andhra Pradesh India
393 D7 **Dharur** Maharashtra India
393 D8 **Dharwad** Karnataka India
392 F5 **Dhaulagiri** *mountain* Nepal
392 F5 **Dhaulpur** Rajasthan India
394 E6 **Dhekelia Sovereign Base Area** Cyprus
379 H3 **Dhemaji** Assam India
393 F7 **Dhenkanal** Orissa India
235 A5 **Dhërmi** Albania
390 F3 **Dhi Qār** *admin. area* Iraq
379 G3 **Dhing** Assam India
393 C7 **Dhola** Gujarat India
392 C6 **Dholka** Gujarat India
307 G3 **Dhoomadeere** Somalia
393 C7 **Dhoraji** Gujarat India
392 C6 **Dhrangadhra** Gujarat India
392 C6 **Dhrol** Gujarat India
393 D7 **Dhule** Maharashtra India
393 E6 **Dhuma** Madhya Pradesh India
392 F5 **Dhunche** Nepal
392 D6 **Dhuri** Madhya Pradesh India
307 I2 **Dhuudo** Somalia
307 H3 **Dhuusa Marreeb** Somalia
376 F5 **Di Linh** Vietnam
235 D8 **Dia** *island* Greece
155 H3 **Diable, Île du (Devil's Island)** *island* French Guiana
163 15 **Diables, Morne aux** *volcano* Dominica
118 K8 **Diablo** Washington USA
132 D2 **Diablo Plateau** Texas USA
128 B2 **Diablo Range** California USA
163 15 **Diablotins, Morne** *volcano* Dominica
235 E8 **Diafani** Greece
300 E6 **Diafarabé** Mali
300 F6 **Diaka** *watercourse* Mali
300 D6 **Diakon** Mali
300 D6 **Dialafara** Mali
300 D6 **Dialakoto** Senegal
163 14 **Diamant, Rocher de** *cape* Martinique
160 F5 **Diamante** Argentina
158 C3 **Diamante Auúl** Peru
158 C1 **Diamante Azul** Peru
425 K6 **Diamantina** *watercourse* Qld Australia
157 D7 **Diamantina** Brazil
157 D6 **Diamantina, Chapada** *region* Brazil
81 O8 **Diamantina Fracture Zone** *underwater feature* Indian Ocean
393 G6 **Diamond Harbour** West Bengal India
124 D5 **Diamond Lake** Oregon USA
300 D6 **Diamou** Mali
380 D4 **Dian Chi** *lake* Yunnan China
122 D2 **Diana, Baie** *bay* Québec Canada
122 D3 **Diana, Lac** *lake* Québec Canada
120 I1 **Diana Lake** Nunavut Canada
310 5b **Diana's Peak** *volcano* St Helena
381 H2 **Dianbu** Anhui China
229 I5 **Diane, Étang de** *lagoon* Corsica France
380 D1 **Dianga** Gansu China
300 E6 **Diangounte Kamara** Mali
157 C5 **Dianópolis** Brazil
304 C3 **Dianra** Côte d'Ivoire
380 C4 **Dianyang** Yunnan China
380 E4 **Diao Jiang** *watercourse* Guangxi Zhuangzu Zizhiqu China
304 E2 **Diapaga** Burkina Faso
235 C7 **Diaporioi** *island* Greece
376 B4 **Diavolo, Mount** Andaman and Nicobar Islands India
130 F3 **Diaz** Arkansas USA
154 B5 **Díaz de Pineda** Ecuador
308 C5 **Diaz Point** *cape* Namibia
306 C5 **Dibaya** Democratic Republic of Congo
308 D5 **Dibeng** South Africa
D'Iberville *see* **Caubvick, Mount** Canada
122 B5 **D'Iberville, Lac** *lake* Québec Canada
373 G6 **Dibiri Island** Papua New Guinea
379 H3 **Dibrugarh** Assam India
154 C2 **Dibulla** Colombia
423 8 **Dick, Mount** Auckland Islands New Zealand
129 L4 **Dickens** Texas USA
125 N3 **Dickinson** North Dakota USA
130 H2 **Dickson** Tennessee USA
232 D5 **Dicomano** Italy
241 F3 **Didcot** Oxfordshire England UK
240 E2 **Diddlebury** Shropshire England UK
301 H3 **Dider** Algeria
307 F2 **Didesa** *watercourse* Ethiopia
300 E6 **Didiéni** Mali
303 F5 **Didigsala** Ethiopia
304 D2 **Didir** Burkina Faso
392 D5 **Didwana** Rajasthan India
225 M5 **Didžiulis** *lake* Lithuania
229 G4 **Die** France
380 D1 **Die Shan** *range* Jiangsu China
304 D2 **Diébougou** Burkina Faso
232 D5 **Diecimo** Italy
161 H5 **Dieciocho de Julio** Uruguay
116 I8 **Diefenbaker, Lake** Saskatchewan Canada
160 D3 **Diego de Almagro** Chile
162 A5 **Diego de Almagro, Isla** *island* Chile
80 L5 **Diego Garcia** *UK territory* Indian Ocean
163 9 **Diego Martin** *admin. area* Trinidad and Tobago
162 C6 **Diego Ramírez, Islas** *island* Chile
162 B5 **Diego Ritchie** Argentina
229 H2 **Diekirch** Luxembourg
300 E6 **Diéma** Mali
226 F3 **Diemantstein** Germany
226 E2 **Diemel** *watercourse* Germany
226 E2 **Diemelsee** *lake* Germany
376 D2 **Điện Biên Phu** Vietnam
376 E3 **Diễn Châu** Vietnam
228 E2 **Dieppe** France
163 19 **Dieppe Bay Town** St Kitts and Nevis
130 D3 **Dierks** Arkansas USA
124 H5 **Dietrich** Idaho USA
229 G4 **Dieulefit** France
229 H2 **Dieuze** France
158 B2 **Diez de Agosto** Peru
305 G2 **Diffa** Niger
306 D3 **Digba** Democratic Republic of Congo
123 F10 **Digby** Nova Scotia Canada
123 E10 **Digby Neck** *peninsula* Nova Scotia Canada
120 H3 **Digges** Manitoba Canada
121 Q1 **Digges Islands** Nunavut Canada
393 G7 **Digha** West Bengal India
125 O7 **Dighton** Kansas USA
229 H4 **Digne** France
226 B4 **Digoin** France
377 J6 **Digos** Philippines
393 D7 **Digras** Maharashtra India
391 L4 **Digri** Pakistan
373 G5 **Digul** *watercourse* Indonesia
122 F4 **Dihourse, Lac** *lake* Québec Canada
307 G3 **Diinsoor** Somalia
229 G3 **Dijon** France
305 H3 **Dik** Chad
237 X3 **Dika, Mys** *cape* Russian Federation
235 E5 **Dikaia** Greece
222 J4 **Dikanäs** Sweden
303 G5 **Dikhil** Djibouti
225 M4 **Dikļi** Latvia
304 C3 **Dikodougou** Côte d'Ivoire
236 R4 **Dikson** Russian Federation
235 D8 **Dikti** *range* Greece
305 G2 **Dikwa** Nigeria
307 F2 **Dila** Ethiopia
372 C6 **Dili** Timor-Leste (East Timor)
301 I5 **Dilia** *watercourse* Niger
376 B4 **Diligent Strait** Andaman and Nicobar Islands India
388 D6 **Dilizhan** Armenia
130 B6 **Dilley** Texas USA
300 E6 **Dilli** Mali
302 D5 **Dilling** Sudan
116 D7 **Dillingham** Alaska USA
119 Q5 **Dillon** *watercourse* Saskatchewan Canada
124 I4 **Dillon** Montana USA
423 E6 **Dillon Cone** *mountain* New Zealand
126 I7 **Dillsboro** Indiana USA
388 E6 **Dilmamedli** Azerbaijan
306 C6 **Dilolo** Democratic Republic of Congo
235 D7 **Dilos** *island* Greece
305 G4 **Dimako** Cameroon
379 G4 **Dimapur** Nagaland India
394 F7 **Dimashq (Damascus)** Syria
379 H5 **Dimawhaso** Myanmar
306 C5 **Dimbelenge** Democratic Republic of Congo
304 D3 **Dimbokro** Côte d'Ivoire
425 L9 **Dimboola** Vic. Australia
388 F2 **Dimitrovgrad** Russian Federation
129 K3 **Dimmitt** Texas USA
377 J5 **Dinagat** *island* Philippines
377 J5 **Dinagat Sound** Philippines
379 F4 **Dinajpur** Bangladesh
228 C2 **Dinan** France
391 H3 **Dīnān Āb** Iran
392 D4 **Dinanagar** Punjab India
301 F6 **Dinangourou** Mali
229 G1 **Dinant** Belgium
390 G3 **Dīnār, Kūh-e** *mountain* Iran
228 C2 **Dinard** France
240 C1 **Dinas** Gwynedd Wales UK
240 C2 **Dinas** Pembrokeshire Wales UK
388 J6 **Dinau** Uzbekistan
307 F2 **Dinchiya** *watercourse* Ethiopia
308 B2 **Dinde** Angola
302 E5 **Dinder** Sudan
302 E5 **Dinder** *watercourse* Sudan
393 E8 **Dindi** *watercourse* Andhra Pradesh India
393 D9 **Dindigul** Tamil Nadu India
309 F4 **Dindiza** Mozambique
392 E6 **Dindori** Madhya Pradesh India
307 E2 **Ding Ding** Sudan
384 F5 **Dingbian** Shaanxi China
381 H2 **Dingcheng** Anhui China
380 F5 **Dingcheng** Hainan China
392 G5 **Dingla** Nepal
245 B4 **Dingle** Ireland
245 B4 **Dingle Bay** Ireland
245 B4 **Dingle Peninsula** Ireland
379 H2 **Dingqing** Xizang Zizhiqu China
381 G1 **Dingtao** Shandong China
304 B2 **Dinguiraye** Guinea
123 H9 **Dingwall** Nova Scotia Canada
244 D3 **Dingwall** Highland Scotland UK
384 E6 **Dingxi** Gansu China
385 G5 **Dingxiang** Shanxi China
385 H5 **Dingzhou** Hebei China
376 E2 **Đình Lập** Vietnam
226 F3 **Dinkelsbühl** Germany
226 E1 **Dinklage** Germany
244 F3 **Dinnet** Aberdeenshire Scotland UK
240 C1 **Dinorwic** Gwynedd Wales UK
125 K6 **Dinosaur** Colorado USA
232 B2 **Dinozé** France
119 R7 **Dinsmore** Saskatchewan Canada
374 E5 **Dintiteladas** Indonesia
128 C2 **Dinuba** California USA
159 I5 **Diorama** Brazil
304 C3 **Dioulatie-Dougou** Côte d'Ivoire
300 C6 **Diouloulou** Senegal
300 E6 **Dioura** Mali
300 C6 **Diourbel** Senegal
379 G4 **Diphu** Assam India
134 C4 **Dipilto** Nicaragua
391 L5 **Diplo** Pakistan
128 G6 **Dipo** Mexico
377 I5 **Dipolog** Philippines
244 C5 **Dippen** Argyll and Bute Scotland UK
119 R5 **Dipper Lake** Saskatchewan Canada
244 D5 **Dipple** South Ayrshire Scotland UK
381 H2 **Dipu** Zhejiang China
154 B3 **Dipurdú** Colombia
391 I4 **Dir** Iran
391 K3 **Dirao** Pakistan
300 F5 **Diré** Mali
307 G2 **Dirē Dawa** Ethiopia
307 G2 **Dirē Dawa** *admin. area* Ethiopia
425 L3 **Direction, Cape** Qld Australia
424 inset **Direction Island (Tikus)** Cocos (Keeling) Islands Australia
235 C6 **Dirfys** *range* Greece
391 K3 **Dirgi** Pakistan
308 D3 **Dirico** Angola
424 D6 **Dirk Hartog Island** WA Australia
301 I5 **Dirkou** Niger
244 F4 **Dirleton** East Lothian Scotland UK
302 D5 **Dirra** Sudan
425 N7 **Dirranbandi** Qld Australia
128 G1 **Dirty Devil** *watercourse* Utah USA
392 C6 **Disa** Gujarat India
436 T2 **Disappointment, Cape** Antarctica
163 8 **Disappointment, Cape** South Georgia
124 C3 **Disappointment, Cape** Washington USA
424 G5 **Disappointment, Lake** WA Australia
423 8 **Disappointment Island** Auckland Islands New Zealand
80 D9 **Discovery Guyot** *underwater feature* Southern Ocean
377 F3 **Discovery Reef** Paracel Islands
229 I3 **Disentis** Switzerland
229 I3 **Disentis Muster** Switzerland
302 E2 **Dishnā** Egypt
Disko *see* **Qeqertarsuaq** Greenland
119 S7 **Disley** Saskatchewan Canada
125 O6 **Dismal** *watercourse* Nebraska USA
437 D2 **Dismal Mountains** Antarctica
225 O5 **Disna** Belarus
379 G3 **Dispur** Assam India
241 I2 **Diss** Norfolk England UK
242 E2 **Distington** Cumbria England UK
161 G5 **Distrito Federal** *admin. area* Argentina
157 C6 **Distrito Federal** *admin. area* Brazil
133 F5 **Distrito Federal** *admin. area* Mexico
377 I5 **Dit** *island* Philippines
304 B2 **Ditinn** Guinea
393 C7 **Diu (Daman & Diu)** Gujarat India
375 J1 **Diuata Mountains** *range* Philippines
377 J5 **Diuata Point** Philippines
228 D5 **Diusse** France
227 G5 **Divača** Slovenia
234 B3 **Divci** Serbia
228 D3 **Dive** *watercourse* France
388 D2 **Diveyevo** Russian Federation
393 E8 **Divi, Point** Andhra Pradesh India
232 G4 **Divičani** Bosnia and Herzegovina
222 K2 **Dividalen** *valley* Norway
377 I3 **Divilican Bay** Philippines
232 H2 **Divín** Slovakia
157 C8 **Divinópolis** Brazil
159 F3 **Divisa, Serra da** *range* Brazil
132 B2 **División del Norte** Mexico
157 B7 **Divisões, Serra das** *range* Brazil
235 A5 **Divjakë** Albania
388 D4 **Divnoye** Russian Federation
304 C3 **Divo** Côte d'Ivoire
230 C4 **Divor, Barragem do** *lake* Portugal
306 C6 **Divuma** Democratic Republic of Congo
125 N6 **Dix** Nebraska USA
126 G6 **Dixon** Illinois USA
118 E5 **Dixon Entrance** British Columbia/Alaska Canada/USA
118 M4 **Dixonville** Alberta Canada
390 F2 **Diyālá** *admin. area* Iraq
394 G6 **Diyarbakır** Turkey
394 G6 **Diyarbakir** *admin. area* Turkey
228 F2 **Dizy** France
306 A3 **Dja** *watercourse* Cameroon
301 I4 **Djado** Niger
222 L4 **Djäkneboda** Sweden
301 H2 **Djamâa** Algeria
305 G5 **Djambala** Congo
305 G4 **Djampiel** Cameroon
301 H4 **Djanet** Algeria
427 15a **Djarrit** Marshall Islands
373 I4 **Djaul Island** Papua New Guinea
302 B5 **Djédaa** Chad
301 G2 **Djelfa** Algeria
301 G2 **Djelfa** *admin. area* Algeria
301 F6 **Djenné** Mali
234 C3 **Djerdap** *region* Serbia
305 G3 **Djerem** *watercourse* Cameroon
301 J6 **Djermaya** Chad
231 J6 **Djeurf** Algeria
304 D2 **Djibo** Burkina Faso
303 G5 **Djibouti** *country* Africa
303 G5 **Djibouti** Djibouti
300 E5 **Djiguéni** Mauritania
231 G6 **Djilali Ben Amar** Algeria
304 C2 **Djinko** *watercourse* Guinea
306 C3 **Djolu** Democratic Republic of Congo
302 B5 **Djombo Kibbit** Chad
304 C3 **Djon** *watercourse* Guinea
305 G4 **Djoua** *watercourse* Congo
305 I3 **Djoubissi** Central African Republic
304 E3 **Djougou** Benin
305 G4 **Djoum** Cameroon
305 G3 **Djoumboli** Cameroon
301 J5 **Djourab, Erg du** *desert* Chad
222 inset **Djúpavík** Iceland
222 inset **Djúpivogur** Iceland
222 K5 **Djupsjö** Sweden
223 M3 **Djupträsket** *lake* Sweden
222 L2 **Djupvik** Norway
224 F4 **Djursland** *region* Denmark
224 I3 **Djursö** *island* Sweden
222 H5 **Djursvallen** Sweden
237 AD4 **Dmitriya Lapteva, Proliv** *strait* Russian Federation
388 F3 **Dmitriyevka** Russian Federation
238 G4 **Dmitrov** Russian Federation
234 G2 **Dmytrivka** Ukraine
388 A2 **Dnepr** *watercourse* Russian Federation
238 E5 **Dneprovo** Russian Federation
238 E5 **Dneprovskoye** Russian Federation
394 C2 **Dnieper** *watercourse* Belarus
394 D2 **Dnipro** *see* **Dnipro** Ukraine
394 D2 **Dnipro (Dniepro)** *watercourse* Ukraine
394 E3 **Dnipropetrovs'k** Ukraine
394 E3 **Dnipropetrovs'ka Oblast'** *admin. area* Ukraine
394 C3 **Dnister** *watercourse* Ukraine
225 O4 **Dno** Russian Federation
376 E3 **Đô Lương** Vietnam
309 F3 **Doa** Mozambique
391 L2 **Doaba** Pakistan
123 E9 **Doaktown** New Brunswick Canada
375 H5 **Doangdoangan Besar** *island* Indonesia
375 H5 **Doangdoangan Kecil** *island* Indonesia
305 H3 **Doba** Chad
232 E3 **Dobbiaco** Italy
225 L4 **Dobele** Latvia
225 L4 **Dobeles** *admin. area* Latvia
372 E4 **Doberai, Jazirah** *peninsula* Indonesia
227 H3 **Dobersberg** Austria
305 G3 **Dobinga** Cameroon
372 E5 **Dobo** Indonesia
232 H4 **Doboj** Bosnia and Herzegovina
131 K5 **Doboy Sound** Georgia USA
234 C3 **Dobra** Romania
234 B3 **Dobra** Serbia
234 H2 **Dobre** Ukraine
225 K6 **Dobre Miasto** Poland
234 E4 **Dobrich** Bulgaria
234 E4 **Dobrich** *admin. area* Bulgaria
232 H4 **Dobrinje** Bosnia and Herzegovina
388 C3 **Dobrinka** Russian Federation
232 H5 **Dobro Polje** Bosnia and Herzegovina
227 J4 **Döbrököz** Hungary
232 H5 **Dobromani** Bosnia and Herzegovina
235 C5 **Dobrošinci** Macedonia
234 G1 **Dobrovody** Ukraine
227 M1 **Dobroye** Belarus
238 F5 **Dobroye** Russian Federation
388 C3 **Dobroye** Russian Federation
387 J2 **Dobroye, Ozero** *lake* Russian Federation
225 N3 **Dobruchi** Russian Federation
234 F3 **Dobruja** *region* Romania
388 G1 **Dobryanka** Russian Federation
234 G1 **Dobryanka** Ukraine
225 P5 **Dobryn'** Belarus
227 H1 **Dobrzany** Poland
227 J1 **Dobrzejewice** Poland
423 C6 **Dobson** *watercourse* New Zealand
131 K2 **Dobson** North Carolina USA
377 H6 **Doc Can** *island* Philippines
154 B3 **Docampó, Ensenada de** *bay* Colombia
157 D7 **Doce** *watercourse* Brazil
244 D4 **Dochart** *watercourse* Scotland UK
Docker River *see* **Kaltukatjara** Australia
241 H2 **Docking** Norfolk England UK
225 J5 **Dockmyr** Sweden
222 K5 **Docksta** Sweden
132 E4 **Doctor Arroyo** Mexico
162 B3 **Doctor Ricardo Rojas** Argentina
392 D4 **Doda** Jammu and Kashmir India/Pakistan
392 D4 **Doda** *watercourse* Jammu and Kashmir India/Pakistan
Dodecanese *see* **Sporades** Greece
125 N3 **Dodge** North Dakota USA
125 O8 **Dodge City** Kansas USA
120 C3 **Dodge Lake** Saskatchewan Canada
240 C4 **Dodman Point** England UK
304 C3 **Dodo** *watercourse* Côte d'Ivoire
307 F5 **Dodoma** Tanzania
307 F5 **Dodoma** *admin. area* Tanzania
125 K2 **Dodson** Montana USA
372 C4 **Dofa** Indonesia
234 E2 **Dofteana** Romania
118 J7 **Dog Creek** British Columbia Canada
163 20 **Dog Island** Anguilla
122 H4 **Dog Island** Newfoundland and Labrador Canada
126 G2 **Dog Lake** Ontario Canada
235 G6 **Döğer** Turkey
232 B4 **Dogliani** Italy
229 K3 **Dogna** Italy
386 G4 **Dōgo** *island* Japan
386 G4 **Dōgo** *mountain* Japan
306 D2 **Dogoba** Sudan
304 D2 **Dogon Plateau** *plain* Burkina Faso
301 G6 **Dogondoutchi** Niger
394 H5 **Doğubeyazıt** Turkey
394 G5 **Doğukaradeniz Dağları** Turkey
163 18 **Dogwood Point** St Kitts and Nevis
379 E3 **Dogxung Zangbo** *watercourse* Xizang Zizhiqu China
372 C3 **Doi** *island* Indonesia
118 K4 **Doig** *watercourse* British Columbia Canada
156 D5 **Dois Irmãos, Serra dos** *range* Brazil
157 A9 **Dois Vizinhos** Brazil
229 G1 **Doische** Belgium
235 C5 **Dojran, Lake** Greece
372 E5 **Doka** Indonesia
302 F5 **Doka** Sudan
224 F2 **Dokka** *watercourse* Norway
304 C2 **Doko** Guinea
235 C7 **Dokos** *island* Greece
229 L1 **Doksy** Czech Republic
394 F3 **Dokuchayevs'k** Ukraine
373 F5 **Dolak, Pulau** *island* Indonesia
125 P4 **Doland** South Dakota USA
240 D2 **Dolau** Powys Wales UK
117 L9 **Dolbeau-Mistassini** Québec Canada
240 C2 **Dolbenmaen** Gwynedd Wales UK
233 G7 **Dolcedorme, Serra** *mountain* Italy
76 O9 **Doldrums Fracture Zone** *underwater feature* Atlantic Ocean
229 G3 **Dole** France
235 B5 **Dolenci** Macedonia
236 M5 **Dolgiy, Ostrov** *island* Russian Federation
225 O3 **Dolgovka** Russian Federation
234 D1 **Dolina** Ukraine
387 I1 **Dolinsk** Russian Federation
306 A4 **Dolisie (Loubomo)** Congo
234 C3 **Dolj** *admin. area* Romania
232 G4 **Doljani** Croatia
244 E4 **Dollar** Clackmannanshire Scotland UK
119 Q8 **Dollard** Saskatchewan Canada
226 D1 **Dollart** *bay* Netherlands
436 U2 **Dolleman Island** Antarctica
242 B3 **Dollys Grove** Ireland
227 I2 **Dolnośląskie** *admin. area* Poland
227 J3 **Dolný Kubín** Slovakia
372 A4 **Dolo** Indonesia
307 G3 **Dolo Odo** Ethiopia
161 G6 **Dolores** Argentina
134 B3 **Dolores** Guatemala
161 G5 **Dolores** Uruguay
125 K8 **Dolores** Colorado USA
129 H1 **Dolores** *watercourse* Colorado USA
132 E4 **Dolores Hidalgo** Mexico
238 C4 **Dolostsy** Russian Federation
227 K5 **Dolovo** Serbia
163 7 **Dolphin, Cape** Falkland Islands
116 H5 **Dolphin and Union Strait** Nunavut Canada
308 B5 **Dolphin Head** *cape* Namibia
240 D1 **Dolwyddelan** Conwy Wales UK
234 D1 **Dolyna** Ukraine
234 F2 **Dolyns'ke** Ukraine
234 E1 **Dolzhok** Ukraine
372 F4 **Dom, Gunung** *mountain* Indonesia
159 G3 **Dom Alexandre** Brazil
161 H4 **Dom Pedrito** Brazil
156 C4 **Dom Pedro** Brazil
305 F3 **Doma** Nigeria
123 F7 **Domagaya Lake** Newfoundland and Labrador Canada
235 F6 **Domaniç** Turkey
232 G5 **Domanovići** Bosnia and Herzegovina
378 D2 **Domar Qu** *watercourse* Xizang Zizhiqu China
388 C5 **Dombaj, Gora** *mountain* Russian Federation
388 H3 **Dombarovskiy** Russian Federation
222 F5 **Dombås** Norway
388 D5 **Dombay** Russian Federation
309 F3 **Dombe** Mozambique
308 B2 **Dombe Grande** Angola
229 G3 **Dombes** *region* France
227 J4 **Dombóvár** Hungary
234 B1 **Dombrád** Hungary
226 B2 **Domburg** Netherlands
118 K6 **Dome Creek** British Columbia Canada
423 E6 **Domett** New Zealand
160 D2 **Domeyko, Cordillera** *range* Chile
228 D2 **Domfront** France
155 F2 **Domingo** Venezuela
135 I4 **Dominica** *country* Caribbean
135 I4 **Dominica Passage** Guadeloupe
135 G3 **Dominican Republic** *country* Caribbean
117 L5 **Dominion, Cape** Nunavut Canada
122 H6 **Dominion Lake** Newfoundland and Labrador Canada
437 L1 **Dominion Range** Antarctica
306 C4 **Domiongo** Democratic Republic of Congo
379 G3 **Domka** Bhutan
238 C3 **Domkino** Russian Federation
307 H2 **Domo** Ethiopia
238 G5 **Domodedovo** Russian Federation
226 E4 **Domodossola** Italy
235 C6 **Domokos** Greece
309 H2 **Domoni** Comoros
238 E2 **Domozhirovo** Russian Federation
229 H2 **Dompaire** France
375 H6 **Dompu** Indonesia
222 K5 **Domsjö** Sweden
160 D6 **Domuyo, Volcán** *volcano* Argentina
227 H4 **Domžale** Slovenia
228 D3 **Don** *watercourse* France
388 D4 **Don** *watercourse* Russian Federation
243 G3 **Don** *watercourse* England UK
244 F3 **Don** *watercourse* Scotland UK
377 J6 **Don Carlos** Philippines
129 L7 **Don Martin** Mexico
128 B2 **Don Pedro Reservoir** California USA
376 C5 **Don Sak** Thailand
129 I4 **Dona** New Mexico USA
242 B3 **Donabate** Ireland
242 A2 **Donagh** Fermanagh Northern Ireland UK
242 C2 **Donaghadee** Ards Northern Ireland UK
242 B2 **Donaghmore** Dungannon Northern Ireland UK
118 M7 **Donald** British Columbia Canada
131 I5 **Donalsonville** Georgia USA
232 F2 **Donau (Danube)** *watercourse* Austria
232 C2 **Donau (Danube)** *watercourse* Germany
243 G3 **Doncaster** South Yorkshire England UK
234 E4 **Donchevo** Bulgaria
393 D7 **Dondaicha** Maharashtra India
308 B1 **Dondo** Angola
309 F3 **Dondo** Mozambique
393 E11 **Dondra Head** *cape* Sri Lanka
245 D2 **Donegal** Ireland
245 E1 **Donegal** *admin. area* Ireland
245 D2 **Donegal Bay** Ireland
245 C4 **Donegal Point** Ireland
394 F3 **Donets'k** Ukraine
394 F3 **Donets'ka Oblast'** *admin. area* Ukraine
376 E3 **Đồng Hà** Vietnam
380 E2 **Dong He** *watercourse* Sichuan China
376 E3 **Đồng Hới** Vietnam
381 G4 **Dong Jiang** *watercourse* Guangdong China
376 E2 **Đồng Mỏ** Vietnam
379 G2 **Dong Qu** *watercourse* Qinghai China

376 E2 **Đồng Văn** Vietnam
305 G3 **Donga** Nigeria
305 G3 **Donga** *watercourse* Nigeria
309 G4 **Dongane, Lagoa** *lake* Mozambique
424 E7 **Dongara** WA Australia
385 J4 **Dongbei Pingyuan (Manchurian Plain)** China
380 D3 **Dongchuan** Yunnan China
380 D3 **Dongchuan** Yunnan China
384 G5 **Dongcun** Shanxi China
380 E5 **Dongfang** Hainan China
385 K4 **Dongfeng** Jilin China
379 G3 **Dongga** Xizang Zizhiqu China
372 A4 **Donggala** Indonesia
383 K6 **Donggi Conag** *lake* Qinghai China
381 G4 **Dongguan** Guangdong China
384 G5 **Dongguan** Shanxi China
385 H5 **Dongguang** Hebei China
380 E2 **Donghe** Sichuan China
376 E3 **Dônghén** Laos
380 E1 **Donghua** Gansu China
380 E3 **Donghuang** Guizhou China
381 H1 **Dongkan** Jiangsu China
380 F3 **Dongkou** Hunan China
380 E4 **Donglan** Guangxi Zhuangzu Zizhiqu China
385 J4 **Dongliao He** *watercourse* Jilin China
380 E4 **Dongmen** Guangxi Zhuangzu Zizhiqu China
385 L4 **Dongning** Heilongjiang China
308 C2 **Dongo** Angola
226 E4 **Dongo** Italy
302 E4 **Dongola** Sudan
126 G8 **Dongola** Illinois USA
306 B3 **Dongou** Congo
381 F3 **Dongping** Hunan China
385 H6 **Dongping** Shandong China
388 I4 **Dongsary Koli** *lake* Kazakhstan
381 H4 **Dongshan Dao** *island* Fujian China
384 G5 **Dongsheng** Nei Mongol Zizhiqu China
381 H2 **Dongtai** Jiangsu China
381 F2 **Dongting Hu** *lake* Hunan China
381 I3 **Dongtou Dao** *island* Zhejiang China
308 D2 **Dongwe** *watercourse* Zambia
380 E2 **Dongxiang** Sichuan China
385 H6 **Dongxiaotun** Hebei China
381 H2 **Dongyang** Zhejiang China
385 I5 **Dongying** Shandong China
241 G2 **Donington** Lincolnshire England UK
130 F2 **Doniphan** Missouri USA
234 C4 **Donji Krivodol** Serbia
232 H4 **Donji Miholjac** Croatia
232 G4 **Donji Mujdžići** Bosnia and Herzegovina
232 G4 **Donji Srb** Croatia
234 C4 **Donji Striževac** Serbia
232 H4 **Donji Svilaj** Bosnia and Herzegovina
379 G4 **Donkamokam** Assam India
379 G5 **Donmanick Islands** Bangladesh
222 H3 **Dønna** *island* Norway
127 P3 **Donnacona** Québec Canada
128 C1 **Donnell Lake** California USA
124 G4 **Donnelly** Idaho USA
125 R4 **Donnelly** Minnesota USA
240 E2 **Donnington** Herefordshire England UK
424 E8 **Donnybrook** WA Australia
242 B3 **Donore** Ireland
230 F2 **Donostia-San Sebastián** Spain
235 D7 **Donoussa** Greece
235 D7 **Donoussa** *island* Greece
226 B3 **Dontilly** France
232 E4 **Donzella, Isola della** *island* Italy
228 E4 **Donzenac** France
226 B4 **Donzy** France
245 B3 **Dooagh** Ireland
242 A2 **Dooish** Omagh Northern Ireland UK
425 K4 **Doomadgee** Qld Australia
242 D1 **Doon** *watercourse* Scotland UK
242 D1 **Doon, Loch** *lake* Scotland UK
245 B3 **Doon Hill** Ireland
245 D3 **Dooneen Bridge** Ireland
245 C3 **Doonyvardan** Ireland
126 H4 **Door Peninsula** Wisconsin USA
226 C1 **Doorn** Netherlands
238 F5 **Dor** Russian Federation
129 K4 **Dora** New Mexico USA
424 G5 **Dora, Lake** WA Australia
232 B4 **Dora Baltea** *watercourse* Italy
240 E4 **Dorchester** Dorset England UK
120 Q6 **Dorchester** Nebraska USA
117 L5 **Dorchester, Cape** Nunavut Canada
308 C4 **Dordabis** Namibia
228 F2 **Dordives** France
228 E4 **Dordogne** *watercourse* France
226 C2 **Dordrecht** Netherlands
308 E6 **Dordrecht** South Africa
228 F4 **Dore** *watercourse* France
119 R5 **Doré Lake** Saskatchewan Canada
119 R5 **Doré Lake** Saskatchewan Canada
226 E1 **Dörentrup** Germany
244 D3 **Dores** Highland Scotland UK
157 C7 **Dores do Indaiá** Brazil
301 F5 **Dorey** Mali
226 G3 **Dorfen** Germany
304 D2 **Dori** Burkina Faso
119 Q5 **Dorintosh** Saskatchewan Canada
241 G3 **Dorking** Surrey England UK
393 E8 **Dornakal** Andhra Pradesh India
232 F3 **Dornava** Slovenia
226 E4 **Dornbirn** Austria
226 D2 **Dorndorf** Germany
228 F3 **Dornes** France
244 C3 **Dornie** Highland Scotland UK
244 D3 **Dornoch** Highland Scotland UK
385 H3 **Dornod** *admin. area* Mongolia
384 G4 **Dornogovi** *admin. area* Mongolia
226 D1 **Dornum** Germany
301 F5 **Doro** Mali
238 E5 **Dorogobuzh** Russian Federation
383 J3 **Döröö Nuur** *lake* Mongolia
222 J4 **Dorotea** Sweden
119 O7 **Dorothy** Alberta Canada
236 K7 **Dorovitsa** Russian Federation
238 F4 **Dorozhayevo** Russian Federation
163 1c **Dorp Rincón** Netherlands Antilles
163 1b **Dorp Sint Willebrordus** Netherlands Antilles
129 M1 **Dorrance** Kansas USA
424 E6 **Dorre Island** WA Australia
241 G1 **Dorrington** Lincolnshire England UK
425 O7 **Dorrigo** NSW Australia
241 E4 **Dorset** *admin. area* England UK
229 G3 **Dortan** France
229 H1 **Dortmund** Germany
394 F6 **Dörtyol** Turkey
390 G2 **Dorūd** Iran
306 D3 **Doruma** Democratic Republic of Congo
225 D3 **Dorupe** Latvia
244 C3 **Dorusduain** Highland Scotland UK
230 D5 **Dos Hermanas** Spain
159 F2 **Dos Marmelos** *watercourse* Brazil
162 D3 **Dos Pozos** Argentina
235 G7 **Döşemealtı** Turkey
226 G1 **Dosse** *watercourse* Germany
305 I3 **Dosséo, Bahr** *watercourse* Chad
301 G6 **Dosso** Niger
301 G6 **Dosso** *admin. area* Niger
391 J4 **Dostinzai** Pakistan
389 L5 **Dostuk** Kyrgyzstan
238 D5 **Dosugovo** Russian Federation
124 E1 **Dot** British Columbia Canada
131 I5 **Dothan** Alabama USA
304 B3 **Douako** Guinea
305 F4 **Douala** Cameroon
228 B2 **Douarnenez** France
301 G6 **Doubèlma** Niger
134 D2 **Double Headed Shot Cays** *island* Bahamas
122 I5 **Double Island** Newfoundland and Labrador Canada
122 I5 **Double Mer** *lake* Newfoundland and Labrador Canada
425 N5 **Double Mountain** Qld Australia
229 G3 **Doubs** *watercourse* France
423 B7 **Doubtful Sound (Patea)** New Zealand
422 E2 **Doubtless Bay** New Zealand
241 H5 **Doudeville** France
300 F6 **Douentza** Mali
423 B8 **Doughboy Bay** New Zealand
163 7 **Douglas** Falkland Islands
242 D2 **Douglas** Isle of Man UK
308 D5 **Douglas** South Africa
244 E5 **Douglas** South Lanarkshire Scotland UK
128 H5 **Douglas** Arizona USA
131 J5 **Douglas** Georgia USA
125 M5 **Douglas** Wyoming USA
118 G6 **Douglas Channel** British Columbia Canada
131 I3 **Douglas Lake** Tennessee USA
125 Q8 **Douglass** Kansas USA
131 I4 **Douglasville** Georgia USA
304 B2 **Dougountouni** Guinea
381 F2 **Douhudi** Hubei China
245 B5 **Doulus Head** *cape* Ireland
305 I3 **Doum** Central African Republic
305 G4 **Doumé** Cameroon
244 E1 **Dounby** Orkney Islands Scotland UK
244 D4 **Doune** Stirling Scotland UK
157 B7 **Dourada, Cachoeirada** *watercourse* Brazil
159 H6 **Douradinho** Brazil
159 H6 **Dourados** Brazil
161 H2 **Dourados** *watercourse* Brazil
305 H2 **Dourbali** Chad
228 F4 **Dourbie** *watercourse* France
228 F2 **Dourdan** France
228 F5 **Dourgne** France
230 C3 **Douro** *watercourse* Portugal
381 G3 **Doushui Shuiku** *lake* Jiangxi China
305 G5 **Doussala** Gabon
228 D2 **Douve** *watercourse* France
301 H2 **Douz** Tunisia
228 E5 **Douze** *watercourse* France
229 G2 **Douzy** France
241 F2 **Dove** *watercourse* England UK
117 R3 **Dove Bugt** *bay* Greenland
125 K8 **Dove Creek** Colorado USA
243 G3 **Dove Holes** Derbyshire England UK
242 E2 **Dovenby** Cumbria England UK
123 L8 **Dover** Newfoundland and Labrador Canada
241 I3 **Dover** Kent England UK
127 N7 **Dover** Delaware USA
127 P5 **Dover** New Hampshire USA
127 N6 **Dover** New Jersey USA
127 K6 **Dover** Ohio USA
241 I3 **Dover, Strait of** France/UK
241 E2 **Doverdale** Worcestershire England UK
241 F2 **Doveridge** Derbyshire England UK
159 H5 **Doverlândia** Brazil
163 11 **Dovers** St Vincent and the Grenadines
222 F6 **Dovre** Norway
222 F5 **Dovre-Sundalsfjella Nasjonalpark** *park* Norway
373 H5 **Dowi** *volcano* Papua New Guinea
374 C3 **Dowi, Tanjung** *cape* Indonesia
391 K2 **Dowlat Yār** Afghanistan
119 O7 **Dowling Lake** Alberta Canada
245 G2 **Down** *admin. area* Northern Ireland UK
124 I5 **Downey** Idaho USA
242 B1 **Downhill** Coleraine Northern Ireland UK
242 C2 **Downpatrick** Down Northern Ireland UK
245 C2 **Downpatrick Head** *cape* Ireland
125 P7 **Downs** Kansas USA
241 G3 **Downside** Surrey England UK
241 F4 **Downton** Wiltshire England UK
118 I6 **Downton, Mount** British Columbia Canada
117 L9 **Dozois, Réservoir** Québec Canada
229 H4 **Drac** *watercourse* France
231 H4 **Drac, Coves del** Spain
225 O6 **Drachkava** Belarus
226 D1 **Drachten** Netherlands
234 D3 **Drăcşani** Romania
222 J2 **Drag** Norway
222 I4 **Dragan** *bay* Sweden
234 D4 **Draganovo** Bulgaria
234 B4 **Dragaš** Kosovo
234 A3 **Draginje** Serbia
235 E8 **Dragonada** *island* Greece
235 D7 **Dragonisi** *island* Greece
155 F2 **Dragons Mouths** *strait* Trinidad and Tobago/Venezuela
234 B4 **Dragoševac** Serbia
225 L2 **Dragsfjärd** Finland
229 H5 **Draguignan** France
234 E1 **Drăguşeni** Romania
124 D5 **Drain** Oregon USA
391 K4 **Drakalo** Pakistan
125 O3 **Drake** North Dakota USA
436 T3 **Drake Passage** *strait* Antarctica
128 A2 **Drakes Bay** California USA
224 F3 **Drammen** Norway
234 F2 **Drânceni** Romania
222 inset **Drangajökull** *mountain* Iceland
229 I1 **Dransfeld** Germany
235 D8 **Drapano, Akra** *cape* Greece
242 B2 **Draperstown** Magherafelt Northern Ireland UK
392 D3 **Drass** Jammu and Kashmir India/Pakistan
232 E3 **Drau** *watercourse* Austria
232 G3 **Drava** *watercourse* Croatia
232 H3 **Dravograd** Slovenia
227 H1 **Drawa** *watercourse* Poland
227 H1 **Drawno** Poland
241 F3 **Draycot Foliat** Swindon England UK
242 A2 **Dreen** Londonderry Northern Ireland UK
240 C3 **Drefach** Carmarthenshire Wales UK
229 K3 **Dreiherrnspitze** *mountain* Austria
373 G4 **Dreikikir** Papua New Guinea
226 D3 **Dreisam** *watercourse* Germany
227 L2 **Drelów** Poland
244 F4 **Drem** East Lothian Scotland UK
373 H4 **Dremsel, Mount** Papua New Guinea
234 C4 **Dren** Bulgaria
234 B2 **Drenovci** Croatia
235 C6 **Drepano, Akra** *cape* Greece
227 G2 **Dresden** Germany
130 G2 **Dresden** Tennessee USA
242 D2 **Dreswick Point** Isle of Man UK
228 E2 **Dreux** France
222 H6 **Drevdagen** Sweden
222 H4 **Drevja** Norway
222 H6 **Drevsjø** Norway
124 E5 **Drews Reservoir** Oregon USA
225 N4 **Drīceni** Latvia
225 N5 **Dridža** *lake* Latvia
127 K2 **Driftwood** Ontario Canada
242 E2 **Drigg** Cumbria England UK
244 C4 **Drimnin** Highland Scotland UK
245 C5 **Drimoleague** Ireland
240 E4 **Drimpton** Dorset England UK
234 A4 **Drin** *watercourse* Albania
245 C3 **Drin** Ireland
245 B3 **Drinagh** Ireland
244 B3 **Drinan** Highland Scotland UK
119 S7 **Drinkwater** Saskatchewan Canada
130 C7 **Driscoll** Texas USA
224 E1 **Driva** *watercourse* Norway
224 F3 **Drøbak** Norway
234 C3 **Drobeta-Turnu Severin** Romania
228 G4 **Drobie** *watercourse* France
227 J1 **Drobin** Poland
234 E1 **Drochia** Moldova
224 H3 **Drögen** *lake* Sweden
245 F3 **Drogheda** Ireland
227 L1 **Drogičin** Belarus
Drogobych *see* **Drohobych** Ukraine
227 L1 **Drohiczyn** Poland
234 C1 **Drohobych** Ukraine
242 B2 **Dromara** Banbridge Northern Ireland UK
245 D4 **Dromcolliher** Ireland
228 D2 **Drôme** *watercourse* France
245 E3 **Dromod** Ireland
242 A2 **Dromore** Omagh Northern Ireland UK
245 B3 **Dromore Head** *cape* Ireland
245 D2 **Dromore West** Ireland
229 H4 **Dronero** Italy
244 D5 **Drongan** East Ayrshire Scotland UK
228 E4 **Dronne** *watercourse* France
117 O5 **Dronning Ingrid Land** Greenland
117 Q3 **Dronning Louise Land** Greenland
228 E4 **Dropt** *watercourse* France
229 L2 **Drosendorf** Austria
391 L2 **Drosh** Pakistan
228 E2 **Droué** France
126 I1 **Drowning** *watercourse* Ontario Canada
245 C4 **Drumadrohid** Ireland
242 A2 **Drumbeg** Ireland
244 F3 **Drumblair** Aberdeenshire Scotland UK
245 E2 **Drumcard** Fermanagh Northern Ireland UK
244 D5 **Drumclog** South Lanarkshire Scotland UK
245 C3 **Drumcoggy** Ireland
242 A2 **Drumcondra** Ireland
245 E3 **Drumconnick** Ireland
245 E3 **Drumcree** Ireland
240 A2 **Drumdangan** Ireland
244 E5 **Drumelzier** Scottish Borders Scotland UK
244 C4 **Drumfern** Highland Scotland UK
245 E1 **Drumfin** Ireland
242 A2 **Drumgoon** Ireland
119 O7 **Drumheller** Alberta Canada
244 E3 **Drumin** Moray Scotland UK
244 D5 **Drumjohn** Dumfries and Galloway Scotland UK
242 D2 **Drumkeeran** Ireland
124 I3 **Drummond** Montana USA
131 M2 **Drummond, Lake** Virginia USA
126 I4 **Drummond Island** Michigan USA
117 L9 **Drummondville** Québec Canada
242 A2 **Drummullagh** Ireland
245 D2 **Drummury** Ireland
245 E3 **Drumna** Ireland
244 D3 **Drumnadrochit** Highland Scotland UK
242 B2 **Drumnasoo** Armagh Northern Ireland UK
245 E3 **Drumone** Ireland
242 A2 **Drumquin** Omagh Northern Ireland UK
242 A3 **Drumroe** Ireland
245 D2 **Drumshanbo** Ireland
242 B2 **Drumshanbo** Cookstown Northern Ireland UK
242 B3 **Drumsru** Ireland
225 L5 **Druskininkai** Lithuania
225 N5 **Druya** Belarus
228 F3 **Druyes** France
389 N4 **Druzhba** Kazakhstan
394 E2 **Druzhba** Ukraine
237 AE5 **Druzhina** Russian Federation
232 G4 **Drvar** Bosnia and Herzegovina
227 J1 **Drwęca** *watercourse* Poland
118 B3 **Dry Bay** Alaska USA
124 F6 **Dry Lake** Nevada USA
124 F5 **Dry Lake Reservoir** Oregon USA
134 D1 **Dry Tortugas** *island* Florida USA
126 E2 **Dryberry Lake** Ontario Canada
225 P5 **Drybin** Belarus
119 U4 **Drybrough** Manitoba Canada
120 I8 **Dryden** Ontario Canada
129 K5 **Dryden** Texas USA
437 L2 **Drygalski Basin** *underwater feature* Ross Sea
163 8 **Drygalski Fjord** South Georgia
437 L1 **Drygalski Ice Tongue** Antarctica
437 G2 **Drygalski Island** Antarctica
242 E1 **Dryhope** Scottish Borders Scotland UK
121 W6 **Drylake** Newfoundland and Labrador Canada
222 E5 **Dryna** Norway
225 O5 **Drysa** *watercourse* Belarus
424 H3 **Drysdale** *watercourse* WA Australia
227 J1 **Drzycim** Poland
305 G3 **Dschang** Cameroon
127 L6 **Du Bois** Pennsylvania USA
121 R7 **Du Glas, Lac** *lake* Québec Canada
127 K2 **Du Gué** *watercourse* Québec Canada
306 C3 **Dua** *watercourse* Democratic Republic of Congo
244 C4 **Duachy** Argyll and Bute Scotland UK
157 B8 **Duartina** Brazil
230 C3 **Duas Igrejas** Portugal
373 H5 **Duau, Mount** Papua New Guinea
229 L1 **Dubá** Czech Republic
120 E1 **Dubawnt Lake** Nunavut Canada
126 G4 **Dubay, Lake** Wisconsin USA
391 H4 **Dubayy (Dubai)** United Arab Emirates
425 N8 **Dubbo** NSW Australia
304 C3 **Dube** *watercourse* Liberia
306 D3 **Dubela** Democratic Republic of Congo
388 G3 **Dubenskiy** Russian Federation
238 H3 **Dubets** Russian Federation
244 C5 **Dubhchladach** Argyll and Bute Scotland UK
229 K1 **Dubí** Czech Republic
225 M5 **Dubičiai** Lithuania
306 D5 **Dubie** Democratic Republic of Congo
227 L2 **Dubienka** Poland
238 C4 **Dubki** Russian Federation
245 F3 **Dublin (Baile Átha Cliath)** Ireland
245 F3 **Dublin** *admin. area* Ireland
131 J4 **Dublin** Georgia USA
130 B4 **Dublin** Texas USA
127 K8 **Dublin** Virginia USA
245 F3 **Dublin Bay** Ireland
238 G4 **Dubna** Russian Federation
238 F2 **Dubno** Russian Federation
127 L2 **Dubois** Québec Canada
124 I4 **Dubois** Idaho USA
125 K5 **Dubois** Wyoming USA
124 F8 **Dubois, Mount** California USA
234 C3 **Dubova** Romania
234 E1 **Dubovaya** Ukraine
388 D3 **Dubovka** Russian Federation
227 I5 **Dubovsko** Bosnia and Herzegovina
388 D4 **Dubovskoye** Russian Federation
232 G4 **Dubrava** Bosnia and Herzegovina
232 G5 **Dubrava** Croatia
238 C4 **Dubrovka** Russian Federation
232 H5 **Dubrovnik** Croatia
238 C4 **Dubrovno** Russian Federation
236 O7 **Dubrovnoye** Russian Federation
225 P5 **Dubrowna** Belarus
119 T7 **Dubuc** Saskatchewan Canada
126 F5 **Dubuque** Iowa USA
427 14 **Duc de Gloucester, Îles du** *islands* French Polynesia
376 F4 **Đức Phổ** Vietnam
376 E5 **Đức Phong** Vietnam
228 D2 **Ducey** France
381 F4 **Ducheng** Guangdong China
125 J6 **Duchesne** Utah USA
119 P7 **Duchess** Alberta Canada
427 11 **Ducie Island** Pitcairn Islands
121 Q5 **Duck Island** Nunavut Canada
119 R6 **Duck Lake** Saskatchewan Canada
119 W3 **Duck Lake Post** Manitoba Canada
241 H5 **Duclair** France
163 14 **Ducos** Martinique
240 E1 **Duddon** Cheshire England UK
229 H2 **Dudelange** Luxembourg
234 B2 **Dudeştii Vechi** Romania
236 S5 **Dudinka** Russian Federation
393 D7 **Dudna** *watercourse* Maharashtra India
236 T4 **Dudypta** *watercourse* Russian Federation
304 C3 **Duékoué** Côte d'Ivoire
374 D4 **Duen, Bukit** *volcano* Indonesia
230 D3 **Dueñas** Spain
224 H5 **Dueodde** *cape* Denmark
230 D3 **Duero** *watercourse* Spain
437 L1 **Dufek Coast** Antarctica
119 T7 **Duff** Saskatchewan Canada
426 1 **Duff Islands** Solomon Islands
244 E3 **Dufftown** Moray Scotland UK
244 E3 **Duffus** Moray Scotland UK
120 H1 **Duffy Lake** Nunavut Canada
229 H4 **Dufourspitze** *mountain* Switzerland
122 C3 **Dufreboy, Lac** *lake* Québec Canada
121 Q2 **Dufrost** Manitoba Canada
121 Q2 **Dufrost, Pointe** *cape* Québec Canada
124 E4 **Dufur** Oregon USA
232 F4 **Duga Resa** Croatia
237 AE7 **Duga-Zapadnaya, Mys** *cape* Russian Federation
238 G5 **Dugna** Russian Federation
373 J6 **Dugumenu Island** Papua New Guinea
390 E6 **Duhrān** Yemen
301 J4 **Duhūn Tārsū** *range* Chad
229 K4 **Duino** Italy
244 C3 **Duirinish** Highland Scotland UK
226 D2 **Duisburg** Germany
154 C3 **Duitama** Colombia
308 F4 **Duiwelskloof** South Africa
381 G1 **Duji -Xiangsha** Anhui China
380 D2 **Dujiangyan** Sichuan China
307 G3 **Dūjuuma** Somalia
306 E2 **Duk Faiwil** Sudan
302 F5 **Dukambio** Eritrea
235 A5 **Dukat** Albania
118 F5 **Duke Island** Alaska USA
373 J5 **Duke of York Island** Papua New Guinea
238 E5 **Dukhovshchina** Russian Federation
305 E2 **Dukku** Nigeria
225 N5 **Dūkštas** Lithuania
308 E4 **Dukwe** Botswana
384 F2 **Dulaanhan** Mongolia
377 J5 **Dulag** Philippines
244 E3 **Dulax** Aberdeenshire Scotland UK
160 F4 **Dulce** *watercourse* Argentina
129 I2 **Dulce** New Mexico USA
134 D5 **Dulce, Golfo** *bay* Costa Rica
225 O6 **Dulëby** Belarus
245 F3 **Duleek** Ireland
238 E5 **Dulevo** Russian Federation
390 F2 **Dulf** Iraq
237 AB5 **Dulgalakh** *watercourse* Russian Federation
384 E3 **Dulgeen** Mongolia
375 G3 **Dulit, Banjuran** *range* Malaysia
308 F5 **Dullstroom** South Africa
234 E4 **Dulovo** Bulgaria
126 E3 **Duluth** Minnesota USA
240 D3 **Dulverton** Somerset England UK
379 H3 **Dum Duma** Assam India
377 I5 **Dumaguete** Philippines
374 D3 **Dumai** Indonesia
377 I4 **Dumali Point** Philippines
377 I5 **Dumaran** *island* Philippines
372 C2 **Dumarchen** *island* Indonesia
130 F4 **Dumas** Arkansas USA
129 L3 **Dumas** Texas USA
162 C6 **Dumas, Península** Chile
424 F8 **Dumbleyung** WA Australia
305 G3 **Dumbo** Cameroon
244 E5 **Dumfries** Dumfries and Galloway Scotland UK
244 D5 **Dumfries and Galloway** *admin. area* Scotland UK
238 F6 **Duminichi** Russian Federation
119 S8 **Dummer** Saskatchewan Canada
226 E1 **Dümmer** *lake* Germany
372 C3 **Dumoga** Indonesia
127 M3 **Dumoine, Lac** *lake* Québec Canada
437 J2 **Dumont d'Urville (France)** *research station* Antarctica
437 J2 **Dumont d'Urville Sea** Antarctica
392 B6 **Dumra** Gujarat India
435 G2 **Dumshaf Abyssal Plain** *underwater feature* Norwegian Sea
302 E1 **Dumyāṭ** Egypt
245 D3 **Dún Gar** Ireland
245 F3 **Dún Laoghaire** Ireland
228 F3 **Dun-le-Palestel** France
228 F3 **Dun-sur-Auron** France
234 B1 **Dunajec** *watercourse* Poland
227 I4 **Dunajská Streda** Slovakia
244 D4 **Dunan** Perth and Kinross Scotland UK
245 F3 **Dunany** Ireland
242 B3 **Dunany Point** Ireland
227 J4 **Dunaújváros** Hungary
234 C4 **Dunavtsi** Bulgaria
237 Z4 **Dunay, Ostrova** *islands* Russian Federation
244 F4 **Dunbar** East Lothian Scotland UK
244 E2 **Dunbeath** Highland Scotland UK
245 F3 **Dunboyne** Ireland
245 F4 **Dunbur** Ireland
242 B3 **Dunbyrne** Ireland
118 J8 **Duncan** British Columbia Canada
129 H4 **Duncan** Arizona USA
130 C3 **Duncan** Oklahoma USA
131 J3 **Duncan** South Carolina USA
121 O6 **Duncan, Cape** Nunavut Canada
121 Q6 **Duncan, Lac** *lake* Québec Canada
376 B5 **Duncan Passage** *strait* Andaman and Nicobar Islands India
135 F2 **Duncan Town** Bahamas
244 F2 **Duncansby Head** *cape* Scotland UK
425 inset **Duncombe Bay** Norfolk Island Australia
245 F4 **Duncormick** Ireland
244 D4 **Duncroist** Stirling Scotland UK
385 H4 **Dundahaote** Nei Mongol Zizhiqu China
245 F2 **Dundalk** Ireland
242 B3 **Dundalk Bay** Ireland
424 G8 **Dundas, Lake** WA Australia
118 F5 **Dundas Island** British Columbia Canada
116 H4 **Dundas Peninsula** Northwest Territories Canada
308 F5 **Dundee** South Africa
244 F4 **Dundee** Dundee Scotland UK
244 F4 **Dundee** *admin. area* Scotland UK
126 J6 **Dundee** Michigan USA
436 U2 **Dundee Island** Antarctica
384 F3 **Dundgovi** *admin. area* Mongolia
306 C5 **Dundo** Angola
244 E6 **Dundrennan** Dumfries and Galloway Scotland UK
242 B2 **Dundrod** Antrim Northern Ireland UK
242 C2 **Dundrum** Down Northern Ireland UK
242 C2 **Dundrum Bay** Northern Ireland UK
119 R7 **Dundurn** Saskatchewan Canada
244 F3 **Dunecht** Aberdeenshire Scotland UK
423 D7 **Dunedin** New Zealand
425 N8 **Dunedoo** NSW Australia
245 D5 **Duneen** Ireland
389 M4 **Dunenbay** Kazakhstan
228 E4 **Dunes** France
124 C5 **Dunes City** Oregon USA
245 E1 **Dunfanaghy** Ireland
244 E4 **Dunfermline** Fife Scotland UK
242 B2 **Dungannon** Dungannon Northern Ireland UK
245 E2 **Dungannon** *admin. area* Northern Ireland UK
392 D5 **Dungargarh** Rajasthan India
301 H6 **Dungas** Niger
241 H4 **Dungeness** *cape* England UK
242 B2 **Dungiven** Londonderry Northern Ireland UK
245 D2 **Dunglow** Ireland
242 B2 **Dungooly** Ireland
306 D3 **Dungu** Democratic Republic of Congo
374 D2 **Dungun** Malaysia
243 H3 **Dunholme** Lincolnshire England UK
381 G3 **Dunhou** Jiangxi China
385 K4 **Dunhua** Jilin China
383 J5 **Dunhuang** Gansu China
425 N6 **Dunkeld** Qld Australia
244 E4 **Dunkeld** Perth and Kinross Scotland UK
129 J4 **Dunken** New Mexico USA
226 B2 **Dunkerque** France
127 L5 **Dunkirk** New York USA
126 J6 **Dunkirk** Ohio USA
125 R6 **Dunlap** Iowa USA
245 F3 **Dunlavin** Ireland
245 F3 **Dunleer** Ireland
241 F3 **Dunley** Hampshire England UK
119 V5 **Dunlop** Manitoba Canada
245 D5 **Dunmanus Bay** Ireland
245 C5 **Dunmanway** Ireland
425 J4 **Dunmarra** NT Australia
245 D3 **Dunmore** Ireland
242 B2 **Dunmore** Cookstown Northern Ireland UK
242 C2 **Dunmore** Down Northern Ireland UK
245 F4 **Dunmore East** Ireland
134 E1 **Dunmore Town** Bahamas
242 A2 **Dunmoyle** Omagh Northern Ireland UK
242 B2 **Dunmurry** Lisburn Northern Ireland UK
125 N3 **Dunn Center** North Dakota USA
244 E2 **Dunnet Bay** Scotland UK
244 E2 **Dunnet Head** *cape* Scotland UK
128 B1 **Dunnigan** California USA
244 E4 **Dunning** Perth and Kinross Scotland UK
125 O6 **Dunning** Nebraska USA
163 7 **Dunnose Head** Falkland Islands
127 L5 **Dunnville** Ontario Canada
244 D5 **Dunoon** Argyll and Bute Scotland UK
122 E4 **Dunphy, Lac** *lake* Québec Canada
244 D6 **Dunragit** Dumfries and Galloway Scotland UK
244 F5 **Duns** Scottish Borders Scotland UK
125 O2 **Dunseith** North Dakota USA
118 I8 **Dunsmuir** British Columbia Canada
124 D6 **Dunsmuir** California USA
241 G3 **Dunstable** Bedfordshire England UK
243 G1 **Dunstan** Northumberland England UK
423 C7 **Dunstan Mountains** New Zealand
240 D3 **Dunster** Somerset England UK
244 B3 **Duntulm** Highland Scotland UK
225 M4 **Dūņu ezers** *lake* Latvia
244 B3 **Dunvegan, Loch** *bay* Scotland UK
244 B3 **Dunvegan Head** *cape* Scotland UK
242 A2 **Dunwish** Omagh Northern Ireland UK
391 L3 **Dunyapur** Pakistan
385 H4 **Duolun** Nei Mongol Zizhiqu China
376 E2 **Duong** *watercourse* Vietnam
376 D5 **Dương Đông** Vietnam
122 B4 **Dupire, Lac** *lake* Québec Canada
234 C4 **Dupnitsa** Bulgaria
125 O4 **Dupree** South Dakota USA
127 L2 **Dupuy** Québec Canada
157 D8 **Duque de Caxias** Brazil
163 10a **Duquesne Bay** Grenada
424 H4 **Durack** *watercourse* WA Australia
394 G6 **Duraklı** Turkey
229 G5 **Durance** *watercourse* France
128 E4 **Durango** Mexico
132 D3 **Durango** Mexico
132 D3 **Durango** *admin. area* Mexico
228 C5 **Durango** Spain
125 L8 **Durango** Colorado USA
154 C3 **Durania** Colombia
234 F4 **Durankulashko Ezero** *lake* Bulgaria
160 F6 **Durañona** Argentina
130 C4 **Durant** Oklahoma USA
228 E4 **Duras** France
161 G5 **Durazno** Uruguay
161 H5 **Durazno** *admin. area* Uruguay
119 U7 **Durban** Manitoba Canada
309 F5 **Durban** South Africa
229 G1 **Durbuy** Belgium
242 F2 **Durdar** Cumbria England UK
232 H4 **Đurđenovac** Croatia
307 I2 **Durdura, Raas** *cape* Somalia
227 K2 **Durdy** Poland
393 E7 **Durg** Chhattisgarh India
392 G6 **Durgapur** West Bengal India
243 G2 **Durham** Durham England UK
243 G2 **Durham** *admin. area* England UK
129 N1 **Durham** Kansas USA
131 L3 **Durham** North Carolina USA
423 6 **Durham, Point** Chatham Islands New Zealand
374 D3 **Duri** Indonesia
375 F4 **Duriansebatang** Indonesia
244 E5 **Durisdeer** Dumfries and Galloway Scotland UK
244 D2 **Durness** Highland Scotland UK
227 I3 **Dürnkrut** Austria
121 Q2 **Durouvray** *watercourse* Québec Canada
235 A5 **Durrës** Albania
235 A5 **Durrësit, Gjiri i** *bay* Albania
245 E4 **Durrow** Ireland
245 B5 **Dursey Island** Ireland
240 E3 **Dursley** Gloucestershire England UK
380 E3 **Duru** Guizhou China
235 F5 **Duru Göl** *lake* Turkey
307 H2 **Durukhsi** Somalia
235 F5 **Durusu** Turkey
383 J3 **Durveljin** Mongolia
372 F4 **d'Urville, Tanjung** *cape* Indonesia
436 U2 **D'Urville Island** Antarctica
423 E5 **D'Urville Island** New Zealand
126 H1 **Dusey** *watercourse* Ontario Canada
380 E3 **Dushan** Guizhou China
389 J6 **Dushanbe** Tajikistan
225 L5 **Dusia** *lake* Lithuania
423 B7 **Dusky Sound** New Zealand
385 M2 **Dusse-Alin', Khrebet** *range* Russian Federation
424 I3 **Dussejour, Cape** WA Australia
229 H1 **Düsseldorf** Germany
118 B2 **Dusty** *watercourse* Yukon Territory Canada
389 J6 **Dŭsty** Tajikistan
374 D4 **Dusunmudo** Indonesia
244 E3 **Duthil** Highland Scotland UK
305 F2 **Dutse** Nigeria
305 F2 **Dutsin Ma** Nigeria
425 L5 **Dutton** *watercourse* Qld Australia
124 J3 **Dutton** Montana USA
383 I3 **Duut** Mongolia
119 S7 **Duval** Saskatchewan Canada
122 B4 **Duvert, Lac** *lake* Québec Canada
245 B2 **Duvillaun More** *island* Ireland
121 Q6 **Duxbury, Lac** *lake* Québec Canada
425 L3 **Duyfken Point** Qld Australia
380 E3 **Duyun** Guizhou China
235 G6 **Düzağaç** Turkey
394 D5 **Düzce** *admin. area* Turkey
223 U4 **Dvinskaya Guba** *bay* Russian Federation
225 M5 **Dviragio ežeras** *lake* Lithuania
232 H3 **Dvory nad Žitavou** Slovakia
307 G3 **Dwaa** *watercourse* Ethiopia
309 F2 **Dwangwa** Malawi
393 B6 **Dwarka** Gujarat India
308 E4 **Dwarsberg** South Africa
424 F8 **Dwellingup** WA Australia
126 G6 **Dwight** Illinois USA
129 N1 **Dwight** Kansas USA
124 G3 **Dworshak Reservoir** Idaho USA
234 E1 **D'yakovtsy** Ukraine
304 E3 **Dyan** *watercourse* Nigeria
242 B2 **Dyan** Dungannon Northern Ireland UK
238 F6 **Dyat'kovo** Russian Federation
162 A4 **Dyer, Cabo** *cape* Chile
117 M5 **Dyer, Cape** Nunavut Canada
127 K4 **Dyer Bay** Ontario Canada
130 G2 **Dyersburg** Tennessee USA
240 C2 **Dyffryn** Gwynedd Wales UK
240 D2 **Dyffryn-Castell** Ceredigion Wales UK
240 D2 **Dyfi** *watercourse* Wales UK
237 AB7 **Dygdy-Sise, Khrebet** *range* Russian Federation
224 H5 **Dygowo** Poland
388 D5 **Dyhtau, Gora** *mountain* Russian Federation
227 I3 **Dyje** *watercourse* Czech Republic
244 F4 **Dykehead** Angus Scotland UK
227 M3 **Dykhtinets** Ukraine
227 K1 **Dylewo** Poland
227 J1 **Dylewska Góra** *mountain* Poland
240 D2 **Dylife** Powys Wales UK
241 H3 **Dymchurch** Kent England UK
126 E2 **Dyment** Ontario Canada
238 E3 **Dymi** Russian Federation
234 G1 **Dymino** Ukraine
225 O2 **Dymovo** Russian Federation
222 inset **Dyrhólaey** *cape* Iceland
222 E5 **Dyrnes** Norway
222 J2 **Dyrøya** *island* Norway
222 J2 **Dyrøyhamn** Norway
425 N5 **Dysart** Qld Australia
245 E3 **Dysart** Ireland
225 N5 **Dysna** *watercourse* Belarus
225 N5 **Dysnų ežeras** *lake* Lithuania
225 N5 **Dysnykščio ežeras** *lake* Belarus
235 B6 **Dytiki Ellada** *admin. area* Greece
235 B5 **Dytiki Makedonia** *admin. area* Greece
237 U5 **Dyupkun, Ozero** *lake* Russian Federation
234 F3 **Dyviziya** Ukraine
384 G4 **Dzamïn Üüd** Mongolia
391 K3 **Dzangali** Afghanistan
310 8b **Dzaoudzi** Mayotte
383 J3 **Dzavhan** *admin. area* Mongolia
388 D2 **Dzerzhinsk** Russian Federation
237 AB8 **Dzhagdy, Khrebet** *range* Russian Federation
385 M2 **Dzhaki-Unakhta Yakbyyana, Khrebet** *range* Russian Federation
237 Z8 **Dzhalinda** Russian Federation
237 Z5 **Dzhardzhan** Russian Federation
384 E2 **Dzhida** *watercourse* Russian Federation
237 AG6 **Dzhigudzhak** Russian Federation
Dzhizak *see* **Jizzax** Uzbekistan
237 AC7 **Dzhugdzhur, Khrebet** *range* Russian Federation
389 M4 **Dzhungarskiy Alatau, Khrebet** *range* Kazakhstan
388 I4 **Dzhusaly** Kazakhstan
388 J6 **Dzhush** Uzbekistan
227 K1 **Działdowo** Poland
227 J2 **Działoszyn** Poland
227 K1 **Dzierzgowo** Poland
133 H4 **Dzilam de Bravo** Mexico
133 H4 **Dzilam González** Mexico
225 N5 **Dzisna** *watercourse* Belarus
133 H4 **Dzitás** Mexico
133 H4 **Dzitbalché** Mexico
225 N5 **Dzjaniski** Belarus
133 H5 **Dzuiché** Mexico
382 G3 **Dzungarian Gate** *pass* Xinjiang Uygur Zizhiqu China
384 D2 **Dzuun Nuur** *lake* Mongolia

E

132 E2 **E. V. Spence Reservoir** Texas USA
120 L7 **Eabamet Lake** Ontario Canada
125 N7 **Eads** Colorado USA
126 E4 **Eagan** Minnesota USA
129 H3 **Eagar** Arizona USA
122 I6 **Eagle** *watercourse* Newfoundland and Labrador Canada
125 L7 **Eagle** Colorado USA
125 Q6 **Eagle** Nebraska USA
163 1a **Eagle Beach** *bay* Aruba
125 O4 **Eagle Butte** South Dakota USA
119 R7 **Eagle Creek** Saskatchewan Canada
120 F6 **Eagle Island** Manitoba Canada
126 E6 **Eagle Lake** Ontario Canada
128 E1 **Eagle Lake** California USA
130 C6 **Eagle Lake** Texas USA
129 J2 **Eagle Nest** New Mexico USA
129 J2 **Eagle Nest Reservoir** New Mexico USA
129 L6 **Eagle Pass** Texas USA
163 7 **Eagle Passage** *strait* Falkland Islands
116 F5 **Eagle Plain** Yukon Territory Canada
124 D5 **Eagle Point** Oregon USA
126 G3 **Eagle River** Michigan USA
126 G4 **Eagle River** Wisconsin USA
243 F3 **Earby** Lancashire England UK
120 G6 **Eardley Lake** Manitoba Canada
241 H2 **Earith** Cambridgeshire England UK
423 B7 **Earl Mountains** New Zealand
241 F2 **Earl Shilton** Leicester England UK
128 C3 **Earlimart** California USA
244 F5 **Earlston** Scottish Borders Scotland UK
123 G10 **Earltown** Nova Scotia Canada
130 B5 **Early** Texas USA

244 E4 **Earn** *watercourse* Scotland UK
244 D4 **Earn, Loch** *lake* Scotland UK
423 C7 **Earnslaw, Mount** New Zealand
129 K3 **Earth** Texas USA
243 G2 **Easby** North Yorkshire England UK
244 C4 **Easdale** Argyll and Bute Scotland UK
243 G2 **Easington** Durham England UK
243 I3 **Easington** East Riding of Yorkshire England UK
245 D2 **Easky** Ireland
131 J3 **Easley** South Carolina USA
425 J3 **East Alligator** *watercourse* NT Australia
437 D1 **East Antarctica** *region* Antarctica
131 L3 **East Arcadia** North Carolina USA
244 D5 **East Ayrshire** *admin. area* Scotland UK
131 I5 **East Bay** Florida USA
130 G6 **East Bay** Louisiana USA
155 G4 **East Berbice-Corentyne** *admin. area* Guyana
126 E4 **East Bethel** Minnesota USA
130 H5 **East Brewton** Alabama USA
135 G2 **East Caicos** *island* Turks and Caicos Islands
422 H3 **East Cape** New Zealand
241 I2 **East Carleton** Norfolk England UK
78 K7 **East Caroline Basin** *underwater feature* Pacific Ocean
381 J2 **East China Sea** Asia
244 E2 **East Clyne** Highland Scotland UK
241 F4 **East Cowes** Isle of Wight England UK
244 D5 **East Dunbartonshire** *admin. area* Scotland UK
307 E2 **East Equatoria** *admin. area* Sudan
116 E5 **East Fork Chandalar** *watercourse* Alaska USA
241 G3 **East Grinstead** West Sussex England UK
423 I0 **East Group** *island* Bounty Islands New Zealand
243 G2 **East Harlsey** North Yorkshire England UK
124 J3 **East Helena** Montana USA
243 H2 **East Heslerton** North Yorkshire England UK
240 E3 **East Huntspill** Somerset England UK
240 D3 **East Ilkerton** Devon England UK
81 N7 **East Indiaman Ridge** *underwater feature* Indian Ocean
373 J6 **East Island** Papua New Guinea
424 inset **East Islet** Ashmore Reef and Cartier Island Australia
241 F3 **East Kennet** Wiltshire England UK
243 G3 **East Keswick** West Yorkshire England UK
244 D5 **East Kilbride** South Lanarkshire Scotland UK
120 I6 **East Lake** Ontario Canada
131 K6 **East Lake Tohopekaliga** Florida USA
126 I5 **East Lansing** Michigan USA
244 F5 **East Linton** East Lothian Scotland UK
127 K6 **East Liverpool** West Virginia USA
244 B3 **East Loch Tarbert** *bay* Scotland UK
308 E6 **East London** South Africa
240 C4 **East Looe** Cornwall England UK
244 F5 **East Lothian** *admin. area* Scotland UK
241 G4 **East Marden** West Sussex England UK
78 L6 **East Mariana Basin** *underwater feature* Pacific Ocean
130 D6 **East Matagorda Bay** Texas USA
126 F6 **East Moline** Illinois USA
243 H3 **East Newton** East Riding of Yorkshire England UK
79 U10 **East Pacific Rise** *underwater feature* Pacific Ocean
120 K4 **East Pen Island** Nunavut Canada
123 I10 **East Point** Nova Scotia Canada
123 H9 **East Point** Prince Edward Island Canada
310 5c **East Point** *cape* St Helena
244 D5 **East Renfrewshire** *admin. area* Scotland UK
131 I3 **East Ridge** Tennessee USA
243 H3 **East Riding of Yorkshire** *admin. area* England UK
127 K8 **East River Mountain** Virginia USA
East Sea *see* **Japan, Sea of**
120 G7 **East Selkirk** Manitoba Canada
237 AI4 **East Siberian Sea** Russian Federation
241 H4 **East Sussex** *admin. area* England UK
81 T9 **East Tasman Plateau** *underwater feature* Tasman Sea
128 H1 **East Tavaputs Plateau** Utah USA
East Timor *see* **Timor-Leste**
245 D1 **East Town** Ireland
241 H4 **Eastbourne** East Sussex England UK
119 Q8 **Eastend** Saskatchewan Canada
244 D3 **Easter Drummond** Highland Scotland UK
79 U10 **Easter Fracture Zone** *underwater feature* Pacific Ocean
Easter Island *see* **Isla de Pascua**
307 F3 **Eastern** *admin. area* Kenya
308 E6 **Eastern Cape** *admin. area* South Africa
Eastern Desert *see* **Aş Şaḩrā' Ash Sharqīyah** Egypt
123 G10 **Eastern Passage** Nova Scotia Canada
119 V6 **Easterville** Manitoba Canada
128 D1 **Eastgate** Nevada USA
130 B4 **Eastland** Texas USA
241 F4 **Eastleigh** Hampshire England UK
117 L8 **Eastmain** *watercourse* Québec Canada
240 E4 **Easton** Dorset England UK
127 M7 **Easton** Maryland USA
128 H3 **Eastport** Idaho USA
127 R4 **Eastport** Maine USA
244 E6 **Eastriggs** Dumfries and Galloway Scotland UK
125 M6 **Eaton** Colorado USA
240 E2 **Eaton upon Tern** Shropshire England UK
131 J4 **Eatonton** Georgia USA
124 D3 **Eatonville** Washington USA
155 H4 **Eau Claire** French Guiana
126 F4 **Eau Claire** Wisconsin USA
117 L7 **Eau Claire, Lac à l'** *lake* Québec Canada
127 N2 **Eau-Jaune, Lac à l'** *lake* Québec Canada
373 G2 **Eauripik** *island* Federated States of Micronesia
81 S4 **Eauripik Atoll** *reef* Caroline Islands
81 S4 **Eauripik Rise** *underwater feature* Pacific Ocean
228 E5 **Eauze** France
373 G7 **Ebagoola** Qld Australia
305 E3 **Eban** Nigeria
308 B2 **Ebanga** Angola
306 C4 **Ebangalakata** Democratic Republic of Congo
233 C9 **Ebba Ksoui** Tunisia
226 G4 **Ebbs** Austria
118 J1 **Ebbutt Hills** Northwest Territories Canada
240 D3 **Ebbw Vale** Blaenau Gwent Wales UK
237 AD6 **Ebe** Russian Federation
305 G4 **Ebebiyin** Equatorial Guinea
227 G4 **Ebene Reichenau** Austria
227 I4 **Ebenfurth** Austria
127 L6 **Ebensburg** Pennsylvania USA
229 J1 **Ebern** Germany
232 F3 **Eberndorf** Austria
227 G1 **Eberswalde** Germany
229 I3 **Ebikon** Switzerland
382 G4 **Ebinur Hu** *lake* Xinjiang Uygur Zizhiqu China
306 C3 **Ebola** *watercourse* Democratic Republic of Congo
233 F6 **Eboli** Italy
305 G4 **Ebolowa** Cameroon
427 I5 **Ebon Atoll** Marshall Islands
306 C3 **Ebonda** Democratic Republic of Congo
305 F3 **Ebonyi** *admin. area* Nigeria
229 J2 **Ebrach** Germany
231 F3 **Ebro** *watercourse* Spain
230 E2 **Ebro, Embalse del** *lake* Spain
229 I1 **Ebsdorf** Germany
237 AF5 **Ebyakh** Russian Federation
244 E5 **Ecclefechan** Dumfries and Galloway Scotland UK
240 E2 **Eccleshall** Staffordshire England UK
163 9 **Ecclesville** Trinidad and Tobago
124 F4 **Echo** Oregon USA
120 J5 **Echoing** *watercourse* Manitoba Canada
120 I5 **Echoing Lake** Ontario Canada
244 F3 **Echt** Aberdeenshire Scotland UK
425 M9 **Echuca** Vic. Australia
230 D5 **Écija** Spain
225 J2 **Eckerö** *island* Finland
122 F3 **Eclipse Harbour** Newfoundland and Labrador Canada
117 L4 **Eclipse Sound** Nunavut Canada
228 E3 **Écommoy** France
157 D7 **Ecoporanga** Brazil
127 M3 **Écorces, Lac aux** *lake* Québec Canada
229 G2 **Écrouves** France
130 G3 **Ecru** Mississippi USA
227 I4 **Écs** Hungary
234 A2 **Ecséd** Hungary
234 B2 **Ecsegfalva** Hungary
154 B5 **Ecuador** *country* South America
228 E3 **Écueillé** France
121 Q3 **Écueils, Pointe aux** *cape* Québec Canada
303 G5 **Ed** Eritrea
302 D5 **Ed Da'ein** Sudan
390 C2 **Ed Daher** Lebanon
302 E5 **Ed Damazin** Sudan
302 E4 **Ed Damer** Sudan
302 D4 **Ed Dueim** Sudan
243 G3 **Edale** Derbyshire England UK
244 F1 **Eday** *island* Scotland UK
244 C2 **Eddrachillis Bay** Scotland UK
118 K6 **Eddy** British Columbia Canada
126 G8 **Eddyville** Kentucky USA
226 C1 **Ede** Netherlands
222 J5 **Ede** Sweden
305 G4 **Edéa** Cameroon
305 E3 **Edebo** Sweden
225 J2 **Edebo** Sweden
222 L3 **Edefors** Sweden
120 G2 **Edehon Lake** Nunavut Canada
157 B7 **Edéia** Brazil
161 H3 **Edelira** Paraguay
425 N9 **Eden** NSW Australia
242 F2 **Eden** *watercourse* England UK
130 B5 **Eden** Texas USA
119 U4 **Eden Lake** Manitoba Canada
126 E4 **Eden Prairie** Minnesota USA
125 K5 **Eden Reservoir** Wyoming USA
241 H3 **Edenbridge** Kent England UK
423 C8 **Edendale** New Zealand
245 E3 **Edenderry** Ireland
119 S7 **Edenwold** Saskatchewan Canada
226 E2 **Eder** *watercourse* Germany
373 F5 **Edera** *watercourse* Indonesia
235 C5 **Edessa** Greece
222 H5 **Edevik** Sweden
130 C6 **Edgar** Texas USA
125 P3 **Edgeley** North Dakota USA
122 F2 **Edgell Island** Nunavut Canada
125 N5 **Edgemont** South Dakota USA
236 F3 **Edgeøya** *island* Norway
129 O1 **Edgerton** Kansas USA
125 Q5 **Edgerton** Minnesota USA
125 L5 **Edgerton** Wyoming USA
119 M7 **Edgewater** British Columbia Canada
126 G7 **Edgewood** Illinois USA
127 K6 **Edinboro** Pennsylvania USA
125 Q2 **Edinburg** North Dakota USA
130 B7 **Edinburg** Texas USA
310 5c **Edinburgh** St Helena
244 E5 **Edinburgh** City of Edinburgh Scotland UK
235 E5 **Edincik** Turkey
234 E1 **Edineţ** Moldova
309 F2 **Edingeni** Malawi
394 C5 **Edirne** *admin. area* Turkey
128 C3 **Edison** California USA
131 K4 **Edisto** *watercourse* South Carolina USA
425 K8 **Edithburgh** SA Australia
243 G1 **Edlingham** Northumberland England UK
130 C3 **Edmond** Oklahoma USA
129 L3 **Edmonson** Texas USA
119 O6 **Edmonton** Alberta Canada
125 P2 **Edmore** North Dakota USA
120 I5 **Edmund Lake** Manitoba Canada
123 D9 **Edmundston** New Brunswick Canada
130 D2 **Edna** Kansas USA
130 C6 **Edna** Texas USA
305 F3 **Edo** *admin. area* Nigeria
233 F6 **Edolo** Italy
235 E6 **Edremit** Turkey
235 E6 **Edremit Körfezi** *bay* Turkey
383 J4 **Edrengiyn Nuruu** Mongolia
119 M6 **Edson** Alberta Canada
160 E5 **Eduardo Castex** Argentina
306 D4 **Edward, Lake** Democratic Republic of Congo
436 T1 **Edward, Mount** Antarctica
436 N1 **Edward VII Peninsula** Antarctica
437 D2 **Edward VIII Bay** Antarctica
132 E2 **Edwards Plateau** Texas USA
242 A2 **Edymore** Strabane Northern Ireland UK
124 D7 **Eel** *watercourse* California USA
308 C3 **Eenhana** Namibia
426 7 **Éfaté** *island* Vanuatu
126 G7 **Effingham** Illinois USA
130 D7 **Effingham** Kansas USA
234 F3 **Eforie** Romania
230 F2 **Ega** *watercourse* Spain
128 E1 **Egan Range** Nevada USA
305 F3 **Egbe** Nigeria
224 I4 **Egby** Sweden
226 G2 **Eger** *watercourse* Germany
234 B2 **Eger** Hungary
80 K7 **Egeria Fracture Zone** *underwater feature* Indian Ocean
424 inset **Egeria Point** Christmas Island Australia
372 D6 **Egeron, Selat** *strait* Indonesia
227 I4 **Egervár** Hungary
222 L2 **Egga** Norway
222 K3 **Eggelats** *lake* Sweden
222 G5 **Eggen** Norway
229 K2 **Eggenfelden** Germany
240 D4 **Eggesford** Devon England UK
244 F1 **Egilsay** *island* Scotland UK
222 inset **Egilsstaðir** Iceland
235 F7 **Eğirdir** Turkey
235 G6 **Eğirdir Gölü** *lake* Turkey
384 E2 **Egiyn Gol** *watercourse* Mongolia
384 I3 **Egizkaratau** *mountain* Kazakhstan
225 N5 **Eglaine** Latvia
228 F4 **Égletons** France
423 B7 **Eglinton** *watercourse* New Zealand
116 H3 **Eglinton Island** Northwest Territories Canada
242 B2 **Eglish** Dungannon Northern Ireland UK
240 D2 **Eglwys Fach** Ceredigion Wales UK
Egmont, Mount *see* **Taranaki, Mount** New Zealand
123 F9 **Egmont Bay** Prince Edward Island Canada
242 E2 **Egremont** Cumbria England UK
226 B3 **Égreville** France
228 E3 **Éguzon** France
237 AL5 **Egvekinot** Russian Federation
302 D2 **Egypt** *country* Africa
226 E3 **Ehingen** Germany
124 F2 **Eholt** British Columbia Canada
131 K4 **Ehrhardt** South Carolina USA
427 I4 **Eiao** *island* French Polynesia
224 D3 **Eiavatn** *lake* Norway
228 C5 **Eibar** Spain
226 F2 **Eichsfeld** *region* Germany
226 F3 **Eichstätt** Germany
79 S3 **Eickelberg Seamount** *underwater feature* Pacific Ocean
222 E5 **Eide** Norway
224 E5 **Eider** *watercourse* Germany
224 E5 **Eiderstedt** *peninsula* Germany
222 F5 **Eidet** Norway
222 I3 **Eidet** Norway
222 E5 **Eidsdal** Norway
222 I2 **Eidsfjord** Norway
224 E1 **Eidsvåg** Norway
222 G4 **Eidsvatnet** *lake* Norway
425 N6 **Eidsvold** Qld Australia
302 E4 **Eidukal, Wādī** *watercourse* Sudan
224 C3 **Eigerøya** *island* Norway
244 B4 **Eigg** *island* Scotland UK
393 C10 **Eight Degree Channel** Maldives
245 C2 **Eighter** Ireland
436 R2 **Eights Coast** Antarctica
424 G4 **Eighty Mile Beach** WA Australia
302 F4 **Eigrim, Jebel** *mountain* Sudan
224 C2 **Eikefjord** Norway
224 E1 **Eikesdalsvatnet** *lake* Norway
244 E3 **Eil** Highland Scotland UK
372 E2 **Eil Malk** *island* Palau
226 G2 **Eilenburg** Germany
155 G4 **Eilerts de Haan Gebergte** *range* Suriname
226 F1 **Eimke** Germany
224 F2 **Eina** Norway
425 M4 **Einasleigh** Qld Australia
425 L4 **Einasleigh** *watercourse* Qld Australia
224 F2 **Einavatnet** *lake* Norway
226 C2 **Eindhoven** Netherlands
376 B3 **Einme** Myanmar
435 D3 **Eirik Ridge** *underwater feature* Atlantic Ocean
158 D2 **Eirunepé** Brazil
229 G2 **Eischen** Luxembourg
308 D3 **Eiseb** *watercourse* Botswana
308 C4 **Eiseb** *watercourse* Namibia
229 J1 **Eisenach** Germany
227 H4 **Eisenerz** Austria
124 H1 **Eisenhower Junction** Alberta Canada
229 L3 **Eisenkappel** Austria
227 I4 **Eisenstadt** Austria
226 F2 **Eisfeld** Germany
229 L2 **Eisgarn** Austria
225 M5 **Eišiškės** Lithuania
229 J1 **Eisleben** Germany
223 E3 **Eislingen** Germany
426 1b **Eita** Kiribati
222 H4 **Eiterstraum** Norway
226 D2 **Eitorf** Germany
231 G4 **Eivissa (Ibiza)** *island* Spain
224 G5 **Ejby** Denmark
231 F2 **Ejea de los Caballeros** Spain
309 H4 **Ejeda** Madagascar
222 H5 **Ejheden** Sweden
154 D2 **Ejido** Venezuela
129 I5 **Ejido de Enriquez** Mexico
132 D2 **Ejido de Majalca** Mexico
132 D2 **Ejido El Cuervo** Mexico
128 G5 **Ejido La Cebolla** Mexico
132 D3 **Ejido La Luz** Mexico
132 B3 **Ejido Naco** Mexico
129 I5 **Ejido Rancho Nuevo** Mexico
225 E5 **Ejstrupholm** Denmark
304 D3 **Ejura** Ghana
133 F5 **Ejutla** Mexico
125 M4 **Ekalaka** Montana USA
237 AF9 **Ekarma, Ostrov** *island* Russian Federation
305 G4 **Ékata** Gabon
224 G3 **Ekenäs** Sweden
384 E5 **E'kenhuduge** Nei Mongol Zizhiqu China
388 G6 **Ekerem** Turkmenistan
423 F5 **Eketahuna** New Zealand
162 C5 **Ekewern** Chile
223 M3 **Ekfors** Sweden
237 AK5 **Ekiatapskiy Khrebet** *range* Russian Federation
389 L3 **Ekibastuz** Kazakhstan
305 F3 **Ekiti** *admin. area* Nigeria
225 L2 **Eknäs** Finland
224 I4 **Eknö** *island* Sweden
305 F3 **Ekok** Cameroon
306 C4 **Ekoli** Democratic Republic of Congo
237 W5 **Ekonda** Russian Federation
305 G4 **Ekouamou** Congo
305 F3 **Ekpoma** Nigeria
308 D5 **Eksteenfontein** South Africa
436 X2 **Ekström Ice Shelf** Antarctica
222 K4 **Ekträsk** Sweden
305 E3 **Eku** *watercourse* Nigeria
306 B4 **Ekukola** Democratic Republic of Congo
306 C4 **Ekuku** Democratic Republic of Congo
306 C4 **Ekumakoko** Democratic Republic of Congo
117 K8 **Ekwan** *watercourse* Ontario Canada
121 N6 **Ekwan Point** Ontario Canada
160 D6 **El Abanico** Chile
301 G2 **El Abiodh Sidi Cheikh** Algeria
160 E3 **El Águila** Mexico
155 F3 **El Alambre** Venezuela
132 D2 **El Álamo** Mexico
301 H2 **El Alia** Algeria
132 E3 **El Alicante** Mexico
158 A2 **El Alto** Peru
154 B4 **El Ángel** Ecuador
231 I5 **El Aouana** Algeria
301 H1 **El Aouinet** Algeria
162 B2 **El Arco** Chile
132 B2 **El Arco** Mexico
301 F1 **El Aricha** Algeria
301 H1 **El Arrouch** Algeria
154 B4 **El Aticito** Colombia
134 C4 **El Ayote** Nicaragua
130 B7 **El Azúca** Mexico
154 C3 **El Bagre** Colombia
132 D3 **El Bajío Grande** Mexico
154 C2 **El Banco** Colombia
230 D3 **El Barco de Ávila** Spain
130 B8 **El Barranco** Mexico
128 F6 **El Barril** Mexico
301 E5 **El Barun** Sudan
302 E4 **El Bauga** Sudan
301 G2 **El Bayadh** Algeria
154 C4 **El Billar** Colombia
230 D6 **El Bioutz** Morocco
162 B3 **El Blanco** Chile
230 E4 **El Bonillo** Spain
231 G6 **El Bordj** Algeria
154 B4 **El Bordo** Colombia
301 H2 **El Borma** Algeria
230 D6 **El Brayach** Morocco
132 B3 **El Bule** Mexico
230 E3 **El Burgo de Osma** Spain
162 C2 **El Caín** Argentina
128 D4 **El Cajon** California USA
162 B5 **El Calafate** Argentina
154 D2 **El Camaral** Venezuela
130 C6 **El Campo** Texas USA
132 D3 **El Canelo** Mexico
132 C3 **El Cantil** Mexico
154 D3 **El Capricho** Colombia
155 F2 **El Cardón** Venezuela
159 F4 **El Carmen** Bolivia
128 F5 **El Carrizal** Mexico
132 D3 **El Carrizo** Mexico
230 E3 **El Casar** Spain
154 B5 **El Castañán** *range* Ecuador
134 C5 **El Castillo de La Concepción** Nicaragua
158 A1 **El Caucho** Peru
154 C4 **El Cayman** Colombia
130 B7 **El Cenizo** Texas USA
128 E4 **El Centro** California USA
162 B4 **El Chaltén** Argentina
132 B2 **El Chinero** Mexico
160 D6 **El Chinque** Argentina
162 C4 **El Chonque** Argentina
155 E2 **El Chorro** Venezuela
154 D2 **El Chuco** Venezuela
132 D2 **El Cielo** Mexico
132 B2 **El Cinco** Mexico
154 C3 **El Cocuy** Colombia
132 D5 **El Colomo** Mexico
132 D3 **El Colorado** Mexico
159 E4 **El Combate** Bolivia
162 C5 **El Cóndor** Argentina
132 D3 **El Consuelo** Mexico
134 D5 **El Copé** Panama
154 C2 **El Copey** Colombia
154 E2 **El Corozo** Venezuela
134 D5 **El Cortezo** Panama
130 B8 **El Coyote** Mexico
162 B3 **El Coyte** Argentina
129 I5 **El Cuarenta** Mexico
230 D3 **El Cubo de Tierra del Vino** Spain
129 J6 **El Cuerva, Laguna** *bay* Mexico
132 D2 **El Cuervo** Mexico
154 D2 **El Cují** Venezuela
162 C2 **El Cuy** Argentina
132 B3 **El Datil, Estero** *lake* Mexico
128 D4 **El Descanso** Mexico
132 B2 **El Desemboque** Mexico
154 D2 **El Diario de Yaracuy** Venezuela
132 B2 **El Doctor** Mexico
154 C4 **El Doncello** Colombia
159 F5 **El Dorado** Bolivia
132 D3 **El Dorado** Mexico
130 E4 **El Dorado** Arkansas USA
125 Q8 **El Dorado** Kansas USA
126 C8 **El Dorado Lake** Kansas USA
130 B8 **El Encinal** Mexico
134 C4 **El Espino de Tepale** Honduras
134 B4 **El Estor** Guatemala
231 I5 **El Eulma** Algeria
301 H1 **El Fahs** Tunisia
155 F2 **El Fangal** Venezuela
301 H2 **El Faouar** Tunisia
162 A2 **El Farellón** *island* Chile
302 D5 **El Fasher** Sudan
132 D2 **El Fortín** Mexico
129 I6 **El Fresno** Mexico
307 G2 **El Fud** Ethiopia
132 C3 **El Fuerte** Mexico
302 D5 **El Fula** Sudan
132 B3 **El Gato, Estero** *lake* Mexico
130 B8 **El Gavilán** Mexico
302 E4 **El Geili** Sudan
302 C5 **El Geneina** Sudan
302 E5 **El Gezira** *admin. area* Sudan
162 B4 **El Ghio** Argentina
301 G2 **El Goléa** Algeria
128 E5 **El Golfo de Santa Clara** Mexico
231 G2 **El Grado, Embalse de** *lake* Spain
132 D5 **El Grullo** Mexico
154 C4 **El Guamo** Colombia
231 J5 **El Guerrah** Algeria
302 F5 **El Gulut** Ethiopia
301 H1 **El Hadjar** Algeria
300 E2 **El Hajeb** Morocco
301 H2 **El Hallail, Oued** *watercourse* Algeria
231 I6 **El Hamel** Algeria
301 H2 **El Hamma** Tunisia
233 D8 **El Haouaria** Tunisia
302 E5 **El Hawata** Sudan
302 B5 **El Hidjer** Chad
133 F4 **El Higo** Mexico
302 D5 **El-Hilla** Sudan
129 J6 **El Jabali** Mexico
129 K7 **El Jabali** Mexico
300 E2 **El Jadida** Morocco
132 D3 **El Jaralito** Mexico
302 E5 **El Jebelein** Sudan
301 I1 **El Jem** Tunisia
162 C3 **El Junco** Argentina
302 E4 **El Kab** Sudan
302 E4 **El Kadada** Sudan
301 H1 **El Kala** Algeria
302 E4 **El Kamlin** Sudan
231 I6 **El Kantara** Algeria
302 E5 **El Kawa** Sudan
300 E2 **El Kelaâ Srarhna** Morocco
307 G2 **El Kerē** Ethiopia
302 D5 **El Lagowa** Sudan
307 F3 **El Lēh** Ethiopia
133 I6 **El Llano** Honduras
132 D3 **El Llano** Mexico
133 F4 **El Llano** Mexico
233 C9 **El Ma el Abiod** Algeria
129 H6 **El Maderal** Mexico
231 J6 **El Mahder** Algeria
162 B3 **El Maitén** Argentina
154 D3 **El Mamón** Venezuela
302 E5 **El Managil** Sudan
301 F3 **El Mansour** Algeria
160 D6 **El Marucho** Argentina
132 E4 **El Matorral** Mexico
154 E4 **El Médano** Colombia
307 G2 **El Medo** Ethiopia
301 H2 **El Meghaïer** Algeria
302 E4 **El Metemma** Sudan
129 K7 **El Mezquite** Mexico
300 C5 **El Mhaïjrat** Mauritania
154 D3 **El Milagro** Venezuela
301 H1 **El Milia** Algeria
154 D4 **El Mirador** Colombia
129 I5 **El Mirador** Mexico
162 C3 **El Mirasol** Argentina
230 E3 **El Molar** Spain
154 C2 **El Molino** Colombia
132 B2 **El Molino** Mexico
128 C3 **El Monte** California USA
154 D2 **El Moral** Mexico
160 E5 **El Morro** *mountain* Argentina
128 H6 **El Novillo** Mexico
302 E5 **El Obeid** Sudan
302 D5 **El Odaiya** Sudan
160 E6 **El Odre** Argentina
130 B9 **El Ojital** Mexico
154 D4 **El Olvido** Colombia
158 B1 **El Oro** *admin. area* Ecuador
132 E3 **El Oro** Mexico
155 E3 **El Oso** Venezuela
301 H2 **El Oued** Algeria
231 I6 **El Outaya** Algeria
162 C3 **El Pajarito** Argentina
132 C3 **El Palmarito** Mexico
159 F4 **El Paraíso** Bolivia
134 C4 **El Paraíso** Honduras
154 C2 **El Paso** Colombia
129 I5 **El Paso** Texas USA
155 F2 **El Patillo** Venezuela
154 C4 **El Pato** Colombia
155 F3 **El Paují** Venezuela
154 C4 **El Paujil** Colombia
128 F4 **El Pedregal** Mexico
154 E4 **El Peligro** Venezuela
160 E3 **El Peñón** Argentina
160 D5 **El Peñón** *mountain* Chile
154 D3 **El Percal** Colombia
231 G3 **El Perelló** Spain
155 F3 **El Pilón** Brazil
129 J5 **El Pino** Mexico
160 F3 **El Pintado** Argentina
230 D4 **El Pintado, Embalse** *lake* Spain
158 A1 **El Plátano** Peru
132 B2 **El Plomo** Mexico
160 D5 **El Plomo, Nevado** *mountain* Chile
162 B4 **El Pluma** Argentina
155 E2 **El Polvero** Venezuela
228 F5 **El Port de la Selva** Spain
154 D3 **El Porvenir** Colombia
128 D4 **El Porvenir** Mexico
129 J5 **El Porvenir** Mexico
132 B3 **El Porvenir** Mexico
132 D2 **El Porvenir** Mexico
134 E5 **El Porvenir** Panama
159 G5 **El Potrero** Bolivia
132 D2 **El Povenir** Mexico
155 F3 **El Prado** Venezuela
134 C4 **El Progreso** Honduras
159 F5 **El Puente** Bolivia
132 B1 **El Puerto** Mexico
162 B3 **El Púlpito** Chile
160 F3 **El Quebrachal** Argentina
155 E2 **El Quebradón** Venezuela
162 C6 **El Quique** Argentina
129 N8 **El Rabón, Laguna** *lake* Mexico
132 D3 **El Ranchito** Mexico
133 I6 **El Rancho** Honduras
230 C5 **El Real de la Jara** Spain
134 E5 **El Real de Santa María** Panama
154 C5 **El Refugio** Colombia
129 L6 **El Remolino** Mexico
130 C3 **El Reno** Oklahoma USA
154 C4 **El Retorno** Colombia
132 E4 **El Retorno** Mexico
133 F3 **El Roble** Mexico
133 H5 **El Roble** Mexico
155 E2 **El Roble** Venezuela
134 C4 **El Rodeo** Honduras
154 A5 **El Rosario** Ecuador
132 D3 **El Rosario** Mexico
132 B2 **El Sacrificio** Mexico
132 B1 **El Sahuaro** Mexico
154 D2 **El Saladillo** Venezuela
162 C4 **El Salado** Argentina
132 D4 **El Salto** Mexico
162 B4 **El Saltón** Chile
134 B4 **El Salvador** *country* Central America
132 B2 **El Salvador** Mexico
132 E3 **El Salvador** Mexico
129 I5 **El Sancho** Mexico
128 G5 **El Sasabe** Mexico
134 C4 **El Sauce** Nicaragua
129 H7 **El Sauz** Mexico
130 B7 **El Sauz** Texas USA
132 A2 **El Sauzal** Mexico
129 K7 **El Socorro** Mexico
154 D2 **El Socorro** Venezuela
132 E3 **El Sol** Mexico
162 C3 **El Sombrero** Argentina
154 E2 **El Sombrero** Venezuela
160 D5 **El Sosneado** Argentina
132 C2 **El Tabacote** Mexico
154 B4 **El Tambo** Colombia
301 H1 **El Tarf** Algeria
301 H1 **El Tarf** *admin. area* Algeria
154 C2 **El Tarra** Colombia
231 H3 **El Ter** *watercourse* Spain
129 I6 **El Terrero** Mexico
132 C2 **El Tigre** Mexico
154 D2 **El Tigre** Venezuela
154 D2 **El Tocuyo** Venezuela
162 B5 **El Toro** Chile
128 F6 **El Toro** Mexico
162 B5 **El Turbio** Argentina
132 D2 **El Uno** Mexico
129 I2 **El Vado Reservoir** New Mexico USA
132 D4 **El Valle** *lake* Mexico
129 H6 **El Vallecito** Mexico
155 E2 **El Vasquero** Venezuela
129 J5 **El Veinticuatro** Mexico
231 G3 **El Vendrell** Spain
129 I7 **El Vergel** Mexico
230 E4 **El Vicario, Embalse de** *lake* Spain
134 C4 **El Viejo** Nicaragua
154 D2 **El Vigía** Venezuela
132 E3 **El Vinatero** Mexico
159 E6 **El Volcán** Bolivia
129 K6 **El Volcan** Mexico
307 G3 **El Wak** Kenya
302 E5 **El Wuz** Sudan
160 F2 **El Yacón** Argentina
163 6a **El Yunque** *volcano* Isla Róbinson Crusoe
132 E3 **El Zacate** Mexico
132 D2 **El Zoco** Mexico
154 C3 **El Zulia** Colombia
162 B5 **El Zurdo** Argentina
235 C7 **Elafonisos** *island* Greece
130 F3 **Elaine** Arkansas USA
423 E5 **Elaine Bay** New Zealand
223 N5 **Elämäjärvi** Finland
223 N5 **Elämäjärvi** *lake* Finland
437 E3 **Elan Bank** *underwater feature* Southern Ocean
235 E8 **Elasa** *island* Greece
235 C6 **Elassona** Greece
373 H2 **Elato** *island* Federated States of Micronesia
394 F5 **Elazığ** Turkey
394 F5 **Elazığ** *admin. area* Turkey
131 H5 **Elba** Alabama USA
232 D5 **Elba, Isola d'** *island* Italy
385 M2 **El'ban** Russian Federation
235 B5 **Elbasan** Albania
227 H2 **Elbe** *watercourse* Czech Republic
226 G2 **Elbe** *watercourse* Germany
126 H7 **Elberfeld** Indiana USA
131 J3 **Elberton** Georgia USA
226 F4 **Elbigenalp** Austria
129 N1 **Elbing** Kansas USA
225 J5 **Elbląg** Poland
119 R7 **Elbow** Saskatchewan Canada
131 M7 **Elbow Cay** Bahamas
119 U6 **Elbow Lake** Saskatchewan Canada
125 R4 **Elbow Lake** Minnesota USA
388 D5 **El'brus, Gora** *mountain* Russian Federation
230 E4 **Elche de la Sierra** Spain
231 F4 **Elche-Elx** Spain
244 E4 **Elcho** Perth and Kinross Scotland UK
231 F4 **Elda** Spain
307 F3 **Eldama Ravine** Kenya
425 inset **Elder, Mount** Macquarie Island Australia
235 F7 **Elderesi** Turkey
157 A8 **Eldorado** Brazil
130 B3 **Eldorado** Oklahoma USA
129 L5 **Eldorado** Texas USA
307 F3 **Eldoret** Kenya
243 F2 **Eldroth** North Yorkshire England UK
130 B3 **Electra** Texas USA
129 I2 **Electra Lake** Colorado USA
162 B4 **Elefantes, Golfo** *bay* Chile
234 B2 **Elek** Hungary
389 O3 **Elekmonar** Russian Federation
307 F4 **Elementeita, Lake** Kenya
162 A4 **Elena, Cabo** *cape* Chile
129 I4 **Elephant Butte** New Mexico USA
132 D1 **Elephant Butte Reservoir** New Mexico USA
436 U2 **Elephant Island** Antarctica
163 7 **Elephant Jason** *island* Falkland Islands
240 D2 **Elerch** Ceredigion Wales UK
156 D4 **Elesbão Veloso** Brazil
134 E1 **Eleuthera** *island* Bahamas
126 F4 **Eleva** Wisconsin USA
373 G5 **Elevala** *watercourse* Papua New Guinea
129 J1 **Elevenmile Canyon Reservoir** Colorado USA
118 C3 **Elfin Cove** Alaska USA
128 H5 **Elfrida** Arizona USA
222 H5 **Elgåhogna** *mountain* Norway
125 O2 **Elgin** Manitoba Canada
244 E3 **Elgin** Moray Scotland UK
126 G5 **Elgin** Illinois USA
124 G4 **Elgin** Oregon USA
130 C5 **Elgin** Texas USA
237 AC5 **El'ginskoye Ploskogor'ye** *region* Russian Federation
244 B3 **Elgol** Highland Scotland UK
307 E3 **Elgon, Mount** Uganda
237 AJ5 **El'gygytgyn, Ozero** *lake* Russian Federation
241 I3 **Elham** Kent England UK
306 C5 **Elias Garcia** Angola
372 D6 **Eliase** Indonesia
129 K4 **Elida** New Mexico USA
303 G5 **Ēlīda'ār** Ethiopia
235 C7 **Elika** Greece
235 C6 **Elikonas** *range* Greece
306 D4 **Elila** Democratic Republic of Congo
306 D4 **Elila** *watercourse* Democratic Republic of Congo
116 C6 **Elim** Alaska USA
225 N2 **Elimäki** Finland
380 E3 **Eling** Guizhou China
122 G3 **Eliot, Mount** Newfoundland and Labrador Canada
306 C4 **Elipa** Democratic Republic of Congo
244 B3 **Elishader** Highland Scotland UK
388 D4 **Elista** Russian Federation
127 N6 **Elizabeth** New Jersey USA
121 R5 **Elizabeth, Lac** *lake* Québec Canada
423 D6 **Elizabeth, Point** New Zealand
131 M2 **Elizabeth City** North Carolina USA
126 I8 **Elizabethtown** Kentucky USA
230 F2 **Elizondo** Spain
124 H2 **Elk** *watercourse* British Columbia Canada
119 S1 **Elk** *watercourse* Northwest Territories Canada
130 H3 **Elk** *watercourse* Alabama USA
128 A1 **Elk** California USA
126 C8 **Elk** *watercourse* Kansas USA
127 K7 **Elk** *watercourse* West Virginia USA
130 D2 **Elk City** Kansas USA
130 B3 **Elk City** Oklahoma USA
128 B1 **Elk Grove** California USA
126 D6 **Elk Horn** Iowa USA
126 I4 **Elk Lake** Michigan USA
125 L6 **Elk Mountain** Wyoming USA
126 I4 **Elk Rapids** Michigan USA
126 E4 **Elk River** Minnesota USA
119 N7 **Elkford** British Columbia Canada
126 I6 **Elkhart** Indiana USA
125 O8 **Elkhart** Kansas USA
130 D5 **Elkhart** Texas USA
119 U8 **Elkhorn** Manitoba Canada
119 N8 **Elko** British Columbia Canada
124 H6 **Elko** Nevada USA
130 H2 **Elkton** Kentucky USA
124 D5 **Elkton** Oregon USA
119 P8 **Elkwater** Alberta Canada
228 C3 **Ellé** *watercourse* France
127 L7 **Elleber Knob** *mountain* West Virginia USA
117 I3 **Ellef Ringnes Island** Nunavut Canada
425 O7 **Ellenborough** NSW Australia
245 F4 **Ellendale** *island* Ireland
125 P4 **Ellendale** North Dakota USA
124 E3 **Ellensburg** Washington USA
127 N6 **Ellenville** New York USA
243 G2 **Ellerbeck** North Yorkshire England UK
240 E2 **Ellesmere** Shropshire England UK
423 E6 **Ellesmere (Te Waihora), Lake** New Zealand
117 K3 **Ellesmere Island** Nunavut Canada
242 F3 **Ellesmere Port** Cheshire England UK
116 I5 **Ellice** *watercourse* Nunavut Canada
131 I3 **Ellijay** Georgia USA
243 G2 **Ellingstring** North Yorkshire England UK
243 G1 **Ellington** Northumberland England UK
126 F8 **Ellington** Missouri USA
425 M4 **Elliot, Mount** Qld Australia
120 H6 **Elliot Lake** Manitoba Canada
126 J3 **Elliot Lake** Ontario Canada
425 J4 **Elliott** NT Australia
125 P7 **Ellis** Kansas USA
118 L8 **Ellison** British Columbia Canada
Ellisras *see* **Lephalale** South Africa
425 J8 **Elliston** SA Australia
130 G5 **Ellisville** Mississippi USA
244 F3 **Ellon** Aberdeenshire Scotland UK
131 K4 **Elloree** South Carolina USA
224 F3 **Ellös** Sweden
119 O5 **Ellscott** Alberta Canada
126 E5 **Ellsworth** Iowa USA
125 P7 **Ellsworth** Kansas USA
130 B3 **Ellsworth, Lake** Oklahoma USA
436 S2 **Ellsworth Land** *plain* Antarctica
436 S1 **Ellsworth Mountains** Antarctica
226 F3 **Ellwangen** Germany
241 H2 **Elm** Cambridgeshire England UK
131 M3 **Elm City** North Carolina USA
120 F8 **Elm Creek** Manitoba Canada
130 B3 **Elm Fork Red** *watercourse* Oklahoma USA
394 E5 **Elma Dağı** Turkey
235 F7 **Elmalı** Turkey
123 G9 **Elmira** Prince Edward Island Canada
127 M5 **Elmira** New York USA
241 E2 **Elmley Castle** Worcestershire England UK
125 J7 **Elmo** Utah USA
130 A2 **Elmwood** Oklahoma USA
228 F5 **Elne** France
222 E5 **Elnesvågen** Norway
119 O7 **Elnora** Alberta Canada
373 I4 **Eloaua Island** Papua New Guinea
305 G4 **Elogo** Congo
128 G4 **Eloy** Arizona USA
245 D3 **Elphin** Ireland

244 C2 **Elphin** Highland Scotland UK
425 N5 **Elphinstone** Qld Australia
160 D4 **Elqui** *watercourse* Chile
244 F3 **Elrick** Aberdeenshire Scotland UK
125 R4 **Elrosa** Minnesota USA
119 Q7 **Elrose** Saskatchewan Canada
232 D5 **Elsa** *watercourse* Italy
243 F1 **Elsdon** Northumberland England UK
226 E3 **Elsenfeld** Germany
232 C2 **Elsenz** *watercourse* Germany
222 L2 **Elsnes** Norway
244 E5 **Elsrickle** South Lanarkshire Scotland UK
226 C2 **Elst** Netherlands
241 G2 **Elsthorpe** Lincolnshire England UK
227 H2 **Elstra** Germany
436 S2 **Eltanin Bay** Antarctica
77 F15 **Eltanin Fracture Zone** *underwater feature* Southern Ocean
388 E3 **El'ton** Russian Federation
388 E3 **El'ton** *lake* Russian Federation
242 F3 **Elton** Cheshire England UK
130 E5 **Elton** Louisiana USA
226 E2 **Eltville** Germany
393 E8 **Eluru** Andhra Pradesh India
222 G6 **Elvål** Norway
244 E5 **Elvanfoot** South Lanarkshire Scotland UK
230 C4 **Elvas** Portugal
222 G6 **Elvdal** Norway
241 H2 **Elveden** Suffolk England UK
224 E2 **Elverum** Norway
243 H3 **Elvington** York England UK
125 P6 **Elwood** Nebraska USA
301 F1 **Elx** Spain
241 H2 **Ely** Cambridgeshire England UK
240 D3 **Ely** Cardiff Wales UK
126 F3 **Ely** Minnesota USA
124 H7 **Ely** Nevada USA
127 J6 **Elyria** Ohio USA
226 E3 **Elz** *watercourse* Germany
226 D2 **Elzbach** *watercourse* Germany
426 7 **Émaé** *island* Vanuatu
223 P4 **Emäjoki** *watercourse* Finland
389 J6 **Emām Şāḩeb** Afghanistan
224 I4 **Emån** *watercourse* Sweden
373 I4 **Emananusa Island** Papua New Guinea
426 7 **Émao** *island* Vanuatu
388 H4 **Emba** Kazakhstan
388 G4 **Emba** *watercourse* Kazakhstan
308 E5 **Embalenhle** South Africa
121 W6 **Embar** Newfoundland and Labrador Canada
237 U5 **Embenchime** *watercourse* Russian Federation
158 D3 **Embira** *watercourse* Brazil
244 E3 **Embo** Highland Scotland UK
157 C7 **Emborcaçao, Represa** *lake* Brazil
229 H4 **Embrun** France
307 F4 **Embu** Kenya
161 J2 **Embu Guaçu** Brazil
308 C3 **Embundo** Angola
225 L4 **Emburga** Latvia
224 D6 **Emden** Germany
235 E7 **Emecik** Turkey
380 D2 **Emeishan** Sichuan China
425 N5 **Emerald** Qld Australia
78 M13 **Emerald Basin** *underwater feature* Southern Ocean
116 H3 **Emerald Isle** Northwest Territories Canada
121 V6 **Emeril** Newfoundland and Labrador Canada
155 H4 **Émerillon, Massif** *range* French Guiana
128 D3 **Emerson Lake** California USA
125 Q5 **Emery** South Dakota USA
124 J7 **Emery** Utah USA
373 G5 **Emeti** Papua New Guinea
224 C2 **Emhjellevatnet** *lake* Norway
301 J5 **Emi Koussi** *mountain* Chad
128 B1 **Emigrant Gap** California USA
232 C4 **Emilia-Romagna** *admin. area* Italy
129 H5 **Emiliano Zapata** Mexico
129 J7 **Emiliano Zapata** Mexico
133 H5 **Emiliano Zapata** Mexico
160 F7 **Emilio Lamarca** Argentina
382 G3 **Emin** Xinjiang Uygur Zizhiqu China
373 I4 **Emirau Island** Papua New Guinea
309 F5 **Emjindini** South Africa
122 C1 **Emma Island** Nunavut Canada
155 G4 **Emma Keten** *range* Suriname
238 G4 **Emmaus** Russian Federation
127 N6 **Emmaus** Pennsylvania USA
425 M7 **Emmdale** NSW Australia
229 H1 **Emmelshausen** Germany
226 D1 **Emmen** Netherlands
226 D2 **Emmerich** Germany
425 M6 **Emmet** Qld Australia
393 D8 **Emmiganuru** Andhra Pradesh India
116 C6 **Emmonak** Alaska USA
241 H2 **Emneth** Norfolk England UK
125 S2 **Emo** Manitoba Canada
234 B2 **Emőd** Hungary
132 C3 **Empalme** Mexico
161 G3 **Empedrado** Argentina
78 M3 **Emperor Seamount** *underwater feature* Pacific Ocean
78 N3 **Emperor Trough** *underwater feature* Pacific Ocean
235 B6 **Empesos** Greece
372 D6 **Emplawas** Indonesia
126 C7 **Emporia** Kansas USA
127 L6 **Emporium** Pennsylvania USA
119 P7 **Empress** Alberta Canada
373 J5 **Empress Augusta Bay** Papua New Guinea
226 D1 **Ems** *watercourse* Germany
226 D1 **Ems-Jade-Kanal** *watercourse* Germany
229 I1 **Emstal** Germany
425 M5 **Emu, Mount** Qld Australia
424 J7 **Emu Junction** SA Australia
302 D5 **En Nahud** Sudan
222 H5 **Enafors** Sweden
244 C2 **Enard Bay** Scotland UK
133 G5 **Encajonado** *watercourse* Mexico
231 G2 **Encamp** Andorra
161 H4 **Encantadas, Serra das** *range* Brazil
161 H3 **Encarnación** Paraguay
130 B6 **Encinal** Texas USA
230 D4 **Encinarejo, Embalse del** *lake* Spain
230 C4 **Encinasola** Spain
128 D4 **Encinitas** California USA
157 D6 **Encruzilhada** Brazil
161 H4 **Encruzilhada do Sul** Brazil
234 B1 **Encs** Hungary
374 D3 **Endau** *watercourse* Malaysia
372 B6 **Ende** Indonesia
372 B6 **Ende** *island* Indonesia
222 G6 **Enden** Norway
426 1 **Enderbury** *island* Kiribati
118 L7 **Enderby** British Columbia Canada
437 D2 **Enderby Abyssal Plain** *underwater feature* Southern Ocean
423 8 **Enderby Island** Auckland Islands New Zealand
437 D2 **Enderby Land** *plain* Antarctica
116 D5 **Endicott Mountains** Alaska USA
158 E3 **Endimari** *watercourse* Brazil
225 N3 **Endla järv** *lake* Estonia
305 G4 **Endom** Cameroon
241 E1 **Endon** Staffordshire England UK
158 C3 **Ene** *watercourse* Peru
424 E7 **Eneabba** WA Australia
388 C5 **Enem** Russian Federation
155 H4 **Énéné Patatpe** Suriname
161 G6 **Energía** Argentina
427 15 **Enewetak Atoll** *reef* Marshall Islands
235 E5 **Enez** Turkey
163 14 **Enfer, Pointe d'** *cape* Martinique
308 B3 **Enfião, Ponta do** *cape* Angola
233 D8 **Enfidaville** Tunisia
241 G3 **Enfield** Greater London England UK
131 M2 **Enfield** North Carolina USA
126 I3 **Engadine** Michigan USA
222 F5 **Engan** Norway
162 D3 **Engaño, Bahía** *bay* Argentina
135 G3 **Engaño, Cabo** *cape* Dominican Republic
387 I2 **Engaru** Japan
222 F5 **Engdal** Norway
222 I3 **Engeløya** *island* Norway
388 E3 **Engel's** Russian Federation
119 R4 **Engemann Lake** Saskatchewan Canada
226 E4 **Engen** Germany
159 G4 **Engenho** Brazil
226 E1 **Enger** Germany
222 H6 **Engerneset** Norway
374 D5 **Enggano** *island* Indonesia
373 I6 **Engineer Group** *island* Papua New Guinea
374 F3 **Engkilili** Malaysia
239 G5 **England** *admin. area* UK
123 J7 **Englee** Newfoundland and Labrador Canada
117 L9 **Englehart** Ontario Canada
119 R3 **Engler Lake** Saskatchewan Canada
125 P8 **Englewood** Kansas USA
126 E1 **English** *watercourse* Ontario Canada
241 G4 **English Channel (La Manche)** *strait* UK/France
436 T2 **English Coast** Antarctica
223 R4 **Engozero** Russian Federation
226 E3 **Engstingen** Germany
225 L4 **Engures ezers** *lake* Latvia
224 I2 **Enhammarsfjärden** *bay* Sweden
130 C2 **Enid** Oklahoma USA
130 G3 **Enid Lake** Mississippi USA
427 15a **Enigu** *island* Marshall Islands
223 O3 **Enijärvi** *lake* Finland
387 I2 **Eniwa** Japan
426 6 **Eniwetak** *island* Marshall Islands
381 G3 **Enjiang** Jiangxi China
237 AD7 **Enkan, Mys** *cape* Russian Federation
226 C1 **Enkhuizen** Netherlands
225 K2 **Enklinge** *island* Finland
380 C4 **Enle** Yunnan China
237 AL5 **Enmelen** Russian Federation
233 F8 **Enna** Italy
119 U2 **Ennadai** Nunavut Canada
120 E2 **Ennadai Lake** Nunavut Canada
305 I2 **Enné, Ouadi** *watercourse* Chad
302 C4 **Ennedi** *range* Chad
242 A3 **Ennell, Lough** *lake* Ireland
228 F4 **Ennezat** France
245 D4 **Ennis** Ireland
124 J4 **Ennis** Montana USA
130 C4 **Ennis** Texas USA
124 J4 **Ennis Lake** Montana USA
245 F4 **Enniscorthy** Ireland
245 D5 **Enniskean** Ireland
245 F3 **Enniskerry** Ireland
245 E2 **Enniskillen** Fermanagh Northern Ireland UK
245 C4 **Ennistymon** Ireland
229 L2 **Enns** Austria
232 E3 **Enns** *watercourse* Austria
232 F3 **Ennstaler Alpen** *range* Austria
223 Q5 **Eno** Finland
374 D4 **Enok** Indonesia
223 P5 **Enonkoski** Finland
223 O4 **Enonkylä** Finland
223 M2 **Enontekiö** Finland
225 O1 **Enonvesi** *bay* Finland
225 O1 **Enonvesi** *lake* Finland
381 F4 **Enping** Guangdong China
135 G3 **Enriquillo, Lago** *lake* Dominican Republic
226 D1 **Enschede** Netherlands
132 A2 **Ensenada** Mexico
380 F2 **Enshi** Hubei China
125 O8 **Ensign** Kansas USA
229 H3 **Ensisheim** France
307 E3 **Entebbe** Uganda
244 E5 **Enterkinfoot** Dumfries and Galloway Scotland UK
131 I5 **Enterprise** Alabama USA
124 G4 **Enterprise** Oregon USA
124 I8 **Enterprise** Utah USA
377 H5 **Enterprise Point** Philippines
154 A3 **Entrada, Punta** *cape* Panama
118 M6 **Entrance** Alberta Canada
228 F4 **Entraygues** France
161 G4 **Entre Ríos** *admin. area* Argentina
157 E5 **Entre Rios** Brazil
230 E3 **Entrepeñas, Embalse de** *lake* Spain
372 E5 **Enu** *island* Indonesia
305 F3 **Enugu** Nigeria
305 F3 **Enugu** *admin. area* Nigeria
154 C3 **Envigado** Colombia
158 D2 **Envira** Brazil
159 G2 **Envira** Brazil
306 C4 **Enyamba** Democratic Republic of Congo
305 H4 **Enyéllé** Congo
232 H3 **Enying** Hungary
232 C2 **Enz** *watercourse* Germany
232 D4 **Enza** *watercourse* Italy
226 G4 **Enzingerboden** Austria
230 C2 **Eo** *watercourse* Spain
386 E4 **Eocheong-do** *island* South Korea
244 A3 **Eolaigearraidh** Na h-Eileanan Siar Scotland UK
233 F7 **Eolie, Isole** *island* Italy
426 6 **Eor** *island* Federated States of Micronesia
226 C1 **Epe** Netherlands
162 D1 **Epecuén, Lago** *lake* Argentina
305 H4 **Epéna** Congo
228 F2 **Épernay** France
124 F3 **Ephrata** Washington USA
426 7 **Epi** *island* Vanuatu
235 C7 **Epidavrou, Kolpos** *bay* Greece
231 F3 **Épila** Spain
229 G3 **Épinac** France
229 H2 **Épinal** France
306 D3 **Epini** Democratic Republic of Congo
225 M2 **Epoo** Finland
127 P5 **Epping** New Hampshire USA
232 C2 **Eppingen** Germany
241 G3 **Epsom** Surrey England UK
228 E2 **Epte** *watercourse* France
308 C4 **Epukiro** Namibia
306 D3 **Epulu** *watercourse* Democratic Republic of Congo
390 G3 **Eqlīd** Iran
305 F5 **Equata** Gabon
306 C3 **Équateur** *admin. area* Democratic Republic of Congo
305 F4 **Equatorial Guinea** *country* Africa
380 C3 **Er Hai** *lake* Yunnan China
300 F2 **Er Rachidia** Morocco
302 E5 **Er Rahad** Sudan
302 E5 **Er Renk** Sudan
302 E5 **Er Roseires** Sudan
302 E5 **Er Ruaat** Sudan
232 D5 **Era** *watercourse* Italy
373 H5 **Era** *watercourse* Papua New Guinea
226 G5 **Eraclea** Italy
375 H1 **Eran Bay** Philippines
134 B4 **Erandique** Honduras
373 G5 **Erave** *watercourse* Papua New Guinea
302 F4 **Erbab, Jebel** *mountain* Sudan
394 G5 **Erciş** Turkey
233 F6 **Ercolano** Italy
232 H3 **Ercsi** Hungary
232 H3 **Érd** Hungary
235 E5 **Erdek Körfezi** *bay* Turkey
394 E6 **Erdemli** Turkey
383 K3 **Erdene** Mongolia
384 G4 **Erdene** Mongolia
383 I3 **Erdeneburen** Mongolia
384 E3 **Erdenedalai** Mongolia
383 J3 **Erdenehairhan** Mongolia
384 E3 **Erdenesant** Mongolia
384 E2 **Erdenet** Mongolia
385 H3 **Erdenetsagaan** Mongolia
384 D3 **Erdenetsogt** Mongolia
234 A3 **Erdevik** Serbia
226 F3 **Erding** Germany
388 E4 **Erdniyevskiy** Russian Federation
228 D3 **Erdre** *watercourse* France
227 J5 **Erdut** Croatia
437 L1 **Erebus, Mount** *volcano* Antarctica
161 H3 **Erechim** Brazil
384 F2 **Eree** Mongolia
385 G2 **Ereen** Mongolia
302 B5 **Eref** Chad
394 D5 **Ereğli** Turkey
394 E6 **Ereğli** Turkey
235 A6 **Ereikoussa** *island* Greece
128 D5 **Eréndira** Mexico
384 G4 **Erenhot** Nei Mongol Zizhiqu China
155 G5 **Erepecu, Lagoa do** *lake* Brazil
307 G2 **Erer** *watercourse* Ethiopia
230 D3 **Eresma** *watercourse* Spain
235 D6 **Eresos** Greece
155 F3 **Erevato** *watercourse* Venezuela
300 F2 **Erfoud** Morocco
226 F2 **Erfurt** Germany
394 F5 **Ergani** Turkey
225 M4 **Ērgeme** Latvia
394 C5 **Ergene** *watercourse* Turkey
235 F5 **Ergili** Turkey
225 M4 **Ērgļi** Latvia
229 G5 **Ergolding** Germany
229 K2 **Ergoldsbach** Germany
125 Q3 **Erhard** Minnesota USA
123 E7 **Éric, Lac** *lake* Québec Canada
232 F7 **Erice** Italy
230 B4 **Ericeira** Portugal
244 D4 **Ericht, Loch** *lake* Scotland UK
130 B3 **Erick** Oklahoma USA
119 V7 **Erickson** Manitoba Canada
125 P6 **Ericson** Nebraska USA
127 K5 **Erie** Pennsylvania USA
127 K5 **Erie, Lake** Canada/USA
244 D5 **Eriff** East Ayrshire Scotland UK
235 E5 **Erikli** Turkey
119 V7 **Eriksdale** Manitoba Canada
224 H4 **Eriksmåla** Sweden
427 15 **Erikub Atoll** *reef* Marshall Islands
235 D6 **Erimitis, Akra** *cape* Greece
130 H2 **Erin** Tennessee USA
163 9 **Erin Point** Trinidad and Tobago
244 C5 **Erines** Argyll and Bute Scotland UK
241 H2 **Eriswell** Suffolk England UK
232 B3 **Eriswil** Switzerland
302 F4 **Eritrea** *country* Africa
224 I3 **Erken** *lake* Sweden
384 F3 **Erkhet Uul** *mountain* Mongolia
229 J6 **Erlangen** Germany
425 K5 **Erldunda** NT Australia
130 E4 **Erling, Lake** Arkansas USA
385 H2 **Ermana, Khrebet** *range* Russian Federation
308 E5 **Ermelo** South Africa
302 D5 **Ermil Post** Sudan
225 M3 **Ermistu järv** *lake* Estonia
235 D7 **Ermoupoli** Greece
230 E2 **Ermúa** Spain
242 A3 **Erne** *watercourse* Ireland
228 D2 **Ernée** France
125 L1 **Ernfold** Saskatchewan Canada
232 G2 **Ernstbrunn** Austria
393 D9 **Erode** Tamil Nadu India
427 15a **Eroj** *island* Marshall Islands
425 L6 **Eromanga** Qld Australia
308 C4 **Erongo** *admin. area* Namibia
373 I6 **Erono** Papua New Guinea
237 AE5 **Erozionnyy** Russian Federation
380 E1 **Erqu** Shaanxi China
228 C2 **Erquy** France
245 B2 **Erris Head** *cape* Ireland
426 7 **Erromango** *island* Vanuatu
229 I2 **Ersbach** Germany
235 B5 **Ersekë** Albania
222 J2 **Ersfjord** Norway
437 B2 **Erskine Iceport** Antarctica
222 L5 **Ersmark/Ume-Ersmark** Sweden
222 L4 **Ersnäs** Sweden
225 L2 **Erstan** *bay* Finland
229 H2 **Erstein** France
388 C3 **Ertil** Russian Federation
383 H3 **Ertix He** *watercourse* Xinjiang Uygur Zizhiqu China
222 M3 **Ertsjärv** Sweden
222 F5 **Ertvågøya** *island* Norway
225 M3 **Eru laht** *bay* Estonia
422 F4 **Erua** New Zealand
155 F3 **Erueda-Tepui** *mountain* Venezuela
305 F3 **Erufa** Nigeria
393 D10 **Eruvadi** Tamil Nadu India
228 D2 **Erve** *watercourse* France
244 C6 **Ervie** Dumfries and Galloway Scotland UK
224 C1 **Ervik** Norway
226 E2 **Ervitte** Germany
240 D2 **Erwood** Powys Wales UK
235 B7 **Erymanthos** *range* Greece
389 Q3 **Erzin** Russian Federation
394 F5 **Erzincan** Turkey
394 F5 **Erzincan** *admin. area* Turkey
394 G5 **Erzurum** Turkey
394 G5 **Erzurum** *admin. area* Turkey
300 D3 **Es Semara** Western Sahara
158 C5 **Esbilla** Peru
377 I5 **Escalante** Philippines
124 J8 **Escalante** Utah USA
128 G2 **Escalante** *watercourse* Utah USA
128 F2 **Escalante Desert** Utah USA
228 E5 **Escales, Pantà d'** *lake* Spain
231 G4 **Escaleta, Punta de la** *cape* Spain
132 D3 **Escalón** Mexico
126 H4 **Escanaba** Michigan USA
133 H5 **Escárcega** Mexico
377 I3 **Escarpada Point** Philippines
229 G2 **Esch-sur-Alzette** Luxembourg
226 F1 **Eschede** Germany
226 E4 **Eschenz** Switzerland
229 H3 **Escholzmatt** Switzerland
226 F2 **Eschwege** Germany
132 E3 **Escobedo** Mexico
135 G3 **Escocesa, Bahía** *bay* Dominican Republic
128 D4 **Escondido** California USA
134 D4 **Escondido, Río** *watercourse* Nicaragua
159 F5 **Escorpión** Bolivia
231 G2 **Escosse** France
436 U2 **Escudero (Chile)** *research station* Antarctica
134 B4 **Escuintla** Guatemala
123 F9 **Escuminac, Point** New Brunswick Canada
305 G4 **Eséke** Cameroon
235 F7 **Eşen** Turkey
235 F7 **Eşen** *watercourse* Turkey
388 G6 **Esenguly** Turkmenistan
388 I6 **Esenmengli** Turkmenistan
224 D6 **Esens** Germany
231 G2 **Esera** *watercourse* Spain
390 G3 **Eşfahān** Iran
390 G2 **Eşfahān** *admin. area* Iran
388 H6 **Esfarāyen** Iran
240 C3 **Esgair** Carmarthenshire Wales UK
390 G2 **Eshehārd** Iran
241 G3 **Esher** Surrey England UK
243 G1 **Eshott** Northumberland England UK
309 F5 **Esikhawini** South Africa
232 E5 **Esino** *watercourse* Italy
309 I4 **Esira** Madagascar
373 I5 **Esis** *watercourse* Papua New Guinea
423 E6 **Esk** *watercourse* New Zealand
242 E1 **Esk** *watercourse* Scotland UK
123 H10 **Eskasoni** Nova Scotia Canada
244 E5 **Eskdalemuir** Dumfries and Galloway Scotland UK
245 E2 **Eske, Lough** *lake* Ireland
121 V6 **Esker** Newfoundland and Labrador Canada
242 A3 **Esker** Ireland
245 C2 **Eskeragh** Ireland
222 inset **Eskifjörður** Iceland
224 I3 **Eskilstuna** Sweden
116 F5 **Eskimo Lakes** Northwest Territories Canada
394 D5 **Eskişehir** *admin. area* Turkey
223 N5 **Eskola** Finland
224 I2 **Eskön** *island* Sweden
245 E2 **Eskragh** Omagh Northern Ireland UK
228 B5 **Esla** *watercourse* Spain
158 D4 **Eslabón, Serranía de** *range* Bolivia
390 F2 **Eslāmābād-e Gharb** Iran
390 G2 **Eslāmshahr** Iran
224 G5 **Eslöv** Sweden
132 E3 **Esmeralda** Mexico
162 A4 **Esmeralda, Isla** *island* Chile
157 C7 **Esmeraldas** Brazil
154 B4 **Esmeraldas** Ecuador
125 P2 **Esmond** North Dakota USA
126 H1 **Esnagami Lake** Ontario Canada
126 I2 **Esnagi Lake** Ontario Canada
154 D1 **Espada, Punta** *cape* Venezuela
228 F4 **Espalion** France
231 G4 **Espalmador, Isla** *island* Spain
132 D3 **España** Mexico
129 I3 **Espanola** New Mexico USA
163 4 **Española, Isla** *island* Archipiélago de Colón (Galapagos Islands)
160 F6 **Espartillar** Argentina
154 C4 **Espejo, Lago** *lake* Colombia
157 D8 **Espera Feliz** Brazil
156 F4 **Esperança** Brazil
310 1b **Esperança, Pico da** *volcano* Azores
424 G8 **Esperance** WA Australia
426 8 **Esperance, Cape** Solomon Islands
156 D3 **Esperantina** Brazil
156 C4 **Esperantinópolis** Brazil
162 B5 **Esperanza** Argentina
129 I6 **Esperanza** Mexico
134 C4 **Esperanza, Sierra la** *range* Honduras
436 U2 **Esperanza (Argentina)** *research station* Antarctica
159 F2 **Espero-em-Deus** Brazil
391 I4 **Espetgi** Iran
230 B4 **Espichel, Cabo** *cape* Portugal
161 I3 **Espigão, Serra do** *range* Brazil
228 F5 **Espiguette, Pointe de l'** *cape* France
154 C3 **Espinal** Colombia
158 C3 **Espinal** Peru
230 D2 **Espinama** Spain
160 D6 **Espinazo del Zorro** Argentina
157 D7 **Espinhaço, Serra do** *range* Brazil
230 B3 **Espinho** Portugal
161 H4 **Espinilho, Serra do** *range* Brazil
155 E2 **Espino** Venezuela
157 D6 **Espinosa** Brazil
159 E2 **Espírito Santo** Brazil
157 D7 **Espírito Santo** *admin. area* Brazil
426 7 **Espíritu Santo** *island* Vanuatu
134 C3 **Espíritu Santo, Bahía del** *bay* Mexico
162 C5 **Espíritu Santo, Cabo** *cape* Argentina
132 C3 **Espíritu Santo, Isla** *island* Mexico
133 H4 **Espita** Mexico
163 5 **Espólon, Punta** *cape* Isla de Pascua (Easter Island)
225 M2 **Espoo** Finland
391 I4 **Espoz** Iran
161 H4 **Espumoso** Brazil
132 C2 **Esqueda** Mexico
162 B3 **Esquel** Argentina
161 G4 **Esquina** Argentina
222 L3 **Esrange** Sweden
232 C2 **Essang** Indonesia
300 E2 **Essaouira** Morocco
304 A2 **Essau** Gambia
305 G4 **Essé** Cameroon
229 G1 **Essen** Belgium
226 D2 **Essen** Germany
424 G6 **Essendon, Mount** WA Australia
155 G4 **Essequibo** *watercourse* Guyana
155 G3 **Essequibo Islands-West Demerara** *admin. area* Guyana
241 H3 **Essex** *admin. area* England UK
163 4 **Essex, Punta** *cape* Archipiélago de Colón (Galapagos Islands)
237 AG7 **Esso** Russian Federation
228 F2 **Essonne** France
223 R6 **Essoyla** Russian Federation
305 G4 **Est** *admin. area* Cameroon
123 H9 **Est, Île de l'** *island* Québec Canada
310 6 **Est, Île de l'** *island* French Southern and Antarctic Lands
123 H8 **Est, Pointe de l'** Québec Canada
230 C2 **Estaca de Bares, Punta da** *cape* Spain
129 I6 **Estacion Consuelo** Mexico
132 E3 **Estación El Fuerte** Mexico
129 L7 **Estacion Golandrinas** Mexico
128 G6 **Estacion Moreno** Mexico
162 D6 **Estados, Isla de los** *island* Argentina
228 F5 **Estagel** France
226 B2 **Estaimpuis** Belgium
226 B2 **Estaires** France
129 I3 **Estancia** New Mexico USA
157 E5 **Estância** Brazil
161 G2 **Estancia Amalia** Paraguay
158 D5 **Estancia Añutani** Bolivia
159 F5 **Estancia Atlantico Norte** Bolivia
159 G5 **Estancia Bella Vista** Bolivia
159 G5 **Estancia Bello Horizonte** Bolivia
161 G2 **Estancia Buena Vista** Paraguay
158 E6 **Estancia Cala Horno** Bolivia
161 G2 **Estancia Campo Sastre** Paraguay
158 E5 **Estancia Catchi Vinto** Bolivia
160 F2 **Estancia Coé Puajhú** Paraguay
159 F5 **Estancia Curiche** Bolivia
160 F2 **Estancia El Dorado** Paraguay
160 F2 **Estancia El Pampero** Paraguay
161 G2 **Estancia Esperanza** Paraguay
161 G2 **Estancia Gómez** Paraguay
159 E5 **Estancia Kayorani** Bolivia
162 C4 **Estancia L. Lorenzo** Argentina
159 F5 **Estancia La Cortina** Bolivia
160 F2 **Estancia Los Caminantes** Paraguay
159 F5 **Estancia Nueva Holanda** Bolivia
159 G5 **Estancia Paquiocito** Bolivia
159 G6 **Estancia Riacho Alegre** Paraguay
159 F4 **Estancia S.S.O.** Bolivia
161 G2 **Estancia San Jorge** Paraguay
159 F5 **Estancia San José** Paraguay
159 F5 **Estancia San Josema** Bolivia
159 G5 **Estancia Santa Rosa** Bolivia
161 G2 **Estancia Santa Teresa** Paraguay
158 D6 **Estancia Sinalaco** Bolivia
158 E6 **Estancia Tambo** Bolivia
161 G2 **Estancia Toldo Cué** Paraguay
161 G2 **Estancia Tomas Cué** Paraguay
161 G2 **Estancia Tres Toritos** Paraguay
158 D5 **Estancia Vinto** Bolivia
129 K7 **Estanque de Leon** Mexico
129 L7 **Estanque de Norias** Mexico
162 A2 **Estaquilla, Punta** *cape* Chile
231 G2 **Estats, Pic d'** *mountain* Spain
123 D9 **Estcourt** Québec Canada
308 E5 **Estcourt** South Africa
226 F5 **Este** Italy
160 E2 **Esteban de Urizar** Argentina
134 C4 **Estelí** Nicaragua
230 E2 **Estella** Spain
130 A3 **Estelline** Texas USA
230 E2 **Estepar** Spain
230 D5 **Estepona** Spain
305 F4 **Esterias, Cape** Gabon
226 B3 **Esternay** France
128 B3 **Estero Bay** California USA
128 F7 **Estero la Bocana** Mexico
160 F2 **Esteros** Paraguay
226 D1 **Esterwegen** Germany
119 T8 **Estevan** Saskatchewan Canada
119 P7 **Esther** Alberta Canada
131 K4 **Estill** South Carolina USA
131 H3 **Estill Springs** Tennessee USA
309 F3 **Estima** Mozambique
228 F2 **Estissac** France
159 G4 **Estivado** Brazil
225 **Estonia** *country* Europe
229 H5 **Estoublon** France
156 A4 **Estragado, Serra do** *range* Brazil
156 D4 **Estreito** Brazil
161 I4 **Estrela** Brazil
128 E5 **Estrella, Punta** *cape* Mexico
230 C4 **Estremoz** Portugal
156 B5 **Estrondo, Serra do** *range* Brazil
305 G4 **Estuaire** *admin. area* Gabon
119 Q7 **Estuary** Saskatchewan Canada
244 inset **Eswick** Shetland Scotland UK
232 H3 **Esztergom** Hungary
122 I6 **Etagaulet Bay** Newfoundland and Labrador Canada
392 E5 **Etah** Uttar Pradesh India
229 G2 **Étain** France
373 J2 **Etall** *island* Federated States of Micronesia
123 H7 **Etamamiou** *watercourse* Québec Canada
228 F2 **Étampes** France
241 I4 **Étaples** France
392 E5 **Etawah** Uttar Pradesh India
120 G4 **Etawney Lake** Manitoba Canada
132 C3 **Etchojoa** Mexico
132 C3 **Etchoropo** Mexico
305 G5 **Etéké** Gabon
225 M2 **Etelä-Suomen** *admin. area* Finland
225 K2 **Eteläjoki** *watercourse* Finland
158 B2 **Eten** Peru
132 E2 **Etéreo** Mexico
125 Q5 **Ethan** South Dakota USA
119 U7 **Ethelbert** Manitoba Canada
307 G2 **Ethiopia** *country* Africa
307 F1 **Ethiopian Highlands** *range* Ethiopia
130 H3 **Ethridge** Tennessee USA
244 D4 **Etive** *watercourse* Scotland UK
244 C4 **Etive, Loch** *lake* Scotland UK
233 F8 **Etna, Monte** *volcano* Italy
224 C3 **Etne** Norway
116 C7 **Etolin Strait** Alaska USA
387 J2 **Etorofu-tō (Ostrov Iturup)** *island* Russian Federation
308 C3 **Etosha Pan** Namibia
305 G4 **Etoumbi** Congo
131 I3 **Etowah** Tennessee USA
241 H5 **Étretat** France
232 B4 **Etroubles** Italy
308 D3 **Etsha** Botswana
426 6 **Ettal** *island* Federated States of Micronesia
229 H2 **Ettelbruck** Luxembourg
244 D3 **Etteridge** Highland Scotland UK
229 I2 **Ettlingen** Germany
423 C7 **Ettrick** New Zealand
244 E5 **Ettrick** Scottish Borders Scotland UK
132 D4 **Etzatlán** Mexico
119 O8 **Etzicom Coulee** *watercourse* Alberta Canada
119 P8 **Etzikom** Alberta Canada
241 I4 **Eu** France
427 10 **'Eua Island** Tonga
426 6 **Euaripik** *island* Federated States of Micronesia
424 I7 **Eucla** WA Australia
127 K6 **Euclid** Ohio USA
123 F7 **Eudistes, Lac des** *lake* Québec Canada
130 F4 **Eudora** Arkansas USA
425 K8 **Eudunda** SA Australia
131 I5 **Eufaula** Alabama USA
130 D3 **Eufaula Lake** Oklahoma USA
124 D4 **Eugene** Oregon USA
128 E7 **Eugenia, Punta** *cape* Mexico
133 H5 **Eugenio Echeverría Castellot** Mexico
230 B2 **Eume, Embalse do** *lake* Spain
425 N5 **Eungella** Qld Australia
129 K4 **Eunice** New Mexico USA
229 H1 **Eupen** Belgium
130 G4 **Eupora** Mississippi USA
228 E2 **Eure** *watercourse* France
126 C8 **Eureka** Kansas USA
124 H2 **Eureka** Montana USA
128 E1 **Eureka** Nevada USA
118 L4 **Eureka River** Alberta Canada
117 K3 **Eureka Sound** Nunavut Canada
425 M9 **Euroa** Vic. Australia
310 6a **Europa, Île** *island* Îles Éparses
160 E6 **Euskadi** Argentina
131 K6 **Eustis** Florida USA
130 H4 **Eutaw** Alabama USA
129 K6 **Eutimias** Mexico
116 G8 **Eutsuk Lake** British Columbia Canada
305 I3 **Euwo** *watercourse* Central African Republic
129 L2 **Eva** Oklahoma USA
158 E4 **Eva Eva, Serranía** *range* Bolivia
225 M2 **Eväjärvi** *lake* Finland
308 C3 **Evale** Angola
158 E3 **Evangelista** Bolivia
118 L8 **Evans** Washington USA
162 A5 **Evans, Isla** *island* Chile
127 M1 **Evans, Lac** *lake* Québec Canada
163 3 **Evans, Punta** *cape* Isla de San Andrés
436 S1 **Evans Ice Stream** Antarctica
436 R2 **Evans Peninsula** Antarctica
117 K6 **Evans Strait** Nunavut Canada
125 J6 **Evanston** Wyoming USA
126 H8 **Evansville** Indiana USA
130 B5 **Evant** Texas USA
126 I5 **Evart** Michigan USA
235 E6 **Evciler** Turkey
241 G1 **Evedon** Lincolnshire England UK
241 F3 **Evenlode** *watercourse* England UK
222 J2 **Evenskjær** Norway
425 J7 **Everard, Lake** SA Australia
379 F3 **Everest, Mount** Xizang Zizhiqu China
392 G5 **Everest, Mount** Nepal
124 D3 **Everett** Washington USA
228 F1 **Evergem** Belgium
132 C5 **Evermann, Cerro** *volcano* Mexico
224 H5 **Everöd** Sweden
224 G2 **Evertsberg** Sweden
241 F2 **Evesham** Worcestershire England UK
241 F2 **Evesham, Vale of** *valley* England UK
223 M5 **Evijärvi** Finland
305 G4 **Evinayong** Equatorial Guinea
224 D3 **Evje** Norway
222 H2 **Evjen** Norway
229 H3 **Evolène** Switzerland
230 C4 **Évora** Portugal
230 C4 **Évora** *admin. area* Portugal
237 AC8 **Evoron, Ozero** *lake* Russian Federation
162 C6 **Evout, Islas** *islands* Chile
228 D2 **Évran** France
228 D3 **Èvre** *watercourse* France
228 E2 **Évreux** France
228 D2 **Évron** France
235 E5 **Evros** *watercourse* Turkey
235 C7 **Evrotas** *watercourse* Greece
235 C6 **Evvoia** *island* Greece
426 4 **Ewa** Nauru
134 E3 **Ewarton** Jamaica
307 F3 **Ewaso Ngiro** *watercourse* Kenya
244 C3 **Ewe, Loch** *bay* Scotland UK
125 P5 **Ewing** Nebraska USA
436 U2 **Ewing Island** Antarctica
305 G5 **Ewo** Congo
158 E3 **Exaltación** Bolivia
240 D4 **Exbourne** Devon England UK
125 J1 **Excel** Alberta Canada
130 H5 **Excel** Alabama USA
308 E5 **Excelsior** South Africa
128 C1 **Excelsior Mountains** Nevada USA
229 J1 **Exdorf** Germany
240 D4 **Exe** *watercourse* England UK
436 P1 **Executive Committee Range** Antarctica
224 G4 **Exen** *lake* Sweden
128 C2 **Exeter** California USA
240 D3 **Exford** Somerset England UK
228 E2 **Exmes** France
240 D4 **Exminster** Devon England UK
240 D3 **Exmoor** England UK
127 N8 **Exmore** Virginia USA
424 E5 **Exmouth** WA Australia
240 D4 **Exmouth** Devon England UK
424 E5 **Exmouth Gulf** WA Australia
81 P6 **Exmouth Plateau** *underwater feature* Indian Ocean
244 inset **Exnaboe** Shetland Scotland UK
235 C5 **Exochi** Greece
123 J8 **Exploits** *watercourse* Newfoundland and Labrador Canada
123 K8 **Exploits, Bay of** Newfoundland and Labrador Canada
119 N7 **Exshaw** Alberta Canada
230 C4 **Extremadura** *admin. area* Spain
305 G2 **Extrême-Nord** *admin. area* Cameroon
156 F4 **Extremoz** Brazil
156 E4 **Exu** Brazil
134 E1 **Exuma Cays** *islands* Bahamas
134 E1 **Exuma Sound** *bay* Bahamas
307 F4 **Eyasi, Lake** Tanzania
241 I2 **Eye** Suffolk England UK
244 F5 **Eyemouth** Scottish Borders Scotland UK
231 I2 **Eyguières** France
222 inset **Eyjafjarðará** *watercourse* Iceland
222 inset **Eyjafjörður** *bay* Iceland
307 H2 **Eyl** Somalia
307 H2 **Eyl** *watercourse* Somalia
228 E4 **Eymoutiers** France
126 E5 **Eyota** Minnesota USA
425 K7 **Eyre North, Lake** SA Australia
425 J8 **Eyre Peninsula** SA Australia
425 K7 **Eyre South, Lake** SA Australia
229 G4 **Eyrieux** *watercourse* France
117 S6 **Eysturoy** *island* Faroe Islands
240 E2 **Eyton** Herefordshire England UK
230 D6 **Ez Zinate** Morocco
308 F5 **Ezakheni** South Africa
132 C2 **Ezcalqui** Mexico
230 E2 **Ezcaray** Spain
162 C2 **Ezequiel Ramos Mexía, Embalse** *lake* Argentina
225 L4 **Ezere** Latvia
234 F4 **Ezerec** Bulgaria
381 G2 **Ezhou** Hubei China

F

427 14a **Faaa** French Polynesia
393 D11 **Faadhippolhu Atoll** Maldives
307 G3 **Faafxadhuun** Somalia
427 14b **Faanui** French Polynesia
231 G2 **Fabian** France
222 J4 **Fäbodliden** Sweden
224 I2 **Fäbodön** *cape* Sweden
232 E5 **Fabriano** Italy
157 D7 **Fabriciano** Brazil
119 P6 **Fabyan** Alberta Canada
243 G2 **Faceby** North Yorkshire England UK
301 I5 **Fachi** Niger
162 B4 **Fachinal** Chile
233 H6 **Faci, Punta** *cape* Italy
162 C3 **Facundo** Argentina
302 C4 **Fada** Chad
304 E2 **Fada N'gourma** Burkina Faso
234 A2 **Fadd** Hungary
116 A6 **Faddeya, Mys** *cape* Russian Federation
237 W3 **Faddeya, Zaliv** *bay* Russian Federation
237 AD3 **Faddeyevskiy, Ostrov** *island* Russian Federation
121 V5 **Faden** Newfoundland and Labrador Canada
389 M2 **Fadikha** *lake* Russian Federation
232 D4 **Faenza** Italy
233 F6 **Faeto** Italy
305 H3 **Fafa** *watercourse* Central African Republic
230 B3 **Fafe** Portugal
307 G2 **Fafen** *watercourse* Ethiopia
304 E2 **Faga** *watercourse* Burkina Faso
427 12c **Fagamalo** Samoa
234 D3 **Făgăraş** Romania
222 I6 **Fågelsjö** Sweden
222 I4 **Fågelsjön** *bay* Sweden
224 H2 **Fågelsjön** *lake* Sweden
224 I2 **Fågelsundet** Sweden
224 E1 **Fagerhaug** Norway
222 L4 **Fagerheden** Sweden
222 J3 **Fagerli** Norway
224 H3 **Fagersta** Sweden
234 C3 **Făget** Romania
305 F2 **Faggo** Nigeria
372 D4 **Fagita** Indonesia
162 C6 **Fagnano, Lago** *lake* Argentina
302 E4 **Fagrinkotti** Sudan
222 inset **Fagurholsmýri** Iceland
310 1b **Faial** *island* Azores
310 1b **Faial, Canal do** *strait* Azores

233 C9 **Faid** Tunisia
229 I3 **Faido** Switzerland
127 M2 **Faillon, Lac** *lake* Québec Canada
244 C3 **Fain** Highland Scotland UK
116 E6 **Fairbanks** Alaska USA
125 Q6 **Fairbury** Nebraska USA
126 D6 **Fairfax** Missouri USA
125 Q8 **Fairfax** Oklahoma USA
131 K4 **Fairfax** South Carolina USA
124 H5 **Fairfield** Idaho USA
125 P6 **Fairfield** Nebraska USA
130 C5 **Fairfield** Texas USA
126 D8 **Fairland** Oklahoma USA
423 D7 **Fairlie** New Zealand
244 D5 **Fairlie** North Ayrshire Scotland UK
126 D5 **Fairmont** Minnesota USA
118 L4 **Fairview** Alberta Canada
126 I4 **Fairview** Michigan USA
125 M3 **Fairview** Montana USA
124 J7 **Fairview** Utah USA
120 J1 **Fairway Island** Nunavut Canada
118 C3 **Fairweather, Mount** British Columbia/Alaska Canada/USA
242 A4 **Fairybush** Ireland
245 D3 **Fairymount** Ireland
426 6 **Fais** *island* Federated States of Micronesia
391 M3 **Faisalabad** Pakistan
125 N4 **Faith** South Dakota USA
233 E6 **Faiti** Italy
392 F5 **Faizabad** Uttar Pradesh India
390 D3 **Fajr, Wādī** *watercourse* Saudi Arabia
376 D3 **Fak Tha** Thailand
427 14 **Fakahina** *island* French Polynesia
422 3 **Fakaofo Village** Tokelau New Zealand
427 14 **Fakarava** *island* French Polynesia
388 F4 **Fakeyevo** Kazakhstan
372 E4 **Fakfak, Pegunungan** *range* Indonesia
234 E4 **Fakija** Bulgaria
232 H4 **Fakovići** Bosnia and Herzegovina
224 G5 **Fakse Bugt** *bay* Denmark
385 J4 **Faku** Liaoning China
304 B3 **Falaba** Sierra Leone
304 E2 **Falagountou** Burkina Faso
244 F5 **Falahill** Scottish Borders Scotland UK
228 D2 **Falaise** France
119 M2 **Falaise Lake** Northwest Territories Canada
379 G4 **Falam** Myanmar
426 8 **Falamae** Solomon Islands
244 D6 **Falbae** Dumfries and Galloway Scotland UK
245 D1 **Falcarragh** Ireland
230 B2 **Falcoeira, Cabo** *cape* Spain
154 D2 **Falcón** *admin. area* Venezuela
133 F3 **Falcón, Presa** *lake* Mexico
232 E5 **Falconara Marittima** Italy
122 F4 **Falcoz** *watercourse* Québec Canada
304 B2 **Falea** Mali
427 12c **Falealupo** Samoa
427 13a **Falefatu** *island* Tuvalu
427 12c **Falelima** Samoa
300 D6 **Falémé** *watercourse* Mali
233 G7 **Falerna** Italy
130 B7 **Falfurrias** Texas USA
118 M5 **Falher** Alberta Canada
224 G4 **Falkenberg** Sweden
244 E4 **Falkirk** Falkirk Scotland UK
244 E5 **Falkirk** *admin. area* Scotland UK
77 N14 **Falkland Escarpment** *underwater feature* Atlantic Ocean
162 F5 **Falkland Islands (Islas Malvinas)** *UK territory* Atlantic Ocean
77 M15 **Falkland Plateau** *underwater feature* Atlantic Ocean
163 7 **Falkland Sound** *strait* Falkland Islands
235 D7 **Falkonera** *island* Greece
127 P6 **Fall River** Massachusetts USA
242 A1 **Fallask** Ireland
244 E5 **Fallford** Dumfries and Galloway Scotland UK
222 L4 **Fällfors** Sweden
436 T2 **Fallières Coast** Antarctica
124 F7 **Fallon** Nevada USA
130 B6 **Falls City** Texas USA
131 L3 **Falls Lake Reservoir** North Carolina USA
131 K3 **Fallston** North Carolina USA
163 18 **Falmouth** Antigua and Barbuda
240 B4 **Falmouth** Cornwall England UK
126 I7 **Falmouth** Kentucky USA
240 B4 **Falmouth Bay** England UK
244 F5 **Falnash** Scottish Borders Scotland UK
300 E6 **Falo** Mali
300 E6 **Falou** Mali
160 D2 **False Chipana, Punta** *cape* Chile
122 D4 **False** *watercourse* Québec Canada
122 J5 **False Cape** Newfoundland and Labrador Canada
231 G3 **Falset** Spain
135 G3 **Falso, Cabo** *cape* Dominican Republic
134 D4 **Falso, Cabo** *cape* Honduras
132 C4 **Falso, Cabo** *cape* Mexico
160 D3 **Falso Azufre** *mountain* Chile
224 G5 **Falster** *island* Denmark
243 F1 **Falstone** Northumberland England UK
224 H2 **Falun** Sweden
372 D4 **Fam, Kepulauan** *island* Indonesia
394 E6 **Famagusta** Cyprus
160 E4 **Famatina** Argentina
160 E4 **Famatina, Sierra de** *range* Argentina
120 H7 **Family Lake** Manitoba Canada
376 D2 **Fan Si Pan** *mountain* Vietnam
300 E6 **Fana** Mali
224 C2 **Fana** Norway
245 E1 **Fanad Head** *cape* Ireland
426 6a **Fananani, Mochun** *strait* Federated States of Micronesia
426 6a **Fanapanges** *island* Federated States of Micronesia
235 E7 **Fanari, Akra** *cape* Greece
304 B2 **Fandanda** Mali
245 F3 **Fane** *watercourse* Ireland
224 G5 **Fanefjord Kirke** *bay* Denmark
235 D8 **Faneromeni, Akra** *cape* Greece
426 6a **Fanew, Mochun** *strait* Federated States of Micronesia
380 F2 **Fang Xian** Hubei China
306 E2 **Fangak** Sudan
427 14 **Fangatau** *island* French Polynesia
427 14 **Fangataufa** *island* French Polynesia
380 E4 **Fangchenggang** Guangxi Zhuangzu Zizhiqu China
380 E2 **Fangdou Shan** *range* Chongqing China
233 C5 **Fango** *watercourse* Corsica France
224 I3 **Fångö** *island* Sweden
385 K3 **Fangzheng** Heilongjiang China
372 D3 **Fani** *island* Indonesia
228 F5 **Fanjeaux** France
244 D3 **Fannich, Loch** *lake* Scotland UK
131 J6 **Fanning Springs** Florida USA
224 E5 **Fanø** *island* Denmark
232 E5 **Fano** Italy
224 E5 **Fanø Bugt** *bay* Denmark
235 C5 **Fanós** Greece
222 I4 **Fånsjön** *lake* Sweden
426 8 **Faore** *island* Solomon Islands
300 D6 **Faraba** Mali
306 D3 **Faradje** Democratic Republic of Congo
309 I4 **Farafangana** Madagascar
300 C6 **Farafenni** Gambia
302 D2 **Farāfirah, Wāḥāt Al** *spring* Egypt
233 D5 **Faraglione, Punta** *cape* Italy
391 J3 **Farāh** Afghanistan
391 J3 **Farāh** *admin. area* Afghanistan
391 J3 **Farāh Rūd** *watercourse* Afghanistan
426 2 **Farallon de Medinilla** *island* Northern Mariana Islands
426 2 **Farallon de Pajaros** *island* Northern Mariana Islands
234 E2 **Faraoani** Romania
388 I6 **Farap** Turkmenistan
373 H1 **Faraulep** *island* Federated States of Micronesia
234 D2 **Farcăul** *mountain* Romania
427 14a **Fareara, Pointe** *cape* French Polynesia
241 F4 **Fareham** Hampshire England UK
427 14a **Farehau** French Polynesia
224 D4 **Farestad** Norway
422 E5 **Farewell, Cape** New Zealand
391 H4 **Farghān** Iran
125 Q3 **Fargo** North Dakota USA
130 B2 **Fargo** Oklahoma USA
389 K6 **Farg'ona** Uzbekistan
389 K6 **Farg'ona** *admin. area* Uzbekistan
126 E4 **Faribault** Minnesota USA
122 C3 **Faribault, Lac** *lake* Québec Canada
392 D5 **Faridabad** Haryana India
392 D4 **Faridkot** Punjab India
379 F4 **Faridpur** Bangladesh
301 K2 **Farigh, Wādī al** *watercourse* Libya
222 I6 **Färila** Sweden
230 B4 **Farilhões, Ilhas** *islands* Portugal
304 A2 **Farim** Guinea-Bissau
391 I2 **Farīmān** Iran
241 F3 **Faringdon** Oxfordshire England UK
156 C4 **Farinha** *watercourse* Brazil
389 K6 **Farkhor** Tajikistan
236 S5 **Farkovo** Russian Federation
244 D2 **Farlary** Highland Scotland UK
235 E7 **Farmakonisi** *island* Greece
121 O3 **Farmer Island** Nunavut Canada
128 C2 **Farmersville** California USA
126 F6 **Farmington** Iowa USA
126 E4 **Farmington** Minnesota USA
130 G3 **Farmington** Mississippi USA
126 F8 **Farmington** Missouri USA
129 H2 **Farmington** New Mexico USA
126 J5 **Farmington Hills** Michigan USA
234 A2 **Farmos** Hungary
127 L8 **Farmville** Virginia USA
232 H3 **Farná** Slovakia
245 E3 **Farnagh** Ireland
241 G3 **Farnborough** Hampshire England UK
240 E1 **Farndon** Cheshire England UK
241 G3 **Farnham** Surrey England UK
118 M7 **Farnham, Mount** British Columbia Canada
243 F3 **Farnworth** Greater Manchester England UK
160 F6 **Faro** Argentina
305 G3 **Faro** *watercourse* Cameroon
116 F6 **Faro** Yukon Territory Canada
230 C5 **Faro** Portugal
230 B5 **Faro** *admin. area* Portugal
135 F5 **Faro, Punta** *cape* Colombia
435 F2 **Faroe Bank** *underwater feature* Atlantic Ocean
435 F2 **Faroe-Iceland Ridge** *underwater feature* Atlantic Ocean
117 S6 **Faroe Islands** *Danish admin. area* North Atlantic Ocean
225 J4 **Fårösund** Sweden
424 E5 **Farquhar, Cape** WA Australia
310 9 **Farquhar Group** *island* Seychelles
244 E3 **Farr** Highland Scotland UK
437 G2 **Farr Bay** Antarctica
244 D3 **Farraline** Highland Scotland UK
245 C4 **Farranfore** Ireland
425 L6 **Farrars** *watercourse* Qld Australia
118 K4 **Farrell Creek** British Columbia Canada
390 G3 **Fārs** *admin. area* Iran
390 G7 **Fartak, Ra's** *cape* Yemen
241 F2 **Farthinghoe** Northamptonshire England UK
157 B8 **Fartura** Brazil
Farvel, Kap *see* **Nunap Isua** Greenland
129 K3 **Farwell** Texas USA
436 R2 **Farwell Island** Antarctica
388 I7 **Fāryāb** *admin. area* Afghanistan
391 H3 **Faryādūn** Iran
391 H4 **Fasā** Iran
244 C3 **Fasag** Highland Scotland UK
244 C3 **Fasagrianach** Highland Scotland UK
233 G7 **Fasana** Italy
233 G6 **Fasano** Italy
427 12c **Fasito'otai** Samoa
224 H3 **Fåsjön** *lake* Sweden
301 I2 **Fassanu** Libya
226 F1 **Faßberg** Germany
372 D4 **Fatagar-Tuting, Tanjung** *cape* Indonesia
304 B2 **Fatala** *watercourse* Guinea
427 13a **Fatato** *island* Tuvalu
392 D5 **Fatehabad** Haryana India
392 D6 **Fatehgarh** Madhya Pradesh India
392 F6 **Fatehpur** Bihar India
392 E6 **Fatehpur** Madhya Pradesh India
392 D5 **Fatehpur** Rajasthan India
392 E5 **Fatehpur** Uttar Pradesh India
392 E6 **Fatehpur** West Bengal India
391 L3 **Fatehpur** Pakistan
388 H7 **Fathabad** Iran
306 E2 **Fathai** Sudan
127 N2 **Father Lake** Québec Canada
300 C6 **Fatick** Senegal
159 H5 **Fátima** Brazil
222 I4 **Fatmomakke** Sweden
300 D6 **Fatoto** Gambia
394 F5 **Fatsa** Turkey
222 I4 **Fättjarn** *lake* Sweden
427 14 **Fatu Hiva** *island* French Polynesia
306 B4 **Fatunda** Democratic Republic of Congo
391 H4 **Fatūyeh** Iran
222 I3 **Faulevatnet** *lake* Norway
125 P4 **Faulkton** South Dakota USA
228 J4 **Fauquembergues** France
118 L8 **Fauquier** British Columbia Canada
426 8 **Fauro** *island* Solomon Islands
222 I3 **Fauske** Norway
241 H5 **Fauville-en-Caux** France
159 F3 **Favela** Brazil
229 H4 **Faverges** France
241 H3 **Faversham** Kent England UK
122 C5 **Favery, Lac** *lake* Québec Canada
229 G2 **Favières** France
120 I6 **Favourable Lake** Ontario Canada
119 N5 **Fawcett** Alberta Canada
126 K6 **Fawn** *watercourse* Ontario Canada
242 A2 **Fawney** Strabane Northern Ireland UK
222 inset **Faxaflói** *bay* Iceland
222 J5 **Faxälven** *watercourse* Sweden
157 B9 **Faxinal** Brazil
305 H2 **Faya** Chad
304 C2 **Faya** *watercourse* Mali
236 P5 **Fayansovyy** Russian Federation
426 7 **Fayaoué** New Caledonia
390 E4 **Fayd** Saudi Arabia
229 H5 **Fayence** France
128 G1 **Fayette** Utah USA
130 D2 **Fayetteville** Arkansas USA
131 L3 **Fayetteville** North Carolina USA
131 H3 **Fayetteville** Tennessee USA
130 C6 **Fayetteville** Texas USA
390 E6 **Fayfā'** Saudi Arabia
229 G3 **Fayl-la-Forêt** France
390 F3 **Faylakā, Jazīrat** *island* Kuwait
426 6 **Fayo** *island* Federated States of Micronesia
130 B7 **Faysville** Texas USA
373 I1 **Fayu** *island* Federated States of Micronesia
232 E4 **Fažana** Croatia
304 E3 **Fazao, Monts** *range* Togo
159 I5 **Fazenda Nova** Brazil
159 G5 **Fazenda Rio Alegre** Brazil
158 E3 **Fazenda São José** Brazil
155 F6 **Fazenda Vista Alegre** Brazil
392 D4 **Fazilka** Punjab India
300 D4 **Fdérik** Mauritania
245 C4 **Feale** *watercourse* Ireland
131 M4 **Fear, Cape** North Carolina USA
244 C3 **Fearnmore** Highland Scotland UK
241 H5 **Fécamp** France
305 F3 **Federal Capital Territory** *admin. area* Nigeria
124 D3 **Federal Way** Washington USA
391 L3 **Federally Administered Tribal Areas** *admin. area* Pakistan
373 I2 **Federated States of Micronesia** *country* Oceania
226 E3 **Federsee** *lake* Germany
224 C2 **Fedje** *island* Norway
389 L2 **Fedorovka** Kazakhstan
388 F3 **Fedorovka** Kazakhstan
237 AD4 **Fëdorovskiy** Russian Federation
225 O4 **Fedosino** Russian Federation
238 H1 **Fedovo** Russian Federation
245 C3 **Feeagh, Lough** *lake* Ireland
245 E2 **Feeny** Limavady Northern Ireland UK
241 H3 **Feering** Essex England UK
426 6a **Fefan** *island* Federated States of Micronesia
224 F5 **Fehmarn** *island* Germany
157 D8 **Feia, Lago** *lake* Brazil
385 H6 **Feicheng** Shandong China
158 D3 **Feijó** Brazil
422 F5 **Feilding** New Zealand
157 E6 **Feira de Santana** Brazil
227 H4 **Feistritz** *watercourse* Austria
159 G4 **Feitoria do Guariroba** Brazil
159 G4 **Feitoria do Orlando** Brazil
159 I4 **Feitoria do Tiné** Brazil
385 H6 **Feixiang** Hebei China
232 H3 **Fejér** *admin. area* Hungary
224 F5 **Fejø** *island* Denmark
232 H3 **Fekeed** Hungary
237 AC7 **Feklistova, Ostrov** *island* Russian Federation
228 E2 **Fel** France
231 H4 **Felanitx** Spain
227 H4 **Feldbach** Austria
226 G1 **Feldberg** Germany
161 G4 **Feliciano** *watercourse* Argentina
393 C11 **Felidhu Atoll** Maldives
240 D2 **Felindre** Powys Wales UK
159 G2 **Felinto** Brazil
133 H5 **Felipe Carrillo Puerto** Mexico
160 F6 **Felipe Solá** Argentina
241 I3 **Felixstowe** Suffolk England UK
232 C2 **Fellbach** Germany
228 F4 **Felletin** France
131 K7 **Fellsmere** Florida USA
232 G3 **Felsőrajk** Hungary
227 K3 **Felsőzsolca** Hungary
240 D4 **Feltham** Somerset England UK
241 I2 **Felthorpe** Norfolk England UK
127 N7 **Felton** Delaware USA
226 F4 **Feltre** Italy
241 H2 **Feltwell** Norfolk England UK
224 F5 **Femer Bælt** *bay* Denmark
224 F5 **Femø** *island* Denmark
224 F3 **Femsjøen** *lake* Norway
222 G5 **Femund** *lake* Norway
222 G6 **Femundsundet** Norway
384 G6 **Fen He** *watercourse* Shanxi China
129 H3 **Fence Lake** New Mexico USA
222 I3 **Fenes** Norway
229 H2 **Fénétrange** France
226 D5 **Fenêtre, Col de** *pass* France/Switzerland
379 G2 **Feng** *mountain* Xizang Zizhiqu China
379 H2 **Feng** *mountain* Xizang Zizhiqu China
381 G4 **Fengcheng** Fujian China
381 H3 **Fengcheng** Fujian China
381 G4 **Fengcheng** Guangdong China
380 E4 **Fengcheng** Guangxi Zhuangzu Zizhiqu China
381 G1 **Fengcheng** Jiangsu China
381 G3 **Fengcheng** Jiangxi China
385 J5 **Fengcheng** Liaoning China
385 I3 **Fenghua** Zhejiang China
385 H5 **Fenghuang** Hebei China
380 E3 **Fengle** Sichuan China
380 D2 **Fengming** Sichuan China
385 I5 **Fengnan** Hebei China
384 G6 **Fengqi** Shaanxi China
379 H4 **Fengqing Fengshan** Yunnan China
381 G5 **Fengqiu** Henan China
381 I5 **Fengrun** Hebei China
381 H3 **Fengshan** Fujian China
381 H4 **Fengshan** Taiwan China
381 G4 **Fengshuba Shuiku** *lake* Guangdong China
385 J2 **Fengshui Shan** *mountain* Heilongjiang China
381 G2 **Fengtai** Anhui China
380 C4 **Fengwei** Yunnan China
385 I3 **Fengxiang** Heilongjiang China
380 E1 **Fengxiang** Shaanxi China
380 C4 **Fengxiang** Yunnan China
381 G4 **Fengyi** Guizhou China
380 D2 **Fengyi** Sichuan China
381 H4 **Fengyüan** Taiwan China
385 H5 **Fengzhen** Nei Mongol Zizhiqu China
385 H5 **Fengzhou** Hebei China
379 G4 **Feni** Bangladesh
373 J5 **Feni Islands** Papua New Guinea
128 E3 **Fenner** California USA
233 C6 **Feno, Capo di** *cape* Corsica France
309 I3 **Fenoarivo Atsinanana** Madagascar
241 H2 **Fens, The** *region* England UK
224 G2 **Fensbol** Sweden
381 H2 **Fenshui Jiang** *watercourse* Zhejiang China
224 F5 **Fensmark** Denmark
243 H3 **Fenton** Nottinghamshire England UK
126 J5 **Fenton** Michigan USA
244 D5 **Fenwick** East Ayrshire Scotland UK
384 G5 **Fenyang** Shanxi China
244 C5 **Feochaig** Argyll and Bute Scotland UK
394 E4 **Feodosiya** Ukraine
244 C5 **Feolin** Argyll and Bute Scotland UK
244 B5 **Feolin Ferry** Argyll and Bute Scotland UK
244 C5 **Feorlan** Argyll and Bute Scotland UK
231 J5 **Fer, Cap de** *cape* Algeria
222 G5 **Feragen** Norway
222 G5 **Feragen** *lake* Norway
238 H3 **Ferapontovo** Russian Federation
426 3 **Ferdinanda, Isla** *island* Archipiélago de Colón (Galapagos Islands)
391 I2 **Ferdows** Iran
235 E5 **Feres** Greece
127 K5 **Fergus** Ontario Canada
125 Q3 **Fergus Falls** Minnesota USA
120 I1 **Ferguson** *watercourse* Nunavut Canada
120 G1 **Ferguson Lake** Nunavut Canada
373 I6 **Fergusson Island** Papua New Guinea
301 H2 **Fériana** Tunisia
394 F6 **Ferikli** Turkey
231 J6 **Ferkane** Algeria
304 C3 **Ferkessedougou** Côte d'Ivoire
232 F3 **Ferlach** Austria
245 E2 **Fermanagh** *admin. area* Northern Ireland UK
121 V6 **Fermont** Québec Canada
230 C3 **Fermoselle** Spain
245 D4 **Fermoy** Ireland
124 D4 **Fern Ridge Reservoir** Oregon USA
230 E4 **Fernandina, Embalse de la** *lake* Spain
131 K5 **Fernandina Beach** Florida USA
77 **Fernando de Noronha** *island* Brazil
159 I6 **Fernandópolis** Brazil
309 H2 **Fernão Veloso** Mozambique
309 H2 **Fernão Veloso, Baía de** *bay* Mozambique
124 C6 **Ferndale** California USA
241 F4 **Ferndown** Dorset England UK
244 E3 **Ferness** Highland Scotland UK
244 B3 **Fernilea** Highland Scotland UK
124 F7 **Fernley** Nevada USA
245 F4 **Ferns** Ireland
123 J7 **Ferolle Point** Newfoundland and Labrador Canada
233 G6 **Ferrandina** Italy
226 F5 **Ferrara** Italy
233 C7 **Ferrato, Capo** *cape* Sardinia Italy
230 B4 **Ferreira do Zêzere** Portugal
244 C3 **Ferrindonald** Highland Scotland UK
130 C4 **Ferris** Texas USA
233 C6 **Ferro, Capo** *cape* Sardinia Italy
310 2 **Ferro, Ilhéu de** *island* Madeira
154 D5 **Ferro Velho** Brazil
230 B2 **Ferrol** Spain
124 J7 **Ferron** Utah USA
233 C7 **Ferru, Monte** *mountain* Sardinia Italy
233 F5 **Ferruccio, Punta di** *cape* Italy
231 H4 **Ferrutx, Cap** *cape* Spain
242 B4 **Ferrybank** Ireland
123 L9 **Ferryland** Newfoundland and Labrador Canada
244 D4 **Fersit** Highland Scotland UK
244 D5 **Ferter** South Ayrshire Scotland UK
125 Q3 **Fertile** Minnesota USA
232 G3 **Fertőrákos** Hungary
230 B2 **Fervenza, Embalse da** *lake* Spain
238 G5 **Ferzikovo** Russian Federation
300 E2 **Fès** Morocco
224 E3 **Feset** Norway
306 B5 **Feshi** Democratic Republic of Congo
125 P3 **Fessenden** North Dakota USA
222 I3 **Festvåg** Norway
372 D4 **Fet Dom, Tanjung** *cape* Indonesia
300 D6 **Fété Bowé** Senegal
234 E3 **Fetești** Romania
242 B4 **Fethard** Ireland
388 F5 **Fetisovo** Kazakhstan
233 E8 **Feto, Capo** *cape* Italy
226 F3 **Feuchtwangen** Germany
122 D3 **Feuilles, Baie aux** *bay* Québec Canada
122 D3 **Feuilles, Lac aux** *lake* Québec Canada
122 C3 **Feuilles, Rivière aux** *watercourse* Québec Canada
241 I5 **Feuquières** France
228 G4 **Feurs** France
222 F5 **Fevåg** Norway
385 L2 **Fevral'sk** Russian Federation
389 K6 **Feyfiābād** Afghanistan
240 D1 **Ffrith** Wrexham Wales UK
160 E3 **Fiambala** *watercourse* Argentina
304 D2 **Fian** Ghana
309 I4 **Fianarantsoa** Madagascar
309 I4 **Fianarantsoa** *admin. area* Madagascar
305 H3 **Fianga** Chad
234 B3 **Fibis** Romania
226 F5 **Ficarolo** Italy
307 F2 **Fichē** Ethiopia
226 G3 **Fichtelnaab** *watercourse* Germany
158 D4 **Fidalgo** *watercourse* Brazil
245 D3 **Fiddaun** Ireland
232 D4 **Fidenza** Italy
226 G4 **Fieberbrunn** Austria
79 T4 **Fieberling Tablemount** *underwater feature* Pacific Ocean
234 D3 **Fieni** Romania
235 A5 **Fier** Albania
229 G4 **Fier** *watercourse* France
234 E3 **Fierbinți-Târg** Romania
245 C4 **Fieries** Ireland
222 I3 **Fierras** *mountain* Sweden
377 G5 **Fiery Cross Reef** Spratly Islands
229 I3 **Fiesch** Switzerland
304 C2 **Fifa** Guinea
244 E4 **Fife** *admin. area* Scotland UK
119 S8 **Fife Lake** Saskatchewan Canada
244 F4 **Fife Ness** *cape* Scotland UK
305 G4 **Fifinda** Cameroon
163 19 **Fifth Cabin** British Columbia Canada
228 F4 **Figeac** France
232 D5 **Figline Valdarno** Italy
159 G5 **Figueira** Brazil
230 B3 **Figueira da Foz** Portugal
230 C3 **Figueira de Castelo Rodrigo** Portugal
230 B3 **Figueiró** Portugal
230 B4 **Figueiró dos Vinhos** Portugal
231 H2 **Figueres** Spain
301 F2 **Figuig** Morocco
305 G3 **Figuil** Cameroon
427 9 **Fiji** *country* Oceania
78 O9 **Fiji Plateau** *underwater feature* Pacific Ocean
307 G2 **Fīk'** Ethiopia
158 D3 **Filadelfia** Bolivia
161 F2 **Filadelfia** Paraguay
304 C2 **Filamana** Mali
234 E4 **Filaretovo** Bulgaria
238 C5 **Filatovo** Belarus
437 G2 **Filchner, Cape** Antarctica
436 V1 **Filchner Ice Shelf** Antarctica
243 H2 **Filey** North Yorkshire England UK
243 H2 **Filey Bay** England UK
235 B6 **Filiates** Greece
301 G6 **Filingué** Niger
234 E2 **Filipeni** Romania
234 D3 **Filipeștii de Pădure** Romania
222 F5 **Fillan** Norway
240 D3 **Filleigh** Devon England UK
119 T8 **Fillmore** Saskatchewan Canada
128 C3 **Fillmore** California USA
235 B5 **Filotas** Greece
232 E5 **Filottrano** Italy
307 G2 **Filtu** Ethiopia
437 A2 **Fimbul Ice Shelf** Antarctica
391 H4 **Fin** Iran
233 F7 **Finale** Italy
232 D4 **Finale Emilia** Italy
244 F4 **Finavon** Angus Scotland UK
225 J2 **Finbo** *island* Finland
225 J2 **Finbofjärden** *bay* Finland
225 K2 **Finby** Finland
307 F2 **Finch'a'ā Hāyk'** *lake* Ethiopia
242 A2 **Findermore** Dungannon Northern Ireland UK
244 E3 **Findhorn** Moray Scotland UK
244 D3 **Findhorn** *watercourse* Scotland UK
119 U8 **Findlay** Manitoba Canada
126 J6 **Findlay** Ohio USA
127 N4 **Fine** New York USA
125 Q3 **Fingal** North Dakota USA
122 G4 **Finger Hill Island** Newfoundland and Labrador Canada
120 I6 **Finger Lake** Ontario Canada
127 M5 **Finger Lakes** New York USA
244 E5 **Fingland** Dumfries and Galloway Scotland UK
309 F3 **Fingoè** Mozambique
235 G7 **Finike** Turkey
235 G7 **Finike Körfezi** *bay* Turkey
129 K8 **Finisterre** Mexico
230 E4 **Finisterre, Embalse de** *lake* Spain
425 J6 **Finke** NT Australia
425 J6 **Finke** *watercourse* NT Australia
126 E2 **Finland** Ontario Canada
223 O3 **Finland** *country* Europe
225 M3 **Finland, Gulf of** Europe
118 I4 **Finlay** *watercourse* British Columbia Canada
425 M8 **Finley** NSW Australia
245 C2 **Finn** *watercourse* Ireland
224 G2 **Finn-Skogne** *island* Norway
242 A3 **Finnea** Ireland
119 O7 **Finnegan** Alberta Canada
224 H3 **Finnerödja** Sweden
222 K2 **Finnkroken** Norway
223 N2 **Finnmark** *admin. area* Norway
223 N2 **Finnmarksvidda** *region* Norway
224 C3 **Finnøy** *island* Norway
222 J2 **Finnsnes** Norway
245 C3 **Finny** Ireland
373 H5 **Finschhafen** Papua New Guinea
224 F2 **Finstad** Norway
234 D2 **Fînţînele** Romania
245 E2 **Fintona** Omagh Northern Ireland UK
244 C3 **Fionn Loch** *lake* Scotland UK
244 B4 **Fionnphort** Highland Scotland UK
423 B7 **Fiordland** *region* New Zealand
119 T6 **Fir** *watercourse* Saskatchewan Canada
119 P4 **Firebag** *watercourse* Alberta Canada
124 E8 **Firebaugh** California USA
120 C2 **Firedrake Lake** Northwest Territories Canada
232 D5 **Firenze (Florence)** Italy
118 H3 **Fireside** British Columbia Canada
118 H4 **Firesteel** *watercourse* British Columbia Canada
304 B3 **Firestone Plantation** *place of interest* Liberia
244 D4 **Firkin** Argyll and Bute Scotland UK
160 F5 **Firmat** Argentina
226 C5 **Firminy** France
238 E4 **Firovo** Russian Federation
393 D8 **Firozabad** Karnataka India
392 E5 **Firozabad** Uttar Pradesh India
392 D4 **Firozpur** Punjab India
391 I5 **Firq** Oman
387 I1 **Firsovo** Russian Federation
244 inset **Firth** Shetland Scotland UK
391 G2 **Fīrūz Kūh** Iran
224 F4 **Fischen** Germany
123 K7 **Fischot Islands** Newfoundland and Labrador Canada
308 C5 **Fish** *watercourse* Namibia
126 E3 **Fish Lake Reservoir** Minnesota USA
127 Q3 **Fish River Lake** Maine USA
125 Q3 **Fisher** Minnesota USA
437 J2 **Fisher Bay** Antarctica
120 G7 **Fisher Bay** Manitoba Canada
437 E2 **Fisher Glacier** *ice* Antarctica
120 G7 **Fisher River** Manitoba Canada
117 K6 **Fisher Strait** Nunavut Canada
309 H4 **Fisherenana** *watercourse* Madagascar
120 H6 **Fishing Lake** Manitoba Canada
131 J2 **Fishtrap Lake** Kentucky USA
222 I4 **Fiskåfjället** *mountain* Sweden
436 U2 **Fiske, Cape** Antarctica
228 F2 **Fismes** France
230 B2 **Fisterra, Cabo** *cape* Spain
127 P5 **Fitchburg** Massachusetts USA
230 F2 **Fitero** Spain
427 12c **Fitiuta** American Samoa
427 12c **Fito, Mount** *volcano* Samoa
301 J6 **Fitri, Lac** *lake* Chad
240 E2 **Fitz** Shropshire England UK
118 H7 **Fitz Hugh Sound** British Columbia Canada
162 C4 **Fitz Roy** Argentina
424 F8 **Fitzgerald** WA Australia
131 J5 **Fitzgerald** Georgia USA
130 C3 **Fitzhugh** Oklahoma USA
424 G4 **Fitzroy** *watercourse* WA Australia
424 H4 **Fitzroy Crossing** WA Australia
163 7 **Fitzroy Settlement** Falkland Islands
127 K4 **Fitzwilliam Island** Ontario Canada
233 E6 **Fiuggi** Italy
233 G7 **Fiume Nicà, Punta** *cape* Italy
233 E6 **Fiumicino** Italy
244 C4 **Fiunary** Highland Scotland UK
423 B7 **Five Fingers Peninsula** New Zealand
163 18 **Five Island Harbour** *bay* Antigua and Barbuda
423 C7 **Five Rivers** New Zealand
232 D4 **Fivizzano** Italy
306 D4 **Fizi** Democratic Republic of Congo
222 I3 **Fjær** Norway
224 D3 **Fjæra** Norway
222 inset **Fjallaskagi** *cape* Iceland
222 I4 **Fjällfjällen** *mountain* Sweden
222 J4 **Fjällsjönäs** Sweden
222 H6 **Fjätervålen** Sweden
222 J2 **Fjelbu** Norway
224 C2 **Fjell** Norway
222 J2 **Fjelldal** Norway
222 K2 **Fjellfrøsvatnet** *lake* Norway
224 E3 **Fjone** Norway
223 M4 **Fjuskön** *island* Sweden
300 E2 **Fkih Ben Salah** Morocco
244 inset **Fladdabister** Shetland Scotland UK
243 G3 **Flagg** Derbyshire England UK
125 N7 **Flagler** Colorado USA
131 K6 **Flagler Beach** Florida USA
128 G3 **Flagstaff** Arizona USA
310 5b **Flagstaff Bay** St Helena
222 J2 **Flakstad** Norway
222 E6 **Flåm** Norway
243 I2 **Flamborough Head** *cape* England UK
162 E2 **Flamenco, Isla** *island* Argentina
125 K6 **Flaming Gorge Reservoir** Wyoming USA
126 E2 **Flanders** Ontario Canada
244 A2 **Flannan Isles** Scotland UK
224 H4 **Flåren** *lake* Sweden
222 K5 **Flärke** Sweden
222 L4 **Flarken** Sweden
125 O3 **Flasher** North Dakota USA
222 H5 **Flåsjön** *lake* Sweden
240 D3 **Flat Holm** *island* England UK
377 G5 **Flat Island** Spratly Islands
163 7 **Flat Jason** *island* Falkland Islands
130 F6 **Flat Lake** Louisiana USA
423 F5 **Flat Point** New Zealand
119 Q5 **Flat Valley** Saskatchewan Canada
119 N5 **Flatbush** Alberta Canada
224 H2 **Flaten** *lake* Sweden
119 N8 **Flathead** *watercourse* Montana USA
124 H3 **Flathead Lake** Montana USA
222 I5 **Flatnor** Sweden
130 C6 **Flatonia** Texas USA
222 H4 **Flått** Norway
425 M3 **Flattery, Cape** Qld Australia
124 C2 **Flattery, Cape** Washington USA
227 H4 **Flattnitz** Austria
127 inset **Flatts Village** Bermuda
422 G4 **Flaxmere** New Zealand
119 T8 **Flaxton** North Dakota USA
119 S8 **Flaxville** Montana USA
162 C4 **Flecha Negra** Argentina
377 I6 **Flecha Point** *island* Philippines
159 G5 **Flechas** Brazil
119 P6 **Fleet** Alberta Canada
241 G3 **Fleet** Hampshire England UK
242 E3 **Fleetwood** Lancashire England UK
222 H3 **Fleinvær** *island* Norway
224 E3 **Flekkerøy** *island* Norway
224 D1 **Flem** Norway
125 N6 **Fleming** Colorado USA
76 N5 **Flemish Cap** *underwater feature* Atlantic Ocean
224 I3 **Flen** Sweden
224 F5 **Flensburger Förde** *bay* Denmark
228 D2 **Flers** France
372 C3 **Flesko, Tanjung** *cape* Indonesia
130 B3 **Fletcher** Oklahoma USA
437 E2 **Fletcher, Cape** Antarctica
425 inset **Fletcher, Mount** Macquarie Island Australia
436 S2 **Fletcher Peninsula** Antarctica
123 J7 **Fleur de Lys** Newfoundland and Labrador Canada
123 F7 **Fleur-de-May, Lac** *lake* Newfoundland and Labrador Canada
228 E5 **Fleurance** France
232 B3 **Fleurier** Switzerland
425 K8 **Fleurieu Peninsula** SA Australia
228 E2 **Fleury** France
228 F5 **Fleury** France
155 F4 **Flexal** Brazil
229 I1 **Flieden** Germany
229 I3 **Flims** Switzerland
119 U5 **Flin Flon** Manitoba Canada
425 L4 **Flinders** *watercourse* Qld Australia
425 L3 **Flinders Group** *islands* Australia
425 J8 **Flinders Island** SA Australia
425 M10 **Flinders Island** Tas. Australia
425 N4 **Flinders Ranges** SA Australia
425 N4 **Flinders Reef** Coral Sea Islands Territory Australia
224 I2 **Flinsjön** *lake* Sweden
242 E3 **Flint** Flintshire Wales UK
131 H3 **Flint** *watercourse* Alabama USA
131 I4 **Flint** *watercourse* Georgia USA
126 J5 **Flint** Michigan USA
426 1 **Flint Island** Kiribati
120 M8 **Flint Lake** Ontario Canada
242 E3 **Flintshire** *admin. area* Wales UK
229 G2 **Flirey** France
241 G2 **Flitton** Bedfordshire England UK
241 J4 **Flixecourt** France
224 G3 **Flo** Sweden
226 B2 **Flobecq** Belgium
228 F3 **Flogny** France
226 G2 **Flöha** Germany
226 G2 **Flöha** *watercourse* Germany
130 H5 **Flomaton** Alabama USA
229 I2 **Flomborn** Germany
242 F2 **Flookburgh** Cumbria England UK
154 C5 **Flor de Agosto** Peru
155 F3 **Flor de Botiquin** Venezuela
159 H6 **Flor de Maio** Brazil
155 F5 **Flora** Brazil
130 F4 **Flora** Mississippi USA
228 F4 **Florac** France
226 C2 **Floreffe** Belgium
Florence *see* **Firenze** Italy
130 H3 **Florence** Alabama USA
128 G4 **Florence** Arizona USA
130 F4 **Florence** Mississippi USA
124 C5 **Florence** Oregon USA
131 L3 **Florence** South Carolina USA
125 Q4 **Florence** South Dakota USA
130 C5 **Florence** Texas USA
126 G4 **Florence** Wisconsin USA
161 G4 **Florencia** Argentina
154 C4 **Florencia** Colombia
228 F5 **Florensac** France
162 D3 **Florentino Ameghino** Argentina
229 G2 **Florenville** Belgium
161 G5 **Flores** *watercourse* Argentina
310 1 **Flores** *island* Azores
134 B3 **Flores** Guatemala
372 B6 **Flores** *island* Indonesia
161 G5 **Flores** *admin. area* Uruguay
375 H5 **Flores, Laut (Flores Sea)** Indonesia
118 H8 **Flores Island** British Columbia Canada
Flores Sea *see* **Flores, Laut** Indonesia
155 E5 **Floresta** Brazil
156 E5 **Floresta** Brazil
157 B8 **Florestópolis** Brazil
130 B6 **Floresville** Texas USA
129 K4 **Florey** Texas USA
156 D4 **Floriano** Brazil
161 I3 **Florianópolis** Brazil
159 F4 **Florida** Bolivia
134 E2 **Florida** Cuba
161 G5 **Florida** Uruguay
161 H5 **Florida** *admin. area* Uruguay
115 **Florida** *admin. area* USA
162 E2 **Florida, Punta** *cape* Argentina
134 D1 **Florida, Straits of** North America
131 K8 **Florida Bay** USA
131 K8 **Florida City** Florida USA
131 K8 **Florida Keys** *islands* USA
162 C4 **Florida Negra** Argentina
154 C3 **Floridablanca** Colombia
233 F8 **Floridia** Italy
126 F7 **Florissant** Missouri USA
222 G5 **Flornes** Norway
224 C2 **Florø** Norway
222 H6 **Flötningen** Sweden
235 E7 **Flouda, Akra** *cape* Greece
131 J4 **Flovilla** Georgia USA
123 J7 **Flower's Cove** Newfoundland and Labrador Canada
126 C5 **Floyd** *watercourse* Iowa USA
129 L4 **Floydada** Texas USA
226 C1 **Fluessen** *lake* Netherlands
224 I2 **Flugen** *lake* Sweden
229 H3 **Flühli** Switzerland
372 C4 **Fluk** Indonesia
224 I2 **Fluren** Sweden
240 B4 **Flushing** Cornwall England UK
231 H2 **Fluvià** *watercourse* Spain
373 G5 **Fly** *watercourse* Papua New Guinea
436 R2 **Flying Fish, Cape** Antarctica
424 inset **Flying Fish Cove** Christmas Island Australia
222 inset **Fnjóská** *watercourse* Iceland
427 10 **Foa** *island* Tonga
162 D4 **Foca, Punta** *cape* Argentina
154 A6 **Foca, Punta** *cape* Peru
244 E3 **Fochabers** Moray Scotland UK
234 E3 **Focșani** Romania
240 D2 **Foel** Powys Wales UK
234 B3 **Foeni** Romania
372 D7 **Fog Bay** Australia
224 I3 **Fogdön** *island* Sweden
301 G3 **Foggaret el Arab** Algeria
233 F6 **Foggia** Italy
372 C4 **Fogi** Indonesia
232 E5 **Foglia** *watercourse* Italy
233 E6 **Foglino, Lago di** *lake* Italy
225 K2 **Föglöfjärden** *bay* Finland
310 4 **Fogo** *island* Cape Verde
310 1a **Fogo, Lagoa do** *lake* Azores
310 4 **Fogo, Mount** *volcano* Cape Verde
123 K8 **Fogo Island** Newfoundland and Labrador Canada

224 E5 **Föhr** *island* Germany
245 C4 **Foiladaun** Ireland
228 E5 **Foix** France
373 F4 **Foja, Pegunungan** *range* Indonesia
305 E2 **Fokku** Nigeria
222 G4 **Folda** *bay* Norway
222 G4 **Foldefjorden** *bay* Norway
234 B2 **Földes** Hungary
130 H5 **Foley** Alabama USA
117 L5 **Foley Island** Nunavut Canada
127 J2 **Foleyet** Ontario Canada
224 D2 **Folgefonna** *lake* Norway
437 H2 **Folger, Cape** Antarctica
232 E5 **Foligno** Italy
222 E5 **Folkestad** Norway
241 I3 **Folkestone** Kent England UK
131 K5 **Folkston** Georgia USA
222 G5 **Follafoss** Norway
222 G5 **Folldal** Norway
130 A2 **Follett** Texas USA
243 G3 **Follifoot** North Yorkshire England UK
222 I5 **Föllinge** Sweden
232 D5 **Follonica** Italy
224 E3 **Follsjå** *lake* Norway
124 E7 **Folsom** California USA
130 F5 **Folsom** Louisiana USA
124 E7 **Folsom Lake** California USA
309 H2 **Fomboni** Comoros
237 W4 **Fomich** *watercourse* Russian Federation
304 C3 **Fon Going** *range* Guinea
163 I3 **Fond Bay** St Lucia
119 R3 **Fond-du-Lac** Saskatchewan Canada
126 G5 **Fond du Lac** Wisconsin USA
233 E6 **Fondi** Italy
230 C3 **Fonfría** Spain
222 G5 **Fongen** *mountain* Norway
230 C2 **Fonsagrada** Spain
154 C2 **Fonseca** Colombia
134 C4 **Fonseca, Golfo de** *bay* Honduras
229 G4 **Fontaine** France
162 B3 **Fontana, Lago** *lake* Argentina
230 D4 **Fontanosas** Spain
118 K3 **Fontas** British Columbia Canada
118 K3 **Fontas** *watercourse* British Columbia Canada
155 E5 **Fonte Boa** Brazil
159 G4 **Fonte do Pau-d'Água** Brazil
159 G4 **Fonte Termal Água Quente** Brazil
123 H7 **Fonteneau, Lac** *lake* Québec Canada
125 J5 **Fontenelle Reservoir** Wyoming USA
222 inset **Fontur** *cape* Iceland
427 10 **Fonualei** *island* Tonga
232 G3 **Fonyód** Hungary
231 G2 **Fonz** Spain
118 M6 **Foothills** Alberta Canada
118 M3 **Footner Lake** Alberta Canada
425 M8 **Forbes** NSW Australia
118 M7 **Forbes, Mount** Alberta/British Columbia Canada
305 F3 **Forcados** Nigeria
232 D2 **Forchheim** Germany
122 F4 **Ford** *watercourse* Québec Canada
245 F4 **Ford** Ireland
244 C4 **Ford** Argyll and Bute Scotland UK
243 G3 **Ford** Derbyshire England UK
240 E2 **Ford** Shropshire England UK
127 F4 **Ford** Kansas USA
424 I3 **Ford, Cape** Australia
436 O1 **Ford Ranges** Antarctica
372 D5 **Fordate** *island* Indonesia
236 B6 **Førdefjorden** *strait* Norway
422 F4 **Fordell** New Zealand
240 D2 **Forden** Powys Wales UK
126 H8 **Fordsville** Kentucky USA
390 G2 **Fordū** Iran
125 Q2 **Fordville** North Dakota USA
242 A3 **Fore** Ireland
304 B3 **Forécariah** Guinea
117 P5 **Forel, Mont** *mountain* Greenland
240 D3 **Foreland Point** England UK
130 D4 **Foreman** Arkansas USA
119 P8 **Foremost** Alberta Canada
130 G4 **Forest** Mississippi USA
131 K3 **Forest Acres** South Carolina USA
126 E5 **Forest City** Iowa USA
130 C4 **Forest Hill** Texas USA
244 E4 **Forest Lodge** Perth and Kinross Scotland UK
241 I4 **Forest-Montiers** France
131 I4 **Forest Park** Georgia USA
241 H3 **Forest Row** East Sussex England UK
121 U8 **Forestville** Québec Canada
228 D4 **Forêt des Landes** *region* France
244 F4 **Forfar** Angus Scotland UK
125 O8 **Forgan** Oklahoma USA
241 I5 **Forges-les-Eaux** France
232 D3 **Forggensee** *lake* Germany
242 B2 **Forkill** Newry and Mourne Northern Ireland UK
124 H3 **Forkland** Alabama USA
124 C3 **Forks** Washington USA
232 E4 **Forlì** Italy
125 Q3 **Forman** North Dakota USA
232 C3 **Formazza** Italy
242 E3 **Formby** Merseyside England UK
231 G4 **Formentera** *island* Spain
231 H4 **Formentor, Cap de** *cape* Spain
241 I5 **Formerie** France
233 E6 **Formia** Italy
161 J2 **Formiga** Brazil
161 G3 **Formosa** Argentina
161 G3 **Formosa** *admin. area* Argentina
157 C6 **Formosa** Brazil
159 H3 **Formosa, Serra** *range* Brazil
157 C5 **Formosa do Rio Preto** Brazil
157 B6 **Formoso** *watercourse* Brazil
230 C3 **Formoso** Portugal
224 F4 **Fornæs** *cape* Denmark
124 F3 **Fornells** Spain
222 J2 **Forneset** Norway
229 K3 **Forno di Zoldo** Italy
309 F4 **Fornos** Mozambique
304 F3 **Foro** Eritrea
234 B3 **Forotic** Romania
156 D3 **Forquilha** Brazil
161 I4 **Forquilhinha** Brazil
244 E3 **Forres** Moray Scotland UK
424 I7 **Forrest** WA Australia
126 G6 **Forrest** Illinois USA
130 F3 **Forrest City** Arkansas USA
119 Q4 **Forrest Lake** Saskatchewan Canada
436 U1 **Forrestal Range** Antarctica
118 E5 **Forrester Island** Alaska USA
222 J5 **Fors** Sweden
222 F4 **Forsa** Norway
129 L4 **Forsan** Texas USA
222 J2 **Forsbakken** Norway
238 A2 **Forsby** Finland
244 E2 **Forsinard** Highland Scotland UK
222 H3 **Forsland** Norway
224 I3 **Forsnäs** Sweden
222 F5 **Forsnes** Norway
225 L2 **Forssa** Finland
227 H2 **Forst** Germany
425 O8 **Forster** NSW Australia
131 J4 **Forsyth** Georgia USA
126 E8 **Forsyth** Missouri USA
125 L3 **Forsyth** Montana USA
162 A3 **Forsyth, Isla** *island* Chile
391 L3 **Fort Abbas** Pakistan
121 O6 **Fort Albany** Ontario Canada
308 E6 **Fort Beaufort** South Africa
116 I9 **Fort Belknap** Montana USA
125 J3 **Fort Benton** Montana USA
124 D7 **Fort Bragg** California USA
119 P3 **Fort Chipewyan** Alberta Canada
125 M6 **Fort Collins** Colorado USA
117 M2 **Fort Conger** Nunavut Canada
129 K5 **Fort Davis** Texas USA
135 I4 **Fort-de-France** Martinique
163 I4 **Fort-de-France, Baie de** *bay* Martinique
131 H5 **Fort Deposit** Alabama USA
126 D5 **Fort Dodge** Iowa USA
127 O5 **Fort Edward** New York USA
123 E9 **Fort Fairfield** Maine USA
118 I5 **Fort Fraser** British Columbia Canada
130 D2 **Fort Gibson Lake** Oklahoma USA
119 U3 **Fort Hall** Manitoba Canada
129 J5 **Fort Hancock** Texas USA
163 10a **Fort Jeudy, Point of** Grenada
124 D6 **Fort Jones** California USA
127 Q3 **Fort Kent** Maine USA
125 M5 **Fort Laramie** Wyoming USA
131 K7 **Fort Lauderdale** Florida USA
118 J2 **Fort Liard** Northwest Territories Canada
119 P4 **Fort MacKay** Alberta Canada
119 O8 **Fort Macleod** Alberta Canada
119 P4 **Fort McMurray** Alberta Canada
116 F5 **Fort McPherson** Northwest Territories Canada
126 F6 **Fort Madison** Iowa USA
241 I4 **Fort-Mahon-Plage** France
131 K7 **Fort Meade** Florida USA
125 N6 **Fort Morgan** Colorado USA
131 K7 **Fort Myers** Florida USA
131 K7 **Fort Myers Beach** Florida USA
118 J3 **Fort Nelson** British Columbia Canada
118 J3 **Fort Nelson** *watercourse* British Columbia Canada
131 I3 **Fort Payne** Alabama USA
125 L3 **Fort Peck Lake** Montana USA
131 K7 **Fort Pierce** Florida USA
125 O4 **Fort Pierre** South Dakota USA
118 M2 **Fort Providence** Northwest Territories Canada
119 T7 **Fort Qu'Appelle** Saskatchewan Canada
119 O2 **Fort Resolution** Northwest Territories Canada
118 I5 **Fort St James** British Columbia Canada
118 K4 **Fort St John** British Columbia Canada
119 O6 **Fort Saskatchewan** Alberta Canada
120 L5 **Fort Severn** Ontario Canada
118 K2 **Fort Simpson** Northwest Territories Canada
119 P2 **Fort Smith** Northwest Territories Canada
130 D3 **Fort Smith** Arkansas USA
129 K5 **Fort Stockton** Texas USA
129 J3 **Fort Sumner** New Mexico USA
131 J4 **Fort Valley** Georgia USA
119 M3 **Fort Vermilion** Alberta Canada
119 Q8 **Fort Walsh** Saskatchewan Canada
131 H5 **Fort Walton Beach** Florida USA
126 I6 **Fort Wayne** Indiana USA
244 C4 **Fort William** Highland Scotland UK
130 C4 **Fort Worth** Texas USA
125 O3 **Fort Yates** North Dakota USA
116 E5 **Fort Yukon** Alaska USA
158 E4 **Fortaleza** Bolivia
158 E3 **Fortaleza** Brazil
231 F3 **Fortanete** Spain
232 D5 **Forte dei Marmi** Italy
424 F5 **Fortescue** *watercourse* WA Australia
244 D4 **Forth** *watercourse* Scotland UK
244 E5 **Forth** South Lanarkshire Scotland UK
244 F4 **Forth, Firth of** *bay* Scotland UK
124 H7 **Fortification Range** Nevada USA
123 E7 **Fortin, Lac** *lake* Québec Canada
160 F2 **Fortín Ávalos Sánchez** Paraguay
160 E2 **Fortín Campero** Argentina
160 F2 **Fortín Coronel Eugenia Garay** Paraguay
159 F5 **Fortín La Victoria** Bolivia
160 F3 **Fortín Lavalle** Argentina
160 F2 **Fortín Pilcomayo** Argentina
160 F2 **Fortín Pozo Hondo** Paraguay
161 G3 **Fortín Sargento Primero Leyes** Argentina
160 E6 **Fortín Uno** Argentina
244 D4 **Fortingall** Perth and Kinross Scotland UK
241 F3 **Forton** Hampshire England UK
242 F3 **Forton** Lancashire England UK
233 F6 **Fortore** *watercourse* Italy
154 D3 **Fortoul** Colombia
423 C8 **Fortrose** New Zealand
244 D3 **Fortrose** Highland Scotland UK
156 C4 **Fortuna** Brazil
124 C6 **Fortuna** California USA
119 T8 **Fortuna** North Dakota USA
234 F3 **Fortuna, Lacul** *lake* Romania
123 K9 **Fortune Bay** Newfoundland and Labrador Canada
391 H4 **Forūr, Jazīreh-ye** *island* Iran
229 G5 **Fos-sur-Mer** France
241 G2 **Fosdyke** Lincolnshire England UK
381 G4 **Foshan** Guangdong China
117 K2 **Fosheim Peninsula** Nunavut Canada
222 G4 **Fosna** *region* Norway
304 D3 **Foso** Ghana
130 B3 **Foss** Oklahoma USA
226 D5 **Fossano** Italy
124 E4 **Fossil** Oregon USA
125 R3 **Fosston** Minnesota USA
242 A4 **Fossy** Ireland
117 Q4 **Foster Bugt** *bay* Greenland
124 F5 **Foster Lake** Oregon USA
241 H3 **Foster Street** Essex England UK
126 J6 **Fostoria** Ohio USA
228 C3 **Fouesnant** France
305 G5 **Fougamou** Gabon
228 D2 **Fougères** France
427 10a **Fo'ui** Tonga
130 E4 **Fouke** Arkansas USA
163 12 **Foul Bay** Barbados
393 E10 **Foul Point** Sri Lanka
304 C2 **Foulabala** Mali
229 G2 **Foulain** France
304 B2 **Foulamôri** Guinea
241 H3 **Foulness Point** England UK
423 D5 **Foulwind, Cape** New Zealand
300 E2 **Foum Zguid** Morocco
310 8a **Foumbouni** Comoros
436 T1 **Foundation Ice Stream** Antarctica
304 E2 **Founougo** Benin
125 M7 **Fountain** Colorado USA
124 G4 **Fountain Hills** Arizona USA
131 J3 **Fountain Inn** South Carolina USA
116 C8 **Four Mountains, Islands of the** Alaska USA
241 H4 **Four Oaks** East Sussex England UK
228 D4 **Fouras** France
123 H10 **Fourchu** Nova Scotia Canada
123 H6 **Fourmont, Lac** *lake* Newfoundland and Labrador Canada
235 B6 **Fourna** Greece
310 7a **Fournaise, Piton de la** *volcano* Réunion
228 F4 **Fournels** France
423 6 **Fournier, Cape** Chatham Islands New Zealand
123 F7 **Fournier, Lac** *lake* Québec Canada
235 E7 **Fournoi** Greece
235 E7 **Fournoi** *island* Greece
228 F3 **Fours** France
243 F1 **Fourstones** Northumberland England UK
118 H4 **Fourth Cabin** British Columbia Canada
304 B2 **Fouta Djallon** *range* Guinea
135 F3 **Foux, Cap-à-** *cape* Haiti
423 B8 **Foveaux Strait** New Zealand
240 C4 **Fowey** *watercourse* England UK
118 F4 **Fowler** British Columbia Canada
125 M7 **Fowler** Colorado USA
436 S1 **Fowler Ice Rise** Antarctica
130 B6 **Fowlerton** Texas USA
240 E2 **Fownhope** Herefordshire England UK
118 I4 **Fox** *watercourse* British Columbia Canada
163 7 **Fox Bay East** Falkland Islands
163 7 **Fox Bay West** Falkland Islands
118 M5 **Fox Creek** Alberta Canada
116 C8 **Fox Islands** Alaska USA
119 U4 **Fox Mine** Manitoba Canada
117 L5 **Foxe Basin** Nunavut Canada
117 K5 **Foxe Channel** Nunavut Canada
117 L6 **Foxe Peninsula** Nunavut Canada
245 C3 **Foxford** Ireland
245 C3 **Foxhall** Ireland
422 F5 **Foxton Beach** New Zealand
119 U7 **Foxwarren** Manitoba Canada
240 E3 **Foy** Herefordshire England UK
162 B3 **Foyel** Argentina
244 D3 **Foyers** Highland Scotland UK
245 E3 **Foygh** Ireland
130 D2 **Foyil** Oklahoma USA
245 E1 **Foyle, Lough** *bay* Northern Ireland UK
245 E2 **Foyle Hill** Londonderry Northern Ireland UK
245 C4 **Foynes** Ireland
230 C2 **Foz** Spain
161 I3 **Foz de Areia, Represa do** *reservoir* Brazil
308 B3 **Foz do Cunene** Angola
161 H3 **Foz do Iguaçu** Brazil
241 F2 **Fradley** Staffordshire England UK
222 E5 **Fræna** *island* Norway
231 G3 **Fraga** Spain
135 F2 **Fraile, Punta del** *cape* Cuba
243 H2 **Fraisthorpe** East Riding of Yorkshire England UK
436 Q1 **Frakes, Mount** Antarctica
437 E2 **Fram Bank** *underwater feature* Antarctica
435 F1 **Fram Basin** *underwater feature* Arctic Ocean
437 D2 **Fram Peak** *mountain* Antarctica
437 E2 **Framnes Mountains** Antarctica
241 G2 **Frampton** Lincolnshire England UK
224 D3 **Framvaren** *bay* Norway
161 J2 **Franca** Brazil
155 H3 **Françaises, Montagnes** *range* Suriname
228 **France** *country* Europe
117 R3 **France, Île de** *island* Greenland
122 G2 **Frances** *watercourse* Yukon Territory Canada
155 G6 **Francês** Brazil
134 D2 **Francés, Punta** *cape* Cuba
122 G2 **Frances Lake** Yukon Territory Canada
Franceville *see* **Masuku** Gabon
240 E2 **Franche** Worcestershire England UK
229 G3 **Franche-Comté** *admin. area* France
122 E5 **Francheville, Lac** *lake* Québec Canada
134 C4 **Francia** Honduras
119 T7 **Francis** Saskatchewan Canada
124 I2 **Francis, Lake** Montana USA
125 P5 **Francis Case, Lake** South Dakota USA
161 H3 **Francisco Beltrão** Brazil
129 K8 **Francisco I. Madero** Mexico
159 H4 **Francisco Lucas** Brazil
157 D7 **Francisco Sá** Brazil
130 B8 **Francisco Villa** Mexico
308 E4 **Francistown** Botswana
118 H5 **François Lake** British Columbia Canada
232 H2 **Francova Lhota** Czech Republic
226 C1 **Franeker** Netherlands
242 A4 **Frankeen's** Ireland
232 C2 **Frankenthal** Germany
126 H6 **Frankfort** Indiana USA
126 I7 **Frankfort** Kentucky USA
227 H1 **Frankfurt** Germany
229 I1 **Frankfurt am Main** Germany
226 F3 **Fränkische Alb** *region* Germany
425 M9 **Frankland, Cape** Tas. Australia
126 F5 **Franklin** Louisiana USA
125 P6 **Franklin** Nebraska USA
127 L6 **Franklin** Pennsylvania USA
130 H3 **Franklin** Tennessee USA
130 C5 **Franklin** Texas USA
127 L7 **Franklin** West Virginia USA
116 G5 **Franklin Bay** Northwest Territories Canada
124 F2 **Franklin D. Roosevelt Lake** Washington USA
437 L1 **Franklin Island** Antarctica
124 H6 **Franklin Lake** Nevada USA
116 G6 **Franklin Mountains** Northwest Territories Canada
423 B7 **Franklin Mountains** New Zealand
127 K6 **Franklin Park** Pennsylvania USA
76 P4 **Franklin Seamount** *underwater feature* Atlantic Ocean
437 L1 **Franklin Shoals** *underwater feature* Ross Sea
117 J4 **Franklin Strait** Nunavut Canada
130 F5 **Franklinton** Louisiana USA
222 H5 **Frankrike** Sweden
130 D4 **Frankston** Texas USA
125 K4 **Frannie** Wyoming USA
121 V8 **Franquelin** Québec Canada
308 B4 **Fransfontein** Namibia
117 R3 **Franske Øer** *island* Greenland
134 M3 **Fransta-Iosifa, Zemlya (Frantz Josef Land)** *island* Russian Federation
222 J5 **Fränsta** Sweden
241 H3 **Frant** East Sussex England UK
236 M3 **Franz Josef Land** *see* **Frantsa-Iosifa, Zemlya**
224 G5 **Franzburg** Germany
233 C7 **Frasca, Capo della** *cape* Sardinia Italy
118 D3 **Fraser** British Columbia Canada
118 J6 **Fraser** *watercourse* British Columbia Canada
122 G4 **Fraser** *watercourse* Newfoundland and Labrador Canada
425 J6 **Fraser Island** Qld Australia
118 I5 **Fraser Lake** British Columbia Canada
122 G5 **Fraser Lake** Newfoundland and Labrador Canada
118 J6 **Fraser Plateau** British Columbia Canada
308 D6 **Fraserburg** South Africa
244 F3 **Fraserburgh** Aberdeenshire Scotland UK
121 O8 **Fraserdale** Ontario Canada
422 G4 **Frasertown** New Zealand
126 I3 **Frater** Ontario Canada
229 I3 **Frauenfeld** Switzerland
161 G5 **Fray Bentos** Uruguay
160 E6 **Fray Luis Beltrán** Argentina
229 H2 **Fraze** France
228 E2 **Frazé** France
242 F3 **Freckleton** Lancashire England UK
232 D4 **Freddi, Monte** *mountain* Italy
126 E4 **Frederic** Wisconsin USA
224 E5 **Fredericia** Denmark
127 M7 **Frederick** Maryland USA
130 B3 **Frederick** Oklahoma USA
125 P4 **Frederick** South Dakota USA
117 P2 **Frederick E. Hyde Fjord** Greenland
127 K2 **Frederick House Lake** Ontario Canada
425 O5 **Frederick Reef** Coral Sea Islands Territory Australia
130 B5 **Fredericksburg** Texas USA
127 M7 **Fredericksburg** Virginia USA
126 F8 **Fredericktown** Missouri USA
123 E10 **Fredericton** New Brunswick Canada
123 E10 **Fredericton Junction** New Brunswick Canada
122 M1 **Frederikshåb Isblink** *ice* Greenland
224 F4 **Frederikshavn** Denmark
163 21 **Frederiksted** US Virgin Islands
128 F2 **Fredonia** Arizona USA
127 L5 **Fredonia** New York USA
222 K4 **Fredrika** Sweden
224 F3 **Fredrikstad** Norway
308 E5 **Free State** *admin. area* South Africa
130 B2 **Freedom** Oklahoma USA
123 L8 **Freels, Cape** Newfoundland and Labrador Canada
119 N5 **Freeman** *watercourse* Alberta Canada
437 I2 **Freeman Point** Antarctica
131 L7 **Freeport** Bahamas
126 G5 **Freeport** Illinois USA
127 O6 **Freeport** New York USA
130 D6 **Freeport** Texas USA
130 B7 **Freer** Texas USA
304 B3 **Freetown** Sierra Leone
310 9a **Frégate** *island* Seychelles
121 R6 **Frégate, Lac de la** *lake* Québec Canada
230 C4 **Fregenal de la Sierra** Spain
Fregon *see* **Kaltjiti** Australia
228 C2 **Fréhel, Cap** *cape* France
222 E5 **Frei** Norway
436 U2 **Frei (Chile)** *research station* Antarctica
229 K1 **Freiberg** Germany
226 G2 **Freiberger Mulde** *watercourse* Germany
226 D4 **Freiburg im Breisgau** Germany
160 C6 **Freire** Chile
226 F3 **Freising** Germany
227 G2 **Freital** Germany
229 H5 **Fréjus** France
424 E8 **Fremantle** WA Australia
240 C3 **Fremington** Devon England UK
124 E8 **Fremont** California USA
125 Q6 **Fremont** Nebraska USA
126 J6 **Fremont** Ohio USA
126 G4 **Fremont** Wisconsin USA
155 H4 **French Guiana** *French department* South America
134 C3 **French Harbor** Honduras
126 H7 **French Lick** Indiana USA
124 E7 **French Meadows Reservoir** California USA
427 I4 **French Polynesia** *French overseas land* Pacific Ocean
126 F3 **French River** Minnesota USA
310 6 **French Southern and Antarctic Lands** *French overseas territory* Indian Ocean/Southern Ocean
126 J8 **Frenchburg** Kentucky USA
116 I9 **Frenchman** *watercourse* Saskatchewan Canada
128 C1 **Frenchman** Nevada USA
127 Q4 **Frenchman Bay** Maine USA
124 E7 **Frenchman Lake** California USA
245 D3 **Frenchpark** Ireland
301 G1 **Frenda** Algeria
232 H2 **Frenštát pod Radhoštěm** Czech Republic
156 B4 **Fresco** *watercourse* Brazil
244 E2 **Fresgoe** Highland Scotland UK
437 K2 **Freshfield, Cape** Antarctica
119 U6 **Freshford** Manitoba Canada
245 D4 **Freshford** Ireland
163 12 **Freshwater Bay** Barbados
162 B3 **Fresia** Chile
226 B2 **Fresnes** France
229 G3 **Fresnes** France
132 E4 **Fresnillo** Mexico
124 F8 **Fresno** California USA
125 J2 **Fresno Reservoir** Montana USA
241 I5 **Fresnoy-Folny** France
226 G1 **Fretzdorf** Germany
231 H4 **Freu, Cap des** *cape* Spain
228 F1 **Frévent** France
425 N10 **Freycinet Peninsula** Tas. Australia
222 E2 **Freyung** Germany
308 B2 **Fria** Guinea
308 B3 **Fria, Cape** Namibia
160 E4 **Frias** Argentina
229 H3 **Fribourg** Switzerland
157 D8 **Friburgo** Brazil
243 H2 **Fridaythorpe** East Riding of Yorkshire England UK
373 G5 **Frieda** *watercourse* Papua New Guinea
129 L1 **Friend** Kansas USA
125 Q6 **Friend** Nebraska USA
227 H4 **Friesach** Austria
163 19 **Frigate Bay** St Kitts and Nevis
241 G3 **Frimley** Surrey England UK
241 I3 **Frinton-on-Sea** Essex England UK
244 F4 **Friockheim** Angus Scotland UK
230 C2 **Friol** Spain
129 K3 **Friona** Texas USA
125 L7 **Frisco** Colorado USA
130 C4 **Frisco** Texas USA
131 H4 **Frisco City** Alabama USA
224 G4 **Frisjön** *lake* Sweden
241 H1 **Friskney** Lincolnshire England UK
129 L3 **Fritch** Texas USA
241 I2 **Fritton** Norfolk England UK
229 I1 **Fritzlar** Germany
232 E3 **Friuli-Venezia Giulia** *admin. area* Italy
242 E3 **Frizington** Cumbria England UK
222 F4 **Froan** *island* Norway
119 T8 **Frobisher** Saskatchewan Canada
117 M6 **Frobisher Bay** Nunavut Canada
119 Q4 **Frobisher Lake** Saskatchewan Canada
242 F3 **Frodsham** Cheshire England UK
120 K5 **Frog** *watercourse* Ontario Canada
222 F4 **Frohavet** *bay* Norway
227 H4 **Frohnleiten** Austria
125 M2 **Froid** Montana USA
228 F2 **Froissy** France
224 J4 **Fröjel** Sweden
388 D3 **Frolovo** Russian Federation
125 K4 **Fromberg** Montana USA
134 E3 **Frome** Jamaica
241 E3 **Frome** Somerset England UK
425 K7 **Frome, Lake** SA Australia
240 E4 **Frome St Quinton** Dorset England UK
230 D2 **Frómista** Spain
122 C6 **Fromont, Lac** *lake* Québec Canada
125 M6 **Front Range** Colorado USA
127 L7 **Front Royal** Virginia USA
122 C2 **Frontenac, Pointe** *cape* Québec Canada
310 3 **Frontera** Canary Islands
132 E3 **Frontera** Mexico
133 G5 **Frontera** Mexico
133 G5 **Frontera, Punta** *cape* Mexico
133 G6 **Frontera Comalapa** Mexico
128 H5 **Fronteras** Mexico
119 Q8 **Frontier** Saskatchewan Canada
228 F5 **Frontignan** France
228 E5 **Fronton** France
222 I2 **Frøskeland** Norway
222 J4 **Frostberget** Sweden
131 K7 **Frostproof** Florida USA
121 R7 **Frotet, Lac** *lake* Québec Canada
224 H3 **Frövi** Sweden
241 F3 **Froxfield** Wiltshire England UK
222 F5 **Frøya** *island* Norway
241 J4 **Fruges** France
125 K7 **Fruita** Colorado USA
127 N7 **Fruitland** Maryland USA
118 M8 **Fruitvale** British Columbia Canada
234 F2 **Frunza** Moldova
Frunze *see* **Bishkek** Kyrgyzstan
161 I2 **Frutal** Brazil
235 E8 **Fry** Greece
227 J3 **Frýdek-Místek** Czech Republic
227 H2 **Frýdlant** Czech Republic
127 P4 **Fryeburg** Maine USA
227 K1 **Frygnowo** Poland
224 G2 **Frysjøen** *lake* Norway
380 E2 **Fu Jiang** *watercourse* Chongqing China
380 D2 **Fu Jiang** *watercourse* Sichuan China
381 H3 **Fu`an** Fujian China
427 10a **Fua'amotu** Tonga
427 13a **Fuafatu** *island* Tuvalu
427 13a **Fuagea** *island* Tuvalu
427 13a **Fualefeke** *island* Tuvalu
427 13a **Fualopa** *island* Tuvalu
226 D4 **Fuans** France
384 E6 **Fucheng** Gansu China
385 H5 **Fucheng** Hebei China
381 H1 **Fucheng** Jiangsu China
384 G6 **Fucheng** Shaanxi China
381 H2 **Fuchun Jiang** *watercourse* Zhejiang China
310 3b **Fuencaliente de la Palma** Canary Islands
230 D5 **Fuengirola** Spain
230 E3 **Fuenlabrada** Spain
230 C4 **Fuente de Cantos** Spain
154 C4 **Fuente de Oro** Colombia
230 D5 **Fuente de Piedra, Laguna de** *lake* Spain
230 D4 **Fuenteovejuna** Spain
230 D5 **Fuentes de Andalucía** Spain
162 B5 **Fuentes del Coyle** Argentina
230 D3 **Fuentesaúco** Spain
134 E5 **Fuerte, Isla** *island* Colombia
310 3d **Fuerteventura** *island* Canary Islands
245 D3 **Fuerty** Ireland
377 I3 **Fuga** *island* Philippines
222 J2 **Fugleberg** Norway
435 H2 **Fugløy Bank** *underwater feature* Barents Sea
222 H3 **Fugløya** *island* Norway
381 G1 **Fugou** Henan China
385 I5 **Fuguo** Shandong China
383 H3 **Fuhai** Xinjiang Uygur Zizhiqu China
226 G2 **Fuhne** *watercourse* Germany
387 H4 **Fuji-san** *volcano* Japan
381 H3 **Fujian** *admin. area* China
385 L3 **Fujin** Heilongjiang China
387 H4 **Fujinomiya** Japan
302 D1 **Fūkah** Egypt
383 H4 **Fukang** Xinjiang Uygur Zizhiqu China
387 G4 **Fukuchiyama** Japan
386 F5 **Fukue-jima** *island* Japan
381 I3 **Fukuei Chiao** *island* Taiwan China
387 H4 **Fukui** Japan
386 F5 **Fukuoka** Japan
386 G4 **Fukuyama** Japan
427 9 **Fulaga** *island* Fiji
224 G2 **Fulan** *watercourse* Sweden
226 E2 **Fulda** Germany
226 E2 **Fulda** *watercourse* Germany
125 R5 **Fulda** Minnesota USA
243 G3 **Fulford** York England UK
241 G3 **Fulham** Greater London England UK
381 H2 **Fuliang** Jiangxi China
380 D2 **Fulin** Sichuan China
380 E2 **Fuling** Chongqing China
163 9 **Fullarton** Trinidad and Tobago
129 L4 **Fullerville** Texas USA
222 F6 **Fullsenn** *lake* Norway
234 C2 **Fülöp** Hungary
126 F7 **Fulton** Missouri USA
127 M5 **Fulton** New York USA
130 C6 **Fulton** Texas USA
127 N5 **Fulton Chain Lakes** New York USA
228 E4 **Fumel** France
427 13a **Funafuti** Tuvalu
427 13a **Funafuti Island** Tuvalu
427 13a **Funagongo** *island* Tuvalu
427 13a **Funamanu** *island* Tuvalu
381 G2 **Funan** Anhui China
310 2 **Funchal** Madeira
154 C2 **Fundación** Colombia
234 D3 **Fundata** Romania
300 B5 **Fundo das Figueiras** Cape Verde
123 E10 **Fundy, Bay of** New Brunswick/Nova Scotia Canada
385 I5 **Funing** Hebei China
226 G5 **Funtana** Croatia
305 F2 **Funtua** Nigeria
154 C3 **Funza** Colombia
244 inset **Funzie** Shetland Scotland UK
385 H5 **Fuping** Hebei China
233 C6 **Furana, Punta** *cape* Sardinia Italy
309 F2 **Furancungo** Mozambique
387 I2 **Furano** Japan
224 C2 **Fure** Norway
224 H4 **Furen** *lake* Sweden
245 C3 **Furmina** Ireland
244 C3 **Furnace** Highland Scotland UK
310 1a **Furnas** Azores
310 1a **Furnas, Lagoa das** *lake* Azores
161 J2 **Furnas, Represa** *reservoir* Brazil
159 H4 **Furnas, Serra das** *range* Brazil
425 N9 **Furneaux Group** *islands* Tas. Australia
381 G3 **Furong** Jiangxi China
234 B2 **Furta** Hungary
159 G6 **Furte Olimpo** Paraguay
226 E3 **Fürth** Germany
226 F3 **Furth** Germany
226 G3 **Furth im Wald** Germany
222 L2 **Furuflaten** Norway
222 L4 **Furuögrund** Sweden
222 F6 **Furusjøen** *lake* Norway
117 K5 **Fury and Hecla Strait** Nunavut Canada
154 C3 **Fusagasuga** Colombia
384 G6 **Fushan** Shanxi China
385 J4 **Fushun** Liaoning China
385 K4 **Fusong** Jilin China
162 B2 **Futa Ruin** Argentina
381 H3 **Futun Xi** *watercourse* Fujian China
426 7 **Futuna** *island* Vanuatu
427 12a **Futuna, Île** *island* Wallis and Futuna
158 D4 **Futuro** Bolivia
302 E1 **Fuwah** Egypt
380 D4 **Fuxian Hu** *lake* Yunnan China
385 J4 **Fuxin** Liaoning China
380 E3 **Fuxing** Guizhou China
381 G2 **Fuyang** Anhui China
381 F4 **Fuyang** Guangxi Zhuangzu Zizhiqu China
381 H2 **Fuyang** Zhejiang China
381 H3 **Fuying Dao** *island* Fujian China
385 J3 **Fuyu** Heilongjiang China
385 M3 **Fuyuan** Heilongjiang China
383 I3 **Fuyun** Xinjiang Uygur Zizhiqu China
381 H3 **Fuzhou** Fujian China
131 I3 **Fyffe** Alabama USA
224 F5 **Fyn** *island* Denmark
244 C5 **Fyne, Loch** *bay* Scotland UK
224 F5 **Fyns Hoved** *cape* Denmark
224 E3 **Fyresdal** Norway
224 E3 **Fyreselv** *watercourse* Norway
224 E3 **Fyresvatn** *lake* Norway
222 I5 **Fyrsjön** *lake* Sweden

G

389 P3 **G. Chureg Tag** *mountain* Russian Federation
307 H2 **Gaalkacyo** Somalia
375 G3 **Gaat** *watercourse* Malaysia
228 E5 **Gabarret** France
228 D5 **Gabas** *watercourse* France
384 D6 **Gabasongduo** Qinghai China
373 G6 **Gabba Island** Australia
128 D1 **Gabbs** Nevada USA
308 B2 **Gabela** Angola
301 I2 **Gabès** Tunisia
302 E3 **Gabgaba, Wādi** *watercourse* Sudan
306 B4 **Gabia** Democratic Republic of Congo
227 J1 **Gąbin** Poland
302 D5 **Gabir** Sudan
422 H4 **Gable End Foreland** *cape* New Zealand
305 G5 **Gabon** *country* Africa
305 F4 **Gabon, Estuaire du** *bay* Gabon
308 E4 **Gaborone** Botswana
235 C5 **Gabrene** Bulgaria
236 T4 **Gabrey, Vozvyshennost'** *range* Russian Federation
122 E1 **Gabriel Island** Nunavut Canada
132 C3 **Gabriel Leyva Solano** Mexico
122 F2 **Gabriel Strait** Nunavut Canada
234 D4 **Gabrovo** *admin. area* Bulgaria
304 B2 **Gabú** Guinea-Bissau
228 E2 **Gacé** France
388 F7 **Gach Sar** Iran
154 C3 **Gachalá** Colombia
154 C3 **Gachetá** Colombia
232 H5 **Gacko** Bosnia and Herzegovina
222 I5 **Gåda** Sweden
393 D8 **Gadag** Karnataka India
373 I6 **Gadaisu** Papua New Guinea
393 E7 **Gadchiroli** Maharashtra India
222 I4 **Gäddede** Sweden
392 C6 **Gadhara** Rajasthan India
393 C7 **Gadhada** Gujarat India
230 E5 **Gádor, Sierra de** *range* Spain
131 I3 **Gadsden** Alabama USA
393 D8 **Gadwal** Andhra Pradesh India
305 H4 **Gadzi** Central African Republic
223 P1 **Gædnjajav'ri** *lake* Norway
228 C2 **Gaël** France
117 Q4 **Gael Hamke Bugt** *bay* Greenland
240 D3 **Gaer** Powys Wales UK
240 E3 **Gaer-fawr** Monmouthshire Wales UK
223 O1 **Gæssejav'ri** *lake* Norway
234 D3 **Găeşti** Romania
233 E6 **Gaeta, Golfo di** *bay* Italy
230 B3 **Gafanha da Nazaré** Portugal
373 H1 **Gaferut** *island* Federated States of Micronesia
131 K3 **Gaffney** South Carolina USA
301 H2 **Gafsa** Tunisia
372 D4 **Gag** *island* Indonesia
305 H3 **Gagal** Chad
238 F5 **Gagarin** Russian Federation
389 J6 **Gagarin** Uzbekistan
129 H4 **Gage** New Mexico USA
130 A3 **Gageby** Texas USA
123 E10 **Gagetown** New Brunswick Canada
224 H2 **Gagnef** Sweden
304 C3 **Gagnoa** Côte d'Ivoire
121 U7 **Gagnon** Québec Canada
379 F4 **Gaibandha** Bangladesh
244 D4 **Gaick Lodge** Highland Scotland UK
390 E2 **Gaida** Iraq
232 E3 **Gail** *watercourse* Austria
129 L4 **Gail** Texas USA
226 E3 **Gaildorf** Germany
228 E5 **Gaillac** France
228 E2 **Gaillon** France
162 D3 **Gaimán** Argentina
131 J6 **Gainesville** Florida USA
131 J3 **Gainesville** Georgia USA
126 E8 **Gainesville** Missouri USA
130 C4 **Gainesville** Texas USA
125 O2 **Gainsborough** Saskatchewan Canada
244 C3 **Gair Loch** *bay* Scotland UK
425 B4 **Gairdner, Lake** SA Australia
244 C3 **Gairloch** Highland Scotland UK
244 E3 **Gairnshiel Lodge** Aberdeenshire Scotland UK
307 F5 **Gairo** Tanzania
223 O1 **Gaissane** *region* Norway
127 M7 **Gaithersburg** Maryland USA
378 E2 **Gaize** Xizang Zizhiqu China
385 J5 **Gaizhou** Liaoning China
225 M4 **Gaiziņkalns** *mountain* Latvia
227 K5 **Gaj** Serbia
386 F6 **Gaja-shima** *island* Japan
305 G2 **Gajiram** Nigeria
308 D5 **Gakarosa** *mountain* South Africa
305 F3 **Gakem** Nigeria
434 N1 **Gakkel Ridge** *underwater feature* Arctic Ocean
227 J5 **Gakovo** Serbia
306 D3 **Gakpi** Democratic Republic of Congo
160 E3 **Galán, Cerro** *mountain* Argentina
307 F4 **Galana** *watercourse* Kenya
374 E3 **Galang Besar** *island* Indonesia
308 C2 **Galangue** Angola
227 I3 **Galanta** Slovakia
79 S8 **Galapagos Fracture Zone** *underwater feature* Pacific Ocean
Galapagos Islands *see* **Colon, Archipiélago de** Ecuador
79 W9 **Galapagos Rise** *underwater feature* Pacific Ocean
79 X8 **Galapagos Seamount** *underwater feature* Pacific Ocean
234 F3 **Galaţi** Romania
234 E3 **Galaţi** *admin. area* Romania
233 H6 **Galatone** Italy
223 N2 **Galbbajávri** *lake* Norway
310 3b **Gáldar** Canary Islands
222 F6 **Galdhøpiggen** *mountain* Norway
300 E6 **Galé** Mali
230 B4 **Galé, Costa da** *region* Portugal
129 I5 **Galeana** Mexico
232 D4 **Galeata** Italy
302 E5 **Galegu** Sudan
375 J3 **Galela** Indonesia
424 D3 **Galena** WA Australia
116 E6 **Galena** Alaska USA
227 G1 **Galenbecker See** *lake* Germany
163 9 **Galeota Point** Trinidad and Tobago
158 E6 **Galera, Pampa** *region* Bolivia
154 A4 **Galera, Punta** *cape* Ecuador
133 F6 **Galera, Punta** *cape* Mexico
154 C2 **Galera, Punta de la** *cape* Colombia
163 9 **Galera Point** Trinidad and Tobago
154 B5 **Galeras, Cordillera de** *range* Ecuador
126 F6 **Galesburg** Illinois USA
372 A5 **Galesong** Indonesia
126 F4 **Galesville** Wisconsin USA

307 G2 **Galeti** *watercourse* Ethiopia
121 O7 **Galeton** Ontario Canada
310 7a **Galets, Pointe des** *cape* Réunion
245 C4 **Galey** *watercourse* Ireland
242 F3 **Galgate** Lancashire England UK
393 H3 **Galguduud** *admin. area* Somalia
157 C6 **Galheirão** *watercourse* Brazil
388 D5 **Gali** Georgia
388 D1 **Galich** Russian Federation
236 J6 **Galichskaya Vozvyshennost'** *range* Russian Federation
230 C2 **Galicia** *admin. area* Spain
305 G3 **Galim** Cameroon
304 A2 **Galinhas, Ilha das** *island* Guinea-Bissau
126 J6 **Galion** Ohio USA
163 I4 **Galion, Baie du** *bay* Martinique
128 G4 **Galiuro Mountains** Arkansas USA
227 G5 **Galižana** Croatia
302 F5 **Gallabat** Sudan
244 A2 **Gallan Head** *cape* Scotland UK
226 E5 **Gallareto** Italy
125 J4 **Gallatin** *watercourse* Montana USA
393 E11 **Galle** Sri Lanka
228 D5 **Gállego** *watercourse* Spain
79 U8 **Gallego Rise** *underwater feature* Pacific Ocean
162 B5 **Gallegos** *watercourse* Argentina
162 A4 **Gallegos, Cabo** *cape* Chile
232 D5 **Galleno** Italy
226 E5 **Gallereto** Italy
245 D5 **Galley Head** *cape* Ireland
232 C4 **Galliate** Italy
244 D4 **Gallin** Perth and Kinross Scotland UK
154 D1 **Gallinas, Punta** *cape* Colombia
226 F5 **Gallio** Italy
233 G6 **Gallipoli** Italy
222 L3 **Gällivare** Sweden
233 E7 **Gallo, Capo** *cape* Italy
129 H3 **Gallo Mountains** New Mexico USA
134 B3 **Gallon Jug** Belize
119 N8 **Galloway** British Columbia Canada
242 D2 **Galloway, Mull of** *cape* Scotland UK
242 A4 **Gallows Hill** Ireland
224 G4 **Gällstad** Sweden
129 H3 **Gallup** New Mexico USA
231 F3 **Gallur** Spain
244 B4 **Galmisdale** Highland Scotland UK
158 E4 **Galo** Bolivia
384 G3 **Galshar** Mongolia
225 L5 **Galstas** *lake* Lithuania
244 D5 **Galston** East Ayrshire Scotland UK
384 D3 **Galt** Mongolia
124 E7 **Galt** California USA
300 D3 **Galtat Zemmour** Western Sahara
224 I3 **Galten** *bay* Sweden
222 J5 **Galtström** Sweden
226 F4 **Galtür** Austria
126 F6 **Galva** Illinois USA
160 C6 **Galvarino** Chile
130 D6 **Galveston** Texas USA
130 D6 **Galveston Bay** Texas USA
130 D6 **Galveston Island** Texas USA
224 I2 **Galvsjön** *lake* Sweden
392 E5 **Galwa** Nepal
245 C3 **Galway** Ireland
245 D3 **Galway** *admin. area* Ireland
245 C3 **Galway Bay** Ireland
372 D4 **Gam** *island* Indonesia
376 E2 **Gâm** *watercourse* Vietnam
162 E2 **Gama, Isla** *island* Argentina
241 I5 **Gamaches** France
305 F3 **Gamana** *watercourse* Nigeria
122 D6 **Gamart, Lac** *lake* Québec Canada
377 J4 **Gamay Bay** Philippines
308 C2 **Gamba** Angola
305 F5 **Gamba** Gabon
307 E2 **Gambēla** Ethiopia
307 E2 **Gambēla Hizboch** *admin. area* Ethiopia
116 B6 **Gambell** Alaska USA
304 A2 **Gambia** *country* Africa
304 B2 **Gambia** *watercourse* Gambia
76 P9 **Gambia Plain** *underwater feature* Atlantic Ocean
304 B2 **Gambie** *watercourse* Guinea
372 D6 **Gambier, Cape** Australia
427 14 **Gambier, Îles** *islands* French Polynesia
123 K8 **Gambo** Newfoundland and Labrador Canada
305 I4 **Gambo** Central African Republic
305 H5 **Gamboma** Congo
305 H4 **Gamboula** Central African Republic
301 H6 **Gamdou** Niger
154 C3 **Gámeza** Colombia
223 M4 **Gammelgården** Sweden
225 J4 **Gammelgarn** Sweden
222 M4 **Gammelstaden** Sweden
308 C4 **Gamsberg** *mountain* Namibia
162 C3 **Gan Gan** Argentina
128 H3 **Ganado** Arizona USA
130 C6 **Ganado** Texas USA
308 B2 **Ganda** Angola
372 A4 **Gandadiwata, Bukit** *mountain* Indonesia
393 E7 **Gandai** Chhattisgarh India
306 C5 **Gandajika** Democratic Republic of Congo
230 B2 **Gándara** Spain
391 K4 **Gandava** Pakistan
123 K8 **Gander** *watercourse* Newfoundland and Labrador Canada
123 K8 **Gander Lake** Newfoundland and Labrador Canada
231 G3 **Gandesa** Spain
392 D6 **Gandhi Sagar** *lake* Madhya Pradesh India
392 C6 **Gandhinagar** Gujarat India
231 F4 **Gandía** Spain
157 E6 **Gandu** Brazil
223 P1 **Gandvik** Norway
392 E5 **Ganga (Ganges)** *watercourse* Uttar Pradesh India
306 D3 **Gangale** Democratic Republic of Congo
392 C5 **Ganganagar** Rajasthan India
392 D5 **Gangapur** Rajasthan India
301 H6 **Gangara** Niger
392 G6 **Gangarampur** West Bengal India
379 H4 **Gangaw** Myanmar
393 D8 **Gangawati** Karnataka India
378 E2 **Gangdise Shan** *range* Xizang Zizhiqu China
228 F5 **Ganges** France
Ganges *see* **Ganga** India
393 H7 **Ganges, Mouths of the** *delta* Bangladesh
81 M3 **Ganges Fan** *underwater feature* Indian Ocean
392 D5 **Gangoh** Uttar Pradesh India
392 G5 **Gangtok** Sikkim India
380 E1 **Gangu** Gansu China
306 C3 **Gangu** *watercourse* Democratic Republic of Congo
372 D4 **Gani** Indonesia
390 G3 **Ganjeh Gūn** Iran
238 E3 **Gan'kovo** Russian Federation
385 J3 **Gannan** Heilongjiang China
228 F3 **Gannat** France
125 K5 **Gannett Peak** Wyoming USA
385 J4 **Gan'qika** Nei Mongol Zizhiqu China
379 G2 **Ganqu** Xizang Zizhiqu China
384 G6 **Ganquan** Shaanxi China
308 C6 **Gansbaai** South Africa
380 D1 **Gansu** *admin. area* China
304 C3 **Ganta** Liberia
307 G3 **Gantama** Somalia
131 H5 **Gantt Lake** Alabama USA
374 F4 **Gantung** Indonesia
305 G3 **Ganye** Nigeria
304 D3 **Ganze** Côte d'Ivoire
381 G3 **Ganzhou** Jiangxi China
380 C2 **Ganzi** Sichuan China
226 G1 **Ganzlin** Germany
301 F5 **Gao** Mali
380 C2 **Gaocheng** Sichuan China
380 F3 **Gaocun** Hunan China
384 E6 **Gaolan** Gansu China
381 G4 **Gaolan Liedao** *island* Guangdong China
380 F2 **Gaoleshan** Hubei China
380 C3 **Gaoligong Shan** *range* Yunnan China
385 I6 **Gaomi** Shandong China
161 G2 **Gaona-cué** Paraguay
385 G6 **Gaoping** Shanxi China
384 D5 **Gaotai** Gansu China
304 D2 **Gaoua** Burkina Faso
304 B2 **Gaoual** Guinea
385 H5 **Gaoyang** Hebei China
385 H5 **Gaoyi** Hebei China
381 H2 **Gaoyou** Jiangsu China
381 H2 **Gaoyou Hu** *lake* Jiangsu China
380 F4 **Gaozhou** Guangdong China
229 H4 **Gap** France
224 G3 **Gapern** *lake* Sweden
222 J2 **Gapøya** *island* Norway
383 I6 **Gar Qu** *lake* Qinghai China
378 D2 **Gar Zangbo** *watercourse* Xizang Zizhiqu China
234 A2 **Gara** Hungary
245 D3 **Gara, Lough** *lake* Ireland
388 I7 **Garabil Belentligi** *lake* Turkmenistan
305 G4 **Garabinzam** Congo
388 G5 **Garabogazköl Aýlagy** *lake* Turkmenistan
134 E5 **Garachiné** Panama
134 E5 **Garachiné, Punta** *cape* Panama
302 E4 **Garada** Sudan
242 B3 **Garadice** Ireland
310 3b **Garafía** Canary Islands
154 C3 **Garagoa** Colombia
388 H6 **Garagum** Turkmenistan
388 I6 **Garagum Kanaly** *watercourse* Turkmenistan
425 N7 **Garah** NSW Australia
391 L2 **Garai** Pakistan
388 I6 **Garamätnyýaz** Turkmenistan
304 D2 **Garango** Burkina Faso
156 E5 **Garanhuns** Brazil
426 2a **Garapan** Northern Mariana Islands
373 I6 **Garara** Papua New Guinea
162 C3 **Garayalde** Argentina
305 I3 **Garba** Central African Republic
307 F3 **Garba Tula** Kenya
307 G3 **Garbahaarrey** Somalia
244 D3 **Garbat** Highland Scotland UK
227 I2 **Garbce** Poland
130 C2 **Garber** Oklahoma USA
244 D3 **Garbole** Highland Scotland UK
157 A6 **Garças, Rio das** *watercourse* Brazil
230 C3 **Garcia** Spain
129 J2 **Garcia** Colorado USA
230 D4 **Garcia de Sola, Embalse de** *lake* Spain
154 B3 **García Gómez** Colombia
161 H2 **Garcias** Brazil
228 F4 **Gard** *watercourse* France
232 D4 **Garda, Lago di** *lake* Italy
223 P2 **Gardajav'ri** *lake* Norway
231 I2 **Gardanne** France
224 I4 **Gårdby** Sweden
124 G5 **Garden City** Idaho USA
125 O8 **Garden City** Kansas USA
129 I5 **Garden City** Texas USA
125 J6 **Garden City** Utah USA
126 I5 **Garden Lake** Ontario Canada
119 O3 **Garden River** Alberta Canada
130 H4 **Gardendale** Alabama USA
244 F3 **Gardenstown** Aberdeenshire Scotland UK
222 H5 **Gärdessjön** *lake* Sweden
235 B6 **Gardiki** Greece
125 J4 **Gardiner** Montana USA
224 E5 **Garding** Germany
391 L2 **Gardiz** Afghanistan
222 I4 **Gärdnäs** Sweden
436 T1 **Gardner Inlet** *bay* Antarctica
224 I5 **Gardno, Jezioro** *lake* Poland
232 D4 **Gardone Riviera** Italy
228 E5 **Gardouch** France
222 I4 **Gärdsjön** *lake* Sweden
222 G5 **Gåre** Norway
244 D4 **Garelochhead** Argyll and Bute Scotland UK
226 E5 **Garessio** Italy
301 H4 **Garet el Djenoun** *mountain* Algeria
233 G6 **Gargano, Testa del** *cape* Italy
126 I3 **Gargantua, Cape** Ontario Canada
388 E6 **Gargar** Iran
222 J4 **Gargnäs** Sweden
392 F6 **Garhwa** Jharkhand India
235 B5 **Gari** Macedonia
391 I4 **Gari Charbān** Iran
118 J8 **Garibaldi, Mount** British Columbia Canada
308 C6 **Garies** South Africa
390 F2 **Garin, Kūh-e** *mountain* Iran
307 F4 **Garissa** Kenya
158 A2 **Garita Garcia** Peru
305 G2 **Garkida** Nigeria
119 U7 **Garland** Manitoba Canada
130 C4 **Garland** Texas USA
244 D5 **Garleffin** South Ayrshire Scotland UK
225 L5 **Garliava** Lithuania
244 D6 **Garlieston** Dumfries and Galloway Scotland UK
388 J6 **Garlyk** Turkmenistan
306 D3 **Garmabe** Sudan
390 G2 **Garmsār** Iran
227 J2 **Garnek** Poland
126 E5 **Garner** Iowa USA
131 L3 **Garner** North Carolina USA
123 K9 **Garnish** Newfoundland and Labrador Canada
245 E3 **Garnish** Ireland
228 E5 **Garonne** *watercourse* France
231 G1 **Garonne, Canal latéral à la** *watercourse* France
307 H2 **Garoowe** Somalia
392 D6 **Garot** Madhya Pradesh India
305 G3 **Garoua** Cameroon
305 G3 **Garoua Boulai** Cameroon
373 I5 **Garove Island** Papua New Guinea
244 B2 **Garrabost** Na h-Eileanan Siar Scotland UK
245 E4 **Garrane** Ireland
245 D3 **Garranlahan** Ireland
160 F6 **Garré** Argentina
245 D4 **Garrison** Ireland
125 O3 **Garrison** North Dakota USA
130 D5 **Garrison** Texas USA
128 E1 **Garrison** Utah USA
242 D1 **Garroch** Dumfries and Galloway Scotland UK
242 C1 **Garron Point** Northern Ireland UK
230 C4 **Garrovillas** Spain
230 F5 **Garrucha** Spain
391 K4 **Garruk** Pakistan
244 D4 **Garry** *watercourse* Scotland UK
117 I5 **Garry Lake** Nunavut Canada
245 F1 **Garryduff** Ballymoney Northern Ireland UK
240 A1 **Garryknock** Ireland
119 Q4 **Garson** *watercourse* Saskatchewan Canada
119 P4 **Garson Lake** Alberta Canada
119 Q4 **Garson Lake** Saskatchewan Canada
242 F3 **Garstang** Lancashire England UK
228 E3 **Gartempe** *watercourse* France
222 F5 **Garten** Norway
240 D2 **Garth** Powys Wales UK
240 D2 **Garthmyl** Powys Wales UK
241 G2 **Garthorpe** Leicester England UK
244 D4 **Gartocharn** West Dunbartonshire Scotland UK
226 F1 **Gartow** Germany
374 E5 **Garut** Indonesia
245 F2 **Garvagh** Coleraine Northern Ireland UK
242 A2 **Garvaghy** Omagh Northern Ireland UK
244 F5 **Garvald** East Lothian Scotland UK
241 H2 **Garveston** Norfolk England UK
423 C7 **Garvie Mountains** New Zealand
227 K2 **Garwolin** Poland
126 H6 **Gary** Indiana USA
127 K8 **Gary** West Virginia USA
224 G5 **Garz** Germany
129 L8 **Garza Garcia** Mexico
130 B8 **Garza Valdez** Mexico
154 C4 **Garzón** Colombia
222 F5 **Gåsbue** Norway
228 E5 **Gascogne** *region* France
228 C5 **Gascogne, Golfe de** *bay* France
130 E2 **Gasconade** *watercourse* Missouri USA
424 F6 **Gascoyne** *watercourse* WA Australia
424 E6 **Gascoyne Junction** WA Australia
78 G9 **Gascoyne Plain** *underwater feature* Pacific Ocean
78 L11 **Gascoyne Tablemount** *underwater feature* Pacific Ocean
302 F4 **Gash** *watercourse* Eritrea
305 G2 **Gashua** Nigeria
244 G3 **Gask** Aberdeenshire Scotland UK
121 O6 **Gasket Island** Nunavut Canada
123 L9 **Gaskiers** Newfoundland and Labrador Canada
227 K1 **Gąsocin** Poland
129 H7 **Gasogachic** Mexico
374 E4 **Gaspar, Selat** *strait* Indonesia
163 9 **Gasparillo** Trinidad and Tobago
123 F8 **Gaspé** Québec Canada
123 F8 **Gaspé, Baie de** *bay* Québec Canada
123 F8 **Gaspé, Cap** *cape* Québec Canada
123 E8 **Gaspésie, Péninsule de la** *peninsula* Québec Canada
304 D2 **Gassan** Burkina Faso
300 C6 **Gassane** Senegal
127 K7 **Gassaway** West Virginia USA
230 D4 **Gasset, Embalse de** *lake* Spain
222 J5 **Gåssjö** Sweden
131 M2 **Gaston, Lake** North Carolina USA
131 K3 **Gastonia** North Carolina USA
162 C3 **Gastre** Argentina
230 C3 **Gata** Spain
230 E5 **Gata, Cabo de** *cape* Spain
394 E6 **Gata, Cape** Cyprus
118 H3 **Gataga** *watercourse* British Columbia Canada
234 B3 **Gătaia** Romania
427 12c **Gataivai** Samoa
225 P3 **Gatchina** Russian Federation
125 O8 **Gate** Oklahoma USA
243 G3 **Gateford** Nottinghamshire England UK
244 D6 **Gatehouse of Fleet** Dumfries and Galloway Scotland UK
242 E2 **Gatesgarth** Cumbria England UK
243 G2 **Gateshead** *admin. area* England UK
243 G2 **Gateshead** Tyne and Wear England UK
117 I4 **Gateshead Island** Nunavut Canada
130 C5 **Gatesville** Texas USA
160 D2 **Gatico** Chile
117 L9 **Gatineau** *watercourse* Québec Canada
380 C2 **Gatong** Xizang Zizhiqu China
377 I3 **Gattaran** Philippines
229 I4 **Gattorna** Italy
134 E5 **Gatún, Lago** *lake* Panama
392 E3 **Gatwan** *watercourse* Jammu and Kashmir India/Pakistan
427 9 **Gau** *island* Fiji
159 H4 **Gaúcha do Norte** Brazil
226 B3 **Gauchy** France
154 D5 **Gaudencio** Colombia
120 G4 **Gauer Lake** Manitoba Canada
225 M4 **Gauja** *watercourse* Latvia
225 N4 **Gaujiena** Latvia
225 G5 **Gaula** *watercourse* Norway
222 E6 **Gaupne** Norway
379 F3 **Gauripur** Bangladesh
379 F3 **Gauripur** Assam India
379 G4 **Gaurnadi** Bangladesh
224 E3 **Gausta** *mountain* Norway
222 I3 **Gausvik** Norway
222 I4 **Gäutan** *bay* Sweden
308 E5 **Gauteng** *admin. area* South Africa
222 F5 **Gautsjøen** *bay* Norway
390 F2 **Gāv Savār** Iran
391 I4 **Gavanak** Iran
237 AG7 **Gavanka** Russian Federation
388 E6 **Gavar** Armenia
228 D5 **Gavarnie** France
391 H4 **Gāvbandi** Iran
235 C8 **Gavdopoula** *island* Greece
235 D8 **Gavdos** *island* Greece
228 D5 **Gave** *watercourse* France
157 D6 **Gavião** *watercourse* Brazil
222 K5 **Gaviksfjärden** *bay* Sweden
128 B3 **Gaviota** California USA
160 F6 **Gaviotas** Argentina
224 I2 **Gävle** Sweden
222 I6 **Gävleborgs** *admin. area* Sweden
224 I2 **Gävlebukten** *bay* Sweden
116 A6 **Gavriila, Bukhta** *bay* Russian Federation
238 H4 **Gavrilov-Yam** Russian Federation
235 D7 **Gavrio** Greece
388 C1 **Gavrlov-Yam** Russian Federation
225 N4 **Gavry** Russian Federation
225 O4 **Gavry** Russian Federation
373 J6 **Gawa Island** Papua New Guinea
392 F6 **Gawan** Jharkhand India
425 K8 **Gawler** SA Australia
425 J8 **Gawler Ranges** SA Australia
305 F3 **Gawu** Nigeria
222 I5 **Gåxsjö** Sweden
222 I5 **Gåxsjön** *lake* Sweden
392 F6 **Gaya** Bihar India
375 G2 **Gaya** *island* Malaysia
305 E2 **Gaya** Niger
305 F2 **Gaya** Nigeria
126 I4 **Gaylord** Michigan USA
425 N6 **Gayndah** Qld Australia
238 G4 **Gaynovo** Russian Federation
236 L6 **Gayny** Russian Federation
122 C5 **Gayot, Lac** *lake* Québec Canada
238 H3 **Gayutino** Russian Federation
241 H2 **Gaywood** Norfolk England UK
390 C3 **Gaza** Gaza Strip (Disputed)
309 F4 **Gaza** *admin. area* Mozambique
391 K4 **Gazan** Pakistan
388 G6 **Gazanjyk** Turkmenistan
373 I4 **Gazelle Channel** *strait* Papua New Guinea
424 inset **Gazert, Cape** Heard Island Australia
306 C3 **Gazi** Democratic Republic of Congo
394 F6 **Gaziantep** Turkey
394 F6 **Gaziantep** *admin. area* Turkey
385 I2 **Gazimurskiy Khrebet** *range* Russian Federation
385 I2 **Gazimurskiy Zavod** Russian Federation
379 G4 **Gazipur** Bangladesh
388 I6 **Gazli** Uzbekistan
388 I5 **Gazojak** Turkmenistan
235 C5 **Gazoros** Greece
232 D4 **Gazzuolo** Italy
306 C3 **Gbadolite** Democratic Republic of Congo
304 C3 **Gbarnga** Liberia
304 E2 **Gbassa** Benin
227 I3 **Gbely** Slovakia
305 F3 **Gboko** Nigeria
225 J5 **Gdańsk** Poland
225 J5 **Gdańsk, Zatoka** *bay* Poland
225 N3 **Gdov** Russian Federation
225 J5 **Gdynia** Poland
245 C5 **Gearha** Ireland
124 D3 **Gearhart** Oregon USA
244 D2 **Gearnsary** Highland Scotland UK
244 A3 **Gearraidh Bhailteas** Na h-Eileanan Siar Scotland UK
243 F2 **Gearstones** North Yorkshire England UK
130 B3 **Geary** Oklahoma USA
222 J5 **Geasjön** *lake* Sweden
304 B2 **Geba** *watercourse* Guinea-Bissau
372 D4 **Gebe** *island* Indonesia
302 F4 **Gebeit** Sudan
302 F3 **Gebeit Mine** Sudan
235 G7 **Gebiz** Turkey
235 F5 **Gebze** Turkey
380 E2 **Gecheng** Chongqing China
374 D4 **Gedang, Gunung** *mountain* Indonesia
302 F5 **Gedaref** Sudan
302 E5 **Gedaref** *admin. area* Sudan
226 E2 **Gedern** Germany
229 G2 **Gedinne** Belgium
235 F6 **Gediz** Turkey
235 E6 **Gediz** *watercourse* Turkey
307 G2 **Gedlegubē** Ethiopia
307 G3 **Gedo** *admin. area* Somalia
307 F2 **Gēdo** Ethiopia
384 G5 **Gedong** Shanxi China
375 F3 **Gedong** Malaysia
228 E5 **Gèdre** France
224 F5 **Gedser** Denmark
224 G5 **Gedser Odde** *cape* Denmark
229 G1 **Geel** Belgium
425 M9 **Geelong** Vic. Australia
383 J6 **Ge'ermu** Qinghai China
303 I5 **Gees Gwardafuy** *cape* Somalia
235 C5 **Gefira** Greece
305 G2 **Geidam** Nigeria
119 S4 **Geikie** *watercourse* Saskatchewan Canada
120 H2 **Geillini** *watercourse* Nunavut Canada
120 H2 **Geillini Lake** Nunavut Canada
222 E5 **Geiranger** Norway
232 D2 **Geisenfeld** Germany
232 B2 **Geisenheim** Germany
306 E4 **Geita** Tanzania
222 J2 **Geitvatnet** *lake* Norway
378 D2 **Geji** Xizang Zizhiqu China
380 D4 **Gejiu** Yunnan China
116 A6 **Geka, Mys** *cape* Russian Federation
306 D2 **Gel** *watercourse* Sudan
233 F8 **Gela** Italy
233 F8 **Gela, Golfo di** *bay* Italy
379 G2 **Geladaindong** *mountain* Qinghai China
307 H2 **Geladī** Ethiopia
375 F4 **Gelam** *island* Indonesia
374 D2 **Gelang, Tanjong** *cape* Malaysia
235 E6 **Gelembe** Turkey
307 G2 **Gelemso** Ethiopia
235 G6 **Gelendost** Turkey
388 C5 **Gelendzhik** Russian Federation
225 L5 **Gelgaudiškis** Lithuania
307 H2 **Gelinsoor** Somalia
391 H4 **Gelkūyeh** Iran
232 G3 **Gelse** Hungary
374 E4 **Gelumbang** Indonesia
225 M5 **Gelvonai** Lithuania
119 O7 **Gem** Alberta Canada
229 G1 **Gembloux** Belgium
305 G3 **Gembu** Nigeria
372 C2 **Gemeh** Indonesia
306 B3 **Gemena** Democratic Republic of Congo
303 G5 **Gemeri Hāyk'** *lake* Ethiopia
235 F7 **Gemiç** Turkey
235 F5 **Gemlik Körfezi** *bay* Turkey
229 K3 **Gemona del Friuli** Italy
228 D4 **Gémozac** France
226 E2 **Gemünden** Germany
307 G2 **Genale** *watercourse* Ethiopia
162 B5 **Gendarme C. Barreto** Argentina
228 G3 **Génelard** France
160 E6 **General Acha** Argentina
160 E5 **General Alvear** Argentina
161 F6 **General Alvear** Argentina
160 F2 **General Ballivián** Argentina
161 G5 **General Belgrano** Argentina
133 F3 **General Bravo** Mexico
159 H4 **General Carneiro** Brazil
132 E3 **General Cepeda** Mexico
160 E7 **General Conesa** Argentina
132 E4 **General Enrique Estrada** Mexico
132 E3 **General Escobedo** Mexico
129 N8 **General Francisco Gonzales Villareal** Mexico
161 G6 **General Guido** Argentina
161 G6 **General Juan Madariaga** Argentina
162 D2 **General Liborio Bernal** Argentina
160 E3 **General Martín Miguel de Güemes** Argentina
162 C3 **General Mosconi** Argentina
161 G3 **General Paz** Argentina
160 F5 **General Pico** Argentina
160 F3 **General Pinedo** Argentina
161 G6 **General Pirán** Argentina
160 E6 **General Roca** Argentina
377 J6 **General Santos** Philippines
133 F3 **General Terán** Mexico
129 I6 **General Trias** Mexico
160 F5 **General Villegas** Argentina
231 F4 **Generalísimo, Embalse del** *lake* Spain
127 M5 **Genesee** *watercourse* New York USA
129 M1 **Geneseo** Kansas USA
125 Q6 **Geneva** Nebraska USA
127 M5 **Geneva** New York USA
224 G4 **Genevad** Sweden
232 B3 **Genève (Geneva)** Switzerland
226 E3 **Gengenbach** Germany
380 C4 **Gengma** Yunnan China
380 C2 **Gengqing** Sichuan China
306 C4 **Gengwa** Democratic Republic of Congo
385 J2 **Genhe** Nei Mongol Zizhiqu China
230 D5 **Genil** *watercourse* Spain
228 E3 **Génillé** France
392 C6 **Genji** Rajasthan India
229 G1 **Genk** Belgium
233 C6 **Gennargentu, Monte del** *mountain* Sardinia Italy
226 C2 **Gennep** Netherlands
162 B3 **Genoa** *watercourse* Argentina
Genoa *see* **Genova** Italy
125 N7 **Genoa** Colorado USA
226 D5 **Genola** Italy
231 H1 **Génolhac** France
229 H3 **Genolier** Switzerland
232 C5 **Genova, Golfo di** *bay* Italy
232 C4 **Genova (Genoa)** Italy
163 4 **Genovesa, Isla** *island* Archipiélago de Colón (Galapagos Islands)
237 AG3 **Genriyetty, Ostrov** *island* Russian Federation
122 E6 **Gensart, Lac** *lake* Québec Canada
228 F1 **Gent** Belgium
374 E5 **Genteng** Indonesia
375 G6 **Genteng** Indonesia
375 G5 **Genteng** *island* Indonesia
226 G1 **Genthin** Germany
127 O3 **Gentilly** Québec Canada
228 E4 **Gentioux** France
373 G4 **Genyem** Indonesia
233 G6 **Genzano di Lucania** Italy
117 Q4 **Geographical Society Øer** *island* Greenland
122 F4 **George** *watercourse* Québec Canada
308 D6 **George** South Africa
123 H10 **George, Cape** Nova Scotia Canada
306 E3 **George, Lake** Uganda
131 K6 **George, Lake** Florida USA
126 I3 **George, Lake** Michigan USA
127 O5 **George, Lake** New York USA
76 Q4 **George Bligh Bank** *underwater feature* Atlantic Ocean
163 7 **George Island** Falkland Islands
423 B7 **George Sound** New Zealand
425 M10 **George Town** Tas. Australia
135 F2 **George Town** Bahamas
134 D3 **George Town** Cayman Islands
374 D2 **George Town** Malaysia
437 J2 **George V Coast** Antarctica
436 T2 **George VI Sound** *strait* Antarctica
130 B6 **George West** Texas USA
76 L5 **Georges Bank** *underwater feature* Atlantic Ocean
310 5a **Georgetown** Ascension
155 G3 **Georgetown** Guyana
163 11a **Georgetown** St Vincent and the Grenadines
126 I7 **Georgetown** Kentucky USA
131 L4 **Georgetown** South Carolina USA
130 C5 **Georgetown** Texas USA
388 D5 **Georgia** *country* Asia
115 **Georgia** *admin. area* USA
124 C2 **Georgia, Gulf of** British Columbia Canada
118 I7 **Georgia, Strait of** British Columbia Canada
127 K4 **Georgian Bay** Ontario Canada
130 H5 **Georgiana** Alabama USA
425 K5 **Georgina** *watercourse* Qld Australia
389 N3 **Georgiyevka** Kazakhstan
388 D5 **Georgiyevsk** Russian Federation
229 K1 **Gera** Germany
235 B7 **Geraki, Akra** *cape* Greece
157 D6 **Geral, Serra** *range* Brazil
116 B4 **Geral'd, Ostrov** *island* Russian Federation
423 D7 **Geraldine** New Zealand
125 J3 **Geraldine** Montana USA
424 E7 **Geraldton** WA Australia
120 L8 **Geraldton** Ontario Canada
229 H2 **Gérardmer** France
232 F2 **Geras** Austria
124 E5 **Gerber Reservoir** Oregon USA
391 H3 **Gerdeh Kūh** Iran
394 E5 **Gerede** Turkey
391 J3 **Gereshk** Afghanistan
230 E5 **Gérgal** Spain
373 H5 **Gerhards, Cape** Papua New Guinea
122 D3 **Gerido, Lac** *lake* Québec Canada
374 D2 **Gerik** Malaysia
125 N6 **Gering** Nebraska USA
227 K3 **Gerlachovský štít** *mountain* Slovakia
226 F4 **Gerlos** Austria
122 E6 **Germaine, Lac** *lake* Québec Canada
117 R3 **Germania Land** *peninsula* Greenland
226 **Germany** *country* Europe
226 C3 **Germay** France
229 I2 **Germersheim** Germany
229 J2 **Gerolzhofen** Germany
240 C4 **Gerrans** Cornwall England UK
231 G2 **Gers** *watercourse* France
228 F4 **Gerzat** France
372 D4 **Geser** Indonesia
373 G6 **Gesoa** Papua New Guinea
222 J5 **Gesunden** *bay* Sweden
225 J2 **Geta** Finland
230 E3 **Getafe** Spain
125 P4 **Gettysburg** South Dakota USA
230 E2 **Getxo** Spain
436 P2 **Getz Ice Shelf** Antarctica
374 C2 **Geumpang** Indonesia
394 G5 **Gevaş** Turkey
235 C5 **Gevgelija** Macedonia
393 D7 **Gevrai** Maharashtra India
222 H5 **Gevsjön** *lake* Sweden
229 H3 **Gex** France
235 E6 **Geyikli** Turkey
374 D6 **Geylang** *admin. area* Singapore
379 G3 **Geylegphug** Bhutan
235 F7 **Geyre** Turkey
128 A1 **Geyserville** California USA
382 E5 **Gez He** *watercourse* Xinjiang Uygur Zizhiqu China
308 D5 **Ghaap Plateau** *plain* South Africa
302 D5 **Ghabeish** Sudan
301 H2 **Ghadāmis** Libya
301 I3 **Ghaddūwah** Libya
392 F5 **Ghaghara** *watercourse* Uttar Pradesh India
302 D5 **Ghalla, Wādi El** *watercourse* Sudan
300 E4 **Ghallamane** *region* Mauritania
304 D3 **Ghana** *country* Africa
308 D4 **Ghanzi** Botswana
308 D4 **Ghanzi** *admin. area* Botswana
302 E4 **Gharb Binna** Sudan
301 G2 **Ghardaïa** Algeria
233 C8 **Ghardimaou** Tunisia
302 E2 **Ghārib, Jabal** *mountain* Egypt
389 K6 **Gharm** Tajikistan
301 I2 **Gharyān** Libya
301 I3 **Ghāt** Libya
392 D7 **Ghatanji** Maharashtra India
426 8 **Ghatere** Solomon Islands
392 F6 **Ghatgan** Orissa India
393 E8 **Ghats, Eastern** *range* Andhra Pradesh India
393 D8 **Ghats, Western** *range* Maharashtra India
301 F1 **Ghazaouet** Algeria
392 D5 **Ghaziabad** Uttar Pradesh India
392 F6 **Ghazipur** Uttar Pradesh India
391 K2 **Ghazni** Afghanistan
391 K2 **Ghazni** *admin. area* Afghanistan
303 G4 **Ghela'elo** Eritrea
232 C4 **Ghemme** Italy
234 D2 **Gheorgheni** Romania
232 E4 **Ghibullo** Italy
234 F2 **Ghidighici, Lacul** *lake* Moldova
234 E2 **Ghimeş-Făget** Romania
233 C5 **Ghisonaccia** Corsica France
393 C7 **Ghogha** Gujarat India
392 F6 **Ghorawal** Uttar Pradesh India
119 N7 **Ghost Lake** Alberta Canada
122 H5 **Ghost Lake** Newfoundland and Labrador Canada
120 K5 **Ghost Lake** Ontario Canada
127 L2 **Ghost Range** Ontario Canada
391 J2 **Ghowr** *admin. area* Afghanistan
391 J2 **Ghowrmāch** Afghanistan
390 E3 **Ghudāf, Wādī al** *watercourse* Iraq
392 F5 **Ghughuli** Uttar Pradesh India
391 M2 **Ghujerab** *watercourse* Pakistan
302 D2 **Ghurd Abū Muharrik** *range* Egypt
301 J3 **Ghuzayyil, Sabkhat** *lake* Libya
376 E5 **Gia Định** Vietnam
376 E3 **Gianh** *watercourse* Vietnam
233 D5 **Giannutri, Isola di** *island* Italy
235 E8 **Gianysada** *island* Greece
233 F8 **Giarratana** Italy
233 F8 **Giarre** Italy
229 H4 **Giaveno** Italy
125 P6 **Gibbon** Nebraska USA
127 inset **Gibb's Hill** Bermuda
307 F2 **Gibe** *watercourse* Ethiopia
233 E8 **Gibellina** Italy
308 C5 **Gibeon** Namibia
230 C5 **Gibraleón** Spain
230 D5 **Gibraltar** *UK overseas territory* Europe
300 E1 **Gibraltar, Strait of** Mediterranean Sea/Atlantic Ocean
243 I3 **Gibraltar Point** England UK
130 E4 **Gibsland** Louisiana USA
424 H5 **Gibson Desert** WA Australia
120 I1 **Gibson Lake** Nunavut Canada
225 L5 **Giby** Poland
232 G3 **Gic** Hungary
383 J3 **Gichgeniyn Nuruu** Mongolia
305 G3 **Gida** Nigeria
307 E2 **Gīdamī** Ethiopia
222 K5 **Gidböle** Sweden
307 F2 **Gīdda** Ethiopia
130 C5 **Giddings** Texas USA
222 K5 **Gideå** Sweden
222 K5 **Gideälven** *watercourse* Sweden
307 F2 **Gīdolē** Ethiopia
228 F3 **Gien** France
229 J2 **Giengen an der Brenz** Germany
234 B3 **Giera** Romania
225 K5 **Gierkiny** Poland
222 J4 **Giertsjaure** *lake* Sweden
Giesecke Isfjord *see* **Kangerlussuaq** Greenland
229 I1 **Gießen** Germany
226 D1 **Gieten** Netherlands
227 K1 **Gietrzwałd** Poland
244 F5 **Gifford** East Lothian Scotland UK
121 Q7 **Gifford, Lac** *lake* Québec Canada
119 N5 **Gift Lake** Alberta Canada
387 H4 **Gifu** Japan
388 D4 **Gigant** Russian Federation
132 D3 **Gigantes** Mexico
244 C5 **Gigha** *island* Scotland UK
234 C4 **Gighera** Romania
233 D5 **Giglio, Isola del** *island* Italy
233 C6 **Giglio, Punta del** *cape* Sardinia Italy
231 H2 **Gignac** France
391 I3 **Giji** Iran
230 D2 **Gijón** Spain
160 F6 **Gil** Argentina
128 F4 **Gila** *watercourse* Arkansas USA
128 F4 **Gila Bend** Arizona USA
388 F7 **Gīlān** *admin. area* Iran
390 F2 **Gīlān-e Gharb** Iran
425 L4 **Gilbert** *watercourse* Qld Australia
122 J6 **Gilbert** *watercourse* Newfoundland and Labrador Canada
128 G4 **Gilbert** Arizona USA
130 F4 **Gilbert** Louisiana USA
426 1 **Gilbert Islands** Kiribati
79 N8 **Gilbert Ridge** *underwater feature* Pacific Ocean
79 Q2 **Gilbert Seamount** *underwater feature* Pacific Ocean
156 C5 **Gilbués** Brazil
125 Q2 **Gilby** North Dakota USA
232 D2 **Gilching** Germany
309 G3 **Gilé** Mozambique
302 D3 **Gilf Kébir Plateau** *plain* Egypt
245 F2 **Gilford** Banbridge Northern Ireland UK
425 N7 **Gilgandra** NSW Australia
391 M2 **Gilgit** Pakistan
391 M2 **Gilgit** *watercourse* Pakistan
375 G6 **Gilimanuk** Indonesia
224 D3 **Gilja** Norway
245 D2 **Gill, Lough** *lake* Ireland
310 5b **Gill Point** *cape* St Helena
224 G4 **Gilleleje** Denmark
423 C6 **Gillespies Beach** New Zealand
130 F3 **Gillett** Arkansas USA
126 G4 **Gillett** Wisconsin USA
125 M4 **Gillette** Wyoming USA
222 I5 **Gillhov** Sweden
121 V5 **Gilling** Newfoundland and Labrador Canada
241 E3 **Gillingham** Dorset England UK
241 H3 **Gillingham** Medway England UK
437 E2 **Gillock Island** Antarctica
127 M4 **Gilmour** Ontario Canada
117 L7 **Gilmour Island** Nunavut Canada
307 E2 **Gilo** *watercourse* Ethiopia
124 E8 **Gilroy** California USA
222 G5 **Gilså** Norway
373 G5 **Giluwe, Mount** Papua New Guinea
240 D3 **Gilwern** Monmouthshire Wales UK
222 J5 **Gim** Sweden
228 E5 **Gimat** France
307 F2 **Gimbi** Ethiopia
232 B3 **Gimel** Switzerland
305 F3 **Gimi** Nigeria
163 I3 **Gimie, Mount** *volcano* St Lucia
223 R5 **Gimoly** Russian Federation
228 E5 **Gimone** *watercourse* France
228 E5 **Gimont** France
372 A4 **Gimpu** Indonesia
425 N6 **Gin Gin** Qld Australia
307 F2 **Ginchi** Ethiopia
303 F4 **Ginda** Eritrea
233 C6 **Ginepro, Punta** *cape* Sardinia Italy
425 E7 **Gingin** WA Australia
377 J5 **Gingoog** Philippines
307 G2 **Ginir** Ethiopia
233 G6 **Ginosa** Italy
230 C2 **Ginzo de Lima** Spain
376 E3 **Gio Linh** Vietnam
233 E6 **Gioia dei Marsi** Italy
233 F7 **Gioia Tauro** Italy
244 B2 **Giosla** Na h-Eileanan Siar Scotland UK
235 D6 **Gioura** *island* Greece
233 G6 **Giovinazzo** Italy
241 I2 **Gipping** Suffolk England UK
393 E7 **Girar** Maharashtra India
127 K6 **Girard** Ohio USA
308 B3 **Giraul** *watercourse* Angola
394 F5 **Giresun** Turkey
394 F5 **Giresun** *admin. area* Turkey
373 H4 **Girgir, Cape** Papua New Guinea
306 B3 **Giri** *watercourse* Democratic Republic of Congo
230 E4 **Giribaile, Embalse de** *lake* Spain
222 I4 **Girisjön** *lake* Sweden
234 B2 **Giriţu de Criş** Romania
225 L5 **Girkalnis** Lithuania
234 E2 **Girleni** Romania
393 D7 **Girna** *watercourse* Maharashtra India
229 H3 **Giromagny** France

154 C3 **Girón** Colombia
231 H3 **Girona** Spain
228 D4 **Gironde** *watercourse* France
228 E5 **Girou** *watercourse* France
243 G2 **Girsby** Darlington England UK
425 M4 **Giru** Qld Australia
161 H4 **Giruá** Brazil
245 D5 **Girvan** South Ayrshire Scotland UK
223 R5 **Girvas** Russian Federation
422 H4 **Gisborne** New Zealand
422 G4 **Gisborne** *admin. area* New Zealand
123 K9 **Gisborne Lake** Newfoundland and Labrador Canada
306 D4 **Gisenyi** Rwanda
224 G4 **Gislaved** Sweden
228 E2 **Gisors** France
233 F5 **Gissi** Italy
225 J3 **Gisslingö** *island* Sweden
306 D4 **Gitega** Burundi
391 M2 **Gittidas** *watercourse* Pakistan
232 C3 **Giubiasco** Switzerland
232 E5 **Giulianova** Italy
234 E3 **Giurgiu** *admin. area* Romania
224 E5 **Give** Denmark
226 C2 **Givet** France
229 G4 **Givors** France
308 F4 **Giyani** South Africa
307 F2 **Giyon** Ethiopia
227 I1 **Gizałki** Poland
426 8 **Gizo** *island* Solomon Islands
225 K5 **Giżycko** Poland
222 E5 **Gjemnes** Norway
222 F6 **Gjendebu** Norway
222 E6 **Gjerde** Norway
224 C2 **Gjerdvik** Norway
222 H3 **Gjerøya** *island* Norway
224 F4 **Gjerrild** Denmark
224 G2 **Gjesåssjøen** *lake* Norway
222 F5 **Gjevilvatn** *lake* Norway
224 E3 **Gjeving** Norway
222 H4 **Gjevsjøen** *lake* Sweden
235 B5 **Gjirokastër** Albania
117 J5 **Gjoa Haven** Nunavut Canada
222 inset **Gjögur** Iceland
222 inset **Gjögurtá** *cape* Iceland
222 F5 **Gjølme** Norway
222 F5 **Gjøra** Norway
222 G5 **Gjota** Norway
224 F2 **Gjøvik** Norway
235 B5 **Gjugjë** Albania
123 I9 **Glace Bay** Nova Scotia Canada
124 G1 **Glacier** British Columbia Canada
118 C3 **Glacier Bay** Alaska USA
122 E2 **Glacier Peak** *volcano* Washington USA
244 C3 **Glackour** Highland Scotland UK
125 P7 **Glade** Kansas USA
130 D4 **Gladewater** Texas USA
222 G4 **Gladstad** Norway
425 N5 **Gladstone** Qld Australia
423 F5 **Gladstone** New Zealand
126 H4 **Gladstone** Michigan USA
119 R5 **Gladue Lake** Saskatchewan Canada
126 I5 **Gladwin** Michigan USA
240 D3 **Glais** Swansea Wales UK
222 G5 **Glåma** *watercourse* Norway
244 E4 **Glamis** Angus Scotland UK
128 E4 **Glamis** California USA
232 G4 **Glamoč** Bosnia and Herzegovina
222 G5 **Glåmos** Norway
226 D3 **Glan** *watercourse* Germany
245 C5 **Glan** Ireland
377 J6 **Glan** Philippines
224 H3 **Glan** *lake* Sweden
245 C5 **Glandart** Ireland
245 E2 **Glangevlin** Ireland
229 I3 **Glarus** Switzerland
240 D2 **Glasbury** Powys Wales UK
244 D3 **Glascarnoch, Loch** *lake* Scotland UK
125 Q7 **Glasco** Kansas USA
245 G2 **Glasdrumman** Newry and Mourne Northern Ireland UK
116 I9 **Glasgow** Montana USA
244 D5 **Glasgow** City of Glasgow Scotland UK
126 I8 **Glasgow** Kentucky USA
126 E7 **Glasgow** Missouri USA
125 L2 **Glasgow** Montana USA
127 L8 **Glasgow** Virginia USA
119 S8 **Glasnevin** Saskatchewan Canada
244 D3 **Glass, Loch** *lake* Scotland UK
127 N7 **Glassboro** New Jersey USA
242 D2 **Glasserton** Dumfries and Galloway Scotland UK
242 F3 **Glasson** Lancashire England UK
240 E3 **Glastonbury** Somerset England UK
242 G2 **Glastry** Ards Northern Ireland UK
130 A2 **Glazier** Texas USA
236 L7 **Glazov** Russian Federation
130 G2 **Gleason** Tennessee USA
300 E5 **Gleïbat Boukenni** Mauritania
119 O7 **Gleichen** Alberta Canada
227 H4 **Gleisdorf** Austria
241 H2 **Glemsford** Suffolk England UK
242 A3 **Glen** Ireland
241 G2 **Glen** *watercourse* England UK
244 D3 **Glen Cannich** *valley* Scotland UK
424 J5 **Glen Helen Resort** NT Australia
244 E5 **Glen Ho** Scottish Borders Scotland UK
425 N7 **Glen Innes** NSW Australia
125 O3 **Glen Ullin** North Dakota USA
245 G2 **Glenarm** Larne Northern Ireland UK
245 F2 **Glenavy** Lisburn Northern Ireland UK
245 E5 **Glenawilling** Ireland
242 A4 **Glenballyvally** Ireland
244 C5 **Glenbarr** Argyll and Bute Scotland UK
244 C5 **Glenbatrick** Argyll and Bute Scotland UK
119 V8 **Glenboro** Manitoba Canada
244 C4 **Glenborrodale** Highland Scotland UK
242 B4 **Glenbrien** Ireland
244 B3 **Glenbrittle** Highland Scotland UK
119 R6 **Glenbush** Saskatchewan Canada
244 C4 **Glenbyre** Highland Scotland UK
127 K5 **Glencoe** Ontario Canada
128 F4 **Glendale** Arizona USA
128 C3 **Glendale** California USA
128 E2 **Glendale** Nevada USA
124 D5 **Glendale** Oregon USA
128 G1 **Glendale** Utah USA
126 H5 **Glendale** Wisconsin USA
425 J7 **Glendambo** SA Australia
245 D4 **Glendine Bridge** Ireland
125 M3 **Glendive** Montana USA
125 M5 **Glendo** Wyoming USA
125 M5 **Glendo Reservoir** Wyoming USA
119 P5 **Glendon** Alberta Canada
242 A1 **Glendooskert** Ireland
155 G3 **Glendor Mountains** Guyana
242 D1 **Glendoune** South Ayrshire Scotland UK
245 E1 **Gleneely** Ireland
242 A2 **Glenfern** Omagh Northern Ireland UK
125 P3 **Glenfield** North Dakota USA
245 D4 **Glengarra Bridge** Ireland
245 C5 **Glengarriff** Ireland
423 E5 **Glenhope** New Zealand
245 C2 **Glenlara** Ireland
245 C2 **Glenlassra River** Ireland
244 F4 **Glenlee** Angus Scotland UK
244 D6 **Glenluce** Dumfries and Galloway Scotland UK
245 E4 **Glenmore** Ireland
245 D4 **Glennahulla Cross** Ireland
116 E6 **Glennallen** Alaska USA
245 E4 **Glennanore** Ireland
245 E4 **Glennaskagh** Ireland
124 H5 **Glenns Ferry** Idaho USA
131 K5 **Glennville** Georgia USA
244 E5 **Glenochar** South Lanarkshire Scotland UK
245 G2 **Glenoe** Larne Northern Ireland UK
118 F4 **Glenora** British Columbia Canada
423 C7 **Glenorchy** New Zealand
242 F2 **Glenridding** Cumbria England UK
244 C5 **Glenrisdell** Argyll and Bute Scotland UK
242 B2 **Glenroan** Strabane Northern Ireland UK
125 M5 **Glenrock** Wyoming USA
244 E4 **Glenrothes** Fife Scotland UK
423 E6 **Glenroy** *watercourse* New Zealand
127 O5 **Glens Falls** New York USA
244 F4 **Glensaugh** Aberdeenshire Scotland UK
244 E6 **Glensone** Dumfries and Galloway Scotland UK
245 D2 **Glenties** Ireland
245 C3 **Glentrasna** Ireland
244 D5 **Glenvernoch** Dumfries and Galloway Scotland UK
425 O6 **Glenwood** Qld Australia
129 H4 **Glenwood** New Mexico USA
128 G1 **Glenwood** Utah USA
229 I3 **Gletsch** Switzerland
222 inset **Glettinganes** *cape* Iceland
224 G5 **Glewitz** Germany
235 C6 **Glifádha** Greece
234 C3 **Glimboca** Romania
245 C4 **Glin** Ireland
238 F6 **Glinishchevo** Russian Federation
227 K1 **Glinojeck** Poland
245 C3 **Glinsce** Ireland
245 D3 **Glinsk** Ireland
241 G2 **Glinton** Peterborough England UK
222 I5 **Glissjöberg** Sweden
222 F6 **Glittertinden** *mountain* Norway
238 C5 **Glivin** Belarus
227 J2 **Gliwice** Poland
128 G4 **Globe** Arizona USA
235 B5 **Globočičko Ezero** *lake* Macedonia
234 E2 **Glodeni** Moldova
227 H4 **Gloggnitz** Austria
227 I2 **Głogów** Poland
222 H3 **Glomfjord** Norway
224 F2 **Glomma** *watercourse* Norway
222 K4 **Glommersträsk** Sweden
224 E2 **Glonde** *lake* Norway
226 F3 **Glonn** *watercourse* Germany
222 L5 **Gloppet** *bay* Finland
76 N4 **Gloria Ridge** *underwater feature* Atlantic Ocean
310 6a **Glorieuses, Îles** *islands* Îles Éparses
243 G3 **Glossop** Derbyshire England UK
130 F5 **Gloster** Mississippi USA
222 H5 **Glöte** Sweden
241 E3 **Gloucester** Gloucestershire England UK
127 P5 **Gloucester** Massachusetts USA
162 B6 **Gloucester, Cabo** *cape* Chile
241 F3 **Gloucestershire** *admin. area* England UK
229 H3 **Glovelier** Switzerland
123 J8 **Glover Island** Newfoundland and Labrador Canada
127 N5 **Gloversville** New York USA
123 K8 **Glovertown** Newfoundland and Labrador Canada
226 G1 **Glöwen** Germany
227 J2 **Główno** Poland
388 D4 **Glubokiy** Russian Federation
389 N3 **Glubokoye** Kazakhstan
224 E5 **Glud** Denmark
238 D6 **Glukhi** Belarus
227 H1 **Głusko** Poland
235 B6 **Glykí** Greece
240 D3 **Glyncorrwg** Neath Port Talbot Wales UK
232 E3 **Gmunden** Austria
222 J5 **Gnarp** Sweden
227 G4 **Gnesau** Austria
224 F4 **Gniben** *cape* Denmark
227 J1 **Gniew** Poland
227 I1 **Gniezno** Poland
234 B4 **Gnjilane** Kosovo
226 G5 **Gnocchetta** Italy
Gnoorganbin *see* **Moreton Island** Australia
424 F8 **Gnowangerup** WA Australia
393 D8 **Goa** *admin. area* India
377 I4 **Goa** Philippines
379 G3 **Goalpara** Assam India
375 H6 **Goang** Indonesia
393 D3 **Goaso** Ghana
163 I8 **Goat Point** Antigua and Barbuda
243 H2 **Goathland** North Yorkshire England UK
307 F2 **Goba** Ethiopia
308 C4 **Gobabis** Namibia
391 I2 **Gōbān** Iraq
307 G2 **Gobele** *watercourse* Ethiopia
154 A6 **Gobernador, Punta** *cape* Peru
162 B3 **Gobernador Costa** Argentina
160 F4 **Gobernador Crespo** Argentina
160 E6 **Gobernador Duval** Argentina
162 B4 **Gobernador Gregores** Argentina
162 B5 **Gobernador Mayer** Argentina
160 F4 **Gobernador Moyano** Argentina
162 C4 **Gobernador Virasoro** Argentina
384 E4 **Gobi** *desert* Mongolia
393 F6 **Gobindpur** Orissa India
235 E6 **Göçbeyli** Turkey
223 M2 **Goccadanjávri** *lake* Norway
226 D2 **Goch** Germany
308 C4 **Gochas** Namibia
229 L1 **Göda** Germany
241 G3 **Godalming** Surrey England UK
393 E7 **Godawari** *watercourse* Andhra Pradesh India
121 V8 **Godbout** Québec Canada
123 E8 **Godbout** *watercourse* Québec Canada
392 G6 **Godda** Jharkhand India
125 Q8 **Goddard** Kansas USA
307 G2 **Godē** Ethiopia
307 F5 **Godegode** Tanzania
222 H4 **Godejorda** Norway
437 B2 **Godel Iceport** Antarctica
241 H5 **Goderville** France
126 F7 **Godfrey** Illinois USA
392 C6 **Godhra** Gujarat India
241 F3 **Godington** Oxfordshire England UK
307 H2 **Godinlabe** Somalia
423 D6 **Godley** *watercourse* New Zealand
130 C4 **Godley** Texas USA
241 H3 **Godmersham** Kent England UK
160 D5 **Godoy Cruz** Argentina
232 G3 **Gödre** Hungary
120 I4 **Gods** *watercourse* Manitoba Canada
120 H5 **Gods Lake** Manitoba Canada
120 H5 **Gods Lake Narrows** Manitoba Canada
120 L1 **Gods Mercy, Bay of** Nunavut Canada
437 E2 **Godspeed Nunataks** *range* Antarctica
224 G3 **Godunovka** Russian Federation
227 L2 **Godziszów** Poland
373 G6 **Goe** Papua New Guinea
226 B2 **Goedereede** Netherlands
117 L8 **Goéland, Lac au** *lake* Québec Canada
117 M7 **Goélands, Lac aux** *lake* Québec Canada
226 B2 **Goes** Netherlands
127 K3 **Gogama** Ontario Canada
126 G3 **Gogebic, Lake** Michigan USA
126 G3 **Gogebic Range** *range* Michigan USA
225 N2 **Gogland, Ostrov** *island* Russian Federation
309 F4 **Gogói** Mozambique
373 H5 **Gogol** *watercourse* Papua New Guinea
238 D5 **Gogolevka** Russian Federation
227 J2 **Gogolin** Poland
234 C3 **Gogoșu** Romania
304 E2 **Gogounou** Benin
306 D2 **Gogrial** Sudan
226 F1 **Göhrde** Germany
158 D2 **Goiabal** Brazil
157 B6 **Goianésia** Brazil
157 B7 **Goiânia** Brazil
157 B6 **Goiás** Brazil
157 B7 **Goiás** *admin. area* Brazil
157 C6 **Goiás, Serra Geral de** *range* Brazil
157 B7 **Goiatuba** Brazil
224 G4 **Göinge** *region* Sweden
226 C2 **Goirle** Netherlands
226 F5 **Goito** Italy
307 F2 **Gojeb** *watercourse* Ethiopia
391 L3 **Gojra** Pakistan
227 J1 **Gójsk** Poland
393 D8 **Gokak** Karnataka India
235 D5 **Gökçeada** *island* Turkey
235 F6 **Gökçek** Turkey
388 G6 **Göklengüy Şorluk** *lake* Turkmenistan
235 E7 **Gökova Körfezi** *bay* Turkey
224 I5 **Göksjön** *lake* Sweden
394 F5 **Göksu Nehri** *watercourse* Turkey
224 E2 **Gol** Norway
232 G3 **Gola** Croatia
392 E5 **Gola Gokaran Nath** Uttar Pradesh India
245 D1 **Gola Island** Ireland
379 G3 **Golaghat** Assam India
227 I1 **Golce** Poland
235 F6 **Gölcük** *watercourse* Turkey
124 C5 **Gold Beach** Oregon USA
118 J7 **Gold Bridge** British Columbia Canada
304 D4 **Gold Coast** West Africa
118 H8 **Gold River** British Columbia Canada
118 M7 **Golden** British Columbia Canada
127 M4 **Golden** Ontario Canada
422 E5 **Golden Bay** New Zealand
130 F6 **Golden Meadow** Louisiana USA
119 Q7 **Golden Prairie** Saskatchewan Canada
124 E4 **Goldendale** Washington USA
128 D2 **Goldfield** Nevada USA
119 Q3 **Goldfields** Saskatchewan Canada
120 J2 **Goldie Lake** Ontario Canada
120 E4 **Goldsand Lake** Manitoba Canada
129 K5 **Goldsmith** Texas USA
130 B5 **Goldthwaite** Texas USA
307 F2 **Golecha** Ethiopia
388 G6 **Golestān** *admin. area* Iran
128 C3 **Goleta** California USA
134 D5 **Golfito** Costa Rica
235 F7 **Gölgeli, Dağları** *range* Turkey
160 E3 **Golgota** Argentina
235 F7 **Gölhisar** Turkey
235 F6 **Goli** *island* Croatia
306 E3 **Goli** Uganda
225 N4 **Goliševa** Latvia
238 G5 **Golitsyno** Russian Federation
229 L3 **Golnik** Slovenia
377 I4 **Golo** *island* Philippines
380 D1 **Golog Shan** *range* Jiangsu China
305 H3 **Golongosso** Central African Republic
235 C5 **Golovchin** Belarus
238 D6 **Golovenchitsy** Belarus
235 G5 **Golovinka** Russian Federation
234 F3 **Golovița, Lacul** *lake* Romania
390 G2 **Golpāyegān** Iran
235 G5 **Gölpazarı** Turkey
244 E3 **Golspie** Highland Scotland UK
232 G4 **Golubić** Croatia
125 N3 **Golva** North Dakota USA
394 G5 **Gölyurt Geçidi** *pass* Turkey
226 G1 **Golzow** Germany
306 E4 **Goma** Uganda
230 E3 **Gómara** Spain
392 E5 **Gomati** *watercourse* Uttar Pradesh India
309 G2 **Gomba** Mozambique
306 D3 **Gombari** Democratic Republic of Congo
305 G2 **Gombe** Nigeria
305 G3 **Gombe** *admin. area* Nigeria
306 E4 **Gombe** *watercourse* Tanzania
235 F7 **Gömbe** Turkey
305 G2 **Gombi** Nigeria
232 D5 **Gombo** Italy
244 B4 **Gometra House** Highland Scotland UK
132 E3 **Gómez Farías** Mexico
132 E3 **Gómez Palacio** Mexico
238 F2 **Gomorovichi** Russian Federation
372 C4 **Gomumu** *island* Indonesia
391 I2 **Gonābād** Iran
135 F3 **Gonaïves** Haiti
237 AA7 **Gonam** *watercourse* Russian Federation
135 F3 **Gonâve, Île de la** *island* Haiti
388 G6 **Gonbad-e Kāvūs** Iran
234 B1 **Gönc** Hungary
392 E5 **Gonda** Uttar Pradesh India
393 C7 **Gondal** Gujarat India
302 F5 **Gonder** Ethiopia
394 G5 **Gonderme Gecidi** *pass* Turkey
305 H3 **Gondey** Chad
393 E7 **Gondiya** Maharashtra India
304 B3 **Gondolahun** Liberia
230 B2 **Gondomar** Spain
229 G2 **Gondrecourt** France
235 E5 **Gönen** Turkey
235 G7 **Gönen** Turkey
308 C3 **Gonga** Angola
379 G3 **Gongb ujiangda** Xizang Zizhiqu China
380 F4 **Gongcheng** Guangxi Zhuangzu Zizhiqu China
379 G3 **Gonggar** Xizang Zizhiqu China
381 G3 **Gongjiang** Jiangxi China
379 G3 **Gongka** Xizang Zizhiqu China
382 G4 **Gongliu** Xinjiang Uygur Zizhiqu China
157 E6 **Gongogi** *watercourse* Brazil
305 G2 **Gongola** *watercourse* Nigeria
305 F5 **Gongoúe** Gabon
379 G3 **Gongtang** Xizang Zizhiqu China
385 J4 **Gongzhuling** Jilin China
233 C7 **Gonnesa** Sardinia Italy
308 E6 **Gonubie** South Africa
125 R3 **Gonvick** Minnesota USA
377 I3 **Gonzaga** Philippines
128 B2 **Gonzales** California USA
130 C6 **Gonzales** Texas USA
127 M8 **Goochland** Virginia USA
130 H4 **Good Hope** Alabama USA
308 C6 **Good Hope, Cape of** South Africa
118 G3 **Good Hope Lake** British Columbia Canada
437 I2 **Goodenough, Cape** Antarctica
373 I6 **Goodenough Island** Papua New Guinea
119 T7 **Goodeve** Saskatchewan Canada
124 H5 **Gooding** Idaho USA
310 7b **Goodlands** Mauritius
130 H2 **Goodlettsville** Tennessee USA
130 G4 **Goodman** Mississippi USA
116 C7 **Goodnews Bay** Alaska USA
425 M7 **Goodooga** NSW Australia
125 O3 **Goodrich** North Dakota USA
119 T8 **Goodwater** Saskatchewan Canada
131 H4 **Goodwater** Alabama USA
129 L2 **Goodwell** Oklahoma USA
240 C2 **Goodwick** Pembrokeshire Wales UK
122 E5 **Goodwood** *watercourse* Québec Canada
226 C2 **Gooik** Belgium
243 H3 **Goole** East Riding of Yorkshire England UK
425 M7 **Goolgowi** NSW Australia
425 K8 **Goolwa** SA Australia
424 F7 **Goomalling** WA Australia
425 N7 **Goondiwindi** Qld Australia
240 B4 **Goonhavern** Cornwall England UK
226 D1 **Goor** Netherlands
122 H6 **Goose** *watercourse* Newfoundland and Labrador Canada
122 H6 **Goose Bay** Newfoundland and Labrador Canada
120 H3 **Goose Creek** Manitoba Canada
131 K4 **Goose Creek** South Carolina USA
163 7 **Goose Green** Falkland Islands
124 E6 **Goose Lake** California USA
240 C4 **Gooseham** Cornwall England UK
229 I2 **Göppingen** Germany
230 E5 **Gor** Spain
227 I2 **Góra** Poland
227 K1 **Góra** Poland
393 E6 **Gorakhpur** Madhya Pradesh India
392 F5 **Gorakhpur** Uttar Pradesh India
232 H5 **Goražde** Bosnia and Herzegovina
238 G6 **Gorbachëvo** Russian Federation
238 C4 **Gorbovo** Russian Federation
388 D1 **Gorchukha** Russian Federation
134 D2 **Gorda, Punta** *cape* Cuba
134 D4 **Gorda, Punta** *cape* Nicaragua
124 C6 **Gorda, Punta** *cape* California USA
131 M7 **Gorda Cay** *island* Bahamas
235 F6 **Gördes** Turkey
131 J4 **Gordon** Georgia USA
125 N5 **Gordon** Nebraska USA
425 M10 **Gordon, Lake** Tas. Australia
119 P4 **Gordon Lake** Alberta Canada
118 L5 **Gordondale** Alberta Canada
425 M4 **Gordonvale** Qld Australia
305 H3 **Goré** Chad
307 F2 **Gore** Ethiopia
423 C8 **Gore** New Zealand
116 D7 **Gore Point** Alaska USA
130 B4 **Goree** Texas USA
238 G5 **Gorelki** Russian Federation
238 E6 **Gorënovo** Russian Federation
126 G8 **Goreville** Illinois USA
245 F4 **Gorey** Ireland
391 I3 **Gorg** Iran
304 D2 **Gorgadji** Burkina Faso
388 G7 **Gorgān** Iran
228 F5 **Gorges** France
154 B4 **Gorgona, Isla** *island* Colombia
232 C5 **Gorgona, Isola di** *island* Italy
302 F5 **Gorgora** Ethiopia
305 G2 **Gorgoram** Nigeria
234 F3 **Gorgova, Lacul** *lake* Romania
129 M1 **Gorham** Kansas USA
127 P4 **Gorham** New Hampshire USA
388 D5 **Gori** Georgia
241 F3 **Goring** Oxfordshire England UK
238 G4 **Goritsy** Russian Federation
226 G5 **Gorizia** Italy
234 C3 **Gorj** *admin. area* Romania
392 F5 **Gorkha** Nepal
236 O5 **Gorki** Russian Federation
388 E1 **Gorki** Russian Federation
238 D4 **Gorki Pathotnaya** Russian Federation
236 J7 **Gor'kovskoye Vodokhranilishche** *lake* Russian Federation
389 M3 **Gor'koye, Ozero** *lake* Russian Federation
389 M3 **Gor'koye Peresheyechnoye** *lake* Russian Federation
227 K3 **Gorlice** Poland
229 L1 **Görlitz** Germany
226 F1 **Gorlosen** Germany
238 H6 **Gorlovo** Russian Federation
130 B4 **Gorman** Texas USA
392 E5 **Gormi** Madhya Pradesh India
229 L4 **Gornje Jelenje** Croatia
227 I4 **Gornji Petrovci** Slovenia
387 O3 **Gorno-Altaysk** Russian Federation
387 I1 **Gornozavodsk** Russian Federation
385 N3 **Gornyak** Russian Federation
385 M2 **Gornyy** Russian Federation
388 E3 **Gornyy** Russian Federation
388 E3 **Gornyy Balykley** Russian Federation
305 I3 **Goro** *watercourse* Central African Republic
226 G5 **Goro** Italy
238 C3 **Gorodishche** Russian Federation
238 H5 **Gorodishchi** Russian Federation
234 F1 **Gorodok** Ukraine
388 D2 **Gorokhovets** Russian Federation
304 D2 **Gorom Gorom** Burkina Faso
372 D5 **Gorong** *island* Indonesia
372 D5 **Gorong, Kepulauan** *island* Indonesia
309 F3 **Gorongosa** Mozambique
309 F3 **Gorongoza, Monte** *mountain* Mozambique
372 B3 **Gorontalo** Indonesia
372 B3 **Gorontalo** *admin. area* Indonesia
162 B5 **Gorra, Cerro** *mountain* Chile
226 D1 **Gorredijk** Netherlands
242 E3 **Gorsedd** Flintshire Wales UK
240 C3 **Gorseinon** Swansea Wales UK
245 D3 **Gort** Ireland
245 C4 **Gortaheera** Ireland
245 C4 **Gortahork** Ireland
240 A2 **Gorteens** Ireland
245 E4 **Gorteeny** Ireland
245 D3 **Gortfree** Ireland
245 C5 **Gortgarriff** Ireland
245 C4 **Gortmore** Ireland
245 D5 **Gortnacrue** Ireland
242 A4 **Gortnagan** Ireland
245 C4 **Gortnaleaha** Ireland
244 B4 **Gorton** Highland Scotland UK
245 D4 **Gortroe** Ireland
245 D3 **Gortskeagh** Ireland
245 C3 **Gorumna Island** Ireland
234 F4 **Gorun** Bulgaria
222 I5 **Görviksjön** *lake* Sweden
387 J2 **Goryacheye, Ozero** *lake* Russian Federation
384 F2 **Goryachinsk (Gremyachinsk)** Russian Federation
225 O5 **Goryany** Belarus
226 G1 **Görzke** Germany
227 H1 **Gorzów Wielkopolski** Poland
232 D3 **Gosaldo** Italy
241 G2 **Gosberton** Lincolnshire England UK
373 I6 **Goschen Strait** Papua New Guinea
224 H5 **Gościno** Poland
241 H3 **Gosfield** Essex England UK
425 N8 **Gosford** NSW Australia
242 E2 **Gosforth** Cumbria England UK
243 G1 **Gosforth** Tyne and Wear England UK
126 I6 **Goshen** Indiana USA
387 I3 **Goshogawara** Japan
391 J4 **Gosht-e 'Olyā** Iran
124 H6 **Goshute Lake** Nevada USA
241 F4 **Gosport** Hampshire England UK
245 E3 **Gossa** *island* Norway
300 C6 **Gossas** Senegal
301 F5 **Gossi** Mali
306 D2 **Gossinga** Sudan
235 B5 **Gostivar** Macedonia
227 J2 **Gostków** Poland
227 I2 **Gostyń** Poland
227 J1 **Gostynin** Poland
224 F3 **Göteborg (Gothenburg)** Sweden
305 G3 **Gotel Mountains** *range* Nigeria
229 J1 **Gotha** Germany
225 J4 **Gothem** Sweden
Gothenburg *see* **Göteborg** Sweden
125 O6 **Gothenburg** Nebraska USA
301 G6 **Gothèye** Niger
225 J4 **Gotland** *island* Sweden
163 1c **Goto Meer** *lake* Netherlands Antilles
229 L3 **Gotovlje** Slovenia
225 J3 **Gotska Sandön** *island* Sweden
386 G4 **Gōtsu** Japan
229 I1 **Göttingen** Germany
222 K5 **Gottne** Sweden
304 C3 **Gouan** *watercourse* Côte d'Ivoire
226 C1 **Gouda** Netherlands
300 D6 **Goudiry** Senegal
301 I6 **Goudoumaria** Niger
160 F5 **Goudra** Argentina
304 C3 **Gouéké** Guinea
119 O6 **Gough Lake** Alberta Canada
117 L9 **Gouin, Réservoir** Québec Canada
304 E3 **Gouka** Benin
425 N8 **Goulburn** NSW Australia
130 F4 **Gould** Arkansas USA
436 O1 **Gould Coast** Antarctica
304 C2 **Goulia** Côte d'Ivoire
305 I2 **Goumbatou** Chad
300 E6 **Goumbou** Mali
305 G3 **Gouna** Cameroon
305 I3 **Gounda** *watercourse* Central African Republic
300 F5 **Goundam** Mali
305 H3 **Goundi** Chad
305 H3 **Gounou-Gaya** Chad
381 I2 **Gouqi Dao** *island* Zhejiang China
301 G1 **Gouraya** Algeria
300 D6 **Gouraye** Mauritania
304 D2 **Gourcy** Burkina Faso
228 E4 **Gourdon** France
301 I6 **Gouré** Niger
228 C2 **Gourin** France
126 I2 **Gourlay Lake** Ontario Canada
241 I5 **Gournay-en-Bray** France
301 J5 **Gouro** Chad
302 B4 **Gouro** Chad
230 C3 **Gouveia** Portugal
127 N4 **Gouverneur** New York USA
229 G1 **Gouvy** Belgium
163 10a **Gouyave** Grenada
228 F3 **Gouzon** France
384 F3 **Gov-ugtaal** Mongolia
425 K3 **Gove Peninsula** NT Australia
237 AI7 **Govena, Poluostrov** *peninsula* Russian Federation
119 Q8 **Govenlock** Saskatchewan Canada
157 D7 **Governador Valadares** Brazil
383 J4 **Govi-Altay** *admin. area* Mongolia
384 E4 **Govi Altayn Nuruu** Mongolia
392 F6 **Govind Ballabh Pant Sagar** *lake* Uttar Pradesh India
392 D4 **Govind Sagar** *lake* Himachal Pradesh India
384 F3 **Govisumber** *admin. area* Mongolia
126 E3 **Gowan** Minnesota USA
126 D7 **Gower** Missouri USA
425 inset **Gower, Mount** Lord Howe Island Australia
118 F6 **Gowgaia Bay** British Columbia Canada
224 I5 **Gowidlino** Poland
245 C3 **Gowla** Ireland
242 B4 **Gowlin** Ireland
391 K3 **Gowmal Kalay** Afghanistan
245 E3 **Gowna, Lough** *lake* Ireland
388 J6 **Gowurdak** Turkmenistan
161 G4 **Goya** Argentina
163 I6 **Goyave** Guadeloupe
425 K6 **Goyder Lagoon** SA Australia
235 G5 **Göynük** Turkey
305 G3 **Goyoum** Cameroon
224 E3 **Gøystvatn** *lake* Norway
302 C5 **Goz-Beïda** Chad
305 I2 **Goz Beïda** Chad
233 F8 **Gozo** *island* Malta
229 I4 **Gozzano** Italy
308 D6 **Graaff-reinet** South Africa
304 C4 **Grabo** Côte d'Ivoire
226 F1 **Grabow** Germany
224 G5 **Grabow** *bay* Germany
227 J1 **Grabów** Poland
227 L1 **Grabówka** Poland
227 J5 **Gračanica** Bosnia and Herzegovina
228 E3 **Graçay** France
124 J5 **Grace** Idaho USA
424 F8 **Grace, Lake** WA Australia
126 H4 **Grace Harbor** Michigan USA
242 B3 **Gracedieu** Ireland
127 M3 **Gracefield** Québec Canada
242 B2 **Gracehill** Ballymena Northern Ireland UK
125 Q4 **Graceville** Minnesota USA
232 B3 **Grächen** Switzerland
134 B4 **Gracias** Honduras
134 D4 **Gracias a Dios, Cabo** *cape* Nicaragua
310 1b **Graciosa** *island* Azores
310 3d **Graciosa** *island* Canary Islands
227 I5 **Gradac** Croatia
232 H4 **Gradačac** Bosnia and Herzegovina
156 B4 **Gradaús, Serra dos** *range* Brazil
235 C5 **Gradec** Macedonia
234 E4 **Gradets** Bulgaria
235 C5 **Gradevo** Bulgaria
234 C4 **Gradište** Serbia
230 C2 **Grado** Spain
130 F3 **Grady** Arkansas USA
229 J2 **Gräfenberg** Germany
245 B4 **Graffee** Ireland
241 G4 **Graffham** West Sussex England UK
245 D2 **Graffy** Ireland
241 G2 **Grafham Water** *lake* England UK
222 H5 **Gräftåvallen** Sweden
425 O7 **Grafton** NSW Australia
125 Q2 **Grafton** North Dakota USA
127 K7 **Grafton** West Virginia USA
118 J4 **Graham** *watercourse* British Columbia Canada
126 F2 **Graham** Ontario Canada
131 L2 **Graham** North Carolina USA
118 E6 **Graham Island** British Columbia Canada
117 J3 **Graham Island** Nunavut Canada
119 N4 **Graham Lake** Alberta Canada
127 Q4 **Graham Lake** Maine USA
436 T2 **Graham Land** *plain* Antarctica
117 L4 **Graham Moore, Cape** Nunavut Canada
308 E6 **Grahamstown** South Africa
245 B4 **Graigue** Ireland
241 H3 **Grain, Isle of** England UK
244 B5 **Grainel** Argyll and Bute Scotland UK
125 O7 **Grainfield** Kansas USA
156 C4 **Grajaú** Brazil
156 C4 **Grajaú** *watercourse* Brazil
227 L1 **Grajewo** Poland
224 E5 **Gram** Denmark
228 E4 **Gramat** France
76 M8 **Gramberg Seamount** *underwater feature* Atlantic Ocean
130 F5 **Gramercy** Louisiana USA
383 K4 **Grampian Mountains** *range* Scotland UK
224 F2 **Gran** Norway
310 3 **Gran Canaria** *island* Canary Islands
135 I9 **Gran Cayo Point** Trinidad and Tobago
154 B4 **Gran Macizo Colombiano** *range* Colombia
158 C3 **Gran Pajonal** *region* Peru
226 D5 **Gran Paradiso** *mountain* Italy
232 B4 **Gran Queyron** *mountain* France/Italy
160 E6 **Gran Salitral** *lake* Argentina
310 3d **Gran Tarajal** Canary Islands
232 B5 **Grana** *watercourse* Italy
134 C5 **Granada** Nicaragua
230 E5 **Granada** Spain
129 H6 **Granados** Mexico
245 E3 **Gránard** Ireland
222 H6 **Granåsen** Norway
222 J4 **Granåsen** Sweden
224 J4 **Granberget** Sweden
222 I5 **Granboda** Sweden
130 C4 **Granbury** Texas USA
130 C4 **Granbury, Lake** Texas USA
127 O4 **Granby** Québec Canada
125 M6 **Granby, Lake** Colorado USA
229 G3 **Grancey** France
126 I5 **Grand** *watercourse* Michigan USA
126 D6 **Grand** *watercourse* Missouri USA
125 O4 **Grand** *watercourse* South Dakota USA
131 M7 **Grand Abaco** *island* Bahamas
163 13 **Grand Anse** St Lucia
232 B4 **Grand Argentier, Le** *mountain* France
131 L7 **Grand Bahama** *island* Bahamas
123 K9 **Grand Bank** Newfoundland and Labrador Canada
76 M5 **Grand Banks of Newfoundland** *underwater feature* Atlantic Ocean
304 D3 **Grand-Bassam** Côte d'Ivoire
126 G2 **Grand Bay** Ontario Canada
304 C4 **Grand Bérébi** Côte d'Ivoire
163 16 **Grand-Bourg** Guadeloupe
128 F2 **Grand Canyon** Arizona USA
134 D3 **Grand Cayman** *island* Cayman Islands
119 P5 **Grand Centre** Alberta Canada
159 F6 **Grand Chaco** *range* Paraguay
163 16 **Grand Cul-de-Sac Marin** *bay* Guadeloupe
123 K8 **Grand Falls-Windsor** Newfoundland and Labrador Canada
118 L8 **Grand Forks** British Columbia Canada
125 Q3 **Grand Forks** North Dakota USA
241 J4 **Grand-Fort-Philippe** France
130 G6 **Grand Gozier Island** Louisiana USA
126 H5 **Grand Haven** Michigan USA
163 16 **Grand Îlet** *island* Guadeloupe
126 H3 **Grand Island** Michigan USA
125 P6 **Grand Island** Nebraska USA
130 G6 **Grand Isle** Louisiana USA
163 7 **Grand Jason** *island* Falkland Islands
125 K7 **Grand Junction** Colorado USA
127 N3 **Grand Lac du Commissaire** *lake* Québec Canada
123 E7 **Grand Lac Germain** *lake* Québec Canada
304 D3 **Grand-lahou** Côte d'Ivoire
123 E10 **Grand Lake** New Brunswick Canada
122 H6 **Grand Lake** Newfoundland and Labrador Canada
125 M6 **Grand Lake** Colorado USA
130 E6 **Grand Lake** Louisiana USA
127 Q3 **Grand Lake Seboeis** Maine USA
127 M3 **Grand Lake Victoria** Québec Canada
228 D3 **Grand-Lieu, Lac de** *lake* France
123 E10 **Grand Manan Island** New Brunswick Canada
126 I3 **Grand Marais** Michigan USA
126 F3 **Grand Marais** Minnesota USA
126 G3 **Grand Portage** Minnesota USA
130 C4 **Grand Prairie** Texas USA
118 I5 **Grand Rapids** British Columbia Canada
119 V6 **Grand Rapids** Manitoba Canada
126 I5 **Grand Rapids** Michigan USA
126 E3 **Grand Rapids** Minnesota USA
163 14 **Grand Rivière** Martinique
163 10a **Grand Roy** Grenada
155 H3 **Grand-Santi** French Guiana
135 I3 **Grand-Terre** *island* Montserrat
125 J5 **Grand Teton** *mountain* Wyoming USA
126 G8 **Grand Tower** Illinois USA
126 I4 **Grand Traverse Bay** Michigan USA
135 G2 **Grand Turk** Turks and Caicos Islands
135 G2 **Grand Turk Island** Turks and Caicos Islands
125 O1 **Grand View** Manitoba Canada
230 C2 **Grandas** Spain
162 C5 **Grande** *watercourse* Argentina
159 F5 **Grande** *watercourse* Bolivia
161 H2 **Grande** Brazil
157 C5 **Grande** *watercourse* Brazil
123 F8 **Grande** *watercourse* Québec Canada
129 J5 **Grande** *watercourse* New Mexico USA
132 D2 **Grande** *watercourse* Texas USA
162 C5 **Grande, Bahía** *bay* Argentina
159 F4 **Grande, Baía** *bay* Brazil
155 F2 **Grande, Boca** *bay* Venezuela
154 E2 **Grande, Cayo** *island* Venezuela
161 H5 **Grande, Cuchilla** *range* Uruguay
157 C8 **Grande, Ilha** *island* Brazil
233 E8 **Grande, Isola** *island* Italy
155 I4 **Grande, Ponta** *cape* Brazil
160 D3 **Grande, Punta** *cape* Chile
160 D2 **Grande, Salar** *pan* Chile
160 E6 **Grande, Salina** *pan* Argentina
159 H5 **Grande, Serra** *range* Brazil
163 16 **Grande-Anse** Guadeloupe
118 L6 **Grande Cache** Alberta Canada
310 8 **Grande Comore (Njazidja)** *island* Comoros
156 B3 **Grande de Gurupa, Ilha** *island* Brazil
160 E2 **Grande de Jujuy, Rio** *watercourse* Argentina
161 H5 **Grande del Durazno, Cuchilla** *range* Uruguay
161 G5 **Grande Inferior, Cuchilla** *range* Uruguay
118 L5 **Grande Prairie** Alberta Canada
157 A6 **Grande Região Centro-Oeste** *region* Brazil
163 9 **Grande Riviere** Trinidad and Tobago
117 L7 **Grande Rivière de la Baleine** *watercourse* Québec Canada
310 7b **Grande Rivière Sud Est** Mauritius
163 16 **Grande-Terre** *island* Guadeloupe
Grande Terre *see* **Mahoré** Mayotte
235 E8 **Grandes** *island* Greece
129 K5 **Grandfalls** Texas USA
436 T2 **Grandidier Channel** *strait* Antarctica
116 H6 **Grandin, Lac** *lake* Northwest Territories Canada
118 F4 **Granduc** British Columbia Canada
124 F3 **Grandview** Washington USA
241 I5 **Grandvilliers** France
231 F3 **Grañén** Spain
160 D5 **Graneros** Chile
245 D4 **Graney, Lough** *lake* Ireland
224 H2 **Grangärde** Sweden
240 A2 **Grange** Ireland
245 D3 **Grange** Ireland
245 E5 **Grange** Ireland
130 C5 **Granger** Texas USA
125 K6 **Granger** Wyoming USA
124 G4 **Grangeville** Idaho USA

222 J5 **Grängsjö** Sweden
224 E2 **Granheim** Norway
222 L3 **Granhult** Sweden
222 J5 **Graninge** Sweden
222 J5 **Graningesjön** *lake* Sweden
118 H5 **Granisle** British Columbia Canada
437 L1 **Granite Harbor** *bay* Antarctica
123 J8 **Granite Lake** Newfoundland and Labrador Canada
125 L5 **Granite Mountains** Wyoming USA
124 F6 **Granite Range** Nevada USA
130 B5 **Granite Shoals** Texas USA
126 I2 **Granitehill Lake** Ontario Canada
423 D5 **Granity** New Zealand
156 D3 **Granja** Brazil
230 D4 **Granja de Torrehermosa** Spain
224 G3 **Gränjön** Sweden
225 P5 **Granki** Russian Federation
134 E2 **Granma** *admin. area* Cuba
224 G3 **Grann** *lake* Sweden
222 J4 **Grannäs** Sweden
130 D3 **Grannis** Arkansas USA
222 K4 **Granö** Sweden
158 B4 **Grano de Oro, Punta** *cape* Peru
160 D6 **Granole** *watercourse* Argentina
226 G1 **Gransee** Germany
242 C2 **Gransha** Larne Northern Ireland UK
222 L3 **Gransjö** Sweden
222 J4 **Gransjön** *lake* Sweden
125 O6 **Grant** Nebraska USA
436 P2 **Grant Island** Antarctica
372 E6 **Grant Island** NT Australia
128 E1 **Grant Range** Nevada USA
241 G2 **Grantham** Lincolnshire England UK
244 E5 **Granton House** Dumfries and Galloway Scotland UK
222 K4 **Granträsket** *lake* Sweden
129 I3 **Grants** New Mexico USA
124 D5 **Grants Pass** Oregon USA
127 L7 **Grantsville** Maryland USA
222 K3 **Granudden** Sweden
119 O8 **Granum** Alberta Canada
242 B2 **Granville** Dungannon Northern Ireland UK
129 H4 **Granville** Arizona USA
125 O2 **Granville** North Dakota USA
117 I7 **Granville Lake** Manitoba Canada
130 D5 **Grapeland** Texas USA
231 J5 **Grarem** Algeria
223 P1 **Grasbakken** Norway
222 F5 **Gråsjøen** *lake* Norway
242 E2 **Grasmere** Cumbria England UK
225 J2 **Gräsö** *island* Sweden
120 F5 **Grass** *watercourse* Manitoba Canada
124 E7 **Grass Valley** California USA
124 E4 **Grass Valley** Oregon USA
119 T5 **Grassberry** *watercourse* Saskatchewan Canada
229 H5 **Grasse** France
127 L2 **Grasset, Lac** *lake* Québec Canada
243 G2 **Grassington** North Yorkshire England UK
222 I5 **Gråssjön** Sweden
224 G3 **Grässjön** *lake* Sweden
423 F5 **Grassmere, Lake** New Zealand
125 K3 **Grassrange** Montana USA
127 K7 **Grassy Knob** *mountain* West Virginia USA
222 I3 **Grasvatnet** *lake* Norway
224 C2 **Gratangen** Norway
227 H4 **Gratkorn** Austria
222 K5 **Grätnäs** Sweden
226 E4 **Graubünden** *admin. area* Switzerland
228 E5 **Graulhet** France
231 G2 **Graus** Spain
161 I4 **Gravataí** Brazil
224 D3 **Gravatn** *lake* Norway
228 D4 **Grave, Pointe de** *cape* France
241 J4 **Gravelines** France
163 I8 **Gravenor Bay** Antigua and Barbuda
241 H3 **Gravesend** Kent England UK
122 H4 **Graveyard Island** Newfoundland and Labrador Canada
135 F3 **Gravois, Pointe-à-** *cape* Haiti
222 G4 **Gravvik** Norway
226 C4 **Gray** France
131 J4 **Gray** Georgia USA
124 G2 **Gray Creek** British Columbia Canada
128 G3 **Gray Mountain** Arizona USA
122 F2 **Gray Strait** Nunavut Canada
241 H3 **Grays** Thurrock England UK
124 C3 **Grays Harbor** Washington USA
124 J5 **Grays Lake** Idaho USA
125 M7 **Grays Peak** Colorado USA
131 K3 **Grayson** Louisiana USA
227 H4 **Graz** Austria
234 E3 **Greaca** Romania
119 R3 **Grease** *watercourse* Saskatchewan Canada
424 I8 **Great Australian Bight** *bay* SA Australia
243 G2 **Great Ayton** North Yorkshire England UK
163 10a **Great Bacolet Point** *cape* Grenada
241 H3 **Great Baddow** Essex England UK
79 Y5 **Great Bahama Bank** *underwater feature* Atlantic Ocean
422 F3 **Great Barrier Island** New Zealand
425 M3 **Great Barrier Reef** Qld Australia
128 E1 **Great Basin** Nevada USA
127 N7 **Great Bay** New Jersey USA
116 G5 **Great Bear Lake** Northwest Territories Canada
125 P7 **Great Bend** Kansas USA
125 Q3 **Great Bend** North Dakota USA
244 B2 **Great Bernera** *island* Scotland UK
245 B4 **Great Blasket Island** Ireland
241 H2 **Great Bradley** Suffolk England UK
242 E2 **Great Broughton** Cumbria England UK
118 I8 **Great Central Lake** British Columbia Canada
376 B4 **Great Coco Island** Andaman and Nicobar Islands India
425 N8 **Great Dividing Range** NSW Australia
425 M5 **Great Dividing Range** Qld Australia
425 M9 **Great Dividing Range** Vic. Australia
126 J4 **Great Duck Island** Ontario Canada
241 H3 **Great Dunmow** Essex England UK
422 E2 **Great Exhibition Bay** New Zealand
135 F2 **Great Exuma** *island* Bahamas
124 J3 **Great Falls** Montana USA
131 M7 **Great Guana Cay** *island* Bahamas
241 H3 **Great Hallingbury** Essex England UK
131 M8 **Great Harbour Cay** *island* Bahamas
123 J7 **Great Harbour Deep** Newfoundland and Labrador Canada
243 F3 **Great Harwood** Lancashire England UK
135 F2 **Great Inagua Island** Bahamas
120 G3 **Great Island** Manitoba Canada
308 D6 **Great Karoo** *plain* South Africa
240 E2 **Great Malvern** Worcestershire England UK
242 E3 **Great Marton** Blackpool England UK
76 P7 **Great Meteor Bank** *underwater feature* Atlantic Ocean
241 F3 **Great Milton** Oxfordshire England UK
243 F3 **Great Mitton** Lancashire England UK
308 C5 **Great Namaqualand** *region* Namibia
376 B6 **Great Nicobar Island** Andaman and Nicobar Islands India
373 G6 **Great North East Channel** *strait* Papua New Guinea
127 L7 **Great North Mountain** Virginia USA
242 E3 **Great Ormes Head** *cape* England UK
241 G2 **Great Ouse** *watercourse* England UK
134 C3 **Great Pedro Bluff** *cape* Jamaica
125 N4 **Great Plains** South Dakota USA
127 Q4 **Great Pond** Maine USA
306 D5 **Great Rift Valley** Africa
307 F5 **Great Ruaha** *watercourse* Tanzania
127 N5 **Great Sacandaga Lake** New York USA
131 L7 **Great Sale Cay** *island* Bahamas
124 I6 **Great Salt Lake** Utah USA
124 I6 **Great Salt Lake Desert** Utah USA
130 B2 **Great Salt Plains Lake** Oklahoma USA
119 Q7 **Great Sand Hills** Saskatchewan Canada
302 C2 **Great Sand Sea** *desert* Libya
424 G4 **Great Sandy Desert** WA Australia
241 H2 **Great Shelford** Cambridgeshire England UK
237 AL8 **Great Sitkin Island** Alaska USA
119 N2 **Great Slave Lake** Northwest Territories Canada
127 inset **Great Sound** *bay* Bermuda
127 O6 **Great South Bay** New York USA
241 H3 **Great Totham** Essex England UK
424 G7 **Great Victoria Desert** WA Australia
436 U2 **Great Wall (China)** *research station* Antarctica
127 R4 **Great Wass Island** Maine USA
376 C5 **Great Western Torres Islands** Myanmar
241 I2 **Great Yarmouth** Norfolk England UK
135 F3 **Greater Antilles** *islands* Caribbean Sea
134 E2 **Greater Bahama Bank** *underwater feature* Atlantic Ocean
241 G3 **Greater London** *admin. area* England UK
375 F5 **Greater Sunda Islands** *islands* Indonesia
241 H4 **Greatstone-on-Sea** Kent England UK
234 C3 **Greci** Romania
224 H3 **Grecken** *bay* Sweden
162 B3 **Greda Este, Cerro** *mountain* Argentina
235 C6 **Greece** *country* Europe
125 M6 **Greeley** Colorado USA
129 O1 **Greeley** Kansas USA
117 K2 **Greely Fiord** Nunavut Canada
131 I2 **Green** *watercourse* Kentucky USA
128 G1 **Green** *watercourse* Utah USA
125 J5 **Green** *watercourse* Wyoming USA
163 I8 **Green Bay** Antigua and Barbuda
126 G4 **Green Bay** Wisconsin USA
126 H4 **Green Bay** Wisconsin USA
134 E2 **Green Cay** *island* Bahamas
119 N5 **Green Court** Alberta Canada
130 E2 **Green Forest** Arkansas USA
424 F7 **Green Head** WA Australia
377 H5 **Green Island Bay** Philippines
373 J5 **Green Islands** Papua New Guinea
130 C6 **Green Lake** Texas USA
125 L7 **Green Mountain Reservoir** Colorado USA
127 O5 **Green Mountains** Vermont USA
240 E3 **Green Ore** Somerset England UK
124 D4 **Green Peter Lake** Oregon USA
125 J7 **Green River** Utah USA
125 K6 **Green River** Wyoming USA
126 I8 **Green River Lake** Kentucky USA
128 G5 **Green Valley** Arizona USA
245 F3 **Greenanstown** Ireland
131 K2 **Greenbrier** *watercourse* West Virginia USA
125 Q2 **Greenbush** Minnesota USA
242 B1 **Greencastle** Ireland
245 F2 **Greencastle** Newry and Mourne Northern Ireland UK
245 E2 **Greencastle** Omagh Northern Ireland UK
126 H7 **Greencastle** Indiana USA
131 J2 **Greeneville** Tennessee USA
241 G2 **Greenfield** Bedfordshire England UK
128 B2 **Greenfield** California USA
126 D6 **Greenfield** Iowa USA
126 G3 **Greenland** Michigan USA
117 N4 **Greenland (Kalaallit Nunaat)** *Danish dependency* Atlantic Ocean
76 R2 **Greenland Abyssal Plain** *underwater feature* Atlantic Ocean
76 S2 **Greenland Fracture Zone** *underwater feature* Atlantic Ocean
435 E2 **Greenland-Iceland Rise** *underwater feature* Atlantic Ocean
117 R4 **Greenland Sea** Greenland
244 E4 **Greenloaning** Perth and Kinross Scotland UK
244 D5 **Greenock** Inverclyde Scotland UK
245 F2 **Greenore** Ireland
245 F4 **Greenore Point** Ireland
424 E7 **Greenough** WA Australia
127 K4 **Greenough Point** Ontario Canada
131 I5 **Greensboro** Florida USA
131 L2 **Greensboro** North Carolina USA
126 I7 **Greensburg** Indiana USA
125 P8 **Greensburg** Kansas USA
244 C3 **Greenstone Point** Scotland UK
304 C3 **Greenville** Liberia
131 H5 **Greenville** Alabama USA
126 G7 **Greenville** Illinois USA
123 D10 **Greenville** Maine USA
130 F4 **Greenville** Mississippi USA
131 M3 **Greenville** North Carolina USA
126 I6 **Greenville** Ohio USA
131 J3 **Greenville** South Carolina USA
130 C4 **Greenville** Texas USA
126 F2 **Greenwater Lake** Ontario Canada
241 G3 **Greenwich** Greater London England UK
130 F4 **Greenwood** Mississippi USA
131 J3 **Greenwood** South Carolina USA
126 F4 **Greenwood** Wisconsin USA
131 J2 **Greer** South Carolina USA
130 E3 **Greers Ferry Lake** Arkansas USA
130 E3 **Greeson, Lake** Arkansas USA
240 E2 **Greete** Shropshire England UK
158 D3 **Gregorio** *watercourse* Brazil
129 K7 **Gregorio A. Garcia** Mexico
425 K4 **Gregory** *watercourse* Qld Australia
424 E7 **Gregory** WA Australia
125 P5 **Gregory** South Dakota USA
130 C7 **Gregory** Texas USA
424 H5 **Gregory, Lake** WA Australia
425 K4 **Gregory Downs** Qld Australia
224 G5 **Greifswald** Germany
224 G5 **Greifswalder Bodden** *bay* Germany
227 H3 **Grein** Austria
226 G2 **Greiz** Germany
394 E6 **Greko, Cap** *cape* Cyprus
223 U2 **Gremikha** Russian Federation
238 H5 **Gremyachev** Russian Federation
224 F4 **Grenå** Denmark
163 10 **Grenada** *country* Caribbean
130 G4 **Grenada** Mississippi USA
130 G4 **Grenada Lake** Mississippi USA
231 G2 **Grenade** France
228 D5 **Grenade-sur-l'Adour** France
135 I4 **Grenadines, The** *islands* St Vincent and the Grenadines
229 H3 **Grenchen** Switzerland
241 F3 **Grendon Underwood** Buckinghamshire England UK
244 F4 **Grenen** *cape* Denmark
244 A3 **Grenitote** Na h-Eileanan Siar Scotland UK
222 inset **Grenivík** Iceland
229 G4 **Grenoble** France
125 N2 **Grenora** North Dakota USA
155 H4 **Grens Gebergte** *range* Brazil
223 Q2 **Grense-Jakobselv** Norway
425 L2 **Grenville, Cape** Qld Australia
229 G5 **Gréoux-les-Bains** France
124 D4 **Gresham** Oregon USA
374 D4 **Gresik** Indonesia
375 G5 **Gresik** Indonesia
222 H4 **Gressåmoen Nasjonalpark** *park* Norway
222 G5 **Gressli** Norway
423 E6 **Greta Valley** New Zealand
244 E6 **Gretna** Dumfries and Galloway Scotland UK
131 I5 **Gretna** Florida USA
130 F6 **Gretna** Louisiana USA
127 L8 **Gretna** Virginia USA
226 D1 **Greven** Germany
229 H2 **Grevenmacher** Luxembourg
229 H2 **Grevenmacher** *admin. area* Luxembourg
423 E5 **Greville Harbour** New Zealand
123 J9 **Grey** *watercourse* Newfoundland and Labrador Canada
130 B6 **Grey Forest** Texas USA
117 N8 **Grey Islands** Newfoundland and Labrador Canada
425 L7 **Grey Range** Qld Australia
125 K4 **Greybull** Wyoming USA
125 K4 **Greybull** *watercourse* Wyoming USA
423 D6 **Greymouth** New Zealand
245 F3 **Greystones** Ireland
423 F5 **Greytown** New Zealand
235 A5 **Grib, Mali** *mountain* Albania
223 S4 **Gridino** Russian Federation
124 E7 **Gridley** California USA
129 O1 **Gridley** Kansas USA
119 T8 **Griffin** Saskatchewan Canada
131 I4 **Griffin** Georgia USA
425 M8 **Griffith** NSW Australia
116 G3 **Griffiths Point** Northwest Territories Canada
229 G4 **Grignan** France
228 D4 **Grignols** France
229 G4 **Grigny** France
234 A4 **Grilë** Albania
425 L10 **Grim, Cape** Tas. Australia
305 I3 **Grimari** Central African Republic
226 G2 **Grimma** Germany
122 H4 **Grimmington Island** Newfoundland and Labrador Canada
222 I5 **Grimnäsfjärden** *bay* Sweden
240 E2 **Grimpo** Shropshire England UK
222 inset **Grimsá** *watercourse* Iceland
243 H3 **Grimsby** North East Lincolnshire England UK
222 inset **Grímsey** *island* Iceland
118 M4 **Grimshaw** Alberta Canada
224 E3 **Grimstad** Norway
222 inset **Grímsvötn** *mountain* Iceland
222 F5 **Grindal** Norway
243 H2 **Grindale** East Riding of Yorkshire England UK
222 inset **Grindavík** Iceland
224 G2 **Grinder** Norway
243 F1 **Grindon** Northumberland England UK
224 E5 **Grindsted** Denmark
134 D5 **Grindstone Bay Chiquita, Punta** *cape* Nicaragua
234 L5 **Griniai** Lithuania
125 L1 **Grinnell** Kansas USA
122 E1 **Grinnell Glacier** Nunavut Canada
117 J3 **Grinnell Peninsula** Nunavut Canada
242 F2 **Grinsdale** Cumbria England UK
224 G3 **Grinstad** Sweden
234 D2 **Grinţieş** Romania
243 G2 **Grinton** North Yorkshire England UK
308 D5 **Griquatown** South Africa
241 I4 **Gris Nez, Cap** *cape* France
117 K3 **Grise Fiord** Nunavut Canada
231 G2 **Grisolles** France
125 O2 **Griswold** Manitoba Canada
244 F2 **Gritley** Orkney Islands Scotland UK
242 E2 **Grizedale** Cumbria England UK
119 Q4 **Grizzly Bear Hills** Saskatchewan Canada
123 K7 **Groais Island** Newfoundland and Labrador Canada
308 D5 **Groblershoop** South Africa
227 L1 **Gródek** Poland
227 I2 **Grodków** Poland
236 C6 **Groen** *watercourse* South Africa
240 D3 **Groesffordd** Powys Wales UK
244 D3 **Groigearraidh** Na h-Eileanan Siar Scotland UK
228 C3 **Groix, Île de** *island* France
227 K2 **Grójec** Poland
228 D3 **Grombalia** Tunisia
232 H5 **Gromiljak** Bosnia and Herzegovina
225 K5 **Gromovo** Russian Federation
120 G3 **Gronbeck Lake** Manitoba Canada
222 L4 **Grönbo** Sweden
222 H4 **Grong** Norway
222 H4 **Grongstadvatnet** *lake* Norway
226 D1 **Groningen** Netherlands
226 D6 **Groningen** *admin. area* Netherlands
155 H3 **Groningen** Suriname
119 S6 **Gronlid** Saskatchewan Canada
222 F5 **Grønnes** Norway
225 J5 **Gronowo Elbląskie** Poland
129 L3 **Groom** Texas USA
128 E2 **Groom Lake** Nevada USA
308 D6 **Groot** *watercourse* South Africa
308 C5 **Groot Karas Berg** *range* Namibia
308 D5 **Grootdrink** South Africa
425 K3 **Groote Eylandt** *island* NT Australia
308 C3 **Grootfontein** Namibia
163 I3 **Gros Islet** St Lucia
123 I7 **Gros Mécatina, Île du** *island* Québec Canada
123 J8 **Gros Morne** *mountain* Newfoundland and Labrador Canada
163 I4 **Gros-Morne** Martinique
163 I3 **Gros Piton** *volcano* St Lucia
125 J5 **Gros Ventre Range** Wyoming USA
226 F4 **Grosio** Italy
240 E3 **Grosmont** Monmouthshire Wales UK
229 G3 **Grosne** *watercourse* France
122 F1 **Gross Island** Nunavut Canada
308 C4 **Gross Ums** Namibia
163 B2 **Grossa, Ponta** *cape* Brazil
231 G4 **Grossa, Punta** *cape* Spain
229 K3 **Großarl** Austria
163 I6 **Grosse Pointe** *cape* Guadeloupe
226 G3 **Große Vils** *watercourse* Germany
224 F5 **Großenbrode** Germany
226 F1 **Großer Graben** *watercourse* Germany
224 F5 **Großer Plöner See** *lake* Germany
227 H4 **Grosser Priel** *mountain* Austria
227 G1 **Großer Selchower See** *lake* Germany
232 D5 **Grosseto** Italy
226 G4 **Großglockner** *mountain* Austria
222 L5 **Grossgrunden** *island* Sweden
227 I3 **Großkrut** Austria
232 C2 **Großostheim** Germany
229 H2 **Grostenquin** France
229 L4 **Grosuplje** Slovenia
78 N5 **Grosvenor Seamount** *underwater feature* Pacific Ocean
122 J5 **Groswater Bay** Newfoundland and Labrador Canada
222 J2 **Grøtavær** Norway
222 I5 **Grötingen** *lake* Sweden
125 P4 **Groton** South Dakota USA
222 K1 **Grøtøy** *island* Norway
232 E5 **Grottammare** Italy
127 L7 **Grottoes** Virginia USA
119 M5 **Grouard** Alberta Canada
228 D2 **Grouin, Pointe du** *cape* France
123 D7 **Groulx, Monts** *range* Québec Canada
118 K5 **Groundbirch** British Columbia Canada
224 E3 **Grova** Norway
126 J7 **Grove City** Ohio USA
130 H5 **Grove Hill** Alabama USA
125 M6 **Grover** Colorado USA
131 K3 **Grover** North Carolina USA
128 B3 **Grover Beach** California USA
130 E6 **Groves** Texas USA
130 D5 **Groveton** Texas USA
389 K5 **Groznoye** Kyrgyzstan
388 E5 **Groznyy** Russian Federation
222 I4 **Grubben** Norway
223 M3 **Grubbnäsudden** Sweden
227 K1 **Grudusk** Poland
227 J1 **Grudziądz** Poland
160 D2 **Gruesa, Punta** *cape* Chile
234 C3 **Gruia** Romania
244 D2 **Gruids** Highland Scotland UK
244 C3 **Gruinard Bay** Scotland UK
244 C3 **Gruinard Island** Scotland UK
228 F5 **Gruissan** France
244 B3 **Grula** Highland Scotland UK
224 G3 **Grumsfjorden** *bay* Sweden
229 I1 **Grünberg** Germany
222 inset **Grundarfjörður** Iceland
222 H5 **Grundsjön** *lake* Sweden
127 J8 **Grundy** Virginia USA
222 J3 **Grunnfjorden** *bay* Norway
234 H1 **Grushkovka** Ukraine
224 C3 **Grutle** Norway
244 inset **Grutness** Shetland Scotland UK
222 I2 **Grubverget** Sweden
129 L2 **Gruver** Texas USA
229 H3 **Gruyères** Switzerland
388 G6 **Gryada Akkyr** Turkmenistan
238 H5 **Gryaznoye** Russian Federation
222 I2 **Grycken** *lake* Sweden
227 H1 **Gryfino** Poland
125 R2 **Grygla** Minnesota USA
235 A5 **Grykë** Albania
224 I3 **Gryt** Sweden
222 J2 **Grytøya** *island* Norway
222 L5 **Grytskäret** *island* Finland
163 8 **Grytviken** South Georgia
384 G6 **Gu Xian** Shanxi China
374 D2 **Gua Musang** Malaysia
162 A2 **Guabún** Chile
154 D3 **Guacamayas** Colombia
134 E2 **Guacanayabo, Golfo de** *bay* Cuba
154 E2 **Guacara** Venezuela
129 I7 **Guachochi** Mexico
230 E5 **Guadahortuna** Spain
230 D5 **Guadajoz** *watercourse* Spain
132 E4 **Guadalajara** Mexico
230 E3 **Guadalajara** Spain
426 8 **Guadalcanal** *admin. area* Solomon Islands
426 8 **Guadalcanal** *island* Solomon Islands
230 E4 **Guadalén** *watercourse* Spain
160 E5 **Guadales** Argentina
230 E4 **Guadalimar** *watercourse* Spain
230 D4 **Guadalmellato, Embalse de** *lake* Spain
230 E4 **Guadalmena** *watercourse* Spain
230 E4 **Guadalmena, Embalse del** *lake* Spain
310 1b **Guadalope** Azores
231 F3 **Guadalope** *watercourse* Spain
230 D5 **Guadalquivir** *watercourse* Spain
132 D2 **Guadalupe de Jesús** Mexico
154 C4 **Guadalupe** Colombia
132 E3 **Guadalupe** Mexico
132 E4 **Guadalupe** Mexico
128 C6 **Guadalupe** *volcano* Mexico
158 B2 **Guadalupe** Peru
128 B3 **Guadalupe** California USA
130 C6 **Guadalupe** *watercourse* Texas USA
128 C6 **Guadalupe, Isla** *island* Mexico
230 D4 **Guadalupe, Sierra de** *range* Spain
129 J7 **Guadalupe de Bahues** Mexico
129 J4 **Guadalupe Mountains** New Mexico USA
132 B1 **Guadalupe Victoria** Mexico
132 D2 **Guadalupe Victoria** Mexico
132 D3 **Guadalupe Victoria** Mexico
132 D3 **Guadalupe y Calvo** Mexico
230 E3 **Guadarrama, Sierra de** *range* Spain
135 I3 **Guadeloupe** *French overseas territory* Caribbean
163 I6 **Guadeloupe** *island* Caribbean
135 I3 **Guadeloupe Passage** Caribbean
230 C4 **Guadiana** *watercourse* Portugal
230 D4 **Guadiana** *watercourse* Spain
134 C2 **Guadiana, Bahía** *bay* Cuba
230 E5 **Guadiana Menor** *watercourse* Spain
230 E5 **Guadix** Spain
162 B3 **Guafo, Boca del** *bay* Chile
155 I5 **Guaíba** Brazil
155 E2 **Guaicupa** Venezuela
158 D5 **Guaiguasi, Cerro** *mountain* Chile
154 D4 **Guainía** *admin. area* Colombia
154 D4 **Guainía** *watercourse* Colombia
155 F3 **Guaiquinima, Cerro** *mountain* Venezuela
157 B8 **Guaíra** Brazil
161 G3 **Guairá** *admin. area* Paraguay
162 B3 **Guaitecas, Islas** *islands* Chile
134 E2 **Guajaba, Cayo** *island* Cuba
154 B3 **Guajará** Brazil
159 E3 **Guajará Mirim** Brazil
154 B5 **Gualaceo** Ecuador
134 C4 **Gualaco** Honduras
128 A1 **Gualala** California USA
134 B4 **Gualán** Guatemala
154 B5 **Gualaquiza** Ecuador
232 E5 **Gualdo Tadino** Italy
161 G5 **Gualeguay** Argentina
161 G4 **Gualeguay** *watercourse* Argentina
162 B3 **Gualjaina** Argentina
426 2 **Guam** *island* Pacific Ocean
426 2 **Guam** *unincorporated US territory* Pacific Ocean
154 C4 **Guamal** Colombia
154 C5 **Guamareyes** Colombia
162 A3 **Guamblin, Isla** *island* Chile
161 H2 **Guamí Taperé** Paraguay
160 F6 **Guaminí** Argentina
154 C3 **Guamo** Colombia
155 E3 **Guampí, Serranía de** *range* Venezuela
132 C3 **Guamúchil** Mexico
385 H5 **Gu'an** Hebei China
155 F3 **Guaña, Cerro** *mountain* Venezuela
158 D3 **Guanabara** Brazil
134 C5 **Guanacaste, Cordillera de** *range* Costa Rica
160 F6 **Guanaco, Cerro** *mountain* Argentina
162 B2 **Guanaco, Cerro del** *mountain* Argentina
134 C2 **Guanahacabibes, Península** Cuba
134 C3 **Guanaja** Honduras
134 C3 **Guanaja, Isla de** *island* Honduras
134 D2 **Guanajay** Cuba
132 E4 **Guanajuato** Mexico
132 E4 **Guanajuato** *admin. area* Mexico
157 D6 **Guanambi** Brazil
158 B3 **Guañape, Punta** *cape* Peru
163 9 **Guanapo** Trinidad and Tobago
154 D2 **Guanare** Venezuela
158 E4 **Guanay** Bolivia
385 H6 **Guancheng** Shandong China
160 D4 **Guandacol** Argentina
134 C2 **Guane** Cuba
380 E2 **Guang'an** Sichuan China
381 G4 **Guangdong** *admin. area* China
380 D2 **Guanghan** Sichuan China
384 E6 **Guanghe** Gansu China
385 J5 **Guanglu Dao** *island* Liaoning China
380 D3 **Guangming** Sichuan China
385 I5 **Guangrao** Shandong China
381 G2 **Guangshui** Hubei China
380 E4 **Guangxi Zhuangzu Zizhiqu** *admin. area* China
380 E2 **Guangyuan** Sichuan China
381 G4 **Guangzhou** Guangdong China
385 H5 **Guangzong** Hebei China
157 D7 **Guanhães** Brazil
155 E3 **Guaniamo, Río** *watercourse* Venezuela
134 D6 **Guánico, Punta** *cape* Panama
134 D2 **Guaniguanico, Cordillera de** *range* Cuba
162 C5 **Guankenken Aike** Argentina
380 F2 **Guanmian Shan** *range* Chongqing China
154 B5 **Guano** Ecuador
155 F2 **Guanoco** Venezuela
380 E3 **Guansuo** Guizhou China
135 F2 **Guantánamo** Cuba
135 F2 **Guantánamo** *admin. area* Cuba
135 F3 **Guantánamo Bay Naval Base (USA)** *US military base* Cuba
385 H6 **Guantao** Hebei China
154 B4 **Guapi** Colombia
154 B4 **Guapí, Bahía de** *bay* Colombia
157 B8 **Guapiaçu** Brazil
157 B7 **Guapó** Brazil
159 F4 **Guapore** *watercourse* Bolivia
161 J2 **Guaraí** Brazil
156 D4 **Guaraciaba do Norte** Brazil
161 I3 **Guaramirim** Brazil
154 B5 **Guaranda** Ecuador
161 J2 **Guaraniaçu** Brazil
161 H3 **Guaraniaçu** Brazil
159 H3 **Guarantã do Norte** Brazil
157 D8 **Guarapari** Brazil
161 I3 **Guarapuava** Brazil
157 E7 **Guaratinga** Brazil
161 J2 **Guaratinguetá** Brazil
161 I3 **Guaratuba** Brazil
161 I3 **Guaratuba, Baía de** *bay* Brazil
158 D4 **Guarayos** Bolivia
158 D4 **Guarayos, Altiplanicie de los** *region* Bolivia
233 E6 **Guarcino** Italy
230 C3 **Guarda** Portugal
230 C3 **Guarda** *admin. area* Portugal
233 E6 **Guardia, Punta della** *cape* Italy
162 D2 **Guardia Mitre** Argentina
162 B6 **Guardián Brito, Isla** *island* Chile
128 E4 **Guardianes de la Patria** Mexico
230 D2 **Guardo** Spain
154 E2 **Guarenas** Venezuela
161 I2 **Guariba** Brazil
154 E2 **Guárico** *admin. area* Venezuela
154 E2 **Guárico** *watercourse* Venezuela
154 E2 **Guarico, Embalse del** *lake* Venezuela
135 F2 **Guarico, Punta** *cape* Cuba
157 C8 **Guarujá** Brazil
157 C8 **Guarulhos** Brazil
132 C3 **Guasave** Mexico
154 B4 **Guascama, Punta** *cape* Colombia
154 D3 **Guasdalito** Venezuela
155 F3 **Guasipati** Venezuela
373 J6 **Guasopa** Papua New Guinea
226 F5 **Guastalla** Italy
134 B4 **Guastatoya** Guatemala
134 B4 **Guatemala** *country* Central America
134 B4 **Guatemala** Guatemala
79 W6 **Guatemala Basin** *underwater feature* Pacific Ocean
154 E2 **Guatire** Venezuela
373 G5 **Guavi** *watercourse* Papua New Guinea
154 C4 **Guaviare** *admin. area* Colombia
154 D4 **Guaviare** *watercourse* Colombia
161 G4 **Guaviraví** Argentina
161 J2 **Guaxupé** Brazil
154 C4 **Guayabero** *watercourse* Colombia
163 9 **Guayaguayare** Trinidad and Tobago
163 9 **Guayaguayare Bay** Trinidad and Tobago
133 F4 **Guayalejo** *watercourse* Mexico
154 E3 **Guayapo, Serranía** *range* Venezuela
154 B5 **Guayaquil** Ecuador
154 A5 **Guayaquil, Golfo de** *bay* Ecuador
159 E3 **Guayaramerín** Bolivia
161 G3 **Guayaybi** Paraguay
161 G3 **Guaycuru** *watercourse* Argentina
132 C3 **Guaymas** Mexico
161 G4 **Guayquiraró** *watercourse* Argentina
160 E2 **Guaytayoc, Lago de** *lake* Argentina
132 C4 **Guazapares** Mexico
134 B4 **Guazapa** El Salvador
302 F5 **Guba** Ethiopia
393 D9 **Gubbi** Karnataka India
232 E5 **Gubbio** Italy
222 K3 **Gubbljaure** *lake* Sweden
227 H2 **Guben** Germany
227 H2 **Gubin** Poland
238 F5 **Gubkin** Russian Federation
305 G2 **Gubio** Nigeria
394 F2 **Gubkin** Russian Federation
381 F2 **Gucheng** Hubei China
381 H2 **Gucheng Hu** *lake* Jiangsu China
384 E3 **Guchin-us** Mongolia
388 H5 **Gudabag** Turkmenistan
393 D9 **Gudalur** Tamil Nadu India
389 K6 **Gudara** Tajikistan
393 F7 **Gudari** Orissa India
224 F2 **Gudbrandsdalen** *valley* Norway
224 H5 **Gudhjem** Denmark
224 I4 **Gudingen** *bay* Sweden
393 D8 **Gudur** Karnataka India
222 E6 **Gudvangen** Norway
229 H3 **Guebwiller** France
127 M2 **Guéguen, Lac** *lake* Québec Canada
304 B3 **Guékédou** Guinea
300 D4 **Guelb er Richât** *mountain* Mauritania
305 H2 **Guelengdeng** Chad
301 H1 **Guelma** Algeria
301 H1 **Guelma** *admin. area* Algeria
300 D3 **Guelmim** Morocco
127 K5 **Guelph** Ontario Canada
228 C2 **Guéméné-sur-Scorff** France
122 B3 **Guentis** Algeria
122 C3 **Guenyveau, Lac** *lake* Québec Canada
228 C3 **Guer** France
162 C5 **Güer Aike** Argentina
305 H2 **Guera** *admin. area* Chad
301 G2 **Guerara** Algeria
305 I2 **Guéréda** Chad
228 E3 **Guéret** France
228 C2 **Guernsey** *British crown dependency* English Channel
125 M5 **Guernsey** Wyoming USA
125 M5 **Guernsey Reservoir** Wyoming USA
300 D5 **Guérou** Mauritania
129 L6 **Guerrero** Mexico
133 F5 **Guerrero** *admin. area* Mexico
129 F2 **Guerrero Negro** Mexico
122 E7 **Guers, Lac** *lake* Québec Canada
231 F2 **Güesa** Spain
226 C4 **Gueugnon** France
304 C3 **Gueyo** Côte d'Ivoire
381 H3 **Gufeng** Fujian China
380 F2 **Gufu** Hubei China
426 2 **Guguan** *island* Northern Mariana Islands
375 H3 **Guguang, Gunung** *mountain* Indonesia
388 I6 **Gugurtli** Uzbekistan
374 E5 **Guhakolak, Tanjung** *cape* Indonesia
161 G2 **Guia Lopes da Laguna** Brazil
76 N9 **Guiana Basin** *underwater feature* Atlantic Ocean
155 F3 **Guiana Highlands** *range* Guyana/Venezuela
304 C3 **Guibéroua** Côte d'Ivoire
380 F4 **Guicheng** Guangxi Zhuangzu Zizhiqu China
301 H6 **Guidan-Roumji** Niger
305 H3 **Guidari** Chad
305 G3 **Guider** Cameroon
301 H6 **Guidiguir** Niger
300 D5 **Guidimaka** *admin. area* Mauritania
380 E3 **Guiding** Guizhou China
381 G3 **Guidong** Hunan China
304 C3 **Guiglo** Côte d'Ivoire
226 B3 **Guignes** France
154 E2 **Güigüe** Venezuela
222 I3 **Guijaurtjärro** *lake* Sweden
381 H2 **Guiji Shan** *range* Zhejiang China
230 D3 **Guijuelo** Spain
241 G3 **Guildford** Surrey England UK
127 Q4 **Guilford** Maine USA
380 F3 **Guilin** Guangxi Zhuangzu Zizhiqu China
121 P6 **Guillaume** *watercourse* Québec Canada
117 L7 **Guillaume Delisle, Lac** *lake* Québec Canada
229 H4 **Guillaumes** France
122 D6 **Guillemot, Lac** *lake* Québec Canada
132 C3 **Guillermo Blake Aguilar, Presa** *lake* Mexico
133 F3 **Guillermo Zúñiga** Mexico
229 H4 **Guillestre** France
310 3a **Güimar** Canary Islands
132 E3 **Guimbalete** Mexico
304 B2 **Guinea** *country* Africa
304 E4 **Guinea, Gulf of** Africa
76 R9 **Guinea Basin** *underwater feature* Atlantic Ocean
304 B2 **Guinea-Bissau** *country* Africa
241 I4 **Guînes** France
134 D2 **Güines** Cuba
123 H6 **Guines, Lac** *lake* Newfoundland and Labrador Canada
228 C2 **Guingamp** France
377 I4 **Guintinua** *island* Philippines
134 C5 **Guiones, Punta** *cape* Costa Rica
380 F4 **Guiping** Guangxi Zhuangzu Zizhiqu China
159 H5 **Guiratinga** Brazil
305 H2 **Guiri** Cameroon
134 E2 **Guisa** Cuba
228 F2 **Guise** France
380 D4 **Guishan** Yunnan China
241 H2 **Guist** Norfolk England UK
230 C2 **Guistolas, Embalse de** *lake* Spain
230 C2 **Guitiriz** Spain
377 J5 **Guiuan** Philippines
380 E3 **Guiyang** Guizhou China
381 F3 **Guiyang** Hunan China
380 E3 **Guizhou** *admin. area* China
228 D4 **Gujan-Mestras** France
391 M2 **Gujar Khan** Pakistan
392 C6 **Gujarat** *admin. area* India
305 G2 **Gujba** Nigeria
384 G5 **Gujiao** Shanxi China
391 M3 **Gujranwala** Pakistan
391 M3 **Gujrat** Pakistan
390 G3 **Gūkān** Iran
384 E5 **Gulang** Gansu China
393 D8 **Gulbarga** Karnataka India
225 N4 **Gulbene** Latvia
225 N4 **Gulbenes** *admin. area* Latvia
122 G3 **Gulch Cape** Newfoundland and Labrador Canada
130 H5 **Gulf Shores** Alabama USA
131 J7 **Gulfport** Florida USA
130 G5 **Gulfport** Mississippi USA
237 Z8 **Gulian** Heilongjiang China
380 E3 **Gulin** Sichuan China
372 D5 **Gulir** Indonesia
389 J6 **Guliston** Uzbekistan
388 C4 **Gulkevichi** Russian Federation
120 K8 **Gull** *watercourse* Ontario Canada
120 K8 **Gull Bay** Ontario Canada
119 O6 **Gull Lake** Alberta Canada
122 H6 **Gull Lake** Newfoundland and Labrador Canada
119 Q7 **Gull Lake** Saskatchewan Canada
126 D3 **Gull Lake** Minnesota USA
244 F4 **Gullane** East Lothian Scotland UK
225 L3 **Gullkronafjärd** *bay* Finland
225 L3 **Gullö** *island* Finland
235 E7 **Güllük Körfezi** *bay* Turkey
242 A4 **Gully Bridge** Ireland
392 D3 **Gulmarg** Jammu and Kashmir India/Pakistan
394 E6 **Gülnar** Turkey
226 G1 **Gülper See** *lake* Germany
235 E6 **Gülpınar** Turkey
389 L4 **Gul'Shat** Kazakhstan
224 F2 **Gulsrud** Norway
307 E3 **Gulu** Uganda
381 G2 **Guluu** Henan China
234 G2 **Gulyanivka** Ukraine
308 D3 **Gumare** Botswana
388 G6 **Gumdag** Turkmenistan
305 F2 **Gumel** Nigeria
230 E3 **Gumiel de Hizán** Spain
392 F6 **Gumla** Jharkhand India
393 F7 **Gumma** Orissa India
305 F2 **Gummi** Nigeria
394 F5 **Gümüşhane** Turkey
394 G5 **Gümüşhane** *admin. area* Turkey
129 N4 **Gun Barrel City** Texas USA
392 D6 **Guna** Madhya Pradesh India
303 F5 **Guna, Mount** *mountain* Ethiopia
380 E2 **Gu'nan** Chongqing China
241 G2 **Gunby** Lincolnshire England UK
306 C3 **Gundji** Democratic Republic of Congo
235 F6 **Güneşli** Turkey
235 F7 **Güney** Turkey
394 G5 **Güney Doğu Toroslar** Turkey
306 B5 **Gungu** Democratic Republic of Congo
308 C2 **Gungue** Angola
388 E5 **Gunib** Russian Federation
120 G6 **Gunisao** *watercourse* Manitoba Canada
120 G6 **Gunisao Lake** Manitoba Canada
232 H4 **Gunja** Croatia
235 F6 **Günlüce** Turkey
119 Q3 **Gunnar** Saskatchewan Canada
222 J4 **Gunnarn** Sweden
223 M4 **Gunnarsfjärden** *bay* Sweden
117 Q5 **Gunnbjørn Fjeld** *mountain* Greenland
425 N7 **Gunnedah** NSW Australia
437 C2 **Gunnerus Bank** *underwater feature* Southern Ocean
437 C2 **Gunnerus Ridge** *underwater feature* Southern Ocean
243 H3 **Gunness** North Lincolnshire England UK
240 C4 **Gunnislake** Cornwall England UK

222 L5 **Gunnismark** Sweden
389 K6 **Gunt** *watercourse* Tajikistan
393 D8 **Guntakal** Andhra Pradesh India
131 H3 **Guntersville Lake** Alabama USA
241 H2 **Gunthorpe** Norfolk England UK
393 E8 **Guntur** Andhra Pradesh India
425 K4 **Gunuang** Qld Australia
375 F3 **Gunung Ayer** Malaysia
372 C5 **Gunungapi** *island* Indonesia
375 H4 **Gunungbatubesar** Indonesia
374 C3 **Gunungsitoli** Indonesia
374 E5 **Gunungsugih** Indonesia
374 C3 **Gunungtua** Indonesia
232 D2 **Günz** *watercourse* Germany
381 G1 **Guo He** *watercourse* Anhui China
381 G1 **Guoyang** Anhui China
380 E1 **Guozhen** Shaanxi China
391 M2 **Gupis** Pakistan
389 K3 **Guraanbular** Mongolia
392 D3 **Gurais** Jammu and Kashmir India/Pakistan
306 D3 **Gurba** *watercourse* Democratic Republic of Congo
392 D4 **Gurdaspur** Punjab India
130 E4 **Gurdon** Arkansas USA
392 D5 **Gurgaon** Haryana India
156 D4 **Gurgueia** *watercourse* Brazil
392 C6 **Gurha** Rajasthan India
155 F3 **Guri, Embalse de** *lake* Venezuela
227 H4 **Gurk** *watercourse* Austria
125 N6 **Gurley** Nebraska USA
303 G5 **Gurmal, Ras** *cape* Eritrea
309 F3 **Guro** Mozambique
388 H7 **Gurpan** Iran
224 C1 **Gurskøy** *island* Norway
235 F5 **Gürsu** Turkey
392 C6 **Guru Sikhar** *mountain* Rajasthan India
309 G3 **Guruè** Mozambique
156 B3 **Gurupá** Brazil
157 B5 **Gurupi** Brazil
155 C3 **Gurupi** *watercourse* Brazil
156 B4 **Gurupi, Serra do** *range* Brazil
155 G4 **Gurupira, Serra do** *range* Brazil
308 F3 **Guruve** Zimbabwe
384 E4 **Gurvan Sayhan Uul** Mongolia
384 G3 **Gurvanbayan** Mongolia
384 E3 **Gurvanbulag** Mongolia
389 F3 **Gurvansaihan** Mongolia
384 E4 **Gurvantes** Mongolia
385 H2 **Gurvanzagal** Mongolia
Gur'yev *see* **Atyrau** Kazakhstan
225 K5 **Gur'yevsk** Russian Federation
227 L3 **Gusakov** Ukraine
305 F2 **Gusau** Nigeria
238 E4 **Gusevo** Russian Federation
388 I7 **Guşgy** Turkmenistan
381 G2 **Gushi** Henan China
381 J3 **Gushikawa** Japan
372 E4 **Gusi** Indonesia
237 AF4 **Gusinaya, Guba** *bay* Russian Federation
435 J2 **Gusinaya Bank** *underwater feature* Barents Sea
384 F2 **Gusinoozërsk** Russian Federation
237 AH4 **Gusmp, Ostrov** *island* Russian Federation
227 I4 **Güssing** Austria
222 J5 **Gussjön** *lake* Sweden
163 I9 **Gustavia** St Barthélemy
118 D3 **Gustavus** Alaska USA
124 E8 **Gustine** California USA
244 inset **Gutcher** Shetland Scotland UK
227 H4 **Gutenstein** Austria
130 C3 **Guthrie** Oklahoma USA
130 A4 **Guthrie** Texas USA
381 H3 **Gutian Shuiku** *lake* Fujian China
133 F4 **Gutiérrez Zamora** Mexico
381 G1 **Guting** Shandong China
126 F5 **Guttenberg** Iowa USA
309 F3 **Gutu** Zimbabwe
383 K3 **Guulin** Mongolia
379 G3 **Guwahati** Assam India
155 G3 **Guyana** *country* South America
381 F3 **Guyang** Hunan China
228 D4 **Guyenne** *region* France
380 F3 **Guyi** Guangxi Zhuangzu Zizhiqu China
129 L2 **Guymon** Oklahoma USA
381 H3 **Guyong** Fujian China
131 J3 **Guyot, Mount** North Carolina USA
425 N7 **Guyra** NSW Australia
131 K4 **Guyton** Georgia USA
385 H4 **Guyuan** Hebei China
384 F6 **Guyuan** Zishiqu China
381 H1 **Guzhen** Anhui China
380 E3 **Guzhou** Guizhou China
129 I5 **Guzmán** Mexico
129 I5 **Guzmán, Laguna de** *bay* Mexico
162 D4 **Guzmán, Punta** *cape* Argentina
388 I6 **G'uzor** Uzbekistan
235 H5 **Gvozd** Montenegro
376 B3 **Gwa** Myanmar
305 F2 **Gwadabawa** Nigeria
391 J4 **Gwadar** Pakistan
392 E5 **Gwalior** Madhya Pradesh India
305 E2 **Gwambara** Nigeria
308 E4 **Gwanda** Zimbabwe
305 F2 **Gwarzo** Nigeria
308 E3 **Gwayi** Zimbabwe
227 I1 **Gwda** *watercourse* Poland
245 D2 **Gweebarra Bay** Ireland
240 B4 **Gweek** Cornwall England UK
245 C2 **Gweesalia** Ireland
308 E3 **Gwembe** Zambia
240 C3 **Gwernogle** Carmarthenshire Wales UK
308 E3 **Gweru** Zimbabwe
308 E3 **Gweru** *watercourse* Zimbabwe
308 E4 **Gweta** Botswana
125 Q3 **Gwinner** North Dakota USA
305 G2 **Gwoza** Nigeria
240 D1 **Gwyddelwern** Denbighshire Wales UK
240 D2 **Gwynedd** *admin. area* Wales UK
240 D2 **Gwystre** Powys Wales UK
229 G3 **Gy** France
224 D3 **Gya** Norway
234 A2 **Gyál** Hungary
235 E7 **Gyali** *island* Greece
383 K6 **Gyaring Hu** *lake* Qinghai China
235 D7 **Gyaros** *island* Greece
236 Q4 **Gyda** Russian Federation
236 Q4 **Gydanskaya Guba** *bay* Russian Federation
236 Q4 **Gydanskiy Poluostrov** *peninsula* Russian Federation
240 D1 **Gyfelia** Wrexham Wales UK
425 O6 **Gympie** Qld Australia
376 B3 **Gyobingauk** Myanmar
227 J4 **Gyöngyös** Hungary
232 G3 **Győr** Hungary
232 G3 **Győr-Moson-Sopron** *admin. area* Hungary
125 L7 **Gypsum** Colorado USA
129 N1 **Gypsum** Kansas USA
119 V7 **Gypsumville** Manitoba Canada
122 D3 **Gyrfalcon Islands** Nunavut Canada
222 E4 **Gyrinosvatnet** *lake* Norway
240 C1 **Gyrn-gôch** Gwynedd Wales UK
234 B2 **Gyula** Hungary
388 D6 **Gyumri** Armenia
224 D3 **Gyvatn** *lake* Norway
388 G6 **Gyzylarbat** Turkmenistan
388 G6 **Gyzyletrek** Turkmenistan
388 G6 **Gyzylgaya** Turkmenistan

H

225 N6 **H. Dzyarzhynskaya** *mountain* Belarus
131 H4 **H. Neely Henry Lake** Alabama USA
379 F3 **Ha** Bhutan
376 E2 **Ha Côi** Vietnam
376 E2 **Hà Đông** Vietnam
382 H4 **Ha-erh-kuo-ssu Ho** *watercourse* Xinjiang Uygur Zizhiqu China
376 E2 **Hạ Long** Vietnam
376 E2 **Hà Nội (Hanoi)** Vietnam
376 E5 **Hà Tiên** Vietnam
376 E3 **Hà Tĩnh** Vietnam
232 F2 **Haag** Austria
437 A2 **Haakon VII Sea** Antarctica
427 I0 **Ha'ano** *island* Tonga
427 I0 **Ha'apai Group** *islands* Tonga
223 N5 **Haapajärvi** Finland
223 O5 **Haapajärvi** *lake* Finland
223 O5 **Haapakoski** Finland
223 N5 **Haapamäki** Finland
225 O1 **Haapaselkä** *lake* Finland
223 N4 **Haapavesi** Finland
225 L3 **Haapsalu** Estonia
232 D2 **Haar** Germany
223 O5 **Haarajoki** Finland
226 C1 **Haarlem** Netherlands
423 C6 **Haast** New Zealand
423 C6 **Haast** *watercourse* New Zealand
307 G3 **Haaway** Somalia
391 K4 **Hab Chauki** Pakistan
383 H3 **Habahe** Xinjiang Uygur Zizhiqu China
390 G6 **Ḩabarūt** Yemen
307 F3 **Habaswein** Kenya
229 G2 **Habay la Neuve** Belgium
379 G4 **Habiganj** Bangladesh
229 L2 **Habry** Czech Republic
391 H5 **Ḩabshān** United Arab Emirates
387 I5 **Hachijō-jima** *island* Japan
387 I3 **Hachinohe** Japan
387 H3 **Hachiro-gata** *lake* Japan
129 H5 **Hachita** New Mexico USA
132 E4 **Hacienda Toribio** Mexico
222 I5 **Hackås** Sweden
245 F4 **Hacketstown** Ireland
245 F3 **Hackett's Cross** Ireland
243 H2 **Hackness** North Yorkshire England UK
222 H5 **Håckren** *bay* Sweden
308 C2 **Haco** Angola
309 F4 **Hacufera** Mozambique
302 F3 **Ḩadāribah, Ra's al** *cape* Sudan
391 I5 **Ḩadd, Ra's al** *cape* Oman
224 C1 **Haddal** Norway
305 G2 **Hadejia** Nigeria
305 G2 **Hadejia** *watercourse* Nigeria
224 F2 **Hadeland** *region* Norway
390 C3 **Hadera** Israel
391 H5 **Ḩadf** United Arab Emirates
393 D7 **Hadgaon** Maharashtra India
393 C12 **Hadhunmathi Atoll** Maldives
302 E1 **Ḩadīd, Jabal** *mountain* Egypt
390 E2 **Ḩadīthah** Iraq
305 G2 **Hadjer Bandala** Chad
305 H2 **Hadjer-Lamis** *admin. area* Chad
224 D2 **Hadlaskar** Norway
126 I5 **Hadley Bay** Nunavut Canada
386 E4 **Hadong** South Korea
243 F1 **Hadrian's Wall** *physical feature* England UK
222 I2 **Hadseløya** *island* Norway
386 E3 **Haeju** North Korea
386 E4 **Haeju-man** *bay* North Korea
223 M1 **Haen** Norway
128 inset **Hā'ena** Hawai'i USA
386 E4 **Haenam** South Korea
385 K3 **Ha`erbin** Heilongjiang China
390 D4 **Ḩafirat Al 'aydā** Saudi Arabia
391 M3 **Hafizabad** Pakistan
379 G4 **Haflong** Assam India
222 inset **Hafnarfjörður** Iceland
222 D4 **Hafslovatnet** *lake* Norway
390 G3 **Haftkel** Iran
222 H6 **Haftorsbygget** Sweden
426 2 **Hagåtña** Guam
224 I4 **Hagby** Sweden
116 C7 **Hagemeister Island** Alaska USA
226 D1 **Hagen** Germany
129 J4 **Hagerman** New Mexico USA
127 M7 **Hagerstown** Maryland USA
228 D5 **Hagetmau** France
222 J5 **Häggdånger** Sweden
224 H2 **Haggen** *lake* Sweden
386 F4 **Hagi** Japan
245 C4 **Hag's Head** *cape* Ireland
119 R6 **Hague** Saskatchewan Canada
241 F5 **Hague, Cap de la** *cape* France
226 D3 **Haguenau** France
422 F3 **Hahei** New Zealand
225 M2 **Hahmajärvi** *lake* Finland
376 F5 **Hai, Hon** *island* Vietnam
376 E2 **Hải Phòng (Haiphong)** Vietnam
381 H2 **Hai'an** Jiangsu China
155 F3 **Haiamatipu Mountains** Guyana
308 C5 **Haib** *watercourse* Namibia
381 G4 **Haicheng** Guangdong China
385 J5 **Haicheng** Liaoning China
384 F6 **Haicheng** Zishiqu China
125 O7 **Haigler** Nebraska USA
380 F5 **Haikou** Hainan China
390 E4 **Ḩā'il** Saudi Arabia
390 E4 **Ḩā'il** *admin. area* Saudi Arabia
117 L9 **Haileybury** Ontario Canada
385 L4 **Hailin** Heilongjiang China
381 F4 **Hailing Dao** *island* Guangdong China
384 F4 **Hailiutu** Nei Mongol Zizhiqu China
241 H4 **Hailsham** East Sussex England UK
385 K3 **Hailun** Heilongjiang China
223 N4 **Hailuoto** Finland
223 N4 **Hailuoto** *island* Finland
381 I2 **Haimen** Jiangsu China
381 J2 **Haimi** Japan
380 F5 **Hainan** *admin. area* China
380 F5 **Hainan** *island* Hainan China
304 B3 **Haindi** Liberia
124 G4 **Haines** Oregon USA
131 K6 **Haines City** Florida USA
118 C2 **Haines Junction** Yukon Territory Canada
227 H3 **Hainfeld** Austria
Haiphong *see* **Hải Phòng** Vietnam
384 E3 **Hairhan** Mongolia
384 E3 **Hairhandulaan** Mongolia
223 O4 **Hairinselkä** *bay* Finland
381 H3 **Haitan Dao** *island* Fujian China
135 F3 **Haiti** *country* Caribbean
128 D2 **Haiwee** California USA
302 F4 **Haiya** Sudan
381 F4 **Haiyan** Guangdong China
381 H2 **Haiyang** Anhui China
385 J6 **Haiyang** Shandong China
385 J5 **Haiyang Dao** *island* Liaoning China
381 I2 **Haiyou** Zhejiang China
385 I6 **Haizhou Wan** *bay* Shandong China
222 H2 **Håja** *island* Norway
391 I5 **Ḩajar, Al** *range* Oman
302 C5 **Ḩajar Banga** Sudan
234 B2 **Hajdú-Bihar** *admin. area* Hungary
227 K4 **Hajdúböszörmény** Hungary
234 B2 **Hajdúszoboszló** Hungary
234 B2 **Hajdúszovát** Hungary
233 C9 **Hajeb el Aioun** Tunisia
391 K4 **Haji Khan** Pakistan
392 F6 **Hajipur** Bihar India
390 E7 **Ḩajjah** Yemen
390 F7 **Ḩajr, Wādī** *watercourse* Yemen
384 G3 **Hajuuuln** Mongolia
379 G4 **Haka** Myanmar
423 B8 **Hakapoua, Lake** New Zealand
423 D7 **Hakataramea** *watercourse* New Zealand
394 G6 **Hakkari** Turkey
394 H6 **Hakkâri** *admin. area* Turkey
387 G4 **Hakken-zan** *mountain* Japan
223 N5 **Häkkilä** Finland
387 I3 **Hakodate** Japan
223 M1 **Hakstabben** Norway
387 H4 **Haku-san** *volcano* Japan
422 4 **Hakupu** Niue New Zealand
387 H4 **Hakusan** Japan
222 J2 **Håkvik** Norway
391 K4 **Hala** Pakistan
394 F6 **Halab (Aleppo)** Syria
390 E5 **Ḩalabān** Saudi Arabia
382 G3 **Halabula** Xinjiang Uygur Zizhiqu China
133 H4 **Halachó** Mexico
422 4 **Halagigie Point** Niue New Zealand
302 F3 **Halaib** Halaib Triangle
302 F3 **Halaib Triangle** *disputed territory* Egypt/Sudan
392 D6 **Halali Reservoir** Madhya Pradesh India
427 12b **Halalo** Wallis and Futuna
377 J6 **Halapitan** Philippines
224 H3 **Hålaveden** *region* Sweden
128 inset **Hālawa** Hawai'i USA
119 T8 **Halbrite** Saskatchewan Canada
233 D3 **Hălchiu** Romania
393 G6 **Haldia** West Bengal India
425 J6 **Hale** *watercourse* NT Australia
129 L3 **Hale Center** Texas USA
241 H3 **Hale Street** Kent England UK
128 inset **Hale'iwa** Hawai'i USA
229 G1 **Halen** Belgium
224 H2 **Halen** *lake* Sweden
241 E2 **Halesowen** West Midlands England UK
241 I2 **Halesworth** Suffolk England UK
130 H3 **Haleyville** Alabama USA
304 D3 **Half Assini** Ghana
425 inset **Halfmoon Bay** Macquarie Island Australia
423 C8 **Halfmoon Bay (Oban)** New Zealand
118 J4 **Halfway** *watercourse* British Columbia Canada
384 E2 **Halganat** Mongolia
385 I3 **Halhgol** Mongolia
385 I3 **Halhin Gol** *watercourse* Mongolia
117 L4 **Haliburton** Ontario Canada
123 G10 **Halifax** Nova Scotia Canada
131 L2 **Halifax** Virginia USA
382 G4 **Halik Shan** *range* Xinjiang Uygur Zizhiqu China
225 L2 **Halikko** Finland
235 E6 **Halilbeyli** Turkey
383 J3 **Haliun** Mongolia
224 G5 **Häljarp** Sweden
223 O5 **Halkokumpu** Finland
227 H4 **Hall** Austria
224 J3 **Hall** Sweden
117 K5 **Hall Beach** Nunavut Canada
373 I1 **Hall Islands** Federated States of Micronesia
117 M6 **Hall Peninsula** Nunavut Canada
222 J5 **Hälla** Sweden
386 E5 **Halla-san** *mountain* South Korea
224 G4 **Halland** *admin. area* Sweden
223 P4 **Hallavaara** Finland
125 P1 **Hallboro** Manitoba Canada
222 J5 **Hällbymagasinet** *lake* Sweden
229 G1 **Halle** Belgium
226 E1 **Halle** Germany
222 I5 **Hallen** Sweden
226 E2 **Hallenburg** Germany
232 D2 **Hallertau** *region* Germany
130 C3 **Hallett** Oklahoma USA
437 L2 **Hallett, Cape** Antarctica
130 C6 **Hallettsville** Texas USA
436 W1 **Halley (UK)** *research station* Antarctica
436 Q2 **Hallgreen, Mount** Antarctica
125 N3 **Halliday** North Dakota USA
224 E5 **Halligen** *island* Germany
224 E2 **Hallingdal** *valley* Norway
224 E2 **Hallingdalselva** *watercourse* Norway
224 E2 **Hallingeberg** Sweden
224 D2 **Hallingskarvet** *region* Norway
125 Q2 **Hallock** Minnesota USA
424 H3 **Halls Creek** WA Australia
224 H3 **Halls Fiskläge** Sweden
225 J4 **Hallstavik** Sweden
225 J2 **Hallviken** Sweden
240 C4 **Hallworthy** Cornwall England UK
372 D3 **Halmahera** *island* Indonesia
372 D4 **Halmahera, Laut** *sea* Indonesia
227 L4 **Halmeu** Romania
224 G3 **Halmøya** *island* Norway
224 G4 **Halmstad** Sweden
224 D2 **Halnefjorden** *lake* Norway
224 F4 **Hals** Denmark
222 F5 **Hals** Norway
222 H3 **Halsa** Norway
240 F2 **Halsall** Lancashire England UK
240 B4 **Halsetown** Cornwall England UK
392 G6 **Halsi** Bihar India
222 C6 **Halsnøy** *island* Norway
222 L5 **Halsön** *island* Finland
241 H3 **Halstead** Essex England UK
223 N5 **Halsua** Finland
223 M5 **Halsuanjärvi** *lake* Finland
423 E6 **Halswell** New Zealand
383 J5 **Haltang He** *watercourse* Qinghai China
222 G5 **Haltdalen** Norway
76 S3 **Halten Bank** *underwater feature* Norwegian Sea
226 D2 **Haltern** Germany
243 H3 **Haltham** Lincolnshire England UK
236 F5 **Haltia** *mountain* Finland
241 F3 **Halton** *admin. area* England UK
390 F2 **Haltūshān** Iran
243 F2 **Haltwhistle** Northumberland England UK
390 G4 **Ḩālūl** *island* Qatar
223 P5 **Haluna** Finland
372 B6 **Halura** *island* Indonesia
392 C6 **Halvad** Gujarat India
391 H2 **Ḩalvān** Iran
226 D2 **Halver** Germany
385 G3 **Halzan** Mongolia
305 H2 **Ham** Chad
229 F2 **Ham** France
244 inset **Ham** Shetland Scotland UK
376 E3 **Hàm Tân** Vietnam
386 G4 **Hamada** Japan
390 F2 **Hamadān** Iran
388 E7 **Hamadān** *admin. area* Iran
301 F2 **Hamaguir** Algeria
394 F6 **Ḩamāh (Hamath)** Syria
387 H4 **Hamam** Turkey
387 H4 **Hamamatsu** Japan
390 G4 **Hamandeh** Iran
224 F2 **Hamar** Norway
222 I2 **Hamarøy** Norway
222 I2 **Hamarøy** *island* Norway
307 G2 **Hamarro Hadad** Ethiopia
Hamath *see* **Ḩamāh** Syria
393 E10 **Hambantota** Sri Lanka
226 E1 **Hamburg** Germany
226 F1 **Hamburg** *admin. area* Germany
127 N6 **Hamburg** New Jersey USA
127 L5 **Hamburg** New York USA
390 E6 **Ḩamḑah** Saudi Arabia
390 D4 **Ḩamḑah, Wādī al** *watercourse* Saudi Arabia
390 F3 **Ḩamdān** Iraq
225 M2 **Hämeenlinna** Finland
226 E1 **Hameln** Germany
386 F3 **Hamgyŏng-Sanmaek** North Korea
386 E3 **Hamhŭng** North Korea
383 J4 **Hami** Xinjiang Uygur Zizhiqu China
235 E5 **Hamidiye** Turkey
425 L5 **Hamilton** *watercourse* Qld Australia
425 J6 **Hamilton** *watercourse* SA Australia
425 L9 **Hamilton** Vic. Australia
127 inset **Hamilton** Bermuda
127 L5 **Hamilton** Ontario Canada
422 F3 **Hamilton** New Zealand
244 D5 **Hamilton** South Lanarkshire Scotland UK
129 N2 **Hamilton** Kansas USA
126 E7 **Hamilton** Missouri USA
124 H3 **Hamilton** Montana USA
127 N5 **Hamilton** New York USA
126 I7 **Hamilton** Ohio USA
130 B5 **Hamilton** Texas USA
130 E3 **Hamilton, Lake** Arkansas USA
425 inset **Hamilton, Mount** Macquarie Island Australia
122 I6 **Hamilton Inlet** Newfoundland and Labrador Canada
123 K8 **Hamilton Sound** Newfoundland and Labrador Canada
302 C1 **Hamīn, Wādī Al** *watercourse* Libya
222 N2 **Hamina** Finland
223 O5 **Haminalahti** Finland
119 U7 **Hamiota** Manitoba Canada
224 D2 **Hamlagrovatnet** *lake* Norway
131 L3 **Hamlet** North Carolina USA
130 A4 **Hamlin** Texas USA
226 D2 **Hamm** Germany
301 I1 **Hammamet** Tunisia
394 F6 **Ḩammāmīyah** Syria
224 H3 **Hammar** Sweden
222 I5 **Hammarnäset** Sweden
224 H5 **Hammarsjön** *lake* Sweden
223 O2 **Hammasjärvi** *lake* Finland
223 P5 **Hammaslahti** Finland
226 E1 **Hamme** *watercourse* Germany
222 K5 **Hammerdal** Sweden
222 I5 **Hammerdalssjön** *lake* Sweden
223 D1 **Hammerfest** Norway
223 M2 **Hammerfest** Norway
424 F5 **Hammersley Range** WA Australia
224 E4 **Hammerum** Denmark
130 B3 **Hammon** Oklahoma USA
126 H6 **Hammond** Indiana USA
130 F5 **Hammond** Louisiana USA
123 J7 **Hammone, Lac** *lake* Québec Canada
222 H4 **Hamn** Norway
223 Q1 **Hamna** Norway
244 inset **Hamnavoe** Shetland Scotland UK
222 L2 **Hamnbukt** Norway
222 L2 **Hamnes** Norway
222 H4 **Hamnøya** *island* Norway
386 E4 **Hampeong** South Korea
241 F3 **Hampshire** *admin. area* England UK
123 F10 **Hampton** New Brunswick Canada
127 P5 **Hampton** New Hampshire USA
127 M8 **Hampton** Virginia USA
305 I2 **Hamra, Ouadi** *watercourse* Chad
302 D5 **Hamrat esh Sheikh** Sudan
241 H3 **Hamstreet** Kent England UK
372 E4 **Hamuku** Indonesia
391 J3 **Hāmūn, Daryācheh-ye** *lake* Iran
391 I4 **Hāmūn-e Jāz Mūrīān** *lake* Iran
391 J3 **Hāmūn Şāberī, Daryācheh-ye** *lake* Iran
241 E4 **Hamworthy** Poole England UK
386 E4 **Hamyang** South Korea
373 J5 **Han Island** Papua New Guinea
381 G4 **Han Jiang** *watercourse* Guangdong China
232 H4 **Han Pijesak** Bosnia and Herzegovina
380 E2 **Han Shui** *watercourse* Shaanxi China
384 E2 **Han-Ula, Gora** *mountain* Russian Federation
373 J5 **Hanahan** Papua New Guinea
226 E2 **Hanau** Germany
384 F4 **Hanbogd** Mongolia
120 J1 **Hanbury Island** Nunavut Canada
118 J7 **Hanceville** British Columbia Canada
381 G3 **Hanchang** Hunan China
384 G6 **Hancheng** Shaanxi China
381 G2 **Hanchuan** Hubei China
125 R4 **Hancock** Minnesota USA
244 C2 **Handa Island** Scotland UK
385 H6 **Handan** Hebei China
307 F5 **Handeni** Tanzania
393 D6 **Handia** Madhya Pradesh India
385 H6 **Handian** Shanxi China
222 H3 **Handnesøya** *island* Norway
222 H5 **Handöl** Sweden
222 I5 **Handsjö** Sweden
119 T8 **Handsworth** Saskatchewan Canada
222 G6 **Hanestad** Norway
380 E2 **Hanfeng** Chongqing China
128 C2 **Hanford** California USA
163 5 **Hanga Roa** Isla de Pascua (Easter Island)
384 E2 **Hangal** Mongolia
383 K3 **Hangayn Nuruu** *range* Mongolia
381 H3 **Hangchuan** Fujian China
Hangö *see* **Hanko** Finland
225 L3 **Hangö östra fjärd** *bay* Finland
225 L3 **Hangö västra fjärd** *bay* Finland
224 I1 **Hångstaörn** *lake* Sweden
385 H5 **Hangu** Tianjin China
391 L2 **Hangu** Pakistan
381 H2 **Hangzhou** Zhejiang China
381 I2 **Hangzhou Wan** *bay* Zhejiang China
384 D2 **Hanh** Mongolia
240 E3 **Hanham** South Gloucestershire England UK
384 E4 **Hanhongor** Mongolia
390 E7 **Ḩanīsh al Kabīr, Jazīrat al** *island* Yemen
424 inset **Hanitch Hill** Christmas Island Australia
375 G4 **Hanjalipan** Indonesia
384 E6 **Hanji** Gansu China
380 E2 **Hanjia** Chongqing China
391 J4 **Hanjīrak** Iran
223 P5 **Hankamäki** Finland
223 O5 **Hankasalem asema** Finland
223 O5 **Hankasalmi** Finland
125 Q3 **Hankinson** North Dakota USA
225 L3 **Hanko (Hangö)** Finland
225 L3 **Hankoniemi** *cape* Finland
235 G6 **Hanköy** Turkey
128 G1 **Hanksville** Utah USA
119 R7 **Hanley** Saskatchewan Canada
125 R4 **Hanley Falls** Minnesota USA
423 E6 **Hanmer Springs** New Zealand
424 H3 **Hann, Mount** WA Australia
119 P7 **Hanna** Alberta Canada
130 B3 **Hanna** Oklahoma USA
125 L6 **Hanna** Wyoming USA
125 P3 **Hannaford** North Dakota USA
121 P7 **Hannah Bay** Ontario Canada
423 C6 **Hannah's Clearing** New Zealand
126 F7 **Hannibal** Missouri USA
226 E1 **Hannover** Germany
229 G1 **Hannut** Belgium
224 H5 **Hanö** *island* Sweden
224 H5 **Hanöbukten** *bay* Sweden
Hanoi *see* **Hà Nội** Vietnam
308 D6 **Hanover** South Africa
127 M7 **Hanover** Pennsylvania USA
162 A5 **Hanover, Isla** *island* Chile
373 J5 **Hanpan, Cape** Papua New Guinea
384 D3 **Hanrai** Mongolia
232 G3 **Hanság** *range* Hungary
381 F3 **Hanshou** Hunan China
126 H8 **Hanson** Kentucky USA
423 6 **Hanson Bay** Chatham Islands New Zealand
226 F1 **Hanstedt** Germany
224 E4 **Hanstholm** Denmark
392 D5 **Hanumangarh** Rajasthan India
393 D9 **Hanur** Karnataka India
384 E3 **Hanuy Gol** *watercourse* Mongolia
380 E2 **Hanyin** Shaanxi China
380 E1 **Hanzhong** Shaanxi China
427 14 **Hao** *reef* French Polynesia
384 E5 **Haomen** Qinghai China
393 G6 **Haora** West Bengal India
128 inset **Hā'ō'ū** Hawai'i USA
301 H2 **Haoud el Hamra** Algeria
223 N4 **Haparanda** Sweden
386 F4 **Hapch'on** South Korea
244 E5 **Hapland** Dumfries and Galloway Scotland UK
379 G3 **Hapoli** Arunachal Pradesh India
241 I2 **Happisburgh** Norfolk England UK
120 H1 **Happotiyik Lake** Nunavut Canada
129 L3 **Happy** Texas USA
390 C3 **Ḩaql** Saudi Arabia
372 E5 **Har** Indonesia
383 K5 **Har Hu** *lake* Qinghai China
385 H3 **Har Nuden** Nei Mongol Zizhiqu China
383 J3 **Har Nuur** *lake* Mongolia
383 I2 **Har-us Nuur** *lake* Mongolia
383 I3 **Har Us Nuur** *lake* Mongolia
222 I5 **Hara** Sweden
238 B6 **Hara Dzyarzhynskaya** *mountain* Belarus
225 M3 **Hara laht** *bay* Estonia
390 G5 **Ḩaraḑ** Saudi Arabia
390 E7 **Ḩaraḑ** Yemen
390 F5 **Ḩaraḑh** Saudi Arabia
238 D5 **Haradok** Belarus
222 L3 **Harads** Sweden
222 E5 **Haram** *island* Norway
387 I4 **Haramachi** Japan
222 E5 **Haramsøya** *island* Norway
392 D3 **Haramukh** *mountain* Jammu and Kashmir India/Pakistan
309 F3 **Harare** Zimbabwe
309 F3 **Harare** *admin. area* Zimbabwe
307 G2 **Hārarī Hizb** *admin. area* Ethiopia
227 L2 **Harasiuki** Poland
301 J2 **Harāwah, Wādī** *watercourse* Libya
305 H2 **Haraz** Chad
302 E4 **Haraza, Jebel** *mountain* Sudan
305 I3 **Haraze-Mangueigne** Chad
222 I4 **Härbergsdalen** Sweden
224 I2 **Harbo** Sweden
126 J5 **Harbor Beach** Michigan USA
241 F2 **Harborne** West Midlands England UK
163 7 **Harbours, Bay of** Falkland Islands
226 E1 **Harburg** Germany
243 H3 **Harby** Nottinghamshire England UK
125 P1 **Harcus** Manitoba Canada
128 F3 **Harcuvar Mountains** Arizona USA
393 D6 **Harda** Madhya Pradesh India
224 D2 **Hardanger vidda** *region* Norway
308 C4 **Hardap** *admin. area* Namibia
241 I4 **Hardelot-Plage** France
375 G2 **Harden, Bukit** *mountain* Indonesia
130 A2 **Hardesty** Oklahoma USA
130 G2 **Hardin** Kentucky USA
124 J4 **Hardin** Montana USA
241 I2 **Hardingham** Norfolk England UK
126 H8 **Hardinsburg** Kentucky USA
116 H6 **Hardisty Lake** Northwest Territories Canada
392 E5 **Hardoi** Uttar Pradesh India
130 B2 **Hardtner** Kansas USA
241 F3 **Hardwick** Oxfordshire England UK
162 C6 **Hardy, Peninsula** Chile
126 I5 **Hardy Dam Pond** Michigan USA
123 K7 **Hare Bay** Newfoundland and Labrador Canada
123 K8 **Hare Bay** Newfoundland and Labrador Canada
224 G3 **Harefjorden** *lake* Sweden
243 G3 **Harehills** West Yorkshire England UK
224 C1 **Hareidlandet** *island* Norway
226 D1 **Haren** Netherlands
307 G2 **Hārer** Ethiopia
243 F2 **Harescough** Cumbria England UK
241 H5 **Harfleur** France
240 D4 **Harford** Devon England UK
307 G2 **Hargele** Ethiopia
307 G2 **Hargeysa** Somalia
234 D2 **Harghita** *admin. area* Romania
125 O2 **Hargrave** Manitoba Canada
241 H2 **Hargrave** Suffolk England UK
384 F5 **Harhatan** Nei Mongol Zizhiqu China
383 I2 **Harhiraa** Mongolia
384 E3 **Harhorin** Mongolia
374 D4 **Hari** *watercourse* Indonesia
225 L3 **Hari Kurk** *bay* Estonia
391 J2 **Hari Rūd** *watercourse* Afghanistan
392 E5 **Haridwar** Uttaranchal India
393 D8 **Harihar** Karnataka India
392 F6 **Hariharpur** Chhattisgarh India
392 C6 **Harij** Gujarat India
391 L2 **Haripur** Pakistan
224 H2 **Härjåsjön** *lake* Sweden
224 G1 **Härjedalen** *valley* Sweden
222 H4 **Harjufjärden** *bay* Sweden
225 M3 **Harjumaa** *admin. area* Estonia
225 N2 **Harjumaa** Finland
223 O5 **Härkajärvi** *lake* Finland
126 D6 **Harlan** Iowa USA
131 J2 **Harlan** Kentucky USA
125 P6 **Harlan County Lake** Nebraska USA
122 F6 **Harlands Landing** Newfoundland and Labrador Canada
241 G2 **Harlaxton** Lincolnshire England UK
240 C2 **Harlech** Gwynedd Wales UK
125 K2 **Harlem** Montana USA
226 C1 **Harlingen** Netherlands
130 C7 **Harlingen** Texas USA
241 H3 **Harlow** Essex England UK
125 K3 **Harlowton** Montana USA
241 H2 **Harlton** Cambridgeshire England UK
235 F6 **Harmancık** Turkey
222 J6 **Harmånger** Sweden
223 P4 **Härmänmäki** Finland
303 G4 **Harmil** *island* Eritrea
126 F2 **Harmon Lake** Ontario Canada
128 B3 **Harmony** California USA
125 F5 **Harney Basin** *pan* Oregon USA
124 F5 **Harney Lake** Oregon USA
243 G1 **Harnham** Northumberland England UK
222 K5 **Härnön** *island* Sweden
222 J5 **Härnösand** Sweden
230 E2 **Haro** Spain
222 J3 **Harö** *island* Sweden
225 N5 **Harodz'ki** Belarus
222 E5 **Harøya** *island* Norway
122 G5 **Harp Lake** Newfoundland and Labrador Canada
393 D8 **Harpanahalli** Karnataka India
222 F6 **Harpefoss** Norway
241 G3 **Harpenden** Hertfordshire England UK
304 C3 **Harper** Liberia
125 P8 **Harper** Kansas USA
128 D3 **Harper Lake** California USA
243 H3 **Harpswell** Lincolnshire England UK
222 L3 **Harrå** Sweden
393 E6 **Harrai** Madhya Pradesh India
222 L3 **Harrejaur** Sweden
127 L2 **Harricanaw** *watercourse* Québec Canada
242 E2 **Harrington** Cumbria England UK
124 F3 **Harrington** Washington USA
117 N8 **Harrington Harbour** Québec Canada
127 inset **Harrington Sound** Bermuda
119 R7 **Harris** Saskatchewan Canada
163 I7 **Harris** Montserrat
244 B4 **Harris** Highland Scotland UK
425 J7 **Harris, Lake** SA Australia
131 K6 **Harris, Lake** Florida USA
423 C7 **Harris Mountains** New Zealand
79 Q3 **Harris Seamount** *underwater feature* Pacific Ocean
126 G8 **Harrisburg** Illinois USA
124 D4 **Harrisburg** Oregon USA
127 M6 **Harrisburg** Pennsylvania USA
308 E5 **Harrismith** South Africa
130 E2 **Harrison** Arkansas USA
126 I4 **Harrison** Michigan USA
125 N5 **Harrison** Nebraska USA
122 J5 **Harrison, Cape** Newfoundland and Labrador Canada
116 D4 **Harrison Bay** Alaska USA
118 K8 **Harrison Hot Springs** British Columbia Canada
118 K8 **Harrison Lake** British Columbia Canada
163 12 **Harrison Point** *cape* Barbados
127 L7 **Harrisonburg** Virginia USA
126 J4 **Harrisville** Michigan USA
127 N4 **Harrisville** New York USA
243 G3 **Harrogate** North Yorkshire England UK
241 G2 **Harrold** Bedfordshire England UK
120 H6 **Harrop Lake** Manitoba Canada
241 G3 **Harrow** Greater London England UK
125 O1 **Harrowby** Manitoba Canada
222 I4 **Harrsjön** Sweden
222 J4 **Harrvik** Sweden
126 E7 **Harry S. Truman Reservoir** Missouri USA
222 J2 **Harstad** Norway
125 M2 **Hart** Saskatchewan Canada
116 F5 **Hart** *watercourse* Yukon Territory Canada
126 H5 **Hart** Michigan USA
129 K3 **Hart** Texas USA
424 H4 **Hart, Mount** WA Australia
124 F5 **Hart Lake** Oregon USA
118 J5 **Hart Range** British Columbia Canada
234 A2 **Harta** Hungary
308 D5 **Hartbees** *watercourse* South Africa
222 J6 **Hårte** Sweden
244 C3 **Hartfield** Highland Scotland UK
127 O6 **Hartford** Connecticut USA
126 H8 **Hartford** Kentucky USA
125 Q5 **Hartford** South Dakota USA
243 G2 **Harthforth** North Yorkshire England UK
240 E1 **Harthill** Cheshire England UK
243 G3 **Harthill** South Yorkshire England UK
241 F1 **Hartington** Derbyshire England UK
123 E9 **Hartland** New Brunswick Canada
123 D10 **Hartland** Maine USA
240 C3 **Hartland Point** England UK
243 G2 **Hartlepool** Hartlepool England UK
243 G2 **Hartlepool** *admin. area* England UK
129 K3 **Hartley** Texas USA
118 G6 **Hartley Bay** British Columbia Canada
129 J1 **Hartsel** Colorado USA
130 H3 **Hartselle** Alabama USA
308 D5 **Hartswater** South Africa
241 G2 **Hartwell** Northamptonshire England UK
131 J3 **Hartwell Lake** South Carolina USA
125 P6 **Harvard** Nebraska USA
424 E8 **Harvey** WA Australia
125 P3 **Harvey** North Dakota USA
129 O1 **Harveyville** Kansas USA
241 I3 **Harwich** Essex England UK
392 D5 **Haryana** *admin. area* India
390 F2 **Harzin** Iran
226 D1 **Hase** *watercourse* Germany
161 G4 **Hasenkamp** Argentina
384 E3 **Hashaat** Mongolia
387 G4 **Hashimoto** Japan
302 D5 **Haskanit** Sudan
130 E3 **Haskell** Arkansas USA
130 B4 **Haskell** Texas USA
423 8 **Haskell Bay** Auckland Islands New Zealand
227 H3 **Haslach an der Mühl** Austria
226 E3 **Haslach im Kinzigtal** Germany
224 H5 **Hasle** Denmark
226 E4 **Hasle** Switzerland
241 G3 **Haslemere** Surrey England UK
224 F5 **Haslev** Denmark
240 E1 **Haslington** Cheshire England UK
228 D5 **Hasparren** France
393 D9 **Hassan** Karnataka India
235 E6 **Hasseki** Turkey
117 J3 **Hassel Sound** Nunavut Canada
222 J5 **Hassela** Sweden
222 J5 **Hasselasjön** *lake* Sweden
425 inset **Hasselborough Bay** Macquarie Island Australia
241 H3 **Hassell Street** Kent England UK
224 I4 **Hassleö** *island* Sweden
229 G1 **Hasselt** Belgium
300 F3 **Hassi el Khebi** Algeria
301 H2 **Hassi Messaoud** Algeria
222 J5 **Hässjö** Sweden
224 G2 **Hassjön** *lake* Sweden
224 G4 **Hässleholm** Sweden
224 H4 **Hasslö** *island* Sweden
232 C2 **Haßloch** Germany
126 E3 **Hassman** Minnesota USA
163 12 **Hastings** Barbados
422 G4 **Hastings** New Zealand
241 H4 **Hastings** East Sussex England UK
126 I5 **Hastings** Michigan USA
126 E4 **Hastings** Minnesota USA
125 P6 **Hastings** Nebraska USA
373 I6 **Hastings Island** Papua New Guinea
224 H3 **Hästnäs** Sweden
225 N2 **Hästön** *island* Finland
224 G4 **Hästveda** Sweden
390 E6 **Ḩasy** Saudi Arabia
376 D6 **Hat Yai** Thailand
391 K4 **Hatachi** Pakistan
384 G4 **Hatanbular** Mongolia
394 F6 **Hatay (Antioch)** Turkey
394 F6 **Hatay** *admin. area* Turkey
127 N6 **Hatboro** Pennsylvania USA
129 I4 **Hatch** New Mexico USA
124 I8 **Hatch** Utah USA
120 D3 **Hatchet Lake** Saskatchewan Canada
130 G3 **Hatchie** *watercourse* Tennessee USA
234 C3 **Hațeg** Romania
381 I4 **Hateruma Shima** *island* Japan
241 G3 **Hatfield** Hertfordshire England UK
243 G3 **Hatfield** South Yorkshire England UK

243 H3 **Hatfield Woodhouse** South Yorkshire England UK
241 F3 **Hatherop** Gloucestershire England UK
392 E5 **Hathras** Uttar Pradesh India
163 1b **Hato, Bocht van** *bay* Netherlands Antilles
392 E6 **Hatta** Madhya Pradesh India
425 L8 **Hattah** Vic. Australia
226 D1 **Hattem** Netherlands
131 N3 **Hatteras, Cape** North Carolina USA
76 K6 **Hatteras Abyssal Plain** *underwater feature* Atlantic Ocean
130 G5 **Hattiesburg** Mississippi USA
125 K1 **Hatton** Saskatchewan Canada
122 F2 **Hatton Headland** Nunavut Canada
376 C4 **Hattras Passage** *strait* Myanmar
224 E5 **Hattstedt** Germany
223 Q5 **Hattuvaara** Finland
223 O4 **Hatulanmäki** Finland
427 14 **Hatutu** *island* French Polynesia
232 H3 **Hatvan** Hungary
307 G2 **Haud** *plain* Ethiopia
224 D3 **Hauge** Norway
224 C3 **Haugesund** Norway
244 E6 **Haugh of Urr** Dumfries and Galloway Scotland UK
222 H3 **Haugland** Norway
222 L1 **Haugnes** Norway
225 M2 **Hauha** *lake* Finland
422 F4 **Hauhungaroa Range** New Zealand
223 Q4 **Haukela** Finland
224 D3 **Haukeligrend** Norway
223 N4 **Haukipudas** Finland
223 P5 **Haukivesi** *bay* Finland
238 B2 **Haukivuori** Finland
222 J2 **Haukøy** *island* Norway
160 F3 **Haumonia** Argentina
422 F3 **Hauraki Gulf** New Zealand
224 H4 **Haurida** Sweden
423 B8 **Hauroko, Lake** New Zealand
229 J3 **Hausham** Germany
Haussez, Iles d' *see* **Mercury Islands** New Zealand
127 Q5 **Haut, Isle au** *island* Maine USA
306 D2 **Haut-Mbomou** *admin. area* Central African Republic
305 G5 **Haut-Ogooué** *admin. area* Gabon
223 P3 **Hautajärvi** Finland
305 I3 **Haute-Kotto** *admin. area* Central African Republic
228 E2 **Haute-Normandie** *admin. area* France
228 D2 **Hauteville-sur-Mer** France
301 G2 **Hauts Plateaux** *range* Algeria
128 inset **Hau'ula** Hawai'i USA
227 G3 **Hauzenberg** Germany
227 K3 **Havaj** Slovakia
Havana *see* **La Habana** Cuba
126 F6 **Havana** Illinois USA
241 G4 **Havant** Hampshire England UK
226 G1 **Havel** *watercourse* Germany
131 M3 **Havelock** North Carolina USA
376 B5 **Havelock Island** Andaman and Nicobar Islands India
226 D1 **Havelte** Netherlands
222 H2 **Håven** Sweden
240 C3 **Haverfordwest** Pembrokeshire Wales UK
241 H2 **Haverhill** Suffolk England UK
127 P5 **Haverhill** Massachusetts USA
393 D8 **Haveri** Karnataka India
222 I5 **Havern** *bay* Sweden
127 O6 **Haverstraw** New York USA
125 P8 **Haviland** Kansas USA
222 H5 **Hävlingen** *lake* Sweden
224 E5 **Havneby** Denmark
223 N1 **Havøya** *island* Norway
223 N1 **Havøysund** Norway
224 I2 **Håvran** *lake* Sweden
235 E6 **Havran** Turkey
125 K2 **Havre** Montana USA
123 H9 **Havre-Aubert** Québec Canada
123 G9 **Havre Aubert, Île du** *island* Québec Canada
123 H9 **Havre-aux-Maisons** Québec Canada
123 G7 **Havre-Saint-Pierre** Québec Canada
234 E1 **Havrylivtsi** Ukraine
222 I4 **Havsnäs** Sweden
128 inset **Hawai'i** *admin. area* USA
78 P5 **Hawaiian Ridge** *underwater feature* Pacific Ocean
79 R5 **Hawaiian Trough** *underwater feature* Pacific Ocean
119 R7 **Hawarden** Saskatchewan Canada
423 E6 **Hawarden** New Zealand
240 D1 **Hawarden** Flintshire Wales UK
125 Q5 **Hawarden** Iowa USA
386 F3 **Hawdae** North Korea
423 C7 **Hawea, Lake** New Zealand
423 C7 **Hawea Flat** New Zealand
422 F4 **Hawera** New Zealand
243 F2 **Hawes** North Yorkshire England UK
243 F2 **Haweswater Reservoir** England UK
244 F5 **Hawick** Scottish Borders Scotland UK
118 M4 **Hawk Hills** Alberta Canada
423 D7 **Hawkdun Range** New Zealand
122 J6 **Hawke** *watercourse* Newfoundland and Labrador Canada
422 G4 **Hawke Bay** New Zealand
425 K7 **Hawker** SA Australia
127 N4 **Hawkesbury** Ontario Canada
130 D4 **Hawkins** Texas USA
241 G3 **Hawkley** Hampshire England UK
135 F1 **Hawks Nest Point** Bahamas
242 F2 **Hawkshead** Cumbria England UK
241 G3 **Hawley** Hampshire England UK
127 N6 **Hawley** Pennsylvania USA
130 B4 **Hawley** Texas USA
243 G3 **Haworth** West Yorkshire England UK
390 F3 **Hawr al Ḥammār** *lake* Iraq
390 E2 **Ḥawrān, Wādī** *watercourse* Iraq
128 C4 **Hawthorne** California USA
303 F5 **Hawzēn** Ethiopia
125 N6 **Haxtun** Colorado USA
425 M8 **Hay** NSW Australia
425 K5 **Hay** *watercourse* NT Australia
119 M2 **Hay** *watercourse* Northwest Territories Canada
240 C4 **Hay** Cornwall England UK
119 P3 **Hay Camp** Alberta Canada
118 L3 **Hay Lake** Alberta Canada
240 D2 **Hay-on-Wye** Powys Wales UK
119 N2 **Hay River** Northwest Territories Canada
125 N5 **Hay Springs** Nebraska USA
372 D4 **Haya** Indonesia
394 F6 **Ḥayāniyah** Syria
391 H5 **Ḥaybi** Oman
394 F3 **Haychur** *watercourse* Ukraine
235 G6 **Haydarlı** Turkey
128 G4 **Hayden** Arizona USA
125 L6 **Hayden** Colorado USA
243 F2 **Haydon Bridge** Northumberland England UK
120 I5 **Hayes** *watercourse* Manitoba Canada
117 J5 **Hayes** *watercourse* Nunavut Canada
125 O6 **Hayes Center** Nebraska USA
117 M3 **Hayes Halvø** *plain* Greenland
303 I5 **Hayf** Yemen
126 E5 **Hayfield** Minnesota USA
303 F5 **Häyk'** Ethiopia
303 F5 **Hayk Hayk** *lake* Ethiopia
302 F4 **Haykota** Eritrea
240 B4 **Hayle** Cornwall England UK
241 F4 **Hayling Island** England UK
391 H6 **Haymā'** Oman
238 B5 **Hayna** Belarus
131 H4 **Hayneville** Alabama USA
119 P7 **Hays** Alberta Canada
125 P7 **Hays** Kansas USA
390 E7 **Ḥays** Yemen
436 N1 **Hays Mountains** Antarctica
125 Q8 **Haysville** Kansas USA
234 F1 **Haysyn** Ukraine
243 H3 **Hayton** East Riding of Yorkshire England UK
234 F1 **Hayvoron** Ukraine
124 D8 **Hayward** California USA
126 F3 **Hayward** Wisconsin USA
241 G4 **Haywards Heath** West Sussex England UK
392 F6 **Hazaribag** Jharkhand India
125 Q4 **Hazel** South Dakota USA
243 F3 **Hazel Grove** Greater Manchester England UK
118 H5 **Hazelton** British Columbia Canada
125 P8 **Hazelton** Kansas USA
125 O3 **Hazelton** North Dakota USA
125 O3 **Hazen** North Dakota USA
117 M2 **Hazen, Lake** Nunavut Canada
117 I3 **Hazen Strait** Northwest Territories/ Nunavut Canada
130 F5 **Hazlehurst** Mississippi USA
241 G3 **Hazlemere** Buckinghamshire England UK
127 N6 **Hazleton** Pennsylvania USA
424 H5 **Hazlett, Lake** WA Australia
385 I4 **He** *lake* Nei Mongol Zizhiqu China
381 F4 **He Jiang** *watercourse* Guangxi Zhuangzu Zizhiqu China
241 H2 **Heacham** Norfolk England UK
424 I7 **Head of Bight** *bay* SA Australia
241 H3 **Headcorn** Kent England UK
130 B3 **Headrick** Oklahoma USA
242 C2 **Headwood** Larne Northern Ireland UK
124 D7 **Healdsburg** California USA
130 C3 **Healdton** Oklahoma USA
116 E6 **Healy** Alaska USA
129 L1 **Healy** Kansas USA
125 J5 **Heaman** Manitoba Canada
241 F1 **Heanor** Derbyshire England UK
424 inset **Heard Island** Indian Ocean
424 inset **Heard Island and McDonald Islands** *Australian territory* Indian Ocean
119 S7 **Hearne** Saskatchewan Canada
130 C5 **Hearne** Texas USA
120 N8 **Hearst** Ontario Canada
436 T2 **Hearst Island** Antarctica
125 N3 **Heart** *watercourse* North Dakota USA
123 H8 **Heath, Pointe** *cape* Québec Canada
241 H4 **Heathfield** East Sussex England UK
130 D3 **Heavener** Oklahoma USA
130 B7 **Hebbronville** Texas USA
123 F10 **Hebbville** Nova Scotia Canada
385 H5 **Hebei** *admin. area* China
128 G3 **Heber** Arizona USA
122 F2 **Hébertville** Québec Canada
125 J4 **Hebgen Lake** Montana USA
385 H6 **Hebi** Henan China
244 B3 **Hebrides, Sea of the** Scotland UK
121 X3 **Hebron** Newfoundland and Labrador Canada
126 H6 **Hebron** Indiana USA
125 Q6 **Hebron** Nebraska USA
129 J2 **Hebron** New Mexico USA
382 H3 **Hebukesai`er** Xinjiang Uygur Zizhiqu China
118 F6 **Hecate Strait** British Columbia Canada
381 H3 **Hecheng** Jiangxi China
381 H3 **Hecheng** Zhejiang China
380 E4 **Hechi** Guangxi Zhuangzu Zizhiqu China
380 E2 **Hechuan** Chongqing China
381 G3 **Hechuan** Jiangxi China
125 P4 **Hecla** South Dakota USA
120 G7 **Hecla Island** Manitoba Canada
425 N5 **Hector, Mount** Qld Australia
423 C7 **Hector Mountains** New Zealand
224 F2 **Hedal** Norway
224 E3 **Heddalsvatnet** *lake* Norway
228 D2 **Hédé** France
222 H5 **Hede** Sweden
222 H6 **Heden** Sweden
223 M3 **Hedenäset** Sweden
222 I2 **Hedesundafjärden** *bay* Sweden
222 H5 **Hedeviken** Sweden
380 F4 **Hedi Shuiku** *lake* Guangdong China
124 E2 **Hedley** British Columbia Canada
130 A3 **Hedley** Texas USA
224 F2 **Hedmark** *admin. area* Norway
243 H3 **Hedon** East Riding of Yorkshire England UK
244 E2 **Heddle** Orkney Islands Scotland UK
390 C3 **Hefa (Haifa)** Israel
381 H2 **Hefei** Anhui China
381 L3 **Hegang** Heilongjiang China
385 L3 **Hegang** Heilongjiang China
222 F5 **Heggem** Norway
222 F6 **Heggenes** Norway
222 H6 **Heggeriset** Norway
222 I3 **Heggmovatnet** *lake* Norway
373 G5 **Hegigio** *watercourse* Papua New Guinea
244 inset **Heglibister** Shetland Scotland UK
222 G5 **Hegra** Norway
380 C4 **Hei Chiang** *watercourse* Yunnan China
384 D5 **Hei He** *watercourse* Gansu China
380 D2 **Hei-shui Ho** *watercourse* Sichuan China
302 E5 **Heiban** Sudan
224 E5 **Heide** Germany
226 E3 **Heidelberg** Germany
308 D6 **Heidelberg** South Africa
308 E5 **Heidelberg** South Africa
130 G5 **Heidelberg** Mississippi USA
385 K2 **Heihe** Heilongjiang China
226 E3 **Heilbronn** Germany
226 G4 **Heiligenblut** Austria
385 K1 **Heilong** *watercourse* Heilongjiang China
385 K3 **Heilongjiang** *admin. area* China
226 F3 **Heilsbronn** Germany
222 inset **Heimaey** *island* Iceland
384 D6 **Heimahe** Qinghai China
373 H4 **Heina Islands** Papua New Guinea
223 O5 **Heinämäki** Finland
223 O5 **Heinävaara** Finland
223 P5 **Heinävesi** Finland
227 H2 **Heinersbrück** Germany
225 N2 **Heinola** Finland
119 P6 **Heinsburg** Alberta Canada
385 J4 **Heishan** Liaoning China
380 D3 **Heishui He** *watercourse* Sichuan China
Heisker Islands *see* **Monach Islands** UK
119 O6 **Heisler** Alberta Canada
225 J4 **Hejde** Sweden
385 H5 **Hejian** Hebei China
380 E3 **Hejiang** Sichuan China
384 G6 **Hejin** Shanxi China
383 H4 **Hejing** Xinjiang Uygur Zizhiqu China
235 G6 **Hekimdağ** Turkey
222 inset **Hekla** *mountain* Iceland
381 H3 **Hekou** Jiangxi China
380 D2 **Hekou** Sichuan China
225 J5 **Hel** Poland
222 H5 **Helagsfjället** *mountain* Sweden
379 G3 **Helam** Arunachal Pradesh India
384 F5 **Helan Shan** *range* Zhishiqu China
226 C2 **Helden** Netherlands
240 D4 **Hele** Devon England UK
126 G2 **Helen Lake** Ontario Canada
130 F3 **Helena** Arkansas USA
124 I3 **Helena** Montana USA
130 B2 **Helena** Oklahoma USA
227 H3 **Helfenberg** Austria
224 H4 **Helgasjön** *lake* Sweden
224 G4 **Helge** *watercourse* Sweden
224 F3 **Helgerød** Norway
224 D5 **Helgoland** *island* Germany
222 K1 **Helgøy** Norway
222 K1 **Helgøy** *island* Norway
222 J5 **Helgum** Sweden
222 J5 **Helgumsjön** *lake* Sweden
222 E2 **Helin** *lake* Norway
384 G5 **Helin`ge`er** Nei Mongol Zizhiqu China
381 H2 **Helixi** Anhui China
222 inset **Hella** Iceland
222 F5 **Helland** Norway
224 D1 **Hellesylt** Norway
224 E3 **Helligskogen** Norway
222 H3 **Helligvær** *island* Norway
230 F4 **Hellín** Spain
222 inset **Hellissandur** Iceland
244 inset **Hellister** Shetland Scotland UK
222 L1 **Hellnes** Norway
222 C3 **Hellvik** Norway
128 B2 **Helm** California USA
391 J3 **Helmand** *admin. area* Afghanistan
226 F2 **Helme** *watercourse* Germany
308 C5 **Helmeringhausen** Namibia
244 E2 **Helmsdale** Highland Scotland UK
244 E2 **Helmsdale** *watercourse* Scotland UK
243 G2 **Helmsley** North Yorkshire England UK
385 L4 **Helong** Jilin China
125 J7 **Helper** Utah USA
234 B4 **Helshan** Albania
224 G4 **Helsingborg** Sweden
224 G4 **Helsinge** Denmark
224 G4 **Helsingør** Denmark
225 M2 **Helsinki** Finland
225 J5 **Helska** *bay* Poland
240 B4 **Helston** Cornwall England UK
245 E4 **Helvick Head** *cape* Ireland
229 J2 **Hemau** Germany
241 G3 **Hemel Hempstead** Hertfordshire England UK
240 C4 **Hemerdon** Devon England UK
128 D4 **Hemet** California USA
119 U5 **Heming Lake** Manitoba Canada
125 N5 **Hemingford** Nebraska USA
240 E3 **Hemington** Somerset England UK
222 K5 **Hemling** Sweden
224 E6 **Hemmoor** Germany
222 H3 **Hemnesberget** Norway
241 I2 **Hemsby** Norfolk England UK
225 J4 **Hemse** Sweden
222 I5 **Hemsjön** *lake* Sweden
222 K5 **Hemsö** Sweden
222 K5 **Hemsön** *island* Sweden
243 G3 **Hemsworth** West Yorkshire England UK
422 F2 **Hen and Chicken Islands** New Zealand
381 F1 **Henan** *admin. area* China
224 F3 **Henån** Sweden
230 E3 **Henares** *watercourse* Spain
233 C9 **Henchir el Fercha** Tunisia
235 G5 **Hendek** Turkey
126 H8 **Henderson** Kentucky USA
130 E5 **Henderson** Louisiana USA
128 E2 **Henderson** Nevada USA
131 L2 **Henderson** North Carolina USA
130 D4 **Henderson** Texas USA
127 M5 **Henderson Bay** New York USA
437 G2 **Henderson Island** Antarctica
427 11 **Henderson Island** Pitcairn Islands
79 T5 **Henderson Seamount** *underwater feature* Pacific Ocean
241 G3 **Hendon** Greater London England UK
391 H4 **Hendorābī, Jazīreh-ye** *island* Iran
241 G4 **Henfield** West Sussex England UK
385 H5 **Heng Shan** *mountain* Shanxi China
385 H5 **Heng Shan** *range* Shanxi China
381 F3 **Hengdong** Hunan China
379 I3 **Hengduan Shan** *range* Xizang Zizhiqu China
381 I2 **Hengsha Dao** *island* Shanghai China
385 H5 **Hengshui** Hebei China
381 G3 **Hengshui** Jiangxi China
381 F3 **Hengyang** Hunan China
380 F4 **Hengzhou** Guangxi Zhuangzu Zizhiqu China
385 H5 **Hengzhou** Hebei China
120 G2 **Heninga Lake** Nunavut Canada
123 K7 **Henley Harbour** Newfoundland and Labrador Canada
241 G3 **Henley-on-Thames** Oxfordshire England UK
241 G2 **Henlow** Bedfordshire England UK
222 I5 **Hennan** Sweden
222 I5 **Hennan** *lake* Sweden
228 C3 **Hennebont** France
126 G6 **Hennepin** Illinois USA
222 I2 **Hennes** Norway
130 C2 **Hennessey** Oklahoma USA
125 R3 **Henning** Minnesota USA
130 G3 **Henning** Tennessee USA
228 F3 **Henrichemont** France
121 N5 **Henrietta Maria, Cape** Ontario Canada
128 G2 **Henrieville** Utah USA
436 T1 **Henry Ice Rise** Antarctica
117 M5 **Henry Kater, Cape** Nunavut Canada
376 B4 **Henry Lawrence Island** Andaman and Nicobar Islands India
128 G1 **Henry Mountains** Utah USA
124 J4 **Henrys Lake** Idaho USA
128 D4 **Henshaw, Lake** California USA
308 B4 **Henties Bay** Namibia
384 G3 **Hentiy** *admin. area* Mongolia
380 E3 **Heping** Guizhou China
380 E3 **Heping** Guizhou China
381 G4 **Hepo** Guangdong China
223 P5 **Heposelkä** *bay* Finland
243 F1 **Hepple** Northumberland England UK
124 F4 **Heppner** Oregon USA
384 G5 **Hequ** Shanxi China
222 inset **Héraðsflói** *bay* Iceland
222 inset **Héraðsvötn** *watercourse* Iceland
425 N4 **Herald Cays** *islands* Coral Sea Islands Territory Australia
422 F4 **Herangi Range** New Zealand
391 J2 **Herāt** Afghanistan
391 J2 **Herāt** *admin. area* Afghanistan
228 F5 **Hérault** *watercourse* France
119 V5 **Herb Lake** Manitoba Canada
119 V5 **Herb Lake Landing** Manitoba Canada
228 E3 **Herbault** France
119 R7 **Herbert** Saskatchewan Canada
423 D7 **Herbert** New Zealand
424 F5 **Herbert, Mount** WA Australia
376 B5 **Herbertabad** Andaman and Nicobar Islands India
245 D4 **Herbertstown** Ireland
228 C3 **Herbignac** France
226 E2 **Herborn** Germany
229 I1 **Herbstein** Germany
120 H4 **Herchmer** Manitoba Canada
129 K6 **Hercules** Mexico
162 D3 **Hércules, Punta** *cape* Argentina
436 P1 **Hercules Dome** *mountain* Antarctica
77 S14 **Herdman Seamount** *underwater feature* Pacific Ocean
240 E2 **Hereford** Herefordshire England UK
129 K3 **Hereford** Texas USA
240 E2 **Herefordshire** *admin. area* England UK
224 E3 **Herefoss** Norway
427 14 **Hereheretue** *island* French Polynesia
422 E2 **Herekino** New Zealand
422 E2 **Herekino Harbour** New Zealand
232 G3 **Herend** Hungary
423 C6 **Heretaniwha Point** New Zealand
229 H3 **Héricourt** France
229 I3 **Herisau** Switzerland
228 F3 **Hérisson** France
436 S1 **Heritage Range** Antarctica
384 G3 **Herlen** Mongolia
384 G3 **Herlen** Mongolia
125 Q4 **Herman** Minnesota USA
424 J5 **Hermannsburg** NT Australia
222 J5 **Hermansjö** Sweden
224 D2 **Hermansverk** Norway
162 F2 **Hermengo, Punta** *cape* Argentina
124 F4 **Hermiston** Oregon USA
425 N4 **Hermit Crab Islet** *island* Coral Sea Islands Territory Australia
373 H4 **Hermit Islands** Papua New Guinea
123 K9 **Hermitage** Newfoundland and Labrador Canada
244 F5 **Hermitage** Scottish Borders Scotland UK
130 E4 **Hermitage** Arkansas USA
123 J9 **Hermitage Bay** Newfoundland and Labrador Canada
125 N5 **Hermosa** South Dakota USA
132 C2 **Hermosillo** Mexico
227 J4 **Hernád** Hungary
227 K3 **Hernád** *watercourse* Hungary
125 O7 **Herndon** Kansas USA
241 I3 **Herne Bay** Kent England UK
122 D4 **Hérodier, Lac** *lake* Québec Canada
226 C2 **Héron** Belgium
423 D6 **Heron, Lake** New Zealand
154 C3 **Herrán** Colombia
224 E3 **Herre** Norway
125 O4 **Herreid** South Dakota USA
226 E3 **Herrenberg** Germany
230 D5 **Herrera** Spain
230 D2 **Herrera de Pisuerga** Spain
230 D4 **Herrera del Duque** Spain
134 C3 **Herrero, Punta** *cape* Mexico
125 P5 **Herrick** South Dakota USA
126 G8 **Herrin** Illinois USA
131 I2 **Herrington Lake** Kentucky USA
119 U4 **Herriot** Manitoba Canada
228 E5 **Hers** *watercourse* France
116 F5 **Herschel Island** Yukon Territory Canada
229 G1 **Herstal** Belgium
241 H4 **Herstmonceux** East Sussex England UK
229 H1 **Herten** Germany
241 G3 **Hertford** Hertfordshire England UK
241 G3 **Hertfordshire** *admin. area* England UK
161 H5 **Herval** Brazil
230 D3 **Hervás** Spain
122 C5 **Hervé, Lac** *lake* Québec Canada
159 E4 **Hervedero** Bolivia
425 O6 **Hervey Bay** Qld Australia
425 O6 **Hervey Bay** Qld Australia
232 C2 **Herxheim** Germany
388 G6 **Hesarcheh** Iran
241 J4 **Hesdin** France
381 F4 **Heshan** Guangdong China
381 F3 **Heshan** Hunan China
380 D2 **Heshan** Sichuan China
385 H5 **Heshun** Shanxi China
383 H4 **Heshuo** Xinjiang Uygur Zizhiqu China
243 G2 **Hesleden** Durham England UK
243 G3 **Heslington** York England UK
128 D3 **Hesperia** California USA
125 K8 **Hesperus Mountain** Colorado USA
118 H8 **Hesquiat** British Columbia Canada
116 F6 **Hess** *watercourse* Yukon Territory Canada
78 N4 **Hess Rise** *underwater feature* Pacific Ocean
224 F4 **Hesselø** *island* Denmark
226 E2 **Hessen** *admin. area* Germany
223 P2 **Hesseng** Norway
243 H3 **Hessle** East Riding of Yorkshire England UK
125 Q7 **Hesston** Kansas USA
222 H3 **Hestmona** *island* Norway
242 E3 **Heswall** Merseyside England UK
124 F8 **Hetch Hetchy Reservoir** California USA
382 F5 **Hetian** Xinjiang Uygur Zizhiqu China
222 I4 **Hetögeln** *bay* Sweden
125 N4 **Hettinger** North Dakota USA
243 G2 **Hetton-le-Hole** Tyne and Wear England UK
244 E3 **Heugh-head** Aberdeenshire Scotland UK
426 8 **Heuru** Solomon Islands
241 G5 **Hève, Cap de la** *cape* France
159 F2 **Hevelândia** Brazil
227 K4 **Heves** Hungary
227 K4 **Heves** *admin. area* Hungary
130 C5 **Hewitt** Texas USA
243 F2 **Hexham** Northumberland England UK
380 C3 **Hexi** Sichuan China
381 H3 **Hexi** Zhejiang China
385 H6 **Heyang** Hebei China
380 F1 **Heyang** Shaanxi China
384 E6 **Heyin** Qinghai China
242 F2 **Heysham** Lancashire England UK
381 G4 **Heyuan** Guangdong China
425 L9 **Heywood** Vic. Australia
424 G3 **Heywood Islands** WA Australia
391 I3 **Hezār, Kūh-e** *mountain* Iran
381 G1 **Heze** Shandong China
380 D3 **Hezhang** Guizhou China
381 F4 **Hezhou** Guangxi Zhuangzu Zizhiqu China
131 K8 **Hialeah** Florida USA
126 D7 **Hiawatha** Kansas USA
126 E3 **Hibbing** Minnesota USA
424 inset **Hibernia Reef** Ashmore Reef and Cartier Island Australia
158 D5 **Hichocollo** Peru
241 G2 **Hickling** Nottinghamshire England UK
160 F2 **Hickmann** Argentina
131 K3 **Hickory** North Carolina USA
131 K3 **Hickory, Lake** North Carolina USA
130 G3 **Hickory Flat** Mississippi USA
422 H3 **Hicks Bay** New Zealand
119 V2 **Hicks Lake** Nunavut Canada
234 C2 **Hida** Romania
387 I2 **Hidaka-sanmyaku** Japan
129 I5 **Hidalgo** Mexico
133 F3 **Hidalgo** Mexico
133 F4 **Hidalgo** *admin. area* Mexico
132 D3 **Hidalgo del Parral** Mexico
227 J4 **Hidas** Hungary
425 M4 **Hidden Valley** Qld Australia
224 G5 **Hiddensee** *island* Germany
234 C2 **Hidişelu de Jos** Romania
224 D3 **Hidra** *island* Norway
426 7 **Hienghène** New Caledonia
310 3 **Hierro** *island* Canary Islands
223 M3 **Hietanen** Sweden
223 P4 **Hietaperä** Finland
386 F5 **Higashi-Suidō** *strait* Japan
230 F2 **Higer, Cabo** *cape* France
130 A2 **Higgins** Texas USA
126 I4 **Higgins Lake** Michigan USA
121 T1 **High Bluff Island** Nunavut Canada
240 D3 **High Bray** Devon England UK
124 E5 **High Desert** Oregon USA
241 H3 **High Garrett** Essex England UK
243 H2 **High Hawsker** North Yorkshire England UK
120 H5 **High Hill Lake** Manitoba Canada
118 M3 **High Level** Alberta Canada
243 G3 **High Peak** *region* England UK
131 L3 **High Point** North Carolina USA
119 O7 **High River** Alberta Canada
131 K3 **High Rock Lake** North Carolina USA
377 I4 **High Rolling Mountains** Philippines
131 J6 **High Springs** Florida USA
241 G3 **High Wycombe** Buckinghamshire England UK
241 F3 **Highclere** Hampshire England UK
240 D2 **Highgate** Powys Wales UK
244 D3 **Highland** *admin. area* Scotland UK
130 F2 **Highland** Arkansas USA
126 D7 **Highland** Kansas USA
131 J3 **Highlands** North Carolina USA
243 G3 **Highlane** Derbyshire England UK
125 P4 **Highmore** South Dakota USA
240 E3 **Highnam** Gloucestershire England UK
119 U5 **Highrock** Manitoba Canada
119 U5 **Highrock Lake** Manitoba Canada
119 S4 **Highrock Lake** Saskatchewan Canada
241 F3 **Highworth** Swindon England UK
132 C3 **Higuera de Zaragoza** Mexico
422 F4 **Hihitahi** New Zealand
225 M2 **Hiidenvesi** *lake* Finland
307 H3 **Hiiraan** *admin. area* Somalia
225 L3 **Hiiumaa** *admin. area* Estonia
225 L3 **Hiiumaa** *island* Estonia
387 H4 **Hikone** Japan
422 F2 **Hikurangi** New Zealand
422 H3 **Hikurangi** *mountain* New Zealand
422 4 **Hikutavake** Niue New Zealand
372 C5 **Hila** Indonesia
372 B5 **Hilahila** Indonesia
119 P7 **Hilda** Alberta Canada
128 F2 **Hildale** Utah USA
229 J1 **Hildburghausen** Germany
226 D2 **Hilden** Germany
226 E1 **Hildesheim** Germany
78 P8 **Hilgard Deep** *underwater feature* Pacific Ocean
374 C3 **Hilialawa** Indonesia
125 P7 **Hill City** Kansas USA
162 E5 **Hill Cove** Falkland Islands
119 O8 **Hill Spring** Alberta Canada
163 12 **Hillaby, Mount** Barbados
437 K1 **Hillary Coast** Antarctica
226 E1 **Hille** Germany
224 G5 **Hillerød** Denmark
240 E3 **Hillesley** Gloucestershire England UK
245 F2 **Hillhead** Banbridge Northern Ireland UK
131 K5 **Hilliard** Florida USA
241 G3 **Hillingdon** Greater London England UK
126 J4 **Hillman** Michigan USA
244 F4 **Hillock** Angus Scotland UK
222 I4 **Hillsand** Sweden
124 D4 **Hillsboro** Oregon USA
135 I4 **Hillsborough** Grenada
123 G9 **Hillsborough Bay** Prince Edward Island Canada
244 inset **Hillside** Shetland Scotland UK
425 M8 **Hillston** NSW Australia
131 K2 **Hillsville** Virginia USA
245 F4 **Hilltown** Ireland
126 I7 **Hillview** Kentucky USA
244 inset **Hillwell** Shetland Scotland UK
128 inset **Hilo** Hawai'i USA
241 G2 **Hilton** Cambridgeshire England UK
241 E4 **Hilton** Dorset England UK
131 K4 **Hilton Head Island** South Carolina USA
436 U2 **Hilton Inlet** *bay* Antarctica
392 D4 **Himachal Pradesh** *admin. area* India
378 E2 **Himalaya** *range* Asia
223 M4 **Himanka** Finland
235 A5 **Himarë** Albania
422 F5 **Himatangi Beach** New Zealand
392 C6 **Himatnagar** Gujarat India
386 F5 **Hime-shima** *island* Japan
387 H4 **Himi** Japan
302 F5 **Himora** Ethiopia
394 F6 **Ḥimş** Syria
374 C3 **Hinako** *island* Indonesia
305 G2 **Hinalé** Cameroon
377 J5 **Hinatuan** Philippines
234 F2 **Hinceşti** Moldova
135 F3 **Hinche** Haiti
425 M4 **Hinchinbrook Island** Qld Australia
241 F2 **Hinckley** Leicester England UK
126 E3 **Hinckley** Minnesota USA
305 G5 **Hinda** Congo
392 D5 **Hindaun** Rajasthan India
241 H2 **Hinderclay** Suffolk England UK
241 G3 **Hindhead** Surrey England UK
126 J8 **Hindman** Kentucky USA
423 D7 **Hinds** New Zealand
123 J8 **Hinds Lake** Newfoundland and Labrador Canada
224 H4 **Hindsen** *lake* Sweden
389 K7 **Hindu Kush** *range* Afghanistan
393 D9 **Hindupur** Andhra Pradesh India
124 F5 **Hines** Oregon USA
118 L4 **Hines Creek** Alberta Canada
131 K5 **Hinesville** Georgia USA
393 E7 **Hinganghat** Maharashtra India
125 J2 **Hingham** Montana USA
393 D7 **Hingoli** Maharashtra India
394 G5 **Hinis** Turkey
225 K1 **Hinjärv** *lake* Finland
222 L5 **Hinjärvträsket** *lake* Finland
224 F4 **Hinnerup** Denmark
222 J2 **Hinnøya** *island* Norway
222 K5 **Hinnsjön** *lake* Sweden
377 I5 **Hinoba-an** Philippines
230 D4 **Hinojosa del Duque** Spain
224 I2 **Hinsen** *lake* Sweden
232 F3 **Hinterstoder** Austria
376 B3 **Hinthada (Henzada)** Myanmar
118 M6 **Hinton** Alberta Canada
130 B3 **Hinton** Oklahoma USA
241 H2 **Hinxton** Cambridgeshire England UK
386 F5 **Hirado-shima** *island* Japan
240 C3 **Hiraeth** Carmarthenshire Wales UK
393 F7 **Hirakud Reservoir** Orissa India
307 F4 **Hiraman** *watercourse* Kenya
392 G6 **Hiranpur** Jharkhand India
381 J4 **Hirara** Japan
307 G2 **Hirna** Ethiopia
240 D2 **Hirnant** Powys Wales UK
387 I3 **Hirosaki** Japan
386 G4 **Hiroshima** Japan
232 D2 **Hirschau** Germany
226 C3 **Hirson** France
234 E3 **Hirşova** Romania
234 F2 **Hirtop** Moldova
224 E4 **Hirtshals** Denmark
223 P3 **Hirvasvaara** Finland
392 D5 **Hisar** Haryana India
235 F6 **Hisarcık** Turkey
384 E3 **Hishigunder** Mongolia
373 H6 **Hisiu** Papua New Guinea
135 G2 **Hispaniola** *island* Caribbean
391 M2 **Hispar Glacier** Pakistan
222 L5 **Hissjön** Sweden
390 E2 **Hit** Iraq
386 F5 **Hita** Japan
387 I4 **Hitachi** Japan
387 I4 **Hitachinaka** Japan
241 G3 **Hitchen** Hertfordshire England UK
155 G3 **Hitia** Guyana
427 14a **Hitiaa** French Polynesia
238 C2 **Hitola** Russian Federation
222 F5 **Hitra** *island* Norway
125 Q3 **Hitterdal** Minnesota USA
226 F1 **Hitzacker** Germany
426 7 **Hiu** *island* Vanuatu
427 14 **Hiva Oa** *island* French Polynesia
121 S5 **Hiver, Lac de l'** *lake* Québec Canada
131 I3 **Hiwassee Lake** Virginia USA
118 J6 **Hixon** British Columbia Canada
241 F2 **Hixon** Staffordshire England UK
131 J5 **Hixtown Swamp** Florida USA
222 L4 **Hjäggböleliden** Sweden
224 F4 **Hjallerup** Denmark
119 Q2 **Hjalmar Lake** Northwest Territories Canada
224 H3 **Hjälmaren** *bay* Sweden
222 inset **Hjalteyri** Iceland
222 I3 **Hjartøya** *island* Norway
222 E6 **Hjelle** Norway
224 F4 **Hjelm** *island* Denmark
224 G5 **Hjelm Bugt** *bay* Denmark
224 D3 **Hjelmeland** Norway
223 N1 **Hjelmsøya** *island* Norway
224 E4 **Hjemitslev** Denmark
222 F5 **Hjerkinn** Norway
224 F4 **Hjørring** Denmark
222 E5 **Hjørungavåg** Norway
376 C3 **Hlaingbwe** Myanmar
234 F3 **Hlavani** Ukraine
376 C3 **Hlegu** Myanmar
234 F2 **Hlinaia** Moldova
227 H3 **Hlinsko** Czech Republic
222 inset **Hlíðarendi** Iceland
227 I3 **Hlohovec** Slovakia
308 E5 **Hlotse** Lesotho
394 E2 **Hlukhiv** Ukraine
234 D1 **Hlyboka** Ukraine
225 N5 **Hlybokaye** Belarus
379 G4 **Hnahthial** Mizoram India
120 G7 **Hnausa** Manitoba Canada
227 J3 **Hnúšťa** Slovakia
304 E3 **Ho** Ghana
376 E5 **Hồ Chí Minh (Saigon)** Vietnam
423 7 **Ho Ho Bay** Snares Islands New Zealand
376 E2 **Hồ Thác Bà** *lake* Vietnam
376 E5 **Hồ Tri an** *watercourse* Vietnam
376 E3 **Hồ Xá** Vietnam
376 E2 **Hòa Bình** Vietnam
308 C4 **Hoachanas** Namibia
308 B3 **Hoanib** *watercourse* Namibia
425 M10 **Hobart** Tas. Australia
130 B3 **Hobart** Oklahoma USA
129 K4 **Hobbs** New Mexico USA
436 O2 **Hobbs Bank** *underwater feature* Amundsen Sea
436 P1 **Hobbs Coast** Antarctica
437 E2 **Hobbs Islands** Antarctica
154 C4 **Hobo** Colombia
224 E4 **Hobro** Denmark
125 K3 **Hobson** Montana USA
131 I4 **Hobson City** Alabama USA
118 K6 **Hobson Lake** British Columbia Canada
307 H2 **Hobyo** Somalia
133 H4 **Hocabá** Mexico
232 C2 **Hochdorf** Germany
308 C4 **Hochfeld** Namibia
226 G4 **Hochgall** *mountain* Italy
386 F3 **Hŏch'ŏn** North Korea
119 W5 **Hockin** Manitoba Canada
234 C1 **Hoczew** Poland
241 G3 **Hoddesdon** Hertfordshire England UK
126 I8 **Hodgenville** Kentucky USA
119 R7 **Hodgeville** Saskatchewan Canada
425 J4 **Hodgson** *watercourse* NT Australia
227 K4 **Hódmezővásárhely** Hungary
307 H1 **Hodmo** *watercourse* Somalia
386 E3 **Hoeyang** North Korea
229 J1 **Hof** Germany
229 I1 **Hofbieber** Germany
222 G4 **Hoffstad** Norway
226 F2 **Hofheim** Germany
222 G4 **Hofles** Norway
308 E6 **Hofmeyr** South Africa
222 inset **Höfn** Iceland
224 I2 **Hofors** Sweden
222 inset **Hofsá** *watercourse* Iceland
222 inset **Hofsjökull** *mountain* Iceland
222 inset **Hofsós** Iceland
386 F4 **Hofu** Japan
222 inset **Höfuðborgarsvæði** *admin. area* Iceland
127 N8 **Hog Island Bay** Virginia USA
163 18 **Hog Point** Antigua and Barbuda
224 G4 **Höganäs** Sweden
424 I3 **Hogarth, Mount** NT Australia
119 Q8 **Hogeland** Montana USA
244 A3 **Hogha Gearraidh** Na h-Eileanan Siar Scotland UK
222 K4 **Högheden** Sweden
222 I4 **Högland** Sweden
224 H3 **Högsjö** Sweden
243 I3 **Hogsthorpe** Lincolnshire England UK
135 F2 **Hogsty Reef** Bahamas
222 H5 **Högvålen** Sweden
383 K3 **Hoh Nuur** *lake* Mongolia
383 I6 **Hoh Xil Shan** *range* Xizang Zizhiqu China
383 K6 **Hoh Yanhu** *lake* Qinghai China
226 E4 **Hohe Freschen** *mountain* Austria
226 F3 **Hohenlinden** Germany
229 K1 **Hohenthurm** Germany
226 G4 **Hoher Dachstein** *mountain* Austria
384 G5 **Hohhot** Nei Mongol Zizhiqu China
224 E5 **Hohn** Germany
304 E3 **Hohoe** Ghana
376 F4 **Hội An** Vietnam
379 G3 **Hojai** Assam India
422 E2 **Hokianga Harbour** New Zealand
423 F5 **Hokio Beach** New Zealand
423 D6 **Hokitika** New Zealand
423 D6 **Hokitika** *watercourse* New Zealand
387 I2 **Hokkaidō** *island* Japan
224 H4 **Hökön** Sweden
423 C8 **Hokonui Hills** New Zealand
222 J2 **Hol** Norway
224 E2 **Hol** Norway
224 G4 **Hol** Sweden
158 D3 **Holanda** Bolivia
159 E4 **Holanda** Bolivia
222 inset **Hólar** Iceland
241 H2 **Holbeach** Lincolnshire England UK
118 G7 **Holberg** British Columbia Canada
383 K2 **Holboo Nuur** *lake* Mongolia
241 H3 **Holborough** Kent England UK
425 M8 **Holbrook** NSW Australia
128 G3 **Holbrook** Arizona USA
125 P6 **Holbrook** Nebraska USA
125 O8 **Holcomb** Kansas USA
222 G4 **Holden** *lake* Norway
243 F3 **Holden** Lancashire England UK
124 I7 **Holden** Utah USA
222 H4 **Holdern** *lake* Sweden
243 H3 **Holderness** *cape* England UK

162 C3 **Holdich** Argentina
135 J4 **Holetown** Barbados
134 E2 **Holguín** Cuba
134 E2 **Holguín** admin. area Cuba
227 I3 **Holíč** Slovakia
227 H2 **Holice** Czech Republic
126 G2 **Holinshead Lake** Ontario Canada
224 G2 **Höljes** Sweden
224 G2 **Höljessjön** lake Sweden
240 C4 **Hollacombe** Devon England UK
119 V8 **Holland** Manitoba Canada
244 F1 **Holland** Orkney Islands Scotland UK
126 H5 **Holland** Michigan USA
374 D4 **Holland Village** admin. area Singapore
244 F1 **Hollandstoun** Orkney Islands Scotland UK
226 F1 **Holle** Germany
224 D3 **Høllen** Norway
241 I2 **Hollesley Bay** England UK
229 J2 **Hollfeld** Germany
436 T2 **Hollick-Kenyon Peninsula** Antarctica
436 Q1 **Hollick-Kenyon Plateau** Antarctica
130 B4 **Holliday** Texas USA
241 H4 **Hollington** East Sussex England UK
130 B3 **Hollis** Oklahoma USA
124 E8 **Hollister** California USA
124 H5 **Hollister** Idaho USA
126 E8 **Hollister** Missouri USA
222 L4 **Hollsvattnet** lake Sweden
226 C1 **Hollum** Netherlands
224 G5 **Höllviken** bay Sweden
125 N7 **Holly** Colorado USA
131 K6 **Holly Hill** Florida USA
131 L3 **Holly Hill** South Carolina USA
131 M3 **Holly Ridge** North Carolina USA
130 G3 **Holly Springs** Mississippi USA
244 D5 **Hollybush** East Ayrshire Scotland UK
423 C7 **Hollyford** New Zealand
423 C7 **Hollyford** watercourse New Zealand
243 I3 **Hollym** East Riding of Yorkshire England UK
245 C3 **Hollymount** Ireland
131 K7 **Hollywood** Florida USA
223 M5 **Holm** Finland
222 H4 **Holm** Norway
222 J5 **Holm** Sweden
224 I4 **Holm** Sweden
234 F2 **Hol'ma** Ukraine
116 H4 **Holman** Northwest Territories Canada
224 D3 **Holmavatn** lake Norway
222 inset **Hólmavík** Iceland
241 G2 **Holme** Cambridgeshire England UK
241 G1 **Holme** Nottinghamshire England UK
437 E2 **Holme Bay** Antarctica
240 E2 **Holme Lacy** Herefordshire England UK
241 H2 **Holme next the Sea** Norfolk England UK
121 T5 **Holmer, Lac** lake Québec Canada
425 N4 **Holmes Reef** Coral Sea Islands Territory Australia
240 A2 **Holmestown** Ireland
243 G3 **Holmfirth** West Yorkshire England UK
222 K4 **Holmfors** Sweden
222 L5 **Holmön** Sweden
222 L5 **Holmön** island Sweden
222 J5 **Holmsjön** bay Sweden
222 I5 **Holmsjön** lake Sweden
222 L5 **Holmsund** Sweden
222 L4 **Holmträsk** Sweden
240 D4 **Holne** Devon England UK
390 C3 **Holon** Israel
308 C5 **Holoog** Namibia
234 G1 **Holovanivs'k** Ukraine
222 G5 **Holøydal** Norway
226 C2 **Holsbeek** Belgium
224 D2 **Holskarvatnet** lake Norway
224 C2 **Holsnøy** island Norway
224 E5 **Holsted** Denmark
131 J2 **Holston** watercourse Tennessee USA
240 C4 **Holsworthy** Devon England UK
222 K2 **Holt** Norway
240 E1 **Holt** Cheshire England UK
241 I2 **Holt** Norfolk England UK
424 F8 **Holt Rock** WA Australia
122 J5 **Holton** Newfoundland and Labrador Canada
222 G5 **Holtsjøen** lake Norway
128 E4 **Holtville** California USA
241 G2 **Holwell** Leicester England UK
226 C1 **Holwerd** Netherlands
242 D3 **Holy Island** England UK
244 D5 **Holy Island** Scotland UK
241 G3 **Holybourne** Hampshire England UK
245 E4 **Holycross** Ireland
242 D3 **Holyhead** Isle of Anglesey Wales UK
242 D3 **Holyhead Bay** Wales UK
125 N6 **Holyoke** Colorado USA
127 O5 **Holyoke** Massachusetts USA
129 M1 **Holyrood** Kansas USA
243 F1 **Holystone** Northumberland England UK
240 B4 **Holywell** Cornwall England UK
242 E3 **Holywell** Flintshire Wales UK
226 E2 **Holzminden** Germany
307 E4 **Homa Bay** Kenya
379 H4 **Homalin** Myanmar
118 I7 **Homathko** watercourse British Columbia Canada
118 I7 **Homathko Icefield** British Columbia Canada
390 G3 **Homāyunshahr** Iran
301 F5 **Hombori** Mali
229 H2 **Homburg** Germany
117 M5 **Home Bay** Nunavut Canada
121 W2 **Home Island** Newfoundland and Labrador Canada
424 inset **Home Island** Cocos (Keeling) Islands Australia
131 J5 **Homeland** Georgia USA
116 D7 **Homer** Alaska USA
130 E4 **Homer** Louisiana USA
126 I5 **Homer** Michigan USA
241 I2 **Homersfield** Norfolk England UK
131 J5 **Homerville** Georgia USA
131 K8 **Homestead** Florida USA
222 H4 **Hommelstø** Norway
222 G5 **Hommelvik** Norway
393 D8 **Homnabad** Karnataka India
234 E2 **Homocea** Romania
133 J2 **Homosassa Bay** Florida USA
228 F5 **Homps** France
394 D2 **Homyel'** Belarus
394 D2 **Homyel'skaya Voblasts'** admin. area Belarus
222 J5 **Hömyra** Sweden
230 F6 **Honaine** Algeria
127 K8 **Honaker** Virginia USA
128 inset **Hōnaunau** Hawai'i USA
393 D8 **Honavar** Karnataka India
154 C3 **Honda** Colombia
154 C1 **Honda, Bahía** bay Colombia
377 H5 **Honda Bay** Philippines
308 C6 **Hondeklipbaai** South Africa
119 N5 **Hondo** Alberta Canada
386 F5 **Hondo** Japan
129 J4 **Hondo** watercourse New Mexico USA
130 B6 **Hondo** Texas USA
134 C4 **Honduras** country Central America
134 C3 **Honduras, Gulf of** Honduras
119 U4 **Hone** Manitoba Canada
224 F2 **Hønefoss** Norway
423 9 **Honey, Mount** Campbell Island New Zealand
124 E6 **Honey Lake** California USA
228 E2 **Honfleur** France
386 E4 **Hong-do** island South Korea
381 G1 **Hong He** watercourse Henan China
381 G4 **Hong Kong (Xianggang)** Hong Kong (XIANGGANG) S.A.R. China
381 G4 **Hong Kong (Xianggang) S.A.R.** admin. area China
379 I5 **Hong Ton** Myanmar
381 G2 **Hong'an** Hubei China
381 G2 **Honghu** Hubei China
380 F3 **Hongjiang** Hunan China
380 E1 **Hongliuwan** Gansu China
381 G3 **Hongmen Shuiku** lake Jiangxi China
385 I6 **Hongning** Shandong China
380 F4 **Hongshui He** watercourse Guangxi Zhuangzu Zizhiqu China
384 G6 **Hongtong** Shanxi China
123 F8 **Honguedo, Détroit d'** strait Québec Canada
386 E3 **Hongwŏn** North Korea
381 H1 **Hongze Hu** lake Jiangsu China
426 8a **Honiara** Solomon Islands
240 D4 **Honiton** Devon England UK
393 D8 **Honnali** Karnataka India
223 O1 **Honningsvåg** Norway
128 inset **Honoka'a** Hawai'i USA
128 inset **Honolulu** Hawai'i USA
128 inset **Honomū** Hawai'i USA
230 E4 **Honrubia** Spain
387 I4 **Honshū** island Japan
128 inset **Honu'apo** Hawai'i USA
124 E4 **Hood, Mount** volcano Oregon USA
373 H6 **Hood Point** Papua New Guinea
224 E5 **Hooge** island Germany
119 M3 **Hoohey Creek** Alberta Canada
245 F4 **Hook Head** cape Ireland
121 N5 **Hook Point** Ontario Canada
130 D4 **Hooks** Texas USA
116 F7 **Hoonah** Alaska USA
125 M8 **Hooper** Colorado USA
116 C6 **Hooper Bay** Alaska USA
125 Q2 **Hoople** North Dakota USA
308 E5 **Hoopstad** South Africa
130 H4 **Hoover** Alabama USA
394 G5 **Hopa** Turkey
118 K8 **Hope** British Columbia Canada
243 G3 **Hope** Derbyshire England UK
240 D4 **Hope** Devon England UK
130 E4 **Hope** Arkansas USA
129 N1 **Hope** Kansas USA
129 J4 **Hope** New Mexico USA
424 G8 **Hope, Lake** WA Australia
244 D2 **Hope, Loch** lake Scotland UK
116 C5 **Hope, Point** Alaska USA
131 L3 **Hope Mills** North Carolina USA
240 E2 **Hope under Dinmore** Herefordshire England UK
122 H5 **Hopedale** Newfoundland and Labrador Canada
133 H5 **Hopelchén** Mexico
236 G3 **Hopen** island Norway
121 U3 **Hopes Advance, Baie** bay Québec Canada
425 L8 **Hopetoun** Vic. Australia
424 G8 **Hopetoun** WA Australia
308 D5 **Hopetown** South Africa
127 M8 **Hopewell** Virginia USA
121 P3 **Hopewell Islands** Nunavut Canada
226 G4 **Hopfgarten** Austria
423 C7 **Hopkins** watercourse New Zealand
424 H6 **Hopkins, Lake** WA Australia
241 I2 **Hopton** Norfolk England UK
241 E2 **Hopton** Staffordshire England UK
308 B2 **Hoque** Angola
124 D3 **Hoquiam** Washington USA
394 G5 **Horasan** Turkey
130 D4 **Horatio** Arkansas USA
226 E3 **Horb am Neckar** Germany
224 G5 **Hörby** Sweden
230 D4 **Horcajo de los Montes** Spain
228 F1 **Hordain** France
224 D2 **Hordaland** admin. area Norway
240 C2 **Horeb** Ceredigion Wales UK
234 C3 **Horezu** Romania
394 F6 **Horgaz** Turkey
383 H3 **Horgo Nuur** lake Mongolia
234 A2 **Horgoš** Serbia
234 D1 **Horhany** range Ukraine
234 F3 **Horia** Romania
156 E4 **Horizonte** Brazil
158 D3 **Horizonte** Brazil
241 H3 **Horkesley Heath** Essex England UK
241 G3 **Horley** Surrey England UK
436 Q1 **Horlick Mountains** Antarctica
391 I3 **Hormak** Iran
158 B3 **Hormigas de Afuera, Islas** islands Peru
391 H4 **Hormoz, Jazireh-ye** island Iran
391 H4 **Hormozgān** admin. area Iran
391 H4 **Hormuz, Strait of** Middle East
227 H3 **Horn** Austria
118 M2 **Horn** watercourse Northwest Territories Canada
222 inset **Horn** cape Iceland
222 H4 **Horn** Norway
224 F2 **Horn** Norway
224 H4 **Horn** Sweden
Horn, Cape see **Hornos, Cabo de** Chile
245 E1 **Horn Head** cape Ireland
118 L1 **Horn Plateau** Northwest Territories Canada
227 K3 **Hornád** watercourse Slovakia
222 inset **Hornafjörður** bay Iceland
222 J3 **Hornavan** bay Sweden
243 H3 **Horncastle** Lincolnshire England UK
222 I3 **Horndal** Norway
240 C4 **Horndon** Devon England UK
427 12 **Horne, Îles** islands Wallis and Futuna
222 K5 **Hörnefors** Sweden
118 L1 **Hornell Lake** Northwest Territories Canada
126 I2 **Hornepayne** Ontario Canada
227 I3 **Horní Benešov** Czech Republic
226 G3 **Horní Bříza** Czech Republic
227 I2 **Horní Jelení** Czech Republic
229 K1 **Horní Jiřetín** Czech Republic
227 H3 **Horní Planá** Czech Republic
222 E6 **Hornindal** Norway
127 I2 **Horning** Norfolk England UK
158 D5 **Horno Chico** Peru
222 J5 **Hornön** Sweden
132 C3 **Hornos** Mexico
162 C6 **Hornos, Cabo de (Cape Horn)** cape Chile
162 C6 **Hornos, Falso Cabo de** cape Chile
162 C6 **Hornos, Isla** island Chile
228 E2 **Hornoy** France
243 H3 **Hornsea** East Riding of Yorkshire England UK
222 J4 **Hornsjö** Sweden
222 K5 **Hörnsjö** Sweden
224 I2 **Hornslandet** cape Sweden
234 F3 **Horodnye** Ukraine
234 G1 **Horodyshche** Ukraine
155 G3 **Horobo** Guyana
385 G3 **Horovlin** Mongolia
161 G2 **Horqueta** Paraguay
240 C4 **Horrabridge** Devon England UK
224 G2 **Horrmunden** lake Sweden
424 inset **Horsburgh Island (Luar)** Cocos (Keeling) Islands Australia
126 I8 **Horse Cave** Kentucky USA
119 V6 **Horse Island** Manitoba Canada
123 K7 **Horse Islands** Newfoundland and Labrador Canada
124 E6 **Horse Lake** California USA
240 C4 **Horsebridge** Devon England UK
118 K6 **Horsefly Lake** British Columbia Canada
245 D3 **Horseleap** Ireland
224 E5 **Horsens** Denmark
124 G5 **Horseshoe Bend** Idaho USA
120 J6 **Horseshoe Lake** Ontario Canada
76 Q6 **Horseshoe Seamounts** underwater feature Atlantic Ocean
425 L9 **Horsham** Vic. Australia
241 G3 **Horsham** West Sussex England UK
226 D1 **Horst** Netherlands
226 D2 **Hörstel** Germany
310 1 **Horta** Azores
224 F3 **Horten** Norway
224 H1 **Horten** lake Sweden
116 G5 **Horton** watercourse Northwest Territories Canada
243 F3 **Horton** Lancashire England UK
126 D7 **Horton** Kansas USA
116 G5 **Horton Lake** Northwest Territories Canada
227 H5 **Horvati** Croatia
227 I4 **Horvátzsidány** Hungary
127 J2 **Horwood Lake** Ontario Canada
394 C2 **Horyn** watercourse Ukraine
307 F2 **Hosai'na K'olito** Ethiopia
241 G2 **Hose** Leicester England UK
375 G3 **Hose, Pegunungan** range Malaysia
224 F2 **Hosen** Norway
391 I3 **Hoseynābād** Iran
393 D6 **Hoshangabad** Madhya Pradesh India
393 D4 **Hoshiarpur** Punjab India
302 F4 **Hoshib** watercourse Sudan
393 D8 **Hospet** Karnataka India
230 D2 **Hospital de Orbigo** Spain
223 P4 **Hossa** Finland
222 K5 **Hössjö** Sweden
162 C6 **Hoste, Isla** island Chile
227 L3 **Hostovice** Slovakia
222 H6 **Höstsätern** Sweden
393 D8 **Hosur** Karnataka India
124 G7 **Hot Creek Range** Nevada USA
130 E3 **Hot Springs** Arkansas USA
124 H3 **Hot Springs** Montana USA
131 J3 **Hot Springs** North Carolina USA
125 N5 **Hot Springs** South Dakota USA
222 I5 **Hotagen** lake Sweden
222 I4 **Hotagsfjällen** island Sweden
387 H4 **Hotaka-dake** volcano Japan
382 F5 **Hotan He** lake Xinjiang Uygur Zizhiqu China
308 D5 **Hotazel** South Africa
118 M4 **Hotchkiss** Alberta Canada
125 L7 **Hotchkiss** Colorado USA
222 J4 **Hoting** Sweden
383 H3 **Hoton Nuur** lake Mongolia
384 E3 **Hotont** Mongolia
77 Q11 **Hotspur Fracture Zone** underwater feature Atlantic Ocean
77 O11 **Hotspur Seamount** underwater feature Atlantic Ocean
116 H5 **Hottah Lake** Northwest Territories Canada
135 F3 **Hotte, Massif de la** range Haiti
308 B5 **Hottentot Bay** bay Namibia
163 5 **Hotuiti** cape Isla de Pascua (Easter Island)
228 C3 **Houat, Île d'** island France
376 D2 **Houayxay** Laos
244 inset **Houbie** Shetland Scotland UK
228 E2 **Houdan** France
226 C3 **Houdelaincourt** France
244 D5 **Houdston** South Ayrshire Scotland UK
228 E4 **Houeillès** France
374 D3 **Hougang** admin. area Singapore
241 G4 **Houghton** West Sussex England UK
126 G3 **Houghton** Michigan USA
126 I4 **Houghton Lake** Michigan USA
422 E2 **Houhora Heads** New Zealand
127 R3 **Houlton** Maine USA
384 G6 **Houma** Shanxi China
427 10a **Houma** Tonga
130 F6 **Houma** Louisiana USA
241 G3 **Hounslow** Greater London England UK
228 D4 **Hourtin et de Carcans, Étang d'** lake France
124 I7 **House Range** Utah USA
244 F1 **Housebay** Orkney Islands Scotland UK
244 inset **Housetter** Shetland Scotland UK
118 H5 **Houston** British Columbia Canada
126 F8 **Houston** Missouri USA
130 D6 **Houston** Texas USA
130 D6 **Houston, Lake** Texas USA
130 D5 **Houston County Lake** Texas USA
121 O6 **Houston Point** Nunavut Canada
424 E7 **Houtman Abrolhos** reef WA Australia
244 E2 **Houton** Orkney Islands Scotland UK
226 C2 **Houyet** Belgium
222 H3 **Hov** Norway
224 F2 **Hov** Norway
234 D1 **Hova Hoverla** mountain Ukraine
383 I2 **Hovd** Mongolia
383 I3 **Hovd** Mongolia
383 H3 **Hovd** Mongolia
383 I3 **Hovd** admin. area Mongolia
224 D3 **Hovda** Norway
222 I2 **Hovden** Norway
224 D3 **Hovden** Norway
224 C2 **Hovden** island Norway
241 G4 **Hove** Brighton and Hove England UK
224 F4 **Hovedstaden** admin. area Denmark
243 I2 **Hoveton** Norfolk England UK
435 G1 **Hovgaard Ridge** underwater feature Greenland Sea
223 M3 **Hovlössjön** lake Sweden
222 F6 **Hovringen** Norway
384 G4 **Hövsgöl** Mongolia
383 K2 **Hövsgöl** admin. area Mongolia
384 D2 **Hövsgöl Nuur** lake Mongolia
384 E4 **Hövüün** Mongolia
302 D4 **Howar, Wādi** watercourse Sudan
125 Q5 **Howard** South Dakota USA
126 G4 **Howard** Wisconsin USA
129 L3 **Howardwick** Texas USA
243 H3 **Howden** East Riding of Yorkshire England UK
130 D3 **Howe** Oklahoma USA
425 N9 **Howe, Cape** NSW Australia
310 6b **Howe, Île** island French Southern and Antarctic Lands
436 O1 **Howe, Mount** mountain Antarctica
126 E1 **Howey** Powys Wales UK
308 F5 **Howick** South Africa
243 G1 **Howick** Northumberland England UK
127 Q4 **Howland** Maine USA
426 1 **Howland Island** USA territory Pacific Ocean
243 H2 **Howsham** North Yorkshire England UK
245 F3 **Howth** Ireland
125 O7 **Hoxie** Kansas USA
226 E2 **Höxter** Germany
244 E2 **Hoy** island Scotland UK
226 E1 **Hoya** Germany
159 E6 **Hoyada** Bolivia
226 F2 **Hoym** Germany
306 D3 **Hoyo, Mount** mountain Democratic Republic of Congo
162 B3 **Hoyo de Epuyén** Argentina
223 P5 **Höytiäinen** lake Finland
376 C3 **Hpa-an** Myanmar
227 H2 **Hradec Králové** Czech Republic
232 G2 **Hranice** Czech Republic
232 F3 **Hrastnik** Slovenia
227 I4 **Hrastovsko** Croatia
222 inset **Hraunhafnartangi** cape Iceland
227 H5 **Hreljin** Croatia
234 F1 **Hristovaia** Moldova
394 B2 **Hrodna** Belarus
394 C2 **Hrodzyenskaya Voblasts'** admin. area Belarus
227 J3 **Hron** watercourse Slovakia
227 L2 **Hrubieszów** Poland
234 A1 **Hruštín** Slovakia
227 I5 **Hrvatska Dubica** Croatia
234 D2 **Hrynyava** Ukraine
379 H4 **Hsenwi** Myanmar
381 H4 **Hsi-Lo Chi** lake Taiwan China
381 H4 **Hsinchu** Taiwan China
380 D4 **Hsing-Yun Hu** lake Yunnan China
381 H4 **Hsinying** Taiwan China
379 H4 **Hsipaw** Myanmar
379 H5 **Hsisaing** Myanmar
381 I4 **Hsuen Shan** mountain Taiwan China
379 G4 **Htantalang** Myanmar
379 H5 **Hti lin** Myanmar
376 C4 **Hua Hin** Thailand
381 H4 **Hua Hsu** island Taiwan China
308 B4 **Huab** watercourse Namibia
154 A5 **Huaca, Punta La** cape Ecuador
159 F4 **Huacaraje** Bolivia
158 D5 **Huachacalla** Bolivia
159 F4 **Huachi, Laguna** lake Bolivia
158 C3 **Huachicña** Peru
129 H5 **Huachinera** Mexico
158 B3 **Huacho** Peru
128 G5 **Huachuca City** Arizona USA
158 B3 **Huacrachuco** Peru
385 H4 **Huade** Nei Mongol Zizhiqu China
385 K4 **Huadian** Jilin China
381 H3 **Huafeng** Fujian China
380 D2 **Huahai** Sichuan China
381 H2 **Huai He** watercourse Anhui China
381 G2 **Huai He** watercourse Jiangsu China
381 H1 **Huai'an** Jiangsu China
381 G1 **Huaibin** Henan China
380 F3 **Huaihua** Hunan China
381 H2 **Huainan** Anhui China
385 H5 **Huaiyang** Hebei China
381 H1 **Huaiyin** Jiangsu China
381 H2 **Huaiyuan** Anhui China
133 F5 **Huajuapan de León** Mexico
129 H6 **Huajumar** Mexico
372 C5 **Huaki** Indonesia
158 D4 **Hualca Hualca, Nevado** mountain Peru
158 C3 **Hualcará, Cerro** mountain Peru
160 E3 **Hualfín** Argentina
381 I4 **Hualien** Taiwan China
158 B3 **Huallaga** watercourse Peru
158 B2 **Huamachuco** Peru
308 C2 **Huambo** Angola
308 C2 **Huambo** admin. area Angola
385 L3 **Huanan** Heilongjiang China
158 B2 **Huancabamba** Peru
162 B3 **Huancache, Sierra** range Argentina
158 C4 **Huancaray** Peru
158 C4 **Huancavelica** Peru
158 C4 **Huancayo** Peru
159 F4 **Huanchaca** Bolivia
159 F4 **Huanchaca, Serranía de** range Bolivia
384 F6 **Huancheng** Gansu China
381 H2 **Huanfeng** Anhui China
381 G1 **Huang He** watercourse Henan China
381 F1 **Huang He** watercourse Jiangsu China
384 F5 **Huang He** watercourse Nei Mongol Zizhiqu China
383 K6 **Huang He** watercourse Qinghai China
385 I5 **Huang He** watercourse Shandong China
380 D1 **Huang He** watercourse Sichuan China
381 H2 **Huang Shan** range Anhui China
381 G2 **Huangchuan** Henan China
385 H5 **Huangcun** Beijing China
381 G4 **Huangguang** Guangdong China
381 H4 **Huanggang Shan** mountain Jiangxi China
385 I5 **Huanghua** Hebei China
380 F4 **Huanghua He** watercourse Guangxi Zhuangzu Zizhiqu China
381 G3 **Huangjianyu** mountain Fujian China
380 D3 **Huangni He** watercourse Yunnan China
381 H2 **Huangshan** Anhui China
380 D2 **Huangshengguan** Sichuan China
381 G2 **Huangshi** Hubei China
160 E6 **Huanguelén** Argentina
384 E6 **Huangyuan** Qinghai China
385 G5 **Huangzhai** Shanxi China
158 C4 **Huanipaca** Peru
385 K4 **Huanren** Liaoning China
158 C4 **Huanta** Peru
160 D6 **Huantraicó, Sierra de** range Argentina
158 B3 **Huánuco** Peru
158 B3 **Huánuco** admin. area Peru
158 E5 **Huanuni** Bolivia
160 D1 **Huara** Chile
158 B3 **Huaraz** Peru
158 B3 **Huarmey** Peru
158 B3 **Huarmey, Bahía** bay Peru
158 B4 **Huarochirí** Peru
158 B1 **Huasaga** Peru
154 B5 **Huasaga** watercourse Peru
158 C2 **Huáscar** Peru
160 D4 **Huasco** Chile
160 D4 **Huasco** watercourse Chile
132 C3 **Huatabampo** Mexico
158 C4 **Huataca** Peru
133 F6 **Huatulco** Mexico
159 E4 **Huatunas, Laguna** lake Bolivia
154 D1 **Huauáriuaha** Colombia
158 B3 **Huaura** Peru
158 B3 **Huaura, Grupo de** island Peru
158 B3 **Huayán** Peru
381 H2 **Huayang** Anhui China
380 F1 **Huayin** Shaanxi China
158 C4 **Huayllampi** Peru
158 C4 **Huaytane, Cerro** mountain Peru
381 G2 **Huayuan** Hubei China
380 F3 **Huayuan** Hunan China
159 E5 **Huayurí** Bolivia
384 E6 **Huazang** Gansu China
380 F4 **Huazhou** Guangdong China
126 F5 **Hubbard** Iowa USA
118 B2 **Hubbard, Mount** Yukon Territory Canada
121 V3 **Hubbard, Pointe** Québec Canada
130 B4 **Hubbard Creek Lake** Texas USA
119 X3 **Hubbart Point** Manitoba Canada
381 F2 **Hubei** admin. area China
393 D8 **Hubli** Karnataka India
234 F1 **Hubnyk** Ukraine
160 E6 **Hucal** Argentina
160 E6 **Hucal, Valle de** valley Argentina
241 F1 **Hucknall** Nottinghamshire England UK
228 F2 **Hucqueliers** France
391 H2 **Hūdar** Iran
243 G3 **Huddersfield** West Yorkshire England UK
385 J3 **Huder** Nei Mongol Zizhiqu China
384 F2 **Huder** Mongolia
224 I2 **Hudiksvall** Sweden
225 N2 **Hudöfjärden** bay Finland
129 M1 **Hudson** Kansas USA
130 D5 **Hudson** Texas USA
125 K5 **Hudson** Wyoming USA
437 K2 **Hudson, Cape** Antarctica
126 D8 **Hudson, Lake** Oklahoma USA
119 Y2 **Hudson Bay** Canada
119 T6 **Hudson Bay** Saskatchewan Canada
127 O5 **Hudson Falls** New York USA
117 Q4 **Hudson Land** plain Greenland
436 R2 **Hudson Mountains** Antarctica
121 S1 **Hudson Strait** Nunavut/Québec Canada
118 J5 **Hudson's Hope** British Columbia Canada
120 H6 **Hudwin Lake** Manitoba Canada
376 E3 **Huế** Vietnam
230 C3 **Huebra** watercourse Spain
162 B2 **Huechulafquén, Lago** lake Argentina
234 C2 **Huedin** Romania
134 B4 **Huehuetenango** Guatemala
132 E4 **Huejuquilla** Mexico
230 E5 **Huelma** Spain
230 C5 **Huelva** Spain
230 E5 **Huéneja** Spain
162 A3 **Huentemó** Chile
230 E5 **Huércal de Almería** Spain
159 E6 **Huerta** Bolivia
132 C3 **Huerta Vieja** Mexico
231 F4 **Huertas, Cabo de las** cape Spain
231 F3 **Huerva** watercourse Spain
230 E5 **Huesa** Spain
231 F2 **Huesca** Spain
163 6a **Huesco Ballena, Punta** cape Isla Róbinson Crusoe
132 E5 **Huetamo de Núñez** Mexico
230 E3 **Huete** Spain
162 A2 **Hueyelhue, Punta** cape Chile
230 D5 **Huezna, Embalse de** lake Spain
302 E5 **Hufeira** Sudan
224 C2 **Huftarøy** island Norway
243 H3 **Huggate** East Riding of Yorkshire England UK
425 M5 **Hughenden** Qld Australia
119 P6 **Hughenden** Alberta Canada
224 C3 **Huglo** island Norway
125 N7 **Hugo** Colorado USA
130 D3 **Hugo** Oklahoma USA
130 D3 **Hugo Lake** Oklahoma USA
125 O8 **Hugoton** Kansas USA
385 H6 **Huguan** Shanxi China
383 J3 **Huhemort** Mongolia
133 H4 **Huhí** Mexico
223 O5 **Huhtilampi** Finland
223 O5 **Huhus** Finland
380 E1 **Hui Xian** Gansu China
422 G4 **Huiarau Range** New Zealand
381 H2 **Huicheng** Anhui China
381 G4 **Huicheng** Guangdong China
386 E3 **Huich'on** North Korea
158 B2 **Huicungo** Peru
380 D3 **Huidong** Sichuan China
154 B5 **Huijin** Peru
308 B3 **Huíla** Angola
308 B2 **Huíla** admin. area Angola
154 C4 **Huila** admin. area Colombia
308 B3 **Huíla, Planalto da** plain Angola
380 D3 **Huili** Sichuan China
385 I5 **Huimin** Shandong China
381 I2 **Huinan** Shanghai China
158 D5 **Huiñaymarca, Lago** lake Bolivia
160 F5 **Huinca Renancó** Argentina
384 E6 **Huining** Gansu China
159 F6 **Huirapitinde** Bolivia
162 B2 **Huiro** Chile
240 C4 **Huish** Devon England UK
244 A3 **Huisinis** Na h-Eileanan Siar Scotland UK
228 E2 **Huisne** watercourse France
162 B3 **Huite** Chile
154 B5 **Huito** Ecuador
225 L2 **Huittinen** Finland
133 F5 **Huitzuco de los Figueroa** Mexico
385 H6 **Huixian** Henan China
133 F5 **Huixquilucan** Mexico
133 G6 **Huixtla** Mexico
380 D3 **Huize** Yunnan China
381 G4 **Huizhou** Guangdong China
223 M3 **Hukanmaa** Sweden
393 D8 **Hukeri** Karnataka India
223 Q4 **Hukkajärvi** Finland
373 H6 **Hula** Papua New Guinea
385 K3 **Hulan** Heilongjiang China
384 F3 **Huld** Mongolia
385 G3 **Hulenbuir** Mongolia
381 G4 **Huliao** Guangdong China
385 L3 **Hulin** Heilongjiang China
224 H4 **Hulingen** lake Sweden
243 H3 **Hull** watercourse England UK
225 L3 **Hullo** Estonia
383 J3 **Hulma Nuur** lake Mongolia
224 H4 **Hult** Sweden
385 I2 **Hulun Buir** Nei Mongol Zizhiqu China
385 I3 **Hulun Nuur** lake Nei Mongol Zizhiqu China
394 F3 **Hulyaypole** Ukraine
385 K2 **Huma** Heilongjiang China
385 K2 **Huma He** watercourse Heilongjiang China
158 C3 **Humaitá** Brazil
129 I7 **Humariza** Mexico
132 D3 **Humaya** watercourse Mexico
308 B3 **Humbe** Angola
243 I3 **Humber, Mouth of the** bay England UK
156 D3 **Humberto de Campos** Brazil
308 C2 **Humbi, Serra** range Angola
130 D6 **Humble** Texas USA
119 S6 **Humboldt** Saskatchewan Canada
126 D6 **Humboldt** Nebraska USA
124 G6 **Humboldt** watercourse Nevada USA
124 C6 **Humboldt Bay** California USA
Humboldt Gletscher see **Sermersuaq** Greenland
124 F7 **Humboldt Lake** Nevada USA
423 C7 **Humboldt Mountains** New Zealand
124 F6 **Humboldt Range** Nevada USA
241 G2 **Humby** Lincolnshire England UK
227 K3 **Humenné** Slovakia
126 E6 **Humeston** Iowa USA
224 I4 **Hummeln** lake Sweden
225 O2 **Hummonselkä** bay Finland
162 B3 **Humos, Isla** island Chile
308 B3 **Humpata** Angola
125 Q6 **Humphrey** Nebraska USA
232 F2 **Humpolec** Czech Republic
223 N5 **Humppi** Finland
225 L2 **Humppila** Finland
424 I3 **Humpty Doo** NT Australia
383 J3 **Humreg** Mongolia
301 J3 **Hūn** Libya
222 inset **Húnaflói** bay Iceland
381 F3 **Hunan** admin. area China
385 L4 **Hunchun** Jilin China
241 F2 **Huncote** Leicester England UK
222 I6 **Hundsjön** lake Sweden
234 C3 **Hunedoara** Romania
234 C3 **Hunedoara** admin. area Romania
229 I1 **Hünfeld** Germany
427 10 **Hunga Ha'apai Island** Tonga
227 J4 **Hungary** country Europe
425 M7 **Hungerford** Qld Australia
241 F3 **Hungerford** West Berkshire England UK
386 E3 **Hŭngnam** North Korea
124 I2 **Hungry Horse Reservoir** Montana USA
222 I5 **Hungsjön** lake Sweden
308 C2 **Hungulo** Angola
244 B3 **Hunish, Rubha** cape Scotland UK
385 K4 **Hunjiang** Jilin China
385 K4 **Hunjiang** watercourse Liaoning China
243 H2 **Hunmanby** North Yorkshire England UK
243 G3 **Hunsingore** North Yorkshire England UK
241 H2 **Hunstanton** Norfolk England UK
243 F2 **Hunstanworth** Durham England UK
393 D9 **Hunsur** Karnataka India
122 H5 **Hunt** watercourse Newfoundland and Labrador Canada
226 E1 **Hunte** watercourse Germany
423 C7 **Hunter** watercourse New Zealand
125 Q3 **Hunter** North Dakota USA
119 R3 **Hunter Creek** Saskatchewan Canada
425 L10 **Hunter Island** Tas. Australia
78 N10 **Hunter Island Ridge** underwater feature Pacific Ocean
423 B7 **Hunter Mountains** New Zealand
379 G5 **Hunters Bay** Myanmar
423 D7 **Hunters Hills, The** range New Zealand
422 F4 **Hunterville** New Zealand
127 N4 **Huntingdon** Québec Canada
241 G2 **Huntingdon** Cambridgeshire England UK
130 G3 **Huntingdon** Tennessee USA
240 D2 **Huntington** Herefordshire England UK
124 G4 **Huntington** Oregon USA
125 J7 **Huntington** Utah USA
127 J7 **Huntington** West Virginia USA
128 D4 **Huntington Beach** California USA
124 F8 **Huntington Lake** California USA
226 E1 **Huntlosen** Germany
422 F3 **Huntly** New Zealand
244 F3 **Huntly** Aberdeenshire Scotland UK
240 E3 **Huntspill** Somerset England UK
131 H3 **Huntsville** Alabama USA
130 E2 **Huntsville** Arkansas USA
130 D5 **Huntsville** Texas USA
133 H4 **Hunucmá** Mexico
227 K4 **Hunya** Hungary
385 H5 **Hunyuan** Shanxi China
381 G1 **Huojia** Henan China
385 I3 **Huolin'gole** Nei Mongol Zizhiqu China
373 H5 **Huon Gulf** bay Papua New Guinea
376 E3 **Hương Khê** Vietnam
223 N5 **Huopana** Finland
381 G2 **Huoqiu** Anhui China
381 G2 **Huoshan** Anhui China
384 G6 **Huozhou** Shanxi China
121 T5 **Hurault, Lac** lake Québec Canada
127 K4 **Hurd, Cape** Ontario Canada
425 inset **Hurd Point** Macquarie Island Australia
224 F2 **Hurdalssjøen** lake Norway
307 I1 **Hurdiyo** Somalia
226 B4 **Huriel** France
383 J5 **Hurleg Hu** lake Qinghai China
245 D4 **Hurler's Cross** Ireland
129 H4 **Hurley** New Mexico USA
384 E4 **Hurmen** Mongolia
128 B2 **Huron** California USA
125 P4 **Huron** South Dakota USA
126 J4 **Huron, Lake** Canada/USA
241 F3 **Hursley** Hampshire England UK
241 H3 **Hurst Green** East Sussex England UK
127 L8 **Hurt** Virginia USA
229 H1 **Hürth** Germany
423 E6 **Hurunui** watercourse New Zealand
119 V2 **Hurwitz Lake** Nunavut Canada
243 G2 **Hurworth-on-Tees** Darlington England UK
224 C2 **Husa** Norway
222 inset **Húsavík** Iceland
241 F2 **Husbands Bosworth** Leicester England UK
222 K4 **Husbondliden** Sweden
384 F2 **Hushaat** Mongolia
116 D5 **Huslia** Alaska USA
225 K2 **Husö** island Finland
224 C2 **Husøy** island Norway
119 O7 **Hussar** Alberta Canada
222 E5 **Hustad** Norway
222 K5 **Husum** Sweden
222 H4 **Husvika** Norway
227 I1 **Huta** Poland
388 G6 **Hūtān** Iran
384 E2 **Hutar-under** Mongolia
118 M3 **Hutch Lake** Alberta Canada
308 D6 **Hutchinson** South Africa
125 Q7 **Hutchinson** Kansas USA
126 D4 **Hutchinson** Minnesota USA
131 K7 **Hutchinson Island** Florida USA
127 K8 **Hutchinson Rock** mountain Virginia USA
384 F2 **Hutel** Mongolia
390 E7 **Ḥūth** Yemen
423 F5 **Hutt** watercourse New Zealand
121 W4 **Hutte Sauvage, Lac de la** lake Québec Canada
243 I3 **Huttoft** Lincolnshire England UK
243 H3 **Hutton** East Riding of Yorkshire England UK
242 F2 **Hutton Roof** Cumbria England UK
383 H4 **Hutubi** Xinjiang Uygur Zizhiqu China
385 H5 **Hutuo He** watercourse Shanxi China
223 M3 **Huuki** Sweden
119 O7 **Huxley** Alberta Canada
229 G1 **Huy** Belgium
381 H2 **Huzhou** Zhejiang China
222 inset **Hvalnes** cape Iceland
222 inset **Hvammsfjörður** bay Iceland
222 inset **Hvammstangi** Iceland
222 inset **Hvannadalshnúkur** mountain Iceland
232 G5 **Hvar** Croatia
222 inset **Hvítá** watercourse Iceland
224 F3 **Hvitsten** Norway
222 inset **Hvolsvöllur** Iceland
386 E3 **Hwach'on** South Korea
308 E3 **Hwange** Zimbabwe
386 E3 **Hwangju** North Korea
386 E4 **Hwasun** South Korea
309 F3 **Hwedza** Zimbabwe
125 O6 **Hyannis** Nebraska USA
383 J2 **Hyaras** Mongolia
383 J2 **Hyargas Nuur** lake Mongolia
227 J3 **Hyby** Slovakia
242 E2 **Hycemoor** Cumbria England UK
131 L2 **Hyco Lake** North Carolina USA
118 E5 **Hydaburg** Alaska USA
423 D7 **Hyde** New Zealand
243 F3 **Hyde** Greater Manchester England UK
120 H2 **Hyde Lake** Nunavut Canada
242 B2 **Hyde Park** Antrim Northern Ireland UK
424 F8 **Hyden** WA Australia
393 E8 **Hyderabad** Andhra Pradesh India
391 K4 **Hyderabad** Pakistan
224 C2 **Hyen** Norway
229 H5 **Hyères** France
229 H5 **Hyères, Îles d'** island France
386 F3 **Hyesan** North Korea
224 F3 **Hyggen** Norway
118 G2 **Hyland** watercourse Yukon Territory Canada
118 G4 **Hyland Post** British Columbia Canada
224 F5 **Hyllekrog** cape Denmark

224 F4 Hyllested Skovgaarde Denmark
119 O5 Hylo Alberta Canada
224 I2 Hyn lake Sweden
386 G4 Hyono-sen volcano Japan
223 N4 Hyry Finland
223 P4 Hyrynjärvi lake Finland
223 P4 Hyrynsalmi Finland
125 L3 Hysham Montana USA
224 G4 Hyssna Sweden
118 L5 Hythe Alberta Canada
241 F4 Hythe Hampshire England UK
241 I3 Hythe Kent England UK
223 O5 Hytölä Finland
386 F5 Hyuga Japan

I

382 G4 I-Li He watercourse Xinjiang Uygur Zizhiqu China
389 M5 I-Li He lake Kazakhstan
301 H4 I-n-Azaoua Niger
301 H5 I-n-Guezzam Algeria
301 G5 I-n-Tebezas Mali
301 F5 I-n-Tilit Mali
157 C6 Iaciara Brazil
158 D3 Iaco watercourse Brazil
157 D6 Iaçu Brazil
373 J5 Iagain Island Papua New Guinea
234 E3 Ialomita admin. area Romania
373 G6 Iamara Papua New Guinea
131 I5 Iamonia, Lake Florida USA
423 D6 Ianthe, Lake New Zealand
373 H5 Iaro watercourse Papua New Guinea
234 E2 Iaşi Romania
234 E2 Iaşi admin. area Romania
130 E5 Iatt, Lake Louisiana USA
155 E5 Iaunari Brazil
305 E3 Ibadan Nigeria
154 C3 Ibagué Colombia
157 B8 Ibaiti Brazil
306 E4 Ibanda Uganda
306 D4 Ibanga Democratic Republic of Congo
234 B4 Ibar watercourse Kosovo
154 B4 Ibarra Ecuador
157 C8 Ibaté Brazil
157 D8 Ibatiba Brazil
390 E7 Ibb Yemen
306 D3 Ibba Sudan
306 D2 Ibba watercourse Sudan
306 C3 Ibembo Democratic Republic of Congo
305 H4 Ibenga watercourse Congo
161 G4 Iberá, Esteros del bay Argentina
158 D3 Iberia Peru
76 Q5 Iberian Plain underwater feature Atlantic Ocean
231 F3 Iberica, Cordillera range Spain
222 J2 Ibestad Norway
118 D2 Ibex Valley Yukon Territory Canada
231 F4 Ibi Spain
157 C7 Ibiá Brazil
156 D3 Ibiapina Brazil
157 E6 Ibicaraí Brazil
157 E6 Ibicuí Brazil
161 G4 Ibicuí Brazil
161 G4 Ibicuí watercourse Brazil
156 E5 Ibimirim Brazil
157 D5 Ibipeba Brazil
157 E6 Ibirataia Brazil
157 C8 Ibirité Brazil
235 E6 İbirler Turkey
161 H4 Ibirubá Brazil
157 B8 Ibitinga Brazil
Ibiza see Eivissa Spain
231 G4 Ibiza Spain
156 D4 Ibjapaba, Serra da range Brazil
235 F7 İblis Burnu cape Turkey
309 H2 Ibo Mozambique
157 D6 Ibotirama Brazil
305 G5 Iboundji Gabon
391 H5 'Ibrī Oman
235 E5 İbrikbaba Turkey
241 F2 Ibstock Leicester England UK
372 C3 Ibu, Gunung mountain Indonesia
377 I2 Ibuhos island Philippines
386 F5 Ibusuki Japan
158 C4 Ica Peru
158 C4 Ica admin. area Peru
238 B4 Iča watercourse Latvia
154 D5 Içá watercourse Brazil
163 9 Icacos Point Trinidad and Tobago
160 D6 Icalma Chile
154 E4 Icana watercourse Brazil
134 E5 Icantí Panama
161 I4 Içara Brazil
156 C3 Icatu Brazil
394 E6 Içel Turkey
394 E6 Içel admin. area Turkey
222 inset Iceland country Europe
435 F2 Icelandic Plateau underwater feature Norwegian Sea
393 D8 Ichalkaranji Maharashtra India
393 F7 Ichchapuram Orissa India
237 W7 Ichëra Russian Federation
237 AI6 Ichigemskiy Khrebet range Russian Federation
159 E5 Ichilo watercourse Bolivia
387 I3 Ichinoseki Japan
386 E3 Ich'on North Korea
386 E4 Ich'ŏn South Korea
241 H2 Icklingham Suffolk England UK
235 F7 İçmeler Turkey
156 E4 Icó Brazil
310 3a Icod de los Vinos Canary Islands
159 F5 Icuati Bolivia
118 D3 Icy Strait Alaska USA
125 R5 Ida Grove Iowa USA
225 N3 Ida-Virumaa admin. area Estonia
305 F4 Idabato Cameroon
130 D4 Idabel Oklahoma USA
305 F3 Idah Nigeria
114 Idaho admin. area USA
124 I5 Idaho Falls Idaho USA
129 L4 Idalou Texas USA
230 C4 Idanha, Barragem da lake Portugal
305 I2 Idd Al-Ghanam Sudan
302 C5 Idd el-Chanam Sudan
307 H2 Iddan Somalia
119 P7 Iddesleigh Alberta Canada
222 L2 Iddon island Norway
131 I4 Ideal Georgia USA
234 D2 Ideciu de Jos Romania
223 S4 Idel' Russian Federation
301 H4 Idelès Algeria
241 H4 Iden East Sussex England UK
383 K3 Ider Mongolia
302 E3 Idfû Egypt
303 F5 Idga Hamus Ethiopia
374 C2 Idi Indonesia
306 B4 Idiofa Democratic Republic of Congo
223 M2 Idivuoma Sweden
388 E6 Idjevan Armenia
224 H2 Idkerberget Sweden
243 H3 Idle watercourse England UK
394 F6 Idlib Syria
307 F5 Idodi Tanzania
222 H6 Idre Sweden
235 G6 İdrisyayla Turkey
225 O4 Idritsa Russian Federation
232 D4 Idro, Lago d' lake Italy
222 I5 Idsjön lake Sweden
232 C1 Idstein Germany
307 F5 Idugalo Tanzania
306 C4 Idumbe Democratic Republic of Congo
237 AB7 Idyum watercourse Russian Federation
381 J3 Ie-shima island Japan
234 D2 Iedu Romania
228 F1 Ieper Belgium
235 D8 Ierapetra Greece
235 D5 Ierissou, Kolpos bay Greece
227 M3 Iernut Romania
223 N2 Iešjav'ri lake Norway
307 F5 Ifakara Tanzania
373 H2 Ifalik island Federated States of Micronesia
309 I4 Ifanadiana Madagascar
305 E3 Ife Nigeria
302 B5 Ifenat Chad
223 O1 Ifjordfjellet region Norway
305 F3 Ifon Nigeria
240 E2 Ifton Heath Shropshire England UK
308 D3 Ifuluta Plain plain Zambia
227 H5 Ig Slovenia
305 F2 Igabi Nigeria
227 I4 Igal Hungary
375 F3 Igan Malaysia
375 F3 Igan watercourse Malaysia
307 E3 Iganga Uganda
157 C8 Igarapava Brazil
156 C3 Igarapé Açu Brazil
156 B3 Igarapé Miri Brazil
156 F4 Igarassu Brazil
236 S5 Igarka Russian Federation
305 F3 Igarra Nigeria
160 F6 Igarzábal Argentina
393 C7 Igatpuri Maharashtra India
305 E3 Igboho Nigeria
305 F3 Igbor Nigeria
394 G5 Iğdir Turkey
394 G5 Iğdir admin. area Turkey
240 E2 Ightfield Shropshire England UK
229 I3 Igis Switzerland
162 F2 Iglesia, Punta cape Argentina
233 C7 Iglesias Sardinia Italy
301 F2 Igli Algeria
117 K5 Igloolik Nunavut Canada
122 H4 Iglosiatik Island Newfoundland and Labrador Canada
122 H4 Iglusuaktalialuk Island Newfoundland and Labrador Canada
120 J8 Ignace Ontario Canada
129 I2 Ignacio Colorado USA
128 G6 Ignacio Ramirez Mexico
132 C3 Ignacio Zaragoza Mexico
132 D2 Ignacio Zaragoza Mexico
225 N5 Ignalina Lithuania
235 E5 İğneada Turkey
394 D5 İğneada Burnu cape Turkey
372 D4 Igom Indonesia
307 E5 Igoma Tanzania
307 E4 Igombe watercourse Tanzania
238 C3 Igomel' Russian Federation
234 D1 Igrovitsa Ukraine
157 B9 Iguaçu watercourse Brazil
161 H3 Iguaçu Falls waterfall Argentina/Brazil
157 D6 Iguaí Brazil
154 C4 Iguaje, Mesas de region Colombia
132 E5 Iguala Mexico
231 G3 Igualada Spain
134 E6 Iguana, Isla island Panama
157 C9 Iguape Brazil
161 H2 Iguatemi Brazil
156 E4 Iguatu Brazil
305 F5 Iguéla Gabon
230 C2 Igueña Spain
154 D2 Igüés Venezuela
159 F6 Iguirayapirurenda Bolivia
307 E4 Igunga Tanzania
426 6 Igup island Federated States of Micronesia
384 D3 Ih Bogd Uul Mongolia
384 E3 Ih-uul Mongolia
393 C10 Ihavandhippolhu Atoll Maldives
306 E4 Ihema, Lac lake Tanzania
301 H3 Iherir Algeria
383 J5 Ihes Nuur lake Mongolia
381 J3 Iheya-shima island Japan
384 G3 Ihhet Mongolia
305 F3 Ihiala Nigeria
228 D3 Iholdy France
309 I4 Ihosy Madagascar
309 I4 Ihosy watercourse Madagascar
235 F6 İhsaniye Turkey
384 E3 Ihtamir Mongolia
423 F5 Ihurua New Zealand
223 N4 Ii Finland
387 H4 Iida Japan
223 O4 Iijärvi lake Finland
223 N4 Iijoki watercourse Finland
223 N3 Iisaku Estonia
225 O5 Iisalmi Finland
225 N2 Iitti Finland
223 P4 Iivaara mountain Finland
223 P4 Iivantiira lake Finland
305 E3 Ijebu-Ode Nigeria
226 D2 IJssel, Oude watercourse Netherlands
226 C1 IJsselmeer bay Netherlands
161 H4 Ijuí Brazil
161 H4 Ijuí watercourse Brazil
225 L2 Ikaalinen Finland
309 I4 Ikalamavony Madagascar
306 C4 Ikanda Democratic Republic of Congo
305 F2 Ikara Nigeria
235 E7 Ikaria island Greece
121 U3 Ikattok, Baie bay Québec Canada
422 G4 Ikawhenua Range New Zealand
305 E3 Ikeja Nigeria
306 C4 Ikela Democratic Republic of Congo
306 B3 Ikelemba watercourse Democratic Republic of Congo
241 I2 Iken Suffolk England UK
305 F5 Ikengué Gabon
305 F3 Ikeni Nigeria
223 J3 Ikesjaure lake Sweden
383 K2 Ikh Bogo Uul mountain Mongolia
234 C4 Ikhtiman Bulgaria
386 F5 Iki island Japan
Iki-Burul see Baga-Burul Russian Federation
306 E4 Ikimba, Lake lake Tanzania
305 E3 Ikire Nigeria
386 F5 Ikitsuki-shima island Japan
306 E5 Ikola Tanzania
305 F3 Ikole Nigeria
305 F3 Ikom Nigeria
309 I4 Ikongo Madagascar
307 E3 Ikoto Sudan
305 G5 Ikoy watercourse Gabon
386 E4 Iksan South Korea
238 G1 Ikshezero, Ozero lake Russian Federation
121 Q2 Iktotat watercourse Québec Canada
307 F5 Ikwiriri Tanzania
233 F9 Il-Ponta ta' Benghajsa cape Malta
158 D5 Ilabaya Peru
306 D5 Ilagala Tanzania
377 I3 Ilagan Philippines
373 I6 Ilai Island Papua New Guinea
223 O5 Ilajanjärvi lake Finland
155 H4 Ilakana Patatpe French Guiana
392 G5 Ilam Nepal
240 E3 Ilam Staffordshire England UK
390 F2 Īlām Iran
390 F2 Īlām admin. area Iran
134 B4 Ilama Honduras
381 I4 Ilan Taiwan China
229 I3 Ilanz Switzerland
304 E3 Ilaro Nigeria
227 J3 Ilava Slovakia
158 D5 Ilave Peru
227 J1 Iława Poland
237 Z6 Ilbenge Russian Federation
240 E3 Ilchester Somerset England UK
235 E6 Ildır Turkey
119 R5 Île-à-la-Crosse Saskatchewan Canada
116 I7 Île-à-la-Crosse, Lac lake Saskatchewan Canada
228 F2 Île-de-France admin. area France
234 E3 Ileana Romania
306 C4 Ilebo Democratic Republic of Congo
394 E6 Ilemin Turkey
245 C5 Ilen watercourse Ireland
307 F3 Ileret Kenya
427 I4 Îles du Vent admin. area French Polynesia
427 I4 Îles Marquises admin. area French Polynesia
427 I4 Îles Sous-le-Vent admin. area French Polynesia
427 I4 Îles Tuamotu-Gambier admin. area French Polynesia
120 H4 Ilford Manitoba Canada
425 M5 Ilfracombe Qld Australia
240 C3 Ilfracombe Devon England UK
225 M5 Ilgis lake Lithuania
157 B8 Ilha Solteira Brazil
159 I6 Ilha Solteira, Represa lake Brazil
161 J2 Ilhabela Brazil
157 E6 Ilhéus Brazil
389 L4 Ili watercourse Kazakhstan
116 D7 Iliamna Lake Alaska USA
235 E6 Ilıca Turkey
307 H2 Ilig, Raas cape Somalia
377 J5 Iligan Philippines
377 J5 Iligan Bay Philippines
377 I3 Iligan Point Philippines
117 Q4 Ilimananngip Nunaa island Greenland
237 W6 Ilimpeya watercourse Russian Federation
377 I4 Ilin island Philippines
389 O3 Il'inka Russian Federation
225 P5 Il'ino Russian Federation
237 AD9 Il'inskiy Russian Federation
387 I1 Il'inskiy Russian Federation
238 F6 Il'inskoye Russian Federation
238 G4 Il'inskoye Russian Federation
238 H4 Il'inskoye Russian Federation
238 H4 Il'inskoye-Khovanskoye Russian Federation
128 inset 'Ilio Point Hawai'i USA
372 C6 Iliomar Timor-Leste (East Timor)
237 AG4 Ilirgytgyn, Ozero lake Russian Federation
229 L4 Ilirska Bistrica Slovenia
225 L5 Il'jinskoe Russian Federation
227 J3 Ilk Hungary
393 D8 Ilkal Karnataka India
241 F2 Ilkeston Derbyshire England UK
243 G3 Ilkley West Yorkshire England UK
229 H2 Ill watercourse France
158 D3 Illampu Bolivia
230 E3 Illana Spain
377 I6 Illana Bay Philippines
160 D4 Illapel Chile
305 F2 Illela Nigeria
301 H6 Illéla Niger
228 F4 Iller watercourse Germany
230 E3 Illescas Spain
225 N3 Illi Estonia
234 G2 Illichivs'k Ukraine
228 E2 Illiers France
245 E1 Illies Ireland
158 E1 Illimani mountain Bolivia
126 G6 Illinois watercourse Illinois USA
234 F1 Illintsi Ukraine
155 G4 Illiwa watercourse Guyana
301 H3 Illizi Algeria
225 L2 Illo Finland
425 I5 Illogwa watercourse NT Australia
230 F3 Illueca Spain
226 F2 Ilm watercourse Germany
222 M5 Ilmajoki Finland
225 P3 Il'men', Ozero lake Russian Federation
229 J1 Ilmenau Germany
241 F2 Ilmer Buckinghamshire England UK
158 D5 Ilo Peru
377 I5 Iloilo Philippines
232 H4 Ilok Croatia
223 O5 Ilomantsi Finland
305 E3 Ilorin Nigeria
232 G4 Ilova Croatia
232 F4 Ilovik island Croatia
388 D3 Ilovlya Russian Federation
227 H2 Iłowa Poland
240 C3 Ilston Swansea Wales UK
243 G2 Ilton North Yorkshire England UK
424 I6 Iltur SA Australia
117 N5 Ilulissat Greenland
117 O5 Ilulissat Gletscher ice Greenland
307 E5 Ilunde Tanzania
307 E5 Ilungu Tanzania
223 N4 Ilveskylä Finland
124 C3 Ilwaco Washington USA
235 E5 Ilyas Burnu cape Turkey
236 M6 Ilych watercourse Russian Federation
225 Q2 Il'ynskiy Russian Federation
232 F3 Ilz Austria
227 K2 Iłża Poland
386 G4 Imabari Japan
155 G5 Imabu watercourse Brazil
156 E4 Imaculada Brazil
388 I7 Imam-baba Turkmenistan
223 R3 Imandra Russian Federation
223 R3 Imandra, Ozero lake Russian Federation
389 J3 Imantau Koli lake Kazakhstan
435 D2 Imarssuak Channel underwater feature Atlantic Ocean
155 F3 Imataca, Serranía de range Venezuela
225 O2 Imatra Finland
154 B4 Imbabura admin. area Ecuador
161 I4 Imbituba Brazil
157 B9 Imbituva Brazil
124 G4 Imbler Oregon USA
238 G3 Imeni Russian Federation
237 AC8 Imeni Peliny Osipenko Russian Federation
385 M2 Imeni Peliny Osipenko Russian Federation
388 H6 Imeni Stalina Turkmenistan
155 E4 Imeri, Serra range Brazil
235 D5 Imeros Greece
307 G2 Īmī Ethiopia
227 M1 Imienin Belarus
120 G2 Imikula Lake Nunavut Canada
121 P3 Imilik, Pointe Québec Canada
386 E4 Imja-do island South Korea
386 E3 Imjin-gang watercourse North Korea
300 C4 Imlili Western Sahara
225 O2 Immalanjärvi lake Finland
224 H4 Immeln lake Sweden
229 I3 Immendingen Germany
243 H3 Immingham North East Lincolnshire England UK
305 F3 Imo admin. area Nigeria
305 F3 Imo watercourse Nigeria
232 D4 Imola Italy
156 C4 Imperatriz Brazil
158 E2 Imperatriz Brazil
232 C5 Imperia Italy
119 S7 Imperial Saskatchewan Canada
128 E4 Imperial California USA
125 O6 Imperial Nebraska USA
119 P5 Imperial Mills Alberta Canada
424 F4 Imperieuse Reef WA Australia
305 H4 Impfondo Congo
379 G4 Imphal Manipur India
228 F3 Imphy France
225 P2 Impilakhti Russian Federation
241 H2 Impington Cambridgeshire England UK
235 F5 İmralı Adası island Turkey
224 C3 Ims Norway
386 E4 Imsil South Korea
226 F4 Imst Austria
237 AA5 Imtenzha Russian Federation
132 C2 Imuris Mexico
377 H5 Imuruan Bay Philippines
301 H3 In Aménas Algeria
301 H4 In Amguel Algeria
376 D4 In Buri Thailand
301 G3 In Salah Algeria
387 H4 Ina Japan
227 H1 Ina watercourse Poland
310 5c Inaccessible Island island St Helena
245 C4 Inagh Ireland
158 D3 Inaiuini watercourse Brazil
159 I3 Inajá, Serra do range Brazil
156 E4 Inambari Peru
158 D4 Iñapari Peru
426 5 Inarajan Guam
234 A2 Inárcs Hungary
223 O2 Inari Finland
223 Q5 Inari Finland
223 O2 Inarijärvi bay Finland
223 O2 Inarijoki watercourse Finland
223 N2 Inarijoki watercourse Norway
231 H4 Inca Spain
242 E3 Ince Blundell Merseyside England UK
394 E4 Ince Burun cape Turkey
245 C4 Inch Ireland
245 C4 Inch Ireland
245 E1 Inch Island Ireland
386 E4 Inch'ŏn South Korea
244 E4 Inchture Perth and Kinross Scotland UK
309 F5 Incomati watercourse Mozambique
302 F5 Inda Silasē Ethiopia
244 B5 Indaal, Loch bay Scotland UK
157 C7 Indaiá watercourse Brazil
157 C8 Indaiatuba Brazil
222 J5 Indalsälven watercourse Sweden
393 C7 Indapur Maharashtra India
379 H4 Indaw Myanmar
379 H4 Indawgyi, Lake Myanmar
128 C2 Independence California USA
126 F5 Independence Iowa USA
126 D8 Independence Kansas USA
126 I7 Independence Kentucky USA
126 D7 Independence Missouri USA
117 P2 Independence Fjord Greenland
124 G6 Independence Mountains Nevada USA
156 D4 Independência Brazil
159 H4 Independência Brazil
158 B4 Independencia, Isla island Peru
385 J3 Inder Nei Mongol Zizhiqu China
388 F4 Inderborskiy Kazakhstan
124 E3 Index Washington USA
393 D8 Indi Karnataka India
378 D4 India country
119 T7 Indian Head Saskatchewan Canada
126 H3 Indian Lake Michigan USA
127 N5 Indian Lake New York USA
81 Indian Ocean
131 K7 Indian River Shores Florida USA
119 V8 Indian Springs Manitoba Canada
128 E2 Indian Springs Nevada USA
114 Indiana admin. area USA
127 L6 Indiana Pennsylvania USA
126 H7 Indianapolis Indiana USA
126 E5 Indianola Iowa USA
130 F4 Indianola Mississippi USA
125 O6 Indianola Nebraska USA
159 G5 Indiarana Brazil
157 E5 Indiaroba Brazil
307 F2 Indibir Ethiopia
236 K5 Indiga Russian Federation
237 AD6 Indigirka watercourse Russian Federation
234 B3 Indija Serbia
128 D4 Indio California USA
392 C5 Indira Gandhi Canal Rajasthan India
426 8 Indispensable Strait Solomon Islands
80 I9 Indomed Fracture Zone underwater feature Southern Ocean
372 E5 Indonesia country Asia
393 D6 Indore Madhya Pradesh India
374 D4 Indragiri watercourse Indonesia
225 M5 Indrajų ežeras lake Lithuania
374 F5 Indramayu Indonesia
374 F5 Indramayu, Tanjung cape Indonesia
374 D4 Indrapura Indonesia
374 D4 Indrapura, Tanjung cape Indonesia
393 E7 Indravati watercourse Chhattisgarh India
228 E3 Indre watercourse France
223 Q1 Indre Kiberg Norway
222 E5 Indre Standal Norway
222 J2 Indre-Tysfjorden bay Norway
222 G4 Indre Vikna island Norway
308 C2 Indungo Angola
391 L3 Indus watercourse Pakistan
80 K2 Indus Fan underwater feature Arabian Sea
126 F6 Industry Illinois USA
130 C6 Industry Texas USA
235 E5 İnecik Turkey
225 M4 Inesis lake Latvia
234 B2 Ineu Romania
235 C5 Inevo Macedonia
132 E5 Infiernillo, Presa lake Mexico
233 F7 Infreschi, Punta degli cape Italy
223 S3 Inga Russian Federation
225 M2 Ingå Finland
301 H5 Ingal Niger
129 L2 Ingalls Kansas USA
306 C4 Inganda Democratic Republic of Congo
225 J3 Ingarö island Sweden
241 H3 Ingatestone Essex England UK
229 I2 Ingelheim Germany
306 B4 Ingende Democratic Republic of Congo
160 F2 Ingeniero Guillermo Nueva Juárez Argentina
162 C2 Ingeniero Jacobacci Argentina
162 B4 Ingeniero Pallavicini Chile
118 I4 Ingenika Mine British Columbia Canada
127 K5 Ingersoll Ontario Canada
425 M4 Ingham Qld Australia
117 M3 Inglefield Land plain Greenland
160 D3 Inglesa, Bahía bay Chile
243 F2 Ingleton North Yorkshire England UK
425 N7 Inglewood Qld Australia
128 C4 Inglewood California USA
131 J6 Inglis Florida USA
385 G2 Ingoda watercourse Russian Federation
379 H4 Ingoka Pum mountain Myanmar
243 I3 Ingoldmells Lincolnshire England UK
125 R2 Ingolf Ontario Canada
117 R2 Ingolf Fjord Greenland
226 F3 Ingolstadt Germany
223 M1 Ingøya island Norway
223 S3 Ingozero, Ozero lake Russian Federation
118 E6 Ingraham Bay British Columbia Canada
392 G6 Ingraj Bazar West Bengal India
243 G1 Ingram Northumberland England UK
130 B5 Ingram Texas USA
437 F2 Ingrid Christensen Coast Antarctica
394 E3 Ingulets watercourse Ukraine
234 H1 Ingulo-Kamenka Ukraine
388 D5 Ingushetiya Respublika admin. area Russian Federation
309 F5 Ingwavuma South Africa
308 E2 Ingwe Zambia
229 H2 Ingwiller France
379 H4 Ingyan Yan Myanmar
309 F5 Inhaca Mozambique
309 F4 Inhafenga Mozambique
309 G4 Inhambane Mozambique
309 F4 Inhambane admin. area Mozambique
157 E5 Inhambupe Brazil
309 F3 Inhaminga Mozambique
157 D7 Inhapim Brazil
309 I2 Inharana Madagascar
235 G5 İnhisar Turkey
156 D4 Inhuma Brazil
157 B7 Inhumas Brazil
225 K2 Iniö island Finland
154 E4 Inírida Colombia
154 D4 Inírida watercourse Colombia
245 F4 Inish Ireland
245 B3 Inishbofin island Ireland
245 C2 Inishcrone Ireland
245 C3 Inisheer island Ireland
245 B2 Inishkea North island Ireland
245 B2 Inishkea South island Ireland
245 C3 Inishmaan island Ireland
245 C3 Inishmore island Ireland
245 D2 Inishmurray island Ireland
245 E1 Inishowen peninsula Ireland
245 F1 Inishowen Head cape Ireland
245 B3 Inishshark island Ireland
245 B4 Inishtooskert island Ireland
245 B3 Inishturk island Ireland
245 B4 Inishvickillane island Ireland
242 A4 Inistioge Ireland
386 F3 Inje South Korea
425 N6 Injune Qld Australia
241 F2 Inkberrow Worcestershire England UK
227 I4 Inke Hungary
223 P4 Inkee Finland
118 E3 Inklin watercourse British Columbia Canada
124 I5 Inkom Idaho USA
423 E6 Inland Kaikoura Range New Zealand
226 G4 Inn watercourse Germany
223 N5 Innala Finland
425 L6 Innamincka SA Australia
224 H4 Innaren lake Sweden
222 I3 Inndyr Norway
244 B4 Inner Hebrides island Scotland UK
310 9 Inner Islands Seychelles
222 G5 Innerdalsvatnet lake Norway
244 E5 Innerleithen Scottish Borders Scotland UK
226 F1 Innerste watercourse Germany
222 L5 Innertavle Sweden
226 F3 Inning Germany
425 M4 Innisfail Qld Australia
119 O6 Innisfail Alberta Canada
386 G4 Innoshima Japan
226 F4 Innsbruck Austria
222 K2 Innset Norway
121 Q3 Innuksuac watercourse Québec Canada
222 E6 Innvikfjorden Norway
245 E3 Inny watercourse Ireland
157 B7 Inocência Brazil
130 D2 Inola Oklahoma USA
235 G6 İnönü Turkey
227 K2 Inowłódz Poland
227 J1 Inowrocław Poland
244 F3 Insch Aberdeenshire Scotland UK
424 D6 Inscription, Cape WA Australia
376 C3 Insein Myanmar
244 D2 Inshore Highland Scotland UK
227 H1 Ińsko, Jezioro lake Poland
236 N5 Inta Russian Federation
242 B3 Intack Ireland
374 D2 Intan, Teluk Malaysia
229 H3 Interlaken Switzerland
126 E2 International Falls Minnesota USA
376 B4 Interview Island Andaman and Nicobar Islands India
134 B4 Intibucá Honduras
161 F4 Intiyaco Argentina
223 V4 Intsy Russian Federation
154 C5 Intuto Peru
121 P3 Inukjuak Québec Canada
162 C5 Inútil, Bahía bay Chile
116 F5 Inuvik Northwest Territories Canada
244 E3 Inver Aberdeenshire Scotland UK
244 C4 Inveraray Argyll and Bute Scotland UK
244 F4 Inverbervie Aberdeenshire Scotland UK
423 C8 Invercargill New Zealand
244 D3 Invercassley Highland Scotland UK
244 D5 Inverclyde admin. area Scotland UK
244 E3 Invereen Highland Scotland UK
425 N7 Inverell NSW Australia
244 E4 Inverey Aberdeenshire Scotland UK
244 C3 Inverie Highland Scotland UK
244 F4 Inverkeilor Angus Scotland UK
244 E4 Inverkeithing Fife Scotland UK
244 D5 Inverkip Inverclyde Scotland UK
244 C4 Inverliever Argyll and Bute Scotland UK
244 C4 Inverliver Argyll and Bute Scotland UK
244 D2 Invernaver Highland Scotland UK
244 D3 Inverness Highland Scotland UK
131 J6 Inverness Florida USA
130 F4 Inverness Mississippi USA
244 F3 Inverurie Aberdeenshire Scotland UK
425 J8 Investigator Group islands SA Australia
81 N5 Investigator Ridge underwater feature Indian Ocean
389 O3 Inya Russian Federation
237 AE6 Inya watercourse Russian Federation
309 F3 Inyangani mountain Zimbabwe
124 F8 Inyo Mountains California USA
128 D3 Inyokern California USA
154 B4 Inzá Colombia
232 E3 Inzell Germany
388 D3 Inzhavino Russian Federation
386 F5 Iō-jima island Japan
235 B6 Ioannina Greece
235 B6 Ioanninon, Limni lake Greece
223 U2 Iokanga Russian Federation
126 D8 Iola Kansas USA
373 J5 Iolasa Island Papua New Guinea
244 B4 Iona island Scotland UK
124 F4 Ione Oregon USA
124 G2 Ione Washington USA
234 D3 Ioneşti Romania
126 I5 Ionia Michigan USA
235 A6 Ionian Islands Greece
235 B7 Ionian Sea Greece
235 A6 Ionioi Nisia island Greece
235 B6 Ionioi Nisoi admin. area Greece
237 AD7 Iony, Ostrov island Russian Federation
373 H5 Iori Papua New Guinea
235 D7 Ios Greece
235 D7 Ios island Greece
118 M5 Iosegun Lake Alberta Canada
236 L6 Iosser Russian Federation
130 E5 Iota Louisiana USA
300 C5 Iouîk Mauritania
114 Iowa admin. area USA
126 F6 Iowa watercourse Iowa USA
126 F6 Iowa City Iowa USA
126 E5 Iowa Falls Iowa USA
129 M4 Iowa Park Texas USA
157 D7 Ipaba Brazil
157 B7 Ipameri Brazil
156 E5 Ipanema watercourse Brazil
157 D7 Ipatinga Brazil
157 B8 Ipauçu Brazil
235 B6 Ipeiros admin. area Greece
394 G5 Ipek Geçidi pass Turkey
227 J3 Ipeľ watercourse Slovakia
308 E5 Ipelegeng South Africa
305 H4 Ipendja watercourse Congo
305 E3 Iperu Nigeria
134 E5 Ipetí Panama
159 H6 Ipezal Brazil
154 B4 Ipiales Colombia
375 I2 Ipil Philippines
377 I6 Ipil Philippines
157 E6 Ipirá Brazil
159 F2 Ipiranga Brazil
155 I5 Ipixuna Brazil
156 A4 Ipixuna watercourse Brazil
374 D2 Ipoh Malaysia
156 F5 Ipojuca Brazil
227 J3 Ipoly watercourse Hungary
157 B7 Iporá Brazil
157 A9 Iporã Brazil
305 I3 Ippy Central African Republic
425 O6 Ipswich Qld Australia
241 I2 Ipswich Suffolk England UK
125 P4 Ipswich South Dakota USA
127 P5 Ipswich Bay Massachusetts USA
156 D4 Ipu Brazil
157 B8 Ipuã Brazil
156 D4 Ipubi Brazil
156 D4 Ipueiras Brazil
374 D4 Ipuh Indonesia
158 D4 Ipuni Bolivia
117 M6 Iqaluit Nunavut Canada
383 J5 Iqe He watercourse Qinghai China
160 D2 Iquique Chile
158 C1 Iquitos Peru
305 I3 Ira Banda Central African Republic
129 L5 Iraan Texas USA
381 I4 Irabu-jima island Japan
158 D3 Iracema Brazil
155 H3 Iracoubo French Guiana
303 F4 Irafayle Eritrea
235 D7 Irakleia island Greece
235 D8 Irakleio Greece
134 D4 Iralaya Honduras
388 G7 Iran country
155 F5 Iranduba Brazil
391 I4 Īrānshahr Iran
132 E4 Irapuato Mexico
390 D3 Iraq country
388 D8 Iraq country Middle East
157 D6 Iraquara Brazil
157 E6 Irará Brazil
156 A3 Iratapuru watercourse Brazil
157 B9 Irati Brazil
372 E4 Irau, Bon mountain Indonesia
134 D5 Irazú, Volcán volcano Costa Rica
225 L4 Irbe Strait Estonia
390 C3 Irbid Jordan
388 I1 Irbit Russian Federation
157 D5 Irecê Brazil
245 E3 Ireland country Europe
127 inset Ireland Islands Bermuda
306 C4 Irema Democratic Republic of Congo
160 F6 Irene Argentina
125 Q5 Irene South Dakota USA
388 I4 Irgiz Kazakhstan
388 H4 Irgiz watercourse Kazakhstan
300 E2 Irherm Morocco
300 E2 Irhil m'Goun mountain Morocco
372 F4 Irian Jaya admin. area Indonesia
372 E4 Irian Jaya Barat admin. area Indonesia
155 G4 Iriau watercourse Brazil
302 C4 Iriba Chad
305 I1 Iriba Chad
155 G4 Iricoumé, Serra range Brazil
234 A3 Irig Serbia
377 I4 Iriga Philippines
388 H3 Iriklinskiy Russian Federation
245 E2 Irineragh Ireland
307 F5 Iringa Tanzania
307 F5 Iringa admin. area Tanzania
381 I4 Iriomote-jima island Japan
156 A4 Iriri watercourse Brazil
156 A5 Iriri Novo watercourse Brazil
245 G3 Irish Sea Ireland/UK
245 E2 Irish Town Omagh Northern Ireland UK
242 B3 Irishford Ireland
156 C3 Irituia Brazil
237 U7 Irkineyeva watercourse Russian Federation
384 E2 Irkut watercourse Russian Federation
237 V8 Irkutsk Russian Federation
237 V7 Irkutskaya Oblast' admin. area Russian Federation
119 P6 Irma Alberta Canada
223 P4 Irnijärvi lake Finland
223 P4 Irninniemi Finland
309 I2 Irodo watercourse Madagascar
126 G4 Iron Mountain Michigan USA
126 G3 Iron River Michigan USA
122 I5 Ironbound Islands Newfoundland and Labrador Canada
126 E3 Ironton Minnesota USA
126 F8 Ironton Missouri USA
126 J7 Ironton Ohio USA
126 F3 Ironwood Michigan USA
377 H5 Iroquis Reef Spratly Islands
125 Q4 Iroquois South Dakota USA
Irrawaddy see Ayeyarwady Myanmar
119 O7 Irricana Alberta Canada
124 F4 Irrigon Oregon USA
225 M4 Irši Latvia
224 I3 Irsta Sweden
236 O7 Irtysh watercourse Russian Federation
389 L2 Irtyshsk Kazakhstan
230 F2 Irún Spain
230 F2 Irurtzun Spain
119 P8 Irvine Alberta Canada
244 D5 Irvine North Ayrshire Scotland UK
128 D4 Irvine California USA
124 C2 Irvines Landing British Columbia Canada
130 C4 Irving Texas USA
126 H8 Irvington Kentucky USA
423 E6 Irwell New Zealand
424 E7 Irwin watercourse WA Australia
124 J5 Irwin Idaho USA
131 J4 Irwinton Georgia USA
305 F2 Isa Nigeria
159 I5 Isaac Portilho Brazil

426 8 **Isabel** *admin. area* Solomon Islands
125 O4 **Isabel** South Dakota USA
377 I6 **Isabela** Philippines
135 G3 **Isabela, Cabo** *cape* Dominican Republic
163 4 **Isabela, Canal** *strait* Archipiélago de Colón (Galapagos Islands)
163 4 **Isabela, Isla** *island* Archipiélago de Colón (Galapagos Islands)
134 C4 **Isabelia, Cordillera** *range* Nicaragua
126 F3 **Isabella** Minnesota USA
128 C3 **Isabella Lake** California USA
236 S3 **Isachenko, Ostrov** *island* Russian Federation
117 I3 **Isachsen, Cape** Nunavut Canada
222 inset **Ísafjarðardjúp** *bay* Iceland
222 inset **Ísafjörður** Iceland
392 D6 **Isagarh** Madhya Pradesh India
386 F5 **Isahaya** Japan
78 L4 **Isakov Seamount** *underwater feature* Pacific Ocean
238 F5 **Isakovo** Russian Federation
227 L5 **Isalniţa** Romania
309 I4 **Isalo, Massif d'** *range* Madagascar
306 D4 **Isambe** Democratic Republic of Congo
306 C4 **Isandja** Democratic Republic of Congo
306 C4 **Isanga** Democratic Republic of Congo
426 7 **Isangel** Vanuatu
306 C3 **Isangi** Democratic Republic of Congo
305 F3 **Isanlu** Nigeria
306 D4 **Isasa** Democratic Republic of Congo
234 G2 **Isayevo** Ukraine
244 inset **Isbister** Shetland Scotland UK
230 D3 **Íscar** Spain
159 E6 **Iscayachi** Bolivia
235 G6 **İscehisar** Turkey
226 F4 **Ischgl** Austria
233 E6 **Ischia, Isola d'** *island* Italy
154 B4 **Iscuande** *watercourse* Colombia
154 B4 **Iscuandé** Colombia
424 G5 **Isdell, Mount** WA Australia
226 B4 **Isdes** France
387 H4 **Ise** Japan
224 F5 **Isefjord** *bay* Denmark
307 E5 **Iseke** Tanzania
226 G4 **Isel** *watercourse* Austria
436 M2 **Iselin Bank** *underwater feature* Southern Ocean
226 E4 **Iselle** Italy
226 G3 **Isen** *watercourse* Germany
232 D4 **Iseo** Italy
229 G4 **Isère** *watercourse* France
155 H3 **Isère, Pointe** *cape* French Guiana
233 F6 **Isernia** Italy
387 H4 **Isesaki** Japan
389 K6 **Isfana** Kyrgyzstan
236 D3 **Isfjorden** *strait* Norway
390 E3 **Ishān Ḩamzah** Iraq
306 D4 **Ishasha** Uganda
236 M6 **Isherim, Gora** *mountain* Russian Federation
155 G4 **Isherton** Guyana
381 I4 **Ishigaki** Japan
381 I4 **Ishigaki-shima** *island* Japan
387 I2 **Ishikari-gawa** *watercourse* Japan
387 I2 **Ishikari-Wan** *bay* Japan
389 K2 **Ishim** Russian Federation
387 I3 **Ishinomaki** Japan
386 G5 **Ishizuchi-san** *volcano* Japan
126 H3 **Ishpeming** Michigan USA
244 C4 **Ishriff** Highland Scotland UK
161 H4 **Isidoro Noblía** Uruguay
389 K2 **Isil'kul'** Russian Federation
306 E5 **Isimbira** Tanzania
237 X8 **Isinga** Russian Federation
385 G2 **Isinga** Russian Federation
307 F3 **Isiolo** Kenya
306 D3 **Isiro** Democratic Republic of Congo
425 M6 **Isisford** Qld Australia
235 E7 **İskandil Burnu** *cape* Turkey
235 F6 **İskenderun Körfezi** *sea* Turkey
394 E5 **Iskilip** Turkey
388 F4 **Iskine** Kazakhstan
389 N2 **Iskitim** Russian Federation
234 C4 **Iskrovci** Serbia
234 C4 **Iskur** *watercourse* Bulgaria
223 N2 **Iškuras** Norway
223 N2 **Iškuras** *mountain* Norway
307 I1 **Iskushuban** Somalia
118 F4 **Iskut** *watercourse* British Columbia Canada
244 E4 **Isla** *watercourse* Scotland UK
163 6a **Isla, Punta** *cape* Isla Róbinson Crusoe
133 H5 **Isla de Aguada** Mexico
163 5 **Isla de Pascua (Easter Island)** *island* Chile
132 D4 **Isla del Bosque** Mexico
154 C5 **Isla Inayuga** Peru
132 D2 **Isla Madero, Presa Fco.** *lake* Mexico
133 I4 **Isla Mujeres** Mexico
134 E5 **Isla Tigre** Panama
158 D1 **Isla Tigre** Peru
161 G3 **Isla Umbú** Paraguay
391 L2 **Islamabad** *admin. area* Pakistan
391 M2 **Islāmābād** Pakistan
391 L4 **Islamgarh** Pakistan
391 L5 **Islamkot** Pakistan
392 D6 **Islamnagar** Madhya Pradesh India
377 H5 **Island Bay** Philippines
119 T5 **Island Falls** Saskatchewan Canada
425 K7 **Island Lagoon** SA Australia
119 O5 **Island Lake** Alberta Canada
120 H6 **Island Lake** Manitoba Canada
126 E3 **Island Lake Reservoir** Minnesota USA
245 G2 **Island Magee** Northern Ireland UK
124 J4 **Island Park** Idaho USA
124 J4 **Island Park Reservoir** Idaho USA
123 J8 **Island Pond** Newfoundland and Labrador Canada
122 I5 **Islands, Bay of** Newfoundland and Labrador Canada
422 F2 **Islands, Bay of** New Zealand
Islas Malvinas *see* **Falkland Islands** Atlantic Ocean
77 P15 **Islas Orcadas Rise** *underwater feature* Atlantic Ocean
244 B5 **Islay** *island* Scotland UK
228 E4 **Isle** *watercourse* France
123 I9 **Isle aux Morts** Newfoundland and Labrador Canada
242 D2 **Isle of Man** *British crown dependency* UK
244 D6 **Isle of Whithorn** Dumfries and Galloway Scotland UK
241 F4 **Isle of Wight** *admin. area* England UK
301 G1 **Isles Baleares** *admin. area* Spain
240 A5 **Isles of Scilly** England UK
240 A5 **Isles of Scilly** *admin. area* England UK
244 inset **Islesburgh** Shetland Scotland UK
241 G3 **Islington** Greater London England UK
241 G2 **Islip** Northamptonshire England UK
229 J2 **Ismaning** Germany
302 E2 **Isnā** Egypt
225 M5 **Išnarų ežeras** *lake* Lithuania
224 F4 **Isny** Germany
229 J3 **Isny im Allgäu** Germany
225 P4 **Iso-Kero** *lake* Finland
223 P4 **Iso-Kiimanen** *lake* Finland
223 O5 **Iso Lamujärvi** *lake* Finland
225 M2 **Iso-Loytäne** *lake* Finland
223 O5 **Iso-Naaklima** *lake* Finland
223 P4 **Iso-Pyhäntä** *lake* Finland
225 M2 **Iso Roine** *lake* Finland
223 O4 **Iso-Syöte** *mountain* Finland
223 P5 **Iso Tipasjärvi** *lake* Finland
223 N3 **Iso Vietonen** *lake* Finland
225 M2 **Isojärven kansallispuisto** *park* Finland
225 M2 **Isojärvi** *lake* Finland
222 L5 **Isojoki** Finland
309 F2 **Isoka** Zambia
225 K2 **Isokari** *island* Finland
223 P4 **Isokumpu** Finland
222 M5 **Isokyrö** Finland
229 H4 **Isola** France
130 F4 **Isola** Mississippi USA
233 E7 **Isola delle Femmine** Italy
233 G7 **Isola di Capo Rizzuto** Italy
225 K2 **Isoma** *island* Finland
306 E5 **Isopa** Tanzania
394 D6 **Isparta** *admin. area* Turkey
234 D1 **Ispas** Ukraine
233 F8 **Ispica** Italy
226 E5 **Ispra** Italy
388 D5 **Ispravnaya** Russian Federation
226 E3 **Ispringen** Germany
390 C3 **Israel** *country*
157 B7 **Israelândia** Brazil
424 G8 **Israelite Bay** WA Australia
225 O4 **Issa** Russian Federation
388 D2 **Issa** Russian Federation
389 L3 **Issen** *lake* Kazakhstan
304 C3 **Issia** Côte d'Ivoire
228 F4 **Issoire** France
232 F4 **Ist** *island* Croatia
238 B4 **Istalsna** Latvia
394 D5 **İstanbul** *admin. area* Turkey
235 F5 **İstanbul Boğazı (Bosporus)** *watercourse* Turkey
222 G6 **Isteren** *lake* Norway
376 C5 **Isthmus of Kra** *sea* Thailand
154 B2 **Isthmus of Panama** *land feature*
389 K6 **Istiqlol, Qullai** *mountain* Tajikistan
154 B3 **Istmina** Colombia
234 B4 **Istok** Kosovo
227 L1 **Istok** Poland
131 K7 **Istokpoga Lake** Florida USA
238 G5 **Istra** Russian Federation
229 G5 **Istres** France
234 F3 **Istria** Romania
223 O5 **Istunmäki** Finland
373 H5 **Isumrud Strait** Papua New Guinea
234 C3 **Isverna** Romania
388 G3 **Isyangulovo** Russian Federation
225 L1 **Itä-Aure** Finland
225 O1 **Itä-Suomen** *admin. area* Finland
157 E5 **Itabaiana** Brazil
158 E2 **Itabaiana** Brazil
157 B8 **Itaberá** Brazil
157 D6 **Itaberaba** Brazil
157 B7 **Itaberaí** Brazil
157 D7 **Itabira** Brazil
157 E6 **Itabuna** Brazil
156 B4 **Itacaiuna** *watercourse* Brazil
156 C5 **Itacajá** Brazil
157 C6 **Itacarambi** Brazil
157 E6 **Itacaré** Brazil
154 D6 **Itacuai** *watercourse* Brazil
161 G3 **Itacurubí del Rosario** Paraguay
157 D6 **Itagi** Brazil
157 E6 **Itagibá** Brazil
157 D7 **Itaguaçu** Brazil
157 D8 **Itaguaí** Brazil
154 C3 **Itagüí** Colombia
157 B8 **Itaí** Brazil
158 E5 **Itaiba** Brazil
156 D4 **Itaim** *watercourse* Brazil
161 H3 **Itaimbey** *watercourse* Paraguay
161 D4 **Itainópolis** Brazil
159 A9 **Itaipu, Represa de** *lake* Brazil
159 H2 **Itaituba** Brazil
161 I3 **Itajaí** Brazil
161 I3 **Itajaí** *watercourse* Brazil
157 B8 **Itajobi** Brazil
157 C8 **Itajubá** Brazil
233 **Italy** *country* Europe
157 E7 **Itamaraju** Brazil
157 D7 **Itamarandiba** Brazil
158 D2 **Itamarati** Brazil
157 D7 **Itambacuri** Brazil
157 D7 **Itambacuri** *watercourse* Brazil
157 D6 **Itambé** Brazil
157 D7 **Itambé, Pico de** *mountain* Brazil
309 H4 **Itampolo** Madagascar
379 G3 **Itanagar** Arunachal Pradesh India
161 H2 **Itanara** Paraguay
157 C9 **Itanhaém** Brazil
159 E2 **Itanhaua** *watercourse* Brazil
157 D7 **Itanhém** Brazil
157 E7 **Itanhém** *watercourse* Brazil
159 F5 **Itani, Serranía de** *range* Bolivia
157 B6 **Itapaci** Brazil
156 E3 **Itapagé** Brazil
159 F2 **Itaparana** *watercourse* Brazil
157 C8 **Itapecerica** Brazil
156 C3 **Itapecuru Mirim** Brazil
157 D8 **Itaperuna** Brazil
157 D6 **Itapetinga** Brazil
157 B8 **Itapetininga** Brazil
157 B8 **Itapeva** Brazil
161 I4 **Itapeva, Lagoa** *lake* Brazil
156 C4 **Itapicuru** *watercourse* Brazil
156 E3 **Itapipoca** Brazil
157 B6 **Itapirapuã** Brazil
157 B8 **Itápolis** Brazil
156 F4 **Itaporanga** Brazil
157 B8 **Itaporanga** Brazil
155 E5 **Itapuã** Brazil
161 I2 **Itapuí** Brazil
157 B6 **Itapuranga** Brazil
161 G4 **Itaqui** Brazil
157 D7 **Itarana** Brazil
157 D6 **Itarantim** Brazil
157 B9 **Itararé** Brazil
393 D6 **Itarsi** Madhya Pradesh India
130 C4 **Itasca** Texas USA
157 C8 **Itatiba** Brazil
157 B8 **Itatinga** Brazil
156 F4 **Itatuba** Brazil
159 I5 **Itauçu** Brazil
157 D4 **Itaueira** Brazil
156 D4 **Itaueira** *watercourse* Brazil
159 H6 **Itaum** Brazil
392 E5 **Itaunja** Uttar Pradesh India
377 I2 **Itbayat** *island* Philippines
235 C6 **Itéa** Greece
235 C6 **Iteas, Kolpos** *bay* Greece
306 D4 **Itebero** Democratic Republic of Congo
389 K3 **Itemgen Koli** *lake* Kazakhstan
307 E5 **Itende** Tanzania
122 N1 **Iterlak** *island* Greenland
127 M5 **Ithaca** New York USA
235 B6 **Ithaki** *island* Greece
306 C3 **Itimbiri** *watercourse* Democratic Republic of Congo
157 D7 **Itinga** Brazil
159 H5 **Itiquira** Brazil
159 H5 **Itiquira** *watercourse* Brazil
157 C8 **Itirapina** Brazil
157 D6 **Itiruçu** Brazil
158 D5 **Itiza** Chile
158 F3 **Itmurinkol'** *lake* Kazakhstan
387 H4 **Itoigawa** Japan
309 I4 **Itomampy** *watercourse* Madagascar
381 J3 **Itoman** Japan
228 E2 **Iton** *watercourse* France
157 D6 **Itororó** Brazil
233 E6 **Itri** Italy
130 F4 **Itta Bena** Mississippi USA
117 Q4 **Ittoqqortoormiit** Greenland
121 S1 **Ittuliuk, Cap** *cape* Québec Canada
157 C8 **Itu** Brazil
377 G5 **Itu Aba Island** Spratly Islands
157 D6 **Ituaçu** Brazil
154 C3 **Ituango** Colombia
157 E6 **Ituberá** Brazil
158 D2 **Itucumã** Brazil
158 D2 **Itui** *watercourse* Brazil
157 B7 **Ituiutaba** Brazil
306 D4 **Itula** Democratic Republic of Congo
307 E5 **Itumba** Tanzania
157 B7 **Itumbiara** Brazil
119 T7 **Ituna** Saskatchewan Canada
156 B4 **Itupiranga** Brazil
157 B7 **Iturama** Brazil
133 H5 **Iturbide** Mexico
306 D3 **Ituri** *watercourse* Democratic Republic of Congo
157 C8 **Ituverava** Brazil
159 E3 **Ituxi** *watercourse* Brazil
161 G3 **Ituzaingo** Argentina
226 F2 **Itz** *watercourse* Germany
224 E6 **Itzehoe** Germany
125 P8 **Iuka** Kansas USA
237 AL5 **Iul'tin** Russian Federation
224 G3 **Ivåg** *lake* Sweden
157 B9 **Ivaí** *watercourse* Brazil
161 I3 **Ivaiporã** Brazil
223 O2 **Ivalo** Finland
223 O2 **Ivalojoki** *watercourse* Finland
227 J4 **Iváncsa** Hungary
234 E1 **Ivane-Puste** Ukraine
425 M8 **Ivanhoe** NSW Australia
127 J2 **Ivanhoe** *watercourse* Ontario Canada
130 G4 **Ivanhoe** Minnesota USA
126 J2 **Ivanhoe Lake** Ontario Canada
232 G4 **Ivanić-Grad** Croatia
234 D1 **Ivano-Frankivs'k** Ukraine
394 C3 **Ivano-Frankivs'ka Oblast'** *admin. area* Ukraine
388 G3 **Ivanovka** Russian Federation
234 G1 **Ivanovka** Ukraine
234 H2 **Ivanovka** Ukraine
234 E4 **Ivanovo** Bulgaria
225 P4 **Ivanovo** Russian Federation
236 J7 **Ivanovo** Russian Federation
238 G3 **Ivanovo** Russian Federation
388 C1 **Ivanovo** Russian Federation
388 C2 **Ivanovskaya** *admin. area* Russian Federation
236 J7 **Ivanovskaya Oblast'** *admin. area* Russian Federation
389 N3 **Ivanovskiy Khrebet** *range* Kazakhstan
128 E3 **Ivanpah Lake** California USA
234 E4 **Ivanski** Bulgaria
388 F3 **Ivanteyevka** Russian Federation
227 M2 **Ivanychi** Ukraine
222 H4 **Ivarrud** Norway
235 E5 **Ivaylovgrad** Bulgaria
234 F1 **Ivcha** Ukraine
236 N6 **Ivdel'** Russian Federation
131 J4 **Ivey** Georgia USA
159 H6 **Ivinheima** Brazil
122 N2 **Ivittuut** Greenland
394 F2 **Ivnya** Russian Federation
309 I4 **Ivohibe** Madagascar
238 F6 **Ivot** Russian Federation
394 E2 **Ivotka** *watercourse* Ukraine
226 D5 **Ivrea** Italy
235 E6 **İvrindi** Turkey
388 D5 **Ivris Ugheltekhili** *pass* Georgia
121 Q1 **Ivujivik** Québec Canada
307 E5 **Ivuna** Tanzania
116 F5 **Ivvavik National Park** Yukon Territory Canada
240 D4 **Ivybridge** Devon England UK
373 I6 **Iwa Island** Papua New Guinea
387 I4 **Iwaki** Japan
386 G4 **Iwakuni** Japan
306 C4 **Iwala** Democratic Republic of Congo
387 I2 **Iwamizawa** Japan
387 I3 **Iwate-san** *volcano* Japan
306 D4 **Iwe** Democratic Republic of Congo
307 F5 **Iwimbi** Tanzania
229 L1 **Iwiny** Poland
305 E3 **Iwo** Nigeria
155 G3 **Iwokrama Mountains** Guyana
225 M6 **Iwye** Belarus
158 D4 **Ixiamas** Bolivia
133 H4 **Ixil** Mexico
132 D4 **Ixtapa** Mexico
132 E5 **Ixtapa** Mexico
132 E5 **Ixtapa, Punta** *cape* Mexico
132 D4 **Ixtlán** Mexico
241 H2 **Ixworth** Suffolk England UK
237 V8 **Iya** *watercourse* Russian Federation
302 D5 **Iyal Bakhit** Sudan
307 E5 **Iyayi** Tanzania
386 G5 **Iyo-nada** *bay* Japan
227 L3 **Iza** Ukraine
134 B4 **Izabal, Lago de** *lake* Guatemala
227 I4 **Ižakovci** Slovenia
133 H4 **Izamal** Mexico
223 V3 **Izba Bol'shaya Bab'ya** Russian Federation
388 E5 **Izberbash** Russian Federation
227 L2 **Izbica** Poland
234 D4 **Izbiceni** Romania
238 B4 **Izborsk** Russian Federation
238 E5 **Izdëshkovo** Russian Federation
390 G3 **Izeh** Iran
381 J3 **Izena-shima** *island* Japan
234 E4 **Izgrev** Bulgaria
388 G2 **Izhevsk** Russian Federation
236 L5 **Izhma** *watercourse* Russian Federation
234 F3 **Izmayil** Ukraine
394 C5 **İzmir** *admin. area* Turkey
235 E6 **İzmir Körfezi** *bay* Turkey
Izmit *see* **Kocaeli** Turkey
230 D5 **Iznajar, Embalse de** *lake* Spain
235 E5 **Iznalloz** Spain
235 F5 **İznik Gölü** *lake* Turkey
238 F5 **Iznoski** Russian Federation
232 E4 **Izola** Slovenia
159 F5 **Izozog, Banados del** *watercourse* Bolivia
234 A2 **Izsák** Hungary
387 I5 **Izu-shotō** *island* Japan
78 K4 **Izu Trench** *underwater feature* Pacific Ocean
386 F4 **Izuhara** Japan
387 G4 **Izumisano** Japan
386 G4 **Izumo** Japan
236 R3 **Izvestiy Ts.I.K., Ostrova** *island* Russian Federation
234 C4 **Izvor** Serbia
234 E4 **Izvorovo** Bulgaria
234 E2 **Izvorul Muntelui, Lacul** *lake* Romania
225 O3 **Izvoz** Russian Federation
394 F3 **Izyum** Ukraine

J

117 O6 **J. A. D. Jensen Nunatakker** *mountain* Greenland
129 L4 **J. B. Thomas, Lake** Texas USA
131 J4 **J. Strom Thurmond Lake** Georgia USA
121 N7 **Jaab Lake** Ontario Canada
225 N2 **Jaala** Finland
225 O4 **Jaalanka** Finland
225 N3 **Jaama** Estonia
225 M3 **Jaamaküla** Estonia
225 N2 **Jääsjärvi** *lake* Finland
373 J5 **Jaba** Papua New Guinea
390 E6 **Jabal Al Ḩijāz** *range* Saudi Arabia
302 E5 **Jabal Bozi** Sudan
391 H6 **Jabal Samhān** *range* Oman
390 E7 **Jabal Zuqar, Jazirat** *island* Yemen
162 E2 **Jabalí, Península** Argentina
392 E6 **Jabalpur** Madhya Pradesh India
226 B2 **Jabbeke** Belgium
233 D9 **Jabinnanah** Tunisia
424 J3 **Jabiru** NT Australia
394 E8 **Jablah** Syria
229 L4 **Jablanac** Croatia
232 H5 **Jablaničko Jezero** *lake* Bosnia and Herzegovina
234 A1 **Jabłonka** Poland
156 F5 **Jaboatão** Brazil
391 H4 **Jabri** Iran
234 A4 **Jabuka** Serbia
374 E4 **Jabung, Tanjung** *cape* Indonesia
158 C3 **Jaburu** Brazil
159 G2 **Jabuti** Brazil
231 F2 **Jaca** Spain
162 B3 **Jacaf, Canal** *strait* Chile
155 E5 **Jacaré** Brazil
157 A6 **Jacaré** Brazil
157 D5 **Jacaré** *watercourse* Brazil
159 G2 **Jacareacanga** Brazil
157 C8 **Jacareí** Brazil
158 D5 **Jacha Jipiña** Bolivia
160 D4 **Jáchal** *watercourse* Argentina
159 E3 **Jaci Paraná** Brazil
159 H4 **Jaciara** Brazil
160 F6 **Jacinto Arauz** Argentina
159 E3 **Jaciparana** *watercourse* Brazil
155 E5 **Jacitara** Brazil
130 E4 **Jack Lee, Lake** Arkansas USA
119 Q6 **Jackfish Lake** Saskatchewan Canada
120 G7 **Jackhead Harbour** Manitoba Canada
121 V1 **Jackman Sound** Nunavut Canada
130 B4 **Jacksboro** Texas USA
241 F1 **Jacksdale** Nottinghamshire England UK
163 I2 **Jackson** Barbados
130 H5 **Jackson** Alabama USA
126 J8 **Jackson** Kentucky USA
126 I5 **Jackson** Michigan USA
133 H1 **Jackson** Mississippi USA
126 G8 **Jackson** Missouri USA
131 K4 **Jackson** South Carolina USA
130 G3 **Jackson** Tennessee USA
125 J5 **Jackson** Wyoming USA
436 T2 **Jackson, Mount** *mountain* Antarctica
423 C6 **Jackson Bay** New Zealand
423 C6 **Jackson Bay** New Zealand
131 J4 **Jackson Lake** Georgia USA
125 J5 **Jackson Lake** Wyoming USA
125 M6 **Jackson Reservoir** Colorado USA
118 F4 **Jacksons** British Columbia Canada
131 K5 **Jacksonville** Florida USA
131 M3 **Jacksonville** North Carolina USA
130 D5 **Jacksonville** Texas USA
131 K5 **Jacksonville Beach** Florida USA
245 D1 **Jackstown** Ireland
135 F3 **Jacmel** Haiti
121 P7 **Jacob Island** Nunavut Canada
128 F2 **Jacob Lake** Arizona USA
391 K4 **Jacobabad** Pakistan
157 D5 **Jacobina** Brazil
240 C4 **Jacobstowe** Devon England UK
423 9 **Jacquemart Island** Campbell Island New Zealand
123 G8 **Jacques-Cartier, Détroit de** *strait* Québec Canada
123 F8 **Jacques-Cartier, Mont** Québec Canada
373 I5 **Jacquinot Bay** Papua New Guinea
128 D4 **Jacumba** California USA
156 B3 **Jacundá** *watercourse* Brazil
157 B9 **Jacupiranga** Brazil
154 D5 **Jacurapa, Parana de** *watercourse* Brazil
227 K2 **Jadachy** Poland
232 H4 **Jadar** Bosnia and Herzegovina
118 G3 **Jade City** British Columbia Canada
226 E1 **Jadebusen** *bay* Germany
224 I2 **Jädraås** Sweden
232 F4 **Jadranovo** Croatia
222 H3 **Jægtvik** Norway
158 B2 **Jaén** Peru
230 E5 **Jaén** Spain
224 C3 **Jæren** *region* Norway
393 C7 **Jafarabad Harbour** Gujarat India
Jaffa *see* **Tel Aviv-Yafo** Israel
425 K9 **Jaffa, Cape** SA Australia
393 E10 **Jaffna** Sri Lanka
393 F7 **Jagdalpur** Chhattisgarh India
226 E3 **Jagst** *watercourse* Germany
393 E7 **Jagtial** Andhra Pradesh India
157 E6 **Jaguaquara** Brazil
161 H5 **Jaguarão** Brazil
161 H5 **Jaguarão** *watercourse* Brazil
157 D5 **Jaguarari** Brazil
161 H4 **Jaguari** *watercourse* Brazil
157 B9 **Jaguariaíva** Brazil
156 E4 **Jaguaribe** Brazil
156 E4 **Jaguaribe** *watercourse* Brazil
156 E4 **Jaguaruana** Brazil
158 B4 **Jaguay** Peru
160 D4 **Jague** *watercourse* Argentina
223 M5 **Jähdyspohja** Finland
390 F7 **Jahniyah** Yemen
232 H5 **Jahorina** *mountain* Bosnia and Herzegovina
391 H4 **Jahrom** Iran
158 B3 **Jahuí, Cerro** *mountain* Peru
156 D4 **Jaicós** Brazil
372 C3 **Jailolo** Indonesia
372 D4 **Jailolo, Selat** *strait* Indonesia
393 D7 **Jaipur** Maharashtra India
392 D5 **Jaipur** Rajasthan India
379 H3 **Jairampur** Assam India
392 C5 **Jaisalmer** Rajasthan India
392 E6 **Jaitwara** Madhya Pradesh India
393 G7 **Jajapur** Orissa India
227 J4 **Ják** Hungary
234 A2 **Jakabszállás** Hungary
223 O4 **Jäkäläyaara** Finland
379 G3 **Jakar** Bhutan
374 E5 **Jakarta** Indonesia
374 E5 **Jakarta** *admin. area* Indonesia
302 C2 **Jakharrah** Libya
227 K3 **Jaklovce** Slovakia
222 K3 **Jäknajaure** *lake* Sweden
372 C6 **Jako** *island* Timor-Leste (East Timor)
222 K2 **Jakobnjargga** *peninsula* Norway
222 J3 **Jakobsbakken** Norway
223 M5 **Jakobstad/Pietarsaari** Finland
305 F3 **Jakpa** Nigeria
129 K4 **Jal** New Mexico USA
391 H5 **Jalah** Oman
389 L6 **Jalal-Abad** Kyrgyzstan
389 K5 **Jalal-Abad** *admin. area* Kyrgyzstan
391 L2 **Jalālābād** Afghanistan
302 E2 **Jalālat al Qiblīyah, Jabal al** *mountain* Egypt
392 F5 **Jalalpur** Uttar Pradesh India
392 D4 **Jalandhar** Punjab India
134 C4 **Jalapa** Nicaragua
133 F5 **Jalapa Enríquez** Mexico
223 M5 **Jalasjärvi** Finland
392 E5 **Jalaun** Uttar Pradesh India
132 D4 **Jalcocotán** Mexico
391 K3 **Jaldak** Afghanistan
157 B8 **Jales** Brazil
393 G7 **Jaleswar** Orissa India
392 F5 **Jaleswar** Nepal
390 F3 **Jalībah** Iraq
305 G3 **Jalingo** Nigeria
132 D4 **Jalisco** *admin. area* Mexico
227 I4 **Jalkovec** Croatia
224 I3 **Jälla** Sweden
224 G4 **Jällunden** *lake* Sweden
393 D7 **Jalna** Maharashtra India
427 15a **Jaloklab** *island* Marshall Islands
230 F3 **Jalón** *watercourse* Spain
392 C6 **Jalor** Rajasthan India
132 E4 **Jalpa** Mexico
379 F3 **Jalpaiguri** West Bengal India
133 F4 **Jalpan** Mexico
133 G5 **Jaltepec** *watercourse* Mexico
302 C2 **Jālū** Libya
427 15 **Jaluit Atoll** *reef* Marshall Islands
307 G3 **Jamaame** Somalia
134 E3 **Jamaica** *country* Caribbean
135 F3 **Jamaica Channel** Caribbean
225 L3 **Jämaja** Estonia
391 I4 **Jamāl Pā'īn** Iran
379 F4 **Jamalpur** Bangladesh
163 1a **Jamanota** *mountain* Aruba
159 H2 **Jamanxim** *watercourse* Brazil
133 F5 **Jamapa** *watercourse* Mexico
159 F3 **Jamari** Brazil
159 F3 **Jamari** *watercourse* Brazil
308 C2 **Jamba** Angola
158 A1 **Jambelí, Punta** *cape* Ecuador
374 D4 **Jambi** Indonesia
374 D4 **Jambi** *admin. area* Indonesia
374 C2 **Jamboaye** *watercourse* Indonesia
375 H2 **Jambongan** *island* Malaysia
375 H4 **Jambu** Indonesia
374 C2 **Jambuair, Tanjung** *cape* Indonesia
125 Q5 **James** *watercourse* South Dakota USA
127 M8 **James** *watercourse* Virginia USA
162 B3 **James, Isla** *island* Chile
121 O6 **James Bay** Ontario/Québec Canada
436 U2 **James Ross Island** Antarctica
117 J5 **James Ross Strait** Nunavut Canada
117 Q4 **Jameson Land** *region* Greenland
425 K8 **Jamestown** SA Australia
310 5b **Jamestown** St Helena
131 I2 **Jamestown** Kentucky USA
127 L5 **Jamestown** New York USA
125 P3 **Jamestown** North Dakota USA
127 K6 **Jamestown** Pennsylvania USA
131 I2 **Jamestown** Tennessee USA
393 E7 **Jamikunta** Andhra Pradesh India
393 D8 **Jamkhandi** Karnataka India
393 D7 **Jamkhed** Maharashtra India
224 E4 **Jammerbugten** *bay* Denmark
224 F5 **Jammerland Bugt** *bay* Denmark
392 D4 **Jammu** Jammu and Kashmir India/Pakistan
392 D3 **Jammu and Kashmir** *admin. area* India
392 C6 **Jamnagar** Gujarat India
393 D7 **Jamner** Maharashtra India
374 E5 **Jampang Kulon** Indonesia
391 L3 **Jampur** Pakistan
223 N5 **Jämsä** Finland
223 M2 **Jämsä** Finland
392 G6 **Jamshedpur** Jharkhand India
224 G1 **Jämtland** *admin. area* Sweden
154 B4 **Jamundí** Colombia
119 T5 **Jan Lake** Saskatchewan Canada
117 S4 **Jan Mayen** *dependency* Norway
435 F2 **Jan Mayen Fracture Zone** *underwater feature* Norwegian Sea
435 F2 **Jan Mayen Ridge** *underwater feature* Norwegian Sea
225 M2 **Janakkala** Finland
392 E6 **Janakpur** Chhattisgarh India
392 F5 **Janakpur** Nepal
157 D6 **Janaúba** Brazil
156 B2 **Janaucú, Ilha** *island* Brazil
158 B2 **Jancala** Peru
391 L2 **Jand** Pakistan
157 B8 **Jandaia do Sul** Brazil
310 H2 **Jandaq** Iran
310 3d **Jandia, Punta** *cape* Canary Islands
158 D2 **Jandiatuba** *watercourse* Brazil
230 D4 **Jándula, Embalse del** *lake* Spain
157 C5 **Janeiro** *watercourse* Brazil
155 H4 **Janemale** French Guiana
244 F4 **Janeston** Angus Scotland UK
126 G5 **Janesville** Wisconsin USA
309 G4 **Jangamo** Mozambique
391 K2 **Jangjay** Afghanistan
227 J1 **Janikowo** Poland
223 Q5 **Janisjoki** *watercourse* Finland
234 A3 **Janja** Bosnia and Herzegovina
223 N5 **Jänkä** Finland
223 M3 **Jänkisjärvi** Sweden
223 P2 **Jankkila** Finland
234 B4 **Jankov Kamen** *mountain* Serbia
227 I2 **Janków** Poland
129 H5 **Janos** Mexico
227 I4 **Jánossomorja** Hungary
227 K2 **Janowiec** Poland
227 K1 **Janowo** Poland
308 D6 **Jansenville** South Africa
222 H5 **Jänsmässholmen** Sweden
162 D3 **Janssen, Bahía** *bay* Argentina
374 B2 **Jantho** Indonesia
157 C6 **Januária** Brazil
228 D2 **Janville** France
228 D3 **Janzé** France
392 D6 **Jaora** Madhya Pradesh India
387 H3 **Japan** *country*
386 G3 **Japan, Sea of (East Sea)** Japan
78 J3 **Japan Basin** *underwater feature* Sea of Japan (East Sea)
78 K4 **Japan Trench** *underwater feature* Pacific Ocean
157 D8 **Japeri** Brazil
223 O5 **Jäppilä** Finland
224 E5 **Japsand** *island* Germany
155 E5 **Japura** *watercourse* Brazil
374 D4 **Japura** Indonesia
379 G3 **Japvo Mount** Assam India
134 E6 **Jaqué** Panama
134 E6 **Jaque, Punta** *cape* Panama
163 I5 **Jaquot, Pointe** *cape* Dominica
157 B6 **Jaraguá** Brazil
157 B9 **Jaraguá do Sul** Brazil
230 D3 **Jaraiz de la Vera** Spain
234 A3 **Jarak** Serbia
162 B3 **Jaramillo** Argentina
162 C4 **Jaramillo** Argentina
155 H5 **Jaraucu** *watercourse* Brazil
156 E3 **Jardim** Brazil
159 G6 **Jardim** Brazil
156 E4 **Jardim de Piranhas** Brazil
156 E4 **Jardim do Seridó** Brazil
134 E2 **Jardines de la Reina, Archipiélago de los** *island* Cuba
222 L2 **Jarga** *island* Norway
383 J3 **Jargalan** Mongolia
384 D3 **Jargalant** Mongolia
384 D3 **Jargalant** Mongolia
384 D3 **Jargalant** Mongolia
384 E2 **Jargalant** Mongolia
384 F3 **Jargalant** Mongolia
383 K3 **Jargalant Uul** *mountain* Mongolia
384 G3 **Jargalthaan** Mongolia
223 N2 **Jårgastak** Norway
228 F3 **Jargeau** France
391 K2 **Jarghān** Afghanistan
223 M3 **Jarhois** Sweden
156 A3 **Jari** *watercourse* Brazil
159 F2 **Jari, Lago** *lake* Brazil
234 E3 **Jariştea** Romania
224 H3 **Järnlunden** *lake* Sweden
224 G3 **Järnsjön** *lake* Sweden
229 G2 **Jarny** France
227 I2 **Jarocin** Poland
224 I5 **Jarosławiec** Poland
222 H5 **Järpen** Sweden
389 J6 **Jarqo'rg'on** Uzbekistan
131 M2 **Jarratt** Virginia USA
228 D2 **Jarron** France
243 G2 **Jarrow** Tyne and Wear England UK
384 F5 **Jartai Yanchi** *lake* Nei Mongol Zizhiqu China
159 F3 **Jaru** Brazil
225 M3 **Järvamaa** *admin. area* Estonia
119 O5 **Jarvie** Alberta Canada
223 O4 **Järvikylä** Finland
127 L5 **Jarvis** Ontario Canada
426 1 **Jarvis Island** *unincorporated US territory* Pacific Ocean
222 I4 **Järvsand** Sweden
392 E5 **Jarwal** Uttar Pradesh India
393 C6 **Jasdan** Gujarat India
227 I5 **Jasenica** Bosnia and Herzegovina
227 H2 **Jasień** Poland
304 E3 **Jasikan** Ghana
227 K3 **Jasiołka** *watercourse* Poland
391 I4 **Jāsk** Iran
227 K3 **Jaśliska** Poland
227 K3 **Jasło** Poland
436 U2 **Jason Peninsula** Antarctica
118 L6 **Jasper** Alberta Canada
130 H4 **Jasper** Alabama USA
130 E3 **Jasper** Arkansas USA
131 J5 **Jasper** Florida USA
126 H7 **Jasper** Indiana USA
126 D8 **Jasper** Missouri USA
130 E5 **Jasper** Texas USA
118 M6 **Jasper National Park** Alberta Canada
227 J3 **Jastrzębie-Zdrój** Poland
227 K4 **Jász-Nagykun-Szolnok** *admin. area* Hungary
232 H3 **Jászberény** Hungary
232 H3 **Jászjákóhalma** Hungary
234 B2 **Jásztelek** Hungary
157 B7 **Jataí** Brazil
161 I2 **Jataizinho** Brazil
393 F7 **Jatani** Orissa India
155 G5 **Jatapu** *watercourse* Brazil
392 E6 **Jatara** Madhya Pradesh India
392 D5 **Jatari** Uttar Pradesh India
159 H6 **Jateí** Brazil
375 F5 **Jatiroto** Indonesia
156 A4 **Jatobá** Brazil
156 E5 **Jatobá** Brazil
157 A8 **Jatobá** Brazil
391 L3 **Jatoi Janubi** Pakistan
222 J6 **Jättholmarna** *island* Sweden
159 F3 **Jatuarana** Brazil
159 E6 **Jatun** Bolivia
158 B3 **Jatun Patay** Peru
158 D4 **Jatunari, Serranía** *range* Bolivia
157 B8 **Jaú** Brazil
155 F5 **Jaú** *watercourse* Brazil
155 F5 **Jauaperi** *watercourse* Brazil
155 H5 **Jauari, Serra** *range* Brazil
155 E5 **Jauató** Brazil
228 F2 **Jaulgonne** France
133 F4 **Jaumave** Mexico
238 B4 **Jaunanna** Latvia
228 E3 **Jaunay-Clan** France
225 N4 **Jaungulbene** Latvia
392 F6 **Jaunpur** Uttar Pradesh India
223 O4 **Jaurakkajärvi** Finland
159 G4 **Jauru** Brazil
159 H5 **Jauru** Brazil
223 P3 **Jaurutunturi** *island* Finland
Java *see* **Jawa** Indonesia
81 P5 **Java Ridge** *underwater feature* Indian Ocean
Java Sea *see* **Jawa, Laut** Indonesia
81 P6 **Java Trench** *underwater feature* Indian Ocean
158 C2 **Javari** *watercourse* Peru
158 C2 **Javari Mirim** *watercourse* Peru
223 O3 **Javarus** Finland
223 O3 **Javarusjärvi** *lake* Finland
384 F2 **Javhlant** Mongolia
162 A4 **Javier, Isla** *island* Chile
234 B4 **Javor** *range* Serbia
227 J3 **Javorie** *mountain* Slovakia
227 I2 **Javorník** Czech Republic
222 L4 **Jävre** Sweden
222 L4 **Jävrefjärden** *bay* Sweden
375 F5 **Jawa, Laut (Java Sea)** Indonesia
374 F6 **Jawa (Java)** *island* Indonesia
374 E5 **Jawa Barat** *admin. area* Indonesia
375 F5 **Jawa Tengah** *admin. area* Indonesia
375 G5 **Jawa Timur** *admin. area* Indonesia
392 C6 **Jawai** *lake* Rajasthan India
390 D3 **Jawf, Al** *admin. area* Saudi Arabia
307 H3 **Jawhar** Somalia
229 M1 **Jawor** Poland
227 K2 **Jawor Solecki** Poland
227 L3 **Jawornik Polski** Poland
227 J2 **Jaworzno** Poland
372 F5 **Jaya, Puncak** *mountain* Indonesia
373 D7 **Jayakwadi Sagar** *lake* Maharashtra India
372 G4 **Jayapura** Indonesia
373 F5 **Jayawijaya, Pegunungan** *range* Indonesia
390 C3 **Jayb, Wādī al** *watercourse* Jordan
130 A4 **Jayton** Texas USA
391 I4 **Jāz Mūrīan** Iran
391 H6 **Jazā'ir Khurīyā' Murīyā** *island* Oman
390 G4 **Jazirat Ḩawār** *island* Bahrain
391 I6 **Jazirat Maşirah** *island* Oman
300 D3 **Jdiriya** Western Sahara
128 E3 **Jean** Nevada USA
130 F6 **Jean Lafitte** Louisiana USA
135 F3 **Jean-Rabel, Pointe** Haiti
121 T2 **Jean-Talon, Pointe** Québec Canada
130 F6 **Jeanerette** Louisiana USA
310 6b **Jeanne d'Arc, Presqu'île** *peninsula* French Southern and Antarctic Lands
127 L6 **Jeannette** Pennsylvania USA
121 V4 **Jeannin, Lac** *lake* Québec Canada
305 E3 **Jebba** Nigeria
234 B3 **Jebel** Romania
388 G6 **Jebel** Turkmenistan
302 D4 **Jebel Abyad Plateau** *desert* Sudan
302 E4 **Jebel Qerri** Sudan
391 K4 **Jebri** Pakistan
374 E4 **Jebus** Indonesia
244 F5 **Jedburgh** Scottish Borders Scotland UK
123 J8 **Jeddore Lake** Newfoundland and Labrador Canada
227 K2 **Jedlińsk** Poland
232 G2 **Jedovnice** Czech Republic
227 K2 **Jędrzejów** Poland
223 O3 **Jeesiö** Finland
223 N3 **Jeesiöjärvi** Finland
226 F1 **Jeetze** *watercourse* Germany
302 C3 **Jef-Jef, Plateau de** *plain* Chad

125 R4 **Jeffers** Minnesota USA
129 J1 **Jefferson** Colorado USA
124 D4 **Jefferson** Oregon USA
127 P4 **Jefferson, Mount** New Hampshire USA
126 E7 **Jefferson City** Missouri USA
305 E2 **Jega** Nigeria
Jeju *see* **Cheju** South Korea
225 M4 **Jēkabpils** Latvia
225 M4 **Jēkabpils** *admin. area* Latvia
436 X2 **Jelbart Ice Shelf** Antarctica
227 J3 **Jelenec** Slovakia
227 H2 **Jelenin** Poland
225 L4 **Jelgava** Latvia
225 L4 **Jelgavas** *admin. area* Latvia
224 F3 **Jeløy** *island* Norway
232 G5 **Jelsa** Croatia
224 D3 **Jelsa** Norway
300 E2 **Jemaa de Mrirt** Morocco
374 E3 **Jemaja** *island* Indonesia
375 G6 **Jember** Indonesia
129 I3 **Jemez Springs** New Mexico USA
305 F3 **Jemma** Nigeria
227 H3 **Jemnice** Czech Republic
427 15 **Jemo** *island* Marshall Islands
375 G4 **Jempang, Danau** *lake* Indonesia
226 F2 **Jena** Germany
130 E5 **Jena** Louisiana USA
391 H4 **Jenāḩ** Iran
309 F2 **Jenda** Malawi
301 H1 **Jendouba** Tunisia
155 I4 **Jenipapo** Brazil
119 P7 **Jenner** Alberta Canada
227 I4 **Jennersdorf** Austria
131 J5 **Jennings** Florida USA
130 E5 **Jennings** Louisiana USA
155 H3 **Jenny** Suriname
163 15 **Jenny Point** *cape* Dominica
375 F5 **Jepara** Indonesia
223 M5 **Jeppo** Finland
157 D6 **Jequié** Brazil
157 D7 **Jequitinhonha** Brazil
157 D7 **Jequitinhonha** *watercourse* Brazil
301 F2 **Jerada** Morocco
374 D3 **Jerantut** Malaysia
135 F3 **Jérémie** Haiti
156 E5 **Jeremoabo** Brazil
307 G2 **Jerer** *watercourse* Ethiopia
375 H6 **Jereweh** Indonesia
230 C5 **Jerez de la Frontera** Spain
230 C4 **Jerez de los Caballeros** Spain
222 K4 **Jerfojaur** Sweden
222 N2 **Jergul** Norway
425 M5 **Jericho** Qld Australia
128 F1 **Jericho** Utah USA
226 G1 **Jerichow** Germany
375 F3 **Jerijeh, Tanjung** *cape* Malaysia
425 M8 **Jerilderie** NSW Australia
227 H2 **Jerischke** Germany
223 N3 **Jerisjärvi** *lake* Finland
227 I2 **Jerka** Poland
128 F3 **Jerome** Arizona USA
124 H5 **Jerome** Idaho USA
159 H5 **Jerônimo** Brazil
245 F2 **Jerrettspass** Newry and Mourne Northern Ireland UK
228 C2 **Jersey** *British crown dependency* UK
127 N6 **Jersey City** New Jersey USA
374 D2 **Jertih** Malaysia
Jerusalem *see* **Yerushalayim (Al Quds)** Israel
425 N8 **Jervis Bay Territory** *admin. area* Australia
118 J8 **Jervis Inlet** British Columbia Canada
373 G6 **Jervis Island** Australia
227 J1 **Jerzwald** Poland
232 F3 **Jesenice** Slovenia
232 G1 **Jeseník** Czech Republic
232 E5 **Jesi** Italy
226 G5 **Jesolo** Italy
379 F4 **Jessore** Bangladesh
131 K5 **Jesup** Georgia USA
135 G5 **Jesús Carranza** Mexico
130 B2 **Jet** Oklahoma USA
304 A2 **Jeta, Ilha de** *island* Guinea-Bissau
119 U4 **Jetait** Manitoba Canada
225 M4 **Jeti** Estonia
157 D8 **Jetibá** Brazil
125 P7 **Jetmore** Kansas USA
227 I3 **Jevišovka** *watercourse* Czech Republic
125 P7 **Jewell** Kansas USA
130 C5 **Jewett** Texas USA
234 A4 **Jezercë, Maja** *mountain* Albania
232 G4 **Jezero** Bosnia and Herzegovina
227 I5 **Jezerski Grad** Bosnia and Herzegovina
227 J1 **Jeżewo** Poland
394 B2 **Jezioro Drestwo** *lake* Poland
392 G6 **Jha Jha** Bihar India
392 D6 **Jhabua** Madhya Pradesh India
391 K4 **Jhal** Pakistan
379 G4 **Jhalokati** Bangladesh
392 D6 **Jhalrapatan** Rajasthan India
391 L3 **Jhang Sadr** Pakistan
392 G5 **Jhanjharpur** Bihar India
392 E6 **Jhansi** Uttar Pradesh India
392 G5 **Jhapa** Bihar India
392 D6 **Jharda** Madhya Pradesh India
393 G6 **Jhargram** West Bengal India
392 F6 **Jharkhand** *admin. area* India
393 F7 **Jharsuguda** Orissa India
391 M3 **Jhelum** Pakistan
391 L3 **Jhelum** *watercourse* Pakistan
379 F4 **Jhenaidah** Bangladesh
393 F6 **Jhinkpani** Jharkhand India
391 L3 **Jhok Bodo** Pakistan
160 F2 **Jhovy** Paraguay
392 D5 **Jhunjhunun** Rajasthan India
159 F3 **Ji-Paraná, Rio** *watercourse* Brazil
379 H2 **Ji Qu** *watercourse* Qinghai China
385 G3 **Ji'an** Jiangxi China
381 K4 **Ji'an** Jilin China
385 H4 **Jia Xian** Henan China
381 G3 **Jiading** Jiangxi China
385 J2 **Jiagedaqi** Heilongjiang China
381 J3 **Jiahe** Hunan China
378 E3 **Jiajia** Xizang Zizhiqu China
383 J6 **Jiajiboluoge** Qinghai China
380 E1 **Jialing Jiang** *watercourse* Jiangsu China
384 G5 **Jialu** Shaanxi China
385 L3 **Jiamusi** Heilongjiang China
381 F4 **Jian Jiang** *watercourse* Guangdong China
227 L5 **Jiana** Romania
385 I5 **Jianchang** Liaoning China
381 H2 **Jiande** Zhejiang China
381 H2 **Jiangdu** Jiangsu China
379 F3 **Jiangga** Xizang Zizhiqu China
380 E2 **Jiangkou** Sichuan China
381 G3 **Jiangkou Shuiku** *lake* Jiangxi China
381 G4 **Jiangmen** Guangdong China
380 D4 **Jiangna** Yunnan China
381 H1 **Jiangsu** *admin. area* China
381 G3 **Jiangxi** *admin. area* China
384 G6 **Jiangxian** Shanxi China
381 H2 **Jiangyan** Jiangsu China
381 H2 **Jiangyin** Jiangsu China
380 D2 **Jiangyou** Sichuan China
379 F3 **Jiangzi** Xizang Zizhiqu China
380 E1 **Jianjun** Shaanxi China
381 H3 **Jian'ou** Fujian China
380 C2 **Jianshe** Sichuan China
380 C3 **Jiantang** Yunnan China
381 H3 **Jianyang** Fujian China
380 D2 **Jianyang** Sichuan China
381 G4 **Jiaocheng** Guangdong China
385 K4 **Jiaohe** Jilin China
380 D3 **Jiaokui** Yunnan China
385 I6 **Jiaonan** Shandong China
385 I6 **Jiaozhou** Shandong China
381 G1 **Jiaozuo** Henan China
381 G4 **Jiapeng Liedao** *island* Guangdong China
382 E5 **Jiashi** Xinjiang Uygur Zizhiqu China
381 H2 **Jiaxing** Zhejiang China
383 K5 **Jiayuguang** Gansu China
390 F5 **Jibal Ţuwayq** *range* Saudi Arabia
424 F7 **Jibberding** WA Australia
234 D3 **Jibert** Romania
301 H6 **Jibiya** Niger
391 H6 **Jibjāt** Oman
159 H5 **Jibóia, Serra da** *range* Brazil
234 C2 **Jibou** Romania
227 L4 **Jichişu de Jos** Romania
227 H2 **Jičín** Czech Republic
390 D5 **Jiddah (Jeddah)** Saudi Arabia
154 C5 **Jidina** Colombia
379 H3 **Jido** Arunachal Pradesh India
381 J3 **Jidong** Heilongjiang China
234 D2 **Jidvieu** Romania
379 H2 **Jiegu** Qinghai China
222 K2 **Jiehkkevarri** *mountain* Norway
385 I6 **Jiehu** Shandong China
236 F5 **Jiek'kevarri** *mountain* Norway
381 G4 **Jieshi Wan** *bay* Guangdong China
381 G1 **Jieshou** Anhui China
384 G5 **Jiexiu** Shanxi China
381 G4 **Jieyang** Guangdong China
305 F2 **Jigawa** *admin. area* Nigeria
383 I6 **Jiggitai Tsho** *lake* Qinghai China
381 H4 **Jih-Yueh T'an** *lake* Taiwan China
227 H3 **Jihlava** Czech Republic
227 H3 **Jihlava** *watercourse* Czech Republic
227 H3 **Jihočeský Kraj** *admin. area* Czech Republic
227 I3 **Jihomoravský Kraj** *admin. area* Czech Republic
301 H1 **Jijel** Algeria
301 H1 **Jijel** *admin. area* Algeria
380 E2 **Jijiang** Chongqing China
307 G2 **Jijiga** Ethiopia
383 H3 **Jili Hu** *lake* Xinjiang Uygur Zizhiqu China
307 G3 **Jilib** Somalia
385 K4 **Jilin** *admin. area* China
385 K4 **Jilin** Jilin China
382 G4 **Jiliyuzi** Xinjiang Uygur Zizhiqu China
222 J4 **Jiltjaur** Sweden
307 F2 **Jima** Ethiopia
134 E2 **Jimaguayu, Embalse de** *lake* Cuba
380 C1 **Jimai** Qinghai China
306 C6 **Jimbe** *watercourse* Zambia
307 F5 **Jimbo** Tanzania
129 J7 **Jiménez** Mexico
132 D2 **Jiménez** Mexico
132 E2 **Jiménez** Mexico
305 G3 **Jimeta** Nigeria
373 H5 **Jimi** *watercourse* Papua New Guinea
385 I6 **Jimo** Shandong China
383 I4 **Jimusa'er** Xinjiang Uygur Zizhiqu China
372 E5 **Jin, Kepulauan** *island* Indonesia
381 G3 **Jin Jiang** *watercourse* Jiangxi China
381 H3 **Jin Xi** *watercourse* Fujian China
380 E2 **Jin'e** Sichuan China
385 H6 **Jinan** Shandong China
380 D3 **Jinbi** Yunnan China
385 E5 **Jincheng** Gansu China
385 G6 **Jincheng** Shanxi China
380 D3 **Jincheng** Sichuan China
380 E2 **Jincheng** Sichuan China
380 D3 **Jincheng** Yunnan China
380 D2 **Jinchuan** Sichuan China
392 D5 **Jind** Haryana India
380 C3 **Jinding** Yunnan China
380 E2 **Jinfo Shan** *mountain* Chongqing China
384 F6 **Jing He** *watercourse* Gansu China
380 E1 **Jing He** *watercourse* Shaanxi China
381 H2 **Jing Xian** Anhui China
384 F6 **Jingchuan** Gansu China
381 H2 **Jingdezhen** Jiangxi China
381 G3 **Jinggangshan** Jiangxi China
382 G4 **Jinghe** Xinjiang Uygur Zizhiqu China
380 C4 **Jinghong** Yunnan China
384 G5 **Jingle** Shanxi China
381 F2 **Jingmen** Hubei China
384 F6 **Jingning** Gansu China
385 I4 **Jingpeng** Nei Mongol Zizhiqu China
380 D4 **Jingping** Yunnan China
380 D3 **Jingxin** Yunnan China
381 H2 **Jingyang** Anhui China
380 E2 **Jingyang** Shaanxi China
385 K4 **Jingyu** Jilin China
380 E1 **Jingyu Nao** *mountain* Shaanxi China
384 E6 **Jingyuan** Gansu China
381 F2 **Jingzhou** Hubei China
381 F2 **Jingzhou** Hubei China
380 D4 **Jinhe** Yunnan China
380 C3 **Jinhua** Yunnan China
381 H2 **Jinhua** Zhejiang China
385 H4 **Jining** Nei Mongol Zizhiqu China
381 G1 **Jining** Shandong China
385 H6 **Jining** Shandong China
381 H4 **Jinjiang** Fujian China
381 H2 **Jinjiazhuang** Anhui China
307 F2 **Jinka** Ethiopia
381 G2 **Jinniu** *mountain* Hubei China
134 C4 **Jinotega** Nicaragua
134 C5 **Jinotepe** Nicaragua
384 F6 **Jinping** Gansu China
380 C4 **Jinping** Yunnan China
380 D4 **Jinping** Yunnan China
380 E3 **Jinsha** Guizhou China
380 C2 **Jinsha Jiang** *watercourse* Xizang Zizhiqu China
380 D3 **Jinsha Jiang** *watercourse* Yunnan China
384 G4 **Jinshan** Nei Mongol Zizhiqu China
385 I4 **Jinshan** Nei Mongol Zizhiqu China
380 D3 **Jinshan** Yunnan China
380 F3 **Jinshi** Hunan China
381 F2 **Jinshi** Hunan China
384 D3 **Jinst** Mongolia
383 K5 **Jinta** Gansu China
381 H2 **Jintan** Jiangsu China
381 I2 **Jintang Shan** *range* Zhejiang China
377 I5 **Jintotolo** *island* Philippines
393 D7 **Jintur** Maharashtra India
385 I5 **Jinxi** Liaoning China
381 G3 **Jinxi Hu** *lake* Jiangxi China
381 G1 **Jinxiang** Shandong China
380 F4 **Jinxiu** Guangxi Zhuangzu Zizhiqu China
380 D2 **Jinyuan** Sichuan China
385 G5 **Jinzhong** Shanxi China
385 J4 **Jinzhou** Liaoning China
380 C2 **Jinzhu** Sichuan China
154 A5 **Jipijapa** Ecuador
132 C2 **Jiquima** Mexico
392 D6 **Jiran** Madhya Pradesh India
159 E3 **Jirau** Brazil
229 L1 **Jiřikov** Czech Republic
307 H2 **Jirriban** Somalia
384 G6 **Jishan** Shanxi China
384 E6 **Jishi** Qinghai China
380 F3 **Jishou** Hunan China
157 E6 **Jitaúna** Brazil
381 F4 **Jitian** Guangdong China
374 D2 **Jitra** Malaysia
234 C3 **Jiu** *watercourse* Romania
381 F3 **Jiucai Ling** *mountain* Guangxi Zhuangzu Zizhiqu China
381 G2 **Jiujiang** Jiangxi China
381 G2 **Jiuling Shan** *range* Jiangxi China
380 E2 **Jiulong** Sichuan China
381 H3 **Jiulong Shan** *mountain* Zhejiang China
383 K5 **Jiuquan** Gansu China
385 J5 **Jiurongcheng** Shandong China
385 K4 **Jiutai** Jilin China
133 F5 **Jiutepec** Mexico
391 J5 **Jiwani, Rās** *cape* Pakistan
385 L3 **Jixi** Heilongjiang China
385 L3 **Jixian** Heilongjiang China
384 G6 **Jixian** Shanxi China
379 G3 **Jixiong** Xizang Zizhiqu China
385 I6 **Jiyang** Shandong China
381 F1 **Jiyuan** Henan China
390 G7 **Jiz', Wādī al** *watercourse* Yemen
390 E7 **Jīzān** *admin. area* Saudi Arabia
390 E7 **Jīzān** Saudi Arabia
385 H6 **Jize** Hebei China
390 D4 **Jizl, Wādī al** *watercourse* Saudi Arabia
389 J6 **Jizzax** Uzbekistan
389 J6 **Jizzax** *admin. area* Uzbekistan
222 G4 **Jøa** *island* Norway
161 I3 **Joaçaba** Brazil
157 D7 **Joaíma** Brazil
300 C6 **Joal-Fadiout** Senegal
156 F4 **João Câmara** Brazil
159 F4 **João Felipe** Brazil
161 H5 **João Maria, Albardão do** *watercourse* Brazil
157 D7 **João Monlevade** Brazil
156 F4 **João Pessoa** Brazil
157 C7 **João Pinheiro** Brazil
160 E3 **Joaquin V. González** Argentina
134 E2 **Jobabo** Cuba
393 D6 **Jobat** Madhya Pradesh India
227 J4 **Jobbágyi** Hungary
131 J3 **Jocassee, Lake** South Carolina USA
223 M3 **Jockfall/Jokk** Sweden
226 E3 **Jockgrim** Germany
159 H2 **Jococa** Brazil
134 C4 **Jocón** Honduras
393 F7 **Joda** Orissa India
230 E5 **Jódar** Spain
392 C5 **Jodhpur** Rajasthan India
78 N4 **Joe Ferguson Seamount** *underwater feature* Pacific Ocean
223 P5 **Joensuu** Finland
426 1a **Joe's Hill** Kiribati
222 H4 **Joesjö** Sweden
387 H4 **Joetsu** Japan
119 O6 **Joffre** Alberta Canada
119 N7 **Joffre, Mount** Alberta/British Columbia Canada
120 M7 **Jog Lake** Ontario Canada
225 N3 **Jõgeva** Estonia
225 N3 **Jõgevamaa** *admin. area* Estonia
386 F4 **Jogji-do** *island* South Korea
121 U4 **Jogues, Lac** *lake* Québec Canada
391 K3 **Johan** Pakistan
131 L3 **Johan Peninsula** Nunavut Canada
308 E5 **Johannesburg** South Africa
391 I4 **Johlū** Iran
124 F4 **John Day** Oregon USA
124 E4 **John Day** *watercourse* Oregon USA
119 N3 **John D'Or Prairie** Alberta Canada
131 L2 **John H. Kerr Reservoir** Virginia USA
125 N7 **John Martin Reservoir** Colorado USA
126 D7 **John Redmond Reservoir** Kansas USA
127 J8 **John W. Flannagan Reservoir** Virginia USA
130 D2 **Johnson** Arkansas USA
125 N7 **Johnson** Kansas USA
130 C3 **Johnson** Oklahoma USA
424 inset **Johnson Bank** Ashmore Reef and Cartier Island Australia
127 N5 **Johnson City** New York USA
131 J2 **Johnson City** Tennessee USA
130 B5 **Johnson City** Texas USA
163 7 **Johnson Harbour Settlement** Falkland Islands
121 P4 **Johnson Island** Nunavut Canada
118 E2 **Johnsons Crossing** Yukon Territory Canada
163 I8 **Johnsons Point** Antigua and Barbuda
131 L4 **Johnsonville** South Carolina USA
240 C3 **Johnston** Pembrokeshire Wales UK
78 P6 **Johnston Atoll** *reef* Pacific Ocean
78 P6 **Johnston Atoll** *unincorporated US territory* Pacific Ocean
244 D5 **Johnstone** Renfrewshire Scotland UK
245 E4 **Johnstown** Ireland
374 D3 **Johor** *admin. area* Malaysia
374 D3 **Johor Bahru** Malaysia
374 D3 **Johore Strait** Singapore
223 O2 **Johtijärvi** *lake* Finland
225 N3 **Jõhvi** Estonia
226 B4 **Joigny** France
130 F3 **Joiner** Arkansas USA
157 B9 **Joinville** Brazil
226 C3 **Joinville** France
436 U2 **Joinville Island** Antarctica
132 C2 **Jojoba** Mexico
225 M2 **Jokela** Finland
117 Q3 **Jokelbugten** *bay* Greenland
223 O5 **Jokijärvi** Finland
223 P4 **Jokijärvi** Finland
223 O4 **Jokikokko** Finland
223 N5 **Jokikylä** Finland
223 P4 **Jokikylä** Finland
223 M5 **Jokipii** Finland
222 K3 **Jokkmokk** Sweden
225 K5 **Jokūbavas** Lithuania
222 inset **Jökulsá á Brú** *watercourse* Iceland
222 inset **Jökulsá á Fjöllum** *watercourse* Iceland
223 N3 **Jolanki** Finland
121 P7 **Jolicoeur** *watercourse* Québec Canada
126 G6 **Joliet** Illinois USA
125 K4 **Joliet** Montana USA
117 L9 **Joliette** Québec Canada
130 B4 **Jolly** Texas USA
377 I6 **Jolo** Philippines
377 I6 **Jolo** *island* Philippines
377 I6 **Jolo Group** *island* Philippines
222 E6 **Jolstavatnet** *lake* Norway
377 I4 **Jomalig** *island* Philippines
375 G5 **Jombang** Indonesia
392 F5 **Jomsom** Nepal
229 I3 **Jona** Switzerland
225 M5 **Jonava** Lithuania
154 B5 **Jondachi** Ecuador
120 J1 **Jones, Cape** Nunavut Canada
436 R2 **Jones Mountains** Antarctica
424 inset **Jones Point** Christmas Island Australia
117 K3 **Jones Sound** Nunavut Canada
130 F3 **Jonesboro** Arkansas USA
130 E4 **Jonesboro** Louisiana USA
130 F5 **Jonesville** Louisiana USA
131 K3 **Jonesville** South Carolina USA
131 J2 **Jonesville** Virginia USA
223 O4 **Jongunjärvi** *lake* Finland
225 M4 **Joniškėlis** Lithuania
225 L4 **Joniškis** Lithuania
223 P5 **Jonkeri** *lake* Finland
224 H4 **Jönköping** Sweden
224 H4 **Jönköping** *admin. area* Sweden
222 G5 **Jonsvatn** *lake* Norway
133 G5 **Jonuta** Mexico
228 D4 **Jonzac** France
126 D8 **Joplin** Missouri USA
129 H7 **Jopopaco** Mexico
390 C3 **Jordan** *country*
125 L3 **Jordan** Montana USA
131 H4 **Jordan Lake** Alabama USA
124 G5 **Jordan Valley** Oregon USA
224 G2 **Jordet** Norway
162 A5 **Jorge, Cabo** *cape* Chile
162 A5 **Jorge Montt, Isla** *island* Chile
162 B4 **Jorge Montt, Ventisquero** *glacier* Chile
379 H3 **Jorhat** Assam India
159 H5 **Jorigue, Serra do** *range* Brazil
226 E1 **Jork** Germany
223 O4 **Jormasjärvi** *lake* Finland
224 H4 **Jormlien** Sweden
223 P4 **Jormua** Finland
222 L4 **Jörn** Sweden
129 I4 **Jornada del Muerto** New Mexico USA
223 O5 **Joroinen** Finland
224 D3 **Jørpeland** Norway
305 F3 **Jos** Nigeria
305 F3 **Jos Plateaux** *plain* Nigeria
377 J6 **Jose Abad Santos** Philippines
162 D2 **José B. Casás** Argentina
159 F4 **José Bonifácio** Brazil
156 D4 **José de Freitas** Brazil
162 B3 **José de San Martín** Argentina
129 K6 **José María Morelos** Mexico
159 G2 **José Santos** Brazil
230 D5 **José Torán, Embalse de** *lake* Spain
124 G4 **Joseph** Oregon USA
124 I7 **Joseph** Utah USA
121 W6 **Joseph, Lac** *lake* Newfoundland and Labrador Canada
424 H3 **Joseph Bonaparte Gulf** WA Australia
128 G3 **Joseph City** Arizona USA
76 Q6 **Josephine Bank** *underwater feature* Atlantic Ocean
392 E4 **Joshimath** Uttaranchal India
130 C4 **Joshua** Texas USA
128 E4 **Joshua Tree National Park** California USA
222 G4 **Jøssund** Norway
222 G4 **Jøssundjorden** *bay* Norway
163 21 **Jost van Dyke Island** British Virgin Islands
222 E6 **Jostedalsbreen Nasjonalpark** *park* Norway
222 E5 **Jøstølen** Norway
222 F6 **Jotunheimen Nasjonalpark** *park* Norway
223 P4 **Joukokylä** Finland
134 E1 **Joulter Cays** *island* Bahamas
390 C2 **Joûnié** Lebanon
119 N5 **Joussard** Alberta Canada
223 P3 **Joutsenaapa** *island* Finland
225 O2 **Joutseno** Finland
223 O3 **Joutsijärvi** Finland
225 L2 **Joutsjärvi** *lake* Finland
157 B7 **Joviânia** Brazil
379 G4 **Jowai** Meghalaya India
388 J6 **Jowzjān** *admin. area* Afghanistan
121 T2 **Joy, Baie** *bay* Québec Canada
133 G6 **Joya, Laguna de la** *lake* Mexico
228 G4 **Joyeuse** France
388 J6 **Jo'ynoy** Uzbekistan
379 F4 **Joypurhat** Bangladesh
227 K1 **Józefów** Poland
160 F6 **Juan A. Pradere** Argentina
132 E3 **Juan Aldama** Mexico
79 T3 **Juan de Fuca Ridge** *underwater feature* Pacific Ocean
160 E6 **Juan de Garay** Argentina
310 6a **Juan de Nova, Île** *island* Îles Éparses
163 1b **Juan Domingo** Netherlands Antilles
160 F6 **Juan E. Barra** Argentina
162 A5 **Juan Guillermos, Isla** *island* Chile
162 C4 **Juan José Albornoz** Argentina
129 H8 **Juan Jose Rios** Mexico
118 F6 **Juan Perez Sound** British Columbia Canada
133 G5 **Juan Rodríguez Clara** Mexico
162 A4 **Juan Stuven, Isla** *island* Chile
222 I5 **Juånäset** Sweden
161 G6 **Juancho** Argentina
135 G3 **Juancho** Dominican Republic
307 F5 **Juani** *island* Tanzania
158 B2 **Juanjuí** Peru
223 P5 **Juankoski** Finland
381 G2 **Juanshui** Hubei China
304 E3 **Juapon** Ghana
159 G3 **Juara** Brazil
129 H5 **Juárez** Mexico
129 L7 **Juárez** Mexico
132 D3 **Juárez** Mexico
132 A1 **Juárez, Sierra de** *range* Mexico
155 F2 **Juasjuillal** Venezuela
158 D2 **Juati** *watercourse* Brazil
157 D5 **Juàzeiro** Brazil
156 E4 **Juazeiro do Norte** Brazil
304 C3 **Juazohn** Liberia
306 E3 **Juba** Sudan
436 U2 **Jubany (Argentina)** *research station* Antarctica
307 G3 **Jubba, Webi** *watercourse* Somalia
307 G3 **Jubbada Dhexe** *admin. area* Somalia
307 G3 **Jubbada Hoose** *admin. area* Somalia
390 D4 **Jubbah** Saudi Arabia
224 E5 **Jübek** Germany
424 H7 **Jubilee Lake** WA Australia
123 K8 **Jubilee Lake** Newfoundland and Labrador Canada
228 D2 **Jublains** France
230 E4 **Júcar** *watercourse* Spain
156 E4 **Jucás** Brazil
132 E4 **Juchipila** *watercourse* Mexico
157 E7 **Jucuruçu** *watercourse* Brazil
156 E4 **Jucurutu** Brazil
229 L3 **Judenburg** Austria
125 K3 **Judith** *watercourse* Montana USA
125 K3 **Judith Gap** Montana USA
381 I2 **Juegang** Jiangsu China
121 Q2 **Juet, Lac** *lake* Québec Canada
222 L3 **Juggijaur** Sweden
425 N8 **Jugiong** NSW Australia
383 K2 **Jugnayn Nuur** *lake* Mongolia
228 C2 **Jugon-les-Lacs** France
390 E7 **Juḩā** Saudi Arabia
391 I4 **Jūhānī** Iran
134 C4 **Juigalpa** Nicaragua
226 D1 **Juist** Germany
157 D8 **Juiz de Fora** Brazil
374 D4 **Jujuhan** *watercourse* Indonesia
160 E2 **Jujuy** *admin. area* Argentina
222 L3 **Jukkasjärvi** *bay* Sweden
159 E5 **Jukumari Bajo** Bolivia
222 H4 **Jule** Norway
437 J2 **Jules, Cape** Antarctica
125 N6 **Julesburg** Colorado USA
125 N6 **Julesburg Reservoir** Colorado USA
158 D5 **Juli** Peru
425 L5 **Julia Creek** Qld Australia
158 D4 **Juliaca** Peru
128 D4 **Julian** California USA
121 Q5 **Julian, Lac** *lake* Québec Canada
163 1b **Julianadorp** Netherlands Antilles
129 J6 **Julimes** Mexico
161 H4 **Júlio de Castilhos** Brazil
223 O2 **Jullamojärvi** *lake* Finland
228 D2 **Julloville** France
381 F2 **Julong Shan** *mountain* Hubei China
385 H5 **Julu** Hebei China
223 P4 **Jumalisjärvi** *lake* Finland
159 F2 **Jumas** Brazil
231 F4 **Jumilla** Spain
391 H2 **Jūmīn** Iran
223 O5 **Juminen** Finland
392 E5 **Jumla** Nepal
306 D2 **Jummayzah** Sudan
306 E2 **Jummayzah** Sudan
155 F3 **Jumpeteri, Cerro** *mountain* Venezuela
393 C7 **Junagadh** Gujarat India
393 F7 **Junagarh** Orissa India
231 G3 **Juncosa** Spain
130 B5 **Junction** Texas USA
125 Q7 **Junction City** Kansas USA
130 E4 **Junction City** Louisiana USA
155 F5 **Jundiá** Brazil
156 F5 **Jundiá** Brazil
385 H5 **Jundu Shan** *range* Beijing China
118 D3 **Juneau** Alaska USA
118 D3 **Juneau Icefield** Alaska USA
225 J3 **Jungfrufjorden** *bay* Sweden
225 K2 **Jungfruskär** *island* Finland
383 H3 **Junggar Pendi** Xinjiang Uygur Zizhiqu China
306 E2 **Jungli Canal** *watercourse* Sudan
306 E2 **Jungoli** *admin. area* Sudan
234 B4 **Junik** Kosovo
160 F5 **Junín** Argentina
160 D1 **Junín** Chile
154 B4 **Junín** Colombia
154 A5 **Junín** Ecuador
158 C3 **Junín** Peru
158 C3 **Junín** *admin. area* Peru
158 B3 **Junín, Lago** *lake* Peru
162 B2 **Junín de los Andes** Argentina
128 F3 **Juniper Mountains** Arkansas USA
226 C3 **Juniville** France
223 M4 **Junkön** *island* Sweden
380 D3 **Junlian** Sichuan China
393 C7 **Junnar** Maharashtra India
129 L5 **Juno** Texas USA
223 M3 **Junosuando** Sweden
222 J5 **Junsele** Sweden
381 G3 **Junshan Hu** *lake* Jiangxi China
159 E6 **Juntas** Bolivia
134 C5 **Juntas** Costa Rica
223 P4 **Juntusranta** Finland
381 H3 **Junxi** Fujian China
225 M4 **Juodupė** Lithuania
223 P5 **Juojärvi** *lake* Finland
223 M3 **Juoksengi** Sweden
223 M3 **Juoksenki** Finland
225 N2 **Juolasvesi** *bay* Finland
223 O4 **Juorkuna** Finland
391 I3 **Jūpār** Iran
157 B8 **Jupiá, Represa** *lake* Brazil
131 K7 **Jupiter** Florida USA
154 D2 **Júptui** Colombia
157 C9 **Juquiá** Brazil
161 J3 **Juquitiba** Brazil
306 D2 **Jur** *watercourse* Sudan
244 B5 **Jura** *island* Scotland UK
244 C5 **Jura, Sound of** *bay* Scotland UK
154 B3 **Juradó** Colombia
225 L5 **Jurbarkas** Lithuania
228 F4 **Jurf** France
424 E7 **Jurien Bay** WA Australia
372 E5 **Juring** Indonesia
225 L4 **Jūrmala** Latvia
225 K3 **Jurmofjärden** *bay* Finland
223 O4 **Jurmu** Finland
381 H2 **Jurong** Jiangsu China
374 B3 **Jurong** *admin. area* Singapore
374 B4 **Jurong, Selat** *strait* Singapore
374 B4 **Jurong Bird Park** Singapore
374 B4 **Jurong Island** *island* Singapore
374 B4 **Jurong Park** Singapore
156 E4 **Juru** Brazil
158 C3 **Juruá** *watercourse* Brazil
159 G3 **Juruena** Brazil
159 G4 **Juruena** Brazil
159 G3 **Juruena** *watercourse* Brazil
155 F3 **Jurumato, Cerro** *mountain* Venezuela
161 I2 **Jurumirim, Represa de** *lake* Brazil
155 I4 **Jurupari, Arquipélago do** *island* Brazil
155 F2 **Jurupú** Venezuela
155 G5 **Juruti** Brazil
155 G5 **Juruti Velho** Brazil
222 L5 **Jurva** Finland
223 N5 **Jurvansalo** Finland
159 I4 **Jussara** Brazil
225 L3 **Jussarö** *island* Finland
229 G3 **Jussey** France
129 L4 **Justiceburg** Texas USA
159 F5 **Justiniano** Bolivia
160 E5 **Justo Daract** Argentina
227 I4 **Juta** Hungary
154 E5 **Jutaí** Brazil
158 D2 **Jutaí** Brazil
158 E1 **Jutaí** *watercourse* Brazil
156 A3 **Jutaí, Serra do** *mountain* Brazil
158 E5 **Jutaulha** Bolivia
226 G1 **Jüterbog** Germany
159 H6 **Juti** Brazil
134 B4 **Jutiapa** Guatemala
134 C4 **Jutiapa** Honduras
159 E1 **Jutica** Brazil
134 C4 **Juticalpa** Honduras
133 I6 **Jutiquile** Honduras
222 J3 **Jutis** Sweden
227 I2 **Jutrosin** Poland
223 P5 **Juuka** Finland
225 M2 **Juupajoki** Finland
223 Q6 **Juurikka** Finland
223 P5 **Juuruvesi** *bay* Finland
224 D3 **Juvatn** *lake* Norway
133 J4 **Juventud, Isla de la** *island* Cuba
159 G6 **Juvi** Brazil
223 P5 **Juvola** Finland
222 H5 **Juvuln** *bay* Sweden
375 F5 **Juwana** Indonesia
385 H6 **Juye** Shandong China
226 C3 **Juzennecourt** France
308 D4 **Jwaneng** Botswana
224 F5 **Jyderup** Denmark
224 E4 **Jylland** *island* Denmark
222 M5 **Jyllinkoski** Finland
223 O5 **Jyrkkä** Finland
223 N5 **Jyväskylä** Finland

K

305 F2 **K. Hausa** Nigeria
382 E6 **K2** *mountain* (disputed)
391 M2 **K2** *mountain* Pakistan
305 E2 **Ka** *watercourse* Nigeria
386 E3 **Ka-do** *island* North Korea
128 inset **Ka Lae** *cape* Hawai'i USA
Ka Tiritiri O Te Moana *see* **Southern Alps** New Zealand
128 inset **Ka'a'awa** Hawai'i USA
307 E3 **Kaabong** Uganda
155 H3 **Kaaimans Hoofd** *cape* Suriname
222 L3 **Kaalasjärvi** Sweden
222 K3 **Kaalasjärvi** *lake* Sweden
223 O2 **Kaamanen** Finland
223 O2 **Kaamasjoki** *watercourse* Finland
128 inset **Ka'anapali** Hawai'i USA
238 B2 **Kääpälä** Finland
223 M2 **Kaaresuvanto** Finland
225 L2 **Kaarina** Finland
223 P2 **Kaarmassaari** *bay* Finland
222 L3 **Kaartijärvi** Sweden
223 P5 **Kaavi** Finland
223 P5 **Kaavinjärvi** *lake* Finland
375 I5 **Kabaena** *island* Indonesia
372 B5 **Kabaena, Selat** *strait* Indonesia
304 B3 **Kabala** Sierra Leone
306 D4 **Kabale** Uganda
155 G3 **Kabalebe** *watercourse* Suriname
306 D5 **Kabalo** Democratic Republic of Congo
373 J5 **Kabaman** Papua New Guinea
306 D5 **Kabamba, Lac** *lake* Democratic Republic of Congo
389 M4 **Kabanbay** Kazakhstan
306 B5 **Kabanga** Democratic Republic of Congo
306 C6 **Kabangu** Democratic Republic of Congo
120 K6 **Kabania Lake** Ontario Canada
374 C3 **Kabanjahe** Indonesia
377 I5 **Kabankalan** Philippines
427 9 **Kabara** *island* Fiji
372 D4 **Kabarai** Indonesia
388 D5 **Kabardino Balkarskaya Resp.** *admin. area* Russian Federation
379 H4 **Kabaw Valley** Myanmar
305 F3 **Kabba** Nigeria
301 I6 **Kabélawa** Niger
126 I2 **Kabenung Lake** Ontario Canada
375 I3 **Kabetan** *island* Indonesia
126 E2 **Kabetogama Lake** Minnesota USA
306 D5 **Kabeya** Democratic Republic of Congo
225 L4 **Kabile** Latvia
376 D4 **Kabin Buri** Thailand
117 K9 **Kabinakagami Lake** Ontario Canada
306 C5 **Kabinda** Democratic Republic of Congo
305 H3 **Kabo** Central African Republic
391 L2 **Kābol** *admin. area* Afghanistan
391 L2 **Kābol (Kābul)** Afghanistan
308 D2 **Kabompo** Zambia
308 D2 **Kabompo** *watercourse* Zambia
375 F3 **Kabong** Malaysia
306 D5 **Kabongo** Democratic Republic of Congo
376 C4 **Kabosa Island** Myanmar
300 C6 **Kabrousse** Senegal
390 E5 **Kabshān** Saudi Arabia
222 J2 **Kåbtajaure** *lake* Sweden
391 I2 **Kabūdeh** Iran
309 F2 **Kabudira** *watercourse* Malawi
Kabul *see* **Kābol** Afghanistan
372 A6 **Kabunduk** Indonesia
375 J3 **Kaburuang** *island* Indonesia
302 E4 **Kabushiya** Sudan
308 E2 **Kabwe** Zambia
306 D5 **Kabwe, Lac** *lake* Democratic Republic of Congo
234 B3 **Kačarevo** Serbia
308 F2 **Kachalola** Zambia
392 B6 **Kachchh, Gulf of** Gujarat India
237 AA6 **Kachkattsy** Russian Federation
379 H4 **Kachin** *admin. area* Myanmar
306 E4 **Kachira, Lake** *lake* Uganda
389 L2 **Kachiry** Kazakhstan
307 F2 **Kachisi** Ethiopia
237 W6 **Kachug** Russian Federation
391 I3 **Kachūli** Iran
309 G3 **Kachulu** Malawi
307 E3 **Kachung** Uganda
394 G5 **Kaçkar Daği** *mountain* Turkey
229 K1 **Kadaň** Czech Republic
376 C4 **Kadan Kyun** Myanmar
375 G5 **Kadapongan** *island* Indonesia
375 I5 **Kadatuang** *island* Indonesia
427 9 **Kadavu** *island* Fiji
427 9 **Kadavu Passage** *strait* Fiji
304 D3 **Kade** Ghana
306 B3 **Kadéï** *watercourse* Central African Republic
392 C6 **Kadi** Gujarat India
304 B2 **Kadiondola, Mount** *mountain* Guinea
393 E8 **Kadiri** Andhra Pradesh India
394 F6 **Kadirli** Turkey
305 I2 **Kadja, Ouadi** *watercourse* Chad
393 C9 **Kadmat Island** Lakshadweep India
125 O5 **Kadoka** South Dakota USA
388 D2 **Kadom** Russian Federation
308 E3 **Kadoma** Zimbabwe
373 H4 **Kadova Island** Papua New Guinea
302 D5 **Kadugli** Sudan
305 F2 **Kaduna** Nigeria
305 F2 **Kaduna** *admin. area* Nigeria
305 F2 **Kaduna** *watercourse* Nigeria
379 H3 **Kadusam** *mountain* Arunachal Pradesh India
238 G3 **Kaduy** Russian Federation
386 E3 **Kaechon** North Korea
300 D5 **Kaédi** Mauritania
123 K8 **Kaegudeck Lake** Newfoundland and Labrador Canada
305 G2 **Kaélé** Cameroon
128 inset **Kaelekū** Hawai'i USA
128 inset **Ka'ena Point** Hawai'i USA
223 Q5 **Käenkoski** Finland
386 E4 **Kaesŏng** North Korea
306 C5 **Kafakumba** Democratic Republic of Congo
388 E6 **Kafan** Armenia
305 F3 **Kafanchan** Nigeria
387 G1 **Kafen** *watercourse* Russian Federation
394 F6 **Kafer ez Zaïta** Syria
372 D4 **Kafiau** *island* Indonesia
235 D6 **Kafireas, Akra** *cape* Greece
223 M2 **Kåfjord** Norway
222 L2 **Kåfjorddalen** Norway
308 E3 **Kafue Flats** Zambia
304 D3 **Kafolo** Côte d'Ivoire
302 E1 **Kafr ash Shaykh** Egypt
306 E3 **Kafu** *watercourse* Uganda
308 E3 **Kafue** *watercourse* Zambia
308 E3 **Kafue Gorge** Zambia
379 F3 **Kaga** Xizang Zizhiqu China
388 G2 **Kaga** Russian Federation
305 H3 **Kaga Bandoro** Central African Republic
127 J4 **Kagawong** Ontario Canada
222 L4 **Kåge** Sweden
222 L4 **Kagefjärd** *bay* Sweden
382 F5 **Kageleke** Xinjiang Uygur Zizhiqu China
222 L1 **Kågen** *island* Norway
306 E4 **Kagera** *admin. area* Tanzania
306 E4 **Kagera** *watercourse* Tanzania
120 K7 **Kagianagami Lake** Ontario Canada
376 B3 **Kagin** Myanmar
394 G5 **Kağızman** Turkey
426 2a **Kagman** Northern Mariana Islands
374 C4 **Kagologolo** Indonesia
305 F3 **Kagoro** Nigeria
386 F5 **Kagoshima** Japan
128 inset **Kahala Point** Hawai'i USA
391 K3 **Kahan** Pakistan
375 J3 **Kahatola** *island* Indonesia
375 G4 **Kahayan** *watercourse* Indonesia
306 B5 **Kahemba** Democratic Republic of Congo
391 I4 **Kahnūj** Iran
304 C3 **Kahnwia** Liberia

128 inset **Kaho'olawe** Hawai'i USA
394 F5 **Kahraman-Maraş** *admin. area* Turkey
394 F6 **Kahramanmaraş** Turkey
391 L3 **Kahror Pakka** Pakistan
128 inset **Kahuā** Hawai'i USA
423 6 **Kahuitara Point** Chatham Islands New Zealand
128 inset **Kahuku Point** Hawai'i USA
128 inset **Kahului** Hawai'i USA
423 E5 **Kahurangi Point** New Zealand
372 E5 **Kai, Kepulauan** *island* Indonesia
372 E5 **Kai Besar** *island* Indonesia
422 F4 **Kai Iwi** New Zealand
372 E5 **Kai Ketjil** *island* Indonesia
305 E3 **Kaiama** Nigeria
373 H5 **Kaiapit** Papua New Guinea
423 E6 **Kaiapoi** New Zealand
128 G2 **Kaibito** Arizona USA
381 G1 **Kaifeng** Henan China
225 N2 **Kaihtula** Finland
380 D4 **Kaihua** Yunnan China
381 H2 **Kaihua** Zhejiang China
162 C6 **Kaiken** Argentina
422 E2 **Kaikohe** New Zealand
423 E6 **Kaikoura** New Zealand
423 E6 **Kaikoura Peninsula** New Zealand
374 B4 **Kailasahar** Tripura India
373 I6 **Kaileuna Island** Papua New Guinea
380 E3 **Kaili** Guizhou China
385 J4 **Kailu** Nei Mongol Zizhiqu China
128 inset **Kailua** Hawai'i USA
128 inset **Kailua-Kona** Hawai'i USA
373 G5 **Kaim** *watercourse* Papua New Guinea
422 F4 **Kaimanawa Mountains** New Zealand
375 G4 **Kaimeer** *island* Indonesia
225 L3 **Käina** Estonia
387 G4 **Kainan** Japan
305 E2 **Kainji Reservoir** *lake* Nigeria
223 M3 **Kainulasjärvi** Sweden
422 F3 **Kaipara Harbour** New Zealand
128 G2 **Kaiparowits Plateau** Utah USA
122 I5 **Kaipokok Bay** Newfoundland and Labrador Canada
372 D4 **Kairatu** Indonesia
373 G4 **Kairiru Island** Papua New Guinea
231 J6 **Kaïs** Algeria
372 E4 **Kais** *watercourse* Indonesia
229 K3 **Kaisergebirge** *range* Austria
226 D3 **Kaiserslautern** Germany
225 M5 **Kaišiadorys** Lithuania
118 E6 **Kaisun** British Columbia Canada
374 E4 **Kait, Tanjung** *cape* Indonesia
223 P3 **Kaita-aapa** *island* Finland
423 C8 **Kaitangata** New Zealand
372 E5 **Kaitanimbar** *island* Indonesia
423 E5 **Kaiteriteri** New Zealand
392 D6 **Kaitha** Madhya Pradesh India
374 F1 **Kaithal** Haryana India
392 D5 **Kaithoon** Rajasthan India
423 E6 **Kaitorete Spit** New Zealand
222 K3 **Kaitumälven** *watercourse* Sweden
422 F4 **Kaivanto** Finland
372 C6 **Kaiwatu** Indonesia
128 inset **Kaiwi Channel** Hawai'i USA
380 E3 **Kaiyang** Guizhou China
385 J4 **Kaiyuan** Liaoning China
380 D4 **Kaiyuan** Yunnan China
381 F3 **Kaiyun** Hunan China
223 O4 **Kajaani** Finland
223 N5 **Kajama** Finland
223 M2 **Kajanki** Finland
307 F4 **Kajiado** Kenya
306 D2 **Kajok** Sudan
232 F2 **Kájov** Czech Republic
305 F2 **Kajuru** Nigeria
158 E4 **Kaka** *watercourse* Bolivia
388 H6 **Kaka** Turkmenistan
423 C8 **Kaka Point** New Zealand
375 H3 **Kakaban** *island* Indonesia
375 I5 **Kakabia** *island* Indonesia
127 M3 **Kakabonga, Lake** Québec Canada
121 P5 **Kakachischuan, Pointe** Québec Canada
126 E2 **Kakagi Lake** Ontario Canada
372 A4 **Kakali** Indonesia
308 D5 **Kakamas** South Africa
307 E3 **Kakamega** Kenya
305 G5 **Kakamoéka** Congo
376 B5 **Kakana** Andaman and Nicobar Islands India
423 D7 **Kakanui** New Zealand
423 D7 **Kakanui Mountains** New Zealand
119 V4 **Kakapawanis** Manitoba Canada
124 C2 **Kakawis** British Columbia Canada
118 E4 **Kake** Alaska USA
222 K3 **Kakel** *bay* Sweden
306 C4 **Kakenge** Democratic Republic of Congo
381 J3 **Kakeroma-jima** *island* Japan
237 AG7 **Kakhtana** Russian Federation
121 R4 **Kakiattualuk, Lac** *lake* Québec Canada
393 F8 **Kakinada** Andhra Pradesh India
118 M2 **Kakisa Lake** Northwest Territories Canada
306 B5 **Kakobola** Democratic Republic of Congo
304 B2 **Kakou** *mountain* Guinea
304 B2 **Kakrima** *watercourse* Guinea
223 O2 **Kakslauttanen** Finland
116 E4 **Kaktovik** Alaska USA
222 I5 **Kakuåsen** Sweden
387 I4 **Kakuda** Japan
307 E3 **Kakuma** Kenya
223 Q5 **Kakunkyulya** Russian Federation
375 G3 **Kakus** *watercourse* Malaysia
118 L5 **Kakwa** *watercourse* Alberta Canada
388 G7 **Kal-e Shur Khar Va Towain** *watercourse* Iran
301 I6 **Kala** Nigeria
306 E5 **Kala** Tanzania
235 C6 **Kala Nera** Greece
Kalaallit Nunaat *see* **Greenland**
233 C9 **Kalaat Khasba** Tunisia
391 L3 **Kalabagh** Pakistan
375 H2 **Kalabakan** Malaysia
307 F3 **Kalabata** *watercourse* Kenya
308 D2 **Kalabo** Zambia
388 D3 **Kalach** Russian Federation
388 D4 **Kalach-na-Donu** Russian Federation
379 G5 **Kaladan** *watercourse* Myanmar
393 D9 **Kaladi** Kerala India
308 D4 **Kalahari Desert** *desert* Botswana
223 N5 **Kalaja** Finland
225 L1 **Kalajäjärvi** *lake* Finland
223 M4 **Kalajoki** Finland
305 E2 **Kalalé** Benin
375 J2 **Kalalusu** *island* Indonesia
391 L2 **Kalam** Pakistan
124 D4 **Kalama** Washington USA
235 C7 **Kalamata** Greece
126 I5 **Kalamazoo** Michigan USA
375 G5 **Kalambau** *island* Indonesia
306 E5 **Kalambo Falls** Tanzania
235 C6 **Kalamítsion** Greece
235 B6 **Kalamos** Greece
235 B6 **Kalamos** *island* Greece
235 B6 **Kalampaka** Greece
375 H3 **Kalampising** Indonesia
389 K6 **Kalān Eylqah** Afghanistan
225 L3 **Kalana** Estonia
394 E3 **Kalanchak** Ukraine
235 C6 **Kalandra** Greece
307 E5 **Kalangali** Tanzania
225 K2 **Kalanti** Finland
375 I5 **Kalao** *island* Indonesia
128 inset **Kalaoa** Hawai'i USA
377 J6 **Kalaong** Philippines
372 B5 **Kalaotoa** *island* Indonesia
374 E4 **Kalapa** Indonesia
128 inset **Kalapana** Hawai'i USA
237 Y7 **Kalar** *watercourse* Russian Federation
390 G3 **Kalār, Kūh-e** *mountain* Iran
238 F4 **Kalashnikovo** Russian Federation
391 J4 **Kalat** Pakistan
391 K3 **Kalat** Pakistan
391 J4 **Kalatāk** Iran
128 inset **Kalaupapa** Hawai'i USA
128 inset **Kalaupapa National Historical Park** Hawai'i USA
393 C6 **Kalavad** Gujarat India
235 E7 **Kalavarda** Greece
379 H5 **Kalaw** Myanmar
379 H4 **Kalawa** Myanmar
379 H4 **Kalay (Mawlaik)** Myanmar
379 H4 **Kalaymyo** Myanmar
391 I6 **Kalbān** Oman
424 E6 **Kalbarri** WA Australia
389 N3 **Kalbinskiy Khrebet** *range* Kazakhstan
227 H5 **Kalce** Slovenia
227 I4 **Káld** Hungary
222 J2 **Kaldfarnes** Norway
379 G3 **Kaldiya Nadi** *watercourse* Assam India
222 I2 **Kaldvåg** Norway
235 F7 **Kale** Turkey
118 L8 **Kaleden** British Columbia Canada
375 I5 **Kaledupa** *island* Indonesia
393 D7 **Kalegaon** Maharashtra India
390 G2 **Kaleh** Iran
388 E7 **Kaleh Gavi** Iran
232 F1 **Kalek** Czech Republic
307 F3 **Kalekol** Kenya
235 D5 **Kaleköy** Turkey
306 C4 **Kalema** Democratic Republic of Congo
306 D5 **Kalemie** Democratic Republic of Congo
222 J5 **Kälen** Sweden
235 B6 **Kaléntzion** Greece
388 F3 **Kalenyy** Kazakhstan
235 D6 **Kalérgon** Greece
223 Q4 **Kalevala** Russian Federation
223 T5 **Kalgachikha** Russian Federation
223 T5 **Kalgachinskoye, Ozero** *lake* Russian Federation
424 G7 **Kalgoorlie-Boulder** WA Australia
232 F4 **Kali** Croatia
393 D7 **Kali** Maharashtra India
392 C4 **Kali** Rajasthan India
392 E4 **Kali** *watercourse* Uttaranchal India
373 H4 **Kali Bay** Papua New Guinea
234 F4 **Kaliakra** *cape* Bulgaria
375 G5 **Kalianget** Indonesia
377 I5 **Kalibo** Philippines
306 D4 **Kalima** Democratic Republic of Congo
375 G4 **Kalimantan** *region* Indonesia
375 F4 **Kalimantan Barat** *admin. area* Indonesia
375 G4 **Kalimantan Selatan** *admin. area* Indonesia
375 G4 **Kalimantan Tengah** *admin. area* Indonesia
375 H3 **Kalimantan Timur** *admin. area* Indonesia
234 B4 **Kalimash** Albania
309 F2 **Kalinda** Zambia
393 F7 **Kalingapatnam** Andhra Pradesh India
225 K5 **Kaliningrad** Russian Federation
225 K5 **Kaliningradskaya Oblast'** *admin. area* Russian Federation
388 D3 **Kalininsk** Russian Federation
232 H5 **Kalinovik** Bosnia and Herzegovina
388 E6 **Kalinovka** Azerbaijan
225 K5 **Kalinovka** Russian Federation
373 I5 **Kalip** Papua New Guinea
124 H2 **Kalispell** Montana USA
227 J2 **Kalisz** Poland
306 E5 **Kaliua** Tanzania
235 D7 **Kalivárion** Greece
223 M4 **Kalix** Sweden
223 M3 **Kalixälven** *watercourse* Sweden
222 L3 **Kalixfors** Sweden
424 I4 **Kalkarindji** NT Australia
126 I4 **Kalkaska** Michigan USA
308 C4 **Kalkfeld** Namibia
235 E6 **Kalkım** Turkey
308 C4 **Kalkrand** Namibia
393 E10 **Kalkudah** Sri Lanka
223 O5 **Kallavesi** *bay* Finland
222 M4 **Kallax** Sweden
224 F3 **Kållekärr** Sweden
223 M4 **Kallfjärden** *bay* Sweden
235 E6 **Kallimasia** Greece
223 O5 **Kallioylä** Finland
235 D5 **Kallísti** Greece
235 C7 **Kallithea** Greece
235 D5 **Kallithéa** Greece
235 B6 **Kallithiron** Greece
223 N3 **Kallo** Finland
227 J4 **Kálló** Hungary
222 K4 **Kallön** Sweden
222 H5 **Kallsjön** *bay* Sweden
222 L5 **Kallsta/Ringsta** Sweden
222 L5 **Kallträsk** Finland
223 P3 **Kallunki** Finland
223 P3 **Kallunkijärvi** *lake* Finland
389 J3 **Kalmakkol** *lake* Kazakhstan
388 J4 **Kalmakkyrgan** *watercourse* Kazakhstan
389 N3 **Kalmanka** Russian Federation
224 I4 **Kalmar** Sweden
224 I4 **Kalmar** *admin. area* Sweden
224 I4 **Kalmarsund** *bay* Sweden
225 N3 **Kalme** Estonia
229 G1 **Kalmthout** Belgium
393 E10 **Kalmunai** Sri Lanka
388 E4 **Kalmykiya Respublika** *admin. area* Russian Federation
234 A1 **Kalna** Slovakia
393 F6 **Kalnai** Chhattisgarh India
225 L4 **Kalnciems** Latvia
234 F1 **Kal'nik** Ukraine
225 L5 **Kalnujai** Lithuania
304 C3 **Kaloa** Côte d'Ivoire
227 J4 **Kalocsa** Hungary
128 inset **Kalohi Channel** Hawai'i USA
392 C6 **Kalol** Gujarat India
393 C6 **Kalol** Gujarat India
306 D4 **Kalole** Democratic Republic of Congo
235 E7 **Kalolimnos** *island* Greece
375 J3 **Kaloma** *island* Indonesia
308 E3 **Kalomo** Zambia
235 B6 **Kalpakio** Greece
393 C10 **Kalpeni Island** Lakshadweep India
393 D9 **Kalpetta** Kerala India
392 E5 **Kalpi** Uttar Pradesh India
224 F5 **Kalsenakke** *island* Denmark
116 D6 **Kaltag** Alaska USA
424 J6 **Kaltjiti (Fregon)** SA Australia
424 I6 **Kaltukatjara (Docker River)** NT Australia
234 B3 **Kaluđerica** Serbia
238 G5 **Kaluga** Russian Federation
375 H5 **Kalukalukuang** *island* Indonesia
375 H4 **Kaluku** Indonesia
375 G3 **Kalulong, Bukit** *mountain* Malaysia
308 E2 **Kalulushi** Zambia
424 H3 **Kalumburu** WA Australia
306 D5 **Kalungwishi** *watercourse* Zambia
391 L3 **Kalur Kot** Pakistan
234 D1 **Kalush** Ukraine
393 E10 **Kalutara** Sri Lanka
238 F5 **Kaluzhskaya Oblast'** *admin. area* Russian Federation
224 C2 **Kalvåg** Norway
222 I3 **Kalvatnet** *lake* Norway
224 G5 **Kalvehave** Denmark
225 K4 **Kalvene** Latvia
129 L1 **Kalvesta** Kansas USA
223 M5 **Kälviä** Finland
225 N2 **Kalvitsa** Finland
222 K4 **Kalvträsk** Sweden
235 E7 **Kalymnos** Greece
235 E7 **Kalymnos** *island* Greece
305 G3 **Kam** *watercourse* Nigeria
388 G2 **Kama** *lake* Russian Federation
305 I2 **Kamaday** Chad
225 M5 **Kamajai** Lithuania
375 G5 **Kamal** Indonesia
391 L3 **Kamalia** Pakistan
128 inset **Kamalō** Hawai'i USA
392 D5 **Kaman** Rajasthan India
389 K3 **Kamandan** *watercourse* Indonesia
155 G4 **Kamani Kreek** *watercourse* Guyana
127 M4 **Kamaniskeg Lake** Ontario Canada
308 B3 **Kamanjab** Namibia
391 J2 **Kamar Zard** Afghanistan
235 B6 **Kamárai** Greece
393 E7 **Kamareddy** Andhra Pradesh India
235 D7 **Kamares** Greece
235 C6 **Kamárion** Greece
235 D5 **Kamariotissa** Greece
304 B3 **Kamaron** Sierra Leone
120 G6 **Kamaskawak** Manitoba Canada
308 E3 **Kamativi** Zimbabwe
305 E2 **Kamba** Nigeria
388 H4 **Kambak-kul'** *lake* Kazakhstan
305 H3 **Kambakota** Central African Republic
424 G7 **Kambalda** WA Australia
393 D10 **Kambam** Tamil Nadu India
374 D4 **Kambang** Indonesia
374 F5 **Kambangan, Nusa** *island* Indonesia
304 B3 **Kambia** Sierra Leone
304 E3 **Kambole** Togo
235 B6 **Kámbos** Greece
306 D6 **Kambove** Democratic Republic of Congo
372 B4 **Kambuno, Bunto** *mountain* Indonesia
302 C1 **Kambūt** Libya
237 AF7 **Kamchatka, Poluostrov** *peninsula* Russian Federation
434 R3 **Kamchatka Basin** *underwater feature* Bering Sea
237 AG7 **Kamchatskiy Kray** *admin. area* Russian Federation
237 AH7 **Kamchatskiy Zaliv** *bay* Russian Federation
234 E4 **Kamchiya** *watercourse* Bulgaria
391 L2 **Kāmdish** Afghanistan
225 O5 **Kamen'** Belarus
234 D4 **Kamen** Bulgaria
306 C5 **Kamende** Democratic Republic of Congo
234 D4 **Kamenets** Bulgaria
238 C6 **Kamenichi** Belarus
232 E4 **Kamenjak, Rt** *cape* Croatia
388 F3 **Kamenka** Kazakhstan
225 O2 **Kamenka** Russian Federation
225 O3 **Kamenka** Russian Federation
238 E5 **Kamenka** Russian Federation
238 F5 **Kamenka** Russian Federation
388 D2 **Kamenka** Russian Federation
234 G2 **Kamenka** Ukraine
238 G4 **Kamenki** Russian Federation
Kamen'naobi *see* **Kamennaobi** Russian Federation
389 N2 **Kamennaobi** Russian Federation
238 H3 **Kamenniki** Russian Federation
223 Q4 **Kamennoye, Ozero** *lake* Russian Federation
237 AF3 **Kamennyy, Mys** *cape* Russian Federation
388 I2 **Kamensk-uralskiy** Russian Federation
227 I5 **Kamensko** Croatia
229 L1 **Kamenz** Germany
392 E4 **Kamet** *mountain* Uttaranchal India
386 F5 **Kami Koshiki-jima** *island* Japan
124 G3 **Kamiah** Idaho USA
227 I1 **Kamieniec** Poland
227 J2 **Kamieńsk** Poland
308 C6 **Kamieskroon** South Africa
120 E1 **Kamilukuak Lake** Nunavut Canada
306 C5 **Kamina** Democratic Republic of Congo
120 H1 **Kaminak Lake** Nunavut Canada
381 J3 **Kaminone-Sho** *island* Japan
387 I4 **Kamisu** Japan
118 K7 **Kamloops** British Columbia Canada
235 B5 **Kamnik** Albania
227 H4 **Kamnik** Slovenia
422 F2 **Kamo** New Zealand
155 G4 **Kamoa Mountains** Guyana
223 M1 **Kamøya** *island* Norway
232 F2 **Kamp** *watercourse* Austria
374 E4 **Kampa** Indonesia
307 E3 **Kampala** Uganda
235 D6 **Kampanos, Akra** *cape* Greece
374 D3 **Kampar** *watercourse* Indonesia
374 D3 **Kampar** Malaysia
374 D3 **Kamparkiri** *watercourse* Indonesia
225 E3 **Kampen** Germany
306 D4 **Kampene** Democratic Republic of Congo
125 Q4 **Kampeska, Lake** South Dakota USA
376 C3 **Kamphaeng Phet** *admin. area* Cambodia
376 C3 **Kamphaeng Phet** Thailand
307 E5 **Kampi Katoto** Tanzania
376 E5 **Kâmpóng Cham** Cambodia
376 E4 **Kâmpóng Chhnăng** Cambodia
374 D2 **Kampong Koh** Malaysia
376 D5 **Kâmpóng Saôm (Sihanoukville)** Cambodia
376 E4 **Kâmpóng Thum** Cambodia
232 F4 **Kampor** Croatia
376 E5 **Kâmpôt** Cambodia
304 D2 **Kampti** Burkina Faso
309 F2 **Kampumbu** Zambia
373 F5 **Kampung** *watercourse* Indonesia
374 D2 **Kampung Gurun** Malaysia
372 E4 **Kamrau, Teluk** *bay* Indonesia
119 U7 **Kamsack** Saskatchewan Canada
304 B2 **Kamsar** Guinea
391 I4 **Kamshahr** Iran
393 E7 **Kamthi** Maharashtra India
126 H2 **Kamuck** *watercourse* Ontario Canada
372 F5 **Kamura** *watercourse* Indonesia
387 K2 **Kamuy, Gora** *volcano* Russian Federation
227 L1 **Kamyanyets** Belarus
225 N6 **Kamyen'** Belarus
388 C4 **Kamyshevatskaya** Russian Federation
388 E3 **Kamyshin** Russian Federation
388 I4 **Kamyshlybash** Kazakhstan
388 E4 **Kamyzyak** Russian Federation
237 U7 **Kan** *watercourse* Russian Federation
306 E2 **Kan** Sudan
121 R5 **Kanaaupscow** *watercourse* Québec Canada
128 F2 **Kanab** *watercourse* Arkansas USA
128 F2 **Kanab** Utah USA
427 9 **Kanacea** *island* Fiji
237 AL8 **Kanaga Island** Alaska USA
122 H5 **Kanairiktok Bay** Newfoundland and Labrador Canada
229 K3 **Kanal** Slovenia
223 N5 **Kanala** Finland
222 I4 **Kanan** Sweden
306 C5 **Kananga** Democratic Republic of Congo
388 E2 **Kanash** Russian Federation
133 H4 **Kanasín** Mexico
127 N4 **Kanata** Ontario Canada
389 N3 **Kanayka** Kazakhstan
387 H4 **Kanazawa** Japan
379 H4 **Kanbalu** Myanmar
304 D2 **Kanbi** *watercourse* Burkina Faso
133 I5 **Kancab-Ché** Mexico
376 C4 **Kanchanaburi** Thailand
376 C4 **Kanchanaburi** *admin. area* Thailand
392 G5 **Kanchenjunga** *mountain* Nepal
391 K3 **Kandahār** Afghanistan
391 K3 **Kandahār** *admin. area* Afghanistan
223 R3 **Kandalaksha** Russian Federation
236 I5 **Kandalakshskiy Zaliv** *bay* Russian Federation
223 S3 **Kandalakshskiya Guba** *bay* Russian Federation
374 C3 **Kandang** Indonesia
375 G4 **Kandangan** Indonesia
372 D6 **Kandar** Indonesia
391 J4 **Kandasol** Pakistan
229 H3 **Kandersteg** Switzerland
391 L4 **Kandhkot** Pakistan
304 E2 **Kandi** Benin
392 G6 **Kandi** West Bengal India
375 I3 **Kandi, Tanjung** *cape* Indonesia
391 K4 **Kandiaro** Pakistan
392 C6 **Kandla** Gujarat India
309 I3 **Kandreho** Madagascar
393 F7 **Kandri** Maharashtra India
393 E9 **Kandukur** Andhra Pradesh India
393 E10 **Kandy** Sri Lanka
237 AF6 **Kandychan** Russian Federation
127 L6 **Kane** Pennsylvania USA
117 M3 **Kane Basin** Greenland
76 N7 **Kane Fracture Zone** *underwater feature* Atlantic Ocean
300 D5 **Kanel** Senegal
301 J6 **Kanem** *admin. area* Chad
128 inset **Kane'ohe** Hawai'i USA
391 K3 **Kaneti** Pakistan
223 U3 **Kanëvka** Russian Federation
388 C4 **Kanevskaya** Russian Federation
232 E4 **Kanfanar** Croatia
308 D4 **Kang** Botswana
380 E1 **Kang Xian** Gansu China
122 N1 **Kangaarsuup Tasersua** *lake* Greenland
117 N5 **Kangaatsiaq** Greenland
304 C2 **Kangaba** Mali
394 F5 **Kangal** Turkey
237 AA6 **Kangalassy** Russian Federation
374 D2 **Kangar** Malaysia
304 C2 **Kangaré** Mali
425 J8 **Kangaroo Island** SA Australia
223 M5 **Kangas** Finland
223 N4 **Kangas** Finland
223 N5 **Kangasaho** Finland
225 N1 **Kangasjärvi** *lake* Finland
223 O4 **Kangaskylä** Finland
223 O2 **Kangaslahti** Finland
223 P5 **Kangaslampi** Finland
385 H4 **Kangbao** Hebei China
386 E3 **Kangdong** North Korea
375 G5 **Kangean, Kepulauan** *island* Indonesia
117 M5 **Kangeeak Point** Nunavut Canada
307 E2 **Kangen** *watercourse* Sudan
117 O6 **Kangeq** *cape* Greenland
122 O2 **Kangeq** *island* Greenland
117 N5 **Kangerlussuaq** Greenland
117 P5 **Kangerlussuaq** *bay* Greenland
117 N4 **Kangerlussuaq (Giesecke Isfjord)** *island* Greenland
117 N5 **Kangerlussuaq (Søndre Strømfjord)** *bay* Greenland
117 O6 **Kangerlussuatsiaq (Lindenow Fjord)** *bay* Greenland
117 Q4 **Kangertittivaq** *bay* Greenland
117 P5 **Kangertittivatsiaq** *bay* Greenland
386 E3 **Kanggye** North Korea
122 M1 **Kangigdlermiut** Greenland
117 Q4 **Kangikajik (Kap Brewster)** *cape* Greenland
122 N2 **Kangilinnguit** Greenland
121 W3 **Kangiqsualujjuaq** Québec Canada
121 T2 **Kangiqsujuaq** Québec Canada
121 T2 **Kangirsuk** Québec Canada
381 G3 **Kangle** Jiangxi China
378 E3 **Kangma** Xizang Zizhiqu China
378 F3 **Kangma** Xizang Zizhiqu China
386 E4 **Kangnyŏng** North Korea
305 G4 **Kango** Gabon
223 M3 **Kangos/Kangosfors** Sweden
223 M3 **Kangosjärvi** Finland
385 J4 **Kangping** Liaoning China
378 D2 **Kangrinboqê Feng** *mountain* Xizang Zizhiqu China
386 F4 **Kangŭng** South Korea
304 C3 **Kani** Côte d'Ivoire
387 H4 **Kani** Japan
379 H4 **Kani** Myanmar
310 8b **Kani Kéli** Mayotte
306 C5 **Kaniama** Democratic Republic of Congo
375 H2 **Kanibongan** Malaysia
423 D6 **Kaniere, Lake** New Zealand
373 H4 **Kaniet Islands** Papua New Guinea
393 E8 **Kanigiri** Andhra Pradesh India
236 K5 **Kanin, Poluostrov** *peninsula* Russian Federation
236 J5 **Kanin Nos** Russian Federation
223 W2 **Kanin Nos, Mys** *cape* Russian Federation
236 J5 **Kaninskiy Bereg** *range* Russian Federation
234 G1 **Kaniv** Ukraine
392 F5 **Kanjiroba** *mountain* Nepal
225 L2 **Kankaanpää** Finland
126 H6 **Kankakee** Illinois USA
304 C2 **Kankan** Guinea
305 F2 **Kankara** Nigeria
304 C2 **Kankelaba** *watercourse* Mali
393 E7 **Kanker** Chhattisgarh India
300 D5 **Kankossa** Mauritania
377 I5 **Kanlaon, Mount** *volcano* Philippines
376 C5 **Kanmaw Kyun** Myanmar
393 D7 **Kannad** Maharashtra India
223 P4 **Kannas** Finland
392 E5 **Kannauj** Uttar Pradesh India
393 D10 **Kanniyakumari** Tamil Nadu India
225 M1 **Kannonjärvi** Finland
223 N5 **Kannonkoski** Finland
393 D9 **Kannur** Kerala India
223 M5 **Kannus** Finland
375 J4 **Kano** *island* Indonesia
305 F2 **Kano** Nigeria
305 F2 **Kano** *admin. area* Nigeria
135 G5 **Kanon, Point** Netherlands Antilles
308 F2 **Kanona** Zambia
389 M3 **Kanonerka** Kazakhstan
129 N1 **Kanopolis Lake** Kansas USA
125 N7 **Kanorado** Kansas USA
124 I7 **Kanosh** Utah USA
375 G3 **Kanowit** Malaysia
386 F5 **Kanoya** Japan
223 S3 **Kanozero, Ozero** *lake* Russian Federation
392 E5 **Kanpur** Uttar Pradesh India
308 E2 **Kansanshi** Zambia
115 **Kansas** *admin. area* USA
126 D7 **Kansas City** Missouri USA
306 D6 **Kansenia** Democratic Republic of Congo
237 U7 **Kansk** Russian Federation
389 Q2 **Kansk** Russian Federation
386 F3 **Kansŏng** South Korea
393 F7 **Kantabanji** Orissa India
238 B1 **Kantala** Finland
376 C6 **Kantang** Thailand
304 E2 **Kantchari** Burkina Faso
116 D6 **Kantishna** *watercourse* Alaska USA
426 1 **Kanton** *island* Kiribati
78 O8 **Kanton Reef** Phoenix Islands
222 M5 **Kantti** Finland
133 H4 **Kantunil** Mexico
133 I4 **Kantunilkin** Mexico
245 D4 **Kanturk** Ireland
391 H2 **Kanūgar** Iran
155 G4 **Kanuku Mountains** Guyana
387 H4 **Kanuma** Japan
308 C5 **Kanus** Namibia
306 D4 **Kanyaru** *watercourse* Burundi
308 E4 **Kanye** Botswana
238 E5 **Kanyutino** Russian Federation
301 H5 **Kao** Niger
427 10 **Kao Island** Tonga
376 D5 **Kaôh Kong** *island* Cambodia
376 D5 **Kaôh Rung** *island* Cambodia
381 H4 **Kaohsiung** Taiwan China
308 B3 **Kaokoveld** *range* Namibia
300 C6 **Kaolack** Senegal
308 D2 **Kaoma** Zambia
234 B4 **Kaona** Serbia
305 I3 **Kaouadja** Central African Republic
128 inset **Kapa'a** Hawai'i USA
235 E6 **Kapaklı** Turkey
389 M4 **Kapal** Kazakhstan
372 C4 **Kapalabuaya** Indonesia
372 C4 **Kapalatmada, Gunung** *mountain* Indonesia
128 inset **Kapalua** Hawai'i USA
304 D3 **Kapandae** Ghana
306 C5 **Kapanga** Democratic Republic of Congo
372 F5 **Kapare** *watercourse* Indonesia
306 E5 **Kapatu** Zambia
373 H5 **Kapau** *watercourse* Papua New Guinea
389 M5 **Kapchagayskoya Vodokhranilishche** *lake* Kazakhstan
307 E3 **Kapchorwa** Uganda
120 H5 **Kapeeseewinik** Manitoba Canada
227 H3 **Kapelln** Austria
235 C7 **Kapello, Akra** *cape* Greece
227 H4 **Kapfenberg** Austria
235 E6 **Kápi** Greece
235 F6 **Kapıdağı Yarımadası** *island* Turkey
306 D3 **Kapili** *watercourse* Democratic Republic of Congo
78 L7 **Kapingamarangi Atoll** *reef* Micronesia
308 E2 **Kapiri Mposhi** Zambia
391 L2 **Kāpīsā** *admin. area* Afghanistan
120 M6 **Kapiskau** *watercourse* Ontario Canada
375 G3 **Kapit** Malaysia
423 F5 **Kapiti Island** New Zealand
155 H4 **Kapiting** Brazil
305 I2 **Kapka, Massif du** *range* Chad
130 E6 **Kaplan** Louisiana USA
372 B6 **Kapondai, Tanjung** *cape* Indonesia
422 F4 **Kaponga** New Zealand
227 I4 **Kaposvár** Hungary
222 H4 **Kappfjällen** *mountain* Norway
386 F3 **Kapsan** North Korea
375 G4 **Kapuas** *watercourse* Indonesia
375 G3 **Kapuas Hulu, Pegunungan** *range* Malaysia
392 D4 **Kapurthala** Punjab India
117 K9 **Kapuskasing** Ontario Canada
119 U3 **Kapuskaypachik** Manitoba Canada
306 D5 **Kaputa** Zambia
425 N7 **Kaputar, Mount** NSW Australia
307 F3 **Kaputir** Kenya
304 E3 **Kara** *watercourse* Benin
236 N5 **Kara** *watercourse* Russian Federation
394 F6 **Kara** Syria
304 E3 **Kara** Togo
389 L5 **Kara-Balta** Kyrgyzstan
388 H6 **Kara-Ker** Turkmenistan
389 K5 **Kara-Köl** Kyrgyzstan
389 L5 **Kara-Koyun** *watercourse* Kyrgyzstan
236 Q3 **Kara Sea** Russian Federation
388 I2 **Karabalyk** Kazakhstan
388 H4 **Karabau** Kazakhstan
235 E5 **Karabiga** Turkey
388 F5 **Karabogaz** Turkmenistan
394 E5 **Karabük** Turkey
235 F5 **Karaburun** Turkey
394 F6 **Karaburun** Turkey
388 H3 **Karabutak** Kazakhstan
235 F5 **Karacabey** Turkey
235 F5 **Karacaköy** Turkey
235 F5 **Karacasu** Turkey
388 D5 **Karachayevo-Cherkesskaya Resp.** *admin. area* Russian Federation
391 K5 **Karachi** Pakistan
235 F7 **Karaçulha** Turkey
393 D8 **Karad** Maharashtra India
227 J5 **Karadaglije** Bosnia and Herzegovina
304 D3 **Karaga** Ghana
237 AH7 **Karaga** Russian Federation
389 L3 **Karaganda** Kazakhstan
389 K4 **Karagandinskaya oblast'** *admin. area* Kazakhstan
389 M4 **Karaganzhal** *lake* Kazakhstan
389 L3 **Karagayly** Kazakhstan
237 AI7 **Karaginskiy, Ostrov** *island* Russian Federation
237 AI7 **Karaginskiy Zaliv** *bay* Russian Federation
389 P3 **Karagos, Gora** *mountain* Russian Federation
389 N3 **Karaguzhikha** Kazakhstan
235 F6 **Karahallı** Turkey
388 G2 **Karaidel'** Russian Federation
393 E9 **Karaikkudi** Tamil Nadu India
375 H3 **Karaitan** Indonesia
388 F7 **Karaj** Iran
390 G2 **Karaj** Iran
227 J5 **Karakaja** Bosnia and Herzegovina
388 I3 **Karakamys** *lake* Kazakhstan
382 F5 **Karakax He** *watercourse* Xinjiang Uygur Zizhiqu China
375 J2 **Karakelong** *island* Indonesia
375 J2 **Karakitang** *island* Indonesia
388 G3 **Karakol** Kazakhstan
389 K5 **Karakol** *watercourse* Kazakhstan
389 M5 **Karakol** Kyrgyzstan
382 F6 **Karakoram Pass** Xinjiang Uygur Zizhiqu China
392 D3 **Karakoram Pass** Jammu and Kashmir India/Pakistan
391 N2 **Karakoram Pass** Pakistan
382 F6 **Karakoram Range** Xinjiang Uygur Zizhiqu China
392 D3 **Karakoram Range** Jammu and Kashmir India/Pakistan
Karaköse *see* **Ağrı** Turkey
235 E6 **Karaköy** Turkey
388 G2 **Karakulino** Russian Federation
389 M4 **Karakum** Kazakhstan
235 F6 **Karakür** Turkey
308 C3 **Karakuwisa** Namibia
235 E6 **Karakuzu** Turkey
301 I6 **Karal** Chad
225 K3 **Karala** Estonia
223 Q5 **Karali** Russian Federation
375 H4 **Karama** *watercourse* Indonesia
394 E6 **Karaman** Turkey
394 E6 **Karaman** *admin. area* Turkey
391 M2 **Karambar Pass** Pakistan
375 H4 **Karambu** Indonesia
423 E5 **Karamea** New Zealand
423 E5 **Karamea** *watercourse* New Zealand
375 G5 **Karamian** *island* Indonesia
382 G5 **Karamiran He** *watercourse* Xinjiang Uygur Zizhiqu China
383 H6 **Karamiran Shankou** *pass* Xinjiang Uygur Zizhiqu China
235 F5 **Karamürsel** Turkey
300 C6 **Karang** Senegal
372 A4 **Karang, Tanjung** *cape* Indonesia
374 E4 **Karangagung** Indonesia
423 C6 **Karangarua** *watercourse* New Zealand
375 G6 **Karangasem** Indonesia
305 G4 **Karangoua** *watercourse* Congo
393 D7 **Karanja** Maharashtra India
393 E7 **Karanja** Maharashtra India
393 E6 **Karanjia** Madhya Pradesh India
223 N5 **Karankajärvi** *lake* Finland
389 L3 **Karaoba** Kazakhstan
235 E7 **Karaova** Turkey
389 L4 **Karaoy** Kazakhstan
394 E6 **Karapinar** Turkey
422 F3 **Karapiro** New Zealand
389 J4 **Karaqoyyn Koli** *lake* Kazakhstan
392 E6 **Karari** Uttar Pradesh India
372 E4 **Karas** *island* Indonesia
308 C5 **Karas** *admin. area* Namibia
238 H4 **Karash** Russian Federation
222 N2 **Kárášjohka** Norway
223 N2 **Karasjokka** *watercourse* Norway
389 L3 **Karasor, Ozero** *lake* Kazakhstan
389 L3 **Karasor Koli** *lake* Kazakhstan
235 G5 **Karasu** Turkey
389 M2 **Karasuk** Russian Federation
389 O4 **Karatal** Kazakhstan
389 M4 **Karatal** *watercourse* Kazakhstan
235 G7 **Karatas Gölü** *lake* Turkey
222 K3 **Karatj** *lake* Sweden
388 G3 **Karatobe** Kazakhstan
388 I3 **Karatomarskoye Vodokhranilishche** *lake* Kazakhstan
386 F5 **Karatsu** Japan
375 J2 **Karatung** *island* Indonesia
389 M4 **Karaul** Kazakhstan
236 R4 **Karaul** Russian Federation
392 D5 **Karauli** Rajasthan India
235 C7 **Karavas** Greece
235 A5 **Karavastasë, Gjiri i** *bay* Albania
238 H4 **Karavayevo** Russian Federation
235 E7 **Karavonisia** *island* Greece
372 E5 **Karawaira, Kepulauan** *island* Indonesia
374 E5 **Karawang, Tanjung** *cape* Indonesia
373 G5 **Karawari** *watercourse* Papua New Guinea
389 K4 **Karazhal** Kazakhstan
389 L4 **Karazhingil** Kazakhstan
390 E3 **Karbalā'** Iraq
390 E3 **Karbalā'** *admin. area* Iraq
222 I6 **Kårböle** Sweden
224 H2 **Kårböleskog** Sweden
227 K4 **Karcag** Hungary
227 K3 **Karcsa** Hungary
227 K1 **Karczew** Poland
234 F4 **Kardam** Bulgaria
235 B7 **Kardamás** Greece
235 B6 **Karditsa** Greece
225 L3 **Kärdla** Estonia
227 I4 **Kardos-ér** *watercourse* Hungary
238 E5 **Kardymovo** Russian Federation
308 D6 **Kareeberge** *range* South Africa
302 E4 **Kareima** Sudan
223 R5 **Karel'skaya Masel'ga** Russian Federation
237 Y8 **Karenga** *watercourse* Russian Federation
392 E6 **Karera** Madhya Pradesh India
305 F2 **Karfi** Nigeria
388 G3 **Kargala** Russian Federation
389 N3 **Kargaly** Kazakhstan
237 AK5 **Karganay** Russian Federation
235 G7 **Kargı** Turkey
392 D3 **Kargil** Jammu and Kashmir India/Pakistan
238 H2 **Kargopol'** Russian Federation
392 E5 **Karhal** Uttar Pradesh India
223 N4 **Karhukangas** Finland
305 G2 **Kari** Nigeria
308 E3 **Kariba** Zimbabwe
308 E3 **Kariba, Lake** *lake* Zimbabwe
387 H2 **Kariba-yama** *volcano* Japan
308 C4 **Karibib** Namibia
308 D6 **Kariega** *watercourse* South Africa
223 N2 **Karigasniemi** Finland
238 B2 **Karijärvi** *lake* Finland
422 E2 **Karikari Peninsula** New Zealand
304 E2 **Karimama** Benin
374 F4 **Karimata** *island* Indonesia
374 F4 **Karimata, Kepulauan** *island* Indonesia
374 F4 **Karimata, Selat** *strait* Indonesia
379 G4 **Karimganj** Assam India
393 E7 **Karimnagar** Andhra Pradesh India
374 D3 **Karimun** *island* Indonesia
375 F5 **Karimungawa, Kepulauan** *island* Indonesia
375 F5 **Karimunjawa** *island* Indonesia
303 H5 **Karin** Somalia
223 N4 **Karinkanta** Finland
422 F3 **Karioi, Mount** *volcano* New Zealand
423 D7 **Karitane** New Zealand
393 C6 **Karjan** Gujarat India
373 H5 **Karkar Island** Papua New Guinea
389 L3 **Karkaralinsk** Kazakhstan
391 K4 **Karkh** Pakistan
235 F7 **Karkinágrion** Greece
394 E4 **Karkinits'ka Zatoka** *sea* Ukraine
225 M2 **Karkkila** Finland
302 E5 **Karkoj** Sudan
390 E2 **Karkūk (Kirkuk)** Iraq
223 P1 **Karlebotn** Norway
226 D2 **Kärlich** Germany
302 E5 **Karling** Sudan
224 H5 **Karlino** Poland
394 E3 **Karlivka** Ukraine
232 F4 **Karlovac** Croatia
226 G2 **Karlovarský Kraj** *admin. area* Czech Republic
234 D4 **Karlovo** Bulgaria
226 G2 **Karlovy Vary** Czech Republic
223 M4 **Karlsborg** Sweden
226 F3 **Karlsfeld** Germany
224 H4 **Karlskrona** Sweden
222 L1 **Karlsøy** *island* Norway
222 I3 **Karlsøyvær** *island* Norway
226 E3 **Karlsruhe** Germany
125 O2 **Karlsruhe** North Dakota USA
224 G3 **Karlstad** Sweden
125 Q2 **Karlstad** Minnesota USA
232 C2 **Karlstadt** Germany
301 G6 **Karma** Niger
305 I1 **Karma, Ouadi** *watercourse* Chad

238 F5 **Karmanovo** Russian Federation
301 J6 **Karme** Chad
224 C3 **Karmøy** *island* Norway
223 N5 **Kärnä** Finland
392 D5 **Karnal** Haryana India
392 E5 **Karnali** *watercourse* Nepal
379 G4 **Karnaphuli Reservoir** Bangladesh
393 D8 **Karnataka** *admin. area* India
130 C6 **Karnes City** Texas USA
227 J1 **Karniszyn** Poland
234 E4 **Karnobat** Bulgaria
224 F3 **Kärnsjön** *lake* Sweden
226 G4 **Kärnten** *admin. area* Austria
308 E3 **Karoi** Zimbabwe
427 9 **Karoko** Fiji
309 F1 **Karonga** Malawi
306 D4 **Karonje** *mountain* Rwanda
222 K4 **Karonsbo** Sweden
391 L3 **Karor** Pakistan
303 F4 **Karora** Eritrea
427 9a **Karorko** Fiji
372 A6 **Karosso, Tanjung** *cape* Indonesia
302 C5 **Karoub** Chad
223 P4 **Kärpänkylä** Finland
235 E8 **Karpathos** *island* Greece
223 Q4 **Karpivaara** Russian Federation
235 E7 **Karpuzlu Barajı** *lake* Turkey
388 H7 **Karrān** Iran
424 F5 **Karratha** WA Australia
224 F5 **Karrebæksminde Bugt** *bay* Denmark
394 G5 **Kars** Turkey
394 G5 **Kars** *admin. area* Turkey
225 N3 **Kärsa** Estonia
223 N4 **Kärsämä** Finland
223 N5 **Kärsämäki** Finland
225 N4 **Kārsava** Latvia
388 F6 **Karshi** Turkmenistan
236 M4 **Karskiye Vorota, Proliv** *strait* Russian Federation
236 Q3 **Karskoye More** *sea* Russian Federation
223 N5 **Karstula** Finland
222 I6 **Karsvall** Sweden
234 A2 **Kartal** Hungary
310 8a **Kartala** *volcano* Comoros
388 H2 **Kartaly** Russian Federation
225 P4 **Kartsevo** Russian Federation
223 O5 **Karttula** Finland
224 J5 **Kartuzy** Poland
225 M3 **Käru** Estonia
425 L4 **Karumba** Qld Australia
223 M3 **Karungi** Sweden
307 E4 **Karungu** Kenya
222 E5 **Kårvåg** Norway
223 M5 **Karvala** Finland
222 M5 **Karvia** Finland
225 L1 **Karvianjärvi** *lake* Finland
225 L2 **Karvianjoki** *watercourse* Finland
227 J3 **Karviná** Czech Republic
223 N5 **Karvoskylä** Finland
393 D8 **Karwar** Karnataka India
392 D6 **Karwar** Madhya Pradesh India
385 H2 **Karymskoye** Russian Federation
236 S7 **Kas** *watercourse* Russian Federation
302 C5 **Kas** Sudan
305 I2 **Kas** Sudan
235 F7 **Kaş** Turkey
224 E4 **Kås** Denmark
224 F7 **Kasaba** Turkey
120 K6 **Kasabonika** Ontario Canada
120 K6 **Kasabonika Lake** Ontario Canada
306 C5 **Kasai** *watercourse* Democratic Republic of Congo
386 G4 **Kasai** Japan
306 C5 **Kasaï-Occidental** *admin. area* Democratic Republic of Congo
306 C4 **Kasaï-Oriental** *admin. area* Democratic Republic of Congo
306 C6 **Kasaji** Democratic Republic of Congo
376 D3 **Kasalin** Thailand
309 F2 **Kasama** Zambia
308 E3 **Kasane** Botswana
306 B4 **Kasangulu** Democratic Republic of Congo
303 F4 **Kasar, Ras** *cape* Eritrea/Sudan
393 D9 **Kasaragod** Kerala India
225 M3 **Kasari** *watercourse* Estonia
223 O2 **Kasariselkä** *bay* Finland
304 B3 **Kasasi** Sierra Leone
120 D2 **Kasba Lake** Northwest Territories/Nunavut Canada
388 J6 **Kasbi** Uzbekistan
306 E2 **Kasempa** Zambia
306 D6 **Kasenga** Democratic Republic of Congo
306 D4 **Kasese** Democratic Republic of Congo
306 E3 **Kasese** Uganda
376 D3 **Kaset Sombun** Thailand
222 J2 **Kasfjord** Norway
392 E5 **Kasganj** Uttar Pradesh India
391 I4 **Kash** Iran
391 I2 **Kashaf Rūd** *watercourse* Iran
390 G2 **Kāshān** Iran
121 O6 **Kashechewan** Ontario Canada
385 E2 **Kashi** Xinjiang Uygur Zizhiqu China
238 G4 **Kashin** Russian Federation
393 F7 **Kashipur** Orissa India
392 E5 **Kashipur** Uttaranchal India
238 H5 **Kashira** Russian Federation
120 K8 **Kashishibog Lake** Ontario Canada
387 H4 **Kashiwazaki** Japan
389 L4 **Kashkanteniz** Kazakhstan
225 Q2 **Kashkany** Russian Federation
223 T3 **Kashkarantsy** Russian Federation
391 I2 **Kāshmar** Iran
391 L4 **Kashmor** Pakistan
154 C2 **Kashure** Colombia
306 D2 **Kashwal** Sudan
372 A4 **Kasimbar** Indonesia
375 I4 **Kasimbar** Indonesia
235 G7 **Kasımlar** Turkey
238 D2 **Kasimov** Russian Federation
306 D3 **Kasingi** Democratic Republic of Congo
375 J4 **Kasiruta** *island* Indonesia
372 D5 **Kasiui** *island* Indonesia
222 K3 **Kaska Kaitumjaure** *lake* Sweden
126 G7 **Kaskaskia** *watercourse* Illinois USA
120 J4 **Kaskattama** *watercourse* Manitoba Canada
222 J3 **Kaskaure** *lake* Sweden
223 O2 **Kaskiinkylä** Finland
222 L5 **Kaskinen** Finland
391 I4 **Kāskūh** Iran
118 M8 **Kaslo** British Columbia Canada
119 U3 **Kasmere Lake** Manitoba Canada
375 G4 **Kasongan** Indonesia
306 D4 **Kasongo** Democratic Republic of Congo
305 H6 **Kasongo-lunda** Democratic Republic of Congo
306 D4 **Kasongo Rive** Democratic Republic of Congo
235 E8 **Kasos** *island* Greece
388 E5 **Kaspiysk** Russian Federation
225 P5 **Kasplya** Russian Federation
394 F6 **KasratFaraj** Syria
393 D6 **Kasrawad** Madhya Pradesh India
302 F4 **Kassala** Sudan
302 F4 **Kassala** *admin. area* Sudan
235 C6 **Kassandras, Akra** *cape* Greece
229 I1 **Kassel** Germany
301 H1 **Kasserine** Tunisia
394 E5 **Kastamonu** Turkey
235 C5 **Kastanea** Greece
232 F4 **Kaštel Žegarski** Croatia
235 E8 **Kastellou, Akra** *cape* Greece
226 F3 **Kastl** Germany
235 B5 **Kastoria** Greece
235 B5 **Kastorias, Limni** *lake* Greece
235 B6 **Kastos** *island* Greece
238 C4 **Kastrova** Belarus
238 E6 **Kastsyukovichy** Belarus
306 E4 **Kasulu** Tanzania
306 D6 **Kasumbulesa** Democratic Republic of Congo
388 E5 **Kasumkent** Russian Federation
122 H5 **Kasungatak Island** Newfoundland and Labrador Canada
309 F2 **Kasungu** Malawi
391 M3 **Kasur** Pakistan
424 I6 **Kata Tjuta (Mount Olga)** *mountain* NT Australia
427 9 **Katafaga** *island* Fiji
305 G2 **Katagum** Nigeria
305 F2 **Katagum** *watercourse* Nigeria
306 C4 **Katako-Kombe** Democratic Republic of Congo
235 B7 **Katakolo, Akra** *cape* Greece
307 E3 **Katakwi** Uganda
306 C5 **Katanda** Democratic Republic of Congo
306 D5 **Katanga** *admin. area* Democratic Republic of Congo
237 V7 **Katanga** *watercourse* Russian Federation
393 E7 **Katangi** Madhya Pradesh India
424 F8 **Katanning** WA Australia
305 F3 **Katcha** Nigeria
376 B6 **Katchall** *island* Andaman and Nicobar Islands India
306 C5 **Katenge** Democratic Republic of Congo
235 C5 **Katerini** Greece
118 E4 **Kates Needle** *mountain* British Columbia/Alaska Canada/USA
242 B2 **Katesbridge** Banbridge Northern Ireland UK
307 F4 **Katesh** Tanzania
309 F2 **Katete** Zambia
393 F6 **Katghora** Chhattisgarh India
379 H4 **Katha** Myanmar
424 J3 **Katherine** NT Australia
392 F5 **Kathmandu** Nepal
119 O7 **Kathryn** Alberta Canada
308 D5 **Kathu** South Africa
392 D4 **Kathua** Jammu and Kashmir India/Pakistan
300 E6 **Kati** Mali
375 G3 **Katibas** *watercourse* Malaysia
374 C4 **Katiet** Indonesia
392 G6 **Katihar** Bihar India
422 F3 **Katikati** New Zealand
308 D3 **Katima Mulilo** Namibia
238 H6 **Katino** Russian Federation
306 C3 **Katiola** Côte d'Ivoire
427 14 **Katiu** *island* French Polynesia
223 M2 **Kätkäsuvanto** Finland
223 M2 **Kätkesuando** Sweden
234 F3 **Katlabukh, Ozero** *lake* Ukraine
116 D7 **Katmai National Park and Preserve** Alaska USA
235 C7 **Kato Kalivia** Greece
235 B6 **Kato Makrinou** Greece
235 D7 **Kato Sounion** Greece
235 E8 **Káto Zákros** Greece
393 E7 **Katol** Maharashtra India
223 M5 **Kåtölandet** *island* Finland
306 C5 **Katombe** Democratic Republic of Congo
235 D7 **Katomeri, Akra** *cape* Greece
306 D5 **Katompi** Democratic Republic of Congo
374 E4 **Katong** *admin. area* Singapore
372 B4 **Katoposa, Gunung** *mountain* Indonesia
235 B6 **Katouna** Greece
227 J2 **Katowice** Poland
393 E6 **Katra** Madhya Pradesh India
235 G7 **Katrancık Dağı** *range* Turkey
244 D4 **Katrine, Loch** *lake* Scotland UK
222 J3 **Kätsak** *lake* Sweden
234 E4 **Katselovo** Bulgaria
305 F2 **Katsina** Nigeria
305 F3 **Katsina** *admin. area* Nigeria
305 F3 **Katsina Ala** Nigeria
121 W3 **Kattaktoc, Cap** *cape* Québec Canada
388 J6 **Kattaqo'rg'on** Uzbekistan
222 H2 **Kåttbo** Sweden
224 F4 **Kattegat** *bay* Denmark
224 I2 **Katterat** Norway
121 S2 **Kattiniq** Québec Canada
307 G3 **Katulo** *watercourse* Kenya
389 O3 **Katun** *watercourse* Russian Federation
130 D6 **Katy** Texas USA
236 Q7 **Katyl'ga** Russian Federation
375 J3 **Kau, Teluk** *bay* Indonesia
128 inset **Kaua'i** *island* Hawai'i USA
128 inset **Kaua'i Channel** Hawai'i USA
226 F4 **Kaufbeuren** Germany
375 H5 **Kaugel** *watercourse* Papua New Guinea
222 M5 **Kauhajoki** Finland
222 M5 **Kauhajoki** *watercourse* Finland
222 L5 **Kauhaneva-Pohjankankas kansallis-puisto** *park* Finland
223 M5 **Kauhava** Finland
223 N3 **Kaukonen** Finland
128 inset **Ka'ula** *island* Hawai'i USA
128 inset **Kaulakahi Channel** Hawai'i USA
223 M3 **Kaulinranta** Finland
308 D3 **Kaulu Plain** *plain* Zambia
128 inset **Kaumalapau** Hawai'i USA
225 L5 **Kaunas** Lithuania
225 L5 **Kaunatava** Lithuania
379 I3 **Kaunglanhpu** Myanmar
225 L5 **Kauno** *admin. area* Lithuania
225 M5 **Kauno marios** *lake* Lithuania
222 E6 **Kaupanger** Norway
128 inset **Kaupō** Hawai'i USA
305 F2 **Kaura-Namoda** Nigeria
223 M5 **Kaustinen** Finland
223 M2 **Kautokeino** Norway
234 B4 **Kavadar** Serbia
235 A5 **Kavajë** Albania
235 E5 **Kavaklı** Turkey
235 C5 **Kavala** Greece
235 D5 **Kavalas, Kolpos** *bay* Greece
393 E8 **Kavali** Andhra Pradesh India
393 C9 **Kavaratti** Lakshadweep India
393 C9 **Kavaratti Island** Lakshadweep India
235 B7 **Kavásilas** Greece
238 E5 **Kavel'shchino** Russian Federation
373 G5 **Kavienanga** Papua New Guinea
373 I4 **Kavieng** Papua New Guinea
308 D3 **Kavimba** Botswana
388 G7 **Kavīr-e Ḥājī 'Ali Qoli** *lake* Iran
235 B6 **Kavos** Greece
308 D2 **Kavungo** Angola
155 H3 **Kaw, Montagnes de** *range* French Guiana
130 C2 **Kaw Lake** Oklahoma USA
387 H4 **Kawagoe** Japan
128 inset **Kawaihae** Hawai'i USA
128 inset **Kawaihoa Point** Hawai'i USA
306 D5 **Kawambwa** Zambia
308 E2 **Kawana** Zambia
393 E7 **Kawardha** Chhattisgarh India
127 L4 **Kawartha Lakes** Ontario Canada
306 D5 **Kawasa** Democratic Republic of Congo
387 H4 **Kawasaki** Japan
422 F3 **Kawau Island** New Zealand
121 V5 **Kawawachikamach** Québec Canada
422 G4 **Kaweka** *mountain* New Zealand
422 G4 **Kaweka Range** New Zealand
128 inset **Kawela** Hawai'i USA
422 F4 **Kawhia** New Zealand
422 F4 **Kawhia Harbour** New Zealand
124 G8 **Kawich Range** Nevada USA
375 H6 **Kawinda** Indonesia
375 J2 **Kawio** *island* Indonesia
372 C2 **Kawio, Kepulauan** *island* Indonesia
379 H4 **Kawlin** Myanmar
302 E3 **Kawm Umbū** Egypt
379 I4 **Kawngmeum** Myanmar
376 C5 **Kawthaung** Myanmar
382 G4 **Kax He** *watercourse* Xinjiang Uygur Zizhiqu China
222 H5 **Kaxås** Sweden
382 F5 **Kaxgar He** *watercourse* Xinjiang Uygur Zizhiqu China
304 D2 **Kaya** Burkina Faso
374 D5 **Kayaapu** Indonesia
394 F6 **Kayabasi** Turkey
379 H5 **Kayah** *admin. area* Myanmar
306 E5 **Kayambi** Zambia
393 D10 **Kayamkulam** Kerala India
375 H3 **Kayan** *watercourse* Indonesia
375 G3 **Kayan-Mentarang, Taman Nasional** *park* Indonesia
372 E1 **Kayangel Atoll** *reef* Palau
125 L5 **Kaycee** Wyoming USA
306 C5 **Kayembe-Mukulu** Democratic Republic of Congo
128 G2 **Kayenta** Arizona USA
300 D6 **Kayes** Mali
300 D6 **Kayes** *admin. area* Mali
376 C3 **Kayin** *admin. area* Myanmar
226 D3 **Kayl** Luxembourg
223 P3 **Käylä** Finland
389 M3 **Kaynar** Kazakhstan
235 G5 **Kaynarca** Turkey
375 J3 **Kayoa** *island* Indonesia
389 L4 **Kayrakty** Kazakhstan
389 L4 **Kayran-kul** *lake* Russian Federation
388 E3 **Kaysatskoye** Russian Federation
155 G4 **Kayser Gebergte** *range* Suriname
394 E5 **Kayseri** Turkey
394 E5 **Kayseri** *admin. area* Turkey
124 J6 **Kaysville** Utah USA
375 I5 **Kayuadi** *island* Indonesia
372 E4 **Kayuagung** Indonesia
374 E4 **Kayumerah, Teluk** *bay* Indonesia
119 S8 **Kayville** Saskatchewan Canada
235 E6 **Kaz Dargi** *mountain* Turkey
237 W7 **Kazachinskoye** Russian Federation
236 O7 **Kazachka** Russian Federation
388 F5 **Kazakhskiy Zaliv** *bay* Kazakhstan
388 I4 **Kazakhstan** *country*
388 I4 **Kazalinsk** Kazakhstan
119 U2 **Kazan** *watercourse* Nunavut Canada
238 F2 **Kazan'** Russian Federation
388 D3 **Kazanskaja** Russian Federation
76 O7 **Kazanskiy Seamount** *underwater feature* Atlantic Ocean
305 F2 **Kazaure** Nigeria
388 D5 **Kazbek, Gora** *mountain* Russian Federation
390 G3 **Kāzerūn** Iran
388 E5 **Kaziyurt** Russian Federation
225 L5 **Kazlų Rūda** Lithuania
229 K2 **Kazněјov** Czech Republic
388 E3 **Kaztalovka** Kazakhstan
306 C5 **Kazumba** Democratic Republic of Congo
387 I3 **Kazuno** Japan
236 O6 **Kazymskiy Mys** Russian Federation
226 E2 **Kdyně** Czech Republic
235 D7 **Kea** *island* Greece
128 inset **Kea'au** Hawai'i USA
245 F2 **Keady** Armagh Northern Ireland UK
158 D5 **Keakeani, Cordillera** *range* Bolivia
243 I3 **Keal Coates** Lincolnshire England UK
128 inset **Kealaikahiki Channel** Hawai'i USA
128 inset **Kealakekua** Hawai'i USA
242 B3 **Kealstown** Ireland
245 G2 **Kearney** Ards Northern Ireland UK
125 P6 **Kearney** Nebraska USA
128 G4 **Kearny** Arizona USA
122 E5 **Keating, Lac** *lake* Québec Canada
122 E5 **Keato, Lac** *lake* Québec Canada
376 E5 **Kêb** Cambodia
394 F5 **Keban Barajı.** *lake* Turkey
305 E2 **Kebbi** *admin. area* Nigeria
300 C5 **Kébémèr** Senegal
301 H2 **Kebili** Tunisia
305 I2 **Kebkabiya** Sudan
222 K3 **Kebnekaise** *mountain* Sweden
244 B2 **Kebock Head** *cape* Scotland UK
307 G2 **K'ebri Dehar** Ethiopia
385 G4 **Kebu'er** Nei Mongol Zizhiqu China
374 F5 **Kebumen** Indonesia
374 D4 **Kebur** Indonesia
234 A2 **Kecel** Hungary
116 G7 **Kechika** *watercourse* British Columbia Canada
235 G7 **Keçiborlu** Turkey
234 A2 **Kecskemét** Hungary
374 D2 **Kedah** *admin. area* Malaysia
225 L5 **Kėdainiai** Lithuania
392 E4 **Kedarnath** Uttaranchal India
305 H2 **Kédédéssé** Chad
305 G3 **Kedei** *watercourse* Cameroon
123 E9 **Kedgwick** New Brunswick Canada
375 G5 **Kediri** Indonesia
385 K3 **Kedong** Heilongjiang China
300 D6 **Kédougou** Senegal
225 R1 **Kedr-Ozero, Ozero** *lake* Russian Federation
374 F3 **Kedukul** Indonesia
374 F5 **Kedungwuni** Indonesia
236 L6 **Kedvavom** Russian Federation
227 J2 **Kędzierzyn-Koźle** Poland
245 C4 **Keel** Ireland
116 G6 **Keele** *watercourse* Northwest Territories Canada
116 F6 **Keele Peak** Yukon Territory Canada
125 M1 **Keeler** Saskatchewan Canada
119 Q5 **Keeley Lake** Saskatchewan Canada
Keeling Islands *see* **Cocos Islands**
381 I3 **Keelung** Taiwan China
128 C3 **Keene** California USA
127 O5 **Keene** New Hampshire USA
244 F4 **Keene** Angus Scotland UK
242 A2 **Keeran** Fermanagh Northern Ireland UK
308 C5 **Keetmanshoop** Namibia
120 K7 **Keezhik Lake** Ontario Canada
235 D5 **Kefalas, Akra** *cape* Greece
235 D5 **Kefalo Burnu** *cape* Turkey
235 E7 **Kefalos** Greece
235 D7 **Kefalos, Akra** *cape* Greece
235 C6 **Kefalovryso** Greece
372 C6 **Kefamenanu** Indonesia
305 F3 **Keffi** Nigeria
235 G5 **Kefken** Turkey
118 M4 **Keg River** Alberta Canada
121 W3 **Keglo Bay** Québec Canada
241 F2 **Kegworth** Leicester England UK
302 E4 **Keheili** Sudan
226 D3 **Kehl** Germany
226 D2 **Kehrig** Germany
379 H5 **Kehsi Mansam** Myanmar
243 G3 **Keighley** West Yorkshire England UK
225 L2 **Keikyä** Finland
225 M3 **Keila** Estonia
244 D4 **Keilator** Stirling Scotland UK
244 C5 **Keillmore** Argyll and Bute Scotland UK
225 N2 **Keipsalo** *island* Finland
130 F3 **Keiser** Arkansas USA
225 K2 **Keistiö** *island* Finland
301 H6 **Keïta** Niger
305 H3 **Keita ou Doka, Bahr** *watercourse* Central African Republic
223 O5 **Keitele** Finland
223 N5 **Keitele** *lake* Finland
223 N5 **Keitelepohja** Finland
425 L9 **Keith** SA Australia
116 G5 **Keith Arm** Northwest Territories Canada
118 K6 **Keithley Creek** British Columbia Canada
427 9a **Keiyasi** Fiji
124 D4 **Keizer** Oregon USA
390 G3 **Kejān** Iran
225 M4 **Ķekava** Latvia
227 K4 **Kékes** *mountain* Hungary
384 G4 **Kekeyiligeng** Nei Mongol Zizhiqu China
375 K4 **Kekik** *island* Indonesia
305 E3 **Kekki Lagoon** *bay* Nigeria
392 D6 **Kekri** Rajasthan India
233 D9 **Kelaa Kebira** Tunisia
307 G2 **K'elafo** Ethiopia
382 G3 **Kelamayi** Xinjiang Uygur Zizhiqu China
384 G5 **Kelan** Shanxi China
375 J4 **Kelang** *island* Indonesia
374 D2 **Kelantan** *admin. area* Malaysia
374 D2 **Kelantan** *watercourse* Malaysia
235 B5 **Këlcyrë** Albania
119 U7 **Keld** Manitoba Canada
243 F2 **Keld** North Yorkshire England UK
243 G3 **Kelfield** North Yorkshire England UK
301 I1 **Kelibia** Tunisia
388 I6 **Kelifskiy Uzboy** *lake* Turkmenistan
373 F4 **Kelila** Indonesia
394 F5 **Kelkit** Turkey
116 G6 **Keller Lake** Northwest Territories Canada
120 H4 **Kellet** Manitoba Canada
116 G4 **Kellett, Cape** Northwest Territories Canada
116 H3 **Kellett Strait** Northwest Territories Canada
119 T7 **Kelliher** Saskatchewan Canada
125 R3 **Kelliher** Minnesota USA
223 N4 **Kello** Finland
236 S6 **Kellog** Russian Federation
222 P4 **Kellojärvi** *lake* Finland
223 O3 **Kelloniemi** Finland
223 P3 **Kelloselkä** Finland
245 E4 **Kells** Ireland
245 F3 **Kells** Ireland
245 F2 **Kells** Ballymena Northern Ireland UK
225 L5 **Kelmė** Lithuania
305 H3 **Kélo** Chad
223 N3 **Kelontekemä** Finland
223 N3 **Kelontekemäjärvi** *lake* Finland
222 L2 **Kelottijärvi** *lake* Sweden
118 L8 **Kelowna** British Columbia Canada
130 B7 **Kelsey** Texas USA
119 W4 **Kelsey** Manitoba Canada
124 C1 **Kelsey Bay** British Columbia Canada
244 F5 **Kelso** Scottish Borders Scotland UK
126 G8 **Kelso** Missouri USA
124 D3 **Kelso** Washington USA
244 E4 **Kelty** Fife Scotland UK
374 D3 **Keluang** Malaysia
375 F4 **Keluang, Tanjung** *cape* Indonesia
223 P3 **Kelujärvi** *lake* Finland
223 Q5 **Kelvä** Finland
241 H3 **Kelvedon** Essex England UK
241 H3 **Kelvedon Hatch** Essex England UK
120 K8 **Kelvin Island** Ontario Canada
387 H2 **Kema** *watercourse* Russian Federation
375 G2 **Kemabung** Malaysia
235 E6 **Kemalpaşa** Turkey
374 D2 **Kemasik** Malaysia
375 F3 **Kembayan** Indonesia
305 I4 **Kembé** Central African Republic
234 A1 **Kemence** Hungary
235 E5 **Kemer** Turkey
235 F7 **Kemer** Turkey
235 G7 **Kemer** Turkey
235 F5 **Kemerburgaz** Turkey
389 O2 **Kemerovo** Russian Federation
236 S7 **Kemerovskaya Oblast'** *admin. area* Russian Federation
389 O2 **Kemerovskayaoblast'** *admin. area* Russian Federation
223 N4 **Kemi** Finland
223 O3 **Kemijärvi** Finland
223 O3 **Kemijärvi** *lake* Finland
223 O3 **Kemijoki** *watercourse* Finland
223 P4 **Kemilä** Finland
389 L5 **Kemin** Kyrgyzstan
125 J6 **Kemmerer** Wyoming USA
232 D2 **Kemnath** Germany
305 H3 **Kémo** *admin. area* Central African Republic
129 M4 **Kemp, Lake** Texas USA
437 D2 **Kemp Coast** Antarctica
436 U2 **Kemp Peninsula** Antarctica
118 M4 **Kemp River** Alberta Canada
223 N4 **Kempele** Finland
237 Y6 **Kempendyay** Russian Federation
130 C5 **Kempner** Texas USA
425 O7 **Kempsey** NSW Australia
241 E2 **Kempsey** Worcestershire England UK
117 L9 **Kempt, Lac** *lake* Québec Canada
226 F4 **Kempten** Germany
240 E2 **Kempton** Shropshire England UK
375 F5 **Kemujan** *island* Indonesia
244 E6 **Ken** *watercourse* Scotland UK
242 D1 **Ken, Loch** *lake* Scotland UK
301 F2 **Kenadsa** Algeria
116 D6 **Kenai** Alaska USA
116 D7 **Kenai Fiords National Park** Alaska USA
116 D7 **Kenai Mountains** Alaska USA
116 D6 **Kenai Peninsula** Alaska USA
374 E5 **Kenam, Tanjung** *cape* Indonesia
122 H6 **Kenamu** *watercourse* Newfoundland and Labrador Canada
375 G6 **Kencong** Indonesia
393 F6 **Kenda** Chhattisgarh India
392 G6 **Kenda** West Bengal India
242 F2 **Kendal** Cumbria England UK
129 L2 **Kendall** Kansas USA
120 L1 **Kendall, Cape** Nunavut Canada
372 B4 **Kendari** Indonesia
375 F4 **Kendawangan** Indonesia
375 F4 **Kendawangan** *watercourse* Indonesia
305 H2 **Kendégué** Chad
226 D2 **Kendel** *watercourse* Netherlands
124 G3 **Kendrick** Idaho USA
130 C6 **Kenedy** Texas USA
130 D5 **Kenefick** Texas USA
304 B3 **Kenema** Sierra Leone
122 I6 **Kenemich** *watercourse* Newfoundland and Labrador Canada
373 G5 **Kenewa** Papua New Guinea
306 B4 **Kenge** Democratic Republic of Congo
379 I5 **Kengtung** Myanmar
308 D5 **Kenhardt** South Africa
300 D6 **Kéniéba** Mali
375 H2 **Keningau** Malaysia
300 E2 **Kénitra** Morocco
240 E2 **Kenley** Shropshire England UK
385 I5 **Kenli** Shandong China
245 C5 **Kenmare** Ireland
245 C5 **Kenmare** *bay* Ireland
125 N2 **Kenmare** North Dakota USA
244 B3 **Kenmore** Na h-Eileanan Siar Scotland UK
244 D4 **Kenmore** Perth and Kinross Scotland UK
240 E3 **Kenn** North Somerset England UK
425 O5 **Kenn Reef** Qld Australia
129 K4 **Kenna** New Mexico USA
127 Q4 **Kennebec** *watercourse* Maine USA
130 H4 **Kennedy** Alabama USA
125 Q2 **Kennedy** Minnesota USA
118 I7 **Kennedy, Mount** British Columbia Canada
379 G4 **Kennedy Peak** *mountain* Myanmar
130 F6 **Kenner** Louisiana USA
241 F3 **Kennet** *watercourse* England UK
241 F3 **Kennet and Avon Canal** England UK
241 H2 **Kennett** Cambridgeshire England UK
130 F2 **Kennett** Missouri USA
124 F3 **Kennewick** Washington USA
121 X5 **Kenney Lake** Newfoundland and Labrador Canada
126 I1 **Kenogami** *watercourse* Ontario Canada
127 P2 **Kénogami, Lac** *lake* Québec Canada
127 K2 **Kenogamissi Lake** Ontario Canada
120 H8 **Kenora** Ontario Canada
119 T8 **Kenosee Lake** Saskatchewan Canada
126 H5 **Kenosha** Wisconsin USA
223 U5 **Kenozero, Ozero** *lake* Russian Federation
223 U5 **Kenozersky National Park** *park* Russian Federation
223 Q5 **Kenraalinkylä** Finland
125 P3 **Kensal** North Dakota USA
125 R4 **Kensington** Minnesota USA
118 K8 **Kent** British Columbia Canada
241 H3 **Kent** *admin. area* England UK
127 K6 **Kent** Ohio USA
129 J5 **Kent** Texas USA
124 D3 **Kent** Washington USA
126 I5 **Kent City** Michigan USA
116 I5 **Kent Peninsula** Nunavut Canada
389 J5 **Kentau** Kazakhstan
389 P3 **Kentegir** *watercourse* Russian Federation
240 D4 **Kentisbeare** Devon England UK
130 G2 **Kenton** Tennessee USA
235 C5 **Kentriki Makedonia** *admin. area* Greece
115 **Kentucky** *admin. area* USA
126 I7 **Kentucky** *watercourse* Kentucky USA
130 G2 **Kentucky Lake** Tennessee USA
123 F10 **Kentville** Nova Scotia Canada
119 U6 **Kenville** Manitoba Canada
307 F3 **Kenya** *country* Africa
307 F3 **Kenya, Mount** *mountain* Kenya
227 I4 **Kenyeri** Hungary
374 D2 **Kenyir, Tasik** *watercourse* Malaysia
389 K3 **Kenzharyk** Kazakhstan
226 D3 **Kenzingen** Germany
126 F6 **Keokuk** Iowa USA
124 I1 **Keoma** Alberta Canada
131 J3 **Keowee, Lake** South Carolina USA
376 E2 **Kép** Vietnam
374 D4 **Kepahiang** Indonesia
375 G6 **Kepanjen** Indonesia
373 F5 **Kepi** Indonesia
235 A5 **Kepi i Rodonit** *cape* Albania
121 W6 **Kepimits Lake** Newfoundland and Labrador Canada
382 F5 **Keping** Xinjiang Uygur Zizhiqu China
227 I2 **Kępno** Poland
163 7 **Keppel Island** Falkland Islands
162 E5 **Keppel Sound** Falkland Islands
244 C3 **Keppoch** Highland Scotland UK
375 F5 **Kepulauan Karimunjawa Marine National Park** Indonesia
374 E3 **Kepulauan Riau** *admin. area* Indonesia
375 J5 **Kepulauan Seribu, Taman Nasional** *park* Indonesia
Kepulauan Seribu Marine National Park *see* **Kepulauan Seribu, Taman Nasional** Indonesia
380 C1 **Kequ** Qinghai China
393 D9 **Kerala** *admin. area* India
373 H5 **Keram** *watercourse* Papua New Guinea
235 D5 **Keramoti** Greece
425 L8 **Kerang** Vic. Australia
235 B6 **Kerasona** Greece
373 I5 **Keravat** Papua New Guinea
374 D4 **Kerbau, Tanjung** *cape* Indonesia
228 C2 **Kerbédic** France
394 F4 **Kerch** Ukraine
306 D2 **Kéré** Central African Republic
302 E5 **Kereimet** Sudan
118 L8 **Keremeos** British Columbia Canada
302 F4 **Keren** Eritrea
133 F1 **Kerens** Texas USA
389 J3 **Kerey Koli** *lake* Kazakhstan
310 6 **Kerguélen, Îles** *island* French Southern and Antarctic Lands
437 F3 **Kerguelen Plateau** *underwater feature* Southern Ocean
235 B7 **Keri** Greece
307 F4 **Kericho** Kenya
422 E2 **Kerikeri** New Zealand
391 I2 **Kerimanj** Iran
374 D4 **Kerinci, Danau** *lake* Indonesia
374 D4 **Kerinci, Gunung** *volcano* Indonesia
374 D4 **Kerinci Seblat, Taman Nasional** *park* Indonesia
307 F3 **Kerio** *watercourse* Kenya
235 C5 **Kerkinitis, Limni** *lake* Greece
235 A6 **Kerkyra** Greece
235 A6 **Kerkyra (Corfu)** *island* Greece
374 E4 **Kerma** Sudan
422 5 **Kermadec Islands** New Zealand
78 O11 **Kermadec Ridge** *underwater feature* Pacific Ocean
78 O11 **Kermadec Trench** *underwater feature* Pacific Ocean
223 P5 **Kermajärvi** *lake* Finland
391 H3 **Kermān** Iran
391 I3 **Kermān** *admin. area* Iran
390 F2 **Kermānshāh** Iran
390 F2 **Kermānshāh** *admin. area* Iran
234 E4 **Kermen** Bulgaria
129 K5 **Kermit** Texas USA
128 C3 **Kern** *watercourse* California USA
304 E2 **Kérou** Benin
304 C3 **Kérouané** Guinea
229 H1 **Kerpen** Germany
437 K1 **Kerr, Cape** Antarctica
244 C4 **Kerrera** *island* Scotland UK
129 K2 **Kerrick** Texas USA
119 Q7 **Kerrobert** Saskatchewan Canada
130 B5 **Kerrville** Texas USA
245 C4 **Kerry** *admin. area* Ireland
240 D2 **Kerry** Powys Wales UK
245 B4 **Kerry Head** *cape* Ireland
307 F2 **Kersa Dek** Ethiopia
242 F1 **Kershopefoot** Cumbria England UK
223 O3 **Kersilö** Finland
118 J6 **Kersley** British Columbia Canada
224 I2 **Kerstinbo** Sweden
374 E4 **Kertapati** Indonesia
374 D2 **Kerteh** Malaysia
235 F6 **Kertil** Turkey
393 D8 **Kerur** Karnataka India
301 F3 **Kerzaz** Algeria
121 O7 **Kesagami** *watercourse* Ontario Canada
121 O7 **Kesagami Lake** Ontario Canada
387 I3 **Kesennuma** Japan
385 K3 **Keshan** Heilongjiang China
389 K7 **Keshem** Afghanistan
393 C7 **Keshod** Gujarat India
393 F7 **Kesinga** Orissa India
223 N4 **Keskikylä** Finland
394 E5 **Keskin** Turkey
223 N4 **Keskipiiri** Finland
225 Q2 **Keskozero** Russian Federation
238 G3 **Kes'ma** Russian Federation
238 G4 **Kesova Gora** Russian Federation
241 I2 **Kessingland** Suffolk England UK
241 I2 **Kessingland Beach** Suffolk England UK
235 F5 **Kestel** Turkey
223 Q3 **Kesten'ga** Russian Federation
223 O4 **Kestilä** Finland
242 E2 **Keswick** Cumbria England UK
124 D6 **Keswick Reservoir** California USA
236 R7 **Ket'** *watercourse* Russian Federation
237 AB7 **Ket-Kap, Khrebet** *range* Russian Federation
236 T5 **Keta, Ozero** *lake* Russian Federation
304 E3 **Keta Lagoon** *bay* Ghana
374 D4 **Ketahun** Indonesia
235 B6 **Ketalliona** *island* Greece
374 D3 **Ketamputih** Indonesia
374 F4 **Ketapang** Indonesia
118 H3 **Ketchika** *watercourse* British Columbia Canada
118 F5 **Ketchikan** Alaska USA
124 H5 **Ketchum** Idaho USA
226 C1 **Ketelmeer** *bay* Netherlands
159 G4 **Ketéroco** Brazil
232 G3 **Kéthely** Hungary
240 E2 **Ketley** Telford and Wrekin England UK
222 N2 **Ketojärvi** *lake* Finland
223 N2 **Ketomella** Finland
237 AF9 **Ketoy, Ostrov** *island* Kuril Islands
387 L1 **Ketoy, Ostrov** *lake* Russian Federation
305 H4 **Ketta** Congo
305 G4 **Kétté** Cameroon
241 G2 **Kettering** Northamptonshire England UK
126 I7 **Kettering** Ohio USA
118 L8 **Kettle** *watercourse* British Columbia Canada
120 K4 **Kettle** *watercourse* Manitoba Canada
124 F2 **Kettle Falls** Washington USA
127 J5 **Kettle Point** Ontario Canada
124 F2 **Kettle River Range** Washington USA
128 C2 **Kettleman City** California USA
243 F2 **Kettlewell** North Yorkshire England UK
375 F3 **Ketungau** *watercourse* Indonesia
374 B2 **Keude Teunom** Indonesia
237 V7 **Keul'** Russian Federation
226 F2 **Keula** Germany
223 N5 **Keurusselkä** *lake* Finland
223 N5 **Keuruu** Finland
304 E3 **Keve** Togo
124 J2 **Kevin** Montana USA
223 O2 **Kevo** Finland
223 P5 **Kevritty** *lake* Finland
425 O7 **Kew** NSW Australia
126 G6 **Kewanee** Illinois USA
126 H4 **Kewaunee** Wisconsin USA
126 G3 **Keweenaw Bay** Michigan USA
126 G3 **Keweenaw Peninsula** Michigan USA
126 H3 **Keweenaw Point** Michigan USA
243 G3 **Kexbrough** South Yorkshire England UK
131 K8 **Key Colony Beach** Florida USA
127 K4 **Key Harbour** Ontario Canada
119 S4 **Key Lake Mine** Saskatchewan Canada
131 K8 **Key Largo** *island* Florida USA
131 K8 **Key West** Florida USA
125 O5 **Keya Paha** *watercourse* South Dakota USA
121 S6 **Keyano** Québec Canada
129 K2 **Keyes** Oklahoma USA
238 C3 **Keykino** Russian Federation
116 A6 **Keyngypil'gyn, Laguna** Russian Federation
240 E3 **Keynsham** Bath and North East Somerset England UK
127 N6 **Keyport** New Jersey USA
118 C3 **Keysall** *watercourse* British Columbia Canada
127 L7 **Keyser** West Virginia USA
126 C8 **Keystone Lake** Oklahoma USA
127 L8 **Keysville** Virginia USA
227 K3 **Kežmarok** Slovakia
308 D4 **Kgalagadi** *admin. area* Botswana
308 E4 **Kgatleng** *admin. area* Botswana
391 H4 **Khabar, Kūh-e** *mountain* Iran
385 M3 **Khabarovsk** Russian Federation
237 AC8 **Khabarovskiy Kray** *admin. area* Russian Federation
388 E2 **Khabary** Russian Federation
390 E7 **Khabb, Wādī** *watercourse* Yemen
391 H3 **Khabr** Iran
390 F7 **Khabt al Aslūm** Yemen
391 K2 **Khadir** Afghanistan
388 C5 **Khadyzhensk** Russian Federation
234 G2 **Khadzhybeys'kyy Lyman** *lake* Ukraine
392 E6 **Khaga** Uttar Pradesh India
379 G4 **Khagrachari** Bangladesh
393 E7 **Khairagarh** Chhattisgarh India
391 K4 **Khairpur** Pakistan
391 L3 **Khairpur** Pakistan
384 E2 **Khaizan Burged Uul** *mountain* Mongolia
389 P2 **Khakasiya** *admin. area* Russian Federation
391 K3 **Khākerān** Afghanistan
308 D4 **Khakhea** Botswana
394 F7 **Khalhale** Syria
388 E5 **Khali-Keloy** Russian Federation
390 F3 **Khalid** Iraq
391 I6 **Khalij Maşirah** *sea* Oman
388 H3 **Khalilovo** Russian Federation
235 C6 **Khálki** Greece
235 C6 **Khalkoútsion** Greece
384 E2 **Khamar-Daban, Khrebet** *range* Russian Federation
392 E6 **Khamaria** Madhya Pradesh India
393 B6 **Khambhaliya** Gujarat India
393 C6 **Khambhat** Gujarat India
393 C7 **Khambhat, Gulf of** Gujarat India
393 D7 **Khamgaon** Maharashtra India
390 E6 **Khamis Mushayt** Saudi Arabia
393 E8 **Khammam** Andhra Pradesh India
237 Y6 **Khampa** Russian Federation
237 Z6 **Khampa** Russian Federation
379 H3 **Khamti** Myanmar
394 F7 **Khan al 'Arus** Syria
393 D7 **Khandwa** Madhya Pradesh India
237 AC6 **Khandyga** Russian Federation
231 J6 **Khangat Sidi Nadji** Algeria
237 Z7 **Khani** Russian Federation
238 G5 **Khanino** Russian Federation

386 G2 **Khanka, Ozero** *lake* Russian Federation
388 H6 **Khankui** Turkmenistan
237 Y5 **Khannya** *watercourse* Russian Federation
392 D6 **Khanpur** Rajasthan India
384 E2 **Khantayn Nuruu Uul** *mountain* Mongolia
236 T5 **Khantayskoye, Ozero** *lake* Russian Federation
236 T5 **Khantayskoye Vodokhranilishche** *lake* Russian Federation
236 O6 **Khanty-Mansiysk** Russian Federation
236 O6 **Khanty-Mansiyskiy Avotomnyy Okrug-Yugra** *admin. area* Russian Federation
237 AD7 **Khanyangda** Russian Federation
376 C5 **Khao Luang** *mountain* Myanmar
376 C5 **Khao Luang** *mountain* Thailand
393 E6 **Khapa** Madhya Pradesh India
385 G2 **Khapcheranga** Russian Federation
391 J2 **Khar Bid** Afghanistan
390 G2 **Khar Rūd** *watercourse* Iran
391 L3 **Khar Tangai Manda** *watercourse* Pakistan
237 W4 **Khara-Tas, Gory** *range* Russian Federation
388 E4 **Kharabali** Russian Federation
393 G6 **Kharagpur** West Bengal India
394 G6 **Kharā'ij** Syria
391 K4 **Kharan** Pakistan
237 AA4 **Kharaulakhskiy Khrebet** *range* Russian Federation
392 E6 **Kharela** Uttar Pradesh India
393 D7 **Khargone** Madhya Pradesh India
391 H4 **Khargū** Iran
393 F7 **Kharhial** Orissa India
391 M3 **Kharian** Pakistan
302 E3 **Khārijah, Wāḥāt Al** *spring* Egypt
237 AG9 **Kharimkotan, Ostrov** *island* Kuril Islands
383 I2 **Kharkhiraa Uul** *mountain* Mongolia
394 F2 **Kharkiv** Ukraine
394 F3 **Kharkivs'ka Oblast'** *admin. area* Ukraine
223 T2 **Kharlovka** Russian Federation
225 P2 **Kharlu** Russian Federation
235 D5 **Kharmanli** Bulgaria
393 F7 **Kharod** Chhattisgarh India
235 C5 **Kharopón** Greece
238 I3 **Kharovsk** Russian Federation
393 F7 **Kharsia** Chhattisgarh India
237 AD4 **Kharstan** Russian Federation
302 E4 **Khartoum** *admin. area* Sudan
237 AA6 **Kharyyalakh** Russian Federation
391 H4 **Khaşab** Oman
388 H6 **Khasar-Kala** Turkmenistan
388 E5 **Khasavyurt** Russian Federation
391 J4 **Khāsh** Iran
388 J6 **Khashdala** Uzbekistan
302 F5 **Khashm el Girba** Sudan
235 D5 **Khaskovo** Bulgaria
235 D4 **Khaskovo** *admin. area* Bulgaria
391 J2 **Khaţţā'i** Iran
237 V4 **Khatanga** Russian Federation
237 V4 **Khatanga** *watercourse* Russian Federation
237 W4 **Khatangskiy Zaliv** *bay* Russian Federation
392 D5 **Khatauli** Uttar Pradesh India
388 J6 **Khatcha** Uzbekistan
389 K6 **Khatlon** *admin. area* Tajikistan
238 G5 **Khatun'** Russian Federation
237 Y6 **Khaty** Russian Federation
237 AK6 **Khatyrka** Russian Federation
391 K2 **Khavāl** Afghanistan
392 B6 **Khavda** Gujarat India
391 J3 **Khāway** Afghanistan
379 G4 **Khawhai** Mizoram India
302 F3 **Khawr Daiat** *spring* Sudan
390 E6 **Khaybar** Saudi Arabia
308 C6 **Khayelitsha** South Africa
376 E3 **Khe Sanh** Vietnam
393 D7 **Khede** Maharashtra India
301 G1 **Khemis Miliana** Algeria
300 E2 **Khemis Zemamra** Morocco
300 E2 **Khemisset** Morocco
301 H1 **Khenchela** Algeria
301 H2 **Khenchela** *admin. area* Algeria
300 E2 **Khenifra** Morocco
301 H1 **Kherrata** Algeria
394 E3 **Kherson** Ukraine
394 E3 **Khersons'ka Oblast'** *admin. area* Ukraine
237 U4 **Kheta** *watercourse* Russian Federation
223 R3 **Khetolambina** Russian Federation
392 D5 **Khetri** Rajasthan India
223 P2 **Kheykhen'yarvi** Russian Federation
225 O2 **Khiitola** Russian Federation
384 G2 **Khilok** Russian Federation
384 G2 **Khilok** *watercourse* Russian Federation
238 G5 **Khimki** Russian Federation
394 F7 **Khirbat Ra's al Wa'r** Syria
238 E5 **Khislavichi** Russian Federation
382 F6 **Khitai Pass** (disputed)
223 S5 **Khizhozero, Ozero** *lake* Russian Federation
238 F5 **Khlepen'** Russian Federation
376 D4 **Khlong Luang** Thailand
376 D4 **Khlung** Thailand
238 F2 **Khmelëzero** Russian Federation
394 C3 **Khmel'nyts'ka Oblast'** *admin. area* Ukraine
234 E1 **Khmel'nyts'kyy** Ukraine
376 E5 **Khoai, Hòn** *island* Vietnam
225 P6 **Khodosy** Belarus
234 C1 **Khodovichi** Ukraine
389 J7 **Kholm** Afghanistan
225 P4 **Kholm** Russian Federation
238 E5 **Kholm-Zhirkovskiy** Russian Federation
238 E4 **Kholmino** Russian Federation
237 AD9 **Kholmsk** Russian Federation
387 I1 **Kholmsk** Russian Federation
225 O5 **Kholomer'ye** Belarus
389 N3 **Kholzun, Khrebet** *range* Russian Federation
308 C4 **Khomas** *admin. area* Namibia
390 G2 **Khomeyn** Iran
389 M2 **Khomutino** *lake* Russian Federation
376 D4 **Khon Buri** Thailand
376 D3 **Khon Kaen** Thailand
383 J3 **Khondlon Uul** *mountain* Mongolia
237 AF6 **Khongo** Russian Federation
388 D5 **Khoni** Georgia
391 H4 **Khonj** Iran
379 H3 **Khonsa** Arunachal Pradesh India
393 C7 **Khopoli** Maharashtra India
387 G1 **Khor** Russian Federation
387 H1 **Khor** *watercourse* Russian Federation
302 E3 **Khor Abu Sunt** *watercourse* Sudan
302 E5 **Khor Dulayb** *watercourse* Sudan
391 I3 **Khorāsān-E Janūbi** *admin. area* Iran
391 I2 **Khorāsān-E Razavi** *admin. area* Iran
388 G6 **Khorāsān-E Shemāli** *admin. area* Iran
376 D3 **Khorat Plateau** Thailand
384 G2 **Khorinsk** Russian Federation
308 B4 **Khorixas** Namibia
394 E2 **Khorol** *watercourse* Ukraine
390 F2 **Khorramābād** Iran
390 F3 **Khorramshahr** Iran
389 K6 **Khorugh** Tajikistan
388 E4 **Khosheutovo** Russian Federation
391 I2 **Khoshk** Iran
238 F6 **Khot'kovo** Russian Federation
238 H4 **Khot'kovo** Russian Federation
234 E1 **Khotyn** Ukraine
391 H4 **Khour Fakkān** United Arab Emirates
300 E2 **Khouribga** Morocco
388 G7 **Khowsh-e Yeylāq** Iran
391 L2 **Khowst** Afghanistan
391 L2 **Khowst** *admin. area* Afghanistan
394 D2 **Khoyniki** Belarus
235 C7 **Khrānoi** Greece
237 AE4 **Khromskaya Guba** *bay* Russian Federation
388 H3 **Khromtau** Kazakhstan
238 H5 **Khruslovka** Russian Federation
234 F1 **Khrystynivka** Ukraine
388 E5 **Khryuk** Russian Federation
308 D4 **Khudumalapye** Botswana
308 D5 **Khuis** Botswana
389 K6 **Khŭjand.** Tajikistan
236 N6 **Khulga** *watercourse* Russian Federation
379 F4 **Khulna** Bangladesh
379 F4 **Khulna** *admin. area* Bangladesh
384 F3 **Khulstayn Uul** *mountain* Mongolia
237 AC8 **Khummi, Ozero** *lake* Russian Federation
390 E2 **Khunayfis** Iraq
382 E6 **Khunjerab Pass** Xinjiang Uygur Zizhiqu China
392 F6 **Khunti** Jharkhand India
392 E6 **Khurai** Madhya Pradesh India
302 D5 **Khureit** Sudan
392 D5 **Khurja** Uttar Pradesh India
225 O6 **Khutor** Belarus
302 D5 **Khuwei** Sudan
391 K4 **Khuzdar** Pakistan
390 F3 **Khūzestān** *admin. area* Iran
388 E3 **Khvalynsk** Russian Federation
388 E6 **Khvar** Iran
238 F5 **Khvashchevka** Russian Federation
390 G4 **Khvormūj** Iran
391 I2 **Khvoshābeh** Iran
388 D6 **Khvoy** Iran
238 F3 **Khvoynaya** Russian Federation
223 Q4 **Khyame** Russian Federation
391 L2 **Khyber Pass** Pakistan
234 C1 **Khyriv** Ukraine
427 9 **Kia** *island* Fiji
373 G5 **Kia** *watercourse* Indonesia
426 8 **Kia** Solomon Islands
425 N8 **Kiama** NSW Australia
377 J6 **Kiamba** Philippines
306 D5 **Kiambi** Democratic Republic of Congo
425 N8 **Kiandra** NSW Australia
223 P4 **Kiantajärvi** *bay* Finland
223 P4 **Kiantajärvi** *lake* Finland
117 N4 **Kiatassuaq** *island* Greenland
235 C6 **Kiato** Greece
134 C4 **Kiauban** Honduras
131 K4 **Kiawah Island** South Carolina USA
224 E4 **Kibæk** Denmark
307 F5 **Kibaha** Tanzania
306 A5 **Kibala** Angola
306 E3 **Kibale** Uganda
306 D3 **Kibali** *watercourse* Democratic Republic of Congo
305 G5 **Kibangou** Congo
392 D4 **Kibar** Himachal Pradesh India
306 D5 **Kibara, Monts** *range* Democratic Republic of Congo
307 F5 **Kibau** Tanzania
307 F5 **Kibaya** Tanzania
223 Q1 **Kiberg** Norway
306 E3 **Kiboga** Uganda
307 F4 **Kiboko** *watercourse* Kenya
306 E4 **Kibondo** Tanzania
307 F2 **Kibre Mengist** Ethiopia
225 K4 **Kiburi** Latvia
223 P1 **Kiby** Norway
234 E4 **Kichevo** Bulgaria
301 G5 **Kidal** Mali
234 G1 **Kidanovka** Ukraine
377 J6 **Kidapawan** Philippines
241 E2 **Kidderminster** Worcestershire England UK
307 E2 **Kidepo** *watercourse* Sudan
300 D6 **Kidira** Senegal
241 F3 **Kidlington** Oxfordshire England UK
422 G4 **Kidnappers, Cape** New Zealand
240 E1 **Kidsgrove** Staffordshire England UK
375 G3 **Kidurong, Tanjong** *cape* Malaysia
224 F5 **Kiel** Germany
126 G5 **Kiel** Wisconsin USA
227 K2 **Kielce** Poland
227 J2 **Kielcza** Poland
243 F1 **Kielder** Northumberland England UK
243 F1 **Kielder Water** *lake* England UK
224 F5 **Kieler Bucht** *bay* Germany
376 E3 **Kiến An** Vietnam
222 L2 **Kiepanjaure** *lake* Sweden
373 J5 **Kiera** Papua New Guinea
227 J2 **Kietrz** Poland
307 F5 **Kifanyo** Tanzania
300 D5 **Kiffa** Mauritania
235 C6 **Kifissos** *watercourse* Greece
306 D4 **Kigali** Rwanda
122 H4 **Kiglapait, Cape** Newfoundland and Labrador Canada
304 C2 **Kignan** Mali
306 D4 **Kigoma** Tanzania
306 E4 **Kigoma** *admin. area* Tanzania
307 F5 **Kigwe** Tanzania
375 G4 **Kihambatang** Indonesia
375 H3 **Kihammawon** Indonesia
128 inset **Kihei** Hawai'i USA
223 M3 **Kihlanki** Finland
223 M3 **Kihlanki** Sweden
225 N3 **Kihlevere** Estonia
223 M5 **Kihniö** Finland
225 M3 **Kihnu** *island* Estonia
387 G5 **Kii-sanchi** Japan
223 N5 **Kiihtelysvaara** Finland
389 K4 **Kiik** Kazakhstan
223 N4 **Kiiminki** Finland
223 N5 **Kiiskilä** Finland
223 N3 **Kiistala** Finland
306 E4 **Kijanebalola, Lake** *lake* Uganda
374 E3 **Kijang** Indonesia
227 K2 **Kije** Poland
234 B4 **Kijevo** Kosovo
307 F5 **Kijunga** *spring* Tanzania
306 D4 **Kikamba** Democratic Republic of Congo
225 O3 **Kikerino** Russian Federation
122 H4 **Kikiktaksoak Island** Newfoundland and Labrador Canada
234 B3 **Kikinda** Serbia
119 O5 **Kikino** Alberta Canada
423 E5 **Kikiwa** New Zealand
122 H4 **Kikkertavak Island** Newfoundland and Labrador Canada
121 V3 **Kikkertoksoak Islands** Nunavut Canada
236 R6 **Kikkiakki** Russian Federation
235 D7 **Kikladhes** *island* Greece
388 E1 **Kiknur** Russian Federation
306 D5 **Kikondja** Democratic Republic of Congo
373 G5 **Kikori** *watercourse* Papua New Guinea
388 D3 **Kikvidze** Russian Federation
306 B5 **Kikwit** Democratic Republic of Congo
224 E3 **Kil** Norway
128 inset **Kilauea Crater** *volcano* Hawai'i USA
232 F2 **Kilb** Austria
245 D5 **Kilbeg** Ireland
245 F3 **Kilberry** Ireland
244 C5 **Kilberry** Argyll and Bute Scotland UK
222 H3 **Kilboghamn** Norway
222 I2 **Kilbotn** Norway
242 B3 **Kilbride Cross Roads** Ireland
242 A4 **Kilbrids Cross Roads** Ireland
245 F4 **Kilcarney** Ireland
244 C5 **Kilchenzie** Argyll and Bute Scotland UK
244 B4 **Kilchoan** Highland Scotland UK
244 B5 **Kilchoman** Argyll and Bute Scotland UK
244 C4 **Kilchrenan** Argyll and Bute Scotland UK
244 C5 **Kilchrist** Argyll and Bute Scotland UK
386 F3 **Kilchu** North Korea
242 C2 **Kilclief** Down Northern Ireland UK
242 B2 **Kilcoo** Down Northern Ireland UK
245 F3 **Kilcoole** Ireland
245 D4 **Kilcor** Ireland
245 E3 **Kilcormac** Ireland
242 A4 **Kilcruise** Ireland
245 F3 **Kilcullen** Ireland
242 B2 **Kilcurly** Ireland
242 B3 **Kildalkey** Ireland
245 F3 **Kildare** Ireland
245 F3 **Kildare** *admin. area* Ireland
123 G9 **Kildare, Cape** Prince Edward Island Canada
244 D3 **Kildary** Highland Scotland UK
240 A2 **Kildavin** Ireland
245 F3 **Kilday** Ireland
236 I5 **Kil'din, Ostrov** *island* Russian Federation
223 R2 **Kil'dinstroy** Russian Federation
242 B2 **Kildoagh** Ireland
124 C2 **Kildonan** British Columbia Canada
244 C5 **Kildonan** North Ayrshire Scotland UK
244 E2 **Kildonan Lodge** Highland Scotland UK
245 C3 **Kildun** Ireland
224 D3 **Kilefjordan** *lake* Norway
388 E2 **Kilemary** Russian Federation
306 D5 **Kilembe** Democratic Republic of Congo
306 D5 **Kileo** Democratic Republic of Congo
224 E3 **Kilevatnet** *lake* Norway
244 D3 **Kilfinnan** Highland Scotland UK
245 D3 **Kilglass** Ireland
243 H2 **Kilham** East Riding of Yorkshire England UK
427 15 **Kili** *island* Marshall Islands
304 E3 **Kilibo** Benin
302 B5 **Kilim** Chad
305 H2 **Kilim** Chad
307 F4 **Kilimanjaro** *admin. area* Tanzania
307 F4 **Kilimanjaro** *volcano* Tanzania
394 F6 **Kilis** Turkey
394 F6 **Kilis** *admin. area* Turkey
234 F3 **Kiliya** Ukraine
245 F4 **Kilkea** Ireland
245 F4 **Kilkee** Ireland
245 C4 **Kilkee** Ireland
245 F2 **Kilkeel** Newry and Mourne Northern Ireland UK
245 D3 **Kilkelly** Ireland
245 E4 **Kilkenny** Ireland
245 E4 **Kilkenny** *admin. area* Ireland
225 N2 **Kilkinkylä** Finland
425 O6 **Kilkivan** Qld Australia
245 B3 **Kill** Ireland
131 N2 **Kill Devil Hills** North Carolina USA
245 E4 **Killadangan** Ireland
245 F3 **Killadreenan** Ireland
245 C2 **Killala** Ireland
245 C2 **Killala Bay** Ireland
126 H2 **Killala Lake** Ontario Canada
245 D4 **Killaloe** Ireland
119 T7 **Killaly** Saskatchewan Canada
245 C4 **Killarney** Ireland
245 C3 **Killary Harbour** Ireland
242 A3 **Killasona** Ireland
245 D3 **Killaun** Ireland
245 C3 **Killavally** Ireland
245 D2 **Killavil** Ireland
119 R8 **Killdeer** Saskatchewan Canada
245 E4 **Killea** Ireland
245 D3 **Killeelaun** Ireland
245 D4 **Killeen** Ireland
130 C5 **Killeen** Texas USA
245 D3 **Killeenaran** Ireland
242 C1 **Killellan** Argyll and Bute Scotland UK
130 H3 **Killen** Alabama USA
245 E4 **Killenaule** Ireland
130 F5 **Killian** Louisiana USA
244 D4 **Killichonan** Perth and Kinross Scotland UK
245 D3 **Killimor** Ireland
244 D4 **Killin** Stirling Scotland UK
245 G2 **Killinchy** Ards Northern Ireland UK
242 B3 **Killiney** Ireland
222 L3 **Killinge** Sweden
245 F4 **Killinick** Ireland
121 W2 **Killiniq** Nunavut Canada
121 W2 **Killiniq Island** Nunavut Canada
223 N5 **Killinkoski** Finland
245 E3 **Killinlahan** Ireland
244 C5 **Killocraw** Argyll and Bute Scotland UK
245 D4 **Killorglin** Ireland
242 B3 **Killosseny** Ireland
245 E4 **Killough** Ireland
245 G2 **Killough** Down Northern Ireland UK
245 D3 **Killower** Ireland
244 B4 **Killunaig** Highland Scotland UK
242 A2 **Killybane** Dungannon Northern Ireland UK
245 D2 **Killybegs** Ireland
242 B2 **Killycolpy** Cookstown Northern Ireland UK
242 B3 **Killyon** Ireland
244 D5 **Kilmacolm** Inverclyde Scotland UK
245 E4 **Kilmacthomas** Ireland
245 C3 **Kilmaine** Ireland
245 D4 **Kilmallock** Ireland
244 B3 **Kilmaluag** Highland Scotland UK
244 B3 **Kilmarie** Highland Scotland UK
244 D5 **Kilmarnock** East Ayrshire Scotland UK
244 C4 **Kilmartin** Argyll and Bute Scotland UK
245 D5 **Kilmartin Upper** Ireland
244 C4 **Kilmelford** Argyll and Bute Scotland UK
242 B3 **Kilmessan** Ireland
388 F2 **Kil'mez** Russian Federation
388 F2 **Kil'mez** Russian Federation
245 F2 **Kilmichael Point** Ireland
245 D4 **Kilmihil** Ireland
245 D5 **Kilmona** Ireland
245 D3 **Kilmore** Ireland
245 F3 **Kilmore** Ireland
245 G2 **Kilmore** Down Northern Ireland UK
245 F4 **Kilmore Quay** Ireland
242 B4 **Kilmurry** Ireland
245 D4 **Kilmurry** Ireland
245 F4 **Kilnacoo** Ireland
244 C4 **Kilninver** Argyll and Bute Scotland UK
243 I3 **Kilnsea** East Riding of Yorkshire England UK
162 D3 **Kilómetro 164** Argentina
244 B4 **Kiloran** Argyll and Bute Scotland UK
307 F5 **Kilosa** Tanzania
240 E3 **Kilpeck** Herefordshire England UK
242 B3 **Kilpedder** Ireland
245 F4 **Kilpierce** Ireland
243 H3 **Kilpin** East Riding of Yorkshire England UK
222 L2 **Kilpisjärvi** *lake* Sweden
223 R2 **Kilp"yavr** Russian Federation
242 B1 **Kilraghts** Ballymoney Northern Ireland UK
242 B2 **Kilrea** Coleraine Northern Ireland UK
245 D3 **Kilreekill** Ireland
245 C4 **Kilrush** Ireland
224 E3 **Kilsfjorden** *bay* Norway
245 E2 **Kilskeery** Omagh Northern Ireland UK
244 D6 **Kilstay** Dumfries and Galloway Scotland UK
393 C9 **Kiltan Island** Lakshadweep India
242 B3 **Kilternan** Ireland
242 A3 **Kiltoom** Ireland
223 O5 **Kiltuanjärvi** *lake* Finland
245 D3 **Kiltullagh** Ireland
306 D5 **Kilubi** *watercourse* Democratic Republic of Congo
245 D3 **Kilvine** Ireland
222 L3 **Kilvo** Sweden
307 F5 **Kilwa Kivinje** Tanzania
305 G3 **Kim** *watercourse* Cameroon
305 H3 **Kim** Chad
373 F5 **Kimaan** Indonesia
375 G2 **Kimanis, Teluk** *bay* Malaysia
223 Q4 **Kimasozero, Ozero** *lake* Russian Federation
425 K8 **Kimba** SA Australia
305 G5 **Kimba** Congo
126 D4 **Kimball** Minnesota USA
125 N6 **Kimball** Nebraska USA
306 B5 **Kimbao** Democratic Republic of Congo
373 I5 **Kimbe** Papua New Guinea
373 I5 **Kimbe Bay** Papua New Guinea
424 H4 **Kimberley** *region* NT Australia
308 D5 **Kimberley** South Africa
124 H5 **Kimberly** Idaho USA
155 G3 **Kimbia** Guyana
422 F5 **Kimbolton** New Zealand
386 F3 **Kim'chaek** North Korea
386 F4 **Kimhae** South Korea
225 L2 **Kimito** *island* Finland
118 M5 **Kimiwan Lake** Alberta Canada
386 E4 **Kimje** South Korea
121 U1 **Kimmirut** Nunavut Canada
387 I2 **Kimobetsu-dake** *volcano* Japan
235 D7 **Kimolos** *island* Greece
305 G5 **Kimongo** Congo
223 Q5 **Kimovaara** Russian Federation
238 H5 **Kimovsk** Russian Federation
300 F6 **Kimparana** Mali
306 A5 **Kimpese** Democratic Republic of Congo
238 G4 **Kimry** Russian Federation
118 H6 **Kimsquit** British Columbia Canada
306 B5 **Kimvula** Democratic Republic of Congo
379 H4 **Kin-u** Myanmar
375 H2 **Kinabalu, Gunung** *mountain* Malaysia
375 H2 **Kinabalu National Park** Malaysia
375 H2 **Kinabatangan** *watercourse* Malaysia
235 E7 **Kinaros** *island* Greece
375 H2 **Kinarut** Malaysia
118 F4 **Kinaskan Lake** British Columbia Canada
116 H8 **Kinbasket Lake** Alberta Canada
118 L6 **Kinbasket Lake** British Columbia Canada
244 E2 **Kinbrace** Highland Scotland UK
119 R8 **Kincaid** Saskatchewan Canada
129 O1 **Kincaid** Kansas USA
244 E4 **Kincardine** Fife Scotland UK
244 D3 **Kincardine** Highland Scotland UK
224 G4 **Kind** *region* Sweden
306 D5 **Kinda** Democratic Republic of Congo
224 H3 **Kinda** *region* Sweden
305 G5 **Kindamba** Congo
227 H4 **Kindberg** Austria
306 A5 **Kindeje** Angola
130 E5 **Kinder** Louisiana USA
127 O5 **Kinderhook** New York USA
119 Q7 **Kindersley** Saskatchewan Canada
304 B2 **Kindia** Guinea
306 D4 **Kindu** Democratic Republic of Congo
388 I3 **Kindykty** *lake* Kazakhstan
388 F2 **Kinel-cherkasy** Russian Federation
424 G4 **King** *watercourse* WA Australia
424 F8 **King, Lake** WA Australia
117 I3 **King Christian Island** Nunavut Canada
128 B2 **King City** California USA
126 D6 **King City** Missouri USA
116 C7 **King Cove** Alaska USA
163 8 **King Edward Point** South Georgia
163 7 **King George Bay** *bay* Falkland Islands
436 U2 **King George Island** Antarctica
121 P4 **King George Islands** Nunavut Canada
163 8 **King Haakon Bay** South Georgia
425 M9 **King Island** Tas. Australia
424 H4 **King Leopold Ranges** WA Australia
436 S1 **King Peak** *mountain* Antarctica
436 R2 **King Peninsula** Antarctica
436 U2 **King Sejong (South Korea)** *research station* Antarctica
117 J5 **King William Island** Nunavut Canada
425 N6 **Kingaroy** Qld Australia
245 D2 **Kingarrow** Ireland
244 C5 **Kingarth** Argyll and Bute Scotland UK
118 H7 **Kingcome** *watercourse* British Columbia Canada
127 P4 **Kingfield** Maine USA
130 C3 **Kingfisher** Oklahoma USA
120 K6 **Kingfisher Lake** *lake* Ontario Canada
241 F3 **Kingham** Oxfordshire England UK
244 E4 **Kinghorn** Fife Scotland UK
225 O3 **Kingisepp** Russian Federation
128 G3 **Kingman** Arizona USA
125 P8 **Kingman** Kansas USA
306 D4 **Kingombe** Democratic Republic of Congo
424 I6 **Kings Canyon Resort** NT Australia
241 H2 **King's Lynn** Norfolk England UK
125 J6 **Kings Peak** Utah USA
123 J8 **King's Point** Newfoundland and Labrador Canada
241 F3 **King's Worthy** Hampshire England UK
240 D4 **Kingsbridge** Devon England UK
128 C2 **Kingsburg** California USA
241 F3 **Kingsclere** Hampshire England UK
425 K8 **Kingscote** SA Australia
241 E3 **Kingscote** Gloucestershire England UK
131 K5 **Kingsland** Georgia USA
243 F3 **Kingsley** Cheshire England UK
131 J2 **Kingsport** Tennessee USA
244 E3 **Kingsteps** Highland Scotland UK
240 E3 **Kingsthorne** Herefordshire England UK
425 inset **Kingston** Norfolk Island Australia
425 M10 **Kingston** Tas. Australia
123 F10 **Kingston** Nova Scotia Canada
127 M4 **Kingston** Ontario Canada
134 E3 **Kingston** Jamaica
423 C7 **Kingston** New Zealand
131 I3 **Kingston** Georgia USA
129 I4 **Kingston** New Mexico USA
127 O6 **Kingston** New York USA
128 F1 **Kingston** Utah USA
241 E3 **Kingston Deverill** Wiltshire England UK
425 K9 **Kingston S.E.** SA Australia
243 H3 **Kingston upon Hull** East Riding of Yorkshire England UK
241 G3 **Kingston upon Thames** Greater London England UK
163 11a **Kingstown** St Vincent and the Grenadines
130 C7 **Kingsville** Texas USA
240 E3 **Kingswood** South Gloucestershire England UK
240 D2 **Kington** Herefordshire England UK
306 B5 **Kingungi** Democratic Republic of Congo
121 X4 **Kingurutik** *watercourse* Newfoundland and Labrador Canada
244 D3 **Kingussie** Highland Scotland UK
306 D6 **Kiniama** Democratic Republic of Congo
235 F6 **Kınık** Turkey
305 G5 **Kinkala** Congo
304 D3 **Kinkene** *watercourse* Côte d'Ivoire
422 F4 **Kinleith** New Zealand
244 D2 **Kinloch** Highland Scotland UK
244 C3 **Kinloch Hourn** Highland Scotland UK
244 D4 **Kinlochard** Stirling Scotland UK
244 C3 **Kinlochewe** Highland Scotland UK
244 C4 **Kinlochmorar** Highland Scotland UK
244 D4 **Kinlochmore** Highland Scotland UK
244 B2 **Kinlochroag** Na h-Eileanan Siar Scotland UK
244 E3 **Kinloss** Moray Scotland UK
224 G4 **Kinna** Sweden
124 G2 **Kinnaird** British Columbia Canada
244 E4 **Kinnaird Ho** Perth and Kinross Scotland UK
223 O1 **Kinnarodden** *cape* Norway
245 E3 **Kinnegad** Ireland
242 E1 **Kinnelhead** Dumfries and Galloway Scotland UK
224 G3 **Kinneviken** *bay* Sweden
223 N5 **Kinnula** Finland
223 O5 **Kinnulanlahti** Finland
120 D4 **Kinoosao** Saskatchewan Canada
121 O7 **Kinosheo** *watercourse* Ontario Canada
119 V7 **Kinosota** Manitoba Canada
244 E3 **Kinrara** Highland Scotland UK
245 D5 **Kinsale** Ireland
163 I7 **Kinsale** Montserrat
119 P6 **Kinsella** Alberta Canada
437 K2 **Kinsey, Cape** Antarctica
306 B4 **Kinshasa** Democratic Republic of Congo
306 B4 **Kinshasa** *admin. area* Democratic Republic of Congo
131 M3 **Kinston** North Carolina USA
225 K5 **Kintai** Lithuania
304 C2 **Kintinian** Guinea
424 I5 **Kintore** NT Australia
244 F3 **Kintore** Aberdeenshire Scotland UK
244 B5 **Kintour** Argyll and Bute Scotland UK
244 B4 **Kintra** Highland Scotland UK
244 C5 **Kintyre, Mull of** *cape* Scotland UK
244 C4 **Kinuachdrachd** Argyll and Bute Scotland UK
121 N5 **Kinushseo** *watercourse* Ontario Canada
119 W6 **Kinusisipi** Manitoba Canada
245 D3 **Kinvara** Ireland
241 E2 **Kinvere** Staffordshire England UK
393 E7 **Kinwat** Maharashtra India
226 E2 **Kinzig** *watercourse* Germany
427 9a **Kioa** *island* Fiji
307 E4 **Kiomboi** Tanzania
223 O5 **Kiorus** *bay* Finland
125 P8 **Kiowa** Kansas USA
306 D4 **Kipaka** Democratic Republic of Congo
127 L3 **Kipawa** Québec Canada
117 L9 **Kipawa, Lac** *lake* Québec Canada
238 H3 **Kipelovo** Russian Federation
307 E5 **Kipembawe** Tanzania
307 E5 **Kipengere Range** *range* Tanzania
306 E5 **Kipili** Tanzania
223 O4 **Kipinä** Finland
125 N1 **Kipling Station** Saskatchewan Canada
116 C7 **Kipnuk** Alaska USA
235 E5 **Kipoi** Greece
235 D5 **Kipos, Akra** *cape* Greece
244 D4 **Kippen** Stirling Scotland UK
389 N2 **Kiprino** Russian Federation
306 D6 **Kipushi** Democratic Republic of Congo
426 8 **Kirakira** Solomon Islands
222 G4 **Kiran** Norway
393 F7 **Kirandul** Chhattisgarh India
300 D5 **Kirané** Mali
235 F6 **Kıranköy** Turkey
235 F6 **Kiraz** Turkey
237 X5 **Kirbey** Russian Federation
225 L3 **Kirbla** Estonia
243 G2 **Kirby** North Yorkshire England UK
130 E5 **Kirbyville** Texas USA
226 E3 **Kirchheim** Germany
394 G5 **Kireçli Geçidi** *pass* Turkey
237 W7 **Kirenga** *watercourse* Russian Federation
235 F7 **Kirenis** *watercourse* Turkey
238 G6 **Kireyevsk** Russian Federation
389 L5 **Kirgizskiy Range** *range* Kyrgyzstan
306 B4 **Kiri** Democratic Republic of Congo
426 1 **Kiribati** *country* Oceania
307 H2 **Kiridh** Somalia
235 E5 **Kırıkkale** *admin. area* Turkey
394 E5 **Kırıkkale** Turkey
238 H3 **Kirillov** Russian Federation
238 C2 **Kirillovskoye** Russian Federation
225 P3 **Kirishi** Russian Federation
426 1 **Kiritimati** *island* Kiribati
373 I6 **Kiriwina Island** Papua New Guinea
242 D2 **Kirk Michael** Isle of Man UK
244 F5 **Kirk Yetholm** Scottish Borders Scotland UK
235 G6 **Kırka** Turkey
244 E6 **Kirkbean** Dumfries and Galloway Scotland UK
242 E2 **Kirkbride** Cumbria England UK
242 D1 **Kirkbride** South Ayrshire Scotland UK
243 H3 **Kirkby** Lincolnshire England UK
242 F2 **Kirkby Stephen** Cumbria England UK
119 O7 **Kirkcaldy** Alberta Canada
244 E4 **Kirkcaldy** Fife Scotland UK
244 D5 **Kirkconnel** Dumfries and Galloway Scotland UK
244 D6 **Kirkcowan** Dumfries and Galloway Scotland UK
244 D6 **Kirkcudbright** Dumfries and Galloway Scotland UK
125 O2 **Kirkella** Manitoba Canada
223 Q2 **Kirkenes** Norway
242 F3 **Kirkham** Lancashire England UK
244 B3 **Kirkibost** Highland Scotland UK
222 inset **Kirkjubæjarklaustur** Iceland
243 F2 **Kirkland** Cumbria England UK
244 D5 **Kirkland** Dumfries and Galloway Scotland UK
117 K9 **Kirkland Lake** Ontario Canada
394 C5 **Kırklareli** *admin. area* Turkey
243 G3 **Kirklees** *admin. area* England UK
126 H6 **Kirklin** Indiana USA
423 D7 **Kirkliston Range** New Zealand
242 D2 **Kirkmaiden** Dumfries and Galloway Scotland UK
244 E4 **Kirkmichael** Perth and Kinross Scotland UK
224 F3 **Kirkøy** *island* Norway
244 E5 **Kirkpatrick** Dumfries and Galloway Scotland UK
243 H3 **Kirkstead** Lincolnshire England UK
126 E6 **Kirksville** Missouri USA
244 F4 **Kirkton** Angus Scotland UK
244 D3 **Kirkton** Highland Scotland UK
244 F3 **Kirkton of Culsalmond** Aberdeenshire Scotland UK
244 E4 **Kirkton of Kingoldrum** Angus Scotland UK
244 F3 **Kirktown of Deskford** Moray Scotland UK
244 F2 **Kirkwall** Orkney Islands Scotland UK
226 D3 **Kirn** Germany
238 F5 **Kirov** Russian Federation
236 L7 **Kirovo-Chepetsk** Russian Federation
388 F1 **Kirovo-Chepetsk** Russian Federation
234 H1 **Kirovohrad** Ukraine
394 D3 **Kirovohrads'ka Oblast'** *admin. area* Ukraine
223 R3 **Kirovsk** Russian Federation
238 D3 **Kirovsk** Russian Federation
236 K7 **Kirovskaya Oblast'** *admin. area* Russian Federation
388 E4 **Kirovskiy** Russian Federation
225 O2 **Kirovskoye** Russian Federation
244 E4 **Kirriemuir** Angus Scotland UK
233 D9 **Kirrouan** Tunisia
236 L7 **Kirs** Russian Federation
394 E5 **Kirşehir** Turkey
394 E5 **Kirşehir** *admin. area* Turkey
241 F3 **Kirtlington** Oxfordshire England UK
222 L3 **Kiruna** Sweden
436 X2 **Kirwan Escarpment** *range* Antarctica
387 H4 **Kiryū** Japan
238 H4 **Kirzhach** Russian Federation
224 H4 **Kisa** Sweden
227 J5 **Kisač** Serbia
307 F5 **Kisaki** Tanzania
306 D3 **Kisangani** Democratic Republic of Congo
306 B4 **Kisantete** Democratic Republic of Congo
306 B5 **Kisantu** Democratic Republic of Congo
375 J5 **Kisar** *island* Indonesia
374 C3 **Kisaran** Indonesia
227 I4 **Kisdobsza** Hungary
389 O2 **Kiselevsk** Russian Federation
225 Q2 **Kisel'nya** Russian Federation
306 C6 **Kisenge** Democratic Republic of Congo
225 M4 **Kišezers** *lake* Latvia
391 H4 **Kish, Jazireh-ye** *island* Iran
392 D5 **Kishangarh** Rajasthan India
305 E3 **Kishi** Nigeria
120 I3 **Kishiayamweekemow** Manitoba Canada
386 F5 **Kishiga-zaki** *island* Japan
120 I6 **Kishikas** *watercourse* Ontario Canada
KishinevChişinău *see* **Chişinău** Moldova
379 G4 **Kishoreganj** Bangladesh
244 C3 **Kishorn, Loch** *bay* Scotland UK
392 D4 **Kishtwar** Jammu and Kashmir India/Pakistan
306 E5 **Kisi** Tanzania
307 E5 **Kisigo** *watercourse* Tanzania
307 E4 **Kisii** Kenya
237 AK8 **Kiska** *island* Alaska USA
118 K5 **Kiskatinaw** *watercourse* British Columbia Canada
119 V5 **Kiskitto Lake** Manitoba Canada
119 V5 **Kiskittogisu Lake** Manitoba Canada
225 L2 **Kisko** Finland
234 B2 **Kiskőre** Hungary
234 A2 **Kiskunhalas** Hungary
235 F6 **Kışla** Turkey
235 F6 **Kışlaköy** Turkey
234 C2 **Kisléta** Hungary
388 D5 **Kislovodsk** Russian Federation
307 G4 **Kismaayo** Somalia
125 O8 **Kismet** Kansas USA
118 G5 **Kispiox** *watercourse* British Columbia Canada
235 C8 **Kissamou, Kolpos** *bay* Greece
304 B3 **Kissidougou** Guinea
131 K7 **Kissimmee, Lake** Florida USA
119 U5 **Kississing Lake** Manitoba Canada
232 C3 **Kißlegg** Germany
234 A2 **Kisszállás** Hungary
234 A2 **Kistelek** Hungary
120 I5 **Kistigan Lake** Manitoba Canada
223 N1 **Kistrand** Norway
307 E4 **Kisumu** Kenya
306 A5 **Kisundi** Democratic Republic of Congo
234 C1 **Kisvárda** Hungary
125 N7 **Kit Carson** Colorado USA
300 E6 **Kita** Mali
386 F5 **Kita-Kyūshū** Japan
390 E6 **Kitāf** Yemen
387 I4 **Kitaibaraki** Japan
307 E3 **Kitale** Kenya
387 I2 **Kitami** Japan
307 E4 **Kitangiri, Lake** *lake* Tanzania
373 I6 **Kitava Island** Papua New Guinea
307 G6 **Kitaya** Tanzania
127 K5 **Kitchener** Ontario Canada
120 L6 **Kitchie Lake** Ontario Canada
121 P7 **Kitchigama** *watercourse* Québec Canada
120 I5 **Kitchisakik** Manitoba Canada
306 C5 **Kiteba** Democratic Republic of Congo
223 Q5 **Kitee** Finland
223 P5 **Kiteenjärvi** *lake* Finland
238 D1 **Kiteenjärvi** *lake* Russian Federation
234 E4 **Kiten** Bulgaria
306 D5 **Kitendwe** Democratic Republic of Congo
307 E3 **Kitgum** Uganda
118 G5 **Kitimat** British Columbia Canada
118 G5 **Kitimat Ranges** British Columbia Canada
223 P3 **Kitka** Finland
223 M3 **Kitkiöjärvi** Sweden
223 M3 **Kitkiöjoki** Sweden
237 AF9 **Kitoboynyy** Kuril Islands
387 K1 **Kitoboynyy** Russian Federation

163 I2 **Kitridge Point** *cape* Barbados
235 C5 **Kítros** Greece
223 Q5 **Kitsi** Finland
222 K3 **Kittajaur** Sweden
225 K2 **Kittamaa** *island* Finland
222 I4 **Kittelfjäll** Sweden
223 N3 **Kittilä** Finland
240 D4 **Kittisford** Somerset England UK
124 E3 **Kittitas** Washington USA
225 L2 **Kitula** Finland
307 F4 **Kitumbeine** *volcano* Tanzania
307 F5 **Kitumbini** Tanzania
307 E5 **Kitunda** Tanzania
306 C5 **Kitunga** Democratic Republic of Congo
308 E2 **Kitwe** Zambia
223 O3 **Kiurujärvi** *lake* Finland
223 O5 **Kiuruvesi** Finland
223 O5 **Kiuruvesi** *lake* Finland
118 E5 **Kiusta** British Columbia Canada
223 N3 **Kivalo** *island* Finland
238 G4 **Kiverichi** Russian Federation
227 M2 **Kivertsi** Ukraine
223 O4 **Kivesjärvi** Finland
223 O4 **Kivesjärvi** *lake* Finland
223 N5 **Kivijärvi** Finland
223 N5 **Kivijärvi** *lake* Finland
223 Q5 **Kivilahti** Finland
223 N3 **Kivilompolo** Finland
306 D4 **Kivu, Lake** *lake* Democratic Republic of Congo
237 AC8 **Kivun, Khrebet** *range* Russian Federation
306 B5 **Kiwaba N'zogi** Angola
373 G6 **Kiwai Island** Papua New Guinea
307 F5 **Kiwawa** Tanzania
422 F5 **Kiwitea** New Zealand
388 E6 **Kiyamaki Dagh** *mountain* Azerbaijan
389 K3 **Kiyevka** Kazakhstan
235 F5 **Kıyıköy** Turkey
382 E5 **Kizil He** *watercourse* Xinjiang Uygur Zizhiqu China
235 F7 **Kızılcabölük** Turkey
235 F7 **Kızılcadağ** Turkey
394 E5 **Kızılırmak** *watercourse* Turkey
388 H3 **Kizil'skoye** Russian Federation
388 C4 **Kiziltashskiy Liman** *lake* Russian Federation
388 E5 **Kizlyar** Russian Federation
388 E5 **Kizlyarskiy Zaliv** *bay* Russian Federation
388 F2 **Kizner** Russian Federation
222 J2 **Kjeldebotn** Norway
222 K2 **Kjerkesjora** Norway
222 J2 **Kjerr** Norway
224 G3 **Kjerret** Norway
222 I3 **Kjerringøy** Norway
222 F5 **Kjerringvåg** Norway
222 K2 **Kjerstad** Norway
223 O1 **Kjøllefjord** Norway
222 J2 **Kjøpsvik** Norway
224 I3 **Kjulaås** Sweden
374 E4 **Klabat, Teluk** *bay* Indonesia
373 F6 **Kladar** Indonesia
226 F1 **Kläden** Germany
375 H2 **Klagan** Malaysia
227 H4 **Klagenfurt** Austria
225 K5 **Klaipėda** Lithuania
225 K5 **Klaipėdos** *admin. area* Lithuania
124 D6 **Klamath** *watercourse* California USA
124 E5 **Klamath Falls** Oregon USA
124 D6 **Klamath Mountains** California USA
238 B2 **Klamila** Finland
375 H3 **Klampo** Indonesia
232 F4 **Klana** Croatia
374 D3 **Klang** Malaysia
424 inset **Klapa Tuju** Cocos (Keeling) Islands Australia
222 K4 **Kläppen** Sweden
222 J5 **Kläppsjö** Sweden
222 G3 **Klarälven** *watercourse* Sweden
375 F5 **Klaten** Indonesia
226 G3 **Klatovy** Czech Republic
222 L2 **Klauvnes** Norway
308 C6 **Klawer** South Africa
118 E5 **Klawock** Alaska USA
304 B3 **Kle** Liberia
227 I1 **Kłecko** Poland
227 J1 **Kleczew** Poland
118 I7 **Kleena Kleene** British Columbia Canada
163 1c **Klein Bonaire** *island* Netherlands Antilles
163 1b **Klein Curaçao** *island* Netherlands Antilles
308 C5 **Klein Karas** Namibia
226 G3 **Kleine Laaber** *watercourse* Germany
222 E5 **Kleive** Norway
304 C2 **Kléla** Mali
234 F1 **Klembivka** Ukraine
232 H4 **Klenje** Serbia
225 O3 **Klenna** Russian Federation
308 E5 **Klerksdorp** South Africa
388 D3 **Kletskaya** Russian Federation
224 H4 **Klevshult** Sweden
226 G1 **Klietz** Germany
234 E4 **Klikach** Bulgaria
238 G4 **Klimatino** Russian Federation
394 D2 **Klimavichy** Belarus
234 F4 **Kliment** Bulgaria
225 O2 **Klimovo** Russian Federation
394 E2 **Klimovo** Russian Federation
238 G5 **Klimovsk** Russian Federation
238 G4 **Klin** Russian Federation
234 B4 **Klina** Kosovo
118 I7 **Klinaklini** *watercourse* British Columbia Canada
238 C6 **Klinok** Belarus
394 E2 **Klintsy** Russian Federation
222 J4 **Klippen** Sweden
308 D6 **Klipplaat** South Africa
238 H5 **Klishino** Russian Federation
227 I2 **Klisino** Poland
234 A3 **Klijajićevo** Serbia
225 M5 **Kljavica** Belarus
232 G4 **Ključ** Bosnia and Herzegovina
225 L3 **Klobbfjärden** *bay* Finland
227 J2 **Kłobuck** Poland
227 K2 **Kłoczew** Poland
227 I2 **Kłodzko** Poland
224 F2 **Kløfta** Norway
235 B5 **Klos** Albania
229 I3 **Klosters** Switzerland
122 B2 **Klotz, Lac** *lake* Québec Canada
426 3 **Kloulklubed** Palau
222 I5 **Klövsjö** Sweden
116 F6 **Kluane Lake** Yukon Territory Canada
118 B2 **Kluane National Park** Yukon Territory Canada
222 L4 **Klubbfors** Sweden
227 J2 **Kluczbork** Poland
388 D5 **Klukhoris Ugheltekhili** *pass* Georgia
227 K1 **Klukowo** Poland
118 C2 **Klukshu** Yukon Territory Canada
118 D3 **Klukwan** Alaska USA
375 H4 **Klumpang, Teluk** *bay* Indonesia
375 G6 **Klungkung** Indonesia
234 A3 **Klupci** Serbia
389 M3 **Klyuchi** Russian Federation
224 K4 **Knaften** Sweden
224 F4 **Knebel** Denmark
120 H5 **Knee Lake** Manitoba Canada
119 R5 **Knee Lake** Saskatchewan Canada
119 O6 **Kneehills Creek** Alberta Canada
229 J2 **Knetzgau** Germany
234 D4 **Knezha** Bulgaria
227 I5 **Knežica** Bosnia and Herzegovina
125 N3 **Knife** *watercourse* North Dakota USA
119 X3 **Knife Delta** Manitoba Canada
118 H7 **Knight Inlet** British Columbia Canada
240 D2 **Knighton** Powys Wales UK
232 G4 **Knin** Croatia
424 F3 **Knob, Cape** WA Australia
245 C4 **Knock** Ireland
245 D3 **Knock** Ireland
245 E4 **Knock** Ireland
243 F2 **Knock** Cumbria England UK
243 F2 **Knock Fell** *mountain* England UK
244 C6 **Knockaldie** Dumfries and Galloway Scotland UK
245 C4 **Knockalough** Ireland
244 C2 **Knockan** Highland Scotland UK
242 B3 **Knockaphrumpa** Ireland
242 A2 **Knockarevan** Fermanagh Northern Ireland UK
244 D3 **Knockban** Highland Scotland UK
242 B4 **Knockbane** Ireland
245 F3 **Knockbride** Ireland
244 D5 **Knockburnie** East Ayrshire Scotland UK
245 D3 **Knockcroghery** Ireland
245 C4 **Knockeencreen** Ireland
244 C5 **Knockenkelly** North Ayrshire Scotland UK
245 D4 **Knocklong** Ireland
245 D4 **Knockmealdown Mountains** Ireland
242 B2 **Knockmore** Lisburn Northern Ireland UK
245 D3 **Knockmoyle** Ireland
245 F1 **Knocknacarry** Moyle Northern Ireland UK
245 C2 **Knocknalina** Ireland
244 D5 **Knocknalling** Dumfries and Galloway Scotland UK
242 A3 **Knocks** Ireland
228 F1 **Knokke-Heist** Belgium
224 G2 **Knon** *lake* Sweden
222 G5 **Knösen** *cape* Sweden
242 D1 **Knowe** Dumfries and Galloway Scotland UK
243 F1 **Knowesgate** Northumberland England UK
244 D5 **Knoweside** South Ayrshire Scotland UK
436 U2 **Knowles, Cape** Antarctica
242 F3 **Knowsley** *admin. area* England UK
427 15 **Knox Atoll** *reef* Marshall Islands
130 B4 **Knox City** Texas USA
437 H2 **Knox Coast** Antarctica
121 W5 **Knox Lake** Newfoundland and Labrador Canada
126 E6 **Knoxville** Iowa USA
131 J3 **Knoxville** Tennessee USA
244 C3 **Knoydart** *cape* Scotland UK
240 D2 **Knucklas** Powys Wales UK
117 M3 **Knud Rasmussen Land** *plain* Greenland
243 F3 **Knutsford** Cheshire England UK
225 P6 **Knyazhitsy** Belarus
308 D6 **Knysna** South Africa
227 L1 **Knyszyn** Poland
387 H1 **Ko, Gora** *mountain* Russian Federation
376 C6 **Ko Adang** *island* Thailand
376 D5 **Ko Chang** Thailand
382 H5 **Ko-hsieh-ko-ta-erh Shui** *watercourse* Xinjiang Uygur Zizhiqu China
387 H5 **Ko-jima** *island* Japan
376 D5 **Ko Kut** Thailand
382 E6 **Ko-le-ching Ho** *watercourse* Xinjiang Uygur Zizhiqu China
392 F5 **Ko-li Ho** *watercourse* Nepal
387 I3 **Ko-numa** *lake* Japan
376 D5 **Ko Phangan** Thailand
376 C5 **Ko Samui** Thailand
376 D5 **Ko Samui** Thailand
381 J2 **Ko-Takara-jima** *island* Japan
386 F6 **Ko-takara-shima** *island* Japan
376 C5 **Ko Tao** Thailand
304 D2 **Koalla** Burkina Faso
307 F5 **Koani** Tanzania
374 E4 **Koba** Indonesia
226 G4 **Kobarid** Slovenia
386 F5 **Kobayashi** Japan
117 O6 **Kobberminebugt** *bay* Greenland
372 C3 **Kobe** Indonesia
387 G4 **Kobe** Japan
307 E2 **Kobecha** Ethiopia
224 G5 **København (Copenhagen)** Denmark
300 E5 **Kobenni** Mauritania
118 K4 **Kobes** British Columbia Canada
381 I3 **Kōbi-sho** *island* Japan
305 H3 **Koblagué** Chad
229 H1 **Koblenz** Germany
307 F5 **K'obo** Ethiopia
306 E3 **Koboko** Uganda
305 I3 **Kobou** *watercourse* Central African Republic
238 F3 **Kobozha** Russian Federation
225 P3 **Kobralovo** Russian Federation
372 E5 **Kobroor** *island* Indonesia
227 M1 **Kobryn** Belarus
116 D5 **Kobuk Valley National Park** Alaska USA
388 D5 **Kobuleti** Georgia
235 G5 **Kocaali** Turkey
235 G7 **Kocaaliler** Turkey
235 F7 **Kocabaş** Turkey
394 D5 **Kocaeli** *admin. area* Turkey
235 F5 **Kocaeli (İzmit)** Turkey
394 D5 **Kocasu** *watercourse* Turkey
235 E4 **Kocayazı** Turkey
232 G5 **Kočerin** Bosnia and Herzegovina
227 H5 **Kočevje** Slovenia
379 F3 **Koch Bihar** West Bengal India
235 D3 **Kochan** Bulgaria
386 E4 **Koch'ang** South Korea
237 V6 **Kochechum** *watercourse* Russian Federation
226 F4 **Kochelsee** *lake* Germany
237 V7 **Kochenga** Russian Federation
226 E3 **Kocher** *watercourse* Germany
393 D10 **Kochi** Kerala India
386 G5 **Kochi** Japan
388 E2 **Kochkurovo** Russian Federation
227 L2 **Kock** Poland
234 A2 **Kocsér** Hungary
237 Y2 **Kodar, Khrebet** *range* Russian Federation
227 L2 **Kodeń** Poland
116 D7 **Kodiak** Alaska USA
116 D7 **Kodiak Island** Alaska USA
434 U3 **Kodiak Seamount** *underwater feature* Pacific Ocean
236 J6 **Kodima** Russian Federation
393 C7 **Kodinar** Gujarat India
223 U5 **Kodino** Russian Federation
304 E2 **Kodjar** Burkina Faso
305 H3 **Kodo** *watercourse* Central African Republic
302 E6 **Kodok** Sudan
306 E2 **Kodok** Sudan
393 D8 **Kodoli** Maharashtra India
234 F1 **Kodyma** Ukraine
226 B2 **Koekelare** Belgium
392 F5 **Koeripur** Uttar Pradesh India
308 C5 **Koës** Namibia
386 E4 **Koesan** South Korea
128 F4 **Kofa Mountains** Arkansas USA
235 E5 **Kofçaz** Turkey
308 D5 **Koffiefontein** South Africa
227 H4 **Köflach** Austria
304 D3 **Koforidua** Ghana
387 H4 **Kōfu** Japan
386 F5 **Koga** Japan
387 H4 **Koga** Japan
121 Q3 **Kogaluc** *watercourse* Québec Canada
121 Q3 **Kogaluc, Baie** *bay* Québec Canada
121 X4 **Kogaluk** *watercourse* Newfoundland and Labrador Canada
224 G5 **Køge Bugt** *bay* Denmark
305 F3 **Kogi** *admin. area* Nigeria
119 V2 **Kognak** *watercourse* Nunavut Canada
304 B2 **Kogon** *watercourse* Guinea
388 I6 **Kogon** Uzbekistan
387 I3 **Kogota** Japan
386 E4 **Kogum-do** *island* South Korea
390 G3 **Kohgīlūyeh Va Būyer Ahmad** *admin. area* Iran
379 H4 **Kohima** Nagaland India
224 E6 **Köhlen** Germany
436 Q1 **Kohler Glacier** Antarctica
436 Q1 **Kohler Range** Antarctica
80 K10 **Kohler Seamount** *underwater feature* Southern Ocean
372 E5 **Kohn** *island* Indonesia
390 E2 **Koi Sanjaq** Iraq
304 B3 **Koidu-Sefadu** Sierra Leone
376 B5 **Koihoa** Andaman and Nicobar Islands India
374 B1 **Koihoa** Tripura India
383 J6 **Koikyim Qu** *watercourse* Qinghai China
373 H4 **Koil Island** Papua New Guinea
310 8a **Koimbani** Comoros
235 C5 **Koimisis** Greece
304 B3 **Koindu** Sierra Leone
223 Q5 **Koitajoki** *watercourse* Finland
223 Q5 **Koitere** *lake* Finland
223 P4 **Koitila** Finland
225 O2 **Koitsanlahti** Finland
223 N3 **Koivu** Finland
223 O5 **Koivujärvi** *lake* Finland
223 P5 **Koivumäki** Finland
223 N4 **Koivuniemi** Finland
223 Q5 **Koivuvaara** Finland
386 F4 **Koje** South Korea
227 I3 **Kojetín** Czech Republic
424 F3 **Kojonup** WA Australia
307 F2 **Koka, Lake** *lake* Ethiopia
127 Q4 **Kokadjo** Maine USA
155 G2 **Kokali Point** *cape* Guyana
225 K3 **Kökar** *island* Finland
388 H4 **Kokaral** Kazakhstan
389 K2 **Kokay** *lake* Kazakhstan
225 L2 **Kokemäenjoki** *watercourse* Finland
375 F5 **Kokenau** Indonesia
308 C5 **Kokerboom** Namibia
155 G3 **Kokerite** Guyana
393 E10 **Kokkilai** Sri Lanka
223 M5 **Kokkola** Finland
222 L5 **Köklot** Finland
222 L5 **Köklot** *island* Finland
225 M4 **Koknese** Latvia
305 E2 **Koko** Nigeria
373 H6 **Kokoda** Papua New Guinea
126 H6 **Kokomo** Indiana USA
308 D4 **Kokong** Botswana
308 E5 **Kokosi** South Africa
304 B3 **Kokoulo** *watercourse* Guinea
389 K3 **Kokpaksor** *lake* Kazakhstan
389 N3 **Kokpekty** Kazakhstan
379 G3 **Kokrajhar** Assam India
238 E3 **Koksan** North Korea
389 K2 **Kokshetau (Kokchetav)** Kazakhstan
228 F1 **Koksijde** Belgium
121 U4 **Koksoak** *watercourse* Québec Canada
308 E6 **Kokstad** South Africa
121 Q3 **Koktac** *watercourse* Québec Canada
389 M5 **Koktal** Kazakhstan
389 M4 **Kokterek** Kazakhstan
389 N3 **Koktuma** Kazakhstan
375 I5 **Koku, Tanjung** *cape* Indonesia
386 F5 **Kokubu** Japan
223 P5 **Kola** *island* Indonesia
223 R2 **Kola** Russian Federation
223 T3 **Kola** *watercourse* Russian Federation
229 L6 **Kolan** Croatia
223 N3 **Kolana** Indonesia
393 E7 **Kolar** Chhattisgarh India
393 E9 **Kolar** Karnataka India
223 M3 **Kolari** Finland
227 J4 **Kolárovo** Slovakia
234 E4 **Kolartsi** Bulgaria
224 H5 **Kolåsen** Sweden
379 G4 **Kolasib** Mizoram India
225 Q2 **Kolatsel'ga** Russian Federation
392 C5 **Kolayat** Rajasthan India
435 E2 **Kolbeinsey Ridge** *underwater feature* Norwegian Sea
227 K1 **Kolbiel** Poland
225 Q2 **Kolchanovo** Russian Federation
238 H4 **Kol'chugino** Russian Federation
235 F6 **Kölcse** Hungary
300 D6 **Kolda** Senegal
225 E5 **Kolding** Denmark
306 C4 **Kole** Democratic Republic of Congo
306 D3 **Kole** Democratic Republic of Congo
426 7 **Kolé** Vanuatu
304 B3 **Kolenté** *watercourse* Guinea
222 L4 **Koler** Sweden
225 M3 **Kolga** Estonia
225 M3 **Kolga Laht** *bay* Estonia
224 C2 **Kolgrov** Norway
236 L5 **Kolguyev, Ostrov** *island* Russian Federation
393 D8 **Kolhapur** Maharashtra India
393 C11 **Kolhumadulu Atoll** Maldives
223 P5 **Koli** *mountain* Finland
223 P5 **Koli kansallispuisto** *park* Finland
304 B2 **Koliba** *watercourse* Guinea-Bissau
223 N5 **Kolima** *lake* Finland
227 H2 **Kolín** Czech Republic
229 K2 **Kolinec** Czech Republic
225 L4 **Kolka** Latvia
224 E4 **Kølkær** Denmark
225 L4 **Kolkasrags** *cape* Latvia
393 G6 **Kolkata** West Bengal India
223 O5 **Kolkku** *lake* Finland
225 N1 **Kolkonjärvi** *lake* Finland
223 O4 **Kollaja** Finland
393 D10 **Kollam** Kerala India
223 M3 **Kölmjärv** Sweden
229 H1 **Köln (Cologne)** Germany
227 J1 **Koło** Poland
307 F4 **Kolo** Tanzania
238 D6 **Kolodezskaya** Belarus
305 G2 **Kolofata** Cameroon
427 12a **Kolofau, Mont** *mountain* Wallis and Futuna
300 E6 **Kolokani** Mali
426 8 **Kolombangara** *island* Solomon Islands
238 H5 **Kolomna** Russian Federation
306 C4 **Kolomonyi** Democratic Republic of Congo
234 D1 **Kolomyya** Ukraine
304 C2 **Kolondieba** Mali
427 10a **Kolonga** Tonga
223 Q4 **Kolongozero, Ozero** *lake* Russian Federation
426 6b **Kolonia** Federated States of Micronesia
375 K3 **Kolorai** *island* Indonesia
375 I5 **Kolowana Watobo, Teluk** *bay* Indonesia
236 R7 **Kolpashevo** Russian Federation
389 N1 **Kolpashevo** Russian Federation
225 P3 **Kolpino** Russian Federation
226 G1 **Kölpinsee** *lake* Germany
235 C7 **Kolpos Epidavrou** *island* Greece
391 K3 **Kolpur** Pakistan
236 I5 **Kol'skiy Poluostrov** *peninsula* Russian Federation
224 I3 **Kolsnaren** *lake* Sweden
224 E3 **Kolsrud** Norway
223 Q2 **Koltakyulya** Russian Federation
222 L3 **Költräsket** *lake* Sweden
162 C4 **Koluel Kayke** Argentina
389 K3 **Koluton** Kazakhstan
223 Q3 **Kolvasozero** Russian Federation
222 G4 **Kolvereid** Norway
223 N1 **Kolvik** Norway
223 R3 **Kolvits, Ozero** *lake* Russian Federation
223 R3 **Kolvitsa** Russian Federation
306 D6 **Kolwezi** Democratic Republic of Congo
237 AG5 **Kolyma** *watercourse* Russian Federation
237 AF4 **Kolymskaya Nizmennost'** *region* Russian Federation
237 AG6 **Kolymskoye Nagor'ye** *mountain* Russian Federation
237 AM5 **Kolyuchinskaya Guba** *cape* Russian Federation
389 N3 **Kolyvan'** Russian Federation
389 M5 **Kol'zhat** Kazakhstan
384 F2 **Koma** *watercourse* Russian Federation
227 K4 **Komádi** Hungary
305 G2 **Komadugu-Gana** *watercourse* Nigeria
223 Q1 **Komagvær** Norway
227 L3 **Komańcza** Poland
237 AI7 **Komandorskiye Ostrova** *island* Russian Federation
120 G7 **Komarno** Manitoba Canada
227 J4 **Komárno** Slovakia
227 J4 **Komárom-Esztergom** *admin. area* Hungary
238 C2 **Komarovo** Russian Federation
238 E3 **Komarovo** Russian Federation
238 E5 **Komary** Russian Federation
387 H4 **Komatsu** Japan
375 I5 **Komba** *island* Indonesia
308 C3 **Kombat** Namibia
306 D4 **Kombe** Democratic Republic of Congo
304 D2 **Kombissiri** Burkina Faso
237 AB6 **Komelëk** Russian Federation
374 E4 **Komering** *watercourse* Indonesia
235 D7 **Komi** Greece
232 G5 **Komin** Croatia
234 G2 **Kominternivs'ke** Ukraine
386 F2 **Komissorovka** *watercourse* Russian Federation
232 G5 **Komiža** Croatia
227 J4 **Komló** Hungary
225 P2 **Kommunary** Russian Federation
389 K6 **Kommunizm, Qullai** *mountain* Kyrgyzstan
427 9 **Komo** *island* Fiji
305 G4 **Komo** *watercourse* Gabon
375 H6 **Komodo** *island* Indonesia
375 H6 **Komodo, Taman Nasional** *park* Indonesia
304 D3 **Komoé** *watercourse* Côte d'Ivoire
305 G5 **Komono** Congo
373 F6 **Komoran** *island* Indonesia
235 D5 **Komotini** Greece
223 N3 **Kompelusvaara** Sweden
234 A2 **Kömpöc** Hungary
235 B6 **Kompotion** Greece
237 V2 **Komsomolets, Ostrov** *island* Russian Federation
237 AC8 **Komsomol'sk-na-Amure** Russian Federation
385 N2 **Komsomol'sk-na-Amure** Russian Federation
388 G4 **Komsomolskiy** Kazakhstan
237 AJ5 **Komsomol'skiy** Russian Federation
388 E4 **Komsomol'skiy** Russian Federation
237 X3 **Komsomol'skoy Pravdy, Ostrova** *island* Russian Federation
238 C2 **Komsomol'skoye** Russian Federation
235 D5 **Komuniga** Bulgaria
392 F6 **Kon** Uttar Pradesh India
379 I4 **Kon Kyan** Myanmar
376 F4 **Kon Tum** Vietnam
393 F7 **Konada** Andhra Pradesh India
388 E5 **Konagkend** Azerbaijan
238 G4 **Konakovo** Russian Federation
389 K7 **Konar** *admin. area* Afghanistan
391 J4 **Konār Bast** Iran
391 I3 **Konārak** Iran
393 G7 **Konarka** Orissa India
235 C4 **Konarsko** Bulgaria
392 E6 **Konch** Uttar Pradesh India
238 F3 **Konchanskoye-Suvorovskoye** Russian Federation
238 F1 **Konchezero** Russian Federation
372 D4 **Konda** Indonesia
236 N6 **Konda** *watercourse* Russian Federation
393 E7 **Kondagaon** Chhattisgarh India
237 AF5 **Kondakova** Russian Federation
307 F4 **Kondoa** Tanzania
373 G6 **Kondomirat** Indonesia
237 AC8 **Kondon** Russian Federation
385 M2 **Kondon** Russian Federation
225 R1 **Kondopoga** Russian Federation
389 J7 **Kondoz** Afghanistan
389 J7 **Kondoz** *admin. area* Afghanistan
238 C2 **Kondrat'yevo** Russian Federation
238 F5 **Kondrovo** Russian Federation
426 7 **Koné** New Caledonia
236 M6 **Konetsbor** Russian Federation
388 H5 **Köneürgench** Turkmenistan
238 H1 **Konëvo** Russian Federation
376 E4 **Kong** *watercourse* Cambodia
305 G3 **Kong** Cameroon
304 D3 **Kong** Côte d'Ivoire
117 P5 **Kong Christian IX Land** *plain* Greenland
117 Q4 **Kong Christian X Land** *plain* Greenland
117 O5 **Kong Frederik IX Land** *plain* Greenland
117 O6 **Kong Frederik VI Kyst** *coast* Greenland
117 Q3 **Kong Frederik VIII Land** *plain* Greenland
117 Q4 **Kong Oscars Fjord** Greenland
117 Q3 **Kong Wilhelm Land** *plain* Greenland
223 N3 **Köngäs** Finland
223 O4 **Kongasjärvi** *lake* Finland
305 I4 **Kongbo** Central African Republic
223 N5 **Konginkangas** Finland
237 AG6 **Konginskiye Gory** *range* Russian Federation
386 E4 **Kongjiu** South Korea
375 H3 **Kongkemul** *mountain* Indonesia
308 D3 **Kongola** Namibia
306 D5 **Kongolo** Democratic Republic of Congo
304 D2 **Kongoussi** Burkina Faso
224 E3 **Kongsberg** Norway
222 I2 **Kongselva** Norway
222 H4 **Kongsmoen** Norway
236 G3 **Kongsøya** *island* Norway
222 J2 **Kongsvik** Norway
224 G2 **Kongsvinger** Norway
224 F5 **Kongsvoll** Norway
382 E5 **Kongur Shan** *mountain* Xinjiang Uygur Zizhiqu China
121 Q3 **Kongut** *watercourse* Québec Canada
237 AF7 **Koni, Poluostrov** *peninsula* Russian Federation
389 K6 **Konibodom** Tajikistan
227 K3 **Konieczna** Poland
226 F1 **Königslutter** Germany
226 G4 **Königssee** *lake* Germany
388 J6 **Konimex** Uzbekistan
227 J1 **Konin** Poland
229 H3 **Köniz** Switzerland
232 G5 **Konjic** Bosnia and Herzegovina
308 C5 **Konkiep** *watercourse* Namibia
306 D6 **Konko** Democratic Republic of Congo
304 B2 **Konkoure** *watercourse* Guinea
237 X7 **Konkudera** Russian Federation
300 F6 **Konna** Mali
223 O5 **Konnevesi** Finland
223 O5 **Konnevesi** *bay* Finland
225 M3 **Kõnnu** Estonia
225 P1 **Konnunvaara** Finland
373 J5 **Konogaiang, Mount** Papua New Guinea
155 F3 **Konoro Village** Guyana
238 I2 **Konosha** Russian Federation
225 P5 **Konoshi** Belarus
394 E2 **Konotop** Ukraine
426 3 **Konrai** Palau
304 B2 **Konrokota** Mali
224 I2 **Könsberg** *cape* Sweden
227 K2 **Końskie** Poland
307 F2 **Konso** Ethiopia
238 H4 **Konstantinovskiy** Russian Federation
227 L1 **Konstantynów** Poland
229 I3 **Konstanz** Germany
305 F2 **Kontagora** Nigeria
305 E2 **Kontagora** *watercourse* Nigeria
225 O1 **Kontiolahti** Finland
223 P5 **Kontkala** Finland
235 D7 **Kontos, Akra** *cape* Greece
223 N3 **Konttajärvi** Finland
223 O4 **Konttila** Finland
394 E6 **Konya** Turkey
394 E5 **Konya** *admin. area* Turkey
234 C4 **Konyavo** Bulgaria
389 L4 **Konyrat** Kazakhstan
389 M5 **Konyrolen** Kazakhstan
389 K2 **Konyukhovo** Kazakhstan
124 H2 **Koocanusa, Lake** Montana USA
424 F7 **Koorda** WA Australia
225 N3 **Koosa Järv** *lake* Estonia
124 J7 **Kooshare m** Utah USA
124 G2 **Kootenie Lake** British Columbia Canada
119 N8 **Kootenay** *watercourse* British Columbia Canada
118 M8 **Kootenay Bay** British Columbia Canada
118 M8 **Kootenay Lake** British Columbia Canada
119 N7 **Kootenay National Park** British Columbia Canada
389 L5 **Kopa** *watercourse* Kazakhstan
309 F2 **Kopa** Zambia
392 F5 **Kopaganj** Uttar Pradesh India
224 I5 **Kopań, Jezioro** *lake* Poland
222 inset **Kópanes** *cape* Iceland
235 B6 **Kopani** Greece
235 C5 **Kopanós** Greece
388 E4 **Kopanovka** Russian Federation
234 B4 **Kopaonik** *range* Kosovo
393 D7 **Kopargaon** Maharashtra India
222 inset **Kópasker** Iceland
234 E1 **Kopayhorod** Ukraine
389 M4 **Kopbirlik** Kazakhstan
232 E4 **Koper** Slovenia
388 H6 **Kopet Dag** *range* Iran
224 H3 **Köping** Sweden
234 A4 **Koplik** Albania
222 K5 **Köpmanholmen** Sweden
238 C3 **Kopor'ye** Russian Federation
393 D8 **Koppal** Karnataka India
222 G6 **Koppang** Norway
222 L2 **Koppangen** Norway
223 O2 **Koppelo** Finland
222 G5 **Kopperå** Norway
234 D4 **Koprivets** Bulgaria
235 G6 **Köprüören** Turkey
223 N4 **Kopsa** Finland
234 D1 **Kopychyntsi** Ukraine
235 B5 **Korab** *mountain* Macedonia
388 C2 **Korablino** Russian Federation
121 Q2 **Korak, Baie** *bay* Québec Canada
235 D7 **Korakas, Akra** *cape* Greece
389 K7 **Korān Va Monjān** Afghanistan
300 F5 **Korarou, Lac** *lake* Mali
393 E7 **Koratla** Andhra Pradesh India
393 F6 **Korba** Chhattisgarh India
301 I1 **Korba** Tunisia
226 E2 **Korbach** Germany
238 F2 **Korbenichi** Russian Federation
234 C3 **Korbovo** Serbia
232 G4 **Korčanica** Bosnia and Herzegovina
235 B5 **Korçë** Albania
232 G5 **Korčula** *island* Croatia
388 F7 **KordestĀn** *admin. area* Iran
234 G2 **Kordon** Ukraine
386 D3 **Korea Bay** North Korea
386 F4 **Korea Strait** Japan
372 D5 **Koreare** Indonesia
238 G5 **Korekozevo** Russian Federation
223 R4 **Korelaksha** Russian Federation
303 F5 **Korem** Ethiopia
301 H6 **Korén Adoua** *watercourse* Niger
223 O4 **Korentokylä** Finland
236 M6 **Korepino** Russian Federation
227 I2 **Korfantów** Poland
235 F5 **Körfez** Turkey
436 T1 **Korff Ice Rise** Antarctica
235 C7 **Korfos** Greece
222 H3 **Korgen** Norway
304 C3 **Korhogo** Côte d'Ivoire
392 B6 **Kori Creek** Gujarat India
223 N5 **Koria** Finland
372 E4 **Korido** Indonesia
300 F5 **Korientzé** Mali
300 F5 **Korienzé, Lac** *lake* Mali
155 G3 **Korikori, Kaap** *cape* Suriname
235 C7 **Korinthos (Corinth)** Greece
235 B5 **Korisós** Greece
235 D7 **Korissia** Greece
232 H5 **Korita** Bosnia and Herzegovina
387 I4 **Kōriyama** Japan
223 Q5 **Korkeakangas** Finland
390 F2 **Korki** Iran
388 I2 **Korkino** Russian Federation
237 AF6 **Korkodon** Russian Federation
237 AG5 **Korkodon** *watercourse* Russian Federation
382 G5 **Korla** Xinjiang Uygur Zizhiqu China
382 H4 **Korla** Xinjiang Uygur Zizhiqu China
155 H4 **Kormontibo** French Guiana
389 N2 **Kornilovo** Russian Federation
388 E3 **Kornyeevka** Russian Federation
304 C3 **Koro** Côte d'Ivoire
427 9 **Koro** *island* Fiji
223 M5 **Koro** Finland
300 F6 **Koro** Mali
427 9a **Koro Sea** Fiji
301 J5 **Koro Toro** Chad
302 B4 **Koro Toro** Chad
373 G5 **Koroba** Papua New Guinea
121 W3 **Koroc** *watercourse* Québec Canada
225 P5 **Korolëvshchina** Russian Federation
427 9a **Korolevu** Fiji
305 H2 **Korom, Bahr** *watercourse* Chad
377 J6 **Koronadal** Philippines
235 B7 **Koroni** Greece
426 3 **Koror** Palau
426 3 **Koror** *island* Palau
227 K4 **Körös** *watercourse* Hungary
373 G5 **Korosameri** *watercourse* Papua New Guinea
394 D2 **Korosten'** Ukraine
427 9a **Korotasere** Fiji
373 J5 **Korovou** Solomon Islands
223 N5 **Korpi** Finland
225 N2 **Korpijärvi** *lake* Finland
223 M3 **Korpilombolo** Sweden
223 Q5 **Korpisel'kya** Russian Federation
223 P5 **Korpivaara** Finland
225 K2 **Korpo** Finland
225 K2 **Korpo** *island* Finland
223 N5 **Korppinen** Finland
237 AD9 **Korsakov** Russian Federation
387 I1 **Korsakov** Russian Federation
227 M2 **Korshev** Ukraine
237 X7 **Korshunovo** Russian Federation
222 J2 **Korsnes** Norway
224 F5 **Korsør** Denmark
222 L4 **Korsträsk** Sweden
222 H5 **Korsvattnet** *lake* Sweden
222 G5 **Korsvegen** Norway
302 E5 **Kortala** Sudan
223 P4 **Kortesalmi** Finland
223 M5 **Kortesjärvi** Finland
302 E4 **Korti** Sudan
228 F1 **Kortrijk** Belgium
223 P5 **Kortteinen** Finland
235 F7 **Koruköy** Turkey
223 P4 **Korvua** Finland
223 P4 **Korvuanjärvi** *lake* Finland
237 AJ6 **Koryakskoye Nagor'ye** *range* Russian Federation
236 K6 **Koryazhma** Russian Federation
235 E7 **Kos** Greece
235 E7 **Kos** *island* Greece
237 AL6 **Kosa Russkaya Koshka** *cape* Russian Federation
393 C7 **Kosamba** Gujarat India
386 E3 **Kosan** North Korea
227 I1 **Kościan** Poland
227 J1 **Kościelec** Poland
130 G4 **Kosciusko** Mississippi USA
425 N9 **Kosciuszko, Mount** NSW Australia
225 M3 **Kose** Estonia
225 N4 **Kose** Estonia
235 B5 **Kosel** Macedonia
235 E6 **Köseler** Turkey
224 G4 **Kösen** *lake* Sweden
389 O3 **Kosh-Agach** Russian Federation
302 E3 **Kosha** Sudan
388 G4 **Koshkar** Kazakhstan
126 G5 **Koshkonong, Lake** Wisconsin USA
227 K3 **Košice** Slovakia
227 K3 **Košický** *admin. area* Slovakia
389 N2 **Kosikha** Russian Federation
222 H5 **Kosjön** *lake* Sweden
222 M5 **Koskenkorva** Finland
223 N4 **Koskenkylä** Finland
223 P4 **Koskenmäki** Finland
223 O2 **Koskenniska** Finland
223 N5 **Koskenpää** Finland
238 E5 **Koski** Russian Federation
225 Q2 **Kos'kovo** Russian Federation
223 M5 **Koskue** Finland
236 K6 **Koslan** Russian Federation
235 C7 **Kosmas** Greece
388 J6 **Koson** Uzbekistan
234 B4 **Kosovo** *country* Europe
234 B4 **Kosovo Polje** *region* Kosovo
234 B4 **Kosovska Mitrovica** Kosovo
426 6 **Kosrae** *admin. area* Federated States of Micronesia
426 6 **Kosrae** *island* Federated States of Micronesia
130 C5 **Kosse** Texas USA
304 C3 **Kossou, Lac de** *lake* Côte d'Ivoire
224 H4 **Kosta** Sweden
227 I5 **Kostajnica** Bosnia and Herzegovina
388 I2 **Kostanay** Kazakhstan
388 I3 **Kostanayskaya Oblast'** *admin. area* Kazakhstan
227 H5 **Kostanjevica** Slovenia
224 F3 **Koster** *island* Sweden
302 E5 **Kosti** Sudan
235 C4 **Kostino** Russian Federation
234 H2 **Kostomarovka** Ukraine
223 Q4 **Kostomuksha** Russian Federation
223 P4 **Kostonjärvi** *lake* Finland
394 C2 **Kostopil'** Ukraine
225 O4 **Kostorovo** Russian Federation
225 O5 **Kostritsa** Belarus
236 J7 **Kostroma** Russian Federation
388 D1 **Kostroma** Russian Federation
388 E1 **Kostromskaya Oblast'** *admin. area* Russian Federation
238 C5 **Kostyuki** Belarus
304 E3 **Kosubosu** Nigeria
223 P5 **Kosula** Finland
224 I5 **Koszalin** Poland
227 K2 **Koszyce** Poland
391 K4 **Kot Diji** Pakistan
393 E8 **Kota** Andhra Pradesh India
393 F6 **Kota** Chhattisgarh India
392 D6 **Kota** Rajasthan India
392 F6 **Kota** Uttar Pradesh India
375 H2 **Kota Belud** Malaysia
374 D2 **Kota Bharu** Malaysia
375 H2 **Kota Kinabalu** Malaysia
375 F3 **Kota Samarahan** Malaysia
374 D3 **Kota Tinggi** Malaysia
374 E5 **Kotaagung** Indonesia
374 C3 **Kotabaru** Indonesia
375 F4 **Kotabaru** Indonesia
375 H4 **Kotabaru** Indonesia
375 G4 **Kotabesi** Indonesia
374 E5 **Kotabumi** Indonesia
372 C3 **Kotabunan** Indonesia
223 N5 **Kotala** Finland
223 P3 **Kotala** Finland
374 C3 **Kotanopan** Indonesia
374 D3 **Kotapinang** Indonesia
374 D3 **Kotatengah** Indonesia
375 F4 **Kotawaringin** Indonesia
375 F4 **Kotawaringin, Teluk** *bay* Indonesia
118 K3 **Kotcho Lake** British Columbia Canada
388 E1 **Kotel'nich** Russian Federation
388 D4 **Kotel'nikovo** Russian Federation

237 AC3 **Kotel'nyy, Ostrov** *island* Russian Federation
394 E2 **Kotel'va** Ukraine
392 F6 **Kothi** Madhya Pradesh India
307 E3 **Kotido** Uganda
237 AD9 **Kotikovo** Russian Federation
223 O4 **Kotila** Finland
223 P4 **Kotiranta** Finland
225 N2 **Kotka** Finland
225 Q2 **Kotkozero** Russian Federation
236 K6 **Kotlas** Russian Federation
116 C6 **Kotlik** Alaska USA
229 L3 **Kotlje** Slovenia
238 F3 **Kotlovan** Russian Federation
238 C3 **Kotly** Russian Federation
307 F3 **Kotome** *watercourse* Kenya
238 N4 **Kotorsko** Bosnia and Herzegovina
304 D3 **Kotouba** Côte d'Ivoire
388 D3 **Kotovo** Russian Federation
388 D3 **Kotovsk** Russian Federation
393 F7 **Kotpad** Chhattisgarh India
392 D5 **Kotputli** Rajasthan India
392 C6 **Kotra** Gujarat India
393 D7 **Kotra** Madhya Pradesh India
392 E6 **Kotra** Uttar Pradesh India
393 E8 **Kottagudem** Andhra Pradesh India
393 D10 **Kottayam** Kerala India
305 I3 **Kotto** *watercourse* Central African Republic
116 C5 **Kotzebue** Alaska USA
116 C5 **Kotzebue Sound** Alaska USA
305 H3 **Kouango** Central African Republic
304 F5 **Kouango, Pointe** Gabon
426 7 **Kouari** New Caledonia
304 B2 **Koubia** Guinea
304 D2 **Koudougou** Burkina Faso
304 D2 **Kouéré** Burkina Faso
301 I6 **Koufey** Niger
235 D7 **Koufonisi** *island* Greece
305 G5 **Kouilou** *admin. area* Congo
305 H3 **Kouki** Central African Republic
305 H3 **Koukourou** Central African Republic
305 I3 **Koukourou** *watercourse* Central African Republic
305 G5 **Koulamoutou** Gabon
305 I2 **Koulba** Chad
302 C5 **Koulbo** Chad
300 E6 **Koulikoro** Mali
300 E6 **Koulikoro** *admin. area* Mali
304 B2 **Kouloun** *watercourse* Guinea
305 G3 **Koum** Cameroon
305 H3 **Kouma** *watercourse* Central African Republic
426 7 **Koumac** New Caledonia
305 G4 **Koumameyong** Gabon
155 I3 **Koumarouman, Pointe** *cape* French Guiana
304 B2 **Koumbia** Guinea
305 I3 **Koumou** *watercourse* Central African Republic
305 H3 **Koumra** Chad
300 D6 **Koundian** Mali
304 D2 **Koundougou** Burkina Faso
300 D6 **Koungheul** Senegal
300 D6 **Kounkané** Senegal
130 D5 **Kountze** Texas USA
385 K4 **Kouqian** Jilin China
304 B2 **Kouragué** Mali
304 C3 **Kourai** *watercourse* Guinea
301 G6 **Kouré** Niger
381 J3 **Kouri-shima** *island* Japan
232 F1 **Kouřim** Czech Republic
155 H3 **Kourou** French Guiana
300 D5 **Koûroudjél** Mauritania
304 D2 **Kourouma** Burkina Faso
304 D2 **Koury** Mali
300 D6 **Koussanar** Senegal
300 D6 **Koussane** Senegal
301 J6 **Kousséri** Chad
235 D7 **Koutalás** Greece
304 C2 **Koutiala** Mali
223 O4 **Kouva** Finland
225 N2 **Kouvola** Finland
304 C2 **Kouya** *watercourse* Guinea
305 H5 **Kouyou** *watercourse* Congo
232 G5 **Kovači** Bosnia and Herzegovina
235 G7 **Kovada Gölü** *lake* Turkey
229 L2 **Kovářov** Czech Republic
238 H2 **Kovarzino** Russian Federation
223 R3 **Kovda** Russian Federation
223 Q3 **Kovdor** Russian Federation
223 Q3 **Kovdozero, Ozero** *lake* Russian Federation
225 P1 **Kovero** Finland
227 K4 **Kövesd** Romania
121 Q2 **Kovik** *watercourse* Québec Canada
121 Q2 **Kovik, Baie** *bay* Québec Canada
234 B3 **Kovilj** Serbia
393 D10 **Kovilpatti** Tamil Nadu India
234 B3 **Kovin** Serbia
223 M5 **Kovjoki** Finland
224 H1 **Kövra** Sweden
237 AH6 **Kovrizhka** Russian Federation
388 D2 **Kovrov** Russian Federation
388 D2 **Kovylkino** Russian Federation
238 G2 **Kovzha** Russian Federation
227 J1 **Kowal** Poland
225 L5 **Kowale Oleckie** Poland
425 L3 **Kowanyama** Qld Australia
227 H2 **Kowary** Poland
381 G4 **Kowloon** Hong Kong (XIANGGANG) S.A.R. China
391 K3 **Kowndalān** Afghanistan
389 L7 **Kowtal-e Ershād Owin** *pass*
391 M2 **Kowtal-e Ershād Owin** *pass* Pakistan
391 L2 **Kowtal-e Khāvāk** *pass* Afghanistan
391 K2 **Kowtal-e Morgh** *pass* Afghanistan
391 K2 **Kowtal-e Shibar** *pass* Afghanistan
391 K2 **Kowtal-e Wonay** *pass* Afghanistan
388 J3 **Koybagbar Koli** *lake* Kazakhstan
235 F7 **Köyceğiz Gölü** *lake* Turkey
236 J5 **Koyda** Russian Federation
223 M5 **Köyhäjoki** Finland
242 B4 **Koyle** Ireland
388 G6 **Koymatdag, Gory** *range* Turkmenistan
223 O3 **Köyry** *lake* Finland
388 C4 **Koysug** Russian Federation
116 C6 **Koyuk** Alaska USA
116 D5 **Koyukuk** *watercourse* Alaska USA
235 E6 **Koyuneli** Turkey
235 E6 **Koyuneri** Turkey
223 Q4 **Koyvas, Ozero** *lake* Russian Federation
238 H3 **Koza** Russian Federation
235 F7 **Kozağacı** Turkey
235 G5 **Kozan** Turkey
394 E6 **Kozan** Turkey
235 B5 **Kozani** Greece
303 G5 **Kozar, Ras** *cape* Eritrea
232 H2 **Kozelník** Slovakia
238 F5 **Kozel'sk** Russian Federation
388 I4 **Kozhabakha** Kazakhstan
393 D9 **Kozhikode** Kerala India
223 U5 **Kozhozero, Ozero** *lake* Russian Federation
223 U5 **Kozhposëlok** Russian Federation
227 K2 **Kozienice** Poland
235 F7 **Kozlar** Turkey
388 D3 **Kozlovka** Russian Federation
238 G4 **Kozlovo** Russian Federation
235 G5 **Kozluca** Turkey
235 F6 **Kozluca** Turkey
394 G5 **Kozluk** Turkey
227 J2 **Koźminek** Poland
388 E2 **Koz'modem'yansk** Russian Federation
234 C4 **Koznitsa** *mountain* Bulgaria
234 D1 **Kozova** Ukraine
387 H4 **Kōzu-shima** *island* Japan
227 H2 **Kozy** Poland
235 E5 **Kozyörük** Turkey
234 G2 **Kozyrka** Ukraine
304 E2 **Kpako** *watercourse* Benin
304 E3 **Kpalimé** Togo
376 C5 **Kra Buri** Thailand
160 F6 **Krabbé** Argentina
224 I3 **Krabbfjärden** *bay* Sweden
225 N4 **Krabi** Estonia
376 C5 **Krabi** *admin. area* Thailand
376 E4 **Krâchéh** Cambodia
222 J4 **Kraddsele** Sweden
234 B3 **Kragujevac** Serbia
374 E5 **Krakatau** *volcano* Indonesia
374 E5 **Krakatau, Taman Nasional** *park* Indonesia
222 K5 **Kråken** Sweden
224 G3 **Kråklingbo** Sweden
222 I3 **Kråkmo** Norway
222 H4 **Kråknes** Norway
227 L3 **Krakovets'** Ukraine
227 J3 **Kraków** Poland
375 G5 **Kraksaan** Indonesia
232 G1 **Králíky** Czech Republic
234 B4 **Kraljevo** Serbia
227 H2 **Královéhradecký Kraj** *admin. area* Czech Republic
394 F3 **Kramators'k** Ukraine
120 E8 **Kramer** North Dakota USA
128 D3 **Kramer Junction** California USA
222 J5 **Kramfors** Sweden
223 Q1 **Krampenes** Norway
235 B6 **Kranea** Greece
374 B2 **Kranji Reservoir** Singapore
227 G4 **Kranjska Gora** Slovenia
125 Q4 **Kranzburg** South Dakota USA
238 F6 **Krapivenskiy** Russian Federation
238 F6 **Krapivna** Russian Federation
238 G6 **Krapivna** Russian Federation
116 B4 **Krasin, Zaliv** *bay* Russian Federation
225 N5 **Krāslava** Latvia
225 N5 **Krāslavas** *admin. area* Latvia
238 D6 **Krasnapollye** Belarus
238 H4 **Krasnaya Plamya** Russian Federation
225 N5 **Krasnaye** Belarus
227 M3 **Krasne** Ukraine
227 L2 **Kraśnik** Poland
385 I2 **Krasnikamensk** Russian Federation
227 F3 **Krasno Polje** Croatia
238 H4 **Krasnoarmeysk** Russian Federation
394 F3 **Krasnoarmeysk** Ukraine
238 F3 **Krasnoborskiy** Russian Federation
388 C4 **Krasnodar** Russian Federation
388 C4 **Krasnodarskiy Kray** *admin. area* Russian Federation
225 P3 **Krasnofarfornyy** Russian Federation
238 C4 **Krasnogorodskoye** Russian Federation
387 I1 **Krasnogorsk** Russian Federation
236 M7 **Krasnokamsk** Russian Federation
388 G1 **Krasnokamsk** Russian Federation
234 F1 **Krasnopil'** Ukraine
236 R5 **Krasnosel'kup** Russian Federation
389 N3 **Krasnoshchekovo** Russian Federation
223 T3 **Krasnoshchel'ye** Russian Federation
236 N7 **Krasnotur'insk** Russian Federation
388 H2 **Krasnoufimsk** Russian Federation
236 N7 **Krasnoural'sk** Russian Federation
236 M6 **Krasnovishersk** Russian Federation
389 M2 **Krasnovishnevoye** *lake* Russian Federation
388 G6 **Krasnovodskiy, Mys** *cape* Turkmenistan
388 G6 **Krasnovodskoye Plato** Turkmenistan
236 T7 **Krasnoyarsk** Russian Federation
389 Q2 **Krasnoyarsk** Russian Federation
237 U6 **Krasnoyarskiy Kray** *admin. area* Russian Federation
389 P2 **Krasnoyarskiy Vodokhranilishche** *lake* Russian Federation
225 O4 **Krasnoye** Russian Federation
225 P5 **Krasnoye** Russian Federation
388 C4 **Krasnoye** Russian Federation
237 AJ6 **Krasnoye, Ozero** *lake* Russian Federation
225 P3 **Krasnoye Selo** Russian Federation
238 F4 **Krasnoye Znamya** Russian Federation
234 H2 **Krasnoznamenka** Ukraine
225 L5 **Krasnoznamensk** Russian Federation
227 L2 **Krasnystaw** Poland
384 F2 **Krasnyy Chikoy** Russian Federation
238 E4 **Krasnyy Gorodok** Russian Federation
238 G3 **Krasnyy Kholm** Russian Federation
388 E3 **Krasnyy Kut** Russian Federation
225 P4 **Krasnyy Luch** Russian Federation
394 F3 **Krasnyy Luch** Ukraine
389 L4 **Krasnyy Oktyabr'** Kazakhstan
238 D3 **Krasnyy Yar** Russian Federation
388 E1 **Krasnyye Baki** Russian Federation
235 B5 **Krastë** Albania
234 E1 **Krasyliv** Ukraine
373 H5 **Kratke Range** Papua New Guinea
373 G4 **Krau** Indonesia
436 X2 **Kraul Mountains** Antarctica
232 H2 **Kravaře** Czech Republic
130 D3 **Krebs** Oklahoma USA
238 H2 **Krechetovo** Russian Federation
225 P3 **Krechevitsy** Russian Federation
229 H1 **Krefeld** Germany
225 M5 **Krekenava** Lithuania
394 E3 **Kremenchuk** Ukraine
394 E3 **Kremenchuts'ka Vodoskhovyshche** *lake* Ukraine
225 N5 **Kremenets** Belarus
394 F3 **Kremennaya** Ukraine
238 F5 **Kremenskoye** Russian Federation
119 P8 **Kremlin** Montana USA
235 C7 **Kremmidi, Akra** *cape* Greece
125 L6 **Kremmling** Colorado USA
234 A4 **Kremna** Serbia
232 F2 **Křemže** Czech Republic
225 O4 **Krenëvo** Russian Federation
116 C8 **Krenitzin Islands** Alaska USA
129 L3 **Kress** Texas USA
237 AD5 **Krest-Mayor** Russian Federation
116 B5 **Kresta, Zaliv** Russian Federation
236 L5 **Krestovka** Russian Federation
237 Y6 **Krestyakh** Russian Federation
225 K5 **Kretinga** Lithuania
226 F4 **Kreuth** Germany
129 K3 **Kribi** Cameroon
129 K3 **Krider** New Mexico USA
229 L3 **Krieglach** Austria
235 B6 **Krikello** Greece
225 O3 **Krikkovo** Russian Federation
305 H3 **Krim-Krim** Chad
227 G1 **Krimml** Austria
227 H2 **Křinec** Czech Republic
235 C6 **Krios, Akrotirio** *cape* Greece
393 E8 **Krishna** *watercourse* Andhra Pradesh India
393 D8 **Krishnagiri** Andhra Pradesh India
393 E9 **Krishnagiri** Tamil Nadu India
392 G6 **Krishnanagar** West Bengal India
224 D3 **Kristiansand** Norway
222 K4 **Kristineberg** Sweden
224 H3 **Kristinehamn** Sweden
222 L5 **Kristinestad/Kristiinankaupunki** Finland
235 C5 **Krithiá** Greece
235 D8 **Kriti (Crete)** *admin. area* Greece
235 D7 **Kritiko Pelago (Sea of Crete)** *sea* Europe
235 D8 **Kritsa** Greece
225 L5 **Kriūkai** Lithuania
234 C4 **Kriva Reka** *watercourse* Macedonia
232 H2 **Krivań** Slovakia
238 E6 **Krivoles** Russian Federation
223 R4 **Krivoy Porog** Russian Federation
223 T6 **Krivtsy** Russian Federation
232 G2 **Křižanov** Czech Republic
232 G3 **Križevci** Croatia
232 F4 **Križpolje** Croatia
232 F4 **Krk** *island* Croatia
232 G4 **Krnjeuša** Bosnia and Herzegovina
227 I2 **Krnov** Czech Republic
227 I2 **Krobia** Poland
224 E2 **Krøderen** *lake* Norway
227 I4 **Krog** Slovenia
223 Q1 **Krognes** Norway
304 C4 **Krohnwodoke** Liberia
222 I4 **Kroken** Norway
222 J5 **Krokfors** Sweden
222 L3 **Krokfors** Sweden
222 I5 **Kroknäs** Sweden
222 I5 **Krokom** Sweden
375 F3 **Krokong** Malaysia
224 J5 **Krokowa** Poland
222 inset **Króksfjarðarnes** Iceland
222 J4 **Kroksjö** Sweden
222 L4 **Kroksjö** Sweden
225 K5 **Krokų Lankos ežeras** *lake* Lithuania
222 I3 **Krokvik** Sweden
394 E2 **Krolevets** Ukraine
232 G2 **Kroměříž** Czech Republic
224 H4 **Krön** *lake* Sweden
229 J1 **Kronach** Germany
119 S7 **Kronau** Saskatchewan Canada
376 D5 **Krŏng Kaôh Kŏng** Cambodia
224 H4 **Kronoberg** *admin. area* Sweden
223 M5 **Kronoby** Finland
237 AH8 **Kronotskiy, Mys** *cape* Russian Federation
237 AH8 **Kronotskiy Poluostrov** *peninsula* Russian Federation
237 AH8 **Kronotskiy Zaliv** *bay* Russian Federation
237 AH8 **Kronotskoye Ozero** *lake* Russian Federation
117 R2 **Kronprins Christian Land** *plain* Greenland
117 P5 **Kronprins Frederik Bjerge** *mountains* Greenland
225 O2 **Kronshtadt** Russian Federation
308 E5 **Kroonstad (Maokeng)** South Africa
388 C4 **Kropotkin** Russian Federation
224 E3 **Kropp** Germany
227 K3 **Krosno** Poland
222 F6 **Krossbu** Norway
227 I2 **Krotoszyn** Poland
227 H5 **Krško** Slovenia
225 O5 **Krucha** Belarus
227 I1 **Krucz** Poland
237 AC9 **Kruglikovo** Russian Federation
387 G1 **Kruglikovo** Russian Federation
225 O5 **Kruhlaye** Belarus
375 D5 **Krui** Indonesia
308 D6 **Kruisfontein** South Africa
235 A5 **Krujë** Albania
225 K5 **Kruklanki** Poland
372 E4 **Krumasye** Indonesia
226 E4 **Krumbach** Germany
226 F3 **Krumbach** Germany
226 F4 **Krün** Germany
376 D4 **Krung Thep (Bangkok)** Thailand
232 H5 **Krupac** Bosnia and Herzegovina
227 J3 **Krupinská planina** *region* Slovakia
234 E4 **Krushevets** Bulgaria
238 C6 **Krushinovka** Belarus
232 G2 **Krušné Hory** *range* Czech Republic
234 D4 **Krūstets** Bulgaria
233 H5 **Krute** Montenegro
232 B3 **Kruth** France
237 AG7 **Krutogorovo** Russian Federation
222 J3 **Krutsjön** *lake* Sweden
222 I4 **Krutvatnet** *lake* Norway
237 AF9 **Kruzenshtenra, Proliv** *strait* Russian Federation
118 D4 **Kruzof Island** Alaska USA
227 M2 **Krylov** Ukraine
76 O8 **Krylov Seamount** *underwater feature* Atlantic Ocean
225 K5 **Krylovo** Russian Federation
388 C4 **Krylovskaya** Russian Federation
237 C5 **Krymsk** Russian Federation
234 B1 **Krynica** Poland
227 L1 **Krynki** Poland
235 B6 **Kryoneri** Greece
224 G2 **Kryptjärn** Sweden
394 E3 **Kryvyy Rih** Ukraine
234 F1 **Kryzhopil'** Ukraine
227 I2 **Krzelów** Poland
227 J2 **Krzepice** Poland
227 J2 **Krzeszowice** Poland
227 L3 **Krzywcza** Poland
301 F3 **Ksabi** Algeria
300 F2 **Ksabi** Morocco
301 G1 **Ksar el Boukhari** Algeria
301 G2 **Ksar el Hirane** Algeria
300 E2 **Ksar el Kebir** Morocco
379 F3 **Ksham Chuu** *watercourse* Xizang Zizhiqu China
233 D9 **Ksour-Essaf** Tunisia
388 D2 **Kstovo** Russian Federation
302 D5 **Ku, Wādī El** *watercourse* Sudan
382 E5 **Ku-shan Ho** *watercourse* Xinjiang Uygur Zizhiqu China
374 C3 **Kuah** Malaysia
375 G2 **Kuala Belait** Brunei
374 D2 **Kuala Krai** Malaysia
375 D2 **Kuala Lipis** Malaysia
374 D3 **Kuala Lumpur** Malaysia
374 D3 **Kuala Lumpur** *admin. area* Malaysia
375 G2 **Kuala Penyu** Malaysia
374 D3 **Kuala Rompin** Malaysia
374 D2 **Kuala Terengganu** Malaysia
375 G4 **Kualakapuas** Indonesia
375 G4 **Kualakuayan** Indonesia
375 G4 **Kualakurun** Indonesia
374 C2 **Kualalangsa** Indonesia
375 G4 **Kualapembuang** Indonesia
375 G4 **Kualasampit** Indonesia
375 G4 **Kualasimpang** Indonesia
374 D4 **Kualatungkal** Indonesia
372 H2 **Kuamut** Malaysia
385 I5 **Kuancheng** Hebei China
372 B3 **Kuandang, Teluk** *bay* Indonesia
385 J5 **Kuandian** Liaoning China
375 D3 **Kuantan** Malaysia
390 E7 **Ku'aydinah** Yemen
388 C4 **Kuban** *watercourse* Russian Federation
234 G2 **Kubanka** Ukraine
222 K5 **Kubbe** Sweden
302 C5 **Kubbum** Sudan
305 I2 **Kubbum** Sudan
238 H3 **Kubenskoye** Russian Federation
238 H3 **Kubenskoye, Ozero** *lake* Russian Federation
224 G5 **Kubitzer Bodden** *bay* Germany
225 O5 **Kublichy** Belarus
373 H5 **Kubor Range** Papua New Guinea
374 F4 **Kubu** Indonesia
375 G6 **Kubu** Indonesia
375 G3 **Kubuang** Indonesia
375 G3 **Kubumesaai** Indonesia
373 H6 **Kubuna** Papua New Guinea
235 A5 **Kuç** Albania
392 D5 **Kuchaman City** Rajasthan India
382 G4 **Kuche** Xinjiang Uygur Zizhiqu China
236 J5 **Kuchema** Russian Federation
392 C5 **Kuchera** Rajasthan India
434 R1 **Kucherov Terrace** *underwater feature* Arctic Ocean
376 E3 **Kuchinarai** Thailand
374 F3 **Kuching** Malaysia
386 F5 **Kuchino-shima** *island* Japan
386 F5 **Kuchinoerabu-jima** *island* Japan
226 G4 **Kuchl** Austria
389 M3 **Kuchukskoye** *lake* Russian Federation
234 G2 **Kuchurhans'ke Vodoskhovyshche** *lake* Ukraine
222 inset **Kúðafljót** *watercourse* Iceland
393 C8 **Kudal** Maharashtra India
374 F4 **Kudangan** Indonesia
374 D3 **Kudap** Indonesia
375 H2 **Kudat** Malaysia
302 E4 **Kudayn** Sudan
372 E5 **Kudene** Indonesia
225 O4 **Kudever'** Russian Federation
225 L5 **Kudirkos Naumiestis** Lithuania
393 D8 **Kudligi** Karnataka India
393 D9 **Kudremukh** *mountain* Karnataka India
238 F6 **Kudryavets** Russian Federation
234 G2 **Kudryavtsevka** Ukraine
305 F3 **Kudu** Nigeria
375 F5 **Kudus** Indonesia
381 I4 **Kueishan Tao** *island* Taiwan China
232 E3 **Kufstein** Austria
117 K5 **Kugaaruk** Nunavut Canada
116 H5 **Kugluktuk** Nunavut Canada
116 F5 **Kugmallit Bay** Northwest Territories Canada
121 O4 **Kugong Island** Nunavut Canada
388 E6 **Kūh-e Sabalān** *mountain* Iran
388 E6 **Kūh-e Sahand** *mountain* Iran
223 O4 **Kuha** Finland
391 J4 **Kūhak** Iran
390 F2 **Kūhdasht** Iran
391 H4 **Kūhej** Iran
388 H7 **Kūhhā-ye Kūhhā Jaftāy** *range* Iran
390 G3 **Kūhhā-ye Zāgros** Iran
389 K6 **Kūhistoni Badakhshon** *admin. area* Tajikistan
225 M2 **Kuhmajärvi** *lake* Finland
223 P4 **Kuhmo** Finland
373 H5 **Kui** Papua New Guinea
376 C4 **Kui Buri** Thailand
223 N5 **Kuikka** Finland
134 C4 **Kuikuina** Nicaragua
308 C4 **Kuiseb** *watercourse* Namibia
308 C2 **Kuito** Angola
382 G4 **Kuitun** Xinjiang Uygur Zizhiqu China
118 D4 **Kuiu Island** Alaska USA
223 O2 **Kuivajärvi** *lake* Finland
223 M3 **Kuivakangas** Sweden
223 N4 **Kuivaniemi** Finland
223 M5 **Kuivasjärvi** *lake* Finland
223 N5 **Kuivasmäki** Finland
225 L3 **Kuivastu** Estonia
227 J1 **Kujawsko-Pomorskie** *admin. area* Poland
391 K4 **Kukai Bent** Pakistan
388 D3 **Kukarki** Russian Federation
223 Q3 **Kukas, Ozero** *lake* Russian Federation
305 G3 **Kukawa** Nigeria
234 B4 **Kukës** Albania
225 M2 **Kukkia** *lake* Finland
223 N5 **Kukko** Finland
223 N4 **Kukkola** Finland
223 N4 **Kukkola** Sweden
227 K1 **Kuklin** Poland
238 H3 **Kukoboy** Russian Federation
128 inset **Kukuihaele** Hawai'i USA
120 J8 **Kukukus Lake** Ontario Canada
304 B3 **Kukuna** Sierra Leone
232 H4 **Kula** Nigeria
234 B3 **Kula** Serbia
379 G3 **Kula Kangri** *mountain* Bhutan
374 C3 **Kulabu, Gunung** *mountain* Indonesia
391 L3 **Kulachi** Pakistan
388 F4 **Kulagino** Kazakhstan
374 D3 **Kulai** Malaysia
391 J4 **Kūlaki** Iran
235 G5 **Kulaklı** Turkey
307 F3 **Kulal, Mount** *mountain* Kenya
388 F5 **Kulaly, Ostrov** *island* Kazakhstan
306 C4 **Kulampanga** Democratic Republic of Congo
388 G5 **Kulandag** *range* Turkmenistan
388 H4 **Kulandy** Kazakhstan
377 I6 **Kulassein** *island* Philippines
237 AC8 **Kul'chi** Russian Federation
391 K2 **Kuldan** Pakistan
225 K4 **Kuldiga** Latvia
225 K4 **Kuldigas** *admin. area* Latvia
118 H5 **Kuldo** British Columbia Canada
306 D4 **Kule** Botswana
388 D2 **Kulebaki** Russian Federation
376 E4 **Kulen** Cambodia
234 F2 **Kulevcha** Ukraine
425 J6 **Kulgera** NT Australia
238 H6 **Kulikovo Pole** Russian Federation
374 D2 **Kulim** Malaysia
424 F8 **Kulin** WA Australia
237 V6 **Kulinda** Russian Federation
119 U7 **Kulish** Manitoba Canada
225 L2 **Kullaa** Finland
224 G4 **Kullen** *cape* Sweden
392 D4 **Kullu** Himachal Pradesh India
125 P3 **Kulm** North Dakota USA
389 K6 **Kŭlob** Tajikistan
238 E3 **Kulotino** Russian Federation
225 L2 **Kulovesi** *bay* Finland
304 D2 **Kulpawn** *watercourse* Ghana
388 G4 **Kulsary** Kazakhstan
223 M2 **Kultima** Finland
222 I4 **Kultsjön** *lake* Sweden
384 E2 **Kultuk** Russian Federation
237 AE6 **Kulu** *watercourse* Russian Federation
373 J6 **Kulumadau** Papua New Guinea
385 J4 **Kulun** Nei Mongol Zizhiqu China
389 M3 **Kulunda** Russian Federation
389 M2 **Kulundinskoye** *lake* Russian Federation
223 O5 **Kulvemäki** Finland
388 I4 **Kulykol'** *lake* Kazakhstan
235 E6 **Kum** *watercourse* Turkey
386 E4 **Küm-Gang** *watercourse* South Korea
388 D5 **Kuma** *watercourse* Russian Federation
372 E4 **Kumafa, Pegunungan** *range* Indonesia
387 H4 **Kumagaya** Japan
374 F4 **Kumai** Indonesia
375 F4 **Kumai, Teluk** *bay* Indonesia
388 H3 **Kumak** Russian Federation
373 F4 **Kumamba, Kepulauan** *island* Indonesia
386 F5 **Kumamoto** Japan
387 H5 **Kumano** Japan
423 D6 **Kumara** New Zealand
423 D6 **Kumara Junction** New Zealand
304 D3 **Kumasi** Ghana
305 F4 **Kumba** Cameroon
235 E5 **Kumbağ** Turkey
393 E8 **Kumbakonam** Tamil Nadu India
373 G6 **Kumbe** Indonesia
373 G5 **Kumbe** *watercourse* Indonesia
392 D6 **Kumbhraj** Madhya Pradesh India
386 E3 **Kumch'on** North Korea
235 G6 **Kumdanlı** Turkey
381 J3 **Kume-shima** *island* Japan
388 F1 **Kumeny** Russian Federation
388 G3 **Kumertau** Russian Federation
422 F3 **Kumeu** New Zealand
386 F3 **Kumgang-san** *mountain* North Korea
392 E6 **Kumhari** Madhya Pradesh India
386 F4 **Kumi** South Korea
225 K2 **Kumlinge** *island* Finland
222 L2 **Kummavuopio** Sweden
226 G1 **Kummerower See** *lake* Germany
305 G2 **Kumo** Nigeria
379 H3 **Kumon Range** Myanmar
223 N5 **Kumpula** Finland
393 D8 **Kumta** Karnataka India
386 E3 **Kumya-man** *bay* North Korea
124 G5 **Kuna** Idaho USA
Kunashir, Ostrov *see* **Kunashiri-tô** Kuril Islands
387 J2 **Kunashiri-tô (Ostrov Kunashir)** *island* Russian Federation
424 H5 **Kunawaritji Community** WA Australia
225 N3 **Kunda** Estonia
379 G3 **Kunda** Assam India
393 E6 **Kunda** Chhattisgarh India
305 H6 **Kunda Dia-Baze** Angola
225 N3 **Kunda Laht** *bay* Estonia
391 K3 **Kundar** *watercourse* Pakistan
393 E8 **Kunderu** *watercourse* Andhra Pradesh India
391 L3 **Kundian** Pakistan
232 D3 **Kundl** Austria
393 C7 **Kundla** Gujarat India
373 K6 **Kundu** Solomon Islands
374 D3 **Kundur** *island* Indonesia
308 B3 **Kunene** *admin. area* Namibia
308 B3 **Kunene** *watercourse* Namibia
223 O1 **Kunes** Norway
118 E5 **Kung** British Columbia Canada
224 F4 **Kungälv** Sweden
237 W4 **Kungasalakh, Ozero** *lake* Russian Federation
389 L5 **Kungey-Alatau** Kyrgyzstan
118 F6 **Kunghit Island** British Columbia Canada
306 B3 **Kungu** Democratic Republic of Congo
388 G1 **Kungur** Russian Federation
376 B3 **Kungyangon** Myanmar
227 K4 **Kunhegyes** Hungary
379 I5 **Kunhing** Myanmar
374 F5 **Kuningan** Indonesia
379 I4 **Kunlon** Myanmar
379 I4 **Kunlong** Myanmar
383 J6 **Kunlun Shan** *range* Qinghai China
383 H6 **Kunlun Shan** *range* Xinjiang Uygur Zizhiqu China
382 G6 **Kunlunshan** *range* Xinjiang Uygur Zizhiqu China
380 D3 **Kunming** Yunnan China
222 H3 **Kunna** Norway
227 H1 **Kunow** Germany
386 E4 **Kunsan** South Korea
237 AE7 **Kuntuk** Russian Federation
424 I3 **Kununurra** WA Australia
305 F2 **Kunya** Nigeria
225 P4 **Kun'ya** Russian Federation
380 D4 **Kunyang** Yunnan China
229 L2 **Kunžak** Czech Republic
381 H3 **Kuocang Shan** *mountain* Zhejiang China
381 H3 **Kuocang Shan** *range* Zhejiang China
222 J3 **Kuoddujaure** *lake* Sweden
223 P5 **Kuohattijärvi** *lake* Finland
225 M2 **Kuohijärvi** *lake* Finland
222 L3 **Kuoksu** Sweden
223 P3 **Kuolayarvi** Russian Federation
225 N2 **Kuolimo** *lake* Finland
222 K3 **Kuollejaur** Sweden
222 K3 **Kuollejaure** *lake* Sweden
223 N5 **Kuona** Finland
223 O5 **Kuopio** Finland
223 Q5 **Kuora** Finland
223 M5 **Kuortane** Finland
225 L1 **Kuortaneenjärvi** *lake* Finland
223 P3 **Kuosku** Finland
372 B6 **Kupang** Indonesia
375 I6 **Kupang, Teluk** *bay* Indonesia
373 I6 **Kupiano** Papua New Guinea
227 H5 **Kupinec** Croatia
234 B3 **Kupinovo** Serbia
225 M5 **Kupiškis** Lithuania
235 E5 **Küplü** Turkey
393 D9 **Kuppam** *watercourse* Kerala India
225 N4 **Kuprava** Latvia
116 F7 **Kupreanof Island** Alaska USA
116 D7 **Kupreanof Point** Alaska USA
229 J1 **Küps** Germany
424 H4 **Kupungarri** WA Australia
225 P4 **Kupuy** Russian Federation
392 D3 **Kupwara** Jammu and Kashmir India/ Pakistan
388 E5 **Kur** *watercourse* Azerbaijan
372 E5 **Kur** *island* Indonesia
390 G4 **Kūr Deh** Iran
388 F6 **Kür Dili Qizilağac Körfazi** *island* Azerbaijan
391 I4 **Kūr Gich** Iran
389 K5 **Kuragaty** *watercourse* Kazakhstan
305 F3 **Kuragwi** Nigeria
388 E5 **Kurakh** Russian Federation
388 G3 **Kurashassayskiy** Kazakhstan
393 E6 **Kurasia** Madhya Pradesh India
422 F4 **Kuratau** New Zealand
386 G4 **Kurayoshi** Japan
389 N4 **Kurchum** Kazakhstan
389 N4 **Kurchum** *watercourse* Kazakhstan
227 J4 **Kurd** Hungary
388 D6 **Kurdistan** *region* Iran
235 D5 **Kŭrdzhali** Bulgaria
235 D5 **Kŭrdzhali** *admin. area* Bulgaria
386 G4 **Kure** Japan
78 O5 **Kure Atoll** *reef US dependency* Pacific Ocean
223 M5 **Kurejoki** Finland
225 L3 **Kuressaare** Estonia
225 K3 **Kurevere** Estonia
388 J2 **Kurgan** Russian Federation
388 I2 **Kurganskaya Oblast'** *admin. area* Russian Federation
225 O3 **Kurgolovo** Russian Federation
372 E4 **Kuri** *watercourse* Indonesia
426 1 **Kuria** *island* Kiribati
222 M5 **Kurikka** Finland
78 K3 **Kuril Basin** *underwater feature* Pacific Ocean
78 L3 **Kuril-Kamchatka Trench** *underwater feature* Pacific Ocean
387 J2 **Kuril'skiye Ostrova (Kuril Islands)** Russian Federation
388 E3 **Kurilovka** Russian Federation
387 J2 **Kuril'sk** Russian Federation
373 F5 **Kurima** Indonesia
225 P5 **Kurino** Belarus
235 F7 **Kürkçüler** Turkey
223 P4 **Kurkijärvi** *lake* Finland
302 E5 **Kurmuk** Sudan
307 E1 **Kurmuk** Sudan
393 E8 **Kurnool** Andhra Pradesh India
386 F5 **Kuro-shima** *island* Japan
119 T7 **Kuroki** Saskatchewan Canada
238 H5 **Kurovskoye** Russian Federation
423 D7 **Kurow** New Zealand
391 K3 **Kurram** Pakistan
391 L2 **Kurram Garhi** Pakistan
222 L3 **Kurravaara** Sweden
225 L4 **Kuršenaj** Lithuania
394 F2 **Kursk** Russian Federation
388 D5 **Kurskaya** Russian Federation
394 E2 **Kurskaya Oblast'** *admin. area* Russian Federation
238 C3 **Kursko** Russian Federation
223 P3 **Kursu** Finland
235 F5 **Kurşunlu** Turkey
223 N3 **Kurtakko** Finland
130 D5 **Kurth Lake** Texas USA
235 F7 **Kurtoğlu Burnu** *cape* Turkey
223 P4 **Kurtto** Finland
389 L5 **Kurty** *watercourse* Kazakhstan
306 D2 **Kuru** *watercourse* Sudan
393 E7 **Kurud** Chhattisgarh India
308 D5 **Kuruman** South Africa
308 D5 **Kuruman** *watercourse* South Africa
386 F5 **Kurume** Japan
384 G1 **Kurumkan** Russian Federation
382 E5 **Kurunduk** *watercourse* Xinjiang Uygur Zizhiqu China
393 E10 **Kurunegala** Sri Lanka
302 E3 **Kurush, Jebel** *range* Sudan
223 P4 **Kurvinen** Finland
236 S4 **Kur'ya** Russian Federation
389 N3 **Kur'ya** Russian Federation
386 E4 **Kurye** South Korea
235 E5 **Kuş Gölü** *lake* Turkey
234 B3 **Kusadak** Serbia
235 E7 **Kuşadası Körfezi** *bay* Greece
389 L4 **Kusak** *watercourse* Kazakhstan
118 C2 **Kusawa Lake** Yukon Territory Canada
388 J6 **Kusaykuduk** Uzbekistan
226 F1 **Kusey** Germany
238 G4 **Kushalino** Russian Federation
238 F5 **Kushereka** Russian Federation
386 F5 **Kushikino** Japan
386 F5 **Kushima** Japan
387 G5 **Kushimoto** Japan
387 J2 **Kushiro** Japan
223 V4 **Kushkushara** Russian Federation
388 H3 **Kushmurun** Kazakhstan
388 J3 **Kushmurun** *lake* Kazakhstan
234 C1 **Kushnytsya** Ukraine
379 F4 **Kushtia** Bangladesh
388 F3 **Kushum** Kazakhstan
234 B3 **Kusiće** Serbia
116 D6 **Kuskokwim** *watercourse* Alaska USA
116 C7 **Kuskokwim Bay** Alaska USA
116 D6 **Kuskokwim Mountains** Alaska USA
222 L4 **Kusmark** Sweden
387 J2 **Kussharo-ko** *lake* Japan
225 K2 **Kustavi** Finland
234 B3 **Kuštilj** Serbia
372 C3 **Kusu** Indonesia
375 G6 **Kuta** Indonesia
374 C2 **Kutabagok** Indonesia
374 C3 **Kutacane** Indonesia
394 D5 **Kütahya** *admin. area* Turkey
375 H3 **Kutai, Taman Nasional** *park* Indonesia
388 D5 **Kutaisi** Georgia
226 E1 **Kutenholz** Germany
232 G4 **Kutina** Croatia
222 J3 **Kutjaure** *lake* Sweden
379 H4 **Kutkai** Myanmar
227 J1 **Kutno** Poland
223 Q2 **Kutovaya** Russian Federation
223 M2 **Kuttanen** Finland
387 I2 **Kuttara-ko** *lake* Japan
130 G2 **Kuttawa** Kentucky USA
379 G5 **Kutubdia Island** Bangladesh
302 C5 **Kutum** Sudan
305 I2 **Kutum** Sudan
389 M5 **Kuturga** Kyrgyzstan
225 L5 **Kutuzovo** Russian Federation
223 O5 **Kuuhankavesi** *lake* Finland
116 H4 **Kuujjua** *watercourse* Northwest Territories Canada
121 U3 **Kuujjuaq** Québec Canada
121 Q5 **Kuujjuarapik** Québec Canada
388 F6 **Kuuli-Mayak** Turkmenistan
223 N5 **Kuusa** Finland
223 N5 **Kuusaa** Finland
223 P4 **Kuusamo** Finland
223 P4 **Kuusamojärvi** *lake* Finland
223 O4 **Kuusiranta** Finland
308 C2 **Kuvango** Angola
238 F4 **Kuvshinovo** Russian Federation
390 F5 **Kuwait** *country*
Kuwait City *see* **Al Kuwayt** Kuwait
236 J5 **Kuya** Russian Federation
389 M2 **Kuybyshev** Russian Federation
387 J2 **Kuybyshevskoye, Ozero** *lake* Russian Federation
389 L4 **Kuygan** Kazakhstan
235 G7 **Kuyucak** Turkey
394 F6 **Kuyulu** Turkey
237 U6 **Kuyumba** Russian Federation
238 F5 **Kuzemki** Russian Federation
238 H3 **Kuzino** Russian Federation
234 A3 **Kuzmin** Serbia
234 C1 **Kuźmina** Poland
236 T6 **Kuz'movka** Russian Federation
388 E2 **Kuznetsk** Russian Federation
234 G2 **Kuznetsovo** Ukraine
227 K2 **Kuźnica** Poland
227 L1 **Kuźnica** Poland
236 I5 **Kuzomen'** Russian Federation
238 H6 **Kuzovka** Russian Federation
223 S3 **Kuzreka** Russian Federation
224 I3 **Kvädö** *island* Sweden
222 L1 **Kvænangen** *bay* Norway
222 J2 **Kvæøya** *island* Norway
222 G5 **Kvål** Norway
222 H2 **Kvalnes** Norway
222 G4 **Kvaløya** *island* Norway
222 K1 **Kvaløysætra** Norway
222 G4 **Kvaløyslétta** Norway
223 M1 **Kvalsund** Norway
222 F6 **Kvam** Norway
222 F5 **Kvanne** Norway
388 E5 **Kvareli** Georgia
388 H3 **Kvarkeno** Russian Federation
224 J4 **Kvarnäkershamn** Sweden
222 J5 **Kvarnbacken** Sweden
222 H4 **Kvarnbergsvattnet** *lake* Sweden
234 D1 **Kvasy** Ukraine
222 G2 **Kvennsjøen** *lake* Norway
222 H4 **Kvesjøen** *lake* Norway
222 L5 **Kvevlax** Finland
116 D7 **Kvichak Bay** Alaska USA
224 G2 **Kvien** *lake* Sweden
224 D3 **Kvifjorden** *lake* Norway
222 J3 **Kvikkjokk** Sweden
222 M5 **Kvimo** Finland
224 D3 **Kvina** *watercourse* Norway
224 D3 **Kvinlog** Norway

222 H6 **Kvisla** Norway
222 E5 **Kvisvik** Norway
224 E3 **Kviteseidvatnet** *lake* Norway
222 L1 **Kvitnes** Norway
236 H2 **Kvitøya** *island* Norway
224 E5 **Kvong** Denmark
306 B4 **Kwa** *watercourse* Democratic Republic of Congo
118 I4 **Kwadacha Wilderness Provincial Park** British Columbia Canada
304 D3 **Kwadwokurom** Ghana
427 I5 **Kwajalein Atoll** *reef* Marshall Islands
379 G4 **Kwakta** Manipur India
155 G3 **Kwakwani** Guyana
307 F4 **Kwale** Kenya
305 F3 **Kwale** Nigeria
155 G4 **Kwamalasamutu** Suriname
309 F5 **Kwamashu** South Africa
372 B3 **Kwandang** Indonesia
308 D3 **Kwando** *watercourse* Botswana
386 E4 **Kwangju** South Korea
306 B4 **Kwango** *watercourse* Democratic Republic of Congo
386 F3 **Kwanmo-bong** *mountain* North Korea
308 E6 **Kwanobuhle** South Africa
305 E3 **Kwara** *admin. area* Nigeria
121 O7 **Kwataboahegan** *watercourse* Ontario Canada
309 F5 **Kwazulu Natal** *admin. area* South Africa
308 E3 **Kwekwe** Zimbabwe
308 D4 **Kweneng** *admin. area* Botswana
306 B5 **Kwenge** *watercourse* Democratic Republic of Congo
227 J1 **Kwidzyn** Poland
303 F5 **Kwīhzā** Ethiopia
373 H6 **Kwikila** Papua New Guinea
227 I1 **Kwilcz** Poland
306 B5 **Kwilu** *watercourse* Democratic Republic of Congo
424 E8 **Kwinana** WA Australia
376 E3 **Kỳ Anh** Vietnam
376 E3 **Kỳ Sơn** Vietnam
376 C4 **Kya-in** Myanmar
305 H3 **Kyabé** Chad
376 B3 **Kyaiklat** Myanmar
376 C3 **Kyaikto** Myanmar
223 U4 **Kyanda** Russian Federation
379 F2 **Kyaring Tsho** *lake* Xizang Zizhiqu China
376 C3 **Kyaukki** Myanmar
379 H4 **Kyaukme** Myanmar
379 H5 **Kyaukpadaung** Myanmar
379 G5 **Kyaukphyu** Myanmar
379 H5 **Kyaukse** Myanmar
376 C3 **Kyauktan** Myanmar
379 G5 **Kyauktaw** Myanmar
376 B3 **Kyaunggon** Myanmar
376 C3 **Kyauktaga** Myanmar
225 L5 **Kybartai** Lithuania
222 I4 **Kycklingvattnet** Sweden
425 M8 **Kyeamba** NSW Australia
307 E5 **Kyela** Tanzania
394 D2 **Kyiv/Kyyiv (Kiev)** Ukraine
394 D2 **Kyivs'ka Oblast** *admin. area* Ukraine
227 I3 **Kyjov** Czech Republic
235 D7 **Kyklades (Cyclades)** *islands* Greece
223 P5 **Kylänlahti** Finland
119 Q7 **Kyle** Saskatchewan Canada
244 C3 **Kyleakin** Highland Scotland UK
226 D2 **Kyll** *watercourse* Germany
235 B7 **Kyllini** Greece
223 O4 **Kylmälä** Finland
235 D6 **Kymi** Greece
238 B2 **Kymi/Länsi-Suomi** *admin. area* Finland
238 B2 **Kymijoki** *watercourse* Finland
235 D6 **Kymis, Akra** *cape* Greece
392 E6 **Kymore** Madhya Pradesh India
118 D2 **Kynocks** Yukon Territory Canada
223 P4 **Kynsivaara** Finland
223 O5 **Kynsivesi** *lake* Finland
425 L5 **Kynuna** Qld Australia
307 E3 **Kyoga, Lake** *lake* Uganda
425 O7 **Kyogle** NSW Australia
386 F4 **Kyŏngju** South Korea
386 F3 **Kyŏngsŏng** North Korea
376 B3 **Kyonpyaw** Myanmar
387 G4 **Kyoto** Japan
235 B7 **Kyparissia** Greece
235 B7 **Kyparissiakos Kolpos** *bay* Greece
235 C6 **Kyra Panagia** *island* Greece
237 AA6 **Kyrbykan** Russian Federation
394 E6 **Kyrenia** Cyprus
237 Z6 **Kyrgyday** Russian Federation
389 L5 **Kyrgyzstan** *country*
226 G1 **Kyritz** Germany
223 N2 **Kyrö** Finland
225 L2 **Kyrö** Finland
222 L5 **Kyrönjoki** *watercourse* Finland
225 L2 **Kyrösjärvi** *lake* Finland
236 M6 **Kyrta** Russian Federation
227 K3 **Kysak** Slovakia
237 Z5 **Kystatyam** Russian Federation
232 H2 **Kysucké Nové Mesto** Slovakia
227 M2 **Kysylyn** Ukraine
237 AB5 **Kytalyktakh** Russian Federation
234 F3 **Kytay, Ozero** *lake* Ukraine
235 C7 **Kythira** Greece
235 C7 **Kythira** *island* Greece
235 D7 **Kythnos** Greece
235 D7 **Kythnos** *island* Greece
223 N4 **Kytökylä** Finland
223 P4 **Kytömäki** Finland
237 X5 **Kyuekh-Bulung** Russian Federation
376 C5 **Kyun Pila** Myanmar
376 C4 **Kyungyi** Myanmar
379 H4 **Kyunhla** Myanmar
118 H7 **Kyuquot** British Columbia Canada
388 G4 **Kyushe** Kazakhstan
387 F5 **Kyūshū** *island* Japan
81 R3 **Kyushu-Palau Ridge** *underwater feature* Pacific Ocean
234 C4 **Kyustendil** *admin. area* Bulgaria
237 AA4 **Kyusyur** Russian Federation
394 D2 **Kyyivs'ka Misto** *admin. area* Ukraine
223 N5 **Kyyjärvi** Finland
223 N5 **Kyyjärvi** *lake* Finland
225 N1 **Kyyvesi** *lake* Finland
388 F5 **Kyzan** Kazakhstan
389 Q3 **Kyzyl** Russian Federation
389 P3 **Kyzyl-Mazhalyk** Russian Federation
389 K6 **Kyzyl-Su** *watercourse* Tajikistan
389 M4 **Kyzylagash** Kazakhstan
388 I5 **Kyzylkum** Uzbekistan
388 J5 **Kyzylorda** Kazakhstan
388 I4 **Kyzylordinskaya Oblast'** *admin. area* Kazakhstan
388 F5 **Kyzylsay** Kazakhstan
389 L3 **Kyzyltas** Kazakhstan
389 K4 **Kyzyltau** Kazakhstan
389 K4 **Kyzylzhar** Kazakhstan

L

154 D2 **La Adjunta** Venezuela
231 F3 **La Almunia de Doña Godina** Spain
133 F3 **La América** Mexico
129 L6 **La Amistad** Mexico
129 H5 **La Angostura, Presa** *lake* Mexico
128 D4 **La Asturiana** Argentina
155 F2 **La Asunción** Venezuela
160 F6 **La Aurora** Argentina
162 C4 **La Bajada** Argentina
230 D2 **La Bañeza** Spain
132 E4 **La Barca** Mexico
125 J5 **La Barge** Wyoming USA
162 B2 **La Barra** Chile
228 C3 **La Barre-de-Monts** France
226 B2 **La Bassée** France
122 C4 **La Bazinière, Lac** *lake* Québec Canada
132 C3 **La Beata** Mexico
131 K7 **La Belle** Florida USA
228 F2 **La Belle Étoile** France
119 O5 **La Biche, Lac** *lake* Alberta Canada
310 3d **La Bocayna** *strait* Canary Islands
162 B3 **La Bolsa** Argentina
129 J7 **La Boquilla de Conchos** Mexico
228 F4 **La Bourboule** France
158 A2 **La Breita** Peru
229 G5 **La Brillanne** France
160 D6 **La Buitrera** Argentina
228 B4 **La Bussière** France
129 I7 **La Buta** Mexico
132 C2 **La Cabaña** Mexico
129 J8 **La Cadena** Mexico
154 D3 **La Calzada** Venezuela
154 D3 **La Campiña** Colombia
128 C3 **La Canada Flintridge** California USA
126 H3 **La Canadienne Point** Ontario Canada
228 F4 **La Canourgue** France
228 F2 **La Capelle** France
160 F5 **La Carlota** Argentina
230 D5 **La Carlota** Spain
155 F3 **La Casa Verde** Venezuela
129 I6 **La Casita** Mexico
159 F5 **La Cautiva** Bolivia
154 E4 **La Ceiba** Colombia
134 C4 **La Ceiba** Honduras
133 F4 **La Ceiba** Mexico
154 D2 **La Ceiba** Venezuela
155 E2 **La Ceiba** Venezuela
154 C3 **La Ceja** Colombia
229 G3 **La Chapelle-de-Guinchay** France
228 E3 **La Châtre** France
229 H3 **La Chaux-de-Fonds** Switzerland
122 B3 **La Chevrotière, Lac** *lake* Québec Canada
134 E5 **La Chorrera** Panama
132 C2 **La Choya** Mexico
128 G5 **La Cienega** Mexico
129 I3 **La Cienega** New Mexico USA
132 E4 **La Cinta** Mexico
229 G5 **La Ciotat** France
226 D5 **La Clusaz** France
160 E3 **La Cocha** Argentina
155 E3 **La Cochinera** Venezuela
160 F6 **La Colina** Argentina
132 E3 **La Colonia** Mexico
132 C2 **La Colorada** Mexico
160 E6 **La Copelina** Argentina
228 E4 **La Coquille** France
119 P5 **La Corey** Alberta Canada
130 B6 **La Coste** Texas USA
228 F4 **La Courtine** France
131 L2 **La Crosse** Virginia USA
124 G3 **La Crosse** Washington USA
126 F5 **La Crosse** Wisconsin USA
161 G4 **La Cruz** Argentina
158 E3 **La Cruz** Bolivia
159 F5 **La Cruz** Bolivia
134 C5 **La Cruz** Costa Rica
132 D4 **La Cruz** Mexico
154 D2 **La Cruz** Venezuela
158 D6 **La Cruz de Pica** Chile
129 K6 **La Cuesta de Malena** Mexico
129 J3 **La Cueva** New Mexico USA
132 C2 **La Cueva de Tres Rios** Mexico
163 I6 **La Désirade** *island* Guadeloupe
310 9a **La Digue** *island* Seychelles
154 C3 **La Dorada** Colombia
162 C2 **La Dulce, Laguna** *lake* Argentina
158 D4 **La Encañada** Peru
133 F4 **La Encarnación** Mexico
162 D2 **La Ensenada** Argentina
155 E4 **La Esmeralda** Venezuela
162 C2 **La Esperanza** Argentina
154 C4 **La Esperanza** Colombia
134 B4 **La Esperanza** Honduras
132 E3 **La Esperanza** Mexico
155 F2 **La Esperanza** Venezuela
158 E4 **La Estación** Bolivia
160 E2 **La Estrella** Argentina
230 D4 **La Estrella** Spain
160 E4 **La Falda** Argentina
228 F2 **La Fère** France
228 E3 **La Ferrière** France
226 B3 **La Ferté-Alais** France
226 B3 **La Ferté-Milon** France
241 I5 **La Feuillie** France
228 D3 **La Flotte** France
122 C5 **La Forest, Lac** *lake* Québec Canada
154 C2 **La Fría** Venezuela
123 G7 **La Galissonnière, Lac** *lake* Québec Canada
159 E4 **La Garganta** Bolivia
129 I2 **La Garita Mountains** Colorado USA
230 E4 **La Gineta** Spain
118 L5 **La Glace** Alberta Canada
241 F5 **La Glacerie** France
133 F3 **La Gloria** Mexico
310 3a **La Gomera, Isla de** *island* Canary Islands
155 F3 **La Gran Sabana** *region* Venezuela
124 F4 **La Grande** Oregon USA
121 Q6 **La Grande 2, Réservoir de** Québec Canada
121 R6 **La Grande 3, Réservoir de** Québec Canada
121 S5 **La Grande 4, Réservoir de** Québec Canada
228 G4 **La Grande-Combe** France
228 G5 **La Grande-Motte** France
123 I7 **La Grande Passe, Île de** *island* Québec Canada
121 P6 **La Grande Rivière** *watercourse* Québec Canada
163 I6 **La Grande Vigie, Pointe de** *cape* Guadeloupe
131 I4 **La Grange** Georgia USA
130 C6 **La Grange** Texas USA
125 M6 **La Grange** Wyoming USA
159 E4 **La Granja** Bolivia
135 G3 **La Granja, Punta de** *cape* Dominican Republic
155 H4 **La Grève** French Guiana
310 8a **La Grille** *volcano* Comoros
135 F5 **La Guajira** *admin. area* Colombia
135 G4 **La Guajira, Península de** *peninsula* Colombia
154 D3 **La Guaracura** Colombia
160 E4 **La Guardia** Argentina
160 D3 **La Guardia** Chile
134 D2 **La Habana** *admin. area* Cuba
134 D2 **La Habana (Havana)** Cuba
160 E5 **La Herradura** Argentina
228 E2 **La Hutte** France
154 C3 **La India** Venezuela
133 F5 **La Isla** Mexico
154 C2 **La Jagua de Ibirico** Colombia
122 E6 **La Jannaye, Lac** *lake* Québec Canada
129 J2 **La Jara** Colorado USA
129 I2 **La Jara** New Mexico USA
129 I2 **La Jara Reservoir** Colorado USA
229 H4 **La Javie** France
134 C4 **La Jicaral** Nicaragua
231 H2 **La Jonquera** Spain
158 E5 **La Joya** Bolivia
129 I6 **La Joya** Mexico
154 C4 **La Julia** Colombia
159 F4 **La Junta** Bolivia
162 B3 **La Junta** Chile
129 I6 **La Junta** Mexico
125 N8 **La Junta** Colorado USA
132 D5 **La Juntas** Mexico
160 F5 **La Laguna** Argentina
310 3a **La Laguna** Canary Islands
129 K7 **La Leche, Lago** *lake* Mexico
154 C4 **La Libertad** Colombia
154 A5 **La Libertad** Ecuador
158 B3 **La Libertad** *admin. area* Peru
160 D5 **La Ligua** Chile
162 B2 **La Lipela** Argentina
154 B4 **La Llanada** Colombia
162 D2 **La Lobería** Argentina
119 Q4 **La Loche, Lac** *lake* Saskatchewan Canada
119 Q4 **La Loche West** Saskatchewan Canada
132 D3 **La Loma** Mexico
133 F3 **La Loma** Mexico
121 P6 **La Longue Pointe** *cape* Québec Canada
228 G1 **La Louvière** Belgium
154 C4 **La Macarena** Colombia
154 C4 **La Macarena, Serranía de** *range* Colombia
154 B5 **La Maná** Ecuador
230 E4 **La Mancha** *region* Spain
La Manche *see* **English Channel** UK/France
162 C4 **La Manchuria** Argentina
132 D4 **La Manga** Mexico
129 K7 **La Margarita del Norte** Mexico
162 C4 **La María** Argentina
154 B4 **La María** Colombia
155 F2 **La Marinera** Venezuela
132 E3 **La Maroma** Mexico
130 D6 **La Marque** Texas USA
134 D5 **La Mesa** Panama
128 D4 **La Mesa** California USA
132 E5 **La Mira Tumbiscatio** Mexico
132 E4 **La Miseria** Mexico
128 D4 **La Mision** Mexico
158 C4 **La Misión** Peru
126 F6 **La Moine** *watercourse* Illinois USA
122 E4 **La Moinerie, Lac** *lake* Québec Canada
154 C4 **La Montañita** Colombia
132 E2 **La Morita** Mexico
127 L2 **La Motte** Québec Canada
229 G4 **La Motte-Servolex** France
230 D3 **La Mudarra** Spain
132 E3 **La Muralla** Mexico
229 G4 **La Mure** France
129 N8 **La Nacha, Laguna** *lake* Mexico
129 J7 **La Navecilla** Mexico
160 D6 **La Negra** Argentina
160 D2 **La Negra** Chile
159 F4 **La Noria** Bolivia
129 H6 **La Norteña** Mexico
310 3d **La Oliva** Canary Islands
310 3a **La Orotava** Canary Islands
158 C3 **La Oroya** Peru
228 F3 **La Pacaudière** France
132 E3 **La Paila** Mexico
310 3 **La Palma** *island* Canary Islands
134 E5 **La Palma** Panama
230 C5 **La Palma** Spain
134 D5 **La Palmas** Panama
228 D4 **La Palmyre** France
160 E6 **La Pampa** *admin. area* Argentina
161 G6 **La Pastora** Argentina
155 F2 **La Pastora** Venezuela
158 D5 **La Paz** Bolivia
158 D4 **La Paz** *admin. area* Bolivia
154 C2 **La Paz** Colombia
134 C4 **La Paz** Honduras
132 C3 **La Paz** Mexico
161 H3 **La Paz** Paraguay
134 C4 **La Paz Centro** Nicaragua
158 B2 **La Peca** Peru
154 D5 **La Pedrera** Colombia
132 D2 **La Pedrera** Mexico
129 J6 **La Perla** Mexico
120 G5 **La Pérouse** Manitoba Canada
163 5 **La Pérouse, Bahía** *bay* Isla de Pascua (Easter Island)
130 C9 **La Pesca** Mexico
134 C4 **La Pimienta** Honduras
163 I5 **La Plaine** Dominica
310 7a **La Plaine des Palmistes** Réunion
133 H6 **La Planes** Honduras
161 G5 **La Plata** Argentina
154 C4 **La Plata** Colombia
126 E6 **La Plata** Missouri USA
154 A5 **La Playa** Peru
119 R5 **La Plonge** Saskatchewan Canada
119 R5 **La Plonge, Lac** *lake* Saskatchewan Canada
231 G2 **La Pobla de Lillet** Spain
231 G2 **La Pobla de Segur** Spain
230 D2 **La Pola de Gordón** Spain
132 B2 **La Polvareda** Mexico
310 7a **La Posession** Réunion
122 B3 **La Potherie, Lac** *lake* Québec Canada
133 F4 **La Poza** Mexico
128 F8 **La Poza Grande** Mexico
126 E3 **La Prairie** Minnesota USA
129 L8 **La Presa** Mexico
130 D4 **La Presa** Mexico
154 D3 **La Primavera** Colombia
230 E2 **La Proveda de Soria** Spain
154 D2 **La Providencia** Venezuela
130 B6 **La Pryor** Texas USA
160 F4 **La Puerta** Argentina
132 E4 **La Punta** Mexico
128 D4 **La Quinta** California USA
230 E3 **La Rasa** Spain
154 E2 **La Raya** Venezuela
160 E6 **La Reforma** Argentina
154 D4 **La Reforma** Colombia
133 F3 **La Reforma** Mexico
133 F3 **La Reforma** Mexico
228 D4 **La Réole** France
132 D3 **La Resolana** Mexico
231 K2 **La Revellata** *cape* Corsica France
160 E4 **La Rioja** Argentina
160 E4 **La Rioja** *admin. area* Argentina
230 E2 **La Rioja** *admin. area* Spain
228 C5 **La Rioja** *region* Spain
230 D2 **La Robla** Spain
230 C4 **La Roca de la Sierra** Spain
228 E4 **La Roche-Chalais** France
229 G1 **La Roche-en-Ardenne** Belgium
229 H3 **La Roche-sur-Foron** France
228 E4 **La Rochefoucauld** France
120 G8 **La Rochelle** Manitoba Canada
228 D3 **La Rochelle** France
230 E4 **La Roda** Spain
123 H7 **La Romaine** Québec Canada
135 G3 **La Romana** Dominican Republic
119 S5 **La Ronge** Saskatchewan Canada
116 I8 **La Ronge, Lac** *lake* Saskatchewan Canada
159 F6 **La Rosa** Bolivia
129 K6 **La Rosita** Mexico
160 F4 **La Rubia** Argentina
128 D4 **La Rumorosa** Mexico
161 G3 **La Sabana** Argentina
132 A1 **La Salina** Mexico
155 F2 **La Salina** Venezuela
310 3d **La Santa** Canary Islands
117 L9 **La Sarre** Québec Canada
228 D4 **La Sauve-Majeure** France
123 K8 **La Scie** Newfoundland and Labrador Canada
231 G3 **La Sènia** Spain
160 D4 **La Serena** Chile
154 D2 **La Solita** Venezuela
228 E3 **La Souterraine** France
229 I4 **La Spezia** Italy
123 I7 **La Tabatière** Québec Canada
132 E4 **La Tapona** Mexico
228 D4 **La Teste** France
232 B4 **La Thuile** Italy
132 D5 **La Tijera** Mexico
132 C4 **La Tinaja** Mexico
154 B4 **La Tola** Colombia
428* E7 **La Touche, Mount** Qld Australia
229 G4 **La Tour-du-Pin** France
228 D4 **La Tremblade** France
163 I4 **La Trinité** Martinique
432* H8 **La Trobe, Mount** Vic. Australia
154 B5 **La Troncal** Ecuador
117 L9 **La Tuque** Québec Canada
162 B2 **La Unión** Chile
154 B4 **La Unión** Colombia
134 C4 **La Unión** Honduras
132 C3 **La Unión** Mexico
132 E5 **La Unión** Mexico
158 A2 **La Unión** Peru
158 B3 **La Unión** Peru
231 F5 **La Unión** Spain
231 F4 **La Vall d'Uxó** Spain
230 D2 **La Vega** Spain
230 D3 **La Vellés** Spain
132 C4 **La Venta** Mexico
230 E3 **La Ventosa** Spain
131 H2 **La Vergne** Tennessee USA
130 B6 **La Vernia** Texas USA
125 M8 **La Veta** Colorado USA
155 F2 **La Victoria** Venezuela
130 C7 **La Villa** Texas USA
160 E3 **La Viña** Argentina
125 Q6 **La Vista** Nebraska USA
155 F2 **La Viuda** Venezuela
229 G4 **La Voulte-sur-Rhône** France
130 C6 **La Ward** Texas USA
132 D3 **La Zarca** Mexico
223 P5 **Laakajärvi** *lake* Finland
225 N3 **Lääne-Virumaa** *admin. area* Estonia
225 L3 **Läänemaa** *admin. area* Estonia
223 O2 **Laanila** Finland
307 H1 **Laas Dawaco** Somalia
307 H2 **Laascaanood** Somalia
225 N4 **Laatre** Estonia
226 E4 **Laax** Switzerland
300 D3 **Laâyoune** Western Sahara
372 B6 **Labala** Indonesia
375 G3 **Labang** Malaysia
427 9a **Labasa** Fiji
228 E4 **Labastide-Murat** France
228 F5 **Labastide-Rouairoux** France
228 E5 **Labastide-Saint-Pierre** France
154 C3 **Labateca** Colombia
432* B5 **Labatt, Point** SA Australia
245 D4 **Labbanacallee** Ireland
222 J3 **Labbas** *lake* Sweden
241 I5 **L'Abbaye** France
227 H2 **Labe** *watercourse* Czech Republic
304 B2 **Labé** Guinea
127 N3 **Labelle** Québec Canada
372 B4 **Labengke** *island* Indonesia
118 D2 **Laberge, Lake** Yukon Territory Canada
160 F6 **Laberinto, Punta** *cape* Argentina
375 G2 **Labi** Brunei
388 C5 **Labinsk** Russian Federation
374 D3 **Labis** Malaysia
390 F5 **Labkah** Saudi Arabia
375 I4 **Labobo** *island* Indonesia
227 I4 **Lábod** Hungary
224 F5 **Laboe** Germany
163 I3 **Laborie** St Lucia
228 D4 **Labouheyre** France
160 F5 **Laboulaye** Argentina
122 G4 **Labrador** *region* Newfoundland and Labrador Canada
121 V6 **Labrador City** Newfoundland and Labrador Canada
117 N7 **Labrador Sea** Canada/Greenland
228 D4 **Labrit** France
374 E4 **Labu** Indonesia
375 G2 **Labuan** Malaysia
375 G2 **Labuan** *admin. area* Malaysia
424 inset **Labuan, Cape** Heard Island Australia
375 I4 **Labuanbajo** Indonesia
385 I2 **Labudalin** Nei Mongol Zizhiqu China
374 D3 **Labuhanbilik** Indonesia
374 C3 **Labuhanhaji** Indonesia
374 C3 **Labuhanruku** Indonesia
377 H6 **Labuk** *watercourse* Malaysia
377 H6 **Labuk, Teluk** *bay* Malaysia
384 E6 **Labuleng** Gansu China
372 A6 **Labunanbajo** Indonesia
376 B3 **Labutta** Myanmar
224 I2 **Läby** Sweden
235 A5 **Laç** Albania
301 I6 **Lac** *admin. area* Chad
123 H7 **Lac, Île du** *island* Québec Canada
127 O2 **Lac-Bouchette** Québec Canada
119 U3 **Lac Brochet** Manitoba Canada
127 O3 **Lac-Chat** Québec Canada
120 G7 **Lac du Bonnet** Manitoba Canada
127 O3 **Lac Edouard** Québec Canada
119 P5 **Lac La Biche** Alberta Canada
118 K7 **Lac la Hache** British Columbia Canada
119 S5 **Lac La Ronge Provincial Park** Saskatchewan Canada
127 L2 **Lac-Lois** Québec Canada
125 R4 **Lac qui Parle** *lake* Minnesota USA
120 N8 **Lac-Ste-Thérèse** Ontario Canada
158 E5 **Laca Jahuira** *watercourse* Bolivia
228 F4 **Lacalm** France
228 D4 **Lacanau** France
228 D4 **Lacanau, Étang de** *lake* France
228 D4 **Lacanau-Océan** France
133 H5 **Lacandón, Laguna** *lake* Mexico
133 H5 **Lacantún** *lake* Mexico
234 A3 **Laćarak** Serbia
231 H2 **Lacaune** France
393 D9 **Laccadive Sea** India
243 H3 **Laceby** North East Lincolnshire England UK
424 G4 **Lacepede Islands** WA Australia
124 D3 **Lacey** Washington USA
391 L2 **Lachi Toi** *watercourse* Pakistan
425 M8 **Lachlan** *watercourse* NSW Australia
227 L1 **Lachowo** Poland
127 N4 **Lachute** Québec Canada
235 G5 **Laçin** Turkey
242 A2 **Lack** Omagh Northern Ireland UK
127 L5 **Lackawanna** New York USA
241 H2 **Lackford** Suffolk England UK
120 H8 **Laclu** Ontario Canada
119 O6 **Lacombe** Alberta Canada
127 P5 **Laconia** New Hampshire USA
163 1c **Lacre Punt** *cape* Netherlands Antilles
163 I4 **Lacroix, Piton** *volcano* Martinique
227 I4 **Lad** Hungary
374 C3 **Ladara** Indonesia
159 G5 **Ladário** Brazil
222 J3 **Låddaure** *lake* Sweden
121 P4 **Laddie Island** Nunavut Canada
225 M4 **Lādes ezers** *lake* Latvia
234 D3 **Lādești** Romania
225 O4 **Ladino** Russian Federation
233 E6 **Ladispoli** Italy
124 D2 **Ladner** British Columbia Canada
392 D5 **Ladnu** Rajasthan India
228 F2 **Ladon** France
225 P2 **Ladozhskoye Ozero** *lake* Russian Federation
162 C5 **Ladrillero, Cabo** *cape* Argentina
162 B5 **Ladrillero, Cerro** *mountain* Chile
162 A4 **Ladrillero, Golfo** *bay* Chile
379 G3 **Ladu** *mountain* Xizang Zizhiqu China
225 K5 **Ladushkin** Russian Federation
238 F2 **Ladva** Russian Federation
117 K3 **Lady Ann Strait** Nunavut Canada
425 N10 **Lady Barron** Tas. Australia
122 G1 **Lady Franklin Island** Nunavut Canada
308 E6 **Lady Frere** South Africa
308 E6 **Lady Grey** South Africa
131 K6 **Lady Lake** Florida USA
437 L2 **Lady Newnes Bay** Antarctica
244 F5 **Ladykirk** Scottish Borders Scotland UK
118 J8 **Ladysmith** British Columbia Canada
308 E5 **Ladysmith** South Africa
126 F4 **Ladysmith** Wisconsin USA
234 F1 **Ladyzhyn** Ukraine
373 H5 **Lae** Papua New Guinea
427 I5 **Lae Atoll** *reef* Marshall Islands
376 C5 **Laem Ao Kham** *island* Thailand
376 C6 **Laem Mum Nok** *island* Thailand
224 H4 **Läen** *lake* Sweden
224 D2 **Lærdalsøyri** Norway
224 F4 **Læsø** *island* Denmark
223 N2 **Lævnasjav'ri** *lake* Norway
223 O2 **Lævvajåk** Norway
131 I4 **Lafayette** Alabama USA
125 M7 **Lafayette** Colorado USA
126 H6 **Lafayette** Indiana USA
130 E5 **Lafayette** Louisiana USA
226 C4 **Laferté** France
305 F3 **Lafia** Nigeria
127 M2 **Laflamme** *watercourse* Québec Canada
122 B2 **Laflamme, Lac** *lake* Québec Canada
227 H4 **Lafnitz** *watercourse* Austria
121 S5 **Laforge** *watercourse* Québec Canada
222 I6 **Laforsen** Sweden
228 E4 **Lafrançaise** France
374 B2 **Laful** Andaman and Nicobar Islands India
245 E1 **Lagacurry** Ireland
373 G5 **Lagaip** *watercourse* Papua New Guinea
388 E4 **Lagan'** Russian Federation
224 H4 **Lagan** *watercourse* Sweden
235 B7 **Lagana, Kolpos** *bay* Greece
222 inset **Lagarfljót** *watercourse* Iceland
157 E5 **Lagarto** Brazil
377 I3 **Lagawe** Philippines
300 D5 **Lagbar** Senegal
305 G3 **Lagdo** Cameroon
306 A2 **Lagdo, Résevoir de** *lake* Cameroon
226 E2 **Lage** Germany
224 E2 **Lågen** *watercourse* Norway
226 E1 **Lägerdorf** Germany
224 H3 **Lagerfors** Sweden
161 I3 **Lages** Brazil
244 D3 **Laggan** Highland Scotland UK
244 D4 **Laggan, Loch** *lake* Scotland UK
222 M5 **Laggars** Finland
307 F3 **Lagh Bogal** *watercourse* Kenya
307 G3 **Lagh Bor** *watercourse* Kenya
391 L2 **Laghmān** *admin. area* Afghanistan
301 G2 **Laghouat** Algeria
162 B3 **Lago Blanco** Argentina
162 B4 **Lago Buenos Aires, Meseta del** *plateau* Argentina
162 B4 **Lago Cardiel** Argentina
156 C4 **Lago da Pedra** Brazil
308 D2 **Lago Dilolo** Angola
162 B3 **Lago Futalaufquen** Argentina
155 I4 **Lago Novo** Brazil
162 B4 **Lago Posadas** Argentina
162 B4 **Lago San Martín** Argentina
162 B3 **Lago Verde** Chile
162 B4 **Lago Viedma** Argentina
310 1a **Lagoa** Azores
155 E4 **Lagoa da Canoa** Brazil
157 C8 **Lagoa da Prata** Brazil
157 C7 **Lagoa Formosa** Brazil
157 E4 **Lagoa Nova** Brazil
161 I4 **Lagoa Vermelha** Brazil
157 C7 **Lagoas** Brazil
376 F7 **Lagong** *island* Indonesia
425 inset **Lagoon, The** *lake* Lord Howe Island Australia
305 E3 **Lagos** Nigeria
305 E3 **Lagos** *admin. area* Nigeria
230 B5 **Lagos** Portugal
132 E4 **Lagos de Moreno** Mexico
305 E3 **Lagos Lagoon** *bay* Nigeria
227 K2 **Łagów** Poland
222 H5 **Lågsjön** *lake* Sweden
377 J6 **Laguilayan** Philippines
128 D4 **Laguna Beach** California USA
230 D2 **Laguna de Negrillos** Spain
134 D4 **Laguna de Perlas** Nicaragua
162 B4 **Laguna Grande** Argentina
162 C3 **Laguna Grande** Argentina
128 D4 **Laguna Niguel** California USA
128 F7 **Laguna San Ignacio** Mexico
237 AL5 **Laguna Tenkergynpil'gyn** *bay* Russian Federation
160 F3 **Laguna Yema** Argentina
158 C3 **Lagunas** Peru
129 J6 **Lagunetas** Mexico
154 D2 **Lagunillas** Venezuela
159 E4 **Lagunita** Brazil
375 H6 **Lahad Datu** Malaysia
245 E4 **Lahagh** Ireland
245 D5 **Lahard** Ireland
374 D4 **Lahat** Indonesia
379 H3 **Lahe** Myanmar
225 L3 **Lahepera Laht** *bay* Estonia
374 C3 **Lahewa** Indonesia
390 F7 **Laḩij** Yemen
388 F6 **Lāhījān** Iran
226 E2 **Lahn** *watercourse* Germany
223 M3 **Lahnajärvi** Sweden
223 M3 **Lahnasuando** Sweden
224 G4 **Laholmsbukten** *bay* Sweden
128 B2 **Lahoma** Oklahoma USA
124 F7 **Lahontan Reservoir** Nevada USA
391 M3 **Lahore** Pakistan
223 P5 **Lahovaara** Finland
226 D3 **Lahr** Germany
391 K3 **Lahri** Pakistan
225 M2 **Lahti** Finland
377 I4 **Lahuy** *island* Philippines
305 H3 **Laï** Chad
373 G5 **Lai** *watercourse* Papua New Guinea
162 C4 **Lai Aike** Argentina
376 D2 **Lai Châu** Vietnam
379 H5 **Lai-hka** Myanmar
380 F4 **Laibin** Guangxi Zhuangzu Zizhiqu China
244 D2 **Laid** Highland Scotland UK
128 inset **Lā'ie** Hawai'i USA
244 B4 **Laig** Highland Scotland UK
228 E2 **L'Aigle** France
226 C4 **Laignes** France
222 M5 **Laihia** Finland
159 E5 **Laikakota** Bolivia
225 O2 **Laikko** Finland
222 K2 **Laimoluokta** *bay* Sweden
223 M3 **Lainio** Sweden
244 D2 **Lairg** Highland Scotland UK
374 D4 **Lais** Indonesia
307 F3 **Laisamis** Kenya
222 J3 **Laisan** *lake* Sweden
228 F4 **Laissac** France
222 J3 **Laisvall** Sweden
225 K2 **Laitila** Finland
225 M3 **Laitse** Estonia
225 N3 **Laiusevälja** Estonia
385 I6 **Laiwu** Shandong China
372 C4 **Laiwui** Indonesia
385 I6 **Laixi** Shandong China
385 I6 **Laiyang** Shandong China
385 H5 **Laiyuan** Hebei China
385 I5 **Laizhou** Shandong China
385 I5 **LaizhouWan** *bay* Shandong China
160 D6 **Laja, Laguna de la** *lake* Chile
154 E4 **Laja Suiza** Venezuela
424 I4 **Lajamanu** NT Australia
156 D5 **Laje** Brazil
156 E5 **Lajedo** Brazil
310 4 **Lajedo dos Espargos** Cape Verde
310 1b **Lajes** Azores
157 D8 **Lajinha** Brazil
129 K6 **Lajitas** Texas USA
234 A2 **Lajosmizse** Hungary
163 I4 **L'Ajoupa-Bouillon** Martinique
222 J4 **Lajsbäck** Sweden
227 I4 **Lajta** *watercourse* Hungary
227 H2 **Łąka** Poland
223 M5 **Lakaluoma** Finland
300 E6 **Lakamané** Mali
426 7 **Lakatoro** Vanuatu
222 L3 **Lakaträsk** Sweden
222 L3 **Lakaträsket** *lake* Sweden
225 I5 **Lakavattnet** Sweden
119 S8 **Lake Alma** Saskatchewan Canada
125 P5 **Lake Andes** South Dakota USA
424 I4 **Lake Argyle Village** WA Australia
129 J4 **Lake Arthur** New Mexico USA
131 J5 **Lake Butler** Florida USA
130 E5 **Lake Charles** Louisiana USA
125 L7 **Lake City** Colorado USA
131 J5 **Lake City** Florida USA
126 I4 **Lake City** Michigan USA
131 J4 **Lake City** South Carolina USA
131 I2 **Lake City** Tennessee USA
116 D6 **Lake Clark National Park and Preserve** Alaska USA
423 D6 **Lake Clearwater** New Zealand
242 E2 **Lake District National Park** England UK
128 D4 **Lake Elsinore** California USA
125 J6 **Lake Fork** *watercourse* Utah USA
130 D4 **Lake Fork Reservoir** Texas USA
128 E3 **Lake Havasu City** Arizona USA
423 C7 **Lake Hawea** New Zealand
130 D6 **Lake Jackson** Texas USA
119 S6 **Lake Lenore** Saskatchewan Canada
126 G3 **Lake Linden** Michigan USA
119 M7 **Lake Louise** Alberta Canada
131 J3 **Lake Lure** North Carolina USA
128 E3 **Lake Mead National Recreation Area** *park* Nevada USA
129 L3 **Lake Meredith National Recreation Area** *park* Texas USA
126 E5 **Lake Mills** Iowa USA
128 G3 **Lake Montezuma** Arizona USA
373 G5 **Lake Murray** Papua New Guinea
131 J5 **Lake Park** Georgia USA
125 R5 **Lake Park** Iowa USA
131 K7 **Lake Placid** Florida USA
127 O4 **Lake Placid** New York USA
130 F4 **Lake Providence** Louisiana USA
124 F6 **Lake Range** Nevada USA
124 D3 **Lake Stevens** Washington USA
129 L3 **Lake Tanglewood** Texas USA
423 D7 **Lake Tekapo** New Zealand
131 L3 **Lake View** South Carolina USA
120 F6 **Lake Winnipeg** Manitoba Canada
427 9 **Lakeba** *island* Fiji
427 9 **Lakeba Passage** *strait* Fiji
373 H6 **Lakekamu** *watercourse* Papua New Guinea
425 M3 **Lakeland** Qld Australia
131 K6 **Lakeland** Florida USA
131 I3 **Lakeland** Tennessee USA
118 G5 **Lakelse Lake** British Columbia Canada
224 G3 **Lakenesjön** *lake* Sweden
424 4 **Lakepa** Niue New Zealand
124 D7 **Lakeport** California USA
306 E2 **Lakes** *admin. area* Sudan
124 C5 **Lakeside** Oregon USA
130 E2 **Lakeview** Arkansas USA
124 E5 **Lakeview** Oregon USA
130 A3 **Lakeview** Texas USA
126 E4 **Lakeville** Minnesota USA
125 M7 **Lakewood** Colorado USA
392 C5 **Lakha** Rajasthan India
225 P2 **Lakhdenpokh'ya** Russian Federation
392 D6 **Lakheri** Rajasthan India
392 E5 **Lakhimpur** Uttar Pradesh India
379 G3 **Lakhipur** Assam India
379 G4 **Lakhipur** Assam India
392 G6 **Lakhisarai** Bihar India
393 E6 **Lakhnadon** Madhya Pradesh India
392 B6 **Lakhpat** Gujarat India
125 O8 **Lakin** Kansas USA
121 N5 **Lakitusaki** *watercourse* Ontario Canada
235 B6 **Lakka** Greece
391 L3 **Lakki Marwat** Pakistan
235 D5 **Lakkoma** Greece
227 I5 **Lakócsa** Hungary
235 C7 **Lakonikos Kolpos** *bay* Greece
376 D6 **Lakor** *island* Indonesia
304 C3 **Lakota** Côte d'Ivoire
125 P2 **Lakota** North Dakota USA
223 N1 **Lakselv/Leavdnja** Norway
393 C9 **Lakshadweep** *admin. area* India
393 C9 **Lakshadweep (Laccadive Islands, India)** Lakshadweep India
379 G4 **Lakshmipur** Bangladesh
222 H4 **Laksjøen** *lake* Norway
222 K2 **Laksvatn** Norway
391 K2 **La'l** Afghanistan
379 G4 **Lalaghat** Assam India
391 K3 **Lālī** Afghanistan
133 G5 **Lalana** *watercourse* Mexico
235 B7 **Lalas** Greece
309 G2 **Lalaua** Mozambique
235 A5 **Lalëzit, Gjiri i** *bay* Albania
303 F5 **Lalibela** Ethiopia
372 C5 **Laliki** Indonesia
230 B2 **Lalín** Spain
372 B4 **Lalindu** *watercourse* Indonesia
392 E6 **Lalitpur** Uttar Pradesh India
222 F6 **Lalm** Norway
379 F4 **Lalmonirhat** Bangladesh

375 I5 Laloa Indonesia
372 C4 Laluin *island* Indonesia
226 G3 Lam Germany
229 I5 Lama Corsica France
236 T5 Lama, Ozero *lake* Russian Federation
229 J4 Lama Mocogno Italy
375 H2 Lamag Malaysia
426 7 Lamap Vanuatu
130 E3 Lamar Arkansas USA
125 N7 Lamar Colorado USA
126 D8 Lamar Missouri USA
226 C3 Lamarche France
373 H5 Lamari *watercourse* Papua New Guinea
160 E6 Lamarque Argentina
229 G4 Lamastre France
228 C2 Lamballe France
161 G3 Lambaré Paraguay
305 G5 Lambaréné Gabon
157 C8 Lambari Brazil
159 I4 Lambari, Serra do *range* Brazil
245 G3 Lambay Island Ireland
158 B2 Lambayeque *admin. area* Peru
Lambell, Mount *see* Gupuluk Australia
375 G4 Lambeng Indonesia
241 H3 Lamberhurst Kent England UK
437 E2 Lambert Glacier Antarctica
308 C6 Lambert's Bay South Africa
424 inset Lambeth Bluff *cape* Heard Island Australia
392 D4 Lambi Punjab India
243 F2 Lambley Northumberland England UK
241 F3 Lambourn West Berkshire England UK
245 B5 Lamb's Head *cape* Ireland
242 B4 Lambstown Ireland
373 I4 Lambu Papua New Guinea
374 C3 Lame Indonesia
305 G3 Lamé Chad
230 C3 Lamego Portugal
162 A2 Lameguapi, Punta *cape* Chile
163 I6 Lamentin Guadeloupe
123 F9 Lamèque New Brunswick Canada
123 F9 Lamèque, Île *island* New Brunswick Canada
129 L4 Lamesa Texas USA
231 G3 L'Ametlla de Mar Spain
233 G7 Lamezia Italy
427 9a Lami Fiji
235 C6 Lamia Greece
373 I6 Lamington, Mount *volcano* Papua New Guinea
372 D4 Lamlam Indonesia
244 C5 Lamlash North Ayrshire Scotland UK
423 C7 Lammerlaw Range New Zealand
223 M5 Lammi Finland
118 K6 Lamming Mills British Columbia Canada
242 A4 Lamoge Ireland
126 E6 Lamoni Iowa USA
124 G3 Lamont Washington USA
240 C4 Lamorran Cornwall England UK
373 H2 Lamotrek *island* Federated States of Micronesia
158 D4 Lampa Peru
376 C3 Lampang Thailand
376 C3 Lampang *admin. area* Thailand
130 B5 Lampasas Texas USA
228 B2 Lampaul-Plouarzel France
132 E3 Lampazos de Naranjo Mexico
233 E9 Lampedusa, Isola di *island* Italy
223 O5 Lamperila Finland
240 C2 Lampeter Ceredigion Wales UK
376 C3 Lamphun Thailand
233 E9 Lampione, Isola di *island* Italy
119 T8 Lampman Saskatchewan Canada
120 H3 Lamprey Manitoba Canada
374 E5 Lampung *admin. area* Indonesia
374 E5 Lampung, Teluk *bay* Indonesia
379 G4 Lamsang Manipur India
223 O4 Lamu Finland
307 G4 Lamu Kenya
307 G4 Lamu Bay Kenya
307 G4 Lamu Island *island* Kenya
381 I4 Lan Yü *island* Taiwan China
226 F4 Lana Italy
128 inset Lāna'i *island* Hawai'i USA
375 J2 Lanao, Lake Philippines
244 E5 Lanark South Lanarkshire Scotland UK
375 H2 Lanas Malaysia
162 D3 Lanaud, Península Argentina
376 C5 Lanbi Kyun Myanmar
379 H2 Lancang Jiang *watercourse* Xizang Zizhiqu China
380 C3 Lancang Jiang *watercourse* Yunnan China
380 C3 Lancang Jiang (Mekong) *water-course* Yunnan China
243 F3 Lancashire *admin. area* England UK
128 C3 Lancaster California USA
126 I8 Lancaster Kentucky USA
126 E6 Lancaster Missouri USA
127 L5 Lancaster New York USA
126 J7 Lancaster Ohio USA
127 M6 Lancaster Pennsylvania USA
131 K3 Lancaster South Carolina USA
242 F3 Lancaster Canal England UK
117 K4 Lancaster Sound Nunavut Canada
424 E7 Lancelin WA Australia
243 G2 Lanchester Durham England UK
233 F5 Lanciano Italy
160 C6 Lanco Chile
436 O1 Land Bay Antarctica
375 F3 Landak *watercourse* Indonesia
226 E3 Landau in der Pfalz Germany
154 C3 Landázuri Colombia
222 H4 Lande Norway
222 I3 Landegode *island* Norway
424 J5 Lander *watercourse* NT Australia
125 K5 Lander Wyoming USA
228 B2 Landerneau France
231 F4 Landete Spain
228 C3 Landévant France
240 B5 Landewednack Cornwall England UK
376 B4 Landfall Island Andaman and Nicobar Islands India
374 D4 Landik, Gunung *mountain* Indonesia
131 K3 Landis North Carolina USA
228 B2 Landivisiau France
228 D2 Landivy France
308 E2 Landless Corner Zambia
222 H5 Landögssjön *lake* Sweden
222 I5 Landön Sweden
228 F4 Landos France
229 I3 Landquart Switzerland
131 J3 Landrum South Carolina USA
240 B4 Land's End *cape* England UK
229 J2 Landsberg am Lech Germany
423 C6 Landsborough *watercourse* New Zealand
226 G3 Landshut Germany
224 G5 Landskrona Sweden
228 B2 Landudec France
240 C4 Landulph Cornwall England UK
128 E1 Lane Nevada USA
243 F2 Lane Head Durham England UK
228 C3 Lanester France
376 E2 Lang Chánh Vietnam
378 D2 Lang Ho *watercourse* Xizang Zizhiqu China
384 F4 Lang Shan *range* Nei Mongol Zizhiqu China
376 E2 Lạng Sơn Vietnam
376 C5 Lang Suan Thailand
379 G3 Lang Zhen Xizang Zizhiqu China
224 E4 Langå Denmark
232 C4 Langan, Punta *cape* Italy
307 F2 Langano, Lake *lake* Ethiopia
380 E2 Langao Shaanxi China
372 B5 Langara Indonesia
162 C4 Lángara, Bahía *bay* Argentina
222 K3 Langas *bay* Sweden
224 G4 Långås Sweden
244 B2 Langavat, Loch *lake* Scotland UK
242 F1 Langburnshiels Scottish Borders Scotland UK
380 E2 Langchi Sichuan China
125 P2 Langdon North Dakota USA
228 F4 Langeac France
302 F4 Langeb *watercourse* Sudan
224 F5 Langeland *island* Denmark
224 F5 Langelands Bælt *bay* Denmark
226 E2 Langen Germany
119 U7 Langenburg Saskatchewan Canada
226 E3 Langenburg Germany
222 I2 Langenes Norway
229 H3 Langenthal Switzerland
236 Q6 Langepas Russian Federation
224 E3 Langesjå *lake* Norway
224 C3 Langevåg Norway
385 H5 Langfang Hebei China
223 M1 Langfjordjøkulen *bay* Norway
118 J8 Langford British Columbia Canada
374 D3 Langgam Indonesia
374 C3 Langgapayung Indonesia
226 E2 Langgöns Germany
224 I3 Långhalsen *bay* Sweden
223 M3 Långheden Sweden
232 D4 Langhirano Italy
379 I5 Langhko Myanmar
244 E5 Langholm Dumfries and Galloway Scotland UK
381 I3 Langji Shan *range* Zhejiang China
222 inset Langjökull *ice* Iceland
374 C2 Langka Indonesia
376 C6 Langkawi *island* Thailand
379 G3 Langkazi Xizang Zizhiqu China
375 J5 Langkesi, Kepulauan *island* Indonesia
375 H2 Langkon Malaysia
128 C2 Langley, Mount California USA
243 G2 Langley Park Durham England UK
425 M6 Langlo Crossing Qld Australia
228 F4 Langogne France
228 D4 Langon France
223 M4 Långön *island* Sweden
222 I2 Langøya *island* Norway
240 E3 Langport Somerset England UK
230 D2 Langreo Spain
226 C4 Langres France
222 K5 Langron Sweden
224 H2 Långrösten *lake* Sweden
119 V7 Langruth Manitoba Canada
374 C2 Langsa Indonesia
224 I2 Långsand Sweden
222 M3 Långsel Sweden
222 G5 Langsjøen *lake* Norway
224 I2 Långsjön *lake* Sweden
222 L5 Långskäret *island* Finland
222 I2 Langslett Norway
129 N3 Langston Oklahoma USA
243 H2 Langtoft East Riding of Yorkshire England UK
243 H2 Langton North Yorkshire England UK
222 L4 Långträsk Sweden
240 C4 Langtree Devon England UK
129 L6 Langtry Texas USA
380 F1 Languan Shaanxi China
226 C5 Languedoc-Roussillon *admin. area* France
162 B3 Languiñeo Argentina
375 H6 Langundu, Tanjung *cape* Indonesia
222 F5 Langvatnet *lake* Norway
222 J5 Långvattnet Sweden
222 H5 Långvattnet *lake* Sweden
222 K5 Långviksmon Sweden
381 H2 Langxi Anhui China
380 E2 Langzhong Sichuan China
393 C8 Lanja Maharashtra India
375 G3 Lanjak, Bukit *mountain* Malaysia
230 E5 Lanjarón Spain
379 G4 Lanka Assam India
393 E7 Lanka Chhattisgarh India
381 G1 Lankao Henan China
228 C2 Lanmeur France
222 I5 Lännässjön *lake* Sweden
222 L2 Lannavaara Sweden
228 E5 Lannemezan France
228 B2 Lannilis France
228 C2 Lannion France
228 C2 Lannion, Baie de *bay* France
228 E4 Lanouaille France
133 H6 Lanquín Guatemala
228 C2 Lanrivain France
127 N6 Lansdale Pennsylvania USA
126 G3 L'Anse Michigan USA
123 J7 L'Anse-au-Loup Newfoundland and Labrador Canada
123 K7 L'Anse aux Meadows Newfoundland and Labrador Canada
127 P2 L'Anse-St-Jean Québec Canada
125 O2 Lansford North Dakota USA
225 L1 Länsi-Suomen *admin. area* Finland
126 I5 Lansing Michigan USA
222 M3 Lansjärv Sweden
227 I3 Lanškroun Czech Republic
229 H4 Lanslebourg-Mont-Cenis France
376 C6 Lanta, Ko *island* Thailand
223 M4 Lantjärv Sweden
385 K3 Lanxi Heilongjiang China
381 H2 Lanxi Zhejiang China
121 Q2 Lanyan, Lac *lake* Québec Canada
230 D3 Lanzahita Spain
310 3d Lanzarote *island* Canary Islands
384 E6 Lanzhou Gansu China
227 F7 Lao *watercourse* Italy
376 D2 Lào Cai Vietnam
377 I3 Laoag Philippines
381 G3 Laodao He *watercourse* Hunan China
385 J4 Laoha He *watercourse* Nei Mongol Zizhiqu China
381 F2 Laohekou Hubei China
245 E3 Laois *admin. area* Ireland
380 C3 Laojie Yunnan China
228 F2 Laon France
376 E3 Laos *country*
385 L4 Laoye Ling *range* Heilongjiang China
376 D3 Lap Lae Thailand
157 B9 Lapa Brazil
377 I6 Lapac *island* Philippines
161 G3 Lapachito Argentina
228 F3 Lapalisse France
134 D4 Lapan Nicaragua
377 I6 Laparan *island* Philippines
228 F3 Lapeyrouse France
238 C6 Lapichy Belarus
225 N2 Lapinjärvi Finland
223 O5 Lapinlahti Finland
223 O5 Lapinsalo Finland
223 R2 Laplandiya Russian Federation
228 F4 Lapleau France
223 V4 Lapominka Russian Federation
119 Q7 Laporte Saskatchewan Canada
125 R3 Laporte Minnesota USA
234 B3 Lapovo Serbia
223 M5 Lappajärvi Finland
223 M5 Lappajärvi *lake* Finland
223 M2 Lappalaisten kesätuvat Finland
225 L2 Lappdalsfjärden *bay* Finland
225 O2 Lappeenranta Finland
222 L5 Lappfjärd Finland
223 M5 Lappfors Finland
223 O3 Lappi *admin. area* Finland
223 O2 Lappland *region* Finland
222 M2 Lappojärvi *lake* Norway
222 L3 Lappträsket *lake* Sweden
Laptev Sea *see* Laptevykh, More Russian Federation
237 AA3 Laptevykh, More (Laptev Sea) *sea* Russian Federation
223 M5 Lapua Finland
223 M5 Lapuanjoki *watercourse* Finland
372 B5 Lapuko Indonesia
125 G3 Lapwai Idaho USA
233 E5 L'Aquila Italy
392 F5 Lar Uttar Pradesh India
391 H4 Lār Iran
157 D2 Lara *admin. area* Venezuela
300 D3 Larabanga Ghana
300 E1 Larache Morocco
242 B3 Laracor Ireland
242 B3 Laragh Ireland
229 G4 Laragne-Montéglin France
391 H4 Lārak, Jazireh-ye *island* Iran
305 H3 Laramanay Chad
125 M6 Laramie Wyoming USA
125 M6 Laramie *watercourse* Wyoming USA
125 M6 Laramie Mountains Colorado USA
157 D7 Laranja da Terra Brazil
159 H4 Laranjal Brazil
159 H4 Laranjeiras do Sul Brazil
372 B6 Larantuka Indonesia
375 I6 Larantuka Indonesia
372 D5 Larat Indonesia
372 E5 Larat *island* Indonesia
301 G1 Larba Algeria
244 C6 Larbrax Dumfries and Galloway Scotland UK
228 E4 L'Arbre France
225 J4 Lärbro Sweden
228 D5 Larceveau France
229 H4 Larche France
229 J4 Lardaro Italy
118 M7 Lardeau British Columbia Canada
124 G1 Lardo British Columbia Canada
235 F7 Lardos Greece
158 B3 Laredo Peru
230 E2 Laredo Spain
130 B7 Laredo Texas USA
234 E1 Larga Moldova
244 D5 Largae Dumfries and Galloway Scotland UK
245 D3 Largan Ireland
131 J7 Largo Florida USA
133 H4 Largo, Cayo *island* Cuba
130 C7 Largo, Laguna *lake* Texas USA
244 D4 Largo Bay Scotland UK
244 D5 Largs North Ayrshire Scotland UK
244 C5 Largybaan Argyll and Bute Scotland UK
242 C1 Largybeg North Ayrshire Scotland UK
233 D8 L'Ariana Tunisia
372 A4 Lariang Indonesia
372 A4 Lariang *watercourse* Indonesia
125 Q3 Larimore North Dakota USA
233 F6 Larino Italy
225 P2 Larionovo Russian Federation
235 C6 Larisa Greece
241 H2 Lark *watercourse* England UK
222 K4 Larkana Pakistan
129 J1 Larkspur Colorado USA
241 H2 Larling Norfolk England UK
228 C3 Larmor-Plage France
394 E6 Larnaka Cyprus
245 G2 Larne Larne Northern Ireland UK
245 G2 Larne *admin. area* Northern Ireland UK
245 G2 Larne Lough *bay* Northern Ireland UK
305 G3 Laro Cameroon
372 B4 Larompong Indonesia
231 G1 Laroque-Timbaut France
228 F4 Laroquebrou France
230 F2 Larraga Spain
228 D5 Larrau France
424 J3 Larrimah NT Australia
123 H10 Larrys River Nova Scotia Canada
437 E2 Lars Christensen Coast Antarctica
436 T2 Larsen Ice Shelf Antarctica
122 F2 Larson Ontario Canada
160 F6 Lartigau Argentina
228 D5 Laruns France
120 H7 Larus Lake Ontario Canada
223 F3 Larvik Norway
125 N7 Las Animas Colorado USA
161 G6 Las Armas Argentina
132 B2 Las Arrastras Mexico
162 B2 Las Bayas Argentina
129 H7 Las Bocas Mexico
132 D3 Las Borregas Mexico
154 E3 Las Carmelitas Venezuela
160 E3 Las Cejas Argentina
162 C3 Las Chapas Argentina
133 G5 Las Choapas Mexico
231 F2 Las Cinco Villas *region* Spain
159 G5 Las Conchas Bolivia
129 I6 Las Cruces Mexico
129 I4 Las Cruces New Mexico USA
129 J5 Las Cuatas Mexico
134 E5 Las Cumbres Panama
159 F5 Las Cutas Bolivia
155 F2 Las Delicias Venezuela
155 E2 Las Dos Quebradas Venezuela
129 L7 Las Esperanzas Mexico
161 G6 Las Flores Argentina
131 E5 Las Guacamayas Mexico
154 C3 Las Guamas Colombia
160 D5 Las Heras Argentina
132 B4 Las Horquetas Argentina
310 3b Las Indias Canary Islands
160 D5 Las Leñas Argentina
134 D5 Las Lomas Panama
158 A2 Las Lomas Peru
160 F3 Las Lomitas Argentina
133 E3 Las Margaritas Mexico
133 H5 Las Margaritas Mexico
135 G3 Las Matas de Farfán Dominican Republic
132 D3 Las Mesitas Mexico
132 D2 Las Mesteñas Mexico
161 G6 Las Nutrias Argentina
160 D6 Las Ovejas Argentina
132 C3 Las Pacas Mexico
310 3b Las Palmas de Gran Canaria Canary Islands
129 J7 Las Pampas Mexico
230 E4 Las Pedroñeras Spain
155 F2 Las Piedritas Venezuela
155 F2 Las Piñas Venezuela
125 F2 Las Plumas Argentina
162 C3 Las Pulgas Argentina
303 H5 Las Qoray Somalia
160 F5 Las Rosas Argentina
310 3d Las Salinas Canary Islands
134 D6 Las Tablas Panama
159 F5 Las Taperas Bolivia
160 E3 Las Termas Argentina
132 B3 Las Tres Vírgenes, Volcán *volcano* Mexico
134 C4 Las Trojes Honduras
134 E2 Las Tunas Cuba
134 E2 Las Tunas *admin. area* Cuba
132 D4 Las Varas Mexico
160 F4 Las Varillas Argentina
128 E2 Las Vegas Nevada USA
129 J3 Las Vegas New Mexico USA
129 J6 Las Víboras Mexico
154 D2 Las Yeritas Venezuela
375 G3 Lasan Indonesia
373 H5 Lasanga Island Papua New Guinea
161 H5 Lascano Uruguay
425 L8 Lascelles Vic. Australia
375 F5 Lasem Indonesia
379 H4 Lashio Myanmar
391 J3 Lashkar Gāh Afghanistan
227 J1 Łasin Poland
372 B4 Lasolo *watercourse* Indonesia
227 G1 Lassan Germany
228 D2 Lassay France
436 T2 Lassiter Coast Antarctica
119 S7 Last Mountain Lake Saskatchewan Canada
160 C6 Lastarria Chile
160 D3 Lastarria, Volcán *volcano* Chile/Argentina
243 H2 Lastingham North Yorkshire England UK
305 G5 Lastoursville Gabon
232 G5 Lastovo *island* Croatia
232 G5 Lastovski Kanal *watercourse* Croatia
376 C4 Lat Yao Thailand
426 8 Lata Solomon Islands
427 12c Lata Mountain American Samoa
154 B5 Latacunga Ecuador
436 S2 Latady Island Antarctica
372 C4 Latalata *island* Indonesia
158 D5 Latarana Chile
427 10 Late Island Tonga
392 F6 Latehar Jharkhand India
229 J5 Latera Italy
392 D6 Lateri Madhya Pradesh India
130 C4 Latham Kansas USA
393 C7 Lathi Gujarat India
392 C5 Lathi Rajasthan India
222 J4 Latikberg Sweden
126 E5 Latimer Iowa USA
233 E6 Latina Italy
242 A2 Latnamard Ireland
424 F4 Latouche Treville, Cape WA Australia
227 K1 Latowicz Poland
222 inset Látrar Iceland
242 A3 Latsey Ireland
243 H3 Latskoye Russian Federation
131 L3 Latta South Carolina USA
228 F5 Lattes France
222 K3 Latunjaure *lake* Sweden
393 D7 Latur Maharashtra India
225 M4 Latvia *country* Europe
78 O9 Lau Basin *underwater feature* Pacific Ocean
244 C4 Laudale Ho Highland Scotland UK
125 O2 Lauder Manitoba Canada
244 F5 Lauder Scottish Borders Scotland UK
225 O4 Lauderi Latvia
226 D2 Lauf an der Pegnitz Germany
226 G4 Laufen Germany
229 H3 Laufen Switzerland
226 E3 Lauffen Germany
117 M3 Lauge Koch Kyst *region* Greenland
222 M5 Lauhavuori *mountain* Finland
222 M1 Laukaa Finland
223 P5 Laukansalo Finland
225 M4 Lauker Sweden
222 L1 Laukøya *island* Norway
223 M1 Laukvik Norway
425 M10 Launceston Tas. Australia
240 C4 Launceston Cornwall England UK
245 C4 Laune *watercourse* Ireland
376 C4 Launglon Myanmar
226 E3 Laupheim Germany
425 M3 Laura Qld Australia
427 15a Laura Marshall Islands
162 C4 Laura, Bahía *bay* Argentina
245 C5 Lauragh Ireland
130 G5 Laurel Mississippi USA
125 K4 Laurel Montana USA
125 Q5 Laurel Nebraska USA
154 D3 Laurel Gacho Colombia
127 L6 Laurel Hill *range* Pennsylvania USA
131 I2 Laurel River Lake Kentucky USA
245 D3 Laurencetown Ireland
424 inset Laurens Peninsula Heard Island Australia
127 P3 Laurentian Highlands Québec Canada
233 F6 Lauria Italy
244 D6 Laurieston Dumfries and Galloway Scotland UK
131 L3 Laurinburg North Carolina USA
126 G3 Laurium Michigan USA
161 I4 Lauro Muller Brazil
229 H3 Lausanne Switzerland
374 F4 Laut *island* Indonesia
375 G4 Laut, Selat *strait* Indonesia
375 G5 Laut Kecil, Kepulauan *island* Indonesia
223 M3 Lautakoski Sweden
160 C6 Lautaro Chile
372 C6 Lautem Timor-Leste (East Timor)
229 H3 Lauterbrunnen Switzerland
427 9 Lauthala *island* Fiji
427 9a Lautoka Fiji
222 G4 Lauvøyfjorden *bay* Norway
222 G4 Lauvsnes Norway
224 C1 Lauvstad Norway
226 D1 Lauwersoog Netherlands
228 E4 Lauzerte France
309 I2 Lava, Nosy *island* Madagascar
129 N6 Lavaca Bay Texas USA
130 B9 Lavaderos Mexico
228 D2 Laval France
228 F4 Laval-Atger France
223 P4 Lavala Finland
391 H4 Lāvān, Jazireh-ye *island* Iran
160 C6 Lavapié, Punta *cape* Chile
231 G1 Lavardac France
391 I3 Lavari Āb Iran
228 E5 Lavaur France
228 E5 Lavelanet France
120 F8 Lavenham Manitoba Canada
241 H2 Lavenham Suffolk England UK
228 E5 Laveno Italy
373 J5 L'Averdy, Cape Papua New Guinea
125 P8 Laverne Oklahoma USA
226 E4 Lavertezzo Switzerland
424 G7 Laverton WA Australia
242 A3 Lavey Ireland
229 I5 Lavezzo, Col de *pass* Corsica France
225 L2 Lavia Finland
130 B9 Lavín Mexico
125 K3 Lavina Montana USA
232 D3 Lavis Italy
237 AI5 Lavka Integralsoyuza Russian Federation
436 T2 Lavoisier Island Antarctica
130 C4 Lavon Lake Texas USA
222 H3 Lávong Norway
131 J3 Lavonia Georgia USA
157 C8 Lavras Brazil
156 E4 Lavras da Mangabeira Brazil
116 B5 Lavrentiya Russian Federation
159 G4 Lavrinhas Brazil
437 H2 Law Dome *plain* Antarctica
121 P7 Lawagamau *watercourse* Ontario Canada
127 L2 Lawagamau Lake Ontario Canada
427 9a Lawaki Fiji
375 H6 Lawang *island* Indonesia
375 G2 Lawas Malaysia
121 N6 Lawashi *watercourse* Ontario Canada
372 B4 Lawata Indonesia
372 B5 Laweele Indonesia
375 K4 Lawin *island* Indonesia
375 G3 Lawit, Gunung *mountain* Indonesia
374 D2 Lawit, Gunung *mountain* Malaysia
243 F2 Lawkland North Yorkshire England UK
120 H4 Lawledge Manitoba Canada
123 K9 Lawn Newfoundland and Labrador Canada
130 B4 Lawn Texas USA
304 D2 Lawra Ghana
126 H7 Lawrence Indiana USA
126 D7 Lawrence Kansas USA
127 P5 Lawrence Massachusetts USA
130 H3 Lawrenceburg Tennessee USA
123 F10 Lawrencetown Nova Scotia Canada
242 B2 Lawrencetown Banbridge Northern Ireland UK
131 J4 Lawrenceville Georgia USA
127 M6 Lawrenceville Pennsylvania USA
128 C2 Laws California USA
131 J5 Lawtey Florida USA
130 B3 Lawton Oklahoma USA
390 C4 Lawz, Jabal al *mountain* Saudi Arabia
118 F5 Lax Kw'alaams British Columbia Canada
230 B2 Laxe, Cabo de *cape* Spain
242 D2 Laxey Isle of Man UK
244 inset Laxo Shetland Scotland UK
226 D3 Laxou France
222 I5 Laxsjö Sweden
224 H3 Laxsjön *lake* Sweden
304 D2 Lay Burkina Faso
228 D3 Lay *watercourse* France
131 H4 Lay Lake Alabama USA
375 G5 Layar, Tanjung *cape* Indonesia
236 K5 Laydënnyy, Mys *cape* Russian Federation
120 F8 Layland Manitoba Canada
158 D4 Layo Peru
228 D3 Layon *watercourse* France
163 11a Layou St Vincent and the Grenadines
379 H4 Layshi Myanmar
124 J6 Layton Utah USA
234 E2 Laza Romania
310 9b Lazare, Pointe *cape* Seychelles
437 A2 Lazarev Sea Southern Ocean
234 B3 Lazarevac Serbia
238 G6 Lazarevo Russian Federation
128 E5 Lázaro Cárdenas Mexico
129 I6 Lázaro Cárdenas Mexico
132 E5 Lázaro Cárdenas Mexico
132 D3 Lázaro Cárdenas, Presa *lake* Mexico
233 E5 Lazio *admin. area* Italy
226 F5 Lazise Italy
234 B3 Laznica Serbia
242 F2 Lazonby Cumbria England UK
227 L4 Lazuri Romania
161 G6 Lazzarino Argentina
228 D4 Le Barp France
228 E3 Le Blanc France
228 E4 Le Bourg France
229 H4 Le Bourg-d'Oisans France
426 7 Le Cap New Caledonia
228 F5 Le Cap d'Agde France
163 I4 Le Carbet Martinique
228 F1 Le Catelet France
228 F5 Le Caylar France
228 F3 Le Châtelet France
226 C3 Le Chesne France
226 C5 Le Cheylard France
228 B2 Le Conquet France
131 J3 Le Conte, Mount Tennessee USA
229 G3 Le Creusot France
241 I4 Le Crotoy France
163 I4 Le Diamant Martinique
228 F3 Le Donjon France
228 E3 Le Dorat France
123 H7 Le Doré, Lac *lake* Québec Canada
122 F3 Le Droit, Pointe *cape* Québec Canada
228 C2 Le Faouët France
163 I4 Le François Martinique
163 I6 Le Gosier Guadeloupe
126 E5 Le Grand Iowa USA
228 E3 Le Grand-Lucé France
228 E2 Le Grand-Quevilly France
228 E2 Le Havre France
163 I4 Le Lamentin Martinique
226 D5 Le Lauzet-Ubaye France
229 H5 Le Lavandou France
229 H3 Le Locle Switzerland
163 I4 Le Lorrain Martinique
228 E3 Le Lude France
162 D6 Le Maire, Estrecho de *strait* Argentina
228 E2 Le Mans France
162 C5 Le Marchand Argentina
163 I4 Le Marin Martinique
228 F4 Le Monastier-sur-Gazeille France
229 H4 Le Monêtier-les-Bains France
163 I4 Le Morne Rouge Martinique
163 I6 Le Moule Guadeloupe
122 D4 Le Moyne, Lac *lake* Québec Canada
231 F1 Le Muret France
229 H5 Le Muy France
228 C3 Le Palais France
228 F3 Le Parcq France
228 E2 Le Péage France
229 G4 Le Péage-de-Roussillon France
119 U3 Le Pensie Manitoba Canada
228 D3 Le Plessis France
226 B4 Le Pondy France
229 G5 Le Pontet France
228 D4 Le Porge France
310 7a Le Port Réunion
163 I4 Le Prêcheur Martinique
226 B2 Le Quesnoy France
163 I4 Le Robert Martinique
126 G6 Le Roy Illinois USA
121 R3 Le Roy, Lac *lake* Québec Canada
226 D4 Le Russey France
163 I4 Le Saint-Esprit Martinique
233 C8 Le Sers Tunisia
231 G2 Le Seu d'Urgell Spain
310 7a Le Tampon Réunion
226 C5 Le Teil France
228 D2 Le Teilleul France
376 E2 Lê Thanh Vietnam
241 I4 Le Touquet-Paris-Plage France
226 D4 Le Tour France
241 H5 Le Trait France
241 I4 Le Tréport France
163 I4 Le Vauclin Martinique
232 E5 Le Ville Italy
373 H6 Lea Lea Papua New Guinea
241 A3 Leabeg Ireland
245 E3 Leabeg Ireland
240 D2 Leabgarrow Ireland
121 V1 Leach Bay Nunavut Canada
125 N4 Lead South Dakota USA
241 G1 Leadenham Lincolnshire England UK
244 E5 Leadhills South Lanarkshire Scotland UK
125 L7 Leadville Colorado USA
126 F8 Leadwood Missouri USA
119 V4 Leaf Rapids Manitoba Canada
130 B6 Leakey Texas USA
244 C4 Lealt Argyll and Bute Scotland UK
244 B3 Lealt Highland Scotland UK
126 J5 Leamington Ontario Canada
124 I7 Leamington Utah USA
245 D5 Leamlara Ireland
124 G1 Leanchoil British Columbia Canada
245 C4 Leane, Lough *lake* Ireland
245 C4 Leanevglissane Ireland
309 I3 Leanja Madagascar
245 C4 Leansaghane Ireland
245 C5 Leap Ireland
131 I5 Leary Georgia USA
241 G3 Leatherhead Surrey England UK
126 D7 Leavenworth Kansas USA
224 I5 Łeba Poland
226 D3 Lebach Germany
305 G5 Lébamba Gabon
234 B4 Lebane Serbia
390 C2 Lebanon *country*
126 I8 Lebanon Kentucky USA
126 E8 Lebanon Missouri USA
127 O5 Lebanon New Hampshire USA
124 D4 Lebanon Oregon USA
127 M6 Lebanon Pennsylvania USA
388 I6 Lebap Welaýaty *admin. area* Turkmenistan
128 C3 Lebec California USA
304 B2 Lébékéré Guinea
117 L9 Lebel-sur-Quévillon Québec Canada
306 C3 Lebo Democratic Republic of Congo
126 D7 Lebo Kansas USA
224 I5 Lębork Poland
308 E4 Lebowakgomo South Africa
230 C5 Lebrija Spain
224 I5 Łebsko, Jezioro *lake* Poland
160 C6 Lebu Chile
154 C3 Lebvrija *watercourse* Colombia
233 H6 Lecce Italy
226 E5 Lecco Italy
231 F3 Lécera Spain
235 B7 Lechaina Greece
132 E3 Leche, Lago La *lake* Mexico
134 E2 Leche, Laguna de *lake* Cuba
381 G3 Lecheng Guangdong China
234 D2 Lechința Romania
243 F2 Leck Lancashire England UK
244 C3 Leckie Highland Scotland UK
130 E5 Lecompte Louisiana USA
306 A4 Léconi Gabon
305 G5 Léconi *watercourse* Gabon
228 E5 Lectoure France
227 L2 Łęczna Poland
374 D3 Ledang, Gunung *mountain* Malaysia
227 I4 Ledava *watercourse* Slovenia
240 E2 Ledbury Herefordshire England UK
230 D3 Ledesma Spain
244 D2 Ledmore Highland Scotland UK
223 Q4 Ledmozero Russian Federation
223 R4 Ledmozero, Ozero *lake* Russian Federation
374 F3 Ledo Indonesia
119 O6 Leduc Alberta Canada
241 F3 Ledwell Oxfordshire England UK
245 C5 Lee *watercourse* Ireland
240 C3 Lee Devon England UK
242 E2 Leece Cumbria England UK
126 D3 Leech Lake Minnesota USA
130 B3 Leedey Oklahoma USA
243 G3 Leeds West Yorkshire England UK
131 H4 Leeds Alabama USA
125 P2 Leeds North Dakota USA
128 F2 Leeds Utah USA
243 F3 Leeds and Liverpool Canal England UK
226 D1 Leek Netherlands
241 E1 Leek Staffordshire England UK
245 C3 Leenane Ireland
241 F2 Lees Derbyshire England UK
243 G3 Lees West Yorkshire England UK
126 D7 Lees Summit Missouri USA
131 I3 Leesburg Alabama USA
131 K6 Leesburg Florida USA
131 I5 Leesburg Georgia USA
126 I6 Leesburg Indiana USA
126 J7 Leesburg Ohio USA
127 M7 Leesburg Virginia USA
226 C1 Leeuwarden Netherlands
424 E8 Leeuwin, Cape WA Australia
81 P8 Leeuwin Sill *underwater feature* Indian Ocean
135 I3 Leeward Islands Caribbean
305 H5 Léfini *watercourse* Congo
235 D8 Lefka Ori *range* Greece
235 B6 Lefkada Greece
235 B6 Lefkada *island* Greece
130 A3 Lefors Texas USA
121 T3 Lefroy *watercourse* Québec Canada
424 G7 Lefroy, Lake WA Australia
119 O6 Legal Alberta Canada
230 E3 Leganés Spain
120 M7 Legarde *watercourse* Ontario Canada
377 I4 Legazpi Philippines
228 D3 Legé France
240 E2 Legion Cross Herefordshire England UK
227 K1 Legionowo Poland
226 F5 Legnago Italy
227 I2 Legnica Poland
374 F5 Legokjawa Indonesia
232 G3 Legrad Croatia
424 G8 LeGrand, Cape WA Australia
228 C2 Léguer *watercourse* France
306 D3 Legwe *watercourse* Democratic Republic of Congo
392 D3 Leh Jammu and Kashmir India/Pakistan
127 N6 Lehighton Pennsylvania USA
234 E3 Lehliu-Gară Romania
222 M5 Lehmäjoki Finland
223 N3 Lehmikumpu Finland
223 P5 Lehmo Finland
125 P3 Lehr North Dakota USA
226 F1 Lehre Germany
226 E1 Lehrte Germany
223 M5 Lehtimäki Finland
225 L3 Lehtma Nina *cape* Estonia
223 O4 Lehtovaara Finland
160 C6 Lehuelán Chile
308 D4 Lehututu Botswana
227 H4 Leibnitz Austria
241 F2 Leicester Leicester England UK
243 G4 Leicester *admin. area* England UK
241 F2 Leicestershire *admin. area* England UK
425 K4 Leichhardt *watercourse* Qld Australia
226 C1 Leiden Netherlands
225 N3 Leie Estonia
226 F1 Leiferde Germany
422 F3 Leigh New Zealand
241 E3 Leigh Gloucestershire England UK
243 F3 Leigh Greater Manchester England UK
125 Q6 Leigh Nebraska USA
425 K7 Leigh Creek SA Australia
241 G3 Leighton Buzzard Bedfordshire England UK
222 K2 Leinavatnet *lake* Norway
226 E1 Leine *watercourse* Germany
223 P4 Leino Finland

225 O2 Leino Finland
424 G6 Leinster WA Australia
245 F4 Leinster, Mount mountain Ireland
240 E2 Leintwardine Herefordshire England UK
222 L3 Leipojärvi Sweden
235 E7 Leipsoi island Greece
226 G2 Leipzig Germany
222 F5 Leira Norway
222 K2 Leirbukta Norway
230 B4 Leiria Portugal
230 B4 Leiria admin. area Portugal
224 C3 Leirvik Norway
241 I2 Leiston Suffolk England UK
225 L3 Leisu Estonia
126 H8 Leitchfield Kentucky USA
244 E5 Leithen Lodge Scottish Borders Scotland UK
423 E6 Leithfield Beach New Zealand
373 G4 Leitre Papua New Guinea
245 D3 Leitrim Ireland
245 E2 Leitrim admin. area Ireland
154 B4 Leiva Colombia
223 P5 Leivonmäki Finland
225 N2 Leivonmäki Finland
381 F3 Leiyang Hunan China
380 F5 Leizhou Guangdong China
380 F5 Leizhou Wan bay Guangdong China
154 C4 Lejanías Colombia
222 G4 Leka island Norway
306 C4 Lekatero Democratic Republic of Congo
305 G5 Lékéti watercourse Congo
300 D5 Lekhcheb Mauritania
225 P5 Lekhovo Russian Federation
305 G5 Lékila Gabon
372 C4 Lekitobi Indonesia
222 E5 Leknes Norway
305 G5 Lékona watercourse Congo
305 G5 Lékoumou admin. area Congo
223 G5 Leksdalsvatn lake Norway
223 U6 Lekshmozero Russian Federation
223 Q5 Leksozero, Ozero lake Russian Federation
222 G5 Leksvik Norway
375 K3 Lelai, Tanjung cape Indonesia
222 H3 Leland Norway
224 G3 Lelång lake Sweden
162 B3 Leleque Argentina
308 C6 Leliefontein South Africa
155 H3 Lelydorp Suriname
226 C1 Lelystad Netherlands
224 E4 Lem Denmark
307 G3 Lema Shilindi Ethiopia
229 H3 Léman, Lac (Lake Geneva) lake Switzerland/France
373 J5 Lemankoa Papua New Guinea
229 H2 Lembach France
375 H6 Lembar Indonesia
225 K5 Lembas Lithuania
228 D5 Lembeye France
375 H3 Lembu Indonesia
374 C2 Lembu, Gunung mountain Indonesia
157 C8 Leme Brazil
223 P4 Lemetinvaara Finland
124 I4 Lemhi watercourse Idaho USA
225 N2 Lemi Finland
117 M6 Lemieux Islands Nunavut Canada
223 N2 Lemmenjoen kansallispuisto park Finland
223 O2 Lemmenjoki Finland
125 N4 Lemmon South Dakota USA
128 C2 Lemoore California USA
118 J5 Lemoray British Columbia Canada
226 B5 Lempdes France
119 Q7 Lemsford Saskatchewan Canada
305 F3 Lemu Nigeria
162 A3 Lemu, Isla island Chile
374 F3 Lemukutan island Indonesia
224 E4 Lemvig Denmark
376 B3 Lemyethna Myanmar
237 X7 Lena watercourse Russian Federation
229 I4 Lena, Capo cape Italy
80 J10 Lena Tablemount underwater feature Southern Ocean
245 C2 Lenadoon Point Ireland
245 E1 Lenan Ireland
375 H6 Lenangguar Indonesia
232 F3 Lenart Slovenia
157 B8 Lençóis Paulista Brazil
306 D3 Lenda watercourse Democratic Republic of Congo
244 D5 Lendalfoot South Ayrshire Scotland UK
223 Q5 Lendery Russian Federation
119 R6 Leney Saskatchewan Canada
372 E4 Lengguru watercourse Indonesia
222 H4 Lenglingen lake Norway
384 E5 Lenglong Ling mountain Gansu China
384 E5 Lenglong Ling range Gansu China
381 F3 Lengshuijiang Hunan China
381 F3 Lengshuitan Hunan China
160 C4 Lengua de Vaca, Punta cape Chile
389 K6 Lenina, Pik mountain Tajikistan
389 K6 Leningrad Tajikistan
225 P3 Leningradskaya Oblast' admin. area Russian Federation
237 AK5 Leningradskiy Russian Federation
389 N3 Leninogorsk Kazakhstan
389 K5 Leninpol' Kyrgyzstan
388 J4 Leninsk Kazakhstan
388 E4 Leninsk Russian Federation
389 O2 Leninsk-Kuznetskiy Russian Federation
238 G5 Leninskiy Russian Federation
226 D4 Lenk Switzerland
234 E1 Lenkovtsy Ukraine
372 D4 Lenmalu Indonesia
242 A2 Lennaght Ireland
226 E2 Lenne watercourse Germany
226 E2 Lennestadt Germany
437 K1 Lennox-King Glacier Antarctica
232 D4 Leno Italy
131 K3 Lenoir North Carolina USA
125 P7 Lenora Kansas USA
119 S6 Lenore Lake Saskatchewan Canada
228 F1 Lens France
237 X6 Lensk Russian Federation
222 F5 Lensvik Norway
388 D5 Lentekhi Georgia
227 I4 Lenti Hungary
223 P4 Lentiira Finland
241 G2 Lenton Lincolnshire England UK
223 P4 Lentua lake Finland
238 G3 Lent'yevo Russian Federation
304 D2 Léo Burkina Faso
118 I5 Leo Creek British Columbia Canada
232 E3 Leoben Austria
228 D4 Léognan France
372 B3 Leok Indonesia
375 I3 Leok Indonesia
130 E3 Leola Arkansas USA
240 E2 Leominster Herefordshire England UK
127 P5 Leominster Massachusetts USA
228 D5 Léon France
132 E4 León Mexico
134 C4 León Nicaragua
230 D2 León Spain
130 C2 Leon Kansas USA
129 N5 Leon watercourse Texas USA
228 D5 Léon, Étang de lake France
132 D2 Leon, Presa Luis L. lake Mexico
162 D3 León, Punta cape Argentina
129 K8 Leon Guzmán Mexico
133 I4 Leona Vicario Mexico
130 C4 Leonard Texas USA
308 C4 Leonardville Namibia
125 Q7 Leonardville Kansas USA
427 12c Leone American Samoa
162 D2 Leone, Valle valley Argentina
233 E5 Leonessa Italy
233 F8 Leonforte Italy
425 M9 Leongatha Vic. Australia
424 G7 Leonora WA Australia
237 AH4 Leont'yeva, Ostrov island Russian Federation
245 B3 Leopardstown Ireland
437 F2 Leopold and Astrid Coast Antarctica
232 G2 Leopoldov Slovakia
234 D3 Leordeni Romania
125 O7 Leoti Kansas USA
119 R6 Leoville Saskatchewan Canada
374 E4 Lepar island Indonesia
241 F4 Lepe Hampshire England UK
122 B2 Lepellé watercourse Québec Canada
308 E4 Lephalala watercourse South Africa
308 E4 Lephalale (Ellisras) South Africa
308 E4 Lephepe Botswana
244 C4 Lephinmore Argyll and Bute Scotland UK
381 H3 Leping Jiangxi China
235 D6 Lepoura Greece
223 M2 Leppäjärvi Finland
223 N5 Leppävesi lake Finland
223 O5 Leppävirta Finland
422 F4 Lepperton New Zealand
238 D2 Leppyasel'kya Russian Federation
389 M4 Lepsy Kazakhstan
235 C5 Leptokarya Greece
300 D5 Leqceïba Mauritania
381 H3 Leqing Zhejiang China
222 G5 Ler Norway
304 D3 Léraba watercourse Burkina Faso
308 E4 Lerala Botswana
436 W1 Lerchenfeld Glacier Antarctica
133 G5 Lerdo de Tejada Mexico
305 G3 Léré Chad
300 F5 Léré Mali
373 F4 Lereh Indonesia
230 F2 Lerín Spain
222 J5 Leringen bay Sweden
132 E4 Lerma watercourse Mexico
230 E2 Lerma Spain
233 C6 Lerno, Monte mountain Sardinia Italy
235 E7 Leros island Greece
224 F3 Lervik Norway
244 inset Lerwick Shetland Scotland UK
229 G4 Les Abrets France
163 16 Les Abymes Guadeloupe
228 D5 Les Aldudes France
310 9 Les Amirantes island Seychelles
163 14 Les Anses-d'Arlets Martinique
231 G3 Les Borges Blanques Spain
135 F3 Les Cayes Haiti
123 C9 Les Éboulements Québec Canada
229 G4 Les Échelles France
123 D8 Les Escoumins Québec Canada
228 D3 Les Essarts France
228 B3 Les Gets France
241 I5 Les Hayons France
135 F3 Les Irois Haiti
229 G3 Les Laumes France
121 V8 Les Méchins Québec Canada
229 G4 Les Mées France
228 D2 Les Pieux France
228 D3 Les Sables-d'Olonne France
163 16 Les Saintes island Guadeloupe
163 14 Les Trois-Îlets Martinique
228 G4 Les Vans France
234 B4 Lešak Kosovo
230 F2 Lesaka Spain
231 H2 L'Escala Spain
228 D5 Lescar France
122 A2 Lesdiguières, Lac lake Québec Canada
380 D2 Leshan Sichuan China
236 K6 Leshukonskoye Russian Federation
232 F2 Lesiów Poland
222 F5 Lesja Norway
223 N4 Leskelä Finland
234 F3 Leski Ukraine
227 I3 Lesko Poland
437 F2 Leskov Island Antarctica
234 B4 Leskovac Serbia
226 C3 Lesmont France
229 L1 Leśna Poland
227 J1 Leśna Jania Poland
237 AH7 Lesnaya Russian Federation
228 B2 Lesneven France
234 A3 Lešnica Serbia
238 E3 Lesnoye Russian Federation
236 T7 Lesosibirsk Russian Federation
308 E5 Lesotho country Africa
386 G2 Lesozavodsk Russian Federation
228 D4 Lesparre-Médoc France
422 5 L'Esperance Rock island Kermadec Islands New Zealand
231 F2 Lesperon France
231 G3 L'Espluga de Francolí Spain
163 G3 Lesser Antilles island Caribbean
116 N5 Lesser Slave watercourse Alberta Canada
116 H7 Lesser Slave Lake Alberta Canada
372 B6 Lesser Sunda Islands Indonesia
121 T2 Lestage watercourse Québec Canada
228 E3 Lesterps France
223 N5 Lestijärvi lake Finland
223 N5 Lestijoki watercourse Finland
372 C3 Lesung, Bukit mountain Indonesia
235 E6 Lesvos island Greece
244 C6 Leswalt Dumfries and Galloway Scotland UK
227 I2 Leszno Poland
123 H9 L'Étang-du-Nord Québec Canada
125 P5 Letcher South Dakota USA
241 G3 Letchworth Hertfordshire England UK
232 G3 Letenye Hungary
379 G4 Letha Myanmar
119 O8 Lethbridge Alberta Canada
155 G4 Lethem Guyana
372 C6 Leti island Indonesia
372 C6 Leti, Kepulauan island Indonesia
308 D4 Letiahau watercourse Botswana
158 D2 Leticia Colombia
385 I5 Leting Hebei China
308 E4 Letlhakane Botswana
308 E4 Letlhakeng Botswana
223 S4 Letnerechenskiy Russian Federation
234 D4 Letnitsa Bulgaria
223 T4 Letniy Navolok Russian Federation
223 S4 Letnyaya Reka Russian Federation
376 B3 Letpadan Myanmar
376 C5 Letsok-aw Kyun Myanmar
224 H2 Letsjön lake Sweden
305 G4 Letta Cameroon
227 G2 Letten lake Sweden
245 C3 Letter Ireland
245 D3 Lettera Ireland
245 E2 Letterkenny Ireland
245 D2 Lettermacaward Ireland
245 C3 Lettermullan Ireland
125 R1 Lettonia Manitoba Canada
374 E3 Letung Indonesia
243 G3 Letwell South Yorkshire England UK
372 D5 Letwurung Indonesia
234 C3 Leu Romania
308 D2 Lèuá Angola
233 H7 Leuca, Capo Santa Maria di cape Italy
228 F5 Leucate France
244 F4 Leuchers Fife Scotland UK
226 D4 Leukerbad Switzerland
244 B2 Leumrabhagh Na h-Eileanan Siar Scotland UK
229 K1 Leuna Germany
128 G3 Leupp Corner Arizona USA
374 C3 Leuser, Gunung mountain Indonesia
229 G1 Leuven Belgium
374 E5 Leuwiliang Indonesia
388 C2 Lev Tolstoy Russian Federation
222 G5 Levanger Norway
232 C4 Levante, Riviera de region Italy
233 E7 Levanzo, Isola di island Italy
223 O3 Leväranta Finland
162 A3 Level, Isla island Chile
129 K4 Levelland Texas USA
119 W5 Leven Manitoba Canada
243 H3 Leven East Riding of Yorkshire England UK
244 E4 Leven Fife Scotland UK
242 F2 Levens Cumbria England UK
244 inset Levenwick Shetland Scotland UK
424 G4 Leveque, Cape WA Australia
423 6 L'Eveque, Cape Chatham Islands New Zealand
226 D2 Leverkusen Germany
241 H1 Leverton Lincolnshire England UK
228 F3 Levet France
227 J3 Levice Slovakia
226 F4 Levico Terme Italy
229 H3 Levier France
423 F5 Levin New Zealand
244 D3 Levishie Highland Scotland UK
235 F7 Levitha island Greece
223 O4 Levo-oja Finland
232 F5 Levrnaka island Croatia
228 E3 Levroux France
234 D4 Levski Bulgaria
427 9a Levuka Fiji
228 D2 Lévy, Cap cape France
372 A6 Lewa Indonesia
379 H5 Lewe Myanmar
125 N6 Lewellen Nebraska USA
127 N7 Lewes Delaware USA
123 K9 Lewin's Cove Newfoundland and Labrador Canada
125 Q2 Lewis Manitoba Canada
129 M2 Lewis Kansas USA
126 C5 Lewis and Clark Lake Nebraska USA
123 I8 Lewis Hills Newfoundland and Labrador Canada
124 I2 Lewis Range Montana USA
130 H3 Lewis Smith Lake Alabama USA
126 H8 Lewisburg Kentucky USA
130 H3 Lewisburg Tennessee USA
127 K8 Lewisburg West Virginia USA
241 G3 Lewisham Greater London England UK
124 G3 Lewiston Idaho USA
127 P4 Lewiston Maine USA
124 J6 Lewiston Utah USA
126 F6 Lewistown Illinois USA
125 K3 Lewistown Montana USA
130 C4 Lewisville Texas USA
131 C4 Lewisville Lake Texas USA
130 F4 Lexington Mississippi USA
125 P6 Lexington Nebraska USA
131 K3 Lexington North Carolina USA
124 F4 Lexington Oregon USA
127 L8 Lexington Virginia USA
126 I7 Lexington-Fayette Kentucky USA
240 C4 Ley Cornwall England UK
310 6b Leygues, Îles island French Southern and Antarctic Lands
242 F3 Leyland Lancashire England UK
228 D4 Leyre watercourse France
229 H3 Leysin Switzerland
377 J5 Leyte Gulf Philippines
240 C4 Lezant Cornwall England UK
235 A5 Lezhë Albania
394 E2 L'gov Russian Federation
379 F3 Lhagoi Kangri mountain Xizang Zizhiqu China
379 G3 Lhasa Xizang Zizhiqu China
227 H3 Lhenice Czech Republic
228 F4 L'Herm France
372 B4 Lhokkruet Indonesia
374 C2 Lhokseumawe Indonesia
374 C2 Lhoksukon Indonesia
379 G3 Lhuntshi Bhutan
379 G3 Lhuntsi Dzong Bhutan
Li Jiang see Dayan China
380 F2 Li Shui watercourse Hunan China
235 B6 Liakas, Akra cape Greece
158 C4 Liamayoc, Cerro mountain Peru
308 D3 Liambezi, Lake lake Botswana
163 I9 Liamuiga, Mount volcano St Kitts and Nevis
381 G4 Lian Jiang lake Guangdong China
380 E3 Liancheng Guizhou China
380 I4 Liancheng Yunnan China
386 G4 Liancourt Rocks island
381 G3 Lianfeng Fujian China
372 B4 Liang Indonesia
375 I4 Liang Indonesia
374 D3 Liang Timur, Gunung mountain Malaysia
377 J5 Lianga Philippines
377 J5 Lianga Bay Philippines
385 G5 Liangcheng Nei Mongol Zizhiqu China
380 E1 Liangdan Gansu China
380 D1 Lianghekou Gansu China
375 G3 Liangpran, Bukit mountain Indonesia
380 E2 Liangshan Chongqing China
385 H6 Liangshan Shandong China
380 F4 Lianjiang Guangdong China
381 G3 Lianjiang Jiangxi China
381 H1 Lianyungang Jiangsu China
381 F4 Lianzhou Guangdong China
380 F4 Lianzhou Guangxi Zhuangzu Zizhiqu China
380 D4 Lianzhu Yunnan China
385 H6 Liaocheng Shandong China
385 J5 Liaodong Wan bay Liaoning China
385 J4 Liaoning admin. area China
385 J4 Liaoyang Liaoning China
385 K4 Liaoyuan Jilin China
116 G7 Liard watercourse British Columbia Canada
118 J2 Liard watercourse Northwest Territories Canada
118 F2 Liard watercourse Yukon Territory Canada
118 I2 Liard Range Northwest Territories Canada
118 H3 Liard River British Columbia Canada
391 K4 Liari Pakistan
374 E4 Liat island Indonesia
244 D3 Liatrie Highland Scotland UK
427 15 Lib island Marshall Islands
154 C3 Líbano Colombia
244 E5 Libberton South Lanarkshire Scotland UK
124 H2 Libby Montana USA
229 J5 Libeccio, Punta cape Italy
306 B3 Libenge Democratic Republic of Congo
227 K1 Liberadz Poland
125 O8 Liberal Kansas USA
227 H2 Liberec Czech Republic
227 H2 Liberecký Kraj admin. area Czech Republic
304 C3 Liberia country Africa
134 C5 Liberia Costa Rica
160 D5 Libertador General Bernardo O'Higgins admin. area Chile
160 E2 Libertador General San Martín Argentina
126 D7 Liberty Missouri USA
127 N6 Liberty New York USA
130 D5 Liberty Texas USA
124 G3 Liberty Lake Washington USA
229 G2 Libin Belgium
375 K4 Libobo, Tanjung cape Indonesia
308 E6 Libode South Africa
307 G3 Liboi Kenya
308 D2 Libonda Zambia
227 H2 Libouchec Czech Republic
228 D4 Libourne France
235 B5 Librazhd Albania
305 F4 Libreville Gabon
301 J3 Libya country Africa
302 C2 Libyan Desert Libya
Libyan Plateau see Aḍ Ḍiffah Egypt
129 I6 Lic. A Lopez Mateos Mexico
394 G5 Lice Turkey
381 H3 Licheng Fujian China
381 H1 Licheng Jiangsu China
385 H6 Licheng Shanxi China
241 F2 Lichfield Staffordshire England UK
309 G2 Lichinga Mozambique
229 J1 Lichte Germany
227 H3 Lichtenau Austria
308 E5 Lichtenburg South Africa
121 R6 Lichteneger, Lac lake Québec Canada
380 E2 Lichuan Hubei China
227 H5 Lička Jesenica Croatia
232 F4 Lički Osik Croatia
126 I7 Licking watercourse Kentucky USA
126 F8 Licking Missouri USA
227 H5 Licko Lešće Croatia
225 M6 Lida Belarus
244 F2 Liddel Orkney Islands Scotland UK
222 J5 Liden Sweden
308 C4 Lidfontein Namibia
241 H2 Lidgate Suffolk England UK
425 inset Lidgbird, Mount Lord Howe Island Australia
224 G3 Lidköping Sweden
232 E4 Lido island Italy
235 C6 Lidoriki Greece
222 I4 Lidsjöberg Sweden
222 K4 Lidträsket lake Sweden
227 J1 Lidzbark Poland
227 H4 Liebenfels Austria
119 Q7 Liebenthal Saskatchewan Canada
129 M1 Liebenthal Kansas USA
227 H2 Lieberose Germany
234 B3 Liebling Romania
226 Liechtenstein country Europe
229 G1 Liège Belgium
223 M2 Liejankijärvi lake Finland
306 C3 Lieki Democratic Republic of Congo
223 O4 Liekola Finland
223 Q5 Lieksa Finland
225 N4 Liel Kalupes ezers lake Latvia
238 B4 Lielais Ludzas lake Latvia
225 L2 Lielax Finland
225 L4 Lielupe watercourse Latvia
225 M4 Lielvārde Latvia
225 K4 Liepāja Latvia
225 K4 Liepājas admin. area Latvia
225 K4 Liepājas ezers lake Latvia
225 K4 Liepene Latvia
225 L5 Lieplaukė Lithuania
225 N4 Liepna Latvia
229 G1 Lier Belgium
226 C4 Liernais France
228 E2 Lierville France
223 N3 Liesjärvi Finland
225 L2 Liesjärvi lake Finland
228 F2 Liesse France
229 H3 Liestal Switzerland
226 C2 Liesveld Netherlands
225 L2 Lieto Finland
225 N/O2 Lietvesi lake Finland
228 E2 Lieurey France
223 O5 Lievestuore Finland
225 M1 Lievestuoreenjärvi lake Finland
228 F1 Liévin France
127 N4 Lièvre watercourse Québec Canada
227 H4 Liezen Austria
306 C3 Lifanga Democratic Republic of Congo
245 F3 Liffey watercourse Ireland
245 E2 Lifford Ireland
228 D2 Liffré France
426 7 Lifou island New Caledonia
427 10 Lifuka island Tonga
225 M4 Ligatne Latvia
377 I4 Ligaya Philippines
235 B6 Ligeni I Butrintit lake Albania
228 F3 Lignières France
125 N2 Lignite North Dakota USA
309 G3 Ligonha watercourse Mozambique
228 E3 Ligueil France
228 E3 Ligugé France
132 C3 Ligui Mexico
232 C4 Liguria admin. area Italy
229 I5 Ligurian Sea Europe
373 J4 Lihir Island Papua New Guinea
223 N5 Lihjamo Finland
425 O4 Lihou Reef Coral Sea Islands Territory Australia
222 H3 Lihovdet island Norway
128 inset Lihu'e Hawai'i USA
160 E6 Lihuel-Calel Argentina
225 L3 Lihula Estonia
225 L3 Liivi laht bay Estonia
380 D4 Lijiang Yunnan China
385 I5 Lijin Shandong China
306 D6 Likasi Democratic Republic of Congo
306 C3 Likati Democratic Republic of Congo
118 K6 Likely British Columbia Canada
306 C4 Likete Democratic Republic of Congo
238 F4 Likhoslavl' Russian Federation
373 F4 Liki island Indonesia
427 15 Likiep Atoll Marshall Islands
306 C3 Likimi Democratic Republic of Congo
372 C6 Likisia Timor-Leste (East Timor)
224 D3 Liknes Norway
305 H4 Likouala admin. area Congo
305 H5 Likouala watercourse Congo
305 H4 Likouala aux Herbes watercourse Congo
238 C3 Likovskoye Russian Federation
224 I3 Likstammen lake Sweden
374 F3 Liku Indonesia
375 G2 Liku Malaysia
422 4 Liku Niue New Zealand
306 C3 Likulu Democratic Republic of Congo
372 C3 Likupang Indonesia
131 I4 Lilburn Georgia USA
229 I5 L'Île-Rousse Corsica France
306 C3 Lileko Democratic Republic of Congo
306 C3 Lilenga Democratic Republic of Congo
78 O4 Liliuokalani Ridge underwater feature Pacific Ocean
225 N2 Liljendal Finland
222 I4 Lill-Björkvattnet bay Sweden
222 K3 Lill-Mattaure lake Sweden
222 L3 Lilla Luleälven lake Sweden
222 K5 Lillarmsjö Sweden
228 F1 Lille France
222 I2 Lille Molla island Norway
241 H5 Lillebonne France
224 F2 Lillehammer Norway
228 F1 Lillers France
224 E3 Lillesand Norway
240 E2 Lilleshall Telford and Wrekin England UK
222 L2 Lillestraumen bay Norway
119 S7 Lillestrom Saskatchewan Canada
222 I6 Lillhärdal Sweden
222 I5 Lillholmsjö Sweden
225 M3 Lilli Estonia
437 K2 Lillie Glacier Antarctica
222 I4 Lilljorn bay Sweden
222 L4 Lillkägeträsk Sweden
222 J4 Lillögda Sweden
118 K7 Lillooet British Columbia Canada
118 J7 Lillooet watercourse British Columbia Canada
118 J7 Lillooet Lake British Columbia Canada
118 J7 Lillooet Range British Columbia Canada
222 K4 Lillsele Sweden
223 M3 Lillselet Sweden
222 I5 Lillsjöhögen Sweden
309 F2 Lilongwe Malawi
309 F2 Lilongwe watercourse Malawi
118 I6 Lily Lake British Columbia Canada
234 C4 Lilyache Bulgaria
425 M9 Lilydale Vic. Australia
305 H3 Lim watercourse Cameroon
234 A4 Lim watercourse Montenegro
158 B4 Lima Peru
158 B3 Lima admin. area Peru
126 I6 Lima Ohio USA
157 D8 Lima Duarte Brazil
124 I4 Lima Reservoir Montana USA
388 C4 Liman Vostochnyy lake Russian Federation
227 K3 Limanowa Poland
159 G2 Limão Brazil
159 H2 Limão Brazil
160 D4 Limarí watercourse Chile
374 E3 Limas Indonesia
394 E6 Limassol Cyprus
245 F1 Limavady Limavady Northern Ireland UK
245 F1 Limavady admin. area Northern Ireland UK
162 C2 Limay watercourse Argentina
228 E2 Limay France
134 C4 Limbaica Nicaragua
375 G2 Limbang Malaysia
377 G6 Limbang watercourse Malaysia
225 M4 Limbaži Latvia
225 M4 Limbažu admin. area Latvia
393 C6 Limbdi Gujarat India
372 B6 Limbung Indonesia
375 G4 Limbungan Indonesia
229 G1 Limburg admin. area Belgium
226 C2 Limburg admin. area Netherlands
232 F3 Limbuš Slovenia
157 C8 Limeira Brazil
245 D4 Limerick Ireland
245 F4 Limerick Ireland
245 D4 Limerick admin. area Ireland
245 D4 Limerick Junction Ireland
133 F2 Limestone, Lake Texas USA
119 V6 Limestone Point Manitoba Canada
134 C4 Limeta Honduras
224 E4 Limfjorden lake Denmark
222 H4 Limingen lake Norway
223 M3 Limingojärvi Sweden
223 N4 Liminka Finland
235 D6 Limnos island Greece
156 B3 Limoeiro do Ajuru Brazil
156 F4 Limoeiro do Norte Brazil
228 E4 Limoges France
228 E4 Limogne France
125 N7 Limon Colorado USA
133 H5 Limones Mexico
226 B3 Limours France
228 E4 Limousin admin. area France
228 F4 Limousin region France
228 F5 Limoux France
309 F4 Limpopo watercourse Mozambique
308 E4 Limpopo admin. area South Africa
308 E4 Limpopo watercourse South Africa
422 4 Limufuafua Point Niue New Zealand
380 D4 Lin`an Yunnan China
222 L3 Linaälven Sweden
222 L3 Linaälven watercourse Sweden
223 Q2 Linakhamari Russian Federation
162 B2 Linao Chile
377 H5 Linapacan island Philippines
160 D5 Linares Chile
133 F3 Linares Mexico
230 E3 Linares Spain
230 E3 Linares, Embalse de lake Spain
235 D6 Linaria Greece
233 E5 Linaro, Capo cape Italy
375 G3 Linau Balui plain Malaysia
241 F1 Linby Nottinghamshire England UK
226 C2 Lincent Belgium
380 F5 Lincheng Hainan China
380 F3 Lincheng Hunan China
381 G3 Linchuan Jiangxi China
436 R1 Linck Nunataks mountain Antarctica
160 F5 Lincoln Argentina
243 H3 Lincoln Lincolnshire England UK
131 H4 Lincoln Alabama USA
126 G6 Lincoln Illinois USA
127 Q4 Lincoln Maine USA
116 H9 Lincoln Montana USA
125 Q6 Lincoln Nebraska USA
125 O3 Lincoln North Dakota USA
127 P4 Lincoln, Mount New Hampshire USA
116 G10 Lincoln City Oregon USA
377 G3 Lincoln Island Paracel Islands
117 N2 Lincoln Sea Canada/Greenland
243 H3 Lincolnshire admin. area England UK
131 J4 Lincolnton Georgia USA
131 K3 Lincolnton North Carolina USA
124 F3 Lind Washington USA
159 I5 Linda Vista Brazil
224 C2 Lindås-Halvøya island Norway
226 G1 Lindau Germany
119 P6 Lindbergh Alberta Canada
159 E5 Linde Bolivia
224 E4 Linde Denmark
425 N5 Lindeman Group island Qld Australia
155 G3 Linden Guyana
130 H4 Linden Alabama USA
128 B1 Linden California USA
Lindenow Fjord see Kangerlussuatsiaq Greenland
224 D4 Lindesnes bay Norway
306 D3 Lindi watercourse Democratic Republic of Congo
307 F5 Lindi Tanzania
307 F5 Lindi admin. area Tanzania
385 J3 Lindian Heilongjiang China
161 G2 Lindo, Monte watercourse Paraguay
224 I2 Lindön island Sweden
385 I4 Lindong Nei Mongol Zizhiqu China
235 F7 Lindos, Akra cape Greece
127 L4 Lindsay Ontario Canada
128 C2 Lindsay California USA
125 Q6 Lindsay Nebraska USA
125 Q7 Lindsborg Kansas USA
243 G3 Lindwell West Yorkshire England UK
426 1 Line Islands Kiribati
391 M2 Line of Control Pakistan
222 F5 Linesøya island Norway
384 G6 Linfen Shanxi China
377 I3 Lingayen Philippines
377 H3 Lingayen Gulf Philippines
380 F1 Lingbao Henan China
381 H1 Lingcheng Anhui China
380 F4 Lingcheng Guangxi Zhuangzu Zizhiqu China
380 F5 Lingcheng Hainan China
380 F3 Lingchuan Guangxi Zhuangzu Zizhiqu China
385 H6 Lingchuan Shanxi China
222 E5 Linge Norway
226 D1 Lingen Germany
241 G3 Lingfield Surrey England UK
374 E4 Lingga island Indonesia
375 F3 Lingga Malaysia
374 E3 Lingga, Kepulauan island Indonesia
383 H6 Linggo Co mountain Xizang Zizhiqu China
385 J4 Linghai Liaoning China
380 E2 Lingjiang Sichuan China
375 H2 Lingkabau Malaysia
375 H3 Lingkas Indonesia
306 C3 Lingomo Democratic Republic of Congo
384 G6 Lingshi Shanxi China
385 H5 Lingshou Hebei China
393 D8 Lingsugur Karnataka India
300 C5 Linguère Senegal
380 F3 Lingui Guangxi Zhuangzu Zizhiqu China
384 F5 Lingwu Zishiqu China
380 F2 Lingxi Hunan China
381 H3 Lingxi Zhejiang China
381 F2 Lingyang Hunan China
385 I4 Lingyuan Liaoning China
381 H1 Linhai Jiangsu China
381 I3 Linhai Zhejiang China
157 D7 Linhares Brazil
384 F5 Linhe Nei Mongol Zizhiqu China
224 J5 Liniewo Poland
381 G3 Linjiang Fujian China
385 K4 Linjiang Jilin China
223 M3 Linkka Sweden
224 H3 Linköping Sweden
385 L3 Linkou Heilongjiang China
225 L4 Linkuva Lithuania
130 B7 Linn Texas USA
223 N5 Linnankylä Finland
223 P5 Linnansaari kansallispuisto park Finland
244 C4 Linnhe, Loch bay Scotland UK
126 E4 Lino Lakes Minnesota USA
233 E9 Linosa, Isola di island Italy
385 H6 Linqing Hebei China
385 I6 Linqu Shandong China
381 G1 Linquan Anhui China
158 D4 Linquipata Peru
157 B8 Lins Brazil
222 H5 Linsell Sweden
381 H1 Linshu Shandong China
309 H4 Linta watercourse Madagascar
380 D1 Lintan Gansu China
119 T6 Lintlaw Saskatchewan Canada
241 H2 Linton Cambridgeshire England UK
125 O3 Linton North Dakota USA
223 N3 Lintula Finland
381 F3 Linwu Hunan China
385 I4 Linxi Nei Mongol Zizhiqu China
384 E6 Linxia Gansu China
384 G5 Linxian Shanxi China
381 F3 Linxiang Hunan China
381 G2 Linxiang Hunan China
308 D3 Linyati Swamp swamp Namibia
381 H1 Linyi Shandong China
385 H5 Linyi Shandong China
380 F1 Linyi Shanxi China
381 G1 Linying Henan China
227 H3 Linz Austria
384 D5 Linze Gansu China
379 H3 Linzhi Xizang Zizhiqu China
385 H6 Linzhou Henan China
375 G3 Lio Matoh Malaysia
227 M2 Lioboml' Ukraine
225 L5 Lioliai Lithuania
309 G3 Lioma Mozambique
228 F5 Lion, Golfe du bay France
162 E5 Lion Point Falkland Islands
118 J8 Lions Bay British Columbia Canada
372 C5 Lioppa Indonesia
373 H4 Liot Island Papua New Guinea
301 I6 Lioua Chad
305 H4 Liouesso Congo
377 I4 Lipa Philippines
130 B4 Lipan Texas USA
227 K3 Lipany Slovakia
234 A3 Lipar Serbia
233 F7 Lipari Italy
233 F7 Lipari, Isola island Italy
374 D3 Lipatkain Indonesia
229 K1 Lipenec Czech Republic
160 E2 Lipeo Argentina
223 P5 Liperi Finland
388 C3 Lipetsk Russian Federation
388 C3 Lipetskaya Oblast' admin. area Russian Federation
158 E6 Lipez, Cordillera de range Bolivia
241 G3 Liphook Hampshire England UK
238 G2 Lipin Bor Russian Federation
225 M4 Lipiniški Latvia
234 B4 Lipkovo Macedonia
225 Q3 Lipnaya Gorka Russian Federation
224 I6 Lipnica Poland
227 I1 Lipnica Poland
227 J1 Lipnica Poland
227 H3 Lipno, Vodní nádrž lake Czech Republic
234 A3 Lipolist Serbia
234 B2 Lipova Romania
234 C3 Lipovu Romania
130 A2 Lipscomb Texas USA
119 T7 Lipton Saskatchewan Canada
304 E2 Liptougou Burkina Faso
238 F5 Liptsy Russian Federation
224 I5 Lipusz Poland
159 E6 Lique, Sierra de range Bolivia
162 B2 Liquiñe Chile
307 E3 Lira Uganda
233 E6 Liri watercourse Italy
231 F4 Liria Spain
372 C3 Lirung Indonesia
245 E4 Lis Ireland
234 D3 Lisa Romania
245 D3 Lisacul Ireland
306 B4 Lisafa Democratic Republic of Congo
306 C3 Lisala Democratic Republic of Congo
155 F5 Lisbão Brazil
245 E2 Lisbellaw Fermanagh Northern Ireland UK
158 D3 Lisboa Bolivia

230 B4 **Lisboa** *admin. area* Portugal
230 B4 **Lisboa (Lisbon)** Portugal
Lisbon *see* **Lisboa** Portugal
125 Q3 **Lisbon** North Dakota USA
245 F2 **Lisburn** Lisburn Northern Ireland UK
245 F2 **Lisburn** *admin. area* Northern Ireland UK
116 C5 **Lisburne, Cape** Alaska USA
245 C3 **Liscarney** Ireland
123 G10 **Liscomb** Nova Scotia Canada
245 D3 **Lisconly** Ireland
381 G4 **Lishi** Jiangxi China
384 G5 **Lishi** Shanxi China
381 H4 **Lishi Liedao** *island* Fujian China
385 J4 **Lishu** Jilin China
381 H3 **Lishui** Zhejiang China
228 E2 **Lisieux** France
225 P2 **Lisiy Nos** Russian Federation
224 H2 **Lisjön** *lake* Sweden
240 C4 **Liskeard** Cornwall England UK
394 F2 **Liski** Russian Federation
245 E2 **Lislap** Omagh Northern Ireland UK
228 E3 **L'Isle-Bouchard** France
228 E5 **L'Isle-en-Dodon** France
229 G5 **L'Isle-sur-la-Sorgue** France
123 D8 **L'Isle-Verte** Québec Canada
242 A2 **Lislea** Ireland
123 C9 **L'Islet** Québec Canada
130 G4 **Lisman** Alabama USA
425 O7 **Lismore** NSW Australia
123 G10 **Lismore** Nova Scotia Canada
245 E4 **Lismore** Ireland
244 C4 **Lismore** *island* Scotland UK
125 R5 **Lismore** Minnesota USA
225 O4 **Lisna, Vozyera** *lake* Belarus
242 B2 **Lisnacree** Newry and Mourne Northern Ireland UK
242 B1 **Lisnagunogue** Moyle Northern Ireland UK
245 E2 **Lisnaskea** Fermanagh Northern Ireland UK
234 F2 **Lisne** Ukraine
232 G4 **Lišnja** Bosnia and Herzegovina
227 H3 **Lišov** Czech Republic
234 G1 **Lisovichi** Ukraine
242 A3 **Lisreagh** Ireland
245 E3 **Lisryan** Ireland
241 G3 **Liss** Hampshire England UK
245 D4 **Lissatunny** Ireland
243 H2 **Lissett** East Riding of Yorkshire England UK
243 H3 **Lissington** Lincolnshire England UK
224 E5 **List** Germany
224 D3 **Lista** *island* Norway
437 K1 **Lister, Mount** *mountain* Antarctica
235 G3 **Lištica** Bosnia and Herzegovina
242 C2 **Listooder** Down Northern Ireland UK
245 C4 **Listowel** Ireland
242 B2 **Listullycurran** Lisburn Northern Ireland UK
222 I5 **Lit/Söre** Sweden
380 C3 **Litang Qu** *watercourse* Sichuan China
126 G7 **Litchfield** Illinois USA
234 E2 **Liteni** Romania
235 D6 **Lithari, Akra** *cape* Greece
425 N8 **Lithgow** NSW Australia
235 E8 **Lithines** Greece
235 D8 **Lithino, Akra** *cape* Greece
235 D6 **Líthion** Greece
225 M5 **Lithuania** *country* Europe
227 M3 **Litiatyn** Ukraine
156 D4 **Litigated Zone** Brazil
237 AL4 **Litke, Mys** *cape* Russian Federation
232 G2 **Litomyšl** Czech Republic
227 I3 **Litovel** Czech Republic
129 N5 **Little** *watercourse* Texas USA
131 M7 **Little Abaco** *island* Bahamas
121 O7 **Little Abitibi** *watercourse* Ontario Canada
127 K2 **Little Abitibi Lake** Ontario Canada
436 N1 **Little America Basin** *bay* Antarctica
376 B5 **Little Andaman** *island* Andaman and Nicobar Islands India
244 C2 **Little Assynt** Highland Scotland UK
131 M7 **Little Bahama Bank** *reef* Bahamas
241 G2 **Little Barford** Bedfordshire England UK
422 F3 **Little Barrier Island** New Zealand
243 F1 **Little Bavington** Northumberland England UK
125 J3 **Little Bell Mountains** Montana USA
125 L4 **Little Bighorn** *watercourse* Montana USA
124 H2 **Little Bitterroot Lake** Montana USA
119 O7 **Little Bow** *watercourse* Alberta Canada
241 G3 **Little Brickhill** Milton Keynes England UK
119 O2/3 **Little Buffalo** *watercourse* Alberta/Northwest Territories Canada
241 G2 **Little Bytham** Lincolnshire England UK
244 C6 **Little Cairnbrock** Dumfries and Galloway Scotland UK
134 D3 **Little Cayman** *island* Cayman Islands
241 H2 **Little Chesterford** Essex England UK
120 H4 **Little Churchill** *watercourse* Manitoba Canada
126 G4 **Little Chute** Wisconsin USA
376 B4 **Little Coco Island** Andaman and Nicobar Islands India
128 G3 **Little Colorado** *watercourse* Arkansas USA
241 F3 **Little Compton** Warwickshire England UK
241 H2 **Little Cornard** Suffolk England UK
120 M7 **Little Current** *watercourse* Ontario Canada
124 E5 **Little Deschutes** *watercourse* Oregon USA
127 O7 **Little Egg Harbor** New Jersey USA
135 F2 **Little Exuma** *island* Bahamas
119 O3 **Little Fishery** Alberta Canada
118 K7 **Little Fort** British Columbia Canada
243 H2 **Little Habton** North Yorkshire England UK
240 B3 **Little Haven** Pembrokeshire Wales UK
241 F2 **Little Haywood** Staffordshire England UK
243 G3 **Little Hucklow** Derbyshire England UK
135 F2 **Little Inagua Island** Bahamas
128 D3 **Little Lake** California USA
130 F6 **Little Lake** Louisiana USA
126 F3 **Little Marais** Minnesota USA
123 H6 **Little Mecatina** *watercourse* Newfoundland and Labrador Canada
244 B3 **Little Minch** *bay* Scotland UK
125 N3/4 **Little Missouri** *watercourse* North Dakota/South Dakota USA
124 E3 **Little Naches** *watercourse* Washington USA
376 B6 **Little Nicobar Island** Andaman and Nicobar Islands India
125 M4 **Little Powder** *watercourse* Montana USA
392 C6 **Little Rann** Gujarat India
119 N3 **Little Red River** Alberta Canada
241 F3 **Little Rissington** Gloucestershire England UK
130 E3 **Little Rock** Arkansas USA
120 I5 **Little Sachigo Lake** Ontario Canada
124 I8 **Little Salt Lake** Utah USA
135 F1 **Little San Salvador** *island* Bahamas
424 G6 **Little Sandy Desert** WA Australia
126 D5 **Little Sioux** *watercourse* Iowa USA
237 AK8 **Little Sitkin Island** *island* Alaska USA
118 M5 **Little Smoky** Alberta Canada
118 M5 **Little Smoky** *watercourse* Alberta Canada
237 AL8 **Little Tanaga Island** Alaska USA
241 F3 **Little Tew** Oxfordshire England UK
241 H2 **Little Thetford** Cambridgeshire England UK
126 I4 **Little Traverse Bay** Michigan USA
120 I7 **Little Vermilion Lake** Ontario Canada
241 H3 **Little Wakering** Essex England UK
125 O5 **Little White** *watercourse* South Dakota USA
243 F3 **Littleborough** Greater Manchester England UK
241 H2 **Littlebury** Essex England UK
128 F2 **Littlefield** Arizona USA
129 K4 **Littlefield** Texas USA
240 C4 **Littleham** Devon England UK
241 G4 **Littlehampton** West Sussex England UK
241 H2 **Littleport** Cambridgeshire England UK
125 M7 **Littleton** Colorado USA
305 G4 **Littoral** *admin. area* Cameroon
309 G2 **Litunde** Mozambique
118 C3 **Lituya Bay** Alaska USA
229 K1 **Litvínov** Czech Republic
238 D6 **Litvinovichi** Belarus
234 C1 **Litynya** Ukraine
225 M3 **Liu** Estonia
381 H2 **Liucheng** Jiangsu China
381 H4 **Liuchiu Yü** *island* Taiwan China
380 E3 **Liuchuan** Guizhou China
385 K4 **Liuhe** Jilin China
381 I2 **Liuheng Dao** *island* Zhejiang China
384 E6 **Liujiaxia** Gansu China
307 E6 **Liuli** Tanzania
380 D1 **Liulin** Gansu China
384 F6 **Liupan Shan** *range* Zishiqu China
309 G3 **Liúpo** Mozambique
308 D2 **Liuwa Plain** *plain* Zambia
381 G4 **Liuxi He** *watercourse* Guangdong China
381 G3 **Liuyang** Hunan China
381 G3 **Liuyang He** *watercourse* Hunan China
380 F4 **Liuzhou** Guangxi Zhuangzu Zizhiqu China
235 D7 **Livada, Akra** *cape* Greece
235 C5 **Livadi** Greece
235 E7 **Livadi** *island* Greece
235 E7 **Livádia** Greece
235 C6 **Livanátai** Greece
225 N4 **Līvāni** Latvia
233 H5 **Livari** Montenegro
228 E2 **Livarot** France
124 E7 **Live Oak** California USA
131 J5 **Live Oak** Florida USA
128 D4 **Live Oak Springs** California USA
163 7 **Lively Island** Falkland Islands
242 F3 **Liverpool** *admin. area* England UK
242 F3 **Liverpool** Merseyside England UK
117 L4 **Liverpool, Cape** Nunavut Canada
116 F5 **Liverpool Bay** Northwest Territories Canada
242 E3 **Liverpool Bay** England UK
306 D5 **Lividjo** *watercourse* Democratic Republic of Congo
121 V6 **Livingston** Newfoundland and Labrador Canada
134 B4 **Livingston** Guatemala
244 E5 **Livingston** West Lothian Scotland UK
130 G4 **Livingston** Alabama USA
124 E8 **Livingston** California USA
126 G7 **Livingston** Illinois USA
125 J4 **Livingston** Montana USA
130 D5 **Livingston, Lake** Texas USA
436 T2 **Livingston Island** Antarctica
308 E3 **Livingstone** Zambia
232 G5 **Livno** Bosnia and Herzegovina
394 F2 **Livny** Russian Federation
223 O4 **Livo** Finland
223 O4 **Livojärvi** *lake* Finland
223 O4 **Livojoki** *watercourse* Finland
130 F5 **Livonia** Louisiana USA
126 J5 **Livonia** Michigan USA
127 M5 **Livonia** New York USA
232 D5 **Livorno** Italy
159 G2 **Livramento** Brazil
157 D6 **Livramento do Brumado** Brazil
228 G4 **Livron-sur-Drôme** France
227 K1 **Liw** Poland
309 F2 **Liwale** *watercourse* Malawi
307 F5 **Liwale** Tanzania
307 F5 **Liwale Juu** Tanzania
385 H5 **Liwu** Hebei China
380 E1 **Lixian** Gansu China
380 D4 **Lixian Jiang** *watercourse* Yunnan China
381 G1 **Lixin** Anhui China
235 B6 **Lixouri** Greece
381 H2 **Liyang** Anhui China
381 H2 **Liyang** Jiangsu China
380 F2 **Liyuan** Hunan China
240 B5 **Lizard** Cornwall England UK
425 M3 **Lizard Island** Qld Australia
240 B5 **Lizard Point** England UK
156 C5 **Lizarda** Brazil
223 S5 **Lizhma** Russian Federation
223 R5 **Lizhmozero, Ozero** *lake* Russian Federation
226 B3 **Lizy** France
234 B3 **Ljig** Serbia
227 H4 **Ljubljana** Slovenia
234 A3 **Ljubovija** Serbia
224 H2 **Ljugaren** *lake* Sweden
225 J4 **Ljugarn** Sweden
222 H5 **Ljungan** *watercourse* Sweden
222 H5 **Ljungdalen** Sweden
222 L4 **Ljuså** Sweden
222 J6 **Ljusdal** Sweden
222 I6 **Ljusnan** *watercourse* Sweden
224 H3 **Ljusnaren** *lake* Sweden
222 H5 **Ljusnedal** Sweden
158 C4 **Llaico** Peru
158 E5 **Llallagua** Bolivia
158 D6 **Llamara, Salar de** *pan* Chile
240 C2 **Llanaber** Gwynedd Wales UK
240 C2 **Llanaelhaiarn** Gwynedd Wales UK
240 D2 **Llanafan-fawr** Powys Wales UK
240 D2 **Llanarmon Dyffryn** Wrexham Wales UK
240 C2 **Llanbadarn-Fawr** Ceredigion Wales UK
242 D3 **Llanbadrig** Isle of Anglesey Wales UK
240 C2 **Llanbedr** Gwynedd Wales UK
240 C2 **Llanbedrog** Gwynedd Wales UK
240 C1 **Llanberis** Gwynedd Wales UK
240 C2 **Llancynfelyn** Ceredigion Wales UK
240 C2 **Llanddeiniol** Ceredigion Wales UK
240 D1 **Llanddoget** Conwy Wales UK
240 D2 **Llandegley** Powys Wales UK
240 D3 **Llandeilo** Carmarthenshire Wales UK
240 C3 **Llandissilio** Pembrokeshire Wales UK
240 D3 **Llandovery** Carmarthenshire Wales UK
240 D2 **Llandrillo** Denbighshire Wales UK
242 E3 **Llandudno** Conwy Wales UK
240 D2 **Llandulas** Powys Wales UK
240 C2 **Llandyssul** Carmarthenshire Wales UK
240 D3 **Llanedeyrn** Cardiff Wales UK
240 C3 **Llanedy** Carmarthenshire Wales UK
240 C3 **Llanegwad** Carmarthenshire Wales UK
240 C3 **Llanelli** Carmarthenshire Wales UK
240 D2 **Llanelwedd** Powys Wales UK
240 C2 **Llanengan** Gwynedd Wales UK
240 D2 **Llanerfyl** Powys Wales UK
230 D2 **Llanes** Spain
240 D2 **Llanfachreth** Gwynedd Wales UK
242 D3 **Llanfaethlu** Isle of Anglesey Wales UK
240 C2 **Llanfair** Gwynedd Wales UK
240 C2 **Llanfair Clydogau** Ceredigion Wales UK
242 E3 **Llanfair Talhaiarn** Conwy Wales UK
240 D2 **Llanfair Waterdine** Shropshire England UK
242 E3 **Llanfairfechan** Conwy Wales UK
240 C2 **Llanfihangel-y-pennant** Gwynedd Wales UK
240 D2 **Llanfyllin** Powys Wales UK
240 D2 **Llangadfan** Powys Wales UK
240 D2 **Llangadwaladr** Powys Wales UK
240 E3 **Llangattock nigh Usk** Monmouthshire Wales UK
242 D3 **Llangefni** Isle of Anglesey Wales UK
240 C2 **Llangeler** Carmarthenshire Wales UK
240 C2 **Llangelynin** Gwynedd Wales UK
240 D1 **Llangernyw** Conwy Wales UK
242 D3 **Llangoed** Isle of Anglesey Wales UK
240 D2 **Llangollen** Denbighshire Wales UK
240 E2 **Llangollen Branch** *watercourse* England UK
240 D2 **Llangower** Gwynedd Wales UK
240 C2 **Llangranog** Ceredigion Wales UK
240 D2 **Llangunllo** Powys Wales UK
240 D2 **Llangurig** Powys Wales UK
240 C2 **Llangwm** Conwy Wales UK
240 C2 **Llangwnadl** Gwynedd Wales UK
240 D3 **Llangynidr** Powys Wales UK
240 D2 **Llangynog** Powys Wales UK
240 D3 **Llanhamlach** Powys Wales UK
240 C3 **Llanilar** Ceredigion Wales UK
240 C2 **Llanina** Ceredigion Wales UK
240 C1 **Llanllechid** Gwynedd Wales UK
240 D2 **Llanllyfni** Gwynedd Wales UK
240 C3 **Llanmiloe** Carmarthenshire Wales UK
130 B5 **Llano** Texas USA
132 D3 **Llano, El** *plain* Mexico
129 J6 **Llano de los Cabellos Mesteños** Mexico
134 D6 **Llano de Piedra** Panama
132 E1 **Llano Estacado** *region* New Mexico USA
240 C2 **Llanon** Ceredigion Wales UK
154 D3 **Llanos** *region*
310 3d **Llanos de Concepción** Canary Islands
240 C3 **Llanrhidian** Swansea Wales UK
242 D3 **Llanrhyddlad** Isle of Anglesey Wales UK
240 B3 **Llanrian** Pembrokeshire Wales UK
240 D1 **Llanrwst** Conwy Wales UK
240 D2 **Llansaintffread in Elvel** Powys Wales UK
240 D1 **Llansannan** Conwy Wales UK
240 C3 **Llansantffraid** Ceredigion Wales UK
240 C2 **Llansawel** Carmarthenshire Wales UK
240 D2 **Llansilin** Powys Wales UK
240 E3 **Llansoy** Monmouthshire Wales UK
242 D3 **Llantrisaint** Isle of Anglesey Wales UK
240 D2 **Llantysilio** Denbighshire Wales UK
240 D2 **Llanuwchllyn** Gwynedd Wales UK
240 D2 **Llanwddyn** Powys Wales UK
240 C1 **Llanwnda** Gwynedd Wales UK
240 D2 **Llanwnog** Powys Wales UK
240 D3 **Llanwrda** Carmarthenshire Wales UK
240 D2 **Llanwrin** Powys Wales UK
240 D2 **Llanwrtyd Wells** Powys Wales UK
240 D2 **Llanyblodwel** Shropshire England UK
240 C2 **Llanychaiarn** Ceredigion Wales UK
240 C2 **Llanycil** Gwynedd Wales UK
240 D2 **Llanycrwys** Carmarthenshire Wales UK
240 D2 **Llanymawddwy** Gwynedd Wales UK
162 B2 **Llao Llao** Argentina
158 B3 **Llata** Peru
231 G2 **Llavorsí** Spain
240 E1 **Llay** Wrexham Wales UK
240 D2 **Lledrod** Ceredigion Wales UK
231 G3 **Lleida** Spain
133 F4 **Llera de Canales** Mexico
230 C4 **Llerena** Spain
160 C6 **Llico** Chile
231 H3 **Lloret de Mar** Spain
154 B3 **Lloró** Colombia
240 D2 **Llowes** Powys Wales UK
118 I4 **Lloyd George, Mount** British Columbia Canada
116 I7 **Lloyd Lake** Saskatchewan Canada
119 P6 **Lloydminster** Saskatchewan Canada
240 D2 **Lloyney** Shropshire England UK
231 H4 **Llucmajor** Spain
160 D3 **Llullaillaco, Volcán** *volcano* Chile
158 C5 **Lluta** Peru
240 C2 **Llwyngwril** Gwynedd Wales UK
240 D2 **Llynclys** Shropshire England UK
240 C3 **Llys-y fran** Pembrokeshire Wales UK
242 E3 **Llysfaen** Conwy Wales UK
227 J1 **Lniano** Poland
376 E2 **Lô** *watercourse* Vietnam
132 D5 **Lo Arado** Mexico
375 H4 **Loa Janan** Indonesia
375 G3 **Loagan Bunut National Park** Malaysia
377 G5 **Loaita Island** Spratly Islands
375 H4 **Loakulu** Indonesia
157 A8 **Loanda** Brazil
306 C5 **Loange** *watercourse* Democratic Republic of Congo
306 A5 **Loango** Democratic Republic of Congo
232 C4 **Loano** Italy
372 B4 **Lobata** Indonesia
308 E5 **Lobatse** Botswana
228 H1 **Löbau** Germany
305 H4 **Lobaye** *admin. area* Central African Republic
305 H3 **Lobaye** *watercourse* Central African Republic
226 C2 **Lobbes** Belgium
305 G4 **Lobe** *watercourse* Cameroon
229 J1 **Lobenstein** Germany
307 E3 **Lobira** Sudan
308 B2 **Lobito** Angola
238 D6 **Lobkovichi** Belarus
226 2 **Löbnitz** Germany
133 F4 **Lobo, Isla de** *island* Mexico
161 G5 **Lobos** Argentina
132 B2 **Lobos, Cabo** *cape* Mexico
132 C3 **Lobos, Isla** *island* Mexico
310 3d **Lobos, Isla de** *island* Canary Islands
162 D3 **Lobos, Punta** *cape* Argentina
158 A2 **Lobos de Afuera, Islas** *islands* Peru
158 A2 **Lobos de Tierra, Isla** *island* Peru
423 E6 **Lobourn** New Zealand
236 N7 **Lobva** Russian Federation
227 I1 **Łobżenica** Poland
376 E5 **Lộc Ninh** Vietnam
229 H4 **Locana** Italy
229 I3 **Locarno** Switzerland
244 A3 **Loch nam Madadh** Na h-Eileanan Siar Scotland UK
244 A3 **Loch Sgioport** Na h-Eileanan Siar Scotland UK
244 C4 **Lochaline** Highland Scotland UK
242 C2 **Lochans** Dumfries and Galloway Scotland UK
244 E5 **Locharbriggs** Dumfries and Galloway Scotland UK
244 E2 **Lochdhu Hotel** Highland Scotland UK
244 C4 **Lochdon** Highland Scotland UK
244 D3 **Lochdrum** Highland Scotland UK
244 E4 **Lochee** Dundee Scotland UK
228 E3 **Loches** France
244 C4 **Lochgilphead** Argyll and Bute Scotland UK
244 D4 **Lochgoilhead** Argyll and Bute Scotland UK
244 C2 **Lochinver** Highland Scotland UK
244 D3 **Lochluichart** Highland Scotland UK
244 E5 **Lochmaben** Dumfries and Galloway Scotland UK
227 J1 **Łochocin** Poland
244 A3 **Lochportain** Na h-Eileanan Siar Scotland UK
244 E2 **Lochside** Highland Scotland UK
244 D3 **Lochy, Loch** *lake* Scotland UK
123 F11 **Lockeport** Nova Scotia Canada
244 E5 **Lockerbie** Dumfries and Galloway Scotland UK
133 I2 **Lockhart** Florida USA
130 C6 **Lockhart** Texas USA
222 I5 **Lockne** Sweden
222 I5 **Locknesjön** *lake* Sweden
129 L3 **Lockney** Texas USA
241 F4 **Locks Heath** Hampshire England UK
243 H2 **Lockton** North Yorkshire England UK
119 S7 **Lockwood** Saskatchewan Canada
126 E8 **Lockwood** Missouri USA
426 5 **Lockwood Terrace** Guam
228 C3 **Locminé** France
228 B2 **Locronan** France
228 B3 **Loctudy** France
233 C6 **Loculi** Sardinia Italy
130 D2 **Locust Grove** Oklahoma USA
241 I2 **Loddon** Norfolk England UK
307 E2 **Lodein** Sudan
228 F5 **Lodève** France
225 Q2 **Lodeynoye Pole** Russian Federation
125 L4 **Lodge Grass** Montana USA
119 N6 **Lodgepole** Alberta Canada
306 C4 **Lodi** Democratic Republic of Congo
226 E5 **Lodi** Italy
124 E7 **Lodi** California USA
222 I3 **Løding** Norway
222 I2 **Lødingen** Norway
306 C4 **Lodja** Democratic Republic of Congo
230 E2 **Lodosa** Spain
229 I3 **Lodrino** Switzerland
307 F3 **Lodwar** Kenya
227 J2 **Łódź** Poland
227 J2 **Łódzkie** *admin. area* Poland
376 D3 **Loei** Thailand
376 D3 **Loei** *admin. area* Thailand
308 C6 **Loeriesfontein** South Africa
384 G5 **Loess Plateau** Nei Mongol Zizhiqu China
384 B3 **Lofa** *watercourse* Liberia
226 B2 **Loffre** France
222 H2 **Lofoten** *island* Norway
222 H5 **Lofssjön** *lake* Sweden
388 D3 **Log** Russian Federation
301 G6 **Loga** Niger
304 E3 **Loga** Sudan
129 K6 **Logan** New Mexico USA
124 I6 **Logan** Utah USA
123 E8 **Logan, Mount** Québec Canada
118 A2 **Logan, Mount** Yukon Territory Canada
118 K7 **Logan Lake** British Columbia Canada
131 H4 **Logan Martin Lake** Alabama USA
118 H2 **Logan Mountains** Yukon Territory Canada
126 H6 **Logansport** Indiana USA
222 K4 **Lögdasjön** *lake* Sweden
222 K4 **Lögdeälven** *watercourse* Sweden
244 E3 **Logie** Moray Scotland UK
307 F3 **Logipi, Lake** Kenya
224 D3 **Logna** *watercourse* Norway
305 H2 **Logne** *watercourse* Chad
305 H3 **Logone-Occidental** *admin. area* Chad
305 H3 **Logone-Oriental** *admin. area* Chad
228 E2 **Logron** France
230 E2 **Logroño** Spain
230 D4 **Logrosán** Spain
224 E4 **Løgstrup** Denmark
426 7 **Loh** *island* Vanuatu
392 D5 **Loharu** Haryana India
228 D3 **Lohéac** France
223 N3 **Lohijärvi** *lake* Finland
225 O2 **Lohilahti** Finland
223 N3 **Lohiniva** Finland
225 M2 **Lohja** Finland
229 I1 **Lohr** Germany
229 L1 **Lohsa** Germany
223 M4 **Lohtaja** Finland
225 N3 **Lohusuu** Estonia
379 H4 **Loi Song** *mountain* Myanmar
379 H5 **Loikaw** Myanmar
306 C4 **Loile** *watercourse* Democratic Republic of Congo
379 H5 **Loilem** Myanmar
225 L2 **Loimijoki** *watercourse* Finland
223 Q6 **Loimola** Russian Federation
228 F3 **Loing** *watercourse* France
228 F3 **Loire** *watercourse* France
228 F3 **Loire, Canal latéral à la** *watercourse* France
224 G5 **Loissin** Germany
224 G6 **Loitz** Germany
154 B5 **Loja** Ecuador
154 B6 **Loja** *admin. area* Ecuador
230 D5 **Loja** Spain
305 G6 **Loje** *watercourse* Angola
372 M2 **Lokachi** Ukraine
306 C3 **Lokaiema** Democratic Republic of Congo
223 O3 **Lokan tekojärvi** *lake* Finland
306 D4 **Lokeli** Democratic Republic of Congo
232 E1 **Loket** Czech Republic
379 H3 **Lokhuni** Nagaland India
308 D4 **Lokhwabe** Botswana
307 F3 **Lokichar** Kenya
307 E3 **Lokichokio** Kenya
306 D4 **Lokila** Democratic Republic of Congo
307 F3 **Lokitaung** Kenya
223 O3 **Lokka** Finland
222 F5 **Lokken** Norway
223 N5 **Lokkiperä** Finland
225 P4 **Loknya** Russian Federation
305 F3 **Loko** Nigeria
305 F3 **Lokoja** Nigeria
306 C4 **Lokolia** Democratic Republic of Congo
306 B4 **Lokolo** *watercourse* Democratic Republic of Congo
306 B3 **Lokomo** Cameroon
306 C4 **Lokoro** *watercourse* Democratic Republic of Congo
304 E3 **Lokossa** Benin
394 E2 **Lokot** Russian Federation
117 M6 **Loks Land** *island* Nunavut Canada
225 M3 **Loksa** Estonia
155 H3 **Loksie Hatti** Suriname
222 H3 **Løkta** *island* Norway
379 G4 **Loktak** *lake* Manipur India
305 G4 **Lokundje** *watercourse* Cameroon
426 8 **Lokuru** Solomon Islands
225 M3 **Lokuta** Estonia
306 C3 **Lokutu** Democratic Republic of Congo
222 L2 **Løkvollen** Norway
306 D2 **Lol** *watercourse* Sudan
308 B2 **Lola** Angola
304 C3 **Lola** Guinea
306 C4 **Lolaka** *watercourse* Democratic Republic of Congo
306 C3 **Lolengi** Democratic Republic of Congo
224 F5 **Lolland** *island* Denmark
226 E2 **Lollar** Germany
372 D3 **Lolobata** Indonesia
372 C3 **Loloda Utara, Kepulauan** *island* Indonesia
305 G4 **Lolodorf** Cameroon
426 7 **Lolowaï** Vanuatu
374 C3 **Lolowau** Indonesia
241 H2 **Lolworth** Cambridgeshire England UK
234 C4 **Lom** Bulgaria
305 G3 **Lom** *watercourse* Cameroon
222 F6 **Lom** Norway
238 H4 **Lom** Russian Federation
376 D3 **Lom Sak** Thailand
129 H1 **Loma** Colorado USA
129 L6 **Loma Alta** Texas USA
132 D2 **Loma Blanca** Mexico
160 D6 **Loma Farías** Argentina
230 F5 **Loma Pelada, Punta de** *cape* Spain
427 9 **Lomaloma** Fiji
306 C4 **Lomami** Democratic Republic of Congo
306 D4 **Lomami** *watercourse* Democratic Republic of Congo
126 E2 **Loman** Minnesota USA
161 G3 **Lomas de Vallejos** Argentina
427 9a **Lomawai** Fiji
227 L2 **Łomazy** Poland
308 D3 **Lomba** *watercourse* Angola
424 G4 **Lombadina** WA Australia
156 B2 **Lombarda, Serra** *range* Brazil
232 C4 **Lombardia (Lombardy)** *admin. area* Italy
245 D4 **Lombardstown** Ireland
Lombardy *see* **Lombardia** Italy
228 F5 **Lombez** France
375 I6 **Lomblen** *island* Indonesia
375 H6 **Lombok** *island* Indonesia
375 G6 **Lombok, Selat** *strait* Indonesia
304 E3 **Lomé** Togo
306 C4 **Lomela** Democratic Republic of Congo
306 C4 **Lomela** *watercourse* Democratic Republic of Congo
232 C4 **Lomello** Italy
130 B5 **Lometa** Texas USA
305 G4 **Lomié** Cameroon
128 C4 **Lomita** California USA
154 C4 **Lomitas** Colombia
229 K1 **Lommatzsch** Germany
229 G1 **Lommel** Belgium
227 I3 **Lomnice** Czech Republic
227 H3 **Lomnice nad Lužnicí** Czech Republic
119 O7 **Lomond** Alberta Canada
244 D4 **Lomond, Loch** *lake* Scotland UK
434 P1 **Lomonosov Ridge** *underwater feature* Arctic Ocean
388 D2 **Lomov** Russian Federation
128 B3 **Lompoc** California USA
222 J4 **Lomselenäs** Sweden
222 J4 **Lomsjökullen** Sweden
227 L1 **Łomża** Poland
224 H4 **Lönashult** Sweden
232 D4 **Lonato** Italy
162 C2 **Lonco Vaca** Argentina
160 C6 **Loncoche** Chile
160 D6 **Loncopué** Argentina
241 I5 **Londinières** France
127 K5 **London** Ontario Canada
426 1a **London** Kiribati
241 G3 **London** Greater London England UK
130 E3 **London** Arkansas USA
126 I8 **London** Kentucky USA
130 B5 **London** Texas USA
163 13 **Londonderry** St Lucia
245 E1 **Londonderry** Londonderry Northern Ireland UK
424 H3 **Londonderry, Cape** WA Australia
157 B8 **Londrina** Brazil
118 K7 **Lone Butte** British Columbia Canada
130 D4 **Lone Oak** Texas USA
128 C2 **Lone Pine** California USA
119 V7 **Lone Spruce** Manitoba Canada
130 D4 **Lone Star** Texas USA
125 M7 **Lone Tree** Colorado USA
130 B3 **Lone Wolf** Oklahoma USA
224 G4 **Lönern** *lake* Sweden
376 C3 **Long** Thailand
240 E3 **Long Ashton** North Somerset England UK
131 L4 **Long Bay** South Carolina USA
128 C4 **Long Beach** California USA
130 G5 **Long Beach** Mississippi USA
124 C3 **Long Beach** Washington USA
241 G2 **Long Bennington** Lincolnshire England UK
127 O6 **Long Branch** New Jersey USA
135 F2 **Long Cay** *island* Bahamas
124 F4 **Long Creek** Oregon USA
241 F2 **Long Eaton** Derbyshire England UK
126 F6 **Long Grove** Iowa USA
375 H3 **Long Ibau** Indonesia
163 18 **Long Island** Antigua and Barbuda
135 F2 **Long Island** Bahamas
127 R4 **Long Island** New Brunswick Canada
123 E10 **Long Island** Nova Scotia Canada
121 P5 **Long Island** Nunavut Canada
373 H5 **Long Island** Papua New Guinea
121 P5 **Long Island Sound** Nunavut/Québec Canada
127 O6 **Long Island Sound** *bay* USA
380 F4 **Long Jiang** *watercourse* Guangxi Zhuangzu Zizhiqu China
120 H3 **Long Lake** Manitoba Canada
120 H7 **Long Lake** Manitoba Canada
123 E9 **Long Lake** New Brunswick Canada
117 K9 **Long Lake** Ontario Canada
127 Q3 **Long Lake** Maine USA
125 O3 **Long Lake** North Dakota USA
375 G3 **Long Lama** Malaysia
241 F2 **Long Marston** Warwickshire England UK
241 H2 **Long Melford** Suffolk England UK
375 G3 **Long Murum** Malaysia
120 F6 **Long Point** Manitoba Canada
123 I8 **Long Point** Newfoundland and Labrador Canada
127 L5 **Long Point** Ontario Canada
423 C8 **Long Point** New Zealand
377 H5 **Long Point** Philippines
127 L5 **Long Point Bay** Ontario Canada
125 R4 **Long Prairie** Minnesota USA
243 F2 **Long Preston** North Yorkshire England UK
123 I9 **Long Range Mountains** Newfoundland and Labrador Canada
425 O4 **Long Reef** Qld Australia
120 H4 **Long Spruce** Manitoba Canada
241 I2 **Long Stratton** Norfolk England UK
241 H2 **Long Sutton** Lincolnshire England UK
375 G3 **Long Teru** Malaysia
380 E1 **Long Xian** Shaanxi China
376 E5 **Long Xuyên** Vietnam
380 E4 **Long'an** Guangxi Zhuangzu Zizhiqu China
380 D2 **Long'an** Sichuan China
308 C2 **Longa** Angola
308 C3 **Longa** *watercourse* Angola
237 AK4 **Longa, Proliv** *strait* Russian Federation
375 G3 **Longagung** Indonesia
375 G3 **Longbawan** Indonesia
375 G3 **Longberini** Indonesia
375 H3 **Longbia** Indonesia
131 J7 **Longboat Key** Florida USA
375 G3 **Longboh** Indonesia
120 H8 **Longbow Lake** Ontario Canada
241 E3 **Longbridge Deverill** Wiltshire England UK
381 G1 **Longcheng** Anhui China
381 G4 **Longcheng** Guangdong China
381 G2 **Longcheng** Jiangxi China
380 D3 **Longchuan** Yunnan China
241 F1 **Longcliffe** Derbyshire England UK
130 B2 **Longdale** Oklahoma USA
384 F6 **Longde** Zishiqu China
241 E2 **Longdon** Worcestershire England UK
226 C4 **Longeau** France
232 D3 **Longega** Italy
229 H4 **Longet, Col de** *pass* France
245 E3 **Longford** Ireland
245 E3 **Longford** *admin. area* Ireland
241 F2 **Longford** West Midlands England UK
245 E4 **Longfordpass North** Ireland
381 G2 **Longgan Hu** *lake* Anhui China
380 E2 **Longgang** Chongqing China
378 E2 **Longge'er** Xizang Zizhiqu China
385 I4 **Longhua** Hebei China
437 K1 **Longhurst, Mount** Antarctica
375 H4 **Longikis** Indonesia
436 U2 **Longing, Cape** Antarctica
375 G4 **Longiram** Indonesia
385 J3 **Longjiang** Heilongjiang China
381 G3 **Longjin** Jiangxi China
385 L4 **Longjing** Jilin China
380 F1 **Longjuzhai** Shaanxi China
375 H3 **Longkabinu** Indonesia
385 I5 **Longkou** Shandong China
120 L8 **Longlac** Ontario Canada
121 Q4 **Longland** *watercourse* Québec Canada
120 H7 **Longlegged Lake** Ontario Canada
125 M6 **Longmont** Colorado USA
241 G3 **Longmoor Camp** Hampshire England UK
381 G4 **Longnan** Jiangxi China
375 G3 **Longnawan** Indonesia
243 G3 **Longnor** Staffordshire England UK
308 C2 **Longonjo** Angola
375 G3 **Longpahangai** Indonesia
120 G2 **Longpre Lake** Nunavut Canada
375 G3 **Longpujungan** Indonesia
380 E3 **Longquan** Guizhou China
381 F3 **Longquan** Hunan China
380 D4 **Longquan** Yunnan China
381 H3 **Longquan** Zhejiang China
122 D5 **Longrais, Lac** *lake* Québec Canada
425 M5 **Longreach** Qld Australia
243 F3 **Longridge** Lancashire England UK
125 M6 **Longs Peak** Colorado USA
380 E3 **Longshan** Guizhou China
380 F3 **Longsheng** Guangxi Zhuangzu Zizhiqu China
380 F3 **Longsheng** Guangxi Zhuangzu Zizhiqu China
380 F4 **Longsheng** Guangxi Zhuangzu Zizhiqu China
384 E5 **Longshou Shan** *range* Nei Mongol Zizhiqu China
242 F3 **Longton** Lancashire England UK
241 E2 **Longton** Stoke-on-Trent England UK
242 F1 **Longtown** Cumbria England UK
228 F1 **Longuenesse** France
119 N7 **Longview** Alberta Canada
130 D4 **Longview** Texas USA
124 D3 **Longview** Washington USA
375 H3 **Longwai** Indonesia
242 B3 **Longwood** Ireland
310 5b **Longwood** St Helena
423 B8 **Longwood Range** New Zealand
118 K6 **Longworth** British Columbia Canada
384 E6 **Longwu** Qinghai China
380 D1 **Longxi** Gansu China
381 G4 **Longxian** Guangdong China
381 H3 **Longxun** Fujian China
381 H3 **Longyan** Fujian China
385 H5 **Longyao** Hebei China
236 3C **Longyearbyen** Svalbard
380 E4 **Longzhou** Guangxi Zhuangzu Zizhiqu China
379 G3 **Longzi** Xizang Zizhiqu China
222 G4 **Lonin** Norway
224 E3 **Lonin** Norway
223 P4 **Lonka** Russian Federation
306 C4 **Lonkonia** *watercourse* Democratic Republic of Congo
226 C3 **Lonny** France
225 N5 **Lonskiya** Belarus
222 inset **Lónsvík** *cape* Iceland
372 D5 **Lontor** *island* Indonesia
159 I2 **Lontra** Brazil
234 C1 **Lónya** Hungary
126 I5 **Looking Glass** *watercourse* Michigan USA
120 N5 **Lookout, Cape** Ontario Canada
131 M3 **Lookout, Cape** North Carolina USA
424 H4 **Looma** WA Australia
125 K2 **Loomis** Saskatchewan Canada
125 P6 **Loomis** Nebraska USA
119 N4 **Loon** *watercourse* Alberta Canada
119 N4 **Loon Lake** Alberta Canada
245 B4 **Loop Head** *cape* Ireland
383 I5 **Lop Nur** *lake* Xinjiang Uygur Zizhiqu China
235 B5 **Lopan** Albania
232 F4 **Lopar** Croatia
388 E5 **Lopatin** Russian Federation
237 AD8 **Lopatina, Gora** *mountain* Russian Federation
388 E3 **Lopatino** Russian Federation
237 AG8 **Lopatka** Russian Federation
237 AG8 **Lopatka, Mys** *cape* Russian Federation
238 C4 **Lopatovo** Russian Federation
307 E2 **Lopaye** Sudan
376 D4 **Lopburi** Thailand
225 L3 **Lõpe** Estonia
240 E4 **Lopen** Somerset England UK
130 B7 **Lopeno** Texas USA
426 7 **Lopévi** *island* Vanuatu

161 G6 **López** Argentina
305 F5 **Lopez, Cape** *cape* Gabon
307 E3 **Lopodi** Sudan
306 C3 **Lopori** *watercourse* Democratic Republic of Congo
222 L1 **Loppa** Norway
222 L1 **Lopphavet** *bay* Norway
225 M2 **Loppijärvi** *lake* Finland
229 I5 **Loppio, Pointe** *mountain* Corsica France
222 I3 **Løpsmarka** Norway
225 O3 **Lopukhinka** Russian Federation
121 V4 **Loquin, Lac** *lake* Québec Canada
119 Q3 **Lorado** Saskatchewan Canada
127 J6 **Lorain** Ohio USA
129 L4 **Loraine** Texas USA
391 K3 **Loralai** Pakistan
155 F2 **Loran, Boca** *bay* Venezuela
243 G1 **Lorbottle** Northumberland England UK
230 F5 **Lorca** Spain
425 inset **Lord Howe Island** Australia
78 M11 **Lord Howe Rise** *underwater feature* Tasman Sea
376 C5 **Lord Loughborough Island** Myanmar
390 G3 **Lordegān** Iran
129 H4 **Lordsburg** New Mexico USA
375 I4 **Lore Lindu, Taman Nasional** *park* Indonesia
119 R7 **Loreburn** Saskatchewan Canada
154 C3 **Lorena** Colombia
373 F5 **Lorentz** *watercourse* Indonesia
129 L4 **Lorenzo** Texas USA
390 F2 **Lorestān** *admin. area* Iran
154 B5 **Loreto** Ecuador
132 C3 **Loreto** Mexico
158 C2 **Loreto** *admin. area* Peru
130 H3 **Loretto** Tennessee USA
154 C2 **Lorica** Colombia
228 C3 **Lorient** France
117 J5 **Lorillard** *watercourse* Nunavut Canada
227 J4 **Lőrinci** Hungary
119 R8 **Loring** Montana USA
237 AM5 **Lorino** Russian Federation
158 D5 **Loripongo** Peru
131 L3 **Loris** South Carolina USA
228 F3 **Lormes** France
393 E6 **Lormi** Chhattisgarh India
244 C4 **Lorn, Firth of** *bay* Scotland UK
154 D4 **Loro** Colombia
304 D2 **Loropeni** Burkina Faso
229 H2 **Lorraine** *admin. area* France
229 H2 **Lorraine** *region* France
129 M1 **Lorraine** Kansas USA
226 B4 **Lorris** France
226 D1 **Lorup** Germany
301 I2 **Lorzot** Tunisia
222 I5 **Los** Sweden
304 B3 **Los, Îles de** *island* Guinea
129 J6 **Los Alamos** Mexico
128 B3 **Los Alamos** California USA
128 G7 **Los Algdones, Estero** Mexico
133 F4 **Los Altos** Mexico
160 D5 **Los Andes** Chile
160 C6 **Los Ángeles** Chile
128 C3 **Los Angeles** California USA
128 C3 **Los Angeles Aqueduct** *watercourse* California USA
162 B4 **Los Antiguos** Argentina
230 E2 **Los Arcos** Spain
124 E8 **Los Banos** California USA
158 D5 **Los Baños** Peru
230 D5 **Los Barrios** Spain
160 F2 **Los Blancos** Argentina
154 D2 **Los Botalones** Venezuela
154 E2 **Los Caballos** Venezuela
160 E4 **Los Cerrillos** Argentina
155 F3 **Los Cerros** Venezuela
154 D3 **Los Cochinos** Venezuela
160 E4 **Los Colorados** Argentina
155 F3 **Los Corrales** Venezuela
159 E4 **Los Cusis** Bolivia
133 H5 **Los Divorciados** Mexico
133 F3 **Los Dos Estados** Mexico
155 F3 **Los Ermitaños** Venezuela
158 E5 **Los Frailes, Cordillera de** *range* Bolivia
128 E8 **Los Gatos** California USA
154 D2 **Los Guarimos** Venezuela
160 D6 **Los Helechos** Argentina
129 M8 **Los Herreras** Mexico
132 C2 **Los Hoyos** Mexico
158 C4 **Los Incas** Peru
130 C7 **Los Indios** Texas USA
129 N8 **Los Indios El Control** Mexico
162 B2 **Los Juncos** Argentina
162 B2 **Los Ladrillos** Chile
160 C6 **Los Lagos** *admin. area* Chile
129 J6 **Los Lamentos** Mexico
310 3b **Los Llanos de Aridane** Canary Islands
129 I3 **Los Lunas** New Mexico USA
154 E2 **Los Mangos** Venezuela
155 E2 **Los Maniritos** Venezuela
134 C4 **Los Marrabios, Cordillera** *range* Nicaragua
162 C2 **Los Menucos** Argentina
132 C3 **Los Mochis** Mexico
132 C4 **Los Molinos** Mexico
162 C2 **Los Monos** Argentina
132 C3 **Los Muertos** Mexico
132 E4 **Los Muertos** Mexico
230 D4 **Los Navalmorales** Spain
132 C4 **Los Palmitos** Colombia
154 C3 **Los Patios** Colombia
154 D5 **Los Patricio** Colombia
159 F5 **Los Portigos** Bolivia
160 D6 **Los Puquios** Chile
129 I3 **Los Ranchos de Albuquerque** New Mexico USA
154 D2 **Los Rastrojos** Venezuela
162 B2 **Los Repollos** Argentina
373 I4 **Los Reyes Islands** Papua New Guinea
162 B2 **Los Ríos** *admin. area* Chile
155 E2 **Los Roques, Islas** *islands* Venezuela
76 L8 **Los Roques Trench** *underwater feature* Caribbean Sea
230 E5 **Los Royos** Spain
132 B2 **Los Sauces** Mexico
162 B3 **Los Tamariscos** Argentina
155 F2 **Los Testigos** *island* Venezuela
160 F3 **Los Tigres** Argentina
159 F5 **Los Troncos** Bolivia
128 F4 **Los Vidrios** Mexico
160 D3 **Los Vientos** Chile
160 D4 **Los Vilos** Chile
154 D2 **Los Zorros** Venezuela
238 B6 **Loša** Belarus
231 F4 **Losa del Obispo** Spain
392 D5 **Losal** Rajasthan India
373 J2 **Losap** *island* Federated States of Micronesia
225 P2 **Losevo** Russian Federation
388 C3 **Losevo** Russian Federation
226 D2 **Losheim** Belgium
229 H1 **Losheim** Germany
227 L1 **Łosinka** Poland
222 J2 **Losivatnet** *lake* Norway
238 F5 **Los'mino** Russian Federation
223 P5 **Losonmäki** Finland
225 R2 **Lososinnoye** Russian Federation
372 C6 **Lospalos** Timor-Leste (East Timor)
244 E3 **Lossiemouth** Moray Scotland UK
222 H5 **Lossnen** *lake* Sweden
124 I4 **Lost River Range** Idaho USA
240 C4 **Lostwithiel** Cornwall England UK
225 P5 **Losvida, Vozyera** *lake* Belarus
226 B5 **Lot** *watercourse* France
160 C6 **Lota** Chile
244 E2 **Lothbeg** Highland Scotland UK
228 E3 **Lothiers** France
306 C4 **Loto** Democratic Republic of Congo
306 C4 **Loto** *watercourse* Democratic Republic of Congo
427 12c **Lotofaga** Samoa
238 F4 **Lotoshino** Russian Federation
308 E4 **Lotsane** *watercourse* Botswana
130 C5 **Lott** Texas USA
224 I4 **Löttorp** Sweden
373 H4 **Lou Island** Papua New Guinea
376 D2 **Louangnamtha** Laos
376 D2 **Louangnamtha** *admin. area* Laos
376 D3 **Louangphabang** Laos
376 D3 **Louangphabang** *range* Laos
Loubomo *see* **Dolisie** Congo
228 C2 **Loudéac** France
381 F3 **Loudi** Hunan China
229 H3 **Loue** *watercourse* France
305 G5 **Louéssé** *watercourse* Congo
384 G5 **Loufan** Shanxi China
300 C5 **Louga** Senegal
228 E5 **Louge** *watercourse* France
242 A3 **Lough** Ireland
245 E1 **Lough Swilly** *bay* Ireland
245 D2 **Loughanure** Ireland
241 F2 **Loughborough** Leicester England UK
245 E4 **Loughcapple Bridge** Ireland
117 I3 **Lougheed Island** Nunavut Canada
245 D2 **Lougheraherk** Ireland
245 D3 **Loughrea** Ireland
241 H3 **Loughton** Essex England UK
225 N2 **Louhivesi** *lake* Finland
118 K7 **Louis Creek** British Columbia Canada
308 E4 **Louis Trichardt** South Africa
121 P5 **Louis-XIV, Pointe** *cape* Québec Canada
126 J7 **Louisa** Kentucky USA
127 L7 **Louisa** Virginia USA
123 I10 **Louisbourg** Nova Scotia Canada
126 D7 **Louisburg** Kansas USA
123 H10 **Louisdale** Nova Scotia Canada
118 F6 **Louise Island** British Columbia Canada
373 J6 **Louisiade Archipelago** *islands* Papua New Guinea
115 **Louisiana** *admin. area* USA
126 F7 **Louisiana** Missouri USA
131 I5 **Louisville** Alabama USA
126 I7 **Louisville** Kentucky USA
125 Q6 **Louisville** Nebraska USA
78 P11 **Louisville Ridge** *underwater feature* Pacific Ocean
223 R3 **Loukhi** Russian Federation
306 B4 **Loukoléla** Democratic Republic of Congo
305 G5 **Loukouo** Congo
230 B5 **Loulé** Portugal
304 C2 **Loulouni** Mali
305 F4 **Loum** Cameroon
120 H7 **Lount Lake** Ontario Canada
229 K1 **Louny** Czech Republic
129 F5 **Loup** *watercourse* France
129 P5 **Loup City** Nebraska USA
121 S4 **Loups Marins, Lacs des** Québec Canada
231 F2 **Lourdes** France
155 I4 **Lourenço** Brazil
230 B3 **Louriçal** Portugal
230 B4 **Lourinhã** Portugal
228 E3 **Loury** France
223 Q5 **Lout, Ozero** *lake* Russian Federation
425 M7 **Louth** NSW Australia
245 F3 **Louth** *admin. area* Ireland
243 H3 **Louth** Lincolnshire England UK
235 D7 **Loutra** Greece
235 C7 **Loutraki** Greece
305 G5 **Louvakou** Congo
226 C3 **Louvois** France
306 D5 **Lovai** *watercourse* Democratic Republic of Congo
222 L4 **Lövånger** Sweden
225 P4 **Lovat'** *watercourse* Russian Federation
222 E6 **Lovatnet** *lake* Norway
222 I4 **Lövberg** Sweden
222 I5 **Lövberga** Sweden
234 D4 **Lovech** Bulgaria
234 D4 **Lovech** *admin. area* Bulgaria
130 D5 **Lovelady** Texas USA
125 M6 **Loveland** Colorado USA
125 K4 **Lovell** Wyoming USA
124 F6 **Lovelock** Nevada USA
226 B2 **Lovendegem** Belgium
119 Q7 **Loverna** Saskatchewan Canada
222 K2 **Lovik** Norway
223 M3 **Lovikka** Sweden
129 J4 **Loving** New Mexico USA
129 K4 **Lovington** New Mexico USA
227 I4 **Lövő** Hungary
222 K3 **Lovos** Sweden
227 H4 **Lovosice** Czech Republic
222 P2 **Lovozero** Russian Federation
223 S3 **Lovozero, Ozero** *lake* Russian Federation
232 F4 **Lovran** Croatia
227 G5 **Lovreć** Croatia
234 B3 **Lovrin** Romania
222 I5 **Lövsjön** *lake* Sweden
222 I4 **Lövstrand** Sweden
308 D2 **Lóvua** Angola
120 M1 **Low, Cape** Nunavut Canada
243 G3 **Low Bradfield** South Yorkshire England UK
243 H3 **Low Burnham** North Lincolnshire England UK
436 T2 **Low Island** Antarctica
424 inset **Low Point** Christmas Island Australia
306 D4 **Lowa** *watercourse* Democratic Republic of Congo
391 L2 **Lowarai Pass** Pakistan
127 P5 **Lowell** Massachusetts USA
124 D5 **Lowell** Oregon USA
118 L8 **Lower Arrow Lake** British Columbia Canada
128 B1 **Lower Bear River Reservoir** California USA
240 D2 **Lower Chapel** Powys Wales UK
119 S4 **Lower Foster Lake** Saskatchewan Canada
241 G3 **Lower Froyle** Hampshire England UK
240 D2 **Lower Hergest** Herefordshire England UK
423 F5 **Lower Hutt** New Zealand
124 E6 **Lower Klamath Lake** California USA
244 B3 **Lower Milovaig** Highland Scotland UK
118 G3 **Lower Post** British Columbia Canada
126 D3 **Lower Red Lake** Minnesota USA
122 F2 **Lower Savage Islands** Nunavut Canada
374 D2 **Lower Seletar Reservoir** Singapore
241 H3 **Lower Stoke** Medway England UK
241 E2 **Lower Strensham** Worcestershire England UK
241 F2 **Lower Tean** Staffordshire England UK
241 I2 **Lowestoft** Suffolk England UK
242 E2 **Loweswater** Cumbria England UK
391 L2 **Lowgar** *admin. area* Afghanistan
243 F2 **Lowgill** Lancashire England UK
227 J1 **Łowicz** Poland
117 J4 **Lowther Island** Nunavut Canada
243 H2 **Lowthorpe** East Riding of Yorkshire England UK
127 N5 **Lowville** New York USA
425 L8 **Loxton** SA Australia
308 D6 **Loxton** South Africa
244 D2 **Loyal, Loch** *lake* Scotland UK
131 J2 **Loyall** Kentucky USA
124 E7 **Loyalton** California USA
426 7 **Loyauté, Îles** *islands* New Caledonia
223 Q6 **Loymola** Russian Federation
234 E4 **Lozarevo** Bulgaria
227 H1 **Łozice** Poland
234 A3 **Loznica** Serbia
234 F3 **Lozova** Ukraine
234 B3 **Lozovik** Serbia
236 N6 **Loz'va** *watercourse* Russian Federation
381 G2 **Lu Hu** *lake* Hubei China
381 H4 **Lu-liao Shui-K'u** *lake* Taiwan China
385 I6 **Lu Shan** *range* Shandong China
381 I4 **Lü Tao** *island* Taiwan China
306 B3 **Lua** *watercourse* Democratic Republic of Congo
306 B3 **Lua-Dekere** *watercourse* Democratic Republic of Congo
159 G2 **Lua Nova** Brazil
306 B3 **Lua Vindu** *watercourse* Democratic Republic of Congo
306 D5 **Luabo** Democratic Republic of Congo
309 G3 **Luabo** Mozambique
308 D2 **Luacano** Angola
306 C5 **Luaco** Angola
Lualaba *see* **Congo** Democratic Republic of Congo
306 D4 **Luama** *watercourse* Democratic Republic of Congo
308 D2 **Luambimba** *watercourse* Zambia
308 D3 **Luampa** Zambia
381 G2 **Lu'an** Anhui China
160 E6 **Luan Toro** Argentina
381 F1 **Luanchuan** Henan China
160 D6 **Luanco** Argentina
230 D2 **Luanco** Spain
306 A5 **Luanda** Angola
308 B1 **Luanda** *admin. area* Angola
308 C2 **Luando** Angola
375 K6 **Luang** *island* Indonesia
308 D2 **Luanginga** *watercourse* Zambia
306 B5 **Luangue** *watercourse* Angola
308 D2 **Luanguinga** *watercourse* Angola
306 E5 **Luangwa** *watercourse* Zambia
385 I5 **Luanping** Hebei China
308 E2 **Luanshya** Zambia
306 D6 **Luapula** *watercourse* Democratic Republic of Congo
308 E2 **Luapula** *admin. area* Zambia
Luar *see* **Horsburgh Island** Australia
230 C2 **Luarca** Spain
306 C6 **Luashi** Democratic Republic of Congo
308 C3 **Luassingua** *watercourse* Angola
308 D2 **Luatamba** Angola
309 G2 **Luatize** *watercourse* Mozambique
308 D2 **Luau** Angola
305 F4 **Luba** Equatorial Guinea
306 B5 **Lubalo** Angola
227 H2 **Lubań** Poland
225 N4 **Lubāna** Latvia
238 B4 **Lubānas ezers** *lake* Latvia
377 I4 **Lubang** *island* Philippines
308 B2 **Lubango** Angola
225 N4 **Lubāns** *lake* Latvia
306 D5 **Lubao** Democratic Republic of Congo
227 L2 **Lubartów** Poland
129 L4 **Lubbock** Texas USA
222 J4 **Lubbträsket** *lake* Sweden
244 D3 **Lubcroy** Highland Scotland UK
224 F6 **Lübeck** Germany
224 F5 **Lübecker Bucht** *bay* Germany
306 C4 **Lubefu** Democratic Republic of Congo
385 I4 **Lubei** Nei Mongol Zizhiqu China
227 L2 **Lubelskie** *admin. area* Poland
388 G3 **Lubenka** Kazakhstan
306 D4 **Lubero** Democratic Republic of Congo
228 E4 **Lubersac** France
227 H1 **Łubianka** Poland
227 M2 **Lubiaż** Ukraine
377 I5 **Lubic** *island* Philippines
119 N4 **Lubicon Lake** Alberta Canada
227 I1 **Lubie, Jezioro** *lake* Poland
227 J1 **Lubień Kujawski** Poland
227 H1 **Lubin** Poland
227 I2 **Lubin** Poland
225 P3 **Lubino** Russian Federation
227 L2 **Lublin** Poland
227 J2 **Lubliniec** Poland
244 C3 **Lubmore** Highland Scotland UK
375 F3 **Lubok Antu** Malaysia
227 I1 **Luboń** Poland
227 J1 **Luboniek** Poland
227 I1 **Łubowo** Poland
230 E5 **Lubrín** Spain
306 D5 **Lubudi** Democratic Republic of Congo
306 C5 **Lubudi** *watercourse* Democratic Republic of Congo
374 D4 **Lubuk Linggau** Indonesia
374 D3 **Lubuksikaping** Indonesia
306 D6 **Lubumbashi** Democratic Republic of Congo
227 H1 **Lubuskie** *admin. area* Poland
306 D4 **Lubutu** Democratic Republic of Congo
306 D4 **Lubutu** *watercourse* Democratic Republic of Congo
308 E2 **Lubwe** Zambia
127 R2 **Luc, Pointe à** *cape* Québec Canada
229 G4 **Luc-en-Diois** France
308 C1 **Lucala** Angola
306 B5 **Lucala** *watercourse* Angola
127 K5 **Lucan** Ontario Canada
245 F3 **Lucan** Ireland
306 C5 **Lucapa** Angola
159 H5 **Lucas** Brazil
129 M1 **Lucas** Kansas USA
155 G5 **Lucas Borges** Brazil
232 D5 **Lucca** Italy
229 L3 **Luče** Slovenia
244 D6 **Luce Bay** Scotland UK
130 G5 **Lucedale** Mississippi USA
157 B8 **Lucélia** Brazil
377 I4 **Lucena** Philippines
230 D5 **Lucena** Spain
231 F3 **Lucena del Cid** Spain
227 J3 **Lučenec** Slovakia
233 F6 **Lucera** Italy
158 D4 **Lucera** Peru
132 D2 **Lucero** Mexico
129 I4 **Lucero, Lake** New Mexico USA
154 B4 **Lucero, Punta** *cape* Ecuador
380 F4 **Lucheng** Guangxi Zhuangzu Zizhiqu China
385 H6 **Lucheng** Shanxi China
380 D2 **Lucheng** Sichuan China
309 G2 **Luchering** *watercourse* Mozambique
238 H4 **Luchki** Russian Federation
238 H2 **Lucho, Ozero** *lake* Russian Federation
226 F1 **Lüchow** Germany
226 E4 **Luchsingen** Switzerland
159 I3 **Luciára** Brazil
155 G4 **Lucie** *watercourse* Suriname
121 P7 **Lucie, Lac** *lake* Québec Canada
159 I5 **Lucilândia** Brazil
159 I3 **Lúcio da Luz** Brazil
375 J5 **Lucipara, Kepulauan** *island* Indonesia
308 B2 **Lucira** Angola
234 E3 **Luciu** Romania
227 G2 **Luckau** Germany
127 K5 **Lucknow** Ontario Canada
392 E5 **Lucknow** Uttar Pradesh India
119 R7 **Lucky Lake** Saskatchewan Canada
228 D3 **Luçon** France
135 F2 **Lucrecia, Cayo** *island* Cuba
306 A5 **Lucunga** Angola
308 D2 **Lucusse** Angola
223 U4 **Luda** Russian Federation
226 F1 **Lüderitz** Germany
308 C5 **Lüderitz** Namibia
127 K4 **Ludgate** Ontario Canada
241 F3 **Ludgershall** Wiltshire England UK
240 B4 **Ludgvan** Cornwall England UK
392 D4 **Ludhiana** Punjab India
306 C5 **Ludimba** *watercourse* Democratic Republic of Congo
126 H5 **Ludington** Michigan USA
240 E2 **Ludlow** Shropshire England UK
128 D3 **Ludlow** California USA
234 C3 **Ludoș** Romania
234 A2 **Ludoško Jezero** *lake* Serbia
226 E3 **Ludwigshafen am Rhein** Germany
227 M2 **Ludyn** Ukraine
225 N4 **Ludza** Latvia
225 N4 **Ludzas** *admin. area* Latvia
306 C5 **Luebo** Democratic Republic of Congo
130 B4 **Lueders** Texas USA
306 D4 **Lueki** Democratic Republic of Congo
306 D4 **Luemba** Democratic Republic of Congo
308 F2 **Luembe** Zambia
308 C2 **Luena** Angola
308 D2 **Luena** *watercourse* Angola
306 D5 **Luena** Democratic Republic of Congo
308 F2 **Luena** Zambia
308 D2 **Luena** *watercourse* Zambia
308 D2 **Luena Flats** *pan* Zambia
308 D3 **Luengué** Angola
380 E1 **Lueyang** Shaanxi China
373 H4 **Luf Island** Papua New Guinea
381 G4 **Lufeng** Guangdong China
380 F3 **Lufeng** Hunan China
306 A5 **Lufico** Angola
306 D5 **Lufila** *watercourse* Democratic Republic of Congo
308 E2 **Lufira, Lac de Retenue de la** *lake* Democratic Republic of Congo
130 D5 **Lufkin** Texas USA
306 A5 **Lufu** Democratic Republic of Congo
308 E1 **Lufubu** Zambia
306 E5 **Lufubu** *watercourse* Zambia
227 J5 **Lug** Croatia
225 O3 **Luga** Russian Federation
229 I3 **Lugano** Switzerland
426 7 **Luganville** Vanuatu
309 G3 **Lugela** *watercourse* Mozambique
309 G2 **Lugenda** *watercourse* Mozambique
240 E2 **Lugg** *watercourse* England UK
379 G2 **Luggudontsen** *mountain* Xizang Zizhiqu China
234 D1 **Lugi** Ukraine
234 F1 **Lugi** Ukraine
222 J5 **Lugnvik** Sweden
232 D4 **Lugo** Italy
230 C2 **Lugo** Spain
234 B3 **Lugoj** Romania
306 D4 **Lugulu** *watercourse* Democratic Republic of Congo
377 I6 **Lugus** Philippines
377 I6 **Lugus** *island* Philippines
225 L2 **Luhalahti** Finland
394 F3 **Luhans'k** Ukraine
394 F3 **Luhans'ka Oblast'** *admin. area* Ukraine
385 I3 **Luhin Sum** Nei Mongol Zizhiqu China
306 D4 **Luhoho** *watercourse* Democratic Republic of Congo
307 F5 **Luhombero** Tanzania
307 F5 **Luhombero** *mountain* Tanzania
380 D2 **Luhua** Sichuan China
306 B5 **Lui** *watercourse* Angola
306 C5 **Luia** Angola
309 F3 **Luia** *watercourse* Mozambique
308 D3 **Luiana** Angola
308 D3 **Luiana** *watercourse* Angola
244 B3 **Luib** Highland Scotland UK
244 D4 **Luibeilt** Highland Scotland UK
309 F4 **Luido** Mozambique
223 P5 **Luikonlahti** Finland
244 C4 **Luing** *island* Scotland UK
308 D2 **Luio** *watercourse* Angola
223 O3 **Luiro** Finland
223 O3 **Luiro** *watercourse* Finland
159 I2 **Luís Gonçalves** Brazil
132 E4 **Luis Moya** Mexico
306 D6 **Luishia** Democratic Republic of Congo
158 C4 **Luisiana** Peru
436 V1 **Luitpold Coast** Antarctica
306 C5 **Luiza** Democratic Republic of Congo
308 D2 **Luizavo** *watercourse* Angola
306 D5 **Luizi** Democratic Republic of Congo
381 H2 **Lujiang** Anhui China
232 F4 **Luka** Croatia
306 A5 **Lukala** Democratic Republic of Congo
308 E2 **Lukanga Swamps** *swamp* Zambia
232 H4 **Lukavac** Bosnia and Herzegovina
306 D5 **Lukenga, Lac** *lake* Democratic Republic of Congo
306 C4 **Lukenie** *watercourse* Democratic Republic of Congo
245 E4 **Lukeswell** Ireland
128 F5 **Lukeville** Mexico
132 B2 **Lukeville** Arizona USA
388 D1 **Lukh** Russian Federation
238 H5 **Lukhovitsy** Russian Federation
425 M3 **Lukin, Mount** Qld Australia
238 F2 **Lukinskaya** Russian Federation
225 K4 **Luknės** Lithuania
381 G3 **Lukou** Hunan China
234 D4 **Lukovit** Bulgaria
227 M2 **Lukovo** Belarus
232 F4 **Lukovo Šugarje** Croatia
227 L2 **Łuków** Poland
388 D2 **Lukoyanov** Russian Federation
372 B4 **Luksagu** Indonesia
225 L5 **Lukšiai** Lithuania
227 K1 **Łukta** Poland
306 D5 **Lukuga** *watercourse* Democratic Republic of Congo
306 A5 **Lukula** Democratic Republic of Congo
308 D2 **Lukulu** Zambia
308 F2 **Lukulu** *watercourse* Zambia
306 D5 **Lukumbi** *watercourse* Democratic Republic of Congo
307 F5 **Lukumburu** Tanzania
306 B5 **Lukuni** Democratic Republic of Congo
426 6 **Lukunor** *island* Federated States of Micronesia
131 J3 **Lula** Georgia USA
388 F1 **Lūlaki** Iran
222 M4 **Luleå** Sweden
235 E5 **Lüleburgaz** Turkey
309 F4 **Lulekani** South Africa
222 J3 **Lulep Jutas** *lake* Sweden
384 G5 **Luliang Shan** *range* Shanxi China
306 D4 **Lulimba** Democratic Republic of Congo
130 C6 **Luling** Texas USA
385 I5 **Lulong** Hebei China
306 B3 **Lulonga** *watercourse* Democratic Republic of Congo
306 C3 **Lulu** *watercourse* Democratic Republic of Congo
427 12b **Lulu Fakahega, Mont** *mountain* Wallis and Futuna
306 C5 **Lulua** *watercourse* Democratic Republic of Congo
241 E4 **Lulworth Camp** Dorset England UK
305 E2 **Luma** Nigeria
308 C2 **Luma Cassai** Angola
375 G6 **Lumajang** Indonesia
391 K2 **Lūmān** Afghanistan
306 D4 **Lumana** Democratic Republic of Congo
225 L3 **Lümanda** Estonia
308 D2 **Lumbala Kaquengue** Angola
308 D2 **Lumbala N'guimbo** Angola
308 D3 **Lumbe** *watercourse* Zambia
119 N8 **Lumberton** British Columbia Canada
131 L3 **Lumberton** North Carolina USA
130 D5 **Lumberton** Texas USA
375 H2 **Lumbis** Indonesia
236 J5 **Lumbovka** Russian Federation
241 J4 **Lumbres** France
118 L7 **Lumby** British Columbia Canada
379 G4 **Lumding** Assam India
235 B5 **Lumi I Osum** *watercourse* Albania
161 G2 **Lumiador, Cordilheira do** *range* Brazil
223 N4 **Lumijoki** Finland
229 G1 **Lummen** Belgium
245 C3 **Lumnagh** Ireland
225 K2 **Lumparn** *bay* Finland
376 E4 **Lumphăt** Cambodia
131 I4 **Lumpkin** Georgia USA
123 L8 **Lumsden** Newfoundland and Labrador Canada
119 S7 **Lumsden** Saskatchewan Canada
423 C7 **Lumsden** New Zealand
306 C7 **Lumulunga** Zambia
308 D3 **Lumuna** *watercourse* Angola
374 D2 **Lumut** Malaysia
375 H4 **Lumut, Gunung** *mountain* Indonesia
374 E4 **Lumut, Tanjung** *cape* Indonesia
308 E2 **Lumwana** Zambia
229 L4 **Lun** Croatia
384 F3 **Lün** Mongolia
159 F2 **Luna** *watercourse* Brazil
231 F2 **Luna** Spain
230 D2 **Luna** *watercourse* Spain
244 F4 **Lunan Bay** Scotland UK
227 L5 **Lunca Cernii de Sus** Romania
234 E2 **Lunca de Jos** Romania
234 D2 **Lunca Ilvei** Romania
118 I8 **Lund** British Columbia Canada
222 G4 **Lund** Norway
224 G5 **Lund** Sweden
243 H3 **Lund** East Riding of Yorkshire England UK
128 E1 **Lund** Nevada USA
308 C1 **Lunda Norte** *admin. area* Angola
308 D2 **Lunda Sul** *admin. area* Angola
120 F7 **Lundar** Manitoba Canada
244 C4 **Lundavra** Highland Scotland UK
309 F2 **Lundazi** Zambia
224 E3 **Lunde** Norway
224 I5 **Lunde** Sweden
222 H3 **Lundeura** *island* Norway
224 D3 **Lundevatn** *lake* Norway
244 F4 **Lundie Castle** Angus Scotland UK
222 I2 **Lundøya** *island* Norway
224 H3 **Lundsfjärden** *bay* Sweden
222 I5 **Lundsjön** Sweden
375 F3 **Lundu** Malaysia
240 C3 **Lundy Island** England UK
243 F2 **Lune** *watercourse* England UK
226 F1 **Lüneburger Heide** *region* Germany
231 I2 **Lunel** France
123 F10 **Lunenburg** Nova Scotia Canada
229 H2 **Lunéville** France
309 H3 **Lunga** Mozambique
426 8a **Lunga Point** Solomon Islands
378 E2 **Lungar Shan** *mountain* Xizang Zizhiqu China
308 C2 **Lunge** Angola
224 G3 **Lungen** *lake* Sweden
304 B3 **Lungi** Sierra Leone
222 K5 **Lungön** *island* Sweden
222 J5 **Lungsjön** Sweden
392 F5 **Lunh** Nepal
392 C6 **Luni** *watercourse* Rajasthan India
128 C1 **Luning** Nevada USA
388 E2 **Lunino** Russian Federation
392 C5 **Lunkaransar** Rajasthan India
244 inset **Lunna** Shetland Scotland UK
222 H5 **Lunnäset** Sweden
226 D1 **Lünne** Germany
308 E2 **Lunsemfwa** *watercourse* Zambia
382 G4 **Luntai** Xinjiang Uygur Zizhiqu China
375 H6 **Lunyuk** Indonesia
380 C1 **Lu'nyung** Sichuan China
227 H4 **Lunz am See** Austria
381 F4 **Luo He** *watercourse* Jiangsu China
381 F4 **Luoding** Guangdong China
380 F5 **Luodou Sha** *island* Guangdong China
381 G1 **Luohe** Henan China
379 F3 **Luojiang** Xizang Zizhiqu China
381 H1 **Luoma Hu** *lake* Jiangsu China
380 F1 **Luonan** Shaanxi China
225 N2 **Luonteri** *bay* Finland
382 F5 **Luopu** Xinjiang Uygur Zizhiqu China
381 G2 **Luoshan** Henan China
223 O2 **Luostari** Russian Federation
223 M5 **Luoto** Finland
223 P1 **Luovtejok** Norway
381 G3 **Luoxiao Shan** *range* Hunan China
380 D4 **Luoxiong** Yunnan China
381 F1 **Luoyang** Henan China
379 G3 **Luozha** Xizang Zizhiqu China
306 A4 **Luozi** Democratic Republic of Congo
308 E3 **Lupane** Zimbabwe
380 D3 **Lupanshui** Guizhou China
375 F3 **Lupar** *watercourse* Malaysia
227 L5 **Lupeni** Romania
135 G3 **Luperón** Dominican Republic
309 G2 **Lupilichi** Mozambique
308 C2 **Lupire** Angola
307 F5 **Lupiro** Tanzania
426 5 **Lupog** Guam
225 P5 **Lupolovo** Belarus
377 J6 **Lupon** Philippines
240 D4 **Luppitt** Devon England UK
129 H3 **Lupton** Arizona USA
380 D2 **Luqiao** Sichuan China
380 D1 **Luqu** Gansu China
229 H3 **Lure** France
131 J3 **Lure, Lake** North Carolina USA
309 G2 **Lureco** *watercourse* Mozambique
306 B5 **Luremo** Angola
228 E3 **Lureuil** France
245 F3 **Lurgan** Ireland
245 F2 **Lurgan** Armagh Northern Ireland UK
158 E5 **Luribay** Bolivia
309 H2 **Lúrio** Mozambique
309 G2 **Lúrio** *watercourse* Mozambique
222 H3 **Lurøya** *island* Norway
245 D5 **Lurrig** Ireland
154 C2 **Luruaco** Colombia
306 D5 **Lusaka** Democratic Republic of Congo
308 E3 **Lusaka** Zambia
308 E3 **Lusaka** *admin. area* Zambia
306 D4 **Lusako** Democratic Republic of Congo
306 D4 **Lusamba** Democratic Republic of Congo
306 C4 **Lusambo** Democratic Republic of Congo
373 I6 **Lusancay Islands and Reefs** Papua New Guinea
306 B4 **Lusanga** Democratic Republic of Congo
306 D4 **Lusangi** Democratic Republic of Congo
118 M6 **Luscar** Alberta Canada
307 F6 **Lusewa** Tanzania
384 E6 **Lushaer** Qinghai China
380 F1 **Lushi** Henan China
235 A5 **Lushnjë** Albania
307 F4 **Lushoto** Tanzania
226 C3 **Lusigny** France
245 F3 **Lusk** Ireland
125 M5 **Lusk** Wyoming USA
232 G5 **Lusnić** Bosnia and Herzegovina
230 B3 **Luso** Portugal
244 D4 **Luss** Argyll and Bute Scotland UK
244 C4 **Lussagiven** Argyll and Bute Scotland UK
229 G4 **Lussan** France
308 B2 **Lussusso** Angola
244 B3 **Lusta** Highland Scotland UK
222 E6 **Luster** Norway
225 N4 **Lusti** Estonia
232 D3 **Lutago** Italy
130 F5 **Lutcher** Louisiana USA
308 D2 **Lutembo** Angola
426 8 **Luti** Solomon Islands
224 F5 **Lütjenburg** Germany
241 G3 **Luton** *admin. area* England UK
241 G3 **Luton** Luton England UK
375 G2 **Lutong** Malaysia
118 M3 **Lutose** Alberta Canada
225 K5 **Lutry** Poland
227 M2 **Luts'k** Ukraine
241 F2 **Lutterworth** Leicester England UK
223 P2 **Lutto** *watercourse* Finland
241 H2 **Lutton** Lincolnshire England UK
242 B3 **Luttrellstown** Ireland
308 D2 **Lutuai** Angola
437 C2 **Lützow-Holm Bay** Antarctica
384 F3 **Luuc** Mongolia
372 B2 **Luuk** Philippines
377 I6 **Luuk** Philippines
225 N2 **Luumäki** Finland
307 G3 **Luuq** Somalia
223 O3 **Luusua** Finland
306 C6 **Luveira** *watercourse* Democratic Republic of Congo
131 H5 **Luverne** Alabama USA
125 Q5 **Luverne** Minnesota USA
225 K2 **Luvia** Finland
306 A5 **Luvo** Angola
223 Q4 **Luvozero** *lake* Russian Federation
308 D2 **Luvuei** Angola
309 F2 **Luwawa** Malawi
307 F5 **Luwegu** *watercourse* Tanzania
307 E3 **Luwero** Uganda
308 E2 **Luwingu** Zambia
372 D3 **Luwo** *island* Indonesia
375 F4 **Luwuhuyu** Indonesia
372 B4 **Luwuk** Indonesia
229 **Luxembourg** *country* Europe
229 H2 **Luxembourg** Luxembourg
229 H3 **Luxeuil-les-Bains** France
228 D4 **Luxey** France
380 C4 **Luxi** Yunnan China
381 I3 **Luxi Dao** *island* Zhejiang China
228 D5 **Luy** *watercourse* France
384 G5 **Luya Shan** *range* Shanxi China
306 D4 **Luyamba** Democratic Republic of Congo
230 C2 **Luyego de Somoza** Spain
381 G1 **Luyi** Henan China
157 C7 **Luz** Brazil
230 C5 **Luz, Costa de la** *region* Spain
236 K6 **Luza** Russian Federation
229 I3 **Luzern (Lucerne)** Switzerland
380 F4 **Luzhai** Guangxi Zhuangzu Zizhiqu China
380 C3 **Luzhang** Yunnan China
225 O2 **Luzhayka** Russian Federation
225 O4 **Luzhitsy** Russian Federation
225 N5 **Luzhki** Belarus
225 O2 **Luzhki** Russian Federation
380 E3 **Luzhou** Sichuan China
157 C7 **Luziânia** Brazil
227 H2 **Lužicka** *watercourse* Czech Republic
156 D3 **Luzilândia** Brazil
224 J5 **Luzino** Poland
227 H3 **Lužnice** *watercourse* Czech Republic
377 I3 **Luzon** *island* Philippines
377 I2 **Luzon Strait** Philippines
228 F3 **Luzy** France
238 G5 **L'va Tolstogo** Russian Federation
234 D1 **L'viv** Ukraine
394 C2 **L'vivs'ka Oblast'** *admin. area* Ukraine
227 I1 **Lwówek** Poland
225 P5 **Lyady** Belarus
237 AC4 **Lyakhovskiye Ostrova** *island* Russian Federation
388 E6 **Lyaki** Azerbaijan
223 T4 **Lyamitskoye Ozero** *lake* Russian Federation
223 T4 **Lyamtsa** Russian Federation
225 P2 **Lyaskelya** Russian Federation
235 D5 **Lyaskovo** Bulgaria
227 M1 **Lyasnaya** Belarus
244 E2 **Lybster** Highland Scotland UK
227 M2 **Lybytiv** Ukraine
129 K2 **Lycan** Colorado USA
225 Q4 **Lychkovo** Russian Federation
222 K4 **Lycksele** Sweden
241 H4 **Lydd** Kent England UK
119 V5 **Lyddal** Manitoba Canada
240 C4 **Lydford** Devon England UK
240 E3 **Lydney** Gloucestershire England UK
118 F6 **Lyell Island** British Columbia Canada
225 O5 **Lyepyel'** Belarus
130 C7 **Lyford** Texas USA
224 D3 **Lygna** *watercourse* Norway
224 G4 **Lygnern** *lake* Sweden
238 E3 **Lykoshino** Russian Federation
125 O2 **Lyleton** Manitoba Canada
223 P4 **Lylykylä** Finland
128 G1 **Lyman** Utah USA
125 J6 **Lyman** Wyoming USA

234 G2 **Lymany** Ukraine
240 E4 **Lyme Bay** England UK
241 F4 **Lymington** Hampshire England UK
240 D4 **Lympstone** Devon England UK
127 L8 **Lynchburg** Virginia USA
425 L4 **Lynd** *watercourse* Qld Australia
124 D2 **Lynden** Washington USA
424 E5 **Lyndon** *watercourse* WA Australia
126 G6 **Lyndon** Illinois USA
127 O4 **Lyndonville** Vermont USA
241 F3 **Lyneham** Wiltshire England UK
222 L2 **Lyngen** *bay* Norway
224 D3 **Lyngna** *lake* Norway
222 L2 **Lyngseidet** Norway
222 G4 **Lyngsnes** Norway
224 D3 **Lyngsvatnet** *lake* Norway
240 D3 **Lynmouth** Devon England UK
243 G1 **Lynmouth** Northumberland England UK
130 H3 **Lynn** Alabama USA
126 I6 **Lynn** Indiana USA
127 P5 **Lynn** Massachusetts USA
118 D3 **Lynn Canal** Alaska USA
131 I5 **Lynn Haven** Florida USA
119 U4 **Lynn Lake** Manitoba Canada
124 I7 **Lynndyl** Utah USA
240 D3 **Lynton** Devon England UK
119 R1 **Lynx Lake** Northwest Territories Canada
224 F5 **Lyø** *island* Denmark
229 G4 **Lyon** France
244 D4 **Lyon** *watercourse* Scotland UK
244 D4 **Lyon, Loch** *lake* Scotland UK
424 E6 **Lyons** *watercourse* WA Australia
125 P7 **Lyons** Kansas USA
126 I6 **Lyons** Ohio USA
244 B5 **Lyrabus** Argyll and Bute Scotland UK
224 H3 **Lyrestad** Sweden
228 F1 **Lys** *watercourse* France
224 F3 **Lysekil** Sweden
224 F3 **Lyseren** *lake* Norway
227 I3 **Lysice** Czech Republic
235 B6 **Lysimachia, Limni** *lake* Greece
227 J1 **Łysomice** Poland
222 F5 **Lysøysund** Norway
229 H3 **Lyss** Switzerland
236 M7 **Lys'va** Russian Federation
388 H1 **Lys'va** Russian Federation
234 G1 **Lysyanka** Ukraine
234 F3 **Lysychans'k** Ukraine
388 D3 **Lysyye Gory** Russian Federation
242 F3 **Lytham** Lancashire England UK
242 E3 **Lytham St Anne's** Lancashire England UK
238 G5 **Lytkarino** Russian Federation
130 B6 **Lytle** Texas USA
227 M2 **Lytovezh** Ukraine
423 E6 **Lyttelton** New Zealand
423 E6 **Lyttelton Harbour** New Zealand
118 K7 **Lytton** British Columbia Canada
225 P3 **Lyuban'** Russian Federation
238 G5 **Lyubertsy** Russian Federation
227 M2 **Lyubeshiv** Ukraine
238 H6 **Lyubimovka** Russian Federation
238 F6 **Lyubitovo** Russian Federation
238 B6 **Lyubyacha** Belarus
238 E3 **Lyubytino** Russian Federation
238 F6 **Lyudinovo** Russian Federation
238 F5 **Lyudkovo** Russian Federation

M

376 E2 **Ma Song** *watercourse* Vietnam
376 B3 **Ma-Ubin** Myanmar
380 D2 **Ma'erkang** Sichuan China
223 N4 **Maakrunni** *island* Finland
222 L5 **Maalahti** Finland
393 C11 **Maalhosmadulu Atoll** Maldives
245 C3 **Maam Cross** Ireland
390 C3 **Ma'ān** Jordan
223 O5 **Maaninka** Finland
223 P5 **Maanselkä** Finland
226 C2 **Maas** *watercourse* Belgium/Netherlands
229 G1 **Maaseik** Belgium
223 P4 **Maaselkä** Finland
154 D1 **Maásimay** Colombia
377 J5 **Maasin** Philippines
226 C2 **Maastricht** Netherlands
427 14a **Maatea** French Polynesia
425 M10 **Maatsuyker Group** *islands* Tas. Australia
223 N5 **Määttälä** Finland
381 G4 **Maba** Guangdong China
372 D3 **Maba** Indonesia
380 D4 **Mabai** Yunnan China
377 I4 **Mabalacat** Philippines
309 F4 **Mabalane** Mozambique
306 D3 **Mabana** Democratic Republic of Congo
390 E7 **Ma'bar** Yemen
155 G2 **Mabaruma** Guyana
308 D3 **Mabebe Depression** *pan* Botswana
379 H4 **Mabein** Myanmar
126 F5 **Mabel** Minnesota USA
124 F1 **Mabel Lake** British Columbia Canada
130 B4 **Mabelle** Texas USA
130 G4 **Maben** Mississippi USA
377 J5 **Mabini** Philippines
243 I3 **Mablethorpe** Lincolnshire England UK
155 H4 **Maboga** Suriname
304 B3 **Mabole** *watercourse* Sierra Leone
124 F3 **Mabton** Washington USA
377 I2 **Mabudis** *island* Philippines
305 F2 **Mabuto** Nigeria
308 D4 **Mabutsane** Botswana
158 B2 **Macabí, Isla** *island* Peru
157 D8 **Macaé** Brazil
230 E5 **Macael** Spain
394 G5 **Macahel Gecidi** *pass* Turkey
130 D3 **McAlester** Oklahoma USA
118 J6 **Macalister** British Columbia Canada
130 B7 **McAllen** Texas USA
117 I5 **McAlpine Lake** Nunavut Canada
127 L2 **Macamic Lake** Québec Canada
375 I5 **Macan, Kepulauan** *island* Indonesia
154 E4 **Macanacape, Laguna** *lake* Venezuela
309 F4 **Macandze** Mozambique
155 I4 **Macapá** Brazil
158 E3 **Macapá** Brazil
154 B6 **Macará** Ecuador
154 D6 **Macaracas** Panama
154 C4 **Macaranaima** Colombia
155 F2 **Macareo, Caño** *watercourse* Venezuela
120 H7 **McArthur Falls** Manitoba Canada
154 B5 **Macas** Ecuador
Macassar Strait *see* **Makassar, Selat** Indonesia
156 E4 **Macau** Brazil
381 G4 **Macau (Aomen)** Macau (AOMEN) S.A.R. China
381 G4 **Macau (Aomen) S.A.R.** *admin. area* China
159 I3 **Macaúba** Brazil
157 D6 **Macaúbas** Brazil
422 5 **Macauley Island** Kermadec Islands New Zealand
154 C4 **Macaya-tunia** *watercourse* Colombia
126 I4 **McBain** Michigan USA
307 I2 **Macbar, Raas** *cape* Somalia
131 K3 **McBee** South Carolina USA
118 K6 **McBride** British Columbia Canada
124 G4 **McCall** Idaho USA
129 K5 **McCamey** Texas USA
124 H5 **McCammon** Idaho USA
436 V1 **McCarthy Inlet** *bay* Antarctica
129 I3 **McCartys** New Mexico USA
124 D3 **McCleary** Washington USA
131 J5 **Macclenny** Florida USA
123 K8 **Maccles Lake** Newfoundland and Labrador Canada
243 F3 **Macclesfield** Cheshire England UK
377 G4 **Macclesfield Bank** *island* Paracel Islands
81 P3 **Macclesfield Bank** *underwater feature* South China Sea
243 F3 **Macclesfield Canal** England UK
437 K1 **McClintock, Mount** *mountain* Antarctica
127 M6 **McClure** Pennsylvania USA
124 E8 **McClure, Lake** California USA
125 O3 **McClusky** North Dakota USA
131 L3 **McColl** South Carolina USA
130 F5 **McComb** Mississippi USA
125 O6 **McConaughy, Lake** Nebraska USA
120 H2 **McConnell** *watercourse* Nunavut Canada
125 O6 **McCook** Nebraska USA
119 R8 **McCord** Saskatchewan Canada
131 J4 **McCormick** South Carolina USA
437 L2 **McCormick, Cape** Antarctica
120 I6 **McCoy Lake** Ontario Canada
130 F3 **McCrory** Arkansas USA
119 V7 **Macdonald** Manitoba Canada
129 K4 **McDonald** New Mexico USA
424 H5 **MacDonald, Lake** WA Australia
124 I2 **McDonald, Lake** Montana USA
437 G2 **McDonald Bay** Antarctica
424 inset **McDonald Island** Heard Island Australia
124 H2 **MacDonald Range** British Columbia Canada
424 J5 **MacDonnell Ranges** NT Australia
131 I4 **McDonough** Georgia USA
309 F4 **McDougal, Lake** *lake* Zimbabwe
119 R6 **Macdowall** Saskatchewan Canada
117 J8 **MacDowell Lake** Ontario Canada
234 B2 **Macea** Romania
235 B5 **Macedonia** *country* Europe
156 F5 **Maceió** Brazil
154 C3 **Maceo** Colombia
232 E5 **Macerata** Italy
425 L5 **McEvoy, Mount** Qld Australia
128 C3 **McFarland** California USA
119 Q3 **MacFarlane** *watercourse* Saskatchewan Canada
242 B1 **Macfinn Lower** Coleraine Northern Ireland UK
125 K1 **McGee** Saskatchewan Canada
130 D3 **McGee Creek Reservoir** Oklahoma USA
124 D1 **McGillivray Falls** British Columbia Canada
245 C5 **Macgillycuddy's Reeks** *range* Ireland
116 D6 **McGrath** Alaska USA
118 K5 **McGregor** British Columbia Canada
118 K5 **McGregor** *watercourse* British Columbia Canada
119 O7 **McGregor Lake** Alberta Canada
124 H3 **McGregor Lake** Montana USA
154 B5 **Machachi** Ecuador
157 C8 **Machado** Brazil
309 F4 **Machaila** Mozambique
154 B5 **Machala** Ecuador
383 K6 **Machali** Qinghai China
375 G3 **Machan** Malaysia
379 H3 **Machanbaw** Myanmar
307 E2 **Machar Marshes** *swamp* Sudan
428* E8 **Machattie, Lake** Qld Australia
120 K7 **Machawaian Lake** Ontario Canada
228 D3 **Machecoul** France
381 G2 **Macheng** Hubei China
123 E10 **Machias** Maine USA
127 R4 **Machias Bay** Maine USA
120 J4 **Machichi** *watercourse* Manitoba Canada
310 2 **Machico** Madeira
308 E3 **Machile** *watercourse* Zambia
393 E8 **Machilipatnam** Andhra Pradesh India
154 C2 **Machiques** Venezuela
244 C5 **Machrihanish** Argyll and Bute Scotland UK
159 E4 **Machupo** *watercourse* Bolivia
240 D2 **Machynlleth** Powys Wales UK
309 F4 **Macia** Mozambique
227 K2 **Maciejowice** Poland
159 G2 **Maciel** Brazil
161 G3 **Maciel** Paraguay
229 I5 **Macinaggio** Corsica France
120 I6 **McInnes Lake** Ontario Canada
126 E2 **McIntosh** Ontario Canada
125 O4 **McIntosh** South Dakota USA
118 E5 **McIntyre Bay** British Columbia Canada
126 G2 **McIntyre Bay** Ontario Canada
425 N5 **Mackay** Qld Australia
119 O4 **MacKay** *watercourse* Alberta Canada
124 I5 **Mackay** Idaho USA
424 H5 **Mackay, Lake** WA Australia
122 F6 **McKay Lake** Newfoundland and Labrador Canada
116 H6 **MacKay Lake** Northwest Territories Canada
126 H2 **McKay Lake** Ontario Canada
436 O1 **Mackay Mountains** Antarctica
426 1 **McKean** *island* Kiribati
126 J8 **McKee** Kentucky USA
118 J5 **Mackenzie** British Columbia Canada
118 J1 **Mackenzie** *watercourse* Northwest Territories Canada
131 H5 **McKenzie** Alabama USA
437 E2 **MacKenzie Bay** Antarctica
116 F5 **Mackenzie Bay** Northwest Territories/Yukon Territory Canada
116 H3 **Mackenzie King Island** Northwest Territories/Nunavut Canada
116 F5 **Mackenzie Mountains** Northwest Territories Canada
116 F5 **Mackenzie River Delta** Northwest Territories Canada
423 C7 **McKerrow, Lake** New Zealand
MacKillop Lake *see* **Yamma Yamma Lake** Australia
126 I4 **Mackinaw City** Michigan USA
425 L5 **McKinlay** Qld Australia
425 K7 **McKinlay, Mount** SA Australia
116 D6 **McKinley, Mt (Denali)** Alaska USA
130 C4 **McKinney** Texas USA
436 U2 **Mackintosh, Cape** Antarctica
130 G5 **McLain** Mississippi USA
125 O4 **McLaughlin** South Dakota USA
130 A3 **McLean** Texas USA
119 S5 **McLennan Lake** Saskatchewan Canada
423 C8 **MacLennan Range** New Zealand
119 N6 **McLeod** *watercourse* Alberta Canada
424 E6 **McLeod, Lake** WA Australia
119 P1 **McLeod Bay** Northwest Territories Canada
118 J5 **McLeod Lake** British Columbia Canada
129 J6 **Maclovio Herrera** Mexico
132 D1 **McMillan, Lake** New Mexico USA
131 I3 **McMinnville** Tennessee USA
125 K1 **McMorran** Saskatchewan Canada
120 H8 **McMunn** Manitoba Canada
118 M7 **McMurdo** British Columbia Canada
437 L1 **McMurdo (USA)** *research station* Antarctica
437 K1 **McMurdo Sound** *strait* Antarctica
121 Q6 **McNab, Lac** *lake* Québec Canada
129 J5 **McNary** Texas USA
245 E2 **Macnean, Upper Lough** *lake* Northern Ireland UK
119 U7 **MacNutt** Saskatchewan Canada
123 F11 **McNutts Island** Nova Scotia Canada
154 E4 **Maco** Bolivia
309 F4 **Maçobere** Mozambique
306 B5 **Macocola** Angola
135 G4 **Macolla, Punta** *cape* Venezuela
233 G7 **Macolone, Punta di** *cape* Italy
126 F6 **Macomb** Illinois USA
131 J4 **Macon** Georgia USA
130 G4 **Macon** Mississippi USA
229 G3 **Mâcon** France
229 G3 **Mâconais** *region* France
308 D2 **Macondo** Angola
245 F1 **Macosquin** Coleraine Northern Ireland UK
230 D3 **Macotera** Spain
163 I4 **Macouba** Martinique
125 N2 **Macoun** Saskatchewan Canada
120 D4 **Macoun Lake** Saskatchewan Canada
309 G4 **Macovane** Mozambique
122 E5 **McPhayden** *watercourse* Newfoundland and Labrador Canada
129 H2 **McPhee Reservoir** Colorado USA
125 Q7 **McPherson** Kansas USA
437 E2 **Macpherson Robertson Land** *plain* Antarctica
425 inset **Macquarie Island** Australia
81 U9 **Macquarie Ridge** *underwater feature* Southern Ocean
120 H1 **MacQuoid Lake** Nunavut Canada
131 J4 **McRae** Georgia USA
120 J7 **McRea Lake** Ontario Canada
374 C3 **MacRitchie Reservoir** Singapore
245 D5 **Macroom** Ireland
116 H5 **McTavish Arm** Northwest Territories Canada
127 L4 **MacTier** Ontario Canada
154 D4 **Macu** Brazil
155 F5 **Macucuau** *watercourse* Brazil
154 C4 **Macuje** Colombia
154 B5 **Macuma** Ecuador
425 K6 **Macumba** *watercourse* SA Australia
154 E4 **Macuruco** Venezuela
154 D4 **Macusani** Peru
118 J6 **McVeigh** Manitoba Canada
119 U4 **McVictor Arm** Northwest Territories Canada
125 P3 **McVille** North Dakota USA
127 Q4 **Macwahoc** Maine USA
309 I4 **Madagascar** *country* Africa
80 J7 **Madagascar Basin** *underwater feature* Indian Ocean
80 I7 **Madagascar Plateau** *underwater feature* Indian Ocean
230 E6 **Madagh** Morocco
307 G3 **Madagoi** *watercourse* Somalia
310 1b **Madalena** Azores
123 H10 **Madame, Isle** *island* Nova Scotia Canada
305 H3 **Madana** Chad
301 H6 **Madaoua** Niger
234 E4 **Madara** Bulgaria
379 G4 **Madaripur** Bangladesh
373 J6 **Madau Island** Papua New Guinea
388 G6 **Madaw** Turkmenistan
127 L4 **Madawaska** Ontario Canada
307 G3 **Madax Gooy** *watercourse* Somalia
379 H4 **Madaya** Myanmar
306 E2 **Madbar** Sudan
229 J4 **Maddalena, Monte** *mountain* Italy
233 F8 **Maddalena, Penisola della** *cape* Italy
377 I3 **Maddela** Philippines
241 F3 **Maddington** Wiltshire England UK
125 P3 **Maddock** North Dakota USA
226 C2 **Made** Netherlands
391 I3 **Mādeh Kariz** Iran
155 F5 **Madeira** *watercourse* Brazil
310 2 **Madeira, Ilha de** *island* Atlantic Ocean
123 H9 **Madeleine, Îles de la** *islands* Québec Canada
240 E2 **Madeley** Staffordshire England UK
240 E2 **Madeley** Telford and Wrekin England UK
126 D4 **Madelia** Minnesota USA
389 M4 **Madeniyet** Kazakhstan
132 C2 **Madera** Mexico
124 E8 **Madera** California USA
226 E4 **Madesimo** Italy
379 F4 **Madhubani** Bihar India
392 E6 **Madhya Pradesh** *admin. area* India
307 F5 **Madibira** Tanzania
158 D4 **Madidi** *watercourse* Bolivia
390 G4 **Madiinat ash Shamāl** Qatar
130 C3 **Madill** Oklahoma USA
306 A5 **Madimba** Angola
306 B4 **Madimba** Democratic Republic of Congo
390 F4 **Madīnah, Al** *admin. area* Saudi Arabia
391 H5 **Madīnat Zāyid** United Arab Emirates
305 G5 **Madingo-Kayes** Congo
305 G5 **Madingou** Congo
305 G3 **Madingrin** Cameroon
309 I3 **Madirovalo** Madagascar
307 G2 **Madiso Shet** *watercourse* Ethiopia
125 K1 **Madison** Saskatchewan Canada
130 H3 **Madison** Alabama USA
130 F3 **Madison** Arkansas USA
131 J5 **Madison** Florida USA
126 I7 **Madison** Indiana USA
126 C7 **Madison** Kansas USA
123 D10 **Madison** Maine USA
125 Q4 **Madison** Minnesota USA
124 J4 **Madison** *watercourse* Montana USA
125 Q6 **Madison** Nebraska USA
126 G5 **Madison** Wisconsin USA
126 H8 **Madisonville** Kentucky USA
375 F5 **Madiun** Indonesia
305 G4 **Madjingo** Gabon
226 G4 **Madling** Austria
426 6b **Madolenihmw** Federated States of Micronesia
226 D3 **Madon** *watercourse* France
225 N4 **Madona** Latvia
225 N4 **Madonas** *admin. area* Latvia
391 I6 **Madrakah, Ra's al** *cape* Oman
Madras *see* **Chennai** India
124 E4 **Madras** Oregon USA
133 F3 **Madre, Laguna** *lake* Mexico
130 C7 **Madre, Laguna** *lake* Texas USA
377 I3 **Madre, Sierra** *range* Philippines
158 D4 **Madre de Dios** *watercourse* Bolivia
158 D3 **Madre de Dios** *admin. area* Peru
162 A5 **Madre de Dios, Archipiélago** *islands* Chile
133 F5 **Madre Del Sur, Sierra** *range* Mexico
132 D4 **Madre Occidental, Sierra** *range* Mexico
129 K7 **Madre Oriental, Sierra** *range* Mexico
230 E3 **Madrid** Spain
230 E3 **Madrid** *admin. area* Spain
125 O6 **Madrid** Nebraska USA
230 E4 **Madridejos** Spain
224 H4 **Madroken** *lake* Sweden
230 D4 **Madrona, Sierra** *range* Spain
230 D4 **Madroñera** Spain
301 I4 **Madrūsah** Libya
375 I5 **Madu** *island* Indonesia
377 I5 **Maducang** *island* Philippines
393 F8 **Madugula** Andhra Pradesh India
375 G5 **Madura** *island* Indonesia
375 G5 **Madura, Selat** *strait* Indonesia
393 E10 **Madurai** Tamil Nadu India
307 E5 **Madyo** Tanzania
308 E3 **Madziwadzido** Zimbabwe
376 C2 **Mae Chan** Thailand
376 C3 **Mae Hong Son** Thailand
379 I4 **Mae Nam Khong** *watercourse* Myanmar
376 C3 **Mae Ramat** Thailand
379 I5 **Mae Sai** Myanmar
376 C3 **Mae Sot** Thailand
376 C3 **Mae Taeng** Thailand
376 C3 **Mae Tha** Thailand
376 C2 **Maeai** Thailand
231 G3 **Maella** Spain
240 D2 **Maesbrook** Shropshire England UK
240 D2 **Maesbury Marsh** Shropshire England UK
240 D3 **Maesteg** Bridgend Wales UK
232 E4 **Maestra, Punta della** *cape* Italy
134 E2 **Maestra, Sierra** *range* Cuba
426 7 **Maéwo** *island* Vanuatu
372 C3 **Mafa** Indonesia
390 E2 **Mafa** Iraq
309 G3 **Mafamede, Ilha de** Mozambique
119 U6 **Mafeking** Manitoba Canada
308 E5 **Mafeteng** Lesotho
373 F4 **Maffin** Indonesia
307 F5 **Mafia Channel** *strait* Tanzania
307 F5 **Mafia** *island* Tanzania
308 E5 **Mafikeng** South Africa
304 B2 **Mafou** *watercourse* Guinea
157 B9 **Mafra** Brazil
230 B4 **Mafra** Portugal
305 G2 **Maga** Cameroon
237 AF7 **Magadan** Russian Federation
237 AF6 **Magadanskaya Oblast'** *admin. area* Russian Federation
307 F4 **Magadi, Lake** Kenya
309 F4 **Magaiza** Mozambique
162 B5 **Magallanes, Estrecho de (Magellan Strait)** *strait* Chile
162 B5 **Magallanes y de la Antártica Chilena** *admin. area* Chile
231 F3 **Magallón** Spain
230 E3 **Magaña** Spain
242 B4 **Maganey** Ireland
154 C2 **Magangué** Colombia
377 J6 **Maganoy** Philippines
301 H6 **Magaria** Niger
373 I6 **Magarida** Papua New Guinea
388 D5 **Magas** Russian Federation
130 E3 **Magazine** Arkansas USA
305 G3 **Magba** Cameroon
385 K1 **Magdagachi** Russian Federation
154 C2 **Magdalena** *admin. area* Colombia
154 C2 **Magdalena** *watercourse* Colombia
132 C2 **Magdalena** Mexico
128 G5 **Magdalena** *watercourse* Mexico
129 I3 **Magdalena** New Mexico USA
132 B3 **Magdalena, Bahía** *bay* Mexico
162 B3 **Magdalena, Isla** *island* Chile
132 B3 **Magdalena, Isla** *island* Mexico
128 G5 **Magdalena de Kino** Mexico
375 H2 **Magdalene, Gunung** *mountain* Malaysia
226 F1 **Magdeburg** Germany
386 F5 **Mage-shima** *island* Japan
130 G5 **Magee** Mississippi USA
375 F5 **Magelang** Indonesia
78 O7 **Magellan Rise** *underwater feature* Pacific Ocean
78 L6 **Magellan Seamounts** *underwater feature* Pacific Ocean
Magellan Strait *see* **Magallanes, Estrecho de** Chile
426 6 **Magererik** *island* Federated States of Micronesia
223 N1 **Magerøya** *island* Norway
375 F5 **Magetan** Indonesia
226 E5 **Maggiorasca, Monte** *mountain* Italy
232 C3 **Maggiore, Lago** *lake* Italy
302 E2 **Maghāghah** Egypt
300 D5 **Maghama** Mauritania
392 F5 **Maghar** Uttar Pradesh India
242 B2 **Maghera** Magherafelt Northern Ireland UK
245 E1 **Magheradrumman** Ireland
242 B2 **Magherafelt** Magherafelt Northern Ireland UK
245 F2 **Magherafelt** *admin. area* Northern Ireland UK
242 C2 **Magheramorne** Larne Northern Ireland UK
242 B2 **Maghereagh Cross** Ireland
390 E5 **Maghib** Saudi Arabia
124 H5 **Magic Reservoir** Idaho USA
307 F5 **Magingo** Tanzania
120 J6 **Magiss Lake** Ontario Canada
119 V7 **Magnet** Manitoba Canada
437 D2 **Magnet Bay** Antarctica
388 H2 **Magnitogorsk** Russian Federation
130 E4 **Magnolia** Arkansas USA
130 F5 **Magnolia** Mississippi USA
133 G2 **Magnolia** Texas USA
118 I3 **Magnum Mine** British Columbia Canada
427 9 **Mago** *island* Fiji
227 J4 **Mágócs** Hungary
309 F3 **Màgoé** Mozambique
127 O4 **Magog** Québec Canada
123 F7 **Magpie** *watercourse* Québec Canada
117 M8 **Magpie, Lac** *lake* Québec Canada
392 G6 **Magra** West Bengal India
302 E5 **Magrur** Sudan
302 D4 **Magrur, Wādi** *watercourse* Sudan
300 D5 **Magta Lakjar** Mauritania
156 B3 **Maguarinho, Cabo** *cape* Brazil
135 F2 **Magüey, Sierra del** *range* Cuba
300 D6 **Magui, Mare de** *lake* Mali
121 S3 **Maguire, Lac** *lake* Québec Canada
305 G2 **Magumeri** Nigeria
308 E3 **Magunge** Zimbabwe
120 H2 **Maguse** *watercourse* Nunavut Canada
120 H2 **Maguse Lake** Nunavut Canada
120 I2 **Maguse Point** Nunavut Canada
119 X2 **Maguse River** Nunavut Canada
379 H5 **Magway** *admin. area* Myanmar
379 H5 **Magway (Magwe)** Myanmar
Magwe *see* **Magway** Myanmar
376 D3 **Maha Sarakham** Thailand
388 E7 **Mahābād** Iran
393 C8 **Mahabaleshwar** Maharashtra India
309 I3 **Mahabe** Madagascar
392 F5 **Mahabharat Range** Nepal
393 E7 **Mahad** Maharashtra India
427 14a **Mahaena** French Polynesia
155 G3 **Mahaica-Berbice** *admin. area* Guyana
155 G3 **Mahaicony Village** Guyana
392 C5 **Mahajan** Rajasthan India
309 I3 **Mahajanga** Madagascar
309 I3 **Mahajanga** *admin. area* Madagascar
309 I3 **Mahajilo** *watercourse* Madagascar
375 G3 **Mahakam** *watercourse* Indonesia
308 E4 **Mahalapye** Botswana
393 F7 **Mahanadi** *watercourse* Chhattisgarh India
393 F7 **Mahanadi** *watercourse* Orissa India
309 I3 **Mahanoro** Madagascar
392 E6 **Maharajpur** Madhya Pradesh India
393 D7 **Maharashtra** *admin. area* India
390 G3 **Mahārlū, Daryācheh-ye** *lake* Iran
125 Q7 **Mahaska** Kansas USA
309 I3 **Mahasolo** Madagascar
309 I4 **Mahatalaky** Madagascar
309 I3 **Mahatsinjo** Madagascar
163 I5 **Mahaut** Dominica
309 I3 **Mahazoma** Madagascar
302 D5 **Mahbub** Sudan
393 E8 **Mahbubnagar** Andhra Pradesh India
301 G1 **Mahdia** Algeria
155 G3 **Mahdia** Guyana
301 I1 **Mahdia** Tunisia
310 9 **Mahé** *island* Seychelles
310 7b **Mahébourg** Mauritius
393 F7 **Mahendragiri** *mountain* Andhra Pradesh India
227 L2 **Maheriv** Ukraine
392 C6 **Mahesana** Gujarat India
392 D6 **Mahi** *watercourse* Rajasthan India
422 G4 **Mahia** New Zealand
422 G4 **Mahia Peninsula** New Zealand
225 P6 **Mahilyow** Belarus
394 D2 **Mahilyowskaya Voblasts'** *admin. area* Belarus
305 E3 **Mahin** Nigeria
427 14a **Mahina** French Polynesia
300 D6 **Mahina** Mali
423 C7 **Mahinerangi, Lake** New Zealand
390 E6 **Mahlal** Saudi Arabia
391 K4 **Mahmud Aulia** Pakistan
391 L2 **Mahmūd-e-Rāqī** Afghanistan
125 R3 **Mahnomen** Minnesota USA
392 E6 **Mahoba** Uttar Pradesh India
231 I4 **Mahón** Spain
123 F10 **Mahone Bay** Nova Scotia Canada
116 G5 **Mahoney Lake** Northwest Territories Canada
245 C4 **Mahoonagh** Ireland
230 F4 **Mahora** Spain
310 8 **Mahoré (Grande Terre)** *island* Mayotte
305 H2 **Mahoua** Chad
301 I2 **Mahrès** Tunisia
379 G4 **Mahur** Assam India
373 J4 **Mahur Island** Papua New Guinea
155 H3 **Mahury, Plateau du** *region* French Guiana
307 F6 **Mahuta** Tanzania
393 C7 **Mahuva** Gujarat India
392 D5 **Mahwa** Rajasthan India
235 E5 **Mahya Dağı** *mountain* Turkey
375 J5 **Mai** *island* Indonesia
306 B4 **Mai-Ndombe, Lac** *lake* Democratic Republic of Congo
426 1 **Maiana** *island* Kiribati
379 G4 **Maibong** Assam India
154 C2 **Maicao** Colombia
127 M1 **Maicasagi, Lac** *lake* Québec Canada
229 H3 **Maîche** France
159 F2 **Maici** *watercourse* Brazil
129 H6 **Maicova** Mexico
155 H5 **Maicuru** *watercourse* Brazil
233 G7 **Maida** Italy
121 S1 **Maiden Island** Nunavut Canada
240 E4 **Maiden Newton** Dorset England UK
244 E5 **Maidencots** South Lanarkshire Scotland UK
241 G3 **Maidenhead** Windsor and Maidenhead England UK
245 G2 **Maidens, The** *islands* Northern Ireland UK
121 X3 **Maidmonts Island** Newfoundland and Labrador Canada
241 H3 **Maidstone** Kent England UK
305 G2 **Maiduguri** Nigeria
241 G2 **Maidwell** Northamptonshire England UK
227 M4 **Maieru** Romania
382 F5 **Maigaiti** Xinjiang Uygur Zizhiqu China
155 E3 **Maigualide, Sierra** *range* Venezuela
392 E6 **Maihar** Madhya Pradesh India
223 N3 **Maijanen** Finland
132 D2 **Maijoma** Mexico
306 D4 **Maiko** *watercourse* Democratic Republic of Congo
372 E5 **Maikoor** *island* Indonesia
244 inset **Mail** Shetland Scotland UK
392 E5 **Mailani** Uttar Pradesh India
374 C4 **Mailepe** Indonesia
227 K5 **Mailovac** Serbia
391 L3 **Mailsi** Pakistan
123 J8 **Main** *watercourse* Newfoundland and Labrador Canada
226 F3 **Main** *watercourse* Germany
245 F2 **Main** *watercourse* Northern Ireland UK
123 J7 **Main Brook** Newfoundland and Labrador Canada
226 F3 **Main-Donau-Kanal** *watercourse* Germany
423 10 **Main Group** *islands* Bounty Islands New Zealand
163 9 **Main Ridge** *range* Trinidad and Tobago
374 C5 **Main Strait** Singapore
235 C7 **Mainalon, Oros** *range* Greece
393 D8 **Maindargi** Maharashtra India
114 **Maine** *admin. area* USA
123 D11 **Maine, Gulf of** Canada/USA
301 I6 **Maïne-Soroa** Niger
226 E3 **Mainhardt** Germany
377 J5 **Mainit, Lake** Philippines
244 inset **Mainland** *island* Scotland UK
392 E5 **Mainpuri** Uttar Pradesh India
244 D3 **Mains of Faillie** Highland Scotland UK
244 F4 **Mains of Kelly** Angus Scotland UK
223 O4 **Mainua** Finland
226 E2 **Mainz** Germany
310 4 **Maio** *island* Cape Verde
161 G6 **Maipú** Argentina
158 C2 **Maipuco** Peru
154 E3 **Maipures** Colombia
379 F3 **Maiqu Zangbo** *watercourse* Xizang Zizhiqu China
162 B2 **Maiquillahue, Punta** *cape* Chile
159 F5 **Mairana** Bolivia
157 D5 **Mairi** Brazil
228 F5 **Maisons** France
229 L2 **Maissau** Austria
226 B3 **Maisse** France
308 E4 **Maitengwe** Botswana
425 N8 **Maitland** NSW Australia
425 K8 **Maitland** SA Australia
437 A2 **Maitri (India)** *research station* Antarctica
134 D4 **Maíz, Islas del** *islands* Nicaragua
134 D4 **Maíz Grande, Isla del** Nicaragua
387 G4 **Maizuru** Japan
232 G4 **Maja** Croatia
390 E6 **Majaba** Saudi Arabia
154 C2 **Majagual** Colombia
222 H4 **Majavatn** Norway
234 B3 **Majdanpek** Serbia
372 A4 **Majene** Indonesia
158 C5 **Majes** *watercourse* Peru
392 F6 **Majgaon** Madhya Pradesh India
381 G1 **Majia He** *watercourse* Henan China
385 I5 **Majia He** *watercourse* Shandong China
384 F5 **Majiawan** Zishiqu China
390 G3 **Majnavā** Iran
425 inset **Major Lake** Macquarie Island Australia
Majorca *see* **Mallorca** Spain
379 H3 **Majuli** Assam India
427 15a **Majuro** Marshall Islands
427 15 **Majuro Atoll** Marshall Islands
427 15a **Majuro Lagoon** Marshall Islands
308 E5 **Majwemasweu** South Africa
234 D1 **Mak** Ukraine
300 D6 **Maka** Senegal
305 G5 **Makabana** Congo
128 inset **Mākaha** Hawai'i USA
305 G5 **Makaka** Congo
306 D4 **Makamba** Burundi
307 E5 **Makambako** Tanzania
389 N4 **Makanchi** Kazakhstan
309 F2 **Makanjila** Malawi
237 AF9 **Makanrushi, Ostrov** *island* Russian Federation
154 D2 **Makaraipaho** Colombia
426 8a **Makarakomburu, Mount** Solomon Islands
305 G2 **Makari** Cameroon
155 G3 **Makari** Guyana
237 AD9 **Makarov** Russian Federation
434 R1 **Makarov Basin** *underwater feature* Arctic Ocean
78 L5 **Makarov Seamount** *underwater feature* Pacific Ocean
232 G5 **Makarska** Croatia
388 E1 **Makar'ye** Russian Federation
306 E5 **Makasa** Zambia
372 A5 **Makassar** Indonesia
375 H4 **Makassar, Selat (Macassar Strait)** Indonesia
388 G4 **Makat** Kazakhstan
307 F5 **Makatapora** Tanzania
427 14 **Makatea** *island* French Polynesia
79 R9 **Makatea** *reef* French Polynesia
309 F5 **Makatini Flats** *plain* South Africa
422 4 **Makefu** Niue New Zealand
427 14 **Makemo** *island* French Polynesia
128 inset **Makena** Hawai'i USA
304 B3 **Makeni** Sierra Leone
426 7 **Makéoné** Vanuatu
306 E4 **Makere** Tanzania
384 E6 **Maketang** Qinghai China
422 G3 **Maketu** New Zealand
308 E4 **Makgadikgadi** *pan* Botswana
388 E5 **Makhachkala** Russian Federation
391 L2 **Makhad** Pakistan
388 F4 **Makhambet** Kazakhstan
387 H4 **Maki** Japan
375 J3 **Makian** *island* Indonesia
426 1 **Makin** *island* Kiribati
119 V7 **Makinak** Manitoba Canada
389 K3 **Makinsk** Kazakhstan
426 8 **Makira** *admin. area* Solomon Islands
390 E5 **Makkah** *admin. area* Saudi Arabia
390 D5 **Makkah (Mecca)** Saudi Arabia
122 I5 **Makkovik** Newfoundland and Labrador Canada
122 I5 **Makkovik, Cape** Newfoundland and Labrador Canada
300 D6 **Mako** Senegal
234 B2 **Makó** Hungary
155 G4 **Makoa, Serra** *range* Brazil
427 9 **Makogai** *island* Fiji
305 G4 **Makokou** Gabon
391 J4 **Makola** Pakistan
307 E5 **Makongolosi** Tanzania
120 J6 **Makoop Lake** Ontario Canada
306 D3 **Makoro** Democratic Republic of Congo
125 O3 **Makoti** North Dakota USA
305 H5 **Makoua** Congo
305 G4 **Makoubi** Congo
234 B4 **Makovac** Kosovo
234 B5 **Makovo** Macedonia
236 S5 **Makovskoye, Ozero** *lake* Russian Federation
235 B6 **Makrakomi** Greece
392 D5 **Makrana** Rajasthan India
227 M2 **Makrany** Belarus
235 B6 **Makri** *island* Greece
235 B7 **Makrisia** Greece
235 D7 **Makronisi** *island* Greece
225 N3 **Mäksa** Estonia
390 F3 **Maksar** Iran
238 F4 **Maksatikha** Russian Federation
236 S7 **Maksimkin Yar** Russian Federation
387 I2 **Makubetsu** Japan
379 H3 **Makum** Assam India
308 D4 **Makunda** Botswana
381 H4 **Makung** Taiwan China
307 F5 **Makunguwiro** Tanzania
393 C11 **Makunudhoo** *island* Maldives
386 F5 **Makurazaki** Japan
305 F3 **Makurdi** Nigeria
119 Q6 **Makwa** Saskatchewan Canada
379 F3 **Mal** West Bengal India
245 C4 **Mal Bay** Ireland
373 H4 **Mal Island** Papua New Guinea
305 H3 **Mala** Central African Republic
158 B4 **Mala** Peru
224 G4 **Mala** Sweden
222 K4 **Malå** Sweden
134 E6 **Mala, Punta** *cape* Panama
227 J3 **Malá Fatra** *range* Slovakia
392 E5 **Mala Kheti** Nepal
131 K7 **Malabar** Florida USA
393 D9 **Malabar Coast** Kerala India
425 inset **Malabar Hill** Lord Howe Island Australia
305 F4 **Malabo** Equatorial Guinea
155 F4 **Malacacheta** Brazil
157 D7 **Malacacheta** Brazil
374 D3 **Malacca, Strait of** Indonesia/Malaysia
124 I5 **Malad City** Idaho USA
225 N5 **Maladzyechna** Belarus
427 12b **Mala'efo'ou** Wallis and Futuna
225 O3 **Malaf'yevka** Russian Federation
154 C3 **Málaga** Colombia
230 D5 **Málaga** Spain
154 B4 **Málaga, Bahía de** *bay* Colombia
306 E5 **Malagarasi** *watercourse* Tanzania
134 E2 **Malagueta, Punta** *cape* Cuba
245 F3 **Malahide** Ireland
234 D3 **Malaia** Romania
309 I4 **Malaimbandy** Madagascar
426 8 **Malaita** *admin. area* Solomon Islands
426 8 **Malaita** *island* Solomon Islands
306 E2 **Malakal** Sudan
427 9a **Malake** *island* Fiji
130 D4 **Malakoff** Texas USA
426 7 **Malakula** *island* Vanuatu
124 F1 **Malakwa** British Columbia Canada
391 M3 **Malakwal** Pakistan
373 G6 **Malam** Papua New Guinea

375 I4 **Malamala** Indonesia
154 C2 **Malambo** Colombia
375 G5 **Malang** Indonesia
309 G2 **Malanga** Mozambique
307 E5 **Malangali** Tanzania
222 K2 **Malangen** Norway
222 K2 **Malangen** bay Norway
308 C1 **Malanje** Angola
308 C1 **Malanje** admin. area Angola
377 H5 **Malanut Bay** Philippines
160 E4 **Malanzán** Argentina
426 7 **Malao** Vanuatu
224 I3 **Mälaren** bay Sweden
155 H4 **Malaripo** Brazil
127 L2 **Malartic, Lac** lake Québec Canada
227 M2 **Malaryta** Belarus
225 P5 **Malashenki** Belarus
375 H5 **Malasoro, Teluk** bay Indonesia
162 C3 **Malaspina** Argentina
118 I8 **Malaspina Strait** British Columbia Canada
375 G4 **Malatayur, Tanjung** cape Indonesia
394 F5 **Malatya** Turkey
394 F5 **Malatya** admin. area Turkey
226 C5 **Malaucène** France
301 H6 **Malawa** Niger
375 H2 **Malawali** island Malaysia
309 F2 **Malawi** country Africa
309 F2 **Malawi, Lake (Lake Nyasa)** lake Malawi/Mozambique
390 D6 **Malāwī Jidārah** Saudi Arabia
222 L5 **Malax** Finland
376 D5 **Malay Peninsula** cape Thailand
225 Q3 **Malaya Vishera** Russian Federation
377 J5 **Malaybalay** Philippines
390 F2 **Malāyer** Iran
374 E3 **Malaysia** country Asia
425 L5 **Malbon** Qld Australia
225 J5 **Malbork** Poland
383 J2 **Malchin** Mongolia
226 G1 **Malchiner See** lake Germany
227 K3 **Malcov** Slovakia
130 G2 **Malden** Missouri USA
426 1 **Malden Island** Kiribati
393 C11 **Maldives** country
241 H3 **Maldon** Essex England UK
161 H5 **Maldonado** Uruguay
161 H5 **Maldonado** admin. area Uruguay
133 F5 **Maldonado, Punta** cape Mexico
161 G2 **Maldonado-cué** Paraguay
232 D3 **Malè** Italy
393 C11 **Male** Maldives
393 C11 **Male Atoll** Maldives
304 C2 **Maléa** Guinea
374 C3 **Malea, Gunung** mountain Indonesia
235 C7 **Maleas, Akra** cape Greece
227 L1 **Malec** Poland
309 G3 **Malei** Mozambique
306 E2 **Malek** Sudan
391 K3 **Malek Din** Afghanistan
305 G5 **Malélé** Congo
309 G2 **Malema** Mozambique
305 F2 **Malendo** watercourse Nigeria
373 J4 **Malendok Island** Papua New Guinea
223 T5 **Malen'ga** Russian Federation
162 D6 **Malengüena, Cabo** cape Argentina
228 F2 **Malesherbes** France
391 K2 **Malestān** Afghanistan
228 C3 **Malestroit** France
426 8 **Malevangga** Solomon Islands
238 H6 **Malevka** Russian Federation
227 M2 **Malevo** Ukraine
233 C7 **Malfatano, Capo** cape Sardinia Italy
222 K4 **Malfjälen** Sweden
302 D4 **Malha** Sudan
243 F2 **Malham** North Yorkshire England UK
124 F5 **Malheur Lake** Oregon USA
101 F5 **Mali** country Africa
380 D4 **Mali** Yunnan China
306 D4 **Mali** Democratic Republic of Congo
427 9a **Mali** island Fiji
379 H3 **Mali** watercourse Myanmar
234 A3 **Mali Iđoš** Serbia
376 C4 **Mali Kyun** Myanmar
232 F4 **Mali Lošinj** Croatia
232 F4 **Mali Lug** Croatia
235 C6 **Maliakos Kolpos** bay Greece
375 J6 **Maliana** Timor-Leste (East Timor)
124 C4 **Malibu** California USA
228 D3 **Malicorne** France
225 N4 **Maliena** Latvia
306 D5 **Malimba, Monts** range Democratic Republic of Congo
374 E5 **Malimping** Indonesia
240 C2 **Malin** Ireland
245 D2 **Malin Beg** Ireland
245 E1 **Malin Head** cape Ireland
377 I5 **Malindang, Mount** mountain Philippines
307 G4 **Malindi** Kenya
222 I6 **Målingen** lake Sweden
234 E2 **Mălini** Romania
227 L1 **Malinniki** Poland
238 H5 **Malino** Russian Federation
372 B3 **Malino, Gunung** mountain Indonesia
388 D3 **Malinovka** Russian Federation
389 M3 **Malinovoye Ozero** Russian Federation
307 F5 **Malinyi** Tanzania
235 D8 **Malion, Kolpos** bay Greece
377 J6 **Malita** Philippines
129 K4 **Maljamar** New Mexico USA
307 G3 **Malka Mari** Kenya
393 E7 **Malkangiri** Orissa India
384 F2 **Malkhanskiy Khrebet** range Russian Federation
227 L1 **Małkinia Górna** Poland
425 N9 **Mallacoota** Vic. Australia
119 P5 **Mallaig** Alberta Canada
244 C3 **Mallaig** Highland Scotland UK
154 B4 **Mallama** Colombia
225 M2 **Mallasvesi** bay Finland
302 E2 **Mallawi** Egypt
117 J6 **Mallery Lake** Nunavut Canada
226 G4 **Mallnitz** Austria
231 H4 **Mallorca (Majorca)** island Spain
225 N1 **Mallos** lake Finland
245 D4 **Mallow** Ireland
240 D2 **Mallwyd** Gwynedd Wales UK
222 G4 **Malm** Norway
222 L3 **Malmberget** Sweden
229 H1 **Malmédy** Belgium
308 C6 **Malmesbury** South Africa
241 E3 **Malmesbury** Wiltshire England UK
222 K4 **Malmesjaure** lake Sweden
224 G5 **Malmö** Sweden
224 I4 **Malmö** island Sweden
224 F3 **Malmöfjord** bay Sweden
163 1c **Malmok** cape Netherlands Antilles
222 I5 **Malmsjön** lake Sweden
388 F2 **Malmyzh** Russian Federation
375 J2 **Malo** island Indonesia
232 G4 **Malo Tičevo** Bosnia and Herzegovina
155 F5 **Maloca** Brazil
155 H4 **Maloca** Brazil
158 D3 **Maloca** Brazil
159 H3 **Maloca Caiabi** Brazil
154 D4 **Maloca Capi Ponta** Brazil
154 D4 **Maloca do Chico** Brazil
155 H4 **Maloca dos Urucuianas** Brazil
154 D4 **Maloca Jutica** Brazil
155 F4 **Maloca Macu** Brazil
154 D4 **Maloca Pacu** Brazil
155 H4 **Maloca Repy** Brazil
159 F4 **Maloca Salamaim** Brazil
154 D4 **Maloca Uacari** Brazil
427 15 **Maloelap Atoll** Marshall Islands
427 9a **Malolo** island Fiji
309 G2 **Malombe, Lake** lake Malawi
227 H2 **Małomice** Poland
131 I5 **Malone** Florida USA
127 N4 **Malone** New York USA
380 D3 **Malong** Yunnan China
306 C6 **Malonga** Democratic Republic of Congo
306 E5 **Malonje** mountain Tanzania
227 J3 **Małopolskie** admin. area Poland
224 C2 **Måløy** Norway
238 G5 **Maloyaroslavets** Russian Federation
387 I1 **Maloye, Ozero** lake Russian Federation
236 L5 **Malozemel'skaya Tundra** region Russian Federation
230 C4 **Malpartida de Plasencia** Spain
154 A4 **Malpelo, Isla de** island Colombia
123 G9 **Malpeque Bay** Prince Edward Island Canada
230 B2 **Malpica** Spain
230 C4 **Malpica do Tejo** Portugal
227 H3 **Malše** watercourse Czech Republic
222 K2 **Målsnes** Norway
222 I5 **Målsta** Sweden
233 F9 **Malta** country Europe
233 F9 **Malta** island Europe
125 L2 **Malta** Montana USA
301 J1 **Malta Channel** strait Malta
308 C4 **Maltahöhe** Namibia
243 I3 **Maltby le Marsh** Lincolnshire England UK
243 H2 **Malton** North Yorkshire England UK
133 F5 **Maltrata** Mexico
375 F3 **Maludam National Park** Malaysia
306 B4 **Maluku** Democratic Republic of Congo
375 K4 **Maluku** admin. area Indonesia
375 J3 **Maluku, Laut (Molucca Sea)** Indonesia
375 J4 **Maluku (Moluccas)** islands Indonesia
375 J3 **Maluku Utara** admin. area Indonesia
224 G2 **Malungsfors** Sweden
377 I6 **Maluso** Philippines
308 E5 **Maluti Mountains** range Lesotho
426 8 **Maluu** Solomon Islands
393 C8 **Malvan** Maharashtra India
240 E2 **Malvern Link** Worcestershire England UK
222 G5 **Malvik** Norway
Malvinas, Islas see **Falkland Islands** Atlantic Ocean
389 M5 **Malybay** Kazakhstan
227 K3 **Mályi** Hungary
237 AH5 **Malyy Anyuy** watercourse Russian Federation
237 AD4 **Malyy Lyakhovskiy, Ostrov** island Russian Federation
237 X3 **Malyy Taymyr, Ostrov** island Russian Federation
388 E3 **Malyy Uzen** watercourse Kazakhstan
389 Q3 **Malyy Yenisey** watercourse Russian Federation
388 D4 **Malyye Derbety** Russian Federation
228 F4 **Malzieu-Ville** France
237 X7 **Mama** Russian Federation
388 F2 **Mamadysh** Russian Federation
308 E5 **Mamafubedu** South Africa
126 I3 **Mamainse Point** Ontario Canada
422 G3 **Mamaku Plateau** New Zealand
300 D5 **Mamari** Senegal
155 H5 **Mamaru, Ilha Grande do** island Brazil
377 J5 **Mambajao** Philippines
305 G3 **Mambal** Cameroon
307 E4 **Mambali** Tanzania
375 H6 **Mambang, Tanjung** cape Indonesia
373 H6 **Mambare** watercourse Papua New Guinea
306 D3 **Mambasa** Democratic Republic of Congo
305 H4 **Mambére** watercourse Central African Republic
305 H4 **Mambéré-Kadéï** admin. area Central African Republic
305 G4 **Mambili** watercourse Congo
308 B3 **Mambonde** watercourse Angola
154 A5 **Mambra, Punta** cape Ecuador
120 J8 **Mameigweiss Lake** Ontario Canada
228 E2 **Mamers** France
305 F3 **Mamfé** Cameroon
155 F5 **Mamiá, Lago** lake Brazil
388 D5 **Mamison Pass** Russian Federation
226 G3 **Mamming** Germany
128 G4 **Mammoth** Arizona USA
125 J4 **Mammoth Hot Springs** Wyoming USA
124 F8 **Mammoth Lakes** California USA
124 F8 **Mammoth Pool Reservoir** California USA
159 E3/4 **Mamoré, Rio** watercourse Brazil/Bolivia
154 E5 **Mamori, Ilhas** island Brazil
304 B2 **Mamou** Guinea
130 E5 **Mamou** Louisiana USA
310 8b **Mamoudzou** Mayotte
309 I3 **Mampikony** Madagascar
304 D3 **Mampong** Ghana
308 B2 **Mamue** Angola
372 A4 **Mamuju** Indonesia
132 E3 **Mamulique** Mexico
304 C3 **Man** Côte d'Ivoire
127 K8 **Man** West Virginia USA
379 G5 **Man-Aung (Cheduba)** Myanmar
379 G5 **Man-aung Kyun** Myanmar
379 E3 **Man Ho** watercourse Xizang Zizhiqu China
163 9 **Man O'War Bay** Trinidad and Tobago
122 H4 **Man O'War Peak** Newfoundland and Labrador Canada
155 H3 **Mana** French Guiana
155 H3 **Mana** watercourse French Guiana
236 T7 **Mana** watercourse Russian Federation
128 inset **Mānā** Hawai'i USA
423 F5 **Mana Island** New Zealand
154 A5 **Manabí** admin. area Ecuador
154 C3 **Manacacias** watercourse Colombia
155 F5 **Manacapuru** Brazil
155 F5 **Manacapuru, Lago Grande de** lake Brazil
233 G6 **Manaccore, Punta di** cape Italy
231 H4 **Manacor** Spain
372 C3 **Manado** Indonesia
134 C4 **Managua** Nicaragua
134 C4 **Managua, Lago de** lake Nicaragua
422 F4 **Manaia** New Zealand
156 E4 **Manaira** Brazil
309 I4 **Manakara** Madagascar
392 D4 **Manali** Himachal Pradesh India
373 H5 **Manam** volcano Papua New Guinea
393 E10 **Manamadurai** Tamil Nadu India
309 I4 **Manambondro** Madagascar
155 F2 **Manamo, Caño** watercourse Venezuela
309 I3 **Mananara** Madagascar
309 I4 **Mananjary** Madagascar
304 C2 **Manankoro** Mali
300 D6 **Manantali, Lac de** lake Mali
309 I4 **Manantenina** Madagascar
423 B7 **Manapouri** New Zealand
423 B7 **Manapouri, Lake** New Zealand
393 D7 **Manar** watercourse Maharashtra India
432* F5 **Manara** NSW Australia
423 F5 **Manaroa** New Zealand
382 H4 **Manas** Xinjiang Uygur Zizhiqu China
383 H3 **Manas Hu** lake Xinjiang Uygur Zizhiqu China
392 F5 **Manaslu** mountain Nepal
125 M8 **Manassa** Colorado USA
382 H4 **Manasu He** watercourse Xinjiang Uygur Zizhiqu China
372 C6 **Manatang** Indonesia
134 E2 **Manatí** Cuba
372 C6 **Manatuto** Timor-Leste (East Timor)
154 C2 **Manaure** Colombia
155 F5 **Manaus** Brazil
394 D6 **Manavgat** Turkey
393 D6 **Manawar** Madhya Pradesh India
302 C5 **Manawashei** Sudan
422 F5 **Manawatu** watercourse New Zealand
372 D5 **Manawoka** island Indonesia
377 J6 **Manay** Philippines
392 G6 **Manbazar** West Bengal India
243 I3 **Manby** Lincolnshire England UK
245 C5 **Manch Bridge** Ireland
230 E5 **Mancha Real** Spain
154 B5 **Manchari** watercourse Peru
Manche, La see **English Channel** UK/France
243 F3 **Manchester** admin. area England UK
243 F3 **Manchester** Greater Manchester England UK
129 N1 **Manchester** Kansas USA
126 J8 **Manchester** Kentucky USA
127 P5 **Manchester** New Hampshire USA
125 P8 **Manchester** Oklahoma USA
243 F3 **Manchester Ship Canal** England UK
233 D5 **Manciano** Italy
228 E5 **Manciet** France
158 C2 **Mâncio Lima** Brazil
158 A2 **Mâncora** Peru
125 K8 **Mancos** Colorado USA
391 J4 **Mand** Pakistan
307 E5 **Manda** Tanzania
307 E6 **Manda** Tanzania
157 A8 **Mandaguaçu** Brazil
374 D4 **Mandah** Indonesia
384 F4 **Mandah** Mongolia
374 D4 **Mandahara** Indonesia
384 F3 **Mandal** Mongolia
224 D3 **Mandal** Norway
373 G5 **Mandala, Puncak** mountain Indonesia
377 I5 **Mandalagan, Mount** volcano Philippines
379 H5 **Mandalay** Myanmar
379 H5 **Mandalay** admin. area Myanmar
384 F3 **Mandalgovi** Mongolia
384 E4 **Mandalovoo** Mongolia
304 C2 **Mandan** watercourse Guinea
125 O3 **Mandan** North Dakota USA
377 I4 **Mandaon** Philippines
375 H4 **Mandar, Teluk** bay Indonesia
305 G2 **Mandara Mountains** range Cameroon
134 C4 **Mandasta** Honduras
125 L4 **Manderson** Wyoming USA
130 F5 **Mandeville** Louisiana USA
392 D4 **Mandi** Himachal Pradesh India
374 D2 **Mandi Angin, Gunung** mountain Malaysia
300 F6 **Mandiakui** Mali
304 C2 **Mandiana** Guinea
309 F3 **Mandié** Mozambique
235 D7 **Mandili** island Greece
309 G2 **Mandimba** Mozambique
304 C2 **Mandingues, Mountains** range Mali
309 F5 **Mandini** South Africa
375 J4 **Mandioli** island Indonesia
305 G5 **Mandji** Gabon
305 F5 **Mandji, Île** island Gabon
393 E6 **Mandla** Madhya Pradesh India
224 E5 **Mandø** island Denmark
392 C5 **Mandor** Rajasthan India
374 F3 **Mandor** Indonesia
306 D3 **Mandoro** Democratic Republic of Congo
309 I3 **Mandoto** Madagascar
391 K3 **Mandowzi** Afghanistan
235 E5 **Mándra** Greece
235 E7 **Mandraki** Greece
309 I4 **Mandrare** watercourse Madagascar
309 I3 **Mandritsara** Madagascar
309 I4 **Mandrosonor** Madagascar
392 D6 **Mandsaur** Madhya Pradesh India
375 H3 **Mandul** island Indonesia
385 H4 **Mandulatu** Nei Mongol Zizhiqu China
424 E8 **Mandurah** WA Australia
392 B6 **Mandvi** Gujarat India
393 D9 **Mandya** Karnataka India
241 H2 **Manea** Cambridgeshire England UK
132 A2 **Maneadero** Mexico
394 C2 **Manevichi** Ukraine
302 E2 **Manfalūṭ** Egypt
233 F6 **Manfredonia** Italy
233 G6 **Manfredonia, Golfo di** bay Italy
157 D6 **Manga** Brazil
306 A5 **Manga Grande** Angola
156 C5 **Mangabeiras, Serra das** range Brazil
306 B4 **Mangai** Democratic Republic of Congo
422 1 **Mangaia** island Cook Islands New Zealand
301 G6 **Mangaïze** Niger
422 E2 **Mangakahia** watercourse New Zealand
379 G3 **Mangaldai** Assam India
234 F4 **Mangalia** Romania
302 H2 **Mangalmé** Chad
393 D9 **Mangalore** Karnataka India
422 E2 **Mangamuka Bridge** New Zealand
306 B5 **Mangando** Angola
422 F4 **Manganuioteao** watercourse New Zealand
372 C3 **Mangarang** Indonesia
427 14 **Mangareva** island French Polynesia
422 F5 **Mangatainoka** New Zealand
392 E6 **Mangawan** Madhya Pradesh India
422 F4 **Mangaweka** New Zealand
422 F3 **Mangawhai Heads** New Zealand
422 F4 **Mangawhero** watercourse New Zealand
224 C2 **Manger** Norway
423 6 **Mangere Island** Chatham Islands New Zealand
374 F4 **Manggar** Indonesia
373 F4 **Manggasi** Indonesia
372 E5 **Manggawitu** Indonesia
372 D5 **Manggur** island Indonesia
130 F4 **Mangham** Louisiana USA
379 H4 **Mangin Range** Myanmar
388 G5 **Mangistauskaya Oblast'** admin. area Kazakhstan
375 H3 **Mangkalihat, Tanjung** cape Indonesia
384 D6 **Manglaqiongtuo** Qinghai China
154 B4 **Manglares, Cabo** cape Colombia
304 E2 **Mango** Togo
304 D3 **Mangodara** Burkina Faso
309 H4 **Mangoky** watercourse Madagascar
375 J4 **Mangole** island Indonesia
375 J4 **Mangole, Selat** strait Indonesia
306 D4 **Mangombe** Democratic Republic of Congo
422 E2 **Mangonui** New Zealand
155 F2 **Mangotín** Venezuela
240 E3 **Mangotsfield** South Gloucestershire England UK
393 C7 **Mangrol** Gujarat India
392 D6 **Mangrol** Rajasthan India
155 E5 **Mangu Karnali** watercourse Nepal
391 K3 **Manguchar** Pakistan
305 I2 **Mangueigne** Chad
161 H5 **Mangueira, Lagoa** lake Brazil
134 C4 **Mangulile** Honduras
130 B3 **Mangum** Oklahoma USA
156 C3 **Mangunça, Ilha** island Brazil
306 D3 **Manguredjipa** Democratic Republic of Congo
244 A2 **Mangurstadh** Na h-Eileanan Siar Scotland UK
388 F5 **Mangyshlakskiy Zaliv** bay Kazakhstan
383 I3 **Manhan** Mongolia
125 Q7 **Manhattan** Kansas USA
124 J4 **Manhattan** Montana USA
157 D8 **Manhuaçu** Brazil
301 I6 **Mani** Chad
154 C3 **Maní** Colombia
235 C7 **Mani** peninsula Greece
305 F2 **Mani** Nigeria
391 I4 **Māni Gaz** Iran
309 I4 **Mania** watercourse Madagascar
306 C5 **Mania-Manu** Democratic Republic of Congo
229 K3 **Maniago** Italy
309 F2 **Maniamba** Mozambique
305 I6 **Maniamuna** Democratic Republic of Congo
121 U7 **Manic Trois, Réservoir** Québec Canada
309 F3 **Manica** Mozambique
309 F3 **Manica** admin. area Mozambique
309 F3 **Manicaland** admin. area Zimbabwe
377 J5 **Manicani** island Philippines
159 F2 **Manicoré** Brazil
159 F2 **Manicoré** watercourse Brazil
121 U8 **Manicouagan** watercourse Québec Canada
306 D4 **Maniema** admin. area Democratic Republic of Congo
120 G7 **Manigotagan** Manitoba Canada
120 G7 **Manigotagan** watercourse Manitoba Canada
392 G6 **Manihari** Bihar India
427 14 **Manihi** island French Polynesia
426 1 **Manihiki** island Cook Islands New Zealand
78 P9 **Manihiki Atoll** reef Cook Islands New Zealand
78 P8 **Manihiki Plateau** underwater feature Pacific Ocean
117 N5 **Maniitsoq** Greenland
306 D6 **Manika** Democratic Republic of Congo
306 D5 **Manika, Plateau de la** plain Democratic Republic of Congo
392 E6 **Manikpur** Uttar Pradesh India
377 I4 **Manila** Philippines
125 K6 **Manila** Utah USA
225 M3 **Manilaid** island Estonia
230 D5 **Manilva** Spain
375 H4 **Manimbaya, Tanjung** cape Indonesia
425 J3 **Maningrida** NT Australia
374 C4 **Maninjau, Danau** lake Indonesia
375 J4 **Manipa** island Indonesia
375 J4 **Manipa, Selat** strait Indonesia
379 H4 **Manipur** admin. area India
394 D5 **Manisa** admin. area Turkey
126 H4 **Manistee** Michigan USA
126 H4 **Manistee** watercourse Michigan USA
126 H3 **Manistique** Michigan USA
126 I3 **Manistique Lake** Michigan USA
120 E5 **Manitoba** admin. area Canada
119 V7 **Manitoba, Lake** Manitoba Canada
130 B3 **Manitou** Oklahoma USA
123 F7 **Manitou, Lac** lake Québec Canada
126 H4 **Manitou Islands** Michigan USA
119 Q6 **Manitou Lake** Saskatchewan Canada
125 M7 **Manitou Springs** Colorado USA
127 J4 **Manitoulin Island** Ontario Canada
121 Q5 **Manitounuk Islands** Nunavut Canada
127 K4 **Manitowaning Bay** Ontario Canada
126 H4 **Manitowish** Wisconsin USA
126 H4 **Manitowoc** Wisconsin USA
159 H3 **Manitsaua-missu** watercourse Brazil
127 N3 **Maniwaki** Québec Canada
154 C3 **Manizales** Colombia
309 H4 **Manja** Madagascar
386 E4 **Manjae-do** island South Korea
309 F4 **Manjalaze** Mozambique
424 F8 **Manjimup** WA Australia
305 F4 **Manjo** Cameroon
393 D7 **Manjra** watercourse Maharashtra India
126 E4 **Mankato** Minnesota USA
377 I3 **Mankayan** Philippines
234 G1 **Man'kivka** Ukraine
304 C3 **Mankono** Côte d'Ivoire
119 R8 **Mankota** Saskatchewan Canada
393 E10 **Mankulam** Sri Lanka
384 F4 **Manlai** Mongolia
231 H3 **Manlleu** Spain
393 D7 **Manmad** Maharashtra India
425 J3 **Mann** watercourse NT Australia
375 D5 **Manna** Indonesia
425 H5 **Mannahill** SA Australia
393 E10 **Mannar, Gulf of** India
121 T5 **Mannessier, Lac** lake Québec Canada
222 J2 **Mannfjorden** bay Norway
232 C2 **Mannheim** Germany
223 M3 **Männikkö** Sweden
245 B3 **Mannin Bay** Ireland
118 M4 **Manning** Alberta Canada
426 1a **Manning, Cape** Kiribati
118 K8 **Manning Provincial Park** British Columbia Canada
241 I3 **Manningtree** Essex England UK
222 M4 **Mannön** island Sweden
233 C6 **Mannu** watercourse Sardinia Italy
233 C6 **Mannu, Capo** cape Sardinia Italy
233 C6 **Mannu, Monte** mountain Sardinia Italy
158 E3 **Mano** Bolivia
304 B3 **Mano** Sierra Leone
309 H3 **Manoba** watercourse Madagascar
158 D3 **Manoel Urbano** Brazil
234 C4 **Manojlovce** Serbia
372 E4 **Manokwari** Indonesia
309 H4 **Manombo** Madagascar
159 F4 **Manomo, Serranía del** range Bolivia
306 D5 **Manono** Democratic Republic of Congo
427 12c **Manono** island Samoa
240 C3 **Manorbier** Pembrokeshire Wales UK
245 D2 **Manorhamilton** Ireland
240 B3 **Manorowen** Pembrokeshire Wales UK
229 G5 **Manosque** France
127 N3 **Manouane** Québec Canada
121 T7 **Manouane** watercourse Québec Canada
121 T7 **Manouane, Lac** lake Québec Canada
233 D8 **Manouba** Tunisia
121 V7 **Manowin, Île** island Québec Canada
386 E3 **Manp'o** North Korea
392 E6 **Manpur** Madhya Pradesh India
426 1 **Manra** island Kiribati
231 G3 **Manresa** Spain
392 D4 **Mansa** Punjab India
308 E2 **Mansa** Zambia
304 A2 **Mansa Konko** Gambia
304 A2 **Mansabá** Guinea-Bissau
378 D2 **Mansarowar Lake** Xizang Zizhiqu China
391 M2 **Mansehra** Pakistan
121 P1 **Mansel Island** Nunavut Canada
241 F1 **Mansfield** Nottinghamshire England UK
130 D3 **Mansfield** Arkansas USA
130 E4 **Mansfield** Louisiana USA
127 O4 **Mansfield, Mount** Vermont USA
379 H4 **Mansi** Myanmar
230 E2 **Mansilla, Embalse de** lake Spain
228 E4 **Mansle** France
304 A2 **Mansôa** Guinea-Bissau
118 I5 **Manson Creek** British Columbia Canada
118 I7 **Mansons Landing** British Columbia Canada
154 C3 **Manta** Colombia
154 A5 **Manta** Ecuador
120 G7 **Mantagao** watercourse Manitoba Canada
377 H5 **Mantalingajan, Mount** mountain Philippines
375 H2 **Mantanani Besar** island Malaysia
119 Q7 **Mantario** Saskatchewan Canada
158 C4 **Mantaro** watercourse Peru
124 E8 **Manteca** California USA
230 C3 **Manteigas** Portugal
157 D7 **Mantenópolis** Brazil
131 N3 **Manteo** North Carolina USA
125 O8 **Manter** Kansas USA
392 G6 **Manteswar** West Bengal India
228 E3 **Manthelan** France
124 J7 **Manti** Utah USA
223 M5 **Mantila** Finland
157 C8 **Mantiqueira, Serra da** range Brazil
241 F3 **Manton** Wiltshire England UK
232 D4 **Mantova** Italy
134 C2 **Mantua** Cuba
223 O4 **Mäntyjärvi** Finland
154 B5 **Manú** Ecuador
158 D4 **Manú** Peru
158 D3 **Manú** watercourse Peru
422 1 **Manuae** island Cook Islands New Zealand
79 Q9 **Manuae** reef French Polynesia
133 F4 **Manuel** Mexico
157 B5 **Manuel Alves** watercourse Brazil
156 C4 **Manuel Alves Grande** watercourse Brazil
132 E2 **Manuel Benavides** Mexico
162 B5 **Manuel Rodriguez, Isla** island Chile
159 F3 **Manuel Tomás** Brazil
159 H2 **Manuelzinho** Brazil
427 14 **Manuhangi** island French Polynesia
375 I4 **Manui** island Indonesia
377 I6 **Manuk Manka** island Philippines
423 F3 **Manukau** New Zealand
422 F3 **Manukau Harbour** New Zealand
373 H4 **Manus Island** Papua New Guinea
125 Q2 **Manvel** North Dakota USA
130 D6 **Manvel** Texas USA
393 D8 **Manvi** Karnataka India
125 M5 **Manville** Wyoming USA
130 E5 **Many** Louisiana USA
128 H2 **Many Farms Lake** Arizona USA
119 P7 **Many Island Lake** Alberta Canada
308 F3 **Manyame, Lake** lake Zimbabwe
307 F4 **Manyara** admin. area Tanzania
307 F4 **Manyara, Lake** lake Tanzania
235 E5 **Manyas** Turkey
119 P8 **Manyberries** Alberta Canada
388 D4 **Manych Gudilo** lake Russian Federation
308 D2 **Manyinga** Zambia
231 F3 **Manzanares** Spain
163 9 **Manzanilla Point** Trinidad and Tobago
134 E2 **Manzanillo** Cuba
132 D5 **Manzanillo** Mexico
134 E5 **Manzanillo, Punta** cape Panama
124 D4 **Manzanita** Oregon USA
232 E4 **Manzano** Italy
228 F4 **Manzat** France
306 B5 **Manzengele** Democratic Republic of Congo
385 I2 **Manzhouli** Nei Mongol Zizhiqu China
233 D8 **Manzil Boū Zalafah** Tunisia
302 E1 **Manzilah, Buḥayrat al** lake Egypt
309 F5 **Manzini** Swaziland
237 W8 **Manzurka** Russian Federation
301 J6 **Mao** Chad
232 H4 **Maoča** Bosnia and Herzegovina
372 F4 **Maoke, Pegunungan** range Indonesia
Maokeng see **Kroonstad** South Africa
380 F4 **Maoming** Guangdong China
380 F2 **Maoping** Hubei China
375 J5 **Maopora** island Indonesia
155 E4 **Mapacú, Cerros** range Venezuela
309 F4 **Mapai** Mozambique
373 G6 **Mapamoiwa** Papua New Guinea
155 G4 **Maparri Mountains** Guyana
133 G6 **Mapastepec** Mexico
373 F5 **Mapi** watercourse Indonesia
158 E3 **Mapiá** Brazil
372 E3 **Mapia, Kepulauan** island Indonesia
155 E4 **Mapiche, Serranía** range Venezuela
132 E3 **Mapimí** Mexico
155 E3 **Mapire** Venezuela
158 D4 **Mapiri** Bolivia
154 C4 **Mapiripán** Colombia
154 D4 **Mapirriare** Colombia
126 D5 **Maple** watercourse Iowa USA
126 I5 **Maple** watercourse Michigan USA
126 C3 **Maple** watercourse North Dakota USA
119 Q8 **Maple Creek** Saskatchewan Canada
126 E4 **Maple Grove** Minnesota USA
130 H4 **Maplesville** Alabama USA
78 M5 **Mapmaker Seamounts** underwater feature Pacific Ocean
425 L2 **Mapoon** Qld Australia
374 E3 **Mapor** island Indonesia
423 D6 **Mapourika, Lake** New Zealand
243 H3 **Mappleton** East Riding of Yorkshire England UK
393 C8 **Mapuca** Goa India
155 G5 **Mapuera** watercourse Brazil
309 F4 **Mapulanguene** Mozambique
375 H2 **Mapun** island Philippines
306 C5 **Mapunda** Democratic Republic of Congo
309 F5 **Maputo** Mozambique
309 F5 **Maputo** admin. area Mozambique
390 G4 **Maqātel** Iran
302 F4 **Maqdam, Ras** cape Sudan
394 F7 **Maqha' ash Shuḥaymī** Syria
390 C4 **Maqnah** Saudi Arabia
300 D4 **Maqteïr** region Mauritania
378 E2 **Maquan He** watercourse Xizang Zizhiqu China
158 C2 **Maquea** Peru
162 C4 **Maqueda, Punta** cape Argentina
306 B5 **Maquela do Zombo** Angola
162 C2 **Maquinchao** Argentina
160 F4 **Mar Chiquita, Laguna** lake Argentina
161 G6 **Mar de Cobo** Argentina
161 G6 **Mar del Plata** Argentina
161 G6 **Mar del Sur** Argentina
133 F3 **Mar Negro, Lago** lake Mexico
307 E4 **Mara** admin. area Tanzania
155 E5 **Maraã** Brazil
156 B4 **Marabá** Brazil
375 G4 **Marabahan** Indonesia
375 H5 **Marabatua** island Indonesia
126 F2 **Maraboeuf Lake** Ontario Canada
304 C3 **Maraboué** watercourse Côte d'Ivoire
156 B2 **Maracá, Ilha de** island Brazil
156 C3 **Maracaçumé** Brazil
157 B8 **Maracaí** Brazil
155 E5 **Maracai, Lago de** lake Brazil
154 D2 **Maracaibo** Venezuela
154 D2 **Maracaibo, Lago de** lake Venezuela
159 H6 **Maracaju** Brazil
159 H6 **Maracaju, Sierra de** range Brazil
156 C3 **Maracanã** Brazil
156 E3 **Maracanaú** Brazil
157 D6 **Maracás** Brazil
154 E2 **Maracay** Venezuela
160 E6 **Maracó Grande, Valle** valley Argentina
301 J3 **Marādah** Libya
301 H6 **Maradi** Niger
301 H6 **Maradi** admin. area Niger
388 E5 **Maraga** Russian Federation
388 E6 **Marāgheh** Iran
156 F5 **Maragogi** Brazil
157 E6 **Maragogipe** Brazil
154 E3 **Marairona, Cerros** range Venezuela
156 B3 **Marajó, Baía de** bay Brazil
156 B3 **Marajó, Ilha de** island Brazil
426 1 **Marakei** island Kiribati
306 D3 **Marakesa** Democratic Republic of Congo
307 F3 **Maralal** Kenya
389 M3 **Maraldy** lake Kazakhstan
305 H3 **Marali** Central African Republic
426 8 **Maramasike** island Solomon Islands
436 U2 **Marambio (Argentina)** research station Antarctica
375 J2 **Marampit** island Indonesia
373 G5 **Maramuni** watercourse Papua New Guinea
234 C2 **Maramureș** admin. area Romania
374 D3 **Maran** Malaysia
128 G4 **Marana** Arizona USA
230 E3 **Maranchón** Spain
388 E6 **Marand** Iran
301 H5 **Marandet** Niger
374 D2 **Marang** Malaysia
156 C4 **Maranhão** admin. area Brazil
157 B6 **Maranhão** watercourse Brazil
230 C4 **Maranhão, Barragem do** lake Portugal
158 B2 **Marañon** watercourse Peru
228 D3 **Marans** France
372 E4 **Maransabadi** island Indonesia
309 F4 **Marão** Mozambique
156 C3 **Marapanim** Brazil
155 G4 **Marapi** watercourse Brazil
374 D4 **Marapi, Gunung** volcano Indonesia
233 C6 **Marargiu, Capo** cape Sardinia Italy
423 C7 **Mararoa** watercourse New Zealand
375 H5 **Marasende** island Indonesia
390 F4 **Marāt** Saudi Arabia
157 D8 **Marataízes** Brazil
117 K9 **Marathon** Ontario Canada
129 K5 **Marathon** Texas USA
235 B7 **Marathopolis** Greece
375 H3 **Maratua** island Indonesia
159 G2 **Marau** Brazil
375 F4 **Marau** Indonesia
157 E6 **Maraú** Brazil
422 H4 **Marau Point** New Zealand
132 E5 **Maravatío** Mexico
160 E4 **Maraves** Argentina
426 8a **Maravovo** Solomon Islands
377 J5 **Marawi** Philippines
391 H5 **Marawwaḥ, Jazirat** island United Arab Emirates
158 C4 **Marayniocc** Peru
240 B4 **Marazion** Cornwall England UK
230 D5 **Marbella** Spain
129 I1 **Marble** Colorado USA
424 F5 **Marble Bar** WA Australia
128 G2 **Marble Canyon** Arizona USA
126 G8 **Marble Hill** Missouri USA
120 J1 **Marble Island** Nunavut Canada
125 J5 **Marbleton** Wyoming USA
226 C4 **Marboz** France
240 E1 **Marbury** Cheshire England UK
224 H1 **Marby** Sweden
308 B3 **Marca, Ponta da** cape Angola
227 I4 **Marcali** Hungary
158 D4 **Marcapata** watercourse Peru
159 E5 **Marcavi** Bolivia
121 V7 **Marcel, Lac** lake Québec Canada
121 U4 **Marcel, Lac** lake Québec Canada
126 E3 **Marcell** Minnesota USA
158 A2 **Marcelo** Peru
241 H2 **March** Cambridgeshire England UK
424 F7 **Marchagee** WA Australia
125 Q2 **Marchand** Manitoba Canada
229 H3 **Marchaux** France
228 E3 **Marche** region France
232 E5 **Marche** admin. area Italy
229 G1 **Marche-en-Famenne** Belgium
230 D5 **Marchena** Spain
163 4 **Marchena, Canal de** strait Archipiélago de Colón (Galapagos Islands)
163 4 **Marchena, Isla** island Archipiélago de Colón (Galapagos Islands)
425 K2 **Marchinbar Island** NT Australia
228 G3 **Marcigny** France
241 I4 **Marck** France
156 D3 **Marco** Brazil
121 P4 **Marcopeet Islands** Nunavut Canada
157 C7 **Marcos** watercourse Brazil
121 S3 **Marcouard, Lac** lake Québec Canada
125 R5 **Marcus** Iowa USA
388 F6 **Mardakyan** Azerbaijan
391 L2 **Mardan** Pakistan
394 G6 **Mardin** Turkey
394 G6 **Mardin** admin. area Turkey
222 I3 **Mårdsel** Sweden
222 K4 **Mårdsele** Sweden
222 I5 **Mårdsjö** Sweden
375 J3 **Mare** island Indonesia
426 7 **Maré** island New Caledonia
394 F6 **Mare'** Syria
232 E5 **Marecchia** watercourse Italy
157 A9 **Marechal Cândido Rondon** Brazil
158 C3 **Marechal Thaumaturgo** Brazil
244 C3 **Maree, Loch** lake Scotland UK
425 M4 **Mareeba** Qld Australia
233 D5 **Maremma** region Italy
300 D6 **Maréna** Mali
126 G5 **Marengo** Illinois USA
390 G2 **Marenjān** Iran
228 D4 **Marennes** France
309 H4 **Marerano** Madagascar
241 H4 **Maresfield** East Sussex England UK
233 E8 **Marettimo, Isola di** island Italy

387 G1 **Marevka** *watercourse* Russian Federation
225 Q4 **Marevo** Russian Federation
129 J5 **Marfa** Texas USA
234 C3 **Marga** Romania
240 D3 **Margam** Neath Port Talbot Wales UK
118 H7 **Margaret Bay** British Columbia Canada
121 V5 **Margaret Hamilton Lake** Newfoundland and Labrador Canada
119 N3 **Margaret Lake** Alberta Canada
424 E8 **Margaret River** WA Australia
160 F6 **Margarita, Isla** *island* Argentina
155 E2 **Margarita, Isla de** *island* Venezuela
241 I3 **Margate** Kent England UK
234 C2 **Mărgău** Romania
233 G6 **Margherita di Savoia** Italy
306 D3 **Margherita Peak** *mountain* Uganda
234 C2 **Marghita** Romania
389 K6 **Marg'ilon** Uzbekistan
377 I6 **Margosatubig** Philippines
436 T2 **Marguerite Bay** Antarctica
394 E3 **Marhanets'** Ukraine
156 F4 **Mari** Brazil
373 G6 **Mari** Papua New Guinea
163 1b **Mari Pompún** Netherlands Antilles
123 F8 **Maria** Québec Canada
427 14 **Maria** *reef* French Polynesia
132 D4 **María Cleofas, Isla** *island* Mexico
154 C2 **María la Baja** Colombia
132 D4 **María Madre, Isla** *island* Mexico
132 D4 **María Magdelena, Isla** *island* Mexico
232 F3 **Maria Neustift** Austria
422 E2 **Maria van Diemen, Cape** New Zealand
161 I2 **Marialva** Brazil
157 D8 **Mariana** Brazil
119 O5 **Mariana Lake** Alberta Canada
78 K6 **Mariana Ridge** *underwater feature* Pacific Ocean
78 K6 **Mariana Trench** *underwater feature* Pacific Ocean
78 K6 **Mariana Trough** *underwater feature* Pacific Ocean
379 H3 **Mariani** Assam India
130 F3 **Marianna** Arkansas USA
131 I5 **Marianna** Florida USA
161 G4 **Mariano Loza** Argentina
160 D6 **Mariano Moreno** Argentina
154 D4 **Mariapiri, Mesa de** *region* Colombia
155 G5 **Mariaqua** *watercourse* Brazil
154 E2 **Mariara** Venezuela
132 D4 **Marías, Islas** *islands* Mexico
154 E3 **Mariata** Venezuela
134 D6 **Mariato, Punta** *cape* Panama
390 F7 **Ma'rib** Yemen
155 F3 **Mariba, Sierra** *range* Venezuela
224 F5 **Maribo** Denmark
128 C3 **Maricopa** California USA
306 D3 **Maridi** Sudan
306 D2 **Maridi** *watercourse* Sudan
154 E5 **Marie** *watercourse* Brazil
436 P1 **Marie Byrd Land** *plain* Antarctica
436 Q2 **Marie Byrd Seamount** *underwater feature* Amundsen Sea
163 I6 **Marie-Galante** *island* Guadeloupe
119 P5 **Marie Lake** Alberta Canada
310 9 **Marie Louis Island** Seychelles
224 H3 **Marieberg** Sweden
222 I5 **Marieby** Sweden
224 I3 **Mariefred** Sweden
225 J2 **Mariehamn/Maarianhamina** Finland
134 D2 **Mariel** Cuba
157 B6 **Mariembero** *watercourse* Brazil
308 C4 **Mariental** Namibia
224 G3 **Mariestadsfjärden** *bay* Sweden
121 Q3 **Mariet** *watercourse* Québec Canada
131 I4 **Marietta** Georgia USA
127 K7 **Marietta** Ohio USA
130 C4 **Marietta** Oklahoma USA
76 P4 **Marietta Seamount** *underwater feature* Atlantic Ocean
119 T7 **Marieval** Saskatchewan Canada
379 G3 **Marigaon** Assam India
229 G5 **Marignane** France
163 I5 **Marigot** Dominica
163 I4 **Marigot** Martinique
163 20 **Marigot** St Martin
163 I3 **Marigot Harbour** *bay* St Lucia
237 Y3 **Marii Pronchishchevoy, Bukhta** *bay* Russian Federation
225 L5 **Marijampolė** Lithuania
225 L5 **Marijampolės** *admin. area* Lithuania
157 D7 **Marilândia** Brazil
157 B8 **Marília** Brazil
155 G6 **Marimari** *watercourse* Brazil
306 B5 **Marimba** Angola
230 B2 **Marín** Spain
374 D4 **Marina Bay** Singapore
233 C7 **Marina di Arbus** Sardinia Italy
238 C6 **Mar''ina Horka** Belarus
377 I4 **Marinduque** *island* Philippines
229 I5 **Marine de Luri** Corsica France
229 I5 **Marine de Sisco** Corsica France
226 A3 **Marines** France
126 H4 **Marinette** Wisconsin USA
157 B8 **Maringá** Brazil
306 C4 **Maringa** *watercourse* Democratic Republic of Congo
230 B3 **Marinha das Ondas** Portugal
230 B4 **Marinha Grande** Portugal
230 B3 **Marinhas** Portugal
426 7 **Marino** Vanuatu
225 O3 **Mar'insko** Russian Federation
159 H4 **Mário Spinelli** Brazil
130 H4 **Marion** Alabama USA
126 I6 **Marion** Indiana USA
126 F5 **Marion** Iowa USA
125 Q7 **Marion** Kansas USA
130 E4 **Marion** Louisiana USA
130 G4 **Marion** Mississippi USA
131 K3 **Marion** North Carolina USA
125 P3 **Marion** North Dakota USA
126 J6 **Marion** Ohio USA
130 B6 **Marion** Texas USA
131 K2 **Marion** Virginia USA
131 K4 **Marion, Lake** South Carolina USA
425 K8 **Marion Bay** SA Australia
125 Q7 **Marion Lake** Kansas USA
301 H4 **Mariou, Adrar** *mountain* Algeria
154 C3 **Maripí** Colombia
377 J5 **Maripipi** *island* Philippines
128 C2 **Mariposa** California USA
154 E3 **Mariposo** Venezuela
372 B3 **Marisa** Indonesia
159 F6 **Mariscal Estigarribia** Paraguay
161 H5 **Mariscala** Uruguay
235 D4 **Maritsa** *watercourse* Bulgaria
394 F3 **Mariupol'** Ukraine
155 F2 **Mariusa, Isla** *island* Venezuela
388 E7 **Marīvān** Iran
377 I4 **Mariveles** Philippines
377 G5 **Mariveles Reef** Spratly Islands
223 O5 **Marjovaara** Finland
224 G4 **Mark** *region* Sweden
126 F7 **Mark Twain Lake** Missouri USA
307 G3 **Marka** Somalia
389 O4 **Markakol'** *lake* Kazakhstan
380 C2 **Markam** Xizang Zizhiqu China
393 E8 **Markapur** Andhra Pradesh India
390 G2 **Markazī** *admin. area* Iran
226 E4 **Markdorf** Germany
226 G1 **Markee** Germany
226 C1 **Marken** *island* Netherlands
308 E4 **Marken** South Africa
226 C1 **Markermeer** *bay* Netherlands
241 G2 **Market Deeping** Lincolnshire England UK
240 E2 **Market Drayton** Shropshire England UK
243 H3 **Market Rasen** Lincolnshire England UK
243 H3 **Market Weighton** East Riding of Yorkshire England UK
245 F2 **Markethill** Armagh Northern Ireland UK
373 H5 **Markham** *watercourse* Papua New Guinea
437 K1 **Markham, Mount** *mountain* Antarctica
227 K1 **Marki** Poland
222 L3 **Markitta** Sweden
244 D5 **Marklach** Dumfries and Galloway Scotland UK
126 I6 **Markle** Indiana USA
305 H3 **Markounda** Central African Republic
236 S6 **Markovo** Russian Federation
304 E2 **Markoye** Burkina Faso
388 E3 **Marks** Russian Federation
130 F3 **Marks** Mississippi USA
226 F2 **Marksuhl** Germany
229 J2 **Markt Bibart** Germany
232 C2 **Marktheidenfeld** Germany
226 F4 **Marktoberdorf** Germany
229 H1 **Marl** Germany
425 J6 **Marla** SA Australia
372 E5 **Marlasi** Indonesia
118 M6 **Marlboro** Alberta Canada
425 N5 **Marlborough** Qld Australia
226 B3 **Marle** France
130 C5 **Marlin** Texas USA
127 K7 **Marlinton** West Virginia USA
241 G3 **Marlow** Buckinghamshire England UK
228 F1 **Marly** France
229 H2 **Marly** France
228 E4 **Marmande** France
235 E5 **Marmara** Turkey
235 E5 **Marmara Adası** *island* Turkey
235 F5 **Marmara Denizi** *bay* Turkey
235 E6 **Marmara Gölü** *lake* Turkey
235 E5 **Marmaraereğlisi** Turkey
235 D6 **Marmarion** Greece
235 E6 **Marmaro** Greece
125 N3 **Marmarth** North Dakota USA
126 D8 **Marmaton** *watercourse* Kansas USA
224 I2 **Marmen** *lake* Sweden
230 D4 **Marmolejo** Spain
127 M4 **Marmora** Ontario Canada
229 G3 **Marnay** France
222 I3 **Mårnes** Norway
388 D5 **Marneuli** Georgia
388 E5 **Marneuli** Georgia
226 F1 **Marnitz** Germany
379 H3 **Marniu** Arunachal Pradesh India
244 F3 **Marnoch** Aberdeenshire Scotland UK
305 H3 **Maro** Chad
309 I3 **Maroantsetra** Madagascar
422 F4 **Marokopa** New Zealand
392 D3 **Marol** Jammu and Kashmir India/Pakistan
391 M2 **Marol** Pakistan
241 I5 **Maromme** France
373 H4 **Maron Island** Papua New Guinea
309 F3 **Marondera** Zimbabwe
228 F4 **Maronne** *watercourse* France
425 O6 **Maroochydore** Qld Australia
372 A5 **Maros** Indonesia
309 I3 **Maroseranana** Madagascar
427 14 **Marotiri, Îles** *islands* French Polynesia
232 E5 **Marotta** Italy
305 G2 **Maroua** Cameroon
309 H3 **Marovoay** Madagascar
309 I3 **Marovolo** Madagascar
79 S9 **Marquesas Fracture Zone** *underwater feature* Pacific Ocean
131 J8 **Marquesas Keys** *islands* Florida USA
126 H3 **Marquette** Michigan USA
130 C5 **Marquez** Texas USA
119 S7 **Marquis** Saskatchewan Canada
163 I3 **Marquis** St Lucia
163 I3 **Marquis, Cape** St Lucia
241 I4 **Marquise** France
427 14 **Marquises, Îles** *islands* French Polynesia
154 E2 **Marquito** Venezuela
305 I2 **Marra, Jebel** *range* Sudan
232 D4 **Marradi** Italy
300 E2 **Marrakech** Morocco
121 V4 **Marralik** *watercourse* Québec Canada
223 N3 **Marrasjärvi** Finland
223 N3 **Marrasjärvi** *lake* Finland
231 H4 **Marratxi** Spain
425 M10 **Marrawah** Tas. Australia
425 K7 **Marree** SA Australia
244 E2 **Marrel** Highland Scotland UK
309 G3 **Marromeu** Mozambique
309 G2 **Marrupa** Mozambique
127 R3 **Mars Hill** Maine USA
131 J3 **Mars Hill** North Carolina USA
302 E2 **Marsá al 'Alam** Egypt
301 J2 **Marsá al Burayqah** Libya
302 D1 **Marsá Maṭrūḥ** Egypt
302 F3 **Marsa' Sha'b** Halaib Triangle
307 F3 **Marsabit** Kenya
233 E8 **Marsala** Italy
425 M8 **Marsden** NSW Australia
243 G3 **Marsden** West Yorkshire England UK
229 F5 **Marseillan** France
229 G5 **Marseille** France
243 F2 **Marsett** North Yorkshire England UK
131 M7 **Marsh Harbour** Bahamas
130 F6 **Marsh Island** *island* Louisiana USA
118 D2 **Marsh Lake** Yukon Territory Canada
243 G3 **Marsh Lane** Derbyshire England UK
119 Q6 **Marshall** Saskatchewan Canada
304 B3 **Marshall** Liberia
130 E3 **Marshall** Arkansas USA
126 H7 **Marshall** Illinois USA
126 I5 **Marshall** Michigan USA
125 R4 **Marshall** Minnesota USA
126 E7 **Marshall** Missouri USA
130 D4 **Marshall** Texas USA
373 I6 **Marshall Bennett Islands** Papua New Guinea
427 15 **Marshall Islands** *country* Pacific Ocean
120 L7 **Marshall Lake** Ontario Canada
126 E5 **Marshalltown** Iowa USA
225 O4 **Marshavitsy** Russian Federation
243 I3 **Marshchapel** Lincolnshire England UK
126 E8 **Marshfield** Missouri USA
126 F4 **Marshfield** Wisconsin USA
226 C3 **Marson** France
222 I4 **Marssjön** *lake* Sweden
224 I3 **Märsta** Sweden
224 F5 **Marstal** Denmark
224 F5 **Marstal Bugt** *bay* Denmark
241 F3 **Marston** Oxfordshire England UK
130 G2 **Marston** Missouri USA
130 C5 **Mart** Texas USA
233 D5 **Marta** *watercourse* Italy
376 C3 **Martaban, Gulf of** Myanmar
305 G3 **Martap** Cameroon
374 E5 **Martapura** Indonesia
305 G2 **Marte** Nigeria
234 E4 **Marten** Bulgaria
120 M7 **Marten Falls** Ontario Canada
234 B2 **Martfű** Hungary
130 B3 **Martha** Oklahoma USA
127 P6 **Marthas Vineyard** *island* Massachusetts USA
228 E4 **Marthon** France
134 D2 **Martí** Cuba
229 H3 **Martigny** Switzerland
229 G5 **Martigues** France
232 H2 **Martin** Slovakia
126 J8 **Martin** Kentucky USA
125 O5 **Martin** South Dakota USA
130 G2 **Martin** Tennessee USA
131 I4 **Martin Lake** Alabama USA
130 D4 **Martin Lake** Texas USA
436 Q2 **Martin Peninsula** Antarctica
234 A3 **Martinci** Serbia
135 I4 **Martinique** *French overseas territory* Caribbean
135 I4 **Martinique Passage** *strait* Caribbean
223 N4 **Martinniemi** Finland
423 B7 **Martins Bay** New Zealand
227 H3 **Martinsberg** Austria
127 M7 **Martinsburg** West Virginia USA
232 E5 **Martinsicuro** Italy
126 H7 **Martinsville** Indiana USA
131 L2 **Martinsville** Virginia USA
155 E5 **Martírio** Brazil
240 E2 **Martley** Worcestershire England UK
240 E4 **Martock** Somerset England UK
422 F5 **Marton** New Zealand
243 G2 **Marton** North Yorkshire England UK
240 D2 **Marton** Shropshire England UK
223 P5 **Martonvaara** Finland
230 E5 **Martos** Spain
116 H6 **Martre, Lac la** *lake* Northwest Territories Canada
223 P3 **Martti** Finland
388 G3 **Martuk** Kazakhstan
372 D5 **Maru** *island* Indonesia
375 G2 **Marudi** Malaysia
375 H2 **Marudu, Teluk** *bay* Malaysia
423 E6 **Maruia** *watercourse* New Zealand
423 E6 **Maruia Springs** New Zealand
225 J3 **Marum** Sweden
373 I5 **Marunga** Papua New Guinea
389 O3 **Marushka** Russian Federation
155 F4 **Marutani, Serra** *range* Brazil
390 G3 **Marv Dasht** Iran
224 E2 **Mårvatn** *lake* Norway
130 F3 **Marvell** Arkansas USA
434 W1 **Marvin Spur** *underwater feature* Arctic Ocean
424 I3 **Mary** *watercourse* NT Australia
388 I6 **Mary** Turkmenistan
424 E5 **Mary Anne Reef** WA Australia
388 I6 **Mary Welaýaty** *admin. area* Turkmenistan
425 O6 **Maryborough** Qld Australia
308 D5 **Marydale** South Africa
119 U8 **Maryfield** Saskatchewan Canada
244 F4 **Marykirk** Aberdeenshire Scotland UK
129 L4 **Maryneal** Texas USA
244 E3 **Marypark** Moray Scotland UK
242 E2 **Maryport** Cumbria England UK
242 D2 **Maryport** Dumfries and Galloway Scotland UK
122 K6 **Mary's Harbour** Newfoundland and Labrador Canada
124 I7 **Marysvale** Utah USA
124 H2 **Marysville** British Columbia Canada
124 F7 **Marysville** California USA
125 Q7 **Marysville** Kansas USA
126 D6 **Maryville** Missouri USA
131 J3 **Maryville** Tennessee USA
154 B3 **Marzo, Cabo** *cape* Colombia
373 J4 **Masahet Island** Papua New Guinea
374 D2 **Masai** Malaysia
307 F4 **Masai Steppe** *plain* Tanzania
306 E4 **Masaka** Uganda
375 G5 **Masalembu Besar** *island* Indonesia
375 G5 **Masalembu Kecil** *island* Indonesia
372 B4 **Masamba** Indonesia
386 F4 **Masan** South Korea
307 F6 **Masasi** Tanzania
134 C5 **Masaya** Nicaragua
377 I4 **Masbate** *island* Philippines
301 G1 **Mascara** Algeria
301 G1 **Mascara** *admin. area* Algeria
80 J6 **Mascarene Basin** *underwater feature* Indian Ocean
80 I7 **Mascarene Plain** *underwater feature* Indian Ocean
80 K6 **Mascarene Plateau** *underwater feature* Indian Ocean
157 E6 **Mascote** Brazil
125 L2 **Masefield** Saskatchewan Canada
372 D6 **Masela** Indonesia
372 D6 **Masela** *island* Indonesia
222 K2 **Måselva** *watercourse* Norway
375 I4 **Masepe** *island* Indonesia
308 E5 **Maseru** Lesotho
307 F2 **Masha** Ethiopia
306 C5 **Mashala** Democratic Republic of Congo
308 F4 **Mashava** Zimbabwe
391 M2 **Masherbrum** *mountain* Pakistan
394 E2 **Mashevo** Ukraine
388 H7 **Mashhad** Iran
309 F3 **Mashonaland Central** *admin. area* Zimbabwe
309 F3 **Mashonaland East** *admin. area* Zimbabwe
308 E3 **Mashonaland West** *admin. area* Zimbabwe
387 J2 **Mashū-ko** *lake* Japan
306 B4 **Masi-Manimba** Democratic Republic of Congo
306 B4 **Masia-Mbio** Democratic Republic of Congo
372 E5 **Masian, Tanjung** *cape* Indonesia
307 E5 **Masimba** Tanzania
372 A4 **Masimbu** Indonesia
375 I5 **Masin** Indonesia
306 E3 **Masindi** Uganda
307 F4 **Masinga Reservoir** *lake* Kenya
377 H4 **Masinloc** Philippines
306 D4 **Masisi** Democratic Republic of Congo
234 D2 **Masivul Ceahlău** *range* Romania
372 D4 **Masiwang** *watercourse* Indonesia
391 J2 **Masjed Negar** Afghanistan
390 G3 **Masjed Soleymān** Iran
245 C3 **Mask, Lough** *lake* Ireland
222 J4 **Maskaure** Sweden
222 J4 **Måskenåive** Sweden
234 E4 **Maslen Nos** *cape* Bulgaria
390 E6 **Masliyah** Saudi Arabia
225 O2 **Maslovo** Russian Federation
223 R5 **Maslozero, Ozero** *lake* Russian Federation
309 J3 **Masoala, Tanjona** *cape* Madagascar
309 I4 **Masomeloka** Madagascar
130 B5 **Mason** Texas USA
423 B8 **Mason Bay** New Zealand
126 E5 **Mason City** Iowa USA
163 9 **Mason Hall** Trinidad and Tobago
118 D2 **Mason Landing** Yukon Territory Canada
375 J4 **Masoni** *island* Indonesia
127 L7 **Masontown** West Virginia USA
223 N1 **Måsøya** *island* Norway
310 3b **Maspalomas** Canary Islands
391 I5 **Masqaṭ (Muscat)** Oman
393 D7 **Massa** Maharashtra India
232 D4 **Massa** Italy
226 G5 **Massa Fiscaglia** Italy
127 P5 **Massachusetts Bay** Massachusetts USA
163 I5 **Massacre** Dominica
124 F6 **Massacre Lake** Nevada USA
301 J6 **Massaguet** Chad
301 J6 **Massakory** Chad
301 J6 **Massalassef** Chad
306 C4 **Massanga** Democratic Republic of Congo
305 G3 **Massangam** Cameroon
306 B5 **Massango** Angola
309 G2 **Massangulo** Mozambique
228 E5 **Massat** France
306 B5 **Massau** Angola
236 N6 **Massava** Russian Federation
303 F4 **Massawa** Eritrea
303 G4 **Massawa Channel** *strait* Eritrea
127 N4 **Massena** New York USA
305 H2 **Massenya** Chad
229 J3 **Masseria** Italy
118 E5 **Masset** British Columbia Canada
118 E6 **Masset Inlet** British Columbia Canada
228 E5 **Masseube** France
228 F4 **Massiac** France
225 M4 **Massiaru** Estonia
308 D2 **Massibi** Angola
228 F4 **Massif Central** *region* France
304 C2 **Massigui** Mali
300 E6 **Massina** Mali
309 F4 **Massingir** Mozambique
309 F4 **Massingir, Barragem de** *lake* Mozambique
125 L7 **Massive, Mount** Colorado USA
437 G2 **Masson Island** Antarctica
232 D5 **Massoncello, Monte** *mountain* Italy
228 B3 **Massy** France
423 F5 **Masterton** New Zealand
235 E6 **Masticho, Akra** *cape* Greece
233 C7 **Màstixi, Punta su** *cape* Sardinia Italy
224 G4 **Mästocka** Sweden
386 F4 **Masuda** Japan
222 M3 **Masugnsbyn** Sweden
305 G5 **Masuku (Franceville)** Gabon
393 D8 **Masur** Maharashtra India
374 D4 **Masurai, Bukit** *mountain* Indonesia
309 F4 **Masvingo** Zimbabwe
309 F4 **Masvingo** *admin. area* Zimbabwe
307 E4 **Maswa** Tanzania
372 E4 **Maswaar** *island* Indonesia
227 L2 **Masyevichy** Belarus
227 H1 **Maszewo** Poland
155 E3 **Mata, Serranía de** *range* Venezuela
162 B4 **Mata Amarilla** Argentina
157 E6 **Mata de São João** Brazil
155 F2 **Mata de Venado** Venezuela
155 F3 **Mata en Medio** Venezuela
308 E3 **Matabeleland North** *admin. area* Zimbabwe
308 E4 **Matabeleland South** *admin. area* Zimbabwe
427 9 **Matacaw Levu** *island* Fiji
127 K2 **Matachewan** Ontario Canada
129 I6 **Matachic** Mexico
385 H3 **Matad** Mongolia
306 A5 **Matadi** Democratic Republic of Congo
129 L3 **Matador** Texas USA
134 C4 **Matagalpa** Nicaragua
121 Q8 **Matagami** Québec Canada
121 Q8 **Matagami, Lac** *lake* Québec Canada
130 C6 **Matagorda Bay** Texas USA
130 C6 **Matagorda Island** Texas USA
130 C6 **Matagorda Peninsula** Texas USA
384 F5 **Mataigou** Zizhiqu China
423 F5 **Mataikona** New Zealand
427 14 **Mataiva** *reef* French Polynesia
374 E3 **Matak** *island* Indonesia
425 M8 **Matakana** NSW Australia
422 G3 **Matakana Island** New Zealand
422 H3 **Matakaoa Point** New Zealand
423 E6 **Matakitaki** *watercourse* New Zealand
308 B2 **Matala** Angola
306 D4 **Matala** Democratic Republic of Congo
235 D8 **Matala** Greece
306 D4 **Matale** Democratic Republic of Congo
393 E10 **Matale** Sri Lanka
162 C3 **Matalinares, Punta** *cape* Argentina
304 B2 **Matam** Senegal
301 H6 **Matameye** Niger
127 M6 **Matamoras** Pennsylvania USA
132 E3 **Matamoros** Mexico
133 F3 **Matamoros** Mexico
375 I4 **Matana, Danau** *lake* Indonesia
377 I6 **Matanal Point** Philippines
307 F5 **Matandu** *watercourse* Tanzania
121 V8 **Matane** Québec Canada
121 V8 **Matane** *watercourse* Québec Canada
154 D3 **Matanegra** Colombia
134 D2 **Matanzas** Cuba
134 D2 **Matanzas** *admin. area* Cuba
157 B8 **Matão** Brazil
159 I3 **Matão, Serra do** *range* Brazil
134 D5 **Matapalo, Cabo** *cape* Costa Rica
128 H6 **Matape** Mexico
127 R2 **Matapédia** *watercourse* Québec Canada
127 R2 **Matapédia, Lac** *lake* Québec Canada
155 G3 **Matappi** Suriname
160 D5 **Mataquito** *watercourse* Chile
223 P5 **Matara** Finland
393 E11 **Matara** Sri Lanka
235 B6 **Mataragka** Greece
375 H6 **Mataram** Indonesia
424 J3 **Mataranka** NT Australia
375 I4 **Matarape, Teluk** *bay* Indonesia
231 H3 **Mataró** Spain
234 C3 **Mătăsari** Romania
375 G5 **Matasiri** *island* Indonesia
223 P5 **Mätäsvaara** Finland
308 E6 **Matatiele** South Africa
423 C8 **Mataura** New Zealand
423 C7 **Mataura** *watercourse* New Zealand
427 12b **Mata'utu** Wallis and Futuna
154 E3 **Mataveni** Venezuela
422 2 **Matavera** Cook Islands New Zealand
163 5 **Mataveri** Isla de Pascua (Easter Island)
120 I5 **Matawak** Manitoba Canada
127 O3 **Matawin Reservoir** Québec Canada
389 M4 **Matay** Kazakhstan
160 D6 **Matazilla, Pampa de la** *range* Argentina
227 L2 **Matcze** Poland
154 D3 **Mate Palma** Colombia
159 F4 **Mateguá** Bolivia
132 E4 **Matehuala** Mexico
427 13a **Mateika** *island* Tuvalu
159 I5 **Mateira, Serra** *range* Brazil
157 A9 **Matelândia** Brazil
232 E5 **Matelica** Italy
163 9 **Matelot** Trinidad and Tobago
308 C3 **Matende** Angola
309 F3 **Matenga** Mozambique
134 C4 **Mateo** Honduras
233 G6 **Matera** Italy
234 A4 **Mateševo** Montenegro
301 H1 **Mateur** Tunisia
224 I1 **Matfors** Sweden
228 D4 **Matha** France
79 U6 **Mathematicians Seamounts** *underwater feature* Pacific Ocean
129 K1 **Matheson** Colorado USA
130 C6 **Mathis** Texas USA
235 A6 **Mathraki** *island* Greece
392 D5 **Mathura** Uttar Pradesh India
377 J6 **Mati** Philippines
307 F4 **Matia** *watercourse* Kenya
391 K4 **Matiari** Pakistan
156 D3 **Matias Olímpio** Brazil
133 G5 **Matías Romero** Mexico
309 H2 **Matibane** Mozambique
156 C3 **Matinha** Brazil
157 D8 **Matipó** Brazil
427 14a **Matiti** French Polynesia
223 Q6 **Matkasel'kya** Russian Federation
308 E4 **Matlabas** *watercourse* South Africa
241 F1 **Matlock** Derbyshire England UK
377 J4 **Matnog** Philippines
159 G4 **Mato Grosso** Brazil
159 H4 **Mato Grosso** *admin. area* Brazil
157 A6 **Mato Grosso, Planalto do** *region* Brazil
159 H5 **Mato Grosso do Sul** *admin. area* Brazil
157 D6 **Mato Verde** Brazil
159 I3 **Mato Verde** Brazil
238 D2 **Matoksa** Russian Federation
309 F5 **Matola** Mozambique
121 U7 **Matonipi** *watercourse* Québec Canada
121 U7 **Matonipi, Lac** *lake* Québec Canada
307 G4 **Matooni, Raas** *cape* Somalia
230 B3 **Matosinhos** Portugal
380 E4 **Matou** Guangxi Zhuangzu Zizhiqu China
229 G3 **Matour** France
305 G5 **Matouti, Pointe** *cape* Gabon
391 I5 **Maṭraḥ** Oman
224 C2 **Matre** Norway
226 G4 **Matrei** Austria
304 B3 **Matru** Sierra Leone
222 I4 **Matsdal** Sweden
309 I4 **Matsiatra** *watercourse* Madagascar
381 H3 **Matsu Tao (Taiwan)** *island* Fujian China
386 G4 **Matsue** Japan
387 H4 **Matsumoto** Japan
387 H4 **Matsusaka** Japan
386 G5 **Matsuyama** Japan
155 H3 **Matta** Suriname
121 N7 **Mattagami** *watercourse* Ontario Canada
160 F5 **Mattaldi** Argentina
131 M3 **Mattamuskeet, Lake** North Carolina USA
127 L3 **Mattawa** Ontario Canada
124 F3 **Mattawa** Washington USA
127 Q3 **Mattawamkeag Lake** Maine USA
232 B3 **Matten** Switzerland
229 H4 **Matterhorn** *mountain* Switzerland
135 F2 **Matthew Town** Bahamas
131 K3 **Matthews** North Carolina USA
423 F5 **Matthews, Mount** New Zealand
390 G5 **Maṭṭī, Sabkhat** United Arab Emirates
223 M2 **Mattiselva** *watercourse* Norway
222 H5 **Mattmar** Sweden
126 G7 **Mattoon** Illinois USA
226 G4 **Mattsee** *lake* Austria
375 F3 **Matu** Malaysia
375 F4 **Matua** Indonesia
237 AF9 **Matua, Ostrov** *island* Russian Federation
393 E10 **Matugama** Sri Lanka
427 9 **Matuku** *island* Fiji
308 C2 **Matumbo** Angola
379 G5 **Matupi** Myanmar
163 9 **Matura** Trinidad and Tobago
163 9 **Matura Bay** Trinidad and Tobago
155 F2 **Maturín** Venezuela
234 G1 **Matusov** Ukraine
375 J2 **Matutuang** *island* Indonesia
230 E2 **Matxitxako, Cabo** *cape* Spain
236 S6 **Matyl'ka** Russian Federation
392 F6 **Mau** Bihar India
392 E5 **Mau** Madhya Pradesh India
392 E6 **Mau** Madhya Pradesh India
392 E6 **Mau Ranipur** Uttar Pradesh India
309 G2 **Maúa** Mozambique
130 C3 **Maud** Oklahoma USA
437 A2 **Maud Rise** *underwater feature* Southern Ocean
437 L1 **Maude, Cape** Antarctica
159 G1 **Maués** Brazil
155 G6 **Maues Acu** *watercourse* Brazil
426 2 **Maug Islands** *islands* Northern Mariana Islands
242 D2 **Maughold Head** *cape* Isle of Man UK
128 inset **Maui** *island* Hawai'i USA
422 1 **Mauke** *island* Cook Islands New Zealand
223 N4 **Maula** Finland
160 D5 **Maule** *admin. area* Chile
160 C5 **Maule** *watercourse* Chile
160 D6 **Maule, Lago de** *lake* Chile
228 D3 **Maulévrier** France
162 B2 **Maullín** Chile
245 C3 **Maum** Ireland
126 I6 **Maumee** *watercourse* Indiana USA
130 E3 **Maumelle, Lake** Arkansas USA
372 B6 **Maumere** Indonesia
308 D3 **Maun** Botswana
232 F4 **Maun** *island* Croatia
128 inset **Mauna Kea** *volcano* Hawai'i USA
128 inset **Mauna Loa** *volcano* Hawai'i USA
128 inset **Maunaloa** Hawai'i USA
392 F6 **Maunath Bhanjan** Uttar Pradesh India
308 E4 **Maunatlala** Botswana
422 2 **Maungaroa** *volcano* Cook Islands New Zealand
379 G5 **Maungdaw (Sinchaigbyin)** Myanmar
376 C4 **Maungmagan Islands** Myanmar
116 G5 **Maunoir, Lac** *lake* Northwest Territories Canada
223 M2 **Maunu** Sweden
121 T7 **Maupertuis, Lac** *lake* Québec Canada
427 14 **Maupihaa** *island* French Polynesia
124 E4 **Maupin** Oregon USA
224 F2 **Maura** Norway
227 K5 **Măureni** Romania
130 F5 **Maurepas, Lake** Louisiana USA
228 F4 **Mauriac** France
424 I7 **Maurice, Lake** SA Australia
310 7b **Mauritius** *country* Indian Ocean
310 7 **Mauritius** *island* Mauritius
233 F6 **Mauro, Monte** *mountain* Italy
228 C2 **Mauron** France
228 F4 **Maurs** France
437 I2 **Maury Bay** Antarctica
435 E3 **Maury Channel** *underwater feature* Atlantic Ocean
227 G3 **Mauth** Germany
228 E5 **Mauvezin** France
228 D3 **Mauzé-sur-le-Mignon** France
309 G2 **Mavago** Mozambique
309 G4 **Mavanza** Mozambique
222 J3 **Mavas** Sweden
222 J3 **Mavasjaure** *lake* Sweden
308 C3 **Mavengue** Angola
308 D3 **Mavinga** Angola
427* G3 **Mavis Reef** WA Australia
234 D3 **Mavrodin** Romania
392 D6 **Mawana** Madhya Pradesh India
306 B5 **Mawanga** Democratic Republic of Congo
376 C5 **Mawdaung Pass** *mountain* Myanmar
422 H4 **Mawhai Point** New Zealand
379 H5 **Mawkme** Myanmar
376 C3 **Mawlamyaing (Moulmein)** Myanmar
390 E4 **Mawqaq** Saudi Arabia
390 E7 **Mawr, Wādī** *watercourse* Yemen
437 E2 **Mawson (Australia)** *research station* Antarctica
437 L2 **Mawson Bank** *underwater feature* Ross Sea
437 E2 **Mawson Coast** Antarctica
437 E2 **Mawson Escarpment** *range* Antarctica
424 inset **Mawson Peak** Heard Island Australia
437 K2 **Mawson Peninsula** Antarctica
125 O3 **Max** North Dakota USA
307 H3 **Maxaas** Somalia
160 E4 **Maxán** Argentina
133 H4 **Maxcanú** Mexico
228 C3 **Maxent** France
118 J3 **Maxhamish Lake** British Columbia Canada
309 G4 **Maxixe** Mozambique
422 F4 **Maxwell** New Zealand
125 O6 **Maxwell** Nebraska USA
129 J2 **Maxwell** New Mexico USA
428* G6 **Maxwelton** Qld Australia
373 G5 **May** *watercourse* Papua New Guinea
437 L1 **May, Cape** Antarctica
244 F4 **May, Isle of** Scotland UK
429* H4 **May, Mount** Qld Australia
429* J7 **May Downs** Qld Australia
134 E3 **May Pen** Jamaica
430* E4 **Maya** WA Australia
374 F4 **Maya** *island* Indonesia
237 AC7 **Maya** *watercourse* Russian Federation
134 B3 **Maya Mountains** Belize
376 B4 **Mayabandar** Andaman and Nicobar Islands India
135 F2 **Mayaguana Island** Bahamas
135 F2 **Mayaguana Passage** Bahamas
135 H3 **Mayagüez** Puerto Rico
301 H6 **Mayahi** Niger
389 K7 **Mayakovskiy, Qullai** *mountain* Tajikistan
234 F2 **Mayaky** Ukraine
306 B5 **Mayala** Democratic Republic of Congo
372 D4 **Mayalibit, Teluk** *bay* Indonesia
386 F3 **Mayang-dong** *island* North Korea
380 E1 **Mayanhe** Gansu China
306 E3 **Mayania** *watercourse* Uganda
430* E6 **Mayanup** WA Australia
163 9 **Mayaro** Trinidad and Tobago
163 9 **Mayaro Bay** Trinidad and Tobago
244 D5 **Maybole** South Ayrshire Scotland UK
303 F5 **Maych'ew** Ethiopia
234 G1 **Maydanets'ke** Ukraine
388 J6 **Maydayobu** Uzbekistan
372 E4 **Mayege** Indonesia
226 D2 **Mayen** Germany
228 D2 **Mayenne** France
379 F2 **Mayer Kangri** *mountain* Xizang Zizhiqu China
228 E3 **Mayet** France
423 D6 **Mayfield** New Zealand
130 C2 **Mayfield** Kansas USA
130 G2 **Mayfield** Kentucky USA
128 G1 **Mayfield** Utah USA
129 J4 **Mayhill** New Mexico USA
389 L3 **Maykain** Kazakhstan
389 M4 **Maykamys** Kazakhstan
388 C5 **Maykop** Russian Federation
389 O3 **Mayma** Russian Federation
237 AC7 **Maymakan** *watercourse* Russian Federation
379 H4 **Maymyo** Myanmar
388 E2 **Mayna** Russian Federation
388 J6 **Maynamak** Uzbekistan
428* F7 **Mayne** *watercourse* Qld Australia
428* F7 **Maynes Peak** *mountain* Qld Australia
237 AK6 **Mayno-Amamkut** Russian Federation
237 AK6 **Mayno-Gytkino** Russian Federation
127 M4 **Maynooth** Ontario Canada
245 F3 **Maynooth** Ireland
162 B3 **Mayo** *watercourse* Argentina
116 F6 **Mayo** Yukon Territory Canada
245 C2 **Mayo** *admin. area* Ireland
163 9 **Mayo** Trinidad and Tobago
131 J5 **Mayo** Florida USA
162 B6 **Mayo, Cerro** *mountain* Chile
377 J6 **Mayo Bay** Philippines
305 G3 **Mayo Belwa** Nigeria
305 G3 **Mayo Darlé** Cameroon
305 G3 **Mayo Godi** *watercourse* Cameroon
305 H2 **Mayo-Kebbi Est** *admin. area* Chad
305 G3 **Mayo-Kebbi Ouest** *admin. area* Chad
159 E4 **Mayo Mayo** Bolivia
131 L2 **Mayo Reservoir** North Carolina USA
305 G5 **Mayoko** Congo
377 I4 **Mayon** *volcano* Philippines
230 C5 **Mayor, Isla** *island* Spain
160 F6 **Mayor Buratovich** Argentina
422 G3 **Mayor Island (Tuhua)** New Zealand
159 F5 **Mayor Pablo Lagerenza** Paraguay
230 D2 **Mayorga** Spain
163 9 **Mayoro-Rio Claro** *admin. area* Trinidad and Tobago
310 6a **Mayotte** *French overseas department* Indian Ocean
377 I3 **Mayraira Point** Philippines
163 11 **Mayreau** St Vincent and the Grenadines
226 F4 **Mayrhofen** Austria
223 M5 **Mäyry** Finland
390 F3 **Maysān** *admin. area* Iraq
385 L2 **Mayskiy** Russian Federation
237 AB8 **Mayskiy, Khrebet** *range* Russian Federation
389 M3 **Mayskoye** Kazakhstan
119 R4 **Mayson Lake** Saskatchewan Canada
377 H5 **Maytiguid** *island* Philippines
375 J3 **Mayu** *island* Indonesia
393 E9 **Mayuram** Tamil Nadu India
125 Q3 **Mayville** North Dakota USA
244 inset **Maywick** Shetland Scotland UK
125 O6 **Maywood** Nebraska USA
237 AB6 **Mayya** Russian Federation
390 E6 **Mayzah** Saudi Arabia
238 G3 **Maza** Russian Federation
308 E3 **Mazabuka** Zambia
156 B3 **Mazagão** Brazil
124 E2 **Mazama** British Columbia Canada
118 K8 **Mazama** Washington USA
228 F5 **Mazamet** France
132 E5 **Mazamitla** Mexico
391 H2 **Mazanābād** Iran
388 F7 **MazandarÂn** *admin. area* Iran
388 J7 **Mazār-e-Sharīf** Afghanistan
382 F5 **Mazar Tag** *mountain* Xinjiang Uygur Zizhiqu China

233 E8 **Mazara del Vallo** Italy
162 C4 **Mazarredo** Argentina
231 F5 **Mazarrón** Spain
155 F3 **Mazaruni** *watercourse* Guyana
132 C2 **Mazatán** Mexico
132 D4 **Mazatlán** Mexico
225 L4 **Mazeikiai** Lithuania
231 G2 **Mazères** France
232 F4 **Mazin** Croatia
127 M4 **Mazinaw Lake** Ontario Canada
225 L4 **Mazirbe** Latvia
128 G6 **Mazocahui** Mexico
306 D4 **Mazomeno** Democratic Republic of Congo
307 F5 **Mazomora** Tanzania
383 J4 **Mazong Shan** *mountain* Gansu China
309 F3 **Mazowe** *watercourse* Zimbabwe
227 K1 **Mazowieckie** *admin. area* Poland
302 D5 **Mazrub** Sudan
225 M4 **Mazsalaca** Latvia
308 E4 **Mazunga** Zimbabwe
394 D2 **Mazyr** Belarus
301 H2 **Mazzouna** Tunisia
305 G3 **Mba** Cameroon
309 F5 **Mbabane** Swaziland
310 8a **Mbachilé** Comoros
300 C6 **Mbacké** Senegal
305 H4 **Mbaïki** Central African Republic
305 G3 **Mbakaou** Cameroon
305 H4 **Mbako** Central African Republic
306 E5 **Mbala** Zambia
305 G4 **Mbalam** Cameroon
307 E3 **Mbale** Uganda
305 H3 **Mbali** Central African Republic
305 I3 **Mbali** *watercourse* Central African Republic
305 G4 **Mbalmayo** Cameroon
426 8a **Mbalo** Solomon Islands
305 G3 **Mbam** *watercourse* Cameroon
305 G5 **Mbama** Congo
307 E6 **Mbamba Bay** Tanzania
306 B4 **Mbandaka** Democratic Republic of Congo
305 G4 **Mbandjok** Cameroon
305 G4 **Mbandza** Congo
305 G4 **Mbang** Cameroon
305 G6 **M'banza Congo** Angola
306 A5 **Mbanza-Ngungu** Democratic Republic of Congo
300 C6 **Mbar** Senegal
306 E4 **Mbarara** Uganda
305 I3 **Mbari** *watercourse* Central African Republic
309 F2 **Mbati** Zambia
373 K5 **Mbava** *island* Solomon Islands
305 G3 **Mbé** Cameroon
305 H5 **Mbé** Congo
308 E3 **Mbembesi** Zimbabwe
307 F5 **Mbemkuru** *watercourse* Tanzania
310 8a **Mbéni** Comoros
305 G3 **Mbere** *watercourse* Cameroon
308 E4 **Mberengwa** Zimbabwe
304 B3 **Mbesi, Lake** Sierra Leone
309 F1 **Mbesuma** Zambia
307 E5 **Mbeya** Tanzania
307 E5 **Mbeya** *admin. area* Tanzania
305 H4 **Mbi** *watercourse* Central African Republic
305 G5 **Mbigou** Gabon
307 E6 **Mbinga** Tanzania
305 G4 **Mbini** *watercourse* Equatorial Guinea
305 G4 **Mbomo** Congo
305 I3 **Mbomou** *admin. area* Central African Republic
305 H5 **Mbon** Congo
306 D3 **Mboro** Democratic Republic of Congo
306 C2 **Mbotou** *watercourse* Central African Republic
305 G3 **Mboula** Cameroon
300 D6 **Mboun** Senegal
300 C6 **Mbour** Senegal
300 D5 **Mbout** Mauritania
305 H3 **Mbrés** Central African Republic
306 C5 **Mbuji-Mayi** Democratic Republic of Congo
306 C5 **Mbuji-Mayi** *watercourse* Democratic Republic of Congo
161 G4 **Mburucuyá** Argentina
427 9a **Mbutha** Fiji
307 F5 **Mchinga** Tanzania
309 F2 **Mchinji** Zambia
120 H4 **M'Clintock** Manitoba Canada
117 I4 **M'Clintock Channel** Nunavut Canada
116 G3 **M'Clure Strait** Northwest Territories Canada
308 E6 **Mdantsane** South Africa
230 D6 **M'diq** Morocco
231 I6 **M'Doukal** Algeria
387 I2 **Me-akan-dake** *volcano* Japan
376 E3 **Mê, Hon** *island* Vietnam
386 F5 **Me-shima** *island* Japan
130 C4 **Mead** Oklahoma USA
128 E2 **Mead, Lake** Nevada USA
116 D5 **Meade** *watercourse* Alaska USA
125 O8 **Meade** Kansas USA
230 B3 **Meadela** Portugal
244 D2 **Meadie, Loch** *lake* Scotland UK
129 K4 **Meadow** Texas USA
124 I7 **Meadow** Utah USA
119 Q5 **Meadow Lake Provincial Park** Saskatchewan Canada
130 C5 **Meadowlakes** Texas USA
130 F5 **Meadville** Mississippi USA
127 K6 **Meadville** Pennsylvania USA
242 F2 **Meal Bank** Cumbria England UK
244 A2 **Mealasta** *island* Scotland UK
230 B3 **Mealhada** Portugal
122 I6 **Mealy Mountains** Newfoundland and Labrador Canada
425 N6 **Meandarra** Qld Australia
118 M3 **Meander River** Alberta Canada
156 C4 **Mearim** *watercourse* Brazil
222 J5 **Meåstrand** Sweden
245 F3 **Meath** *admin. area* Ireland
245 E3 **Meathas Troim** Ireland
372 E4 **Mebo, Gunung** *mountain* Indonesia
306 A5 **Mebridege** *watercourse* Angola
375 G6 **Mebulu, Tanjung** *cape* Indonesia
155 F3 **Mecalineta** Brazil
309 G3 **Mecanhelas** Mozambique
Mecca *see* **Makkah** Saudi Arabia
307 G2 **Mechāra** Ethiopia
229 G1 **Mechelen** Belgium
231 G6 **Mecheraa Asfa** Algeria
426 3 **Mecherchar** *island* Palau
301 F2 **Mecheria** Algeria
226 D2 **Mechernich** Germany
301 J6 **Mechimére** Chad
389 J4 **Mechkey-sor** *lake* Kazakhstan
226 G1 **Mecklenburg-Vorpommern** *admin. area* Germany
224 F5 **Mecklenburger Bucht** *bay* Germany
309 G2 **Meconta** Mozambique
309 G2 **Mecuburi** *watercourse* Mozambique
309 H2 **Mecúfi** Mozambique
309 G2 **Mecula** Mozambique
230 C3 **Meda** Portugal
232 F4 **Medak** Croatia
393 E7 **Medak** Andhra Pradesh India
374 C3 **Medan** Indonesia
375 H6 **Medang** *island* Indonesia
154 D2 **Médanos, Istmo de** *peninsula* Venezuela
162 D4 **Medanosa, Punta** *cape* Argentina
119 V5 **Medard** Manitoba Canada
393 E10 **Medawachchiya** Sri Lanka
301 G1 **Médéa** Algeria
301 G1 **Médéa** *admin. area* Algeria
157 D7 **Medeiros Neto** Brazil
154 C3 **Medellín** Colombia
222 J5 **Medelpad** *region* Sweden
301 I2 **Medenine** Tunisia
300 C5 **Mederdra** Mauritania
235 F7 **Medet** Turkey
125 Q8 **Medford** Oklahoma USA
124 D5 **Medford** Oregon USA
126 F4 **Medford** Wisconsin USA
235 D5 **Médhousa** Greece
306 E2 **Medi** Sudan
160 E5 **Media Luna** Argentina
134 E2 **Media Luna** Cuba
230 F5 **Media Naranja, Punta de la** *cape* Spain
157 A9 **Medianeira** Brazil
231 G2 **Mediano, Embalse de** *lake* Spain
124 G3 **Medical Lake** Washington USA
232 D4 **Medicina** Italy
125 L6 **Medicine Bow** Wyoming USA
125 L6 **Medicine Bow Mountains** Wyoming USA
119 P7 **Medicine Hat** Alberta Canada
125 M2 **Medicine Lake** Montana USA
125 P8 **Medicine Lodge** Kansas USA
129 M3 **Medicine Park** Oklahoma USA
157 D7 **Medina** Brazil
377 J5 **Medina** Philippines
127 L5 **Medina** New York USA
130 G3 **Medina** Tennessee USA
162 D2 **Medina, Ensenada de** *bay* Argentina
230 E2 **Medina de Pomar** Spain
230 D3 **Medina del Campo** Spain
300 D6 **Medina Gounas** Senegal
393 G6 **Medinipur** West Bengal India
160 D6 **Medio, Chihuido** *mountain* Argentina
132 D2 **Medio Camino** Mexico
154 C5 **Mediodía** Colombia
76 U6 **Mediterranean Ridge** *underwater feature* Mediterranean Sea
220 **Mediterranean Sea** Europe
231 H6 **Medjedel** Algeria
231 J5 **Medjez Sfa** Algeria
222 L4 **Medle** Sweden
238 F4 **Mednoye** Russian Federation
237 U3 **Mednyy, Mys** *cape* Russian Federation
237 AI8 **Mednyy, Ostrov** *island* Russian Federation
126 F7 **Medora** Illinois USA
125 N3 **Medora** North Dakota USA
225 K5 **Medovoye** Russian Federation
231 G6 **Medrissa** Algeria
222 H5 **Medstugan** Sweden
227 I5 **Medumajdan** Croatia
234 B4 **Medveda** Serbia
237 AH4 **Medvezh'i, Ostrov** *island* Russian Federation
236 T4 **Medvezhiy Yar** Russian Federation
387 H1 **Medvezh'ya, Gora** *mountain* Russian Federation
236 H6 **Medvezh'yegorsk** Russian Federation
241 H3 **Medway** *admin. area* England UK
234 C1 **Medyka** Ukraine
238 F5 **Medyn'** Russian Federation
424 F6 **Meekatharra** WA Australia
125 L6 **Meeker** Colorado USA
245 D3 **Meelick** Ireland
123 J8 **Meelpaeg Lake** Newfoundland and Labrador Canada
245 D2 **Meenacross** Ireland
225 N3 **Meerapalu** Estonia
226 C2 **Meerhout** Belgium
392 D5 **Meerut** Uttar Pradesh India
125 K4 **Meeteetse** Wyoming USA
240 C4 **Meeth** Devon England UK
307 F3 **Mēga** Ethiopia
307 F3 **Mega Escarpment** *range* Ethiopia
307 G2 **Megalo** Ethiopia
426 7 **Mégam** Vanuatu
235 B6 **Meganisi** *island* Greece
130 B4 **Megargel** Texas USA
393 G7 **Megasini** *mountain* Orissa India
379 G4 **Meghalaya** *admin. area* India
127 M2 **Mégiscane, Lac** *lake* Québec Canada
390 B2 **Megisti** *island* Greece
238 F3 **Megletsy** Russian Federation
225 Q2 **Megrega** Russian Federation
225 Q2 **Megrozero** Russian Federation
227 L5 **Mehadia** Romania
223 O1 **Mehamn** Norway
391 K4 **Mehar** Pakistan
424 F5 **Meharry, Mount** WA Australia
392 F5 **Mehdawal** Uttar Pradesh India
234 C3 **Mehedinți** *admin. area* Romania
224 E3 **Meheia** Norway
392 G6 **Meherpur** West Bengal India
225 N3 **Mehikoorma** Estonia
227 K4 **Méhkerék** Hungary
390 F2 **Mehrān** Iran
223 N4 **Mehtäkylä** Finland
391 L2 **Mehtar Lām** Afghanistan
160 C6 **Mehuín** Chile
381 G2 **Meicheng** Anhui China
305 G3 **Meidougou** Cameroon
240 D2 **Meifod** Powys Wales UK
245 F2 **Meigh** Newry and Mourne Northern Ireland UK
117 I2 **Meighen Island** Nunavut Canada
244 E4 **Meigle** Perth and Kinross Scotland UK
131 I5 **Meigs** Georgia USA
385 K4 **Meihekou** Jilin China
380 E3 **Meijiang** Guizhou China
381 G3 **Meijiang** Jiangxi China
379 H5 **Meiktila** Myanmar
222 L1 **Meiland** Norway
381 G3 **Meilin** Jiangxi China
230 C2 **Meira** Spain
229 I3 **Meiringen** Switzerland
381 G2 **Meishan** Anhui China
380 D2 **Meishan** Sichuan China
381 G2 **Meishan Shuiku** *lake* Anhui China
124 D6 **Meiss Lake** California USA
226 G2 **Meißen** Germany
380 D2 **Meixing** Sichuan China
381 G4 **Meizhou** Guangdong China
381 H3 **Meizhou Dao** *island* Fujian China
160 E4 **Mejicana** *mountain* Argentina
134 B4 **Mejicanos** El Salvador
162 D2 **Mejillón, Punta** *cape* Argentina
160 D2 **Mejillones** Chile
160 D2 **Mejillones, Bahía** *bay* Chile
427 I5 **Mejit Island** Marshall Islands
305 E3 **Mejo** Nigeria
305 G4 **Mékambo** Gabon
303 F5 **Mekane Selam** Ethiopia
303 F5 **Mek'elē** Ethiopia
225 Q2 **Mekhbaza** Russian Federation
300 C5 **Mékhé** Senegal
391 J3 **Mekhtar** Pakistan
300 E2 **Meknès** Morocco
376 E5 **Mekong** *watercourse* Cambodia
380 C4 **Mekong** *watercourse* Yunnan China
376 E4 **Mekong** *watercourse* Laos
376 E3 **Mekong** *watercourse* Thailand
375 I5 **Mekongga, Teluk** *bay* Indonesia
223 Q5 **Mekrijärvi** *lake* Finland
306 C2 **Mela, Mount** Central African Republic
226 F4 **Melago** Italy
374 D3 **Melaka** Malaysia
374 D3 **Melaka** *admin. area* Malaysia
375 G2 **Melalap** Malaysia
374 E4 **Melalo, Tanjung** *cape* Indonesia
78 M7 **Melanesian Basin** *underwater feature* Pacific Ocean
235 D6 **Melanios, Akra** *cape* Greece
235 B6 **Melátai** Greece
375 G4 **Melawi** *watercourse* Indonesia
124 G5 **Melba** Idaho USA
244 B2 **Melbost Borve** Na h-Eileanan Siar Scotland UK
425 M9 **Melbourne** Vic. Australia
241 F2 **Melbourne** Derbyshire England UK
130 F2 **Melbourne** Arkansas USA
131 K6 **Melbourne** Florida USA
241 E4 **Melbury Abbas** Dorset England UK
162 B3 **Melchor, Isla** *island* Chile
129 L7 **Melchor Múzquiz** Mexico
388 H4 **Meldikol** *lake* Kazakhstan
224 E5 **Meldorfer Bucht** *bay* Germany
302 C6 **Mélé** Central African Republic
305 I3 **Mélé** Central African Republic
120 G7 **Meleb** Manitoba Canada
426 3 **Melekeok** Palau
309 G3 **Melela** *watercourse* Mozambique
234 B3 **Melenci** Serbia
388 D2 **Melenki** Russian Federation
388 G3 **Meleuz** Russian Federation
121 T4 **Mélèzes, Rivière aux** *watercourse* Québec Canada
305 H2 **Melfi** Chad
233 F6 **Melfi** Italy
222 H3 **Melfjorden** Norway
119 S6 **Melfort** Saskatchewan Canada
230 B2 **Melgaço** Portugal
230 D2 **Melgar de Fernamental** Spain
386 F2 **Melgunovka** *watercourse* Russian Federation
120 I1 **Meliadine Lake** Nunavut Canada
226 E5 **Melide** Switzerland
235 C5 **Meliki** Greece
230 E6 **Melilla** *autonomous Spanish city* Africa
234 C3 **Melinești** Romania
162 B3 **Melinka** Chile
375 H4 **Melintang, Danau** *lake* Indonesia
235 D8 **Melissa, Akra** *cape* Greece
394 E3 **Melitopol'** Ukraine
227 H3 **Melk** Austria
307 F3 **Melka Guba** Ethiopia
241 E3 **Melksham** Wiltshire England UK
232 D4 **Mella** *watercourse* Italy
223 N3 **Mellakoski** Finland
231 G6 **Mellakou** Algeria
302 C5 **Mellam** Sudan
224 G3 **Mellan Fryken** *bay* Sweden
222 H5 **Mellanfjärden** *bay* Sweden
222 K5 **Mellansel** Sweden
222 I5 **Mellansjö** Sweden
228 D3 **Melle** France
226 E1 **Melle** Germany
126 F3 **Mellen** Wisconsin USA
222 M4 **Mellerstön** *island* Sweden
125 P4 **Mellette** South Dakota USA
233 F9 **Mellieħa** Malta
425 O4 **Mellish Reef** Qld Australia
302 D5 **Mellit** Sudan
437 E2 **Mellor Glacier** *ice* Antarctica
240 E3 **Mells** Somerset England UK
224 I4 **Mellstaby** Sweden
226 E1 **Mellum** *island* Germany
243 F2 **Melmerby** Cumbria England UK
243 G2 **Melmerby** North Yorkshire England UK
227 H2 **Mělník** Czech Republic
225 O2 **Mel'nikovo** Russian Federation
225 O3 **Mel'nitsy** Russian Federation
161 H5 **Melo** Uruguay
309 G2 **Meloco** Mozambique
372 B6 **Melolo** Indonesia
394 G3 **Melovoye** Ukraine
222 H3 **Meløya** *island* Norway
116 D5 **Melozitna** *watercourse* Alaska USA
222 inset **Melrakkanes** *cape* Iceland
123 G10 **Melrose** Nova Scotia Canada
244 F5 **Melrose** Scottish Borders Scotland UK
125 R4 **Melrose** Minnesota USA
129 K3 **Melrose** New Mexico USA
125 L3 **Melstone** Montana USA
223 N3 **Meltaus** Finland
222 G5 **Meltingvatnet** *lake* Norway
131 I3 **Melton Hill Lake** Tennessee USA
241 G2 **Melton Mowbray** Leicester England UK
223 N3 **Meltosjärvi** Finland
309 G2 **Meluco** Mozambique
226 B3 **Melun** France
244 C3 **Melvaig** Highland Scotland UK
126 D7 **Melvern Lake** Kansas USA
244 E2 **Melvich** Highland Scotland UK
119 T7 **Melville** Saskatchewan Canada
130 F5 **Melville** Louisiana USA
425 M3 **Melville, Cape** Qld Australia
377 H6 **Melville, Cape** Philippines
122 I6 **Melville, Lake** Newfoundland and Labrador Canada
116 G5 **Melville Hills** Northwest Territories Canada
424 I2 **Melville Island** NT Australia
116 H3 **Melville Island** Northwest Territories/Nunavut Canada
117 K5 **Melville Peninsula** Nunavut Canada
130 B5 **Melvin** Texas USA
245 D2 **Melvin, Lough** *lake* Ireland
226 E5 **Melzo** Italy
375 G4 **Memala** Indonesia
309 H2 **Memba** Mozambique
373 F4 **Memberamo** *watercourse* Indonesia
372 A6 **Memboro** Indonesia
230 C4 **Membrio** Spain
225 M4 **Mēmele** *watercourse* Latvia
226 F4 **Memmingen** Germany
374 F3 **Mempawah** Indonesia
126 E6 **Memphis** Missouri USA
130 G3 **Memphis** Tennessee USA
130 A3 **Memphis** Texas USA
127 O4 **Memphremagog, Lake** Québec Canada
394 E2 **Mena** Ukraine
130 D3 **Mena** Arkansas USA
125 R3 **Menahga** Minnesota USA
242 D3 **Menai Bridge** Gwynedd Wales UK
301 G5 **Ménaka** Mali
372 C4 **Menanga** Indonesia
309 I4 **Menarandra** *watercourse* Madagascar
130 B5 **Menard** Texas USA
77 G14 **Menard Fracture Zone** *underwater feature* Pacific Ocean
230 D4 **Menasalbas** Spain
374 E4 **Mendanau** *island* Indonesia
374 E3 **Mendarik** *island* Indonesia
375 G4 **Mendawai** Indonesia
375 G4 **Mendawai** *watercourse* Indonesia
228 F4 **Mende** France
307 F2 **Mendebo** *plain* Ethiopia
434 S1 **Mendeleyev Abyssal Plain** *underwater feature* Arctic Ocean
434 S1 **Mendeleyev Ridge** *underwater feature* Arctic Ocean
229 H1 **Menden** Germany
130 G5 **Mendenhall** Mississippi USA
116 C7 **Mendenhall, Cape** Alaska USA
235 F6 **Menderes** Turkey
231 G6 **Mendes** Algeria
157 D8 **Mendes** Brazil
133 F3 **Méndez** Mexico
119 Q7 **Mendham** Saskatchewan Canada
307 F2 **Mendī** Ethiopia
240 E3 **Mendip Hills** England UK
129 I7 **Mendoceño** Mexico
124 C6 **Mendocino, Cape** California USA
124 D7 **Mendocino, Lake** California USA
79 R3 **Mendocino Fracture Zone** *underwater feature* Pacific Ocean
126 I5 **Mendon** Michigan USA
124 E8 **Mendota** California USA
126 G5 **Mendota, Lake** Wisconsin USA
160 D5 **Mendoza** Argentina
160 D5 **Mendoza** *admin. area* Argentina
158 C3 **Mendoza** Peru
235 E6 **Menemen** Turkey
228 F1 **Menen** Belgium
426 4 **Meneng Point** Nauru
235 E8 **Menetes** Greece
233 E8 **Menfi** Italy
305 G3 **Meng** *watercourse* Cameroon
380 F4 **Meng Jiang** *watercourse* Guangxi Zhuangzu Zizhiqu China
380 E3 **Meng Jiang** *watercourse* Guizhou China
385 I6 **Meng Shan** *range* Shandong China
375 G2 **Mengalum** *island* Malaysia
381 G1 **Mengcheng** Anhui China
226 E3 **Mengen** Germany
374 E5 **Menggala** Indonesia
375 G4 **Mengkatip** Indonesia
372 B4 **Mengkoka, Gunung** *mountain* Indonesia
380 D4 **Mengla** Yunnan China
380 C4 **Menglang** Yunnan China
380 C4 **Menglian** Yunnan China
380 D4 **Menglie** Yunnan China
380 C4 **Mengmao Zhen** Yunnan China
380 C4 **Mengmeng** Yunnan China
305 G4 **Mengong** Cameroon
380 F4 **Mengshan** Guangxi Zhuangzu Zizhiqu China
381 F3 **Mengshan** *mountain* Hunan China
380 C4 **Mengsuo** Yunnan China
385 I6 **Mengyin** Shandong China
381 F1 **Mengzhou** Henan China
121 V5 **Menihek** Newfoundland and Labrador Canada
121 V5 **Menihek Lakes** Newfoundland and Labrador Canada
425 L8 **Menindee** NSW Australia
425 L8 **Menindee Lake** NSW Australia
425 K8 **Meningie** SA Australia
237 Z5 **Menkere** Russian Federation
125 Q5 **Menno** South Dakota USA
244 E5 **Mennock** Dumfries and Galloway Scotland UK
130 B2 **Meno** Oklahoma USA
235 C5 **Menoikion Oros** *range* Greece
126 H4 **Menominee** *watercourse* Michigan USA
308 C2 **Menongue** Angola
230 C5 **Menor, Isla** *island* Spain
231 I4 **Menorca (Minorca)** *island* Spain
301 F2 **Menouarar** Algeria
229 G4 **Mens** France
375 H3 **Mensalong** Indonesia
237 AD8 **Men'shikova, Ostrov** *island* Russian Federation
243 G3 **Menston** West Yorkshire England UK
374 D3 **Mentakab** Malaysia
375 H3 **Mentarang** *watercourse* Indonesia
374 C4 **Mentawai, Kepulauan** *island* Indonesia
374 C4 **Mentawai, Selat** *strait* Indonesia
158 B4 **Mentiroso, Islas** *islands* Peru
374 E4 **Mentok** Indonesia
229 H5 **Menton** France
127 K6 **Mentor** Ohio USA
160 E6 **Menucos** Argentina
375 G2 **Menumbok** Malaysia
375 H3 **Menyapa, Gunung** *mountain* Indonesia
301 H1 **Menzel Bourguiba** Tunisia
233 D9 **Menzel Chaker** Tunisia
233 C8 **Menzel Jemil** Tunisia
301 I1 **Menzel Temime** Tunisia
424 G7 **Menzies** WA Australia
437 E2 **Menzies, Mount** Antarctica
226 E4 **Menziken** Switzerland
241 H3 **Meopham** Kent England UK
132 D2 **Meoqui** Mexico
306 A5 **Mepala** Angola
388 D5 **Mepists'karo, Mt** *mountain* Georgia
309 F2 **Meponda** Mozambique
226 D1 **Meppel** Netherlands
226 D1 **Meppen** Germany
231 F3 **Mequinenza, Embalse de** *lake* Spain
228 E3 **Mer** France
130 F4 **Mer Rouge** Louisiana USA
375 H3 **Merah** Indonesia
222 G5 **Meråker** Norway
126 F7 **Meramec** *watercourse* Missouri USA
226 F4 **Merano** Italy
375 F5 **Merapi, Gunung** *volcano* Indonesia
123 K9 **Merasheen Island** Newfoundland and Labrador Canada
222 L3 **Merasjärvi** Sweden
232 C4 **Merate** Italy
308 D4 **Meratswe** *watercourse* Botswana
375 G4 **Meratus, Pegunungan** *range* Indonesia
374 D3 **Merbau** Indonesia
229 H4 **Mercantour, Parc National du** *park* France
154 C5 **Merced** Ecuador
124 E8 **Merced** California USA
160 D4 **Mercedario, Cerro** *mountain* Argentina
161 G4 **Mercedes** Argentina
161 G5 **Mercedes** Argentina
161 G5 **Mercedes** Uruguay
422 F3 **Mercer** New Zealand
422 F3 **Mercury Bay** New Zealand
422 F3 **Mercury Islands (Iles d'Haussez)** New Zealand
117 M6 **Mercy, Cape** Nunavut Canada
228 C2 **Merdrignac** France
243 F3 **Mere** Cheshire England UK
241 E3 **Mere** Wiltshire England UK
426 7 **Méré Lava** *island* Vanuatu
162 E5 **Meredith, Cape** Falkland Islands
129 L3 **Meredith, Lake** Texas USA
307 H3 **Mereeg** Somalia
394 F3 **Merefa** Ukraine
422 F3 **Meremere** New Zealand
422 F4 **Meremere** New Zealand
234 D3 **Mereniidesus** Romania
228 F2 **Méréville** France
238 G3 **Merëzha** Russian Federation
388 F3 **Mergenevo** Kazakhstan
305 G2 **Méri** Cameroon
232 B4 **Méribel** France
235 E5 **Meriç** Turkey
125 K1 **Merid** Saskatchewan Canada
133 H4 **Mérida** Mexico
230 C4 **Mérida** Spain
154 D2 **Mérida** Venezuela
154 D2 **Mérida** *admin. area* Venezuela
154 D2 **Mérida, Cordillera de** *range* Venezuela
241 F2 **Meriden** West Midlands England UK
127 O6 **Meriden** Connecticut USA
125 R5 **Meriden** Iowa USA
124 G5 **Meridian** Idaho USA
130 G4 **Meridian** Mississippi USA
130 C5 **Meridian** Texas USA
125 N7 **Meridith, Lake** Colorado USA
301 F2 **Meridja** Algeria
228 D4 **Mérignac** France
228 E5 **Mérigon** France
225 K2 **Merikarvia** Finland
229 L2 **Měřín** Czech Republic
222 F6 **Meringsdalen** Norway
372 E2 **Merir** *island* Palau
375 G3 **Merit** Malaysia
426 5 **Merizo** Guam
130 A4 **Merkel** Texas USA
225 M5 **Merkys** *watercourse* Lithuania
228 E1 **Merlimont-Plage** France
424 F4 **Mermaid Reef** WA Australia
125 P6 **Merna** Nebraska USA
301 H1 **Merouana** Algeria
302 E4 **Merowe** Sudan
424 F7 **Merredin** WA Australia
126 E8 **Merriam Woods** Missouri USA
244 D5 **Merrick** *mountain* Scotland UK
126 G4 **Merrill** Wisconsin USA
126 F4 **Merrillan** Wisconsin USA
125 O5 **Merriman** Nebraska USA
118 K7 **Merritt** British Columbia Canada
125 O5 **Merritt Reservoir** Nebraska USA
425 N8 **Merriwa** NSW Australia
130 E5 **Merryville** Louisiana USA
231 F6 **Mers el Hadjad** Algeria
303 G5 **Mersa Fatma** Eritrea
229 H2 **Mersch** Luxembourg
241 H3 **Mersea Island** England UK
226 F2 **Merseburg** Germany
243 F3 **Mersey** *watercourse* England UK
374 D3 **Mersing** Malaysia
375 G3 **Mersing, Bukit** *mountain* Malaysia
225 L4 **Mērsrags** *cape* Latvia
392 D5 **Merta City** Rajasthan India
240 D2 **Merthyr Cynog** Powys Wales UK
240 D3 **Merthyr Tydfil** Merthyr Tydfil Wales UK
240 D3 **Merthyr Tydfil** *admin. area* Wales UK
230 C5 **Mértola** Portugal
241 H2 **Merton** Norfolk England UK
301 H4 **Mertoutek** Algeria
437 J2 **Mertz Glacier Tongue** *ice* Antarctica
129 L5 **Mertzon** Texas USA
226 B3 **Méru** France
307 F3 **Meru** Kenya
307 F4 **Meru, Mount** *volcano* Tanzania
375 G6 **Meru Betiri, Taman Nasional** *park* Indonesia
375 H4 **Meruat, Tanjung** *cape* Indonesia
155 F3 **Merume Mountains** Guyana
375 H2 **Merutai** Malaysia
242 B4 **Mervyn** Ireland
308 D6 **Merweville** South Africa
124 D4 **Merwin, Lake** Washington USA
226 B3 **Méry** France
436 U2 **Merz Peninsula** Antarctica
394 E5 **Merzifon** Turkey
226 D3 **Merzig** Germany
372 D3 **Mesa** Indonesia
128 G4 **Mesa** Arizona USA
124 F3 **Mesa** Washington USA
129 I7 **Mesa de Coloradas** Mexico
129 H6 **Mesa Tres Rios** Mexico
126 E3 **Mesabi Range** Minnesota USA
121 P7 **Mésaconane, Pointe** Québec Canada
233 G6 **Mesagne** Italy
374 E3 **Mesanak** *island* Indonesia
306 D4 **Mesaraba** Democratic Republic of Congo
132 E1 **Mescalero Ridge** *range* New Mexico USA
222 J4 **Meselefors** Sweden
426 6a **Meseong** *island* Federated States of Micronesia
230 D3 **Meseta** *region* Spain
154 C4 **Mesetas** Colombia
121 R7 **Mesgouez, Lac** *lake* Québec Canada
238 F5 **Meshchovsk** Russian Federation
129 I4 **Mesilla** New Mexico USA
233 B9 **Meskiana** Algeria
241 I5 **Mesnières-en-Bray** France
232 C3 **Mesocco** Switzerland
232 E4 **Mesola** Italy
235 B6 **Mesolongi** Greece
235 B6 **Mesolongiou, Limnothalassa** *bay* Greece
235 A6 **Mesongi** Greece
163 11a **Mesopotamia** St Vincent and the Grenadines
222 H3 **Mesøy** Norway
128 E2 **Mesquite** Nevada USA
130 C4 **Mesquite** Texas USA
128 E3 **Mesquite Lake** California USA
391 H2 **Meşr** Iran
301 G2 **Messaad** Algeria
309 G2 **Messalo** *watercourse* Mozambique
228 D5 **Messanges** France
222 L3 **Messaure** Sweden
222 G6 **Messelt** Norway
162 A4 **Messier, Canal** *strait* Chile
233 F7 **Messina** Italy
235 C7 **Messiniakos Kolpos** *bay* Greece
229 I3 **Meßkirch** Germany
236 Q5 **Messoyakha** *watercourse* Russian Federation
232 C2 **Meßstetten** Germany
235 C5 **Mesta** Bulgaria
235 C5 **Mesta** *watercourse* Bulgaria
226 F1 **Mestlin** Germany
232 G1 **Město Albrechtice** Czech Republic
227 I3 **Město Libavá** Czech Republic
235 D6 **Meston, Akra** *cape* Greece
232 E4 **Mestre** Italy
374 E4 **Mesuji** *watercourse* Indonesia
226 C4 **Mesvres** France
154 C4 **Meta** *admin. area* Colombia
135 G6 **Meta, Rio** *watercourse* Colombia/Venezuela
121 U1 **Meta Incognita Peninsula** Nunavut Canada
123 K8 **Meta Pond** Newfoundland and Labrador Canada
234 C2 **Metaliferi, Munții** *range* Romania
124 G2 **Metaline Falls** Washington USA
232 H5 **Metaljka** Montenegro
225 P3 **Metallostroy** Russian Federation
160 E3 **Metán** Argentina
375 G4 **Metangai** Indonesia
309 F2 **Metangula** Mozambique
234 A4 **Metanjac** Montenegro
309 G2 **Metarica** Mozambique
235 E5 **Metaxades** Greece
122 G6 **Metchin** *watercourse* Newfoundland and Labrador Canada
302 F5 **Metema** Ethiopia
80 F9 **Meteor Seamount** *underwater feature* Southern Ocean
235 B6 **Meteora** *monastery* Greece
133 F5 **Metepec** Mexico
373 I4 **Meteran** Papua New Guinea
226 B2 **Météren** France
134 E5 **Metetí** Panama
243 H3 **Metheringham** Lincolnshire England UK
244 F3 **Methlick** Aberdeenshire Scotland UK
423 D6 **Methven** New Zealand
244 E4 **Methven** Perth and Kinross Scotland UK
241 H2 **Methwold** Norfolk England UK
120 J8 **Metionga Lake** Ontario Canada
118 M3 **Metis** Alberta Canada
119 P6 **Metiskow** Alberta Canada
309 G2 **Metoro** Mozambique
374 E5 **Metro** Indonesia
223 P4 **Metsäkylä** Finland
225 M4 **Metsapoole** Estonia
158 C3 **Metsoquiari Alto** Peru
131 J4 **Metter** Georgia USA
307 F2 **Metu** Ethiopia
375 G3 **Metulang** Indonesia
375 H3 **Metut** Indonesia
229 H2 **Metz** France
232 B2 **Metzervisse** France
228 C2 **Meu** *watercourse* France
374 C2 **Meulaboh** Indonesia
229 H2 **Meurthe** *watercourse* France
229 G1 **Meuse** *watercourse* Belgium
229 G2 **Meuse** *watercourse* France
240 C4 **Mevagissey** Cornwall England UK
380 D1 **Mêwa** Sichuan China
243 G3 **Mexborough** South Yorkshire England UK
130 C5 **Mexia** Texas USA
156 B3 **Mexiana, Ilha** *island* Brazil
132 B1 **Mexicali** Mexico
128 H2 **Mexican Hat** Utah USA
128 H2 **Mexican Water** Arizona USA
132 C5 **Mexico** *country* North America
126 F7 **Mexico** Missouri USA
133 F5 **México** *admin. area* Mexico
134 B1 **Mexico, Gulf of** Caribbean
76 I7 **Mexico Basin** *underwater feature* Gulf of Mexico
México City *see* **Ciudad de México** Mexico
244 E2 **Mey** Highland Scotland UK
388 E6 **Meyāneh** Iran
391 K2 **Meydān Shahr** Afghanistan
226 G1 **Meyenburg** Germany
127 L7 **Meyersdale** Pennsylvania USA
229 G4 **Meylan** France
240 C2 **Meyllteyrn** Gwynedd Wales UK
391 J2 **Meymaneh** Afghanistan
390 G2 **Meymeh** Iran
237 AK6 **Meynypil'gyno** Russian Federation
305 G4 **Meyo Centre** Cameroon
125 L2 **Meyronne** Saskatchewan Canada
226 B5 **Meyrueis** France
133 G5 **Mezcalapa** *lake* Mexico
228 F5 **Mèze** France
236 J5 **Mezen'** Russian Federation
236 J5 **Mezen'** *watercourse* Russian Federation
228 G4 **Mézenc, Mount** *mountain* France
236 J5 **Mezenskaya Guba** *bay* Russian Federation
237 U4 **Mezenskiy** Russian Federation
236 L4 **Mezhdusharskiy, Ostrov** *island* Russian Federation
388 H2 **Mezhozernyy** Russian Federation
118 G4 **Meziadin Lake** British Columbia Canada
227 H4 **Mežica** Slovenia
229 G4 **Mézilhac** France
228 E4 **Mézin** France
227 K4 **Mezőcsát** Hungary
227 K4 **Mezőkeresztes** Hungary
226 F4 **Mezzano** Italy
226 G5 **Mezzogoro** Italy
307 E4 **Mfangano Island** *island* Uganda
305 G4 **Mfou** Cameroon
225 P3 **Mga** Russian Federation
237 AD8 **Mgachi** Russian Federation
244 B5 **Mhàil, Rubh' a'** *cape* Scotland UK
393 D8 **Mhasvad** Maharashtra India
244 D3 **Mhòr, Loch** *lake* Scotland UK
393 D6 **Mhow** Madhya Pradesh India
379 G5 **Mi** *watercourse* Myanmar
386 F4 **Mi-shima** *island* Japan
376 E2 **Mia Sơn** Vietnam
244 B2 **Miabhaig** Na h-Eileanan Siar Scotland UK
227 L2 **Miączyn** Poland
133 F5 **Miahuatlán** Mexico
305 H3 **Miaméré** Central African Republic
128 G4 **Miami** Arizona USA
131 K8 **Miami** Florida USA
126 D8 **Miami** Oklahoma USA
130 A3 **Miami** Texas USA
131 K8 **Miami Beach** Florida USA
126 I7 **Miamisburg** Ohio USA
390 F3 **Mian Āb** Iran
391 L3 **Mian Channun** Pakistan
381 F1 **Mianchi** Henan China
388 E7 **Miāndoāb** Iran
375 J2 **Miangas** *island* Indonesia
377 J6 **Miangas (Indonesia)** *island* Indonesia
380 D3 **Mianning** Sichuan China
391 L3 **Mianwali** Pakistan
380 D2 **Mianyang** Sichuan China
380 D2 **Mianzhu** Sichuan China
381 H4 **Miaoli** Taiwan China
309 I3 **Miarinarivo** Madagascar
388 H2 **Miass** Russian Federation
224 I5 **Miastko** Poland
306 C5 **Mibalaie** Democratic Republic of Congo
234 D2 **Mica** Romania
160 D2 **Mica, Cerro de** *mountain* Chile
118 L6 **Mica Creek** British Columbia Canada
118 I4 **Mica Peak** British Columbia Canada
135 F2 **Micarro, Sierra de** *range* Cuba
309 G3 **Micaúne** Mozambique
131 J5 **Miccosukee, Lake** Florida USA
373 H5 **Michael, Mount** Papua New Guinea
227 K3 **Michalovce** Slovakia
227 L1 **Michałowo** Poland
119 Q4 **Michel** Saskatchewan Canada
226 F2 **Michelau** Germany
229 I2 **Michelstadt** Germany
380 C3 **Micheng** Yunnan China
119 O7 **Michichi** Alberta Canada
126 G3 **Michigamme Reservoir** Michigan USA
114 **Michigan** *admin. area* USA
126 H4 **Michigan, Lake** Michigan USA
126 H6 **Michigan City** Indiana USA
122 I5 **Michinappi Lake** Newfoundland and Labrador Canada
162 B3 **Michinmahuida, Volcán** *volcano* Chile
126 I3 **Michipicoton** Ontario Canada
126 I3 **Michipicoton Bay** Ontario Canada
126 H3 **Michipicoton Island** Ontario Canada
132 E5 **Michoacán** *admin. area* Mexico
388 C3 **Michurinsk** Russian Federation
222 L5 **Mickelsörarna** *island* Finland
222 L4 **Mickelsträsk** Sweden
243 F2 **Mickle Fell** *mountain* England UK

243 G3 **Micklefield** West Yorkshire England UK
163 I3 **Micoud** St Lucia
373 I2 **Micronesia, Federated States of** *country* Oceania
76 N7 **Mid-Atlantic Ridge** *underwater feature* Atlantic Ocean
81 M5 **Mid-Indian Basin** *underwater feature* Indian Ocean
80 K5 **Mid-Indian Ridge** *underwater feature* Indian Ocean
78 M6 **Mid-Pacific Mountains** *underwater feature* Pacific Ocean
78 N6 **Mid-Pacific Seamount** *underwater feature* Pacific Ocean
244 inset **Mid Yell** Shetland Scotland UK
374 E3 **Midai** *island* Indonesia
125 N2 **Midale** Saskatchewan Canada
244 F1 **Midbea** Orkney Islands Scotland UK
226 B2 **Middelburg** Netherlands
308 D6 **Middelburg** South Africa
308 E5 **Middelburg** South Africa
226 C2 **Middelharnis** Netherlands
228 F1 **Middelkerke** Belgium
124 E6 **Middle Alkali Lake** California USA
79 W6 **Middle America Trench** *underwater feature* Pacific Ocean
376 B4 **Middle Andaman** *island* Andaman and Nicobar Islands India
123 J8 **Middle Arm** Newfoundland and Labrador Canada
135 G2 **Middle Caicos** *island* Turks and Caicos Islands
124 E7 **Middle Fork Feather** *watercourse* California USA
119 S4 **Middle Foster Lake** Saskatchewan Canada
163 I9 **Middle Island** St Kitts and Nevis
424 inset **Middle Islet** Ashmore Reef and Cartier Island Australia
119 S6 **Middle Lake** Saskatchewan Canada
241 F3 **Middle Winterslow** Wiltshire England UK
125 R2 **Middlebro** Manitoba Canada
425 inset **Middlegate** Norfolk Island Australia
423 D7 **Middlemarch** New Zealand
240 E4 **Middlemarsh** Dorset England UK
425 N5 **Middlemount** Qld Australia
243 G2 **Middlesbrough** Middlesbrough England UK
243 G2 **Middlesbrough** *admin. area* England UK
243 G2 **Middlesmoor** North Yorkshire England UK
123 F10 **Middleton** Nova Scotia Canada
243 F2 **Middleton** Cumbria England UK
243 G3 **Middleton** North Yorkshire England UK
241 F2 **Middleton** Warwickshire England UK
130 G3 **Middleton** Tennessee USA
126 G5 **Middleton** Wisconsin USA
241 F2 **Middleton Cheney** Northamptonshire England UK
128 A1 **Middletown** California USA
127 N6 **Middletown** New York USA
126 I7 **Middletown** Ohio USA
300 F2 **Midelt** Morocco
241 G4 **Midhurst** West Sussex England UK
225 F5 **Midi, Canal du** *watercourse* France
228 F4 **Midi-Pyrénées** *admin. area* France
424 F7 **Midland** WA Australia
127 L4 **Midland** Ontario Canada
126 I5 **Midland** Michigan USA
125 O4 **Midland** South Dakota USA
129 K5 **Midland** Texas USA
308 E3 **Midlands** *admin. area* Zimbabwe
244 E5 **Midlothian** *admin. area* Scotland UK
224 E6 **Midlum** Germany
124 H1 **Midnapore** Alberta Canada
309 I4 **Midongy Atsimo** Madagascar
228 D5 **Midou** *watercourse* France
228 D5 **Midouze** *watercourse* France
226 C1 **Midsland** Netherlands
224 D1 **Midsund** Norway
244 F4 **Midtown of Barras** Aberdeenshire Scotland UK
124 G4 **Midvale** Idaho USA
118 L8 **Midway** British Columbia Canada
131 K5 **Midway** Georgia USA
78 O5 **Midway Islands** *unincorporated US territory* Pacific Ocean
130 C3 **Midwest City** Oklahoma USA
394 G6 **Midyat** Turkey
305 G4 **Midyobo** Equatorial Guinea
234 C4 **Midzhur** *mountain* Serbia
227 K2 **Miechów** Poland
227 H1 **Miedwie, Jezioro** *lake* Poland
227 L2 **Międzyrzec Podlaski** Poland
223 M3 **Miekojärvi** *lake* Sweden
228 E5 **Miélan** France
227 K2 **Mielec** Poland
307 F5 **Miembwe** Tanzania
224 H4 **Mien** *lake* Sweden
425 M10 **Miena** Tas. Australia
390 C3 **Miépe Ramon** Israel
133 F3 **Mier** Mexico
230 D2 **Mieres** Spain
232 B2 **Miesau** Germany
232 D3 **Miesbach** Germany
307 G2 **Mī'ēso** Ethiopia
227 I1 **Mieszków** Poland
227 H1 **Mieszkowice** Poland
225 O2 **Miettilä** Finland
229 K5 **Migliano** Italy
228 E3 **Migné** France
232 C5 **Mignole, Pointe di** *cape* Corsica France
307 E4 **Migori** Kenya
133 F5 **Miguel Alemán, Presa** *lake* Mexico
157 D4 **Miguel Alves** Brazil
132 E3 **Miguel Auza** Mexico
157 D5 **Miguel Calmon** Brazil
133 F5 **Miguel de la Madrid, Presa** *lake* Mexico
132 C3 **Miguel Hidalgo, Presa** *lake* Mexico
157 B8 **Miguelópolis** Brazil
234 E3 **Mihai Bravu** Romania
234 C3 **Mihajlovac** Serbia
235 G6 **Mihalıççık** Turkey
227 M4 **Mihești de Câmpie** Romania
305 H3 **Mihi** *watercourse* Central African Republic
307 F6 **Mihumo Chini** Tanzania
225 N5 **Mikhalishki** Belarus
238 H5 **Mikhaylov** Russian Federation
437 F2 **Mikhaylov Island** Antarctica
389 L2 **Mikhaylovka** Kazakhstan
389 M5 **Mikhaylovka** Kyrgyzstan
384 E2 **Mikhaylovka** Russian Federation
388 D3 **Mikhaylovka** Russian Federation
234 G1 **Mikhaylovka Pervaya** Ukraine
389 M3 **Mikhaylovskiy** Russian Federation
238 G5 **Mikhnëvo** Russian Federation
235 D5 **Miki** Greece
225 P1 **Mikitänjärvi** *lake* Finland
225 N2 **Mikkeli** Finland
222 K1 **Mikkelvik** Norway
119 N4 **Mikkwa** *watercourse* Alberta Canada
232 G3 **Mikosszéplak** Hungary
235 B5 **Mikra Prespa, Limni** *lake* Greece
235 C5 **Mikra Volvi** Greece
235 C6 **Mikrón Elevtherokhórion** Greece
225 P5 **Mikulino** Russian Federation
234 D1 **Mikulintsy** Ukraine
307 F5 **Mikumi** Tanzania
236 L6 **Mikun'** Russian Federation
387 H4 **Mikuni** Japan
387 H4 **Mikuni Sanmyaku** Japan
387 H5 **Mikura-jima** *island* Japan
301 H1 **Mila** Algeria
301 H1 **Mila** *admin. area* Algeria
126 E4 **Milaca** Minnesota USA
393 C10 **Miladhunmadulu Atoll** Maldives
156 E4 **Milagres** Brazil
154 C4 **Milán** Colombia
Milan *see* **Milano** Italy
131 J4 **Milan** Georgia USA
130 C2 **Milan** Kansas USA
125 R4 **Milan** Minnesota USA
129 I3 **Milan** New Mexico USA
306 B5 **Milando** Angola
226 E5 **Milano (Milan)** Italy
235 E7 **Milas** Turkey
233 F7 **Milazzo** Italy
233 F7 **Milazzo, Capo di** *cape* Italy
125 Q4 **Milbank** South Dakota USA
118 G6 **Milbanke Sound** British Columbia Canada
127 R4 **Milbridge** Maine USA
119 R7 **Milden** Saskatchewan Canada
425 L8 **Mildura** Vic. Australia
303 G5 **Milē** Ethiopia
163 I2 **Mile and a Quarter** Barbados
303 G5 **Milē Wenz** *watercourse* Ethiopia
390 F2 **Mileh Sar** Iran
240 A2 **Milehouse** Ireland
227 L1 **Milejczyce** Poland
307 F6 **Milepa** Mozambique
425 N6 **Miles** Qld Australia
130 A5 **Miles** Texas USA
125 M3 **Miles City** Montana USA
388 D1 **Mileshino** Russian Federation
119 S8 **Milestone** Saskatchewan Canada
245 D4 **Milestone** Ireland
229 L2 **Milevsko** Czech Republic
238 F6 **Mileyevo** Russian Federation
245 E1 **Milford** Ireland
127 N7 **Milford** Delaware USA
125 Q6 **Milford** Nebraska USA
130 C4 **Milford** Texas USA
124 I7 **Milford** Utah USA
240 B3 **Milford Haven** Pembrokeshire Wales UK
125 Q7 **Milford Lake** Kansas USA
423 B7 **Milford Sound** New Zealand
423 B7 **Milford Sound** New Zealand
159 F3 **Milho** Brazil
427 I5 **Mili Atoll** Marshall Islands
301 G1 **Miliana** Algeria
232 H4 **Milići** Bosnia and Herzegovina
424 I2 **Milikapiti** NT Australia
233 C6 **Milis** Sardinia Italy
232 H5 **Miljevina** Bosnia and Herzegovina
119 P8 **Milk** *watercourse* Alberta Canada
119 Q8 **Milk** *watercourse* Montana USA
302 E4 **Milk, Wādī El** *watercourse* Sudan
119 O8 **Milk River** Alberta Canada
124 D4 **Mill City** Oregon USA
241 I2 **Mill Green** Norfolk England UK
127 M6 **Mill Hall** Pennsylvania USA
436 T2 **Mill Inlet** *bay* Antarctica
437 G2 **Mill Island** Antarctica
117 L6 **Mill Island** Nunavut Canada
163 I8 **Mill Reef** Antigua and Barbuda
228 F5 **Millas** France
228 F4 **Millau** France
117 J9 **Mille Lacs, Lac des** *lake* Ontario Canada
126 E3 **Mille Lacs Lake** Minnesota USA
131 J4 **Milledgeville** Georgia USA
131 K4 **Millen** Georgia USA
125 P6 **Miller** Nebraska USA
125 P4 **Miller** South Dakota USA
388 C4 **Millerovo** Russian Federation
423 C7 **Millers Flat** New Zealand
126 I7 **Millersburg** Kentucky USA
127 K6 **Millersburg** Ohio USA
127 M6 **Millerstown** Pennsylvania USA
124 F8 **Millerton Lake** California USA
119 O6 **Millet** Alberta Canada
244 C5 **Milleur Point** Scotland UK
228 F4 **Millevaches** France
245 F2 **Millford** Armagh Northern Ireland UK
244 C5 **Millhouse** Argyll and Bute Scotland UK
130 C5 **Millican** Texas USA
425 L9 **Millicent** SA Australia
242 E1 **Milliganton** Dumfries and Galloway Scotland UK
125 M6 **Milliken** Colorado USA
130 G3 **Millington** Tennessee USA
117 M9 **Millinocket** Maine USA
158 D6 **Milliri, Cerro** *mountain* Bolivia
245 G2 **Millisle** Ards Northern Ireland UK
425 N6 **Millmerran** Qld Australia
242 E2 **Millom** Cumbria England UK
130 G4 **Millport** Alabama USA
245 F4 **Millrad** Ireland
130 G5 **Millry** Alabama USA
125 L5 **Mills** Wyoming USA
118 L2 **Mills Lake** Northwest Territories Canada
245 C4 **Millstreet** Ireland
243 F2 **Millthrop** Cumbria England UK
242 B4 **Milltown** Ireland
245 D3 **Milltown** Ireland
242 B2 **Milltown** Armagh Northern Ireland UK
245 G2 **Milltown** Larne Northern Ireland UK
242 B2 **Milltown** Newry and Mourne Northern Ireland UK
123 K9 **Milltown-Head of Bay d'Espoir** Newfoundland and Labrador Canada
245 C4 **Milltown Malbay** Ireland
130 E4 **Millwood Lake** Arkansas USA
230 F3 **Milmarcos** Spain
232 G5 **Milna** Croatia
244 E4 **Milnathort** Perth and Kinross Scotland UK
373 I6 **Milne Bay** Papua New Guinea
131 I4 **Milner** Georgia USA
122 E6 **Milner Lake** Newfoundland and Labrador Canada
125 Q1 **Milner Ridge** Manitoba Canada
129 K4 **Milnesand** New Mexico USA
242 F2 **Milnthorpe** Cumbria England UK
119 O7 **Milo** Alberta Canada
304 C2 **Milo** *watercourse* Guinea
307 E5 **Milo** Tanzania
127 Q4 **Milo** Maine USA
234 B4 **Miločaj** Serbia
128 inset **Milolii** Hawai'i USA
235 D7 **Milos** Greece
235 D7 **Milos** *island* Greece
235 A5 **Milot** Albania
227 M1 **Milovidy** Belarus
227 J3 **Milówka** Poland
425 L7 **Milparinka** NSW Australia
129 I8 **Milpas Viejas** Mexico
124 E8 **Milpitas** California USA
244 F5 **Milsington** Scottish Borders Scotland UK
123 F10 **Milton** Nova Scotia Canada
127 L5 **Milton** Ontario Canada
423 C8 **Milton** New Zealand
242 D2 **Milton** Dumfries and Galloway Scotland UK
244 C3 **Milton** Highland Scotland UK
244 E4 **Milton** Perth and Kinross Scotland UK
130 H5 **Milton** Florida USA
126 E6 **Milton** Iowa USA
127 O4 **Milton** Vermont USA
241 G2 **Milton Keynes** Milton Keynes England UK
241 G2 **Milton Keynes** *admin. area* England UK
126 D3 **Miltona, Lake** Minnesota USA
125 Q7 **Miltonvale** Kansas USA
381 G3 **Miluo** Hunan China
126 H5 **Milwaukee** Wisconsin USA
389 L4 **Milyblak** Kazakhstan
373 J5 **Mimias, Cape** Papua New Guinea
120 K7 **Miminiska Lake** Ontario Canada
228 D4 **Mimizan** France
228 D4 **Mimizan-Plage** France
305 G5 **Mimongo** Gabon
159 H6 **Mimoso** Brazil
157 D8 **Mimoso do Sul** Brazil
381 H3 **Min Jiang** *watercourse* Fujian China
380 D2 **Min Jiang** *watercourse* Sichuan China
380 F2 **Min'an** Hunan China
380 E3 **Min'gu** Guizhou China
132 E3 **Mina** Mexico
390 D5 **Minā** Saudi Arabia
121 W4 **Mina, Lac** *lake* Québec Canada
134 D4 **Mina Columbus** Nicaragua
230 C5 **Mina de São Domingos** Portugal
160 D3 **Mina la Casualidad** Argentina
160 D6 **Mina La Escondida** Argentina
391 I4 **Mīnāb** Iran
120 F5 **Minago** *watercourse* Manitoba Canada
375 I3 **Minahasa, Semenanjung** *peninsula* Indonesia
225 P2 **Minala** Russian Federation
386 F5 **Minamata** Japan
235 F7 **Minare** Turkey
374 D3 **Minas** Indonesia
161 H5 **Minas** Uruguay
154 D4 **Minas, Cerros** *range* Colombia
154 B4 **Minas, Serranía de las** *range* Colombia
123 F10 **Minas Basin** Nova Scotia Canada
123 F10 **Minas Channel** Nova Scotia Canada
132 E3 **Minas de Barroterán** Mexico
161 H4 **Minas de Corrales** Uruguay
159 I5 **Minas Gerais** *admin. area* Brazil
157 D7 **Minas Novas** Brazil
132 D5 **Minatitlán** Mexico
133 G5 **Minatitlán** Mexico
379 H5 **Minbu** Myanmar
119 P6 **Minburn** Alberta Canada
379 G5 **Minbya** Myanmar
244 C2 **Minch, The** *strait* Scotland UK
132 E3 **Minchaca** Mexico
158 B1 **Minchana** Peru
377 J6 **Mindanao** *island* Philippines
379 G5 **Mindat** Myanmar
229 J2 **Mindel** *watercourse* Germany
226 F3 **Mindelheim** Germany
310 4 **Mindelo** Cape Verde
127 L4 **Minden** Ontario Canada
125 P6 **Minden** Nebraska USA
222 H4 **Mindlandet** *island* Norway
379 H5 **Mindon** Myanmar
377 I4 **Mindoro** *island* Philippines
386 F4 **Mine** *volcano* Japan
242 B4 **Mine Bridge** Ireland
245 E5 **Mine Head** *cape* Ireland
240 D3 **Minehead** Somerset England UK
157 A7 **Mineiros** Brazil
233 F8 **Mineo** Italy
130 B4 **Mineral Wells** Texas USA
232 D4 **Minerbe** Italy
159 F5 **Mineros** Bolivia
124 I7 **Minersville** Utah USA
382 E5 **Ming-tieh-kai Ho** *watercourse* Xinjiang Uygur Zizhiqu China
306 D6 **Minga** Democratic Republic of Congo
309 F2 **Minga** Zambia
388 E6 **Mingäçevir Su Anbari** *lake* Azerbaijan
305 I3 **Mingala** Central African Republic
123 F7 **Mingan** Québec Canada
123 G7 **Mingan** *watercourse* Québec Canada
388 I5 **Mingbuloq** Uzbekistan
424 E7 **Mingenew** WA Australia
381 F2 **Mingfeng** Hubei China
381 H2 **Mingguang** Anhui China
379 H4 **Mingin** Myanmar
422 G4 **Minginui** New Zealand
230 F4 **Minglanilla** Spain
385 K3 **Mingshui** Heilongjiang China
307 G6 **Mingueri** Mozambique
385 K4 **Mingyue** Jilin China
381 G2 **Mingzhou** Shaanxi China
376 E3 **Minh Hóa** Vietnam
381 G3 **Minhe** Jiangxi China
379 H5 **Minhla** Myanmar
234 C4 **Minićevo** Serbia
393 C10 **Minicoy Island** Lakshadweep India
124 I5 **Minidoka** Idaho USA
225 K5 **Minija** *watercourse* Lithuania
304 C3 **Mininian** Côte d'Ivoire
119 U7 **Minitonas** Manitoba Canada
122 H6 **Minipi** *watercourse* Newfoundland and Labrador Canada
122 H6 **Minipi Lake** Newfoundland and Labrador Canada
120 J7 **Miniss Lake** Ontario Canada
230 E3 **Ministra, Sierra** *range* Spain
162 C2 **Ministro Ramos Mexía** Argentina
158 D5 **Miñita** Chile
425 J3 **Miniyeri (Hodgson Downs)** NT Australia
Minjerriba *see* **North Stradbroke Island** Australia
380 D3 **Minjian** Sichuan China
372 E6 **Minjilang** NT Australia
118 M2 **Mink Lake** Northwest Territories Canada
384 D5 **Minle** Gansu China
305 F3 **Minna** Nigeria
437 L1 **Minna Bluff** Antarctica
381 I4 **Minna-jima** *island* Japan
125 Q7 **Minneapolis** Kansas USA
126 E4 **Minneapolis** Minnesota USA
125 O8 **Minneola** Kansas USA
126 E4 **Minnesota** *watercourse* Minnesota USA
126 D4 **Minnewaska, Lake** Minnesota USA
125 P2 **Minnewaukan** North Dakota USA
120 J8 **Minnitaki Lake** Ontario Canada
230 B2 **Miño** *watercourse* Spain
126 F3 **Minong** Wisconsin USA
Minorca *see* **Menorca** Spain
125 O2 **Minot** North Dakota USA
302 D1 **Minqār al Majabirah** *mountain* Egypt
384 E5 **Minqin** Gansu China
390 E4 **Minsafa** Saudi Arabia
225 N6 **Minsk** Belarus
227 K1 **Mińsk Mazowiecki** Poland
394 C2 **Minskaya Voblasts'** *admin. area* Belarus
241 H3 **Minster** Kent England UK
305 G4 **Minta** Cameroon
382 E5 **Mintaka Pass** Xinjiang Uygur Zizhiqu China
391 M1 **Mintaka Pass** Pakistan
243 H3 **Minting** Lincolnshire England UK
244 F3 **Mintlaw** Aberdeenshire Scotland UK
125 O2 **Minto** Manitoba Canada
123 E9 **Minto** New Brunswick Canada
125 Q2 **Minto** North Dakota USA
121 R8 **Minto, Lac** *lake* Québec Canada
437 L2 **Minto, Mount** Antarctica
116 H4 **Minto Inlet** Northwest Territories Canada
305 G4 **Mintom II** Cameroon
119 S8 **Minton** Saskatchewan Canada
389 P2 **Minusinsk** Russian Federation
305 G4 **Minvoul** Gabon
380 D1 **Minxian** Gansu China
126 I4 **Mio** Michigan USA
118 K6 **Miocene** British Columbia Canada
244 B4 **Miodar** Highland Scotland UK
229 G4 **Mions** France
228 D4 **Mios** France
234 D3 **Mioveni** Romania
390 D3 **Miqt** Jordan
383 H4 **Miquan** Xinjiang Uygur Zizhiqu China
123 J9 **Miquelon** St Pierre and Miquelon
123 J9 **Miquelon** *island* St Pierre and Miquelon
226 G5 **Mira** Italy
230 B3 **Mira** Portugal
230 B5 **Mira** *watercourse* Portugal
161 G2 **Mirabeau** Paraguay
230 C4 **Mirabel** Spain
157 C7 **Mirabela** Brazil
157 C9 **Miracatu** Brazil
156 B5 **Miracema do Tocantins** Brazil
156 C4 **Mirador** Brazil
228 E4 **Miradoux** France
154 C3 **Miraflores** Colombia
154 D4 **Miraflores** Colombia
157 D8 **Miraí** Brazil
391 L3 **Miram Shah** Pakistan
133 F3 **Miramar** Mexico
133 F4 **Miramar** Mexico
158 D5 **Miramar** Peru
131 K8 **Miramar** Florida USA
229 G5 **Miramas** France
228 D4 **Mirambeau** France
123 F9 **Miramichi** New Brunswick Canada
123 F9 **Miramichi Bay** New Brunswick Canada
391 I4 **Mīrān Sū** Iran
162 C5 **Miranda** Argentina
159 G6 **Miranda** Brazil
159 G6 **Miranda** *watercourse* Brazil
154 B4 **Miranda** Colombia
155 E2 **Miranda** *admin. area* Venezuela
160 D2 **Miranda, Sierra** *range* Chile
230 E2 **Miranda de Ebro** Spain
226 F5 **Mirandola** Italy
157 B8 **Mirandópolis** Brazil
161 I2 **Mirante, Serra do** *range* Brazil
235 B5 **Miras** Albania
391 H6 **Mirbāṭ** Oman
228 E3 **Mirebeau** France
229 H2 **Mirecourt** France
228 E5 **Mirepoix** France
234 C2 **Mireșu Mare** Romania
375 G2 **Miri** Malaysia
301 H6 **Miria** Niger
393 E8 **Mirialguda** Andhra Pradesh India
425 N6 **Miriam Vale** Qld Australia
161 H5 **Mirim, Lagoa** *lake* Brazil
372 E4 **Mirimiri** Indonesia
161 G4 **Miriñay** *watercourse* Argentina
159 F2 **Miriti** Brazil
154 D5 **Miritiparana** *watercourse* Colombia
391 J3 **Mirjāveh** Iran
234 C4 **Mirkovo** Bulgaria
227 H5 **Mirna** Slovenia
437 G2 **Mirny (Russia)** *research station* Antarctica
237 X6 **Mirnyy** Russian Federation
227 M1 **Mironim** Belarus
232 F2 **Mirotice** Czech Republic
234 C4 **Mirovyane** Bulgaria
226 G1 **Mirow** Germany
391 L4 **Mirpur Khas** Pakistan
391 K5 **Mirpur Sakro** Pakistan
307 H2 **Mirsale** Somalia
226 G7 **Mirto Crosia** Italy
235 C7 **Mirtoö Pelagos** *sea* Greece
308 F3 **Miruro** Mozambique
379 G4 **Mirzaganj** Bangladesh
392 F6 **Mirzapur** Uttar Pradesh India
232 E5 **Misa** *watercourse* Italy
133 F5 **Misantla** Mexico
305 G2 **Misau** Nigeria
387 I3 **Misawa** Japan
377 G5 **Mischief Reef** Spratly Islands
227 L5 **Mischii** Romania
123 F9 **Miscou Island** New Brunswick Canada
376 B6 **Misha** Andaman and Nicobar Islands India
374 B1 **Misha** Tripura India
306 E5 **Mishamo** Tanzania
385 L3 **Mishan** Heilongjiang China
390 G3 **Mishān-e 'Olyā** Iran
387 H4 **Mishima** Japan
225 P5 **Mishutki** Belarus
223 O3 **Misijärvi** *lake* Finland
120 J6 **Misikeyask Lake** Ontario Canada
373 J6 **Misima Island** Papua New Guinea
128 F6 **Mision Santa Gertrudis** Mexico
161 G2 **Misión Yalve Sanga** Paraguay
161 H3 **Misiones** *admin. area* Argentina
161 G3 **Misiones** *admin. area* Paraguay
161 H3 **Misiones, Sierra de** *range* Argentina
232 H3 **Miske** Hungary
154 A1 **Miskitos, Cayos** *island* Nicaragua
234 B1 **Miskolc** Hungary
227 H4 **Mislinja** Slovenia
158 D4 **Mismi, Nevado** *mountain* Peru
229 L4 **Mišnjak** Croatia
372 D4 **Misool** *island* Indonesia
126 F3 **Misquah Hills** *range* Minnesota USA
301 J2 **Mişrātah** Libya
159 G2 **Missão** Brazil
304 C2 **Misseni** Mali
228 C3 **Missillac** France
121 N8 **Missinaibi** *watercourse* Ontario Canada
117 K9 **Missinaibi Lake** Ontario Canada
119 S5 **Missinipe** Saskatchewan Canada
125 O5 **Mission** South Dakota USA
130 B7 **Mission** Texas USA
128 D4 **Mission Bay** California USA
128 D4 **Mission Viejo** California USA
119 T6 **Missipuskiow** *watercourse* Saskatchewan Canada
300 D6 **Missira** Senegal
120 M6 **Missisa** *watercourse* Ontario Canada
120 M6 **Missisa Lake** Ontario Canada
121 P7 **Missisicabi** *watercourse* Québec Canada
115 **Mississippi** *admin. area* USA
130 F3 **Mississippi** *watercourse* Arkansas USA
130 F5 **Mississippi** *watercourse* Louisiana USA
126 D3 **Mississippi** *watercourse* Minnesota USA
130 F5 **Mississippi** *watercourse* Mississippi USA
126 G8 **Mississippi** *watercourse* Missouri USA
130 G6 **Mississippi Delta** Louisiana USA
127 M4 **Mississippi Lake** Ontario Canada
130 G5 **Mississippi Sound** Mississippi USA
159 E2 **Missões** Brazil
124 I3 **Missoula** Montana USA
300 F2 **Missour** Morocco
115 **Missouri** *admin. area* USA
126 F7 **Missouri** *watercourse* Missouri USA
119 S8 **Missouri** *watercourse* Montana USA
126 D6 **Missouri** *watercourse* Nebraska USA
125 P5 **Missouri** *watercourse* South Dakota USA
130 D6 **Missouri City** Texas USA
125 R6 **Missouri Valley** Iowa USA
120 I1 **Mistake Bay** Nunavut Canada
123 G7 **Mistanipisipou** *watercourse* Québec Canada
127 L2 **Mistaouac, Lac** *lake* Québec Canada
121 S7 **Mistassibi** *watercourse* Québec Canada
121 T7 **Mistassibi Nord-Est** *watercourse* Québec Canada
121 S8 **Mistassini** *watercourse* Québec Canada
121 S7 **Mistassini, Lac** *lake* Québec Canada
121 X5 **Mistastin Lake** Newfoundland and Labrador Canada
119 T6 **Mistatim** Saskatchewan Canada
224 I4 **Misterhult** Sweden
134 D3 **Misteriosa Bank** *reef* Caribbean
240 E4 **Misterton** Somerset England UK
120 J4 **Mistikokan** *watercourse* Manitoba Canada
121 W5 **Mistinibi, Lac** *lake* Québec Canada
121 U6 **Mistinic, Lac** *lake* Québec Canada
160 F2 **Mistol Marcado** Argentina
233 F8 **Mistretta** Italy
235 C6 **Mistros** Greece
119 W4 **Mistuhekasookun** Manitoba Canada
120 E3 **Misty Lake** Manitoba Canada
306 C4 **Misumba** Democratic Republic of Congo
232 E3 **Misurina** Italy
222 I3 **Misvær** Norway
222 I3 **Misværfjorden** *bay* Norway
158 D4 **Mita** Peru
132 D4 **Mita, Punta de** *cape* Mexico
307 F6 **Mitande** Mozambique
302 F4 **Mitatib** Sudan
240 E3 **Mitcheldean** Gloucestershire England UK
425 M6 **Mitchell** Qld Australia
425 L3 **Mitchell** *watercourse* Qld Australia
240 B4 **Mitchell** Cornwall England UK
126 H7 **Mitchell** Indiana USA
125 N6 **Mitchell** Nebraska USA
124 E4 **Mitchell** Oregon USA
125 P5 **Mitchell** South Dakota USA
131 J3 **Mitchell, Mount** North Carolina USA
131 H4 **Mitchell Lake** Alabama USA
424 I2 **Mitchell Point** NT Australia
242 A1 **Mitchells Town** Ireland
305 G4 **Mitémélé** *watercourse* Equatorial Guinea
162 A4 **Mitford, Cabo** *cape* Chile
391 L5 **Mithi** Pakistan
391 L4 **Mithrau** Pakistan
235 E6 **Mithymna** Greece
375 K3 **Miti** *island* Indonesia
422 1 **Mitiaro** *island* Cook Islands New Zealand
236 K5 **Mitina** Russian Federation
387 I4 **Mito** Japan
158 C3 **Mitoc, Cerro** *mountain* Peru
307 F5 **Mitole** Tanzania
235 C5 **Mitrašinci** Macedonia
423 F5 **Mitre** *mountain* New Zealand
162 D6 **Mitre, Península** *peninsula* Argentina
423 B7 **Mitre Peak** *mountain* New Zealand
309 H2 **Mitsamiouli** Comoros
309 I2 **Mitsio, Nosy** *island* Madagascar
387 H4 **Mitsuke** Japan
222 H5 **Mittådalen** Sweden
226 F1 **Mittellandkanal** *watercourse* Germany
229 J2 **Mittelneufnach** Germany
226 F4 **Mittenwald** Germany
226 G4 **Mittersill** Austria
229 K2 **Mitterteich** Germany
154 D4 **Mitú** Colombia
306 D5 **Mitumba, Chaîne des** *range* Democratic Republic of Congo
306 D5 **Mitumba, Monts** *range* Uganda
306 D4 **Mitwaba** Democratic Republic of Congo
305 G4 **Mitzic** Gabon
241 F2 **Mixbury** Oxfordshire England UK
134 B4 **Mixco** Guatemala
305 F2 **Miya** Nigeria
387 H4 **Miyake-jima** *island* Japan
387 I3 **Miyako** Japan
381 J4 **Miyako-jima** *island* Japan
381 J4 **Miyako Rettō** *island* Japan
388 G4 **Miyaly** Kazakhstan
386 F6 **Miyazaki** Japan
386 G4 **Miyoshi** Japan
385 H5 **Miyun** Beijing China
307 F2 **Mizan Teferi** Ethiopia
301 I2 **Mizdah** Libya
245 G4 **Mizen Head** *cape* Ireland
384 G5 **Mizhi** Shaanxi China
234 C4 **Miziya** Bulgaria
379 G4 **Mizoram** *admin. area* India
159 E5 **Mizque** Bolivia
387 I3 **Mizusawa** Japan
222 K5 **Mjällom** Sweden
222 I3 **Mjelde** Norway
222 L5 **Mjölefjärden** *bay* Sweden
224 D2 **Mjølfell** Norway
222 K1 **Mjølvik** Norway
224 C2 **Mjømna** Norway
224 G4 **Mjörn** *lake* Sweden
224 F2 **Mjøsa** *lake* Norway
222 K5 **Mjösjöby** Sweden
222 H4 **Mjøsundvatnet** *lake* Norway
307 F5 **Mkokotoni** Tanzania
307 F5 **Mkondoa** *watercourse* Tanzania
307 F4 **Mkujani** Tanzania
307 E5 **Mkurusi** Tanzania
308 E2 **Mkushi** Zambia
227 H2 **Mladá Boleslav** Czech Republic
232 G4 **Mlaka** Croatia
306 E5 **Mlala Hills** *range* Tanzania
307 F5 **Mlandizi** Tanzania
227 K1 **Mława** Poland
227 I2 **Mleczno** Poland
307 F5 **Mligasi** *watercourse* Tanzania
310 8b **Mlima Benara** *mountain* Mayotte
232 G5 **Mljet** *island* Croatia
375 F5 **Mlonggo** Indonesia
230 J2 **Młynek** Poland
308 E4 **Mmashoro** Botswana
305 F3 **Mo** *watercourse* Cameroon
304 E3 **Mo** *watercourse* Ghana
222 J5 **Mo** Sweden
224 G3 **Mo** Sweden
304 E3 **Mo** *watercourse* Togo
222 I3 **Mo i Rana** Norway
135 F2 **Moa** Cuba
375 J6 **Moa** *island* Indonesia
425 L2 **Moa Island** Qld Australia
125 K7 **Moab** Utah USA
427 9 **Moala** *island* Fiji
423 D6 **Moana** New Zealand
245 E3 **Moate** Ireland
309 F3 **Moatize** Mozambique
422 F4 **Moawhango, Lake** New Zealand
306 D5 **Moba** Democratic Republic of Congo
387 I4 **Mobara** Japan
390 G3 **Mobārakeh** Iran
305 I4 **Mobaye** Central African Republic
126 E7 **Moberly** Missouri USA
118 K5 **Moberly Lake** British Columbia Canada
130 G5 **Mobile** Alabama USA
130 H5 **Mobile Bay** Alabama USA
130 H5 **Mobile Point** Alabama USA
432* F2 **Moble** Qld Australia
125 O4 **Mobridge** South Dakota USA
135 G3 **Moca** Dominican Republic
156 B3 **Mocajuba** Brazil
309 H3 **Moçambique** Mozambique
427 9 **Moce** *island* Fiji
160 C6 **Mocha, Isla** *island* Chile
159 E6 **Mochará, Cordillera de** *range* Bolivia
240 D2 **Mochdre** Powys Wales UK
227 J1 **Mochowo** Poland
308 E4 **Mochudi** Botswana
309 H2 **Mocímboa da Praia** Mozambique
309 G2 **Mocímboa do Rovuma** Mozambique
224 H4 **Möckeln** *lake* Sweden
226 G2 **Mockrehna** Germany
155 G4 **Moco-Moco Village** Guyana
154 B4 **Mocoa** Colombia
157 C8 **Mococa** Brazil
309 G4 **Mocoduene** Mozambique
129 I8 **Mocorito** Mexico
234 F2 **Mocra** Moldova
132 E4 **Moctezuma** Mexico
309 G3 **Mocuba** Mozambique
242 B4 **Mocurry Bridge** Ireland
229 H4 **Modane** France
392 C6 **Modasa** Gujarat India
229 G1 **Modave** Belgium
240 D4 **Modbury** Devon England UK
226 F5 **Modena** Italy
128 F2 **Modena** Utah USA
124 E8 **Modesto** California USA
233 F8 **Modica** Italy
308 E4 **Modimolle** South Africa
227 H2 **Modła** Poland
227 H1 **Modlęcin** Poland
227 L2 **Modliborzyce** Poland
372 E5 **Modowi** Indonesia
227 H4 **Modriach** Austria
232 H4 **Modriča** Bosnia and Herzegovina
227 H5 **Modruš** Croatia
425 M9 **Moe** Vic. Australia
309 G3 **Moebase** Mozambique
379 H4 **Moegaung** Myanmar
422 F3 **Moehau** *mountain* New Zealand
379 H4 **Moehnyin** Myanmar
375 K4 **Moelijk** *island* Indonesia
306 B3 **Moekoe** *watercourse* Democratic Republic of Congo
224 E3 **Moel** *watercourse* Norway
242 D3 **Moelfre** Isle of Anglesey Wales UK
222 K2 **Moen** Norway
155 H3 **Moengo** Suriname
128 G2 **Moenkopi** Arizona USA
423 D7 **Moeraki Point** New Zealand
229 H1 **Moers** Germany
244 E5 **Moffat** Dumfries and Galloway Scotland UK
125 M8 **Moffat** Colorado USA
392 D4 **Moga** Punjab India
Mogadishu *see* **Muqdisho** Somalia
230 C3 **Mogadouro** Portugal
387 H3 **Mogami-gawa** *lake* Japan
310 3b **Mogán** Canary Islands
385 M2 **Mogdy** Russian Federation
156 F4 **Mogeiro** Brazil
227 I1 **Mogilno** Poland
232 E5 **Mogliano** Italy
237 Y8 **Mogocha** Russian Federation
385 I1 **Mogocha** Russian Federation
384 E3 **Mogod** Mongolia
379 H4 **Mogok** Myanmar
128 G3 **Mogollon Plateau** Arizona USA
162 A4 **Mogotes, Cabo** *cape* Chile
237 AE4 **Mogotoyevo, Ozero** *lake* Russian Federation
305 H2 **Mogroum** Chad
118 J7 **Moha** British Columbia Canada
234 A3 **Mohács** Hungary
393 E7 **Mohala** Chhattisgarh India
308 E6 **Mohales Hoek** Lesotho
125 O2 **Mohall** North Dakota USA
301 G1 **Mohammadia** Algeria
300 E2 **Mohammedia** Morocco
128 F4 **Mohawk** Arizona USA
392 E6 **Mohdra** Madhya Pradesh India
385 J1 **Mohe** Heilongjiang China
237 Z8 **Mohe** Nei Mongol Zizhiqu China
310 8 **Mohéli (Mwali)** *island* Comoros
116 C6 **Mohican, Cape** Alaska USA
245 E3 **Mohill** Ireland
390 G4 **Mohkdān** Iran
223 Q5 **Möhkö** Finland
226 D4 **Möhlin** Switzerland
226 E2 **Möhnesee** *lake* Germany
435 G2 **Mohns Ridge** *underwater feature* Norwegian Sea
127 N6 **Mohnton** Pennsylvania USA
307 F5 **Mohoro** Tanzania
224 D3 **Moi** Norway
231 H3 **Moià** Spain
244 C4 **Moidart** *cape* Scotland UK
230 C3 **Moimenta da Beira** Portugal
244 C5 **Moineruadh** Argyll and Bute Scotland UK
234 E2 **Moinești** Romania
245 F2 **Moira** Armagh Northern Ireland UK
227 M4 **Moisei** Romania
121 V7 **Moisie** *watercourse* Québec Canada
223 P4 **Moisiovaara** Finland
305 H3 **Moïssala** Chad
157 C7 **Moitinha** Brazil
225 J3 **Möja** *island* Sweden
129 K7 **Mojada, Sierra** *range* Mexico
128 C3 **Mojave** California USA
128 D3 **Mojave Desert** California USA
128 E3 **Mojave National Preserve** *park* California USA
157 C8 **Moji Mirim** Brazil
380 D4 **Mojiang** Yunnan China
120 K7 **Mojikit Lake** Ontario Canada
227 G4 **Mojstrana** Slovenia
227 J3 **Mojtín** Slovakia
156 B3 **Moju** Brazil
156 B3 **Moju** *watercourse* Brazil
422 F4 **Mokau** New Zealand
422 F4 **Mokau** *watercourse* New Zealand
224 G2 **Møkeren** *lake* Norway
423 E5 **Mokihinui** *watercourse* New Zealand
426 6 **Mokil** *island* Federated States of Micronesia
222 H5 **Mokkavatnet** *lake* Norway
301 I1 **Moknine** Tunisia
379 H3 **Mokokchung** Nagaland India
305 G2 **Mokolo** Cameroon
306 C4 **Mokombe** *watercourse* Democratic Republic of Congo
308 E4 **Mokopane** South Africa

386 E4 **Mokp'o** South Korea
234 B4 **Mokra Gora** *range* Kosovo
234 B3 **Mokrin** Serbia
388 E3 **Mokrous** Russian Federation
238 G6 **Mokroye** Russian Federation
223 N5 **Möksy** Finland
305 F3 **Mokwa** Nigeria
234 B3 **Mol** Serbia
379 H3 **Mol Len** *mountain* Nagaland India
119 S5 **Molanosa** Saskatchewan Canada
233 C6 **Molara, Isola** *island* Sardinia Italy
226 F5 **Molare** Italy
228 E5 **Molas** France
232 F4 **Molat** Croatia
232 F4 **Molat** *island* Croatia
372 B4 **Molawe** Indonesia
240 D1 **Mold** Flintshire Wales UK
389 M3 **Moldary** Kazakhstan
222 E5 **Molde** Norway
234 F2 **Moldova** *country* Europe
234 D2 **Moldova** *watercourse* Romania
227 K5 **Moldova Nouă** Romania
234 D3 **Moldoveanu, Vârful** *mountain* Romania
234 E2 **Moldovei, Câmpia** *region* Romania
234 C2 **Moldovenești** Romania
304 D3 **Mole** *watercourse* Ghana
307 E5 **Mole** Tanzania
241 G3 **Mole** *watercourse* England UK
373 H4 **Mole Island** Papua New Guinea
228 B2 **Molène, Île de** *island* France
308 E4 **Molepolole** Botswana
241 G2 **Molesworth** Cambridgeshire England UK
225 M5 **Molėtai** Lithuania
233 G6 **Molfetta** Italy
372 B3 **Molibagu** Indonesia
160 D5 **Molina** Argentina
160 D5 **Molina** Chile
230 F3 **Molina de Aragón** Spain
231 F4 **Molinar, Embalse del** *lake* Spain
130 C2 **Moline** Kansas USA
159 E5 **Molinero** Bolivia
233 F8 **Molini, Capo** *cape* Italy
163 10a **Molinière Point** *cape* Grenada
128 E6 **Molino Lacy** Mexico
123 E3 **Molinos** Argentina
162 B2 **Molinos** Chile
230 D4 **Molinos de Matachel, Embalse de los** *lake* Spain
306 E5 **Moliro** Democratic Republic of Congo
233 F6 **Molise** *admin. area* Italy
223 N3 **Molkojärvi** *lake* Finland
226 G4 **Möll** *watercourse* Austria
240 D3 **Molland** Devon England UK
235 B5 **Mollas** Albania
224 G4 **Mölle** Sweden
155 E5 **Molle Punco** Bolivia
424 F7 **Mollerin** WA Australia
231 G3 **Mollerussa** Spain
121 R5 **Mollet, Lacs** *lake* Québec Canada
121 T5 **Molleville, Lac** *lake* Québec Canada
435 G1 **Molloy Deep** *underwater feature* Greenland Sea
307 F4 **Molo** Kenya
309 G3 **Molocue** *watercourse* Mozambique
437 D2 **Molodezhnaya (Russia)** *research station* Antarctica
238 C3 **Molodi** Russian Federation
238 E4 **Molodoy Tud** Russian Federation
238 F4 **Mologa** *watercourse* Russian Federation
128 inset **Moloka'i** *island* Hawai'i USA
79 S5 **Molokai Fracture Zone** *underwater feature* Pacific Ocean
238 G3 **Molokovo** Russian Federation
159 G2 **Molongó** Brazil
308 D5 **Molopo** *watercourse* South Africa
235 C6 **Molos** Greece
305 H4 **Moloundou** Cameroon
234 F2 **Molovata** Moldova
226 C4 **Moloy** France
222 L5 **Molpe** Finland
120 G5 **Molson Lake** Manitoba Canada
372 D5 **Molu** *island* Indonesia
Molucca Sea *see* **Maluku, Laut** Indonesia
Moluccas *see* **Maluku** Indonesia
309 G3 **Molumbo** Mozambique
380 C2 **Moluo** Xizang Zizhiqu China
225 Q4 **Molvotitsy** Russian Federation
306 D6 **Molwe** Democratic Republic of Congo
423 C8 **Molyneaux Bay** New Zealand
306 C5 **Moma** Democratic Republic of Congo
309 G3 **Moma** Mozambique
237 AD5 **Moma** *watercourse* Russian Federation
373 F5 **Momats** *watercourse* Indonesia
156 E4 **Mombaça** Brazil
232 E5 **Mombaroccio** Italy
307 F4 **Mombasa** Kenya
306 B4 **Momboyo** *watercourse* Democratic Republic of Congo
159 H5 **Mombuca, Serra da** *range* Brazil
373 F6 **Mombum** Indonesia
391 I3 **Mo'menābād, Kūh-e** *mountain* Iran
427 9a **Momi** Fiji
226 C2 **Momignies** Belgium
154 C2 **Mompós** Colombia
237 AE5 **Momskiy Khrebet** *range* Russian Federation
224 G5 **Møn** *island* Denmark
379 H3 **Mon** Nagaland India
376 C3 **Mon** *admin. area* Myanmar
163 I3 **Mon Repos** St Lucia
135 H3 **Mona, Isla** *island* Puerto Rico
134 D5 **Mona, Punta** *cape* Costa Rica
135 G3 **Mona Passage** *strait* Dominican Republic
124 J7 **Mona Reservoir** Utah USA
244 A3 **Monach Islands (Heisker Islands)** Scotland UK
229 H5 **Monaco** *country* Europe
229 H5 **Monaco** Monaco
244 D3 **Monadhliath Mountains** Scotland UK
222 M5 **Monafjärd** *bay* Finland
155 F2 **Monagas** *admin. area* Venezuela
245 F2 **Monaghan** Ireland
245 F2 **Monaghan** *admin. area* Ireland
240 A2 **Monale** Ireland
244 C3 **Monar, Loch** *lake* Scotland UK
119 O8 **Monarch** Alberta Canada
118 I7 **Monarch Mountain** British Columbia Canada
159 F5 **Monas** Bolivia
118 L7 **Monashee Mountains** British Columbia Canada
233 G7 **Monasterace** Italy
301 I1 **Monastir** Tunisia
238 D5 **Monastyrshchina** Russian Federation
234 D1 **Monastyrs'ka** Ukraine
305 G4 **Monatélé** Cameroon
242 B4 **Monatore** Ireland
305 G3 **Monboré** Cameroon
227 H3 **Mönchdorf** Austria
223 R3 **Monchegorsk** Russian Federation
226 D2 **Mönchengladbach** Germany
230 B5 **Monchique** Portugal
119 R8 **Monchy** Saskatchewan Canada
132 E3 **Monclova** Mexico
228 D3 **Moncoutant** France
123 F9 **Moncton** New Brunswick Canada
161 H3 **Mondai** Brazil
125 Q6 **Mondamin** Iowa USA
230 E3 **Mondéjar** Spain
233 E7 **Mondello** Italy
301 J6 **Mondo** Chad
306 C4 **Mondombe** Democratic Republic of Congo
230 C2 **Mondoñedo** Spain
126 F4 **Mondovi** Wisconsin USA
307 F4 **Monduli** Tanzania
384 D2 **Mondy** Russian Federation
305 F3 **Mone** *watercourse* Cameroon
234 C2 **Moneasa** Romania
231 F3 **Monegrillo** Spain
231 F3 **Monegros, Los** *region* Spain
235 C7 **Monemvasia** Greece
387 I1 **Moneron, Ostrov** *island* Russian Federation
127 L6 **Monessen** Pennsylvania USA
230 C4 **Monesterio** Spain
229 G4 **Monestier-de-Clermont** France
245 E4 **Moneygall** Ireland
245 F2 **Moneymore** Cookstown Northern Ireland UK
232 C4 **Monferrato** *region* Italy
379 I5 **Mong Hsat** Myanmar
379 I5 **Mong Hsu** Myanmar
379 H5 **Mong Ne** Myanmar
379 I5 **Mong Ping** Myanmar
379 I4 **Mong Yai** Myanmar
379 I5 **Mong Yang** Myanmar
306 C3 **Monga** Democratic Republic of Congo
306 B3 **Mongala** *watercourse* Democratic Republic of Congo
306 E2 **Mongalla** Sudan
379 G3 **Mongar** Bhutan
306 C3 **Mongemputu** Democratic Republic of Congo
233 E7 **Mongerbino, Capo** *cape* Italy
424 F7 **Mongers Lake** WA Australia
373 H5 **Mongi** *watercourse* Papua New Guinea
379 H5 **Mongkaing** Myanmar
302 B5 **Mongo** Chad
383 K3 **Mongolia** *country*
384 D4 **Mongolian Plateau** Mongolia
305 G4 **Mongomo** Equatorial Guinea
305 G2 **Mongonu** Nigeria
302 C5 **Mongororo** Chad
305 H4 **Mongoumba** Central African Republic
379 I5 **Mongpayak** Myanmar
308 D3 **Mongu** Zambia
308 C3 **Mongua** Angola
305 G3 **Mônguel** Mauritania
379 I5 **Mongyang** Myanmar
383 I3 **Monh Hajrhan** *mountain* Mongolia
226 F3 **Monheim** Germany
244 E5 **Moniaive** Dumfries and Galloway Scotland UK
119 P7 **Monitor** Alberta Canada
124 G7 **Monitor Range** Nevada USA
245 D3 **Monivea** Ireland
310 2 **Moniz, Porto** Madeira
134 C4 **Monjarás** Honduras
306 C4 **Monjuku** Democratic Republic of Congo
377 J6 **Monkayo** Philippines
309 F2 **Monkey Bay** Malawi
424 E6 **Monkey Mia** WA Australia
227 L1 **Mońki** Poland
240 C4 **Monkleigh** Devon England UK
306 C4 **Monkoto** Democratic Republic of Congo
240 D3 **Monksilver** Somerset England UK
240 E3 **Monmouth** Monmouthshire Wales UK
124 D4 **Monmouth** Oregon USA
118 J7 **Monmouth Mountain** British Columbia Canada
240 E3 **Monmouthshire** *admin. area* Wales UK
119 Q6 **Monnery** *watercourse* Saskatchewan Canada
223 Q5 **Mönni** Finland
426 8 **Mono** *island* Solomon Islands
304 E3 **Mono** *watercourse* Togo
134 D5 **Mono, Punta del** *cape* Nicaragua
128 C2 **Mono Lake** California USA
225 N2 **Monola** Finland
126 G5 **Monona** Wisconsin USA
233 G6 **Monopoli** Italy
234 D2 **Monor** Romania
163 9 **Monos** *island* Trinidad and Tobago
423 B7 **Monowai, Lake** New Zealand
376 B3 **Monoy** Myanmar
228 E4 **Monpazier** France
231 F3 **Monreal del Campo** Spain
131 J4 **Monroe** Georgia USA
130 E4 **Monroe** Louisiana USA
126 J6 **Monroe** Michigan USA
131 K3 **Monroe** North Carolina USA
126 G5 **Monroe** Wisconsin USA
126 H7 **Monroe Lake** Indiana USA
130 H5 **Monroeville** Alabama USA
304 B3 **Monrovia** Liberia
228 F1 **Mons** Belgium
224 G5 **Møns Klint** *cape* Denmark
230 C3 **Monsagro** Spain
157 E7 **Monsarás, Ponta de** *cape* Brazil
226 D2 **Monschau** Germany
156 D4 **Monsenhor Gil** Brazil
158 E6 **Monserrate** Bolivia
154 E3 **Monserrate** Colombia
304 C3 **Monsoro** *watercourse* Guinea
229 H4 **Mont, Col du** *pass* Italy
127 P3 **Mont-Apica** Québec Canada
130 D6 **Mont Belvieu** Texas USA
229 H4 **Mont Cenis, Lac du** *lake* France
228 D5 **Mont-de-Marsan** France
127 N3 **Mont-Laurier** Québec Canada
123 F8 **Mont-Louis** Québec Canada
228 F5 **Mont-Louis** France
241 I5 **Mont-St-Aignan** France
155 H3 **Mont Valérien** French Guiana
229 H1 **Montabaur** Germany
373 I5 **Montagu Harbour** *bay* Papua New Guinea
124 D6 **Montague** California USA
126 H5 **Montague** Michigan USA
162 A4 **Montague, Isla** *island* Chile
116 E6 **Montague Island** Alaska USA
228 D3 **Montaigu** France
231 F3 **Montalbán** Spain
230 E4 **Montalbo** Spain
301 J1 **Montalto** *mountain* Italy
229 H5 **Montalto Ligure** Italy
234 C4 **Montana** Bulgaria
234 C4 **Montana** *admin. area* Bulgaria
114 **Montana** *admin. area* USA
163 1c **Montaña** Netherlands Antilles
310 3d **Montaña Clara, Isla de** *island* Canary Islands
154 D3 **Montañas del Totumo** Colombia
157 D7 **Montanha** Brazil
230 B4 **Montargil, Barragem de** *lake* Portugal
228 E4 **Montauban** France
229 G3 **Montbard** France
228 F4 **Montbazens** France
229 H3 **Montbéliard** France
226 C5 **Montbrison** France
123 H7 **Montcevelles, Lac** *lake* Québec Canada
228 G2 **Montcornet** France
228 E4 **Montcuq** France
228 F2 **Montdidier** France
160 F6 **Monte, Laguna del** *lake* Argentina
155 H5 **Monte Alegre** Brazil
157 B7 **Monte Alegre de Minas** Brazil
157 B8 **Monte Aprazível** Brazil
162 C5 **Monte Aymond** Argentina
157 D6 **Monte Azul** Brazil
424 E5 **Monte Bello Islands** WA Australia
158 C2 **Monte Belo** Brazil
229 H5 **Monte-Carlo** Monaco
157 C7 **Monte Carmelo** Brazil
308 E4 **Monte Christo** South Africa
160 E5 **Monte Comans** Argentina
158 D2 **Monte Cristo** Brazil
226 G4 **Monte Croce Carnia, Passo di** *pass* Italy
162 C5 **Monte Dinero** Argentina
132 E4 **Monte Escobedo** Mexico
162 C5 **Monte León** Argentina
162 C5 **Monte León, Isla** *island* Argentina
160 D4 **Monte Patria** Chile
160 F3 **Monte Quemado** Argentina
233 C6 **Monte Rossu, Capo** *cape* Sardinia Italy
157 E5 **Monte Santo** Brazil
159 F3 **Monte Santo** Brazil
233 C6 **Monte Santu, Capo di** *cape* Sardinia Italy
125 L8 **Monte Vista** Colorado USA
159 F5 **Monteagudo** Bolivia
231 F4 **Montealegre del Castillo** Spain
228 E5 **Montech** France
154 A5 **Montecristi** Ecuador
233 D5 **Montecristo, Isola di** *island* Italy
232 E5 **Montefalco** Italy
134 E3 **Montego Bay** Jamaica
156 E4 **Monteiro** Brazil
229 G4 **Montélimar** France
230 B4 **Montemor-o-Nova** Portugal
133 F3 **Montemorelos** Mexico
228 D4 **Montendre** France
232 H5 **Montenegro** *country* Europe
309 G2 **Montepuez** Mozambique
309 G2 **Montepuez** *watercourse* Mozambique
124 E8 **Monterey** California USA
124 D8 **Monterey Bay** California USA
154 C2 **Montería** Colombia
159 F5 **Montero** Bolivia
154 C3 **Monterrey** Colombia
132 E3 **Monterrey** Mexico
156 C4 **Montes Altos** Brazil
157 D7 **Montes Claros** Brazil
160 F6 **Montes de Oca** Argentina
233 F6 **Montesarchio** Italy
230 D3 **Montesclaros** Spain
228 E5 **Montesquiou** France
232 D5 **Montevarchi** Italy
161 G5 **Montevideo** Uruguay
125 R4 **Montevideo** Minnesota USA
125 O8 **Montezuma** Kansas USA
231 H2 **Montgó, Cala** *cape* Spain
131 H4 **Montgomery** Alabama USA
229 H3 **Monthey** Switzerland
229 G2 **Monthois** France
233 C6 **Monti** Sardinia Italy
131 J5 **Monticello** Florida USA
131 J4 **Monticello** Georgia USA
126 F5 **Monticello** Iowa USA
131 I2 **Monticello** Kentucky USA
130 F5 **Monticello** Mississippi USA
125 K8 **Monticello** Utah USA
126 G5 **Monticello** Wisconsin USA
232 D4 **Montichiari** Italy
161 G4 **Montiel, Cuchilla de** *range* Argentina
228 E4 **Montignac** France
228 F2 **Montigny** France
127 M2 **Montigny, Lac de** *lake* Québec Canada
230 B4 **Montijo** Portugal
230 C4 **Montijo** Spain
134 D6 **Montijo, Golfo de** *lake* Panama
230 D5 **Montilla** Spain
308 B2 **Montipa** Angola
159 I5 **Montividiu** Brazil
241 H5 **Montivilliers** France
228 F3 **Montluçon** France
228 F3 **Montmarault** France
119 T7 **Montmartre** Saskatchewan Canada
229 H4 **Montmélian** France
229 H5 **Montmeyan** France
228 E2 **Montmirail** France
228 E3 **Montmorillon** France
425 N6 **Monto** Qld Australia
223 O5 **Montola** Finland
230 F3 **Montón** Spain
230 D4 **Montoro, Embalse de** *lake* Spain
124 J5 **Montpelier** Idaho USA
125 P3 **Montpelier** North Dakota USA
127 O4 **Montpelier** Vermont USA
228 F5 **Montpellier** France
228 E4 **Montpon-Ménestérol** France
226 C4 **Montpont** France
127 O4 **Montreal** Québec Canada
126 F3 **Montreal** Wisconsin USA
126 J3 **Montreal** *watercourse* Ontario Canada
119 S5 **Montréal** *watercourse* Saskatchewan Canada
226 C4 **Montréal** France
126 I3 **Montreal Island** Ontario Canada
228 E5 **Montréjeau** France
228 F3 **Montrésor** France
241 I4 **Montreuil** France
229 H3 **Montreux** Switzerland
229 G3 **Montrevel-en-Bresse** France
118 M8 **Montrose** British Columbia Canada
244 F4 **Montrose** Angus Scotland UK
130 F4 **Montrose** Arkansas USA
125 L7 **Montrose** Colorado USA
121 V8 **Monts, Pointe des** *cape* Québec Canada
228 E3 **Monts-sur-Guesnes** France
228 F4 **Montsalvy** France
228 G3 **Montsauche** France
163 I7 **Montserrat** *UK territory* Caribbean
163 I7 **Montserrat** Montserrat
228 D2 **Montsûrs** France
124 F4 **Monument** Oregon USA
129 K4 **Monument** *watercourse* Texas USA
122 G1 **Monumental Island** Nunavut Canada
379 H4 **Monywa** Myanmar
226 E5 **Monza** Italy
308 E3 **Monze** Zambia
231 G3 **Monzón** Spain
232 D4 **Monzone** Italy
130 C5 **Moody** Texas USA
308 C5 **Mooifontein** Namibia
127 L8 **Moomaw, Lake** West Virginia USA
425 L7 **Moomba** SA Australia
124 E6 **Moon Lake** California USA
127 J2 **Moonbeam** Ontario Canada
425 M4 **Moongobulla** Qld Australia
425 N6 **Moonie** Qld Australia
79 R5 **Moonless Mountains** *underwater feature* Pacific Ocean
245 D3 **Moor** Ireland
372 E4 **Moor, Kepulauan** *island* Indonesia
424 E7 **Moora** WA Australia
125 M4 **Moorcroft** Wyoming USA
224 D6 **Moordorf** Germany
124 I5 **Moore** Idaho USA
125 K3 **Moore** Montana USA
130 C3 **Moore** Oklahoma USA
128 G1 **Moore** Utah USA
424 F7 **Moore, Lake** WA Australia
437 K1 **Moore Embayment** *bay* Antarctica
131 K7 **Moore Haven** Florida USA
425 N4 **Moore Reefs** Coral Sea Islands Territory Australia
427 14a **Moorea** *island* French Polynesia
242 B2 **Moorefield** Armagh Northern Ireland UK
130 B2 **Mooreland** Oklahoma USA
122 H4 **Moores Harbour** Newfoundland and Labrador Canada
131 M7 **Moores Island** Bahamas
131 K3 **Mooresville** North Carolina USA
245 F2 **Moorfields** Ballymena Northern Ireland UK
125 Q3 **Moorhead** Minnesota USA
308 C6 **Moorreesburg** South Africa
121 O7 **Moose** *watercourse* Ontario Canada
120 G7 **Moose Island** Manitoba Canada
119 S7 **Moose Jaw** Saskatchewan Canada
119 S7 **Moose Jaw** *watercourse* Saskatchewan Canada
119 V6 **Moose Lake** Manitoba Canada
126 E3 **Moose Lake** Minnesota USA
121 O7 **Moose River** Ontario Canada
127 Q4 **Moosehead Lake** Maine USA
119 V7 **Moosehorn** Manitoba Canada
127 P4 **Moosilauke, Mount** New Hampshire USA
119 U7 **Moosomin** Saskatchewan Canada
121 O7 **Moosonee** Ontario Canada
309 G3 **Mopeia** Mozambique
308 D4 **Mopipi** Botswana
300 F6 **Mopti** Mali
300 F6 **Mopti** *admin. area* Mali
391 K3 **Moqor** Afghanistan
158 D5 **Moquegua** Peru
158 D5 **Moquegua** *admin. area* Peru
155 E2 **Moquetico** Venezuela
227 J4 **Mór** Hungary
305 G2 **Mora** Cameroon
230 B4 **Mora** Portugal
230 E4 **Mora** Spain
224 H2 **Mora** Sweden
126 E4 **Mora** Minnesota USA
160 D5 **Mora, Cerro** *mountain* Chile
231 F3 **Mora de Rubielos** Spain
234 A4 **Morača** *watercourse* Montenegro
159 H2 **Morada Bom Lugar** Brazil
392 E5 **Moradabad** Uttar Pradesh India
309 H3 **Morafenobe** Madagascar
232 H5 **Morakovo** Montenegro
230 C3 **Moraleja** Spain
154 B4 **Morales** Colombia
154 C2 **Morales** Colombia
134 B4 **Morales** Guatemala
130 C6 **Morales** Texas USA
133 F4 **Morales, Laguna de** *lake* Mexico
309 I3 **Moramanga** Madagascar
130 B4 **Moran** Texas USA
155 F2 **Moranacas, Islas** *islands* Venezuela
427 14 **Morane** *reef* French Polynesia
134 E3 **Morant Point** Jamaica
244 C4 **Morar** Highland Scotland UK
244 C4 **Morar, Loch** *lake* Scotland UK
229 H3 **Morat, Lac de** *lake* Switzerland
230 E3 **Morata de Tajuña** Spain
230 F4 **Moratalla** Spain
393 E10 **Moratuwa** Sri Lanka
227 H4 **Moravče** Slovenia
234 B3 **Moravița** Romania
234 C4 **Moravitsa** Bulgaria
227 J3 **Morávka** Czech Republic
227 I3 **Moravská Třebová** Czech Republic
227 J3 **Moravskoslezský Kraj** *admin. area* Czech Republic
424 F7 **Morawa** WA Australia
155 G2 **Morawhanna** Guyana
227 K2 **Morawica** Poland
227 J2 **Morawin** Poland
244 E3 **Moray** *admin. area* Scotland UK
244 E3 **Moray Firth** *bay* Scotland UK
226 D3 **Morbach** Germany
392 C6 **Morbi** Gujarat India
310 6b **Morbihan, Golfe du** *bay* French Southern and Antarctic Lands
228 D4 **Morcenx** France
154 D2 **Mórchipa** Venezuela
241 G2 **Morcott** Rutland England UK
238 H5 **Mordves** Russian Federation
244 D2 **More, Loch** *lake* Scotland UK
224 D1 **Møre og Romsdal** *admin. area* Norway
125 N4 **Moreau** *watercourse* South Dakota USA
130 F5 **Moreauville** Louisiana USA
244 F5 **Morebattle** Scottish Borders Scotland UK
242 F2 **Morecambe** Lancashire England UK
242 E2 **Morecambe Bay** England UK
425 N7 **Moree** NSW Australia
228 E3 **Morée** France
228 E3 **Morefield** Highland Scotland UK
379 H4 **Moreh** Manipur India
241 I3 **Morehall** Kent England UK
373 G6 **Morehead** *watercourse* Papua New Guinea
130 G2 **Morehouse** Missouri USA
159 F3 **Moreira Cabral, Serra** *range* Brazil
125 M2 **Moreland** Saskatchewan Canada
132 E5 **Morelia** Mexico
425 L5 **Morella** Qld Australia
231 F3 **Morella** Spain
129 I7 **Morelos** Mexico
133 F5 **Morelos** *admin. area* Mexico
392 E5 **Morena** Madhya Pradesh India
230 D5 **Morena, Sierra** *range* Spain
160 D2 **Moreno, Bahía** *bay* Chile
162 D3 **Moreno, Isla** *island* Argentina
162 B5 **Moreno, Ventisquero** *glacier* Argentina
128 D4 **Moreno Valley** California USA
233 C6 **Mores** Sardinia Italy
242 E2 **Moresby** Cumbria England UK
118 E6 **Moresby Island** British Columbia Canada
228 C5 **Morestel** France
240 D4 **Moretonhampstead** Devon England UK
229 H3 **Morez** France
240 C2 **Morfa** Pembrokeshire Wales UK
240 C3 **Morfa-Bach** Carmarthenshire Wales UK
240 C2 **Morfa Nefyn** Gwynedd Wales UK
130 F6 **Morgan City** Louisiana USA
128 E3 **Morgan Hill** California USA
389 P3 **Morgan Tajga** *mountain* Russian Federation
154 E3 **Morganito** Venezuela
126 H8 **Morgantown** Kentucky USA
127 L7 **Morgantown** West Virginia USA
230 B5 **Morgavel, Barragem de** *lake* Portugal
229 H3 **Morges** Switzerland
232 E4 **Morgo, Isola** *island* Italy
226 D3 **Morhange** France
123 G7 **Morhiban, Lac de** *lake* Québec Canada
129 I3 **Moriarty** New Mexico USA
304 C3 **Moribaya** Guinea
118 H5 **Morice Lake** British Columbia Canada
118 H5 **Moricetown** British Columbia Canada
391 L2 **Morich** Pakistan
155 F2 **Morichal** Venezuela
154 D4 **Morichal Viejo** Colombia
155 E2 **Morichalito** Venezuela
244 D3 **Morie, Loch** *lake* Scotland UK
373 G5 **Morigio Island** Papua New Guinea
305 F2 **Moriki** Nigeria
226 E2 **Moringen** Germany
225 P4 **Morino** Russian Federation
119 O6 **Morinville** Alberta Canada
387 I3 **Morioka** Japan
426 7 **Moriou** Vanuatu
155 F4 **Moriru** Brazil
244 D3 **Moriston** *watercourse* Scotland UK
223 M3 **Morjärv** Sweden
388 E2 **Morki** Russian Federation
238 G4 **Morkiny Gory** Russian Federation
237 X5 **Morkoka** *watercourse* Russian Federation
222 H6 **Mörkret** Sweden
228 C2 **Morlaix** France
118 E2 **Morley** *watercourse* Yukon Territory Canada
243 G2 **Morley** Durham England UK
243 G3 **Morley** West Yorkshire England UK
126 G8 **Morley** Missouri USA
118 E2 **Morley River** Yukon Territory Canada
128 G3 **Mormon Lake** Arizona USA
124 H5 **Mormon Reservoir** Idaho USA
163 I6 **Morne-à-l'Eau** Guadeloupe
163 I5 **Morne Raquette** Dominica
119 O6 **Morningside** Alberta Canada
425 K4 **Mornington Island** Qld Australia
391 K4 **Moro** Pakistan
377 I6 **Moro Gulf** Philippines
373 H5 **Morobe** Papua New Guinea
306 E3 **Morobo** Sudan
300 E2 **Morocco** *country* Africa
158 B3 **Morococha** Peru
245 D4 **Moroe** Ireland
307 F5 **Morogoro** Tanzania
307 F5 **Morogoro** *admin. area* Tanzania
308 D5 **Morokweng** South Africa
134 C4 **Morolica** Honduras
375 J5 **Moromaho** *island* Indonesia
309 H4 **Morombe** Madagascar
134 E2 **Morón** Cuba
154 D2 **Morón** Venezuela
384 D2 **Mörön** Mongolia
158 B1 **Morona** *watercourse* Peru
154 B5 **Morona-Santiago** *admin. area* Ecuador
309 H4 **Morondava** Madagascar
304 C3 **Morondo** Côte d'Ivoire
309 H2 **Moroni** Comoros
309 D3 **Moronou** Côte d'Ivoire
425 O7 **Moroo** NSW Australia
237 AG7 **Moroshechnoye** Russian Federation
375 K3 **Morotai** *island* Indonesia
375 K3 **Morotai, Selat** *strait* Indonesia
307 E3 **Moroto** Uganda
223 P2 **Morottaja** Finland
372 B4 **Morowali** Indonesia
388 D4 **Morozovsk** Russian Federation
245 D5 **Morozzo** Italy
243 G1 **Morpeth** Northumberland England UK
394 E6 **Morphou** Cyprus
157 B7 **Morrinhos** Brazil
423 F5 **Morrinsville** New Zealand
132 D2 **Morrión** Mexico
130 H4 **Morris** Alabama USA
126 G6 **Morris** Illinois USA
125 R4 **Morris** Minnesota USA
117 P2 **Morris Jesup, Kap** *cape* Greenland
435 E1 **Morris Jesup Rise** *underwater feature* Arctic Ocean
131 I3 **Morrison** Tennessee USA
128 F4 **Morristown** Arizona USA
131 J2 **Morristown** Tennessee USA
134 C5 **Morrito** Nicaragua
304 B3 **Morro** *watercourse* Sierra Leone
160 D3 **Morro, Punta** *cape* Chile
154 A5 **Morro, Punta del** *cape* Ecuador
157 B8 **Morro Agudo** Brazil
128 B3 **Morro Bay** California USA
310 3d **Morro del Jable** Canary Islands
157 D5 **Morro do Chapéu** Brazil
158 A2 **Mórrope** Peru
158 B2 **Morropón** Peru
156 C5 **Morros** Brazil
154 C2 **Morrosquillo, Golfo de** *bay* Colombia
309 G3 **Morrumbala** Mozambique
309 G4 **Morrumbene** Mozambique
224 H4 **Morrumsån** *watercourse* Sweden
224 E4 **Mors** *cape* Denmark
388 D2 **Morsansk** Russian Federation
437 I2 **Morse, Cape** Antarctica
233 C5 **Morsetta, Capo della** *cape* Corsica France
234 C1 **Morshyn** Ukraine
393 E7 **Morsi** Maharashtra India
223 S5 **Morskaya Masel'ga** Russian Federation
120 H8 **Morson** Ontario Canada
233 C9 **Morsott** Algeria
241 H2 **Morston** Norfolk England UK
228 D2 **Mortain** France
240 C3 **Morte Point** England UK
229 H3 **Morteau** France
240 G3 **Mortehoe** Devon England UK
229 I5 **Mortella, Punta** *cape* Corsica France
233 F7 **Mortelle** Italy
132 D3 **Mortero** Mexico
160 F4 **Morteros** Argentina
157 A6 **Mortes, Rio das** *watercourse* Brazil
224 I4 **Mörtfors** Sweden
134 E5 **Morti** Panama
241 F3 **Mortimer** West Berkshire England UK
373 J2 **Mortlock Islands** Federated States of Micronesia
241 G2 **Morton** Lincolnshire England UK
126 G6 **Morton** Illinois USA
130 G4 **Morton** Mississippi USA
129 K4 **Morton** Texas USA
124 D3 **Morton** Washington USA
228 E2 **Mortrée** France
222 I5 **Mörtsjön** Sweden
222 I5 **Mörtsjön** *lake* Sweden
163 9 **Moruga** Trinidad and Tobago
425 N8 **Moruya** NSW Australia
425 M6 **Morven** Qld Australia
131 J5 **Morven** Georgia USA
240 E2 **Morville** Shropshire England UK
425 M9 **Morwell** Vic. Australia
225 P2 **Mor'ye** Russian Federation
238 F5 **Mosal'sk** Russian Federation
225 O5 **Mosar** Belarus
222 I5 **Mosätt** Sweden
Moscow *see* **Moskva** Russian Federation
124 G3 **Moscow** Idaho USA
125 O9 **Moscow** Kansas USA
437 H2 **Moscow University Ice Shelf** Antarctica
242 F2 **Mosedale** Cumbria England UK
308 D5 **Moselebe** *watercourse* Botswana
229 H2 **Moselle** *watercourse* France
226 D2 **Moselle** *watercourse* Germany
123 G10 **Moser River** Nova Scotia Canada
124 F3 **Moses Lake** Washington USA
159 E5 **Mosetenes, Cordillera de** *range* Bolivia
159 F5 **Mosevi** Bolivia
236 K5 **Moseyevo** Russian Federation
423 D7 **Mosgiel** New Zealand
223 R3 **Mosha** Russian Federation
391 H2 **Moshajari** Iran
308 D5 **Moshaweng** *watercourse* South Africa
225 N3 **Moshchnyy, Ostrov** *island* Russian Federation
238 F3 **Moshenskoye** Russian Federation
305 E3 **Moshi** *watercourse* Nigeria
307 F4 **Moshi** Tanzania
225 P5 **Moshkany** Belarus
373 J5 **Mosigo** Papua New Guinea
306 C3 **Mosite** Democratic Republic of Congo
222 H4 **Mosjøen** Norway
237 AD8 **Moskal'vo** Russian Federation
222 H3 **Mosken** *island* Norway
222 H2 **Moskenesøy** *island* Norway
222 K4 **Moskosel** Sweden
238 G4 **Moskovskaya Oblast'** *admin. area* Russian Federation
389 K6 **Moskva** Tajikistan
238 G5 **Moskva (Moscow)** Russian Federation
234 E2 **Moșna** Romania
242 B3 **Mosney Camp** Ireland
426 7 **Moso** *island* Vanuatu
226 F4 **Moso in Passiria** Italy
158 D4 **Mosoc Llacta** Peru
227 I4 **Mosoni-Duna** *watercourse* Hungary
129 K3 **Mosquero** New Mexico USA
231 F3 **Mosqueruela** Spain
133 I6 **Mosquitia** *region* Honduras
134 E5 **Mosquito, Punta** *cape* Panama
131 K6 **Mosquito Lagoon** Florida USA
116 F7 **Mosquito Lake** Alaska USA
134 D4 **Mosquitos, Costa de** *region* Nicaragua
134 D5 **Mosquitos, Golfo de los** *bay* Panama
224 F3 **Moss** Norway
130 C4 **Moss Lake** Texas USA
225 K2 **Mossalafjärd** *bay* Finland
244 F3 **Mossat** Aberdeenshire Scotland UK
119 S8 **Mossbank** Saskatchewan Canada
423 C7 **Mossburn** New Zealand
308 D6 **Mossel Bay** South Africa
308 D6 **Mossel Bay** *bay* South Africa
305 G5 **Mossendjo** Congo
425 M8 **Mossgiel** NSW Australia
226 E3 **Mössingen** Germany
425 M4 **Mossman** Qld Australia
224 I2 **Mössön** Sweden
156 F4 **Mossoró** Brazil
119 T5 **Mossy** *watercourse* Saskatchewan Canada
124 D3 **Mossyrock** Washington USA
235 D5 **Most** Bulgaria
232 E3 **Most na Soči** Slovenia
301 G1 **Mostaganem** Algeria
301 G1 **Mostaganem** *admin. area* Algeria
232 G5 **Mostar** Bosnia and Herzegovina
161 I4 **Mostardas, Ponta de** *cape* Brazil
310 1a **Mosteiros** Azores
227 H2 **Mostek** Czech Republic
234 E3 **Mostiștea, Lacul** *lake* Romania
230 E3 **Móstoles** Spain
119 Q5 **Mostoos Hills** Saskatchewan Canada
389 N2 **Mostovoye** *lake* Russian Federation
234 G2 **Mostovoye** Ukraine
227 L2 **Mosty** Poland
375 H2 **Mostyn** Malaysia
242 E3 **Mostyn** Flintshire Wales UK
224 E3 **Møsvatnet** *lake* Norway
302 F5 **Mot'a** Ethiopia
230 E4 **Mota del Cuervo** Spain
426 7 **Mota Lava** *island* Vanuatu
305 H4 **Motaba** *watercourse* Congo
134 B4 **Motagua** *watercourse* Guatemala
224 H3 **Motala** Sweden
241 E3 **Motcombe** Dorset England UK
306 B3 **Motenge-Boma** Democratic Republic of Congo
392 E6 **Moth** Uttar Pradesh India
244 E5 **Motherwell** North Lanarkshire Scotland UK
375 J3 **Moti** *island* Indonesia
392 F5 **Motihari** Bihar India
230 F4 **Motilla del Palancar** Spain
222 J4 **Mötingselberget** Sweden
422 G3 **Motiti Island** New Zealand
125 R3 **Motley** Minnesota USA
379 I4 **Motlong** Myanmar
155 F3 **Motó** Venezuela
308 D4 **Motokwe** Botswana
373 J6 **Motorina Island** Papua New Guinea
230 E5 **Motril** Spain
234 E1 **Motrunki** Ukraine
125 N3 **Mott** North Dakota USA
233 E4 **Motta di Livenza** Italy
233 G6 **Mottola** Italy
422 G3 **Motu** *watercourse* New Zealand
423 E5 **Motueka** New Zealand
423 E6 **Motunau Beach** New Zealand
379 H3 **Motuo** Xizang Zizhiqu China
158 B2 **Motupe** Peru
427 9 **Moturiki** *island* Fiji
422 2 **Mototapu** *island* Cook Islands New Zealand
422 F4 **Motutere** New Zealand
306 B3 **Mouali Gbangba** Congo
437 L2 **Moubray Bay** Antarctica
121 U6 **Mouchalagane** *watercourse* Québec Canada
229 G3 **Mouchard** France
135 G2 **Mouchoir Bank** Turks and Caicos Islands
135 G2 **Mouchoir Passage** Turks and Caicos Islands
300 D5 **Moudjéria** Mauritania
229 H3 **Moudon** Switzerland
305 G5 **Mouenda** Gabon
225 L2 **Mouhijärvi** *lake* Finland
304 D2 **Mouhoun** *watercourse* Burkina Faso
304 D3 **Mouhoun (Black Volta)** *watercourse* Ghana
305 G5 **Mouila** Gabon
305 I3 **Mouka** Central African Republic
425 M8 **Moulamein** NSW Australia
230 C6 **Moulay-Bousselham** Morocco
163 I3 **Moule a Chique, Cape** St Lucia
228 F3 **Moulilherne** France
228 F3 **Moulins** France
228 E3 **Moulismes** France
Moulmein *see* **Mawlamyaing** Myanmar
243 F3 **Moulton** Cheshire England UK
130 C6 **Moulton** Texas USA
436 P1 **Moulton, Mount** *mountain* Antarctica
131 J5 **Moultrie** Georgia USA
131 K4 **Moultrie, Lake** South Carolina USA
379 G4 **Moulvibazar** Bangladesh
244 E4 **Moulzie** Angus Scotland UK
305 G5 **Mounana** Gabon

130 F4 **Mound Bayou** Mississippi USA
305 H3 **Moundou** Chad
126 G8 **Mounds** Illinois USA
130 C3 **Mounds** Oklahoma USA
305 G3 **Mounguel** Cameroon
223 M3 **Mounioälveri** *watercourse* Sweden
304 B3 **Mount, Cape** *cape* Liberia
124 D4 **Mount Angel** Oregon USA
128 C6 **Mount Augusta** *volcano* Isla Guadeloupe Mexico
425 K8 **Mount Barker** SA Australia
424 F8 **Mount Barker** WA Australia
425 inset **Mount Bates** Norfolk Island Australia
245 D3 **Mount Bellew Bridge** Ireland
423 F5 **Mount Bruce** New Zealand
126 H7 **Mount Carmel** Illinois USA
124 F1 **Mount Cartier** British Columbia Canada
118 J7 **Mount Currie** British Columbia Canada
118 F4 **Mount Edziza Provincial Park** British Columbia Canada
80 J4 **Mount Error** *underwater feature* Indian Ocean
374 C4 **Mount Faber Park** Singapore
308 E6 **Mount Frere** South Africa
425 L9 **Mount Gambier** SA Australia
126 J6 **Mount Gilead** Ohio USA
242 A2 **Mount Hamilton** Strabane Northern Ireland UK
130 E3 **Mount Ida** Arkansas USA
425 K5 **Mount Isa** Qld Australia
127 L7 **Mount Jackson** Virginia USA
131 H2 **Mount Juliet** Tennessee USA
117 L9 **Mount-Laurier** Québec Canada
424 F7 **Mount Magnet** WA Australia
128 C2 **Mount Montgomery** Nevada USA
425 N5 **Mount Morgan** Qld Australia
123 I8 **Mount Moriah** Newfoundland and Labrador Canada
242 A3 **Mount Nugent** Ireland
130 G5 **Mount Olive** Mississippi USA
425 N5 **Mount Ossa** Qld Australia
123 L9 **Mount Pearl** Newfoundland and Labrador Canada
126 I5 **Mount Pleasant** Michigan USA
131 L4 **Mount Pleasant** South Carolina USA
130 H3 **Mount Pleasant** Tennessee USA
130 D4 **Mount Pleasant** Texas USA
124 J7 **Mount Pleasant** Utah USA
127 N6 **Mount Pocono** Pennsylvania USA
126 H5 **Mount Prospect** Illinois USA
118 L6 **Mount Robson Provincial Park** British Columbia Canada
124 D6 **Mount Shasta** California USA
423 D6 **Mount Somers** New Zealand
127 M6 **Mount Union** Pennsylvania USA
130 H5 **Mount Vernon** Alabama USA
126 G7 **Mount Vernon** Illinois USA
126 I8 **Mount Vernon** Kentucky USA
127 J6 **Mount Vernon** Ohio USA
235 B6 **Mounta, Akra** *cape* Greece
154 A1 **Mountain** Colombia
125 Q2 **Mountain** North Dakota USA
120 D6 **Mountain Cabin** Saskatchewan Canada
131 J3 **Mountain City** Georgia USA
131 K2 **Mountain City** Tennessee USA
130 C5 **Mountain City** Texas USA
126 E8 **Mountain Grove** Missouri USA
130 E2 **Mountain Home** Arkansas USA
124 H5 **Mountain Home** Idaho USA
118 M6 **Mountain Park** Alberta Canada
130 B3 **Mountain Park** Oklahoma USA
155 G4 **Mountain Point** Guyana
119 O8 **Mountain View** Alberta Canada
128 inset **Mountain View** Hawai'i USA
126 F8 **Mountain View** Missouri USA
125 J6 **Mountain View** Wyoming USA
116 C6 **Mountain Village** Alaska USA
129 I3 **Mountainair** New Mexico USA
130 D3 **Mountainburg** Arkansas USA
244 E5 **Mountbenger** Scottish Borders Scotland UK
241 H4 **Mountfield** East Sussex England UK
245 E2 **Mountfield** Omagh Northern Ireland UK
245 E2 **Mountjoy** Omagh Northern Ireland UK
245 E3 **Mountmellick** Ireland
245 E4 **Mountrath** Ireland
240 B4 **Mount's Bay** England UK
155 F5 **Moura** Brazil
230 C4 **Moura** Portugal
230 C4 **Mourão** Portugal
302 C4 **Mourdi, Dépression du** *pan* Chad
300 E6 **Mourdiah** Mali
228 D5 **Mourenx** France
235 D6 **Mourtzeflos, Akra** *cape* Greece
228 F1 **Mouscron** Belgium
373 H4 **Mouse Island** Papua New Guinea
305 H2 **Mousgougou** Chad
301 J6 **Moussoro** Chad
229 H5 **Moustiers-Sainte-Marie** France
376 B4 **Mouth of the Ayeyarwady (Irrawaddy)** *bay* Myanmar
229 H3 **Mouthe** France
391 K5 **Mouths of the Indus** *sea* Pakistan
229 H4 **Moûtiers** France
422 G3 **Moutohora Island** New Zealand
372 B3 **Moutong** Indonesia
310 8 **Moutsamoudou** Comoros
228 F2 **Mouy** France
305 G5 **Mouyondzi** Congo
301 J6 **Mouzarak** Chad
222 K2 **Movik** Norway
245 E1 **Moville** Ireland
125 Q5 **Moville** Iowa USA
155 G3 **Mowasi Mountains** Guyana
245 F2 **Mowhan** Armagh Northern Ireland UK
308 D2 **Moxico** *admin. area* Angola
156 E5 **Moxotó** *watercourse* Brazil
245 F2 **Moy** Ireland
245 D2 **Moy** *watercourse* Ireland
245 F2 **Moy** Dungannon Northern Ireland UK
244 D4 **Moy** Highland Scotland UK
245 F2 **Moyad** Newry and Mourne Northern Ireland UK
307 F3 **Moyalē** Kenya
242 B1 **Moyarget** Moyle Northern Ireland UK
121 X5 **Moyen, Lac** *lake* Québec Canada
305 H3 **Moyen-Chari** *admin. area* Chad
305 G5 **Moyen-Ogooué** *admin. area* Gabon
229 H2 **Moyenvic** France
237 V5 **Moyero** *watercourse* Russian Federation
119 N8 **Moyie** British Columbia Canada
119 M8 **Moyie Springs** Idaho USA
245 F1 **Moyle** *admin. area* Northern Ireland UK
245 E2 **Moyle** Strabane Northern Ireland UK
240 C2 **Moylgrove** Pembrokeshire Wales UK
242 B3 **Moynalty** Ireland
245 D3 **Moyne** Ireland
375 H6 **Moyo** *island* Indonesia
158 B2 **Moyobamba** Peru
245 C3 **Moyour Bridge** Ireland
306 E4 **Moyowosi** *watercourse* Tanzania
301 J6 **Moyto** Chad
382 F5 **Moyu** Xinjiang Uygur Zizhiqu China
389 L4 **Moyynty** Kazakhstan
309 F3 **Mozambique** *country* Africa
309 H3 **Mozambique Channel** *strait* Mozambique/Madagascar
80 H9 **Mozambique Escarpment** *underwater feature* Indian Ocean
80 H8 **Mozambique Plateau** *underwater feature* Indian Ocean
157 B6 **Mozarlândia** Brazil
230 B3 **Mozelos** Portugal
226 E5 **Mozzanica** Italy
306 C5 **Mpama** *watercourse* Congo
306 F5 **Mpanda** Tanzania
308 E3 **Mpandamatenga** Botswana
305 G3 **Mpem** *watercourse* Cameroon
300 E6 **Mpessoba** Mali
309 F2 **Mpika** Zambia
305 H4 **Mpoko** *watercourse* Central African Republic
307 F5 **Mponde** *watercourse* Tanzania
309 F2 **Mponela** Malawi
308 E2 **Mpongwe** Zambia
305 E5 **Mporokoso** Zambia
304 D3 **Mpraeso** Ghana
306 E5 **Mpui** Tanzania
306 E5 **Mpulungu** Zambia
308 E5 **Mpumalanga** *admin. area* South Africa
305 I5 **Mpungu** Democratic Republic of Congo
307 F6 **Mpurukasese** Tanzania
308 F6 **Mqanduli** South Africa
232 G4 **Mrakovica** Bosnia and Herzegovina
227 J5 **Mramor** Bosnia and Herzegovina
232 H5 **Mratinje** Montenegro
379 G5 **Mrauk-U (Myohaung)** Myanmar
229 L4 **Mrkopalj** Croatia
227 K1 **Mroków** Poland
301 I1 **M'Saken** Tunisia
307 F5 **Msangasi** *watercourse* Tanzania
227 M1 **Mscibava** Belarus
227 G2 **Mšec** Czech Republic
227 H2 **Mšeno** Czech Republic
234 D1 **Mshanets** Ukraine
301 G1 **M'Sila** Algeria
301 G1 **M'Sila** *admin. area* Algeria
238 F4 **Msta** Russian Federation
225 Q3 **Mstinskiy Most** Russian Federation
227 K3 **Mszana Dolna** Poland
227 K2 **Mszczonów** Poland
307 F3 **Mtelo** *mountain* Kenya
307 F4 **Mtito Andei** Kenya
310 8b **Mtsamgamouji** Mayotte
238 G6 **Mtsensk** Russian Federation
388 D5 **Mtskheta** Georgia
309 F5 **Mtubatuba** South Africa
307 G6 **Mtwara** Tanzania
307 F6 **Mtwara** *admin. area* Tanzania
379 H4 **Mu-Se** Myanmar
427 10a **Mu'a** Tonga
309 G2 **Muaguide** Mozambique
309 F2 **Mualadzi** Mozambique
156 B3 **Muaná** Brazil
306 A5 **Muanda** Democratic Republic of Congo
376 E2 **Muang Et** Laos
376 D2 **Muang Hiam** Laos
376 D3 **Muang Hôngsa** Laos
376 D2 **Muang Houn** Laos
376 D2 **Muang Hup** Laos
376 D2 **Muang Khoa** Laos
376 E4 **Muang Khôngxédôn** Laos
376 D2 **Muang La** Laos
376 E3 **Muang Mahaxai** Laos
376 D2 **Muang Meung** Laos
376 D2 **Muang Namo** Laos
376 D2 **Muang Ngoy** Laos
376 E3 **Muang Nong** Laos
376 D2 **Muang Ou Tai** Laos
376 D2 **Muang Paktha** Laos
376 D3 **Muang Phiang** Laos
376 E3 **Muang Phin** Laos
376 E2 **Muang Sing** Laos
376 E3 **Muang Songkhon** Laos
376 D3 **Muang Thadua** Laos
376 D2 **Muang Xon** Laos
376 D2 **Muangxay** Laos
309 F3 **Muanza** Mozambique
374 D3 **Muar** Malaysia
374 D3 **Muar** *watercourse* Malaysia
375 G2 **Muara** Brunei
375 H3 **Muara Pantai** *island* Indonesia
375 H3 **Muaraatap** Indonesia
374 D4 **Muarabeliti** Indonesia
375 G3 **Muarabemlelakidau** Indonesia
374 D4 **Muarabulian** Indonesia
374 D4 **Muarabungo** Indonesia
374 E5 **Muaradua** Indonesia
374 D4 **Muaraenim** Indonesia
375 G4 **Muarainu** Indonesia
375 H4 **Muarajawa** Indonesia
375 H4 **Muarakaman** Indonesia
374 D4 **Muaralabuh** Indonesia
374 D4 **Muaralakitan** Indonesia
375 H3 **Muaralasan** Indonesia
375 G4 **Muaralaung** Indonesia
375 H3 **Muaras Reef** Indonesia
374 D4 **Muarasabak** Indonesia
375 H3 **Muarasengajan** Indonesia
374 C4 **Muarasiberut** Indonesia
374 C4 **Muarasigep** Indonesia
374 C3 **Muarasipongi** Indonesia
374 D4 **Muaratebo** Indonesia
375 G4 **Muarateweh** Indonesia
375 H3 **Muarawahau** Indonesia
375 J4 **Muari** *island* Indonesia
391 K5 **Muāri, Rās** *cape* Pakistan
309 G3 **Muatua** Mozambique
306 E3 **Mubende** Uganda
305 G2 **Mubi** Nigeria
388 J6 **Muborak** Uzbekistan
372 E4 **Mubrani** Indonesia
374 E3 **Mubur** *island* Indonesia
306 B5 **Mucaba, Serra** *range* Angola
155 F4 **Mucajaí** *watercourse* Brazil
155 F4 **Mucajaí, Serra do** *range* Brazil
309 F3 **Mucanha** *watercourse* Mozambique
226 D2 **Much** Germany
240 E2 **Much Wenlock** Shropshire England UK
310 3b **Muchachos, Roque de los** *volcano* Canary Islands
158 E4 **Muchanes** Bolivia
158 E4 **Muchani, Serranía de** *range* Bolivia
242 B4 **Muchwood Cross Roads** Ireland
244 B4 **Muck** *island* Scotland UK
309 H2 **Mucojo** Mozambique
308 D2 **Muconda** Angola
308 B3 **Mucope** Angola
308 C3 **Mucope** *watercourse* Angola
309 G3 **Mucubela** Mozambique
159 E2 **Mucuim** *watercourse* Brazil
306 C6 **Mucumbo** *watercourse* Zambia
309 F3 **Mucumbura** Mozambique
154 D2 **Mucumpiz** Venezuela
308 C2 **Mucundi** Angola
309 G3 **Mucupia** Mozambique
155 F5 **Mucura** Brazil
157 E7 **Mucuri** Brazil
157 E7 **Mucuri** *watercourse* Brazil
157 D7 **Mucurici** Brazil
308 D2 **Mucussueje** Angola
124 I5 **Mud Lake** Idaho USA
126 B4 **Mud Lake Reservoir** South Dakota USA
118 J6 **Mud River** British Columbia Canada
374 D2 **Muda** *watercourse* Malaysia
244 D2 **Mudale** Highland Scotland UK
385 L4 **Mudanjiang** Heilongjiang China
232 C2 **Mudau** Germany
240 C3 **Muddiford** Devon England UK
222 L3 **Muddus nationalpark** *park* Sweden
125 N8 **Muddy Creek Reservoir** Colorado USA
393 D8 **Mudgal** Karnataka India
393 D7 **Mudhol** Andhra Pradesh India
393 D8 **Mudhol** Karnataka India
390 F7 **Mūdiyah** Yemen
119 R4 **Mudjatik** *watercourse* Saskatchewan Canada
393 D7 **Mudkhed** Maharashtra India
310 3b **Mudo, Punta del** *cape* Canary Islands
376 C3 **Mudon** Myanmar
235 E4 **Mŭdrets** Bulgaria
307 H2 **Mudug** *admin. area* Somalia
235 G5 **Mudurnu** Turkey
235 G5 **Mudurnu** *watercourse* Turkey
223 U5 **Mud'yuga** Russian Federation
309 G2 **Mueda** Mozambique
309 F2 **Muende** Mozambique
162 B4 **Muerte, Meseta de la** *plateau* Argentina
381 G3 **Mufu Shan** *mountain* Hunan China
308 E2 **Mufulira** Zambia
383 J6 **Mug Qu** *watercourse* Qinghai China
306 E5 **Mugewo** Tanzania
394 D6 **Muğla** *admin. area* Turkey
302 D5 **Muhagiriya** Sudan
382 G6 **Muhala** Xinjiang Uygur Zizhiqu China
306 D5 **Muhala** Democratic Republic of Congo
391 L4 **Muhammad Ashraf** Pakistan
302 F3 **Muhammad Qol** Sudan
307 E5 **Muhesi** *watercourse* Tanzania
229 H1 **Mühlberg** Germany
229 L2 **Mühldorf** Austria
437 A2 **Mühlig-Hofmann Mountains** Antarctica
232 F2 **Mühlviertel** *region* Austria
223 N5 **Muhola** Finland
223 O4 **Muhos** Finland
225 L3 **Muhu** *island* Estonia
307 E6 **Muhukuru** Tanzania
309 G2 **Muhula** Mozambique
306 D4 **Muhulu** Democratic Republic of Congo
307 F6 **Muhuwesi** *watercourse* Tanzania
376 E5 **Mui Ca Mau** *island* Vietnam
376 F5 **Mui Ca Na** *island* Vietnam
376 F5 **Mui Kê Ga** *island* Vietnam
376 E3 **Mui Rôn** *island* Vietnam
244 E4 **Muick, Loch** *lake* Scotland UK
309 G2 **Muidumbe** Mozambique
308 D2 **Muié** Angola
242 A2 **Muine Bheag** Ireland
244 E4 **Muir** Aberdeenshire Scotland UK
244 D4 **Muirhill** North Lanarkshire Scotland UK
244 D5 **Muirkirk** East Ayrshire Scotland UK
154 A4 **Muisne** Ecuador
309 G2 **Muite** Mozambique
223 P5 **Mujejärvi** Finland
376 C6 **Muk, Ko** *island* Thailand
375 G3 **Mukah** Malaysia
375 G3 **Mukah** *watercourse* Malaysia
306 C5 **Mukanga** Democratic Republic of Congo
376 E3 **Mukdahan** Thailand
243 F2 **Muker** North Yorkshire England UK
426 3 **Mukeru** Palau
120 M6 **Muketei** *watercourse* Ontario Canada
238 H4 **Mukhanovo** Russian Federation
227 L1 **Mukhavets** Belarus
387 H1 **Mukhen** Russian Federation
124 D3 **Mukilteo** Washington USA
424 F7 **Mukinbudin** WA Australia
374 D4 **Mukomuko** Indonesia
388 J6 **Mukry** Turkmenistan
392 D4 **Muktsar** Punjab India
306 D5 **Mukunsa** Zambia
306 E5 **Mukupa Kaoma** Zambia
388 G4 **Mukur** Kazakhstan
120 G6 **Mukutawa** *watercourse* Manitoba Canada
393 C11 **Mulaku Atoll** Maldives
389 M4 **Mulaly** Kazakhstan
385 K3 **Mulan** Heilongjiang China
309 G2 **Mulanje Mountains** Malawi
155 F5 **Mulato** Brazil
129 H6 **Mulatos** Mexico
163 I5 **Mulâtre, Pointe** *cape* Dominica
130 E3 **Mulberry** Arkansas USA
117 D4 **Mulchatna** *watercourse* Alaska USA
160 C6 **Mulchén** Chile
235 D5 **Muldava** Bulgaria
226 G2 **Mulde** *watercourse* Germany
132 C3 **Mulegé** Mexico
383 I4 **Mulei** Xinjiang Uygur Zizhiqu China
375 I6 **Mules** *island* Indonesia
232 D3 **Mules** Italy
130 B3 **Muleshoe** Texas USA
309 G3 **Mulevala** Mozambique
230 E5 **Mulhacén** *mountain* Spain
229 H3 **Mulhouse** France
375 F4 **Mulia** Indonesia
427 12c **Mulifanua** Samoa
385 L4 **Muling** Heilongjiang China
393 D9 **Mulki** Karnataka India
244 C4 **Mull** *island* Scotland UK
244 F1 **Mull Head** *cape* Scotland UK
242 B3 **Mullagh** Ireland
245 F3 **Mullagh** Ireland
245 B3 **Mullaghglass** Ireland
245 C2 **Mullaghnacross** Ireland
393 E10 **Mullaittivu** Sri Lanka
245 E3 **Mullanalaghta** Ireland
245 D2 **Mullany's Cross** Ireland
125 O5 **Mullen** Nebraska USA
375 G3 **Müller, Pegunungan** *range* Indonesia
126 I4 **Mullet Lake** Michigan USA
424 E7 **Mullewa** WA Australia
226 D4 **Müllheim** Germany
122 H5 **Mulligan** *watercourse* Newfoundland and Labrador Canada
130 B5 **Mullin** Texas USA
245 E3 **Mullingar** Ireland
131 L3 **Mullins** South Carolina USA
129 M2 **Mullinville** Kansas USA
388 F2 **Mullovka** Russian Federation
224 G4 **Mullsjö** Sweden
225 L3 **Mullutu laht** *lake* Estonia
308 C3 **Mulondo** Angola
308 D3 **Mulongo Plain** *plain* Zambia
245 C3 **Mulrany** Ireland
224 G4 **Mulseryd** Sweden
393 E7 **Multai** Madhya Pradesh India
391 L3 **Multan** Pakistan
236 P6 **Multanovy** Russian Federation
223 N5 **Multia** Finland
154 B5 **Multitud** Ecuador
375 G2 **Mulu, Gunung** *mountain* Malaysia
306 D5 **Mulumbe, Monts** *range* Democratic Republic of Congo
125 Q8 **Mulvane** Kansas USA
125 P1 **Mulvihill** Manitoba Canada
242 A2 **Mulvin** Strabane Northern Ireland UK
236 N6 **Mulym'ya** Russian Federation
306 C3 **Muma** Democratic Republic of Congo
393 C7 **Mumbai** Maharashtra India
308 D2 **Mumbeji** Zambia
240 D3 **Mumbles Head** *cape* Wales UK
308 B2 **Mumbondo** Angola
308 C2 **Mumbué** Angola
308 E2 **Mumbwa** Zambia
373 H5 **Mumeng** Papua New Guinea
307 E3 **Mumias** Kenya
Muminabad *see* **Leningrad** Tajikistan
155 G4 **Mumpututu, Serra** *range* Brazil
388 E4 **Mumra** Russian Federation
372 E5 **Mun** Indonesia
386 F4 **Mun-yeŏng** South Korea
375 I5 **Muna** *island* Indonesia
237 Z5 **Muna** *watercourse* Russian Federation
375 I5 **Muna, Selat** *strait* Indonesia
237 Y5 **Munakan** *watercourse* Russian Federation
375 G6 **Muncar** Indonesia
232 D2 **München (Munich)** Germany
118 I3 **Muncho Lake** British Columbia Canada
118 I3 **Muncho Lake Provincial Park** British Columbia Canada
126 I6 **Muncie** Indiana USA
308 B3 **Munda** Angola
392 D5 **Munda** Rajasthan India
426 8 **Munda** Solomon Islands
237 AE5 **Mundar** Russian Federation
158 C3 **Mundaú** Brazil
241 I2 **Mundesley** Norfolk England UK
241 H2 **Mundford** Norfolk England UK
392 B6 **Mundra** Gujarat India
306 E2 **Mundri** Sudan
373 I5 **Mundua Island** Papua New Guinea
425 N6 **Mundubbera** Qld Australia
159 G2 **Mundurucus** Brazil
392 C5 **Mundwa** Rajasthan India
230 E4 **Munera** Spain
392 E6 **Mungaoli** Madhya Pradesh India
309 F3 **Mungári** Mozambique
306 D3 **Mungbere** Democratic Republic of Congo
384 F3 **Mungenmort** Mongolia
392 G6 **Munger** Bihar India
425 K7 **Mungeranie** SA Australia
374 F3 **Munggresak, Tanjung** *cape* Indonesia
228 C5 **Mungia** Spain
425 N7 **Mungindi** NSW Australia
308 C2 **Mungo** Angola
389 P3 **Mungun Tayga, Gora** *mountain* Russian Federation
385 G3 **Munhahaan** Mongolia
308 C2 **Munhango** Angola
383 I3 **Munhehairhan** Mongolia
427 9 **Munia** *island* Fiji
Munich *see* **München** Germany
125 P2 **Munich** North Dakota USA
154 D3 **Municipio de Arauquita** Venezuela
230 D3 **Muñico** Spain
231 F3 **Muniesa** Spain
126 H3 **Munising** Michigan USA
162 C5 **Munizaga** Chile
424 F5 **Munjina** WA Australia
119 W5 **Munk** Manitoba Canada
223 P2 **Munkelva** Norway
302 D2 **Munkhafaḍ al Qaṭṭārah** *pan* Egypt
384 D2 **Munku-Sardyk, Gora** *mountain* Russian Federation
389 R3 **Munku-Sasan, Gora** *mountain* Russian Federation
389 K3 **Munly** *mountain* Kazakhstan
226 F2 **Münnerstadt** Germany
423 6 **Munning, Point** Chatham Islands New Zealand
162 B5 **Muñoz Gamero, Península de** *peninsula* Chile
120 F3 **Munroe Lake** Manitoba Canada
386 E4 **Munsan** South Korea
372 B5 **Munse** Indonesia
379 G4 **Munshiganj** Bangladesh
226 D3 **Munster** France
226 D2 **Münster** Germany
127 Q3 **Munsungan Lake** Maine USA
222 I4 **Munsvattnet** Sweden
306 D5 **Mununga** Zambia
126 I3 **Munuscong Lake** Michigan USA
309 F3 **Munyati** *watercourse* Zimbabwe
223 M3 **Muodoslompolo** Sweden
223 P4 **Muojärvi** *lake* Finland
376 E2 **Mường Khương** Vietnam
376 D2 **Mường Tè** Vietnam
376 E3 **Mường Xén** Vietnam
223 M3 **Muonio** Finland
223 M3 **Muonionalusta** Sweden
222 L3 **Muorjevaara** Sweden
308 C3 **Mupa** Angola
309 G3 **Mupa** *watercourse* Mozambique
309 E3 **Mupfure** *watercourse* Zimbabwe
302 E4 **Muqaddam, Wādī** *watercourse* Sudan
390 F2 **Muqaq** Iraq
307 H3 **Muqdisho (Mogadishu)** Somalia
227 G4 **Mur** *watercourse* Austria
157 B6 **Mura** Brazil
232 G3 **Mura** *watercourse* Croatia
374 B3 **Murai Reservoir** Singapore
387 H3 **Murakami** Japan
162 B4 **Murallón, Cerro** *mountain* Argentina
227 K3 **Muráň** Slovakia
236 K7 **Murashi** Russian Federation
225 M3 **Muraste** Estonia
228 F4 **Murat** France
394 G5 **Murat Nehri** *watercourse* Turkey
228 F5 **Murat-sur-Vèbre** France
235 E5 **Muratlı** Turkey
227 H4 **Murau** Austria
302 F3 **Murayr, Jazīrat** *island* Egypt
302 D1 **Muraysah, Ra's Al** *cape* Libya
226 E5 **Murazzano** Italy
393 C7 **Murbad** Maharashtra India
424 E6 **Murchison** WA Australia
424 E6 **Murchison** *watercourse* WA Australia
423 E5 **Murchison** New Zealand
130 D4 **Murchison** Texas USA
121 Q1 **Murchison, Cape** Nunavut Canada
437 L2 **Murchison, Mount** *mountain* Antarctica
424 F6 **Murchison, Mount** WA Australia
120 K7 **Murchison Island** Ontario Canada
231 F5 **Murcia** Spain
230 F5 **Murcia** *admin. area* Spain
230 F4 **Murcia** *region* Spain
118 K4 **Murdale** British Columbia Canada
125 O5 **Murdo** South Dakota USA
123 F8 **Murdochville** Québec Canada
235 F5 **Mürefte** Turkey
384 G3 **Muren** Mongolia
154 D5 **Mureru, Ilhas** *island* Brazil
234 D2 **Mureş** *admin. area* Romania
234 D2 **Mureş** *watercourse* Romania
228 E5 **Muret** France
388 D5 **Muret** Georgia
234 F3 **Murfatlar** Romania
130 E3 **Murfreesboro** Arkansas USA
131 H3 **Murfreesboro** Tennessee USA
226 E3 **Murg** *watercourse* Germany
391 J2 **Murgap** *watercourse* Afghanistan
424 J2 **Murgenella** NT Australia
391 L3 **Murgha Kibzai** Pakistan
230 E2 **Murgia** Spain
422 2 **Muri** Cook Islands New Zealand
375 F5 **Muria, Gunung** *mountain* Indonesia
157 D8 **Muriaé** Brazil
228 A5 **Murias de Paredes** Spain
156 F5 **Murici** Brazil
308 D1 **Muriege** Angola
374 F3 **Murih** *island* Indonesia
373 J1 **Murilo** *island* Federated States of Micronesia
154 B3 **Murindó** Colombia
234 A4 **Murino** Montenegro
245 B4 **Murirrigane** Ireland
222 L3 **Murjek** Sweden
236 H5 **Murmansk** Russian Federation
435 I2 **Murmansk Rise** *underwater feature* Barents Sea
236 H5 **Murmanskaya Oblast'** *admin. area* Russian Federation
223 R2 **Murmashi** Russian Federation
226 F4 **Murnau** Germany
231 F4 **Muro del Alcoy** Spain
309 I4 **Murodava** *watercourse* Madagascar
388 D2 **Murom** Russian Federation
387 I2 **Muroran** Japan
230 B2 **Muros** Spain
436 Q1 **Murphy, Mount** Antarctica
437 J2 **Murphy Bay** Antarctica
121 X3 **Murphy Head** Newfoundland and Labrador Canada
126 G8 **Murphysboro** Illinois USA
134 C4 **Murra** Nicaragua
244 E2 **Murra** Orkney Islands Scotland UK
425 M8 **Murray** *watercourse* NSW Australia
425 K8 **Murray** *watercourse* SA Australia
118 K5 **Murray** *watercourse* British Columbia Canada
130 G2 **Murray** Kentucky USA
130 C4 **Murray, Lake** Oklahoma USA
131 K3 **Murray, Lake** South Carolina USA
425 K8 **Murray Bridge** SA Australia
79 R4 **Murray Fracture Zone** *underwater feature* Pacific Ocean
424 inset **Murray Hill** Christmas Island Australia
373 G6 **Murray Island** Australia
119 P8 **Murray Lake** Alberta Canada
373 G5 **Murray Range** Papua New Guinea
308 D6 **Murraysburg** South Africa
391 M2 **Murree** Pakistan
226 E3 **Murrhardt** Germany
245 C3 **Murrisk** Ireland
233 F8 **Murro di Porco, Capo** *cape* Italy
245 C3 **Murrough** Ireland
425 M8 **Murrumbidgee** *watercourse* NSW Australia
309 G3 **Murrupula** Mozambique
393 D7 **Murtajapur** Maharashtra India
229 H3 **Murten** Switzerland
232 F5 **Murter** Croatia
118 L6 **Murtle Lake** British Columbia Canada
223 P4 **Murtovaara** Finland
158 D3 **Muru** *watercourse* Brazil
134 C4 **Murubila** Nicaragua
375 G3 **Murud, Gunung** *mountain* Malaysia
237 V5 **Murukta** Russian Federation
375 G3 **Murung** *watercourse* Indonesia
422 G4 **Murupara** New Zealand
427 14 **Mururoa** *reef* French Polynesia
159 G1 **Murutinga** Brazil
130 D4 **Murvaul, Lake** Texas USA
392 E6 **Murwara** Madhya Pradesh India
301 I3 **Murzūq** Libya
394 G5 **Muş** Turkey
394 G5 **Muş** *admin. area* Turkey
308 E3 **Musa** *watercourse* Zambia
225 L4 **Mūša** *watercourse* Lithuania
302 E2 **Mūsá, Jabal (Mount Sinai)** *mountain* Egypt
303 G5 **Mūsa Ālī** *mountain* Eritrea
393 G6 **Musabani** Jharkhand India
306 C4 **Musadi** Democratic Republic of Congo
234 C4 **Musala** *mountain* Bulgaria
374 C3 **Musala** *island* Indonesia
304 B3 **Musala** Sierra Leone
386 F2 **Musan** North Korea
391 H4 **Musandam, Ra's** *cape* Oman
126 F6 **Muscatine** Iowa USA
229 H1 **Müschi** Germany
373 G4 **Muschu Island** Papua New Guinea
130 H3 **Muscle Shoals** Alabama USA
120 H7 **Musclow Lake** Ontario Canada
127 Q5 **Muscongus Bay** Maine USA
306 E5 **Muse** Tanzania
306 C5 **Musenge** Democratic Republic of Congo
306 D4 **Musenge** Democratic Republic of Congo
123 L8 **Musgrave Harbour** Newfoundland and Labrador Canada
424 I6 **Musgrave Ranges** SA Australia
306 C4 **Mushenge** Democratic Republic of Congo
306 B4 **Mushie** Democratic Republic of Congo
224 F5 **Musholm Bugt** *bay* Denmark
306 D6 **Mushoshi** Democratic Republic of Congo
374 E4 **Musi** *watercourse* Indonesia
158 C4 **Musi** Peru
78 P4 **Musicians Seamounts** *underwater feature* Pacific Ocean
390 E5 **Musiddah** Saudi Arabia
308 F4 **Musina** South Africa
126 G2 **Muskeg Lake** Ontario Canada
118 L6 **Muskeg River** Alberta Canada
126 G5 **Muskego** Wisconsin USA
126 H5 **Muskegon** *watercourse* Michigan USA
130 D3 **Muskogee** Oklahoma USA
120 J6 **Muskrat Dam** Ontario Canada
120 J6 **Muskrat Dam Lake** Ontario Canada
118 J3 **Muskwa** *watercourse* British Columbia Canada
118 I4 **Muskwa Ranges** British Columbia Canada
119 V4 **Muskwesi** *watercourse* Manitoba Canada
302 F4 **Musmar** Sudan
225 M5 **Musninkai** Lithuania
308 E2 **Musofu** Zambia
307 E4 **Musoma** Tanzania
306 C5 **Musongoie** Democratic Republic of Congo
123 H7 **Musquaro, Lac** *lake* Québec Canada
123 G10 **Musquodoboit Harbour** Nova Scotia Canada
373 I4 **Mussau Island** Papua New Guinea
244 E5 **Musselburgh** East Lothian Scotland UK
125 K3 **Musselshell** *watercourse* Montana USA
308 C2 **Mussende** Angola
228 E4 **Mussidan** France
308 D2 **Mussuma** Angola
308 D2 **Mussuma** *watercourse* Angola
226 C4 **Mussy-sur-Seine** France
225 N2 **Mustamaa** *island* Finland
130 C3 **Mustang** Oklahoma USA
222 L5 **Mustasaari** Finland
388 G3 **Mustayevo** Russian Federation
383 I3 **Muste** Mongolia
162 C2 **Musters** Argentina
162 C3 **Musters, Lago** *lake* Argentina
163 I1 **Mustique** St Vincent and the Grenadines
135 I4 **Mustique** *island* St Vincent and the Grenadines
223 P2 **Mustola** Finland
120 M7 **Muswabik Lake** Ontario Canada
425 N8 **Muswellbrook** NSW Australia
227 K3 **Muszyna** Poland
394 E6 **Mut** Turkey
225 L2 **Mutala** Finland
422 4 **Mutalau** Niue New Zealand
308 E2 **Mutanda** Zambia
309 F3 **Mutare** Zimbabwe
154 B3 **Mutatá** Colombia
391 I5 **Muṭayli'** Oman
427 14b **Mute, Motu** *island* French Polynesia
390 F3 **Muthanná, Al** *admin. area* Iraq
244 E4 **Muthill** Perth and Kinross Scotland UK
373 G5 **Muting** Indonesia
309 F4 **Mutirikwi, Lake** *lake* Zimbabwe
154 B3 **Mutis** Colombia
372 C6 **Mutis, Gunung** *mountain* Indonesia
309 F3 **Mutoko** Zimbabwe
306 C5 **Mutoto** Democratic Republic of Congo
309 H2 **Mutsamudu** Comoros
306 C6 **Mutshatsha** Democratic Republic of Congo
387 I3 **Mutsu** Japan
387 I3 **Mutsu-wan** *bay* Japan
425 M5 **Muttaburra** Qld Australia
245 C4 **Mutton Island** Ireland
309 G2 **Mutúali** Mozambique
426 8 **Mutuavi** *island* Solomon Islands
157 E6 **Mutuípe** Brazil
157 D7 **Mutum** Brazil
159 H6 **Mutum** Brazil
154 D6 **Mutum** *watercourse* Brazil
159 E3 **Mutumparaná** Brazil
393 E10 **Mutur** Sri Lanka
372 E4 **Muturi** *watercourse* Indonesia
223 O2 **Mutusjärvi** *lake* Finland
238 B3 **Muuga** Estonia
223 N5 **Muurame** Finland
223 N5 **Muurasjärvi** Finland
223 N5 **Muurasjärvi** *lake* Finland
223 N5 **Muuratjärvi** *lake* Finland
223 N3 **Muurola** Finland
223 P5 **Muuruvesi** Finland
373 I6 **Muwa Island** Papua New Guinea
380 D3 **Muxi** Sichuan China
230 B2 **Muxía** Spain
308 B1 **Muxima** Angola
223 Q5 **Muyezerskiy** Russian Federation
306 E4 **Muyinga** Burundi
388 H5 **Mŭynoq** Uzbekistan
309 F2 **Muyombe** Zambia
159 E5 **Muyu Khuchi** Bolivia
305 F4 **Muyuka** Cameroon
382 H6 **Muz Tag** *mountain* Xinjiang Uygur Zizhiqu China
391 M2 **Muzaffarabad** Pakistan
391 L3 **Muzaffargarh** Pakistan
392 D5 **Muzaffarnagar** Uttar Pradesh India
392 F5 **Muzaffarpur** Bihar India
382 G4 **Muzat He** *watercourse* Xinjiang Uygur Zizhiqu China
309 F3 **Muze** Mozambique
236 N5 **Muzhi** Russian Federation
154 C3 **Muzo** Colombia
132 E3 **Múzquiz** Mexico
382 F6 **Muztag** *mountain* Xinjiang Uygur Zizhiqu China
382 E5 **Muztagata** *mountain* Xinjiang Uygur Zizhiqu China
305 G4 **Mvangan** Cameroon
306 D2 **Mvolo** Sudan
305 G4 **Mvoung** *watercourse* Gabon
307 F5 **Mvuha** Tanzania
308 F3 **Mvuma** Zimbabwe
Mwali *see* **Mohéli** Comoros
307 F4 **Mwanga** Tanzania
306 D6 **Mwangalala** Democratic Republic of Congo
307 E5 **Mwanisenga** Tanzania
426 8 **Mwaniwowo** Solomon Islands
306 D5 **Mwanza** Democratic Republic of Congo
309 F3 **Mwanza** Malawi
307 E4 **Mwanza** Tanzania
307 E4 **Mwanza** *admin. area* Tanzania
306 C5 **Mwanzangoma** *watercourse* Democratic Republic of Congo
306 C4 **Mweka** Democratic Republic of Congo
307 F4 **Mwele** Tanzania
308 E2 **Mwenda** Zambia
306 C5 **Mwene-Biji** Democratic Republic of Congo
306 C5 **Mwene-Ditu** Democratic Republic of Congo
308 E2 **Mwense** Zambia
306 D5 **Mweru, Lake** *lake* Democratic Republic of Congo
306 D5 **Mweru Wantipa, Lake** Zambia
308 E3 **Mwezi** *watercourse* Zambia
306 C5 **Mwilambwe** Democratic Republic of Congo
307 F4 **Mwingi** Kenya
308 D2 **Mwinilunga** Zambia
376 E5 **Mỹ Tho** Vietnam
225 N5 **Myadzye, Vozyeral** *lake* Belarus
379 H5 **Myaing** Myanmar
225 O4 **Myakishevo** Russian Federation
237 AF6 **Myakit** Russian Federation
238 H3 **Myaksa** Russian Federation
376 B3 **Myanaung** Myanmar
223 T4 **Myandozero, Ozero** *lake* Russian Federation
383 I3 **Myangad** Mongolia
384 E3 **Myangan Ugalfat Uul** *mountain* Mongolia
376 C2 **Myanmar** *country*
223 Q3 **Myantyuniyemi** Russian Federation
238 F5 **Myatlevo** Russian Federation
376 B3 **Myaungmya** Myanmar
222 inset **Mýdalsjökull** *mountain* Iceland
379 G5 **Myebon** Myanmar
379 H5 **Myede (Aunglan)** Myanmar
376 C4 **Myeik (Mergui)** Myanmar
376 C5 **Myeik Kyunzu** *island* Myanmar
379 H5 **Myingyan** Myanmar
376 C4 **Myinmoletkat** *mountain* Myanmar
379 H4 **Myitkyina** Myanmar
379 H5 **Myittha** Myanmar
232 G2 **Myjava** Slovakia
227 I3 **Myjava** *watercourse* Slovakia
224 E3 **Mykle** *lake* Norway
222 E5 **Myklebost** Norway
222 I3 **Myklebostad** Norway
394 E3 **Mykolaïvs'ka Oblast'** *admin. area* Ukraine
227 J3 **Mykolajiw** Ukraine
234 G2 **Mykolayiv** Ukraine
234 G2 **Mykolayivka** Ukraine
235 D7 **Mykonos** *island* Greece
234 D1 **Mykulychyn** Ukraine
238 B2 **Myllykoski** Finland

223 N5 **Myllymäki** Finland
235 C7 **Mylopotamos** Greece
379 G4 **Mymensingh** Bangladesh
389 L4 **Mynaral** Kazakhstan
237 AB6 **Myndagay** Russian Federation
238 B5 **Myory** Belarus
224 E3 **Myra** Norway
222 I2 **Myre** Norway
222 I2 **Myre** Norway
222 G5 **Myrhaug** Norway
222 L4 **Myrheden** Sweden
235 D6 **Myrina** Greece
222 L5 **Myrkky** Finland
222 I2 **Myrland** Norway
222 G5 **Myrmoen** Norway
222 inset **Mýrnatangi** cape Iceland
234 G1 **Myronivka** Ukraine
245 C5 **Myross** Ireland
131 L4 **Myrtle Beach** South Carolina USA
124 D5 **Myrtle Creek** Oregon USA
124 C5 **Myrtle Point** Oregon USA
235 D8 **Myrtos** Greece
222 I5 **Myrviken** Sweden
237 AL5 **Mys Schmidta** Russian Federation
223 R2 **Mys Skorbeyevskiy** Russian Federation
236 P4 **Mys Taran** Russian Federation
238 H4 **Myshkin** Russian Federation
238 C6 **Myshkovichi** Belarus
227 H1 **Myślibórskie, Jezioro** lake Poland
393 D9 **Mysore** Karnataka India
237 AG5 **Mysovaya** Russian Federation
227 K1 **Myszyniec** Poland
388 D2 **Myt** Russian Federation
235 B6 **Mytikas** Greece
235 E6 **Mytilini** Greece
238 F5 **Mytishchino** Russian Federation
234 E1 **Mytki** Ukraine
232 H2 **Mýtna** Slovakia
125 J6 **Myton** Utah USA
222 inset **Mývatn** lake Iceland
307 F5 **Mziha** Tanzania
309 F2 **Mzimba** Malawi
309 F2 **Mzuzu** Malawi

N

244 B2 **Na h-Eileanan Siar** admin. area Scotland UK
376 E2 **Na Hang** Vietnam
244 B2 **Na Hearadh** island Scotland UK
376 D3 **Na Klang** Thailand
244 C3 **na Sealga, Loch** lake Scotland UK
244 C5 **na Tràille, Rubha** cape Scotland UK
376 E3 **Na Wa** Thailand
226 G3 **Naab** watercourse Germany
128 inset **Nā'ālehu** Hawai'i USA
306 D2 **Na'am** watercourse Sudan
301 F2 **Naama** Algeria
223 P4 **Naamankajärvi** lake Finland
223 L2 **Naantali** Finland
225 Q5 **Naarva** Finland
245 F3 **Naas** Ireland
377 I5 **Nabas** Philippines
390 C2 **Nabatîyé et Tahta** Lebanon
224 I4 **Nabbelund** Sweden
388 F2 **Naberezhnyye Chelny** Russian Federation
116 E6 **Nabesna** Alaska USA
301 I1 **Nabeul** Tunisia
390 E7 **Nabī Shu'ayb, Jabal an** mountain Yemen
307 E3 **Nabilatuk** Uganda
372 E4 **Nabire** Indonesia
123 G7 **Nabisipi** watercourse Québec Canada
304 D2 **Nabou** Burkina Faso
427 9a **Nabouwalu** Fiji
243 G3 **Naburn** York England UK
307 E4 **Nabuyongo Island** island Tanzania
309 H2 **Nacala** Mozambique
134 C4 **Nacaome** Honduras
309 G2 **Nacaroa** Mozambique
158 E3 **Nacebe** Bolivia
232 F2 **Načeradec** Czech Republic
129 N8 **Nacha, Laguna La** bay Mexico
388 E4 **Nachalovo** Russian Federation
122 D4 **Nachicapau, Lac** lake Québec Canada
392 C5 **Nachna** Rajasthan India
376 B5 **Nachuge** Andaman and Nicobar Islands India
121 X3 **Nachvak Fiord** Newfoundland and Labrador Canada
128 B3 **Nacimiento Reservoir** California USA
123 E10 **Nackawic** New Brunswick Canada
226 G1 **Nackel** Germany
132 C2 **Naco** Mexico
130 D5 **Nacogdoches** Texas USA
128 H5 **Nacozari de Garcia** Mexico
132 C2 **Nacozari Viejo** Mexico
241 I2 **Nacton** Suffolk England UK
427 9 **Nacula** island Fiji
245 D4 **Nadanuller Beg** Ireland
304 D2 **Nadawali** Ghana
222 E6 **Naddvik** Norway
427 9a **Nadi** Fiji
427 9a **Nadi Bay** Fiji
392 C6 **Nadiad** Gujarat India
301 F1 **Nador** Morocco
238 F2 **Nadporozh'ye** Russian Federation
427 9a **Naduri** Fiji
227 M3 **Nadvirna** Ukraine
223 S5 **Nadvoitsy** Russian Federation
224 F2 **Næren** lake Norway
222 G4 **Nærøy** island Norway
243 H2 **Nafferton** East Riding of Yorkshire England UK
235 B6 **Nafpaktos** Greece
235 C7 **Nafplio** Greece
390 D4 **Nafūd, An** Saudi Arabia
379 G2 **Nag Qu** watercourse Xizang Zizhiqu China
389 Q3 **Nag. Sangilen** Russian Federation
377 I4 **Naga** Philippines
386 F5 **Naga-shima** island Japan
120 M8 **Nagagami** watercourse Ontario Canada
126 I2 **Nagagami Lake** Ontario Canada
387 H3 **Nagai** Japan
379 H3 **Nagaland** admin. area India
387 H4 **Nagano** Japan
387 H4 **Nagaoka** Japan
379 G3 **Nagaon** Assam India
393 E9 **Nagappattinam** Tamil Nadu India
392 E6 **Nagar** Madhya Pradesh India
300 D5 **Nagara** Mali
393 D10 **Nagarcoil** Tamil Nadu India
393 E8 **Nagarjuna. Sagar** lake Andhra Pradesh India
386 F5 **Nagasaki** Japan
222 J5 **Nagasjön** lake Sweden
386 F4 **Nagato** Japan
392 C5 **Nagaur** Rajasthan India
393 F7 **Nagavali** watercourse Andhra Pradesh India
392 D6 **Nagda** Madhya Pradesh India
129 I2 **Nageezi** New Mexico USA
222 J5 **Naggen** Sweden
307 E3 **Nagichot** Sudan
392 E5 **Nagina** Uttar Pradesh India
392 E5 **Nagla** Uttaranchal India
392 E5 **Nagma** Nepal
238 H4 **Nagor'ye** Russian Federation
393 C7 **Nagothana** Maharashtra India
387 H4 **Nagoya** Japan
307 E3 **Nagpotpot** Sudan
392 E7 **Nagpur** Maharashtra India
393 E7 **Nagri** Chhattisgarh India
131 N3 **Nags Head** North Carolina USA
225 K2 **Nagu** Finland
135 G3 **Nagua** Dominican Republic
121 T2 **Nagvaraaluk, Lac** lake Québec Canada
234 B1 **Nagyhalász** Hungary
232 H3 **Nagykőrös** Hungary
232 H2 **Nagylóc** Hungary
381 J3 **Naha** Japan
388 G7 **Nahaldan** Iran
118 J2 **Nahanni Butte** plain Northwest Territories Canada
118 I2 **Nahanni National Park Reserve** Northwest Territories Canada
118 J2 **Nahanni Range** Northwest Territories Canada
230 E3 **Naharros** Spain
391 I5 **Nahdah** Oman
226 D3 **Nahe** watercourse Germany
385 J3 **Nahe Zhen** Heilongjiang China
394 F6 **Nahr al Furāt** watercourse Syria
390 F3 **Nahr Dijlah** watercourse Iraq
158 C3 **Nahuas** Peru
162 B2 **Nahuel Huapí, Lago** lake Argentina
160 E5 **Nahuel Mapá** Argentina
162 C2 **Nahuel Niyeu** Argentina
131 K5 **Nahunta** Georgia USA
377 I4 **Naic** Philippines
132 D3 **Naica** Mexico
119 S6 **Naicam** Saskatchewan Canada
392 G6 **Naihati** West Bengal India
383 J6 **Naij Gol He** watercourse Qinghai China
372 B6 **Naikliu** Indonesia
240 E3 **Nailsea** North Somerset England UK
241 E3 **Nailsworth** Gloucestershire England UK
122 H4 **Nain** Newfoundland and Labrador Canada
391 H3 **Nā'īn** Iran
427 9a **Naindi** Fiji
392 E5 **Nainital** Uttaranchal India
393 E6 **Nainpur** Madhya Pradesh India
392 D6 **Nainwa** Rajasthan India
427 9 **Nairai** island Fiji
244 E3 **Nairn** Highland Scotland UK
307 F4 **Nairobi** Kenya
307 F4 **Nairobi Area** admin. area Kenya
225 M3 **Naissaar** island Estonia
427 9 **Naitaba** island Fiji
307 F4 **Naivasha** Kenya
307 F4 **Naivasha, Lake** Kenya
390 G3 **Najafābād** Iran
230 E2 **Nájera** Spain
385 J3 **Naji** Nei Mongol Zizhiqu China
390 E5 **Najrān** Saudi Arabia
390 F6 **Najrān** admin. area Saudi Arabia
386 E4 **Naju** South Korea
386 F5 **Nakadori-shima** island Japan
304 D2 **Nakambé** watercourse Burkina Faso
386 G4 **Nakano-shima** island Japan
307 F6 **Nakapanya** Tanzania
386 F5 **Nakatsu** Japan
303 F4 **Nakfa** Eritrea
386 G2 **Nakhodka** Russian Federation
376 D4 **Nakhon Pathom** Thailand
376 E3 **Nakhon Phanom** Thailand
376 D4 **Nakhon Ratchasima** Thailand
376 D4 **Nakhon Sawan** Thailand
376 C5 **Nakhon Si Thammarat** Thailand
376 D5 **Nakhon Srithammarat** admin. area Thailand
376 D3 **Nakhon Thai** Thailand
118 E3 **Nakina** watercourse British Columbia Canada
120 L7 **Nakina** Ontario Canada
306 E4 **Nakivali, Lake** Uganda
116 D7 **Naknek** Alaska USA
307 E5 **Nakonde** Zambia
386 F6 **Nakono-shima** island Japan
234 B3 **Nakovo** Serbia
304 D2 **Nakpanduri** Ghana
224 F5 **Nakskov** Denmark
222 I5 **Näkten** lake Sweden
307 F4 **Nakuru** Kenya
118 M7 **Nakusp** British Columbia Canada
384 F3 **Nalaih** Mongolia
223 O5 **Nälämtöjärvi** lake Finland
309 F4 **Nalázi** Mozambique
234 F3 **Nalbant** Romania
379 G3 **Nalbari** Assam India
388 D5 **Nal'chik** Russian Federation
222 I5 **Nälden** Sweden
393 D8 **Naldurg** Maharashtra India
393 E8 **Nalgonda** Andhra Pradesh India
223 P4 **Näljänkä** Finland
235 G5 **Nallıhan** Turkey
121 S2 **Nallusarqituq, Lac** lake Québec Canada
301 I2 **Nālūt** Libya
376 E2 **Nam Định** Vietnam
376 D3 **Nam Ngum Reservoir** Laos
309 G2 **Namacala** Mozambique
308 C3 **Namacunde** Angola
309 G3 **Namacurra** Mozambique
390 G2 **Namak, Daryācheh-ye** lake Iran
374 E4 **Namang** Indonesia
307 F4 **Namanga** Kenya
389 K5 **Namangan** Uzbekistan
389 K6 **Namangan** admin. area Uzbekistan
306 E3 **Namanyere** Tanzania
309 G2 **Namapa** Mozambique
308 C5 **Namaqualand** region South Africa
426 7 **Namaram** Vanuatu
372 E5 **Namaripi, Tanjung** cape Indonesia
373 G5 **Namas** Indonesia
372 E4 **Namber** Indonesia
307 F5 **Nambiranji** Tanzania
425 O6 **Nambour** Qld Australia
425 O7 **Nambucca Heads** NSW Australia
379 G2 **Namco** lake Xizang Zizhiqu China
222 H4 **Namdalen** region Norway
225 J3 **Nämdö** island Sweden
427 I5 **Namdrik Atoll** Marshall Islands
427 9 **Namenalala** island Fiji
232 H2 **Námestovo** Slovakia
309 G3 **Nametil** Mozambique
119 U5 **Namew Lake** Saskatchewan Canada
379 H4 **Namhsan** Myanmar
309 G2 **Namialo** Mozambique
308 C4 **Namib Desert** Namibia
308 B3 **Namibe** Angola
308 B3 **Namibe** admin. area Angola
308 C4 **Namibia** country Africa
80 F7 **Namibia Abyssal Plain** underwater feature Atlantic Ocean
387 I4 **Namie** Japan
309 G3 **Namiroe** watercourse Mozambique
223 P2 **Nammijärvi** lake Finland
373 J2 **Namoluk** island Federated States of Micronesia
304 E3 **Namon** Togo
373 I1 **Namonuito** island Federated States of Micronesia
81 T4 **Namonuito Atoll** reef Caroline Islands
118 M4 **Nampa** Alberta Canada
124 G5 **Nampa** Idaho USA
300 E5 **Nampala** Mali
386 E3 **Namp'o** North Korea
374 D2 **Nampong Pangkal Kalong** Malaysia
309 G3 **Nampula** Mozambique
309 G2 **Nampula** admin. area Mozambique
372 C4 **Namrole** Indonesia
379 H3 **Namsai** Arunachal Pradesh India
379 H5 **Namsang** Myanmar
222 H4 **Namsen** watercourse Norway
222 G4 **Namsos** Norway
222 H4 **Namsskogan** Norway
222 H4 **Namsvatn** Norway
237 AA6 **Namtsy** Russian Federation
379 H4 **Namtu** Myanmar
118 H7 **Namu** British Columbia Canada
427 I5 **Namu Atoll** Marshall Islands
427 9 **Namuka-i-Lau** island Fiji
309 G3 **Namuli, Monte** mountain Mozambique
309 G2 **Namuno** Mozambique
372 D5 **Namwaan** island Indonesia
308 E3 **Namwala** Zambia
386 E4 **Namwŏn** South Korea
237 AB5 **Namy** Russian Federation
377 G5 **Namyit Island** Spratly Islands
227 H2 **Namysłów** Poland
376 D3 **Nan** Thailand
376 D3 **Nan** admin. area Thailand
426 6b **Nan Madol** ruins Federated States of Micronesia
381 G3 **Nan'an** Jiangxi China
305 G3 **Nana** Cameroon
305 H3 **Nana** watercourse Central African Republic
305 H3 **Nana** watercourse Chad
305 H3 **Nana Bakassa** Central African Republic
306 C6 **Nana Candundo** Angola
305 H3 **Nana-Grébizi, Préfecture de la** admin. area Central African Republic
305 H3 **Nana-Mambéré** admin. area Central African Republic
387 I3 **Nanae** Japan
118 J8 **Nanaimo** British Columbia Canada
387 H4 **Nanao** Japan
381 H4 **Nan'ao Dao** island Guangdong China
158 C1 **Nanay** watercourse Peru
380 E3 **Nanbai** Guizhou China
381 G3 **Nanchang** Jiangxi China
381 I5 **Nanchangshan** Shandong China
380 E2 **Nanchong** Sichuan China
374 B2 **Nancowry** island Andaman and Nicobar Islands India
376 B6 **Nancowry** island Andaman and Nicobar Islands India
228 D4 **Nancras** France
229 H2 **Nancy** France
423 B7 **Nancy Sound** New Zealand
392 E4 **Nanda Devi** mountain Uttaranchal India
392 E4 **Nanda Kot** mountain Uttaranchal India
380 E4 **Nandan** Guangxi Zhuangzu Zizhiqu China
134 C5 **Nandayure** Costa Rica
393 D7 **Nanded** Maharashtra India
309 F4 **Nandi** Zimbabwe
393 E8 **Nandikotkur** Andhra Pradesh India
380 F5 **Nandu** watercourse Hainan China
393 D7 **Nandurbar** Maharashtra India
393 E8 **Nandyal** Andhra Pradesh India
391 M2 **Nanga Parbat** mountain Pakistan
375 G3 **Nangah Bunut** Indonesia
375 F4 **Nangah Dedai** Indonesia
375 G4 **Nangah Embaloh** Indonesia
375 F3 **Nangah Kantuk** Indonesia
375 G3 **Nangah Kemangai** Indonesia
375 F3 **Nangah Ketungau** Indonesia
375 F4 **Nangah Pinoh** Indonesia
375 G4 **Nangah Serawai** Indonesia
375 G3 **Nangah Suruk** Indonesia
375 G3 **Nangah Tempuai** Indonesia
377 I5 **Nangalao** island Philippines
307 F6 **Nanganga** Tanzania
391 L2 **Nangarhār** admin. area Afghanistan
375 F4 **Nangataman** Indonesia
375 F4 **Nangatayap** Indonesia
304 E3 **Nangbéto, Retenue de** lake Togo
229 F2 **Nangis** France
382 F6 **Nangong Kangri** Xinjiang Uygur Zizhiqu China
386 E3 **Nangnim-sanmaek** North Korea
307 E3 **Nangolet** Sudan
385 H5 **Nangong** Hebei China
223 P2 **Nangujärvi** lake Finland
223 O2 **Nanguvuono** bay Finland
385 H4 **Nanhaoqian** Hebei China
391 H3 **Nānī Ghūnd** Afghanistan
118 H6 **Nanika Lake** British Columbia Canada
390 G3 **Nanizak** Iran
381 I3 **Nanji Shan** range Zhejiang China
380 C3 **Nanjian** Yunnan China
380 E2 **Nanjiang** Sichuan China
381 F4 **Nanjie** Guangdong China
381 H2 **Nanjing** Jiangsu China
309 G1 **Nanjirinji** Tanzania
381 G3 **Nankang** Jiangxi China
386 G5 **Nankoku** Japan
308 C3 **Nankova** Angola
392 D4 **Nankun** mountain Jammu and Kashmir India/Pakistan
426 6b **Nanlaud** mountain Federated States of Micronesia
385 H6 **Nanle** Henan China
381 H2 **Nanling** Anhui China
380 F4 **Nanliu Jiang** watercourse Guangxi Zhuangzu Zizhiqu China
385 I6 **Nanma** Shandong China
379 F3 **Nanmulinxue** Xizang Zizhiqu China
380 E3 **Nanning** Guangxi Zhuangzu Zizhiqu China
424 E8 **Nannup** WA Australia
117 O6 **Nanortalik** Greenland
380 D4 **Nanpan Jiang** watercourse Yunnan China
392 E5 **Nanpara** Uttar Pradesh India
381 F4 **Nanpeng Dao** island Guangdong China
385 H5 **Nanpi** Hebei China
381 H3 **Nanping** Fujian China
380 D1 **Nanping** Sichuan China
381 H3 **Nanpu** Fujian China
381 I2 **Nanqiao** Shanghai China
381 H3 **Nanri Dao** island Fujian China
381 F4 **Nansan Dao** island Guangdong China
381 J3 **Nansei-shotō (Ryukyu Islands, Japan)** Japan
434 N1 **Nansen Basin** underwater feature Arctic Ocean
117 O2 **Nansen Land** region Greenland
117 J2 **Nansen Sound** bay Nunavut Canada
380 D4 **Nansha** Yunnan China
377 G5 **Nanshan Island** Spratly Islands
381 G4 **Nanshui Shuiku** lake Guangdong China
237 AD7 **Nansikan, Ostrov** island Russian Federation
307 E4 **Nansio** Tanzania
121 R2 **Nantais, Lac** lake Québec Canada
240 C2 **Nantcwnlle** Ceredigion Wales UK
228 D3 **Nantes** France
240 D1 **Nantglyn** Denbighshire Wales UK
374 D5 **Nanti, Bukit** mountain Indonesia
228 E3 **Nantiat** France
127 M6 **Nanticoke** Pennsylvania USA
119 O7 **Nanton** Alberta Canada
381 H2 **Nantong** Jiangsu China
381 H4 **Nant'ou** Taiwan China
436 U2 **Nantucket Inlet** bay Antarctica
127 Q6 **Nantucket Island** Massachusetts USA
127 P6 **Nantucket Sound** bay Massachusetts USA
309 G2 **Nantulo** Mozambique
240 E1 **Nantwich** Cheshire England UK
427 9 **Nanuku Passage** strait Fiji
427 9a **Nanukuloa** Fiji
426 1 **Nanumanga** island Tuvalu
426 1 **Nanumea** island Tuvalu
157 D7 **Nanuque** Brazil
372 C2 **Nanusa, Kepulauan** island Indonesia
380 D3 **Nanxi** Sichuan China
380 D4 **Nanxi He** watercourse Yunnan China
381 G3 **Nanxiong** Guangdong China
381 F2 **Nanyang** Henan China
381 G1 **Nanyang Hu** lake Shandong China
381 H2 **Nanyi Hu** lake Anhui China
387 I3 **Nanyo** Japan
307 F3 **Nanyuki** Kenya
379 H3 **Nanyung** Myanmar
381 H4 **Nanzhao** Fujian China
381 F1 **Nanzhao** Henan China
381 F2 **Nanzhou** Hunan China
231 G4 **Nao, Cabo de la** cape Spain
161 H4 **Não Me Toque** Brazil
121 T6 **Naococane, Lac** lake Québec Canada
379 F4 **Naogaon** Bangladesh
375 G3 **Naong, Bukit** mountain Malaysia
392 D4 **Naoshehra** Jammu and Kashmir India/Pakistan
235 D7 **Naousa** Greece
380 F5 **Naozhou Dao** island Guangdong China
124 D7 **Napa** California USA
309 G2 **Napaha** Mozambique
116 H5 **Napaktulik Lake** Nunavut Canada
161 G6 **Napaleofú** Argentina
236 P4 **Napalkovo** Russian Federation
372 E4 **Napanwainami** Indonesia
392 C5 **Napasar** Rajasthan India
127 P6 **Napeague Bay** New York USA
126 G6 **Naperville** Illinois USA
123 J7 **Napetipi** watercourse Québec Canada
379 I4 **Naphan** Myanmar
376 D3 **Naphèng** Laos
372 E4 **Napido** Indonesia
422 G4 **Napier** New Zealand
424 I4 **Napier, Mount** NT Australia
437 D2 **Napier Mountains** Antarctica
119 U8 **Napinka** Manitoba Canada
Naples see **Napoli** Italy
131 K7 **Naples** Florida USA
125 K6 **Naples** Utah USA
380 E4 **Napo** Guangxi Zhuangzu Zizhiqu China
154 B5 **Napo** watercourse Ecuador
154 C5 **Napo** watercourse Peru
125 P3 **Napoleon** North Dakota USA
233 F6 **Napoli (Naples)** Italy
160 F6 **Napostá** Argentina
427 14 **Napuka** island French Polynesia
388 E7 **Naqadeh** Iran
154 D4 **Naquén, Serranía** range Colombia
225 J4 **När** Sweden
392 B6 **Nara** Gujarat India
300 E5 **Nara** Mali
129 K3 **Nara Visa** New Mexico USA
225 N5 **Narach, Vozyera** lake Belarus
425 K7 **Naracoorte** SA Australia
383 H3 **Naran** Mongolia
383 I2 **Naranbulag** Mongolia
154 B5 **Naranjal** Ecuador
154 B5 **Naranjal** Peru
155 C3 **Naranjo** Costa Rica
133 F4 **Naranjos** Mexico
376 D6 **Narathiwat** Thailand
376 D6 **Narathiwat** admin. area Thailand
379 G4 **Narayanganj** Bangladesh
393 E6 **Narayanganj** Madhya Pradesh India
234 D1 **Narayev** Ukraine
240 C3 **Narbeth** Pembrokeshire Wales UK
228 F5 **Narbonne** France
241 H2 **Narborough** Norfolk England UK
230 C2 **Narcea** watercourse Spain
376 B4 **Narcondam Island** Andaman and Nicobar Islands India
118 J6 **Narcosli Creek** British Columbia Canada
373 I5 **Narega Island** Papua New Guinea
224 G2 **Naren** lake Sweden
76 L7 **Nares Deep** underwater feature Sargasso Sea
117 L3 **Nares Strait** Canada/Greenland
227 M1 **Narew** watercourse Belarus
227 L1 **Narew** Poland
227 L1 **Narew** watercourse Poland
227 L1 **Narewka** Poland
393 D8 **Nargund** Karnataka India
223 O5 **Närhilä** Finland
379 G4 **Naria** Bangladesh
154 B4 **Nariño** admin. area Colombia
129 G7 **Narizon, Punta** cape Mexico
392 D4 **Narkanda** Himachal Pradesh India
223 O3 **Narkaus** Finland
224 H3 **Närke** region Sweden
223 M3 **Narken** Sweden
393 D6 **Narmada** watercourse Madhya Pradesh India
392 D5 **Narnaul** Haryana India
233 E5 **Narni** Italy
377 I5 **Naro** island Philippines
238 G5 **Naro-Fominsk** Russian Federation
307 F4 **Narok** Kenya
230 B2 **Narón** Spain
388 D2 **Narovchat** Russian Federation
426 7 **Narovorovo** Vanuatu
222 L5 **Närpes** Finland
425 N7 **Narrabri** NSW Australia
244 C4 **Narrachan** Argyll and Bute Scotland UK
425 M8 **Narrandera** NSW Australia
118 K5 **Narraway** watercourse British Columbia Canada
424 F8 **Narrogin** WA Australia
425 N8 **Narromine** NSW Australia
119 S5 **Narrow Hills Provincial Park** Saskatchewan Canada
117 O6 **Narsarsuaq** Greenland
122 N1 **Narsatsiaat** Greenland
224 H2 **Närsen** lake Sweden
379 G4 **Narsingdi** Bangladesh
234 E3 **Năruja** Romania
227 K1 **Naruszewo** Poland
225 O3 **Narva** Estonia
223 M2 **Närvä** Sweden
225 N3 **Narva Bay** Estonia
238 B3 **Narva Zaliv** bay Russian Federation
222 J2 **Narvik** Norway
392 D5 **Narwana** Haryana India
236 L5 **Nar'yan-Mar** Russian Federation
389 O4 **Narymskiy Khrebet** range Kazakhstan
389 L5 **Naryn** Kyrgyzstan
389 L5 **Naryn** admin. area Kyrgyzstan
389 L5 **Naryn** watercourse Kyrgyzstan
305 F3 **Nasarawa** Nigeria
154 C5 **Nasayá** Colombia
222 I6 **Näsberg** Sweden
155 F4 **Nascente** Brazil
129 H2 **Naschitti** New Mexico USA
240 E3 **Nash** Newport Wales UK
130 B2 **Nash** Oklahoma USA
154 B5 **Nashicta** Ecuador
393 C7 **Nashik** Maharashtra India
125 L2 **Nashua** Montana USA
127 P5 **Nashua** New Hampshire USA
130 E4 **Nashville** Arkansas USA
126 G7 **Nashville** Illinois USA
125 P8 **Nashville** Kansas USA
130 **Nashville** Tennessee USA
304 D2 **Nasia** Ghana
304 D2 **Nasia** watercourse Ghana
232 H4 **Našice** Croatia
375 F3 **Nasilat** Indonesia
307 E2 **Nasir** Sudan
302 E3 **Nāşir, Buḩayrat** lake Egypt
392 D5 **Nasirabad** Rajasthan India
391 J4 **Nasirabad** Pakistan
391 K4 **Nasirabad** Pakistan
391 I3 **Nask** Iran
122 G5 **Naskaupi** watercourse Newfoundland and Labrador Canada
224 I3 **Näsnaren** lake Sweden
233 F7 **Naso** Italy
306 D6 **Nasondoye** Democratic Republic of Congo
427 9a **Nasorolevu** mountain Fiji
393 E7 **Naspur** Andhra Pradesh India
116 G7 **Nass** watercourse British Columbia Canada
223 M2 **Näšša** island Norway
305 F3 **Nassarawa** admin. area Nigeria
134 E1 **Nassau** Bahamas
422 1 **Nassau** island Cook Islands New Zealand
127 O5 **Nassau** New York USA
426 1 **Nassau Island** Cook Islands New Zealand
131 K5 **Nassau Sound** Florida USA
127 N8 **Nassawadox** Virginia USA
226 F4 **Nassereith** Austria
304 D3 **Nassian** Côte d'Ivoire
117 N5 **Nassuttooq** bay Greenland
222 J4 **Nästansjö** Sweden
117 L7 **Nastapoca** watercourse Québec Canada
117 L7 **Nastapoka Islands** Nunavut Canada
222 I5 **Nästelsjön** lake Sweden
225 M2 **Nastola** Finland
377 I4 **Nasugbu** Philippines
225 L3 **Nasva** Estonia
225 P4 **Nasva** Russian Federation
308 E4 **Nata** Botswana
308 E4 **Nata** watercourse Botswana
154 C4 **Natagaima** Colombia
156 F4 **Natal** Brazil
159 F2 **Natal** Brazil
124 H2 **Natal** British Columbia Canada
374 C3 **Natal** Indonesia
80 H8 **Natal Basin** underwater feature Indian Ocean
130 B6 **Natalia** Texas USA
122 G6 **Natashquan** watercourse Newfoundland and Labrador Canada
123 H7 **Natashquan** Québec Canada
123 H7 **Natashquan** watercourse Québec Canada
123 H7 **Natashquan, Pointe de** Québec Canada
123 H7 **Natashquan Est** watercourse Québec Canada
130 E5 **Natchez** Louisiana USA
130 F5 **Natchez** Mississippi USA
130 E5 **Natchitoches** Louisiana USA
229 H3 **Naters** Switzerland
427 9a **Natewa Bay** Fiji
376 B3 **Nathaingchaung** Myanmar
231 H3 **Nati, Punta** cape Spain
304 E3 **Natia-Boani** Burkina Faso
425 L9 **Natimuk** Vic Australia
118 I5 **Nation** watercourse British Columbia Canada
128 D4 **National City** California USA
155 H3 **Nationale** French Guiana
304 E2 **Natitingou** Benin
121 N1 **Native Bay** Nunavut Canada
159 E4 **Natividad** Bolivia
132 B3 **Natividad, Isla** island Mexico
157 C5 **Natividade** Brazil
379 H5 **Natmauk** Myanmar
379 H5 **Natogyi** Myanmar
129 M1 **Natoma** Kansas USA
129 H6 **Nátora** Mexico
379 F4 **Natore** Bangladesh
387 I3 **Natori** Japan
307 F4 **Natron, Lake** lake Tanzania
376 B3 **Nattalin** Myanmar
393 E9 **Nattam** Tamil Nadu India
222 L3 **Nattavaara** Sweden
223 N2 **Nattvatnet** lake Norway
121 T4 **Natuak, Lac** lake Québec Canada
122 F5 **Natuashish** Newfoundland and Labrador Canada
374 E3 **Natuna, Kepulauan** island Indonesia
374 F3 **Natuna Besar** island Indonesia
424 E8 **Naturaliste, Cape** WA Australia
81 P8 **Naturaliste Plateau** underwater feature Indian Ocean
125 K7 **Naturita** Colorado USA
226 F4 **Naturno** Italy
308 C4 **Nauchas** Namibia
307 F7 **Nauela** Mozambique
161 I3 **Naufragados, Ponta dos** cape Brazil
377 I4 **Naujan, Lake** lake Philippines
225 L4 **Naujoji Akmenė** Lithuania
392 C5 **Naukh** Rajasthan India
242 B3 **Naul** Ireland
308 B3 **Naulila** Angola
373 I4 **Nauna Island** Papua New Guinea
160 D6 **Naunaucó, Sierra** range Argentina
379 H3 **Naung-Mon** Myanmar
388 E5 **Naurskaya** Russian Federation
426 4 **Nauru** island Nauru
426 4 **Nauru** country Pacific Ocean
427 9a **Nausori** Fiji
222 K3 **Nausta** Sweden
222 K3 **Naustajaure** lake Sweden
222 K3 **Nautijaur** Sweden
225 K2 **Nautimaa** island Finland
133 F4 **Nautla** Mexico
223 P2 **Nautsi** Russian Federation
224 C2 **Nautsund** Norway
391 L2 **Nāv** Afghanistan
306 D3 **Nava** watercourse Democratic Republic of Congo
132 E2 **Nava** Mexico
232 B4 **Nava, Colle di** pass Italy
230 D3 **Nava de la Asunción** Spain
228 F5 **Navacelles, Cirque de** point of interest France
230 D4 **Navahermosa** Spain
129 I2 **Navajo Reservoir** New Mexico USA
230 D3 **Navalcán** Spain
245 F3 **Navan** Ireland
225 O5 **Navapolatsk** Belarus
237 AK6 **Navarin, Mys** cape Russian Federation
162 C6 **Navarino, Isla** island Chile
222 J5 **Navarn** lake Sweden
230 F2 **Navarra** admin. area Spain
228 D5 **Navarra** region Spain
228 C5 **Navarrete** Spain
130 C5 **Navarro Mills Lake** Texas USA
231 G3 **Navàs** Spain
230 C4 **Navas del Madroño** Spain
129 N5 **Navasota** watercourse Texas USA
135 F3 **Navassa Islands** US territory Caribbean
122 M1 **Navdlúnguaq** bay Greenland
230 C3 **Nave de Haver** Portugal
244 D2 **Naver** watercourse Scotland UK
244 D2 **Naver, Loch** lake Scotland UK
160 E5 **Navia** Argentina
230 C2 **Navia** Spain
230 C2 **Navia** watercourse Spain
230 C2 **Navia de Suarna** Spain
160 D5 **Navidad** Chile
130 C6 **Navidad** watercourse Texas USA
135 G2 **Navidad Bank** underwater feature Atlantic Ocean
229 G3 **Navilly** France
157 A8 **Naviraí** Brazil
226 F4 **Navis** Austria
427 9 **Naviti** island Fiji
373 G6 **Naviu Island** Papua New Guinea
388 J6 **Navoiy** Uzbekistan
388 I5 **Navoiy** admin. area Uzbekistan
129 H7 **Navojoa** Mexico
132 D3 **Navolato** Mexico
238 H1 **Navolok** Russian Federation
224 H4 **Nävragöl** Sweden
304 D2 **Navrongo** Ghana
393 C7 **Navsari** Gujarat India
427 9a **Navua** Fiji
427 9a **Navua** watercourse Fiji
391 K2 **Naw-e Tondaki** Afghanistan
394 F7 **Nawá** Syria
391 L4 **Nawa Kot** Pakistan
379 F4 **Nawabganj** Bangladesh
391 K4 **Nawabshah** Pakistan
392 F6 **Nawada** Bihar India
392 D5 **Nawalgarh** Rajasthan India
391 L3 **Nawan Kot** Pakistan
393 C7 **Nawapur** Maharashtra India
379 H4 **Nawngcho** Myanmar
388 E6 **Naxçhevan'** Azerbaijan
235 D7 **Naxos** island Greece
393 F7 **Nayagarh** Orissa India
132 D4 **Nayarit** admin. area Mexico
427 9 **Nayau** island Fiji
391 K2 **Naylowr** Afghanistan
387 I2 **Nayoro** Japan
379 H5 **Naypyidaw** Myanmar
309 G2 **Nayuchi** Malawi
157 E6 **Nazaré** Brazil
230 B4 **Nazaré** Portugal
129 K3 **Nazareth** Texas USA
80 K6 **Nazareth Bank** underwater feature Indian Ocean
426 7 **Nazareth-Rantis** Vanuatu
132 D3 **Nazas** Mexico
158 C4 **Nazca** Peru
79 Y9 **Nazca Ridge** underwater feature Pacific Ocean
381 K3 **Naze** Japan
241 I3 **Naze, The** cape England UK
390 C3 **Nazerat (Nazareth)** Israel
379 H3 **Nazira** Assam India
225 P3 **Naziya** Russian Federation
118 J6 **Nazko** British Columbia Canada
118 J6 **Nazko** watercourse British Columbia Canada
307 F2 **Nazrēt** Ethiopia
389 K2 **Nazyvayevsk** Russian Federation
300 D5 **Nbâk** Mauritania
306 D5 **Nchelenge** Zambia
308 D4 **Ncojane** Botswana
307 E4 **Ndala** Tanzania
308 B1 **N'dalantando** Angola
304 E3 **Ndali** Benin
305 I3 **Ndanda** Central African Republic
300 C5 **Ndande** Senegal
375 I6 **Ndao** island Indonesia
305 F3 **Ndeji** Nigeria
305 I3 **Ndélé** Central African Republic
305 G5 **Ndendé** Gabon
305 H3 **Ndim** Central African Republic
305 G5 **Ndindi** Gabon
300 C6 **Ndioum Guènt** Senegal
305 H2 **N'Djamena** Chad
305 I3 **Ndji** watercourse Central African Republic
305 G5 **Ndjolé** Gabon
305 F5 **Ndogo, Lagune** lake Gabon
305 G3 **Ndok** Cameroon
308 E2 **Ndola** Zambia
305 G3 **Ndop** Cameroon
304 D3 **Ndouci** Côte d'Ivoire
305 H3 **Ndoumbou** Central African Republic
235 A5 **Ndroq** Albania
426 7 **Ndui Ndui** Vanuatu
426 8a **Nduindui** Solomon Islands
307 F6 **Ndumbwe** Tanzania
306 D3 **Nduye** watercourse Democratic Republic of Congo
235 D6 **Nea Artaki** Greece
235 C5 **Nea Efesos** Greece
235 C5 **Nea Kerdylia** Greece
235 C7 **Nea Kios** Greece
235 B6 **Nea Manolás** Greece
235 C5 **Nea Poteidaia** Greece
235 B6 **Nea Selévkia** Greece
245 F2 **Neagh, Lough** lake Northern Ireland UK
118 I8 **Neah Bay** Washington USA
121 Q2 **Neakongut, Baie** bay Québec Canada
245 C3 **Neale** Ireland
425 J6 **Neales** watercourse SA Australia
234 E2 **Neanmţ** admin. area Romania
235 C7 **Neapoli** Greece
237 AJ8 **Near Islands** Alaska USA
240 D3 **Neath** Neath Port Talbot Wales UK
240 D3 **Neath Port Talbot** admin. area Wales UK
304 D2 **Nebbou** Burkina Faso
372 B6 **Nebe** Indonesia
227 H5 **Nebljusi** Croatia
238 E3 **Nebolchi** Russian Federation
114 **Nebraska** admin. area USA
233 F8 **Nebrodi, Monti** range Italy
306 D3 **Nebulu** Democratic Republic of Congo
426 7 **Nécé** New Caledonia
126 F4 **Necedah** Wisconsin USA
118 I6 **Nechako** watercourse British Columbia Canada
130 D5 **Neches** watercourse Texas USA
154 C2 **Nechí** Colombia
135 F6 **Nechí** watercourse Colombia
227 G1 **Nechlin** Germany
231 J5 **Nechmeya** Algeria
226 E3 **Neckar** watercourse Germany
78 O6 **Necker Ridge** underwater feature Pacific Ocean

161 G6 **Necochea** Argentina
154 B2 **Necoclí** Colombia
306 A4 **Necuto** Angola
225 O5 **Nedal'** Belarus
222 H5 **Nedalshytta** Norway
234 D4 **Nedan** Bulgaria
222 J5 **Nedansjö** Sweden
238 G5 **Nedel'noye** Russian Federation
130 E6 **Nederland** Texas USA
225 M5 **Nedingis** *lake* Lithuania
121 S4 **Nedlouc** *watercourse* Québec Canada
224 G3 **Nedre Fryken** *bay* Sweden
224 E2 **Nedre Hermdalsvatn** *lake* Norway
222 L3 **Nedre Kuouka** Sweden
224 H3 **Nedre Malingbosjön** *lake* Sweden
224 E3 **Nedre Tokke** *lake* Norway
226 D1 **Neede** Netherlands
241 I2 **Needham Market** Suffolk England UK
118 L8 **Needles** British Columbia Canada
128 E3 **Needles** California USA
241 F4 **Needles, The** *cape* England UK
129 K3 **Needmore** Texas USA
130 D6 **Needville** Texas USA
119 V8 **Neelin** Manitoba Canada
161 G3 **Ñeembucú** *admin. area* Paraguay
392 D6 **Neemuch** Madhya Pradesh India
119 V7 **Neepawa** Manitoba Canada
117 L4 **Neergaard Lake** Nunavut Canada
119 N5 **Neerlandia** Alberta Canada
226 F1 **Neetze** Germany
303 F5 **Nefas Mewch'a** Ethiopia
301 H2 **Nefta** Tunisia
388 F6 **Nefteçal** Azerbaijan
388 F3 **Neftegorsk** Russian Federation
388 G2 **Neftekamsk** Russian Federation
236 P6 **Nefteyugansk** Russian Federation
301 H1 **Nefza** Tunisia
306 B5 **Negage** Angola
300 E6 **Négala** Mali
375 G4 **Negara** Indonesia
375 G6 **Negara** Indonesia
375 G4 **Negara** *watercourse* Indonesia
307 F2 **Negēlē** Ethiopia
374 D3 **Negeri Sembilan** *admin. area* Malaysia
308 B2 **Negola** Angola
309 G2 **Negomane** Mozambique
393 E10 **Negombo** Sri Lanka
235 C5 **Negotino** Macedonia
129 J3 **Negra** New Mexico USA
162 C6 **Negra, Punta** *cape* Chile
160 D3 **Negra, Salar Punta** *lake* Chile
157 A7 **Negra, Serra** *range* Brazil
376 B4 **Negrais, Cape** Myanmar
232 D4 **Negrar** Italy
230 E5 **Negratín, Embalse de** *lake* Spain
230 B2 **Negreira** Spain
227 L4 **Negreni** Romania
301 H2 **Négrine** Algeria
160 E6 **Negro** *watercourse* Argentina
159 F4 **Negro** *watercourse* Bolivia
157 B9 **Negro** *watercourse* Brazil
161 G3 **Negro** *watercourse* Paraguay
161 H5 **Negro** *watercourse* Uruguay
129 N8 **Negro, Lago Mar** *bay* Mexico
160 E6 **Negro Muerto** Argentina
160 E6 **Negro Muerto, Laguna** *lake* Argentina
377 I5 **Negros** *island* Philippines
126 I2 **Negwazu Lake** Ontario Canada
234 E3 **Nehoiu** Romania
308 C3 **Nehone** Angola
383 L4 **Nei Mongol Zizhiqu** *admin. area* China
427 10 **Neiafu** Tonga
223 P2 **Neiden** Norway
119 R7 **Neidpath** Saskatchewan Canada
310 7a **Neiges, Piton des** *volcano* Réunion
380 E2 **Neijiang** Sichuan China
126 F4 **Neillsville** Wisconsin USA
79 R10 **Neilson Reef** French Polynesia
244 D5 **Neilston** East Renfrewshire Scotland UK
227 H2 **Neiße** *watercourse* Poland
154 C4 **Neiva** Colombia
120 G3 **Nejanilini Lake** Manitoba Canada
307 F2 **Nejo** Ethiopia
307 F2 **Nek'emte** Ethiopia
120 D4 **Nekweaga Bay** Saskatchewan Canada
230 C3 **Nelas** Portugal
224 E3 **Nelaug** *lake* Norway
237 AF5 **Nelemnoye** Russian Federation
238 E4 **Nelidovo** Russian Federation
125 P5 **Neligh** Nebraska USA
237 AC7 **Nel'kan** Russian Federation
223 P2 **Nellim** Finland
393 E8 **Nellore** Andhra Pradesh India
160 F4 **Nelson** Argentina
120 G5 **Nelson** *watercourse* Manitoba Canada
423 E5 **Nelson** New Zealand
243 F3 **Nelson** Lancashire England UK
128 E3 **Nelson** Nevada USA
373 I6 **Nelson, Cape** Papua New Guinea
162 A5 **Nelson, Estrecho** *strait* Chile
118 I3 **Nelson Forks** British Columbia Canada
119 V5 **Nelson House** Manitoba Canada
125 L2 **Nelson Reservoir** Montana USA
309 F5 **Nelspruit** South Africa
373 J2 **Nema** *island* Federated States of Micronesia
388 F1 **Nema** Russian Federation
300 E5 **Néma** Mauritania
225 L5 **Neman** Russian Federation
126 J3 **Nemegos** Ontario Canada
126 J3 **Nemegosenda Lake** Ontario Canada
227 J4 **Németkér** Hungary
121 Q7 **Némiscau** Québec Canada
121 Q7 **Némiscau** *watercourse* Québec Canada
121 Q7 **Némiscau, Lac** *lake* Québec Canada
226 B3 **Nemours** France
387 J2 **Nemuro** Japan
227 L2 **Nemyriv** Ukraine
385 K2 **Nen Jiang** *watercourse* Heilongjiang China
162 B2 **Nena, Punta** *cape* Chile
245 D4 **Nenagh** Ireland
116 E6 **Nenana** Alaska USA
426 8 **Nendö** *island* Solomon Islands
241 G2 **Nene** *watercourse* England UK
236 M5 **Nenetskiy Avtonomnyy Okrug** *admin. area* Russian Federation
427 14 **Nengo-Nengo** *island* French Polynesia
385 K2 **Nenjiang** Heilongjiang China
223 U4 **Nenokса** Russian Federation
426 6a **Nenom, Mochun** *strait* Federated States of Micronesia
134 B4 **Nentón** Guatemala
235 C6 **Neo Monastiri** Greece
426 6a **Neoch** *reef* Federated States of Micronesia
126 D8 **Neodesha** Kansas USA
235 B6 **Néos Oropós** Greece
126 D8 **Neosho** *watercourse* Kansas USA
126 D8 **Neosho** Missouri USA
129 O2 **Neosho Falls** Kansas USA
129 O1 **Neosho Rapids** Kansas USA
237 W7 **Nepa** Russian Federation
237 W7 **Nepa** *watercourse* Russian Federation
392 F5 **Nepal** *country*
392 E5 **Nepalganj** Nepal
124 J7 **Nephi** Utah USA
117 M9 **Nepisiguit** *watercourse* New Brunswick Canada
306 D3 **Nepoko** *watercourse* Democratic Republic of Congo
131 K5 **Neptune Beach** Florida USA
436 U1 **Neptune Range** Antarctica
233 E5 **Nera** *watercourse* Italy
237 AE6 **Nera** *watercourse* Russian Federation
228 E4 **Nérac** France
425 O7 **Nerang** Qld Australia
385 H2 **Nerchinsk** Russian Federation
385 I2 **Nerchinskiy Khrebet** *range* Russian Federation
240 D1 **Nercwys** Flintshire Wales UK
224 H2 **Nerdе Gärdsjö** Sweden
222 F5 **Nerdvika** Norway
228 D4 **Néré** France
225 M4 **Nereta** Latvia
232 H5 **Neretva** *watercourse* Bosnia and Herzegovina
122 N2 **Neria** Greenland
122 N2 **Neria** *bay* Greenland
308 D3 **Neriquinha** Angola
225 M5 **Neris** *watercourse* Lithuania
116 D7 **Nerka, Lake** Alaska USA
223 M5 **Nerkoonjärvi** *lake* Finland
238 G4 **Nerl'** Russian Federation
222 E5 **Nerland** Norway
224 C1 **Nerlandsøy** *island* Norway
154 A6 **Ñermete, Punta** *cape* Peru
226 B4 **Nérondes** France
237 AG5 **Nerpich'ye, Ozero** *lake* Russian Federation
230 E4 **Nerpio** Spain
234 F3 **Nerushay** Ukraine
230 C5 **Nerva** Spain
226 G5 **Nervesa** Italy
229 I4 **Nervi** Italy
237 Z7 **Neryungri** Russian Federation
226 C1 **Nes** Netherlands
236 J5 **Nes'** Russian Federation
224 E2 **Nesbyen** Norway
227 H2 **Neschwitz** Germany
234 E4 **Nesebŭr** Bulgaria
222 F5 **Neset** Norway
222 E5 **Nesjestranda** Norway
222 G5 **Nesjøen** *lake* Norway
120 L6 **Neskantaga** Ontario Canada
222 inset **Neskaupstaður** Iceland
116 B5 **Neskynpil'gyn, Laguna** Russian Federation
226 B3 **Nesle** France
222 H3 **Nesna** Norway
222 H3 **Nesøya** *island* Norway
244 D3 **Ness, Loch** *lake* Scotland UK
125 P7 **Ness City** Kansas USA
223 P1 **Nesseby** Norway
118 D3 **Nesselrode, Mount** British Columbia/Alaska Canada/USA
121 S8 **Nestaocano** *watercourse* Québec Canada
228 E5 **Neste** *watercourse* France
225 L5 **Nesterov** Russian Federation
238 H3 **Nesterovo** Russian Federation
242 E3 **Neston** Cheshire England UK
241 E3 **Neston** Wiltshire England UK
235 D5 **Nestos** *watercourse* Greece
234 F2 **Nestoyita** Ukraine
224 D3 **Nesvatn** *lake* Norway
303 I5 **Nët** Yemen
390 C3 **Netanya** Israel
242 E1 **Nether Dalgliesh** Scottish Borders Scotland UK
240 C3 **Nethercott** Devon England UK
226 **Netherlands** *country* Europe
135 G4 **Netherlands Antilles** *Dutch autonomous country* Caribbean
242 B4 **Nethertown** Ireland
244 E3 **Nethy Bridge** Highland Scotland UK
118 J2 **Netla** Northwest Territories Canada
233 G7 **Neto** *watercourse* Italy
232 F2 **Netolice** Czech Republic
229 I1 **Netphen** Germany
379 G4 **Netrakona** Bangladesh
227 H5 **Netretić** Croatia
126 E2 **Nett Lake** Minnesota USA
229 G2 **Nettancourt** France
117 L5 **Nettilling Lake** Nunavut Canada
241 H3 **Nettlestead** Kent England UK
130 G3 **Nettleton** Mississippi USA
233 C6 **Nettuno, Grotta di** Sardinia Italy
226 F3 **Neu-Ulm** Germany
229 I3 **Neuberg an der Mürz** Austria
227 H4 **Neubruck** Austria
229 H3 **Neuchâtel** Switzerland
226 D4 **Neuchâtel, Lac de** *lake* Switzerland
119 T7 **Neudorf** Saskatchewan Canada
226 E3 **Neuenstein** Germany
226 D3 **Neuf-Brisach** France
229 G2 **Neufchâteau** Belgium
226 C3 **Neufchâteau** France
241 I5 **Neufchâtel-en-Bray** France
227 H4 **Neuhaus** Austria
226 F2 **Neuhaus am Rennweg** Germany
229 I1 **Neuhof** Germany
226 C4 **Neuilly** France
232 G5 **Neum** Bosnia and Herzegovina
229 J2 **Neumarkt in der Oberpfalz** Germany
436 X2 **Neumayer (Germany)** *research station* Antarctica
224 E5 **Neumünster** Germany
376 D3 **Neun** *watercourse* Laos
227 I4 **Neunkirchen** Austria
236 Q4 **Neupokoyeva, Ostrov** *island* Russian Federation
227 H3 **Neupölla** Austria
160 D6 **Neuquén** Argentina
162 C2 **Neuquén** *admin. area* Argentina
160 D6 **Neuquén** *watercourse* Argentina
131 M3 **Neuse** *watercourse* North Carolina USA
226 D2 **Neuss** Germany
226 G1 **Neustrelitz** Germany
228 F4 **Neuvic d'Ussel** France
228 E3 **Neuville** France
228 F2 **Neuvy** France
224 E6 **Neuwerk** *island* Germany
114 **Nevada** *admin. area* USA
126 D8 **Nevada** Missouri USA
162 C3 **Nevada, Sierra** *range* Argentina
160 D3 **Nevada, Sierra** *mountain* Chile
230 E5 **Nevada, Sierra** *range* Spain
124 E7 **Nevada, Sierra** *range* California USA
124 E7 **Nevada City** California USA
160 D5 **Nevado, Cerro** *mountain* Argentina
225 N5 **Nevaišiu** *mountain* Lithuania
391 K3 **Nevay Deh** Afghanistan
225 L4 **Neveja** Latvia
227 H3 **Neveklov** Czech Republic
225 O4 **Nevel'** Russian Federation
227 M2 **Nevel'** Ukraine
237 AD9 **Nevel'sk** Russian Federation
387 I1 **Nevel'sk** Russian Federation
237 AD8 **Nevel'skogo, Proliv** *strait* Russian Federation
237 Z8 **Never** Russian Federation
385 J1 **Never** Russian Federation
223 M1 **Neverfjord** Norway
228 F3 **Nevers** France
425 M7 **Nevertire** NSW Australia
305 F4 **Neves** São Tomé and Príncipe
240 I2 **Nevill Bay** Nunavut Canada
119 R8 **Neville** Saskatchewan Canada
388 D5 **Nevinnomyssk** Russian Federation
163 19 **Nevis** *island* St Kitts and Nevis
125 R3 **Nevis** Minnesota USA
423 C7 **Nevis Crossing** New Zealand
163 19 **Nevis Peak** *volcano* St Kitts and Nevis
227 L3 **Nevitske** Ukraine
394 E5 **Nevşehir** Turkey
394 E5 **Nevşehir** *admin. area* Turkey
155 G4 **New** *watercourse* Guyana
244 E6 **New Abbey** Dumfries and Galloway Scotland UK
241 G3 **New Addington** Greater London England UK
118 G5 **New Aiyansh** British Columbia Canada
126 I7 **New Albany** Indiana USA
241 F3 **New Alresford** Hampshire England UK
155 G3 **New Amsterdam** Guyana
127 P6 **New Bedford** Massachusetts USA
436 U2 **New Bedford Inlet** *bay* Antarctica
131 M3 **New Bern** North Carolina USA
243 G1 **New Bewick** Northumberland England UK
126 E7 **New Bloomfield** Missouri USA
130 D4 **New Boston** Texas USA
130 B6 **New Braunfels** Texas USA
242 B4 **New Bridge** Ireland
245 E4 **New Bridge** Ireland
119 P7 **New Brigden** Alberta Canada
373 I5 **New Britain** *island* Papua New Guinea
127 O6 **New Britain** Connecticut USA
78 L8 **New Britain Trench** *underwater feature* Solomon Sea
131 I5 **New Brockton** Alabama USA
241 I2 **New Buckenham** Norfolk England UK
245 E2 **New Buildings** Londonderry Northern Ireland UK
426 7 **New Caledonia** *French territorial collectivity* Pacific Ocean
78 M10 **New Caledonia Basin** *underwater feature* Pacific Ocean
121 F8 **New Carlisle** Québec Canada
125 L7 **New Castle** Colorado USA
126 I7 **New Castle** Kentucky USA
127 K6 **New Castle** Pennsylvania USA
242 E2 **New Cowper** Cumbria England UK
244 D5 **New Cumnock** East Ayrshire Scotland UK
129 L4 **New Deal** Texas USA
244 F3 **New Deer** Aberdeenshire Scotland UK
392 D5 **New Delhi** Delhi India
118 M8 **New Denver** British Columbia Canada
243 G3 **New Edlington** South Yorkshire England UK
125 Q4 **New Effington** South Dakota USA
76 L6 **New England Seamounts** *underwater feature* Atlantic Ocean
126 F7 **New Florence** Missouri USA
241 G4 **New Forest** *region* England UK
426 8 **New Georgia** *island* Solomon Islands
373 K6 **New Georgia Group** *island* Solomon Islands
426 8 **New Georgia Sound** *strait* Solomon Islands
126 G5 **New Glarus** Wisconsin USA
123 G10 **New Glasgow** Nova Scotia Canada
163 9 **New Grant** Trinidad and Tobago
373 G5 **New Guinea** *island* Papua New Guinea
78 J8 **New Guinea Trench** *underwater feature* Pacific Ocean
302 F4 **New Halfa** Sudan
373 I4 **New Hanover** *island* Papua New Guinea
308 F5 **New Hanover** South Africa
124 I8 **New Harmony** Utah USA
127 O6 **New Haven** Connecticut USA
126 I6 **New Haven** Indiana USA
78 M9 **New Hebrides Bank** *underwater feature* Pacific Ocean
78 N10 **New Hebrides Trench** *underwater feature* Pacific Ocean
129 L4 **New Home** Texas USA
373 J4 **New Ireland** *island* Papua New Guinea
163 7 **New Island** Falkland Islands
127 L6 **New Kensington** Pennsylvania USA
134 E3 **New Kingston** Jamaica
125 O3 **New Leipzig** North Dakota USA
126 F5 **New Lisbon** Wisconsin USA
130 E5 **New Llano** Louisiana USA
127 O6 **New London** Connecticut USA
126 F6 **New London** Iowa USA
125 R4 **New London** Minnesota USA
126 F7 **New London** Missouri USA
126 G4 **New London** Wisconsin USA
244 D6 **New Luce** Dumfries and Galloway Scotland UK
130 G2 **New Madrid** Missouri USA
127 L7 **New Market** Virginia USA
124 G4 **New Meadows** Idaho USA
115 **New Mexico** *admin. area* USA
241 G3 **New Mill** Hertfordshire England UK
243 F3 **New Mills** Derbyshire England UK
240 D2 **New Mills** Powys Wales UK
241 F3 **New Milton** Hampshire England UK
424 F7 **New Norcia** WA Australia
130 F6 **New Orleans** Louisiana USA
244 F3 **New Pitsligo** Aberdeenshire Scotland UK
422 F4 **New Plymouth** New Zealand
131 J6 **New Port Richey** Florida USA
134 E1 **New Providence** *island* Bahamas
240 C2 **New Quay** Ceredigion Wales UK
240 D2 **New Radnor** Powys Wales UK
127 O6 **New Rochelle** New York USA
125 P3 **New Rockford** North Dakota USA
241 H4 **New Romney** Kent England UK
245 F4 **New Ross** Ireland
242 A3 **New Row** Ireland
125 O3 **New Salem** North Dakota USA
119 O6 **New Sarepta** Alberta Canada
244 E4 **New Scone** Perth and Kinross Scotland UK
425 M7 **New South Wales** *admin. area* Australia
129 O1 **New Strawn** Kansas USA
116 D7 **New Stuyahok** Alaska USA
130 D5 **New Summerfield** Texas USA
245 E3 **New Town** Ireland
125 N3 **New Town** North Dakota USA
126 D4 **New Ulm** Minnesota USA
130 D5 **New Waverly** Texas USA
123 L8 **New-Wes-Valley** Newfoundland and Labrador Canada
123 K8 **New World Island** Newfoundland and Labrador Canada
241 F3 **New Yatt** Oxfordshire England UK
124 F6 **New Year Lake** Nevada USA
114 **New York** *admin. area* USA
127 N6 **New York** New York USA
422 E4 **New Zealand** *country* Oceania
78 M13 **New Zealand Plateau** *underwater feature* Southern Ocean
244 F1 **Newark** Orkney Islands Scotland UK
130 F3 **Newark** Arkansas USA
127 N7 **Newark** Delaware USA
127 N6 **Newark** New Jersey USA
127 J6 **Newark** Ohio USA
124 H7 **Newark Lake** Nevada USA
241 G1 **Newark-upon-Trent** Nottinghamshire England UK
126 I5 **Newaygo** Michigan USA
124 D4 **Newberg** Oregon USA
130 G2 **Newbern** Tennessee USA
131 J6 **Newberry** Florida USA
126 I3 **Newberry** Michigan USA
131 K3 **Newberry** South Carolina USA
128 D3 **Newberry Springs** California USA
243 G1 **Newbiggin-by-the-Sea** Northumberland England UK
131 J4 **Newborn** Georgia USA
240 C1 **Newborough** Isle of Anglesey Wales UK
119 O5 **Newbrook** Alberta Canada
244 F3 **Newburgh** Aberdeenshire Scotland UK
244 E4 **Newburgh** Fife Scotland UK
241 F3 **Newbury** West Berkshire England UK
127 P5 **Newburyport** Massachusetts USA
242 F2 **Newby Bridge** Cumbria England UK
425 N8 **Newcastle** NSW Australia
242 B4 **Newcastle** Ireland
245 F3 **Newcastle** Ireland
308 E5 **Newcastle** South Africa
163 19 **Newcastle** St Kitts and Nevis
245 G2 **Newcastle** Down Northern Ireland UK
130 C3 **Newcastle** Oklahoma USA
125 M5 **Newcastle** Wyoming USA
240 C2 **Newcastle Emlyn** Carmarthenshire Wales UK
240 E1 **Newcastle-under-Lyme** Staffordshire England UK
243 G1 **Newcastle upon Tyne** *admin. area* UK
243 G2 **Newcastle upon Tyne** Tyne and Wear England UK
244 F5 **Newcastleton** Scottish Borders Scotland UK
129 H2 **Newcomb** New Mexico USA
125 O1 **Newdale** Manitoba Canada
241 G3 **Newdigate** Surrey England UK
125 P4 **Newell** South Dakota USA
119 P7 **Newell, Lake** Alberta Canada
121 V1 **Newell Sound** Nunavut Canada
130 F4 **Newellton** Louisiana USA
116 C7 **Newenham, Cape** Alaska USA
125 Q2 **Newfolden** Minnesota USA
127 P5 **Newfound Lake** New Hampshire USA
123 I8 **Newfoundland** *island* Newfoundland and Labrador Canada
122 G3 **Newfoundland and Labrador** *admin. area* Canada
76 N5 **Newfoundland Basin** *underwater feature* Atlantic Ocean
76 N6 **Newfoundland Rise** *underwater feature* Atlantic Ocean
119 N8 **Newgate** British Columbia Canada
241 H4 **Newhaven** East Sussex England UK
241 H4 **Newick** East Sussex England UK
129 J3 **Newkirk** New Mexico USA
130 B3 **Newkirk** Oklahoma USA
425 M5 **Newlands** Qld Australia
424 F5 **Newman** WA Australia
126 H7 **Newman** Illinois USA
424 F5 **Newman, Mount** WA Australia
245 C4 **Newmarket** Ireland
241 H2 **Newmarket** Suffolk England UK
242 B2 **Newmills** Dungannon Northern Ireland UK
244 D3 **Newmills** Highland Scotland UK
131 I4 **Newnan** Georgia USA
241 G2 **Newnham** Hertfordshire England UK
240 A1 **Newpark** Ireland
135 G4 **Newport** Netherlands Antilles
243 H3 **Newport** East Riding of Yorkshire England UK
241 H2 **Newport** Essex England UK
241 F4 **Newport** Isle of Wight England UK
244 E2 **Newport** Highland Scotland UK
240 E2 **Newport** Newport Wales UK
240 E2 **Newport** Telford and Wrekin England UK
240 E3 **Newport** *admin. area* Wales UK
130 F3 **Newport** Arkansas USA
126 I7 **Newport** Kentucky USA
131 M3 **Newport** North Carolina USA
124 C4 **Newport** Oregon USA
127 M6 **Newport** Pennsylvania USA
127 P6 **Newport** Rhode Island USA
131 J3 **Newport** Tennessee USA
127 O4 **Newport** Vermont USA
127 M8 **Newport News** Virginia USA
241 G2 **Newport Pagnell** Milton Keynes England UK
240 B4 **Newquay** Cornwall England UK
245 F2 **Newry** Newry and Mourne Northern Ireland UK
245 F2 **Newry and Mourne** *admin. area* Northern Ireland UK
243 F3 **Newsholme** Lancashire England UK
244 C5 **Newton** North Ayrshire Scotland UK
241 G2 **Newton** Northamptonshire England UK
244 F5 **Newton** Scottish Borders Scotland UK
126 G7 **Newton** Illinois USA
126 E6 **Newton** Iowa USA
125 Q7 **Newton** Kansas USA
127 P5 **Newton** Massachusetts USA
130 G4 **Newton** Mississippi USA
127 N6 **Newton** New Jersey USA
130 E5 **Newton** Texas USA
240 D4 **Newton Abbot** Devon England UK
131 L3 **Newton Grove** North Carolina USA
244 F4 **Newton of Boysack** Angus Scotland UK
241 I2 **Newton St Faith** Norfolk England UK
244 D6 **Newton Stewart** Dumfries and Galloway Scotland UK
240 C3 **Newton Tracey** Devon England UK
244 F3 **Newtonhill** Aberdeenshire Scotland UK
245 E4 **Newtown** Ireland
242 F2 **Newtown** Cumbria England UK
241 F3 **Newtown** Hampshire England UK
241 E2 **Newtown** Herefordshire England UK
244 D3 **Newtown** Highland Scotland UK
240 D2 **Newtown** Powys Wales UK
245 E2 **Newtown Butler** Fermanagh Northern Ireland UK
244 F5 **Newtown St Boswells** Scottish Borders Scotland UK
242 B3 **Newtown Trim** Ireland
245 G2 **Newtownabbey** Newtownabbey Northern Ireland UK
245 G2 **Newtownabbey** *admin. area* Northern Ireland UK
245 G2 **Newtownards** Ards Northern Ireland UK
245 E2 **Newtownstewart** Strabane Northern Ireland UK
133 I2 **Newville** Alabama USA
121 V1 **Ney Harbour** Nunavut Canada
120 I5 **Ney Lake** Ontario Canada
388 D1 **Neya** Russian Federation
240 C3 **Neyland** Pembrokeshire Wales UK
391 H3 **Neyriz** Iran
391 H4 **Neyriz** Iran
388 H7 **Neyshābūr** Iran
393 E9 **Neyveli** Tamil Nadu India
382 F4 **Nezah** Ontario Canada
133 F5 **Nezahualcóyotl** Mexico
133 G5 **Nezahualcóyotl, Presa** *lake* Mexico
225 O3 **Nezhadovo** Russian Federation
234 D1 **Nezvys'ko** Ukraine
376 E3 **Nga Sơn** Vietnam
375 F3 **Ngabang** Indonesia
305 H5 **Ngabé** Congo
372 E5 **Ngabordamlu, Tanjung** *cape* Indonesia
423 D5 **Ngakawau** New Zealand
305 G2 **Ngala** Nigeria
372 C3 **Ngalipaeng** Indonesia
372 B6 **Ngalu** Indonesia
375 I6 **Ngalu** Indonesia
305 H2 **Ngam** Chad
301 J6 **Ngama** Chad
308 D3 **Ngamaseri** *watercourse* Botswana
305 G4 **Ngambé** Cameroon
308 D4 **Ngami, Lake** *lake* Botswana
376 E2 **Ngân Sơn** Vietnam
300 C6 **Nganda** Senegal
378 E2 **Ngangla Ringco** *lake* Xizang Zizhiqu China
378 D2 **Nganglong Kangri** *mountain* Xizang Zizhiqu China
306 D4 **Nganji** Democratic Republic of Congo
305 G3 **Ngaoundéré** Cameroon
374 E5 **Ngaras** Indonesia
426 3 **Ngardmau** Palau
422 F3 **Ngaruawahia** New Zealand
422 2 **Ngatangiia** Cook Islands New Zealand
426 6 **Ngatik** *island* Federated States of Micronesia
306 A3 **Ngato** Cameroon
375 F5 **Ngawi** Indonesia
423 F5 **Ngawi** New Zealand
376 C4 **Ngayanni Kyauk Taung** *mountain* Myanmar
305 G4 **Ngbala** Congo
426 3 **Ngcheangel** *island* Palau
426 3 **Ngercheluk** Palau
426 3 **Ngeriuns** *island* Palau
426 3 **Ngeruktabel** *island* Palau
427 9a **Nggamea** *island* Fiji
426 8 **Nggatokae** *island* Solomon Islands
426 8a **Nggela Pile** *island* Solomon Islands
426 8a **Nggela Sule** *island* Solomon Islands
372 C6 **Ngilmina** Indonesia
375 G6 **Ngliyep** Indonesia
376 E4 **Ngoc Linh** *mountain* Vietnam
372 C3 **Ngofakiaha** Indonesia
305 G4 **Ngoïla** Cameroon
305 H5 **Ngoko** Congo
305 H4 **Ngoko** *watercourse* Congo
308 D3 **Ngoma** Botswana
307 E5 **Ngomba** Tanzania
305 G4 **Ngomedzap** Cameroon
305 G3 **Ngong** Cameroon
307 E5 **Ngongo** Tanzania
383 K6 **Ngoring Hu** *lake* Qinghai China
306 B4 **Ngoso** Democratic Republic of Congo
305 H4 **Ngoto** Central African Republic
306 D2 **Ngouanga** *watercourse* Central African Republic
305 G4 **Ngoulemakong** Cameroon
305 G5 **Ngounié** *admin. area* Gabon
305 G5 **Ngounié** *watercourse* Gabon
301 J6 **Ngoura** Chad
301 J6 **Ngouri** Chad
301 I5 **Ngourti** Niger
305 G4 **Ngoyeboma** Congo
307 D4 **Ngozi** Burundi
307 E4 **Ngudu** Tanzania
305 G3 **Nguia Bouar** Central African Republic
301 I6 **Nguigmi** Niger
424 I2 **Nguiu** NT Australia
425 J3 **Ngukurr** NT Australia
372 F1 **Ngulu** *island* Federated States of Micronesia
426 7 **Nguna** *island* Vanuatu
309 F4 **Ngundu** Zimbabwe
422 F2 **Ngunguru Bay** New Zealand
375 I6 **Ngunju, Tanjung** *cape* Indonesia
375 G6 **Ngunut** Indonesia
305 G2 **Nguru** Nigeria
376 E2 **Nguyên Bình** Vietnam
308 E3 **Ngweze** *watercourse* Zambia
376 F4 **Nha Trang** Vietnam
308 D4 **Nhabe** *watercourse* Botswana
309 F3 **Nhacolo** Mozambique
309 F3 **Nhamatanda** Mozambique
155 G5 **Nhamundá** Brazil
155 G5 **Nhamundá** *watercourse* Brazil
308 C2 **N'harea** Angola
158 C5 **Nhecolândia** Brazil
308 B2 **Nhia** *watercourse* Angola
425 L9 **Nhill** Vic. Australia
308 D3 **Nhoma** Namibia
161 H4 **Nhu Pora** Brazil
425 K3 **Nhulunbuy** NT Australia
382 G5 **Ni-ya He** *watercourse* Xinjiang Uygur Zizhiqu China
385 J3 **Ni'erji** Nei Mongol Zizhiqu China
304 D3 **Niablé** Côte d'Ivoire
127 L5 **Niagara Falls** New York USA
127 L5 **Niagara Falls** *waterfall* New York USA
304 C2 **Niagassola** Guinea
375 G3 **Niah** Malaysia
375 G3 **Niah National Park** Malaysia
300 E6 **Niamey** Niger
300 D6 **Niamina** Mali
372 C2 **Niampak** Indonesia
384 E6 **Nianbo** Qinghai China
304 C2 **Niandan Koro** Guinea
304 C3 **Niandati** *watercourse* Guinea
307 F5 **Niangandu** Tanzania
306 D3 **Niangara** Democratic Republic of Congo
304 D2 **Niangoloko** Burkina Faso
130 E2 **Niangua** *watercourse* Missouri USA
304 B2 **Niantan** *watercourse* Guinea
381 G2 **Nianyushan Shuiku** *lake* Henan China
305 G5 **Niari** *admin. area* Congo
374 C3 **Nias** *island* Indonesia
309 G2 **Niassa** *admin. area* Mozambique
233 B6 **Nibaru, Punta de lu** *cape* Italy
120 K6 **Nibinamik** Ontario Canada
120 K6 **Nibinamik Lake** Ontario Canada
426 4 **Nibok** Nauru
225 K4 **Nica** Latvia
134 C4 **Nicaragua** *country* Central America
134 C5 **Nicaragua, Lago de** *lake* Nicaragua
127 Q4 **Nicatous Lake** Maine USA
229 H5 **Nice** France
131 H5 **Niceville** Florida USA
237 AE4 **Nichalakh** Russian Federation
127 T6 **Nichicun, Lac** *lake* Québec Canada
386 F5 **Nichinan** Japan
392 F5 **Nichlaul** Uttar Pradesh India
134 D2 **Nicholas Channel** Cuba
126 I8 **Nicholasville** Kentucky USA
131 J5 **Nicholls** Georgia USA
134 E1 **Nicholls Town** Bahamas
126 J3 **Nicholson** Ontario Canada
133 I4 **Nichupte, Laguna** *lake* Mexico
129 J5 **Nickel Creek Station** Texas USA
155 G3 **Nickerie** *admin. area* Suriname
125 P7 **Nickerson** Kansas USA
376 B6 **Nicobar Islands (India)** India
127 N2 **Nicobi Lake** Québec Canada
129 I6 **Nicolas Bravo** Mexico
133 H5 **Nicolás Bravo** Mexico
233 F8 **Nicosia** Italy
394 E6 **Nicosia (Lefkosia)** Cyprus
233 F7 **Nicotera** Italy
134 C5 **Nicoya** Costa Rica
134 C5 **Nicoya, Golfo de** *lake* Costa Rica
134 C5 **Nicoya, Península de** *peninsula* Costa Rica
309 G3 **Nicuadala** Mozambique
123 J9 **Nid à l'Aigle, Cap du** *cape* St Pierre and Miquelon
225 K5 **Nida** Lithuania
227 K2 **Nida** *watercourse* Poland
243 G2 **Nidd** *watercourse* England UK
226 E2 **Nidda** Germany
226 E2 **Nidda** *watercourse* Germany
243 G2 **Nidderdale** *valley* England UK
224 E3 **Nidelva** *watercourse* Norway
377 H5 **Nido, El** Philippines
237 V6 **Nidym** *watercourse* Russian Federation
227 K1 **Nidzica** Poland
233 C7 **Niedda, Punta** *cape* Sardinia Italy
233 C6 **Nieddu, Capo** *cape* Sardinia Italy
227 H3 **Niederösterreich** *admin. area* Austria
226 E1 **Niedersachsen** *admin. area* Germany
379 E3 **Nielamu** Xizang Zizhiqu China
392 F5 **Nielamu** Nepal
305 H3 **Niem** Central African Republic
306 D5 **Niemba** Democratic Republic of Congo
227 I2 **Niemcza** Poland
223 P3 **Niemelä** Finland
223 Q5 **Niemijärvi** Finland
223 M3 **Niemis** Sweden
222 M3 **Niemisel** Sweden
223 N5 **Niemisvesi** *lake* Finland
300 D6 **Niéri Ko** *watercourse* Senegal
226 D2 **Niers** *watercourse* Germany
223 N3 **Niesi** Finland
227 H2 **Niesky** Germany
227 M1 **Nieśwież** Poland
227 J1 **Nieszawa** Poland
162 B3 **Nieto** Argentina
222 L3 **Nietsakjaure** *lake* Sweden
155 H3 **Nieuw Amsterdam** Suriname
81 M8 **Nieuw Amsterdam Fracture Zone** *underwater feature* Indian Ocean
155 G3 **Nieuw Nickerie** Suriname
163 1b **Nieuwpoort** Netherlands Antilles
159 E4 **Nieve** Bolivia
132 E4 **Nieves** Mexico
310 3b **Nieves, Pico de las** *volcano* Canary Islands
372 D4 **Nif** Indonesia
394 E6 **Niğde** Turkey
394 E6 **Niğde** *admin. area* Turkey
305 F2 **Niger** *country* Africa
304 C2 **Niger** *watercourse* Guinea
300 E6 **Niger** *watercourse* Mali
301 G6 **Niger** *watercourse* Niger
305 F4 **Niger** *watercourse* Nigeria
80 E4 **Niger Fan** *underwater feature* Gulf of Guinea
305 F2 **Nigeria** *country* Africa
244 D3 **Nigg** Highland Scotland UK
244 D3 **Nigg Bay** Scotland UK
423 C7 **Nightcaps** New Zealand
127 K2 **Nighthawk Lake** Ontario Canada
310 5c **Nightingale Island** St Helena
162 B2 **Nihue, Punta** *cape* Chile
387 H4 **Nii-jima** *island* Japan
387 H4 **Niigata** Japan
386 G5 **Niihama** Japan
128 inset **Ni'ihau** *island* Hawai'i USA
387 I2 **Niikappu-gawa** *lake* Japan
386 G4 **Niimi** Japan
223 P5 **Niinivaara** Finland
223 O5 **Niinivesi** *bay* Finland
230 E5 **Nijar** Spain
234 A3 **Nijemci** Croatia
226 C1 **Nijkerk** Netherlands
226 C2 **Nijmegen** Netherlands
226 D1 **Nijverdal** Netherlands
235 C6 **Nikaia** Greece
422 2 **Nikao** Cook Islands New Zealand
236 H5 **Nikel'** Russian Federation
235 B5 **Niki** Greece
238 H2 **Nikiforovo** Russian Federation
375 J6 **Nikiniki** Indonesia
120 J6 **Nikip Lake** Ontario Canada
235 C5 **Nikitas** Greece
388 D2 **Nikitino** Russian Federation
235 B5 **Nikodim** Macedonia
388 D5 **Nikolayevka** Russian Federation
238 D6 **Nikolayevka** Ukraine
388 E3 **Nikolayevsk** Russian Federation
237 AD8 **Nikolayevsk-na-Amure** Russian Federation
236 K7 **Nikol'sk** Russian Federation
388 E2 **Nikol'sk** Russian Federation
238 H3 **Nikol'skiy Torzhok** Russian Federation
238 G3 **Nikol'skoye** Russian Federation
306 E4 **Nikonga** *watercourse* Tanzania
394 E3 **Nikopol'** Ukraine
235 D7 **Nikouria** *island* Greece
232 H5 **Nikšić** Montenegro
426 1 **Nikumaroro** *island* Kiribati
426 1 **Nikunau** *island* Kiribati
302 E2 **Nil, Nahr an (Nile)** *watercourse* Egypt
302 E4 **Nil, Nahr an (Nile)** *watercourse* Sudan
372 D5 **Nila** *island* Indonesia
223 O5 **Nilakka** *lake* Finland
393 C11 **Nilandhoo Atoll** Maldives
Nile *see* **Nil, Nahr an** Africa
302 E4 **Nile** *admin. area* Sudan
382 G4 **Nileke** Xinjiang Uygur Zizhiqu China
126 H6 **Niles** Michigan USA
133 I5 **Nilivaara** Sweden
437 E2 **Nilsen Bay** Antarctica
392 D6 **Nimbahera** Rajasthan India
229 G5 **Nimes** France
234 D2 **Nimigea de Sur** Romania
118 H7 **Nimpkish** *watercourse* British Columbia Canada
118 H7 **Nimpkish Lake** British Columbia Canada
437 K1 **Nimrod Glacier** *ice* Antarctica
391 J3 **Nimrūz** *admin. area* Afghanistan
225 N3 **Nina** Estonia
390 E2 **Ninawā** *admin. area* Iraq
121 V4 **Ninawawe, Lac** *lake* Québec Canada
308 D2 **Ninda** Angola
425 N7 **Nindigully** Qld Australia
393 C10 **Nine Degree Channel** *strait* Lakshadweep India
243 F2 **Ninebanks** Northumberland England UK
119 V8 **Ninette** Manitoba Canada
422 E2 **Ninety Mile Beach** New Zealand
81 M5 **Ninetyeast Ridge** *underwater feature* Indian Ocean
162 D3 **Ninfas, Punta** *cape* Argentina
380 D4 **Ning'er** Yunnan China
385 L4 **Ning'an** Heilongjiang China
381 I2 **Ningbo** Zhejiang China
381 H3 **Ningde** Fujian China
381 I2 **Ninghai** Zhejiang China
381 I5 **Ninghe** Tianjin China
305 F2 **Ningi** Nigeria
385 H5 **Ningjin** Shandong China
381 G1 **Ningling** Henan China
380 E2 **Ningqiang** Shaanxi China
380 E1 **Ningshan** Shaanxi China
380 E2 **Ningwu** Shanxi China
380 E1 **Ningxia Huizu Zizhiqu** *admin. area* China
385 H6 **Ningyang** Shandong China
376 E2 **Ninh Bình** Vietnam
376 F4 **Ninh Hòa** Vietnam
373 H4 **Ninigo Group** *island* Papua New Guinea
130 C3 **Ninnekah** Oklahoma USA
437 J2 **Ninnis Glacier Tongue** *ice* Antarctica
387 I3 **Ninohe** Japan
153 I5 **Niños Héroes de Chapultepec** Mexico
228 G1 **Ninove** Belgium
159 H6 **Nioaque** Brazil

125 P5 **Niobrara** *watercourse* Nebraska USA
117 R3 **Nioghalvfjerdsfjorden** *bay* Greenland
300 E6 **Niono** Mali
300 E5 **Nioro** Mali
300 C6 **Nioro du Rip** Senegal
228 D3 **Niort** France
373 G5 **Nipa** Papua New Guinea
393 D8 **Nipani** Karnataka India
135 F2 **Nipe, Bahía de** *bay* Cuba
309 G2 **Nipepe** Mozambique
393 D7 **Niphad** Maharashtra India
126 G2 **Nipigon, Lake** Ontario Canada
126 H2 **Nipigon Bay** Ontario Canada
119 Q5 **Nipin** *watercourse* Saskatchewan Canada
309 G3 **Nipiodi** Mozambique
123 F9 **Nipisiguit Bay** New Brunswick Canada
127 L3 **Nipissing, Lake** Ontario Canada
121 V7 **Nipissis, Lac** *lake* Québec Canada
121 W7 **Nipisso, Lac** *lake* Québec Canada
157 B6 **Niquelândia** Brazil
134 E2 **Niquero** Cuba
393 D8 **Nira** *watercourse* Maharashtra India
160 D6 **Ñire-Có** Argentina
136 B3 **Ñirehuao** Chile
393 E7 **Nirmal** Andhra Pradesh India
225 N4 **Nirza** Latvia
234 B4 **Niš** Serbia
234 C4 **Nišava** *watercourse* Serbia
244 F5 **Nisbet House** Scottish Borders Scotland UK
233 F8 **Niscemi** Italy
234 C4 **Niševac** Serbia
386 G4 **Nishino-shima** *island* Japan
127 M3 **Nishkotea Lake** Québec Canada
392 F5 **Nisi Khola** Nepal
156 F4 **Nísia Floresta** Brazil
223 O4 **Niskanselkä** *bay* Finland
120 K4 **Niskibi** *watercourse* Ontario Canada
223 M5 **Niskos** Finland
125 N4 **Nisland** South Dakota USA
224 G4 **Nissan** *watercourse* Sweden
373 J5 **Nissan Island** Papua New Guinea
224 E3 **Nisser** *lake* Norway
223 O5 **Nissilä** Finland
224 E4 **Nissum Bredning** *bay* Denmark
224 F2 **Nistru** *watercourse* Moldova
235 E7 **Nisyros** *island* Greece
121 T6 **Nitchequon** Québec Canada
161 K2 **Niterói** Brazil
244 D5 **Nith** *watercourse* Scotland UK
372 C6 **Nitibe** Timor-Leste (East Timor)
241 F4 **Niton** Isle of Wight England UK
119 N6 **Niton Junction** Alberta Canada
227 J3 **Nitra** Slovakia
227 J3 **Nitriansky** *admin. area* Slovakia
226 B4 **Nitry** France
223 O2 **Nitsijärvi** *bay* Finland
427 I2 **Niuafo'ou** *island* Tonga
427 I2 **Niuatoputapu** *island* Tonga
380 C3 **Niujing** Yunnan China
225 O2 **Niukkala** Finland
380 D3 **Niulan Jiang** *watercourse* Yunnan China
128 inset **Niuli'i** Hawai'i USA
426 1 **Niutao** *island* Tuvalu
381 I2 **Niutou Shan** *range* Zhejiang China
427 10a **Niutoua** Tonga
224 G5 **Nivå** Denmark
225 P2 **Niva** Russian Federation
223 N5 **Nivala** Finland
228 D5 **Nive** *watercourse* France
229 G1 **Nivelles** Belgium
228 F3 **Nivernais, Canal du** *watercourse* France
223 R3 **Nivskiy** Russian Federation
392 D5 **Niwai** Rajasthan India
392 E6 **Niwari** Madhya Pradesh India
126 E8 **Nixa** Missouri USA
379 I2 **Nixia** Sichuan China
130 C6 **Nixon** Texas USA
Niyazoba *see* **Nizovaya** Azerbaijan
381 I3 **Niyu Shan** *range* Zhejiang China
375 F3 **Niyut, Gunung** *mountain* Indonesia
238 F3 **Niz** Russian Federation
379 G3 **Niz Hajo** Assam India
393 D7 **Nizam Sagar** *lake* Andhra Pradesh India
393 E7 **Nizamabad** Andhra Pradesh India
388 D2 **Nizhegorodskaya** *admin. area* Russian Federation
236 J7 **Nizhegorodskaya Oblast'** *admin. area* Russian Federation
223 T4 **Nizhmozero** Russian Federation
237 AH7 **Nizhne-Ozërnaya** Russian Federation
237 U8 **Nizhneudinsk** Russian Federation
389 R2 **Nizhneudinsk** Russian Federation
236 Q6 **Nizhnevartovsk** Russian Federation
223 Q4 **Nizhneye Kuyto, Ozero** *lake* Russian Federation
388 D4 **Nizhniy Chir** Russian Federation
388 C3 **Nizhniy Mamon** Russian Federation
236 J7 **Nizhniy Novgorod** Russian Federation
388 D2 **Nizhniy Novgorod** Russian Federation
236 M7 **Nizhniy Tagil** Russian Federation
388 H1 **Nizhniy Tagil** Russian Federation
236 L6 **Nizhniy Voch** Russian Federation
236 K7 **Nizhniy Yenangsk** Russian Federation
237 U7 **Nizhnyaya Poyma** Russian Federation
389 R2 **Nizhnyaya Poyma** Russian Federation
237 U6 **Nizhnyaya Tunguska** *watercourse* Russian Federation
388 H1 **Nizhnyaya Tura** Russian Federation
236 J5 **Nizhnyaya Zolotitsa** Russian Federation
225 N5 **Nizina Polatskaya** *region* Belarus
227 I2 **Nizina Śląska** *region* Poland
396 F6 **Nizip** Turkey
232 H2 **Nízke Tatry** *range* Slovakia
116 A6 **Nizkiy, Mys** *cape* Russian Federation
225 P5 **Nizkobor'ye** Belarus
388 E5 **Nizovaya** Azerbaijan
391 I5 **Nizwa'** Oman
222 K3 **Njavve** Sweden
Njazidja *see* **Grande Comore** Comoros
307 F5 **Njinjo** Tanzania
308 D3 **Njoko** *watercourse* Zambia
307 E5 **Njombe** Tanzania
307 E5 **Njombe** *watercourse* Tanzania
224 H4 **Njudung** *region* Sweden
222 J5 **Njurundabommen/Njurunda** Sweden
305 G4 **Nkam** *watercourse* Gabon
305 G5 **Nkayi** Congo
309 F2 **Nkhata Bay** Malawi
309 F2 **Nkhotakota** Malawi
305 G4 **Nkolabona** Gabon
305 F5 **Nkomi, Lagune** *lake* Gabon
306 E5 **Nkondwe** Tanzania
305 F4 **Nkongsamba** Cameroon
306 E5 **Nkundi** Tanzania
308 C3 **Nkurenkuru** Namibia
306 E3 **Nkusi** *watercourse* Uganda
304 E3 **Nkwanta** Ghana
304 C3 **Nlaklan** Liberia
379 H4 **Nmai** *watercourse* Myanmar
379 G4 **Noakhali** Bangladesh
116 D5 **Noatak** *watercourse* Alaska USA
116 C5 **Noatak National Preserve** *park* Alaska USA
245 F3 **Nobber** Ireland
127 K4 **Nobel** Ontario Canada
386 F5 **Nobeoka** Japan
126 H6 **Noblesville** Indiana USA
159 G4 **Nobres** Brazil
232 E5 **Nocera Umbra** Italy
132 E4 **Nochistlán** Mexico
233 G6 **Noci** Italy
425 L6 **Nockatunga** Qld Australia
130 C4 **Nocona** Texas USA
162 D4 **Nodales, Bahía de los** *bay* Argentina
126 D6 **Nodaway** *watercourse* Missouri USA
127 K3 **Noelville** Ontario Canada
224 H4 **Noen** *lake* Sweden
224 F5 **Noer** Germany
132 C2 **Nogales** Mexico
132 C2 **Nogales** Arizona USA
226 F5 **Nogara** Italy
236 T6 **Noginsk** Russian Federation
238 H5 **Noginsk** Russian Federation
425 M6 **Nogoa** *watercourse* Qld Australia
161 G5 **Nogoyá** *watercourse* Argentina
227 J4 **Nógrád** *admin. area* Hungary
229 H2 **Nohfelden** Germany
386 E4 **Nohwa-do** *island* South Korea
127 M3 **Noire** *watercourse* Québec Canada
228 C3 **Noirmoutier, Île de** *island* France
387 H4 **Nojiri-ko** *lake* Japan
391 J4 **Nok Kundi** Pakistan
426 8 **Noka** Solomon Islands
392 F6 **Nokha** Bihar India
392 C5 **Nokha** Rajasthan India
391 I4 **Nokhowch, Kūh-e** *mountain* Iran
237 Y7 **Nokhtuysk** Russian Federation
372 B4 **Nokilalaki, Gunung** *mountain* Indonesia
119 S7 **Nokomis** Saskatchewan Canada
301 I6 **Nokou** Chad
304 E3 **Nokoue, Lac** *lake* Benin
379 G4 **Nokrek Peak** *mountain* Meghalaya India
305 H4 **Nola** Central African Republic
233 F6 **Nola** Italy
226 C4 **Nolay** France
232 C4 **Noli, Capo di** *cape* Italy
131 H2 **Nolin Lake** Kentucky USA
388 F1 **Nolinsk** Russian Federation
373 G5 **Nomad** *watercourse* Papua New Guinea
240 D4 **Nomansland** Devon England UK
121 O6 **Nomansland Point** Ontario Canada
230 D3 **Nombela** Spain
162 C5 **Nombre, Cabo** *cape* Argentina
132 D4 **Nombre de Dios** Mexico
116 C6 **Nome** Alaska USA
229 H2 **Nomexy** France
384 F4 **Nomgon** Mongolia
235 C7 **Nómia** Greece
224 H4 **Nömmen** *lake* Sweden
427 10 **Nomuka** *island* Tonga
426 6 **Nomwin** *island* Federated States of Micronesia
119 Q2 **Nonacho Lake** Northwest Territories Canada
228 E2 **Nonancourt** France
232 D4 **Nonantola** Italy
116 D7 **Nondalton** Alaska USA
376 D3 **Nong Bua Lamphu** Thailand
385 M3 **Nong Jiang** *watercourse* Heilongjiang China
376 D3 **Nong Khai** Thailand
376 D4 **Nong Phai** Thailand
385 K4 **Nong'an** Jilin China
384 G5 **Nongchang** *mountain* Shaanxi China
224 H3 **Nöngen** *lake* Sweden
379 G4 **Nongkhlaw** Meghalaya India
309 F5 **Nongoma** South Africa
374 E3 **Nongsa** Indonesia
374 G5 **Nongsapura** Indonesia
379 G4 **Nongstoin** Meghalaya India
304 B2 **Nono** *watercourse* Guinea
426 1 **Nonouti** *island* Kiribati
386 E4 **Nonsan** South Korea
130 E4 **Nonsuch** Manitoba Canada
163 18 **Nonsuch Bay** Antigua and Barbuda
376 D4 **Nonthaburi** Thailand
228 E4 **Nontron** France
116 D7 **Nonvianuk Lake** Alaska USA
229 I5 **Nonza** Corsica France
125 N2 **Noonan** North Dakota USA
424 F7 **Noondie, Lake** WA Australia
163 1a **Noord** Aruba
163 1a **Noordkaap** *cape* Aruba
135 G4 **Noordpunt** *cape* Netherlands Antilles
116 C5 **Noorvik** Alaska USA
425 O6 **Noosa Heads** Qld Australia
124 B2 **Nootka** British Columbia Canada
118 H8 **Nootka Island** British Columbia Canada
118 H8 **Nootka Sound** British Columbia Canada
222 M5 **Nopankylä** Finland
224 I3 **Nora** Sweden
389 K6 **Norak** Tajikistan
118 H6 **Noralee** British Columbia Canada
132 F4 **Norcasia** Colombia
125 O7 **Norcatur** Kansas USA
305 G3 **Nord** *admin. area* Cameroon
121 R4 **Nord, Rivière du** *watercourse* Québec Canada
306 D4 **Nord-Kivu** *admin. area* Democratic Republic of Congo
222 K1 **Nord-Kvaløy** *island* Norway
224 F2 **Nord-Mesna** *lake* Norway
224 E5 **Nord-Ostsee-Kanal** *watercourse* Germany
305 G3 **Nord-Ouest** *admin. area* Cameroon
228 F1 **Nord-Pas-de-Calais** *admin. area* France
222 L1 **Nord-Rekvik** Norway
222 H4 **Nord-Trøndelag** *admin. area* Norway
222 K4 **Nordanås** Sweden
222 J5 **Nordanede** Sweden
222 J5 **Nordankäl** Sweden
241 J4 **Nordausques** France
236 F3 **Nordaustlandet** *island* Norway
222 F5 **Nordbotn** Norway
223 M2 **Nordbotn** Norway
224 E5 **Nordby** Denmark
119 M6 **Nordegg** Alberta Canada
241 H2 **Nordelph** Norfolk England UK
226 D1 **Norden** Germany
243 F3 **Norden** Greater Manchester England UK
237 U3 **Nordenshel'da, Arkipelag** *islands* Russian Federation
437 L1 **Nordenskjöld Basin** *underwater feature* Ross Sea
226 D1 **Norderney** *island* Germany
224 F6 **Norderstedt** Germany
306 C5 **Nordeste** Angola
224 C2 **Nordfjordeid** Norway
229 J1 **Nordhausen** Germany
224 E4 **Nordjylland** *admin. area* Denmark
236 G2 **Nordkapp** *cape* Norway
236 G4 **Nordkinnhalvøya** *cape* Norway
222 K2 **Nordkjosbotn** Norway
223 O1 **Nordkynhalvøya** *peninsula* Norway
222 I3 **Nordland** *admin. area* Norway
222 H4 **Nordli** Norway
229 F3 **Nördlingen** Germany
222 K5 **Nordmaling** Sweden
224 D2 **Nordmannslågen** *lake* Norway
224 H2 **Nordmannvik** Norway
222 I2 **Nordmela** Norway
222 H6 **Nordomsjön** Sweden
226 D1 **Nordradde** *watercourse* Germany
222 I3 **Nordre-Bjøllåvatn** *lake* Norway
224 F2 **Nordre Osa** *watercourse* Norway
226 D2 **Nordrhein-Westfalen** *admin. area* Germany
222 G4 **Nordskjør** Norway
222 I3 **Nordskot** Norway
237 X4 **Nordvik** Russian Federation
222 F5 **Nordvika** Norway
222 H3 **Nordvikfjellet** *island* Norway
245 E4 **Nore** *watercourse* Ireland
224 E2 **Nore** Norway
245 E4 **Nore Bridge** Ireland
231 H2 **Norfeu, Cap de** *cape* Spain
241 H2 **Norfolk** *admin. area* England UK
125 Q5 **Norfolk** Nebraska USA
425 M10 **Norfolk** Tas. Australia
127 M8 **Norfolk** Virginia USA
425 inset **Norfolk Island** *Australian territory* Pacific Ocean
78 M10 **Norfolk Ridge** *underwater feature* Pacific Ocean
130 E2 **Norfork Lake** Arkansas USA
226 D1 **Norg** Netherlands
119 V7 **Norgate** Manitoba Canada
118 R8 **Norge** Saskatchewan Canada
130 C7 **Norias** Texas USA
236 S5 **Noril'sk** Russian Federation
131 L2 **Norlina** North Carolina USA
126 G6 **Normal** Illinois USA
425 L4 **Norman** *watercourse* Qld Australia
130 C3 **Norman** Oklahoma USA
131 K3 **Norman, Lake** North Carolina USA
423 8 **Norman Inlet** Auckland Islands New Zealand
131 J5 **Norman Park** Georgia USA
116 G5 **Norman Wells** Northwest Territories Canada
Normandes, Îles *see* **Channel Islands** UK
228 E2 **Normandie (Normandy)** *region* France
Normandy *see* **Normandie** France
129 L6 **Normandy** Texas USA
130 C5 **Normangee** Texas USA
425 L4 **Normanton** Qld Australia
127 L2 **Normetal** Québec Canada
129 I7 **Norogachic** Mexico
310 6b **Noroît, Baie du** *bay* French Southern and Antarctic Lands
222 inset **Norðurfjörður** Iceland
222 inset **Norðurland Vestra** *admin. area* Iceland
130 E4 **Norphlet** Arkansas USA
119 T7 **Norquay** Saskatchewan Canada
160 D6 **Ñorquín** Argentina
162 B2 **Ñorquinco** Argentina
224 I2 **Norr-Bränningen** *lake* Sweden
224 F3 **Norr Bullaresjön** *lake* Sweden
224 H2 **Norr Hörken** *lake* Sweden
224 H2 **Norra Barken** *bay* Sweden
222 K3 **Norra Bergnäs** Sweden
222 J6 **Norra Dellen** *lake* Sweden
224 I3 **Norra Finnö** *island* Sweden
222 I4 **Norra Fjällnäs** Sweden
222 K4 **Norra Malånäs** Sweden
224 I4 **Norra Näsby** Sweden
222 I5 **Norra Skärvången** Sweden
222 I4 **Norra Storfjället** *island* Sweden
222 I4 **Norråker** Sweden
224 I2 **Norrala** Sweden
224 H3 **Norrälgen** *lake* Sweden
224 H4 **Norraryd** Sweden
222 J4 **Norrbäck** Sweden
222 J4 **Norrberg** Sweden
222 I5 **Norrböle** Sweden
222 L3 **Norrbotten** *admin. area* Sweden
222 K4 **Norrbyberg** Sweden
224 E4 **Nørre Alslev** Denmark
224 E4 **Nørre Lyngby** Denmark
224 E4 **Nørre Vorupør** Denmark
222 J5 **Norrfjärden** Sweden
225 K2 **Norrhavet** *bay* Finland
123 K8 **Norris Arm** Newfoundland and Labrador Canada
126 G8 **Norris City** Illinois USA
131 J2 **Norris Lake** Tennessee USA
123 J8 **Norris Point** Newfoundland and Labrador Canada
224 I3 **Norrköping** Sweden
224 I3 **Norrköpings Bukten** *bay* Sweden
222 L5 **Norrnäs** Finland
222 J5 **Norrstig** Sweden
225 J3 **Norrtälje** Sweden
424 G8 **Norseman** WA Australia
224 H3 **Norsholm** Sweden
224 E3 **Norsjø** *lake* Norway
222 K4 **Norsjö** Sweden
117 R3 **Norske Øer** *island* Greenland
222 L1 **Norskehavet** *bay* Norway
426 7 **Norsup** Vanuatu
163 5 **Norte, Cabo** *cape* Isla de Pascua (Easter Island)
156 B2 **Norte, Canal do** *watercourse* Brazil
162 A3 **Norte, Punta** *cape* Chile
163 6a **Norte, Punta** *cape* Isla Róbinson Crusoe
159 G3 **Norte, Serra do** *range* Brazil
154 C2 **Norte de Santander** *admin. area* Colombia
161 G6 **Norte del Cabo San Antonio, Punta** *cape* Argentina
121 X4 **North** *watercourse* Newfoundland and Labrador Canada
437 L2 **North, Cape** Antarctica
123 H9 **North, Cape** Nova Scotia Canada
127 O5 **North Adams** Massachusetts USA
376 B4 **North Andaman** *island* Andaman and Nicobar Islands India
119 N1 **North Arm** Northwest Territories Canada
163 7 **North Arm** Falkland Islands
131 K4 **North Augusta** South Carolina USA
121 W3 **North Aulatsivik Island** Newfoundland and Labrador Canada
244 D5 **North Ayrshire** *admin. area* Scotland UK
377 H5 **North Balabac Strait** Philippines
119 Q6 **North Battleford** Saskatchewan Canada
121 U1 **North Bay** Nunavut Canada
127 L3 **North Bay** Ontario Canada
117 K7 **North Belcher Islands** Nunavut Canada
124 E2 **North Bend** British Columbia Canada
244 F4 **North Berwick** East Lothian Scotland UK
126 D2 **North Branch** Ontario Canada
126 E4 **North Branch** Minnesota USA
376 B5 **North Brother Island** Andaman and Nicobar Islands India
135 G2 **North Caicos** *island* Turks and Caicos Islands
123 G9 **North Cape** Prince Edward Island Canada
423 11 **North Cape** Antipodes Islands New Zealand
423 9 **North Cape** Campbell Island New Zealand
163 8 **North Cape** South Georgia
422 E2 **North Cape (Otou)** New Zealand
117 J8 **North Caribou Lake** Ontario Canada
120 J6 **North Caribou Lake** Ontario Canada
115 **North Carolina** *admin. area* USA
243 H3 **North Cave** East Riding of Yorkshire England UK
244 C5 **North Channel** Northern Ireland/Scotland UK
131 L4 **North Charleston** South Carolina USA
126 H5 **North Chicago** Illinois USA
385 H6 **North China Plain** Shandong China
243 H3 **North Cliffe** East Riding of Yorkshire England UK
118 J8 **North Cowichan** British Columbia Canada
241 H2 **North Creake** Norfolk England UK
114 **North Dakota** *admin. area* USA
243 H3 **North Dalton** East Riding of Yorkshire England UK
245 G2 **North Down** *admin. area* Northern Ireland UK
241 H3 **North Downs** *range* England UK
308 E4 **North-East** *admin. area* Botswana
423 7 **North East Island** Snares Islands New Zealand
243 H3 **North East Lincolnshire** *admin. area* England UK
424 inset **North East Point** Christmas Island Australia
426 1a **North East Point** Kiribati
307 G3 **North-Eastern** *admin. area* Kenya
422 F4 **North Egmont** New Zealand
135 F1 **North End Point** Bahamas
130 C2 **North Enid** Oklahoma USA
244 F4 **North Esk** *watercourse* Scotland UK
162 E5 **North Falkland Sound** Falkland Islands
78 N9 **North Fiji Basin** *underwater feature* Pacific Ocean
241 I3 **North Foreland** *cape* England UK
119 N8 **North Fork** *watercourse* British Columbia Canada
124 H2 **North Fork Flathead** *watercourse* Montana USA
129 M3 **North Fork Red** *watercourse* Oklahoma USA
121 O7 **North French** *watercourse* Ontario Canada
163 19 **North Friar's Bay** St Kitts and Nevis
425 J2 **North Goulburn Island** NT Australia
243 H2 **North Grimston** North Yorkshire England UK
425 O7 **North Haven** NSW Australia
425 inset **North Head** Lord Howe Island Australia
422 F3 **North Head** New Zealand
119 W2 **North Henik Lake** Nunavut Canada
307 F3 **North Horr** Kenya
243 H3 **North Hykeham** Lincolnshire England UK
422 E3 **North Island** New Zealand
310 9a **North Island** Seychelles
131 L4 **North Island** South Carolina USA
377 I5 **North Islet** Philippines
435 I2 **North Kanin Basin** *underwater feature* Barents Sea
424 inset **North Keeling Island** Cocos (Keeling) Islands Australia
243 H3 **North Kelsey** Lincolnshire England UK
244 D3 **North Kessock** Highland Scotland UK
243 H3 **North Killingholme** North Lincolnshire England UK
120 G3 **North Knife** *watercourse* Manitoba Canada
117 J7 **North Knife Lake** Manitoba Canada
119 W3 **North Knife Lake** Manitoba Canada
386 F3 **North Korea** *country*
379 H3 **North Lakhimpur** Assam India
244 E5 **North Lanarkshire** *admin. area* Scotland UK
128 E2 **North Las Vegas** Nevada USA
243 H3 **North Lincolnshire** *admin. area* England UK
130 E3 **North Little Rock** Arkansas USA
241 F2 **North Littleton** Worcestershire England UK
125 P6 **North Loup** Nebraska USA
125 O5 **North Loup** *watercourse* Nebraska USA
126 D4 **North Mankato** Minnesota USA
241 G3 **North Marston** Buckinghamshire England UK
163 11 **North Mayreau Channel** *strait* St Vincent and the Grenadines
131 K8 **North Miami** Florida USA
240 D3 **North Molton** Devon England UK
120 E5 **North Moose Lake** Manitoba Canada
131 L4 **North Myrtle Beach** South Carolina USA
118 I1 **North Nahanni** *watercourse* Northwest Territories Canada
124 J6 **North Ogden** Utah USA
240 D3 **North Petherton** Somerset England UK
125 O6 **North Platte** Nebraska USA
125 N6 **North Platte** *watercourse* Nebraska USA
163 12 **North Point** *cape* Barbados
310 9b **North Point** *cape* Seychelles
310 5c **North Point** *cape* St Helena
435 **North Pole** Arctic
116 E6 **North Pole** Alaska USA
131 J7 **North Port** Florida USA
124 G4 **North Powder** Oregon USA
377 F3 **North Reef** Paracel Islands
376 B4 **North Reef Island** Andaman and Nicobar Islands India
119 X3 **North River** Manitoba Canada
243 F3 **North Rode** Cheshire England UK
244 F1 **North Ronaldsay** *island* Scotland UK
119 N6 **North Saskatchewan** *watercourse* Alberta Canada
119 R6 **North Saskatchewan** *watercourse* Saskatchewan Canada
241 J2 **North Sea** Northern Europe
119 U3 **North Seal** *watercourse* Manitoba Canada
376 B5 **North Sentinel Island** Andaman and Nicobar Islands India
244 C4 **North Shian** Argyll and Bute Scotland UK
422 F3 **North Shore** New Zealand
116 D5 **North Slope** *region* Alaska USA
243 I3 **North Somercotes** Lincolnshire England UK
240 E3 **North Somerset** *admin. area* England UK
245 C3 **North Sound** Ireland
244 F1 **North Sound, The** Scotland UK
120 I6 **North Spirit Lake** Ontario Canada
122 J5 **North Stag Islands** Newfoundland and Labrador Canada
243 F2 **North Stainmore** Cumbria England UK
118 M4 **North Star** Alberta Canada
422 E3 **North Taranaki Bight** New Zealand
244 F4 **North Tarbrax** Angus Scotland UK
116 G8 **North Thompson** *watercourse* British Columbia Canada
127 O4 **North Troy** Vermont USA
121 O6 **North Twin Island** Nunavut Canada
243 F1 **North Tyne** *watercourse* England UK
243 G1 **North Tyneside** *admin. area* England UK
North Uist *see* **Uibhist a Tuath** UK
118 J8 **North Vancouver** British Columbia Canada
119 O4 **North Wabasca Lake** Alberta Canada
308 D3 **North-West** *admin. area* Botswana
308 E5 **North West** *admin. area* South Africa
424 E5 **North West Cape** WA Australia
423 8 **North West Cape** Auckland Islands New Zealand
391 L2 **North-West Frontier** *admin. area* Pakistan
424 inset **North West Point** Christmas Island Australia
426 1a **North West Point** *cape* Kiribati
122 H6 **North West River** Newfoundland and Labrador Canada
308 E2 **North-Western** *admin. area* Zambia
243 H2 **North York Moors** *region* England UK
243 G2 **North Yorkshire** *admin. area* England UK
424 F7 **Northam** WA Australia
240 C3 **Northam** Devon England UK
424 E7 **Northampton** WA Australia
241 G2 **Northampton** Northamptonshire England UK
437 L2 **Northampton, Mount** *mountain* Antarctica
241 G2 **Northamptonshire** *admin. area* England UK
437 G2 **Northcliffe Glacier** *ice* Antarctica
240 C4 **Northcott** Cornwall England UK
377 G5 **Northeast Cay** *island* Spratly Islands
117 P3 **Northeast Greenland National Park** Greenland
423 9 **Northeast Harbour** Campbell Island New Zealand
79 T7 **Northeast Pacific Basin** *underwater feature* Pacific Ocean
135 F2 **Northeast Point** Bahamas
134 E1 **Northeast Providence Channel** Bahamas
304 D3 **Northern** *admin. area* Ghana
309 F2 **Northern** *admin. area* Zambia
391 M2 **Northern Areas** *admin. area* Pakistan
306 D2 **Northern Bahr-el-Ghazal** *admin. area* Sudan
308 D5 **Northern Cape** *admin. area* South Africa
422 1 **Northern Cook Islands** Cook Islands New Zealand
302 D4 **Northern Darfur** *admin. area* Sudan
119 W4 **Northern Indian Lake** Manitoba Canada
242 B2 **Northern Ireland** *admin. area* UK
302 D4 **Northern Kordofan** *admin. area* Sudan
426 2 **Northern Mariana Islands** *US territory* Pacific Ocean
424 I4 **Northern Territory** *admin. area* Australia
126 E4 **Northfield** Minnesota USA
125 N2 **Northgate** North Dakota USA
126 I3 **Northland Station** Ontario Canada
240 C4 **Northlew** Devon England UK
125 R3 **Northome** Minnesota USA
130 H4 **Northport** Alabama USA
124 G2 **Northport** Washington USA
437 I2 **Norths Highland** *region* Antarctica
243 G1 **Northumberland** *admin. area* England UK
425 K9 **Northumberland, Cape** SA Australia
425 N5 **Northumberland Islands** Qld Australia
117 M9 **Northumberland Strait** Nova Scotia/Prince Edward Island Canada
131 L3 **Northwest** North Carolina USA
76 N4 **Northwest Atlantic Mid-Ocean Canyon** *underwater feature* Atlantic Ocean
78 L4 **Northwest Pacific Basin** *underwater feature* Pacific Ocean
135 F2 **Northwest Point** Bahamas
131 M7 **Northwest Providence Channel** Bahamas
78 I9 **Northwest Shelf** *underwater feature* Indian Ocean
116 G6 **Northwest Territories** *admin. area* Canada
243 F3 **Northwich** Cheshire England UK
434 T1 **Northwind Abyssal Plain** *underwater feature* Arctic Ocean
434 T1 **Northwind Escarpment** *underwater feature* Arctic Ocean
434 T1 **Northwind Ridge** *underwater feature* Arctic Ocean
125 Q3 **Northwood** North Dakota USA
123 F10 **Norton** New Brunswick Canada
241 E3 **Norton** Gloucestershire England UK
241 H2 **Norton** Suffolk England UK
241 G4 **Norton** West Sussex England UK
125 P7 **Norton** Kansas USA
308 F3 **Norton** Zimbabwe
240 D3 **Norton Fitzwarren** Somerset England UK
240 E2 **Norton in Hales** Shropshire England UK
126 H5 **Norton Shores** Michigan USA
116 C6 **Norton Sound** Alaska USA
223 N3 **Norvajärvi** *lake* Finland
436 X2 **Norvegia, Cape** Antarctica
128 C4 **Norwalk** California USA
126 J6 **Norwalk** Ohio USA
222 F5 **Norway** *country* Europe
435 G2 **Norwegian Basin** *underwater feature* Norwegian Sea
117 J3 **Norwegian Bay** Nunavut Canada
117 R5 **Norwegian Sea** Iceland/Norway
243 H3 **Norwell** Nottinghamshire England UK
241 I2 **Norwich** Norfolk England UK
127 O6 **Norwich** Connecticut USA
244 inset **Norwick** Shetland Scotland UK
127 M4 **Norwood** Ontario Canada
125 K7 **Norwood** Colorado USA
126 E8 **Norwood** Missouri USA
387 H3 **Noshiro** Japan
244 F2 **Noss Head** *cape* Scotland UK
157 E5 **Nossa Senhora da Glória** Brazil
154 E4 **Nossa Senhora da Guia** Brazil
308 C4 **Nossob** *watercourse* Namibia
308 D5 **Nossop** *watercourse* Botswana
309 I4 **Nosy-varika** Madagascar
227 I4 **Noszlop** Hungary
227 I1 **Noteć** *watercourse* Poland
119 V5 **Notigi** Manitoba Canada
118 L4 **Notikewin** *watercourse* Alberta Canada
235 D7 **Notio Aigaio** *admin. area* Greece
233 F8 **Noto, Golfo di** *bay* Italy
387 J2 **Notoro-ko** *lake* Japan
223 Q2 **Notozero, Ozero** *lake* Russian Federation
117 M9 **Notre Dame, Monts** *range* Québec Canada
123 K8 **Notre Dame Bay** Newfoundland and Labrador Canada
304 E3 **Notsé** Togo
240 D3 **Nottage** Bridgend Wales UK
121 P7 **Nottaway** *watercourse* Québec Canada
131 I3 **Nottely Lake** Georgia USA
241 F2 **Nottingham** *admin. area* England UK
241 F2 **Nottingham** Nottingham England UK
121 Q1 **Nottingham Island** Nunavut Canada
243 G3 **Nottinghamshire** *admin. area* England UK
131 M2 **Nottoway** *watercourse* Virginia USA
300 C4 **Nouâdhibou** Mauritania
300 C5 **Nouakchott** Mauritania
300 C5 **Nouâmghâr** Mauritania
122 C5 **Noue, Lac de la** *lake* Québec Canada
426 7 **Nouméa** New Caledonia
304 D2 **Nouna** Burkina Faso
305 G4 **Nouna** *watercourse* Gabon
223 P3 **Nousu** Finland
123 E8 **Nouvelle** Québec Canada
426 7 **Nouvelle Calédonie** *island* New Caledonia
122 B1 **Nouvelle-France, Cap de** *cape* Québec Canada
241 I4 **Nouvion** France
227 I4 **Nova** Hungary
159 F3 **Nova, Serra** *range* Brazil
159 I3 **Nova Amélia** Brazil
157 A8 **Nova Andradina** Brazil
227 J3 **Nová Baňa** Slovakia
306 A5 **Nova Caipemba** Angola
159 I4 **Nova Crixás** Brazil
156 F4 **Nova Cruz** Brazil
159 G5 **Nova Dourados** Brazil
309 F4 **Nova Golegã** Mozambique
232 E4 **Nova Gorica** Slovenia
157 D8 **Nova Iguaçu** Brazil
157 A8 **Nova Londrina** Brazil
309 F4 **Nova Mambone** Mozambique
159 G3 **Nova Monte Verde** Brazil
159 G4 **Nova Olímpia** Brazil
159 G1 **Nova Olinda** Brazil
159 H2 **Nova Olinda** Brazil
159 G1 **Nova Olinda do Norte** Brazil
157 C7 **Nova Ponte, Represa** *lake* Brazil
161 I4 **Nova Prata** Brazil
227 I5 **Nova Rača** Croatia
156 D4 **Nova Russas** Brazil
117 M10 **Nova Scotia** *admin. area* Canada
157 E5 **Nova Soure** Brazil
234 E1 **Nova Ushytsya** Ukraine
234 A4 **Nova Varoš** Serbia
157 D7 **Nova Venécia** Brazil
227 M2 **Nova Verba** Ukraine
158 F7 **Nova Viçosa** Brazil
158 E1 **Nova Vida** Brazil
157 A6 **Nova Xavantina** Brazil
227 L5 **Novaci** Romania
227 J3 **Nováky** Slovakia
232 F4 **Novalja** Croatia
127 L4 **Novar** Ontario Canada
226 E5 **Novara** Italy
124 D7 **Novato** California USA
388 F4 **Novaya Kazanka** Kazakhstan
225 Q2 **Novaya Ladoga** Russian Federation
237 AE3 **Novaya Sibir', Ostrov** *island* Russian Federation
223 R2 **Novaya Titovka** Russian Federation
236 M4 **Novaya Zemlya** *island* Russian Federation
435 J2 **Novaya Zemlya Trough** *underwater feature* Karskoye More (Kara Sea)
234 E1 **Nove Selo** Ukraine
227 J4 **Nové Zámky** Slovakia
225 P4 **Novgorodskaya Oblast'** *admin. area* Russian Federation
227 K5 **Novi Bečej** Serbia
226 E5 **Novi Ligure** Italy
234 A3 **Novi Sad** Serbia
130 B5 **Novice** Texas USA
232 E4 **Novigrad** Croatia
387 I1 **Novikovo** Russian Federation
159 E5 **Novillero** Bolivia
154 B3 **Nóvita** Colombia
238 H3 **Novlenskoye** Russian Federation
156 B2 **Novo, Lago** *lake* Brazil
159 E3 **Novo Apuá** Brazil
159 F2 **Novo Aripuanã** Brazil
157 D7 **Novo Cruzeiro** Brazil
159 I6 **Novo Horizonte** Brazil
227 H5 **Novo Mesto** Slovenia
234 B3 **Novo Miloševo** Serbia
159 H3 **Novo Mundo** Brazil
234 A3 **Novo Orahovo** Serbia
156 D4 **Novo Oriente** Brazil
154 E5 **Novo Paraíso** Brazil
235 C5 **Novo Selo** Macedonia
388 F3 **Novo-sergiyevskiy** Russian Federation
238 F5 **Novoaleksandrovskiy** Russian Federation
389 N2 **Novoaltaysk** Russian Federation
388 D3 **Novoanninskiy** Russian Federation
394 E3 **Novoaya Kakhovka** Ukraine
389 K6 **Novobod** Tajikistan
388 E2 **Novocheboksarsk** Russian Federation
388 C4 **Novocherkassk** Russian Federation
389 K3 **Novodolinka** Kazakhstan
238 F5 **Novodugino** Russian Federation
236 J6 **Novodvinsk** Russian Federation
388 E5 **Novokayakent** Russian Federation
238 C5 **Novokhovansk** Russian Federation
389 O2 **Novokuznetsk** Russian Federation
437 A2 **Novolazarevskaya (Russia)** *research station* Antarctica
225 O5 **Novolukoml'** Belarus
238 H5 **Novomoskovsk** Russian Federation
394 E3 **Novomoskovs'k** Ukraine
234 G1 **Novomyrhorod** Ukraine
388 H3 **Novoorsk** Russian Federation
394 F3 **Novopskov** Ukraine
388 C5 **Novorossiysk** Russian Federation
389 K3 **Novorybinka** Kazakhstan
238 C4 **Novorzhev** Russian Federation
235 A5 **Novoselë** Albania
225 O5 **Novosëlki** Belarus
238 C3 **Novosel'ye** Russian Federation
234 E1 **Novoselytsya** Ukraine
389 N2 **Novosibirsk** Russian Federation
389 M2 **Novosibirskaya Oblast'** *admin. area* Russian Federation
237 AE3 **Novosibirskiye Ostrova** *island* Russian Federation
394 F2 **Novosil'** Russian Federation
225 P4 **Novosokol'niki** Russian Federation
234 G2 **Novosvetlovka** Ukraine
388 H3 **Novotroitsk** Russian Federation
238 E6 **Novotroitskoye** Russian Federation
388 H3 **Novoural'sk** Russian Federation
388 E3 **Novouzensk** Russian Federation
234 G2 **Novovasil'yevka** Ukraine
227 M2 **Novovolyns'k** Ukraine
237 AA8 **Novovoskresenovka** Russian Federation
385 K2 **Novovoskresenovka** Russian Federation
234 C1 **Novoye Misto** Ukraine
389 M3 **Novoyegor'yevskoye** Russian Federation
236 L6 **Novozhilovskaya** Russian Federation
232 G4 **Novska** Croatia
227 I3 **Nový Jičín** Czech Republic
225 N5 **Novy Pahost** Belarus
237 W4 **Novyy** Russian Federation
236 L5 **Novyy Bor** Russian Federation
394 E3 **Novyy Buh** Ukraine
238 D6 **Novyy Bykhov** Belarus
394 D1 **Novyy Rozdil** Ukraine
236 Q5 **Novyy Urengoy** Russian Federation
385 L2 **Novyy Urgal** Russian Federation
234 G2 **Novyye Bilyari** Ukraine
391 J3 **Now Bahār** Iran
391 I2 **Now Deh** Afghanistan
227 I2 **Nowa Brzeźnica** Poland
227 I2 **Nowa Ruda** Poland
227 L2 **Nowa Sarzyna** Poland
227 H2 **Nowa Sól** Poland
227 L1 **Nowa Wieś Ełcka** Poland

227 J1 **Nowe** Poland
227 K1 **Nowiny** Poland
120 E1 **Nowleye Lake** Nunavut Canada
227 K1 **Nowogród** Poland
425 N8 **Nowra** NSW Australia
227 L2 **Nowy Lubliniec** Poland
227 K3 **Nowy Sącz** Poland
227 J3 **Nowy Targ** Poland
120 F2 **Nowyak Lake** Nunavut Canada
124 H3 **Noxon Reservoir** Montana USA
130 G4 **Noxubee** *watercourse* Mississippi USA
305 G4 **Noya** *watercourse* Gabon
389 R3 **Noyan-khol'** *lake* Russian Federation
228 E3 **Noyant** France
228 G3 **Noyers** France
123 I7 **Noyrot, Lac** *lake* Québec Canada
386 F5 **Nozaki-jima** *island* Japan
228 D3 **Nozay** France
229 H3 **Nozeroy** France
305 H5 **Nsa** Congo
306 B4 **Nsambi** Democratic Republic of Congo
305 G4 **Nsoc** Equatorial Guinea
308 E2 **Nsombo** Zambia
305 F3 **Nsukka** Nigeria
308 D2 **Ntambu** Zambia
306 B4 **Ntandembele** Democratic Republic of Congo
309 F2 **Ntcheu** Malawi
305 G4 **Ntem** *watercourse* Gabon
305 F4 **Ntoum** Gabon
306 E4 **Ntungamo** Uganda
309 G2 **Ntwetwe Pan** Botswana
380 C4 **Nu Jiang** *watercourse* Yunnan China
376 I6 **Nuakata Island** Papua New Guinea
372 C3 **Nuangan** Indonesia
393 F7 **Nuaparha** Orissa India
223 O4 **Nuasjärvi** *bay* Finland
302 E5 **Nuba Mountains** *range* Sudan
302 D4 **Nubian Desert** Sudan
302 E3 **Nubian Monuments** *point of interest* Egypt
160 D6 **Ñuble** *watercourse* Chile
372 F4 **Nuboai** Indonesia
118 H8 **Nuchatlitz Inlet** British Columbia Canada
238 G4 **Nudol'** Russian Federation
130 B6 **Nueces** *watercourse* Texas USA
119 V3 **Nueltin Lake** Manitoba/Nunavut Canada
162 C6 **Nueva, Isla** *island* Chile
161 H3 **Nueva Alborada** Paraguay
133 F3 **Nueva Ciudad Guerrero** Mexico
158 D4 **Nueva Cruz** Peru
155 E2 **Nueva Esparta** *admin. area* Venezuela
161 G2 **Nueva Germania** Paraguay
134 D2 **Nueva Gerona** Cuba
154 C2 **Nueva Granada** Colombia
134 C5 **Nueva Guinea** Nicaragua
160 C6 **Nueva Imperial** Chile
161 G3 **Nueva Italia** Paraguay
154 B4 **Nueva Loja** Ecuador
162 B3 **Nueva Lubecka** Argentina
161 G5 **Nueva Palmira** Uruguay
160 F3 **Nueva Pompeya** Argentina
160 F6 **Nueva Roma** Argentina
132 E3 **Nueva Rosita** Mexico
160 C6 **Nueva Toltén** Chile
160 F5 **Nueve de Julio** Argentina
134 E2 **Nuevitas, Bahia de** *bay* Cuba
162 D3 **Nuevo, Golfo** *bay* Argentina
134 C4 **Nuevo Amanecer** Nicaragua
132 D2 **Nuevo Casas Grandes** Mexico
130 B7 **Nuevo Ciudad Guerrero** Mexico
154 C5 **Nuevo Horizonte** Peru
158 B4 **Nuevo Imperial** Peru
132 E5 **Nuevo Italia de Ruiz** Mexico
133 F3 **Nuevo Laredo** Mexico
133 F3 **Nuevo León** *admin. area* Mexico
159 E5 **Nuevo Mundo** Bolivia
158 C3 **Nuevo Mundo** Peru
133 F3 **Nuevo Padilla** Mexico
133 F4 **Nuevo Progreso** Mexico
129 K7 **Nuevo Reforma** Mexico
132 B2 **Nuevo Uruapan** Mexico
307 H2 **Nugaal** *admin. area* Somalia
423 C8 **Nugget Point** New Zealand
426 8a **Nughu Island** *island* Solomon Islands
224 G2 **Nuguren** *lake* Norway
373 J4 **Nuguria Islands** Papua New Guinea
392 D5 **Nuh** Haryana India
422 G4 **Nuhaka** New Zealand
427 13 **Nui** *island* Tuvalu
376 E2 **Nui Con Voi** Vietnam
116 D4 **Nuiqsut** Alaska USA
118 J5 **Nukko Lake** British Columbia Canada
427 14 **Nuku Hiva** *island* French Polynesia
427 10a **Nuku'alofa** Tonga
427 13 **Nukufetau** *island* Tuvalu
427 13 **Nukulaelae** *island* Tuvalu
422 3 **Nukunonu** *island* Tokelau New Zealand
422 3 **Nukunonu Village** Tokelau New Zealand
427 10a **Nukunuku** Tonga
78 L7 **Nukuoro Atoll** *reef* Micronesia
388 H5 **Nukus** Uzbekistan
427 14 **Nukutavake** *island* French Polynesia
427 14 **Nukutipipi** *island* French Polynesia
116 D6 **Nulato** Alaska USA
231 F4 **Nules** Spain
424 G5 **Nullagine** WA Australia
424 G5 **Nullagine** *watercourse* WA Australia
424 H7 **Nullarbor Plain** WA Australia
424 I7 **Nullarbor Roadhouse** SA Australia
121 Q3 **Nuluarniavik, Lac** *lake* Québec Canada
385 I4 **Nulu'erhu Shan** *range* Liaoning China
372 E4 **Num** *island* Indonesia
305 G3 **Numan** Nigeria
306 D2 **Numatinna** *watercourse* Sudan
387 H4 **Numazu** Japan
374 E3 **Numbing** *island* Indonesia
425 J3 **Numbulwar** NT Australia
224 E2 **Numedal** *valley* Norway
225 M2 **Numminen** Finland
122 H5 **Nunaksaluk Island** Newfoundland and Labrador Canada
119 X3 **Nunalla** Manitoba Canada
117 O7 **Nunap Isua (Kap Farvel)** *cape* Greenland
122 O2 **Nunarsuit** *island* Greenland
122 M1 **Nunasarnaq** *island* Greenland
121 Q4 **Nunavik** *region* Québec Canada
116 I5 **Nunavut** *admin. area* Canada
154 C3 **Nunchía** Colombia
424 J7 **Nundroo** SA Australia
241 F2 **Nuneaton** Warwickshire England UK
424 F7 **Nungarin** WA Australia
120 I7 **Nungesser Lake** Ontario Canada
309 G2 **Nungo** Mozambique
116 C6 **Nunivak Island** Alaska USA
223 N2 **Nunnanen** Finland
231 G4 **Nunó, Cap** *cape* Spain
158 D4 **Ñuñoa** Peru
245 G2 **Nuns Quarter** Ards Northern Ireland UK
375 H2 **Nunukan** *island* Indonesia
380 E2 **Nuojiang** Sichuan China
223 Q5 **Nuorajärvi** *bay* Finland
223 O4 **Nuoritta** Finland
233 C6 **Nuoro** Sardinia Italy
223 O4 **Nuorunka** Finland
301 J4 **Nuqayy, Jabal** *range* Libya
390 E4 **Nuqrah** Saudi Arabia
227 L1 **Nur** Poland
389 L4 **Nura** Kazakhstan
390 F2 **Nūrabād** Iran
232 C4 **Nure** *watercourse* Italy
305 C5 **Nurei** Sudan
391 L2 **Nūrestān** *admin. area* Afghanistan
132 C2 **Nuri** Mexico
374 F4 **Nuri, Teluk** *bay* Indonesia
388 F2 **Nurlat** Russian Federation
238 F2 **Nurlaty** Russian Federation
222 M3 **Nurmasuanto** Sweden
223 P5 **Nurmes** Finland
223 Q5 **Nurmijärvi** Finland
223 M5 **Nurmo** Finland
226 F3 **Nürnberg** Germany
372 A5 **Nusa Tenggara Barat** *admin. area* Indonesia
372 B6 **Nusa Tenggara Timur** *admin. area* Indonesia
372 E5 **Nusawulan** Indonesia
394 G6 **Nusaybin** Turkey
372 D4 **Nusela, Kepulauan** *island* Indonesia
234 D2 **Nuşeni** Romania
222 H2 **Nusfjord** Norway
391 K3 **Nushki** Pakistan
122 H4 **Nutak** Newfoundland and Labrador Canada
116 B5 **Nutauge, Laguna** *lagoon* Russian Federation
116 B5 **Nutepel'men** Russian Federation
391 K4 **Nuttal** Pakistan
117 N4 **Nuugaatsiaap Tunua** *bay* Greenland
117 N6 **Nuuk** Greenland
223 O3 **Nuupas** Finland
427 14a **Nuupere, Pointe** *cape* French Polynesia
384 D4 **Nuur** *lake* Mongolia
117 N4 **Nuussuaq** *peninsula* Greenland
223 O4 **Nuutila** Finland
223 O2 **Nuvusskaidi** Finland
223 O2 **Nuvvus** Finland
392 F5 **Nuwakot** Nepal
308 C6 **Nuwerus** South Africa
305 H3 **Nwa** Cameroon
305 H3 **Nya** *watercourse* Chad
305 G4 **Nyabessan** Cameroon
424 F8 **Nyabing** WA Australia
307 F3 **Nyahururu** Kenya
379 G2 **Nyainqentanglha Shan** *range* Xizang Zizhiqu China
222 K5 **Nyåker** Sweden
236 N6 **Nyaksimvol'** Russian Federation
302 C5 **Nyala** Sudan
309 F3 **Nyamapanda** Zimbabwe
306 D2 **Nyamlell** Sudan
307 F6 **Nyamtumbo** Tanzania
236 I2 **Nyandoma** Russian Federation
236 J6 **Nyandomskiy Rayon** *range* Russian Federation
379 F2 **Nyang Qu** *lake* Xizang Zizhiqu China
379 G3 **Nyang Qu** *watercourse* Xizang Zizhiqu China
305 G5 **Nyanga** *admin. area* Gabon
309 F3 **Nyanga** Zimbabwe
307 F5 **Nyangolo** Tanzania
306 E4 **Nyantakara** Tanzania
307 E4 **Nyanza** *admin. area* Kenya
306 D4 **Nyanza Lac** Burundi
232 H3 **Nyárlőrinc** Hungary
307 E6 **Nyasa, Lake** Africa
379 H5 **Nyaung-U** Myanmar
376 C3 **Nyaunglebin** Myanmar
224 F5 **Nyborg** Denmark
222 L5 **Nyby** Finland
223 N1 **Nyby** Norway
222 I5 **Nyby** Sweden
222 H3 **Nybyn** Sweden
305 G4 **Nyé** *watercourse* Gabon
117 N2 **Nyeboe Land** *region* Greenland
307 F4 **Nyeri** Kenya
237 AM6 **Nygchigen, Mys** *cape* Russian Federation
222 I4 **Nyhem** Sweden
222 I5 **Nyhem** Sweden
306 E2 **Nyiel** Sudan
309 F2 **Nyika Plateau** *plain* Malawi
309 F2 **Nyimba** Zambia
227 L4 **Nyírbogát** Hungary
234 B2 **Nyíregyháza** Hungary
234 B1 **Nyirtura** Hungary
223 N4 **Nykälä** Finland
222 M5 **Nykarleby/Uusikaarlepy** Finland
224 F5 **Nykøbing** Denmark
224 I3 **Nyköping** Sweden
222 J5 **Nyland** Sweden
222 K5 **Nyliden** Sweden
425 M8 **Nymagee** NSW Australia
227 H2 **Nymburk** Czech Republic
224 I3 **Nynäshamn** Sweden
425 M7 **Nyngan** NSW Australia
227 L1 **Nyoman** *watercourse* Belarus
305 G4 **Nyong** *watercourse* Cameroon
229 G4 **Nyons** France
232 E2 **Nýrsko** Czech Republic
229 K2 **Nýrsko, Vodní nádrž** *lake* Czech Republic
223 P2 **Nyrud** Norway
227 I2 **Nysa** Poland
224 G3 **Nysäter** Sweden
224 G3 **Nysockensjön** *lake* Sweden
124 G5 **Nyssa** Oregon USA
224 F5 **Nysted** Denmark
222 F6 **Nystova** Norway
225 M2 **Nytkyn** *lake* Finland
223 Q4 **Nyuk, Ozero** *lake* Russian Federation
237 Z7 **Nyukzha** *watercourse* Russian Federation
306 D5 **Nyunzu** Democratic Republic of Congo
375 H3 **Nyurang** Indonesia
237 Y6 **Nyurba** Russian Federation
237 X6 **Nyuya** *watercourse* Russian Federation
223 M1 **Nyvoll** Norway
234 D1 **Nyzhniv** Ukraine
305 I3 **Nzako** Central African Republic
305 G5 **Nzambi** Congo
307 E4 **Nzega** Tanzania
304 C3 **Nzérékoré** Guinea
306 A5 **N'zeto** Angola
304 D3 **Nzi** *watercourse* Côte d'Ivoire
306 D6 **Nzilo, Lac** *lake* Democratic Republic of Congo
304 C3 **Nzo** *watercourse* Côte d'Ivoire
304 C3 **Nzoo** Guinea
306 E3 **Nzoro** *watercourse* Democratic Republic of Congo
Nzwani *see* **Angouan** Comoros

O

230 C2 **O Barco** Spain
230 B2 **O Castro** Spain
222 K4 **Ö Kikkejaure** *lake* Sweden
386 G5 **Ō-Shima** *island* Japan
130 D2 **O The Cherokees, Lake** Oklahoma USA
130 D4 **O' the Pines, Lake** Texas USA
244 B5 **Oa, Mull of** *cape* Scotland UK
125 P5 **Oacoma** South Dakota USA
241 F2 **Oadby** Leicester England UK
128 inset **O'ahu** *island* Hawai'i USA
125 L6 **Oak Creek** Colorado USA
130 A4 **Oak Creek Reservoir** Texas USA
130 H2 **Oak Grove** Kentucky USA
129 N4 **Oak Grove** Texas USA
130 F2 **Oak Grove Heights** Arkansas USA
124 D2 **Oak Harbor** Washington USA
131 K6 **Oak Hill** Florida USA
127 K8 **Oak Hill** West Virginia USA
131 K2 **Oak Island** North Carolina USA
119 U8 **Oak Lake** Manitoba Canada
126 H3 **Oak Lawn** Illinois USA
126 H6 **Oak Park** Illinois USA
125 P1 **Oak Point** Manitoba Canada
131 I3 **Oak Ridge** Tennessee USA
125 O1 **Oakburn** Manitoba Canada
130 E5 **Oakdale** Louisiana USA
125 Q5 **Oakdale** Nebraska USA
240 E2 **Oakengates** Telford and Wrekin England UK
125 P3 **Oakes** North Dakota USA
124 G3 **Oakesdale** Washington USA
425 N6 **Oakey** Qld Australia
245 F3 **Oakfield** Ireland
241 G2 **Oakham** Rutland England UK
128 C2 **Oakhurst** California USA
120 F7 **Oakland** Manitoba Canada
124 D8 **Oakland** California USA
126 G7 **Oakland** Illinois USA
126 D6 **Oakland** Iowa USA
130 G3 **Oakland** Mississippi USA
130 C3 **Oakland** Oklahoma USA
124 D5 **Oakland** Oregon USA
241 F3 **Oakley** Buckinghamshire England UK
124 I5 **Oakley** Idaho USA
125 O7 **Oakley** Kansas USA
130 H4 **Oakman** Alabama USA
424 G5 **Oakover** *watercourse* WA Australia
124 D5 **Oakridge** Oregon USA
126 H7 **Oaktown** Indiana USA
422 F2 **Oakura** New Zealand
120 F8 **Oakville** Manitoba Canada
124 D3 **Oakville** Washington USA
125 O5 **Oakwood** Texas USA
423 D7 **Oamaru** New Zealand
422 E4 **Oaonui** New Zealand
128 F1 **Oasis** Utah USA
425 M4 **Oasis Roadhouse** Qld Australia
437 K2 **Oates Coast** Antarctica
133 F5 **Oaxaca** Mexico
236 O5 **Ob'** *watercourse* Russian Federation
389 N3 **Ob** *watercourse* Russian Federation
437 K2 **Ob' Bay** Antarctica
80 J10 **Ob' Tablemount** *underwater feature* Southern Ocean
126 I2 **Oba Lake** Ontario Canada
373 F5 **Obaa** Indonesia
126 I2 **Obakamiga Lake** Ontario Canada
127 M2 **Obalski Lake** Québec Canada
387 G4 **Obama** Japan
Oban *see* **Halfmoon Bay** New Zealand
305 F3 **Oban** Nigeria
244 C4 **Oban** Argyll and Bute Scotland UK
305 F3 **Oban Hills** *range* Nigeria
389 K6 **Obanbori Qayroqum** *lake* Tajikistan
127 N2 **Obatogamau** *watercourse* Québec Canada
127 N2 **Obatogamau Lake** Québec Canada
222 L5 **Obbola** Sweden
234 D2 **Obcina Feredeului** *region* Romania
118 M6 **Obed** Alberta Canada
225 M5 **Obeliai** Lithuania
232 C2 **Ober-Olm** Germany
232 D3 **Oberau** Germany
232 D2 **Oberbaar** Germany
232 C2 **Oberkirch** Germany
125 O7 **Oberlin** Kansas USA
130 E5 **Oberlin** Louisiana USA
229 H2 **Obernai** France
226 G3 **Oberösterreich** *admin. area* Austria
227 I4 **Oberpullendorf** Austria
226 F4 **Oberstaufen** Germany
226 F4 **Oberstdorf** Germany
226 G4 **Obertrumer See** *lake* Austria
227 I4 **Oberwart** Austria
375 J4 **Obi** *island* Indonesia
305 F3 **Obi** Nigeria
387 I2 **Obihiro** Japan
375 J4 **Obilatu** *island* Indonesia
229 K2 **Obing** Germany
386 G2 **Oblachnaya, Gora** *mountain* Russian Federation
388 D4 **Oblivskaya** Russian Federation
126 H7 **Oblong** Illinois USA
385 L3 **Obluchye** Russian Federation
238 G5 **Obninsk** Russian Federation
306 D2 **Obo** Central African Republic
303 G5 **Obock** Djibouti
234 F1 **Obodivka** Ukraine
306 D4 **Obokote** Democratic Republic of Congo
372 E4 **Obome** Indonesia
126 G2 **Obonga Lake** Ontario Canada
227 K3 **Oborín** Slovakia
234 D4 **Oborishte** Bulgaria
388 G6 **Oboy** Turkmenistan
394 F2 **Oboyan'** Russian Federation
392 F6 **Obra** Uttar Pradesh India
234 A3 **Obrež** Serbia
134 B4 **O'Brien** Texas USA
227 H5 **Obrov** Slovenia
227 H5 **Obrtići** Bosnia and Herzegovina
162 D6 **Observatorio, Isla** *island* Argentina
425 N4 **Observatory Cay** Coral Sea Islands Territory Australia
118 F5 **Observatory Inlet** British Columbia Canada
388 E2 **Obshaovka** Russian Federation
236 P5 **Obskaya Guba** *bay* Russian Federation
304 D3 **Obuasi** Ghana
304 F3 **Obudu** Nigeria
234 E4 **Obzor** Bulgaria
235 E5 **Ocakı** Turkey
131 J6 **Ocala** Florida USA
132 E3 **Ocampo** Mexico
133 F4 **Ocampo** Mexico
154 C2 **Ocaña** Colombia
230 E4 **Ocaña** Spain
124 E4 **Ocara** Brazil
154 B3 **Occidental, Cordillera** *range* Colombia
158 C4 **Occidental, Cordillera** *range* Peru
244 E2 **Occumster** Highland Scotland UK
127 N7 **Ocean City** New Jersey USA
118 H6 **Ocean Falls** British Columbia Canada
76 O6 **Oceanographer Fracture Zone** *underwater feature* Atlantic Ocean
128 D4 **Oceanside** California USA
426 5 **Oceanview** Guam
426 6a **Ocha** *island* Federated States of Micronesia
234 G2 **Ochakiv** Ukraine
387 H4 **Ochi-gata** *lake* Japan
244 D5 **Ochiltree** East Ayrshire Scotland UK
129 J6 **Ochoa** Texas USA
125 P1 **Ochre River** Manitoba Canada
244 E4 **Ochtertyre** Perth and Kinross Scotland UK
226 D1 **Ochtrup** Germany
131 J5 **Ocilla** Georgia USA
131 K6 **Ocklawaha Lake** Florida USA
244 B4 **Ockle** Highland Scotland UK
131 J5 **Ocmulgee** *watercourse* Georgia USA
234 E1 **Ocniţa** Moldova
158 C5 **Ocoña** *watercourse* Peru
131 J4 **Oconee** *watercourse* Georgia USA
126 H4 **Oconto** Wisconsin USA
133 G6 **Ocós** Guatemala
133 G5 **Ocosingo** Mexico
134 C4 **Ocotal** Nicaragua
133 F5 **Ocotlán** Mexico
227 K4 **Öcsöd** Hungary
241 F5 **Octeville** France
134 D6 **Ocú** Panama
309 G2 **Ocua** Mozambique
154 E2 **Ocumare del Tuy** Venezuela
224 G4 **Od** Sweden
304 D3 **Oda** Ghana
386 G4 **Ōda** Japan
302 F3 **Oda, Jebel** *mountain* Sudan
373 F5 **Odammun** *watercourse* Indonesia
387 I3 **Ōdate** Japan
387 H4 **Odawara** Japan
120 H4 **O'Day** Manitoba Canada
224 D2 **Odda** Norway
119 V5 **Oddhill** Manitoba Canada
130 C7 **Odem** Texas USA
230 B5 **Odemira** Portugal
235 E6 **Ödemiş** Turkey
224 F5 **Odense** Denmark
224 F5 **Odense Fjord** *bay* Denmark
226 F2 **Oder** *watercourse* Germany
232 E4 **Oderzo** Italy
234 G2 **Odesa** Ukraine
394 D3/4 **Odes'ka Oblast'** *admin. area* Ukraine
119 T7 **Odessa** Saskatchewan Canada
125 Q4 **Odessa** Minnesota USA
126 E7 **Odessa** Missouri USA
129 K5 **Odessa** Texas USA
124 F3 **Odessa** Washington USA
389 K2 **Odesskoye** Russian Federation
228 C2 **Odet** *watercourse* France
230 C5 **Odiel** *watercourse* Spain
304 C3 **Odienné** Côte d'Ivoire
238 G5 **Odintsovo** Russian Federation
230 B4 **Odivelas, Barragem de** *lake* Portugal
436 U2 **Odom Inlet** *bay* Antarctica
228 D2 **Odon** *watercourse* France
424 H4 **O'Donnell** *watercourse* WA Australia
129 L5 **O'Donnell** Texas USA
227 H1 **Odra** *watercourse* Poland
224 F4 **Odrus** *watercourse* Sudan
227 I3 **Odry** Czech Republic
241 F3 **Odstock** Wiltshire England UK
232 H4 **Odžaci** Serbia
232 H6 **Odžak** Montenegro
225 M4 **Odzes Ezers** *lake* Latvia
309 F3 **Odzi** *watercourse* Zimbabwe
156 D4 **Oeiras** Brazil
158 D3 **Oeiras do Pará** Brazil
125 N5 **Oelrichs** South Dakota USA
229 K1 **Oelsnitz** Germany
126 F5 **Oelwein** Iowa USA
427 11 **Oeno Island** Pitcairn Islands
386 E4 **Oeraro-do** *island* South Korea
226 F3 **Oettingen** Germany
229 J2 **Oettingen in Bayern** Germany
226 F4 **Oetz** Austria
226 F1 **Oetzen** Germany
122 B5 **Oeufs, Lac des** *lake* Québec Canada
126 G7 **O'Fallon** Illinois USA
233 F6 **Ofanto** *watercourse* Italy
373 F5 **Ofe** *watercourse* Nigeria
233 E5 **Ofena** Italy
305 E3 **Offa** Nigeria
245 E3 **Offaly** *admin. area* Ireland
232 C1 **Offenbach am Main** Germany
125 P8 **Offerle** Kansas USA
160 D2 **Oficina Sara** Chile
235 E7 **Ofidoussa** *island* Greece
162 A4 **Ofqui, Istmo de** *peninsula* Chile
224 E3 **Ofte** Norway
427 12c **Ofu** *island* American Samoa
387 I3 **Ōfunato** Japan
375 G3 **Oga** *watercourse* Indonesia
387 H3 **Oga** Japan
307 H2 **Ogaden** *plain* Ethiopia
387 H4 **Ōgaki** Japan
125 O6 **Ogallala** Nebraska USA
374 E4 **Ogan** *watercourse* Indonesia
387 I3 **Ogawara-ko** *lake* Japan
305 E3 **Ogbomosho** Nigeria
125 Q7 **Ogden** Kansas USA
124 J6 **Ogden** Utah USA
127 N4 **Ogdensburg** New York USA
224 E3 **Øgdern** *lake* Norway
427 9 **Ogea Driki** *island* Fiji
131 J4 **Ogeechee** *watercourse* Georgia USA
119 S8 **Ogema** Saskatchewan Canada
224 E3 **Ogge** *lake* Norway
232 C4 **Oggiono** Italy
387 H4 **Ogi** Japan
119 V7 **Ogilvie** Manitoba Canada
116 F5 **Ogilvie** *watercourse* Yukon Territory Canada
116 F6 **Ogilvie Mountains** Yukon Territory Canada
162 C6 **Oglander, Bahía** *bay* Chile
233 B9 **Oglat Oulad Mahboub** Algeria
382 H6 **Oglung He** *watercourse* Xizang Zizhiqu China
229 G3 **Ognon** *watercourse* France
372 B3 **Ogoamas, Gunung** *mountain* Indonesia
305 F3 **Ogoja** Nigeria
120 M7 **Ogoki** Ontario Canada
120 K7 **Ogoki** *watercourse* Ontario Canada
120 L7 **Ogoki Lake** Ontario Canada
120 K7 **Ogoki Reservoir** Ontario Canada
305 G5 **Ogooué** *watercourse* Congo
305 G5 **Ogooué** *watercourse* Gabon
305 G4 **Ogooué-Ivindo** *admin. area* Gabon
305 G5 **Ogooué-Lolo** *admin. area* Gabon
305 F5 **Ogooué-Maritime** *admin. area* Gabon
225 M4 **Ogre** Latvia
225 M4 **Ogres** *admin. area* Latvia
234 D3 **Ogrezeni** Romania
305 E3 **Ogun** *admin. area* Nigeria
305 E3 **Ogun** *watercourse* Nigeria
388 F6 **Ogurja Ada** *island* Turkmenistan
422 G4 **Ohaaki** New Zealand
423 B7 **Ohai** New Zealand
422 G4 **Ohakuri** New Zealand
301 H3 **Ohanet** Algeria
308 C3 **Ohangwena** *admin. area* Namibia
119 O6 **Ohaton** Alberta Canada
423 C7 **Ohau, Lake** New Zealand
127 I2 **Ohey** Belgium
160 D2 **O'Higgins** Chile
163 5 **O'Higgins, Cabo** *cape* Isla de Pascua (Easter Island)
162 B4 **O'Higgins, Cerro** *mountain* Chile
163 6a **O'Higgins, Punta** *cape* Isla Róbinson Crusoe
436 U2 **O'Higgins (Chile)** *research station* Antarctica
422 F4 **Ohingaiti** New Zealand
114 **Ohio** *admin. area* USA
126 G8 **Ohio** *watercourse* Illinois USA
126 J7 **Ohio** *watercourse* Indiana USA
126 J7 **Ohio** *watercourse* Kentucky USA
127 K7 **Ohio** *watercourse* Ohio USA
436 Q1 **Ohio Range** Antarctica
229 I1 **Ohm** *watercourse* Germany
222 I5 **Öhn** Sweden
427 10a **'Ohonua** Tonga
226 G2 **Ohře** *watercourse* Czech Republic
235 B5 **Ohrid** Macedonia
235 B5 **Ohrid, Lake** Macedonia
226 E3 **Öhringen** Germany
223 M3 **Ohtanajärvi** Sweden
223 M5 **Ohtola** Finland
422 F4 **Ohura** New Zealand
235 D7 **Oia** Greece
230 B3 **Oiã** Portugal
156 A2 **Oiapoque** *watercourse* Brazil
155 I4 **Oiapoque** French Guiana
155 H4 **Oiapoque** *watercourse* French Guiana
155 I3 **Oiapoque, Baía do** *bay* French Guiana
121 P6 **Oies, Baie des** *bay* Québec Canada
127 P3 **Oies, Ile aux** *island* Québec Canada
223 N4 **Oijärvi** Finland
387 I2 **Oikamanae-numa** *lake* Japan
223 O3 **Oikarainen** Finland
130 C2 **Oilton** Oklahoma USA
235 C6 **Oinoi** Greece
235 E6 **Oinoússai** Greece
228 F2 **Oise** *watercourse* France
241 I5 **Oisemont** France
135 J4 **Oistins** Barbados
386 F5 **Oita** Japan
235 C6 **Oiti** *mountain* Greece
223 M5 **Oivu** Finland
223 M5 **Öja** Finland
224 I3 **Öja** *island* Sweden
128 C3 **Ojai** California USA
223 N4 **Ojakylä** Finland
224 I2 **Öjaren** *lake* Sweden
222 I5 **Öjarssjön** *lake* Sweden
224 G2 **Öje** Sweden
222 L4 **Öjebyn** Sweden
160 E5 **Ojeda** Argentina
222 J5 **Öjen** *lake* Sweden
127 L4 **Ojibway Bay** Ontario Canada
132 D2 **Ojinaga** Mexico
222 I6 **Öjingen** *lake* Sweden
132 D2 **Ojito** Mexico
132 C2 **Ojo de Agua de Elías** Mexico
132 B3 **Ojo de Liebre, Laguna** *lake* Mexico
129 J6 **Ojo del Carrizo** Mexico
305 F3 **Oju** Nigeria
222 H6 **Öjvasseln** Sweden
373 G5 **Ok Tedi** *watercourse* Papua New Guinea
238 H5 **Oka** *watercourse* Russian Federation
308 C4 **Okahandja** Namibia
423 E6 **Okains Bay** New Zealand
122 H4 **Okak Islands** Newfoundland and Labrador Canada
308 C4 **Okakarara** Namibia
118 L8 **Okanagan Falls** British Columbia Canada
118 L7 **Okanagan Lake** British Columbia Canada
393 E10 **Okanda** Sri Lanka
305 G5 **Okandja** Gabon
305 G4 **Okano** *watercourse* Gabon
124 F1 **Okanogan** British Columbia Canada
124 F2 **Okanogan** Washington USA
375 H4 **Okaoka** Indonesia
391 M3 **Okara** Pakistan
130 C3 **Okarche** Oklahoma USA
423 D6 **Okarito** New Zealand
423 D6 **Okarito Lagoon** New Zealand
130 G4 **Okatibbee Lake** Mississippi USA
422 E4 **Okato** New Zealand
308 D3 **Okavango** *watercourse* Botswana
308 C3 **Okavango** *admin. area* Namibia
308 D3 **Okavango Delta** *swamp* Botswana
423 6 **Okawa Point** Chatham Islands New Zealand
386 G4 **Okayama** Japan
305 E3 **Oke-Iho** Nigeria
131 K7 **Okeechobee** Florida USA
131 K7 **Okeechobee, Lake** Florida USA
130 B2 **Okeene** Oklahoma USA
240 C4 **Okehampton** Devon England UK
130 C3 **Okemah** Oklahoma USA
305 F3 **Okene** Nigeria
226 F1 **Oker** *watercourse* Germany
237 AD8 **Okha** Russian Federation
392 G5 **Okhaldhunga** Nepal
237 AD7 **Okhotsk** Russian Federation
387 J1 **Okhotsk, Sea of (Okhotskoye More)** Russian Federation
237 AC6 **Okhotskiy Perevoz** Russian Federation
223 Q4 **Okhtan"yarvi, Ozero** *lake* Russian Federation
394 E2 **Okhtyrka** Ukraine
225 Q4 **Okhvat** Russian Federation
386 G4 **Oki-shotō** *island* Japan
422 F2 **Okiato** New Zealand
381 J3 **Okinawa** Japan
381 J3 **Okinawa-shotō** *island* Japan
381 J3 **Okino-erabu** Japan
381 J3 **Okino-erabu-shima** *island* Japan
305 E3 **Okitipupa** Nigeria
115 **Oklahoma** *admin. area* USA
130 C3 **Oklahoma City** Oklahoma USA
232 G5 **Oklaj** Croatia
130 D3 **Okmulgee** Oklahoma USA
302 F3 **Ōkō, Wādī** *watercourse* Sudan
308 C4 **Okombahe** Namibia
227 L2 **Okopy Nowy** Poland
119 O7 **Okotoks** Alberta Canada
305 H5 **Okoyo** Congo
227 H3 **Okříšky** Czech Republic
227 K2 **Oksa** Poland
223 M3 **Oksajärvi** Sweden
223 N5 **Oksakoski** Finland
373 G5 **Oksapmin** Papua New Guinea
224 E5 **Oksby** Denmark
222 E5 **Oksenøya** *island* Norway
223 M1 **Øksfjord** Norway
223 M1 **Øksfjordjøkulen** *bay* Norway
236 L5 **Oksino** Russian Federation
222 G4 **Øksnes** Norway
222 I2 **Øksneshamn** Norway
426 2a **Okso Takpochao** *mountain* Northern Mariana Islands
236 I6 **Oksovskiy** Russian Federation
222 I3 **Okstindan** *mountain* Norway
130 D3 **Oktaha** Oklahoma USA
379 H5 **Oktwin** Myanmar
238 G4 **Oktyabr'** Russian Federation
223 S3 **Oktyabr'skiy** Russian Federation
237 AG8 **Oktyabr'skiy** Russian Federation
238 H5 **Oktyabr'skiy** Russian Federation
388 G2 **Oktyabr'skiy** Russian Federation
237 U3 **Oktyabr'skoy Revolyutsii, Ostrov** *island* Russian Federation
238 E3 **Okulovka** Russian Federation
387 H2 **Okushiri-tō** *volcano* Japan
305 F3 **Okuta** Nigeria
308 D4 **Okwa** *watercourse* Botswana
305 F3 **Okwa** *watercourse* Nigeria
222 inset **Olafsfjörður** Iceland
222 inset **Ólafsvík** Iceland
393 E9 **Olakkur** Tamil Nadu India
118 L8 **Olalla** British Columbia Canada
128 C2 **Olancha** California USA
134 C4 **Olanchito** Honduras
224 I4 **Öland** *island* Sweden
224 I4 **Ölands Norra Udde** *cape* Sweden
224 I4 **Ölands Sodra Udde** *cape* Sweden
223 Q3 **Olanga** Russian Federation
160 E2 **Olaroz Chico** Argentina
125 L7 **Olathe** Colorado USA
126 D7 **Olathe** Kansas USA
160 F6 **Olavarría** Argentina
154 B3 **Olave** Colombia
227 I2 **Oława** Poland
229 K1 **Olbernhau** Germany
233 C6 **Olbia** Sardinia Italy
234 B2 **Olcea** Romania
229 J2 **Olching** Germany
134 E2 **Old Bahama Channel** *strait* Cuba
302 E4 **Old Dongola** Sudan
119 P3 **Old Fort** *watercourse* Alberta Canada
118 H5 **Old Fort** British Columbia Canada
131 J2 **Old Fort** North Carolina USA
119 N1 **Old Fort Providence** Northwest Territories Canada
119 N1 **Old Fort Rae** Northwest Territories Canada
116 D7 **Old Harbor** Alaska USA
245 D5 **Old Head of Kinsale** *cape* Ireland
131 H2 **Old Hickory Lake** Tennessee USA
242 F2 **Old Hutton** Cumbria England UK
241 H1 **Old Leake** Lincolnshire England UK
308 E2 **Old Mkushi** Zambia
123 L8 **Old Perlican** Newfoundland and Labrador Canada
245 E4 **Old Pike Bridge** Ireland
163 I8 **Old Road** Antigua and Barbuda
163 I9 **Old Road Town** St Kitts and Nevis
240 A2 **Old Ross** Ireland
240 A2 **Old Town** Ireland
243 F1 **Old Town** Northumberland England UK
127 Q4 **Old Town** Maine USA
125 M1 **Old Wives** Saskatchewan Canada
119 S7 **Old Wives Lake** Saskatchewan Canada
245 F3 **Oldbawn** Ireland
241 E2 **Oldbury** West Midlands England UK
240 E3 **Oldcastle** Monmouthshire Wales UK
222 F5 **Olden** Norway
226 E1 **Oldenburg** Germany
224 E5 **Oldenswort** Germany
222 L2 **Olderdalen** Norway
222 L1 **Olderfjord** Norway
222 E6 **Oldevatnet** *lake* Norway
245 F3 **Oldgrange** Ireland
243 F3 **Oldham** Greater Manchester England UK
245 C4 **Oldmill Bridge** Ireland
242 A4 **Oldtown** Ireland
240 D3 **Oldways End** Devon England UK
127 L5 **Olean** New York USA
225 L5 **Olecko** Poland
232 C4 **Oleggio** Italy
230 C4 **Oleiros** Portugal
237 Z7 **Olekma** *watercourse* Russian Federation
237 Y8 **Olekminskiy Stanovik** *range* Russian Federation
234 H1 **Oleksandrivka** Ukraine
234 F2 **Oleksiyivka** Ukraine
229 G1 **Olen** Belgium
224 C3 **Ølen** Norway
223 R2 **Olenegorsk** Russian Federation
237 X5 **Olenëk** Russian Federation
237 Y5 **Olenëk** *watercourse* Russian Federation
237 Z4 **Olenekskiy Zaliv** *bay* Russian Federation
238 E4 **Olenino** Russian Federation
223 S3 **Olenitsa** Russian Federation
236 Q4 **Oleniy, Ostrov** *island* Russian Federation
389 L3 **Olenty** *watercourse* Kazakhstan
228 D4 **Oléron, Île d'** *island* France
227 I2 **Oleśnica** Poland
232 G2 **Olešnice** Czech Republic
227 J2 **Olesno** Poland
375 H6 **Olet Tongo** *mountain* Indonesia
228 F5 **Olette** France
226 D2 **Olfen** Germany
121 Q8 **Olga, Lac** *lake* Québec Canada
Olga, Mount *see* **Kata Tjuta** Australia
435 H1 **Olga Basin** *underwater feature* Barents Sea
229 I4 **Olgiate Comasco** Italy
Ölgiy *see* **Ulgii** Mongolia
383 I3 **Ölgiy** Mongolia
230 C5 **Olhão** Portugal
223 N4 **Olhava** Finland
308 C4 **Olifants** *watercourse* Namibia
308 D5 **Olifantshoek** South Africa
156 F5 **Olinda** Brazil
157 E5 **Olindina** Brazil
377 I5 **Olingan** Philippines
224 H2 **Olingskog** Sweden
230 F2 **Olite** Spain
231 F4 **Oliva** Spain
130 G3 **Olive Branch** Mississippi USA
157 C8 **Oliveira** Brazil
157 D6 **Oliveira dos Brejinhos** Brazil
156 E5 **Olivença** Brazil
230 C4 **Olivenza** Spain
118 L8 **Oliver** British Columbia Canada
119 T4 **Oliver Lake** Saskatchewan Canada
228 E3 **Olivet** France
125 R4 **Olivia** Minnesota USA
423 C7 **Olivine Range** New Zealand
159 I5 **Olivo Peres** Brazil
229 I3 **Olivone** Switzerland
234 D1 **Oliyiv** Ukraine
384 F5 **Oljoq** Nei Mongol Zizhiqu China
224 D2 **Øljuvatnet** *lake* Norway
234 B1 **Olka** Slovakia
388 D3 **Olkhovka** Russian Federation
225 K2 **Olkiluoto** *island* Finland
130 E5 **Olla** Louisiana USA
244 inset **Ollaberry** Shetland Scotland UK
158 D6 **Ollagüe, Volcán** *volcano* Chile
231 F4 **Olleria** Spain
240 E2 **Ollerton** Shropshire England UK
223 P3 **Ollila** Finland
160 D4 **Ollita, Cordillera de** *range* Argentina
160 D4 **Ollitas** *mountain* Argentina
223 Q5 **Öllölä** Finland
232 B3 **Ollon** Switzerland
222 I5 **Ollsta** Sweden
229 H2 **Olm** Luxembourg
389 K6 **Olmaliq** Uzbekistan
230 D3 **Olmedo** Spain
307 F4 **Olmoti** *volcano* Tanzania
241 G2 **Olney** Milton Keynes England UK
130 B4 **Olney** Texas USA
123 H7 **Olomane** *watercourse* Québec Canada
227 I3 **Olomouc** Czech Republic
227 I3 **Olomoucký Kraj** *admin. area* Czech Republic
225 Q2 **Olonets** Russian Federation
377 I4 **Olongapo** Philippines
375 G4 **Olongliko** Indonesia
228 D3 **Olonne-sur-Mer** France
231 H2 **Olonzac** France
228 D5 **Oloron-Sainte-Marie** France
427 12c **Olosega** *island* American Samoa
231 H2 **Olot** Spain
385 H2 **Olovyannaya** Russian Federation
237 AH5 **Oloyskiy Khrebet** *range* Russian Federation
226 D2 **Olpe** Germany
126 C7 **Olpe** Kansas USA
226 E2 **Olsberg** Germany
234 C1 **Olszanica** Poland
227 K2 **Olszany** Poland
227 K1 **Olsztyn** Poland
234 D3 **Olt** *admin. area* Romania

234 D3 **Olt** *watercourse* Romania
224 D3 **Oltedal** Norway
229 H3 **Olten** Switzerland
234 E3 **Olteniţa** Romania
234 E3 **Oltina, Lacul** *lake* Romania
129 K3 **Olton** Texas USA
394 G5 **Oltu** Turkey
381 H4 **Olun Pi** *island* Taiwan China
230 E5 **Olula del Río** Spain
130 B3 **Olustee** Oklahoma USA
223 O4 **Olvasjärvi** Finland
230 D5 **Olvera** Spain
230 E4 **Olvera, Embalse de** *lake* Spain
235 E8 **Olymbos** Greece
124 D3 **Olympia** Washington USA
124 D3 **Olympic Mountains** Washington USA
235 C5 **Olympos** *mountain* Greece
394 E6 **Olympus, Mount** *mountain* Cyprus
237 AI6 **Olyutorskiy** Russian Federation
237 AJ7 **Olyutorskiy, Mys** *cape* Russian Federation
237 AJ6 **Olyutorskiy Poluostrov** *peninsula* Russian Federation
237 AI6 **Olyutorskiy Zaliv** *bay* Russian Federation
302 F5 **Om Hajēr** Eritrea
245 E2 **Omagh** *admin. area* Northern Ireland UK
245 E2 **Omagh** Omagh Northern Ireland UK
125 R6 **Omaha** Nebraska USA
308 C4 **Omaheke** *admin. area* Namibia
124 F2 **Omak Lake** Washington USA
385 N2 **Omal'skiy Khrebet** *range* Russian Federation
393 E9 **Omalur** Tamil Nadu India
391 H4 **Oman** *country*
391 I5 **Oman, Gulf of**
422 E2 **Omapere** New Zealand
422 E2 **Omapere, Lake** New Zealand
423 C7 **Omarama** New Zealand
121 P5 **Omarolluk Sound** Nunavut Canada
232 G4 **Omarska** Bosnia and Herzegovina
308 C4 **Omaruru** Namibia
158 B4 **Omas** Peru
308 C4 **Omatako** *watercourse* Namibia
308 C4 **Omatjete** Namibia
306 B2 **Ombella-M'poko** *admin. area* Central African Republic
241 E2 **Ombersley** Worcestershire England UK
224 C3 **Ombo** *island* Norway
374 C3 **Ombolata** Indonesia
305 F5 **Omboué** Gabon
302 E4 **Omdurman** Sudan
387 H4 **Ome** Japan
232 C4 **Omegna** Italy
425 M9 **Omeo** Vic. Australia
242 B2 **Omerbank** Ballymoney Northern Ireland UK
235 F5 **Ömerli Barajı** *lake* Turkey
134 C5 **Ometepe, Isla de** *island* Nicaragua
133 F5 **Ometepec** Mexico
245 B3 **Omey Island** Ireland
390 G3 **Omīdīyeh** Iran
233 C5 **Omigna, Punta d'** *cape* Corsica France
225 K2 **Ominaisfjärden** *bay* Finland
118 I5 **Omineca** *watercourse* British Columbia Canada
118 H4 **Omineca Mountains** British Columbia Canada
232 G5 **Omiš** Croatia
232 F4 **Omišalj** Croatia
308 C4 **Omitara** Namibia
117 I4 **Ommanney Bay** Nunavut Canada
224 G4 **Ömmern** *lake* Sweden
384 E4 **Ömnögovi** *admin. area* Mongolia
307 F2 **Omo** *watercourse* Ethiopia
134 B4 **Omoa** Honduras
237 AB4 **Omoloy** *watercourse* Russian Federation
389 L2 **Omsk** Russian Federation
236 P7 **Omskaya Oblast'** *admin. area* Russian Federation
237 AG6 **Omsukchanskiy Khrebet** *range* Russian Federation
305 F3 **Omu-aran** Nigeria
305 F3 **Omuo** Nigeria
386 F5 **Omura** Japan
308 B3 **Omusati** *admin. area* Namibia
386 F5 **Omuta** Japan
230 E2 **Oña** Spain
128 H6 **Onabas** Mexico
130 D5 **Onalaska** Texas USA
126 F5 **Onalaska** Wisconsin USA
120 L8 **Onaman Lake** Ontario Canada
126 E3 **Onamia** Minnesota USA
372 A4 **Onang** Indonesia
305 G5 **Onangué, Lac** *lake* Gabon
127 K3 **Onaping-Levack** Ontario Canada
225 M2 **Onas landet** *island* Finland
117 L9 **Onatchiway, Lac** *lake* Québec Canada
129 J3 **Onava** New Mexico USA
125 Q5 **Onawa** Iowa USA
160 F5 **Oncativo** Argentina
242 D2 **Onchan** Isle of Man UK
386 E3 **Onch'ŏn** North Korea
308 B3 **Oncócua** Angola
228 E3 **Oncques** France
231 F4 **Onda** Spain
308 C3 **Ondangwa** Namibia
231 G4 **Ondara** Spain
228 C5 **Ondarroa** Spain
157 C6 **Ondas** *watercourse* Brazil
308 E3 **Ondava** *watercourse* Slovakia
308 D6 **Onderstedorings** South Africa
308 C3 **Ondjiva** Angola
305 F3 **Ondo** Nigeria
305 F3 **Ondo** *admin. area* Nigeria
384 G3 **Öndörhaan** Mongolia
223 R5 **Ondozero** Russian Federation
223 R5 **Ondozero, Ozero** *lake* Russian Federation
427 14 **One, Motu** *island* French Polynesia
424 G4 **One Arm Point** *cape* WA Australia
427 9 **Oneata** *island* Fiji
236 I6 **Onega** Russian Federation
236 I6 **Onega** *watercourse* Russian Federation
127 N5 **Oneida** New York USA
131 I2 **Oneida** Tennessee USA
127 N5 **Oneida Lake** New York USA
159 F3 **Oneide** Brazil
125 P5 **O'Neill** Nebraska USA
237 AG9 **Onekotan, Ostrov** *island* Kuril Islands
159 F5 **Oñema** Bolivia
306 C4 **Onema Ututu** Democratic Republic of Congo
223 T4 **Onezhskaya Guba** *bay* Russian Federation
236 I6 **Onezhskiy Poluostrov** *peninsula* Russian Federation
238 F2 **Onezhskoye Ozero** *lake* Russian Federation
393 F7 **Ong** *watercourse* Orissa India
376 E5 **Ông Đốc** *watercourse* Vietnam
422 F4 **Ongarue** New Zealand
308 D6 **Ongers** *watercourse* South Africa
386 E4 **Ongjin** North Korea
393 E8 **Ongole** Andhra Pradesh India
385 H3 **Ongon** Mongolia
240 E2 **Onibury** Shropshire England UK
125 O4 **Onida** South Dakota USA
163 1c **Onima** Netherlands Antilles
372 D4 **Onin, Djazirah** *peninsula* Indonesia
121 T7 **Onistagane, Lac** *lake* Québec Canada
305 F3 **Onitsha** Nigeria
223 P3 **Onkamo** Finland
223 P3 **Onkamojärvi** *lake* Finland
225 L2 **Onkijoki** Finland
223 O5 **Onkivesi** *bay* Finland
237 X5 **Onkuchakh** Russian Federation
427 9 **Ono** *island* Fiji
426 1 **Onotoa** *island* Kiribati
426 6 **Onoun** *island* Federated States of Micronesia
222 H3 **Onøya** Norway
230 B2 **Ons, Illa de** *island* Spain
224 F2 **Onsaker** Norway
308 C5 **Onseepkans** South Africa
424 E5 **Onslow** WA Australia
131 M3 **Onslow Bay** North Carolina USA
241 G3 **Onslow Village** Surrey England UK
387 H4 **Ontake-san** *mountain* Japan
117 J8 **Ontario** *admin. area* Canada
128 D3 **Ontario** California USA
124 G4 **Ontario** Oregon USA
127 M5 **Ontario, Lake** Canada/USA
231 F4 **Ontinyent** Spain
223 P4 **Ontojärvi** *lake* Finland
126 G3 **Ontonagon** Michigan USA
387 I2 **Ōnuma** *lake* Japan
163 2 **Onverwacht** Suriname
437 K1 **Onyx** *watercourse* Antarctica
425 J6 **Oodnadatta** SA Australia
307 H2 **Oodweyne** Somalia
126 D8 **Oolagahl Lake** Oklahoma USA
424 I7 **Ooldea** SA Australia
118 F6 **Oona River** British Columbia Canada
126 H5 **Oostburg** Wisconsin USA
228 F1 **Oostende** Belgium
228 F1 **Oostkamp** Belgium
163 1b **Oostpunt** *cape* Netherlands Antilles
118 H6 **Ootsa Lake** British Columbia Canada
125 J6 **Opal** Wyoming USA
306 C4 **Opala** Democratic Republic of Congo
227 H3 **Opařany** Czech Republic
423 E5 **Oparara** New Zealand
127 L2 **Opasatica Lake** Québec Canada
120 I6 **Opasquia Lake** Ontario Canada
126 J2 **Opastika** Ontario Canada
121 R7 **Opataca, Lac** *lake* Québec Canada
121 Q7 **Opataouaga, Lac** *lake* Québec Canada
229 L4 **Opatija** Croatia
227 I3 **Opava** Czech Republic
127 J2 **Opawica Lake** Québec Canada
126 J2 **Opazatika Lake** Ontario Canada
238 F3 **Opechenskiy Posad** Russian Federation
131 I4 **Opelika** Alabama USA
130 E5 **Opelousas** Louisiana USA
127 N2 **Opémisca Lake** Québec Canada
127 L4 **Opeongo Lake** Ontario Canada
226 E5 **Opera** Italy
226 C2 **Opglabbeek** Belgium
125 L2 **Opheim** Montana USA
423 C7 **Ophir** New Zealand
374 C3 **Ophir, Gunung** *volcano* Indonesia
229 K4 **Opicina** Italy
128 inset **Opihikao** Hawai'i USA
121 R6 **Opinaca** *watercourse* Québec Canada
121 Q6 **Opinaca, Réservoir** Québec Canada
121 N5 **Opinnagau** *watercourse* Ontario Canada
120 M6 **Opinnagau Lake** Ontario Canada
121 V6 **Opiscotéo, Lac** *lake* Québec Canada
226 C1 **Opmeer** Netherlands
305 F4 **Opobo** Nigeria
225 O4 **Opochka** Russian Federation
121 V6 **Opocopa** Newfoundland and Labrador Canada
227 K2 **Opoczno** Poland
227 I2 **Opole** Poland
227 J2 **Opolskie** *admin. area* Poland
422 G4 **Opotiki** New Zealand
422 G4 **Opoutama** New Zealand
131 H5 **Opp** Alabama USA
224 E5 **Oppdal** Norway
222 F5 **Oppdal Herad** Norway
224 C2 **Oppedal** Norway
222 F5 **Opphaug** Norway
224 F2 **Opphus** Norway
233 G6 **Oppido Lucano** Italy
224 E2 **Oppland** *admin. area* Norway
222 F5 **Oppsal** Norway
119 U5 **Optic Lake** Manitoba Canada
129 L2 **Optima** Oklahoma USA
129 L2 **Optima Lake** Oklahoma USA
129 J3 **Optimo** New Mexico USA
423 D6 **Opuha Lake** New Zealand
422 E4 **Opunake** New Zealand
308 B3 **Opuwo** Namibia
232 G5 **Opuzen** Croatia
388 J6 **Oqtosh** Uzbekistan
234 B2 **Oradea** Romania
228 E4 **Oradour-sur-Vayres** France
234 B4 **Orahovac** Kosovo
232 G4 **Orahovica** Croatia
392 E6 **Orai** Uttar Pradesh India
223 O3 **Orajärvi** *lake* Finland
422 G4 **Orakei Korako** New Zealand
223 O3 **Orakylä** Finland
301 F1 **Oran** Algeria
154 C5 **Orán** Peru
379 G3 **Orang** Assam India
386 F3 **Ŏrang** North Korea
425 N8 **Orange** NSW Australia
229 G4 **Orange** France
308 C5 **Orange** *watercourse* Namibia
308 D5 **Orange** *watercourse* South Africa
128 D4 **Orange** California USA
130 E5 **Orange** Texas USA
155 I3 **Orange, Cabo** *cape* Brazil
77 T12 **Orange Cone** *underwater feature* Atlantic Ocean
128 C2 **Orange Cove** California USA
130 C7 **Orange Grove** Texas USA
163 3 **Orange Hill** Isla de San Andrés
163 11a **Orange Hill** St Vincent and the Grenadines
131 J6 **Orange Lake** Florida USA
131 K5 **Orange Park** Florida USA
134 B3 **Orange Walk** Belize
131 K4 **Orangeburg** South Carolina USA
373 I6 **Orangerie Bay** Papua New Guinea
304 A2 **Orango** *island* Guinea-Bissau
304 A2 **Orango-Zinho** *island* Guinea-Bissau
233 C6 **Orani** Sardinia Italy
155 H4 **Oranje Gebergte** *range* Suriname
308 C5 **Oranjemund** Namibia
135 G4 **Oranjestad** Aruba
163 19 **Oranjestad** Netherlands Antilles
308 E4 **Orapa** Botswana
227 I5 **Orašac** Bosnia and Herzegovina
227 L5 **Orăştioara de Sus** Romania
222 M5 **Oravainen** Finland
222 K4 **Öravan** Sweden
234 B3 **Oraviţa** Romania
228 F5 **Orb** *watercourse* France
229 H3 **Orbe** Switzerland
228 E2 **Orbec** France
233 E5 **Orbetello** Italy
228 F5 **Orbieu** *watercourse* France
230 C2 **Orbigo** *watercourse* Spain
425 N9 **Orbost** Vic. Australia
224 I2 **Örbyhus** Sweden
436 V2 **Orcadas (Argentina)** *research station* Antarctica
230 E4 **Orcera** Spain
125 L7 **Orchard City** Colorado USA
228 E3 **Orches** France
131 K7 **Orchid Island** Florida USA
226 B2 **Orchies** France
155 E2 **Orchila, Isla** *island* Venezuela
229 I5 **Orchina, Punta d'** *cape* Corsica France
229 H4 **Orcières** France
424 I3 **Ord** *watercourse* WA Australia
125 P6 **Ord** Nebraska USA
224 D3 **Ørdalsvatn** *lake* Norway
230 B2 **Órdenes** Spain
394 F5 **Ordu** Turkey
394 F5 **Ordu** *admin. area* Turkey
230 E2 **Orduña** Spain
125 N7 **Ordway** Colorado USA
305 E3 **Ore** Nigeria
224 D3 **Øre** *lake* Norway
241 H4 **Ore** East Sussex England UK
130 D4 **Ore City** Texas USA
222 K5 **Öreälven** *watercourse* Sweden
224 H3 **Örebro** Sweden
224 H3 **Örebro** *admin. area* Sweden
225 P3 **Oredezh** Russian Federation
114 **Oregon** *admin. area* USA
126 G5 **Oregon** Illinois USA
126 J6 **Oregon** Ohio USA
124 D4 **Oregon City** Oregon USA
225 J2 **Öregrund** Sweden
225 J2 **Öregrundsgrepen** *bay* Sweden
238 C4 **Orekhovichi** Russian Federation
238 H5 **Orekhovo-Zuyevo** Russian Federation
394 F2 **Orel** Russian Federation
237 AD8 **Orel', Ozero** *lake* Russian Federation
154 B5 **Orellana** *admin. area* Ecuador
230 D4 **Orellana, Embalse de** *lake* Spain
230 D4 **Orellana la Vieja** Spain
124 J6 **Orem** Utah USA
224 H4 **Ören** *lake* Sweden
235 E7 **Ören** Turkey
388 G3 **Orenburg** Russian Federation
388 G3 **Orenburgskaya Oblast'** *admin. area* Russian Federation
161 G6 **Orense** Argentina
224 G3 **Öresjö** *lake* Sweden
224 H2 **Oresjön** *lake* Sweden
235 E5 **Orestiada** Greece
423 C7 **Oreti** *watercourse* New Zealand
422 F3 **Orewa** New Zealand
121 W6 **Oreway** Newfoundland and Labrador Canada
235 C5 **Orfanou, Kolpos** *bay* Greece
241 I2 **Orford** Suffolk England UK
241 I2 **Orford Ness** *cape* England UK
235 E7 **Orfos, Akra** *cape* Greece
128 F4 **Organ Pipe Cactus National Monument** *park* Arizona USA
235 D5 **Organi** Greece
158 A2 **Órganos Chico, Punta** *cape* Peru
229 G3 **Orgelet** France
230 E5 **Orgiva** Spain
391 L3 **Orgūn-e Kalān** Afghanistan
235 F6 **Orhaneli** Turkey
235 F5 **Orhangazi** Turkey
235 E5 **Orhaniye** Turkey
235 F7 **Orhanlı** Turkey
235 F2 **Orhei** Moldova
384 E3 **Orhon** Mongolia
384 E3 **Orhon** *admin. area* Mongolia
384 E3 **Orhon Gol** *watercourse* Mongolia
384 E3 **Orhontuul** Mongolia
233 G6 **Oria** Italy
230 E2 **Oria** *watercourse* Spain
118 L8 **Orient** Washington USA
126 G2 **Orient Bay** Ontario Canada
301 F2 **Oriental** *admin. area* Morocco
131 M3 **Oriental** North Carolina USA
160 E2 **Oriental, Cordillera** *range* Bolivia
154 C3 **Oriental, Cordillera** *range* Colombia
158 D4 **Oriental, Cordillera** *range* Peru
160 F6 **Oriente** Argentina
159 E3 **Oriente** Brazil
159 F5 **Oriente, Llanos del** *region* Bolivia
230 F3 **Orihuela del Tremedal** Spain
235 A5 **Orikum** Albania
394 E3 **Oril** *watercourse* Ukraine
121 S6 **Orillat, Lac** *lake* Québec Canada
127 L4 **Orillia** Ontario Canada
225 M2 **Orimattila** Finland
224 E1 **Orinin** Ukraine
154 E3 **Orinoco** *watercourse* Colombia/Venezuela
155 F2 **Orinoco Delta** Venezuela
373 G6 **Oriomo** Papua New Guinea
119 P8 **Orion** Alberta Canada
126 F6 **Orion** Illinois USA
125 Q3 **Oriska** North Dakota USA
127 N5 **Oriskany** New York USA
222 M5 **Orismala** Finland
393 F7 **Orissa** *admin. area* India
233 C7 **Oristano** Sardinia Italy
233 C7 **Oristano, Golfo di** *bay* Sardinia Italy
242 B3 **Oristown** Ireland
225 L2 **Orisuo** Finland
154 B4 **Orito** Colombia
225 M2 **Orivesi** Finland
223 P5 **Orivesi** *bay* Finland
155 H5 **Oriximiná** Brazil
133 F5 **Orizaba** Mexico
133 F4 **Orizatlán** Mexico
157 B7 **Orizona** Brazil
234 D4 **Orizovo** Bulgaria
222 F5 **Orkanger** Norway
224 H4 **Örken** *lake* Sweden
222 F5 **Orkla** *watercourse* Norway
308 E5 **Orkney** South Africa
244 E1 **Orkney Islands** Scotland UK
244 E1 **Orkney Islands** *admin. area* Scotland UK
129 K5 **Orla** Texas USA
124 D7 **Orland** California USA
126 H6 **Orland Park** Illinois USA
131 K6 **Orlando** Florida USA
234 D4 **Orlea** Romania
161 I4 **Orleans** Brazil
228 E3 **Orléans** France
127 O4 **Orleans** Vermont USA
127 O3 **Orléans, Canal d'** *watercourse* France
227 H3 **Orlík, Vodní nádrž** *lake* Czech Republic
388 E3 **Orlov Gay** Russian Federation
385 K2 **Orlovka** *watercourse* Russian Federation
234 F3 **Orlovka** Ukraine
394 F2 **Orlovskaya Oblast'** *admin. area* Russian Federation
227 M1 **Orlya** Belarus
235 G5 **Ormanlı** Turkey
232 B4 **Ormea** Italy
222 E3 **Orménion** Greece
235 C5 **Ormilia** Greece
377 J5 **Ormoc** Philippines
422 G5 **Ormondville** New Zealand
222 J4 **Ormsjön** *lake* Sweden
242 F3 **Ormskirk** Lancashire England UK
222 F6 **Ormtjernkampen Nasjonalpark** *park* Norway
229 H3 **Ornans** France
228 D2 **Orne** *watercourse* France
222 E6 **Ørnes** Norway
222 H3 **Ørnes** Norway
233 F6 **Orneta** Italy
225 J3 **Ornö** *island* Sweden
222 K5 **Örnsköldsvik** Sweden
225 L3 **Örö** *island* Finland
128 G4 **Oro Valley** Arizona USA
154 D3 **Orocué** Colombia
304 D2 **Orodara** Burkina Faso
384 D4 **Orog Nuur** *lake* Mongolia
129 I4 **Orogrande** New Mexico USA
427 14a **Orohena** *volcano* French Polynesia
373 J2 **Oroluk** *island* Federated States of Micronesia
426 6 **Oroluk** *reef* Federated States of Micronesia
232 H4 **Orom** Serbia
158 B2 **Oromina** Peru
307 G2 **Oromiya** *admin. area* Ethiopia
123 E10 **Oromocto** New Brunswick Canada
123 E10 **Oromocto Lake** New Brunswick Canada
305 F4 **Oron** Nigeria
426 1 **Orona** *island* Kiribati
78 O8 **Orona** *reef* Phoenix Islands
123 D10 **Orono** Maine USA
244 B4 **Oronsay** *island* Scotland UK
158 D4 **Oropesa** Peru
377 I5 **Oroquieta** Philippines
156 E4 **Orós** Brazil
156 E4 **Orós, Açude** *lake* Brazil
233 C6 **Orosei, Golfo di** *bay* Sardinia Italy
230 B2 **Oroso** Spain
232 H3 **Orosházy** Hungary
233 C6 **Orotelli** Sardinia Italy
237 AC4 **Orotko, Ozero** *lake* Russian Federation
234 C1 **Orov** Ukraine
124 E7 **Oroville** California USA
124 F2 **Oroville** Washington USA
124 E7 **Oroville, Lake** California USA
76 N4 **Orphan Knoll** *underwater feature* Atlantic Ocean
228 E2 **Orphin** France
241 H3 **Orpington** Greater London England UK
154 B3 **Orpúa** Colombia
385 J2 **Orqohan** Nei Mongol Zizhiqu China
224 H4 **Orrefors** Sweden
225 N2 **Orrengrund** *island* Finland
233 F6 **Orria** Italy
244 D3 **Orrin Reservoir** *lake* Scotland UK
222 H6 **Orrmosjön** *lake* Sweden
242 E2 **Orroland** Dumfries and Galloway Scotland UK
425 K8 **Orroroo** SA Australia
127 K4 **Orrville** Ontario Canada
224 H2 **Orsa** Sweden
222 K5 **Örsbäck** Sweden
224 I3 **Örsbacken** *bay* Sweden
225 P5 **Orsha** Belarus
238 G4 **Orsha** Russian Federation
229 H3 **Orsières** Switzerland
224 H4 **Örsjö** Sweden
224 I2 **Orsjön** *bay* Sweden
224 G2 **Örsjön** *lake* Sweden
388 H3 **Orsk** Russian Federation
225 J2 **Örskär** *island* Sweden
222 M3 **Orslandet** *island* Finland
234 C3 **Orşova** Romania
389 L4 **Orta-bakanas** *watercourse* Kazakhstan
235 G6 **Ortaca** Turkey
235 E7 **Ortaköy** Turkey
233 E5 **Orte** Italy
230 C2 **Ortegal, Cabo** *cape* Spain
222 H5 **Orten** *lake* Sweden
388 I7 **Ortepa** Afghanistan
228 D5 **Orthez** France
242 E2 **Orthwaite** Cumbria England UK
157 B9 **Ortigueira** Brazil
230 C2 **Ortigueira** Spain
128 G6 **Ortíz** Mexico
243 F2 **Orton** Cumbria England UK
241 G2 **Orton** Northamptonshire England UK
233 F5 **Ortona** Italy
125 Q4 **Ortonville** Minnesota USA
222 K4 **Örträsk** Sweden
222 K4 **Örträskjön** *lake* Sweden
226 F1 **Örtze** *watercourse* Germany
237 AA5 **Orulgan, Khrebet** *range* Russian Federation
388 E6 **Orūmīyeh** Iran
158 E5 **Oruro** Bolivia
158 E5 **Oruro** *admin. area* Bolivia
224 F3 **Orust** *island* Sweden
391 K3 **Orūzgān** *admin. area* Afghanistan
232 E5 **Orvieto** Italy
233 C6 **Orvili, Punta** *cape* Sardinia Italy
436 T1 **Orville Coast** Antarctica
235 C5 **Orvilos** *range* Greece
229 K5 **Orvinio** Italy
394 E2 **Orzhitsa** *watercourse* Ukraine
232 C4 **Orzinuovi** Italy
300 D3 **Orzola** Spain
222 G5 **Os** Norway
222 G5 **Osa** Norway
134 C5 **Osa, Península de** *lake* Costa Rica
119 T8 **Osage** Saskatchewan Canada
126 E5 **Osage** Iowa USA
126 F7 **Osage** *watercourse* Missouri USA
126 E7 **Osage Beach** Missouri USA
387 G4 **Ōsaka** Japan
125 R4 **Osakis** Minnesota USA
126 D4 **Osakis, Lake** Minnesota USA
229 I5 **Osani** Corsica France
234 B4 **Osaonica** Serbia
161 J2 **Osasco** Brazil
81 M6 **Osborn Plateau** *underwater feature* Indian Ocean
125 P7 **Osborne** Kansas USA
119 V5 **Osborne Lake** Manitoba Canada
227 J3 **Oščadnica** Slovakia
129 I6 **Oscar Soto Maynez** Mexico
126 E6 **Osceola** Iowa USA
244 B3 **Ose** Highland Scotland UK
234 A3 **Osečina** Serbia
225 P2 **Osel'ki** Russian Federation
222 G4 **Osen** Norway
224 F2 **Osensjøen** *lake* Norway
231 F3 **Osera** Spain
243 G3 **Osgodby** North Yorkshire England UK
389 K6 **Osh** Kyrgyzstan
389 K6 **Osh** *admin. area* Kyrgyzstan
308 C3 **Oshakati** Namibia
308 C3 **Oshana** *admin. area* Namibia
127 L5 **Oshawa** Ontario Canada
223 U6 **Oshevenskiy Pogost** Russian Federation
308 C3 **Oshikango** Namibia
308 C3 **Oshikoto** *admin. area* Namibia
308 C3 **Oshikuku** Namibia
308 C3 **Oshivelo** Namibia
125 N6 **Oshkosh** Nebraska USA
126 G4 **Oshkosh** Wisconsin USA
305 E3 **Oshogbo** Nigeria
238 F2 **Oshtinskiy Pogost** Russian Federation
390 G2 **Oshtorān Kūh** *mountain* Iran
306 B4 **Oshwe** Democratic Republic of Congo
234 D3 **Osica de Sus** Romania
227 J1 **Osie** Poland
227 J1 **Osięciny** Poland
227 J1 **Osiek** Poland
227 H1 **Osiek, Jezioro** *lake* Poland
232 H4 **Osijek** Croatia
234 D4 **Osikovitsa** Bulgaria
116 G7 **Osilinka** *watercourse* British Columbia Canada
232 E5 **Osimo** Italy
225 P5 **Osinovka** Belarus
234 B3 **Osipaonica** Serbia
308 C4 **Osire** Namibia
392 C5 **Osiyan** Rajasthan India
222 I5 **Ösjön** *bay* Sweden
126 E6 **Oskaloosa** Iowa USA
224 I4 **Oskarshamn** Sweden
119 R6 **Oskélanéo** Saskatchewan Canada
224 F3 **Oslo** Norway
224 F2 **Oslo** *admin. area* Norway
373 G5 **Oslobip** Papua New Guinea
223 N3 **Osma** Finland
393 D7 **Osmanabad** Maharashtra India
394 F6 **Osmaniye** Turkey
394 F6 **Osmaniye** *admin. area* Turkey
223 O4 **Osmankajärvi** *lake* Finland
225 O3 **Os'mino** Russian Federation
238 D6 **Osmolovichi** Belarus
225 L3 **Osmussaar** *island* Estonia
125 P3 **Osnabrock** North Dakota USA
226 E1 **Osnabrück** Germany
120 J7 **Osnaburgh House** Ontario Canada
228 F2 **Osny** France
306 D4 **Oso** *watercourse* Democratic Republic of Congo
226 G4 **Osoppo** Italy
232 F4 **Osor** Croatia
162 B2 **Osorno** Chile
230 D2 **Osorno** Spain
162 B3 **Osorno, Volcán** *volcano* Chile
225 O6 **Osovets** Belarus
118 L8 **Osoyoos** British Columbia Canada
224 C2 **Osøyri** Norway
118 I4 **Ospika** *watercourse* British Columbia Canada
229 J4 **Ospitaletto** Italy
425 M3 **Osprey Reef** Coral Sea Islands Territory Australia
226 C2 **Oss** Netherlands
227 K2 **Ossa** Poland
235 C5 **Óssa** Greece
425 M10 **Ossa, Mount** Tas. Australia
230 E4 **Ossa de Montiel** Spain
228 E5 **Osse** *watercourse* France
305 F3 **Osse** *watercourse* Nigeria
243 G3 **Ossett** West Yorkshire England UK
227 G4 **Ossiacher See** *lake* Austria
126 F5 **Ossian** Iowa USA
121 W6 **Ossokmanuan Reservoir** Newfoundland and Labrador Canada
131 K5 **Ossabaw Sound** Georgia USA
232 F4 **Oštarije** Croatia
238 F5 **Ostashëvo** Russian Federation
238 E4 **Ostashkov** Russian Federation
222 I5 **Östavall** Sweden
224 G2 **Østby** Norway
226 E1 **Oste** *watercourse* Germany
422 F3 **Ostend** New Zealand
238 E5 **Oster** Russian Federation
226 F1 **Osterburg** Germany
224 F4 **Österby** Denmark
224 G2 **Österdalälven** *bay* Sweden
222 G6 **Østerdalen** *valley* Norway
224 H3 **Östergötland** *admin. area* Sweden
224 E4 **Østerild** Denmark
224 H5 **Østerlars** Denmark
222 J4 **Östernoret** Sweden
224 C2 **Osterøya** *region* Norway
222 I5 **Östersund** Sweden
224 F3 **Østfold** *admin. area* Norway
225 J2 **Östhammar** Sweden
222 J5 **Östloning** Sweden
224 G2 **Östmark** Sweden
222 L5 **Östnäs** Sweden
222 L5 **Östra Gloppet** *bay* Finland
224 I3 **Östra Hjälmaren** *bay* Sweden
224 I3 **Östra Husby** Sweden
222 J4 **Östra Mullejaure** *lake* Sweden
224 G5 **Östra Ringsjön** *lake* Sweden
224 I3 **Östra Silen** *lake* Sweden
227 J3 **Ostrava** Czech Republic
232 H5 **Oštrelj** Bosnia and Herzegovina
227 J1 **Ostróda** Poland
394 F2 **Ostrogozhsk** Russian Federation
227 K1 **Ostrołęka** Poland
227 H2 **Ostroměř** Czech Republic
234 D4 **Ostrov** Bulgaria
234 E3 **Ostrov** Romania
225 O4 **Ostrov** Russian Federation
234 C4 **Ostroveni** Romania
225 O5 **Ostrovno** Belarus
237 AH7 **Ostrovnoy** Russian Federation
237 AG6 **Ostrovnoy, Mys** *cape* Russian Federation
388 D1 **Ostrovskoye** Russian Federation
227 K1 **Ostrów Mazowiecka** Poland
227 K2 **Ostrowiec Świętokrzyski** Poland
227 I2 **Ostrzeszów** Poland
233 G6 **Ostuni** Italy
229 H2 **Ostwald** France
227 L2 **Osuchy** Poland
238 F4 **Osuga** Russian Federation
120 L7 **O'Sullivan Lake** Ontario Canada
386 F5 **Ōsumi-Shotō** *island* Japan
305 E3 **Osun** *admin. area* Nigeria
230 D5 **Osuna** Spain
157 B8 **Osvaldo Cruz** Brazil
126 D8 **Oswego** Kansas USA
127 M5 **Oswego** New York USA
240 D2 **Oswestry** Shropshire England UK
227 J2 **Oświęcim** Poland
237 Z4 **Ot-Siyen** Russian Federation
161 I3 **Otacílio Costa** Brazil
121 N6 **Otadaonanis** *watercourse* Ontario Canada
423 D7 **Otago Harbour** New Zealand
423 D7 **Otago Peninsula** New Zealand
225 K2 **Otajärvi** *lake* Finland
423 F5 **Otaki** New Zealand
423 F5 **Otaki Beach** New Zealand
422 G4 **Otane** New Zealand
387 I2 **Otaru** Japan
423 C8 **Otautau** New Zealand
154 B4 **Otavalo** Ecuador
308 C3 **Otavi** Namibia
423 D7 **Otekaieke** New Zealand
127 D4 **Otelnuk, Lac** *lake* Québec Canada
234 C3 **Oţelu Roşu** Romania
225 N3 **Otepää** Estonia
225 N3 **Otepää Kõrgustik** *range* Estonia
223 O4 **Oterma** Finland
223 O4 **Otermajärvi** *lake* Finland
241 H3 **Otford** Kent England UK
384 E3 **Otgon** Mongolia
383 K3 **Otgon Tenger Uul** *mountain* Mongolia
124 F3 **Othello** Washington USA
119 R3 **Otherside** *watercourse* Saskatchewan Canada
235 C6 **Othris** *mountain* Greece
372 A4 **Oti** Indonesia
224 H3 **Oti** Sweden
423 E6 **Otira** *watercourse* New Zealand
125 N6 **Otis** Colorado USA
129 M1 **Otis** Kansas USA
122 C6 **Otish, Monts** *range* Québec Canada
126 J5 **Otisville** Michigan USA
308 C3 **Otjikondo** Namibia
308 C4 **Otjimbingwe** Namibia
308 C4 **Otjinene** Namibia
308 C3 **Otjitambi** Namibia
308 C4 **Otjiwarongo** Namibia
308 C4 **Otjosondu** Namibia
308 C3 **Otjozondjupa** *admin. area* Namibia
243 G3 **Otley** West Yorkshire England UK
232 G2 **Otnice** Czech Republic
426 8 **Otong Java** *island* Solomon Islands
302 E5 **Otoro, Jebel** *mountain* Sudan
120 J7 **Otoskwin** *watercourse* Ontario Canada
119 T6 **Otosquen** Saskatchewan Canada
Otou *see* **North Cape** New Zealand
224 D3 **Otra** *watercourse* Norway
163 1 **Otrabanda** Netherlands Antilles
238 G6 **Otradinskiy** Russian Federation
238 D3 **Otradnoye** Russian Federation
233 H6 **Otranto** Italy
233 H6 **Otranto, Capo d'** *cape* Italy
233 H6 **Otranto, Strait of** Italy
126 I4 **Otsego Lake** Michigan USA
304 E3 **Otta** Nigeria
222 F6 **Otta** *watercourse* Norway
222 F6 **Ottavatn** *bay* Norway
127 N4 **Ottawa** Ontario Canada
127 L3 **Ottawa** *watercourse* Ontario Canada
126 G6 **Ottawa** Illinois USA
126 D7 **Ottawa** Kansas USA
126 I6 **Ottawa** Ohio USA
126 H2 **Otter Head** *cape* Ontario Canada
121 O7 **Otter Rapids** Ontario Canada
125 R3 **Otter Tail Lake** Minnesota USA
240 D4 **Otterford** Somerset England UK
222 E5 **Otterøya** *island* Norway
240 D4 **Otterton** Devon England UK
224 F5 **Otterup** Denmark
240 D4 **Ottery St Mary** Devon England UK
229 G1 **Ottignies** Belgium
224 I2 **Ottnaren** *lake* Sweden
373 H5 **Otto, Mount** Papua New Guinea
117 K2 **Otto Fiord** Nunavut Canada
226 F4 **Ottobeuren** Germany
226 E5 **Ottone** Italy
222 K4 **Ottonträsk** Sweden
126 I6 **Ottoville** Ohio USA
222 H5 **Ottsjön** *lake* Sweden
126 E6 **Ottumwa** Iowa USA
126 E2 **Otukamamoan Lake** Ontario Canada
305 F3 **Otukpa** Nigeria
160 F3 **Otumpa** Argentina
158 B2 **Otuzco** Peru
162 A5 **Otway, Bahía** *bay* Chile
425 L9 **Otway, Cape** Vic. Australia
227 K1 **Otwock** Poland
226 F4 **Ötztal** *valley* Austria
376 D2 **Ou** *watercourse* Laos
376 D2 **Ou Nua** Laos
301 H6 **Ouacha** Niger
130 E4 **Ouachita** *watercourse* Arkansas USA
130 F5 **Ouachita** *watercourse* Louisiana USA
130 E3 **Ouachita, Lake** Arkansas USA
130 D3 **Ouachita Mountains** Oklahoma USA
426 7 **Ouăco** New Caledonia
300 C5 **Ouâd Nâga** Mauritania
305 I3 **Ouadda** Central African Republic
305 I2 **Ouaddaï** *admin. area* Chad
304 D2 **Ouagadougou** Burkina Faso
304 D2 **Ouahigouya** Burkina Faso
306 C2 **Ouaka** *admin. area* Central African Republic
306 C2 **Ouaka** *watercourse* Central African Republic
304 E3 **Ouake** Benin
300 E5 **Oualâta** Mauritania
300 D6 **Oualia** Mali
301 G6 **Ouallam** Niger
305 I3 **Ouanda Djailé** Central African Republic
305 H3 **Ouandago** Central African Republic
305 I4 **Ouango** Central African Republic
304 C3 **Ouangolo-Dougou** Côte d'Ivoire
228 F3 **Ouanne, L'** *watercourse* France
306 D2 **Ouara** *watercourse* Central African Republic
300 E6 **Ouardé** Mali
304 E2 **Ouargaye** Burkina Faso
301 H2 **Ouargla** Algeria
301 G5 **Ouaritoufoulout** Mali
300 E2 **Ouarzazate** Morocco
121 S8 **Ouasiemsca** *watercourse* Québec Canada
301 G5 **Ouatagouna** Mali
228 F1 **Oudenaarde** Belgium
376 D2 **Oudomxai** *admin. area* Laos
228 D3 **Oudon** *watercourse* France
308 D6 **Oudtshoorn** South Africa
301 G2 **Oued Lili** Algeria
231 G6 **Oued Tlelat** Algeria
300 E2 **Oued Zem** Morocco
233 B8 **Oued Zenati** Algeria
426 7 **Ouégoa** New Caledonia
304 D3 **Ouéllé** Côte d'Ivoire
304 E3 **Ouémé** *watercourse* Benin
228 B2 **Ouessant, Île d'** *island* France
305 H4 **Ouesso** Congo
305 G3 **Ouest** *admin. area* Cameroon
310 6b **Ouest, Île de l'** *island* French Southern and Antarctic Lands
123 F8 **Ouest, Pointe de l'** *cape* Québec Canada
300 E2 **Ouezzane** Morocco
229 G1 **Ouffet** Belgium
245 C3 **Oughterard** Ireland
305 H3 **Ouham** *admin. area* Central African Republic
305 H3 **Ouham** *watercourse* Central African Republic
305 H3 **Ouham** *watercourse* Chad
305 H3 **Ouham-Pendé** *admin. area* Central African Republic
301 F2 **Oujda** Morocco
231 G5 **Oulad Bou Djemaa** Algeria
223 N4 **Oulainen** Finland
223 P3 **Oulankajoki** *watercourse* Finland
245 F4 **Oulart** Ireland
304 E2 **Oulé** *watercourse* Burkina Faso
304 C3 **Oulé** *watercourse* Guinea
301 H2 **Ouled Djellal** Algeria
305 G3 **Ouli** Cameroon
305 I2 **Oulou, Bahr** *watercourse* Central African Republic
243 G2 **Oulston** North Yorkshire England UK
241 I2 **Oulton** Suffolk England UK
223 N4 **Oulu** Finland
223 O4 **Oulujärvi** *bay* Finland
223 N4 **Oulujoki** *watercourse* Finland
223 O4 **Oulun** *admin. area* Finland
226 D5 **Oulx** Italy
302 C4 **Oum Chalouba** Chad
233 B9 **Oum el Bouaghi** Algeria
301 H1 **Oum el Bouaghi** *admin. area* Algeria
305 H2 **Oum-Hadjer** Chad
231 I6 **Oum Ladjoul** Algeria
301 H3 **Ounane, Djebel** *mountain* Algeria
300 E2 **Ounara** Morocco
223 M2 **Ounasjärvi** *lake* Finland
223 N3 **Ounasjoki** *watercourse* Finland
223 N2 **Ounastunturi** *island* Finland
241 G2 **Oundle** Northamptonshire England UK
119 T8 **Oungre** Saskatchewan Canada
302 C4 **Ounianga -Kebir** Chad
305 H3 **Ouogo** Central African Republic
308 D4 **Our** *watercourse* Botswana
226 D3 **Our** *watercourse* Luxembourg
225 K2 **Ouransaaristo** *island* Finland
229 G2 **Ource** *watercourse* France
304 B2 **Ouré-Kaba** Guinea
156 C3 **Ourém** Brazil
230 B4 **Ourém** Portugal
230 C2 **Ourense** Spain
156 D4 **Ouricuri** Brazil
157 B8 **Ourinhos** Brazil

157 C5 **Ouro** *watercourse* Brazil
157 D8 **Ouro Preto** Brazil
159 F3 **Ouro Preto do Oeste** Brazil
159 G4 **Ouro Verde** Brazil
123 G8 **Ours, Cap de l'** *cape* Québec Canada
226 C2 **Ourthe** *watercourse* Belgium
244 E2 **Ousdale** Highland Scotland UK
241 H2 **Ousden** Suffolk England UK
243 G3 **Ouse** *watercourse* England UK
228 E5 **Oust** France
228 C3 **Oust** *watercourse* France
243 I3 **Out Newton** East Riding of Yorkshire England UK
223 O2 **Outakoski** Finland
123 D8 **Outardes, Rivière aux** *watercourse* Québec Canada
123 D7 **Outardes Quatre, Réservoir** Québec Canada
300 F2 **Outat Oulad el Haj** Morocco
435 F2 **Outer Bailey** *underwater feature* Atlantic Ocean
126 F3 **Outer Island** Wisconsin USA
243 F2 **Outhgill** Cumbria England UK
308 C4 **Outjo** Namibia
223 P5 **Outokumpu** Finland
423 D7 **Outram** New Zealand
228 E1 **Outreau** France
241 H2 **Outwell** Cambridgeshire England UK
426 7 **Ouvéa** *island* New Caledonia
229 G4 **Ouvèze** *watercourse* France
241 H5 **Ouville-la-Rivière** France
425 L8 **Ouyen** Vic. Australia
226 E5 **Ovada** Italy
163 5 **Ovahí, Caleta** *bay* Isla de Pascua (Easter Island)
427 9 **Ovalau** *island* Fiji
305 G4 **Ovan** Gabon
224 H2 **Ovanåker** Sweden
230 B3 **Ovar** Portugal
373 K5 **Ovau** *island* Solomon Islands
234 B3 **Ovča** Serbia
154 C2 **Ovejas** Colombia
160 E5 **Ovejas, Cerro de las** *mountain* Argentina
305 G4 **Oveng** Cameroon
241 H2 **Over** Cambridgeshire England UK
244 E5 **Over Dalgliesh** Scottish Borders Scotland UK
241 F3 **Over Kiddington** Oxfordshire England UK
241 F3 **Over Wallop** Hampshire England UK
222 I5 **Överammer** Sweden
222 F5 **Overås** Norway
224 F3 **Överby** Sweden
119 T6 **Overflowing** *watercourse* Saskatchewan Canada
119 U6 **Overflowing River** Manitoba Canada
222 K2 **Øvergard** Norway
222 I5 **Överhogdal** Sweden
223 M3 **Överkalix** Sweden
222 L4 **Överklinten** Sweden
126 D7 **Overland Park** Kansas USA
424 E6 **Overlander Roadhouse** WA Australia
222 L5 **Övermark** Finland
223 M3 **Övermorjärv** Sweden
160 D5 **Overo, Volcán** *volcano* Argentina
222 K4 **Överrödå** Sweden
244 E6 **Overton** Dumfries and Galloway Scotland UK
241 F3 **Overton** Hampshire England UK
240 E2 **Overton** Wrexham Wales UK
130 D4 **Overton** Texas USA
223 M3 **Övertorneå** Sweden
222 I3 **Överuman** *lake* Sweden
234 F3 **Ovidiu** Romania
135 G3 **Oviedo** Dominican Republic
230 D2 **Oviedo** Spain
224 G1 **Oviksfjällen** *range* Sweden
225 K4 **Ovišī** Latvia
384 E3 **Övörhangay** *admin. area* Mongolia
222 J5 **Övra** Sweden
222 I3 **Övre Ältsvattnet** *lake* Sweden
223 N2 **Övre Anarjokka Nasjonalpark** *park* Norway
222 E6 **Øvre Årdal** Norway
222 I4 **Övre Boksjön** *lake* Sweden
222 K2 **Øvre Dividal Nasjonalpark** *park* Norway
222 H4 **Øvre Fiplingvatnet** *lake* Norway
224 G2 **Övre Fryken** *lake* Sweden
224 E2 **Øvre Hein** *lake* Norway
222 L2 **Övre Soppero** Sweden
222 L4 **Övre Tväråsel** Sweden
222 J5 **Övsjöbyn** Sweden
222 E5 **Ovstrup** Denmark
423 C8 **Owaka** New Zealand
305 H5 **Owando** Congo
387 H4 **Owase** Japan
126 D8 **Owasso** Oklahoma USA
126 E4 **Owatonna** Minnesota USA
423 E5 **Owen, Mount** New Zealand
80 J3 **Owen Fracture Zone** *underwater feature* Indian Ocean
376 C5 **Owen Island** Myanmar
423 E5 **Owen River** New Zealand
127 K4 **Owen Sound** Ontario Canada
373 H6 **Owen Stanley Range** Papua New Guinea
305 F3 **Owena** *watercourse* Nigeria
305 F4 **Owendo** Gabon
245 C2 **Owenduff** Ireland
124 F8 **Owens** *watercourse* California USA
128 C2 **Owens Lake** California USA
126 H8 **Owensboro** Kentucky USA
305 F3 **Owerri** Nigeria
245 D1 **Owey Island** Ireland
422 F4 **Owhango** New Zealand
163 11a **Owia Bay** St Vincent and the Grenadines
241 G3 **Owlswick** Buckinghamshire England UK
241 H3 **Owmby** Lincolnshire England UK
126 I5 **Owosso** Michigan USA
124 G5 **Owyhee** *watercourse* Oregon USA
124 G5 **Owyhee, Lake** Oregon USA
245 D2 **Ox Mountains** Ireland
158 C3 **Oxapampa** Peru
222 inset **Öxarfjörður** *bay* Iceland
119 T8 **Oxbow** Saskatchewan Canada
126 E2 **Oxdrift** Ontario Canada
235 B6 **Oxeia** *island* Greece
241 E3 **Oxenton** Gloucestershire England UK
423 E6 **Oxford** New Zealand
241 F3 **Oxford** Oxfordshire England UK
131 I4 **Oxford** Alabama USA
130 F2 **Oxford** Arkansas USA
125 Q8 **Oxford** Kansas USA
130 G3 **Oxford** Mississippi USA
127 N5 **Oxford** New York USA
131 L2 **Oxford** North Carolina USA
126 I7 **Oxford** Ohio USA
120 H5 **Oxford Lake** Manitoba Canada
241 F3 **Oxfordshire** *admin. area* England UK
224 G5 **Oxie** Sweden
133 H4 **Oxkutzcab** Mexico
128 C3 **Oxnard** California USA
241 G3 **Oxted** Surrey England UK
241 F1 **Oxton** Nottinghamshire England UK
244 F5 **Oxton** Scottish Borders Scotland UK
235 D6 **Oxylithos** Greece
375 F3 **Oya** Malaysia
375 G3 **Oya** *watercourse* Malaysia
229 H4 **Oyace** Italy
158 D3 **Oyague** Peru
118 L7 **Oyama** British Columbia Canada
387 H4 **Oyama** Japan
222 F6 **Øyangen** *lake* Norway
155 H4 **Oyapock** *watercourse* French Guiana
224 D3 **Øyarvatn** *lake* Norway
389 N4 **Oychilik** Kazakhstan
222 F6 **Øye** Norway
305 G4 **Oyem** Gabon
119 P7 **Oyen** Alberta Canada
222 H4 **Øyevatnet** *lake* Norway
222 J2 **Øyjorda** Norway
244 D3 **Oykel Bridge** Highland Scotland UK
224 F3 **Øymarksjøen** *lake* Norway
305 H5 **Oyo** Congo
305 E3 **Oyo** *admin. area* Nigeria
158 B3 **Oyón** Peru
229 G3 **Oyonnax** France
389 L6 **Oytal** Kyrgyzstan
222 G5 **Øyungen** *lake* Norway
237 AF5 **Oyusardakh** Russian Federation
394 G5 **Özalp** Turkey
377 I5 **Ozamiz** Philippines
131 I5 **Ozark** Alabama USA
126 E8 **Ozark** Missouri USA
130 E3 **Ozark Lake** Arkansas USA
126 E8 **Ozark Plateau** Missouri USA
126 E7 **Ozarks, Lake of the** Missouri USA
227 K3 **Ózd** Hungary
238 C6 **Ozerany** Belarus
238 F3 **Ozerevo** Russian Federation
238 E5 **Ozerishche** Russian Federation
234 F3 **Ozerne** Ukraine
237 AH7 **Ozernoy, Zaliv** *bay* Russian Federation
387 I1 **Ozerskiy** Russian Federation
238 H5 **Ozëry** Russian Federation
124 C2 **Ozette Lake** Washington USA
120 K6 **Ozhiski Lake** Ontario Canada
237 AE5 **Ozhogino** Russian Federation
237 AE5 **Ozhogino, Ozero** *lake* Russian Federation
227 M3 **Ozhydiv** Ukraine
238 F3 **Ozinki** Russian Federation
129 L5 **Ozona** Texas USA
227 J2 **Ozorków** Poland
305 F3 **Ozoro** Nigeria
386 G5 **Ozu** Japan
388 D5 **Ozurgeti** Georgia

P

386 E3 **P-aro Ho** *lake* South Korea
304 D2 **Pâ** Burkina Faso
381 H4 **Pa-Chao Tao** *island* Taiwan China
376 C3 **Pa Daet** Thailand
378 D2 **Pa-li Ho** *watercourse* Xizang Zizhiqu China
380 C4 **Pa-pien Ho** *watercourse* Yunnan China
382 H4 **Pa-yin-kou Ho** *watercourse* Xinjiang Uygur Zizhiqu China
223 O2 **Paaddos** Finland
223 N5 **Pääjärvi** Finland
222 M2 **Pääjärvi** *lake* Finland
426 7 **Paama** *island* Vanuatu
117 O6 **Paamiut** Greenland
229 Q4 **Paanayarvi National Park** Russian Federation
229 J2 **Paar** *watercourse* Germany
163 1a **Paardenbaai** *bay* Aruba
308 C6 **Paarl** South Africa
223 O2 **Paatari** *lake* Finland
223 O4 **Paatinjärvi** *lake* Finland
223 N4 **Paavola** Finland
244 A4 **Pabaigh** *island* Scotland UK
244 A3 **Pabbay** *island* Scotland UK
375 H5 **Pabbiring, Kepulauan** *island* Indonesia
132 C3 **Pabellones, Ensenada** *lake* Mexico
227 J2 **Pabianice** Poland
158 D4 **Pablo Amaya** Bolivia
379 F4 **Pabna** Bangladesh
123 F8 **Pabos** Québec Canada
123 F8 **Pabos Mills** Québec Canada
225 M5 **Pabradė** Lithuania
156 D5 **Pacae** Peru
159 I1 **Pacajá** Brazil
155 I5 **Pacajá** *watercourse* Brazil
155 F3 **Pacaraimã, Serra** *range* Brazil
158 B2 **Pacasmayo, Punta** *cape* Peru
156 B3 **Pacatuba** Brazil
162 A5 **Pacheco, Isla** *island* Chile
235 D7 **Pacheia** *island* Greece
388 D2 **Pachelma** Russian Federation
129 I6 **Pachera** Mexico
233 F8 **Pachino** Italy
158 C4 **Pachiri** Peru
158 C3 **Pachitea** *watercourse* Peru
154 C3 **Pacho** Colombia
392 F5 **Pachperwa** Uttar Pradesh India
133 F4 **Pachuca** Mexico
126 F7 **Pacific** Missouri USA
436 O2 **Pacific-Antarctic Ridge** *underwater feature* Southern Ocean
124 E8 **Pacific Grove** California USA
118 I8 **Pacific Rim National Park** British Columbia Canada
375 G5 **Pacinan, Tanjung** *cape* Indonesia
375 G5 **Paciran** Indonesia
375 F6 **Pacitan** Indonesia
425 L7 **Packsaddle** NSW Australia
154 D4 **Pacoa** Colombia
159 G3 **Paçoca** Brazil
158 D5 **Pacocha** Peru
134 E5 **Pacora** Panama
229 L2 **Pacov** Czech Republic
159 E2 **Pacovalzinho** Brazil
227 J1 **Pacyna** Poland
377 J6 **Padada** Philippines
391 K3 **Padag Road** Pakistan
375 I5 **Padamarang** *island* Indonesia
155 E4 **Padamo, Rio** *watercourse* Venezuela
392 C5 **Padampur** Rajasthan India
375 B5 **Padang** Indonesia
374 D3 **Padang** Indonesia
374 D4 **Padang** *island* Indonesia
374 D3 **Padang Endau** Malaysia
374 D4 **Padangpanjang** Indonesia
374 C3 **Padangsidempuan** Indonesia
374 F4 **Padangtikar** Indonesia
374 F4 **Padangtikar** *island* Indonesia
223 R5 **Padany** Russian Federation
375 G2 **Padas** *watercourse* Malaysia
155 F4 **Padauari** *watercourse* Brazil
224 E5 **Padborg** Denmark
393 C6 **Paddhari** Gujarat India
241 H3 **Paddock Wood** Kent England UK
119 S6 **Paddockwood** Saskatchewan Canada
375 I4 **Padeabesar** *island* Indonesia
235 B5 **Padej** Serbia
130 C3 **Paden** Oklahoma USA
226 E2 **Paderborn** Germany
234 C3 **Padeş** Romania
307 E3 **Padibe** Uganda
243 F3 **Padiham** Lancashire England UK
159 E5 **Padilla** Bolivia
234 B3 **Padina** Serbia
222 J3 **Padjelanta** *range* Sweden
222 J3 **Padjelanta nationalpark** *park* Sweden
120 G2 **Padlei** Nunavut Canada
223 S5 **Padmozero, Ozero** *lake* Russian Federation
226 F5 **Padova** Italy
393 C6 **Padra** Gujarat India
306 A5 **Padrão, Ponta** *cape* Angola
157 B6 **Padre Bernardo** Brazil
130 C7 **Padre Island** Texas USA
157 D7 **Padre Paraíso** Brazil
230 B2 **Padrón** Spain
392 C6 **Padru** Rajasthan India
233 C6 **Padru** Sardinia Italy
240 C4 **Padstow** Cornwall England UK
126 G8 **Paducah** Kentucky USA
130 A3 **Paducah** Texas USA
427 14a **Paea** French Polynesia
386 E4 **Paegnyŏng-do** *island* North Korea
385 K4 **Paektu San** *mountain* Jilin China
386 F2 **Paektu San** *mountain* North Korea
422 G3 **Paengaroa** New Zealand
422 F3 **Paeroa** New Zealand
309 F4 **Pafuri** South Africa
232 F4 **Pag** Croatia
159 H2 **Paga-Conta** Brazil
377 I6 **Pagadian** Philippines
374 D4 **Pagai Selatan** *island* Indonesia
374 D4 **Pagai Utara** *island* Indonesia
426 2 **Pagan** *island* Northern Mariana Islands
232 D5 **Paganico** Italy
374 D5 **Pagaralam** Indonesia
235 C6 **Pagasitikos Kolpos** *bay* Greece
375 G4 **Pagatan** Indonesia
376 C4 **Pagawyun** Myanmar
155 F3 **Pagé** Brazil
128 G2 **Page** Arizona USA
125 Q3 **Page** North Dakota USA
131 K3 **Pageland** South Carolina USA
374 E4 **Pagerdewa** Indonesia
163 8 **Paget, Mount** South Georgia
235 C6 **Pagkalos, Akra** *cape* Greece
232 B2 **Pagny** France
426 5 **Pago Bay** Guam
427 12 **Pago Pago** American Samoa
125 L8 **Pagosa Springs** Colorado USA
163 15 **Pagua Pointe** *cape* Dominica
126 I2 **Pagwachuan Lake** Ontario Canada
373 G5 **Pagwi** Papua New Guinea
128 inset **Pāhala** Hawai'i USA
392 D4 **Pahalgam** Jammu and Kashmir India/Pakistan
374 D2 **Pahang** *admin. area* Malaysia
374 D3 **Pahang** *watercourse* Malaysia
423 F5 **Pahaoa** New Zealand
134 D4 **Páhara, Laguna** *lake* Nicaragua
391 L3 **Paharpur** Pakistan
234 A2 **Páhi** Hungary
423 B8 **Pahia** New Zealand
423 B8 **Pahia Point** New Zealand
422 F5 **Pahiatua** New Zealand
223 O4 **Pahkakoski** Finland
223 O5 **Pahkamäki** Finland
128 inset **Pāhoa** Hawai'i USA
131 K7 **Pahokee** Florida USA
124 H8 **Pahranagat Range** Nevada USA
124 E2 **Pahrump** Nevada USA
128 G8 **Pahute Mesa** *range* Nevada USA
305 G3 **Pai** *watercourse* Nigeria
381 H4 **Pai-Sha Tao** *island* Taiwan China
159 G5 **Paiaguás** Brazil
244 A3 **Paible** Na h-Eileanan Siar Scotland UK
157 A8 **Paiçandu** Brazil
381 H3 **Paich'üan Liehtao (Taiwan)** *island* Taiwan China
154 C4 **Paicol** Colombia
225 M3 **Paide** Estonia
240 D4 **Paignton** Torbay England UK
225 M2 **Päijänne** *bay* Finland
305 F3 **Paiko** Nigeria
129 K8 **Paila** Mexico
376 D4 **Pailin** Cambodia
158 D4 **Pailipaya** Bolivia
158 E3 **Pailita** Bolivia
158 C4 **Pailitas** Colombia
159 F5 **Pailón** Bolivia
154 C3 **Paime** Colombia
228 C2 **Paimpol** France
374 D4 **Painan** Indonesia
127 K6 **Painesville** Ohio USA
225 L2 **Painio** *lake* Finland
121 P6 **Paint Hills Bay** Québec Canada
119 W5 **Paint Lake** Manitoba Canada
130 B5 **Paint Rock** Texas USA
128 G3 **Painted Desert** Arkansas USA
126 J8 **Paintsville** Kentucky USA
154 C3 **Paipa** Colombia
244 B2 **Pairc** Na h-Eileanan Siar Scotland UK
426 7 **Païromé** New Caledonia
230 E2 **País Vasco** *admin. area* Spain
244 D5 **Paisley** Renfrewshire Scotland UK
124 E5 **Paisley** Oregon USA
223 O5 **Paisua** Finland
426 7 **Paita** New Caledonia
158 A2 **Paita** Peru
158 A2 **Paita, Bahía de** *bay* Peru
375 H2 **Paitan, Teluk** *bay* Malaysia
393 D7 **Paithan** Maharashtra India
223 M2 **Paittasjärvi** Sweden
222 K3 **Paittasjärvi** *lake* Sweden
159 F3 **Paixão, Serra da** *range* Brazil
223 M3 **Pajala** Sweden
154 A5 **Paján** Ecuador
160 D2 **Pajancha** Chile
310 3d **Pajara** Canary Islands
162 C4 **Pajarito, Puerto** *bay* Argentina
160 D4 **Pájaros, Islotes** *island* Chile
307 E3 **Pajule** Uganda
223 O5 **Pajuskylä** Finland
225 N3 **Pajusti** Estonia
373 H4 **Pak Island** Papua New Guinea
376 C5 **Pak Nam Chumphon** Thailand
125 J2 **Pak-oghkee** Alberta Canada
376 D3 **Pak-Ou** Laos
376 D5 **Pak Phanang** Thailand
376 D6 **Pak Phayun** Thailand
227 I4 **Páka** Hungary
374 D2 **Paka** Malaysia
393 E9 **Pakala** Andhra Pradesh India
155 F3 **Pakaraima Mountains** Guyana
223 O5 **Pakarila** Finland
126 F2 **Pakashkan Lake** Ontario Canada
376 D3 **Pakbèng** Laos
376 C5 **Pakchan** *watercourse* Myanmar
133 H5 **Pakchén** Mexico
162 A4 **Pakenham, Cabo** *cape* Chile
223 Q4 **Pakhomova-Vara** Russian Federation
305 F2 **Paki** Nigeria
375 H6 **Pakijangan, Tanjung** *cape* Indonesia
426 6 **Pakin** *island* Federated States of Micronesia
225 K2 **Pakinainen** *island* Finland
391 J4 **Pakistan** *country*
120 H5 **Pakitahokansik** Manitoba Canada
379 H5 **Pakokku** Myanmar
227 J1 **Pakość** Poland
119 P8 **Pakowki Lake** Alberta Canada
391 M3 **Pakpattan** Pakistan
232 G4 **Pakrac** Croatia
225 L5 **Pakruojis** Lithuania
234 A2 **Paks** Hungary
391 L2 **Paktīā** *admin. area* Afghanistan
391 K3 **Paktikā** *admin. area* Afghanistan
392 G6 **Pakur** Jharkhand India
120 I7 **Pakwash Lake** Ontario Canada
120 D6 **Pakwaw Lake** Saskatchewan Canada
376 D3 **Pakxan** Laos
376 E4 **Pakxe** Laos
376 D2 **Pakxèng** Laos
305 G3 **Pala** Chad
374 E5 **Palabuhanratu, Teluk** *bay* Indonesia
135 F2 **Palacca Point** *cape* Bahamas
130 C6 **Palacios** Texas USA
393 E8 **Palacole** Andhra Pradesh India
231 H3 **Palafrugell** Spain
233 F8 **Palagonia** Italy
235 C8 **Palaiochora** Greece
235 B6 **Palaiochórion** Greece
235 B6 **Palairou, Ormos** *bay* Greece
393 D9 **Palakkad** Kerala India
308 D4 **Palamakoloi** Botswana
372 C4 **Palamea** Indonesia
231 H3 **Palamós** Spain
392 D4 **Palampur** Himachal Pradesh India
377 I3 **Palanan Bay** Philippines
234 G2 **Palanca** Moldova
393 E7 **Palandur** Maharashtra India
391 I3 **Palangān, Kūh-e** *mountain* Iran
375 G4 **Palangkaraya** Indonesia
393 D9 **Palani** Tamil Nadu India
392 C6 **Palanpur** Gujarat India
372 A5 **Palanro** Indonesia
308 E4 **Palapye** Botswana
126 G5 **Palatine** Illinois USA
237 AF6 **Palatka** Russian Federation
131 K6 **Palatka** Florida USA
233 C6 **Palau** Sardinia Italy
132 E3 **Palau** Mexico
372 E2 **Palau** *country* Oceania
78 J7 **Palau Trench** *underwater feature* Pacific Ocean
377 I3 **Palaui** *island* Philippines
374 E5 **Palausekopong, Tanjung** *cape* Indonesia
377 H5 **Palawan** *island* Philippines
78 H7 **Palawan Trough** *underwater feature* South China Sea
229 I5 **Palazzo, Punta** *cape* Corsica France
226 E5 **Palazzolo** Italy
159 E6 **Palca Grande** Bolivia
129 M1 **Palco** Kansas USA
227 K2 **Palczew** Poland
225 M3 **Paldiski** Estonia
240 D2 **Pale** Gwynedd Wales UK
372 B3 **Paleleh** Indonesia
374 E4 **Palembang** Indonesia
162 B3 **Palena** Chile
162 B3 **Palena, Lago** *lake* Argentina
230 D2 **Palencia** Spain
133 H5 **Palenque** Mexico
135 G3 **Palenque, Punta** *cape* Dominican Republic
392 E6 **Palera** Madhya Pradesh India
160 E3 **Palermo** Argentina
233 E7 **Palermo** Italy
158 D2 **Palestina** Brazil
160 D2 **Palestina** Chile
130 F3 **Palestine** Arkansas USA
130 D5 **Palestine** Texas USA
130 D4 **Palestine, Lake** Texas USA
155 H3 **Palétuviers, Pointe des** *cape* French Guiana
393 C7 **Palghar** Maharashtra India
161 I3 **Palhoça** Brazil
392 C6 **Pali** Rajasthan India
392 E6 **Pali** Uttar Pradesh India
375 G5 **Paliat** *island* Indonesia
232 H3 **Palić** Serbia
227 J4 **Palicko Jezero** *lake* Serbia
225 O5 **Palik** Belarus
426 6b **Palikir** Federated States of Micronesia
377 J6 **Palimbang** Philippines
233 F6 **Palinuro, Capo** *cape* Italy
235 D5 **Paliouri** Greece
235 C6 **Paliouri, Akra** *cape* Greece
235 B6 **Paliouria** Greece
125 K7 **Palisade** Colorado USA
229 G2 **Paliseul** Belgium
393 C7 **Palitana** Gujarat India
133 G5 **Palizada** Mexico
233 F8 **Palizzi** Italy
223 O4 **Paljakka** *mountain* Finland
393 E10 **Palk Bay** Sri Lanka
393 E10 **Palk Strait** India
225 M2 **Pälkänevesi** *lake* Finland
222 L3 **Pålkem** Sweden
238 C4 **Palkino** Russian Federation
392 F6 **Palkot** Jharkhand India
245 E3 **Pallas** Ireland
245 D4 **Pallas Green** Ireland
223 M2 **Pallas-Yllästunturin Kansallispuisto** *park* Finland
223 N2 **Pallasjärvi** *lake* Finland
388 E3 **Pallasovka** Russian Federation
158 E5 **Pallini** Bolivia
423 F5 **Palliser, Cape** New Zealand
423 F5 **Palliser Bay** New Zealand
392 D5 **Pallu** Rajasthan India
131 K6 **Palm Bay** Florida USA
163 1a **Palm Beach** *bay* Aruba
128 E4 **Palm Springs** Florida USA
125 C6 **Palma** *watercourse* Brazil
309 H2 **Palma** Mozambique
231 H4 **Palma** Spain
230 D5 **Palma del Río** Spain
158 E4 **Palma Seca** Bolivia
135 F2 **Palma Soriano** Cuba
161 H5 **Palmar, Punta del** *cape* Uruguay
155 F5 **Palmares** Brazil
161 I4 **Palmares do Sul** Brazil
157 B5 **Palmas** Brazil
157 B9 **Palmas** Brazil
304 C4 **Palmas, Cape** *cape* Liberia
134 D5 **Palmas Bellas** Panama
157 D6 **Palmas de Monte Alto** Brazil
128 C3 **Palmdale** California USA
157 B9 **Palmeira** Brazil
161 H3 **Palmeira das Missões** Brazil
156 D4 **Palmeirais** Brazil
159 G5 **Palmeiras** Brazil
157 C6 **Palmeiras** *watercourse* Brazil
157 B7 **Palmeiras de Goiás** Brazil
308 B1 **Palmeirinhas, Ponta das** *cape* Angola
373 G5 **Palmer** *watercourse* Papua New Guinea
116 E6 **Palmer** Alaska USA
125 Q7 **Palmer** Kansas USA
125 P6 **Palmer** Nebraska USA
130 C4 **Palmer** Texas USA
436 T2 **Palmer (USA)** *research station* Antarctica
436 T2 **Palmer Archipelago** *island* Antarctica
436 T2 **Palmer Land** *plain* Antarctica
424 I3 **Palmerston** NT Australia
127 K5 **Palmerston** Ontario Canada
427 11 **Palmerston** *island* Cook Islands New Zealand
423 D7 **Palmerston** New Zealand
422 F5 **Palmerston North** New Zealand
131 J7 **Palmetto** Florida USA
163 18 **Palmetto Point** Antigua and Barbuda
131 M8 **Palmetto Point** Bahamas
154 E4 **Palmira** Bolivia
154 B4 **Palmira** Colombia
163 10a **Palmiste Bay** Grenada
161 G5 **Palmitas** Uruguay
126 H7 **Palmyra** Indiana USA
126 F7 **Palmyra** Missouri USA
78 P7 **Palmyra Atoll** *unincorporated US territory* Pacific Ocean
393 G7 **Palmyras Point** Orissa India
244 E6 **Palnackie** Dumfries and Galloway Scotland UK
155 F2 **Palo Blanco** Venezuela
130 B4 **Palo Pinto, Lake** Texas USA
160 F3 **Palo Santo** Argentina
163 9 **Palo Seco** Trinidad and Tobago
128 E4 **Palo Verde** California USA
375 F3 **Paloh** Malaysia
222 L3 **Palohuornas** Sweden
223 M2 **Palojärvi** *lake* Finland
223 M2 **Palojoensuu** Finland
223 O5 **Palokangas** Finland
223 P5 **Palomäki** Finland
132 E3 **Palomas, Lago de** *lake* Mexico
372 B4 **Palopo** Indonesia
231 F5 **Palos, Cabo de** *cape* Spain
157 A9 **Palotina** Brazil
158 C4 **Palpa** Peru
224 E2 **Pålsbufjorden** *bay* Norway
222 L4 **Pålsträsk** Sweden
223 O4 **Paltamo** Finland
223 O4 **Paltaniemi** Finland
223 O4 **Paltaselkä** *bay* Finland
238 F6 **Pal'tso** Russian Federation
372 A4 **Palu** Indonesia
225 M5 **Paluknys** Lithuania
393 E9 **Palur** Tamil Nadu India
226 G4 **Paluzza** Italy
376 C4 **Palwa** Myanmar
392 D5 **Palwal** Haryana India
304 E2 **Pama** Burkina Faso
305 H4 **Pama** *watercourse* Central African Republic
375 I6 **Pamana, Pulau** *island* Indonesia
374 E5 **Pamanukan** Indonesia
310 8b **Pamanzi (Petite Terre)** *island* Mayotte
309 G4 **Pambarra** Mozambique
372 A3 **Pambero** Indonesia
119 R8 **Pambrun** Saskatchewan Canada
372 F4 **Pamdai** Indonesia
375 G5 **Pamekasan** Indonesia
374 E5 **Pameungpeuk** Indonesia
235 E6 **Pamfylla** Greece
227 I4 **Pamhagen** Austria
228 E5 **Pamiers** France
389 K6 **Pamir** *lake* Tajikistan
131 N3 **Pamlico Sound** North Carolina USA
127 P2 **Pamouscachiou, Lac** *lake* Québec Canada
129 L3 **Pampa** Texas USA
158 C4 **Pampa Blanca** Peru
162 C3 **Pampa de Agnia** Argentina
160 F3 **Pampa de Infierno** Argentina
158 c2 **Pampa del Sacramento** *range* Peru
162 C3 **Pampa Pelada** *region* Argentina
158 C4 **Pampa Redonda** Peru
229 H4 **Pamparato** Italy
160 E5 **Pampas** *region* Argentina
158 C4 **Pampas** Peru
158 C4 **Pampas** *watercourse* Peru
158 D2 **Pampeiro** Brazil
228 F4 **Pampelonne** France
310 7b **Pamplemousses** Mauritius
127 L8 **Pamplin** Virginia USA
154 C3 **Pamplona** Colombia
230 F2 **Pamplona/Irunea** Spain
426 8 **Pamua** Solomon Islands
375 H4 **Pamukan, Teluk** *bay* Indonesia
235 G5 **Pamukova** Turkey
127 M8 **Pamunkey** *watercourse* Virginia USA
244 F2 **Pan** Orkney Islands Scotland UK
160 D3 **Pan de Azúcar** Chile
161 H5 **Pan de Azúcar** Uruguay
233 C7 **Pan di Zucchero, Scoglio** *island* Sardinia Italy
379 G2 **Pana** Xizang Zizhiqu China
305 G5 **Pana** Gabon
133 H4 **Panaba** Mexico
128 E2 **Panaca** Nevada USA
127 K3 **Panache, Lake** Ontario Canada
234 D2 **Panaci** Romania
392 E6 **Panagar** Madhya Pradesh India
374 E5 **Panaitan** *island* Indonesia
235 B6 **Panaitolikon** *range* Greece
393 C8 **Panaji** Goa India
134 D5 **Panama** *country* Central America
134 E5 **Panamá** Panama
154 B2 **Panamá, Bahía de** *bay* Panama
154 B3 **Panamá, Golfo de** *bay* Panama
79 X7 **Panama Basin** *underwater feature* Pacific Ocean
134 D5 **Panama Canal** Panama
131 I5 **Panama City** Florida USA
161 H4 **Panambi** Brazil
128 D2 **Panamint Range** California USA
373 J6 **Panapompom Island** Papua New Guinea
374 F3 **Panarik** Indonesia
373 J6 **Panatinane Island** Papua New Guinea
373 J6 **Panawina Island** Papua New Guinea
377 I5 **Panay** *island* Philippines
228 E4 **Panazol** France
124 H7 **Pancake Range** Nevada USA
234 B3 **Pančevo** Serbia
121 W6 **Panchia Lake** Newfoundland and Labrador Canada
381 I4 **Panchiao** Taiwan China
129 H5 **Pancho Villa** Mexico
234 B4 **Pančicev Vrh** *mountain* Serbia
375 G3 **Pancingapan, Bukit** *mountain* Indonesia
234 B2 **Pâncota** Romania
372 F4 **Pandaidori, Kepulauan** *island* Indonesia
377 J4 **Pandan** Philippines
374 D4 **Pandan, Selat** *strait* Singapore
374 B4 **Pandan Reservoir** Singapore
375 G4 **Pandang** Indonesia
424 inset **Pandang, Pulu** *island* Cocos (Keeling) Islands Australia
157 C6 **Pandeiros** *watercourse* Brazil
393 D8 **Pandharpur** Maharashtra India
393 E7 **Pandhurna** Madhya Pradesh India
158 E3 **Pando** *admin. area* Bolivia
240 D2 **Pandy** Gwynedd Wales UK
240 E3 **Pandy** Monmouthshire Wales UK
225 M5 **Panevėžio** *admin. area* Lithuania
225 M5 **Panevėžys** Lithuania
241 H3 **Panfield** Essex England UK
225 L3 **Panga** Estonia
427 10 **Pangai** Tonga
305 G5 **Pangala** Congo
307 F5 **Pangani** *watercourse* Tanzania
241 F3 **Pangbourne** West Berkshire England UK
375 H4 **Pangean** Indonesia
426 8 **Panggoe** Solomon Islands
306 D4 **Pangi** Democratic Republic of Congo
375 G5 **Pangkah, Tanjung** *cape* Indonesia
375 F4 **Pangkalanbuun** Indonesia
374 C3 **Pangkalanlunang** Indonesia
374 E4 **Pangkalpinang** Indonesia
372 B4 **Pangkalsiang, Tanjung** *cape* Indonesia
117 M5 **Pangnirtung** Nunavut Canada
306 A5 **Pango Aluquem** Angola
158 C4 **Pangoa** Peru
305 I3 **Pangonda** Central African Republic
160 C6 **Panguipulli** Chile
124 I8 **Panguitch** Utah USA
374 C3 **Panguruan** Indonesia
377 I6 **Pangutaran** *island* Philippines
377 I6 **Pangutaran Group** *island* Philippines
129 L3 **Panhandle** Texas USA
306 D5 **Pania-Mwanga** Democratic Republic of Congo
372 F4 **Paniai, Danau** *lake* Indonesia
235 D5 **Panichkovo** Bulgaria
426 7 **Panié, Mont** *mountain* New Caledonia
238 F4 **Panino** Russian Federation
238 G2 **Paninskaya** Russian Federation
154 B5 **Panintsa** Peru
392 D5 **Panipat** Haryana India
160 D6 **Paniri, Cerro** *mountain* Chile
377 H5 **Panitan** Philippines
391 K2 **Panjāb** Afghanistan
389 J6 **Panjakent** Tajikistan
Panjang *see* **West Island** Australia
374 E5 **Panjang** Indonesia
375 H3 **Panjang** *island* Indonesia
374 D3 **Panjang, Selat** *strait* Indonesia
234 B3 **Panjevac** Serbia
391 J4 **Panjgur** Pakistan
385 J4 **Panjin** Liaoning China
391 L2 **Panjshir** *admin. area* Afghanistan
223 O5 **Panka** Finland
223 Q5 **Pankajärvi** *lake* Finland
223 Q5 **Pankakoski** Finland
234 G3 **Pankasz** Hungary
387 I2 **Panke-to** *lake* Japan
392 F6 **Panki** Jharkhand India
238 D3 **Pankovka** Russian Federation
225 P5 **Pan'kovo** Russian Federation
305 F3 **Pankshin** Nigeria
380 D3 **Panlian** Sichuan China
392 E6 **Panna** Madhya Pradesh India
391 L4 **Pano Aqil** Pakistan
157 B8 **Panorama** Brazil
126 D6 **Panorama Lake** Iowa USA
235 D8 **Panormos** Greece
393 E9 **Panruti** Tamil Nadu India
379 I6 **Pansam** Myanmar
385 K4 **Panshi** Jilin China
380 D3 **Panshui** Guizhou China
240 D2 **Pant-y-dwr** Powys Wales UK
231 G2 **Pantà d'Escales** *lake* Spain
375 H4 **Pantai** Indonesia
374 D2 **Pantai Remis** Malaysia
159 G5 **Pantanal** *region* Brazil
222 M5 **Päntäne** Finland
375 J6 **Pantar** *island* Indonesia
233 D8 **Pantelleria** Italy
233 D8 **Pantelleria, Isola di** *island* Italy
233 G6 **Pantenecianni, Punta** *cape* Italy
243 H3 **Panton** Lincolnshire England UK
222 M5 **Panttila** Finland
306 B4 **Panu** Democratic Republic of Congo
133 F4 **Pánuco** Mexico
393 C7 **Panvel** Maharashtra India
380 D3 **Panzhihua** Sichuan China
306 B5 **Panzi** Democratic Republic of Congo
134 B4 **Panzós** Guatemala
233 G7 **Paola** Italy
126 D7 **Paola** Kansas USA
125 L7 **Paonia Reservoir** Colorado USA
427 14a **Paopao** French Polynesia
305 H3 **Paoua** Central African Republic
227 I4 **Pápa** Hungary
128 inset **Pāpā** Hawai'i USA
233 F6 **Papa, Monte del** *mountain* Italy
244 F1 **Papa Westray** *island* Scotland UK
128 inset **Pāpa'aloa** Hawai'i USA
157 C7 **Papagaios** Brazil
155 F2 **Papagayos, Islas** *islands* Venezuela
128 inset **Pāpa'ikou** Hawai'i USA
422 F3 **Papakura** New Zealand
133 F5 **Papaloapan** *lake* Mexico
422 G3 **Papamoa Beach** New Zealand
132 E5 **Papanoa, Morro de** *cape* Mexico
133 F4 **Papantla de Olarte** Mexico
375 G2 **Papar** Malaysia
427 14a **Papara** French Polynesia
393 F7 **Paparhahandi** Orissa India
423 D6 **Paparoa Range** New Zealand
235 D7 **Papas, Akra** *cape* Greece
158 A2 **Papayal** Peru
427 14a **Papeete** French Polynesia
158 E5 **Papel Pampa** Bolivia
226 D1 **Papenburg** Germany
427 14a **Papenoo** French Polynesia
427 14a **Papeotai** French Polynesia
225 K5 **Papes Ezers** *lake* Latvia
222 inset **Papey** *island* Iceland
394 E6 **Paphos** Cyprus
244 inset **Papil** Shetland Scotland UK
225 L4 **Papilė** Lithuania
125 Q6 **Papillion** Nebraska USA
225 M4 **Papilys** Lithuania
227 L3 **Papín** Slovakia
372 E5 **Papisoi, Tanjung** *cape* Indonesia
124 H8 **Papoose Lake** Nevada USA
160 D3 **Paposo** Chile
134 C4 **Paptalaya** Honduras
373 H6 **Papua, Gulf of** Papua New Guinea
373 H5 **Papua New Guinea** *country* Oceania
160 D5 **Papudo** Chile
424 I6 **Papulankutja (Blackstone)** WA Australia
376 C3 **Papun** Myanmar
160 D2 **Paquica, Cabo** *cape* Chile
391 I4 **Par Kūh** Iran
131 K4 **Par Pond** South Carolina USA
159 H2 **Pará** *admin. area* Brazil
375 J3 **Para** *island* Indonesia
155 H3 **Para** *admin. area* Suriname
155 I5 **Pará, Ilha do** *island* Brazil
156 B3 **Pará, Rio do** *watercourse* Brazil
157 C7 **Pará de Minas** Brazil
226 E5 **Parabiago** Italy
155 G6 **Paracari** *watercourse* Brazil
158 B4 **Paracas, Península de** *peninsula* Peru
157 C7 **Paracatu** Brazil
157 C7 **Paracatu** *watercourse* Brazil
377 G3 **Paracel Islands (Disputed)**
391 L2 **Parachinar** Pakistan
125 K7 **Parachute** Colorado USA
156 E3 **Paracuru** Brazil
393 G7 **Paradip** Orissa India
127 M2 **Paradis** Québec Canada
122 J6 **Paradise** *watercourse* Newfoundland and Labrador Canada
163 10a **Paradise** Grenada
155 G3 **Paradise** Guyana
124 E7 **Paradise** California USA
122 J6 **Paradise River** Newfoundland and Labrador Canada
119 P6 **Paradise Valley** Alberta Canada
372 A6 **Parado** Indonesia
156 C3 **Paragominas** Brazil
124 I8 **Paragonah** Utah USA
130 F2 **Paragould** Arkansas USA
159 F4 **Paragua** *watercourse* Bolivia
155 F3 **Paragua** *watercourse* Venezuela
157 E6 **Paraguaçu** *watercourse* Brazil
154 D2 **Paraguaná, Península de** *peninsula* Venezuela
159 G5 **Paraguay** *watercourse* Brazil
161 G2 **Paraguay** *watercourse* Paraguay
161 G2 **Paraguay** *country* South America
160 F6 **Paragüil** Argentina
155 F3 **Paraí-tepuí** Venezuela
156 E4 **Paraíba** *admin. area* Brazil
156 D4 **Paraibano** Brazil
159 F3 **Paraíso** Brazil
155 H5 **Paraíso** Brazil
157 A7 **Paraíso** Brazil

159 G2 **Paraíso** Brazil
135 G3 **Paraíso** Dominican Republic
133 G5 **Paraíso** Mexico
156 B5 **Paraíso do Tocantins** Brazil
160 F6 **Paraje El Gavilán** Argentina
161 G2 **Paraje Tuyuyú** Paraguay
422 F3 **Parakai** New Zealand
222 L3 **Parakka** Sweden
304 E3 **Parakou** Benin
393 F7 **Paralakhemundi** Orissa India
235 C7 **Paralia Tyrou** Greece
373 G6 **Parama Island** Papua New Guinea
155 H3 **Paramaribo** Suriname
156 D4 **Parambu** Brazil
157 D5 **Paramirim** *watercourse* Brazil
237 AG8 **Paramushir, Ostrov** *island* Kuril Islands
160 F4 **Paraná** Argentina
161 G3 **Paraná** *watercourse* Argentina
161 I3 **Paraná** *admin. area* Brazil
157 C6 **Paraná** *watercourse* Brazil
157 C6 **Paranã** Brazil
157 C6 **Paranã, Serra Geral do** *range* Brazil
155 G5 **Paraná Madeirinha** *watercourse* Brazil
154 E5 **Parana Mirim Pirajuanana** *watercourse* Brazil
157 B9 **Paranaguá** Brazil
157 B7 **Paranaíba** Brazil
157 B7 **Paranaíba** *watercourse* Brazil
157 B8 **Paranapanema** Brazil
157 B8 **Paranapanema** *watercourse* Brazil
161 I3 **Paranapiacaba, Serra** *range* Brazil
157 A8 **Paranavaí** Brazil
372 D4 **Parang** *island* Indonesia
377 I6 **Parang** Philippines
161 H2 **Paranhos** Brazil
393 E10 **Paranki Aru** *watercourse* Sri Lanka
427 14 **Paraoa** *island* French Polynesia
157 C7 **Paraopeba** *watercourse* Brazil
423 F5 **Paraparaumu** New Zealand
159 F5 **Parapeti** *watercourse* Bolivia
426 8 **Parara** *island* Solomon Islands
130 B7 **Paras** Mexico
392 F7 **Parasi** Chhattisgarh India
392 F6 **Parasi** Jharkhand India
235 E8 **Paraspori, Akra** *cape* Greece
158 C3 **Paratari** Brazil
157 C8 **Parati** Brazil
157 D6 **Paratinga** Brazil
156 B4 **Parauapebas** *watercourse* Brazil
156 A3 **Parauaquara, Serra** *mountain* Brazil
159 G2 **Parauari** *watercourse* Brazil
157 B7 **Paraúna** Brazil
379 F4 **Parbatipur** Bangladesh
393 D7 **Parbhani** Maharashtra India
227 J2 **Parcice** Poland
234 E1 **Parcova** Moldova
393 C7 **Pardi** Gujarat India
234 F3 **Pardina** Romania
161 G6 **Pardo** Argentina
159 E3 **Pardo** Bolivia
161 H2 **Pardo** *watercourse* Brazil
424 F5 **Pardoo Roadhouse** WA Australia
227 H2 **Pardubice** Czech Republic
227 I3 **Pardubický Kraj** *admin. area* Czech Republic
159 G4 **Parecis** Brazil
159 F4 **Parecis, Serra dos** *range* Brazil
310 3d **Pared, Puerto de la** *bay* Canary Islands
162 B4 **Pared Norte, Cerro** *mountain* Chile
162 B4 **Pared Sur, Cerro** *mountain* Chile
230 D2 **Paredes de Nava** Spain
160 D5 **Pareditas** Argentina
160 C5 **Paredones** Chile
156 E4 **Parelhas** Brazil
228 F4 **Pareloup, Lac de** *lake* France
426 6a **Parem** *island* Federated States of Micronesia
237 AH6 **Paren'** *watercourse* Russian Federation
422 E2 **Parengarenga Harbour** New Zealand
127 M2 **Parent, Lac** *lake* Québec Canada
423 D7 **Pareora** New Zealand
372 A5 **Parepare** Indonesia
225 P4 **Parfino** Russian Federation
393 D8 **Pargi** Andhra Pradesh India
310 2 **Pargo, Ponta do** *cape* Madeira
154 E3 **Parguaza, Serranía de** *range* Venezuela
163 I8 **Parham** Antigua and Barbuda
163 9 **Paria, Gulf of** Trinidad and Tobago
155 F2 **Paria, Gulf of** Venezuela
155 F2 **Paria, Península de** *peninsula* Venezuela
374 D4 **Pariaman** Indonesia
155 E5 **Parica, Lago** *lake* Brazil
155 I4 **Paricás** Brazil
159 F2 **Paricatuba, Lago** *lake* Brazil
154 A2 **Parida, Isla** *island* Panama
160 D2 **Parihuana, Laguna** *lake* Bolivia
238 C2 **Parikkala** Finland
391 K4 **Pariko** Pakistan
155 E4 **Parima, Serra** *range* Venezuela
158 D5 **Parinacota, Nevado** *mountain* Chile
158 A2 **Pariñas, Punta** *cape* Peru
423 C6 **Paringa** *watercourse* New Zealand
423 C6 **Paringa, Lake** New Zealand
234 C2 **Parîngul Mare, Vîrful** *mountain* Romania
155 G5 **Parintins** Brazil
157 C9 **Pariquera Açu** Brazil
127 K5 **Paris** Ontario Canada
228 F2 **Paris** France
426 1a **Paris** *ruins* Kiribati
124 J5 **Paris** Idaho USA
126 H7 **Paris** Illinois USA
130 G2 **Paris** Tennessee USA
130 D4 **Paris** Texas USA
126 I3 **Parisienne, Ile** *island* Ontario Canada
374 D2 **Parit Buntar** Malaysia
134 D5 **Parita** Panama
388 H2 **Parizh** Russian Federation
245 D2 **Park** Ireland
245 F4 **Park** Ireland
129 L1 **Park** Kansas USA
125 Q4 **Park Falls** Wisconsin USA
126 F8 **Park Hills** Missouri USA
125 R3 **Park Rapids** Minnesota USA
125 Q2 **Park River** North Dakota USA
223 M3 **Parkajoki** Sweden
223 M3 **Parkalompolo** Sweden
234 G2 **Parkantsy** Ukraine
122 I6 **Parke Lake** Newfoundland and Labrador Canada
128 E3 **Parker** Arizona USA
125 M7 **Parker** Colorado USA
124 J5 **Parker** Idaho USA
125 Q5 **Parker** South Dakota USA
127 K7 **Parkersburg** West Virginia USA
425 N8 **Parkes** NSW Australia
241 I3 **Parkeston** Essex England UK
244 E5 **Parkgate** Dumfries and Galloway Scotland UK
127 K5 **Parkhill** Ontario Canada
222 K3 **Parkijaure** *bay* Sweden
223 N5 **Parkkila** Finland
223 N5 **Parkkima** Finland
119 O7 **Parkland** Alberta Canada
119 U8 **Parkman** Saskatchewan Canada
128 B2 **Parkside** California USA
127 N8 **Parksley** Virginia USA
125 Q5 **Parkston** South Dakota USA
118 I8 **Parksville** British Columbia Canada
391 M2 **Parkutta** Pakistan
163 9 **Parlatuvier** Trinidad and Tobago
393 D7 **Parli** Maharashtra India
393 C8 **Parli Vaijnath** Maharashtra India
128 C2 **Parlier** California USA
227 F5 **Parma** Italy
232 D4 **Parma** *watercourse* Italy
124 G5 **Parma** Idaho USA
130 G2 **Parma** Missouri USA
127 K6 **Parma** Ohio USA
156 D3 **Parnaíba** Brazil
156 C4 **Parnaíba** *watercourse* Brazil
77 O10 **Parnaíba Ridge** *underwater feature* Atlantic Ocean
156 C5 **Parnaibinha** *watercourse* Brazil
154 D4 **Parnaíuicava** Brazil
156 E5 **Parnamirim** Brazil
156 D4 **Parnarama** Brazil
235 C6 **Parnassos** *mountain* Greece
423 E6 **Parnassus** New Zealand
232 H2 **Părnica** Slovakia
235 C7 **Parnon Oros** *range* Greece
225 M3 **Pärnu** Estonia
225 M3 **Pärnu** *watercourse* Estonia
225 M3 **Pärnu Laht** *bay* Estonia
225 M3 **Pärnumaa** *admin. area* Estonia
379 F3 **Paro Dzong** Bhutan
393 D7 **Parola** Maharashtra India
158 D6 **Paroma, Cerro** *mountain* Bolivia
425 M6 **Paroo** *watercourse* NSW Australia
235 D7 **Paros** *island* Greece
124 I8 **Parowan** Utah USA
229 H4 **Parpaillon** *range* France
160 D6 **Parral** Chile
132 E3 **Parras** Mexico
230 D2 **Parres** Spain
240 E4 **Parrett** *watercourse* England UK
130 H4 **Parrish** Alabama USA
134 C5 **Parrita** Costa Rica
123 F10 **Parrsboro** Nova Scotia Canada
116 G4 **Parry, Cape** Northwest Territories Canada
117 K5 **Parry Bay** Nunavut Canada
116 H4 **Parry Channel** Nunavut Canada
116 H3 **Parry Islands** Northwest Territories/Nunavut Canada
118 E5 **Parry Passage** British Columbia Canada
127 K4 **Parry Sound** Ontario Canada
226 F3 **Parsberg** Germany
225 K5 **Paršežeria Ežeras** *lake* Lithuania
125 N3 **Parshall** North Dakota USA
225 P5 **Parshino** Belarus
118 J5 **Parsnip** *watercourse* British Columbia Canada
124 G1 **Parson** British Columbia Canada
241 H2 **Parson Drove** Cambridgeshire England UK
126 D8 **Parsons** Kansas USA
130 G3 **Parsons** Tennessee USA
127 L7 **Parsons** West Virginia USA
223 O5 **Partala** Finland
233 E8 **Partanna** Italy
222 J3 **Pårtefjällen** *mountain* Sweden
228 D3 **Parthenay** France
235 C7 **Parthénion** Greece
126 J2 **Parthia** Ontario Canada
384 F3 **Partizan** Mongolia
227 J3 **Partizánske** Slovakia
243 I3 **Partney** Lincolnshire England UK
242 E2 **Parton** Cumbria England UK
244 D5 **Parton** Dumfries and Galloway Scotland UK
240 D3 **Partrishow** Powys Wales UK
245 C3 **Partry** Ireland
393 D7 **Partur** Maharashtra India
424 G8 **Paru** NT Australia
156 A3 **Paru** *watercourse* Brazil
155 E3 **Parú, Serranía** *range* Venezuela
155 G4 **Paru de Oeste** *watercourse* Brazil
391 J4 **Pārūd** Iran
155 F3 **Paruima Mission** Guyana
155 F3 **Parupá** Venezuela
426 8 **Paruru** Solomon Islands
234 G2 **Parutyne** Ukraine
391 K2 **Parvān** *admin. area* Afghanistan
391 K4 **Parwan** Pakistan
241 F1 **Parwich** Derbyshire England UK
227 J2 **Parzymiechy** Poland
391 J2 **Pasāband** Afghanistan
128 C3 **Pasadena** California USA
130 D6 **Pasadena** Texas USA
154 A5 **Pasado, Cabo** *cape* Ecuador
154 B5 **Pasaje** Ecuador
393 F6 **Pasan** Chhattisgarh India
372 A4 **Pasangkayu** Indonesia
379 H5 **Pasanglaw** Myanmar
374 D4 **Pasarbantal** Indonesia
374 D4 **Pasarseblat** Indonesia
374 D5 **Pasarseluma** Indonesia
372 B5 **Pasarwajo** Indonesia
223 O2 **Pasasjärvi** *lake* Finland
127 N2 **Pascagama** *watercourse* Québec Canada
130 G5 **Pascagoula** Mississippi USA
134 C4 **Pascale** Honduras
158 C3 **Pasco** *admin. area* Peru
124 F3 **Pasco** Washington USA
157 E7 **Pascoal, Monte** *mountain* Brazil
424 inset **Pascoe Passage** Ashmore Reef and Cartier Island Australia
374 E5 **Paseh** Indonesia
227 G1 **Pasewalk** Germany
120 C3 **Pasfield Lake** Saskatchewan Canada
225 Q2 **Pasha** Russian Federation
238 F2 **Pashozero** Russian Federation
388 J6 **Pashxo'rt** Uzbekistan
225 O4 **Pasiene** Latvia
379 H3 **Pasighat** Arunachal Pradesh India
374 D3 **Pasir Gudang** Malaysia
374 D2 **Pasir Mas** Malaysia
374 inset **Pasir Panjang** *admin. area* Singapore
374 E3 **Pasir Ris** *admin. area* Singapore
374 E3 **Pasir Ris Park** Singapore
374 D3 **Pasirpengarayan** Indonesia
391 J4 **Paskūh** Iran
424 G8 **Pasley, Cape** WA Australia
223 N3 **Pasmajärvi** Finland
223 N2 **Pasmajärvi** *lake* Finland
160 F6 **Pasman** Argentina
391 J4 **Pasni** Pakistan
372 D4 **Paso** Indonesia
154 D3 **Paso de Guajibo** Venezuela
154 D2 **Paso de Las Dos Bocas** Venezuela
154 D3 **Paso de Los Bellacos** Venezuela
160 D6 **Paso de Los Indios** Argentina
161 G5 **Paso de Los Toros** Uruguay
161 G3 **Paso de Patria** Paraguay
132 E2 **Paso de San Antonio** Mexico
162 B4 **Paso del Águila** Argentina
154 E2 **Paso del Ganado** Venezuela
133 F5 **Paso del Macho** Mexico
154 D3 **Paso del Toro** Colombia
154 E2 **Paso El Caballo** Venezuela
155 F2 **Paso El Jabal** Venezuela
162 C4 **Paso Gobernador Gregores** Argentina
162 B3 **Paso Guenguel** Argentina
161 G3 **Paso Horqueta** Paraguay
162 B2 **Paso Limay** Argentina
154 E3 **Paso Mayor** Argentina
155 F2 **Paso Nuevo** Venezuela
162 B4 **Paso Rodolfo Roballos** Argentina
125 M1 **Pasqua** Saskatchewan Canada
116 I8 **Pasquia Hills** Saskatchewan Canada
242 A3 **Pass of Kilbride** Ireland
375 J6 **Passabe** Timor-Leste (East Timor)
245 F4 **Passage East** Ireland
245 D5 **Passage West** Ireland
159 G2 **Passagem** Brazil
156 D4 **Passagem Franca** Brazil
155 F5 **Passarão, Ilhas** *island* Brazil
226 G3 **Passau** Germany
229 H3 **Passavant** France
233 F8 **Passero, Capo** *cape* Italy
161 H4 **Passo Fundo** Brazil
161 H4 **Passo Real, Barragem** *lake* Brazil
157 C8 **Passos** Brazil
227 H1 **Passow** Germany
377 F3 **Passu Keah** *island* Paracel Islands
229 H4 **Passy** France
225 N5 **Pastavy** Belarus
154 B5 **Pastaza** *admin. area* Ecuador
154 B5 **Pastaza** *watercourse* Ecuador
154 B4 **Pasto** Colombia
159 F2 **Pasto Grande** Brazil
133 F6 **Pastoría, Laguna de** *lake* Mexico
159 E6 **Pastos** Bolivia
162 B3 **Pastos Blancos** Argentina
156 C4 **Pastos Bons** Brazil
129 J3 **Pastura** New Mexico USA
232 D4 **Pasubio, Monte** *mountain* Italy
375 G5 **Pasuruan** Indonesia
225 M4 **Pasvalys** Lithuania
225 L4 **Pašvitinys** Lithuania
234 A2 **Pásztó** Hungary
130 D4 **Pat Mayse Lake** Texas USA
158 D4 **Pata** Bolivia
305 I3 **Pata** Central African Republic
377 I6 **Pata** *island* Philippines
300 D6 **Pata** Senegal
158 C4 **Pata Corral** Peru
158 E5 **Patacamaya** Bolivia
160 D2 **Patache, Punta** *cape* Chile
162 B4 **Patagonia** *region* Argentina
128 G5 **Patagonia** Arizona USA
374 D5 **Patah, Gunung** *mountain* Indonesia
230 B4 **Pataias** Portugal
391 I3 **Patambar** Iran
122 C6 **Patamisk, Lac** *lake* Québec Canada
393 E7 **Patan** Chhattisgarh India
392 C6 **Patan** Gujarat India
393 E6 **Patan** Madhya Pradesh India
392 F5 **Patan** Nepal
223 M5 **Patanan tekojärvi** *lake* Finland
305 F3 **Patani** Nigeria
123 E8 **Patapédia** *watercourse* Québec Canada
158 C3 **Patarcocha, Cerro** *mountain* Peru
234 E3 **Pătârlagele** Romania
155 G3 **Pataro** *watercourse* Guyana
225 N3 **Pataste** Estonia
228 E2 **Patay** France
127 O6 **Patchogue** New York USA
240 E3 **Patchway** South Gloucestershire England UK
307 G4 **Paté** *island* Kenya
133 I2 **Pate Lake** Florida USA
Patea *see* **Doubtful Sound** New Zealand
422 F4 **Patea** New Zealand
305 F3 **Pategi** Nigeria
243 G2 **Pateley Bridge** North Yorkshire England UK
227 I1 **Paterek** Poland
232 E3 **Paternion** Austria
233 F6 **Paternopoli** Italy
124 F2 **Pateros** Washington USA
232 E2 **Patersdorf** Germany
119 V5 **Paterson** Manitoba Canada
127 N6 **Paterson** New Jersey USA
423 C8 **Paterson Inlet** New Zealand
393 F6 **Pathalgaon** Chhattisgarh India
392 D4 **Pathankot** Punjab India
393 D7 **Pathardi** Maharashtra India
393 F6 **Patharia** Madhya Pradesh India
376 B3 **Pathein (Bassein)** Myanmar
125 L5 **Pathfinder Reservoir** Wyoming USA
375 G5 **Pathiu** Thailand
376 D4 **Pathum Thani** Thailand
375 F5 **Pati** Indonesia
426 5 **Pati Point** Guam
392 D4 **Patiala** Punjab India
372 C4 **Patinti, Selat** *strait* Indonesia
235 E7 **Patmos** Greece
235 E7 **Patmos** *island* Greece
392 F6 **Patna** Bihar India
393 F7 **Patnagarh** Orissa India
394 G5 **Patnos** Turkey
157 A9 **Pato Branco** Brazil
393 D7 **Patoda** Maharashtra India
126 H7 **Patoka Lake** Indiana USA
223 N3 **Patokoski** Finland
237 Y7 **Patomskoye Nagor'ye** *region* Russian Federation
307 E3 **Patongo** Uganda
235 A5 **Patos** Albania
156 E4 **Patos** Brazil
161 I4 **Patos, Lagoa dos** *lake* Brazil
157 C7 **Patos de Minas** Brazil
160 E4 **Patquía** Argentina
235 B6 **Patra** Greece
154 D2 **Patrecitos** Venezuela
119 P7 **Patricia** Alberta Canada
129 K4 **Patricia** Texas USA
162 A4 **Patricio Lynch, Isla** *island* Chile
243 H3 **Patrington** East Riding of Yorkshire England UK
436 S1 **Patriot Hills (Chile)** *research station* Antarctica
157 C7 **Patrocínio** Brazil
372 A5 **Pattalasang** Indonesia
376 D6 **Pattani** Thailand
242 F2 **Patterdale** Cumbria England UK
124 E8 **Patterson** California USA
131 J5 **Patterson** Georgia USA
426 7 **Patteson Passage** *strait* Vanuatu
392 F6 **Patti** Uttar Pradesh India
233 F7 **Patti** Italy
233 F7 **Patti, Golfo di** *bay* Italy
393 D8 **Pattikonda** Andhra Pradesh India
423 6 **Pattison, Cape** Chatham Islands New Zealand
79 U4 **Patton Escarpment** *underwater feature* Pacific Ocean
79 R2 **Patton Seamount** *underwater feature* Pacific Ocean
393 E9 **Pattukkottai** Tamil Nadu India
116 G7 **Pattullo, Mount** British Columbia Canada
156 E4 **Patu** Brazil
119 R5 **Patuanak** Saskatchewan Canada
154 B5 **Patuca** Ecuador
134 C4 **Patuca** *watercourse* Honduras
134 C4 **Patuca, Punta** *cape* Honduras
393 D7 **Patur** Maharashtra India
127 M7 **Patuxent** *watercourse* Maryland USA
436 T1 **Patuxent Range** Antarctica
223 O5 **Patvinsuo Kansallispuisto** *park* Finland
132 E5 **Pátzcuaro, Lago de** *lake* Mexico
228 D5 **Pau** France
157 E6 **Pau Brasil** Brazil
159 G5 **Pau Prêto** Brazil
422 F3 **Pauanui** New Zealand
155 H3 **Paubasoe** Suriname
234 C2 **Păuca** Romania
158 D4 **Paucartambo** Peru
228 D4 **Pauillac** France
158 E2 **Pauini** Brazil
158 D2 **Pauini** *watercourse* Brazil
379 H5 **Pauk** Myanmar
379 H5 **Paukhaung** Myanmar
379 G5 **Pauktaw** Myanmar
240 B4 **Paul** Cornwall England UK
122 H4 **Paul Island** Newfoundland and Labrador Canada
116 G5 **Paulatuk** Northwest Territories Canada
128 F3 **Paulden** Arizona USA
156 F4 **Paulista** Brazil
156 E5 **Paulo Afonso** Brazil
309 F5 **Paulpietersburg** South Africa
127 M8 **Pauls Crossroads** Virginia USA
376 C3 **Paung** Myanmar
379 H4 **Paungbyin** Myanmar
376 B3 **Paungde** Myanmar
393 E7 **Pauni** Maharashtra India
392 E4 **Pauri** Uttaranchal India
226 G1 **Pausin** Germany
222 J4 **Pauträsk** Sweden
222 J4 **Pauträsket** *lake* Sweden
128 inset **Pa'uwela** Hawai'i USA
427 13a **Pava** *island* Tuvalu
223 P2 **Pavdejarvi** *lake* Finland
390 F2 **Paveh** Iran
238 H6 **Pavelets** Russian Federation
241 G2 **Pavenham** Bedfordshire England UK
226 E5 **Pavia** Italy
118 K7 **Pavilion** British Columbia Canada
118 H5 **Pavilly** France
227 M2 **Pavitstsye** Belarus
238 E5 **Pavlinovo** Russian Federation
234 F1 **Pavlivka** Ukraine
389 L3 **Pavlodar** Kazakhstan
389 M3 **Pavlodarskaya Oblast'** *admin. area* Kazakhstan
116 C7 **Pavlof Volcano** Alaska USA
389 L2 **Pavlogradka** Russian Federation
394 E3 **Pavlohrad** Ukraine
389 K3 **Pavlovka** Kazakhstan
388 G2 **Pavlovka** Russian Federation
225 J5 **Pavlovo** Russian Federation
388 D2 **Pavlovo** Russian Federation
131 J5 **Pavo** Georgia USA
225 M5 **Pavoverė** Lithuania
426 8 **Pavuvu** *island* Solomon Islands
225 O3 **Pavy** Russian Federation
121 R3 **Pavy, Lac** *lake* Québec Canada
306 D3 **Pawa** Democratic Republic of Congo
374 B5 **Pawai, Pulau** *island* Singapore
375 F4 **Pawan** *watercourse* Indonesia
126 C8 **Pawhuska** Oklahoma USA
119 U5 **Pawistik** Manitoba Canada
227 K1 **Pawłowo** Poland
125 O7 **Pawnee** *watercourse* Kansas USA
125 Q8 **Pawnee** Oklahoma USA
130 C6 **Pawnee** Texas USA
125 Q6 **Pawnee City** Nebraska USA
125 P7 **Pawnee Rock** Kansas USA
127 P6 **Pawtucket** Rhode Island USA
376 C4 **Pawut** Myanmar
129 N1 **Paxico** Kansas USA
235 B6 **Paxoi** Greece
235 B6 **Paxoi** *island* Greece
131 H5 **Paxton** Florida USA
126 G6 **Paxton** Illinois USA
236 N5 **Pay-Khoy, Khrebet** *range* Russian Federation
372 C3 **Payahe** Indonesia
374 D4 **Payakumbuh** Indonesia
154 B4 **Payán** Colombia
388 J6 **Payariq** Uzbekistan
229 H3 **Payerne** Switzerland
124 G4 **Payette** Idaho USA
121 U3 **Payne, Baie** *bay* Québec Canada
117 L7 **Payne, Lac** *lake* Québec Canada
424 F7 **Paynes Find** WA Australia
125 R4 **Paynesville** Minnesota USA
375 G3 **Payong, Tanjong** *cape* Malaysia
228 D3 **Pays de la Loire** *admin. area* France
161 G5 **Paysandú** Uruguay
161 G5 **Paysandú** *admin. area* Uruguay
128 G3 **Payson** Arizona USA
119 U5 **Payuk** Manitoba Canada
160 D6 **Payún, Cerro** *volcano* Argentina
393 D9 **Payyannur** Kerala India
132 C3 **Paz, Bahía de la** *bay* Mexico
160 D1 **Paz, Cerro de** *mountain* Chile
155 E5 **Paz, Ponta** *cape* Brazil
394 G5 **Pazar** Turkey
234 D4 **Pazardzhik** *admin. area* Bulgaria
235 F6 **Pazarlar** Turkey
232 E4 **Pazin** Croatia
227 J3 **Pcim** Poland
427 10a **Pea** Tonga
157 A8 **Peabiru** Brazil
125 Q7 **Peabody** Kansas USA
116 H7 **Peace** *watercourse* Alberta Canada
116 G7 **Peace** *watercourse* British Columbia Canada
131 J7 **Peace** *watercourse* Florida USA
119 M3 **Peace Point** Alberta Canada
118 O4 **Peace River** Alberta Canada
241 G4 **Peacehaven** East Sussex England UK
128 F3 **Peach Springs** Arizona USA
118 L8 **Peachland** British Columbia Canada
131 I4 **Peachtree City** Georgia USA
426 1 **Peak, The** *mountain* Ascension
243 G3 **Peak District National Park** England UK
377 H5 **Peaked Point** Philippines
222 L2 **Peäldujävri** *lake* Finland
128 D3 **Pearblossom** California USA
230 C2 **Peares, Embalse dos** *lake* Spain
130 F4 **Pearl** Mississippi USA
133 H2 **Pearl** *watercourse* Mississippi USA
78 O5 **Pearl and Hermes Atoll** *reef* USA
128 inset **Pearl Harbor** Hawai'i USA
130 B6 **Pearland** Texas USA
130 D6 **Pearsall** Texas USA
131 I5 **Pearson** Georgia USA
377 G5 **Pearson Reef** Spratly Islands
117 I3 **Peary Channel** Nunavut Canada
117 O2 **Peary Land** *region* Greenland
130 B3 **Pease** *watercourse* Texas USA
120 M5 **Peawanuck** Ontario Canada
309 G3 **Pebane** Mozambique
163 7 **Pebble Island** Falkland Islands
375 F5 **Pecangakan** Indonesia
157 D7 **Peçanha** Brazil
234 F3 **Peceneaga** Romania
121 P6 **Pêche, Rivière la** *watercourse* Québec Canada
234 E3 **Pechea** Romania
223 Q2 **Pechenga** Russian Federation
234 D1 **Pechenizhyn** Ukraine
236 M5 **Pechora** Russian Federation
236 M6 **Pechora** *watercourse* Russian Federation
236 M5 **Pechorskaya Guba** *bay* Russian Federation
236 M5 **Pechorskoye More** *sea* Russian Federation
225 N4 **Pechory** Russian Federation
234 B2 **Pecica** Romania
234 B3 **Peciu Nou** Romania
304 A2 **Pecixe, Ilha de** *island* Guinea-Bissau
233 C7 **Pecora, Capo** *cape* Sardinia Italy
233 D5 **Pecoraro, Punta del** *cape* Italy
129 J3 **Pecos** New Mexico USA
129 J3 **Pecos** *watercourse* New Mexico USA
129 K5 **Pecos** Texas USA
129 K5 **Pecos** *watercourse* Texas USA
226 B2 **Pecq** Belgium
227 J4 **Pécs** Hungary
238 F2 **Pedasel'ga** Russian Federation
134 D6 **Pedasí** Panama
425 M10 **Pedder, Lake** Tas. Australia
308 E6 **Peddie** South Africa
135 G3 **Pedernales** Dominican Republic
130 B5 **Pedernales** *watercourse* Texas USA
160 D3 **Pedernales, Salar de** *pan* Chile
224 H5 **Pedersker** Denmark
223 M5 **Pedersöre** Finland
372 C3 **Pediwang** Indonesia
155 E5 **Pedra** Brazil
157 D7 **Pedra Azul** Brazil
233 C6 **Pedra Bianca, Punta** *cape* Sardinia Italy
156 E4 **Pedra Branca** Brazil
159 F3 **Pedra Branca** Brazil
155 I4 **Pedra Branca do Amapari** Brazil
300 B5 **Pedra Lume** Cape Verde
159 F4 **Pedras Negras** Brazil
157 C8 **Pedregulho** Brazil
155 I5 **Pedreira** Brazil
156 B5 **Pedro Afonso** Brazil
79 Y6 **Pedro Bank** *underwater feature* Caribbean Sea
154 A5 **Pedro Carbo** Ecuador
132 E3 **Pedro Carrizales** Mexico
156 D4 **Pedro II** Brazil
161 H2 **Pedro Juan Caballero** Paraguay
160 F6 **Pedro Luro** Argentina
230 E5 **Pedro-Martínez** Spain
156 F4 **Pedro Velho** Brazil
231 F3 **Pedrola** Spain
131 L3 **Pee Dee** *watercourse* South Carolina USA
244 E5 **Peebles** Scottish Borders Scotland UK
118 K4 **Peejay** British Columbia Canada
116 F5 **Peel** *watercourse* Yukon Territory Canada
242 D2 **Peel** Isle of Man UK
423 D6 **Peel Forest** New Zealand
117 J4 **Peel Sound** Nunavut Canada
227 G1 **Peene** *watercourse* Germany
229 G1 **Peer** Belgium
119 S8 **Peerless** Montana USA
119 N6 **Peers** Alberta Canada
125 N6 **Peetz** Colorado USA
235 B5 **Péfkos** Greece
235 E5 **Pegalajar** Spain
423 B8 **Pegasus, Port** New Zealand
423 E6 **Pegasus Bay** New Zealand
232 D2 **Pegnitz** Germany
230 B4 **Pego do Altar, Barragem do** *lake* Portugal
Pegu *see* **Bago** Myanmar
372 E3 **Pegun** *island* Indonesia
241 I3 **Pegwell Bay** England UK
304 E2 **Péhonko** Benin
160 F5 **Pehuajó** Argentina
381 G1 **Peicheng** Jiangsu China
244 B3 **Peinchorran** Highland Scotland UK
162 B5 **Peineta, Cerro** *mountain* Argentina
232 D3 **Peio** Italy
238 B3 **Peipsi Järve** *lake* Estonia
235 C7 **Peiraias** Greece
226 F4 **Peiting** Germany
157 B6 **Peixe** *watercourse* Brazil
161 J2 **Peixoto, Represa** *lake* Brazil
374 E3 **Pejantan** *island* Indonesia
375 F5 **Pekalongan** Indonesia
374 D3 **Pekan** Malaysia
374 D3 **Pekanbaru** Indonesia
223 N5 **Pekankylä** Finland
223 M3 **Pekanpää** Finland
121 V6 **Pékans** *watercourse* Québec Canada
423 E6 **Peketa** New Zealand
126 G6 **Pekin** Illinois USA
Peking *see* **Beijing** China
223 O3 **Pekkala** Finland
238 E6 **Peklino** Russian Federation
237 AJ5 **Pekul'ney, Khrebet** *range* Russian Federation
162 B3 **Pelados, Cerros** *mountain* Argentina
233 E9 **Pelagie, Isole** *island* Italy
235 B5 **Pelagonija** *region* Macedonia
374 D3 **Pelalawan** Indonesia
374 E4 **Pelapis** *island* Indonesia
391 K4 **Pelar** Pakistan
375 H3 **Pelawanbesar** Indonesia
154 C2 **Pelaya** Colombia
158 D4 **Pelechuco** Bolivia
163 14 **Pelée, Montagne** *volcano* Martinique
426 3 **Peleliu** *island* Palau
375 I4 **Peleng** *island* Indonesia
372 B4 **Peleng, Selat** *strait* Indonesia
374 B4 **Peleng, Teluk** *bay* Indonesia
306 C4 **Pelenge** Democratic Republic of Congo
130 H4 **Pelham** Alabama USA
131 I5 **Pelham** Georgia USA
227 H3 **Pelhřimov** Czech Republic
122 B3 **Pélican, Lac du** *lake* Québec Canada
163 I8 **Pelican Bay** Antigua and Barbuda
119 O5 **Pelican Lake** Alberta Canada
126 E2 **Pelican Lake** Minnesota USA
119 O5 **Pelican Mountains** Alberta Canada
119 T5 **Pelican Narrows** Saskatchewan Canada
125 Q3 **Pelican Rapids** Minnesota USA
154 B5 **Pelileo** Ecuador
132 D2 **Pelillo** Mexico
235 B5 **Pelister** *mountain* Macedonia
131 H4 **Pell City** Alabama USA
235 C5 **Pélla** Greece
308 C5 **Pella** South Africa
162 D2 **Pellegrini, Lago** *lake* Argentina
373 G4 **Pelleluhu Islands** Papua New Guinea
232 E4 **Pellestrina, Isola di** *island* Italy
232 B4 **Pellice** *watercourse* Italy
223 N3 **Pello** Finland
224 E5 **Pellworm** *island* Germany
116 F6 **Pelly** *watercourse* Yukon Territory Canada
117 J5 **Pelly Bay** Nunavut Canada
118 F1 **Pelly Lakes** Yukon Territory Canada
118 E2 **Pelly Mountains** Yukon Territory Canada
375 H5 **Pelokang** *island* Indonesia
235 C7 **Peloponnisos** *admin. area* Greece
233 F7 **Peloro, Capo** *cape* Italy
423 E5 **Pelorus** *watercourse* New Zealand
423 E5 **Pelorus Sound** New Zealand
161 H4 **Pelotas** Brazil
223 N2 **Peltovuoma** Finland
127 Q4 **Pemadumcook Lake** Maine USA
379 G3 **Pemagatsel** Bhutan
372 B4 **Pemali, Tanjung** *cape* Indonesia
374 F3 **Pemangkat** Indonesia
374 C3 **Pematangsiantar** Indonesia
309 H2 **Pemba** Mozambique
307 F5 **Pemba Island** Tanzania
307 F5 **Pemba North** *admin. area* Tanzania
307 F5 **Pemba South** *admin. area* Tanzania
124 D1 **Pemberton Meadows** British Columbia Canada
119 M6 **Pembina** *watercourse* Alberta Canada
125 Q2 **Pembina** North Dakota USA
126 H4 **Pembine** Wisconsin USA
373 F5 **Pembre** Indonesia
240 C3 **Pembrey** Carmarthenshire Wales UK
240 E2 **Pembridge** Herefordshire England UK
127 M4 **Pembroke** Ontario Canada
163 9 **Pembroke** Trinidad and Tobago
240 C3 **Pembroke** Pembrokeshire Wales UK
131 K4 **Pembroke** Georgia USA
130 H2 **Pembroke** Kentucky USA
121 O1 **Pembroke, Cape** Nunavut Canada
131 K7 **Pembroke Pines** Florida USA
240 C3 **Pembrokeshire** *admin. area* Wales UK
375 G4 **Pembuanghulu** Indonesia
241 H3 **Pembury** Kent England UK
229 K2 **Pemfling** Germany
375 F4 **Pemuar** Indonesia
393 C7 **Pen** Maharashtra India
379 G5 **Pen** *watercourse* Myanmar
240 C1 **Pen-y-groes** Gwynedd Wales UK
240 D1 **Pen-y-stryt** Denbighshire Wales UK
129 I6 **Peña Blanca** Mexico
154 B4 **Peña Colorada** Colombia
230 E2 **Peñacerrada** Spain
230 D3 **Peñafiel** Spain
163 9 **Penal** Trinidad and Tobago
163 9 **Penal-Débé** *admin. area* Trinidad and Tobago
230 E3 **Peñalara, Pico** *mountain* Spain
156 C3 **Penalva** Brazil
372 E5 **Penambulai** *island* Indonesia
157 B8 **Penápolis** Brazil
230 D3 **Peñaranda de Bracamonte** Spain
230 E4 **Peñarroya, Embalse de** *lake* Spain
240 D3 **Penarth** Vale of Glamorgan Wales UK
162 C5 **Peñas, Cabo** *cape* Argentina
230 D2 **Peñas, Cabo de** *cape* Spain
162 A4 **Penas, Golfo de** *bay* Chile
155 F2 **Peñas, Punta** *cape* Venezuela
127 M6 **Penbrook** Pennsylvania USA
240 C2 **Penbryn** Ceredigion Wales UK
240 C2 **Pencarreg** Carmarthenshire Wales UK
124 G2 **Pend Oreille, Lake** Idaho USA
305 H3 **Pendé** *watercourse* Central African Republic
304 B3 **Pendembu** Sierra Leone
156 E4 **Pendências** Brazil
240 C3 **Pendine** Carmarthenshire Wales UK
124 F4 **Pendleton** Oregon USA
374 D4 **Pendopo** Indonesia
393 E6 **Pendra** Chhattisgarh India
306 D4 **Pene-Mende** Democratic Republic of Congo
374 F4 **Penebangan** *island* Indonesia
381 H4 **P'eng-Hu Tao** *island* Taiwan China
393 E7 **Penganga** *watercourse* Maharashtra India
308 F4 **Penge** South Africa
374 F3 **Pengiki** *island* Indonesia
385 I5 **Penglai** Shandong China
161 I3 **Penha** Brazil
228 B2 **Penhir, Pointe de** *cape* France
230 B4 **Peniche** Portugal
244 E5 **Penicuik** Midlothian Scotland UK
375 G6 **Penida** *island* Indonesia
229 K1 **Penig** Germany
231 G3 **Peñíscola** Spain
233 F8 **Penisola Magnisi** *cape* Italy
243 G3 **Penistone** South Yorkshire England UK
133 G5 **Peñitas, Presa** *lake* Mexico
156 C5 **Penitente, Serra do** *range* Brazil
238 G6 **Pen'kovo** Russian Federation
227 H1 **Penkun** Germany
240 C2 **Penllech** Gwynedd Wales UK
240 D1 **Penmachno** Conwy Wales UK
240 D2 **Penmaenpool** Gwynedd Wales UK
228 B3 **Penmarch** France
228 B3 **Penmarch, Pointe de** *cape* France
242 D3 **Penmon** Isle of Anglesey Wales UK
393 E9 **Pennadam** Tamil Nadu India
240 D2 **Pennal** Gwynedd Wales UK
119 Q7 **Pennant** Saskatchewan Canada
240 C2 **Pennant** Ceredigion Wales UK
240 D2 **Pennant** Powys Wales UK
240 D2 **Pennant-Melangell** Powys Wales UK
240 C3 **Pennard** Swansea Wales UK
229 K5 **Penne** Italy
233 G6 **Penne, Punta** *cape* Italy
437 M2 **Pennel Bank** *underwater feature* Ross Sea
437 L2 **Pennell Coast** Antarctica
425 K8 **Penneshaw** SA Australia
131 K6 **Penney Farms** Florida USA
243 F2 **Pennines** *range* England UK
127 K7 **Pennsboro** West Virginia USA
114 **Pennsylvania** *admin. area* USA
118 K6 **Penny** British Columbia Canada
437 K1 **Penny Point** Antarctica
120 I4 **Pennycutaway** *watercourse* Manitoba Canada
238 E4 **Peno** Russian Federation
127 Q4 **Penobscot** *watercourse* Maine USA
127 Q4 **Penobscot Bay** Maine USA
425 L9 **Penola** SA Australia
132 D3 **Peñón Blanco** Mexico
231 G4 **Peñón de Ifach** *cape* Spain
424 J7 **Penong** SA Australia
134 D5 **Penonomé** Panama
240 C2 **Penrhos** Gwynedd Wales UK
240 D3 **Penrhos** Powys Wales UK
422 1 **Penrhyn (Tongareva)** *island* Cook Islands New Zealand
79 Q8 **Penrhyn Atoll** *reef* Cook Islands New Zealand
79 Q8 **Penrhyn Basin** *underwater feature* Pacific Ocean
425 N8 **Penrith** NSW Australia
242 F2 **Penrith** Cumbria England UK
240 B4 **Penryn** Cornwall England UK
130 H5 **Pensacola** Florida USA
130 H5 **Pensacola Bay** Florida USA
436 U1 **Pensacola Mountains** Antarctica
159 H4 **Pensão Sêca** Brazil
392 D4 **Pensi La** *pass* Jammu and Kashmir India/Pakistan
375 H2 **Pensiangan** Malaysia
122 K6 **Pensons Arm** Newfoundland and Labrador Canada
235 B5 **Pentalofos** Greece
426 7 **Pentecost** *island* Vanuatu
121 V7 **Pentecôte** *watercourse* Québec Canada
118 L8 **Penticton** British Columbia Canada
425 M5 **Pentland** Qld Australia
244 E2 **Pentland Firth** *bay* Scotland UK
244 E5 **Pentland Hills** *range* Scotland UK
244 F2 **Pentland Skerries** *island* Scotland UK
242 D3 **Pentraeth** Isle of Anglesey Wales UK
240 D2 **Pentre** Powys Wales UK
240 D3 **Pentre-bâch** Powys Wales UK
240 C3 **Pentre Galar** Pembrokeshire Wales UK
240 C3 **Pentre-Morgan** Carmarthenshire Wales UK
240 D1 **Pentrefoelas** Conwy Wales UK
126 H5 **Pentwater** Michigan USA
225 M3 **Penu** Estonia
374 E4 **Penuba** Indonesia
374 E4 **Penuguan** Indonesia
374 D2 **Penunjuk, Tanjung** *cape* Malaysia
240 C2 **Penuwch** Ceredigion Wales UK
129 K5 **Penwell** Texas USA
240 D2 **Peny-bryn** Gwynedd Wales UK
240 D2 **Penybont** Powys Wales UK
240 D2 **Penybontfawr** Powys Wales UK
119 R2 **Penylan Lake** Northwest Territories Canada
242 D3 **Penysarn** Isle of Anglesey Wales UK
372 C5 **Penyu, Kepulauan** *island* Indonesia
374 F5 **Penyu, Tulek** *bay* Indonesia

388 E2 **Penza** Russian Federation
125 M1 **Penzance** Saskatchewan Canada
240 B4 **Penzance** Cornwall England UK
226 F4 **Penzberg** Germany
388 D3 **Penzenskaya Oblast'** *admin. area* Russian Federation
237 AI6 **Penzhina** *watercourse* Russian Federation
237 AH6 **Penzhinskaya Guba** *bay* Russian Federation
237 AI6 **Penzhinskiy Khrebet** *range* Russian Federation
226 G1 **Penzlin** Germany
128 F4 **Peoria** Arizona USA
126 G6 **Peoria** Illinois USA
129 K4 **Pep** New Mexico USA
235 B5 **Pepellash** Albania
121 S7 **Pépeshquasati** *watercourse* Québec Canada
437 J2 **Pépin, Cape** Antarctica
161 H3 **Pepiri Guaçú** *watercourse* Argentina
235 E5 **Peplos** Greece
154 C3 **Peque** Colombia
132 B3 **Pequeña, Punta** *cape* Mexico
157 D6 **Pequeno, Verde** *watercourse* Brazil
126 D3 **Pequot Lakes** Minnesota USA
232 G3 **Pér** Hungary
223 O3 **Perä-Posio** Finland
374 D2 **Perak** *admin. area* Malaysia
225 K1 **Perälä** Finland
230 D4 **Peraleda del Zaucejo** Spain
231 F3 **Perales del Alfambra** Spain
160 F6 **Peralta** Argentina
230 F2 **Peralta** Spain
235 D8 **Perama** Greece
223 N4 **Perämeri Kansallispuisto** *park* Finland
307 F6 **Peramiho** Tanzania
223 P4 **Peranka** Finland
223 N5 **Perânne** *lake* Finland
223 M5 **Peräseinäjoki** Finland
374 C3 **Perbaungan** Indonesia
123 F8 **Percé** Québec Canada
228 E2 **Perche, Collines du** *range* France
232 G2 **Perchtoldsdorf** Austria
244 F3 **Percie** Aberdeenshire Scotland UK
424 H5 **Percival Lakes** WA Australia
126 G7 **Percy** Illinois USA
156 C5 **Perdida** *watercourse* Brazil
161 G2 **Perdido, Serra do** *range* Brazil
130 H5 **Perdido Bay** Alabama USA
161 J2 **Perdões** Brazil
234 C1 **Perechyn** Ukraine
238 F5 **Peredel** Russian Federation
154 C3 **Pereira** Colombia
157 B8 **Pereira Barreto** Brazil
388 D3 **Perelazovskiy** Russian Federation
388 F3 **Perelyub** Russian Federation
437 H2 **Peremenny, Cape** Antarctica
234 F1 **Peremoga** Ukraine
393 C9 **Peremul Par** *island* Lakshadweep India
238 G5 **Peremyshl'** Russian Federation
158 C3 **Perené** Peru
234 F2 **Peresecina** Moldova
238 H4 **Pereslavl' Zalesskiy** Russian Federation
227 M2 **Perespa** Ukraine
234 D3 **Peretu** Romania
389 L6 **Pereval Akbaytal** *pass* Tajikistan
382 F4 **Pereval Bedel'** *pass* Xinjiang Uygur Zizhiqu China
389 M5 **Pereval Bedel'** *pass* Kyrgyzstan
389 L6 **Pereval Chyyyrchyk Asnuusu** *pass* Kyrgyzstan
382 E5 **Pereval Karaart** *pass* Xinjiang Uygur Zizhiqu China
389 L6 **Pereval Karaart** *pass* Tajikistan
388 E5 **Pereval Khalakhurkats** *pass* Russian Federation
382 E5 **Pereval Kipchak** *pass* Xinjiang Uygur Zizhiqu China
389 L6 **Pereval Kipchak** *pass* Kyrgyzstan
388 D5 **Pereval Klukhorskiy** *pass* Russian Federation
388 D5 **Pereval Sharivtsek** *pass* Russian Federation
389 L6 **Pereval Taldyk** *pass* Kyrgyzstan
382 E5 **Pereval Turugart** *pass* Xinjiang Uygur Zizhiqu China
389 L6 **Pereval Turugart** *pass* Kyrgyzstan
389 L6 **Pereval Urum-Bash** *pass* Kyrgyzstan
388 D2 **Perevoz** Russian Federation
234 F1 **Pereyma** Ukraine
227 H3 **Perg** Austria
160 F5 **Pergamino** Argentina
229 K5 **Pergola** Italy
125 R3 **Perham** Minnesota USA
374 D2 **Perhentian Besar, Pulao** *island* Malaysia
376 D6 **Perhentian Besar, Pulau** *island* Malaysia
223 N5 **Perho** Finland
223 M5 **Perhonjoki** *watercourse* Finland
127 P2 **Péribonka** *watercourse* Québec Canada
123 C7 **Péribonka, Lac** *lake* Québec Canada
160 E3 **Perico** Argentina
134 D2 **Perico** Cuba
128 G4 **Peridot** Arizona USA
228 D2 **Périers** France
228 E4 **Périgueux** France
154 C2 **Perija, Sierra de** *range* Venezuela
225 E5 **Perino** Italy
159 F3 **Periquitos** Brazil
234 D3 **Periș** Romania
234 E3 **Perișoru** Romania
235 D6 **Peristera** *island* Greece
235 C6 **Peristerio** Greece
162 B4 **Perito Moreno** Argentina
235 B6 **Perivolion** Greece
374 E4 **Perkat, Tanjung** *cape* Indonesia
227 M1 **Perkavičy** Belarus
130 C3 **Perkins** Oklahoma USA
154 B2 **Perlas, Archipiélago de las** *island* Panama
134 D4 **Perlas, Laguna de** *lake* Nicaragua
134 D4 **Perlas, Punta de** *cape* Nicaragua
226 F1 **Perleberg** Germany
125 Q3 **Perley** Minnesota USA
234 B3 **Perlez** Serbia
374 D2 **Perlis** *admin. area* Malaysia
236 M7 **Perm'** Russian Federation
388 G1 **Perm'** Russian Federation
235 B5 **Përmet** Albania
236 M7 **Permskiy Kray** *admin. area* Russian Federation
232 F4 **Permuda** Croatia
229 L4 **Permuda** *island* Croatia
225 N2 **Pernaja** Finland
156 E5 **Pernambuco** *admin. area* Brazil
77 P10 **Pernambuco Plain** *underwater feature* Atlantic Ocean
77 O10 **Pernambuco Seamounts** *underwater feature* Atlantic Ocean
232 F4 **Pernat** Croatia
234 C4 **Pernik** *admin. area* Bulgaria
227 H4 **Pernitz** Austria
223 O3 **Pernu** Finland
133 F5 **Perote** Mexico
387 I2 **Perouse Strait, La** Russian Federation
228 F5 **Perpignan** France
375 H3 **Perpuk, Tanjung** *cape* Indonesia
160 C6 **Perquenco** Chile
240 B4 **Perranporth** Cornwall England UK
120 I7 **Perrault Lake** Ontario Canada
425 L6 **Perrier, Mount** Qld Australia
128 D4 **Perris** California USA
129 J3 **Perro, Laguna de** *lake* New Mexico USA
228 C2 **Perros-Guirec** France
226 D4 **Perroy** Switzerland
131 J5 **Perry** Florida USA
131 J4 **Perry** Georgia USA
126 F7 **Perry** Missouri USA
130 C2 **Perry** Oklahoma USA
437 I2 **Perry Bay** Antarctica
126 J6 **Perrysburg** Ohio USA
130 A2 **Perryton** Texas USA
130 E3 **Perryville** Arkansas USA
126 G8 **Perryville** Missouri USA
224 H2 **Persbo** Sweden
423 9 **Perseverance Harbour** Campbell Island New Zealand
159 E3 **Perseverancia** Bolivia
159 F4 **Perseverancia** Bolivia
127 M3 **Pershing Lake** Québec Canada
241 E2 **Pershore** Worcestershire England UK
224 I4 **Persnäs** Sweden
424 E7 **Perth** WA Australia
127 M4 **Perth** Ontario Canada
244 E4 **Perth** Perth and Kinross Scotland UK
244 D4 **Perth and Kinross** *admin. area* Scotland UK
81 O7 **Perth Basin** *underwater feature* Indian Ocean
223 U4 **Pertominsk** Russian Federation
229 G5 **Pertuis** France
158 C3 **Peru** *country* South America
126 H6 **Peru** Indiana USA
160 E6 **Perú** Argentina
79 X9 **Peru Basin** *underwater feature* Pacific Ocean
79 Y10 **Peru-Chile Trench** *underwater feature* Pacific Ocean
234 A4 **Perućac** Serbia
232 E5 **Perugia** Italy
157 C9 **Peruíbe** Brazil
223 N3 **Perunkajärvi** Finland
228 F1 **Péruwelz** Belgium
389 K3 **Pervomayka** Kazakhstan
388 D2 **Pervomaysk** Russian Federation
234 G1 **Pervomays'k** Ukraine
389 N3 **Pervomayskiy** Kazakhstan
388 H6 **Pervomayskiy** Turkmenistan
388 E2 **Pervomayskoye** Russian Federation
238 F3 **Pes'** Russian Federation
375 F4 **Pesaguan** Indonesia
375 F4 **Pesaguan** *watercourse* Indonesia
232 E5 **Pesaro** Italy
156 B2 **Pescada, Ponta da** *cape* Brazil
128 A2 **Pescadero** California USA
158 C5 **Pescadores, Punta** *cape* Peru
163 9 **Pescadores, Punta** *cape* Venezuela
233 F5 **Pescara** Italy
234 F1 **Peschana** Ukraine
223 S5 **Peschanoye** Russian Federation
387 J2 **Peschanoye, Ozero** *lake* Russian Federation
388 F5 **Peschanyy, Mys** *cape* Kazakhstan
237 Y4 **Peschanyy, Ostrov** *island* Russian Federation
233 G6 **Peschici** Italy
233 E5 **Pescina** Italy
134 D6 **Pesé** Panama
391 L2 **Peshawar** Pakistan
235 B5 **Peshkopi** Albania
222 L3 **Peske** Sweden
238 H5 **Peski** Russian Federation
226 C4 **Pesmes** France
238 H3 **Pesochnoye** Russian Federation
128 G6 **Pesqueira** Mexico
228 D4 **Pessac** France
226 G1 **Pessin** Germany
227 J4 **Pest** *admin. area* Hungary
238 F3 **Pestovo** Russian Federation
237 AG6 **Pëstraya Dresva** Russian Federation
436 N1 **Pestrud Bank** *underwater feature* Ross Sea
132 E5 **Petacalco, Bahía** *bay* Mexico
225 N2 **Petäiskylä** Finland
223 O2 **Petäjäsaaret** *island* Finland
223 N5 **Petäjävesi** Finland
130 G5 **Petal** Mississippi USA
235 D7 **Petalida, Akra** *cape* Greece
374 D3 **Petaling Jaya** Malaysia
235 D7 **Petalioi** *island* Greece
124 D7 **Petaluma** California USA
228 G2 **Pétange** Luxembourg
375 H4 **Petangis** Indonesia
134 B3 **Petapa** Guatemala
154 E2 **Petare** Venezuela
132 E5 **Petatlán** Mexico
132 E5 **Petatlán, Morro de** *cape* Mexico
309 F2 **Petauke** Zambia
127 M4 **Petawawa** Ontario Canada
126 G4 **Petenwell Lake** Wisconsin USA
436 R2 **Peter I Island** *Norwegian dependency* Antarctica
120 I1 **Peter Lake** Nunavut Canada
119 Q4 **Peter Pond Lake** Saskatchewan Canada
126 J2 **Peterbell** Ontario Canada
425 K8 **Peterborough** Vic. Australia
127 L4 **Peterborough** Ontario Canada
241 G2 **Peterborough** *admin. area* England UK
241 G2 **Peterborough** Peterborough England UK
127 P5 **Peterborough** New Hampshire USA
244 C3 **Peterburn** Highland Scotland UK
240 E2 **Peterchurch** Herefordshire England UK
244 F3 **Peterculter** Aberdeen Scotland UK
244 G3 **Peterhead** Aberdeenshire Scotland UK
243 G2 **Peterlee** Durham England UK
117 Q4 **Petermann Bjerg** *mountain* Greenland
117 M2 **Petermann Gletscher** *ice* Greenland
160 D5 **Peteroa, Volcán** *volcano* Chile
122 C3 **Peters, Lac** *lake* Québec Canada
240 C4 **Peters Marland** Devon England UK
122 E1 **Peters Point** Nunavut Canada
229 I1 **Petersberg** Germany
118 E4 **Petersburg** Alaska USA
125 P6 **Petersburg** Nebraska USA
125 O3 **Petersburg** North Dakota USA
129 L4 **Petersburg** Texas USA
130 H2 **Petersburg** Virginia USA
127 L7 **Petersburg** West Virginia USA
437 H2 **Petersen Bank** *underwater feature* Southern Ocean
241 G3 **Petersfield** Hampshire England UK
127 K8 **Peterstown** West Virginia USA
242 B3 **Petersville** Ireland
234 B1 **Petervására** Hungary
123 K8 **Peterview** Newfoundland and Labrador Canada
225 O4 **Peti** Russian Federation
163 I6 **Petit-Bourg** Guadeloupe
163 I6 **Petit-Canal** Guadeloupe
163 I6 **Petit Cul-de-Sac Marin** *bay* Guadeloupe
121 S4 **Petit Lac des Loups Marins** *lake* Québec Canada
121 W6 **Petit Lac Joseph** *lake* Newfoundland and Labrador Canada
121 V7 **Petit Lac Manicouagan** *lake* Québec Canada
123 I7 **Petit Mécatina** *watercourse* Québec Canada
123 I7 **Petit Mécatina, Île du** *island* Québec Canada
163 I3 **Petit Piton** *volcano* St Lucia
231 G5 **Petit Port** Algeria
127 P3 **Petit-Rivière** Québec Canada
123 F9 **Petit-Rocher** New Brunswick Canada
163 9 **Petit Valley** Trinidad and Tobago
123 F10 **Petitcodiac** New Brunswick Canada
127 O2 **Petite Lièvre** *watercourse* Québec Canada
310 7b **Petite Rivière Noire, Piton de la** *volcano* Mauritius
135 I4 **Petite Rivière Salée** Martinique
163 I5 **Petite Savane Point** *cape* Dominica
Petite Terre *see* **Pamanzi** Mayotte
163 I6 **Petite Terre, Îles de la** *islands* Guadeloupe
118 L3 **Petitot** *watercourse* Alberta Canada
118 J2 **Petitot** *watercourse* Northwest Territories Canada
121 V5 **Petitsikapau Lake** Newfoundland and Labrador Canada
223 Q5 **Petkeljärvi Kansallispuisto** *park* Finland
223 O3 **Petkula** Finland
133 H4 **Peto** Mexico
126 I6 **Petoskey** Michigan USA
120 I6 **Petownikip Lake** Ontario Canada
386 F2 **Petra Velikogo, Zaliv** *island* Russian Federation
436 P1 **Petras, Mount** *mountain* Antarctica
225 O2 **Petraselkä** *bay* Finland
423 6 **Petre Bay** Chatham Islands New Zealand
230 F4 **Petrer** Spain
234 D3 **Petrești** Romania
128 H3 **Petrified Forest National Park** Arizona USA
227 L5 **Petrila** Romania
232 G4 **Petrinja** Croatia
227 L4 **Petriș** Romania
234 G2 **Petrivka** Ukraine
160 D4 **Petro, Cerro de** *mountain* Chile
225 O3 **Petrodvorets** Russian Federation
129 I3 **Petroglyph National Monument** *park* New Mexico USA
230 F4 **Pétrola, Laguna Salada de** *lake* Spain
130 B3 **Petrolia** Texas USA
156 D5 **Petrolina** Brazil
157 B7 **Petrolina de Goiás** Brazil
389 L2 **Petropavlovka** Russian Federation
Petropavlovsk *see* **Petropavlovskiy** Kazakhstan
389 K2 **Petropavlovsk** Kazakhstan
237 AG8 **Petropavlovsk-Kamchatskiy** Russian Federation
388 J2 **Petropavlovskiy** Kazakhstan
157 D8 **Petrópolis** Brazil
76 P5 **Petrov Fracture Zone** *underwater feature* Atlantic Ocean
223 P5 **Petrovaara** Finland
234 B3 **Petrovac** Serbia
235 B5 **Petrovci** Croatia
238 E6 **Petrovichi** Russian Federation
388 E3 **Petrovsk** Russian Federation
384 F2 **Petrovsk-zabaykalskiy** Russian Federation
234 F3 **Petrovs'ke** Ukraine
238 G5 **Petrovskiy** Russian Federation
223 S5 **Petrovskiy Yam** Russian Federation
238 G4 **Petrovskoye** Russian Federation
388 C3 **Petrovskoye** Russian Federation
388 G2 **Petrovskoye** Russian Federation
223 R2 **Petrozavodsk** Russian Federation
223 O2 **Petsikko** Finland
245 E2 **Pettigo** Fermanagh Northern Ireland UK
389 J2 **Petukhovo** Russian Federation
238 H5 **Petushki** Russian Federation
241 G4 **Petworth** West Sussex England UK
227 G3 **Peuerbach** Austria
374 C2 **Peuetsagu, Gunung** *volcano* Indonesia
121 P6 **Peuplier, Rivière du** *watercourse* Québec Canada
223 O3 **Peurasuvanto** Finland
222 J3 **Peuraure** Sweden
222 J3 **Peuraure** *lake* Sweden
374 C2 **Peureula** Indonesia
237 AJ5 **Pevek** Russian Federation
241 H4 **Pevensey Bay** East Sussex England UK
241 F3 **Pewsey** Wiltshire England UK
224 D6 **Pewsum** Germany
229 G5 **Peyrehorade** France
226 B5 **Peyreleau** France
228 E4 **Peyrissac** France
129 J1 **Peyton** Colorado USA
228 F5 **Pézenas** France
391 L3 **Pezu** Pakistan
229 J3 **Pfaff, Wilder** *mountain* Austria
130 C5 **Pflugerville** Texas USA
226 E3 **Pforzheim** Germany
226 E4 **Pfullendorf** Germany
226 F4 **Pfunds** Austria
226 E3 **Pfungstadt** Germany
376 D4 **Phai Sali** Thailand
309 F4 **Phalaborwa** South Africa
392 C5 **Phalodi** Rajasthan India
229 H2 **Phalsbourg** France
393 D8 **Phaltan** Maharashtra India
376 F5 **Phan Rí Cửa** Vietnam
376 F5 **Phan Thiết** Vietnam
376 C5 **Phangnga** Thailand
392 G5 **Phaplu** Nepal
376 B3 **Phapon (Pyapon)** Myanmar
130 B7 **Pharr** Texas USA
376 E2 **Phát Diệm** Vietnam
376 D6 **Phatt-Halung** *admin. area* Thailand
376 C5 **Phayao** Thailand
376 D3 **Phayao** *admin. area* Thailand
376 D4 **Phayuha Khiri** Thailand
379 H4 **Phek** Nagaland India
130 B5 **Phelps Lake** Saskatchewan Canada
131 M3 **Phelps Lake** North Carolina USA
131 I4 **Pheonix City** Alabama USA
376 D3 **Phetchabun** Thailand
376 C4 **Phetchaburi** Thailand
376 E4 **Phiafai** Laos
376 D3 **Phichit** Thailand
376 D3 **Phichit** *admin. area* Thailand
130 G4 **Philadelphia** Mississippi USA
131 M3 **Philadelphia** Pennsylvania USA
302 E3 **Philae** *ruin* Egypt
240 C4 **Philham** Devon England UK
125 O4 **Philip** South Dakota USA
425 inset **Philip Island** Norfolk Island Australia
116 E5 **Philip Smith Mountains** Alaska USA
229 G1 **Philippeville** Belgium
127 K7 **Philippi** West Virginia USA
78 I6 **Philippine Basin** *underwater feature* Philippine Sea
377 J3 **Philippine Sea** Philippines
78 I6 **Philippine Trench** *underwater feature* Philippine Sea
377 J4 **Philippines** *country*
163 20 **Philipsburg** Netherlands Antilles
124 I3 **Philipsburg** Montana USA
242 B3 **Philipstown** Ireland
392 D4 **Phillaur** Punjab India
130 C3 **Phillips** Oklahoma USA
126 F4 **Phillips** Wisconsin USA
117 K2 **Phillips Inlet** Nunavut Canada
125 P7 **Phillipsburg** Kansas USA
127 N6 **Phillipsburg** Pennsylvania USA
127 O5 **Philmont** New York USA
124 D4 **Philomath** Oregon USA
119 P5 **Philomena** Alberta Canada
131 K2 **Philpott Lake** Virginia USA
376 D3 **Phitsanulok** Thailand
376 E5 **Phnum Pénh (Phnom Penh)** Cambodia
132 B1 **Phoenix** Arizona USA
426 1 **Phoenix Islands** Kiribati
376 D4 **Phon** Thailand
376 D2 **Phong Thô** Vietnam
376 D2 **Phongsali** Laos
376 D2 **Phongsali** *admin. area* Laos
376 D3 **Phonhong** Laos
376 D3 **Phonsavan** Laos
244 E3 **Phorp** Moray Scotland UK
376 E4 **Phouphieng Bolovens** Laos
376 C5 **Phra Thong, Ko** *island* Thailand
376 D3 **Phrae** Thailand
376 E3 **Phú Bài** Vietnam
376 D3 **Phu Khieo** Thailand
376 D3 **Phu Kra Dung** Thailand
376 E3 **Phú Lộc** Vietnam
376 E2 **Phủ Lý** Vietnam
376 D5 **Phu Quoc, Đao** *island* Vietnam
376 E2 **Phủ Yên** Vietnam
308 D4 **Phuduhudu** Botswana
376 C6 **Phuket** Thailand
376 C5 **Phuket** *admin. area* Thailand
376 C6 **Phuket, Ko** *island* Thailand
393 F7 **Phulabani** Orissa India
376 E4 **Phumi Kâmpóng Trâlach** Cambodia
376 E4 **Phumi Mlu Prey** Cambodia
376 D4 **Phumi Sâmraông** Cambodia
308 E5 **Phuthaditjhaba** South Africa
376 D4 **Phutthaisong** Thailand
379 G5 **Pi** *watercourse* Myanmar
157 C9 **Piaçabuçu** Brazil
226 E5 **Piacenza** Italy
123 C7 **Piacouadie, Lac** *lake* Québec Canada
226 F5 **Piadena** Italy
121 P5 **Piagochioui** *watercourse* Québec Canada
422 F3 **Piako** *watercourse* New Zealand
156 E4 **Piancó** Brazil
232 D5 **Pianella** Italy
384 G5 **Pianguan** Shanxi China
226 F5 **Pianoro** Italy
233 F5 **Pianosa, Isola** *island* Italy
426 6a **Pianu, Mochun** *strait* Federated States of Micronesia
119 Q8 **Piapot** Saskatchewan Canada
227 H1 **Piasek** Poland
234 E2 **Piatra Neamț** Romania
156 D4 **Piauí** *admin. area* Brazil
156 D4/5 **Piauí** *watercourse* Brazil
232 E3 **Piave** *watercourse* Italy
233 F8 **Piazza Armerina** Italy
302 E2 **Pibor** *watercourse* Sudan
307 E2 **Pibor Post** Sudan
126 H2 **Pic** *watercourse* Ontario Canada
159 F5 **Picacho, Serrania El** *range* Bolivia
154 B4 **Picacho Bujío** *mountain* Colombia
160 F2 **Picada Catorce de Mayo** Paraguay
234 A2 **Picán** Croatia
228 F2 **Picardie** *admin. area* France
130 G5 **Picayune** Mississippi USA
158 D5 **Pichalo, Punta** *cape* Chile
130 D2 **Picher** Oklahoma USA
392 E6 **Pichhor** Madhya Pradesh India
160 E6 **Pichi Mahuida** Argentina
158 D4 **Pichigua** Peru
154 B3 **Pichimá** Colombia
158 B5 **Pichincha, Volcán** *volcano* Ecuador
158 D5 **Pichu Pichu, Nevado de** *mountain* Peru
133 G5 **Pichucalco** Mexico
125 O3 **Pick City** North Dakota USA
243 G3 **Pickburn** South Yorkshire England UK
130 G4 **Pickens** Mississippi USA
130 G4 **Pickensville** Alabama USA
120 F4 **Pickerel Lake** Ontario Canada
243 H2 **Pickering** North Yorkshire England UK
243 H2 **Pickering, Vale of** *valley* England UK
126 I3 **Pickford** Michigan USA
243 G2 **Pickhill** North Yorkshire England UK
120 J7 **Pickle Lake** Ontario Canada
243 F3 **Pickmere** Cheshire England UK
125 Q6 **Pickrell** Nebraska USA
125 P5 **Pickstown** South Dakota USA
130 G3 **Pickwick Lake** Mississippi USA
310 1 **Pico** *island* Azores
233 E6 **Pico** Italy
154 A5 **Pico, Punta** *cape* Peru
160 C3 **Pico de Salamanca** Argentina
310 1b **Pico Negro, Punta** *cape* Azores
158 D4 **Pico Tres, Nevado** *mountain* Peru
156 D4 **Picos** Brazil
158 B2 **Picota** Peru
123 G10 **Pictou** Nova Scotia Canada
123 G10 **Pictou Island** Nova Scotia Canada
119 O8 **Picture Butte** Alberta Canada
156 E4 **Picuí** Brazil
160 D6 **Picún Leufú** Argentina
388 C5 **Picunda** Georgia
391 J4 **Pidarak** Pakistan
310 8a **Pidjani** Comoros
234 H1 **Pidlisne** Ukraine
238 F2 **Pid'ma** Russian Federation
393 E10 **Pidurutalagala** *mountain* Sri Lanka
154 B3 **Pié de Pató** Colombia
129 H3 **Pie Town** New Mexico USA
227 K1 **Piecki** Poland
310 1b **Piedade** Azores
154 C3 **Piedecuesta** Colombia
Piedmont *see* **Piemonte** Italy
126 F8 **Piedmont** Missouri USA
130 C3 **Piedmont** Oklahoma USA
162 B3 **Piedra Blanca** Chile
162 C4 **Piedra Clavada** Argentina
162 B2 **Piedra del Águila** Argentina
160 F6 **Piedra Echada** Argentina
230 D4 **Piedrabuena** Spain
230 C2 **Piedrafita** Spain
154 C4 **Piedras** Colombia
161 G5 **Piedras, Punta** *cape* Argentina
158 D3 **Piedras, Río de Las** *watercourse* Peru
132 E2 **Piedras Negras** Mexico
223 N4 **Piehinki** Finland
223 O5 **Pieksämäki** Finland
225 N1 **Pieksänjärvi** *lake* Finland
230 E2 **Pielagas** Spain
223 O5 **Pielavesi** Finland
223 O5 **Pielavesi** *lake* Finland
223 P5 **Pielinen** *bay* Finland
222 J3 **Pieljekaise National Park** *park* Sweden
232 B4 **Piemonte** *admin. area* Italy
227 M3 **Pieniaki** Ukraine
227 H2 **Pieńsk** Poland
232 D5 **Pienza** Italy
244 C4 **Pier** Highland Scotland UK
227 J1 **Pieranie** Poland
124 H3 **Pierce** Idaho USA
120 I5 **Pierce Lake** Ontario Canada
161 G6 **Pieres** Argentina
125 O5 **Pierre** South Dakota USA
228 E4 **Pierre-Buffière** France
127 K2 **Pierre Lake** Ontario Canada
241 I5 **Pierrepont** France
163 9 **Pierreville** Trinidad and Tobago
119 U8 **Pierson** Manitoba Canada
131 K6 **Pierson** Florida USA
222 K3 **Piertinjaure** Sweden
126 D4 **Pierz** Minnesota USA
227 K2 **Pierzchnica** Poland
222 J3 **Pieskehaure** *lake* Sweden
227 H1 **Pieski** Poland
227 I3 **Piešťany** Slovakia
308 F5 **Piet Retief** South Africa
308 F5 **Pietermaritzburg** South Africa
233 F6 **Pietracatella** Italy
226 D5 **Pietraporzio** Italy
229 J5 **Pietrasanta** Italy
233 F6 **Pietre Nere, Punta** *cape* Italy
234 C3 **Pietroasa** Romania
234 D4 **Pietroșani** Romania
234 D2 **Pietrosul** *mountain* Romania
227 H2 **Pietrzyków** Poland
232 E3 **Pieve di Cadore** Italy
229 K4 **Pieve di Soligo** Italy
310 5c **Pig Beach** St Helena
126 G2 **Pigeon** *watercourse* Ontario Canada
163 I6 **Pigeon** Guadeloupe
126 J5 **Pigeon** Michigan USA
423 E6 **Pigeon Bay** New Zealand
119 O6 **Pigeon Lake** Alberta Canada
232 B5 **Pigna** Italy
233 F6 **Pignola** Italy
238 E5 **Pigulino** Russian Federation
422 F3 **Piha** New Zealand
223 O5 **Pihkainmäki** Finland
223 O4 **Pihkala** Finland
225 O2 **Pihlajavesi** *lake* Finland
223 N5 **Pihtipudas** Finland
223 N4 **Piippola** Finland
223 P4 **Piispajärvi** *lake* Finland
133 G6 **Pijijiapan** Mexico
238 F3 **Pikalëvo** Russian Federation
120 H7 **Pikangikum Lake** Ontario Canada
225 L4 **Pikeliai** Lithuania
426 6 **Pikelot** *island* Federated States of Micronesia
125 M7 **Pikes Peak** Colorado USA
126 J7 **Piketon** Ohio USA
127 J8 **Pikeville** Kentucky USA
131 I3 **Pikeville** Tennessee USA
377 J6 **Pikit** Philippines
305 H4 **Pikounda** Congo
119 W5 **Pikwitonei** Manitoba Canada
226 G5 **Pila** Italy
227 I1 **Piła** Poland
161 G3 **Pilagá** *watercourse* Argentina
162 C2 **Pilahué** Argentina
392 D5 **Pilani** Rajasthan India
156 D5 **Pilão Arcado** *watercourse* Brazil
160 F4 **Pilar** Argentina
161 G3 **Pilar** Paraguay
377 I4 **Pilar** Philippines
162 A5 **Pilar, Cabo** *cape* Chile
157 C8 **Pilar do Sul** Brazil
377 I6 **Pilas** *island* Philippines
230 C5 **Pilas** Spain
228 D4 **Pilat, Dune du** *dunes* France
227 I2 **Piława** Poland
424 F7 **Pilbara** *region* WA Australia
162 B2 **Pilcaniyeu** Argentina
227 H2 **Pilchowicie, Jezioro** *lake* Poland
159 F6 **Pilcomayo** *watercourse* Bolivia
160 F2 **Pilcomayo** *watercourse* Paraguay
227 I1 **Pile, Jezioro** *lake* Poland
308 F4 **Pilgrims Rest** South Africa
243 H3 **Pilham** Lincolnshire England UK
160 E2 **Pili, Cerro** *mountain* Chile
392 E5 **Pilibhit** Uttar Pradesh India
227 J2 **Pilica** *watercourse* Poland
155 G4 **Pilinawa** Guyana
232 H3 **Pilis** Hungary
154 B3 **Piliza** Colombia
154 B5 **Pillaro** Ecuador
240 C4 **Pillaton** Cornwall England UK
240 D2 **Pilleth** Powys Wales UK
425 N7 **Pilliga** NSW Australia
242 F3 **Pilling** Lancashire England UK
124 D7 **Pillsbury, Lake** California USA
225 P6 **Pil'nya** Belarus
160 D6 **Pilolil** Argentina
230 D2 **Piloña** Spain
119 V8 **Pilot Mound** Manitoba Canada
124 F4 **Pilot Rock** Oregon USA
240 E4 **Pilsdon** Dorset England UK
Pilsen *see* **Plzeň** Czech Republic
242 A4 **Piltown** Ireland
222 K4 **Pilträsk** Sweden
237 AD8 **Pil'tun, Zaliv** *bay* Russian Federation
234 B2 **Pilu** Romania
236 P6 **Pim** Russian Federation
128 H4 **Pima** Arizona USA
128 G6 **Pimas** Mexico
159 F3 **Pimenta Bueno** Brazil
156 D4 **Pimenteiras** Brazil
159 F4 **Pimenteiras do Oeste** Bolivia
158 B2 **Pimentel** Peru
393 C7 **Pimpri Chinchwad** Maharashtra India
227 M1 **Pina** *watercourse* Belarus
231 F3 **Pina** Spain
132 B2 **Pinacate, Sierra del** *mountain* Mexico
392 E5 **Pinahat** Uttar Pradesh India
128 H4 **Pinaleno Mountains** Arkansas USA
154 C4 **Piñalito** Colombia
377 I4 **Pinamalayan** Philippines
374 D2 **Pinang** *admin. area* Malaysia
374 D2 **Pinang** *island* Malaysia
375 H2 **Pinangah** Malaysia
374 D4 **Pinangteluk** Indonesia
231 H4 **Pinar, Cap des** *cape* Spain
134 D2 **Pinar del Río** Cuba
134 D2 **Pinar del Rio** *admin. area* Cuba
154 B5 **Piñas** Ecuador
377 I4 **Pinatubo, Mount** *volcano* Philippines
120 H7 **Pinawa** Manitoba Canada
241 G2 **Pinchbeck** Lincolnshire England UK
124 I2 **Pincher** Alberta Canada
119 O8 **Pincher Creek** Alberta Canada
154 B5 **Pincho** Ecuador
159 G4 **Pindaiuval** Brazil
156 F5 **Pindaival** Brazil
156 C4 **Pindaré** *watercourse* Brazil
156 C3 **Pindaré Mirim** Brazil
379 H5 **Pindaya** Myanmar
157 D5 **Pindobaçu** Brazil
235 B6 **Pindos Oros** *range* Greece
159 G2 **Pindoval** Brazil
392 E6 **Pindrawa** Rajasthan India
118 J5 **Pine** *watercourse* British Columbia Canada
119 U7 **Pine** *watercourse* Manitoba Canada
128 G3 **Pine** Arizona USA
127 N7 **Pine Beach** New Jersey USA
119 T5 **Pine Bluff** Saskatchewan Canada
130 F3 **Pine Bluff** Arkansas USA
125 M6 **Pine Bluffs** Wyoming USA
424 I3 **Pine Creek** NT Australia
130 D3 **Pine Creek Lake** Oklahoma USA
120 G7 **Pine Dock** Manitoba Canada
124 F8 **Pine Flat Reservoir** California USA
130 H5 **Pine Hill** Alabama USA
130 C5 **Pine Island** Texas USA
436 R2 **Pine Island Bay** Antarctica
436 R1 **Pine Island Glacier** *ice* Antarctica
131 J7 **Pine Island Sound** Florida USA
119 N2 **Pine Point** Northwest Territories Canada
125 N5 **Pine Ridge** Nebraska USA
119 U7 **Pine River** Manitoba Canada
119 R5 **Pine River** Saskatchewan Canada
118 J5 **Pine Valley** British Columbia Canada
231 H3 **Pineda** Spain
128 G3 **Pinedale** Arizona USA
125 K5 **Pinedale** Wyoming USA
236 K6 **Pinega** *watercourse* Russian Federation
124 G3 **Pinehurst** Idaho USA
130 E5 **Pinehurst** Texas USA
120 K6 **Pineimuta** *watercourse* Ontario Canada
235 B6 **Pineios** *watercourse* Greece
130 E5 **Pineland** Texas USA
131 J7 **Pinellas Park** Florida USA
131 K4 **Pineridge** South Carolina USA
226 D5 **Pinerolo** Italy
233 F5 **Pineto** Italy
128 H3 **Pinetop-Lakeside** Arizona USA
131 J4 **Pineview** Georgia USA
130 E5 **Pineville** Louisiana USA
126 D8 **Pineville** Missouri USA
127 K8 **Pineville** West Virginia USA
126 D2 **Pinewood** Minnesota USA
120 H8 **Piney** Manitoba Canada
229 G2 **Piney** France
131 J6 **Piney Point** Florida USA
384 E6 **Ping'an** Qinghai China
380 E3 **Pingba** Guizhou China
381 G3 **Pingchuan** Fujian China
385 H5 **Pingding** Shanxi China
381 F1 **Pingdingshan** Henan China
381 G3 **Pingdu** Jiangxi China
385 I6 **Pingdu** Shandong China
426 6 **Pingelap** *island* Federated States of Micronesia
385 I5 **Pinggu** Beijing China
380 E3 **Pinghu** Guizhou China
381 I2 **Pinghu** Zhejiang China
380 F4 **Pingle** Guangxi Zhuangzu Zizhiqu China
380 F2 **Pingli** Shaanxi China
384 F6 **Pingliang** Gansu China
384 F5 **Pingluo** Zishiqu China
380 E4 **Pingma** Guangxi Zhuangzu Zizhiqu China
380 F4 **Pingnan** Guangxi Zhuangzu Zizhiqu China
310 6 **Pingouins, Île des** *island* French Southern and Antarctic Lands
385 I5 **Pingquan** Hebei China
385 H5 **Pingshan** Hebei China
380 D3 **Pingshan** Yunnan China
385 H5 **Pingshu** Hebei China
381 H3 **Pingtan** Fujian China
381 H4 **P'ingtung** Taiwan China
122 G3 **Pingkuskoak, Mount** Newfoundland and Labrador Canada
380 E3 **Pingxi** Guizhou China
384 F6 **Pingxiang** Gansu China
380 E4 **Pingxiang** Guangxi Zhuangzu Zizhiqu China
381 G3 **Pingxiang** Jiangxi China
384 G5 **Pingyao** Shanxi China
385 I6 **Pingyi** Shandong China
385 H5 **Pingyuan** Shandong China
380 C4 **Pingyuan** Yunnan China
380 E3 **Pingzhaio** Guizhou China
157 B9 **Pinhão** Brazil
156 C3 **Pinheiro** Brazil
161 H4 **Pinheiro Machado** Brazil
159 H1 **Pinhel** Brazil
230 C3 **Pinhel** Portugal
374 C3 **Pini** *island* Indonesia
373 J5 **Pinipel Island** Papua New Guinea
131 M3 **Pink Hill** North Carolina USA
118 J4 **Pink Mountain** British Columbia Canada
227 I4 **Pinka** *watercourse* Austria
227 I4 **Pinkafeld** Austria
379 H4 **Pinlebu** Myanmar
242 D1 **Pinminnoch** South Ayrshire Scotland UK
244 D5 **Pinmore** South Ayrshire Scotland UK
425 L8 **Pinnaroo** SA Australia
235 D5 **Pinnes, Akra** *cape* Greece
229 I5 **Pino** Corsica France
160 D6 **Pino Hachado** Argentina
230 C3 **Pinofranqueado** Spain
375 F4 **Pinoh** *watercourse* Indonesia
132 D3 **Pinole** Mexico
124 D8 **Pinole** California USA
230 E5 **Pinos Puente** Spain
231 F4 **Pinoso** Spain
133 F5 **Pinotepa Nacional** Mexico
426 7 **Pins, Île des** *island* New Caledonia
394 C2 **Pinsk** Belarus
128 H3 **Pinta** Arizona USA
163 4 **Pinta, Canal de** *strait* Archipiélago de Colón (Galapagos Islands)
163 4 **Pinta, Isla** *island* Archipiélago de Colón (Galapagos Islands)
159 I4 **Pintado** *watercourse* Brazil
223 O4 **Pintamo** Finland
375 H2 **Pintasan** Malaysia
159 E5 **Pinto** Bolivia
162 B4 **Pinturas** *watercourse* Argentina
123 J7 **Pinware** Newfoundland and Labrador Canada
244 D5 **Pinwherry** South Ayrshire Scotland UK
230 C3 **Pinzio** Portugal
163 4 **Pinzón, Isla** *island* Archipiélago de Colón (Galapagos Islands)
377 I4 **Pio Duran** Philippines
156 D4 **Pio IX** Brazil
156 C3 **Pio XII** Brazil
128 E2 **Pioche** Nevada USA
306 D5 **Piodi** Democratic Republic of Congo
232 D5 **Piombino** Italy
79 S4 **Pioneer Fracture Zone** *underwater feature* Pacific Ocean
124 I4 **Pioneer Mountains** Montana USA
236 S3 **Pioner, Ostrov** *island* Russian Federation
422 F4 **Piopio** New Zealand
233 F6 **Pioppi** Italy
155 F5 **Piorini, Lago** *lake* Brazil
226 D5 **Piossasco** Italy
232 E4 **Piove di Sacco** Italy
424 I6 **Pipalyatjara** SA Australia
160 E4 **Pipanaco, Salar de** *lake* Argentina
241 F2 **Pipe Ridware** Staffordshire England UK
235 D6 **Piperi** *island* Greece
120 J6 **Pipestone** *watercourse* Ontario Canada
125 Q5 **Pipestone** Minnesota USA
126 E2 **Pipestone Lake** Ontario Canada
305 I3 **Pipi** *watercourse* Central African Republic
234 E2 **Pipirig** Romania
123 C8 **Pipmuacan, Réservoir** *lake* Québec Canada
119 S5 **Piprell Lake** Saskatchewan Canada
393 D6 **Pipri** Madhya Pradesh India
393 D7 **Pipri** Maharashtra India
228 D3 **Pipriac** France
119 V5 **Pipun** Manitoba Canada
235 A5 **Piqeras** Albania
157 C8 **Piquete** Brazil
158 C4 **Piquicha** Peru
159 F6 **Piquirenda** Paraguay
157 A9 **Piquiri** *watercourse* Brazil

389 J7 **Pir Nakhchir** Afghanistan
392 D4 **Pir Panjal Range** Jammu and Kashmir India/Pakistan
391 I3 **Pir Shūrān** *mountain* Iran
157 B7 **Piracanjuba** Brazil
157 C8 **Piracicaba** Brazil
156 D3 **Piracuruca** Brazil
157 B9 **Piraí do Sul** Brazil
154 E4 **Piraiuara** Brazil
157 B8 **Piraju** Brazil
157 B8 **Pirajuí** Brazil
162 B4 **Pirámide, Cerro** *mountain* Chile
226 G5 **Piran** Slovenia
161 G3 **Pirané** Argentina
155 H5 **Piranga, Serra da** *range* Brazil
159 H2 **Piranhaquara** Brazil
155 E5 **Piranhas** Brazil
157 B7 **Piranhas** Brazil
156 C3 **Pirapemas** Brazil
157 B8 **Pirapó** *watercourse* Brazil
157 C7 **Pirapora** Brazil
157 B8 **Pirapozinho** Brazil
159 E2 **Pirapucu** Brazil
135 F2 **Pirates Well** Bahamas
159 H6 **Piratini** Brazil
156 B2 **Piratuba, Lago** *lake* Brazil
155 G5 **Piratucu** *watercourse* Brazil
121 T7 **Piraube, Lac** *lake* Québec Canada
162 C3 **Piré Mahuida, Sierra** *range* Argentina
162 B2 **Pirehueico** Chile
157 B6 **Pirenópolis** Brazil
157 B7 **Pires do Rio** Brazil
158 D4 **Pirhua, Cerro** *mountain* Peru
156 C3 **Piriá** *watercourse* Brazil
161 G3 **Piribebuy** Paraguay
373 F5 **Pirimapun** Indonesia
235 C5 **Pirin** *range* Bulgaria
156 D4 **Piripiri** Brazil
159 G5 **Pirizeiro** Brazil
424 I2 **Pirlangimpi** NT Australia
229 H2 **Pirmasens** Germany
227 G2 **Pirna** Germany
244 C5 **Pirnmill** North Ayrshire Scotland UK
163 I6 **Pirogue** Guadeloupe
422 F3 **Pirongia** New Zealand
422 F3 **Pirongia** *volcano* New Zealand
234 C4 **Pirot** Serbia
228 D2 **Pirou** France
128 H5 **Pirtleville** Arizona USA
241 G3 **Pirton** Hertfordshire England UK
372 D4 **Piru** Indonesia
375 K4 **Piru, Teluk** *bay* Indonesia
232 D5 **Pisa** Italy
423 C7 **Pisa Range** New Zealand
372 D4 **Pisang** *island* Indonesia
372 D4 **Pisang, Kepulauan** *island* Indonesia
158 B4 **Pisco** Peru
234 C2 **Pişcolt** Romania
227 H3 **Písek** Czech Republic
380 D3 **Pisha** Sichuan China
382 F5 **Pishan** Xinjiang Uygur Zizhiqu China
234 F1 **Pishchanka** Ukraine
375 I5 **Pising** Indonesia
128 B3 **Pismo Beach** California USA
304 B3 **Piso, Lake** *lake* Liberia
159 F4 **Piso Firme** Bolivia
158 C2 **Pisqui** *watercourse* Peru
160 D3 **Pissis, Cerro** *mountain* Argentina
228 D4 **Pissos** France
223 P4 **Pista** *watercourse* Finland
229 J5 **Pistoia** Italy
120 I1 **Pistol Bay** Nunavut Canada
235 A5 **Pistull** Albania
240 C2 **Pistyll** Gwynedd Wales UK
230 D3 **Pisuerga** *watercourse* Spain
227 K1 **Pisz** Poland
227 L2 **Piszczac** Poland
124 E6 **Pit** *watercourse* California USA
121 W6 **Pitaga** Newfoundland and Labrador Canada
154 C4 **Pital** Colombia
134 C5 **Pital** Costa Rica
154 B4 **Pitalito** Colombia
157 B9 **Pitanga** Brazil
157 C7 **Pitangui** Brazil
159 F4 **Pitari, Lagoa** *lake* Brazil
427 11 **Pitcairn Island** Pacific Ocean
427 11 **Pitcairn Islands** *UK overseas territory* Pacific Ocean
240 E2 **Pitchford** Shropshire England UK
222 L4 **Piteå** Sweden
222 L4 **Piteälven** *watercourse* Sweden
388 D2 **Pitelino** Russian Federation
388 E3 **Piterka** Russian Federation
234 D3 **Piteşti** Romania
226 B3 **Pithiviers** France
427 14b **Piti Aau, Motu** *island* French Polynesia
156 F4 **Pitimbu** Brazil
132 B2 **Pitiquito** Mexico
223 K2 **Pitkäluoto** Finland
225 P2 **Pitkyaranta** Russian Federation
225 P2 **Pitkyayarvi** Russian Federation
244 E4 **Pitlochry** Perth and Kinross Scotland UK
244 F3 **Pitmedden** Aberdeenshire Scotland UK
305 G3 **Pitoa** Cameroon
380 D2 **Pitong** Sichuan China
163 I3 **Pitons, Anse des** *bay* St Lucia
244 F4 **Pitscottie** Fife Scotland UK
241 G2 **Pitsford Reservoir** England UK
118 G6 **Pitt Island** British Columbia Canada
423 6 **Pitt Island (Rangiauria)** Chatham Islands New Zealand
118 J8 **Pitt Lake** British Columbia Canada
423 6 **Pitt Strait** Chatham Islands New Zealand
244 D3 **Pittentrail** Highland Scotland UK
244 F4 **Pittenweem** Fife Scotland UK
126 D8 **Pittsburg** Kansas USA
130 D3 **Pittsburg** Texas USA
127 L6 **Pittsburgh** Pennsylvania USA
126 F7 **Pittsfield** Illinois USA
123 D10 **Pittsfield** Maine USA
127 O5 **Pittsfield** Massachusetts USA
307 F5 **Pitu** *watercourse* Tanzania
120 M7 **Pitukupi Lake** Ontario Canada
226 F4 **Pitztal** *valley* Austria
157 C8 **Piuí** Brazil
373 J5 **Piul Island** Papua New Guinea
157 D8 **Piúma** Brazil
158 A2 **Piura** Peru
158 A2 **Piura** *admin. area* Peru
158 A2 **Piura** *watercourse* Peru
124 I7 **Piute Reservoir** Utah USA
159 G4 **Piúva** Brazil
121 N7 **Pivabiska** *watercourse* Ontario Canada
234 F1 **Pivdennyy Buh** *watercourse* Ukraine
227 H5 **Pivka** Slovenia
232 H4 **Pivnice** Serbia
232 H5 **Pivško Jezero** *lake* Montenegro
133 H5 **Pixoyal** Mexico
230 D5 **Pizarra** Spain
154 B3 **Pizarro** Colombia
305 F3 **Pizhi** Nigeria
388 E1 **Pizhma** Russian Federation
381 H1 **Pizhou** Jiangsu China
233 G7 **Pizzo** Italy
233 F5 **Pizzo, Punta di** *cape* Italy
229 K5 **Pizzuto, Monte** *mountain* Italy
222 K4 **Pjesker** *lake* Sweden
226 G1 **Plaaz** Germany
159 H1 **Placas** Brazil
123 L9 **Placentia** Newfoundland and Labrador Canada
123 K9 **Placentia Bay** Newfoundland and Labrador Canada
129 H1 **Placerville** Colorado USA
234 D4 **Plachkovtsi** Bulgaria
158 E3 **Plácido de Castro** Bolivia
244 C5 **Pladda** *island* Scotland UK
126 F5 **Plain** Wisconsin USA
130 E4 **Plain Dealing** Louisiana USA
126 H7 **Plainfield** Indiana USA
126 G4 **Plainfield** Wisconsin USA
131 I4 **Plains** Georgia USA
125 O8 **Plains** Kansas USA
129 K4 **Plains** Texas USA
125 Q5 **Plainview** Nebraska USA
129 L3 **Plainview** Texas USA
125 P7 **Plainville** Kansas USA
226 A3 **Plaisir** France
374 E4 **Plaju** Indonesia
235 D5 **Plaka** Greece
235 D8 **Pláka** Greece
235 D5 **Plaka, Akra** *cape* Greece
119 O5 **Plamondon** Alberta Canada
375 H6 **Plampang** Indonesia
129 J7 **Plan de Ayala** Mexico
231 I2 **Plan-de-Cuques** France
232 E2 **Planá** Czech Republic
135 F2 **Plana Cays** *island* Bahamas
154 C4 **Planadas** Colombia
157 C6 **Planaltina** Brazil
155 H5 **Planalto Maracanaquará** *region* Brazil
234 B3 **Plandište** Serbia
154 C2 **Planeta Rica** Colombia
226 G3 **Plánice** Czech Republic
162 D2 **Planicie de los Vientos** *region* Argentina
130 C4 **Plano** Texas USA
235 B7 **Plános** Greece
226 F4 **Plansee** *lake* Austria
131 J6 **Plant City** Florida USA
131 K7 **Plantation** Florida USA
230 C3 **Plasencia** Spain
227 H5 **Plaški** Croatia
235 B5 **Plasnica** Macedonia
123 E9 **Plaster Rock** New Brunswick Canada
232 E2 **Plasy** Czech Republic
154 B5 **Plata, Isla de La** *island* Ecuador
162 B3 **Plata, Lago La** *lake* Argentina
160 D3 **Plata, Punta** *cape* Chile
161 G5 **Plata, Río de la** *watercourse* Argentina
158 C3 **Platanal** Peru
233 E8 **Platani** *watercourse* Italy
235 B6 **Plataria** Greece
305 F3 **Plateau** *admin. area* Nigeria
382 G6 **Plateau of Tibet** Xizang Zizhiqu China
305 H5 **Plateaux** *admin. area* Congo
236 F2 **Platen, Kap** *cape* Norway
132 E4 **Plateros** Mexico
227 L1 **Platerów** Poland
238 C4 **Platishino** Russian Federation
231 H3 **Platja d'Aro** Spain
119 Q7 **Plato** Saskatchewan Canada
154 C2 **Plato** Colombia
125 L8 **Platoro Reservoir** Colorado USA
125 O6 **Platte** *watercourse* Nebraska USA
125 P5 **Platte** South Dakota USA
310 9 **Platte Island** Seychelles
125 M6 **Platteville** Colorado USA
126 F5 **Platteville** Wisconsin USA
226 G3 **Plattling** Germany
127 O4 **Plattsburgh** New York USA
226 G1 **Plau am See** Germany
226 G2 **Plauen** Germany
226 G1 **Plauer See** *lake* Germany
234 A4 **Plav** Montenegro
227 K3 **Plavnica** Slovakia
227 F4 **Plavnik** *island* Croatia
236 R4 **Plavnikovye, Ostrova** *island* Russian Federation
238 G6 **Plavsk** Russian Federation
376 F4 **Plây Ku** Vietnam
310 3d **Playa Blanca** Canary Islands
132 E5 **Playa Corrida de San Juan, Punta** *cape* Mexico
154 E4 **Playa de Candela** Venezuela
310 3a **Playa de la Americas** Canary Islands
310 3b **Playa de Mogán** Canary Islands
133 I4 **Playa del Carmen** Mexico
310 3b **Playa del Ingles** Canary Islands
155 E2 **Playa e Riedra, Embalse** *lake* Venezuela
154 C5 **Playa Paiche** *region* Peru
162 B2 **Playa Pilolcura** Chile
155 G2 **Playa Point** *cape* Guyana
310 3b **Playa Puerto Rico** Canary Islands
132 B2 **Playa Unión** Mexico
154 B5 **Playas** Ecuador
129 H5 **Playas Lake** New Mexico USA
241 I2 **Playford** Suffolk England UK
119 V6 **Playgreen Lake** Manitoba Canada
125 O2 **Plaza** North Dakota USA
128 F4 **Pleasant, Lake** Arizona USA
118 C3 **Pleasant Camp** Alaska USA
131 I3 **Pleasant Hill** Tennessee USA
423 D7 **Pleasant Point** New Zealand
133 F1 **Pleasant Valley** Texas USA
119 S6 **Pleasantdale** Saskatchewan Canada
126 D7 **Pleasanton** Kansas USA
130 B6 **Pleasanton** Texas USA
120 N7 **Pledger Lake** Ontario Canada
228 G1 **Pleinfeld** Germany
226 G2 **Pleiße** *watercourse* Germany
234 C3 **Pleniţa** Romania
425 K5 **Plenty** *watercourse* NT Australia
125 M2 **Plentywood** Montana USA
236 J6 **Plesetsk** Russian Federation
238 H3 **Pleshcheevo Ozero National Park** Russian Federation
228 C2 **Pleslin** France
238 F5 **Plëso** Russian Federation
227 M5 **Pleşoiu** Romania
227 I2 **Pleszew** Poland
121 T7 **Plétipi, Lac** *lake* Québec Canada
228 E3 **Pleumartin** France
234 D4 **Pleven** Bulgaria
125 M3 **Plevna** Montana USA
225 L4 **Plienciems** Latvia
235 G3 **Plieran** *watercourse* Malaysia
225 K5 **Plikiai** Lithuania
225 L4 **Plinkšių ežeras** *lake* Lithuania
225 O5 **Plisa** Belarus
232 H5 **Pljevlja** Montenegro
227 J1 **Płock** Poland
234 B4 **Pločnik** Serbia
228 C3 **Ploemeur** France
228 C2 **Ploeuc** France
234 E3 **Ploieşti** Romania
235 E6 **Plomari** Greece
228 F4 **Plomb du Cantal** *mountain* France
229 H3 **Plombières-les-Bains** France
227 H1 **Płoń, Jezioro** *lake* Poland
228 B3 **Plonéour-Lanvern** France
227 K1 **Płońsk** Poland
234 F1 **Plop** Moldova
234 F2 **Plopi** Moldova
234 G2 **Plopiş** Romania
234 C3 **Plopşoru** Romania
225 P4 **Ploskosh'** Russian Federation
238 F2 **Plotichno** Russian Federation
228 C2 **Plouaret** France
228 C3 **Plouay** France
228 C2 **Plougasnou** France
228 B2 **Plougastel-Daoulas** France
228 C2 **Plouha** France
228 C3 **Plouharnel** France
235 D4 **Plovdiv** Bulgaria
235 D5 **Plovdiv** *admin. area* Bulgaria
126 G4 **Plover** Wisconsin USA
240 E2 **Plowden** Shropshire England UK
228 B3 **Plozévet** France
241 H3 **Pluckley** Kent England UK
120 G8 **Plum Coulee** Manitoba Canada
125 P1 **Plumas** Manitoba Canada
245 E2 **Plumbridge** Strabane Northern Ireland UK
130 E3 **Plumerville** Arkansas USA
227 I3 **Plumlov** Czech Republic
124 G3 **Plummer** Idaho USA
125 Q3 **Plummer** Minnesota USA
308 E4 **Plumtree** Zimbabwe
241 G2 **Plungar** Leicester England UK
225 L5 **Plungė** Lithuania
227 J2 **Pluszkiejmy** Poland
132 C2 **Plutarco Elías Calles, Presa** *lake* Mexico
135 I3 **Plymouth** Montserrat
163 9 **Plymouth** Trinidad and Tobago
240 C4 **Plymouth** *admin. area* England UK
240 C4 **Plymouth** Plymouth England UK
126 H6 **Plymouth** Indiana USA
126 E4 **Plymouth** Minnesota USA
124 I6 **Plymouth** Utah USA
240 D4 **Plymtree** Devon England UK
225 O3 **Plyussa** Russian Federation
226 G3 **Plzeň (Pilsen)** Czech Republic
226 G3 **Plzeňský Kraj** *admin. area* Czech Republic
227 I1 **Pniewy** Poland
304 D2 **Pô** Burkina Faso
232 D4 **Po** *watercourse* Italy
232 E4 **Po, Delta del** Italy
375 F3 **Po, Tanjong** *cape* Malaysia
379 E3 **Po Ho** *watercourse* Xizang Zizhiqu China
157 D8 **Poá** Brazil
132 E3 **Poanas** Mexico
382 F4 **Pobeda Peak** *mountain* Xinjiang Uygur Zizhiqu China
232 E2 **Poběžovice** Czech Republic
227 I1 **Pobiedziska** Poland
224 I5 **Pobrzeże Koszalińskie** *region* Poland
130 F2 **Pocahontas** Arkansas USA
156 C4 **Poção de Pedras** Brazil
130 C3 **Pocasset** Oklahoma USA
124 I5 **Pocatello** Idaho USA
238 E5 **Pochinok** Russian Federation
386 F3 **Poch'ŏn** North Korea
122 H5 **Pocket Knife Lake** Newfoundland and Labrador Canada
227 G3 **Pocking** Germany
243 H3 **Pocklington** East Riding of Yorkshire England UK
157 E5 **Poço Verde** Brazil
157 D6 **Poções** Brazil
127 N7 **Pocomoke City** Maryland USA
159 D5 **Poconchile** Chile
159 G5 **Poconé** Brazil
157 C8 **Poços de Caldas** Brazil
134 D5 **Pocrí** Panama
234 B2 **Pocsaj** Hungary
235 C5 **Podareš** Macedonia
225 P4 **Podberez'ye** Russian Federation
225 P4 **Podberez'ye** Russian Federation
238 C4 **Podborov'ye** Russian Federation
232 G4 **Podbrđde** Bosnia and Herzegovina
232 G4 **Podbrdo** Bosnia and Herzegovina
227 H4 **Podčetrtek** Slovenia
225 P4 **Poddor'ye** Russian Federation
389 M5 **Podeba Peak** *mountain* Kyrgyzstan
227 H1 **Podelzig** Germany
232 H5 **Podgorica** Montenegro
236 R7 **Podgornoye** Russian Federation
389 N1 **Podgornoye** Russian Federation
237 AE9 **Podgornyy** Kuril Islands
387 K2 **Podgornyy** Russian Federation
234 C1 **Podhorod'** Slovakia
232 G5 **Podhum** Bosnia and Herzegovina
393 E8 **Podile** Andhra Pradesh India
234 D2 **Podişul Transilvaniei (Transylvanian Basin)** *region* Romania
232 G2 **Podivín** Czech Republic
227 K2 **Podkarpackie** *admin. area* Poland
238 H5 **Podkhozheye** Russian Federation
235 D5 **Podkova** Bulgaria
238 B6 **Podkozel'ye** Belarus
227 L1 **Podlaskie** *admin. area* Poland
234 E2 **Podoleni** Romania
238 G5 **Podol'sk** Russian Federation
300 D5 **Podor** Senegal
234 D1 **Podorozhnoye** Ukraine
238 F2 **Podporozh'ye** Russian Federation
225 O4 **Podsevy** Russian Federation
158 A2 **Poechos, Reservorio** *lake* Peru
309 G4 **Poelela, Lagoa** *lake* Mozambique
234 C2 **Poeni** Romania
308 C5 **Pofadder** South Africa
394 E2 **Pogar** Russian Federation
229 J5 **Poggio Alti** *mountain* Italy
232 D5 **Poggibonsi** Italy
232 E5 **Poggiodomo** Italy
227 H3 **Pöggstall** Austria
237 AD8 **Pogibi** Russian Federation
234 B4 **Pogled** *mountain* Serbia
238 F4 **Pogoreloye** Russian Federation
235 B5 **Pogradec** Albania
372 B4 **Poh** Indonesia
386 F4 **P'ohang** South Korea
225 F5 **Pohangina** New Zealand
223 O4 **Pohjanmaa** *region* Finland
223 O3 **Pohjaslahti** Finland
223 P4 **Pohjavaara** Finland
225 N1 **Pohjois-Virmas** *lake* Finland
426 6 **Pohnpei** *admin. area* Federated States of Micronesia
426 6 **Pohnpei** *island* Federated States of Micronesia
227 K3 **Pohorelá** Slovakia
234 F1 **Pohrebyshche** Ukraine
392 D6 **Pohri** Madhya Pradesh India
234 D3 **Poiana Mărului** Romania
306 C4 **Poie** Democratic Republic of Congo
234 D2 **Poienile de Sub Munte** Romania
372 C3 **Poigar** Indonesia
155 H4 **Poimró** Brazil
437 H2 **Poinsett, Cape** Antarctica
126 C4 **Poinsett, Lake** South Dakota USA
130 D4 **Point** Texas USA
124 D7 **Point Arena** California USA
130 F6 **Point au Fer Island** Louisiana USA
424 I3 **Point Blaze** NT Australia
424 E5 **Point Cloates** WA Australia
163 9 **Point Fortin** Trinidad and Tobago
163 9 **Point Fortin** *admin. area* Trinidad and Tobago
116 C5 **Point Hope** Alaska USA
116 H5 **Point Lake** Northwest Territories Canada
123 K9 **Point Lance** Newfoundland and Labrador Canada
116 C5 **Point Lay** Alaska USA
424 G8 **Point Malcolm** WA Australia
127 N6 **Point Pleasant** New Jersey USA
127 J7 **Point Pleasant** West Virginia USA
228 F4 **Point Sublime** France
123 E8 **Pointe-à-la-Croix** Québec Canada
163 I5 **Pointe-à-Peine** *cape* Dominica
163 9 **Pointe-à-Pierre** Trinidad and Tobago
163 I6 **Pointe-à-Pitre** Guadeloupe
127 K4 **Pointe au Baril Station** Ontario Canada
123 D8 **Pointe-Lebel** Québec Canada
163 I5 **Pointe Michel** Dominica
305 G5 **Pointe-Noire** Congo
163 I6 **Pointe-Noire** Guadeloupe
241 G2 **Pointon** Lincolnshire England UK
128 inset **Poipu** Hawai'i USA
226 D5 **Poirino** Italy
424 F4 **Poissonnier Point** WA Australia
121 W6 **Poissons** *watercourse* Newfoundland and Labrador Canada
226 C3 **Poissons** France
226 B3 **Poissy** France
228 E3 **Poitiers** France
228 E3 **Poitou** *region* France
228 D4 **Poitou-Charentes** *admin. area* France
310 9 **Poivre Islands** Seychelles
241 I5 **Poix-de-Picardie** France
226 C3 **Poix-Terron** France
227 I1 **Pojezierze Pomorskie** *region* Poland
129 I3 **Pojoaque** New Mexico USA
392 C5 **Pokaran** Rajasthan India
422 F3 **Pokeno** New Zealand
392 F5 **Pokhara** Nepal
223 N2 **Pokka** Finland
306 D3 **Poko** Democratic Republic of Congo
238 F5 **Pokrov** Russian Federation
389 K5 **Pokrovka** Kyrgyzstan
234 G2 **Pokrovka** Ukraine
234 G2 **Pokrovs'ke** Ukraine
388 C4 **Pokrovskoye** Russian Federation
227 H5 **Pokupsko** Croatia
391 K2 **Pol-e 'Alam** Afghanistan
390 F2 **Pol-e Dokhtar** Iran
389 J7 **Pol-e Khomri** Afghanistan
225 P4 **Pola** Russian Federation
230 D2 **Pola de Laviana** Spain
230 D2 **Pola de Lena** Spain
230 C2 **Pola de Somiedo** Spain
232 G5 **Polače** Croatia
227 J1 **Poland** *country* Europe
426 1a **Poland** Kiribati
227 K2 **Połaniec** Poland
158 D6 **Polapi, Cerro** *mountain* Chile
436 V1 **Polar Plateau** Antarctica
225 O5 **Polatsk** Belarus
244 D5 **Polbae** Dumfries and Galloway Scotland UK
244 C2 **Polbain** Highland Scotland UK
222 L3 **Polcirkeln** Sweden
160 D6 **Polcura** Chile
224 I5 **Pólczno** Poland
223 U5 **Pole** Russian Federation
434 O1 **Pole Abyssal Plain** *underwater feature* Arctic Ocean
372 D4 **Polee** *island* Indonesia
241 H4 **Polegate** East Sussex England UK
121 Q3 **Polemond** *watercourse* Québec Canada
225 K5 **Polessk** Russian Federation
372 A4 **Polewali** Indonesia
227 K4 **Polgár** Hungary
305 G3 **Poli** Cameroon
235 B5 **Poliçan** Albania
233 F7 **Policastro, Golfo di** *bay* Italy
227 H1 **Police** Poland
227 I3 **Polička** Czech Republic
233 G6 **Policoro** Italy
229 G3 **Poligny** France
235 C5 **Polikrapion** Greece
377 I4 **Polillo** *island* Philippines
377 I4 **Polillo Islands** Philippines
233 G7 **Polistena** Italy
232 H5 **Polje** Bosnia and Herzegovina
232 G5 **Polje** Croatia
227 I2 **Polkowice** Poland
131 K3 **Polkton** North Carolina USA
244 D2 **Polla** Highland Scotland UK
393 D9 **Pollachi** Tamil Nadu India
226 E2 **Polle** Germany
224 C3 **Pollestad** Norway
119 P7 **Pollockville** Alberta Canada
245 E4 **Pollrone** Ireland
242 B4 **Pollshane** Ireland
423 C7 **Pollux, Mount** New Zealand
223 P1 **Polmak** Norway
222 O2 **Polmakvatnet** *lake* Finland
227 I1 **Polne** Poland
126 G6 **Polo** Illinois USA
394 F3 **Pologi** Ukraine
308 E4 **Polokwane** South Africa
377 J6 **Polomolok** Philippines
225 O4 **Polonoye** Russian Federation
225 O5 **Polota** Belarus
237 AC5 **Polousnyy, Kryazh** *range* Russian Federation
227 L5 **Polovragi** Romania
240 C2 **Polperro** Cornwall England UK
240 C4 **Polruan** Cornwall England UK
124 H3 **Polson** Montana USA
232 H2 **Poltár** Slovakia
394 E3 **Poltava** Ukraine
394 E3 **Poltavs'ka Oblast'** *admin. area* Ukraine
389 K2 **Poludino** Kazakhstan
393 E9 **Polur** Tamil Nadu India
225 N3 **Põlva** Estonia
129 I3 **Polvadera** New Mexico USA
225 N3 **Põlvamaa** *admin. area* Estonia
223 P5 **Polvela** Finland
223 P5 **Polvijärvi** Finland
235 D7 **Polyaigos** *island* Greece
388 C5 **Polyana** Russian Federation
234 C1 **Polyana** Ukraine
223 R2 **Polyarnyy** Russian Federation
236 N5 **Polyarnyy Ural** *range* Russian Federation
223 R3 **Polyarnyye Zori** Russian Federation
235 C5 **Polygyros** Greece
372 E4 **Pom** Indonesia
158 B3 **Pomabamba** Peru
232 D5 **Pomarance** Italy
225 L2 **Pomarkku** Finland
232 H3 **Pomáz** Hungary
156 E4 **Pombal** Brazil
230 B4 **Pombal** Portugal
235 D8 **Pómbia** Greece
155 G3 **Pomeroon Point** *cape* Guyana
155 G3 **Pomeroon-Supenaam** *admin. area* Guyana
242 B2 **Pomeroy** Cookstown Northern Ireland UK
124 G3 **Pomeroy** Washington USA
233 E6 **Pomezia** Italy
308 D5 **Pomfret** South Africa
234 G1 **Pomichna** Ukraine
126 E8 **Pomme de Terre Lake** Missouri USA
224 H5 **Pommersche Bucht** *bay* Germany
223 O3 **Pomokaira** *island* Finland
128 D3 **Pomona** California USA
126 D7 **Pomona Lake** Kansas USA
234 E4 **Pomoriysko Ezero** *lake* Bulgaria
227 I1 **Pomorskie** *admin. area* Poland
131 K7 **Pompano Beach** Florida USA
157 C7 **Pompeéu** Brazil
159 G2 **Pompeu** Brazil
133 H4 **Pomuch** Mexico
120 I5 **Ponask Lake** Ontario Canada
125 Q8 **Ponca City** Oklahoma USA
135 G3 **Ponce** Puerto Rico
131 K8 **Ponce De Leon Bay** Florida USA
125 L7 **Poncha Springs** Colorado USA
121 Q7 **Poncheville, Lac** *lake* Québec Canada
125 Q8 **Pond Creek** Oklahoma USA
117 L4 **Pond Inlet** Nunavut Canada
154 C2 **Ponedera** Colombia
232 C5 **Ponente, Riviera di** *coast* Italy
426 7 **Ponérihouen** New Caledonia
238 E6 **Ponetovka** Russian Federation
230 C2 **Ponferrada** Spain
376 D3 **Pong** Thailand
305 F4 **Pongara, Pointe** *cape* Gabon
422 G5 **Pongaroa** New Zealand
386 F4 **Ponghwa** South Korea
306 D2 **Pongo** *watercourse* Sudan
309 F5 **Pongola** South Africa
304 D2 **Poni** *watercourse* Burkina Faso
227 I2 **Poniec** Poland
372 B4 **Ponindilisa, Tanjung** *cape* Indonesia
225 P5 **Ponizov'ye** Russian Federation
393 D9 **Ponnani** Kerala India
372 E5 **Pono** Indonesia
119 O6 **Ponoka** Alberta Canada
375 F5 **Ponorogo** Indonesia
377 I5 **Ponot** Philippines
236 J5 **Ponoy** Russian Federation
236 I5 **Ponoy** *watercourse* Russian Federation
372 B4 **Ponrang** Indonesia
121 U5 **Pons** *watercourse* Québec Canada
228 D4 **Pons** France
229 G1 **Pont-à-Celles** Belgium
229 H2 **Pont-à-Mousson** France
240 C3 **Pont Antwn** Carmarthenshire Wales UK
229 G3 **Pont-d'Ain** France
228 F4 **Pont-de-Salars** France
231 G2 **Pont de Suert** Spain
228 B3 **Pont-l'Abbé** France
240 D2 **Pont-Rhyd** Powys Wales UK
229 G4 **Pont-St-Esprit** France
310 1b **Ponta da Divisão** Brazil
310 1b **Ponta da Ilha** *cape* Azores
310 1b **Ponta da Terra** *cape* Azores
310 1a **Ponta Delgada** Azores
310 1b **Ponta do Arrife** *cape* Azores
310 1b **Ponta do Pico** *volcano* Azores
310 2 **Ponta do Sol** Madeira
157 B9 **Ponta Grossa** Brazil
159 H6 **Ponta Porã** Brazil
228 D5 **Pontacq** France
157 B8 **Pontal** Brazil
156 D5 **Pontal** *watercourse* Brazil
157 B9 **Pontal do Paraná** Brazil
157 B7 **Pontalina** Brazil
240 D3 **Pontardawe** Neath Port Talbot Wales UK
240 C3 **Pontardulais** Carmarthenshire Wales UK
229 H3 **Pontarlier** France
228 F4 **Pontaumur** France
121 Q7 **Pontax** *watercourse* Québec Canada
130 F5 **Pontchartrain, Lake** Louisiana USA
228 C3 **Pontchâteau** France
157 A7 **Ponte Branca** Brazil
159 G4 **Ponte de Pedra** Brazil
230 B4 **Ponte de Sor** Portugal
233 C5 **Ponte-Leccia** Corsica France
157 D8 **Ponte Nova** Brazil
230 B2 **Ponteareas** Spain
226 G4 **Pontebba** Italy
243 G3 **Pontefract** West Yorkshire England UK
159 H5 **Ponteira** Brazil
119 R8 **Ponteix** Saskatchewan Canada
243 G1 **Ponteland** Northumberland England UK
240 D2 **Ponterwyd** Ceredigion Wales UK
159 G4 **Pontes e Lacerda** Brazil
240 E2 **Pontesbury** Shropshire England UK
230 B2 **Pontevedra** Spain
126 G6 **Pontiac** Illinois USA
374 F4 **Pontianak** Indonesia
226 B4 **Pontigny** France
228 D2 **Pontmain** France
157 D5 **Ponto Novo** Brazil
119 V5 **Ponton** Manitoba Canada
228 D5 **Pontonx-sur-l'Adour** France
245 C3 **Pontoon** Ireland
232 C4 **Pontremoli** Italy
229 I3 **Pontresina** Switzerland
240 D2 **Pontrhydfendigaid** Ceredigion Wales UK
240 E3 **Pontrilas** Herefordshire England UK
240 D3 **Pontsticill** Powys Wales UK
240 D3 **Pontypridd** Rhondda Cynon Taff Wales UK
422 F3 **Ponui Island** New Zealand
233 E6 **Ponza, Isola di** *island* Italy
233 E6 **Ponziane, Isole** *island* Italy
425 J8 **Poochera** SA Australia
305 G5 **Pool** *admin. area* Congo
240 D2 **Pool Quay** Powys Wales UK
240 F4 **Poole** *admin. area* England UK
241 F4 **Poole** Poole England UK
241 F4 **Poole Bay** England UK
244 C3 **Poolewe** Highland Scotland UK
425 L8 **Pooncarie** NSW Australia
158 E5 **Poopó** Bolivia
158 E5 **Poopó, Lago** *lake* Bolivia
422 F2 **Poor Knights Islands** New Zealand
225 N3 **Pööra** Estonia
119 U2 **Poorfish Lake** Nunavut Canada
379 H5 **Popa, Mount** *mountain* Myanmar
225 K4 **Pope** Latvia
234 C2 **Popeşti** Romania
241 F3 **Popham** Hampshire England UK
120 G6 **Poplar** *watercourse* Manitoba Canada
125 M2 **Poplar** Montana USA
125 M2 **Poplar** *watercourse* Montana USA
126 F3 **Poplar** Wisconsin USA
126 F8 **Poplar Bluff** Missouri USA
118 G1 **Poplar Creek** British Columbia Canada
120 H6 **Poplar Hill** Ontario Canada
130 G5 **Poplarville** Mississippi USA
375 F6 **Popoh** Indonesia
233 E5 **Popoli** Italy
426 8a **Popomanaseu, Mount** Solomon Islands
232 H5 **Popov Do** Montenegro
225 O4 **Popovka** Russian Federation
238 G5 **Popovka** Russian Federation
238 H2 **Popovka** Russian Federation
154 B4 **Popayán** Colombia
227 K3 **Poprad** Slovakia
133 G5 **Poptún** Guatemala
422 G5 **Porangahau** New Zealand
157 B6 **Porangatu** Brazil
227 M1 **Porazava** Belarus
393 B7 **Porbandar** Gujarat India
118 F6 **Porcher Island** British Columbia Canada
226 G5 **Porcia** Italy
157 D8 **Porciúncula** Brazil
157 C6 **Porcos** *watercourse* Brazil
234 C2 **Porcsalma** Hungary
230 D5 **Porcuna** Spain
116 E5 **Porcupine** *watercourse* Alaska USA
122 J6 **Porcupine, Cape** Newfoundland and Labrador Canada
76 Q5 **Porcupine Abyssal Plain** *underwater feature* Atlantic Ocean
76 Q4 **Porcupine Bank** *underwater feature* Atlantic Ocean
119 T6 **Porcupine Plain** Saskatchewan Canada
228 C2 **Pordic** France
229 J3 **Pordoi, Passo** *pass* Italy
154 D3 **Pore** Colombia
232 E4 **Poreč** Croatia
157 B8 **Porecatu** Brazil
225 P4 **Porech'ye** Russian Federation
238 F5 **Porech'ye** Russian Federation
238 G3 **Porech'ye** Russian Federation
238 H4 **Porech'ye-Rybnoye** Russian Federation
162 D2 **Pórfido, Punta** *cape* Argentina
304 E2 **Porga** Benin
225 K2 **Pori** Finland
244 D3 **Porin** Highland Scotland UK
423 F5 **Porirua** New Zealand
222 K3 **Porjus** Sweden
225 O4 **Porkhov** Russian Federation
225 M3 **Porkkala** *peninsula* Finland
225 M3 **Porkkalafjärden** *bay* Finland
155 F2 **Porlamar** Venezuela
240 D3 **Porlock** Somerset England UK
230 D2 **Porma** *watercourse* Spain
228 B5 **Porma, Embalse de** *lake* Spain
234 D1 **Pormortsy** Ukraine
425 L3 **Pormpuraaw** Qld Australia
228 C3 **Pornic** France
222 L2 **Porojärvi** *lake* Finland
223 P3 **Porokylä** Finland
237 AD9 **Poronaysk** Russian Federation
375 G5 **Porong** Indonesia
376 E4 **Porông** *watercourse* Cambodia
235 B6 **Poros** Greece
235 C7 **Poros** Greece
223 R5 **Porosozero** Russian Federation
227 K4 **Poroszló** Hungary
223 Q2 **Porovaara** Russian Federation
234 E4 **Poroy** Bulgaria
232 F4 **Porozina** Croatia
437 I2 **Porpoise Bay** Antarctica
423 C8 **Porpoise Bay** New Zealand
229 H3 **Porrentruy** Switzerland
245 C3 **Porridgetown** Ireland
223 O1 **Porsangen** *bay* Norway
223 N1 **Porsangerhalvøya** *peninsula* Norway
374 C3 **Porsea** Indonesia
222 L3 **Porsi** Sweden
235 G6 **Porsuk** *watercourse* Turkey
235 G6 **Porsuk Barajı** *lake* Turkey
306 E3 **Port** Democratic Republic of Congo
245 D2 **Port** Ireland
222 O2 **Port** Norway
118 I8 **Port Alberni** British Columbia Canada
422 F3 **Port Albert** New Zealand
118 D4 **Port Alexander** Alaska USA
308 E6 **Port Alfred** South Africa
118 H7 **Port Alice** British Columbia Canada
130 F5 **Port Allen** Louisiana USA
124 D2 **Port Angeles** Washington USA
244 C4 **Port Appin** Argyll and Bute Scotland UK
425 M10 **Port Arthur** Tas. Australia
130 E6 **Port Arthur** Texas USA
244 B5 **Port Askaig** Argyll and Bute Scotland UK
123 I8 **Port au Port Bay** Newfoundland and Labrador Canada
123 I8 **Port au Port Peninsula** Newfoundland and Labrador Canada
135 F3 **Port-au-Prince** Haiti
425 K8 **Port Augusta** SA Australia
126 J4 **Port Austin** Michigan USA
310 6b **Port-aux-Français** French Southern and Antarctic Lands
231 H2 **Port-Barcarès** France
130 F5 **Port Barre** Louisiana USA
376 B5 **Port Blair** Andaman and Nicobar Islands India
123 K8 **Port Blandford** Newfoundland and Labrador Canada
425 L9 **Port Campbell** Vic. Australia
121 V7 **Port-Cartier** Québec Canada
422 F3 **Port Charles** New Zealand
244 B5 **Port Charlotte** Argyll and Bute Scotland UK
118 E6 **Port Clements** British Columbia Canada
423 B8 **Port Craig** New Zealand
123 F8 **Port-Daniel, Baie de** Québec Canada
374 D3 **Port Dickson** Malaysia
425 M4 **Port Douglas** Qld Australia
118 F5 **Port Edward** British Columbia Canada
308 F6 **Port Edward** South Africa
308 E6 **Port Elizabeth** South Africa
163 11 **Port Elizabeth** St Vincent and the Grenadines
244 B5 **Port Ellen** Argyll and Bute Scotland UK
242 D2 **Port Erin** Isle of Man UK
118 G5 **Port Essington** British Columbia Canada
240 C3 **Port-Eynon** Swansea Wales UK
422 F3 **Port Fitzroy** New Zealand
305 F5 **Port-Gentil** Gabon
130 F5 **Port Gibson** Mississippi USA
305 F4 **Port Harcourt** Nigeria
118 H7 **Port Hardy** British Columbia Canada
423 E5 **Port Hardy** New Zealand
123 H10 **Port Hawkesbury** Nova Scotia Canada
424 F5 **Port Hedland** WA Australia
127 O4 **Port Henry** New York USA
127 L5 **Port Hope** Ontario Canada
122 J6 **Port Hope Simpson** Newfoundland and Labrador Canada
163 7 **Port Howard** Falkland Islands
127 J5 **Port Huron** Michigan USA
130 C7 **Port Isabel** Texas USA
228 C3 **Port-Joinville** France
228 F5 **Port-la-Nouvelle** France
377 I6 **Port Languyan** Philippines
130 C6 **Port Lavaca** Texas USA
127 N5 **Port Leyden** New York USA
425 J8 **Port Lincoln** SA Australia
244 D6 **Port Logan** Dumfries and Galloway Scotland UK
127 L4 **Port Loring** Ontario Canada
163 I6 **Port-Louis** Guadeloupe
310 7b **Port Louis** Mauritius
118 H7 **Port McNeill** British Columbia Canada
425 O7 **Port Macquarie** NSW Australia
134 E3 **Port Maria** Jamaica
118 J8 **Port Mellon** British Columbia Canada
123 F8 **Port-Menier** Québec Canada
116 C7 **Port Moller** Alaska USA
244 B4 **Port Mor** Highland Scotland UK
373 H6 **Port Moresby** Papua New Guinea
123 F11 **Port Mouton Island** Nova Scotia Canada
244 B3 **Port na Long** Highland Scotland UK
244 B2 **Port nan Giuran** Na h-Eileanan Siar Scotland UK
244 A3 **Port nan Long** Na h-Eileanan Siar Scotland UK
135 F2 **Port Nelson** Bahamas
120 I4 **Port Nelson** Manitoba Canada
124 B1 **Port Neville** British Columbia Canada
244 B2 **Port Nis** Na h-Eileanan Siar Scotland UK
308 C5 **Port Nolloth** South Africa
163 9 **Port of Spain** Trinidad and Tobago
163 9 **Port of Spain** *admin. area* Trinidad and Tobago
422 G3 **Port Ohope** New Zealand
131 K6 **Port Orange** Florida USA
124 C5 **Port Orford** Oregon USA
127 L4 **Port Perry** Ontario Canada

425 K8 **Port Pirie** SA Australia
240 C4 **Port Quin** Cornwall England UK
118 I8 **Port Renfrew** British Columbia Canada
127 K5 **Port Rowan** Ontario Canada
131 K4 **Port Royal** South Carolina USA
131 K4 **Port Royal Sound** South Carolina USA
131 I6 **Port Saint Joe** Florida USA
229 G5 **Port-St-Louis-du-Rhône** France
131 K7 **Port Saint Lucie** Florida USA
242 D2 **Port St Mary** Isle of Man UK
126 J5 **Port Sanilac** Michigan USA
123 J7 **Port Saunders** Newfoundland and Labrador Canada
308 F6 **Port Shepstone** South Africa
163 7 **Port Stephens** Falkland Islands
302 F4 **Port Sudan** Sudan
240 D3 **Port Talbot** Neath Port Talbot Wales UK
228 F5 **Port-Vendres** France
426 7 **Port-Vila** Vanuatu
223 R2 **Port-Vladimir** Russian Federation
422 F3 **Port Waikato** New Zealand
425 K8 **Port Wakefield** SA Australia
126 H5 **Port Washington** Wisconsin USA
244 D6 **Port William** Dumfries and Galloway Scotland UK
126 F3 **Port Wing** Wisconsin USA
310 4a **Porta Gouveia** Cape Verde
244 C5 **Portachoillan** Argyll and Bute Scotland UK
159 F5 **Portachuelo** Bolivia
154 B4 **Portachuelo, Cordillera** *range* Colombia
245 F2 **Portadown** Armagh Northern Ireland UK
126 I5 **Portage** Michigan USA
124 I6 **Portage** Utah USA
120 F8 **Portage La Prairie** Manitoba Canada
127 Q3 **Portage Lake** Maine USA
242 A1 **Portahack** Ireland
125 N2 **Portal** North Dakota USA
230 C4 **Portalegre** Portugal
230 C4 **Portalegre** *admin. area* Portugal
129 K3 **Portales** New Mexico USA
230 C2 **Portas, Embalse das** *lake* Spain
244 C5 **Portavadie** Argyll and Bute Scotland UK
245 G2 **Portavogie** Ards Northern Ireland UK
228 D2 **Portbail** France
127 L7 **Porte Crayon, Mount** West Virginia USA
155 G5 **Porteira** Brazil
156 B5 **Portel** Brazil
230 C4 **Portel** Portugal
130 D3 **Porter** Oklahoma USA
119 R4 **Porter Lake** Saskatchewan Canada
118 F3 **Porter Landing** British Columbia Canada
163 11a **Porter Point** *cape* St Vincent and the Grenadines
128 C2 **Porterville** California USA
240 B3 **Portfield Gate** Pembrokeshire Wales UK
244 E2 **Portgower** Highland Scotland UK
240 D3 **Porth** Rhondda Cynon Taff Wales UK
240 B4 **Porthleven** Cornwall England UK
240 C4 **Portholland** Cornwall England UK
240 B4 **Porthoustock** Cornwall England UK
240 C3 **Porthyrhyd** Carmarthenshire Wales UK
233 C6 **Porticcio** Corsica France
230 D3 **Portillo** Spain
230 B5 **Portimão** Portugal
223 O3 **Portimo** Finland
231 G4 **Portinatx** Spain
240 E3 **Portishead** North Somerset England UK
244 F3 **Portknockie** Moray Scotland UK
425 L9 **Portland** Vic. Australia
130 F4 **Portland** Arkansas USA
127 P5 **Portland** Maine USA
124 D4 **Portland** Oregon USA
130 C7 **Portland** Texas USA
123 J7 **Portland Creek Pond** Newfoundland and Labrador Canada
240 E4 **Portland Harbour** England UK
118 F5 **Portland Inlet** British Columbia Canada
422 G4 **Portland Island** New Zealand
163 12 **Portland Point** Jamaica
425 L3 **Portland Roads** Qld Australia
245 E3 **Portlaoise** Ireland
245 E4 **Portlaw** Ireland
244 F3 **Portlethen** Aberdeenshire Scotland UK
134 E3 **Portmore** Jamaica
123 D8 **Portneuf-sur-Mer** Québec Canada
237 V4 **Portnyagino, Ozero** *lake* Russian Federation
156 D3 **Porto** Brazil
233 C5 **Porto** Corsica France
230 B3 **Porto** Portugal
230 B3 **Porto** *admin. area* Portugal
156 A4 **Porto Alegre** Brazil
161 I4 **Porto Alegre** Brazil
157 A8 **Porto Alegre** Brazil
158 E3 **Pôrto Alegre** Brazil
159 F4 **Porto Amarante** Brazil
308 B2 **Porto Amboim** Angola
154 E5 **Porto Antunes** Brazil
155 I4 **Pôrto Arari** Brazil
232 D5 **Porto Azzurro** Italy
157 A8 **Pôrto Barra do Ivinheima** Brazil
161 I3 **Porto Belo** Brazil
159 F3 **Pôrto Bicentenário** Brazil
159 H3 **Pôrto Cajueiro** Brazil
159 H5 **Pôrto Cedro** Brazil
159 H2 **Pôrto da Lontra** Brazil
159 F4 **Pôrto da Telha** Brazil
157 A6 **Pôrto de Meinacos** Brazil
156 A3 **Pôrto de Moz** Brazil
159 H4 **Pôrto do Angico** Brazil
159 H5 **Pôrto do Massacás** Brazil
159 F4 **Pôrto do Palhal** Brazil
159 G2 **Pôrto do Sará** Brazil
159 G5 **Pôrto dos Gaúchos** Brazil
159 H4 **Pôrto dos Meinacos** Brazil
233 E8 **Porto Empedocle** Italy
159 G4 **Porto Esperança** Brazil
159 G4 **Porto Esperidião** Brazil
157 C8 **Pôrto Feliz** Brazil
155 H5 **Pôrto Franco** Brazil
156 C4 **Pôrto Franco** Brazil
159 H4 **Pôrto Fundação** Brazil
159 H2 **Pôrto Fundo** Brazil
155 I4 **Pôrto Grande** Brazil
235 C7 **Pórto Káyio** Greece
159 G5 **Pôrto Manduri** Brazil
159 G6 **Pôrto Murtinho** Brazil
157 B5 **Porto Nacional** Brazil
304 E3 **Porto-Novo** Benin
310 4 **Porto Novo** Cape Verde
155 H4 **Pôrto Poet** Brazil
161 H2 **Porto Primavera, Represa** *lake* Brazil
232 E5 **Porto Recanati** Italy
232 E5 **Porto San Giorgio** Italy
229 K5 **Porto Sant'Elpidio** Italy
310 2 **Porto Santo, Ilha de** *island* Madeira
159 I3 **Pôrto São Domingos** Brazil
159 G5 **Pôrto São José Velho** Brazil
157 E7 **Pôrto Seguro** Brazil
159 G4 **Pôrto Tenente Marques** Brazil
233 C6 **Porto Torres** Sardinia Italy
157 B9 **Pôrto União** Brazil
159 F3 **Pôrto Velho** Brazil
159 I3 **Pôrto Velho** Brazil
158 C3 **Pôrto Walter** Brazil
134 E5 **Portobelo** Panama
222 L5 **Pörtom** Finland
159 F5 **Porton** Bolivia
154 A5 **Portoviejo** Ecuador
244 C6 **Portpatrick** Dumfries and Galloway Scotland UK
245 F3 **Portrane** Ireland
240 B4 **Portreath** Cornwall England UK
244 B3 **Portree** Highland Scotland UK
245 F1 **Portrush** Coleraine Northern Ireland UK
245 E1 **Portsalon** Ireland
241 F4 **Portsmouth** Hampshire England UK
127 P5 **Portsmouth** New Hampshire USA
126 J7 **Portsmouth** Ohio USA
127 M8 **Portsmouth** Virginia USA
127 P5 **Portsmouth Harbor** New Hampshire USA
244 F3 **Portsoy** Aberdeenshire Scotland UK
245 F1 **Portstewart** Coleraine Northern Ireland UK
223 O2 **Porttipahdan Tekojärvi** *lake* Finland
230 C4 **Portugal** *country* Europe
154 D2 **Portuguesa** *admin. area* Venezuela
154 C4 **Portuguesa, Nevado** *mountain* Peru
245 D3 **Portumna** Ireland
245 C2 **Porturlin** Ireland
127 L5 **Portville** New York USA
242 D2 **Portyerrock** Dumfries and Galloway Scotland UK
162 B5 **Porvenir** Chile
225 M2 **Porvoo/Borgå** Finland
223 N2 **Por'ya Guba** Russian Federation
230 D4 **Porzuna** Spain
228 F2 **Posad** Russian Federation
230 D2 **Posada** Spain
161 H3 **Posadas** Argentina
162 B4 **Posadas, Lago** *lake* Argentina
437 F2 **Posadowsky Bay** Antarctica
229 J3 **Poschiavo** Switzerland
154 C4 **Posco** Peru
162 C5 **Posesión, Bahía** *bay* Argentina
238 H3 **Poshekhon'ye Volodarsk** Russian Federation
223 P3 **Posio** Finland
223 P3 **Posionjärvi** *lake* Finland
372 B4 **Poso** Indonesia
375 I4 **Poso** *watercourse* Indonesia
372 B4 **Poso, Teluk** *bay* Indonesia
386 E4 **Posŏng** South Korea
389 N3 **Pospelikha** Russian Federation
130 C6 **Posse** Brazil
305 H3 **Possel** Central African Republic
310 6 **Possession, Île de la** *island* French Southern and Antarctic Lands
163 8 **Possession Bay** South Georgia
130 B4 **Possum Kingdom Lake** Texas USA
129 L4 **Post** Texas USA
124 G3 **Post Falls** Idaho USA
233 E5 **Posta** Italy
233 F6 **Posta Piana** Italy
301 G4 **Poste Weygand (Balise 250)** Algeria
226 G5 **Postioma** Italy
308 D5 **Postmasburg** South Africa
159 H3 **Pôsto Alto Manissaua** Brazil
159 H2 **Pôsto Cocraimoro** Brazil
159 H2 **Pôsto Curua** Brazil
159 F4 **Pôsto Fiscal Rolim de Moura** Brazil
159 H4 **Pôsto Indígena Batovi** Brazil
232 G5 **Posušje** Bosnia and Herzegovina
372 B6 **Pota** Indonesia
126 J3 **Potagannissing Bay** Michigan USA
132 C3 **Potam** Mexico
133 G5 **Potaro-Siparuni** *admin. area* Guyana
308 E5 **Potchefstroom** South Africa
233 D1 **Potcoava** Romania
130 B6 **Poteet** Texas USA
388 E3 **Potemkino** Russian Federation
233 F6 **Potenza** Italy
233 F6 **Potenza** *watercourse* Italy
233 E5 **Potenza Picena** Italy
423 B8 **Poteriteri, Lake** New Zealand
230 D2 **Potes** Spain
130 B6 **Poth** Texas USA
156 D4 **Poti** *watercourse* Brazil
388 D5 **Poti** Georgia
232 G5 **Potirna** Croatia
305 G2 **Potiskum** Nigeria
222 L2 **Potka** Norway
126 G4 **Potlatch** Idaho USA
426 7 **Potnarvin** Vanuatu
232 G5 **Potoci** Bosnia and Herzegovina
234 F1 **Potoki** Ukraine
126 F6 **Potomac** Illinois USA
127 M7 **Potomac** *watercourse* Virginia USA
127 M7 **Potomac** *watercourse* West Virginia USA
234 A1 **Pôtor** Slovakia
304 B3 **Potoru** Sierra Leone
159 E5 **Potosí** Bolivia
160 E2 **Potosí** *admin. area* Bolivia
134 C5 **Potosí** Nicaragua
126 F8 **Potosi** Missouri USA
126 F5 **Potosi** Wisconsin USA
159 G5 **Potrerito de la Noria** Bolivia
159 F5 **Potrero** Bolivia
154 C4 **Potrero** Colombia
127 N2 **Potrincourt Lake** Québec Canada
226 G1 **Potsdam** Germany
393 F7 **Pottangi** Orissa India
126 D7 **Pottawatomie** *watercourse* Kansas USA
125 N6 **Potter** Nebraska USA
121 W1 **Potter Island** Nunavut Canada
241 E3 **Potterne** Wiltshire England UK
241 G3 **Potters Bar** Hertfordshire England UK
244 F3 **Potterton** Aberdeenshire Scotland UK
245 E4 **Pottlerath** Ireland
122 J5 **Pottles Bay** Newfoundland and Labrador Canada
241 G2 **Potton** Bedfordshire England UK
130 E3 **Pottsville** Arkansas USA
127 M6 **Pottsville** Pennsylvania USA
393 E10 **Pottuvil** Sri Lanka
125 Q8 **Potwin** Kansas USA
228 D3 **Pouancé** France
118 K5 **Pouce Coupe** British Columbia Canada
310 7b **Poudre d'Or** Mauritius
127 O6 **Poughkeepsie** New York USA
226 B4 **Pouilly** France
127 O2 **Poularies** Québec Canada
245 C5 **Poulgorm Bridge** Ireland
127 P2 **Poulin-de-Courval, Lac** *lake* Québec Canada
423 D6 **Poulter** *watercourse* New Zealand
241 F3 **Poulton** Gloucestershire England UK
242 F3 **Poulton-le-Fylde** Lancashire England UK
426 7 **Poum** New Caledonia
235 D6 **Pounta, Akra** *cape* Greece
235 C6 **Pourion** Greece
160 F6 **Pourtalé** Argentina
157 C8 **Pouso Alegre** Brazil
159 G3 **Pouso Alegre** Brazil
223 P4 **Poussu** Finland
376 D4 **Poŭthĭsăt** Cambodia
304 D2 **Pouy-Tenga** Burkina Faso
228 D3 **Pouzauges** France
231 I1 **Pouzilhac** France
223 S5 **Povenets** Russian Federation
422 G4 **Poverty Bay** New Zealand
234 A3 **Povlen, Mali** *mountain* Serbia
230 B3 **Póvoa de Varzim** Portugal
388 D3 **Povorino** Russian Federation
386 G2 **Povorotnyy, Mys** *island* Russian Federation
127 L3 **Powassan** Ontario Canada
128 D4 **Poway** California USA
125 L4 **Powder** *watercourse* Wyoming USA
126 J6 **Powell** Ohio USA
125 K4 **Powell** Wyoming USA
128 G2 **Powell, Lake** Utah USA
425 J5 **Powell, Mount** NT Australia
118 I7 **Powell Lake** British Columbia Canada
134 E1 **Powell Point** Bahamas
118 I8 **Powell River** British Columbia Canada
131 J2 **Powell River** Tennessee USA
245 D5 **Power Head** *cape* Ireland
125 N2 **Powers Lake** North Dakota USA
120 G7 **Powerview** Manitoba Canada
127 M8 **Powhatan** Virginia USA
241 E2 **Powick** Worcestershire England UK
227 I1 **Powidz** Poland
240 D2 **Powys** *admin. area* Wales UK
159 H4 **Poxoréo** Brazil
426 7 **Poya** New Caledonia
374 A3 **Poyan Reservoir** Singapore
381 G3 **Poyang** Jiangxi China
381 G2 **Poyang Hu** *lake* Jiangxi China
385 K2 **Poyarkovo** Russian Federation
126 G4 **Poygan, Lake** Wisconsin USA
245 F2 **Poyntz Pass** Armagh Northern Ireland UK
230 B2 **Poyo** Spain
235 F6 **Poyrazdamları** Turkey
223 N2 **Pöyrisjärvi** *lake* Finland
225 N2 **Pöyry** Finland
225 L2 **Pöytyä** Finland
133 F4 **Poza Rica** Mexico
232 G4 **Požega** Croatia
235 K5 **Pozezdrze** Poland
238 C4 **Pozherevitsy** Russian Federation
394 E2 **Pozhnya** *watercourse* Ukraine
227 I1 **Poznań** Poland
227 I4 **Poznanovec** Croatia
230 E5 **Pozo Alcón** Spain
160 F2 **Pozo Anta** Paraguay
155 F3 **Pozo Azul** Venezuela
159 F4 **Pozo Blanco** Bolivia
161 G2 **Pozo Colorado** Paraguay
159 G5 **Pozo de Buey** Paraguay
160 E3 **Pozo Hondo** Argentina
230 D4 **Pozoblanco** Spain
230 D4 **Pozohondo** Spain
162 D2 **Pozos, Punta** *cape* Argentina
158 C3 **Pozuzo** Peru
233 F8 **Pozzallo** Italy
233 F8 **Pozzillo, Lago di** *lake* Italy
233 C6 **Pozzo di Borgo, Punta di** *mountain* Corsica France
233 F6 **Pozzuoli** Italy
233 F6 **Pozzuolo** Italy
304 D3 **Pra** *watercourse* Ghana
373 F6 **Prabumulih** Indonesia
230 B4 **Pracana, Barragem de** *lake* Portugal
227 F4 **Prachatice** Czech Republic
230 C2 **Prada, Embalse de** *lake* Spain
227 I2 **Praděd** *mountain* Czech Republic
228 F4 **Pradelles** France
154 B4 **Pradera** Colombia
228 F5 **Prades** France
157 E7 **Prado** Brazil
154 C4 **Prado** Colombia
Prague *see* **Praha** Czech Republic
227 H2 **Praha** *admin. area* Czech Republic
227 H2 **Praha (Prague)** Czech Republic
232 D3 **Prahecq** France
234 D3 **Prahova** *admin. area* Romania
227 L5 **Prahovo** Serbia
310 4a **Praia** Cape Verde
310 1b **Praia da Vitória** Azores
309 F5 **Praia do Bilene** Mozambique
310 1b **Praia do Norte** Azores
155 F5 **Praia do Vinte e Oito** Brazil
157 C9 **Praia Grande** Brazil
234 D2 **Praid** Romania
310 1b **Prainha** Azores
155 I5 **Prainha** Brazil
156 A3 **Prainha** Brazil
124 F4 **Prairie City** Oregon USA
129 L3 **Prairie Dog Town Fork of the Red** *watercourse* Texas USA
126 F5 **Prairie du Chien** Wisconsin USA
125 P7 **Prairie View** Kansas USA
376 D4 **Prakhon Chai** Thailand
376 C4 **Pran Buri** Thailand
225 M3 **Prangli** *island* Estonia
134 D4 **Pranza** Nicaragua
374 C3 **Prapat** Indonesia
310 9a **Praslin** *island* Seychelles
163 13 **Praslin** St Lucia
162 A4 **Prat, Isla** *island* Chile
157 B8 **Prata** Brazil
157 B7 **Prata** *watercourse* Brazil
392 D6 **Pratapgarh** Rajasthan India
392 E6 **Pratapgarh** Uttar Pradesh India
381 G5 **Pratas Island** China
232 D5 **Prato** Italy
228 F5 **Prats-de-Mollo-la-Preste** France
125 P8 **Pratt** Kansas USA
434 U3 **Pratt Seamount** *underwater feature* Pacific Ocean
131 H4 **Prattville** Alabama USA
229 G3 **Prauthoy** France
230 C2 **Pravia** Spain
227 I2 **Prawików** Poland
132 D2 **Praxédis Guerrero** Mexico
375 H6 **Praya** Indonesia
225 O5 **Prazaroki** Belarus
376 E4 **Preah** *watercourse* Cambodia
238 E5 **Prechistoye** Russian Federation
227 I5 **Predavac** Croatia
227 G4 **Predlitz** Austria
226 G4 **Predoi** Italy
232 H5 **Predolje** Bosnia and Herzegovina
232 F4 **Predošćica** Croatia
242 F3 **Preesall** Lancashire England UK
224 F5 **Preetz** Germany
121 N1 **Prefontaine, Cape** Nunavut Canada
122 K5 **Pregolya** *watercourse* Russian Federation
232 F3 **Pregrada** Croatia
225 N4 **Preiļi** Latvia
225 N4 **Preiļu** *admin. area* Latvia
127 L2 **Preissac, Lac** *lake* Québec Canada
232 F1 **Přelouč** Czech Republic
232 E4 **Premantura** Croatia
228 F3 **Prémery** France
118 F4 **Premier** British Columbia Canada
130 B7 **Premont** Texas USA
227 J3 **Prenčov** Slovakia
234 F2 **Prenistrului, Dealurile** *range* Moldova
126 F4 **Prentice** Wisconsin USA
130 G5 **Prentiss** Mississippi USA
237 AI8 **Preobrazhenskoye** Russian Federation
376 B4 **Preparis Island** Andaman and Nicobar Islands India
376 B4 **Preparis North Channel** Andaman and Nicobar Islands India
376 B4 **Preparis South Channel** Andaman and Nicobar Islands India
232 G2 **Přerov** Czech Republic
224 G5 **Prerow** Germany
233 G6 **Presciutto, Punta** *cape* Italy
128 F3 **Prescott** Arizona USA
130 E4 **Prescott** Arkansas USA
124 F3 **Prescott** Washington USA
128 F3 **Prescott Valley** Arizona USA
423 B8 **Preservation Inlet** New Zealand
125 O5 **Presho** South Dakota USA
160 F3 **Presidencia Roque Sáenz Peña** Argentina
79 R10 **President Thiers Seamount** *underwater feature* Pacific Ocean
157 B8 **Presidente Bernardes** Brazil
156 C4 **Presidente Dutra** Brazil
157 A8 **Presidente Epitácio** Brazil
161 G2 **Presidente Hayes** *admin. area* Paraguay
159 F3 **Presidente Médici** Brazil
157 A6 **Presidente Murtinho** Brazil
157 B8 **Presidente Prudente** Brazil
157 B8 **Presidente Venceslau** Brazil
132 D4 **Presidio** *watercourse* Mexico
129 J6 **Presidio** Texas USA
227 K3 **Prešov** Slovakia
227 K3 **Prešovský** *admin. area* Slovakia
235 D5 **Prespa** *mountain* Bulgaria
235 B5 **Prespa, Lake** Macedonia
127 Q3 **Presque Isle** Maine USA
163 14 **Presqu'île la Caravelle** Martinique
120 J8 **Press Lake** Ontario Canada
228 E3 **Pressac** France
228 D3 **Pressath** Germany
242 E3 **Prestatyn** Denbighshire Wales UK
222 I2 **Presteid** Norway
240 D2 **Presteign** Powys Wales UK
240 E2 **Presthope** Shropshire England UK
242 F3 **Preston** Lancashire England UK
244 F5 **Preston** Scottish Borders Scotland UK
124 J5 **Preston** Idaho USA
129 M2 **Preston** Kansas USA
126 E5 **Preston** Minnesota USA
241 F2 **Preston on Stour** Warwickshire England UK
244 F5 **Prestonpans** East Lothian Scotland UK
126 J8 **Prestonsburg** Kentucky USA
436 N1 **Prestrud Inlet** *bay* Antarctica
244 D5 **Prestwick** South Ayrshire Scotland UK
157 C7 **Preto** *watercourse* Brazil
155 G5 **Preto da Eva** *watercourse* Brazil
159 F2 **Preto do Igapo-acu** *watercourse* Brazil
308 E5 **Pretoria (Tshwane)** South Africa
228 F3 **Préveranges** France
125 N6 **Prewitt Reservoir** Colorado USA
376 E5 **Prey Vêng** Cambodia
232 F4 **Prezid** Croatia
232 F4 **Prezid** Slovenia
385 I2 **Priargunsk** Russian Federation
116 C7 **Pribilof Islands** Alaska USA
232 H4 **Priboj** Bosnia and Herzegovina
234 A4 **Priboj** Serbia
234 C4 **Priboj** Serbia
227 L2 **Priborovo** Belarus
125 J7 **Price** Utah USA
125 J7 **Price** *watercourse* Utah USA
376 B4 **Price, Cape** Andaman and Nicobar Islands India
130 H3 **Priceville** Alabama USA
130 G5 **Prichard** Alabama USA
163 10a **Prickly Bay** Grenada
163 10a **Prickly Point** *cape* Grenada
241 H2 **Prickwillow** Cambridgeshire England UK
240 E3 **Priddy** Somerset England UK
234 B4 **Pridvorica** Serbia
230 E3 **Priego** Spain
225 L4 **Priekule** Latvia
225 K5 **Priekulė** Lithuania
226 G4 **Prien** Germany
225 L5 **Prienai** Lithuania
308 D5 **Prieska** South Africa
244 C3 **Priest Island** Scotland UK
124 G3 **Priest Lake** Idaho USA
124 F3 **Priest Rapids Lake** Washington USA
227 J3 **Prievidza** Slovakia
238 E6 **Prigory** Russian Federation
232 F4 **Prijeboj** Croatia
234 A4 **Prijepolje** Serbia
234 B4 **Prijevor** Serbia
304 D3 **Prikro** Côte d'Ivoire
235 B5 **Prilep** Macedonia
225 P4 **Priluki** Russian Federation
238 H3 **Priluki** Russian Federation
231 G4 **Prima, Punta** *cape* Spain
232 E2 **Přimda** Czech Republic
162 D2 **Primera Angostura** Argentina
160 F4 **Primero** *watercourse* Argentina
129 L7 **Primero de Mayo** Mexico
132 A1 **Primo Tapia** Mexico
225 O2 **Primorsk** Russian Federation
394 E4 **Primorskiy** Ukraine
384 F2 **Primorskiy Khrebet** *range* Russian Federation
237 AB10 **Primorskiy Kray** *admin. area* Russian Federation
225 K5 **Primor'ye** Russian Federation
119 Q5 **Primrose Lake** Saskatchewan Canada
119 Q6 **Prince** Saskatchewan Canada
119 S6 **Prince Albert** Saskatchewan Canada
308 D6 **Prince Albert** South Africa
437 K1 **Prince Albert Mountains** Antarctica
119 R5 **Prince Albert National Park** Saskatchewan Canada
116 H4 **Prince Albert Peninsula** Northwest Territories Canada
116 H4 **Prince Albert Sound** Northwest Territories Canada
116 G4 **Prince Alfred, Cape** Northwest Territories Canada
117 L5 **Prince Charles Island** Nunavut Canada
437 E2 **Prince Charles Mountains** Antarctica
122 C2 **Prince-de-Galles, Cap du** *cape* Québec Canada
80 H9 **Prince Edward Fracture Zone** *underwater feature* Southern Ocean
123 G9 **Prince Edward Island** *admin. area* Canada
118 J6 **Prince George** British Columbia Canada
117 I3 **Prince Gustaf Adolf Sea** Nunavut Canada
437 C2 **Prince Harald Coast** Antarctica
116 C5 **Prince of Wales, Cape** Alaska USA
120 H3 **Prince of Wales Fort** Manitoba Canada
425 L2 **Prince of Wales Island** Qld Australia
117 J4 **Prince of Wales Island** Nunavut Canada
118 E5 **Prince of Wales Island** Alaska USA
116 H4 **Prince of Wales Strait** Northwest Territories Canada
437 C2 **Prince Olav Coast** Antarctica
116 H3 **Prince Patrick Island** Northwest Territories Canada
117 J4 **Prince Regent Inlet** Nunavut Canada
118 F5 **Prince Rupert** British Columbia Canada
163 15 **Prince Rupert Bay** Dominica
116 E6 **Prince William Sound** Alaska USA
241 G3 **Princes Risborough** Buckinghamshire England UK
163 9 **Princes Town** Trinidad and Tobago
163 9 **Princes Town** *admin. area* Trinidad and Tobago
156 E4 **Princesa Isabel** Brazil
127 N7 **Princess Anne** Maryland USA
437 A2 **Princess Astrid Coast** Antarctica
437 F2 **Princess Elizabeth Land** *plain* Antarctica
436 X2 **Princess Martha Coast** Antarctica
437 B2 **Princess Ragnhild Coast** Antarctica
118 G6 **Princess Royal Island** British Columbia Canada
118 K8 **Princeton** British Columbia Canada
126 G6 **Princeton** Illinois USA
126 H8 **Princeton** Kentucky USA
126 E6 **Princeton** Missouri USA
240 D4 **Princetown** Devon England UK
128 inset **Princeville** Hawai'i USA
305 F4 **Príncipe** *island* São Tomé and Príncipe
118 F6 **Principe Channel** British Columbia Canada
124 E4 **Prineville** Oregon USA
124 E4 **Prineville Reservoir** Oregon USA
125 N5 **Pringle** South Dakota USA
374 E5 **Pringsewu** Indonesia
134 D4 **Prinzapolka** Nicaragua
425 inset **Prion Lake** Macquarie Island Australia
230 B2 **Prior, Cabo** *cape* Spain
241 F2 **Priors Marston** Warwickshire England UK
225 O2 **Priozersk** Russian Federation
236 N6 **Pripolyarnyy Ural** *range* Russian Federation
223 Q2 **Prirechnyy** Russian Federation
234 E4 **Priseltsi** Bulgaria
394 F2 **Pristen** Russian Federation
234 B4 **Priština** Kosovo
125 N8 **Pritchett** Colorado USA
392 E6 **Prithvipur** Madhya Pradesh India
121 V1 **Pritzler Harbour** Nunavut Canada
229 G4 **Privas** France
122 E4 **Privert, Lac** *lake* Québec Canada
234 D1 **Privetnoye** Ukraine
388 D1 **Privolzhsk** Russian Federation
388 E3 **Privolzhskiy** Russian Federation
388 E3 **Privolzhskoye** Russian Federation
234 B4 **Prizren** Kosovo
233 E8 **Prizzi** Italy
232 G4 **Prnjavor** Bosnia and Herzegovina
234 A3 **Prnjavor** Serbia
244 B5 **Proaig** Argyll and Bute Scotland UK
375 G5 **Probolinggo** Indonesia
240 C4 **Probus** Cornwall England UK
118 M8 **Procter** British Columbia Canada
130 B4 **Proctor Lake** Texas USA
393 E8 **Proddatur** Andhra Pradesh India
121 Q2 **Profond, Pointe du** *cape* Québec Canada
154 C5 **Progreso** Ecuador
129 I5 **Progreso** Mexico
132 B1 **Progreso** Mexico
133 H4 **Progreso** Mexico
225 K5 **Prokhladnoye** Russian Federation
388 D5 **Prokhladnyy** Russian Federation
237 AC7 **Prokof'yeva, Ostrov** *island* Russian Federation
235 C6 **Prokopion** Greece
389 O2 **Prokopyevsk** Russian Federation
234 B4 **Prokuplje** Serbia
225 P3 **Proletariy** Russian Federation
157 B8 **Promissão** Brazil
159 H5 **Promissão** Brazil
161 I2 **Promissão, Represa** *lake* Brazil
158 B3 **Promontorio Salinas** *cape* Peru
225 P6 **Pronya** *watercourse* Belarus
118 I4 **Prophet** *watercourse* British Columbia Canada
118 J3 **Prophet River** British Columbia Canada
157 E5 **Propriá** Brazil
224 G5 **Prorer Wiek** *bay* Germany
425 N5 **Proserpine** Qld Australia
227 J2 **Prosna** *watercourse* Poland
163 12 **Prospect** Barbados
131 K3 **Prosperity** South Carolina USA
310 5b **Prosperous Bay** St Helena
227 I2 **Prószków** Poland
125 P8 **Protection** Kansas USA
235 D5 **Proti** Greece
232 F2 **Protivín** Czech Republic
236 O6 **Protochnyye** Russian Federation
238 G5 **Protvino** Russian Federation
229 H5 **Provence-Alpes-Côte d'Azur** *admin. area* France
126 H8 **Providence** Kentucky USA
127 P6 **Providence** Rhode Island USA
124 J6 **Providence** Utah USA
310 9 **Providence Island** Seychelles
154 C3 **Providencia** Colombia
132 C2 **Providencia** Mexico
163 2 **Providencia, Isla de (Colombia)** *island* Colombia
159 F3 **Providência, Serra da** *range* Brazil
135 F2 **Providenciales Island** Turks and Caicos Islands
306 D3 **Province Orientale** *admin. area* Democratic Republic of Congo
228 F2 **Provins** France
124 J6 **Provo** Utah USA
119 P6 **Provost** Alberta Canada
304 D3 **Pru** *watercourse* Ghana
157 B9 **Prudentópolis** Brazil
243 G2 **Prudhoe** Northumberland England UK
238 E5 **Prudki** Russian Federation
226 D2 **Prüm** Germany
226 D2 **Prüm** *watercourse* Germany
233 C5 **Prunelli-di-Fiumorbo** Corsica France
232 H2 **Pruské** Slovakia
227 J1 **Pruszcz** Poland
227 K1 **Pruszków** Poland
234 E2 **Prut** *watercourse* Moldova
234 E1 **Prut** *watercourse* Romania
234 D1 **Prut** *watercourse* Ukraine
225 N5 **Prūto Ežeras** *lake* Belarus
225 Q2 **Pryazha** Russian Federation
437 F2 **Prydz Bay** Antarctica
394 E2 **Pryluky** Ukraine
227 K1 **Przasnysz** Poland
227 I1 **Przechlewo** Poland
227 I2 **Przeczów** Poland
227 J2 **Przedbórz** Poland
227 H2 **Przemków** Poland
227 L3 **Przemyśl** Poland
227 L2 **Przeworsk** Poland
227 K2 **Przysucha** Poland
227 K2 **Przytyk** Poland
224 J5 **Przywidz** Poland
235 D6 **Psara** Greece
235 D6 **Psara** *island* Greece
235 C6 **Psaromita, Akra** *cape* Greece
235 D6 **Psathoura** *island* Greece
388 C5 **Psebay** Russian Federation
235 D8 **Pseira** *island* Greece
394 E2 **Psel** *watercourse* Russian Federation
235 E7 **Pserimos** *island* Greece
388 C5 **Pshada** Russian Federation
235 D8 **Psiloritis** *mountain* Greece
225 O4 **Pskov** Russian Federation
225 N3 **Pskov, Lake** *lake* Russian Federation
225 O4 **Pskovskaya Oblast'** *admin. area* Russian Federation
394 E2 **Ps'ol** *watercourse* Ukraine
232 E1 **Pšov** Czech Republic
227 H1 **Pszczew** Poland
227 J3 **Pszczyna** Poland
121 T4 **Ptarmigan** *watercourse* Québec Canada
235 C6 **Pteleos** Greece
227 H4 **Ptuj** Slovenia
380 D4 **Pu-la Ho** *watercourse* Yunnan China
373 G4 **Pua** *watercourse* Papua New Guinea
375 I4 **Puah** *island* Indonesia
128 inset **Puakō** Hawai'i USA
160 F6 **Puan** Argentina
427 12c **Pu'apu'a** Samoa
379 G2 **Pubao** Xizang Zizhiqu China
158 E6 **Puca Apacheta** Bolivia
158 C1 **Pucacuro** Peru
158 C3 **Pucallpa** Peru
158 D5 **Pucapacheta, Cerro** *mountain* Peru
158 E5 **Pucara** Bolivia
158 E6 **Pucara** Bolivia
227 L2 **Puchaczów** Poland
380 F1 **Pucheng** Shaanxi China
388 D2 **Puchezh** Russian Federation
386 E4 **Puch'ŏn** South Korea
377 I5 **Pucio Point** Philippines
225 J5 **Pucka, Zatoka** *bay* Poland
223 O4 **Pudasjärvi** Finland
380 E3 **Puding** Guizhou China
236 Q7 **Pudino** Russian Federation
378 E2 **Pudog Zangbo** *watercourse* Xizang Zizhiqu China
223 T6 **Pudozh** Russian Federation
380 D3 **Pudu He** *watercourse* Yunnan China
393 E9 **Puducherry** Puducherry India
422 2 **Pue** Cook Islands New Zealand
133 F5 **Puebla** Mexico
133 F5 **Puebla** *admin. area* Mexico
230 D5 **Puebla, Embalse de la** *lake* Spain
230 D4 **Puebla de Alcocer** Spain
230 E3 **Puebla de Beleña** Spain
230 C2 **Puebla de Brollón** Spain
230 D4 **Puebla de Don Rodrigo** Spain
230 D2 **Puebla de Lillo** Spain
230 C4 **Puebla de Obando** Spain
125 M7 **Pueblo** Colorado USA
230 E5 **Pueblo de Don Fadrique** Spain
154 C4 **Pueblo de Indios** Colombia
154 B3 **Pueblo Libre** Peru
160 F6 **Pueblo Nuevo** Argentina
154 C2 **Pueblo Nuevo** Colombia
158 B2 **Pueblo Nuevo** Peru
134 B4 **Pueblo Nuevo Tiquisate** Guatemala
163 2 **Pueblo Viejo** Isla de Providencia
134 D5 **Pueblo Viejo** Panama
154 D2 **Pueblo Viejo** Venezuela
133 F4 **Pueblo Viejo, Laguna de** *lake* Mexico
132 C3 **Pueblo Yaqui** Mexico
160 E6 **Puelches** Argentina
160 E6 **Puelén** Argentina
230 D5 **Puente-Genil** Spain
230 D4 **Puente Nuevo, Embalse de** *lake* Spain
228 C5 **Puente Viesgo** Spain
230 F5 **Puentes, Embalse de** *lake* Spain
230 C2 **Puentes de Garcia Rodriguez** Spain
129 I3 **Puerco** *watercourse* New Mexico USA
132 C2 **Puerta Cajón** Mexico
160 F2 **Puerta de Díaz** Argentina
128 E5 **Puertecitos** Mexico
154 C5 **Puerto** Peru
162 B3 **Puerto Aguirre** Chile
162 B3 **Puerto Aisén** Chile
159 F4 **Puerto Alegre** Bolivia
154 D5 **Puerto Alfonso** Colombia
134 D5 **Puerto Armuelles** Panama
155 F3 **Puerto Arturo** Venezuela
154 B4 **Puerto Asís** Colombia
154 E3 **Puerto Ayacucho** Venezuela
163 4 **Puerto Ayora** Archipiélago de Colón (Galapagos Islands)
161 G2 **Puerto Bahía Negra** Paraguay
163 4 **Puerto Baquerizo Moreno** Archipiélago de Colón (Galapagos Islands)
134 B4 **Puerto Barrios** Guatemala
154 C5 **Puerto Benjamín García** Colombia
154 C3 **Puerto Berrío** Colombia
129 H5 **Puerto Blanca** Mexico
129 I7 **Puerto Blanco** Mexico
154 C3 **Puerto Boyacá** Colombia
158 C3 **Puerto Breu** Peru
134 D4 **Puerto Cabezas** Nicaragua
162 B3 **Puerto Cahacabuco** Chile
154 D5 **Puerto Caimán** Colombia
132 C3 **Puerto Cancún** Mexico
128 E6 **Puerto Canoas** Mexico
154 C5 **Puerto Carlos** Colombia
135 H6 **Puerto Carreño** Colombia
134 C3 **Puerto Castilla** Honduras
154 C2 **Puerto Catatumbo** Venezuela
158 B2 **Puerto Chicama** *bay* Peru
162 B3 **Puerto Cisnes** Chile
162 C5 **Puerto Coig** Argentina
154 C2 **Puerto Colombia** Colombia
154 D4 **Puerto Colombia** Colombia
154 E4 **Puerto Colombia** Venezuela
154 C4 **Puerto Concordia** Colombia
134 C4 **Puerto Cortés** Honduras
154 C4 **Puerto Cuba** Colombia
162 B5 **Puerto Curtze** Chile
310 3a **Puerto de la Cruz** Canary Islands
300 C3 **Puerto de la Estaca** Spain
310 3 **Puerto de Rosario** Canary Islands
158 E4 **Puerto de Tumupasa** Bolivia
310 3d **Puerto del Rosario** Canary Islands
162 D4 **Puerto Deseado** Argentina
158 B2 **Puerto Díaz** Peru
134 B4 **Puerto El Triunfo** El Salvador
154 B2 **Puerto Escondido** Colombia
132 C3 **Puerto Escondido** Mexico
133 F6 **Puerto Escondido** Mexico
134 D5 **Puerto Escondido** Panama
162 D6 **Puerto Español** Argentina
158 D3 **Puerto Estirón de Marcos** Peru
158 D3 **Puerto Fortaleza** Peru
154 B5 **Puerto Francisco de Orellanas** Ecuador
158 C2 **Puerto Franco** Peru
154 C3 **Puerto Gaitán** Colombia
154 C5 **Puerto Grau** Peru
162 B4 **Puerto Guadal** Chile
158 D5 **Puerto Guaqui** Bolivia
158 D4 **Puerto Heath** Bolivia
154 C4 **Puerto Huitoto** Colombia
154 B5 **Puerto Ila** Ecuador
162 B4 **Puerto Ingeniero Ibáñez** Chile
163 6a **Puerto Inglés** *bay* Isla Róbinson Crusoe
160 F2 **Puerto Irigoyen** Argentina
158 D4 **Puerto Leguía** Peru
154 C5 **Puerto Leguízamo** Colombia
134 D4 **Puerto Lempira** Honduras
159 F4 **Puerto Leytón** Bolivia
133 B2 **Puerto Libertad** Mexico
154 D3 **Puerto Limón** Colombia
134 D5 **Puerto Limón** Costa Rica
162 D2 **Puerto Lobos** Argentina
128 F5 **Puerto Lobos** Mexico
230 F5 **Puerto Lumbreras** Spain
133 G6 **Puerto Madero** Mexico
162 D3 **Puerto Madryn** Argentina
158 C3 **Puerto Mairo** Peru
158 D4 **Puerto Maldonado** Peru
159 E4 **Puerto Márquez** Bolivia
154 C4 **Puerto Mercedes** Colombia
154 E3 **Puerto Miranda** Venezuela
162 B2 **Puerto Montt** Chile

154 D5 **Puerto Nariño** Colombia
162 B5 **Puerto Natales** Chile
159 E5 **Puerto Nuevo** Bolivia
154 D4 **Puerto Nuevo** Colombia
134 E2 **Puerto Padre** Cuba
132 D2 **Puerto Palomas** Mexico
158 B1 **Puerto Pardo** Peru
158 C2 **Puerto Parinari** Peru
159 F4 **Puerto Pastos** Bolivia
154 D4 **Puerto Peñalito** Colombia
132 B2 **Puerto Peñasco** Mexico
158 B3 **Puerto Perdido** *bay* Peru
162 D3 **Puerto Pirámides** Argentina
158 B3 **Puerto Pisana** Peru
159 F6 **Puerto Potosí** Bolivia
377 H5 **Puerto Princesa** Philippines
154 C4 **Puerto Príncipe** Colombia
162 C5 **Puerto Progreso** Chile
162 C5 **Puerto Puyuguapi** Chile
162 B3 **Puerto Quellón** Chile
159 G5 **Puerto Quijarro** Bolivia
162 C6 **Puerto Remolino** Argentina
154 C5 **Puerto Reyes** Colombia
135 H3 **Puerto Rico** *unincorporated US territory* Caribbean
154 C4 **Puerto Rico** Colombia
76 L8 **Puerto Rico Trench** *underwater feature* Atlantic Ocean
154 D3 **Puerto Rondón** Colombia
161 G3 **Puerto Rosario** Paraguay
158 E3 **Puerto Ruiz** Bolivia
162 D2 **Puerto San Antonio Este** Argentina
134 B4 **Puerto San José** Guatemala
158 B3 **Puerto Santa** Peru
162 C5 **Puerto Santa Cruz** Argentina
135 F5 **Puerto Santander** Colombia
154 C5 **Puerto Santander** Colombia
154 C2 **Puerto Santander** Venezuela
132 A2 **Puerto Santo Tomás** Mexico
159 F6 **Puerto Sucre** Bolivia
158 C2 **Puerto Supay** Peru
158 B3 **Puerto Supe** Peru
158 D4 **Puerto Tahuantinsuyo** Peru
162 B4 **Puerto Tranquilo** Chile
154 C3 **Puerto Triunfo** Colombia
154 C5 **Puerto Triunfo** Peru
132 D4 **Puerto Vallarta** Mexico
163 4 **Puerto Velasco Ibarra** Archipiélago de Colón (Galapagos Islands)
154 C5 **Puerto Victoria** Colombia
159 F4 **Puerto Viejo** Bolivia
160 D3 **Puerto Viejo** Chile
163 4 **Puerto Villamil** Archipiélago de Colón (Galapagos Islands)
162 C3 **Puerto Visser** Argentina
154 C3 **Puerto Wilches** Colombia
162 B5 **Puerto Yartou** Chile
154 C4 **Puerto Yavilla** Colombia
162 B5 **Puerto Zenteno** Chile
230 D4 **Puertollano** Spain
161 G2 **Puesto Alambique** Paraguay
154 C5 **Puesto Arturo** Peru
160 F2 **Puesto Bullain** Paraguay
160 F2 **Puesto Curupayty** Paraguay
160 F2 **Puesto Dorado** Paraguay
161 G2 **Puesto González** Paraguay
160 F2 **Puesto Jabalí** Paraguay
158 D4 **Puesto Moscoso** Bolivia
160 F2 **Puesto Pavón** Paraguay
161 G2 **Puesto Santa Rosa** Paraguay
427 14a **Pueu** French Polynesia
132 D4 **Puga** Mexico
388 E3 **Pugachev** Russian Federation
392 C5 **Pugal** Rajasthan India
380 D3 **Puge** Sichuan China
229 H5 **Puget-sur-Argens** France
233 G6 **Puglia** *admin. area* Italy
163 5 **Puhi** *volcano* Isla de Pascua (Easter Island)
223 O4 **Puhos** Finland
227 L5 **Pui** Romania
306 D2 **Puig** Sudan
231 G3 **Puig-reig** Spain
228 F1 **Puisieux** France
234 F3 **Puiu, Lacul** *lake* Romania
304 B3 **Pujehun** Sierra Leone
424 inset **Puji, Tanjong** *cape* Cocos (Keeling) Islands Australia
154 B5 **Pujilí** Ecuador
158 D5 **Pujocucho** Peru
386 E3 **Pujon** North Korea
386 E3 **Pujon-ho** *lake* North Korea
423 D7 **Pukaki** *watercourse* New Zealand
423 D6 **Pukaki, Lake** New Zealand
426 1 **Pukapuka** *island* Cook Islands New Zealand
427 14 **Pukapuka** *island* French Polynesia
223 Q4 **Pukari** Finland
427 14 **Pukarua** *island* French Polynesia
224 H4 **Pukavik** Sweden
224 H4 **Pukavikbukten** *bay* Sweden
386 F3 **Pukch'ŏng** North Korea
234 A4 **Pukë** Albania
422 F3 **Pukekohe** New Zealand
423 E6 **Puketeraki Range** New Zealand
423 C8 **Puketi** New Zealand
422 G5 **Puketoi Range** New Zealand
238 I1 **Puksa** Russian Federation
232 E4 **Pula** Croatia
232 G3 **Pula** Hungary
233 C7 **Pula** Sardinia Italy
233 C7 **Pula, Capo di** *cape* Sardinia Italy
235 A5 **Pulaj** Albania
378 D2 **Pulan** Xizang Zizhiqu China
385 J5 **Pulandian** Liaoning China
375 G4 **Pulangpisau** Indonesia
373 I2 **Pulap** *island* Federated States of Micronesia
375 I5 **Pulasi** *island* Indonesia
127 M5 **Pulaski** New York USA
127 K8 **Pulaski** Virginia USA
373 F5 **Pulau** *watercourse* Indonesia
374 C4 **Pulautelo** Indonesia
227 K2 **Puławy** Poland
227 L2 **Pulemets** Ukraine
229 K3 **Pulfero** Italy
240 E1 **Pulford** Cheshire England UK
393 E7 **Pulgaon** Maharashtra India
240 E4 **Pulham** Dorset England UK
226 D2 **Pulheim** Germany
393 E9 **Pulicat Lake** Andhra Pradesh India
372 C3 **Pulisan, Tanjung** *cape* Indonesia
223 N2 **Pulju** Finland
223 O5 **Pulkonkoski** Finland
124 G3 **Pullman** Washington USA
226 D4 **Pully** Switzerland
372 D2 **Pulo Anna** *island* Palau
376 C5 **Pulo Buda** Myanmar
377 I3 **Pulog, Mount** *mountain* Philippines
223 R2 **Pulozero** Russian Federation
223 S5 **Pulozero, Ozero** *lake* Russian Federation
119 U7 **Pulp River** Manitoba Canada
230 F5 **Pulpí** Spain
132 C3 **Púlpito, Punta** *cape* Mexico
227 G2 **Pulsnitz** *watercourse* Germany
222 L2 **Pulsujärvi** Sweden
426 6 **Pulusuk** *island* Federated States of Micronesia
373 I2 **Puluwat** *island* Federated States of Micronesia
392 D4 **Pulwama** Jammu and Kashmir India/Pakistan
307 E4 **Puma** Tanzania
158 C4 **Pumacahuanca** Peru
158 C4 **Pumasillo, Cerro** *mountain* Peru
380 E4 **Pumiao** Guangxi Zhuangzu Zizhiqu China
159 E5 **Puna** Bolivia
154 A5 **Puná, Isla** *island* Ecuador
427 14a **Punaauia** French Polynesia
423 D6 **Punakaiki** New Zealand
379 F3 **Punakha** Bhutan
393 D10 **Punalur** Kerala India
393 C5 **Punasar** Rajasthan India
232 F4 **Punat** Croatia
159 E5 **Punata** Bolivia
392 D4 **Punch** Jammu and Kashmir India/Pakistan
309 F4 **Punda Maria** South Africa
393 C7 **Pune** Maharashtra India
225 M2 **Punelia** *lake* Finland
374 D3 **Punggol** *admin. area* Singapore
386 F3 **P'ungsan** North Korea
306 D4 **Punia** Democratic Republic of Congo
159 E5 **Punilla** Bolivia
160 D4 **Punilla, Cordillera de la** *range* Chile
392 D4 **Punjab** *admin. area* India
391 L3 **Punjab** *admin. area* Pakistan
225 O2 **Punkaharju** Finland
391 M2 **Punmah Glacier** Pakistan
119 S7 **Punnichy** Saskatchewan Canada
158 D4 **Puno** Peru
158 D5 **Puno** *admin. area* Peru
128 F7 **Punta Abreojos** Mexico
160 F6 **Punta Alta** Argentina
162 B5 **Punta Arenas** Chile
154 D2 **Punta Cardón** Venezuela
158 C5 **Punta Colorada** Peru
132 C3 **Punta Coyote** Mexico
160 D4 **Punta de Díaz** Chile
160 D5 **Punta del Agua** Argentina
310 3a **Punta del Hidalgo** Canary Islands
162 B5 **Punta del Monte** Argentina
162 D3 **Punta Delgada** Argentina
134 B3 **Punta Gorda** Belize
131 J7 **Punta Gorda** Florida USA
134 C4 **Punta Piedra** Honduras
132 B3 **Punta Prieta** Mexico
233 F8 **Punta Secca** Italy
230 C5 **Punta Umbría** Spain
310 3b **Puntagorda** Canary Islands
134 C5 **Puntarenas** Costa Rica
305 F4 **Puntas, Cabo dos** *cape* Equatorial Guinea
132 B2 **Puntas Coloradas** Mexico
158 C2 **Puntilla** Peru
154 A5 **Puntilla, La** *cape* Ecuador
154 D2 **Punto Fijo** Venezuela
127 L6 **Punxsutawney** Pennsylvania USA
223 O4 **Puokio** Finland
223 O4 **Puolanka** Finland
222 L3 **Puoltikasvaara** Sweden
223 M3 **Puostijärvi** *lake* Sweden
222 L3 **Puottaure** Sweden
159 E5 **Pupayoj** Bolivia
232 G5 **Pupnat** Croatia
422 E5 **Puponga** New Zealand
158 E2 **Pupunha** Brazil
158 C4 **Puquio** Peru
236 Q5 **Pur** *watercourse* Russian Federation
236 S4 **Pura** *watercourse* Russian Federation
392 E5 **Puranpur** Uttar Pradesh India
160 C6 **Puraquina** Chile
373 H5 **Purari** *watercourse* Papua New Guinea
130 C3 **Purcell** Oklahoma USA
118 M7 **Purcell Mountains** British Columbia Canada
126 E8 **Purdy** Missouri USA
373 H4 **Purdy Islands** Papua New Guinea
225 M3 **Purekkari Neem** *cape* Estonia
160 C6 **Purén** Chile
422 F4 **Pureora** New Zealand
422 F4 **Pureora** *volcano* New Zealand
129 K2 **Purgatoire** *watercourse* Colorado USA
393 E7 **Puri** Chhattisgarh India
393 F7 **Puri** Orissa India
376 B4 **Purian Point** Myanmar
154 C4 **Purificación** Colombia
132 D5 **Purificación** Mexico
133 F3 **Purificación** *watercourse* Mexico
236 S4 **Purinskoye, Ozero** *lake* Russian Federation
222 K3 **Purkijaur** *lake* Sweden
393 D7 **Purna** Maharashtra India
154 C5 **Purna Susa** Colombia
223 T4 **Purnema** Russian Federation
392 G6 **Purnia** Bihar India
222 L3 **Purnu** Sweden
223 P4 **Purnuvaara** Finland
119 P8 **Purple Springs** Alberta Canada
162 B2 **Purranque** Chile
154 D1 **Purruruhu** Colombia
240 E3 **Purton** Gloucestershire England UK
241 F3 **Purton** Wiltshire England UK
241 F3 **Purton Stoke** Wiltshire England UK
121 S2 **Purtuniq** Québec Canada
159 F4 **Purubi** Bolivia
375 G4 **Puruk Cahu** Indonesia
392 G6 **Puruliya** West Bengal India
154 B4 **Purún, Punta de** *cape* Colombia
158 E3 **Purus** *watercourse* Brazil
373 G6 **Purutu Island** Papua New Guinea
225 O2 **Puruvesi** *bay* Finland
233 G3 **Purvis** Mississippi USA
375 F5 **Purwodadi** Indonesia
374 F5 **Purwokerto** Indonesia
375 G5 **Purworejo** Indonesia
241 G2 **Pury End** Northamptonshire England UK
386 F2 **Puryŏng** North Korea
375 F3 **Pusa** Malaysia
393 D7 **Pusad** Maharashtra India
386 F4 **Pusan (Busan)** South Korea
375 H4 **Pusat Damai** Indonesia
127 Q4 **Pushaw Lake** Maine USA
237 AG8 **Pushchino** Russian Federation
238 G5 **Pushchino** Russian Federation
392 D5 **Pushkar** Rajasthan India
238 D3 **Pushkin** Russian Federation
238 C4 **Pushkinskiye Gory** Russian Federation
223 T4 **Pushlakhta** Russian Federation
127 M2 **Puskitamika Lake** Québec Canada
227 K2 **Pustków** Poland
234 C1 **Pustomyty** Ukraine
237 AH6 **Pustoretsk** Russian Federation
225 O4 **Pustoška** Russian Federation
223 S5 **Pustoye, Ozero** *lake* Russian Federation
227 K4 **Pusztaföldvár** Hungary
372 C6 **Putain** Indonesia
375 H2 **Putalan** Malaysia
379 H3 **Putao (Fort Hertz)** Myanmar
422 F4 **Putaruru** New Zealand
422 G4 **Putauaki** *volcano* New Zealand
381 H3 **Putian** Fujian China
158 D4 **Putina** Peru
375 F4 **Puting, Tanjung** *cape* Indonesia
225 P6 **Putki** Belarus
223 O3 **Putkivaara** Finland
133 F5 **Putla de Guerrero** Mexico
226 G1 **Putlitz** Germany
234 B1 **Putnok** Hungary
373 J5 **Putoo** Papua New Guinea
381 I2 **Puto Shan** *range* Zhejiang China
237 U5 **Putorana, Plato** *region* Russian Federation
225 K2 **Putsaari** *island* Finland
229 H2 **Puttelange** France
154 C4 **Putumayo** *admin. area* Colombia
154 C5 **Putumayo** *watercourse* Colombia
154 C5 **Putumayo** *watercourse* Peru
375 G3 **Putusibau** Indonesia
234 D2 **Putyla** Ukraine
128 inset **Pu'uanahulu** Hawai'i USA
223 P5 **Puukari** Finland
223 M4 **Puukkofjärden** *bay* Sweden
223 N4 **Puukkokumpu** Finland
225 N2 **Puula** *lake* Finland
225 O2 **Puumala** Finland
128 inset **Pu'uwai** Hawai'i USA
121 Q2 **Puvirnituq** *bay* Québec Canada
121 Q2 **Puvirnituq** *watercourse* Québec Canada
121 Q3 **Puvirnituq, Baie de** Québec Canada
121 Q2 **Puvirnituq, Lac de** *lake* Québec Canada
126 F8 **Puxico** Missouri USA
156 F4 **Puxinanã** Brazil
228 F4 **Puy-Guillaume** France
124 D3 **Puyallup** Washington USA
385 H5 **Puyang** Hebei China
385 H6 **Puyang** Henan China
381 H2 **Puyang** Zhejiang China
162 B2 **Puyehue** Chile
228 F5 **Puylaurens** France
154 B5 **Puyo** Ecuador
386 E4 **Puyŏ** South Korea
423 B8 **Puysegur Point** New Zealand
162 B3 **Puyuguapi, Canal** *strait* Chile
225 L4 **Puzes Ezers** *lake* Latvia
231 F4 **Puzol** Spain
307 F5 **Pwani** *admin. area* Tanzania
240 B3 **Pwllcrochan** Pembrokeshire Wales UK
240 C2 **Pwllheli** Gwynedd Wales UK
237 AF7 **P'yagina, Poluostrov** *peninsula* Russian Federation
236 Q6 **Pyakupur** *watercourse* Russian Federation
223 U3 **Pyalitsa** Russian Federation
223 S5 **Pyal'ma** Russian Federation
225 Q1 **Pyal'vozero** Russian Federation
223 Q3 **Pyaozero, Ozero** *lake* Russian Federation
223 Q4 **Pyaozerskiy** Russian Federation
236 T4 **Pyasina** *watercourse* Russian Federation
236 S5 **Pyasino, Ozero** *lake* Russian Federation
236 R4 **Pyasinskiy Zaliv** *bay* Russian Federation
238 C3 **Pyatchino** Russian Federation
379 H5 **Pyawbwe** Myanmar
376 B3 **Pyay (Prome)** Myanmar
238 F3 **Pyazhelka** Russian Federation
238 F2 **Pyazhiyeva Sel'ga** Russian Federation
225 N2 **Pyhäjärvi** *bay* Finland
223 P5 **Pyhäjärvi** *lake* Finland
223 N3 **Pyhäjoki** Finland
223 N4 **Pyhäjoki** *watercourse* Finland
223 N2 **Pyhältö** Finland
223 N4 **Pyhänkoski** Finland
223 O4 **Pyhäntä** Finland
225 K2 **Pyhäranta** Finland
223 N5 **Pyhäsalmi** Finland
223 P5 **Pyhäselkä** Finland
225 P1 **Pyhäselkä** *bay* Finland
225 L2 **Pyhäjärvi** *lake* Finland
379 H4 **Pyin-U-Lwin** Myanmar
379 H5 **Pyinmana** Myanmar
240 D3 **Pyle** Bridgend Wales UK
223 N5 **Pylkönmäki** Finland
235 B7 **Pylos** Greece
225 K2 **Pyntäinen** Finland
386 E3 **Pyŏktong** North Korea
386 E4 **P'yongil-do** *island* South Korea
386 E3 **P'yŏngsan** North Korea
386 E4 **P'yŏngt'aek** South Korea
386 E3 **Pyongyang** North Korea
129 K5 **Pyote** Texas USA
124 F6 **Pyramid Lake** Nevada USA
227 M2 **Pyratyn** Ukraine
231 G2 **Pyrenees** *range* France/Spain
235 D6 **Pyrgi** Greece
235 B5 **Pyrgoi** Greece
235 D8 **Pyrgos** Greece
227 H1 **Pyrzyce** Poland
236 K7 **Pyshchug** Russian Federation
225 N4 **Pytalovo** Russian Federation
376 C3 **Pyu** Myanmar
392 F5 **Pyuthan** Nepal
240 C4 **Pyworthy** Devon England UK
225 M1 **Pyyrinlahti** Finland

Q

390 C3 **Qā'al Jafr** *watercourse* Jordan
117 M3 **Qaanaaq** Greenland
390 F3 **Qādisiyah, Al** *admin. area* Iraq
391 I2 **Qā'en** Iran
122 O2 **Qaersuarssuk** *island* Greenland
390 F3 **Qafās** Iraq
390 G5 **Qaffāy, Al** *island* United Arab Emirates
385 J3 **Qagan Nuur** *lake* Jilin China
385 H4 **Qagan Nuur** *lake* Nei Mongol Zizhiqu China
383 K6 **Qaidam He** *watercourse* Qinghai China
302 E5 **Qala'en Nahl** Sudan
391 K2 **Qalagai** Afghanistan
391 K3 **Qalāt** Afghanistan
390 E6 **Qal'at Bīshah** Saudi Arabia
391 K2 **Qal'eh-ye Khān** Afghanistan
391 J2 **Qal'eh-ye Now** Afghanistan
121 R3 **Qalluviartuuq, Lac** *lake* Québec Canada
389 K2 **Qalybek Koli** *lake* Kazakhstan
117 J6 **Qamanirjuaq Lake** Nunavut Canada
388 J6 **Qamashi** Uzbekistan
302 B1 **Qaminis** Libya
303 H5 **Qandala** Somalia
388 E7 **Qanqanlu** Iran
390 F3 **Qāpi** Iran
117 O6 **Qaqortoq** Greenland
122 M1 **Qaqqarsuaq** *mountain* Greenland
391 K2 **Qarah Bāgh** Afghanistan
388 H4 **Qarakol** *lake* Kazakhstan
389 M3 **Qarakol** *lake* Kazakhstan
302 D1 **Qārat al Mashrūkah** *mountain* Egypt
307 H2 **Qardho** Somalia
390 G2 **Qareh Chāy** *watercourse* Iran
388 H3 **Qarghaly Bogeni** *lake* Kazakhstan
383 H5 **Qarqan He** *watercourse* Xinjiang Uygur Zizhiqu China
388 J6 **Qarqin** Afghanistan
388 J6 **Qarshi** Uzbekistan
388 J6 **Qashqadaryo** *admin. area* Uzbekistan
117 N5 **Qasigiannguit** Greenland
390 E4 **Qaşim, Al** *admin. area* Saudi Arabia
384 G5 **Qasq** Nei Mongol Zizhiqu China
301 J2 **Qaşr Aḩmad** Libya
302 D2 **Qaşr al Farāfirah** Egypt
302 C1 **Qaşr al Qarn** *point of interest* Libya
302 C1 **Qaşr ash Shaqqah** *point of interest* Libya
301 J2 **Qaşr Bū Hādī** Libya
302 E3 **Qaşr Ibrim** *point of interest* Egypt
122 O2 **Qassimiut** Greenland
122 N1 **Qassit** *bay* Greenland
390 E7 **Qa'tabah** Yemen
390 G5 **Qatar** *country*
388 F7 **Qazvīn** Iran
427 9 **Qele Levu** *island* Fiji
117 N5 **Qeqertarsuaq** Greenland
122 N1 **Qeqertarsuaq** Greenland
117 N5 **Qeqertarsuaq (Disko)** *island* Greenland
122 M1 **Qeqertarsuatsiaat** Greenland
117 N4 **Qeqertarsuatsiaq** *island* Greenland
117 N5 **Qeqertarsuup Tunua** *bay* Greenland
391 H4 **Qeshm** Iran
391 H4 **Qeshm, Jazīreh-ye** *island* Iran
381 G1 **Qi Xian** Henan China
384 D6 **Qiabuqia** Qinghai China
380 E1 **Qian He** *watercourse* Shaanxi China
385 J5 **Qian Shan** *range* Liaoning China
380 E1 **Qian Xian** Shaanxi China
385 I5 **Qian'an** Hebei China
385 J4 **Qian'an** Jilin China
385 J3 **Qianguozhen** Jilin China
380 E2 **Qianjiang** Chongqing China
381 F2 **Qianjiang** Hubei China
380 F3 **Qianling** Hunan China
380 E3 **Qianxi** Guizhou China
380 E1 **Qianyang** Shaanxi China
384 G6 **Qiaoshan** Shaanxi China
384 E6 **Qiaotou** Qinghai China
380 D3 **Qiaowa** Sichuan China
380 D3 **Qiaozhuang** Sichuan China
388 E7 **Qidar** Iran
382 H5 **Qiemo** Xinjiang Uygur Zizhiqu China
302 E2 **Qifţ** Egypt
381 H2 **Qike** Heilongjiang China
385 K2 **Qike** Heilongjiang China
117 M5 **Qikiqtarjuaq** Nunavut Canada
117 Q3 **Qikirtajuaq Island** Nunavut Canada
391 J4 **Qila Safed** Pakistan
121 Q3 **Qilalugalik, Lac** *lake* Québec Canada
385 I4 **Qilaotu Shan** *range* Hebei China
383 K5 **Qilian Shan** *range* Gansu China
383 J5 **Qilian Shan** *range* Qinghai China
117 U3 **Qimusseriarsuaq** *bay* Greenland
380 E1 **Qin Ling** *range* Jiangsu China
302 E2 **Qinā** Egypt
302 E2 **Qinā, Wādī** *watercourse* Egypt
380 E1 **Qin'an** Gansu China
381 G3 **Qincheng** Jiangxi China
380 F2 **Qing Jiang** *watercourse* Hubei China
385 J3 **Qing'an** Heilongjiang China
384 F6 **Qingcheng** Gansu China
385 I6 **Qingdao** Shandong China
385 H6 **Qingfeng** Henan China
385 K3 **Qinggang** Heilongjiang China
379 H2 **Qinghai** *admin. area* China
384 D6 **Qinghai Hu** *lake* Qinghai China
383 K6 **Qinghai Nanshan** *range* Qinghai China
383 I3 **Qinghe** Xinjiang Uygur Zizhiqu China
381 H1 **Qingkou** Jiangsu China
380 E3 **Qinglong** Guizhou China
385 I5 **Qinglong** Hebei China
381 I2 **Qingpu** Shanghai China
381 G2 **Qingquan** Hubei China
385 K3 **Qingshan** Heilongjiang China
384 G5 **Qingshuihe** Nei Mongol Zizhiqu China
384 F5 **Qingtongxia** Zizhiqu China
384 E6 **Qingyuan** Gansu China
381 G4 **Qingyuan** Guangdong China
385 J4 **Qingyuan** Liaoning China
385 H5 **Qingzhou** Hebei China
385 I6 **Qingzhou** Shandong China
385 I5 **Qinhuangdao** Hebei China
385 I6 **Qinjiang** Jiangxi China
381 G3 **Qinjiang** Jiangxi China
384 G6 **Qinshui** Shanxi China
385 G6 **Qinxian** Shanxi China
380 E4 **Qinzhou** Guangxi Zhuangzu Zizhiqu China
380 E4 **Qinzhou Wan** *bay* Guangxi Zhuangzu Zizhiqu China
380 F5 **Qionghai** Hainan China
379 G3 **Qiongjie** Xizang Zizhiqu China
380 D2 **Qionglai** Sichuan China
380 F5 **Qiongshan** Hainan China
380 D2 **Qiongxi** Sichuan China
380 F5 **Qiongzhou Haixia (Hainan Strait)** Hainan China
385 J3 **Qiqihar** Heilongjiang China
122 D3 **Qirniraujaq, Pointe** *cape* Québec Canada
383 I4 **Qitai** Xinjiang Uygur Zizhiqu China
385 L3 **Qitaihe** Heilongjiang China
381 H2 **Qiupu** *watercourse* Anhui China
385 F6 **Qixia** Shandong China
381 H3 **Qixing Liedao** *island* Fujian China
389 K3 **Qiyakty Koli** *lake* Kazakhstan
390 F2 **Qom** Iran
390 G2 **Qom Rūd** *watercourse* Iran
382 G6 **Qong Muztag** *mountain* Xinjiang Uygur Zizhiqu China
388 H4 **Qopasor Koli** *lake* Kazakhstan
389 K6 **Qo'qon** Uzbekistan
388 I6 **Qorako'l** Uzbekistan
388 F5 **Qoraqalpog'iston** *admin. area* Uzbekistan
390 F2 **Qorveh** Iran
391 K2 **Qosh Tirdawān** Afghanistan
388 J6 **Qo'shrabot** Uzbekistan
391 H3 **Qoṭrom** Iran
391 J6 **Qo'ytosh** Uzbekistan
161 I4 **Quadros, Lagoa dos** *lake* Brazil
424 F8 **Quairading** WA Australia
118 I8 **Qualicum Beach** British Columbia Canada
425 M7 **Quambone** NSW Australia
376 E2 **Quan Đao Cô Tô** *island* Vietnam
376 E5 **Quan Đao Nam Du** *island* Vietnam
376 E5 **Quan Đao Trà Bản** *island* Vietnam
376 E2 **Quan Hóa** Vietnam
130 B3 **Quanah** Texas USA
163 I5 **Quanery, Anse** *bay* Dominica
376 E2 **Quảng Uyên** Vietnam
381 G3 **Quanjiang** Jiangxi China
381 H4 **Quanzhou** Fujian China
380 F3 **Quanzhou** Guangxi Zhuangzu Zizhiqu China
119 S7 **Qu'Appelle** *watercourse* Saskatchewan Canada
121 U2 **Quaqtaq** Québec Canada
161 G4 **Quaraí** *watercourse* Brazil
305 F3 **Quarar** *watercourse* Nigeria
244 inset **Quarff** Shetland Scotland UK
230 B5 **Quarteira** Portugal
232 E5 **Quarto** Italy
120 H1 **Quartzite Lake** Nunavut Canada
128 E4 **Quartzsite** Arizona USA
240 E2 **Quatford** Shropshire England UK
154 E5 **Quati Parana** *watercourse* Brazil
163 11 **Quatre, Île à** *island* St Vincent and the Grenadines
310 7b **Quatre Bornes** Mauritius
161 I3 **Quatro Barras** Brazil
310 1b **Quatro Ribeiras** Azores
118 G7 **Quatsino Sound** British Columbia Canada
240 E2 **Quatt** Shropshire England UK
388 H6 **Qūchān** Iran
389 I4 **Qudaykol** *lake* Kazakhstan
376 E3 **Quế Phong** Vietnam
425 N8 **Queanbeyan** NSW Australia
127 P3 **Québec** Québec Canada
117 L8 **Québec** *admin. area* Canada
159 H6 **Quebra Côco** Brazil
161 G4 **Quebracho** Uruguay
160 E3 **Quebracho Coto** Argentina
134 D5 **Quebrada Canoa** Panama
152 F5 **Quebrada Honda** Venezuela
154 C3 **Quebradona, Embalse** *lake* Colombia
162 A2 **Quedal, Cabo** *cape* Chile
437 L1 **Queen Alexandra Range** Antarctica
118 I7 **Queen Bess, Mount** British Columbia Canada
118 E6 **Queen Charlotte** British Columbia Canada
163 7 **Queen Charlotte Bay** Falkland Islands
118 E6 **Queen Charlotte Islands** British Columbia Canada
118 G7 **Queen Charlotte Sound** British Columbia Canada
118 H7 **Queen Charlotte Strait** British Columbia Canada
126 E6 **Queen City** Missouri USA
130 D4 **Queen City** Texas USA
128 G4 **Queen Creek** Arizona USA
116 H2 **Queen Elizabeth Islands** Nunavut Canada
437 K1 **Queen Elizabeth Mountains** Antarctica
437 C2 **Queen Fabiola Mountains** Antarctica
437 G2 **Queen Mary Coast** Antarctica
310 5c **Queen Mary's Peak** *volcano* St Helena
163 8 **Queen Maud Bay** South Georgia
117 I5 **Queen Maud Gulf** Nunavut Canada
437 B2 **Queen Maud Land** *plain* Antarctica
437 L1 **Queen Maud Mountains** Antarctica
117 J3 **Queens Channel** Nunavut Canada
308 E3 **Queen's Mine** Zimbabwe
243 G3 **Queensbury** West Yorkshire England UK
425 L5 **Queensland** *admin. area* Australia
81 T6 **Queensland Plateau** *underwater feature* Coral Sea
423 C7 **Queenstown** Tas. Australia
119 M10 **Queenstown** Alberta Canada
423 C7 **Queenstown** New Zealand
374 C4 **Queenstown** *admin. area* Singapore
308 E6 **Queenstown** South Africa
381 I3 **Queerao** *island* Zhejiang China
160 E6 **Quehué** Argentina
162 B3 **Queilén** Chile
156 B3 **Queimada, Ilha** *island* Brazil
157 E5 **Queimadas** Brazil
159 H6 **Queiroz** Brazil
306 B5 **Quela** Angola
228 D3 **Quélaines** France
309 G3 **Quelimane** Mozambique
158 C4 **Quellococha** Peru
306 A5 **Quelo** Angola
230 B4 **Queluz** Portugal
159 G1 **Quem Diria** Brazil
308 D2 **Quembo** *watercourse* Angola
160 F6 **Quemú-Quemú** Argentina
241 I4 **Quend-Plage-les-Pins** France
241 F3 **Quenington** Gloucestershire England UK
134 C5 **Quepos** Costa Rica
160 F6 **Quequén Salado** *watercourse* Argentina
158 E5 **Querarani** Bolivia
158 A2 **Querecotillo** Peru
159 H4 **Querência** Brazil
157 A8 **Querência do Norte** Brazil
132 E4 **Querétaro** Mexico
133 F4 **Querétaro** *admin. area* Mexico
132 C2 **Querobabi** Mexico
134 C5 **Quesada** Costa Rica
118 J6 **Quesnel** British Columbia Canada
118 J6 **Quesnel** *watercourse* British Columbia Canada
118 K6 **Quesnel Lake** British Columbia Canada
135 F2 **Quest, Pointe** *cape* Haiti
129 J2 **Questa** New Mexico USA
126 F2 **Quetico** Ontario Canada
162 C2 **Quetrequile** Argentina
391 K3 **Quetta** Pakistan
134 B4 **Quetzaltenango** Guatemala
308 B2 **Queve** *watercourse* Angola
154 B5 **Quevedo** Ecuador
127 M2 **Quévillon, Lac** *lake* Québec Canada
228 D4 **Queyrac** France
377 H5 **Quezon** Philippines
377 I4 **Quezon City** Philippines
385 H6 **Qufu** Shandong China
244 E2 **Quholm** Orkney Islands Scotland UK
308 B2 **Quibala** Angola
154 B3 **Quibdó** Colombia
126 C2 **Quibell** Ontario Canada
228 C3 **Quiberon** France
228 C3 **Quiberon, Baie de** *bay* France
306 B5 **Quibocolo** Angola
308 B2 **Quibor** Venezuela
158 C4 **Quichuaña** Peru
118 H5 **Quick** British Columbia Canada
306 B5 **Quiculungo** Angola
241 H2 **Quidenham** Norfolk England UK
162 B2 **Quidico** Chile
118 E2 **Quiet Lake** Yukon Territory Canada
119 N6 **Quigley** Alberta Canada
308 B3 **Quihita** Angola
162 C2 **Quila Mahuida, Altiplanicie del** *region* Argentina
160 D6 **Quilachanquil** Argentina
134 C4 **Quilalí** Nicaragua
162 A3 **Quilán, Cabo** *cape* Chile
162 A3 **Quilán, Isla** *island* Chile
158 D4 **Quilca, Nevado** *mountain* Peru
308 B2 **Quilenda** Angola
308 B2 **Quilengues** Angola
160 D6 **Quili Malal** Argentina
119 S7 **Quill Lakes** Saskatchewan Canada
228 F5 **Quillan** France
160 D5 **Quillota** Chile
158 B4 **Quilmaná** Peru
161 G5 **Quilmes** Argentina
425 M6 **Quilpie** Qld Australia
160 D5 **Quilpué** Chile
306 B5 **Quimbele** Angola
158 E5 **Quime** Bolivia
160 F3 **Quimilí** Argentina
228 B3 **Quimper** France
228 C3 **Quimperlé** France
245 D4 **Quin** Ireland
377 I4 **Quinalasag** *island* Philippines
124 D3 **Quinault** *watercourse* Washington USA
158 D4 **Quince Mil** Peru
154 C3 **Quinchía** Colombia
131 I5 **Quincy** Florida USA
127 P5 **Quincy** Massachusetts USA
126 F7 **Quincy** Missouri USA
124 F3 **Quincy** Washington USA
160 E5 **Quines** Argentina
309 H3 **Quinga** Mozambique
229 G3 **Quingey** France
116 C7 **Quinhagak** Alaska USA
155 E3 **Quiniqua, Serranía** *range* Venezuela
160 F6 **Quiñihual** Argentina
377 I5 **Quiniluban** *island* Philippines
154 B4 **Quinindé** *watercourse* Ecuador
130 C4 **Quinlan** Texas USA
124 F6 **Quinn** *watercourse* Nevada USA
124 H7 **Quinn Canyon Range** Nevada USA
133 H5 **Quintana Roo** *admin. area* Mexico
230 E4 **Quintanar de la Orden** Spain
230 E3 **Quintanar de la Sierra** Spain
160 E5 **Quinto** *watercourse* Argentina
231 F3 **Quinto** Spain
127 L3 **Quinze, Lac des** *lake* Québec Canada
309 H2 **Quionga** Mozambique
156 E5 **Quipapá** Brazil
160 C6 **Quirihue** Chile
129 H7 **Quiriego** Mexico
308 C2 **Quirima** Angola
155 F5 **Quirimiri, Lago** *lake* Brazil
157 B7 **Quirinópolis** Brazil
160 F5 **Quiroga** Argentina
132 E5 **Quiroga** Mexico
230 C2 **Quiroga** Spain
154 D2 **Quisiro** Venezuela
228 G5 **Quissac** France
308 C2 **Quissongo** Angola
134 D4 **Quita Sueño Bank** *reef* Colombia
308 C2 **Quitapa** Angola
129 L3 **Quitaque** Texas USA
309 H2 **Quiterajo** Mozambique
160 F3 **Quitilipi** Argentina
131 J5 **Quitman** Georgia USA
130 G4 **Quitman** Mississippi USA
130 D4 **Quitman** Texas USA
154 B5 **Quito** Ecuador
128 F5 **Quitovac** Mexico
160 C6 **Quitratúe** Chile
156 E4 **Quixadá** Brazil
159 F3 **Quixadá** Brazil
156 E4 **Quixeramobim** Brazil
156 E4 **Quixeré** Brazil
380 E2 **Qujiang** Sichuan China
380 D3 **Qujing** Yunnan China
383 J6 **Qumar He** *watercourse* Qinghai China
424 E6 **Quobba** WA Australia
117 J6 **Quoich** *watercourse* Nunavut Canada
244 C3 **Quoich, Loch** *lake* Scotland UK
126 F2 **Quorn** Ontario Canada
390 C2 **Quornet es Sauda** *mountain* Lebanon
389 J6 **Qūrghonteppa** Tajikistan
121 V3 **Qurlutuq** *watercourse* Québec Canada
391 I5 **Quryāt** Oman
302 E2 **Quş** Egypt
380 D2 **Qushan** Sichuan China
379 G3 **Qushui** Xizang Zizhiqu China
379 G3 **Qusong** Xizang Zizhiqu China
389 L3 **Qutau** *mountain* Kazakhstan
117 L2 **Quttinirpaaq National Park** Nunavut Canada
390 E2 **Quwasi** Iraq
384 F6 **Quwu Shan** *range* Gansu China
379 F3 **Quxia** Xizang Zizhiqu China
376 E3 **Quỳ Châu** Vietnam
376 E4 **Quy Nhơn** Vietnam
380 F3 **Quyang** Hunan China
376 D2 **Quỳnh Nhai** Vietnam
385 H6 **Quzhou** Hebei China
381 H3 **Quzhou** Zhejiang China
389 J3 **Qypshaq Koli** *lake* Kazakhstan
389 L2 **Qyzylqaq Koli** *lake* Kazakhstan

R

131 I4 **R. L. Harris Reservoir** Alabama USA
376 C5 **Ra, Ko** *island* Thailand
227 H4 **Raab** *watercourse* Austria
223 N4 **Raahe** Finland
223 P5 **Rääkkylä** Finland
375 G5 **Raas** *island* Indonesia
244 C3 **Raasay** *island* Scotland UK
223 N2 **Raattama** Finland
227 H5 **Rab** Croatia
227 I4 **Rába** *watercourse* Hungary
305 F2 **Rabah** Nigeria
302 E5 **Rabak** Sudan
372 E5 **Rabal** Indonesia
228 E5 **Rabastens** France
233 F9 **Rabat** Malta
300 E2 **Rabat** Morocco
424 I5 **Rabbit Flat Roadhouse** NT Australia
119 T3 **Rabbit Lake Mine** Saskatchewan Canada
118 L2 **Rabbitskin** *watercourse* Northwest Territories Canada
227 I3 **Rábca** *watercourse* Austria
222 J4 **Råberg** Sweden
238 E4 **Rabezha** Russian Federation
427 9a **Rabi** *island* Fiji
163 4 **Rábida, Isla** *island* Archipiélago de Colón (Galapagos Islands)
390 D5 **Rābigh** Saudi Arabia
379 G5 **Rabnabad Islands** Bangladesh
310 1a **Rabo de Peixe** Azores
133 F3 **Rabón, Laguna El** *lake* Mexico
234 C3 **Rabrovo** Bulgaria
234 A3 **Rača** Bosnia and Herzegovina
234 D3 **Răcari** Romania
135 F2 **Raccoon Cay** *island* Bahamas
232 F3 **Rače** Slovenia
123 L9 **Race, Cape** Newfoundland and Labrador Canada
376 E5 **Rạch Giá** Vietnam
376 C6 **Racha Noi, Ko** *island* Thailand
376 C6 **Racha Yai, Ko** *island* Thailand
133 F3 **Rachal** Texas USA
238 G3 **Rachevo** Russian Federation
126 H5 **Racine** Wisconsin USA
126 J2 **Racine Lake** Ontario Canada
118 I3 **Racing** *watercourse* British Columbia Canada
227 M5 **Racoviţa** Romania
225 L6 **Raczki** Poland
154 B2 **Rada, Punta de la** *cape* Colombia
162 C3 **Rada Tilly** Argentina
234 B4 **Radan** *region* Serbia
227 G2 **Rådasjön** *lake* Sweden
226 G3 **Radbuza** *watercourse* Czech Republic
238 G4 **Radchenko** Russian Federation
126 I8 **Radcliff** Kentucky USA
243 F3 **Radcliffe** Greater Manchester England UK
224 F3 **Råde** Norway
229 K1 **Radebeul** Germany
127 K8 **Radford** Virginia USA
392 C6 **Radhanpur** Gujarat India
155 F4 **Radiador** Brazil
229 J4 **Radici, Foce delle** *pass* Italy
121 Q6 **Radisson** Québec Canada
119 M7 **Radium Hot Springs** British Columbia Canada
163 9 **Radix, Point** Trinidad and Tobago
436 R1 **Radlinski, Mount** *mountain* Antarctica
227 H4 **Radlje ob Dravi** Slovenia
222 L3 **Rådnejaure** *lake* Sweden
234 D4 **Radnevo** Bulgaria
238 F3 **Radogoshcha** Russian Federation
227 K2 **Radom** Poland
234 C4 **Radomir** Bulgaria
227 J2 **Radomsko** Poland
227 K2 **Radoszyce** Poland
235 E5 **Radovets** Bulgaria
234 C4 **Radovnica** Serbia
224 C2 **Radøy** *island* Norway
240 E3 **Radstock** Bath and North East Somerset England UK
234 F2 **Rădulenii Vechi** Moldova
119 S8 **Radville** Saskatchewan Canada
227 L3 **Radymno** Poland
392 E5 **Rae Bareli** Uttar Pradesh India
119 M1 **Rae-Edzo** Northwest Territories Canada

117 K5 **Rae Isthmus** Nunavut Canada
131 L3 **Raeford** North Carolina USA
226 D2 **Raeren** Belgium
423 C7 **Raes Junction** New Zealand
424 G7 **Raeside, Lake** WA Australia
422 F4 **Raetihi** New Zealand
160 F4 **Rafaela** Argentina
305 I4 **Rafaï** Central African Republic
233 E8 **Raffadali** Italy
244 C2 **Raffin** Highland Scotland UK
308 F3 **Raffingora** Zimbabwe
390 E3 **Rafḥā** Saudi Arabia
233 D8 **Rafrāf** Tunisia
391 H3 **Rafsanjān** Iran
223 M1 **Rafsbotn** Norway
119 U5 **Rafter** Manitoba Canada
229 I3 **Rafz** Switzerland
306 D2 **Raga** Sudan
306 D2 **Raga** *watercourse* Sudan
225 M4 **Ragana** Latvia
377 J6 **Ragang, Mount** *mountain* Philippines
377 I4 **Ragay Gulf** Philippines
135 F2 **Ragged Island** Bahamas
163 I2 **Ragged Point** *cape* Barbados
245 D2 **Raghly** Ireland
392 C5 **Raghu Nathpura** Rajasthan India
422 F3 **Raglan** New Zealand
240 E3 **Raglan** Monmouthshire Wales UK
422 F3 **Raglan Harbour** New Zealand
423 E5 **Raglan Range** New Zealand
224 G3 **Råglanda** Sweden
222 J3 **Rago Nasjonalpark** *park* Norway
222 J4 **Rågoliden** Sweden
154 C3 **Ragonvalia** Colombia
226 G1 **Ragösen** Germany
121 U8 **Ragueneau** Québec Canada
222 J5 **Ragunda** Sweden
233 F8 **Ragusa** Italy
225 M5 **Raguva** Lithuania
302 E5 **Rahad** *watercourse* Sudan
302 C5 **Rahad el Berdi** Sudan
305 I2 **Rahad el Berdi** Sudan
223 O2 **Rahajärvi** *lake* Finland
305 F2 **Rahama** Nigeria
245 E3 **Raheen** Ireland
303 G5 **Raheita** Eritrea
391 L4 **Rahimyar Khan** Pakistan
242 A3 **Rahincuill** Ireland
223 M4 **Rahja** Finland
245 G2 **Raholp** Down Northern Ireland UK
231 G6 **Rahouia** Algeria
160 D6 **Rahue** *mountain* Chile
160 D6 **Rahué** Argentina
393 D7 **Rahuri** Maharashtra India
423 E5 **Rai Valley** New Zealand
233 E5 **Raiano** Italy
374 E3 **Raibu** *island* Indonesia
393 D8 **Raichur** Karnataka India
392 F6 **Raidih** Jharkhand India
392 G6 **Raiganj** West Bengal India
393 F7 **Raigarh** Chhattisgarh India
393 F7 **Raighar** Orissa India
375 I6 **Raijua** *island* Indonesia
126 F4 **Railroad Valley** Nevada USA
122 D6 **Raimbault, Lac** *lake* Québec Canada
226 F3 **Rain** Germany
118 L3 **Rainbow Lake** Alberta Canada
124 D3 **Rainier** Washington USA
372 C2 **Rainis** Indonesia
243 F3 **Rainow** Cheshire England UK
126 E2 **Rainy Lake** Ontario Canada
117 J9 **Rainy River** Ontario Canada
225 K1 **Raippaluoto (Vallgrund)** *island* Finland
393 E7 **Raipur** Chhattisgarh India
392 D5 **Raipur** Rajasthan India
427 15a **Rairik** Marshall Islands
223 O3 **Räisälä** Finland
392 D6 **Raisen** Madhya Pradesh India
223 O4 **Raiskio** Finland
244 E4 **Raith** Perth and Kinross Scotland UK
427 14 **Raivavae** *island* French Polynesia
393 E7 **Raj Nandgaon** Chhattisgarh India
375 G5 **Raja** *island* Indonesia
374 C3 **Raja, Ujung** *cape* Indonesia
372 D4 **Raja Ampat, Kepulauan** *island* Indonesia
374 E5 **Rajabasa, Gunung** *volcano* Indonesia
393 E8 **Rajahmundry** Andhra Pradesh India
223 O3 **Rajala** Finland
393 F7 **Rajam** Andhra Pradesh India
225 M2 **Rajamäki** Finland
375 F3 **Rajang** Malaysia
375 G3 **Rajang** *watercourse* Malaysia
391 L3 **Rajanpur** Pakistan
393 E8 **Rajapur** Andhra Pradesh India
392 C5 **Rajasthan** *admin. area* India
222 I4 **Rajastrand/Söfors** Sweden
392 D4 **Rajauri** Jammu and Kashmir India/Pakistan
392 G5 **Rajbiraj** Nepal
392 D6 **Rajgarh** Madhya Pradesh India
374 E4 **Rajik** Indonesia
386 F2 **Rajin** North Korea
234 B4 **Rajince** Serbia
227 I3 **Rajka** Hungary
393 C6 **Rajkot** Gujarat India
393 G7 **Rajnagar** Orissa India
393 C7 **Rajpipla** Gujarat India
393 D7 **Rajpur** Madhya Pradesh India
392 C6 **Rajsamand** Rajasthan India
379 F4 **Rajshahi** Bangladesh
379 F4 **Rajshahi** *admin. area* Bangladesh
393 C7 **Rajula** Gujarat India
426 1 **Rakahanga** *island* Cook Islands New Zealand
306 E4 **Rakai** Uganda
423 D6 **Rakaia** *watercourse* New Zealand
423 E6 **Rakaia Huts** New Zealand
234 B1 **Rakamaz** Hungary
391 M2 **Rakaposhi** *mountain* Pakistan
378 D2 **Rakas Lake** Xizang Zizhiqu China
225 N6 **Rakaw** Belarus
241 G3 **Rake** West Sussex England UK
227 H5 **Rakek** Slovenia
376 B3 **Rakhine** *admin. area* Myanmar
379 H5 **Rakhine Yoma** Myanmar
234 D1 **Rakhiv** Ukraine
225 P2 **Rakh'ya** Russian Federation
427 9a **Rakiraki** Fiji
374 F5 **Rakit** *island* Indonesia
394 E2 **Rakitnoye** Russian Federation
232 H4 **Rakitovica** Croatia
225 N3 **Rakke** Estonia
307 H2 **Rako** Somalia
308 D4 **Rakops** Botswana
227 J3 **Rakovà** Slovakia
227 K2 **Raków** Poland
223 M3 **Räktjärv** *lake* Sweden
388 F5 **Rakushechnyy, Mys** *cape* Kazakhstan
222 G5 **Råkvåg** Norway
225 N3 **Rakvere** Estonia
224 H4 **Ralången** *lake* Sweden
130 G4 **Raleigh** Mississippi USA
131 L3 **Raleigh** North Carolina USA
131 M3 **Raleigh Bay** North Carolina USA
124 I2 **Raley** Alberta Canada
227 L3 **Ralivka** Ukraine
122 E3 **Ralleau, Lac** *lake* Québec Canada
310 6b **Rallier du Baty, Péninsule** *peninsula* French Southern and Antarctic Lands
129 L4 **Ralls** Texas USA
234 B3 **Ram** Serbia
134 C4 **Rama** Nicaragua
159 F3 **Rama-Rama** Brazil
393 F8 **Ramachandrapuram** Andhra Pradesh India
159 G5 **Ramada del Pato** Bolivia
158 E5 **Ramadilla** Bolivia
160 D2 **Ramaditas** Chile
393 E7 **Ramagundam** Andhra Pradesh India
125 M7 **Ramah** Colorado USA
392 D5 **Raman** Punjab India
393 D9 **Ramanagaram** Karnataka India
393 E10 **Ramanathapuram** Tamil Nadu India
393 C8 **Ramas, Cape** Goa India
244 B3 **Ramasaig** Highland Scotland UK
308 E5 **Ramatlabama** South Africa
222 H2 **Ramberg** Norway
229 H2 **Rambervillers** France
393 F7 **Rambha** Orissa India
228 E2 **Rambouillet** France
373 H4 **Rambutyo Island** Papua New Guinea
393 D8 **Ramdurg** Karnataka India
240 C4 **Rame** Cornwall England UK
240 C4 **Rame Head** *cape* England UK
123 J9 **Ramea** Newfoundland and Labrador Canada
123 J9 **Ramea Islands** Newfoundland and Labrador Canada
392 G5 **Ramechhap** Nepal
238 G4 **Rameshki** Russian Federation
393 E10 **Rameswaram** Tamil Nadu India
393 F6 **Ramgarh** Chhattisgarh India
392 F6 **Ramgarh** Jharkhand India
393 C8 **Ramgarh** Maharashtra India
392 C5 **Ramgarh** Rajasthan India
390 G3 **Rāmhormoz** Iran
425 J3 **Ramingining** NT Australia
162 A5 **Ramírez, Isla** *island* Chile
307 G2 **Ramis** *watercourse* Ethiopia
392 F6 **Ramkola** Chhattisgarh India
302 C3 **Ramlat Rabyānah** *desert* Libya
390 C3 **Ramm, Jabal** *mountain* Jordan
224 E4 **Ramme** Denmark
392 E5 **Ramnagar** Uttar Pradesh India
234 D3 **Râmnicu Vâlcea** Romania
394 F2 **Ramon** Russian Federation
129 J3 **Ramon** New Mexico USA
126 D8 **Ramona** Oklahoma USA
125 Q4 **Ramona** South Dakota USA
132 E3 **Ramos Arizpe** Mexico
161 G6 **Ramos Otero** Argentina
229 J3 **Ramosch** Switzerland
242 E2 **Rampside** Cumbria England UK
393 E7 **Rampur** Andhra Pradesh India
392 D4 **Rampur** Himachal Pradesh India
392 E6 **Rampur** Madhya Pradesh India
393 F7 **Rampur** Orissa India
392 C6 **Rampur** Rajasthan India
392 E5 **Rampur** Uttar Pradesh India
379 G5 **Ramree** Myanmar
379 G5 **Ramree Island** Myanmar
224 H3 **Ramsberg** Sweden
243 F3 **Ramsbottom** Greater Manchester England UK
222 J5 **Ramsele** Sweden
242 D2 **Ramsey** Isle of Man UK
241 G2 **Ramsey** Cambridgeshire England UK
240 B3 **Ramsey Island** Wales UK
241 G2 **Ramsey St Marys** Cambridgeshire England UK
379 G3 **Ramsing** *mountain* Xizang Zizhiqu China
222 I5 **Ramsjö** Sweden
222 J2 **Ramsund** Norway
393 F7 **Ramtek** Chhattisgarh India
373 H5 **Ramu** *watercourse* Papua New Guinea
222 J5 **Ramvik** Sweden
305 G2 **Ran** Nigeria
222 I3 **Rana** *watercourse* Norway
392 D6 **Rana Pratap Sagar** *lake* Madhya Pradesh India
372 B6 **Ranaka, Gunung** *volcano* Indonesia
392 D6 **Ranapur** Madhya Pradesh India
375 H2 **Ranau** Malaysia
374 D5 **Ranau, Danau** *lake* Indonesia
160 D5 **Rancagua** Chile
228 F5 **Rance** *watercourse* France
159 I6 **Rancharia** Brazil
118 F2 **Rancheria** Yukon Territory Canada
129 I5 **Rancheria** Mexico
129 I7 **Rancheria Valerio** Mexico
125 L4 **Ranchester** Wyoming USA
392 F6 **Ranchi** Jharkhand India
132 D3 **Rancho Benton** Mexico
132 D3 **Rancho de Agujas** Mexico
132 D2 **Rancho de las Lilas** Mexico
132 E3 **Rancho El Altos** Mexico
132 E2 **Rancho El Milagro** Mexico
132 A2 **Rancho El Salado** Mexico
132 A2 **Rancho Grande** Mexico
132 B2 **Rancho Guadalupe** Mexico
132 C2 **Rancho La Junta** Mexico
132 C2 **Rancho La Noria** Mexico
132 D3 **Rancho La Puerta** Mexico
132 C2 **Rancho Los Cabezones** Mexico
128 D4 **Rancho Mirage** California USA
132 C2 **Rancho Monumento** Mexico
132 B2 **Rancho Pozo Hielo Estrella** Mexico
132 D2 **Rancho San Francisco** Mexico
132 E3 **Rancho Santa Fe** Mexico
159 H6 **Rancho São Francisco** Brazil
133 F3 **Rancho Sol de Mayo** Mexico
159 E5 **Rancho Tarueca** Bolivia
134 D2 **Rancho Veloz** Cuba
132 E4 **Rancho Verde** Mexico
154 D2 **Ranchogrande** Colombia
162 B2 **Ranco, Lago** *lake* Chile
303 G5 **Randa** Djibouti
130 B7 **Randado** Texas USA
126 D3 **Randall** Minnesota USA
228 F3 **Randan** France
222 H5 **Rånddalen** Sweden
224 F4 **Randers** Denmark
222 K3 **Randijaur** Sweden
222 K3 **Randijaure** *bay* Sweden
229 H3 **Randogne** Switzerland
125 Q5 **Randolph** Nebraska USA
127 L5 **Randolph** New York USA
123 L8 **Random Island** Newfoundland and Labrador Canada
372 F4 **Randowaya** Indonesia
222 F6 **Randsverk** Norway
222 M4 **Råneå** Sweden
222 L3 **Råneälven** *watercourse* Sweden
222 G4 **Ranemsletta** Norway
228 D2 **Rânes** France
119 P6 **Ranfurly** Alberta Canada
423 D7 **Ranfurly** New Zealand
379 G4 **Rangamati** Bangladesh
379 G3 **Rangapara** Assam India
422 F4 **Rangataua** New Zealand
423 6 **Rangatira Island** Chatham Islands New Zealand
422 E2 **Ranganu Harbour** New Zealand
127 P4 **Rangeley** Maine USA
125 K6 **Rangely** Colorado USA
130 B4 **Ranger** Texas USA
126 J3 **Ranger Lake** Ontario Canada
379 G3 **Rangia** Assam India
Rangiora *see* **Pitt Island** New Zealand
423 E6 **Rangiora** New Zealand
427 14 **Rangiputa** New Zealand
427 14 **Rangiroa** *island* French Polynesia
422 G4 **Rangitaiki** New Zealand
422 G4 **Rangitaiki** *watercourse* New Zealand
423 D7 **Rangitata** New Zealand
423 D6 **Rangitata** *watercourse* New Zealand
422 G4 **Rangitikei** *watercourse* New Zealand
423 F5 **Rangitoto Islands** New Zealand
374 E5 **Rangkasbitung** Indonesia
380 C2 **Rangke** Sichuan China
379 H3 **Rangku** Arunachal Pradesh India
386 E3 **Rangnim** North Korea
379 F4 **Rangpur** Bangladesh
374 D3 **Rangsang** *island* Indonesia
392 C6 **Rani** Rajasthan India
393 D8 **Ranibennur** Karnataka India
392 G6 **Raniganj** West Bengal India
392 F6 **Ranijula Peak** *mountain* Chhattisgarh India
392 C6 **Raniwara** Rajasthan India
390 E2 **Rāniyah** Iraq
425 K5 **Ranken** *watercourse* NT Australia
224 G3 **Ränken** *lake* Sweden
129 L5 **Rankin** Texas USA
120 I1 **Rankin Inlet** Nunavut Canada
392 B6 **Rann of Kachchh** Gujarat India
225 N3 **Ranna** Estonia
244 D4 **Rannoch Moor** *region* Scotland UK
224 G3 **Rannsjön** *lake* Sweden
225 N3 **Rannu** Estonia
305 F2 **Rano** Nigeria
309 I4 **Ranohira** Madagascar
121 O7 **Ranoke** Ontario Canada
393 C6 **Ranoli** Gujarat India
223 M4 **Rånön** *island* Sweden
426 8 **Ranonnga** *island* Solomon Islands
376 D6 **Ranot** Thailand
309 I4 **Ranotsara Avatatra** Madagascar
222 I4 **Ransarn** *lake* Sweden
372 E4 **Ransiki** Indonesia
224 G2 **Ransjön** *lake* Sweden
125 P7 **Ransom** Kansas USA
224 I3 **Ransta** Sweden
223 M3 **Rantajärvi** Sweden
223 P5 **Rantasalmi** Finland
375 G4 **Rantau** Indonesia
374 D3 **Rantau** *island* Indonesia
374 D3 **Rantaukampar** Indonesia
375 G4 **Rantaupanjang** Indonesia
375 H4 **Rantauprapat** Indonesia
375 G4 **Rantaupulut** Indonesia
372 B4 **Rantemario, Gunung** *mountain* Indonesia
126 G6 **Rantoul** Illinois USA
238 F4 **Rantsevo** Russian Federation
223 N4 **Rantsila** Finland
223 O4 **Ranua** Finland
426 7 **Ranwas** Vanuatu
385 M3 **Raohe** Heilongjiang China
229 H2 **Raon-l'Étape** France
232 D4 **Raossi** Italy
223 S **Raoul Island** Kermadec Islands New Zealand
385 J4 **Raoyang He** *watercourse* China
427 14 **Rapa** *island* French Polynesia
225 L5 **Rapa** Poland
393 C6 **Rapar** Gujarat India
160 D5 **Rapel** *watercourse* Chile
162 A4 **Râper, Cabo** *cape* Chile
117 M5 **Raper, Cape** Nunavut Canada
245 E2 **Raphoe** Ireland
125 O1 **Rapid City** Manitoba Canada
125 N4 **Rapid City** South Dakota USA
119 Q5 **Rapid View** Saskatchewan Canada
225 M3 **Rapla** Estonia
223 M3 **Raplamaa** *admin. area* Estonia
225 N2 **Rapojärvi** *lake* Finland
156 C4 **Raposa** Brazil
375 H4 **Rappang** Indonesia
222 J3 **Rappen** *lake* Sweden
389 K6 **Rāqh** Afghanistan
127 N5 **Raquette Lake** New York USA
309 G3 **Raraga** *watercourse* Mozambique
427 14 **Raroia** *island* French Polynesia
229 H3 **Raron** Switzerland
422 1 **Rarotonga** *island* Cook Islands New Zealand
390 F7 **Ra's al Kalb** Yemen
391 H4 **Ra's al Khaymah** United Arab Emirates
233 C9 **Râs el Aïoun** Algeria
301 F2 **Râs el Ma** Algeria
300 F5 **Râs el Mâ** Mali
302 E2 **Ra's Ghārib** Egypt
229 L4 **Raša** Croatia
377 H5 **Rasa** *island* Philippines
162 D2 **Rasa, Punta** *cape* Argentina
162 D4 **Rasa Chica, Isla** *island* Argentina
223 O5 **Räsälä** Finland
310 3a **Rasca, Punta de la** *cape* Canary Islands
226 G2 **Raschau** Germany
234 F2 **Rașcov** Moldova
225 L5 **Raseiniai** Lithuania
384 E2 **Rashaant** Mongolia
302 E5 **Rashad** Sudan
245 F2 **Rasharkin** Ballymoney Northern Ireland UK
302 E1 **Rashid** Egypt
390 F3 **Rashnūdi** Iran
388 F6 **Rasht** Iran
234 D3 **Rășinari** Romania
232 G3 **Rasinja** Croatia
225 O1 **Rasivaara** Finland
243 G2 **Raskelf** North Yorkshire England UK
117 J5 **Rasmussen Basin** Nunavut Canada
234 D3 **Râșnov** Romania
310 4 **Raso** *island* Cape Verde
424 H7 **Rason, Lake** WA Australia
234 E3 **Rasova** Romania
234 C4 **Rasovo** Bulgaria
392 F6 **Rasra** Uttar Pradesh India
237 AF9 **Rasshua, Ostrov** *island* Kuril Islands
387 L1 **Rasshua, Ostrov** *lake* Russian Federation
388 D3 **Rasskazovo** Russian Federation
237 AF5 **Rassokha** *watercourse* Russian Federation
226 E3 **Rastatt** Germany
222 L2 **Råsto** *island* Sweden
222 L2 **Råstojaure** *lake* Sweden
234 C4 **Rastu** Romania
222 I3 **Råsvalen** *lake* Sweden
373 H4 **Rat Island** Papua New Guinea
237 AK8 **Rat Island** Alaska USA
119 V4 **Rat Lake** Manitoba Canada
119 O2 **Rat River** Northwest Territories Canada
422 F4 **Rata** New Zealand
244 C3 **Ratagan** Highland Scotland UK
374 E5 **Ratai, Gunung** *mountain* Indonesia
222 L5 **Ratan** Sweden
222 I5 **Rätan** Sweden
392 D5 **Ratangarh** Rajasthan India
392 F7 **Ratanpur** Chhattisgarh India
392 C6 **Ratanpur** Gujarat India
392 E6 **Rath** Uttar Pradesh India
245 D4 **Ráth Luirc** Ireland
245 F3 **Rathangan** Ireland
242 B4 **Rathanna** Ireland
126 E6 **Rathbun Lake** Iowa USA
240 A1 **Rathconnellwood** Ireland
245 F3 **Rathcoole** Ireland
242 B3 **Rathcor** Ireland
245 F3 **Rathcore** Ireland
245 D4 **Rathcormack** Ireland
245 F4 **Rathdrum** Ireland
379 G5 **Rathedaung** Myanmar
242 B3 **Rathfeigh** Ireland
245 F2 **Rathfriland** Newry and Mourne Northern Ireland UK
245 D4 **Rathkeale** Ireland
245 F1 **Rathlin Island** Northern Ireland UK
243 F2 **Rathmell** North Yorkshire England UK
245 E1 **Rathmelton** Ireland
245 C4 **Rathmore** Ireland
245 E1 **Rathmullan** Ireland
245 F4 **Rathnageeragh** Ireland
245 F4 **Rathnew** Ireland
245 C4 **Rathomin Bridge** Ireland
242 A3 **Rathowen** Ireland
245 F3 **Rathtroane** Ireland
245 F4 **Rathvilly** Ireland
392 D6 **Ratlam** Madhya Pradesh India
240 E2 **Ratlinghope** Shropshire England UK
393 C8 **Ratnagiri** Maharashtra India
393 E10 **Ratnapura** Sri Lanka
227 M2 **Ratne** Ukraine
225 M6 **Ratnyčia** Lithuania
245 F3 **Ratoath** Ireland
129 J2 **Raton** New Mexico USA
236 R6 **Ratta** Russian Federation
244 E2 **Rattar** Highland Scotland UK
244 G3 **Rattray Head** *cape* Scotland UK
223 N3 **Rattosjärvi** *lake* Finland
244 E4 **Rattray** Perth and Kinross Scotland UK
222 L5 **Ratu** Sweden
225 N2 **Ratula** Finland
118 E4 **Ratz, Mount** British Columbia/Alaska Canada/USA
226 F1 **Ratzeburger See** *lake* Germany
375 K3 **Rau** *island* Indonesia
225 L5 **Râu-de-Mori** Romania
234 D3 **Râu Sadului** Romania
374 D3 **Raub** Malaysia
161 G6 **Rauch** Argentina
237 AI5 **Rauchua** *watercourse* Russian Federation
162 B3 **Rauco** Chile
223 O3 **Raudanjoki** Finland
223 O5 **Raudanvesi** *lake* Finland
223 N5 **Raudaskylä** Finland
121 W5 **Raude, Lac** *lake* Québec Canada
222 F5 **Raudsand** Norway
222 I3 **Raudvatnet** *lake* Norway
222 inset **Raufarhöfn** Iceland
223 N3 **Rauhala** Finland
158 B3 **Raujunte, Nevado** *mountain* Peru
222 I4 **Raukasjön** *lake* Sweden
225 K2 **Rauma** Finland
225 M4 **Rauna** Latvia
241 G2 **Raunds** Northamptonshire England UK
422 F4 **Raurimu** New Zealand
393 F6 **Raurkela** Orissa India
387 J2 **Rausu-dake** *volcano* Japan
234 F2 **Raut** *watercourse* Moldova
223 O5 **Rautalampi** Finland
222 K3 **Rautas** Sweden
222 K2 **Rautasjärvi** *lake* Sweden
223 P5 **Rautavaara** Finland
225 L5 **Rautavesi** *bay* Finland
225 M2 **Rautavesi** *lake* Finland
223 N4 **Rautio** Finland
225 O2 **Rautjärvi** Finland
222 I3 **Rauvatn** Norway
232 F5 **Rava** *island* Croatia
227 L2 **Rava-Rus'ka** Ukraine
233 E8 **Ravanusa** Italy
391 H3 **Rāvar** Iran
389 K6 **Ravat** Kyrgyzstan
127 O5 **Ravena** New York USA
130 F2 **Ravenden** Arkansas USA
242 E2 **Ravenglass** Cumbria England UK
241 I2 **Raveningham** Norfolk England UK
226 G5 **Ravenna** Italy
126 J8 **Ravenna** Kentucky USA
125 P6 **Ravenna** Nebraska USA
130 C4 **Ravenna** Texas USA
226 E4 **Ravensburg** Germany
243 H2 **Ravenscar** North Yorkshire England UK
119 Q8 **Ravenscrag** Saskatchewan Canada
425 M4 **Ravenshoe** Qld Australia
240 E1 **Ravensmoor** Cheshire England UK
424 G8 **Ravensthorpe** WA Australia
243 F2 **Ravenstonedale** Cumbria England UK
391 M3 **Ravi** *watercourse* Pakistan
130 C3 **Ravia** Oklahoma USA
228 F5 **Raviège, Lac de la** *lake* France
117 Q5 **Ravn, Kap** *cape* Greenland
227 H4 **Ravne** Slovenia
232 H4 **Ravno Selo** Serbia
222 K5 **Rävsön** Sweden
222 J3 **Råvvejaure** *lake* Sweden
243 H2 **Raw** North Yorkshire England UK
227 K2 **Rawa Mazowiecka** Poland
426 1 **Rawaki** *island* Kiribati
391 M2 **Rawalpindi** Pakistan
390 E2 **Rawandoz** Iraq
374 D4 **Rawas** *watercourse* Indonesia
392 D6 **Rawatbhata** Rajasthan India
392 D5 **Rawatsar** Rajasthan India
119 U5 **Rawebb** Manitoba Canada
422 E2 **Rawene** New Zealand
422 F4 **Rawhiti** New Zealand
376 C6 **Rawi, Ko** *island* Thailand
227 I2 **Rawicz** Poland
424 H7 **Rawlinna** WA Australia
125 L6 **Rawlins** Wyoming USA
162 D3 **Rawson** Argentina
436 N1 **Rawson Mountains** Antarctica
245 E1 **Ray** Ireland
125 N2 **Ray** North Dakota USA
123 I9 **Ray, Cape** Newfoundland and Labrador Canada
131 J5 **Ray City** Georgia USA
119 W2 **Ray Lake** Nunavut Canada
130 C4 **Ray Roberts Lake** Texas USA
375 G4 **Raya, Bukit** *mountain* Indonesia
393 E8 **Rayachoti** Andhra Pradesh India
393 D8 **Rayadurg** Andhra Pradesh India
393 F7 **Rayagada** Orissa India
385 L2 **Raychikhinsk** Russian Federation
238 G3 **Rayda** Russian Federation
237 AF9 **Raykoke, Ostrov** *island* Russian Federation
235 D5 **Raykovo** Bulgaria
243 F1 **Raylees** Northumberland England UK
119 O8 **Raymond** Alberta Canada
124 D3 **Raymond** Washington USA
425 N8 **Raymond Terrace** NSW Australia
130 C7 **Raymondville** Texas USA
126 D7 **Raymore** Missouri USA
423 8 **Raynal, Mount** Auckland Islands New Zealand
437 D2 **Rayner Glacier** Antarctica
128 G6 **Rayón** Mexico
133 F4 **Rayón** Mexico
133 G5 **Rayón** Mexico
376 D4 **Rayong** Thailand
223 M5 **Räyrinki** Finland
127 M6 **Raystown Lake** Pennsylvania USA
126 D7 **Raytown** Missouri USA
130 F4 **Rayville** Louisiana USA
391 L3 **Razani** Pakistan
234 E3 **Războieni** Romania
232 G4 **Razboj** Bosnia and Herzegovina
388 D6 **Razdan** Armenia
391 I3 **Razeh** Iran
390 G2 **Razeqan** Iran
234 E4 **Razgrad** Bulgaria
234 E4 **Razgrad** *admin. area* Bulgaria
234 F3 **Razim, Lacul** *lake* Romania
225 N4 **Rāznas** *lake* Latvia
238 E6 **Razrytoye** Russian Federation
228 D3 **Ré, Île de** *island* France
241 H2 **Reach** Cambridgeshire England UK
124 C1 **Read Island** British Columbia Canada
241 G3 **Reading** *admin. area* England UK
241 G3 **Reading** Reading England UK
127 N6 **Reading** Pennsylvania USA
243 F2 **Reagill** Cumbria England UK
157 E5 **Real** *watercourse* Brazil
230 B3 **Real** Portugal
157 A9 **Realeza** Brazil
160 E5 **Realicó** Argentina
132 C2 **Realito** Mexico
228 F5 **Réalmont** France
427 14 **Reao** *island* French Polynesia
244 E2 **Reay** Highland Scotland UK
233 C8 **Rebaa Oulad Yahia** Tunisia
226 B3 **Rebais** France
222 K1 **Rebbenesøy** *island* Norway
132 C2 **Rebeico** Mexico
372 E5 **Rebi** Indonesia
223 Q5 **Reboly** Russian Federation
230 C3 **Rebordelo** Portugal
230 B2 **Rebordelo** Spain
389 N2 **Rebrikha** Russian Federation
235 B5 **Reç** Albania
162 A5 **Recalada, Isla** *island* Chile
232 E5 **Recanati** Italy
230 E3 **Recas** Spain
229 G3 **Recey-sur-Ource** France
231 G6 **Rechaïga** Algeria
225 P4 **Rechane** Russian Federation
424 G8 **Recherche, Archipelago of the** WA Australia
238 D6 **Rechitsa** Belarus
234 E4 **Rechitsa** Bulgaria
234 D1 **Rechka** Ukraine
394 D2 **Rechytsa** Belarus
227 H5 **Rečica** Croatia
156 F5 **Recife** Brazil
308 E6 **Recife, Cape** South Africa
226 D2 **Recklinghausen** Germany
232 D4 **Recoaro Terme** Italy
377 I6 **Recodo** Philippines
161 G4 **Reconquista** Argentina
436 W1 **Recovery Glacier** Antarctica
157 D8 **Recreio** Brazil
159 F2 **Recreio** Brazil
154 C5 **Recreo** Peru
128 F2 **Rector** Arkansas USA
241 I3 **Reculver** Kent England UK
227 H1 **Recz** Poland
227 J2 **Ręczno** Poland
130 E4 **Red** *watercourse* Louisiana USA
125 Q3 **Red** *watercourse* Minnesota USA
126 C3 **Red** *watercourse* North Dakota USA
123 J7 **Red Bay** Newfoundland and Labrador Canada
124 D6 **Red Bluff** California USA
129 K5 **Red Bluff Reservoir** Texas USA
126 G7 **Red Bud** Illinois USA
125 L7 **Red Cliff** Colorado USA
120 I5 **Red Cross Lake** Manitoba Canada
119 O6 **Red Deer** Alberta Canada
119 N7 **Red Deer** *watercourse* Alberta Canada
119 T6 **Red Deer** *watercourse* Saskatchewan Canada
118 K5 **Red Deer Creek** British Columbia Canada
119 U6 **Red Deer Lake** Manitoba Canada
119 N4 **Red Earth Creek** Alberta Canada
242 A3 **Red Gate** Ireland
130 B2 **Red Hills** *range* Kansas USA
123 J8 **Red Indian Lake** Newfoundland and Labrador Canada
123 K9 **Red Island** Newfoundland and Labrador Canada
120 I7 **Red Lake** Ontario Canada
128 E3 **Red Lake** Arizona USA
126 C3 **Red Lake** *watercourse* Minnesota USA
125 K6 **Red Lake** Wyoming USA
125 Q3 **Red Lake Falls** Minnesota USA
125 K4 **Red Lodge** Montana USA
129 J2 **Red River** New Mexico USA
126 G2 **Red Rock** Ontario Canada
125 Q8 **Red Rock** Oklahoma USA
390 D5/6 **Red Sea** Middle East
302 F4 **Red Sea** *admin. area* Sudan
127 K7 **Red Spruce Knob** *mountain* West Virginia USA
120 I5 **Red Sucker Lake** Manitoba Canada
119 O6 **Red Willow** Alberta Canada
122 H5 **Red Wine** *watercourse* Newfoundland and Labrador Canada
126 E4 **Red Wing** Minnesota USA
222 F5 **Redalen** Norway
374 D2 **Redang** *island* Malaysia
119 R6 **Redberry Lake** Saskatchewan Canada
243 H3 **Redbourne** North Lincolnshire England UK
244 D3 **Redburn** Highland Scotland UK
243 F1 **Redburn** Northumberland England UK
243 G2 **Redcar** Redcar and Cleveland England UK
243 H2 **Redcar and Cleveland** *admin. area* England UK
124 D6 **Redding** California USA
241 F2 **Redditch** Worcestershire England UK
227 I4 **Réde** Hungary
156 B4 **Redenção** Brazil
156 E4 **Redenção** Brazil
301 H2 **Redeyef** Tunisia
125 P4 **Redfield** South Dakota USA
121 V6 **Redfir Lake** Newfoundland and Labrador Canada
240 A1 **Redford** Ireland
130 E2 **Redford** Texas USA
163 9 **Redhead** Trinidad and Tobago
245 D3 **Redhill** Ireland
241 G3 **Redhill** Surrey England UK
238 G4 **Redkino** Russian Federation
128 D3 **Redlands** California USA
241 F4 **Redlynch** Wiltshire England UK
124 E4 **Redmond** Oregon USA
124 D2 **Redmond** Washington USA
226 F3 **Rednitz** *watercourse* Germany
228 C3 **Redon** France
135 I3 **Redonda** *island* Antigua and Barbuda
163 9 **Redonda, Isla** *island* Venezuela
163 5 **Redonda, Punta** *cape* Isla de Pascua (Easter Island)
230 B2 **Redondela** Spain
230 C3 **Redondo** Portugal
160 E2 **Redondo, Cerro** *mountain* Chile
121 V5 **Redore** Newfoundland and Labrador Canada
244 C3 **Redpoint** Highland Scotland UK
129 H4 **Redrock** New Mexico USA
240 B4 **Redruth** Cornwall England UK
373 H6 **Redscar Bay** Papua New Guinea
118 J5 **Redstone** British Columbia Canada
116 G6 **Redstone** *watercourse* Northwest Territories Canada
129 H1 **Redvale** Colorado USA
119 O6 **Redwater** Alberta Canada
130 D4 **Redwater** Texas USA
244 E4 **Redwells** Fife Scotland UK
125 R4 **Redwood Falls** Minnesota USA
245 E3 **Ree, Lough** *lake* Ireland
126 I5 **Reed City** Michigan USA
119 U5 **Reed Lake** Manitoba Canada
125 N3 **Reeder** North Dakota USA
241 I2 **Reedham** Norfolk England UK
128 C2 **Reedley** California USA
243 H3 **Reedness** East Riding of Yorkshire England UK
124 C5 **Reedsport** Oregon USA
436 P1 **Reedy Glacier** Antarctica
130 G2 **Reelfoot Lake** Tennessee USA
245 B5 **Reenard Cross** Ireland
226 D2 **Rees** Germany
423 C7 **Rees** *watercourse* New Zealand
162 E5 **Rees Harbour** Falkland Islands
124 G6 **Reese** *watercourse* Nevada USA
243 G2 **Reeth** North Yorkshire England UK
242 A4 **Reevanagh** Ireland
130 H4 **Reform** Alabama USA
133 H5 **Reforma** Mexico
424 inset **Refuge, Port** Cocos (Keeling) Islands Australia
162 B3 **Refugio, Isla** *island* Chile
227 H1 **Rega** *watercourse* Poland
230 D6 **Regaïa** Morocco
226 G3 **Regen** *watercourse* Germany
156 D4 **Regeneração** Brazil
226 G3 **Regensburg** Germany
226 G3 **Regenstauf** Germany
125 N3 **Regent** North Dakota USA
157 B8 **Regente Feijó** Brazil
301 G3 **Reggane** Algeria
232 D5 **Reggello** Italy
233 F7 **Reggio di Calabria** Italy
226 F5 **Reggio nell'Emilia** Italy
234 D2 **Reghin** Romania
156 B1 **Regina** Brazil
119 S7 **Regina** Saskatchewan Canada
119 S7 **Regina Beach** Saskatchewan Canada
160 D5 **Región Metropolitana** *admin. area* Chile
233 G7 **Regione Calabria** *region* Italy
157 C9 **Registro** Brazil
157 B6 **Registro do Araguaia** Brazil
224 H3 **Regna** Sweden
389 J6 **Regor** Tajikistan
244 E3 **Regoul** Highland Scotland UK
223 Q4 **Regozero** Russian Federation
232 E1 **Rehau** Germany
392 E6 **Rehli** Madhya Pradesh India
308 C4 **Rehoboth** Namibia
127 N7 **Rehoboth Bay** Delaware USA
127 N7 **Rehoboth Beach** Delaware USA
373 I5 **Reibeck Bay** Papua New Guinea
121 X3 **Reichel Head** Newfoundland and Labrador Canada
229 H2 **Reichshoffen** France
244 C3 **Reidh, Rubha** *cape* Scotland UK
131 J4 **Reidsville** Georgia USA
131 L2 **Reidsville** North Carolina USA
244 C2 **Reiff** Highland Scotland UK
241 G3 **Reigate** Surrey England UK
231 I2 **Reillanne** France
226 C3 **Reims** France
162 A5 **Reina Adelaida, Archipiélago de la** *island* Chile
119 T5 **Reindeer** *watercourse* Saskatchewan Canada
119 W6 **Reindeer Island** Manitoba Canada
120 D4 **Reindeer Lake** Manitoba/Saskatchewan Canada
222 H3 **Reine** Norway
422 E2 **Reinga, Cape** New Zealand
226 E3 **Reinheim** Germany
222 J3 **Reinoksvatnet** *lake* Norway
230 D2 **Reinosa** Spain
222 K2 **Reinøy** *island* Norway
223 N1 **Reinøya** *island* Norway
224 F2 **Reinsvatnet** *lake* Norway
222 E5 **Reinsvik** Norway
223 M2 **Reisa Nasjonalpark** *park* Norway
223 M2 **Reisadalen Nasjonal Park** *park* Norway
222 L2 **Reisaelva** *watercourse* Norway
226 G3 **Reisbach** Germany
223 N5 **Reisjärvi** Finland
244 E2 **Reiss** Highland Scotland UK
222 G5 **Reitan** Norway
308 E5 **Reitz** South Africa
224 H3 **Rejmyre** Sweden
Rekohua *see* **Chatham Island** New Zealand
224 C2 **Reksteren** *island* Norway
238 D6 **Rekta** Belarus
222 J3 **Rekvatnet** *lake* Norway
225 L5 **Rėkyvos ežeras** *lake* Lithuania
238 C3 **Rel'** Russian Federation
245 C5 **Releagh** Ireland
125 P5 **Reliance** South Dakota USA
301 G1 **Relizane** Algeria
301 G1 **Relizane** *admin. area* Algeria
232 H3 **Rém** Hungary
301 I2 **Remada** Tunisia
158 C3 **Remanso** Brazil
159 F2 **Remanso** Brazil
423 C7 **Remarkables, The** *range* New Zealand
158 D2 **Remate de Males** Brazil
375 F5 **Rembang** Indonesia
375 F5 **Rembang, Teluk** *bay* Indonesia
222 I4 **Remdalen** Sweden
132 D3 **Remedios, Los** *watercourse* Mexico
134 B4 **Remedios, Punta** *cape* El Salvador
230 B2 **Remedios, Punta dos** *cape* Spain
226 D1 **Remels** Germany
234 D2 **Remetea** Romania
227 I4 **Remetinec** Croatia
127 J2 **Remi Lake** Ontario Canada
310 9 **Remire Island** Seychelles
155 H3 **Remire-Montjoly** French Guiana
229 H2 **Remiremont** France
222 J5 **Remmarbäcken** Sweden
158 C4 **Remolino** Peru
229 G5 **Remoulins** France
374 E3 **Rempang** *island* Indonesia
226 D2 **Remscheid** Germany
126 D5 **Remsen** Iowa USA
127 N5 **Remsen** New York USA
155 H4 **Remure** Brazil
226 C5 **Rémuzat** France
224 F2 **Rena** Norway
222 G5 **Rena** *watercourse* Norway
228 D3 **Renac** France
436 T2 **Renaud Island** Antarctica
232 E4 **Renče** Slovenia
383 K2 **Renchinlhumbe** Mongolia
126 G7 **Rend Lake** Illinois USA
225 L4 **Renda** Latvia
380 D3 **Rende** Yunnan China
233 G7 **Rende** Italy
426 8 **Rendova** *island* Solomon Islands
123 D7 **René-Levasseur, Île** *island* Québec Canada
226 B2 **Renesse** Netherlands
244 D5 **Renfrewshire** *admin. area* Scotland UK
222 H3 **Renga** *island* Norway
393 F7 **Rengali Reservoir** Orissa India
374 E5 **Rengasdengklok** Indonesia
374 D4 **Rengat** Indonesia
381 G3 **Renhua** Guangdong China
380 E3 **Renhuai** Guizhou China
234 F3 **Reni** Ukraine
162 B3 **Reñihué** Chile
244 B3 **Renish Point** Scotland UK
121 O7 **Renison** Ontario Canada
425 L8 **Renmark** SA Australia
222 F5 **Rennebu** Norway
426 8 **Rennell** *island* Solomon Islands
162 B5 **Rennell, Islas** *island* Chile

426 8 **Rennell and Bellona** *admin. area* Solomon Islands
118 E6 **Rennell Sound** British Columbia Canada
425 J4 **Renner Springs** NT Australia
228 D2 **Rennes** France
224 C3 **Rennesøy** *island* Norway
437 K2 **Rennick Bay** Antarctica
437 K2 **Rennick Glacier** Antarctica
437 L2 **Rennick Trough** *underwater feature* Southern Ocean
119 S2 **Rennie Lake** Northwest Territories Canada
243 G1 **Rennington** Northumberland England UK
118 M5 **Reno** Alberta Canada
232 D4 **Reno** *watercourse* Italy
124 F7 **Reno** Nevada USA
130 C4 **Reno** Texas USA
127 M6 **Renovo** Pennsylvania USA
385 H5 **Renqiu** Hebei China
222 K2 **Rensjön** Sweden
222 L4 **Renström** Sweden
235 B6 **Rentina** Greece
124 D3 **Renton** Washington USA
392 F6 **Renukut** Uttar Pradesh India
372 B6 **Reo** Indonesia
304 D2 **Réo** Burkina Faso
158 C3 **Repartición** Peru
158 D5 **Repartición** Peru
159 F3 **Repartimento** Brazil
388 I6 **Repetek** Turkmenistan
222 L5 **Replot** Finland
222 L5 **Replotfjärden** *island* Finland
223 N2 **Repokaira** *island* Finland
422 G4 **Reporoa** New Zealand
126 E8 **Republic** Missouri USA
124 F2 **Republic** Washington USA
159 F4 **República** Brazil
125 Q7 **Republican** *watercourse* Kansas USA
117 K5 **Repulse Bay** Nunavut Canada
158 C2 **Requena** Peru
231 F4 **Requena** Spain
155 E3 **Requena** Venezuela
228 F4 **Réquista** France
224 F5 **Rerik** Germany
245 C5 **Rerrin** Ireland
131 I3 **Resaca** Georgia USA
232 D4 **Resana** Italy
162 A4 **Rescue, Punta** *cape* Chile
79 BB6 **Researcher Ridge** *underwater feature* Atlantic Ocean
157 C8 **Resende** Brazil
157 B9 **Reserva** Brazil
158 D3 **Reserva Extrema** Brazil
162 C5 **Reserva Fiscal** Chile
119 T6 **Reserve** Saskatchewan Canada
129 H4 **Reserve** New Mexico USA
238 C4 **Reshëty** Russian Federation
388 F7 **Reshteh-ye Kūhhā-ye Alborz** *range* Iran
161 G3 **Resistencia** Argentina
234 B3 **Reşiţa** Romania
234 A4 **Resnik** Montenegro
117 J4 **Resolute** Nunavut Canada
122 F5 **Résolution, Lac** *lake* Québec Canada
122 F2 **Resolution Island** Nunavut Canada
423 B7 **Resolution Island** New Zealand
159 H5 **Resolvido** Brazil
240 C4 **Resourie** Highland Scotland UK
157 D7 **Resplendor** Brazil
388 C5 **Respublika Adygeya** *admin. area* Russian Federation
388 G2 **Respublika Bashkortostan** *admin. area* Russian Federation
237 X8 **Respublika Buryatiya** *admin. area* Russian Federation
388 E5 **Respublika Dagestan** *admin. area* Russian Federation
236 H6 **Respublika Kareliya** *admin. area* Russian Federation
236 L6 **Respublika Komi** *admin. area* Russian Federation
388 E2 **Respublika Mariy El** *admin. area* Russian Federation
388 D2 **Respublika Mordoviya** *admin. area* Russian Federation
237 AA6 **Respublika Sakha** *admin. area* Russian Federation
388 D5 **Respublika Severnaya Osetiya** *admin. area* Russian Federation
388 F2 **Respublika Tatarstan** *admin. area* Russian Federation
123 E9 **Restigouche** *watercourse* New Brunswick/Québec Canada
125 O2 **Reston** Manitoba Canada
244 F5 **Reston** Scottish Borders Scotland UK
134 B4 **Retalhuleu** Guatemala
422 F4 **Retaruke** New Zealand
228 D4 **Retaud** France
243 H3 **Retford** Nottinghamshire England UK
226 C3 **Rethel** France
235 D8 **Rethymno** Greece
226 C2 **Retie** Belgium
228 D3 **Retiers** France
154 D5 **Retiro** Brazil
159 G5 **Retiro** Brazil
159 G5 **Retiro Carrapatinho** Brazil
159 H5 **Retiro Central** Brazil
159 H5 **Retiro do Buriti** Brazil
159 G5 **Retiro do Presidente** Brazil
159 H6 **Retiro Monte Belo** Brazil
227 H3 **Retz** Austria
226 G1 **Reuden** Germany
228 F3 **Reuilly** France
310 7a **Réunion** *French overseas department* Indian Ocean
310 7 **Réunion** *island* Indian Ocean
231 G3 **Reus** Spain
374 C3 **Reusam** *island* Indonesia
226 C2 **Reusel** Netherlands
229 I3 **Reuss** *watercourse* Switzerland
226 E3 **Reutlingen** Germany
229 J3 **Reutte** Austria
223 S3 **Revda** Russian Federation
228 F5 **Revel** France
436 T2 **Revelle Inlet** *bay* Antarctica
118 L7 **Revelstoke** British Columbia Canada
118 L7 **Revelstoke, Lake** British Columbia Canada
309 G2 **Révia** Mozambique
132 C5 **Revillagigedo, Islas** *island* Mexico
118 F5 **Revillagigedo Channel** Alaska USA
118 F5 **Revillagigedo Island** Alaska USA
226 C3 **Revin** France
229 K1 **Řevničov** Czech Republic
226 F4 **Revò** Italy
223 N4 **Revonlahti** Finland
223 N1 **Revsbotn** *bay* Norway
222 J2 **Revsnes** Norway
224 I4 **Revsudden** Sweden
222 I5 **Revsund** Sweden
222 I5 **Revsundssjön** *bay* Sweden
309 F3 **Revubue** *watercourse* Mozambique
232 I2 **Revúca** Slovakia
392 E6 **Rewa** Madhya Pradesh India
119 O6 **Reward** Saskatchewan Canada
392 D5 **Rewari** Haryana India
436 S2 **Rex, Mount** *mountain* Antarctica
124 J5 **Rexburg** Idaho USA
125 O7 **Rexford** Kansas USA
124 H2 **Rexford** Montana USA
154 B2 **Rey, Isla del** *island* Panama
129 K7 **Rey, Lago del** *lake* Mexico
132 E3 **Rey, Laguna del** *watercourse* Mexico
222 inset **Reyðarfjörður** *bay* Iceland
158 E3 **Reyes** Bolivia
124 D7 **Reyes, Point** California USA
158 B4 **Reyes, Punta** *cape* Peru
222 inset **Reykholt** Iceland
222 inset **Reykjahlíð** Iceland
435 E2 **Reykjanes Ridge** *underwater feature* Atlantic Ocean
222 inset **Reykjanestá** *cape* Iceland
222 inset **Reykjavík** Iceland
125 R2 **Reynolds** Manitoba Canada
131 I4 **Reynolds** Georgia USA
126 H6 **Reynolds** Indiana USA
125 Q3 **Reynolds** North Dakota USA
133 F3 **Reynosa** Mexico
240 C4 **Rezare** Cornwall England UK
225 N4 **Rēzekne** Latvia
225 N4 **Rēzeknes** *admin. area* Latvia
379 H2 **Rezhaka** Xizang Zizhiqu China
234 F2 **Rezina** Moldova
235 F5 **Rezovo** Bulgaria
232 D4 **Rezzato** Italy
232 B4 **Rezzo** Italy
125 N3 **Rhame** North Dakota USA
240 D2 **Rhandir-mwyn** Carmarthenshire Wales UK
240 D2 **Rhayader** Powys Wales UK
226 D2 **Rhede** Germany
229 H2 **Rhein** *watercourse* France
226 D3 **Rheinau** Germany
226 D1 **Rheine** Germany
226 D3 **Rheinland-Pfalz** *admin. area* Germany
240 D1 **Rhewl** Denbighshire Wales UK
127 O6 **Rhinebeck** New York USA
126 G4 **Rhinelander** Wisconsin USA
226 G1 **Rhinkanal** *watercourse* Germany
306 E3 **Rhino Camp** Uganda
226 G1 **Rhinow** Germany
240 C2 **Rhiw** Gwynedd Wales UK
232 C4 **Rho** Italy
Rhodes *see* **Rodos** Greece
235 D5 **Rhodope Mountains** *range* Bulgaria
130 C4 **Rhome** Texas USA
240 D3 **Rhondda** Rhondda Cynon Taff Wales UK
240 D3 **Rhondda Cynon Taff** *admin. area* Wales UK
229 G4 **Rhône** *watercourse* France
162 A3 **Rhone, Puerto** *bay* Chile
229 G4 **Rhône-Alpes** *admin. area* France
240 D3 **Rhoose** Vale of Glamorgan Wales UK
240 C3 **Rhos** Carmarthenshire Wales UK
242 E3 **Rhôs-on-Sea** Conwy Wales UK
240 C2 **Rhós-y-llan** Gwynedd Wales UK
240 D2 **Rhosgoch** Powys Wales UK
240 D1 **Rhosllanerchrugog** Wrexham Wales UK
242 D3 **Rhosneigr** Isle of Anglesey Wales UK
240 C3 **Rhossili** Swansea Wales UK
301 H1 **Rhoufi** Algeria
244 D4 **Rhu** Argyll and Bute Scotland UK
242 E3 **Rhuallt** Denbighshire Wales UK
244 C5 **Rhubodach** Argyll and Bute Scotland UK
242 E3 **Rhuddlan** Denbighshire Wales UK
240 C2 **Rhydcymmerau** Carmarthenshire Wales UK
240 C2 **Rhydlios** Gwynedd Wales UK
242 E3 **Rhyl** Denbighshire Wales UK
240 D3 **Rhymney** Caerphilly Wales UK
244 F3 **Rhynie** Aberdeenshire Scotland UK
305 F4 **Riaba** Equatorial Guinea
156 C4 **Riachão** Brazil
157 C5 **Riachão das Neves** Brazil
157 F5 **Riachão do Jacuipe** Brazil
157 D6 **Riacho de Santana** Brazil
162 E2 **Riachos, Islas de los** *island* Argentina
157 B6 **Rialma** Brazil
231 G3 **Rialp, Pantà de** *lake* Spain
379 G3 **Riang** Arunachal Pradesh India
230 B2 **Rianjo** Spain
229 G5 **Rians** France
392 D4 **Riasi** Jammu and Kashmir India/Pakistan
222 G5 **Riasten** *lake* Norway
374 D3 **Riau** *admin. area* Indonesia
226 D4 **Riaz** Switzerland
231 G3 **Riba-roja, Pantà de** *lake* Spain
230 C2 **Ribadeo** Spain
230 D2 **Ribadesella** Spain
231 G2 **Ribagorça** *region* Spain
234 D4 **Ribaritsa** Bulgaria
157 A8 **Ribas do Rio Pardo** Brazil
230 B4 **Ribatejo** *region* Portugal
309 G2 **Ribáuè** Mozambique
243 F2 **Ribble** *watercourse* England UK
243 F2 **Ribblesdale** *valley* England UK
243 F3 **Ribchester** Lancashire England UK
225 E5 **Ribe** Denmark
157 B9 **Ribeira** *watercourse* Brazil
230 B3 **Ribeira** Portugal
310 2 **Ribeira Brava** Madeira
310 4a **Ribeira da Barca** Cape Verde
157 E5 **Ribeira do Pombal** Brazil
310 1a **Ribeira Grande** Azores
310 4a **Ribeira Prata** Cape Verde
156 F5 **Ribeirão** Brazil
159 E3 **Ribeirão** Brazil
157 B9 **Ribeirão Branco** Brazil
157 B6 **Ribeirão Cascalheira** Brazil
159 I3 **Ribeirão Crisostomo** *watercourse* Brazil
157 C8 **Ribeirão Preto** Brazil
233 E8 **Ribera** Italy
230 B2 **Ribera** Spain
230 D3 **Ribera del Fresno** Spain
228 E4 **Ribérac** France
159 E3 **Riberalta** Bolivia
232 H4 **Ribnica** Bosnia and Herzegovina
227 H4 **Ribnica** Slovenia
227 H5 **Ribnica** Slovenia
234 F2 **Rîbniţa** Moldova
232 D5 **Ribolla** Italy
119 P6 **Ribstone** Alberta Canada
387 I2 **Ribun tō** *island* Japan
154 B4 **Ricaurte** Ecuador
233 F6 **Riccia** Italy
128 E3 **Rice** California USA
130 C4 **Rice** Texas USA
127 L4 **Rice Lake** Ontario Canada
126 F4 **Rice Lake** Wisconsin USA
162 B5 **Rice Trevor, Islas** *island* Chile
131 K5 **Riceboro** Georgia USA
119 P5 **Rich Lake** Alberta Canada
126 E2 **Richan** Ontario Canada
119 R6 **Richard** Saskatchewan Canada
131 J3 **Richard B. Russell Lake** Georgia USA
309 F5 **Richards Bay** South Africa
119 R3 **Richards Lake** Saskatchewan Canada
119 P3 **Richardson** *watercourse* Alberta Canada
119 P3 **Richardson Lake** Alberta Canada
116 F5 **Richardson Mountains** Northwest Territories/Yukon Territory Canada
423 C7 **Richardson Mountains** New Zealand
125 N3 **Richardton** North Dakota USA
123 J7 **Riche, Point** Newfoundland and Labrador Canada
128 E3 **Richelieu** France
126 C2 **Richer** Manitoba Canada
125 M3 **Richey** Montana USA
124 H5 **Richfield** Idaho USA
124 I7 **Richfield** Utah USA
245 F2 **Richill** Armagh Northern Ireland UK
131 I4 **Richland** Georgia USA
126 I5 **Richland** Michigan USA
124 G4 **Richland** Oregon USA
130 C5 **Richland** Texas USA
124 F3 **Richland** Washington USA
131 J3 **Richland Balsam** *mountain* North Carolina USA
126 F5 **Richland Center** Wisconsin USA
130 B5 **Richland Springs** Texas USA
127 K8 **Richlands** Virginia USA
425 L5 **Richmond** Qld Australia
118 J8 **Richmond** British Columbia Canada
127 O4 **Richmond** Québec Canada
308 D6 **Richmond** South Africa
163 11a **Richmond** St Vincent and the Grenadines
124 D8 **Richmond** California USA
126 I7 **Richmond** Indiana USA
126 I8 **Richmond** Kentucky USA
130 F4 **Richmond** Louisiana USA
127 M8 **Richmond** Virginia USA
423 E5 **Richmond Range** New Zealand
127 N5 **Richmondville** New York USA
119 Q7 **Richmound** Saskatchewan Canada
245 E3 **Richmount Hill** Ireland
130 E4 **Richwood** Louisiana USA
127 K7 **Richwood** West Virginia USA
241 G3 **Rickmansworth** Hertfordshire England UK
125 K8 **Rico** Colorado USA
230 D3 **Ricobayo, Embalse de** *lake* Spain
390 E7 **Ridā'** Yemen
437 E2 **Riddell Nunataks** *range* Antarctica
232 B3 **Riddes** Switzerland
124 D5 **Riddle** Oregon USA
225 L4 **Rideļi** Latvia
120 M7 **Ridge** *watercourse* Ontario Canada
128 D3 **Ridgecrest** California USA
119 S6 **Ridgedale** Saskatchewan Canada
130 F4 **Ridgeland** Mississippi USA
131 K4 **Ridgeland** South Carolina USA
127 K5 **Ridgetown** Ontario Canada
131 L2 **Ridgeway** Virginia USA
126 G5 **Ridgeway** Wisconsin USA
125 L7 **Ridgway** Colorado USA
234 A3 **Riđica** Serbia
119 U7 **Riding Mountain National Park** Manitoba Canada
241 G2 **Ridlington** Rutland England UK
243 F1 **Ridsdale** Northumberland England UK
222 J3 **Riebnes** *lake* Sweden
154 D3 **Riecito** *watercourse* Venezuela
226 G3 **Ried** Austria
222 I2 **Riedern** Germany
226 E3 **Riedlingen** Germany
228 B5 **Riego de la Vega** Spain
222 G5 **Rien** *lake* Norway
229 K1 **Riesa** Germany
233 F8 **Riesi** Italy
308 D6 **Rietbron** South Africa
308 D5 **Rietfontein** South Africa
233 E5 **Rieti** Italy
228 E5 **Rieumes** France
231 H1 **Rieupeyroux** France
243 G2 **Rievaulx** North Yorkshire England UK
229 H5 **Riez** France
381 G3 **Rifeng** Jiangxi China
124 D3 **Riffe Lake** Washington USA
125 L7 **Rifle** Colorado USA
307 F3 **Rift Valley** *admin. area* Kenya
301 I6 **Rig-Rig** Chad
225 M4 **Riga** Latvia
225 L4 **Riga, Gulf of** Estonia/Latvia
225 M4 **Rigas** *admin. area* Latvia
124 J5 **Rigby** Idaho USA
244 B3 **Rigg** Highland Scotland UK
124 H4 **Riggins** Idaho USA
244 E5 **Righead** Dumfries and Galloway Scotland UK
122 I5 **Rigolet** Newfoundland and Labrador Canada
244 E5 **Rigside** South Lanarkshire Scotland UK
225 L3 **Riguldi** Estonia
225 M2 **Riihimäki** Finland
223 O3 **Riipijärvi** *lake* Finland
436 W2 **Riiser-Larsen Basin** *underwater feature* Southern Ocean
436 W2 **Riiser-Larsen Ice Shelf** Antarctica
437 C2 **Riiser-Larsen Peninsula** Antarctica
437 B2 **Riiser-Larsen Sea** Antarctica
225 M3 **Riisipere** Estonia
225 K2 **Riispyy** Finland
223 P4 **Riitakylä** Finland
305 F2 **Rijau** Nigeria
232 F4 **Rijeka** Croatia
379 F3 **Rikaze** Xizang Zizhiqu China
223 P5 **Rikkavesi** *lake* Finland
379 H3 **Rikor** Arunachal Pradesh India
387 I3 **Rikuzentakata** Japan
234 C4 **Rila** *range* Bulgaria
228 E3 **Rillé** France
305 F2 **Rima** *watercourse* Nigeria
390 E4 **Rimah, Wādī ar** *watercourse* Saudi Arabia
427 I4 **Rimatara** *island* French Polynesia
374 E4 **Rimau** *island* Indonesia
227 J3 **Rimavská Baňa** Slovakia
119 N6 **Rimbey** Alberta Canada
232 E4 **Rimini** Italy
392 D3 **Rimo Glacier** Jammu and Kashmir India/Pakistan
123 D8 **Rimouski** Québec Canada
123 D8 **Rimouski** *watercourse* Québec Canada
124 E3 **Rimrock Lake** Washington USA
244 D2 **Rimsdale, Loch** *lake* Scotland UK
375 H6 **Rinca** *island* Indonesia
162 C5 **Rincón** Argentina
132 E4 **Rincón de Romos** Mexico
230 F2 **Rincón de Soto** Spain
161 G5 **Rincón del Bonete, Lago artificial de** *lake* Uruguay
163 7 **Rincon Grande Settlement** Falkland Islands
222 F5 **Rindal** Norway
235 D7 **Rineia** *island* Greece
242 B4 **Ring** Ireland
224 I3 **Ringarum** Sweden
392 D5 **Ringas** Rajasthan India
245 G2 **Ringboy** Ards Northern Ireland UK
224 F5 **Ringe** Denmark
222 G6 **Ringebu** Norway
224 D2 **Ringedalsvatnet** *lake* Norway
244 D6 **Ringford** Dumfries and Galloway Scotland UK
131 I4 **Ringgold** Louisiana USA
224 D5 **Ringkøbing Fjord** *lake* Denmark
241 I2 **Ringland** Norfolk England UK
130 C3 **Ringling** Oklahoma USA
224 G2 **Ringnäs** Sweden
242 B3 **Ringsend** Ireland
245 F1 **Ringsend** Coleraine Northern Ireland UK
224 I3 **Ringsön** *island* Sweden
241 G2 **Ringstead** Northamptonshire England UK
224 F5 **Ringsted** Denmark
241 F4 **Ringwood** Hampshire England UK
241 I3 **Ringwould** Kent England UK
225 O2 **Rinkilä** Finland
244 C6 **Rinns of Galloway** *peninsula* Scotland UK
226 E1 **Rinteln** Germany
158 D5 **Río Blanco** Bolivia
134 C4 **Río Blanco** Nicaragua
129 I1 **Rio Blanco** Colorado USA
155 F2 **Río Bonito** Venezuela
162 B5 **Río Bote** Argentina
162 F3 **Rio Branco** Brazil
159 G4 **Rio Branco** Brazil
133 F3 **Río Bravo** Mexico
130 B7 **Rio Bravo** Texas USA
159 H6 **Rio Brilhante** Brazil
157 D8 **Rio Casca** Brazil
134 E2 **Río Cauto** Cuba
162 B2 **Río Chico** Argentina
162 C4 **Río Chico** Argentina
162 B3 **Río Cisnes** Chile
157 C8 **Rio Claro** Brazil
160 C6 **Río Claro** Chile
163 9 **Rio Claro** Trinidad and Tobago
162 E2 **Río Colorado, Delta del** *region* Argentina
160 E5 **Río Cuarto** Argentina
157 D8 **Rio das Ostras** Brazil
309 G4 **Rio das Pedras** Mozambique
157 D8 **Rio de Janeiro** Brazil
161 K2 **Rio de Janeiro** *admin. area* Brazil
134 D6 **Río de Jesús** Panama
133 G5 **Río de Teapa** Mexico
124 C6 **Rio Dell** California USA
161 I3 **Rio do Sul** Brazil
134 C4 **Río Esteban** Honduras
162 C5 **Río Gallegos** Argentina
162 C5 **Río Grande** Argentina
158 E6 **Río Grande** Bolivia
161 H5 **Rio Grande** Brazil
160 D2 **Río Grande** Chile
132 E4 **Río Grande** Mexico
160 E3 **Río Grande, Salar de** *pan* Argentina
130 B7 **Rio Grande City** Texas USA
156 E4 **Rio Grande do Norte** *admin. area* Brazil
161 H4 **Rio Grande do Sul** *admin. area* Brazil
125 L8 **Rio Grande Reservoir** Colorado USA
77 O13 **Rio Grande Rise** *underwater feature* Atlantic Ocean
162 B4 **Río Guenguel, Pampa del** *region* Argentina
130 C7 **Rio Hondo** Texas USA
160 E3 **Río Hondo, Embalse** *lake* Argentina
133 H4 **Río Lagartos** Mexico
230 B4 **Rio Maior** Portugal
232 D5 **Rio Manso, Represa do** *lake* Brazil
232 D5 **Rio Marina** Italy
162 B3 **Río Mayo** Argentina
160 F3 **Río Muerto** Argentina
132 C3 **Río Muerto** Mexico
158 E5 **Río Mulatos** Bolivia
157 B9 **Rio Negrinho** Brazil
162 C2 **Río Negro** *admin. area* Argentina
159 F6 **Rio Negro** Brazil
161 G5 **Río Negro** *admin. area* Uruguay
154 D5 **Rio Novo** Brazil
161 H4 **Rio Pardo** Brazil
157 D6 **Rio Pardo de Minas** Brazil
162 B3 **Río Pico** Argentina
157 B8 **Rio Pomba** Brazil
157 C7 **Rio Preto, Serra do** *range* Brazil
129 I3 **Rio Rancho** New Mexico USA
157 E5 **Rio Real** Brazil
160 E5 **Río Tercero** Argentina
156 F4 **Rio Tinto** Brazil
159 I5 **Rio Verde** Brazil
159 H5 **Rio Verde de Mato Grosso** Brazil
154 C2 **Río Viejo** Colombia
130 C4 **Rio Vista** Texas USA
158 C4 **Riobamba** Ecuador
231 F3 **Riodeva** Spain
154 C2 **Ríohacha** Colombia
158 B2 **Rioja** Peru
159 I5 **Riolândia** Brazil
228 F4 **Riom** France
228 F4 **Riom-ès-Montagnes** France
154 C3 **Rionegro** Colombia
233 F6 **Rionero in Vulture** Italy
388 D5 **Rioni** *watercourse* Georgia
228 G3 **Riorges** France
154 B3 **Riosucio** Colombia
154 C3 **Riosucio** Colombia
229 G4 **Riotord** France
119 R3 **Riou Lake** Saskatchewan Canada
158 E3 **Riozinho** Brazil
156 A4 **Riozinho** *watercourse* Brazil
232 F4 **Ripač** Bosnia and Herzegovina
232 D5 **Ripalti, Punta dei** *cape* Italy
241 F1 **Ripley** Derbyshire England UK
243 G2 **Ripley** North Yorkshire England UK
130 G3 **Ripley** Mississippi USA
126 J7 **Ripley** Ohio USA
130 C2 **Ripley** Oklahoma USA
130 G3 **Ripley** Tennessee USA
231 H2 **Ripoll** Spain
243 G2 **Ripon** North Yorkshire England UK
158 C4 **Riquillacasa, Cerro** *mountain* Peru
228 F2 **Ris-Orangis** France
232 H5 **Risan** Montenegro
306 D4 **Risasa** Democratic Republic of Congo
224 I4 **Risbäck** Sweden
222 I6 **Risbrunn** Sweden
240 E2 **Risbury** Herefordshire England UK
241 H2 **Risby** Suffolk England UK
240 D3 **Risca** Caerphilly Wales UK
154 A2 **Risco** Panama
222 F5 **Rise** Norway
243 H3 **Rise** East Riding of Yorkshire England UK
243 H3 **Riseholme** Lincolnshire England UK
241 G2 **Riseley** Bedfordshire England UK
392 E4 **Rishikesh** Uttaranchal India
387 I2 **Rishiri-tō** *island* Japan
387 I2 **Rishiri-zan** *volcano* Japan
130 B4 **Rising Star** Texas USA
118 J7 **Riske Creek** British Columbia Canada
244 E5 **Riskinhope** Scottish Borders Scotland UK
228 E2 **Risle** *watercourse* France
222 K4 **Risliden** Sweden
130 E4 **Rison** Arkansas USA
224 E3 **Risør** Norway
222 I2 **Risøyhamn** Norway
226 E3 **Riß** *watercourse* Germany
222 I4 **Rissjön** *lake* Sweden
222 I5 **Rissna** Sweden
225 M3 **Risti** Estonia
223 Q2 **Ristikent** Russian Federation
223 P3 **Ristilä** Finland
223 N5 **Ristinselkä** *bay* Finland
234 B3 **Ristovac** Serbia
222 L3 **Risträsk** Sweden
224 G3 **Risveden** *region* Sweden
156 F4 **Rita** Brazil
129 K3 **Rita Blanca** *watercourse* Texas USA
376 B4 **Ritchie's Archipelago** Andaman and Nicobar Islands India
426 5 **Ritidian Point** Guam
308 C3 **Rito** Angola
436 X2 **Ritscher Upland** *plain* Antarctica
378 D2 **Ritu** Xizang Zizhiqu China
124 F3 **Ritzville** Washington USA
373 J6 **Riu, Mount** Papua New Guinea
225 N2 **Riutanselkä** *bay* Finland
223 O2 **Riutula** Finland
229 J4 **Riva** Italy
160 D5 **Rivadavia** Argentina
160 F3 **Rivadavia** Argentina
226 E5 **Rivanazzano** Italy
241 F3 **Rivar** Wiltshire England UK
134 C5 **Rivas** Nicaragua
229 G4 **Rive-de-Gier** France
304 C3 **River Cess** Liberia
131 H5 **River Falls** Alabama USA
123 F10 **River Hebert** Nova Scotia Canada
128 B1 **River Reservoir** California USA
160 F6 **Rivera** Argentina
161 H4 **Rivera** Uruguay
161 H4 **Rivera** *admin. area* Uruguay
124 E8 **Riverbank** California USA
242 B4 **Riverchapel** Ireland
131 I4 **Riverdale** Georgia USA
119 R7 **Riverhurst** Saskatchewan Canada
162 A3 **Rivero, Isla** *island* Chile
119 U7 **Rivers** Manitoba Canada
305 F4 **Rivers** *admin. area* Nigeria
119 S8 **Rivers, Lake of the** Saskatchewan Canada
118 H7 **Rivers Inlet** British Columbia Canada
245 F3 **Riversdale** Ireland
423 G5 **Riversdale Beach** New Zealand
128 D4 **Riverside** California USA
124 F2 **Riverside** Washington USA
125 M6 **Riverside Reservoir** Colorado USA
124 J6 **Riverton** Utah USA
125 K5 **Riverton** Wyoming USA
229 G4 **Rives** France
130 C7 **Riviera** Texas USA
131 K7 **Riviera Beach** Florida USA
127 O3 **Rivière-à-Pierre** Québec Canada
127 O2 **Rivière-au-Doré** Québec Canada
123 F7 **Rivière-au-Tonnerre** Québec Canada
310 7b **Rivière de Rempart** Mauritius
310 7b **Rivière des Anguilles** Mauritius
123 D9 **Rivière-du-Loup** Québec Canada
123 C9 **Rivière Ouelle** Québec Canada
121 V8 **Rivière-Pentecôte** Québec Canada
123 F7 **Rivière-St-Jean** Québec Canada
163 14 **Rivière-Salée** Martinique
234 G1 **Rivne** Ukraine
394 C2 **Rivne** Ukraine
394 C2 **Rivnens'ka Oblast'** *admin. area* Ukraine
242 A2 **Rivory** Ireland
308 D3 **Rivungo** Angola
386 F3 **Riwon** North Korea
390 E5 **Riyāḍ, Ar** *admin. area* Saudi Arabia
391 G2 **Rizāb-e Mayām** Iran
394 G5 **Rize** Turkey
394 G5 **Rize** *admin. area* Turkey
385 I6 **Rizhao** Shandong China
233 G7 **Rizzuto, Capo** *cape* Italy
224 D3 **Rjuven** *region* Norway
300 C5 **Rkîz** Mauritania
230 E3 **Roa** Spain
163 5 **Roa, Punta** *cape* Isla de Pascua (Easter Island)
242 A3 **Roachtown** Ireland
163 21 **Road Town** British Virgin Islands
222 E5 **Roald** Norway
222 J5 **Röan** Sweden
125 K7 **Roan Plateau** Colorado USA
228 G3 **Roanne** France
133 I1 **Roanoke** Georgia USA
131 M2 **Roanoke** *watercourse* North Carolina USA
127 L8 **Roanoke** Virginia USA
131 M2 **Roanoke Rapids** North Carolina USA
132 E1 **Roaring Springs** Texas USA
245 C5 **Roaringwater Bay** Ireland
234 D3 **Roata de Jos** Romania
134 C3 **Roatán** Honduras
134 C3 **Roatán, Isla de** *island* Honduras
391 H2 **Robāṭ-e Khān** Iran
391 I2 **Robāṭ-e Mūreshq** Iran
391 I2 **Robāṭ-e Samangān** Iran
118 M6 **Robb** Alberta Canada
131 L3 **Robbins** North Carolina USA
425 K9 **Robe** SA Australia
424 E5 **Robe** *watercourse* WA Australia
307 F2 **Robē** Ethiopia
226 F5 **Robecco** Italy
437 J2 **Robert, Cape** Antarctica
437 D2 **Robert Glacier** Antarctica
129 L5 **Robert Lee** Texas USA
130 D3 **Robert S. Kerr Reservoir** Oklahoma USA
131 J4 **Roberta** Georgia USA
244 F5 **Roberton** Scottish Borders Scotland UK
122 C2 **Roberts, Lac** *lake* Québec Canada
437 K2 **Roberts Butte** *plain* Antarctica
308 C6 **Robertson** South Africa
123 I7 **Robertson, Lac** *lake* Québec Canada
437 L2 **Robertson Bay** Antarctica
121 P5 **Robertson Bay** Nunavut Canada
436 U2 **Robertson Island** Antarctica
304 B3 **Robertsport** Liberia
242 A4 **Robertstown** Ireland
117 L9 **Roberval** Québec Canada
117 N2 **Robeson Channel** Canada/Greenland
225 N5 **Robežnieki** Latvia
244 B2 **Robhanais, Rubha** *cape* Scotland UK
243 H2 **Robin Hood's Bay** North Yorkshire England UK
425 K4 **Robinson** *watercourse* NT Australia
130 C5 **Robinson** Texas USA
163 6a **Róbinson Crusoe, Isla** *island* Juan Fernández Archipiélago
123 I8 **Robinsons** *watercourse* Newfoundland and Labrador Canada
425 L8 **Robinvale** Vic. Australia
119 U7 **Roblin** Manitoba Canada
159 G5 **Roboré** Bolivia
230 E3 **Robregordo** Spain
119 Q8 **Robsart** Saskatchewan Canada
118 L6 **Robson, Mount** British Columbia Canada
130 A4 **Roby** Texas USA
232 F4 **Roč** Croatia
230 B4 **Roca, Cabo da** *cape* Portugal
162 C6 **Roca Nassau** *island* Chile
133 G5 **Roca Partida, Punta** *cape* Mexico
233 H6 **Roca Vecchia** Italy
132 B3 **Rocas Alijos** *island* Mexico
233 G6 **Rocca Imperiale** Italy
233 F6 **Roccadaspide** Italy
233 F8 **Roccalumera** Italy
233 E6 **Roccamonfina** Italy
232 D5 **Roccastrada** Italy
233 G7 **Roccella Ionica** Italy
160 F6 **Rocha** Argentina
161 H5 **Rocha** Uruguay
161 H5 **Rocha** *admin. area* Uruguay
230 B5 **Rocha, Barragem do Monte da** *lake* Portugal
243 F3 **Rochdale** Greater Manchester England UK
230 C5 **Roche, Cabo** *cape* Spain
229 G4 **Roche-la-Molière** France
132 D3 **Rochéachic** Mexico
127 M2 **Rochebaucourt** Québec Canada
228 E4 **Rochechouart** France
229 G1 **Rochefort** Belgium
228 D4 **Rochefort** France
121 S3 **Rochefort, Lac** *lake* Québec Canada
131 J5 **Rochelle** Georgia USA
119 O2 **Rocher River** Northwest Territories Canada
163 17 **Roche's Bluff** *cape* Montserrat
228 D3 **Rocheservière** France
425 M9 **Rochester** Vic. Australia
241 H3 **Rochester** Medway England UK
243 F1 **Rochester** Northumberland England UK
126 E4 **Rochester** Minnesota USA
127 P5 **Rochester** New Hampshire USA
127 M5 **Rochester** New York USA
130 B4 **Rochester** Texas USA
126 J5 **Rochester Hills** Michigan USA
242 A4 **Rochestown** Ireland
241 H3 **Rochford** Essex England UK
126 C5 **Rock** *watercourse* Minnesota USA
423 C7 **Rock and Pillar Range** New Zealand
118 I7 **Rock Bay** British Columbia Canada
124 F2 **Rock Creek** British Columbia Canada
127 M7 **Rock Hall** Maryland USA
126 G2 **Rock Harbor** Michigan USA
131 K3 **Rock Hill** South Carolina USA
130 D3 **Rock Island** Oklahoma USA
124 E3 **Rock Island** Washington USA
125 P2 **Rock Lake** North Dakota USA
124 G3 **Rock Lake** Washington USA
245 F1 **Rock Port** Moyle Northern Ireland UK
125 M6 **Rock River** Wyoming USA
134 E1 **Rock Sound** Bahamas
128 F3 **Rock Springs** Arizona USA
125 K6 **Rock Springs** Wyoming USA
125 Q5 **Rock Valley** Iowa USA
437 J2 **Rock X** *island* Antarctica
76 Q4 **Rockall Bank** *underwater feature* Atlantic Ocean
76 Q4 **Rockall Rise** *underwater feature* Atlantic Ocean
124 D4 **Rockaway Beach** Oregon USA
244 E6 **Rockcliffe** Dumfries and Galloway Scotland UK
130 C5 **Rockdale** Texas USA
436 P1 **Rockefeller Plateau** *plain* Antarctica
229 H2 **Rockenhausen** Germany
244 E3 **Rockfield** Highland Scotland UK
126 G5 **Rockford** Illinois USA
126 E5 **Rockford** Iowa USA
126 I6 **Rockford** Ohio USA
125 M2 **Rockglen** Saskatchewan Canada
425 N5 **Rockhampton** Qld Australia
424 E8 **Rockingham** WA Australia
126 B2 **Rocklake** North Dakota USA
123 D10 **Rockland** Maine USA
131 K6 **Rockledge** Florida USA
127 M3 **Rockliffe** Ontario Canada
124 E7 **Rocklin** California USA
163 9 **Rockly Bay** Trinidad and Tobago
131 I4 **Rockmart** Georgia USA
127 N4 **Rockport** Ontario Canada
126 H8 **Rockport** Indiana USA
126 J4 **Rockport** Michigan USA
130 C6 **Rockport** Texas USA
129 L5 **Rocksprings** Texas USA
155 G3 **Rockstone** Guyana
129 J1 **Rockvale** Colorado USA
242 A4 **Rockview** Ireland
126 H7 **Rockville** Indiana USA
128 F2 **Rockville** Utah USA
130 B3 **Rocky** Oklahoma USA
125 N7 **Rocky Ford** Colorado USA
131 M3 **Rocky Mount** North Carolina USA
119 N6 **Rocky Mountain House** Alberta Canada
118 H3 **Rocky Mountains** Alberta/British Columbia Canada
129 J2 **Rocky Mountains** Colorado USA
124 I3 **Rocky Mountains** Montana USA
125 K6 **Rocky Mountains** Wyoming USA
124 D2 **Rocky Point** British Columbia Canada
425 inset **Rocky Point** Norfolk Island Australia
226 C3 **Rocroi** France
226 F2 **Rodach** *watercourse* Germany
226 D3 **Rodalben** Germany
224 F5 **Rødby** Denmark
242 B4 **Roddenagh** Ireland
123 J7 **Roddickton** Newfoundland and Labrador Canada
224 E5 **Rødding** Denmark
224 E5 **Rødekro** Denmark
231 F2 **Rodellar** Spain
224 E5 **Rodenäs** Germany
224 F3 **Rødenessjøen** *lake* Norway
160 D4 **Rodeo** Argentina
132 D3 **Rodeo** Mexico
129 H5 **Rodeo** New Mexico USA
120 H7 **Roderick Lake** Ontario Canada
226 D4 **Rodersdorf** Switzerland
158 E6 **Rodespampa** Bolivia
229 K1 **Rodewisch** Germany
228 F4 **Rodez** France
225 J3 **Rödhamnsfjärden** *bay* Finland
235 C5 **Rodholívos** Greece
226 G3 **Roding** Germany
241 H3 **Roding** *watercourse* England UK
389 M3 **Rodino** Russian Federation
236 M5 **Rodionovo** Russian Federation
241 E3 **Rodmarton** Gloucestershire England UK
227 M4 **Rodna** Romania
422 F3 **Rodney, Cape** New Zealand
163 13 **Rodney Bay** St Lucia
388 H3 **Rodnikovka** Kazakhstan
238 E6 **Rodnya** Belarus
238 F4 **Rodnya** Russian Federation
235 A5 **Rodonit, Gjiri i** *bay* Albania
235 F7 **Rodos (Rhodes)** Greece
235 F7 **Rodos (Rhodes)** *island* Greece
222 H3 **Rødøy** Norway
222 L1 **Rødøy** *island* Norway
222 H3 **Rodøya** *island* Norway
222 H4 **Rødøya** *island* Norway
310 7 **Rodrigues, Île** *island* Mauritius
80 K6 **Rodrigues Ridge** *underwater feature* Indian Ocean
222 G4 **Rødseidet** Norway
224 E2 **Rødungen** *lake* Norway
224 G5 **Rødvig** Denmark
245 F1 **Roe** *watercourse* Northern Ireland UK
424 G4 **Roebuck Roadhouse** WA Australia
308 E4 **Roedtan** South Africa
226 C/D2 **Roer** *watercourse* Netherlands
117 K6 **Roes Welcome Sound** Nunavut Canada
228 F1 **Roeselare** Belgium
232 G5 **Rogač** Croatia
238 G4 **Rogachëvo** Russian Federation
158 E4 **Rogagua, Laguna** *lake* Bolivia
159 E4 **Rogaguado, Laguna** *lake* Bolivia
224 D3 **Rogaland** *admin. area* Norway
244 D2 **Rogart** Highland Scotland UK
227 H4 **Rogaška Slatina** Slovenia
227 I4 **Rogašovci** Slovenia
241 G3 **Rogate** West Sussex England UK
232 H5 **Rogatica** Bosnia and Herzegovina
226 F1 **Rogätz** Germany
224 G2 **Røgden** *lake* Sweden
222 H5 **Rogen** *lake* Sweden
127 L3 **Roger, Lac** *lake* Québec Canada
118 M7 **Rogers** British Columbia Canada
130 C5 **Rogers** Texas USA
126 J4 **Rogers City** Michigan USA
128 D3 **Rogers Lake** California USA
123 F9 **Rogersville** New Brunswick Canada
121 P5 **Roggan** *watercourse* Québec Canada
121 Q5 **Roggan, Lac** *lake* Québec Canada
163 5 **Roggeveen, Cabo** *cape* Isla de Pascua (Easter Island)
79 W10 **Roggeveen Basin** *underwater feature* Pacific Ocean
222 I3 **Rognan** Norway
238 E6 **Rognedino** Russian Federation

232 F5 **Rogoznica** Croatia
224 H2 **Rogsjön** *lake* Sweden
124 C5 **Rogue** *watercourse* California USA
427 15a **Roguron** *island* Marshall Islands
228 C2 **Rohan** France
124 D7 **Rohnert Park** California USA
226 D4 **Rohr** Switzerland
229 H2 **Rohrbach-lès-Bitche** France
391 K4 **Rohri Canal** *watercourse* Pakistan
392 D4 **Rohru** Himachal Pradesh India
392 D5 **Rohtak** Haryana India
376 D3 **Roi-Et** Thailand
231 F5 **Roig, Cabo** *cape* Spain
225 M2 **Roine** *bay* Finland
379 H3 **Roing** Arunachal Pradesh India
223 P2 **Roiro** *island* Finland
228 F2 **Roisel** France
225 L4 **Roja** Latvia
162 B3 **Rojas, Isla** *island* Chile
133 F4 **Rojo, Cabo** *cape* Mexico
135 H3 **Rojo, Cabo** *cape* Puerto Rico
374 D3 **Rokan** *watercourse* Indonesia
225 M5 **Rokiškis** Lithuania
222 F5 **Røkkem** Norway
222 I3 **Røkland** Norway
222 L4 **Roknäs** Sweden
234 G1 **Rokytne** Ukraine
120 G8 **Roland** Manitoba Canada
310 6b **Roland, Île du** *island* French Southern and Antarctic Lands
224 E4 **Rold** Denmark
224 D3 **Røldalsvatnet** *lake* Norway
154 B3 **Roldanillo** Colombia
125 P2 **Rolette** North Dakota USA
222 J2 **Rolla** *island* Norway
125 O8 **Rolla** Kansas USA
126 F8 **Rolla** Missouri USA
125 P2 **Rolla** North Dakota USA
425 N6 **Rolleston** Qld Australia
423 D6 **Rolleston Range** New Zealand
127 L3 **Rollet** Québec Canada
126 I8 **Rolling Fork** *watercourse* Kentucky USA
130 F4 **Rolling Fork** Mississippi USA
222 H3 **Rolvåg** Norway
223 M1 **Rolvsøya** *island* Norway
425 N6 **Roma** Qld Australia
375 J5 **Roma** *island* Indonesia
233 E6 **Roma (Rome)** Italy
131 L4 **Romain, Cape** South Carolina USA
123 G7 **Romaine** *watercourse* Québec Canada
227 F2 **Romaldkirk** Durham England UK
234 C4 **Roman** Bulgaria
226 C5 **Romanche** *watercourse* France
77 P10 **Romanche Fracture Zone** *underwater feature* Atlantic Ocean
77 P10 **Romanche Gap** *underwater feature* Atlantic Ocean
122 E4 **Romanet, Lac** *lake* Québec Canada
234 D3 **Romania** *country* Europe
232 H5 **Romanija** Bosnia and Herzegovina
131 K8 **Romano, Cape** Florida USA
134 E2 **Romano, Cayo** *island* Cuba
237 X8 **Romanovka** Russian Federation
385 G1 **Romanovka** Russian Federation
225 K5 **Romanovo** Russian Federation
229 G4 **Romans-sur-Isère** France
116 C6 **Romanzof, Cape** Alaska USA
229 H2 **Rombas** France
373 F4 **Rombebai, Danau** *lake* Indonesia
377 I4 **Romblon** *island* Philippines
Rome *see* **Roma** Italy
131 I3 **Rome** Georgia USA
127 N5 **Rome** New York USA
222 L4 **Romelsön** *island* Sweden
125 M8 **Romeo** Colorado USA
227 F2 **Romerike** *region* Norway
241 H3 **Romford** Greater London England UK
300 E2 **Rommani** Morocco
127 L7 **Romney** West Virginia USA
394 E2 **Romny** Ukraine
224 E5 **Rømø** *island* Denmark
374 D3 **Rompin** *watercourse* Malaysia
223 P5 **Romppala** Finland
226 E2 **Romrod** Germany
241 F4 **Romsey** Hampshire England UK
224 F3 **Rømsjøen** *lake* Norway
234 C3 **Romuli** Romania
393 D8 **Ron** Karnataka India
376 C5 **Ron Phibun** Thailand
244 C1 **Rona** *island* Scotland UK
227 M4 **Rona de Sus** Romania
124 H3 **Ronan** Montana USA
222 I4 **Rönäs** Sweden
244 A3 **Ronay** *island* Scotland UK
134 E4 **Roncador, Cay** *island* Colombia
159 I4 **Roncador, Serra do** *range* Brazil
127 K8 **Ronceverte** West Virginia USA
230 D5 **Ronda** Spain
159 F4 **Ronda das Salinas** Brazil
159 G4 **Ronda do Sul** Brazil
222 F6 **Rondane** *range* Norway
222 F6 **Rondane Nasjonalpark** *park* Norway
224 F4 **Rønde** Denmark
163 I5 **Ronde, Pointe** *cape* Dominica
135 I4 **Ronde Island** Grenada
159 F3 **Rondônia** *admin. area* Brazil
159 H5 **Rondonópolis** Brazil
224 C2 **Rong** Norway
380 F3 **Rong Jiang** *watercourse* Guangxi Zhuangzu Zizhiqu China
376 D3 **Rong Kwang** Thailand
381 H2 **Rongcheng** Anhui China
380 F4 **Rongcheng** Guangxi Zhuangzu Zizhiqu China
385 H5 **Rongcheng** Hebei China
381 F2 **Rongcheng** Hubei China
385 J5 **Rongcheng** Shandong China
427 15 **Rongelap Atoll** *reef* Marshall Islands
222 H4 **Røngen** *bay* Norway
427 15 **Rongerik Atoll** *reef* Marshall Islands
381 G3 **Rongjiang** Jiangxi China
381 G2 **Rongjiawan** Hunan China
380 F3 **Rongshui** Guangxi Zhuangzu Zizhiqu China
427 14a **Roniu** *volcano* French Polynesia
223 P5 **Rönkönvaara** Finland
224 F4 **Rönnäng** Sweden
222 J4 **Rönnäs** Sweden
224 H5 **Rønne** Denmark
436 T2 **Ronne Entrance** *strait* Antarctica
436 U1 **Ronne Ice Shelf** Antarctica
224 H4 **Ronneby** Sweden
222 L4 **Rönnskär** *island* Sweden
228 F1 **Ronse** Belgium
159 H4 **Ronuro** *watercourse* Brazil
372 E4 **Rooin** *island* Indonesia
310 5c **Rookery Point** *cape* St Helena
243 H3 **Roos** East Riding of Yorkshire England UK
159 F3 **Roosevelt** *watercourse* Brazil
130 B3 **Roosevelt** Oklahoma USA
125 K6 **Roosevelt** Utah USA
118 I3 **Roosevelt, Mount** British Columbia Canada
436 M1 **Roosevelt Island** Antarctica
223 N5 **Roosinpohja** Finland
245 E1 **Roosky** Ireland
225 M3 **Roosna-Alliku** Estonia
245 D5 **Rooves Beg** Ireland
224 I2 **Ropen** *lake* Sweden
425 J3 **Roper** *watercourse* NT Australia
131 M3 **Roper** North Carolina USA
425 J3 **Roper Bar** NT Australia
129 K4 **Ropesville** Texas USA
222 L2 **Ropi** *mountain* Finland
227 J3 **Ropice** Czech Republic
225 O3 **Ropsha** Russian Federation
229 H4 **Roquebillière** France
231 H2 **Roquebrun** France
231 H2 **Roquecourbe** France
231 F1 **Roquefort** France
222 G5 **Rørа** Norway
244 E2 **Rora Head** *cape* Scotland UK
155 F4 **Roraima** *admin. area* Brazil
155 F3 **Roraima, Monte** *mountain* Venezuela
155 F4 **Rorainópolis** Brazil
224 E3 **Rore** *bay* Norway
392 D5 **Rori** Haryana India
224 F4 **Rörö** Sweden
222 G5 **Røros** Norway
222 I3 **Rørstad** Norway
222 G4 **Rørvik** Norway
234 G1 **Ros'** *watercourse* Ukraine
135 F2 **Rosa, Lake** Bahamas
132 C3 **Rosa, Punta** *cape* Mexico
154 B4 **Rosa Zárate** Ecuador
230 B3 **Rosal** Spain
230 C5 **Rosal de la Frontera** Spain
132 D2 **Rosales** Mexico
124 G3 **Rosalia** Washington USA
163 5 **Rosalia, Punta** *cape* Isla de Pascua (Easter Island)
163 I5 **Rosalie** Dominica
134 D3 **Rosalind Bank** *underwater feature* Caribbean
128 C3 **Rosamond Lake** California USA
222 I5 **Rosången** *lake* Sweden
229 G4 **Rosans** France
244 E3 **Rosarie** Moray Scotland UK
160 F5 **Rosario** Argentina
158 E6 **Rosario** Bolivia
158 E4 **Rosario** Bolivia
129 H7 **Rosario** Mexico
154 C2 **Rosario** Venezuela
134 D2 **Rosario, Cayo del** *island* Cuba
134 C3 **Rosario Bank** *underwater feature* Caribbean
160 E3 **Rosario de la Frontera** Argentina
160 E3 **Rosario de Lerma** Argentina
158 C4 **Rosario de Yauca** Peru
161 G5 **Rosario del Tala** Argentina
161 H4 **Rosário do Sul** Brazil
159 G4 **Rosário Oeste** Brazil
132 A1 **Rosarito** Mexico
245 F4 **Rosbercon** Ireland
125 P4 **Roscoe** South Dakota USA
129 L4 **Roscoe** Texas USA
228 C2 **Roscoff** France
245 D3 **Roscommon** Ireland
245 D3 **Roscommon** *admin. area* Ireland
242 A4 **Rosconnell Bridge** Ireland
245 E4 **Roscrea** Ireland
233 H5 **Rose** Montenegro
78 P9 **Rose Atoll** *reef* American Samoa
310 7b **Rose Belle** Mauritius
118 F6 **Rose Harbour** British Columbia Canada
131 L3 **Rose Hill** North Carolina USA
118 H5 **Rose Lake** British Columbia Canada
118 F5 **Rose Point** British Columbia Canada
135 I4 **Roseau** Dominica
125 R2 **Roseau** Minnesota USA
119 O7 **Rosebud** Alberta Canada
119 O7 **Rosebud** *watercourse* Alberta Canada
130 C5 **Rosebud** Texas USA
124 D5 **Roseburg** Oregon USA
119 O7 **Rosedale** Alberta Canada
243 H2 **Rosedale Abbey** North Yorkshire England UK
302 E5 **Roseires Reservoir** *lake* Sudan
130 F5 **Roseland** Louisiana USA
241 H4 **Roselands** East Sussex England UK
126 C2 **Rosenfeld** Manitoba Canada
232 E3 **Rosenheim** Germany
125 G6 **Rosepine** Louisiana USA
231 H2 **Roses** Spain
231 H2 **Roses, Golfo de** *bay* Spain
232 E5 **Roseto degli Abruzzi** Italy
245 F3 **Rosetown** Ireland
124 E7 **Roseville** California USA
126 F6 **Roseville** Illinois USA
308 C5 **Rosh Pinah** Namibia
388 C2 **Roshal** Russian Federation
234 F2 **Roshcha** Ukraine
225 O2 **Roshchino** Russian Federation
244 C4 **Roshven** Highland Scotland UK
232 D5 **Rosia** Italy
227 M5 **Roșia** Romania
227 I3 **Rosice** Czech Republic
234 B2 **Roșiori** Romania
233 C3 **Roskeeda** Ireland
245 D2 **Roskeeragh Point** Ireland
224 G5 **Roskilde** Denmark
235 A5 **Roskovec** Albania
238 E6 **Roslavl'** Russian Federation
224 E4 **Roslev** Denmark
223 R2 **Roslyakova** Russian Federation
124 E3 **Roslyn** Washington USA
126 H2 **Roslyn Lake** Ontario Canada
230 C4 **Rosmaninhal** Portugal
235 B5 **Rosoman** Macedonia
234 F1 **Rososha** Ukraine
228 C3 **Rosporden** France
120 G8 **Ross** Manitoba Canada
245 C4 **Ross** Ireland
423 D6 **Ross** New Zealand
242 D2 **Ross** Dumfries and Galloway Scotland UK
130 C5 **Ross** Texas USA
310 6b **Ross, Mont** *volcano* French Southern and Antarctic Lands
425 inset **Ross, Point** Norfolk Island Australia
436 M1 **Ross Bank** *underwater feature* Ross Sea
121 V6 **Ross Bay Junction** Newfoundland and Labrador Canada
245 E4 **Ross Bridge** Ireland
245 C5 **Ross Carbery** Ireland
424 inset **Ross Hill** Christmas Island Australia
436 M1 **Ross Ice Shelf** Antarctica
437 L1 **Ross Island** Antarctica
119 V5 **Ross Island** Manitoba Canada
124 E2 **Ross Lake** Washington USA
130 G4 **Ross R. Barnett Reservoir** Mississippi USA
436 M1 **Ross Sea** Antarctica
245 D2 **Rossan Point** Ireland
233 G7 **Rossano** Italy
245 D2 **Rossbeg** Ireland
119 U7 **Rossburn** Manitoba Canada
127 L4 **Rosseau Lake** Ontario Canada
373 J6 **Rossel Island** Papua New Guinea
242 A2 **Rossgeir** Ireland
242 C2 **Rossglass** Down Northern Ireland UK
123 F10 **Rossignol, Lake** Nova Scotia Canada
245 D2 **Rossinver** Ireland
224 G4 **Rossjön** *lake* Sweden
224 D3 **Rosskreppfjorden** *lake* Norway
118 M8 **Rossland** British Columbia Canada
245 F4 **Rosslare Harbour** Ireland
245 F4 **Rosslare Point** Ireland
242 A2 **Rosslea** Fermanagh Northern Ireland UK
245 D2 **Rossnowlagh** Ireland
300 C5 **Rosso** Mauritania
233 C5 **Rosso, Capo** *cape* Corsica France
233 E9 **Rosso, Monte** *mountain* Italy
222 J5 **Rossön** Sweden
394 F2 **Rossosh'** Russian Federation
222 H4 **Røssvatnet** *lake* Norway
119 W6 **Rossville** Manitoba Canada
222 F5 **Rossvoll** Norway
222 H3 **Røst** Norway
222 H3 **Røst** *island* Norway
435 G2 **Røst Bank** *underwater feature* Norwegian Sea
222 K2 **Rosta** Norway
222 K2 **Rostavatn** *lake* Norway
119 R6 **Rosthern** Saskatchewan Canada
224 G5 **Rostock** Germany
222 L2 **Rostonsölkä** *range* Sweden
238 H4 **Rostov** Russian Federation
388 C4 **Rostov-na-Donu** Russian Federation
388 C4 **Rostovskaya** *admin. area* Russian Federation
222 I4 **Röströmssjön** *lake* Sweden
222 H5 **Røstvollen** Norway
234 F3 **Roșu, Lacul** *lake* Romania
222 I3 **Røsvik** Norway
222 L4 **Rosvik** Sweden
131 I3 **Roswell** Georgia USA
129 J4 **Roswell** New Mexico USA
426 2 **Rota** *island* Northern Mariana Islands
372 B6 **Rote, Selat** *strait* Indonesia
226 E1 **Rotenburg an der Wümme** Germany
226 F3 **Roth** Germany
241 H4 **Rother** *watercourse* England UK
436 T2 **Rothera (United Kingdom)** *research station* Antarctica
243 G3 **Rotherham** South Yorkshire England UK
241 G3 **Rotherwick** Hampshire England UK
244 E3 **Rothes** Moray Scotland UK
123 F10 **Rothesay** New Brunswick Canada
244 C5 **Rothesay** Argyll and Bute Scotland UK
436 T2 **Rothschild Island** Antarctica
241 G2 **Rothwell** Northamptonshire England UK
372 B6 **Roti** Indonesia
372 B6 **Roti, Pulau** *island* Indonesia
223 O5 **Rotimo** *lake* Finland
422 F4 **Rotoaira, Lake** New Zealand
422 G4 **Rotoiti** New Zealand
422 G4 **Rotoiti, Lake** New Zealand
422 F4 **Rotorangi, Lake** New Zealand
423 E5 **Rotoroa, Lake** New Zealand
422 G4 **Rotorua** New Zealand
422 G4 **Rotorua, Lake** New Zealand
422 F3 **Rotowaro** New Zealand
226 G3 **Rott** *watercourse* Germany
244 E4 **Rottal** Angus Scotland UK
226 G3 **Rottenburg** Germany
226 C2 **Rotterdam** Netherlands
226 E3 **Röttingen** Germany
224 H4 **Rottnen** *lake* Sweden
226 E3 **Rottweil** Germany
160 F6 **Rotura del Colorado** *watercourse* Argentina
222 I5 **Rötviken** Sweden
231 J5 **Rouached** Algeria
228 F1 **Roubaix** France
225 L3 **Rõude** Estonia
228 E2 **Rouen** France
229 H3 **Rouffach** France
228 D3 **Rougé** France
121 S6 **Rouget, Lac** *lake* Québec Canada
423 C7 **Rough Ridge** *range* New Zealand
126 H8 **Rough River Lake** Kentucky USA
231 G5 **Rouina** Algeria
119 S7 **Rouleau** Saskatchewan Canada
127 M4 **Round Lake** Ontario Canada
127 O5 **Round Lake** New York USA
128 D1 **Round Mountain** Nevada USA
130 B5 **Round Mountain** Texas USA
123 J8 **Round Pond** *lake* Newfoundland and Labrador Canada
130 C5 **Round Rock** Texas USA
122 C6 **Roundeyed, Lac** *lake* Québec Canada
125 K3 **Roundup** Montana USA
244 E1 **Rousay** *island* Scotland UK
245 E2 **Rousky** Omagh Northern Ireland UK
228 F5 **Roussillon** *region* France
122 B2 **Routel, Lac** *lake* Québec Canada
226 B4 **Rouy** France
117 L9 **Rouyn-Noranda** Québec Canada
384 F6 **Rouyuan** Gansu China
223 O3 **Rovala** Finland
223 N3 **Rovaniemi** Finland
222 F5 **Rovde** *lake* Norway
227 M1 **Rovbitsk** Belarus
394 F3 **Roveńki** Russian Federation
394 F3 **Roven'ky** Ukraine
226 F5 **Roverbella** Italy
235 C6 **Rovial** Greece
376 E4 **Rôviĕng Tbong** Cambodia
226 F5 **Rovigo** Italy
232 E4 **Rovinj** Croatia
225 N3 **Rovisuvanto** Finland
223 Q5 **Rovkul'skoye, Ozero** *lake* Russian Federation
388 E3 **Rovnoye** Russian Federation
426 7 **Rowa Islands** *island* Vanuatu
120 I8 **Rowan Lake** Ontario Canada
241 E3 **Rowde** Wiltshire England UK
242 E3 **Rowen** Conwy Wales UK
117 L5 **Rowley Island** Nunavut Canada
424 F4 **Rowley Shoals** *reef* WA Australia
240 E3 **Rowlstone** Herefordshire England UK
304 A2 **Roxa** *island* Guinea-Bissau
377 H5 **Roxas** Philippines
377 I3 **Roxas** Philippines
377 I4 **Roxas** Philippines
131 L2 **Roxboro** North Carolina USA
163 9 **Roxborough** Trinidad and Tobago
423 C7 **Roxburgh** New Zealand
425 K7 **Roxby Downs** SA Australia
224 H3 **Roxen** *lake* Sweden
130 F5 **Roxie** Mississippi USA
230 C5 **Roxo, Barragem do** *lake* Portugal
241 G2 **Roxton** Bedfordshire England UK
130 D4 **Roxton** Texas USA
124 C1 **Roy** British Columbia Canada
129 J3 **Roy** New Mexico USA
124 I6 **Roy** Utah USA
163 7 **Roy Cove** Falkland Islands
125 R5 **Royal** Iowa USA
163 8 **Royal Bay** South Georgia
126 H6 **Royal Center** Indiana USA
377 G6 **Royal Charlotte Reef** Spratly Islands
124 F3 **Royal City** Washington USA
241 F2 **Royal Leamington Spa** Warwickshire England UK
437 K1 **Royal Society Range** Antarctica
241 H3 **Royal Tunbridge Wells** Kent England UK
126 G3 **Royale, Isle** *island* Michigan USA
228 D4 **Royan** France
229 G4 **Roybon** France
228 F4 **Royère** France
222 H4 **Røyrvik** Norway
222 F6 **Røysheim** Norway
241 G2 **Royston** Hertfordshire England UK
243 G3 **Royston** South Yorkshire England UK
131 J3 **Royston** Georgia USA
121 S5 **Roz, Lac** *lake* Québec Canada
234 B4 **Rožaje** Montenegro
227 M1 **Rózanka** Belarus
230 C2 **Rozas, Embalse de las** *lake* Spain
234 G2 **Rozdil'na** Ukraine
129 M1 **Rozel** Kansas USA
238 G4 **Rozhdestveno** Russian Federation
388 F2 **Rozhdestveno** Russian Federation
234 F1 **Rozhnyatovka** Ukraine
227 M2 **Rozhyshche** Ukraine
122 D2 **Rozière, Baie de** *bay* Québec Canada
227 K1 **Rozogi** Poland
234 A4 **Rrapë** Albania
235 A5 **Rrapëza-Rshat** Albania
388 D3 **Rtishchevo** Russian Federation
227 L5 **Rtkovo** Serbia
381 G2 **Ru`ning** Henan China
240 D2 **Ruabon** Wrexham Wales UK
308 B3 **Ruacana** Namibia
422 G4 **Ruahine Range** New Zealand
422 F2 **Ruakaka** New Zealand
422 G4 **Ruakituri** *watercourse* New Zealand
240 B5 **Ruan Minor** Cornwall England UK
422 F4 **Ruapehu, Mount** *volcano* New Zealand
423 C8 **Ruapuke Island** New Zealand
309 F2 **Ruarwe** Malawi
422 H3 **Ruatoria** New Zealand
307 F5 **Ruawa** Tanzania
422 F3 **Ruawai** New Zealand
390 G6 **Rub' Al Khālī, Ar** Saudi Arabia
232 D4 **Rubano** Italy
222 K2 **Rubben** *island* Norway
307 F5 **Rubeho** Tanzania
306 D3 **Rubi** *watercourse* Democratic Republic of Congo
157 B6 **Rubiataba** Brazil
226 F5 **Rubiera** Italy
389 N3 **Rubtsovsk** Russian Federation
116 D6 **Ruby** Alaska USA
119 T6 **Ruby Beach** Saskatchewan Canada
124 H6 **Ruby Lake** Nevada USA
124 H6 **Ruby Mountains** Nevada USA
225 K4 **Rucava** Latvia
381 G4 **Rucheng** Guangdong China
381 G3 **Rucheng** Hunan China
223 V3 **Ruch'i** Russian Federation
225 O3 **Ruch'i** Russian Federation
132 D4 **Rucias** Mexico
127 L7 **Ruckersville** Virginia USA
241 H3 **Ruckinge** Kent England UK
388 G6 **Rūd-e Atrak** *watercourse* Iran
390 G3 **Rūd-e Beshar** *watercourse* Iran
391 I2 **Rūd-e Kāl Shūr** *watercourse* Iran
390 F3 **Rūd-e Kārūn** *watercourse* Iran
391 H3 **Rūd-e Kor** *watercourse* Iran
390 G4 **Rūd-e Mand** *watercourse* Iran
390 G4 **Rūd-e Shur** *watercourse* Iran
391 I2 **Rūd Jām** *watercourse* Iran
229 K4 **Ruda** Italy
225 M5 **Rudamina** Lithuania
391 I4 **Rūdān** Iran
234 B4 **Rudare** Serbia
225 O3 **Ruddilovo** Russian Federation
119 U5 **Ruddock** Manitoba Canada
227 H5 **Rude** Croatia
224 F5 **Rude** Denmark
234 F1 **Rude Selo** Ukraine
225 M5 **Rūdiškės** Lithuania
390 G3 **Rūdkhāneh-ye Helleh** *watercourse* Iran
388 E6 **Rudkhaneh-ye Qotur** *lake* Iran
234 C1 **Rudky** Ukraine
227 I2 **Rudna** Poland
225 M5 **Rudnia** Lithuania
234 B4 **Rudnica** Serbia
227 K2 **Rudnik** Poland
227 J2 **Rudniki** Poland
227 L2 **Rudno** Poland
225 O3 **Rudno** Russian Federation
225 O6 **Rudnya** Belarus
225 P5 **Rudnya** Belarus
225 Q4 **Rudnya** Russian Federation
238 D5 **Rudnya** Russian Federation
388 D3 **Rudnya** Russian Federation
227 M2 **Rudnya** Ukraine
388 I3 **Rudnyy** Kazakhstan
130 C7 **Rudolph** Texas USA
388 F6 **Rūdsar** Iran
238 B6 **Rudzyensk** Belarus
228 E1 **Rue** France
232 B3 **Rue** Switzerland
230 D3 **Rueda** Spain
125 L7 **Ruedi Reservoir** Colorado USA
302 E5 **Rufa'a** Sudan
229 J5 **Rufeno, Monte** *mountain* Italy
228 E3 **Ruffec** France
226 C5 **Ruffieux** France
307 F5 **Rufiil** *watercourse* Tanzania
160 F5 **Rufino** Argentina
308 E3 **Rufunsa** Zambia
124 E4 **Rufus** Oregon USA
240 D2 **Rug** Denbighshire Wales UK
381 H2 **Rugao** Jiangsu China
241 F2 **Rugby** Warwickshire England UK
125 P2 **Rugby** North Dakota USA
241 F2 **Rugeley** Staffordshire England UK
224 G5 **Rügen** *island* Germany
240 E3 **Rugeway** South Gloucestershire England UK
228 E2 **Rugles** France
223 R4 **Rugozero** Russian Federation
306 D5 **Rugurfu** *watercourse* Tanzania
307 F5 **Ruhangino** Tanzania
226 F1 **Rühen** Germany
306 D4 **Ruhengeri** Rwanda
227 G2 **Ruhland** Germany
225 L4 **Ruhnu** Estonia
225 L4 **Ruhnu** *island* Estonia
226 D2 **Ruhr** *watercourse* Germany
307 F5 **Ruhudji** *watercourse* Tanzania
381 H3 **Rui`an** Zhejiang China
380 F1 **Ruicheng** Shanxi China
129 J6 **Ruidosa** Texas USA
129 J4 **Ruidoso** New Mexico USA
129 J4 **Ruidoso Downs** New Mexico USA
223 N3 **Ruikka** Finland
228 F4 **Ruines** France
121 U4 **Ruisseau-Highfall** *watercourse* Québec Canada
310 2 **Ruivo, Pico** *volcano* Madeira
132 D4 **Ruiz** Mexico
132 D2 **Ruiz Cortines** Mexico
234 C4 **Rujen** *mountain* Macedonia
225 M4 **Rūjiena** Latvia
391 H4 **Rūk** Iran
223 P5 **Rukavesi** *bay* Finland
225 O4 **Rukovo** Russian Federation
372 C5 **Rukua** Indonesia
306 E5 **Rukwa** *admin. area* Tanzania
307 E5 **Rukwa, Lake** *lake* Tanzania
222 I6 **Rulbo** Sweden
130 B4 **Rule** Texas USA
130 F4 **Ruleville** Mississippi USA
375 J7 **Rulhieres, Cape** Australia
380 F3 **Rulin** Hunan China
380 C2 **Rulong** Sichuan China
225 N5 **Rum** Belarus
227 I4 **Rum** Hungary
244 B3 **Rum** *island* Scotland UK
135 F2 **Rum Cay** *island* Bahamas
305 F2 **Ruma** Nigeria
234 A3 **Ruma** Serbia
390 F4 **Rumāḩ** Saudi Arabia
306 D2 **Rumbek** Sudan
372 E4 **Rumberpon** *island* Indonesia
230 E4 **Rumblar, Embalse del** *lake* Spain
240 C4 **Rumford** Cornwall England UK
223 P5 **Rummukkala** Finland
223 P5 **Rumo** Finland
387 I2 **Rumoi** Japan
306 D4 **Rumonge** Burundi
309 F2 **Rumphi** Malawi
391 J4 **Rumra** Pakistan
307 F3 **Rumuruti** Kenya
372 D5 **Run** *island* Indonesia
245 C5 **Runalunn** Ireland
423 D6 **Runanga** New Zealand
422 G3 **Runaway, Cape** New Zealand
134 E3 **Runaway Bay** Jamaica
234 C3 **Runcu** Romania
224 C1 **Runde** *island* Norway
309 F4 **Runde** *watercourse* Zimbabwe
222 K2 **Rundhaug** Norway
308 C3 **Rundu** Namibia
375 J5 **Runduma** *island* Indonesia
222 K5 **Rundvik** Sweden
306 E5 **Rungwa** Tanzania
307 E5 **Rungwa** *watercourse* Tanzania
307 E5 **Rungwe** *mountain* Tanzania
234 B4 **Runica** Macedonia
225 J3 **Runmarö** *island* Sweden
224 H2 **Runn** *lake* Sweden
129 K3 **Running Water** *watercourse* Texas USA
224 I4 **Runnö** *island* Sweden
426 6 **Ruo** *island* Federated States of Micronesia
223 N3 **Ruokojärvi** Finland
223 O3 **Ruopsa** Finland
383 H5 **Ruoqiang** Xinjiang Uygur Zizhiqu China
223 O5 **Ruotaanmäki** Finland
225 M2 **Ruotsalainen** *lake* Finland
225 L1 **Ruovesi** *bay* Finland
229 L4 **Rupa** Croatia
379 G3 **Rupa** Arunachal Pradesh India
162 B2 **Rupanco, Lago** *lake* Chile
309 F2 **Rupashe** *watercourse* Malawi
374 D3 **Rupat** *island* Indonesia
234 D2 **Rupea** Romania
121 P7 **Rupert** *watercourse* Québec Canada
124 I5 **Rupert** Idaho USA
121 P7 **Rupert, Baie de** *bay* Québec Canada
436 O1 **Rupert Coast** Antarctica
307 F5 **Rupia** Tanzania
307 F6 **Ruponda** Tanzania
226 G1 **Ruppiner See** *lake* Germany
393 G7 **Rupsa** Orissa India
234 D4 **Ruptsi** Bulgaria
155 G4 **Rupununi** *watercourse* Guyana
226 D2 **Rur** *watercourse* Germany
427 14 **Rurutu** *island* French Polynesia
309 F3 **Rusape** Zimbabwe
234 D4 **Ruse** Bulgaria
245 F3 **Rush** Ireland
125 P7 **Rush Center** Kansas USA
241 F3 **Rushall** Wiltshire England UK
385 J6 **Rushan** Shandong China
241 G2 **Rushden** Northamptonshire England UK
126 F5 **Rushford** Minnesota USA
309 F3 **Rushinga** Zimbabwe
379 H3 **Rushon** Arunachal Pradesh India
241 G2 **Rushton** Northamptonshire England UK
241 E1 **Rushton Spencer** Staffordshire England UK
119 S7 **Rushville** Saskatchewan Canada
126 F6 **Rushville** Illinois USA
126 I7 **Rushville** Indiana USA
130 D5 **Rusk** Texas USA
222 J5 **Ruske** Sweden
225 P2 **Ruskeala** Russian Federation
222 K4 **Ruskele** Sweden
224 H4 **Rusken** *lake* Sweden
223 P5 **Ruskila** Finland
225 K5 **Rusnė** Lithuania
225 L3 **Russarö** *island* Finland
244 C3 **Russel** Highland Scotland UK
119 U7 **Russell** Manitoba Canada
125 P7 **Russell** Kansas USA
125 R4 **Russell** Minnesota USA
117 J4 **Russell Island** Nunavut Canada
119 U4 **Russell Lake** Manitoba Canada
119 S4 **Russell Lake** Saskatchewan Canada
126 I8 **Russell Springs** Kentucky USA
130 H3 **Russellville** Alabama USA
130 E3 **Russellville** Arkansas USA
130 H2 **Russellville** Kentucky USA
223 M1 **Russeluft** Norway
222 L2 **Russelv** Norway
222 I5 **Russfjärden** *bay* Sweden
124 D7 **Russian** *watercourse* California USA
238 E4 **Russian Federation** *country*
387 I1 **Russian Federation** *country* Russian Federation
389 L2 **Russkaya Polyana** Russian Federation
237 U3 **Russkiy, Ostrov** *island* Russian Federation
237 AE4 **Russkoye Ust'ye** Russian Federation
227 I4 **Rust** Austria
391 K4 **Rustam Khan Shahr** Pakistan
391 I5 **Rustāq** Oman
308 E5 **Rustenburg** South Africa
130 E4 **Ruston** Louisiana USA
227 H2 **Ruszów** Poland
225 L2 **Rutajärvi** *lake* Finland
306 D4 **Rutana** Burundi
230 D5 **Rute** Spain
308 F4 **Rutenga** Zimbabwe
229 I1 **Rüthen** Germany
127 L3 **Rutherglen** Ontario Canada
244 E2 **Ruthers of Howe** Highland Scotland UK
226 E4 **Rüthi** Switzerland
240 D1 **Ruthin** Denbighshire Wales UK
125 Q4 **Ruthton** Minnesota USA
244 E6 **Ruthwell** Dumfries and Galloway Scotland UK
227 L1 **Rutki** Poland
241 G2 **Rutland** *admin. area* England UK
125 Q3 **Rutland** North Dakota USA
127 O5 **Rutland** Vermont USA
376 B5 **Rutland Island** Andaman and Nicobar Islands India
241 G2 **Rutland Water** *lake* England UK
232 B4 **Rutor, Testa del** *mountain* Italy
223 N4 **Ruukki** Finland
223 Q5 **Ruunaa** Finland
223 Q5 **Ruunaanjärvi** *lake* Finland
225 N4 **Ruusmäe** Estonia
223 P3 **Ruuvaoja** Finland
307 F6 **Ruvuma** *watercourse* Mozambique
307 F6 **Ruvuma** *admin. area* Tanzania
390 D3 **Ruwayshid, Wādī** *watercourse* Jordan
157 D6 **Ruy Barbosa** Brazil
238 G5 **Ruza** Russian Federation
388 J3 **Ruzayevka** Kazakhstan
388 D2 **Ruzayevka** Russian Federation
227 M1 **Ruzhany** Belarus
381 F1 **Ruzhou Zhen** Henan China
234 F1 **Ruzhyn** Ukraine
232 G5 **Ružić** Croatia
225 N4 **Ružina** Latvia
234 A2 **Rusza** Hungary
306 E4 **Rwanda** *country* Africa
306 E3 **Rwenzori** *range* Uganda
306 E4 **Rweru, Lake** *lake* Rwanda
224 E4 **Ry** Denmark
238 F5 **Ryabiki** Russian Federation
225 O2 **Ryabovo** Russian Federation
238 E5 **Ryabtsevo** Russian Federation
234 E4 **Ryakhovo** Bulgaria
130 C3 **Ryan** Oklahoma USA
129 J5 **Ryan** Texas USA
244 D6 **Ryan, Loch** *bay* Scotland UK
225 O5 **Ryasna** Belarus
388 C2 **Ryazan'** Russian Federation
388 C2 **Ryazanskaya Oblast'** *admin. area* Russian Federation
236 H5 **Rybachiy, Poluostrov** *peninsula* Russian Federation
389 N4 **Rybach'ye** Kazakhstan
389 L5 **Rybach'ye** Kyrgyzstan
234 H2 **Rybal'che** Ukraine
389 L4 **Rybalka Tas-aral** Kazakhstan
238 H3 **Rybinsk** Russian Federation
238 H3 **Rybinskoye Vodokhranilishche** *lake* Russian Federation
227 J2 **Rybnik** Poland
227 J1 **Rybno** Poland
227 K1 **Rybno** Poland
227 K1 **Rybno** Poland
225 J6 **Rychliki** Poland
227 I2 **Rychnov nad Kněžnou** Czech Republic
227 J1 **Rychwał** Poland
225 N5 **Rychy, Vozyera** *lake* Belarus
118 L5 **Rycroft** Alberta Canada
436 S2 **Rydberg Peninsula** Antarctica
241 F4 **Ryde** Isle of Wight England UK
241 H4 **Rye** East Sussex England UK
241 H4 **Rye Bay** England UK
241 H4 **Rye Harbour** East Sussex England UK
124 F6 **Rye Patch Reservoir** Nevada USA
242 A3 **Ryefield** Ireland
241 E3 **Ryeford** Gloucestershire England UK
125 K3 **Ryegate** Montana USA
243 H3 **Ryehill** East Riding of Yorkshire England UK
241 G2 **Ryhall** Rutland England UK
227 K2 **Ryki** Poland
119 O6 **Ryley** Alberta Canada
394 E2 **Ryl'sk** Russian Federation
425 N8 **Rylstone** NSW Australia
227 I3 **Rýmařov** Czech Republic
240 E4 **Ryme Intrinseca** Dorset England UK
224 H4 **Rymmen** *lake* Sweden
224 H2 **Rymnäsbodarna** Sweden
223 T2 **Rynda** Russian Federation
225 N2 **Ryökäsvesi** *lake* Finland
386 E3 **Ryong-yŏn** North Korea
387 H3 **Ryōtsu** Japan
227 J1 **Rypin** Poland
227 I1 **Rytel** Poland
243 G3 **Ryther** North Yorkshire England UK
223 O4 **Rytinki** Finland
223 O5 **Rytky** Finland
241 F2 **Ryton on Dunsmore** Warwickshire England UK
234 B1 **Rytro** Poland
224 H5 **Rytterknægten** *mountain* Denmark
78 I5 **Ryukyu Trench** *underwater feature* Pacific Ocean
225 P2 **Ryuttyu** Russian Federation
227 L2 **Rzeszów** Poland
227 H1 **Rzewnowo** Poland
227 J2 **Rzgón** Poland
238 F4 **Rzhev** Russian Federation

S

226 C1 **'s-Gravenhage (The Hague)** Netherlands
226 C2 **'s-Hertogenbosch** Netherlands
376 D3 **Sa** Thailand
376 E5 **Sa Déc** Vietnam
231 H4 **Sa Dragonera** *island* Spain
376 F4 **Sa Huỳnh** Vietnam
376 D4 **Sa Kaeo** Thailand
376 D2 **Sa Pa** Vietnam
305 G4 **Saa** Cameroon
426 8 **Sa'a** Solomon Islands
225 M2 **Sääksjärvi** Finland
225 L2 **Sääksjärvi** *lake* Finland
224 G5 **Saal** Germany
226 F2 **Saale** *watercourse* Germany
229 H2 **Saales** France
228 E2 **Saâne** *watercourse* France
232 B3 **Saanen** Switzerland
118 J8 **Saanich** British Columbia Canada
226 D3 **Saarbrücken** Germany
225 L4 **Sääre** Estonia
225 L3 **Saaremaa** *admin. area* Estonia
225 L3 **Saaremaa** *island* Estonia
223 N3 **Saarenkylä** Finland
223 O3 **Saari-Kämä** Finland
223 O4 **Saariharju** Finland
223 N5 **Saarijärvi** Finland
225 M1 **Saarijärvi** *lake* Finland
223 M3 **Saaripudas** Finland
223 O2 **Saariselka** *island* Finland
223 O2 **Saariselkä** Finland
226 D3 **Saarland** *admin. area* Germany
122 O2 **Saarloq** Greenland
229 H2 **Saarlouis** Germany
244 C3 **Saasaig** Highland Scotland UK
229 H2 **Saasenheim** France
223 O3 **Sääskilahti** Finland
159 I2 **Saba** Brazil
163 20 **Saba** *island* Netherlands Antilles
232 H4 **Šabac** Serbia
231 H3 **Sabadell** Spain
387 H4 **Sabae** Japan
375 H2 **Sabah** *admin. area* Malaysia
374 D3 **Sabak** Malaysia
375 H5 **Sabalana** *island* Indonesia
375 H5 **Sabalana, Kepulauan** *archipelago* Indonesia
154 C5 **Sabana** Colombia
154 D4 **Sabana** Colombia
155 H3 **Sabana** Suriname
134 D2 **Sabana, Archipiélago de** *islands* Cuba
154 C3 **Sabana de Torres** Colombia
135 G3 **Sabana Yegua** Dominican Republic
154 C3 **Sabanalarga** Colombia
133 H5 **Sabancuy** Mexico
134 B3 **Sabancuy, Bancos de** *reef* Mexico
155 F3 **Sabaneta** Venezuela
155 F2 **Sabaneta, Punta** *cape* Venezuela
373 F5 **Sabang** Indonesia
374 B2 **Sabang** Indonesia
134 E5 **Sabanitas** Panama
304 E3 **Sabari** Ghana
393 E7 **Sabari** *watercourse* Chhattisgarh India
375 H5 **Sabaru** *island* Indonesia
372 B4 **Sabbang** Indonesia
301 I3 **Sabhā** Libya
309 F4 **Sabi** *watercourse* Zimbabwe
302 F4 **Sabidana, Jebel** *mountain* Sudan
309 F5 **Sabie** Mozambique
308 F5 **Sabie** South Africa
225 L4 **Sabile** Latvia
126 J7 **Sabina** Ohio USA
130 B6 **Sabinal** Texas USA
134 E2 **Sabinal, Cayo** *island* Cuba
231 F2 **Sabiñánigo** Spain
132 E3 **Sabinas** Mexico
132 E3 **Sabinas** *watercourse* Mexico
132 E3 **Sabinas Hidalgo** Mexico
130 E5 **Sabine** *watercourse* Louisiana USA
130 D4 **Sabine** *watercourse* Texas USA
121 S3 **Sabine, Lac** *lake* Québec Canada

130 E6 **Sabine Lake** Louisiana USA
227 K3 **Sabinov** Slovakia
121 U5 **Sable** *watercourse* Québec Canada
123 F11 **Sable, Cape** Nova Scotia Canada
131 K8 **Sable, Cape** Florida USA
123 I11 **Sable Island** Nova Scotia Canada
228 D3 **Sablé-sur-Sarthe** France
127 P2 **Sables, Rivière aux** *watercourse* Québec Canada
229 G5 **Sablon, Pointe du** *cape* France
230 C3 **Sabor** *watercourse* Portugal
127 M3 **Sabourin, Lac** *lake* Québec Canada
372 E4 **Sabra, Tanjung** *cape* Indonesia
301 I2 **Sabrātah** Libya
228 D4 **Sabres** France
437 H2 **Sabrina Coast** Antarctica
377 I2 **Sabtang** *island* Philippines
388 F6 **Sabu Chal** Iran
372 D4 **Sabuda** *island* Indonesia
230 C3 **Sabugal** Portugal
126 F5 **Sabula** Iowa USA
372 B4 **Sabulu** Indonesia
374 C4 **Sabulubek** Indonesia
375 G5 **Sabunten** *island* Indonesia
390 E6 **Şabyā** Saudi Arabia
388 H7 **Sabzevār** Iran
391 I4 **Sabzvārān** Iran
124 F3 **Sacajawea, Lake** Washington USA
154 C3 **Sácama** Colombia
162 C3 **Sacanana** Argentina
305 H6 **Sacandica** Angola
134 B4 **Sacapulas** Guatemala
233 E6 **Sacco** *watercourse* Italy
230 E3 **Sacedón** Spain
154 C4 **Sachene** Colombia
120 J5 **Sachigo** *watercourse* Ontario Canada
120 I6 **Sachigo Lake** Ontario Canada
386 F4 **Sach'on** South Korea
116 G4 **Sachs Harbour** Northwest Territories Canada
229 K1 **Sachsen** *admin. area* Germany
226 F2 **Sachsen-Anhalt** *admin. area* Germany
227 H1 **Sachsendorf** Germany
391 K3 **Sachu** Pakistan
232 E4 **Sacile** Italy
123 F10 **Sackville** New Brunswick Canada
125 L2 **Saco** Montana USA
157 C7 **Sacramento** Brazil
124 E7 **Sacramento** California USA
124 E7 **Sacramento** *watercourse* California USA
129 J4 **Sacramento Mountains** New Mexico USA
230 E5 **Sacratif, Cabo** *cape* Spain
154 B5 **Sacraurcu** *mountain* Ecuador
233 F6 **Sacro, Monte** *mountain* Italy
234 C2 **Săcueni** Romania
159 G4 **Sacuriuina** *watercourse* Brazil
310 8b **Sada** Mayotte
308 E6 **Sada** South Africa
231 F2 **Sádaba** Spain
394 F6 **Şadad** Syria
390 E7 **Şa'dah** Yemen
375 H4 **Sadang** *watercourse* Indonesia
376 D6 **Sadao** Thailand
375 F4 **Sadau** Indonesia
391 L2 **Sadda** Pakistan
222 K3 **Saddajaure** *bay* Sweden
244 C5 **Saddell** Argyll and Bute Scotland UK
241 F2 **Saddington** Leicester England UK
118 L5 **Saddle Hills** Alberta Canada
376 B4 **Saddle Peak** *mountain* Andaman and Nicobar Islands India
154 B4 **Sade** Ecuador
242 F2 **Sadgill** Cumbria England UK
391 H6 **Şadḩ** Oman
307 F2 **Sadi** Ethiopia
300 D6 **Sadiola** Mali
379 H3 **Sadiya** Assam India
130 C4 **Sadler** Texas USA
163 I9 **Sadlers** St Kitts and Nevis
230 B4 **Sado** *watercourse* Portugal
387 H4 **Sadoga-shima** *island* Japan
375 F3 **Sadong** *watercourse* Malaysia
234 F2 **Sadova** Moldova
234 C4 **Sadova** Romania
234 G2 **Sadova** Ukraine
388 D4 **Sadovoye** Russian Federation
393 D7 **Sadri** Madhya Pradesh India
227 H2 **Sadská** Czech Republic
222 J3 **Sädvajaure** *lake* Sweden
222 J3 **Sädvaluspen** Sweden
373 H4 **Sae Islands** Papua New Guinea
222 E5 **Sæbø** Norway
224 F4 **Sæby** Denmark
230 D2 **Saelices del Rio** Spain
226 D1 **Saerbeck** Germany
222 G4 **Sætervika** Norway
304 D2 **Safané** Burkina Faso
390 E5 **Şaffāqah** Saudi Arabia
224 G3 **Säffle** Sweden
128 H4 **Safford** Arizona USA
241 H2 **Saffron Walden** Essex England UK
300 E2 **Safi** Morocco
390 E7 **Safi** Yemen
237 AK6 **Safonovo** Russian Federation
238 E5 **Safonovo** Russian Federation
386 F5 **Saga** Japan
379 H5 **Sagaing** Myanmar
379 H4 **Sagaing** *admin. area* Myanmar
126 J2 **Saganash Lake** Ontario Canada
227 H2 **Sagar** Germany
393 D8 **Sagar** Karnataka India
392 E6 **Sagar** Madhya Pradesh India
393 G7 **Sagar Island** West Bengal India
237 AA4 **Sagastyyr** Russian Federation
116 E5 **Sagavanirktok** *watercourse* Alaska USA
377 I5 **Sagay** Philippines
222 K2 **Sagelvvatnet** *lake* Norway
222 J3 **Saggat** *bay* Sweden
225 J2 **Saggöfjärden** *bay* Finland
126 J5 **Saginaw** Michigan USA
126 J4 **Saginaw Bay** Michigan USA
388 G4 **Sagiz** Kazakhstan
388 G4 **Sagiz** *watercourse* Kazakhstan
122 G3 **Saglek Bay** Newfoundland and Labrador Canada
375 I4 **Sago** *island* Indonesia
159 F3 **Sagrada Paixão, Serra da** *range* Brazil
230 B5 **Sagres** Portugal
230 B5 **Sagres, Ponta de** *cape* Portugal
390 E6 **Sagrit** Saudi Arabia
134 D2 **Sagua la Grande** Cuba
125 L7 **Saguache** Colorado USA
129 I7 **Saguarachi** Mexico
128 G4 **Saguaro National Park** Arizona USA
123 C8 **Saguenay** *watercourse* Québec Canada
227 J3 **Ságújfalu** Hungary
231 F4 **Sagunto** Spain
227 J4 **Ságvár** Hungary
392 D6 **Sagwara** Rajasthan India
388 F5 **Sagyndyk, Mys** *cape* Kazakhstan
154 C2 **Sahagún** Colombia
230 D2 **Sahagún** Spain
391 H5 **Şaḩam** Oman
241 H2 **Saham Hills** Norfolk England UK
392 E5 **Sahanpur** Uttar Pradesh India
300 E4 **Sahara** *desert* North Africa
392 D5 **Saharanpur** Uttar Pradesh India
390 G5 **Sahbā', Wādī as** *watercourse* Saudi Arabia
235 E5 **Şahin** Turkey
391 M3 **Sahiwal** Pakistan
390 F2 **Sahneh** Iran
223 N5 **Sahrajärvi** Finland
118 J3 **Sahtaneh** *watercourse* British Columbia Canada
132 C2 **Sahuarachic** Mexico
132 C2 **Sahuaripa** Mexico
128 G5 **Sahuarita** Arizona USA
132 B2 **Sahuaro** Mexico
379 H2 **Sahuteng** Qinghai China
155 H4 **Saï** French Guiana
376 D6 **Sai Buri** Thailand
373 G6 **Saibai Island** Australia
301 G2 **Saïda** Algeria
301 G2 **Saïda** *admin. area* Algeria
390 C2 **Saïda (Sidon)** Lebanon
388 E7 **Sā'īdābād** Iran
301 F1 **Saïdia** Morocco
379 F4 **Saidpur** Bangladesh
379 G4 **Saiha** Mizoram India
384 E3 **Saihan** Mongolia
384 E3 **Saihan-ovoo** Mongolia
385 G4 **Saihan Tal** Nei Mongol Zizhiqu China
384 G4 **Saihandulaan** Mongolia
223 P3 **Saija** Finland
386 F5 **Saiki** Japan
380 C2 **Sailaitang** Qinghai China
229 G4 **Saillans** France
372 D4 **Sailolof** Indonesia
225 O2 **Saimaa** *lake* Finland
223 P5 **Säimen** Finland
132 E4 **Saín Alto** Mexico
121 S5 **Saindon, Lacs** *lakes* Québec Canada
244 F5 **St Abb's Head** *cape* Scotland UK
228 F5 **St-Affrique** France
240 B4 **St Agnes** Cornwall England UK
240 A5 **St Agnes** *island* England UK
229 G4 **St-Agrève** France
228 E3 **St-Aignan** France
241 G3 **St Albans** Hertfordshire England UK
241 E4 **St Alban's Head** *cape* England UK
119 O6 **St Albert** Alberta Canada
127 O3 **St-Alexis-des-Monts** Québec Canada
226 B5 **Saint-Amans-la-Lozère** France
231 H2 **Saint-Amans-Soult** France
120 F7 **St Ambroise** Manitoba Canada
228 G4 **St-Ambroix** France
229 H2 **Saint-Amé** France
229 G3 **St-Amour** France
123 D9 **St-André** Québec Canada
228 E3 **Saint-André** France
310 7a **Saint-André** Réunion
155 G3 **Saint Andrew Point** *cape* Guyana
131 K5 **Saint Andrew Sound** Georgia USA
123 E10 **St Andrews** New Brunswick Canada
244 F4 **St Andrews** Fife Scotland UK
244 F4 **St Andrews Bay** Scotland UK
241 E5 **St Anne** Alderney Channel Islands UK
117 M9 **Saint-Anne-des-Monts** Québec Canada
242 E1 **St Ann's** Dumfries and Galloway Scotland UK
123 H9 **St Anns Bay** Nova Scotia Canada
126 E5 **Saint Ansgar** Iowa USA
123 K7 **St Anthony** Newfoundland and Labrador Canada
124 J5 **Saint Anthony** Idaho USA
123 F9 **Saint-Antoine** New Brunswick Canada
228 E4 **Saint-Antonin** France
423 E6 **St Arnaud Range** New Zealand
242 E3 **St Asaph** Denbighshire Wales UK
123 I7 **St-Augustin** Québec Canada
131 K6 **Saint Augustine** Florida USA
131 K6 **Saint Augustine Beach** Florida USA
123 I7 **St-Augustine Nord-Ouest** *watercourse* Québec Canada
240 C4 **St Austell** Cornwall England UK
240 C4 **St Austell Bay** England UK
228 F4 **Saint-Bard** France
135 I3 **St Barthélemy** *French overseas collectivity* Caribbean
163 I9 **St Barthélemy** *island* St Barthélemy
423 C7 **St Bathans Range** New Zealand
228 E5 **St-Béat** France
242 E2 **St Bees Head** *cape* England UK
226 B4 **Saint Benin** France
310 7a **Saint-Benoît** Réunion
229 G2 **Saint-Blin** France
240 E3 **St Briavels** Gloucestershire England UK
123 K9 **St Bride's** Newfoundland and Labrador Canada
240 B3 **St Bride's Bay** Wales UK
228 C2 **St-Brieuc** France
228 C2 **St-Brieuc, Baie de** *bay* France
119 S6 **St Brieux** Saskatchewan Canada
127 L5 **St Catharines-Niagara** Ontario Canada
130 G5 **Saint Catherine, Lake** Louisiana USA
163 10a **St Catherine, Mount** *volcano* Grenada
127 inset **St Catherine Point** Bermuda
241 F4 **St Catherine's Point** England UK
131 K5 **Saint Catherines Sound** Georgia USA
228 E4 **St-Céré** France
229 H3 **Saint-Cergue** Switzerland
228 F4 **St-Cernin** France
229 G5 **St-Chamas** France
229 G4 **St-Chamond** France
126 F7 **Saint Charles** Missouri USA
228 F4 **St-Chély-d'Apcher** France
127 J5 **St Clair, Lake** Ontario Canada
128 G4 **Saint Clair, Lake** Arizona USA
229 G3 **St-Claude** France
163 16 **Saint-Claude** Guadeloupe
240 C3 **Saint Clears** Wales UK
228 D3 **Saint-Clément-des-Baleines** France
126 D4 **Saint Cloud** Minnesota USA
244 G3 **St Combs** Aberdeenshire Scotland UK
229 G4 **St Cristol, Plateau de** *region* France
123 E10 **St Croix** *watercourse* Canada/USA
163 21 **St Croix** *island* US Virgin Islands
126 E4 **Saint Croix Falls** Wisconsin USA
228 F5 **Saint-Cyprien-Plage** France
127 N2 **Saint-Cyr** *watercourse* Québec Canada
123 C8 **Saint-David-de-Falardeau** Québec Canada
163 10a **St David's** Grenada
240 B3 **St David's** Pembrokeshire Wales UK
240 B3 **St David's Head** *cape* Wales UK
127 inset **St David's Island** Bermuda
228 F2 **St-Denis** France
310 7a **Saint-Denis** Réunion
228 D3 **Saint-Denis-d'Oléron** France
228 D2 **Saint-Denis-le-Gast** France
240 E3 **St Devereux** Herefordshire England UK
229 H2 **St-Dié** France
226 C3 **St-Dizier** France
240 C2 **St Dogmells** Pembrokeshire Wales UK
125 Q6 **Saint Edward** Nebraska USA
226 C5 **St-Égrève** France
116 E7 **St Elias, Cape** Alaska USA
116 E6 **St Elias, Mount** Alaska USA
118 A2 **St Elias Mountains** British Columbia/Yukon Territory/Alaska Canada/USA
126 G7 **Saint Elmo** Illinois USA
228 F3 **St-Éloy-les-Mines** France
228 D4 **Saint-Émilion** France
240 B4 **St Erth** Cornwall England UK
229 G4 **St-Étienne** France
229 G4 **Saint-Étienne-les-Orgues** France
135 I3 **St Eustatius** *island* Netherlands Antilles
123 D8 **St-Fabien** Québec Canada
228 D3 **Saint-Félix** France
244 G3 **St Fergus** Aberdeenshire Scotland UK
229 H4 **Saint-Firmin** France
229 I5 **St-Florent** Corsica France
228 F2 **St-Florentin** France
228 F4 **St-Flour** France
228 E3 **Saint-Flovier** France
122 C3 **St-Fond** *watercourse* Québec Canada
127 Q3 **St Francis** *watercourse* Canada/USA
125 O7 **Saint Francis** Kansas USA
123 L9 **St Francis, Cape** Newfoundland and Labrador Canada
308 D6 **St Francis, Cape** South Africa
127 P4 **St Francis, Lake** Québec Canada
130 F5 **Saint Francisville** Louisiana USA
163 16 **Saint-François** Guadeloupe
123 C8 **Saint-Fulgence** Québec Canada
229 I3 **St Gallen** Switzerland
228 E5 **St-Gaudens** France
228 E3 **St-Gaultier** France
127 P2 **St-Gédéon** Québec Canada
226 B5 **St-Geniez-d'Olt** France
425 N7 **St George** Qld Australia
127 inset **St George** Bermuda
131 K4 **Saint George** South Carolina USA
128 F2 **Saint George** Utah USA
373 J5 **Saint George, Cape** Papua New Guinea
124 C6 **St George, Point** California USA
116 C7 **St George Island** Alaska USA
131 I6 **Saint George Sound** Florida USA
127 P3 **St-Georges** Québec Canada
135 I4 **St George's** Grenada
123 I8 **St George's Bay** Newfoundland and Labrador Canada
123 H10 **St George's Bay** Nova Scotia Canada
376 B6 **St George's Channel** Andaman and Nicobar Islands India
245 G4 **St George's Channel** *strait* Ireland/UK
373 J5 **Saint George's Channel** *strait* Papua New Guinea
119 Q5 **St George's Hill** Saskatchewan Canada
127 inset **St George's Island** Bermuda
122 B2 **St-Germain, Lac** *lake* Québec Canada
241 F5 **Saint-Germain-des-Vaux** France
240 C4 **St Germans** Cornwall England UK
228 F1 **Saint-Ghislain** Belgium
228 C3 **St-Gildas, Pointe de** *cape* France
228 E5 **St-Girons** France
228 D5 **Saint-Girons-en-Marensin** France
240 C3 **St Govan's Head** *cape* Wales UK
127 O3 **St-Grégoire** Québec Canada
240 D2 **Saint Harmon** Powys Wales UK
310 5b **St Helena** *British overseas territory* Atlantic Ocean
310 5b **St Helena** *island* Atlantic Ocean
308 C6 **St Helena Bay** *bay* South Africa
131 K4 **Saint Helena Sound** South Carolina USA
425 N10 **St Helens** Tas. Australia
242 F3 **St Helens** *admin. area* England UK
124 D4 **Saint Helens** Oregon USA
228 C2 **St Helier** Jersey Channel Islands UK
127 P3 **St-Henri-de-Lévis** Québec Canada
125 Q3 **Saint Hilaire** Minnesota USA
228 F3 **Saint-Hilaire-près Pionsat** France
226 B4 **Saint-Honoré** France
117 L9 **Saint-Hyacinthe** Québec Canada
126 I4 **Saint Ignace** Michigan USA
124 H3 **Saint Ignatius** Montana USA
240 C3 **St Ishmael** Carmarthenshire Wales UK
241 G2 **St Ives** Cambridgeshire England UK
240 B4 **St Ives** Cornwall England UK
240 B4 **St Ives Bay** England UK
125 Q2 **Saint James** Manitoba Canada
228 D2 **St-James** France
126 F8 **Saint James** Missouri USA
118 F7 **St James, Cape** British Columbia Canada
423 E6 **St James Range** New Zealand
117 L9 **St-Jean, Lac** *lake* Québec Canada
228 C3 **St-Jean-de-Monts** France
135 F3 **Saint-Jean du Sud** Haiti
228 D5 **St-Jean-Pied-de-Port** France
123 C9 **St-Jean-Port-Joli** Québec Canada
127 O4 **St-Jean-sur-Richelieu** Québec Canada
127 N4 **St-Jérôme** Québec Canada
130 C4 **Saint Jo** Texas USA
124 H3 **St Joe** *watercourse* Idaho USA
123 E10 **St John** New Brunswick Canada
123 E9 **St John** *watercourse* Canada/USA
304 C3 **St John** *watercourse* Liberia
163 21 **St John** *island* US Virgin Islands
125 P8 **Saint John** Kansas USA
123 K8 **St John, Cape** Newfoundland and Labrador Canada
123 J7 **St John Bay** Newfoundland and Labrador Canada
123 E10 **St John Harbour** New Brunswick Canada
123 J7 **St John Island** Newfoundland and Labrador Canada
163 18 **Saint John's** Antigua and Barbuda
123 L9 **St John's** Newfoundland and Labrador Canada
129 H3 **Saint Johns** Arizona USA
126 I5 **Saint Johns** Michigan USA
135 I3 **Saint John's Flat** Netherlands Antilles
163 18 **Saint John's Harbour** *bay* Antigua and Barbuda
245 D2 **St John's Point** Ireland
245 G2 **St John's Point** Northern Ireland UK
163 17 **St John's Village** Montserrat
163 14 **Saint-Joseph** Martinique
426 7 **Saint Joseph** New Caledonia
310 7a **Saint-Joseph** Réunion
163 9 **Saint Joseph** Trinidad and Tobago
126 D7 **Saint Joseph** Missouri USA
120 J7 **St Joseph, Lake** Ontario Canada
131 I6 **Saint Joseph Bay** Florida USA
310 9 **Saint Joseph Island** Seychelles
130 C7 **St Joseph Island** Texas USA
131 J6 **Saint Joseph Sound** Florida USA
127 P3 **St-Josephe-de-Beauce** Québec Canada
245 C4 **Saint Joseph's** Ireland
228 F4 **Saint-Julien-aux-Bois** France
228 E4 **St-Junien** France
240 B4 **St Just** Cornwall England UK
228 D5 **Saint-Justin** France
240 B4 **St Keverne** Cornwall England UK
163 19 **St Kitts** *island* St Kitts and Nevis
135 I3 **St Kitts and Nevis** *country* Caribbean
228 E5 **St-Lary-Soulan** France
125 Q1 **Saint-Laurent** Manitoba Canada
231 H2 **St-Laurent-de-Cerdans** France
231 H2 **St-Laurent-de-la-Salanque** France
155 H3 **Saint-Laurent-du-Maroni** French Guiana
241 H5 **Saint-Laurent-en-Caux** France
425 N5 **St Lawrence** Qld Australia
163 12 **St Lawrence** Barbados
123 K9 **St Lawrence** Newfoundland and Labrador Canada
123 D8 **St Lawrence** *watercourse* Canada/USA
241 H3 **St Lawrence** Essex England UK
125 P4 **Saint Lawrence** South Dakota USA
123 H9 **St Lawrence, Cape** Nova Scotia Canada
123 G8 **St Lawrence, Gulf of** Canada
116 B6 **St Lawrence Island** Alaska USA
125 O1 **Saint Lazare** Manitoba Canada
124 G1 **Saint Leon** British Columbia Canada
228 E4 **St-Léonard-de-Noblat** France
310 7a **Saint-Leu** Réunion
240 B4 **St Levan** Cornwall England UK
122 K6 **St Lewis** Newfoundland and Labrador Canada
122 J6 **St Lewis** *watercourse* Newfoundland and Labrador Canada
122 K6 **St Lewis Sound** Newfoundland and Labrador Canada
228 E5 **Saint-Lizier** France
228 D2 **St-Lô** France
119 S6 **St Louis** Saskatchewan Canada
163 16 **Saint-Louis** Guadeloupe
310 7a **Saint-Louis** Réunion
300 C5 **St-Louis** Senegal
126 I5 **Saint Louis** Michigan USA
126 F7 **Saint Louis** Missouri USA
123 F9 **Saint-Louis-de-Kent** New Brunswick Canada
229 H3 **St-Loup-sur-Semouse** France
163 13 **St Lucia** *country* Caribbean
309 F5 **St Lucia** South Africa
309 F5 **St Lucia, Lake** *lake* South Africa
135 I4 **St Lucia Channel** St Lucia
123 K7 **St Lunaire-Griquet** Newfoundland and Labrador Canada
228 D3 **St-Maixent-l'École** France
228 C2 **St-Malo, Golfe de** *bay* France
228 G5 **Saint-Mamert-du-Gard** France
135 F3 **Saint-Marc** Haiti
135 F3 **St-Marc, Canal de** *strait* Haiti
155 H4 **St Marcel, Mont** *mountain* French Guiana
119 R8 **St Marie** Montana USA
124 G3 **St Maries** Idaho USA
163 10a **St Mark Bay** Grenada
245 F3 **Saint Marnocks** Ireland
163 20 **St Martin** *French overseas collectivity* Caribbean
163 20 **St Martin** *island* Caribbean
163 14 **St-Martin, Cap** *cape* Martinique
120 F7 **St Martin, Lake** Manitoba Canada
228 D3 **St-Martin-de-Ré** France
240 A5 **St Martin's** *island* England UK
379 G5 **St Martin's Island** Myanmar
231 G2 **St-Martory** France
119 O8 **St Mary** *watercourse* Alberta Canada
119 M8 **St Mary** *watercourse* British Columbia Canada
119 O8 **St Mary** Montana USA
123 E10 **St Mary, Cape** Nova Scotia Canada
373 H6 **Saint Mary, Mount** Papua New Guinea
425 K7 **St Mary Peak** *mountain* SA Australia
124 I2 **St Mary Reservoir** Alberta Canada
244 F2 **St Mary's** Orkney Islands Scotland UK
163 9 **Saint Marys** Trinidad and Tobago
240 A5 **St Mary's** *island* England UK
131 K5 **Saint Marys** Georgia USA
127 L6 **Saint Marys** Pennsylvania USA
123 K9 **St Mary's, Cape** Newfoundland and Labrador Canada
123 L9 **St Mary's Bay** Newfoundland and Labrador Canada
423 D7 **St Marys Range** New Zealand
228 B2 **St-Mathieu, Pointe de** *cape* France
116 B6 **St Matthew Island** Alaska USA
373 I4 **Saint Matthias Group** *island* Papua New Guinea
228 F2 **St-Maur-des-Fossés** France
240 B4 **St Mawes** Cornwall England UK
229 G5 **St-Maximin-la-Ste-Baume** France
228 D4 **St-Médard-en-Jalles** France
227 G4 **St Michael im Lungau** Austria
240 E2 **St Michaels** Worcestershire England UK
228 B2 **St-Michel, Réservoir de** *lake* France
229 H4 **St-Michel-de-Maurienne** France
117 L9 **Saint-Michel-des-Saints** Québec Canada
229 G2 **St-Mihiel** France
244 F4 **St Monans** Fife Scotland UK
232 C3 **St Moritz** Switzerland
241 G2 **St Neots** Cambridgeshire England UK
240 B3 **St Nicholas** Pembrokeshire Wales UK
241 I5 **Saint-Nicolas-d'Aliermont** France
229 L3 **St Nikolai** Austria
226 B2 **St-Omer** France
127 Q3 **St-Pacôme** Québec Canada
228 D5 **St-Palais** France
123 D9 **St-Pamphile** Québec Canada
123 D9 **St-Pascal** Québec Canada
127 M3 **St-Patrice, Lac** *lake* Québec Canada
163 17 **Saint Patrick's** Montserrat
119 P6 **St Paul** Alberta Canada
123 J7 **St Paul** *watercourse* Québec Canada
155 H3 **Saint-Paul** French Guiana
304 B3 **St Paul** *watercourse* Liberia
310 7a **Saint-Paul** Réunion
116 B7 **St Paul** Alaska USA
237 AM7 **St Paul** *island* Alaska USA
126 D8 **Saint Paul** Kansas USA
126 E4 **Saint Paul** Minnesota USA
125 P6 **Saint Paul** Nebraska USA
131 J2 **Saint Paul** Virginia USA
304 E3 **St Paul, Cape** Ghana
310 6 **Saint-Paul, Île** *island* French Southern and Antarctic Lands
123 H9 **St Paul Island** Nova Scotia Canada
116 B7 **St Paul Island** Alaska USA
228 G4 **Saint-Paul-le-Jeune** France
163 19 **Saint Paul's** Saint Kitts and Nevis
131 L3 **Saint Pauls** North Carolina USA
123 J8 **St Paul's Inlet** Newfoundland and Labrador Canada
427 11a **St Paul's Point** *cape* Pitcairn Islands
224 E5 **St Peter-Ording** Germany
228 C2 **St Peter Port Guernsey** Channel Islands UK
123 G9 **St Peters** Prince Edward Island Canada
126 F7 **Saint Peters** Missouri USA
St Petersburg *see* **Sankt-Peterburg** Russian Federation
131 J7 **Saint Petersburg** Florida USA
310 7a **Saint-Philippe** Réunion
155 H4 **Saint Pierre** French Guiana
163 14 **Saint-Pierre** Martinique
310 7a **Saint-Pierre** Réunion
123 J9 **St-Pierre** St Pierre and Miquelon
123 J9 **St-Pierre, Île** *island* St Pierre and Miquelon
127 O3 **St-Pierre, Lac** *lake* Québec Canada
123 F8 **St-Pierre, Pointe** *cape* Québec Canada
123 J9 **St Pierre and Miquelon** *French overseas territorial collectivity* North America
228 D4 **St-Pierre-d'Oléron** France
241 F5 **Saint-Pierre-Église** France
310 9 **Saint Pierre Island** Seychelles
120 G8 **St-Pierre-Jolys** Manitoba Canada
228 F3 **St-Pierre-le-Moûtier** France
240 C4 **St Pinnock** Cornwall England UK
127 L3 **St Placide** Québec Canada
228 C2 **St-Pol-de-Léon** France
227 H3 **St Pölten** Austria
231 H2 **St-Pons-de-Thomières** France
228 F3 **St-Pourçain-sur-Sioule** France
123 E9 **St-Quentin** New Brunswick Canada
228 F2 **St-Quentin** France
229 G4 **Saint-Rambert-d'Albon** France
127 P3 **St-Raphaël** Québec Canada
231 J2 **St-Raphaël** France
127 P3 **St-Raymond** Québec Canada
228 D2 **St-Rémy** France
228 F3 **Saint-Révérien** France
241 I4 **Saint-Riquier** France
241 I5 **St-Saëns** France
228 F3 **Saint-Satur** France
228 E3 **Saint-Savin** France
228 F5 **Saint-Sernin-sur-Rance** France
228 D5 **St-Sever** France
123 D9 **St-Siméon** Québec Canada
131 K5 **Saint Simons Sound** Georgia USA
127 O2 **St-Stanislas** Québec Canada
127 R4 **St Stephen** Maine USA
131 L4 **Saint Stephen** South Carolina USA
228 E5 **St-Sulpice** France
228 D4 **St-Symphorien** France
127 K5 **St Thomas** Ontario Canada
163 21 **St Thomas** *island* US Virgin Islands
127 O3 **St-Tite** Québec Canada
127 P3 **St-Tite-des-Caps** Québec Canada
229 H5 **St-Tropez** France
229 H5 **St-Tropez, Cap de** *cape* France
229 G1 **St-Truiden** Belgium
229 G4 **St-Vallier** France
228 D3 **Saint-Varent** France
227 H4 **St Veit an der Glan** Austria
226 D5 **St-Vincent** Italy
163 11 **St Vincent** *island* St Vincent and the Grenadines
125 Q2 **Saint Vincent** Minnesota USA
425 K8 **St Vincent, Gulf** SA Australia
135 I4 **St Vincent and the Grenadines** *country* Caribbean
135 I4 **St Vincent Passage** St Vincent and the Grenadines
131 I6 **Saint Vincent Sound** Florida USA
119 Q6 **St Walburg** Saskatchewan Canada
240 E3 **St Weonards** Herefordshire England UK
228 E4 **Saint-Yrieix-la-Perche** France
123 C9 **St-Zacharie** Québec Canada
125 Q2 **Sainte Anne** Manitoba Canada
155 H3 **Sainte-Anne** French Guiana
163 16 **Sainte-Anne** Guadeloupe
163 14 **Sainte-Anne** Martinique
119 N6 **Ste Anne, Lac** *lake* Alberta Canada
121 V8 **Sainte-Anne-des-Monts** Québec Canada
127 O4 **Ste-Anne-des-Plaines** Québec Canada
127 N3 **Ste-Anne-du-Lac** Québec Canada
310 9b **Sainte Anne Island** Seychelles
305 F5 **Ste-Catherine, Pointe** *cape* Gabon
228 E1 **Sainte-Cécile-Plage** France
127 P3 **Ste-Claire** Québec Canada
229 H3 **Sainte-Croix** Switzerland
229 H5 **Ste-Croix, Lac de** *lake* France
228 E4 **Ste-Foy-la-Grande** France
126 F8 **Sainte Genevieve** Missouri USA
123 D9 **Ste-Hélène** Québec Canada
228 D3 **Ste-Hermine** France
127 P3 **Ste-Justine** Québec Canada
127 Q2 **Ste-Luce** Québec Canada
163 14 **Sainte-Luce** Martinique
127 O3 **Ste-Madeleine** Québec Canada
163 16 **Sainte-Marguerite** Guadeloupe
163 16 **Sainte-Marie** Guadeloupe
163 14 **Sainte-Marie** Martinique
229 H2 **Sainte-Marie-aux-Mines** France
233 D8 **Sainte Marie du Zit** Tunisia
229 H5 **Sainte-Maxime** France
163 17 **Sainte-Rose** Montserrat
310 7a **Sainte-Rose** Réunion
119 V7 **Sainte-Rose-du-Lac** Manitoba Canada
310 7a **Sainte-Suzanne** Réunion
127 O3 **Ste-Thècle** Québec Canada
228 D4 **Saintes** France
228 G5 **Stes Maries, Golfe des** *bay* France
229 G5 **Stes-Maries-de-la-Mer** France
245 G2 **Saintfield** Down Northern Ireland UK
384 F3 **Saintsagaan** Mongolia
160 D6 **Sainuco** Argentina
228 E2 **Sainville** France
392 E4 **Saipal** *mountain* Nepal
426 2 **Saipan** Northern Mariana Islands
426 2 **Saipan** *island* Northern Mariana Islands
426 3 **Saipan** Palau
379 G4 **Sairang** Mizoram India
160 E2 **Sairecábur, Cerro** *mountain* Chile
231 H2 **Saissac** France
387 H4 **Saitama** Japan
386 F5 **Saito** Japan
379 G4 **Saitual** Mizoram India
223 M2 **Saivomuotka** Sweden
384 F4 **Saiwusu** Nei Mongol Zizhiqu China
158 D5 **Sajama, Nevado** *mountain* Bolivia
379 F3 **Sajia** Xizang Zizhiqu China
234 B3 **Šajkaš** Serbia
227 K3 **Sajó** *watercourse* Hungary
159 E5 **Sajpuco** Bolivia
308 D6 **Sak** *watercourse* South Africa
225 N3 **Saka** Estonia
307 F2 **Saka** Ethiopia
225 K4 **Saka** Latvia
222 L3 **Sakajärvi** Sweden
390 D3 **Sakākā** Saudi Arabia
375 H5 **Sakala** *island* Indonesia
121 Q6 **Sakami** Québec Canada
121 R6 **Sakami** *watercourse* Québec Canada
121 Q6 **Sakami, Lac** *lake* Québec Canada
306 D6 **Sakania** Democratic Republic of Congo
422 3 **Sakaofo** *island* Tokelau New Zealand
235 E5 **Sakar** *range* Bulgaria
373 H5 **Sakar Island** Papua New Guinea
309 H4 **Sakaraha** Madagascar
235 G5 **Sakarya** *admin. area* Turkey
235 G5 **Sakarya (Adapazırı)** Turkey
387 H3 **Sakata** Japan
127 J3 **Sakatawi Lake** Ontario Canada
386 E3 **Sakchu** North Korea
389 M2 **Sakhalin** *lake* Russian Federation
237 AD8 **Sakhalin, Ostrov** *island* Russian Federation
237 AD8 **Sakhalinskaya Oblast'** *admin. area* Russian Federation
237 AD8 **Sakhalinskiy Zaliv** *bay* Russian Federation
Saki *see* **Sheki** Azerbaijan
225 L5 **Šakiai** Lithuania
374 C5 **Sakijang Bendera, Pulau** *island* Singapore
374 D5 **Sakijang Pelepah, Pulau** *island* Singapore
391 K3 **Sakīr Gharūna** *mountain* Pakistan
373 G6 **Sakiramke** Indonesia
381 I4 **Sakishima-shotō** *island* Japan
223 P3 **Säkkilänvaara** Finland
225 L3 **Sakla** Estonia
376 E3 **Sakon Nakhon** Thailand
388 I4 **Saksaulskiy** Kazakhstan
387 H4 **Saku** Japan
386 F5 **Sakura-jima** *volcano* Japan
120 J6 **Sakwaso Lake** Ontario Canada
225 L2 **Säkylä** Finland
310 4 **Sal** *island* Cape Verde
135 H5 **Sal, Cayo de** *island* Venezuela
134 C4 **Sal, Punta** *cape* Honduras
134 D2 **Sal Cay** *island* Bahamas
154 A5 **Sal Chico, Punta** *cape* Peru
310 4 **Sal Rei** Cape Verde
79 W10 **Sala y Gómez Ridge** *underwater feature* Pacific Ocean
375 I4 **Salabangka, Kepulauan** Indonesia
225 M4 **Salacgrīva** Latvia
160 D3 **Salada, Bahía** *bay* Chile
162 C3 **Salada, Gran Laguna** *lake* Argentina
128 E4 **Salada, Laguna** *lake* Mexico
161 G5 **Saladillo** Argentina
160 F5 **Saladillo** *watercourse* Argentina
160 F4 **Salado** *watercourse* Argentina
160 D3 **Salado** *watercourse* Chile
161 G4 **Salado, Lago** *lake* Argentina
160 D3 **Salado, Nevado Ojos del** *mountain* Argentina
304 D3 **Salaga** Ghana
132 B1 **Salaga, Laguna** *lake* Mexico
390 E2 **Şalaḩ Ad Dīn** *admin. area* Iraq
223 O5 **Salahmi** Finland
427 12c **Sala'ilua** Samoa
234 C2 **Sălaj** *admin. area* Romania
308 D4 **Salajwe** Botswana
301 J6 **Salal** Chad
302 F3 **Salâla** Sudan
391 H6 **Şalālah** Oman
223 N5 **Salamajärvi kansallispuisto** *park* Finland
160 D4 **Salamanca** Chile
132 E4 **Salamanca** Mexico
230 D3 **Salamanca** Spain
127 L5 **Salamanca** New York USA
162 C3 **Salamanca, Pampa de** *region* Argentina
309 F5 **Salamanga** Mozambique
305 I2 **Salamat** *admin. area* Chad
305 H3 **Salamat, Bahr** *watercourse* Chad
373 H5 **Salamaua** Papua New Guinea
427 12c **Salamumu** Samoa
384 G5 **Salaqi** Nei Mongol Zizhiqu China
160 E3 **Salar de Pocitos** Argentina
391 I3 **Sālārābād** Iran
230 C2 **Salas** Spain
230 E2 **Salas de los Infantes** Spain
231 H2 **Salasc** France
375 F5 **Salatiga** Indonesia
376 E4 **Salavan** Laos
158 B3 **Salaverry** Peru
372 D4 **Salawati** *island* Indonesia
393 B6 **Salaya** Gujarat India
160 F6 **Salazar** Argentina
310 7a **Salazie** Réunion
228 F3 **Salbris** France
158 C4 **Salcantay, Nevado** *mountain* Peru
132 C2 **Salcedo** Mexico
234 C3 **Salcia** Romania
240 D4 **Salcombe** Devon England UK
235 F7 **Salda Gölü** *lake* Turkey
230 D2 **Saldaña** Spain
308 C6 **Saldanha** South Africa
225 L4 **Saldus** Latvia
225 L4 **Saldus** *admin. area* Latvia
425 M9 **Sale** Vic. Australia
243 F3 **Sale** Greater Manchester England UK
375 H6 **Saleh, Teluk** *bay* Indonesia
427 12c **Sale'imoa** Samoa
236 O5 **Salekhard** Russian Federation
427 12c **Salelologa** Samoa
393 E9 **Salem** Tamil Nadu India
163 17 **Salem** Montserrat
240 C3 **Salem** Carmarthenshire Wales UK
130 F2 **Salem** Arkansas USA
126 G8 **Salem** Kentucky USA
126 F8 **Salem** Missouri USA
127 K6 **Salem** Ohio USA
124 D4 **Salem** Oregon USA
125 Q5 **Salem** South Dakota USA
127 K8 **Salem** Virginia USA
224 H4 **Salen** *bay* Sweden
233 F6 **Salerno** Italy
233 F6 **Salerno, Golfo di** *bay* Italy
159 I3 **Sales** Brazil
223 O5 **Sälevä** *lake* Finland
243 F3 **Salford** Greater Manchester England UK
157 E5 **Salgado** Brazil
223 M2 **Salgganjávri** *lake* Norway
227 J3 **Salgótarján** Hungary
156 E5 **Salgueiro** Brazil
384 F2 **Salhit** Mongolia
160 E4 **Sali** *watercourse* Argentina
232 F5 **Sali** Croatia
245 C3 **Saliahoona** Ireland
375 J3 **Salibabu** *island* Indonesia
163 9 **Salibea** Trinidad and Tobago
125 M7 **Salida** Colorado USA
228 D5 **Salies-de-Béarn** France
394 C2 **Salihorsk** Belarus
121 Q4 **Salikuit Islands** Nunavut Canada
309 F2 **Salima** Malawi
375 H3 **Salimbatu** Indonesia
230 C2 **Salime, Embalse de** *lake* Spain
379 H5 **Salin** Myanmar
125 Q7 **Salina** Kansas USA
124 J7 **Salina** Utah USA
133 G5 **Salina Cruz** Mexico
160 D5 **Salina Llancanelo** *lake* Argentina
135 F2 **Salina Point** Bahamas
157 D7 **Salinas** Brazil
154 A5 **Salinas** Ecuador
132 E4 **Salinas** Mexico
124 E8 **Salinas** California USA
128 B2 **Salinas** *watercourse* California USA
158 B3 **Salinas, Bahía** *bay* Peru
231 F4 **Salinas, Laguna de** *lake* Spain
160 E4 **Salinas, Pampas de las** *lake* Argentina
135 G3 **Salinas, Punta** *cape* Dominican Republic
154 A5 **Salinas, Punta** *cape* Ecuador
163 6a **Salinas, Punta** *cape* Isla Róbinson Crusoe
159 G4 **Salinas, Serra das** *range* Brazil
158 B4 **Salinas de Otuma** Peru
160 E4 **Salinas Grandes** *lake* Argentina
244 E4 **Saline** Fife Scotland UK
130 E3 **Saline** *watercourse* Arkansas USA
125 P7 **Saline** *watercourse* Kansas USA
163 9 **Saline Bay** Trinidad and Tobago
130 E5 **Saline Lake** Louisiana USA
158 A2 **Salinera Colán** Peru
231 H4 **Salines, Cap de Ses** *cape* Spain
135 I5 **Salines, Point** Grenada
379 H5 **Salingyi** Myanmar
226 C4 **Salins** France
163 15 **Salisbury** Dominica
241 F3 **Salisbury** Wiltshire England UK
127 N7 **Salisbury** Maryland USA
121 Q1 **Salisbury Island** Nunavut Canada
426 5 **Salisbury Junction** Guam
241 F3 **Salisbury Plain** England UK
124 H2 **Salish Mountains** Montana USA
234 D2 **Săliştea de Sus** Romania
132 E3 **Salitillo** Mexico
158 A2 **Salitral** Peru
157 D5 **Salitre** *watercourse* Brazil
160 D3 **Salitrosa** *watercourse* Chile
125 Q5 **Salix** Iowa USA
224 H4 **Saljen** *lake* Sweden
234 F1 **Sal'kovo** Ukraine
223 P3 **Salla** Finland
158 D4 **Sallalli** Peru
229 H4 **Sallanches** France
224 E4 **Salling** *cape* Denmark
242 B3 **Sallins** Ireland
222 J3 **Sallohaure** *lake* Sweden

121 R1 Salluit Québec Canada
302 D1 Sallûm, Khalîj as bay Egypt/Libya
245 D5 Sally Port Ireland
392 F5 Sallyana Nepal
225 P2 Salmi Russian Federation
223 P3 Salmivaara Finland
118 M8 Salmo British Columbia Canada
123 F9 Salmon watercourse New Brunswick Canada
124 I4 Salmon Idaho USA
124 H4 Salmon watercourse Idaho USA
118 L7 Salmon Arm British Columbia Canada
424 G8 Salmon Gums WA Australia
124 H4 Salmon River Mountains Idaho USA
223 S3 Sal'nitsa Russian Federation
306 B3 Salo Central African Republic
225 L2 Salo Finland
230 F4 Salobral, Laguna del lake Spain
225 M4 Saločiai Lithuania
154 D3 Saloma Colombia
163 I4 Salomon, Cap cape Martinique
228 G2 Salon France
392 E5 Salon Uttar Pradesh India
229 G5 Salon-de-Provence France
306 C4 Salonga watercourse Democratic Republic of Congo
235 D5 Salonikos, Akra cape Greece
118 F3 Saloon British Columbia Canada
230 C4 Salorino Spain
227 I4 Šalovci Slovenia
225 N2 Salpausselkä range Finland
159 F2 Salsa, Igarape Cabeceira do watercourse Brazil
160 E4 Salsacate Argentina
231 G3 Salsadella Spain
222 G4 Salsbruket Norway
228 F5 Salses-le-Château France
119 O3 Salt watercourse Alberta Canada
241 E2 Salt Staffordshire England UK
128 G4 Salt watercourse Arkansas USA
126 F7 Salt watercourse Missouri USA
129 J5 Salt Flat Texas USA
129 M2 Salt Fork Arkansas watercourse Kansas USA
129 L3 Salt Fork Red watercourse Texas USA
124 J6 Salt Lake City Utah USA
124 I7 Salt Marsh Lake Utah USA
119 O2 Salt River Northwest Territories Canada
124 E7 Salt Springs Reservoir California USA
128 C1 Salt Wells Nevada USA
160 E3 Salta Argentina
160 E3 Salta admin. area Argentina
240 C4 Saltash Cornwall England UK
119 T7 Saltcoats Saskatchewan Canada
244 D5 Saltcoats North Ayrshire Scotland UK
222 I3 Saltdalen valley Norway
222 I3 Saltdalselva watercourse Norway
222 I3 Saltdalsfjorden bay Norway
245 F4 Saltee Islands Ireland
222 I3 Saltfjellet-Svartisen Nasjonalpark park Norway
243 I3 Saltfleetby St Clement Lincolnshire England UK
224 G5 Saltholm island Denmark
235 G6 Saltık Turkey
132 E3 Saltillo Mexico
130 G3 Saltillo Mississippi USA
244 E2 Saltness Orkney Islands Scotland UK
160 F5 Salto Argentina
157 C8 Salto Brazil
161 G4 Salto Uruguay
161 G4 Salto admin. area Uruguay
133 G5 Salto de Agua Mexico
161 H3 Salto del Guairá Paraguay
161 G4 Salto Grande, Embalse de lake Argentina
157 A9 Salto Osório, Represa lake Brazil
222 K3 Saltoluokta Sweden
243 H2 Salton North Yorkshire England UK
128 E4 Salton Sea California USA
159 E5 Saltos Bolivia
423 D6 Saltwater Lagoon New Zealand
388 C2 Saltyki Russian Federation
131 K4 Saluda South Carolina USA
375 I4 Salue Timpaus, Selat strait Indonesia
375 I4 Saluebesar island Indonesia
377 I5 Salug Philippines
392 D6 Salumbar Rajasthan India
393 F7 Salur Andhra Pradesh India
226 D5 Saluzzo Italy
162 A5 Salvación, Bahía bay Chile
160 E4 Salvador Argentina
154 D4 Salvador Bolivia
157 E6 Salvador Brazil
130 F6 Salvador, Lake Louisiana USA
163 7 Salvador, Port Falkland Islands
135 G3 Salvaleón de Higüey Dominican Republic
132 E4 Salvatierra Mexico
228 C5 Salvatierra Spain
230 B2 Salvora, Illa de island Spain
240 E4 Salway Ash Dorset England UK
163 9 Salybia Trinidad and Tobago
226 F2 Salza watercourse Germany
226 G4 Salzach watercourse Austria
226 G4 Salzburg Austria
226 G4 Salzburg admin. area Austria
226 F1 Salzgitter Germany
226 F1 Salzwedel Germany
392 C5 Sam Rajasthan India
130 D5 Sam Rayburn Reservoir Texas USA
376 E3 Sầm Sơn Vietnam
373 G4 Sama Atoll reef Papua New Guinea
129 I7 Samachic Mexico
391 I5 Şamad Oman
228 D5 Samadet France
374 E4 Samak, Tanjung cape Indonesia
390 E6 Samakh Saudi Arabia
374 F3 Samalantan Indonesia
377 I6 Samales Group island Philippines
237 AN8 Samalga Pass strait Alaska USA
302 E2 Samâlûţ Egypt
135 G3 Samaná, Cabo cape Dominican Republic
135 F2 Samana Cay island Bahamas
158 B3 Samanco, Bahía lake Peru
389 J7 SamangĀn admin. area Afghanistan
235 F5 Samanlı Dağları range Turkey
121 S8 Samaqua watercourse Québec Canada
377 J5 Samar Sea Philippines
134 C5 Sámara Costa Rica
388 F2 Samara Russian Federation
373 I6 Samarai Papua New Guinea
375 H4 Samarinda Indonesia
388 J6 Samarqand Uzbekistan
388 J6 Samarqand admin. area Uzbekistan
390 E2 Sāmarrā' Iraq
388 F3 Samarskaya Oblast' admin. area Russian Federation
389 N3 Samarskoye Kazakhstan
227 M2 Samary Ukraine
392 F6 Samastipur Bihar India
158 E3 Samaúma Brazil
306 C3 Samba Democratic Republic of Congo
375 G4 Samba watercourse Indonesia
306 B5 Samba Caju Angola
375 H3 Sambaliung Pergunungan range Indonesia
393 F7 Sambalpur Orissa India
309 H3 Sambao watercourse Madagascar
372 B5 Sambapolulu, Gunung mountain Indonesia
375 F4 Sambar, Tanjung cape Indonesia
374 F3 Sambas Indonesia
309 J2 Sambava Madagascar
392 E5 Sambhal Uttar Pradesh India
392 D5 Sambhar Salt Lake Rajasthan India
375 H3 Sambit island Indonesia
156 D4 Sambito watercourse Brazil
308 C2 Sambo Angola
375 H4 Samboja Indonesia
160 F5 Samborombon watercourse Argentina
161 G5 Samborombón, Bahía bay Argentina
241 F2 Sambourne Warwickshire England UK
386 F4 Samch'ŏk South Korea
379 G8 Samdrup Jongkhar Bhutan
307 F4 Same Tanzania
226 A2 Samer France
308 E2 Samfya Zambia
303 I5 Samhah island Yemen
375 I3 Samia, Tanjung cape Indonesia
386 F3 Samjiyŏn North Korea
223 M5 Sammatti Finland
301 I3 Samnū Libya
427 12c Samoa country Pacific Ocean
78 P9 Samoa Basin underwater feature Pacific Ocean
226 D4 Samoëns France
232 G2 Šamorín Slovakia
235 E7 Samos Greece
235 E7 Samos island Greece
230 C2 Samos Spain
374 C3 Samosir island Indonesia
235 D5 Samothraki island Greece
234 D4 Samovodene Bulgaria
388 D3 Samoylovka Russian Federation
304 D3 Sampa Ghana
160 E5 Sampacho Argentina
375 G5 Sampang Indonesia
240 D4 Sampford Arundel Somerset England UK
240 D4 Sampford Courtenay Devon England UK
240 D4 Sampford Peverell Devon England UK
375 G4 Sampit Indonesia
375 G4 Sampit watercourse Indonesia
375 G4 Sampit, Teluk strait Indonesia
372 B5 Sampolawa Indonesia
120 I6 Sampson Lake Ontario Canada
154 C2 Sampués Colombia
373 J5 Sampun Papua New Guinea
306 D5 Sampwe Democratic Republic of Congo
303 F5 Samrē Ethiopia
222 G5 Samsjøen lake Norway
224 G4 Sämsjön lake Sweden
224 F5 Samsø island Denmark
127 L8 Samson Alabama USA
386 E3 Samsu North Korea
394 F5 Samsun Turkey
394 F5 Samsun admin. area Turkey
379 F8 Samtse Bhutan
379 G4 Samurou Manipur India
376 D4 Samut Prakan Thailand
376 E4 San watercourse Cambodia
300 F6 San Mali
227 L3 San watercourse Poland
230 B2 San Adrián, Cabo de cape Spain
154 B4 San Agustin Colombia
128 E6 San Agustin Mexico
377 J6 San Agustin, Cape Philippines
129 I4 San Agustin, Plains of New Mexico USA
154 C3 San Alberto Colombia
161 H3 San Alberto Paraguay
129 I4 San Andreas Mountains New Mexico USA
159 E4 San Andrés Bolivia
154 A1 San Andrés Colombia
163 3 San Andrés Isla de San Andrés
163 3 San Andrés, Isla de island Colombia
133 F4 San Andres, Laguna de lake Mexico
228 B5 San Andrés del Rabanedo Spain
129 L5 San Angelo Texas USA
154 C2 San Antero Colombia
158 D4 San Antón Peru
160 D3 San Antonia Chile
133 H5 San Antonio Belize
159 E5 San Antonio Bolivia
160 D5 San Antonio Chile
154 C5 San Antonio Colombia
158 C1 San Antonio Peru
377 I4 San Antonio Philippines
128 B2 San Antonio watercourse California USA
131 J6 San Antonio Florida USA
129 I4 San Antonio New Mexico USA
130 B6 San Antonio Texas USA
129 N6 San Antonio watercourse Texas USA
154 E4 San Antonio Venezuela
134 C2 San Antonio, Cabo de cape Cuba
231 G4 San Antonio, Cabo de cape Spain
133 F5 San Antonio, Isla island Ecuador
162 D2 San Antonio, Puerto bay Argentina
231 G4 San Antonio Abad Spain
377 H5 San Antonio Bay Philippines
130 C6 San Antonio Bay Texas USA
132 D2 San Antonio de Bravo Mexico
134 C4 San Antonio de Cusicancha Peru
129 L8 San Antonio de las Alazanas Mexico
160 E3 San Antonio de los Cobres Argentina
158 E5 San Antonio de Nor Kala Bolivia
159 E4 San Antonio de Rivera Bolivia
162 D2 San Antonio Oeste Argentina
128 B3 San Antonio Reservoir California USA
160 E4 San Augustin de Valle Fértil Argentina
130 D5 San Augustine Texas USA
159 E4 San Bartolo Bolivia
162 D6 San Bartolomé, Cabo cape Argentina
230 C5 San Bartolomé de la Torre Spain
232 E5 San Benedetto del Tronto Italy
132 C5 San Benedicto, Isla island Mexico
134 B3 San Benito Guatemala
130 C7 San Benito Texas USA
132 B2 San Benito, Islas island Mexico
128 D3 San Bernardino California USA
128 D3 San Bernardino Mountains California USA
160 D5 San Bernardo Chile
132 C3 San Bernardo Mexico
160 E4 San Blas Argentina
162 D2 San Blas Argentina
132 D4 San Blas Mexico
134 E5 San Blas, Archipiélago de islands Panama
134 E5 San Blas, Cordillera de range Panama
134 E5 San Blas, Punta cape Panama
158 E4 San Borja Bolivia
159 E3 San Borja Bolivia
128 F7 San Bruno Mexico
132 C3 San Buenaventura Mexico
160 D5 San Carlos Argentina
159 F5 San Carlos Bolivia
160 D6 San Carlos Chile
163 7 San Carlos Falkland Islands
130 B8 San Carlos Mexico
134 C5 San Carlos Nicaragua
161 G2 San Carlos Paraguay
161 G2 San Carlos watercourse Paraguay
377 I5 San Carlos Philippines
154 C2 San Carlos Venezuela
160 F6 San Carlos de Bolívar Argentina
154 C4 San Carlos de Guaroa Colombia
154 D2 San Carlos del Zulia Venezuela
128 G4 San Carlos Reservoir Arizona USA
233 E8 San Cataldo Italy
128 D4 San Clemente California USA
230 E5 San Clemente, Embalse de lake Spain
161 G6 San Clemente del Tuyú Argentina
132 A1 San Clemente Island California USA
426 8 San Cristobal island Solomon Islands
160 F4 San Cristóbal Argentina
160 D2 San Cristóbal Chile
134 D2 San Cristóbal Cuba
161 H3 San Cristóbal Paraguay
154 C3 San Cristóbal Venezuela
163 4 San Cristóbal, Isla islands Archipiélago de Colón (Galapagos Islands)
300 C3 San Cristóbal de la Laguna Spain
133 G5 San Cristóbal de las Casas Mexico
159 F5 San Diablo, Serranía range Bolivia
154 C2 San Diego Colombia
132 A1 San Diego California USA
130 B7 San Diego Texas USA
162 D6 San Diego, Cabo cape Argentina
128 D4 San Diego Bay California USA
132 D3 San Diego de Alcalo Mexico
132 E4 San Diego de la Unión Mexico
132 E3 San Dionisio Mexico
229 K4 San Donà di Piave Italy
132 D4 San Elizario Texas USA
134 C4 San Esteban Honduras
129 K6 San Esteban Mexico
162 A4 San Estéban, Golfo bay Chile
132 B2 San Esteban, Isla island Mexico
233 E6 San Felice Circeo Italy
160 D5 San Felipe Chile
154 E4 San Felipe Colombia
132 B2 San Felipe Mexico
132 E4 San Felipe Mexico
154 D2 San Felipe Venezuela
162 C5 San Felipe, Bahía bay Chile
133 J4 San Felipe, Cayos de island Cuba
133 H5 San Felipe, Laguna lake Mexico
129 I7 San Felipe de Jesus Mexico
135 G3 San Felipe de Puerto Plata Dominican Republic
134 D5 San Félix Panama
161 G5 San Félix Uruguay
129 J7 San Fermin Mexico
161 G5 San Fernando Argentina
160 D5 San Fernando Chile
133 F3 San Fernando Mexico
377 I3 San Fernando Philippines
163 9 San Fernando Trinidad and Tobago
163 9 San Fernando admin. area Trinidad and Tobago
128 C3 San Fernando California USA
133 E3 San Fernando de Apure Venezuela
160 E4 San Fernando del Valle de Catamarca Argentina
154 C5 San Fernendo Peru
163 9 San Francique Trinidad and Tobago
160 F4 San Francisco Argentina
159 F5 San Francisco Bolivia
154 D5 San Francisco Colombia
134 C5 San Francisco Costa Rica
134 B4 San Francisco El Salvador
129 H5 San Francisco Mexico
133 F5 San Francisco Panama
377 J5 San Francisco Philippines
124 D8 San Francisco California USA
129 H4 San Francisco watercourse New Mexico USA
154 A4 San Francisco, Cabo de cape Ecuador
128 A2 San Francisco Bay California USA
129 J8 San Francisco de Asis Mexico
133 I6 San Francisco de Coray Honduras
135 G3 San Francisco de Macoris Dominican Republic
162 C4 San Francisco de Paula, Cabo cape Argentina
133 E4 San Francisco del Rincón Mexico
231 G4 San Francisco Javier Spain
154 B3 San Francisco Solano, Punta cape Colombia
128 F6 San Francisquito Mexico
154 B4 San Gabriel Ecuador
133 F5 San Gabriel Casa Blanca Mexico
128 D3 San Gabriel Mountains California USA
160 F6 San Germán Argentina
154 C3 San Gil Colombia
226 G5 San Giorgio di Nogaro Italy
162 D3 San Gregorio, Bahía bay Argentina
129 K6 San Guillermo Mexico
132 B3 San Hipólito, Punta cape Mexico
134 B3 San Ignacio Belize
159 F4 San Ignacio Bolivia
132 D4 San Ignacio Mexico
158 B2 San Ignacio Peru
132 B3 San Ignacio, Laguna lake Mexico
154 B4 San Ignacio, Punta cape Colombia
159 E4 San Ignacio de Moxo Bolivia
159 F5 San Ignacio de Velasco Bolivia
132 E2 San Ildefonso Mexico
377 I4 San Ildefonso, Cape Philippines
377 I3 San Ildefonso Peninsula cape Philippines
134 D5 San Isidro Costa Rica
128 F7 San Isidro Mexico
129 I5 San Isidro Mexico
130 B7 San Isidro Texas USA
161 H3 San Isidro de Curuguaty Paraguay
154 C2 San Jacinto Colombia
377 I4 San Jacinto Philippines
128 D4 San Jacinto California USA
161 G4 San Jaime Argentina
231 F5 San Javier Spain
133 G5 San Jerónimo Ixtepec Mexico
159 F4 San Joaquin watercourse Bolivia
159 E4 San Joaquín Bolivia
161 G3 San Joaquín Paraguay
124 E8 San Joaquin California USA
124 E8 San Joaquin watercourse California USA
129 K3 San Jon New Mexico USA
160 F4 San Jorge Argentina
154 C4 San Jorge Colombia
426 8 San Jorge island Solomon Islands
162 C4 San Jorge, Golfo bay Argentina
377 I4 San Jose Philippines
377 I4 San Jose Philippines
377 J6 San Jose Philippines
124 E8 San Jose California USA
126 G6 San Jose Illinois USA
161 G6 San José Argentina
158 E4 San José Bolivia
159 F2 San José Brazil
160 C6 San José Chile
154 B4 San José Colombia
134 C5 San José Costa Rica
134 B3 San José Guatemala
134 C4 San José Honduras
128 G7 San José Mexico
133 F4 San José Mexico
231 F4 San José Spain
161 G5 San José admin. area Uruguay
162 D3 San José, Cabo cape Argentina
162 D3 San José, Golfo bay Argentina
132 C3 San José, Isla island Mexico
134 E5 San José, Isla island Panama
133 F5 San José de Bácum Mexico
128 G6 San José de Baviácora Mexico
134 C4 San José de Bocay Nicaragua
377 I5 San Jose de Buenavista Philippines
155 E3 San José de Camani Venezuela
132 B3 San José de Castro Mexico
161 G4 San José de Feliciano Argentina
155 E2 San José de Guanipa Venezuela
160 D4 San José de Jáchal Argentina
129 I6 San José de la Ermita Mexico
128 E6 San José de las Palomas Mexico
161 G5 San José de Mayo Uruguay
154 E2 San José de Tiznados Venezuela
132 E3 San José del Aguaje Mexico
160 F3 San José del Boquerón Argentina
159 E4 San José del Carrito Bolivia
154 C4 San José del Guaviare Colombia
134 C4 San José del Potrero Honduras
129 N6 San Jose Island Texas USA
160 D4 San Juan Argentina
160 D4 San Juan admin. area Argentina
158 E4 San Juan Bolivia
310 3a San Juan Canary Islands
162 B5 San Juan Chile
133 F3 San Juan watercourse Mexico
154 C5 San Juan Peru
135 H3 San Juan Puerto Rico
163 9 San Juan Trinidad and Tobago
129 H2 San Juan watercourse Utah USA
162 D6 San Juan, Cabo cape Argentina
305 F4 San Juan, Cabo cape Equatorial Guinea
154 C4 San Juan, Llanos de region Colombia
134 E2 San Juan, Loma region Cuba
134 B4 San Juan, Punta lake El Salvador
163 5 San Juan, Punta cape Isla de Pascua (Easter Island)
163 2 San Juan, Punta cape Isla de Providencia
163 6a San Juan Bautista Isla Róbinson Crusoe
161 G3 San Juan Bautista Paraguay
158 C4 San Juan Bautista Peru
132 D4 San Juan de Abajo Mexico
154 C4 San Juan de Arama Colombia
154 D2 San Juan de Colón Venezuela
154 C2 San Juan de Guía, Cabo de cape Colombia
154 B4 San Juan de La Costa Colombia
310 3a San Juan de la Rambla Canary Islands
154 D2 San Juan de los Cayos Venezuela
154 E2 San Juan de los Morros Venezuela
154 B2 San Juan de Urabá Colombia
154 C2 San Juan del Cesar Colombia
134 C5 San Juan del Norte Nicaragua
134 D5 San Juan del Norte, Bahía de bay Nicaragua
133 E4 San Juan del Río Mexico
134 C5 San Juan del Sur Nicaragua
158 D4 San Juan Grande Peru
124 D2 San Juan Islands Washington USA
163 9 San Juan-Laventille admin. area Trinidad and Tobago
129 I2 San Juan Mountains Colorado USA
132 E3 San Juan Nepomuceno Mexico
133 H4 San Juan Ote Mexico
134 B4 San Juan Sacatepéquez Guatemala
128 F7 San Juanico Mexico
128 F7 San Juanico, Laguna Mexico
132 B3 San Juanico, Punta cape Mexico
129 I7 San Juanito Mexico
132 D4 San Juanito, Isla island Mexico
162 C4 San Julián Argentina
162 C4 San Julián, Bahía bay Argentina
162 C4 San Julián, Gran Bajo de region Argentina
160 F4 San Justo Argentina
161 G2 San Lázaro Paraguay
132 B3 San Lázaro, Cabo cape Mexico
130 C5 San Leanna Texas USA
232 E5 San Leo Italy
230 E3 San Leonardo de Yagüe Spain
154 B4 San Lorenz de Esmeraldas Ecuador
161 G4 San Lorenzo Argentina
159 F4 San Lorenzo Bolivia
154 C4 San Lorenzo Colombia
134 C4 San Lorenzo Honduras
129 I6 San Lorenzo Mexico
158 D4 San Lorenzo Peru
154 A5 San Lorenzo, Cabo cape Ecuador
132 B2 San Lorenzo, Isla island Mexico
162 C4 San Lorenzo, Monte mountain Argentina
159 F5 San Lorenzo, Serranía range Bolivia
230 E4 San Lorenzo de la Parrilla Spain
233 C7 San Lotemzo, Capo cape Sardinia Italy
129 J6 San Lucas Mexico
132 C4 San Lucas Mexico
128 B2 San Lucas California USA
154 C3 San Lucas, Serranía de range Colombia
160 E5 San Luis Argentina
160 E5 San Luis admin. area Argentina
135 F2 San Luis Cuba
134 B3 San Luis Guatemala
134 C4 San Luis Honduras
163 3 San Luis Isla de San Andrés
132 B2 San Luis Mexico
158 C4 San Luis Peru
125 M8 San Luis Colorado USA
132 B2 San Luís, Isla island Mexico
159 F4 San Luis, Laguna lake Bolivia
154 D2 San Luis, Sierra de range Venezuela
133 F5 San Luis Acatlán Mexico
132 E4 San Luis de la Paz Mexico
129 J8 San Luis del Cordero Mexico
128 B3 San Luis Obispo California USA
132 E4 San Luis Potosí Mexico
132 E4 San Luis Potosí admin. area Mexico
128 E4 San Luis Reservoir California USA
128 D4 San Luis Rey watercourse California USA
132 B1 San Luis Río Colorado Mexico
132 B2 San Luisito Mexico
161 G6 San Manuel Argentina
129 I4 San Marcial New Mexico USA
132 C3 San Marcial, Punta cape Mexico
233 E8 San Marco, Capo cape Italy
158 E4 San Marcos Bolivia
159 E6 San Marcos Bolivia
154 C2 San Marcos Colombia
133 F5 San Marcos Mexico
158 B2 San Marcos Peru
128 D4 San Marcos California USA
130 C6 San Marcos Texas USA
132 C3 San Marcos, Isla island Mexico
232 E5 San Marino San Marino
160 D5 San Martin Argentina
159 F4 San Martín watercourse Bolivia
162 C5 San Martín Chile
154 C4 San Martín Colombia
158 B2 San Martín admin. area Peru
133 G5 San Martín, Volcán volcano Mexico
436 T2 San Martín (Argentina) research station Antarctica
162 B2 San Martín de los Andes Argentina
377 I3 San Mateo Philippines
129 I3 San Mateo New Mexico USA
154 B4 San Mateo, Bahía bay Ecuador
154 C2 San Mateo, Serranía de range Colombia
133 G5 San Mateo del Mar Mexico
134 B4 San Mateo Ixtatán Guatemala
129 I4 San Mateo Mountains New Mexico USA
159 G5 San Matías Brazil
162 D2 San Matías, Golfo bay Argentina
229 H4 San Mauro Torinese Italy
229 K4 San Michele al Tagliamento Italy
160 E6 San Miguel Argentina
159 F5 San Miguel Bolivia
159 F4 San Miguel watercourse Bolivia
154 B4 San Miguel Colombia
154 B5 San Miguel Ecuador
154 B4 San Miguel watercourse Ecuador
132 C2 San Miguel Mexico
134 E5 San Miguel Panama
161 G3 San Miguel Paraguay
158 C4 San Miguel Peru
134 E5 San Miguel, Golfo de bay Panama
377 I4 San Miguel Bay Philippines
158 B3 San Miguel de Cauri Peru
132 C2 San Miguel de Horcasitas watercourse Mexico
160 E3 San Miguel de Tucumán Argentina
158 E4 San Miguel del Bala Bolivia
161 G5 San Miguel del Monte Argentina
128 B3 San Miguel Island California USA
377 H6 San Miguel Islands Philippines
132 D3 San Miguel Papasquiaro Mexico
133 G5 San Miguel Quetzaltepec Mexico
158 D3 San Miguelito Bolivia
134 C5 San Miguelito Nicaragua
134 E5 San Miguelito Panama
134 B4 San Miquel El Salvador
134 D2 San Nicolás Cuba
134 C4 San Nicolás Honduras
155 E2 San Nicolás Venezuela
158 C4 San Nicolás, Bahía bay Peru
160 F5 San Nicolás de los Arroyos Argentina
132 E3 San Nicolás de los Garzas Mexico
310 3b San Nicolás de Tolentino Canary Islands
128 C4 San Nicolas Island California USA
129 I8 San Nicolas Sitio de Arriba Mexico
154 C2 San Onofre Colombia
162 C6 San Pablo Argentina
162 B2 San Pablo Chile
154 C2 San Pablo Colombia
377 I4 San Pablo Philippines
132 B3 San Pablo, Punta cape Mexico
129 I7 San Pablo Balleza Mexico
161 G3 San Pablo de Ycuámandyyú Paraguay
233 F8 San Paolo Italy
132 D5 San Patricio Mexico
161 G5 San Pedro Argentina
134 C3 San Pedro Belize
159 E6 San Pedro Bolivia
132 C3 San Pedro Mexico
129 H5 San Pedro watercourse Mexico
161 G3 San Pedro admin. area Paraguay
158 D3 San Pedro Peru
128 G4 San Pedro watercourse Arkansas USA
304 C4 San Pédro Côte d'Ivoire
162 A2 San Pedro, Bahía bay Chile
160 E2 San Pedro, Nevado de mountain Argentina
134 D5 San Pedro, Punta lake Costa Rica
129 H5 San Pedro, Rio de watercourse Mexico
128 C4 San Pedro Channel California USA
128 H6 San Pedro de la Cueva Mexico
129 K8 San Pedro de las Colonias Mexico
135 G3 San Pedro de Macorís Dominican Republic
230 D3 San Pedro de Rozados Spain
154 B2 San Pedro de Urabá Colombia
161 G3 San Pedro de Ycuamandiyú Paraguay
129 J8 San Pedro del Gallo Mexico
161 G3 San Pedro del Paraná Paraguay
228 C5 San Pedro Manrique Spain
128 E5 San Pedro Martir Mexico
133 F6 San Pedro Pochutla Mexico
134 B4 San Pedro Sula Honduras
130 C7 San Perlita Texas USA
232 D5 San Piero in Bagno Italy
229 I4 San Pietro Vara Italy
132 B2 San Quintín Mexico
132 A2 San Quintín, Cabo cape Mexico
160 D5 San Rafael Argentina
158 D4 San Rafael Peru
124 D8 San Rafael California USA
125 J7 San Rafael watercourse Utah USA
128 C3 San Rafael Mountains California USA
159 F4 San Ramón Bolivia
134 C5 San Ramón Costa Rica
158 C3 San Ramón Peru
232 B5 San Remo Italy
133 H5 San Román Mexico
154 D1 San Román, Cabo cape Venezuela
426 2a San Roque Northern Mariana Islands
128 E7 San Roque, Punta cape Mexico
130 B5 San Saba Texas USA
161 G4 San Salvador Argentina
135 F1 San Salvador island Bahamas
134 B4 San Salvador El Salvador
163 4 San Salvador, Isla island Archipiélago de Colón (Galapagos Islands)
160 E3 San Salvador de Jujuy Argentina
233 F5 San Salvo Italy
162 C5 San Sebastián Argentina
162 C5 San Sebastián, Cabo cape Argentina
310 3a San Sebastián de la Gomera Canary Islands
133 F5 San Sebastián Zinacatepec Mexico
233 F6 San Severo Italy
128 B3 San Simeon California USA
129 H4 San Simon Arizona USA
159 F4 San Simón Bolivia
160 D5 San Vicente Chile
162 D6 San Vicente, Cabo cape Argentina
230 C4 San Vicente de Alcántara Spain
154 C3 San Vicente de Chucurí Colombia
154 C4 San Vicente del Caguán Colombia
232 D5 San Vincenzo Italy
230 C3 San Vitero Spain
134 D5 San Vito Costa Rica
233 G6 San Vito, Capo cape Italy
233 E7 San Vito lo Capo Italy
154 D4 San Yanaro Colombia
133 F3 San Ygnacio Mexico
130 B7 San Ygnacio Texas USA
129 I3 San Ysidro New Mexico USA
132 B3 San Zacharías Mexico
390 E7 Şan'ā' admin. area Yemen
390 E7 Şan'ā' (Sanaa) Yemen
307 H1 Sanaag admin. area Somalia
304 D2 Sanaba Burkina Faso
436 X2 SANAE IV (South Africa) research station Antarctica
244 B5 Sanaigmore Argyll and Bute Scotland UK
116 C8 Sanak Island Alaska USA
132 D3 Sanalona, Presa lake Mexico
390 E5 Sanām Saudi Arabia
375 J4 Sanana island Indonesia
392 C6 Sanand Gujarat India
390 F2 Sanandaj Iran
300 E6 Sanando Mali
234 B3 Sânandrei Romania
161 I3 Sananduva Brazil
305 G4 Sananga watercourse Cameroon
304 C2 Sanankoroba Mali
154 D2 Sanare Abajo Venezuela
373 I6 Sanaroa Island Papua New Guinea
426 6a Sanat island Federated States of Micronesia
393 D6 Sanawad Madhya Pradesh India
125 P3 Sanborn North Dakota USA
228 F3 Sancerre France
230 D3 Sanchidrián Spain
392 C6 Sanchore Rajasthan India
377 J5 Sanco Point Philippines
375 J1 Sanco Point cape Philippines
228 F3 Sancoins France
230 C5 Sancti Petri, Isla island Spain
134 E2 Sancti Spíritus Cuba
134 E2 Sancti Spíritus admin. area Cuba
230 C3 Sancti-Spíritus Spain
243 H3 Sancton East Riding of Yorkshire England UK
125 K1 Sanctuary Saskatchewan Canada
228 F4 Sancy, Puy de mountain France
119 P5 Sand watercourse Alberta Canada
224 F2 Sand Norway
373 G4 Sand watercourse Papua New Guinea
308 E4 Sand watercourse South Africa
222 L4 Sand Sweden
393 C9 Sand Cay island Lakshadweep India
310 9 Sand Cay island Seychelles
125 O6 Sand Hills Nebraska USA
116 C6 Sand Islands Alaska USA
120 H7 Sand Lake Ontario Canada
116 C7 Sand Point Alaska USA
130 C2 Sand Springs Oklahoma USA
387 G4 Sanda Japan
244 C5 Sanda Island Scotland UK
391 K4 Sandadkot Pakistan
375 F4 Sandai Indonesia
244 C3 Sandaig Highland Scotland UK
375 H2 Sandakan Malaysia
375 H2 Sandakan, Teluk bay Malaysia
225 R1 Sandal, Ozero lake Russian Federation
390 E6 Şandalīyah Saudi Arabia
233 C7 Sandalo, Capo cape Sardinia Italy
376 E4 Sândân Cambodia
308 D2 Sandando Angola
244 F1 Sanday Sound Scotland UK
240 E1 Sandbach Cheshire England UK
222 L2 Sandbukt Norway
224 F3 Sande Norway
224 C3 Sandeid Norway
425 inset Sandell Bay Macquarie Island Australia
224 F2 Sander Norway
437 D2 Sandercock Nunataks mountain Antarctica
129 K5 Sanderson Texas USA
131 J4 Sandersville Georgia USA
130 G5 Sandersville Mississippi USA
222 I2 Sandes Norway
243 F2 Sandford Cumbria England UK
437 I2 Sandford Glacier Antarctica
244 F1 Sandgarth Orkney Islands Scotland UK
222 inset Sandgerði Iceland
244 D6 Sandhead Dumfries and Galloway Scotland UK
222 I3 Sandhornøya island Norway
241 G3 Sandhurst Bracknell Forest England UK
394 F6 Şandi Syria
305 I4 Sandiki watercourse Central African Republic
235 G6 Sandıklı Turkey
392 E5 Sandila Uttar Pradesh India
374 D4 Sanding island Indonesia
227 H3 Sandl Austria
222 J5 Sandnäset Sweden
222 I2 Sandnes Norway
224 C3 Sandnes Norway
244 inset Sandness Shetland Scotland UK
222 H3 Sandnessjøen Norway
306 C5 Sandoa Democratic Republic of Congo
159 I4 Sandolândia Brazil
227 K2 Sandomierz Poland
241 E2 Sandon Staffordshire England UK
223 M4 Sandön island Sweden
154 B4 Sandoná Colombia
234 B2 Sándorfalva Hungary
238 G3 Sandovo Russian Federation
372 E4 Sandow Indonesia
241 F4 Sandown Isle of Wight England UK
222 K1 Sandoy island Faroe Islands
124 G2 Sandpoint Idaho USA
244 F1 Sandquoy Orkney Islands Scotland UK
244 A4 Sandray island Scotland UK
120 G7 Sandridge Manitoba Canada
224 D3 Sandsavatnet lake Norway
424 F7 Sandstone WA Australia
126 E3 Sandstone Minnesota USA
222 J2 Sandstrand Norway
393 F7 Sandur watercourse Chhattisgarh India
126 J5 Sandusky Michigan USA
126 J6 Sandusky Ohio USA
222 F6 Sandvatnet lake Norway
308 C6 Sandveld plain South Africa
222 K2 Sandvik Norway
224 I4 Sandvik Sweden
224 F3 Sandvika Norway
224 I2 Sandviken Sweden
243 F4 Sandwell admin. area England UK
241 I3 Sandwich Kent England UK
122 J6 Sandwich Bay Newfoundland and Labrador Canada
244 inset Sandwick Shetland Scotland UK
241 G2 Sandy Bedfordshire England UK
119 T5 Sandy Bay Saskatchewan Canada
134 C3 Sandy Bay Honduras
425 inset Sandy Bay Macquarie Island Australia
425 O6 Sandy Cape Qld Australia
127 M5 Sandy Creek New York USA
122 K6 Sandy Hook Newfoundland and Labrador Canada
126 J7 Sandy Hook Kentucky USA
122 K6 Sandy Islands Newfoundland and Labrador Canada
119 O5 Sandy Lake Alberta Canada
123 J8 Sandy Lake Newfoundland and Labrador Canada
120 I6 Sandy Lake Ontario Canada
119 R4 Sandy Lake Saskatchewan Canada
119 T5 Sandy Narrows Saskatchewan Canada
310 5c Sandy Point cape St Helena
245 F3 Sandyford Ireland
388 I6 Sandyklygum lake Turkmenistan
230 E2 Sanfelices Spain
222 H5 Sånfjället mountain Sweden
222 H5 Sånfjället nationalpark park Sweden
424 F6 Sanford watercourse WA Australia
120 G8 Sanford Manitoba Canada
129 J2 Sanford Colorado USA
131 L3 Sanford North Carolina USA
129 L3 Sanford Texas USA
386 F4 Sang-do island South Korea
308 C2 Sanga Angola
300 F6 Sanga Mali
222 J5 Sånga Sweden
393 D7 Sangamner Maharashtra India
391 K3 Sangan Pakistan
237 AA6 Sangar Russian Federation
304 B2 Sangarédi Guinea
392 D5 Sangaria Rajasthan India
235 C7 Sángas Greece
305 G3 Sangbé Cameroon
377 I6 Sangboy Islands Philippines
306 D5 Sange Democratic Republic of Congo
391 K2 Sange Shāndeh Afghanistan
375 H6 Sangeang island Indonesia
234 D2 Sângeorz-Băi Romania
128 C2 Sanger California USA
130 C4 Sanger Texas USA
375 H6 Sanggar, Teluk bay Indonesia

375 F3 **Sanggau** Indonesia
374 F3 **Sanggauledo** Indonesia
375 J3 **Sanggeluhang** *island* Indonesia
305 H4 **Sangha** *admin. area* Congo
305 H4 **Sangha** *watercourse* Congo
305 H4 **Sangha-Mbaéré** *admin. area* Central African Republic
375 J3 **Sangihe, Kepulauan** *island* Indonesia
223 O4 **Sanginkylä** Finland
375 J3 **Sangir** *island* Indonesia
383 K2 **Sangiyn Dalay Nuur** *lake* Mongolia
386 F4 **Sangju** South Korea
375 G5 **Sangkapura** Indonesia
375 H3 **Sangkulirang** Indonesia
375 H3 **Sangkulirang, Teluk** *bay* Indonesia
392 D8 **Sangli** Maharashtra India
392 D6 **Sangod** Rajasthan India
393 D8 **Sangola** Maharashtra India
154 B5 **Sangolquí** Ecuador
372 D3 **Sangowo** Indonesia
129 J2 **Sangre de Cristo Range** Colorado/New Mexico USA
163 9 **Sangre Grande** Trinidad and Tobago
163 9 **Sangre Grande** *admin. area* Trinidad and Tobago
155 G2 **Sangretal Bay** Guyana
379 G3 **Sangri** Xizang Zizhiqu China
233 F5 **Sangro** *watercourse* Italy
222 J4 **Sangsjön** *lake* Sweden
386 E4 **Sangtae-do** *island* South Korea
119 N6 **Sangudo** Alberta Canada
159 G3 **Sangue, Rio do** *watercourse* Brazil
228 D4 **Sanguinet** France
162 C4 **Sanguineto, Bahía** *bay* Argentina
304 B2 **Sangulana** Guinea
309 F4 **Sangutane** *watercourse* Mozambique
389 K6 **Sangvor** Tajikistan
385 H5 **Sangyuan** Hebei China
304 C2 **Sanhala** Côte d'Ivoire
380 E3 **Sanhe** Guizhou China
302 E2 **Sanhûr** Egypt
235 C5 **Sani** Greece
131 J7 **Sanibel** Florida USA
131 J7 **Sanibel Island** Florida USA
155 H3 **Saniki** Suriname
127 P4 **Sanikiluaq** Nunavut Canada
158 E5 **Sanipaya** Bolivia
227 L4 **Sanislău** Romania
224 G5 **Sanitz** Germany
380 F3 **Sanjiang** Guizhou China
384 D6 **Sanjiaocheng** Qinghai China
376 C3 **Sankamphaeng** Thailand
304 B3 **Sankanbiaiwa** *mountain* Guinea
304 C2 **Sankarani** *watercourse* Guinea
232 F3 **Sankt Aegyd am Neuwalde** Austria
229 K2 **Sankt Florian** Austria
226 E4 **Sankt Gallen** Switzerland
226 E3 **Sankt Georgen** Germany
229 H1 **Sankt Goar** Germany
224 H5 **Sankt Olof** Sweden
225 P3 **Sankt-Peterburg (St Petersburg)** Russian Federation
306 C4 **Sankuru** *watercourse* Democratic Republic of Congo
394 F6 **Şanlıurfa** Turkey
394 F6 **Şanlıurfa** *admin. area* Turkey
233 C7 **Sanluri** Sardinia Italy
381 I3 **Sanmen Wan** *bay* Zhejiang China
381 F1 **Sanmenxia** Henan China
381 H3 **Sanming** Fujian China
244 B4 **Sanna** Highland Scotland UK
122 N2 **Sannerut** *island* Greenland
237 AC4 **Sannikova, Proliv** *strait* Russian Federation
244 C5 **Sannox** North Ayrshire Scotland UK
227 L3 **Sanok** Poland
300 E5 **Sanpaka** Mali
376 C3 **Sanpatong** Thailand
244 E5 **Sanquhar** Dumfries and Galloway Scotland UK
163 9 **Sans Souci** Trinidad and Tobago
304 B2 **Sansale** Guinea
300 E6 **Sansanding** Mali
381 F4 **Sanshui** Guangdong China
232 G4 **Sanski Most** Bosnia and Herzegovina
304 C2 **Sanso** Mali
422 F5 **Sanson** New Zealand
384 E3 **Sant** Mongolia
384 F2 **Sant** Mongolia
232 C4 **Sant' Anna, Punta** *cape* Italy
231 G3 **Sant Carles de la Ràpita** Spain
231 G3 **Sant Jordi, Golfo de** *bay* Spain
231 G3 **Sant Mateu** Spain
154 B4 **Santa Ana** Colombia
154 A5 **Santa Ana** Ecuador
134 B4 **Santa Ana** El Salvador
134 B3 **Santa Ana** Guatemala
134 C4 **Santa Ana** Honduras
129 I8 **Santa Ana** Mexico
158 C4 **Santa Ana** Peru
426 8 **Santa Ana** *island* Solomon Islands
128 D4 **Santa Ana** California USA
129 I3 **Santa Ana Pueblo** New Mexico USA
130 B5 **Santa Anna** Texas USA
159 G4 **Santa Bárbara** Brazil
154 C3 **Santa Bárbara** Colombia
134 B4 **Santa Bárbara** Guatemala
134 B4 **Santa Bárbara** Honduras
132 D3 **Santa Bárbara** Mexico
231 G3 **Santa Bárbara** Spain
128 C3 **Santa Barbara** California USA
310 1b **Santa Bárbara, Serra de** *volcano* Azores
161 H2 **Santa Bárbara, Serra de** *range* Brazil
128 B3 **Santa Barbara Channel** California USA
230 C5 **Santa Bárbara de Casa** Spain
135 G3 **Santa Bárbara de Samaná** Dominican Republic
128 C4 **Santa Barbara Island** California USA
157 C8 **Santa Branca** Brazil
160 D3 **Santa Catalina** Chile
132 A1 **Santa Catalina, Gulf of** California USA
163 2 **Santa Catalina, Isla de** *island* Isla de Providencia
128 C4 **Santa Catalina Island** California USA
161 I3 **Santa Catarina** *admin. area* Brazil
128 I3 **Santa Catarina** Mexico
159 H6 **Santa Catarina, Serra** *range* Brazil
163 1b **Santa Caterina** Netherlands Antilles
161 I3 **Santa Cecília** Brazil
233 H6 **Santa Cesarea Terme** Italy
154 D5 **Santa Clara** Colombia
134 E2 **Santa Clara** Cuba
132 E3 **Santa Clara** Mexico
132 D2 **Santa Clara** *watercourse* Mexico
158 B2 **Santa Clara** Peru
129 H4 **Santa Clara** New Mexico USA
128 F2 **Santa Clara** Utah USA
128 C3 **Santa Clara, Barragem de** *lake* Portugal
163 6 **Santa Clara, Isla** *island* Juan Fernández Archipiélago
128 C3 **Santa Clarita** California USA
231 H3 **Santa Coloma de Gramanet** Spain
233 F8 **Santa Croce, Capo** *cape* Italy
163 4 **Santa Cruz** Archipiélago de Colón (Galapagos Islands)
162 C4 **Santa Cruz** *admin. area* Argentina
162 B5 **Santa Cruz** *watercourse* Argentina
163 1a **Santa Cruz** Aruba
159 F5 **Santa Cruz** Bolivia
160 F2 **Santa Cruz** *admin. area* Bolivia
159 G5 **Santa Cruz** Brazil
310 4a **Santa Cruz** Cape Verde
160 D5 **Santa Cruz** Chile
134 C5 **Santa Cruz** Costa Rica
310 2 **Santa Cruz** Madeira
128 G5 **Santa Cruz** Mexico
133 H5 **Santa Cruz** Mexico
377 H4 **Santa Cruz** Philippines
377 I4 **Santa Cruz** Philippines
124 D8 **Santa Cruz** California USA
163 4 **Santa Cruz, Isla** *island* Archipiélago de Colón (Galapagos Islands)
132 C3 **Santa Cruz, Isla** *island* Mexico
162 C5 **Santa Cruz, Puerto** *bay* Argentina
157 E7 **Santa Cruz Cabrália** Brazil
230 E2 **Santa Cruz de Bezana** Spain
135 G3 **Santa Cruz de El Seibo** Dominican Republic
310 1b **Santa Cruz de Graciosa** Azores
310 3b **Santa Cruz de la Palma** Canary Islands
310 3a **Santa Cruz de Tenerife** Canary Islands
134 D2 **Santa Cruz del Norte** Cuba
156 E4 **Santa Cruz do Capibaribe** Brazil
157 B8 **Santa Cruz do Rio Pardo** Brazil
161 H4 **Santa Cruz do Sul** Brazil
128 C4 **Santa Cruz Island** California USA
133 F5 **Santa Cruz Xoxocotlán** Mexico
129 J8 **Santa Domingo** Mexico
230 E3 **Santa Domingo de Silos** Spain
158 E4 **Santa Elena** Bolivia
154 A5 **Santa Elena** Ecuador
154 A5 **Santa Elena** *admin. area* Ecuador
133 H4 **Santa Elena** Mexico
154 C5 **Santa Elena** Peru
154 A5 **Santa Elena, Bahía de** *bay* Ecuador
134 C5 **Santa Elena, Cabo** *cape* Costa Rica
159 H5 **Santa Elvira** Brazil
230 D4 **Santa Eufemia** Spain
233 F7 **Santa Eufemia, Golfo di** *bay* Italy
231 F3 **Santa Eulalia** Spain
231 G4 **Santa Eulalia del Río** Spain
160 F4 **Santa Fe** Argentina
160 F4 **Santa Fe** *admin. area* Argentina
377 I4 **Santa Fe** Philippines
129 J3 **Santa Fe** New Mexico USA
134 E5 **Santa Fé** Panama
163 4 **Santa Fé, Isla** *island* Archipiélago de Colón (Galapagos Islands)
157 B8 **Santa Fé do Sul** Brazil
131 J6 **Santa Fe Lake** Florida USA
154 B3 **Santa Genoveva de Docorodó** Colombia
159 H5 **Santa Helena** Brazil
157 B7 **Santa Helena de Goiás** Brazil
132 E3 **Santa Inés** Mexico
154 D2 **Santa Inés** Venezuela
156 C3 **Santa Inês** Brazil
162 B5 **Santa Inés, Isla** *island* Chile
160 E6 **Santa Isabel** Argentina
159 G5 **Santa Isabel** Brazil
163 2 **Santa Isabel** Isla de Providencia
132 B2 **Santa Isabel** Mexico
426 8 **Santa Isabel** *island* Solomon Islands
154 E2 **Santa Isabel** Venezuela
132 B2 **Santa Isabel, Sierra** *range* Mexico
155 E5 **Santa Isabel do Rio Negro** Brazil
161 G4 **Santa Lucia** *watercourse* Argentina
154 C2 **Santa Lucía** Colombia
154 C5 **Santa Lucía** Colombia
154 A5 **Santa Lucía** Ecuador
158 D4 **Santa Lucía** Peru
162 A5 **Santa Lucía, Cabo** *cape* Chile
128 B2 **Santa Lucia Range** California USA
159 H5 **Santa Luisa, Serra de** *range* Brazil
156 C4 **Santa Luzia** Brazil
310 4 **Santa Luzia** *island* Cape Verde
230 B3 **Santa Luzia, Barragem de** *lake* Portugal
159 F3 **Santa Luzia d'Oeste** Brazil
160 F4 **Santa Margarita** Argentina
128 B3 **Santa Margarita** California USA
132 B3 **Santa Margarita, Isla** *island* Mexico
310 1 **Santa Maria** *island* Azores
159 F4 **Santa María** Bolivia
161 H4 **Santa Maria** Brazil
310 4 **Santa Maria** Cape Verde
132 D2 **Santa María** *watercourse* Mexico
163 1b **Santa Maria** Netherlands Antilles
161 G3 **Santa María** Paraguay
377 I3 **Santa Maria** Philippines
128 B3 **Santa Maria** California USA
426 7 **Santa Maria** *island* Vanuatu
308 B2 **Santa Maria, Cabo de** *cape* Angola
309 F5 **Santa Maria, Cabo de** *cape* Mozambique
230 C5 **Santa Maria, Cabo de** *cape* Portugal
135 F2 **Santa Maria, Cape** Bahamas
134 E2 **Santa María, Cayo** *island* Cuba
163 4 **Santa María, Isla** *island* Archipiélago de Colón (Galapagos Islands)
160 C6 **Santa María, Isla** *island* Chile
133 F5 **Santa María Asunción Tlaxiaco** Mexico
156 E5 **Santa Maria da Boa Vista** Brazil
157 C6 **Santa Maria da Vitória** Brazil
154 C2 **Santa María de Ipire** Venezuela
132 E3 **Santa María de Mohovano** Mexico
228 B5 **Santa María del Páramo** Spain
132 E4 **Santa María del Río** Mexico
233 F6 **Santa Maria di Castellabate** Italy
156 C3 **Santa Maria do Pará** Brazil
157 D7 **Santa Maria do Suaçuí** Brazil
230 D3 **Santa María la Real de Nieva** Spain
133 F6 **Santa María Xadani** Mexico
233 F7 **Santa Marina Salina** Italy
154 C2 **Santa Marta** Colombia
128 F7 **Santa Marta** Mexico
230 C4 **Santa Marta** Spain
154 C2 **Santa Marta, Cienaga Grande de** *lake* Colombia
154 C2 **Santa Marta, Sierra Nevada de** *range* Colombia
230 D3 **Santa Marta de Tormes** Spain
128 C3 **Santa Monica Bay** California USA
128 C3 **Santa Monica Mountains National Recreation Area** *park* California USA
230 D3 **Santa Olalla** Spain
128 C3 **Santa Paula** California USA
156 D4 **Santa Quitéria** Brazil
156 D3 **Santa Quitéria do Maranhão** Brazil
158 C3 **Santa Rita** Brazil
154 D4 **Santa Rita** Colombia
132 C4 **Santa Rita** Mexico
155 F3 **Santa Rita** Venezuela
155 G5 **Santa Rita, Ilha** *island* Brazil
157 A8 **Santa Rita do Pardo** Brazil
160 E6 **Santa Rosa** Argentina
159 F6 **Santa Rosa** Bolivia
159 F3 **Santa Rosa** Brazil
161 H3 **Santa Rosa** Brazil
162 B2 **Santa Rosa** Chile
163 1b **Santa Rosa** Netherlands Antilles
161 G3 **Santa Rosa** Paraguay
158 B3 **Santa Rosa** Peru
128 F4 **Santa Rosa** Arizona USA
124 D7 **Santa Rosa** California USA
129 J3 **Santa Rosa** New Mexico USA
130 C7 **Santa Rosa** Texas USA
154 D2 **Santa Rosa** Venezuela
134 C3 **Santa Rosa, Punta** *cape* Mexico
154 E4 **Santa Rosa de Amanadona** Venezuela
134 B4 **Santa Rosa de Copán** Honduras
158 C3 **Santa Rosa de Dinamarca** Peru
154 C3 **Santa Rosa de Osos** Colombia
159 F5 **Santa Rosa del Sara** Bolivia
154 C3 **Santa Rosa del Sur** Colombia
128 B4 **Santa Rosa Island** California USA
154 C5 **Santa Rosa Menaje** Colombia
128 D4 **Santa Rosa Mountains** California USA
124 G6 **Santa Rosa Range** Nevada USA
130 H5 **Santa Rosa Sound** Florida USA
132 B3 **Santa Rosalía** Mexico
155 E3 **Santa Rosalía** Venezuela
128 E6 **Santa Rosalita** Mexico
160 F3 **Santa Sylvina** Argentina
230 B3 **Santa Tecla** *region* Portugal
425 J6 **Santa Teresa** NT Australia
159 G5 **Santa Teresa** Bolivia
157 B6 **Santa Teresa** *watercourse* Brazil
130 B8 **Santa Teresa** Mexico
154 E2 **Santa Teresa** Venezuela
154 B6 **Santa Teresita** Ecuador
128 F7 **Santa Tomas** Mexico
159 E6 **Santa Victoria, Sierra** *range* Argentina
157 B7 **Santa Vitória** Brazil
161 H5 **Santa Vitória do Palmar** Brazil
128 C3 **Santa Ynez** *watercourse* California USA
230 D5 **Santaella** Spain
233 D5 **Sant'Agostino, Punta** *cape* Italy
380 E2 **Santai** Sichuan China
157 E5 **Santaluz** Brazil
375 H4 **Santan** Indonesia
375 H4 **Santan, Tanjung** *cape* Indonesia
156 B3 **Santana** Brazil
310 2 **Santana** Madeira
161 H4 **Santana, Coxilha de** *range* Brazil
161 H4 **Santana da Boa Vista** Brazil
156 D3 **Santana do Acaraú** Brazil
156 B5 **Santana do Araguaia** Brazil
161 H4 **Santana do Livramento** Brazil
156 E4 **Santana do Matos** Brazil
154 C3 **Santander** *admin. area* Colombia
230 E2 **Santander** Spain
133 F3 **Santander Jiménez** Mexico
229 I4 **Sant'Angelo Lodigiano** Italy
233 C7 **Sant'Antioco** Sardinia Italy
229 I5 **Sant'Appiano, Monte** *mountain* Corsica France
124 J7 **Santaquin** Utah USA
155 H5 **Santarém** Brazil
230 B4 **Santarém** Portugal
230 B4 **Santarém** *admin. area* Portugal
134 E2 **Santaren Channel** Bahamas
128 D4 **Santee** California USA
131 J3 **Santeetlah Lake** North Carolina USA
232 E4 **Sant'Erasmo, Isola** *island* Italy
232 C4 **Sant'Erasmo, Punta** *cape* Italy
161 H4 **Santiago** Brazil
310 4 **Santiago** *island* Cape Verde
160 D5 **Santiago** Chile
154 B4 **Santiago** *watercourse* Ecuador
132 E3 **Santiago** Mexico
134 D5 **Santiago** Panama
161 G3 **Santiago** Paraguay
377 I3 **Santiago** Philippines
162 A5 **Santiago, Cabo** *cape* Chile
132 D4 **Santiago, Grande de** *watercourse* Mexico
305 F4 **Santiago, Punta** *cape* Equatorial Guinea
159 G5 **Santiago, Serranía de** *range* Bolivia
158 B3 **Santiago de Chuco** Peru
230 B2 **Santiago de Compostela** Spain
135 F2 **Santiago de Cuba** Cuba
134 E3 **Santiago de Cuba** *admin. area* Cuba
133 F4 **Santiago de la Peña** Mexico
135 G3 **Santiago de los Caballeros** Dominican Republic
158 D4 **Santiago de Pacaguaras** Bolivia
160 E3 **Santiago del Estero** Argentina
160 F3 **Santiago del Estero** *admin. area* Argentina
310 3a **Santiago del Teide** Canary Islands
159 F5 **Santiago del Torno** Bolivia
132 D4 **Santiago Ixcuintla** Mexico
133 F5 **Santiago Miahuatlán** Mexico
129 K6 **Santiago Mountains** Texas USA
132 D3 **Santiago Papasquiaro** Mexico
120 N1 **Santianna Point** Nunavut Canada
381 I3 **Santiao Chiao** *island* Taiwan China
230 C3 **Santibáñez el Bajo** Spain
372 B3 **Santigi** Indonesia
375 I3 **Santigi, Tanjung** *cape* Indonesia
383 J3 **Santmargants** Mongolia
310 2 **Santo, Porto** Madeira
230 C4 **Santo Aleixo** Portugal
157 E6 **Santo Amaro** Brazil
161 I3 **Santo Amaro da Imperatriz** Brazil
157 B8 **Santo Anastácio** Brazil
157 C8 **Santo André** Brazil
230 B4 **Santo André** Portugal
161 H4 **Santo Ângelo** Brazil
156 F5 **Santo Antão** Brazil
310 4 **Santo Antão** *island* Cape Verde
305 F4 **Santo António** São Tomé and Príncipe
156 F4 **Santo Antônio** Brazil
159 I5 **Santo Antônio da Barra** Brazil
156 A3 **Santo Antônio da Cachoeira** Brazil
159 I3 **Santo Antônio da Solta** Brazil
157 E6 **Santo Antônio de Jesus** Brazil
154 E5 **Santo Antônio do Içá** Brazil
159 G4 **Santo Antônio do Leverger** Brazil
161 J2 **Santo Antônio do Monte** Brazil
157 A9 **Santo Antônio do Sudoeste** Brazil
156 B3 **Santo Antônio do Tauá** Brazil
159 F4 **Santo Domingo** Bolivia
135 G3 **Santo Domingo** Dominican Republic
154 B4 **Santo Domingo** Ecuador
129 L6 **Santo Domingo** Mexico
132 D4 **Santo Domingo** Mexico
133 H5 **Santo Domingo** *watercourse* Mexico
154 B4 **Santo Domingo de los Colorados** Ecuador
133 G5 **Santo Domingo Tehuantepec** Mexico
157 E6 **Santo Estêvão** Brazil
233 F8 **Santo Pietro** Italy
232 D3 **Santo Stino di Livenza** Italy
230 B3 **Santo Tirso** Portugal
159 G5 **Santo Tomás** Bolivia
128 D5 **Santo Tomás** Mexico
134 C4 **Santo Tomás** Nicaragua
158 C4 **Santo Tomas** Peru
161 G4 **Santo Tomé** Argentina
162 B3 **Santo Victoria** Chile
231 F3 **Santolea, Embalse de** *lake* Spain
241 H2 **Santon Downham** Norfolk England UK
230 E2 **Santoña** Spain
233 E6 **Sant'Onofrio** Italy
161 J2 **Santos** Brazil
77 N12 **Santos Plateau** *underwater feature* Atlantic Ocean
380 F5 **Sanya** Hainan China
380 E1 **Sanyuan** Shaanxi China
306 B5 **Sanza Pombo** Angola
381 G4 **Sanzao Dao** *island* Guangdong China
159 G5 **São Benedito** Brazil
156 D3 **São Benedito do Rio Preto** Brazil
156 C3 **São Bento** Brazil
156 E4 **São Bento** Brazil
159 E2 **São Bernado** Brazil
156 D3 **São Bernardo** Brazil
161 H4 **São Borja** Brazil
158 D3 **São Brás** Brazil
157 C8 **São Carlos** Brazil
157 C6 **São Desidério** Brazil
157 A8 **São Domingos** Brazil
159 F3 **São Domingos** *watercourse* Brazil
310 4a **São Domingos** Cape Verde
230 B5 **São Domingos** Portugal
156 C4 **São Domingos do Maranhão** Brazil
155 F5 **São Felipe** Brazil
157 D6 **São Felipe** Brazil
230 B3 **São Félix da Marinha** Portugal
157 B5 **São Félix do Araguaia** Brazil
156 B4 **São Félix do Xingu** Brazil
157 D8 **São Fidélis** Brazil
310 4 **São Filipe** Cape Verde
157 C6 **São Francisco** Brazil
157 D6 **São Francisco** *watercourse* Brazil
161 I3 **São Francisco, Ilha de** *island* Brazil
161 H4 **São Francisco de Assis** Brazil
161 I4 **São Francisco de Paula** Brazil
161 H4 **São Gabriel** Brazil
154 E5 **São Gabriel da Cachoeira** Brazil
156 B4 **São Geraldo do Araguaia** Brazil
159 H5 **São Gonçalo** Brazil
156 F4 **São Gonçalo do Amarante** Brazil
157 C7 **São Gotardo** Brazil
155 F4 **São Gregório** Brazil
159 H5 **São Jerônimo, Serra de** *range* Brazil
159 G5 **São João** Brazil
156 C3 **São João, Ilhas de** *island* Brazil
159 F3 **São João, Serra de** *range* Brazil
157 D8 **São João da Barra** Brazil
157 C8 **São João da Boa Vista** Brazil
157 C6 **São João da Ponte** Brazil
156 C3 **São João de Pirabas** Brazil
159 I5 **São João do Aporé** Brazil
156 B4 **São João do Araguaia** Brazil
157 D6 **São João do Paraíso** Brazil
156 D5 **São João do Piauí** Brazil
305 F4 **São João dos Angolares** São Tomé and Príncipe
156 D4 **São João dos Patos** Brazil
157 D7 **São João Evangelista** Brazil
157 D8 **São João Nepomuceno** Brazil
161 I4 **São Joaquim** Brazil
310 1 **São Jorge** *island* Azores
310 2 **São Jorge, Ponta de** *cape* Madeira
158 D2 **São José** Brazil
158 E3 **São José** Brazil
159 H6 **São José** Brazil
156 E5 **São José da Tapera** Brazil
159 F2 **São José de Cuxo** Brazil
156 C3 **São José de Ribamar** Brazil
156 E4 **São José do Belmonte** Brazil
157 A6 **São José do Couto** Brazil
156 F4 **São José do Egito** Brazil
159 G5 **São José do Piquiri** Brazil
157 B8 **São José do Rio Preto** Brazil
157 C8 **São José dos Campos** Brazil
157 B9 **São José dos Pinhais** Brazil
158 C2 **São Leopoldo** Brazil
158 C3 **São Lorentino** Brazil
157 C8 **São Lourenço** Brazil
159 H5 **São Lourenço** Brazil
310 2 **São Lourenço, Ponta de** *cape* Madeira
157 B7 **São Lourenço, Serra** *range* Brazil
161 I4 **São Lourenço do Sul** Brazil
157 A9 **São Lourenço d'Oeste** Brazil
156 C3 **São Luís** Brazil
159 H5 **São Luís** Brazil
157 B7 **São Luís de Montes Belos** Brazil
157 C8 **São Luís do Quitunde** Brazil
155 F4 **São Luiz** Brazil
161 H4 **São Luiz Gonzaga** Brazil
161 I4 **São Marcos** Brazil
157 C7 **São Marcos** *watercourse* Brazil
310 1b **São Mateus** Azores
157 E7 **São Mateus** Brazil
156 C4 **São Mateus do Maranhão** Brazil
157 B9 **São Mateus do Sul** Brazil
310 1 **São Miguel** *island* Azores
155 I4 **São Miguel** Brazil
156 F4 **São Miguel** Brazil
157 B6 **São Miguel do Araguaia** Brazil
156 C3 **São Miguel do Guamá** Brazil
157 A9 **São Miguel do Iguaçu** Brazil
310 4 **São Nicolau** *island* Cape Verde
157 C8 **São Paulo** Brazil
161 I2 **São Paulo** *admin. area* Brazil
154 D5 **São Paulo de Olivença** Brazil
157 C8 **São Pedro** Brazil
156 E5 **São Pedro** *watercourse* Brazil
230 B4 **São Pedro da Cadeira** Portugal
161 H4 **São Pedro do Sul** Brazil
156 C4 **São Raimundo das Mangabeiras** Brazil
156 D5 **São Raimundo Nonato** Brazil
310 1b **São Roque do Pico** Azores
310 1b **São Sebastião** Azores
159 F3 **São Sebastião** Brazil
157 C8 **São Sebastião, Ilha de** *island* Brazil
309 G4 **São Sebastião, Ponta** *cape* Mozambique
157 C8 **São Sebastião do Paraíso** Brazil
161 H4 **São Sepé** Brazil
157 C8 **São Simão** Brazil
157 B7 **São Simão, Barragem de** *lake* Brazil
230 B5 **São Teotónio** Portugal
305 F4 **São Tomé** São Tomé and Príncipe
305 F5 **São Tomé** *island* São Tomé and Príncipe
157 D8 **São Tomé, Cabo de** *cape* Brazil
305 F4 **São Tomé and Príncipe** *country* Africa
310 4 **São Vicente** *island* Cape Verde
310 2 **São Vicente** Madeira
230 B5 **São Vicente, Cabo de** *cape* Portugal
159 G4 **São Vicente, Serra de** *range* Brazil
135 G3 **Saona, Isla** *island* Dominican Republic
226 C4 **Saône** *watercourse* France
393 E7 **Saoner** Maharashtra India
121 P7 **Saouayane, Pointe** *cape* Québec Canada
157 C5 **Sapão** *watercourse* Brazil
372 D4 **Saparua** Indonesia
154 E5 **Sapateiro, Lago** *lake* Brazil
375 H6 **Sape, Selak** *strait* Indonesia
305 F3 **Sapele** Nigeria
131 K5 **Sapelo Sound** Georgia USA
238 C2 **Sapernoye** Russian Federation
132 D3 **Sapién** Mexico
235 B7 **Sapientza** *island* Greece
134 E6 **Sapo, Serranía del** *range* Panama
158 B2 **Saposoa** Peru
225 K2 **Säppi** *island* Finland
387 I2 **Sapporo** Japan
233 F6 **Sapri** Italy
238 D5 **Saprinovichi** Belarus
386 E4 **Sapsi-do** *island* South Korea
223 P4 **Sapsolampi** Finland
377 J6 **Sapu** Philippines
375 G5 **Sapudi** *island* Indonesia
130 C3 **Sapulpa** Oklahoma USA
375 G5 **Sapulu** Indonesia
375 H2 **Sapulut** Malaysia
391 I2 **Sāq** Iran
122 O2 **Saqqamiut** Greenland
388 E7 **Saqqez** Iran
158 C2 **Saquena** Peru
391 J3 **Sar Banāder** Afghanistan
388 J7 **Sar-e Pol** Afghanistan
391 K2 **Sar-E Pol** *admin. area* Afghanistan
162 C5 **Sara** Argentina
304 D2 **Sara** Burkina Faso
158 C4 **Sara Sara, Nevado** *mountain* Peru
376 D4 **Saraburi** Thailand
376 D4 **Saraburi** *admin. area* Thailand
233 E7 **Saraceno, Punta del** *cape* Italy
388 I7 **Sarahs** Turkmenistan
388 D2 **Sarai** Russian Federation
225 K4 **Saraiäi** Latvia
393 F7 **Saraipali** Chhattisgarh India
223 O4 **Säräisniemi** Finland
159 I4 **Saraiva** Brazil
235 B4 **Saraj** Macedonia
223 O4 **Sarajärvi** Finland
232 H5 **Sarajevo** Bosnia and Herzegovina
235 C6 **Sarakiniko, Akra** *cape* Greece
235 D6 **Sarakino** *island* Greece
388 G3 **Saraktash** Russian Federation
130 G5 **Saraland** Alabama USA
225 O3 **Saralog** Russian Federation
379 H4 **Saramati** *mountain* Myanmar
228 E3 **Saran** France
389 K3 **Saran'** Kazakhstan
375 F4 **Saran, Gunung** *mountain* Indonesia
234 B2 **Sáránd** Hungary
377 J6 **Sarangani** Philippines
377 J6 **Sarangani** *island* Philippines
377 J6 **Sarangani Bay** Philippines
377 J6 **Sarangani Islands** Philippines
388 E2 **Saransk** Russian Federation
237 AC9 **Sarapul'skoye** Russian Federation
385 M3 **Sarapul'skoye** Russian Federation
131 J7 **Sarasota** Florida USA
131 J7 **Sarasota Bay** Florida USA
392 E5 **Saraswati** *watercourse* Uttaranchal India
125 L6 **Saratoga** Wyoming USA
127 O5 **Saratoga Lake** New York USA
375 F3 **Saratok** Malaysia
388 E3 **Saratov** Russian Federation
388 E3 **Saratovskaya Oblast'** *admin. area* Russian Federation
391 J4 **Sarāvān** Iran
375 G3 **Sarawak** *admin. area* Malaysia
394 H5 **Saray** Turkey
300 D6 **Saraya** Senegal
235 F7 **Sarayköy** Turkey
235 E5 **Saraylar** Turkey
227 I1 **Sarbia** Poland
234 A2 **Sárbogárd** Hungary
244 E2 **Sarclet** Highland Scotland UK
126 D8 **Sarcoxie** Missouri USA
389 K7 **Sard Āb** *pass* Afghanistan
391 K3 **Sardāgh** Afghanistan
230 B5 **Sardão, Cabo** *cape* Portugal
392 D5 **Sardarshahr** Rajasthan India
233 C6 **Sardegna** *admin. area* Italy
307 F3 **Sardendida Plain** *plain* Kenya
134 C5 **Sardinal** Costa Rica
131 K4 **Sardis** Georgia USA
130 G3 **Sardis** Mississippi USA
130 G3 **Sardis Lake** Mississippi USA
222 J3 **Sareks nationalpark** *park* Sweden
222 J3 **Sarektjåkkå** *mountain* Sweden
375 G4 **Sarempaka, Gunung** *mountain* Indonesia
130 E4 **Sarepta** Louisiana USA
229 I3 **Sargans** Switzerland
76 L7 **Sargasso Sea** Atlantic Ocean
158 B1 **Sargento Puño** Peru
129 I1 **Sargents** Colorado USA
391 L3 **Sargodha** Pakistan
389 L4 **Sargumei** Kazakhstan
305 H3 **Sarh** Chad
304 C3 **Sarhala** Côte d'Ivoire
388 G7 **Sārī** Iran
235 B6 **Saría** Greece
235 E8 **Saría** *island* Greece
225 N5 **Sariai** Lithuania
372 I6 **Sariba Island** Papua New Guinea
372 E4 **Saribi, Tanjung** *cape* Indonesia
128 G5 **Saric** Mexico
426 2 **Sarigan** *island* Northern Mariana Islands
375 F3 **Sarikei** Malaysia
235 E7 **Sarıkemer** Turkey
235 E5 **Sarıköy** Turkey
235 F7 **Sarılar** Turkey
374 B2 **Sarimbun Reservoir** Singapore
425 N5 **Sarina** Qld Australia
231 F3 **Sariñena** Spain
307 G3 **Sarinleey** Somalia
302 C2 **Sarīr Kalanshiyū Ar Ramlī Al Kabīr** *desert* Libya
386 E3 **Sariwŏn** North Korea
235 G5 **Sarıyar Barajı** *lake* Turkey
228 C2 **Sark** *island* Channel Islands UK
222 J3 **Sårkåjaure** *lake* Norway
389 M4 **Sarkand** Kazakhstan
392 C5 **Sarkari Tala** Rajasthan India
223 M3 **Särkijärvi** Finland
223 M5 **Särkijärvi** *lake* Finland
235 G6 **Şarkikaraağaç** Turkey
225 O2 **Särkisalmi** Finland
235 E6 **Şarköy** Turkey
126 B2 **Sarles** North Dakota USA
373 F4 **Sarmi** Indonesia
162 C3 **Sarmiento** Argentina
162 B5 **Sarmiento, Lago** *lake* Chile
162 B6 **Sarmiento, Monte** *mountain* Chile
234 C3 **Sarmizegetusa** Romania
240 D2 **Sarn** Powys Wales UK
222 H6 **Särna** Sweden
232 E5 **Sarnano** Italy
392 F6 **Sarnath** Uttar Pradesh India
240 C2 **Sarnau** Ceredigion Wales UK
229 I3 **Sarnen** Switzerland
393 E6 **Sarni** Madhya Pradesh India
127 J5 **Sarnia** Ontario Canada
227 G1 **Sarnow** Germany
372 B4 **Saroako** Indonesia
374 D4 **Sarolangun** Indonesia
387 J2 **Saroma-ko** *lake* Japan
373 G6 **Sarone** Indonesia
235 E5 **Saros Körfezi** *bay* Turkey
236 O5 **Saroto** Russian Federation
388 D2 **Sarova** Russian Federation
390 F2 **Sarpol-e Ẓahāb** Iran
224 F3 **Sarpsborg** Norway
228 C5 **Sarracín** Spain
226 D3 **Sarralbe** France
229 H2 **Sarre-Union** France
229 H2 **Sarrebourg** France
229 H2 **Sarreguemines** France
300 E6 **Sarro** Mali
233 C7 **Sarròch** Sardinia Italy
383 I3 **Sarsai** Mongolia
244 D2 **Sarsgrum** Highland Scotland UK
242 A4 **Sart Cross Roads** Ireland
233 C6 **Sartène** Corsica France
228 D3 **Sarthe** *watercourse* France
235 C5 **Sarti** Greece
229 I4 **Sartirana Lomellina** Italy
225 M5 **Sartų Ežeras** *lake* Lithuania
236 N6 **Sartyn'ya** Russian Federation
235 E6 **Saruhanlı** Turkey
223 M5 **Sarvikas** Finland
223 P5 **Sarvikumpu** Finland
222 H5 **Särvsjö** Sweden
392 D5 **Sarwar** Rajasthan India
225 N5 **Sar"ya** Belarus
388 H4 **Sarybasat** Kazakhstan
394 E4 **Sarych, Mys** *cape* Ukraine
388 H5 **Sarygamysh Köli** *lake* Turkmenistan
389 L3 **Sarykiyak** Kazakhstan
Sarykomey *see* **Sargumei** Kazakhstan
388 I3 **Sarykopa** *lake* Kazakhstan
388 I3 **Saryqopa Koli** *lake* Kazakhstan
389 L4 **Saryshagan** Kazakhstan
389 K4 **Sarysu** *watercourse* Kazakhstan
388 F3 **Saryumir** Kazakhstan
388 I7 **Saryýazy Suwhowdany** *lake* Turkmenistan
228 C3 **Sarzeau** France
161 J2 **Sarzedo** Brazil
389 M3 **Sarzhal** Kazakhstan
235 C4 **Sasa** Macedonia
307 G2 **Sasabeneh** Ethiopia
120 H7 **Sasaginnigak Lake** Manitoba Canada
374 C3 **Sasak** Indonesia
426 8 **Sasamungga** Solomon Islands
375 H6 **Sasar, Tanjung** *cape* Indonesia
392 F6 **Sasaram** Bihar India
159 E5 **Sasasama** Bolivia
234 D2 **Saschiz** Romania
234 C3 **Săsciori** Romania
234 E2 **Sascut** Romania
227 J4 **Sásd** Hungary
386 F5 **Sasebo** Japan
116 I8 **Saskatchewan** *admin. area* Canada
119 S6 **Saskatchewan** *watercourse* Saskatchewan Canada
119 R6 **Saskatoon** Saskatchewan Canada
237 X4 **Saskylakh** Russian Federation
388 D2 **Sasovo** Russian Federation
304 C4 **Sass Town** Liberia
223 N3 **Sassali** Finland
223 O3 **Sassalinjärvi** *lake* Finland
304 C4 **Sassandra** Côte d'Ivoire
304 C3 **Sassandra** *watercourse* Côte d'Ivoire
233 C6 **Sassari** Sardinia Italy
226 E5 **Sassello** Italy
373 G6 **Sassie Island** Australia
232 D4 **Sasso Marconi** Italy
232 E5 **Sassoferrato** Italy
389 M4 **Sasyqköl** *lake* Kazakhstan
300 D6 **Satadougou** Mali
392 E6 **Satai** Madhya Pradesh India
393 D7 **Satana** Maharashtra India
234 E1 **Sataniv** Ukraine
125 O8 **Satanta** Kansas USA
230 C3 **Satão** Portugal
393 D8 **Satara** Maharashtra India
237 AB5 **Satara** Russian Federation
426 6 **Satawal** *island* Federated States of Micronesia
306 C3 **Satéma** Democratic Republic of Congo
375 H5 **Satengar** *island* Indonesia
222 K3 **Satihaure** *lake* Sweden
158 C3 **Satipo** Peru
304 D2 **Satiri** Burkina Faso
154 C3 **Sativanorte** Colombia
388 H2 **Satka** Russian Federation
379 F4 **Satkhira** Bangladesh
392 E6 **Satna** Madhya Pradesh India
234 B1 **Sátoraljaújhely** Hungary
235 C5 **Satovcha** Bulgaria
224 F6 **Satow** Germany
426 6 **Satowan** *island* Federated States of Micronesia
389 J4 **Satpayev** Kazakhstan
393 D7 **Satpura Range** Madhya Pradesh India
130 G5 **Satsuma** Alabama USA
386 F6 **Satsunan-shotō** *island* Japan
376 D4 **Sattahip** Thailand
223 M3 **Sattajärvi** Sweden
222 L3 **Satter** Sweden
240 D4 **Satterleigh** Devon England UK
392 D3 **Satti** Jammu and Kashmir India/Pakistan
234 C2 **Satu Mare** Romania
234 C2 **Satu Mare** *admin. area* Romania
375 G4 **Satui** Indonesia
376 D4 **Satuk** Thailand
376 C6 **Satun** *admin. area* Thailand
155 F3 **Sauata** Brazil
375 G5 **Saubi** *island* Indonesia
132 B1 **Sauceda Mountains** Arizona USA
132 D2 **Saucillo** Mexico
224 D3 **Sauda** Norway
222 inset **Sauðárkrókur** Iceland
390 F5 **Saudi Arabia** *country*
159 G4 **Saueruina** *watercourse* Brazil
126 H5 **Saugatuck** Michigan USA
244 F5 **Saughtree** Scottish Borders Scotland UK
228 F4 **Saugues** France
155 G5 **Sauiá** Brazil
228 D4 **Saujon** France
126 D4 **Sauk Rapids** Minnesota USA
223 P5 **Saukko** Finland
225 L2 **Saukkola** Finland
223 N3 **Saukkoriipi** Finland
372 E4 **Saukorem** Indonesia
245 G2 **Saul** Down Northern Ireland UK
155 H4 **Saül** French Guiana
224 E3 **Sauland** Norway
228 E3 **Sauldre** *watercourse* France
229 I2 **Saulgau** Germany
226 C4 **Saulieu** France
229 G4 **Sault** France
228 D5 **Sault-de-Navailles** France
126 I3 **Sault Ste Marie** Ontario Canada
226 D4 **Saulx** France
229 H3 **Saulxures** France
389 J2 **Saumalkol (Volodarskoye)** Kazakhstan
228 D3 **Saumur** France
223 P5 **Saunajärvi** *lake* Finland
223 O3 **Saunavaara** Finland
436 N1 **Saunders Coast** Antarctica
163 7 **Saunders Island** Falkland Islands
240 C3 **Saundersfoot** Pembrokeshire Wales UK
389 O4 **Saur, Khrebet** *range* Kazakhstan
222 inset **Saurbær** Iceland
373 I5 **Sauren** Papua New Guinea
308 D1 **Saurimo** Angola
134 C4 **Sausa** Honduras
372 E4 **Sausapor** Indonesia
308 C2 **Sautar** Angola
135 I4 **Sauteurs** Grenada
222 L3 **Sautusjärvi** *lake* Sweden
121 S6 **Sauvolles, Lac** *lake* Québec Canada
228 F4 **Sauxillanges** France
160 F2 **Sauzal** Paraguay
228 E3 **Sauzé-Vaussais** France
232 H4 **Sava** *watercourse* Bosnia and Herzegovina
232 G4 **Sava** *watercourse* Croatia
233 G6 **Sava** Italy
427 12 **Savai'i** *island* Samoa
222 G5 **Savalen** *lake* Norway
304 E3 **Savalou** Benin
121 T7 **Savane** *watercourse* Québec Canada
309 G3 **Savane** Mozambique
163 1a **Savaneta** Aruba
130 D3 **Savanna** Oklahoma USA
131 K4 **Savannah** Georgia USA
131 J3 **Savannah** *watercourse* South Carolina USA
134 C3 **Savannah Bight** Honduras
376 E3 **Savannakhet** Laos
126 F2 **Savanne** Ontario Canada
120 J7 **Savant Lake** Ontario Canada
222 L5 **Sävar** Sweden
235 E6 **Savaştepe** Turkey

308 C3 **Savate** Angola
228 E5 **Save** *watercourse* France
309 F3 **Save** *watercourse* Zimbabwe
304 E3 **Savé** Benin
390 G2 **Sāveh** Iran
224 G4 **Säven** *lake* Sweden
228 D3 **Savenay** France
228 E5 **Saverdun** France
229 H2 **Saverne** France
223 O5 **Säviä** Finland
229 H3 **Savièse** Switzerland
226 F5 **Savigno** Italy
223 P5 **Savijärvi** Finland
223 P5 **Savikylä** Finland
229 H4 **Savines-le-Lac** France
388 E3 **Savinka** Russian Federation
394 F3 **Savintsy** Ukraine
223 O4 **Saviselkä** Finland
232 H5 **Šavnik** Montenegro
426 8 **Savo** *island* Solomon Islands
120 M8 **Savoff** Ontario Canada
118 K7 **Savona** British Columbia Canada
226 E5 **Savona** Italy
163 1b **Savonet** Netherlands Antilles
225 O2 **Savonlinna** Finland
223 P5 **Savonranta** Finland
116 B6 **Savoonga** Alaska USA
424 G5 **Savory** *watercourse* WA Australia
372 B6 **Savu** Indonesia
372 B6 **Savu** *island* Indonesia
372 B6 **Savu, Kepulauan** *island* Indonesia
Savu Sea *see* **Sawu, Laut** Indonesia
232 E4 **Savudrija** Croatia
223 P3 **Savukoski** Finland
427 9a **Savusavu Bay** Fiji
308 D3 **Savuti** Botswana
379 H5 **Saw** Myanmar
394 G6 **Şawāb, Wādī aş** Syria
372 D4 **Sawai, Teluk** *bay* Indonesia
392 D6 **Sawai Madhopur** Rajasthan India
375 G4 **Sawan** Indonesia
376 C3 **Sawankhalok** Thailand
125 L7 **Sawatch Range** Colorado USA
119 U4 **Sawbill** Manitoba Canada
121 V6 **Sawbill** Newfoundland and Labrador Canada
391 H6 **Sawdā', As** *island* Oman
390 E6 **Sawdā, Jabal** *mountain* Saudi Arabia
302 E2 **Sawhāj** Egypt
376 B5 **Sawi Bay** Andaman and Nicobar Islands India
304 D3 **Sawla** Ghana
241 F2 **Sawley** Derbyshire England UK
391 H6 **Şawqirah** Oman
241 H2 **Sawston** Cambridgeshire England UK
379 I3 **Sawt-Law** Myanmar
425 O7 **Sawtell** NSW Australia
124 H5 **Sawtooth Range** Idaho USA
124 E2 **Sawtooth Ridge** Washington USA
375 I6 **Sawu, Laut (Savu Sea)** Indonesia
125 P8 **Sawyer** Kansas USA
125 O2 **Sawyer** North Dakota USA
231 F4 **Sax** Spain
155 G3 **Saxakalli** Guyana
225 J3 **Saxarfjorden** *bay* Sweden
425 L4 **Saxby** *watercourse* Qld Australia
241 I2 **Saxham Street** Suffolk England UK
243 H3 **Saxilby** Lincolnshire England UK
241 I2 **Saxmundham** Suffolk England UK
229 H2 **Saxon-Sion** France
300 F6 **Say** Mali
301 G6 **Say** Niger
388 G5 **Say-utes** Kazakhstan
80 K6 **Saya de Malha Bank** *underwater feature* Indian Ocean
372 D3 **Sayafi** *island* Indonesia
389 M4 **Sayak** Kazakhstan
393 C7 **Sayan** Gujarat India
389 P3 **Sayano-Shushenskoye Vodokhranilishche** *lake* Russian Federation
389 P3 **Sayanskiy Khrebet** *range* Russian Federation
388 I6 **Saýat** Turkmenistan
134 B3 **Sayaxché** Guatemala
388 E4 **Saykhin** Kazakhstan
303 G5 **Saylac** Somalia
126 E6 **Saylorville Lake** Iowa USA
223 N5 **Säynätsalo** Finland
382 G4 **Sayram Hu** *lake* Xinjiang Uygur Zizhiqu China
130 B3 **Sayre** Oklahoma USA
132 E5 **Sayula** Mexico
133 G5 **Sayula de Alemán** Mexico
390 F7 **Say'ūn** Yemen
118 I7 **Sayward** British Columbia Canada
237 AC5 **Sayylyk** Russian Federation
236 H3 **Sázava** Czech Republic
227 H3 **Sázava** *watercourse* Czech Republic
391 M2 **Sazin** Pakistan
238 F3 **Sazonovo** Russian Federation
301 F3 **Sbaa** Algeria
301 H1 **Sbeitla** Tunisia
228 C2 **Scaër** France
242 E2 **Scafell Pike** *mountain* England UK
243 H3 **Scalby** East Riding of Yorkshire England UK
233 F7 **Scalea** Italy
233 F7 **Scalea, Capo** *cape* Italy
242 F2 **Scalehouses** Cumbria England UK
242 E2 **Scales** Cumbria England UK
244 inset **Scalloway** Shetland Scotland UK
244 C3 **Scalpay** *island* Scotland UK
243 H3 **Scamblesby** Lincolnshire England UK
116 C6 **Scammon Bay** Alaska USA
244 C4 **Scamodale** Highland Scotland UK
243 H2 **Scampston** North Yorkshire England UK
119 O7 **Scandia** Alberta Canada
306 B5 **Scandica** Angola
233 C5 **Scandola, Pointe** *cape* Corsica France
232 D5 **Scansano** Italy
244 E2 **Scapa Flow** *bay* Scotland UK
124 D4 **Scappoose** Oregon USA
244 F1 **Scar** Orkney Islands Scotland UK
244 C4 **Scarba** *island* Scotland UK
163 9 **Scarborough** Trinidad and Tobago
243 H2 **Scarborough** North Yorkshire England UK
377 H4 **Scarborough Shoal** *island* Philippines
244 D5 **Scariff Island** Ireland
244 B4 **Scarinish** Highland Scotland UK
244 A2 **Scarp** *island* Scotland UK
228 F1 **Scarpe** *watercourse* France
245 D4 **Scarriff** Ireland
243 H3 **Scartho** North East Lincolnshire England UK
245 F2 **Scarva** Armagh Northern Ireland UK
123 I9 **Scatarie Island** Nova Scotia Canada
244 D3 **Scatraig** Highland Scotland UK
427 9 **Scatterbreak Channel** *strait* Fiji
243 H3 **Scawby** North Lincolnshire England UK
119 Q7 **Sceptre** Saskatchewan Canada
226 F1 **Schaalsee** *lake* Germany
229 I3 **Schaffhausen** Switzerland
226 C1 **Schagen** Netherlands
226 G3 **Schardenberg** Austria
226 G3 **Schärding** Austria
224 E6 **Scharhörn** *island* Germany
229 I3 **Schattdorf** Switzerland
126 G5 **Schaumburg** Illinois USA
226 E3 **Schefflenz** Germany
227 H3 **Scheibbs** Austria
234 C3 **Schela** Romania
124 H7 **Schell Creek Range** Nevada USA
226 C2 **Schelle** Belgium
127 O5 **Schenectady** New York USA
126 H6 **Schererville** Indiana USA
130 B6 **Schertz** Texas USA
226 E4 **Schesaplana** *mountain* Austria/Switzerland
229 J2 **Scheßlitz** Germany
244 D4 **Schiehallion** *mountain* Scotland UK
229 I3 **Schiers** Switzerland
226 F1 **Schilde** *watercourse* Germany
229 H2 **Schiltigheim** France
226 D3 **Schirmeck** France
233 F8 **Schisò, Capo** *cape* Italy
227 G4 **Schladming** Austria
229 K3 **Schleching** Germany
224 E5 **Schlei** *bay* Germany
229 H1 **Schleiden** Germany
373 I4 **Schleinitz Range** Papua New Guinea
226 F2 **Schleiz** Germany
224 E5 **Schleswig-Holstein** *admin. area* Germany
226 F2 **Schleusingen** Germany
226 E2 **Schlitz** Germany
163 I4 **Schœlcher** Martinique
129 M1 **Schoenchen** Kansas USA
235 D7 **Schoinoussa** *island* Greece
127 L4 **Schomberg** Ontario Canada
226 G3 **Schomberg** Germany
227 G1 **Schöneiche Berlin** Germany
226 G3 **Schönsee** Germany
127 Q4 **Schoodic Lake** Maine USA
226 C1 **Schoorl** Netherlands
226 E3 **Schorndorf** Germany
163 1b **Schottegat** *bay* Netherlands Antilles
373 H5 **Schrader Range** Papua New Guinea
229 I2 **Schramberg** Germany
227 H3 **Schrems** Austria
127 O5 **Schroon Lake** New York USA
226 E4 **Schruns** Austria
119 P7 **Schuler** Alberta Canada
245 C5 **Schull** Ireland
130 D3 **Schulter** Oklahoma USA
128 C1 **Schurz** Nevada USA
125 Q6 **Schuyler** Nebraska USA
226 F3 **Schwabach** Germany
226 E3 **Schwäbisch Hall** Germany
226 E2 **Schwalm** *watercourse* Germany
229 I3 **Schwanden** Switzerland
375 G4 **Schwaner, Pegunungan** *range* Indonesia
224 E5 **Schwansen** *peninsula* Germany
437 D2 **Schwartz Range** Antarctica
226 F2 **Schwarza** *watercourse* Germany
226 G2 **Schwarze Elster** *watercourse* Germany
229 J3 **Schwaz** Austria
227 H1 **Schwedt** Germany
230 D3 **Schweich** Germany
226 F2 **Schweinfurt** Germany
229 I3 **Schwyz** Switzerland
233 E8 **Sciacca** Italy
244 D2 **Sciberscross** Highland Scotland UK
233 F8 **Scicli** Italy
228 E2 **Scie** *watercourse* France
126 I8 **Science Hill** Kentucky USA
233 F7 **Scilla** Italy
126 J7 **Scioto** *watercourse* Ohio USA
128 F1 **Scipio** Utah USA
124 I7 **Scipio Lake** Utah USA
233 C6 **Scirocco, Punta di** *cape* Sardinia Italy
119 U7 **Sclater** Manitoba Canada
240 C3 **Scleddau** Pembrokeshire Wales UK
125 M2 **Scobey** Montana USA
124 J7 **Scofield Reservoir** Utah USA
233 C6 **Scoglietti, Punta** *cape* Sardinia Italy
242 B2 **Scolboa** Antrim Northern Ireland UK
241 I2 **Scole** Norfolk England UK
233 C6 **Scomunica, Punta della** *mountain* Sardinia Italy
244 B3 **Sconser** Highland Scotland UK
130 G4 **Scooba** Mississippi USA
233 C5 **Scopa, Punta alla** *cape* Corsica France
226 E5 **Scopello** Italy
117 Q4 **Scoresby Land** *plain* Greenland
228 C2 **Scorff** *watercourse* France
243 G2 **Scotch Corner** North Yorkshire England UK
245 F2 **Scotch Street** Armagh Northern Ireland UK
245 E2 **Scotch Town** Omagh Northern Ireland UK
243 H3 **Scothern** Lincolnshire England UK
127 L4 **Scotia** Ontario Canada
125 P6 **Scotia** Nebraska USA
127 O5 **Scotia** New York USA
436 U3 **Scotia Sea** Antarctica
244 **Scotland** *admin. area* UK
130 B4 **Scotland** Texas USA
119 Q8 **Scotsguard** Saskatchewan Canada
119 Q6 **Scott** Saskatchewan Canada
130 E5 **Scott** Louisiana USA
118 G7 **Scott, Cape** British Columbia Canada
437 L1 **Scott Base (New Zealand)** *research station* Antarctica
125 O7 **Scott City** Kansas USA
437 K1 **Scott Coast** Antarctica
437 G2 **Scott Glacier** Antarctica
117 L4 **Scott Inlet** Nunavut Canada
118 G7 **Scott Islands** British Columbia Canada
119 R3 **Scott Lake** Saskatchewan Canada
437 D2 **Scott Mountains** Antarctica
81 Q6 **Scott Plateau** *underwater feature* Indian Ocean
424 G3 **Scott Reef** WA Australia
243 H3 **Scotter** Lincolnshire England UK
244 F5 **Scottish Borders** *admin. area* Scotland UK
243 G2 **Scotton** North Yorkshire England UK
163 I5 **Scotts Head** *cape* Dominica
124 D8 **Scotts Valley** California USA
125 N6 **Scottsbluff** Nebraska USA
131 H3 **Scottsboro** Alabama USA
126 I7 **Scottsburg** Indiana USA
425 M10 **Scottsdale** Tas. Australia
128 G4 **Scottsdale** Arizona USA
127 L8 **Scottsville** Virginia USA
126 H5 **Scottville** Michigan USA
244 C2 **Scourie** Highland Scotland UK
244 inset **Scousburgh** Shetland Scotland UK
245 E3 **Scrabby** Ireland
244 E2 **Scrabster** Highland Scotland UK
125 D5 **Scranton** Iowa USA
125 N3 **Scranton** North Dakota USA
127 N6 **Scranton** Pennsylvania USA
241 I2 **Scratby** Norfolk England UK
131 K5 **Screven** Georgia USA
373 G4 **Screw** *watercourse* Papua New Guinea
242 F3 **Scropton** Derbyshire England UK
163 20 **Scrub Island** Anguilla
127 L4 **Scugog, Lake** Ontario Canada
243 H3 **Scunthorpe** North Lincolnshire England UK
229 J3 **Scuol** Switzerland
244 A3 **Scurrival Point** Scotland UK
234 D3 **Scurtu Mare** Romania
234 A4 **Scutari, Lake** Albania
234 E3 **Scutelnici** Romania
126 F2 **Sea Gull Lake** Minnesota USA
127 N7 **Sea Isle City** New Jersey USA
134 I3 **Sea Lion Islands** Falkland Islands
241 I2 **Sea Palling** Norfolk England UK
245 D5 **Sea View** Ireland
157 D6 **Seabra** Brazil
131 K4 **Seabrook Island** South Carolina USA
245 E2 **Seacor** Ireland
130 C6 **Seadrift** Texas USA
241 H4 **Seaford** East Sussex England UK
425 N5 **Seaforth** Qld Australia
130 C4 **Seagoville** Texas USA
243 G2 **Seaham** Durham England UK
121 W6 **Seahorse** Newfoundland and Labrador Canada
120 H3 **Seal** *watercourse* Manitoba Canada
436 X2 **Seal Bay** Antarctica
310 5c **Seal Bay** St Helena
123 J8 **Seal Cove** Newfoundland and Labrador Canada
122 H5 **Seal Lake** Newfoundland and Labrador Canada
130 C6 **Sealy** Texas USA
244 D5 **Seamill** North Ayrshire Scotland UK
128 E3 **Searchlight** Nevada USA
126 I3 **Searchmont** Ontario Canada
130 F3 **Searcy** Arkansas USA
128 D3 **Searles** California USA
128 D3 **Searles Lake** California USA
123 D10 **Searsport** Maine USA
242 E2 **Seascale** Cumbria England UK
124 E8 **Seaside** California USA
124 D4 **Seaside** Oregon USA
242 E2 **Seathwaite** Cumbria England UK
240 D4 **Seaton** Devon England UK
241 G2 **Seaton** Rutland England UK
243 G1 **Seaton Delaval** Northumberland England UK
437 D2 **Seaton Glacier** Antarctica
243 H3 **Seaton Ross** East Riding of Yorkshire England UK
163 I8 **Seatons** Antigua and Barbuda
124 D3 **Seattle** Washington USA
243 G2 **Seave Green** North Yorkshire England UK
241 F4 **Seaview** Isle of Wight England UK
423 E6 **Seaward Kaikoura Range** New Zealand
372 B6 **Seba** Indonesia
127 P5 **Sebago Lake** Maine USA
375 H4 **Sebakung** Indonesia
375 G4 **Sebamban** Indonesia
375 G4 **Sebangan, Teluk** *bay* Indonesia
374 E3 **Sebangka** *island* Indonesia
374 C5 **Sebarok, Pulau** *island* Singapore
122 H6 **Sebaskachu** *watercourse* Newfoundland and Labrador Canada
160 F4 **Sebastián Elcano** Argentina
132 B2 **Sebastián Vizcaíno, Bahía** *bay* Mexico
127 Q4 **Sebasticook Lake** Maine USA
Sebastopol *see* **Sevastopol'** Ukraine
375 F4 **Sebayan, Bukit** *mountain* Indonesia
302 F4 **Sebderat** Eritrea
301 F2 **Sebdou** Algeria
127 Q4 **Sebec Lake** Maine USA
300 E6 **Sébékoro** Mali
235 G5 **Seben** Turkey
227 L5 **Sebeş** Romania
227 K4 **Sebes-Körös** *watercourse* Hungary
374 E5 **Sebesi** *island* Indonesia
238 C3 **Sebezhsky National Park** *park* Russian Federation
234 C2 **Sebiş** Romania
374 D4 **Seblat, Gunung** *mountain* Indonesia
127 Q4 **Seboeis Lake** Maine USA
127 Q4 **Seboomook Lake** Maine USA
126 H8 **Sebree** Kentucky USA
131 K7 **Sebring** Florida USA
377 J6 **Sebu** Philippines
375 G3 **Sebuah** Malaysia
155 F3 **Sebucán** Venezuela
375 H4 **Sebuku** *island* Indonesia
375 H4 **Sebuku** *watercourse* Indonesia
375 H3 **Sebuku, Teluk** *bay* Indonesia
375 F3 **Sebuyau** Malaysia
372 E4 **Sebyar** *watercourse* Indonesia
162 B4 **Seca, Laguna** *lake* Argentina
132 D2 **Sección Alsacia** Mexico
132 C5 **Sección Gap** Argentina
162 B3 **Sección Tapera** Chile
227 J2 **Secemin** Poland
229 G2 **Séchault** France
121 U6 **Séchelles, Lac** *lake* Québec Canada
118 J8 **Sechelt** British Columbia Canada
158 A2 **Sechura** Peru
158 A2 **Sechura, Ensenada de** *bay* Peru
228 F1 **Seclin** France
128 G3 **Second Mesa** Arizona USA
228 D3 **Secondigny** France
310 4 **Secos, Ilhéus** *island* Cape Verde
423 B7 **Secretary Island** New Zealand
393 E8 **Secunderabad** Andhra Pradesh India
234 B2 **Secusigiu** Romania
225 M4 **Seda** Latvia
126 E7 **Sedalia** Missouri USA
229 G2 **Sedan** France
126 C8 **Sedan** Kansas USA
129 K2 **Sedan** New Mexico USA
242 F2 **Sedbergh** Cumbria England UK
245 D4 **Sedboro** Ireland
423 F5 **Seddon** New Zealand
229 G4 **Séderon** France
125 Q8 **Sedgwick** Kansas USA
300 C6 **Sédhiou** Senegal
226 G4 **Sedico** Italy
119 S7 **Sedley** Saskatchewan Canada
128 G3 **Sedona** Arizona USA
301 H1 **Sedrata** Algeria
124 D2 **Sedro-Woolley** Washington USA
375 H3 **Sedulang** Indonesia
225 L5 **Šeduva** Lithuania
228 D2 **Sée** *watercourse* France
119 N7 **Seebe** Alberta Canada
120 I6 **Seeber Lake** Ontario Canada
226 G4 **Seeboden** Austria
229 I3 **Seedorf** Switzerland
229 J3 **Seefeld in Tirol** Austria
226 F1 **Seehausen** Germany
436 R1 **Seelig, Mount** *mountain* Antarctica
228 E2 **Sées** France
226 F2 **Seesen** Germany
235 E6 **Seferihisar** Turkey
300 D6 **Séféto** Mali
391 G4 **Sefīdār, Kūh-e** *mountain* Iran
234 B3 **Sefkerin** Serbia
308 E4 **Sefophe** Botswana
300 F2 **Sefrou** Morocco
423 E6 **Sefton** New Zealand
242 F3 **Sefton** *admin. area* England UK
423 D6 **Sefton, Mount** New Zealand
307 G2 **Segag** Ethiopia
300 D6 **Ségala** Mali
222 G6 **Segalstad** Norway
375 H2 **Segama** *watercourse* Malaysia
374 D3 **Segamat** Malaysia
227 L5 **Segarcea** Romania
305 E2 **Ségbana** Benin
372 E4 **Sege** Indonesia
372 A5 **Segeri** Indonesia
236 H6 **Segezha** Russian Federation
231 I6 **Seggana** Algeria
426 8 **Seghe** Solomon Islands
231 H5 **Seghouane** Algeria
222 L1 **Seglvik** Norway
233 E6 **Segni** Italy
379 G2 **Segong** Xizang Zizhiqu China
231 F4 **Segorbe** Spain
300 E6 **Ségou** Mali
300 E6 **Ségou** *admin. area* Mali
154 C3 **Segovia** Colombia
223 R5 **Segozerskoye, Ozero** *lake* Russian Federation
231 G3 **Segre** *watercourse* Spain
228 E2 **Ségrie** France
237 AM8 **Seguam Island** Alaska USA
301 I4 **Séguédine** Niger
304 C3 **Séguéla** Côte d'Ivoire
304 D2 **Séguénéga** Burkina Faso
130 C6 **Seguin** Texas USA
132 B3 **Segunda Etapa** Mexico
160 F4 **Segundo** *watercourse* Argentina
230 F4 **Segura** *watercourse* Spain
230 E5 **Segura, Sierra de** *range* Spain
161 G6 **Segurola** Argentina
308 D4 **Sehithwa** Botswana
226 E1 **Sehnde** Germany
375 J4 **Seho** *island* Indonesia
392 D6 **Sehore** Madhya Pradesh India
373 I6 **Sehulea** Papua New Guinea
391 K4 **Sehwan** Pakistan
230 C3 **Seia** Portugal
231 J6 **Seïar** Algeria
125 N7 **Seibert** Colorado USA
228 D3 **Seiche** *watercourse* France
222 G4 **Seierstad** Norway
121 U6 **Seignelay** *watercourse* Québec Canada
228 D5 **Seignosse** France
379 H5 **Seikpyu** Myanmar
223 M1 **Seiland** *island* Norway
223 M1 **Seilandsjøkelen** *bay* Norway
228 E4 **Seilhac** France
229 H2 **Seille** *watercourse* France
224 C2 **Seim** Norway
234 F3 **Seimeni** Romania
228 B2 **Sein, Île de** *island* France
223 M5 **Seinäjärvi** *lake* Finland
223 M5 **Seinäjoki** Finland
223 M5 **Seinäjoki** *watercourse* Finland
228 E2 **Seine** *watercourse* France
228 D2 **Seine, Baie de la** *bay* France
76 Q6 **Seine Abyssal Plain** *underwater feature* Atlantic Ocean
76 Q6 **Seine Seamount** *underwater feature* Atlantic Ocean
234 C2 **Seini** Romania
223 O3 **Seipäjärvi** Finland
375 G4 **Seipinang** Indonesia
225 L5 **Seirijis** *lake* Lithuania
241 E2 **Seisdon** Staffordshire England UK
425 L2 **Seisia** Qld Australia
375 H4 **Sejaka** Indonesia
374 F3 **Sejangkung** Indonesia
224 F5 **Sejerby** Denmark
224 F5 **Sejerø** *island* Denmark
224 F5 **Sejerø Bugt** *bay* Denmark
158 E4 **Sejeruma, Serranía** *range* Bolivia
225 L5 **Sejny** Poland
376 D3 **Seka** Thailand
375 G4 **Sekadau** Indonesia
375 H3 **Sekatak, Teluk** *bay* Indonesia
374 D4 **Sekayu** Indonesia
380 C2 **Seke** Sichuan China
235 F7 **Seki** *watercourse* Turkey
381 I3 **Sekibi-sho** *island* Japan
223 L2 **Sekkemo** Norway
379 G4 **Sekmai Bazar** Manipur India
308 D4 **Sekoma** Botswana
304 D4 **Sekondi** Ghana
303 F5 **Sek'ot'a** Ethiopia
374 D3 **Sekudai** Malaysia
374 F3 **Sekura** Indonesia
222 G5 **Sela** Norway
124 E3 **Selah** Washington USA
375 H4 **Selakau** Indonesia
374 F3 **Selalang** Malaysia
374 D3 **Selangor** *admin. area* Malaysia
373 I4 **Selapiu Island** Papua New Guinea
233 C7 **Selargius** Sardinia Italy
375 G5 **Selatan, Tanjung** *cape* Indonesia
374 D4 **Selatpanjang** Indonesia
116 C5 **Selawik** Alaska USA
375 I5 **Selayar** *island* Indonesia
375 I5 **Selayar, Selat** *strait* Indonesia
226 G2 **Selb** Germany
224 C2 **Selbjørn** *island* Norway
222 G5 **Selbustrand** Norway
243 G3 **Selby** North Yorkshire England UK
125 O4 **Selby** South Dakota USA
127 N7 **Selbyville** Delaware USA
234 A4 **Selcë** Albania
235 E7 **Selçuk** Turkey
125 O7 **Selden** Kansas USA
116 D7 **Seldovia** Alaska USA
372 D4 **Sele** Indonesia
233 F6 **Sele** *watercourse* Italy
308 E4 **Selebi Phikwe** Botswana
307 F5 **Selegu** *mountain* Tanzania
237 AB8 **Selemdzhinsk** Russian Federation
385 M1 **Selemdzhinskiy Khrebet** *range* Russian Federation
235 F6 **Selendi** Turkey
306 B4 **Selenge** Democratic Republic of Congo
384 E2 **Selenge** Mongolia
384 E2 **Selenge** *admin. area* Mongolia
384 E2 **Selenge Moron** *watercourse* Mongolia
235 A5 **Selenicë** Albania
237 AD5 **Selennyakh** *watercourse* Russian Federation
229 H2 **Sélestat** France
222 L4 **Selet** Sweden
225 O2 **Seleznëvo** Russian Federation
225 P5 **Selezni** Russian Federation
222 inset **Selfoss** Iceland
125 O3 **Selfridge** North Dakota USA
238 C6 **Seliba** Belarus
300 D5 **Sélibabi** Mauritania
128 F3 **Seligman** Arizona USA
126 D8 **Seligman** Missouri USA
225 O4 **Selikhnovo** Russian Federation
305 I4 **Selim** Central African Republic
302 D3 **Selima** *spring* Sudan
237 AB7 **Selingde** Russian Federation
304 C2 **Sélingué, Lac de** *lake* Mali
300 D6 **Selinnkegni** Mali
238 E4 **Selishche** Russian Federation
235 C4 **Selishte** Bulgaria
225 M3 **Seliste** Estonia
234 C4 **Selište** Serbia
374 E4 **Seliu** *island* Indonesia
238 E4 **Selizharovo** Russian Federation
224 C1 **Selje** Norway
224 D3 **Seljestad** Norway
224 E3 **Seljordsvatnet** *lake* Norway
223 P3 **Selkälä** Finland
120 G7 **Selkirk** Manitoba Canada
118 L7 **Selkirk Mountains** British Columbia/Idaho Canada/USA
240 E3 **Sellack** Herefordshire England UK
135 F3 **Selle, Massif de la** *range* Haiti
228 E3 **Selles** France
229 G3 **Sellières** France
241 I3 **Sellindge** Kent England UK
128 G5 **Sells** Arizona USA
127 K3 **Sellwood** Ontario Canada
237 AC4 **Sellyakhskaya Guba** *bay* Russian Federation
227 I5 **Sellye** Hungary
130 H4 **Selma** Alabama USA
128 C2 **Selma** California USA
131 L3 **Selma** North Carolina USA
130 G3 **Selmer** Tennessee USA
232 G3 **Selnica** Croatia
227 I4 **Selo** Slovenia
228 E3 **Selommes** France
375 H6 **Selong** Indonesia
229 G3 **Selongey** France
241 G4 **Selsey** West Sussex England UK
241 G4 **Selsey Bill** *cape* England UK
222 J5 **Seltjäm/Seltjärn** Sweden
238 F6 **Sel'tso** Russian Federation
372 D5 **Selu** *island* Indonesia
374 E2 **Seluan** *island* Indonesia
228 D2 **Sélune** *watercourse* France
229 J3 **Selva** Italy
222 F5 **Selva** Norway
159 E3 **Selvas** *region* Brazil
155 E3 **Selvas** *region* Venezuela
124 H3 **Selway** *watercourse* Idaho USA
425 L5 **Selwyn** Qld Australia
119 S2 **Selwyn Lake** Northwest Territories Canada
116 I7 **Selwyn Lake** Saskatchewan Canada
118 F1 **Selwyn Mountains** Northwest Territories/Yukon Territory Canada
426 7 **Selwyn Strait** Vanuatu
234 D2 **Selyatyn** Ukraine
227 H4 **Selzthal** Austria
309 F3 **Semacueza** Mozambique
372 E4 **Semai** *island* Indonesia
374 C5 **Semakau, Pulau** *island* Singapore
374 E5 **Semangka, Teluk** *bay* Indonesia
119 S7 **Semans** Saskatchewan Canada
375 F3 **Semarang** Indonesia
375 H4 **Semaras** Indonesia
392 F6 **Semaria** Chhattisgarh India
375 F3 **Sematan** Malaysia
375 I6 **Semau** *island* Indonesia
375 H4 **Semayang, Danau** *lake* Indonesia
306 E4 **Sembabule** Uganda
375 H3 **Sembakung** *watercourse* Indonesia
374 C2 **Sembawang** *admin. area* Singapore
305 G4 **Sembé** Congo
394 H6 **Semdinli** *mountain* Turkey
227 J5 **Semeljci** Croatia
238 H4 **Semendyayevo** Russian Federation
388 D2 **Semenov** Russian Federation
223 T6 **Semënovo** Russian Federation
238 F5 **Semënovskoye** Russian Federation
238 H3 **Semënovskoye** Russian Federation
374 D3 **Semenyih** Malaysia
241 H2 **Semer** Suffolk England UK
375 G6 **Semeru, Gunung** *volcano* Indonesia
235 E5 **Semetli** Turkey
227 H5 **Semič** Slovenia
237 AJ8 **Semichi Islands** Alaska USA
116 D7 **Semidi Islands** Alaska USA
238 I3 **Semigorodnyaya** Russian Federation
375 G4 **Semilat** Indonesia
394 F2 **Semiluki** Russian Federation
125 L5 **Seminoe Reservoir** Wyoming USA
129 K4 **Seminole** Texas USA
131 I5 **Seminole, Lake** Georgia USA
389 M3 **Semipalatinsk** Kazakhstan
377 I4 **Semirara** *island* Philippines
390 G3 **Semiron** Iran
375 F3 **Semitau** Indonesia
389 L3 **Semizbugy** Kazakhstan
238 E5 **Semlëvo** Russian Federation
241 E3 **Semley** Wiltshire England UK
120 H5 **Semmens Lake** Manitoba Canada
391 H2 **Semnān** Iran
388 G7 **Semnān** *admin. area* Iran
375 H2 **Sempang Mangayau, Tanjong** *cape* Malaysia
375 H2 **Semporna** Malaysia
375 G6 **Sempu** *island* Indonesia
229 G3 **Semur-en-Auxios** France
376 E4 **Sên** *watercourse* Cambodia
158 D3 **Sena Madureira** Brazil
157 B7 **Senador Canedo** Brazil
158 E3 **Senador Guiomard** Brazil
156 B3 **Senador José Porfírio** Brazil
156 E4 **Senador Pompeu** Brazil
303 F5 **Sen'afe** Eritrea
375 H2 **Senaja** Malaysia
374 B6 **Senang, Pulau** *island* Singapore
308 D3 **Senanga** Zambia
375 F3 **Senaning** Indonesia
231 I2 **Sénas** France
387 I3 **Sendai** Japan
226 D2 **Senden** Germany
393 D7 **Sendhwa** Madhya Pradesh India
374 D3 **Senebui, Tanjung** *cape* Indonesia
227 J3 **Senec** Slovakia
125 Q7 **Seneca** Kansas USA
126 D8 **Seneca** Missouri USA
124 F4 **Seneca** Oregon USA
127 M5 **Seneca Lake** New York USA
229 G1 **Seneffe** Belgium
300 D6 **Senegal** *country* Africa
300 D5 **Sénégal** *lake* Mauritania
233 C6 **Senetosa, Capu di** *cape* Corsica France
126 I3 **Seney** Michigan USA
306 E5 **Senga Hill** Zambia
375 H3 **Sengata** Indonesia
307 E4 **Sengerema** Tanzania
373 G4 **Senggi** Indonesia
388 E2 **Sengiley** Russian Federation
388 F5 **Sengirli, Mys** *cape* Kazakhstan
374 D3 **Sengkang** *admin. area* Singapore
162 C3 **Senguer** *watercourse* Argentina
308 E3 **Sengwa** *watercourse* Zimbabwe
227 I3 **Senica** Slovakia
160 D6 **Senillosa** Argentina
235 G6 **Senirkent** Turkey
233 G6 **Senise** Italy
232 F4 **Senj** Croatia
222 J2 **Senja** *island* Norway
234 B4 **Senje** Serbia
381 I3 **Senkaku-shotō (disputed)** *island* Disputed
304 C3 **Senko** Guinea
119 Q6 **Senlac** Saskatchewan Canada
308 D5 **Senlac** South Africa
228 F2 **Senlis** France
376 E4 **Senmonorom** Cambodia
302 E5 **Sennar** Sudan
302 E5 **Sennar** *admin. area* Sudan
223 S6 **Sennaya Guba** Russian Federation
240 B4 **Sennen** Cornwall England UK
234 D4 **Sennik** Bulgaria
225 O5 **Senno** Belarus
234 F4 **Senokos** Bulgaria
229 H2 **Senones** France
133 H5 **Señor** Mexico
389 O3 **Senrinskiy Khrebet** *range* Russian Federation
226 B3 **Sens** France
134 B4 **Sensuntepeque** El Salvador
389 N3 **Sentas** Kazakhstan
227 H4 **Šentilj** Slovenia
128 F4 **Sentinel** Arizona USA
130 B3 **Sentinel** Oklahoma USA
118 J5 **Sentinel Peak** British Columbia Canada
436 S1 **Sentinel Range** Antarctica
374 D5 **Sentosa** *island* Singapore
120 I2 **Sentry Island** Nunavut Canada
373 G4 **Senu** *watercourse* Papua New Guinea
305 F4 **Senye** Equatorial Guinea
375 H3 **Senyiur** Indonesia
386 F4 **Seongju** South Korea
393 E6 **Seoni** Madhya Pradesh India
393 E6 **Seoni Chhapara** Madhya Pradesh India
393 D6 **Seoni Malwa** Madhya Pradesh India
375 H5 **Sepanjang** *island* Indonesia
129 H4 **Separ** New Mexico USA
423 E5 **Separation Point** New Zealand
375 H3 **Sepasu** Indonesia
159 E3 **Sepatini** *watercourse* Brazil
375 F3 **Sepauk** Indonesia
228 F3 **Sépeaux** France
426 8 **Sepi** *island* Solomon Islands
373 G5 **Sepik** *watercourse* Papua New Guinea
386 E3 **Sep'o** North Korea
225 K5 **Sępopol** Poland
379 G3 **Seppa** Arunachal Pradesh India
121 V7 **Sept-Îles** Québec Canada
135 G3 **Septentrional, Cordillera** *range* Dominican Republic
308 D3 **Sepupa** Botswana
374 E5 **Seputih** *watercourse* Indonesia
131 I3 **Sequatchie** *watercourse* Tennessee USA
230 D3 **Sequillo** *watercourse* Spain
128 C2 **Sequoia National Park** California USA
372 D5 **Sera** *island* Indonesia
388 D3 **Serafimovich** Russian Federation
129 J3 **Serafina** New Mexico USA
229 G1 **Seraing** Belgium
372 D4 **Seram** *island* Indonesia
375 K4 **Seram, Laut (Ceram Sea)** Indonesia
372 F4 **Serami** Indonesia
374 E5 **Serang** Indonesia
374 D3 **Serangoon** *admin. area* Singapore
374 E3 **Serangoon Harbour** Singapore
374 F3 **Serasan** *island* Indonesia
374 F3 **Serasan, Selat** *strait* Indonesia
232 D5 **Seravezza** Italy
374 F3 **Seraya** *island* Indonesia
234 B3 **Serbia** *country* Serbia
234 E1 **Serbinovtsy** Ukraine
234 G2 **Serbka** Ukraine
379 G4 **Serchhip** Mizoram India
303 G5 **Serdo** Ethiopia
388 D3 **Serdobsk** Russian Federation
116 B5 **Serdtse-Kamen', Mys** *cape* Russian Federation
238 C3 **Serebryanka** Russian Federation
387 J2 **Serebryanoye, Ozero** *lake* Russian Federation
238 H5 **Serebryany Prudy** Russian Federation
238 F5 **Sereda** Russian Federation
388 D1 **Sereda** Russian Federation
238 C3 **Seredka** Russian Federation
234 C1 **Seret** Ukraine
228 F3 **Serein** *watercourse* France
300 C6 **Serekunda** Gambia
374 D3 **Seremban** Malaysia
230 D4 **Serena, Embalse de la** *lake* Spain
230 D4 **Serena, La** *region* Spain
307 E4 **Serengeti Plain** *plain* Tanzania
308 F2 **Serenje** Zambia
228 C3 **Sérent** France
159 E6 **Sereré** Bolivia
234 D1 **Seret** *watercourse* Ukraine
235 D7 **Serfopoula** *island* Greece
388 E2 **Sergach** Russian Federation
385 H3 **Sergelen** Mongolia
223 T5 **Sergievo** Russian Federation
236 O6 **Serginskiy** Russian Federation
157 E5 **Sergipe** *admin. area* Brazil
238 H4 **Sergiyev Posad** Russian Federation
234 G2 **Sergiyivka** Ukraine
223 T3 **Sergozero, Ozero** *lake* Russian Federation
375 G2 **Seria** Brunei
375 F3 **Serian** Malaysia
374 E5 **Seribu, Kepulauan** *island* Indonesia
374 C3 **Seribudolok** Indonesia
235 D7 **Serifos** *island* Greece
122 D5 **Sérigny** *watercourse* Québec Canada
122 D5 **Sérigny, Lac** *lake* Québec Canada
305 I2 **Seringa** *watercourse* Central African Republic
156 B4 **Seringa, Serra da** *range* Brazil
158 D3 **Seringal Sacado** Brazil
424 G3 **Seringapatam Reef** WA Australia
235 F7 **Serinhisar** Turkey
373 G6 **Serki** Papua New Guinea
226 B3 **Sermaises** France
372 D6 **Sermata** *island* Indonesia
372 D6 **Sermata, Kepulauan** *island* Indonesia
117 M3 **Sermersuaq (Humboldt Gletscher)** *glacier* Greenland
122 N2 **Sermersuut** *island* Greenland
122 N2 **Sermilik** *bay* Greenland
230 C3 **Sernancelhe** Portugal
388 F2 **Sernovodsk** Russian Federation
388 F2 **Sernur** Russian Federation
227 K1 **Serock** Poland
163 1a **Seroe Colorado** Aruba
230 E5 **Serón** Spain
308 D3 **Seronga** Botswana
231 G3 **Serós** Spain
236 N7 **Serov** Russian Federation
308 E4 **Serowe** Botswana
230 C5 **Serpa** Portugal
155 G5 **Serpa, Ilha de** *island* Brazil
127 P2 **Serpent** *watercourse* Québec Canada
300 E6 **Serpent, Vallée du** *valley* Mali
424 I7 **Serpentine Lakes** SA Australia
163 9 **Serpent's Mouth** *strait* Trinidad and Tobago
238 F5 **Serpeysk** Russian Federation
238 G5 **Serpukhov** Russian Federation
157 D8 **Serra** Brazil
157 B6 **Serra da Mesa, Represa** *lake* Brazil
233 E8 **Serradifalco** Italy
233 C7 **Serramanna** Sardinia Italy
157 C8 **Serrana** Brazil
134 E4 **Serrana Bank** *reef* Colombia
134 D4 **Serranilla Bank** *underwater feature* Caribbean Sea
310 1b **Serrata** Azores
228 F2 **Serre** *watercourse* France
229 G4 **Serres** France
235 C5 **Serres** Greece
160 E4 **Serrezuela** Argentina
157 E5 **Serrinha** Brazil
159 H6 **Serrito** Brazil
157 D7 **Serro** Brazil
233 G7 **Sersale** Italy
230 B4 **Sertã** Portugal
156 E5 **Sertânia** Brazil
157 B8 **Sertanópolis** Brazil
375 F4 **Sertung** *island* Indonesia
372 D5 **Serua** *island* Indonesia
374 C2 **Seruai** Indonesia
374 F4 **Serutu** *island* Indonesia
375 G4 **Seruyan** *watercourse* Indonesia
225 N5 **Servach** *watercourse* Belarus
384 D4 **Serven Uul** *mountain* Mongolia
232 E5 **Servigliano** Italy
372 C6 **Serwaru** Indonesia
116 B5 **Serykh Gusey, Ostrova** *island* Russian Federation
375 H6 **Sesayap** Indonesia
375 H3 **Sesayap** *watercourse* Indonesia
306 B3 **Sese** Democratic Republic of Congo
120 J7 **Seseganaga Lake** Ontario Canada
230 E3 **Seseña** Spain
308 B3 **Sesfontein** Namibia
238 E6 **Seshcha** Russian Federation
308 D3 **Sesheke** Zambia
230 B4 **Sesimbra** Portugal
223 M4 **Seskarö** Sweden

242 A2 **Seskinore** Omagh Northern Ireland UK
134 B4 **Sesori** El Salvador
308 D2 **Sessa** Angola
222 J2 **Sessaya** *island* Norway
226 F2 **Seßlach** Germany
232 E3 **Sesto** Italy
226 E5 **Sesto Calende** Italy
225 L5 **Šeštokai** Lithuania
229 I4 **Sestri Levante** Italy
226 D5 **Sestriere** Italy
225 O2 **Sestroretsk** Russian Federation
229 J3 **Sesvenna, Piz** *mountain* Italy/Switzerland
386 F5 **Setaka** Japan
228 F5 **Sète** France
157 C7 **Sete Lagoas** Brazil
222 K2 **Setermoen** Norway
310 1a **Setes Cicades, Caldeira das** *lake* Azores
224 D3 **Setesdal** *valley* Norway
301 H1 **Sétif** Algeria
301 H1 **Sétif** *admin. area* Algeria
241 F4 **Setley** Hampshire England UK
118 J7 **Seton Portage** British Columbia Canada
222 I3 **Setså** Norway
300 E2 **Settat** Morocco
305 F5 **Setté Cama** Gabon
237 AC6 **Sette-Daban, Khrebet** *range* Russian Federation
224 F3 **Setten** *lake* Norway
119 V5 **Setting Lake** Manitoba Canada
243 F2 **Settle** North Yorkshire England UK
424 inset **Settlement** Christmas Island Australia
304 E3 **Setto** Benin
228 G3 **Settons, Lac des** *lake* France
230 B3 **Setúbal** Portugal
230 B4 **Setúbal** *admin. area* Portugal
228 D4 **Seudre** *watercourse* France
228 D4 **Seugne** *watercourse* France
226 C3 **Seuil-d'Argonne** France
222 J3 **Seukojaure** *lake* Sweden
120 I7 **Seul, Lac** *lake* Ontario Canada
374 B2 **Seulimeum** Indonesia
226 C4 **Seurre** France
388 E6 **Sevana Lich** *lake* Armenia
234 E4 **Sevar** Bulgaria
300 F6 **Sévaré** Mali
235 A5 **Sevaster** Albania
394 E4 **Sevastopol'** Ukraine
225 O2 **Sevast'yanovo** Russian Federation
229 I3 **Sevelen** Switzerland
242 A4 **Seven** Ireland
130 F4 **Seven Devils Lake** Arkansas USA
122 G3 **Seven Islands Bay** Newfoundland and Labrador Canada
240 D3 **Seven Sisters** Neath Port Talbot Wales UK
130 B6 **Seven Sisters** Texas USA
125 Q1 **Seven Sisters Falls** Manitoba Canada
241 H3 **Sevenoaks** Kent England UK
119 P8 **Sevenpersons** Alberta Canada
237 AI6 **Sever** Russian Federation
228 F4 **Sévérac-le-Château** France
157 B8 **Severinia** Brazil
161 H4 **Severino Ribeiro** Brazil
120 I6 **Severn** *watercourse* Ontario Canada
423 E6 **Severn** *mountain* New Zealand
308 D5 **Severn** South Africa
240 E2 **Severn** *watercourse* England/Wales UK
120 J6 **Severn Lake** Ontario Canada
236 S5 **Severnaya** *watercourse* Russian Federation
236 N6 **Severnaya Sos'va** *watercourse* Russian Federation
237 W3 **Severnaya Zemlya** *island* Russian Federation
237 X7 **Severo-Baykal'-skoye Nagor'ye** *region* Russian Federation
389 O3 **Severo-Chuyskiy Khr** *mountain* Russian Federation
389 K2 **Severo-Kazakhstanskaya Oblast'** *admin. area* Kazakhstan
237 U4 **Severo-Sibirskaya Nizmennost'** *region* Russian Federation
238 H5 **Severo-Zadonsk** Russian Federation
236 I6 **Severodvinsk** Russian Federation
236 H5 **Severomorsk** Russian Federation
130 C2 **Severy** Kansas USA
223 P2 **Sevettijärvi** Finland
128 F1 **Sevier** *watercourse* Utah USA
128 F1 **Sevier Bridge Reservoir** Utah USA
128 F1 **Sevier Desert** Utah USA
128 F1 **Sevier Lake** Utah USA
230 D5 **Sevilla** Spain
305 G4 **Sevilla de Niefang** Equatorial Guinea
234 D4 **Sevlievo** Bulgaria
232 F3 **Sevnica** Slovenia
226 B3 **Sevran** France
234 E4 **Sevrei** Mongolia
304 B3 **Sewa** *watercourse* Sierra Leone
118 E6 **Sewall** British Columbia Canada
131 K7 **Sewall's Point** Florida USA
116 E6 **Seward** Alaska USA
125 Q6 **Seward** Nebraska USA
116 C5 **Seward Peninsula** Alaska USA
373 G6 **Sewerimabu** Papua New Guinea
118 L5 **Sexsmith** Alberta Canada
129 J7 **Sextin** Mexico
236 P4 **Sēyakha** Russian Federation
236 O4 **Sēyakha** *watercourse* Russian Federation
133 H5 **Seyaplaya** Mexico
133 H5 **Seybaplaya** Mexico
310 9 **Seychelles** *country* Indian Ocean
310 9b **Seychellois, Morne** *mountain* Seychelles
388 I6 **Seÿdi** Turkmenistan
222 inset **Seyðisfjörður** Iceland
235 G6 **Seyitgazi** Turkey
235 F6 **Seyitömer** Turkey
394 F2 **Seym** *watercourse* Russian Federation
425 M9 **Seymour** Vic. Australia
126 I7 **Seymour** Indiana USA
130 B4 **Seymour** Texas USA
163 4 **Seymour, Isla** *islands* Archipiélago de Colón (Galapagos Islands)
120 G7 **Seymourville** Manitoba Canada
229 H4 **Seyne** France
229 H4 **Seynod** France
235 E6 **Seyrek** Turkey
229 G4 **Seyssel** France
391 K3 **Seyyed Bûs** Afghanistan
232 E4 **Sežana** Slovenia
226 B3 **Sézanne** France
235 D8 **Sfakion** Greece
234 D3 **Sfântu Gheorghe** Romania
301 I2 **Sfax** Tunisia
233 C7 **Sferracavallo, Capo** *cape* Sardinia Italy
235 C8 **Sfinárion** Greece
244 A4 **Sgallairidh** Na h-Eileanan Siar Scotland UK
381 G3 **Sha Xi** *lake* Fujian China
381 H3 **Sha Xi** *watercourse* Fujian China
380 E1 **Shaanxi** *admin. area* China
126 G6 **Shabbona** Illinois USA
307 H3 **Shabeellaha Dhexe** *admin. area* Somalia
307 G3 **Shabeellaha Hoose** *admin. area* Somalia
307 H3 **Shabeelle, Webi** *watercourse* Somalia
388 C4 **Shabel'sk** Russian Federation
234 F4 **Shabla** Bulgaria
234 F4 **Shabla** *cape* Bulgaria
121 V6 **Shabo** Newfoundland and Labrador Canada
122 E6 **Shabogamo Lake** Newfoundland and Labrador Canada
120 K7 **Shabuskwia Lake** Ontario Canada
382 F5 **Shache** Xinjiang Uygur Zizhiqu China
381 H3 **Shacheng** Fujian China
381 H3 **Shacheng Gang** *lake* Fujian China
119 Q7 **Shackleton** Saskatchewan Canada
437 K1 **Shackleton** Antarctica
437 G2 **Shackleton Ice Shelf** Antarctica
437 L1 **Shackleton Inlet** *bay* Antarctica
436 W1 **Shackleton Range** Antarctica
390 F3 **Shādegān** Iran
125 N4 **Shadehill Reservoir** South Dakota USA
388 I2 **Shadrinsk** Russian Federation
302 E2 **Shadwan Island** Egypt
124 D5 **Shady Cove** Oregon USA
130 D3 **Shady Point** Oklahoma USA
126 H6 **Shafer, Lake** Indiana USA
437 K2 **Shafer Peak** *mountain* Antarctica
128 C3 **Shafter** California USA
129 J6 **Shafter** Texas USA
241 E3 **Shaftesbury** Dorset England UK
424 inset **Shag Island** Heard Island Australia
423 D7 **Shag Point** New Zealand
120 L5 **Shagamu** *watercourse* Ontario Canada
120 L5 **Shagamu Lake** Ontario Canada
389 Q3 **Shagonar** Russian Federation
373 D3 **Shah Alam** Malaysia
391 J3 **Shāh Fūlādi** *mountain* Afghanistan
393 E5 **Shahabad** Andhra Pradesh India
393 D8 **Shahabad** Karnataka India
393 E5 **Shahabad** Uttar Pradesh India
391 J4 **Shāhābād** Iran
391 H4 **Shahābi** Iran
393 D7 **Shahada** Maharashtra India
234 G3 **Shahany, Ozero** *lake* Ukraine
391 K4 **Shahdadpur** Pakistan
392 E6 **Shahdol** Madhya Pradesh India
385 H6 **Shahe** Hebei China
392 E6 **Shahganj** Madhya Pradesh India
390 G4 **Shahid** Iran
392 E5 **Shahjahanpur** Uttar Pradesh India
393 C6 **Shahpur** Gujarat India
393 D8 **Shahpur** Karnataka India
391 K4 **Shahpur** Pakistan
391 K4 **Shahpur Chakar** Pakistan
392 D6 **Shahpura** Rajasthan India
391 H3 **Shahr-e Bābak** Iran
391 H3 **Shahr-e Kord** Iran
390 G3 **Shahrezā** Iran
389 J6 **Shahriston** Tajikistan
390 E3 **Sha'ib Ḩisb** *watercourse* Iraq
391 K3 **Shaighalu** Pakistan
391 K3 **Shaikh Salar** Pakistan
154 B5 **Shaimi, Cordillera de** *range* Peru
392 D6 **Shajapur** Madhya Pradesh India
308 D3 **Shakawe** Botswana
130 H3 **Shakespeare Island** Ontario Canada
120 K8 **Shakespeare Island** Ontario Canada
391 F5 **Shakhbūt** Oman
238 F4 **Shakhovskaya** Russian Federation
238 G5 **Shakhs, Ras** *cape* Eritrea
389 K3 **Shakhtinsk** Kazakhstan
388 C4 **Shakhty** Russian Federation
305 E3 **Shaki** Nigeria
116 C5 **Shaktoolik** Alaska USA
307 F2 **Shala, Lake** Ethiopia
389 M3 **Shalakterek** *lake* Kazakhstan
238 I1 **Shalakusha** Russian Federation
241 F3 **Shalbourne** Wiltshire England UK
389 M3 **Shalday** Kazakhstan
241 H3 **Shalford** Essex England UK
383 J6 **Shaliu He** *watercourse* Qinghai China
384 D5 **Shaliuhe** Qinghai China
388 F3 **Shalkar** *lake* Kazakhstan
388 H4 **Shalkar (Shalqar)** Kazakhstan
388 I3 **Shalkar-karashatau** *lake* Kazakhstan
131 L4 **Shallotte** North Carolina USA
437 E2 **Shallow Bay** Antarctica
129 L4 **Shallowater** Texas USA
Shalqar *see* **Shalkar** Kazakhstan
380 C2 **Shalulie Shan** *range* Sichuan China
379 H3 **Shaluni** *mountain* Xizang Zizhiqu China
307 E5 **Shama** *watercourse* Tanzania
384 F2 **Shamaat** Mongolia
120 I5 **Shamattawa** Manitoba Canada
120 M5 **Shamattawa** *watercourse* Ontario Canada
306 E2 **Shambe** Sudan
307 F2 **Shambu** Ethiopia
127 M6 **Shamokin** Pennsylvania USA
225 Q2 **Shamoksha** Russian Federation
119 R7 **Shamrock** Saskatchewan Canada
130 A3 **Shamrock** Texas USA
391 I5 **Shams, Jabal** *mountain* Oman
309 F3 **Shamva** Zimbabwe
379 H5 **Shan** *admin. area* Myanmar
379 H5 **Shan Plateau** Myanmar
384 F5 **Shanba** Nei Mongol Zizhiqu China
381 H4 **Shancheng** Fujian China
242 B2 **Shanco** Ireland
384 E5 **Shandan** Gansu China
381 H1 **Shandong** *admin. area* China
385 I6 **Shandong** *admin. area* China
391 L2 **Shandur Pass** Pakistan
308 E3 **Shangani** *watercourse* Zimbabwe
380 E3 **Shangchao** Guangxi Zhuangzu Zizhiqu China
381 G2 **Shangcheng** Henan China
381 F4 **Shangchuan Dao** *island* Guangdong China
384 E6 **Shangchuankou** Qinghai China
385 H4 **Shangdu** Nei Mongol Zizhiqu China
381 I2 **Shanghai** *admin. area* China
381 I2 **Shanghai** Shanghai China
380 C3 **Shangpa** Yunnan China
381 H2 **Shangpai** Anhui China
381 G1 **Shangqiu** Henan China
381 H3 **Shangrao** Jiangxi China
154 C3 **Shangri-Lá** Colombia
382 F5 **Shangyou Shuiku** *lake* Xinjiang Uygur Zizhiqu China
385 K3 **Shangzhi** Heilongjiang China
380 F1 **Shangzhou** Shaanxi China
384 F6 **Shanhe** Gansu China
391 K4 **Shank** Pakistan
392 G5 **Shankarpur** Bihar India
242 B3 **Shankill** Ireland
241 F4 **Shanklin** Isle of Wight England UK
242 B3 **Shanlis Cross Roads** Ireland
245 D4 **Shannon** Ireland
245 D4 **Shannon** *watercourse* Ireland
130 G3 **Shannon** Mississippi USA
245 C4 **Shannon, Mouth of the** *bay* Ireland
120 E3 **Shannon Lake** Manitoba Canada
437 F1 **Shannon Øer** *island* Greenland
383 I4 **Shanshan** Xinjiang Uygur Zizhiqu China
237 AC7 **Shantarskiye Ostrova** *island* Russian Federation
392 G6 **Shantipur** West Bengal India
381 G4 **Shantou** Guangdong China
423 D6 **Shantytown** New Zealand
158 B2 **Shanusi** Peru
381 G4 **Shanwei** Guangdong China
381 F1 **Shanxi** *admin. area* China
380 F1 **Shanyang** Shaanxi China
385 G5 **Shanyin** Shanxi China
381 G4 **Shaoguan** Guangdong China
381 H3 **Shaowu** Fujian China
381 H2 **Shaoxing** Zhejiang China
242 F2 **Shap** Cumbria England UK
154 C5 **Shapajal** Peru
306 C4 **Shapembe** Democratic Republic of Congo
380 D2 **Shaping** Sichuan China
244 F1 **Shapinsay** *island* Scotland UK
122 H5 **Shapio Lake** Newfoundland and Labrador Canada
225 P3 **Shapki** Russian Federation
238 C4 **Shapkino** Russian Federation
390 F4 **Shaqrā'** Saudi Arabia
302 D5 **Sharafa** Sudan
391 J4 **Sharak** Pakistan
391 K2 **Sharan** Afghanistan
391 K3 **Sharan Jogizai** Pakistan
391 H6 **Sharbithāt, Ra's** *cape* Oman
389 J5 **Shardara Bogeni** *lake* Uzbekistan
388 H7 **Shāreh** Iran
383 J3 **Sharga** Mongolia
384 D4 **Sharga Morit Uul** *mountain* Mongolia
387 J2 **Sharidake** *volcano* Japan
384 F2 **Sharingol** Mongolia
424 E6 **Shark Bay** WA Australia
238 B5 **Sharkawshchyna** Belarus
302 E2 **Sharm ash Shaykh** Egypt
130 B2 **Sharon** Kansas USA
125 Q3 **Sharon** North Dakota USA
127 K6 **Sharon** Pennsylvania USA
125 O7 **Sharon Springs** Kansas USA
126 I7 **Sharonville** Ohio USA
238 D6 **Sharoyevka** Belarus
125 P4 **Sharpe, Lake** South Dakota USA
120 I5 **Sharpe Lake** Manitoba Canada
120 H7 **Sharpstone Lake** Ontario Canada
391 M3 **Sharqpur** Pakistan
236 K7 **Shar'ya** Russian Federation
308 E4 **Shashe** Botswana
308 E4 **Shashe** *watercourse* Zimbabwe
124 D6 **Shasta, Mount** *volcano* California USA
124 D6 **Shasta Lake** California USA
238 E5 **Shatalovo** Russian Federation
234 E1 **Shatava** Ukraine
130 B2 **Shattuck** Oklahoma USA
238 H5 **Shatura** Russian Federation
240 C4 **Shaugh Prior** Devon England UK
119 Q8 **Shaunavon** Saskatchewan Canada
125 L7 **Shavano, Mount** Colorado USA
124 F8 **Shaver Lake** California USA
223 Q5 **Shaverki** Russian Federation
130 F4 **Shaw** Mississippi USA
126 G4 **Shawano** Wisconsin USA
126 G4 **Shawano Lake** Wisconsin USA
240 E2 **Shawbury** Shropshire England UK
117 L9 **Shawinigan** Québec Canada
130 C3 **Shawnee** Oklahoma USA
118 J8 **Shawnigan Lake** British Columbia Canada
382 G4 **Shaya** Xinjiang Uygur Zizhiqu China
390 C4 **Shaybārā** *island* Saudi Arabia
302 E5 **Shaykh Jok** Sudan
238 F5 **Shaykovka** Russian Federation
389 K6 **Shazud** Tajikistan
227 M1 **Shchara** *watercourse* Belarus
238 G5 **Shchëkino** Russian Federation
236 L5 **Shchel' yayur** Russian Federation
238 F5 **Shchelkanovo** Russian Federation
238 H5 **Shchelkovo** Russian Federation
389 M3 **Shcherbakty** Kazakhstan
238 H3 **Shchetinskoye** Russian Federation
238 H5 **Shchurovo** Russian Federation
389 O3 **Shebalino** Russian Federation
126 F2 **Shebandowan** Ontario Canada
240 C4 **Shebbear** Devon England UK
394 F2 **Shebekino** Russian Federation
388 J7 **Sheberghān** Afghanistan
126 H5 **Sheboygan** Wisconsin USA
126 H5 **Sheboygan Falls** Wisconsin USA
387 I1 **Shebunino** Russian Federation
123 F9 **Shediac** New Brunswick Canada
123 F9 **Shediac Bay** New Brunswick Canada
245 E3 **Sheelin, Lough** *lake* Ireland
118 H7 **Sheemahant** *watercourse* British Columbia Canada
124 G6 **Sheep Creek Reservoir** Nevada USA
308 F5 **Sheepmoor** South Africa
245 C5 **Sheep's Head** *cape* Ireland
240 C4 **Sheepwash** Devon England UK
241 H3 **Sheerness** Kent England UK
123 G10 **Sheet Harbour** Nova Scotia Canada
243 G3 **Sheffield** South Yorkshire England UK
129 L5 **Sheffield** Texas USA
123 J8 **Sheffield Lake** Newfoundland and Labrador Canada
241 F3 **Shefford Woodlands** West Berkshire England UK
393 D7 **Shegaon** Maharashtra India
236 R7 **Shegarka** *watercourse* Russian Federation
307 G2 **Shēh Husēn** Ethiopia
119 T7 **Sheho** Saskatchewan Canada
244 C2 **Sheigra** Highland Scotland UK
302 F5 **Shek Husen** Ethiopia
126 I2 **Shekak** *watercourse* Ontario Canada
389 K5 **Sheker** Kyrgyzstan
391 M3 **Shekhupura** Pakistan
388 E5 **Sheki** Azerbaijan
238 H3 **Sheksna** Russian Federation
389 N2 **Shelabolikha** Russian Federation
237 AJ4 **Shelagskiy, Mys** *cape* Russian Federation
126 E7 **Shelbina** Missouri USA
123 F11 **Shelburne** Nova Scotia Canada
126 H5 **Shelby** Michigan USA
130 F4 **Shelby** Mississippi USA
124 J2 **Shelby** Montana USA
131 K3 **Shelby** North Carolina USA
126 I7 **Shelbyville** Indiana USA
126 E7 **Shelbyville** Missouri USA
131 H3 **Shelbyville** Tennessee USA
126 G7 **Shelbyville, Lake** Illinois USA
240 D4 **Sheldon** Devon England UK
125 R5 **Sheldon** Iowa USA
126 D8 **Sheldon** Missouri USA
125 Q3 **Sheldon** North Dakota USA
237 V8 **Shelekhov** Russian Federation
237 AG7 **Shelikhova, Zaliv** *bay* Russian Federation
116 D7 **Shelikof Strait** Alaska USA
119 R6 **Shell Lake** Saskatchewan Canada
119 R6 **Shellbrook** Saskatchewan Canada
118 J6 **Shelley** British Columbia Canada
124 I5 **Shelley** Idaho USA
131 I5 **Shellman** Georgia USA
125 Q3 **Shelly** Minnesota USA
238 H2 **Shelokhovskaya** Russian Federation
118 M7 **Shelter Bay** British Columbia Canada
127 O6 **Shelton** Connecticut USA
124 D3 **Shelton** Washington USA
238 F2 **Sheltozero** Russian Federation
238 F2 **Shemenichi** Russian Federation
379 G3 **Shemgang** Bhutan
389 N3 **Shemonaikha** Kazakhstan
385 H6 **Shen Xian** Shandong China
384 G5 **Shenchi** Shanxi China
302 E4 **Shendi** Sudan
379 H2 **Shengda** Xizang Zizhiqu China
304 B3 **Shenge** Sierra Leone
235 B5 **Shëngjergj** Albania
235 A5 **Shëngjin** Albania
383 H4 **Shengli Daban** *pass* Xinjiang Uygur Zizhiqu China
380 C3 **Shengping** Yunnan China
236 J6 **Shenkursk** Russian Federation
304 C3 **Shenkwehn** *watercourse* Liberia
384 G5 **Shenmu** Shaanxi China
380 F4 **Shentang Shan** *mountain* Guangxi Zhuangzu Zizhiqu China
385 J4 **Shenyang** Liaoning China
385 H5 **Shenze** Hebei China
379 F2 **Shenzha** Xizang Zizhiqu China
381 G4 **Shenzhen** Guangdong China
392 C6 **Sheoganj** Rajasthan India
392 D6 **Sheopur** Madhya Pradesh India
436 O2 **Shepard Island** Antarctica
126 I5 **Shepherd** Michigan USA
130 D5 **Shepherd** Texas USA
425 M9 **Shepparton** Vic. Australia
241 H3 **Sheppey, Isle of** England UK
240 E3 **Shepton Mallet** Somerset England UK
388 E7 **Shera** Iran
117 K4 **Sherard, Cape** Nunavut Canada
243 G2 **Sheraton** Durham England UK
240 E4 **Sherborne** Dorset England UK
304 B3 **Sherbro Island** Sierra Leone
117 L9 **Sherbrooke** Québec Canada
127 N5 **Sherburne** New York USA
245 F3 **Shercock** Ireland
302 E4 **Shereiq** Sudan
130 E3 **Sheridan** Arkansas USA
128 B1 **Sheridan** California USA
124 I4 **Sheridan** Montana USA
125 L4 **Sheridan** Wyoming USA
117 M2 **Sheridan, Cape** Nunavut Canada
241 I2 **Sheringham** Norfolk England UK
245 C5 **Sherkin Island** Ireland
392 E5 **Sherkot** Uttar Pradesh India
126 G7 **Sherman** Illinois USA
127 L5 **Sherman** New York USA
130 C4 **Sherman** Texas USA
117 J5 **Sherman Basin** Nunavut Canada
436 R2 **Sherman Island** Antarctica
125 P6 **Sherman Reservoir** Nebraska USA
127 Q4 **Sherman Station** Maine USA
244 D3 **Sherramore** Highland Scotland UK
119 U5 **Sherridon** Manitoba Canada
245 F2 **Sherrigrim** Dungannon Northern Ireland UK
130 E3 **Sherwood** Arkansas USA
126 I6 **Sherwood** Ohio USA
119 O6 **Sherwood Park** Alberta Canada
126 J4 **Sheshegwaning** Ontario Canada
245 C2 **Sheskin** Ireland
118 F3 **Sheslay** British Columbia Canada
238 H4 **Shestikhino** Russian Federation
235 A5 **Shetaj** Albania
158 C2 **Shetebo** Peru
126 D4 **Shetek, Lake** Minnesota USA
244 inset **Shetland** *admin. area* Scotland UK
244 inset **Shetland Islands** Scotland UK
388 F5 **Shetpe** Kazakhstan
Shevchenko *see* **Aktau** Kazakhstan
388 H4 **Shevchenko, Zaliv** *lake* Kazakhstan
234 F3 **Shevchenkove** Ukraine
125 R3 **Shevlin** Minnesota USA
237 Y6 **Sheya** Russian Federation
125 P3 **Sheyenne** North Dakota USA
126 B3 **Sheyenne** *watercourse* North Dakota USA
388 E7 **Sheykhlar** Iran
225 P4 **Sheykino** Russian Federation
244 B3 **Shiant Islands** Scotland UK
237 AG9 **Shiashkotan, Ostrov** *island* Kuril Islands
390 F7 **Shibām** Yemen
384 G6 **Shibao** Shaanxi China
387 H4 **Shibata** Japan
237 AA8 **Shibazhan** Heilongjiang China
120 K6 **Shibogama Lake** Ontario Canada
387 I2 **Shibunotsunai-to** *lake* Japan
381 H3 **Shicheng** Fujian China
385 J5 **Shicheng Dao** *island* Liaoning China
385 J6 **Shidao** Shandong China
389 L3 **Shiderty** *watercourse* Kazakhstan
244 C4 **Shiel, Loch** *lake* Scotland UK
244 C3 **Shiel Bridge** Highland Scotland UK
425 K3 **Shield, Cape** NT Australia
244 C3 **Shieldaig** Highland Scotland UK
380 D2 **Shifang** Sichuan China
240 E2 **Shifnal** Shropshire England UK
390 G6 **Shiḩan, Wādī** *watercourse* Yemen
382 H4 **Shihezi** Xinjiang Uygur Zizhiqu China
307 H2 **Shiikh** Somalia
235 A5 **Shijak** Albania
381 G4 **Shijiao** Guangdong China
385 H5 **Shijiazhuang** Hebei China
381 H2 **Shijiu Hu** *lake* Jiangsu China
120 J8 **Shikag Lake** Ontario Canada
387 I2 **Shikaribetsu-ko** *lake* Japan
391 K4 **Shikarpur** Pakistan
308 D3 **Shikela** *watercourse* Zambia
387 H4 **Shikine-jima** *island* Japan
392 E5 **Shikohabad** Uttar Pradesh India
386 G5 **Shikoku** *island* Japan
386 G5 **Shikoku-sanchi** Japan
381 G4 **Shikongkong** *mountain* Guangdong China
387 J2 **Shikontan-tō (Ostrov Shikotan)** *island* Russian Federation
387 I2 **Shikotsu-ko** *lake* Japan
388 H3 **Shil'da** Russian Federation
243 G2 **Shildon** Durham England UK
391 H3 **Shileh** Iran
392 G5 **Shiliguri** West Bengal India
379 F3 **Shiliguri** *admin. area* West Bengal India
380 F5 **Shiliu** Hainan China
385 H2 **Shilka** *watercourse* Russian Federation
392 E4 **Shilla** *mountain* Himachal Pradesh India
244 A3 **Shillay** *island* Scotland UK
245 F4 **Shillelagh** Ireland
304 B3 **Shilling, Cape** *cape* Sierra Leone
127 K2 **Shillington** Ontario Canada
379 G4 **Shillong** Meghalaya India
388 E3 **Shil'naya Balka** Kazakhstan
125 P2 **Shilo** Manitoba Canada
384 G6 **Shilou** Shanxi China
238 H6 **Shilovo** Russian Federation
388 C2 **Shilovo** Russian Federation
383 K3 **Shiluustei** Mongolia
237 AA8 **Shimanovsk** Russian Federation
380 C3 **Shimen** Yunnan China
392 D4 **Shimla** Himachal Pradesh India
386 F5 **Shimo Koshiko-jima** *island* Japan
387 H4 **Shimoda** Japan
393 D9 **Shimoga** Karnataka India
386 F5 **Shimonoseki** Japan
225 P3 **Shimsk** Russian Federation
244 D2 **Shin, Loch** *lake* Scotland UK
384 D3 **Shina-under** Mongolia
391 H5 **Shināş** Oman
390 E2 **Shindir** Iraq
384 D4 **Shinejust** Mongolia
130 C6 **Shiner** Texas USA
306 C4 **Shinga** Democratic Republic of Congo
241 I2 **Shingle Street** Suffolk England UK
126 H3 **Shingleton** Michigan USA
389 M4 **Shingozha** Kazakhstan
387 G5 **Shingu** Japan
391 K3 **Shinkay** Afghanistan
158 D4 **Shintuya** Peru
386 E3 **Shinwŏn** North Korea
307 E4 **Shinyanga** Tanzania
307 E4 **Shinyanga** *admin. area* Tanzania
387 I3 **Shiogama** Japan
387 G5 **Shiono-misaki** *island* Japan
127 N7 **Ship Bottom** New Jersey USA
123 G10 **Ship Harbour East** Nova Scotia Canada
381 G2 **Shipai** Anhui China
238 H4 **Shipilovo** Russian Federation
380 D4 **Shiping** Yunnan China
122 G5 **Shipiskan Lake** Newfoundland and Labrador Canada
123 F9 **Shippegan** New Brunswick Canada
127 M6 **Shippensburg** Pennsylvania USA
127 L6 **Shippenville** Pennsylvania USA
129 H2 **Shiprock** New Mexico USA
121 T8 **Shipshaw** *watercourse* Québec Canada
241 F2 **Shipston on Stour** Warwickshire England UK
240 E2 **Shipton** Shropshire England UK
237 AH8 **Shipunskiy, Mys** *cape* Russian Federation
380 E3 **Shiqian** Guizhou China
381 G4 **Shiqiao** Guangdong China
380 E1 **Shiquan** Shaanxi China
378 D2 **Shiquan He** *watercourse* Xizang Zizhiqu China
378 D2 **Shiquanhe** Xizang Zizhiqu China
389 J6 **Shir Khan** Afghanistan
389 P2 **Shira** *lake* Russian Federation
387 I3 **Shiragami-dake** *volcano* Japan
387 H4 **Shirane-san** *mountain* Japan
387 I2 **Shiraoi** Japan
436 N1 **Shirase Bank** *underwater feature* Ross Sea
436 N1 **Shirase Coast** Antarctica
437 C2 **Shirase Glacier** Antarctica
390 G3 **Shirāz** Iran
393 D7 **Shirdi** Maharashtra India
309 F3 **Shire** *watercourse* Malawi
243 G3 **Shirebrook** Derbyshire England UK
241 F1 **Shirland** Derbyshire England UK
241 F2 **Shirley** West Midlands England UK
163 18 **Shirley, Cape** Antigua and Barbuda
234 C4 **Shiroki Dol** Bulgaria
234 G2 **Shirokolanovka** Ukraine
237 AC4 **Shirokostan, Poluostrov** *peninsula* Russian Federation
393 D7 **Shirpur** Maharashtra India
434 R3 **Shirshov Ridge** *underwater feature* Bering Sea
388 H6 **Shirvān** Iran
116 C8 **Shishaldin Volcano** Alaska USA
381 H4 **Shishi** Fujian China
116 C5 **Shishmaref** Alaska USA
235 C5 **Zrnovci** Macedonia
234 A2 **Zsámbék** Hungary
226 G2 **Zschortau** Germany
389 K7 **Zu** Afghanistan
154 E2 **Zuata** *watercourse* Venezuela
227 J3 **Zuberec** Slovakia
234 B4 **Zubin Potok** Kosovo
238 G6 **Zubkovo** Russian Federation
388 D2 **Zubova Polyana** Russian Federation
388 F2 **Zubovka** Russian Federation
225 P5 **Zubovo** Belarus
238 G2 **Zubovo** Russian Federation
227 L2 **Zubowice** Poland
238 F4 **Zubtsov** Russian Federation
234 B4 **Žuč** Serbia
232 D3 **Zuckerhütl** *mountain* Austria
230 E2 **Zudaire** Spain
231 F3 **Zuera** Spain
230 C5 **Zufre** Spain
230 C5 **Zufre, Embalse de** *lake* Spain
229 I3 **Zug** Switzerland
388 D5 **Zugdidi** Georgia
305 F2 **Zugu** Nigeria
380 E1 **Zuitou** Shaanxi China
230 D4 **Zújar** *watercourse* Spain
227 L2 **Żuków** Poland
154 D2 **Zulia** *admin. area* Venezuela
226 D2 **Zülpich** Germany
228 F1 **Zulte** Belgium
228 C5 **Zumaia** Spain
436 T1 **Zumberge Coast** Antarctica
226 C2 **Zundert** Netherlands
379 H4 **Zunheboto** Nagaland India
385 I5 **Zunhua** Hebei China
129 H3 **Zuni Mountains** New Mexico USA
129 H3 **Zuni Pueblo** New Mexico USA
380 E3 **Zunyi** Guizhou China
385 H5 **Zuoquan** Shanxi China
385 G5 **Zuoyun** Shanxi China
232 H4 **Županja** Croatia
302 C3 **Zurgh, Jabal** *mountain* Libya
229 I3 **Zürich** Switzerland
227 J1 **Żuromin** Poland
154 A4 **Zurones, Punta** *cape* Ecuador
305 F2 **Zuru** Nigeria
232 D2 **Zusam** *watercourse* Germany
387 H4 **Zushi** Japan
226 F1 **Züsow** Germany
232 F5 **Žut** *island* Croatia
229 L4 **Žuta Lokva** Croatia
384 G4 **Zuunebayan** Mongolia
384 E3 **Zuunebayan-ylaan** Mongolia
383 J2 **Zuunegov** Mongolia
383 J2 **Zuunehangai** Mongolia
384 F3 **Zuunmod** Mongolia
225 L5 **Žuvintas** *lake* Lithuania
301 I2 **Zuwārah** Libya
388 F1 **Zuyevka** Russian Federation
424 E6 **Zuytdorp Cliffs** WA Australia
225 O3 **Zvad** Russian Federation
238 E6 **Zvenchatka** Belarus
234 C4 **Zverino** Bulgaria
225 M5 **Žverno ežeras** *lake* Lithuania
235 E4 **Zvezdets** Bulgaria
225 M4 **Zvirgzde** Latvia
308 F4 **Zvishavane** Zimbabwe
227 J3 **Zvolen** Slovakia
232 H4 **Zvornik** Bosnia and Herzegovina
304 C3 **Zwedru** Liberia
229 H3 **Zweisimmen** Switzerland
227 H3 **Zwettl** Austria
229 K1 **Zwickau** Germany
226 G2 **Zwickauer Mulde** *watercourse* Germany
227 L2 **Zwierzyniec** Poland
226 G3 **Zwiesel** Germany
226 D1 **Zwolle** Netherlands
130 E5 **Zwolle** Louisiana USA
226 G2 **Zwönitz** Germany
227 K1 **Żyrardów** Poland
237 AF5 **Zyryanka** Russian Federation
389 N3 **Zyryanovsk** Kazakhstan
227 L2 **Żyrzyn** Poland
227 J3 **Żywiec** Poland
385 H6 **Zoucheng** Shandong China
300 D4 **Zouérat** Mauritania
234 F1 **Zozov** Ukraine
384 E3 **Zrdenemandan** Mongolia
234 B3 **Zrenjanin** Serbia
231 J6 **Zribet Ahmed** Algeria
381 F2 **Shishou** Hubei China
238 H3 **Shishovka** Russian Federation
242 C1 **Shiskine** North Ayrshire Scotland UK
154 B5 **Shitihuaca** Ecuador
384 F3 **Shivee Gov** Mongolia
126 I7 **Shively** Kentucky USA
392 D6 **Shivpuri** Madhya Pradesh India
393 C6 **Shivrajpur** Gujarat India
309 F2 **Shiwa Ngandu** Zambia
384 G5 **Shiwan** Shaanxi China
380 F2 **Shiyan** Hubei China
388 I3 **Shiyli** *lake* Kazakhstan
381 H1 **Shizilu** Shandong China
384 F5 **Shizuishan** Zishiqu China
387 I2 **Shizunai** Japan
387 H4 **Shizuoka** Japan
238 H5 **Shkin'** Russian Federation
227 L3 **Shklo** Ukraine
388 D3 **Shklovo** Russian Federation
225 P5 **Shklow** Belarus
234 A4 **Shkodër** Albania
235 B5 **Shkumbin** *watercourse* Albania
238 D3 **Shlissel'burg** Russian Federation
234 F1 **Shlyakhova** Ukraine
236 S2 **Shmidta, Ostrov** *island* Russian Federation
237 AD8 **Shmidta, Poluostrov** *peninsula* Russian Federation
225 O5 **Sho, Vozyera** *lake* Belarus
119 U7 **Shoal Lake** Manitoba Canada
120 H8 **Shoal Lake** Ontario Canada
120 G7 **Shoal Lakes** Manitoba Canada
386 G4 **Shobara** Japan
386 G4 **Shodo-shima** *island* Japan
127 N6 **Shoemakersville** Pennsylvania USA
388 I6 **Shofirkon** Uzbekistan
236 P4 **Shokal'skogo, Ostrov** *island* Russian Federation
389 L3 **Sholaksor** *lake* Kazakhstan
223 R4 **Shomba** Russian Federation
223 R4 **Shombozero, Ozero** *lake* Russian Federation
388 H4 **Shomishkol'** Kazakhstan
77 S14 **Shona Ridge** *underwater feature* Atlantic Ocean
379 G3 **Shongar Dzong** Bhutan
126 D3 **Shooks** Minnesota USA
240 C4 **Shop** Cornwall England UK
238 H4 **Shopsha** Russian Federation
389 L3 **Shoptykol'** Kazakhstan
391 K4 **Shoran** Pakistan
121 N1 **Shoran Bay** Nunavut Canada
388 E6 **Shorbachy** Azerbaijan
389 J6 **Sho'rchi** Uzbekistan
124 D3 **Shoreline** Washington USA
308 D3 **Shorobe** Botswana
389 K3 **Shortandy** Kazakhstan
426 8 **Shortland** *island* Solomon Islands
388 I4 **Shoshkakol** *lake* Kazakhstan
128 D3 **Shoshone** California USA
124 H5 **Shoshone** Idaho USA
125 J4 **Shoshone Lake** Wyoming USA
124 G6 **Shoshone Mountains** Nevada USA
308 E4 **Shoshong** Botswana
125 K5 **Shoshoni** Wyoming USA
394 E2 **Shostka** Ukraine
423 C7 **Shotover** *watercourse* New Zealand
241 F2 **Shotteswell** Warwickshire England UK
385 I6 **Shouguang** Shandong China
385 H5 **Shouyang** Shanxi China
128 G3 **Show Low** Arizona USA
302 F5 **Showak** Sudan
236 J5 **Shoyna** Russian Federation
238 I2 **Shozhma** Russian Federation
234 G1 **Shpola** Ukraine
234 F1 **Shpykiv** Ukraine
240 E2 **Shrawardine** Shropshire England UK
130 E4 **Shreveport** Louisiana USA
241 F2 **Shrewley** Warwickshire England UK
240 E2 **Shrewsbury** Shropshire England UK
393 C7 **Shrivardhan** Maharashtra India
245 C4 **Shrone** Ireland
241 H2 **Shropham** Norfolk England UK
240 E2 **Shropshire** *admin. area* England UK
245 C3 **Shruthair** Ireland
389 L5 **Shu** Kazakhstan
385 K3 **Shuangcheng** Heilongjiang China
384 G5 **Shuanghuyu** Shaanxi China
380 F3 **Shuangjiang** Hunan China
385 J4 **Shuangliao** Jilin China
385 K4 **Shuangyang** Jilin China
385 L3 **Shuangyashan** Heilongjiang China
381 G2 **Shuangzhong** Jiangxi China
302 C1 **Shu'bah, Wādi ash** *watercourse* Libya
388 J4 **Shubar-tengiz** *lake* Kazakhstan
388 G3 **Shubarkuduk** Kazakhstan
381 G2 **Shucheng** Anhui China
381 H1 **Shucheng** Jiangsu China
382 E5 **Shufu** Xinjiang Uygur Zizhiqu China
238 F3 **Shugozero** Russian Federation
238 E5 **Shui** Russian Federation
382 F4 **Shuiding** Xinjiang Uygur Zizhiqu China
381 H2 **Shuihu** Anhui China
380 E1 **Shuiluocheng** Gansu China
381 G4 **Shuizhai** Guangdong China
385 K4 **Shulan** Jilin China
382 E5 **Shule** Xinjiang Uygur Zizhiqu China
383 K5 **Shule He** *watercourse* Gansu China
388 J7 **Shūlgareh** Afghanistan
384 G5 **Shulinzhao** Nei Mongol Zizhiqu China
126 F5 **Shullsburg** Wisconsin USA
238 G3 **Shulma** Russian Federation
225 P3 **Shum** Russian Federation
116 C8 **Shumagin Islands** Alaska USA
308 E3 **Shumba** Zimbabwe
234 E4 **Shumen** *admin. area* Bulgaria
388 I2 **Shumikha** Russian Federation
237 AG8 **Shumshu, Ostrov** *island* Kuril Islands
381 G4 **Shunde** Guangdong China
223 S5 **Shun'ga** Russian Federation
388 C1 **Shunga** Russian Federation
381 F3 **Shunling** Hunan China
385 H5 **Shunyi** Beijing China
223 Q4 **Shuopolaksha, Ozero** *lake* Russian Federation
130 G4 **Shuqualak** Mississippi USA
388 F6 **Shuraabad** Azerbaijan
391 H2 **Shūrab** Iran
388 H6 **Shurak** Iran
389 L3 **Shureksor Koli** *lake* Kazakhstan
388 J6 **Shurguzar** Uzbekistan
390 G3 **Shūrjestān** Iran
308 E3 **Shurugwi** Zimbabwe
388 I6 **Shuruk** Uzbekistan
390 F3 **Shūsh** Iran
390 F3 **Shūshtar** Iran
118 L7 **Shuswap Lake** British Columbia Canada
223 S6 **Shuya** Russian Federation
388 D2 **Shuya** Russian Federation
116 D7 **Shuyak Island** Alaska USA
223 S4 **Shuyeretskoye** Russian Federation
225 O4 **Shvanibakhovo** Russian Federation
379 H4 **Shwebo** Myanmar
376 B3 **Shwedaung** Myanmar
379 H4 **Shwego** Myanmar
376 C3 **Shwegyin** Myanmar
379 H4 **Shweli** *watercourse* Myanmar
379 H4 **Shweudaung** *mountain* Myanmar
389 L3 **Shybyndy Koli** *lake* Kazakhstan
389 L3 **Shyganak** *lake* Kazakhstan
389 K5 **Shymkent (Chimkent)** Kazakhstan
238 B6 **Shyshchytsy** Belarus
376 D4 **Si Racha** Thailand
376 E4 **Si Sa Ket** Thailand
372 E5 **Sia** Indonesia
244 B2 **Siabost** Na h-Eileanan Siar Scotland UK
374 C3 **Siabu** Indonesia
391 M2 **Siachen Glacier** Pakistan
244 B2 **Siadar Uarach** Na h-Eileanan Siar Scotland UK
391 J2 **Siāhkāki** Afghanistan
374 D3 **Siak** *watercourse* Indonesia
391 M3 **Sialkot** Pakistan
373 H5 **Sialum** Papua New Guinea

155 E3 **Siamacu, Sabana** *region* Venezuela
374 E3 **Siantan** *island* Indonesia
155 E4 **Siapa** *watercourse* Venezuela
377 J5 **Siargao** *island* Philippines
377 I6 **Siasi** Philippines
377 I6 **Siasi** *island* Philippines
377 I5 **Siaton** Philippines
372 C3 **Siau** *island* Indonesia
225 L5 **Šiauliai** Lithuania
225 L5 **Šiaulių** *admin. area* Lithuania
134 E2 **Sibanicú** Cuba
154 C3 **Sibaté** Colombia
388 H3 **Sibay** Russian Federation
309 F5 **Sibaya, Lake** *lake* South Africa
119 P7 **Sibbald** Alberta Canada
232 F5 **Šibenik** Croatia
154 C4 **Siberia** Colombia
Siberia *see* **Sibir'** Russian Federation
434 Q1 **Siberia Abyssal Plain** *underwater feature* Arctic Ocean
374 C4 **Siberut** *island* Indonesia
374 C4 **Siberut, Selat** *strait* Indonesia
374 C4 **Siberut, Taman Nasional** *park* Indonesia
373 G6 **Sibidiri** Papua New Guinea
374 B3 **Sibigo** Indonesia
237 W/X5 **Sibir' (Siberia)** *region* Russian Federation
236 Q4 **Sibiryakova, Ostrov** *island* Russian Federation
305 G5 **Sibiti** Congo
234 D3 **Sibiu** Romania
234 D3 **Sibiu** *admin. area* Romania
241 H3 **Sible Hedingham** Essex England UK
125 R5 **Sibley** Iowa USA
130 E4 **Sibley** Louisiana USA
154 E5 **Sibó** Brazil
374 C3 **Sibolga** Indonesia
374 C3 **Siborongborong** Indonesia
379 H3 **Sibsagar** Assam India
241 H1 **Sibsey** Lincolnshire England UK
375 F3 **Sibu** Malaysia
377 I6 **Sibuco** Philippines
377 I6 **Sibuguey Bay** Philippines
305 H3 **Sibut** Central African Republic
375 G2 **Sibuti** Malaysia
377 H6 **Sibutu** *island* Philippines
377 H6 **Sibutu Passage** *strait* Philippines
377 I4 **Sibuyan** *island* Philippines
377 I4 **Sibuyan Sea** Philippines
128 G5 **Sibyl** Arizona USA
234 C2 **Sic** Romania
118 L7 **Sicamous** British Columbia Canada
377 I3 **Sicapoo, Mount** *mountain* Philippines
158 C5 **Sicera** Peru
234 C4 **Sićevo** Serbia
380 E4 **Sicheng** Guangxi Zhuangzu Zizhiqu China
234 B3 **Sichevița** Romania
379 J2 **Sichuan** *admin. area* China
229 G5 **Sicié, Cap** *cape* France
233 E8 **Sicilia** *admin. area* Italy
233 F8 **Sicilia** *island* Italy
233 E8 **Sicilian Channel** Mediterranean Sea
241 H2 **Sicklesmere** Suffolk England UK
134 C4 **Sicsayeri** Honduras
234 D2 **Siculeni** Romania
234 A3 **Šid** Serbia
119 S1 **Sid Lake** Northwest Territories Canada
375 F3 **Sidas** Indonesia
240 D4 **Sidbury** Devon England UK
245 F3 **Siddan** Ireland
392 C6 **Siddhapur** Gujarat India
242 E2 **Siddick** Cumbria England UK
243 F3 **Siddington** Cheshire England UK
393 E7 **Siddipet** Andhra Pradesh India
235 G7 **Side** Turkey
222 L5 **Sideby** Finland
373 I6 **Sideia Island** Papua New Guinea
222 K5 **Sidensjö** Sweden
233 G7 **Siderno** Italy
235 E8 **Sideros, Akra** *cape* Greece
240 D4 **Sidford** Devon England UK
392 E5 **Sidhauli** Uttar Pradesh India
392 E6 **Sidhi** Madhya Pradesh India
231 G6 **Sidi** Algeria
301 G1 **Sidi Aïssa** Algeria
301 G1 **Sidi Ali** Algeria
231 F6 **Sidi Ali Boussidi** Algeria
302 D1 **Sidi Barrâni** Egypt
231 F6 **Sidi Bel Abbes** Algeria
301 F2 **Sidi Bel Abbes** *admin. area* Algeria
231 G6 **Sidi Bou Bekeur** Algeria
301 H2 **Sidi Bou Zid** Tunisia
233 C8 **Sidi Ferjani** Tunisia
300 D3 **Sidi Ifni** Morocco
300 E2 **Sidi Kacem** Morocco
301 G2 **Sidi Khaled** Algeria
231 H6 **Sidi Ladjel** Algeria
300 E2 **Sidi Slimane** Morocco
300 E2 **Sidi Smaïl** Morocco
374 C3 **Sidikalang** Indonesia
241 H4 **Sidley** East Sussex England UK
436 P1 **Sidley, Mount** *mountain* Antarctica
240 D4 **Sidmouth** Devon England UK
118 J8 **Sidney** British Columbia Canada
125 P2 **Sidney** Manitoba Canada
126 D6 **Sidney** Iowa USA
125 M3 **Sidney** Montana USA
125 N6 **Sidney** Nebraska USA
126 I6 **Sidney** Ohio USA
131 J3 **Sidney Lanier, Lake** Georgia USA
304 C2 **Sido** Mali
372 B3 **Sidoan** Indonesia
375 G5 **Sidoarjo** Indonesia
379 H5 **Sidoktaya** Myanmar
130 F4 **Sidon** Mississippi USA
225 L5 **Sidory** Poland
159 H6 **Sidrolândia** Brazil
222 I5 **Sidsjö** Sweden
222 K4 **Siebnesjaure** *lake* Sweden
227 L1 **Siedlce** Poland
226 D2 **Sieg** *watercourse* Germany
229 I1 **Siegen** Germany
222 J3 **Sieldutjåkkå** *watercourse* Sweden
373 I4 **Siemens, Cape** Papua New Guinea
227 L1 **Siemiatycze** Poland
376 E4 **Siĕmpang** Cambodia
376 D4 **Siĕmréab** Cambodia
380 E4 **Si'en** Guangxi Zhuangzu Zizhiqu China
232 D5 **Siena** Italy
227 L2 **Sieniawa** Poland
227 L2 **Sienica Różana** Poland
227 K2 **Sienno** Poland
227 J2 **Sieradz** Poland
226 D4 **Sierentz** France
230 D2 **Siero** Spain
227 J1 **Sierpc** Poland
162 D2 **Sierra, Punta** *cape* Argentina
162 C3 **Sierra Chata** Argentina
162 C2 **Sierra Colorada** Argentina
160 D2 **Sierra Gorda** Chile
162 D2 **Sierra Grande** Argentina
304 B3 **Sierra Leone** *country* Africa
76 Q9 **Sierra Leone Basin** *underwater feature* Atlantic Ocean
76 P9 **Sierra Leone Rise** *underwater feature* Atlantic Ocean
128 C3 **Sierra Madre Mountains** California USA
129 K7 **Sierra Mojada** Mexico
162 C3 **Sierra Nevada** Argentina
162 D2 **Sierra Pailemán** Argentina
132 E4 **Sierra Vieja** Mexico
128 G5 **Sierra Vista** Arizona USA
127 N3 **Siesta, Lac de la** *lake* Québec Canada
158 B2 **Siete de Junio** Peru
234 D2 **Șieu-Odorhei** Romania
223 N5 **Sievi** Finland
303 G5 **Sifeni** Ethiopia
235 D7 **Sifnos** *island* Greece
301 F1 **Sig** Algeria
223 S4 **Sig** Russian Federation
235 E6 **Sığacık Körfezi** *bay* Turkey
427 9a **Sigatoka** Fiji
374 C4 **Sigep, Tanjung** *island* Indonesia
222 I2 **Sigerfjord** Norway
240 D4 **Sigford** Devon England UK
117 N4 **Sigguup Nunaa** *region* Greenland
374 B2 **Sigli** Indonesia
222 inset **Siglufjörður** Iceland
232 D5 **Signa** Italy
241 F3 **Signet** Oxfordshire England UK
226 C3 **Signy-l'Abbaye** France
374 C4 **Sigoisooinan** Indonesia
126 E6 **Sigourney** Iowa USA
235 D6 **Sigri** Greece
232 B3 **Sigriswil** Switzerland
230 E3 **Sigüenza** Spain
304 C2 **Siguiri** Guinea
225 M4 **Sigulda** Latvia
124 J7 **Sigurd** Utah USA
374 C3 **Sihabuhabu, Gunung** *mountain* Indonesia
394 G5 **Sıhanköy** Turkey
393 C7 **Sihor** Gujarat India
392 E6 **Sihor** Madhya Pradesh India
381 F4 **Sihui** Guangdong China
223 N4 **Siikajoki** Finland
223 N4 **Siikajoki** *watercourse* Finland
225 N1 **Siilinjärvi** Finland
394 G6 **Siirt** Turkey
394 G6 **Siirt** *admin. area* Turkey
426 6a **Siis** *island* Federated States of Micronesia
381 I2 **Sijiao Shan** *range* Zhejiang China
390 E2 **Sijin** Iraq
374 D4 **Sijunjung** Indonesia
426 8 **Sikaiana** *island* Solomon Islands
374 D4 **Sikakap** Indonesia
118 J4 **Sikanni Chief** British Columbia Canada
392 D5 **Sikar** Rajasthan India
391 L2 **Sikārām Sar** *mountain* Afghanistan
304 C2 **Sikasso** Mali
304 C2 **Sikasso** *admin. area* Mali
235 C5 **Sikea** Greece
222 L4 **Sikeå** Sweden
372 B5 **Sikeli** Indonesia
126 G8 **Sikeston** Missouri USA
222 L4 **Sikfors** Sweden
376 D4 **Sikhiu** Thailand
387 H1 **Sikhote-Alin** Russian Federation
237 AC9 **Sikhote Alin** *range* Russian Federation
155 H4 **Sikini** French Guiana
235 D7 **Sikinos** *island* Greece
222 E6 **Sikkelbreen** *glacier* Norway
392 G5 **Sikkim** *admin. area* India
227 J5 **Siklós** Hungary
372 C3 **Siko** *island* Indonesia
308 D3 **Sikongo** Zambia
222 J4 **Siksele** Sweden
222 J4 **Siksjö** Sweden
222 J4 **Siksjö/Siksjöhöjden** Sweden
237 Z5 **Siktyakh** Russian Federation
375 H2 **Sikuati** Malaysia
230 C2 **Sil** *watercourse* Spain
225 L5 **Šilalė** Lithuania
232 D3 **Silandro** Italy
130 G5 **Silas** Alabama USA
225 L5 **Šilavotas** Lithuania
376 B6 **Silawaih Agam** *mountain* Indonesia
377 I5 **Silay** Philippines
232 F5 **Silba** Croatia
379 G4 **Silchar** Assam India
120 H4 **Silcox** Manitoba Canada
235 F5 **Şile** Turkey
242 E2 **Silecroft** Cumbria England UK
235 D5 **Silen** Bulgaria
226 E4 **Silenen** Switzerland
131 L3 **Siler City** North Carolina USA
393 E8 **Sileru** *watercourse* Andhra Pradesh India
301 G4 **Silet** Algeria
389 K3 **Sileti Bögeni** *lake* Kazakhstan
389 L2 **Siletitengiz Koli** *lake* Kazakhstan
124 D4 **Siletz** Oregon USA
392 E5 **Silgarhi** Nepal
379 G3 **Silghat** Assam India
310 9a **Silhouette** *island* Seychelles
240 C2 **Silian** Ceredigion Wales UK
301 H1 **Siliana** Tunisia
394 E6 **Silifke** Turkey
237 X5 **Siligir** *watercourse* Russian Federation
307 G1 **Silil** *watercourse* Somalia
427 12c **Silisili, Mount** *volcano* Samoa
234 D3 **Siliştea** Romania
234 E4 **Silistra** *admin. area* Bulgaria
235 F5 **Silivri** Turkey
224 H2 **Siljan** *lake* Sweden
224 F2 **Siljuberget** Norway
231 F4 **Silla** Spain
225 N3 **Sillamäe** Estonia
223 M5 **Sillanpää** Finland
232 D4 **Sillara, Monte** *mountain* Italy
224 G2 **Sillerö** Sweden
304 D2 **Silli** Burkina Faso
393 D7 **Sillod** Maharashtra India
228 C2 **Sillon de Talbert** *peninsula* France
242 E2 **Silloth** Cumbria England UK
222 J5 **Sillre** Sweden
224 I2 **Sillvik** Sweden
244 F3 **Sillyearn** Moray Scotland UK
373 I6 **Silo Silo** Papua New Guinea
130 D2 **Siloam Springs** Arkansas USA
394 G6 **Silopi** Turkey
222 J2 **Silsand** Norway
130 D5 **Silsbee** Texas USA
120 H5 **Silsby Lake** Manitoba Canada
125 L7 **Silt** Colorado USA
124 C5 **Siltcoos Lake** Oregon USA
119 S7 **Silton** Saskatchewan Canada
375 F3 **Siluas** Indonesia
238 B4 **Siļukalns** Latvia
305 F3 **Siluko** Nigeria
305 F3 **Siluko** *watercourse* Nigeria
224 G5 **Silvåkra** Sweden
394 G5 **Silvan** Turkey
157 B7 **Silvânia** Brazil
393 C7 **Silvassa** Dadra and Nagar Haveli India
119 V7 **Silver Bay** Manitoba Canada
126 F3 **Silver Bay** Minnesota USA
129 H4 **Silver City** New Mexico USA
125 M7 **Silver Cliff** Colorado USA
118 L7 **Silver Creek** British Columbia Canada
125 Q6 **Silver Creek** Nebraska USA
127 L5 **Silver Creek** New York USA
126 G2 **Silver Islet** Ontario Canada
126 I6 **Silver Lake** Indiana USA
126 E7 **Silver Lake** Missouri USA
124 E5 **Silver Lake** Oregon USA
124 D3 **Silver Lake** Washington USA
126 G2 **Silver Mountain** Ontario Canada
128 D2 **Silver Peak Range** Nevada USA
128 C1 **Silver Springs** Nevada USA
241 F2 **Silverstone** Northamptonshire England UK
118 K8 **Silvertip Mountain** British Columbia Canada
425 L7 **Silverton** NSW Australia
118 M8 **Silverton** British Columbia Canada
240 D4 **Silverton** Devon England UK
125 L8 **Silverton** Colorado USA
129 L3 **Silverton** Texas USA
119 U7 **Silverwood** Manitoba Canada
230 B5 **Silves** Portugal
233 F5 **Silvi** Italy
240 E2 **Silvington** Shropshire England UK
121 Q5 **Silvy, Lac** *lake* Québec Canada
237 AD4 **Sil'yeyaki** Russian Federation
238 H4 **Sima** Russian Federation
238 C6 **Simanovichi** Belarus
235 C5 **Simantra** Greece
380 C4 **Simao** Yunnan China
157 E5 **Simão Dias** Brazil
377 I4 **Simara** *island* Philippines
117 L9 **Simard, Lac** *lake* Québec Canada
235 F6 **Simav** *watercourse* Turkey
132 E6 **Simba, Volcán** *volcano* Chile
229 K2 **Simbach am Inn** Germany
235 D5 **Simbâta** Romania
373 J4 **Simberi Island** Papua New Guinea
305 J2 **Simbi, Ouadi** *watercourse* Chad
426 8 **Simbo** *island* Solomon Islands
127 K5 **Simcoe** Ontario Canada
127 L4 **Simcoe, Lake** Ontario Canada
392 F6 **Simdega** Jharkhand India
374 E3 **Simei** *admin. area* Singapore
237 W6 **Simenga** Russian Federation
234 C3 **Simeria** Romania
233 F8 **Simeto** *watercourse* Italy
374 C3 **Simeulue** *island* Indonesia
128 C3 **Simi Valley** California USA
392 E5 **Simikot** Nepal
376 C5 **Similan, Ko** *island* Thailand
118 K8 **Similkameen** *watercourse* British Columbia Canada
305 I3 **Simindou** Central African Republic
154 C3 **Simití** Colombia
235 C5 **Simitli** Bulgaria
307 E4 **Simiyu** *watercourse* Tanzania
125 M7 **Simla** Colorado USA
229 H2 **Simmern** Germany
130 F5 **Simmesport** Louisiana USA
119 Q8 **Simmie** Saskatchewan Canada
225 L5 **Simnas** Lithuania
223 N4 **Simo** Finland
156 D4 **Simões** Brazil
223 O3 **Simojärvi** *lake* Finland
223 N4 **Simojoki** *watercourse* Finland
155 H3 **Simon** French Guiana
118 L5 **Simonette** *watercourse* Alberta Canada
119 U5 **Simonhouse** Manitoba Canada
240 D3 **Simonsbath** Somerset England UK
224 I3 **Simonstorp** Sweden
374 E4 **Simpang** Indonesia
374 D2 **Simpang Empat** Malaysia
374 D3 **Simpang Renggam** Malaysia
225 O2 **Simpelejärvi** *lake* Finland
156 D4 **Simplício Mendes** Brazil
119 S7 **Simpson** Saskatchewan Canada
119 P8 **Simpson** Montana USA
425 J6 **Simpson Desert** NT Australia
119 O2 **Simpson Islands** Northwest Territories Canada
124 G7 **Simpson Park Mountains** Nevada USA
117 K5 **Simpson Peninsula** Nunavut Canada
131 J3 **Simpsonville** South Carolina USA
122 F6 **Sims Lake** Newfoundland and Labrador Canada
124 E4 **Simtustus, Lake** Oregon USA
374 C4 **Simuk** *island* Indonesia
225 N3 **Simuna** Estonia
375 F3 **Simunjan** Malaysia
377 H6 **Simunul** *island* Philippines
237 AF9 **Simushir, Ostrov** *island* Kuril Islands
387 L1 **Simushir, Ostrov** *island* Russian Federation
377 G5 **Sin Cowe Island** Spratly Islands
162 B5 **Sin Nombre, Peninsula** *peninsula* Chile
158 D4 **Sina** Peru
307 H2 **Sina Dhaqa** Somalia
374 C3 **Sinabang** Indonesia
374 C3 **Sinabung** *volcano* Indonesia
302 E2 **Sinai** *peninsula* Egypt
Sinai, Mount *see* **Mûsa, Jabal** Egypt
234 D3 **Sinaia** Romania
132 D3 **Sinaloa** *admin. area* Mexico
132 D3 **Sinaloa** *watercourse* Mexico
132 C3 **Sinaloa de Leyva** Mexico
301 I2 **Sīnāwin** Libya
391 J2 **Sinay** Afghanistan
308 E3 **Sinazongwe** Zambia
379 H5 **Sinbaungwe** Myanmar
154 C2 **Sincé** Colombia
154 C2 **Sincelejo** Colombia
Sinchaingbyin *see* **Maungdaw** Myanmar
119 U8 **Sinclair** Manitoba Canada
125 L6 **Sinclair** Wyoming USA
131 J4 **Sinclair, Lake** Georgia USA
155 G3 **Sinclair Landing** Guyana
234 C2 **Sincraiu** Romania
392 D6 **Sind** *watercourse* Madhya Pradesh India
309 F2 **Sinda** Zambia
374 E5 **Sindangbarang** Indonesia
372 B6 **Sindeh, Teluk** *bay* Indonesia
232 C2 **Sindelfingen** Germany
393 D8 **Sindgi** Karnataka India
391 K4 **Sindh** *admin. area* Pakistan
393 D8 **Sindhnur** Karnataka India
302 C4 **Sindi, Wādi** *watercourse* Sudan
233 C6 **Sindia** Sardinia Italy
235 F6 **Sındırgı** Turkey
304 E2 **Sinende** Benin
127 N7 **Sinepuxent Bay** Maryland USA
230 B5 **Sines** Portugal
230 B5 **Sines, Cabo de** *cape* Portugal
223 N3 **Sinettä** Finland
223 N3 **Sinettäjärvi** *lake* Finland
373 I5 **Sinewit, Mount** Papua New Guinea
304 C3 **Sinfra** Côte d'Ivoire
302 E5 **Singa** Sudan
392 E5 **Singahi Bhiraura** Uttar Pradesh India
374 D3 **Singapore** *country*
374 D3 **Singapore** Singapore
374 C3 **Singapore Island** Singapore
374 E5 **Singapore Strait** Singapore
375 G6 **Singaraja** Indonesia
427 12a **Singavé** Wallis and Futuna
427 12a **Singavé, Mont** *mountain* Wallis and Futuna
376 D4 **Singburi** *admin. area* Thailand
232 C3 **Singen** Germany
234 E3 **Singeru** Romania
307 E4 **Singida** Tanzania
307 E5 **Singida** *admin. area* Tanzania
372 B5 **Singkang** Indonesia
374 D4 **Singkarak** Indonesia
374 F3 **Singkawang** Indonesia
374 E4 **Singkep** *island* Indonesia
374 C3 **Singkil** Indonesia
374 C3 **Singkuang** Indonesia
224 F3 **Singlefjorden** *bay* Norway
425 J6 **Singleton** NSW Australia
225 J2 **Singö** *island* Sweden
222 J5 **Singsjön** *lake* Sweden
222 I5 **Singsjön/Slåttön** Sweden
376 D2 **Sinh Hồ** Vietnam
386 E3 **Sinhŭng** North Korea
388 H3 **Siniy Shikhan** Russian Federation
232 G5 **Sinj** Croatia
386 E4 **Sinji-do** *island* South Korea
302 F4 **Sinkat** Sudan
386 E3 **Sinmi-do** *island* North Korea
226 E2 **Sinn** *watercourse* Germany
155 H3 **Sinnamary** French Guiana
155 H3 **Sinnamary, Fleuve** *watercourse* French Guiana
234 F3 **Sinoie, Lacul** *lake* Romania
394 E5 **Sinop** Turkey
394 E5 **Sinop** *admin. area* Turkey
305 E3 **Sinou** Nigeria
386 F3 **Sinp'o** North Korea
232 C3 **Sins** Switzerland
234 D2 **Sinsimion** Romania
237 AA6 **Sinsk** Russian Federation
226 C2 **Sint-Amands** Belgium
163 1b **Sint Christoffelberg** *mountain* Netherlands Antilles
163 20 **Sint Eustatius** *island* Netherlands Antilles
163 20 **Sint Maarten** *Netherlands territory* Caribbean
163 20 **Sint Maarten** *island* Netherlands Antilles
163 1a **Sint Nicolaas** Aruba
375 F3 **Sintang** Indonesia
130 C6 **Sinton** Texas USA
238 G4 **Sintsovo** Russian Federation
154 C2 **Sinu** *watercourse* Colombia
385 J5 **Sinŭiju** Liaoning China
307 H2 **Sinujif** Somalia
374 E5 **Sinumbra** Indonesia
226 E3 **Sinzheim** Germany
229 H1 **Sinzig** Germany
224 J2 **Sió** *watercourse* Hungary
377 I6 **Siocon** Philippines
227 J5 **Siófok** Hungary
229 H3 **Sion** Switzerland
245 E2 **Sion Mills** Strabane Northern Ireland UK
122 M1 **Sioraq** *plain* Greenland
228 F4 **Sioule** *watercourse* France
125 Q5 **Sioux Center** Iowa USA
125 Q5 **Sioux City** Iowa USA
125 Q5 **Sioux Falls** South Dakota USA
120 J7 **Sioux Lookout** Ontario Canada
126 D5 **Sioux Rapids** Iowa USA
158 C4 **Sipaci** Peru
375 H2 **Sipadan, Pulau** *island* Malaysia
155 H4 **Sipaliwini** *admin. area* Suriname
375 F3 **Sipang, Tanjong** *cape* Malaysia
163 9 **Siparia** Trinidad and Tobago
163 9 **Siparia** *admin. area* Trinidad and Tobago
158 E5 **Sipe Sipe** Bolivia
154 B3 **Sipí** Colombia
385 J4 **Siping** Jilin China
375 G2 **Sipitang** Malaysia
119 W5 **Sipiwesk** Manitoba Canada
119 W5 **Sipiwesk Lake** Manitoba Canada
436 P2 **Siple, Mount** *mountain* Antarctica
436 N1 **Siple Coast** Antarctica
436 P2 **Siple Island** Antarctica
377 I4 **Sipocot** Philippines
223 N4 **Sipola** Finland
232 G4 **Šipovo** Bosnia and Herzegovina
130 H4 **Sipsey** *watercourse* Alabama USA
374 C4 **Sipura** *island* Indonesia
374 C4 **Sipura, Selat** *strait* Indonesia
303 I5 **Şiqirah** Yemen
377 I5 **Siquijor** *island* Philippines
134 D5 **Siquirres** Costa Rica
118 K6 **Sir Alexander, Mount** British Columbia Canada
390 G5 **Şīr Banī Yās** *island* United Arab Emirates
391 H4 **Şīr Bū Nu'āyr (UAE)** *island* United Arab Emirates
425 K3 **Sir Edward Pellew Group** *islands* NT Australia
424 H3 **Sir Graham Moore Islands** WA Australia
376 C5 **Sir J. Malcolm Island** Myanmar
118 H1 **Sir James MacBrien, Mount** Northwest Territories Canada
118 M7 **Sir Sandford, Mount** British Columbia Canada
118 L6 **Sir Wilfrid Laurier, Mount** British Columbia Canada
393 D9 **Sira** Karnataka India
224 D3 **Sira** Norway
224 D3 **Sira** *watercourse* Norway
233 F8 **Siracusa (Syracuse)** Italy
379 F4 **Sirajganj** Bangladesh
231 G6 **Sirat** Algeria
304 E2 **Sirba** *watercourse* Burkina Faso
158 D5 **Sircajahuira** Peru
391 I3 **Sirch** Iran
224 D3 **Sirdalsvatn** *lake* Norway
118 M8 **Sirdar** British Columbia Canada
389 J6 **Sirdaryo** Uzbekistan
389 J6 **Sirdaryo** *admin. area* Uzbekistan
307 F2 **Sirê** Ethiopia
373 H5 **Sirebi** *watercourse* Papua New Guinea
126 E4 **Siren** Wisconsin USA
234 D1 **Siret** *watercourse* Ukraine
392 G5 **Sirha** Nepal
234 B2 **Şiria** Romania
234 A3 **Sirig** Serbia
375 F3 **Sirik, Tanjong** *cape* Malaysia
372 E4 **Siriwo** *watercourse* Indonesia
391 H3 **Sīrjān** Iran
223 N3 **Sirkka** Finland
223 N3 **Sirkkakoski** Finland
223 O1 **Sirma** Norway
392 D6 **Sirmaur** Madhya Pradesh India
117 K4 **Sirmilik National Park** Nunavut Canada
392 E6 **Sirmour** Madhya Pradesh India
234 D3 **Şirna** Romania
394 G6 **Şırnak** Turkey
394 G6 **Şırnak** *admin. area* Turkey
392 C6 **Sirohi** Rajasthan India
374 C3 **Sirombu** Indonesia
307 E3 **Sironko** Uganda
393 E7 **Sirpur** Andhra Pradesh India
391 H4 **Sirrī, Jazīreh-ye** *island* Iran
392 D5 **Sirsa** Haryana India
393 E7 **Sirsa** Maharashtra India
392 F6 **Sirsa** Uttar Pradesh India
392 F6 **Sirsi** Chhattisgarh India
393 D8 **Sirsi** Karnataka India
392 D6 **Sirsi** Madhya Pradesh India
393 E7 **Sirsilla** Andhra Pradesh India
306 E3 **Sirsiri** Sudan
393 D7 **Sirur** Maharashtra India
225 M4 **Širvęnos ežeras** *lake* Lithuania
225 M5 **Širvintos** Lithuania
232 G4 **Sisak** Croatia
229 K4 **Šišan** Croatia
230 E4 **Sisante** Spain
385 I6 **Sishui** Shandong China
388 E6 **Sisiani Lerrnants** *pass* Azerbaijan
117 N5 **Sisimiut** Greenland
119 U5 **Sisipuk Lake** Manitoba Canada
126 G3 **Siskiwit Bay** Michigan USA
222 I3 **Sisovatnet** *lake* Norway
128 B3 **Sisquoc** *watercourse* California USA
226 D4 **Sissach** Switzerland
223 M5 **Sissala** Finland
373 G4 **Sissano** Papua New Guinea
125 Q4 **Sisseton** South Dakota USA
123 E9 **Sisson Branch Reservoir** New Brunswick Canada
226 B3 **Sissonne** France
391 J3 **Sīstān Daryācheh-ye** *watercourse* Afghanistan
391 I4 **Sīstān Va Balūchestān** *admin. area* Iran
229 G4 **Sisteron** France
376 B5 **Sisters Islands** Andaman and Nicobar Islands India
222 F5 **Sistranda** Norway
234 E3 **Sita Buzăului** Romania
392 D6 **Sitamau** Madhya Pradesh India
309 I3 **Sitampiky** Madagascar
380 E3 **Sitang** Guizhou China
392 E6 **Sitapur** Madhya Pradesh India
392 E5 **Sitapur** Uttar Pradesh India
222 J3 **Sitasjaure** *lake* Sweden
235 C5 **Sithonia** *peninsula* Greece
155 F5 **Sítio Castanhal** Brazil
155 F4 **Sítio do Pino** Brazil
159 H4 **Sítio Novo** Brazil
159 F3 **Sítio Paraná** Brazil
116 F7 **Sitka** Alaska USA
234 B4 **Sitnica** *watercourse* Kosovo
222 K3 **Sitojaure** *lake* Sweden
302 D2 **Sitrah** Egypt
226 C1 **Sittard** Netherlands
241 H3 **Sittingbourne** Kent England UK
302 F5 **Sittona** Eritrea
379 G5 **Sittwe (Akyab)** Myanmar
375 G5 **Situbondo** Indonesia
372 B5 **Siumpu** *island* Indonesia
427 12c **Si'umu** Samoa
372 B4 **Siuna** Indonesia
134 C4 **Siuna** Nicaragua
225 M2 **Siuntio** Finland
225 L4 **Šiupyliai** Lithuania
392 G6 **Siuri** West Bengal India
223 O4 **Siuruanjoki** *watercourse* Finland
234 F3 **Siutghiol, Lacul** *lake* Romania
234 A3 **Sivac** Serbia
393 D10 **Sivakasi** Tamil Nadu India
237 AA8 **Sivaki** Russian Federation
223 P5 **Sivakka** Finland
394 F5 **Sivas** Turkey
394 F5 **Sivas** *admin. area* Turkey
235 F6 **Sivaslı** Turkey
300 D5 **Sivé** Mauritania
225 P3 **Siverskiy** Russian Federation
302 D2 **Siwah** Egypt
302 D2 **Siwah, Wāḩāt** *lake* Egypt
392 F5 **Siwan** Bihar India
392 C6 **Siwana** Rajasthan India
229 G5 **Six-Fours-les-Plages** France
163 12 **Six Men's Bay** Barbados
134 D5 **Sixaola** Costa Rica
243 H3 **Sixhills** Lincolnshire England UK
381 H1 **Sixian** Anhui China
245 E2 **Sixmilecross** Omagh Northern Ireland UK
226 D4 **Sixt** France
302 F3 **Siyāl, Jazā'ir** *island* Sudan
380 E4 **Siyang** Guangxi Zhuangzu Zizhiqu China
308 D3 **Siyowe** *watercourse* Zambia
228 B2 **Sizun** France
224 F5 **Sjælland** *island* Denmark
222 K3 **Sjaunjaape** *island* Sweden
224 E3 **Sjåvatnet** *lake* Norway
222 L3 **Sjisjka** Sweden
224 E2 **Sjoa** *watercourse* Norway
222 G4 **Sjøåsen** Norway
224 G5 **Sjöbo** Sweden
222 E5 **Sjøholt** Norway
224 E4 **Sjørup** Denmark
222 J2 **Sjøvegan** Norway
222 I4 **Sjulsåsen** Sweden
222 F6 **Skåbu** Norway
394 E3 **Skadovs'k** Ukraine
222 H5 **Skækervatnet** *lake* Norway
117 R3 **Skærfjorden** *bay* Greenland
222 inset **Skagafjörður** *bay* Iceland
222 inset **Skagaströnd** Iceland
222 inset **Skagatá** *cape* Iceland
222 G4 **Skage** Norway
224 F4 **Skagen** Denmark
224 H3 **Skagern** *lake* Sweden
236 C7 **Skagerrak** *strait* Norway
224 I4 **Skäggenäs** *island* Sweden
124 E2 **Skagit** *watercourse* Washington USA
116 F7 **Skagway** Alaska USA
223 N1 **Skáiddajávri** *lake* Norway
223 N1 **Skáidi** Norway
244 D2 **Skail** Highland Scotland UK
235 C7 **Skála** Greece
227 J2 **Skała** Poland
235 D6 **Skala Eresou** Greece
235 D5 **Skala Marion** Greece
222 I5 **Skålan** Sweden
224 G4 **Skälderviken** *bay* Sweden
232 G2 **Skalica** Slovakia
234 E4 **Skalitsa** Bulgaria
223 Q1 **Skallelv** Norway
222 J5 **Skallsjön** *lake* Sweden
222 I4 **Skalmodal** Sweden
235 D5 **Skaloti** Greece
222 H5 **Skalsvattnet** *lake* Sweden
224 G4 **Skåne** *admin. area* Sweden
222 J4 **Skansholm** Sweden
235 D6 **Skantzoura** *island* Greece
224 G3 **Skåpafors** Sweden
224 I3 **Skåra** Sweden
222 J2 **Skarberget** Norway
232 F4 **Škarda** *island* Croatia
222 K4 **Skarda** Sweden
391 M2 **Skardu** Pakistan
224 E4 **Skarp-Salling** Denmark
222 F5 **Skarsøy** *island* Norway
222 F6 **Skarstind** *mountain* Norway
222 J4 **Skarvsjön** *lake* Sweden
227 K2 **Skaryszew** Poland
224 G2 **Skasen** *lake* Norway
229 K2 **Skašov** Czech Republic
224 H2 **Skattungen** *lake* Sweden
225 L5 **Skaudvilė** Lithuania
224 E4 **Skave** Denmark
224 G3 **Skaven** Sweden
244 inset **Skaw** Shetland Scotland UK
227 J3 **Skawina** Poland
300 C4 **Skaymat** Western Sahara
118 F6 **Skedans** British Columbia Canada
225 J3 **Skedviken** *lake* Sweden
224 H3 **Skedvisjön** *lake* Sweden
118 G5 **Skeena** *watercourse* British Columbia Canada
118 G4 **Skeena Mountains** British Columbia Canada
222 inset **Skeggjastaðir** Iceland
243 I3 **Skegness** Lincolnshire England UK
222 G4 **Skei** Norway
234 B3 **Skela** Serbia
234 A4 **Skelani** Bosnia and Herzegovina
155 G3 **Skeldon** Suriname
308 B3 **Skeleton Coast** *region* Namibia
222 L4 **Skellefteå** Sweden
222 K4 **Skellefteälven** *watercourse* Sweden
222 L4 **Skelleftebukten** *bay* Sweden
222 L4 **Skelleftehamn** Sweden
245 B5 **Skelligs Rocks** Ireland
129 L3 **Skellytown** Texas USA
244 D5 **Skelmorlie** North Ayrshire Scotland UK
118 E6 **Skelu Bay** British Columbia Canada
244 F1 **Skelwick** Orkney Islands Scotland UK
232 G4 **Skender Vakuf** Bosnia and Herzegovina
240 E3 **Skenfrith** Monmouthshire Wales UK
235 C5 **Skepastón** Greece
222 J5 **Skeppshamn** Sweden
244 C5 **Skeroblingarry** Argyll and Bute Scotland UK
245 F3 **Skerries** Ireland
245 F2 **Skerries** Armagh Northern Ireland UK
227 L3 **Skhidni Karpaty** *range* Ukraine
301 I2 **Skhira** Tunisia
238 G5 **Skhodnya** Russian Federation
224 F3 **Ski** Norway
235 C6 **Skiathos** *island* Greece
126 D8 **Skiatook** Oklahoma USA
222 L2 **Skibotn** Norway
227 M1 **Skidal'** Belarus
242 E2 **Skiddan** *mountain* England UK
118 F6 **Skidegate Inlet** British Columbia Canada
130 C6 **Skidmore** Texas USA
224 E3 **Skien** Norway
227 L2 **Skierbieszów** Poland
222 K3 **Skierfajaure** *bay* Sweden
227 K2 **Skierniewice** Poland
301 H1 **Skikda** Algeria
301 H1 **Skikda** *admin. area* Algeria
224 H4 **Skillingaryd** Sweden
235 B7 **Skinari, Akra** *cape* Greece
242 E2 **Skinburness** Cumbria England UK
118 F6 **Skincuttle Inlet** British Columbia Canada
222 inset **Skinnastaður** Iceland
392 D4 **Skio** Jammu and Kashmir India/Pakistan
243 F3 **Skipton** North Yorkshire England UK
241 G2 **Skirbeck** Lincolnshire England UK
244 E2 **Skirza** Highland Scotland UK
222 K2 **Skitenelv** Norway
224 E4 **Skive** Denmark
222 G5 **Skjækra** *watercourse* Norway
224 G2 **Skjærberget** Norway
222 F6 **Skjåk** Norway
222 inset **Skjálfandafljót** *watercourse* Iceland
222 inset **Skjálfandi** *bay* Iceland
222 H4 **Skjåvika** Norway
222 H4 **Skjelbreid** Norway
222 G5 **Skjelstad** Norway
224 E5 **Skjern** Denmark
222 I3 **Skjerstad** Norway
222 L1 **Skjervøy** Norway
222 L1 **Skjervøy** *island* Norway
222 K2 **Skjold** Norway
222 E6 **Skjolden** Norway
222 J2 **Skjomen** Norway
223 O3 **Skjutövn-Omr** *island* Finland
237 Z4 **Sklad** Russian Federation
389 K6 **Skobeleva, Pik** *mountain* Kyrgyzstan
222 J2 **Skodbergvatnet** *lake* Norway
222 E5 **Skodje** Norway
232 F3 **Škofja Loka** Slovenia
223 N2 **Skoganvarre** Norway
223 P2 **Skogerøya** *island* Norway
223 P2 **Skogfoss** Norway
224 G3 **Skoghall** Sweden
222 G5 **Skogn** Norway
222 K1 **Skogsfjord** Norway
240 B3 **Skokholm Island** Wales UK
126 H5 **Skokie** Illinois USA
234 C1 **Skole** Ukraine
223 M4 **Skomakarfjärden** *bay* Sweden
240 B3 **Skomer Island** Wales UK
234 F1 **Skomoroshki** Ukraine
222 I3 **Skonseng** Norway
119 N8 **Skookumchuck** British Columbia Canada
235 C6 **Skopelos** Greece
235 C6 **Skopelos** *island* Greece
235 B4 **Skopje** Macedonia
227 I2 **Skorogoszcz** Poland
224 C2 **Skorpa** Norway
224 C2 **Skorpa** *island* Norway
222 J5 **Skorped** Sweden
224 E4 **Skørping** Denmark
224 E3 **Skottevik** Norway
235 C6 **Skourta** Greece
224 G3 **Skövde** Sweden
385 J1 **Skovorodino** Russian Federation
127 Q4 **Skowhegan** Maine USA
119 V7 **Skownan** Manitoba Canada
235 C5 **Skra** Greece
232 F4 **Skrad** Croatia
222 L3 **Skröven** Sweden
309 F4 **Skukuza** South Africa
222 K5 **Skuleskogens nationalpark** *park* Sweden
222 E5 **Skuløya** *island* Norway
222 K2 **Skulsfjord** Norway
227 J1 **Skulsk** Poland
225 M4 **Skulte** Latvia
126 F6 **Skunk** *watercourse* Iowa USA
225 K4 **Skuodas** Lithuania
223 N1 **Skuotanjar'ga** *peninsula* Norway
222 inset **Skútustaðir** Iceland
222 I2 **Skutvika** Norway
234 F1 **Skvyra** Ukraine
235 C5 **Skydra** Greece
244 B3 **Skye** *island* Scotland UK
124 E3 **Skykomish** Washington USA
235 D6 **Skyros** Greece
235 D6 **Skyros** *island* Greece
436 S1 **Skytrain Ice Rise** Antarctica
225 N5 **Slabodka** Belarus
242 B3 **Slade** Ireland
222 K4 **Slagnäs** Sweden
243 F3 **Slaidburn** Lancashire England UK
224 H3 **Slaka** Sweden
374 F5 **Slamet, Gunung** *volcano* Indonesia
227 K3 **Slaná** *watercourse* Slovakia
245 F3 **Slane** Ireland
227 K3 **Slanec** Slovakia
234 E4 **Slannik** *range* Bulgaria
232 G5 **Slano** Croatia
225 O3 **Slantsy** Russian Federation
227 H2 **Slaný** Czech Republic
130 A2 **Slapout** Oklahoma USA
222 J3 **Slappejaure** *lake* Sweden
222 K4 **Släppträsket** *lake* Sweden
241 F2 **Slapton** Northamptonshire England UK
227 J2 **Śląskie** *admin. area* Poland
126 H2 **Slate Islands** Ontario Canada
232 G4 **Slatina** Bosnia and Herzegovina
232 G4 **Slatina** Croatia
232 G2 **Slatinice** Czech Republic
234 C3 **Slătioara** Romania
129 L4 **Slaton** Texas USA
130 F5 **Slaughter** Louisiana USA
130 C3 **Slaughterville** Oklahoma USA
116 H7 **Slave** *watercourse* Alberta/Northwest Territories Canada
304 E3 **Slave Coast** Africa
119 N5 **Slave Lake** Alberta Canada
389 M3 **Slavgorod** Russian Federation
238 G4 **Slavnoye** Russian Federation
387 K2 **Slavnoye, Ozero** *lake* Russian Federation
227 H3 **Slavonice** Czech Republic
232 H4 **Slavonski Brod** Croatia
125 R5 **Slayton** Minnesota USA
245 B4 **Slea Head** *cape* Ireland
241 G2 **Sleaford** Lincolnshire England UK

244 C3 **Sleat, Sound of** bay Scotland UK
119 R5 **Sled Lake** Saskatchewan Canada
130 F3 **Sledge** Mississippi USA
117 L7 **Sleeper Islands** Nunavut Canada
243 H2 **Sleights** North Yorkshire England UK
375 F5 **Sleman** Indonesia
222 K4 **Sleng** lake Sweden
436 W1 **Slessor Glacier** Antarctica
224 C3 **Sletta** bay Norway
224 F4 **Sletterhage** cape Denmark
130 G5 **Slidell** Louisiana USA
224 E2 **Slidrefjord** bay Norway
222 I3 **Sliergaise** mountain Sweden
242 B2 **Slieve** Ireland
245 E1 **Slievebane** Ireland
245 E4 **Slieveroe** Ireland
244 B3 **Sligachan** Highland Scotland UK
245 D2 **Sligo** Ireland
245 D2 **Sligo** admin. area Ireland
245 D2 **Sligo Bay** Ireland
134 D4 **Slilmasía** Nicaragua
231 H6 **Slim** Algeria
240 E3 **Slimbridge** Gloucestershire England UK
232 D3 **Slingia** Italy
244 F3 **Slioch** Aberdeenshire Scotland UK
422 F3 **Slipper Island** New Zealand
222 G5 **Slipra** Norway
225 J4 **Slite** Sweden
234 E4 **Sliven** Bulgaria
232 F4 **Slivnica** Croatia
234 C4 **Slivnitsa** Bulgaria
227 J1 **Śliwice** Poland
225 N5 **Sloboda** Belarus
225 P5 **Sloboda** Russian Federation
234 E3 **Slobozia Bradului** Romania
124 G2 **Slocan Lake** British Columbia Canada
226 D1 **Slochteren** Netherlands
118 E3 **Sloko** watercourse British Columbia Canada
227 K2 **Słomniki** Poland
423 C8 **Slope Point** New Zealand
241 G3 **Slough** admin. area England UK
241 G3 **Slough** Slough England UK
227 K5 **Slovac** Serbia
224 C2 **Slovåg** Norway
227 J3 **Slovakia** country Europe
227 M1 **Slovatyche** Belarus
227 H5 **Slovenia** country
234 D1 **Slovita** Ukraine
236 S3 **Slozhnyy, Ostrov** island Russian Federation
227 H1 **Słubice** Poland
394 C2 **Sluch** watercourse Ukraine
226 B2 **Sluis** Netherlands
227 H5 **Slunj** Croatia
224 I5 **Słupsk** Poland
238 B6 **Slutsk** Belarus
245 B3 **Slyne Head** cape Ireland
384 E2 **Slyudyanka** Russian Federation
130 E4 **Smackover** Arkansas USA
224 H4 **Småland** region Sweden
222 G5 **Småland** Norway
224 F5 **Smålandsfarvandet** bay Denmark
241 I2 **Smallburgh** Norfolk England UK
240 E4 **Smallridge** Devon England UK
122 F6 **Smallwood Reservoir** Newfoundland and Labrador Canada
225 N5 **Smalvas ežeras** lake Lithuania
232 F3 **Šmartno** Slovenia
223 M4 **Småskären** island Sweden
119 S6 **Smeaton** Saskatchewan Canada
225 O3 **Smerdi** Russian Federation
244 E2 **Smerral** Highland Scotland UK
127 L6 **Smethport** Pennsylvania USA
227 H2 **Smidary** Czech Republic
385 M3 **Smidovich** Russian Federation
227 M2 **Smidyn** Ukraine
234 G1 **Smila** Ukraine
119 Q7 **Smiley** Saskatchewan Canada
130 C6 **Smiley** Texas USA
235 D5 **Smilyan** Bulgaria
234 D4 **Smirdioasa** Romania
229 L1 **Smiřice** Czech Republic
234 E4 **Smirnenski** Bulgaria
237 AD9 **Smirnykh** Russian Federation
119 N5 **Smith** Alberta Canada
118 H3 **Smith** watercourse British Columbia Canada
127 K4 **Smith, Cape** Ontario Canada
116 G5 **Smith Arm** Northwest Territories Canada
117 L3 **Smith Bay** Nunavut Canada
116 D4 **Smith Bay** Alaska USA
125 P7 **Smith Center** Kansas USA
436 Q1 **Smith Glacier** Antarctica
436 T2 **Smith Island** Antarctica
117 L6 **Smith Island** Nunavut Canada
131 M4 **Smith Island** North Carolina USA
131 L2 **Smith Mountain Lake** Virginia USA
118 H3 **Smith River** British Columbia Canada
117 L3 **Smith Sound** Canada/Greenland
118 H5 **Smithers** British Columbia Canada
131 L3 **Smithfield** North Carolina USA
127 L7 **Smithfield** Pennsylvania USA
127 M4 **Smiths Falls** Ontario Canada
126 H8 **Smiths Grove** Kentucky USA
424 inset **Smithson Bight** bay Christmas Island Australia
425 M10 **Smithton** Tas. Australia
126 E7 **Smithton** Missouri USA
131 I5 **Smithville** Georgia USA
130 G3 **Smithville** Mississippi USA
130 C5 **Smithville** Texas USA
238 E5 **Smogiri** Russian Federation
123 H9 **Smokey, Cape** Nova Scotia Canada
232 G5 **Smokvica** Croatia
116 H8 **Smoky** watercourse Alberta Canada
425 J8 **Smoky Bay** SA Australia
120 D6 **Smoky Burn** Saskatchewan Canada
121 N7 **Smoky Falls** Ontario Canada
125 O7 **Smoky Hill** watercourse Kansas USA
125 P7 **Smoky Hills** Kansas USA
222 F5 **Smøla** island Norway
388 F3 **Smolenka** Russian Federation
238 E5 **Smolensk** Russian Federation
238 E5 **Smolenskaya Oblast'** admin. area Russian Federation
238 E5 **Smolensko-Moskovskaya Vozvyshennost** region Russian Federation
238 E5 **Smolenskoe Poozerye National Park** Russian Federation
234 G1 **Smolino** Ukraine
235 P6 **Smolitsa** Belarus
235 D5 **Smolyan** admin. area Bulgaria
234 C4 **Smolyanovtsi** Bulgaria
225 P5 **Smolyany** Belarus
117 K9 **Smooth Rock Falls** Ontario Canada
120 E7 **Smoothrock Lake** Ontario Canada
119 R5 **Smoothstone** watercourse Saskatchewan Canada
119 R5 **Smoothstone Lake** Saskatchewan Canada
227 M2 **Smorzhiv** Ukraine
234 E1 **Smotrych** Ukraine
224 G5 **Smygehamn** Sweden
436 S2 **Smyley Island** Antarctica
163 7 **Smylie Channel** Falkland Islands
131 H3 **Smyrna** Tennessee USA
242 D2 **Snaefell** mountain Isle of Man UK
222 inset **Snæfellsjökull** mountain Iceland
234 E3 **Snagov, Lacul** lake Romania
241 H2 **Snailwell** Cambridgeshire England UK
243 G3 **Snaith** East Riding of Yorkshire England UK
124 G3 **Snake** watercourse Idaho USA
124 F3 **Snake** watercourse Washington USA
124 H7 **Snake Range** Nevada USA
118 J3 **Snake River** British Columbia Canada
124 I5 **Snake River Plain** Idaho USA
243 G2 **Snape** North Yorkshire England UK
241 I2 **Snape** Suffolk England UK
225 L2 **Snappertuna** Finland
223 M5 **Snåre** Finland
423 B9 **Snares, The** islands New Zealand
124 L6 **Snaring** watercourse Alberta Canada
222 H4 **Snåsa** Norway
222 H4 **Snåsvatnet** bay Norway
240 D2 **Snead** Powys Wales UK
241 F3 **Snead** Alabama USA
226 C1 **Sneek** Netherlands
245 C5 **Sneem** Ireland
122 H5 **Snegamook Lake** Newfoundland and Labrador Canada
121 W5 **Snelgrove Lake** Newfoundland and Labrador Canada
422 F3 **Snells Beach** New Zealand
241 H2 **Snettisham** Norfolk England UK
234 C1 **Snina** Slovakia
118 M5 **Snipe Lake** Alberta Canada
234 E1 **Snitkov** Ukraine
244 B3 **Snizort, Loch** bay Scotland UK
222 F5 **Snøhetta** mountain Norway
238 E6 **Snopot'** Russian Federation
222 F5 **Snota** mountain Norway
222 H3 **Snøtinden** mountain Norway
127 N7 **Snow Hill** Maryland USA
436 U2 **Snow Hill Island** Antarctica
119 U5 **Snow Lake** Manitoba Canada
124 H6 **Snow Water Lake** Nevada USA
116 I6 **Snowbird Lake** Northwest Territories Canada
240 C1 **Snowdon** mountain Wales UK
240 D1 **Snowdonia National Park** Wales UK
119 Q1 **Snowdrift** watercourse Northwest Territories Canada
128 G3 **Snowflake** Arizona USA
425 K8 **Snowtown** SA Australia
124 I6 **Snowville** Utah USA
135 F2 **Snug Corner** Bahamas
376 C5 **Snuŏl** Cambodia
130 B3 **Snyder** Oklahoma USA
129 L4 **Snyder** Texas USA
127 L7 **Snyder Knob** mountain West Virginia USA
386 E4 **So-do** island South Korea
372 D4 **Soabuwe** Indonesia
154 C3 **Soacha** Colombia
223 M2 **Soadnojávri** lake Norway
309 I3 **Soalala** Madagascar
391 L2 **Soan** watercourse Pakistan
386 E4 **Soan-do** island South Korea
225 P1 **Soanlahti** Russian Federation
124 F3 **Soap Lake** Washington USA
373 G5 **Soari** watercourse Papua New Guinea
309 H4 **Soaserana** Madagascar
372 C3 **Soasiu** Indonesia
154 C3 **Soatá** Colombia
244 B3 **Soay** island Scotland UK
308 C2 **Soba Matias** Angola
386 E4 **Sobaek-sanmaek** South Korea
159 E4 **Soberante** Bolivia
222 I2 **Søberg** Norway
373 G4 **Sobger** watercourse Indonesia
227 K2 **Sobienie-Jeziory** Poland
388 C2 **Sobinka** Russian Federation
237 AG8 **Sobolevo** Russian Federation
227 K2 **Sobolew** Poland
227 K2 **Sobótka** Poland
156 D5 **Sobradinho, Represa de** lake Brazil
156 D3 **Sobral** Brazil
230 E2 **Sobrón, Embalse de** lake Spain
376 E5 **Sóc Trăng** Vietnam
388 C5 **Sochi** Russian Federation
386 E4 **Sŏch'ŏn** South Korea
427 I4 **Societé, Îles de la** island French Polynesia
131 L3 **Society Hill** South Carolina USA
243 G2 **Sockburn** Darlington England UK
234 B2 **Socodor** Romania
227 K5 **Socol** Romania
160 D3 **Socompa** Chile
157 D3 **Socompa, Volcán** volcano Chile
157 C8 **Socorro** Brazil
154 C3 **Socorro** Colombia
129 K7 **Socorro** Mexico
377 J5 **Socorro** Philippines
129 I3 **Socorro** New Mexico USA
129 I5 **Socorro** Texas USA
132 C5 **Socorro, Isla** island Mexico
154 C3 **Socotá** Colombia
Socotra see **Suquṭrā** Yemen
230 F4 **Socovos** Spain
118 J6 **Soda Creek** British Columbia Canada
128 C3 **Soda Lake** California USA
124 J5 **Soda Springs** Idaho USA
223 O3 **Sodankylä** Finland
131 I3 **Soddy-Daisy** Tennessee USA
224 I4 **Söderåkra** Sweden
224 H3 **Söderälgen** lake Sweden
225 L3 **Söderby** Estonia
225 J2 **Söderfjärden** bay Finland
224 I2 **Söderhamn** Sweden
224 J3 **Södermanland** admin. area Sweden
224 I3 **Södertälje** Sweden
222 L5 **Söderudden** Finland
302 D5 **Sodiri** Sudan
307 F2 **Sodo** Ethiopia
224 H2 **Södra Barken** bay Sweden
225 K1 **Södra Björkön** island Finland
224 F3 **Södra Bullaresjön** lake Sweden
224 I2 **Södra Dellen** lake Sweden
224 I3 **Södra Enby** Sweden
224 I3 **Södra Finnö** island Sweden
222 J4 **Södra Insjö** Sweden
224 F3 **Södra Kornsjön** lake Sweden
225 J2 **Södra Kvarken** bay Sweden
222 J4 **Södra Storfjället** island Sweden
222 J4 **Södra Tresund** Sweden
222 L5 **Södra Vallgrund** Finland
227 H5 **Sodražica** Slovenia
375 J6 **Soë** Indonesia
309 G3 **Sofala** admin. area Mozambique
Sofia see **Sofiyah** Bulgaria
309 I3 **Sofia** watercourse Madagascar
234 F2 **Sofia** Moldova
235 C7 **Sofiko** Greece
234 C4 **Sofiya** admin. area Bulgaria
234 C4 **Sofiya (Sofia)** Bulgaria
234 G1 **Sofiyevka** Ukraine
234 G1 **Sofiyivka** Ukraine
237 AB8 **Sofiysk** Russian Federation
222 J2 **Søfjord** Norway
223 Q4 **Sofporog** Russian Federation
235 E7 **Sofrana** island Greece
238 G4 **Sofrino** Russian Federation
379 G2 **Sog Qu** watercourse Xizang Zizhiqu China
154 C3 **Sogamoso** Colombia
154 C3 **Sogamoso** watercourse Colombia
373 H5 **Sogeram** watercourse Papua New Guinea
389 J6 **Soghd** admin. area Tajikistan
224 D2 **Sogn og Fjordane** admin. area Norway
222 E6 **Sogndalsfjøra** Norway
224 C2 **Sognefjorden** bay Norway
224 C2 **Sognesjøen** bay Norway
307 F3 **Sogo Hills** plain Kenya
377 J5 **Sogod** Philippines
377 J5 **Sogod Bay** Philippines
235 E6 **Soğucak** Turkey
235 F7 **Söğüt** Turkey
235 G5 **Söğüt** Turkey
386 E5 **Sŏgwip'o** South Korea
Sohag see **Sawhāj** Egypt
241 H2 **Soham** Cambridgeshire England UK
234 E3 **Sohatu** Romania
386 E4 **Soheugsan-do** island South Korea
384 F2 **Sohor, Gora** mountain Russian Federation
386 E3 **Sohung** North Korea
226 G1 **Soignies** Belgium
234 C3 **Şoimuş** Romania
223 N5 **Soini** Finland
223 P5 **Soisalo** island Finland
228 F2 **Soissons** France
392 C6 **Sojat** Rajasthan India
227 I4 **Söjtör** Hungary
308 E4 **Sojwe** Botswana
386 F3 **Sokch'o** South Korea
306 C5 **Sokele** Democratic Republic of Congo
388 C5 **Sokhumi** Georgia
227 M2 **Sokil** Ukraine
223 M5 **Soklot** Finland
224 E2 **Sokna** Norway
234 B4 **Sokobanja** Serbia
304 E3 **Sokodé** Togo
238 I3 **Sokol** Russian Federation
387 I1 **Sokol** Russian Federation
232 H5 **Sokolac** Bosnia and Herzegovina
227 L1 **Sokolany** Poland
300 E6 **Sokolo** Mali
227 L1 **Sokołów Podlaski** Poland
227 L3 **Sokolya** Ukraine
300 C6 **Sokone** Senegal
223 P2 **Sokosti** mountain Finland
305 F2 **Sokoto** Nigeria
305 F2 **Sokoto** admin. area Nigeria
305 F2 **Sokoto** watercourse Nigeria
227 K3 **Sol'** Slovakia
388 G3 **Sol-iletsk** Russian Federation
306 D5 **Sola** Democratic Republic of Congo
377 I3 **Solana** Philippines
128 D4 **Solana Beach** California USA
423 B8 **Solander Islands** New Zealand
156 F4 **Solânea** Brazil
161 G6 **Solanet** Argentina
154 C4 **Solano** Colombia
129 J3 **Solano** New Mexico USA
162 C3 **Solano, Bahía** bay Argentina
393 D8 **Solapur** Maharashtra India
226 E5 **Solaro** Italy
372 C3 **Solat, Gunung** mountain Indonesia
227 H4 **Solčava** Slovenia
229 I5 **Solche, Pointe de** cape Corsica France
154 B5 **Soldado Luna** Peru
237 AI6 **Soldatovo** Russian Federation
229 I3 **Sölden** Austria
126 D5 **Soldier** watercourse Iowa USA
116 D6 **Soldotna** Alaska USA
227 K2 **Solec nad Wisłą** Poland
160 F4 **Soledad** Argentina
154 C2 **Soledad** Colombia
128 B2 **Soledad** California USA
155 E3 **Soledad** Venezuela
132 E3 **Soledad de Abajo** Mexico
132 E4 **Soledad Díez Gutiérrez** Mexico
161 H4 **Soledade** Brazil
388 D4 **Solenoye** Russian Federation
224 F2 **Solensjøen** lake Norway
241 F4 **Solent, The** strait England UK
233 C6 **Solenzara** Corsica France
304 D2 **Solenzo** Burkina Faso
222 L5 **Solf** Finland
224 H4 **Solgen** lake Sweden
232 D4 **Soliera** Italy
241 F2 **Solihull** West Midlands England UK
236 M7 **Solikamsk** Russian Federation
233 D8 **Soliman** Tunisia
226 D2 **Solingen** Germany
308 C4 **Solitaire** Namibia
224 G3 **Söljeflagen** bay Sweden
232 E4 **Solkan** Slovenia
222 J5 **Sollefteå** Sweden
224 I3 **Sollentuna** Sweden
231 H4 **Sóller** Spain
222 G4 **Sollsvika** Norway
238 G4 **Solnechnogorsk** Russian Federation
375 F5 **Solo** watercourse Indonesia
223 O2 **Solojärvi** lake Finland
374 D4 **Solok** Indonesia
125 Q7 **Solomon** Kansas USA
373 K5 **Solomon Islands** country Oceania
373 I5 **Solomon Sea** Papua New Guinea
127 Q4 **Solon** Maine USA
127 K6 **Solon** Ohio USA
126 F3 **Solon Springs** Wisconsin USA
388 J4 **Solonchak Arys** lake Kazakhstan
388 H6 **Solonchakovye Vpadiny Unguz** lake Turkmenistan
389 N3 **Soloneshnoye** Russian Federation
372 B6 **Solor** island Indonesia
372 B6 **Solor, Kepulauan** island Indonesia
427 12c **Solosolo** Samoa
229 H3 **Solothurn** Switzerland
234 C2 **Solotvyno** Ukraine
223 S4 **Solovetskiy** Russian Federation
223 S4 **Solovetskiye Ostrova** island Russian Federation
238 E5 **Solov'yëvo** Russian Federation
385 J1 **Solov'yevsk** Russian Federation
235 F5 **Sölöz** Turkey
222 G4 **Solsem** Norway
223 G3 **Solsona** Spain
234 A2 **Solt** Hungary
226 E1 **Soltau** Germany
389 O3 **Solton** Russian Federation
225 P3 **Sol'tsy** Russian Federation
235 B5 **Solunska Glava** mountain Macedonia
128 B3 **Solvang** California USA
224 H4 **Sölvesborg** Sweden
222 E6 **Solvorn** Norway
244 E6 **Solway Firth** bay Scotland UK
308 E2 **Solwezi** Zambia
392 C6 **Som** Rajasthan India
372 I4 **Soma** Japan
228 F1 **Somain** France
80 J5 **Somali Basin** underwater feature Indian Ocean
307 I1 **Somali Peninsula** peninsula Somalia
307 H2 **Somalia** country Africa
307 F5 **Somanga** Tanzania
391 I2 **Sombā** Iran
229 G3 **Sombernon** France
232 H4 **Sombor** Serbia
132 E4 **Sombrerete** Mexico
163 20 **Sombrero** island Anguilla
374 B2 **Sombrero Channel** strait India
376 B6 **Sombrero Channel** Andaman and Nicobar Islands India
160 F2 **Sombrero Negro** Argentina
161 I4 **Sombrio** Brazil
161 I4 **Sombrio, Lagoa do** lake Brazil
226 C2 **Someren** Netherlands
225 L2 **Somerniemi** Finland
127 N7 **Somers Point** New Jersey USA
127 inset **Somerset** Bermuda
240 E3 **Somerset** admin. area England UK
129 I1 **Somerset** Colorado USA
126 I8 **Somerset** Kentucky USA
127 J7 **Somerset** Ohio USA
130 B6 **Somerset** Texas USA
308 E6 **Somerset East** South Africa
127 inset **Somerset Island** Bermuda
117 J4 **Somerset Island** Nunavut Canada
308 C6 **Somerset West** South Africa
241 F3 **Somerton** Oxfordshire England UK
240 E3 **Somerton** Somerset England UK
128 E4 **Somerton** Arizona USA
127 N6 **Somerville** New Jersey USA
130 G3 **Somerville** Tennessee USA
130 C5 **Somerville** Texas USA
129 N5 **Somerville Lake** Texas USA
234 C2 **Someș** watercourse Romania
234 C2 **Someșu Cald** watercourse Romania
234 C2 **Someșu Mic** watercourse Romania
238 F3 **Somino** Russian Federation
222 K2 **Sommarøy** Norway
222 J2 **Sommarøy** island Norway
228 E1 **Somme** watercourse France
228 E1 **Somme, Baie de la** bay France
224 H4 **Sommen** lake Sweden
228 G5 **Sommières** France
228 E3 **Sommières-du-Clain** France
222 H4 **Sømna** island Norway
227 I4 **Somogy** admin. area Hungary
427 9a **Somosomo** Fiji
134 C4 **Somotillo** Nicaragua
134 C4 **Somoto** Nicaragua
393 F7 **Sompeta** Andhra Pradesh India
227 J1 **Sompolno** Poland
241 G4 **Sompting** West Sussex England UK
162 C2 **Somuncurá, Meseta de** plateau Argentina
392 F6 **Son** watercourse Madhya Pradesh India
376 D2 **Sơn La** Vietnam
231 H4 **Son Servera** Spain
226 F5 **Sona** Italy
134 D5 **Soná** Panama
237 AC8 **Sonakh** Russian Federation
389 K3 **Sonaly** Kazakhstan
389 K3 **Sonaly** Kazakhstan
392 E6 **Sonar** watercourse Madhya Pradesh India
379 H3 **Sonari** Assam India
386 F2 **Sŏnbong** North Korea
386 E3 **Sonch'ŏn** North Korea
230 E2 **Soncillo** Spain
226 F4 **Sondalo** Italy
223 R5 **Sondaly** Russian Federation
224 E5 **Sønderbo** Denmark
224 E4 **Sondervig** Denmark
122 N2 **Søndre Strøre** island Greenland
Søndre Strømfjord see **Kangerlussuaq** Greenland
393 F7 **Sonepur** Orissa India
224 E2 **Soneren** lake Norway
305 G4 **Song** Gabon
375 G3 **Song** Malaysia
376 F4 **Sông Cầu** Vietnam
376 E2 **Song Da (Black)** watercourse Vietnam
376 E2 **Song Hong (Red)** watercourse Vietnam
380 D4 **Song Ko** watercourse Yunnan China
389 L5 **Song-Kol** lake Kyrgyzstan
385 I5 **Song Ling** range Liaoning China
376 D2 **Sông Mã** Vietnam
381 F1 **Song Xian** Henan China
304 E3 **Songaw Lagoon** bay Ghana
380 F2 **Songbai** Hubei China
307 F6 **Songea** Tanzania
224 D3 **Songevatnet** lake Norway
386 E3 **Sŏnggan** North Korea
373 G4 **Songgato** watercourse Indonesia
385 L3 **Songhua Jiang** watercourse Heilongjiang China
386 E3 **Songhwa** North Korea
383 J3 **Songino** Mongolia
393 D7 **Songir** Maharashtra India
376 D6 **Songkhla** Thailand
376 D3 **Songkhram** watercourse Thailand
376 D6 **Songkla** admin. area Thailand
380 C3 **Songmai** Sichuan China
386 E4 **Sŏngnam** South Korea
386 E3 **Songnim** North Korea
307 F5 **Songo Songo** island Tanzania
380 D2 **Songpan** Sichuan China
380 E3 **Songshan** Guizhou China
380 F3 **Songtao** Guizhou China
307 E5 **Songwe** watercourse Tanzania
386 E3 **Songwŏn** North Korea
380 D3 **Songyang** Yunnan China
385 J3 **Songyuan** Jilin China
381 H3 **Songyuan** Zhejiang China
381 F2 **Songzi** Hubei China
392 F6 **Sonhat** Chhattisgarh India
392 D5 **Sonipat** Haryana India
158 E6 **Soniquera** Bolivia
223 N3 **Sonka** Finland
223 O5 **Sonkajärvi** Finland
223 O5 **Sonkari** lake Finland
391 K4 **Sonmiani** Pakistan
229 J1 **Sonneberg** Germany
119 R6 **Sonningdale** Saskatchewan Canada
156 C5 **Sono** watercourse Brazil
132 C2 **Sonora** admin. area Mexico
132 C2 **Sonora** watercourse Mexico
128 B2 **Sonora** California USA
129 L5 **Sonora** Texas USA
132 B2 **Sonoyta** Mexico
390 F2 **Sonqor** Iran
230 E4 **Sonseca** Spain
154 C3 **Sonsón** Colombia
224 E2 **Sønstevatn** lake Norway
229 I1 **Sontra** Germany
307 H2 **Sool** admin. area Somalia
161 G4 **Sopas** watercourse Uruguay
122 D1 **Soper** watercourse Nunavut Canada
131 J4 **Soperton** Georgia USA
372 D3 **Sopi, Tanjung** cape Indonesia
234 F1 **Sopin** Ukraine
235 B5 **Sopište** Macedonia
306 D2 **Sopo** watercourse Sudan
387 K2 **Sopochnoye, Ozero** lake Russian Federation
235 B5 **Sopot** Albania
225 J5 **Sopot** Poland
234 B3 **Şopotu Nou** Romania
223 O3 **Soppela** Finland
227 H4 **Sopron** Hungary
392 D3 **Sopur** Jammu and Kashmir India/Pakistan
372 C3 **Soputan, Gunung** volcano Indonesia
426 6a **Sopweru, Mochun** strait Federated States of Micronesia
222 H3 **Sør-Arnøy** Norway
224 H2 **Sör Hörken** lake Sweden
388 G4 **Sor Kaydak** lake Kazakhstan
388 G4 **Sor Mertvyy Kultuk** lake Kazakhstan
224 F2 **Sør-Mesna** lake Norway
437 B2 **Sør Rondane Mountains** Antarctica
222 G5 **Sør-Trøndelag** admin. area Norway
222 L1 **Sør Tverrfjord** Norway
222 F2 **Sør Varanger Herad** Norway
233 E6 **Sora** Italy
393 F7 **Sorada** Orissa India
222 J5 **Söråker** Sweden
222 H3 **Sørarnøy** island Norway
158 D4 **Sorata** Bolivia
158 C4 **Soraya** Peru
230 F5 **Sorbas** Spain
226 F5 **Sorbolo** Italy
223 M4 **Sörbrändöfjärden** bay Sweden
222 J5 **Sörbygden** Sweden
237 AB6 **Sordoginskiy Khrebet** range Russian Federation
127 O3 **Sorel** Québec Canada
117 L9 **Sorel-Tracy** Québec Canada
425 M10 **Sorell** Tas. Australia
226 E5 **Soresina** Italy
373 K5 **Sorezaru Point** Solomon Islands
222 I3 **Sörfjärden** bay Sweden
224 I3 **Sørfjordmoen** Norway
224 I1 **Sörfors** Sweden
231 I1 **Sorgues** France
231 H2 **Sorgues** watercourse France
230 E3 **Soria** Spain
161 G5 **Soriano** admin. area Uruguay
374 C3 **Sorikmarapi** volcano Indonesia
158 B2 **Soritor** Peru
236 D3 **Sørkappøya** cape Norway
389 L3 **Sorkopa** lake Kazakhstan
222 H3 **Sørland** Norway
222 F5 **Sørleka** island Norway
222 H4 **Sørli** Norway
222 J2 **Sørli** Norway
244 D5 **Sorn** East Ayrshire Scotland UK
224 F5 **Sorø** Denmark
393 G7 **Soro** Orissa India
163 1c **Sorobon** Netherlands Antilles
234 F1 **Soroca** Moldova
157 C8 **Sorocaba** Brazil
388 G3 **Sorochinsk** Russian Federation
223 G3 **Sorokino** Russian Federation
373 G1 **Sorol** island Federated States of Micronesia
305 G3 **Sorombéo** Cameroon
372 D4 **Sorong** Indonesia
156 B4 **Sororó** watercourse Brazil
307 E3 **Soroti** Uganda
223 M1 **Sørøya** island Norway
230 B4 **Sorraia** watercourse Portugal
130 F5 **Sorrento** Louisiana USA
222 J2 **Sorrollnes** Norway
222 K2 **Sorruisa** Norway
225 N1 **Sorsavesi** lake Finland
222 J4 **Sorsele** Sweden
224 G2 **Sörsjön** Sweden
233 C6 **Sorso** Sardinia Italy
377 J4 **Sorsogon** Philippines
231 G2 **Sort** Spain
225 P2 **Sortavala** Russian Federation
222 I2 **Sortland** Norway
222 G5 **Sørungen** lake Norway
222 H3 **Sørvær** Norway
222 H3 **Sørvågen** Norway
222 H5 **Sörvattnet** Sweden
222 J2 **Sørvik** Norway
222 G5 **Sørvika** Norway
222 I5 **Sörviken** Sweden
231 G1 **Sos** France
231 F2 **Sos del Rey Católico** Spain
386 E4 **Sŏsan** South Korea
121 Q7 **Soscumica, Lac** lake Québec Canada
225 O3 **Sosedno** Russian Federation
227 H5 **Sošice** Croatia
394 E2 **Soskovo** Russian Federation
237 W6 **Sosna** Russian Federation
394 F2 **Sosna** watercourse Russian Federation
160 D5 **Sosneado** mountain Argentina
227 I1 **Sośnica** Poland
238 C3 **Sosnitsy** Russian Federation
237 M3 **Sosniv** Ukraine
236 L6 **Sosnogorsk** Russian Federation
223 S4 **Sosnovets** Russian Federation
389 M3 **Sosnovka** Kazakhstan
389 L5 **Sosnovka** Kyrgyzstan
223 V3 **Sosnovka** Russian Federation
223 H3 **Sosnovka** Russian Federation
388 D2 **Sosnovka** Russian Federation
223 O5 **Sosnovo** Russian Federation
225 O4 **Sosnovo** Russian Federation
225 P2 **Sosnovo** Russian Federation
223 R4 **Sosnovyy** Russian Federation
223 O3 **Sosnovyy Bor** Russian Federation
236 R6 **Sosnovyy Bor** Russian Federation
227 J2 **Sosnowiec** Poland
223 N4 **Soso** Finland
229 H5 **Sospel** France
305 H4 **Sosso** Central African Republic
227 H4 **Šoštanj** Slovenia
133 G3 **Sosúa** Dominican Republic
310 4 **Sotavento, Ilhas do** island Cape Verde
224 F3 **Sotefjorden** bay Sweden
162 C2 **Sotera, Laguna** lake Argentina
159 E3 **Soterio** watercourse Brazil
223 P4 **Sotkamo** Finland
160 E4 **Soto** Argentina
163 1b **Soto** Netherlands Antilles
133 F4 **Soto La Marina** Mexico
133 F4 **Soto La Marina** watercourse Mexico
231 F2 **Sotonera, Embalse de** lake Spain
304 E3 **Sotouboua** Togo
230 D2 **Sotresgudo** Spain
224 H3 **Sottern** lake Sweden
133 H4 **Sotuta** Mexico
305 G4 **Souanké** Congo
304 C3 **Soubré** Côte d'Ivoire
163 I3 **Soucis** St Lucia
423 E5 **Soucis, Cape** New Zealand
126 E3 **Soudan** Minnesota USA
305 F4 **Souellaba, Pointe** cape Cameroon
228 F3 **Souesmes** France
229 H2 **Soufflenheim** France
235 E5 **Soufli** Greece
163 16 **Soufrière** volcano Guadeloupe
163 17 **Soufrière** volcano Montserrat
163 I3 **Soufrière** St Lucia
163 11a **Soufrière** volcano St Vincent and the Grenadines
301 G1 **Sougueur** Algeria
228 E4 **Souillac** France
229 G2 **Souilly** France
301 H1 **Souk Ahras** Algeria
301 H1 **Souk Ahras** admin. area Algeria
230 D6 **Souk-el-Arba-des-Beni-Hassan** Morocco
233 C8 **Souk-El Khemis** Tunisia
301 G6 **Soukoukoutane** Niger
386 E4 **Sŏul (Seoul)** South Korea
228 D4 **Soulac-sur-Mer** France
243 F2 **Soulby** Cumbria England UK
232 B3 **Soultz** France
229 G1 **Soumagne** Belgium
231 F2 **Soumoulou** France
424 G4 **Sound** watercourse WA Australia
240 E1 **Sound** Cheshire England UK
240 C4 **Sound, The** bay England UK
376 B4 **Sound Island** Andaman and Nicobar Islands India
119 P7 **Sounding Creek** Alberta Canada
300 C6 **Soungrougrou** watercourse Senegal
390 C2 **Soûr (Tyre)** Lebanon
301 G1 **Sour el Ghozlane** Algeria
228 D2 **Sourdeval** France
156 B3 **Soure** Brazil
230 B3 **Soure** Portugal
119 U8 **Souris** Manitoba Canada
119 U8 **Souris** watercourse Manitoba Canada
119 T8 **Souris** watercourse Saskatchewan Canada
123 G9 **Souris** Prince Edward Island Canada
125 O2 **Souris** watercourse North Dakota USA
235 C6 **Sourpi** Greece
156 E4 **Sousa** Brazil
230 C4 **Sousel** Portugal
301 I1 **Sousse** Tunisia
228 D5 **Soustons** France
228 D5 **Soustons, Étang de** lake France
305 E2 **Souta** watercourse Benin
308 D6 **South Africa** country Africa
424 J3 **South Alligator** watercourse NT Australia
436 T3 **South America** continent
376 B5 **South Andaman** island Andaman and Nicobar Islands India
122 H4 **South Aulatsivik Island** Newfoundland and Labrador Canada
425 J7 **South Australia** admin. area Australia
81 R8 **South Australian Basin** seabed
244 D5 **South Ayrshire** admin. area Scotland UK
242 D1 **South Balloch** South Ayrshire Scotland UK
120 I7 **South Bay** Ontario Canada
127 J4 **South Baymouth** Ontario Canada
126 H6 **South Bend** Indiana USA
124 D3 **South Bend** Washington USA
118 H6 **South Bentinck** British Columbia Canada
131 L2 **South Boston** Virginia USA
240 D4 **South Brent** Devon England UK
123 J8 **South Brook** Newfoundland and Labrador Canada
376 B5 **South Brother Island** Andaman and Nicobar Islands India
425 M10 **South Bruny Island** Tas. Australia
423 B8 **South Cape (Whiore)** New Zealand
115 **South Carolina** admin. area USA
243 H3 **South Cave** East Riding of Yorkshire England UK
241 F3 **South Cerney** Gloucestershire England UK
127 K7 **South Charleston** West Virginia USA
243 G1 **South Charlton** Northumberland England UK
377 G4 **South China Sea**
377 G4 **South China Sea** Asia
126 D8 **South Coffeyville** Oklahoma USA
114 **South Dakota** admin. area USA
131 K6 **South Daytona** Florida USA
244 B2 **South Dell** Na h-Eileanan Siar Scotland UK
241 G4 **South Downs** range England UK
308 E4 **South-East** admin. area Botswana
425 M10 **South East Cape** Tas. Australia
426 1a **South East Point** Kiribati
78 N10 **South Fiji Basin** underwater feature Pacific Ocean
78 O10 **South Fiji Ridge** underwater feature Pacific Ocean
241 I3 **South Foreland** cape England UK
125 L8 **South Fork** Colorado USA
125 N7 **South Fork Republican** watercourse Colorado USA
124 D6 **South Fork Trinity** watercourse California USA
163 19 **South Friar's Bay** Saint Kitts and Nevis
437 H1 **South Geomagnetic Pole** Antarctica
163 8 **South Georgia** island South Georgia
163 8 **South Georgia** territory UK
77 N15 **South Georgia Ridge** underwater feature Scotia Sea
240 E3 **South Gloucestershire** admin. area England UK
244 B3 **South Harris** island Scotland UK
241 G4 **South Harting** West Sussex England UK
125 Q8 **South Haven** Kansas USA
126 H5 **South Haven** Michigan USA
425 inset **South Head** Lord Howe Island Australia
422 F3 **South Head** New Zealand
117 J6 **South Henik Lake** Nunavut Canada
131 I2 **South Hill** Virginia USA
78 K5 **South Honshu Ridge** underwater feature Pacific Ocean
307 F3 **South Horr** Kenya
437 H3 **South Indian Basin** underwater feature Southern Ocean
423 C6 **South Island** New Zealand
424 inset **South Island (Atas)** Cocos (Keeling) Islands Australia
377 H5 **South Islet** Philippines
163 7 **South Jason** island Falkland Islands
424 inset **South Keeling Islands** Cocos (Keeling) Islands Australia
119 W3 **South Knife** watercourse Manitoba Canada
119 W3 **South Knife Lake** Manitoba Canada
386 F4 **South Korea** country
241 G1 **South Kyme** Lincolnshire England UK
124 F7 **South Lake Tahoe** California USA
244 E5 **South Lanarkshire** admin. area Scotland UK
241 I2 **South Lopham** Norfolk England UK
125 P6 **South Loup** watercourse Nebraska USA
437 J1 **South Magnetic Pole** Antarctica
241 H4 **South Malling** East Sussex England UK
131 K8 **South Miami** Florida USA
240 D3 **South Molton** Devon England UK
117 J8 **South Moose Lake** Manitoba Canada
127 M7 **South Mountains** Pennsylvania USA
118 H2 **South Nahanni** watercourse Northwest Territories Canada
134 E3 **South Negril Point** cape Jamaica
78 M10 **South New Hebrides Trench** underwater feature Pacific Ocean
243 H3 **South Newbald** East Riding of Yorkshire England UK
436 U2 **South Orkney Islands** UK territory Antarctica
130 C7 **South Padre Island** Texas USA
426 1a **South Passage** strait Kiribati
240 E4 **South Petherton** Somerset England UK
129 L3 **South Plains** Texas USA
135 F2 **South Point** Bahamas
163 12 **South Point** cape Barbados
424 inset **South Point** Christmas Island Australia
130 G6 **South Point** Louisiana USA
437 F1 **South Pole** Antarctica
127 P5 **South Portland** Maine USA
241 H2 **South Raynham** Norfolk England UK
243 I3 **South Reston** Lincolnshire England UK
127 L4 **South River** Ontario Canada
244 F2 **South Ronaldsay** island Scotland UK
436 V2 **South Sandwich Fracture Zone** underwater feature Atlantic Ocean
119 P7 **South Saskatchewan** watercourse Alberta/Saskatchewan Canada
119 W3 **South Seal** watercourse Manitoba Canada
436 U2 **South Shetland Islands** Antarctica
77 L16 **South Shetland Trough** underwater feature Southern Ocean
125 Q5 **South Sioux City** Nebraska USA
124 E4 **South Sister** volcano Oregon USA
78 M9 **South Solomon Trench** underwater feature Pacific Ocean
243 I3 **South Somercotes** Lincolnshire England UK
117 L5 **South Spicer Island** Nunavut Canada
241 G2 **South Stoke** Lincolnshire England UK
422 F4 **South Taranaki Bight** bay New Zealand

81 S9 **South Tasman Rise** *underwater feature* Southern Ocean
128 G4 **South Tucson** Arizona USA
121 P6 **South Twin Island** Nunavut Canada
243 G2 **South Tyneside** *admin. area* England UK
119 O5 **South Wabasca Lake** Alberta Canada
424 inset **South West Bay** Heard Island Australia
425 M10 **South West Cape** Tas. Australia
423 B8 **South West Cape** New Zealand
426 1a **South West Point** Kiribati
425 inset **South West Point** Macquarie Island Australia
310 5b **South West Point** *cape* St Helena
130 G6 **South West Point** Louisiana USA
425 O7 **South West Rocks** NSW Australia
129 M4 **South Wichita** *watercourse* Texas USA
122 K6 **South Wolf Island** Newfoundland and Labrador Canada
241 H3 **South Woodham Ferrers** Essex England UK
241 H2 **South Wootton** Norfolk England UK
241 F2 **Southam** Warwickshire England UK
127 K4 **Southampton** Ontario Canada
241 F4 **Southampton** *admin. area* England UK
241 F4 **Southampton** Southampton England UK
127 O6 **Southampton** New York USA
120 L1 **Southampton Island** Nunavut Canada
130 G3 **Southaven** Mississippi USA
241 H3 **Southborough** Kent England UK
423 E6 **Southbridge** New Zealand
423 9 **Southeast Harbour** Campbell Island New Zealand
81 M9 **Southeast Indian Ridge** *seabed*
79 W12 **Southeast Pacific Basin** *underwater feature* Pacific Ocean
135 F2 **Southeast Point** Bahamas
244 C5 **Southend** Argyll and Bute Scotland UK
241 H3 **Southend** *admin. area* England UK
241 H3 **Southend-on-Sea** Southend England UK
119 T4 **Southend Reindeer** Saskatchewan Canada
308 D4 **Southern** *admin. area* Botswana
309 G2 **Southern** *admin. area* Malawi
308 E3 **Southern** *admin. area* Zambia
423 D6 **Southern Alps (Ka Tiritiri O Te Moana)** *range* New Zealand
131 M8 **Southern Bight** *bay* Bahamas
422 1 **Southern Cook Islands** Cook Islands New Zealand
424 F7 **Southern Cross** WA Australia
302 D5 **Southern Darfur** *admin. area* Sudan
123 L9 **Southern Harbour** Newfoundland and Labrador Canada
119 V4 **Southern Indian Lake** Manitoba Canada
302 E5 **Southern Kordofan** *admin. area* Sudan
308 D3 **Southern Lueti** *watercourse* Zambia
436 F3 **Southern Ocean**
131 L3 **Southern Pines** North Carolina USA
131 N2 **Southern Shores** North Carolina USA
240 D3 **Southerndown** Vale of Glamorgan Wales UK
241 H2 **Southery** Norfolk England UK
119 S7 **Southey** Saskatchewan Canada
134 E3 **Southfield** Jamaica
126 J5 **Southfield** Michigan USA
118 I7 **Southgate** *watercourse* British Columbia Canada
241 H3 **Southminster** Essex England UK
241 I2 **Southolt** Suffolk England UK
425 M10 **Southport** Tas. Australia
242 E3 **Southport** Merseyside England UK
131 M4 **Southport** North Carolina USA
243 H3 **Southrey** Lincolnshire England UK
131 H4 **Southside** Alabama USA
244 F2 **Southtown** Orkney Islands Scotland UK
240 E4 **Southwell** Dorset England UK
241 G1 **Southwell** Nottinghamshire England UK
377 G5 **Southwest Cay** *island* Spratly Islands
80 J8 **Southwest Indian Ridge** *seabed*
79 S12 **Southwest Pacific Basin** *underwater feature* Pacific Ocean
241 I2 **Southwold** Suffolk England UK
222 L3 **Soutojärvi** *lake* Sweden
234 D2 **Sovata** Romania
225 K5 **Sovetsk** Russian Federation
237 AD9 **Sovetskaya Gavan'** Russian Federation
225 O2 **Sovetskiy** Russian Federation
236 R5 **Sovetskoye, Ozero** *lake* Russian Federation
222 E5 **Søvik** Norway
222 E5 **Sövik** Norway
232 G5 **Sovra** Croatia
308 E4 **Sowa** Botswana
308 E4 **Sowa Pan** *pan* Botswana
120 J8 **Sowden Lake** Ontario Canada
242 F2 **Sowerby Row** Cumbria England UK
308 E5 **Soweto** South Africa
389 K6 **So'x** Tajikistan
386 E4 **Soyang-ho** *lake* South Korea
306 A5 **Soyo** Angola
234 E4 **Sozopol** Bulgaria
226 C2 **Spa** Belgium
163 1a **Spaans Lagoen** *bay* Aruba
163 1b **Spaanse Water** *bay* Netherlands Antilles
436 T2 **Spaatz Island** Antarctica
237 AE7 **Spafar'yeva, Ostrov** *island* Russian Federation
230 E4 **Spain** *country* Europe
119 S6 **Spalding** Saskatchewan Canada
241 G2 **Spalding** Lincolnshire England UK
241 G2 **Spaldwick** Cambridgeshire England UK
227 G3 **Spálené Poříčí** Czech Republic
225 M4 **Spalviškiai** Lithuania
241 G2 **Spanby** Lincolnshire England UK
229 I1 **Spangenberg** Germany
124 G3 **Spangle** Washington USA
125 M8 **Spanish Peaks** Colorado USA
163 18 **Spanish Point** Antigua and Barbuda
163 21 **Spanish Town** British Virgin Islands
134 E3 **Spanish Town** Jamaica
242 E2 **Spark Bridge** Cumbria England UK
131 J5 **Sparks** Georgia USA
126 G6 **Sparland** Illinois USA
155 H3 **Sparouine, Montagnes de la** *range* Suriname
Sparta *see* **Sparti** Greece
131 K2 **Sparta** North Carolina USA
131 I3 **Sparta** Tennessee USA
126 F5 **Sparta** Wisconsin USA
131 K3 **Spartanburg** South Carolina USA
235 C7 **Sparti (Sparta)** Greece
233 G8 **Spartivento, Capo** *cape* Italy
243 F2 **Spartylea** Northumberland England UK
119 N8 **Sparwood** British Columbia Canada
238 F5 **Spas-Demensk** Russian Federation
238 G4 **Spas-Ugol** Russian Federation
238 F5 **Spass** Russian Federation
386 G2 **Spassk-Dal'niy** Russian Federation
223 R5 **Spasskaya Guba** Russian Federation
225 P3 **Spasskaya Polist'** Russian Federation
389 J3 **Spasskoye** Kazakhstan
235 C7 **Spathi, Akra** *cape* Greece
118 G4 **Spatsizi Plateau Provincial Wilderness Park** British Columbia Canada
122 K6 **Spear Harbour** Newfoundland and Labrador Canada
119 R4 **Spear Lake** Saskatchewan Canada
242 A3 **Spear Vale** Ireland
126 D4 **Spearfish** South Dakota USA
129 L2 **Spearman** Texas USA
125 P8 **Spearville** Kansas USA
163 7 **Speedwell Island** Falkland Islands
243 H2 **Speeton** North Yorkshire England UK
227 H4 **Speikkogel** *mountain* Austria
307 E4 **Speke Gulf** *bay* Tanzania
126 H7 **Spencer** Indiana USA
126 D5 **Spencer** Iowa USA
125 P5 **Spencer** Nebraska USA
131 K3 **Spencer** North Carolina USA
116 C5 **Spencer, Point** Alaska USA
425 K8 **Spencer Gulf** SA Australia
121 P6 **Spencer Island** Nunavut Canada
118 K7 **Spences Bridge** British Columbia Canada
243 G2 **Spennymoor** Durham England UK
224 E2 **Sperillen** *lake* Norway
126 C2 **Sperling** Manitoba Canada
233 C7 **Sperone, Capo** *cape* Sardinia Italy
242 A2 **Sperrin** Strabane Northern Ireland UK
130 D2 **Sperry** Oklahoma USA
235 C7 **Spetses** *island* Greece
244 D3 **Spey** *watercourse* Scotland UK
244 E3 **Spey Bay** Moray Scotland UK
244 E3 **Spey Bay** Scotland UK
226 E3 **Speyer** Germany
163 9 **Speyside** Trinidad and Tobago
227 L2 **Spiczyn** Poland
127 K4 **Spider Bay** Ontario Canada
436 I2 **Spieden, Cape** Antarctica
226 D1 **Spiekeroog** *island* Germany
229 H3 **Spiez** Switzerland
222 L3 **Spikberg** Sweden
222 L1 **Spildra** *island* Norway
226 G4 **Spilimbergo** Italy
119 M7 **Spillimacheen** British Columbia Canada
243 I3 **Spilsby** Lincolnshire England UK
391 K3 **Spin Buldak** Afghanistan
229 G2 **Spincourt** France
232 C4 **Spinetta** Italy
124 G3 **Spirit Lake** Idaho USA
126 D5 **Spirit Lake** Iowa USA
118 L5 **Spirit River** Alberta Canada
238 F4 **Spirovo** Russian Federation
227 K3 **Spišská Stará Ves** Slovakia
227 K3 **Spišské Vlachy** Slovakia
424 inset **Spit Bay** Heard Island Australia
424 inset **Spit Point** Heard Island Australia
236 E3 **Spitsbergen** *island* Norway
435 H1 **Spitsbergen Bank** *underwater feature* Barents Sea
435 F1 **Spitsbergen Fracture Zone** *underwater feature* Greenland Sea
225 N3 **Spitsino** Russian Federation
226 G4 **Spittal** Austria
242 D2 **Spittal** Dumfries and Galloway Scotland UK
240 C3 **Spittal** Pembrokeshire Wales UK
229 K3 **Spittal an der Drau** Austria
244 E4 **Spittal of Glenshee** Perth and Kinross Scotland UK
225 M2 **Spjutsund** Finland
130 D5 **Splendora** Texas USA
232 G5 **Split** Croatia
121 P4 **Split Island** Nunavut Canada
119 W4 **Split Lake** Manitoba Canada
124 G3 **Spokane** Washington USA
232 E5 **Spoleto** Italy
126 F6 **Spoon** *watercourse* Illinois USA
126 F4 **Spooner** Wisconsin USA
235 E7 **Sporades (Dodecanese)** *island* Greece
227 M1 **Sporavskaye, Vozyera** *lake* Belarus
222 I5 **Sporrsjön** *bay* Sweden
122 K6 **Spotted Island** Newfoundland and Labrador Canada
124 G3 **Sprague** Washington USA
377 F5 **Spratly Island** Spratly Islands
377 G5 **Spratly Islands (Disputed)**
124 F4 **Spray** Oregon USA
227 G1 **Spree** *watercourse* Germany
224 F5 **Sprenge** Germany
243 H3 **Spridlington** Lincolnshire England UK
119 O8 **Spring Coulee** Alberta Canada
126 F5 **Spring Green** Wisconsin USA
126 F5 **Spring Grove** Minnesota USA
131 L3 **Spring Lake** North Carolina USA
128 E2 **Spring Mountains** Nevada USA
119 Q3 **Spring Point** Saskatchewan Canada
163 7 **Spring Point** Falkland Islands
126 E5 **Spring Valley** Minnesota USA
308 C5 **Springbok** South Africa
126 I7 **Springboro** Ohio USA
128 F2 **Springdale** Utah USA
124 G2 **Springdale** Washington USA
129 J2 **Springer** New Mexico USA
130 C3 **Springer** Oklahoma USA
129 H3 **Springerville** Arizona USA
423 D6 **Springfield** New Zealand
125 N8 **Springfield** Colorado USA
131 K4 **Springfield** Georgia USA
126 G7 **Springfield** Illinois USA
126 I8 **Springfield** Kentucky USA
127 O5 **Springfield** Massachusetts USA
125 R4 **Springfield** Minnesota USA
126 E8 **Springfield** Missouri USA
126 J7 **Springfield** Ohio USA
124 D4 **Springfield** Oregon USA
130 H2 **Springfield** Tennessee USA
129 J2 **Springfield, Lake** Illinois USA
308 E6 **Springfontein** South Africa
123 F10 **Springhill** Nova Scotia Canada
118 J7 **Springhouse** British Columbia Canada
129 K3 **Springlake** Texas USA
423 E6 **Springs Junction** New Zealand
425 N6 **Springsure** Qld Australia
130 C4 **Springtown** Texas USA
125 P5 **Springview** Nebraska USA
127 L5 **Springville** New York USA
124 J6 **Springville** Utah USA
119 Q7 **Springwater** Saskatchewan Canada
224 E2 **Sprogen** *lake* Norway
222 G4 **Sprova** Norway
119 R6 **Spruce** *watercourse* Saskatchewan Canada
127 L7 **Spruce Knob** *mountain* West Virginia USA
131 J3 **Spruce Pine** North Carolina USA
128 F1 **Spry** Utah USA
233 G7 **Spulico, Capo** *cape* Italy
129 L4 **Spur** Texas USA
126 C2 **Spurgrave** Manitoba Canada
243 I3 **Spurn Head** *cape* England UK
116 D6 **Spurr, Mount** Alaska USA
423 E6 **Spy Glass Point** New Zealand
125 O1 **Spy Hill** Saskatchewan Canada
227 K1 **Spychowo** Poland
127 Q3 **Squa Pan Lake** Maine USA
118 J8 **Squamish** British Columbia Canada
118 J7 **Squamish** *watercourse* British Columbia Canada
127 Q3 **Square Lake** Maine USA
124 F1 **Squilax** British Columbia Canada
233 G7 **Squillace** Italy
233 G7 **Squillace, Golfo di** *bay* Italy
120 N7 **Squirrel** *watercourse* Ontario Canada
375 F5 **Sragen** Indonesia
245 C2 **Srah** Ireland
245 E4 **Srahbaun** Ireland
245 D5 **Sraleigh** Ireland
375 F5 **Srandakan** Indonesia
245 E1 **Srath** Ireland
234 B4 **Srbica** Kosovo
376 D5 **Srê Âmbĕl** Cambodia
232 H4 **Srebrenik** Bosnia and Herzegovina
234 E4 **Sredets** Bulgaria
237 AG7 **Sredinnyy, Khrebet** *range* Russian Federation
234 D4 **Sredna Gora** *range* Bulgaria
238 G6 **Sredne Russkaya Vozvyshennost'** *region* Russian Federation
237 W6 **Sredne-Sibirskoye Ploskogor'ye** *range* Russian Federation
237 AF9 **Srednego, Ostrov** *island* Kuril Islands
387 L1 **Srednego, Ostrov** *lake* Russian Federation
237 AF5 **Srednekolymsk** Russian Federation
223 Q4 **Sredneye Kuyto, Ozero** *lake* Russian Federation
385 L2 **Sredniy Urgal** Russian Federation
237 AF7 **Sredniy Urgal** Russian Federation
237 AB8 **Sredniy Urgal** Russian Federation
234 B3 **Srednjevo** Serbia
234 D4 **Srednogorie** Bulgaria
237 AH6 **Srednyaya Itkana** Russian Federation
391 K3 **Sreh Chânhând Tânah** Afghanistan
227 I1 **Śrem** Poland
376 D4 **Srêng** *watercourse* Cambodia
385 F1 **Sretensk** Russian Federation
393 E10 **Sri Jayewardenepura Kotte** Sri Lanka
393 E10 **Sri Lanka** *country*
393 E9 **Sriharikota Island** Andhra Pradesh India
392 G6 **Srinagar** Bihar India
392 D3 **Srinagar** Jammu and Kashmir India/Pakistan
392 G6 **Srirampur** Jharkhand India
389 O3 **Srostki** Russian Federation
234 B3 **Srpska Crnja** Serbia
222 H5 **Staa/Sta** Sweden
425 L4 **Staaten** *watercourse* Qld Australia
222 F5 **Stabben** *island* Norway
223 N1 **Stabbursdalen Nasjonalpark** *park* Norway
224 E4 **Staby** Denmark
244 D2 **Stack, Loch** *lake* Scotland UK
244 D1 **Stack Skerry** *island* Scotland UK
240 C3 **Stackpole** Pembrokeshire Wales UK
226 B2 **Staden** Belgium
224 C1 **Stadhavet** *bay* Norway
224 C1 **Stadlandet** *island* Norway
227 L1 **Stadniki** Poland
226 E2 **Stadtallendorf** Germany
229 J2 **Stadtbergen** Germany
226 F2 **Stadtilm** Germany
226 D2 **Stadtkyll** Germany
232 C3 **Stäfa** Switzerland
244 B3 **Staffin** Highland Scotland UK
241 E2 **Stafford** Staffordshire England UK
125 P8 **Stafford** Kansas USA
243 G3 **Staffordshire** *admin. area* England UK
242 B2 **Staffordstown** Antrim Northern Ireland UK
233 E8 **Stagnone, Punta dello** *cape* Italy
222 G6 **Stai** Norway
225 M4 **Staicele** Latvia
243 G3 **Stainburn** North Yorkshire England UK
243 G2 **Staindrop** Durham England UK
241 G3 **Staines** Surrey England UK
162 B5 **Staines, Peninsula** *peninsula* Chile
243 F2 **Stainforth** North Yorkshire England UK
243 G2 **Stainton** North Yorkshire England UK
243 H2 **Staintondale** North Yorkshire England UK
244 D6 **Stairhaven** Dumfries and Galloway Scotland UK
227 L3 **Stakčín** Slovakia
225 M5 **Stakliškės** Lithuania
234 B4 **Stalać** Serbia
240 E4 **Stalbridge** Dorset England UK
229 H3 **Stalden** Switzerland
233 G7 **Staletti, Punta di** *cape* Italy
241 I2 **Stalham** Norfolk England UK
243 F2 **Stalling Busk** North Yorkshire England UK
Stallingrad *see* **Volgograd** Russian Federation
222 L2 **Stalojaure** *lake* Sweden
222 I4 **Stalon** Sweden
227 L2 **Stalowa Wola** Poland
225 N5 **Stalti** Latvia
125 M1 **Stalwart** Saskatchewan Canada
241 G2 **Stamford** Lincolnshire England UK
127 O6 **Stamford** Connecticut USA
130 B4 **Stamford** Texas USA
130 B4 **Stamford, Lake** Texas USA
243 H3 **Stamford Bridge** North Yorkshire England UK
124 E7 **Stampede Reservoir** California USA
308 C4 **Stampriet** Namibia
222 I3 **Stamstik** Norway
222 H2 **Stamsund** Norway
126 D6 **Stanberry** Missouri USA
240 F4 **Stanbridge** Dorset England UK
436 W1 **Stancomb-Wills Glacier** Antarctica
119 O8 **Stand Off** Alberta Canada
119 O7 **Standard** Alberta Canada
308 E5 **Standerton** South Africa
243 F3 **Standish** Greater Manchester England UK
393 D9 **Stanely** *lake* Tamil Nadu India
241 H2 **Stanfield** Norfolk England UK
124 F4 **Stanfield** Oregon USA
241 G2 **Stanford** Bedfordshire England UK
126 I8 **Stanford** Kentucky USA
123 I3 **Stanford** Montana USA
128 C2 **Stanford, Mount** California USA
241 F3 **Stanford in the Vale** Oxfordshire England UK
224 F2 **Stange** Norway
436 S2 **Stange Sound** *strait* Antarctica
309 F5 **Stanger** South Africa
241 H2 **Stanhoe** Norfolk England UK
243 F2 **Stanhope** Durham England UK
241 G2 **Stanion** Northamptonshire England UK
232 F5 **Stankovci** Croatia
118 K6 **Stanley** British Columbia Canada
123 E9 **Stanley** New Brunswick Canada
163 7 **Stanley** Falkland Islands
243 G2 **Stanley** Durham England UK
244 E4 **Stanley** Perth and Kinross Scotland UK
124 H4 **Stanley** Idaho USA
125 N2 **Stanley** North Dakota USA
119 S5 **Stanley Mission** Saskatchewan Canada
308 E4 **Stanmore** Zimbabwe
237 Y7 **Stanovoye Nagor'ye** *region* Russian Federation
229 I3 **Stans** Switzerland
241 H3 **Stansted Mountfitchet** Essex England UK
425 N7 **Stanthorpe** Qld Australia
241 F2 **Stanton** Gloucestershire England UK
241 H2 **Stanton** Suffolk England UK
126 J8 **Stanton** Kentucky USA
130 G3 **Stanton** Tennessee USA
129 L4 **Stanton** Texas USA
240 E2 **Stanton Long** Shropshire England UK
241 F2 **Stanton on the Wolds** Nottinghamshire England UK
241 F2 **Stanton under Bardon** Leicester England UK
242 F2 **Stanwix** Cumbria England UK
226 F4 **Stanzach** Austria
234 A3 **Stapar** Serbia
226 D1 **Staphorst** Netherlands
241 H3 **Staplehurst** Kent England UK
125 R3 **Staples** Minnesota USA
242 B3 **Staplestown** Ireland
240 E2 **Stapleton** Herefordshire England UK
125 O6 **Stapleton** Nebraska USA
227 K2 **Stąporków** Poland
223 N1 **Stappane** *island* Norway
238 F6 **Star'** Russian Federation
131 L3 **Star** North Carolina USA
130 F4 **Star City** Arkansas USA
235 C5 **Star Dojran** Macedonia
227 L1 **Stara Kamionka** Poland
234 D4 **Stara Planina** *range* Bulgaria
227 L3 **Stara Sil'** Ukraine
234 F3 **Stara Synyava** Ukraine
234 I3 **Stará Turá** Slovakia
234 F3 **Stara Ushytsya** Ukraine
227 M2 **Stara Vyzhivka** Ukraine
227 K1 **Stara Wieś** Poland
234 D4 **Stara Zagora** Bulgaria
234 D4 **Stara Zagora** *admin. area* Bulgaria
227 K2 **Starachowice** Poland
223 Q2 **Staraya** Russian Federation
225 O5 **Staraya Byelitsa** Belarus
225 P3 **Staraya Russa** Russian Federation
225 P4 **Staraya Toropa** Russian Federation
120 G8 **Starbuck** Manitoba Canada
125 R4 **Starbuck** Minnesota USA
124 F3 **Starbuck** Washington USA
426 1 **Starbuck Island** Kiribati
240 D4 **Starcross** Devon England UK
227 I2 **Staré Město** Czech Republic
238 B6 **Staritsa** Belarus
238 F4 **Staritsa** Russian Federation
238 C3 **Staritsy** Russian Federation
130 D2 **Stark** Kansas USA
125 M8 **Starkville** Colorado USA
130 G4 **Starkville** Mississippi USA
125 P2 **Starkweather** North Dakota USA
226 F4 **Starnberger See** *lake* Germany
235 B5 **Staro Gradsko** Macedonia
234 E4 **Staro Oryakhovo** Bulgaria
235 B4 **Staro Slano** Bosnia and Herzegovina
389 N3 **Staroaleyskoye** Russian Federation
394 F3 **Starobelsk** Ukraine
394 E2 **Starodub** Russian Federation
234 E1 **Starokostyantyniv** Ukraine
238 H5 **Staroletovo** Russian Federation
236 K7 **Staroverscheskaya** Russian Federation
225 O3 **Staroye Gorkolovo** Russian Federation
388 C2 **Staroyur'yevo** Russian Federation
242 D1 **Starr** East Ayrshire Scotland UK
237 AE6 **Starry Eschan** Russian Federation
240 D4 **Start Bay** England UK
240 D4 **Start Point** England UK
235 D5 **Startsevo** Bulgaria
125 J6 **Starvation Reservoir** Utah USA
227 L2 **Stary Dzików** Poland
227 K3 **Stary Sącz** Poland
234 D1 **Staryy Oleksynets'** Ukraine
394 F2 **Staryy Oskol** Russian Federation
234 E1 **Staryy Ostropil'** Ukraine
234 C1 **Staryy Sambir** Ukraine
238 G3 **Staryye Yagnitsy** Russian Federation
127 M6 **State College** Pennsylvania USA
130 G5 **State Line** Mississippi USA
131 K4 **Statesboro** Georgia USA
131 K3 **Statesville** North Carolina USA
241 G2 **Stathe** Somerset England UK
302 E4 **Station No. 10** Sudan
302 E3 **Station No. 5** Sudan
302 E3 **Station No. 6** Sudan
233 G6 **Statte** Italy
224 C3 **Stavanger** Norway
234 A3 **Stave** Serbia
118 J8 **Stave Lake** British Columbia Canada
423 D6 **Staveley** New Zealand
242 F2 **Staveley** Cumbria England UK
243 G3 **Staveley** Derbyshire England UK
243 G2 **Staveley** North Yorkshire England UK
226 C2 **Stavelot** Belgium
119 O7 **Stavely** Alberta Canada
224 F3 **Stavern** Norway
234 D4 **Stavertsi** Bulgaria
234 G2 **Stavki** Ukraine
227 M2 **Stavky** Ukraine
226 C1 **Stavoren** Netherlands
388 D4 **Stavropol'** Russian Federation
388 D4 **Stavropol'skiy Kray** *admin. area* Russian Federation
235 D8 **Stavros, Akra** *cape* Greece
235 B5 **Stavroskiádion** Greece
234 F2 **Stavrove** Ukraine
225 J3 **Stavsnäs** Sweden
234 G1 **Stavyshche** Ukraine
425 L9 **Stawell** Vic. Australia
227 L1 **Stawiski** Poland
227 J2 **Stawiszyn** Poland
238 F6 **Staykі** Russian Federation
240 D2 **Staylittle** Powys Wales UK
127 K4 **Stayner** Ontario Canada
124 D4 **Stayton** Oregon USA
118 J3 **Steamboat** British Columbia Canada
125 L6 **Steamboat Springs** Colorado USA
243 G2 **Stean** North Yorkshire England UK
240 E3 **Steart** Somerset England UK
116 C6 **Stebbins** Alaska USA
234 D1 **Stebni** Ukraine
234 C1 **Stebnik** Ukraine
243 G3 **Steel Bank** South Yorkshire England UK
131 H4 **Steele** Alabama USA
125 P3 **Steele** North Dakota USA
436 U2 **Steele Island** Antarctica
126 F8 **Steeleville** Missouri USA
229 G1 **Steenbergen** Netherlands
124 F5 **Steens Mountains** Oregon USA
117 N3 **Steenstrup Gletscher** *glacier* Greenland
424 L9 **Steep Point** WA Australia
119 V7 **Steep Rock** Manitoba Canada
126 F2 **Steep Rock Lake** Ontario Canada
241 G2 **Steeple Gidding** Cambridgeshire England UK
163 7 **Steeple Jason** *island* Falkland Islands
126 F2 **Steeprock Lake** Ontario Canada
436 M1 **Steershead Crevasses** *valley* Antarctica
234 F2 **Ştefan Vodă** Moldova
436 E2 **Stefansson Bay** Antarctica
117 I4 **Stefansson Island** Nunavut Canada
162 C3 **Steffen, Cerro** *mountain* Argentina
234 C2 **Ştei** Romania
227 H4 **Steiermark** *admin. area* Austria
222 I3 **Steigen** Norway
226 F3 **Stein** Germany
244 B3 **Stein** Highland Scotland UK
227 G4 **Stein an der Enns** Austria
229 J3 **Steinach** Austria
226 E2 **Steinau** Germany
120 G8 **Steinbach** Manitoba Canada
159 H4 **Steinen** *watercourse* Brazil
226 D1 **Steinfurter Aa** *watercourse* Germany
226 F4 **Steingaden** Germany
308 C4 **Steinhausen** Namibia
226 E1 **Steinhuder Meer** *lake* Germany
222 G4 **Steinkjer** Norway
308 C5 **Steinkopf** South Africa
222 E5 **Steinshamn** Norway
223 P2 **Steinsjærnes** Norway
224 C2 **Steinslandsvatnet** *lake* Norway
234 F3 **Stejaru** Romania
228 G1 **Stekene** Belgium
389 M2 **Steklyannoye** *lake* Russian Federation
308 D5 **Stella** South Africa
226 F1 **Stelle** Germany
224 I4 **Stenåsa** Sweden
226 C3 **Stenay** France
222 K2 **Stenbacken** Sweden
226 F1 **Stendal** Germany
225 L4 **Stende** Latvia
224 H4 **Stengårdshultasjön** *lake* Sweden
234 B3 **Stenjevac** Serbia
224 J4 **Stenkumla** Sweden
244 inset **Stenness** Shetland Scotland UK
235 E8 **Steno Karpathou** *bay* Greece
235 C7 **Stenon** Greece
224 H4 **Stensjön** *lake* Sweden
222 K3 **Stenträsk** Sweden
244 B2 **Steòrnabhagh** Na h-Eileanan Siar Scotland UK
234 E1 **Stepanki** Ukraine
225 O4 **Stepankino** Russian Federation
238 H5 **Stepanshchino** Russian Federation
238 G4 **Stepantsevo** Russian Federation
232 H5 **Stepen** Bosnia and Herzegovina
232 E2 **Stephansposching** Germany
125 Q2 **Stephen** Minnesota USA
130 E4 **Stephens** Arkansas USA
163 7 **Stephens, Port** *bay* Falkland Islands
423 F5 **Stephens Island** New Zealand
120 H4 **Stephens Lake** Manitoba Canada
118 D3 **Stephens Passage** Alaska USA
126 H4 **Stephenson** Michigan USA
436 T2 **Stephenson, Mount** *mountain* Antarctica
130 B4 **Stephenville** Texas USA
123 I8 **Stephenville Crossing** Newfoundland and Labrador Canada
388 D5 **Stepnoye** Russian Federation
389 N3 **Stepnoye** *lake* Russian Federation
389 K3 **Stepnyak** Kazakhstan
238 F4 **Stepurino** Russian Federation
235 C6 **Sterea Ellada** *admin. area* Greece
308 D6 **Sterling** South Africa
125 N6 **Sterling** Colorado USA
126 G6 **Sterling** Illinois USA
125 P7 **Sterling** Kansas USA
126 I4 **Sterling** Michigan USA
124 J7 **Sterling** Utah USA
129 L5 **Sterling City** Texas USA
126 J5 **Sterling Heights** Michigan USA
388 G2 **Sterlitamak** Russian Federation
235 C7 **Sterna** Greece
224 E2 **Sternbusjøen** *lake* Norway
223 T6 **Steshëvskaya** Russian Federation
241 H2 **Stetchworth** Cambridgeshire England UK
229 L1 **Štětí** Czech Republic
373 I5 **Stettin Bay** Papua New Guinea
227 H1 **Stettiner Haff (Zalew Szczeciński)** *bay* Poland
119 O6 **Stettler** Alberta Canada
127 K6 **Steubenville** Ohio USA
241 G3 **Stevenage** Hertfordshire England UK
126 G4 **Stevens Point** Wisconsin USA
131 I3 **Stevenson** Alabama USA
120 H6 **Stevenson Lake** Manitoba Canada
244 D5 **Stevenston** North Ayrshire Scotland UK
126 H5 **Stevensville** Michigan USA
124 H3 **Stevensville** Montana USA
224 G5 **Stevns Klint** *cape* Denmark
118 G5 **Stewart** British Columbia Canada
119 S6 **Stewart Creek** Saskatchewan Canada
423 C8 **Stewart Island** New Zealand
117 K5 **Stewart Lake** Nunavut Canada
126 F6 **Stewart Lake** Illinois USA
119 R7 **Stewart Valley** Saskatchewan Canada
244 D5 **Stewarton** East Ayrshire Scotland UK
126 E5 **Stewartville** Minnesota USA
123 G10 **Stewiacke** Nova Scotia Canada
241 G4 **Steyning** West Sussex England UK
308 E6 **Steynsburg** South Africa
227 H3 **Steyr** Austria
227 H4 **Steyr** *watercourse* Austria
227 H2 **Stěžery** Czech Republic
227 K2 **Stężyca** Poland
229 I4 **Stezzano** Italy
241 H2 **Stibbard** Norfolk England UK
240 C4 **Sticker** Cornwall England UK
243 I3 **Stickford** Lincolnshire England UK
241 H1 **Stickney** Lincolnshire England UK
125 P5 **Stickney** South Dakota USA
226 C1 **Stiens** Netherlands
241 H2 **Stiffkey** Norfolk England UK
222 H3 **Stigen** *island* Norway
226 F5 **Stiglia** Italy
233 G6 **Stigliano** Italy
118 F4 **Stikine** British Columbia Canada
118 F4 **Stikine** *watercourse* British Columbia Canada
118 F3 **Stikine Plateau** British Columbia Canada
129 L5 **Stiles** Texas USA
130 C5 **Stillhouse Hollow Lake** Texas USA
130 C2 **Stillwater** Oklahoma USA
124 F7 **Stillwater Range** Nevada USA
127 N5 **Stillwater Reservoir** New York USA
233 G7 **Stilo** Italy
233 G7 **Stilo, Punta** *cape* Italy
241 G2 **Stilton** Cambridgeshire England UK
129 L3 **Stinnett** Texas USA
235 C5 **Štip** Macedonia
119 O8 **Stirling** Alberta Canada
127 M4 **Stirling** Ontario Canada
244 D4 **Stirling** *admin. area* Scotland UK
244 E4 **Stirling** Stirling Scotland UK
124 H3 **Stites** Idaho USA
234 B1 **Štítnik** Slovakia
243 H3 **Stixwould** Lincolnshire England UK
223 M1 **Stjernøya** *island* Norway
222 G5 **Stjørdalselva** *watercourse* Norway
222 G5 **Stjørdalshalsen** Norway
224 G2 **Støa** Norway
227 I1 **Stobno** Poland
232 G5 **Stobreč** Croatia
222 J6 **Stocka** Sweden
241 F3 **Stockbridge** Hampshire England UK
130 C6 **Stockdale** Texas USA
119 T7 **Stockholm** Saskatchewan Canada
224 J3 **Stockholm** Sweden
125 Q4 **Stockholm** South Dakota USA
240 D4 **Stockland** Devon England UK
243 F3 **Stockport** Greater Manchester England UK
77 O11 **Stocks Seamount** *underwater feature* Atlantic Ocean
222 L5 **Stöcksjö** Sweden
124 E8 **Stockton** California USA
126 F5 **Stockton** Illinois USA
125 P7 **Stockton** Kansas USA
126 E8 **Stockton** Missouri USA
130 E2 **Stockton Lake** Missouri USA
243 G2 **Stockton-on-Tees** *admin. area* England UK
243 G2 **Stockton-on-Tees** Stockton-on-Tees England UK
240 E2 **Stockton on Teme** Worcestershire England UK
132 E2 **Stockton Plateau** Texas USA
227 K1 **Stoczek** Poland
227 K2 **Stoczek Łukowski** Poland
227 G3 **Stod** Czech Republic
222 J5 **Stöde** Sweden
222 J5 **Stödesjön** *lake* Sweden
238 E5 **Stodolishche** Russian Federation
376 E4 **Stœng Trêng** Cambodia
244 C2 **Stoer** Highland Scotland UK
244 C2 **Stoer, Point of** *cape* Scotland UK
387 J2 **Stokap, Gora** *volcano* Russian Federation
241 G2 **Stoke Albany** Northamptonshire England UK
241 H2 **Stoke By Clare** Suffolk England UK
240 E2 **Stoke Heath** Shropshire England UK
241 I2 **Stoke Holy Cross** Norfolk England UK
240 E2 **Stoke Lacy** Herefordshire England UK
241 E1 **Stoke-on-Trent** *admin. area* England UK
241 E1 **Stoke-on-Trent** Stoke-on-Trent England UK
241 E3 **Stoke Orchard** Gloucestershire England UK
240 E2 **Stoke Prior** Herefordshire England UK
241 E2 **Stoke Prior** Worcestershire England UK
162 B6 **Stokes, Bahía** *bay* Chile
425 L10 **Stokes Point** Tas. Australia
240 E2 **Stokesay** Shropshire England UK
241 I2 **Stokesby** Norfolk England UK
243 G2 **Stokesley** North Yorkshire England UK
222 F4 **Stokkøya** *island* Norway
222 G4 **Stokksund** Norway
222 I2 **Stokmarknes** Norway
232 G5 **Stolac** Bosnia and Herzegovina
389 N3 **Stolbourkha** Kazakhstan
238 G5 **Stolbovaya** Russian Federation
237 AC4 **Stolbovoy, Ostrov** *island* Russian Federation
240 D3 **Stolford** Somerset England UK
394 C2 **Stolin** Belarus
224 C3 **Stolmen** *island* Norway
234 E2 **Stolniceni-Prăjescu** Romania
234 D3 **Stolnici** Romania
227 J1 **Stolno** Poland
224 D2 **Stolsheimen** *island* Norway
155 G3 **Stondansie Projekt** *lake* Suriname
240 E3 **Stone** Gloucestershire England UK
241 H3 **Stone** Kent England UK
241 E2 **Stone** Staffordshire England UK
240 E3 **Stone Allerton** Somerset England UK
244 F4 **Stone of Morphie** Aberdeenshire Scotland UK
242 A4 **Stoneen** Ireland
243 H2 **Stonegrave** North Yorkshire England UK
127 P3 **Stoneham** Québec Canada
243 F1 **Stonehaugh** Northumberland England UK
244 F4 **Stonehaven** Aberdeenshire Scotland UK
425 L6 **Stonehenge** Qld Australia
118 J6 **Stoner** British Columbia Canada
241 F3 **Stonesfield** Oxfordshire England UK
130 E4 **Stonewall** Louisiana USA
130 G4 **Stonewall** Mississippi USA
130 C3 **Stonewall** Oklahoma USA
240 E3 **Stoney Stratton** Somerset England UK
241 F2 **Stoneygate** Leicester England UK
222 J2 **Stonglandseidet** Norway
122 K6 **Stony Island** Newfoundland and Labrador Canada
120 G7 **Stony Mountain** Manitoba Canada
119 S3 **Stony Rapids** Saskatchewan Canada
244 inset **Stonybreck** Shetland Scotland UK
245 F2 **Stonyford** Lisburn Northern Ireland UK
310 5c **Stonyhill Point** *cape* St Helena
121 N7 **Stooping** *watercourse* Ontario Canada
222 I4 **Stor-Björkvattnet** *bay* Sweden
222 I4 **Stor-Byvattnet** *lake* Sweden
222 J4 **Stor Dainan** *lake* Sweden
222 K5 **Stor Degersjön** *lake* Sweden
222 J5 **Stor-Finnsjön** *lake* Sweden
224 I4 **Stor Laison** *lake* Sweden
222 J5 **Stor-Laxsjön** *lake* Sweden
222 K3 **Stor-Mattaure** *lake* Sweden
222 H5 **Stor-Stensjön** *lake* Sweden
222 L4 **Stor-Teuger** *lake* Sweden
222 I5 **Stor-Valsjön** *lake* Sweden
224 H3 **Stora** Sweden
224 I3 **Stora Ålö** *island* Sweden
224 I4 **Stora Alvaret** *region* Sweden
222 J4 **Stora Arasjön** *lake* Sweden
224 I4 **Stora Askö** *island* Sweden
224 G3 **Stora Bör** *lake* Sweden
224 G4 **Stora Färgen** *lake* Sweden
222 I5 **Stora Foskvattnet** *lake* Sweden
224 G3 **Stora Gla** *lake* Sweden
222 J5 **Stora Grundsjön** *lake* Sweden
224 G3 **Stora Hästefjorden** *lake* Sweden
224 I4 **Stora Karlsö** *island* Sweden
222 K4 **Stora Kvammarn** *lake* Sweden
224 F3 **Stora Le** *lake* Sweden
222 K3 **Stora Lulevatten** *bay* Sweden
224 H3 **Stora Rängen** *lake* Sweden
222 K3 **Stora Sjöfallet** *waterfall* Sweden
222 J3 **Stora Sjöfallets nationalpark** *park* Sweden
222 J4 **Stora Skyrsjön** *lake* Sweden
222 J5 **Stora Tågsjön** *lake* Sweden
222 K5 **Stora Tällvattnet** *lake* Sweden
224 I3 **Stora Värtan** *bay* Sweden
224 I3 **Storåga** *watercourse* Norway
222 F5 **Storås** Norway
222 K4 **Storavan** *bay* Sweden
223 M5 **Storbacka** Finland
222 H6 **Storbäcken** Sweden
222 K4 **Storberg** Sweden
224 C3 **Stord** *island* Norway
222 L1 **Stordalen** Norway
222 G5 **Stordalsfjorden** *bay* Norway
232 F3 **Store** Slovenia
224 C2 **Store Kalsøy** *island* Norway
117 R3 **Store Koldewey** *island* Greenland
222 G5 **Store Korssjøen** *lake* Norway
223 M1 **Store Kvalfjord** Norway
224 G5 **Store Lyngby** Denmark
222 H4 **Store Majavatnet** *lake* Norway
222 I3 **Store Malvatnet** *lake* Norway
222 I2 **Store Molla** *island* Norway
222 H4 **Store Namsvatnet** *lake* Norway
223 P2 **Store Sametti** *lake* Norway
224 C2 **Store Sotra** *island* Norway
223 N1 **Store Tamsøya** *island* Norway
224 D3 **Store Urevatnet** *lake* Norway
222 I3 **Storeakersvatnet** *lake* Norway
222 G5 **Støren** Norway
222 I2 **Storfjärden** *bay* Sweden
222 K2 **Storfjord** Norway
222 E5 **Storfjorden** *lake* Norway
224 H3 **Storfors** Sweden
224 I3 **Storforshei** Norway
222 F5 **Storfosna** *island* Norway
222 I4 **Storfulvurn** *lake* Sweden
222 I3 **Storglomvatnet** *lake* Norway

224 H2 **Storhamrasjön** *lake* Sweden
222 I5 **Storhögen** Sweden
222 I3 **Storjord** Norway
222 I3 **Storjorda** Norway
222 I4 **Storjorm** *bay* Sweden
222 J4 **Storjuktan** *lake* Sweden
224 I2 **Storjungfrun** *island* Sweden
222 J4 **Storkågeträsk** *lake* Sweden
116 I4 **Storkerson Peninsula** Nunavut Canada
225 K2 **Storklyndan** *island* Finland
225 K2 **Storlandet** *island* Finland
222 H5 **Storlien** Sweden
126 D5 **Storm Lake** Iowa USA
120 I8 **Stormy Lake** Ontario Canada
222 F5 **Storodden** Norway
223 M4 **Storöhamn** Sweden
222 K5 **Storön** *island* Sweden
222 H3 **Storøya** *island* Norway
223 M2 **Storpellinge** *island* Finland
241 G4 **Storrington** West Sussex England UK
223 M1 **Storsandes** Norway
222 H5 **Storsätern** Sweden
222 H5 **Storsjö** Sweden
224 F2 **Storsjøen** *lake* Norway
222 I5 **Storsjön** *bay* Sweden
226 I6 **Storsjön** *lake* Sweden
222 I4 **Storsjouten** *lake* Sweden
222 L2 **Storslett** Norway
222 K2 **Storsteinnes** Norway
222 L4 **Storsund** Sweden
119 U8 **Storthoaks** Saskatchewan Canada
222 J4 **Storuman** Sweden
222 J4 **Storuman** *lake* Sweden
222 J4 **Storväktaren** *lake* Sweden
222 H4 **Storvatnet** *lake* Norway
222 J4 **Storvindeln** *lake* Sweden
226 F2 **Stößen** Germany
222 H3 **Støtvær** *island* Norway
119 T8 **Stoughton** Saskatchewan Canada
126 G5 **Stoughton** Wisconsin USA
244 C4 **Stoul** Highland Scotland UK
241 I3 **Stour** *watercourse* England UK
120 H6 **Stout Lake** Ontario Canada
244 F1 **Stove** Orkney Islands Scotland UK
241 H3 **Stow** Lincolnshire England UK
244 F5 **Stow** Scottish Borders Scotland UK
127 K6 **Stow** Ohio USA
240 D2 **Stowe** Shropshire England UK
241 H2 **Stowmarket** Suffolk England UK
227 M2 **Stoyaniv** Ukraine
234 E4 **Stozher** Bulgaria
226 G5 **Stra** Italy
226 G2 **Straach** Germany
245 E2 **Strabane** *admin. area* Northern Ireland UK
245 E2 **Strabane** Strabane Northern Ireland UK
234 E3 **Strachina, Lacul** *lake* Romania
244 C4 **Strachur** Argyll and Bute Scotland UK
234 C4 **Stradalovo** Bulgaria
245 E3 **Stradbally** Ireland
226 E5 **Stradella** Italy
126 E8 **Strafford** Missouri USA
425 M10 **Strahan** Tas. Australia
245 F1 **Straid** Moyle Northern Ireland UK
245 G2 **Straid** Newtownabbey Northern Ireland UK
224 H4 **Stråken** *lake* Sweden
227 G3 **Strakonice** Czech Republic
234 E4 **Straldzha** Bulgaria
242 A2 **Stralongford** Omagh Northern Ireland UK
224 G5 **Stralsund** Germany
245 E3 **Stramillian** Ireland
241 F2 **Stramshall** Staffordshire England UK
245 E2 **Stranagalwilly** Strabane Northern Ireland UK
227 H3 **Strančice** Czech Republic
222 E5 **Stranda** Norway
222 E4 **Strandafjord** *bay* Norway
224 D2 **Strandavatnet** *lake* Norway
224 F4 **Strandby** Denmark
245 G2 **Strangford Lough** *bay* Northern Ireland UK
245 E2 **Stranorlar** Ireland
244 C6 **Stranraer** Dumfries and Galloway Scotland UK
234 E3 **Străoane** Romania
229 H2 **Strasbourg** France
125 M1 **Strasbourg Station** Saskatchewan Canada
227 G1 **Strasburg** Germany
125 O3 **Strasburg** North Dakota USA
226 F2 **Straßberg** Germany
127 K5 **Stratford** Ontario Canada
422 F4 **Stratford** New Zealand
130 C3 **Stratford** Oklahoma USA
129 K2 **Stratford** Texas USA
126 F4 **Stratford** Wisconsin USA
241 F3 **Stratford Tony** Wiltshire England UK
241 F2 **Stratford-upon-Avon** Warwickshire England UK
244 E2 **Strath** Highland Scotland UK
244 D5 **Strathaven** South Lanarkshire Scotland UK
121 T1 **Strathcona Islands** Nunavut Canada
118 I8 **Strathcona Provincial Park** British Columbia Canada
244 C3 **Strathkanaird** Highland Scotland UK
119 O7 **Strathmore** Alberta Canada
244 D2 **Strathmore** *watercourse* Scotland UK
244 D2 **Strathnavar** *valley* Scotland UK
425 O6 **Strathpine** Qld Australia
127 K5 **Strathroy** Ontario Canada
244 D2 **Strathy Point** Scotland UK
235 C5 **Stratoni** Greece
240 C4 **Stratton** Cornwall England UK
240 E4 **Stratton** Dorset England UK
125 N7 **Stratton** Colorado USA
125 O6 **Stratton** Nebraska USA
222 F5 **Straum** Norway
222 I2 **Straume** Norway
224 E3 **Straume** Norway
222 I3 **Straumen** Norway
227 G1 **Strausberg** Germany
125 J6 **Strawberry Reservoir** Utah USA
130 B4 **Strawn** Texas USA
227 G3 **Strážný** Czech Republic
425 J8 **Streaky Bay** SA Australia
245 E3 **Streamstown** Ireland
120 M6 **Streatfield Lake** Ontario Canada
241 F3 **Streatley** West Berkshire England UK
126 G6 **Streator** Illinois USA
227 H3 **Středočeský Kraj** *admin. area* Czech Republic
245 E3 **Street** Ireland
243 H2 **Street** North Yorkshire England UK
240 E3 **Street** Somerset England UK
125 P3 **Streeter** North Dakota USA
227 L5 **Strehaia** Romania
229 K1 **Strehla** Germany
227 L3 **Strelki** Ukraine
238 F2 **Strelkovo** Russian Federation
223 U3 **Strel'na** Russian Federation
225 O4 **Stremutka** Russian Federation
240 D4 **Strete** Devon England UK
240 E2 **Stretford** Herefordshire England UK
241 E2 **Stretton** Staffordshire England UK
117 S6 **Streymoy** *island* Faroe Islands
226 G3 **Střibro** Czech Republic
244 F3 **Strichen** Aberdeenshire Scotland UK
127 K2 **Strickland** Ontario Canada
373 G5 **Strickland** *watercourse* Papua New Guinea
226 C2 **Strijen** Netherlands
235 C5 **Strimonas** *watercourse* Greece
222 G5 **Strindfjorden** *bay* Norway
222 I3 **Strindvatnet** *lake* Norway
130 C3 **Stringtown** Oklahoma USA
222 K4 **Strittjomvare** Sweden
232 G5 **Striževo** Bosnia and Herzegovina
234 F1 **Strizhavka** Ukraine
388 F1 **Strizhi** Russian Federation
162 B4 **Strobel, Laguna** *lake* Argentina
162 D2 **Stroeder** Argentina
222 K4 **Ström** Sweden
244 E2 **Stroma, Island of** Scotland UK
222 J4 **Strömåker** Sweden
222 I2 **Strømaren** *lake* Sweden
222 J6 **Strömbacka** Sweden
233 F7 **Stromboli, Isola** *island* Italy
244 C3 **Stromeferry** Highland Scotland UK
222 J4 **Strömnäs** Sweden
244 E2 **Stromness** Orkney Islands Scotland UK
163 8 **Stromness Bay** South Georgia
222 J6 **Strömsbruk** Sweden
125 Q6 **Stromsburg** Nebraska USA
222 K2 **Strømsmo** Norway
222 I3 **Strømsnes** Norway
224 F3 **Strömstad** Sweden
222 I5 **Strömsund** Sweden
244 D4 **Stronachlachar** Stirling Scotland UK
244 D2 **Stronechrubie** Highland Scotland UK
244 D2 **Stronenaba** Highland Scotland UK
130 E4 **Strong** Arkansas USA
373 H5 **Strong, Mount** Papua New Guinea
125 Q7 **Strong City** Kansas USA
244 F1 **Stronsay** *island* Scotland UK
244 C4 **Strontian** Highland Scotland UK
245 B1 **Stroove** Ireland
227 K3 **Stropkov** Slovakia
227 H3 **Stropnice** *watercourse* Czech Republic
226 D5 **Stroppo** Italy
241 E3 **Stroud** Gloucestershire England UK
119 R6 **Struan** Saskatchewan Canada
224 E4 **Struer** Denmark
238 C3 **Strugi-Krasnyye** Russian Federation
308 D6 **Struisbaai** South Africa
245 E2 **Strule** *watercourse* Northern Ireland UK
232 D2 **Strullendorf** Germany
235 C5 **Struma** *watercourse* Bulgaria
240 B2 **Strumble Head** *cape* Wales UK
234 F3 **Strumok** Ukraine
235 C5 **Strumyani** Bulgaria
238 H4 **Strunino** Russian Federation
127 K6 **Struthers** Ohio USA
121 P6 **Strutton Islands** Nunavut Canada
234 D4 **Stryama** Bulgaria
308 D5 **Strydenburg** South Africa
119 N8 **Stryker** Montana USA
224 E2 **Strykken** *lake* Norway
227 J2 **Strykowo** Poland
227 I1 **Strykowo** Poland
222 K4 **Stryksele** Sweden
222 E6 **Stryn** Norway
224 D2 **Strynsvatnet** *lake* Norway
227 J3 **Stryszawa** Poland
234 G2 **Stryukovo** Ukraine
234 C1 **Stryy** Ukraine
234 C1 **Stryy** *watercourse* Ukraine
227 I1 **Strzałkowo** Poland
425 K7 **Strzelecki Desert** SA Australia
227 J1 **Strzelno** Poland
227 K1 **Strzyże** Poland
227 K3 **Strzyżów** Poland
131 K7 **Stuart** Florida USA
126 D6 **Stuart** Iowa USA
125 P5 **Stuart** Nebraska USA
130 C3 **Stuart** Oklahoma USA
131 K2 **Stuart** Virginia USA
118 I5 **Stuart Lake** British Columbia Canada
423 B7 **Stuart Mountains** New Zealand
425 J6 **Stuart Well** NT Australia
120 G8 **Stuartburn** Manitoba Canada
241 F4 **Stubbington** Hampshire England UK
163 11a **Stubbs** St Vincent and the Grenadines
394 C2 **Stubia** *watercourse* Ukraine
234 A2 **Štubik** Serbia
234 C3 **Studena** Bulgaria
238 E6 **Studenets** Russian Federation
241 F4 **Studland** Dorset England UK
224 I3 **Studsvik** Sweden
226 G1 **Stuer** Germany
224 H1 **Stugun** Sweden
222 G5 **Stugusjøen** *lake* Norway
222 I3 **Stuhr** Germany
120 I5 **Stull Lake** Ontario Canada
234 D2 **Stulpicani** Romania
126 B3 **Stump Lake** North Dakota USA
222 M2 **Stuorajávri** *mountain* Norway
223 P2 **Stuorát Golmmesjávri** *lake* Finland
223 O1 **Stuore Sopmir** *lake* Norway
232 H4 **Stupari** Bosnia and Herzegovina
238 H5 **Stupino** Russian Federation
243 H3 **Sturgate** Lincolnshire England UK
436 L2 **Sturge Island** Antarctica
126 E7 **Sturgeon** Missouri USA
119 W6 **Sturgeon Bay** Manitoba Canada
126 I4 **Sturgeon Bay** Michigan USA
126 H4 **Sturgeon Bay** Wisconsin USA
118 M5 **Sturgeon Heights** Alberta Canada
118 M5 **Sturgeon Lake** Alberta Canada
120 J5 **Sturgeon Lake** Ontario Canada
119 T7 **Sturgis** Saskatchewan Canada
126 H8 **Sturgis** Kentucky USA
126 I6 **Sturgis** Michigan USA
125 N4 **Sturgis** South Dakota USA
225 L4 **Stūri** Latvia
224 H4 **Stürkö** Sweden
241 H2 **Sturmer** Essex England UK
241 E4 **Sturminster Newton** Dorset England UK
234 A2 **Štúrovo** Slovakia
233 C6 **Sturraggia, Capo sa** *cape* Sardinia Italy
424 I4 **Sturt** *watercourse* NT Australia
425 K6 **Sturt Stony Desert** SA Australia
308 E6 **Stutterheim** South Africa
226 E3 **Stuttgart** Germany
130 F3 **Stuttgart** Arkansas USA
222 inset **Stykkishólmur** Iceland
227 M2 **Styr** *watercourse* Ukraine
375 G3 **Suai** Malaysia
372 C6 **Suai** Timor-Leste (East Timor)
154 C3 **Suaita** Colombia
302 F4 **Suakin** Sudan
302 F4 **Suakin Archipelago** *island* Sudan
386 E3 **Suan** North Korea
306 C5 **Suana** Democratic Republic of Congo
132 C2 **Suaqui Grande** Mexico
154 B4 **Suárez** Colombia
373 I6 **Suau** Papua New Guinea
304 D4 **Sub-Comoé** *admin. area* Côte d'Ivoire
374 E5 **Subang** Indonesia
379 G3 **Subankhata** Assam India
307 E2 **Sūbāt** *watercourse* Sudan
374 F3 **Subi Besar** *island* Indonesia
125 O8 **Sublette** Kansas USA
124 D4 **Sublimity** Oregon USA
234 A2 **Subotica** Serbia
241 I2 **Subourne** Suffolk England UK
307 F4 **Subougo** *mountain* Kenya
245 D4 **Subulter** Ireland
119 Q7 **Success** Saskatchewan Canada
128 C2 **Success, Lake** California USA
228 D3 **Sucé** France
234 E2 **Suceava** Romania
234 E2 **Suceava** *admin. area* Romania
232 G4 **Sučevići** Croatia
225 J5 **Suchacz** Poland
227 H1 **Suchań** Poland
133 G6 **Suchiate** Mexico
227 L1 **Suchowola** Poland
234 D2 **Suciu de Sus** Romania
245 D3 **Suck** *watercourse* Ireland
240 E2 **Suckley** Worcestershire England UK
373 H6 **Suckling, Cape** Papua New Guinea
373 I6 **Suckling, Mount** Papua New Guinea
159 E5 **Sucre** Bolivia
154 B4 **Sucre** Colombia
154 C2 **Sucre** Colombia
154 C2 **Sucre** *admin. area* Colombia
154 A5 **Sucre** Ecuador
155 F2 **Sucre** *admin. area* Venezuela
163 3 **Sucre, Cayo** *island* Isla de San Andrés
154 B5 **Sucúa** Ecuador
155 F4 **Sucuba** Brazil
154 B5 **Sucumbíos** *admin. area* Ecuador
159 G2 **Sucunduri** *watercourse* Brazil
159 H5 **Sucuriu** *watercourse* Brazil
154 C5 **Sucusari** Peru
305 G4 **Sud** *admin. area* Cameroon
123 G8 **Sud, Pointe du** *cape* Québec Canada
310 9b **Sud, Pointe du** *cape* Seychelles
306 D4 **Sud-Kivu** *admin. area* Democratic Republic of Congo
305 F3 **Sud-Ouest** *admin. area* Cameroon
123 G8 **Sud-Ouest, Pointe du** *cape* Québec Canada
238 G3 **Suda** Russian Federation
394 E4 **Sudak** Ukraine
302 D5 **Sudan** *country* Africa
129 K3 **Sudan** Texas USA
127 K3 **Sudbury** Ontario Canada
241 H2 **Sudbury** Suffolk England UK
227 M2 **Sudche** Ukraine
128 B3 **Sudden** California USA
222 K4 **Suddesjaur** Sweden
226 F1 **Sude** *watercourse* Germany
224 E5 **Süderoogsand** *island* Germany
227 H2 **Sudety** *region* Poland
391 H5 **Sudi** Oman
388 D1 **Sudislavl** Russian Federation
373 G7 **Sudley** QLD Australia
388 C2 **Sudogda** Russian Federation
222 L3 **Sudok** Sweden
374 B5 **Sudong, Pulau** *island* Singapore
302 E2 **Sudr** Egypt
388 E5 **Sudur** Azerbaijan
222 inset **Suðurland** *admin. area* Iceland
222 inset **Suðurnes** *admin. area* Iceland
117 S6 **Suðuroy** *island* Faroe Islands
306 D2 **Sue** *watercourse* Sudan
Suez, Gulf of *see* **Suways, Khalij as** Egypt
302 E1 **Suez Canal** *watercourse* Egypt
373 H4 **Suf Island** Papua New Guinea
119 P7 **Suffield** Alberta Canada
241 I2 **Suffolk** *admin. area* England UK
131 M2 **Suffolk** Virginia USA
125 N7 **Sugar City** Colorado USA
130 D6 **Sugar Land** Texas USA
310 5b **Sugar Loaf Point** *cape* St Helena
392 F5 **Sugauli** Bihar India
377 J5 **Sugbuhan Point** Philippines
119 T5 **Suggi Lake** Saskatchewan Canada
374 D3 **Sugi** Indonesia
240 E2 **Sugnall** Staffordshire England UK
379 G4 **Sugnu** Manipur India
377 H6 **Sugut** *watercourse* Malaysia
377 H6 **Sugut, Tanjong** *cape* Malaysia
307 F3 **Suguta** *watercourse* Kenya
383 J5 **Suhai Hu** *lake* Qinghai China
234 D4 **Suhaia** Romania
234 D4 **Suhaia, Lacul** *lake* Romania
391 H5 **Şuḩār** Oman
384 F2 **Sühbaatar** Mongolia
385 H3 **Sühbaatar** *admin. area* Mongolia
393 C9 **Suheli Par** *island* Lakshadweep India
229 J1 **Suhl** Germany
232 G4 **Suhopolje** Croatia
381 F4 **Sui Jiang** *watercourse* Guangdong China
381 H4 **Sui'an** Fujian China
159 H3 **Suiá-Missu** *watercourse* Brazil
232 G5 **Šuica** Bosnia and Herzegovina
381 G3 **Suicheng** Fujian China
380 F4 **Suicheng** Guangdong China
385 L4 **Suifenhe** Heilongjiang China
385 J3 **Suihua** Heilongjiang China
223 M2 **Suijavaara** Sweden
388 K3 **Suileng** Heilongjiang China
380 E2 **Suining** Sichuan China
223 P3 **Suininki** *lake* Finland
386 E3 **Suip-ch'on** *watercourse* South Korea
229 G2 **Suippe** *watercourse* France
245 E4 **Suir** *watercourse* Ireland
128 A1 **Suisun** California USA
381 G1 **Suixi** Anhui China
385 I5 **Suizhong** Liaoning China
382 G2 **Suizhou** Hubei China
159 F4 **Sujalito** Bolivia
392 D5 **Sujangarh** Rajasthan India
391 K5 **Sujawal** Pakistan
385 I5 **Suji** Hebei China
374 E5 **Sukabumi** Indonesia
374 E5 **Sukadana** Indonesia
375 F4 **Sukadana, Teluk** *bay* Indonesia
375 F5 **Sukaraja** Indonesia
375 F4 **Sukaramai** Indonesia
375 H2 **Sukau** Malaysia
386 E3 **Sukch'ŏn** North Korea
392 D6 **Suket** Rajasthan India
223 O5 **Sukeva** Finland
237 Y5 **Sukhana** Russian Federation
225 P6 **Sukhari** Belarus
227 M1 **Sukhinichi** Belarus
238 F5 **Sukhinichi** Russian Federation
238 H6 **Sukhodol'skiy** Russian Federation
236 J7 **Sukhona** *watercourse* Russian Federation
376 C3 **Sukhothai** Thailand
376 C3 **Sukhothai** *admin. area* Thailand
373 G6 **Suki** Papua New Guinea
302 E5 **Suki** Sudan
223 R5 **Sukkozero** Russian Federation
391 K4 **Sukkur** Pakistan
376 C4 **Sukon, Ko** *island* Thailand
387 H1 **Sukpay** *watercourse* Russian Federation
238 F4 **Sukromlya** Russian Federation
308 C4 **Suses** Namibia
237 AF6 **Suksukan** Russian Federation
386 G5 **Sukumo** Japan
372 B6 **Sukun** *island* Indonesia
222 H5 **Sul** Norway
224 C2 **Sula** *island* Norway
236 L5 **Sula** *watercourse* Russian Federation
372 C5 **Sula, Kepulauan** *island* Indonesia
223 Q5 **Sula, Ozero** *lake* Russian Federation
244 B1 **Sula Sgeir** *island* Scotland UK
391 L3 **Sulaiman Range** Pakistan
385 E5 **Sulak** Russian Federation
222 G5 **Sulåmoen** Norway
375 H6 **Sulat** *island* Indonesia
377 J5 **Sulat** Philippines
372 B4 **Sulawesi (Celebes)** *island* Indonesia
372 A4 **Sulawesi Barat** *admin. area* Indonesia
372 A4 **Sulawesi Selatan** *admin. area* Indonesia
372 B4 **Sulawesi Tengah** *admin. area* Indonesia
372 B5 **Sulawesi Tenggara** *admin. area* Indonesia
372 C3 **Sulawesi Utara** *admin. area* Indonesia
390 D5 **Sulaym** Saudi Arabia
390 F2 **Sulaymānīyah, As** *admin. area* Iraq
390 F5 **Sulayyimah** Saudi Arabia
390 F4 **Şulbūkh** Saudi Arabia
224 D3 **Suldal** Norway
224 D3 **Suldalsvatnet** *lake* Norway
244 D1 **Sule Skerry** *island* Scotland UK
227 H1 **Sulęcin** Poland
305 F3 **Suleja** Nigeria
227 J2 **Sulejów** Poland
375 H3 **Suleman, Teluk** *bay* Indonesia
222 F5 **Sulfjorden** *bay* Norway
227 M1 **Sulichevo** Belarus
234 F3 **Sulina** Romania
226 E1 **Sulingen** Germany
222 J3 **Sulitjelma** *mountain* Norway
225 M2 **Sulkava** Finland
223 O5 **Sulkavanjärvi** Finland
223 M5 **Sulkavankylä** Finland
158 A2 **Sullana** Peru
245 C5 **Sullane** *watercourse* Ireland
235 F6 **Süller** Turkey
126 G7 **Sullivan** Illinois USA
118 H7 **Sullivan Bay** British Columbia Canada
119 O7 **Sullivan Lake** Alberta Canada
240 D3 **Sully** Vale of Glamorgan Wales UK
126 E6 **Sully** Iowa USA
227 I2 **Sulmierzyce** Poland
235 E5 **Sülöğlu** Turkey
130 E5 **Sulphur** Louisiana USA
130 C3 **Sulphur** Oklahoma USA
130 D4 **Sulphur Springs** Texas USA
128 F1 **Sulphurdale** Utah USA
126 J3 **Sultan** Ontario Canada
301 K2 **Sultan** Libya
124 E3 **Sultan** Washington USA
392 F5 **Sultanpur** Uttar Pradesh India
236 K6 **Sul'tsa** Russian Federation
306 C4 **Sulu** Democratic Republic of Congo
377 I6 **Sulu Archipelago** Philippines
78 I7 **Sulu Basin** *underwater feature* Sulu Sea
377 H6 **Sulu Sea** Philippines
377 J5 **Suluan** *island* Philippines
389 K6 **Sülüktü** Kyrgyzstan
301 K2 **Sulūq** Libya
302 C1 **Sulūq** Libya
393 E9 **Suluru** Andhra Pradesh India
389 L6 **Suluu-Istik** *watercourse* Tajikistan
222 H5 **Sulviken** Sweden
388 E3 **Sulyayevka** Russian Federation
436 N1 **Sulzberger Bay** Antarctica
226 F3 **Sulzemoos** Germany
234 B3 **Šumadija** Serbia
375 H4 **Sumaianyar** Indonesia
307 G2 **Sumalē** *admin. area* Ethiopia
157 C8 **Sumaré** Brazil
236 S6 **Sumarokovo** Russian Federation
373 G4 **Sumasuma Island** Papua New Guinea
374 D4 **Sumatera (Sumatra)** *island* Indonesia
374 D4 **Sumatera Barat** *admin. area* Indonesia
374 D4 **Sumatera Selatan** *admin. area* Indonesia
374 C3 **Sumatera Utara** *admin. area* Indonesia
Sumatra *see* **Sumatera** Indonesia
226 G3 **Šumava** *range* Czech Republic
375 H6 **Sumba** *island* Indonesia
306 B3 **Sumba, Île** *island* Democratic Republic of Congo
375 H6 **Sumba, Selat** *strait* Indonesia
388 G6 **Sumbar** *watercourse* Turkmenistan
375 H6 **Sumbawa** *island* Indonesia
375 H6 **Sumbawabesar** Indonesia
306 E5 **Sumbawanga** Tanzania
308 B2 **Sumbe** Angola
374 F5 **Sumber** Indonesia
384 F3 **Sumber** Mongolia
385 I3 **Sumber** Mongolia
374 D4 **Sumbing, Gunung** *volcano* Indonesia
306 E5 **Sumbu** Zambia
304 B3 **Sumbuya** Sierra Leone
156 E4 **Sumé** Brazil
227 I4 **Sümeg** Hungary
375 G5 **Sumenep** Indonesia
388 F5 **Sumgait** Azerbaijan
225 N1 **Sumiainen** Finland
390 E4 **Sumlah** Saudi Arabia
223 N5 **Summasjärvi** *lake* Finland
244 C2 **Summer Isles** Scotland UK
124 E5 **Summer Lake** Oregon USA
308 C4 **Summerdown** Namibia
129 K3 **Summerfield** Texas USA
245 F3 **Summerhill** Ireland
118 L8 **Summerland** British Columbia Canada
123 G9 **Summerside** Prince Edward Island Canada
131 K4 **Summerton** South Carolina USA
242 A3 **Summerville** Ireland
130 F5 **Summit** Mississippi USA
130 D3 **Summit** Oklahoma USA
125 Q4 **Summit** South Dakota USA
118 I3 **Summit Lake** British Columbia Canada
423 E6 **Sumner, Lake** New Zealand
129 J3 **Sumner, Lake** New Mexico USA
118 E4 **Sumner Strait** Alaska USA
238 G2 **Sumozero, Ozero** *lake* Russian Federation
372 A5 **Sumpangbinangae** Indonesia
379 H3 **Sumrabum** Myanmar
130 G5 **Sumrall** Mississippi USA
223 P4 **Sumsa** Finland
394 E2 **Sum'ska Oblast'** *admin. area* Ukraine
223 S4 **Sumskiy Posad** Russian Federation
131 K4 **Sumter** South Carolina USA
392 D3 **Sumur** Jammu and Kashmir India/Pakistan
394 E2 **Sumy** Ukraine
308 E5 **Sun City** South Africa
124 H5 **Sun Valley** Idaho USA
393 F7 **Sunabeda** Orissa India
387 I2 **Sunagawa** Japan
392 D6 **Sunaj** Madhya Pradesh India
392 D4 **Sunam** Punjab India
379 G4 **Sunamganj** Bangladesh
127 O5 **Sunapee Lake** New Hampshire USA
305 G3 **Sunati** *watercourse* Nigeria
131 I2 **Sunbright** Tennessee USA
125 R4 **Sunburg** Minnesota USA
124 J2 **Sunburst** Montana USA
425 M9 **Sunbury** Vic. Australia
241 G3 **Sunbury** Surrey England UK
160 F4 **Sunchales** Argentina
160 F3 **Suncho Corral** Argentina
386 E4 **Sunch'ŏn** South Korea
225 K2 **Sund** Finland
222 I3 **Sund** Sweden
222 I5 **Sund** Sweden
224 F3 **Sund** Sweden
374 E5 **Sunda, Selat** *strait* Indonesia
81 O4 **Sunda Shelf** *seabed*
222 F5 **Sundan** Norway
125 M4 **Sundance** Wyoming USA
392 D4 **Sundar Nagar** Himachal Pradesh India
224 F5 **Sundby** Denmark
223 M5 **Sundby** Finland
243 G2 **Sunderland** *admin. area* England UK
243 G2 **Sunderland** Tyne and Wear England UK
226 E2 **Sundern** Germany
222 H5 **Sundet** Sweden
222 K4 **Sundö** Sweden
222 M4 **Sundom** Sweden
129 K4 **Sundown** Texas USA
119 N7 **Sundre** Alberta Canada
224 J4 **Sundre** Sweden
127 L4 **Sundridge** Ontario Canada
222 J5 **Sundsvall** Sweden
222 K5 **Sundsvallsbukten** *bay* Sweden
224 G4 **Sundsvoll** Norway
126 I5 **Sunfield** Michigan USA
128 G4 **Sunflower** Arizona USA
130 F4 **Sunflower** Mississippi USA
375 F3 **Sungai Ayak** Indonesia
374 D2 **Sungai Petani** Malaysia
374 D3 **Sungaiapit** Indonesia
374 D3 **Sungaiguntung** Indonesia
374 F4 **Sungaikakap** Indonesia
374 E4 **Sungailiat** Indonesia
374 D4 **Sungaipenuh** Indonesia
374 F3 **Sungaipinyuh** Indonesia
374 F3 **Sungairaya** Indonesia
374 E4 **Sungaipadang** Indonesia
374 B2 **Sungei Buloh Nature Park** Singapore
374 D3 **Sunggal** Indonesia
372 A5 **Sungguminasa** Indonesia
309 F3 **Sungo** Mozambique
374 E4 **Sungsang** Indonesia
394 E5 **Sungurlu** Turkey
233 C6 **Suni** Sardinia Italy
129 I5 **Sunland Park** New Mexico USA
222 G4 **Sunnan** Norway
224 H2 **Sunnansjö** Sweden
222 E5 **Sunndalen** *valley* Norway
222 F5 **Sunndalsøra** Norway
222 I5 **Sunne** Sweden
224 G3 **Sunnemo** Sweden
119 P7 **Sunnynook** Alberta Canada
128 E1 **Sunnyside** Nevada USA
125 J7 **Sunnyside** Utah USA
124 E3 **Sunnyside** Washington USA
124 D8 **Sunnyvale** California USA
124 J2 **Sunray** Texas USA
131 K7 **Sunrise** Florida USA
159 G5 **Sunsas, Serranía** *range* Bolivia
130 E5 **Sunset** Louisiana USA
130 C4 **Sunset** Texas USA
131 L4 **Sunset Beach** North Carolina USA
237 AD6 **Suntar Khayata, Khrebet** *range* Russian Federation
225 M4 **Suntaži** Latvia
391 J4 **Suntsar** Pakistan
307 F2 **Suntu** Ethiopia
386 E4 **Sunwi-do** *island* North Korea
385 K2 **Sunwu** Heilongjiang China
304 D3 **Sunyani** Ghana
223 N5 **Suolahti** Finland
237 X4 **Suolama** *watercourse* Russian Federation
223 P4 **Suolijärvi** Finland
223 O4 **Suolijärvi** *lake* Finland
223 O2 **Suolisjärvi** *lake* Finland
223 P2 **Suolisvuono** *bay* Finland
222 O1 **Suolojav'ri** *lake* Norway
223 N2 **Suomijärvi** *bay* Finland
223 P4 **Suomussalmi** Finland
384 E6 **Suonaihai** Qinghai China
384 E6 **Suonan** Gansu China
223 O5 **Suonenjoki** Finland
376 E5 **Suong** Cambodia
225 N2 **Suontee** *lake* Finland
223 O5 **Suontienselkä** *lake* Finland
222 K3 **Suorva** Sweden
223 N3 **Šuosjav'ri** Norway
223 N5 **Suotuperä** Finland
225 Q1 **Suoyarvi** Russian Federation
225 Q1 **Suoyarvi, Ozero** *lake* Russian Federation
158 B3 **Supe** Peru
128 G4 **Superior** Arizona USA
124 H3 **Superior** Montana USA
125 P6 **Superior** Nebraska USA
126 E3 **Superior** Wisconsin USA
133 G5 **Superior, Laguna** *lake* Mexico
126 H3 **Superior, Lake** Canada/USA
376 D4 **Suphan Buri** Thailand
376 C4 **Suphanburi** *admin. area* Thailand
233 E6 **Supino** Italy
372 E4 **Supiori** *island* Indonesia
436 U1 **Support Force Glacier** Antarctica
386 E3 **Supung** North Korea
227 L4 **Supuru de Jos** Romania
390 E6 **Sūq al 'Ajamah** Saudi Arabia
302 D5 **Şuq'at Al Jamal** Sudan
381 H1 **Suqian** Jiangsu China
303 I5 **Suquṭrá (Socotra)** *islands* Yemen
391 I5 **Şūr** Oman
163 5 **Sur, Cabo** *cape* Isla de Pascua (Easter Island)
128 A2 **Sur, Point** California USA
163 3 **Sur, Punta** *cape* Isla de San Andrés
388 E2 **Sura** Russian Federation
388 E2 **Sura** *watercourse* Russian Federation
391 K4 **Surab** Pakistan
375 G5 **Surabaya** Indonesia
224 I3 **Surahammar** Sweden
234 E3 **Surania** Romania
375 F5 **Surakarta** Indonesia
372 A4 **Suramana** Indonesia
232 H2 **Šurany** Slovakia
425 N6 **Surat** Qld Australia
393 C7 **Surat** Gujarat India
423 C8 **Surat Bay** New Zealand
376 C5 **Surat Thani** Thailand
376 C5 **Surat Thani** *admin. area* Thailand
392 C5 **Suratgarh** Rajasthan India
394 E2 **Surazh** Russian Federation
233 H6 **Surbo** Italy
392 C6 **Surendranagar** Gujarat India
127 N7 **Surf City** New Jersey USA
131 M3 **Surf City** North Carolina USA
425 O7 **Surfers Paradise** Qld Australia
241 G2 **Surfleet** Lincolnshire England UK
393 C7 **Surgana** Maharashtra India
228 D3 **Surgères** France
236 P6 **Surgut** Russian Federation
236 S6 **Surgutikha** Russian Federation
391 H3 **Sūrīān** Iran
393 E8 **Suriapet** Andhra Pradesh India
377 J5 **Surigao** Philippines
377 J5 **Surigao Strait** Philippines
376 D4 **Surin** Thailand
376 D4 **Surin** *admin. area* Thailand
155 H3 **Suriname** *country* South America
154 D3 **Suripa** *watercourse* Venezuela
392 F5 **Surkhet** Nepal
223 P2 **Surnujärvi** *lake* Finland
223 P2 **Surnuvuono** *bay* Finland
158 D5 **Suropa** Bolivia
388 D4 **Surovikino** Russian Federation
159 E3 **Surprêsa** Brazil
118 E3 **Surprise** British Columbia Canada
128 F4 **Surprise** Arizona USA
127 N2 **Surprise, Lac** *lake* Québec Canada
125 M2 **Surprise Valley** Saskatchewan Canada
118 J8 **Surrey** British Columbia Canada
241 G3 **Surrey** *admin. area* England UK
119 U8 **Surrey** North Dakota USA
388 E2 **Surskoye** Russian Federation
301 J2 **Surt** Libya
301 J2 **Surt, Khalij** *bay* Libya
222 inset **Surtsey** *island* Iceland
154 E5 **Surubim** Brazil
155 F4 **Surucucus, Serra dos** *range* Brazil
387 H4 **Suruga-wan** *bay* Japan
374 D4 **Surulangun** Indonesia
155 G4 **Surumatra** Guyana
129 I8 **Surutato** Mexico
388 J6 **Surxondaryo** *admin. area* Uzbekistan
154 C3 **Susa** Colombia
226 D5 **Susa** Italy
232 G5 **Sušac** *island* Croatia
232 F4 **Susak** *island* Croatia
386 G5 **Susaki** Japan
225 P3 **Susanino** Russian Federation
233 H5 **Šušanj** Montenegro
124 E6 **Susanville** California USA
226 G3 **Sušice** Czech Republic
238 C4 **Šuškova** Latvia
222 I4 **Susna** *watercourse* Norway
392 D6 **Susner** Madhya Pradesh India
381 G2 **Susong** Anhui China
154 A4 **Suspiro, Punta** *cape* Ecuador
231 H3 **Susqueda, Pantà de** *lake* Spain
160 E2 **Susques** Argentina
123 F10 **Sussex** New Brunswick Canada
309 F3 **Sussundenga** Mozambique
118 H4 **Sustut** *watercourse* British Columbia Canada
307 F4 **Susua** *mountain* Kenya
426 8 **Susubona** Solomon Islands
375 H2 **Susul** Malaysia
426 2a **Susupe** Northern Mariana Islands
235 F6 **Susurluk** Turkey
227 J1 **Susz** Poland
389 P3 **Sut-khol', Ozero** *lake* Russian Federation
383 J3 **Sutay Uul** *mountain* Mongolia
240 C4 **Sutcombe** Devon England UK
235 G7 **Sütçüler** Turkey
308 D6 **Sutherland** South Africa
125 O6 **Sutherland** Nebraska USA
423 B7 **Sutherland Sound** New Zealand
124 D5 **Sutherlin** Oregon USA
392 D4 **Sutlej** *watercourse* Punjab India
225 O4 **Sutoki** Russian Federation
124 E7 **Sutter Creek** California USA
241 G2 **Sutterton** Lincolnshire England UK
120 M1 **Sutton** *watercourse* Nunavut Canada
127 L4 **Sutton** Ontario Canada
120 M5 **Sutton** *watercourse* Ontario Canada
242 B3 **Sutton** Ireland
241 G3 **Sutton** Greater London England UK
241 I2 **Sutton** Norfolk England UK
243 H3 **Sutton** Nottinghamshire England UK
240 E2 **Sutton** Shropshire England UK
241 I2 **Sutton** Suffolk England UK
125 Q6 **Sutton** Nebraska USA
241 G2 **Sutton Bassett** Northamptonshire England UK
241 H2 **Sutton Bridge** Lincolnshire England UK
241 F2 **Sutton Coldfield** West Midlands England UK
241 F1 **Sutton in Ashfield** Nottinghamshire England UK
120 M5 **Sutton Lake** Ontario Canada
243 I3 **Sutton on Sea** Lincolnshire England UK
243 H3 **Sutton-on-Trent** Nottinghamshire England UK
241 H2 **Sutton St Edmund** Lincolnshire England UK
241 E3 **Sutton Veny** Wiltshire England UK
241 F3 **Sutton Wick** Oxfordshire England UK
300 D6 **Sutukoba** Gambia
237 AB5 **Sutun'ya** Russian Federation
116 D7 **Sutwik Island** Alaska USA
426 8 **Su'u** Solomon Islands
306 E2 **Suud** *swamp* Sudan
225 L3 **Suur Katel** *bay* Estonia
225 N4 **Suur Munamägi** *mountain* Estonia
223 Q5 **Suuri Onkamojärvi** *lake* Finland
223 P5 **Suurijärvi** *lake* Finland
427 9a **Suva** Fiji
235 B5 **Suva Gora** *range* Macedonia
234 B4 **Suva Reka** Kosovo
223 O3 **Suvanto** Finland
223 P5 **Suvasvesi** *bay* Finland
233 G7 **Suvero, Capo** *cape* Italy
238 G5 **Suvorov** Russian Federation
234 H2 **Suvorovka** Ukraine
375 G4 **Suwakong** Indonesia
225 L5 **Suwałki** Poland
131 J5/6 **Suwannee** *watercourse* Georgia/Florida USA
386 F6 **Suwanose-jima** *island* Japan
422 1 **Suwarrow Atoll** *reef* Cook Islands New Zealand
302 E2 **Suways, Khalij as (Gulf of Suez)** *bay* Egypt
386 E4 **Suwŏn** South Korea
381 G1 **Suyahu Shuiku** *lake* Henan China
389 N3 **Suykbulak** Kazakhstan
238 D2 **Suystamo** Russian Federation
388 F5 **Suz, Mys** *cape* Kazakhstan
387 H4 **Suzaka** Japan
157 C8 **Suzano** Brazil
388 C2 **Suzdal** Russian Federation
381 G1 **Suzhou** Anhui China
381 H2 **Suzhou** Jiangsu China
387 H4 **Suzuka** Japan
229 J4 **Suzzara** Italy
224 H2 **Svabensverk** Sweden
223 O1 **Sværholtklubben** *cape* Norway
223 O1 **Sværholthalvøya** *peninsula* Norway
236 D3 **Svalbard** *island* Norway
236 D3 **Svalbard** *Norway territory* Norway
234 C1 **Svalyava** Ukraine
222 J4 **Svanabyn** Sweden
222 L3 **Svanisträsket** *lake* Sweden
222 K3 **Svannäs** Sweden
222 C2 **Svanøy** Norway
224 C2 **Svanøy** *island* Norway
223 Q2 **Svanvik** Norway
222 L3 **Svappavaara** Sweden
238 E4 **Svapushcha** Russian Federation
222 inset **Svartá** *watercourse* Iceland
224 H3 **Svartå** Sweden
224 D3 **Svartevatn** *lake* Norway
222 I3 **Svartisen** *island* Norway
225 J3 **Svartlöga** *island* Sweden
225 J3 **Svartlögafjärden** *bay* Sweden
224 I2 **Svartnäs** Sweden
225 J3 **Svartsö** *island* Sweden
223 M3 **Svartträsk** Sweden
222 J4 **Svärtträsk/Gunnarsberg** Sweden
227 M2 **Svaryn'** Belarus
394 F3 **Svatove** Ukraine
376 D4 **Svay Chék** Cambodia
388 E1 **Svecha** Russian Federation
225 M5 **Svėdasai** Lithuania
222 K5 **Svedje** Sweden
222 I5 **Sveg** Sweden
222 I5 **Svegsjön** *lake* Sweden
224 C3 **Sveio** Norway
225 K5 **Švėkšna** Lithuania
224 F5 **Svendborg** Denmark
222 H4 **Svenningdal** Norway
222 K2 **Svensby** Norway
222 L4 **Svensbyfjärden** *bay* Sweden
236 G3 **Svenskøya** *island* Norway
222 I5 **Svenstavik** Sweden
225 M5 **Švenčionys** *watercourse* Lithuania
394 F3 **Sverdlovs'k** Ukraine

236 N7 **Sverdlovskaya Oblast'** *admin. area* Russian Federation
117 J3 **Sverdrup Channel** Nunavut Canada
236 Q4 **Sverdrupa, Ostrov** *island* Russian Federation
388 D4 **Svetlograd** Russian Federation
223 P2 **Svetlyy** Russian Federation
388 H3 **Svetlyy** Russian Federation
388 D4 **Svetlyy Yar** Russian Federation
225 O2 **Svetogorsk** Russian Federation
227 K3 **Svidník** Slovakia
226 G3 **Švihov** Czech Republic
225 L3 **Sviibi** Estonia
232 G5 **Svilaja** *region* Croatia
235 E5 **Svilengrad** Bulgaria
224 H4 **Svinhult** Sweden
234 C3 **Sviniţa** Romania
225 N5 **Svir, Vozyera** *lake* Belarus
225 Q2 **Sviritsa** Russian Federation
225 N5 **Svirkos** Lithuania
225 Q2 **Svir'stroy** Russian Federation
234 D4 **Svishtov** Bulgaria
227 M1 **Svislach** Belarus
238 C6 **Svislach** *watercourse* Belarus
238 C6 **Svisloch'** Belarus
238 D5 **Svistovichi** Russian Federation
227 K3 **Svit** Slovakia
227 I3 **Svitava** *watercourse* Czech Republic
232 G2 **Svitavy** Czech Republic
234 D4 **Svoboda** Bulgaria
385 K2 **Svobodnyy** Russian Federation
234 C4 **Svođe** Serbia
227 J4 **Svodín** Slovakia
232 G4 **Svodna** Bosnia and Herzegovina
234 C4 **Svoge** Bulgaria
232 H4 **Svojat** Bosnia and Herzegovina
222 I2 **Svolvær** Norway
232 G2 **Svratka** Czech Republic
234 C4 **Svrljig** Serbia
225 N5 **Svyantsyanskiya Hrady** *region* Belarus
435 K1 **Svyataya Anna Fan** *underwater feature* Arctic Ocean
435 K1 **Svyataya Anna Trough** *underwater feature* Arctic Ocean
227 N1 **Svyatitsa** Belarus
236 J5 **Svyatoy Nos, Mys** *cape* Russian Federation
225 Q2 **Svyatozero** Russian Federation
225 N5 **Svyalionys** Lithuania
241 F2 **Swadlincote** Derbyshire England UK
241 H2 **Swaffham** Norfolk England UK
426 1 **Swains Island** American Samoa
308 C4 **Swakop** *watercourse* Namibia
308 B4 **Swakopmund** Namibia
243 F2 **Swale** *watercourse* England UK
310 5c **Swales Fell** *volcano* St Helena
243 H3 **Swallow** Lincolnshire England UK
377 G6 **Swallow Reef** Spratly Islands
121 U5 **Swampy Bay** *watercourse* Québec Canada
121 N6 **Swan** *watercourse* Ontario Canada
425 L8 **Swan Hill** Vic. Australia
119 N5 **Swan Hills** Alberta Canada
134 D3 **Swan Islands** Honduras
118 G5 **Swan Lake** British Columbia Canada
125 P2 **Swan Lake** Manitoba Canada
120 J5 **Swan Lake** Ontario Canada
126 D4 **Swan Lake** Minnesota USA
124 I3 **Swan Lake** Montana USA
119 T6 **Swan Plain** Saskatchewan Canada
425 K8 **Swan Reach** SA Australia
119 U6 **Swan River** Manitoba Canada
126 E3 **Swan River** Minnesota USA
124 J5 **Swan Valley** Idaho USA
306 D6 **Swana-Mume** Democratic Republic of Congo
241 F4 **Swanage** Dorset England UK
241 H3 **Swanley** Kent England UK
425 N8 **Swansea** NSW Australia
425 N10 **Swansea** Tas. Australia
240 D3 **Swansea** Swansea Wales UK
240 D3 **Swansea** *admin. area* Wales UK
131 K4 **Swansea** South Carolina USA
240 D3 **Swansea Bay** Wales UK
125 O6 **Swanson Reservoir** Nebraska USA
127 O4 **Swanton** Vermont USA
243 G1 **Swarland** Northumberland England UK
391 I2 **Swat** *watercourse* Pakistan
309 F5 **Swaziland** *country* Africa
222 J4 **Sweden** *country* Europe
124 D4 **Sweet Home** Oregon USA
126 E7 **Sweet Springs** Missouri USA
240 C4 **Sweetshouse** Cornwall England UK
130 A4 **Sweetwater** Texas USA
125 K5 **Sweetwater** *watercourse* Wyoming USA
227 I2 **Świdnica** Poland
227 L2 **Świdnik** Poland
227 J1 **Świecie** Poland
227 J1 **Świekatowo** Poland
227 J2 **Święta Anna** Poland
227 K2 **Świętokrzyskie** *admin. area* Poland
119 R7 **Swift Current** Saskatchewan Canada
124 D3 **Swift Reservoir** Washington USA
118 F2 **Swift River** Yukon Territory Canada
226 C1 **Swifterbant** Netherlands
241 F3 **Swindon** *admin. area* England UK
241 E3 **Swindon** Gloucestershire England UK
241 F3 **Swindon** Swindon England UK
241 G2 **Swineshead** Lincolnshire England UK
245 D3 **Swinford** Ireland
242 B4 **Swinn** Ireland
244 F5 **Swinton** Scottish Borders Scotland UK
226 **Switzerland** *country* Europe
244 B4 **Swordle** Highland Scotland UK
245 F3 **Swords** Ireland
236 P5 **Syaday-Kharvuta** Russian Federation
237 AD5 **Syagannakh** Russian Federation
237 Z5 **Syalakh** Russian Federation
223 R6 **Syamozero, Ozero** *lake* Russian Federation
225 Q2 **Syas'stroy** Russian Federation
388 E1 **Syava** Russian Federation
245 B4 **Sybil Point** Ireland
238 F5 **Sychëvka** Russian Federation
238 C6 **Sychkovo** Belarus
227 J2 **Syców** Poland
225 K2 **Sydänmaa** Finland
224 E5 **Syddanmark** *admin. area* Denmark
425 N8 **Sydney** NSW Australia
124 D2 **Sydney** British Columbia Canada
123 H9 **Sydney** Nova Scotia Canada
425 inset **Sydney Bay** Norfolk Island Australia
124 B2 **Sydney Inlet** British Columbia Canada
120 H7 **Sydney Lake** Ontario Canada
123 H9 **Sydney Mines** Nova Scotia Canada
241 G1 **Syerston** Nottinghamshire England UK
394 F3 **Syeverodonets'k** Ukraine
235 C7 **Sykea** Greece
125 P3 **Sykeston** North Dakota USA
236 L6 **Syktyvkar** Russian Federation
131 H4 **Sylacauga** Alabama USA
222 H5 **Sylarna** *mountain* Norway
240 C3 **Sylen** Carmarthenshire Wales UK
379 G4 **Sylhet** Bangladesh
379 G4 **Sylhet** *admin. area* Bangladesh
224 E5 **Sylt** *island* Germany
222 E5 **Sylte** Norway
131 J3 **Sylva** North Carolina USA
120 G7 **Sylvan** Manitoba Canada
125 P7 **Sylvan Grove** Kansas USA
119 N6 **Sylvan Lake** Alberta Canada
119 S6 **Sylvania** Saskatchewan Canada
131 K4 **Sylvania** Georgia USA
126 J6 **Sylvania** Ohio USA
129 M2 **Sylvia** Kansas USA
118 I3 **Sylvia, Mount** British Columbia Canada
244 inset **Symbister** Shetland Scotland UK
235 E7 **Symi** Greece
235 E7 **Symi** *island* Greece
244 D5 **Symington** South Ayrshire Scotland UK
224 E2 **Syndin** *lake* Norway
224 E3 **Syndle** *lake* Norway
240 C2 **Synod Inn** Ceredigion Wales UK
234 G1 **Synyukha** *watercourse* Ukraine
436 C2 **Syowa (Japan)** *research station* Antarctica
Syracuse *see* **Siracusa** Italy
125 O8 **Syracuse** Kansas USA
125 Q6 **Syracuse** Nebraska USA
127 M5 **Syracuse** New York USA
388 I4 **Syrdarya** *watercourse* Kazakhstan
388 I4 **Syrdarya** *watercourse* Kazakhstan
223 N5 **Syri** Finland
394 F6 **Syria** *country*
394 F6 **Syria** *country* Middle East
235 E7 **Syrna** *island* Greece
238 D5 **Syrokorenskiye Lipki** Russian Federation
235 D7 **Syros** *island* Greece
224 I4 **Syrsan** *lake* Sweden
224 D2 **Sysenvatnet** *lake* Norway
223 O5 **Sysmä** *lake* Finland
224 G2 **Sysslebäck** Sweden
389 Q3 **Systyg-Khem** Russian Federation
223 M2 **Syväjärvi** Finland
223 O5 **Syvänsi** *lake* Finland
223 P5 **Syväri** *lake* Finland
223 O2 **Sysijärvi** *lake* Finland
388 E2 **Syzran** Russian Federation
227 L4 **Szabolcs-Szatmár-Bereg** *admin. area* Hungary
227 J2 **Szadek** Poland
373 G5 **Szaga Lake** Papua New Guinea
227 J5 **Szajk** Hungary
227 J5 **Szalánta** Hungary
234 B1 **Szalonna** Hungary
227 L4 **Szamos** *watercourse* Hungary
232 H3 **Szank** Hungary
227 I4 **Szany** Hungary
234 B2 **Szarvas** Hungary
227 H1 **Szczecin** Poland
Szczeciński, Zalew *see* **Stettiner Haff** Poland
227 J2 **Szczekociny** Poland
225 N5 **Szczerby** Belarus
227 L1 **Szczuczyn** Poland
225 K5 **Szczurkowo** Russian Federation
227 K1 **Szczytno** Poland
227 J2 **Szczyty** Poland
234 A1 **Szécsény** Hungary
234 B2 **Szeged** Hungary
227 K4 **Szeghalom** Hungary
234 B1 **Székely** Hungary
234 A2 **Székesfehérvár** Hungary
234 A2 **Szekszárd** Hungary
224 J5 **Szemud** Poland
234 B1 **Szendrő** Hungary
232 H3 **Szentendre** Hungary
234 B2 **Szentes** Hungary
227 I4 **Szentőrinc** Hungary
227 I4 **Szigetvár** Hungary
227 H2 **Szklarska Poręba** Poland
227 K4 **Szolnok** Hungary
232 G3 **Szombathely** Hungary
227 J4 **Szorosad** Hungary
227 L1 **Sztabin** Poland
227 I1 **Szubin** Poland
227 K2 **Szydłów** Poland
227 K2 **Szydłowiec** Poland
227 J2 **Szynkielów** Poland

T

381 H4 **Ta Hsu** *island* Taiwan China
376 E5 **Ta Khmau** Cambodia
382 G5 **Ta-li-mu Ho (Tarim He)** *watercourse* Xinjiang Uygur Zizhiqu China
119 N8 **Ta Ta Creek** British Columbia Canada
244 C3 **Taagan** Highland Scotland UK
377 I4 **Taal, Lake** *lake* Philippines
372 E5 **Taam** *island* Indonesia
158 D5 **Taapacá, Cerro** *mountain* Chile
223 N3 **Taapajärvi** Finland
227 J4 **Tab** Hungary
302 D5 **Tabago Hills** Sudan
129 J6 **Tabalaopa** Mexico
158 B2 **Tabalosos** Peru
375 G6 **Tabanan** Indonesia
375 H3 **Tabang** Indonesia
373 I4 **Tabar Islands** Papua New Guinea
301 H1 **Tabarka** Tunisia
391 H2 **Ţabas** Iran
132 E4 **Tabasco** Mexico
133 G5 **Tabasco** *admin. area* Mexico
302 E5 **Tabat** Sudan
158 D2 **Tabatinga** Brazil
161 I2 **Tabatinga** Brazil
301 F3 **Tabelbala** Algeria
301 H2 **Taberdga** Algeria
372 E5 **Taberfane** Indonesia
224 H4 **Taberg** Sweden
242 B4 **Taberlomina** Ireland
163 I9 **Tabernacle** Saint Kitts and Nevis
230 E5 **Tabernas** Spain
125 J6 **Tabiona** Utah USA
374 D4 **Tabir** *watercourse* Indonesia
156 F4 **Tabira** Brazil
426 1 **Tabiteuea** *island* Kiribati
154 E2 **Tablantico** Venezuela
162 A3 **Tablaruca, Punta** *cape* Chile
377 I4 **Tablas** *island* Philippines
160 D4 **Tablas, Cabo** *cape* Chile
377 I4 **Tablas Strait** Philippines
231 H5 **Tablat** Algeria
123 H8 **Table, Cap de la** *cape* Québec Canada
310 7a **Table, Pointe de la** *cape* Réunion
122 J6 **Table Bay** Newfoundland and Labrador Canada
373 I6 **Table Bay** Papua New Guinea
422 H4 **Table Cape** New Zealand
123 K6 **Table Head** Newfoundland and Labrador Canada
376 B4 **Table Island** Andaman and Nicobar Islands India
126 E8 **Table Rock Lake** Missouri USA
425 M4 **Tabletop, Mount** Qld Australia
230 C2 **Taboada** Spain
238 G5 **Tabolovo** Russian Federation
227 H3 **Tábor** Czech Republic
237 AE4 **Tabor** Russian Federation
125 Q5 **Tabor** South Dakota USA
131 L3 **Tabor City** North Carolina USA
307 E5 **Tabora** Tanzania
307 E5 **Tabora** *admin. area* Tanzania
236 N7 **Taborinskiy** Russian Federation
304 C4 **Tabou** Côte d'Ivoire
388 E6 **Tabriz** Iran
426 1 **Tabuaeran** *island* Kiribati
373 G5 **Tabubil** Papua New Guinea
230 F3 **Tabuenca** Spain
377 I3 **Tabuk** Philippines
390 C4 **Tabūk** Saudi Arabia
390 D4 **Tabūk** *admin. area* Saudi Arabia
374 B4 **Tabulan** Indonesia
374 C3 **Tabuyung** Indonesia
426 7 **Tabwémasana, Mount** *volcano* Vanuatu
224 J3 **Täby** Sweden
155 H4 **Tacalé** Brazil
132 E5 **Tacámbaro de Codallos** Mexico
133 G6 **Tacaná, Volcán** *volcano* Mexico
382 G3 **Tacheng** Xinjiang Uygur Zizhiqu China
379 I5 **Tachileik** Myanmar
154 D3 **Táchira** *admin. area* Venezuela
232 E2 **Tachov** Czech Republic
372 B5 **Tacipi** Indonesia
159 F2 **Taciua, Lago** *lake* Brazil
377 J5 **Tacloban** Philippines
158 D5 **Tacna** Peru
158 D5 **Tacna** *admin. area* Peru
160 F3 **Taco Pozo** Argentina
124 D3 **Tacoma** Washington USA
309 G3 **Tacuane** Mozambique
159 G5 **Tacuara** Bolivia
158 E4 **Tacuaral, Serranía de** *range* Bolivia
161 G3 **Tacuaras** Paraguay
161 H4 **Tacuarembó** Uruguay
161 H5 **Tacuarembó** *admin. area* Uruguay
161 H5 **Tacuarí** *watercourse* Uruguay
161 G2 **Tacuatí** Paraguay
129 H6 **Tacupeto** Mexico
377 J6 **Tacurong** Philippines
156 F4 **Tacutu** *watercourse* Brazil
243 G3 **Tadcaster** North Yorkshire England UK
303 G5 **Tadjourah** Djibouti
303 G5 **Tadjourah, Golfe de** *bay* Djibouti
301 G2 **Tadjrouna** Algeria
241 F3 **Tadley** Hampshire England UK
119 T7 **Tadmore** Saskatchewan Canada
394 F6 **Tadmur (Palmyra)** Syria
154 B3 **Tadó** Colombia
119 V3 **Tadoule Lake** Manitoba Canada
123 D8 **Tadoussac** Québec Canada
386 E4 **Taejŏn** South Korea
386 E4 **Taean** South Korea
386 F3 **Taebaek sanmaek** South Korea
386 E4 **Taebu-do** *island* South Korea
386 E3 **T'aech'ŏn** North Korea
386 E4 **Taech'ong-do** *island* North Korea
386 E3 **Taedong-gang** *watercourse* North Korea
386 F4 **Taegu** South Korea
386 E3 **Taegwan** North Korea
386 E3 **Taehung** North Korea
386 E3 **Taehwa-do** *island* North Korea
386 E4 **Taenanji-do** *island* South Korea
386 F4 **T'aepaek** South Korea
386 E4 **Taeyonp'yong-do** *island* South Korea
427 12 **Tafahi** *island* Tonga
230 F2 **Tafalla** Spain
231 J6 **Tafassour** Algeria
375 E6 **Tafermaar** Indonesia
240 D3 **Taff** *watercourse* Wales UK
160 E3 **Tafi Viejo** Argentina
222 E5 **Tafjord** Norway
300 E3 **Tafraoute** Morocco
390 G2 **Tafresh** Iran
124 F1 **Taft** British Columbia Canada
391 H3 **Taft** Iran
128 C3 **Taft** California USA
130 C7 **Taft** Texas USA
222 L5 **Täftefjärden** *bay* Sweden
376 B6 **Tafwap** Andaman and Nicobar Islands India
427 12c **Taga** Samoa
234 D2 **Taga** Romania
391 J4 **Tagas** Pakistan
377 I5 **Tagbilaran** Philippines
378 E2 **Tagchagpu Ri** *mountain* Xizang Zizhiqu China
301 F2 **Taghit** Algeria
245 F4 **Taghmon** Ireland
118 D2 **Tagish** Yukon Territory Canada
118 D3 **Tagish Lake** British Columbia Canada
232 E3 **Tagliamento** *watercourse* Italy
232 E4 **Tagliamento, Punta** *cape* Italy
377 I5 **Tagolo Point** Philippines
388 H5 **Tagta** Turkmenistan
388 I7 **Tagtabazar** Turkmenistan
157 C6 **Taguatinga** Brazil
373 J6 **Tagula** Papua New Guinea
373 J6 **Tagula Island** Papua New Guinea
377 J6 **Tagum** Philippines
Tagus *see* **Tejo** Portugal
118 L7 **Tahaetkun Mountain** British Columbia Canada
374 D2 **Tahan, Gunung** *mountain* Malaysia
301 H4 **Tahat, Mont** *mountain* Algeria
385 J2 **Tahe** Heilongjiang China
427 14 **Tahiti** *island* French Polynesia
427 14a **Tahiti Iti** French Polynesia
427 14a **Tahiti Nui** French Polynesia
124 C5 **Tahkenitch Lake** Oregon USA
225 L3 **Tahkuna Nina** *cape* Estonia
130 D3 **Tahlequah** Oklahoma USA
118 F3 **Tahltan** British Columbia Canada
124 E7 **Tahoe, Lake** California USA
116 I4 **Tahoe Lake** Nunavut Canada
129 L4 **Tahoka** Texas USA
301 H6 **Tahoua** Niger
118 H8 **Tahsis** British Columbia Canada
302 E2 **Ţahţā** Egypt
235 F6 **Tahtaköprü** Turkey
118 H6 **Tahtsa Lake** British Columbia Canada
158 D3 **Tahuamanu** *watercourse* Bolivia
427 14 **Tahuata** *island* French Polynesia
372 C3 **Tahulandang** *island* Indonesia
372 C3 **Tahuna** Indonesia
304 C3 **Taï** Liberia
376 D3 **Tai** Thailand
381 H2 **Tai Hu** *lake* Jiangsu China
385 I6 **Tai Shan** *range* Shandong China
385 I6 **Tai'an** Shandong China
380 E1 **Taibai Shan** *mountain* Shaanxi China
385 J5 **Taibao D** *mountain* Shandong China
381 I5 **T'aichung** Taiwan China
423 D7 **Taieri** *watercourse* New Zealand
423 D8 **Taieri Mouth** New Zealand
380 E3 **Taigong** Guizhou China
385 H5 **Taihang Shan** *range* Hebei China
385 H6 **Taihang Shan** *range* Shanxi China
422 F4 **Taihape** New Zealand
381 G1 **Taihe** Anhui China
381 F4 **Taihe** Guangdong China
380 E2 **Taihe** Sichuan China
381 G2 **Taihu** Anhui China
385 J3 **Taikang** Heilongjiang China
376 B3 **Taikkyi** Myanmar
385 J3 **Tailai** Heilongjiang China
374 C4 **Taileleo** Indonesia
237 U6 **Taimba** Russian Federation
223 N5 **Taimoniemi** Finland
304 D3 **Tain** *watercourse* Ghana
244 D3 **Tain** Highland Scotland UK
381 H4 **T'ainan** Taiwan China
235 C7 **Tainaro, Akra** *cape* Greece
158 C4 **Taino** Peru
157 D6 **Taiobeiras** Brazil
373 J5 **Taiof Island** Papua New Guinea
372 B4 **Taipa** Indonesia
223 N4 **Taipale** Finland
223 O4 **Taipaleenharju** Finland
381 H4 **T'aipao** Taiwan China
381 I3 **T'aipei** Taiwan China
381 G4 **Taiping** Guangdong China
380 E4 **Taiping** Guangxi Zhuangzu Zizhiqu China
374 D2 **Taiping** Malaysia
423 D6 **Taipo** *watercourse* New Zealand
156 F4 **Taipu** Brazil
385 H6 **Taiqian** Henan China
386 F6 **Taira-shima** *island* Japan
242 D1 **Tairlaw** South Ayrshire Scotland UK
422 F3 **Tairua** New Zealand
374 D4 **Tais** Indonesia
381 F4 **Taishan** Guangdong China
381 H3 **Taishun** Zhejiang China
374 D4 **Taitaitanopo** *island* Indonesia
162 A4 **Taitao, Península de** *peninsula* Chile
423 E6 **Taitapu** New Zealand
158 E2 **Taititu** Brazil
381 I4 **T'aitung** Taiwan China
381 H4 **Taitung Shan** *range* Taiwan China
223 P4 **Taivalkoski** Finland
381 H4 **Taiwan** *admin. area* China
381 H4 **Taiwan** *island* Taiwan China
381 H4 **Taiwan Strait** Taiwan China
381 H2 **Taixing** Jiangsu China
132 E5 **Taixtan** Mexico
302 E5 **Taiyara** Sudan
389 K2 **Taiynsha (Krasnoarmeysk)** Kazakhstan
385 G5 **Taiyuan** Shanxi China
385 G6 **Taiyue Shan** *range* Shanxi China
381 H2 **Taizhou** Jiangsu China
381 I3 **Taizhou** Zhejiang China
390 E7 **Ta'izz** Yemen
388 H6 **Taj Ed Din** Iran
162 A3 **Tajamar, Punta** *cape* Chile
301 H3 **Tajarḥī** Libya
230 E3 **Tajera, Embalse de la** *lake* Spain
158 E4 **Tajibo** Bolivia
389 K6 **Tajikistan** *country*
387 H4 **Tajimi** Japan
129 I6 **Tajirachic** Mexico
230 E3 **Tajo** *watercourse* Spain
159 E6 **Tajsara, Cordillera de** *range* Bolivia
230 E3 **Tajuña** *watercourse* Spain
376 C3 **Tak** Thailand
376 C3 **Tak** *admin. area* Thailand
427 I5 **Taka Atoll** Marshall Islands
388 E7 **Takāb** Iran
381 J3 **Takabanare-jima** *island* Japan
307 G3 **Takabba** Kenya
436 Q1 **Takahe, Mount** *mountain* Antarctica
387 I3 **Takahoko-numa** *lake* Japan
423 E5 **Takaka** New Zealand
372 A5 **Takalar** Indonesia
155 G3 **Takama** Guyana
310 9b **Takamaka** Seychelles
386 G4 **Takamatsu** Japan
386 F5 **Takanabe** Japan
387 H4 **Takaoka** Japan
422 G5 **Takapau** New Zealand
381 K2 **Takara-jima** *island* Japan
427 14 **Takaroa** *island* French Polynesia
308 D4 **Takatshwane** Botswana
422 F3 **Takatu Point** New Zealand
386 F5 **Take-shima** *island* Japan
374 C2 **Takengon** Indonesia
224 H3 **Tåkern** *lake* Sweden
388 F7 **Tākestān** Iran
376 E5 **Takêv** Cambodia
389 K7 **Takhār** *admin. area* Afghanistan
231 G6 **Takhemaret** Algeria
118 D2 **Takhini** Yukon Territory Canada
118 C2 **Takhini** *watercourse* Yukon Territory Canada
391 J3 **Takht** Afghanistan
391 L3 **Takht-i-Sulaiman** *mountain* Pakistan
388 D4 **Takhta** Russian Federation
301 H6 **Takiéta** Niger
119 U5 **Takipy** Manitoba Canada
375 G4 **Takisung** Indonesia
423 B7 **Takitimu Mountains** New Zealand
387 I3 **Takizawa** Japan
387 J2 **Takkobu-numa** *lake* Japan
118 H5 **Takla Lake** British Columbia Canada
118 I5 **Takla Landing** British Columbia Canada
382 G5 **Taklamakan Desert** Xinjiang Uygur Zizhiqu China
Taklamakan Shamo *see* **Taklamakan Desert** China
304 D4 **Takoradi** Ghana
304 E3 **Takpamba** Togo
118 E3 **Taku** British Columbia Canada
118 E3 **Taku** *watercourse* British Columbia Canada
376 C5 **Takua Pa** Thailand
305 F3 **Takum** Nigeria
306 B4 **Takundi** Democratic Republic of Congo
422 1 **Takutea** *island* Cook Islands New Zealand
222 K2 **Takvatnet** *lake* Norway
121 S7 **Takwa** *watercourse* Québec Canada
392 D6 **Tal** Madhya Pradesh India
391 L2 **Tal** Pakistan
240 C2 **Tal-gareg** Ceredigion Wales UK
383 I3 **Tal Nuur** *lake* Mongolia
242 E3 **Tal-y-Cafn** Conwy Wales UK
240 D2 **Tal-y-llyn** Gwynedd Wales UK
240 C1 **Tal-y-sarn** Gwynedd Wales UK
161 H5 **Tala** Uruguay
225 O5 **Talachyn** Belarus
242 E3 **Talacre** Flintshire Wales UK
427 10a **Talafo'ou** Tonga
162 C3 **Talagapa** Argentina
393 C7 **Talaja** Gujarat India
130 D2 **Talala** Oklahoma USA
134 D5 **Talamanca, Cordillera de** *range* Costa Rica
374 F5 **Talang** Indonesia
374 D4 **Talang, Gunung** *volcano* Indonesia
134 C3 **Talanga** Honduras
374 E4 **Talangbatu** Indonesia
374 E4 **Talangbetutu** Indonesia
229 G3 **Talant** France
391 L2 **Talar Kandao** *pass* Pakistan
158 A2 **Talara** Peru
158 A2 **Talara, Bahía de** *bay* Peru
389 K5 **Talas** Kyrgyzstan
389 K5 **Talas** *admin. area* Kyrgyzstan
389 K5 **Talas** *watercourse* Kyrgyzstan
373 I5 **Talasea** Papua New Guinea
238 E5 **Talashkino** Russian Federation
393 C7 **Talasri** Maharashtra India
372 C2 **Talaud, Kepulauan** *island* Indonesia
230 F4 **Talave, Embalse de** *lake* Spain
230 D4 **Talavera de la Reina** Spain
373 I5 **Talawe, Mount** *volcano* Papua New Guinea
392 E6 **Talbehat** Uttar Pradesh India
117 L3 **Talbot Inlet** Nunavut Canada
118 F5 **Talbot Lake** Manitoba Canada
131 I4 **Talbotton** Georgia USA
160 D5 **Talca** Chile
160 C6 **Talcahuano** Chile
130 D4 **Talco** Texas USA
238 G4 **Taldom** Russian Federation
389 M5 **Taldy-su** Kyrgyzstan
389 M5 **Taldykorgan** Kazakhstan
389 K3 **Taldysay** Kazakhstan
234 D3 **Talea** Romania
228 D4 **Talence** France
240 D2 **Talerddig** Powys Wales UK
389 M5 **Talgar** Kazakhstan
240 D3 **Talgarth** Powys Wales UK
302 F4 **Talguharai** Sudan
225 M3 **Tali** Estonia
306 E2 **Tali Post** Sudan
372 C4 **Taliabu** *island* Indonesia
226 D5 **Taliard** France
377 J5 **Talibon** Philippines
130 D3 **Talihina** Oklahoma USA
393 D8 **Talikota** Karnataka India
155 H4 **Talimã** Brazil
377 I5 **Talisay** Philippines
375 H3 **Talisayan** Indonesia
244 B3 **Talisker** Highland Scotland UK
238 H3 **Talitsy** Russian Federation
375 H6 **Taliwang** Indonesia
116 D6 **Talkeetna** Alaska USA
390 E2 **Tall 'Afar** Iraq
391 J3 **Tall Kala** Afghanistan
244 C3 **Talladale** Highland Scotland UK
131 H4 **Talladega** Alabama USA
131 I5 **Tallahassee** Florida USA
244 D5 **Tallaminnoch** South Ayrshire Scotland UK
242 B3 **Tallanstown** Ireland
131 I4 **Tallapoosa** Georgia USA
229 H4 **Tallard** France
240 D3 **Talley** Carmarthenshire Wales UK
118 H6 **Tallheo** British Columbia Canada
225 M3 **Tallinn** Estonia
223 Q4 **Talloreka** Russian Federation
245 D4 **Tallow** Ireland
130 F4 **Tallulah** Louisiana USA
223 O5 **Talluskylä** Finland
125 N2 **Talmage** Saskatchewan Canada
228 D4 **Talmont** France
236 S5 **Talnakh** Russian Federation
394 D3 **Tal'ne** Ukraine
306 E1 **Talodi** Sudan
426 5 **Talofofo** Guam
130 B2 **Taloga** Oklahoma USA
237 AE7 **Talon** Russian Federation
389 K7 **Tāloqān** Afghanistan
436 K2 **Talos Dome** *mountain* Antarctica
388 C3 **Talovaya** Russian Federation
117 J5 **Taloyoak** Nunavut Canada
163 9 **Talparo** Trinidad and Tobago
385 I3 **Talping Ling** *mountain* Nei Mongol Zizhiqu China
131 I5 **Talquin, Lake** Florida USA
240 C2 **Talsarn** Ceredigion Wales UK
240 C2 **Talsarnau** Gwynedd Wales UK
225 L4 **Talsi** Latvia
225 L4 **Talsu** *admin. area* Latvia
160 D3 **Taltal** Chile
119 O2 **Taltson** *watercourse* Northwest Territories Canada
374 D3 **Talu** Indonesia
372 B3 **Taludaa** Indonesia
372 D4 **Taluti, Teluk** *bay* Indonesia
223 M1 **Talvik** Norway
242 D3 **Talwrn** Isle of Anglesey Wales UK
240 D3 **Talybont** Powys Wales UK
376 D3 **Tam Kỳ** Vietnam
230 D2 **Tama** Spain
126 E6 **Tama** Iowa USA
375 G3 **Tama Abu, Banjaran** *range* Malaysia
388 D3 **Tamala** Russian Federation
304 D3 **Tamale** Ghana
375 F4 **Tamalung** Indonesia
230 C3 **Tamames** Spain
375 G5 **Taman** Indonesia
426 1 **Tamana** *island* Kiribati
300 E2 **Tamanar** Morocco
156 F5 **Tamandaré** Brazil
159 I5 **Tamandaré** Brazil
161 G6 **Tamangueyú** Argentina
301 I3 **Tamanhint** Libya
300 E6 **Tamani** Mali
386 G4 **Tamano** Japan
301 H4 **Tamanrasset** Algeria
240 C4 **Tamar** *watercourse* England UK
163 7 **Tamar Harbour** *bay* Falkland Islands
154 C3 **Tamara** Colombia
131 K7 **Tamarac** Florida USA
310 7b **Tamarin** Mauritius
234 E4 **Tamarino** Bulgaria
231 G3 **Tamarite de Litera** Spain
160 D2 **Tamarugel, Pampa de** *region* Chile
227 L2 **Tamashowka** Belarus
227 J4 **Tamási** Hungary
133 F3 **Tamaulipas** *admin. area* Mexico
132 E5 **Tamazula de Gordiano** Mexico
300 D6 **Tambacounda** Senegal
375 I5 **Tambalongang** *island* Indonesia
375 F4 **Tambanmunjul** Indonesia
304 E2 **Tambao** Burkina Faso
157 C8 **Tambaú** Brazil
372 B5 **Tambea** Indonesia
374 E3 **Tambelan, Kepulauan** *island* Indonesia
374 E3 **Tambelan Besar** *island* Indonesia
375 G5 **Tamberu** Indonesia
158 E6 **Tambillo** Bolivia
158 B2 **Tambillo** Peru
158 C5 **Tambillo** Peru
160 D4 **Tambillos, Nevados de los** *range* Chile
372 A2 **Tambisan** Malaysia
375 H2 **Tambisan** Malaysia
425 M6 **Tambo** Qld Australia
158 C4 **Tambo** Peru
158 C5 **Tambo** *watercourse* Peru
304 C3 **Tambo, Lac de** *lake* Côte d'Ivoire
158 B3 **Tambo del Sol** Peru
158 A2 **Tambo Grande** Peru
154 D5 **Tambo Yaguas** Peru
154 D5 **Tambo Yanayacu** Peru
309 H3 **Tambohorano** Madagascar
372 B4 **Tamboli** Indonesia
158 D4 **Tambopata** Peru
158 D4 **Tambopata** *watercourse* Peru
308 B3 **Tambor** Angola
375 H6 **Tambora, Gunung** *volcano* Indonesia
156 D4 **Tamboril** Brazil
388 D3 **Tambov** Russian Federation
388 D3 **Tambovskaya Oblast'** *admin. area* Russian Federation
230 B2 **Tambre** *watercourse* Spain
375 H3 **Tambu, Teluk** *bay* Indonesia
375 H2 **Tambulanan, Bukit** *mountain* Malaysia
306 D2 **Tambura** Sudan
375 H2 **Tambuyukon, Gunung** *mountain* Malaysia
300 D5 **Tâmchekket** Mauritania
389 L5 **Tamchy** Kyrgyzstan
388 H3 **Tamdy** Kazakhstan
154 D3 **Tame** Colombia
129 I8 **Tameapa** Mexico
230 C3 **Tâmega** *watercourse* Portugal/Spain
162 B4 **Tamel Aike** Argentina
235 D7 **Tamelos, Akra** *cape* Greece
243 F3 **Tameside** *admin. area* England UK
301 H5 **Tamgak, Adrar** *mountain* Niger
389 J4 **Tamgaly** *lake* Kazakhstan
304 B2 **Tamgué, Massif du** *mountain* Guinea
133 F4 **Tamiahua** Mexico
133 F4 **Tamiahua, Laguna de** *lake* Mexico
374 C2 **Tamiang** *watercourse* Indonesia
374 C2 **Tamiang, Ujung** *cape* Indonesia
393 E9 **Tamil Nadu** *admin. area* India
390 E2 **Ta'mim, At** *admin. area* Iraq
375 G4 **Taminglayang** Indonesia
234 B3 **Tamiš** *watercourse* Serbia
223 U4 **Tamitsa** Russian Federation
245 F2 **Tamlaght** Magherafelt Northern Ireland UK
231 J5 **Tamlouka** Algeria
225 N2 **Tammijärvi** *lake* Finland
225 N2 **Tammio** *island* Finland
224 I2 **Tämnaren** *lake* Sweden
234 C3 **Tamnič** Serbia
301 G6 **Tamou** Niger
131 J7 **Tampa** Florida USA
129 N1 **Tampa** Kansas USA
131 J7 **Tampa Bay** Florida USA
374 E5 **Tampang** Indonesia
225 L2 **Tampere** Finland
132 B2 **Tampico** Mexico
133 F4 **Tampico** Mexico
374 D3 **Tampin** Malaysia
374 E3 **Tampines** *admin. area* Singapore
372 B5 **Tampo** Indonesia
227 G4 **Tamsweg** Austria
379 H4 **Tamu** Myanmar
426 5 **Tamuning** Guam
425 N7 **Tamworth** NSW Australia
241 F2 **Tamworth** Staffordshire England UK
386 E4 **Tanyang** South Korea
389 L4 **Tan** Kazakhstan
301 H3 **Tan Emellel** Algeria
381 F4 **Tan Jiang** *watercourse* Guangdong China
376 E3 **Tân Kỳ** Vietnam
300 D3 **Tan-Tan** Morocco
307 G4 **Tana** *watercourse* Kenya
223 P1 **Tana Bru** Norway
302 F5 **T'ana Hāyk'** *lake* Ethiopia
387 G5 **Tanabe** Japan
157 B8 **Tanabi** Brazil
234 E2 **Tanacu** Romania
223 P1 **Tanafjorden** *bay* Norway
237 AL8 **Tanaga Island** Alaska USA
374 F5 **Tanah, Tanjung** *cape* Indonesia
374 D2 **Tanah Merah** Malaysia
374 C4 **Tanahbala** *island* Indonesia
375 H4 **Tanahgrogot** Indonesia
375 I5 **Tanahjampea** *island* Indonesia
375 H3 **Tanahkuning** Indonesia
374 C4 **Tanahmasa** *island* Indonesia
374 D3 **Tanahputih** Indonesia
379 H3 **Tanaing** Myanmar
375 H5 **Tanakeke** *island* Indonesia
392 E5 **Tanakpur** Uttaranchal India
236 Q4 **Tanama** *watercourse* Russian Federation
424 I5 **Tanami Desert** NT Australia
116 D5 **Tanana** Alaska USA
116 E6 **Tanana** *watercourse* Alaska USA
309 H4 **Tanandava** Madagascar
223 P1 **Tananes** Norway
377 I4 **Tanauan** Philippines
241 H5 **Tancarville** France
381 H1 **Tancheng** Shandong China
386 F3 **Tanch'ŏn** North Korea
304 D3 **Tanda** Côte d'Ivoire
393 D6 **Tanda** Madhya Pradesh India
392 F5 **Tanda** Uttar Pradesh India
234 C3 **Tanda** Serbia
300 F5 **Tanda, Lac** *lake* Mali
377 J5 **Tandag** Philippines
375 H2 **Tandek** Malaysia
301 F5 **Tanderiouel** *watercourse* Mali
161 G6 **Tandil** Argentina
161 G6 **Tandil, Sierra del** *range* Argentina
305 H3 **Tandjilé** *admin. area* Chad
224 G2 **Tandö** Sweden
391 K4 **Tando Adam** Pakistan
391 K4 **Tando Allahyar** Pakistan
391 K5 **Tando Bago** Pakistan
245 F2 **Tandragee** Armagh Northern Ireland UK
377 I6 **Tandubatu** *island* Philippines
386 F5 **Tanega-shima** *island* Japan
222 G5 **Tanem** Norway
372 B5 **Tanete** Indonesia
372 C4 **Taneti** *island* Indonesia
245 E3 **Tang** Ireland
381 H3 **Tang Yu** *island* Fujian China
307 F5 **Tanga** Tanzania
307 F5 **Tanga** *admin. area* Tanzania
373 J4 **Tanga Islands** Papua New Guinea
393 E10 **Tangalla** Sri Lanka
306 D5 **Tanganyika, Lake** Tanzania
156 F4 **Tangará** Brazil
222 H5 **Tångböle** Sweden
381 F3 **Tangdukou** Hunan China
436 D2 **Tange Promontory** *peninsula* Antarctica
224 F2 **Tangen** Norway
300 E1 **Tanger (Tangier)** Morocco
300 E1 **Tanger-Tétouan** *admin. area* Morocco
374 E5 **Tangerang** Indonesia
379 G2 **Tanggula (Dangla) Shan** *range* Xizang Zizhiqu China
379 G2 **Tanggula Shan** *mountain* Xizang Zizhiqu China
379 G2 **Tanggula Shankou** *pass* Xizang Zizhiqu China
385 I5 **Tanghai** Hebei China
381 F2 **Tanghe** Henan China
391 L2 **Tangi** Pakistan
Tangier *see* **Tanger** Morocco
422 F5 **Tangimoana** New Zealand
130 F5 **Tangipahoa** Louisiana USA
372 B4 **Tangkelemboke, Gunung** *mountain* Indonesia
374 E5 **Tangkittebak, Gunung** *mountain* Indonesia
379 G3 **Tangla** Assam India
393 E7 **Tangla** Maharashtra India
379 F2 **Tanglha Range** Xizang Zizhiqu China
422 E2 **Tangowahine** New Zealand
374 B2 **Tangse** Indonesia
385 I5 **Tangshan** Hebei China
392 E3 **Tangtse** Jammu and Kashmir India/Pakistan
154 B4 **Tangua** Colombia
304 E2 **Tanguiéta** Benin
381 G4 **Tangxi Shuiku** *lake* Guangdong China
379 I4 **Tangyan** Myanmar
385 H6 **Tangyin** Henan China
385 L3 **Tangyuan** Heilongjiang China
157 D6 **Tanhaçu** Brazil
223 O3 **Tanhua** Finland
225 O2 **Tani** Finland
379 H2 **Taniantaweng Shan** *range* Xizang Zizhiqu China
372 D6 **Tanimbar, Kepulauan** *island* Indonesia
155 E3 **Tanimiña** Venezuela
224 H2 **Tåningen** *lake* Sweden
376 C4 **Tanintharyi** *admin. area* Myanmar
372 E4 **Tanisapata** Indonesia
372 D4 **Taniwel** Indonesia
374 D3 **Tanjong Karang** Malaysia
374 D3 **Tanjong Malim** Malaysia
375 G4 **Tanjung** Indonesia
374 F2 **Tanjung Belungkor**
375 F4 **Tanjung Puting, Taman Nasional** *park* Indonesia
374 D4 **Tanjungagung** Indonesia
375 H4 **Tanjungaru** Indonesia
375 H3 **Tanjungbalai** Indonesia
372 C4 **Tanjungbaliha** Indonesia
374 D3 **Tanjungbatu** Indonesia

375 H3 **Tanjungbuayabuaya** *island* Indonesia
374 E4 **Tanjungpandan** Indonesia
374 E3 **Tanjungpinang** Indonesia
374 C3 **Tanjungpura** Indonesia
374 E4 **Tanjungraja** Indonesia
375 H3 **Tanjungredeb** Indonesia
374 F4 **Tanjungsaleh** *island* Indonesia
374 F4 **Tanjungsatai** Indonesia
375 H3 **Tanjungselor** Indonesia
375 F4 **Tanjungwaringin** Indonesia
223 O2 **Tankapirtti** Finland
242 B4 **Tankardstown** Ireland
304 D3 **Tankuw** *watercourse* Ghana
381 H2 **Tanmu Shan** *range* Zhejiang China
226 F2 **Tann** Germany
426 7 **Tanna** *island* Vanuatu
222 H5 **Tännäs** Sweden
222 H5 **Tänndalen** Sweden
226 F2 **Tanne** Germany
118 L8 **Tanner, Mount** British Columbia Canada
223 N4 **Tannila** Finland
126 F2 **Tannin** Ontario Canada
389 P3 **Tannu-Ola, Khrebet** *range* Russian Federation
390 G4 **Tannūrah, Ra's** *cape* Saudi Arabia
304 D3 **Tano** *watercourse* Ghana
392 C5 **Tanot** Rajasthan India
301 H6 **Tânout** Niger
300 E2 **Tanout Ou Filal, Tizi** *pass* Morocco
393 C7 **Tansa** *watercourse* Maharashtra India
392 F5 **Tansen** Nepal
302 E1 **Ţanţā** Egypt
379 H5 **Tantabin** Myanmar
229 H2 **Tantonville** France
381 I2 **Tantou Shan** *range* Zhejiang China
118 F6 **Tanu** British Columbia Canada
307 F4 **Tanu** *watercourse* Kenya
393 E8 **Tanuku** Andhra Pradesh India
224 F3 **Tanumshede** Sweden
425 K8 **Tanunda** SA Australia
240 D2 **Tanygrisiau** Gwynedd Wales UK
237 AK5 **Tanyurer** *watercourse* Russian Federation
307 E5 **Tanzania** *country* Africa
118 F3 **Tanzilla** *watercourse* British Columbia Canada
384 E6 **Tao He** *watercourse* Gansu China
380 D1 **Tao He** *watercourse* Jiangsu China
381 I2 **Taohua Dao** *island* Zhejiang China
381 F3 **Taohuajiang** Hunan China
385 J3 **Taonan** Jilin China
427 15 **Taongi Atoll** *island* Marshall Islands
233 F8 **Taormina** Italy
129 J2 **Taos** New Mexico USA
300 F4 **Taoudenni** Mali
231 G5 **Taougrite** Algeria
301 F2 **Taourirt** Morocco
384 E6 **Taoyang** Gansu China
381 I4 **T'aoyüan** Taiwan China
381 H2 **Taozhou** Anhui China
133 G6 **Tapachula** Mexico
159 F5 **Tapado** Bolivia
374 D2 **Tapah** Malaysia
159 G2 **Tapajós** *watercourse* Brazil
374 C3 **Tapaktuan** Indonesia
161 F6 **Tapalqué** Argentina
374 D4 **Tapan** Indonesia
155 H4 **Tapanahoni** *lake* Suriname
423 C7 **Tapanui** New Zealand
374 C3 **Tapanuli, Teluk** *bay* Indonesia
155 H5 **Tapará, Ilha Grande do** *island* Brazil
155 H5 **Tapará, Serra do** *range* Brazil
372 C4 **Tapat** *island* Indonesia
159 E2 **Tapauá** *watercourse* Brazil
157 A8 **Tapejara** Brazil
161 H4 **Tapejara** Brazil
159 G5 **Tapenema** Bolivia
155 F5 **Tapera** Brazil
156 E4 **Taperoá** Brazil
157 E6 **Taperoá** Brazil
304 C3 **Tapeta** Liberia
376 D3 **Taphan Hin** Thailand
393 D7 **Tapi** *watercourse* Madhya Pradesh India
393 D7 **Tapi** *watercourse* Maharashtra India
162 B5 **Tapi Aike** Argentina
377 I6 **Tapiantana Group** *island* Philippines
375 F4 **Tapinbini** Indonesia
373 H6 **Tapini** Papua New Guinea
223 O3 **Tapionniemi** Finland
157 D5 **Tapiramutá** Brazil
157 B5 **Tapirapé** *watercourse* Brazil
155 E4 **Tapirapecó, Sierra** *range* Venezuela
159 G4 **Tapirapuã** Brazil
159 G4 **Tapirapuã, Serra do** *range* Brazil
392 G5 **Taplejung** Nepal
304 E2 **Tapoa** *watercourse* Burkina Faso
232 G3 **Tapolca** Hungary
372 A4 **Tappalang** Indonesia
124 F1 **Tappen** British Columbia Canada
125 P3 **Tappen** North Dakota USA
387 H3 **Tappi-numa** *lake* Japan
422 F3 **Tapu** New Zealand
423 E5 **Tapuae-o-Uenuku** *mountain* New Zealand
422 H3 **Tapuaeroa** *watercourse* New Zealand
377 I6 **Tapul** *island* Philippines
377 I6 **Tapul Group** *island* Philippines
374 C3 **Tapulonanjing** *mountain* Indonesia
391 H6 **Ţāqah** Oman
159 H5 **Taquari** Brazil
161 I4 **Taquari** Brazil
159 H5 **Taquari, Serra do** *range* Brazil
157 B8 **Taquaritinga** Brazil
157 B8 **Taquarituba** Brazil
162 C3 **Taquetrén, Laguna** *lake* Argentina
232 E4 **Tar** Croatia
234 A2 **Tar** Hungary
131 M3 **Tar** *watercourse* North Carolina USA
234 A4 **Tara** *watercourse* Montenegro
305 G3 **Taraba** *admin. area* Nigeria
305 G3 **Taraba** *watercourse* Nigeria
301 I2 **Tarābulus (Tripoli)** Libya
234 F3 **Taraclia** Moldova
301 I3 **Tarāghin** Libya
154 D4 **Taraira** Brazil
310 3d **Tarajalejo** Canary Islands
375 H3 **Tarakan** Indonesia
375 H3 **Tarakan** *island* Indonesia
235 G5 **Taraklı** Turkey
381 I4 **Tarama-jima** *island* Japan
372 C6 **Taramana** Indonesia
392 D6 **Tarana** Madhya Pradesh India
392 D5 **Taranagar** Rajasthan India
422 F4 **Taranaki** *admin. area* New Zealand
422 F4 **Taranaki (Egmont), Mount** *volcano* New Zealand
230 E3 **Tarancón** Spain
244 A3 **Taransay** *island* Scotland UK
244 A3 **Taransay, Sound of** *bay* Scotland UK
233 G6 **Taranto** Italy
233 G7 **Taranto, Golfo di** *bay* Italy
423 D7 **Taranui** New Zealand
158 D5 **Tarapacá** *admin. area* Chile
426 8 **Tarapaina** Solomon Islands
154 B5 **Tarapoa** Ecuador
158 B2 **Tarapoto** Peru
391 H5 **Ţaraq** United Arab Emirates
229 G4 **Tarare** France
161 G5 **Tarariras** Uruguay
229 G5 **Tarascon** France
228 E5 **Tarascon-sur-Ariège** France
234 G1 **Tarashcha** Ukraine
234 G1 **Tarasovka** Ukraine
236 K5 **Tarasovo** Russian Federation
301 H3 **Tarat** Algeria
159 E5 **Tarata** Bolivia
426 1b **Taratai** Kiribati
426 1b **Taratai** *island* Kiribati
158 D3 **Tarauacá** Brazil
158 D2 **Tarauacá** *watercourse* Brazil
427 14a **Taravao** French Polynesia
426 1 **Tarawa** *island* Kiribati
373 G4 **Tarawai Island** Papua New Guinea
422 G4 **Tarawera** New Zealand
422 G4 **Tarawera, Lake** New Zealand
422 G4 **Tarawera, Mount** *volcano* New Zealand
389 K5 **Taraz (Zhambyl)** Kazakhstan
230 F3 **Tarazona** Spain
230 F4 **Tarazona de la Mancha** Spain
382 F3 **Tarbagatai Shan** *range* Xinjiang Uygur Zizhiqu China
389 N4 **Tarbagatai Shan** *range* Kazakhstan
389 N4 **Tarbagatavy, Khrebet** *range* Kazakhstan
389 N4 **Tarbagatay** Kazakhstan
244 E3 **Tarbat Ness** *cape* Scotland UK
245 C4 **Tarbert** Ireland
228 E5 **Tarbes** France
244 C2 **Tarbet** Highland Scotland UK
244 D5 **Tarbolton** South Ayrshire Scotland UK
131 M3 **Tarboro** North Carolina USA
425 J7 **Tarcoola** SA Australia
228 D5 **Tardets-Sorholus** France
228 E4 **Tardoire** *watercourse* France
425 O7 **Taree** NSW Australia
223 M3 **Tärendö** Sweden
390 E6 **Ţarfā, Ra's at** *cape* Saudi Arabia
302 E2 **Ţarfā, Wādī aţ** *watercourse* Egypt
300 D3 **Tarfaya** Morocco
244 F4 **Tarfside** Angus Scotland UK
230 D6 **Targa** Morocco
227 K1 **Targowo** Poland
234 E3 **Târgu Bujor** Romania
234 C3 **Târgu Jiu** Romania
234 D2 **Târgu-Mureş** Romania
234 E2 **Târgu Secuiesc** Romania
300 F2 **Targuist** Morocco
301 I2 **Tarhūnah** Libya
384 E2 **Tarialan** Mongolia
154 D4 **Tariana** Brazil
384 D3 **Tariat** Mongolia
391 H5 **Ţarif** United Arab Emirates
230 D5 **Tarifa** Spain
230 D6 **Tarifa, Punta de** *cape* Spain
377 I3 **Tarigtig Point** Philippines
159 E6 **Tarija** Bolivia
160 E2 **Tarija** *admin. area* Bolivia
231 H6 **Tarik Ibn Ziad** Algeria
372 F4 **Tariku** *watercourse* Indonesia
390 G7 **Tarim** Yemen
382 H4 **Tarim He** *watercourse* Xinjiang Uygur Zizhiqu China
132 E4 **Tarimoro** Mexico
391 K3 **Tarin Kowt** Afghanistan
373 F4 **Taritatu** *watercourse* Indonesia
223 N5 **Tarjannevesi** *bay* Finland
236 Q6 **Tarko-Sale** Russian Federation
238 D3 **Tarkovichi** Russian Federation
304 D3 **Tarkwa** Ghana
377 I4 **Tarlac** Philippines
242 F3 **Tarleton** Lancashire England UK
227 M4 **Târlişua** Romania
158 C3 **Tarma** Peru
245 C4 **Tarmon** Ireland
228 E5 **Tarn** *watercourse* France
222 I4 **Tärnaby** Sweden
391 K3 **Tarnak Rūd** *watercourse* Afghanistan
222 I4 **Tärnasjön** *lake* Sweden
222 E5 **Tårnes** Norway
223 Q2 **Tårnet** Norway
224 H4 **Tärnö** *island* Sweden
227 K2 **Tarnobrzeg** Poland
232 H3 **Tárnok** Hungary
228 D5 **Tarnos** France
227 K3 **Tarnov** Slovakia
227 K5 **Târnova** Romania
227 K2 **Tarnów** Poland
227 I1 **Tarnówka** Poland
232 C4 **Taro** *watercourse* Italy
391 H4 **Ţarom** Iran
379 G3 **Tarong** Xizang Zizhiqu China
425 N6 **Taroom** Qld Australia
224 E5 **Tarp** Germany
234 C1 **Tarpa** Hungary
131 J6 **Tarpon Springs** Florida USA
154 C5 **Tarqui** Peru
233 D5 **Tarquinia** Italy
222 J3 **Tarradalen** *valley* Sweden
310 4a **Tarrafal** Cape Verde
231 G3 **Tarragona** Spain
222 K3 **Tårrajaur** Sweden
241 E4 **Tarrant Gunville** Dorset England UK
423 C7 **Tarras** New Zealand
231 G3 **Tàrrega** Spain
244 E3 **Tarrel** Highland Scotland UK
224 F4 **Tårs** Denmark
301 J4 **Tarso Emissi** *mountain* Chad
394 E6 **Tarsus** Turkey
160 F2 **Tartagal** Argentina
232 D4 **Tartaro, Fiume** *watercourse* Italy
155 I4 **Tartarugal Grande** Brazil
228 D5 **Tartas** France
225 N3 **Tartu** Estonia
225 N3 **Tartumaa** *admin. area* Estonia
394 E6 **Tartus** Syria
422 G4 **Taruarau** *watercourse* New Zealand
157 B8 **Tarumã** Brazil
388 E5 **Tarumovka** Russian Federation
238 G5 **Tarusa** Russian Federation
376 C6 **Tarutao, Ko** *island* Thailand
374 C3 **Tarutung** Indonesia
234 F2 **Tarutyne** Ukraine
222 F5 **Tarva** *island* Norway
223 O5 **Tarvaala** Finland
222 F5 **Tarvahavet** *bay* Norway
225 L2 **Tarvainen** Finland
237 AD6 **Tas-Kystabyt, Khrebet** *range* Russian Federation
237 AB4 **Tas-Tumus** Russian Federation
129 H7 **Tasajeras** Mexico
301 I3 **Tasāwah** Libya
388 J5 **Tasbuget** Kazakhstan
132 D2 **Táscate** Mexico
127 L2 **Taschereau** Québec Canada
375 G2 **Tasek Merimbun National Park** Brunei
118 J7 **Taseko Lakes** British Columbia Canada
389 K5 **Tash-Kömür** Kyrgyzstan
382 E5 **Tashiku'ergan** Xinjiang Uygur Zizhiqu China
391 H3 **Tashk, Daryācheh-ye** *lake* Iran
Tashkent *see* **Toshkent** Uzbekistan
225 K4 **Tāši** Latvia
121 T3 **Tasialujjuaq, Lac** *lake* Québec Canada
121 R3 **Tasiat, Lac** *lake* Québec Canada
374 F5 **Tasikmalaya** Indonesia
121 U3 **Tasiujaq** Québec Canada
121 X4 **Tasiuyak Tasialua Lake** Newfoundland and Labrador Canada
222 I4 **Tåsjö** Sweden
222 I4 **Tåsjön** *lake* Sweden
389 M4 **Taskesken** Kazakhstan
389 R3 **Taskyl-Sajtyg, Gora** *mountain* Russian Federation
423 E5 **Tasman** *admin. area* New Zealand
423 E5 **Tasman Bay** New Zealand
78 K13 **Tasman Fracture Zone** *underwater feature* Tasman Sea
423 E5 **Tasman Mountains** New Zealand
425 M10 **Tasman Peninsula** Tas. Australia
78 L11 **Tasman Plain** *underwater feature* Tasman Sea
425 P8 **Tasman Sea** Oceania
425 M10 **Tasmania** *admin. area* Tas. Australia
234 A2 **Tass** Hungary
301 H5 **Tassara** Niger
121 S3 **Tassialouc, Lac** *lake* Québec Canada
117 P5 **Tassiilaq** Greenland
304 E2 **Tassiné** *watercourse* Benin
121 Q7 **Tast, Lac du** *lake* Québec Canada
389 N4 **Tastau, Gora** *mountain* Kazakhstan
118 E6 **Tasu Sound** British Columbia Canada
426 8 **Tasure** Solomon Islands
232 H3 **Tát** Hungary
300 E3 **Tata** Morocco
372 C6 **Tata Mailau, Gunung** *mountain* Timor-Leste (East Timor)
227 J4 **Tatabánya** Hungary
234 A2 **Tataháza** Hungary
427 14 **Tatakoto** *island* French Polynesia
123 G10 **Tatamagouche** Nova Scotia Canada
426 8 **Tatamba** Solomon Islands
301 I2 **Tataouine** Tunisia
232 F4 **Tatar Varoš** Croatia
234 E1 **Tătăraşeni, Lacul** *lake* Romania
234 F3 **Tatarbunary** Ukraine
235 G6 **Tatarlı** Turkey
225 P5 **Tatarsk** Russian Federation
237 AD9 **Tatarskiy Proliv** *strait* Russian Federation
234 E3 **Tătarul, Lacul** *lake* Romania
375 G3 **Tatau** Malaysia
373 J4 **Tatau Island** Papua New Guinea
384 F2 **Tataurovo** Russian Federation
372 E4 **Tatawa** Indonesia
162 A5 **Tate, Cabo** *cape* Chile
387 H4 **Tateyama** Japan
387 H4 **Tateyama** *volcano* Japan
118 M2 **Tathlina Lake** Northwest Territories Canada
390 E6 **Tathlith** Saudi Arabia
390 E6 **Tathlīth, Wādī** *watercourse* Saudi Arabia
425 N9 **Tathra** NSW Australia
159 F6 **Tatí** Bolivia
119 W2 **Tatinnai Lake** Nunavut Canada
388 E3 **Tatishchevo** Russian Federation
379 H5 **Tatkon** Myanmar
118 I7 **Tatla Lake** British Columbia Canada
118 H4 **Tatlatui Provincial Park** British Columbia Canada
118 I7 **Tatlayoko Lake** British Columbia Canada
120 J4 **Tatnam, Cape** Manitoba Canada
118 G4 **Tatogga** British Columbia Canada
234 A1 **Tatry, Nízke** *range* Slovakia
118 C3 **Tatshenshini** *watercourse* British Columbia Canada
388 D4 **Tatsinskiy** Russian Federation
157 C8 **Tatuí** Brazil
129 K4 **Tatum** New Mexico USA
130 D4 **Tatum** Texas USA
394 G5 **Tatvan** Turkey
240 E4 **Tatworth** Somerset England UK
427 12 **Tau** *island* American Samoa
156 D4 **Tauá** Brazil
426 6a **Tauanap, Mochun** *strait* Federated States of Micronesia
157 C8 **Taubaté** Brazil
226 E3 **Tauber** *watercourse* Germany
229 J2 **Tauberzell** Germany
388 F5 **Tauchik** Kazakhstan
229 H3 **Täuffelen** Switzerland
306 E2 **Taufikia** Sudan
422 G4 **Tauhara** *volcano* New Zealand
422 F4 **Taumarunui** New Zealand
422 G5 **Taumatawhakatangihangakoauauo tamateapokai-whenuakitanatahu** *mountain* New Zealand
308 D5 **Taung** South Africa
379 H5 **Taungdwingyi** Myanmar
379 H5 **Taunggyi** Myanmar
376 C3 **Taunggyi Tanen** *watercourse* Thailand
376 C4 **Taungnyo Range** Myanmar
379 H5 **Taungup** Myanmar
391 L3 **Taunsa** Pakistan
240 D3 **Taunton** Somerset England UK
127 P6 **Taunton** Massachusetts USA
422 G4 **Taupo** New Zealand
422 F4 **Taupo, Lake** New Zealand
422 F2 **Taupo Bay** New Zealand
78 L11 **Taupo Tablemount** *underwater feature* Tasman Sea
225 L5 **Tauragė** Lithuania
225 L5 **Tauragės** *admin. area* Lithuania
154 C3 **Tauramena** Colombia
422 G3 **Tauranga** New Zealand
373 H5 **Tauri** *watercourse* Papua New Guinea
233 G7 **Taurianova** Italy
233 H7 **Taurisano** Italy
225 M4 **Taurkalne** Latvia
422 E2 **Tauroa Point** New Zealand
225 L4 **Tausalo ežeras** *lake* Lithuania
427 14a **Tautira** French Polynesia
223 N4 **Tauvo** Finland
235 E6 **Tavaklı** Turkey
120 I1 **Tavani** Nunavut Canada
229 H3 **Tavannes** Switzerland
230 B3 **Tavarede** Portugal
156 E4 **Tavares** Brazil
223 Q3 **Tavayarvi, Ozero** *lake* Russian Federation
236 O7 **Tavda** Russian Federation
241 I2 **Taverham** Norfolk England UK
307 F4 **Taveta** Kenya
427 9 **Taveuni** *island* Fiji
230 C5 **Tavira** Portugal
230 C5 **Tavira, Ilha de** *cape* Portugal
240 C4 **Tavistock** Devon England UK
389 M3 **Tavolzhan** Kazakhstan
235 F6 **Tavşanlı** Turkey
427 9a **Tavua** Fiji
240 D4 **Taw** *watercourse* England UK
393 E6 **Tawa** *lake* Madhya Pradesh India
375 H2 **Tawai, Bukit** *mountain* Malaysia
427 9a **Tawake** Fiji
130 C4 **Tawakoni, Lake** Texas USA
379 G3 **Tawang** Arunachal Pradesh India
126 J4 **Tawas City** Michigan USA
119 O5 **Tawatinaw** Alberta Canada
119 O5 **Tawatinaw** *watercourse* Alberta Canada
375 H2 **Tawau** Malaysia
375 H2 **Tawau, Teluk** *bay* Malaysia
302 D5 **Taweisha** Sudan
377 I6 **Tawi Tawi** *island* Philippines
302 C5 **Tawila** Sudan
222 I5 **Tåxan** Sweden
133 F5 **Taxco** Mexico
244 E4 **Tay** *watercourse* Scotland UK
244 D4 **Tay, Loch** *lake* Scotland UK
376 E5 **Tây Ninh** Vietnam
377 I4 **Tayabas Bay** Philippines
375 F4 **Tayan** Indonesia
372 E5 **Tayandu** Indonesia
372 E5 **Tayandu** *island* Indonesia
372 D5 **Tayandu, Kepulauan** *island* Indonesia
391 I2 **Taybād** Iran
223 R2 **Taybola** Russian Federation
307 G3 **Tayeeglow** Somalia
235 E5 **Tayfur** Turkey
389 O2 **Tayga** Russian Federation
237 AH6 **Taygonos, Mys** *cape* Russian Federation
237 AH6 **Taygonos, Poluostrov** *peninsula* Russian Federation
128 G3 **Taylor** Arizona USA
130 E4 **Taylor** Arkansas USA
126 J5 **Taylor** Michigan USA
125 P6 **Taylor** Nebraska USA
130 C5 **Taylor** Texas USA
125 L7 **Taylor Park Reservoir** *park* Colorado USA
130 G5 **Taylorsville** Mississippi USA
131 K3 **Taylorsville** North Carolina USA
124 J6 **Taylorsville** Utah USA
126 G7 **Taylorville** Illinois USA
390 D4 **Taymā'** Saudi Arabia
237 U6 **Taymura** *watercourse* Russian Federation
236 T5 **Taymyr** Russian Federation
237 V4 **Taymyr, Ozero** *lake* Russian Federation
237 V3 **Taymyr, Poluostrov** *peninsula* Russian Federation
241 F3 **Taynton** Oxfordshire England UK
244 C4 **Taynuilt** Argyll and Bute Scotland UK
132 D3 **Tayoltita** Mexico
244 B5 **Tayovullin** Argyll and Bute Scotland UK
244 F4 **Tayport** Fife Scotland UK
237 U7 **Tayshet** Russian Federation
377 H5 **Taytay** Philippines
377 H5 **Taytay Bay** Philippines
375 F5 **Tayu** Indonesia
155 F3 **Tayucay** Venezuela
236 R5 **Taz** *watercourse* Russian Federation
300 F2 **Taza** Morocco
300 F2 **Taza-Al Hoceima-Taounate** *admin. area* Morocco
387 I3 **Tazawa-ko** *lake* Japan
119 Q2 **Tazin** *watercourse* Northwest Territories Canada
119 Q3 **Tazin Lake** Saskatchewan Canada
302 C2 **Tāzirbū** Libya
236 P5 **Tazovskaya Guba** *bay* Russian Federation
236 Q5 **Tazovskiy** Russian Federation
301 H4 **Tazrouk** Algeria
300 E2 **Tazzarine** Morocco
388 D5 **T'bilisi** Georgia
388 D5 **Tbilisi** Georgia
304 E3 **Tchamba** Togo
304 E3 **Tchaourou** Benin
118 I5 **Tchentlo Lake** British Columbia Canada
304 E3 **Tchetti** Benin
305 G5 **Tchibanga** Gabon
301 H5 **Tchighozérine** Niger
301 H5 **Tchin-Tabaradene** Niger
305 G3 **Tcholliré** Cameroon
130 F4 **Tchula** Mississippi USA
225 J5 **Tczew** Poland
423 B7 **Te Anau** New Zealand
423 B7 **Te Anau, Lake** New Zealand
422 H3 **Te Araroa** New Zealand
422 G4 **Te Aute** New Zealand
422 F4 **Te Awamutu** New Zealand
422 G4 **Te Awanga** New Zealand
422 E2 **Te Hapua** New Zealand
422 G4 **Te Haroto** New Zealand
422 F3 **Te Henga (Bethells Beach)** New Zealand
422 G3 **Te Kaha** New Zealand
422 E2 **Te Kao** New Zealand
422 G4 **Te Karaka** New Zealand
422 E3 **Te Kopuru** New Zealand
422 F4 **Te Kuiti** New Zealand
427 2 **Te Manga** *volcano* Cook Islands New Zealand
422 E2 **Te Paki** New Zealand
423 D6 **Te Pirita** New Zealand
422 G3 **Te Puke** New Zealand
422 G4 **Te Teko** New Zealand
423 B8 **Te Waewae Bay** New Zealand
Te Waihora *see* **Ellesmere, Lake** New Zealand
422 G4 **Te Whaiti** New Zealand
155 E5 **Tea** *watercourse* Brazil
125 Q5 **Tea** South Dakota USA
133 H4 **Teabo** Mexico
132 D4 **Teacapán** Mexico
129 K4 **Teague** New Mexico USA
130 C5 **Teague** Texas USA
427 14a **Teahupoo** French Polynesia
163 7 **Teal Inlet** Falkland Islands
243 H3 **Tealby** Lincolnshire England UK
426 1b **Teaoraereke** Kiribati
133 G5 **Teapa** Mexico
427 14a **Teavaro** French Polynesia
373 F4 **Teba** Indonesia
230 D5 **Teba** Spain
301 G6 **Tébarat** Niger
374 F3 **Tebas** Indonesia
243 F2 **Tebay** Cumbria England UK
375 F3 **Tebedu** Malaysia
301 H1 **Tébessa** Algeria
301 H2 **Tébessa** *admin. area* Algeria
374 C3 **Tebingtinggi** Indonesia
374 D4 **Tebingtinggi** Indonesia
160 D2 **Tebinquiche, Laguna** *lake* Chile
374 D4 **Tebo** *watercourse* Indonesia
301 H1 **Tébourba** Tunisia
301 H1 **Téboursouk** Tunisia
132 E5 **Tecalitlán** Mexico
132 A1 **Tecate** Mexico
228 F5 **Tech** *watercourse* France
304 D3 **Techiman** Ghana
235 B6 **Techniti Limni Kremaston** *lake* Greece
162 B3 **Tecka** Argentina
132 F5 **Tecoanapa** Mexico
133 H4 **Tecoh** Mexico
128 E4 **Tecolote** Mexico
132 D4 **Tecolotlán** Mexico
132 E5 **Tecomán** Mexico
133 F5 **Tecomate, Laguna** *lake* Mexico
129 H6 **Tecoriname** Mexico
132 C2 **Tecoripa** Mexico
133 E5 **Tecpán de Galeana** Mexico
133 G5 **Tecpatán** Mexico
132 D4 **Tecuala** Mexico
125 Q6 **Tecumseh** Nebraska USA
130 G3 **Ted** Somalia
161 G6 **Tedín Uriburu** Argentina
388 H6 **Tedzhenskiy Oazis** *watercourse* Turkmenistan
134 D4 **Tee Kamp** Nicaragua
129 K5 **Teec Nos Pos** Arizona USA
389 P3 **Teeli** Russian Federation
223 P4 **Teeriranta** Finland
243 F2 **Tees** *watercourse* England UK
243 G2 **Tees Bay** England UK
243 F2 **Teesdale** *valley* England UK
383 J3 **Teetsenuul** Mongolia
427 13a **Tefala** *island* Tuvalu
155 E4 **Tefé** Brazil
159 E2 **Tefé** *watercourse* Brazil
155 E5 **Tefé, Lago** *lake* Brazil
235 F7 **Tefenni** Turkey
241 E3 **Teffont Magna** Wiltshire England UK
374 F5 **Tegal** Indonesia
226 D2 **Tegelen** Netherlands
222 J5 **Tegelträsket** *lake* Sweden
305 F2 **Tegina** Nigeria
388 I3 **Tegissor Koli** *lake* Kazakhstan
234 B2 **Téglás** Hungary
240 C3 **Tegryn** Pembrokeshire Wales UK
426 7 **Tégua** *island* Vanuatu
162 B2 **Teguilda** Chile
134 C4 **Tegucigalpa** Honduras
301 H5 **Teguidda-n-Tessoumt** Niger
310 3d **Teguise** Canary Islands
128 C3 **Tehachapi** California USA
124 D6 **Tehama** California USA
117 J5 **Tehek Lake** Nunavut Canada
304 D3 **Téhini** Côte d'Ivoire
225 M2 **Tehinselkä** *bay* Finland
127 K4 **Tehkummah** Ontario Canada
390 G2 **Tehrān** Iran
388 F7 **Tehrān** *admin. area* Iran
392 E4 **Tehri** Uttaranchal India
133 F5 **Tehuacán** Mexico
132 C2 **Tehuachi** Mexico
133 G6 **Tehuantepec, Golfo de** *bay* Mexico
133 G5 **Tehuantepec, Istmo de** *region* Mexico
79 W6 **Tehuantepec Ridge** *underwater feature* Pacific Ocean
162 C4 **Tehuelches** Argentina
310 3a **Teide, Pico de** *volcano* Canary Islands
240 D4 **Teignmouth** Devon England UK
225 L2 **Teisko** Finland
302 E4 **Teiti** Sudan
156 E4 **Teixeira** Brazil
230 C3 **Teixoso** Portugal
129 K8 **Tejaban de la Rosita** Mexico
375 G6 **Tejakula** Indonesia
388 H6 **Tejen** Turkmenistan
310 3a **Tejina** Canary Islands
230 C4 **Tejo (Tagus)** *watercourse* Portugal
132 E5 **Tejupan, Punta** *cape* Mexico
125 Q6 **Tekamah** Nebraska USA
423 D7 **Tekapo** *watercourse* New Zealand
423 D6 **Tekapo, Lake** New Zealand
133 H4 **Tekax de Álvaro Obregón** Mexico
389 J5 **Teke** Kazakhstan
389 K2 **Teke Koli** *lake* Kazakhstan
388 H4 **Tekeli** Kazakhstan
382 F4 **Tekes He** *watercourse* Xinjiang Uygur Zizhiqu China
382 G4 **Tekesi** Xinjiang Uygur Zizhiqu China
227 L5 **Tekija** Serbia
382 F6 **Tekiliktag** *mountain* Xinjiang Uygur Zizhiqu China
394 C5 **Tekirdağ** *admin. area* Turkey
393 F7 **Tekkali** Andhra Pradesh India
374 F3 **Tekong, Pulau** *island* Singapore
374 F3 **Tekong Kechil, Pulau** *island* Singapore
372 B4 **Teku** Indonesia
390 C3 **Tel Aviv-Yafo** Israel
306 D6 **Tela** Democratic Republic of Congo
134 C4 **Tela** Honduras
388 E5 **T'elavi** Georgia
227 H3 **Telč** Czech Republic
236 G2 **Tel'ch'ye** Russian Federation
234 D2 **Telciu** Romania
310 3b **Telde** Canary Islands
306 C3 **Tele** *watercourse* Democratic Republic of Congo
374 C3 **Tele** Indonesia
375 G4 **Telegapulang** Indonesia
130 B5 **Telegraph** Texas USA
222 K3 **Telejaur** Sweden
427 13a **Telele** *island* Tuvalu
157 B9 **Telêmaco Borba** Brazil
224 E3 **Telemark** *admin. area* Norway
375 H3 **Telen** *watercourse* Indonesia
235 E7 **Telendos** *island* Greece
234 D3 **Teleorman** *admin. area* Romania
301 H4 **Telertheba, Djebel** *mountain* Algeria
159 H4 **Teles Pires** *watercourse* Brazil
163 10a **Telescope Point** *cape* Grenada
389 O3 **Teletskoye, Ozero** *lake* Russian Federation
424 G5 **Telfer** WA Australia
120 H8 **Telford** Manitoba Canada
240 E2 **Telford** Telford and Wrekin England UK
127 N6 **Telford** Pennsylvania USA
240 E2 **Telford and Wrekin** *admin. area* England UK
226 F4 **Telfs** Austria
226 D2 **Telgte** Germany
134 C4 **Telica** Nicaragua
304 B2 **Télimélé** Guinea
234 D4 **Telish** Bulgaria
227 K3 **Telkibánya** Hungary
118 H5 **Telkwa** British Columbia Canada
116 C5 **Teller** Alaska USA
162 C4 **Tellier** Argentina
226 C2 **Tellin** Belgium
154 C4 **Tello** Colombia
383 K3 **Telmen** Mongolia
383 K3 **Telmen Nuur** *lake* Mongolia
374 C4 **Telok Blangah** *admin. area* Singapore
162 C3 **Telsen** Argentina
225 L5 **Telšiai** Lithuania
225 L5 **Telšiai** *admin. area* Lithuania
375 F4 **Telukbatang** Indonesia
374 D4 **Telukbayur** Indonesia
374 C3 **Telukdalam** Indonesia
374 D4 **Telukkuantan** Indonesia
375 F4 **Telukmelano** Indonesia
375 E4 **Teluknaga** Indonesia
374 C3 **Teluknibung** Indonesia
374 F4 **Telukpakedai** Indonesia
393 E10 **Telulla** Sri Lanka
304 D3 **Tema** Ghana
426 1b **Temaiku** *island* Kiribati
374 F3 **Temaju** *island* Indonesia
160 D4 **Temas de Socos** Chile
132 D4 **Temascal** Mexico
427 14 **Tematangi** *island* French Polynesia
237 U5 **Tembenchi** *watercourse* Russian Federation
374 D4 **Tembesi** *watercourse* Indonesia
374 D4 **Tembilahan** Indonesia
308 E5 **Tembisa** South Africa
306 B5 **Tembo Aluma** Angola
309 F2 **Tembwe** Zambia
240 E2 **Teme** *watercourse* England UK
128 D4 **Temecula** California USA
376 D6 **Temengor, Tasik** *lake* Malaysia
375 F5 **Teméra** Mali
374 D3 **Temerloh** Malaysia
374 E3 **Temiang** *island* Indonesia
374 D2 **Temiang, Bukit** *mountain* Malaysia
372 D4 **Teminabuan** Indonesia
389 K3 **Temirtau** Kazakhstan
121 T7 **Témiscamie** *watercourse* Québec Canada
127 L3 **Témiscaming** Québec Canada
127 L3 **Témiscamingue, Lac** *lake* Québec Canada
123 D9 **Témiscouata, Lac** *lake* Québec Canada
238 F5 **Temkino** Russian Federation
223 N4 **Temmes** Finland
388 D2 **Temnikov** Russian Federation
425 M8 **Temora** NSW Australia
132 C2 **Temósachic** Mexico
426 8 **Temotu** *admin. area* Solomon Islands
133 H4 **Temozón** Mexico
128 G4 **Tempe** Arizona USA
154 C5 **Tempestad** Peru
374 D4 **Tempino** Indonesia
233 C6 **Tempio Pausania** Sardinia Italy
130 C5 **Temple** Texas USA
240 C2 **Temple Bar** Ceredigion Wales UK
425 L3 **Temple Bay** Qld Australia
241 I3 **Temple Ewell** Kent England UK
133 J2 **Temple Terrace** Florida USA
245 E4 **Templemore** Ireland
242 A1 **Templemoyle** Ireland
245 E4 **Templetuohy** Ireland
245 E2 **Tempo** Fermanagh Northern Ireland UK
133 F4 **Tempoal** *watercourse* Mexico
133 F4 **Tempoal de Sánchez** Mexico
238 G4 **Tempy** Russian Federation
229 G1 **Temse** Belgium
160 C6 **Temuco** Chile
423 D7 **Temuka** New Zealand
380 D3 **Temuli** Sichuan China
388 H3 **Temyasovo** Russian Federation
224 D6 **Ten Boer** Netherlands
376 A5 **Ten Degree Channel** Andaman and Nicobar Islands India
123 K8 **Ten Mile Pond** Newfoundland and Labrador Canada
125 L4 **Ten Sleep** Wyoming USA
131 K8 **Ten Thousand Islands** Florida USA
154 B5 **Tena** Ecuador
133 H4 **Tenabó** Mexico
225 L2 **Tenala** Finland
229 G4 **Tenay** France
240 E2 **Tenbury Wells** Worcestershire England UK
240 C3 **Tenby** Pembrokeshire Wales UK
228 G4 **Tence** France
303 G5 **Tendaho** Ethiopia
229 H4 **Tende** France
229 H4 **Tende, Colle di** *pass* France
302 E5 **Tendelti** Sudan
301 F2 **Tendrara** Morocco
310 3 **Tenerife** *island* Canary Islands
301 G1 **Ténès** Algeria
375 J3 **Tenga** Indonesia
375 H5 **Tengah, Kepulauan** *island* Indonesia
380 F4 **Tengcheng** Guangxi Zhuangzu Zizhiqu China
380 C3 **Tengchong** Yunnan China
388 F5 **Tenge** Kazakhstan
372 D5 **Tenggara, Kepulauan** *island* Indonesia
375 H4 **Tenggarong** Indonesia
384 E5 **Tengger Shamo** Nei Mongol Zizhiqu China
376 D6 **Tenggol** *island* Malaysia
375 H2 **Tenghilan** Malaysia
389 L3 **Tengiz** *lake* Kazakhstan
381 H1 **Tengzhou** Shandong China
161 E3 **Teniente López** Peru
160 F2 **Teniente Ochoa** Paraguay
160 F6 **Teniente Origone** Argentina
158 B2 **Teniente Pinglo** Peru
124 D2 **Tenino** Washington USA
393 D10 **Tenkasi** Tamil Nadu India
306 D6 **Tenke** Democratic Republic of Congo
116 B5 **Tenkergynpil'gyn, Laguna** *lake* Russian Federation
130 D3 **Tenkiller Ferry Lake** Oklahoma USA
304 D2 **Tenkodogo** Burkina Faso
124 C5 **Tenmile Lake** Oregon USA
232 E5 **Tenna** *watercourse* Italy
233 E8 **Tenna, Punta** *cape* Italy
224 G2 **Tennänget** Sweden
425 J4 **Tennant Creek** NT Australia
115 **Tennessee** *admin. area* USA
130 G2 **Tennessee** *watercourse* Kentucky/Tennessee USA
229 G1 **Tenneville** Belgium
222 J2 **Tennevoll** Norway
131 J4 **Tennille** Georgia USA
223 P3 **Tenniöjoki** *watercourse* Finland
160 D5 **Teno** Chile
310 3a **Teno, Punta de** *cape* Canary Islands
375 G2 **Tenom** Malaysia
133 H5 **Tenosique de Pino Suárez** Mexico
124 G3 **Tensed** Idaho USA
125 R3 **Tenstrike** Minnesota USA
388 H4 **Tentekor** *lake* Kazakhstan
388 I3 **Tentekor Koli** *lake* Kazakhstan
372 B4 **Tentena** Indonesia
241 H3 **Tenterden** Kent England UK
425 N7 **Tenterfield** NSW Australia
372 B3 **Tentolomatinan, Gunung** *mountain* Indonesia
230 B2 **Teo** Spain
132 E4 **Teocaltiche** Mexico
157 A8 **Teodoro Sampaio** Brazil
157 D7 **Teófilo Otoni** Brazil
377 I6 **Teomabal** *island* Philippines
392 E6 **Teonthar** Madhya Pradesh India
133 G5 **Teopisca** Mexico
235 B5 **Teovo** Macedonia
304 D3 **Tepa** Ghana
375 J5 **Tepa** Indonesia
422 4 **Tepa Point** Niue New Zealand
132 E5 **Tepalcatepec** Mexico
223 N2 **Tepasto** Finland
132 D3 **Tepehuanes** Mexico
309 G2 **Tepere** Mozambique
133 F4 **Tepetzintla** Mexico
375 H3 **Tepianlangsat** Indonesia
132 D4 **Tepic** Mexico
158 C2 **Tepiche** *watercourse* Peru
226 G3 **Teplá** Czech Republic
227 G2 **Teplice** Czech Republic
238 G6 **Teplogorka** Russian Federation
238 H6 **Tëploye** Russian Federation
132 B2 **Tepoca, Punta** *cape* Mexico
129 I7 **Tepórachi** Mexico
427 14 **Tepoto** *island* French Polynesia
223 N3 **Tepsa** Finland
427 13a **Tepuka** *island* Tuvalu
131 K7 **Tequesta** Florida USA
132 E4 **Tequila** Mexico
231 H2 **Ter** *watercourse* Spain
226 D1 **Ter Apel** Netherlands
301 G6 **Téra** Niger
230 C2 **Tera** *watercourse* Spain
426 1 **Teraina** *island* Kiribati
306 E2 **Terakeka** Sudan
382 E6 **Teram Kangri Peak** *mountain* (disputed)
391 M2 **Teram Kangri Peak** *mountain* Pakistan
232 E5 **Teramo** Italy
225 K4 **Tērande** Latvia
162 B3 **Terao** Chile
227 L2 **Teratyn** Poland
372 D5 **Terbang Selatan** *island* Indonesia
372 D5 **Terbang Utara** *island* Indonesia
374 E5 **Terbanggi-besar** Indonesia
310 1b **Terceira** *island* Azores
155 H4 **Terceiro Acampamento** Brazil
160 F5 **Tercero** *watercourse* Argentina
389 R3 **Tere-khol'** *lake* Russian Federation
238 F6 **Tereben'** Russian Federation
234 C1 **Tereblya** Ukraine
238 H5 **Terebush** Russian Federation
227 L5 **Teregova** Romania
388 D5 **Terek** *watercourse* Russian Federation
389 J4 **Terekty** Kazakhstan
388 E2 **Teren'ga** Russian Federation
374 D2 **Terengganu** *admin. area* Malaysia
238 E5 **Terenino** Russian Federation

159 H6 **Terenos** Brazil
374 F4 **Terentang** Indonesia
226 F4 **Terento** Italy
234 E1 **Tereshpol'** Ukraine
156 D4 **Teresina** Brazil
154 D4 **Teresita** Colombia
157 D8 **Teresópolis** Brazil
376 B5 **Teressa** *island* Andaman and Nicobar Islands India
234 C1 **Teresva** Ukraine
230 C5 **Terges, Ribeira de** *watercourse* Portugal
390 E7 **Terifa** Yemen
223 M5 **Terjärv** Finland
232 D3 **Terlano** Italy
120 I1 **Term Point** Nunavut Canada
394 F5 **Terme** Turkey
233 E8 **Termini Imerese** Italy
133 H5 **Términos, Laguna de** *lake* Mexico
301 I5 **Termit-Kaoboul** Niger
389 J6 **Termiz**
372 C3 **Ternate** Indonesia
121 U6 **Ternay, Lac** *lake* Québec Canada
229 L3 **Ternberg** Austria
387 H2 **Terney** Russian Federation
233 E5 **Terni** Italy
232 G3 **Ternitz** Austria
234 F1 **Ternivka** Ukraine
234 C3 **Ternopil's'ka Oblast'** *admin. area* Ukraine
234 G1 **Ternovka** Ukraine
394 E2 **Terny** Ukraine
237 AE9 **Terpeniya, Mys** *cape* Russian Federation
237 AD9 **Terpeniya, Zaliv** *bay* Russian Federation
161 H2 **Terra Boa** Brazil
308 D5 **Terra Firma** South Africa
157 D6 **Terra Nova** Brazil
436 L1 **Terra Nova Bay** Antarctica
157 A8 **Terra Rica** Brazil
157 B8 **Terra Roxa** Brazil
155 G5 **Terra Santa** Brazil
118 G5 **Terrace** British Columbia Canada
233 E6 **Terracina** Italy
231 G2 **Terradets, Pantà de** *lake* Spain
222 H2 **Terråk** Norway
130 C4 **Terral** Oklahoma USA
231 H3 **Terrassa** Spain
228 E5 **Terraube** France
163 I6 **Terre-de-Bas** Guadeloupe
163 I6 **Terre-de-Bas** *island* Guadeloupe
163 I6 **Terre-de-Haut** Guadeloupe
163 I6 **Terre-de-Haut** *island* Guadeloupe
126 H7 **Terre Haute** Indiana USA
127 H3 **Terrebonne Bay** Louisiana USA
130 C4 **Terrell** Texas USA
162 E5 **Terrible, Cape** Falkland Islands
162 B5 **Terromontos, Pampa de** *region* Chile
130 F4 **Terry** Mississippi USA
125 M3 **Terry** Montana USA
130 D5 **Terryglass** Ireland
226 C1 **Terschelling** *island* Netherlands
233 C7 **Tertenia** Sardinia Italy
224 E5 **Tertius** *island* Germany
154 C4 **Teruel** Colombia
231 F3 **Teruel** Spain
224 E4 **Tervel** Bulgaria
223 O5 **Tervo** Finland
223 N3 **Tervola** Finland
225 P2 **Tervu** Russian Federation
227 H4 **Terz** Austria
383 J2 **Tes** Mongolia
129 N1 **Tescott** Kansas USA
304 D3 **Teselima** Ghana
302 F4 **Teseney** Eritrea
116 D4 **Teshekpuk Lake** Alaska USA
384 E2 **Teshig** Mongolia
132 C3 **Tesia** Mexico
118 E2 **Teslin** Yukon Territory Canada
118 D2 **Teslin** *watercourse* Yukon Territory Canada
118 E3 **Teslin Lake** British Columbia Canada
234 D3 **Teslui** Romania
157 A7 **Tesouro** Brazil
225 P3 **Tësovo-Netyl'skiy** Russian Federation
225 P3 **Tesovskiy** Russian Federation
301 G4 **Tessalit** Mali
301 H6 **Tessaoua** Niger
224 E2 **Tesse** *lake* Norway
226 E4 **Tesserete** Switzerland
309 F4 **Tessolo** Mozambique
241 F3 **Test** *watercourse* England UK
301 H1 **Testour** Tunisia
228 F5 **Têt** *watercourse* France
118 I6 **Tetachuck Lake** British Columbia Canada
160 D2 **Tetas, Punta** *cape* Chile
241 E3 **Tetbury** Gloucestershire England UK
240 E2 **Tetchill** Shropshire England UK
309 F3 **Tete** Mozambique
309 F3 **Tete** *admin. area* Mozambique
426 8 **Tetepare** *island* Solomon Islands
123 D7 **Tétépisca, Lac** *lake* Québec Canada
226 D3 **Téterchen** France
226 G1 **Teterow** Germany
243 H3 **Tetford** Lincolnshire England UK
133 H4 **Tetiz** Mexico
243 H3 **Tetney** Lincolnshire England UK
124 I3 **Teton** *watercourse* Montana USA
125 J5 **Teton Range** Wyoming USA
300 E1 **Tétouan** Morocco
223 U3 **Tetrino** Russian Federation
226 E4 **Tettnang** Germany
388 E2 **Tetyushi** Russian Federation
160 F3 **Teuco** *watercourse* Argentina
233 C7 **Teulada** Sardinia Italy
231 G4 **Teulada** Spain
120 G7 **Teulon** Manitoba Canada
372 D5 **Teun** *island* Indonesia
374 B2 **Teunom** *watercourse* Indonesia
223 M3 **Teurajärvi** Sweden
161 I4 **Teutônia** Brazil
424 G7 **Teutonic** WA Australia
222 L5 **Teuva** Finland
427 14b **Tevairoa** *island* French Polynesia
233 E5 **Tevere** *watercourse* Italy
241 H2 **Teversham** Cambridgeshire England UK
244 F5 **Teviot** *watercourse* Scotland UK
244 F5 **Teviothead** Scottish Borders Scotland UK
224 I2 **Tevsjön** *bay* Sweden
375 G4 **Tewah** Indonesia
375 G4 **Teweh** *watercourse* Indonesia
244 F4 **Tewel** Aberdeenshire Scotland UK
241 E3 **Tewkesbury** Gloucestershire England UK
244 B5 **Texa** *island* Scotland UK
130 C6 **Texana, Lake** Texas USA
133 G1 **Texarkana** Arkansas USA
130 D4 **Texarkana** Texas USA
425 N7 **Texas** Qld Australia
115 **Texas** *admin. area* USA
130 D6 **Texas City** Texas USA
226 C1 **Texel** *island* Netherlands
129 L2 **Texhoma** Oklahoma USA
129 K3 **Texico** New Mexico USA
129 K2 **Texline** Texas USA
130 C3 **Texoma, Lake** Oklahoma USA
308 E5 **Teyateyaneng** Lesotho
229 K5 **Tezio, Monte** *mountain* Italy
133 F5 **Teziutlán** Mexico
379 G3 **Tezpur** Assam India
379 H3 **Tezu** Arunachal Pradesh India
376 D2 **Tha** *watercourse* Laos
117 J6 **Tha-anne** *watercourse* Nunavut Canada
376 D3 **Tha Bo** Thailand
308 E5 **Thaba Putsoa** *mountain* Lesotho
376 B3 **Thabaung** Myanmar
308 E4 **Thabazimbi** South Africa
130 C4 **Thackerville** Oklahoma USA
376 D2 **Thafa** Laos
376 E2 **Thái Bình** Vietnam
376 E3 **Thái Hòa** Vietnam
376 E2 **Thái Nguyên** Vietnam
376 D3 **Thailand** *country*
376 D5 **Thailand, Gulf of** Thailand
393 D7 **Thair** Maharashtra India
379 F3 **Thakurgaon** Bangladesh
391 L2 **Thal** Pakistan
301 H1 **Thala** Tunisia
120 G7 **Thalberg** Manitoba Canada
226 F2 **Thale** Germany
376 D6 **Thale Luang** *lake* Thailand
229 K1 **Thalheim** Germany
124 E2 **Thalia** British Columbia Canada
308 E4 **Thamaga** Botswana
388 I3 **Thaman-akkol** *lake* Kazakhstan
391 H6 **Thamarit** Oman
427 9a **Thambia** *island* Fiji
241 G3 **Thame** Buckinghamshire England UK
241 G3 **Thame** *watercourse* England UK
422 F3 **Thames** New Zealand
241 F3 **Thames** *watercourse* England UK
422 F3 **Thames, Firth of** *bay* New Zealand
376 C5 **Than Kyun** Myanmar
376 D2 **Than Uyên** Vietnam
376 C4 **Thanbyuzayat** Myanmar
379 H5 **Thandaung** Myanmar
376 B3 **Thandwe** Myanmar
392 D5 **Thanesar** Haryana India
376 E3 **Thanh Chương** Vietnam
376 E3 **Thanh Hóa** Vietnam
393 E9 **Thanjavur** Tamil Nadu India
376 C3 **Thanlwin (Salween)** *watercourse* Myanmar
376 C3 **Thanlyin** Myanmar
229 H3 **Thann** France
391 K4 **Thano Ahmad Khan** Pakistan
120 G2 **Thaolintoa Lake** Nunavut Canada
376 C5 **Thap Sakae** Thailand
392 C5 **Thar Desert** Rajasthan India
392 C6 **Thara** Gujarat India
392 C6 **Tharad** Gujarat India
307 F4 **Tharaka** Kenya
425 L7 **Thargomindah** Qld Australia
390 E2 **Tharthār, Wādī ath** *watercourse* Iraq
235 D5 **Thasos** Greece
235 D5 **Thasos** *island* Greece
376 E2 **Thát Khê** Vietnam
376 E3 **That Phanom** Thailand
241 F3 **Thatcham** West Berkshire England UK
128 H4 **Thatcher** Arizona USA
376 C3 **Thaton** Myanmar
391 K5 **Thatta** Pakistan
241 H3 **Thaxted** Essex England UK
130 G3 **Thaxton** Mississippi USA
376 C4 **Thayawthadangyi Kyun** Myanmar
126 D8 **Thayer** Kansas USA
130 F2 **Thayer** Missouri USA
379 H5 **Thayet** Myanmar
125 J5 **Thayne** Wyoming USA
379 H5 **Thazi** Myanmar
163 20 **The Bottom** Netherlands Antilles
373 J6 **The Calvados Chain** *island* Papua New Guinea
242 B4 **The Cedars** Ireland
244 D3 **The Craigs** Highland Scotland UK
163 I2 **The Crane** Barbados
242 A3 **The Downs** Ireland
242 B1 **The Drones** Ballymoney Northern Ireland UK
425 K2 **The English Companys Islands** NT Australia
241 H2 **The Fens** England UK
245 F3 **The Five Roads** Ireland
390 G4 **The Gulf**
The Hague *see* **Den Haag/'s-Gravenhage** Netherlands
130 C5 **The Hills** Texas USA
423 D7 **The Hunters Hills** *range* New Zealand
425 inset **The Lagoon** Lord Howe Island Australia
245 F4 **The Little Crosses** Ireland
244 C2 **The Minch** *strait* Scotland UK
163 19 **The Narrows** *strait* Saint Kitts and Nevis
244 F1 **The North Sound** Scotland UK
119 U6 **The Pas** Manitoba Canada
310 5a **The Peak** *mountain* Ascension
245 E3 **The Pigeons** Ireland
423 C7 **The Remarkables** *range* New Zealand
245 D4 **The Rodney** Ireland
424 C2 **The Settlement** Christmas Island Australia
163 21 **The Settlement** British Virgin Islands
242 B2 **The Sheddings** Ballymena Northern Ireland UK
245 F2 **The Six Towns** Magherafelt Northern Ireland UK
423 B9 **The Snares** *islands* New Zealand
119 T5 **The Two Rivers** Saskatchewan Canada
163 20 **The Valley** Anguilla
130 C3 **The Village** Oklahoma USA
228 E1 **The Weald** *region* England UK
126 I3 **Theano Point** Ontario Canada
128 F4 **Theba** Arizona USA
125 O6 **Thedford** Nebraska USA
233 C9 **Thelepte** Tunisia
116 I6 **Thelon** *watercourse* Northwest Territories Canada
229 J1 **Themar** Germany
122 D6 **Thémines** *watercourse* Québec Canada
228 D3 **Thénezay** France
229 G1 **Thenia** Algeria
301 G1 **Theniet El Had** Algeria
228 E4 **Thenon** France
121 Q7 **Théodat, Lac** *lake* Québec Canada
425 N6 **Theodore** Qld Australia
119 T7 **Theodore** Saskatchewan Canada
132 C1 **Theodore Roosevelt Lake** Arizona USA
228 F3 **Théols** *watercourse* France
228 F2 **Thérain** *watercourse* France
310 9b **Thérèse, Île** *island* Seychelles
235 C5 **Thermaïkos Kolpos** *bay* Greece
228 D5 **Thermes-d'Armagnac** France
436 W1 **Theron Mountains** Antarctica
116 G4 **Thesiger Bay** Northwest Territories Canada
235 B6 **Thessalia** *admin. area* Greece
235 C5 **Thessaloniki** Greece
241 H2 **Thetford** Norfolk England UK
127 P3 **Thetford Mines** Québec Canada
229 H4 **Théus** France
229 G1 **Theux** Belgium
117 L7 **Thévenet, Lac** *lake* Québec Canada
226 B3 **Thiais** France
120 H4 **Thibaudeau** Manitoba Canada
130 F6 **Thibodaux** Louisiana USA
120 D2 **Thief Lake** Minnesota USA
125 Q2 **Thief River Falls** Minnesota USA
436 R1 **Thiel Mountains** Antarctica
226 F5 **Thiene** Italy
228 F4 **Thiers** France
121 R3 **Thiersant, Lac** *lake* Québec Canada
300 C6 **Thiès** Senegal
307 F4 **Thika** Kenya
393 C10 **Thiladhunmathi Atoll** Maldives
300 D5 **Thilogne** Senegal
379 F3 **Thimphu** Bhutan
222 inset **Þingeyri** Iceland
222 inset **Þingvallavatn** *lake* Iceland
376 D3 **Thinkèo** Laos
303 G5 **Thio** Eritrea
426 7 **Thio** New Caledonia
235 D7 **Thira** *island* Greece
235 D7 **Thirasia** *island* Greece
243 G2 **Thirsk** North Yorkshire England UK
393 D10 **Thiruvananthapuram** Kerala India
393 E9 **Thiruvarur** Tamil Nadu India
222 inset **Þistilfjörður** *bay* Iceland
235 C6 **Thisvi** Greece
377 G5 **Thitu Island** Spratly Islands
376 E4 **Thiu Kaho Phanom Dong Rak** Thailand
235 C6 **Thívai** Greece
228 E4 **Thiviers** France
222 inset **Þjórsá** *watercourse* Iceland
120 E3 **Thlewiaza** *watercourse* Manitoba Canada
376 D5 **Thô Chu, Dao** *island* Vietnam
119 Q2 **Thoa** *watercourse* Northwest Territories Canada
376 C3 **Thoen** Thailand
376 D3 **Thoeng** Thailand
308 F4 **Thohoyandou** South Africa
158 E5 **Thola Palca** Bolivia
226 C2 **Tholen** Netherlands
235 B7 **Tholón** Greece
130 B3 **Thomas** Oklahoma USA
240 C3 **Thomas Chapel** Pembrokeshire Wales UK
126 E7 **Thomas Hill Reservoir** Missouri USA
117 J2 **Thomas Hubbard, Cape** Nunavut Canada
245 D3 **Thomas Street** Ireland
131 I4 **Thomaston** Georgia USA
130 H5 **Thomasville** Alabama USA
131 J5 **Thomasville** Georgia USA
229 H1 **Thommen** Belgium
135 G3 **Thomonde** Haiti
119 W5 **Thompson** Manitoba Canada
125 Q3 **Thompson** North Dakota USA
124 H3 **Thompson Falls** Montana USA
118 H7 **Thompson Sound** British Columbia Canada
128 H1 **Thompson Springs** Utah USA
126 G8 **Thompsonville** Illinois USA
116 H4 **Thomsen** *watercourse* Northwest Territories Canada
244 E3 **Thomshill** Moray Scotland UK
425 L6 **Thomson** *watercourse* Qld Australia
131 J4 **Thomson** Georgia USA
423 C7 **Thomson Mountains** New Zealand
423 B7 **Thomson Sound** New Zealand
232 B4 **Thônes** France
226 D4 **Thônex** Switzerland
229 H3 **Thonon-les-Bains** France
129 H3 **Thoreau** New Mexico USA
222 inset **Þórisvatn** *lake* Iceland
222 inset **Þorlákshöfn** Iceland
243 G2 **Thormanby** North Yorkshire England UK
243 G2 **Thornaby on Tees** Stockton-on-Tees England UK
240 E3 **Thornbury** South Gloucestershire England UK
130 C5 **Thorndale** Texas USA
241 I2 **Thorndon** Suffolk England UK
243 H3 **Thorne** South Yorkshire England UK
118 E5 **Thorne Bay** Alaska USA
241 G2 **Thorney** Peterborough England UK
242 B2 **Thornford** Ireland
240 E4 **Thornford** Dorset England UK
243 G3 **Thornhill** Derbyshire England UK
244 E5 **Thornhill** Dumfries and Galloway Scotland UK
244 D4 **Thornhill** Stirling Scotland UK
242 A4 **Thornpack** Ireland
242 E2 **Thornthwaite** Cumbria England UK
240 A1 **Thornton** Ireland
243 E3 **Thornton** Lancashire England UK
130 E4 **Thornton** Arkansas USA
128 B1 **Thornton** California USA
241 G1 **Thornton le Fen** Lincolnshire England UK
243 H3 **Thornton le Moor** Lincolnshire England UK
132 E2 **Thorntonville** Texas USA
241 F1 **Thorpe** Derbyshire England UK
241 I2 **Thorpeness** Suffolk England UK
222 inset **Þórshöfn** Iceland
224 E4 **Thorsminde** Denmark
240 D4 **Thorverton** Devon England UK
228 D3 **Thouars** France
379 H4 **Thoubal** Manipur India
228 D3 **Thouet** *watercourse* France
228 F2 **Thourotte** France
128 C3 **Thousand Oaks** California USA
241 G2 **Thrapston** Northamptonshire England UK
124 J4 **Three Forks** Montana USA
380 F2 **Three Gorges Dam** Hubei China
380 E2 **Three Gorges Reservoir** Chongqing China
119 O7 **Three Hills** Alberta Canada
78 N11 **Three Kings Basin** *underwater feature* Pacific Ocean
422 E2 **Three Kings Islands** New Zealand
128 G4 **Three Points** Arizona USA
304 D4 **Three Points, Cape** *cape* Ghana
129 I4 **Three Rivers** New Mexico USA
130 B6 **Three Rivers** Texas USA
240 A2 **Three Wells** Ireland
241 G2 **Threekingham** Lincolnshire England UK
243 F2 **Thringarth** Durham England UK
243 G2 **Thrintoft** North Yorkshire England UK
393 D9 **Thrissur** Kerala India
130 B4 **Throckmorton** Texas USA
243 G1 **Thropton** Northumberland England UK
424 G6 **Throssell, Lake** WA Australia
118 M8 **Thrums** British Columbia Canada
241 F3 **Thruxton** Hampshire England UK
376 E4 **Thu Bon** *watercourse* Vietnam
307 F4 **Thua** *watercourse* Kenya
376 D2 **Thuận Châu** Vietnam
425 L3 **Thud Point** Qld Australia
228 G4 **Thueyts** France
229 G1 **Thuin** Belgium
119 O3 **Thultue Lake** Alberta Canada
229 H3 **Thun** Switzerland
117 K9 **Thunder Bay** Ontario Canada
126 G2 **Thunder Bay** Ontario Canada
126 J4 **Thunder Bay** Michigan USA
119 R7 **Thunder Creek** Saskatchewan Canada
130 C3 **Thunderbird, Lake** Oklahoma USA
124 F8 **Thunderbolt Peak** California USA
376 C5 **Thung Song** Thailand
376 E3 **Thường Xuân** Vietnam
243 G3 **Thurcroft** South Yorkshire England UK
226 A1 **Thurgarton** Norfolk England UK
226 F2 **Thüringen** *admin. area* Germany
226 F2 **Thüringer Wald** *region* Germany
241 G2 **Thurlby** Lincolnshire England UK
245 E4 **Thurles** Ireland
226 F2 **Thurnau** Germany
241 H3 **Thurnham** Kent England UK
241 G2 **Thurning** Northamptonshire England UK
241 H3 **Thurrock** *admin. area* England UK
425 L2 **Thursday Island** Qld Australia
127 N4 **Thurso** Ontario Canada
244 E2 **Thurso** Highland Scotland UK
244 E2 **Thurso** *watercourse* Scotland UK
436 R2 **Thurston Island** Antarctica
229 I3 **Thusis** Switzerland
118 H4 **Thutade Lake** British Columbia Canada
241 I2 **Thuxton** Norfolk England UK
243 F2 **Thwaite** North Yorkshire England UK
436 Q2 **Thwaites Glacier Tongue** *ice* Antarctica
243 H2 **Thwing** East Riding of Yorkshire England UK
224 E4 **Thy** *cape* Denmark
224 E4 **Thyborøn** Denmark
235 E7 **Thymaina** *island* Greece
301 G5 **Ti-n-Azabo** Mali
425 J5 **Ti-Tree** NT Australia
381 G2 **Tiancheng** Hubei China
380 E2 **Tianchi** Sichuan China
380 D3 **Tiandiba** Sichuan China
156 D3 **Tianguá** Brazil
385 I5 **Tianjin** *admin. area* China
385 I5 **Tianjin** Tianjin China
304 D2 **Tiankoura** Burkina Faso
380 E4 **Tianlin** Guangxi Zhuangzu Zizhiqu China
381 H3 **Tianma** Zhejiang China
381 G2 **Tianmen** Hubei China
385 I4 **Tianshan** Nei Mongol Zizhiqu China
380 E1 **Tianshui** Gansu China
381 I2 **Tiantai** Zhejiang China
381 G2 **Tiantang** Anhui China
385 I4 **Tianyi** Nei Mongol Zizhiqu China
385 H5 **Tianzhen** Shanxi China
301 G1 **Tiaret** Algeria
301 G2 **Tiaret** *admin. area* Algeria
310 3d **Tias** Canary Islands
427 12c **Ti'avea** Samoa
154 C3 **Tibacuy** Colombia
157 B9 **Tibagi** Brazil
157 B8 **Tibagi** *watercourse* Brazil
154 C3 **Tibaná** Colombia
234 E2 **Țibana** Romania
305 G3 **Tibati** Cameroon
240 E3 **Tibberton** Gloucestershire England UK
304 C3 **Tibé, Pic de** *mountain* Guinea
301 G3 **Tiberghamine** Algeria
301 J4 **Tibesti** *desert* Libya
Tibet *see* **Xizang Zizhiqu** China
425 L7 **Tibooburra** NSW Australia
392 F5 **Tibrikot** Nepal
224 H3 **Tibro** Sweden
154 C2 **Tibú** Colombia
154 B3 **Tibuga, Ensenada** *bay* Colombia
135 F3 **Tiburon** Haiti
134 E5 **Tiburón, Cabo** *cape* Colombia
132 B2 **Tiburón, Isla** *island* Mexico
234 E4 **Ticha** Bulgaria
127 M4 **Tichborne** Ontario Canada
121 S7 **Tichégami** *watercourse* Québec Canada
125 L1 **Tichfield** Saskatchewan Canada
300 E5 **Tichit** Mauritania
300 D4 **Tichla** Western Sahara
229 I3 **Ticino** *watercourse* Switzerland
240 E2 **Ticklerton** Shropshire England UK
243 H3 **Tickton** East Riding of Yorkshire England UK
133 H4 **Ticul** Mexico
158 C3 **Ticumpina** Peru
425 M9 **Tidal River** Vic. Australia
241 F3 **Tidcombe** Wiltshire England UK
127 R3 **Tide Head** New Brunswick Canada
240 E3 **Tidenham** Gloucestershire England UK
224 H4 **Tidersrum** Sweden
300 D5 **Tidjikja** Mauritania
123 G10 **Tidnish** Nova Scotia Canada
372 C3 **Tidore** *island* Indonesia
245 C4 **Tiduff** Ireland
241 F3 **Tidworth** Wiltshire England UK
304 C3 **Tiébissou** Côte d'Ivoire
385 J4 **Tiefa** Liaoning China
226 G3 **Tiefenbach** Germany
226 C2 **Tiel** Netherlands
300 C6 **Tiel** Senegal
385 K3 **Tieli** Heilongjiang China
385 J4 **Tieling** Liaoning China
376 E5 **Tien Giang (Mekong)** *watercourse* Vietnam
376 E2 **Tiến Hải** Vietnam
382 F4 **Tien Shan** *range* Xinjiang Uygur Zizhiqu China
304 C3 **Tienigboue** Côte d'Ivoire
223 Q5 **Tiensuu** Finland
228 E2 **Tiercé** France
224 I2 **Tierp** Sweden
129 I2 **Tierra Amarilla** New Mexico USA
230 C4 **Tierra Barros** *region* Spain
133 F5 **Tierra Colorada** Mexico
162 C6 **Tierra del Fuego** *admin. area* Argentina
154 B2 **Tierralta** Colombia
132 E4 **Tierranueva** Mexico
230 D4 **Tiétar** *watercourse* Spain
157 B8 **Tietê** *watercourse* Brazil
228 D3 **Tiffauges** France
126 J6 **Tiffin** Ohio USA
131 J5 **Tifton** Georgia USA
372 C4 **Tifu** Indonesia
230 E6 **Tifzioune** Morocco
375 G2 **Tiga** *island* Malaysia
426 7 **Tiga, Île** *island* New Caledonia
305 F2 **Tiga Reservoir** *lake* Nigeria
310 3b **Tigalate** Canary Islands
377 I4 **Tigaon** Philippines
374 D4 **Tigapuluh, Pegunungan** *range* Indonesia
388 F5 **Tigen** Kazakhstan
118 M8 **Tiger** Washington USA
234 F2 **Tigheciului, Dealurile** *range* Moldova
234 F2 **Tighina** Moldova
372 F5 **Tigi, Danau** *lake* Indonesia
237 AG7 **Tigil'** *watercourse* Russian Federation
389 N3 **Tigiretskiy Khrebet** *range* Russian Federation
305 G3 **Tignère** Cameroon
226 D5 **Tignes** France
123 F9 **Tignish** Prince Edward Island Canada
426 8 **Tigoa** Solomon Islands
302 F5 **Tigray** *admin. area* Ethiopia
158 B2 **Tigre** Peru
158 C2 **Tigre** *watercourse* Peru
158 D4 **Tigre, Serranía del** *range* Bolivia
390 F3 **(Tigris)** *watercourse* Iraq
300 C5 **Tiguent** Mauritania
301 G5 **Tiguezefene** Niger
302 E2 **Tih, Jabal at** *desert* Egypt
223 O5 **Tihilä** Finland
133 F4 **Tihuatlán** Mexico
223 P5 **Tiilikkajärvi kansallispuisto** *park* Finland
392 D5 **Tijara** Rajasthan India
160 C6 **Tijeral** Chile
129 I3 **Tijeras** New Mexico USA
301 I2 **Tiji** Libya
425 L3 **Tijou Reef** Qld Australia
132 A1 **Tijuana** Mexico
161 I3 **Tijucas, Baía de** *bay* Brazil
157 B7 **Tijuco** *watercourse* Brazil
134 B3 **Tikal** Guatemala
392 E6 **Tikamgarh** Madhya Pradesh India
116 D6 **Tikchik Lake** Alaska USA
305 H3 **Tikem** Chad
238 H4 **Tikhmenevo** Russian Federation
388 C4 **Tikhoretsk** Russian Federation
225 Q3 **Tikhvin** Russian Federation
238 G2 **Tikhvinskaya Gryada** *range* Russian Federation
79 S9 **Tiki Basin** *underwater feature* Pacific Ocean
134 D4 **Tikiraya** Honduras
231 I5 **Tikjda** Algeria
223 N5 **Tikkakoski** Finland
122 G4 **Tikkoatokak Bay** Newfoundland and Labrador Canada
422 G4 **Tikokino** New Zealand
426 1 **Tikopia** *island* Solomon Islands
393 F7 **Tikra** *watercourse* Orissa India
390 E2 **Tikrit** Iraq
223 R4 **Tiksha** Russian Federation
223 Q3 **Tiksheozero, Ozero** *lake* Russian Federation
Tikus *see* **Direction Island** Cocos (Keeling) Islands Australia
133 G5 **Tila** Mexico
372 B3 **Tilamuta** Indonesia
392 F6 **Tilaya** *lake* Jharkhand India
226 C2 **Tilburg** Netherlands
127 J5 **Tilbury** Ontario Canada
241 H3 **Tilbury** Thurrock England UK
160 E2 **Tilcara** Argentina
126 G7 **Tilden** Illinois USA
125 Q5 **Tilden** Nebraska USA
130 B6 **Tilden** Texas USA
301 G5 **Tilemsès** Niger
301 G6 **Tillabéri** Niger
301 G6 **Tillabéri** *admin. area* Niger
124 C4 **Tillamook Bay** Oregon USA
124 C4 **Tillamook Head** *cape* Oregon USA
374 B1 **Tillanchang Dwip** *island* Andaman and Nicobar Islands India
376 B5 **Tillanchong** *island* Andaman and Nicobar Islands India
229 G3 **Tille** *watercourse* France
119 P7 **Tilley** Alberta Canada
301 G5 **Tillia** Niger
228 E3 **Tilly** France
121 R6 **Tilly, Lac** *lake* Québec Canada
244 F3 **Tillyfar** Aberdeenshire Scotland UK
244 F3 **Tillyfourie** Aberdeenshire Scotland UK
235 E7 **Tilos** *island* Greece
235 E7 **Tilos, Akra** *cape* Greece
241 F3 **Tilshead** Wiltshire England UK
240 E2 **Tilstock** Shropshire England UK
240 E1 **Tilston** Cheshire England UK
225 N4 **Tilža** Latvia
224 E4 **Tim** Denmark
394 F2 **Tim** Russian Federation
127 L3 **Timagami** Ontario Canada
127 L3 **Timagami, Lake** Ontario Canada
310 3d **Timanfaya, Parque Nacional de** *park* Canary Islands
234 F1 **Timanovka** Ukraine
236 L6 **Timanskiy Kryazh** *region* Russian Federation
310 1b **Timão, Pico** *volcano* Azores
423 D7 **Timaru** New Zealand
233 E3 **Timau** Italy
130 F6 **Timbalier Bay** Louisiana USA
300 E5 **Timbedgha** Mauritania
119 S5 **Timber Bay** Saskatchewan Canada
424 I3 **Timber Creek** NT Australia
125 O4 **Timber Lake** South Dakota USA
129 L3 **Timbercreek Canyon** Texas USA
154 B4 **Timbiquí, Bahía de** *bay* Colombia
156 D4 **Timbiras** Brazil
154 B4 **Timbiré** Ecuador
234 D3 **Timboești** Romania
372 A2 **Timbun Mata** *island* Malaysia
301 H1 **Timgad** Algeria
301 H5 **Timia** Niger
154 C5 **Timicurillo** Peru
301 G3 **Timimoun** Algeria
237 AF5 **Timir-Atakh-Tas** Russian Federation
234 B3 **Timiș** *admin. area* Romania
234 B3 **Timiș** *watercourse* Romania
127 L3 **Timiskaming Station** Québec Canada
234 B3 **Timișoara** Romania
236 N6 **Timkapaul'** Russian Federation
117 K9 **Timmins** Ontario Canada
131 L3 **Timmonsville** South Carolina USA
234 C3 **Timna** Romania
234 C4 **Timok** *watercourse* Serbia
238 G3 **Timokhino** Russian Federation
245 F4 **Timolin** Ireland
156 D4 **Timon** Brazil
233 C6 **Timone, Punta** *cape* Sardinia Italy
375 J6 **Timor** *island* Timor-Leste (East Timor)
372 C6 **Timor-Leste (East Timor)** *country*
372 C6 **Timor Sea** Indonesia/Australia
78 I8 **Timor Trough** *underwater feature* Timor Sea
157 D7 **Timóteo** Brazil
301 F3 **Timoudi** Algeria
375 G4 **Timpah** Indonesia
129 K2 **Timpas** Colorado USA
130 D5 **Timpson** Texas USA
237 AA7 **Timpton** *watercourse* Russian Federation
222 J5 **Timrå** Sweden
131 H3 **Tims Ford Lake** Tennessee USA
244 A2 **Timsgearraidh** Na h-Eileanan Siar Scotland UK
238 G2 **Timshino** Russian Federation
388 J3 **Timtuir Koli** *lake* Kazakhstan
302 C1 **Tin, Ra's at** *cape* Libya
425 O6 **Tin Can Bay** Qld Australia
423 B8 **Tin Range** New Zealand
377 J6 **Tinaca Point** Philippines
377 I4 **Tinaga** *island* Philippines
245 F4 **Tinahely** Ireland
310 3d **Tinajo** Canary Islands
426 8 **Tinakula** *volcano* Solomon Islands
372 A4 **Tinambung** Indonesia
154 D2 **Tinaquillo** Venezuela
234 B2 **Tinca** Romania
304 E2 **Tindangou** Burkina Faso
310 3d **Tindaya** Canary Islands
300 E3 **Tindouf** Algeria
302 C5 **Tiné** Sudan
229 H4 **Tinée** *watercourse* France
230 C2 **Tineo** Spain
300 E2 **Tinerhir** Morocco
300 E3 **Tinfouchy** Algeria
375 G3 **Tinggi** *island* Malaysia
304 B3 **Tingi Mountains** *range* Guinea
158 C3 **Tingo María** Peru
304 C2 **Tingréla** Côte d'Ivoire
224 H4 **Tingsryd** Sweden
160 D5 **Tinguiririca, Volcán** *volcano* Chile
222 F5 **Tingvoll** Norway
244 E1 **Tingwall** Orkney Islands Scotland UK
373 I4 **Tingwon Group** *islands* Papua New Guinea
373 I4 **Tingwon Island** Papua New Guinea
381 G3 **Tingzhou** Fujian China
376 E3 **Tĩnh Gia** Vietnam
376 E2 **Tĩnh Túc** Vietnam
157 E6 **Tinharé, Ilha de** *island* Brazil
426 2 **Tinian** *island* Northern Mariana Islands
121 R3 **Tininnirusiq, Lac** *lake* Québec Canada
422 G4 **Tiniroto** New Zealand
375 G3 **Tinjar** *watercourse* Malaysia
374 E5 **Tinjil** *island* Indonesia
245 F5 **Tinkerslane** Ireland
304 C2 **Tinkisso** *watercourse* Guinea
224 E3 **Tinnoset** Norway
224 E3 **Tinnsjo** *lake* Norway
245 D3 **Tinny Park** Ireland
160 E4 **Tinogasta** Argentina
372 B3 **Tinombo** Indonesia
235 D7 **Tinos** Greece
235 D7 **Tinos** *island* Greece
231 F5 **Tiñoso, Cabo** *cape* Spain
373 J5 **Tinputz** Papua New Guinea
228 F2 **Tinqueux** France
379 H3 **Tinsukia** Assam India
240 C4 **Tintagel** Cornwall England UK
300 D5 **Tintâne** Mauritania
375 H3 **Tintang** Indonesia
301 G4 **Tintejert, Adrar** *mountain* Algeria
240 E3 **Tintern Parva** Monmouthshire Wales UK
160 F3 **Tintina** Argentina
230 C5 **Tinto** *watercourse* Spain
235 G5 **Tinui** New Zealand
125 N2 **Tioga** North Dakota USA
154 B5 **Tioloma** *mountain* Ecuador
301 F4 **Tiom** Indonesia
374 E3 **Tioman** *island* Malaysia
160 D2 **Tiomonte** Chile
127 L6 **Tionesta** Pennsylvania USA
372 D5 **Tioor** *island* Indonesia
304 E2 **Tioribougou** Mali
301 F6 **Tiou** Burkina Faso
301 F1 **Tipasa** Algeria
223 P4 **Tipasoja** Finland
301 G1 **Tipaza** *admin. area* Algeria
134 C4 **Tipitapa** Nicaragua
245 D4 **Tipperary** Ireland
245 D4 **Tipperary** *admin. area* Ireland
244 F4 **Tipperty** Aberdeenshire Scotland UK
128 C2 **Tipton** California USA
126 H6 **Tipton** Indiana USA
125 P7 **Tipton** Kansas USA
130 B3 **Tipton** Oklahoma USA
130 G2 **Tiptonville** Tennessee USA
241 H3 **Tiptree** Essex England UK
393 D9 **Tiptur** Karnataka India
155 G4 **Tipuru Village** Brazil
132 E5 **Tiquicheo** Mexico
154 D4 **Tiquie** *watercourse* Brazil
154 C2 **Tiquisio** Colombia
154 B3 **Tira-Cerveja** Brazil
156 C3 **Tiracambu, Serra do** *range* Brazil
161 J2 **Tiradentes** Brazil
Tirana *see* **Tiranë** Albania
235 A5 **Tiranë (Tirana)** Albania
226 F4 **Tirano** Italy
379 I3 **Tirap** Arunachal Pradesh India
234 F2 **Tiraspol** Moldova
423 G5 **Tiraumea** New Zealand
235 E6 **Tire** Turkey
244 B4 **Tiree** *island* Scotland UK
391 L2 **Tirich Mir** *mountain* Pakistan
392 E4 **Tirido** Jammu and Kashmir India/ Pakistan
154 E4 **Tiriquin** Venezuela
241 E3 **Tirley** Gloucestershire England UK
226 G4 **Tirol** *admin. area* Austria
234 B3 **Tirol** Romania
305 I3 **Tiroungoulou** Central African Republic
229 K2 **Tirschenreuth** Germany
393 G7 **Tirtol** Orissa India
162 B2 **Tirúa, Cabo** *cape* Chile
393 E9 **Tiruchchirappalli** Tamil Nadu India
393 D10 **Tirumangalam** Tamil Nadu India
393 D10 **Tirunelveli** Tamil Nadu India
393 E9 **Tirupati** Andhra Pradesh India
393 D9 **Tiruppur** Tamil Nadu India
393 D9 **Tirur** Kerala India
393 E9 **Tirutturaippundi** Tamil Nadu India
393 D10 **Tiruvalla** Kerala India
393 E9 **Tiruvannamalai** Tamil Nadu India
393 E9 **Tiruvottiyur** Tamil Nadu India
234 B4 **Tisa** *watercourse* Serbia
241 E3 **Tisbury** Wiltshire England UK
119 S6 **Tisdale** Saskatchewan Canada
225 O4 **Tishino** Russian Federation
232 F1 **Tišice** Czech Republic
224 G2 **Tisjön** *lake* Sweden
301 H4 **Tiska, Mont** *mountain* Algeria
224 E2 **Tisleifjorden** *lake* Norway
234 C3 **Tismana** Romania
222 K2 **Tisnes** Norway
232 H2 **Tisovec** Slovakia
301 G1 **Tissemsilt** Algeria
301 G1 **Tissemsilt** *admin. area* Algeria
379 F3 **Tista** *watercourse* West Bengal India
223 M4 **Tistersöfjärden** *bay* Sweden
222 H4 **Tisvatnet** *lake* Norway
Tisza *see* **Tysa**
234 B3 **Tisza** *watercourse* Serbia
227 L3 **Tisza** *watercourse* Ukraine
227 K4 **Tiszabura** Hungary
227 K3 **Tiszadob** Hungary
227 K4 **Tiszakécske** Hungary
227 K3 **Tiszalök** Hungary
234 B2 **Tiszaörs** Hungary
234 B2 **Tiszasas** Hungary
300 H4 **Tit** Algeria
379 H3 **Titabar** Assam India
436 I1 **Titan Dome** *mountain* Antarctica
304 D2 **Titao** Burkina Faso
241 F4 **Titchfield** Hampshire England UK
234 B3 **Titel** Serbia
234 D3 **Titești** Romania
158 D4 **Titicaca, Lago** *lake* Peru
422 2 **Titikaveka** Cook Islands New Zealand
221 C7 **Tititea (Mount Aspiring)** New Zealand
393 F7 **Titlagarh** Orissa India
240 E2 **Titley** Herefordshire England UK
235 B5 **Titov Vrv** *mountain* Macedonia
222 F5 **Titran** Norway
126 I5 **Tittabawassee** *watercourse* Michigan USA
229 J2 **Titting** Germany
306 D3 **Titule** Democratic Republic of Congo
391 I3 **Titūn** Iran
131 K6 **Titusville** Florida USA
127 L6 **Titusville** Pennsylvania USA
244 B2 **Tiumpan Head** *cape* Scotland UK
374 E4 **Tiung, Tanjung** *island* Indonesia
307 F4 **Tiva** *watercourse* Kenya
300 C6 **Tivaouane** Senegal
233 H5 **Tivat** Montenegro
224 H3 **Tived** Sweden
240 E1 **Tiverton** Cheshire England UK
240 D4 **Tiverton** Devon England UK
163 10a **Tivoli** Grenada
233 E6 **Tivoli** Italy
302 D4 **Tiwal** *watercourse* Sudan
377 I4 **Tiwi** Philippines
372 B5 **Tiworo, Selat** *strait* Indonesia
241 E2 **Tixall** Staffordshire England UK
372 E5 **Tiyo, Pegunungan** *range* Indonesia
391 H4 **Tizaj** Iran
132 E4 **Tizapán el Alto** Mexico
301 G1 **Tizi Ouzou** Algeria
301 G1 **Tizi Ouzou** *admin. area* Algeria

133 H4 **Tizimín** Mexico
382 F5 **Tiznap He** *watercourse* Xinjiang Uygur Zizhiqu China
300 E3 **Tiznit** Morocco
155 G3 **Tjakkatjakka Ston** Suriname
222 K3 **Tjaktjajaure** *lake* Sweden
222 J3 **Tjålmejaure** *lake* Sweden
222 K3 **Tjåmotis** Sweden
222 K3 **Tjåmotisjaure** *bay* Sweden
222 J5 **Tjärn** Sweden
222 K3 **Tjäura** Sweden
222 J3 **Tjeggelvas** *bay* Sweden
222 J2 **Tjeldøya** *island* Norway
222 F5 **Tjelle** Norway
232 H5 **Tjentište** Bosnia and Herzegovina
226 C1 **Tjeukemeer** *lake* Netherlands
222 J3 **Tjidtjak** *range* Sweden
222 J3 **Tjockö** *island* Sweden
224 F3 **Tjörn** *island* Sweden
224 G5 **Tjörnarp** Sweden
222 H4 **Tjøtta** Norway
424 H6 **Tjukayirla Roadhouse** WA Australia
222 J4 **Tjulträsk** Sweden
224 H4 **Tjurken** *lake* Sweden
224 F4 **Tjuvkil** Sweden
224 N2 **Tjuvö** Finland
379 G4 **Tlabung** Mizoram India
132 E3 **Tlahualilo de Zaragoza** Mexico
132 E4 **Tlajomulco de Zúñiga** Mexico
132 E5 **Tlalchapa** Mexico
133 F5 **Tlalnepantla** Mexico
133 F5 **Tlanalapan** Mexico
133 F4 **Tlanchinol** Mexico
133 F5 **Tlapa de Comonfort** Mexico
132 E5 **Tlaquepaque** Mexico
132 E4 **Tlatenango de Sánchez Román** Mexico
133 F5 **Tlaxcala** Mexico
133 F5 **Tlaxcala** *admin. area* Mexico
301 F2 **Tlemcen** Algeria
301 F2 **Tlemcen** *admin. area* Algeria
231 J6 **Tletz** Algeria
215 J6 **Tlidjen** Algeria
227 J3 **Tlmače** Slovakia
227 K1 **Tłuszcz** Poland
301 J3 **Tmassah** Libya
387 H4 **To-shima** *island* Japan
374 D3 **Toa Payoh** *admin. area* Singapore
244 inset **Toab** Shetland Scotland UK
118 H3 **Toad** *watercourse* British Columbia Canada
118 I3 **Toad River** British Columbia Canada
309 I3 **Toamasina** Madagascar
309 I3 **Toamasina** *admin. area* Madagascar
379 H2 **Toba** Xizang Zizhiqu China
387 H4 **Toba** Japan
391 K4 **Toba** Pakistan
374 C3 **Toba, Danau** *lake* Indonesia
131 I5 **Tobaccoville** North Carolina USA
163 9 **Tobago** *admin. area* Trinidad and Tobago
163 9 **Tobago** *island* Trinidad and Tobago
372 D4 **Tobalai** *island* Indonesia
230 F4 **Tobarra** Spain
386 G5 **Tobe** Japan
155 F2 **Tobe Jube, Bahía** *bay* Venezuela
155 F2 **Tobejuba, Punta** *cape* Venezuela
242 B3 **Tober** Ireland
245 D2 **Tobercurry** Ireland
245 D3 **Toberdan** Ireland
244 B4 **Tobermory** Highland Scotland UK
244 C4 **Toberonochy** Argyll and Bute Scotland UK
242 B4 **Toberpatrick** Ireland
372 D3 **Tobi** *island* Palau
125 Q6 **Tobias** Nebraska USA
157 E5 **Tobias Barreto** Brazil
119 T6 **Tobin Lake** Saskatchewan Canada
374 E4 **Toboali** Indonesia
300 B3 **Tobokani Point** *cape* Liberia
388 I3 **Tobol** *watercourse* Kazakhstan
388 I2 **Tobol** *watercourse* Russian Federation
236 O7 **Tobol'sk** Russian Federation
304 E2 **Tobré** Benin
236 L5 **Tobseda** Russian Federation
244 B2 **Tobson** Na h-Eileanan Siar Scotland UK
224 G3 **Tobyn** Sweden
158 B3 **Tocache Nuevo** Peru
158 E4 **Tocahuara** Bolivia
154 C3 **Tocaima** Colombia
156 C4 **Tocantinópolis** Brazil
156 B5 **Tocantins** *admin. area* Brazil
156 B5 **Tocantins** *watercourse* Brazil
131 J3 **Toccoa** Georgia USA
232 C3 **Toce** *watercourse* Italy
234 F2 **Tochylove** Ukraine
240 E3 **Tockington** South Gloucestershire England UK
224 F3 **Töcksfors** Sweden
163 9 **Toco** Trinidad and Tobago
134 C4 **Tocoa** Honduras
155 F4 **Tocobiren, Serra** *range* Brazil
160 D2 **Toconce** Chile
160 D2 **Tocopilla** Chile
160 E2 **Tocorpuri, Cerros de** *mountain* Chile
154 D2 **Tocuyo, Río** *watercourse* Venezuela
224 E1 **Todalen** Norway
222 F5 **Todalsfjellet** *island* Norway
425 J6 **Todd** *watercourse* NT Australia
241 F3 **Toddington** Gloucestershire England UK
372 C4 **Todeli** Indonesia
241 F2 **Todenham** Gloucestershire England UK
242 F2 **Todhills** Cumbria England UK
244 D4 **Todholes** Stirling Scotland UK
234 E2 **Todireşti** Romania
243 F3 **Todmorden** West Yorkshire England UK
157 E6 **Todos os Santos, Bahia de** *bay* Brazil
160 E2 **Todos Santos** Bolivia
132 C4 **Todos Santos** Mexico
389 Q3 **Todzha** *lake* Russian Federation
245 C5 **Toe Head** *cape* Ireland
244 A3 **Toe Head** *cape* Scotland UK
119 O6 **Tofield** Alberta Canada
121 C2 **Tofino** British Columbia Canada
241 G2 **Toft** Cambridgeshire England UK
244 inset **Toft** Shetland Scotland UK
224 H2 **Toftan** *lake* Sweden
224 H2 **Toftbyn** Sweden
126 F3 **Tofte** Minnesota USA
224 H3 **Toften** *lake* Sweden
224 E5 **Tofterup** Denmark
224 E5 **Toftlund** Denmark
427 10 **Tofua** *island* Tonga
307 G2 **Tog Wajaale** Ethiopia
426 7 **Toga** *island* Vanuatu
307 H2 **Togdheer** *admin. area* Somalia
307 H1 **Togga Miriye** *watercourse* Somalia
242 B3 **Togher** Ireland
116 C7 **Togiak** Alaska USA
372 B4 **Togian** *island* Indonesia
372 B4 **Togian, Kepulauan** *islands* Indonesia
232 E2 **Töging** Germany
302 F4 **Tognuf** Eritrea
304 E3 **Togo** *country* Africa
373 G6 **Togo** Papua New Guinea
304 C3 **Togobala** Guinea
383 H5 **Tograsay He** *watercourse* Xinjiang Uygur Zizhiqu China
389 N2 **Toguchin** Russian Federation
Toguz *see* **Togyz** Kazakhstan
388 H4 **Togyz** Kazakhstan
392 D5 **Tohana** Haryana India
427 14a **Tohiea** *volcano* French Polynesia
394 H5 **Tohil** Turkey
223 Q5 **Tohmajärvi** Finland
225 P1 **Tohmajärvi** *lake* Finland
223 N5 **Toholampi** Finland
131 K6 **Tohopekaliga Lake** Florida USA
225 M3 **Tohvri** Estonia
422 4 **Toi** Niue New Zealand
225 L2 **Toijala** Finland
372 B4 **Toili** Indonesia
232 C4 **Toirano** Italy
223 M5 **Toisvesi** *lake* Finland
223 O5 **Toivakka** Finland
223 O5 **Toivala** Finland
128 D1 **Toiyabe Range** Nevada USA
235 B5 **Tojaci** Macedonia
372 B4 **Tojo** Indonesia
158 D4 **Tojuyo** Peru
158 C4 **Tojyanca** Peru
116 E6 **Tok** Alaska USA
155 G4 **Toka Village** Guyana
422 F4 **Tokaanu** New Zealand
387 I2 **Tokachi-dake** *volcano* Japan
387 H4 **Tokamachi** Japan
302 F4 **Tokar** Sudan
388 D3 **Tokarevka** Russian Federation
232 F2 **Tokari** Russian Federation
232 H2 **Tokarnia** Poland
381 J3 **Tokashiki-shima** *island* Japan
394 F5 **Tokat** Turkey
394 F5 **Tokat** *admin. area* Turkey
386 E3 **Tŏkch'ŏn** North Korea
422 3 **Tokelau** *NZ territory* Pacific Ocean
227 K3 **Toki** Poland
394 E3 **Tokmak** Ukraine
389 L5 **Tokmok** Kazakhstan
234 A2 **Tokod** Hungary
422 F5 **Tokomaru** New Zealand
422 H4 **Tokomaru Bay** New Zealand
422 F4 **Tokoroa** New Zealand
304 C3 **Tokounou** Guinea
223 Q5 **Tokrajärvi** Finland
223 U5 **Toksha-Kuznetsova** Russian Federation
116 C6 **Toksook Bay** Alaska USA
225 P2 **Toksovo** Russian Federation
389 N4 **Tokty** Kazakhstan
427 10 **Toku Island** Tonga
235 F6 **Tokul** Turkey
381 J3 **Tokuno-jima** *mountain* Japan
386 G3 **Tokushima** Japan
387 H4 **Tōkyō** Japan
426 6a **Tol** *island* Federated States of Micronesia
422 H4 **Tolaga Bay** New Zealand
309 I5 **Tôlanaro** Madagascar
130 C4 **Tolar** Texas USA
160 E3 **Tolar, Cerro** *mountain* Argentina
244 B2 **Tolastaidh** Na h-Eileanan Siar Scotland UK
383 I3 **Tolbo** Mongolia
383 I3 **Tolbo Nuur** *lake* Mongolia
436 T1 **Tolchin, Mount** *mountain* Antarctica
157 A9 **Toledo** Brazil
160 D3 **Toledo** Chile
230 D4 **Toledo** Spain
126 G7 **Toledo** Illinois USA
126 J6 **Toledo** Ohio USA
124 D4 **Toledo** Oregon USA
230 E4 **Toledo, Montes de** *range* Spain
130 E5 **Toledo Bend Reservoir** Louisiana USA
377 I5 **Toledo City** Philippines
229 K5 **Tolentino** Italy
231 I6 **Tolga** Algeria
222 G5 **Tolga** Norway
309 H4 **Toliara** Madagascar
309 H4 **Toliara** *admin. area* Madagascar
372 B3 **Tolitoli, Teluk** *bay* Indonesia
224 G4 **Tolken** *lake* Sweden
225 J5 **Tolkmicko** Poland
225 K5 **Tolko** Poland
243 G3 **Toll Bar** South Yorkshire England UK
244 G3 **Toll of Birness** Aberdeenshire Scotland UK
241 E4 **Tollard Royal** Wiltshire England UK
226 G1 **Tollense** *watercourse* Germany
243 G2 **Tollerton** North Yorkshire England UK
244 B2 **Tolmachan** Na h-Eileanan Siar Scotland UK
225 O3 **Tolmachevo** Russian Federation
234 A2 **Tolna** Hungary
227 J4 **Tolna** *admin. area* Hungary
125 P3 **Tolna** North Dakota USA
373 H5 **Tolo, Teluk** *bay* Indonesia
375 F5 **Tolokiwa Island** Papua New Guinea
223 N3 **Tolonen** Finland
373 D2 **Tolonuu** *island* Indonesia
230 E2 **Tolosa** Spain
223 Q5 **Tolosenmäki** Finland
241 E4 **Tolpuddle** Dorset England UK
385 E4 **Tolsan-do** *island* South Korea
385 J5 **Tolshan Dao** *island* Liaoning China
244 B2 **Tolsta Head** *cape* Scotland UK
237 AG7 **Tolstoy, Mys** *cape* Russian Federation
154 C2 **Tolú** Colombia
133 F5 **Toluca** Mexico
223 P3 **Tolva** Finland
244 E3 **Tolvah** Highland Scotland UK
223 Q3 **Tolvand, Ozero** *lake* Russian Federation
223 S5 **Tolvuya** Russian Federation
388 F2 **Tol'yatti** Russian Federation
389 O2 **Tom** *watercourse* Russian Federation
422 E2 **Tom Bowling Bay** New Zealand
424 F5 **Tom Price** WA Australia
116 E6 **Tom White, Mount** *mountain* Alaska USA
304 D2 **Toma** Burkina Faso
119 N6 **Tomahawk** Alberta Canada
126 G4 **Tomahawk** Wisconsin USA
234 F2 **Tomai** Moldova
387 I2 **Tomakomai** Japan
124 D7 **Tomales Bay** California USA
372 C4 **Tomani** Malaysia
427 9 **Tomanivi** *mountain* Fiji
230 B4 **Tomar** Portugal
387 I1 **Tomari** Russian Federation
158 E5 **Tomás Barrón** Bolivia
161 G4 **Tomás Gomensoro** Uruguay
234 F1 **Tomashpil'** Ukraine
227 L2 **Tomaszów Lubelski** Poland
227 K2 **Tomaszów Mazowiecki** Poland
244 E3 **Tomatin** Highland Scotland UK
132 D5 **Tomatlán** Mexico
159 G4 **Tombador, Serra do** *range* Brazil
130 D5 **Tomball** Texas USA
426 8 **Tombe** Solomon Islands
229 J5 **Tombe, Punta le** *cape* Italy
130 G4 **Tombigbee** *watercourse* Alabama USA
130 G3 **Tombigbee** *watercourse* Mississippi USA
306 A5 **Tomboco** Angola
300 F5 **Tombouctou (Timbuktu)** Mali
128 G5 **Tombstone** Arizona USA
308 B3 **Tombua** Angola
244 E4 **Tomchulan** Perth and Kinross Scotland UK
244 E3 **Tomdow** Moray Scotland UK
387 I3 **Tome** Japan
309 F4 **Tome** Mozambique
156 B3 **Tomé Açu** Brazil
372 B5 **Tomea** *island* Indonesia
232 G4 **Tomina** Bosnia and Herzegovina
304 B3 **Tominé** *watercourse* Guinea
372 B4 **Tomini, Teluk** *bay* Indonesia
300 F6 **Tominian** Mali
230 B3 **Tomiño** Spain
244 E3 **Tomintoul** Moray Scotland UK
222 H3 **Tomma** *island* Norway
244 E3 **Tomnaven** Moray Scotland UK
154 D3 **Tomo** *watercourse* Colombia
129 I6 **Tomochic** Mexico
306 B3 **Tomori** Central African Republic
235 B5 **Tomorit, Maja e** *mountain* Albania
426 1 **Tömotu Noi** *island* Solomon Islands
237 W7 **Tompa** Russian Federation
372 B4 **Tompira** Indonesia
119 Q7 **Tompkins** Saskatchewan Canada
372 A4 **Tompo** Indonesia
128 C2 **Toms Place** California USA
389 N2 **Tomsk** Russian Federation
236 R7 **Tomskaya Oblast'** *admin. area* Russian Federation
240 C2 **Ton-fanau** Gwynedd Wales UK
231 H3 **Tona** Spain
132 D3 **Tónachic** Mexico
133 G5 **Tonalá** Mexico
156 E3 **Tonantins** Brazil
233 C6 **Tonara** Sardinia Italy
124 F2 **Tonasket** Washington USA
127 L5 **Tonawanda** New York USA
154 B4 **Tonchigüe** Ecuador
230 B3 **Tondela** Portugal
300 D6 **Tondidji** Mali
240 D3 **Tondu** Bridgend Wales UK
242 B1 **Tonduff** Moyle Northern Ireland UK
240 E3 **Tone** *watercourse* England UK
436 Q1 **Toney Mountain** *mountain* Antarctica
373 H4 **Tong Island** Papua New Guinea
427 10 **Tonga** *country* Oceania
306 E2 **Tonga** Sudan
78 O9 **Tonga Trench** *underwater feature* Pacific Ocean
309 F5 **Tongaat** South Africa
427 10a **Tongamama'o** Tonga
422 F4 **Tongaporutu** New Zealand
Tongareva *see* **Penrhyn** Cook Islands New Zealand
426 7 **Tongariki** *island* Vanuatu
422 F4 **Tongariro, Mount** *volcano* New Zealand
427 10a **Tongatapu** *island* Tonga
427 10 **Tongatapu Group** *islands* Tonga
381 G2 **Tongbai** Henan China
381 G2 **Tongcheng** Anhui China
Tongchuan *see* **Santai** China
380 F1 **Tongchuan** Shaanxi China
386 E4 **Tongduch'ŏn** South Korea
229 G1 **Tongeren** Belgium
381 G4 **Tonggu Zhang** *mountain* Guangdong China
386 F4 **Tonghae** South Korea
381 G3 **Tonghai** Jiangxi China
385 K3 **Tonghe** Heilongjiang China
385 K4 **Tonghua** Jilin China
385 L3 **Tongjiang** Heilongjiang China
386 E3 **Tongjoson-man** *bay* North Korea
380 E4 **Tongle** Guangxi Zhuangzu Zizhiqu China
385 J4 **Tongliao** Nei Mongol Zizhiqu China
381 H2 **Tongling** Anhui China
381 H2 **Tonglu** Zhejiang China
426 7 **Tongoa** *island* Vanuatu
162 A3 **Tongoi, Bahía** *bay* Chile
304 D2 **Tongomayél** Burkina Faso
160 D4 **Tongoy** Chile
377 I6 **Tongquil** *island* Philippines
380 F3 **Tongren** Guizhou China
380 F5 **TongShi** Hainan China
383 J6 **Tongtian He** *lake* Qinghai China
383 J6 **Tongtian He** *watercourse* Qinghai China
379 H2 **Tongtian He** *watercourse* Sichuan China
244 D2 **Tongue** Highland Scotland UK
125 L4 **Tongue** *watercourse* Montana USA
304 B2 **Tongué** Guinea
244 D2 **Tongue Bay** Scotland UK
134 E1 **Tongue of the Ocean** *strait* Bahamas
125 L4 **Tongue River Reservoir** Montana USA
384 F6 **Tongxin** Zizhiqu China
381 G1 **Tongxu** Henan China
386 F4 **T'ongyŏng** South Korea
385 J4 **Tongyu** Jilin China
385 H5 **Tongzhou** Beijing China
381 I2 **Tongzhou** Jiangsu China
380 D3 **Tongzilin** Sichuan China
383 J3 **Tonhul** Mongolia
154 E4 **Tonina** Venezuela
306 D2 **Tonj** Sudan
392 D5 **Tonk** Rajasthan India
125 Q8 **Tonkawa** Oklahoma USA
125 N1 **Tonkin** Saskatchewan Canada
376 F2 **Tonkin, Gulf of** Vietnam
376 E4 **Tônlé Sap** *lake* Cambodia
228 D4 **Tonnay-Boutonne** France
228 D4 **Tonnay-Charente** France
228 F4 **Tonneins** France
126 G2 **Tonnere, Pointe au** *cape* Ontario Canada
228 F3 **Tonnerre** France
222 H3 **Tonnes** Norway
387 I3 **Tōno** Japan
426 6a **Tonoas** *island* Federated States of Micronesia
160 F2 **Tonono** Argentina
128 F4 **Tonopah** Arizona USA
128 D1 **Tonopah** Nevada USA
134 D6 **Tonosí** Panama
308 E4 **Tonota** Botswana
224 F3 **Tønsberg** Norway
304 C3 **Toobli** Liberia
245 D3 **Toomard** Ireland
245 C3 **Toombeola** Ireland
242 B2 **Toome** Antrim Northern Ireland UK
425 M6 **Toompine** Qld Australia
131 J4 **Toomsboro** Georgia USA
245 D3 **Toomyvara** Ireland
427 14b **Toopua, Motu** *island* French Polynesia
245 B5 **Toor** Ireland
242 B1 **Toor** Ballymoney Northern Ireland UK
245 C4 **Toorboney** Ireland
245 C3 **Tooreen** Ireland
245 C3 **Tooreengarve** Ireland
425 N6 **Toowoomba** Qld Australia
424 I4 **Top Springs** NT Australia
238 G3 **Topalki** Russian Federation
234 F3 **Topalu** Romania
128 F1 **Topaz Slough** *lake* Utah USA
389 N3 **Topchikha** Russian Federation
243 G2 **Topcliffe** North Yorkshire England UK
126 D7 **Topeka** Kansas USA
238 H5 **Topkanovo** Russian Federation
389 O2 **Topki** Russian Federation
118 H5 **Topley** British Columbia Canada
234 C4 **Topli Do** Serbia
234 D2 **Toplița** Romania
310 1b **Topo** Azores
128 E3 **Topock** Arizona USA
158 D5 **Topohoco** Bolivia
234 B3 **Topola** Serbia
232 H2 **Topoľčany** Slovakia
234 E4 **Topolchane** Bulgaria
237 AC6 **Topolinyy** Russian Federation
132 C3 **Topolobampo** Mexico
234 B3 **Topolovățu Mare** Romania
235 E4 **Topolovgrad** Bulgaria
235 D5 **Topolovo** Bulgaria
234 D3 **Toporu** Romania
223 Q4 **Topozero** Russian Federation
223 R4 **Topozero, Ozero** *lake* Russian Federation
127 R4 **Topsfield** Maine USA
240 D4 **Tor Bay** England UK
233 G7 **Torano Castello** Italy
155 H3 **Torarica Meer** *lake* Suriname
222 M3 **Torasjärvi** Sweden
244 B4 **Torastan** Highland Scotland UK
158 D5 **Torata** Peru
244 E3 **Torbain** Moray Scotland UK
235 E6 **Torbalı** Turkey
391 I2 **Torbat-e Ḩeydarīyeh** Iran
391 I2 **Torbat-e Jām** Iran
240 D4 **Torbay** *admin. area* England UK
238 F5 **Torbeyevo** Russian Federation
240 D4 **Torbryan** Devon England UK
119 T6 **Torch** *watercourse* Saskatchewan Canada
227 M2 **Torchyn** Ukraine
241 I5 **Torcy-le-Grand** France
234 B3 **Torda** Serbia
230 D3 **Tordesillas** Spain
227 J5 **Tordinci** Croatia
244 D3 **Tore** Highland Scotland UK
223 M4 **Töre** Sweden
231 H2 **Torelló** Spain
372 B4 **Toreo** Indonesia
240 D3 **Torfaen** *admin. area* Wales UK
224 D2 **Torfinnsvatnet** *lake* Norway
226 G2 **Torgau** Germany
383 K2 **Torgon Nuur** *lake* Mongolia
224 H4 **Torhamn** Sweden
224 I4 **Torhamns Udde** *cape* Sweden
381 J3 **Tori-shima** *island* Japan
154 B4 **Toribío** Colombia
230 E3 **Torija** Spain
226 D5 **Torino** Italy
159 H5 **Toriparu** Brazil
307 E3 **Torit** Sudan
156 E5 **Toritama** Brazil
157 A7 **Torixoreu** Brazil
225 N3 **Torma** Estonia
223 O5 **Tormälä** Finland
223 O2 **Törmänen** Finland
223 N4 **Törmäperä** Finland
223 N3 **Törmäsjärvi** *lake* Finland
230 D3 **Tormes** *watercourse* Spain
224 H4 **Törn** *lake* Sweden
124 H2 **Tornado Mountain** British Columbia Canada
227 K3 **Tornaľa** Slovakia
230 D3 **Tornavacas** Spain
244 F3 **Tornaveen** Aberdeenshire Scotland UK
222 L3 **Torneälven** *watercourse* Sweden
222 K2 **Torneträsk** *bay* Sweden
122 F3 **Torngat Mountains** Newfoundland and Labrador/Québec Canada
223 N4 **Tornio** Finland
234 A3 **Tornjoš** Serbia
160 F6 **Tornquist** Argentina
154 B3 **Toro** Colombia
230 D3 **Toro** Spain
306 E3 **Toro** Uganda
224 I3 **Törö** *island* Sweden
160 D4 **Toro, Cerro del** *mountain* Argentina
154 D3 **Toro Pintado** Venezuela
301 G6 **Torodi** Niger
237 AC8 **Torom** Russian Federation
162 C3 **Torongeñeu, Sierra de** *range* Argentina
127 L5 **Toronto** Ontario Canada
130 D2 **Toronto** Kansas USA
130 D2 **Toronto Lake** Kansas USA
227 I4 **Torony** Hungary
225 P4 **Toropets** Russian Federation
307 E3 **Tororo** Uganda
158 C4 **Torome** Peru
394 E6 **Toros Dağları** Turkey
159 E5 **Torotoro** Bolivia
224 G4 **Torpa** Sweden
224 I3 **Torpfjön** *bay* Sweden
244 F3 **Torphins** Aberdeenshire Scotland UK
240 C4 **Torpoint** Cornwall England UK
222 J5 **Torpshammar** Sweden
161 H4 **Torquato Severo** Brazil
119 T8 **Torquay** Saskatchewan Canada
240 D4 **Torquay** Torbay England UK
244 B3 **Torran** Highland Scotland UK
128 C4 **Torrance** California USA
129 J3 **Torrance** New Mexico USA
230 B4 **Torrão** Portugal
230 D4 **Torre de Abraham, Embalse de la** *lake* Spain
230 D5 **Torre del Águila, Embalse de la** *lake* Spain
226 D5 **Torre Pellice** Italy
230 D4 **Torrecampo** Spain
230 E2 **Torrecilla en Cameros** Spain
159 E5 **Torrecillas** Bolivia
230 E5 **Torredonjimeno** Spain
230 D3 **Torrejón el Rubio** Spain
230 E3 **Torrelaguna** Spain
232 D5 **Torrenieri** Italy
425 K7 **Torrens, Lake** SA Australia
132 E3 **Torreón** Mexico
230 C4 **Torreorgaz** Spain
161 I4 **Torres** Brazil
230 D2 **Torres, Cabo** *cape* Spain
426 7 **Torres Islands** *island* Vanuatu
230 B4 **Torres Novas** Portugal
425 L2 **Torres Strait** Australia
230 B4 **Torres Vedras** Portugal
124 J7 **Torrey** Utah USA
222 I5 **Torrflonäs** Sweden
373 G4 **Torricelli Mountains** *range* Papua New Guinea
240 C4 **Torridge** *watercourse* England UK
244 C3 **Torridon** Highland Scotland UK
230 D4 **Torrijos** Spain
244 B3 **Torrin** Highland Scotland UK
224 H1 **Torringen** *lake* Sweden
119 O7 **Torrington** Alberta Canada
125 M5 **Torrington** Wyoming USA
222 L3 **Torrivaara** Sweden
222 H5 **Torrön** *bay* Sweden
224 H3 **Torrvarpen** *lake* Sweden
225 O2 **Torsa** *lake* Finland
222 H5 **Torsborg** Sweden
117 S6 **Tórshavn** Faroe Islands
222 J2 **Torsken** Norway
222 M5 **Torsön** *island* Finland
222 K1 **Torsvåg** Norway
222 E5 **Torsvatnet** *lake* Norway
234 A2 **Törtel** Hungary
128 G4 **Tortilla Flat** Arizona USA
389 L3 **Tortkuduk** Kazakhstan
163 21 **Tortola** *island* British Virgin Islands
223 M3 **Tortola** Finland
155 F2 **Tortola, Isla** *island* Venezuela
230 D3 **Tórtoles de Esgueva** Spain
233 C7 **Tortoli** Sardinia Italy
226 E5 **Tortona** Italy
231 G3 **Tortosa** Spain
231 G3 **Tortosa, Cap de** *cape* Spain
135 F2 **Tortue, Île de la** *island* Haiti
155 H3 **Tortue, Monts** *range* French Guiana
163 4 **Tortuga, Isla** *island* Archipiélago de Colón (Galapagos Islands)
128 G7 **Tortuga, Isla** *island* Mexico
155 E2 **Tortuga, Isla La** *island* Venezuela
154 B4 **Tortugas, Golfo** *bay* Colombia
372 D4 **Torubi** *island* Indonesia
372 B4 **Torue** Indonesia
234 C1 **Torun'** Ukraine
227 J1 **Toruń** Poland
224 G4 **Torup** Sweden
242 E2 **Torver** Cumbria England UK
222 E5 **Torvik** Norway
222 E5 **Torvikbukt** Norway
223 O3 **Torvinen** Finland
245 D1 **Tory Island** Ireland
238 F4 **Torzhok** Russian Federation
154 A5 **Tosagua** Ecuador
386 E3 **T'osan** North Korea
222 H4 **Tosbotn** Norway
308 D5 **Tosca** South Africa
132 C3 **Tosca, Punta** *cape* Mexico
244 C3 **Toscaig** Highland Scotland UK
232 D5 **Toscana** *admin. area* Italy
233 D5 **Toscano, Arcipelago** *islands* Italy
222 H4 **Tosenfjorden** *bay* Norway
389 J6 **Toshkent** *admin. area* Uzbekistan
389 K5 **Toshkent (Tashkent)** Uzbekistan
225 P3 **Tosno** Russian Federation
383 J5 **Toson Hu** *lake* Qinghai China
222 H5 **Tossåsen** Sweden
224 G3 **Tösse** Sweden
245 F2 **Tossy** Ireland
160 F4 **Tostado** Argentina
241 H2 **Tostock** Suffolk England UK
237 X4 **Tostuya** Russian Federation
234 B2 **Tószeg** Hungary
154 C3 **Tota, Laguna de** *lake* Colombia
224 D3 **Totak** *lake* Norway
393 E10 **Totapola** *mountain* Sri Lanka
423 E5 **Totaranui** New Zealand
244 D2 **Totegan** Highland Scotland UK
308 D4 **Toteng** Botswana
241 I5 **Tôtes** France
426 6a **Totiw** *island* Federated States of Micronesia
234 B2 **Tótkomlós** Hungary
241 F4 **Totland** Isle of Wight England UK
240 D4 **Totnes** Devon England UK
155 G3 **Totness** Suriname
120 K6 **Totogan Lake** Ontario Canada
134 B4 **Totonicapán** Guatemala
158 D5 **Totora** Bolivia
160 E4 **Totoralejos** Argentina
154 B4 **Totoró** Colombia
304 C3 **Totota** Liberia
427 9 **Totoya** *island* Fiji
388 F3 **Totskoye** Russian Federation
222 G4 **Tøttdal** Norway
241 G3 **Tottenham** Greater London England UK
241 H2 **Tottington** Norfolk England UK
241 F4 **Totton** Hampshire England UK
386 G4 **Tottori** Japan
300 D4 **Touajil** Mauritania
304 C3 **Touba** Côte d'Ivoire
300 C6 **Touba** Senegal
300 D6 **Toubéré Bafal** Senegal
300 E2 **Toubkal, Jbel** *mountain* Morocco
305 H3 **Touboro** Cameroon
228 F3 **Toucy** France
231 J6 **Touffana** Algeria
304 D2 **Tougan** Burkina Faso
304 D2 **Tougouri** Burkina Faso
426 7 **Touho** New Caledonia
300 D5 **Touil** Mauritania
301 G2 **Touil, Oued** *watercourse* Algeria
300 E6 **Toukoto** Mali
304 E2 **Toukountouna** Benin
229 G2 **Toul** France
304 C3 **Touléplеu** Côte d'Ivoire
381 H4 **Touliu** Taiwan China
123 E7 **Toulnustouc** *watercourse* Québec Canada
229 G5 **Toulon** France
226 C4 **Toulon-sur-Arroux** France
228 E5 **Toulouse** France
301 I4 **Toummo** Libya
304 C3 **Toumodi** Côte d'Ivoire
379 H5 **Toungoo** Myanmar
228 E2 **Touques** *watercourse* France
304 C3 **Toura, Monts** *range* Côte d'Ivoire
230 B2 **Toural** Spain
301 J6 **Tourba** Chad
228 F1 **Tourcoing** France
230 B2 **Touriñán, Cabo** *cape* Spain
241 F5 **Tourlaville** France
228 F1 **Tournai** Belgium
226 B3 **Tournan** France
228 E5 **Tournay** France
229 G4 **Tournon-sur-Rhône** France
226 C4 **Tournus** France
156 F4 **Touros** Brazil
305 G3 **Touroua** Cameroon
228 E2 **Tourouvre** France
228 E3 **Tours** France
231 I2 **Tourves** France
228 E2 **Toury** France
231 F4 **Tous, Embalse de** *lake* Spain
301 J4 **Toussidé, Pic** *mountain* Chad
425 inset **Toutcher, Cape** Macquarie Island Australia
119 V7 **Toutes Aides** Manitoba Canada
308 D6 **Touwsriver** South Africa
226 G2 **Toužim** Czech Republic
384 F3 **Tov** *admin. area* Mongolia
238 F5 **Tovarkovo** Russian Federation
238 H6 **Tovarkovskiy** Russian Federation
224 E3 **Tovdalselv** *watercourse* Norway
162 D3 **Tovita, Isla** *island* Argentina
234 D1 **Tovste** Ukraine
243 G2 **Tow Law** Durham England UK
387 I3 **Towada-ko** *lake* Japan
372 B5 **Towari** Indonesia
241 G2 **Towcester** Northamptonshire England UK
118 I6 **Towdystan** British Columbia Canada
242 A4 **Tower Bridge** Ireland
129 K1 **Towner** Colorado USA
125 O2 **Towner** North Dakota USA
123 J4 **Townsend** Montana USA
120 H1 **Townsend Lake** Nunavut Canada
162 B6 **Townshend, Punta** *cape* Chile
425 M4 **Townsville** Qld Australia
372 B4 **Towori, Teluk** *bay* Indonesia
391 K3 **Towrzi** Afghanistan
240 C2 **Towyn** Ceredigion Wales UK
387 I2 **Tōya-ko** *lake* Japan
132 D3 **Toyachic** Mexico
129 K5 **Toyah** Texas USA
387 H4 **Toyama** Japan
227 M2 **Toykut** Ukraine
387 H4 **Toyokawa** Japan
386 G4 **Toyooka** Japan
223 M5 **Töysä** Finland
382 G6 **Toze Kangri** *mountain* Xizang Zizhiqu China
301 H2 **Tozeur** Tunisia
390 E2 **Tozkhurmato** Iraq
388 D5 **Tqvarch'eli** Georgia
376 E2 **Trà Linh** Vietnam
376 E5 **Trà Vinh** Vietnam
230 C3 **Trabazos** Spain
390 C2 **Trâblous (Tripoli)** Lebanon
225 M5 **Traby** Belarus
394 F5 **Trabzon** Turkey
394 F5 **Trabzon** *admin. area* Turkey
123 F9 **Tracadie-Sheila** New Brunswick Canada
158 D2 **Tracoá** Brazil
125 R4 **Tracy** Minnesota USA
226 E5 **Tradate** Italy
435 G2 **Traena Bank** *underwater feature* Norwegian Sea
222 H3 **Trænfjorden** *bay* Norway
126 E5 **Traer** Iowa USA
233 C6 **Traessu, Monte** *mountain* Sardinia Italy
123 G10 **Trafalgar** Nova Scotia Canada
230 C5 **Trafalgar, Cabo de** *cape* Spain
243 F3 **Trafford** *admin. area* England UK
131 K7 **Trafford, Lake** Florida USA
162 B2 **Trafful, Lago** *lake* Argentina
230 F3 **Tragacete** Spain
234 E2 **Traian** Romania
162 B3 **Traiguén** Chile
118 M8 **Trail** British Columbia Canada
117 Q4 **Traill Øer** *island* Greenland
156 E5 **Traipu** Brazil
154 D5 **Traíra, Serrania de** *range* Colombia
156 E3 **Trairi** Brazil
225 M5 **Trakai** Lithuania
225 M5 **Trakai** *region* Lithuania
235 C7 **Trakhila** Greece
245 C4 **Tralee** Ireland
245 C4 **Tralee Bay** Ireland
376 E2 **Trạm Tấu** Vietnam
245 E4 **Tramore** Ireland
245 E4 **Tramore Bay** Ireland
233 F6 **Tramutola** Italy
224 H3 **Tranås** Sweden
160 E3 **Trancas** Argentina
132 E4 **Trancoso** Mexico
376 C6 **Trang** Thailand
376 C6 **Trang** *admin. area* Thailand
372 E5 **Trangan** *island* Indonesia
233 G6 **Trani** Italy
309 I4 **Tranomaro** Madagascar
222 I2 **Tranøy** Norway
161 H4 **Tranqueras** Uruguay
228 D2 **Trans** France
436 K1 **Transantarctic Mountains** Antarctica
234 D2 **Transilvaniei, Câmpia** *region* Romania
224 G2 **Transtrand** Sweden
234 D3 **Transylvanian Alps** *range* Romania
Transylvanian Basin *see* **Podișul Transilvaniei** Romania
244 E2 **Trantlemore** Highland Scotland UK
160 E6 **Trapalcó** Argentina
160 D6 **Trapatrapa** Chile
154 E3 **Trapichote** Venezuela
124 E1 **Trapp Lake** British Columbia Canada
229 J1 **Trappstadt** Germany
425 M9 **Traralgon** Vic. Australia
158 D2 **Trarú** Brazil
230 C3 **Trás-os-Montes** *region* Portugal
379 G3 **Trashigang** Bhutan
232 E5 **Trasimeno, Lago** *lake* Italy
222 L5 **Träskvik** Finland
130 E3 **Traskwood** Arkansas USA
376 D5 **Trat** *admin. area* Thailand
160 D6 **Trayén** Argentina
227 H3 **Traun** Austria
229 K3 **Traunsee** *lake* Austria
229 K3 **Traunstein** Germany
229 J4 **Travagliato** Italy
233 G6 **Trave, Punta de** *cape* Italy
128 C2 **Traver** California USA
126 I4 **Traverse City** Michigan USA
122 H6 **Traverspine** *watercourse* Newfoundland and Labrador Canada
133 F2 **Travis, Lake** Texas USA
232 G4 **Travnik** Bosnia and Herzegovina
226 E5 **Travo** Italy
240 C2 **Trawsfynydd, Llyn** *lake* Wales UK
390 D3 **Ţraybīl** Iraq
229 H4 **Trbuk** Bosnia and Herzegovina
240 C2 **Tre-groes** Ceredigion Wales UK
240 D2 **Tre-Taliesin** Ceredigion Wales UK
240 C3 **Tre-Vaughan** Carmarthenshire Wales UK
242 A2 **Treantagh** Ireland
244 B3 **Treaslane** Highland Scotland UK
373 J5 **Treasury Islands** Solomon Islands
226 G1 **Trebbin** Germany
224 G5 **Trebel** *watercourse* Germany
227 H3 **Třebíč** Czech Republic
229 L4 **Trebnje** Slovenia
232 F2 **Třeboň** Czech Republic
240 D3 **Treborough** Somerset England UK
240 D3 **Trecastle** Powys Wales UK
240 D3 **Tredegar** Blaenau Gwent Wales UK
377 G3 **Tree Island** Paracel Islands
240 B4 **Treen** Cornwall England UK
224 E5 **Treene** *watercourse* Germany
240 D2 **Trefeglwys** Powys Wales UK
226 F2 **Treffurt** Germany
240 B3 **Trefgarn Owen** Pembrokeshire Wales UK
240 C2 **Trefilan** Ceredigion Wales UK
242 E3 **Trefnant** Denbighshire Wales UK
240 D1 **Trefriw** Conwy Wales UK
240 D2 **Tregaron** Ceredigion Wales UK
240 C4 **Tregoney** Cornwall England UK
228 C2 **Tréguier** France
240 D2 **Tregynon** Powys Wales UK
119 V8 **Treherne** Manitoba Canada
384 F1 **Trehgolwi Gorez** *mountain* Russian Federation
244 D4 **Treig, Loch** *lake* Scotland UK
228 E4 **Treignac** France
161 H5 **Treinta y Tres** Uruguay
161 H5 **Treinta y Tres** *admin. area* Uruguay
225 I5 **Trekilen** Sweden
229 H4 **Tréla Tête, Aiguilles de** *mountain* France
162 D3 **Trelew** Argentina
240 E3 **Trelleck** Monmouthshire Wales UK
240 D2 **Trelystan** Powys Wales UK
227 I4 **Trema** Croatia
240 C2 **Tremadog** Gwynedd Wales UK
240 C2 **Tremadog Bay** Wales UK
240 C4 **Tremail** Cornwall England UK
119 V7 **Tremaine** Manitoba Canada
240 C4 **Trematon** Cornwall England UK
118 I5 **Trembleur Lake** British Columbia Canada
157 D6 **Tremedal** Brazil
129 J3 **Trementina** New Mexico USA
233 F5 **Tremiti, Isole** *islands* Italy
124 I6 **Tremonton** Utah USA
231 G2 **Tremp** Spain
240 B4 **Trenance** Cornwall England UK
227 J3 **Trenčiansky** *admin. area* Slovakia
232 H2 **Trenčín** Slovakia
224 E4 **Trend** Denmark
232 G4 **Trenkovo** Croatia
160 F5 **Trenque Lauquen** Argentina
241 F2 **Trent** *watercourse* England, UK
240 E4 **Trent** Dorset England UK
125 Q5 **Trent** South Dakota USA
130 A4 **Trent** Texas USA
241 E2 **Trent Vale** Stoke-on-Trent England UK
131 M3 **Trent Woods** North Carolina USA
232 D2 **Trentino-Alto Adige** *admin. area* Italy
224 F4 **Trento** Italy
131 I6 **Trenton** Florida USA
131 J4 **Trenton** Georgia USA
126 E6 **Trenton** Missouri USA
127 N6 **Trenton** New Jersey USA

130 G3 Trenton Tennessee USA
130 C4 Trenton Texas USA
123 L9 Trepassey Newfoundland and Labrador Canada
123 L9 Trepassey Bay Newfoundland and Labrador Canada
160 F6 Tres Arroyos Argentina
157 B9 Três Barras Brazil
159 G4 Três Barras Brazil
159 F2 Tres Casas, Lago lake Brazil
162 C4 Tres Cerros Argentina
157 C8 Três Corações Brazil
158 D5 Tres Cruces Bolivia
160 D4 Tres Cruces Chile
161 H3 Três de Maio Brazil
230 E6 Tres Forcas, Cap cape Morocco
160 F3 Tres Isletas Argentina
157 B8 Três Lagoas Brazil
162 B4 Tres Lagos Argentina
157 C7 Três Marias, Represa de lake Brazil
162 A4 Tres Montes, Cabo cape Chile
162 A4 Tres Montes, Península peninsula Chile
132 E5 Tres Palos Mexico
133 F5 Tres Palos, Laguna lake Mexico
161 H3 Três Passos Brazil
133 G6 Tres Picos Mexico
160 F6 Tres Picos, Cerro mountain Argentina
129 J2 Tres Piedras New Mexico USA
162 B1 Tres Pinos Chile
128 E5 Tres Pozos Mexico
162 D4 Tres Puntas, Cabo cape Argentina
134 B3 Tres Puntas, Cabo de cape Guatemala
157 D8 Três Rios Brazil
240 A5 Tresco island England UK
225 F5 Tresfjord Norway
244 B4 Treshnish Highland Scotland UK
233 F6 Tresino, Punta cape Italy
235 B5 Treska watercourse Macedonia
225 N4 Treski Estonia
230 E2 Trespaderne Spain
244 E4 Tressait Perth and Kinross Scotland UK
228 E3 Tresson France
227 H3 Třešť Czech Republic
238 E4 Trestino Russian Federation
238 F4 Trestna Russian Federation
243 H3 Treswell Nottinghamshire England UK
222 L2 Tretta Norway
222 G6 Tretten Norway
127 N2 Trève, Lac La lake Québec Canada
162 B3 Trevelín Argentina
228 D3 Trèves France
229 K5 Trevi Italy
240 B3 Trevine Pembrokeshire Wales UK
226 G5 Treviso Italy
230 C3 Trevões Portugal
240 C2 Trevor Gwynedd Wales UK
240 B4 Trevose Head cape England UK
425 N8 Trewilga NSW Australia
240 C4 Trewithian Cornwall England UK
240 B4 Trewolla Cornwall England UK
240 C4 Trewornan Cornwall England UK
232 B3 Treyvaux Switzerland
226 E5 Trezzo Italy
234 C4 Trgovište Serbia
235 E7 Tria Nisia island Greece
425 M10 Triabunna Tas. Australia
228 D3 Triaize France
122 K6 Triangle Newfoundland and Labrador Canada
379 H3 Triangle, The region Myanmar
235 F7 Trianta Greece
119 T8 Tribune Saskatchewan Canada
125 O7 Tribune Kansas USA
160 E5 Trica Có Argentina
160 D6 Tricao Malal Argentina
226 G4 Tricesimo Italy
228 E5 Trie-sur-Baïse France
227 H4 Trieben Austria
226 D3 Trier Germany
227 G5 Trieste Italy
228 C2 Trieux watercourse France
234 E2 Trifeşti Romania
235 B6 Trikala Greece
225 M4 Trikāta Latvia
394 E6 Trikomo Cyprus
373 F5 Trikora, Puncak mountain Indonesia
232 G5 Trilj Croatia
242 A2 Trillick Omagh Northern Ireland UK
230 E3 Trillo Spain
245 F3 Trim Ireland
241 I2 Trimingham Norfolk England UK
241 I3 Trimley St Mary Suffolk England UK
229 I3 Trimmis Switzerland
154 A5 Trinchera, Punta cape Ecuador
393 E10 Trincomalee Sri Lanka
156 D4 Trindade Brazil
157 B7 Trindade Brazil
77 Trindade, Ilha da island Brazil
77 Trindade, Ilha da island Brazil
241 G3 Tring Hertfordshire England UK
159 E4 Trinidad Bolivia
154 D3 Trinidad Colombia
134 E2 Trinidad Cuba
134 B4 Trinidad Honduras
163 9 Trinidad island Trinidad and Tobago
161 G5 Trinidad Uruguay
124 C6 Trinidad California USA
125 M8 Trinidad Colorado USA
162 A4 Trinidad, Golfo bay Chile
162 E2 Trinidad, Isla island Argentina
135 I5 Trinidad and Tobago country Caribbean
233 E8 Trinità, Lago della lake Italy
233 G6 Trinitapoli Italy
155 H3 Trinité, Montagnes de la range French Guiana
123 L8 Trinity Newfoundland and Labrador Canada
124 D6 Trinity watercourse California USA
131 L3 Trinity North Carolina USA
130 D5 Trinity Texas USA
130 C5 Trinity watercourse Texas USA
117 N9 Trinity Bay Newfoundland and Labrador Canada
116 D7 Trinity Islands Alaska USA
374 B1 Trinkat island Andaman and Nicobar Islands India
376 B5 Trinkat island Andaman and Nicobar Islands India
302 F4 Trinkitat Sudan
226 E5 Trino Italy
233 F6 Triolo watercourse Italy
131 I3 Trion Georgia USA
233 G7 Trionto, Capo cape Italy
374 C2 Tripa watercourse Indonesia
235 C7 Tripoli Greece
232 E5 Triponzo Italy
235 B7 Tripotama Greece
229 J1 Triptis Germany
379 G4 Tripura admin. area India
123 I7 Triquet, Lac lake Québec Canada
226 F4 Trisanna watercourse Austria
224 E5 Trischen island Germany
310 5c Tristan da Cunha island St Helena
304 A2 Tristao, Îles island Guinea-Bissau
310 2 Tristão, Ponta do cape Madeira
245 C2 Tristia Ireland
234 D2 Tritenii de Jos Romania
123 K8 Triton Newfoundland and Labrador Canada
372 E4 Triton, Teluk bay Indonesia
377 F4 Triton Island Paracel Islands
159 E3 Triunfo Bolivia
159 F3 Triunfo Brazil
133 H5 Triunfo Mexico
233 F6 Trivento Italy
232 G4 Trn Bosnia and Herzegovina
227 I3 Trnava Slovakia
227 I3 Trnavský admin. area Slovakia
234 C3 Trnjane Serbia
233 H5 Trnovo Bosnia and Herzegovina
373 I6 Trobriand Islands Papua New Guinea
119 O7 Trochu Alberta Canada
121 P6 Trodely Island Nunavut Canada
240 C2 Troedyraur Ceredigion Wales UK
227 H4 Trofaiach Austria
232 B4 Trofarello Italy
222 H4 Trofors Norway
232 G5 Trogir Croatia
234 D4 Troianul Romania
121 R7 Troilus, Lac lake Québec Canada
135 J4 Trois-Bassins Réunion
123 D8 Trois-Pistoles Québec Canada
163 I5 Trois Pitons, Morne volcano Dominica
127 O3 Trois-Rivières Québec Canada
163 I6 Trois-Rivières Guadeloupe
229 H1 Troisvierges Luxembourg
388 I2 Troitsk Russian Federation
388 D4 Troitskoye Russian Federation
389 N3 Troitskoye Russian Federation
133 I6 Trojas Honduras
222 G5 Trolla Norway
223 O1 Trollbukta Norway
224 G3 Trollhättan Sweden
222 E5 Trolltindan mountain Norway
155 G5 Trombetas watercourse Brazil
310 6a Tromelin, Île French Southern and Antarctic Lands
162 D1 Tromen, Volcán volcano Argentina
224 E3 Tromøya island Norway
224 G5 Tromper Wiek bay Germany
308 E6 Trompsburg South Africa
222 K2 Troms admin. area Norway
222 K2 Tromsø Norway
222 K2 Tromvik Norway
244 inset Trondavoe Shetland Scotland UK
222 G5 Trondheim Norway
222 G5 Trondheimsfjorden bay Norway
222 H4 Trones Norway
379 G3 Trongsa Bhutan
232 E5 Tronto watercourse Italy
228 E3 Trôo France
244 D5 Troon South Ayrshire Scotland UK
226 C2 Trooz Belgium
238 F5 Troparëvo Russian Federation
157 C6 Tropeiros, Serra dos range Brazil
124 I8 Tropic Utah USA
132 C3 Troquero Mexico
236 M5 Trosh Russian Federation
119 S8 Trossachs Saskatchewan Canada
394 E2 Trostyanets' Ukraine
222 E2 Trotuş watercourse Romania
135 F3 Trou du Nord Haiti
163 I3 Trou Gras Point cape St Lucia
163 11a Troumaka St Vincent and the Grenadines
130 D4 Troup Texas USA
244 F3 Troup Head cape Scotland UK
119 N4 Trout watercourse Alberta Canada
128 F1 Trout Creek Utah USA
118 K2 Trout Lake Northwest Territories Canada
120 I7 Trout Lake Ontario Canada
123 I8 Trout River Newfoundland and Labrador Canada
242 F2 Troutbeck Cumbria England UK
124 D4 Troutdale Oregon USA
241 E3 Trowbridge Wiltshire England UK
241 I2 Trowse Newton Norfolk England UK
Troy see Truva Turkey
131 I5 Troy Alabama USA
126 J5 Troy Michigan USA
124 H2 Troy Montana USA
126 I6 Troy Ohio USA
127 M6 Troy Pennsylvania USA
130 G2 Troy Tennessee USA
130 C5 Troy Texas USA
234 D4 Troyan Bulgaria
228 G2 Troyes France
234 G2 Troyits'ke Ukraine
232 G5 Trpanj Croatia
234 B4 Trpezi Montenegro
233 H5 Trsa Montenegro
227 J3 Trstená Slovakia
234 B3 Trstenik Serbia
119 S8 Truax Saskatchewan Canada
229 H3 Trub Switzerland
230 C2 Truchas Spain
124 E7 Truckee California USA
238 E4 Trud Russian Federation
388 E4 Trudfront Russian Federation
229 G3 Trugny France
154 B3 Trujillo Colombia
134 C4 Trujillo Honduras
158 B3 Trujillo Peru
230 D4 Trujillo Spain
154 D2 Trujillo Venezuela
154 D2 Trujillo admin. area Venezuela
234 C1 Trukhanov Ukraine
240 D4 Trull Somerset England UK
374 C3 Trumon Indonesia
241 H2 Trumpington Cambridgeshire England UK
224 E2 Trun France
229 I3 Trun Switzerland
234 C4 Trŭn Bulgaria
241 I2 Trunch Norfolk England UK
376 E2 Trùng Khánh Vietnam
376 E5 Trùng Lón, Hòn island Vietnam
123 G10 Truro Nova Scotia Canada
240 B4 Truro Cornwall England UK
375 H2 Trus Madi, Gunung mountain Malaysia
375 G2 Trusan Malaysia
375 G2 Trusan watercourse Malaysia
241 F2 Trusley Derbyshire England UK
131 H4 Trussville Alabama USA
234 D4 Trŭstenik Bulgaria
224 F4 Trustrup Denmark
118 J4 Trutch British Columbia Canada
129 I4 Truth or Consequences New Mexico USA
235 E6 Truva (Troy) site Turkey
228 F4 Truyère watercourse France
235 B6 Trygon Greece
131 J3 Tryon North Carolina USA
422 F3 Tryphena New Zealand
235 D6 Trypiti, Akra cape Greece
224 G2 Trysil Norway
224 F2 Trysilelva watercourse Norway
227 I1 Trzcianka Poland
227 L1 Trzcianne Poland
227 H1 Trzciel Poland
227 H1 Trzcińsko Zdrój Poland
227 H2 Trzebień Poland
227 H1 Trzebież Poland
227 I2 Trzebnica Poland
227 I1 Trzemeszno Poland
227 H4 Tržič Slovenia
383 J3 Tsagaan Nuur lake Mongolia
385 H3 Tsagaan Ovoo Mongolia
384 D2 Tsagaan Uul mountain Mongolia
384 F3 Tsagaandelger Mongolia
384 F2 Tsagaannuul Mongolia
383 I2 Tsagaannuur Mongolia
388 E4 Tsagan-Nur Russian Federation
383 J3 Tsaganhairhan Mongolia
222 J3 Tsäkkok island Sweden
131 J6 Tsala Apopka Lake Florida USA
305 G5 Tsama Congo
235 B6 Tsamantas Greece
238 C3 Tsapel'ka Russian Federation
384 E2 Tsaraan-uure Mongolia
383 J3 Tsaraanchuluut Mongolia
383 J2 Tsaraanhairhan Mongolia
383 K2 Tsaraannuur Mongolia
309 I3 Tsaramandroso Madagascar
309 I3 Tsarantanana Madagascar
392 D4 Tsarap Lingti Chu watercourse Jammu and Kashmir India/Pakistan
309 I2 Tsaratanama, Massif du range Madagascar
234 E4 Tsarev Brod Bulgaria
234 E4 Tsarevo Bulgaria
383 I3 Tsast Uul mountain Mongolia
388 D4 Tsatsa Russian Federation
308 D4 Tsau Botswana
118 I4 Tsay Keh Dene British Columbia Canada
125 O3 Tschida, Lake North Dakota USA
383 J3 Tseel Mongolia
384 F3 Tseel Mongolia
389 O2 Tselinnoye Russian Federation
238 F6 Tsementnyy Russian Federation
383 I3 Tsengel Mongolia
384 D2 Tsengel Mongolia
384 E3 Tsenher Mongolia
383 I3 Tsetseg Mongolia
383 J3 Tsetseg Nuur lake Mongolia
308 D4 Tsetseng Botswana
190 D2 Tsetserleg Mongolia
384 E3 Tsetserleg Mongolia
304 E3 Tsévié Togo
308 D5 Tshabong Botswana
306 C5 Tshala Democratic Republic of Congo
306 A4 Tshela Democratic Republic of Congo
306 C4 Tshenge-Oshwe Democratic Republic of Congo
306 C5 Tshibala Democratic Republic of Congo
306 C5 Tshibuka Democratic Republic of Congo
306 C5 Tshibwika Democratic Republic of Congo
306 C5 Tshikapa Democratic Republic of Congo
306 C5 Tshilenge Democratic Republic of Congo
308 F4 Tshipise South Africa
306 C5 Tshisenge Democratic Republic of Congo
306 C5 Tshitanzu Democratic Republic of Congo
392 E4 Tsho Moriri lake Jammu and Kashmir India/Pakistan
306 D5 Tshofa Democratic Republic of Congo
308 E3 Tsholotsho Zimbabwe
308 D4 Tshootsha Botswana
306 C4 Tshupa watercourse Democratic Republic of Congo
Tshwane see Pretoria South Africa
388 D4 Tsimlyansk Russian Federation
388 D4 Tsimlyanskoye Vodokhranilishche lake Russian Federation
308 D5 Tsineng South Africa
309 I3 Tsinjoarivo Madagascar
308 C3 Tsintsabis Namibia
309 I5 Tsiombe Madagascar
237 X8 Tsipa watercourse Russian Federation
237 AC7 Tsipanda Russian Federation
237 X8 Tsipikan Russian Federation
309 I3 Tsiribihina watercourse Madagascar
309 I3 Tsiroanomandidy Madagascar
309 I4 Tsitondroina Madagascar
118 I6 Tsitsutl Peak British Columbia Canada
388 D5 Ts'khinvali Georgia
308 D3 Tsodilo Hills range Botswana
308 E6 Tsolo South Africa
308 E6 Tsomo South Africa
238 B4 Tsooru Estonia
383 J3 Tsort Mongolia
387 H4 Tsu Japan
388 E4 Tsubu Russian Federation
387 I3 Tsugarū-kaikyō strait Japan
308 C3 Tsumeb Namibia
308 D3 Tsumkwe Namibia
387 H4 Tsuru Japan
387 I2 Tsuru-numa lake Japan
387 H4 Tsuruga Japan
386 G5 Tsurugi-san volcano Japan
387 H3 Tsuruoka Japan
386 F4 Tsushima island Japan
386 G4 Tsuyama Japan
308 D4 Tswaane Botswana
223 R2 Tsypnavolok Russian Federation
230 C3 Tua watercourse Portugal
374 E5 Tua, Tanjung cape Indonesia
422 F3 Tuakau New Zealand
245 D3 Tuam Ireland
423 E5 Tuamarina New Zealand
376 D2 Tuần Giáo Vietnam
374 C3 Tuangku island Indonesia
158 D4 Tuanuni Bolivia
388 C5 Tuapse Russian Federation
375 H2 Tuaran Malaysia
374 A4 Tuas admin. area Singapore
427 12c Tuasivi Samoa
375 G5 Tuban Indonesia
375 G3 Tubau Malaysia
377 H5 Tubbataha Reefs Philippines
245 D4 Tubber Ireland
245 E4 Tubbrid Ireland
306 C5 Tubeya-Dita Democratic Republic of Congo
377 I6 Tubigan island Philippines
230 E2 Tubilla del Agua Spain
228 G1 Tubize Belgium
304 B3 Tubmanburg Liberia
427 9 Tubou Fiji
238 G1 Tubozero, Ozero lake Russian Federation
302 C1 Tubruq Libya
427 14 Tubuaï island French Polynesia
427 14 Tubuaï, Îles islands French Polynesia
134 E5 Tubualá Panama
132 C2 Tubutama Mexico
154 D4 Tucana Brazil
157 E5 Tucano Brazil
162 B1 Tucapel, Punta cape Chile
159 G5 Tucavaca watercourse Bolivia
232 G5 Tučepi Croatia
228 F5 Tuchan France
132 D3 Tucheachi Mexico
118 G2 Tuchitua Yukon Territory Canada
238 G5 Tuchkovo Russian Federation
118 I3 Tuchodi watercourse British Columbia Canada
227 I1 Tuchola Poland
227 K3 Tuchów Poland
128 G4 Tucson Arizona USA
162 B4 Tucu Tucu Argentina
156 B3 Tucumã Brazil
160 E3 Tucumán admin. area Argentina
129 K3 Tucumcari New Mexico USA
158 B2 Túcume Peru
155 F2 Tucupita Venezuela
156 B3 Tucuruí Brazil
156 B4 Tucuruí, Represa de lake Brazil
230 F2 Tudela Spain
122 F5 Tudor, Lac lake Québec Canada
225 P5 Tudorovo Belarus
225 N3 Tudulinna Estonia
305 F2 Tudun Wada Nigeria
230 C3 Tuela watercourse Portugal
379 H3 Tuensang Nagaland India
156 B3 Tueré watercourse Brazil
394 F5 Tufanbeyli Turkey
379 F3 Tufanganj West Bengal India
234 E3 Tufeşti Romania
228 E2 Tuffé France
79 R3 Tufts Plain underwater feature Pacific Ocean
241 G2 Tugby Leicester England UK
240 E2 Tugford Shropshire England UK
383 J3 Tugreg Mongolia
375 H3 Tuguan Maputi island Indonesia
377 I3 Tuguegarao Philippines
385 H5 Tuguiwula Nei Mongol Zizhiqu China
237 AC8 Tugur Russian Federation
Tuhua see Mayor Island New Zealand
235 B5 Tuin Macedonia
155 E5 Tuina Brazil
310 3d Tuineje Canary Islands
379 G4 Tuivaw watercourse Mizoram India
225 M4 Tūja Latvia
158 E5 Tujuria Bolivia
388 H2 Tukan Russian Federation
372 C5 Tukangbesi, Kepulauan island Indonesia
121 P4 Tukarak Island Nunavut Canada
234 C1 Tukhol'ka Ukraine
422 G4 Tukituki watercourse New Zealand
302 C1 Tūkrah Libya
116 F5 Tuktoyaktuk Northwest Territories Canada
116 G5 Tuktut Nogait National Park Northwest Territories Canada
225 L4 Tukuma admin. area Latvia
225 L4 Tukums Latvia
237 AA8 Tukuringra, Khrebet range Russian Federation
388 E5 Tukuy-Mekteb Russian Federation
427 12c Tula American Samoa
133 F4 Tula Mexico
238 G5 Tula Russian Federation
436 D2 Tula Mountains Antarctica
426 8 Tulagi Solomon Islands
383 I6 Tulagt Ar Gol watercourse Qinghai China
383 K5 Tulai He watercourse Gansu China
383 K5 Tulai Nanshan range Gansu China
124 E2 Tulameen British Columbia Canada
133 F4 Tulancingo Mexico
374 E5 Tulangbawang watercourse Indonesia
234 B4 Tulare Serbia
128 C2 Tulare California USA
125 P4 Tulare South Dakota USA
128 C3 Tulare Lake Bed California USA
129 I4 Tularosa New Mexico USA
132 D1 Tularosa Valley New Mexico USA
393 F7 Tulasi mountain Chhattisgarh India
390 D2 Ţulayḩah Iraq
154 B4 Tulcan Ecuador
234 F3 Tulcea Romania
234 F3 Tulcea admin. area Romania
244 E4 Tulchan Lodge Angus Scotland UK
234 F1 Tul'chyn Ukraine
133 F5 Tulcingo del Valle Mexico
158 D5 Tulduni Chile
124 E6 Tule Lake Sump California USA
124 E6 Tulelake California USA
120 F1 Tulemalu Lake Nunavut Canada
130 C6 Tuleta Texas USA
229 G4 Tulette France
308 E4 Tuli watercourse Zimbabwe
129 L3 Tulia Texas USA
116 G6 Tulita Northwest Territories Canada
245 D3 Tulla Ireland
244 D4 Tulla, Loch lake Scotland UK
245 E1 Tullagh Ireland
242 B3 Tullaghanoge Ireland
131 H3 Tullahoma Tennessee USA
245 C5 Tullakeel Ireland
425 M8 Tullamore NSW Australia
245 E3 Tullamore Ireland
228 E4 Tulle France
222 K2 Tulleng Norway
222 I5 Tulleråsen Sweden
244 C4 Tullich Argyll and Bute Scotland UK
244 E3 Tullich Highland Scotland UK
245 C4 Tullig Ireland
232 G2 Tulln Austria
128 B2 Tulloch Reservoir California USA
245 F4 Tullow Ireland
425 M4 Tully Qld Australia
127 M5 Tully New York USA
245 F3 Tullyallen Ireland
242 B3 Tullygowan Ireland
245 D4 Tullylease Ireland
242 C2 Tullymurry Down Northern Ireland UK
242 B4 Tullytusk Ireland
245 C3 Tullywee Bridge Ireland
234 E3 Tulnici Romania
160 D2 Túlor Chile
223 Q5 Tulos Russian Federation
223 Q5 Tulos, Ozero lake Russian Federation
236 M6 Tulpan Russian Federation
223 P3 Tulppio Finland
130 D2 Tulsa Oklahoma USA
118 E3 Tulsequah British Columbia Canada
392 F5 Tulsipur Nepal
238 G6 Tul'skaya Oblast' admin. area Russian Federation
155 F4 Tulu-Tuloi, Serra range Brazil
154 B3 Tuluá Colombia
383 I4 Tulufan Xinjiang Uygur Zizhiqu China
133 I4 Tulum Mexico
237 V8 Tulun Russian Federation
373 J5 Tulun Islands Papua New Guinea
375 F6 Tulungagung Indonesia
377 H5 Tuluran island Philippines
388 C2 Tuma Russian Federation
373 I6 Tuma Island Papua New Guinea
154 B4 Tumaco Colombia
154 B4 Tumaco, Bahía de bay Colombia
223 S2 Tumannyy Russian Federation
238 F5 Tumanovo Russian Federation
237 AC4 Tumat Russian Federation
238 F2 Tumazy Russian Federation
306 C4 Tumba Democratic Republic of Congo
224 I3 Tumba Sweden
306 B4 Tumba, Lac lake Democratic Republic of Congo
375 G4 Tumbangmiri Indonesia
375 G4 Tumbangsamba Indonesia
375 G4 Tumbangsenamang Indonesia
375 F4 Tumbangtiti Indonesia
160 E2 Tumbaya Argentina
158 A1 Tumbes Peru
154 A5 Tumbes admin. area Peru
118 K5 Tumbler Ridge British Columbia Canada
425 K8 Tumby Bay SA Australia
385 L4 Tumen Jilin China
385 G3 Tumentsogt Mongolia
384 D2 Tumerbular Mongolia
372 A2 Tumindao island Philippines
119 U7 Tummel Manitoba Canada
244 D4 Tummel Bridge Perth and Kinross Scotland UK
374 D2 Tumpat Malaysia
372 B4 Tumpu, Gunung mountain Indonesia
393 E7 Tumsar Maharashtra India
304 D2 Tumu Ghana
Tumuc-Humac Mountains see Tumucumaque, Serra Brazil
155 H4 Tumucumaque, Serra (Tumuc-Humac) range Brazil
393 F7 Tumudibandh Orissa India
304 D3 Tuna Ghana
135 H3 Tuna, Punta cape Puerto Rico
154 D4 Tunahí, Sierra range Colombia
154 C4 Tunaima, Laguna lake Colombia
159 E6 Tunal Bolivia
383 K2 Tunamal Nuur lake Mongolia
163 9 Tunapuna Trinidad and Tobago
163 9 Tunapuna-Piarco admin. area Trinidad and Tobago
160 F6 Tunas, Sierra del las range Argentina
302 D2 Tunaydah Egypt
394 F5 Tunceli Turkey
394 F5 Tunceli admin. area Turkey
380 F5 Tunchang Hainan China
425 O8 Tuncurry NSW Australia
307 E5 Tunduma Tanzania
307 F6 Tunduru Tanzania
234 D4 Tundzha watercourse Bulgaria
384 D2 Tunel Mongolia
305 F3 Tunga Nigeria
385 I1 Tungir watercourse Russian Federation
375 H2 Tungku Malaysia
222 inset Tungnaá watercourse Iceland
118 G2 Tungsten Northwest Territories Canada
223 R4 Tunguda Russian Federation
222 inset Tungufljót watercourse Iceland
237 AA6 Tunguskhaya Russian Federation
236 T6 Tunguskoye Plato region Russian Federation
372 E5 Tunguwatu Indonesia
384 F3 Tunhel Mongolia
130 F3 Tunica Mississippi USA
301 I1 Tunis Tunisia
233 D8 Tunis, Golfe de bay Tunisia
301 H2 Tunisia country Africa
154 C3 Tunja Colombia
131 I3 Tunnel Hill Georgia USA
224 E2 Tunnhovdfjorden bay Norway
225 O2 Tunnila Finland
222 H4 Tunnsjøen lake Norway
222 I5 Tunnvågen Sweden
224 F5 Tunø island Denmark
224 D2 Tunsbergdalsvatnet lake Norway
243 G2 Tunstall North Yorkshire England UK
156 C4 Tuntum Brazil
122 H4 Tunungayualok Island Newfoundland and Labrador Canada
121 Q3 Tunusualuk, Lac lake Québec Canada
160 D5 Tunuyán Argentina
160 E5 Tunuyán watercourse Argentina
379 G4 Tunzang Myanmar
381 H1 Tuo He watercourse Anhui China
380 D4 Tuodian Yunnan China
378 D2 Tuoding Xizang Zizhiqu China
385 I5 Tuoji Dao island Shandong China
380 F3 Tuojiang Hunan China
381 F3 Tuojiang Hunan China
384 G5 Tuoketuo Nei Mongol Zizhiqu China
383 H4 Tuokexun Xinjiang Uygur Zizhiqu China
382 G3 Tuoli Xinjiang Uygur Zizhiqu China
222 L3 Tuolpukka Sweden
223 N4 Tuomioja Finland
380 E4 Tuoniang Jiang watercourse Guangxi Zhuangzu Zizhiqu China
382 H3 Tuoputiereke Xinjiang Uygur Zizhiqu China
383 I6 Tuotuo He watercourse Qinghai China
245 D5 Tuough Bridge Ireland
157 B8 Tupã Brazil
427 14 Tupai island French Polynesia
159 F2 Tupana watercourse Brazil
155 F4 Tupari Brazil
130 C3 Tupelo Oklahoma USA
157 B8 Tupi Paulista Brazil
238 E6 Tupichino Belarus
238 E5 Tupik Russian Federation
385 I1 Tupik Russian Federation
159 G1 Tupinambarama, Ilha island Brazil
225 O3 Tupisyno Russian Federation
159 E6 Tupiza Bolivia
118 K5 Tupper British Columbia Canada
127 N4 Tupper Lake New York USA
388 I6 Tuprakkala Turkmenistan
385 J3 Tuquan Nei Mongol Zizhiqu China
234 A2 Tura Hungary
379 G4 Tura Meghalaya India
237 V6 Tura Russian Federation
388 J1 Tura watercourse Russian Federation
390 E5 Turabah Saudi Arabia
390 E5 Turabah, Wādī watercourse Saudi Arabia
158 C4 Turajaja Peru
237 Z4 Turakh Russian Federation
422 F5 Turakina New Zealand
423 F5 Turakirae Head New Zealand
234 A3 Turalići Bosnia and Herzegovina
373 G5 Turama watercourse Papua New Guinea
237 AB8 Turana, Khrebet range Russian Federation
422 F4 Turangi New Zealand
234 A1 Turany Slovakia
391 I6 Tur'at Maşirah sea Oman
227 J2 Turawskie, Jezioro lake Poland
225 M3 Turba Estonia
154 C2 Turbaco Colombia
391 J4 Turbat Pakistan
131 L4 Turbeville South Carolina USA
227 K2 Turbia Poland
244 C4 Turbiskill Argyll and Bute Scotland UK
154 B2 Turbo Colombia
234 C3 Turceni Romania
223 U5 Turchasovo Russian Federation
158 D5 Turco Bolivia
234 F3 Turcoaia Romania
158 E4 Turcocala Bolivia
238 H6 Turdey Russian Federation
245 E1 Ture Ireland
230 D3 Turégano Spain
427 14 Tureia island French Polynesia
227 J1 Turek Poland
225 M2 Turenki Finland
244 F3 Turfgate Aberdeenshire Scotland UK
388 I3 Turgay Kazakhstan
389 K3 Turgay Kazakhstan
388 I4 Turgay watercourse Kazakhstan
383 I2 Turgen Mongolia
383 I2 Turgen Uul mountain Mongolia
127 L2 Turgeon watercourse Québec Canada
127 L2 Turgeon, Lac lake Québec Canada
234 E4 Tŭrgovishte Bulgaria
394 F5 Turhal Turkey
233 G6 Turi Italy
225 M3 Türi Estonia
231 F4 Turia watercourse Spain
156 C3 Turiaçu Brazil
156 C3 Turiaçu watercourse Brazil
156 C3 Turiaçu, Baía de bay Brazil
307 F5 Turiani Tanzania
227 K5 Turija Serbia
155 F2 Turimiquire, Serrania de range Venezuela
119 O8 Turin Alberta Canada
388 I1 Turinsk Russian Federation
227 M2 Turiys'k Ukraine
232 G5 Turjaci Croatia
227 H5 Turjak Slovenia
234 C1 Turka Ukraine
307 F3 Turkana, Lake lake Kenya
235 E7 Türkbükü Turkey
241 F3 Turkdean Gloucestershire England UK
235 E5 Türkeli Adası island Turkey
389 J5 Turkestan Kazakhstan
234 B2 Túrkeve Hungary
394 E5 Turkey country Asia
129 L3 Turkey Texas USA
388 D3 Turki Russian Federation
388 I6 Türkmenabat Turkmenistan
388 F6 Türkmenbaşy Turkmenistan
388 F6 Türkmenbaşy Aýlagy bay Turkmenistan
388 H6 Turkmenistan country
135 G2 Turks and Caicos Islands British overseas territory Caribbean
135 G2 Turks Islands Turks and Caicos Islands
135 G2 Turks Islands Passage channel Turks and Caicos Islands
225 L2 Turku/Åbo Finland
124 E8 Turlock California USA
157 D7 Turmalina Brazil
227 K3 Turňa nad Bodvou Slovakia
422 G5 Turnagain, Cape New Zealand
373 G6 Turnagain Island Australia
240 E2 Turnastone Herefordshire England UK
122 I5 Turnavik Islands Newfoundland and Labrador Canada
119 U6 Turnberry Manitoba Canada
244 D5 Turnberry South Ayrshire Scotland UK
134 C3 Turneffe Islands Belize
119 Q8 Turner Montana USA
119 N7 Turner Valley Alberta Canada
242 B4 Turner's Ireland
304 B3 Turners Peninsula peninsula Sierra Leone
241 E4 Turners Puddle Dorset England UK
227 H4 Türnitz Austria
119 Q4 Turnor Lake Saskatchewan Canada
227 H2 Turnov Czech Republic
125 P8 Turon Kansas USA
227 K1 Turośl Poland
227 I1 Turowo Poland
Turpan see Tulufan China
129 I1 Turquoise Lake Colorado USA
227 G4 Turrach Austria
130 F3 Turrell Arkansas USA
244 D4 Turret Bridge Highland Scotland UK
134 D5 Turrialba Costa Rica
244 F3 Turriff Aberdeenshire Scotland UK
390 F2 Tursāq Iraq
388 H5 Türtkŭl Uzbekistan
126 F3 Turtle Flambeau lake Wisconsin USA
375 H2 Turtle Islands Philippines
119 Q6 Turtle Lake Saskatchewan Canada
126 E4 Turtle Lake Wisconsin USA
119 Q6 Turtleford Saskatchewan Canada
236 R5 Turukhan watercourse Russian Federation
236 S5 Turukhansk Russian Federation
235 G7 Turunçova Turkey
388 G4 Turush Kazakhstan
157 B7 Turvo watercourse Brazil
227 M2 Tur'ya Ukraine
234 A1 Turzovka Slovakia
234 C2 Tusa Romania
160 E2 Tusaquilla Argentina
130 H4 Tuscaloosa Alabama USA
130 H4 Tuscaloosa, Lake Alabama USA
233 D5 Tuscania Italy
127 M6 Tuscarora Mountains Pennsylvania USA
126 G7 Tuscola Illinois USA
130 B4 Tuscola Texas USA
131 J2 Tusculum Tennessee USA
130 H3 Tuscumbia Alabama USA
229 I5 Tuselli, Punta alli cape Corsica France
222 G5 Tuset Norway
242 E1 Tushielaw Scottish Borders Scotland UK
384 F2 Tushig Mongolia
225 L5 Tushino Russian Federation
130 C3 Tushka Oklahoma USA
225 N2 Tuskas Finland
131 I4 Tuskegee Alabama USA
222 J2 Tussøya island Norway
222 I4 Tustervatnet lake Norway
222 E5 Tustna island Norway
227 K2 Tuszów Narodowy Poland
391 J2 Tuta Afghanistan
391 J2 Tūtachī Afghanistan
422 G4 Tutaekuri watercourse New Zealand
427 13a Tutaga island Tuvalu
241 F2 Tutbury Staffordshire England UK
393 E10 Tuticorin Tamil Nadu India
422 G4 Tutira New Zealand
375 G2 Tutoh watercourse Malaysia
156 D3 Tutóia Brazil
236 T5 Tutonchana watercourse Russian Federation
237 T5 Tutonchana, Vozvyshennost' range Russian Federation
375 G2 Tutong Brunei
234 E2 Tutova Romania
118 D3 Tutshi Lake British Columbia Canada
130 C3 Tuttle Oklahoma USA
126 C7 Tuttle Creek Lake Kansas USA
222 J3 Tutturjaure lake Sweden
122 O2 Tuttutooq island Greenland
129 I6 Tutuaca Mexico
372 C6 Tutuala Timor-Leste (East Timor)
427 12 Tutuila island American Samoa
422 F2 Tutukaka New Zealand
308 E4 Tutume Botswana
426 8a Tutumu Solomon Islands
158 D5 Tutupaca, Volcán volcano Peru
130 F3 Tutwiler Mississippi USA
225 L3 Tuudi Estonia
223 N3 Tuuliharju Finland
223 Q5 Tuupovaara Finland
225 O1 Tuusjärvi Finland
225 O2 Tuusjärvi lake Finland
223 P5 Tuusniemi Finland
163 5 Tuutapu volcano Isla de Pascua Z(Easter Island)
426 13 Tuvalu country Oceania
436 S2 Tuve, Mount mountain Antarctica
384 G3 Tuvshinshiree Mongolia
384 E3 Tuvshruuleh Mongolia
427 9 Tuvuca island Fiji
126 C2 Tuxedo Manitoba Canada
125 M1 Tuxford Saskatchewan Canada
243 H3 Tuxford Nottinghamshire England UK
133 G5 Tuxtla Gutiérrez Mexico
376 E4 Tuỳ Đức Vietnam
376 F4 Tuy Hòa Vietnam
118 F3 Tuya Lake British Columbia Canada
394 E5 Tuz Gölü lake Turkey
235 E7 Tuzburgazı Turkey
388 E1 Tuzha Russian Federation
233 H5 Tuzi Montenegro
232 H4 Tuzla Bosnia and Herzegovina
235 E5 Tuzla Turkey
235 G6 Tuzlukçu Turkey
234 C1 Tuzsér Hungary
224 G4 Tvååker Sweden
222 K4 Tvärålund Sweden
222 J4 Tväråträsk Sweden
224 E3 Tvedestrand Norway
238 F4 Tver' Russian Federation
222 K2 Tverrfjellet island Norway

238 E4 **Tverskaya Oblast'** *admin. area* Russian Federation
224 F4 **Tversted** Denmark
232 H2 **Tvrdošín** Slovakia
227 I2 **Twardogóra** Poland
244 E1 **Twatt** Orkney Islands Scotland UK
308 C5 **Twee Rivier** Namibia
127 M4 **Tweed** Ontario Canada
242 E1 **Tweed** *watercourse* Scotland UK
244 E5 **Tweedsmuir** Scottish Borders Scotland UK
118 H6 **Tweedsmuir Provincial Park** British Columbia Canada
241 G2 **Twenty** Lincolnshire England UK
128 D3 **Twentynine Palms** California USA
123 K8 **Twillingate** Newfoundland and Labrador Canada
124 I4 **Twin Bridges** Montana USA
132 E2 **Twin Buttes Reservoir** Texas USA
131 J4 **Twin City** Georgia USA
124 H5 **Twin Falls** Idaho USA
123 K8 **Twin Lakes** Newfoundland and Labrador Canada
129 I1 **Twin Lakes Reservoir** Colorado USA
308 E2 **Twingi** Zambia
124 E2 **Twisp** Washington USA
226 D1 **Twist** Germany
226 E2 **Twiste** Germany
128 B3 **Twitchell Reservoir** California USA
310 5a **Two Boats Village** Ascension
128 B3 **Two Buttes Reservoir** Colorado USA
119 M5 **Two Creeks** Alberta Canada
163 18 **Two Feet Bay** Antigua and Barbuda
128 G3 **Two Guns** Arizona USA
126 F3 **Two Harbors** Minnesota USA
119 P6 **Two Hills** Alberta Canada
120 J6 **Two River Lake** Ontario Canada
126 H4 **Two Rivers** Wisconsin USA
132 D1 **Two Rivers Reservoir** New Mexico USA
423 D6 **Two Thumb Range** New Zealand
227 J2 **Tworóg** Poland
241 F3 **Twyford** Hampshire England UK
241 G2 **Twyford** Leicester England UK
241 E2 **Twyning** Gloucestershire England UK
240 D3 **Twynllanan** Carmarthenshire Wales UK
240 D2 **Ty-nant** Gwynedd Wales UK
131 J5 **Ty Ty** Georgia USA
234 C1 **Tyachiv** Ukraine
238 G1 **Tyagozero, Ozero** *lake* Russian Federation
224 E2 **Tyberton** Herefordshire England UK
227 J2 **Tychy** Poland
118 D4 **Tyee** Alaska USA
118 G2 **Tyers** *watercourse* Yukon Territory Canada
224 H2 **Tyfors** Sweden
237 AA8 **Tygda** Russian Federation
224 E2 **Tyin** *lake* Norway
227 K3 **Tylawa** Poland
222 G5 **Tyldal** Norway
126 F4 **Tyler** Minnesota USA
130 D4 **Tyler** Texas USA
130 F5 **Tylertown** Mississippi USA
234 G2 **Tylihul's'kyy Lyman** *lake* Ukraine
237 AB8 **Tyl'skiy Khrebet** *range* Russian Federation
236 R6 **Tym** *watercourse* Russian Federation
224 H5 **Tymień** Poland
116 A6 **Tymna, Laguna** Russian Federation
242 B2 **Tynan** Armagh Northern Ireland UK
237 Z7 **Tynda** Russian Federation
125 Q1 **Tyndall** Manitoba Canada
125 Q5 **Tyndall** South Dakota USA
222 J5 **Tynderö** Sweden
244 D4 **Tyndrum** Stirling Scotland UK
243 G2 **Tyne** *watercourse* England UK
123 G9 **Tyne Valley** Prince Edward Island Canada
224 G2 **Tyngsjö** Sweden
223 N4 **Tynkä** Finland
234 G1 **Tynovka** Ukraine
222 G5 **Tynset** Norway
223 N4 **Typpö** Finland
223 N3 **Typpyrä** Finland
223 P4 **Tyräjärvi** *lake* Finland
223 P4 **Tyrävaara** Finland
227 L3 **Tyrawa Wołoska** Poland
224 F2 **Tyrifjorden** *bay* Norway
385 L2 **Tyrma** Russian Federation
385 L2 **Tyrma** *watercourse* Russian Federation
223 N4 **Tyrnävä** Finland
130 A2 **Tyrone** Oklahoma USA
127 L6 **Tyrone** Pennsylvania USA
130 F3 **Tyronza** Arkansas USA
119 V5 **Tyrrell** Manitoba Canada
229 J5 **Tyrrhenian Sea** Italy
237 AC6 **Tyry** *watercourse* Russian Federation
Tysa *see* **Tisza**
234 C/D1 **Tysa** *watercourse* Ukraine
224 C3 **Tysnesøy** *island* Norway
224 C2 **Tysse** Norway
224 I3 **Tystberga** Sweden
241 E3 **Tytherton Lucas** Wiltshire England UK
225 L5 **Tytuvėnai** Lithuania
237 F5 **Tyub-Karagan, Mys** *cape* Kazakhstan
389 K2 **Tyukalinsk** Russian Federation
237 Y6 **Tyukyan** *watercourse* Russian Federation
388 F4 **Tyulen'i Ostrova** *island* Kazakhstan
388 G3 **Tyul'gan** Russian Federation
388 J1 **Tyumen'** Russian Federation
236 O7 **Tyumenskaya Oblast'** *admin. area* Russian Federation
237 AB6 **Tyungyulyu** Russian Federation
389 Q3 **Tyva** *admin. area* Russian Federation
240 D2 **Tywi** *watercourse* Wales UK
240 C2 **Tywyn** Gwynedd Wales UK
154 B5 **Tzungüi** Ecuador

U

386 E5 **U-do** *island* South Korea
427 14 **Ua Huka** *island* French Polynesia
427 14 **Ua Pu** *island* French Polynesia
155 F3 **Uacauyén** Venezuela
UAE *see* **United Arab Emirates**
134 E5 **Ualá** Honduras
155 F3 **Uaray, Sierra de** *range* Venezuela
155 E5 **Uarini** Brazil
155 E3 **Uasadi, Cerros** *range* Venezuela
155 G5 **Uatumã** *watercourse* Brazil
156 E5 **Uauá** Brazil
155 F3 **Uaua, Cerro** *mountain* Venezuela
154 E4 **Uaupés** *watercourse* Brazil
234 B3 **Ub** Serbia
157 D8 **Ubá** Brazil
305 G2 **Uba** Nigeria
373 I5 **Ubai** Papua New Guinea
392 D6 **Ubaidullaganj** Madhya Pradesh India
157 E6 **Ubaitaba** Brazil
156 D3 **Ubajara** Brazil
306 B3 **Ubangi** *watercourse* Central African Republic
305 H4 **Ubangi** *watercourse* Congo
154 C3 **Ubaque** Colombia
157 E6 **Ubatã** Brazil
154 C3 **Ubaté** Colombia
157 C8 **Ubatuba** Brazil
391 L4 **Ubauro** Pakistan
229 H4 **Ubaye** *watercourse* France
390 E3 **Ubayyiḍ, Wādī al** Iraq
386 F5 **Ube** Japan
230 E4 **Úbeda** Spain
157 C7 **Uberaba** Brazil
157 B7 **Uberlândia** Brazil
372 F5 **Ubia, Gunung** *mountain* Indonesia
374 E3 **Ubin, Pulau** *island* Singapore
389 M2 **Ubinskoye** *lake* Russian Federation
234 C1 **Ubľa** Slovakia
162 C3 **Ubledo, Laguna** *lake* Argentina
232 G5 **Ubli** Croatia
232 H5 **Ubli** Montenegro
376 E4 **Ubon Ratchathani** Thailand
230 D5 **Ubrique** Spain
375 G6 **Ubud** Indonesia
306 D4 **Ubundu** Democratic Republic of Congo
134 C4 **Ucacabatla** Honduras
388 I6 **Üçajy** Turkmenistan
158 C3 **Ucayali** *admin. area* Peru
158 C3 **Ucayali** *watercourse* Peru
230 E3 **Uceda** Spain
237 U6 **Uchami** Russian Federation
237 T6 **Uchami** *watercourse* Russian Federation
389 M4 **Ucharal** Kazakhstan
158 B3 **Uchiza** Peru
389 K5 **Uchqurghon** Uzbekistan
237 AB7 **Uchur** *watercourse* Russian Federation
241 H4 **Uckfield** East Sussex England UK
124 C2 **Ucluelet** British Columbia Canada
235 E6 **Üçpınar** Turkey
233 F7 **Ucria** Italy
133 H5 **Ucum** Mexico
237 AB8 **Uda** *watercourse* Russian Federation
388 E4 **Udachnoye** Russian Federation
237 X5 **Udachnyy** Russian Federation
392 C6 **Udaipur** Rajasthan India
392 E6 **Udaipura** Madhya Pradesh India
390 E4 **Ūdākh** Saudi Arabia
393 E10 **Udangudi** Tamil Nadu India
393 E8 **Udayagiri** Andhra Pradesh India
232 F4 **Udbina** Croatia
224 F5 **Udby** Denmark
224 F5 **Udbyhøj** Denmark
224 F3 **Uddevalla** Sweden
224 G3 **Uddheden** Sweden
244 E5 **Uddington** South Lanarkshire Scotland UK
222 J4 **Uddjaure** *bay* Sweden
226 C2 **Uden** Netherlands
393 D7 **Udgir** Maharashtra India
392 D4 **Udhampur** Jammu and Kashmir India/Pakistan
226 G4 **Udine** Italy
436 P3 **Udintsev Fracture Zone** *underwater feature* Southern Ocean
236 L7 **Udmurtskaya Respublika** *admin. area* Russian Federation
237 Y7 **Udokan, Khrebet** *range* Russian Federation
238 F4 **Udomlya** Russian Federation
376 D3 **Udon Thani** Thailand
426 6a **Udot** *island* Federated States of Micronesia
222 K3 **Udtja** Sweden
393 D9 **Udupi** Karnataka India
237 AD8 **Udyl', Ozero** *lake* Russian Federation
237 Y4 **Udzha** Russian Federation
375 I4 **Uëbonti** Indonesia
227 H1 **Uecker** *watercourse* Germany
387 H4 **Ueda** Japan
372 B4 **Uekuli** Indonesia
306 D3 **Uele** *watercourse* Democratic Republic of Congo
237 Y4 **Uele** *watercourse* Russian Federation
116 C5 **Uelen** Russian Federation
237 AL5 **Uel'kal** Russian Federation
226 F1 **Uelzen** Germany
383 I3 **Uench** Mongolia
306 D3 **Uere** *watercourse* Democratic Republic of Congo
226 E1 **Uetersen** Germany
226 F1 **Uetze** Germany
388 G2 **Ufa** Russian Federation
240 D4 **Uffculme** Devon England UK
240 E2 **Uffington** Shropshire England UK
241 I2 **Ufford** Suffolk England UK
308 B4 **Ugab** *watercourse* Namibia
225 L4 **Ugāle** Latvia
306 E5 **Ugalla** *watercourse* Tanzania
306 E3 **Uganda** *country* Africa
234 B4 **Ugao** Serbia
233 H7 **Ugento** Italy
388 D5 **Ugheltekhili Nakra** *pass* Georgia
230 E5 **Ugíjar** Spain
229 H4 **Ugine** France
122 G3 **Ugjuktok Fiord** Newfoundland and Labrador Canada
390 E4 **'Uglah** Saudi Arabia
237 AD9 **Uglegorsk** Russian Federation
238 H4 **Uglich** Russian Federation
232 F4 **Ugljan** Croatia
238 E3 **Uglovka** Russian Federation
389 M3 **Uglovskoye** Russian Federation
116 A6 **Ugol'naya, Bukhta** *bay* Russian Federation
238 F5 **Ugra** Russian Federation
238 F5 **Ugra National Park** Russian Federation
234 B3 **Ugrinovci** Serbia
237 Y5 **Ugumun** Russian Federation
234 D4 **Ugŭrchin** Bulgaria
235 F6 **Uğurluca** Turkey
234 C1 **Uh** *watercourse* Slovakia
227 I3 **Uherské Hradiště** Czech Republic
232 G2 **Uherský Brod** Czech Republic
226 G3 **Úhlava** *watercourse* Czech Republic
227 L2 **Uhniv** Ukraine
229 H4 **Uia Bessanese** *mountain* France
244 A3 **Uibhist a Tuath (North Uist)** *island* Scotland UK
225 L4 **Ûibzde** Latvia
244 B3 **Uig** Highland Scotland UK
306 B5 **Uíge** Angola
306 B5 **Uíge** *admin. area* Angola
427 10 **'Uiha Island** Tonga
386 E3 **Ŭiju** North Korea
388 G3 **Uil** Kazakhstan
388 G3 **Uil** *watercourse* Kazakhstan
223 Q5 **Uimaharju** Finland
128 F2 **Uinkaret Plateau** Arkansas USA
125 J6 **Uinta Mountains** Utah USA
156 E4 **Uiraúna** Brazil
308 B4 **Uis Mine** Namibia
244 B4 **Uisken** Highland Scotland UK
308 E6 **Uitenhage** South Africa
226 D1 **Uithuizen** Netherlands
226 E4 **Uitikon** Switzerland
122 G3 **Uivak, Cape** Newfoundland and Labrador Canada
427 15 **Ujae Atoll** Marshall Islands
426 15 **Ujelang Atoll** Marshall Islands
227 K4 **Újfehértó** Hungary
387 G4 **Uji** Japan
372 E5 **Ujir** *island* Indonesia
392 D6 **Ujjain** Madhya Pradesh India
234 B2 **Újkígyós** Hungary
375 G3 **Ujohbilang** Indonesia
227 I1 **Ujście** Poland
374 E5 **Ujung Kulon, Taman Nasional** *park* Indonesia
UK *see* **United Kingdom**
237 AH7 **Uka** Russian Federation
393 C7 **Ukai Sagar** *lake* Gujarat India
122 H5 **Ukasiksalik Island** Newfoundland and Labrador Canada
305 F2 **Ukata** Nigeria
381 K3 **Uke-shima** *island* Japan
237 AJ6 **Ukelayat** Russian Federation
236 L6 **Ukhta** Russian Federation
426 8 **Uki** *island* Solomon Islands
124 D7 **Ukiah** California USA
124 F4 **Ukiah** Oregon USA
307 E5 **Ukimbo** Tanzania
117 J5 **Ukkusiksalik National Park** Nunavut Canada
238 F6 **Ukolitsa** Russian Federation
223 P2 **Ukonselkä** *lake* Finland
234 G1 **Ukraine** *country* Europe
238 G1 **Uksh-Ozero** *lake* Russian Federation
236 K6 **Uktym** Russian Federation
308 B2 **Uku** Angola
386 F5 **Uku-shima** *island* Japan
307 E3 **Ukutat** *watercourse* Uganda
225 O5 **Ula** *watercourse* Belarus
235 F7 **Ula** Turkey
384 E4 **Ulaan Nuur** *lake* Mongolia
384 F3 **Ulaanbaatar (Ulan Bator)** Mongolia
383 I2 **Ulaangom** Mongolia
383 I2 **Ulaanhus** Mongolia
383 K2 **Ulaanuul** Mongolia
237 AB5 **Ulaga** Russian Federation
237 AC6 **Ulakhan-Bom, Khrebet** *range* Russian Federation
237 AE6 **Ulakhan-Chistay, Khrebet** *range* Russian Federation
384 F5 **Ulan** Nei Mongol Zizhiqu China
384 F5 **Ulan Buh Shamo** Nei Mongol Zizhiqu China
237 W8 **Ulan-Burgasy, Khrebet** *range* Russian Federation
388 D4 **Ulan-Erge** Russian Federation
384 G4 **Ulan Hua** Nei Mongol Zizhiqu China
388 E4 **Ulan-Khol** Russian Federation
384 F5 **Ulan Suhai** *lake* Nei Mongol Zizhiqu China
384 F2 **Ulan-Ude** Russian Federation
384 G4 **Ulan-ull** Mongolia
385 J3 **Ulanhot** Nei Mongol Zizhiqu China
227 L2 **Ulanów** Poland
426 8 **Ulawa** *island* Solomon Islands
373 I5 **Ulawun, Mount** *volcano* Papua New Guinea
237 AD6 **Ul'beya** *watercourse* Russian Federation
158 D3 **Ulbio** Brazil
244 E2 **Ulbster** Highland Scotland UK
243 H3 **Ulceby Skitter** North Lincolnshire England UK
386 F4 **Ulchin** South Korea
233 H6 **Ulcinj** Montenegro
224 G5 **Uie näbbe** *cape* Sweden
385 G2 **Ulety** Russian Federation
235 A5 **Ulëz** Albania
226 D2 **Ulft** Netherlands
383 I2 **Ulgii** Mongolia
383 J3 **Uliastai** Mongolia
227 L3 **Ulič** Slovakia
426 3 **Ulimang** Palau
306 D4 **Ulindi** *watercourse* Democratic Republic of Congo
426 6 **Ulithi** *island* Federated States of Micronesia
227 K5 **Uljma** Serbia
223 N4 **Uljuan tekojärvi** *lake* Finland
118 I6 **Ulkatcho** British Columbia Canada
389 K2 **Ulken Qaraoy Koli** *lake* Kazakhstan
223 N4 **Ulkokrunni** *island* Finland
230 B2 **Ulla** *watercourse* Spain
425 N8 **Ulladulla** NSW Australia
244 C3 **Ullapool** Highland Scotland UK
224 G4 **Ullared** Sweden
222 L3 **Ullatti** Sweden
223 M5 **Ullava** Finland
223 N5 **Ullavanjärvi** *lake* Finland
222 K4 **Ullbergsträsk** Sweden
232 H3 **Üllés** Hungary
230 E2 **Ullibarri, Embalse de** *lake* Spain
244 B3 **Ullinish** Highland Scotland UK
162 B5 **Ulloa, Península** *peninsula* Chile
222 K2 **Ullsfjorden** *bay* Norway
242 F2 **Ullswater** *lake* England UK
226 E3 **Ulm** Germany
225 K4 **Ulmale** Latvia
227 L4 **Ulmeni** Romania
234 F2 **Ulmu** Moldova
224 E2 **Ulnes** Norway
232 H5 **Ulog** Bosnia and Herzegovina
237 AF4 **Ulovo** Russian Federation
222 L2 **Uløya** *island* Norway
386 F4 **Ulreuno-do** *island* South Korea
227 G3 **Ulrichsberg** Austria
222 I5 **Ulriksfors** Sweden
243 H3 **Ulrome** East Riding of Yorkshire England UK
224 E2 **Ulsåk** Norway
386 F4 **Ulsan** South Korea
226 F2 **Ulster** *watercourse* Germany
222 I2 **Ulsvåg** Norway
222 K3 **Ultevis** *mountain* Sweden
158 C2 **Ultraoriental, Cordillera** *range* Peru
372 C3 **Ulu** Indonesia
237 AA6 **Ulu** Russian Federation
375 G2 **Ulu Temburong National Park** Brunei
374 D3 **Ulu Tiram** Malaysia
133 I6 **Ulua** *watercourse* Honduras
235 F5 **Ulubat Gölü** *lake* Turkey
235 F6 **Ulubey** Turkey
235 G6 **Uluborlu** Turkey
235 F5 **Uludağ** *mountain* Turkey
309 F5 **Ulundi** South Africa
383 H3 **Ulungur Hu** *lake* Xinjiang Uygur Zizhiqu China
424 I6 **Uluru (Ayers Rock)** *mountain* NT Australia
244 C4 **Uluvalt** Highland Scotland UK
422 4 **Uluvehi Landing** Niue New Zealand
244 B4 **Ulva** *island* Scotland UK
242 E2 **Ulverston** Cumbria England UK
224 H3 **Ulvettern** *bay* Sweden
225 N3 **Ulvi** Estonia
225 K2 **Ulvila** Finland
222 K5 **Ulvön** *island* Sweden
237 AD7 **Ul'ya** *watercourse* Russian Federation
238 G3 **Ul'yanikha** Russian Federation
234 G1 **Ul'yanovka** Ukraine
238 F6 **Ul'yanovo** Russian Federation
388 E2 **Ul'yanovsk** Russian Federation
388 E2 **Ul'yanovskaya Oblast'** *admin. area* Russian Federation
125 O8 **Ulysses** Kansas USA
384 D3 **Ulziit** Mongolia
384 E3 **Ulziit** Mongolia
384 E3 **Ulziit** Mongolia
384 F4 **Ulziit** Mongolia
384 G3 **Ulziit** Mongolia
306 D3 **Uma** Democratic Republic of Congo
232 E4 **Umag** Croatia
305 F3 **Umaisha** Nigeria
426 6a **Uman** *island* Federated States of Micronesia
133 H4 **Umán** Mexico
234 G1 **Uman'** Ukraine
160 D4 **Umango, Cerro** *mountain* Argentina
372 E5 **Umari** Indonesia
156 E4 **Umarizal** Brazil
393 F7 **Umarkot** Orissa India
391 L4 **Umarkot** Pakistan
426 5 **Umatac** Guam
131 K6 **Umatilla** Florida USA
124 F4 **Umatilla** Oregon USA
223 S3 **Umba** Russian Federation
425 K3 **Umbakumba** NT Australia
306 C2 **Umbelasha** *watercourse* Sudan
372 B4 **Umbele** *island* Indonesia
232 E5 **Umbertide** Italy
373 H5 **Umboi** *island* Papua New Guinea
223 S3 **Umbozero, Ozero** *lake* Russian Federation
229 J3 **Umbrail, Piz** *mountain* Italy/Switzerland
232 E5 **Umbria** *admin. area* Italy
373 I4 **Umbukul** Papua New Guinea
308 E3 **Ume** *watercourse* Zimbabwe
222 L5 **Umeå** Sweden
222 K4 **Umeälven** *watercourse* Sweden
126 D1 **Umfreville Lake** Ontario Canada
122 G4 **Umiakovik Lake** Newfoundland and Labrador Canada
117 O6 **Umiiviip Kangertiva** *bay* Greenland
128 inset **'Umikoa** Hawai'i USA
121 Q4 **Umiujaq** Québec Canada
309 F5 **Umlazi** South Africa
390 D5 **Umm al Birak** Saudi Arabia
391 H4 **Umm al Qaywayn** United Arab Emirates
390 D5 **Umm 'Amāyin** Saudi Arabia
302 C1 **Umm ar Rizam** Libya
391 H5 **Umm as Samim** Oman
390 G4 **Umm ash Shubrum** Qatar
302 D5 **Umm Badr** Sudan
302 D5 **Umm Bel** Sudan
302 E5 **Umm Dam** Sudan
302 D5 **Umm Dhibbān** Sudan
301 J3 **Umm Farud** Libya
302 D5 **Umm Keddada** Sudan
390 D4 **Umm Lajj** Saudi Arabia
302 D5 **Umm Marahik** Sudan
390 F3 **Umm Qaṣr** Iraq
302 D5 **Umm Qawzayn** Sudan
390 E6 **Umm Raḥṭā'** Saudi Arabia
302 E5 **Umm Ruwaba** Sudan
302 D1 **Umm Sa'ad** Libya
305 I1 **Umm Saggat, Wadi** *watercourse* Sudan
302 E5 **Umm Saiyala** Sudan
390 G4 **Umm Ṣalāl Muḥammad** Qatar
390 D5 **Umm Samā'** Saudi Arabia
302 D5 **Umm Shugeira** Sudan
390 D5 **Umm Sidrah** Saudi Arabia
224 G5 **Ummanz** *island* Germany
116 C8 **Umnak Island** Alaska USA
222 J4 **Umnassjön** *lake* Sweden
384 G3 **Umnegelder** Mongolia
237 U5 **Umnym, Khrebet** *range* Russian Federation
309 G2 **Umpuhua** Mozambique
235 G6 **Umraniye** Turkey
393 E7 **Umred** Maharashtra India
393 E7 **Umri** Andhra Pradesh India
372 E4 **Umsini, Gunung** *mountain* Indonesia
308 E6 **Umtata** South Africa
305 F3 **Umuahia** Nigeria
157 A8 **Umuarama** Brazil
308 E6 **Umzimkulu** South Africa
308 E4 **Umzingwani** *watercourse* Zimbabwe
308 F6 **Umzinto** South Africa
232 G4 **Una** *watercourse* Bosnia and Herzegovina
157 E6 **Una** Brazil
393 C7 **Una** Gujarat India
392 D4 **Una** Himachal Pradesh India
223 U4 **Una** Russian Federation
131 J4 **Unadilla** Georgia USA
157 C7 **Unaí** Brazil
116 C6 **Unalakleet** Alaska USA
116 C8 **Unalaska** Alaska USA
116 C8 **Unalaska Island** Alaska USA
309 G2 **Unango** Mozambique
426 6 **Unanu** *island* Federated States of Micronesia
160 E6 **Unanué** Argentina
154 E2 **Unare** *watercourse* Venezuela
155 E2 **Unare, Laguna de** *lake* Venezuela
223 N3 **Unari** Finland
223 N3 **Unari** *lake* Finland
372 B4 **Unauna** *island* Indonesia
231 F2 **Uncastillo** Spain
129 I1 **Uncompahgre** *watercourse* Colorado USA
125 L7 **Uncompahgre Peak** Colorado USA
125 K7 **Uncompahgre Plateau** Colorado USA
224 H3 **Unden** *lake* Sweden
224 H3 **Undenäs** Sweden
384 D3 **Under-ulaan** Mongolia
383 J2 **Underhangai** Mongolia
222 H5 **Undersåker** Sweden
384 F3 **Undershil** Mongolia
384 F3 **Undershireet** Mongolia
125 O3 **Underwood** North Dakota USA
386 F2 **Undok** North Korea
238 H1 **Undozero, Ozero** *lake* Russian Federation
372 B6 **Undu, Tanjung** *cape* Indonesia
372 D4 **Undur** Indonesia
225 K3 **Undva Nina** *cape* Estonia
155 E5 **Uneiuxi** *watercourse* Brazil
223 T5 **Unezhma** Russian Federation
375 F5 **Ungaran** Indonesia
122 B3 **Ungava, Péninsule d'** *peninsula* Québec Canada
122 D3 **Ungava Bay** Québec Canada
234 E2 **Ungheni** Moldova
234 D3 **Ungheni** Romania
234 D3 **Ungra** Romania
154 B2 **Unguía** Colombia
225 M4 **Ungura ezers** *lake* Latvia
234 E2 **Ungureni-Hora** Romania
307 G4 **Ungwana Bay** Kenya
392 D6 **Unhel** Madhya Pradesh India
232 F1 **Unhošť** Czech Republic
156 D4 **União** Brazil
157 B9 **União da Vitória** Brazil
159 I5 **União de Minas** Brazil
159 H3 **União do Sul** Brazil
131 J2 **Unicoi** Tennessee USA
232 G2 **Uničov** Czech Republic
227 J2 **Uniejów** Poland
232 F4 **Unije** Croatia
232 F4 **Unije** *island* Croatia
426 6a **Unikar, Mochun** *strait* Federated States of Micronesia
116 C8 **Unimak Island** Alaska USA
155 F5 **Unini** *watercourse* Brazil
160 E5 **Unión** Argentina
163 10a **Union** Grenada
161 G3 **Unión** Paraguay
126 F7 **Union** Missouri USA
125 R6 **Union** Nebraska USA
124 G4 **Union** Oregon USA
131 K3 **Union** South Carolina USA
127 K8 **Union** West Virginia USA
377 G5 **Union Atoll** Spratly Islands
131 I4 **Union City** Georgia USA
127 L6 **Union City** Pennsylvania USA
130 G2 **Union City** Tennessee USA
132 D5 **Unión de Tula** Mexico
124 E3 **Union Gap** Washington USA
133 G5 **Unión Hidalgo** Mexico
163 10 **Union Island** Grenada
135 I4 **Union Island** St Vincent and the Grenadines
131 J4 **Union Point** Georgia USA
131 I4 **Union Springs** Alabama USA
128 B1 **Union Valley Reservoir** California USA
308 D6 **Uniondale** South Africa
130 H4 **Uniontown** Alabama USA
130 D2 **Uniontown** Kansas USA
127 L7 **Uniontown** Pennsylvania USA
124 G3 **Uniontown** Washington USA
126 J5 **Unionville** Michigan USA
126 E6 **Unionville** Missouri USA
391 H5 **United Arab Emirates** *country*
239 F4 **United Kingdom (UK)** *country* Europe
114 **United States of America (USA)** *country* North America
117 K2 **United States Range** Nunavut Canada
119 Q6 **Unity** Saskatchewan Canada
306 D2 **Unity** *admin. area* Sudan
308 B4 **Unjab** *watercourse* Namibia
392 C6 **Unjha** Gujarat India
222 H4 **Unkervatnet** *lake* Norway
392 E5 **Unnao** Uttar Pradesh India
224 G4 **Unnaryd** Sweden
224 G4 **Unnen** *lake* Sweden
224 H2 **Unntorp** Sweden
223 P5 **Unnukka** *bay* Finland
386 E3 **Ŭnsan** North Korea
222 M5 **Untamala** Finland
392 F6 **Untari** Jharkhand India
226 G4 **Untertilliach** Austria
227 G1 **Unterueckersee** *lake* Germany
118 F4 **Unuk** *watercourse* British Columbia Canada
394 F5 **Ünye** Turkey
388 D1 **Unzha** Russian Federation
236 J7 **Unzha** *watercourse* Russian Federation
233 D5 **Uomo, Capo d'** *cape* Italy
155 F3 **Uonán** Venezuela
376 E2 **Uông Bí** Vietnam
381 I3 **Uotsuri-shima** *island* Japan
134 C5 **Upala** Costa Rica
156 E4 **Upanema** Brazil
155 F2 **Upata** Venezuela
241 F3 **Upavon** Wiltshire England UK
306 D5 **Upemba, Lac** *lake* Democratic Republic of Congo
225 L4 **Upenieki** Latvia
117 N4 **Upernavik** Greenland
125 O2 **Upham** North Dakota USA
377 J6 **Upi** Philippines
227 I2 **Úpice** Czech Republic
308 D5 **Upington** South Africa
225 M2 **Upinniemi** Finland
240 E3 **Upleadon** Gloucestershire England UK
393 C7 **Upleta** Gujarat India
240 E4 **Uplyme** Devon England UK
225 N4 **Upmala** Latvia
222 J3 **Upmas** *lake* Sweden
223 Q3 **Upoloksha** Russian Federation
426 1 **Upolu** *island* Samoa
128 inset **'Upolu Point** Hawai'i USA
124 G1 **Upper Arrow Lake** British Columbia Canada
422 G4 **Upper Atiamuri** New Zealand
130 H3 **Upper Bear Creek Reservoir** Alabama USA
241 G2 **Upper Benefield** Northamptonshire England UK
244 F4 **Upper Birnie** Aberdeenshire Scotland UK
240 C2 **Upper Borth** Ceredigion Wales UK
244 E2 **Upper Camster** Highland Scotland UK
240 D2 **Upper Chapel** Powys Wales UK
127 N4 **Upper Chateaugay Lake** New York USA
243 F2 **Upper Denton** Cumbria England UK
119 S4 **Upper Foster Lake** Saskatchewan Canada
120 I7 **Upper Goose Lake** Ontario Canada
243 H2 **Upper Helmsley** North Yorkshire England UK
244 E5 **Upper Howecleuch** South Lanarkshire Scotland UK
241 F1 **Upper Hulme** Staffordshire England UK
123 E9 **Upper Kent** New Brunswick Canada
124 E5 **Upper Klamath Lake** Oregon USA
118 D2 **Upper Laberge** Yukon Territory Canada
128 A1 **Upper Lake** California USA
118 G2 **Upper Liard** Yukon Territory Canada
242 A2 **Upper Lough Erne** *lake* Northern Ireland UK
126 E2 **Upper Manitou Lake** Ontario Canada
163 9 **Upper Manzanilla** Trinidad and Tobago
423 E5 **Upper Moutere** New Zealand
123 G10 **Upper Musquodoboit** Nova Scotia Canada
307 E2 **Upper Nile** *admin. area* Sudan
374 C3 **Upper Peirce Reservoir** Singapore
126 D2 **Upper Red Lake** Minnesota USA
127 N4 **Upper Saranac Lake** New York USA
374 C3 **Upper Seletar Reservoir** Singapore
241 F3 **Upper Slaughter** Gloucestershire England UK
241 F4 **Upper Street** Hampshire England UK
423 E5 **Upper Takaka** New Zealand
155 G4 **Upper Takutu-Upper Essequibo** *admin. area* Guyana
120 J6 **Upper Windigo Lake** Ontario Canada
224 G3 **Upphärad** Sweden
241 G2 **Uppingham** Rutland England UK
224 I3 **Uppsala** Sweden
224 I2 **Uppsala** *admin. area* Sweden
126 F2 **Upsala** Ontario Canada
243 G2 **Upsall** North Yorkshire England UK
123 E9 **Upsalquitch** *watercourse* New Brunswick Canada
131 N2 **Upshur Bay** Virginia USA
425 M4 **Upstart, Cape** Qld Australia
245 D5 **Upton** Ireland
240 C4 **Upton** Cornwall England UK
241 E4 **Upton** Dorset England UK
241 F4 **Upton** Hampshire England UK
241 I2 **Upton** Norfolk England UK
243 H3 **Upton** Nottinghamshire England UK
240 D3 **Upton** Somerset England UK
126 I8 **Upton** Kentucky USA
125 M4 **Upton** Wyoming USA
240 E3 **Upton Bishop** Herefordshire England UK
240 D4 **Upton Pyne** Devon England UK
241 E3 **Upton St Leonards** Gloucestershire England UK
241 E3 **Upton Scudamore** Wiltshire England UK
241 H2 **Upwell** Cambridgeshire England UK
241 G2 **Upwood** Cambridgeshire England UK
225 L5 **Upyna** Lithuania
223 R2 **Ura-Guba** Russian Federation
154 B2 **Urabá, Golfo de** *bay* Colombia
227 H1 **Urad** Poland
155 F3 **Uraday** Venezuela
225 M2 **Urajärvi** *lake* Finland
388 F4 **Ural** *watercourse* Kazakhstan
388 H3 **Ural** *watercourse* Russian Federation
425 N7 **Uralla** NSW Australia
237 AA8 **Uralovka** Russian Federation
388 F3 **Ural'sk** Kazakhstan
388 H2 **Ural'skiy Khrebet** *range* Russian Federation
306 E5 **Urambo** Tanzania
393 D8 **Uran Islampur** Maharashtra India
425 M8 **Urana** NSW Australia
425 K5 **Urandangi** Qld Australia
130 E5 **Urania** Louisiana USA
119 Q3 **Uranium City** Saskatchewan Canada
155 F4 **Uraricaa** *watercourse* Brazil
155 F4 **Uraricoera** *watercourse* Brazil
233 C7 **Uras** Sardinia Italy
393 D8 **Uravakonda** Andhra Pradesh India
388 E2 **Urazovka** Russian Federation
126 G6 **Urbana** Illinois USA
126 J6 **Urbana** Ohio USA
229 K5 **Urbania** Italy
156 D3 **Urbano Santos** Brazil
232 E5 **Urbino** Italy
233 C5 **Urbino, Étang d'** *lake* Corsica France
227 I3 **Určice** Czech Republic
158 D4 **Urcos** Peru
388 E4 **Urda** Kazakhstan
154 B5 **Urdaneta** Ecuador
377 I4 **Urdaneta** Philippines
228 D5 **Urdos** France
389 N4 **Urdzhar** Kazakhstan
243 G2 **Ure** *watercourse* England UK
372 E4 **Urema** *watercourse* Indonesia
236 K7 **Uren'** Russian Federation
422 F4 **Urenui** New Zealand
426 7 **Uréparapara** *island* Vanuatu
132 C2 **Ures** Mexico
383 J3 **Urgamal** Mongolia
388 H5 **Urganch** Uzbekistan
235 E6 **Urganlı** Turkey
384 G4 **Urgen** Mongolia
244 B3 **Urgha** Na h-Eileanan Siar Scotland UK
394 E5 **Ürgüp** Turkey
223 P2 **Urho Kekkosen kansallispuisto** *park* Finland
303 F5 **Uri Wenz** *watercourse* Ethiopia
154 C4 **Uribe** Colombia
162 A5 **Uribe, Canal** *strait* Chile
154 C2 **Uribia** Colombia
227 L5 **Uricani** Romania
126 E7 **Urich** Missouri USA
384 E3 **Uringuur** Mongolia
158 C4 **Urinpay** Peru
129 I7 **Urique** Mexico
158 C2 **Urituyacu** *watercourse* Peru
234 D2 **Uriu** Romania
226 C1 **Urk** Netherlands
388 E5 **Urkarakh** Russian Federation
163 18 **Urlings** Antigua and Barbuda
305 F3 **Uromi** Nigeria
223 S5 **Urosozero** Russian Federation
389 K6 **Ŭroteppa** Tajikistan
388 D5 **Urozhaynoye** Russian Federation
243 G2 **Urra** North Yorkshire England UK
154 B3 **Urrao** Colombia
162 E2 **Urre Lauquen, Laguna** *lake* Argentina
230 E2 **Urrúnaga, Embalse de** *lake* Spain
133 F5 **Ursulo Galván** Mexico
222 L4 **Ursviken** Sweden
227 J1 **Urszulewo** Poland
388 H3 **Urtazym** Russian Federation
157 B6 **Uruaçu** Brazil
157 B6 **Uruana** Brazil
128 D5 **Uruapan** Mexico
159 F2 **Uruapiara, Lago** *lake* Brazil
159 H1 **Uruará** Brazil
158 C4 **Urubamba** *watercourse* Peru
159 F4 **Urubichá** Bolivia
155 G5 **Urubu** *watercourse* Brazil
155 G5 **Urucará** Brazil
394 E2 **Urucje** Russian Federation
159 E2 **Urucu** *watercourse* Brazil
157 E6 **Uruçuca** Brazil
156 C4 **Uruçuí** Brazil
156 C5 **Uruçuí, Serra do** *range* Brazil
156 C4 **Uruçuí Preto** *watercourse* Brazil
157 C6 **Urucuia** *watercourse* Brazil
155 H5 **Urucuricaia, Ilha** *island* Brazil
155 G5 **Urucurituba** Brazil
161 G4 **Uruguaiana** Brazil
161 G5 **Uruguay** *watercourse* Argentina
161 G5 **Uruguay** *country* South America
159 E6 **Uruguayito** Bolivia
372 E2 **Urukthapel** *island* Palau
154 D2 **Urumaco** Venezuela
388 D5 **Urup** Russian Federation
237 AF9 **Urup, Ostrov** *island* Kuril Islands
387 K1 **Urup, Ostrov** *island* Russian Federation
157 B8 **Urupês** Brazil
237 Z8 **Urusha** Russian Federation
306 E5 **Uruwira** Tanzania
158 C4 **Uruysaccasa** Peru
226 B3 **Ury** France
389 O3 **Uryl** Kazakhstan
236 K7 **Urzhum** Russian Federation
163 21 **US Virgin Islands** *unincorporated US territory* Caribbean
386 F5 **Usa** Japan
USA *see* **United States of America** North America
236 M5 **Usa** *watercourse* Russian Federation
394 D5 **Uşak** *admin. area* Turkey
225 O6 **Usakino** Belarus
308 C4 **Usakos** Namibia
436 K2 **Usarp Mountains** Antarctica
390 E4 **'Usaylab** Saudi Arabia
163 7 **Usborne, Mount** Falkland Islands
234 B4 **Ušće** Serbia
224 H6 **Usedom** *island* Germany
424 E6 **Useless Loop** WA Australia
307 E4 **Usengi** Kenya
225 O5 **Ushachy** Belarus
236 Q2 **Ushakova, Ostrov** *island* Russian Federation
237 AL4 **Ushakovskoye** Russian Federation
390 G3 **Ūshan** Iran
119 T6 **Usherville** Saskatchewan Canada
237 AK5 **Ushkan'iy, Gory** *range* Russian Federation
389 Q3 **Ushpe-khol'** *lake* Russian Federation
388 F5 **Ushtagan** Kazakhstan
389 M4 **Ushtobe** Kazakhstan
162 C6 **Ushuaia** Argentina
237 AH5 **Ushurakchan, Khrebet** *range* Russian Federation
225 L4 **Uši** Latvia
155 I4 **Usina Taparabo** Brazil
226 E2 **Usingen** Germany
373 H5 **Usino** Papua New Guinea
120 L5 **Usiske** *watercourse* Ontario Canada
118 G5 **Usk** British Columbia Canada
240 E3 **Usk** Monmouthshire Wales UK
240 D3 **Usk** *watercourse* Wales UK
240 D3 **Usk Reservoir** *lake* Wales UK
224 C3 **Uskedalen** Norway
224 H3 **Usken** *lake* Sweden
388 C3 **Usman'** Russian Federation
225 P5 **Usmyn'** Russian Federation
238 C6 **Usokhi** Belarus
237 V8 **Usol'ye-Sibirskoye** Russian Federation
387 I3 **Usoriyama-ko** *lake* Japan
160 D5 **Uspallata** Argentina
389 M3 **Uspenka** Kazakhstan
389 K4 **Uspenskiy** Kazakhstan

388 D5 **Uspenskiy** Russian Federation
228 F4 **Ussel** France
386 G2 **Ussuri** *watercourse* Russian Federation
386 F2 **Ussuriysk** Russian Federation
237 AJ5 **Ust'-Belaya** Russian Federation
237 W6 **Ust'-Chayka Zimor'ye** Russian Federation
236 L6 **Ust'-Chërnaya** Russian Federation
237 V7 **Ust' Ilimsk** Russian Federation
237 V7 **Ust'-Ilimskiy Vodokhranilishche** *lake* Russian Federation
236 P7 **Ust' Ishim** Russian Federation
237 AH7 **Ust'-Kamchatsk** Russian Federation
389 N3 **Ust'-Kamenogorsk (Öskemen)** Kazakhstan
237 Y8 **Ust'-Karenga** Russian Federation
385 I2 **Ust'-Karsk** Russian Federation
237 AG7 **Ust'-Khayryuzovo** Russian Federation
237 W7 **Ust' Kut** Russian Federation
388 C4 **Ust'-Labinsk** Russian Federation
236 M5 **Ust' Lyzha** Russian Federation
236 L6 **Ust' Nem** Russian Federation
237 AD6 **Ust' Nera** Russian Federation
237 AB8 **Ust' Niman** Russian Federation
237 Y4 **Ust'-Olenëk** Russian Federation
237 AE6 **Ust' Omchug** Russian Federation
384 E1 **Ust'-Ordynskiy** Russian Federation
237 V8 **Ust-Ordynskiy Buryatskiy AO** *admin. area* Russian Federation
236 S7 **Ust'-Ozernoye** Russian Federation
236 T7 **Ust'-Pit** Russian Federation
236 R5 **Ust'-Port** Russian Federation
238 E2 **Ust'-Sara** Russian Federation
237 AB6 **Ust'-Tatta** Russian Federation
236 M6 **Ust' Un'ya** Russian Federation
236 M5 **Ust' Usa** Russian Federation
237 AG7 **Ust'-Voyampolka** Russian Federation
237 AC4 **Ust' Yansk** Russian Federation
236 O5 **Ust'-Yuribey** Russian Federation
227 G2 **Ústecký Kraj** *admin. area* Czech Republic
232 C3 **Uster** Switzerland
224 E2 **Ustevatn** *lake* Norway
227 H2 **Ústí nad Labem** Czech Republic
234 F2 **Ustia** Moldova
232 H5 **Ustibar** Bosnia and Herzegovina
233 E7 **Ustica, Isola di** *island* Italy
224 I5 **Ustka** Poland
389 N3 **Ustokamenogorskoye Vodokhranilishche** *lake* Kazakhstan
235 E4 **Ustrem** Bulgaria
227 L3 **Ustrzyki Dolne** Poland
227 L3 **Ustrzyki Górne** Poland
134 E5 **Ustupo** Panama
238 H3 **Ust'ye** Russian Federation
227 M2 **Ustyluh** Ukraine
227 N3 **Ustynivka** Ukraine
238 F3 **Ustyutskoye** Russian Federation
238 G3 **Ustyuzhna** Russian Federation
372 B6 **Usu** *island* Indonesia
134 B4 **Usulután** El Salvador
225 O5 **Usvyach'ye, Vozyera** *lake* Belarus
225 O4 **Usvyach'ye, Vozyera** *lake* Russian Federation
225 P5 **Usvyaty** Russian Federation
372 F5 **Uta** Indonesia
372 F5 **Uta** *watercourse* Indonesia
114 **Utah** *admin. area* USA
124 J6 **Utah Lake** Utah USA
223 O4 **Utajärvi** Finland
375 H6 **Utan** Indonesia
222 J5 **Utanede** Sweden
158 B3 **Utcuyacu** Peru
125 R5 **Ute** Iowa USA
231 F3 **Utebo** Spain
308 D3 **Utembo** *watercourse* Angola
225 M5 **Utena** Lithuania
225 M5 **Utenos** *admin. area* Lithuania
237 AJ5 **Utesiki** Russian Federation
307 F5 **Utete** Tanzania
376 C4 **Uthai Thani** *admin. area* Thailand
222 F5 **Uthaug** Norway
159 G4 **Utiariti** Brazil
125 O7 **Utica** Kansas USA
130 F4 **Utica** Mississippi USA
127 N5 **Utica** New York USA
127 J6 **Utica** Ohio USA
231 F4 **Utiel** Spain
422 F4 **Utiku** New Zealand
116 H7 **Utikuma Lake** Alberta Canada
389 P2 **Utinoye** *watercourse* Russian Federation
427 I5 **Utirik Atoll** Marshall Islands
134 C4 **Utla-Almuk** Honduras
224 H4 **Utlängan** *island* Sweden
224 D2 **Utne** Norway
386 F5 **Uto** Japan
225 J3 **Utö** *island* Sweden
240 D4 **Uton** Devon England UK
225 P3 **Utorgosh** Russian Federation
162 D1 **Utracán, Valle de** *valley* Argentina
392 F5 **Utraula** Uttar Pradesh India
226 C1 **Utrecht** Netherlands
154 B3 **Utria, Ensenada de** *bay* Colombia
223 O2 **Utsjoki** Finland
222 H3 **Utskarpen** Norway
436 E2 **Utstikkar Bay** Antarctica
388 E4 **Utta** Russian Federation
392 E5 **Uttar Pradesh** *admin. area* India
376 D3 **Uttaradit** Thailand
376 D3 **Uttaradit** *admin. area* Thailand
392 E5 **Uttaranchal** *admin. area* India
392 E4 **Uttarkashi** Uttaranchal India
226 G4 **Uttendorf** Austria
127 L4 **Utterson** Ontario Canada
222 K4 **Utterträsk** Sweden
241 F2 **Uttoxeter** Staffordshire England UK
237 AB5 **Uttyakh** Russian Federation
426 1 **Utupua** *island* Solomon Islands
158 E6 **Uturuncu, Cerro** *mountain* Bolivia
222 G4 **Utvorda** Norway
385 G3 **Uulbayan** Mongolia
117 N4 **Uummannaq** Greenland
117 N4 **Uummannaq Fjord** Greenland
223 N5 **Uurainen** Finland
223 O5 **Uurainen** *lake* Finland
383 I2 **Uureg Nuur** *lake* Mongolia
225 M3 **Uuri** Estonia
222 M5 **Uuro** Finland
225 K2 **Uusikaupunki** Finland
308 B3 **Uutapi** Namibia
223 P4 **Uva** Finland
234 A4 **Uvac** Serbia
131 J4 **Uvalda** Georgia USA
130 B6 **Uvalde** Texas USA
238 F5 **Uvarovka** Russian Federation
388 D3 **Uvarovo** Russian Federation
426 1 **Uvea** *island* Wallis and Futuna
235 E6 **Üvecik** Turkey
155 E2 **Uveral** Venezuela
306 E5 **Uvinza** Tanzania
383 I2 **Uvs** *admin. area* Mongolia
383 I2 **Uvs Nuur** *lake* Mongolia
306 C4 **Uvungo** Democratic Republic of Congo
386 G5 **Uwajima** Japan
373 F5 **Uwebu** Indonesia
302 D3 **Uweinat, Jebel** *mountain* Sudan
374 E3 **Uwi** *island* Indonesia
373 G5 **Uwimmerah** *watercourse* Indonesia
127 L4 **Uxbridge** Ontario Canada
241 G3 **Uxbridge** Greater London England UK
237 AD5 **Uyandi** Russian Federation
384 E3 **Uyanga** Mongolia
236 T7 **Uyar** Russian Federation
244 inset **Uyeasound** Shetland Scotland UK
236 R3 **Uyedineniya, Ostrov** *island* Russian Federation
305 F3 **Uyo** Nigeria
306 E4 **Uyowa** Tanzania
379 H4 **Uyu** *watercourse* Myanmar
158 E6 **Uyuni** Bolivia
158 E6 **Uyuni, Salar de** *pan* Bolivia
388 H5 **Uzbekistan** *country*
388 G6 **Uzboy** *watercourse* Turkmenistan
162 C3 **Uzcudun** Argentina
227 K5 **Uzdin** Serbia
227 K1 **Uzdowo** Poland
228 E4 **Uzerche** France
229 G4 **Uzès** France
394 D2 **Uzh** *watercourse* Ukraine
234 C1 **Uzhhorod** Ukraine
234 C1 **Uzhok** Ukraine
225 P5 **Uzkoye** Russian Federation
234 F3 **Uzlina, Lacul** *lake* Romania
238 H6 **Uzlovaya** Russian Federation
225 L5 **Uzlovoye** Russian Federation
234 A3 **Uzovnica** Serbia
235 E6 **Uzun Ada** *island* Turkey
235 E5 **Uzunköprü** Turkey
225 L5 **Užventis** Lithuania
232 C3 **Uzwil** Switzerland

V

132 C1 **V-Cross-T Lake** New Mexico USA
305 I3 **Va** *watercourse* Central African Republic
223 N5 **Vaajakoski** Finland
223 O4 **Vaala** Finland
223 O3 **Vaalajärvi** Finland
223 O3 **Vaalajärvi** *lake* Finland
225 N2 **Vaalimaa** Finland
226 D2 **Vaals** Netherlands
223 M3 **Vaaranperä** Sweden
223 O5 **Vaaraslahti** Finland
228 E3 **Vaas** France
222 L5 **Vaasa** Finland
222 M5 **Vaasa** *admin. area* Finland
225 M1 **Väätäiskylä** Finland
232 H3 **Vác** Hungary
161 I4 **Vacaria** Brazil
162 B4 **Vacas, Sierra de las** *range* Argentina
124 E7 **Vacaville** California USA
223 R5 **Vacha** Russian Federation
135 F3 **Vache, Île-à-** *island* Haiti
122 B2 **Vachon** *watercourse* Québec Canada
393 C7 **Vada** Maharashtra India
225 J3 **Väddö** *island* Sweden
124 D3 **Vader** Washington USA
224 F3 **Väderöfjorden** *bay* Sweden
224 E3 **Vadfoss** Norway
238 E5 **Vadino** Russian Federation
388 D2 **Vadinsk** Russian Federation
129 J2 **Vadito** New Mexico USA
393 C6 **Vadodara** Gujarat India
225 M5 **Vadokliai** Lithuania
223 P1 **Vadsø** Norway
224 H3 **Vadstena** Sweden
226 E4 **Vaduz** Liechtenstein
224 C2 **Værlandet** *island* Norway
222 H3 **Værøy** *island* Norway
224 C3 **Våg** Norway
236 J6 **Vaga** *watercourse* Russian Federation
222 F6 **Vågåmo** Norway
117 S6 **Vágar** *island* Faroe Islands
222 F6 **Vågåvatn** *bay* Norway
224 D4 **Våge** Norway
223 P2 **Vagge** Norway
224 I3 **Väggö** *island* Sweden
426 8 **Vaghena** *island* Solomon Islands
230 B3 **Vagos** Portugal
224 C2 **Vagsøy** *island* Norway
225 N4 **Vagula Järv** *lake* Estonia
232 G2 **Váh** *watercourse* Slovakia
223 N5 **Vahanka** Finland
225 M2 **Vaheri** Finland
427 14 **Vahitahi** *island* French Polynesia
390 G2 **Vahnabad** Iran
436 V1 **Vahsel Bay** Antarctica
225 L2 **Vahto** Finland
130 G4 **Vaiden** Mississippi USA
228 D2 **Vaiges** France
163 5 **Vaihu** Isla de Pascua (Easter Island)
393 D7 **Vaijapur** Maharashtra India
225 L3 **Väike-Pakri** *island* Estonia
222 K3 **Vaikijaur** Sweden
222 K3 **Vaikijaur** *lake* Sweden
125 L7 **Vail** Colorado USA
373 H5 **Vailala** *watercourse* Papua New Guinea
228 F2 **Vailly** France
228 F3 **Vailly-sur-Sauldre** France
222 J3 **Vaimok** *lake* Sweden
225 N4 **Vainava** Latvia
427 10a **Vaini** Tonga
238 B4 **Vainova** Latvia
393 D7 **Vairag** Maharashtra India
229 G4 **Vaison-la-Romaine** France
427 14b **Vaitape** French Polynesia
427 14a **Vaitunanaa** French Polynesia
427 13 **Vaitupu** *island* Tuvalu
427 12b **Vaitupu** Wallis and Futuna
222 K3 **Vajmat** Sweden
234 A3 **Vajska** Serbia
227 I5 **Vajszló** Hungary
305 I3 **Vakaga** *admin. area* Central African Republic
224 H2 **Vakern** Sweden
389 K6 **Vakhsh** *watercourse* Tajikistan
222 K3 **Vakkotavarekåtan** Sweden
234 A2 **Vál** Hungary
127 N3 **Val-David** Québec Canada
229 G2 **Val-de-Meuse** France
232 B4 **Val-d'Isère** France
117 L9 **Val-d'Or** Québec Canada
127 M2 **Val-Laflamme** Québec Canada
119 R8 **Val Marie** Saskatchewan Canada
226 C4 **Val-Suzon** France
235 C5 **Valandovo** Macedonia
222 L2 **Valanhamn** Norway
227 J3 **Valaská Belá** Slovakia
235 D6 **Valaxa** *island* Greece
227 M5 **Vâlcea** *admin. area* Romania
162 C2 **Valcheta** Argentina
127 O4 **Valcourt** Québec Canada
229 H3 **Valdahon** France
238 F6 **Valdaisky National Park** Russian Federation
238 E4 **Valday** Russian Federation
238 E4 **Valdayskaya Vozvyshennost** *region* Russian Federation
230 D4 **Valdecañas, Embalse de** *lake* Spain
230 E5 **Valdeinfierno, Embalse de** *lake* Spain
230 E4 **Valdepeñas** Spain
230 D3 **Valderaduey** *watercourse* Spain
230 D2 **Valderas** Spain
233 E7 **Valderice** Italy
222 E5 **Valderøya** Norway
231 G3 **Valderrobres** Spain
162 D3 **Valdés, Caleta** *bay* Argentina
162 D3 **Valdés, Península** *peninsula* Argentina
154 B4 **Valdez** Ecuador
116 E6 **Valdez** Alaska USA
162 B2 **Valdivia** Chile
436 E2 **Valdivia Abyssal Plain** *underwater feature* Southern Ocean
232 D4 **Valdobbiadene** Italy
131 J5 **Valdosta** Georgia USA
124 G5 **Vale** Oregon USA
222 I5 **Våle** Sweden
230 C4 **Vale da Amoreira** Portugal
230 C3 **Vale de Espinho** Portugal
159 H4 **Vale dos Sonhos** Brazil
240 D3 **Vale of Glamorgan** *admin. area* Wales UK
234 E3 **Valea Argovei** Romania
227 L4 **Valea Ierii** Romania
227 L4 **Valea lui Mihai** Romania
234 D2 **Valea Lungă** Romania
234 D3 **Valea Mare-Pravăț** Romania
234 E3 **Valea Mărului** Romania
118 L6 **Valemount** British Columbia Canada
157 D8 **Valença** Brazil
157 E6 **Valença** Brazil
156 D4 **Valença do Piauí** Brazil
228 E4 **Valence** France
228 E5 **Valence-sur-Baïse** France
154 B2 **Valencia** Colombia
377 J6 **Valencia** Philippines
231 F4 **Valencia** Spain
163 8 **Valencia** Trinidad and Tobago
154 D2 **Valencia** Venezuela
231 F4 **Valencia, Golfo de** *bay* Spain
230 D2 **Valencia de Don Juan** Spain
230 D4 **Valencia de las Torres** Spain
245 B5 **Valencia Island** Ireland
231 F4 **Valenciana** *admin. area* Spain
230 C4 **Valencid del Mombuey** Spain
228 F1 **Valenciennes** France
229 J5 **Valentano** Italy
157 E5 **Valente** Brazil
229 H3 **Valentigney** France
156 D4 **Valentim, Serra do** *range* Brazil
132 D2 **Valentín Gómez Farías** Mexico
128 F3 **Valentine** Arizona USA
125 O5 **Valentine** Nebraska USA
129 J5 **Valentine** Texas USA
226 E5 **Valenza** Italy
154 D2 **Valera** Venezuela
159 H5 **Valério** Brazil
224 D3 **Valevatnet** *lake* Norway
225 N4 **Valgamaa** *admin. area* Estonia
225 N3 **Valgma** Estonia
118 M8 **Valhalla Provincial Park** British Columbia Canada
124 I2 **Valier** Montana USA
233 C6 **Valinco, Golfe de** *bay* Corsica France
234 C2 **Vâlișoara** Romania
223 O4 **Välitalo** Finland
234 A3 **Valjevo** Serbia
225 N4 **Valka** Latvia
225 M4 **Valkas** *admin. area* Latvia
238 D2 **Valkeavaara** Finland
225 M5 **Valkininkai** Lithuania
394 E3 **Valky** Ukraine
436 C1 **Valkyrie Dome** *mountain* Antarctica
225 J4 **Vall** Sweden
231 F3 **Vall d'Alba** Spain
224 H3 **Valla** Sweden
230 D3 **Valladolid** Spain
234 C2 **Vállaj** Hungary
122 D6 **Vallard, Lac** *lake* Québec Canada
233 F6 **Vallata** Italy
222 H5 **Vallbo** Sweden
222 E5 **Valldal** Norway
160 D4 **Valle Cura, Río de** *watercourse* Argentina
232 B4 **Valle d'Aosta** *admin. area* Italy
160 E6 **Valle Daza** Argentina
155 E2 **Valle de La Pascua** Venezuela
132 D3 **Valle de Olivos** Mexico
132 B3 **Valle de Vizcaíno** Mexico
154 B4 **Valle del Cauca** *admin. area* Colombia
154 B4 **Valle del Guamuez** Colombia
133 F3 **Valle Hermoso** Mexico
134 C4 **Valle Kuikuinita** Nicaragua
128 E5 **Valle La Trinidad** Mexico
134 C4 **Vallecillo** Honduras
129 M7 **Vallecillo** Mexico
160 E4 **Vallecito** Argentina
129 I2 **Vallecito Reservoir** Colorado USA
154 C2 **Valledupar** Colombia
159 E5 **Vallegrande** Bolivia
124 D7 **Vallejo** California USA
233 E8 **Vallelunga Pratameno** Italy
222 J5 **Vallen** Sweden
160 D4 **Vallenar** Chile
222 I4 **Vallenäs** Sweden
228 D3 **Vallet** France
233 F9 **Valletta** Malta
245 C2 **Valley** Ireland
242 D3 **Valley** Isle of Anglesey Wales UK
131 I4 **Valley** Alabama USA
125 Q6 **Valley** Nebraska USA
125 Q8 **Valley Center** Kansas USA
125 Q3 **Valley City** North Dakota USA
127 K3 **Valley East** Ontario Canada
126 D7 **Valley Falls** Kansas USA
377 I3 **Valley Head** *cape* Philippines
130 C5 **Valley Mills** Texas USA
128 B1 **Valley Springs** California USA
130 C4 **Valley View** Texas USA
118 M5 **Valleyview** Alberta Canada
Vallgrund *see* **Raippaluoto** Finland
130 D4 **Valliant** Oklahoma USA
124 G2 **Vallican** British Columbia Canada
224 G5 **Vällinge** Sweden
222 J4 **Vallnäs** Sweden
224 I4 **Vällö** *island* Sweden
229 H3 **Vallorbe** Switzerland
231 G3 **Valls** Spain
222 H5 **Valmåsen** Sweden
225 M4 **Valmiera** Latvia
225 M4 **Valmieras** *admin. area* Latvia
241 H5 **Valmont** France
222 G4 **Valøya** Norway
225 N5 **Valozhyn** Belarus
157 B8 **Valparaíso** Brazil
160 D5 **Valparaíso** Chile
160 D5 **Valparaíso** *admin. area* Chile
154 C4 **Valparaíso** Colombia
132 E4 **Valparaíso** Mexico
126 H6 **Valparaiso** Indiana USA
230 C3 **Valparaiso, Embalse de** *lake* Spain
228 B5 **Valporquero, Cuevas de** Spain
232 H4 **Valpovo** Croatia
228 F5 **Valras-Plage** France
372 F6 **Vals, Tanjung** *cape* Indonesia
393 C7 **Valsad** Gujarat India
222 I4 **Valsjöbyn** Sweden
222 I4 **Valsjön** *bay* Sweden
222 L5 **Valsörarna** *island* Finland
308 D5 **Valspan** South Africa
224 G3 **Valstad** Sweden
223 P5 **Valtimo** Finland
394 F2 **Valuyki** Russian Federation
230 E4 **Valverde de Júcar** Spain
230 C3 **Valverde del Fresno** Spain
234 D2 **Vama** Romania
234 D3 **Vama Buzăului** Romania
232 G1 **Vamberk** Czech Republic
235 L2 **Vammala** Finland
235 D8 **Vamos** Greece
235 E6 **Vamvakas, Akra** *cape* Greece
394 G5 **Van** Turkey
394 G5 **Van** *admin. area* Turkey
240 D2 **Van** Powys Wales UK
130 D4 **Van** Texas USA
127 O3 **Van Bruyssel** Québec Canada
130 D3 **Van Buren** Arkansas USA
127 R3 **Van Buren** Maine USA
126 F8 **Van Buren** Missouri USA
376 F4 **Vân Canh** Vietnam
372 F4 **Van Daalen** *watercourse* Indonesia
424 I2 **Van Diemen, Cape** NT Australia
424 I2 **Van Diemen Gulf** NT Australia
394 G5 **Van Gölü (Lake Van)** *lake* Turkey
129 J5 **Van Horn** Texas USA
376 F4 **Vạn Ninh** Vietnam
372 F4 **Van Rees, Pegunungan** *range* Indonesia
308 D5 **Van Zylsrus** South Africa
388 D6 **Vanadzor** Armenia
225 M2 **Vanajavesi** *lake* Finland
124 C2 **Vananda** British Columbia Canada
121 R2 **Vanasse, Lac** *lake* Québec Canada
427 14 **Vanavana** *island* French Polynesia
127 R4 **Vanceboro** Maine USA
131 M3 **Vanceboro** North Carolina USA
126 J7 **Vanceburg** Kentucky USA
118 J8 **Vancouver** British Columbia Canada
124 D4 **Vancouver** Washington USA
124 C2 **Vancouver Island** British Columbia Canada
437 K1 **Vanda, Lake** Antarctica
126 F7 **Vandalia** Missouri USA
225 N4 **Vandāni** Latvia
118 I5 **Vanderhoof** British Columbia Canada
308 D5 **Vanderkloof** South Africa
425 K3 **Vanderlin Island** NT Australia
224 G3 **Vanderydvattnet** *lake* Sweden
229 H2 **Vandoeuvre-lès-Nancy** France
127 O3 **Vandry** Québec Canada
222 H3 **Vandved** *island* Norway
224 G3 **Vänern** *bay* Sweden
224 E2 **Vang** Norway
436 T2 **Vang, Mount** *mountain* Antarctica
309 I4 **Vangaindrano** Madagascar
225 M4 **Vangaži** Latvia
241 H3 **Vange** Essex England UK
222 J5 **Vängel** Sweden
222 G5 **Vangshylla** Norway
224 D2 **Vangsvatnet** *lake* Norway
222 J2 **Vangsvik** Norway
119 R8 **Vanguard** Saskatchewan Canada
426 8 **Vangunu** *island* Solomon Islands
225 M2 **Vanhanselkä** *bay* Finland
393 C7 **Vani** Maharashtra India
222 K4 **Vänjaurbäck** Sweden
234 C3 **Vânjule Mare** Romania
237 AL5 **Vankarem** Russian Federation
116 B5 **Vankarem, Laguna** *lagoon* Russian Federation
225 L2 **Vankavesi** *bay* Finland
222 K1 **Vanna** *island* Norway
222 K1 **Vannareid** Norway
222 K5 **Vännäs** Sweden
222 K5 **Vännäsby** Sweden
228 F2 **Vanne** *watercourse* France
228 C3 **Vannes** France
122 E5 **Vannes, Lac** *lake* Québec Canada
222 L4 **Vånören** *island* Sweden
308 C6 **Vanrhynsdorp** South Africa
117 K5 **Vansittart Island** Nunavut Canada
224 H3 **Vänstern** *lake* Sweden
125 M2 **Vantaa** Finland
125 L2 **Vantage** Saskatchewan Canada
223 O3 **Vanttausjärvi** *lake* Finland
223 O3 **Vanttauskoski** Finland
427 9 **Vanua Balavu** *island* Fiji
426 7 **Vanua Lava** *island* Vanuatu
427 9 **Vanua Levu** *island* Fiji
427 9 **Vanua Vatu** *island* Fiji
426 7 **Vanuatu** *country* Oceania
376 D3 **Vanviang** Laos
426 7 **Vao** New Caledonia
230 C2 **Vao, Embalse de** *lake* Spain
227 I2 **Vápenná** Czech Republic
234 F1 **Vapnyarka** Ukraine
229 H4 **Var** *watercourse* France
310 1a **Vara, Pico da** *mountain* Azores
158 C2 **Varadero** Peru
226 D5 **Varaita** *watercourse* Italy
223 N3 **Varajärvi** Finland
225 N4 **Varakļāni** Latvia
224 G2 **Varaldsjøen** *lake* Sweden
224 D2 **Varaldsøy** *region* Norway
304 D3 **Varalé** Côte d'Ivoire
390 G2 **Varāmin** Iran
392 F6 **Varanasi** Uttar Pradesh India
223 P1 **Varangerbotn** Norway
223 Q2 **Varangerfjorden** *bay* Norway
223 P1 **Varangerhalvøya** *peninsula* Norway
233 F6 **Varano, Lago di** *lake* Italy
232 C4 **Varazze** Italy
224 G4 **Varberg** Sweden
235 B6 **Varda** Greece
391 K2 **Vardak** *admin. area* Afghanistan
393 E8 **Vardannapet** Andhra Pradesh India
235 B5 **Vardar** *watercourse* Macedonia
224 E5 **Varde** Denmark
388 E6 **Vardenis** Armenia
234 D4 **Vardim** Bulgaria
229 I5 **Vardiola, Cap** *cape* Corsica France
225 M3 **Vardja** Estonia
223 Q1 **Vardø** Norway
226 E1 **Varel** Germany
304 A2 **Varela** Guinea-Bissau
229 H3 **Varen** Switzerland
241 H5 **Varengeville-sur-Mer** France
226 B4 **Varennes** France
226 E5 **Varese** Italy
234 C2 **Vârfurile** Romania
224 G3 **Vårgårda** Sweden
160 D5 **Vargas** Argentina
154 E2 **Vargas** *admin. area* Venezuela
156 E5 **Vargem** *watercourse* Brazil
234 D2 **Vârghiș** Romania
157 C8 **Varginha** Brazil
222 L4 **Vargön** *island* Sweden
224 C3 **Varhaug** Norway
235 D7 **Vari** Greece
227 K4 **Variaș** Romania
227 J3 **Varín** Slovakia
224 H3 **Väringen** *lake* Sweden
235 B5 **Vàris** Greece
225 N3 **Varja** Estonia
222 I4 **Värjaren** *lake* Sweden
222 K3 **Varjisträsk** Sweden
156 D4 **Varjota** Brazil
223 O5 **Varkaus** Finland
225 J3 **Värmdolandet** *island* Sweden
224 G3 **Varmeln** *lake* Sweden
224 G3 **Värmland** *admin. area* Sweden
224 G3 **Värmlandsnäs** *peninsula* Sweden
234 E4 **Varna** Bulgaria
234 E4 **Varna** *admin. area* Bulgaria
224 H4 **Värnamo** Sweden
224 G2 **Värnäs** Sweden
223 P1 **Varnesodden** *cape* Norway
225 L5 **Varniai** Lithuania
227 H2 **Varnsdorf** Czech Republic
225 N5 **Varnyany** Belarus
223 P3 **Värriö** Finland
158 E3 **Varsovia** Bolivia
240 D3 **Varteg** Torfaen Wales UK
223 P4 **Vartius** Finland
394 G5 **Varto** Turkey
222 L4 **Varuträsket** *lake* Sweden
225 K4 **Värve** Latvia
236 Q6 **Var'yegan** Russian Federation
161 H3 **Várzea** *watercourse* Brazil
157 C7 **Várzea da Palma** Brazil
159 G4 **Várzea Grande** Brazil
157 C6 **Varzelândia** Brazil
232 C4 **Varzi** Italy
236 I5 **Varzino** Russian Federation
389 J6 **Varzob** Tajikistan
223 T3 **Varzuga** Russian Federation
226 B4 **Varzy** France
227 I4 **Vas** *admin. area* Hungary
222 I5 **Vås** Sweden
427 13a **Vasafua** *island* Tuvalu
223 P3 **Vasaraperä** Finland
227 L3 **Vásárosnamény** Hungary
225 N3 **Vasavere** Estonia
230 E2 **Vasca, Costa** *region* Spain
227 L4 **Vașcău** Romania
241 I5 **Vascoeuil** France
163 8 **Vashel, Cape** South Georgia
234 D1 **Vashkivtsi** Ukraine
236 O6 **Vashnël** Russian Federation
390 F2 **Vasiān** Iran
227 J5 **Vašica** Serbia
223 O2 **Vasikkaselkä** *bay* Finland
235 D5 **Vasil Kolarov, Yazovir** *reservoir* Bulgaria
238 F4 **Vasil'yevskiy Mokh** Russian Federation
229 I5 **Vasina, Pointe de la** *cape* Corsica France
426 1a **Vaskess Bay** Kiribati
225 J4 **Väskinde** Sweden
225 L2 **Vaskio** Finland
223 M5 **Vaskivesi** *bay* Finland
225 N3 **Vasknarva** Estonia
223 O2 **Vaskojoki** *watercourse* Finland
238 E5 **Vas'kovo** Russian Federation
234 E2 **Vaslui** Romania
234 E2 **Vaslui** *admin. area* Romania
127 M2 **Vassan** Québec Canada
125 R2 **Vassar** Manitoba Canada
126 J5 **Vassar** Michigan USA
222 H6 **Vassbo** Sweden
224 H2 **Vässinjärvi** *lake* Sweden
224 I3 **Vassunda** Sweden
222 I4 **Västansjö** Sweden
225 M3 **Vastemõisa** Estonia
222 J3 **Vastenjaure** *lake* Sweden
224 I3 **Västerås** Sweden
224 I3 **Västeråsfjärden** *bay* Sweden
222 J4 **Västerbotten** *admin. area* Sweden
224 G2 **Västerdalälven** *watercourse* Sweden
222 J3 **Västerfjäll** Sweden
224 J4 **Västergarn** Sweden
222 J5 **Västernorrland** *admin. area* Sweden
224 G4 **Vastersjön** *lake* Sweden
224 I4 **Västervik** Sweden
223 N5 **Vastinki** Finland
223 P5 **Västinniemi** Finland
224 I3 **Västmanland** *admin. area* Sweden
233 F5 **Vasto** Italy
224 G4 **Västra Fegen** *lake* Sweden
222 I4 **Västra Fiskåvattnet** *lake* Sweden
224 G3 **Västra Götaland** *admin. area* Sweden
222 K4 **Västra Kikkejaure** *lake* Sweden
224 G3 **Västra Örten** *lake* Sweden
224 G5 **Västra Ringsjön** *lake* Sweden
224 G3 **Västra Silen** *lake* Sweden
222 I4 **Västra Tåsjö** Sweden
222 L5 **Västra Yttermark** Finland
224 I4 **Västrum** Sweden
238 B3 **Vastse-Kuuste** Estonia
225 N4 **Vastseliina** Estonia
225 N3 **Vasula** Estonia
223 M5 **Vasunmäki** Finland
227 I4 **Vasvár** Hungary
394 D2 **Vasyl'kiv** Ukraine
236 Q7 **Vasyugan** *watercourse* Russian Federation
228 E3 **Vatan** France
225 Q1 **Vatchelskoye, Ozero** *lake* Russian Federation
244 B3 **Vaternish Point** Scotland UK
235 C7 **Vathí** Greece
235 E7 **Vathy** Greece
233 E6 **Vatican City** *country* Europe
233 F7 **Vaticano, Capo** *cape* Italy
117 R6 **Vatnajökull** *ice* Iceland
224 D3 **Vatndalsvatnet** *lake* Norway
222 inset **Vatneyri** Iceland
222 inset **Vatnsdalsá** *watercourse* Iceland
225 J3 **Vätö** *island* Sweden
427 9 **Vatoa** *island* Fiji
309 I3 **Vatomandry** Madagascar
392 C6 **Vatrak** *watercourse* Gujarat India
244 B3 **Vatten** Highland Scotland UK
224 H3 **Vättern** *bay* Sweden
427 9 **Vatu Vara** *island* Fiji
427 9a **Vatukoula** Fiji
427 9a **Vatulele** *island* Fiji
234 G1 **Vatutine** Ukraine
237 AJ6 **Vatyna** Russian Federation
226 C3 **Vaubecourt** France
229 G2 **Vaucouleurs** France
129 J3 **Vaughn** New Mexico USA
122 C5 **Vaulezar, Lac** *lake* Québec Canada
154 D4 **Vaupés** *admin. area* Colombia
154 D4 **Vaupés (Uaupés)** *watercourse* Brazil/Colombia
228 G5 **Vauvert** France
241 F5 **Vauville** France
229 G2 **Vaux-sur-Sûre** Belgium
392 C6 **Vav** Gujarat India
224 E2 **Vavatn** *lake* Norway
427 10 **Vava'u Group** *island* Tonga
427 10 **Vava'u Island** Tonga
118 L7 **Vavenby** British Columbia Canada
222 K2 **Vavetjåkka nationalpark** *park* Sweden
227 M1 **Vawkavysk** Belarus
119 Q6 **Vawn** Saskatchewan Canada
224 I2 **Växbo** Sweden
225 J3 **Vaxholm** Sweden
224 H4 **Växjö** Sweden
223 Q2 **Vaydaguba** Russian Federation
236 M4 **Vaygach** Russian Federation
236 N4 **Vaygach, Ostrov** *island* Russian Federation
223 O2 **Väylä** Finland
223 M3 **Väylänpää** Sweden
223 O4 **Väyrylä** Finland
235 E5 **Vaysal** Turkey
157 C7 **Vazante** Brazil
232 H2 **Važec** Slovakia
226 C5 **Veauche** France
125 Q4 **Veblen** South Dakota USA
222 L4 **Vebomark** Sweden
226 D1 **Vecht** *watercourse* Germany
226 E1 **Vechta** Germany
310 3b **Vecindario** Canary Islands
230 D3 **Vecinos** Spain
225 N4 **Veclaicene** Latvia
227 J4 **Vecsés** Hungary
225 N4 **Vecumi** Latvia
222 J5 **Veda** Sweden
393 E9 **Vedaranniyam** Tamil Nadu India
224 G4 **Veddige** Sweden
234 D3 **Vedea** *watercourse* Romania
222 I4 **Vedjeön** Sweden
225 Q2 **Vedlozero** Russian Federation
232 G4 **Vedro Polje** Croatia
244 inset **Veensgarth** Shetland Scotland UK
225 L3 **Veere** Estonia
226 B2 **Veere** Netherlands
222 H4 **Vefsna** *watercourse* Norway
222 G4 **Vega** *island* Norway
129 K3 **Vega** Texas USA
230 C2 **Vega de Espinareda** Spain
230 E4 **Vega del Jabalón, Embalse de la** *lake* Spain
436 U2 **Vega Island** Antarctica
158 A2 **Vega Moro** Peru
129 I1 **Vega Reservoir** Colorado USA
155 E2 **Vega Vieja** Venezuela
154 C3 **Vegachí** Colombia
230 C2 **Vegadeo** Spain
225 L4 **Vegeriai** Lithuania
224 E4 **Vegger** Denmark
233 G6 **Veglie** Italy
119 O6 **Vegreville** Alberta Canada
225 M2 **Vehkajärvi** *lake* Finland
223 P5 **Vehmersalmi** Finland
161 G3 **Veinticinco de Diciembre** Paraguay
160 E6 **Veinticinco de Mayo** Argentina
225 L5 **Veisiejai** *lake* Lithuania
222 E6 **Veitastrondvatnet** *lake* Norway
224 E5 **Vejle** Denmark
225 K2 **Vekara** *island* Finland
154 C1 **Vela, Cabo de la** *cape* Colombia
310 1b **Velas** Azores
134 C5 **Velas, Cabo** *cape* Costa Rica
160 E4 **Velasco, Sierra de** *range* Argentina
234 B1 **Veľaty** Slovakia
161 H5 **Velázquez** Uruguay
308 C6 **Velddrif** South Africa
226 D2 **Velen** Germany
227 J4 **Velencei-tó** *lake* Hungary
235 B5 **Veles** Macedonia
232 F2 **Velešín** Czech Republic
154 C3 **Vélez** Colombia
230 D5 **Vélez-Málaga** Spain
230 E5 **Vélez-Rubio** Spain
157 C7 **Velhas** *watercourse* Brazil
155 G5 **Velho Mocambo de Santana** Brazil
388 E5 **Velichayevskoye** Russian Federation
232 G4 **Velika** Croatia
227 M2 **Velika Hlusha** Ukraine
232 F4 **Velika Kladuša** Bosnia and Herzegovina
234 B3 **Velika Plana** Serbia
237 AJ6 **Velikaya** *watercourse* Russian Federation
223 S5 **Velikaya Guba** Russian Federation
227 H5 **Velike Lašče** Slovenia
234 B3 **Veliki Crljeni** Serbia
232 G5 **Veliki Drvenik** *island* Croatia
227 K5 **Veliki Gaj** Serbia
234 C4 **Veliki Izvor** Serbia
234 B4 **Veliki Kupci** Serbia
238 C3 **Velikino** Russian Federation
234 C1 **Velikiy Lyuben'** Ukraine
225 P3 **Velikiy Novgorod** Russian Federation
236 K6 **Velikiy Ustyug** Russian Federation
225 P4 **Velikiye-Luki** Russian Federation
227 K5 **Veliko Laole** Serbia
227 K5 **Veliko Selo** Serbia
394 C4 **Veliko Tŭrnovo** Bulgaria
238 E4 **Velikooktyabr'skiy** Russian Federation
232 H4 **Velimirovac** Croatia
240 C2 **Velindre-farchog** Pembrokeshire Wales UK
300 D6 **Vélingara** Senegal
229 K5 **Velino, Monte** *mountain* Italy
225 P5 **Velizh** Russian Federation
227 I3 **Velká Bíteš** Czech Republic
227 J3 **Veľká Fatra** *range* Slovakia
226 G3 **Velká Hleďsebe** Czech Republic
227 K3 **Veľká Ida** Slovakia
234 A1 **Veľká Udiča** Slovakia
227 J3 **Velké Karlovice** Czech Republic
227 I2 **Velké Poříčí** Czech Republic
236 D3 **Velkomstpynten** *cape* Norway
232 H2 **Veľký Krtíš** Slovakia
227 I4 **Veľký Meder** Slovakia
426 8 **Vella Lavella** *island* Solomon Islands
233 E6 **Velletri** Italy
226 E2 **Vellmar** Germany
393 E9 **Vellore** Tamil Nadu India
226 C1 **Velsen** Netherlands
236 J6 **Vel'sk** Russian Federation
236 K5 **Vel't** Russian Federation
224 G2 **Velta** Norway
125 O2 **Velva** North Dakota USA
229 L1 **Velvary** Czech Republic
235 C5 **Velvendos** Greece
234 C1 **Velyatyn** Ukraine
234 F2 **Velyka Mykhaylivka** Ukraine
227 L3 **Velyki Luchky** Ukraine
234 F2 **Velykopoloske** Ukraine
234 C1 **Velykyy Bereznyy** Ukraine
76 N8 **Vema Fracture Zone** *underwater feature* Atlantic Ocean
80 F8 **Vema Seamount** *underwater feature* Atlantic Ocean
80 K6 **Vema Trench** *underwater feature* Indian Ocean
224 E4 **Vemb** Denmark
222 H5 **Vemdalen** Sweden
224 G5 **Ven** *island* Sweden
224 H4 **Vena** Sweden
229 I5 **Venaco** Corsica France
154 C3 **Venadillo** Colombia
134 D5 **Venado, Isla del** *island* Nicaragua
160 F5 **Venado Tuerto** Argentina
233 F6 **Venafro** Italy
125 N6 **Venango** Nebraska USA
226 D5 **Venaria** Italy
229 H4 **Venasca** Italy
229 H5 **Vence** France
230 E3 **Vencías, Embalse de las** *lake* Spain
225 K5 **Venckai** Lithuania
230 B4 **Vendas Novas** Portugal
228 D4 **Vendays-Montalivet** France
228 D3 **Vendée** *region* France
224 I2 **Vendelsjön** *lake* Sweden
229 G2 **Vendeuvre-sur-Barse** France
163 10a **Vendôme** Grenada
154 D4 **Venecia** Colombia
223 O4 **Veneheitto** Finland
223 N3 **Venejärvi** Finland
223 M5 **Veneskoski** Finland
124 D4 **Veneta** Oregon USA
116 E5 **Venetie** Alaska USA
223 N5 **Venetjoen tekojärvi** *lake* Finland
232 D4 **Veneto** *admin. area* Italy
223 N5 **Venetpalo** Finland
238 H5 **Venëv** Russian Federation
232 E4 **Venezia, Golfo di** *bay* Italy
232 E4 **Venezia (Venice)** Italy
135 H6 **Venezuela** *country* South America
154 D2 **Venezuela, Golfo de** *bay* Venezuela
76 L8 **Venezuelan Basin** *underwater feature* Caribbean Sea
223 O4 **Vengasaho** Finland
222 K2 **Vengsøya** *island* Norway
393 C8 **Vengurla** Maharashtra India
116 D7 **Veniaminof Volcano** Alaska USA
Venice *see* **Venezia** Italy
131 J7 **Venice** Florida USA
229 G4 **Vénissieux** France
224 G2 **Venjan** Sweden
224 G2 **Venjanssjön** *lake* Sweden
393 E9 **Venkatagiri** Andhra Pradesh India
119 U7 **Venlaw** Manitoba Canada
240 D4 **Venn Ottery** Devon England UK
224 D3 **Vennesla** Norway

233 F6 **Venosa** Italy
222 I3 **Venset** Norway
226 F4 **Vent** Austria
225 K4 **Venta** *watercourse* Latvia
225 L4 **Venta** Lithuania
225 L5 **Venta** *watercourse* Lithuania
162 D6 **Ventana, Punta** *cape* Argentina
230 D5 **Ventas de Zafarraya** Spain
158 D5 **Ventilla** Bolivia
134 D5 **Ventisqueros, Cerro** *mountain* Costa Rica
241 F4 **Ventnor** Isle of Wight England UK
233 E6 **Ventotene, Isola** *island* Italy
225 K4 **Ventspils** Latvia
225 K4 **Ventspils** *admin. area* Latvia
154 E3 **Ventuari** *watercourse* Venezuela
130 C4 **Venus** Texas USA
425 J8 **Venus Bay** SA Australia
132 E3 **Venustiano Carranza** Mexico
132 E3 **Venustiano Carranza, Presa** *lake* Mexico
229 K3 **Venzone** Italy
225 M5 **Vepriai** Lithuania
223 P5 **Vepsä** Finland
223 P5 **Vepsänjärvi** *lake* Finland
160 F4 **Vera** Argentina
230 F5 **Vera** Spain
162 D3 **Vera, Bahía** *bay* Argentina
157 D6 **Vera Cruz** Brazil
133 F5 **Veracruz** Mexico
133 F5 **Veracruz** *admin. area* Mexico
154 D4 **Veradal** Colombia
222 H5 **Veravatnet** *lake* Sweden
227 M2 **Verba** Ukraine
229 H3 **Verbier** Switzerland
238 G4 **Verbilki** Russian Federation
226 E5 **Vercelli** Italy
163 I9 **Verchild's Mountain** *volcano* St Kitts and Nevis
222 H5 **Verdal** *island* Norway
222 G5 **Verdalsøra** Norway
159 I4 **Verde** Brazil
157 A7 **Verde** *watercourse* Brazil
161 G2 **Verde** *watercourse* Paraguay
128 G3 **Verde** *watercourse* Arkansas USA
230 C2 **Verde, Costa** *region* Spain
162 E2 **Verde, Península** *peninsula* Argentina
158 C4 **Verdecocha, Cerro** *mountain* Peru
130 B3 **Verden** Oklahoma USA
130 C2 **Verdigris** *watercourse* Kansas USA
129 O2 **Verdigris** *watercourse* Oklahoma USA
157 B7 **Verdinho, Serra do** *range* Brazil
238 E5 **Verdino** Russian Federation
229 H5 **Verdon** *watercourse* France
229 G2 **Verdun** France
119 T7 **Veregin** Saskatchewan Canada
225 O5 **Veremeyevo** Belarus
234 C3 **Verendin** Romania
238 C6 **Vereytsy** Belarus
304 B2 **Verga, Cap** *cape* Guinea
161 H5 **Vergara** Uruguay
229 J4 **Vergato** Italy
127 O4 **Vergennes** Vermont USA
225 N3 **Vergi** Estonia
238 H4 **Verigino** Russian Federation
230 C3 **Verín** Spain
225 N3 **Veriora** Estonia
237 AG8 **Verkhne Kolpakora Urochishche** Russian Federation
237 X7 **Verkhneangarskiy Khrebet** *range* Russian Federation
223 Q2 **Verkhnetulomskiy** Russian Federation
223 Q4 **Verkhneye Kuyto, Ozero** *lake* Russian Federation
223 S5 **Verkhneye Volozero, Ozero** *lake* Russian Federation
388 E4 **Verkhniy Baskunchak** Russian Federation
388 D5 **Verkhniy Chegem** Russian Federation
223 S3 **Verkhniy Vyalozërskiy** Russian Federation
388 E3 **Verkhniy Yeruslan** Russian Federation
237 AA7 **Verkhnyaya Amga** Russian Federation
234 D1 **Verkhnyaya Lipitsa** Ukraine
236 J6 **Verkhnyaya Toyma** Russian Federation
238 G4 **Verkhnyaya Troitsa** Russian Federation
234 D1 **Verkhovyna** Ukraine
237 AB5 **Verkhoyanskiy Khrebet** *range* Russian Federation
389 N3 **Verkhuba** Kazakhstan
227 M2 **Verkhy** Ukraine
226 E2 **Verl** Germany
125 K1 **Verlo** Saskatchewan Canada
222 F5 **Verma** Norway
228 F2 **Vermand** France
156 E4 **Vermelho** *watercourse* Brazil
228 F3 **Vermenton** France
227 K5 **Vermeş** Romania
232 D3 **Vermiglio** Italy
119 P6 **Vermilion** *watercourse* Alberta Canada
130 F6 **Vermilion Bay** Louisiana USA
126 E3 **Vermilion Lake** Minnesota USA
126 E3 **Vermilion Range** *range* Minnesota USA
125 S2 **Vermillion** Ontario Canada
125 Q5 **Vermillion** South Dakota USA
126 C5 **Vermillion** *watercourse* South Dakota USA
235 B5 **Vermio** *range* Greece
163 11a **Vermont** St Vincent and the Grenadines
114 **Vermont** *admin. area* USA
234 A4 **Vermosh** Albania
394 E2 **Vern** *watercourse* Ukraine
436 T2 **Vernadsky (Ukraine)** *research station* Antarctica
125 K6 **Vernal** Utah USA
229 H3 **Vernayaz** Switzerland
127 K3 **Verner** Ontario Canada
226 D4 **Vernier** Switzerland
118 L7 **Vernon** British Columbia Canada
228 E2 **Vernon** France
131 I5 **Vernon** Florida USA
130 B3 **Vernon** Texas USA
124 I6 **Vernon** Utah USA
121 R3 **Vernon, Lac** *lake* Québec Canada
130 E5 **Vernon Lake** Louisiana USA
163 I6 **Vernou** Guadeloupe
232 B2 **Verny** France
131 K7 **Vero Beach** Florida USA
235 C5 **Veroia** Greece
229 H4 **Verolengo** Italy
126 E3 **Veroli** Italy
226 F5 **Verona** Italy
125 P3 **Verona** North Dakota USA
130 F6 **Verret, Lake** Louisiana USA
228 F2 **Versailles** France
126 I7 **Versailles** Indiana USA
126 I7 **Versailles** Kentucky USA
229 H3 **Versoix** France
229 H3 **Versoix** Switzerland
300 C6 **Vert, Cap** *cape* Senegal
158 D2 **Vertentes** Brazil
134 E2 **Vertientes** Cuba
160 E2 **Vertientes Sulfhídricas** Bolivia
228 D3 **Vertou** France
228 G2 **Vertus** France
224 G4 **Verum** Sweden
229 G1 **Verviers** Belgium
119 S8 **Verwood** Saskatchewan Canada
241 F4 **Verwood** Dorset England UK
235 C5 **Véryi** Greece
223 N5 **Vesanka** Finland
223 O5 **Vesanto** Finland
227 I4 **Vése** Hungary
238 G5 **Veselëvo** Russian Federation
388 D4 **Veselovskoye Vodokhranilishche** *lake* Russian Federation
225 J5 **Vesëloye** Russian Federation
225 M2 **Vesijako** *lake* Finland
225 M2 **Vesijärvi** *lake* Finland
225 L3 **Veskijärv** *lake* Estonia
223 O2 **Veskoniemi** Finland
228 F2 **Vesle** *watercourse* France
225 P2 **Vesnino** Russian Federation
229 H3 **Vesoul** France
157 D7 **Vespasiano** Brazil
226 E5 **Vespolate** Italy
224 G4 **Vessigebro** Sweden
224 D3 **Vest-Agder** *admin. area* Norway
224 D3 **Vestbygd** Norway
236 D5 **Vesterålen** *island* Norway
122 N2 **Vesterland** *island* Greenland
222 inset **Vestfirðir** *admin. area* Iceland
222 I3 **Vestfjorden** *bay* Norway
224 E3 **Vestfjorden** *lake* Norway
224 F3 **Vestfold** *admin. area* Norway
436 F2 **Vestfold Hills** *range* Antarctica
222 inset **Vestmannaeyjar** Iceland
117 Q6 **Vestmannaeyjar** *island* Iceland
222 E5 **Vestnes** Norway
226 F5 **Vestone** Italy
224 C3 **Vestre Bokn** *island* Norway
223 P1 **Vestre Jakobselv** Norway
436 X2 **Veststraumen Glacier** *ice* Antarctica
222 inset **Vesturland** *admin. area* Iceland
222 G5 **Vestvik** Norway
238 G3 **Ves'yegonsk** Russian Federation
227 I4 **Veszprém** Hungary
227 I4 **Veszprém** *admin. area* Hungary
234 B2 **Vésztő** Hungary
427 9 **Vetavuaa** *island* Fiji
223 M5 **Veteli** Finland
235 B5 **Vetersko** Macedonia
388 E1 **Vetluga** Russian Federation
234 E4 **Vetovo** Bulgaria
234 D4 **Vetren** Bulgaria
235 C4 **Vetren** Macedonia
234 E4 **Vetrino** Bulgaria
227 H2 **Vetschau** Germany
223 O2 **Vetsijärvi** *lake* Finland
223 O2 **Vetsikko** Finland
222 L3 **Vettasjärvi** Sweden
222 L3 **Vettasjärvi** *lake* Sweden
241 H5 **Veules-les-Roses** France
241 H5 **Veulettes-sur-Mer** France
228 F1 **Veurne** Belgium
222 E5 **Vevang** Norway
426 8 **Veve, Mount** *volcano* Solomon Islands
307 E2 **Veveno** *watercourse* Sudan
229 H3 **Vevey** Switzerland
226 D4 **Vex** Switzerland
222 M5 **Vexala** Finland
225 O3 **Veymarn** Russian Federation
229 G4 **Veynes** France
228 F3 **Vézelay** France
228 E4 **Vézère** *watercourse* France
223 T4 **Vezhmozero, Ozero** *lake* Russian Federation
394 E5 **Vezirköprü** Turkey
222 J5 **Vi** Sweden
228 E2 **Viabon** France
159 E6 **Viacha** Bolivia
226 F5 **Viadana** Italy
373 H4 **Viai Island** Papua New Guinea
161 I4 **Viamão** Brazil
160 F5 **Viamonte** Argentina
162 C6 **Viamonte** Argentina
130 D3 **Vian** Oklahoma USA
156 C3 **Viana** Brazil
230 E2 **Viana** Spain
230 C4 **Viana do Alentejo** Portugal
230 B3 **Viana do Castelo** *admin. area* Portugal
229 H2 **Vianden** Luxembourg
373 D3 **Viangchan (Vientiane)** Laos
157 B7 **Vianópolis** Brazil
223 N4 **Viantie** Finland
230 D5 **Viar** *watercourse* Spain
230 D5 **Viareggio** Italy
225 K2 **Viasvesi** *bay* Finland
228 F4 **Viaur** *watercourse* France
233 G7 **Vibo Valentia** Italy
130 B7 **Viboras** Texas USA
224 E4 **Viborg** Denmark
228 E2 **Vibraye** France
126 F8 **Viburnum** Missouri USA
231 H3 **Vic** Spain
228 E5 **Vic-en-Bigorre** France
228 E5 **Vic-Fezensac** France
228 F4 **Vic-sur-Cère** France
132 C3 **Vicam** Mexico
230 E5 **Vícar** Spain
158 A2 **Vice** Peru
156 F4 **Vicência** Brazil
128 E4 **Vicente Guerrero** Mexico
132 B2 **Vicente Guerrero** Mexico
132 E4 **Vicente Guerrero** Mexico
130 B9 **Vicente Guerrero, Presa** *lake* Mexico
226 F5 **Vicenza** Italy
154 D3 **Vichada** *admin. area* Colombia
154 D3 **Vichada** *watercourse* Colombia
161 H4 **Vichadero** Uruguay
228 F3 **Vichy** France
130 B2 **Vici** Oklahoma USA
130 A5 **Vick** Texas USA
128 F4 **Vicksburg** Arizona USA
130 F4 **Vicksburg** Mississippi USA
155 F4 **Viçosa** Brazil
157 D8 **Viçosa** Brazil
156 B2 **Viçosa, Ilha** *island* Brazil
156 E3 **Viçosa do Ceará** Brazil
234 D2 **Vicovu de Jos** Romania
234 D2 **Vicovu de Sus** Romania
119 U7 **Victor** Manitoba Canada
126 E6 **Victor** Iowa USA
127 M5 **Victor** New York USA
436 C2 **Victor, Mount** *mountain* Antarctica
124 J2 **Victor Bay** Antarctica
425 K8 **Victor Harbor** SA Australia
160 F5 **Victoria** Argentina
425 L9 **Victoria** *admin. area* Australia
424 I3 **Victoria** *watercourse* NT Australia
159 G5 **Victoria** Bolivia
118 J8 **Victoria** British Columbia Canada
123 L9 **Victoria** Newfoundland and Labrador Canada
123 G9 **Victoria** Prince Edward Island Canada
160 C6 **Victoria** Chile
233 F8 **Victoria** Malta
310 9 **Victoria** Seychelles
125 P7 **Victoria** Kansas USA
130 C6 **Victoria** Texas USA
162 B3 **Victoria, Isla** *island* Chile
307 E4 **Victoria, Lake** *lake* Uganda
379 G5 **Victoria, Mount** Myanmar
373 H6 **Victoria, Mount** Papua New Guinea
117 L3 **Victoria and Albert Mountains** Nunavut Canada
120 G7 **Victoria Beach** Manitoba Canada
117 O2 **Victoria Fjord** Greenland
116 H4 **Victoria Island** Northwest Territories/Nunavut Canada
123 J8 **Victoria Lake** Newfoundland and Labrador Canada
436 K1 **Victoria Land** *plain* Antarctica
306 E3 **Victoria Nile** *watercourse* Uganda
423 E6 **Victoria Range** New Zealand
424 I4 **Victoria River Downs** NT Australia
424 I3 **Victoria River Roadhouse** NT Australia
127 L4 **Victoria Road** Ontario Canada
308 D6 **Victoria West** South Africa
377 I5 **Victorias** Philippines
117 L9 **Victoriaville** Québec Canada
160 E3 **Victorica** Argentina
128 D3 **Victorville** California USA
120 H1 **Victory Lake** Nunavut Canada
160 D4 **Vicuña** Chile
160 E5 **Vicuna Mackenna** Argentina
155 I5 **Vida Nova** Brazil
128 E3 **Vidal** California USA
128 E3 **Vidal Junction** California USA
225 L4 **Vidāle** Latvia
131 J4 **Vidalia** Georgia USA
130 F5 **Vidalia** Louisiana USA
227 L1 **Vidamlya** Belarus
229 H5 **Vidauban** France
130 C6 **Vidaurri** Texas USA
224 E4 **Videbæk** Denmark
222 inset **Víðidalsá** *watercourse* Iceland
230 C4 **Vidigueira** Portugal
234 C4 **Vidin** *admin. area* Bulgaria
225 J3 **Vidinge** *island* Sweden
230 C2 **Vidio, Cabo** *cape* Spain
392 D6 **Vidisha** Madhya Pradesh India
225 Q2 **Vidlitsa** Russian Federation
238 G5 **Vidnoye** Russian Federation
130 D5 **Vidor** Texas USA
224 G4 **Vidöstern** *lake* Sweden
232 G4 **Vidovci** Croatia
232 H4 **Vidovice** Bosnia and Herzegovina
234 D3 **Vidraru, Lacul** *lake* Romania
231 H3 **Vidrieres** Spain
224 H3 **Vidsel** Sweden
228 D3 **Vie** *watercourse* France
162 D2 **Viedma** Argentina
162 B4 **Viedma, Lago** *lake* Argentina
162 B4 **Viedma, Ventisquero** *glacier* Argentina
163 I5 **Vieille Case** Dominica
230 B4 **Vieira de Leiria** Portugal
228 C5 **Vieja** *region* Spain
129 J5 **Vieja, Sierra** *range* Texas USA
225 P5 **Vieki** Finland
223 P5 **Viekinjärvi** *lake* Finland
231 G2 **Vielha** Spain
229 G1 **Vielsalm** Belgium
226 F2 **Vienenburg** Germany
126 G8 **Vienna** Illinois USA
127 M7 **Vienna** Virginia USA
127 K7 **Vienna** West Virginia USA
229 G4 **Vienne** France
228 E3 **Vienne** *watercourse* France
135 H3 **Vieques** Puerto Rico
135 H3 **Vieques** *island* Puerto Rico
223 O5 **Vieremä** Finland
228 F3 **Vierzon** France
132 E3 **Viesca** Mexico
225 M4 **Viesīte** Latvia
233 G6 **Vieste** Italy
376 E2 **Việt Trì** Vietnam
222 K3 **Vietas** Sweden
376 E3 **Vietnam** *country*
163 I6 **Vieux-Bourg** Guadeloupe
163 I6 **Vieux-Fort** Guadeloupe
155 F1 **Vieux Fort** St Lucia
163 I6 **Vieux Fort, Pointe du** *cape* Guadeloupe
155 H3 **Vieux Grand-Santi** French Guiana
163 I6 **Vieux-Habitants** Guadeloupe
229 G4 **Vif** France
132 E3 **Viga, Cerro de la** *mountain* Mexico
377 I3 **Vigan** Philippines
226 E5 **Vigevano** Italy
222 I5 **Vigge** Sweden
156 B3 **Vigia** Brazil
230 C4 **Vigia, Barragem da** *lake* Portugal
154 B3 **Vigía del Fuerte** Colombia
229 K5 **Vignanello** Italy
226 F5 **Vignola** Italy
233 F5 **Vignola, Punta** *cape* Italy
233 C6 **Vignola Mare l'Agnata** Sardinia Italy
230 B2 **Vigo** Spain
241 E2 **Vigo** Worcestershire England UK
224 C1 **Vigra** *island* Norway
232 B2 **Vigy** France
223 N4 **Vihanti** Finland
391 L3 **Vihari** Pakistan
228 D3 **Vihiers** France
391 L3 **Vihowa** Pakistan
225 O1 **Vihtari** Finland
225 M2 **Vihti** Finland
225 M2 **Vihtijärvi** Finland
225 L2 **Viiala** Finland
223 M3 **Viikusjärvi** Sweden
223 P5 **Viinijärvi** *lake* Finland
223 Q2 **Viişoara** Romania
223 P5 **Viitaniemi** Finland
223 N5 **Viitasaari** Finland
225 N3 **Viitna** Estonia
392 D6 **Vijainagar** Rajasthan India
393 E8 **Vijayawada** Andhra Pradesh India
154 B4 **Vijes** Colombia
222 inset **Vík** Iceland
222 H3 **Vik** Norway
223 O3 **Vikajärvi** Finland
392 D4 **Vikasnagar** Uttaranchal India
222 E5 **Vike** Norway
372 C6 **Vikeke** Timor-Leste (East Timor)
224 H2 **Viken** Sweden
224 H3 **Vikern** *lake* Sweden
238 D5 **Vikhra** *watercourse* Russian Federation
235 C5 **Vikhren** *mountain* Bulgaria
119 P6 **Viking** Alberta Canada
224 G4 **Vikna** *island* Norway
234 D1 **Vikno** Ukraine
222 G4 **Vikøyri** Norway
222 K2 **Vikran** Norway
224 C2 **Viksdalsvatnet** *lake* Norway
222 J5 **Viksjö** Sweden
224 I2 **Viksjön** *lake* Sweden
222 F5 **Vikum** Norway
159 G4 **Vila Bela da Santíssima Trindade** Brazil
154 D5 **Vila Bittencourt** Colombia
154 D5 **Vila Calmon** Brazil
159 F1 **Vila Camará** Brazil
310 4 **Vila da Ribeira Brava** Cape Verde
160 F4 **Vila de María** Argentina
156 F4 **Vila do Conde** Brazil
310 4 **Vila do Maio** Cape Verde
230 C3 **Vila Flor** Portugal
230 B4 **Vila Franca de Xira** Portugal
310 1a **Vila Franca do Campo** Azores
159 G2 **Vila Nova** Brazil
310 4 **Vila Nova Sintra** Cape Verde
159 H4 **Vila Paredão** Brazil
155 F4 **Vila Pereira** Brazil
230 B3 **Vila Praia de Âncora** Portugal
230 C3 **Vila Real** Portugal
230 C3 **Vila Real** *admin. area* Portugal
230 C5 **Vila Real de Santo António** Portugal
159 I3 **Vila Rica** Brazil
155 F4 **Vila Tepequém** Brazil
159 I4 **Vila Velha** Brazil
157 D8 **Vila Velha** Brazil
230 C4 **Vila Viçosa** Portugal
158 C3 **Vilacamba, Cordillera** *range* Peru
310 3a **Vilaflor** Canary Islands
231 G3 **Vilafranca del Penedès** Spain
228 C3 **Vilaine** *watercourse* France
309 H3 **Vilanandro, Tanjona** *cape* Madagascar
309 G4 **Vilankulos** Mozambique
231 G3 **Vilanova i la Geltrú** Spain
158 D5 **Vilaque** Bolivia
230 B3 **Vilar do Paraíso** Portugal
125 N8 **Vilas** Colorado USA
222 I3 **Vilasund** Sweden
160 C6 **Vilcún** Chile
224 E4 **Vildbjerg** Denmark
230 C3 **Vilela** Portugal
222 J4 **Vilhelmina** Sweden
159 F4 **Vilhena** Brazil
235 C6 **Vilia** Greece
237 AG6 **Viliga-Kushka** Russian Federation
225 N5 **Viliya** *watercourse* Belarus
225 M3 **Viljandi** Estonia
225 M3 **Viljandimaa** *admin. area* Estonia
308 E5 **Viljoenskroon** South Africa
223 P5 **Viljolahti** Finland
225 L5 **Vilkaviškis** Lithuania
225 M4 **Viļķene** Latvia
225 L5 **Vilkija** Lithuania
236 Q4 **Vil'kitskogo, Ostrov** *island* Russian Federation
237 V3 **Vil'kitskogo, Proliv** *strait* Russian Federation
132 D2 **Villa Ahumada** Mexico
160 F3 **Villa Ángela** Argentina
154 D2 **Villa Bruzual** Venezuela
134 B4 **Villa Canales** Guatemala
160 E4 **Villa Carlos Paz** Argentina
162 B4 **Villa Cerro Castillo** Chile
134 D2 **Villa Clara** *admin. area* Cuba
133 D5 **Villa Corzo** Mexico
158 B3 **Villa Culebras** Peru
132 E5 **Villa de Álvarez** Mexico
132 F4 **Villa de Cos** Mexico
132 E4 **Villa de Cura** Venezuela
129 L8 **Villa de Garcia** Mexico
161 G5 **Villa del Carmen** Uruguay
230 D3 **Villa del Prado** Spain
230 D5 **Villa del Río** Spain
154 C3 **Villa del Rosario** Colombia
160 E4 **Villa Dolores** Argentina
161 G3 **Villa Florida** Paraguay
132 E4 **Villa Guerrero** Mexico
132 D4 **Villa Hidalgo** Mexico
160 E5 **Villa Huidobro** Argentina
159 F6 **Villa Ingavi** Bolivia
132 C3 **Villa Insurgentes** Mexico
128 F6 **Villa Jesus Maria** Mexico
132 C3 **Villa Juárez** Mexico
160 D4 **Villa Krause** Argentina
162 B3 **Villa Mañihuales** Chile
160 F5 **Villa María** Argentina
162 B2 **Villa Mascardi** Argentina
129 J7 **Villa Matamoros** Mexico
160 E5 **Villa Mercedes** Argentina
134 B4 **Villa Nueva** Guatemala
155 F2 **Villa Nueva** Venezuela
161 G4 **Villa Ocampo** Argentina
132 D3 **Villa Ocampo** Mexico
160 F4 **Villa Ojo de Agua** Argentina
161 G3 **Villa Oliva** Paraguay
132 D3 **Villa Orestes Pereyra** Mexico
154 B4 **Villa Rica** Colombia
158 C3 **Villa Rica** Peru
160 E4 **Villa San Martín** Argentina
232 E3 **Villa Santina** Italy
161 H5 **Villa Sara** Uruguay
160 D4 **Villa Unión** Argentina
132 D4 **Villa Unión** Mexico
132 E2 **Villa Unión** Mexico
160 E5 **Villa Valeria** Argentina
159 F5 **Villa Yapacaní** Bolivia
230 E2 **Villabona** Spain
230 D3 **Villabrágima** Spain
230 D3 **Villacastín** Spain
227 G4 **Villach** Austria
233 C7 **Villacidro** Sardinia Italy
230 D2 **Villada** Spain
230 D2 **Villadiego** Spain
232 C3 **Villadossola** Italy
233 E8 **Villafrati** Italy
230 E3 **Villafruela** Spain
154 B4 **Villagarzón** Colombia
163 6a **Villagra, Bahía** *bay* Isla Róbinson Crusoe
161 G4 **Villaguay** Argentina
133 G5 **Villahermosa** Mexico
230 E4 **Villahermosa** Spain
228 D2 **Villaines-la-Juhel** France
223 P5 **Villala** Finland
230 C2 **Villalba** Spain
230 E3 **Villalba de la Sierra** Spain
161 G3 **Villalbín** Paraguay
129 L7 **Villaldama** Mexico
230 D2 **Villalón de Campos** Spain
160 F6 **Villalonga** Argentina
233 C7 **Villamar** Sardinia Italy
230 D5 **Villamartín** Spain
159 F6 **Villamontes** Bolivia
230 E2 **Villano, Cabo** *cape* Spain
154 D3 **Villanueva** Colombia
132 E4 **Villanueva** Mexico
230 D4 **Villanueva de Córdoba** Spain
230 D4 **Villanueva de la Serena** Spain
230 C4 **Villanueva del Fresno** Spain
227 J5 **Villány** Hungary
230 E4 **Villapalacios** Spain
233 C7 **Villaputzu** Sardinia Italy
230 C3 **Villar de Peralonso** Spain
230 C4 **Villar del Rey** Spain
230 C4 **Villar del Rey, Embalse de** *lake* Spain
229 G4 **Villard-de-Lans** France
160 F6 **Villarino Viejo** Argentina
233 F8 **Villarosa** Italy
230 D2 **Villarramiel** Spain
160 C6 **Villarrica** Chile
161 G3 **Villarrica** Paraguay
160 C6 **Villarrica, Lago** *lake* Chile
162 C2 **Villarrica, Volcán** *volcano* Chile
230 E4 **Villarrobledo** Spain
226 C5 **Villars-les-Dombes** France
231 J2 **Villars-sur-Var** France
230 D3 **Villatoro** Spain
154 C3 **Villavicencio** Colombia
228 B5 **Villaviciosa** Spain
154 C4 **Villavieja** Colombia
160 E2 **Villazón** Argentina
226 D3 **Villé** France
228 F4 **Villefort** France
228 E5 **Villefranche-de-Lauragais** France
228 F4 **Villefranche-de-Panat** France
228 F4 **Villefranche-de-Rouergue** France
229 G4 **Villefranche-sur-Saône** France
162 D3 **Villegas, Valle** *valley* Argentina
229 H3 **Villeneuve** Switzerland
228 D5 **Villeneuve-de-Marsan** France
228 F3 **Villeneuve-sur-Allier** France
228 E4 **Villeneuve-sur-Lot** France
228 F5 **Villepinte** France
228 F4 **Villeréal** France
127 P3 **Villeroy** Québec Canada
226 C2 **Villers-la-Ville** Belgium
229 H3 **Villersexel** France
228 E4 **Villesèque** France
154 C3 **Villeta** Colombia
229 G4 **Villeurbanne** France
308 E5 **Villiers** South Africa
225 J3 **Villinge** *island* Sweden
230 D2 **Villodrigo** Spain
226 G5 **Villorba** Italy
225 M5 **Vilniaus** *admin. area* Lithuania
225 M5 **Vilnius** Lithuania
158 E5 **Viloco** Bolivia
225 M1 **Vilppula** Finland
229 J3 **Vils** Austria
226 F3 **Vils** *watercourse* Germany
234 G1 **Vil'shanka** Ukraine
234 G1 **Vil'shanka** *watercourse* Ukraine
226 G3 **Vilshofen** Germany
232 H5 **Vilusi** Montenegro
158 D4 **Viluyo** Peru
229 G1 **Vilvoorde** Belgium
238 B4 **Viļyaka** Latvia
388 E6 **Vilyashchay** *watercourse* Azerbaijan
225 N5 **Vilyeyskaye, Vozyera** *lake* Belarus
237 Y6 **Vilyuy** *watercourse* Russian Federation
237 Z6 **Vilyuysk** Russian Federation
237 X5 **Vilyuyskoye Plato** *region* Russian Federation
237 X6 **Vilyuyskoye Vodokhranilishche** *lake* Russian Federation
230 B2 **Vimianzo** Spain
230 C4 **Vimieiro** Portugal
230 C3 **Vimioso** Portugal
224 H4 **Vimmerby** Sweden
223 M5 **Vimpeli** Finland
227 G3 **Vimperk** Czech Republic
305 H3 **Vina** *watercourse* Cameroon
160 D5 **Viña del Mar** Chile
160 D5 **Viña Sausiño** Chile
231 G3 **Vinaròs** Spain
226 C5 **Vinay** France
224 G4 **Vinberg** Sweden
122 B5 **Vincelotte, Lac** *lake* Québec Canada
126 H7 **Vincennes** Indiana USA
436 H2 **Vincennes Bay** Antarctica
425 inset **Vincent Point** Norfolk Island Australia
154 B5 **Vinces** Ecuador
160 D4 **Vinchina** Argentina
229 J5 **Vinci** Italy
222 J3 **Vindelälven** *watercourse* Sweden
222 K4 **Vindelgransele** Sweden
222 K4 **Vindeln** Sweden
393 D6 **Vindhya Range** Madhya Pradesh India
225 J3 **Vindö** *island* Sweden
224 I3 **Vindommen** *lake* Sweden
127 N7 **Vineland** New Jersey USA
228 E3 **Vineuil** France
234 B2 **Vinga** Romania
222 G5 **Vingelen** Norway
376 E3 **Vinh** Vietnam
376 F5 **Vinh Cam Rahn** *bay* Vietnam
376 E5 **Vinh Châu** Vietnam
376 E3 **Vinh Lộc** Vietnam
376 E5 **Vinh Long** Vietnam
376 E5 **Vinh Rach Giá** *bay* Vietnam
376 E2 **Vinh Thuc, Đao** *island* Vietnam
376 E2 **Vinh Tuy** Vietnam
376 F4 **Vinh Van Phong** *bay* Vietnam
230 C3 **Vinhais** Portugal
227 H5 **Vinica** Slovenia
436 S1 **Vinison Mastif** *mountain* Antarctica
126 D8 **Vinita** Oklahoma USA
224 D2 **Vinje** Norway
222 I3 **Vinknes** Norway
232 H4 **Vinkovci** Croatia
227 K3 **Vinné** Slovakia
238 F2 **Vinnitsy** Russian Federation
394 D3 **Vinnyts'ka Oblast'** *admin. area* Ukraine
394 D3 **Vinnytsya** Ukraine
224 I4 **Vinö** *island* Sweden
234 D4 **Vinogradets** Bulgaria
222 F6 **Vinsternes** Norway
222 F6 **Vinstra** Norway
222 F6 **Vinstra** *watercourse* Norway
118 K7 **Vinsulla** British Columbia Canada
234 E3 **Vintileasca** Romania
224 I2 **Vintjärn** Sweden
158 E5 **Vinto** Bolivia
126 E5 **Vinton** Iowa USA
130 E5 **Vinton** Louisiana USA
129 I5 **Vinton** Texas USA
127 L8 **Vinton** Virginia USA
234 C3 **Vinţu de Jos** Romania
230 E3 **Vinuesa** Spain
393 E8 **Vinukonda** Andhra Pradesh India
126 F6 **Viola** Illinois USA
130 C2 **Viola** Kansas USA
436 U2 **Violante Inlet** *bay* Antarctica
308 C5 **Vioolsdrif** South Africa
232 E4 **Vipava** *watercourse* Slovenia
232 D3 **Vipiteno** Italy
232 F4 **Vir** Croatia
232 F4 **Vir** *island* Croatia
377 J4 **Virac** Philippines
392 C6 **Viramgam** Gujarat India
236 I6 **Virandozero** Russian Federation
393 F7 **Virar** Maharashtra India
391 L5 **Virawah** Pakistan
223 Q5 **Virda** Russian Federation
119 U8 **Virden** Manitoba Canada
129 H4 **Virden** New Mexico USA
228 D2 **Vire** *watercourse* France
224 H4 **Viren** *lake* Sweden
225 N4 **Vireši** Latvia
162 C5 **Vírgenes, Cabo** *cape* Argentina
128 E2 **Virgin** *watercourse* Nevada USA
128 F2 **Virgin** Utah USA
135 H3 **Virgin Gorda** *island* Virgin Islands
Virgin Islands (UK) *see* **British Virgin Islands** Virgin Islands
135 H3 **Virgin Islands (USA)** *US territory* Caribbean
128 F2 **Virgin Mountains** Arkansas USA
245 E3 **Virginia** Ireland
308 E5 **Virginia** South Africa
115 **Virginia** *admin. area* USA
126 F7 **Virginia** Illinois USA
126 E3 **Virginia** Minnesota USA
127 N8 **Virginia Beach** Virginia USA
427 9a **Viria** Fiji
222 J3 **Virihaure** *lake* Sweden
232 G3 **Virje** Croatia
223 O4 **Virkkunen** Finland
223 O5 **Virmanpää** Finland
223 O5 **Virmas** *lake* Finland
223 O5 **Virmasvesi** *bay* Finland
225 N2 **Virolahden Kirkonkylä** Finland
232 G4 **Virovitica** Croatia
233 H5 **Virpazar** Montenegro
223 M5 **Virrat** Finland
158 B2 **Virrey Nuevo** Peru
224 H4 **Virserum** Sweden
223 P2 **Virtaniemi** Finland
225 M1 **Virtasalmi** Finland
229 G2 **Virton** Belgium
234 C3 **Virtop** Romania
158 B3 **Virú** Peru
238 B3 **Viru-Kabala** Estonia
232 G5 **Vis** Croatia
232 G5 **Vis** *island* Croatia
308 D6 **Vis** *watercourse* South Africa
128 C2 **Visalia** California USA
393 C7 **Visavadar** Gujarat India
377 I5 **Visayan Islands** Philippines
377 I5 **Visayan Sea** Philippines
226 E1 **Visbek** Germany
224 F4 **Visborg** Denmark
224 J4 **Visby** Sweden
116 H4 **Viscount Melville Sound** *strait* Northwest Territories/Nunavut Canada
229 G1 **Visé** Belgium
234 A4 **Višegrad** Bosnia and Herzegovina
229 K3 **Visentin, Col** *mountain* Italy
156 C3 **Viseu** Brazil
230 C3 **Viseu** Portugal
230 C3 **Viseu** *admin. area* Portugal
393 F8 **Vishakhapatnam** Andhra Pradesh India
234 F3 **Vishnëvoye** Ukraine
225 N5 **Vishnewskaye, Vozyera** *lake* Belarus
222 K4 **Viskasjön** *lake* Sweden
392 C6 **Visnagar** Gujarat India
229 L4 **Višnja Gora** Slovenia
227 H2 **Višňova** Czech Republic
229 H3 **Visp** Switzerland
222 J4 **Vispsjön** *lake* Sweden
235 B6 **Vissani** Greece
393 E8 **Vissannapeta** Andhra Pradesh India
224 H4 **Vissjön** *lake* Sweden
232 E5 **Visso** Italy
128 D4 **Vista** California USA
155 E5 **Vista Alegre** Brazil
159 G5 **Vista Alegre** Brazil
154 C4 **Vista Hermosa** Colombia
224 G3 **Visten** *lake* Sweden
222 L4 **Vistheden** Sweden
235 D5 **Vistonias, Ormos** *bay* Greece
235 D5 **Vistonida, Limni** *lake* Greece
225 L5 **Vištytis** Lithuania
225 L5 **Vištytis** *lake* Russian Federation
234 D4 **Vit** *watercourse* Bulgaria
393 D8 **Vita** Maharashtra India
391 L3 **Vitakri** Pakistan
222 L4 **Vitberget** Sweden
225 O5 **Vitebsk/Vitsyebskaya Voblasts'** *admin. area* Belarus
154 C3 **Viterbo** Colombia
233 E5 **Viterbo** Italy
235 B5 **Vithkuq** Albania
427 9 **Viti Levu** *island* Fiji
427 9a **Viti Levu Bay** Fiji
373 H5 **Vitiaz Strait** Papua New Guinea
159 E6 **Vitichi** Bolivia
230 C3 **Vitigudino** Spain
237 X7 **Vitim** Russian Federation
237 Y8 **Vitim** *watercourse* Russian Federation
385 G1 **Vitimskoye Ploskogor'ye** Russian Federation
237 X8 **Vitimskoye Ploskogor'ye** *region* Russian Federation
232 G5 **Vitina** Bosnia and Herzegovina
235 C7 **Vitina** Greece
235 B5 **Vitolište** Macedonia
158 C5 **Vitor** *watercourse* Peru
157 D8 **Vitória** Brazil
157 D6 **Vitória da Conquista** Brazil
230 E2 **Vitoria-Gasteiz** Spain
77 O12 **Vitória Seamount** *underwater feature* Atlantic Ocean
158 D3 **Vitória Velha** Brazil
154 C4 **Vitorino Freire** Brazil
228 D2 **Vitré** France
229 G5 **Vitrolles** France
225 P5 **Vitsyebsk** Belarus
222 L3 **Vittangi** Sweden
222 L2 **Vittangijaure** *lake* Sweden
229 G3 **Vitteaux** France
229 G2 **Vittel** France
222 L4 **Vittjärv** Sweden
233 F8 **Vittoria** Italy
226 G5 **Vittorio Veneto** Italy
223 M3 **Vittvattnet** Sweden
78 N9 **Vityaz Trench** *underwater feature* Pacific Ocean
231 F4 **Viver** Spain
230 C2 **Vivero** Spain
232 C4 **Viverone, Lago di** *lake* Italy
237 U5 **Vivi** *watercourse* Russian Federation
120 G8 **Vivian** Manitoba Canada
130 E4 **Vivian** Louisiana USA
373 I6 **Vivigani** Papua New Guinea
161 G6 **Vivoratá** Argentina
427 9 **Viwa** *island* Fiji
158 D4 **Vizcachane** Peru
158 E6 **Vizcachilla** Bolivia
132 B3 **Vizcaíno, Sierra** *range* Mexico
230 E2 **Vizcaya, Golfo de** *bay* Spain
235 E5 **Vize** Turkey
236 Q3 **Vize, Ostrov** *island* Russian Federation
393 F7 **Vizianagaram** Andhra Pradesh India
122 B3 **Vizien** *watercourse* Québec Canada
227 G5 **Vižinada** Croatia
223 Q3 **Viziyarvi, Ozero** *lake* Russian Federation
235 A5 **Vjosë** *watercourse* Albania
234 E3 **Vlădeni** Romania
234 F3 **Vlădeşti** Romania
234 C4 **Vladičin Han** Serbia
388 D5 **Vladikavkaz** Russian Federation
236 J7 **Vladimir** Russian Federation
388 C2 **Vladimirskaya** *admin. area* Russian Federation
238 H4 **Vladimirskaya Oblast'** *admin. area* Russian Federation
386 F2 **Vladivostok** Russian Federation
238 H3 **Vladychnoye** Russian Federation
235 B7 **Vlakhópoulon** Greece
234 B4 **Vlase** Serbia
232 H4 **Vlasenica** Bosnia and Herzegovina
227 H3 **Vlašim** Czech Republic
234 C4 **Vlasinsko Jezero** *lake* Serbia
389 P2 **Vlas'yevo** *lake* Russian Federation
226 C1 **Vlieland** *island* Netherlands
226 B2 **Vlissingen** Netherlands
235 C6 **Vlochos** Greece
235 A5 **Vlorë** Albania
235 A5 **Vlorës, Gjiri i** *bay* Albania
226 E1 **Vlotho** Germany
227 G3 **Vltava** *watercourse* Czech Republic
388 I6 **Vobkent** Uzbekistan
235 E4 **Voden** Bulgaria
234 G1 **Vodjanoye** Ukraine
223 T5 **Vodla** Russian Federation
238 G1 **Vodlozero, Ozero** *lake* Russian Federation
223 T5 **Vodlozerskiy National Park** Russian Federation
227 H3 **Vodňany** Czech Republic
229 K4 **Vodnjan** Croatia
226 D2 **Voerde** Germany
226 E5 **Voghera** Italy
222 F5 **Vognill** Norway
229 K2 **Vohenstrauß** Germany
309 I4 **Vohilava** Madagascar
309 I5 **Vohimena, Tanjon'i** *cape* Madagascar
307 F4 **Voi** Kenya
307 F4 **Voi** *watercourse* Kenya
227 M5 **Voiceşti** Romania
229 G2 **Void-Vacon** France
225 M3 **Võidu** Estonia
234 C3 **Voineasa** Romania
229 G2 **Voire** *watercourse* France
229 G4 **Voiron** France
227 H4 **Voitsberg** Austria
225 M3 **Võivaku** Estonia
224 E5 **Vojens** Denmark
222 J4 **Vojmsjön** *lake* Sweden
232 F4 **Vojnić** Croatia
227 H4 **Vojnik** Slovenia

373 H4 **Vokeo Island** Papua New Guinea
223 Q4 **Voknavolok** Russian Federation
238 B5 **Volas, Vozyera** *lake* Belarus
158 E6 **Volcán, Cerro** *volcano* Argentina
162 F1 **Volcán, Sierra del** *range* Argentina
128 inset **Volcano** Hawai'i USA
389 M3 **Volchikha** Russian Federation
222 E5 **Volda** Norway
238 H4 **Volga** Russian Federation
238 H4 **Volga** *watercourse* Russian Federation
125 Q4 **Volga** South Dakota USA
388 D4 **Volgodonsk** Russian Federation
238 G4 **Volgograd** Russian Federation
388 D3 **Volgogradskaya** *admin. area* Russian Federation
235 B7 **Volimai** Greece
234 F2 **Volintiri** Moldova
232 G5 **Voljevac** Bosnia and Herzegovina
227 H4 **Völkermarkt** Austria
225 Q3 **Volkhov** Russian Federation
225 Q3 **Volkov** *watercourse* Russian Federation
225 O6 **Volma** Belarus
394 E3 **Vol'n'ansk** Ukraine
394 F3 **Volnovakha** Ukraine
237 T4 **Volochanka** Russian Federation
234 E1 **Volochys'k** Ukraine
238 H3 **Vologda** Russian Federation
238 G3 **Vologodskaya Oblast'** *admin. area* Russian Federation
238 F4 **Volokolamsk** Russian Federation
238 H3 **Volokoslavinskoye** Russian Federation
236 K5 **Volokovaya** Russian Federation
223 R5 **Voloma** Russian Federation
235 C6 **Volos** Greece
238 I2 **Voloshka** Russian Federation
225 O3 **Voloshovo** Russian Federation
225 O5 **Volosovo** Belarus
238 C3 **Volosovo** Russian Federation
225 P4 **Volot** Russian Federation
227 L3 **Volovets'** Ukraine
238 H6 **Volovo** Russian Federation
225 P2 **Voloyarvi** Russian Federation
238 F5 **Voloye** Russian Federation
223 S5 **Volozero, Ozero** *lake* Russian Federation
388 E3 **Vo'lsk** Russian Federation
304 E3 **Volta** *watercourse* Ghana
304 D3 **Volta, Lake** *lake* Ghana
232 D5 **Volterra** Italy
229 I4 **Voltri** Italy
223 M5 **Voltti** Finland
233 F6 **Volturno** *watercourse* Italy
162 E1 **Voluntad** Argentina
235 C5 **Volvi, Limni** *lake* Greece
394 C2 **Volyns'ka Oblast'** *admin. area* Ukraine
388 E2 **Volzhsk** Russian Federation
388 D4 **Volzhskiy** Russian Federation
224 G5 **Vombsjön** *lake* Sweden
427 9a **Vomo** *island* Fiji
234 D4 **Voneshta Voda** Bulgaria
131 I3 **Vonore** Tennessee USA
225 N3 **Võõpsu** Estonia
222 inset **Vopnafjörður** Iceland
222 inset **Vopnafjörður** *bay* Iceland
225 M5 **Voranava** Belarus
226 E4 **Vorarlberg** *admin. area* Austria
235 B5 **Voras** *range* Macedonia
235 D6 **Voreio Aigaio** *admin. area* Greece
223 S5 **Vorenzha** Russian Federation
435 G2 **Voring Plateau** *underwater feature* Norwegian Sea
379 G3 **Vorjing** *mountain* Xizang Zizhiqu China
379 H3 **Vorjing** *mountain* Arunachal Pradesh India
236 N5 **Vorkuta** Russian Federation
225 L3 **Vormsi** *island* Estonia
388 C3 **Vorob'yevka** Russian Federation
238 F5 **Vorob'yëvo** Russian Federation
162 F2 **Vorohué, Punta** *cape* Argentina
394 F2 **Voronezh** Russian Federation
394 F2 **Voronezh** *watercourse* Russian Federation
388 C3 **Voronezhskaya Oblast'** *admin. area* Russian Federation
435 L1 **Voronin Trough** *underwater feature* Arctic Ocean
237 U3 **Voronina, Ostrov** *island* Russian Federation
435 F1 **Voronov Plateau** *underwater feature* Arctic Ocean
225 O3 **Voronovo** Russian Federation
234 G1 **Voronoye** Ukraine
234 H2 **Vorontsovka** Ukraine
237 AE5 **Vorontsovo** Russian Federation
225 P5 **Vorony** Belarus
227 M3 **Voronyaky** *region* Ukraine
238 E5 **Vorot'kovo** Russian Federation
388 E2 **Vorotynets** Russian Federation
436 B2 **Vorposten Peak** *mountain* Antarctica
222 L2 **Vorterøy** *island* Norway
225 N3 **Võrtsjärv** *lake* Estonia
225 N4 **Võru** Estonia
389 K6 **Voruk** Tajikistan
225 N4 **Võrumaa** *admin. area* Estonia
229 H2 **Vosges** *range* France
238 H4 **Voshchazhnikovo** Russian Federation
225 L5 **Vosiliškis** Lithuania
235 B5 **Voskopojë** Albania
238 H5 **Voskresensk** Russian Federation
234 H2 **Voskresens'ke** Ukraine
238 G3 **Voskresenskoye** Russian Federation
388 E2 **Voskresenskoye** Russian Federation
388 G2 **Voskresenskoye** Russian Federation
223 R2 **Vosmus** Russian Federation
234 H2 **Vossiyatskoye** Ukraine
236 I5 **Vostochnaya Litsa** Russian Federation
389 N4 **Vostochno-Kazakstanskaya Oblast'** *admin. area* Kazakhstan
237 AH4 **Vostochno-Sibirskoye More** *sea* Russian Federation
237 U8 **Vostochnyy Sayan** *range* Russian Federation
437 G1 **Vostok, Lake** Antarctica
436 H1 **Vostok (Russia)** *research station* Antarctica
426 1 **Vostok Island** Kiribati
225 M3 **Võsu** Estonia
426 7 **Vot Tandé** *island* Vanuatu
227 H3 **Votice** Czech Republic
388 G1 **Votkinsk** Russian Federation
426 7 **Votlo** Vanuatu
235 B6 **Votonosion** Greece
226 C3 **Voué** France
230 C3 **Vouga** *watercourse* Portugal
229 G3 **Vougeot** France
235 C8 **Voukolies** Greece
228 D3 **Vouvant** France
235 C8 **Vouxa, Akrotirio** *cape* Greece
229 G2 **Vouziers** France
228 E2 **Voves** France
306 D2 **Vovondo** *watercourse* Central African Republic
223 Q4 **Voynitsa** Russian Federation
426 8 **Voza** Solomon Islands
238 H2 **Vozhe, Ozero** *lake* Russian Federation
238 I2 **Vozhega** Russian Federation
389 K3 **Voznesenka** Kazakhstan
238 F2 **Voznesen'ye** Russian Federation
234 G2 **Voznesens'k** Ukraine
389 K2 **Vozvyshenka** Kazakhstan
224 E4 **Vrå** Denmark
224 G4 **Vrå** Sweden
234 C4 **Vrachesh** Bulgaria
234 G2 **Vradiyivka** Ukraine
234 E3 **Vrancea** *admin. area* Romania
237 AL4 **Vrangelya, Ostrov** *island* Russian Federation
233 H5 **Vranj** Montenegro
234 B4 **Vranje** Serbia
235 A5 **Vrap** Albania
234 C3 **Vrata** Romania
234 B4 **Vratnica** Macedonia
234 C4 **Vratsa** *admin. area* Bulgaria
232 G4 **Vrbanja** Bosnia and Herzegovina
227 J5 **Vrbanja** Croatia
232 G4 **Vrbas** *watercourse* Bosnia and Herzegovina
234 A3 **Vrbas** Serbia
227 I5 **Vrbaška** Bosnia and Herzegovina
232 G4 **Vrbovljani** Croatia
232 F4 **Vrbovsko** Croatia
227 H2 **Vrchlabí** Czech Republic
227 K5 **Vrčin** Serbia
227 H3 **Vrdy** Czech Republic
308 C6 **Vredenburg** South Africa
308 C6 **Vredendal** South Africa
155 G3 **Vreed en Hoop** Guyana
232 F5 **Vrgada** *island* Croatia
232 G5 **Vrgorac** Croatia
227 I5 **Vrhopolje** Bosnia and Herzegovina
227 H5 **Vrhovine** Croatia
235 B7 **Vrisai** Greece
224 G3 **Vristulven** *lake* Sweden
235 B6 **Vromonas** *island* Greece
241 I4 **Vron** France
235 B5 **Vronterón** Greece
235 B6 **Vrosina** Greece
234 B3 **Vršac** Serbia
232 E4 **Vrsar** Croatia
232 F4 **Vrsi** Croatia
225 O3 **Vruda** Russian Federation
232 F5 **Vrulje** Croatia
235 B5 **Vrutok** Macedonia
308 D5 **Vryburg** South Africa
308 F5 **Vryheid** South Africa
227 I3 **Vsetín** Czech Republic
116 C8 **Vsevidof, Mount** Alaska USA
225 P3 **Vsevolozhsk** Russian Federation
376 E2 **Vụ Bản** Vietnam
427 9 **Vuagava** *island* Fiji
306 D3 **Vube** Democratic Republic of Congo
234 D4 **Vǔbel** Bulgaria
226 C2 **Vught** Netherlands
227 H4 **Vuhred** Slovenia
227 J5 **Vuka** Croatia
234 C4 **Vukan** Bulgaria
232 H4 **Vukovar** Croatia
308 E5 **Vukuzakhe** South Africa
377 G3 **Vuladdore Reef** Paracel Islands
119 O7 **Vulcan** Alberta Canada
233 F7 **Vulcano, Isola** *island* Italy
234 E4 **Vǔlchidol** Bulgaria
227 M5 **Vulturești** Romania
234 E3 **Vulturu de Jos** Romania
376 E5 **Vũng Tàu** Vietnam
427 9a **Vunindawa** Fiji
427 9 **Vunisei** Fiji
116 F5 **Vuntut National Park** Yukon Territory Canada
222 J3 **Vuoggatjålmjaure** *lake* Sweden
223 O2 **Vuogojarvi** *lake* Finland
225 N2 **Vuohijärvi** *lake* Finland
223 O3 **Vuojärvi** Finland
222 K3 **Vuojat** Sweden
223 P4 **Vuokatti** Finland
223 P4 **Vuokkijärvi** *lake* Finland
223 P5 **Vuokko** Finland
222 K3 **Vuolep Kaitumjaure** *lake* Sweden
223 N3 **Vuolijoki** Finland
222 L3 **Vuollerim** Sweden
222 K3 **Vuollerim** *bay* Sweden
223 M3 **Vuomajärvi** Sweden
223 N2 **Vuontisjärvi** Finland
223 P2 **Vuopioniemi** Finland
223 P3 **Vuori-Yarvi, Ozero** *lake* Russian Federation
223 N5 **Vuorilahti** Finland
223 P4 **Vuosanganjärvi** *lake* Finland
225 M1 **Vuosjärvi** *lake* Finland
223 P3 **Vuosnayarvi, Ozero** *lake* Russian Federation
223 O3 **Vuostimo** Finland
225 O1 **Vuotjärvi** *lake* Finland
223 O2 **Vuotso** Finland
222 L3 **Vuottas** Sweden
223 O4 **Vuottolahti** Finland
223 P3 **Vuotunki** Finland
223 M5 **Vurpăr** Romania
225 N5 **Vustsye** Belarus
234 E2 **Vutcani** Romania
234 F2 **Vvedenka** Ukraine
223 S3 **Vyalozero, Ozero** *lake* Russian Federation
393 C7 **Vyara** Gujarat India
223 Q5 **Vyartsilya** Russian Federation
236 L7 **Vyatka** *watercourse* Russian Federation
238 C6 **Vyaz'ma** Belarus
238 F5 **Vyaz'ma** Russian Federation
388 D3 **Vyazovka** Russian Federation
388 E4 **Vyazovka** Russian Federation
238 C6 **Vyaz'ye** Belarus
225 N5 **Vyazyn'** Belarus
238 C4 **Vybor** Russian Federation
225 O2 **Vyborg** Russian Federation
236 K6 **Vychegda** *watercourse* Russian Federation
225 O5 **Vydritsa** Belarus
225 O5 **Vyesnitsk** Belarus
223 S5 **Vygozero, Ozero** *lake* Russian Federation
234 C1 **Vyhorlat** *mountain* Slovakia
225 P5 **Vykhodtsy** Belarus
388 D2 **Vyksa** Russian Federation
234 F3 **Vylkove** Ukraine
227 L3 **Vylok** Ukraine
236 L6 **Vym'** *watercourse* Russian Federation
236 O6 **Vyngapur** Russian Federation
234 D1 **Vynnyky** Ukraine
238 E4 **Vypolzovo** Russian Federation
225 O3 **Vyra** Russian Federation
225 P3 **Vyritsa** Russian Federation
240 D2 **Vyrnwy, Lake** Wales UK
388 C4 **Vyselki** Russian Federation
238 C4 **Vyshgorodok** Russian Federation
234 C1 **Vyshkove** Ukraine
238 F4 **Vyshkovo** Russian Federation
238 F4 **Vyshniy-Volochek** Russian Federation
225 O3 **Vyskatka** Russian Federation
225 P4 **Vyskod'** Russian Federation
232 G2 **Vyškov** Czech Republic
227 H3 **Vysočina Kraj** *admin. area* Czech Republic
227 L1 **Vysokaye** Belarus
237 AE3 **Vysokiy, Mys** *cape* Russian Federation
238 B4 **Vysokiy Most** Russian Federation
238 H4 **Vysokovo** Russian Federation
238 G4 **Vysokovsk** Russian Federation
238 F4 **Vysokoye** Russian Federation
232 G2 **Vytegra** Russian Federation
237 AI6 **Vyvenka** *watercourse* Russian Federation
234 D1 **Vyzhnytsya** Ukraine
387 I1 **Vzmor'ye** Russian Federation

W

131 K2 **W. Kerr Scott Reservoir** North Carolina USA
304 D2 **Wa** Ghana
307 G3 **Waajid** Somalia
120 H6 **Waasagomach** Manitoba Canada
306 E2 **Waat** Sudan
373 G5 **Waawoi** *watercourse* Papua New Guinea
120 L7 **Wababimiga Lake** Ontario Canada
120 K7 **Wabakimi Lake** Ontario Canada
119 N6 **Wabamun Lake** Alberta Canada
116 H7 **Wabasca** *watercourse* Alberta Canada
126 I6 **Wabash** Indiana USA
126 H7 **Wabash** *watercourse* Indiana USA
120 L7 **Wabassi** *watercourse* Ontario Canada
242 E2 **Waberthwaite** Cumbria England UK
302 E3 **Wabi, Wādi** *watercourse* Sudan
307 G2 **Wabi Gestro** *watercourse* Ethiopia
307 G2 **Wabi Shēbelē** *watercourse* Ethiopia
120 I8 **Wabigoon Lake** Ontario Canada
120 M7 **Wabimeig Lake** Ontario Canada
373 J6 **Waboma Island** Papua New Guinea
119 V5 **Wabowden** Manitoba Canada
227 J1 **Wąbrzeźno** Poland
381 G2 **Wabu-hu** *lake* Anhui China
373 G6 **Wabuda Island** Papua New Guinea
120 M5 **Wabuk Point** Ontario Canada
121 V6 **Wabush** Newfoundland and Labrador Canada
128 C1 **Wabuska** Nevada USA
131 L3 **Waccamaw, Lake** North Carolina USA
133 J2 **Waccasassa Bay** Florida USA
307 F3 **Wach'īlē** Ethiopia
226 E2 **Wächtersbach** Germany
121 W7 **Waco** Québec Canada
130 C5 **Waco** Texas USA
130 C5 **Waco Lake** Texas USA
125 P7 **Waconda Lake** Kansas USA
391 K4 **Wad** Pakistan
302 D5 **Wad Banda** Sudan
302 D5 **Wad Hassib** Sudan
302 E5 **Wad Medani** Sudan
302 E4 **Wad Rawa** Sudan
301 J3 **Waddān** Libya
226 C1 **Waddeneilanden** *region* Netherlands
425 M8 **Waddi** NSW Australia
127 N3 **Waddington** Québec Canada
127 N4 **Waddington** New York USA
118 I7 **Waddington, Mount** British Columbia Canada
122 F5 **Wade Lake** Newfoundland and Labrador Canada
240 E4 **Wadeford** Somerset England UK
119 T7 **Wadena** Saskatchewan Canada
125 R3 **Wadena** Minnesota USA
226 D3 **Wadern** Germany
226 E2 **Wadersloh** Germany
131 K3 **Wadesboro** North Carolina USA
424 I3 **Wadeye** NT Australia
393 D7 **Wadgaon** Maharashtra India
123 L8 **Wadham Islands** Newfoundland and Labrador Canada
305 I2 **Wadi Fira** *admin. area* Chad
302 E3 **Wādī Halfa** Sudan
305 I2 **Wadibra** *watercourse* Sudan
119 S5 **Wadin Bay** Saskatchewan Canada
131 I4 **Wadley** Alabama USA
131 J4 **Wadley** Georgia USA
227 J3 **Wadowice** Poland
127 K6 **Wadsworth** Ohio USA
393 D7 **Wadwani** Maharashtra India
130 C6 **Waelder** Texas USA
436 P1 **Waesche, Mount** *mountain* Antarctica
385 J5 **Wafangdian** Liaoning China
372 C4 **Waflia** Indonesia
244 E2 **Wag** Highland Scotland UK
373 G4 **Wagasu** *watercourse* Papua New Guinea
226 E1 **Wagenfeld** Germany
155 G3 **Wageningen** Suriname
162 A4 **Wager, Isla** *island* Chile
117 K5 **Wager Bay** Nunavut Canada
425 M8 **Wagga Wagga** NSW Australia
424 F8 **Wagin** WA Australia
125 P5 **Wagner** South Dakota USA
129 J3 **Wagon Mound** New Mexico USA
130 D3 **Wagoner** Oklahoma USA
227 H1 **Wągrowiec** Poland
128 F1 **Wah Wah Mountains** Utah USA
304 D2 **Wahabu** Ghana
372 D4 **Wahai** Indonesia
304 E3 **Wahala** Togo
122 C6 **Wahemen, Lac** *lake* Québec Canada
128 inset **Wahiawā** Hawai'i USA
304 C2 **Wahiré** Côte d'Ivoire
125 Q6 **Wahoo** Nebraska USA
125 Q3 **Wahpeton** North Dakota USA
302 C2 **Wāḥūt Jalū** Libya
128 inset **Waiakoa** Hawai'i USA
422 H3 **Waiapu** *watercourse* New Zealand
423 C7 **Waiatoto** *watercourse* New Zealand
423 E6 **Waiau** New Zealand
423 E6 **Waiau** *watercourse* New Zealand
227 H3 **Waidhofen** Austria
372 B6 **Waienga-one** *bay* Indonesia
372 D4 **Waigama** Indonesia
372 D4 **Waigeo** *island* Indonesia
422 F3 **Waiheke Island** New Zealand
422 F3 **Waihi** New Zealand
422 F3 **Waihi Beach** New Zealand
423 D6 **Waiho** *watercourse* New Zealand
423 E5 **Waihopai** *watercourse* New Zealand
372 A6 **Waikabubak** Indonesia
423 C7 **Waikaia** New Zealand
423 C7 **Waikaka** New Zealand
423 F5 **Waikanae** New Zealand
422 F3 **Waikare, Lake** New Zealand
422 G4 **Waikaremoana, Lake** New Zealand
422 F4 **Waikato** *admin. area* New Zealand
422 F3 **Waikato** *watercourse* New Zealand
423 C8 **Waikawa** New Zealand
372 A6 **Waikelo** Indonesia
128 inset **Waiki'i** Hawai'i USA
422 G4 **Waikite Valley** New Zealand
423 D7 **Waikouaiti** New Zealand
423 E6 **Waikuku Beach** New Zealand
128 inset **Wailua** Hawai'i USA
422 G4 **Waimana** *watercourse* New Zealand
372 A6 **Waimanguar** Indonesia
422 G4 **Waimarama** New Zealand
423 D7 **Waimate** New Zealand
128 inset **Waimea** Hawai'i USA
426 8 **Wainaworasi** Solomon Islands
243 I3 **Wainfleet All Saints** Lincolnshire England UK
372 B6 **Waingapu** Indonesia
155 G3 **Waini** *watercourse* Guyana
155 G2 **Waini Point** *cape* Guyana
423 F5 **Wainuioru** New Zealand
116 C4 **Wainwright** Alaska USA
422 F4 **Waiouru** New Zealand
372 F4 **Waipa** Indonesia
128 inset **Waipahu** Hawai'i USA
423 C8 **Waipapa Point** New Zealand
423 E6 **Waipara** New Zealand
119 N7 **Waiparous** Alberta Canada
422 G4 **Waipawa** New Zealand
422 G4 **Waipawa** *watercourse* New Zealand
422 H4 **Waipiro Bay** New Zealand
422 E2 **Waipoua Settlement** New Zealand
422 F2 **Waipu** New Zealand
422 G4 **Waipukurau** New Zealand
422 G4 **Wairakei** New Zealand
423 E5 **Wairau** *watercourse* New Zealand
306 E3 **Wairingo** *watercourse* Uganda
422 G4 **Wairoa** New Zealand
422 G4 **Wairoa** *watercourse* New Zealand
372 B6 **Wairunu** Indonesia
423 D6 **Waitaha** *watercourse* New Zealand
422 G4 **Waitahanui** New Zealand
423 C7 **Waitahuna** New Zealand
422 F3 **Waitakere** New Zealand
423 D7 **Waitaki** *watercourse* New Zealand
422 F2 **Waitangi** New Zealand
422 F4 **Waitara** New Zealand
422 F4 **Waitara** *watercourse* New Zealand
422 F5 **Waitarere** New Zealand
436 Q2 **Waite, Cape** Antarctica
425 inset **Waite, Mount** Macquarie Island Australia
422 E2 **Waitiki Landing** New Zealand
422 F3 **Waitoa** New Zealand
422 F4 **Waitomo Caves** New Zealand
422 F4 **Waitotara** New Zealand
422 F4 **Waitotara** *watercourse* New Zealand
124 F3 **Waitsburg** Washington USA
422 F3 **Waiuku** New Zealand
373 I6 **Waiwa** Papua New Guinea
422 F3 **Waiwera** New Zealand
387 H4 **Wajima** Japan
307 G3 **Wajir** Kenya
306 C3 **Waka** Democratic Republic of Congo
307 F2 **Waka** Ethiopia
372 B6 **Waka** Indonesia
372 C4 **Waka, Tanjung** *cape* Indonesia
155 G4 **Wakadanawa** Brazil
423 E5 **Wakamarama Range** New Zealand
387 G4 **Wakasa-wan** *bay* Japan
423 C7 **Wakatipu, Lake** New Zealand
119 S6 **Wakaw** Saskatchewan Canada
427 9 **Wakaya** *island* Fiji
373 F4 **Wakde** *island* Indonesia
131 L3 **Wake Forest** North Carolina USA
418 **Wake Island** *unincorporated US territory* Pacific Ocean
125 P7 **WaKeeney** Kansas USA
423 E5 **Wakefield** New Zealand
243 G3 **Wakefield** West Yorkshire England UK
126 G3 **Wakefield** Michigan USA
127 M8 **Wakefield** Virginia USA
122 B2 **Wakeham, Baie** *bay* Québec Canada
376 B3 **Wakema** Myanmar
241 G2 **Wakerley** Northamptonshire England UK
129 N2 **Wakita** Oklahoma USA
387 I2 **Wakkanai** Japan
373 I5 **Wako** Papua New Guinea
119 V8 **Wakopa** Manitoba Canada
308 C2 **Waku Kungo** Angola
122 E5 **Wakuach, Lac** *lake* Québec Canada
127 K1 **Wakwayowkastic** *watercourse* Ontario Canada
306 D2 **Wal Athiang** Sudan
372 B5 **Walanae** *watercourse* Indonesia
227 I2 **Wałbrzych** Poland
425 N7 **Walcha** NSW Australia
226 F4 **Walchensee** *lake* Germany
241 I2 **Walcott** Norfolk England UK
124 I5 **Walcott, Lake** Idaho USA
229 G1 **Walcourt** Belgium
227 I1 **Wałcz** Poland
232 C3 **Wald** Switzerland
307 F3 **Walde** *watercourse* Ethiopia
119 R7 **Waldeck** Saskatchewan Canada
229 I1 **Waldeck** Germany
125 L6 **Walden** Colorado USA
125 L6 **Walden Reservoir** Colorado USA
226 D3 **Waldkirch** Germany
226 E4 **Waldkirch** Switzerland
226 G3 **Waldkraiburg** Germany
131 J6 **Waldo** Florida USA
124 D5 **Waldo Lake** Oregon USA
124 C4 **Waldport** Oregon USA
130 D3 **Waldron** Arkansas USA
436 H2 **Waldron, Cape** Antarctica
227 H3 **Waldviertel** *region* Austria
372 B4 **Walea, Selat** *strait* Indonesia
372 B4 **Waleakodi** *island* Indonesia
240 D2 **Wales** *admin. area* UK
128 G1 **Wales** Utah USA
122 C2 **Wales Island** Nunavut Canada
243 H3 **Walesby** Nottinghamshire England UK
304 D2 **Walewale** Ghana
126 F6 **Walford** Iowa USA
425 N7 **Walgett** NSW Australia
436 Q1 **Walgreen Coast** Antarctica
125 Q2 **Walhalla** North Dakota USA
306 D4 **Walikale** Democratic Republic of Congo
372 E5 **Walir** *island* Indonesia
373 G4 **Walis Island** Papua New Guinea
243 F3 **Walkden** Greater Manchester England UK
126 I5 **Walker** Michigan USA
125 R3 **Walker** Minnesota USA
131 L7 **Walker Cay** Bahamas
163 7 **Walker Creek** Falkland Islands
120 G5 **Walker Lake** Manitoba Canada
128 C1 **Walker Lake** Nevada USA
436 R2 **Walker Mountains** Antarctica
127 K4 **Walkerton** Ontario Canada
125 N5 **Wall** South Dakota USA
124 F3 **Walla Walla** Washington USA
125 O6 **Wallace** Nebraska USA
131 M3 **Wallace** North Carolina USA
119 N5 **Wallace Mountain** Alberta Canada
127 J5 **Wallaceburg** Ontario Canada
423 C8 **Wallacetown** New Zealand
425 K8 **Wallaroo** SA Australia
242 E3 **Wallasey** Merseyside England UK
229 I2 **Walldürn** Germany
308 C6 **Wallekraal** South Africa
127 N6 **Wallenpaupack, Lake** Pennsylvania USA
130 D5 **Waller** Texas USA
226 G3 **Wallersdorf** Germany
226 G4 **Wallersee** *lake* Austria
229 J3 **Wallgau** Germany
163 11a **Wallilabou** St Vincent and the Grenadines
241 F3 **Wallingford** Oxfordshire England UK
427 12 **Wallis, Îles** *island* Wallis and Futuna
427 12 **Wallis and Futuna** *French overseas territory* Pacific Ocean
124 G4 **Wallowa Lake** Oregon USA
244 inset **Walls** Shetland Scotland UK
224 E5 **Wallsbüll** Germany
242 E2 **Walney, Isle of** England UK
126 D6 **Walnut** Iowa USA
130 G3 **Walnut** Mississippi USA
131 K2 **Walnut Cove** North Carolina USA
131 M3 **Walnut Creek** North Carolina USA
130 F2 **Walnut Ridge** Arkansas USA
130 C4 **Walnut Springs** Texas USA
424 F8 **Walpole** WA Australia
125 O2 **Walpole** Saskatchewan Canada
121 P6 **Walrus, Pointe** *lake* Québec Canada
121 N1 **Walrus Island** Nunavut Canada
243 G4 **Walsall** *admin. area* England UK
241 F2 **Walsall** West Midlands England UK
125 M8 **Walsenburg** Colorado USA
125 J2 **Walsh** Alberta Canada
125 N8 **Walsh** Colorado USA
241 H2 **Walsham le Willows** Suffolk England UK
226 E1 **Walsrode** Germany
131 I5 **Walter F. George Reservoir** Georgia USA
131 K4 **Walterboro** South Carolina USA
130 B3 **Walters** Oklahoma USA
80 I8 **Walters Shoal** *underwater feature* Indian Ocean
125 Q5 **Walthill** Nebraska USA
131 K5 **Walthourville** Georgia USA
240 D2 **Walton** Powys Wales UK
129 N1 **Walton** Kansas USA
240 C3 **Walton East** Pembrokeshire Wales UK
308 B4 **Walvis Bay** Namibia
80 E7 **Walvis Ridge** *underwater feature* Atlantic Ocean
243 F1 **Walwick** Northumberland England UK
240 B3 **Walwyn's Castle** Pembrokeshire Wales UK
306 E3 **Wamala, Lake** Uganda
304 D3 **Wamanfo** Ghana
372 E5 **Wamar** *island* Indonesia
306 D3 **Wamba** Democratic Republic of Congo
306 B5 **Wamba** *watercourse* Democratic Republic of Congo
305 F3 **Wamba** Nigeria
373 F5 **Wamena** Indonesia
378 E2 **Wamo Zangbo** *watercourse* Xizang Zizhiqu China
120 H8 **Wampum** Manitoba Canada
134 C4 **Wampusirpi** Honduras
125 L6 **Wamsutter** Wyoming USA
372 C4 **Wamulan** Indonesia
379 I5 **Wan Singpyin** Myanmar
391 L3 **Wana** Pakistan
425 M7 **Wanaaring** NSW Australia
423 C7 **Wanaka** New Zealand
423 C7 **Wanaka, Lake** New Zealand
163 1c **Wanapa** Netherlands Antilles
127 K3 **Wanapitei Lake** Ontario Canada
134 C4 **Wanblán** Nicaragua
423 D7 **Wanbrow, Cape** New Zealand
302 F5 **Wancha** Ethiopia
372 B5 **Wanci** Indonesia
372 F4 **Wandai** Indonesia
155 G3 **Wandaik Village** Guyana
117 R2 **Wandel Sea** Greenland
119 O5 **Wandering River** Alberta Canada
380 C4 **Wanding** Yunnan China
425 N6 **Wandoan** Qld Australia
373 H5 **Wandokai** Papua New Guinea
241 G3 **Wandsworth** Greater London England UK
130 C3 **Wanette** Oklahoma USA
226 F2 **Wanfried** Germany
376 D3 **Wang Saphung** Thailand
306 D3 **Wanga** Democratic Republic of Congo
422 F4 **Wanganui** New Zealand
423 D6 **Wanganui** *watercourse* New Zealand
425 M9 **Wangaratta** Vic. Australia
304 D3 **Wangasi-turu** Ghana
385 I6 **Wangcon** Shandong China
379 F3 **Wangdi Phodrang** Bhutan
385 H5 **Wangdu** Hebei China
372 B6 **Wanggamet, Gunung** *mountain* Indonesia
372 E4 **Wanggar** *watercourse* Indonesia
372 B5 **Wangiwangi** *island* Indonesia
381 G2 **Wangjiang** Anhui China
385 K3 **Wangkui** Heilongjiang China
126 J3 **Wangoon Lake** Ontario Canada
385 L4 **Wangqing** Jilin China
381 H1 **Wangying** Jiangsu China
393 E7 **Wani** Maharashtra India
134 C4 **Waní** Nicaragua
306 D3 **Wanie Rukula** Democratic Republic of Congo
426 8 **Wanione** Solomon Islands
392 C6 **Wankaner** Gujarat India
307 G3 **Wanlaweyn** Somalia
119 U5 **Wanless** Manitoba Canada
241 F2 **Wanlip** Leicester England UK
380 F5 **Wanning** Hainan China
241 G2 **Wansford** Peterborough England UK
380 F3 **Wanshan** Guizhou China
422 G5 **Wanstead** New Zealand
241 F3 **Wantage** Oxfordshire England UK
127 K3 **Wanup** Ontario Canada
380 E2 **Wanyuan** Sichuan China
229 G1 **Wanze** Belgium
381 H2 **Wanzhi** Anhui China
380 E2 **Wanzhou** Chongqing China
226 F1 **Wanzleben** Germany
126 I6 **Wapakoneta** Ohio USA
120 J5 **Wapaseese** *watercourse* Ontario Canada
119 S5 **Wapawekka Lake** Saskatchewan Canada
119 V4 **Wapawsik** Manitoba Canada
120 K6 **Wapekeka** Ontario Canada
119 U7 **Wapella** Saskatchewan Canada
126 F6 **Wapello** Iowa USA
120 J7 **Wapikaimaski Lake** Ontario Canada
120 I5 **Wapikani** *watercourse* Manitoba Canada
120 L6 **Wapikopa Lake** Ontario Canada
118 L5 **Wapiti** *watercourse* Alberta Canada
240 E3 **Wapley** South Gloucestershire England UK
372 F4 **Wapoga** *watercourse* Indonesia
372 C4 **Wapotih** Indonesia
130 F2 **Wappapello, Lake** Missouri USA
373 G5 **Wapumba Island** Papua New Guinea
117 J7 **Wapusk National Park** Manitoba Canada
123 I7 **Wapustagamau, Lac** *lake* Québec Canada
380 D1 **Waqên** Sichuan China
227 L3 **Wara** Poland
304 B3 **Wara Wara Mountains** *range* Sierra Leone
306 D2 **Warab** Sudan
306 D2 **Warab** *admin. area* Sudan
372 D4 **Warakaraket** *island* Indonesia
424 I6 **Warakurna Roadhouse** WA Australia
307 G2 **Warandab** Ethiopia
393 E8 **Warangal** Andhra Pradesh India
241 G2 **Warboys** Cambridgeshire England UK
119 N6 **Warburg** Alberta Canada
425 K6 **Warburton** *watercourse* SA Australia
424 H6 **Warburton** WA Australia
226 D2 **Warche** *watercourse* Belgium
226 C3 **Warcq** France
425 M6 **Ward** *watercourse* Qld Australia
423 F5 **Ward** New Zealand
130 F3 **Ward** Arkansas USA
436 T2 **Ward, Mount** *mountain* Antarctica
118 F5 **Ward Cove** Alaska USA
373 I6 **Ward Hunt Strait** Papua New Guinea
308 E5 **Warden** South Africa
124 F3 **Warden** Washington USA
119 P7 **Wardlow** Alberta Canada
372 E4 **Wardo** Indonesia
129 K2 **Ware** Texas USA
241 E4 **Wareham** Dorset England UK
372 F4 **Waren** Indonesia
241 G2 **Waresley** Cambridgeshire England UK
425 N5 **Warginburra Peninsula** Qld Australia
373 I6 **Wari Island** Papua New Guinea
425 N7 **Warialda** NSW Australia
372 E5 **Warilau** *island* Indonesia
224 F6 **Warin** Germany
243 F1 **Wark** Northumberland England UK
422 F3 **Warkworth** New Zealand
243 G2 **Warlaby** North Yorkshire England UK
128 D1 **Warm Springs** Nevada USA
124 F5 **Warm Springs Reservoir** Oregon USA
372 E4 **Warmandi** Indonesia
225 K5 **Warmia** *region* Poland
241 G2 **Warmington** Northamptonshire England UK
227 K1 **Warminsko-Mazurskie** *admin. area* Poland
226 E1 **Warmsen** Germany
224 G5 **Warnemünde** Germany
119 O8 **Warner** Alberta Canada
130 D3 **Warner** Oklahoma USA
125 P4 **Warner** South Dakota USA
124 E6 **Warner Mountains** California USA
131 J4 **Warner Robins** Georgia USA
159 F5 **Warnes** Bolivia
372 F4 **Waropen, Teluk** *bay* Indonesia
373 G5 **Waropko** Indonesia
120 F6 **Warpath** *watercourse* Manitoba Canada
425 M6/7 **Warrego** *watercourse* NSW/Qld Australia
127 K3 **Warren** Ontario Canada
245 F1 **Warren** Moyle Northern Ireland UK
130 E4 **Warren** Arkansas USA
126 I6 **Warren** Indiana USA
126 J5 **Warren** Michigan USA
125 Q2 **Warren** Minnesota USA
127 K6 **Warren** Ohio USA
127 L6 **Warren** Pennsylvania USA
242 B2 **Warrenpoint** Newry and Mourne Northern Ireland UK
126 G7 **Warrensburg** Illinois USA
126 E7 **Warrensburg** Missouri USA
131 J4 **Warrenton** Georgia USA
124 D3 **Warrenton** Oregon USA
127 M7 **Warrenton** Virginia USA
305 F3 **Warri** Nigeria
423 D7 **Warrington** New Zealand
243 F3 **Warrington** *admin. area* England UK
425 L9 **Warrnambool** Vic. Australia
125 R2 **Warroad** Minnesota USA
389 K7 **Warsaj** Afghanistan
Warsaw *see* **Warszawa** Poland
126 F6 **Warsaw** Illinois USA
126 I6 **Warsaw** Indiana USA
126 E7 **Warsaw** Missouri USA
127 L5 **Warsaw** New York USA
131 L3 **Warsaw** North Carolina USA
127 J6 **Warsaw** Ohio USA
127 M8 **Warsaw** Virginia USA
241 F1 **Warslow** Staffordshire England UK
119 O5 **Warspite** Alberta Canada
227 K1 **Warszawa (Warsaw)** Poland
227 J2 **Warta** Poland
227 H1 **Warta** *watercourse* Poland
243 H3 **Warter** East Riding of Yorkshire England UK
119 Q7 **Wartime** Saskatchewan Canada
242 F2 **Warton** Lancashire England UK
393 E7 **Warud** Maharashtra India
134 C4 **Warunta** Honduras
373 G4 **Waruta** *watercourse* Indonesia
425 O7 **Warwick** Qld Australia
130 C3 **Warwick** Oklahoma USA
127 P6 **Warwick** Rhode Island USA
241 F2 **Warwickshire** *admin. area* England UK
119 N8 **Wasa** British Columbia Canada
425 L2 **Wasaga** Qld Australia
127 L4 **Wasaga Beach** Ontario Canada
125 P1 **Wasagaming** Manitoba Canada
305 F2 **Wasagu** Nigeria
426 7 **Wasaka** Vanuatu
128 G1 **Wasatch Range** Utah USA
128 C3 **Wasco** California USA
124 E4 **Wasco** Oregon USA
305 F3 **Wase** *watercourse* Nigeria
119 Q6 **Waseca** Saskatchewan Canada
126 E4 **Waseca** Minnesota USA
241 H2 **Wash, The** *bay* England UK
125 O3 **Washburn** North Dakota USA
126 F3 **Washburn** Wisconsin USA
243 G2 **Washfold** North Yorkshire England UK
240 D4 **Washford Pyne** Devon England UK
393 D7 **Washim** Maharashtra India
241 G4 **Washington** West Sussex England UK
114 **Washington** *admin. area* USA
127 M7 **Washington** District of Columbia USA
131 J4 **Washington** Georgia USA
126 G6 **Washington** Illinois USA
126 H7 **Washington** Indiana USA
126 F6 **Washington** Iowa USA
125 Q7 **Washington** Kansas USA
130 E5 **Washington** Louisiana USA
126 F7 **Washington** Missouri USA
131 M3 **Washington** North Carolina USA
127 K6 **Washington** Pennsylvania USA
128 F2 **Washington** Utah USA
436 L2 **Washington, Cape** Antarctica
130 F4 **Washington, Lake** Mississippi USA
127 P4 **Washington, Mount** New Hampshire USA
126 H4 **Washington Island** Wisconsin USA
117 M2 **Washington Land** *region* Greenland
163 1c **Washington Slagbaai National Park** Netherlands Antilles
130 A3 **Washita** *watercourse* Texas USA
124 F7 **Washoe Lake** Nevada USA
120 G7 **Washow Bay** Manitoba Canada
124 F3 **Washtucna** Washington USA
116 E6 **Wasilla** Alaska USA
304 E3 **Wasimi** Nigeria
372 E5 **Wasir** *island* Indonesia
372 C5 **Wasiri** Indonesia
390 F3 **Wāsiṭ** *admin. area* Iraq
120 G4 **Waskaiowaka Lake** Manitoba Canada
119 R6 **Waskesiu Lake** Saskatchewan Canada
134 C4 **Waslala** Nicaragua
227 I2 **Wąsosz** Poland
134 D4 **Waspam** Nicaragua
241 F2 **Wasperton** Warwickshire England UK
134 C4 **Waspuk** Nicaragua
243 G2 **Wass** North Yorkshire England UK
300 D6 **Wassadou** Senegal
131 K5 **Wassaw Sound** *strait* Georgia USA
304 B2 **Wassou** Guinea
229 G2 **Wassy** France
242 E2 **Wast Water** *lake* England UK
373 H5 **Wasu** Papua New Guinea
373 G6 **Wasua** Papua New Guinea
128 C1 **Wasuk Range** Nevada USA
121 R8 **Waswanipi** Québec Canada
121 Q8 **Waswanipi, Lac** *lake* Québec Canada
127 K2 **Watabeag Lake** Ontario Canada
123 I7 **Watagheistic, Île** *island* Québec Canada
372 B5 **Watampone** Indonesia
155 G3 **Watamung Mountains** Guyana
131 J2 **Watauga Lake** Tennessee USA
240 D3 **Watchet** Somerset England UK
122 G3 **Watchman Island** Newfoundland and Labrador Canada
126 F2 **Watcomb** Ontario Canada
134 E2 **Water Cays** *island* Bahamas
119 N7 **Water Valley** Alberta Canada
129 L5 **Water Valley** Texas USA
244 E5 **Waterbeck** Dumfries and Galloway Scotland UK
308 C4 **Waterberg** Namibia
127 O6 **Waterbury** Connecticut USA
127 O4 **Waterbury** Vermont USA

120 C3 **Waterbury Lake** Saskatchewan Canada
131 K3 **Wateree Lake** South Carolina USA
241 F1 **Waterfall** Staffordshire England UK
425 inset **Waterfall Lake** Macquarie Island Australia
245 E4 **Waterford** Ireland
245 E4 **Waterford** *admin. area* Ireland
119 S3 **Waterfound** *watercourse* Saskatchewan Canada
245 D4 **Watergrasshill** Ireland
242 E1 **Waterhead** Dumfries and Galloway Scotland UK
120 F6 **Waterhen Lake** Manitoba Canada
119 Q5 **Waterhen Lake** Saskatchewan Canada
119 Q5 **Waterhen Lake** Saskatchewan Canada
229 G1 **Waterloo** Belgium
304 B3 **Waterloo** Sierra Leone
163 9 **Waterloo** Trinidad and Tobago
244 C3 **Waterloo** Highland Scotland UK
126 F7 **Waterloo** Illinois USA
126 E5 **Waterloo** Iowa USA
119 Q3 **Waterloo Lake** Saskatchewan Canada
241 F4 **Waterlooville** Hampshire England UK
244 E3 **Waterside** Aberdeenshire Scotland UK
126 G3 **Watersmeet** Michigan USA
124 I2 **Waterton Park** Alberta Canada
125 Q4 **Watertown** South Dakota USA
126 G5 **Watertown** Wisconsin USA
245 B5 **Waterville** Ireland
127 Q4 **Waterville** Maine USA
126 E4 **Waterville** Minnesota USA
127 N5 **Waterville** New York USA
124 E3 **Waterville** Washington USA
126 H5 **Watervliet** Michigan USA
127 O5 **Watervliet** New York USA
241 G3 **Watford** Hertfordshire England UK
125 N3 **Watford City** North Dakota USA
120 D4 **Wathaman** *watercourse* Saskatchewan Canada
126 D7 **Wathena** Kansas USA
118 M5 **Watino** Alberta Canada
127 M5 **Watkins Glen** New York USA
241 F3 **Watlington** Oxfordshire England UK
372 D5 **Watmuri** Indonesia
130 B3 **Watonga** Oklahoma USA
119 S7 **Watrous** Saskatchewan Canada
129 J3 **Watrous** New Mexico USA
306 D3 **Watsa** Democratic Republic of Congo
126 H6 **Watseka** Illinois USA
306 C4 **Watsi** Democratic Republic of Congo
306 C4 **Watsi Kengo** Democratic Republic of Congo
119 S6 **Watson** Saskatchewan Canada
436 O1 **Watson Escarpment** *range* Antarctica
118 G2 **Watson Lake** Yukon Territory Canada
124 E8 **Watsonville** California USA
436 J2 **Watt Bay** Antarctica
241 J4 **Watten** France
244 E2 **Watten, Loch** *lake* Scotland UK
232 D3 **Wattens** Austria
120 F2 **Watterson Lake** Nunavut Canada
241 H2 **Watton** Norfolk England UK
131 I3 **Watts Bar Lake** Tennessee USA
372 D5 **Watubela, Kepulauan** *island* Indonesia
372 B6 **Watumanuk, Tanjung** *cape* Indonesia
372 B4 **Watuwila, Bukit** *mountain* Indonesia
372 E4 **Wau** Indonesia
306 D2 **Wau** Sudan
306 D2 **Wau** *watercourse* Sudan
126 C4 **Waubay Lake** South Dakota USA
125 R3 **Waubun** Minnesota USA
425 J5 **Wauchope** NT Australia
131 K7 **Wauchula** Florida USA
125 R2 **Waugh** Manitoba Canada
126 H5 **Waukegan** Illinois USA
126 G5 **Waukesha** Wisconsin USA
130 C2 **Waukomis** Oklahoma USA
126 F5 **Waukon** Iowa USA
125 O6 **Wauneta** Nebraska USA
126 G5 **Waupun** Wisconsin USA
130 C3 **Waurika** Oklahoma USA
130 B3 **Waurika Lake** Oklahoma USA
126 G4 **Wausau** Wisconsin USA
126 G4 **Wausaukee** Wisconsin USA
241 I2 **Waveney** *watercourse* England UK
422 F4 **Waverley** New Zealand
126 E5 **Waverly** Iowa USA
126 E7 **Waverly** Missouri USA
125 Q6 **Waverly** Nebraska USA
127 M6 **Waverly** Pennsylvania USA
130 H2 **Waverly** Tennessee USA
131 I4 **Waverly Hall** Georgia USA
241 G1 **Wavre** Belgium
376 C3 **Waw** Myanmar
126 I3 **Wawa** Ontario Canada
305 E3 **Wawa** Nigeria
121 Q5 **Wawa, Lac** *lake* Québec Canada
120 K6 **Wawakapewin** Ontario Canada
119 V8 **Wawanesa** Manitoba Canada
126 F2 **Wawang Lake** Ontario Canada
134 C4 **Wawina** Honduras
372 B4 **Wawo** Indonesia
119 T8 **Wawota** Saskatchewan Canada
130 C4 **Waxahachie** Texas USA
131 K3 **Waxhaw** North Carolina USA
229 H1 **Waxweiler** Germany
424 G6 **Way, Lake** WA Australia
374 E5 **Way Kambas, Taman Nasional** *park* Indonesia
427 9 **Waya** *island* Fiji
372 D3 **Wayag** *island* Indonesia
134 C4 **Wayawás** Nicaragua
131 J5 **Waycross** Georgia USA
372 C4 **Wayhaya** Indonesia
372 C4 **Waykilo** Indonesia
126 I5 **Wayland** Michigan USA
127 M5 **Wayland** New York USA
134 C4 **Waylaska** Nicaragua
130 C3 **Wayne** Oklahoma USA
131 K4 **Waynesboro** Georgia USA
130 H3 **Waynesboro** Tennessee USA
127 L7 **Waynesboro** Virginia USA
126 E8 **Waynesville** Missouri USA
131 J3 **Waynesville** North Carolina USA
125 P8 **Waynoka** Oklahoma USA
305 G2 **Waza** Cameroon
392 F6 **Wazirganj** Bihar India
120 J6 **Weagamow Lake** Ontario Canada
228 E1 **Weald, The** *region* England UK
243 F2 **Wear** *watercourse* England UK
243 F2 **Wear Head** Durham England UK
304 B3 **Weasua** Liberia
130 B3 **Weatherford** Oklahoma USA
126 E8 **Weaubleau** Missouri USA
120 G6 **Weaver Lake** Manitoba Canada
243 F3 **Weaverham** Cheshire England UK
119 Q7 **Webb** Saskatchewan Canada
131 I5 **Webb** Alabama USA
130 F4 **Webb** Mississippi USA
127 K3 **Webbwood** Ontario Canada
78 J8 **Weber Basin** *underwater feature* Banda Sea
129 K3 **Weber City** New Mexico USA
226 F1 **Weberin** Germany
125 Q4 **Webster** South Dakota USA
126 E5 **Webster City** Iowa USA
125 P7 **Webster Reservoir** Kansas USA
227 K2 **Węchadłow** Poland
372 C3 **Weda** Indonesia
372 D3 **Weda, Teluk** *bay* Indonesia
436 V2 **Weddell Abyssal Plain** *underwater feature* Weddell Sea
163 7 **Weddell Island** Falkland Islands
436 V2 **Weddell Sea** Southern Ocean
423 D7 **Wedderburn** New Zealand
226 E1 **Wedel** Germany
240 E3 **Wedmore** Somerset England UK
241 E2 **Wednesbury** West Midlands England UK
131 I4 **Wedowee** Alabama USA
372 E5 **Weduar, Tanjung** *cape* Indonesia
425 N7 **Wee Waa** NSW Australia
124 D6 **Weed** California USA
372 D4 **Weeim** *island* Indonesia
243 H3 **Weel** East Riding of Yorkshire England UK
229 G1 **Weert** Netherlands
229 I3 **Weesen** Switzerland
425 N7 **Weetaliba** NSW Australia
425 M8 **Weethalle** NSW Australia
241 F2 **Weethley** Warwickshire England UK
241 H2 **Weeting** Norfolk England UK
118 G6 **Weewanie** British Columbia Canada
426 6 **Weey** *island* Federated States of Micronesia
226 F2 **Wegeleben** Germany
374 B2 **Weh, Pulau** *island* Indonesia
302 F5 **Wehni** Ethiopia
226 D4 **Wehr** Germany
380 E1 **Wei He** *watercourse* Jiangsu China
385 I5 **Weichang** Hebei China
227 H1 **Weichensdorf** Germany
227 H4 **Weichselboden** Austria
381 G2 **Weidoushan Shuiku** *lake* Hubei China
385 I6 **Weifang** Shandong China
385 J5 **Weihai** Shandong China
381 G1 **Weihui** Henan China
226 E3 **Weil** Germany
226 E2 **Weil** *watercourse* Germany
226 F2 **Weilburg** Germany
226 E2 **Weimar** Germany
130 C6 **Weimar** Texas USA
380 F1 **Weinan** Shaanxi China
130 F3 **Weiner** Arkansas USA
130 B4 **Weinert** Texas USA
226 E3 **Weinheim** Germany
425 L3 **Weipa** Qld Australia
124 H3 **Weippe** Idaho USA
380 E1 **Weiqu** Shaanxi China
130 G4 **Weir** Mississippi USA
129 N5 **Weir** Texas USA
131 K6 **Weir, Lake** Florida USA
120 H4 **Weir River** Manitoba Canada
127 K6 **Weirton** Ohio USA
124 G4 **Weiser** Idaho USA
380 C3 **Weishan** Yunnan China
381 H1 **Weishan Hu** *lake* Shandong China
381 G1 **Weishi** Henan China
131 I3 **Weiss Lake** Alabama USA
226 G2 **Weiße Elster** *watercourse* Germany
226 G4 **Weißensee** *lake* Austria
226 F2 **Weißer Main** *watercourse* Germany
381 H2 **Weitang** Zhejiang China
227 H3 **Weitra** Austria
119 R4 **Weitzel Lake** Saskatchewan Canada
384 E6 **Weiyuan** Qinghai China
380 C4 **Weiyuan** Yunnan China
227 H4 **Weiz** Austria
380 F4 **Weizhou Dao** *island* Guangxi Zhuangzu Zizhiqu China
423 E6 **Weka Pass** New Zealand
423 E5 **Wekakura Point** New Zealand
119 V5 **Wekusko** Manitoba Canada
119 V5 **Wekusko Lake** Manitoba Canada
243 H2 **Welburn** North Yorkshire England UK
126 D8 **Welch** Oklahoma USA
127 K8 **Welch** West Virginia USA
240 C4 **Welcombe** Devon England UK
303 F5 **Weldiya** Ethiopia
224 I6 **Wełdkowo** Poland
130 C3 **Weleetka** Oklahoma USA
241 F2 **Welford** Northamptonshire England UK
79 R2 **Welker Seamount** *underwater feature* Pacific Ocean
307 F2 **Welk'it'ē** Ethiopia
308 E5 **Welkom** South Africa
243 G2 **Well** North Yorkshire England UK
301 G6 **Wèlla Sofon Gari** Niger
241 G2 **Welland** *watercourse* England UK
425 K2 **Wellesley Islands** Qld Australia
241 G1 **Wellingore** Lincolnshire England UK
425 N8 **Wellington** NSW Australia
124 C2 **Wellington** British Columbia Canada
127 M5 **Wellington** Ontario Canada
423 F5 **Wellington** New Zealand
423 F5 **Wellington** *admin. area* New Zealand
240 D4 **Wellington** Somerset England UK
126 B6 **Wellington** Colorado USA
125 Q8 **Wellington** Kansas USA
128 C1 **Wellington** Nevada USA
130 A3 **Wellington** Texas USA
125 J7 **Wellington** Utah USA
162 A4 **Wellington, Archipiélago** *island* Chile
162 A4 **Wellington, Isla** *island* Chile
423 F5 **Wellington Harbour** New Zealand
245 F4 **Wellingtonbridge** Ireland
129 K4 **Wellman** Texas USA
240 E3 **Wells** Somerset England UK
124 H6 **Wells** Nevada USA
127 N5 **Wells** New York USA
130 D5 **Wells** Texas USA
424 G6 **Wells, Lake** WA Australia
424 H4 **Wells, Mount** WA Australia
118 K6 **Wells Gray Provincial Park** British Columbia Canada
120 E4 **Wells Lake** Manitoba Canada
127 M6 **Wellsboro** Pennsylvania USA
241 F2 **Wellsborough** Leicester England UK
422 F3 **Wellsford** New Zealand
126 I4 **Wellston** Michigan USA
127 J7 **Wellston** Ohio USA
130 C3 **Wellston** Oklahoma USA
126 D7 **Wellsville** Kansas USA
127 M5 **Wellsville** New York USA
127 K6 **Wellsville** Ohio USA
124 J6 **Wellsville** Utah USA
128 E4 **Wellton** Arizona USA
241 H2 **Welney** Norfolk England UK
128 inset **Welokā** Hawai'i USA
227 H3 **Wels** Austria
130 E5 **Welsh** Louisiana USA
240 B3 **Welsh Hook** Pembrokeshire Wales UK
240 D2 **Welshpool** Powys Wales UK
242 E2 **Welton** Cumbria England UK
243 H3 **Welton le Wold** Lincolnshire England UK
307 H2 **Welwel** Ethiopia
241 G3 **Welwyn Garden City** Hertfordshire England UK
226 E3 **Welzheim** Germany
306 C4 **Wema** Democratic Republic of Congo
307 E4 **Wembere** *watercourse* Tanzania
118 L5 **Wembley** Alberta Canada
241 G3 **Wembley** Greater London England UK
307 G2 **Wemell** *watercourse* Ethiopia
121 P6 **Wemindji** Québec Canada
381 G1 **Wen Xian** Henan China
385 H5 **Wen'an** Hebei China
124 E3 **Wenatchee** Washington USA
124 E3 **Wenatchee Mountains** Washington USA
379 F2 **Wenbu** Xizang Zizhiqu China
157 B8 **Wenceslau Braz** Brazil
380 E2 **Wenchang** Sichuan China
380 F5 **Wenchang** Hainan China
304 E2 **Wenchiki** Ghana
124 H5 **Wendell** Idaho USA
385 J5 **Wendeng** Shandong China
372 E4 **Wendesi** Indonesia
304 B2 **Wéndou Mbôrou** Guinea
241 G3 **Wendover** Buckinghamshire England UK
124 H6 **Wendover** Utah USA
240 B4 **Wendron** Cornwall England UK
126 J3 **Wenebegon Lake** Ontario Canada
380 D2 **Wenehuan** Sichuan China
381 G3 **Wenfeng** Jiangxi China
241 I2 **Wenhaston** Suffolk England UK
380 D3 **Wenjiang** Sichuan China
380 D4 **Wenlan** Yunnan China
381 I3 **Wenling** Zhejiang China
426 6 **Weno** Federated States of Micronesia
426 6a **Weno** *island* Federated States of Micronesia
380 D3 **Wenping** Yunnan China
380 E2 **Wenquan** Chongqing China
381 G2 **Wenquan** Hubei China
382 G4 **Wenquan** Xinjiang Uygur Zizhiqu China
243 F2 **Wensleydale** *valley* England UK
382 F4 **Wensu** Xinjiang Uygur Zizhiqu China
241 H2 **Wensum** *watercourse* England UK
243 G3 **Wentbridge** West Yorkshire England UK
240 E2 **Wentnor** Shropshire England UK
425 L8 **Wentworth** NSW Australia
125 Q5 **Wentworth** South Dakota USA
119 N3 **Wentzel Lake** Alberta Canada
381 F1 **Wenxi** Shanxi China
380 D2 **Wenxian** Gansu China
381 F3 **Wenxing** Hunan China
303 F5 **Wenz** *spring* Ethiopia
381 H3 **Wenzhou** Zhejiang China
240 E2 **Weobley** Herefordshire England UK
308 E5 **Wepener** South Africa
306 D2 **Wer Ping** Sudan
227 G1 **Werbellinsee** *lake* Germany
226 G2 **Werbig** Germany
308 D5 **Werda** Botswana
229 K1 **Werdau** Germany
226 G1 **Werder** Germany
307 H2 **Werdër** Ethiopia
226 D2 **Werdohl** Germany
226 G4 **Werfen** Austria
372 E4 **Weri** Indonesia
226 D1 **Werlte** Germany
229 K1 **Wermsdorf** Germany
226 E3 **Wern** *watercourse* Germany
232 E2 **Wernberg-Köblitz** Germany
229 I2 **Wertheim** Germany
155 F3 **Werushima Range** Guyana
228 F1 **Wervik** Belgium
372 D6 **Werwaru** Indonesia
226 D2 **Wesel** Germany
226 E1 **Weser** *watercourse* Germany
163 I5 **Wesley** Dominica
127 R4 **Wesley** Maine USA
227 K2 **Wesoła** Poland
227 K1 **Wesołowo** Poland
425 K2 **Wessel, Cape** NT Australia
425 J2 **Wessel Islands** NT Australia
125 P4 **Wessington Springs** South Dakota USA
130 F5 **Wesson** Mississippi USA
130 C5 **West** Texas USA
241 H2 **West Acre** Norfolk England UK
126 G5 **West Allis** Wisconsin USA
436 Q1 **West Antarctica** *region* Antarctica
390 C3 **West Bank (Disputed)** *admin. area* Asia
241 H2 **West Barsham** Norfolk England UK
122 J5 **West Bay** Newfoundland and Labrador Canada
130 G6 **West Bay** Louisiana USA
126 G5 **West Bend** Wisconsin USA
379 F4 **West Bengal** *admin. area* India
242 C1 **West Bennan** North Ayrshire Scotland UK
241 H3 **West Bergholt** Essex England UK
241 F3 **West Berkshire** *admin. area* England UK
241 H2 **West Bilney** Norfolk England UK
130 H4 **West Blocton** Alabama USA
241 F2 **West Bromwich** West Midlands England UK
135 F2 **West Caicos** *island* Turks and Caicos Islands
423 B7 **West Cape** New Zealand
78 J7 **West Caroline Basin** *underwater feature* Pacific Ocean
243 G1 **West Chevington** Northumberland England UK
423 D6 **West Coast** *admin. area* New Zealand
374 C4 **West Coast Park** Singapore
131 K4 **West Columbia** South Carolina USA
241 G4 **West Dean** West Sussex England UK
241 H2 **West Dereham** Norfolk England UK
126 E6 **West Des Moines** Iowa USA
244 F4 **West Drums** Angus Scotland UK
244 D4 **West Dunbartonshire** *admin. area* Scotland UK
131 L7 **West End** Bahamas
131 L7 **West End Point** Bahamas
125 Q3 **West Fargo** North Dakota USA
373 H1 **West Fayu** *island* Federated States of Micronesia
130 D3 **West Fork** Arkansas USA
123 E10 **West Grand Lake** Maine USA
241 F3 **West Grimstead** Wiltshire England UK
241 F2 **West Haddon** Northamptonshire England UK
243 H3 **West Halton** North Lincolnshire England UK
127 O6 **West Haven** Connecticut USA
125 R2 **West Hawk Lake** Manitoba Canada
130 F3 **West Helena** Arkansas USA
244 B4 **West Hynish** Highland Scotland UK
436 F2 **West Ice Shelf** Antarctica
241 F3 **West Ilsley** West Berkshire England UK
135 H3 **West Indies** *island* Caribbean
376 B4 **West Island** Andaman and Nicobar Islands India
424 inset **West Island (Panjang)** Cocos (Keeling) Islands Australia
424 inset **West Islet** Ashmore Reef and Cartier Island Australia
425 O5 **West Islet** Qld Australia
124 J6 **West Jordan** Utah USA
242 E3 **West Kirby** Merseyside England UK
126 H6 **West Lafayette** Indiana USA
130 C5 **West Lake Hills** Texas USA
241 F3 **West Lavington** Wiltshire England UK
126 J8 **West Liberty** Kentucky USA
244 E5 **West Linton** Scottish Borders Scotland UK
240 C4 **West Looe** Cornwall England UK
127 K5 **West Lorne** Ontario Canada
244 E5 **West Lothian** *admin. area* Scotland UK
241 E4 **West Lulworth** Dorset England UK
308 D2 **West Lunga** *watercourse* Zambia
78 J6 **West Mariana Basin** *underwater feature* Atlantic Ocean
130 F3 **West Memphis** Arkansas USA
241 H3 **West Mersea** Essex England UK
122 H5 **West Mistake Lake** Newfoundland and Labrador Canada
241 H2 **West Newton** Norfolk England UK
308 E4 **West Nicholson** Zimbabwe
126 D5 **West Okoboji Lake** Iowa USA
131 K7 **West Palm Beach** Florida USA
126 F8 **West Plains** Missouri USA
123 H11 **West Point** Nova Scotia Canada
130 G4 **West Point** Mississippi USA
125 Q6 **West Point** Nebraska USA
127 M8 **West Point** Virginia USA
131 I4 **West Point Lake** Georgia USA
119 M5 **West Prairie** *watercourse* Alberta Canada
240 C4 **West Putford** Devon England UK
118 I6 **West Road** *watercourse* British Columbia Canada
241 H2 **West Roe** Suffolk England UK
241 H2 **West Rudham** Norfolk England UK
243 F2 **West Stonesdale** North Yorkshire England UK
241 G4 **West Sussex** *admin. area* England UK
243 G2 **West Tanfield** North Yorkshire England UK
226 C1 **West-Terschelling** Netherlands
245 D1 **West Town** Ireland
126 F5 **West Union** Iowa USA
127 K7 **West Union** West Virginia USA
124 J6 **West Valley City** Utah USA
114 **West Virginia** *admin. area* USA
124 H6 **West Wendover** Nevada USA
425 M8 **West Wyalong** NSW Australia
125 J4 **West Yellowstone** Montana USA
377 G5 **West York Island** Spratly Islands
118 L8 **Westbank** British Columbia Canada
126 F4 **Westboro** Wisconsin USA
127 P5 **Westbrook** Maine USA
129 L4 **Westbrook** Texas USA
240 E2 **Westbury** Shropshire England UK
125 M2 **Westby** Montana USA
244 E5 **Wester Deans** Scottish Borders Scotland UK
243 H2 **Westerdale** North Yorkshire England UK
224 E5 **Westerland** Germany
307 E3 **Western** *admin. area* Kenya
426 8 **Western** *admin. area* Solomon Islands
308 D2 **Western** *admin. area* Zambia
424 F6 **Western Australia** *admin. area* Australia
306 D2 **Western Bahr-el-Ghazal** *admin. area* Sudan
308 D6 **Western Cape** *admin. area* South Africa
423 7 **Western Chain** *island* Snares Islands New Zealand
305 I2 **Western Darfur** *admin. area* Sudan
424 inset **Western Entrance** *port* Cocos (Keeling) Islands Australia
306 D2 **Western Equatoria** *admin. area* Sudan
373 H4 **Western Island** Papua New Guinea
127 K4 **Western Islands** *island* Ontario Canada
302 D5 **Western Kordofan** *admin. area* Sudan
123 F10 **Western Shore** Nova Scotia Canada
226 D2 **Westerwald** *region* Germany
244 inset **Westerwick** Shetland Scotland UK
241 H4 **Westfield** East Sussex England UK
127 L5 **Westfield** New York USA
126 G5 **Westfield** Wisconsin USA
244 F3 **Westhill** Aberdeenshire Scotland UK
124 D2 **Westholme** British Columbia Canada
125 O2 **Westhope** North Dakota USA
241 I2 **Westleton** Suffolk England UK
119 O5 **Westlock** Alberta Canada
425 N6 **Westmar** Qld Australia
245 E3 **Westmeath** *admin. area* Ireland
127 M7 **Westminster** Maryland USA
131 H2 **Westmoreland** Tennessee USA
128 E4 **Westmorland** California USA
375 G2 **Weston** Malaysia
423 D7 **Weston** New Zealand
241 G4 **Weston** Hampshire England UK
243 H3 **Weston** Nottinghamshire England UK
240 E2 **Weston** Shropshire England UK
124 F4 **Weston** Oregon USA
127 K7 **Weston** West Virginia USA
126 G4 **Weston** Wisconsin USA
121 P6 **Weston Island** Nunavut Canada
241 F2 **Weston Subedge** Gloucestershire England UK
240 E3 **Weston-super-Mare** North Somerset England UK
241 F2 **Weston Underwood** Derbyshire England UK
240 E3 **Westonzoyland** Somerset England UK
129 O1 **Westphalia** Kansas USA
163 7 **Westpoint Island** Falkland Islands
245 C3 **Westport** Ireland
423 D5 **Westport** New Zealand
125 P4 **Westport** South Dakota USA
124 C3 **Westport** Washington USA
163 1b **Westpunt** *cape* Netherlands Antilles
119 U6 **Westray** Manitoba Canada
244 E1 **Westray Firth** *bay* Scotland UK
244 F5 **Westruther** Scottish Borders Scotland UK
130 D3 **Westville** Oklahoma USA
242 E2 **Westward** Cumbria England UK
240 C3 **Westward** Devon England UK
130 F6 **Westwego** Louisiana USA
118 L7 **Westwold** British Columbia Canada
423 B7 **Wet Jacket Arm** *bay* New Zealand
121 P5 **Wetalltok Bay** Nunavut Canada
372 D5 **Wetan** *island* Indonesia
372 C5 **Wetar** *island* Indonesia
372 C6 **Wetar, Selat** *strait* Indonesia
119 O6 **Wetaskiwin** Alberta Canada
307 F5 **Wete** Tanzania
127 M2 **Wetetnagami Lake** Québec Canada
242 F2 **Wetheral** Cumbria England UK
243 G3 **Wetherby** West Yorkshire England UK
120 G5 **Wetikoweskwattam** Manitoba Canada
379 H4 **Wetlet** Myanmar
227 L3 **Wetlina** Poland
129 J1 **Wetmore** Colorado USA
226 D2 **Wetter** Germany
241 F1 **Wetton** Staffordshire England UK
130 C3 **Wetumka** Oklahoma USA
131 H4 **Wetumpka** Alabama USA
243 H2 **Wetwang** East Riding of Yorkshire England UK
130 C3 **Wewoka** Oklahoma USA
245 F4 **Wexford** Ireland
245 F4 **Wexford** *admin. area* Ireland
245 F4 **Wexford Harbour** Ireland
241 G3 **Wey** *watercourse* England UK
126 G4 **Weyauwega** Wisconsin USA
226 E1 **Weyhe** Germany
123 F10 **Weymouth** Nova Scotia Canada
240 E4 **Weymouth** Dorset England UK
134 E1 **Weymyss Bight** Bahamas
422 G3 **Whakaari-White Island** *volcano* New Zealand
422 G3 **Whakatane** New Zealand
422 G4 **Whakatane** *watercourse* New Zealand
376 C5 **Whale Bay** Myanmar
243 G3 **Whaley Bridge** Derbyshire England UK
422 F2 **Whananaki** New Zealand
422 F5 **Whangaehu** New Zealand
422 F4 **Whangaehu** *watercourse* New Zealand
422 F3 **Whangamata** New Zealand
422 F4 **Whanganui** *watercourse* New Zealand
422 E5 **Whanganui Inlet** New Zealand
422 F3 **Whangaparaoa** New Zealand
422 E2 **Whangape** New Zealand
422 E2 **Whangape, Lake** New Zealand
422 E2 **Whangape Harbour** New Zealand
422 F3 **Whangapoua Harbour** New Zealand
422 F2 **Whangarei** New Zealand
422 F2 **Whangarei Harbour** New Zealand
422 E2 **Whangaroa** New Zealand
422 F2 **Whangaruru** New Zealand
422 F2 **Whangaruru Harbour** New Zealand
121 Q5 **Whapmagoostui** Québec Canada
423 E6 **Whareama** New Zealand
243 F2 **Wharfe** *watercourse* England UK
243 G2 **Wharfedale** *valley* England UK
130 C6 **Wharton** Texas USA
436 K1 **Wharton, Mount** Antarctica
81 O6 **Wharton Basin** *underwater feature* Indian Ocean
423 D6 **Whataroa** *watercourse* New Zealand
244 D6 **Whauphill** Dumfries and Galloway Scotland UK
126 F6 **Wheatland** Iowa USA
125 M5 **Wheatland** Wyoming USA
125 M6 **Wheatland Reservoir** Wyoming USA
125 Q4 **Wheaton** Minnesota USA
126 D8 **Wheaton** Missouri USA
241 E2 **Wheaton Aston** Staffordshire England UK
240 D3 **Wheddon Cross** Somerset England UK
122 E4 **Wheeler** *watercourse* Québec Canada
124 D4 **Wheeler** Oregon USA
130 A3 **Wheeler** Texas USA
130 H3 **Wheeler Lake** Alabama USA
128 C3 **Wheeler Ridge** California USA
127 K6 **Wheeling** West Virginia USA
241 F3 **Whelford** Gloucestershire England UK
243 G2 **Whenby** North Yorkshire England UK
Whenua Hou *see* **Codfish Island** New Zealand
241 F2 **Whetstone** Leicester England UK
128 G5 **Whetstone** Arizona USA
243 G2 **Whickham** Tyne and Wear England UK
240 D4 **Whiddon Down** Devon England UK
245 C5 **Whiddy Island** *island* Ireland
244 G3 **Whinnyfold** Aberdeenshire Scotland UK
241 G3 **Whipsnade** Bedfordshire England UK
154 B4 **Whiskey** Colombia
120 E3 **Whiskey Jack Lake** Manitoba Canada
124 I2 **Whisky Gap** Alberta Canada
118 J7 **Whistler** British Columbia Canada
241 F1 **Whiston** Staffordshire England UK
131 M2 **Whitakers** North Carolina USA
242 E2 **Whitbeck** Cumbria England UK
123 L9 **Whitbourne** Newfoundland and Labrador Canada
240 E2 **Whitbourne** Herefordshire England UK
243 H2 **Whitby** North Yorkshire England UK
241 F3 **Whitchurch** Hampshire England UK
240 E3 **Whitchurch** Herefordshire England UK
240 E2 **Whitchurch** Shropshire England UK
127 L5 **Whitchurch-Stouffville** Ontario Canada
240 E4 **Whitcombe** Dorset England UK
130 F3 **White** *watercourse* Arkansas USA
125 K6 **White** *watercourse* Colorado USA
126 H7 **White** *watercourse* Indiana USA
128 E2 **White** *watercourse* Nevada USA
125 N5 **White** *watercourse* South Dakota USA
240 D4 **White Ball** Somerset England UK
123 J8 **White Bay** Newfoundland and Labrador Canada
122 I6 **White Bear** *watercourse* Newfoundland and Labrador Canada
119 Q7 **White Bear** Saskatchewan Canada
122 H4 **White Bear Island** Newfoundland and Labrador Canada
122 I5 **White Bear Lake** Newfoundland and Labrador Canada
124 G4 **White Bird** Idaho USA
128 G2 **White Canyon** Utah USA
130 F5 **White Castle** Louisiana USA
125 M1 **White City** Saskatchewan Canada
129 N1 **White City** Kansas USA
425 L7 **White Cliffs** NSW Australia
129 L3 **White Deer** Texas USA
119 S6 **White Fox** Saskatchewan Canada
130 E3 **White Hall** Arkansas USA
122 G3 **White Handkerchief, Cape** Newfoundland and Labrador Canada
123 H9 **White Hill** Nova Scotia Canada
436 D2 **White Island** Antarctica
117 K5 **White Island** Nunavut Canada
126 I2 **White Lake** Ontario Canada
127 M4 **White Lake** Ontario Canada
130 E6 **White Lake** Louisiana USA
125 P5 **White Lake** South Dakota USA
125 P5 **White Lake** South Dakota USA
116 C6 **White Mountain** Alaska USA
128 C2 **White Mountain** California USA
White Nile *see* **Abiad, Bahr el** Sudan
302 E5 **White Nile** *admin. area* Sudan
130 E4 **White Oak Lake** Arkansas USA
126 F2 **White Otter Lake** Ontario Canada
131 J2 **White Pine** Tennessee USA
128 E1 **White Pine Range** Nevada USA
126 H8 **White Plains** Kentucky USA
127 O6 **White Plains** New York USA
126 I2 **White River** Ontario Canada
125 O5 **White River** South Dakota USA
128 E1 **White River Valley** Nevada USA
118 J8 **White Rock** British Columbia Canada
124 E4 **White Salmon** Washington USA
White Sea *see* **Beloye More** Russian Federation
130 C4 **White Settlement** Texas USA
129 H4 **White Signal** New Mexico USA
131 J5 **White Springs** Florida USA
122 C1 **White Strait** Nunavut Canada
125 J3 **White Sulphur Springs** Montana USA
304 D2 **White Volta** *watercourse* Ghana
240 A2 **Whitechurch** Ireland
423 D6 **Whitecliffs** New Zealand
119 N5 **Whitecourt** Alberta Canada
120 H7 **Whitedog** Ontario Canada
126 E3 **Whiteface** *watercourse* Minnesota USA
129 K4 **Whiteface** Texas USA
126 E3 **Whiteface Reservoir** Minnesota USA
242 A1 **Whitefield** Ireland
124 H2 **Whitefish** Montana USA
127 J3 **Whitefish Bay** Ontario Canada
126 I3 **Whitefish Bay** Michigan USA
120 I5 **Whitefish Lake** Manitoba Canada
129 L3 **Whiteflat** Texas USA
240 C3 **Whiteford Point** Wales UK
245 D4 **Whitegate** Ireland
245 E4 **Whitehall** Ireland
244 F1 **Whitehall** Orkney Islands Scotland UK
124 I4 **Whitehall** Montana USA
126 J7 **Whitehall** Ohio USA
127 K7 **Whitehall** West Virginia USA
126 F4 **Whitehall** Wisconsin USA
242 E2 **Whitehaven** Cumbria England UK
244 F3 **Whitehills** Aberdeenshire Scotland UK
118 D2 **Whitehorse** Yukon Territory Canada
120 H8 **Whitemouth** Manitoba Canada
126 D2 **Whitemouth** *watercourse* Manitoba Canada
126 D2 **Whitemouth Lake** Manitoba Canada
118 L4 **Whitemud** *watercourse* Alberta Canada
244 D2 **Whiten Head** *cape* Scotland UK
241 F3 **Whiteparish** Wiltshire England UK
129 J4 **Whites City** New Mexico USA
245 F3 **Whites Town** Ireland
118 H6 **Whitesail Lake** British Columbia Canada
119 N3 **Whitesand** *watercourse* Alberta Canada
119 T7 **Whitesand** *watercourse* Saskatchewan Canada
130 C4 **Whitesboro** Texas USA
131 I4 **Whitesburg** Georgia USA
242 B2 **Whitesides Corner** Ballymena Northern Ireland UK
240 D4 **Whitestaunton** Somerset England UK
244 C5 **Whitestone** Argyll and Bute Scotland UK
120 J7 **Whitestone Lake** Ontario Canada
126 H8 **Whitesville** Kentucky USA
127 K8 **Whitesville** West Virginia USA
119 S8 **Whitetail** Montana USA
131 L3 **Whiteville** North Carolina USA
130 G3 **Whiteville** Tennessee USA
126 G5 **Whitewater** Wisconsin USA
134 D1 **Whitewater Bay** Florida USA
120 K7 **Whitewater Lake** Ontario Canada
243 F3 **Whitewell** Lancashire England UK
119 T7 **Whitewood** Saskatchewan Canada
130 C4 **Whitewright** Texas USA
243 F2 **Whitfield** Northumberland England UK
119 U6 **Whithorn** Manitoba Canada
244 D6 **Whithorn** Dumfries and Galloway Scotland UK
118 E3 **Whiting** *watercourse* Alaska USA
127 R4 **Whiting** Maine USA
244 C5 **Whiting Bay** North Ayrshire Scotland UK
241 H2 **Whitington** Norfolk England UK
119 R6 **Whitkow** Saskatchewan Canada
125 J2 **Whitla** Alberta Canada
240 C3 **Whitland** Carmarthenshire Wales UK
131 K3 **Whitmire** South Carolina USA
436 Q1 **Whitmore Mountains** Antarctica
127 L4 **Whitney** Ontario Canada
240 D2 **Whitney** Herefordshire England UK
130 C5 **Whitney, Lake** Texas USA
128 C2 **Whitney, Mount** California USA
127 N5 **Whitney Point** New York USA
244 F5 **Whitnmuir** Scottish Borders Scotland UK
242 E2 **Whitrigg** Cumbria England UK
240 C4 **Whitsand Bay** England UK
240 E3 **Whitson** Newport Wales UK
241 I3 **Whitstable** Kent England UK
425 N4 **Whitsunday Group** *islands* Qld Australia
243 G1 **Whittingham** Northumberland England UK
240 D2 **Whittington** Shropshire England UK
241 G2 **Whittlesey** Cambridgeshire England UK
241 H2 **Whittlesford** Cambridgeshire England UK
240 D2 **Whitton** Powys Wales UK
243 G3 **Whitwell** Derbyshire England UK
120 C2 **Wholdaia Lake** Northwest Territories Canada
425 K8 **Whyalla** SA Australia
123 H10 **Whycocomagh** Nova Scotia Canada
386 E4 **Wi-do** *island* South Korea
155 G3 **Wiapri** Guyana
244 A3 **Wiay** *island* Scotland UK
125 M3 **Wibaux** Montana USA
241 F2 **Wibtoft** Warwickshire England UK
303 F5 **Wich'alē** Ethiopia
125 Q8 **Wichita** Kansas USA
227 K2 **Wichta** Poland
244 E2 **Wick** Highland Scotland UK
240 D3 **Wick** Vale of Glamorgan Wales UK
241 G2 **Wicken** Northamptonshire England UK
128 F4 **Wickenburg** Arizona USA
424 F8 **Wickepin** WA Australia
130 D3 **Wickes** Arkansas USA
129 K5 **Wickett** Texas USA
241 H3 **Wickford** Essex England UK
424 F5 **Wickham** WA Australia
241 F4 **Wickham** Hampshire England UK
425 L9 **Wickham, Cape** Tas. Australia
162 E5 **Wickham Heights** *range* Falkland Islands
241 I2 **Wickham Market** Suffolk England UK
241 H2 **Wickhambrook** Suffolk England UK
124 E5 **Wickiup Reservoir** Oregon USA
126 G8 **Wickliffe** Kentucky USA
245 F4 **Wicklow** Ireland
245 F4 **Wicklow** *admin. area* Ireland
245 G4 **Wicklow Head** *cape* Ireland
245 F3 **Wicklow Mountains** Ireland
241 I2 **Wickmere** Norfolk England UK
227 J2 **Widawa** Poland
373 J5 **Wide Bay** Papua New Guinea
240 D4 **Widecombe in the Moor** Devon England UK
436 B2 **Widerøe, Mount** Antarctica
119 N5 **Widewater** Alberta Canada
372 D4 **Widi, Kepulauan** *island* Indonesia
242 F3 **Widnes** Merseyside England UK
242 C2 **Widows Row** Newry and Mourne Northern Ireland UK
240 D4 **Widworthy** Devon England UK
227 I1 **Więcbork** Poland
226 D2 **Wied** *watercourse* Germany
121 P4 **Wiegand Island** Nunavut Canada
226 D2 **Wiehl** Germany
224 G5 **Wiek** Germany
227 I1 **Wiele** Poland
227 I1 **Wieleń** Poland
227 I1/2 **Wieleńskie, Jezioro** *lake* Poland
227 I1 **Wielichowo** Poland
227 I1 **Wielimie, Jezioro** *lake* Poland
227 H1 **Wielkie, Jezioro** *lake* Poland
227 I1 **Wielkopolskie** *admin. area* Poland
226 B2 **Wielsbeke** Belgium
227 J2 **Wieluń** Poland
227 I3 **Wien** *admin. area* Austria
232 G2 **Wien (Vienna)** Austria
227 I3 **Wiener Neudorf** Austria
227 L2 **Wieprz** *watercourse* Poland
224 I5 **Wieprza** *watercourse* Poland
227 K2 **Wierzchosławice** Poland
227 I1 **Wierzchowo, Jezioro** *lake* Poland
229 I1 **Wiesbaden** Germany
226 E1 **Wietze** Germany
243 F3 **Wigan** Greater Manchester England UK
130 G5 **Wiggins** Mississippi USA
241 F3 **Wigginton** Oxfordshire England UK
243 F2 **Wigglesworth** North Yorkshire England UK
241 F4 **Wight, Isle of** England UK
240 E2 **Wigmore** Herefordshire England UK
243 H3 **Wigsley** Nottinghamshire England UK
242 E2 **Wigton** Cumbria England UK
244 D6 **Wigtown** Dumfries and Galloway Scotland UK
242 D2 **Wigtown Bay** Scotland UK
119 N8 **Wigwam** *watercourse* British Columbia Canada
129 J1 **Wigwam** Colorado USA
120 K6 **Wigwascence Lake** Ontario Canada
227 I2 **Wijewo** Poland
303 F5 **Wik'ro** Ethiopia

232 C3 **Wila** Switzerland
125 Q6 **Wilber** Nebraska USA
127 L4 **Wilberforce** Ontario Canada
423 D6 **Wilberforce** *watercourse* New Zealand
425 K2 **Wilberforce, Cape** NT Australia
124 F3 **Wilbur** Washington USA
241 H2 **Wilburton** Cambridgeshire England UK
130 D3 **Wilburton** Oklahoma USA
241 H2 **Wilby** Norfolk England UK
425 L7 **Wilcannia** NSW Australia
240 E3 **Wilcrick** Newport Wales UK
436 K2 **Wild, Cape** Antarctica
125 K3 **Wild Horse Lake** Montana USA
124 H6 **Wild Horse Reservoir** Nevada USA
227 H4 **Wildalpen** Austria
226 G1 **Wildberg** Germany
119 W5 **Wilde** Manitoba Canada
373 F5 **Wildeman** *watercourse* Indonesia
124 G5 **Wilder** Idaho USA
127 M7 **Wilderness** Virginia USA
118 M6 **Wildhay** *watercourse* Alberta Canada
125 N2 **Wildrose** North Dakota USA
241 F2 **Wilford** Nottingham England UK
373 H5 **Wilhelm, Mount** Papua New Guinea
436 G2 **Wilhelm II Coast** Antarctica
436 F2 **Wilhelm II Land** *plain* Antarctica
155 G4 **Wilhelmina Gebergte** *range* Suriname
226 F4 **Wilhelmsdorf** Germany
224 E6 **Wilhelmshaven** Germany
127 N6 **Wilkes-Barre** Pennsylvania USA
436 H2 **Wilkes Land** *plain* Antarctica
131 K2 **Wilkesboro** North Carolina USA
244 E3 **Wilkhaven** Highland Scotland UK
436 T2 **Wilkins Coast** Antarctica
436 T2 **Wilkins Sound** *strait* Antarctica
127 L6 **Wilkinsburg** Pennsylvania USA
131 J5 **Willacoochee** Georgia USA
124 D4 **Willamina** Oregon USA
124 C3 **Willapa Bay** Washington USA
126 E8 **Willard** Missouri USA
129 I3 **Willard** New Mexico USA
124 I6 **Willard** Utah USA
128 H4 **Willcox** Arizona USA
132 C1 **Willcox Playa** *pan* Arizona USA
135 G4 **Willemstad** Netherlands Antilles
243 H2 **Willerby** North Yorkshire England UK
240 D2 **Willersley** Herefordshire England UK
241 H3 **Willesborough Lees** Kent England UK
119 Q3 **William** *watercourse* Saskatchewan Canada
425 L9 **William, Mount** Vic. Australia
423 C8 **William, Port** New Zealand
130 H4 **William "Bill" Dannelly Reservoir** Alabama USA
425 K7 **William Creek** SA Australia
122 F2 **William-Smith, Cap** *cape* Québec Canada
379 G4 **Williamnagar** Meghalaya India
424 F8 **Williams** WA Australia
128 F3 **Williams** Arizona USA
124 D7 **Williams** California USA
125 R2 **Williams** Minnesota USA
436 L2 **Williams, Cape** Antarctica
436 E2 **Williams, Point** Antarctica
125 L7 **Williams Fork Reservoir** Colorado USA
134 E1 **Williams Island** Bahamas
118 J6 **Williams Lake** British Columbia Canada
120 J7 **Williams Lake** Ontario Canada
81 M10 **Williams Seamount** *underwater feature* Southern Ocean
126 E6 **Williamsburg** Iowa USA
129 O1 **Williamsburg** Kansas USA
131 I2 **Williamsburg** Kentucky USA
129 I4 **Williamsburg** New Mexico USA
127 M8 **Williamsburg** Virginia USA
131 J2 **Williamson** West Virginia USA
128 C2 **Williamson, Mount** California USA
436 H2 **Williamson Glacier** *ice* Antarctica
127 M7 **Williamsport** Maryland USA
127 M6 **Williamsport** Pennsylvania USA
131 M3 **Williamston** North Carolina USA
126 I7 **Williamstown** Kentucky USA
229 H1 **Willich** Germany
163 I8 **Willikies** Antigua and Barbuda
119 O6 **Willingdon** Alberta Canada
241 H4 **Willingdon** East Sussex England UK
119 M7 **Willingdon, Mount** Alberta Canada
229 I1 **Willingen** Germany
243 H3 **Willingham by Stowe** Lincolnshire England UK
243 G2 **Willington** Durham England UK
163 8 **Willis Islands** South Georgia
425 N4 **Willis Islets** Coral Sea Islands Territory Australia
308 D6 **Williston** South Africa
131 J6 **Williston** Florida USA
125 N2 **Williston** North Dakota USA
131 K4 **Williston** South Carolina USA
116 G7 **Williston Lake** British Columbia Canada
240 D3 **Williton** Somerset England UK
124 D7 **Willits** California USA
119 T8 **Willmar** Saskatchewan Canada
125 R4 **Willmar** Minnesota USA
118 L6 **Willmore Wilderness Provincial Park** Alberta Canada
163 I8 **Willoughby Bay** Antigua and Barbuda
118 K6 **Willow** *watercourse* British Columbia Canada
116 E6 **Willow** Alaska USA
130 B3 **Willow** Oklahoma USA
125 M2 **Willow Bunch** Saskatchewan Canada
125 M2 **Willow Bunch Lake** Saskatchewan Canada
125 O2 **Willow City** North Dakota USA
119 O7 **Willow Creek** Alberta Canada
124 G6 **Willow Creek Reservoir** Nevada USA
118 L1 **Willow Lake** Northwest Territories Canada
125 Q4 **Willow Lake** South Dakota USA
126 G4 **Willow Reservoir** Wisconsin USA
126 F8 **Willow Springs** Missouri USA
125 N1 **Willowbrook** Saskatchewan Canada
118 J1 **Willowlake** *watercourse* Northwest Territories Canada
308 D6 **Willowmore** South Africa
124 D7 **Willows** California USA
308 E6 **Willowvale** South Africa
130 D4 **Wills Point** Texas USA
425 K8 **Willunga** SA Australia
241 F2 **Wilmcote** Warwickshire England UK
127 N7 **Wilmington** Delaware USA
131 M3 **Wilmington** North Carolina USA
126 J7 **Wilmington** Ohio USA
126 I8 **Wilmore** Kentucky USA
130 F4 **Wilmot** Arkansas USA
125 Q4 **Wilmot** South Dakota USA
243 F3 **Wilmslow** Cheshire England UK
241 F2 **Wilnecote** Staffordshire England UK
425 K7 **Wilpena** SA Australia
425 L6 **Wilson** *watercourse* Qld Australia
120 I1 **Wilson** *watercourse* Nunavut Canada
130 F3 **Wilson** Arkansas USA
130 F5 **Wilson** Louisiana USA
131 M3 **Wilson** North Carolina USA
130 C3 **Wilson** Oklahoma USA
129 L4 **Wilson** Texas USA
162 B6 **Wilson, Cabo** *cape* Chile
117 K5 **Wilson, Cape** Nunavut Canada
124 F3 **Wilson Creek** Washington USA
436 K2 **Wilson Hills** *range* Antarctica
129 M1 **Wilson Lake** Kansas USA
425 M9 **Wilsons Promontory** *peninsula* Vic. Australia
125 O6 **Wilsonville** Nebraska USA
124 D4 **Wilsonville** Oregon USA
226 E1 **Wilstedt** Germany
224 E6 **Wilster** Germany
226 D1 **Wilsum** Germany
227 H2 **Wilthen** Germany
240 E3 **Wilton** Herefordshire England UK
240 D3 **Wilton** Somerset England UK
241 F3 **Wilton** Wiltshire England UK
127 P4 **Wilton** Maine USA
125 O3 **Wilton** North Dakota USA
241 F3 **Wiltshire** *admin. area* England UK
229 G2 **Wiltz** Luxembourg
424 G6 **Wiluna** WA Australia
120 F5 **Wimapedi** *watercourse* Manitoba Canada
125 P3 **Wimbledon** North Dakota USA
241 H2 **Wimblington** Cambridgeshire England UK
119 O7 **Wimborne** Alberta Canada
241 F4 **Wimborne St Giles** Dorset England UK
241 I4 **Wimereux** France
131 I6 **Wimico, Lake** Florida USA
229 H2 **Wimmenau** France
226 D4 **Wimmis** Switzerland
134 C4 **Wina** Nicaragua
118 M5 **Winagami Lake** Alberta Canada
126 H6 **Winamac** Indiana USA
240 E3 **Wincanton** Somerset England UK
241 H4 **Winchelsea** East Sussex England UK
127 N4 **Winchester** Ontario Canada
423 D7 **Winchester** New Zealand
241 F3 **Winchester** Hampshire England UK
124 G3 **Winchester** Idaho USA
126 I8 **Winchester** Kentucky USA
126 J7 **Winchester** Ohio USA
127 L7 **Winchester** Virginia USA
116 F5 **Wind** *watercourse* Yukon Territory Canada
125 K5 **Wind** *watercourse* Wyoming USA
125 K5 **Wind River Range** Wyoming USA
127 L6 **Windber** Pennsylvania USA
119 N7 **Windermere** British Columbia Canada
242 E2 **Windermere** *lake* England UK
308 C4 **Windhoek** Namibia
120 I6 **Windigo** *watercourse* Ontario Canada
127 O2 **Windigo** *watercourse* Québec Canada
120 J6 **Windigo Lake** Ontario Canada
125 Q7 **Windom** Kansas USA
125 R5 **Windom** Minnesota USA
130 D4 **Windom** Texas USA
425 L6 **Windorah** Qld Australia
436 G2 **Winds, Bay of** Antarctica
425 N8 **Windsor** NSW Australia
123 F10 **Windsor** Nova Scotia Canada
126 J5 **Windsor** Ontario Canada
127 O4 **Windsor** Québec Canada
241 G3 **Windsor** Windsor and Maidenhead England UK
124 D7 **Windsor** California USA
131 M3 **Windsor** North Carolina USA
131 M2 **Windsor** Virginia USA
241 G3 **Windsor and Maidenhead** *admin. area* England UK
308 D5 **Windsorton** South Africa
119 T7 **Windthorst** Saskatchewan Canada
130 B4 **Windthorst** Texas USA
423 I1 **Windward Islands** Antipodes Islands New Zealand
135 F2 **Windward Passage** *marine channel* Caribbean
423 D6 **Windwhistle** New Zealand
424 F8 **Windy Harbour** WA Australia
245 F3 **Windy Harbour** Ireland
120 E2 **Windy Lake** Nunavut Canada
120 F8 **Windygates** Manitoba Canada
125 P2 **Windygates** North Dakota USA
379 H4 **Wine-maw** Myanmar
119 P5 **Winefred Lake** Alberta Canada
155 G3 **Wineperu** Guyana
119 N6 **Winfield** Alberta Canada
130 H4 **Winfield** Alabama USA
125 Q8 **Winfield** Kansas USA
131 I2 **Winfield** Tennessee USA
130 D4 **Winfield** Texas USA
127 K7 **Winfield** West Virginia USA
240 D2 **Winforton** Herefordshire England UK
125 O3 **Wing** North Dakota USA
243 G1 **Wingates** Northumberland England UK
Wingellina *see* **Irrunytju** Australia
125 R3 **Winger** Minnesota USA
127 K5 **Wingham** Ontario Canada
372 C6 **Wini** Indonesia
125 K3 **Winifred** Montana USA
120 L5 **Winisk** *watercourse* Ontario Canada
120 L6 **Winisk Lake** Ontario Canada
129 K5 **Wink** Texas USA
128 G4 **Winkelman** Arizona USA
226 G3 **Winklarn** Germany
120 G8 **Winkler** Manitoba Canada
226 G4 **Winklern** Austria
118 M8 **Winlaw** British Columbia Canada
124 D3 **Winlock** Washington USA
126 G5 **Winnebago, Lake** Wisconsin USA
124 F6 **Winnemucca** Nevada USA
124 F6 **Winnemucca Lake** Nevada USA
125 P5 **Winner** South Dakota USA
125 K3 **Winnett** Montana USA
130 E5 **Winnfield** Louisiana USA
120 D3 **Winnibigoshish, Lake** Minnesota USA
120 G8 **Winnipeg** Manitoba Canada
120 G7 **Winnipeg** *watercourse* Manitoba Canada
117 J8 **Winnipeg, Lake** Manitoba Canada
120 G7 **Winnipeg Beach** Manitoba Canada
119 V7 **Winnipegosis** Manitoba Canada
117 J8 **Winnipegosis, Lake** Manitoba Canada
127 P5 **Winnipesaukee, Lake** New Hampshire USA
130 F4 **Winnsboro** Louisiana USA
122 G6 **Winokapau Lake** Newfoundland and Labrador Canada
128 G3 **Winona** Arizona USA
125 O7 **Winona** Kansas USA
126 F4 **Winona** Minnesota USA
130 G4 **Winona** Mississippi USA
126 F8 **Winona** Missouri USA
130 D4 **Winona** Texas USA
226 D1 **Winschoten** Netherlands
226 E1 **Winsen** Germany
243 F3 **Winsford** Cheshire England UK
240 D3 **Winsford** Somerset England UK
242 F2 **Winskill** Cumbria England UK
241 G3 **Winslow** Buckinghamshire England UK
128 G3 **Winslow** Arizona USA
125 Q6 **Winslow** Nebraska USA
240 E3 **Winson** Gloucestershire England UK
241 F1 **Winster** Derbyshire England UK
131 K2 **Winston-Salem** North Carolina USA
224 D6 **Winsum** Netherlands
131 K6 **Winter Garden** Florida USA
131 K6 **Winter Park** Florida USA
226 E2 **Winterberg** Germany
241 E4 **Winterborne Kingston** Dorset England UK
240 E4 **Winterborne Steepleton** Dorset England UK
241 F3 **Winterbourne Bassett** Wiltshire England UK
241 F3 **Winterbourne Dauntsey** Wiltshire England UK
123 D10 **Winterport** Maine USA
130 B5 **Winters** Texas USA
126 D6 **Winterset** Iowa USA
229 I3 **Winterthur** Switzerland
123 L9 **Winterton** Newfoundland and Labrador Canada
241 I2 **Winterton-on-Sea** Norfolk England UK
131 M3 **Winterville** North Carolina USA
243 I3 **Winthorpe** Lincolnshire England UK
123 D10 **Winthrop** Maine USA
126 D4 **Winthrop** Minnesota USA
124 E2 **Winthrop** Washington USA
425 L5 **Winton** Qld Australia
423 C8 **Winton** New Zealand
131 M2 **Winton** North Carolina USA
241 G2 **Winwick** Cambridgeshire England UK
243 F3 **Winwick** Warrington England UK
226 F2 **Wipper** *watercourse* Germany
374 E4 **Wiralaga** Indonesia
372 E4 **Wiriagar** *watercourse* Indonesia
241 F1 **Wirksworth** Derbyshire England UK
372 D5 **Wirmaf** Indonesia
242 E3 **Wirral** *admin. area* England UK
426 6a **Wisas** *island* Federated States of Micronesia
241 H2 **Wisbech** Cambridgeshire England UK
123 D10 **Wiscasset** Maine USA
114 **Wisconsin** *admin. area* USA
126 F5 **Wisconsin** *watercourse* Wisconsin USA
126 G5 **Wisconsin Dells** Wisconsin USA
436 P1 **Wisconsin Range** Antarctica
126 G4 **Wisconsin Rapids** Wisconsin USA
131 J2 **Wise** Virginia USA
119 R7 **Wiseton** Saskatchewan Canada
119 T7 **Wishart** Saskatchewan Canada
244 E5 **Wishaw** North Lanarkshire Scotland UK
125 P3 **Wishek** North Dakota USA
307 H2 **Wisil Dabarow** Somalia
227 K2 **Wisła** *watercourse* Poland
227 K3 **Wisłoka** *watercourse* Poland
224 F6 **Wismar** Germany
130 F5 **Wisner** Louisiana USA
125 Q6 **Wisner** Nebraska USA
241 I4 **Wissant** France
229 H2 **Wissembourg** France
241 H2 **Wissey** *watercourse* England UK
240 E2 **Wistanstow** Shropshire England UK
118 H6 **Wistaria** British Columbia Canada
130 D3 **Wister** Oklahoma USA
130 D3 **Wister Lake** Oklahoma USA
241 G2 **Wistow** Cambridgeshire England UK
243 G3 **Wistow** North Yorkshire England UK
308 E5 **Witbank** South Africa
308 C5 **Witbooisvlei** Namibia
119 R6 **Witchekan Lake** Saskatchewan Canada
241 G1 **Witham** *watercourse* England UK
241 H3 **Witham** Essex England UK
241 H3 **Withcall** Lincolnshire England UK
241 G2 **Withcote** Leicester England UK
126 F4 **Withee** Wisconsin USA
243 I3 **Withernsea** East Riding of Yorkshire England UK
241 H2 **Withersfield** Suffolk England UK
242 F2 **Witherslack** Cumbria England UK
241 F3 **Withington** Gloucestershire England UK
240 E2 **Withington** Herefordshire England UK
243 F3 **Withnell** Lancashire England UK
240 D3 **Withypool** Somerset England UK
123 L9 **Witless Bay** Newfoundland and Labrador Canada
241 G3 **Witley** Surrey England UK
241 F3 **Witney** Oxfordshire England UK
227 J1 **Witonia** Poland
126 G7 **Witt** Illinois USA
227 H2 **Wittichenau** Germany
226 F1 **Wittingen** Germany
226 D3 **Wittlich** Germany
128 F4 **Wittmann** Arizona USA
224 G5 **Wittow** *island* Germany
226 G1 **Wittstock** Germany
373 I5 **Witu Islands** Papua New Guinea
308 C4 **Witvlei** Namibia
240 D3 **Wiveliscombe** Somerset England UK
120 H4 **Wivenhoe** Manitoba Canada
241 H3 **Wivenhoe** Essex England UK
134 C4 **Wiwili** Nicaragua
241 H2 **Wixoe** Essex England UK
130 C5 **Wixon Valley** Texas USA
155 H3 **W.J. van Blommestein Meer** *lake* Suriname
227 K1 **Wkra** *watercourse* Poland
224 J5 **Władysławowo** Poland
227 J1 **Włocławek** Poland
227 J2 **Włoszczowa** Poland
226 F1 **Wöbbelin** Germany
241 G3 **Woburn** Bedfordshire England UK
425 M9 **Wodonga** Vic. Australia
226 C1 **Woerden** Netherlands
232 B2 **Woerth** France
436 A2 **Wohlthat Mountains** Antarctica
241 I4 **Woincourt** France
373 H6 **Woitape** Papua New Guinea
227 K3 **Wojaszówka** Poland
227 J1 **Wójcin** Poland
372 E5 **Wokam** *island* Indonesia
379 H3 **Wokha** Nagaland India
118 L5 **Woking** Alberta Canada
241 G3 **Woking** Surrey England UK
241 G3 **Wokingham** *admin. area* England UK
227 L2 **Wola Obszańska** Poland
227 J2 **Wolbrom** Poland
126 I6 **Wolcottville** Indiana USA
243 H3 **Wold Newton** North East Lincolnshire England UK
227 G1 **Woldegk** Germany
373 G2 **Woleai** *island* Federated States of Micronesia
78 K7 **Woleai Atoll** *reef* Caroline Islands
305 G4 **Woleu-Ntem** *admin. area* Gabon
119 P5 **Wolf** *watercourse* Alberta Canada
118 E2 **Wolf** *watercourse* Yukon Territory Canada
126 D7 **Wolf** *watercourse* Kansas USA
126 G4 **Wolf** *watercourse* Wisconsin USA
163 4 **Wolf, Isla** *island* Archipiélago de Colón (Galapagos Islands)
163 4 **Wolf, Volcán** *volcano* Archipiélago de Colón (Galapagos Islands)
118 F2 **Wolf Lake** Yukon Territory Canada
125 L4 **Wolf Mountains** Montana USA
125 M2 **Wolf Point** Montana USA
226 G2 **Wolfen** Germany
229 I3 **Wolfenschiessen** Switzerland
241 H2 **Wolferton** Norfolk England UK
129 L4 **Wolfforth** Texas USA
226 G4 **Wolfgangsee** *lake* Austria
240 C3 **Wolf's Castle** Pembrokeshire Wales UK
227 H4 **Wolfsberg** Austria
226 F1 **Wolfsburg** Germany
227 G3 **Wolfsegg am Hausruck** Austria
229 H3 **Wolfwil** Switzerland
229 I3 **Wolhusen** Switzerland
227 H1 **Wolin** Poland
162 C6 **Wollaston, Isla** *island* Chile
119 T3 **Wollaston Lake** Saskatchewan Canada
119 T3 **Wollaston Lake** Saskatchewan Canada
116 H5 **Wollaston Peninsula** Northwest Territories/Nunavut Canada
425 K4 **Wollogorang** NT Australia
425 N8 **Wollongong** NSW Australia
304 B3 **Wologizi Mountains** Liberia
227 L3 **Wołosate** Ukraine
227 I2 **Wołów** Poland
119 T7 **Wolseley** Saskatchewan Canada
125 P4 **Wolsey** South Dakota USA
243 G2 **Wolsingham** Durham England UK
117 L6 **Wolstenholme, Cap** *cape* Québec Canada
226 D1 **Wolvega** Netherlands
241 F3 **Wolvercote** Oxfordshire England UK
243 F4 **Wolverhampton** *admin. area* England UK
241 E2 **Wolverhampton** West Midlands England UK
119 M4 **Wolverine** *watercourse* Alberta Canada
241 G2 **Wolverton** Milton Keynes England UK
243 H2 **Wombleton** North Yorkshire England UK
243 G3 **Wombwell** South Yorkshire England UK
372 E4 **Wondiwoi, Pegunungan** *mountain* Indonesia
386 E4 **Wŏnju** South Korea
375 F5 **Wonosari** Indonesia
375 F5 **Wonosobo** Indonesia
372 C6 **Wonreli** Indonesia
386 E3 **Wŏnsan** North Korea
425 M9 **Wonthaggi** Vic. Australia
119 R8 **Wood** *watercourse* Saskatchewan Canada
436 L2 **Wood Bay** Antarctica
116 H7 **Wood Buffalo National Park** Alberta/Northwest Territories Canada
241 I2 **Wood Dalling** Norfolk England UK
123 G10 **Wood Islands** Prince Edward Island Canada
119 R8 **Wood Mountain** Saskatchewan Canada
125 P6 **Wood River** Nebraska USA
241 G2 **Wood Walton** Cambridgeshire England UK
372 F7 **Woodah, Isle** NT Australia
131 K5 **Woodbine** Georgia USA
125 Q7 **Woodbine** Kansas USA
424 inset **Woodbine Bank** Ashmore Reef and Cartier Island Australia
423 E5 **Woodbourne** New Zealand
425 O1 **Woodburn** NSW Australia
124 D4 **Woodburn** Oregon USA
131 I4 **Woodbury** Georgia USA
127 N7 **Woodbury** New Jersey USA
131 H3 **Woodbury** Tennessee USA
118 G5 **Woodcock** British Columbia Canada
241 F3 **Woodcott** Hampshire England UK
242 B4 **Woodenbridge** Ireland
244 E5 **Woodfoot** Dumfries and Galloway Scotland UK
128 C1 **Woodfords** California USA
242 B3 **Woodfort** Ireland
243 H3 **Woodhall Spa** Lincolnshire England UK
128 C2 **Woodlake** California USA
123 E10 **Woodland** Maine USA
131 M2 **Woodland** North Carolina USA
124 D4 **Woodland** Washington USA
125 M7 **Woodland Park** Colorado USA
120 G7 **Woodlands** Manitoba Canada
374 C2 **Woodlands** *admin. area* Singapore
373 J6 **Woodlark Island** Papua New Guinea
120 G8 **Woodridge** Manitoba Canada
241 H2 **Woodrising** Norfolk England UK
424 I6 **Woodroffe, Mount** SA Australia
131 J3 **Woodruff** South Carolina USA
425 J4 **Woods, Lake** NT Australia
117 J9 **Woods, Lake of the** Canada/USA
122 F5 **Woods Lake** Newfoundland and Labrador Canada
130 C6 **Woodsboro** Texas USA
127 K7 **Woodsfield** Ohio USA
128 G1 **Woodside** Utah USA
130 B4 **Woodson** Texas USA
425 M4 **Woodstock** Qld Australia
123 E9 **Woodstock** New Brunswick Canada
127 K5 **Woodstock** Ontario Canada
241 F3 **Woodstock** Oxfordshire England UK
126 G5 **Woodstock** Illinois USA
242 A4 **Woodstown** Ireland
422 F5 **Woodville** New Zealand
131 H3 **Woodville** Alabama USA
130 F5 **Woodville** Mississippi USA
130 D5 **Woodville** Texas USA
130 B2 **Woodward** Oklahoma USA
130 E5 **Woodworth** Louisiana USA
377 G3 **Woody Island** Paracel Islands
119 T5 **Woody Lake** Saskatchewan Canada
240 E2 **Woofferton** Herefordshire England UK
241 E4 **Wool** Dorset England UK
240 C3 **Woolacombe** Devon England UK
240 E3 **Woolaston** Gloucestershire England UK
240 E2 **Woolhope** Herefordshire England UK
241 E4 **Woolland** Dorset England UK
436 R1 **Woollard, Mount** *mountain* Antarctica
121 S7 **Woollett, Lac** *lake* Québec Canada
240 E2 **Woolstaston** Shropshire England UK
425 K7 **Woomera** SA Australia
127 P5 **Woonsocket** Rhode Island USA
240 E2 **Woonton** Herefordshire England UK
243 G1 **Wooperton** Northumberland England UK
424 E6 **Wooramel Roadhouse** WA Australia
127 K6 **Wooster** Ohio USA
241 G2 **Wooton** Northamptonshire England UK
241 F3 **Wootton Bassett** Wiltshire England UK
241 F2 **Wootton Wawen** Warwickshire England UK
307 G1 **Woqooyi Galbeed** *admin. area* Somalia
229 H3 **Worben** Switzerland
308 C6 **Worcester** South Africa
241 E2 **Worcester** Worcestershire England UK
127 P5 **Worcester** Massachusetts USA
241 E2 **Worcestershire** *admin. area* England UK
240 E2 **Worfield** Shropshire England UK
226 G4 **Wörgl** Austria
372 E5 **Workai** *island* Indonesia
242 E2 **Workington** Cumbria England UK
243 G3 **Worksop** Nottinghamshire England UK
226 C1 **Workum** Netherlands
243 I3 **Worlaby** Lincolnshire England UK
125 L5 **Worland** Wyoming USA
240 E1 **Worleston** Cheshire England UK
241 H2 **Worlington** Suffolk England UK
228 F1 **Wormhout** France
226 E3 **Worms** Germany
240 C3 **Worms Head** *cape* Wales UK
229 L2 **Wörnharts** Austria
241 I4 **Wornicourt** France
226 F3 **Wörnitz** *watercourse* Germany
232 C2 **Wörrstadt** Germany
241 I2 **Worstead** Norfolk England UK
241 I3 **Worth** Kent England UK
229 I2 **Wörth** Germany
129 N5 **Wortham** Texas USA
227 H4 **Wörther See** *lake* Austria
163 12 **Worthing** Barbados
241 G4 **Worthing** West Sussex England UK
125 R5 **Worthington** Minnesota USA
126 J6 **Worthington** Ohio USA
372 C4 **Wosi** Indonesia
372 D5 **Wotap** *island* Indonesia
425 I5 **Wotje Atoll** Marshall Islands
240 C4 **Wotter** Devon England UK
372 B4 **Wotu** Indonesia
375 I5 **Wowoni** *island* Indonesia
375 I5 **Wowoni, Selat** *strait* Indonesia
374 C2 **Woyla** *watercourse* Indonesia
227 J2 **Woźniki** Poland
243 H3 **Wragby** Lincolnshire England UK
434 Q1 **Wrangel Abyssal Plain** *underwater feature* Arctic Ocean
118 E4 **Wrangell** Alaska USA
118 E4 **Wrangell Island** Alaska USA
116 E6 **Wrangell Mountains** Alaska USA
118 A2 **Wrangell-St Elias National Park and Preserve** Alaska USA
241 H1 **Wrangle** Lincolnshire England UK
244 C2 **Wrath, Cape** Scotland UK
243 H3 **Wrawby** North Lincolnshire England UK
240 E3 **Wraxall** Somerset England UK
125 N6 **Wray** Colorado USA
425 O5 **Wreck Reefs** Coral Sea Islands Territory Australia
426 1a **Wrecks, Bay of** Kiribati
243 H2 **Wrelton** North Yorkshire England UK
240 E1 **Wrenbury** Cheshire England UK
241 I2 **Wreningham** Norfolk England UK
131 J4 **Wrens** Georgia USA
119 O8 **Wrentham** Alberta Canada
240 E1 **Wrexham** *admin. area* Wales UK
240 E1 **Wrexham** Wrexham Wales UK
423 C8 **Wreys Bush** New Zealand
125 M5 **Wright** Wyoming USA
436 Q2 **Wright Inlet** *bay* Antarctica
436 Q2 **Wright Island** Antarctica
130 D4 **Wright Patman Lake** Texas USA
127 K5 **Wright Point** Ontario Canada
437 K1 **Wright Valley** Antarctica
130 E3 **Wrightsville** Arkansas USA
131 J4 **Wrightsville** Georgia USA
116 G6 **Wrigley** Northwest Territories Canada
436 P2 **Wrigley Gulf** *bay* Antarctica
227 I2 **Wrocław** Poland
227 I2 **Wroniniec** Poland
241 F3 **Wroughton** Swindon England UK
241 F4 **Wroxall** Isle of Wight England UK
119 U8 **Wroxton** Saskatchewan Canada
227 H1 **Września** Poland
227 I2 **Wschowa** Poland
380 E2 **Wu Jiang** *watercourse* Chongqing China
382 H3 **Wu-mu-ha-ko Yen-tse** *lake* Xinjiang Uygur Zizhiqu China
380 F2 **Wu Shan** *range* Hubei China
381 H4 **Wu'an** Fujian China
424 F7 **Wubin** WA Australia
385 K4 **Wuchang** Heilongjiang China
381 G3 **Wuchang Hu** *lake* Anhui China
381 H2 **Wucheng** Anhui China
385 H5 **Wucheng** Shandong China
381 H4 **Wuchiu Yü (Taiwan)** *island* Taiwan China
380 F4 **Wuchuan** Guangdong China
385 K3 **Wudalianchi** Heilongjiang China
385 I4 **Wudan** Nei Mongol Zizhiqu China
305 F2 **Wudil** Nigeria
425 J8 **Wudinna** SA Australia
380 D1 **Wudu** Gansu China
380 F2 **Wufeng** Hubei China
380 D3 **Wufeng** Yunnan China
381 G1 **Wugang** Henan China
380 F3 **Wugang** Hunan China
381 G3 **Wugong Shan** *mountain* Jiangxi China
384 F5 **Wuhai** Nei Mongol Zizhiqu China
381 G2 **Wuhan** Hubei China
381 H1 **Wuhe** Anhui China
381 H2 **Wuhu** Anhui China
385 H5 **Wuji** Hebei China
381 H2 **Wujiang** Jiangsu China
305 F3 **Wukari** Nigeria
380 D4 **Wuliang Shan** *range* Yunnan China
372 D5 **Wuliaru** *island* Indonesia
380 F3 **Wuling Shan** *range* Hunan China
385 H3 **Wuliyasitai** Nei Mongol Zizhiqu China
372 D5 **Wulmasa** Indonesia
383 H3 **Wulumuqi** Xinjiang Uygur Zizhiqu China
372 D5 **Wulur** Indonesia
305 G3 **Wum** Cameroon
381 G3 **Wumei Shan** *mountain* Jiangxi China
380 E4 **Wuming** Guangxi Zhuangzu Zizhiqu China
226 E1 **Wümme** *watercourse* Germany
306 E2 **Wunagak** Sudan
379 H5 **Wundwin** Myanmar
229 I1 **Wünnenberg** Germany
120 K6 **Wunnummin Lake** Ontario Canada
120 K6 **Wunnummin Lake** Ontario Canada
226 E1 **Wunstorf** Germany
379 H4 **Wuntho** Myanmar
226 D2 **Wupper** *watercourse* Germany
308 C6 **Wuppertal** South Africa
384 F6 **Wuqi** Shaanxi China
382 E5 **Wuqia** Xinjiang Uygur Zizhiqu China
381 G1 **Wuquan** Henan China
305 F2 **Wurno** Nigeria
127 N6 **Wurtsboro** New York USA
229 J1 **Wurzbach** Germany
232 C2 **Würzburg** Germany
229 K1 **Wurzen** Germany
380 D1 **Wushan** Gansu China
382 F4 **Wushi** Xinjiang Uygur Zizhiqu China
426 7 **Wusi** Vanuatu
80 D8 **Wüst Seamount** *underwater feature* Atlantic Ocean
226 G1 **Wusterwitz** Germany
382 G4 **Wusu** Xinjiang Uygur Zizhiqu China
385 H5 **Wutai Shan** *range* Shanxi China
373 G4 **Wuvulu Island** Papua New Guinea
384 E5 **Wuwei** Gansu China
380 F2 **Wuxi** Chongqing China
381 I2 **Wuxi** Jiangsu China
380 F2 **Wuxia** Chongqing China
385 G6 **Wuxiang** Shanxi China
380 F4 **Wuxuan** Guangxi Zhuangzu Zizhiqu China
381 G2 **Wuxue** Hubei China
380 E3 **Wuyang** Guizhou China
385 H5 **Wuyi** Hebei China
381 G3 **Wuyi Shan** *range* Fujian China
381 H3 **Wuyishan** Fujian China
384 F4 **Wuyuan** Nei Mongol Zizhiqu China
381 G2 **Wuyue Shuiku** *lake* Henan China
384 F5 **Wuzhong** Zishiqu China
381 F4 **Wuzhou** Guangxi Zhuangzu Zizhiqu China
381 F4 **Wuzhu Zhou** *island* Guangdong China
77 T13 **Wyandot Seamount** *underwater feature* Atlantic Ocean
425 M6 **Wyandra** Qld Australia
241 G2 **Wyberton** Lincolnshire England UK
240 E1 **Wybunbury** Cheshire England UK
241 F2 **Wychnor** Staffordshire England UK
240 E3 **Wye** *watercourse* England/Wales UK
240 E4 **Wyke Regis** Dorset England UK
241 F3 **Wylye** Wiltshire England UK
119 R7 **Wymark** Saskatchewan Canada
125 Q6 **Wymore** Nebraska USA
424 I3 **Wyndham** WA Australia
423 C8 **Wyndham** New Zealand
162 B5 **Wyndham, Monte** *mountain* Chile
245 D4 **Wyndham's Bridge** Ireland
125 Q3 **Wyndmere** North Dakota USA
118 M8 **Wynndel** British Columbia Canada
130 F3 **Wynne** Arkansas USA
130 C3 **Wynnewood** Oklahoma USA
116 H4 **Wynniatt Bay** Northwest Territories Canada
126 C8 **Wynona** Oklahoma USA
119 S7 **Wynyard** Saskatchewan Canada
114 **Wyoming** *admin. area* USA
126 F5 **Wyoming** Iowa USA
126 I5 **Wyoming** Michigan USA
125 J5 **Wyoming Range** Wyoming USA
425 N8 **Wyong** NSW Australia
241 E2 **Wyre Piddle** Worcestershire England UK
241 F2 **Wysall** Nottinghamshire England UK
227 K2 **Wyśmierzyce** Poland
227 L2 **Wysokie** Poland
227 L1 **Wysokie Mazowieckie** Poland
227 J2 **Wyszanów** Poland
227 K1 **Wyszków** Poland
227 K1 **Wyszogród** Poland
131 K2 **Wytheville** Virginia USA
435 F2 **Wyville-Thomson Ridge** *underwater feature* Atlantic Ocean

X

308 C1 **Xá-Muteba** Angola
303 I5 **Xaafuun** Somalia
307 I1 **Xaafuun, Raas** *cape* Somalia
379 F3 **Xab Qu** *watercourse* Xizang Zizhiqu China
308 D4 **Xade** Botswana
309 F5 **Xai-Xai** Mozambique
376 D3 **Xainabouli** *admin. area* Laos
307 H2 **Xalin** Somalia
376 E3 **Xam Tai** Laos
156 B4 **Xambioá** Brazil
376 E2 **Xamnua** Laos
308 D4 **Xanagas** Botswana
376 D3 **Xanakham** Laos
378 D2 **Xang Qu** *watercourse* Xizang Zizhiqu China
308 B3 **Xangongo** Angola
226 D2 **Xanten** Germany
235 D5 **Xanthi** Greece
158 D3 **Xapuri** Brazil
307 H3 **Xarardheere** Somalia
231 G4 **Xarraca, Punta** *cape* Spain
384 D2 **Xatgal** Mongolia
231 F4 **Xàtiva** Spain
308 D4 **Xau, Lake** *lake* Botswana
161 I2 **Xavantes, Represa de** *lake* Brazil
157 B5 **Xavantes, Serra dos** *range* Brazil
378 E2 **Xaxa Zangbo** *watercourse* Xizang Zizhiqu China
376 D3 **Xayabouli** Laos
376 D2 **Xeng** *watercourse* Laos
126 J7 **Xenia** Ohio USA
155 F4 **Xeriuini** *watercourse* Brazil
230 C2 **Xermade** Spain
380 E2 **Xi He** *watercourse* Sichuan China
380 F4 **Xi Jiang** *watercourse* Guangdong China
381 G2 **Xi Xian** Henan China
380 E1 **Xi'an** Shaanxi China
381 F1 **Xia Xian** Shanxi China
381 H1 **Xia Zhen** Shandong China
380 D2 **Xia'er** Sichuan China
385 I5 **Xiabancheng** Hebei China
385 H6 **Xiajin** Shandong China
381 H4 **Xiamen** Fujian China
381 H4 **Xiamen** Fujian China
381 F3 **Xiang Jiang** *lake* Hunan China
381 F3 **Xiang Jiang** *watercourse* Hunan China
381 G1 **Xiangcheng** Henan China
380 C3 **Xiangcheng** Yunnan China
379 H2 **Xiangda** Qinghai China
381 F2 **Xiangfan** Hubei China
384 G6 **Xiangfen** Shanxi China
380 F2 **Xiangfeng** Hubei China
381 H2 **Xianghe** Anhui China
381 G3 **Xiangjiang** Jiangxi China
376 D3 **Xiangkhoang** Laos
376 D3 **Xiangkhoang Plateau** Laos
380 E2 **Xiangkou** Chongqing China
384 G6 **Xiangning** Shanxi China
378 D2 **Xiangquan He** *watercourse* Xizang Zizhiqu China
380 C4 **Xiangshan** Yunnan China
381 H1 **Xiangshui** Jiangsu China
381 F3 **Xiangtan** Hunan China
385 H6 **Xiangyuan** Shanxi China
381 H3 **Xianju** Zhejiang China
381 G2 **Xianjuemiao Shuiku** *lake* Hubei China
381 G2 **Xianning** Hubei China
380 D2 **Xianshui** Sichuan China
380 C2 **Xianshui He** *watercourse* Sichuan China
381 G2 **Xiantao** Hubei China
381 H3 **Xianxia Ling** *range* Fujian China
380 E1 **Xianyang** Shaanxi China
385 K3 **Xiao Hinggan Ling** *range* Heilongjiang China
380 D3 **Xiao Jiang** *watercourse* Yunnan China
381 H3 **Xiao Xi** *lake* Zhejiang China
385 J5 **Xiaochangshan Dao** *island* Liaoning China
381 G2 **Xiaogan** Hubei China
381 G3 **Xiaogang** Jiangxi China
380 F4 **Xiaojiang** Guangxi Zhuangzu Zizhiqu China
380 F4 **Xiaojiang Shuiku** *lake* Guangxi Zhuangzu Zizhiqu China
381 F3 **Xiaopu** Hunan China
385 J4 **Xiaoshi** Liaoning China
381 H4 **Xiaoxi** Fujian China
381 F2 **Xiaoxita** Hubei China
384 G5 **Xiaoyi** Shanxi China
380 D2 **Xiaqiong** Sichuan China
380 C2 **Xiasi** Sichuan China
379 F3 **Xiasima** Xizang Zizhiqu China
381 G3 **Xiayang** Hunan China
381 G1 **Xiayi** Henan China
380 D3 **Xichang** Sichuan China
385 H5 **Xicheng** Hebei China
381 F1 **Xichuan** Henan China
379 F3 **Xiege'er** Xizang Zizhiqu China
380 F5 **Xieyang Dao** *island* Guangxi Zhuangzu Zizhiqu China
381 G1 **Xifei He** *watercourse* Anhui China
384 F6 **Xifeng** Gansu China
385 J4 **Xifeng** Liaoning China
384 F5 **Xiji** Ningxia Zizhiqu China
380 E1 **Xihan Shui** *watercourse* Jiangsu China
380 D3 **Xihe Shuiku** *lake* Yunnan China
380 E1 **Xihe Xian** Gansu China
381 G1 **Xihua** Henan China
384 F6 **Xihuachi** Gansu China
381 G2 **Xilang Hu** *lake* Hubei China

385 I4 **Xiliao** *lake* Nei Mongol Zizhiqu China
383 K6 **Xiligou** Qinghai China
385 H4 **Xilinhaote** Nei Mongol Zizhiqu China
385 J1 **Xilinji** Heilongjiang China
133 F4 **Xilitla** Mexico
384 F5 **Xin** Nei Mongol Zizhiqu China
381 G3 **Xin Jiang** *watercourse* Jiangxi China
381 H2 **Xin'an** Anhui China
381 F1 **Xin'an** Henan China
380 E3 **Xin'an** Guizhou China
381 H2 **Xinanjiang Shuiku** *lake* Zhejiang China
385 H4 **Xinbaolage** Nei Mongol Zizhiqu China
385 K4 **Xinbin** Liaoning China
381 F2 **Xinchang** Zhejiang China
381 H3 **Xincheng** Fujian China
381 F4 **Xincheng** Guangdong China
380 E4 **Xincheng** Guangxi Zhuangzu Zizhiqu China
380 D3 **Xincheng** Sichuan China
380 C2 **Xindu** Sichuan China
380 D2 **Xindu** Sichuan China
381 G4 **Xinfeng Jiang** *lake* Guangdong China
384 G5 **Xing Xian** Shanxi China
385 I5 **Xingcheng** Hebei China
385 I5 **Xingcheng** Liaoning China
308 C1 **Xinge** Angola
385 H5 **Xinghe** Nei Mongol Zizhiqu China
381 H2 **Xinghua** Jiangsu China
381 H3 **XinghuaWan** *bay* Fujian China
383 H4 **Xingjiang Uygur Zizhiqu** *admin. area* China
385 I5 **Xinglong** Hebei China
381 G4 **Xingning** Guangdong China
380 E3 **Xingren** Guizhou China
380 E3 **Xingshan** Guizhou China
385 H5 **Xingtai** Hebei China
156 A4 **Xingu** *watercourse* Brazil
381 G1 **Xingyang** Henan China
380 D3 **Xingyi** Guizhou China
385 H4 **Xinhaote** Nei Mongol Zizhiqu China
382 G4 **Xinhe** Xinjiang Uygur Zizhiqu China
381 G4 **Xinhua** Guangdong China
380 D3 **Xinhua** Sichuan China
380 E4 **Xinhua** Yunnan China
380 F3 **Xinhuang** Hunan China
381 F4 **Xinhui** Guangdong China
385 I4 **Xinhui** Nei Mongol Zizhiqu China
384 E6 **Xining** Qinghai China
385 H5 **Xinji** Hebei China
381 G2 **Xinji** Henan China
381 E3 **Xinjin** Sichuan China
380 E4 **Xinjing** Guangxi Zhuangzu Zizhiqu China
385 I4 **Xinkai He** *watercourse* Nei Mongol Zizhiqu China
385 H5 **Xinle** Hebei China
380 F2 **Xinling** Hubei China
380 D2 **Xinmian** Sichuan China
385 J4 **Xinmin** Liaoning China
384 F6 **Xinning** Gansu China
380 E4 **Xinning** Guangxi Zhuangzu Zizhiqu China
380 E2 **Xinning** Sichuan China
381 G2 **Xinshi** Hubei China
380 D3 **Xinshiba** Sichuan China
385 I6 **Xintai** Shandong China
381 G1 **Xinxiang** Henan China
381 G2 **Xinyang** Henan China
381 F2 **Xinye** Henan China
380 F4 **Xinyi** Guangdong China
381 H1 **Xinyi** Jiangsu China
381 G3 **Xinyu** Jiangxi China
383 K5 **Xinyuan** Qinghai China
382 H4 **Xinyuan** Xinjiang Uygur Zizhiqu China
384 F5 **Xinzhao Shan** *mountain* Nei Mongol Zizhiqu China
380 E4 **Xinzhou** Guangxi Zhuangzu Zizhiqu China
381 G2 **Xinzhou** Hubei China
385 G5 **Xinzhou** Shanxi China
381 H4 **Xiongdi Yu** *island* Fujian China
381 H3 **Xiongshi** Jiangxi China
385 H5 **Xiongzhou** Hebei China
385 H5 **Xiping** Shanxi China
381 H3 **Xiping** Zhejiang China
157 D5 **Xique Xique** Brazil
158 D2 **Xirua** *watercourse* Brazil
380 D4 **Xisa** Yunnan China
384 F5 **Xishanzui** Nei Mongol Zizhiqu China
304 B2 **Xitole** Guinea-Bissau
381 G2 **Xiu Shui** *watercourse* Jiangxi China
381 G3 **Xiugu** Jiangxi China
380 D4 **Xiushan** Yunnan China
381 I2 **Xiushan Dao** *island* Zhejiang China
385 J5 **Xiuyan** Liaoning China
384 G5 **Xiuyan** Shaanxi China
378 E3 **Xixabangma Feng** *mountain* Xizang Zizhiqu China
381 F1 **Xixia** Henan China
384 G6 **Xixian** Shanxi China
384 G6 **Xixian** *mountain* Shanxi China
380 E2 **Xixiang** Shaanxi China
381 H3 **Xiyang Dao** *island* Fujian China
380 E4 **Xiyang Jiang** *watercourse* Yunnan China
379 F2 **Xizang Zizhiqu** *admin. area* China
133 H5 **Xkanhá** Mexico
388 H5 **Xo'jayli** Uzbekistan
388 H5 **Xorazm** *admin. area* Uzbekistan
133 H5 **Xpujil** Mexico
381 H2 **Xuancheng** Anhui China
385 H5 **Xuanhua** Hebei China
380 E3 **Xuanwei** Yunnan China
381 G1 **Xuchang** Henan China
381 H2 **Xucheng** Jiangsu China
307 G3 **Xuddur** Somalia
307 H2 **Xudun** Somalia
380 C3 **Xue Shan** *range* Yunnan China
384 G5 **Xuejiawan** Nei Mongol Zizhiqu China
384 E6 **Xueshan** *mountain* Gansu China
381 G3 **Xujiang** Jiangxi China
385 K2 **Xun He** *watercourse* Heilongjiang China
379 G2 **Xung Qu** *watercourse* Xizang Zizhiqu China
385 H6 **Xunxian** Henan China
380 F2 **Xunyang** Shaanxi China
380 E1 **Xunyi** Shaanxi China
380 F5 **Xuwen** Guangdong China
380 E3 **Xuyong** Sichuan China
381 H1 **Xuzhou** Jiangsu China
235 D5 **Xylagani** Greece

Y

380 D2 **Ya'an** Sichuan China
372 C4 **Yaba** Indonesia
305 F4 **Yabassi** Cameroon
304 C3 **Yabayo** Côte d'Ivoire
161 G3 **Yabebyry** Paraguay
307 F3 **Yabēlo** Ethiopia
159 F4 **Yabeta** Bolivia
234 D4 **Yablanitsa** Bulgaria
234 E4 **Yablanovo** Bulgaria
237 AI5 **Yablon** *watercourse* Russian Federation
385 G2 **Yablon Ovyy Khrebet** *range* Russian Federation
225 P2 **Yablonovka** Russian Federation
237 X8 **Yablonovyy Khrebet** *range* Russian Federation
234 D1 **Yabluniv** Ukraine
234 D1 **Yablun'ka** Ukraine
305 E2 **Yabo** Nigeria
384 E5 **Yabrai Shan** *range* Nei Mongol Zizhiqu China
154 C5 **Yabuyanos** Peru
427 9 **Yacata** *island* Fiji
380 F5 **Yacha** Hainan China
124 C4 **Yachats** Oregon USA
380 E3 **Yachi He** *lake* Guizhou China
124 D4 **Yacolt** Washington USA
154 E3 **Yacuaray** Venezuela
160 F2 **Yacuiba** Argentina
159 E4 **Yacuma** *watercourse* Bolivia
161 G3 **Yacyretá Apipé, Embalse** *lake* Paraguay
388 H6 **Yadak** Iran
393 D8 **Yadgir** Karnataka India
393 D8 **Yadiki** Andhra Pradesh India
388 E2 **Yadrin** Russian Federation
381 I4 **Yaeyama Rettō** *island* Japan
301 I2 **Yafran** Libya
427 9 **Yagasa** *island* Fiji
235 F6 **Yağcılar** Turkey
436 T3 **Yaghan Basin** *underwater feature* Southern Ocean
223 Q5 **Yaglyayarvi** Russian Federation
388 G6 **Yagman** Turkmenistan
238 F6 **Yagodnoye** Russian Federation
305 H2 **Yagoua** Cameroon
134 E2 **Yaguajay** Cuba
161 H4 **Yaguari** *watercourse* Uruguay
154 D5 **Yaguas** Peru
128 H6 **Yagui** *watercourse* Mexico
306 C3 **Yahila** Democratic Republic of Congo
306 C4 **Yahisuli** Democratic Republic of Congo
119 M8 **Yahk** British Columbia Canada
132 E4 **Yahualica** Mexico
306 C3 **Yahuma** Democratic Republic of Congo
376 C4 **Yai (Ye)** Myanmar
387 H4 **Yaita** Japan
310 3d **Yaiza** Canary Islands
387 H4 **Yaizu** Japan
133 G5 **Yajalón** Mexico
373 G4 **Yakamul** Papua New Guinea
116 A5 **Yakan, Mys** *cape* Russian Federation
385 I2 **Yakeshi** Nei Mongol Zizhiqu China
124 E3 **Yakima** Washington USA
234 C4 **Yakimovo** Bulgaria
306 C3 **Yakiri** Democratic Republic of Congo
388 J6 **Yakkabog'** Uzbekistan
391 J4 **Yakmach** Pakistan
304 D2 **Yako** Burkina Faso
306 C3 **Yakoma** Democratic Republic of Congo
306 C3 **Yakonga** Democratic Republic of Congo
386 F5 **Yaku-shima** *island* Japan
387 I2 **Yakumo** Japan
118 B3 **Yakutat** Alaska USA
118 A3 **Yakutat Bay** Alaska USA
237 AA6 **Yakutsk** Russian Federation
379 G2 **Yala** Xizang Zizhiqu China
304 D2 **Yala** Ghana
393 E10 **Yala** Sri Lanka
376 D6 **Yala** Thailand
376 D6 **Yala** *admin. area* Thailand
304 C3 **Yalakoro** Guinea
424 I7 **Yalata Roadhouse** SA Australia
118 K8 **Yale** British Columbia Canada
126 J5 **Yale** Michigan USA
124 D4 **Yale Lake** Washington USA
304 D2 **Yalgo** Burkina Faso
424 F7 **Yalgoo** WA Australia
306 C4 **Yali** Democratic Republic of Congo
306 C3 **Yalibongo** Democratic Republic of Congo
305 I3 **Yalinga** Central African Republic
133 H4 **Yalkubul, Punta** *cape* Mexico
304 D2 **Yallo** Burkina Faso
425 M8 **Yallock** NSW Australia
305 H3 **Yaloké** Central African Republic
380 D3 **Yalong Jiang** *watercourse* Sichuan China
235 F5 **Yalova** *admin. area* Turkey
394 D4 **Yalpugh, Ozero** *lake* Ukraine
394 E4 **Yalta** Ukraine
234 E1 **Yaltushkiv** Ukraine
385 K4 **Yalu** *watercourse* Jilin China
306 C3 **Yalufi** Democratic Republic of Congo
388 J2 **Yalutorovsk** Russian Federation
306 C4 **Yaluwe** Democratic Republic of Congo
235 G6 **Yalvaç** Turkey
237 AC8 **Yam-Alin', Khrebet** *range* Russian Federation
163 5 **Yama, Punta** *cape* Isla de Pascua (Easter Island)
127 O3 **Yamachiche** Québec Canada
386 F4 **Yamaguchi** Japan
236 O4 **Yamal, Poluostrov** *peninsula* Russian Federation
236 P5 **Yamalo-Nenetskiy Avtonomnyy Okrug** *admin. area* Russian Federation
384 G2 **Yamarovka** Russian Federation
134 G3 **Yamasá** Dominican Republic
425 O7 **Yamba** NSW Australia
304 B2 **Yambering** Guinea
154 D4 **Yambí, Mesa de** *region* Colombia
306 D3 **Yambio** Sudan
307 F2 **Yambo** Ethiopia
234 E4 **Yambol** Bulgaria
234 E4 **Yambol** *admin. area* Bulgaria
158 B2 **Yambrasbamba** Peru
236 R4 **Yambuto, Ozero** *lake* Russian Federation
158 B3 **Yamcay, Cerro** *mountain* Peru
372 D5 **Yamdena** *island* Indonesia
376 B3 **Yamethin** Myanmar
377 I2 **Y'Ami** *island* Philippines
373 F5 **Yamin, Puncak** *mountain* Indonesia
304 C3 **Yamoussoukro** Côte d'Ivoire
125 L6 **Yampa** Colorado USA
125 K6 **Yampa** *watercourse* Colorado USA
234 F1 **Yampil'** Ukraine
372 D4 **Yamtu, Tanjung** *cape* Indonesia
392 D4 **Yamunanagar** Haryana India
393 E10 **Yan Oya** *watercourse* Sri Lanka
385 I5 **Yan Shan** *range* Hebei China
384 G6 **Yan'an** Shaanxi China
234 C4 **Yana** Bulgaria
237 AB5 **Yana** *watercourse* Russian Federation
304 B3 **Yana** Sierra Leone
373 I6 **Yanaba Island** Papua New Guinea
158 B3 **Yanacancha** Peru
158 B3 **Yanahuanca** Peru
393 F8 **Yanam** Puducherry India
158 D4 **Yanama** Peru
158 D4 **Yanaoca** Peru
388 G2 **Yanaul** Russian Federation
154 C5 **Yanayacu** Peru
390 D5 **Yanbu' al Baḥr** Saudi Arabia
131 L2 **Yanceyville** North Carolina USA
381 H1 **Yancheng** Jiangsu China
380 D2 **Yancheng** Sichuan China
380 D2 **Yancheng** Sichuan China
424 E7 **Yanchep** WA Australia
384 F5 **Yanchi** Zishiqu China
384 G6 **Yanchuan** Shaanxi China
304 E3 **Yanda** Togo
380 D2 **Yandao** Sichuan China
426 7 **Yandé, Île** *island* New Caledonia
427 9a **Yandua** *island* Fiji
238 E2 **Yanega** Russian Federation
304 C2 **Yanfolila** Mali
380 D4 **Yang-Tsung Hai** *lake* Yunnan China
305 I3 **Yangalia** Central African Republic
306 C3 **Yangambi** Democratic Republic of Congo
381 F4 **Yangcheng** Guangdong China
380 E3 **Yangchuan** Guizhou China
381 F4 **Yangchun** Guangdong China
427 9 **Yangganga** *island* Fiji
385 H5 **Yanggao** Shanxi China
384 F5 **Yanghe** Zishiqu China
389 K5 **Yangiqŭrghon** Uzbekistan
389 K5 **Yangiyŭl** Uzbekistan
381 F4 **Yangjiang** Guangdong China
381 G4 **Yangming** Guangdong China
376 C3 **Yangon** *admin. area* Myanmar
376 C3 **Yangon (Rangoon)** Myanmar
223 T5 **Yangory** Russian Federation
223 R5 **Yangozero, Ozero** *lake* Russian Federation
385 H5 **Yangqu Shan** *mountain* Shanxi China
385 H5 **Yangquan** Shanxi China
380 F4 **Yangshuo** Guangxi Zhuangzu Zizhiqu China
Yangtze *see* **Jinsha** China
380 E1 **Yanguan** Gansu China
230 E2 **Yanguas** Spain
385 I5 **Yangxin** Shandong China
386 F3 **Yangyang** South Korea
381 H2 **Yangzhou** Jiangsu China
380 E1 **Yangzhou** Shaanxi China
159 D4 **Yani** Bolivia
223 S5 **Yanishpole** Russian Federation
223 Q6 **Yanis''yarvi, Ozero** *lake* Russian Federation
385 L4 **Yanji** Jilin China
380 D3 **Yanjing** Sichuan China
380 D3 **Yanjing** Yunnan China
237 Y7 **Yankan, Khrebet** *range* Russian Federation
304 D4 **Yankoman** Ghana
380 E2 **Yankou** Sichuan China
125 Q5 **Yankton** South Dakota USA
237 AD4 **Yano-Indigirskaya Nizmennost'** *region* Russian Federation
237 AC6 **Yano-Oymyakonskoye Nagor'ye** *region* Russian Federation
234 C1 **Yanoshi** Ukraine
236 R5 **Yanov-Stan** Russian Federation
383 H4 **Yanqi** Xinjiang Uygur Zizhiqu China
385 H5 **Yanqing** Beijing China
385 K3 **Yanshou** Heilongjiang China
237 AB5 **Yanskiy** Russian Federation
237 AB4 **Yanskiy Zaliv** *bay* Russian Federation
385 J5 **Yantai** Shandong China
225 J5 **Yantarnyy** Russian Federation
234 D4 **Yantra** *watercourse* Bulgaria
154 B5 **Yantzaza** Ecuador
427 9a **Yanutua** *island* Fiji
241 F3 **Yanworth** Gloucestershire England UK
384 G6 **Yanzhang** Shaanxi China
385 H6 **Yanzhou** Shandong China
387 G4 **Yao** Japan
381 E1 **Yao Xian** Shaanxi China
376 C6 **Yao Yai, Ko** *island* Thailand
381 H2 **Yaodu** Anhui China
306 A3 **Yaoundé** Cameroon
426 6 **Yap** *admin. area* Federated States of Micronesia
426 6 **Yap** *island* Federated States of Micronesia
78 J7 **Yap Trench** *underwater feature* Pacific Ocean
155 E5 **Yapacani** *watercourse* Bolivia
158 A2 **Yapato, Punta** *cape* Peru
372 F4 **Yapen** *island* Indonesia
372 E4 **Yapen, Selat** *strait* Indonesia
161 G4 **Yapeyú** Argentina
425 L4 **Yappar** *watercourse* Qld Australia
373 G5 **Yapsiei** Papua New Guinea
427 9 **Yaqeta** *island* Fiji
132 C2 **Yaqui** *watercourse* Mexico
134 E2 **Yara** Cuba
154 D2 **Yaracuy** *admin. area* Venezuela
388 H6 **Yaradzhi** Turkmenistan
235 F7 **Yaraş** Turkey
235 F6 **Yarbasan** Turkey
240 D4 **Yarcombe** Devon England UK
394 D6 **Yardımcı Burnu** *cape* Turkey
241 I2 **Yare** *watercourse* England UK
159 G5 **Yaré** Bolivia
426 4 **Yaren District** Nauru
154 C4 **Yari** *watercourse* Colombia
306 D6 **Yaring** Thailand
154 D2 **Yaritagua** Venezuela
382 E5 **Yarkant He** *watercourse* Xinjiang Uygur Zizhiqu China
379 F3 **Yarlung Zangbo Jiang** *watercourse* Xizang Zizhiqu China
243 G2 **Yarm** Stockton-on-Tees England UK
234 E1 **Yarmolyntsi** Ukraine
123 E11 **Yarmouth** Nova Scotia Canada
241 F4 **Yarmouth** Isle of Wight England UK
388 E1 **Yarnsk** Russian Federation
227 M2 **Yaroslavichi** Ukraine
238 E1 **Yaroslavl'** Russian Federation
388 C1 **Yaroslavl'** Russian Federation
238 H3 **Yaroslavskaya Oblast'** *admin. area* Russian Federation
388 C1 **Yaroslavskaya Oblast'** *admin. area* Russian Federation
236 P5 **Yarro-To** Russian Federation
244 F5 **Yarrowford** Scottish Borders Scotland UK
238 E5 **Yartsevo** Russian Federation
154 C3 **Yarumal** Colombia
383 J3 **Yaruu** Mongolia
160 D2 **Yarvicoya, Cerro** *mountain* Chile
234 E1 **Yaryshev** Ukraine
306 C4 **Yasa** Democratic Republic of Congo
237 AF5 **Yasachnaya** *watercourse* Russian Federation
390 G5 **Yāsāt, Al** *island* United Arab Emirates
238 C6 **Yasen'** Belarus
305 F2 **Yashi** Nigeria
382 G6 **Yashil Tsho** *lake* Xizang Zizhiqu China
388 G1 **Yashkul'** Russian Federation
238 G5 **Yasnogorsk** Russian Federation
376 E4 **Yasothon** Thailand
425 N8 **Yass** NSW Australia
305 E2 **Yassine** *watercourse* Benin
225 P4 **Yasski** Russian Federation
389 L6 **Yassy** *watercourse* Kyrgyzstan
390 G3 **Yāsūj** Iran
227 M1 **Yasyel'da** *watercourse* Belarus
159 E3 **Yata** *watercourse* Bolivia
301 G6 **Yatakala** Niger
240 E3 **Yate** South Gloucestershire England UK
426 7 **Yaté** New Caledonia
119 M3 **Yates** *watercourse* Alberta Canada
120 G1 **Yathkyed Lake** Nunavut Canada
306 C3 **Yatolema** Democratic Republic of Congo
379 H5 **Yatsauk** Myanmar
387 H4 **Yatsuga-take** *volcano* Japan
387 F5 **Yatsushiro** Japan
240 E3 **Yatton** North Somerset England UK
135 H3 **Yauco** Puerto Rico
158 B3 **Yauya** Peru
393 D7 **Yaval** Maharashtra India
389 K6 **Yavan** Tajikistan
154 D4 **Yavaraté** Brazil
132 C3 **Yávaros** Mexico
393 E7 **Yavatmal** Maharashtra India
134 E5 **Yaviza** Panama
227 L3 **Yavoriv** Ukraine
234 C1 **Yavory** Ukraine
382 G5 **Yawatongguz He** *watercourse* Xinjiang Uygur Zizhiqu China
304 B3 **Yawri Bay** *bay* Sierra Leone
241 G2 **Yaxley** Cambridgeshire England UK
306 C4 **Yayama** Democratic Republic of Congo
235 E6 **Yaylaköy** Turkey
391 H3 **Yazd** Iran
391 H3 **Yazd** *admin. area* Iran
238 F3 **Yazhelbitsy** Russian Federation
235 E7 **Yazıköy** Turkey
130 F4 **Yazoo City** Mississippi USA
227 H4 **Ybbs** *watercourse* Austria
161 G2 **Yby Yaú** Paraguay
161 G3 **Ybycuí** Paraguay
224 F5 **Yderby** Denmark
224 E5 **Yding Skovhøj** *mountain* Denmark
224 H4 **Ydrefors** Sweden
379 G5 **Ye Kyun** Myanmar
379 H4 **Ye-u** Myanmar
127 N7 **Yeadon** Pennsylvania USA
240 D4 **Yealmpton** Devon England UK
385 I4 **Yebaishou** Liaoning China
301 J4 **Yebbi Bou** Chad
302 B3 **Yebbi Bou** Chad
231 F2 **Yebra de Basa** Spain
231 F4 **Yecla** Spain
132 C2 **Yécora** Mexico
379 H5 **Yedashe** Myanmar
307 F2 **YeDedub Bihēroch Bihēresboch na Hizboch** *admin. area* Ethiopia
243 H2 **Yedingham** North Yorkshire England UK
238 E4 **Yedrovo** Russian Federation
238 B5 **Yedy** Belarus
307 G3 **Yeed** Somalia
372 D4 **Yef Lio** Indonesia
238 F3 **Yefimovskiy** Russian Federation
238 H6 **Yefremov** Russian Federation
389 L3 **Yegindybulak** Kazakhstan
238 H5 **Yegor'yevsk** Russian Federation
306 E3 **Yei** Sudan
306 E3 **Yei** *watercourse* Sudan
304 D3 **Yeji** Ghana
306 C3 **Yekana** Democratic Republic of Congo
388 H2 **Yekaterinburg** Russian Federation
387 J2 **Yekateriny, Proliv** *lake* Russian Federation
389 M4 **Yekiasha** Kazakhstan
306 C3 **Yekokora** *watercourse* Democratic Republic of Congo
118 I5 **Yekooche** British Columbia Canada
388 D3 **Yelan'** Russian Federation
234 G2 **Yelanets'** Ukraine
238 D2 **Yelatma** Russian Federation
393 D8 **Yelbarga** Karnataka India
160 B3 **Yelcho, Lago** *lake* Chile
235 E6 **Yeleğen** Turkey
238 F6 **Yelenskiy** Russian Federation
394 F2 **Yelets** Russian Federation
238 E3 **Yeligovo** Russian Federation
300 D5 **Yélimané** Mali
237 AD8 **Yelizavety, Mys** *cape* Russian Federation
237 AG8 **Yelizovo** Russian Federation
388 F2 **Yelkhovka** Russian Federation
393 D8 **Yellapur** Karnataka India
242 B3 **Yellow Furze** Ireland
119 S8 **Yellow Grass** Saskatchewan Canada
126 E4 **Yellow Lake** Minnesota USA
381 I1 **Yellow Sea (Huang Hai)**
242 B4 **Yellowford** Ireland
119 N1 **Yellowknife** Northwest Territories Canada
125 J4 **Yellowstone** *watercourse* Montana USA
125 J4 **Yellowstone Lake** Wyoming USA
130 E2 **Yellville** Arkansas USA
124 D3 **Yelm** Washington USA
236 T4 **Yel'nya** Russian Federation
236 S6 **Yeloguy** *watercourse* Russian Federation
389 N4 **Yel'tay** Kazakhstan
240 C4 **Yelverton** Devon England UK
117 K2 **Yelverton Bay** Nunavut Canada
305 F3 **Yelwa** Nigeria
383 J5 **Yema He** *watercourse* Gansu China
383 J5 **Yema Nanshan** *range* Gansu China
131 K4 **Yemassee** South Carolina USA
390 F7 **Yemen** *country*
225 O5 **Yemenets** Russian Federation
305 G4 **Yen** Cameroon
376 E2 **Yên Bái** Vietnam
376 E2 **Yên Châu** Vietnam
376 E2 **Yên Viên** Vietnam
223 Q3 **Yëna** Russian Federation
305 F3 **Yenagoa** Nigeria
394 F3 **Yenakiyevo** Ukraine
379 H5 **Yenangyaun** Myanmar
372 E4 **Yende** Indonesia
304 D3 **Yendi** Ghana
305 G5 **Yénéganou** Congo
306 C4 **Yenge** *watercourse* Democratic Republic of Congo
304 B3 **Yengema** Sierra Leone
382 E5 **Yengisar** Xinjiang Uygur Zizhiqu China
380 C3 **Yengsheng** Yunnan China
235 E6 **Yenice** Turkey
235 E6 **Yenicekent** Turkey
235 E6 **Yenifoça** Turkey
235 E6 **Yenihisar** Turkey
235 F6 **Yeniköy** Turkey
235 G7 **Yenimahalle** Turkey
235 F5 **Yenişehir** Turkey
235 F6 **Yenişehir** Turkey
236 T7 **Yenisey** *watercourse* Russian Federation
236 T7 **Yeniseysk** Russian Federation
236 T7 **Yeniseyskiy Kryazh** *range* Russian Federation
236 R4 **Yeniseyskiy Zaliv** *bay* Russian Federation
229 G4 **Yenne** France
223 T2 **Yenozero, Ozero** *lake* Russian Federation
240 E4 **Yeo** *watercourse* England UK
424 H6 **Yeo Lake** WA Australia
386 E4 **Yeongheung-do** *island* South Korea
240 E4 **Yeovil** Somerset England UK
132 C2 **Yepachic** Mexico
236 P5 **Yepoko** Russian Federation
425 N5 **Yeppoon** Qld Australia
388 H6 **Yerbent** Turkmenistan
388 D6 **Yerevan** Armenia
389 L3 **Yereymentau** Kazakhstan
124 F7 **Yerington** Nevada USA
236 Q6 **Yerkalnadeypur** *watercourse* Russian Federation
234 G1 **Yerky** Ukraine
235 E5 **Yerlisu** Turkey
435 G1 **Yermak Plateau** *underwater feature* Arctic Ocean
436 K2 **Yermak Point** Antarctica
238 H3 **Yermakovo** Russian Federation
236 L5 **Yermitsa** Russian Federation
129 J7 **Yermo** Mexico
238 G5 **Yermolino** Russian Federation
237 Z8 **Yerofey Pavlovich** Russian Federation
237 AI5 **Yeropol** Russian Federation
228 F2 **Yerres** *watercourse* France
238 E6 **Yershichi** Russian Federation
388 E3 **Yershov** Russian Federation
236 K6 **Yërtom** Russian Federation
238 I2 **Yertsevo** Russian Federation
158 B3 **Yerupajá, Nevado** *mountain* Peru
390 C3 **Yerushaylim/Al Quds (Jerusalem)** West Bank (Disputed)
241 H5 **Yerville** France
240 D4 **Yes Tor** *mountain* England UK
231 F2 **Yesa, Embalse de** *lake* Spain
379 H5 **Yesagyo** Myanmar
238 F4 **Yesenovichi** Russian Federation
389 M5 **Yesik** Kazakhstan
388 J3 **Yesil'** Kazakhstan
238 D5 **Yessentuki** Russian Federation
237 V5 **Yessey** Russian Federation
237 V5 **Yessey, Ozero** *lake* Russian Federation
243 G1 **Yetlington** Northumberland England UK
425 N7 **Yetman** NSW Australia
228 C3 **Yeu, Île d'** *island* France
225 P5 **Yevdokimovichi** Belarus
394 E4 **Yevpatoriya** Ukraine
237 AB9 **Yevreyskaya** *admin. area* Russian Federation
385 L3 **Yevreyskaya Avtonomnaya Oblast'** *admin. area* Russian Federation
304 E3 **Yewa** *watercourse* Nigeria
388 C4 **Yeysk** Russian Federation
380 F2 **Yezhou** Hubei China
380 F2 **Yezhou** Hubei China
161 H3 **Ygatimí** Paraguay
228 D5 **Ygos-Saint-Saturnin** France
237 Y6 **Ygyatta** *watercourse* Russian Federation
161 H3 **Yhú** Paraguay
385 K3 **Yi'an** Heilongjiang China
380 D3 **Yibin** Sichuan China
381 F2 **Yichang** Hubei China
381 F2 **Yicheng** Hubei China
384 G6 **Yicheng** Shanxi China
381 F1 **Yichuan** Henan China
385 K3 **Yichun** Heilongjiang China
381 G3 **Yichun** Jiangxi China
381 F2 **Yidu** Hubei China
235 G5 **Yığılca** Turkey
426 5 **Yigo** Guam
381 H3 **Yijiang** Jiangxi China
384 G6 **Yijun** Shaanxi China
385 L3 **Yilan** Heilongjiang China
394 F5 **Yıldız Dağı** *mountain* Turkey
380 D3 **Yili He** *watercourse* Yunnan China
380 D4 **Yilong Hu** *lake* Yunnan China
381 F1 **Yima** Henan China
373 G4 **Yimi** *watercourse* Papua New Guinea
235 C6 **Yimnón** Greece
384 G4 **Yin Shan** *range* Nei Mongol Zizhiqu China
384 F5 **Yinchuan** Zishiqu China
379 H2 **Yinduo** Xizang Zizhiqu China
385 H5 **Ying Xian** Shanxi China
381 G2 **Yingcheng** Hubei China
381 G4 **Yingde** Guangdong China
380 F5 **Yinggen** Hainan China
385 J5 **Yingkou** Liaoning China
381 G2 **Yingshang** Anhui China
381 H3 **Yingtan** Jiangxi China
305 G4 **Yingui** Cameroon
381 G3 **Yining** Jiangxi China
382 G4 **Yining** Xinjiang Uygur Zizhiqu China
379 H4 **Yinmabin** Myanmar
379 H2 **Yi'ong Zangbo** *watercourse* Xizang Zizhiqu China
307 F2 **Yirga Alem** Ethiopia
307 F2 **Yirga Ch'efē** Ethiopia
306 E2 **Yirol** Sudan
380 D4 **Yisa** Yunnan China
381 H1 **Yishan** Jiangsu China
385 I6 **Yishui** Shandong China
374 D2 **Yishun** *admin. area* Singapore
384 E5 **Yitiaoshan** Gansu China
385 K4 **Yitong** Jilin China
383 J4 **Yiwu** Xinjiang Uygur Zizhiqu China
380 D4 **Yiwu** Yunnan China
381 H2 **Yiwu** Zhejiang China
381 F1 **Yiyang** Henan China
381 F3 **Yiyang** Hunan China
381 F3 **Yizhang** Hunan China
381 H2 **Yizheng** Jiangsu China
380 E4 **Yizhou** Guangxi Zhuangzu Zizhiqu China
385 H5 **Yizhou** Hebei China
385 J4 **Yizhou** Liaoning China
225 L2 **Yläne** Finland
223 N4 **Yli-Ii** Finland
223 N4 **Yli-Kitka** *lake* Finland
223 N5 **Yli-Lesti** Finland
223 M2 **Yli-Muonio** Finland
223 P3 **Yli-Suolijärvi** *lake* Finland
223 M5 **Ylihärmä** Finland
223 N4 **Ylikärppä** Finland
223 O4 **Ylikiiminki** Finland
223 M3 **Ylinenjärvi** Finland
223 N3 **Ylipää** Finland
222 M5 **Ylistaro** Finland
223 M3 **Ylitornio** Finland
223 N4 **Ylivieska** Finland
223 N4 **Ylivirre** Finland
222 H4 **Ylvingen** Norway
222 H4 **Ylvingen** *island* Norway
117 Q3 **Ymer Nunatak** *mountain* Greenland
117 Q4 **Ymer Øer** *island* Greenland
118 M8 **Ymir** British Columbia Canada
223 G3 **Ymsen** *lake* Sweden
224 H3 **Yngen** *lake* Sweden
389 K4 **Yntaly** Kazakhstan
240 D3 **Ynysddu** Caerphilly Wales UK
130 C6 **Yoakum** Texas USA
305 G2 **Yobe** *admin. area* Nigeria
387 I2 **Yobetsu-dake** *volcano* Japan
303 G5 **Yoboki** Djibouti
159 E5 **Yocalla** Bolivia
240 E2 **Yockleton** Shropshire England UK
129 J1 **Yoder** Colorado USA
125 M6 **Yoder** Wyoming USA
373 F5 **Yodom** Indonesia
373 F5 **Yofor** Indonesia
375 F5 **Yogyakarta** Indonesia
375 F6 **Yogyakarta** *admin. area* Indonesia
118 M7 **Yoho National Park** British Columbia Canada
386 F4 **Yōju** South Korea
305 H4 **Yokadouma** Cameroon
243 H3 **Yokefleet** East Riding of Yorkshire England UK
305 G3 **Yoko** Cameroon
381 J3 **Yokoate-shima** *island* Japan
387 H4 **Yokohama** Japan
387 I3 **Yokote** Japan
392 D4 **Yol** Himachal Pradesh India
305 G3 **Yola** Nigeria
306 C4 **Yolombo** Democratic Republic of Congo
388 I6 **Yolöten** Turkmenistan
154 C4 **Yomaira** Colombia
305 G5 **Yombi** Gabon
305 C3 **Yomou** Guinea
379 G3 **Yomtam** Arunachal Pradesh India
373 F5 **Yomuka** Indonesia
228 D3 **Yon** *watercourse* France
426 5 **Yona** Guam
386 G4 **Yonago** Japan
381 I4 **Yonaguni Jima** *island* Japan
386 E4 **Yonan** North Korea
124 D5 **Yoncalla** Oregon USA
381 H3 **Yong'an** Fujian China
380 E2 **Yongchang** Chongqing China
384 E5 **Yongchang** Gansu China
384 E6 **Yongdeng** Gansu China
380 D3 **Yongding** Yunnan China
386 F4 **Yŏngdŏk** South Korea
381 F3 **Yongfeng** Hunan China
380 F4 **Yongfu** Guangxi Zhuangzu Zizhiqu China
386 E4 **Yŏnggwang** South Korea
384 G6 **Yonghe** Shanxi China
386 E3 **Yŏnghŭng** North Korea
380 F1 **Yongji** Shanxi China
380 E3 **Yongjing** Guizhou China
386 F4 **Yŏngju** South Korea
380 F1 **Yongle** Shaanxi China
381 G3 **Yongning** Jiangxi China
380 E1 **Yongqing** Gansu China
385 H5 **Yongqing** Hebei China
386 F4 **Yŏngwol** South Korea
380 E3 **Yongxi** Guizhou China
381 G3 **Yongxing** Hunan China
380 E3 **Yongyang** Guizhou China
381 F3 **Yongzhou** Hunan China
304 B3 **Yonibana** Sierra Leone
127 O6 **Yonkers** New York USA
228 F2 **Yonne** *watercourse* France
300 D5 **Yonoféré** Senegal
386 F3 **Yŏnsa** North Korea
154 C3 **Yopal** Colombia
243 G3 **York** *admin. area* England UK
243 G3 **York** York England UK
130 G4 **York** Alabama USA
125 Q6 **York** Nebraska USA
127 M7 **York** Pennsylvania USA
131 K3 **York** South Carolina USA
131 M2 **York** *watercourse* Virginia USA
425 L2 **York, Cape** Qld Australia
162 A5 **York, Isla Duque de** *island* Chile
120 I4 **York Factory** Manitoba Canada
119 W4 **York Landing** Manitoba Canada
424 H3 **York Sound** WA Australia
127 M6 **York Springs** Pennsylvania USA
425 K8 **Yorke Peninsula** SA Australia
243 H2 **Yorkshire Wolds** *region* England UK
119 T7 **Yorkton** Saskatchewan Canada
130 C6 **Yorktown** Texas USA
134 C4 **Yoro** Honduras
381 J3 **Yoro-shima** *island* Japan
387 H4 **Yoroi-gata** *lake* Japan
381 J3 **Yoron-jima** *island* Japan
304 D2 **Yorosso** Mali
240 E2 **Yorton** Shropshire England UK
306 C3 **Yoseki** Democratic Republic of Congo
128 C2 **Yosemite National Park** California USA
128 C2 **Yosemite Village** California USA
388 E2 **Yoshkar-Ola** Russian Federation
386 E5 **Yoso-do** *island* South Korea
386 E4 **Yosu** South Korea
154 B4 **Yotoco** Colombia
154 C2 **Yotójohoin** Colombia
380 E4 **You Jiang** *watercourse* Guangxi Zhuangzu Zizhiqu China
380 F3 **You Shui** *watercourse* Hunan China
381 H3 **You Xi** *watercourse* Fujian China
381 G3 **You Xian** Hunan China
231 F6 **Youb** Algeria
380 C4 **Youdian** Yunnan China
380 D1 **Youganning** Qinghai China
245 E5 **Youghal** Ireland
245 E5 **Youghal Bay** Ireland
304 B2 **Youkounkoun** Guinea
243 G3 **Youlgreave** Derbyshire England UK
425 N8 **Young** NSW Australia
119 S7 **Young** Saskatchewan Canada
161 G5 **Young** Uruguay
423 6 **Young, Cape** Chatham Islands New Zealand
131 J3 **Young Harris** Georgia USA
436 K2 **Young Island** Antarctica
422 G4 **Young Nicks Head** *cape* New Zealand
127 K6 **Youngstown** Ohio USA
127 L6 **Youngsville** Pennsylvania USA
127 L6 **Youngwood** Pennsylvania USA
300 F5 **Youvarou** Mali
121 Q2 **Youville, Monts D'** *mountains* Québec Canada
381 H3 **Youxi** Fujian China
385 L3 **Youyi** Heilongjiang China
225 N2 **Yövesi** *bay* Finland
425 M6 **Yowah** Qld Australia
241 F2 **Yoxall** Staffordshire England UK
241 I2 **Yoxford** Suffolk England UK
394 E5 **Yozgat** Turkey
394 E5 **Yozgat** *admin. area* Turkey
225 L2 **Ypäjä** Finland
161 G2 **Ypané** *watercourse* Paraguay
241 H5 **Yport** France
223 N4 **Yppäri** Finland
126 J5 **Ypsilanti** Michigan USA
223 P4 **Ypykkä** Finland
161 G6 **Yraízoz** Argentina
128 B5 **Yreka** California USA
373 I6 **Ysabel Channel** *strait* Papua New Guinea
240 D1 **Ysbyty Ifan** Conwy Wales UK
228 G4 **Yssingeaux** France
224 G5 **Ystad** Sweden
240 D3 **Ystalyfera** Powys Wales UK
240 D2 **Ystrad Ffin** Carmarthenshire Wales UK
240 D3 **Ystradfellte** Powys Wales UK
389 M5 **Ysyk-Köl** *admin. area* Kyrgyzstan
389 M5 **Ysyk-Köl** *lake* Kyrgyzstan
244 F3 **Ythan** *watercourse* Scotland UK
240 D2 **Ytre Frønningan** Norway
223 O1 **Ytre Korsnes** Norway
224 E3 **Ytre Ramse** Norway
222 inset **Ytri-Rangá** *watercourse* Iceland
222 I5 **Ytterån** Sweden
222 I5 **Ytterhogdal** Sweden
223 M5 **Ytterjeppo** Finland
224 G2 **Yttermalung** Sweden
222 K5 **Yttre Lemelsjön** *lake* Sweden
237 AB6 **Ytyk-Kyuyel'** Russian Federation
372 D4 **Yu** *island* Indonesia
381 H4 **Yu Shan** *mountain* Taiwan China
381 H4 **Yu-Weng Tao** *island* Taiwan China
385 H5 **Yu Xian** Shanxi China
380 F3 **Yuan Jiang** *watercourse* Hunan China
380 D4 **Yuan Jiang** *watercourse* Yunnan China
381 G3 **Yuan Shui** *watercourse* Jiangxi China
380 F3 **Yuanbao Shan** *mountain* Guangxi Zhuangzu Zizhiqu China
380 E1 **Yuanjiazhuang** Shaanxi China
385 J2 **Yuanlin** Nei Mongol Zizhiqu China
380 F3 **Yuanling** Hunan China
380 D3 **Yuanma** Yunnan China
385 G5 **Yuanping** Shanxi China
383 J5 **Yuanquan** Gansu China
381 G4 **Yuanshan** Guangdong China
373 H5 **Yuat** *watercourse* Papua New Guinea
124 E7 **Yuba City** California USA
307 F2 **Yubdo** Ethiopia
128 D3 **Yucaipa** California USA
154 C4 **Yucalito** Colombia
133 H4 **Yucatán** *admin. area* Mexico
134 B3 **Yucatán, Península de** *region* Mexico
79 X5 **Yucatan Basin** *underwater feature* Caribbean Sea

134 C2 **Yucatán Channel** Mexico
128 E3 **Yucca** Arizona USA
128 D3 **Yucca Valley** California USA
385 H6 **Yucheng** Shandong China
385 J2 **Yudi Shan** *mountain* Nei Mongol Zizhiqu China
238 G4 **Yudino** Russian Federation
388 G6 **Yüdkā** Iran
237 AC6 **Yudoma-Krestovskaya** Russian Federation
380 D3 **Yuecheng** Sichuan China
383 J6 **Yuegaitan** Qinghai China
385 L3 **Yuelai** Heilongjiang China
424 I5 **Yuendumu** NT Australia
382 E5 **Yuepuhu** Xinjiang Uygur Zizhiqu China
381 G2 **Yueyang** Hunan China
380 E2 **Yueyang** Sichuan China
237 AC7 **Yugorenok** Russian Federation
236 N5 **Yugorskiy Poluostrov** *peninsula* Russian Federation
236 J6 **Yugra** *watercourse* Russian Federation
381 H2 **Yuhang** Zhejiang China
380 C3 **Yuhu** Yunnan China
381 I3 **Yuhuan** Zhejiang China
381 I3 **Yuhuan Dao** *island* Zhejiang China
385 I6 **Yuhuang Ding (Tai Shan)** *mountain* Shandong China
380 D2 **Yujin** Sichuan China
237 AG5 **Yukagirskoye Ploskogor'ye** *region* Russian Federation
235 F6 **Yukari Mezit** Turkey
235 E6 **Yukarıbey** Turkey
238 C4 **Yukhavichy** Belarus
238 F2 **Yukhmachi** Russian Federation
238 F5 **Yukhnov** Russian Federation
225 P4 **Yukhovo** Russian Federation
306 B4 **Yuki** Democratic Republic of Congo
225 P2 **Yukki** Russian Federation
116 E6 **Yukon** *watercourse* Yukon Territory Canada
116 D6 **Yukon** *watercourse* Alaska USA
116 E5 **Yukon-Charley Rivers National Preserve** *park* Alaska USA
116 C6 **Yukon River Delta** Alaska USA
116 E6 **Yukon Territory** *admin. area* Canada
394 H6 **Yüksekova** Turkey
386 F5 **Yukuhashi** Japan
424 I6 **Yulara** NT Australia
388 H3 **Yuldybayevo** Russian Federation
424 F5 **Yule** *watercourse* WA Australia
436 L2 **Yule Bay** Antarctica
382 H4 **Yuli** Xinjiang Uygur Zizhiqu China
380 F4 **Yulin** Guangxi Zhuangzu Zizhiqu China
384 G5 **Yulin** Shaanxi China
162 B3 **Yulton, Lago** *lake* Chile
223 R4 **Yuma** Russian Federation
128 E4 **Yuma** Arizona USA
125 N6 **Yuma** Colorado USA
388 G3 **Yumaguzino** Russian Federation
159 F6 **Yumao, Cerros de** *range* Bolivia
306 B4 **Yumbi** Democratic Republic of Congo
154 B4 **Yumbo** Colombia
383 K5 **Yumen** Gansu China
380 F2 **Yun Xian** Hubei China
237 AM8 **Yunaska Island** Alaska USA
380 F1 **Yuncheng** Shanxi China
235 C4 **Yundola** Bulgaria
380 D3 **Yunfu** Sichuan China
380 C3 **Yunhe** Yunnan China
381 H3 **Yunhe** Zhejiang China
381 H4 **Yunling** Fujian China
381 G2 **Yunmeng** Hubei China
380 D4 **Yunnan** *admin. area* China
425 K8 **Yunta** SA Australia
385 H4 **Yunwu Shan** *mountain* Beijing China
380 F2 **Yunxi** Hubei China
380 E3 **Yunxi** Sichuan China
380 E2 **Yunyang** Chongqing China
160 C6 **Yupehue** Chile
380 E3 **Yuping** Guizhou China
380 D4 **Yuping** Yunnan China
159 F6 **Yuquirendita** Bolivia
158 D5 **Yura** Peru
225 M5 **Yuratsishki** Belarus
235 F6 **Yüreğil** Turkey
389 N2 **Yurga** Russian Federation
236 Q4 **Yuribey** Russian Federation
236 P5 **Yuribey** *watercourse* Russian Federation
158 B2 **Yurimaguas** Peru
237 U7 **Yurokhta** Russian Federation
236 K5 **Yuroma** Russian Federation
236 O7 **Yurovsk** Russian Federation
158 E5 **Yuruma** Bolivia
382 F6 **Yurungkax He** *watercourse* Xinjiang Uygur Zizhiqu China
238 E5 **Yury** Russian Federation
238 H4 **Yur'yev-Pol'skiy** Russian Federation
134 C4 **Yuscarán** Honduras
223 Q4 **Yushkozero** Russian Federation
385 K4 **Yushu** Jilin China
388 J7 **Yūsof Mirzā'ī** Afghanistan
388 E4 **Yusta** Russian Federation
381 F3 **Yutan** Hunan China
125 Q6 **Yutan** Nebraska USA
385 I5 **Yutian** Hebei China
381 H3 **Yutou Dao** *island* Fujian China
161 G3 **Yuty** Paraguay
226 D3 **Yutz** France
380 E3 **Yuxi** Guizhou China
380 D4 **Yuxi** Yunnan China
381 I2 **Yuyao** Zhejiang China
154 B4 **Yuyero** Colombia
387 I3 **Yuzawa** Japan
388 D2 **Yuzha** Russian Federation
234 G2 **Yuzhne** Ukraine
387 I1 **Yuzhno-Kamyshovyy Khrebet** *range* Russian Federation
389 J5 **Yuzhno-Kazakhstanskaya Oblast'** *admin. area* Kazakhstan
237 X7 **Yuzhno-Muyskiy Khrebet** *range* Russian Federation
237 AD9 **Yuzhno Sakhalinsk** Russian Federation
387 I1 **Yuzhno Sakhalinsk** Russian Federation
389 N2 **Yuzhnyy** Russian Federation
237 AG7 **Yuzhnyy, Mys** *cape* Russian Federation
389 O3 **Yuzhnyy Altay, Khrebet** *range* Kazakhstan
384 E6 **Yuzhong** Gansu China
385 H5 **Yuzhou** Hebei China
381 G1 **Yuzhou** Henan China
229 H3 **Yverdon** Switzerland
241 H5 **Yvetot** France
226 C2 **Yvoir** Belgium
379 H5 **Ywangan** Myanmar
224 I4 **Yxern** *lake* Sweden
225 J3 **Yxlan** *island* Sweden
388 H5 **Ÿylanly** Turkmenistan
228 F3 **Yzeure** France

Z

379 H2 **Za Qu** *watercourse* Qinghai China
384 E3 **Zaamar** Mongolia
384 E3 **Zaamar Uul** *mountain* Mongolia
226 C1 **Zaanstad** Netherlands
230 D6 **Zaaroura** Morocco
234 B3 **Žabalj** Serbia
234 B3 **Žabari** Serbia
390 E7 **Zabid** Yemen
232 H5 **Žabljak** Montenegro
232 G4 **Žabno** Croatia
227 K2 **Żabno** Poland
391 K3 **Zābol** *admin. area* Afghanistan
391 J3 **Zābol** Iran
227 M2 **Zabolottsy** Ukraine
238 D3 **Zaborov'ye** Russian Federation
225 O5 **Zabor'ye** Belarus
225 P5 **Zabor'ye** Russian Federation
234 B2 **Zābrani** Romania
304 D2 **Zabre** Burkina Faso
232 G2 **Zábřeh** Czech Republic
232 G5 **Zabrišće** Bosnia and Herzegovina
227 J2 **Zabrze** Poland
227 K3 **Zabrzeż** Poland
227 H4 **Zabukovica** Slovenia
388 F4 **Zaburunye** Kazakhstan
134 B4 **Zacapa** Guatemala
132 E5 **Zacapú** Mexico
132 E4 **Zacatecas** Mexico
132 E4 **Zacatecas** *admin. area* Mexico
235 B7 **Zacharo** Greece
130 F5 **Zachary** Louisiana USA
225 O5 **Zachist'ye** Belarus
227 H1 **Zachodniopomorskie** *admin. area* Poland
226 G1 **Zachow** Germany
227 H2 **Žacléř** Czech Republic
133 F4 **Zacualtipán** Mexico
376 C5 **Zadetkale Kyun** Myanmar
376 C5 **Zadetkyi Kyun** Myanmar
126 J2 **Zadi Lake** Ontario Canada
227 J2 **Zadzim** Poland
302 E2 **Za'farānah** Egypt
392 D4 **Zafarwal** Punjab India
234 E3 **Zafirovo** Bulgaria
230 C4 **Zafra** Spain
229 K3 **Žaga** Slovenia
373 G6 **Zagai Island** Qld Australia
233 E6 **Zagarolo** Italy
301 I1 **Zaghouan** Tunisia
235 C3 **Zagkliveri** Greece
233 E4 **Zagon** Romania
235 C6 **Zagorá** Greece
300 E2 **Zagora** Morocco
227 H4 **Zagorci** Slovenia
232 F4 **Zagreb** Croatia
380 D2 **Zagu'nao** Sichuan China
379 F2 **Zagungngomar** *mountain* Xizang Zizhiqu China
227 K4 **Zagyva** *watercourse* Hungary
391 I3 **Zāhedān** Iran
393 D8 **Zahirabad** Andhra Pradesh India
300 C2 **Zahlé** Lebanon
226 G2 **Zahna** Germany
225 N4 **Zaiceva** Latvia
234 F2 **Zaim** Moldova
162 B2 **Zaina Yegua** Argentina
230 E6 **Zaïo** Morocco
306 A5 **Zaire** *admin. area* Angola
394 B3 **Zakarpats'ka Oblast'** *admin. area* Ukraine
388 E5 **Zakataly** Azerbaijan
238 H5 **Zakharovo** Russian Federation
394 B2 **Zakhidnyy Buh** *watercourse* Ukraine
390 E1 **Zakho** Iraq
238 C5 **Zakhodni Dzvina** *watercourse* Belarus
223 T2 **Zakhrebetnoye** Russian Federation
305 F3 **Zaki Biam** Nigeria
227 L2 **Zaklików** Poland
227 J2 **Zakopane** Poland
227 K1 **Zakroczym** Poland
227 L2 **Zakrzówek** Poland
234 E1 **Zakupne** Ukraine
235 B7 **Zakynthos** *island* Greece
227 I4 **Zala** *admin. area* Hungary
227 I4 **Zala** *watercourse* Hungary
227 I4 **Zalaegerszeg** Hungary
227 I4 **Zalakomár** Hungary
232 G3 **Zalalövő** Hungary
230 C5 **Zalamea la Real** Spain
305 G2 **Zalanga** Nigeria
385 J3 **Zalantun** Nei Mongol Zizhiqu China
237 V8 **Zalari** Russian Federation
389 S2 **Zalari** Russian Federation
234 C2 **Zalău** Romania
227 H4 **Žalec** Slovenia
234 B1 **Zalesie** Poland
238 G3 **Zales'ye** Russian Federation
227 J1 **Zalewo** Poland
390 E5 **Zalim** Saudi Arabia
302 C5 **Zalingei** Sudan
225 K5 **Zalivino** Russian Federation
234 H2 **Zaliznyy Port** Ukraine
234 D1 **Zaliztsi** Ukraine
228 C5 **Zalla** Spain
225 L5 **Žaltytis** *lake* Lithuania
225 P4 **Zaluch'ye** Russian Federation
376 B3 **Zalun** Myanmar
234 C2 **Zam** Romania
301 G6 **Zama** Niger
118 L3 **Zama Lake** Alberta Canada
158 C4 **Zamaca** Peru
381 J3 **Zamami-jima** *island* Japan
392 F6 **Zamania** Uttar Pradesh India
309 G3 **Zambeze** *watercourse* Mozambique
306 C6 **Zambezi** *watercourse* Angola
306 C6 **Zambezi** Zambia
308 D2 **Zambezi** *watercourse* Zambia
308 E3 **Zambezi Escarpment** *range* Zambia
309 G3 **Zambezia** *admin. area* Mozambique
308 E2 **Zambia** *country* Africa
377 I6 **Zamboanga** Philippines
227 L1 **Zambrów** Poland
309 F3 **Zambué** Mozambique
227 H2 **Zamek Czocha** *lake* Poland
305 F2 **Zamfara** *admin. area* Nigeria
305 F2 **Zamfara** *watercourse* Nigeria
154 B6 **Zamora** Ecuador
133 I6 **Zamora** Honduras
154 B5 **Zamora** *watercourse* Peru
230 D3 **Zamora** Spain
154 B6 **Zamora-Chinchipe** *admin. area* Ecuador
132 E5 **Zamora de Hidalgo** Mexico
227 L2 **Zamość** Poland
238 D4 **Zamoshki** Russian Federation
390 D5 **Zamrat 'Aqabah** Saudi Arabia
154 D4 **Zamuro, Punta** *cape* Venezuela
155 F3 **Zamuro, Sierra del** *range* Venezuela
158 B2 **Zaña** Peru
305 G5 **Zanaga** Congo
230 E4 **Záncara** *watercourse* Spain
127 J7 **Zanesville** Ohio USA
159 G5 **Zanetti** Brazil
304 C2 **Zangasso** Mali
305 I4 **Zangba** Central African Republic
305 F2 **Zango** Nigeria
382 H6 **Zangser Kangri** *mountain* Xizang Zizhiqu China
385 H5 **Zanhuang** Hebei China
388 E7 **Zanjān** Iran
388 E7 **Zanjān** *admin. area* Iran
162 D2 **Zanjón de Oyuela** Argentina
392 D4 **Zanskar** *watercourse* Jammu and Kashmir India/Pakistan
225 L4 **Zante** Latvia
304 C2 **Zantié Bougou** Mali
236 E7 **Zanul'ye** Russian Federation
307 F5 **Zanzibar** Tanzania
307 F5 **Zanzibar Island** *island* Tanzania
307 F5 **Zanzibar North** *admin. area* Tanzania
307 F5 **Zanzibar South and Central** *admin. area* Tanzania
307 F5 **Zanzibar West** *admin. area* Tanzania
387 I3 **Zaō-zan** *volcano* Japan
238 G5 **Zaokskoye** Russian Federation
305 H3 **Zaorosongou** Central African Republic
381 F3 **Zaoshi** Hunan China
225 Q2 **Zaostrov'ye** Russian Federation
381 F2 **Zaoyang** Hubei China
389 Q2 **Zaozernyy** Russian Federation
238 H4 **Zaozer'ye** Russian Federation
381 H1 **Zaozhuang** Shandong China
125 O3 **Zap** North Dakota USA
234 B4 **Zapadna Morava** *watercourse* Serbia
225 Q4 **Zapadnaya Dvina** Russian Federation
388 C4 **Zapadno Kapitalnaya** Russian Federation
388 F3 **Zapadno-Kazakhstanskaya Oblast'** *admin. area* Kazakhstan
237 AD9 **Zapadno Sakhalinskiye Gory** *range* Russian Federation
236 Q6 **Zapadno-Sibirskaya Ravnina** *mountain* Russian Federation
116 A4 **Zapadnyy, Mys** Russian Federation
223 S2 **Zapadnyy Kil'din** Russian Federation
389 P3 **Zapadnyy Sayan** *range* Russian Federation
160 D6 **Zapala** Argentina
162 E2 **Zapaleri, Cerro** *mountain* Chile
130 B7 **Zapata** Texas USA
162 B5 **Zapata, Cerro** *mountain* Chile
134 D2 **Zapata, Peninsula de** *peninsula* Cuba
154 C3 **Zapatoca** Colombia
154 C2 **Zapatosa, Cienaga de** *lake* Colombia
129 J7 **Zapién** Mexico
158 D5 **Zapiga** Chile
77 N14 **Zapiola Ridge** *underwater feature* Atlantic Ocean
77 P13 **Zapiola Seamount** *underwater feature* Atlantic Ocean
225 O3 **Zapol'ye** Russian Federation
132 E4 **Zapopan** Mexico
394 E3 **Zaporizhzhya** Ukraine
394 E3 **Zaporiz'ka Oblast'** *admin. area* Ukraine
225 P2 **Zaporozhskoye** Russian Federation
233 F6 **Zapponeta** Italy
227 M1 **Zaprudy** Belarus
Zaqatala *see* **Zakataly** Azerbaijan
384 D3 **Zar** Mongolia
154 D3 **Zaracure** Colombia
388 I5 **Zarafshon** Uzbekistan
154 C3 **Zaragoza** Colombia
132 D2 **Zaragoza** Mexico
230 E3 **Zaragoza** Spain
235 D6 **Zárakes** Greece
391 H3 **Zarand** Iran
391 J3 **Zaranj** Afghanistan
225 N5 **Zarasai** Lithuania
161 G5 **Zárate** Argentina
154 C2 **Zárate, Cienaga de** *watercourse* Colombia
230 E2 **Zarautz** Spain
238 H5 **Zaraysk** Russian Federation
155 E2 **Zaraza** Venezuela
223 Q3 **Zarechensk** Russian Federation
227 M1 **Zarechka** Belarus
225 O5 **Zarech'ye** Belarus
118 E4 **Zarembo Island** Alaska USA
391 K3 **Zarghūn Shahr** Afghanistan
305 F2 **Zaria** Nigeria
227 K2 **Żarnów** Poland
227 J2 **Żarnowiec** Poland
224 I5 **Żarnowieckie, Jezioro** *lake* Poland
238 E3 **Zarubino** Russian Federation
225 P5 **Zaruby** Belarus
234 F1 **Zarudyntsy** Ukraine
154 B5 **Zaruma** Ecuador
158 A1 **Zarumilla** Peru
227 H2 **Żary** Poland
237 AC3 **Zarya, Proliv** *strait* Russian Federation
388 H4 **Zarya Oktyabrya** Kazakhstan
238 C3 **Zaryabinka** Russian Federation
310 3d **Zarza, Pico de la** *mountain* Canary Islands
301 H3 **Zarzaïtine** Algeria
154 B3 **Zarzal** Colombia
301 I2 **Zarzis** Tunisia
230 B2 **Zas** Spain
223 Q3 **Zasheek** Russian Federation
238 C4 **Zasitino** Russian Federation
225 N5 **Zaslawskaye Vodaskhovishcha** *lake* Belarus
227 H3 **Zásmuky** Czech Republic
234 D1 **Zastavna** Ukraine
308 E6 **Zastron** South Africa
227 G2 **Žatec** Czech Republic
227 J3 **Zator** Poland
234 F2 **Zatyshshya** Ukraine
225 M4 **Zaube** Latvia
234 A4 **Zaumsko** Serbia
227 L3 **Zavadka** Ukraine
436 F2 **Zavadovskiy Island** Antarctica
235 B5 **Zavalinë** Albania
130 D5 **Zavalla** Texas USA
234 D1 **Zavalov** Ukraine
390 G2 **Zavāreh** Iran
391 G2 **Zavāreh** Iran
383 J3 **Zavhan** Mongolia
383 J3 **Zavhanmandal** Mongolia
227 M2 **Zavidov** Ukraine
227 N1 **Zavine** Belarus
385 L2 **Zavitinsk** Russian Federation
234 A3 **Zavlaka** Serbia
389 N2 **Zavodskoy** Russian Federation
232 G3 **Zavrč** Slovenia
237 AF7 **Zav'yalova, Ostrov** *island* Russian Federation
227 J2 **Zawadzkie** Poland
227 J2 **Zawiercie** Poland
301 J3 **Zawilah** Libya
301 K2 **Zāwiyat Masūs** Libya
227 J3 **Zawoja** Poland
227 I2 **Zawonia** Poland
227 I3 **Zaya** *watercourse* Austria
390 G3 **Zāyandeh Rūd** *watercourse* Iran
225 P5 **Zaykovo** Belarus
389 N4 **Zaysan** Kazakhstan
389 N4 **Zaysan, Ozero** *lake* Kazakhstan
238 C2 **Zaytsevo** Russian Federation
134 E2 **Zaza, Presa** *lake* Cuba
155 D2 **Zazárida** Venezuela
234 D1 **Zbarazh** Ukraine
227 H1 **Zbąszynek** Poland
227 I1 **Zbąszyńskie, Jezioro** *lake* Poland
234 A4 **Zboriste** *mountain* Serbia
234 D1 **Zboriv** Ukraine
227 K3 **Zborowice** Poland
227 L1 **Zbucz** Poland
226 G2 **Žďár** Czech Republic
227 H3 **Žďár nad Sázavou** Czech Republic
232 G4 **Zdenci** Croatia
232 F1 **Zdiby** Czech Republic
227 H5 **Zdihovo** Croatia
227 H1 **Zdroisko** Poland
227 J1 **Zduny** Poland
227 J2 **Zdzieszowice** Poland
240 D4 **Zeal Monachorum** Devon England UK
119 R7 **Zealandia** Saskatchewan Canada
426 2 **Zealandia Bank** *island* Northern Mariana Islands
241 E3 **Zeals** Wiltshire England UK
124 B2 **Zeballos** British Columbia Canada
233 F8 **Żebbuġ** Malta
131 I4 **Zebulon** Georgia USA
232 F4 **Zeča** *island* Croatia
227 H1 **Zechin** Germany
425 M10 **Zeehan** Tas. Australia
226 B2 **Zeeland** *admin. area* Netherlands
308 E5 **Zeerust** South Africa
304 E3 **Zegbeli** Ghana
227 K3 **Żegocina** Poland
125 M1 **Zehner** Saskatchewan Canada
424 H5 **Zeil, Mount** NT Australia
225 M4 **Žeimelis** Lithuania
225 L5 **Žeimiai** Lithuania
227 G2 **Zeisholz** Germany
229 K1 **Zeitz** Germany
225 O2 **Zelënaya Roshcha** Russian Federation
225 R3 **Zelenoborskiy** Russian Federation
238 C2 **Zelenogorsk** Russian Federation
225 K5 **Zelenogradsk** Russian Federation
234 E1 **Zelënyye Kurilovtsy** Ukraine
226 G3 **Železná Ruda** Czech Republic
227 H4 **Železniki** Slovenia
394 E2 **Zeleznogorsk** Russian Federation
301 G2 **Zelfana** Algeria
226 D1 **Zelhem** Netherlands
235 B5 **Želino** Macedonia
235 C6 **Zelio** Greece
227 H3 **Želivka, Vodní nádrž** *lake* Czech Republic
226 D4 **Zell** Germany
226 D4 **Zell** Switzerland
232 E3 **Zell am See** Austria
232 D3 **Zell am Ziller** Austria
226 E4 **Zellersee** *bay* Germany
227 J2 **Zelów** Poland
227 H4 **Zeltweg** Austria
225 M5 **Želva** Lithuania
234 C4 **Zemen** Bulgaria
234 E2 **Zemeş** Romania
388 D2 **Zemetchino** Russian Federation
306 D2 **Zémio** Central African Republic
236 M3 **Zemlya Frantsa-Iosifa** *island* Russian Federation
301 G1 **Zemmora** Algeria
238 E4 **Zemtsy** Russian Federation
130 B2 **Zenda** Kansas USA
391 I4 **Zendeh, Kūh-e** *mountain* Iran
391 J2 **Zendeh Jān** Afghanistan
381 G4 **Zeng Jiang** *watercourse* Guangdong China
381 G4 **Zengcheng** Guangdong China
232 G4 **Zenica** Bosnia and Herzegovina
81 O7 **Zenith Plateau** *underwater feature* Indian Ocean
231 H6 **Zenzach** Algeria
232 H4 **Žepče** Bosnia and Herzegovina
131 J6 **Zephyrhills** Florida USA
382 F5 **Zepu** Xinjiang Uygur Zizhiqu China
226 G2 **Zerbst** Germany
383 I3 **Zereg** Mongolia
388 H3 **Zerenda** Kazakhstan
301 H2 **Zeribet el Oued** Algeria
234 B2 **Zerind** Romania
389 N3 **Zerkalnoye** *lake* Russian Federation
229 J3 **Zernez** Switzerland
388 C4 **Zernograd** Russian Federation
235 B5 **Zerqan** Albania
154 C3 **Zetaquira** Colombia
234 D2 **Zetea** Romania
226 D1 **Zetel** Germany
237 H1 **Zeva** *watercourse* Russian Federation
226 E1 **Zeven** Germany
232 D4 **Zevio** Italy
385 K1 **Zeya** Russian Federation
385 K1 **Zeya Dam** Russian Federation
237 AA8 **Zeyskoye Vodokhranilishche** *lake* Russian Federation
230 C3 **Zêzere** *watercourse* Portugal
390 C2 **Zgharta** Lebanon
227 J2 **Zgierz** Poland
227 K1 **Zgniłocha** Poland
227 M1 **Zhabinka** Belarus
388 F4 **Zhailma** Kazakhstan
388 I3 **Zhaksy-alakol'** *lake* Kazakhstan
388 I3 **Zhaksy-kylysh** *lake* Kazakhstan
389 L3 **Zhalauly Koli** *lake* Kazakhstan
389 K3 **Zhaltyr** Kazakhstan
389 M3 **Zhaltyr** Kazakhstan
388 G4 **Zhamansor** Kazakhstan
388 K3 **Zhamantuz** *lake* Kazakhstan
389 K4 **Zhambyl** Kazakhstan
389 K5 **Zhambylskaya oblast'** *admin. area* Kazakhstan
379 H3 **Zhamu** Xizang Zizhiqu China
389 N3 **Zhanaozen** Kazakhstan
388 I4 **Zhanay** Kazakhstan
388 F4 **Zhanbay** Kazakhstan
385 H4 **Zhangbei** Hebei China
381 H3 **Zhangcheng** Fujian China
380 C4 **Zhangfeng** Yunnan China
380 D2 **Zhanggu** Sichuan China
385 K4 **Zhangguangcai Ling** *range* Heilongjiang China
380 E1 **Zhangjiachuan** Gansu China
380 F2 **Zhangjiajie** Hunan China
385 H5 **Zhangjiakou** Hebei China
381 F3 **Zhangjiang** Hunan China
384 F5 **Zhangjiapan** Shaanxi China
381 H3 **Zhangping** Fujian China
381 G3 **Zhangshu** Jiangxi China
385 J4 **Zhangwu** Liaoning China
384 D5 **Zhangye** Gansu China
381 H4 **Zhangzhou** Fujian China
385 J5 **Zhangzi Dao** *island* Liaoning China
381 F4 **Zhanjiang** Guangdong China
237 AG3 **Zhannetty, Ostrov** *island* Russian Federation
388 G4 **Zhanterek** Kazakhstan
389 K3 **Zhanybekshalkar** *lake* Kazakhstan
380 D2 **Zhao Zhen** Sichuan China
385 K3 **Zhaodong** Heilongjiang China
381 G3 **Zhaojne** Jiangxi China
380 F4 **Zhaoping** Guangxi Zhuangzu Zizhiqu China
381 F4 **Zhaoqing** Guangdong China
380 E1 **Zhaoren** Shaanxi China
382 G4 **Zhaosu** Xinjiang Uygur Zizhiqu China
380 D3 **Zhaotong** Yunnan China
385 K3 **Zhaoyuan** Heilongjiang China
385 I5 **Zhaoyuan** Shandong China
385 K3 **Zhaozhou** Heilongjiang China
225 N5 **Zhardzyazhzha** Belarus
388 G4 **Zharkamys** Kazakhstan
238 E5 **Zharkovskiy** Russian Federation
388 I3 **Zharman Koli** *lake* Kazakhstan
394 D3 **Zhashkiv** Ukraine
380 F1 **Zhashui** Shaanxi China
379 G3 **Zhatang** Xizang Zizhiqu China
380 E3 **Zhaxi** Yunnan China
389 K4 **Zhayrem** Kazakhstan
238 E4 **Zhdanovo** Russian Federation
381 G1 **Zhecheng** Henan China
380 C4 **Zhedao** Yunnan China
381 H3 **Zhejiang** *admin. area* China
388 J3 **Zhekekol** *lake* Kazakhstan
236 O3 **Zhelaniya, Mys** *cape* Russian Federation
389 L2 **Zhelezinka** Kazakhstan
236 L6 **Zheleznodorozhnyy** Russian Federation
381 G2 **Zhelin Shuiku** *lake* Jiangxi China
380 E4 **Zhelou** Guizhou China
380 F3 **Zhenbao Ding** *mountain* Guangxi Zhuangzu Zizhiqu China
385 H5 **Zhengkou** Hebei China
381 G1 **Zhengzhou** Henan China
385 J3 **Zhenlai** Jilin China
380 E3 **Zhenning** Guizhou China
380 F2 **Zhenping** Shaanxi China
384 G6 **Zhenw-udong** Shaanxi China
381 G2 **Zhenyang** Henan China
384 F6 **Zhenyuan** Gansu China
388 H3 **Zhety-kol''** *lake* Russian Federation
238 C4 **Zhevloki** Russian Federation
388 J4 **Zhezdi Bogeni** *lake* Kazakhstan
389 J4 **Zhezkazgan** Kazakhstan
238 C4 **Zhgilëvo** Russian Federation
225 O3 **Zhglino** Russian Federation
381 H2 **Zhicheng** Zhejiang China
237 W8 **Zhigalovo** Russian Federation
380 F3 **Zhijiang** Hunan China
380 E3 **Zhijin** Guizhou China
234 C4 **Zhilentsi** Bulgaria
238 G6 **Zhilino** Russian Federation
237 X4 **Zhillinda** Russian Federation
381 F4 **Zhilong** Guangdong China
154 B5 **Zhimbrue** Ecuador
380 D1 **Zhiqingsongduo** Qinghai China
238 E6 **Zhiryatino** Russian Federation
388 I3 **Zhitikara** Kazakhstan
225 O2 **Zhitkovo** Russian Federation
388 E4 **Zhitkur** Russian Federation
381 G4 **Zhiwan Dao** *island* Guangdong China
238 F6 **Zhizdra** Russian Federation
394 D2 **Zhlobin** Belarus
391 L3 **Zhob** Pakistan
120 G8 **Zhoda** Manitoba Canada
225 O5 **Zhodzina** Belarus
237 AF3 **Zhokhova, Ostrov** *island* Russian Federation
384 G5 **Zhong-yang** Shanxi China
380 D3 **Zhong`an** Yunnan China
380 E3 **Zhongcheng** Sichuan China
380 D3 **Zhongcheng** Yunnan China
380 E3 **Zhongduo** Chongqing China
380 E3 **Zhonghe** Chongqing China
381 G4 **Zhongshan** Guangdong China
381 F4 **Zhongshan** Guangxi Zhuangzu Zizhiqu China
436 F2 **Zhongshan (China)** *research station* Antarctica
380 D3 **Zhongshu** Yunnan China
380 D4 **Zhongshu** Yunnan China
380 E1 **Zhongtai** Gansu China
384 F5 **Zhongwei** Zishiqu China
380 D3 **Zhongxin** Yunnan China
381 H1 **Zhongxing** Jiangsu China
381 G4 **Zhongyang Liedao** *island* Guangdong China
227 M2 **Zhorany** Ukraine
234 F1 **Zhornishche** Ukraine
225 O5 **Zhortay** Belarus
389 K3 **Zhosaly** *lake* Kazakhstan
380 E2 **Zhou He** *watercourse* Sichuan China
379 H2 **Zhoujun** Qinghai China
381 G1 **Zhoukou** Henan China
380 E2 **Zhoukou** Sichuan China
380 D1 **Zhouqu** Gansu China
381 I2 **Zhoushan Dao** *island* Zhejiang China
234 H1 **Zhovnino** Ukraine
227 M3 **Zhovtantsi** Ukraine
234 D1 **Zhovten'** Ukraine
234 F3 **Zhovtyy Yar** Ukraine
385 J5 **Zhuanghe** Liaoning China
381 I3 **Zhuangyuan'ao** *island* Zhejiang China
385 I6 **Zhucheng** Shandong China
381 G4 **Zhuhai** Guangdong China
381 H2 **Zhuji** Zhejiang China
381 I2 **Zhujia Jian** *island* Zhejiang China
238 E6 **Zhukovka** Russian Federation
238 G5 **Zhukovo** Russian Federation
238 H5 **Zhukovskiy** Russian Federation
381 G2 **Zhumadian** Henan China
380 D1 **Zhuogenima** Gansu China
385 H5 **Zhuolu** Hebei China
385 H5 **Zhuozhou** Hebei China
384 F5 **Zhuozi Shan** *mountain* Nei Mongol Zizhiqu China
385 G5 **Zhuozishan** Nei Mongol Zizhiqu China
389 K3 **Zhuravlevka** Kazakhstan
380 F2 **Zhushan** Hubei China
380 F2 **Zhushan** Hubei China
380 F2 **Zhuxi** Hubei China
381 G3 **Zhuzhou** Hunan China
227 M2 **Zhyryche** Ukraine
394 D2 **Zhytomyr** Ukraine
394 D2 **Zhytomyrs'ka Oblast'** *admin. area* Ukraine
381 F3 **Zi Shui** *lake* Hunan China
304 C3 **Zia Town** Liberia
304 C3 **Ziama** *mountain* Guinea
227 J3 **Žiar nad Hronom** Slovakia
385 I6 **Zibo** Shandong China
230 C4 **Zibreira** Portugal
227 H4 **Žice** Slovenia
381 G4 **Zicheng** Guangdong China
234 E4 **Zidarovo** Bulgaria
391 K4 **Zidi** Pakistan
225 L4 **Židikai** Lithuania
155 H4 **Zidok** French Guiana
234 E3 **Ziduri** Romania
227 I2 **Ziębice** Poland
225 K5 **Zięby** Poland
227 H2 **Zielona Góra** Poland
227 J1 **Zieluń** Poland
226 B2 **Zierikzee** Netherlands
226 G1 **Ziesar** Germany
225 M5 **Žiežmariai** Lithuania
302 E1 **Ziftá** Egypt
376 B3 **Zigon** Myanmar
380 D2 **Zigong** Sichuan China
300 C6 **Ziguinchor** Senegal
226 G2 **Žihle** Czech Republic
384 D6 **Ziketan** Qinghai China
238 F6 **Zikeyevo** Russian Federation
391 I4 **Zīkūkī** Iran
394 E5 **Zile** Turkey
225 N4 **Zīle** Latvia
227 J3 **Žilina** Slovakia
379 F2 **Ziling Tsho** *lake* Xizang Zizhiqu China
227 J3 **Žilinsky** *admin. area* Slovakia
301 J3 **Zillah** Libya
124 E3 **Zillah** Washington USA
225 O4 **Zilupe** Latvia
237 V8 **Zima** Russian Federation
133 F4 **Zimapán** Mexico
133 F5 **Zimatlán de Álvarez** Mexico
308 E3 **Zimbabwe** *country* Africa
227 L4 **Zimbor** Romania
391 K2 **Zin** Afghanistan
305 G2 **Zina** Cameroon
132 E5 **Zinapécuaro** Mexico
301 H6 **Zinder** Niger
301 H6 **Zinder** *admin. area* Niger
307 F5 **Zinga Mulika** Tanzania
226 B2 **Zingem** Belgium
224 G5 **Zingst** *island* Germany
154 E6 **Zinho** *watercourse* Brazil
304 D2 **Ziniaré** Burkina Faso
390 F7 **Zinjibār** Yemen
394 E2 **Zin'kiv** Ukraine
234 E1 **Zin'kov** Ukraine
300 E6 **Zinzana** Mali
163 I9 **Zion** St Kitts and Nevis
304 E3 **Zion** *watercourse* Togo
128 F2 **Zion National Park** Utah USA
120 J7 **Zionz Lake** Ontario Canada
132 E5 **Zirándaro** Mexico
392 D6 **Zirapur** Madhya Pradesh India
225 K4 **Ziras** Latvia
233 C8 **Zirba** Tunisia
227 I4 **Zirc** Hungary
232 F3 **Žiri** Slovenia
232 F5 **Žirje** Croatia
232 F5 **Žirje** *island* Croatia
391 H5 **Zirkūh (UAE)** *island* United Arab Emirates
226 F4 **Zirl** Austria
225 M5 **Žirnajų ežeras** *lake* Lithuania
229 J2 **Zirndorf** Germany
379 G3 **Ziro** Arunachal Pradesh India
227 I3 **Zistersdorf** Austria
234 B3 **Žitište** Serbia
156 C4 **Zitiua** *watercourse* Brazil
234 B4 **Žitkovac** Serbia
234 B4 **Žitni Potok** Serbia
380 E2 **Zitong** Chongqing China
229 L1 **Zittau** Germany
232 H4 **Živinice** Bosnia and Herzegovina
307 F2 **Ziway** Ethiopia
307 F2 **Ziway, Lake** Ethiopia
384 F6 **Ziwu Ling** *mountain* Gansu China
381 G3 **Zixing** Hunan China
385 H5 **Ziya He** *watercourse* Hebei China
381 H2 **Ziyang** Jiangxi China
380 E2 **Ziyang** Shaanxi China
380 D2 **Ziyang** Sichuan China
229 I3 **Zizers** Switzerland
234 D4 **Zlataritsa** Bulgaria
227 J3 **Zlaté Moravce** Slovakia
234 A4 **Zlatibor** Serbia
234 A4 **Zlatibor** *range* Serbia
234 C2 **Zlatna** Romania
232 G3 **Zlatná na Ostrove** Slovakia
388 H2 **Zlatoust** Russian Federation
237 AB8 **Zlatoustovsk** Russian Federation
385 M1 **Zlatoustovsk** Russian Federation
225 K4 **Zlēkas** Latvia
227 I3 **Zlín** Czech Republic
227 I3 **Zlínský Kraj** *admin. area* Czech Republic
301 I2 **Zliţan** Libya
232 F2 **Zliv** Czech Republic
227 H2 **Złotoryja** Poland
232 H4 **Zmajevac** Croatia
389 N3 **Zmeinogorsk** Russian Federation
394 F3 **Zmiyiv** Ukraine
227 L2 **Znamenka** Belarus
389 M3 **Znamenka** Kazakhstan
238 F6 **Znamenskoye** Russian Federation
227 I3 **Znojmo** Czech Republic
226 C1 **Zoetermeer** Netherlands
226 E5 **Zogno** Italy
307 F5 **Zoissa** Tanzania
392 D3 **Zoji La** *pass* Jammu and Kashmir India/Pakistan
131 K7 **Zolfo Springs** Florida USA
234 D1 **Zolochiv** Ukraine
237 AA8 **Zolotaya Gora** Russian Federation
234 H1 **Zolotonosha** Ukraine
234 D1 **Zolotyy Potik** Ukraine
227 L2 **Żołynia** Poland
234 A2 **Zomba** Hungary
309 G3 **Zomba** Malawi
389 J6 **Zomin** Uzbekistan
378 E3 **Zongga** Xizang Zizhiqu China
306 D3 **Zongia** Democratic Republic of Congo
306 B3 **Zongo** Democratic Republic of Congo
394 D5 **Zonguldak** Turkey
394 D5 **Zonguldak** *admin. area* Turkey
233 C6 **Zonza** Corsica France
230 D4 **Zorita** Spain
158 A1 **Zorritos** Peru
227 M2 **Zosin** Poland
301 J4 **Zouar** Chad

CREDITS

Key: (t) top of page; (tl) top left of page; (tr) top right of page, (b) bottom of page; (bl) bottom left of page; (br) bottom right of page; (l) left side of page; (r) right side of page; (c) center of page; (cl) center left of page; (cr) center right of page.

All image from Getty Images library unless otherwise noted.

NASA: 25(l); 28(c); 28(b); 29(tr); 29(cr); 29(br); 38(t); 44(bl) NASA; 43(tl) NASA Jet Propulsion Laboratory (NASA-JPL); 25(t), 25(cr) NASA/GSFC/METI/ERSDAC/JAROS, and U.S./Japan ASTER Science Team; 28(t) Manned Spacecraft Center; 29(t) NASA/JPL-Caltech/R. Hurt (SSC); 29(bl) NASA/JPL-Caltech/T. Pyle (SSC)

ESO: 28(b)

Millennium House: 70(l), 88(c), 91(t), 92(tl), 99(t), 97(t), 99(r), 104(t), 143(t), 143(c), 145(t), 145(b), 147(t), 171(t), 171(c), 176(b), 176(l), 183(b), 184(b), 188(t), 188(c), 189(r), 196(c), 200(t), 205(t), 205(r), 206(t), 213(r), 213(b), 216(l), 254(r), 232(b), 318(t), 330(t), 331(c), 345(t), 349(t), 349(r), 401(t), 402(b), 403(br), 408(b), 440(c);

ACKNOWLEDGEMENTS

The publisher would like to thank the following organizations:

Environmental Systems Research Institute, Inc. (ESRI); Digital Chart of the World; U.S. Board on Geographic Names (BGN); ; U.S. Geological Survey (USGS); The Permanent Committee on Geographical Names (PCGN); United Nations (UN) Cartographic Unit; United Nations Food and Agriculture Organisation (FAO); United Nations Statistical Division; United Nations Group of Experts on Geographical Names (UNGEGN); Natural Resources Canada; Geographix; World Gazetteer © Stefan Helders www.world-gazetteer.com; U.S. Geological Survey's EROS Data Center (EDC), 1996, (GTOPO30 relief); The CGIAR Consortium for Spatial Information (CGIAR-CSI), (SRTM90 relief); GEBCO Digital Atlas published by the British Oceanographic Data Centre on behalf of the Intergovernmental Oceanographic Commission of UNESCO and the International Hydrographic Organisation, 2008; The CIA World Factbook, 2008; Geoscience Australia; Robert J. Hijmans, Susan Cameron, and Juan Parra, at the Museum of Vertebrate Zoology, University of California, Berkeley; Peter Jones and Andrew Jarvis (CIAT), and Karen Richardson (Rainforest CRC) (WorldClim database); National Climatic Data Centre, U.S. Department of Commerce; Centre for International Earth Science Information Network (CIESIN); TeleGeography Research Group-PriMetrica Inc. www.telegeography.com; World Wildlife Fund (WWF); American Geological Institute (AGI); Australian Bureau of Statistics; Survey of India: Committee for Geographical Names of Australasia (CGNA); Perry-Castaneda Library (PCL), University of Texas; Gwillim Law, www.statoids.com